The **Rough Guide** to

West Africa

W9-AMJ-318

written and researched by

Richard Trillo and Jim Hudgens

this edition updated by

**Alan Duncan, Anita Ferruzzi, Emma Gregg, Alex Hannaford,
Kate Hawkings, Hilary Heuler, Nana Luckham, Lone
Mouritsen, Roger Norum, Henry Stedman, Richard Trillo,
Ross Velton and Jeremy Weate**

ROUGH
GUIDES

NEW YORK · LONDON · DELHI

www.roughguides.com

Contents

Colour section   1

Introduction 6
The geographical picture 9
Where to go 11
When to go 15

Basics   17

Getting there........................... 19
Red tape and visas 29
Info and media....................... 33
Maps and books 34
Health 37
Costs, money, banks 45
Getting around....................... 48
Accommodation...................... 54
Eating and drinking................. 57
Communications..................... 61
Public holidays and
  festivals 63
Crime and safety.................... 64
Cultural hints........................... 68
Living and working
  in West Africa 70
Travellers with disabilities 71
Gender issues and sexual
  attitudes 72
Wildlife and national parks....... 75
People and languages 77
Travellers' French.................... 82
Practicalities 87

Guide   89

❶ Mauritania 91
❷ Senegal.............................. 153
❸ The Gambia 263
❹ Mali 321
❺ Cape Verde 431
❻ Guinea-Bissau 511
❼ Guinea 559
❽ Sierra Leone...................... 639
❾ Burkina Faso...................... 705
❿ Ghana 783
⓫ Togo.................................. 883
⓬ Benin................................. 949
⓭ Niger 1007
⓮ Nigeria 1069
⓯ Cameroon 1217

Travel store   1339

Small print & Index   1345

West African food plants colour section
following p.400

Arts and crafts colour
section following p.848

◀◀ Green mangoes ◀ Bani River, Mopti, Mali

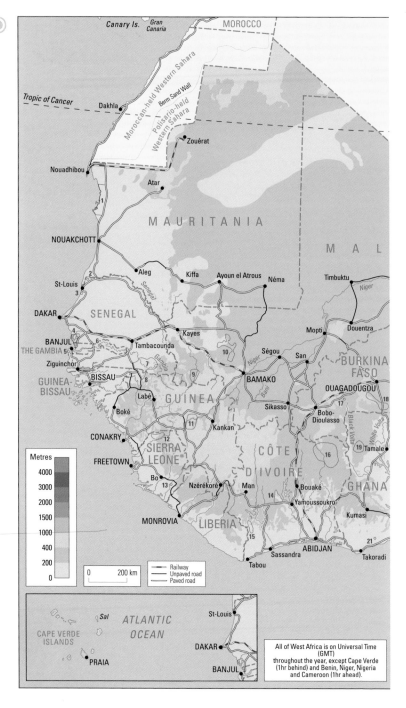

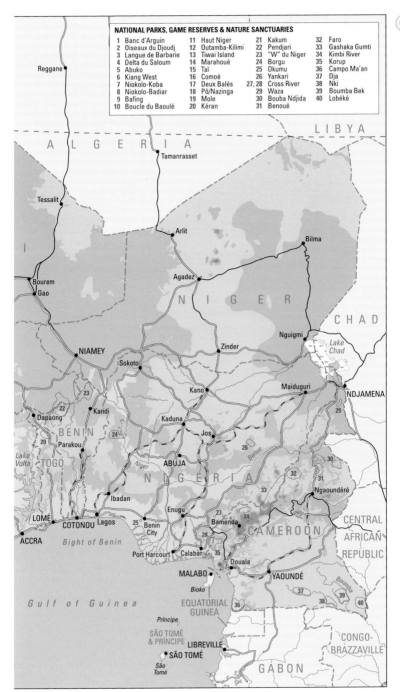

NATIONAL PARKS, GAME RESERVES & NATURE SANCTUARIES

1	Banc d'Arguin	11	Haut Niger	21	Kakum
2	Oiseaux du Djoudj	12	Outamba-Kilimi	22	Pendjari
3	Langue de Barbarie	13	Tiwai Island	23	"W" du Niger
4	Delta du Saloum	14	Marahoué	24	Borgu
5	Abuko	15	Taï	25	Okumu
6	Kiang West	16	Comoé	26	Yankari
7	Niokolo-Koba	17	Deux Balés	27, 28	Cross River
8	Niokolo-Badiar	18	Pô/Nazinga	29	Waza
9	Bafing	19	Mole	30	Bouba Ndjida
10	Boucle du Baoulé	20	Kéran	31	Benoué

32	Faro
33	Gashaka Gumti
34	Kimbi River
35	Korup
36	Campo Ma'an
37	Dja
38	Nki
39	Boumba Bek
40	Lobéké

Introduction to

West Africa

The physical and cultural diversity of West Africa would be hard to exaggerate. Ranging from shifting sand-dunes to dense and uncharted tropical forest, this is also one of the world's most complex regions in cultural and geopolitical terms, comprising seventeen countries, from tiny Gambia to giant Nigeria, with a total area and population not far off that of the United States. Every country has distinctive attributes and attractions, and whether you get to know just one or travel widely across the region, West Africa offers opportunities for discovery and true adventure which are increasingly hard to find elsewhere.

 Most West African countries are fragile entities, blocks of territory divided up at the whim or convenience of the colonial powers – Britain, France, Germany and Portugal. With the exception of Liberia, none of them are more than two generations old as modern nation-states, and many are riven by traditional ethnic divisions that often set the interior apart from the more prosperous coastal regions. As well as one or more official languages, most have lingua-franca trading languages and a multiplicity of tribal languages, often transcending borders and more meaningful to people than the country on their ID cards. For behind the mosaic of modern states lies a more organic pattern – the West Africa of old nations built over hundreds of years, the societies the Europeans began to infiltrate in the sixteenth century and came to dominate by the end of the nineteenth. This was the West Africa of the Mali and Songhai empires; the Yoruba city-states and Hausa emirates of Nigeria; the Mossi kingdoms of Burkina Faso; the Asante empire in Ghana; the Wolof states of Senegal; the Muslim theocracy of Fouta Djalon in Guinea; the Bamiléké chiefdoms of Cameroon; and many more. From this older perspective, the countries of today, granted their independence between 1957 and 1975, are imposters, fixed in place by European powers. Although the national borders are established, and nationalism is a part of each country's social fabric, the richness and variety of West Africa only comes into

focus with some understanding of its historical past, and one of the aims of this guide is to bring that depth of culture to the fore.

Some of the biggest pleasures of West Africa, however, are the small things. You'll encounter a degree of good humour, vitality and openness which can make the relatively cold insularity of Western cultures seem absurd. Entering a shop or starting a conversation with a stranger without proper greetings and hand-shaking becomes inconceivable. If you stumble in the street, passers-by will tell you "sorry" or some similar expression of condolence for which no adequate translation exists in English. You're never ignored in West Africa; you say hello a hundred times a day.

This intimacy – a sense of barriers coming down – sharpens the most everyday events and eases the more mundane hardships. There's no question, travel itself is rarely easy. Going by bus or shared taxi, you'll be crushed for hours, subjected to mysterious delays and halts at police roadblocks, jolted over potholes, and left in strange towns in the middle of the night. The sheer physicality never lets up: cold water, dry skin and clean clothes take on the status of unattainable luxuries.

You can travel in more comfortable conditions, certainly, by hiring an air-conditioned 4x4

Fact file

• West Africa's 17 nations cover a total **area** of 6.5 million square kilometres – roughly the same area as the contiguous USA, minus Texas. The total **population** of the region is around 250 million people, giving an average density of just 38 people per square kilometre – a little higher than the USA, but way below European or Asian averages. Nearly half of all West Africans are Nigerians, and many smaller countries have populations no greater than a large metropolitan area in Europe or North America.

• Most West Africans scrape a living from **subsistence agriculture**. The region has few **exports**: oil is the principal revenue-earner for Nigeria; cocoa and gold are very important for Ghana; several countries have phosphate reserves; Sierra Leone's brutal civil war was about control of its diamond fields; Mali, Burkina and Benin rely on the cotton crop; Niger has uranium.

• Chronic **indebtedness** is common to the whole region, which owes a total of something over $75 billion to rich world lenders. Yet put in the global perspective, this figure – which averages out to more than $300 for every adult and child – is equivalent to just two months of the USA's annual defence expenditure for 2007 of $450 billion.

• While the region has seen economic improvements in the 1990s, **living standards** have fallen over the last decade in Cameroon, Guinea-Bissau, Liberia, Niger, Nigeria, Sierra Leone and Togo – the same countries which have endured the worst periods of undemocratic rule since the early 1990s. On the other hand, Benin, Cape Verde, Ghana, Mali and Senegal have led the way with relatively fair, multiparty elections.

.e with a driver, by flying whenever possible and by only staying in towns
good hotels. But never has a "Rough Guide" been more appropriate:
just cannot buy yourself insulation from West Africa's realities, fortunately
perhaps. Whether you pay a lot or a little, travel can often feel like one big
breakdown, with things confusingly delayed, mysteriously missing or just not
happening, interrupted by sporadic bursts of progress. And you can be so focused
on the mechanics of travel that you miss experiencing the place, so that the "real"
West Africa might sometimes seem elusive.

The material hardships do provide a background, however, against which
every observation and experience stands out with clarity. Once you get used
to the practicalities, the sensuous impact of Africa is undeniable: the brilliance
of red earth and emerald vegetation in the forest areas; the intricate smells of
food cooking, charcoal smoke and damp soil; the towering clouds that fill the
skies at the start of the rains; the villages of sun-baked mud houses, smoothed
and moulded together like pottery; the singing rhythm of voices speaking tonal
languages; and the cool half-hour before dawn on the banks of the Niger, when
the soft clunk of cowbells rises in a haze of dust from the watering herds. These
are the images that stay, long after the horrendous journeys and delays have
become amusing anecdotes.

The Niger River

The Niger – at 4030km Africa's
third longest river after the
Nile and the Congo – rises in
the hilly country on the border
between Sierra Leone and
Guinea. Already a large river as
it flows north through Guinea, it
spreads in Mali into innumerable
shallow watercourses to create
a vast inland delta. The river
then reaches the very fringes
of the Sahara in northern Mali,

where immense sand-dunes rise on the riverbank behind snorting hippos,
before turning south to flow determinedly through Niger and down to its true
delta, the vast expanse of mangroves and creeks in southern Nigeria.

The Niger is the only West African river with a highly developed trading
economy reliant upon its annual flood: much of Mali is utterly dominated by
this seasonal cycle and during the short high-water season after the rains,
the river is a pulsing artery between Bamako and Gao. Many visitors take
the opportunity to travel on the river for a few days – an experience that is
nothing if not memorable, and can be enchanting if you're lucky. Pressure on
the upper reaches of the river and its tributaries, however, for irrigation and
hydroelectricity, are having a serious impact on river transport, as it becomes
too shallow to navigate.

What to eat – and what to avoid

West African food and drink is, for the most part, fairly familiar and, where not, it's easy to get used to. Chillies are used widely but sauces are not usually fearsomely hot. Most of the tropical fruits you'd expect are widely available (see the colour section on food plants and fruit). Rice or a root crop is the staple diet, traditionally eaten around the communal bowl, accompanied by vegetables and protein sources – fish, chicken, mutton, beef or bush meat – as available. Bush meat is the term for the products of the hunt, and

usually means cane rat (a large herbivorous rodent), gazelle, or monkey – though occasionally snails and other invertebrates make an appearance.

In recent years, monkeys and apes have been massively over-exploited as a ready market for dried and smoked bush meat has emerged in the cities, and even overseas. Not only is improperly prepared primate meat a conduit for potentially lethal epidemics, but the pressure on primate populations and habitats, even within protected areas, is rapidly leading to a crisis over the future of many species. Just as you wouldn't buy ivory carvings, it's best to avoid eating monkey meat. For full food and drink information, see p.57.

The geographical picture

With the exception of the extreme north of Mauritania and Mali, the whole of West Africa lies entirely in the tropics. Physically, the region consists predominantly of **savannah**, gently undulating plains of tree-scattered grasslands. As you head north, the vegetation thins and the patches of sand grow larger as you traverse the **Sahel** – an Arabic word meaning edge or coast, referring to the fringes of the Sahara desert. The **Sahara** accounts for much of the three northernmost countries of the region, Mauritania, Mali and Niger.

Topographically, although most countries have their **highlands**, these are generally rugged hills rather than mountain ranges. The most mountainous parts of West Africa are Guinea's **Fouta Djalon**, Niger's **Aïr Massif**, and the highlands of eastern Nigeria and western Cameroon, where **Mount Cameroon** peaks at a respectable 4000m and the summit, close to the equator, is usually icy. The big river of West Africa is the **Niger**, which flows in a

▼ Cape Verde coastline

How far, how fast?

The first recommendation is to give yourself time. While it's easy to plan an optimistic itinerary covering a large part of West Africa in a few weeks, this is an immense region with poor communications, and you should always assume journeys will take longer than the map might suggest. Moreover, the rewards become thinner the faster you go, and beyond a certain pace, the point of being there is lost in the pursuit of the next goal. While it may be hard to stop moving completely or limit yourself to a small corner, that's exactly the way to get the most out of your trip – and incidentally also gives you the chance to put something back in. In such a poor region, the idea of reciprocity is one worth keeping. Haste and intolerance tend to lead to disaster: patience and generosity always pay off.

By far the most satisfying way of visiting West Africa is overland, traversing the yawning expanse of the Sahara, arriving in the dry northern reaches of the Sahel – these days most likely in Mauritania – to the ravishing shock of an alien culture, and then adapting to a new climate, new landscapes and new ways of behaving. A popular and viable route starts in Dakar or Banjul, heads east to Bamako on a paved road and turns south through Burkina Faso and Ghana to Accra for the flight home. If you don't intend to take in Senegal or The Gambia, allow a week to ten days from arrival on the west coast to arrival in Bamako and at least another four weeks to take in some of Mali, Burkina and Ghana. If you're flying out to the Cape Verde Islands or travelling in Guinea, Guinea-Bissau or Sierra Leone, allow at least two weeks extra for each country. Senegal, Burkina Faso and Ghana are relatively predictable and you can get anywhere in these countries in a couple of days. In Mauritania, Mali and Niger, visits to the desert need plenty of flexibility. Togo and Benin are straightforward enough, with main roads getting to most parts, as is Nigeria, which has a well-developed transport infrastructure. Finally, Cameroon is much more variable, with speedy travel and terrific delays quite possible on the same route, the latter particularly frequent if you head into the remote forest regions of the southeast.

If you're travelling alone – and it's really the best way if you want to get to know West Africa rather than your travelling companions – it may be useful to know about the main travellers' crossroads in the region, where you might team up for a while or swap experiences: these are Nouadhibou at the edge of the desert, Banjul in The Gambia, the Basse Casamance district in Senegal, Bamako and Mopti in Mali, Bobo-Dioulasso in Burkina Faso, Cotonou in Benin, Accra – or virtually anywhere west along the coast – in Ghana, and Limbé or Maroua in Cameroon.

▲ Tuareg camels, Mali

huge arc from the border of Sierra Leone, through Guinea and Mali to the very fringes of the Sahara before turning south through Nigeria and into the Atlantic. Among other notable rivers are the **Senegal**, which separates that country from Mauritania and Mali; the **Gambia**, flowing through Senegal and The Gambia; the **Black Volta**, **White Volta** and **Pendjari**, which flow into Ghana's vast artificial **Lake Volta**, behind the Akosombo dam; and the **Benue**, which flows down from northern Cameroon to join the Niger in central Nigeria.

As for the scenic environment, expectations of tropical forest are usually disappointed, at least to begin with. While the natural vegetation across the whole southern coastal belt is **rainforest** – with a gap in the Ghana-Togo area where grasslands come down to the coast – by far the commonest scene in the densely populated parts is a desolate, bush-stripped landscape where dust and bare earth figure heavily. True rainforest is still present in scattered parts of Ghana, Guinea, Sierra Leone, Liberia, Côte d'Ivoire and southeast Nigeria and it fills much of southern Cameroon. Guinea also features beautiful savannah lands, as does Burkina Faso. Along the coast, creeks and mangroves make many parts inaccessible, though there are some excellent beaches.

Where to go

Choosing where to go is no easy task: the region offers so much and Africa is likely to confound many of your expectations and assumptions. In the main section of the Guide, the individual country introductions and highlights boxes give an idea of what to look forward to. However, at the risk of reinforcing stereotypes, it's possible to make a few

Getting over culture shock

The desperate poverty of West Africa may come as a shock, especially if you fly in to a big city and have little experience of the developing world: try to give yourself a day or two to adjust before plunging into exhausting work or travels. At the same time, try not to be disappointed by the tawdry banality of the cities: countless barefoot children in cast-off clothes (often bought from second-hand clothes traders who sell the items donated to Western charities); urban roadsides ankle-deep in plastic cold-drinks bags; everything worn out and inadequate, covered in a grimy paste of dust and diesel exhaust. But then, as you leave the city, be prepared to have your breath taken away: by termite mounds, baobab trees and traditional architecture; or by stands of rainforest resounding with birdsong and flecked with confetti-like butterflies; and by tantalizing side-roads of red earth disappearing into the bush. At some point, you should head off down one of those and explore off the beaten track. Once you get a few kilometres away from the towns and main roads, a much more satisfying version of West Africa starts to appear, one in which people have plenty of time, the old ways are respected, and traditional dress and culture much more the norm. Every country has small ethnic groups who pursue lifestyles somewhat removed from modern society – see the individual chapters for details on visiting.

generalizations about the feel of the countries.

Of the eleven Francophone, **ex-French colonies**, the two nations most dominated by French culture and language are Senegal and Cameroon, and their relatively Westernized cities are inclined to be hustly. **Senegal** is an obvious choice as a base from which to launch travels: facilities are much better than in many parts of the region and the verdant **Basse Casamance** district has a network of village-based accommodation. **Cameroon** – which is English-speaking in the west – blends magnificent scenery and national parks with an extraordinary richness of culture, running the whole African gamut from "Pygmy" hunting camps to Arabic-speaking trading towns, and taking in the colourful kingdoms of the western highlands. **Côte d'Ivoire**, or Ivory Coast – formerly the first choice in the region for French expat postings – has been traumatized by its north–south civil war and, although its mélange of traditional and modern, African and French, is a compelling mix, it cannot be recommended as a destination until unity and reconciliation are fully established, and it's not covered in this edition.

Vast, land-locked **Mali** is blessed with the great inland delta of the Niger River and, again, striking cultural contrasts – the old **Islamic cities** of Gao, Timbuktu and Djenné (on, or near the river), and the magnificent **Dogon country** along the rocky Bandiagara escarpment.

Music

West Africa's musical traditions have become world-famous through the voices and CDs of Youssou N'Dour and Salif Keita. From Senegal's powerful *mbalax* and home-grown hip-hop to the soaring sound of the guitar bands of Mali and Guinea; from Ghana's sweet-natured highlife to Nigeria's percussion-based musical steam engines, *fuji* and *juju*, West Africa is a music hothouse. This rich culture is not difficult to track down – relatively casual or domestic drumming for example is almost a constant accompaniment, especially in rural areas. The role of *griot* or praise-singer is widespread, the professional musician caste always on the scene at parties, particularly weddings and funerals. All over the Mande cultural realm (in other words from Mali to southern Senegal and across most of Guinea and northern Côte d'Ivoire), the griot is known as *jali* or *jeli*, and plays the *kora*, a lustrous-sounding instrument in the harp family. You should also listen out for the *bala*, or *balafon*, a large wooden xylophone with gourd resonators. In the way of musicians the world over, the old repertoire of Mande *kora* songs has been modernized and expanded for guitar, drums and synth.

Late night in any city from Wednesday to Sunday, and especially at the end of the month when workers have been paid, you should be able to find clubs with live music, often starting after midnight. Dakar, Bamako and Lagos are three of the most promising cities to explore, where you can see the stars on their home turf.

Other Francophone countries include the narrow strips of **Togo** and **Benin**, the latter being especially easy-going; the laid-back, former revolutionary republic of **Burkina Faso**; and the remote and dramatic expanses of **Mauritania** and **Niger**. Perhaps the most impressive of the *pays francophones* is the republic of **Guinea**, with only a thin intrusion of European culture, a low population density and superb landscapes.

Four of the West African countries are **former British colonies**, divided from each other by the speed of the French invasion in the nineteenth century. **The**

▼ Timbuktou

13

Gambia is an easy place to set out from, a tiny holiday destination that offers a very accessible gateway to the region. The distinctive personality of **Ghana** provides flamboyant cultural experiences: its splendid, palm-lined coast, dotted with old European slave-trading forts, a handful of good wildlife sanctuaries and government support to the tourist industry, make it one of West Africa's most promising countries for travel. **Sierra Leone** is also hugely likeable, and although it has always been a more demanding destination, it has some of the best beaches in the world – only minutes away from the raffish tumble of Freetown – and seems to have put its years of civil war firmly behind it. **Nigeria**, despite an ostensibly democratic government, seems barely aware of its tourism potential. There are, however, big travel incentives inland – in the fine uplands of the plateau, the old cities of the north and the wildlife reserves in the east, to mention just three areas. It's a difficult country to come to terms

Religion

Although it's easy enough to observe that Islam, Christianity and "animism" – a catchall term for original traditional religious practice – are the three religions of West Africa, the facts on the ground are more complicated. Islam or Christianity often overlie the older religion, with elements of both incorporated into religious practices. The most devoutly Muslim countries are Mauritania, Senegal, The Gambia, Mali and Niger, where adherence ranges from 85 to 99 percent. At the other extreme, in Ghana, Togo, Benin and Cameroon, Muslims make up around 20 percent or less of the population. Christianity has made the biggest inroads in Sierra Leone, Togo, Nigeria and Cameroon, where 30 to 40 percent are church-goers, and in Liberia, which is more than 60 percent Christian. Nigeria is the one country where fundamentalist Islam is gaining ground, several northern states in the republic having instituted sharia law – though still with a fairly light touch – much to the consternation of the federal government.

Traditional religious practice varies greatly between ethnic groups, but a distant supreme being is the norm, combined with a multitude of spiritual entities, represented by, or actually living in, parts of the natural world – animal and plant species, hills or caves, rivers and lakes. At the same time, people's ancestors are part of the community in a way that Westerners find hard to grasp. They have control over people's lives, and to ignore their needs – assuaged through regular sacrifices, celebrations and libations – is as risky as ignoring the requirements of a demanding grandfather or grandmother.

with, but once you're away from Lagos with its unnerving reputation, there's no denying the overall ease and even tranquillity which accompany travels here. The same cannot be said for **Liberia** – a former vassal state of the USA, nominally independent since 1847 – which is struggling to recover after fifteen years of conflict, confusion and economic breakdown. Like Côte d'Ivoire, it has been omitted from this edition.

The **former Portuguese colonies** are West Africa's least-known destinations, though that is changing fast in the case of the Cape Verde Islands. These beguiling, volcanic outcrops and desert islands in the mid-Atlantic have a scenery, lifestyle

▲ Tellem architecture, Youga-Dogourou, Mali

and growing watersports reputation, that make them hard to leave. **Guinea-Bissau** has its own island highlights, the Bijagós – luxuriant green forests in the warm, inshore sea, as different from the Cape Verdes as it's possible to imagine.

When to go

The big consideration is humidity and particularly the timing of the rainy seasons, rather than the heat: temperatures, in fact, only occasionally climb very much higher than you might experience in Europe and only rarely match the sheer hell of a hot day in Washington DC or Houston.

Broadly, the **rains** come mostly between April and October. Although travel is rarely out of the question during the rains, it's obviously not an ideal time, as minor roads, which are usually just dirt tracks, can become quagmires, and transport may grind to a halt. **Climate change** seems to be having an impact, as the devastating floods of 2007 attest, but the seasonality of the climate

Wildlife

In general the central and eastern parts of West Africa have better game-viewing opportunities than the far west, but you won't see many of the large mammals typical of the African plains – such as elephant, giraffe, buffalo and lion. They were fairly widespread until the early twentieth century, but today they can only realistically be seen in protected reserves and national parks, where their survival is precarious. The primates (West Africa has two dozen species of monkey and ape) are also threatened – by bush-meat hunting and habitat destruction – but you're bound to see monkeys at some point in your travels and there are districts where baboons are a common sight at the roadside. Gorilla-tracking in southeast Nigeria and Cameroon is still barely established and there aren't as yet any habituated groups. Otherwise, big-animal experiences include camels, always domesticated and usually hobbled to stop them straying, which you'll soon grow accustomed to seeing all across the Sahel; hippos, which are quite noticeably dispersed in suitable habitats across the whole region; and, surprisingly perhaps, crocodiles, which you can see in every country except Cape Verde, either in sacred crocodile pools, where the reptiles are pampered and commonly believed to bring good luck, or on riverbanks, where you should beware of them (and hippos). If the large wildlife is slightly thin on the ground, West Africa's birdlife is stunningly rich and rewarding, as is the region's profusion of lizards, frogs, and harmless invertebrates, from alien-looking mantids to spectacular butterflies. For more on the region's fauna and national parks, see p.75.

is broadly unaltered. If you're planning extended overland travels of several months, the best time to go is September, as you can be pretty sure of dry weather everywhere from mid-November to the end of January. However, it's as well to be aware of the unpleasant, dust-laden **harmattan** wind that blows southwest across the region, directly out of the Sahara, during the dry season, especially from November to March, and which can bring a miasma-like haze to the landscape for days on end.

Basics

Basics

Getting there 19

Red tape and visas 29

Info and media 33

Maps and books 34

Health 37

Costs, money, banks 45

Getting around 48

Accommodation 54

Eating and drinking 57

Communications 61

Public holidays and festivals 63

Crime and safety 64

Cultural hints 68

Living and working in West Africa 70

Travellers with disabilities 71

Gender issues and sexual attitudes 72

Wildlife and national parks 75

People and languages 77

Travellers' French 82

Practicalities 87

Getting there

The most straightforward – and usually the least expensive – way to get to West Africa is by air. If you have the time, though, making your way partly overland, either with your own vehicle or using a combination of public and any other available transport along the way, offers real rewards of its own and can be an unbeatable introduction to the region. For more local detail, including arrivals from neighbouring countries, see the individual country chapters.

Airline **seasons** for West Africa vary considerably from country to country but most fares don't vary much with the time of year. Most student and youth fares, however, do have a seasonal structure to tie in with summer and Christmas holiday periods. Book as far in advance as you can: some routes get full to capacity at peak periods, especially Christmas, and discounted seats are often snapped up quickly.

You can sometimes cut costs by going through a **specialist flight agent** – either a consolidator, who buys up blocks of tickets from the airlines and sells them at a discount, or a **discount agent**, who in addition to dealing with discounted flights, may also offer special student and youth fares and a range of other travel-related services. Some agents specialize in **charter flights**, which may be cheaper than anything available on a scheduled flight, but departure dates are fixed and the range of destinations very limited.

Depending on where you're starting out from, you may find it cheaper to pick up a **package deal** from a tour operator than to book flights and accommodation separately, even if you only stay in your pre-booked hotel for a night or two before setting off elsewhere. "**Overland tours**" – a catch-all which covers most of the organized holidays that don't *feel* like packages – are covered separately on p.23. Not all of them are overland the entire way – the "fly-out, tour-around-by-truck, fly-back" option is increasingly popular.

Flying **"open jaw"** – out to one city and back from another – is sometimes possible but usually more expensive.

Flights from the UK, Ireland and Europe

The most reliable, nonstop **scheduled flights** from London to West Africa are with British Airways, which serves Dakar, Accra, Lagos and Abuja; Astraeus, flying to Accra, Freetown or Sal (the schedule is sometimes cancelled); Virgin Atlantic, flying to Lagos; and the various holiday airlines flying to The Gambia and Cape Verde. If you're flying to Accra and are willing to put up with patchy punctuality and service, Ghana International Airlines is reasonably good value.

Otherwise you'll need to fly via **mainland Europe** or an African air-travel hub. The airline with the busiest West Africa schedule is Air France, which serves the major Francophone cities, routing all flights through Paris, but Brussels Airlines and Royal Air Maroc are also useful. The French charter company Point-Afrique is a useful, cheaper alternative and offers flexible open-jaw arrangements to unusual destinations such as Gao, Mopti and Ouagadougou.

Generally, return economy fares fall somewhere between £350 and £750, with one-ways rarely less than £200, but charter flight deals, with or without an accommodation package, can be cheaper. The only West African country served by regular **charter flights** from the UK is The Gambia, with services from London Gatwick, Bristol, Manchester and East Midlands. Fares range from £170–625, depending on the season and the length of stay. Special promotions are sometimes introduced to fill seats, and these can be really excellent value. All this makes The Gambia a reasonably conven-ient entry point to the region. The Gambia is also a good exit point: you can buy one-way tickets for charter flights back to the UK from specialist tour company The Gambia Experience.

There are no direct flights from **Ireland** to West Africa: the best routings are via Paris on Air France, via London on British Airways or via Amsterdam on KLM (overnight stay sometimes required).

Flights from the US and Canada

Currently the only **direct flights from North America** to West Africa are from Boston to Praia with TACV Cabo Verde Airlines, from New York to Dakar with South African Airways or from New York to Accra with Delta. There's not much to choose between the fares for direct flights and those that involve a change of plane, and possibly a stopover, in Europe or North Africa. Typical return fares fall in the US$1200–2200/Can$1260–2300 range; to reduce costs, try combining a discounted flight to London with a cheap charter flight to Banjul.

If you plan to break your journey, remember to check the luggage limits for each leg – they are usually less generous on Europe-to-Africa flights than trans-Atlantic.

Fly less – stay longer! Travel and climate change

Climate change is the single biggest issue facing our planet. It is caused by a build-up in the atmosphere of carbon dioxide and other greenhouse gases, which are emitted by many sources – including planes. Already, flights account for around 3–4 percent of human-induced global warming: that figure may sound small, but it is rising year on year and threatens to counteract the progress made by reducing greenhouse emissions in other areas.

Rough Guides regard travel, overall, as a global benefit, and feel strongly that the advantages to developing economies are important, as are the opportunities for greater contact and awareness among peoples. But we all have a responsibility to limit our personal "carbon footprint". That means giving thought to how often we fly and what we can do to redress the harm our trips create.

Flying and climate change

Pretty much every form of motorized travel generates CO_2, but planes are particularly bad offenders, releasing large volumes of greenhouse gases at altitudes where their impact is far more harmful. Flying also allows us to travel much further than we would contemplate doing by road or rail, so the emissions attributable to each passenger become truly shocking. For example, one person taking a return flight between Europe and California produces the equivalent impact of 2.5 tonnes of CO_2 – similar to the yearly output of the average UK car.

Less harmful planes may evolve but it will be decades before they replace the current fleet – which could be too late to avoid climate chaos. In the meantime, there are limited options for concerned travellers: to reduce the amount we travel by air (take fewer trips, stay longer!), to avoid night flights (when plane contrails trap heat from Earth but can't reflect sunlight back to space), and to make the trips we do take "climate neutral" via a carbon offset scheme.

Carbon offset schemes

Offset schemes run by ⓦ www.climatecare.org, ⓦ www.carbonneutral.com and others allow you to "neutralize" the greenhouse gases you are responsible for releasing. Their websites have simple calculators that let you work out the impact of any flight. Once that's done, you can pay to fund projects that will reduce future carbon emissions by an equivalent amount (such as the distribution of low-energy light bulbs and cooking stoves in developing countries). Please take the time to visit our website and make your trip climate neutral:

ⓦ www.roughguides.com/climatechange

Flights from Australia and New Zealand

From Australia and New Zealand, you're best advised to fly **via Europe** for the best choice of routes to West Africa. An alternative is to fly via Johannesburg, which is served by direct flights from Sydney and Perth with Qantas and South African Airways; then in Jo'burg you can connect to a South African Airways flight to Accra, Dakar or Lagos.

Flights from the rest of Africa

Travelling between West African countries is covered in the Basics section of each chapter in this book.

From **southern Africa**, the most direct and reliable routes to West Africa are from Johannesburg to Accra, Dakar or Lagos with South African Airways. Cameroon Airlines flies from Johannesburg to Douala, with connecting flights to Bamako, Cotonou and Lagos.

From **East Africa**, Nairobi is the natural hub for flights; Kenya Airways fly from here to Accra, Bamako, Cotonou, Dakar, Douala, Freetown, Lagos, Monrovia and Yaoundé, and Cameroon Airlines run a service to Douala via Kinshasa. Ethiopian Airlines fly from Addis Ababa to Bamako and Douala.

From **North Africa**, Royal Air Maroc connects Casablanca to Accra, Bamako, Conakry, Cotonou, Dakar, Lomé, Niamey and Nouakchott; Tunisair has a direct flight from Tunis to Dakar and Nouakchott; EgyptAir flies from Cairo to Accra and Lagos; and Afriqiyah flies from Tripoli to a number of West African capitals.

From the **Canary Islands**, TACV runs a weekly flight from Las Palmas in Gran Canaria to Praia, Cape Verde.

Airlines

Afriqiyah Libya ☏ +218 21/444 9734, ⊛ www .afriqiyah.aero. Flights via Tripoli to Accra, Bamako, Cotonou, Douala, Kano, Lomé, Lagos, Niamey and Ouagadougou.

Air Canada ☏ 1-888/247-2262, UK ☏ 0871/220 1111, Republic of Ireland ☏ 01/679 3958, Australia ☏ 1300/655 767, New Zealand ☏ 0508/747 767; ⊛ www.aircanada.com. Flights from Canada to

Europe, with connections to West Africa with partner airlines.

Air France US ☏ 1-800/237-2747, Canada ☏ 1-800/667-2747, UK ☏ 0870/142 4343, Australia ☏ 1300/390 190, SA ☏ 0861/340 340; ⊛ www.airfrance.com. Flights from North American, European and Australasian cities via Paris to Bamako, Conakry, Cotonou, Dakar, Douala, Lagos, Lomé, Niamey, Nouakchott, Ouagadougou and Yaoundé.

Air Mauritanie France ☏ +33 1/825 825 496, ⊛ www.airmauritanie.mr. Flights from Paris Charles de Gaulle to Nouakchott, with connections to Nouadhibou, Bamako and Dakar, plus a service from Las Palmas to Nouadhibou and to Nouakchott.

Air New Zealand Australia ☏ 13 24 76, New Zealand ☏ 0800/737 000, UK ☏ 0800/028 4149, US ☏ 1-800-262/1234, Canada ☏ 1-800-663/5494; ⊛ www.airnz.co.nz. Flights from Auckland to London and Europe for connections to West Africa.

Air Sénégal International France ☏ +33 1/56 64 14 00, ⊛ www.air-senegal-international.com. Flights to Dakar from Paris Orly, Marseille, Lyon, Brussels, Madrid and Johannesburg.

Alitalia US ☏ 1-800/223-5730, Canada ☏ 1-800/361-8336, UK ☏ 0870/544 8259, Republic of Ireland ☏ 01/677 5171, New Zealand ☏ 09/308 3357, SA ☏ 11/721 4500; ⊛ www.alitalia.com. Flights via Milan to Accra, Dakar and Lagos.

American ☏ 1-800/433-7300, UK ☏ 0845/7789 789, Republic of Ireland ☏ 01/602 0550, Australia ☏ 1800/673 486, New Zealand ☏ 0800/445 442, ⊛ www.aa.com. Flights from the US to Europe, for connections to West Africa on partner airlines.

Astraeus US ☏ 410/659-7776, UK ☏ 01293/874380 or ☏ 01293/579000; ⊛ www .flystar.com. Flights from London Gatwick to Accra, Freetown, Monrovia and, in Cape Verde, Sal, Boa Vista and São Vicente.

Bellview UK ☏ 020/7372 3770, ⊛ www .flybellviewair.com. Nigerian airline flying from London and Johannesburg to Lagos and Douala, with onward flights to Abuja, Accra, Banjul, Conakry, Dakar, Freetown, Kano and Monrovia.

British Airways US and Canada ☏ 1-800/ AIRWAYS, UK ☏ 0870/850 9850, Republic of Ireland ☏ 1890/626 747, Australia ☏ 1300/767 177, New Zealand ☏ 09/966 9777, South Africa ☏ 114/418 600, ⊛ www.ba.com. Direct flights from London to Abuja, Accra, Dakar and Lagos, with onward flights to Freetown.

Brussels US ☏ 1-516/740-5200, Canada ☏ 1-866/308-2230, UK ☏ 0870/735 2345, Republic of Ireland ☏ 01/844 6006, Australia ☏ 02/9767 4305; ⊛ www.brusselsairlines.com. Flights to Banjul, Conakry, Dakar, Douala, Freetown, Monrovia and Yaoundé via Brussels.

Cameroon France ☏1/43 12 30 10. Operates services to Douala from Paris, Kinshasa, Nairobi and Johannesburg, with connections to Bamako, Cotonou and Lagos.

Condor Germany ☏+49 1805/576 7757, ⓦwww.condor.com. No service from London, but will take bookings for their flights from Frankfurt to Banjul and Sal.

Continental US and Canada ☏1-800/523-3273, UK ☏0845/607 6760, Republic of Ireland ☏1890/925 252, Australia ☏02/9244 2242, New Zealand ☏09/308 3350, International ☏1800/231 0856; ⓦwww.continental.com. Flights from the US to Europe, for connections to West Africa with KLM.

Delta US and Canada ☏1-800/221-1212, UK ☏0845/600 0950, Republic of Ireland ☏1850/882 031 or 01/407 3165, Australia ☏1300/302 849, New Zealand ☏09/977 2232; ⓦwww.delta.com. Flights from JFK to Accra, and also from North America to Paris, to connect with Air France services to West Africa.

EgyptAir US ☏1-800/334-6787 or 1-212/315-0900, Canada ☏1-416/960-0009, UK ☏020/7734 2343, Australia ☏1300/309 767, SA ☏11/8804 1267/8/9; ⓦwww.egyptair.com.eg. Flights via Cairo to Accra and Lagos.

Ethiopian US ☏1-800/445-2733, UK ☏020/8987 7000; ⓦwww.ethiopianairlines.com. Flights from New York, Washington and London via Addis Ababa to Bamako and Dakar.

First Choice UK ☏0871/200 7799, ⓦwww.firstchoice.co.uk. Flights from London Gatwick, Bristol, East Midlands and Manchester to Banjul.

Ghana International UK ☏020/7100 1165, ⓦwww.fly-ghana.com. Direct flights from London Gatwick to Accra, with a connecting flight to Lagos.

Iberia US ☏1-800/772-4642, UK ☏0870/609 0500, Republic of Ireland ☏0818/462 000, SA ☏011/884 5909; ⓦwww.iberia.com. Flights from New York, Chicago, Miami and London to Dakar via Madrid and Las Palmas.

Kenya US and Canada ☏1-866/536-9224, Australia ☏02/9767 4310, UK ☏01784/888 222, SA ☏11/881 9795; ⓦwww.kenya-airways.com. Flies from Nairobi to Accra, Bamako, Cotonou, Dakar, Douala, Freetown, Lagos, Monrovia and Yaoundé.

KLM US and Canada ☏1-800/225-2525, UK ☏0870/507 4074, Republic of Ireland ☏1850/747 400, Australia ☏1300/392 192, New Zealand ☏09/921 6040, SA ☏11/961 6727; ⓦwww.klm.com. Flights from Amsterdam to Abuja, Accra, Bamako, Dakar, Kano, Lagos and Yaoundé.

Monarch UK ☏0870/040 5040, ⓦwww.flymonarch.com. Flights from London Gatwick to Banjul.

MyTravel UK ☏0870/241 5333, ⓦwww.mytravel.com. Flights from London Gatwick and Manchester to Banjul.

Point Afrique France ☏+33 4/75 97 20 40, ⓦwww.point-afrique.com. Handy travel agency operating their own charter flights from France to West Africa, mainly in the winter. Routes include Paris to Atar (Mauritania), Bamako, Dakar, Gao (Mali), Mopti (Mali), Niamey, Ouagadougou and Cap Skirring (Senegal). They also have a convenient, inexpensive service for obtaining visas.

Qantas US and Canada ☏1-800/227-4500, UK ☏0845/774 7767, Republic of Ireland ☏01/407 3278, Australia ☏13 13 13, New Zealand ☏0800/808 767 or 09/357 8900, SA ☏11/441 8550; ⓦwww.qantas.com. Flights to Europe or South Africa for connections to West Africa.

Royal Air Maroc US ☏1-800/344-6726, Canada ☏1-800/361 7508, UK ☏0207/307 5800; ⓦwww.royalairmaroc.com. Flights from New York, Montréal and London via Casablanca to Accra, Bamako, Conakry, Cotonou, Dakar, Lomé, Niamey and Nouakchott.

South African US and Canada ☏1-800/722-9675, UK ☏0870/747 1111, Australia ☏1800/221 699, New Zealand ☏09/977 2237, SA ☏11/978 1111; ⓦwww.flysaa.com. Flights from New York to Dakar and from Johannesburg to Accra, Dakar and Lagos.

Swiss US ☏1-877/3797-947, Canada ☏1-877/559-7947, UK ☏0845/601 0956, Republic of Ireland ☏1890/200 515, Australia ☏1300/724 666, New Zealand ☏09/977 2238, SA ☏0860/040 506; ⓦwww.swiss.com. Services via Zurich to Douala and Yaoundé.

TACV US ☏617/472-2431, UK ☏01964/536 191, France ☏+33 1/56 79 13 13, Portugal ☏+351 21/323-0555, Cape Verde ☏+238/260 82 00. Direct flights from Boston to Praia and from London, Manchester, Lisbon, Paris and other European cities to Sal and Praia.

TAP US and Canada ☏1-800/221-7370, UK ☏0845/601 0932, Australia and NZ ☏02/9244 2344, SA ☏11/455 4907; ⓦwww.flytap.com. Flights from Lisbon to Bissau, Dakar, Praia and Sal.

Thomas Cook UK ☏0870/516 8242, ⓦwww.flythomascook.com. Flights from London Gatwick, Bristol, East Midlands and Manchester to Banjul.

Thomsonfly UK ☏0870/190 0737, ⓦwww.thomsonfly.com. Flights from London Gatwick and Manchester to Banjul (November to March) and Sal.

Tunisair UK ☏020/7734 7644, ⓦwww.tunisair.com.tn. Flies from Tunis to Nouakchott, Dakar and Bamako.

United US ☏1-800/UNITED-1, UK ☏0845/844 4777, Australia ☏13 17 77; ⓦwww.united.com.

Flights to Europe for onward connections to West Africa.

Virgin Atlantic US ☎ 1-800/821-5438, UK ☎ 0870/380 2007, Australia ☎ 1300/727 340, SA ☎ 11/340 3400; ⓦ www.virgin-atlantic.com. Flights from major US cities to London Heathrow, and from Heathrow to Lagos.

Agents

The following **general travel agents** sell flight tickets; some also holidays. For information on package-holiday specialists, see below; for information on adventure and other specialist tours, see p.24.

Africa Travel Centre UK ☎ 0845/450 1520, ⓦ www.africatravel.co.uk. Helpful and resourceful Africa specialists offering flights, packages, overland tours, books, maps and advice.

Apex Travel Republic of Ireland ☎ 01/241 8000, ⓦ www.apextravel.ie. Long-haul flight specialists.

Co-op Travel Care UK ☎ 0871 574 8762, ⓦ www.travelcareonline.com. Flights and holidays around the world.

Educational Travel Center US ☎ 1-800/747-5551 or 608/256-5551, ⓦ www.edtrav.com. Student/youth discount agent.

Flight Centres Australia ☎ 13 31 33 or 02/9235 3522, ⓦ www.flightcentre.com.au; New Zealand ☎ 0800/243 544 or 09/358 4310, ⓦ www .flightcentre.co.nz. General travel agent.

Joe Walsh Tours Republic of Ireland ☎ 01/676 0991, ⓦ www.joewalshtours.ie. General budget-fares agent.

North South Travel UK ☎ 01245/608 291, ⓦ www.northsouthtravel.co.uk. Friendly, competitive travel agency, offering discounted fares worldwide. Profits are used to support projects in the developing world, especially the promotion of sustainable tourism.

STA Travel US ☎ 1-800/781-4040, UK ☎ 0871/2300 040, Australia ☎ 134 STA, New Zealand ☎ 0800/474 400, SA ☎ 0861/781 781; ⓦ www.statravel.com. Worldwide specialists in low-cost flights and tours for students and under-26s, though other customers welcome.

Trailfinders UK ☎ 0845/058 5858, Republic of Ireland ☎ 01/677 7888, Australia ☎ 1300/780 212; ⓦ www.trailfinders.com. One of the best-informed and most efficient agents for independent travellers.

Travelbag UK ☎ 0800/804 8911, ⓦ www .travelbag.co.uk. Discount flights worldwide.

Travel Cuts Canada ☎ 1-866/246-9762, US ☎ 1-800/592-2887; ⓦ www.travelcuts.com. Canadian student-travel organization.

USIT Republic of Ireland ☎ 01/602 1600, ⓦ www .usitnow.ie. Student and youth travel specialists.

Package tour operators

The Gambia is the best-known West African **package destination** from the UK. Most travel agents will have a choice of brochures which include it, and it's a good place to go if you're looking for a short winter holiday, with plenty of sun and a low-key African atmosphere that is not over-exploited. Most departures are scheduled for November to May but a few operators offer summer departures (during the rainy season), which are generally cheaper than the winter season.

The **Cap Skiring** coast in Senegal is as popular a package destination for the French as The Gambia is for the British.

While **Cape Verde** has been attracting Italian and German holidaymakers for some years, British and Irish tourists are beginning to join them in rapidly increasing numbers, flying direct to the islands from the UK.

For information on adventure and other specialist tours, see below.

The Cape Verde Experience UK ☎ 0845/330 2046, ⓦ www.capeverdeexperience.co.uk. Cape Verde beach holidays and island-hopping tours.

Cape Verde Travel UK ☎ 0845/270 2006, ⓦ www.capeverdetravel.com. Cape Verde specialists, with a good variety of options, including some unusual places to stay.

The Gambia Experience UK ☎ 0845/330 4567, ⓦ www.gambia.co.uk. Gambia specialist with a strong commitment to the country. Clear, honest brochure including far more Gambian hotels than any other operator and, uniquely, year-round departures from Gatwick, Bristol, East Midlands and Manchester.

Overland, adventure and specialist tours

The agents and tour companies in this section typically offer "packages" which exclude flights; by making your own travel arrangements, you can join them from any point on the globe.

It can be worth investigating one of the more inexpensive expeditions advertised in the travel pages of UK and European papers. These are often just private trips hoping to minimize costs by taking others. Scrutinizing their literature gives a good indication of their probable preparedness and real know-how. If their prospectus looks cheap or hasty, forget it.

As a destination for specialist **American operators**, West Africa is little known in comparison with East and southern Africa. You will, however, find a few **"Roots" and African heritage tours** aimed directly at African-Americans.

Although West Africa is less well known for its wildlife than other parts of the continent, it's extremely attractive to ornithologists, who have a number of specialist **bird-watching trips** to choose from.

Adventure Center US ☎1-800/228-8747 or 510/654-1879, ⓦwww.adventure-center.com. Hiking and "soft adventure" specialists. Options include two weeks in Ghana ($2295) or Senegal and The Gambia ($1870), and several tours through Mali taking in Bamako, Timbuktu and the Pays Dogon ($1370–4195). Prices exclude flights.

Adventures Abroad US and Canada ☎1-800/665-3998 or 360/775-9925, UK ☎0114/247 3400, ⓦwww.adventures-abroad .com. Adventure specialists, with a good programme of small-group two- to four-week tours. Countries include Benin, Ghana, Mali, Senegal and Togo; from US$4000–7000, excluding flights.

African Trails UK ☎020/8422 5545, ⓦwww .africantrails.co.uk. From the UK to Cape Town by truck in a 23-week camping safari, driving through Mali, Burkina Faso, Ghana, Togo, Benin, Nigeria and Cameroon, with the option of extending through other parts of Africa.

Africa Travel Centre UK ☎0845/450 1520, ⓦwww.africatravel.co.uk. Agent for several overland tour companies.

Alken Tours US ☎1-800/327-9974 or 718/856-9100, ⓦwww.alkentours.com. Travel company with a specialist division for flights and trips to Africa, including heritage, ecological and cultural tours, plus bespoke itineraries.

Avian Adventures UK ☎01384/372 103, ⓦwww .avianadventures.co.uk. Small-group bird-watching trips to The Gambia and Senegal.

Batafon Arts UK ☎01273/605 791, ⓦwww .batafonarts.co.uk. Drum and dance holidays in Guinea and The Gambia.

Bicycle Africa US ☎1-206/767-0848, ⓦwww .ibike.org/bikeafrica. Easy-going small-group cycling tours that visit many West African countries between Oct & Dec.

Birdfinders UK ☎01258/839 066, ⓦwww .birdfinders.co.uk. Expertly guided bird-watching tours, including two-week trips to The Gambia, Ghana and Cameroon.

Bukima Adventure UK ☎01772/741600, Australia ☎07/4776 0062, New Zealand ☎0800/428 5462, Canada ☎604/892 2240, ⓦwww.bukima.com. 22-week trips across Africa by truck, passing through West Africa.

Dragoman Overland UK ☎01728/861 133, ⓦwww.dragoman.com. Highly experienced operator offering personal and creative extended overland journeys in purpose-built expedition vehicles, plus shorter camping safaris and trips to West African music festivals.

Dreamweaver Travel US ☎715/425-1037, ⓦwww.dreamweavertravel.net. Small community-based cultural- and adventure-travel company. West Africa offerings include trips to Niger, Cameroon and Mali's Festival au Désert.

Exodus UK ☎0845/863 9600, ⓦwww.exodus .co.uk. Environmentally and culturally aware adventure tour operator taking small groups on overland trips, including a 15-day cultural tour of Benin.

ElderTreks US and Canada ☎1-800/741-7956, UK ☎0808/234 1714; ⓦwww.eldertreks.com. Small-group adventures for the over-50s, including a three-week cultural tour of Mali and Burkina Faso (US$5595).

Explore Worldwide UK ☎0870/333 4001, ⓦwww.explore.co.uk. Interesting selection of small-group cultural tours, treks and safaris, visiting Benin, Burkina Faso, The Gambia, Ghana, Mali, Togo and Senegal; less rugged in style than some of the more youth-oriented overland operators, with hotel accommodation rather than camping in most cases.

Fulani Travel UK ☎01341/421 969. Innovative West Africa specialist with a range of tours including festivals, riding in the Dogon country, Dakar to Douala and Ghana, Togo and Benin.

Guerba UK ☎01373/826 611, ⓦwww.guerba .co.uk. One of the best adventure-travel specialists, with a great deal of African experience; options include overland trips to Timbuktu and the Festival au Désert in Mali.

Hidden Gambia UK ☎01285/861839, ⓦwww .hiddengambia.com. Unique, customized tours of coastal and upriver Gambia.

The Imaginative Traveller UK ☎0800/316 2717, ⓦwww.imaginative-traveller.com. Adventure holidays, including two-week tours of Mali, of Senegal and The Gambia, and of Ghana, Togo and Benin.

Journeys International US ☎1-800/255-8735 or 734/665-4407, ⓦwww.journeys-intl.com. Two-week guided tours of Ghana, Togo and Benin for US$4695 and of Mali for US$2650–2800 excluding flights.

Mountain Travel Sobek US ☎1-888/MTSOBEK or 1-510/594-6000, ⓦwww.mtsobek.com. Adventure-travel specialists with trips to take you well off the beaten track, getting around by a mixture of 4x4, hiking, river and camel. Options

Overlanding within West Africa

The practical information at the beginning of each country chapter has details on overland arrival **from that country's neighbours**, including transport availability, road conditions and the kind of treatment you might expect from border officials. As a general rule, borders close at dusk and sometimes on public holidays, but increasingly the busiest borders are open 24/7.

include 15 days in Mali and Burkina Faso, from US$4390, and 16 days in Ghana, Togo and Benin (from US$4190, excluding flights).
Responsible Travel UK ☎ 01273/600030, ⓦ www.responsibletravel.com. Trips and homestays that have been vetted for their sustainable tourism credentials. Burkina Faso, Cameroon, The Gambia, Ghana, Mali and Niger are among the countries covered.
Spector Travel US ☎ 617/338-0111, ⓦ www .spectortravel.com. Well-connected travel agency and flight broker, dealing only with Africa, offering cultural tours.
Turtle Tours US ☎ 888/299-1439, ⓦ www .turtletours.com. Tours to many West African countries, with a focus on tribes and cultural events.
Wilderness Travel ☎ 1-800/368-2794 or 510/558-2488, ⓦ www.wildernesstravel.com. Specialists in worldwide hiking, cultural and wildlife adventures, offering an 18-day tour of Mali and Burkina Faso ($5195), visiting the Dogon, Lobi and Gourunsi.

Overlanding from Europe

From Morocco's Mediterranean coast, the Sahara is just a day's drive to the south – and a couple of days will see you well into the heart of it. Overlanding from Europe takes a good deal of research and preparation, but is the best way to get to the region if you want to become fully immersed in the identities and landscapes of West Africa: as you finally arrive on the far side of the sea of sand and rock, the first sensations of another world are ones that endure.

If you're setting off on extensive travels, especially if you plan to hitchhike and use public transport, you should aim to be in North Africa in September and across the Sahara in October. Throughout most of the region, this gives you at least six months before you can realistically expect to be rained upon. You should also be careful to obtain the most up-to-date information about road conditions and

political developments in the region. Talk to returning travellers and keep up with the news – the BBC's Africa pages are an excellent general source of information (ⓦ news.bbc.co.uk/1/hi/world/Africa).

Trans-Saharan routes

The safest and most popular overland route between North and West Africa takes you through Morocco, Western Sahara and Mauritania, then into Senegal. Travelling south, you should pick up a Mauritanian visa in Casablanca then hug the **Atlantic coast** through southern Morocco, enter Mauritania near the mineral port of Nouadhibou and loop inland, following the road down to Nouakchott and on to Dakar. This route is now paved and practically problem-free; there's an unsealed stretch through the minefield around the Western Sahara–Mauritania border (convoys used to lead vehicles past this) but as long as you stick to the well-worn tracks there should be no danger. Although scenically less impressive than the Algerian Sahara, the terrain is relatively easy on vehicles, as past participants in the annual Plymouth–Banjul Challenge (ⓦ www.plymouth-banjul.co.uk) will testify – this trans-Sahara expedition is only open to vehicles which cost their owners £100 or less and are happy to auction them for charity on arrival in Banjul.

The two classic trans-Saharan routes – the eastern **Route du Hoggar** through Tamanrasset to Agadez in Niger, and the western **Route du Tanezrouft** from Adrar to Gao in Mali – are not to be attempted lightly. Beset by banditry for many years, they became extremely dangerous with the outbreak of civil war in Algeria in 1992, and were closed for some time. They're now officially open but at the time of writing, early 2008, are considered very risky; bandits operate in the Algeria–Mali border region and there have been numerous armed robberies of tourists, carjackings and even kidnappings for ransom.

Which is not to say that during the life of this edition the situation might not improve. To attempt the crossing, you need to be in a convoy with official Algerian guides. The Route du Hoggar, the easier of the two, can be picked up by driving south from Algiers, or, preferably, starting from Tunis, driving southwest into Algiers and turning south at Ghardaia. The Route du Tanezrouft takes you through a volatile part of the border region and is not recommended. A third Algerian route via Tindouf, further west, has been formally closed to tourists since the 1970s, as are the routes from Libya into Algeria or Niger.

Travelling **northward** from Senegal to Morocco along the Atlantic route, you need to obtain a vehicle permit from the Moroccan embassy in Nouakchott; it's not possible to do this at the consulate in Nouadhibou.

Driving to West Africa

Driving to West Africa isn't a difficult feat in itself, and many people complete the journey with unmodified road vehicles. Obviously, high ground clearance is important if you're going to tackle the desert pistes, as is good structural and mechanical condition – and sound knowledge of your vehicle. Local mechanics are most familiar with Mercedes, Peugeot, Renault and Land Rover models, and spares for these are far more likely to be available than for other vehicles. Equipping yourself efficiently is essential and you should take a GPS.

All motorized travellers (whether on two or four wheels) agree that the comfort and independence of their own vehicle is a mixed blessing. It can, if you let it, insulate you from the life of Africa; it's a permanent security headache, especially in towns; and it says one thing – **money** – to everyone you meet along the way. You can feel like a travel-ling circus after a few weeks of this. Taking account of fuel, maintenance and insurance, it is also a fairly expensive business. And unless you have someone aboard who knows the vehicle inside out (and even then), any serious breakdown can be immensely tedious and costly. Travelling in a **convoy** of at least two vehicles cuts down on the chances of getting stranded if disaster strikes.

The outstanding **advantages** of taking your own vehicle are that you can get off the beaten track (assuming the vehicle is sturdy enough) and visit areas that see even a local vehicle only once in a toddler's lifetime. To a great extent, you can actually avoid towns and cities, or at least avoid staying overnight in them by driving out into the wilderness and camping.

One consideration can't be stressed enough: give yourself **time**. Rushing around in Africa is a bad enough idea using local transport. But to try to drive in your own vehicle with a fixed number of days and weeks is to court disaster. Allow a month to head in a leisurely fashion from the Mediterranean to sub-Saharan Africa. It's simply not worth the work, in any case, to rush through at a breakneck pace.

Good **books** for drivers heading to West Africa include *Africa By Road* by Charlie Shackell and Illya Bracht, and *Sahara Overland* by Rough Guide–author Chris Scott (see also Chris's website ⓦwww .sahara-overland.com for useful, regularly updated information).

Selling your vehicle

A good way to cut the cost of overland travel to West Africa is to take a vehicle along with you for sale; all sorts of cars and jeeps are worth more in Africa. The UK, unfortunately, is not the best place to buy (prices are high and the steering wheel is on the wrong side).

If you intend to sell your vehicle in West Africa, your best investment would be a three-year-old left-hand-drive diesel **Peugeot 505** *familiale* estate car or a **Mercedes saloon**. Most of these will end up in service as *taxis brousse* – shared "bush taxis". **Mercedes commercial vans** are also much in demand. **Twin-cab pick-ups** sell like hot cakes and **4x4s** are also very popular. It's worth bearing in mind that Senegal discour-ages the import of cars that are more than five years old; to bring one into the country, you'll have to pay a high import duty.

Where you sell the vehicle can depend on how well it is still working. Selling the car earlier than planned and hitching a lift with other travellers is always an option.

In **Senegal**, **Mali**, **Burkina Faso** and most West African countries there is no problem selling a foreign car; any problems will be faced by the buyer when he registers it locally. In **Mauritania** the car's details are entered into your passport; if you sell the vehicle, it is vital to go with the buyer to the customs office to fill in the paperwork and pay the import duty that will allow you to leave the country without the vehicle. Some purchasers will suggest driving down to the Senegalese border at Rosso to evade Mauritanian duty, but you should be very suspicious of that: Rosso, on the Senegal River, is a confusing border at the best of times and it is easy to get ripped off here. You'd be better off just driving across yourself and selling the vehicle without any customs hassle in Senegal. The worst countries in which to sell a car are **Ghana** and **Nigeria**, which require a carnet (see opposite). Bear in mind that as you near the coast you will start to compete with imports that arrive, rather less depreciated, by ship.

Wherever you make the sale, it is a good idea to draw up a very basic **contract** and get the buyer to sign it. Regardless of its legal worth, such a document could act in your favour – and certainly won't hurt – in case of any disputes later on.

Vehicle documentation

Travelling by private vehicle drastically increases the **red tape** you'll have to deal with. First and foremost, you must be able to produce the vehicle's *carte grise*, its international registration certificate. Effectively making your car's logbook obsolete once in Africa, the *carte grise* states ownership, country of registration and the registration, chassis and engine numbers – all of which can be checked thoroughly at borders. In the UK, a *carte grise* can be issued by the AA or RAC on production of the vehicle's logbook and payment of a small fee. It's useful to carry a few photocopies of the *carte grise* as well. If you're not the owner of the car you're driving, you'll require a **notified document** (*attestation du propriétaire* in French) stating permission to use the car.

You'll also need an **international driving licence** – issued by your motoring organization at home. They will be able to advise whether the countries on your itinerary require you to have a particular format of licence. Spare copies can be useful, as it's the first thing police will confiscate in the event of a traffic offence and you won't get far without one.

A **carnet**, issued by the AA or the RAC in the UK, is also taken by many motorists. These documents allow you to temporarily import your car into a country without, in theory, paying import duties or a deposit. Depending on how many pages you require, they cost around £55–65, and you'll have to place a bank guarantee (usually twice the value of your car) or cash deposit before a carnet will be issued (though it's possible to take out insurance to cover this deposit). Most West African countries will issue a document that will allow **temporary importation** – in Senegal a *passavant*, in Mali a *laissez-passer*, while Mauritanian officials just write the car details in your passport. However there is almost always a fee to be paid for these documents, and a carnet also speeds your passage through borders. In West Africa only **Nigeria** and **Ghana** absolutely require a carnet. If you plan to **sell your car**, of course, a carnet is the last thing you need: if the vehicle isn't correctly stamped in and out of each country you'll lose your deposit.

Motor **insurance** is obligatory and varies in cost. Motorbike insurance costs approximately half that for cars, and commercial vehicles (including minibuses with eight passenger seats) twice as much. Morocco and Tunisia are covered by the European "**Green Card**" scheme (often free; ask your insurance company), without which you will have to buy insurance at the border (about £30 for ten days). Both Mauritania and Senegal require drivers to buy into their national insurance schemes, but most other countries in West Africa are covered by a **carte brune**, an insurance policy that can be taken out in any ECOWAS member state (see ⓦ www.brown-card.ecowas.int/).

UK and Ireland

RAC UK ☎ 0800/550 055, ⓦ www.rac.co.uk.
AA UK ☎ 0800/444 500, ⓦ www.theaa.com.
AA Ireland Dublin ☎ 01/617 9999, ⓦ www .aaireland.ie.

US and Canada

AAA ☎1-800/222-4357, ⓦ www.aaa.com.
CAA ☎613/247-0117, ⓦ www.caa.ca.

Australia and New Zealand

AAA Australia ☎02/6247 7311, ⓦ www.aaa
.asn.au.
New Zealand AA New Zealand ☎0800/500-222,
ⓦ www.aa.co.nz.

Local transport and hitchhiking

If you're going to travel under your own
steam, it's worth considering a cheap,
one-way flight to Morocco, The Gambia or
the Canary Islands to get started. Bearing
in mind the possible cost of even a small
number of days of travel through Europe, this
can be a positive saving.

In the **Canary Islands**, you might check
around the marinas for anyone headed to
Cape Verde, Banjul or Dakar by yacht. During
the east–west transatlantic-crossing season,
roughly from October to March, hundreds
make the journey. Even without experience,
it's possible to get a berth in exchange for
some basic crewing and boat chores. Expect
to pay the skipper for your keep.

From Las Palmas, Air Mauritanie operate
flights to **Nouadhibou** (€270 for a one-
month return) and **Nouakchott** (€315).
Another option might be to travel from Las
Palmas by cargo vessel, which, after some
bargaining with a ship captain, shouldn't
cost more than €25.

If you have the stamina to keep **hitchhiking** and are prepared to camp out
and take on board the security risks that
travelling this way can pose, you can get
to West Africa by thumbing your way

through France and Spain to North Africa
at remarkably little cost. Algeciras is the
cheapest and easiest embarkation point
for Morocco with plenty of ferries every
day to Tangier and the Spanish enclave of
Ceuta. The ease of hitchhiking in Morocco
compensates for the common misery of the
roadside in southern Europe, though in the
far southern regions of Morocco you'll need
to be lucky, as there's no public transport
to the Mauritanian border. Travellers without
their own transport here will have to find lifts
with overlanders (free and often fun) or the
occasional truck, which will generally charge
you. Car sellers may have room for hitchers,
but tourist vehicles are usually packed to
the gills.

Cycling

If you have enough energy, and more
importantly (assuming you're reasonably fit)
enough **time**, it's quite feasible to consider
cycling through Europe in the summer,
down through Morocco in the autumn,
loading your machine aboard a lorry for the
hardest part of the Sahara crossing and
then cycling where your fancy takes you
through the dry season.

It is of course possible to take a sturdy
touring bike, or even use a locally bought
roadster. A tourer is much faster on the
main roads and a fit cyclist could expect
to cover 120km a day or more. But you're
likely to suffer more from broken spokes
and punctures at unexpected potholes and
you're much less free to leave the highways.
Some routes and regions for which a
mountain bike is ideal are beyond the scope
of other bikes. More cycling practicalities are
detailed on p.53.

Red tape and visas

Visa regulations in West Africa are notoriously fickle and hard to pin down, though at the time of writing, eleven of the countries covered in this book – Mali, Niger, Burkina Faso, Cape Verde, Guinea-Bissau, Guinea, Ghana, Togo, Benin, Nigeria and Cameroon – require all non–West African visitors to have visas. Furthermore, all visitors to West Africa require a full ten-year passport, which should remain valid for at least six months beyond the end of the trip. Allow at least one blank page per country to be visited. For more detail, see individual country chapters.

If you need to state your occupation when applying for a visa, try to avoid declaring yourself a journalist, photographer or anything that might be misconstrued as indicating curiosity in matters of state. Bear in mind also that a visa only constitutes "permission to apply to enter". This isn't mere pedantry. You can be turned away despite having a visa (for arriving on a one-way ticket, for example, in the case of Cameroon) and the length of **validity** of a visa may bear no relation to how long you're actually allowed to stay in the country when you arrive. It's almost always possible to **extend** a first stay, but note that in several countries it can be a serious matter if you overstay without extending.

Further kinds of red tape which may entangle you on your travels involve international vaccination certificates (see p.37), vehicle documentation if you're driving (see p.27) and photography permits (see the practical information in each chapter for more on this). Happily, much of this irksome bureaucracy has begun to vanish with the increasing democratization of most countries in the region.

Visas before departure

If you're flying out to a limited number of countries on a short trip, you should apply for visas in advance. If you'll be away for longer, note that few visas remain valid beyond three months, and that certain countries, notably Nigeria and Cameroon, will generally only issue visas in the passport-holder's country of residence, or at the nearest embassy representing that country. Although costly, it may make sense to obtain visas for these West African countries before you leave, let

them expire, and then apply for new visas later on at the relevant embassies in West Africa – often the presence of expired visas for these countries in your passport can be a help in getting new ones.

To get a visa in your home country you'll fairly often be asked to provide evidence of a return air ticket and occasionally have to show an invitation or a covering letter stating the purpose of your trip. **Tourist visas** and **business visas** are always distinct. The latter usually require a letter from your company and often a letter from an African contact. It may be worth asking for a **multiple-entry visa** (which often costs more) – it saves a lot of hassle should you need to re-enter one West African country from a neighbouring state. If you need a visa for a country which doesn't have a representative in your home country, note that personal applications made by mail to an embassy abroad can take several months to process.

West African embassies

UK and Ireland

Benin The Honorary Consul, Millennium House, Humber Rd, near Staples Corner, London NW2 6DW ☏020/8954 8800.

Cameroon 84 Holland Park, London W11 3SB ☏020/7727 0771.

Cape Verde Honorary Consul João Roberto, 18-20 Stanley St, Liverpool L1 6AF ☏0151/236 0206.

The Gambia 57 Kensington Court, London W8 5DG ☏020/7937 6316.

Ghana 13 Belgrave Square, London SW1X 8PN ☏020/7235 4142; Consular Section: 104 Highgate Hill, London N6 5HE ☏020/8342 8686.

Guinea 48 Onslow Gardens, London SW7 3PY ☏020/7594 4811.

Guinea-Bissau Honorary Consul Mabel Figueiredo da Fonseca Smith, PO Box 393, Tunbridge Wells, Kent TN4 9YZ ☎01892/530478.

Liberia 2 Pembridge Place, London W2 4XB ☎020/7221 1036.

Mauritania 8 Carlos Place, London W1K 3AS ☎020/7478 9323.

Morocco 49 Queen's Gate Gardens, London SW7 5NE ☎020/7581 5001; Consular Section: Diamond House, 97-99 Praed St, London W2 ☎020/7724 0719.

Nigeria UK: Nigeria House, 9 Northumberland Ave, London WC2N 5BX ☎020/7839 1244, ⓦwww.nigeriahc.org.uk; Consular Section: 56–57 Fleet St, London EC4 ☎020/7353 3776. Republic of Ireland: 56 Leeson Park, Dublin 6 ☎1/660 4366.

Senegal 39 Marloes Rd, London W8 6LA ☎020/7938 4048, ⓦwww.senegalembassy.com.

Sierra Leone 41 Eagle St, Holborn, London WC1R 4TL ☎020/7404 0140, ⓦwww.slhc-uk.org.uk.

Mainland Europe

As Burkina Faso, Mali, Niger and Togo don't have their own representation in the UK or Republic of Ireland, we've listed their diplomatic missions in mainland Europe below.

Burkina Faso 16 pl Guy d'Arezzo, 1180 Brussels ☎2/345 9912, ⓦwww .ambassadeduburkina.be.

Mali 89 rue du Cherche-Midi, 75006 Paris ☎01/48.07.85.85; 487 av Moliére, 1050 Brussels ☎2/345 7432.

Niger 154 rue de Longchamp, 75116 Paris ☎01/45.04.80.60.

Togo 8 rue Alfred-Roll, 75017 Paris ☎01/43.80.12.13.

US

Benin 2124 Kalorama Rd NW, Washington DC 20008 ☎202/232-6656; 222 Florence Ave, Inglewood CA 90301 ☎310/754-2000.

Burkina Faso 2340 Massachusetts Ave NW, Washington DC 20008 ☎202/332-5577, ⓦwww .burkinaembassy-usa.org; 115 E 73rd St, New York, NY 10021 ☎212/288-7515; 214 23rd St, Santa Monica CA 90402 ☎310/393-2531; 1527 Robert E Lee Blvd, New Orleans LA 70122 ☎504/284-6351.

Cameroon 2349 Massachusetts Ave NW, Washington DC 20008 ☎202/265-8790; 147 Terra Vista, San Francisco CA 94115 ☎415/921-5372.

Cape Verde 3415 Massachusetts Ave NW, Washington DC 20007 ☎202/965-6820; 535

Boylston St, Boston MA 02116 ☎617/353-0014, ⓦwww.capeverdeusa.org.

Côte d'Ivoire 2424 Massachusetts Ave NW, Washington DC 20008 ☎202/797-0300; Pier 23, San Francisco CA 94111 ☎415/391-0176.

The Gambia 1115 15th St NW, Washington DC 20005 ☎202/785-1399; 11718 Barrington Court 130, Los Angeles CA 90077 ☎310/274-5084.

Ghana 3512 International Drive NW, Washington DC 20008 ☎202/686-4520, ⓦwww.ghana-embassy .org; 19 E 47th St, New York NY 10017 ☎212/832-1300; Honorary Consul Jack Webb, 3434 Locke Lane, Houston, Texas ☎713/960-8806.

Guinea 2112 Leroy Place NW, Washington DC 20008 ☎202/483-9420; 3505 S Side Blvd 5, Jacksonville, FL 32216 ☎904/564-1628.

Guinea-Bissau 15929 Yukon Lane, Rockville MD 20855 ☎301/947-3958.

Liberia 5201 16th St NW, Washington DC 20011 ☎202/723-0437.

Mali 2130 R St NW, Washington DC 20008 ☎202/332-2249.

Mauritania 2129 Leroy Place NW, Washington DC 20008 ☎202/232-5700; 211 E 43rd St, New York NY 10017 ☎212/986-7963.

Morocco 1601 21st St NW, Washington DC 20009 ☎202/462-7979; 10 E 40th St, New York NY 10016 ☎212/758-2625.

Niger 2204 R St NW, Washington DC 20008 ☎202/483-4224, ⓦwww.nigerembassyusa.org; 417 E 50th St, New York NY 10022 ☎212/421-3260.

Nigeria 3519 International Court NW, Washington DC 20008 ☎202/986-8400, ⓦwww.nigeriaembassyusa.org; 828 Second Ave, New York NY 10017 ☎212/808-0301, ⓦwww .nigeriahouse.com.

Senegal 2112 Wyoming Ave NW, Washington DC 20008 ☎202/234-0540; 271 W 125th St, New York NY 10027 ☎917/493-8950.

Sierra Leone 1701 19th St NW, Washington DC 20009 ☎202/939-9261; 245 E 49th St, New York, NY 10017 ☎212/688-1656.

Togo 2208 Massachusetts Ave NW, Washington DC 20008 ☎202/234-4212.

Canada

Benin 58 Glebe Ave, Ottawa ON K1S 2C3 ☎613/233-4429.

Burkina Faso 48 Range Rd, Ottawa ON K1N 8J4 ☎613/238-4796, ⓦwww.ambaburkina -canada.org.

Cameroon 170 Clemow Ave, Ottawa ON K1S 2B4 ☎613/865-1664.

Cape Verde 123 York View Drive, Etobicoke, Toronto ON M8Z 2G5 ☎416/252-9881.

Ghana 1 Clemow Ave, Ottawa ON K1S 2A9
☎613/236-0871.
Guinea 483 Wilbrod St, Ottawa ON K1N 6N1
☎613/789-8444.
Liberia 1080 Beaver Hall Hill, Suite 1720, Montreal
PQ H2Z 1S8 ☎514/871-4741.
Mali 50 Goulburn Ave, Ottawa ON K1N 8C8
☎613/232-1501, ⓦwww.ambamalicanada.org.
Morocco 38 Range Rd, Ottawa ON K1N 8J4
☎613/236-7391, ⓦwww.ambassade-maroc
.ottawa.on.ca.
Niger 38 Blackburn Ave, Ottawa ON K1N 8A3,
☎613/232-4291.
Nigeria 295 Metcalfe St, Ottawa ON K2P 1R9
☎613/236-0521.
Senegal 57 Marlborough Ave, Ottawa ON K1N 8E8
☎613/238-6392.
Togo 12 Range Rd, Ottawa ON K1N 8J3
☎613/238-5916.

Australia and New Zealand

In either country, the only West African states with their own consulate are Ghana, at Level 14, Suite 1404, 370 Pitt St, Sydney (☎02/9283 2961, ⓦwww.ghanacg .com.au), and **Cameroon**, at 65 Bingara Rd, Beecroft, NSW 2119 (☎02/9989 8414, ⓦwww.cameroonconsul.com). You can obtain visas for **Burkina Faso**, **Côte d'Ivoire**, **Mauritania**, **Senegal** and **Togo** from the French Consulate General, Level 26, St Martins Tower, 31 Market St, Sydney, NSW 2000 (☎02/9268 2432, ⓦwww .ambafrance-au.org).

South Africa

Few West African consulates or embassies have opened here as yet. **Nigeria**'s consulate general is at 16 Rivonia Rd, Illovo, 2196 Johannesburg (☎011/442 3620, ⓦwww .nigeria.co.za). For **Mali**, go to Suite 106, Infotech Building, 1090 Arcadia St, Hatfield, 0083 Pretoria (☎012/342 7464). **Côte d'Ivoire** and **Ghana** also have representation in Pretoria (respectively ☎012/342 6913 and 342 5847).

Visa services

If you're in a hurry to secure a visa, or antici-pate some kind of hassle getting one, it may be worth considering a commercial **visa service**. They will do all the legwork for a set fee, after you've signed the application forms

and mailed them your passport. You still need to plan ahead of course – try to ascertain how long the agency will take to obtain the visa, and finish the paperwork suitably early. If you happen to be travelling with Point-Afrique (see p.22), note that they offer an inexpensive visa service to passengers.

Given the additional expense of using an agency, however, it makes sense to focus their services on obtaining those visas which you know you won't be able to obtain in West Africa itself. In that specific instance, however, note that you can sometimes avoid using an agency as it may be okay to organize your visa on arrival (this facility is more often available at the airport than to overland arrivals; see below).

UK

CIBT Ground Floor, 4–8 Rodney St, London N1 9JH ☎0870/890 0185, ⓦwww.uk.cibt.com. You can check your visa requirements online and order the visas you need for a handling fee of £35–55 each, plus the cost of the visa and delivery.

US

CIBT ☎1-800/929-2428, ⓦwww.us.cibt.com. Offices in Chicago, Houston, LA, Miami, New York, San Francisco and Washington DC.
Travisa ☎1-800/222-2589, ⓦwww.travisa.com. Offices in Washington DC, Chicago, San Francisco, Detroit and New York.

Visas along the way

On an **overland trip**, it would be simplest to pick up the visas you need along the way – were it not for the fact that some West African embassies in the region may refuse to issue visas to passport holders who could have obtained them in their home country. A further obstacle – though one that's steadily diminishing – is the lack of representation for a number of countries which have very few embassies (Guinea-Bissau and Burkina Faso, for example). You'll need to take visa availability into account when planning your itinerary. Certain nationalities will have hassles getting some of these, so it's worth trying at the first opportunity. Take plenty of passport **photos** – allow three or four for each visa you expect to need.

In the country chapters of this guide, addresses for embassies and consulates

have been given in the "Listings" section at the end of each capital city. Once you've located the embassy in question (where you've any choice, it's the consulate or consular section you need to go to), obtaining visas should be fairly straightforward in most cases and is often a good deal easier and cheaper than sorting things out at home. Nevertheless, you ought to be prepared for an average wait of two to three days from application to delivery, and have a handy hotel address to use as your intended address in the country (nothing too slummy).

A **letter of introduction** from your own embassy is sometimes required (this can usually be provided on the spot, for a fee). Countries for which a letter of introduction is either helpful or mandatory include Mauritania, Guinea, Cameroon and Nigeria, but it's hard to generalize as rules and norms vary greatly from embassy to embassy.

The person whose signature is required for the visa is invariably the **consul**. If you're being delayed or messed around, ask to see him or her in person. If you get stonewalled, or you're in a hurry and told to come back next week, try putting in an hour or two in the waiting room. This often has miraculous effects.

Visa fees can be high (up to £70/$140 or more) and they sometimes vary mysteriously from one applicant to the next, not always depending on nationality. Also, check what you can get for your money – in some cases it costs the same for a thirty-day single-entry visa as it does for a three-month multiple-entry visa, but frequently you'll only be given what you ask for. Visas are often issued with revenue stamps stuck in your passport, or a sum of money indicated in handwriting. The value should be what you paid. If it differs,

it's worth complaining and asking for a receipt (there may have been an accidental overpayment).

In cities where the following countries have no direct representation, visas for **Mauritania**, **Senegal**, **Burkina Faso** and **Togo** may be available from the **French embassy**; there's a large French embassy in pretty well every country in the region.

A few West African countries issue (or have an official policy to issue – not the same thing) **visas on arrival** at the airport, particularly in cases where the passenger is arriving from a country with no embassy. Details are given in the relevant country chapters. Don't risk it unless you have to (and check that the airline won't refuse you boarding if you don't have the required visa), as it always delays the arrival formalities.

Visa Touristique Entente

Burkina Faso, Togo, Benin, Niger and Côte d'Ivoire have now instituted a system, the **Visa Touristique Entente**, whereby you can buy a single visa (for CFA25,000, or around £30/$60) from any of their embassies, which covers one entry to every country in the group. This is a dramatic saving on buying individual visas, but strangely, a number of consulates of these countries seem unaware of the arrangement, insisting it doesn't operate.

It does, as Bob (US) emailed to tell Rough Guides:

"It includes all five countries, including Burkina Faso and absolutely no hassle at any of the borders – they all knew exactly what it was. I was worried because it does not mention the countries on the visa but as I said all was okay."

Info and media

Those few tourist offices that exist outside the region are usually attached to embassies or airlines and rarely offer much in the way of useful advice. Much more useful is the wide variety of websites and news services, some of which have replaced the newspapers from which they emerged. Useful local websites are flagged up in each country chapter.

Websites

Government travel advice
Australian Department of Foreign Affairs Ⓦ www.smartraveller.gov.au.
British Foreign & Commonwealth Office Ⓦ www.fco.gov.uk/travel.
Canadian Department of Foreign Affairs Ⓦ www.voyage.gc.ca.
US State Department Travel Advisories Ⓦ www.travel.state.gov.

News and general information
153 Club Ⓦ www.manntaylor.com/153.html. Club with useful quarterly newsletter for travellers to the "153" region (153 being the number of the old Michelin North and West Africa map).
Africa Centre Ⓦ www.africacentre.org. American site with news and information from and about Africa.
Africa Confidential Ⓦ www.africa-confidential .com. Website from the publishers of a subscription-only fortnightly newsletter with solid inside information.
The Africa Guide Ⓦ www.africaguide.com. Informative general-interest site covering the whole African continent.
Afrol Ⓦ www.afrol.com. News and links.
AllAfrica Ⓦ www.allafrica.com. Excellent searchable database of news from the African press: the best African news site.
Jeune Afrique Ⓦ www.jeuneafrique.com. Hard-hitting French-language West African news and features magazine site.
Travel Africa Ⓦ www.travelafricamag.com. Features for travellers and armchair travellers alike; strong on wildlife and safari destinations.

The blog for this guide
For travel updates, news links and general information, check out Ⓦ theroughguidetowestafrica .blogspot.com.

West Africa Review Ⓦ www.westafricareview .com. Features, essays and interviews.

African music and culture
AfricanCraft Ⓦ www.africancraft.com. A showcase for African artists and craftspeople, mainly from West Africa, with articles to read and items to buy.
Africa on Roots World Ⓦ www.rootsworld.com /africa. Features about the African music scene and audio clips from African musicians.

Libraries and resource centres

UK
Africa Centre 38 King St, London WC2E 8JT ☎ 020/7836 1973, Ⓦ www.africacentre.org.uk.
Royal Geographical Society 1 Kensington Gore, London SW7 2AR Ⓦ www.rgs.org. Helpful Expedition Advisory Service (☎ 020/7591 3030) provides a wealth of information, including maps and technical guides.
School of Oriental and African Studies Library Thornhaugh St, Russell Square, London WC1H 0XG ☎ 020/7637 2388, Ⓦ www.soas.ac .uk/library. A vast collection of books, journals and maps.

US
Boston University African Studies Center Ⓦ www.bu.edu/africa.
Center for African Studies, University of Florida Ⓦ web.africa.ufl.edu.
Herskovits Library of African Studies, Northwestern University Ⓦ www.library .northwestern.edu/africana.
Howard University African American Studies Library Ⓦ www. howard.edu/library/assist/guides /afroam.htm.
Indiana University African Studies Program Ⓦ www.indiana.edu/~libsalc/african.
Institute of African Studies, Columbia University Ⓦ www.columbia.edu/cu/ias.

Michigan State University Africana Collection Ⓦ www2.lib.msu.edu/general/collections /africana.jsp.
University of Illinois Center for African Studies Ⓦ www.afrst.uiuc.edu.

Newspapers

There was a rebirth of the **local press** in West Africa with the movement towards multiparty democracy in the early 1990s. Countries which formerly had almost no newspapers now have a thriving **press**, though critical and independent editors can still find themselves in serious trouble with governments – or government figures – who are uncomfortable with scrutiny of their policies or personal behaviour.

The **local press** in West Africa isn't likely to give you much of an idea of what's going on in the rest of the world. The practical information at the beginning of each country chapter tries to uncover the best and most intrepid of the output. Some British and European newspapers, plus the *Herald Tribune* and *USA Today*, are often available in the lobbies of the more expensive big-city hotels, together with *Time*, *Newsweek* and *Jeune Afrique*. You'll find some of them, too, on sale a few days later from street vendors.

Radio and TV

National and local **radio stations** have blossomed in recent years, along with the print media. It's now common to have a few local stations, though, as with the press, they're frequently subject to all sorts of harassment. Most West African countries have **TV stations**, usually with a rather uninspired mix of deeds and words from government ministers and imported soaps and movies. VHS video rental and satellite TV have swept across the region.

If you're travelling for any length of time, it's a good idea to invest in a pocket-sized short-wave radio. The **BBC World Service** is a real institution in parts of West Africa, and produces several excellent Africa Service programmes, including the morning magazine **Network Africa** and the vital **Focus on Africa**, broadcast in the afternoon and evening Monday to Friday. You can also listen to the BBC in French, Hausa and Portuguese. BBC World Service can also be heard on FM in a number of cities, including Accra, Bamako, Cotonou, Dakar, Freetown, Lagos and Ouagadougou. For details of current schedules and frequencies, check Ⓦ www.bbc.co.uk/worldservice. With a short-wave radio you can also pick up the **Voice of America** (Ⓦ www.voa.gov) and other international broadcasters.

Maps and books

Maps of countries and cities in West Africa are almost always expensive and hard to obtain in the region itself – buy those you need in advance of your trip if you can get them. Books included here cover two or more countries: for titles relating to specific countries, see the "Books" section in each chapter.

Maps of West Africa

Until 2007, the single most useful item to take on a trip through West Africa would have been the **Michelin map 741** *Africa North and West*. The 2007-revised edition of the old Michelin 953/153 map, it takes account of most new roads, showing water and fuel sources, roads liable to flood, ferry crossings and a mass of other details at a scale of 1cm to 40km (1 inch to 63 miles). It covers all of northwest Africa with the exception of southern Cameroon (which appears on their 746 *Africa Central and South*). In 2007, however, the German travel publisher **Reise Know-How** brought out two excellent new maps of the region: *West Africa: Coastal*

Countries and *West Africa: Sahel Countries* – both double-sided, 1:2.2m (in other words 1cm=22km, which is almost twice the scale of the Michelin map) and, most usefully, printed on virtually indestructible plastic paper which will survive a pounding for several months while you carry them around. The maps are much more detailed than the Michelin and indications are they're more accurate too.

For individual countries, the **French Institut Géographique National** (⑩www.ign.fr) has maps for a number of West African countries (though note that in terms of scale – and updatedness – the Reise Know-How maps are equal or superior for several countries). The IGN 1:1,000,000 **topographical surveys** published in the 1960s are still available as print-offs from their French headquarters. There's further information about country mapping in each chapter.

Books about West Africa

As for **books**, while there's a substantial volume of reading material on West Africa, its subject matter and authorship is very unevenly distributed. By far the largest body of literature in English comes from Nigeria, with its hundreds of novelists and academics. Understandably enough, most of the literature from and about Francophone West Africa is in French. For pre-departure reading, probably the best foretaste is provided by West African fiction – much of which is available in paperback in Heinemann's **African Writers Series**.

Country-specific reading lists appear in the Basics at the start of each chapter. In the following general listings, books marked ⵊ are especially recommended.

Series publications

African Historical Dictionaries If you're seriously looking to find out about a country, this series (⑩www.scarecrowpress.com) is what you need. They have titles on many African countries, covering names, places and events in detail. Brand-new, they're super-expensive ($100-plus), so check out amazon or abebooks.com.

ⵊ **Heinemann African Writers Series**
AWS titles were in the vanguard of African fiction-publishing in English and totalled 359 titles as a print series before concluding in 2003. Find them

in libraries and secondhand bookstores, or online at ⑩tinyurl.com/29qc8k.

Travel bibliographies

Louis Taussig *Resource Guide to Travel in Sub-Saharan Africa Vol. 1 East and West Africa.* Published in 1994, extraordinarily detailed country-by-country coverage of every published source and resource.

Travelogues and related literature

Peter Biddlecombe *French Lessons in Africa.* Like an uninvited companion, businessman Biddlecombe rattles out his observations on Francophone West Africa so fast, it seems, there's barely the time to notice the contradictions. Funny, warm and light.

ⵊ **Thomas Coraghassen Boyle** *Water Music.* Lengthy, meticulous – and at times outrageously funny – fictionalization of Mungo Park's explorations. Boyle's vision of the West Africa (and Britain) of two centuries ago is utterly captivating. Essential in situ reading for those long roadside waits: if you only take one book, take this.

Jens Finke *Chasing the Lizard's Tail: By bicycle across the Sahara.* Entertaining and insightful travelogue, recounting Rough Guide–author Finke's journey from Morocco to a sudden end in Banjul, Gambia.

Mark Jenkins *To Timbuktu: A Journey Down the Niger.* Well-written and likeable – though admittedly macho – kayaking adventures.

David Lamb *The Africans.* This was a bestseller, but Lamb's fly-in, fly-out technique is a statistical rant couched in Cold War rhetoric – and, even when ostensibly uncovering a pearl of wisdom, he can be unpleasantly offensive.

Michael Palin *Sahara.* Amusing account of Palin's travels for the BBC-TV series. Features the photography of Basil Pao, which gives a wonderful flavour of Senegal, Mali and Niger (more of which is found in his own coffee-table book *Inside Sahara*).

Mungo Park *Travels into the Interior of Africa.* Absorbing account of the then youthful Scottish traveller's two journeys (1795–97 and 1805) along the Niger.

Pamela Watson *Esprit de Battuta: Alone Across Africa on a Bicycle.* Muscular, modern travelogue-diary, that takes the Australian author from Senegal to Cameroon and beyond – very strong on anecdotal highs and lows.

History

Most histories cover the whole continent, and, inevitably, jump from place to place: Boahen, or Davidson, Buah & Ajayi are the easiest to follow, and are well complemented by various historical and cultural atlases.

The African continent

A.E. Afigbo et al *The Making of Modern Africa, Vol. 1 Nineteenth Century, Vol. 2 Twentieth Century.* A detailed, illustrated guide, putting West Africa in the continental context up until the first big changes after independence.

Cheik Anta Diop *Pre-Colonial Black Africa.* First published in the 1950s, Diop asserts that the origins of Western civilization, as well as African, began in Africa. The work encouraged a whole generation to reinterpret the past from an African perspective.

Basil Davidson *Africa in History.* Lucidly argued and readable summary of Africa's dominant nineteenth- and twentieth-century events.

Christopher Hibbert *Africa Explored: Europeans in the Dark Continent, 1769–1889.* Entertaining read, devoted in large part to the "discovery" of West Africa.

West Africa

Adu Boahen et al *Topics in West African History.* An excellent introduction to basic themes in West African history, written in a clear and concise fashion by one of Ghana's most respected historians.

🏃 **Basil Davidson et al** *A History of West Africa 1000–1800.* Clear, wide-ranging and readable.

J.B. Webster et al *West Africa since 1800: The Revolutionary Years.* An excellent companion to Davidson above.

Historical atlases

Brian Catchpole and L.A. Akinjogbin *A History of West Africa in Maps and Diagrams.* A remarkable and highly recommended encapsulation of the region's history from ancient times to the 1980s.

Colin McEvedy *Penguin Atlas of African History.* Useful for placing West Africa, and the whole continent, in context, and for getting to grips with some of the names and themes. Fifty-nine maps of Africa with facing text.

Land, people and society

Thomas D. Blakely et al (eds) *Religion in Africa: Experience & Expression.* Thorough examination of religion in Africa and the diaspora.

🏃 **R.J. Harrison Church** *West Africa.* Formerly the standard geography reference – traditional in approach. Excellent and unexpectedly absorbing.

Betty Laduke *Africa: Women's Art, Women's Lives.* Laduke turns her worldwide focus on women's art to Africa to examine the pottery of Mali, Cameroon and Togo; bead-making in Cameroon; wall painting

in Burkina Faso; and textiles and leather-working in the Sahel.

Patrick R. McNaughton *The Mande Blacksmiths: Knowledge, Power, and Art in West Africa.* Accessible scholarship that deals with both the aesthetic qualities of ironworking and its social implications for Mande peoples.

Robert Farris Thompson *Flash of the Spirit: African and Afro-American Art and Philosophy.* "Art history to dance by" in the words of the *Philadelphia Inquirer*'s reviewer, and this is a unique book, illuminating the art and philosophy that connects the black worlds on both sides of the Atlantic. Big on Yoruba and Dan-Homey roots. Lots of illustrations.

Claudia Zaslavsky *Africa Counts: Number and Pattern in African Culture.* A unique, extraordinary book, with a chapter on *warri* games (see **p.69**).

Arts

Stephen Belcher *Epic Traditions in Africa.* Elements of epic poetry described, followed by colourful narratives from across the continent in translation. Includes texts from the Sunjata and literary traditions of the Mande and Fula.

Margaret Courtney-Clarke *African Canvas.* Sumptuous colour photos bring out vivid details of exterior and interior house painting by women in a number of countries.

Susan Denyer *African Traditional Architecture.* Rewarding study, featuring hundreds of photos (most of them old) and a wealth of detailed line drawings.

Werner Gillon *A Short History of African Art.* A substantial study despite the name, though inevitably still very selective.

🏃 **Elian Girard et al** *Colons: Statuettes Habillées d'Afrique de l'Ouest.* Fascinating illustrations of a little-known genre of sculpture: statues of Africans dressed in European clothes.

Thomas A. Hale *Griots and Griottes: Masters of Words and Music.* A comprehensive look at griots – male and female – of Niger, Mali, Senegal and The Gambia and their roles as historians, genealogists, diplomats, musicians and advisors.

Michael Huet *The Dance, Art and Ritual of Africa.* Remarkable photos of ceremonies and costume, captured with an exceptional clarity and power.

David Kerr *African Popular Theatre: From Pre-Colonial Times to the Present Day.* Includes sections on masquerade and concert party.

Esi Sagay *African Hairstyles.* What they're called, and how to do them; a wonderful little book.

Jan Vansina *Art History in Africa.* Readable theorizing by an interesting French anthropologist.

🏃 **Deide Von Schaewen (photography), Frederic Coudere & Laurence Dougier** *Inside Africa: South and West.* A massive and sumptuous volume from Taschen, which brings a style consciousness to hundreds of photos of African architecture and house interiors, including eleven West African countries.

Music

Francis Bebey *African Music: A People's Art.* First published in French in 1969, this is an excellent and well-illustrated ethnomusicological survey, concentrating on Francophone Africa.

Wolfgang Bender *Sweet Mother: Modern African Music.* A cultural history of African urban music. Includes an extensive bibliography and discography.

 Simon Broughton, Mark Ellingham and John Lusk (eds) *The Rough Guide to World Music: Vol 1 Africa & the Middle East.* Third edition of *The Rough Guide to World Music*, published in 2006, with detailed articles covering most West African countries, plus hundreds of potted artist biographies and CD reviews.

Samuel Charters *The Roots of the Blues: An African Search.* Charters' serendipitous journey (Gambia, Senegal, Mali) aimed to find the blues' roots in West Africa. While he failed, his other discoveries make great reading.

Food

Daniel K. Abbiw *Useful Plants of Ghana.* Unusual reference guide to plants, organized by use – as food, fuel and medicine. Highly recommended for impoverished volunteers.

Jessica B. Harris *The Africa Cookbook: Tastes of a Continent.* Africa-wide collection of recipes for streetside samplings (bean cakes and fried plantains) and full-course meals.

J.G. Vaughan and C.A. Geissler *The New Oxford Book of Food Plants.* Covers most of the fruit and veg that will come your way in West Africa.

Natural history

T. Haltenorth and H. Diller *A Field Guide to the Mammals of Africa.*
W. Serle and G. Morel *A Field Guide to the Birds of West Africa.* Both these are highly recommended if you're keen enough to have binoculars with you.

Map and book retailers

African Books Collective UK ☎01866/349110, ⓦwww.africanbookscollective.com. Thousands of updated titles from more than forty independent, state and university publishers in West Africa.
Distant Lands US ☎1-800/310-3220, ⓦwww.distantlands.com.
Globe Corner Bookstore US ☎1-617/497-6277, ⓦwww.globecorner.com.
Mapland Australia ☎03/9670 4383, ⓦwww.mapland.com.au.
Map Link US ☎1-800/962-1394, ⓦwww.maplink.com.
The Map Shop Australia ☎08/8231 2033, ⓦwww.mapshop.net.au.
MapWorld New Zealand ☎0800/627 967 or 03/374 5399, ⓦwww.mapworld.co.nz.
Stanfords UK ☎0117/929 9966, ⓦwww.stanfords.co.uk.
The Travel Bookshop UK ☎020/7229 5260, ⓦwww.thetravelbookshop.co.uk.
The Travel Bug Bookstore Canada ☎604/737-1122, ⓦwww.travelbugbooks.ca.
World of Maps Canada ☎1-800/214-8524, ⓦwww.worldofmaps.com.

Health

There's no reason to expect to get ill in West Africa, but there are plenty of opportunities to do so if you're unlucky or careless. The most likely hazards are stomach problems and malaria. Health details for each country, with a brief rundown on local problems and issues, are given in each chapter.

Although you may never actually be asked to present them, the only officially required **international vaccination certificates** are for yellow fever and cholera. In certain countries – Benin, Burkina Faso, Cameroon, Ghana, Niger, Sierra Leone and Togo – a **yellow fever** certificate is always a requirement, even if you're flying in direct from Europe. Several others require the yellow fever certificate if you're staying for longer than two weeks, and all of them require the certificate if you've arrived by way of an area that's classified by the World Health Organization as infected – details online at ⓦ www.who.int/en – but in practice that includes any neighbouring West African country.

The **cholera** certificate is a bureaucratic rather than a health issue. Many doctors who keep up with tropical medicine don't recommend the cholera jab. However, there have been cases of border officials demanding to see a cholera certificate, even though possession of one is not an entry requirement for any country; and during an epidemic, international bus companies may need to see proof that you've received the vaccination when taking a cross-border trip. Some doctors will quite willingly provide a cholera certificate (while discreetly indicating on it that you haven't had the jab) – it seems to do the job at borders and airports.

If you lose a vaccination certificate, you can buy blank ones in many stationery stores. Explain your situation at a hospital or clinic and have it stamped and signed by someone (there'll probably be a small charge).

Vaccinations

Plan ahead: some inoculations need to be administered a few weeks in advance of your travels, and some can't be administered together. **Polio** is now more or less eliminated in the region but it's still worth checking that you're covered.

A **yellow fever** jab is essential; there are no specific drugs to cure the disease, which takes a few days to develop into liver failure and kills about fifty percent of its victims. Though epidemics are very rare, there have been outbreaks in recent years in Senegal and Guinea. The jabs are good for ten years and confer high immunity. A yellow fever certificate becomes valid only ten days after you've had the shot.

You shouldn't consider major travels without a **typhoid vaccination** (which lasts three years and protects you from this disease of infected food or water) or a **tetanus** booster which protects you against a disease occasionally picked up through infected wounds (even minor ones).

It is also worth getting vaccinated against **hepatitis A**, which protects you for up to ten years against this common form of

Insurance

You'd do well to take out a **travel insurance policy** before travelling to cover against theft, loss and illness or injury. Before paying for a new policy, however, it's worth checking whether you are already covered: some all-risks home insurance policies may cover your possessions when overseas, and many private medical schemes include cover when abroad.

After exhausting the possibilities above, you might want to contact a specialist travel insurance company. A typical travel insurance policy usually provides cover for the loss of baggage, tickets and – up to a certain limit – cash or cheques, as well as cancellation or curtailment of your journey. Most of them exclude so-called dangerous sports unless an extra premium is paid. Many policies can be chopped and changed to exclude coverage you don't need – for example, sickness and accident benefits can often be excluded or included at your discretion. If you do take medical coverage, ascertain whether benefits will be paid as treatment proceeds or only after return home, and whether there is a 24-hour medical emergency number. When securing baggage cover, make sure that the per-article limit – typically under £500/$750 – will cover your most valuable possession. If you need to make a claim, you should keep receipts for medicines and medical treatment, and in the event you have anything stolen, you must obtain an official statement from the police.

One thing to check: if you enter a country against the official advice of your government (see p.33), your policy may become invalid – the policy small print will cover that, but you can always call for advice and there is flexibility where the entire country is not a no-go zone.

Rough Guides Travel Insurance

Rough Guides has teamed up with Columbus Direct to offer you **travel insurance** that can be tailored to suit your needs. Products include a low-cost **backpacker** option for long stays; a **short break** option for city getaways; a typical **holiday package** option; and others. There are also annual **multi-trip** policies for those who travel regularly. Different sports and activities (trekking, skiing, etc) can usually be covered if required.

See our website (ⓦwww.roughguidesinsurance.com) for eligibility and purchasing options. Alternatively, UK residents should call ☎0870/033 9988; Australians should call ☎1300/669 999 and New Zealanders should call ☎0800/55 9911. All other nationalities should call ☎+44 870/890 2843.

---

the disease, spread by contaminated food and water. It's a lot less unpleasant having the jabs than catching the disease, which seriously damages your liver and can leave it permanently scarred. The only problem with the hepatitis A course is its cost and the fact that you need to have the first shot at least two weeks before departure.

Hepatitis B, like HIV, is caught through unprotected sexual contact or through the transfer of blood products, usually from shared needles. There is a vaccination, but it's usually only given to people at risk, such as health workers.

The risks of contracting **cholera** are negligible unless you find yourself living in the middle of an epidemic. The vaccine is rarely available, let alone given, but border officials can occasionally still ask for it. Doctors and health services usually offer a **waiver form** that looks like an international vaccination certificate and invariably does the trick.

Immunization against **meningitis** is a good precaution if you're planning extensive travels – outbreaks have occurred in recent years in Nigeria and Burkina Faso.

Malaria

Malaria (*le paludisme* or "*palu*" in French) is caused by a parasite carried in the saliva of *Anopheles* mosquitoes, which can be distinguished by their rather eager head-down position. The parasite is transmitted to humans by the female mosquito, which prefers to bite in the evening. Malaria has a variable **incubation period** of a few days to several weeks, so you can become ill long after being bitten. If you go down with malaria, you'll probably know: the fever, shivering and headaches are something like severe flu and come in waves, usually beginning in the early evening. Malaria is not infectious but it can be dangerous, and even fatal if not treated quickly.

Protection against malaria is absolutely essential in tropical Africa, where the disease is endemic everywhere below the altitude of 1500m. As well as taking a few common-sense measures to **avoid being bitten** (see below), it's vital to be prepared with a course of **preventive tablets**. Outlined below are some of the drugs available, though it's important to discuss the various options with your doctor before deciding which one, or which combination, to take. It's worth noting here that the strain of the malarial parasite commonly found in West Africa, **falciparum**, is both especially severe and often resistant to treatment with chloroquine. **Pregnant women** are at particular risk from the complications of falciparum malaria and need to explore the issue very carefully with their doctor when planning a trip.

Antimalarial drugs

The range of antimalarial drugs available includes **chloroquine**-based tablets (sold under names including Nivaquin and Aralen), **proguanil**-based Paludrine and **pyrimethamine**-based Daraprim and Fansidar. Depending on where you live, you can buy some or all of these without a prescription at a pharmacy before you travel. In West Africa itself, they can be bought in small shops and from street drug stalls all over, though the drugs used with chloroquine-resistant malaria are only available in big towns. When taking any of these tablets to prevent malaria, it's important to keep a routine and cover the period before and after your trip with doses.

Mefloquine (sold as Lariam) has been controversial. Although highly effective, and taken only weekly, about one in four users report neuropsychiatric side-effects ranging from nightmares to depression and paranoia. If you want to use it, you're recommended to start several weeks before your trip, and switch to another drug if necessary.

An excellent, relatively new drug, **atovaquone** (sold as Malarone), has to be taken daily, but can be started a day before you travel and discontinued just a week after you leave the malarial zone. It has few noted side-effects and is recommended by many doctors, but it is the most expensive option.

If you don't mind using an antibiotic as prophylaxis, you could consider **doxycycline**, which is effective against falciparum malaria and can be started just a day before entering a malarial zone A possibly useful side-effect is the protection it can offer against traveller's diarrhoea; on the downside, the steady consumption of antibiotics is generally not advised, and it can make your skin more susceptible to sunburn.

Note that the only completely safe antimalarial for pregnant women and infants is **quinine**, usually used only as treatment.

Mosquito nets and repellents

Sleep under a **mosquito net** when possible – they're inexpensive to buy locally – and burn **mosquito coils** (which you can buy everywhere, though don't use Cock Brand or Lion Brand as these are said to contain the insecticide DDT and are banned in many countries).

Electric mosquito destroyers, which you fit with a pad every night, are less pungent than mosquito coils but more expensive – and you need electricity. The devices that emit a high-frequency **sound** are worthless.

Whenever the mosquitoes are particularly bad, cover exposed skin with a repellent. DEET (short for **diethyltoluamide**) is the base of most of the synthetic ones. So-called "Neat Deet" works well, and you could try soaking wrist and ankle bands in the stuff, diluted 1:9 with water. Beware though: DEET is corrosive and can chew through plastics and artificial fibres.

An excellent, natural, alternative repellent is **citronella oil**, or citronella-based creams of sprays, but they do tend to lose effectiveness quickly.

Treatment of malaria

If you notice the onset of any fever, the priority is to seek **treatment**. Delay can be very risky, and significant numbers of overly casual travellers die of the disease every year. Be aware that the symptoms of malaria can be cyclic, and that after a day or two of improvement you may be knocked out again. It's very important to reduce the fever and drink plenty of clean water.

Ideally, confirm your diagnosis by getting to a doctor and having a blood test to identify the strain. If you cannot get to a doctor, your options for **self-medication** will depend on which drugs are available. Take either four atovaquone (Malarone) tablets daily for three days; or 20mg of mefloquine (Lariam) per kilo of body weight in one or two doses (ie if you weigh 60kg, take 1200mg all at once or in two doses of 600mg). An alternative to these drugs is to take 600mg of quinine, twice a day for seven days, followed at the end of the course by three pyrimethamine-based tablets.

Bilharzia

Schistosomiasis – also known as **bilharzia** – is potentially very nasty, though easily curable. The disease comes from tiny flukes which live in freshwater snails and, as part of their life cycle, leave their hosts and burrow into animal or human skin to multiply in the bloodstream. The snails themselves favour only stagnant water, though the flukes can be swept downstream. While it's possible to pick it up from one brief contact, the risk of contracting bilharzia is fairly low unless you repeatedly come into contact with infected water. If infected, you'll get a slightly itchy rash an hour or two later where the flukes have entered the skin. Bilharzia is most prevalent in the Sahel regions and particularly in artificial lakes. If you have severe abdominal pains and pass blood – the first symptoms occur after four to six weeks – see a doctor.

As regards avoiding the disease, the usual recommendation is never to swim in, wash with, drink or even touch lake or river water that's not been vouched for. On a long trip out in the bush though, this isn't always possible, particularly if you're staying with local people. Snail-free water that has been standing for two days, or has been boiled or chemically treated, is safe, as is brackish water.

Sleeping sickness

Sleeping sickness (**trypanosomiasis**) is mainly a disease of wild animals, but also affects cattle and horses and, to a much lesser extent, people. It's carried by tsetse flies that crowd streams and riverbanks in deep-bush areas. **Tsetse flies** are determined, brutish insects with a painful bite (at rest, their wings fold straight along the abdomen, one on top of the other). They are attracted to large moving objects such as elephants or Land Rovers and you sometimes encounter them when they fly in the windows of vehicles driving through game parks.

Infection is extremely uncommon among travellers – fortunately, because the drugs used to treat it aren't very sophisticated. But a boil which suddenly appears, several days after a tsetse-fly bite, might indicate an infection you should get examined. Untreated, sleeping sickness results in infections of the central nervous system and drowsiness.

Digestive ailments

In many places in West Africa, the water you drink will have come from a tap and is likely to be clean. Since bad water is the most likely cause of **diarrhoea**, you should be cautious of drinking rain- or well-water. If you're visiting for a short time only, it makes sense to be scrupulous – purifying tablets and/or boiling kills most bugs. If you want to be absolutely safe, **purification**, a two-stage process involving both filtration and sterilization, gives the most complete treatment. Portable water-purifiers start from pocket-sized units weighing 60 grams.

For **longer stays**, and especially if you're travelling widely, think of re-educating your stomach rather than fortifying it. It's virtually impossible to travel around the region without exposing yourself to strange bugs from time to time. Take it easy at first, don't overdo the fruit (and wash it in clean, safe water before peeling), don't keep food too long and be very wary of salads. Ironically, perhaps, your chances of picking up stomach bugs are considerably reduced if you stick to inexpensive street restaurants serving one or two freshly prepared dishes (places popular with local people are a good bet), whereas tourist restaurants with a range of dishes on the menu sometimes carelessly thaw and refreeze food, which is often the cause of digestive complaints.

If you do have a serious stomach upset, 24 hours of nothing but boiled water may rinse it out. The important thing is to replace lost fluids. You can make up a **rehydration mix** with four heaped teaspoons of sugar or honey and half a teaspoon of salt dissolved in a litre of water. Most stomach upsets resolve themselves, but if the diarrhoea seems to be getting worse – or you have to travel a long distance while stricken – any pharmacy should have name-brand antidiarrhoea remedies. These (Lomotil, codeine phosphate, etc) shouldn't be overused: a day's worth of doses is about the most you should take.

Antibiotics and antidiarrhoeal drugs shouldn't be used as preventives – this is potentially very dangerous – and you should also avoid jumping for antibiotics at the first sign of trouble. They annihilate what's nicely known as your gut flora (most of which you want to keep). By the time you're considering their use, you should really seek a doctor. If you've definitely got blood in your diarrhoea and it's impossible to see a doctor, then this is the time to take a course of the antibiotic **metronidazole** (commonly sold as Flagyl) – you'll have to get this on prescription before your trip and take it with you.

If you use **oral contraceptives**, don't forget an alternative method to fall back on if you have a stomach upset or take a course of antibiotics, as either can leave you unprotected for the rest of the month.

Other diseases and complaints

Many people get a bout of **prickly heat** rash at first, before they've acclimatized. It's an inflammation of the sweat ducts caused by excessive perspiration which doesn't dry off. A cool shower, **talcum powder** and cotton clothes should help.

On the subject of heat, it's important not to overdose on **sunshine** – at least in the first week or two. The powerful heat and bright light can mess up your system. A hat and sunglasses are necessities. Some people sweat heavily and lose a lot of **salt**; salt tablets, however, are unnecessary – simply sprinkle extra **salt** on your food. Even if you're not a great perspirer, it's important to keep a healthy salt balance. The body can't function without it and it's not uncommon to experience sudden exhaustion a few days after arrival in a hot climate.

STDs, HIV and AIDS

The only other real likelihood of your encountering a serious disease in West Africa is if it's **sexually transmitted**. Assorted venereal diseases are widespread, particularly in the larger towns, and the HIV virus which causes AIDS (known as SIDA in Francophone countries) is alarmingly prevalent and spreading all the time. **Condoms** are available from most pharmacies, or alternatively from some clinics and dispensaries, but they tend

---

Dental care

Make sure that you have a thorough **dental check-up** before leaving and take extra care of your teeth while in West Africa. Stringy meat, acid fruit and too many soft drinks are some of the hazards. As well as your normal routine, floss and brush at least once in the middle of each day. You could also get into the habit of using a fresh "toothbrush stick" cut from a branch, as many locals do. Some varieties (on sale at markets) contain a plaque-destroying enzyme. Get into the habit of chewing gum after eating – even sweet varieties quickly lose their sugar and are soon performing a useful function on your teeth.

If you lose a filling and aren't inclined to see a dentist locally, try and get hold of some **gutta percha**, a natural latex available from some pharmacies; you heat it and then pack it in the hole as a temporary filling. Your dentist could get you some to take with you. **Emergency dental packs** are available from many vaccination centres.

to be expensive or of dubious manufacture, so it's better to take some with you.

On the associated topic of receiving **blood transfusions** or injections in an emergency, you might want to carry a sterile emergency kit to be used by a doctor if you get into trouble. Usually, however, such treatment can only be offered in a hospital environment where most staff are now only too familiar with the need for sterile equipment and fresh needles.

Injuries and animal hazards

Take more care than usual over minor **cuts and scrapes** – the most trivial scratch can become a throbbing infection if you ignore it. As for animal attacks, West African **dogs** are usually sad and skulking and pose little threat though, like captive **monkeys**, they may carry rabies. **Snakes** are common but the vast majority are harmless, and to see one at all you'll need to search stealthily – walk heavily and they obligingly disappear. For reassurance about larger beasts, see p.75.

As for bugs: **scorpions** and **spiders** abound but are hardly ever seen unless you go turning over rocks or logs. Scorpion stings are painful but almost never fatal (walking around at night in bare feet or sandals is the commonest way to get one), while nearly all African spiders – including the large orb spiders that weave huge webs – are completely harmless. The large, unnervingly fast and active **solifugids** (also known as camel spiders or wind scorpions) will only bite if handled – and why would you try to handle one? – but they have no venom at all.

Medical treatment

If you need **medical treatment** in West Africa, you'll discover a frightening lack of well-equipped **hospitals**. In each country, we've tried to indicate which are the best and to give general practitioners and dentists in city "Listings". Blood and urine tests can be performed locally, but for serious treatment you're almost certain to want to come home.

Moderate injuries can be treated locally. In some remote areas, there are **missions** which may have clinics, and these are usually the first recourse. If you require treatment, it's normally proficient and the charges low, though comforts fairly rudimentary.

Travel health centres and resources

For a good **book** on health, get hold of the *Rough Guide to Travel Health* by Dr Nick Jones. If you're living in West Africa – especially if you need to treat yourself or others – the classic *Where There is No Doctor* by David Werner is well worth obtaining.

Websites

ⓦ **www.fitfortravel.scot.nhs.uk** UK NHS website carrying information about travel-related diseases and how to avoid them.
ⓦ **www.istm.org** The website of the International Society for Travel Medicine, with a full list of clinics specializing in international travel health.
ⓦ **www.masta.org** Largest UK network of travel clinics offers the option to buy downloadable health advice specific to the countries you intend to visit.
ⓦ **www.tripprep.com** US. Provides an online-only database of necessary vaccinations for most countries, as well as destination and medical service-provider information.

UK

Hospital for Tropical Diseases Travel Clinic London ⓦ www.thehtd.org. Pre-travel and post-travel advice, jabs and treatment; consultations £15 (by appointment Mon–Fri 9am–5pm).
Liverpool School of Tropical Medicine ⓦ www.liv.ac.uk/lstm. Pre-travel and post-travel advice, jabs and treatment: no appointment required Mon–Fri 9am–noon; by appointment only Mon–Thurs afternoons.
Nomad Travel Clinics London, Bristol and Southampton ⓦ www.nomadtravel.co.uk. Advice, vaccinations, prescriptions and medical kits from friendly staff.
Trailfinders Travel Clinic London ⓦ www.trailfinders.com. No appointment necessary.

Ireland

Tropical Medical Bureau Dublin ⓦ www.tmb.ie/ Comprehensive vaccinations service.

US and Canada

Canadian Society for International Health Ottawa ⓦ www.csih.org. Includes a directory of Canadian travel-health centres.

A medicine bag

There's no need to take a mass of drugs and remedies you'll probably never use. Various items, however, are immensely useful, and well worth buying in advance, especially for a long trip. If you're interested in herbal and other natural remedies, you'll find a wealth of natural cures in markets. You'll have to rely on intuition, common sense and persistent enquiries to judge whether they're worth trying.

Paracetamol Safer than aspirin for pain and fever relief.

Water-purifying (chlorine) tablets or iodine tincture Both taste foul but do the trick, iodine more efficiently than chlorine (and iodine can double as an antiseptic). Ascorbic acid (vitamin C) can be used to neutralize the taste of iodine.

Antimalarial tablets Enough for prophylactic use, plus extra in case of attack.

Antibiotics Amoxicillin (sold as Amoxyl) is a moderate-spectrum antibacterial drug useful against many infections and ciprofloxacin (sold as Ciproxin, among others) can feel like a life-saver in a bowel crisis. Both should only be used as a last resort when you cannot see a doctor and are normally prescription drugs only.

Antidiarrhoeal medication Codeine phosphate (prescription only) or co-phenotrope (sold as Lomotil).

Antifungal powder Clotrimazole (sold as Canestan) is good for sweaty crevices.

Antiseptic cream Creams in tubes invariably squeeze out sooner or later (transfer to a small container).

Alcohol swabs Paper medi-swabs are invaluable for cleaning wounds, insect bites and infections.

Sticking plaster, steri-strip wound closures, sterile gauze dressing, micropore tape You don't need much of this stuff, and you can buy it in most capital cities.

Lip balm Invaluable in dry climates.

Thermometer Very useful. Ideally you'll be 37°C. A forehead thermometer is unbreakable and gives a ready reckoning.

Contact lens solution Hard to find in West Africa.

Centers for Disease Control & Prevention US ⓦwwwn.cdc.gov/travel. Consultation service on immunizations and treatment of diseases for people travelling to developing countries.
International Association for Medical Assistance to Travellers (IAMAT) New York and Guelph, Ontario ⓦwww.iamat.org. Nonprofit, supported by donations.
International SOS Assistance US ⓦwww.internationalsos.com. Members receive pre-trip medical referral info, as well as overseas emergency services designed to complement travel-insurance coverage.

MEDJET Assistance US ⓦwww.medjetassistance.com. Annual membership programme ($225 for individuals, $350 for families) which flies members home or to the hospital of their choice in a medically equipped jet.
Travel Medicine US ⓦwww.travmed.com. Sells travel-health products and books.

Australia and New Zealand

Travellers' Medical and Vaccination Centres ⓣ1300/658844, ⓦwww.tmvc.com.au. Network of clinics covering most major cities in both countries, plus online travel health information.

Costs, money, banks

It's perhaps surprising to find that, in general, West Africa is an expensive part of the world. Mere survival can be dirt cheap, but anything like a Euro-American life-style costs as much, if not more, than in Europe or America. There are important generalities about money in West Africa, but see the individual country chapters for details of the local situation.

In between these extremes you can use the cheapest transport, eat market food and spend nights either camping in the bush, staying with people or in budget hotels. Travelling like this, it's possible to get by on **£400/$800 a month** (though £800/$1600 split between two gets you more value for money). It's clearly much harder to keep costs down in cities such as Dakar or Yaoundé, where a panoply of tempting comforts and consumables is available in every direction and where it's hard to avoid staying in **hotels** – likely to be your biggest single expense.

As a very general guide, a twin room in a very cheap and basic hotel can usually be had for under £10/$20, but only very rarely for under £5/$10. Long-distance **road transport** works out, on average, at about £1.50–4/$3–8 per 100km, though it varies with the quality and speed of the vehicle. **Train** travel, if it's an option, tends to be cheaper and **river travel** more expensive. As for **food**, you can usually fill yourself with calories for under £1/$2 if you eat street food or at a market or lorry-park chop house.

At the other end of the scale, **tourist-class** or **international standard hotels** are predictably expensive in most cities (reckon £50–100/$100–200), and **car rental** rates are some of the highest in the world: across most of the region, a rate in excess of £100/$200 a day for a regular saloon (sedan) or compact is normal.

Bargaining

General stores, groceries and supermarkets invariably have **fixed prices**. Transport costs are usually subject to state or syndicate control and almost always fixed, but baggage can be haggled over. Pretty well every other service (including budget hotel rooms in most countries) can and should be **bargained** over – it's the normal way of conducting business; moreover every time you pay an unreasonable price for goods or services you contribute to local inflation.

Bargaining is often just a case of showing reluctance to pay what you're told is the going rate, and in turn getting some sort of "discount". There's enormous flexibility around a few immutable rules. The most important is never to engage in bargaining if you've no intention of buying the item at any price. To offer what you thought was a silly price and then refuse to pay it can cause grave offence. Nor should you embark on negotiations when you're in a hurry, or if you are feeling less than one hundred percent – it can be an exhausting business.

When negotiating, don't automatically assume you're in the clutches of a rip-off artist. Concepts of **honour** are very important, and stalls are often minded by friends and relatives with whom, if you're quick and convincing, you can sometimes strike real bargains.

Most importantly, men should make **physical contact** – hand-clasping (a

Student cards

An **International Student Identity Card** (ISIC; ⓦ www.isic.org) is no guarantee of cheap deals, but is worth waving for many payments (airlines, railways, museum entrance fees) you may make. If you are a student, it's useful also to have a rubber-stamped letter substantiating the fact.

prolonged handshake) is usually enough to emphasize a point. Be as jocular as possible and don't be shy of making a big scene – the bluffing and mock outrage on both sides is part of the fun. Women can't pursue these negotiating tactics in quite the same way, except when buying from women – invariably much tougher anyway.

Getting down to **figures**, try to delay the moment when you have to name your price. When you hear "One hundred, how much you pay?", say nothing. It's amazing how often the seller's price drops way below your expectation before you've made any offer, so forget the standard "offer-a-third-come-up-to-a-half" formulas. If you seem to have reached a stalemate, a bored companion tugging your sleeve is always a help. But if you do arrive at an unbridgeable gap you can always drop the matter and come by later.

Currencies

Nine different currencies are used in the West African countries covered in this book. The currency of all the **Francophone** countries in West Africa, with two exceptions, is the **CFA franc**. There are in fact two types of CFA (pronounced "seffa" or "siffa", and standing for Communauté Financière de l'Afrique). Most of the Francophone West African states, except Mauritania and Guinea, are members of the Union Monétaire Ouest Africaine, and these countries use one variety of CFA franc, as does Guinea-Bissau, though not itself Francophone. Cameroon's currency is also CFA, but of a different regional grouping, the Communauté Économique et Monétaire Financière de l'Afrique Centrale – which includes Chad, the Central African Republic, Gabon, Equatorial Guinea and Republic of the Congo.

CFA francs are guaranteed by the French treasury and have a fixed value of CFA655.957 to €1. CFAs come in 1, 5, 10, 25, 50, 100 and 250 **coins,** and **notes** of 500, 1000, 2500, 5000 and 10,000, making this easily the most convenient African currency.

Although of equal value, the two types of CFA can't be spent outside their own region, and cannot be interchanged in

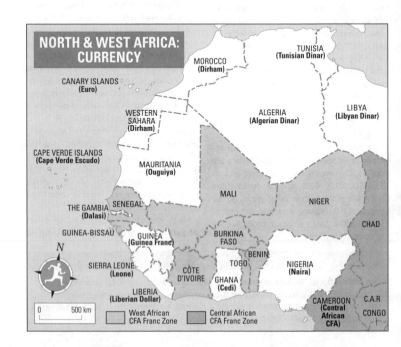

NORTH & WEST AFRICA: CURRENCY

TUNISIA **(Tunisian Dinar)**

MOROCCO **(Dirham)**

CANARY ISLANDS **(Euro)**

WESTERN SAHARA **(Dirham)**

ALGERIA **(Algerian Dinar)**

LIBYA **(Libyan Dinar)**

CAPE VERDE ISLANDS **(Cape Verde Escudo)**

MAURITANIA **(Ouguiya)**

MALI

NIGER

CHAD

THE GAMBIA **(Dalasi)**

SENEGAL

GUINEA-BISSAU

GUINEA **(Guinea Franc)**

BURKINA FASO

N

SIERRA LEONE **(Leone)**

CÔTE D'IVOIRE

BENIN

TOGO

GHANA **(Cedi)**

NIGERIA **(Naira)**

LIBERIA **(Liberian Dollar)**

CAMEROON **(Central African CFA)**

C.A.R

CONGO

0   500 km

☐ West African CFA Franc Zone   ☐ Central African CFA Franc Zone

Exchange rates

At the time of writing (Feb 2008) the following official exchange rates apply:

	£1 =	€1 =	$1 =
CFA franc	880	656	451
Cape Verde escudo	146	109	75
Ghana cedi	1.94	1.40	0.98
Gambian dalasi	44.4	32.8	22.4
Guinean franc	8425	6251	4294
Mauritanian ouguiya	496	370	254
Nigerian naira	231	172	118
Sierra Leonean leone	5810	4328	2970

any bank in the region either. Because of French backing, the CFA is a relatively hard currency – major banks in Europe will sometimes exchange CFA francs at their euro equivalent – and currency laws in the countries which use it are generally relaxed. In theory there are limits to the value of CFA you can export, even from one CFA state to another, but in practice these are very rarely enforced and wouldn't inconvenience normal travellers.

The countries **outside the franc zone** have their own, usually weaker ("soft") currencies. Mauritania uses the **ouguiya**; Cape Verde the Cape Verdean **escudo** (pegged to the euro); The Gambia the **dalasi**; Guinea the **Guinean franc**; Ghana the **cedi**; Sierra Leone the **leone**; and Nigeria the **naira.** West Africa's English-speaking countries are in discussion over the formation of a new monetary union, the West African Monetary Zone, with a common currency, but this is likely to be some years away.

Banks and exchange

West Africa is still largely a **cash-based economy** and the infrastructure for card payment services to function easily is only beginning to appear.

West African **banking systems** are generally slow and limited and the capital cities are by far the best places to change money. It's always a good idea to check out the local **forex bureaux** or *bureaux de change*, which are invariably more efficient than the banks, and sometimes offer a better rate. You will always need your passport.

Debit and credit cards

The simplest way to get local cash is to make withdrawals using your current account (checking account) **debit card** from ATMs – these are gradually springing up in towns – and the flat transaction fee is usually fairly small.

Credit cards can be a handy back-up for **cash advances** either at an ATM or a bank counter. However, don't count on getting a cash advance anywhere outside the CFA zone (though it is possible in the odd location). Even in Francophone capitals you'll have to find the right bank. Remember a credit-card cash advance is a loan, with interest accruing daily from the date of withdrawal. **Visa** and **MasterCard** are the only widely recognized cards and can increasingly be used for payment at high-end hotels and restaurants and other businesses. Other cards have next to no recognition.

Traveller's cheques

Traveller's cheques have never been an easy solution to carrying money in West Africa (waiting half a day for the local bank to get the call from head office with the rate of exchange used to be a regular travel pastime), and now that ATMs and card-payment services are emerging, their days are numbered. If you choose to take them, you'll find only certain banks will exchange them. Euros are the preferred currency for traveller's cheques, and sometimes the only one that a bank will change. In addition, some large hotels will take traveller's cheques (again preferably in euros), but very few other businesses will accept them. Banks often require to see the **receipt** for the original purchase of the cheques. Make sure you keep a record of the serial numbers safe and separate from the cheques themselves. In the event that traveller's cheques are lost or stolen, the issuing company will expect you to report the loss immediately.

Cash

Cash euros are widely acceptable as payment in the CFA countries, though prices tend to be marked up a little over the CFA656-to-the-euro official rate. Like traveller's cheques, **denominations** of euros, pounds and/or dollars that you carry should be as small as you can manage, bearing in mind the bulk that a large sum of local cash is likely to amount to. If you take US$50 or €50 notes for convenience, make sure you have plenty of smaller bills as well. A small stash of really low-value hard-currency notes (US$1 and €5) is always useful.

Where CFA countries border non-CFA countries, your surplus CFA cash can't be changed in the banks, but it can generally be changed with ease in the street or at a shop on

the **parallel market** or "black market" – which is no longer considered an illegal activity in the liberalized economies of most countries in the region. If you do use the parallel market, avoid literally standing in the street for the transaction: either use a shop-based currency trader (just ask around), or adjourn to a shop or somewhere similar and count everything before handing over your cash.

Wiring money

Having **money "wired" from home** is easy, but because of the cost – around 5 percent in fees – is probably still a last resort. Money is usually only paid out in the local currency. Using the companies' websites, you can wire money to yourself, from any Internet café, paying on your credit card and picking it up at your nominated local agent.

MoneyGram International UK ☎0800/8971 8971, US ☎1-800/926-3947, Canada ☎1-800/933-3278, ⓦwww.moneygram.com.
Western Union US and Canada ☎1-800/325-6000, Australia ☎1800/501 500, New Zealand ☎09/270 0050, UK ☎0800/833 833, Republic of Ireland ☎1800/395 395, ⓦwww.westernunion.com.

Getting around

Private car ownership isn't common in West Africa, and most local people rely on public transport, lifts (hitchhiking) or walking to get around. While road transport is a good way to travel cheaply in the company of ordinary Africans you might not otherwise encounter, it can test your patience and powers of endurance. It's a mistake to set yourself a rigid timetable when planning extensive travels in the region, since delays on all modes of transport are commonplace and even flight bookings are not guaranteed.

What follows here is a general user's guide to West African transport. Information about transport conditions in each country is given in the "Getting around" section of the practical information at the beginning of each chapter.

Bush taxis

The classic form of West African public transport is the **bush taxi** (*taxi brousse* in French, plus numerous local terms). Bush taxis are nearly all licensed passenger vehicles, serving approved routes at fixed rates. Many even have notional schedules, though these are never published and rarely adhered to.

The vehicle itself can vary from a reasonably comfortable Peugeot estate car (station wagon) seating five or six plus driver, to the same thing seating nine or ten in discomfort, to a converted **Japanese pick-up** with slat-wood benches and a canvas awning jammed with fifteen people or more. A basket of chickens stuffed under the bench, and maybe a goat or two tied to the roof are regular fare-paying additions. Larger, French **box vans**, increasingly replaced by Japanese and Korean **minibuses**, are no less zoo-like, though padded benches or seats help, as does the extra ventilation. Most vehicles have roof-rack luggage carriers and a more expensive seat or two at the front, next to the driver.

Peugeot taxis generally sell their places and drive straight from A to B, if possible without stopping. They often do the trip in half the time it takes a more beat-up bush taxi, which may drop people off and take fares en route. But the converted pick-ups (*bâchés* in French, after their tarpaulins) are often the only way to get to more obscure destinations, or to travel on the roughest roads; not surprisingly, they're cheaper.

Beware of inadvertently **chartering** a bush taxi (a *déplacement* in French) which some drivers will assume you, as a foreign visitor, require (or they'll pretend to assume it). When you charter the vehicle, you're paying for all the seats.

Given that it's rare to undertake any journey over 20km in West Africa without encountering a posse of uniforms at the side of the road, you should pay some attention to the condition of driver and vehicle before deciding to give him your custom. A neatly turned-out Peugeot with a well-tied load is likely to pause for a greeting and move on. Conversely, a bruised and shaken *camion bâché* (a covered pick-up) with nineteen passengers, no lights and the contents of someone's house on the roof may be detained for some hours.

Bush taxis are probably the most dangerous vehicles on the roads, so don't be afraid to make a very big fuss if the driver

appears to have lost all sense. Ask and then shout at him to slow down (say "*lentement!*" in French – gently, slowly) and try to enlist the support of fellow travellers – though this is rarely forthcoming. In Peugeots it's nice to have a couple of cassettes for the stereo. In any vehicle, and in most parts of West Africa, sharing some kola nuts goes down well (see *West African food plants* colour section). Lastly, if you're in a van with an engine mounted underneath the front cab, be sure not to sit near it – you'll melt.

Taxi parks

Most towns have a **taxi park** ("garage", "motor park", "station", "stand", *gare routière*, *autogare*) where vehicles assemble to fill with passengers. Larger towns may have several, each serving different routes and usually located on the relevant road out, at the edge of town.

Practice varies slightly from country to country, but generally when you go to the taxi park, you'll find you're quickly surrounded by **taxi scouts** trying to get you into their vehicle. This can be frustrating and sometimes unnerving – when there's lots of competition and you're physically mobbed. It pays to behave robustly and to know exactly where you're going, and the names of any towns en route or beyond. It's often the case that your destination is not where all the vehicles are headed. You may have to change, or get out earlier.

The ideal **time to travel** is early in the morning. By a couple of hours after sunrise the best vehicles have gone. In many parts there won't be another until the next day.

Before long on your travels, you'll run into a situation where you seem to be the only passenger in a vehicle you were assured was about to leave. It's true your presence will encourage others to join you – which is why they wanted you there in the first place. But sometimes it's better to forget over-ambitious travel plans (especially any time after noon) or to take a shorter journey with a vehicle that really is about to go. Taxi parks are full of interest for up to an hour or so, but a half-day spent acting as passenger bait is a waste of time.

As for **fares**: in order to guarantee you'll stay and attract others, drivers, owners and scouts will often try to get you to pay up front. Again, practice varies from country to country. Your luggage tied on the roof generally ought to be sufficient sign of your good faith and, unless you see others paying, it's always best to delay, if only because breakdowns are quite frequent and if you've already paid, you would need a refund. Make sure you pay the right person when you do. It's common for small offices or booths at the taxi park to issue tickets on behalf of one or more operators.

Overcharging passengers is almost unheard of. It's your **luggage** that will cost you if you don't argue fiercely about how small, light and streamlined it is. Local fellow passengers are just as likely to suffer but in fact are not in such a good position to create a scene as you are: shout, compare and contrast; tell the crowd how he's trying to kill you with his grasping ways. Make them laugh; make him happy to give you a good price. If you get nowhere, go to one side with him and be conspiratorial – this sometimes works because people like to show off business acumen and it draws attention again. You shouldn't have to pay more than **one third** (normally much less) of your fare for a backpack or large bag. Remember, you can argue forever about what you're *going* to pay, but once you've paid it, the argument is over.

During long waits it's a good idea to keep an eye on your luggage. Anything

---

Whether travelling by bus or bush taxi, it's worth considering your general direction through the trip and **which side to sit on** for the shadiest ride. This is especially important on dirt roads when the combination of slow, bumpy ride, dust and fierce sun can be horrible. If you're travelling on a busy dirt road with lots of other traffic, you don't want to be seated on the left of the vehicle in any case. A final note of warning: on some air-conditioned buses the windows are designed not to be opened and if the air conditioning then doesn't work, you're in for an uncomfortable ride to say the least: get a seat at the front, and on the shady side.

---

tied on the roof is safe, but taxi parks are notorious haunts for **thieves**, and small bags sometimes get grabbed through open windows. Keep valuables round your neck. Don't worry unduly, however, if the vehicle, while waiting to fill, and with booked passengers scattered around, suddenly takes off with all your gear on top. While it's obviously a good idea to make a mental note of the vehicle number plate, you should avoid causing offence by appearing anxious. Often nobody will know where they've gone (probably to fill up with fuel), but they will be back.

Buses

Bus travel is usually more comfortable and less expensive than going by bush taxi, though certain manifestations are little better than gigantic bush taxis and not always much faster.

The big advantage of most buses is having your own seat (even Peugeot bush taxis usually sell more places than there are seats) and being able to buy tickets in advance for a departure at a set time. Having bought a ticket, leave a small item of no value on a seat to reserve it (like a bottle of water) and avoid having to wait inside the vehicle. Even on buses, there's still some room for discussion over the cost of transporting your luggage, but it's rarely a big issue.

Lorries and trucks

Although it's usually against the law, on all main routes – and in the remotest regions too – you'll be able to travel by **lorry**. Pick up a lift in small villages or along the road: because of its illegality, you'll rarely find a truck ride in a large town. You need to know the equivalent bush-taxi or bus fares and distances or you'll find yourself **paying** over the odds. Once aboard, you can expect the lorry to stop at every checkpoint to pay bribes – slow progress.

There's sometimes a spare seat or two in the cab, but more often space in the back. **Travelling in the back** of enclosed, panelled vehicles is pretty miserable, but many older trucks are open at the back with wood-frame sides. When loaded with suitable cargo, these can be a delight to travel in.

You get great views and even, on occasions, a comfortable ride in a recumbent position. Do bear in mind your safety however (look out for low branches) and avoid getting the driver in trouble with the police by being conspicuous or foolhardy.

Travelling in an **empty goods lorry** on bad roads can be close to intolerable, but because they aren't carrying paying freight, they are often available. They go much faster unladen and you're typically forced to stand and clasp the sides as the vehicle smashes through potholes. Lorries often drive late into the night too – if you're being carried outside, especially in hilly regions, be sure to have **something warm to wear** for later.

Hitchhiking

The majority of rural people in West Africa get around by **waving down a vehicle**, but they invariably pay, whether in a truck or in a private car. Private vehicles are still comparatively rare and usually full. **Travelling for free** is often considered to be rather improper and most people will assume your car has broken down. There's some sense, however, in hitching in and out of large cities, especially if you can't find a bus or taxi. The kinds of drivers who respond positively are usually foreign-educated business types or expats.

Hitching **techniques** need to be exuberant. A modest thumb in the air is more likely to be interpreted as a friendly, or rude, gesture than a request. Beckon the driver to stop with your palm. You'll feel like a policeman but that doesn't matter. Always explain first if you can't – or won't – pay, and don't be surprised if you're left at the side of the road.

The best chances for conventional hitching are in Senegal, Niger and Nigeria. Hitching with overland tourists can be a good change of pace, and – if you're in the right vicinity – it can throw you in with people visiting game parks and other relatively inaccessible attractions.

Trains

In colonial times, there was a French plan to push a **railway** across the Sahara, linking Algiers with Dakar. Had it succeeded, it might

have altered today's network, in which only two of the eight West African railway systems cross borders. And of those systems most are no more than single lines running from the coast to the interior.

In practice only three lines are much used by travellers: in Cameroon between **Yaoundé and Ngaoundéré**; the Océan-Niger line between **Bamako and Dakar**; and – until recent troubles – the line between **Abidjan and Ouagadougou**. Although other railway lines exist, not all of them are running and some are freight-only. Travelling by train in West Africa is usually slower than road and, while you can always get street food through the windows at stations, you should take your own drinking water for the duration. Toilets are rarely usable by the time you've left the city.

Ferries

There are hundreds of small, hand-hauled or spluttering diesel ferries pulling people and vehicles across the rivers of West Africa. But proper river transport is very limited. The most interesting **ferry services** run on the Niger River in Mali, from the height of the rainy season to a couple of months after it finishes. Apart from the Ghanaian services on Lake Volta and The Gambian service across the mouth of the Gambia River from Banjul to Barra, there are few other significant car ferries operating in the region.

On the Niger, more or less anywhere between Kouroussa in Guinea and Niamey in Niger, you can usually negotiate a passage in a **pirogue** (a dug-out or plank canoe) or a **pinasse** (a larger, motorized freight-carrying vessel) at any time of year, but in parts of Mali this has now become extremely expensive.

There's virtually no scheduled regional **sea transport** except for ferries connecting the Cape Verde islands with each other (and occasionally Dakar), and minor shipping on the coasts of Senegal, Guinea-Bissau, Sierra Leone, Nigeria and Cameroon.

Flights

At the time of writing, the only West African interstate **airlines** are Ghana International, Cameroon Airlines and Air Sénégal International, which together more or less cover the region. Others (the larger of which operate interstate services) include Air Burkina, Air Ivoire, Bellview, Air Mauritanie and TACV of Cape Verde. Several "national airlines" are virtually defunct. Everywhere, with the new market-economic thrust of recent years, private entrepreneurs are setting up small airlines of light and medium-sized aircraft. Most flights on these airlines are operated on a charter basis, though sometimes with regularity, so you can buy a seat, in effect, from the charterer.

Flights **between West African countries** are expensive, and travel by air not automatically the quickest option. Beware of lower-than-expected baggage allowances on some internal flights.

There's little unofficial discounting of fares; most tickets get sold at the approved fares, though in some cases you'll find it hard to discover what those fares are. If you possess an ISIC student card it's always worth requesting a **student reduction**.

Always book as soon as you can and rebook if plans change, rather than wait until you're certain. This also gives you leverage in terms of personal recognition at the airline office, and bookings don't require a deposit as a rule. Be utterly sceptical of a "confirmed seat" until you're sitting in it. Arrive at the airport long before the flight if you've any doubt about the status of your booking, and always **reconfirm your seat** in person two days before the flight.

Car rental

Car rental is available in nearly every capital city, at most of the larger airports and in one or two provincial towns in a number of countries. You are normally expected to **take a driver** with the car (indeed the insurance cover may only be for a car rented with driver), which doesn't make much difference to the price and can work out brilliantly. Whether you're driving or being driven, you should have an **international driving licence** with you (see p.27). Good drivers are more like guides and, if they know the country or region well, can save you lots of time and hassle. Doing the driving yourself will not really save you any money and, in any case, having a driver means no parking or security concerns, no dealing with city traffic

and someone else to cope with breakdown problems.

Don't automatically assume the vehicle is roadworthy. **Before setting off**, have a look at the engine and tyres and don't leave without checking water, battery and spare tyre (preferably two, with the means to change them) and making sure you've a few tools. If you're driving off the main roads, it's important to keep jerry cans of water and spare fuel on board. As for breakdowns, local mechanics are usually excellent and can apply creative ingenuity to the most disastrous situations. But spare parts, tools and proper equipment are rare away from the main highways – and not really common along them.

There are several other points to bear in mind. First, rented cars cannot as a rule be driven into **neighbouring countries**. And some firms insist on **four-wheel-drive** (4x4) if you'll be departing from surfaced highways – which can be astronomically expensive.

An alternative is to consider simply **renting a taxi** on a daily basis. Pay for the fuel separately and settle every other question – including the driver's bed and board – in advance. However good the price, don't take on a vehicle that's unsafe, or a driver you don't like and can't communicate with.

Motorcycle rental is less common than car rental, but available in some cities. However, if you have some experience, it is well worth considering buying a machine in West Africa, avoiding the expense and paperwork of riding or shipping a bike all the way from Europe. In Mali, for example, reliable and economical Honda 125s are widely available and make ideal machines, if not overloaded (and you shouldn't find it too hard to find a buyer for your motorbike at the end of your trip).

Avis ⓦ www.avis.com. Senegal, The Gambia, Mali, Cape Verde, Guinea, Burkina Faso, Ghana, Togo, Benin, Niger, Nigeria and Cameroon.

Europcar ⓦ www.europcar.co.uk. Mauritania, Senegal, The Gambia, Mali, Cape Verde, Guinea-Bissau, Guinea, Sierra Leone, Burkina Faso, Ghana, Togo, Benin, Niger and Nigeria.

Hertz ⓦ www.hertz.com. Senegal, Mali, Cape Verde, Benin, Nigeria, Cameroon and Ghana.

National ⓦ www.nationalcar.com. Senegal, Burkina Faso and Benin.

Rules of the road

When driving, beware of unexpected rocks and ditches – not to mention animals and people – on the road. It's accepted practice to honk your horn stridently to warn pedestrians.

All of West Africa **drives on the right**, though in reality vehicles keep to the best part of the road until they have to pass each other (fatefully positioned potholes account for many head-on collisions). Right-hand and left-hand **signals** are conventionally used to say "please overtake" or "don't overtake", but you shouldn't assume the driver in front of you can see the road ahead. In fact, never assume anything about the behaviour of other drivers.

As a foreigner, you're unlikely to be kept for long by **police** or other security forces at the roadside, but you should never pass a checkpoint or barrier without stopping and waiting to be waved on. Nor should you ever drive anywhere without all your **documents**.

Cycling

In many ways **cycling** is the ideal form of transport in West Africa, giving you total independence. A bike gives scope for exploring off the beaten track and getting round cities. Routes that can't be used by motor vehicles – even motorcycles – because they're too rough, or involve crossing rivers, are all accessible. With a tough mountain-bike, you can explore off the roads altogether, using bush paths. You can camp out all the time if you wish, or take your bike into hotel rooms with you. If you get tired of pedalling, you have the simple option of transporting your bike on top of a bush taxi or bus (reckon on paying about half-fare) or even "cycle-hitching".

Depending on your fitness and enthusiasm, expect to cycle around 1000km a month, including at least two days off for every three on the road. During periods when you're basically cycling from A to B (often on a paved road, which is somewhat slow on a mountain bike), you'll find 40–50km in the early morning and 20–30km more in the afternoon is plenty.

Finding and carrying **water** is a daily chore on a long cycle trip. You'll need at least one five-litre container per person per day, and more if you're camping out and want a quick shower, but you shouldn't often need to carry it full.

If time is limited, you can **fly your bike** to West Africa. To avoid paying excess-baggage charges, you contact the airline in advance, pack as many heavy items into your hand luggage as possible and arrive several hours before the flight to get to know the check-in staff. It's rare that you'll be obliged to pay any excess-baggage charge and few airlines will insist your bike be boxed or bagged, but it's best to turn the handlebars into the frame and tie them down, invert the pedals and deflate the tyres.

Out on the road, you'll probably want to **carry your gear** in panniers. These are fiendishly inconvenient when not attached to the bike, however, and you might consider sacrificing ideal load-bearing and stream-lining for a backpack you can lash down on the rear carrier; you'll probably have to do this anyway if you buy a bike locally. Using the kind of cane used for local cane furniture, plus lashings made from inner-tube rubber strips, you can create your own highly un-aerodynamic carrier, with room for a box of food and a gallon of water underneath.

With a bike from home, remember to take a battery **lighting system** (dynamo lighting is a pain) as it's surprising how often you'll need it. The front light doubles as a torch and getting batteries is no problem.

It's worth taking a U-bolt **cycle lock**: in towns, where it's essential you lock the bike, you'll always find something to lock it to – out in the bush it's less important. Alternatively, you can improvise with a padlock and chain in a piece of hosepipe, which you can buy and fix up in any market.

One final, *essential* piece of kit: on busy roads a **rear-view mirror** is indispensable.

Apart from the commonest parts, **spares for mountain bikes** are rare in West Africa. But take only what you're sure to need – spare tubes, spare spokes and a good tool kit. If you need to do anything major, you can always borrow large spanners and other heavy equipment. Don't bother with spare tyres if you're going for under six months. On a long trip, it's worth talking to a reputable dealer before you leave so that, in an emergency, you can email for a part to be sent out by courier.

You can forgo any hassles associated with having an expensive bike by **buying** one locally. There are bike shops and market areas devoted to cycling in most large towns. Ouagadougou in Burkina Faso has long been one of the cheapest places to buy, with a vast area devoted to bikes and good secondhand possibilities from about £50/$100. You should be able to get a new bike for under £100/$200.

You can **rent bicycles and mopeds** in a number of places. But they're not usually well-adapted for touring, although they often have carriers. Anywhere you fancy cycling, however, you can often make informal arrangements to lease a bike for a few days.

Walking and riding

Clearly, if you're hardy and not tied to any schedule, you can simply **walk** in West Africa. All over the region, you'll come across local people walking vast distances because they have no money *at all* to pay for transport. If you're hiking for a few days you can fall in with them (if you can manage to keep up), but their French or English may well be limited.

From a more recreational angle, a number of **hiking possibilities** throughout West Africa are covered in the country chapters, mostly in upland and mountainous regions.

Using a **beast of burden** for your travels is an attractive idea. Unfortunately, **horses** succumb quickly in the more southern tsetse-fly regions, and a horse in good shape is expensive. If you know what to look for and how to care for a horse, the most promising districts are sub-Sahelian – most of southern Mali, Burkina Faso, southern Niger, northern Nigeria and further south into highland Cameroon. If you ride south towards the coast, however, and sell your animal, it's likely to end up in a pot.

Mules are a lot tougher (they're used to long treks), cheaper and will happily go further south in the dry season. You'd need three mules between two with luggage, however. Then there are **camels** (dromedaries: *méharis* in Arabic or *chameaux* in French). It's not impossible to join a caravan in the desert or northern Sahel, though fewer and fewer such journeys are made these days. But buying, equipping and travelling with your own animals is not to be undertaken lightly even by the most qualified romantic.

Accommodation

There's not a huge diversity of accommodation options in West Africa. A good range of hotels is found only in the cities, and in several countries even hotels are rather uncommon outside the capital. Hostels of various kinds are usually an urban phenomenon, often permanently full and not to be relied upon, and there are no IYHA youth hostels. *Campements*, found in several of the French-speaking countries, are basically rustic motels, usually in the bush. The options of staying with local people or camping in the bush are usually there, depending on how you travel. Organized campgrounds are rare.

Hotels

In capitals and large towns, you'll want, and probably be obliged, to stay in hotels. There tends to be a gap between the expensive places and the dives, and you sometimes need to look hard to find something good at a reasonable price. If you're splurging, there's usually a clutch of international establishments bookable from abroad. Local star ratings are not much used and, in any case, about as hopeless an indication of value for money as anywhere else.

Accommodation price codes

All accommodation prices in this book are coded according to the following scale. Prices refer to the rate you can expect to pay for a room with two beds or some-times a double bed for two people. Single rooms, or single occupancy, will normally cost at least two-thirds of the twin-occupancy rate. Bear in mind that only the most expensive establishments have a set rate for every room and there's often a chance to negotiate a better deal. In most countries, for a very simple but decent twin room with clean sheets, air conditioning and bathroom, expect to pay upwards of £10–15/$20–30 (❸). You can often get a fairly mediocre place, usually without air conditioning and usually without hot water, for about £5–10/$10–20 (❷). Many hotels in the ❽ bracket run to $200 or more.

❶ Under £5/$10
❷ £5–10/$10–20
❸ £10–15/$20–30
❹ £15–20/$30–40

❺ £20–30/$40–60
❻ £30–40/$60–80
❼ £40–50/$80–100
❽ Over £50/$100

The few mid-range hotels are usually well-run and nice enough places to stay. But small-town hotels – and of course the cheapest joints in the cities – are usually equated with drinking and prostitution. Rooms are often taken for an hour or two only, and there may well be a gang of women and toddlers permanently in residence. Don't be put off unduly. These can be fun places to stay – and by no means all are intimidating places for female travellers – though you may have to pick a room carefully (not easy) for anything like a quiet night.

Inexpensive hotels

In inexpensive hotels, always ask to see the room first and don't be surprised if it looks like a tornado's passed through, especially in the morning before it's been cleaned. Always ask for fresh clean sheets and towel if you're not happy with them. If you suspect bedbugs may lurk behind the plaster, pull the beds away from the wall; keeping the light on deters them.

It's always worth **haggling** over the price of a room, and check there'll be no extra tax on top. If there's air conditioning or a fan but no electricity, ask for a discount. You usually pay on taking the room and may have to leave your passport with the person in charge if there's no registration card to fill out. Use discretion about leaving your keys with the management and, if your door locks by padlock, use your own

and check the fixture. Finally, in highland regions or during the *harmattan* (the wind that blows in the Sahel region in December and January), it's normally expected you'll ask for a bucket of hot water to supple-ment the cold tap or well – but it may not be offered.

Hostels, campements and resthouses

Although there are no internationally affiliated youth hostels in West Africa, you'll find **YMCA** and **YWCA hostels** in several Anglophone cities which are usually permanently full of students and single professionals. If you can get in, they're great places to meet people and, though they're generally run by slightly pious types, there are few limiting restrictions on what you do and when.

For non-camping travellers, alternative types of "hotel" accommodation are popular options in the rural areas. **Campements**, in French-speaking countries, have a fairly loose definition. They're certainly not campsites, though you can sometimes camp at them, but represent more the modern equivalent of a colonial caravan-

---

The following abbreviations have been used in accommodation reviews:

a/c: air conditioning, air-conditioned
s/c: self-contained or en suite, with private shower or bath, and toilet
B&B: Bed and breakfast

serai or "encampment" in the bush, often associated with game parks and areas of natural beauty. They tend to consist of huts or small room blocks made of local materials (often mud bricks and thatch) with shared washing and toilet facilities. At the top end they're effectively motels. At their most innovative, in Senegal, where some are known as CTRIs (*campements touristiques rurals integrés* – "rurally integrated"), they are built with government loans by local villagers in order to host independent travellers.

In the English-speaking countries a network of government **resthouses**, for the use of officials on tour, is theoretically at the disposal of travellers when rooms aren't occupied. There's a similar network of government "villas" in Guinea. In fact, these places are very often unused for long periods and need a good airing. Water and electricity are often turned off or disconnected. First, in any case, you have to find the caretaker to open up.

Lastly, there are the resthouses associated with the **NGOs** – the aid, development, voluntary and other nongovernmental organizations, including the US Peace Corps (some 1400 of whose graduate volunteers are on placements in thirteen West African countries at any one time) and, somewhat thinly these days, **missions**. If you're travelling extensively, you may find these alternatives helpful and generous. In some cases – a few of the Peace Corps resthouses, for example – there's a special tariff for "outsiders". But in general you'll be staying explicitly as a guest, using facilities intended for others. Where such arrangements are based on informal invitations and strictly word-of-mouth, we've usually kept them that way and not included them in the Guide.

Camping

The few **campsites** that exist in West Africa are covered in the main country chapters. There are some in Mali, Mauritania and Niger, one or two on the coast in Togo and virtually no others. If you're bringing a tent, bring the lightest one you can afford; there are lots of good models around these days with snap-together aluminium frames. Or, if the prices put you off, consider making your own with rip-stop nylon and fine nylon netting – not as hard to do as it sounds if you have any skill with a sewing machine.

Camping rough depends much on your style of travel. Clearly, if you're driving your own vehicle it's only necessary to find a good spot for the night. Don't assume you can always do this anonymously. A vehicle in the deep bush is unusual and noisy, and people will flock round to watch you. Bush camping is easier if you're cycling or walking. For safety's sake, always get right away from the main road to avoid being accidentally run over or exciting the interest of occasional motorized bandits. You may still be visited by delegations of machete-wielding villagers, especially if you light a fire, but confirmation that you're harmless is usually their first concern. Some cigarettes or a cup of tea breaks any ice. If you're travelling by public transport, however, it's a lot harder to camp effectively night after night. Vehicles go from town to town and it's rare to be dropped off at just the right spot in between, all ready and supplied for a night under the stars. Walking out of town in search of a place to camp – it can be miles – is an exercise which soon palls.

In more heavily populated or farmed districts, it's usually best to ask someone before pitching a tent. Out in the wilds, hard or thorny ground is likely to be the only obstacle. Fill your water bottles from a village before looking for a site. During the dry season, you'll rarely have trouble finding wood for a small fire so a **stove** isn't absolutely necessary, though it can be very useful for wet or barren conditions. You can find *camping gaz* butane cartridges in most capital cities. Petrol stoves are more convenient once you've shelled out for them. If you're cycle-camping, a small kerosene lamp is perfectly feasible. Be sure to buy kerosene (*pétrole* in French) however, and not petrol/gasoline (*essence*). Wild animals pose little threat (see p.75) and night-time noises, especially in forest regions – some spectacularly eerie and sinister shrieks and calls – merely add to the atmosphere.

Staying with people

All over West Africa you'll run into people who want to put you up for the night. A warm, but more noticeably, a *dutiful* **hospitality** characterizes most of these contacts and it's often difficult to know how to repay such kindness, particularly since it often seems so disruptive of family life, with you set up in the master bedroom and kids sent running for special things for the guest. While it's impossible to generalize, for female guests a trip to the market with the woman or women of the household is an opportunity to pay for everything. Men can't do this, but buying a sack of rice or a big bundle of yams (get it delivered by barrow or porter) makes a generous gift.

Eating and drinking

West Africa has little in the way of well-defined cuisines, in large part because supplies are erratic, recipes aren't written down, and thus no two meals are ever quite the same. Nevertheless, there's a considerable variety of culinary pleasures and an infinite range of intoxicating drinks. Describing it all is complicated by the variety of terms used for common ingredients. For a broad rundown on the fruit, vegetables and cereals of the region, see the *West African food plants* colour section.

Where to eat

If you're lucky enough to be staying **with a family**, you're likely to experience consistently well-prepared and tasty food – though according to their means this may depend on how much you contribute. In homes, or when travelling on long-distance trucks or by trading canoe, people eat around a **communal dish** (in strictly Islamic regions always males at one, females at another, and generally finishing in order of age, the eldest first). Because of this, and because the cash economy is still relatively undeveloped, restaurants, where customers sit down and buy meals for themselves, are not all that common.

Don't assume you can't eat well at the cheapest **street food and market stalls** however. The secret is to eat early – this means late morning (11am–noon) and dusk (5–6pm), when most people eat and food is fresh. Street food isn't usually a takeaway – there's often a table and benches, plastic bowls, spoons and cold water. Anything extra you want – soft drinks, instant coffee – can be fetched for you from nearby.

If you want to eat in more privacy, most towns, even the smallest, have at least one or two **basic restaurants** (sometimes called **chop houses** in the Anglophone countries). Much of the menu is likely to be unavailable, however, and there's probably more cause for hesitation over what you eat in small restaurants where you can't be certain of the freshness or provenance of your food, than there is from street stalls where it all has to be cooked before your eyes.

Large towns have a larger choice of restaurants and relatively fewer street-food options. Dining on chop-house cooking at inflated prices in a silver-service restaurant seems odd at first, but can be a real treat. Throughout the Guide, phone numbers for restaurants are given where **reservations** are advised. The eating-out alternative to African food, in cities, is usually **French** or vaguely **European**, **Chinese** or **Middle Eastern**. **Lebanese** fast-food joints are as common as burger franchises in the US, and serve up snacks and sandwiches, especially *chawarma* (or *shawarma*) – which, like doner kebabs, consists of shreds of barbecued compressed mutton cut from a roll, then wrapped in pitta bread or French bread.

Vegetarian West Africa

West Africa makes no concessions to vegetarians. Eating on the street or in any category of restaurant, is unrewarding: animal protein is the focus of most dishes, and even where it's apparently absent there's likely to be some meat stock somewhere (rice is often cooked in it, or animal fat is added to the vegetables). This means, if you're strictly vegetarian, you're mostly going to have to stick to market fruit and veg and any food you cook for yourself.

Groundnuts (peanuts) – found boiled as well as roasted – and locally made **peanut butter** are a good source of vegetable protein. **Milk** in various forms (and milk powder) and **hard-boiled eggs** are usually obtainable. Cheese is largely unheard of, except in its processed, foil-packaged variety. **Bread** and canned margarine are available everywhere.

Vegetarians who are the guests of African families have a hard time – with such status attached to meat, vegetarianism is regarded as an untenable philosophy. Avoiding meat is particularly trying if you consent to have eggs with every meal instead, as you can find yourself presented with six or more, specially prepared for you, every day.

Food

Most meals consist of a pile of the staple starch diet plus a sauce or stew often called "soup". The **staple** varies geographically. **Rice** predominates everywhere from Mauritania to Liberia and across the Sahel. **Root crops** (varieties of yam and cassava) and **plantains** figure heavily along the coast from Côte d'Ivoire through Nigeria to Cameroon. In the Sahara, **couscous**, tiny grains of durum wheat, is common.

Sauces can be based on **palm oil** (thick and copper-coloured, all along the coast from The Gambia south and eastwards); **groundnut paste** (peanut butter, found mostly in Sahelian regions); **okra** ("gumbo" or "ladies' fingers" – five-sided, green pods with a high slime content); various **beans**, and the **leaves** of sweet potatoes and cassava among others. All of them are usually heavily spiced, often with **chillies** – "hot pepper" – though it's rarely too much. Only southern Nigeria is really dangerous territory for tender mouths. There's a multitude of names in different languages for the same few staples and vegetables – the *West African food plants* colour section attempts to clarify things a little.

The more expensive, or festive, "sauces" (often more like stews) have an emphasis on their animal-protein content. **Fish** and **mutton** are probably the most common. **Beef** tends to be reserved for special occasions. **Chicken** is pricey, but a favourite meat for guests. **Pork** is very localized and hogs foraging at the roadside are a sure sign you're in a non-Islamic district. **Eggs** are always available, especially as omelettes.

Various kinds of **"bush meat"** are widely eaten except in the most devoutly Muslim regions, and often bought and sold. Large, herbivorous rodents ("bush rat", "grass-cutter", "agouti") are the commonest and usually delicious, but porcupines, antelopes, even cats, dogs and giant snails are eaten in various parts of West Africa. Whatever else they consist of, sauces are made with **bouillon cubes**.

Bush meat can be delicious, but avoid eating any kind of **primate**: the bush-meat trade is decimating the populations of several species of monkey, as well as chimpanzee and gorilla. Badly cooked primate meat can also spread dangerous viruses to the human population. Moreover, bush meat trapped with organophosphate-laced bait has in the past resulted in serious illness and fatalities, so you might want to ask local people to recommend somewhere to try bush meat, rather than heading for the nearest chop house.

Street food

Street food varies widely from country to country and regionally too, and is covered in more detail for each country. One snack that's pretty well universal is the **brochette** (*suya* in Hausa) – a tiny stick of kebab meat.

This is often eaten as a sandwich in a piece of French bread.

Although common, **bread** isn't a staple food in West Africa, but more of a luxury, often something to eat on long journeys. Different kinds tend to conform to the colonial recipes. In the Francophone countries it's a *baguette* – a French stick – though rarely as long or as crunchy as the real thing. In the Anglophone countries you have to search hard to find good bread. Mostly it's sponge-like white stuff, sometimes very sweet, and even dyed an unappetizing yellow or pink.

In the French-speaking countries you're likely to adopt the habit of eating **breakfast** in the street. Practice and adroitness vary, but in several countries you'll get excellent hot, whipped instant coffee with *pain beurre* (and real butter) for a set price of about 60p/$1.20. But be ready with appropriate French if you want your coffee black or without sugar. As coffee is sometimes made with sweetened condensed milk, white-no-sugar can be a problem.

Vegetables and cereals

Some of the major West African vegetables and cereals are covered in the *West African food plants* colour section – including **cassava**, **yams** and **groundnuts**, **millet**, **sorghum** and **rice**.

Besides these, and the crops listed below, other common food plants include **onions** and **tomatoes** (available everywhere, even in the driest districts, but often tiny and sold in piles of four), **lettuces** (wash very carefully), short but tasty **cucumbers**, **avocados** (wonderful, huge specimens in Cameroon), **tiger nuts** (*chufa* – tiny tubers), **pigeon peas** (small, round, brown-and-white beans), **white haricot**, **lima** and **butter beans**, and various kinds of **gourd**, **pumpkin** and **squash**. Certain types of melon are good only for their large, oily seeds, commonly known by the Yoruba name, **egusi**, and widely used when crushed to flavour soups.

Aubergine (eggplant) Grown on garden plots all over and come in many shapes and colours (round, white, yellow, red) but rarely in the large, purple variety familiar in the West. Known variously as "garden eggs" or "bitter balls", they can be identified as aubergines by the star-shaped, leathery, leafy bits at the stalk end.

Cowpeas (black-eye beans) The commonest type of bean, cowpeas come in many varieties and are grown throughout the region. They're usually dried and stored for use, or made into flour, but you often see them freshly harvested in their long, pale pods. Mashed cowpeas are used for *akara* – "deep-fried balls" sold nearly everywhere. Common names include *wake* and *niebe*.

Groundnut (peanut, monkey nut) Known as *arachide* or *cacahouètes* in French, groundnuts are grown widely to be used as the basis of sauces, and you'll see little dollops of peanut butter – on leaves or in plastic sachets – for sale in markets everywhere.

Maize (corn) Known as *maïs* in French, corn is grown a lot in forest-region clearings, and used widely on the cob as a stop-gap and a roasted or boiled snack. Maize flour is used quite extensively in some parts as a staple – in Ghana for fermented corn dough (*kenkey*) for example.

Potatoes Unless specified as "Irish", potatoes are usually the **sweet** variety with pink skins, known as *patate* in French – and in the US, confusingly, as "yams". They're grown in mounds and ridges and have a mass of creeping vines. The leaves are edible and widely used. Regular, Irish potatoes only grow in West Africa above an altitude of about 1200m.

Fruit

Perhaps the most satisfying eating in West Africa is **fruit**. There's a magnificent variety in the markets south of the Sahel, though even in the drier regions you'll find citrus most of the year, mangoes in season and the odd pawpaw. Besides the ones we've listed below, you'll also come across **starfruit** (attractively shaped but tasteless), **custard apples** or **soursops** (lovely pear-drop flavour in the roughly heart-shaped, green fruit) and **mangosteens** (amazing taste inside the small, round, brownish fruit with very thick skin). Towards the Sahara you get **dates** in all their different grades and, lastly, at certain times and places, quite a variety of **wild-collected fruit**, some of which (like the *ditak* in Senegal) is particularly good. **Sugar cane**, sometimes sold in markets, isn't actually a fruit; you simply strip off the shiny outside and chomp on the pith, which oozes sucrose.

For information about West Africa's **bananas**, **plantains**, **papaya**, **oranges** and **cashew nuts**, see the *West African food plants* colour section.

Coconut The familiar brown "nuts" of coconut shies are contained within a thick husk and the whole thing is green and about the size of a football. Coconuts are very hard to open without a machete, but all along the coast (they won't grow easily above 500m) you'll have the opportunity to try them in several satisfying stages as the flesh changes from a thin jelly to a thick layer of coconut. They're not seasonal.

Grapefruit African varieties are often exceptionally sweet and big. Leave the segments to dry for a while and peel off the inner skins to reveal hundreds of little packets of grapefruit juice. A fine pleasure.

Guava Don't buy unripe ones – guavas should have a very strongly perfumed scent. The best ones have pink flesh.

Mango Available and rightly esteemed everywhere, mangoes come in hundreds of varieties. The mango season coincides with the end of the dry season and the first rains (roughly March–June depending on where you are). They're expensive at first and rapidly drop in price until they're two a penny (sometimes literally). Whole villages devote themselves to eating and selling the fruit. The very best, found in southern Cameroon, are long and narrow with bright green skins and very firm, orange, stringless flesh.

Pineapple Commonest in coastal districts of Ghana and eastwards to Cameroon. Available throughout the dry season.

Drinking

Probably the most widely consumed beverage in the region – after water – is **green tea** (in reality yellow). Rock sugar in huge lumps, China tea leaves and water are brought to the boil in a little kettle on a handful of coals, then poured out repeatedly to infuse and froth the brew. The tea has to be Green Gunpowder – a tin or packet of which makes a very good gift. In the Sahel, from Senegal to northern Cameroon, green tea is an essential part of every day and no long journey is completed without it. It's common further south, too, in all regions where Islam predominates. It's traditional to drink three glasses – strong and bitter, sweet and full-bodied, and sweet and mild.

Apart from instant coffee (invariably Nescafé), **coffee** is less popular, and real coffee rare except in big hotels. Various **infusions** are locally common. One which has wide popularity in the western part of West Africa (as a base for mixing in a lot of *lait concentré sucré*) is *kenkeliba* (also spelled "quinceliba" and various other ways). *Kenkeliba* is mild and indifferently nutty when mixed with sweet milk or just on its own, but don't mistake it for water and have instant coffee added – the mixture has a revolting flavour.

When you can't get cold water, **soft drinks** – especially fizzy orange and lemonade and Coke – are permanent stand-bys and in remote areas any establishment with electricity is almost bound to have a fridge of battered bottles (bottles are always returned to the wholesaler, so *never* take the bottle away – it's stealing). Supermarkets and most general stores carry large plastic bottles of **drinking water**. On the street, however, you'll often see locally made **fruit juices**, cold water and ices, in plastic bags, sold by children from buckets of ice. Ginger is refreshing, as too is the white sherbet made from baobab fruits. They're safe to drink in areas where you're already drinking the local water with no ill-effects (the same rule of thumb applies to locally bottled soft drinks).

Bissap (hibiscus flower) juice is another thirst-quenching drink, particularly when still frozen (ask for *bissap formé* in French). Since the flowers are boiled in water to extract the juice, it's probably the best choice for delicate stomachs.

Beer and spirits

The most noticeable drink in the region is **beer**, and almost every country has at least one brewery. Nigeria has many, and a whole host of competing brands. Only the Islamic Republic of Mauritania is dry. The beer usually comes in 35cl, half-litre or 70cl bottles and is mostly strong, gassy, sometimes quite bitter in flavour and, most of the time, cold (as is **Guinness**, brewed by local branches of European breweries).

However, bottled beer is extremely expensive for the majority of local people and it can therefore sometimes be difficult to find in smaller villages. As an alternative, the local traditional **home-made beers** are well worth experiencing. Available under many different names, they're as varied in taste and colour as the ingredients used – basically a fermented mash of sugar and cereal (usually sorghum, maize or millet), sometimes with herbs and roots for flavouring. The results are cloudy, frothy and often strong. Always made by women, home-made beer is usually drunk in the round, each person taking their turn with the dipper, from a central calabash.

In coastal parts, **palm wine** is produced from palm sap which, after tapping, ferments in a day from a pleasant, mildly intoxicating juice to a ripe and pungent brew with seriously destabilizing qualities. The flavour is aromatic and slightly acidic. The most common palms tapped are the stumpy, dark-green oil palms, which also produce the glossy red-brown palm nuts for palm oil. Taller borassus and coconut palms can also be tapped, but rarely are.

Spirits distilled from home made beer, palm wine or sugar-cane juice are locally much in evidence across the region (in Ghana, Cameroon, Burkina Faso, Nigeria and Cape Verde for example) and normally only alcoholically dangerous, rather than actually denatured with unknown toxic additives, as in other parts of Africa. But beware nevertheless.

Imported spirits are excessively expensive. **Imported beer**, too, is rarely worth the price. Cheap French **wine**, on the other hand, is fairly affordable in Senegal (unless you live in France, in which case it'll seem extortionate) where you can often buy it from ordinary general stores.

Communications

The postman never comes in West Africa. Mail is sorted into PO Boxes (BP in French, CP in Portuguese) or sometimes into Private Mail Bags (PMB). The lower the number, usually, the older the address – sometimes a useful indication of credentials when making bookings or enquiries. Street addresses are often buildings, or blocks – *Immeuble* in French, often abbreviated to *Imm*.

Mail

In French-speaking countries the post office is called the **PTT** (*Postes, Télécommunications et Télédiffusion*) or **Hôtel des Postes**, in English-speaking countries, the **GPO** and in Portuguese-speaking countries the Correio or **CTT**. Post offices in Francophone countries usually have separate counters (*guichets*) for different services, so make sure you're in the right line. In Europe, allow two weeks for post sent to West Africa to be received and one week to ten days to receive mail from West Africa. Elsewhere, allow three days longer.

If you have **urgent mail** to send, the best place is usually not the main post office but the airport, from where mail is often sent on the next flight out. There may not be much of a post office, just a mail box. For **parcels**, use a courier service like DHL, rather than post.

To receive mail by Poste Restante, it's best to have it sent to a **capital city**, not just in order to maximize your chances of getting it, but to speed up delivery (the service to provincial towns can be very slow). Most main post offices have a poste restante counter. An alternative to Poste Restante is your **embassy** or **high commission**: some will hold mail for up to three months.

Internet

Every large West African town now has at least one **Internet café** – even in some medium-sized towns there are now dozens – though the state of the hardware and reliability of connections varies hugely, and some areas suffer frequent power cuts.

Your email address is likely to be much in demand – a stack of small cards or address labels is very useful.

Useful dialling codes

To **call home** from West Africa, you dial the international access code, which is usually 00, followed by your country code – see the list below – then the number you want, omitting any initial zero:

UK: 44
Ireland: 353
US and Canada: 1

Australia: 61
New Zealand: 64
South Africa: 27

North and West African country codes

Algeria 213
Benin 229
Burkina Faso 226
Cameroon 237
Cape Verde 238
Côte d'Ivoire 225
The Gambia 220
Ghana 233
Guinea 224
Guinea-Bissau 245
Liberia 231

Libya 218
Mali 223
Mauritania 222
Morocco 212
Niger 227
Nigeria 234
Senegal
Sierra Leone 232
Togo 228
Tunisia 216

Phones and mobiles

Landline calls from West Africa are generally straightforward. In most areas, **phonecards** have replaced cumbersome counter procedures for making international calls and phone booths or telecentres are set up in many cities.

Reverse charge or collect calls ("PCV" in French) are possible from most countries, or you can arrange in advance to *receive* a call at a certain time and number.

West African **mobile networks** have roaming agreements with many foreign mobile service providers, so if your home mobile phone has international roaming switched on, it will work in most urban areas and increasingly in the countryside, too. A useful website is ⓦwww .gsmworld.com/roaming, showing coverage and roaming partners, country by country. Before you leave home, it's wise to find out about your provider's charges for making

and receiving calls in the countries you'll be visiting.

In nearly all West African countries, it's possible to buy a local **SIM card** and pay-as-you-go scratch cards in order to use your mobile phone on the local network. These rarely cost more than £5/$10. Remove your phone's SIM card and store it safely, then use the new card (and your temporary number). Of course, your usual number will be unavailable to your home contacts (unless you take a second phone). Using a local SIM card saves a great deal of money for you and your local contacts if you're mainly expecting to use your phone to make and receive calls within the country itself. If your phone is programmed to be used exclusively on your home mobile network it will need to be unlocked – most phone shops can do that easily.

Finally, of course, you can use **Skype** when it's installed (as it often is) at Internet café terminals.

Public holidays and festivals

In addition to the main Christian and Islamic religious festivals, each country in West Africa has its own national holidays, listed in the practical information at the start of each country chapter. These are rarely as established as you would find, for example, in Europe. Some, commemorating no longer respected events, are quietly ignored. Traditional, community festivals, connected either to annual agricultural cycles or to life-cycle events, are more attractive but less accessible. Details are given chapter by chapter wherever possible.

Islamic holidays

Each West African country, with the exception of Cape Verde, has a significant Muslim population. Islam is the dominant religion in most, but Mauritania is the only nation to dub itself an Islamic Republic. In other countries, Muslim holy days are variably observed – devoutly in strictly Muslim districts, perhaps only vaguely in the capital city.

The **Islamic calendar** dates from 622 AD, the "Year of the Hijra" (dates measured with respect to this are denoted AH), when the Prophet fled from Mecca to Medina. It uses a lunar system, the Islamic year divided into twelve months of 29 or 30 days (totalling 354 days), thus the dates of Islamic festivals shift forward by around eleven days every year, relative to the Gregorian calendar.

The **principal events** to be aware of are the ten days of the Muslim New Year which

Islamic festivals

In calendar order, the Muslim months are: Muharram, Safar, Rabia al-Awwal, Rabia al-Thany, Jumada-al-Awwal, Jumada al-Thany, Rajab, Sha'aban, Ramadan, Shawwal, Dhu al Qi'dah and Dhu al-Hijjah. The Gregorian dates given below are approximate, as the Islamic months begin when the new moon is sighted. Muslim month dates are given in parentheses.

New Year's Day (1st of Muharram)
Dec 29, 2008
Dec 18, 2009
Dec 7, 2010
Nov 26, 2011
Nov 15, 2012

Ashoura (10th of Muharram)
Jan 18, 2008
Jan 7, 2009
Dec 27, 2009
Dec 16, 2010
Dec 6, 2011

Mouloud/Maulidi (12th of Rabia al-Thany)
Mar 20, 2008
Mar 9, 2009
Feb 26, 2010
Feb 15, 2011
Feb 4, 2012

Beginning of Ramadan (1st of Ramadan)
Sept 1, 2008
Aug 21, 2009
Aug 11, 2010
Aug 1, 2011
July 20, 2012

Id al-Fitr/Id al-Sighir (1st of Shawwal)
Sept 30, 2008
Sept 21, 2009
Sept 10, 2010
Aug 31, 2011
Aug 19, 2012

Tabaski/Id al-Kabir/Id al-Adha (10th of Dhu al-Hijja)
Dec 8, 2008
Nov 27, 2009
Nov 17 2010
Nov 6, 2011
Oct 26, 2012

starts with the month of Moharem (**Ashoura**, on Moharem 10th, celebrates, among other events, Adam and Eve's first meeting after leaving Paradise), the **Prophet Muhammad's birthday** (known as Mouloud or Maulidi), the month-long fast of **Ramadan** and the feast of relief which follows immediately after it (known as Id al-Fitr or Id al-Sighir), and the **Feast of the Sacrifice** or Tabaski, which coincides with the annual hajj pilgrimage to Mecca, when every Muslim family with the means to do so slaughters a sheep in the Abrahamic tradition.

The last of these festivals (known as the *fête des moutons* in French) can be a lot of fun. As for **Ramadan**, fasting applies throughout the daylight hours and covers every pleasure (food, drink, tobacco and sex). While non-Muslims are not expected to observe the fast, it's highly affronting in strict Muslim areas to contravene publicly. Instead, switch to the night shift, as everyone else does, with special soup to break the fast at dusk, and applied eating and entertainment through the night.

Christian holidays

Christmas and (to a much lesser extent) **Easter** are observed as religious ceremonies in Christian areas and, on a more or less secular, national basis, in every country. If you can't find a bank or post office open, you'll have no trouble finding street food and some transport.

Christmas and **New Year** are occasions for street parades and carnival festivities in a number of cities. On the downside, Christmas is a time to avoid contact, as far as possible, with people in uniform. This most applies to the police in the English-speaking countries, where a misappropriated tradition of "Christmas Boxes" – seasonal gratuities – survives and is relentlessly cultivated from mid-December to the middle of January.

Lastly, both Guinea-Bissau and Cape Verde have inherited and elaborated upon the Portuguese–Brazilian institution of **Carnaval** and host float parades and street festivals in February or March. Shrove Tuesday (**Mardi Gras**) takes place on the following dates:

Feb 5, 2008
Feb 24, 2009
Feb 16, 2010
March 8, 2011
Feb 21, 2012.

Crime and safety

It's easy to exaggerate the potential hassles and disasters of travel in West Africa. True, there's a scattering of urban locations, easily enough pinpointed, where snatch robberies and muggings are common. But most of the region carries minimal risk to personal safety compared to Europe and North America. The main problems are sneak thieving and corrupt people in uniforms. The first can be avoided with care, while dealing with corruption (which is becoming less of a problem as democracy and accountability make inroads into the region) can become a game once you know the rules.

If you're heading for remote regions, to hike for example, it's worth leaving details of your trip with your embassy, high commission or honorary consul.

Theft and scams

If you get mugged, it will be over in an instant and you're not likely to be hurt. But

Big-city survival

Pickpocketing can happen anywhere – usually the work of pocket-high thieves, hanging around in markets or other crowded places. Make sure your valuables are secure. **Heavier attacks** usually take place in specific areas of the city – downtown shopping streets, docks and waterfront, city-centre parks and central markets. Don't feel unduly intimidated at transport parks – these are full of tough young men working as drivers or ticket sellers, who tend to be on the lookout for threats to their passengers – or in the lower-income suburbs and slums away from the city centre, where people just aren't used to travellers.

When walking – assuming you have money or valuables on you – have a destination in mind and stay alert. Keep your hands to yourself. Loose hands are likely to be caught and in disreputable areas a handshake from a stranger in the street, or a item pressed into your hand, or some murmured offer or suggestion can foreshadow an more aggressive act. If you want to give off strong defensive vibes, hands in pockets or round the straps of a backpack are effective, as are dark glasses.

Steer clear of creepy-looking street sharks in jeans and running shoes (every robbery ends in a sprint). And never allow yourself to be steered down an alley or between parked cars.

the hassles, and worse, that gather as soon as you try to do something about it, make it doubly imperative not to let it happen in the first place. Robbers and pickpockets caught red-handed are usually dealt with summarily by the crowd, so when you shout "thief" (*voleur* in French), be swift to intercede once you've retrieved your belongings.

Obviously, if you flaunt the trappings of wealth where there's urban poverty, somebody will want to remove them. There's less risk in leaving your valuables in a securely locked hotel room or, judiciously, with the management. If you clearly have nothing on you (this means not wearing jewellery or an expensive-looking wristwatch), you're unlikely to feel, or be, threatened.

Public transport rarely produces scare stories. Apart from the standard of driving, which is another matter, you haven't much to worry about on the roads in most areas (exceptions are noted in the country chapters).

If you're flying into West Africa, or arriving overland in your first big city, it's obviously wise to be particularly cautious for the first day or two. There's always a lot going on and it's important to distinguish between harmlessly robust, up-front interaction (commonly part of the public-transport scene) and more dangerous preludes. At the risk of sensationalism, the box above

("Big-city survival") outlines some good strategies for looking after yourself in Dakar, Lagos, Douala or Yaoundé – the most difficult to deal with. Accra, Banjul, Bissau, Nouakchott and Ouagadougou are more relaxed, while Bamako, Conakry, Cotonou, Freetown, Lomé and Niamey fall somewhere in between.

In one or two cities, **scams** which play on your conscience have begun to appear: a favourite is the "student agitator" routine, in which you get chatting to a friendly young person and either give him a little money, or exchange addresses. As soon as he's gone, a group of heavies arrives, claiming to be undercover police and informing you that you have been observed planning seditious activities/talking to a terrorist for which you could be arrested – or you could instead pay a fine now. Make a big, public fuss and insist on going to the police station with someone in uniform – they will disappear. On a more general note, any stranger who approaches you asking whether you recognize him ("Tu me reconnais?" in French), is likely to be setting up some scam or another.

Don't feel victimized: every rural immigrant coming to the city for the first time goes through exactly the same process, and many will be considerably less streetwise than you. Finally, don't forget that fellow travellers are as likely – or as unlikely – to rip you off as anyone else.

Reporting crime

If you are the victim of crime, usually the first reaction is to go to the **police**. Unless, however, you've lost irreplaceable property or a lot of money (and cash is virtually irretrievable), think twice about doing this. The police in West Africa rarely do something for nothing – even stamping an insurance form may cost you – and you should consider the ramifications if you and they set off to try to catch the culprits. If you're not certain of their identities, pointing the finger of suspicion at people is the worst possible thing to do. If they're arrested, as they probably will be, a night in the cells usually means a beating and confiscation of their possessions.

In smaller towns, or where you have some contacts, a workable alternative to police involvement is to offer a reward or enlist **traditional help** in searching for your stolen belongings. Various diviners and traditional doctors operate nearly everywhere. If the culprits get to hear of what you're doing you're likely to get some of your stuff back. Local people will often go out of their way to help.

Dealing with the police

West African **police forces** vary considerably from one country to the next. For example, in Guinea-Bissau they're not excessively corrupt but can be unnervingly conscientious and pedantic, while in Guinea they're outrageously on the make and seemingly unfazed by the question of upholding actual laws. Most police forces constitute a separate entity from the rest of the people: they have their own compounds and staff villages and receive – or procure – subsidized rations and services.

While it's wise to avoid the police as far as possible, the notion of "control" remains highly developed in the vast majority of West African countries, even where you're no longer obliged to check in at the local police station in every town. Checks on the movement of people (police and security services) and goods (customs, *douanes*) take place at junctions and along highways in most countries. Many capital cities have major checkpoints on their access roads.

If you have official business with the police, smiles and handshakes always help, as do terms of address like "sir", officer" or (in a French-speaking country) "*mon commandant*". If you're expected to give a bribe (see box) – as you often are – wait for it to be hinted at. Having said that, note that drug possession or infringements of customs laws can easily land you a large fine or worse, and deportation. Don't expect to buy yourself easily out of this kind of trouble.

In **unofficial dealings**, the police, especially in remote outposts, can sometimes go out of their way to help you with food, transportation and accommodation. Try to reciprocate. Police salaries are always low and often months overdue, and they rely on unofficial income to get by.

Offences you might commit

Never go out without **identification**. You don't have to carry a passport at all times, but a photocopy of the first few pages in a plastic wallet is very useful. Not carrying an ID (*carte d'identité*, *papiers* or *pièces* in French) is usually against the law.

Be warned that failure to observe the following points of **public etiquette** can get you arrested or force you to pay a bribe:

• Stand still on any occasion a national anthem is played or a flag raised or lowered. If you see others suddenly cease all activity, do the same.

• Pull off the road completely if motorcycle outriders and limos appear, or stand still. This usually means the president is coming by.

• Never destroy banknotes, no matter how worthless they may be.

Drugs offences

Grass (marijuana, cannabis) is the biggest illegal drug in the region, much cultivated (clandestinely) and as much an object of confused opprobrium and fascination as anywhere else in the world. Many social problems are routinely attributed to smoking the "grass that kills" and it's widely believed to cause insanity. In practice, if you indulge discreetly, it's not likely to get you into trouble. The usual result of a fortuitous bust is on-the-spot fines all round.

Bribery

If you find yourself confronting an implacable person in uniform, you don't have to give in to tacit demands for gifts or money. The golden rule is to **keep talking**. Most laws, including imaginary ones about the importation of backpacks, the possession of two cameras or the writing of diaries, are there to be discussed rather than enforced. If you haven't got all day, a *dash* or **"small present"** – couched in exactly those terms – is all it usually takes to resolve matters, though you should haggle over it as you would any payment. The equivalent of a pound or a couple of dollars is often enough to oil small wheels.

If you can't, or won't, give gifts to officials, give words. On extensive West African travels, you have literally hundreds of police, army, customs, immigration and security checkpoints to cross. You'll sail through ninety percent of them, and with patience and good humour, the other ten percent can be negotiated relatively painlessly too. When you know they know your "infraction" is bogus, keep joking, keep pleading and hang on. If you think you may be in breach of a law (or someone's interpretation of it) you might suggest paying the "fine" (*amende*) immediately, or "coming to an agreement" (*faire arrangement* or *s'arranger* in French). And always keep in mind that everyone is fair game. Indeed, sometimes you'll find that locals are asked to pay bribes (for passport stamps at border checkpoints, for example) when tourists are not.

If you're **driving**, you'll rarely be forced to pay sweeteners, except sometimes on entry to and exit from the country. Travelling by lorry or bush taxi, you'll note it's the driver who pays. If you're singled out, *remind them* it's the driver who pays. Avoid any show of temper – aggressive travellers always have the worst police stories.

An altogether different state of affairs exists with **heroin** and **cocaine**, which are smuggled though West Africa en route to Europe (often inside hapless female mules). Some of the consignments get on to the streets of the capitals, together with the associated tensions and paranoia. Stay well clear: very long prison sentences and the death penalty are not unknown for those convicted of involvement in the trade.

Cameras and the state

At the risk of generalizing, West Africa is hostile to the camera's probing eye (for more on the subject of photography, see p.69). There are people, often teachers or civil servants, who may take it upon themselves to protect the state from your unwelcome inspection and ask you to stop taking pictures, or report you to the police. And there are the security forces themselves, who will often hassle you if they see you taking photographs – usually on the pretext that you are taking pictures of them.

This advice isn't intended to cause alarm, and plenty of travellers complete their trips with not a camera opened. Disturbing encounters are, however, not infrequent. You shouldn't take photos of anything that could be construed as **strategic** or **military** – including any kind of army or police building, police or military vehicles and uniforms, prisons, airports, harbours, ferries, bridges, broadcasting installations, national flags or, of course, presidents. Officially, this is seen as a "risk to state security", but some countries are specifically ill-disposed to tourists taking photographs of scenes reflecting poverty. With this kind of discretionary caveat, you can more or less rule out photography in the towns if you behave with rigid correctness. The Gambia, Senegal and Cape Verde are the least uptight about these subjects; Mali, Burkina Faso and Ghana are also sufficiently familiar with tourists for it rarely to be an issue; Cameroon and Nigeria are notoriously touchy. Finally, **digital camcorders** generally attract less attention than still cameras, especially if you shoot using a monitor rather than an eyepiece.

Cultural hints

You can't hope to avoid social gaffes on a West African stay, but humour and tolerance aren't lacking, so you won't be left to stew in embarrassment. Getting it right really takes an upbringing, but people are delighted when you make the effort.

Greetings

Greetings are fundamental – no conversation starts without one. This means a handshake followed by polite enquiries, even as you enter a shop. Traditionally, such exchanges can last a minute or two, and you'll often hear them performed in a formal, incantatory manner between two men. Long greetings help subsequent negotiations. In French or English you can swap something like "How are you?" "Fine, how's the day?" "Fine, how's business?" "Fine, how's the family?", "Fine, thank God". It's usually considered polite, while someone is speaking to you at length, to grunt in the affirmative, or say thank you at short intervals. Breaks in conversation are filled with more greetings.

Shaking hands is normal between all men present, on arrival and departure. Women shake hands with each other, but with men only in more sophisticated contexts. Soul-brother handshakes and variations on the finger snap are popular among young men. Less natural for Westerners (certainly for men) is an unconscious ease in physical contact. Male visitors need to get used to holding hands with strangers as they're shown around the house, or guided down the street and, on public transport, to hands and limbs draped naturally wherever feels most comfortable.

Social norms

Be aware of the **left hand rule**. Traditionally the left hand is reserved for unhygienic acts and the right for eating and touching, or passing things to others. Like many "rules" it's very often broken: don't think about it then.

Unless you want to provoke a confrontation, never **point** with your finger: it's the equivalent of an obscene gesture. For similar reasons, beckoning is done with the palm down, not up. **Hissing** ("Tsss!") is an ordinary way to attract a stranger's attention. You'll get a fair bit of it, and it's quite in order to hiss at the waiter in a restaurant.

Answering anything in the negative is often considered impolite. If you're asking questions, don't ask closed, yes-no ones. And try not to phrase things in the negative ("Isn't the lorry leaving?") because the answer will often be "Yes…" ("…it isn't leaving"). Be on the lookout, too, for a host of **unexpected turns of phrase** which often pop up in West African English. "I am coming," for example, is often said by someone just as they leave your company – which means they're going, but coming back.

Don't be put off by apparent shiftiness in **eye contact**, especially if you're talking to someone much younger than you. It's fairly normal for those deferring to others to avoid direct looks.

Beggars

Beggars are part of town life, though not as much as you might realistically expect. Most are visibly destitute and many are blind, or victims of polio or accidents, or lepers, or homeless mothers and children. Some have established pitches, others keep on the move. They are harassed by the police and often rounded up. Many people give to the same beggar on a regular basis and, of course, **alms-giving** is a requirement of Islam, supposed to benefit the donor. Keep small change handy all the time for this purpose – it will hardly dent your expenses. There's no question of confusing real beggars with the incessant demands – in the more touristy parts of several of the Francophone countries – for "*cadeaux*", usually from children. These you simply have to devise strategies to deal with. Like heat and mosquitoes, they seem to trouble new arrivals most.

Clothes

People in West Africa are generally very clothes-conscious. Ragged clothes and long hair on men don't go down well. Avoid absolutely any military-style, or army surplus, gear; camouflage prints are out. **Cotton** is obviously the best material to wear from a practical point of view. Dirty-looking colours are best and clothes should be tough enough to stand repeated hand washing. Mostly you'll want to wear the minimum, but pack at least one warm jacket or fleece. Though you can buy clothes as you go, they'll rarely be less expensive than at home. Even "junk clothes" – "deadmen's clothes" shipped in bulk from Europe and the US – which you'll find in every town, may be less pricey bought nearer to source. If you fancy kitting yourself up in local style, both cloth and tailoring are inexpensive. However you dress, pack a set of "smart" clothes for difficult embassies and other important occasions. Forget about water-proofs: all that plastic and nylon is too hot. You won't go out in the rain, and if you do, you'll get wet anyway.

Gifts

It's very useful to have some **tokens** to give to people. Postcards of sights from home are appreciated by people who have little or no chance of possessing colour pictures. Pictures of you and your family are of tremendous value, too, while school kids are also delighted with ballpoint pens. However, you might consider visiting a school more formally, rather than just handing them out. Kola nuts (see the *West African food plants* colour section) are appreciated as gifts, especially by village elders.

Warri

Also spelt *wole*, *ouril* or *oware*, this ancient **game** for two is played all over Africa. It involves two opposing rows of holes, either on a wooden board or just dug in the sand, and a handful each of seeds, cowries or pebbles. The rules vary locally but the principle is always the same. Seeds are deposited in each hole and then the players take turns to pick up a pile from one of their holes and "sow" them, usually one by one, around the board. Depending on the rules, the hole the last seed is sown into determines the continuation of play, and, if it makes up a certain number of seeds in that hole, then they're captured. The player with the most seeds at the end, wins. It's a game that's devastatingly simple and, at the same time, mathematically highly complex in its endless chain of cause and effect – think Fibonacci numbers in the dust.

Time-keeping

Although many people wear watches they're essentially jewellery: notions of time and duration are pretty hazy. Outside the cities, dusk and dawn are the significant markers. You'll soon find you, too, are judging time by the sun, and reckoning how long before dark.

People and things in West Africa are usually late. That said, if you try to anticipate **delays** you'll be caught out. Scheduled transport does leave on time at least some of the time. More importantly, transport may leave *early* if it's full. Even planes have been known to take off before schedule.

Note that in remote areas, if a driver tells you he's going somewhere "today", it doesn't necessarily mean he expects to *reach* there today. Always allow extra time. There's no better way to ruin West African travel than to attempt to rush it.

Photographing people

West Africa is immensely photogenic but to get good pictures takes skill and confidence, and a considerable amount of cultural sensitivity. Photos from Africa are full of examples of people who didn't want to be photographed. That you might have taken some of their soul is not a real explanation, but it's a good metaphor.

There are two options if you want to get **photos of people**. First, you can adopt a gleefully robust (or blithely arrogant) approach, take pictures before anyone knows it's happened and deal with the problems after the event. But this is the kind of crass behaviour that will almost inevitably get you into trouble and spread bad feeling in your wake.

Far better is to **ask people first**. Summoning the confidence and grace to ask to take people's portraits, and to accept refusal with equanimity, is at least half the affair. If they insist on posing, so be it. Try to come to terms with the reality of your position: you can't be a fly on the wall.

Be prepared to **pay** something or to send a print if your subjects have addresses. If you're motivated to take a lot of pictures of people, you should seriously consider lugging along an instant camera and as much instant film as you can muster, in order to offer a portrait on-the-spot – many people have never had a photo of themselves. A family you've stayed with is unlikely to refuse a photo session and may even ask for it. The same people might be furious if you jumped off the bus and immediately started taking photos, or worse, stayed on the bus and did it through the window.

Living and working in West Africa

There are plenty of opportunities for skilled professionals to take up temporary contracts in many West African countries. But in general there is no way you can informally work your way through West Africa. Direct, personal approaches to the appropriate ministry or NGO might open some doors. But underemployment is a serious problem and work-permit regulations everywhere make your getting a salary nearly impossible without pulling strings. You usually sign a declaration that you won't seek work when you obtain the visa or fill in the arrival card.

Voluntary work is more likely. Bed and board in return for your help is sometimes available on development projects, in schools or through voluntary agencies, but such arrangements are entirely informal and word-of-mouth. Teachers, particularly those qualified to teach English to speakers of other languages, information technologists and engineers have the best chances.

As for furthering your education in West Africa, some universities which run courses in African studies offer **study-abroad programmes** to certain countries.

Useful contacts

Details of **organizations** to contact at home are given below. Note that you may need to involve yourself in fundraising activities in order to participate in some voluntary schemes.

UK and Ireland

AFS UK ⓦ www.afsuk.org. Volunteer projects in a number of countries, including Ghana.

British Council ⓦ www.britishcouncil.org. Provides English-language teachers with training opportunities, teaching resources, networking opportunities and work placements, worldwide.
Earthwatch Institute ⓦ www.earthwatch .org. Long-established international charity with environmental and archeological research projects worldwide, including (occasionally) West Africa. Participation mainly as a paying volunteer (pricey) but fellowships for teachers and students available.
Field Studies Council Overseas ⓦ www .fscoverseas.org.uk. Respected educational charity with more than twenty years' experience of organizing specialized holidays with study-tour visits worldwide.
i to i International Projects ⓦ www.i-to-i.com. Gap-year/career-break voluntourism project operator and TEFL training provider offering voluntary teaching, conservation, business and medical placements abroad, including Ghana.
International House ⓦ www.ihlondon.com. Head office for reputable English-teaching organization which offers training and recruits for teaching positions abroad.

VSO (Voluntary Service Overseas) Ⓦ www.vso
.org.uk. Highly respected charity that sends qualified
professionals to spend two years or more working
for local wages on projects benefiting developing
countries. Placements – primarily teachers and health
professionals – are available throughout Anglophone
West Africa.

US and Canada

AFS Intercultural Programs Ⓦ www.afs
.org/usa, Ⓦ www.afscanada.org. Runs experiential
programmes in many countries, including Ghana,
aimed at fostering international understanding for
teenagers and adults.
Association for International Practical Training
Ⓦ www.aipt.org. Summer internships for students who
have completed at least two years of college in science,
agriculture, engineering or architecture; placements
available in Ghana, Nigeria and Sierra Leone.
Council on International Educational
Exchange (CIEE) Ⓦ www.ciee.org. Summer,
semester and academic-year programmes in a
number of countries including West African.
Earthwatch Institute Ⓦ www.earthwatch.org.
(See opposite.)
Experiment in International Living
Ⓦ www.usexperiment.org. Summer programme
for high-school students, including a five-week
programme in Ghana.

Peace Corps Ⓦ www.peacecorps.gov. Accepts
applications from US citizens over the age of 18 for
voluntary field work in some sixty areas of speciality,
including in most West African nations – though there
is little choice in where you're posted.
School for International Training Ⓦ www
.sit.edu. Runs accredited college semesters
abroad, comprising language and cultural studies,
homestays and other academic work, with
opportunities in Senegal, Cameroon, Ghana
and Mali.

Australia and New Zealand

Australian Volunteers International
Ⓦ www.australianvolunteers.com. Postings for
up to two years in developing countries including
(occasionally) West African.
Earthwatch Australia ℡ 03/9682 6828,
Ⓦ www.earthwatch.org/australia. (See opposite.)

West Africa

Save the Earth Network Accra, Ghana
℡ 021/667791, Ⓔ eben_nsten@hotmailyahoo
.com. Volunteer programmes, including reforestation
projects, orphanage work, and rural school and library
construction.
Suntaa-Nuntaa Wa, Ghana Ⓦ www
.suntaa-nuntaa.myweb.nl. Tree-planting project,
providing local women with fruit and fuel wood.

Travellers with disabilities

Although by no means easy, travelling around West Africa does not pose insurmountable problems for people with disabilities. Attitudes to disabled people are
not particularly positive, but disabled foreigners are rarely seen, so you will score
highly for novelty.

Government provision for disabled needs is
almost completely absent, and facilities for
wheelchair or frame users are non-existent
(and wheelchairs virtually unknown) – though
most hotels are single storey or have ground-
floor rooms. Getting around in a wheelchair
on half-paved or unpaved roads, or over soft
sandy streets, is extremely hard work, while
cabs are typically unmodified European or
Japanese saloons. Intercity travel is even
tougher, though in some countries, the

quality of long-distance buses can be well up
to international standards. You'll at least have
no problems recruiting local help.

Visiting game parks and historical sites
is problematic unless you have private
transport. Historical and archeological sites
are often barely maintained, or at least
require some climbing of steps or hiking
through a bit of bush. In the case of the
parks, it's difficult not only to reach them, but
to figure out how to get around them when

you arrive. Guided tours in safari vehicles with good suspension are rare.

UK and Ireland

Door to Door UK ⓦ www.dptac.gov.uk /door-to-door. Internet resource providing transport and travel information for the disabled and those with mobility problems.

Irish Wheelchair Association Ireland ⓣ 01/818 6400, ⓦ www.iwa.ie. Useful information provided about travelling abroad with a wheelchair.

US and Canada

Access-Able ⓦ www.access-able.com. Online resource for travellers with disabilities.

Mobility International USA ⓦ www.miusa.org. Information and referral services, access guides, tours and exchange programmes.

Society for the Advancement of Travelers with Handicaps (SATH) ⓦ www.sath.org. Non-profit educational organization which actively represents travellers with disabilities.

Australia and New Zealand

National Disability Services ⓦ www.nds .org.au. Provides lists of travel agencies and tour operators for people with disabilities.

DPA New Zealand ⓦ www.dpa.org.nz. Resource centre with lists of travel agencies and tour operators for people with disabilities.

Gender issues and sexual attitudes

Male egos in West Africa are softened by reserves of humour and women can travel widely on their own or with each other, without the major problems sometimes experienced in parts of Asia and Latin America. That's not to say that women don't experience unreasonable overtures from men in West Africa – as anywhere – but threats to personal safety arising from the fact of being a woman are rarer and the overall social climate is generally easy-going.

Much of what applies to women travellers in West Africa applies equally to **men**, though of course questions of personal safety and intimidation don't arise in the same way. It's common enough for women, and especially unmarried girls, to flirt with strangers. And many town bars and hotels are patronized by women who more or less make a living from **prostitution**. This is traditionally not the secretive and exploitative transaction of the West and pimps are generally unknown. **Sexually transmitted diseases**, and the HIV virus, are rife, however. Attitudes in West Africa are awake to this new reality, but you should be aware of the very real risks – and be prepared with condoms for the occasion – if you accept one of the many propositions you're likely to receive.

Women travellers

Travelling on your own or with another woman companion is by turns frustrating and rewarding. You'll usually be welcomed with generous hospitality, though occasionally you'll seem to get a run of harassment and hassles because of your gender. It's as well to know, if you're overlanding from Europe, that the biggest difficulties will occur in North Africa – especially Morocco – and that Muslim regions south of the Sahara are altogether different.

On **public transport** a single woman traveller causes quite a stir and fellow passengers don't want to see you badly treated. They'll speak up on your behalf and get you a good seat or argue with the driver over your baggage payments. You can speak your mind, be open and direct, and nobody takes offence. Fellow male passengers always assume protective roles. This can be helpful but is sometimes annoyingly restrictive and occasionally leads to misunderstandings.

Women get offers of **accommodation** in people's homes more often than male

Sexual attitudes

Don't make any assumptions about puritanism on the basis of Islamic society in West Africa. It's the Church which has successfully repressed sexuality. Otherwise, sexual attitudes are liberal (though you'll rarely see open displays of affection between men and women), all adults are regarded as naturally sexually active, and sex is openly discussed – except in the presence of children. It's rarely the subject of personal hangups either, though sexual violence is surely as prevalent in families as it is anywhere. If you travel with an opposite-sex partner, you'll find the relationship tends to insulate you from people of the opposite sex – though not completely.

Gay life
Beyond the big cities, **homosexuality** is more or less invisible. People from a more traditional African background almost always deny it exists, find the notion laughable or childish, or describe it as a phase or a harmless peculiarity. As for the legality of gay sex, most countries, including all the Anglophone ex-colonies, inherited the laws of 1950s Europe and have hardly changed – though in practice prosecutions are rare. For gay male visitors, the only parts of the region you'll find like-minded company are the big capital cities and the resort areas. Gay women can't hope to find any hint of a lesbian community anywhere. There's further, local information in each country chapter

travellers (and most of them without strings attached). And, if you're staying in less reputable hotels, there'll often be female company – employees, family, residents – to look after you.

Dress

The **clothes** you wear and the way you look and behave get noticed by everyone and they're more important if you don't appear to have a male escort. Your head and everything from waist to ankles are the sensitive zones, particularly in Islamic regions. Long, loose **hair** is seen as extraordinarily provocative, doubly so if blonde. Pay attention to these areas by keeping your hair fairly short or tied up (or by wearing a scarf) and wearing long skirts or, at a pinch, very baggy trousers.

In the heat it can be hard to be that disciplined, however, so if you have to wear shorts, try to make them long ones. If you find it's too hot to wear a bra, it's not going to interest anybody. Breasts aren't an important issue (legs are traditionally covered and much more of interest for African men) and topless bathing is tolerated by hotel pools and on tourist beaches. If you'll be travelling much on rough roads, however, you'll need a bra for support.

Propositions
Flirting is universal in West Africa and in practice almost impossible to avoid. If a man asks you to "come and see where I live", he means you should come and see where he and you are going to sleep together. You'll have no shortage of offers and they're usually easy to turn down if you refuse as frankly as you're asked: unwanted physical advances are rare. But it always helps to avoid offence and preserve a friendship if you make your intentions (or lack of them) clear from the outset. If you're not with a man, a fictitious husband in the background, much as you might prefer to avoid the ploy, is always useful – though it may well be met with such responses as "Tell your husband you have to go outside for some air."

All this can be fun: there's really no reason you can't spend an evening dancing and talking and still go back to your bed alone and unharassed.

Meeting other women

It's often very difficult **getting to know women** in West Africa. Most contact is mediated, at least initially, through their male relatives, with whom you'll take on the role of honorary man, at least in the way you're treated socially. In the small towns and

The status of West African women

Despite widespread paper commitments to women's rights, West Africa remains a powerfully male-dominated part of the world. Women do the large proportion of productive labour and most subsistence agriculture is in their hands, though this varies among different ethnic groups. **Matrilineal cultures**, which once held sway over large parts of the region, are on the decline, under joint assault by paternalistic Islam and Christianity. Matrilineal inheritance doesn't, in any case, necessarily imply *matriarchal* social structures but simply inheritance by a man from his mother's brother rather than his own father.

Women have the explicit support of government ministries (for what it's worth) in very few countries; in others there's often a nongovernmental women's organization working to improve the lot of mothers, agricultural labourers and crafts workers. **Women's groups** flourish in some countries, occasionally under the aegis of a government ministry – though in several they've hardly taken off. Where they exist, they're concerned more with improvement of incomes, education, health and nutrition than with social or political emancipation. Professional market women usually run their own informal unions in the cities.

Current major women's **issues** in West Africa are primarily concerned with rights over their bodies – contraception, abortion and the practices of genital mutilation. Few West African countries have successful **family planning** programmes; men remain unwilling to cooperate by using condoms and women are pushed out-of-date pills at market stalls. **Abortion** is virtually a taboo subject in some parts, though abortions by traditional methods (and less traditional backstreet operations) are believed to be widely performed. Few governments permit abortion on demand.

Female genital mutilation or FGM – often still known, in a classic bit of male "anthropologese" as "female circumcision" – is widespread and occurs to some degree in every mainland West African country. It's traditionally carried out by female practitioners on the occasion of a girl's initiation into womanhood. Today, although on the decline, it's also performed under anaesthetic in hospital and often at an early age. It varies from clitoridectomy to excision of the inner labia to excision of most of the outer labia as well (a major operation known as infibulation which, in West Africa, is almost confined to Mali).

All these issues are complex. Both contraception and abortion (especially as encouraged by Western development agencies) are topics which can incense women as well as men, so be wary of crashing into conversation. In the case of genital mutilation, women campaigning to eradicate the practices have met resistance from traditionalist women. And mutilations can't be analyzed just in terms of male sexual demands (a tighter vaginal opening, reduced female sexual response and consequent presumed fidelity). Unfortunately, it's an issue that many governments would prefer not to address: while Burkina Faso, Côte d'Ivoire, Ghana, Guinea, Senegal and Togo have all passed laws to ban FGM, Mali and Sierra Leone, which have some of the highest rates in West Africa, have yet to bring the issue to the top of the agenda. Plan International's excellent paper is well worth looking at: ⓦtinyurl.com/2bpwdq.

villages women are usually less educated than men and rarely speak English or French. They don't hang out in bars and restaurants either and are much more often to be found in their compounds working hard. Their fortitude as housewives is something to behold – always in total control of the family's food and comfort, from chopping wood to selling home-made produce in order to make ends meet. Even school-educated professional women dominate their household affairs and make sure everything runs smoothly. The extended family and the use of the younger girls as helpers is a major contribution. Men are away a great deal of the time.

For their part, West African women will try to picture themselves in your position, travelling around *your* homeland – a scenario that most find hard to imagine in a world in which family obligations are everything. Conveying the fact that you, too, have a family and a home is a good way of reducing the barriers of incomprehension but, assuming you're over 15, explaining the absence of husband and children is normally impossible. You can either invent some or expect sympathy instead – and perhaps the offer of fertility medicine.

Wildlife and national parks

West Africa doesn't have the game reserves and wildlife concentrations of East or southern Africa, though it does offer a number of major national parks that are worth taking in if you're an enthusiastic naturalist. Outside these, too, it's possible to see a good variety of Africa's birds and mammals in habitats ranging from desert and savannah to dry woodland, flooded watercourses, mangrove swamps and dense, moist forest – both lowland and mountain.

Travelling by public transport, it always pays to spend a little more on a seat in the front. That way you can reckon on seeing a lot more wildlife, mostly crossing or flying over the road.

Wildlife

The large animals you'll see most often out on the road, or in the bush, are **monkeys** and **baboons**. **Gazelles** and other small antelope are also quite common, especially in the Sahel. Larger grazing animals are localized and unusual sights. Along the Niger north of Niamey there are **giraffes**, and **buffalo** inhabit pockets of forest and thick bush in various parts.

Elephants survive in dwindling numbers in a surprising number of countries – across most of West Africa in fact – but are in such a dire predicament that little international effort is being made to save those isolated pockets still hanging on against the poachers in the remote bush. Park boundaries aren't always much of a safeguard. The **black rhino** has never inhabited more than the far east of the region and recent surveys suggest that the last few in Cameroon's northern parks have now been wiped out.

None of these animals, even outside the confines of the parks, poses any threat to you as a traveller, even if you choose to camp out and hike or cycle. More threatening

Ivory

Ivory is for sale in many West African cities, much of it carved in Hong Kong, and bracelets and bangles are widely touted. It seems it's still a viable way to earn a living and will likely remain so as long as ivory itself remains unstigmatized. Avoid it (failing to do so could bring serious trouble on returning home, where importing ivory is, in most countries, illegal).

wildlife – the big cats, crocodiles, hippos – are very localized. You're extremely unlikely to see any large predators outside the parks. And even in a national park, seeing a **lion**, **cheetah** or **leopard** in West Africa is cause for some celebration. **Crocodiles** are hard to spot and are mercilessly hunted where they live (except in controlled village pools where they are the object of veneration in many countries) because they do occasionally grab people at the water's edge. You should be somewhat cautious by rivers and lakes. **Hippos**, too, have a deservedly dangerous reputation, especially when accidentally trapped on dry land or panicked in the water while dozing. You're quite likely to see them from a boat on the Niger River in Mali, along the upper Gambia, or in Cameroon.

Another supposedly dangerous animal – the **gorilla** – is really very timid. Western lowland gorillas live in the remote, southern forests of Cameroon and across the border in Nigeria in the Cross River National Park. **Chimpanzees** also survive here, as well as much further to the west, in patches of remote forest from Senegal to Côte d'Ivoire, but their existence is threatened by deforestation.

Spiders, **scorpions** and various other multi-legged invertebrates are less often encountered than you might expect, or fear. **Butterflies** – as many as a thousand different species in some districts – are extensive and colourful, especially in the lowland forests.

Lizards are common everywhere, and you'll soon become familiar with the vigorous push-ups of the red-headed, male **rock agama**. Some towns seem to be positively swarming with them, no doubt in proportion to the insect supply. Large lizards (all species are quite harmless) include the **monitors**, of which the grey-and-yellow Nile monitor grows to an impressive 2m. Nile monitors live near water, but you sometimes see them

dashing across the road. **Chameleons**, too, are often seen making, in their case, painfully slow progress across the road – or, wafer-thin, squashed on the tarmac. In some areas, at night, little house **geckos** come out like translucent aliens to scuttle across the ceiling and walls in their useful pursuit of moths and mosquitoes.

West Africa's **birdlife** is astonishingly diverse – nearly eleven hundred species ranging from the ostrich to the diminutive pygmy woodpecker. Characteristic sights are the urbanite pied crows of the Sahel and savannah; the electric-blue Abyssinian rollers, perched on telephone wires in the grasslands; the marvellous, lurching flight of hornbills swooping across the road in forest areas; and the quite unmistakable flocks of grey parrots, in dense bush along the coast.

National parks

Most countries have some sort of national park network, though in several it consists of just the one park. The most important in the west are Mauritania's **Banc d'Arguin** (for sea and migratory birds), Senegal's **Niokolo-Koba** (large savannah and forest mammals) and Sierra Leone's **Tiwai Island Nature Reserve** and **Gola National Park** (primates).

In central West Africa there's Ghana's surprisingly good **Mole Game Reserve** and **Kakum National Park** (with its famous treetop walkway), Benin's **Pendjari** (excellent game-viewing), and the **Parc National du "W" du Niger**, which extends across the borders of Benin, Burkina Faso and Niger on a bend of the Niger River.

Nigeria and Cameroon have probably the best parks in West Africa. Nigeria's prime savannah reserve, **Yankari National Park**, has well-organized game-viewing and good quantities of animals, while the new **Cross River National Park** is a remote rainforest gorilla refuge. Across the border in Cameroon is the **Korup National Park**. Cameroon's numerous other parks include **Waza National Park** in the floodlands near Lake Chad, which for faunal diversity and herds of elephant is the best in West Africa.

Entrance fees, **seasonality** (many parks are closed during the rains) and **facilities** vary considerably. Some of the smaller parks and reserves – in The Gambia and southern Senegal for example – are low-key enough to permit entrance on foot. Vital, if you're visiting parks, is a pair of good, light **binoculars**.

People and languages

Whether called peoples, ethnic groups, nations or tribes, West Africans have a multiplicity of racial and cultural origins. Distinctions would be simple if similarities in physical appearance were recognizable in those who speak the same language and share a common culture: the term "tribe" tends to imply this kind of stereotype. But tribes are rarely closed units: appearance, language and culture nearly always overlap and, even in the past, families often contained members of different language groups. Over the last fifty years or so, tribal identities have broken down still further, partly replaced by broader class, political and national ones.

The most enduring and meaningful social marker is, in fact, **language**. A person's "mother tongue" is still important as an index of social identity and a tribe is best defined as a group of people sharing a common first language. Many people speak two or three languages (their own plus French or English and sometimes a third or fourth regional lingua franca like Hausa, Bamana or Krio). And for an increasing number, especially in the cities, the old metropolitan languages – French, English or Portuguese – have become their first language. It's worth knowing something of the linguistic connections and differences – apart from being fascinating in itself – if you want to get to grips with what can otherwise seem an unfathomable cultural region.

Names and groups

West Africa is the most linguistically complex region in the world. There are dozens of **major languages** and literally hundreds of less important languages and distinct dialects. Some four hundred of these are spoken in Nigeria alone. Most of West

Africa's languages are viable and thriving and very few are in any danger of extinction.

Most West Africans speak languages of one of three great groups – a southern area of wide affinity, now traditionally called **"Niger-Congo"**; a northern area of wider affinity, which has become known as **"Afro-Asiatic"**; **Mande**, a group which doesn't fit in either set; and **Songhai** – again, a standalone group that goes back a long way. African language classification (the attempt to assess the way the languages are presumed to have evolved from common ancestral languages) is immensely complicated and linguists have recently tried to get away from the notion of "families" of languages, as it may transpire they have elements in common through long association rather than shared ancestry.

For an outsider, the confusion is exacerbated by the fact that, until European colonization, almost none of these languages was written (today, many are written, the vast majority of them in the Roman alphabet, albeit sometimes with additional phonetic symbols). In the early days, even the language and ethnic **names** first recorded

WEST AFRICA: MAIN LANGUAGES

500 km

0

National Languages
Mauritania (Fr/Ar)   Mali (Fr)
Senegal (Fr)   Burkina Faso (Fr)
The Gambia (Eng)   Ghana (Eng)
Guinea-Bissau (Port)   Togo (Fr)
Guinea (Fr)   Benin (Fr)
Sierra Leone (Eng)   Niger (Fr)
Liberia (Eng)   Algeria (Ar/Fr)
Côte d'Ivoire (Fr)   Nigeria (Eng)
                       Cameroon (Fr/Eng)

Hassaniya Arabic

MAURITANIA

Tamashek

Tamashek

ALGERIA

NIGER

Kanuri

Hausa

Hausa

Songhai

Tamashek

Dogon

MALI

Senoufo Lobi

BURKINA
FASO

Mossi

Bantoid

Nupe

Tiv

CAMEROON

Fang

Bamiléké

Ewondo

Idoma

Igbo

Edo

Ijo

NIGERIA

Yoruba

BENIN

TOGO

Eve Fon

Ga

Twi

GHANA

Fante

Akan

CÔTE
D'IVOIRE

Dan

Kru

LIBERIA

Malinke

GUINEA

Bamana

Susu

Temne

Mende

SIERRA
LEONE

SENEGAL

Wolof

THE
GAMBIA

GUINEA-
BISSAU

N

West Atlantic Languages

Fula

Mixed Fula, Adamawa &
Chadic Languages

Mande Languages

Kwa Languages

Voltaic Languages

Bantu & Bantoid Languages

varied according to ...
the researchers and t...
asked. Often enoug...
name of the language a...
speak it are genuinely ...
the name in common usage ...
French may be different (for examp...
and Toucouleur) and the name by w...
language group is known may depen...
the linguistic context – analagous to Germa...
Deutsch and *Allemand*.

In this guide, the aim is to be as consistent and simple as possible, without sweeping distinctions away. Generally, the names we've used are the **names** used locally (for example Malinké in Guinea, Mandinka in The Gambia). On the other hand, the variety of names for the widespread people and language often called **Fulani** is so diverse – Peul, Peulh, Fulfulde, Fulbe, Foulah, Pulaar, Fula and many more – that we've gone for simple **Fula** throughout the book except in Nigeria, where "Fulani" is in common usage.

Later in this section, you'll find a broad and highly selective breakdown of West Africa's people and language groups into separate ethno-linguistic identities. These lists are intended to provide anchorages for the different names you're likely to encounter (and include every language or ethnic group mentioned in the book). The intention is to help work out who relates to whom (or whose languages are related), rather than to provide a rigid classification. Names in brackets are either alternative names for the same group or alternative spellings or pronunciations; additional names separated by commas are very closely related, distinguishable dialects. Names in inverted commas are major languages with closely related subgroups.

In trying to work out where everyone fits in, it helps to keep a flexible attitude to **spellings** (try pronouncing the word in as many ways as possible). Two sets of much interchanged sounds are the **p**, **b**, **v**, **f**, **w** set and the **d**, **gh**, **r**, **l** set. Anything spelled "qu" might just as well be spelt "kw" or, for that matter, "cou" or "kou". Likewise, "j" is commonly spelt "dy" or "di" in French transcription. The French were keen on apostrophes everywhere, too – take the singer Youssou N'Dour's name, for

...
of s...
pictu...
so-calle... ...erts
include W... ...uages, which
this groupin... ...Fula, are part of ... fairly distantly related
to Bantu. Also ...art of the group is the **Kwa subfamily** of language clusters, which include the **Akan languages** (of which the Asante are the most famous speakers), the **Ewe languages** of Ghana and Togo, and the **Yoruba** and **Igbo** language-groups of Benin and Nigeria. To the north, the **Voltaic subfamily** of language clusters includes the **Senoufo**, **More** and **Lobi** groups of Côte d'Ivoire, Ghana and Burkina.

Many of the languages in the Niger-Congo group have **class systems** (something like genders in French in that everything must agree) with up to twenty or more classes – Bantu languages, with their elegantly structured grammars, are the classic examples. Many of these languages are also **tonal** – in which the pitch of a spoken word determines its meaning – and extra notations are often necessary when writing them properly. Yoruba, with its mass of diacritics over vowels, is a good example.

Afro-Asiatic (the northern area of wider affinity)

The **Afro-Asiatic group** includes most of the languages of North Africa and the Middle East, including Hebrew, Arabic, Berber and Tamashek (the language of the Tuareg). The most important languages in the area as far as West Africa is concerned are known as "Chadic", the biggest of which is **Hausa**, spoken by some twenty million people as a

Grebo
Krahn
Bakwe
Bassa

"Edo" group
Edo
Bini (Benin)
Isoko, Urhobo (Sobo)
Kukuruku

"Igbo" group
Igbo (Ibo), Onitsha

"Yoruba" group
Yoruba, Oyo
Egba
Ijebu
Ekiti
Ife
Bunu
Itsekiri
Ana

"Nupe" group
Nupe
Igbira
Gwari, Koro

"Idoma" group
Idoma
Igala
Egede
Iyala

...ango

More (Mole)
Mossi
Dagomba (Dagbani)
Mamprusi
Wala

Gurma
Gourmantché
Bassari, Tchamba
Moba

Habe
Bobo, Bwaba, Kos, Siby

Dogon

"Tem" group
Tem (Kotokoli, Cotocoli)
Kabré (Kabyé), Logba,
Tamberma, Lamba

"Bargu" group
Bargu (Bariba)
Somba (Betammaribe)
Yowa

Kwa languages

"Kru" group
Bete
Dida

..., Peul
...roro, Tukulo...
Wolof, Wo...
Temne
Ser...

... (Diola), Fonyi, Bandial
Balante
Pepel, Manjak (Manjago)
Gola
Baga
Tenda, Bassari
Bijagó (Bidyago)

Voltaic languages

"Senoufo" group
Senoufo, Djimini, Karaboro
Minianka

"Grusi" group
Grusi (Gourounsi), Kassena
(Kassem), Sissala
Dagara (Dagarti)
Lilse, Fulse (Kurumba)
Frafra (Fare-fare)
Builsa
Wagala

first language. Languages in this group are mostly non-tonal and classless, though many have masculine and feminine genders.

Arabic dialects – Hassaniya cluster
Berabish, Imragen, Kunta (Kounta), Regeibat, Rehian, Tajakant, Arosien, Trarza, Zenaga, Chorfa, Tichit, Choa (Shua)

Chadic languages
Hausa, Adrawa, Tazarawa
Angas
Bura
Kotoko (Longone)
Tangale
Mandara (Wandala)
Kapsiki (Margi)

Matakam (Mafa)
Mauri
Wakura
Toupouri (Tuburi)
Wajawa
Gude
Gerawa
Guizica, Mofou
Podoko
Bata
Mousgoum (Musgu)

Berber languages
Tamashek (Tuareg, Touareg)

Saharan languages
Kanouri (Kanuri, Beriberi)

"Twi" languages

Akan group
Twi (Asante)
Fante
Baoulé
Agni
Abron
Akwapim
Guang

"Ewe" group
Ewe, Ang-lo
Fon, Adja, Xwala, Xuéda, Maxi
Ga-Adangme
Mina, Popo
Gun, Tofinu

Central Togo languages
Akposso

Lagoon languages
Abé
Ajukru
Abidji
Alladian
Assini, Nzima
Ebrie

Eastern Nigritic languages

Adamawa
Fali
Massa
Mbum
Mundang

Namshi
Chamba
Longuda
Mumuye
Vere
Yungur

"Ijo" languages
Ijo (Ijaw)
Brass
Kalabari

Bantoid languages
Ibibio, Efik, Anang
Mada
Katab
Boki
Kamberi
Birom
Ekoi, Oban
Orri, Ukelle
Korup
Dukakari
Jerawa
Anyang
Basa-Kaduna
Yergum
Jukun
Ogoni

Macro-Bantu languages
Tiv
Jarawa

Bozo
Kagoro

Peripheral Mand
Mende (Ge
Kpelle (G
Vai (G
D

B **BASICS** | Trav

and languages

...gom
Bandop
Tikar

North-Western Bantu
Bulu, Ewondo (Yaoundé)
Beti, Fang, Eton
Gbaya
Sango-Ngbandi
Bakundu
Duala (Douala)
Bassa, Bakoko
Batanga
Bakweri, Bimbia

Mande

The **Mande cluster of languages** doesn't belong to either area of wider affinity and, linguistically, it's on a classification level with both of them. The languages in this group are closely related and very old. Geographically, they're quite compact and appear to be centred in the Mali–Guinea border region – which, fascinatingly, was also the heartland of the old Mande/Manding/Mali empire. From the linguistic point of view, the "nuclear Mande" family includes **Bamana**, **Malinké** (Mandinka), **Susu** and **Dyula**. This group is also known as "Mande-Tan" (after their word for "ten"). The languages of "Peripheral Mande" (or "Mande-Fu"), which deviate much

more from the heartland languages, and from each other, include languages of Guinea, Sierra Leone and Liberia, such as **Mende**, **Dan-Gio** and **Vai**. Tones are important in this southern section, but less so in the more mainstream Mande languages.

Nuclear Mande languages
Malinké (Mandinka, Mandingo)
Bambara (Bamana)
Soninke (Sarakolé)
Susu (Sousou)
Dyula (Dioula)
Koranko
Diallonke (Yalunka)
Kasonke
Konyanke

...de languages

...e)
...inas)
...h, Gio (Dan-Gio), Mano, Guro
Loma (Toma), Buzi
Samo
Bussa (Busa)
Ngere (Guerze)
Kono
Sia
Loko
Gbande

Songhai

The **Songhai** of the middle Niger River are another old imperial people: their languages – **Songhai** (Sonray), **Dendi** and **Djerma** (Zerma) are quite distinct from any others in Africa.

Language courses and other reading

There is little available on West African – or even African – languages in the sense of general background, but you will find various phrasebooks and some language-learning material.

Pierre Alexandre *Languages and Language in Africa.* Surprisingly entertaining tour of the arcane world of African linguistics, led by a magnificently enthusiastic, French professor.

E.C. Rowlands *Teach Yourself Yoruba* and **Charles H. Kraft and H.M. Kirk-Greene** *Teach Yourself Hausa.*

US State Department Foreign Service Institute *Audio-Forum Basic Courses.* A number of self-instructional language courses available from ⓦ www.audioforum.com. Priced at $220–300, each one comes with a textbook and cassettes. Languages available include the Senegambian dialect of Fula, Hausa, Igbo, More, Twi and Yoruba.

Travellers' French

Apart from some specialized vocabulary, there's little that non-fluent speakers will find characteristic about West African French beyond the accent. As with English spoken as a second language, West African French has the rhythmic and tonal colouring of the speaker's mother tongue. It's generally a lot easier to understand than French as spoken in France, because it's more vigorously pronounced. And the French colonists encouraged the use of French far more than the British, so that, assuming you have at least some French, there are fewer language problems in the *pays francophones*.

Useful vocabulary

In the glossary at the end of this section, we've put together a mix of pertinent words and expressions, together with some French and West African street slang and a few historical terms, which have found their way into West African French.

Basic terms and phrases

aujourd'hui	today
hier	yesterday
demain	tomorrow
le matin	in the morning
l'après-midi	in the afternoon
le soir	in the evening
maintenant	now
plus tard	later
à une heure	at one o'clock
à trois heures	at three o'clock
à dix heures et demie	at ten-thirty
à midi	at midday
un homme	man

une femme	woman
ici	here
là	there
ceci	this one
celà	that one
ouvert	open
fermé	closed
grand	big
petit	small
plus	more
moins	less
un peu	a little
beaucoup	a lot
bon marché	cheap
cher	expensive
bon	good
mauvais	bad
chaud	hot
froid	cold

Talking to people

Pardon	Excuse me
Vous parlez anglais?	Do you speak English?
Comment ça se dit en Français?	How do you say it in French?
Comment vous appelez-vous?	What's your name?
Je m'appelle …	My name is …
Je suis anglais[e]	I'm English/
irlandais[e]	Irish/
écossais[e]	Scottish/
gallois[e]	Welsh/
américain[e]	American/
australien[ne]	Australian/
canadien[ne]	Canadian/
néo-zélandais[e]	a New Zealander
oui	yes
non	no
Je comprends	I understand
Je ne comprends pas	I don't understand
s'il vous plaît, parlez moins vite?	Can you speak slower?
d'accord	OK/agreed
s'il vous plaît	please
merci	thank you
bonjour	hello
au revoir	goodbye
bonjour	good morning /afternoon
bonsoir	good evening
bonne nuit	good night
Comment allez-vous?/ Ça va?	How are you?
Très bien, merci	Fine, thanks
Je ne sais pas	I don't know
Allons-y	Let's go
à demain	See you tomorrow
à bientôt	See you soon
Pardon, Madame/ je m'excuse	Sorry
Fichez-moi la paix!	Leave me alone (aggressive)
Aidez-moi, s'il vous plaît	Please help me

Finding the way

autobus, bus, car	bus
voiture	car
bâteau	boat
chaloupe	launch/motorboat
avion	plane
Il part à quelle heure?	What time does it leave?
Il arrive à quelle heure?	What time does it arrive?
un billet pour …	a ticket to …
vente de billets /guichet	ticket office
combien de kilomètres?	how many kilometres?
combien d'heures?	how many hours?
à pied	on foot
Vous allez où?	Where are you going?
Je vais à …	I'm going to …
Je voudrais descendre à …	I want to get off at …
la route pour …	the road to …
près/pas loin	near
loin	far
à gauche	left
à droite	right
tout droit	straight on
l'autre côté de	on the other side of
à l'angle de	on the corner of
à côté de	next to
derrière	behind
devant	in front of
avant	before
après	after
sous	under
traverser	to cross
pont	bridge

Other needs

médecin	doctor
Je ne me sens pas bien	I don't feel well
médicaments	medicines
ordonnance	prescription
Je suis malade	I feel sick
J'ai mal à la tête	headache
mal à l'estomac	stomach ache
règles	period
douleur	pain
ça fait mal	it hurts
pharmacie	chemist
boulangerie	bakery
alimentation	food shop
supermarché	supermarket
manger	to eat
boire	to drink
banque	bank
argent	money
avec	with
sans	without

Questions and requests

The simplest way of asking a question is to start with *s'il vous plaît* (please), then name the thing you want in an interrogative tone of voice. For example:

| S'il vous plaît, la boulangerie? | Where is the bakery? |
| S'il vous plaît, la route pour Bobo? | Which way is it to Bobo? |

Similarly with requests:

S'il vous plaît, une chambre pour deux	We'd like a room for two
S'il vous plaît, un kilo d'oranges?	Can I have a kilo of oranges?
où?	Where?
comment?	How?
combien?	How many/ how much?
quand?	When?
pourquoi?	Why?
à quelle heure?	At what time?
quel est?	What is/which is?

Accommodation

une chambre pour une/deux personnes	a room for one/ two people
un lit double	a double bed
une chambre avec douche	a room with a shower
Je peux la voir?	Can I see it?
une chambre sur la cour	a room on the courtyard
une chambre sur la rue	a room over the street
premier (1er) étage	first floor
deuxième (2éme) étage	second floor
avec vue	with a view
clef	key
repasser	to iron
faire la lessive	do laundry
draps	sheets
calme	quiet
bruyant	noisy
eau chaude	hot water
eau froide	cold water
le petit déjeuner	breakfast

Days and dates

janvier	January
février	February
mars	March
avril	April
mai	May
juin	June
juillet	July
août	August
septembre	September
octobre	October
novembre	November
décembre	December
dimanche	Sunday
lundi	Monday
mardi	Tuesday
mercredi	Wednesday
jeudi	Thursday
vendredi	Friday
samedi	Saturday
le premier août	August 1
le deux mars	March 2
le quatorze juillet	July 14
le vingt-trois novembre	November 23

Numbers

un	1
deux	2
trois	3
quatre	4
cinq	5
six	6
sept	7
huit	8
neuf	9
dix	10
onze	11
douze	12
treize	13
quatorze	14
quinze	15
seize	16
dix-sept	17
dix-huit	18
dix-neuf	19
vingt	20
vingt-et-un	21
vingt-deux	22
trente	30
quarante	40
cinquante	50
soixante	60
soixante-dix	70
soixante-quinze	75
quatre-vingts	80
quatre-vingt-dix	90
quatre-vingt-quinze	95
cent	100
cent-et-un	101
deux cents	200
trois cents	300
cinq cents	500
mille	1000
deux milles	2000
cinq milles	5000
un million	1,000,000

A traveller's glossary

amende	fine, penalty
atelier	workshop, studio
bâché	pick-up van, (lit. "tarpaulined")
balise	beacon or cairn, usually in the desert
banco	mud and straw mixture for building

barrage	road block, barrier
barraquer	to stop, rest awhile, camp
berline	saloon car
bic	disposable pen
biche	doe, gazelle, pet
bidonville	slum, shantytown
bonne arrivée	favoured greeting in Francophone Africa
bord	fortress (Arabic)
bordelle	prostitute, pick-up
borne	kilometre marker, "kilometre"
bouffer	to eat
break	estate car, station wagon
bricolage	the art of preserving equipment or making something out of nothing
brousse	countryside, the bush
buvette	outside bar, refreshments stall
cadeauter	to give a present; children may tell you, "il faut me cadeauter"
caféman	coffee, bread and omelette man
campement	budget motel or country guesthouse
canari	clay pot for storing cool water
carte d'identité	identity card
carte routière	road map
case	hut, small house
chef	boss, chief
chômer	to be unemployed
cinq cent quatre	Peugeot 504
climatisée	air-conditioned (room)
colon	a colonial
commander	ask someone to do something/order at a restaurant
contrôle	checkpoint
coupe-coupe	machete
coupers de route	roadside bandits
dancing	dance floor, disco
dépannage	breakdown service
depuis	a long time
devises	money or (hard) currency

discuter	to discuss, negotiate
doux	good (even a hot pepper soup, far from mild, can be *doux*)
eau potable	drinking water
en panne	out of order, broken down
escalier	washboard road-surface
escroc	swindler, conman
exigé	required, demanded
faisable	feasible, doable
féticheur	religious man with a knowledge of the ways of the spirits
fiche	form, document to fill in
flic	cop, policeman
fréquenter	to go to school
fric	cash, dosh
fromager	silk-cotton (kapok) tree
garé	parked, not in use
gare routière	motor transport station
gare ferroviaire	railway station
gargote	cheap restaurant or chop house
gaté	spoiled, broken, needing repair
gênant	bothersome, a hassle
gîte (d'étape)	boarding house, inn (staging post)
goudron	tar, tarmac
gri-gri	charm, amulet, juju
griot	traditional musician, storyteller, court minstrel
hivernage	rainy season
HLM	"low rent housing" (council flats)
Immeuble (Imm.)	Building
insh'allah	if Allah wills it (hopefully)
intéressant	good, enjoyable; eg a film or the food you're eating
lampe tempête	hurricane lamp, kerosene lamp
livres sterling	pounds sterling
machin	thingamajig, whatsitsname
mairie	town hall, city hall
maison de passage/passe	boarding house used as a brothel
marigot	creek
marque	make or brand (eg vehicle or spare part)
mec	guy, fellow
moustiquaire	mosquito net/mosquito screen
occasion	a seat or place in a bush taxi
ornières	wheel ruts
paillote	straw hut, sun shade, thatched awning
palétuviers	mangroves
palu/paludisme	malaria
patron/chef	boss, chief, mister
phacochère	warthog
pièces	identity papers
pirogue	dugout canoe
piste	track, trail
préfet/sous-préfet	administrative prefect/assistant prefect (equivalent of district commissioner and assistant)
quatre-quatre	four-wheel-drive
récolte	harvest
régler	to sort out, settle up, pay up
renseignements	information, details
route bitumée	surfaced road
SIDA	AIDS
sofa	nineteenth-century Muslim cavalry
source (d'eau)	spring, water source
sous	money
sucrerie	mineral or soft drink
sympa/sympathique	nice, friendly
tampon	rubber stamp
tata	fortress (Mande)
tôle ondulée	corrugated iron, washboard
tourner	to go out, go dancing, hang out

| triptyque | triptych; a document in three folds | truc | thing, whatsit |
| trop | more often means "very" than "too much" | ventilée | "ventilated" – a room with a fan |

Practicalities

Camera matters

If you take a camera, make sure you have a **dust-proof bag** to keep it in, and take spare **batteries**, too. Memory cards and film are pricey so bring all you need – or transfer your files to CD at an Internet café.

Electricity

The mains supply is usually 220V AC 50Hz with European two-pin sockets in Francophone and Lusophone countries and British three-pin sockets in the Anglophone countries. It's common for electricity supplies to be restricted in West Africa, especially where hydroelectric power stations are responsible for providing power, which can make the end of the dry season – the very time when air conditioning and cold drinks are most welcome – particularly trying.

Laundry

Washing is always done by hand, in a stream with flat rocks by preference. You won't find self-service laundries, but there are plenty of people willing to do the job. Even the smallest hotel can arrange it. If you have any choice, dry your clothes indoors. Avoid spreading them on the ground if you can – they may be infested by the tumbu fly which lays its eggs on wet clothes. Ironing kills the eggs.

Packing essentials

In no particular order, and not all essential, the following items all prove useful.

Pocket dictionary or phrasebook Extremely useful; Rough Guides publishes French and Portuguese dictionary phrasebooks.

Binoculars Even the small, fold-up ones are invaluable for game- and bird-watching.

Multipurpose penknife Essential, but avoid ones with blades longer than a palm-width, which are sometimes confiscated (and remember to pack it in your hold luggage when flying).

Torch (flashlight) Essential for night visits to the long drop where there is no electricity (on those occasions, carrying it all the time when you don't need it will seem a small price to pay).

Padlock Vital in cheap hotels where doors don't lock properly.

Plastic bags Invaluable – bin liners to keep dust off clothes, small sealable ones to protect cameras and film.

GPS Incredibly useful in remote regions, even though there is yet no large-scale digital mapping for West Africa.

Camping gas stove Light and handy: cylinders are sold somewhere in every West African capital.

Sheet sleeping bag Sew up a sheet. The essential for budget hotel travel.

Sleeping bag Only useful if you're climbing mountains since you'll sleep on top of it nine times out of ten. Get the best, most compressible bag you can afford.

Tampons and contraceptives Expensive and often only available in cities.

Footwear Take the lightest, toughest, best-ventilated pair of boots you can afford.

Purse, pouch, wallet

However you decide to carry your few most valuable items – **passport**, **credit cards**, **memory cards**, **cash** – do so in a way that secures them to you as comfortably as possible. Large, external "bumbags" or "fanny packs" attract attention and can be slashed and grabbed, while purses hanging round the neck under a shirt

87

are also unsafe. The best place is under your waistband, against your hip and strapped to your belt (remember to wrap any paperwork or cash in a plastic bag to save it from sweat damage). Whatever you decide, do not take a wallet in your back pocket.

Time

Most of West Africa is on Greenwich Mean Time (GMT). Cape Verde is one hour behind while Benin, Niger, Nigeria and Cameroon are all one hour ahead. The 24hr clock is widely used in the French- and Portuguese-speaking countries. The 12hr system is usual in the English-speaking countries.

Toilet paper

This is usually provided by the user of the facilities rather than the owner; local people generally prefer to wash with a plastic kettle or jug of water.

Guide

Guide

1 Mauritania 91

2 Senegal 153

3 The Gambia 263

4 Mali 321

5 Cape Verde 431

6 Guinea-Bissau 511

7 Guinea 559

8 Sierra Leone 639

9 Burkina Faso 705

10 Ghana 783

11 Togo 883

12 Benin 949

13 Niger 1007

14 Nigeria 1069

15 Cameroon 1217

Mauritania

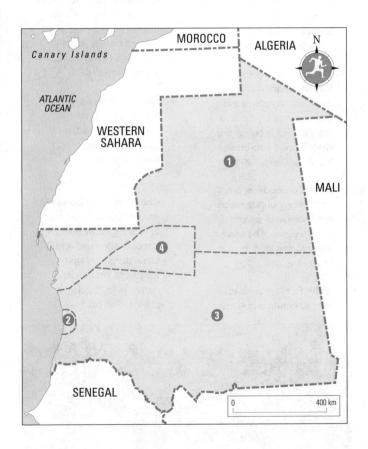

Highlights	92	**1.2** Nouakchott	127
Introduction and Basics	93	**1.3** Southern Mauritania	136
1.1 Nouadhibou and the north	119	**1.4** The Adrar	145

Mauritania highlights

✳ **The ore trains** Immortalized in Michael Palin's *Sahara*, these are some of the longest trains in the world, and a popular means of transport between Nouadhibou and the Adrar. See p.125

✳ **The Banc d'Arguin National Park** A natural reserve with ochre sand dunes sweeping out into the sea, this is one of the world's great bird-breeding sites. See p.126

✳ **Desert crocodiles**, small populations of Nile crocodiles survive in several remote oases. The easiest place to see them is near Moudjéria. See p.138

✳ **Tichit** Remote oasis town with elaborate architecture and an ethnic mix that epitomizes Mauritania. See p.141

✳ **Oualata** Ancient, forgotten caravan town, worth the trek for its remarkable painted buildings, set in a rubble of centuries-old stone. See p.143

✳ **Terjit** A fertile oasis near Atar, sheltered by cliffs and with a secluded *campement* and fine bathing pools. See p.145

✳ **Chinguetti and Ouadane** Ancient Saharan centres of learning, now boasting atmospheric ruins and some gorgeous landscapes of ergs (dunes) and regs (rocky desert plains). See pp.149–151

▲ Moorish reception ceremony

Introduction and Basics

Mauritania, once well off the map for most travellers to Africa, and still rarely covered by the media, can come as a surprising discovery if you're on the overland trail south from Morocco, or if you simply make the effort to visit from elsewhere in West Africa. Pleasantly laid-back, spacious and physically comfortable because of its dry climate, the country is also scenically dramatic in several regions and culturally complex, with its rock paintings, medieval mosques, alluring ancient caravanserai oases and deep-rooted class structure.

Bordered by Senegal, Mali, Morocco and Algeria, Mauritania was referred to by French colonialists as *Le Grand Vide* ("The Great Void"), but the country's name comes from its dominant ethnic group, the **Moors**, who speak the **Hassaniya** dialect of Arabic and are traditionally nomadic.

People

The Moors are broadly divided into "white" **Bidan**, who claim Arab and Berber ancestors from North Africa and Arabia, and "black" **Haratin**, whose physical ancestry lies in Saharan and sub-Saharan Africa and who were subjugated and "Arabized" by the Bidan. Traditionally, the Haratin were vassals to the noble classes, but some Haratin elevated themselves into an independent caste which owed no tribute. The formal abolition of slavery in 1980 decreed that all "ex-slaves" (formerly called Abid) were henceforth to be known as "Haratin" – a source of offence to

"real Haratin" and of confusion to outsiders.

This characterization oversimplifies the make-up of a very diverse and multifaceted population. **Social status** in Mauritania is considerably more than a question of skin colour. The white Moor community is divided broadly into Hassanes (noble families), Zouaya (or Tolba, the pious maraboutic caste) and Zenaga vassals (herders and cultivators). Status among black Moor families tends to be determined by their length of association and degree of intermarriage with white Moors, thereby blurring racial distinctions.

You can get an initial fix on the social complexities of Moorish society from the **position of women**, which is less rigidly defined than in most Arabic-speaking countries. Women may travel alone, drink tea with men, take an active part in male-dominated conversations and breast-feed their children in public; they rarely cover their faces, though they always cover their hair. The Berber and African heritage is apparent

Facts and figures

The **République Islamique de Mauritanie** (often shortened to RIM) covers more than a million square kilometres, more than four times the size of the United Kingdom and nearly as big as California and Texas combined. Approximately half the country is covered in sand, and with around 3.1 million people, it has one of the lowest **population** densities in the world. There's heavy migration to the towns, to the south, and abroad, however, while the eastern third of Mauritania is designated *zone vide* (empty quarter). Life expectancy stands at 44 years for men, 47 years for women. Mauritania's **foreign debt** is currently some £1.3 billion ($2.5 billion; the price of two Stealth Bomber aircraft) – quite a bit more than its annual GDP but a relatively minor figure in global terms. **President Sidi Ould Cheikh Abdallahi** heads up the country's first properly democratic government. **Oil** was recently discovered off the Mauritanian coast – a welcome supplement to Mauritania's beleaguered economy dominated by iron ore and fisheries – and the Australian-run operation began pumping in 2006.

in these freedoms, which indicate the relative superficiality of the country's Arabic culture. In political matters, however, women's freedom is widely curtailed.

You'll quickly notice almost all Moors retain traditional names. Ould and Mint mean "son of" and "daughter of" in Hassaniya: hence Mokhtar Ould Daddah, Dimi Mint Abba.

Outside the Moorish community, the remaining forty percent of the population are southerners – *Soudaniens* in Mauritanian phraseology – speaking **Fula** (Pulaar), **Wolof** or **Soninké**, and mostly farming and herding near the Senegalese and Malian borders

where life is dominated by the Senegal River. In Mauritania, the Fula-speakers of the Tukulor (spelt Toucouleur by the French) and Fula ethnic groups are known jointly as **Hal-Pulaar**.

In addition, Mauritania has a considerable population of African **immigrant workers**, from as far afield as Guinea and Nigeria. Some have come to work, while others are on their way north, fuelled by fictitious stories in their homelands of ships travelling direct to Europe from Mauritania. Many end up in Nouadhibou, hoping for a passage to the Canary Islands, or transport into Morocco.

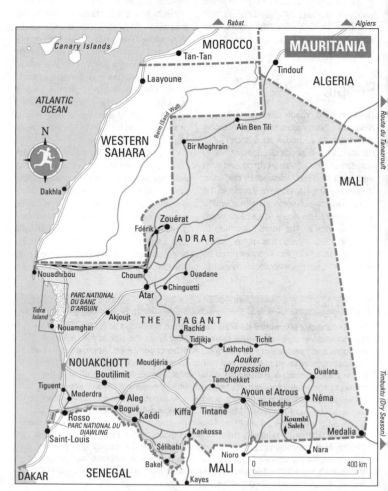

Photography

People tend to be suspicious of cameras and prefer not to have their pictures taken, but the reaction is not normally heavy. However, be careful in Nouakchott; check before snapping and avoid all broad street scenes – there's often an upset. In particular avoid the university area and the ministries on Avenue Abdel Nasser. There is no photography permit. Film in Nouakchott is expensive and unreliably stored.

Where to go

As much of the land is dry and inhospitable and the tourism infrastructure negligible, **travel targets** in Mauritania are easily pinpointed. Starting from Nouakchott and the coast, two roads cut across the country. The first road leads to the central **Adrar region**, where a rugged landscape softened by rolling dunes shelters some ancient towns and oases – **Atar**, **Terjit**, the UNESCO heritage towns of **Chinguetti** and **Ouadane** – and a rich archeological past, embodied in the stone tools and rock paintings found all over the region.

The other road is the desperate-sounding **Route de l'Espoir** (Road of Hope), which leads part of the way to the **Tagant region**, and the ancient towns of **Tidjikja**, **Rashid** and UNESCO-listed **Tichit**. The Route de l'Espoir also provides the easiest access to the colourful town of **Oualata** (the fourth UNESCO site in the country) and the ruins of Koumbi Saleh, the latter once capital of the ancient Ghana empire.

Nouakchott, the capital, is a nearly inevitable but unremarkable transit point, while **Nouadhibou**, the second city, is the point of entry to West Africa for overland vehicles coming from Morocco and Europe, or for travellers arriving from the Canary Islands by air. The two-hundred-wagon **iron-ore train** linking Nouadhibou with central Mauritania makes for an unusual trip. Nouakchott and Nouadhibou, incidentally, both have **beaches** that seem to go on forever.

Wherever you go in Mauritania, you'll find a release from the freneticism of lands further south, and **travel conditions** generally more peaceful than elsewhere in West Africa. The worthwhile goals make travelling around attractive, and the desert journeys are a fair substitute for actually crossing the Sahara.

When to go

When to visit is conditional more on burning temperatures than disruptive rainfall. The coast is cooled by sea breezes, but you'd probably want to avoid the interior between April and October (see the climate table for Atar, and remember these figures are averages: the thermometer often pips 50°C in the shade). The **southwest** gets oppressive humidity and occasional cloudbursts between July and October. At this time of year dirt roads can be cut – especially near the Senegal River – and transport off the paved highway can be very difficult. January and February are Mauritania's windiest months, when hopes for romantic desert nights are often dashed by fierce sandstorms.

Getting there from the rest of Africa

Most of the international flights into Mauritania arrive in the capital, **Nouakchott**. Return trips from Dakar are run several times a week by Tunisair and Air Mauritanie. Air Mauritanie also flies from **Cotonou** via **Abidjan** five times a week and from **Bamako**, also five times a week.

As for flights from North Africa, flying out of **Casablanca** you can choose from Royal Air Maroc or Air Mauritanie, though if you want to head back by this route as well, Royal Air Maroc's fares are better value.

> For details on **getting to Mauritania from outside Africa**, plus important practical information applying to all West African countries, covering health, transport, cultural hints and more, see Basics, pp.19–28.

Average temperatures and rainfall

	Jan	Feb	Mar	Apr	May	June	July	Aug	Sept	Oct	Nov	Dec
Nouakchott												
Temperatures °C												
Min (night)	14	15	17	18	21	23	23	24	24	22	18	13
Max (day)	29	31	32	32	34	33	32	32	34	33	32	28
Rainfall mm	0	3	0	0	0	3	13	104	23	10	3	0
Days with rainfall	0	1	0	0	0	1	1	3	3	1	1	0
Nouadhibou												
Temperatures °C												
Min (night)	12	13	14	14	15	16	18	20	20	19	16	14
Max (day)	26	28	27	27	28	30	27	30	33	30	28	25
Rainfall mm	0	0	0	0	0	0	0	0	8	12	3	10
Atar												
Temperatures °C												
Min (night)	12	13	17	19	22	27	25	26	26	23	17	13
Max (day)	31	33	34	39	40	42	43	42	42	38	33	29
Rainfall mm	3	0	0	0	0	3	8	30	28	3	3	0

There are also two flights a week each from **Algiers** with Air Algérie and from **Tunis** with Tunisair.

For details of **Canary Island connections**, see Basics, p.28.

Entering the country **overland**, you'll generally find Mauritanian **border officials** straight-dealing, if occasionally pedantic, but seldom ostentatiously corrupt. Across the country, *postes de contrôle* may thoroughly check foreign-drivers' paperwork and occasionally expect or demand a "*cadeau*".

Overland from Morocco

The southbound route from Morocco, currently the only viable way of entering West Africa overland from North Africa, is straightforward, though distances between petrol stations are huge, and it's not uncommon for places to run out of fuel, so fill up your tank and jerry cans at every opportunity.

If you're travelling by public transport, you'll find scheduled bus and taxi services as far south as **Dakhla** in Western Sahara and occasionally even as far as the village of **Bir Gandouz** near the Mauritanian border. Assuming you don't strike lucky with a Bir Gandouz vehicle, the best place to find a lift from Dakhla is *Camping Moussaffir*, a favourite overlander's stopover located 500m before the first checkpoint to the north of town. Alternatively, wander around hotels and camp sites in Dakhla and ask who's going south or try hitching a ride with the Mauritanian traders at the first police checkpoint north of town (the price to Nouadhibou should be around €20). If all else fails, a shared taxi the 400-odd kilometres to the border probably won't break the bank. Two recommended places to stay in Dakhla are the *Hôtel Doubs* and the *Al Mouakouama*.

From Dakhla, the first ninety percent of the road south to Nouadhibou is in reasonable condition, much of it paved. Make sure you stock up with enough fuel, food and water to last at least two days. Some travellers try to get from Dakhla to Nouadhibou in a day, but it's better to leave Dakhla in the afternoon and spend the night at *Café Restaurant Motel Dakmar* (aka *Barba's*; ☏028 897 961; ❷), an excellent, airy hotel just 80km from the Mauritanian border. It's also possible to **camp** at Fort Guerguarat near the border itself, which closes at 6pm.

The tarmac comes to an end here as you enter no-man's-land, the road degenerating into 8km of rough bitumen interspersed with soft sand, surrounded by **mines**. Make sure you keep to well-marked tracks as the mines are still live; many choose to hire a guide, though it's far from essential.

At the **Mauritanian border** you will have your vehicle details entered into your passport, sign a declaration promising not to sell your car in Mauritania and pay fees of €10.00/UM3500 at the police post and €15.00/UM5200 at the customs, as well as a motor insurance premium (3 days €6/UM2000; 10 days €10/UM3100; 1 month €30/UM10100). These figures are for ordinary cars: 4x4 cover is roughly 50 percent dearer. Beware of fudging on your dates: your insurance will be frequently checked south of Nouadhibou.

From the border it takes a few hours to negotiate just 50km of sandy track, dotted with various checkpoints and sand traps; the last of these is cleared a few kilometres north of Nouadhibou. Information on Nouadhibou itself starts on p.119.

For more detailed information on this route, see Chris Scott's Ⓦ www.sahara-overland .com or the same Sahara specialist's classic guide *Sahara Overland* (Trailblazer), or join one of the online user groups for the Plymouth–Banjul rally (Ⓦ www .plymouth-banjul.co.uk), whose participants post up-to-date tips on the route and the borders.

Overland from Mali

Routes into Mauritania from Mali are only **from the south**: there are no official border crossings on Mauritania's long eastern frontier. The principal crossing is Bamako–Nioro–Ayoun which is gradually being upgraded on the Bamako–Nioro stretch and already paved from Nioro to Ayoun.

The Tuareg conflict in Mali (see p.344), though now over, affected security in south-eastern Mauritania and there have been reports of banditry being a problem. Keep your ears open and don't proceed without being sure the route is safe. There's a lack of banks in eastern Mauritania, so you will have to change money unofficially. This border is little used by travellers and you may not have to pay the fees that travellers are stung for arriving from Morocco and Senegal. If you're driving, however, you will need to get vehicle **insurance**.

Overland from Senegal

If you make the crossing at the right place, getting into Mauritania from Senegal can be the most hassle-free of all borders. The main crossing point from Senegal is **Rosso**, near the mouth of the Senegal River. The car ferry regularly makes the five-minute crossing (but expect it to take up to an hour to load and unload). During the three-hour lunch break, the ferry doesn't operate and the small currency-exchange booth on the Mauritanian side is also closed. If you're on foot, you can take a pirogue across.

Rosso's notoriously inefficient and corrupt officials make the other major crossing, the **Diama barrage** road, north of St-Louis and west of Rosso, the preferred route for many, though parts of this road are rocky and some of it can be washed out if the rains have come. Rosso is open from 8am to noon and from 3pm to 6pm. Officially, Diama is open from 8am to 6pm, but as the station is essentially manned round-the-clock, getting across after hours becomes a question of how much monetary *cadeau* you're willing to part with. Other, much less used, crossings, not open to vehicles, are at **Bogué**, near Aleg, and at **Gouray**, near Sélibabi; in both locations you'll need to take a pirogue across the river.

Travellers using public transport can sometimes avoid the sundry **taxes and "fees"** that officials levy as you leave Senegal and enter Mauritania, but if you're driving your own vehicle, you'll certainly need to purchase Mauritanian insurance (which at Rosso seems to cost UM5000 for ten days), and you'll probably be hit for further payments per person both on leaving Senegal and on entering Mauritania before you can go on your way. Leaving Senegal, these consist of a CFA4000 dam toll and CFA2500 per person plus CFA2500 per car to clear Customs. In Mauritania, the fees are UM1000 to clear Immigration, UM2000 for Customs and UM500 in local commune tax. You'll be delighted to know that the fees add up to €10 per person on each side of the river – and they accept euros.

Red tape and visas

Visas are required by most nationalities except West Africans. In countries without Mauritanian representation, it is often possible to obtain a visa at the French embassy or consulate – almost always easier than applying for one after you've left your own country – though Europeans should be aware that pan-Schengen visas may not be accepted for entry by Mauritanian officials, whatever the issuing embassy might tell you. If you're travelling overland, you should have no trouble getting a visa at the border – a method that is usually much cheaper than the consulates anyway.

Otherwise, to obtain a visa outside your country of residence, you may have to show a letter of introduction from your embassy and an international air ticket. Some Mauritanian embassies will direct you to get a visa for the "country of embarkation" (in other words a visa for the country you'll be leaving immediately before entering Mauritania). Visa prices and durations vary considerably from embassy to embassy and even from one applicant to the next. As of early 2008, the Mauritanian embassy in London was charging £42 for a visa, while in New York the fee was $100 and in Paris it was €30. Ask the price, get a receipt, and check what you've paid against the revenue stamps stuck into your passport. In several embassies, a little discussion about Mauritania's historic sites can break the ice and lower the price. Mauritanian officials were formerly quite keen on health certificates and often required you to show your **yellow fever certificate** at borders and checkpoints, though this rarely happens these days.

Mauritanian visas in Morocco

If you're planning to travel south into Mauritania along the Atlantic coast of Morocco, and you can't manage to get a visa in your home country, you can purchase one in **Casablanca**, though the price is the same as getting it at the Mauritanian border. The Mauritanian **consulate** in Casablanca is on 382 Route d'El Jadida (☎022 257 373). You'll need to bring your passport plus a photocopy of the key pages, as well as two photos and the visa fee (€20 for a one-month visa). If you bring these when the consulate is open in the morning (Mon–Thurs 9–10.30am, Fri 9am–noon), you should be able to pick up the visa in the afternoon between 2pm and 4pm. Note that visas are valid from the day you apply, rather than your date of arrival in Mauritania.

Other red tape

Large towns have **control posts on entrance roads** where your particulars (*pièces*) will be recorded. Smaller places don't, and it's up to you to find the man on duty and proffer your passport.

To save time, particularly if you are in a group, it is a good idea to write your travel itinerary on a piece of paper (officials will ask for a *fiche*) with the names of all in your party, their passport numbers and nationalities. Make numerous photocopies of this and pass it on at each police checkpoint. If you're driving, you may, in exceptional circumstances, have your vehicle thoroughly searched.

Other regulations of note include laws governing the sale and consumption of **alcohol** – it's illegal except in licensed bars, restaurants and hotels. No booze can legally be brought into the country and those who have attempted to do so in recent years have been slapped with €500 fines and have even spent a night in jail – not to be recommended.

Note also that exporting Mauritanian **currency** is illegal, though it's hard to see why you would want to.

Info, websites, maps

There are no Mauritanian tourist offices, but detailed French-language guides to various regions, including the Adrar and the Tagant are produced by the French Cultural Centre, and can be found in larger hotels and bookshops in Nouakchott.

Websites

The **Internet** isn't exactly overflowing with sites about Mauritania. Three worthwhile urls are:

@**tinyurl.com/2su7c7** Stanford University's annotated links for Mauritania. Good place to start.

ⓦ**www.mauritania.mr** Decent French and Arabic info site, though with a strong official line.
ⓦ**www.terremauritanie.com** Tourism site with up-to-date info on accommodation options.

Maps

The **IGN** 1:2,500,000 (1993) **map** of Mauritania has too small a scale to be useful for serious exploration; it's also quite out of date and leaves off several key, newer routes. IGN's 1:200,000 series covers the whole country, in theory, but obtaining sheets isn't very straightforward (see p.35). The best general map is probably the new **Reise Know-How** *Westafrika: Sahelländer* at 1:2,200,000, printed on durable plastic paper, up to date and quite detailed for its scale.

The media

Since free elections in 1992 the press has been liberalized and there are now a good dozen **daily papers**, mostly in Arabic. Titles come and go frequently, and though most papers tend to serve up the same bland mix of news and articles about drought and the doings of the elite, one or two are startlingly anti-establishment: *La Tribune* and *L'Éveil* are the most widely read. The two papers produced by the official press agency are *Horizons* (in French) and *Chaab* (in Arabic). You'll find French-language newspapers and magazines around Nouakchott and Nouadhibou, and occasionally even an English-language *Economist* or *Herald Tribune* in the Librairie Vents du Sud.

The state-run **Radio Mauritanie** and **TV Mauritanie** network broadcasts in French and Hassaniya, with some programmes in Fula, Wolof and Sarakolé/Soninké. **Television** has exploded in recent years, and even the electricity-starved *bidonvilles* around Nouakchott have battery-driven TVs. The news and "cultural" programmes you'd expect are interrupted by the occasional French soccer match. Most hotels, even down-market ones, have a satellite dish and can receive a variety of international channels. In 2007, the BBC began 24-hour Arabic broadcasts on FM in Nouakchott (106.9m) and Nouadhibou (102.4m)

Health

The most critical feature of travel in Mauritania from a **health** aspect is the size of the country and the isolation of most settlements. You'll often be very far off the beaten track, and here, even more than anywhere else in West Africa, you should have repatriation insurance in case of an accident or sudden illness.

Treat **water** with suspicion – reserves are usually low, and domestic animals depend on them too. It's good practice to carry a five-litre container and refill it at every opportunity. Fresh camel or goat's **milk** (*zrig*) is often offered to guests and it's probably best to limit your consumption, Even in the case of fresh Zebu cow's milk, the risk of TB is very low, but brucellosis and hepatitis A can be contracted from infected milk.

The **malaria** risk in Mauritania is generally thought to be slight, except along the Senegal River, where it's as high as anywhere in West Africa. Roughly north of a line from Nouakchott to Tidjikja it's not reckoned to occur at all, but there are still plenty of mosquitoes about and it would be stupid to break your course of antimalarial pills for just a short stay in the country.

Hospitals and treatment facilities outside Nouakchott are strapped. The north, apart from Atar and Nouadhibou, has almost no public health service, and although some of the southern towns have regional hospitals or health centres, these should be seen as a last resort – and a further burden on local provision if you require treatment. A much better option is to go to a private clinic – consultation fees start at around UM2000. **Pharmacies**, however, are a major growth industry in Nouakchott and in the interior, and these days they're often well stocked.

Sanitary towels and disposable nappies are on sale in Nouakchott and upcountry.

Costs, money, banks

Mauritania's currency is the **ouguiya** (UM, Oug, Ug). Notes come in denominations of UM100, UM200, UM500 and UM1000, with coins of UM1, UM5, UM10 and UM20. Banks, once free to set their own **exchange rates**, now primarily offer the same (typically UM500 = £1, UM370 = €1, UM250 = $1), so you're not likely to lose much while changing money – unless you do it at Nouakchott or Nouadhibou airport, where rates are abominably poor.

Costs

Daily **living costs** in Mauritania are somewhat higher than in Senegal or Mali. If you like a beer, you'll find Mauritania one of the most expensive countries in the world, and there's no avoiding high **transport costs** (see "Getting around"). If you're staying in cheap hotels, eating in small restaurants, sticking to water or soft drinks and using public transport, you could survive on £20/$40 a day (more easily if there are two or more of you), but most people won't be able to manage on much less than £40/$80 per person, and if you want to stay in much more comfortable accommodation, eat well and rent a car (expensive in Mauritania), you could easily be looking at £100/$200 a day.

Banks and exchange

Although the export and import of ouguiya is prohibited, there's only a limited black market in the currency, more useful for convenience than profit; you'll find very little difference between the rates at banks or on the street. Outside of Nouakchott, **banks** are found in the larger towns, including Atar, Ayoun el Atrous, Bogué, Kaédi, Kiffa, Néma, Rosso,

Sélibabi, Tintâne and Zouérat. **Bureaux de change** and even black-market street traders can also give official receipts for changed money, and both are far more efficient than banks. Rates at city hotels tend to shave a percent or two off the official rate.

The preferred hard currency is the euro: and best rates will be obtained for crisp €100 bills in large quantities. Note that the **CFA franc** is not accepted by banks or hotels, though you may still be able to change CFA unofficially. Note also that towns in the interior are notoriously short of **small change**, and many shops and taxis can rarely give change for a UM1000 note, so make sure you stock up on low-denomination notes (you can change UM1000s to smaller bills at the Banque Centrale de Mauritanie).

It has become quite difficult to find places that will take **traveller's cheques**, though in the major cities most bureaux de change and some banks will do so, but you may have difficulty in the interior. American Express no longer have any representatives in Mauritania. The major **credit cards** are accepted by a few airlines and hotels in the capital, with your charge written out in US$ but calculated at unfavourable rates. Credit-card cash advances can be arranged through certain travel agencies in Nouakchott (see p.135), though also at unfavourable exchange rates.

ATMs have barely started being installed in Mauritania and you'll search long and hard anywhere outside Nouakchott or Nouadhibou.

Getting around

Most transport in Mauritania is by **4x4**, though bush taxis operate on the main highways, and there is a new coach-style bus service between Nouadhibou and Nouakchott. The **railway system** – a single

---

Fuel prices

Fuel costs around UM225 per litre for diesel (gasoil) and UM290 for petrol (super). The further you go from Nouakchott, the higher the prices – with the exception of Nouadhibou, which has the cheapest fuel in the country – so stock up before you leave the cities. Remember your fuel consumption will go up when driving in sand.

line for the iron-ore train in the far north – is more an adventure than a standard form of transport, but it's still a useful link between Nouadhibou and Choum, which is a good gateway to the Atar region.

Road transport

The main form of long-distance public transport – between Rosso and Nouakchott, along the **Route de l'Espoir**, and Nouakchott to Atar – is a nine-seater **Peugeot 504** *taxi brousse*, though it's not unusual to have a choice of vehicles available. The best days to travel by bush taxi are Mondays, Thursdays and Saturdays. Few people travel on a Friday, so you may have to spend ages for a vehicle to fill up before you leave. Be prepared for long, dust-blown journeys, frequent breakdowns, lack of water, and no toilet stops. Road journeys **off the main routes** are arduous, with soft sand the recurring problem; conditions are detailed where relevant.

Fares are normally paid in advance. As a broad guide, expect to pay around £2/$4 per 100km on tarred roads and up to twice as much on dirt roads and desert tracks. Prices are fixed on what could be considered "scheduled runs", and you won't be overcharged; baggage, as usual, is another matter. If you want to get to out-of-the-way sites and towns, transport costs can quickly become exorbitant. The cheapest option is to wait for a vehicle that's going anyway.

Note that you normally pay for a particular **seat** in the vehicle, so choose carefully: try to work out where the sun will be during your journey and sit on the other side. Also avoid the seats over the back axle, which can be much higher, giving you a lot less headroom. Riding in the back of trucks, along these same routes, is slower and even less comfortable, but a good deal cheaper.

Given the lack of health-care provision in Mauritania, it's especially sensible to **avoid night-time travel** – with its attendant risks of stray camels on the roads and unilluminated oncoming vehicles – and to be wary of **dangerous vehicles** being used for relatively rough desert and mountain passages. In the north and east, spare parts for vehicles are very hard to obtain and many are driven long after their use-by dates. It's a good idea to check with the driver of a taxi before getting in just to be sure he's carrying a spare tyre – some drivers don't bother, as it takes up valuable luggage space.

Routes and fares

Atar–Chinguetti daily; 2–3hr; UM2000
Atar–Choum 3–6 daily; 3hr; UM2500
Atar–Ouadane 3–6 weekly; 4hr; UM2900
Nouakchott–Aleg 3–6 daily; 4hr; UM2000
Nouakchott–Atar up to 12 daily; 6hr; UM3500
Nouakchott–Ayoun el Atrous at least 1 daily; 13hr; UM6000
Nouakchott–Kaédi several daily; 6hr; UM5000
Nouakchott–Kiffa 3–6 daily; 9hr; UM4000
Nouakchott–Nouadhibou 2–6 weekly; 6hr; UM3000
Nouakchott–Rosso frequent; 3hr; UM2000
Nouakchott–Sélibabi 1 or 2 daily; 18hr; UM6000
Nouakchott–Tidjikja 1 or 2 daily; 10hr; UM4500

Driving

Car rental is as expensive as you'd expect. Since there's pressure to take a driver at little extra cost, it's often indistinguishable from a personalized "safari" arrangement. Count on about UM15,000 a day for a 4x4, including driver but excluding fuel. Keep your fuel tanks and spare jerry cans full. Note that distances between towns are marked by small stone kilometre posts known as *piquets* and coincidentally referred to as "PK", short for Point Kilometre, which is often the only local reference, as in the village at PK70, or the turning at PK15.

The best roads are in the southern parts of the country southeast of the capital and along the Senegalese border. If you're **driving** yourself, you should treat Mauritania north of the Route de l'Espoir exactly as you would a trans-Saharan track; in many respects, because of the scarcity of other travellers, the routes are tougher and more dangerous. The track between the Tagant plateau and the Adrar (connecting Tidjikja with Atar), and the myriad tracks along the coast, are notorious for vehicles getting stuck. If you have no room to carry a local guide (never a problem to find), don't set off on a little-used trail into the desert. The Mauritanians are not used to tourists' follies and nobody will prevent you from going – or think to search for you if you don't arrive.

Rail travel

If you are travelling by public – or available – transport and your point of arrival is Nouadhibou, then Mauritania's only **train** is a good way into the country (see p.125). You can hop off in Choum, and take a *taxi brousse* to Atar, on the Adrar plateau, only 120km away.

Air travel

At one time, **air travel** made sense if you were short on time – one-way domestic flights averaged around UM13,000 and there are airports in all the large towns, as well as airstrips at Chinguetti and Néma – but since 2005 the national airline Air Mauritanie has suspended all internal flights except for a single Nouadhibou–Nouakchott route. A new carrier, **Mauritania Airways**, was due to begin limited services by early 2008, but nothing was concrete at the time of writing. Check with airline offices in Nouakchott or Nouadhibou for the latest news.

Accommodation

Mauritania's better **hotels** generally resemble Moroccan or Middle Eastern establishments, while cheaper lodgings (often called *auberges*) offer shared rooms, often designed for three people. The minimum price you can expect to pay for a room is about UM1000, less if you opt for a mattress only and sleep on the roof. The choice of hotels and *auberges* is extremely limited outside Nouakchott, Nouadhibou, Atar and Chinguetti.

Inexpensive hotels (❶–❷) typically offer a couple of thin mattresses on the floor (or one-man, sleeping-bag-sized tents) with or without electric lighting. Many of the tourist-oriented places may also offer accommodation either in a **tikit**, a traditional Moorish stone hut, generally roomy and quite cool during the day, or a **khaima**, a spacious and breezy low-hanging tent used by nomads and camel herders, often featuring a mat-covered floor and cushions spread about inside. *Khaimas* are usually offered as the cheapest overnight options within *auberges*.

Rooms at **mid-range establishments** (❸–❺) have beds rather than mattresses, and also offer a fan and possibly self-contained (s/c) rooms, with bathrooms en suite. Included in this category are **maisons d'hôtes**, which in Mauritania essentially function as higher-end *auberges*, offering a little more class and comfort.

Above this price range there aren't many hotels to choose from, but those that exist have very comfortable rooms with TV, airconditioning (a/c) and usually a small fridge. Whatever the price bracket, determined haggling can bring discounts, especially for longer stays.

Moorish **hospitality** being legendary, you may well be put up across the country by taxi drivers and other casual acquaintances. In this situation, never offer money as a gift – it may cause great offence, however poor the hosts. Instead, stock up on pocket knives, watches, cigarettes, lighters, and bags of tea, sugar or instant coffee, all of which are suitable gifts before you venture far from major towns.

Camping out, as long as you have access to water, is a fine option and except in rare cases (noted in the Guide), quite safe. A tent can be useful to keep off the

---

Accommodation price codes

All accommodation prices in this chapter are coded according to the following scale, whose equivalent in pounds sterling/US dollars is used throughout the book. Prices refer to the rate you can expect to pay for a room with two or three beds, or sleeping spaces. Single rooms, or single occupancy, will normally cost at least two-thirds of the twin-occupancy rate. For further details, see p.55.

❶ Under UM2700 (under £5/$10)
❷ UM2700–UM5400 (£5–10/$10–20)
❸ UM5400–UM8100 (£10–15/$20–30)
❹ UM8100–UM10,800 (£15–20/$30–40)
❺ UM10,800–UM16,200 (£20–30/$40–60)
❻ UM16,200–UM21,600 (£30–40/$60–80)
❼ UM21,600–UM27,000 (£40–50/$80–100)
❽ Over UM27,000 (over £50/$100)

desert wind, and a mosquito net is essential at certain times of year, but otherwise you can sleep under the night sky and watch the shooting stars.

Eating and drinking

Mauritania doesn't come up with much food that's memorable, but the variety is increasing. **Restaurants** don't thrive outside Nouakchott and Nouadhibou, though there are chop-house eating places in most towns, sometimes run by immigrants from other parts of West Africa.

Main meals are invariably **rice**- or **couscous**-based, and **bread** (French style) is usually in good supply. **Mutton, camel meat** and **chicken** are standard fare, as too is **fish**, usually dried and recooked. Outside influences are apparent in Mauritanian cuisine: you may be served Senegalese *chep-bu-jen* (rice and fish), Lebanese-style grilled *chawarma* (pressed mutton slices), or Moroccan couscous dishes and *tajine* stews. If you eat with Mauritanians, **milk** (fresh, known as *zrig* – often diluted and sweetened, or curdled, can figure prominently.

Vegetarian travellers in Mauritania have quite a hard time of it. Quantities of **eggs** are served to non-flesh-eaters in homes and restaurants. Outside large towns, basic vegetables such as potatoes, carrots and onions can be found only in settlements with an adequate water supply. Nouakchott has many stalls with a good selection of local and European **fruit**, though you'll pay around UM300/kg for the former and UM500/kg for the latter. Otherwise, **fruit** is limited to **dates** – cheapest after the August and September harvest – and a small range of imports from Spain, Morocco, Senegal or Mali, plus what's grown in the far south of Mauritania itself.

Drinking is a serious business – not alcohol, which is illegal except at some licensed establishments in Nouakchott and Nouadhibou, but **tea**. Moors take their green tea seriously and often. Even more so than in Mali or Niger, a few small glasses of scalding, bitter-sweet yellow froth are part of the daily round. There's invariably a shortage of glasses: pass yours back to the tea-maker as soon as you've drained it, and make sure you drain it well, because it can cause offence to Mauritanians if you leave the dregs behind. It's also not the done thing to leave before the third glass has been drunk – or to hang around after the glasses have been washed up and cleared away.

When you do find the occasional licensed bar, a **beer** will cost you at least UM1000, and up to UM2000 in some restaurants.

Opening hours, public holidays and festivals

The working week traditionally runs from **Sunday to Thursday**, but since 2005, the official weekend is Saturday and Sunday, with many businesses closing early on Friday for prayers. Offices are usually open roughly between 8am and any time from 1.30pm to 4pm. Shops also open at 8am (except for groceries, which often open as early as 7am), closing for a long break at lunch time and opening again from the late afternoon until about 7.30pm.

Apart from those holidays decreed by the Islamic lunar calendar, Mauritania's **public holidays** are: January 1, February 26 (National Reunification Day), May 1 (Labour Day), May 25 (African Liberation Day), November 28 (National Day) and December 12 (anniversary of the 1984 coup). December 25 is a holiday for some businesses, though most shops stay open.

The country's major **festival** is the Guetna, or date festival, held in July and August, when nomadic families leave their camps and towns and gather in various desert oases for a variety of (nonreligious) festivities.

The **Festival International des Musiques Nomades** (⊛ www.musiquesnomades .com) is a week-long festival of Mauritanian and African music held each year in early April; it's the best opportunity bar none for hearing the breadth of Mauritania's rich musical tradition.

Communications

The main **post offices** are in Nouakchott and Nouadhibou, and most towns (except

Tichit, Ouadane and Oualata) have telephone shops. **Poste restante** is reliable but slow. Airmail delivery to and from Europe typically takes anything between a week and 18 days; postcards and airmails to Europe or the USA cost UM370.

Phoning or faxing abroad varies in efficiency, and there are frequent problems getting through to Mauritania from abroad. Note that Mauritanian phone numbers have no area codes. Rates are roughly UM200 per minute to Francophone West Africa and the Middle East, UM250 per minute to the USA and UM290 per minute to Europe. In all cases, the cost between 3pm and 10pm is about twenty percent less than from 7am to 3pm, and from 10pm until 7am it's a third less than the daytime rate. On Friday, phoning at any time costs just a quarter of the daytime rate on other days of the week.

Mauritania is covered by two **mobile-phone** companies: Mattel (ⓦwww.mattel.mr) and Mauritel (ⓦwww.mauritel.mr). Mauritel is the most widely used and has the best coverage, though there are numerous parts of the country where service is nonexistent or close to it. If you're here for more than just a few days, consider buying a local SIM card (*abonnement*) for UM3000 (with UM1000 credit) to make calls on a local network. You can do this with any of the turbaned phone-card hawkers around the major towns. Be aware though that rates can still run high and you may easily use UM1000 of credit with just a few calls. On the whole, coverage is good within the capital, and while it exists in other major centres of the country, including Zouérat, Atar, and Ayoun el Atrous, it tends to be spotty.

Internet cafés, excellent value at about UM200/hr, have taken the country by storm, though connection speeds vary considerably and there's frequent loss of service.

Crafts and shopping

Mauritania is famous for stylishly refined **carpets**, woven in Nouakchott. Sadly these are impractical purchases for most travellers, as are the brass-fitted, dark-stained wooden chests and camel saddles (*rahla*). But there's quite a desirable selection of jewellery in silver and ebony, tobacco pipes and pouches, sandals and good-value printed cotton cloth.

In the Adrar and Tagant, children and market-sellers hawk Neolithic **stone arrowheads and tools** that they find in the sand. It's never clear how old these are (certain tribes were hunting with stone tools until historical times), nor how rare or valuable, but judging by the large piles often offered, not very. You should nonetheless establish that exporting them will not upset officials, as it does in some countries. You may be offered medieval glass trading beads as well, though these are becoming internationally sought after and increasingly rare. Modern copies are available.

Crime and safety

As noted under "Visas and red tape", Mauritania is **report-to-the-police** territory. If you fail to do so, you could have an uncomfortable dressing-down when they apprehend you.

The country's general **safety record** is good, with little of the urban hassle that blights the city experience in some other countries. Out on the roads, banditry is very rare and few reports are received of travellers getting into trouble here (but see p.114). However, there is a problem with vehicle theft in Nouadhibou.

Emergencies

Police ☎17. There are no national numbers for fire or ambulance.

Gender issues and sexual attitudes

Women travellers can expect a combination of chivalry and pestering, though not too much of the latter. Covering your **hair** is an effective way of cooling ardour: Moorish women never let their scarves slip. Equally, it is advisable to dress conservatively: exposing your legs and arms will be seen as a provocation. It's natural that you'll spend a fair amount of time, like everyone else in Mauritania, **lying on mattresses** on the ground. It's useful to know, then, that lying either on your back or your stomach is considered highly suggestive; Moorish women invariably lie on their sides, supporting their head with a hand.

Surprisingly perhaps, while much of Moorish society still seems deeply traditional and conservative, and female circumcision is still practised, the subject of **sex** is openly discussed among women, especially in the cities (if, as a female visitor you find yourself with French-speaking young women – or even if you speak a little Hassaniya yourself – the conversation can take remarkable turns). Urban men, too, are beginning to accept a realignment of sexual attitudes, with the expectation that the ideal marriageable woman should be fat – in fact deliberately fattened by her female relatives – no longer seen as the norm. Affairs, "love-marriages" and divorces are increasingly common, and the bride price (paid to the woman or her family) is less often stipulated.

It's also useful to know that it's difficult to get **tampons** outside Nouakchott, though sanitary pads are widely available.

For **male visitors**, it's perhaps a relief to know that you're unlikely to be hustled much by **prostitutes**. **Gay men** will want to know that Mauritanian law stipulates the death penalty by stoning for homosexuality. An informal and low-key gay culture survives nonetheless – and there have never been any executions – although there is no public gay scene of any kind. And remember that although men can often be seen walking hand in hand, this has no sexual connotation.

Entertainment and sports

Independent **artistic expression** is rather rare in Mauritania, in part a reflection of the nomadic culture, where crafts were generally the preserve of specific castes, and in part the result of the Islamic disapproval of representational art. Poetry was the only widespread artistic activity, and even then rarely written down.

Theatre is all but nonexistent, but **cinema** has two leading lights, one being the exiled director **Med Hondo**. Hondo's 1969 film *Soleil Ô* was a bleak mix of *cinéma vérité* and weird set-pieces, dealing with African immigrants in France; more recently he made the impressive historical epic *Sarraounia*, about a queen who resisted both the colonialists and the Muslims. Mauritania's other top director, the Moscow-trained **Abderrahmane Sissako**, made his name with *Heremakono*, in 2003, and won the Lumière award with *Bamako* in 2006 (see p.353).

Music is an increasingly important aspect of Mauritania's national identity, with a number of singers and groups having achieved international success. There's a brief rundown on p.115.

Sport

Sport has never been an important part of Mauritanian culture. **Football** is popular, but there's not much fanaticism, few noteworthy overseas players and generally weak performances from the national squad, who occasionally make a good showing in West Africa's Amílcar Cabral Cup (as in 1995 when they hosted and were runners-up), but have never qualified for the African Nations Cup.

Wildlife and national parks

Mauritania's **wildlife** has been depleted by hunting and the spread of the desert. Formerly, the south had a good cross-section of West African savannah animal, including elephant, hippo, giraffe, cheetah, leopard, lion and several species of antelope. Now all that remain of these are a few leopards, though lions do still occasionally wander into southern Mauritania from Mali.

More common **desert species** include striped hyena, jackal, fennec fox, wild cat and wild sheep. Less common species found only in the south include gazelle, ostrich (near Néma), patas monkey and baboon. You'll see plenty of camels, but these, like all of Africa's dromedaries, are domesticated.

The uninhabited eastern desert is one of the last refuges of the endangered **addax antelope**. Another extraordinary survivor is the **crocodile**, found in a clutch of isolated pools hundreds of miles from the nearest permanent river (see p.141). The sea off the coast of Nouadhibou is home to the world's largest remaining colony of very rare **Mediterranean monk seals**.

For **bird-watchers**, the country's biggest potential attraction is the migratory birdlife of the isolated sandbanks and seashore in the **Parc National du Banc d'Arguin** (see p.126), south of Nouadhibou. The park is administered from Nouadhibou where there's a permit-issuing office for suitably-equipped birders. Another good place for seeing birds is the **Parc National Diawling** on the north bank of the Senegal River (see p.137).

A brief history of Mauritania

Contemporary **Mauritania** doesn't coincide with the ancient "Mauretania Tingitana", a region confined to present-day Morocco and western Algeria, and annexed to the Roman Empire by Claudius in 42 AD. The events and processes that led to the creation of the République Islamique de Mauritanie are taken up below with the arrival of the first Europeans. Accounts of some of the little-known early history of the region are scattered throughout the Guide.

European contact

Direct contact with Europeans began in 1445, when **Portuguese explorers** under Nuno Tristão sighted a habitation at the Arguin Islands and promptly took 29 captives back to Portugal as slaves. At about the same time, the **Hassane Arabs** from Yemen were moving into the northern parts of the territory, subjugating the largely Berber-speaking population, spreading the use of the Hassaniya language, and creating the cultural complex that became **Moorish society**.

Early Portuguese efforts to conduct a trade in slaves and gold were not hugely successful. Instead, acacia-tree gum used in the manufacture of food and drugs (called "gum arabic" because it was originally exported to Europe by Red Sea Arabs) soon became the main item of commerce, most of it coming from the southwest region, near the mouth of the Senegal River.

When Portuguese commercial influence waned in the seventeenth century, the **gum trade** fuelled intense rivalry between French, Dutch and English trading houses. The Dutch pulled out in 1727, but Anglo-French competition (and war) continued until 1857, when the British withdrew from the region in exchange for the French ceding them Albreda Island in the Gambia River. Even alone, the **French** had to use force to impress their control over the gum trade on the Moors, in order to hold a profit.

Throughout the seventeenth and eighteenth centuries, the French had also been more successful than the Portuguese in whipping up the **slave trade**. From their main base at **St-Louis** at the mouth of the Senegal River, they sent foreign goods upriver, ensuring a supply of slaves from the feuding and rigidly class-stratified societies of the interior. Mauritania's involvement in this trade was heavy, and the class structure of the southern agricultural districts was set in aspic by the capture of non-Arabic-speaking peoples, who were sold down the river by their captors in exchange for firearms, cloth and sugar.

But the slave trade didn't account for the slow **decline in trans-Saharan commerce**. This came about through the increasing imposition of Arab (later Arab-Berber) rule throughout the territory during the seventeenth century. By 1800, most of today's Mauritania was divided into competing **"emirates"** – Trarza, Brakna, Adrar and Tagant – which were highly organized internally but had little in the way of constructive foreign relations, and were inimical to commercial links between their domains. The French at St-Louis were able to take advantage of these divisions, and actively promoted **civil war** in order to divert ordinary trade, as well as the slave victims of battle, in their direction.

French expansion up the Senegal River and gathering French interest in Morocco and Algeria led, towards the end of the nineteenth century, to the strategic penetration of the Mauritanian interior, with "protection" and "pacification" offered to local people. The **assassination of Xavier Coppolani**, a French commander, at Tidjikja in 1905, ended a period of relatively peaceful expansion and brought down a five-year reign of terror in the territory. The Adrar was occupied in 1908, the Hodh (in the southeast) in 1911. The next year, France reached an agreement with Spain over respective spheres of influence in the Western Sahara region. In 1920 **la Mauritanie** became a colony of French West Africa. "Police actions" against nomadic guerilla resistance continued throughout the north till 1933, when complete "pacification" was finally achieved.

Western Sahara and the Polisario war

The colony of **Spanish Sahara** was acquired by Spain in a succession of Franco-Spanish conventions between 1886 and 1912. The motivation for coveting this wedge of gravel plains and low hills (about the size of Britain) sprang from a desire to join in the "scramble for Africa", a sense of wounded imperial pride at the loss of the South American colonies, and the proximity of the Spanish Canary Islands.

Villa Cisneros (Dakhla) and La Guera were the only Spanish bases until 1934, when the first foothold was established in the interior. However, **Africa Occidental Española** had no apparent economic potential and General Franco didn't waste money on it. By 1952 there were only 216 civilian employees, 24 telephones and 366 schoolchildren in the entire territory.

The Provincia de Sahara (as it became) with its capital El Ayoun (built in 1940), was ruled as a **military colony** where, as in Spain, political expression was ruthlessly crushed.

In 1966, the UN insisted on the right to **self-determination** for the colony. But a survey of Spanish Sahara's **phosphate reserves** in the early 1960s had indicated vast deposits of up to ten billion tonnes, and Spain was soon digging in. Although there had been armed resistance to Spanish occupation in the late 1950s in the wake of Morocco's independence, urban anti-colonial demonstrations began only in June 1970, when troops fired on marchers in El Ayoun and hundreds more were arrested – and subsequently disappeared.

Polisario

The **Polisario Front** was born in Zouérat in Mauritania on May 10, 1973, spurred into existence by Spain's continued occupation and the threats posed by competing claims from Mauritania and Morocco. Meanwhile, Spain was planning a process of decolonization and independence to thwart Polisario's growing influence, with blueprints for limited self-rule, a referendum, and a state-sponsored Sahrawi National Unity Party of Sahrawi moderates. King Hassan of Morocco put pressure on Spain to reconsider their plans and came to an agreement with Mauritania over partitioning Western Sahara. However, the International Court of Justice upheld the Sahrawis' right to self-determination. This was not enough to stop the **Green March** orchestrated by King Hassan of Morocco, involving 350,000 Moroccans marching, Korans in hand, into the Western Sahara to claim their country's so-called historical right to the territory.

After Franco's death in 1975, Spain agreed to pull out of Western Sahara, leaving the territory to Morocco, Mauritania and the Spanish-installed Djemaa council – a body of conservative, urban Sahrawis through whom they had ruled. Although the UN continued to uphold resolutions on Western Sahara, a UN delegation in 1976 decided that the turmoil in the territory was so great that there was no way the Sahrawis could be properly consulted. A guerilla war between Polisario and Morocco now began in earnest. More than half the population fled the country – old people, women and children to Algerian refugee camps around **Tindouf**, and men to join Polisario. The **Sahrawi Arab Democratic Republic** was proclaimed by Polisario – in exile in Tindouf, Algeria – on February 27, 1976.

The path to independence

The French invested almost nothing in Mauritania's future, administering it as a part of Senegal and counting on nomadic conservatism to look after the population in traditional ways. The country was used by the French as a **buffer zone** protecting their more valuable assets in Senegal and Soudan (Mali), and as a place of internal exile for political agitators from their other colonies.

Mauritania at war

From the beginning Polisario concentrated on knocking Mauritania out of the picture, thus breaking the Morocco–Mauritania alliance. There were repeated, humiliating losses for Mauritania; the iron-ore railway was under constant threat; foreigners working at the mines were kidnapped; and Polisario twice mounted daring raids on the outskirts of Nouakchott itself, shelling the presidential palace. Mauritania was crippled by debt, doubt and drought, and its war was an undignified fiasco. For President Ould Daddah, the situation had become untenable, and he was relieved of his post in July 1978. The new regime sued for peace with Polisario the following year.

Stalemate

In the 1980s, Morocco pulled back its front line to Dakhla and the northwest of Western Sahara (the so-called "useful triangle" containing the phosphate fields), while building an immensely long, defensive, earthworks wall known as the *berm*, that now encloses ninety percent of the territory.

In early 1991 a shaky **ceasefire** was agreed on the understanding that a referendum on the question of independence for the people of the territory would be held. But the UN-monitored process of identifying eligibility to vote has been lengthy and inconclusive. Moreover, Morocco has done a "West Bank", pumping resources – and 150,000 Moroccan **settlers** – into the region, in order to try to obviate a democratic solution for the indigenous people.

In 1997, Morocco was forced by a combination of US and UN pressure to accept face-to-face meetings with Polisario, brokered by the UN. As a result, an agreement was signed laying out the rules for registration to vote in the referendum. The process soon broke down, however, as tens of thousands made fraudulent claims of indigenous Sahrawi status, coached by Moroccan officials.

Between 1997 and 2003, UN Special Envoy, former US Secretary of State James Baker worked on a plan of staged autonomy and Moroccan withdrawal, but ultimately the **Baker plan** failed to break the deadlock, with Morocco and Polisario alternating in their rejection–acceptance of proposals.

The 9/11 attacks completely changed the landscape. Playing on Western – and Moroccan – fears of terrorist networks in the Sahara, **King Mohammed VI** of Morocco offered the Sahrawis autonomy under a Moroccan Royal Council – flatly ruled out by the Algiers-based Sahrawi government-in-exile.

Deadlock reigns. And the prospects for full **Sahrawi independence** are not good, especially since the modernizing Moroccan king is seen as a key war-on-terror ally by Britain and the US. Talks in the US in 2007 got nowhere.

Meanwhile, more than 100,000 Sahrawis languish – as they have for more than thirty years – in refugee camps in Algeria, where food is rationed and medical care limited.

There's a good website and two excellent blogs addressing Western Sahara, all in English:

ⓦ www.wsahara.net
ⓦ w-sahara.blogspot.com
ⓦ www.onehumportwo.blogspot.com.

In 1956, **Morocco** achieved independence, with King Hassan V's ruling group wanting to see the reconstruction of a "greater Morocco" that included much of Mauritania. The claims had repercussions in Mauritania, where an extreme Moorish nationalist movement took shape, fighting to hive off part, if not all, of Mauritania to Morocco, which it believed was the true homeland of all Moors.

In the 1957 Territorial Assembly elections (the first with universal suffrage), the unaffiliated Union Progressiste Mauritanienne – Mauritania's first indigenous political party – won 33 out of 34 seats. **Mokhtar Ould Daddah**, a young, white Moor lawyer with considerable French support (he was de Gaulle's son-in-law), was elected vice-president of Mauritania's first governing council (the French governor was president). Like the Moroccans, he was territorially ambitious, calling on the people of the **Spanish Sahara** to unite with his own in a "great economic and spiritual Mauritania".

On November 28, 1958, Mauritania became an autonomous republic within the French community and the **République Islamique de Mauritanie** was proclaimed. A national election held in 1959 gave Ould Daddah the post of prime minister, after his Parti du Regroupement Mauritanien won every seat in the new National Assembly, and on November 28, 1960, Mauritania became an independent nation-state, with Ould Daddah as president.

Ould Daddah's presidency

With the founding of the new capital of Nouakchott, the development of the Fdérik iron-ore mines and the completion of the railway to Nouadhibou in 1963, Mauritania's economic future looked fairly bright. But at the same time Ould Daddah set about eliminating **political opponents**, forming a one-party state run by his new Parti du Peuple Mauritanien (**PPM**).

In the south and among the non-Arabic-speaking population, expectations raised by independence from France gave way to resentment and indignation. In 1966, Arabic was made the compulsory teaching medium in schools. Ensuing **riots** in Nouakchott were summarily suppressed and laws swiftly enacted to ban all discussion of racial conflict. The country had come close to civil war, but Arabization continued, with a 1968 law putting **Hassaniya** on a co-footing with French as dual official languages.

The government was intent on integrating the trade-union movement into the PPM, a move which angered **teachers** and **miners** particularly, and led to strikes and demonstrations. For two months in 1971 there was a complete shut-down of iron-ore production. The force of government repression, and the determination of the ruling party to silence the opposition led to the creation of clandestine political movements and a simmering groundswell of anti-government feeling. Through much of this first decade of independence, however, foreign-affairs issues served to dampen the opposition.

During the 1960s, support from the other Arab states for Morocco's claim over Mauritania had resulted in very few of them recognizing Mauritania. But in 1969 came Morocco's formal recognition of Mauritania. Increasing Islamic radicalization and a slackening of ties with France, coupled with growing links with Algeria and a clear state socialist programme were the natural consequences. The huge iron-ore complex at Fdérik/Zouérat was nationalized and the country withdrew from the CFA-franc zone to bring in its own currency, the **ouguiya**.

Spain's decision to withdraw its garrisons from the Western Sahara plunged Mauritania into a **war with the Polisario** (see box, p.108), which proved the downfall of Ould Daddah.

The Lieutenant-Colonels

On the night of July 9, 1978, a quiet and bloodless **coup** ousted Mokhtar Ould

Daddah. The coup's leaders dissolved the PPM and announced the formation of a **Comité Militaire de Redressement National** (**CMRN**) – "to save the country from ruin and dismemberment" – under the chairmanship of Chief of Staff Lt-Col **Moustapha Ould Salek**.

Ould Salek tried to bring Polisario and Morocco together for a negotiated settlement, but the terms suited neither party. When Polisario's kidnapping of a Mauritanian prefect pushed Mauritania into a **peace treaty** with Polisario in August 1979, Morocco immediately moved into the territory vacated by Mauritanian troops. Meanwhile, at home, Ould Salek was confronted by outbreaks of racial conflict, student agitation, and factional strife in the CMRN. Ould Salek resigned and was replaced as president by Lt-Col **Mohamed Louly**, whose prime minister, Lt-Col **Mohamed Khouna Haidalla**, in turn staged another palace coup in January 1980, to take control of government.

Haidalla's five years as head of state saw an overall improvement in foreign relations, but a deterioration in the domestic situation. Internally, Mauritania's most dramatic event – as far as the rest of the world was concerned – was the formal **abolition of slavery** in 1980. This may have been intended to forestall links between the Dakar-based black opposition and supporters of exiled white-Moor groups in Paris, and also to divert attention away from the increasingly blatant racial discrimination against the Soudanien southerners, but the effect of the pronouncement was in fact to focus world attention on the brutal military dictatorship Mauritania had become.

For a short time in 1980–81, President Haidalla experimented with **political relaxation**. He formed a civilian government led by Prime Minister Ahmed Ould Bneijara, and drew up a draft constitution recommending a democratic multiparty system. But rumours of a **Libyan-backed plot**, and then a genuine **coup attempt** by the **Parti Islamique** of former

government ministers operating from Morocco, shook the democracy idea apart. Having executed the coup leaders, the CMSN appointed a new prime minister, Lt-Col **Maawiya Sid'Ahmed Ould Taya**, and remilitarized the government.

Meanwhile, a severe **drought** in 1983 brought tens of thousands of famine-stricken nomads virtually to the door of the Presidential Palace in Nouakchott; opposition groups continued to fight a war of words in France, Morocco and Senegal; and Mauritanian–Moroccan relations were further strained with Haidalla's recognition of the Sahrawi Arab Democratic Republic early in 1984. An attempted coup in February 1982 and a successful one in December 1984 succeeded in toppling Haidalla's government and resulted in the prime minister Ould Taya taking over as president.

Ould Taya: progress and reaction

With World Bank and IMF support, **President Ould Taya** adopted a programme of economic recovery with heavy emphasis on fishing and agriculture. Targets were set (and reached), and creditors were evidently impressed by Ould Taya's abandonment of some of the capital-intensive industrial schemes set up by Haidalla to the detriment of basic infrastructure and rural development. Iron ore remained a major source of foreign exchange, but in the late 1980s the **fisheries** came to be seen as a more flexible resource.

But the government's agenda was set by political rather than economic concerns. In 1986, a tract in French entitled *Manifesto of the Oppressed Black Mauritanian: From Civil War to National Liberation Struggle, 1966–86* made the rounds among students and staff at the National Language Institute. It was the work of the Dakar-based **African Liberation Forces of Mauritania** (**FLAM**). Twenty prominent southerners were arrested and jailed on charges of "undermining national unity". Widespread rioting and destruction subsequently took place in Nouakchott and Nouadhibou, and thirteen of those involved were also jailed. Strict **Islamic law** was subsequently introduced.

In 1987, dozens of Fula-speaking Tukulor officers were arrested on charges of insurrection. Three of them were executed and most of the rest were given long jail terms. This blow against the southerners was followed by a purge of Tukulor army officers, with more than five hundred dismissals.

The 1990 race riots

Events finally boiled over in April 1989, triggered by a minor incident on an island on the Senegal River, near Bakel, in which Mauritanian cows owned by Hal-Pulaars (Fula) were supposed to have ruined Senegalese vegetable gardens owned by Soninkés. The Senegalese Soninkés crossed over into Mauritania, and during the ensuing dispute a Mauritanian border guard killed a Senegalese. Thirteen Senegalese were arrested and taken to Sélibabi in Mauritania, which led to attacks on Mauritanian shops in Bakel on the Senegalese side.

Within days, violence had spread to other Senegalese towns, resulting in the deaths of dozens of Mauritanians, while thousands more were driven out as their shops and homes were ransacked. In Dakar, the entire Mauritanian community sheltered in the Grande Mosquée and the Mauritanian embassy. In Mauritania there were even more savage attacks on Senegalese and other black Africans as security forces and lynch mobs of Haratins hunted for southerners. Both governments were quick to condemn killings by the other side, but neither took decisive action to control the violence.

A massive dual **air evacuation**, with international assistance, began as it emerged that up to two hundred Senegalese had died in Nouakchott. As the exodus from Mauritania went on (in the event, there was only a limited flight of Mauritanians from Senegal), it became clear that among those leaving were large numbers of indigenous southern Mauritanians – whom the regime now routinely refers to as "Senegalese" but who are largely **Hal-Pulaar** (Fula-speakers) – many of whom were being forcibly expelled. The government was taking the opportunity to banish up to twenty thousand potential opponents and reduce the proportion of non-Moorish Mauritanians, who had been claiming for several years that they were in the majority.

In November 1990 the government announced there had been a coup attempt, fostered by Senegal. More than three hundred southerners were picked up by the authorities, and never seen again. Most southerners remaining in any positions of responsibility in the civil service were sacked over the next few months.

The 1990–91 **Gulf War** drew the world's attention away from the horrors of Mauritania's human rights record. But the country's military rulers had long been allies of Iraq (Iraqi military advisors are believed to have helped organize the pogroms against Fula villages in the south), and the government stood behind Saddam Hussein throughout the conflict. This alliance put severe strains on Mauritania's relations with Morocco and, of more immediate economic consequence, France. In this light, Ould Taya's pragmatic move to adopt a democratic constitution, when faced with the possibility of complete isolation, was hardly questioned: every other Francophone state in West Africa was undergoing the same process.

The multiparty era

Southerner political groups (and Muslim fundamentalists) boycotted the **referendum** on a multiparty constitution, arguing they hadn't been consulted in drawing up the document, which in practice banned political parties based on religion. Despite only a twenty percent turnout, the "yes" vote was carried into practice, Mauritania becoming a multiparty state on July 20, 1991, with a president as head of state and a prime minister running the country's affairs for him.

In 1992, the **presidential and legislative elections** were marred by fraud. The presidency was won by the former military leader, Ould Taya, despite the best efforts of his main rival, Ahmed Ould Daddah (half-brother of the country's first president) to have the results annulled by the supreme court.

In 1993, the government declared an amnesty for perpetrators of the 1989–90 racial violence. Officially, all seventy-thousand-odd **Mauritanian refugees** in Senegal were encouraged to return home, though in practice, few had any papers, job or land to return to.

Mauritania mended relations with **Senegal** and **Mali** and the three countries have tried to cooperate on cracking down on banditry and smuggling in the border areas. More than forty thousand Tuareg refugees who fled Mali during the Tuareg rebellion left their refugee camp in Mauritania to return home in 1997. Relations with France, however, where the press often spotlights Mauritania's poor human rights record, are not good.

Mauritania's relations with **the rest of the Muslim world**, meanwhile, went through convulsions. After the isolation the country experienced during the Gulf War, especially from Morocco, Mauritania began a process of distancing itself from **Baghdad**. Meanwhile, the decision to start diplomatic relations with **Israel** led to a break-up with **Libya**, formerly an important source of economic assistance, but always an uncomfortably overbearing ally. The establishment of an Israeli embassy in 2000, though widely unpopular with the Mauritanian people, is indicative of the government's pro-Western stance.

After **elections in October 1997**, the Parti Républicain Démocratique et Social (**PRDS**) had 71 of the 79 seats in the Assembly. There was a handful of independent (nonaligned) legislators but only one opposition member of the Assembly, from Action pour Change (**AC**), a party formed mainly to lobby for the rights of Haratin ex-slaves.

Slavery remains a sensitive issue, and brings international attention. In 1998, several human rights activists were arrested after their participation in a French TV documentary on the subject, and AC demonstrations to protest their treatment were met with police violence and more detentions. In 2003 and 2007, laws were passed making slave ownership punishable with a prison sentence of up to ten years – previous laws had abolished the practice but provided no punishment for it – but so far no one has actually been prosecuted. Meanwhile, Amnesty International continues to be banned from conducting slavery research in Mauritania.

The new millennium

Mauritania's economic woes seemed to be solved when **offshore oil reserves** of up to 120 million barrels were discovered near Nouakchott in 2001. An Australian drilling firm was granted a majority stake-holding in the project after committing to an investment of $600 million in drilling infrastructure.

On the political front, too, the new millennium heralded big changes. After an attempted coup by disgruntled troops nearly brought down President Ould Taya in 2003, he went on to be re-elected later that year in a disputed ballot. The plotting continued, and in August 2005 he was finally ousted.

The **Military Council for Justice and Democracy**, made up of various military officials, took power and immediately appointed an interim government to oversee the transition to genuine democracy, with **Colonel Ely Ould Mohamed Vall** at the helm. The coup and regime change were applauded in most quarters locally, but there was international scepticism and censure, culminating in the suspension of Mauritania from the African Union.

For his part, Vall had big plans. He promised to free the press, restore **basic rights** to all Mauritanians and hold **elections** within two years – elections which he promised neither he nor any of his junta would be allowed to contest. By the time the two years were up, the press and judiciary were largely independent and a new constitution granted basic liberties to all citizens, along with term-limits intended to prevent the rise of future dictatorships. Indeed, such significant changes had taken place in the country's public institutions that few Mauritanians wanted Vall to leave office.

Legislative elections in late 2006 paved the way for a more or less peaceful presidential election which was judged essentially free and fair by EU and other independent electoral observers – though not without instances of vote-buying and corruption. An economist, **Sidi Ould Cheikh Abdallahi** – virtually unknown before he announced his candidacy the year before – beat 18 other candidates to win with 53 percent of the votes and become Mauritania's first genuinely democratically elected president. President Abdallahi has a majority in both houses of parliament and, very importantly, the tacit **support of the military**.

Upon taking office, Abdallahi emphasized the virtues of tolerance and reconciliation, condemned the violence of the dark years of 1989–91 and promised to permanently eradicate slavery. In June 2007, he and his cabinet even voted to take a 25 percent pay cut.

But one issue that still faces the country is **Islamic fundamentalism**.

Despite the country's Islamic Republic label, with a legal system strongly influenced by the *sharia* (Islamic law), the government has been making strong efforts to distance itself from fundamentalism. The activities of a number of Islamic groups in the country have been curtailed and Islamic leaders arrested. The army receives financial assistance from the United States as part of its Pan-Sahel Initiative to combat Islamic cells presumed to be operating in the Sahara.

Yet unlike other countries' treatment of suspected radicals, Mauritania has not abandoned its democratic values and the new government seems determined to learn from the mistakes of Taya's regime, and to prove their new democratic credentials. In June 2007, twenty suspected Islamic radicals who had been arrested on suspicion of terrorist activities were released for lack of evidence. But the pressure to clamp down remains: the murder of four French tourists by extremist Islamic gunmen near Aleg in December 2007 led to the cancellation of the 2008 Dakar Rally.

On the surface a certain stability is apparent, but the future for Mauritania is uncertain. Income from fishing has declined markedly and iron-ore output has dropped as demand shrinks. And even **oil revenues** have proved uncertain. Yet despite slow progress, Mauritanians seem prepared to give President Abdallahi and his government a generous honeymoon period: they have waited a long time for some measure of freedom and justice in this factionalised country. If the army can just stick to its job, Mauritania may yet succeed.

Music

The professional musical caste in Mauritania are called **igaouen** or **iggiw**. In the past they depended, like the *jeli* in Mali, on the patronage of big men and nobles. The more flexible, modern *igaouen* repertoire includes complex songs of Middle Eastern character and others simple enough to be taken up in chorus by the audience. The music is based on a sophisticated modal system derived from Arab musical theory, known as the "white and black ways", associated with white and black Moorish culture.

Khalifa Ould Eide and Dimi Mint Abba

Khalifa and Dimi, together with Dimi's two daughters, were the first Mauritanian group to tour in the English-speaking world, in the mid-1980s.

Moorish Music from Mauritania (World Circuit). A beautiful and evocative CD – note the flamenco-style hand-clapping.

Malouma

Malouma is in a league of her own, a hereditary *ardin*-playing griot and modern singer at the same time, who, while singing exclusively in the Hassaniya dialect of Arabic, shows no obedience to Moorish musical strictures or social norms: she also sits in the Mauritanian senate.

Desert of Eden (Shanachie). Highly accessible, jazz-inflected debut CD. The *ardin* shines through to distinctive effect.

Dunya (Marabi). Locally recorded, and it shows, with most of the focus on Malouma's intense voice.

Nour (Marabi). Most recent outing, from 2007, showcasing her Mauritanian singer-songwriter credentials in a bluesy context.

Tahra

Born in Néma in southeastern Mauritania in 1959, Tahra Mint Hembara is a hereditary griot (her aunt was the famous Lekhdera Mint Ahmed Zeidane), who has been steeped in Moorish musical tradition since the age of 10.

Yamen Yamen (EMI). This 1989 album, with Jean-Philippe Rykiel on synth, tested the stretchability of classic musical traditions on the world stage. An intriguing album of Mooro-tech.

Traditional Moorish instruments

Examples of some of these instruments can be seen in Nouakchott's museum.

Ardin Ten- to fourteen-stringed women's harp, played with a calabash acting as a drum.

Daghumma Slender, hollowed-out gourd with a necklace, which acts as a rattle.

Tidinit Lute with two long strings on which the melody is played, and two short ones which give a fixed drone-like rhythm; played by men.

Tobol Large kettle drum, used by women in times of danger to warn men out in the fields or in the *palmeraies*.

Books

Literature in English on Mauritania is minimal, particularly as regards books focusing exclusively on the country, and there's next to nothing in translation from French or Arabic. For good general titles, including some with a strong Mauritanian connection, see p.35.

Samuel Cotton *Silent Terror*. An all-too-rare investigation of the complex issue of slavery in contemporary Mauritania and Senegal.

Lauren Goodsmith *The Children of Mauritania*. Ex–Peace Corps volunteer writes a charming story about a Pulaar boy from the Senegal river valley, and a Moor girl from the Atar region, with excellent pictures.

Peter Hudson *Travels in Mauritania*. Absorbing travelogue detailing a two-month trek across the country in 1988.

Odette du Puigaudeau *Barefoot in Mauritania* (1937). The author

(1894–1991) and her female companion took camels across "the land of death" – a ramble through a Mauritania that hardly knew it existed.

Antoine de Saint-Exupéry *Wind, Sand and Stars*. Not well-known in the Anglophone world, but a cult hero in France, Saint-Exupéry was a pioneering pilot on the Casablanca–Dakar postal run – and also wrote beautifully.

Ronald Segal *Islam's Black Slaves: The Other Black Diaspora*. Though sometimes dry, this is a powerful overview of modern African slavery, with an emphasis on Mauritania and Sudan.

Language

Mauritania's most widespread language is **Hassaniya Arabic**, and although many people speak **French**, it is less popular – and slightly less widely acceptable – than it once was. However, both are widely used in media, administration and education. Other languages are mostly concentrated in the non-Moorish regions of the far south and include **Fula** or Fulfulde, **Wolof** and **Soninké** or Sarakolé. Few people speak English, though this is slowly changing in Nouakchott and Nouadhibou.

Hassaniya

Hassaniya, the sole language of the Moors, is a language that differs considerably from other North African Arabic dialects and retains a large Berber vocabulary. In 1991 it became, controversially, the official language of the country, usurping the less divisive French for many purposes.

Greetings and civilities

Moorish Mauritanians have an elaborate greeting ritual which they go through with resignation or enthusiasm depending on their mood. Farewells, on the other hand, are brief and free of sentiment. A phrase for "Please" is never used. "Ski" (with a short "i") is an expression of satisfaction, usually followed by a hand slap.

Iyak la bas	Greetings (hope nothing's wrong with you)
La bas	Nothing's wrong

The above is usually followed by numerous utterances of iyak, eg:

Iyak mo a ve	Hope you have no sickness

If you want to end the iyak sequence try:

Ma rahbeh	So be it
Mah salaam	Goodbye
Sh'halak	How are you? (informal)
Ilhamdillah	Praise be to God (often added to the end of sentences)
Salaam alaikum	Peace be with you
Alaikum salaam	And peace also with you

Other phrases

Minayn…?	Where is…?
Anta min minayn?	Where are you from?
Waqt shin hoo?	What time is it?
Kaavi	That's okay/enough (eg on being served food)
Bismilah	In the name of God (said before eating or starting an activity)
ahey	yes
abdei	no
walahi	yes/by God
wahai	come here
subh	tomorrow
yaames	yesterday

ilyom	today
Ana nymshee shawr	I am going to
Ana min	I'm from
Oostralia	Australia
Bretanya	Britain
Kanada	Canada
Irelanda	Ireland
New Zeeland	New Zealand
Amreeka	USA
vondeg	hotel
an dak?	do you have?
khalig?	is there?
ilma'	water
lukeel	food
nsara (pl. nasrani)	white person
zaiyn	good
zaiyn hatta	very good
maw zaiyn	not good
baash?	how much is?
ingus shwei?	a little less? (requesting to lower the price)
shwei shwei	a little (or slowly)
Ana stuk fait	I am full
Ana v'tran	I am tired (male)
Ana v'trana	I am tired (female)
Beshawr	Take it easy

Numbers

1	wahid
2	ethnayn
3	athlath
4	arba'a
5	hamsa
6	setta
7	seb'a
8	thimayna
9	tesa'a
10	ashara

Glossary

Adrar Mountain

Aftout Seasonal water course or flood zone; depression between sand dunes

Ain Spring

Aklé Zone of jumbled, live dunes

Al ma' Water

Attay Mauritanian tea

Barkane Mobile, crescent-shaped dune with characteristic crest

Barrad Teapot

Batha/Baten Sandy oued or valley

Birr Well

Boubou Loose cotton shirt or cloak

Cheikh Elder respected for his knowledge

Chemama Flood plain of the Senegal River

Cherif Person who claims descent from the Prophet Muhammad

Dahr/dhar Fault line (cliffs or escarpment)

Dar House or dwelling

Erg District of shifting ("live") sand dunes.

Fesh Sand dune

Girba Goatskin water bag

Guelb Isolated mountain or peak; crater

Guelta Pond or small lake, sometimes augmented by a spring

Guetna Date harvest (July & Aug)

Hal-Pulaar Fula-speaking people, including Fula and Tukulor

Hammada Stony plateau

Houli Man's headscarf, turban

Kas Drinking glass

Kedia Long tableland, mesa

Khaima Tent

Ksar Fort

L'msal Prayer ground

Marabout Holy man from a marabout tribe

M'borou Bread

Mechoui Grilled lamb prepared on feast days

Méharée Camel safari

Nsara Nazarene/Christian; white person (pl. *nasrani*)

Oued River bed

Reg Flat gravel, windblown stony plain

Rifi Hot wind from the north

Sebkha Dry, salt plain

Sirwal Loose, cotton pantaloons

Tabel Tea tray

Tamourt Long, wooded depression, flooded during the rainy season

Tell Hill covering the ruins of a former settlement

Tifinagh Ancient Libyan/Berber writing

Tikit Temporary round hut constructed during the *guetna* (also used in some *auberges*)

Tishtar Dried meat

Toubab Foreigner, European, white person (non-Moorish areas)

Wilaya Administrative region

Zrig Sweet, diluted milk given in welcome and supposed to cure many aches and pains

1.1
Nouadhibou and the north

For travellers arriving by road from Morocco, **Nouadhibou**, Mauritania's second city, comes as an unlikely first taste of West Africa. Isolated north and south by desert, and only recently connected by road with the rest of the country, it is far removed not just from Africa, but from the rest of Mauritania too. The main draws of this region for travellers are the immensely long **iron–ore railway** from Nouadhibou to **Zouérat** via **Choum**, and the immense **Banc d'Arguin National Park**, on the coast between Nouadhibou and Nouakchott, which is one of the best-birdwatching sites in Africa.

Moving on from Nouadhibou

The **iron-ore train** for **Choum** (for taxis on to Atar) and **Zouérat** is described on p.125. You can **fly** to Nouakchott with Air Mauritanie (3 weekly), or to Las Palmas (3 weekly; UM92,000 return).

By road

The Mauritanian road network was notably improved in 2005 when the 470km **tarmac road** between Nouadhibou and Nouakchott was completed, replacing what used to be a desert-only route. The downside for the Mauritanian tourist industry is that overlanders can now leave Morocco in the morning, drive straight through Mauritania, and arrive in Senegal the same night, thus eliminating the need for any stopover. If you take the new road, fill your tank and jerry cans as there are no petrol stations en route, and do not drive it at night. There's a comfortable daily bus operated by El Bouragh Transport (☏574 89 64 or 623 17 19; UM4500), which departs at 3pm from a lot just beyond the airport and arrives in Nouakchott 5½hr later. Otherwise, Nouakchott-bound shared taxis leave from Garage Nouakchott Numerowat (UM100 by taxi from the city centre); passengers pay UM5000 for the six-hour journey. Another, more adventurous alternative is making a **desert drive by convoy**, for which you'll need to club together with a group of other overlanders (try hanging around *Chez Abba*) and hire a guide, preferably one who has been vouched for: expect to pay him about UM90,000 for the two-to-three-day trip for up to five vehicles. The last third of the journey runs along the shoreline and cannot be done at high tide, so you'll need to talk to local fishermen about tide times, and plan your route accordingly. Be aware that you should seek permission at the gendarmerie to do this journey in your own car, and you'll have to pay entrance fees for the Banc d'Arguin National Park (see p.126).

Fewer vehicles drive north between Nouadhibou and Moroccan-occupied Western Sahara than in the opposite direction. UK, US and most European citizens don't need a visa for Morocco. Other nationalities can obtain one at the consulate in Nouadhibou (see p.124) or at the embassy in Nouakchott (see p.135). Be aware of the dangers of **mines** from south of the border as far as just beyond Fort Guerguarat in Western Sahara: stick to used tracks or hire a local guide.

Nouadhibou

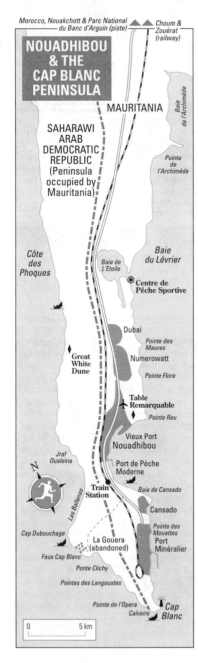

Morocco, Nouakchott & Parc National du Banc d'Arguin (piste)

Choum & Zouérat (railway)

NOUADHIBOU & THE CAP BLANC PENINSULA

MAURITANIA

SAHARAWI ARAB DEMOCRATIC REPUBLIC (Peninsula occupied by Mauritania)

Baie de l'Archiméde

Pointe de l'Archiméde

Côte des Phoques

Baie de L'Etoile

Baie du Lévrier

⊚ Centre de Pêche Sportive

Dubai

Pointe des Maures

Great White Dune

Numerowatt

Pointe Flore

Table Remarquable

Pointe Reu

Vieux Port Nouadhibou

Jraf Oualeina

Port de Pêche Moderne

Train Station

Baie de Cansado

Cansado

Cap Dubouchage

La Gouera (abandoned)

Pointe des Mouettes

Port Minéralier

Faux Cap Blanc

Ponte Clichy

Pointes des Langoustes

Pointe de l'Opera

Calveire

Cap Blanc

0   5 km

Set on the eastern side of the Cap Blanc peninsula, a finger of desert pointing into the sea towards the south, **NOUADHIBOU** ("Jackal's Well") is the first point of entry for overlanding travellers from Europe. It is a pale, flat, industrial city-satellite of Mauritania, where bars are permitted (or rather, the authorities usually turn a blind eye to alcohol), and the mix on the streets adds African, Mediterranean and Oriental traces to the predominant billowing azure robes of locals and rural immigrants. Besides the busy **central market**, the area's wonderful **beaches**, century-old shipwrecks and extraordinary wave- and wind-formed **scenery**, on both sides of the peninsula, are the most obvious attractions. Moreover, Nouadhibou's proximity to the ocean makes the city one of the most comfortable places in the country – indeed, it can be chilly here in January at night and first thing in the morning.

Arrivals, orientation and city transport

Nouadhibou is widely spread out and has four distinct districts. The first as you enter the city is **Dubai**, a recent residential suburb financed with Gulf money and buzzing with ambitious construction projects and upscale housing enclaves. Next comes the older, and messier quarter of **Numerowat**, home to the majority of Nouadhibou's inhabitants. The various quarters of Numerowat are identified by *robinets* ("Premier Robinet", "Deuxième Robinet" and so on) according to the nearest public water standpipe, which come at 500-metre intervals along the surfaced road to downtown Nouadhibou. Downtown itself is known as **Ville**, with all the usual services and shops and the city's main market. To the south of the city centre, a full 10km further on, is the iron-ore company's dormitory town of **Cansado** ("Sleepy" in Spanish).

Formalities for **overlanders in their own vehicles** arriving from Morocco all take place at the border itself (see p.98) and the laborious process of having your passport stamped by the police in town has all been done away with. Having arrived, the priority is to find a safe place to park for the night (see "Accommodation", below).

The **airport** is northeast of the centre (flight information on ☏574 59 02), from where it's a twenty-minute walk or a UM300 taxi ride to the centre – no shared taxis ply this route.

Lastly, should you happen to arrive on the iron-ore **train**, the passenger wagon stops at the derelict rubbish-filled **station** on the way south out of downtown Nouadhibou. Wait by the road on the other side of the station to get a shared taxi to the town centre (UM100).

Standard fares apply for **shared taxis** around town – UM50 for any journey in the downtown area or up the tarmac to Numerowat; UM50 in the same areas, but going off-road; UM100 from town to the port or vice versa; and UM60 to anywhere in Cansado.

Accommodation

There's a decent range of accommodation in Nouadhibou, though only one place, the *Mauritalia*, that stands out. In view of the town's reputation for vehicle theft, overlanders should place a priority on secure parking.

Auberge du Sahara west of bd Médian, downtown (turn off bd Médian by the *Merou* restaurant and take the second right to find it: it isn't well signposted). ☏623 01 77 ℮aubergechezmomo @yahoo.fr. This intimate place feels like a mini-youth hostel and offers clean, quiet rooms, plenty of hot water, and access to a kitchen. There's also a roof-terrace barbecue where Berber soirées are occasionally arranged, a useful notice board giving information and advice on onward travel, and large garages and secure parking, which make it popular with overlanders. The owner is helpful and well informed. ❷

Camping Baie du Levrier bd Médian, downtown ☏574 65 36 ℮alilevrier2003@yahoo.fr. This sandy spot is small but clean and good for overlanders, offering free, secure parking, a pleasant communal area, warm water and helpful staff. There's no charge to park your vehicle. UM1000 per person to sleep under their tent, otherwise ❸.

Centre de Pêche Sportive 14km north of Nouadhibou at Baie de l'Etoile ☏644 73 75 or 574 61 67. Surf-casting is the big affair at this rustic fishing lodge. Rooms have verandahs onto the sea, there's a pleasant boardwalk right out to the water and they grill up catches of the day (from UM2000). It's good value, but you're really cut off without your own vehicle. Call or fax ahead to get picked up from the airport on arrival, or take a taxi (UM1000). ❺

Chez Abba bd Médian, downtown, behind the colourful mural ☏574 98 96 ℮auberge.abba @caramail.com. Hostel offering double and triple rooms around a comfortable, airy lounge area. Secure parking and friendly atmosphere help compensate for the often overstretched facilities and sporadic hot water. Camping is possible in the guarded compound at the rear. Tent or car camping UM1500 per person, *khaimas* UM2000, rooms ❸.

Maghreb between bds Maritime and Médian, downtown ☎574 55 24. Quiet hotel with rooms arranged cloister-like around a garden. Parking available. ❸

Mauritalia bd Maritime, north of the centre in Quartier Dubai ☎574 32 18 or 644 35 23 ⓔmaur.italia@caramail.com. Spic-and-span new place with large, clean, comfortable, a/c rooms all presided over by a friendly and helpful Mauritanian–Italian couple who also run a great

Italian restaurant next door that serves Carlsberg beer. ❽

Oasian 10km south of town at Cansado, overlooking the bay ☎574 27 00 ⓕ574 09 53. Once the best hotel in Nouadhibou, it now feels terribly dated and is primarily patronized by foreign oil workers and diplomatic personnel. It's far from the action, but if you reserve ahead, a courtesy bus will meet you at the airport. Rooms are en suite and have satellite TV, a/c and minibar, plus there's a bar and restaurant. ❻

Résidence Didi bd Maritime, Quartier Dubai ☎574 74 72. A new addition to Nouadhibou's more upscale offerings, with fully-furnished, very clean, apartment-style accommodation featuring large and luxurious beds. ❼

The city and around

Nouadhibou's **Grand Marché** (daily 8am–7pm) teems with cloth-sellers, tailors and silversmiths. Also worthy of exploration nearby is the wind-sculpted **table remarquable**, just east of the main airport runway, while down towards the sea from the fresh fish market, you can wander through what's left of the *village canarien*, once the Canary Islanders' settlement of **Tcherka** or Thiarka. To the south of the town, on the way to Cansado, is an atmospheric **ship's graveyard** of abandoned fishing hulks, scuppered for sometimes fraudulent insurance claims, though a €26-million EU-sponsored initiative is intended to rid the coast of these rusting carcasses over the next several years.

Further afield, 13km north of town, on the east side of the peninsula, there's delightful, sheltered swimming in the almost enclosed **Baie de l'Étoile**, whose lagoon gets packed with locals on weekend afternoons and evenings. With your own transport (you could get a taxi from town for UM1000, in which case you'll probably want to arrange for it to come back for you later in the day), head east from Numerowat to the edge of the lagoon, then follow the track north past the place where camels are butchered, and continue, keeping to the left of the creek (a good place for bird-watching). The track leads you to the *Centre de Pêche Sportive*, the place to try your hand at surf-casting or night fishing, with boat excursions (UM9000) and rod and bait rental (UM4500) available; their visitors' book and cabinet of fishing trophies testify to the richness of the waters here. They have a 100-metre pontoon from which boats transport you across the lagoon (UM1500) to a secluded beach with dunes. Don't cross the railway line to go exploring the beaches on the western side of the peninsula – there are still mines hidden in the sand over there.

The Nouadhibou area is home to the world's largest colony of very **rare Mediterranean monk seals** (*phoques moines*), which you may see if you go down to the lighthouse at **Cap Blanc**. In appearance they resemble young elephant seals, growing to more than 2.5m in length. Their valuable oil and skin has led to widespread extermination, but hunting them is now forbidden. To visit Cap Blanc, you'll need to get a permit from the Banc d'Arguin Park office (UM1200; see p.126). Park guides are available for UM3000 a day and taxis will take you there for UM2000. At Cap Blanc itself, you can ease yourself down the cliffs by using the fixed ropes provided, giving access to some fine beaches and the possibility of seal-spotting.

Eating and nightlife

There's a fair number of cheap **restaurants** near the central market; standard lunchtime fare is rice and fish, with perhaps couscous and camel meat in the evening, and you can eat well for less than UM300. In addition, a handful of pricier

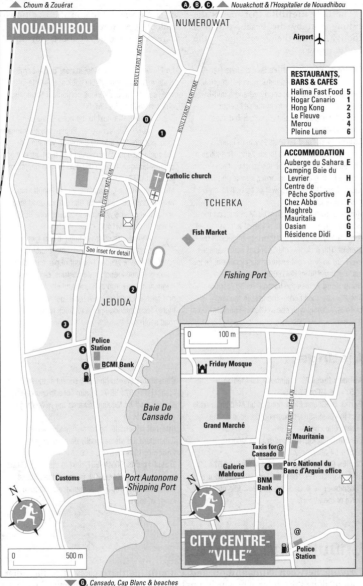

NOUADHIBOU

NUMEROWAT

Airport ✈

BOULEVARD MÉDIAN

BOULEVARD MARITIME

Ⓓ

Ⓞ❶

✝ Catholic church

TCHERKA

✉

See inset for detail

Fish Market ■

Ⓞ

Fishing Port

❷

JEDIDA

❸

Ⓔ

Police
Station

Ⓕ   ⛽ BCMI Bank

*Baie De
Cansado*

Customs

*Port Autonome
-Shipping Port*

N

**RESTAURANTS,
BARS & CAFÉS**
Halima Fast Food **5**
Hogar Canario **1**
Hong Kong **2**
Le Fleuve **3**
Merou **4**
Pleine Lune **6**

ACCOMMODATION
Auberge du Sahara **E**
Camping Baie du
  Levrier **H**
Centre de
  Pêche Sportive **A**
Chez Abba **F**
Maghreb **D**
Mauritalia **C**
Oasian **G**
Résidence Didi **B**

0 ———— 100 m

❺

🕌 Friday Mosque

BOULEVARD MÉDIAN

Grand Marché

Air
Mauritania

Taxis for @
Cansado

Galerie
Mahfoud   ❻   Parc National du
Banc d'Arguin office

BNM
Bank   Ⓗ   ✉

@

⛽   Police
Station

N

**CITY CENTRE-
"VILLE"**

0 ———— 500 m

▼ Ⓖ, Cansado, Cap Blanc & beaches

international restaurants and cafés, including a half-dozen or so Chinese joints and even a burger bar, are available if you want a taste of home. Though officially non-alcoholic, a few of these places offer the chance to liven up an otherwise dull evening with expensive beer and, if you're lucky, wine. If you're self-catering, several quite good **supermarkets** can be found along the main tarmac road, Boulevard Médian, and you can buy fish in the old fishing-port area behind the stadium.

The only **nightlife** that merits the term is *La Sirène* disco, in the traditional fishing port by the beach, which serves alcohol to foreigners. Most visitors, though, spend their evenings at the few restaurants that sell beer, nursing a bottle or two.

Centre de Pêche Sportive Baie d'Étoile (see p.122 for directions). Peaceful, remote fisherman's retreat with a charming courtyard and a laid-back feel that's worlds away from the city centre. UM1000 for a burger and a drink, fish dishes UM1000–2500.

Halima Fast Food bd Médian where Premièr Robinet meets Deuxième (open 24hr). The kitchen shares the same space as the spartan dining room, but they serve good *chawarma*, steaks and fish meals from UM1000, as well as tasty, thin-style pizzas (UM3000).

Hogar Canario just west of bd Maritime, on the northern side of town. The classiest address in town and Nouadhibou's only white-tablecloth restaurant. The reclusive old Spaniard who manages this hard-to-find spot ensures tasty chicken, chops and *calamari* (from UM1800).

Hong Kong Across the harbour on bd Maritime. The Chinese food here – the best in the city – is quite appetizing, with cheap Chinese beers to wash it down.

Le Fleuve west of bd Médian near the *Auberge du Sahara*. Cheikh, the affable cook at this hole in the wall, serves large, delicious portions of Senegalese chicken and fish for UM700.

Mauritalia next to the hotel of the same name, Quartier Dubai. Superb Mediterranean food, prepared by a jovial Sardinian woman. The spaghetti Bolognese is cooked just right, as is the creamy lasagne, though the cold Danish beers are pricey at UM2500.

Merou bd Médian, near *Chez Abba*. Popular place with an uninspiring interior that serves good Asian and global cuisine with a half-decent wine list. Mains start at UM1400.

Plein Lune off bd Médian. If you ignore the flies and the sporadic electricity, this great *pâtisserie* wouldn't be out of place in Paris, with very good French-style pastries, cakes and baguettes. They also do steak and chicken mains and sausage rolls which you can get to go – a highly recommended place to stock up for the road south.

Listings

Airline offices Air Mauritanie, bd Médian ℡ 574 54 49 or 574 45 51.
Banks BMCI and BNM, both on bd Médian, usually give the best rates, though not as good as the bureaux de change.
Car rental SOGETRA Voyages, bd Médian ℡ 574 54 58.
Clinics Clinique Er Raja on bd Médian (℡ 574 90 95 or 636 25 12). The new, Spanish-built Centre l'Hospitalier de Nouadhibou is a few kilometres north of the airport.

Consulates French honorary consul at the Alliance Française ℡ 574 58 71 ⓦ afm.nouadhibou.free.fr; Morocco, off bd Médian, towards the *Hôtel Maghreb* ℡ 574 50 84.
Internet Cybercafé, bd Médian (daily 8am–1pm), Cybertbera, bd Médian (daily 9am–midnight).
Police ℡ 18 or ℡ 574 54 00.
Travel agents SOMASERT, next to the *Hôtel Oasian* in Cansado (℡ 574 90 42), is one of the biggest tourism enterprises in Mauritania, and offers a range of tours.

Choum and Zouérat

Driving between Nouadhibou and Choum (northern gateway to the Adrar region) along the sandy route which runs by the tracks is not recommended without a guide (UM30,000), as half-buried cast-off lengths of track can cause terminal damage to your vehicle. The route crosses areas of sandy dunes, which a 4x4 should be able to cover in two days. Avoid areas north of the railway line due to the mines along the border with Western Sahara. In the past, some drivers chose to put their vehicles on the train, which is still possible, but really not worth considering now that Nouadhibou is not much more than a long day's drive from the Adrar region via the new paved road to Nouakchott.

The iron-ore trains

The **iron-ore trains**, the heaviest in the world, carry on average 22,000 tonnes of crushed rock in a chain of more than 250 wagons that can extend up to 3km long (and travels at a painfully slow 30kph for much of the route). **Schedules** depend partly on the speed of extraction at the mines, and on unpredictable hold-ups – damaged rails, engine failure and even, in the past, attacks by Polisario guerillas from Western Sahara – and travellers need to recognise that ore is the priority, not passengers.

In principle, three trains a day go from Nouadhibou to Zouérat (and vice versa), but the only one with a **passenger carriage** leaves Nouadhibou at 2.30pm, passing through Choum at 2am and arriving in Zouérat at 7am. The return journey departs Zouérat at noon, calling at Choum at 5pm and arriving in Nouadhibou at 6am the next morning. In the passenger carriage, you could go for a **seat** or a **couchette** – given the length of the journey, taking the latter would be advisable, though don't expect anything too clean. **Fares** (for seat/couchette) are: Nouadhibou–Zouérat UM1000/2200; Nouadhibou–Choum UM800/2000; Choum–Zouérat UM400/1000. Riding on top of the ore wagons is free – and you'll discover why, as the dust works its way into your soul. If you choose this option, buy flour sacks from a local patisserie to protect your baggage, take a *houli* to wrap round your head, and have something warm for later in the night, when it can get remarkably cold.

If, for whatever reason, you want to put your vehicle on the train, you'll need to contact the Société Nationale Industrielle et Minière in Nouadhibou (☎574 10 15 or 574 17 54 ⓦwww.snim.com) several days in advance. Nouadhibou–Zouérat prices start at UM22,000 for a car, and you can stay in your vehicle, strapped to the wagon.

The 700km journey generally passes without incident, with several stops to allow trains going the other way to pass. If you pick the right compartment you could find yourself sharing endless cups of tea and learning Hassaniya. The interest outside the carriage, however, even on a clear moonlit night, is minimal.

A **luxury train**, sans iron-ore wagons, and with an observation carriage and cabins, also runs periodically between Choum and Zouérat. For more details, visit the Mauritania section of ⓦwww.cheminsdesable.com.

On the border with Western Sahara, **CHOUM** consists of a string of restaurants and crash-out houses where Nouadhibou-bound passengers snooze through the afternoon, waiting for the train. Arriving in Choum by taxi from Atar, leave your bags in the taxi; when the train arrives, you'll be driven alongside to meet the passenger wagon. As the train may be more than 2km long and often sets off within minutes, this is a taxi fare worth paying.

Zouérat

The **route impériale**, the old military road, continues north from Choum to what is now the garrison town of Fdérik. East of Fdérik it's tarmac to **ZOUÉRAT**, the economic and political heart of the far north. If you're driving, you'll need to drive on the left on this section of road until the town boundary, then change to the right. The iron-ore train from Nouadhibou and Choum gets in at around 7am and departs at noon, arriving at Choum around 5pm and back to Nouadhibou around 6am. Tours of the spectacular mining operations can be arranged relatively easily – and cheaply – from the *Hôtel Oasian* (☎544 06 05 ⓕ544 03 15 ⑤), essentially a company resthouse – rooms have private bathroom and kitchenette – with a restaurant serving tasty local and Spanish food. A cheaper option is to stay in the clean *Hôtel Tiris*, in front of the BMC bank (☎544 06 68 ⓕ544 01 57 ⑤). Nearby, *Le Palmier* is a good central restaurant serving a few inexpensive mains and some cakes; camel steak with fries costs UM1000.

The Imragen – fishing in the desert with dolphins

The Banc d'Arguin National Park contains the seven villages of the 1000-strong **Imragen** (literally, "those who gather life"), whose survival on these shores is entirely dependent on an extractive economy; even most water has to be trucked into the villages from Nouakchott or Nouadhibou. The traditional harvest of **yellow mullet** is caught in November, when huge shoals of fish spawn amid the sea grass in the shallows. By what appears to be a remarkable feat of cooperation between humans and animals, the catch is brought to shore with the assistance of dolphins. Summoned by the Imragen beating the water surface from the shore, the dolphins drive the fish to the beach, where the mullet provide a feast for them and a tremendous haul for the villagers – Jacques Cousteau once came here to study their unique techniques. Recent research suggests that yellow mullet may actually like swimming underneath pods of dolphins, so that the only human intervention is to signal to the dolphins the fish trap that is at their disposal. In any event, it's an extraordinary occasion, a spectacular chaos of leaping fish, thrashing cetaceans and ducking fishermen. Other Imragen fishing methods are less successful: the Imragen aren't skilled boat-builders and they have nothing much to build with; they only have a few small vessels. Another windfall is provided by the literally hundreds of ships scuppered offshore for insurance purposes, the vessels supplying fuel, building materials and occasionally more interesting bounty for the Imragen.

Banc d'Arguin National Park

Between Nouadhibou and the capital, the UNESCO World Heritage Site of **Parc National du Banc d'Arguin** (ⓦ www.mauritania.mr/pnba) is one of Africa's richest marine and littoral ecosystems. Seals and jackals, breeding turtles and rare gazelles, striped hyenas, fennec foxes, several species of dolphins and huge shoals of spawning fish all thrive here. It is the only home of the **Imragen**, an isolated group of Berber-speaking fishing people (see box). The 12,000-square-kilometre park also constitutes one of the world's great **Palearctic wintering sites**, with estimates of many millions of shorebirds and other varieties, totalling more than 200 species, present on the spits and sandbanks at any one time (more than two million broadbilled sandpipers have been recorded here alone). **Breeding residents** include flamingos, pelicans, white-breasted and reed cormorants, several species of tern, grey-headed and slender-billed gulls and, on the dry shore, the rare Sudan golden sparrow.

Wintering species from Europe, Greenland and Siberia, seen in greatest numbers from December to February, include several hundred thousand black terns, plus Eurasian spoonbills, ringed and grey plovers, bar-tailed godwits, redshanks and several species of heron and egret.

The national park requires a major outlay to visit, though the entry fee itself is a reasonable UM1200 per person per day. Although the park has an office in Nouakchott (see p.135), it's easier to make arrangements at the PNBA head office, on Boulevard Médian in Nouadhibou (ⓣ574 57 74), where guides are available. You'll still need your own 4x4 vehicle to reach the area, calling at either of two Imragen villages: **IWIK** (aka Iouik), 200km south of Nouadhibou, or **NOUAMGHAR** (aka Mamghar), about 250km south of Nouadhibou; the latter has petrol and clean water facilities.

For real bird-watching you'll most likely need to rent a boat to go out among the shallow seas, sand shoals and islets, which will cost you upwards of UM20,000; this can be done in Tessit or Iwik (Iwik faces the biggest, permanent island of **Tidra**, which is home to about two hundred endangered and graceful **dorcas gazelle**). Otherwise, you can visit the **Thila peninsula**, which is a haven for water fowl. Almost every village provides limited camping facilities (without water, so be sure to bring enough for your journey). The **campsite** at **Cape Tafarit** (from ❸ for furnished tents) is especially recommended; they serve superb fish **meals** for under UM1000. There's also superb wild camping at the remote **Cape Tagabit**.

1.2

Nouakchott

W hipped by sandstorms for more than two hundred days a year, Mauritania's capital, **NOUAKCHOTT**, lives up to its Hassaniya name, "place of the winds". This is the biggest city in the Sahara, a sprawling place of more than a million inhabitants – over a third of the country's population. Once you're settled in, it's hard to dislike; you can wander around more or less unhassled, and despite its growth problems there's a certain ease in the wide, tree-lined streets bordered by drifts of sand.

The site of the new city of Nouakchott was nominated by Bidan elders in 1957, who chose to raise it near a French military post on the old imperial road – previously the Mauritanian capital was in St-Louis, in present-day Senegal. With funds limited and formal independence pressing, the city was hastily planned and constructed for an anticipated final population of 50,000. In 1969 the first great Sahel drought tipped the country into crisis, setting off an exodus to the city and a sharp decline in the number of nomads. By 1980 the immigrant influx had pushed it past 150,000, and since then it has since grown almost tenfold. Today its burgeoning masses have long exceeded what Nouakchott can comfortably hold.

Arrivals, orientation, information

The **airport** is in the Ksar district, northeast of the city centre. Facilities are limited to a small bank with worse exchange rates than anywhere else in town, a newsagent, a café and car rental agency. Airport **flight information** is on ✆525 83 19. When leaving the country, be wary of airport policemen offering to "help" you through

---

Nouakchott surface arrivals and departures

Drivers arriving from Nouadhibou via the beach route are introduced to Nouakchott by the thatched cottages of *Terjit Camping*, 4km from the city centre. Most drivers these days will be coming down the new Nouadhibou–Nouakchott highway from Morocco, or up from Rosso through the endless shanties south of the city.

Most **taxis brousse** arrive and leave from garages on the outskirts of Nouakchott:

Ksar gare routière in the Ksar district on the northeast side of the city serves destinations in **southeast Mauritania**, including Aleg (4hr; UM2000), Kiffa (9hr; UM4000), Tidjikja (10hr; UM4500), and Ayoun el Atrous (13hr; UM6000).

Garage Rosso, 7km south of the centre, has services to Rosso (at least 3hr; UM2000).

Garage Sélibabi, south of the centre, near the Moroccan mosque, serves Kaédi (6hr; UM5000) and Sélibabi (18hr; UM6000).

Garage Atar, 2km north of the airport, serves Atar (6hr; UM3500), Choum (8hr; UM3500) and Zouérat (at least 12hr; UM5500).

Garage Nouadhibou in the Cinquième district, southwest of the centre, runs all the services to Nouadhibou (5hr; UM3000), and in the same quarter is **Garage Cinquième**, serving Keur Massène (3hr; UM1500).

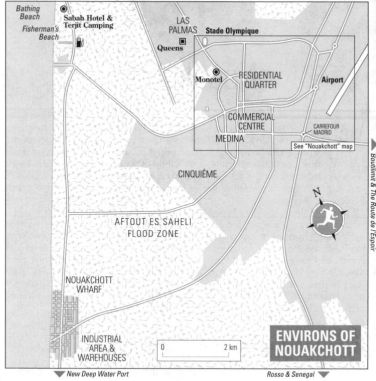

Bathing Beach
Sabah Hotel & Terjit Camping
Fisherman's Beach
LAS PALMAS
Stade Olympique
Queens
Monotel
RESIDENTIAL QUARTER
Airport
COMMERCIAL CENTRE
MEDINA
CARREFOUR MADRID
See "Nouakchott" map
CINQUIÉME
AFTOUT ES SAHELI FLOOD ZONE
N
NOUAKCHOTT WHARF
0   2 km
INDUSTRIAL AREA & WAREHOUSES

ENVIRONS OF NOUAKCHOTT

departure formalities, only then to demand a monetary gift. Official **airport taxis** charge around UM500 into the city centre, but if you can manage to lug your luggage as far as the large roundabout outside the airport, you'll easily find an ordinary taxi willing to take you to the centre for only UM200.

The **layout** of Nouakchott can be confusing at first, and there are no viewpoints from which to get your bearings. The city's main street, **Avenue Abdel Nasser**, runs east–west from just south of the Ksar district, through the centre, **La Capitale**, and out to the ocean, 5km away. Cutting across this road at right angles are **Avenue Kennedy** and **Avenue Charles de Gaulle**, which connect the affluent, ambassadorial and expat quarter of **Tavrak Zeina** on the northern edge of La Capitale to the extensive commercial districts of the Cinquième Arrondissement in the south (Nouakchott is divided into numbered **arrondissements**, subdivided into alphabetical blocks called **îlots**). Most hotels, restaurants and shops are within a short walking distance of the Kennedy–Nasser intersection and this district is likely to be your main focus for the time you're in town.

Helping the police

"Watch out for policemen who want to supplement their income as you struggle through airport departure formalities. One helpful policeman assisted me through the process and duly asked for €10."

David Dixon, UK

City transport and information

Nouakchott doesn't have any publicly run transport services. Ordinary **taxis** (normally Mercedes or Peugeots) will take you around town for UM200 and to the outskirts for UM300. Alternatively, you can travel along set routes using one of the battered old Renault **shared taxis** (*taxis tout droit* or "straight ahead taxis") for UM50 per hop.

The city still has no organized tourist **information** service. For flight information, see "Arrivals", above, and for information about airlines, car rental, national parks and travel agents, see "Listings" on p.134.

If you're wondering about **safety**, you'll find the atmosphere in most parts of Nouakchott relaxed and friendly, and there are no areas in the city centre that have a real off-limits reputation, even late in the evening. Muggings have occurred on the beach in recent years, however, and you shouldn't go there at night.

Accommodation

The range of accommodation available in Nouakchott is much better than anywhere else in the country. Besides a decent range of hotels and hostels, there are reasonable, if weathered **apartments** to choose from, sleeping up to three, at *Semiramis Appartements*, at the end of Avenue Kennedy nearest the church (☎529 13 97 or 627 06 03 ⓦwww.hotelsemiramis.mr ➐) – especially good value if you hanker for your own kitchen and a lounge with TV. *Semiramis* is usually filled with various embassy and NGO characters, and the prices are very negotiable.

For beachside **camping**, favoured by overlanders with their own vehicles, head to *Terjit Camping*, adjacent to the uninspiring and little-used *Hôtel Sabah*, about 1km north of the turning for the Plage du Pêcheurs. Here there are charming, basic but clean three-person beach huts set among dunes, with fine views of the sea and fishing boats (☎631 04 57 or 660 88 95; camping UM1200 per person, or huts ➋).

All the **hotels** and **hostels** reviewed below are in the **Capitale** area. The **Monotel** remains a Nouakchott landmark (still marked on the map, top left, near the French embassy), but has been out of commission as a hotel for some years.

Auberge La Dune opposite Air France on av Kennedy ☎525 62 74 ⓕ525 37 36. Homely hostel, with parking, several delightful shady courtyards and a handful of nicely tiled rooms with fans or a/c. The owner is an expert guide and can manage most nooks and crannies of the country. Dorm beds UM2500, rooms ➎.

Auberge Menata off av Charles de Gaulle ☎636 94 50. The clean shared-bath and en-suite rooms at this great budget spot have a/c and, you can make use of the kitchen (though you're best opting for their excellent fish dinners). The charming French manager is a font of information about the country. Rooftop *khaimas* from UM1500, rooms ➋.

Auberge Nomades just off av Charles de Gaulle near the Naftec petrol station ☎529 13 85 ⓕ525 11 61. Clean, friendly and well-located sandy courtyard right by the city's cheapest eating places. Accommodation is under a canvas awning or in simple, slightly tatty rooms with a/c and mostly shared baths (only one has a private toilet); parking is available. Dorm or tent bed UM1500, rooms ➌.

El Amane av Abdel Nasser ☎525 21 78 ⓦwww .toptechnology.mr/elamane. While the airy,

"modern" rooms may be less atmospheric than in *auberges* (they have a/c and TV but little in the way of style) this is still the city's best downtown mid-range hotel. Run by an efficient, matronly French woman, it features a leafy courtyard and a good French restaurant serving alcohol. ➎

Halima off av Charles de Gaulle ☎525 79 20 ⓔreservation@hotelhalima.com. The decor and feel here is similar to the much pricier *Mercure*, though rooms in the main hotel are rather small, so ask to stay in the newer annexe where they're larger. Staff are cordial, and there/s an on-site café and free Wi-Fi. ➑

Maison d'hôtes Jeloua in a quiet street in Tavrak Zeina ☎525 09 14 or 636 94 50 ⓦwww.escales-mauritanie.com/jeloua. Run by the same friendly and well-connected Franco-Mauritanian couple who own the *Menata*, this quiet collection of rooms is great if you want to take a rest from the chummy, travellers' caravan scene prevalent at many budget spots. The seven simple, elegant rooms are done up with traditional wood and leather *objets*. One of the most spotless places to stay in town. ➍

🏃 **Mercure Nouakchott Marhaba** av Abdel Nasser ☎ 529 50 50 ⓦ www.mercure .com. The smartest hotel in the country, this newly-renovated upscale choice offers tiled furniture, impressive African art on the walls and an outdoor pool. They even take credit cards. ⑧

Novotel Nouakchott Tfeila av Charles De Gaulle ☎ 525 74 00 ⓦ www.novotel.com. Don't be turned off by the gaudy peach facade of this luxury option in the centre. Although it doesn't exude quite the same class as the *Mercure*, the rooms here are the cleanest you'll find in the city, beds are comfortable and, for better or worse, the staff are tirelessly deferential. The good-sized pool, decent restaurant and helpful concierge all add to the comforts, as does the Wi-Fi spot in the bar. ⑧

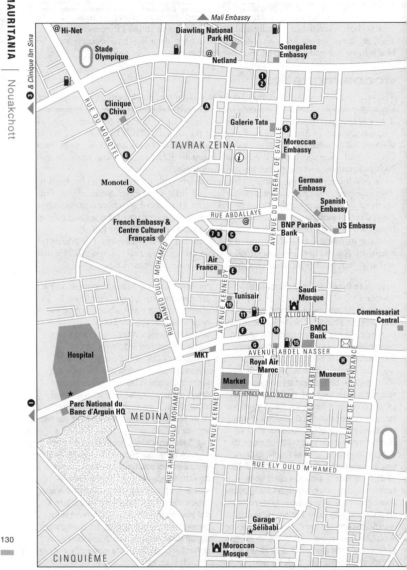

The City

It's quickly apparent that Nouakchott doesn't spill over with things to see and do – even the city's three main mosques are hardly worth more than a snapshot. There are, however, some very rewarding local **markets** and various **artisanal centres**, while the most obvious destination is the **beach**, though it's not as safe as it once was.

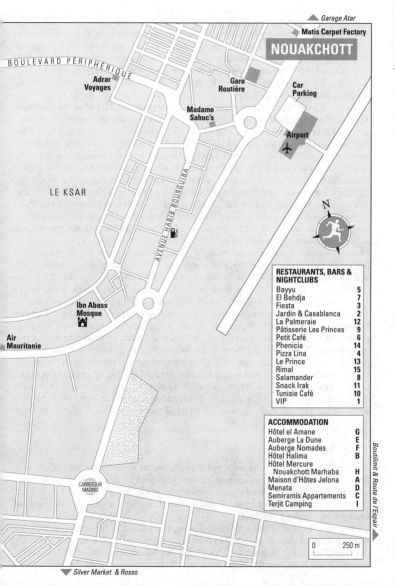

Garage Atar

Matis Carpet Factory

NOUAKCHOTT

BOULEVARD PÉRIPHÉRIQUE

Adrar Voyages

Gare Routiére

Car Parking

Madame Sahuc's

Airport

LE KSAR

AVENUE HABIB BOURGUIBA

N

Ibn Abass Mosque

Air Mauritanie

RESTAURANTS, BARS & NIGHTCLUBS

Bayyu	5
El Behdja	7
Fiesta	3
Jardin & Casablanca	2
La Palmeraie	12
Pâtisserie Les Princes	9
Petit Café	6
Phenicia	14
Pizza Lina	4
Le Prince	13
Rimal	15
Salamander	8
Snack Irak	11
Tunisie Café	10
VIP	1

ACCOMMODATION

Hôtel el Amane	G
Auberge La Dune	E
Auberge Nomades	F
Hôtel Halima	B
Hôtel Mercure Nouakchott Marhaba	H
Maison d'Hôtes Jelona	A
Menata	D
Semiramis Appartements	C
Terjit Camping	I

Boutilimit & Route de l'Espair

CARREFOUR MADRID

0   250 m

131

Silver Market & Rosso

In the centre itself, the national **museum** (Mon–Thurs 8am–5pm, Fri 8am–2pm, Sat & Sun 8am–4pm; ℡525 18 62; UM500), behind the *Marhaba* in the Maison du Parti du Peuple, is well worth a visit. It contains a fine collection of trade beads, arrowheads and pottery, with the oldest artefacts to your left as you enter. Upstairs, past the centuries-old door from remote Oualata and the huge elephant's tusk found near Zouérat, are ethnographic collections on nomads and their way of life.

Markets and crafts shopping

The **silver market** (Foire Artisanale, or *maharat* in Arabic) is a short taxi ride out of town on the Rosso road. Although the place is usually rather empty, there's an impressive array of silver-inlaid ebony chests, Tuareg earrings and bracelets, as well as wood carvings and masks. Take a look behind the booths and you'll see craftsmen in small workshops making intricate jewellery out of silver and ebony. Don't forget to browse round the **large building** at one end of the market, as it has a good collection of cushions, bags, teapots and pottery: the fairly high prices here are set by the women's co-operative in Terjit which produces the items and as a result there's little haggling, but you can buy similar items more cheaply in Chinguetti (p.149)

The city's **general markets** are worth wandering around. The **Marché Capitale**, south of Avenue Abdel Nasser and between avenues Kennedy and de Gaulle, is a good place to **change money** in a pinch, and is also the place to buy the flowing blue **dra'as** or **boubous** (from UM25,000 for a good-quality one) or turban-like **haoulis** (around UM1800) worn by men, which are a must if you're heading for the desert. For a colourful body-length **malahfa**, as worn by women, you can expect to pay from UM4000. At the back of this market is a women's centre where the speciality is **embroidery**, while at the southeastern corner of the market, steps lead down to the **Marché Industriel Tichit**, which houses two-dozen-odd purveyors of jewellery, cushions and the like. Clustering between the Marché Capitale and the intersection of Avenue Abdel Nasser are usually a bunch of pushy **souvenir-sellers**; if you don't want to buy, just give them a firm no and move on.

Southwest of the centre, at the **Marché Cinquième**, you can shuffle along sandy lanes between tubs of home-made peanut butter and buckets of dried and fresh fish, and a wealth of good fabric, including exceptionally fine-weave lightweight muslin in attractive prints. A clutch of medicine and *gris-gris* sellers, with their displays of monkeys' and birds' feet and lizard and turtle heads, make for macabre browsing.

In the opposite direction from the centre, near the airport, is **Madam Suhuc's boutique** (℡525 14 29), a tiny showroom selling tie-dyed batiks, wall hangings, purses and so on at decent prices, many of which are made by local prisoners as part of their rehabilitation. To get there by car or taxi take a right turn down a tiny lane (see the map) and the boutique is in the garden of a private house, on your left.

Further out, past the airport roundabout on the road to Atar, opposite the entrance to the military airport, is **Matis**, a carpet factory set up as a women's income development initiative. They produce finely woven camelhair rugs and carpets in subtle desert colours with rigorous geometrical patterns – though prices start from UM30,000 even for a small rug.

The beach

Although a number of muggings and thefts in recent years have scared many away from the beach, it's still a recommended visit: just don't carry money or unnecessary valuables with you, and ideally go in a group. To get to the beach, take a shared taxi (UM50) from the car park by the hospital west of the city centre, or try to haggle an ordinary taxi down to UM300.

Once you've crossed the wasteland that separates the city from the sea, there's a solid phalanx of dunes, then an impressively straight sweep of fine sand stretching north and south to the horizon. The **Plage des Pêcheurs** is crowded and atmospheric all the time, mostly with Pulaar and Wolof fishermen, but the best time to visit is at around 5pm, when the boats come in against the setting sun, and there are cold-drink kiosks and stalls selling freshly fried fish with hot sauce. If you get here early in the morning, you might even try to negotiate a day-long trip out with a fishing boat (UM5000).

For **swimming and lounging around**, head north of the Plage des Pêcheurs to *Hôtel Sabah* and *Terjit Camping*. Apart from the hotel *paillotes*, there's no shade, so bring plenty of sunscreen. Besides the 4x4s which thunder up and down on the beach with little regard for bathers, occasional hazards include strong currents and stinging jellyfish, and it's best to ask local people what conditions are like before you plunge in.

Eating and drinking

Eating in Nouakchott is better than anywhere else in Mauritania, and apart from good Mauritanian fare, there's a small range of international cuisine on offer, including Mexican, Moroccan and Lebanese. Some places that don't serve alcohol are relaxed about you bringing your own bottle. There are also several **fast-food outlets** on rue Alioune, linking Avenue Kennedy with Avenue Charles de Gaulle (the most popular of which are *Snack Irak* and *Le Prince*, both serving generous portions of *chawarma* for UM500, plus burgers, beans, falafel and grilled chicken): most of them keep the TV on at maximum decibels and remain open well past midnight. Avoid the less-than-fresh salads.

Restaurants

Bayyu av Charles de Gaulle ☎694 79 84. One of the capital's growing number of Asian restaurants, this well-run Chinese place tends to be popular with locals during the day, though Europeans dominate at night. Mains start at UM2000; try the dumplings or the *fruits de mer*. Live music on weekend evenings.

El Bahdja next to the Catholic church on rue Mbdallaye (turn after the bakery) ☎529 52 77 (open till 1am). Bring your own bottle. Excellent Moroccan *tajines* and a host of fish dishes from UM1500, though service can be a bit slow. A new café at the front offers drinks and nibbles.

La Dune at *Auberge La Dune*, opposite Air France on av Kennedy. Typically one dish of the day, such as spaghetti Bolognese, for UM1500, or omelettes for UM400.

Fiesta Las Palmas ☎529 33 28 (closed Sun). Tacos, chimichangas, burritos – the whole enchilada at this authentic Mexican spot a few kilometres west of the centre. The affable owner ensures that mains (from UM2500) are very tasty, and some of them quite spicy.

Hôtel El Amane av Abdel Nasser ☎525 37 65. Good, moderately-priced French food and the best steaks in town.

Jardin off bd Périphérique, next to *VIP* ☎655 40 59 (daily 5pm–midnight). The real draw of this expensive dinner spot is eating in the luxuriantly planted *paillotes* in the verdant grounds. The food is French with an African touch and the clientele

tends to be entirely expat. Several times a week they put on live music in their *Casablanca/Sans Souci* club.

La Palmeraie next to the UN compound on rue Ahmed Ould Hamed ☎525 73 44. Sophisticated French patisserie with a fine garden. The bread and cakes (UM100–300) are superb, and the salads and lamb chops (from UM1500) are also quite tasty. Daily 7.30am–2.30pm & 5pm–midnight.

Pâtisserie Les Princes corner of av Kennedy and rue Abou Baker (daily 6am–1am). The fresh bread and baguettes at this simple bakery are among the best you'll find in the city.

Petit Café rue du Monotel. Trendy café-bar with gateaux and good pancakes.

Phenicia rue Mamadou Konaté on the left as you approach from the BCI Bank ☎525 25 75 (daily noon–midnight). Popular with locals and featuring a varied European and North African menu, including the best couscous in town. A secluded a/c room at the back caters for groups. Main dishes around UM1500, omelettes UM400–1000. Their speciality is the lamb *tajine* (UM1200).

Pizza Lina rue du Monotel ☎525 86 62 (daily 10am–11pm). The oldest restaurant in the country remains one of the most popular, especially among expats and trendy Mauritanians. The pizzas (from UM1500) are thin and good – try the *Jamil* prepared with crème fraîche. They also serve good ice cream.

Rimal av Abdel Nasser, but difficult to find as the sign is almost completely obscured by vegetation

☎525 48 32. Though rather run-down, *Rimal* has a pleasant terrace and has long been popular among diners on a tight budget, and serves good couscous, fried chicken and fish dishes – the *sole à la crème* (UM950) is a good bet.

Tunisie Café av Kennedy next to Tunis Air (daily 7.30am–3am). Low-key, simple terrace café with Maghrebi tea, sweet and savoury crêpes, and hubble-bubble pipes (UM600).

Yo-yo alcohol

"It's not very logical that an Islamic republic still allows the selling of alcohol. Sometimes the police come, close places and threaten restaurant-owners who have tried to cheat the rule and even imprison them (a French and a Vietnamese). Then the restaurants obey and wait for things to calm down. It's a yo-yo situation, up and down."

Joelle Fichter, Switzerland

Nightlife

Mauritania is officially dry, but while **bars** don't advertise, finding alcohol in the capital isn't difficult. Some restaurants serve beer, but licensed clubs are much cheaper (though still pricey) places for a drink.

Most of the capital's nightlife revolves around a handful of **discos** that attract the NGO, UN and embassy crowds. The **French Cultural Centre** on rue Ahmed Ould Mohamed (☎525 25 46) puts on regular **concerts** and **films**. *Casablanca* (aka *Sans Souci*) in the *Jardin* restaurant off Boulevard Périphérique, is the best spot to catch **live music**. Next door, *VIP* is full of black lights and occasionally a few dodgy characters. Other clubs include *Salamander*, just next door to *El Bahdja*, which is fairly upscale, while *Queens*, about 500m beyond the stadium on the road to Nouadhibou, is the newest addition to the nightlife scene – a large, dimly-lit place playing lots of hip-hop.

If you're in town in April, be sure to check out the Festival de Musique Nomade (ⓦ www.musiquesnomades.com), where big-name and local African musicians play at venues throughout the city.

Listings

Airlines Air Algérie, av Abdel Nasser, next to Star petrol station ☎525 35 69; Air France/KLM, av Kennedy ☎525 39 16; Air Mauritanie, av Abdel Nasser, east of the post office ☎525 09 09; Air Sénégal, c/o Agence Maghrébine de Voyage, av Charles de Gaulle ☎525 05 84; Royal Air Maroc, corner av Abdel Nasser and av Charles de Gaulle ☎525 35 64; Tunisair, next to Librairie Vents du Sud on av Kennedy ☎525 87 62.

Banks The Banque Mauritanienne pour le Commerce International (BMCI) and the Banque Nationale de Mauritanie (BNM) can take ages to change money. They're open Mon–Thurs 9am–12.30pm, Fri 9–11am. The BNP Paribas, just east of av Charles de Gaulle, is planning to install an ATM. Out of hours, your best bet is to try one

of the many bureaux de change along av Abdel Nasser. Alternatively, wander around the Marché Capitale and let the black-market money changers find you – the rate tends to be slightly better than the bureaux.

Bookshops Librairie Vents du Sud (Mon–Sat 8am–1pm, 4–7pm; ☎525 20 84), av Kennedy just down from Air France, is the best, though everything is in French. A few scholarly and photographic books on Mauritanian culture and nature can be found at the French Cultural Centre, next to the French embassy. Alternatively, check the more tourist-oriented offerings at the *Marhaba* hotel's boutique.

Car parts and mechanics Garage Express, bd Périphérique (☎525 75 48), is used by many aid agencies to fix their Toyotas. You could also try

Adama Sow, an English-speaking mechanic who works for the US embassy (☎633 30 71), though he tends not to work weekends. Parts for most makes of 4x4s are on sale in the vicinity of the *gare routière* in the Ksar district.

Car rental Prices per day including driver but excluding fuel for the smallest town-car runabouts are around UM11,000; Toyota Hilux 4x4s go for around UM15,000 per day, but all prices are negotiable. One of the cheapest places is Wefa (☎525 49 01 ℱ525 50 09), on the corner of rue Alioune and av Charles de Gaulle, but there are nearly a dozen others in the vicinity. For self-drive, check out Europcar, though be aware that this will cost you around UM20,000 per day due to the extra insurance cost. They have main offices just north of the intersection of rue Alioune and av Charles de Gaulle (☎651 64 08, ℮europcar@mauritel.mr) and a small branch at the airport.

Cinemas While cinemas exist, they rarely seem to be screening much of anything these days. The Oasis is all but closed down, while the Galaxy, behind the Stade Olympique, screens little more than the odd football match. The best bet is probably the Centre Culturel Français Saint-Exupéry (the French Cultural Centre ☎525 25 46), which shows a variety of movies several times a week for UM200.

Embassies and consulates Canada, av Charles de Gaulle ☎525 40 09; France, rue Ahmed Ould Hamed ☎529 96 96 ℗www.france-mauritanie.mr (issues visas for Côte d'Ivoire, Burkina Faso, Togo and CAR); Mali, rue Palais des Congrès ☎525 40 78; Morocco, av Charles de Gaulle ☎525 14 11; Senegal, bd Périphérique ☎525 72 90; UK Honorary Consul, Mr Sidi Ahmed Ould Abeidna, SOGECO, rte de l'Aéroport ☎525 83 31 or 630 12 17 ℮sogeco@opt.mr; US, adjacent to the Presidential Palace ☎525 26 60.

Emergencies Police ☎17; Gendarmerie ☎525 25 18; Fire ☎525 43 10; Hôpital National ☎525 85 13.

Hospitals and clinics West of the centre, the main hospital (Centre National l'Hospitalier ☎525 85 13) is helpful, but over-stretched. Though the hours are limited, the best spot to find an English-speaking doctor is Cabinet Madame Sherif (☎525 15 71; Mon–Fri 8am–noon & 4–6.30pm; UM6000 per consultation), near the French embassy. Otherwise, for 24hr service, there are three recommended clinics: Clinique Ibn Sina (☎525 08 88), on the left after the first roundabout west of the stadium, was built in 2006 and is the best in the city; Clinique Kissi (☎529 27 27), a few minutes from the Monotel Hotel, is primarily a gynecological clinic, but they will deal with other problems

and there's usually someone who speaks a bit of English; Clinique Chiva, off rue du Monotel (☎525 13 25 or 525 80 80), is a bit more expensive than the others, but adequate.

Internet access Nouakchott has dozens of a/c Internet cafés, most of which charge around UM200 per hour and are open until around midnight The fastest connection in the city is at Hi-Net, next to the Olympic stadium. Netland, across from the Senegales embassy, is also very reputable. Otherwise, there are several along the bd Périphérique, between av Charles de Gaulle and rue du Monotel, or try av Kennedy off the rue Alioune intersection. The café at the *Hôtel Halima* has free Wi-Fi.

National Park offices The Parc National du Banc d'Arguin has an office on av Abdel Nasser, near the hospital (☎525 85 41 ℮priba@mauritania.mr). The Parc National Diawling office (☎525 69 22 ℗www.pn-diawling.mr) is near the Senegalese embassy, just north of the bd Périphérique; book here to visit the park, though you pay at the park itself.

Pharmacy Pharmacie Kennedy on av Kennedy opposite Air France (Mon–Sat 8.15am–1.30pm, 4–9pm ☎525 36 93). There is occasionally someone speaking a bit of English.

Post office The "Hôtel des Postes" is on av Abdel Nasser (Mon–Thurs 8am–2.30pm & 3–4pm, Fri 8am–noon). Collecting poste-restante mail depends on the availability of the bureau clerk but is otherwise efficient and costs UM100 per item. To mail abroad, post your stamped item into the unlikely-looking slot marked "étranger" on the side of the building facing the *Marhaba*.

Swimming pools The pool at the *Marhaba* (8am–6pm; UM2200 for non-guests or non-diners) has pleasant, grassy surroundings, but it tends to be an uncomfortable place to swim or sunbathe for women. There is also a pool at the *Novotel*, though it doesn't have such a nice setting.

Telephones Calls abroad are most easily made from the numerous *télécentres* around town (where you can also send faxes and make photocopies; there are several at the intersection of av Charles de Gaulle and av Abdel Nasser. Be sure the shopkeeper sets the meter to zero before you begin. The cost to Europe or the USA is around UM300/minute.

Travel agents MKT (El Majabat El Koubra Tours), Îlot S76, av Abdel Nasser, west of the av Kennedy intersection (☎529 12 55 ℗www.mktours.net), is the biggest travel agent in Mauritania, handling all hotel bookings, and able to arrange tours anywhere. Adrar Voyages, at the Ksar end of bd Périphérique (☎525 17 17 ℗www.adrarvoyages.mr), and ATV on av Charles de Gaulle (☎525 15 75

ⓔatv@compunet.mr), are also both recommended, as is Secutour (ⓣ525 23 82 or 642 69 00), next to *Rimal* restaurant. Alal Amatlich (ⓣ647 88 68) is run by a French woman who's been in Mauritania for more than a decade and knows the Adrar like the back of her hand.

Visas You can extend your visa at the Commissariat Central, off av Abdel Nasser, east of the post office. Besides your passport along with the UM10,000 fee, two passport-sized photos are sometimes requested, though it depends on who's working.

1.3

Southern Mauritania

Southern Mauritania is the most densely populated part of the country, its major settlements connected by the 1099km Brazilian-built **Route de l'Espoir.** This *transmauritanienne* highway has certainly opened up the isolated southeast, bringing the far-flung regional capital of **Néma** within two days' drive of Nouakchott. There's a grim irony to the name, though. Instead of spreading wealth to the provinces, the "Road of Hope" has sucked them dry, offering swift escape from the parched countryside to the even less hopeful Nouakchott shanties – where the nomads and impoverished farmers can only sit and wait.

South of the Route de l'Espoir the population is largely non-Arabic-speaking, and the land is dry savannah and bush, with irrigated rice and millet lands near the Senegal river. The area around **Rosso**, on the north bank of the river, is of more than just border-crossing interest, with a hunting lodge at **Keur Massène**, and rich birdlife at the **Diawling National Park**. North of the Route de l'Espoir itself is the fascinating upland region of the **Tagant**, containing the Moorish caravan towns of **Rachid, Tidjikja** and **Tichit**. **Oualata**, in the far east, north of Néma, is also highly recommended for its unusual architecture, though you'll need plenty of time to get there.

For Bamako in **Mali**, various tracks cut south from the Route de l'Espoir: the one from Timbedgha to Nara passes near the site of **Koumbi Saleh**, probable capital of the ancient kingdom of Ghana. The best route to Mali from this region, however, is provided by the new paved road from Ayoun to Nioro.

Rosso and the southwest

ROSSO, with its ferry crossing point across the Senegal River, is a major gateway to the rest of West Africa, and there's even talk of building a bridge for the crossing, thus completing the trans-Saharan overland road running all the way from Morocco to The Gambia. The town has something of an ominous feel about it, with unscrupulous characters poised to swindle, so take care.

The *gare routière* is 500m north of the ferry port, an arrangement that seems to have been designed to allow the town's *calèche* drivers the opportunity to flog you a ride in their horse-drawn buggies (UM100). To **change money**, there's a bank on the north side of the border gates, and bureaux de change between the border gates and the ferry port. If you must **stay**, the safest bet is the *Hôtel Al Asmaa* (ⓣ556 90 29 ⓕ556 91 39 ❸), not the cleanest lodgings in the world but the rooms at least offer

Crossing into Senegal

At Rosso, the **Senegal River** border crossing is open from 8am to noon and again from 3pm to 6pm. Foot passengers can opt to go by the car ferry that does four crossings a day (UM50, though sometimes free) or in one of the more frequent shared pirogues (UM300). The police will try to charge you UM1000 to "facilitate" your exit, and arguing with them isn't really worth the hassle. There are also established fees and taxes to pay when crossing this border, on both sides. For the full breakdown, see p.159.

Alternatively, if Rosso sounds grim (and it is, rather), there is another crossing into Senegal at the **Diama** dam, south of Diawling and roughly 100km west of Rosso. This dirt road is by far the preferred route if you're with your own transport: although parts of the road are rough, the Diama border is smaller, friendlier and much less chaotic than Rosso, and the crossing is a straightforward drive across the dam itself. (For directions see "Keur Massène and Diawling National Park", below).

private facilities; in comparison the dirt-cheap *Restaurant de Fleuve* (**①**), nearer to the port, vaguely recalls a war zone.

Heading north, you're unlikely to be stuck for **transport to Nouakchott** as *taxis brousse* leave all day until as late as midnight, completing the run in three hours (UM1200) over a pleasant landscape of dunes and acacia-covered sand hills.

If you're travelling in your own 4x4, you could deviate from the highway some 20km north of Rosso to visit **MEDERDRA**, an old gum-arabic centre at the heart of what was once the kingdom of Trarza. It is now renowned for wood and silver craftsmanship.

Keur Massène and Diawling National Park

Just south of *Hôtel Al Asmaa* in Rosso, directly opposite a building signed "Taamin", is the start of an 84km track to the village of **KEUR MASSÈNE**, the nearby **Diawling National Park** and the dam (*barrage*) at **Diama**, the track following the artificial dyke which separates the river from its flood plain.

The *Keur Massène Lodge* (☎645 71 82; bookings through the travel agents MKT in Nouakchott, see p.135; full board **❼**), is 9km from Keur Massène itself. It doesn't feel at all like the rest of Mauritania, situated as it is on the edge of a lake with large trees and a grassy lawn. It's a wonderful place to relax after the stresses of the crossing from Senegal or to visit as an excursion from Nouakchott, and it makes the ideal base for a foray to the Diawling National Park. Accommodation consists of a/c huts with bathroom. If you're here between December and February, you may find you're sharing the place with parties of hunters from France who have come to shoot the numerous **warthogs** (*phacochères*) that roam the neighbouring swamps. This is also the best time for bird-watching in the Diawling National Park.

Allow an hour and a half to reach the lodge from Rosso by public transport: a shared *taxi brousse* to Keur Massène village costs UM500 per person, or you can hire the whole taxi for UM3000–4000. If you only manage to get as far as the village, call the lodge and have them pick you up. Making your own way here from Nouakchott by 4x4, you can bypass Rosso using a shortcut at PK37 (37km north of Rosso) about 100km south of Nouakchott.

The **Parc National du Diawling** (ⓦwww.pn-diawling.mr; see p.135 for park office details; entrance UM1000) was established in 1991 in the wake of the decimation of the environment of the lower Senegal delta, largely caused by the construction of two dams. To get to the park entrance from Keur Massène, go back to the dyke and turn right. Now that the pre-dam flood cycle has been restored (sluice gates have been installed to enable temporary flooding of the flood plain), there has been a massive increase in bird populations and the park now has significant numbers of **wetland birds**, including pelicans, herons, black storks, spoonbills and flamingos, as well as plenty of **warthogs** and **jackals**. Local people have also benefited, with spectacular recoveries of fisheries and an improvement in grazing.

The park **headquarters** are an hour's journey from the lodge, the drive taking you through most of the park – depending on the season, the vistas will be of vast flooded lakes or ponds. You can pay UM1200 per person to stay the night in the staff house, or the park's staff will put up a large Mauritanian-style six-person tent for UM3000. Whatever you decide, you'll need mosquito nets as the insects are insufferable here. Simple meals can be arranged for UM300. From Diawling you can take a guide around the park, visit the beach (only 30km away) or ask a fisherman to take you out on the lake.

To Kaédi and Sélibabi

A less than engrossing two-hour drive from Nouakchott, **BOUTILIMIT**, a Moorish caravanserai with a large, permanent **market**, is the first major settlement along the Route de l'Espoir. The religious capital of the country, Boutilimit is renowned for the collection of religious manuscripts housed at its Koranic school, whose library is among the richest and most important of its kind in Mauritania, and for its crafts – goat- and camel-hair rugs, and silverware.

KAÉDI, some 200km to the southeast (reached initially by a paved road beginning just before **ALEG**, then an eastward turn on to another paved road at **BOGUÉ**), is Mauritania's fourth largest town, and a major market centre – it's a good place to buy cloth. A high percentage of Kaédi's people are settled, or semi-settled, Tukulor, whose white, long-horn zebu cattle can be seen roaming everywhere in the Gorgol and Guidimaka districts, to the southeast. The Alliance Française in Kaédi has some information to hand out on the region. For somewhere **to stay** here, the best option is the *Hôtel Faboly* (☎656 86 82 ❺), as close to the centre as you'll want to be, with clean a/c rooms and good meals for UM2000. Alternatively, the *case de passage* of SONADER (Société National pour le Développement Rural ❸), is a little further away from the centre of town and you have to share facilities, but the price is right considering the rooms are a/c.

Heading southeast from Kaédi towards isolated **SÉLIBABI**, Mauritania's southernmost and least typical town, is difficult in the dry season and usually impossible if it rains – it's right in the middle of the wettest part of the country – although several *taxis brousse* try to maintain a transport network between one flooded river tributary and another. The journey is not made any easier by the impressive number of checkpoints along this "border" road, though the beautiful landscape and exotic bird-life compensate for these hassles.

The Tagant

The **Tagant** is a region of barren, stony plateaux, the remote location of some of Mauritania's oldest towns, several of which are notoriously hard to reach. It takes nine hours to get to **Tidjikja** from Nouakchott by 4x4, the road paved all the way except for a 45-kilometre stretch between Sangrafa and Letfatar, just west of Moudjéria. *Taxis brousse* run to Tidjikja from Nouakchott's *gare routière*, or you could catch a flight – there's a weekly service from the capital. The caravan route **north from Tidjikja** to **the Adrar plateau** – a journey of 470km – is best undertaken in a convoy of at least two high-clearance 4x4s and (essentially) an experienced guide; it's better to drive north than south, because you're travelling "with the sand".

If you're approaching the Tagant from the west, the plateau first appears near **MOUDJÉRIA** (6hr from Nouakchott), with a short, steep climb to the top after you have passed the town. At sunset, the panorama over Moudjéria and the sea of dunes beyond is nothing less than breathtaking. Another 20km further on is the **Tamourt En Na'aj**, one of the finest wooded valleys in Mauritania. The road

The crocodiles of the Sahara

The writers of ancient Greece and Rome, including Herodotus and Pliny the Elder, mentioned the existence of crocodiles in the Sahara, but these accounts were not confirmed until the tantalizing discovery of fresh crocodile footprints in southern Algeria in 1864. Subsequently two more isolated populations were discovered, one in the Tagant plateau and the other in the Ennedi Mountains of northern Chad. The last Algerian desert crocodile was shot in 1924, and the Mauritanian population had been thought extinct since the 1930s. However, in the late 1990s Saharan crocodiles were rediscovered in Mauritania.

These reptiles are **Nile crocodiles** (*Crocodylus niloticus*), though at less than 2.5m in length, they're much smaller (and also less aggressive) than their counterparts which dwell in rivers and lakes. The Saharan crocodiles live in caves and burrows during the dry season, and migrate in search of water to breed.

crosses the valley by a small bridge – which turns into a ford during the brief wet season.

To see a sliver of sub-Saharan Africa in the desert, turn south just after the bridge, and hire a local to guide you to the **pools of Matmata**. The track leads past several villages, and beyond **DAR ES SALAAM** (you'll recognize the village by the large boulders dotted among the houses), the track crosses a small palm grove and a sandy wadi before mounting a rocky platform. At the top of the platform you'll see numerous circular buildings, thought to be **granaries** dating back at least 2000 years. Continue on and take a left turn when you reach a junction; eventually the track leads down into a wadi strewn with large boulders dotted, from October to February, with seasonal pools. The rest of the journey down the wadi can only be done on foot. Look out for the tracks of small **crocodiles** and **Nile monitor lizards** along the edges of the pools as you go along. As you descend, the wadi comes to an abrupt halt at the head of a large cliff forming the back of a stupendous horseshoe-shaped gorge. From here, look out for the crocodiles, which normally rest on a ledge on your right. You should also look out for **rock hyraxes** among the boulders, troops of **patas monkeys** playing on the sand dunes, and flocks of **grey hornbills** in the trees. During the rains the cliff becomes a massive waterfall tumbling down into the crescent-shaped muddy lake below.

Tidjikja and beyond

A 300-year-old bastion of conservative Bidan ideology, **TIDJIKJA** was founded by Moorish exiles from the Adrar, who planted the *palmeraies* for which it's still famous. The town subsequently prospered due to its position on the caravan trade route between Atar and Oualata.

As with other towns in the area, Tidjikja is split by a sizeable **wadi**, which runs wet for a few days at most each year. On the southwest of town, where you arrive, are most of the modern administrative blocks; the gendarmerie, where you should register your presence, is before the wadi on the right. The interest, though, lies up the slope in the **old town** on the northeast bank of the wadi, a fifteen-minute walk away, where it surrounds the Friday mosque, with palm groves and a jumble of houses spreading on either side. The houses, massively constructed out of dressed stone, cemented with and sometimes clad in clay, with flat roofs and palm-trunk waterspouts to drain storm water, display the ornamental *kefya* – triangular niches – that can be seen in various forms right across the Sahelian belt. Rooms are narrow, owing to the lack of long, strong beams, and focus inwards on interior courtyards.

The **airport** is a short distance west of town. The newest accommodation in town is the *Auberge Oudyan* (☎641 40 17 ⓦ www.sahara-oudyan-riv.com ❷), a group of colourful rooms and *khaimas* with western-style toilets, all overseen by an affable

French–Mauritanian couple who are knowledgeable about tours in the area. An alternative is the *Auberge des Caravanes* (☎569 92 25 ⓕ569 92 25 ❸), whose offerings include air-conditioned *tikits*, located at the point where the paved road ends in the north of town; the owner can arrange for the hire of a 4x4 for UM17,000 per day. Also central is the *Auberge Phare du Désert* (☎563 29 29 ❸), slightly smaller but a little cheaper and with hot showers. Other services in Tidjikja include a bank, a post office, a market and a couple of Internet cafés.

Rachid

Northwest of Tidjikja, the first settlement on the route to the Adrar, **RACHID**, is only 38km away, and is more interesting and more photogenic than Tidjikja itself. Several large rocky outcrops form an impressive backdrop to the town, best seen at sunrise or sunset. The deserted **old town**, on a hill separated from modern Rachid by a sandy wadi, was founded in 1723 as a Kounta Bedouin citadel, its piratical tradesmen preying on the caravans wending their way south from the Adrar to Tidjikja. At the foot of modern Rachid is the *Auberge Eraha*, a clean and comfortable place with a kitchen which guests can use, and a small secure parking area (☎529 36 12 ❷, or UM1000 per person to sleep on the roof). The stone track that winds its way up from the *auberge* offers a superb view of the old town.

East of Tidjikja: Tichit and around

The route east from Tidjikja is clear enough to the Rehian stronghold of **LECKCHEB** (a few windblown huts, some tents and a military post), but then the

---

The people of Tichit

Founded around 1150 AD, Tichit once had a population variously estimated at between 6000 and 100,000. Today, however, the number of inhabitants has dropped to around 500, as more families leave each year and more houses are smothered by sand. Nevertheless, the basic ethnic divisions are still visible, encapsulating the ethnic complexity of Mauritania.

The biggest and most economically active group, who call themselves **Masena**, are concentrated on the south side of the town, towards the modern administrative quarter. They are probably descendants of the black peoples who lived all over the Sahara in earlier, more prosperous times, and who were pushed south into oases like Tichit (and Oualata) by the expansion of the desert – and by the Berbers. Wealthy Masena families used to keep slaves, known as **Abid** or **Ould Bella**, and most of these chose to hang on to their traditional way of life even after they were formally freed in 1982, working six days a week in their former masters' gardens or households, in return for their basic needs. Today the Abid form a separate group in Tichit, living in a ghetto in the east of the town. Many have mixed to some extent with Tichit's **Haratin Moors**, whose status as black freed slaves is much longer established, and who continue to enjoy a superior social status owing to their piety and long association with the Bidan Moors.

The Bidan Moors in Tichit are called **Chorfa**, a title indicating a claim to be descended from the Prophet Muhammad. Arabized Berbers who had established themselves in these parts by the ninth century, the Chorfa were originally part of the Zenaga group of Berber-speaking peoples. They are concentrated on the north side of Tichit, around the fourteenth-century mosque.

The final group in Tichit's tiny social realm are the **Rehian**, nomadic Bedouin Arabs who pass through the town to sell meat or take part in the date harvest. They move their tents around with the grazing, as much as 200km either way along the escarpment.

Despite this ethno-linguistic complexity, census returns from Tichit record 99 percent of the population as "Moor", meaning Hassaniya-speaking people – a reflection, perhaps, of the assumption that to identify oneself with any other ethnic group is politically suspect.

piste deteriorates. To the west of Tichit, the line of cliffs fades away and there's a sea of dunes in which to get stuck and lost. Eventually the track descends to the edge of the Aoukar depression, where it winds along the base of the scarp. Keep a look-out for **gazelles** on the way. You'd be lucky to get a lift here for the 12-hour route from Tidjikja; the alternative is to rent a vehicle from the *Auberge des Caravanes* – allow up to UM45,000 for the whole trip, but bargain furiously.

Once a centre for Islamic art and culture, **TICHIT** remains one of Mauritania's most interesting towns, dramatically located at the foot of the Tichit escarpment, and boasting some of the finest **Tagant architecture**, besides preserving the remnants of a complex ethnic division in its town plan. Only two or three dozen **houses** in the whole town are in reasonable condition, but these display a more elaborate and purer architecture than that seen in Tidjikja. Local stone of three different colours is used – greenish stone for the Chorfa quarter in the north; more crumbly, red stone used in the ruinous Masena quarter on the south side; and finely cut, hard, white stone, used only for the most prestigious buildings. The *kefya* ornamental niches are intricate, and the doors of a few of the old residences are still marvellously solid, with heavy, hobnailed bolts and latches made of wood from Mali. Sadly, the skills needed to maintain the buildings are fading, and few people are prepared to invest the time and energy needed.

Be sure to visit the town's mosque, known for its decoration, as well as any of several old **libraries** and the town's **museum**, which contains a few religious manuscripts and other interesting artefacts, including old doors, books and bits of weaponry. There are several *palmeraies* south of the town, between the houses and the **Aoukar depression** which, until about 1000 BC, was a vast reed-covered lake supporting a large population, though is smothered now in dunes and saltpans and is a refuge for the rare **addax** antelope. The salt from the saltpans blows into the palm groves and coats the dates, making them inedible – so the people of Tichit have to spend the last two months of the ripening season painstakingly washing the crop with well-water. The joy of the actual harvest, or *guetna*, makes Tichit one of the best places to be at that time. There is a single *auberge* in town, providing a handful of well-kept rooms (❷) with shared squat toilets; it's just next to the gendarmerie.

Beyond Tichit: to Agrijit and Oualata

If you manage to reach Tichit without your own vehicle, you could be stranded here for several days. You couldn't ask for much more adventure – unless, that is, you're determined to go further and make a full circle by taking on the three days and 400km of *piste*-driving **from Tichit to Oualata** (see p.143). This represents a major desert crossing, and the police in Tichit will make sure you're part of a convoy of at least two vehicles and have a guide. Mostly sandy, the *piste* follows the old caravan route around the Tichit and Oualata escarpments, with good wells at fairly regular intervals – Toujinet, Aratâne, Oujaf, Tagourâret, Hâssi Fouîni – and occasionally ascending the scarp to a kind of *Lost World* scene on top. You're unlikely to see other vehicles along the way. A less daunting forty-kilometre run east of Tichit leads to the nearly deserted and sand-swamped ruins of **Agrijit** – showing what Tichit itself is doomed to become.

The far southeast

East of the Route de l'Espoir's high point on the Tagant plateau – the **Passe de Djoûk** – is the scrappy, teeming administrative town of **KIFFA**, now the second most populated town in the country following the sedentarization of many of Mauritania's nomadic pastoralists. Of the town's several **hotels**, the best is the reasonably new *Maison d'Hôtes* (❺), centrally located by the taxi garage. Less appealing, though perfectly acceptable, is the clean *Auberge Le Phare du Désert* (☎644 24 21 ✉pharerim@yahoo .fr ❺), located in the eastern part of town, which has bright, Tuareg-styled rooms with

Kiffa beads

Trade beads (see *Arts and crafts* colour section) were used in many parts of West Africa before the arrival of the first Europeans. Most were manufactured in the Middle East and Europe, particularly in Venice but there were also **local bead-making centres** across West Africa, especially in southeast Mauritania, of which Kiffa is perhaps the oldest example. Here, they may have been making diamond or pyramid shaped glass beads since the thirteenth century or even earlier. The technique is based on pounding and grinding broken bottle glass and pottery shards, mixing the powder with spittle, shaping and decorating the beads and then firing them on an open fire until the powder melts and fuses. At one time, beads had **symbolic significance** – as indicators of wealth and status. These days, most are made for the limited tourist trade. The Beads of Africa website ⓦseqf.club.fr has interesting background and photos.

a/c and private baths, and a large, carpeted tent area for hanging out. They also have excursions on offer and room prices tend to be negotiable. Slightly pricier (and with less character) are the large rooms at the concrete, bungalow-style *El Emel,* on the left past the gendarmerie just before you get to Kiffa (☎563 26 37 ⓕ563 26 38 ❸). Prices for meals at these places run upwards of UM2000, but you can eat well in town at local African stalls for a few hundred ouguiyas. The **airport** is a few kilometres west of town.

The road from Kiffa to **Ayoun el Atrous** is very scenic by Mauritanian standards, with some fantastic **rock sculptures** just before Ayoun itself. If you happen to stop by a *guelta*, keep an eye open for small **crocodiles** disguised as logs and groups of **baboons** scrambling over rocks. Those in search of the ruins of **Aoudaghost** (see box below) should take the track heading north off the road about 12km west of **TINTÂNE**. This leads to the town of **Tamchekket**, from where you will need a guide to take you to the ruins.

Ayoun el Atrous

AYOUN EL ATROUS is a more attractive town than most others along the road, its pink and red sandstone buildings set amid numerous small natural rock formations. If you're into collecting old trade beads, you'll enjoy the **market**. The town is

Aoudaghost and the Ghana Empire

Aoudaghost (modern name Tegdaoust) was once a great trans-Saharan trading city on the edge of what was then grassland. Its inhabitants were probably speakers of a Mande language like Soninké. From perhaps 500 BC, caravans of horses and bullocks used to arrive from Marrakech and the Roman Empire's Mediterranean shores. By the third century AD, the domestication of the camel had improved the viability of the trans-Saharan trade and Aoudaghost flourished on the commerce through most of the first millennium AD, in later years repulsing Berber Almoravid attempts to subjugate and convert it to Islam. The rapidly expanding empire of Ghana – no relation to the modern state and focussed on Oualata and Koumbi Saleh – captured the town around 1050. Within a decade, however, Ghana's Muslim western neighbour, **Tekrur**, helped the Berber Almoravids to invade and convert Ghana. By early in the twelfth century, the Berbers were leaving again, and over the next century both Tekrur and Ghana were swallowed up by the mightier empire of Mali to the east. Aoudaghost was rebuilt in the sixteenth and seventeenth centuries, and then finally deserted. Today, it's only as interesting as the most recent excavations, and not easily visited (being so hard to find), unless a dig is in progress.

also the starting point for one of the three principal routes to **Mali**, a straightforward three-hour drive to Nioro (plus border delays) on a newly paved road.

The *Hôtel Aioun*, on the right just before the Garde National (☎515 10 55 or 650 28 32 ❹), has overpriced, en-suite, a/c rooms, though it's quite clean and the view from the top floor is appealing. A cheaper alternative, 2km east of town, is the *Auberge Saada-Tenzah* (☎515 19 00 or 648 60 99 ❸), a series of clean, thatched-roof bungalows with either fan or a/c. Ask for the massive *suite présidentielle*. An attached restaurant serves very good local dishes from UM1500.

Koumbi Saleh

The putative capital of the Ghana Empire, **KOUMBI SALEH** is the most important medieval site in West Africa, though archeologists have barely scratched its huge extent, which unfortunately means that unless you've got a shovel there's not much to see. If you're bent on visiting the ruins, press on to **TIMBEDGHA** (Timbedra) and then aim for the Malian town of Nara from there. The site is some 65km southeast of Timbedgha, close to the main route to Nara, and there's a chance of getting there by ordinary *taxi brousse* bound for the border, as long as you're prepared to pay a little extra for the diversion.

Koumbi Saleh is estimated to have had a population of about 30,000, which would have made it one of the largest cities in the world at the time. The Arab geographer Al-Bakri, writing in 1067, described a conurbation of two towns, a northern one with twelve mosques, and, 10km to the south, the royal town of **al-Ghala**, with huts arranged concentrically around a palace. Between the two, along the royal road, was a continuous "suburb" of houses. Curiously, although traces of the royal part of Koumbi Saleh have been found, the royal quarter doesn't appear to have been constructed in stone. The main part of town is more impressive, successive excavations having uncovered massive stone houses, an enormous mosque, and flagstone floors covering a more ancient layer of buildings.

Néma and Oualata

The *transmauritanienne* ends with a whimper at the woebegone town of **NÉMA**, a cluster of shops and workshops surrounding a gritty wadi. The **old town** is worth a visit if you have time to kill, with some Oualata-style buildings, though without the paintings and in a worse state of repair. The basic *Auberge Moulaye Omar* behind the market offers simple rooms with breakfast included in the rate (☎650 34 89 ❷), but for something more upscale, try the *Hotel N'Gady* (☎513 09 00 ❼) at the entrance to town, a newly-built complex of large, comfortable, a/c rooms, all with private baths, set around a pleasant, sculptured courtyard. The attached restaurant serves excellent food.

There's **transport** to Nouakchott and Ayoun in the main *taxi brousse* garage at the western end of town, and there are two *pistes* leading south from Néma to Nara in Mali – but these should only be attempted in convoy. For Oualata, you'll need to ask around town to see if anyone is going that direction: wander through the maze of streets north of the wadi and ask for the shop of Mohammed Lemine De'de, who drives to Oualata most evenings around 5pm. He charges UM3000 in the front and half price to cling onto the goods at the back. It's a beautiful but bone-shattering and chaotic four-hour ride over the ninety kilometres, mostly in the dark, and you'll need to wrap up if you're travelling in winter.

Oualata

One of the most remote towns in Mauritania, **OUALATA** (sometimes spelled Walata, ⓦ www.walata.org) owes its glamour to the amazingly beautiful bas-relief ornamentation of its house walls. The decorations, of gypsum, white and red clay, and indigo, are designed and applied by the women, and although they're personal works, they share certain motifs and a thoroughgoing exuberance. Inside the houses, the effects created can be stunning; the doors are highly stylized as well, the best ones studded with copper and silver.

The town's origins go back to the eleventh century, to the heyday of the Ghana Empire, when this settlement was a Soninké town called Birou. It was destroyed in 1076 by the Almoravids, then re-founded in 1224 by Moorish merchants fleeing from Koumbi Saleh. It rose to a fame equal to that of Timbuktu and Djenné, and features in medieval European maps of Africa. At its zenith, skins, ivory, slaves, gold and kola nuts passed through to reach Arab markets in North Africa. The town faded with the decline in the great trans-Saharan commerce at the end of the seventeenth century, but it has kept its worldwide eminence as a centre of **Islamic scholarship**, the basis of long-term rivalry with Timbuktu. There are only twenty places in its Koranic school, creating a permanent waiting list of anything up to ten years. In recent years, the Mauritanian government, assisted by a Spanish NGO, has made significant efforts to preserve the city through a number of agricultural and tourism development projects.

You'll need to take a guide to see the interiors of houses; people will accost you to offer their services for a half or full day. One of the more interesting houses is that of Bati, the town's marabout, who traces his ancestry back eight hundred years to the founder of the town. His house is typical of many in Oualata, with a sculpted entrance leading to a small room with stone seats at either end, where business would have been transacted or children taught. This room opens onto a courtyard surrounded by several rooms, with steps leading up to more rooms and other compounds. The reception room, off one of the upper courtyards, has carpets spread on stick frames on both sides, instead of the mattresses used elsewhere in Mauritania. Note the fine white sand sprinkled deliberately on the floor and the numerous niches used for Koranic manuscripts and oil lamps.

If you're really into religious manuscripts, ask to see the **manuscript museum**, which has drawers full of more than fifteen hundred ancient Korans and other books, the oldest dating back to the year 999. Don't forget to visit the **Maison des femmes**, where you can buy miniature replicas of a Oualata house with its courtyard and rooms. You can also go on a camel safari and visit several nearby sites holding some evocative ancient rock paintings. Any of the *auberges* in town will happily organize a tour.

There is no shortage of **auberges**, with all of them serving **food** (around UM2000 for a full meal); date-stuffed pigeon is the region's speciality. Opposite the gendarmerie, where you should register once you arrive, is the friendly *Bon Accueil* (T513 03 19 or 641 80 59 ❷), which features twelve rooms, proper toilets and showers and a large parking area. Inside the medina just by the museum is the more comfortable *Ksar Walata* (T644 88 25 or 661 73 82 ❺), with comfortable beds and decorated rooms. Cheapest of all is the basic *Auberge de l'Amitié*, near the old mosque (❷), whose affable owner cooks up superb local cuisine and runs inexpensive guided tours of the town.

1.4

The Adrar

Breaking through the sands of the Sahara, the **Adrar plateau** is Mauritania's most outstanding region. Though nowhere higher than 1000m, the gaunt, brown scenery is strikingly clawed into deep **gorges** and sheer, cliff-edged **mesas**, surrounded by wind-carried **live dunes**. Known in Arabic as the *Trab el Hajra* ("land of stone"), the region's oasis towns were well on the beaten path of caravans in the Middle Ages, but their importance declined once Europeans set up trading posts along the West African coast. Today, the town of **Atar**, plus a handful of villages, and the ancient settlements of **Chinguetti** and **Ouadane**, account for almost half the population; the economy rests on camels and date-palm oases (and increasingly tourism). The ubiquity of Neolithic stone tools – some remarkably small and fine – adds further interest to the area.

To Atar

The sealed Nouakchott–Atar road is efficient, taxis taking about six hours to complete the journey, usually stopping at the copper- and gold-mining centre of **AKJOUJT** on the way for food and petrol. If you've opted to take the sandy, wadi *piste*, you can stop at a small oasis 5km outside of Atar, where you can eat for a few hundred ouguiyas in a gardened *campement*.

Alternatively, you could overnight en route at the lush oasis of **TERJIT**, off the Nouakchott–Atar road and only 25km south of Atar. The track to Terjit is on the right if you are coming from Nouakchott, next to the first police checkpoint; from here it's a rough twelve-kilometre ride past forbidding cliffs to the village, which has a car park at the top end. You enter a world of vegetable gardens, date palms and tiny waterfalls nestling between the cliffs of a narrow gorge. The premier spot to stay here is the new *Auberge Sahara* (☏546 6180 half-board ❺), consisting of rooms in *tikits*. Another 800m further on is the much simpler *Oasis Touristique de Terjit* (❶), which offers tents by a sandy stream below a massive cliff draped in maidenhair ferns and stalactites. Past here the track leads on to several bathing pools – the lower two fed by warm springs – and on up the cliff, passing an upper cold-water pool before reaching the top of the plateau, from where there are spectacular views of Terjit. If you do decide to take a dip, avoid using shampoo or soap to reduce the impact on the environment. At night, look out for small glow-worms by the stream between the campsite and the pools.

Continue a tough 35km further south via the impressive **Passe de Tourvine** (off the Terjit–Atar track) and you come to **OUJEFT**, another oasis with its share of archeological and paleontological relics, like many spots in the Adrar. You can loop back northwest to the delightful *palmeraie* of **TOUNGAD** before rejoining the Nouakchott–Atar road.

Atar and around

From the edge of the plateau the road commences a winding ascent through rocky hills to **ATAR**, the largest settlement in the northern interior. Modern

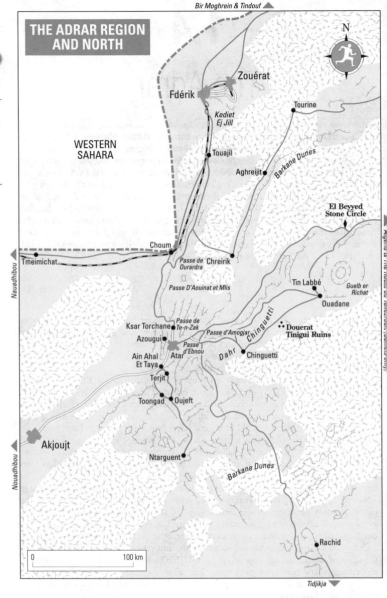

buildings and offices are fairly few, but this is a surprisingly energetic place, boosted in the winter by visitors arriving on Point-Afrique charter flights from Paris and Marseilles. Although the town does have a maze of old buildings, a *palmeraie* and a mosque dating from 1674, there are better examples of each in the surrounding towns and villages, so most travellers use Atar as base for the several worthwhile excursions in the vicinity, or as a staging post on the journey to Chinguetti (see p.149).

The centre of Atar is on the Chinguetti road (the second right from the main roundabout if you're approaching from Nouakchott). North of this is the old Ksar quarter with its crumbling buildings. If you head west (left) from the roundabout you cross a **dyke** which separates the main part of town from its *palmeraie* and the Séguélil wadi.

Between the Ksar and the Chinguetti road is a *quartier* of smiths who make everything from jewellery to saddle fittings; also here is a specialist leather shop. Things tend to pick up once the market gets going, and tobacco, dried dates and other foods are bought and sold with excitement. The town's central **museum** (daily 9am–noon & 3–8pm daily; UM800) has a motley collection of medicinal plants and Mauritanian cultural artefacts, but there's a much more engrossing collection of similar items 13km north of town at the **Museum Touezekt** (Ⓦwww.maisondarts .mr; UM1000), though the exhibits are not labelled. If the museum is closed, beckon one of the kids playing around the town to fetch the key.

Practicalities

The **airport** is on the southeastern edge of town, 3km from the centre; Point-Afrique flights arrive and depart every Sunday, resulting in an influx of tour groups on Saturday and Sunday. The rest of the week you might have a whole *auberge* to yourself, when you can try to bargain prices down. Pick-ups and *taxis brousse* for **Chinguetti** depart from Garage Chinguetti, in front of the *Restaurant Marrakech* (UM1500). There are also daily taxis from Garage Atar, 300m southeast of the main roundabout, to Nouakchott and to **Choum for the train to Nouadhibou** (see p.125), the latter a rough trip some 100km north, with beautiful scenery much of the way (3hr; UM2500). Choum taxi-drivers in Atar will ensure you get to the train on time. Before setting off for Choum, buy food for the journey, and take as much fresh water as you can – supplies on the train vary from limited to nonexistent and the water at Choum itself is unpalatably salty.

Accommodation and eating

Given that Atar is Mauritania's premiere tourist destination, there are accommodation options for all budgets, though note that a few are closed between May and September. Most places will arrange **meals** for about UM1000. For a great European meal, visit the *Restaurant de l'Amitié*, a real find of a place run by a lovely old French woman who offers loads of hospitality and excellent three-course meals (from UM2800) in a very clean setting (be sure to try the honey crêpes). Otherwise, there's a handful of Senegalese, Guinean and Malian restaurants such as the clean(ish) *Chez Hawaa*, found in the side-streets off the road just north of here, where a bowl of rice and fish will set you back just a few hundred ouguiyas.

Auberge Dar Salam on the Choum road at the edge of town ☎546 46 22 Ⓔcherif.dginde @caramail.fr. Simple, musty rooms with a/c are set around sandy grounds that aren't always the cleanest. Alternatively, two can pay UM2400 to stay in a *tikit*, one of the thatched huts used during the date harvest. ❷

Auberge du Désert on the eastern edge of town on the way to the airport ☎546 46 35 or 631 06 17 Ⓔmohdoua@yahoo.fr. Rooms and tents with mattresses on the floor. Staff are pleasant and there's Internet access too. Mid-week, singles pay half-price for a twin. ❷

Auberge Monod 250m east of the main roundabout ☎546 42 36. While there's little of the desert aesthetic about this weathered business-like mainstay, the spacious a/c rooms all offer private bath and hot showers. It's in a great location just a few paces from the market, and while there's no common room for lounging about, there is a small terrace for breakfast (UM1000 extra). ❹

Auberge Tivoujar 3km out of town on the Nouakchott road ☎678 13 42 Ⓦwww .vuedenhaut.com. Atar's newest hotel is also its most spectacular. Run by a knowledgeable French-man, it has both stone *tikits* and rooms, the latter with private baths, as well as a pebbled garden and a fine *paillote* for reading and relaxing. Service is impeccable, with staff well-placed to organize a variety of tours throughout the Adrar, including hot-air-ballooning trips (€180) and excursions for disabled visitors. ❸

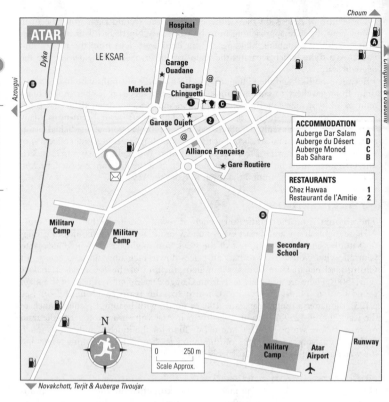

Novakchott, Terjit & Auberge Tivoujar

Bab Sahara on the road to Azougui, past the wadi ☎ 647 39 66 ✉ justusbuma@yahoo.com. An airy, funky place with loads of bohemian charm, this clean, hostel-like find is run by a gregarious Dutchman, and features stone *tikits* decked out in traditional colours (#1 has a comfy double bed), several tents, a great covered patio and a fine collection of ancient wooden doors. Vehicle owners have to pay UM300 to park (and there's an in-house mechanic). *Tikits* ❸ or *khaimas* ❷.

Around Atar

Most excursions around Atar require 4x4 or camel, and you'll get the best feel for the region if you try a bit of both. One of the best trips you can do in the vicinity – and one which an ordinary vehicle can manage – is to head 11km northwest of Atar to the ruins of **AZOUGUI**, once the Almoravid capital of the Adrar. In the eleventh century, this was the Berber base from which the Almoravid holy warriors launched raids on the Ghana-Empire town of Aoudaghost (see p.142), and the Ghana cities of Oualata and Koumbi Saleh. Having swept through the southern fringes of the desert, they turned north for their second great invasion, into Morocco and decadent Andalucían Iberia.

A taxi to Azougui will cost about UM3000. To get there on your own, take the westbound road from the main roundabout, cross the dyke and *palmeraie*, ascend the Tarazi pass and from there you'll be able to see Azougui nestled between massive cliffs, banked by apricot-coloured dunes. The remains of the town's **citadel** are still visible, though there's little else to see apart from a few stone walls. Equally humble is the **necropolis** of Imam Hadrami, one of the eleventh-century warriors and still a centre of pilgrimage for Mauritanians. Both sites are near the mosque. Perhaps more interesting are the seventh-century **rock carvings** on a large boulder in the northwestern corner of the village, across the sandy wadi. On the other side of the village, past the necropolis, is *Auberge Oued Illij*, which has **rooms**, tents or thatched *tikits* (all ❶); or try the simpler *Foum Chor* (☎647 39 66 ❶), run by the folks at the *Bab Sahara* in Atar.

Ten kilometres east of Atar there are ancient **stone circles**, and 20km north of the town, on a paved section of the road to Choum, is **Ksar Torchane**, an attractive oasis. Even further afield, between Terjit and Chinguetti, is the 1800-metre-diameter **meteorite crater** of Tenoumer – the meteor crashed here between 10,000 and 20,000 years ago – for which you'll need a guide.

Chinguetti and Ouadane

Chinguetti is the single most visited site in Mauritania, an accolade it owes to its mosque, ancient libraries and sand-smothered old town. Fewer people reach **Ouadane**, though it is just as interesting in its own way and remains one of the most photogenic towns in the Sahara. Travel by *taxi brousse* to either town can involve a fair amount of waiting, especially for the latter.

From Atar to Chinguetti

It's about 120km from Atar to Chinguetti, the trip taking between two and four hours depending on your vehicle and which of the two routes you use. Heading east out of Atar, you'll find the main road swings north to Choum; continue east, and the road forks after about 10km. The more straightforward route here is to keep right and you'll ascend the **Ebnou Pass**. About 1km from the top of the pass is a gendarmerie, and then it's another hour's driving on a stony *piste* before you reach Chinguetti.

With your own 4x4, however, you can opt for the longer but more impressive route through the **Amogjar pass**: take the left branch of the fork 10km from Atar and bear right at subsequent forks. After a steeply twisting series of hairpins, you reach the head of the Amogjar wadi, a gorge which gives onto a further incline and the Amogjar pass. In the interest of safety, it's standard practice for passengers to get out and walk the steepest ascents and descents. Among the sandstone massifs you'll see gun emplacements and the remains of military posts from the Polisario war. Up at the top squats the incongruous shell of "Fort Saganne", a fake built for the movie of that name in 1985. Up at around 800m, a couple of kilometres after the final climb, you pass a conical rock stack on the left, 50m or so in height. Under an overhang near the top of the stack there are some intriguing red-coloured **rock paintings** of lanky figures. Also look out for the 50cm-long **spiny-tailed uromastyx lizards** (*dhub*) which scamper into holes and crevices as you pass. Harmless vegetarians, they subsist between rains by drawing on reserves of fat in their spiky club-like tails, which they use to guard their tunnels.

Chinguetti

Whichever route you use to reach **CHINGUETTI** from Atar, you'll pass the turning for the upper route to Ouadane (see p.151), 10km before entering the "modern quarter" of Chinguetti, the beginning of which is marked by a diminutive **city gate**, two minaret-like pillars of rocks on either side of the stretch of paved road that takes you into town. On this side of the town, the main building – in fact Chinguetti's most striking structure – is the former French Foreign Legion **fortress**, demarcating the French military's first settlement here and used in the movie *Fort Saganne*, starring Gérard Dépardieu, about the Legion's exploits in Algeria. The fortress doubled as film set and film-crew accommodation and is now the *Hôtel Fort Saganne*. Non-guests can ask to climb the battlements for an excellent view of the town and the dunes that threaten to engulf it.

Cross the sandy wadi to the south and you come to the older part of Chinguetti, a **UNESCO World Heritage Site**. Once the most venerated town in Mauritania – the country itself was once known as *Belad Shinqit* ("The Land of Chinguetti") – it was a centre of learning, an assembly point for the pilgrimage to Mecca and a city on the trans-Saharan caravan route, with its eleven mosques and 20,000 inhabitants. Its glory past, Chinguetti is now a small island of ruins in a sea of sand, dominated by an ugly, modern water tower. From the water tower, turn right, negotiating the dunes, to enter the town's most venerable quarter, the **Ksar** or old town, dating back to the thirteenth century or possibly older. Most of the buildings here are of stone, including the winsome, weathered old **mosque**, which is off-limits to *nasrani*. Happily, you can get fine views of it – complete with the five ostrich eggs atop its squat thirteenth-century minaret, and much of its interior courtyard – from the tops of the dunes that have engulfed neighbouring alleys. The narrow alleys around the mosque are home to six ancient **Koranic libraries**, each of which typically charges UM1000 entry; the Bibliothèque Ehel Hamoni is considered to have the best collection. The "*donnez-moi un cadeau*" brigade, who are out in some force in this area, will happily show you where the libraries are.

Relics of a much more ancient history can be bought in the **market**, near the defunct *Hôtel Fort Saganne*. Extraordinarily fine, small **flint arrowheads** seem to be two a penny, as do the **barbs** that may have been used for fishing in a long-ago Adrar of forests and streams. These items are collected by children in the dunes, and you may come across a few yourself if you take a **camel ride** into the desert: Cheikh Ould Amar, owner of the *Auberge Rose des Sables* (☏746 67 63), can arrange this with prices starting at UM4000 per day. If this isn't a viable option, you can rent a 4x4 with driver for a trip to the desert (from about UM20,000, excluding fuel).

Accommodation and restaurants

Hotels and *auberges* in Chinguetti have burgeoned in recent years, with a handful of great budget options, many of which do well to meld a traditional aesthetic with solid construction and some modern amenities. All levy a UM200 tourist tax which is added to the rates they quote. Those listed here provide meals, typically UM600 for breakfast, and UM1000–1500 for lunch or dinner; but there's no reason why you can't stay in one *auberge* and eat in another. There are also a few *restos* in town, the newest of which is the *Restaurant Marocain*, just across the string of African art boutiques in the centre, serving tasty sandwiches, meat dishes and good (cheeseless) pizzas from UM500.

Auberge des Caravanes on the left as you enter town from Atar ☏ 526 42 71 or 630 45 11. Natty place with two dozen rooms with mattresses on the floor. There is a carpeted common area under a massive *khaima*, and the terrace is pleasant and airy, with good views. Tends to be quite busy with tour groups. ❷

Auberge Rose des Sables just after the service station on the road into town ☏ 540 01 48. This down-at-heel lodging right in the centre of town features weathered *tikits* and *khaimas* that share clean toilets and showers. The owner is well-connected, knowledgeable and eager to help – especially if help involves organizing an excursion out to the sands. ❶

Auberge La Vieille Ville near the old mosque. Basic accommodation with parking. ❷

Eden on the left after you pass the town "gate" on the way in from Atar ☏ 540 00 14 ⓔ mahmoudeden@yahoo.fr. Architecturally enchanting place that, with its authentic Berber touches and meticulously styled interiors, might best be characterized as a boutique *campement*. ❷

Maison de Bien Être on the left as you enter town from Atar ☏ 540 02 03. Rooms and *khaimas* surround a delightful terraced garden and retain various original features such as an *echeylaal* – a beam used for drawing water from a well – plus antique doors in one room. They do good couscous, too. ❷

Le Maure Bleu east of the water tower ☏ 540 01 54 ⓦ www.maurebleu.com. Hands down the nicest spot in Chinguetti and one that raises the bar for most accommodation in the country. The thatched and stone rooms are colourful and comfortable with Berber-styled linens, the Western toilets are clean and the cook makes outstanding Euro-Mauritanian cuisine. Run by an ever-knowledgeable Frenchwoman with decades of Mauritania experience. Breakfast included. ❹

Mille et Une Nuits a few hundred metres east of *Le Maure Bleu* in the dunes at the edge of town. This nicely laid out place features a dozen or so simply-designed *tikits* all connected by a pleasant stone walkway. The Sahara is literally in your backyard here – and when the winds pick up, it often ends up on your front doorstep. ❷

Ouadane and Tin Labbé

OUADANE ("city of two wadis") was founded in 1147 by Berbers of the Ida-u-el-Hadj tribe. Its reputation, beyond the limits of the West African empires, as an important **caravan crossroads and trading centre** for gold, salt and dates lasted nearly four hundred years. There was even a **Portuguese trading post** here as long ago as 1487, busily intercepting the trade for the main Portuguese base on the coast at Arguin Island. Ouadane's fortunes waned, unevenly, as it first succumbed to the onslaught of the sixteenth-century Saadian prince, Ahmed el Mansour of Morocco, who took control of the trans-Saharan trade and diluted much of the town's influence, and then lost its remaining economic power when the Alaouites invaded, also from the north, two centuries later. Over recent years, a Portuguese NGO has partially restored a number of original stone buildings from the rubble, including Ouadane's ancient mosque, its founders' homes and the main town gates, and there are more restorations planned for the future, funds permitting.

Ouadane practicalities

The well-marked main route to Ouadane branches off the Atar–Chinguetti road, 10km west of Chinguetti, from where it's a couple of hours on stony *piste* through featureless desert before you arrive. There is also an eastern, lesser-used route to Ouadane, though this is a sandy, wadi-course for high-clearance 4x4s only. Guides are essential on the latter route due to the shifting nature of the dunes. If you can't find a vehicle going to Ouadane from Chinguetti, take a *taxi brousse* for Atar, and flag down any vehicles going in the opposite direction as you drive (tell your driver, who should help); with luck, you'll find one heading to Ouadane rather than Chinguetti. If you haven't found any transport to Ouadane an hour out of Chinguetti, by which time you'll have reached the gendarmerie at the top of the Ebnou Pass, you may need to get out and wait by the road, though note that there may only be a couple of Ouadane-bound vehicles each day during the winter, and sometimes none at all at other times of year.

Once you're finally on the road to Ouadane, after several hours of dull stony desert, you glimpse your destination clinging to a steep escarpment. The town is quite extraordinary, collapsing in ruins amid the jumble of rocks from which it was constructed eight hundred years ago. If you arrive in the middle of the day, with no shadows to define the buildings, you may not even notice them stacked along the scarp until you're almost upon them. Without doubt, the best time to arrive is in the evening when the setting sun bathes the ruins in pink light: no Saharan town is more spectacular than this.

The best approach to tour the **old town** is to start low at the *palmeraie*, where you enter via the old town gate next to a fortified well, then work upwards through the rubble. The ruins, with their modest wooden doors, granaries and ornamental niches, are still redolent of the prosperity this settlement had centuries ago. Guided tours in English aren't easy to find – check with the *Ouadane Agoueidir* – but if you have some French, you'll easily be able to find someone to show you around (UM1000). Once at the top, sites of interest include the **old mosque**, several ancient manuscript libraries and a smallish museum run by Sidi Ould Abidine Sidi

The Guelb er Richat

Nearly fifty kilometres in diameter, the **Guelb er Richat** is the largest crater in Mauritania. Indeed, it is such a massive feature of African geography in this part of the planet that it has become a positioning landmark for space-shuttle crews. The crater consists of layers of solid rock that run around in concentric, ringed ridges – up to 200m high in some places – with the valleys between filled in with sand. Initially believed to be the aftermath of a meteorite crash, geologists have now proved that the symmetrical uplifts of land are the result of eroded magma rock fused with even older, sedimentary rock. It lies an easily navigable 40km by 4x4, northeast of Ouadane. Take a guide.

(℡632 74 59), which holds assorted archeological and ethnographic odds and ends. All the sites cost UM1000 each to visit.

If you're arriving by the main route, you'll approach the town along a wadi; on the right at the foot of the escarpment is the efficiently run *Auberge Ouadane Agoueidir* (℡546 20 38 ⓦwww.serendib.com/wadane; room only ❷ or full board ❺) with comfy beds in *tikits* (room #3 has an all-too-rare double bed), clean cooking facilities, clean Western toilets and fine views of the old town. But for sheer charm, continue on to ⚐ *Chez Zaida*, where the chummy owner operates a few basic rooms set in a sea of sand (℡546 20 28 ⓔzaida.vasque@yahoo.fr ❶). On the right, at the top of a rocky hill, is the *Hôtel Palace*, with super views of the old city and a variety of rooms offering private facilities (❸). The track continues up the escarpment to the old gendarmerie, opposite which you'll find the friendly *Auberge Vereni* (℡525 54 14 ❷), offering quaint shared rooms and tents; out of all the *auberges*, it's the closest to the old town. All *auberges* provide decent meals for around UM1500 – the *Vereni* even do savoury wheat pancakes called *ksour*, a Ouadane speciality.

Tin Labbé

Only 7km northwest of Ouadane, on the *piste* that curls round the mountain of Guelb er Richat (see box), lies the semi-troglodytic village of **TIN LABBÉ**, where natural rock shelters and crevices have been incorporated into the cluster of stone and mud houses. If you've made it all the way to Ouadane, it would seem a waste of a chance not to walk up the wadi to see it. If you don't fancy the trek, you can hire camels for the ride at *Ouadane Agoueidir* for UM1800 per day, plus UM2600 for the services of the camel driver.

On arrival in Tin Labbé, look around among the tumble of huge boulders down by the vegetable gardens and you'll find interesting rock paintings. There's writing here too, in both Arabic script and the archaic Tifinagh script of the Tuareg, a writing that traces its roots to a Libyan alphabet of the fourth century BC. While here, stop for a bite to eat at the central *Campement des Dattiers*, which also has a few inexpensive rooms (❶).

Senegal

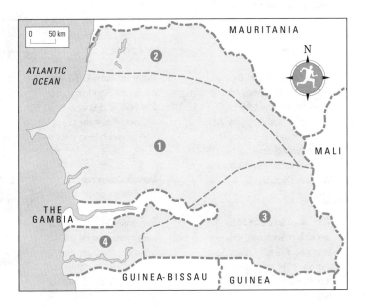

ATLANTIC
OCEAN

MAURITANIA

N

MALI

THE
GAMBIA

GUINEA-BISSAU

GUINEA

0   50 km

Highlights 154
Introduction and Basics 155
2.1 Dakar, Cap Vert and central Senegal 197

2.2 The north and east 228
2.3 Niokolo-Koba and the southeast 238
2.4 Basse Casamance 244

Senegal highlights

✳ **Dakar** Despite all the hustle and bustle, Dakar's great restaurants, lively markets, outstanding music and dance scene and alluring sandy beaches give other African capitals a run for their money. See p.197

✳ **Île de Gorée** Once the nucleus of the West African slave trade, this UNESCO-protected island lures with pastel-coloured mansions and flower-draped alleys that are especially beguiling in the early morning. See p.214

✳ **The Saloum delta** Meander through mangroves in a pirogue or simply enjoy the quiet life on one of the Saloum's enchanting islands. See p.222

✳ **St-Louis** France's entrancing old colonial capital offers heaps of faded elegance, some great beaches, easy access to two national parks and an internationally renowned jazz festival to boot. See p.228

✳ **Pays Bassari** Little-visited corner of Senegal, where low hills and unspoilt villages make for great hiking and biking country. See p.243

✳ **Basse Casamance** Despite its occasional troubles, Casamance remains easily the most seductive part of the country, with lush forests, sensational beaches and the friendliest of people, the Jola. See p.244

▲ Baobab

Introduction and Basics

Senegal is the most French-influenced of all West Africa's Francophone countries. In 1658 the island of St-Louis became the first part of the continent to be colonized by the French, and there's an enduring relationship between the two countries. Partly as a result of this pervasive Europeanism – and in recent years a growing American cultural influence – you could breeze through Senegal and hardly notice anything distinctive about it. It is one of West Africa's biggest holiday destinations, with a fair number of beach hotels and holiday clubs, mostly catering to French visitors.

As soon as you start scraping away the French skin, however, a far more fascinating creature is revealed. The **Muslim marabouts** (see p.184) wield exceptional power in Senegal, commanding bloc votes at elections and even directing the course of the economy by their injunctions to followers. Although Islam in Senegal is quite different from its North African counterpart, the idea of a future Islamic state, perhaps of a moderate variety akin to Mauritania, doesn't seem wholly fanciful. The name of **Touba**, the holy city of one of the most powerful Muslim brotherhoods, is one you'll see all over the country, incorporated into numerous names and signs.

French style and deeply felt **Islam** coexist with extraordinary success, though both elements are relatively recent introductions to most of Senegal. Islam did not have a wide reach until the end of the nineteenth century, while the French, although long-established in key towns on the coast, finally subdued parts of the interior as recently as the 1920s. Neither French culture nor Islam has much to tell about **Casamance**, however, the region of the far south beyond The Gambia, where a completely different tribal and social structure prevails, strongly Christianized in parts, but also distinctively indigenous.

From the **travel and tourism** perspective, Senegal is better organized than its neighbours: it's a country that is easy to get around, and one that is familiar with, and officially supportive of, independent travel. And it's also one of West Africa's less expensive countries for visitors. Although the **Casamance conflict** has delayed the growth in tourism, the country still attracts around half a million visitors a year.

People

The people of Senegal are dominated by the biggest language group, the **Wolof**, who figure prominently in government and business and control the Mouride brotherhood. A clutch of Wolof kingdoms used to cover the heart of Senegal – an area now largely under fields of all-important **groundnuts** – in a highly stratified society based on class and caste differences.

The first Muslims were the **Tukulor** and the closely related **Fula** – people whose kingdom was in the northeast, which is still their heartland. The **Mandinka**, too, were widely converted to Islam before the Wolof. In the southwest, the **Serer** (Sérère) and **Jola** (or Diola) resisted Islam until the twentieth century – in parts they still do, preferring their indigenous religions – and they maintained more egalitarian, clan-based societies than the Wolof or the Muslim peoples. Christian missions have had a limited impact.

Photography

Officially there are few problems with a camera in Senegal: you can even take pictures of the presidential guards and palace, though you should ask first. But you'll certainly hurt people's feelings if you take their pictures without permission, and in many areas, high prices will be demanded.

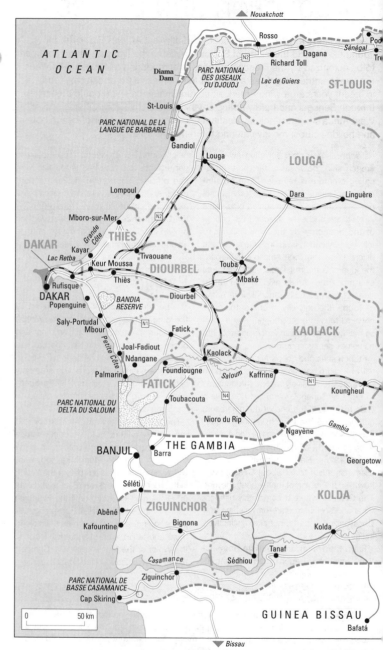

ATLANTIC
OCEAN

▲ Nouakchott

Rosso

Dagana

Sénégal

Pod

Tr

Richard Toll

N2

Diama
Dam

PARC NATIONAL
DES OISEAUX
DU DJOUDJ

Lac de Guiers

ST-LOUIS

St-Louis

PARC NATIONAL DE LA
LANGUE DE BARBARIE

Gandiol

Louga

LOUGA

Lompoul

Dara

Linguère

Mboro-sur-Mer

N2

DAKAR

Kayar

Grande Côte

THIÈS

Lac Retba

Keur Moussa

Tivaouane

DIOURBEL

Touba

Mbaké

Thiès

Rufisque

DAKAR

Popenguine

BANDIA
RESERVE

Diourbel

Saly-Portudal

Mbour

Petite Côte

N1

Fatick

KAOLACK

Joal-Fadiout

Ndangane

Kaolack

Palmarin

Foundiougne

Saloum

Kaffrine

N1

Koungheul

FATICK

Toubacouta

N4

Nioro du Rip

Ngayène

Gambia

PARC NATIONAL DU
DELTA DU SALOUM

BANJUL

Barra

THE GAMBIA

Georgetow

Séléti

ZIGUINCHOR

KOLDA

Abéné

Bignona

N4

Kafountine

Kolda

Casamance

Tanaf

Sédhiou

PARC NATIONAL DE
BASSE CASAMANCE

Ziguinchor

Cap Skiring

GUINEA BISSAU

0   50 km

Bafatá

▼ Bissau

Today, most language groups are increasingly subject to **"Wolofization"** and a national Senegalese identity is emerging as people move to Dakar and other towns. More resilient have been the people of the south – the Jola of Casamance and scattered, largely non-Muslim, communities of Bassari, Bainuk, Konyagi and Jalonké.

Where to go

Senegal is one of the flattest countries in West Africa, rising to barely 500m in the Fouta Djalon foothills in the far southeast. Two main rivers, the Senegal and the Casamance, roughly mark the country's north and south limits, and the southern region is sliced through by The Gambia – the result of an asinine colonial carve-up in the 1890s. While there is a certain degree of scenic variety, the country is most interesting at the cultural level.

The south, effectively screened from Dakar by The Gambia, provides the biggest attraction for travellers. The forests and mangrove creeks of the **Basse Casamance**, and the exceptional **beaches** of the short southern coastline, are the biggest pull – these combined with the largely non-Muslim culture of the Jola. However, the conflict between Casamance separatists means that some parts of the region are occasionally off-limits, and you should keep abreast of the situation

if you intend to travel there. In the southeast, the **Niokolo-Koba National Park** is one of the best game reserves in West Africa, and from here it is well worth the effort to push on into the remote southeast corner of the country with its rugged hills and traditional Bassari villages.

The attractions further **north** are round the edges: along the coast or up the Senegal River. **Dakar** – probably unavoidable, definitely two-faced – is a place to enter with some degree of mental preparation, if not actual caution. Yet for all its tough character, there are rewards in the city itself, and a number of good day-trips are possible in the area of the capital. **St-Louis** is another ambiguous case, either wonderfully charged with atmosphere or depressingly run-down – as it strikes you. The upriver towns, small outposts along the Mauritanian border, are stopovers rather than ends in themselves.

When to go

Senegal's **climate** is one of the best in West Africa, with a short rainy season (*l'hivernage*) between June and September (or until Oct in the south) and a dry period between December and April. The winds tend to blow warm and humid from the southwest during the rainy season, then hot, dry and dusty from the northeast and the Sahara (a wind known

Fact file

La République du Sénégal has a **population** of more than 12.5 million people in an **area** of 196,000 square kilometres – roughly the size of England and Scotland combined, or half as big as California.

The country's **foreign debt** totals nearly £2 billion ($3.7 billion), a massive figure in the West African context, and more than twice the annual value of its exports – though not even one percent of the US's annual defence budget. Traditionally, the groundnut industry has formed the basis of Senegal's economy, but fishing, phosphate mining and tourism now rival it as the principal sources of foreign exchange.

Senegal's **political system**, a presidential democracy, is the longest-established multiparty democracy in West Africa, dating from 1981. Senegal is also one of the freest countries in the region, with a reasonably good human-rights record.

The origins of the country's **name** are obscure: the Wolof have an apocryphal account of its derivation, in which a witless explorer gestures across the Senegal River and asks some fishermen what it's called. "That? That's our boat," they reply – *li suñu gal le*. In fact the name probably derives from the **Sanhaja** Berbers who frequently raided the river region and were known by the early Portuguese explorers as *Azanaga*.

Work and study

Though by no means easy, Dakar is one place in West Africa where you could quite possibly find a job if you're prepared to settle in for a while. The most likely openings are English teaching (approach the British-Senegalese Institute; see p.213) and – if you have very good French – translating, secretarial and other office jobs, or working in upmarket stores. Most are strictly unofficial – making friends with the expat communities will help. Try contacting Sénévolu (℡775 59 67 35 ⓦwww .senevolu.mypage.org), a Senegalese organization promoting community tourism, with homestay programmes enabling volunteers to gain work experience or attend culture and language classes.

as the *harmattan*) during the dry season. Early in the dry season, in December and January, Dakar and St-Louis can be surprisingly cool, especially at night. Through the rains, however, Dakar's combination of high humidity and city pollution can be pretty oppressive.

The weather needn't alter your travel plans as a rule, but you'll find some of the **national parks** closed during the wet season until tracks become passable again.

Getting there from the rest of Africa

Dakar is a common starting and finishing post for overland travels, and in many ways the city feels like a stepping stone between Europe or North America and Africa.

Senegal has become something of an **overland** terminus and departure point, as well as a crossroads for travellers using the Atlantic route across Mauritania.

Flights within Africa

The most useful **flights** from **North Africa** are from Tunis on Tunisair via Nouakchott and from Casablanca on Royal Air Maroc or Air Sénégal International. There are direct flights to Dakar from almost every capital city in **West Africa**, including: daily or almost daily flights from Abidjan, Bamako, Banjul, Bissau and Conakry; and at least weekly from other cities, including Praia on the Cape Verde Islands, which has several flights a week. From **Johannesburg**, South African Airways operates a daily service to Dakar. Ethiopian Airlines and Kenya Airways are the main carriers linking Dakar with **East Africa**, via their hubs at **Addis Ababa** and **Nairobi**.

Overland from Mauritania

From **Nouakchott**, Mauritania's low-key capital, it's just over 200km on a reasonable paved road to the Senegalese border at **Rosso**, where a motor barge transports vehicles across the Senegal River. Rosso can be a big hassle, however, with a lot of people out to make a quick buck out of unwary tourists, and you might prefer to cross much further downstream at the **Diama dam road bridge**, near St-Louis, though public transport is uncertain as far as the border. There are other official crossing points from Mauritania further upriver, of which the main ones are **Kaédi** and **Bakel/Gouray**, though they can't take vehicles: they usually use large pirogues.

If you're driving your own vehicle and crossing at Rosso, you'll certainly be hit for various **"border fees"** on both sides of the river (travellers using public transport are sometimes overlooked, and other crossing points can be more casual about the fees). The fees amount to about €10 per person on each side of the river. On the Mauritanian side they consist of UM1000 to clear Immigration, UM2000 for Customs and UM500 in local commune tax. On the Senegalese side, the fees are CFA4000 dam toll, and CFA2500 per person (plus CFA2500 per car) to clear Customs. If you don't have the right currency, you can pay in euros, which they seem to prefer – and the fees tend to be rounded off to €10 per

For details on **getting to Senegal from outside Africa**, plus important practical information applying to all West African countries, covering health, transport, cultural hints and more, see Basics, pp.19–28.

Average temperatures and rainfall

Dakar
Temperatures °C

	Jan	Feb	Mar	Apr	May	June	July	Aug	Sept	Oct	Nov	Dec
Min (night)	18	17	18	18	20	23	24	24	24	24	23	19
Max (day)	26	27	27	27	29	31	31	31	32	32	30	27
Rainfall mm	0	0	0	0	0	18	89	254	132	38	3	8
Days with rainfall	0	0	0	0	0	2	7	13	11	3	0	1

Ziguinchor
Temperatures °C

	Jan	Feb	Mar	Apr	May	June	July	Aug	Sept	Oct	Nov	Dec
Min (night)	17	17	19	20	22	24	23	23	23	23	21	18
Max (day)	33	34	35	35	35	33	31	30	31	31	32	31
Rainfall mm	0	3	0	0	12	142	406	559	338	160	8	0

person, so it feels more like a simple bribe to be allowed to pass than anything else. It's reasonable to ask for receipts. The border fees are also payable at Diama (which has no formal currency exchange).

Drivers who need to buy vehicle insurance for Senegal can get it most cost-effectively on the Mauritanian side (10 days, around UM5000).

As for onward travel, from the Senegalese side of the river at Rosso, it's 100km to St-Louis, which takes a couple of hours. If you're using public transport, reckon on CFA100 for a seat in a shared taxi to Rosso's *gare routière*, and then CFA2000 for a seat to St-Louis.

From the Senegalese side at the Diama crossing it's another 30km to St-Louis. Public transport to the highway can be hit and miss, however.

Overland from Mali

In the past, people arriving overland **from Mali** tended to do so on the **Océan-Niger train** from Bamako. After many years in the doldrums as anything like a functioning, reliable service, there have recently been some improvements – or perhaps, more accurately, a slowdown in the rate of decline – and you should once again be able to count on at least taking the train.

There are no longer any formal timetables, but the plan is for a train to run in each direction about once a week, or at least three times a month, taking up to 48 hours to cover the 1200km. Further details and fares are given in the "Overland from Senegal" section

in the Mali chapter (p.330), and departure arrangements are covered in the "Surface arrivals and departures" boxes for Dakar (p.200) and Bamako (p.360).

The biggest contributing factor in the decline of the railway is the paving of the **road from Bamako to Dakar** which means that the journey can be done relatively comfortably by bus or taxi in around 18 hours straight, or two days with an overnight in Kayes or Tambacounda.

Overland from Guinea-Bissau and Guinea

The principal paved route **from Guinea-Bissau** crosses into Senegal at **São Domingos**, just south of Ziguinchor. Lesser crossings include Farim to Tanaf and Bafatá to Kolda.

Entering Senegal **from Guinea**, Koundara to Tambacounda is the usual route. A couple of spidery routes further east make the Labé–Kédougou crossing increasingly viable for suitable vehicles. You can expect daily transport except in the rainy season, when road problems will cause lengthy delays. See p.621 for route details.

Overland from The Gambia

Travelling **from Banjul** to Dakar involves a ferry ride to Barra on the north bank of the Gambia River. From here, there are usually two buses a day direct to Dakar. If you don't get on one of these (and Senegalese–Gambian relations sometimes mean the service is suspended), the journey involves a couple of changes of bush taxi, including one short hop across no-man's-land at the border. The route is described in more detail in The Gambia chapter, on p.268.

To head south from Banjul **to Ziguinchor**, you need to take a bush taxi from the main taxi park in Serrekunda market to the border at **Séléti**, about an hour away, where there's usually little hassle. Make sure the Gambian officials stamp you in the right direction though – "Arrival" or "Departure". From Séléti, bush taxis run regularly to Ziguinchor (2hr) and less often to the low-key resorts at Abéné and Kafountine (1hr).

Red tape and visas

US and Canadian citizens and most EU passport holders (recent EU accession states excluded) do not need visas to visit Senegal. Most **non-EU passport holders**, including Australians and New Zealanders, do need visas, which can be issued quickly from Senegalese embassies or consulates.

Once in the country, **police checks** on tourists are cursory and even if you're driving, you shouldn't experience any difficulties at the occasional roadblock.

Note: **vehicles more than five years old** are often refused entry into Senegal. Some travellers have been allowed to continue to Banjul only in convoy.

Info, websites, maps

You can gather a reasonable pile of tourist leaflets and basic maps from your nearest Senegalese embassy. They may have copies of the free monthly listings and adverts pamphlet *Le Dakarois*, also available in Dakar itself. The only proper overseas tourist bureaux are in New York, at Suite 3118, 350 Fifth Avenue (☎212/279-1953 ⓦwww .senegal-tourism.com), and in Paris at 14 av Robert Schuman (☎01.47.05.30.73 ⓦwww .tourisme-senegal.com).

Websites

There's a growing body of online information about Senegal: good general **websites**

The blog for this guide

For **travel updates**, news links and general information, check out ⓦtheroughguidetowestafrica .blogspot.com.

include:
ⓦ www.au-senegal.com
ⓦ www.senegal-online.com
Both these sites include plenty of practical and cultural information, as well as good links.
ⓦ **www.gouv.sn** This Senegalese government website is also a useful resource.

Maps

You're best advised to stock up on **maps** before you get to Senegal, where they're thin on the ground. The IGN **Senegal** map at 1cm:10km is useful, and its companion 1cm:100m **Dakar** is handy in the city, but both are pretty out of date and superseded by Reise Know-How's sturdy 1cm:5.5km double-sided plastic map and Editions Laure Kane's *Dakar* map (1cm:160m), which is less detailed than the old IGN of the city centre, but perfect for the suburbs.

The media

The Senegalese **press** is relatively well developed, with a number of daily papers. *Le Soleil* – nominally independent but effectively the voice of government – has plenty of local news but not much international coverage; other dailies include *Wal Fadjri L'Aurore* and *Sud Quotidien*.

If your French is up to it, *Le Cafard Liberé* (named after the Parisian satirical mag) is a weekly breath of fresher air. Paris-based weeklies available include *Le Temoin*, *Nouvelle Horizon* and *Jeune Afrique*

Language politics are reflected in Senegalese government **radio**. French is the official language but programmes reflect the linguistic diversity of the country, with broadcasting in Wolof, Fula, Serer, Mandinka, Jola and Sarakolé/Soninké. The number of stations has increased considerably over recent years. Radio Sénégal (750MW) carries Dakar information and, on Friday afternoons, news about music and shows, and you can also pick up Sud-FM (98.5FM), Dakar-FM (94.5FM), Nostalgie (90.3FM) playing French and African music from the 1970s and 1980s) and Walf-FM (99.1FM), a more recent addition and the most popular station. The BBC World Service is available in Dakar on 105.6FM.

TV, predominantly in French, is available all over the country. Apart from the government station, RTS, there are also pay-TV channels such as the local Canal Horizons, the French satellite channel TV5, CNN, C-Span and various Arabic channels.

Health

One of the most comfortable countries in West Africa, Senegal doesn't pose too many health problems to travellers. It's mostly dry, seasonally mild (at least along the central and north coast), and has a relatively well-developed health-care infrastructure, with clinics and well-stocked pharmacies in major towns. A **yellow fever certificate** is in theory required if you're arriving from an infected area.

Dakar used to be the place to convalesce from the diseases of the interior. Nowadays, however, if you're getting over something, perhaps you should find a resting-up spot away from the city, which has the country's highest **typhoid** levels – attributed to exhaust fumes, industrial air pollution and the 1400 tonnes of garbage produced every day.

If you're basing yourself – or staying some time – in the Dakar area, especially during the cool, dry season from December to March, you may want to seek local advice about the necessity of **malaria** prophylaxis (see p.40 for more on the subject). Local doctors often insist it's more harmful than beneficial, and many expat residents don't bother. However, as soon as you move on, heading into the interior, especially in forested or watered areas, you expose yourself to risk again, a risk that is higher if you've broken your course.

Town **water** from taps is normally fine, though bottled water is widely available and not too expensive bought from shops, though from hotels and bars much more so.

As in the other Sahel countries, seasonal drought means insufficient washing-water. Away from large towns, try to check on the provenance of the water used (if any) to wash your plate and glass in eating-houses.

Water-borne schistosomiasis (**bilharzia**) poses no threat in the brackish tidal waters of the lower Casamance, Saloum and Senegal rivers, which do not harbour it (though the lower reaches of the Senegal are much less brackish, and thus more dangerous, now that dams are in operation upstream). Make sure, nevertheless, that you're sufficiently downriver for it to be salty before plunging in.

Costs, money, banks

Senegal is part of the **CFA franc zone** (rates of exchange roughly £1=CFA880, $1=CFA450, €1=CFA656). Senegal isn't generally expensive: **accommodation** will cost you from around CFA10,000/day in Dakar for a basic twin room (about £10/US$20) and less outside the capital. Long-distance travel on **public transport**, when you've taken an average-sized bag into account, usually costs around CFA1500 per100km. An ISIC student card can be useful for reduced entry fees to sites and museums, and is worth trying for possible **discounts** on trains and planes.

Credit and debit cards are of more use than in other West African countries, with Visa and MasterCard the most widely accepted at banks and ATMs, as well as at car-rental companies and the smarter hotels, restaurants and shops. As in other CFA countries, it makes sense to carry some of your money in euro **traveller's cheques** for the security these offer, though changing them can be difficult in much of the country, so be sure to have a few cash dollars or euros on you outside of Dakar and the bigger towns. **Western Union** money transfers can be arranged at most banks and post offices.

The commonest **banks** in Senegal are SGBS, BICIS and CBAO, which have branches in most major towns and some smaller ones. SGBS and CBAO can arrange **cash advances** on Visa and MasterCard, BICIS on Visa only. Traveller's cheques can

Fuel prices

In mid-2007, fuel costs were CFA560/litre for diesel, CFA730/litre for petrol – high for West Africa.

be bought using Amex through Senegal Tours in Dakar (see p.213).

Banks open and close early, and often have a long lunch break from around noon to 2.30pm. The only out-of-hours exchange facilities are the (usually exploitative) hotel desks, but 24hr bank **ATMs** can be found in large towns such as Dakar, St-Louis, Mbour, Thiès, Kaolack and Ziguinchor.

Getting around

Compared with many parts of West Africa, Senegal is easy to get around: bush taxis will get you nearly everywhere; plane, train and even boat are all viable options, and hitching is possible in some areas. Senegal has one of West Africa's better tarred **road networks**, with more than 4000km of paved roads; for the rest, flat landscapes make for lots of passable, if monotonous and dusty, *pistes*.

Taxis brousse and buses

Most public transport is by **taxi brousse**. This may be (in descending order of price) a seven-seat Peugeot 504 (known as a *sept places*), a *car* (usually a white, ageing Mercedes minibus), a *camion bâché* (covered pick-up van) or a *car rapide* (blue-and-yellow minibus). You'll travel most comfortably in a 504, as long as you're not squashed in the back or very tall, and these are also the fastest vehicles. Minibuses are better for shorter journeys and give more opportunity to soak up Senegalese life. In recent years, the Mouride brotherhood has started operating forty-plus-seater buses, known as **cars mourides**, on a few popular routes, usually leaving very early in the morning. Elsewhere, buses are not likely to figure much in your travels apart from in Dakar, where there's a decent bus system.

Autogares (or **gares routières**) are usually well organized, and the drivers (or their assistants) will always find you before you find them. Most of the motorable roads

on the IGN and Reise Know-How maps get at least one vehicle of some description every day.

Routes

The busiest road in the country is the **Dakar–Kaolack–Ziguinchor** route, part of which forms the *transgambienne* highway. The route involves crossing the Gambia River between Farafenni and Soma, where you may have to wait for a place on the ferry. Droves of *taxis brousse* use this route (departure is early morning, journey time 7hr-plus). The old route to **Ziguinchor via Barra and Banjul** is much less important as a transit route.

Thiès, a little way east of the capital, is an important transport hub, with a constant stream of vehicles running up from Dakar (1hr) until late in the day. With a morning departure from Dakar you can also go straight through to **St-Louis** (at least 3hr) and **Rosso** (at least 5hr). St-Louis is the transport focus of the north, with departures all day for **Rosso**, **Richard Toll** and **Dakar**, though destinations further upriver are served only by a few early-morning departures and usually require vehicle changes.

A good number of vehicles make a living on the **Tambacounda** road – because the train service is so undependable. You can easily make it there in a day from the capital if you get down to the Dakar *autogare* early. Continuing to the **Kédougou** district in far-southeastern Senegal, you'll be relying mostly on Tambacounda-based vehicles. The **Tambacounda–Ziguinchor** road is mostly quiet, so you'll need to make an early start.

Fares

Current **Peugeot fares** from Dakar are:
Kaolack CFA2850
Karang (for Banjul) CFA5000
Kédougou CFA12500
Kolda CFA9000
Mbour CFA1300
Rosso CFA6000

St-Louis CFA4000
Tambacounda CFA7500
Thiès CFA1200
Touba CFA2850
Ziguinchor CFA7500

Travelling in 12-seater minibuses is about fifteen percent cheaper; 25-seater minibuses are about 25 percent cheaper.

In Senegal it's usual to **pay** the driver before the journey has finished, and often before it's even started. Don't pay, however, unless the vehicle is at least half-full and other passengers have done so. It's also best to find out what the fare should be ahead of time, though if you are overcharged, it's more likely to be by way of a **baggage supplement**, which should be haggled over vigorously and knocked down to no more than ten percent.

Car rental

Car rental is expensive and really only worth considering for special targets which might otherwise be inaccessible (national parks, for example), and even then most realistically for a group of three or four travellers. The **main agents** for Avis (the biggest), Hertz, National and Europcar provide the guarantee of a reputable name and the chance to pay by card, but the all-in cost for a Peugeot 205 or something similar, assuming 1000km, will work out at £500/$1000 or so per week. These companies don't allow driving off the paved highways, and require you to be at least 23. National driving licences, held for either one or two years, are sufficient, but don't be surprised if an **international drivers' licence** is specifically demanded if you're stopped.

If you're not insistent on going with a big-name firm, it's worth checking out some of the **local car-rental places**, which are usually willing to negotiate, can be persuaded to give you unlimited mileage and aren't so fussy about off-road driving. They may work out less than half the price of the big agencies. A weekend is frequently the best deal, and a convenient length of time for many trips. Don't forget possible extras (*frais non-inclus*), such as collision damage waiver and twenty percent tax.

Trains

There's only one main railway line: the **Océan-Niger service** via Thiès, Diourbel

and Tambacounda (see p.160 for details), though it's unlikely you'd want to use this much as bush taxis are so much quicker. The **northern service**, which used to run daily between Dakar and St-Louis, remains indefinitely suspended.

Hitching

Because of the number of private vehicles and expats in Senegal, and a relatively high volume of tourist traffic, **hitching** on some of the main routes is an option worth trying. Moreover, if you're stuck on a minor turnoff, trying to wave down passing vehicles is less frustrating than simply waiting for the day's *taxi brousse* service. As ever in West Africa, you may well be expected to pay, so enquire about the likely cost at the start – some drivers may ask for payment at a much higher rate than on public transport.

In decreasing order of feasibility, there are fair chances of lifts around the Dakar suburbs, to destinations on the coasts north and south of Dakar; and from Tambacounda to Dakar and into the Niokolo-Koba National Park. There are also reasonable hitching opportunities in Basse Casamance, especially for foreigners.

Flights

Air Sénégal International (Ⓦ www.air-senegal-international.com), co-owned by Royal Air Maroc and the Senegalese government, operates a few flights around the country from Dakar. There's a daily flight to **Ziguinchor**, four flights a week to **Cap Skiring**, mostly at the weekend (40min) and regular flights to St-Louis (30min) and Tambacounda (1hr). **Fares** are CFA55,000 to Ziguinchor and Cap Skiring, though occasional promotional fares can reduce this by half.

Boats

A number of pleasure boats ply the waters of the Saloum, Senegal and Casamance deltas; if you're interested, staying in the right hotels in those areas will give you access. The *Bou El Mogdad* (which used to run from St-Louis inland as far as Kayes in the 1950s) has recently been recommissioned to run weekly St-Louis–Podor cruises (see p.235).

There's no public ferry service along the Senegal or Casamance rivers, though you can usually cross by pirogue and there's ample opportunity to make local ad hoc **river transport** arrangements. The Senegal is navigable all year by small boats as far upstream as Kidira, the Casamance as far upstream as Sédhiou.

The **Dakar–Ziguinchor sea route** has been besieged by calamity and cancellation: first with the devastating 2002 sinking of the **MV Joola** in a storm off the coast of The Gambia, in which more than 1800 people drowned (twice the passenger limit for the vessel), then with the suspension of the high-speed **Kassoumay** catamaran. The *Joola* disaster was a national catastrophe and caused great bitterness from the people of Casamance towards the Dakar government whose negligence was seen as responsible. The **MV Wilis** was put into service in 2005 with two sailings a week (one-way fares from around CFA15,000). See p.200 for full details.

Other options

A characteristically Senegalese form of transport is the horse- or mule-drawn two-wheel buggy called a **calèche**, which you'll see all over the country. They're often used as town taxis in smaller places, ferrying goods and people between their homes and businesses and the *autogare*.

You can rent **bicycles** at various places along the Petite Côte, around St-Louis and in Basse Casamance. Often they're not in particularly good condition, but they make

be very comfortable, offering a wider ran... facilities. Not all of the moderate-... hotels include breakfast in their r... newer places tend to.

Campements

Generally offering... the low-end h... **campeme**... small h... rest...

Hotels

Most large towns have several decent **hotels**. If you're arriving overland, you'll find Senegalese establishments on the whole plush and heavily Europeanized. In the higher price brackets, if they're not actually part of a chain, they're very often French- or Lebanese-owned and/or managed. And a surprising number of quite modest places turn out to have French hands behind the scenes.

The most basic lodgings (typically ❷–❸; the few ❶ places are likely to be brothels) may well be shabby and without air conditioning or private facilities. Mid-range places (❹–❻) offer unremarkable amenities at the lower end of the scale, though otherwise you can expect a clean, air-conditioned room with a shower and toilet, along with a restaurant and possibly a pool. Upmarket places (❼ & ❽) will

---

Accommodation price codes

All accommodation prices in this chapter are coded according to the following scale, whose equivalent in pounds sterling/US dollars is used throughout the book. Prices refer to the rate you can expect to pay for a room with two beds, including taxes. Single rooms, or single occupancy, will normally cost at least two-thirds of the twin-occupancy rate. Some resort hotels have two rates – high season from November to Easter, and low season roughly from May to October – in which case the price codes apply to the higher rate. For further details, see p.55.

❶ Under CFA5000 (under £5/$10)
❷ CFA5000–10,000 (£5–10/$10–20)
❸ CFA10,000–15,000 (£10–15/$20–30)
❹ CFA15,000–20,000 (£15–20/$30–40)

❺ CFA20,000–30,000 (£20–30/$40–60)
❻ CFA30,000–40,000 (£30–40/$60–80)
❼ CFA40,000–50,000 (£40–50/$80–100)
❽ Over CFA50,000 (over £50/$100)

...ge of
...d-better
...tes, but the

...a little more character than
...tels are Senegal's ubiquitous
...ts, usually comprising a cluster of
...ts or bungalows around a bigger bar/
...aurant building. Originally, *campements*
...ended to offer a more basic alternative to
hotels but many now offer mid-range or even
luxury rooms.

An important and gratifying exception to
the ordinary *campements* is the network of
campements touristiques rurals integrés
(**CTRIs**) in Casamance, introduced in the
1970s to bring tourist money to the rural
economy (see box, p.251).

Camping

Senegal has no formal **campsites**, though a
few *campements* have small areas set aside
for tents. Camping out in the bush is normally
feasible, as the country has a fairly indulgent
attitude to the eccentricities of foreigners;
the French community has been doing it
for years. Be sure, though, that you're out
of any urban "zone of influence" where you
might conceivably be putting yourself at risk
of robbery. The Dakar region, and the towns
in the groundnut basin – Thiès, Diourbel and
Kaolack – are areas to avoid, as are most of
the beaches.

Staying with people frequently comes out
of efforts to camp on their land – even if it's
not demarcated. Rewarding areas for such
contacts lie throughout southern Senegal
east of Ziguinchor – a region which, except
for the Niokolo-Koba park, gets very few
visitors, and virtually none who stay.

Eating and drinking

Senegal has some of West Africa's best
food, giving opportunities for everything from
serious dining to snacking on street food.
Restaurants in the larger towns and main
hotels incline towards French style, offering
a *menu* (three courses or more, and usually
a choice) and a *plat du jour* (main dish only).

Predictably there's lots of tough steak and
chips, heavy sauces and imported canned
food. For a *menu* expect to pay CFA5000–
6000, and upward of CFA2000 for the *plat*
on its own.

There are some decent French restaurants,
and a few other exotic eating-houses as well,
but with a few exceptions they're an unmem-
orable lot. More worthwhile – certainly in
Dakar – are the cheaper local eating places,
known as **gargotes**, and distinguished by
multicoloured ribbons over the doorways.
Here, you'll almost always find one simple
Senegalese staple, and perhaps omelettes,
on offer, which will never cost you more than
CFA1000. The better venues are covered in
the chapter.

Most **indigenous Senegalese food** bears
heavy North African and Middle Eastern influences, with lots of fish, mutton and Lebanese
snacks. If you've been travelling elsewhere in
West Africa you'll notice the near absence
of plantains and root crops, and palm oil is
used much less than in the southern coastal
countries. The **basics**, though, as everywhere, are a staple – usually rice – and spicy
sauces, though the key word is aroma rather
than pungency.

Riz jollof – a mound of vegetables and meat
in an oily tomato sauce on rice, named after
the old Wolof kingdom – is common here,
as it is all over West Africa. The national dish,
eaten every day by millions of Senegalese, is
chep-bu-jen (spelled variously as *cep-bou-
dien*, *tiéboudienne* and *thiebujen*), Wolof for
"rice-with-fish". This can be anything from
plain rice with boiled fish and a few carrots
to a glorious kind of paella with spiced rice
and half a dozen vegetables. There's no fixed
recipe, but it's virtually the only common meal
that usually comes with vegetables.

Stuffed fish (**poisson farci**), which is an
ingredient of the best *chep-bu-jen*, is associated with St-Louis and sometimes denoted
à la saint-louisienne. Done properly, the
result can be delicious. The usual choice of
fish is mullet, filleted and flayed, leaving the
skin whole; the flesh is then chopped finely,
spiced and herbed, sewn up inside the skin
and the whole package baked.

Varieties of **yassa** – a Casamançais dish
– are characteristic of most menus too.
Traditionally it uses **chicken**, but fish is also

Wolof food terms

The list below will help you ask for and identify food in out-of-the-way places. For more Wolof, see p.193.

bey/sikket	goat	suukar	sugar
chep/maalo	rice	suuna	bulrush millet
chere	couscous/millet	tomate	tomato
chwi	stew	xiif	hunger
dom/garap	fruit	xorom	salt
dugub	millet	yappa	meat
gejj	dried fish	yappi xar	mutton
genar	chicken		
gerte	groundnuts	There are various wild fruits, sold seasonally in the markets:	
jen	fish		
jernat	sorghum millet	ditak	oval, pebble-like fruit, with thin, dry skin and aromatic, acid green flesh surrounding a fibrous seed, sometimes made into a drink; very common in Casamance
kaani	hot pepper		
lem	honey		
lemnad	soft drink		
makka	corn		
mar	thirst		
mbaam	pork		
mbum	boiled leaves		
mburu	bread		
meew	fresh milk	solom	brown, pea-sized berry, with furry (edible) skin and a black seed
nag	beef		
ndox	water		
nen	egg		
nex-na	good (referring to food)	cerise	tart, green "cherry"
		nuul	fruit from oil nut palm tree
nyam dunde	food		
nyebe	beans	dimbu	medium-sized, green, soft fruit with a vegetable taste
sangara	alcohol, spirits		
soble	onions		
soow	sour milk		

common, and any animal ingredient qualifies so long as it is marinated at length in lemon juice, pepper and onions.

Sauces include **mafé** and **domodah**, based loosely around tomatoes and groundnuts. *Domodah*, so peanutty in The Gambia, is sometimes nut-less in Senegal. Both are best with beef or fish. **Soupe kanje** is a sauce made from okra with fish and palm oil.

You'll come across lots of places serving **couscous** (or *basi-salete*), though this is traditionally considered a festive meal and eaten at the Muslim New Year. Comprising steamed grains of millet flour with a smothering of vegetables, mutton and gravy, it's best by far when you're very hungry. **Méchoui**, a whole roast sheep, is one for Tabaski – the *fête des moutons*.

Away from the main growing areas in the south, **fruit** tends to be expensive: you're looking at oranges imported from Morocco, Ivoirian pineapples and French apples. The best fruit is found in the Casamance, where you should look out for unusual wild fruits in the markets (see the "Wolof food terms" box).

Breakfast and snacks

The great French bequest is their **bread**, consumed in vast quantities. *Pain beurre* and *café au lait* is the ubiquitous **breakfast** and roadside snack, often with real butter. Be warned, though, that in some places the Nescafé is made with **kenkeliba** (see p.60); specify "made with water" if you want Nescafé proper. *Kenkeliba* bars are known as **tangana** – which literally means "it's hot".

For **snacks** in towns you'll often end up in a **chawarma bar** – a dependable stand-by, and very cheap. Alternatives include *merguez* (spicy sausage), *kofta* (meat balls), *fataya* (mince and onion pies), *nems* (like a pancake roll made of vermicelli pastry) and **brochettes** of grilled meat.

In the suburbs and countryside the **dibiterie** takes over. Roadside or market stalls, *dibiteries* are really butcher's shops, where you can choose your hunk of flesh which is then chopped and barbecued on the spot and served with a few slithers of raw onion. It's said that flies are attracted to the best cuts, so take their choice as a recommendation.

Drinking

Flag is Senegal's **beer**, and not at all bad. It comes in bottles of a third of a litre and two-thirds of a litre, and the price depends on where you buy it – any bar that sells only the small size is going to be expensive. A quite acceptable alternative, assuming you're in need of refreshment rather than intoxication, is the less-alcoholic Gazelle (large size only), which tends to be one of the cheapest bottled drinks you can buy.

Wine is available in groceries in most town centres, and tends to be about twice the French price. **Palm wine** costs next to nothing but to get some, you need to be in Casamance and friendly with the owner of a tree.

Nonalcoholic alternatives to bottled sodas and mineral water are plastic bags of **iced fruit drinks**: hibiscus syrup (*bisap*), ginger water, **bouille** (sherbety baobab juice) or tamarind juice. If you're interested in unusual tastes, seek out **njamban** – a concoction of tamarind juice, smoked fish, salt and cayenne pepper. Mellower are **thiacry**, a mixture of couscous, sour milk and sugar that's closer to a dessert than a drink, and **lakh** – millet, sour milk, sugar and orange water. Sahelian **tea** – tongue-liftingly bitter-sweet – is another much-loved refreshment just about everywhere.

Communications

Post offices (PTTs; typically Mon–Fri 7.30am–4pm plus Sat morning) operate with grinding, morose efficiency. Senegalese mail is expensive, and sending things overseas from Dakar (where the central PTT has long hours) is slow. Getting mail at **poste restante** may require infinite patience: letters commonly take two to three weeks to find their box in the Dakar poste restante, and are then only held for a month.

Internet cafés have sprung up all over the country, even in out-of-the-way places, reflecting the enthusiasm with which the Senegalese have adopted to life online. **Prices** in big cities such as Dakar, St-Louis and Thiès are a very reasonable CFA500/hr, rising to CFA2000/hr in smaller towns, where connection speeds are also usually slower.

Phones and faxes

Centres téléphoniques, or *télécentres*, can be found just about everywhere, even in the smallest villages. Calls are made from a metered booth and paid for when you hang up – the **price** is measured in units and varies significantly from place to place (CFA75–100 per unit), so shop around. Note that Senegalese phone numbers don't have area codes. **Phoning home** costs around CFA600 per minute to Europe, and a little more to the US. **Fax machines** are also often available for receipt and transmission at the same centres.

Mobile phone coverage is very good in Senegal, especially in larger towns and cities, though network dropouts in less densely populated areas are not uncommon. The two main GSM phone operators, Orange and Tigo, have roaming agreements with most big foreign operators, though calls made this way are expensive. If you're going to be in the country for any length of time, there's no reason not to do like the locals and hook up to a **local network**: you can buy SIM cards for both networks for CFA3000 (which come with CFA1500 credit). While calling rates to Senegalese numbers are similar on both networks – approx CFA100 per minute – Orange's coverage is slightly better. Top-up cards (**cartes de recharge**) can be bought at most kiosks and from hawkers on the street and come in denominations of CFA1000–CFA25,000.

Senegal's **IDD** country code is ☎221.

Opening hours, public holidays and festivals

Shops are open from Monday to Friday between 8am and noon and again from 2.30pm to 6pm, while on Saturdays they're generally open between 8am and noon. Banks follow roughly the same hours but close earlier in the afternoon. Most other offices are open from Monday to Friday between 7.30am and 4pm without a break. Many establishments, including some restaurants, close one day a week – museums usually on Monday.

Apart from Christian and Islamic holidays, during which time all official and most business doors will be closed (see p.63), Senegal also has the following holidays:

National Day April 4 (independence within the Mali Federation declared)
Labour Day May 1
Independence Day June 20
Assumption Aug 15

There's also considerable unofficial disruption to normal hours and services at the time of **Magal** – the annual Mouride pilgrimage to Touba, which falls on the 18th of Safar, 48 days after the Islamic new year – ie around February 27, 2008, February 15, 2009, February 4, 2010, and January 24, 2011. Public transport all over Senegal is severely affected in the days before and after Magal, with many drivers preferring to do pilgrim business only.

As well as the festivals mentioned below, Senegal increasingly has a full calendar of events of all kinds, which means that no matter when you visit, there'll be something going on. And whether you're interested or not, it's always worth remembering the annual **Dakar rally** (ⓦ www.dakar.com), which usually finishes its speedy race from Europe in the capital in February, a week or two after setting off, creating disruption and a run on rooms and other facilities (see p.203).

Music festivals

Like neighbouring Mali, which set a benchmark with its Festival au Désert, Senegal has a growing calendar of **music festivals**. There are several which have achieved calendar status, and one or two which either don't always happen, or happen so rarely as to make it necessary to recommend a big rain check before launching any travel plans around them. **Dak'Art Biennal** falls into the former category (though a hot tip at the time of writing has 9 May to 9 June 2008 as the next event), while the increasingly mythical **Ziguinchor Carnival** falls far into the latter, with the last (and only) sighting apparently in 1979. RIP.

Blues du Fleuve Singer Baaba Maal launched this annual music festival in 2006, in his home town of Podor, with a follow-up in Matam in 2007 (ⓦ www .festivallesbluesdufleuve.com). The line-up is more or less exclusively Senegalese. Recommended.

St-Louis International Jazz Festival Every year, since 1992, this music and culture extravaganza takes over the town in May, often with suitably international jazz stars headlining (ⓦ www .saintlouisjazz.com).

Abéné festival There's often a big party around carnival time in the Casamance seaside village of Abéné. Alnaniking UK may have details (ⓦ www .alnaniking.co.uk).

Kafountine festival Like Abéné, the neighbouring (and larger) beachside village of Kafountine, in northern Casamance, hosts an annual music festival, usually in Feb. Some years it's bigger than Abéné's, and some years smaller.

Traditional festivals

One St-Louis and Gorée institution is the **Fanals** parade, featuring the decorated lanterns (*fanals*) that slaves used to carry in front of wealthy mixed-race women (*signares*) on their way to Christmas Mass. Competition developed between *quartiers* to produce the most elaborate lamp, the rivalry becoming so intense that the events were banned in 1953 after violence between the teams; it wasn't until 1970 that parades were revived in St-Louis. Impressive **pirogue races** also take place from time to time, notably again in St-Louis.

Festivals in the south

In Basse Casamance and in the Bassari country beyond the Niokolo-Koba National Park, a **seasonal cycle of festivals** and ritual events still dominates the cultural sphere, though to a diminishing extent. The events listed below in sequential order are all worth checking out; most take place towards the end of the dry season.

Olugu (March). Jubilant entry of Bassari initiates who underwent Nit the previous year, signifying their re-integration as adults.

Fityay (March–April). Ritual appeasement of the spirit Beliba, supplicated to look after the people of Essil (the region around Enampore) through the dry months.

Nit (end of April). Ritual battle in the Bassari villages of Ebarak, Etiolo and Kote, with masked attacks on boys undergoing initiation.

Ufulung Dyendena (May). Throughout the kingdom of Essil, this ritual propitiation of rain spirits takes place before and after rice planting.

Synaaka (May). "Circumcision" of Jola girls, during which the initiates are instructed in retreat for a week; widespread partying for everyone else.

Zulane (May & June). Festival of the royal priest of Oussouye.

Futampaf (May & June). This initiation of adolescent Jola boys into adulthood, commencing and concluding with major celebrations.

Kunyalen (May & June). Three days of ritual performed to ensure Jola female fertility and the protection of newborn infants.

Ekonkon (June). Traditional dances in Oussouye.

Bukut (June). Initiation ceremony taking place in each Jola village roughly every twenty years.

Wrestling (June & July). In Tionk-Essil, the start of the rains is a traditional time for bouts of *lutte*.

Homebel (Oct). After the rains, wrestling bouts for girls around Oussouye.

Beweng or Epit (Nov & Dec). A two-day harvest festival in Basse Casamance, when the spirits are asked to sanction the transfer of the rice crop to the granaries. Each head of household donates a sheaf.

Ebunay (every two years). A festival in the Oussouye district involving all the women of the village; there are female (*bugureb*) dances in the first week, followed by the enthronement of a ritual priestess.

Crafts and shopping

Senegal doesn't stand out as a country in which to buy **handicrafts**, but you'll find a number of hole-in-the-wall curio shops in Dakar, where some musty old **relics** can be unearthed and argued over. Officially sanctioned *centres artisanals* tend to be touristic setups, where you can see the stuff being made (carved statues and masks, model pirogues, paintings on glass, sand

paintings) but where you might not want to buy it. **Cloth** *pagnes* are generally cheaper than in The Gambia, with Dakar's suburban markets being the best places for a good deal. **Jewellery**, in variety and notably in silver, is usually a good buy. If you'd like to buy superb **tapestry** work, go to Thiès, where you can see some of the best weavers in the world at work (see p.224).

Crime and safety

Be **security-conscious** on first arriving in Dakar (see p.201 for more): this is a city where too many new arrivals are robbed, usually in a snatch-and-run attack. The rest of the country is as safe as anywhere, though you should remain alert in the bigger towns – and you should keep tabs on the situation in Basse Casamance before heading there (see p.246 for more on this).

The **police** are of two main types – machine-gun-toting, brown-uniformed *gendarmes* and blue-togged *agents de police* who operate the occasional countryside road blocks. The latter, though generally not into bothering tourists, will pull you in if you're not carrying any identification, in which case you can be held for 24 hours and fined – this sort of thing happens quite often. If you're out at night and would rather not take your passport, keep a photocopy and another piece of ID with you.

Gender issues and sexual attitudes

Dakar's fairly active **women's movement** is coordinated through the Fédération des Groupements Féminins. Long-standing and continued French influence has been superficially helpful to women in terms of career opportunities. The central issue of institutional female genital mutilation – made illegal in Senegal in 1999 but still performed

Emergencies

Police ☏17; ambulance ☏18; no national fire service number.

in some communities – is being tackled by a pan-African organization who have their headquarters in Dakar, the Commission Internationale pour l'abolition des mutilations sexuelles (CAMS).

The **Wolof** tend to be exceptionally beautiful people, and unafraid of marrying out of their own communities, which tends to strengthen their already dominant position. **Prostitution** has a rather lower profile than, for example, in The Gambia.

Gay attitudes seem relatively relaxed, in Dakar at least: Avenue Georges Pompidou and Ngor beach on the north side of the peninsula are well-known (discreet) cruising areas for *goor-jigeen* (Wolof: "man-woman"). While on the statute book, homosexuality for men and women remains illegal, there is a widespread acceptance of it in Wolof culture, but on condition it remains largely hidden and is not openly expressed.

Entertainment and sport

Unlike a number of countries where organized entertainments can be somewhat inaccessible to outsiders, Senegal has plenty of **spectator sport**, in addition to **theatre** and **cinema** – and Senegalese **music** can come as a revelation after the foreign imports that tend to be heard in some neighbouring countries. Major stadium gigs are held in Dakar, Ziguinchor and elsewhere, and you can find big names playing in Dakar's clubs – the atmosphere is always electric, and tickets aren't expensive. For more on the music scene, see p.187.

Sports

Senegal's "national sport" is Senegambian wrestling, or **la lutte** (see box, p.315), a furious jostling of oiled and charm-laden poseurs trying to get each other down in the dust: it's fun to watch, though best at a small venue. The Casamançais style is less violent than the Wolof brawls.

If anything, **football** (soccer) is even more popular than wrestling, particularly since Senegal thrillingly reached the quarter-finals

of the 2002 World Cup, beating France in the opening game. Everywhere you'll see stickers, posters and T-shirts depicting Senegal's star players, and the locals avidly follow the French league, where most of the team play, on television.

Cinema

Senegal's **film** directors have always struggled for funds and relied heavily on the state despite, in some cases, international critical acclaim. But at least a Senegalese film industry exists. There's a more detailed account on p.190.

Theatre

Theatre doesn't make much impression outside Dakar, where there is a small, active theatre community based around the Senegal National Theatre Company and the institutional Théâtre Daniel Sorano. Foreign cultural centres in Dakar, St-Louis and Ziguinchor may have something worth a look; where appropriate they're listed in the chapter.

Wildlife and national parks

Senegal isn't well endowed with large animals. Until the 1980s there were still elephants along remoter parts of the river in the north, but it now looks like that isolated population has died out. In Niokolo-Koba National Park you can see **western giant elands** and good numbers of **crocodiles** and **hippos**, plus, if you're very lucky, **elephants** and **lions**. There is also an outside chance of seeing **chimpanzees** at the northernmost tip of their range – a small population hangs on here. Senegalese **birdlife** is satisfying and much easier to see: the coast boasts some of the best spots in the world for watching Palearctic winter migrants, in particular the **Langue de Barbarie**, **Oiseaux du Djoudj** and **Delta du Saloum** national parks. For further information contact the Ministry of the Environment and Ecological Protection (BP 4055, Dakar; ☏338 89 02 34 ℉338 32 21 80 ⓦwww.environnement.gouv.sn).

A brief history of Senegal

The earliest real **history of Senegal**, from about 1300 AD, comes from the oral accounts of the aristocracy of the Wolof kingdom of Jolof, in the centre of the country. Jolof fragmented into a number of small Wolof kingdoms which, together with Casamance, had frequent contacts with Portuguese traders after 1500. In 1658, the French settled on an island at the mouth of the Senegal River, which they named St-Louis, after Louis XIV. This account picks up the story from there. For the history of Islam in Senegal, see the section on the Muslim brotherhoods on pp.184–186.

French inroads

By 1659 the trading fort of **St-Louis** was properly established, buying in **slaves** and **gum arabic** – the first a product of upriver raids, the second a valuable extract from acacia trees, used in medicine and textile manufacture.

The permanent French presence at St-Louis stimulated the slave trade to a level at which it began to dominate the Senegal valley's economy, prompting a frenzy of warfare for profit in the region's indigenous states. Wolof rulers (the *damel*) and their warriors (the *ceddo*) were spurred to raid their own peasantry for slaves. In the 1670s a popular jihad by Muslim marabouts, rebelling against this social **cannibalism** of the traditionalist Wolof elite, was suppressed with the help of French soldiers and guns. Henceforth Wolof of all classes found themselves trapped between Islamic reformers and mercenary Europeans.

18th-century St-Louis

Throughout the eighteenth century St-Louis thrived and increasingly absorbed the Wolof people of Walo state, which occupied the area between Richard Toll and the coast. The Wolof had not been converted to Islam: on the contrary, the intermarriage of Wolof women and French Catholics created an exclusive miniature society, to a large extent run by the mixed-race matriarchs known as **signares**.

By the time of the French Revolution, St-Louis had a population of 7000, of whom a large proportion, including the mayor, were *métis* (mixed race). In deference to French blood – and also to post-revolutionary notions of the rights of man – the people of St-Louis and Gorée, the island near Dakar, were accorded most of the privileges of **French citizenship**, including, after 1848, the right to elect a deputy to the National Assembly in Paris – a right later extended to the mainland *communes* of Rufisque and Dakar.

Omar Tall

In the interior, developments were taking place that would shape the future of the modern state. In 1776 a league of **Tukulor marabouts** from north of the Senegal River overthrew the Fula dynasty of Denianke in **Fouta Toro** on the south bank, a region the dynasty had ruled for more than 250 years. They were replaced by a reforming government of Muslim clerics (known as *almamys*) who, with fundamentalist zeal, dispatched warrior-missionaries to spread Islam across the western part of the subcontinent.

The greatest of these expansionists was **Omar Tall**. On his way to Mecca in the 1820s, Tall was initiated into the **Tijaniya brotherhood**, which was founded in Morocco in the late eighteenth century. He was appointed the Tijani chief khalif for the region and travelled extensively, gathering a huge following. By the early 1850s Tall had carved out a vast **empire** centred on **Ségou** in present-day Mali and stretching as far east as Timbuktu, though his ambitions to expand westwards to the coast were soon thwarted by the French.

French conquest

In the 1820s, after the **abolition of slavery**, Governor Baron Roger had tried unsuccessfully to develop agriculture upriver at Richard Toll with a view to French settlement. **Louis Faidherbe**, appointed governor in 1854, saw no mileage in that approach to imperialism. Instead he annexed the Wolof kingdom of **Walo** and brutally subjugated the Mauritanians of Trarza, who had long frustrated French ambitions to control the gum arabic trade. To pay for the military campaigns, the first harvests of **groundnuts** were shipped to French soap and oil factories. In 1857 a deal was struck with the headman of the Lebu village of **Daxar** (Dakar) – which became the administrative capital of French West Africa for the next hundred years – and further settlements were established along the coast at Rufisque and elsewhere. He also strengthened the forts along the river at **Podor**, **Matam** and **Bakel**, which repulsed El Hadj Omar Tall's repeated attacks and provided bases for the French expansion across the Sahel. It was also Faidherbe who founded the **Tirailleurs sénégalais** (West African Infantry), the firepower behind France's "civilizing mission" across West Africa and as far afield as Madagascar.

Omar Tall was killed in 1864, besieged in the Bandiagara escarpment in present-day Dogon country, his Ségou Empire still landlocked. His son **Amadu Sefu** continued his reign.

After Omar Tall's death, **Ma Ba**, a senior disciple, carried on the work of the Tijaniya with a clutch of Soninké (Sarakolé) followers. They led and sponsored jihads against non-Muslim Mandinka along the Gambia River ("**The Soninke-Marabout Wars**"), and also converted most of the Wolof kings to Islam, goading them into individual armed resistance against the French. But a united front of Wolof states proved impossible to achieve. In 1867 Ma Ba died in a battle with the **Serer**-speaking state of Sine, marking a temporary halt in the advance of Islam and leaving the Serer to a different evangelical fate with the Christian missions.

As Wolof leaders were converted, however, pushing their people – or sometimes pushed by them – into accepting Islam, so **conflict with the French** became, with increasing clarity, a conflict between Muslims and infidels. Humiliated by their 1871 defeat in the Franco–Prussian War, the French found new reserves of aggression. And despite the marabouts' powers of mobilization, the French grip on the territory grew tighter every year through the 1880s. The Wolof armies were defeated one by one, and the old authority structures – already weakened by the imposition of Islam – were dismantled as each kingdom was annexed to France.

Wolof capitulation

By now the French were irreversibly committed to making Senegal pay for itself and to administering directly the whole of their West African territory. **Lat Dior**, the ruler of **Kayor**, was ignored when he appealed to the French not to build the Dakar to St-Louis railway through his kingdom, and the line was opened in 1885, despite sabotage by Lat Dior and his *ceddo*. That same year the **Berlin Congress** divided the African spoils among the European powers, splitting Senegal with the creation of The Gambia and formally ratifying France's sovereignty over her possessions. Lat Dior was killed at Dekhlé the following year, and became one of Senegal's folk heroes.

Another Wolof *damel*, **Alboury N'Diaye** (Alboury of Jolof), at first allied himself with the French at St-Louis against Amadu Sefu's Ségou Empire to the east, even undertaking to facilitate the building of the ambitious, and never-completed, railway to Bakel. But, along with his distant cousin Lat Dior, Alboury had been converted to Islam in 1864, and he was secretly in contact with Amadu Sefu. He later became violently opposed to French expansion, allying his kingdom with the Ségou Empire, leading fanatical attacks and trying to expand Ségou even further to the east. His own kingdom, whose capital was **Yang Yang**, was formally annexed by the French in 1889 – the last Wolof kingdom to lose its independence; Ségou itself fell in 1892, and Alboury died in exile in Dosso, Niger, in 1902.

French administration

As everywhere in the early years of Afrique Occidentale Française (**AOF**), the French stressed their **mission civilatrice** – their supposedly peaceful aim of bringing French civilization to black Africa. It was only in Senegal that this was accompanied by any real manifestation of assimilationist ideals, and even here, it was only in the four *communes* that French citizenship was available. Through the rest of Senegal and AOF, most people had the status of *sujet* – subject – and were at the mercy of the hated **indigénat**, or "native justice" code, under which they were ruled by the local *commandant* – the equivalent of a district commissioner – who could impose summary fines and imprisonment. The *indigénat* and a mass of oppressive legislation, including tax provisions, compulsory labour and restrictions on movement, were mostly operated through *chefs de canton* ("district chiefs") nominated by, and answerable to, the *commandant*. The chiefs were frequently corrupt and almost always regarded as collaborators. The only legitimate leadership in the countryside came from the **marabouts** (see p.184).

Blaise Diagne and the marabouts

In marked contrast to the interior, Dakar, Gorée, Rufisque and St-Louis elected a territorial assembly – the **conseil général**, which controlled the budget for the whole of Senegal – and a deputy to the Paris National Assembly. In 1914 **Blaise Diagne**, a customs official from Gorée, became the first black deputy (previous deputies had been mixed race), a post he was to hold until his death in 1934.

The tone of Diagne's career was set early on when he offered to recruit Senegalese soldiers for the French war effort in exchange for legislation guaranteeing the political rights of the black *commune* residents – rights which the colonial administration was keen to erode. Laws were passed confirming that they were full citizens of France. As far as Diagne was concerned, only further **assimilation** could better the lot of Africans. He saw Senegal's fate as inextricably linked to that of France.

Outside the *communes* the Senegalese still had hopes of redemption through their marabouts, but the warrior evangelists of the nineteenth century were gone. In their place, men like **Amadou Bamba** – founder of the Mouride brotherhood – and **Malick Sy** – leader of the biggest Wolof dynasty of the Tijaniya – bought their religious independence by coopting their followers in the colonial process, organizing recruitment drives and providing support to Senegalese politicians in the *communes*. Blaise Diagne's election owed much to support from the Mouride brotherhood, who counted on him to raise his voice on their behalf. The marabouts also encouraged the **cultivation of groundnuts**, a crop that quickly exhausted the soil, was totally dependent on the rains, forced farmers to buy food they would otherwise have grown for themselves and – as groundnut prices fell while others rose – led to falling living standards. In return the marabouts were given the administration's support in their land disputes with Fula cattle-herders. By the end of the 1930s a system of **reciprocal patronage** between marabouts and government was established, and two out of three *sujets* were growing groundnuts.

After Diagne

Diagne was succeeded as deputy by Galandou Diouf, a less-enthusiastic assimilationist. His main rival was **Amadou Lamine Guèye**, Africa's first black lawyer, who came to prominence by demanding the extension of citizenship to the *sujets*. Already elected mayor of St-Louis in 1925, he forged strong links with the French Socialist party and, in 1936, founded the Senegalese branch of the **Section Française de l'Internationale Ouvrière** (SFIO), Africa's first modern political party. When the French Socialists came to power and conceded some limited rights to non-citizens – the right to form trade unions for example – he began organizing among *sujets* in the backcountry towns.

World War II

With the outbreak of **World War II**, political life virtually ceased as the citizens' rights in the *communes* were abrogated, the country was scoured for supplies and the social advances of the prewar government were swiftly negated. The Allies blockaded Vichy-ruled Dakar as Churchill and de Gaulle's **"Operation Menace"** attempted to rally the AOF to the war. Senegal was starved of imports, causing enormous suffering in the groundnut regions. Peasants were forced to switch to subsistence crops, and for the first time were encouraged by the colonial administration to do so.

After two years of Vichy control, the colonial administration turned to the Allies and for the rest of the war the country was an important logistical base for the Free French – though political rights were not restored until 1945. During the Allied occupation, an agricultural campaign – **"Battle for Groundnuts"** – was launched, which extracted more from the country, economically, than Vichy had.

Promises and blunders

The **Brazzaville Conference** of 1944 prepared the ground for major changes in France's relations with its colonies. A fairer deal for Africans, allowing them more administrative involvement, was the main theme, partly in recognition of the part played by them during the war, partly because France's credibility as a great and munificent nation was in question. The underlying aim was the reconstruction of postwar France and the incorporation of all its territories as integral parts of the Republic. The possibility of independence was explicitly ruled out. Yet there was a clear call for "Equal Rights for Equal Sacrifices", a reference to the 200,000 Africans who were recruited to the war, the 100,000 who fought and the 25,000 who died.

Events in Senegal brought citizens and *sujets* closer together. At the end of 1944 at **Camp Thiaroye**, outside Dakar, demobilized West African soldiers just returned from Europe refused to be transported to Bamako without their back pay. When a general was taken hostage, French soldiers were ordered to open fire. Forty Senegalese were killed, many more were injured and a number of survivors sentenced to long jail terms.

Then, in 1945, the **vote for women** was finally won in France, but in the four *communes* only white women were enfranchised, a discrimination that under Blaise Diagne's 1915 guarantee should have been impossible.

Although the women's-vote decision was shortly repealed, both these events sullied relations with France and added fuel to growing demands for radical reforms.

The rise of Senghor

"To speak of independence is to reason with the head on the ground and the feet in the air; it is not to reason at all. It is to advance a false problem."

Léopold Sédar Senghor, Strasbourg, 1950

Early in 1945 a commission was set up to look into ways of organizing a new Constituent Assembly for the French colonies. One of the two black Africans to sit on it was a 38-year-old Senegalese

Catholic, **Léopold Sédar Senghor**, who was chosen because, despite having lived almost continuously in France since 1928, he was the first African to achieve the rank of *agrégé* (the highest teaching qualification), and was in addition a war veteran and a *sujet*. Moreover, he was a Christian Serer rather than a Wolof and had close contacts with the French administration.

In October 1945 **elections** were held to two electoral colleges of the Assembly, one for citizens and one for *sujets*. **Lamine Guèye**, now mayor of Dakar and seen as the most experienced black politician in French West Africa, successfully rallied various political groups to form a popular front and was elected to the first electoral college. **Senghor**, fresh back from France, was easily voted to the second college – even though few Senegalese knew who he was.

Reforms and advances

Though not without hindrance, **reforms** were rapidly pushed through: the *indigénat* was abolished, as was forced labour. Even more significant, Lamine Guèye succeeded in raising the status of all *sujets* to that of citizen.

Senghor meanwhile was emerging from Lamine Guèye's political tutelage within the SFIO, campaigning to extend the role of the peasants in the interior, for increased financial credits and improvements in health and education in the overseas territories, and supporting the 1947–48 **railway workers' strike** for non-racial pay differentials on the Dakar–Bamako line. In 1948 Senghor formed his own party, the **Bloc Démocratique Sénégalais** (BDS), and became leader of an association of African deputies – the Indépendants d'Outre-Mer.

The postwar reforms and the rise to power of the BDS in the early 1950s soon transformed Senegalese **politics**, even if the economy remained heavily dependent on the fickleness of the groundnut harvest. Senghor's party capitalized greatly on its leader's ex-*sujet* status and the credibility this

brought him with the newly politicized peasantry. Senghor also took advantage of maraboutic favour to impress on business interests his influence over the groundnut economy. The **marabouts**, formerly an important behind-the-scenes factor, were becoming political focal points themselves. Lamine Guèye's SFIO meanwhile struggled for support in the urban centres beyond the four *communes* and continued to ignore the countryside, to his party's cost.

The third political grouping, a loose association of **Marxist intellectuals**, trade unionists and students, tended to see the established politicians as too closely wedded to Paris. Their calls for independence were drowned by the clamour for fairer assimilation.

The **Loi Cadre** ("Blueprint Law") of 1956 was a step in both directions. Self-government was instituted for each of the overseas territories. But there was not to be the widely desired **federation** of territories with a capital in Dakar. And defence, higher education and currency would still be issues debated in Paris.

The UPS and the 1958 referendum

Senghor continued to build a power base, drawing his support from the marabouts, the business community and **Mamadou Dia**'s socialist movement. He also attempted to make an alliance with Felix Houphouët-Boigny's Rassemblement Démocratique Africain in Côte d'Ivoire, arguing the need for federation. When this was blocked by Houphouët, the BDS moved left and changed its name to Bloc Populaire Sénégalais, taking with it the **Mouvement autonome de Casamance** – the regional independence movement for Casamance which had grown out of the final "pacification" in the region little more than a decade earlier. Mamadou Dia became prime minister in the new territorial government of 1957 after the defeat of Lamine Guèye's SFIO. His party subsequently merged with the BPS and the

Union Progressiste Sénégalaise (**UPS**) was born.

The UPS was soon split by the coming to power of **de Gaulle** in 1958 and his intransigent offer of either immediate independence and severance from the French Union or continued self-government within the French Union. It was a critical choice and one that Senghor was unwilling to make. Mindful of French economic clout as well as his support among the marabouts and their mistrust of the party left-wing, he ultimately sacrificed a section of young UPS radicals (who immediately formed their own party) and made sure that Senegal's vote to continue the Union was Yes. With this, Lamine Guèye and even Mamadou Dia were in accord. But trade unionists, intellectuals and Casamance separatists were mostly alienated and disappointed at the submission to de Gaulle. Modern Senegalese politics have their roots in the 1958 referendum.

Independence

Senghor still favoured an independent, Dakar-led federation of states. Working with the ex-territory of Soudan (now Mali) and others, the **Mali Federation** was formed to further this end. However, by the time it was constituted in April 1959, the federation's members were reduced to Mali and Senegal – an unworkable alliance given the influence of Dakar. But it was pursued nonetheless.

Lamine Guèye was now elected president of the new territorial assembly, Modibo Keita of Mali president of the Federal Government and Mamadou Dia vice-president. In September, inspired by Guinea's secession, the Mali Federation lobbied France for independence. In a *volte-face* that amazed most observers, de Gaulle conceded that total independence should not, after all, deny a country the right to remain within the French Union. On April 4, 1960 (now National Day), the principle of independence for the Mali Federation was declared, and on June 20, 1960, **independence** was proclaimed.

On August 20, 1960, the Mali Federation suddenly broke down over the election of a president. The Senegalese had insisted on Senghor for this role, having begun to distrust Bamako's rigorous Marxist policies. Senegal proclaimed its **independence from Mali** the same day, arresting Modibo Keita and sending him back to Bamako in a sealed train wagon. Mali refused to recognize the new **Republic of Senegal** and for three years the Dakar–Bamako railway was unused. To this day there remains a degree of rivalry between the two countries, especially in matters of football and music.

Senghor as president

Senghor took the presidency of the new republic, keeping Mamadou Dia as his prime minister. Senghor's formulation of **négritude**, Senegal's nationalism, was blended with his motto: "*Assimiler, pas être assimilés*", urging Africans to assimilate European culture, not be assimilated by it. On this foundation, Senghor and the UPS built the ideology of **African socialism**, which amounted to a tacit defence of the status quo in its emphasis on consensus. Dia, whose own politics remained to the left of Senghor's, failed to find a balance between the business community and the radical left, and succeeded only in irritating the French. In 1962, Senghor had him arrested (he was sentenced to life imprisonment after an alleged coup attempt in which the army came to Senghor's rescue), and relations with France began to prosper.

The one-party state

The rest of the decade saw the government growing increasingly right-wing. In 1963 a **revised constitution** was approved, strengthening the role of the president and effectively forcing radical opposition underground. **Cheikh Anta Diop**'s Bloc des Masses Sénégalaises (BMS), the most powerful group the opposition could legally muster, was smashed by a massive and disputed UPS victory in the elections of that year. **Riots** in the aftermath of the elections were put down by troops, with many deaths – the first serious smear on Senegal's hitherto spotless reputation. The BMS was banned and the remaining opposition had by 1966 been forced into the UPS or harassed out of existence.

Farmers were badly hit by the abolition of French subsidies for groundnut prices in 1967, while most town dwellers were no better off than they had been before independence. In May 1968 **trade unionists** and **students protested** at the government's complacency, confronting it with the charge of neo-imperialism. Senghor confronted the protesters with the army. Further strikes were followed by some concessions, then the government tried to force the unions into its own muzzled national confederation of workers.

Repeated crises slackened at the end of the decade when Senghor revived the post of prime minister – given to Abdou Diouf in 1970. After further university unrest in 1973, Senghor banned the teachers' union and jailed some of the activists. The party was renamed the **Parti Socialiste** (PS), a cosmetic alteration that convinced few.

Democratic reforms

In 1974, a cautious new liberalism was initiated with the release of ex-PM Mamadou Dia from twelve years in detention. Soon after, the **Parti Démocratique Sénégalais** (PDS), led by lawyer **Maître Abdoulaye Wade**, was allowed to register, and by 1976 various brands of liberal and social democracy were on offer, as well as a legal Marxist-Leninist party, which attracted a small number of radicals. A flood of political handouts and newssheets hit the streets. Anta Diop and Mamadou Dia were banned from forming parties, but not excluded from discussion.

By 1978, Senghor – now in his late 60s – was spending more time on poetry and the Académie française than running Senegal, and he began to groom

Abdou Diouf, now vice-president, for leadership. Diouf was already taking responsibility for executive decisions and his status grew as he gained support from the major aid institutions for his austere management of the economy.

A sideshow in the late 1970s was the **militant Tijaniya dynasty** of Ahmet Khalif Niasse. Niasse went into exile in Libya allegedly intending to organize for an Islamic state in Senegal, which led to the cutting of diplomatic relations. The Libyan connection resurfaced across the border in The Gambia, where the "coup attempt" of October 1980 reportedly had the same roots. President Jawara invoked the two countries' historic relationship, and Senegalese troops were sent in.

Diouf in power

Senghor, the first African president to retire voluntarily, passed the presidency to Diouf on January 1, 1981. At first it was feared that Diouf's uncharismatic style would be insufficient to carry him, but **opposition groups** were hopeful he would lift remaining restrictions on political activities. Their hopes were soon fulfilled: Cheikh Anta Diop's Rassemblement National Démocratique (RND) was legalized, and Dia founded the Mouvement Démocratique Populaire (MDP). Wade's PDS relinquished its role as the focal point of opposition and actually lost a few members in a purge of pro-Libyan sympathizers.

Diouf increased his popularity by launching an **anti-corruption drive** focusing on his own cabinet and by firing Senghor's "barons". And traditional supporters of the government – the moderate Muslim masses – were gratified to have a president at last who spoke Wolof as his mother tongue and peppered his speeches with Koranic references.

The July 1981 coup in **The Gambia** served as the most severe test of Diouf's nerve in his first year in office. President Jawara called him from London to ask

Senegal to restore him to power, which the Senegalese army accomplished with considerable bloodshed. A Senegalese detachment stayed in The Gambia until the late 1980s. The spectre of an unfriendly and destabilizing power taking control in The Gambia galvanized Diouf to do something about the dormant **Senegambia confederation** (see p.279). In December 1981 an agreement was ratified and a Senegambian parliament met for its first session in 1983. The Gambia, with no army and little to offer Senegal except a headache and its river, was always going to be the passive partner in a relationship that finally collapsed in 1989.

The Senegalese **economy**, meanwhile, continued to decline. Although the state groundnut-buying monopoly was dissolved in 1980 after years of corruption and inefficiency, low prices and disastrous harvests that year and in 1984 meant no perceptible improvement for peasant farmers. **Fishing** was pushed into first place as a foreign-exchange earner, with **tourism** second and groundnuts third.

The **1988 election** saw the first display of really serious political and social unrest during Diouf's presidency: an ominously quiet polling day was followed by violent riots in Dakar. Diouf declared a **state of emergency**; tanks and tear gas came onto the streets; a dusk-to-dawn curfew was in force for three weeks; and Abdoulaye Wade, who claimed to have been defeated by a rigged poll, was arrested. His trial and conviction on charges of incitement to subvert the state triggered further unrest, which was later quelled by his own, characteristically conciliatory, remarks.

Diouf, however, later banished any inference of a pact between him and Wade and set about making **changes to the electoral system**, ostensibly to guarantee fairer elections. In practice these adjustments delayed local elections and enraged Wade and the main opposition alliance, **Sopi** ("Change"), who accused Diouf of perpetuating the distortion of the democratic process by vested interests and vote buying.

Even the intense dissatisfaction with the political scene was overshadowed during the **Senegal–Mauritania crisis** of April 1989 to October 1990. Triggered by a land dispute on the border, local fighting flared into racial conflict as Mauritanian shopkeepers (the 300,000-strong mainstay of Senegal's retail trade) were hounded out of Senegal, hundreds killed and their stores looted. An international operation assisted refugees to return to Nouakchott, while Senegalese immigrants in Mauritania (who were even more violently and systematically attacked) returned to Senegal. Tens of thousands of Fula-speaking Mauritanians ("southerners" in Mauritanian parlance) also came – the Nouakchott government had taken the opportunity to expel them at the same time. The borders between the two countries closed, and a cloud of deep mutual mistrust hung over the two governments through much of the next decade.

The 1990s

On the political front, the dominant theme of the 1990s – viewed from Dakar, at least, if not from Ziguinchor – was a low-level, grumbling discontent with the inertia of the Parti Socialiste, which several times boiled up into riots.

Like those of 1988, the **elections of February 1993** were again the subject of condemnation by Abdoulaye Wade over alleged photocopied registration papers, multiple voting and other ploys. In the presidential ballot Diouf won overall, though Wade came out in front in the main urban areas of Dakar and Thiès. Three months later in the National Assembly elections, Wade's PDS obtained less than a quarter of the seats while the PS won more than two-thirds on a turnout of well under half the electorate. Wade claimed that if the election had been conducted fairly, the PDS would have been in the lead. Days after announcing the results the vice-chief of the electoral commission, **Babacar Sèye**, was assassinated. The perpetrators remain unknown (a previously unheard-of "Armée du Peuple" claimed responsibility) but it was Abdoulaye Wade and three associates who were arrested without charge. One of them, **Mody Sy**, was kept in jail for more than a year.

The **devaluation of the CFA franc** in February 1994 – supported by Diouf, and partly engineered by him – was particularly hard on the poor. Later that year, in a mass rally for democracy in Dakar, led by the **Tijaniya brotherhood**'s fundamentalist-leaning youth organization Daira al Moustarchidines wal Moustarchidates, militant protestors precipitated a riot and then rounded on the security forces, killing six policemen in a frenzied attack.

Wade and six senior opposition figures on the march were among a group of 177 people arrested for incitement to violence, though most were eventually released. As a result, a new opposition alliance, Bokk Sopi Sénégal ("Uniting to Change Senegal"), was formed in

The Casamance conflict

The reawakening of separatist feeling in Casamance was signalled by sporadic **demonstrations** there throughout the 1980s, often put down at a cost of many lives and with hundreds in detention. In 1990, serious armed conflict erupted as the military wing of the **Mouvement des Forces Démocratiques de la Casamance** (MFDC) went into action. By 1993, in advance of the presidential and legislative elections (boycotted by the MFDC), there were five thousand troops in Casamance and the region was under military control. That year saw a ceasefire agreement and the release of many prisoners by the government, but hostilities flared up again in the southern districts at the end of 1994. Despite the establishment of a **Commission Nationale de Paix**, the army and air force retaliated with bombing raids and manhunts through the forest, in a sporadic, tit-for-tat war which has continued ever since.

The MFDC claim that Casamance existed as a separate territory before the French colonial era, and a large part of the movement's membership wants independence from Senegal. The MFDC is split loosely into the Front Nord, based to the north of Baila and Bignona, and the more extreme Front Sud, focused on the villages along the Guinea-Bissau border. The MFDC was led by **Abbé Augustine Diamacouné Senghor** until his death in January 2007, though during the decade prior to his death his influence had waned as the movement disintegrated into various factions.

The violence in Casamance severely damaged the **Cap Skiring tourist industry** throughout the 80s and 90s, but ordinary villagers suffered the most as the MFDC guerillas abandoned their original aims. By the late 1990s banditry and control of the lucrative local **cannabis** crop were more important to most fighters in the bush than political principles. The MFDC began to turn on itself and retired or disenchanted guerillas were murdered by active units. Despite pleas from Diamacouné Senghor to desist, **mines** (smuggled in from Guinea-Bissau) were laid on minor roads and farm tracks, particularly between Ziguinchor and Cap Skiring, killing and maiming hundreds. Amnesty International accused both sides of terrorizing local people.

Hopes of a peaceful resolution to the conflict rose when President Wade came to power and launched negotiations in December 2000 with most of the MFDC faction leaders. Peace agreements signed in 2001 and 2004 – in which the MFDC modified its position – were intended to end the separatist struggle. Former rebels and MFDC dissidents were responsible for fighting in 2006, which, along with the MFDC's internal divisions, undermined the credibility of the agreements. Sporadic conflict escalated once again in the region following the 2007 elections, with several deaths attributed to land mines, rebel attacks and shootings. At the time of writing, there were still occasional reports of highway banditry along the borders, while the interior of the Casamance region itself appeared largely secure.

September 1994 from Wade's PDS, **Landing Savané**'s communist And-Jëf–Parti Africaine pour la Démocratie et le Socialisme (AJ–PADS) and Mamadou Dia's Mouvement pour le Socialisme et l'Unité (MSU).

Despite their opposition status, in 1995 Wade and six PDS colleagues took **cabinet posts** in the national government on the invitation of Abdou Diouf – the better for Diouf to deal with the charismatic and outspoken Wade behind closed doors than across the barricades. This was not the first time that Wade had accepted a cabinet post, and his credentials as a man of the people – resigning from government to campaign against Diouf at each election, then returning to the cabinet on Diouf's invitation after losing the poll – looked to be wearing thin.

In February 1998, the PS again won a resounding victory in National Assembly elections, but there were signs that the party was running into trouble. Divisions started to emerge in late 1997, when **Djibo Laity Ka** and other senior figures within the party formed a breakaway faction called the Mouvement pour le Renouveau Démocratique (MRD); Ka was suspended from the party and a few months later he resigned, denouncing the PS for corruption and electoral fraud. In 1999, **Moustapha Niasse**, a former foreign minister, also broke ranks, criticizing Diouf and announcing his candidature for the 2000 presidential election; he was promptly expelled from the PS and formed his own party, the Alliance des Forces de Progrès (AFP).

The opposition, meanwhile, was also busy manoeuvring for another attempt to dislodge Diouf. After once again resigning from government in 1998, Wade was nominated in March 1999 by a left-wing alliance of opposition parties to be their joint presidential candidate.

The 2000 presidential election

As the 2000 presidential election approached, tensions were running high in Senegal, and the country seemed ripe for change. Young people in particular mobilized during the election campaign to work against Diouf, with students going on strike and returning to the regions to tell their elders how much they were struggling under PS rule. On election day, the talk on the streets was of possible civil war if the PS tried to rig the vote or Diouf somehow managed to win.

In the event, Diouf – with 41.3 percent of the vote – failed to win an overall majority, resulting in a **second-round vote** with the second-placed Wade (31 percent). A large part of the PS vote had gone to Niasse, who now threw his weight behind Wade. Already supported by prominent left-wingers such as **Landing Savané** and influential members of the **Mouride brotherhood**, Wade went on to gain a substantial victory, garnering 58.5 percent of the second-round vote. Both the election itself, which was described as free, fair and transparent by international observers, and Diouf's gracious acceptance of defeat, enhanced Senegal's reputation as one of Africa's more stable democracies.

The Wade era

Following his victory, Wade set about consolidating his position. Having rewarded Niasse for his support by making him prime minister, Wade went on to dismiss him in March 2001 and replaced him with the lower-profile **Mame Madior Boye**, Senegal's first female prime minister. Wade's mandate was strengthened further when his PDS-led **Sopi coalition** won a landslide victory in the April 2001 **parliamentary elections**.

Wade started his presidency positively, reaffirming his commitment to democracy by pushing through a revised constitution in January 2001, which reduced the presidential term of office from seven to five years and transferring some of the president's powers to the prime minister. He cut an

"Barça ou barsax" – Spain's hellish allure

One of the biggest issues in Senegal today is not taking place at home: "To Barcelona or to hell" is a common Wolof expression that has become emblematic of the record numbers of Senegalese fleeing to Europe. Many of these attempts take place in rickety wooden fishing boats that regularly capsize or sink – drowning dozens of migrants – before they reach the Canary Islands. Despite the bodies washing up regularly on Spanish shores, the numbers attempting the passage have surged. In 2006, more than 30,000 illegal migrants set off, an estimated 6000 of whom died or went missing – a six-fold increase on 2005. In 2007 the numbers were expected to double again to 60,000 migrants and possibly more than 10,000 lost.

For many Senegalese families, shipping a son off to Europe by sea is seen as an opportunity to obtain foreign currency for the family back home, as often for economic advancement as from salvation from abject poverty.

Senegal receives EU support to buy equipment to monitor vessels that might be trafficking migrants. In 2006, a pan-European maritime surveillance force, Frontex, was created to help reduce the number of migrant boats making it into international waters. But the organization has so far only been able to stage small-scale patrols off the coast of West Africa. Moreover, human-rights groups fear that such measures will only result in more deaths, as desperate migrants leave under more dire conditions and attempt to avoid surveillance by making longer, more perilous journeys.

Most recently, Spanish businesses have launched government-approved programmes engaging directly with Senegal to hire workers for European jobs in the fishing, construction and hospitality industries. With more than €25million in development aid, Spain has created job centres in several African countries to filter potential emigrants, ultimately providing a path toward legal immigration in Europe. The initiative is also intended to rid West Africa of people-traffickers.

In an era of conservative immigration policies, in which European countries such as France have adopted less integrationist measures such as offering money to migrant families to return home, Spain's efforts have had some very positive benefits. It remains to be seen whether the model will encourage other European countries to think more liberally about accepting migrants – ultimately necessary if any marked dent is to be made on illegal immigration.

---

impressive figure on the international stage, leading Africa's response to the **September 11 attacks** on America by calling for an African "pact against terrorism". A couple of months later, in December 2001, Wade led Senegal in mourning the death of its first president, Léopold Senghor.

Prospects and threats

Ironically, the wave of hope that first swept Wade to power has turned out to be his biggest problem, as he and his government struggle to meet voters' unrealistically high expectations. At the start of the new century, Senegal's industry was in steep decline, relying heavily on imported raw materials; agricultural diversification was still needed; education was a shambles after years of class boycotts and strikes; and society was increasingly divided between employees of the state – the state pays ten times the national average – and those who have to rely for their income on the private sector or the informal and subsistence economy. Since coming to power, Wade has declared his commitment to liberalizing the economy, clamping down on **corruption** and developing **infrastructure**. But progress has been frustratingly slow, and as the role of the public sector has declined in line with Wade's reform programme, so **unemployment** has grown. The **Casamance** conflict has rumbled on (see box, p.180), despite Wade's promise to find a rapid solution when he took office.

The country's mood was further hit by the **sinking** of the MV *Joola* in 2002, which led to Wade sacking the whole cabinet, including Mame Madior Boye, whom he replaced with his close aide and PDS stalwart **Idrissa Seck**. But within two years, Seck, long considered the presidential heir apparent, had been accused of siphoning millions of dollars from government's coffers. He was removed from office in April 2004 and imprisoned for nearly seven months. Although eventually cleared of the charges for lack of evidence, his fall from grace and alienation from Wade, despite reconciliation attempts, did nothing to bolster the president's standing.

In the February 2007 presidential elections, despite angry opposition denunciations of Wade's new voting district demarcations, a slew of poll boycotts and a call to cancel the vote, Seck and more than a dozen other contenders were defeated by Wade, securing him a **second term** as president – at the age of 80. His longevity has won him the moniker *Gorgui*, an affectionate Wolof term of respect for elders, and one he made liberal use of in his campaign advertisements. In June 2007, after dissolving his cabinet after elections to the legislative assembly, Wade announced the installation of **Cheikh Hadjibou Soumaré**, a former budget minister,

as prime minister. Both will serve until 2012, provided Wade maintains his good health.

So far, Wade's rule has not been entirely smooth sailing: many Senegalese are preoccupied with the **cost of living** and particularly the high cost of health care. Despite budget pressures, the government is committed to several large-scale projects intended to accelerate modernization, including a new international airport for Dakar, a new toll autoroute between Thiès and Dakar and improvements to Dakar's port.

Whatever anyone might say about Wade's victory, the election itself was a victory for **voter turnout**. More than 75 percent of eligible voters (nearly 3.5 million) came out to cast their ballots – a record for Senegal and a benchmark for West Africa.

These days, the Senegalese have become highly politicized; many voters who boycotted the 2007 legislative elections did so as a mark of **discontent with Wade**. Voters are deeply sceptical of his motives in building a new airport and trying to move the capital to Lompoul, between Dakar and St-Louis. But the mood of cynicism in some quarters also arises from a belief in the rightness of political accountability that has rarely been evident in West Africa. Many see that in itself as a sign of a healthy democracy.

The Muslim brotherhoods

Ligey si top, yala la bok
"Work is part of religion"

Amadou Bamba, founder of Mouridism

Any real insight into modern Senegal requires an understanding of the country's extraordinarily influential **Muslim brotherhoods**. You won't stay here long without noticing – in the names on the bush taxis, the signs on the village shops and the flocks of multicoloured disciples – that something very unusual lies in the dusty heart of Senegalese society.

Origins

The Muslim **brotherhoods** are in conflict with original, Arabian, Islam, which says everyone has a direct relationship with God. They resulted from the religion's spread to the Berber peoples of northwest Africa, the brotherhoods flourishing in these class-based societies where it was natural to think that certain men should be gifted with divine insight, able to perform miracles and bestow blessings.

One of the earliest dynasties of Moroccan Muslims to make permanent contact with the people south of the desert was the **Almoravid** (whence marabout: holy leader/saint) who, in the twelfth century, made conversions in the kingdom of **Tekrur** in northeast Senegal. In the fifteenth century, the **Qadiriya** brotherhood was introduced south of the Sahara and, by the end of the eighteenth century, was firmly based near Timbuktu. Stressing **charity**, **humility** and **piety**, Qadirism made no exclusive demands of its followers and recruited from all ethnic groups. A local Qadiri offshoot, the **Layen** brotherhood, was founded in the late nineteenth century as an exclusively Lebu-speaking order in the Cap Vert district near Dakar.

Another order, the **Tijaniya**, crossed the desert early in the nineteenth century and was spread over Senegal by the proselytizing warlord Omar Tall. Tijaniya laid less stress on humility than earlier orders. Indeed, its Moroccan founder Al-Tijani had claimed direct contact with the Prophet Muhammad and, as a consequence, his followers were forbidden allegiance to any other orders. The brotherhood rapidly recruited the mass of Tukulor-speakers in northeast Senegal. Tukulor marabouts – notably the forefathers of the hugely influential **Sy** and **Mbacke** families – were largely responsible for the later conversion of the Wolof.

Marabouts and the French

The interplay between the brotherhoods and the French was complicated. Allegiances often cut through ties of birth and language, so that, typically, peasants found themselves in alliance with the marabouts against their own, traditional rulers who tended to conspire with the French. Moreover, "pacification" by the French often resulted in more fertile ground for the spread of Islam.

By the early 1900s, with the conversion to Islam of even the most resistant traditional rulers, a new establishment of **vested interests** had been founded, uniting the French and the marabouts. Although the Tijaniya traditionally had a core of fundamentalist, anti-French sentiment, the order soon adjusted to the material realities of colonialism. The latest and greatest brotherhood, the **Mouridiya** – exclusively rural and Senegalese – came, in practice, to be a bastion of the status quo.

Mouridism

The Mouridiya was founded in 1887 by **Amadou Bamba**, nephew of the Wolof king Lat Dior, and a member of the influential Mbacke family. An offshoot of the Qadiriya brotherhood, Mouridiya initially attracted many former anti-colonial fighters inspired by its discipline and dynamism, and by the charisma of Bamba.

Rumours of an armed insurrection from his court at Touba terrified the French ("We cannot tolerate a state within a state") and Bamba was twice exiled by the authorities – though these banishments served only to increase his standing at home. Mouride folk history places great emphasis on Bamba's anti-colonial credentials, but soon after his return to Senegal in 1907 (a return celebrated in the annual Magal pilgrimage), he was striking deals with the authorities and trusting in the slow wheels of political reform. He was also amassing a personal fortune.

One of Bamba's early disciples, **Ibra Fall**, though not a gifted Koranic student, was devoted to the marabout. Bamba gave him an axe and told him to work for God with that. Sheikh Ibra Fall went on to found the fanatically slavish **Baye Fall**. Today, these dread-locked devotees in patchwork robes have their own khalif but are exempt from study and even from fasting at Ramadan.

The founding of Baye Fall signalled a radical shift in religious thought, making **labour** a virtue and bringing Mouridism into the very heart of contemporary life. Among Mourides (whose name means "the hopeful") there's a universal belief that hard work is the key to paradise. Bamba is credited with announcing "If you work for me I shall pray for you" and even the five daily prayers are seen as less important than toiling in the groundnut fields. The colonial authorities and the Mouride marabouts (mostly from wealthy, landed families) soon found areas of agreement.

The brotherhoods today

With a few exceptions, the brotherhoods have rooted firmly in the safest political ground. The government, while insisting that the state and political processes are strictly secular, lavishes publicity and patronage on the marabouts for delivering votes. In 1968 the chief khalif instructed Mouride university students to disobey the strike call, and for the next thirty years, **presidential elections** were heavily influenced by the usual maraboutic injunctions. It has long been an irony of Senegalese politics – and frustrating for the country's liberal movers and shakers – that Senegal, with its highly developed democratic structures, should find true democracy repeatedly brushed aside by the mass of its people in exchange for the grace of God.

Cooperation between the government and the brotherhoods has survived the transfer of power from the long-ruling Parti Socialiste to Wade and his Sopi coalition (the Mouride brotherhood's endorsement of Wade was vital in helping him win). As the country enjoys its fifth decade of independence, there are few signs of the link between politics and the brotherhoods breaking down. Yet the relationship remains one of latent mistrust, and even if many of those involved profit through it, the potential for a reactionary and anti-secular revolt against the government has always been there, as the Mouride brotherhood is conservative and rigorously hierarchical.

Economically, the Mouride connection with groundnuts remains, on the whole, solid, with the religious elite supported by the harvest and the boundless offerings of their followers. Many senior and middle-ranking Mouride disciples today form a **new business class**. Even French-educated businessmen would rather become disciples of respected marabouts than short-cut the system. Over a dozen Mourides are multibillionaires in CFA francs (worth up to £100 million/$200 million) and Lebanese entrepreneurs find that business is increasingly out of their hands.

Smuggling has been profitable too, not least in the Mouride capital **Touba** itself, where the absence of government agents brought racketeering on a grand scale. All the hardware of Western consumerism, and even alcohol and arms, was widely available until the chief khalif, under pressure from Dakar, admitted that Mouridism was in danger of losing its soul, and allowed *gendarmes* into the holy city. The black market is clandestine again, but still funnels huge quantities of money and goods between Senegal and The Gambia.

The **Magal** pilgrimage to Touba has become the traditional occasion when the president reiterates his support for the Mourides and his appreciation of the benefits they have brought Senegal. In turn, the chief khalif is expected to emphasize to his millions of followers the sanctity of the groundnut harvest, the importance of not rocking the boat and their duty to support stable government. The implicit message is that a vote against the government would be a vote against the khalif, and therefore against God. The Tijaniya **Gamou** gatherings, in Tivaouane and Kaolack, are smaller-scale versions of the Magal, and similar back-slapping is the order of the day.

The **succession** to the position of chief khalif is a time of crisis in every brotherhood, since the relationship between the voters and the elected government hangs very heavily on the words of the marabouts. The current Mouride chief khalif, **Serigne Saliou Mbacke**, is considered to be less interested in worldly matters than his predecessor, and therefore less likely to throw his weight behind political campaigning.

Since the death of the last Tijaniya chief khalif, Abdoul Aziz Sy, in 1997, there have been dynastic quarrels within that brotherhood, and the current elderly Tijaniya chief khalif, **Serigne Mansour Sy**, born in 1916, also has a reputation for independent thinking. These facts have worried successive governments, concerned as they are about the potential for a rise of **fundamentalism** in Senegal.

The issue of fundamentalism is further complicated by the fact that Mourides form a majority of the Senegalese **diaspora** abroad. Mourides comprise, for example, eighty percent of the street peddlers who sell fake designer bags and sunglasses in Italy – living followers of Bamba's teachings on self-reliance. These Mouride confrères, many of whom go to Senegal at least annually, are steadily gaining influence economically through their remittances, although politically they are something of an unknown quantity. Once the current Mouride chief khalif dies, he is due to be succeeded by Amadou Bamba's oldest grandson. There is much talk in Touba, however, of a **change** from the Mbacke being good for the brotherhood. And talk of change worries Dakar.

Music

While traditional **griots** are less and less to be seen, many Senegalese musicians are internationally known. **Youssou N'Dour** is the biggest star, but he's just one of many.

Folk music

Senegalese **folk music** is heavily influenced by the traditions of the Mande heartland to the east. You're most likely to hear Wolof, Fula, Tukulor (Toucouleur) and Serer music in the north and Mandinka, Jola and Balante music in Casamance.

In the south, listen out for the huge double-xylophones or **balo** of the **Balante**, played by two people facing each other. You may hear them, but you'll have difficulty seeing them, because they're invariably surrounded by a jostle of whooping and clapping women.

The best-known **drums** are the Wolof **tama** and **sabar** (both used to great effect by Youssou N'Dour and his band). Drums of all shapes and sizes are in great abundance in Senegal and are, traditionally, the only instruments that can be played by absolutely anyone. Wrestling matches offer fine opportunities to hear some first-class drumming – in snatches. The wrestlers bring their own drummers to support them and the drum teams jog and pace around the arena, competing with each other with cacophonous dedication.

Modern music

The **modern music** scene in Senegal has been dominated for many years by **mbalax**, the sound of which is all-pervasive in the country. Mbalax grew up as a melding of traditional rhythms and griot praise-singing with the harmonies and syncopated drumming of Afro-Cuban music that made its way back to Africa from the 1950s onwards. By the time the tinny, rhythmic guitar and resounding saxophone were added, this music had come to define the sound of Senegal. The genre has been shaped and contoured by no-one more than the singer **Youssou N'Dour**, with his soaring voice, backed by his band, **Super Étoile de Dakar**. Youssou's *mbalax* features frenetic rhythms with bursts of *tama* (battered by **Assane Thiam**) and complex time signatures.

Of the many other superb musicians around, **Baaba Maal**, a conservatoire-trained Tukulor singer from Podor, is also internationally renowned.

In recent years, homegrown **hip-hop**, largely in Wolof but with quips in French and English, has been a huge phenomenon in Senegal and is growing abroad, especially in France. **Positive Black Soul** was the first group to break internationally, and helped inspire a generation of new rappers, including Dakar-based **Daara J**, **Pee Froiss**, **Pacotille**, **BMG44** and **Didier Awadi** – himself a former member of Positive Black Soul.

In addition to the many purely African groups, US-born, Senegal-raised **Akon** has achieved international acclaim, as has the Senegalese–French rapper **MC Solaar**.

Compilations

Streets of Dakar – Génération Boul Falé (Stern's). Gutsy, invigorating overview, showcasing a wealth of artists, from the earthy neo-traditional sounds of Fatou Guewel and Gambian *kora* duo Tata and Salaam to rap and super-charged nouveau *mbalax* from Assane Ndiaye and Lemzo Diamono.

The Rough Guide to the Music of Senegal and The Gambia (World Music Network). Features hits by Youssou and Cheikh Lô, as well as interesting songs by lesser-known artists.

The Rough Guide to Youssou N'Dour and Etoile de Dakar

(World Music Network). Some of the strongest *mbalax* material by Youssou and his band.

Youssou N'Dour

Youssou is one of the outstanding African music stars of his generation, yet at home in Dakar he still plays regularly at his club, *Thiossane*. His huge body of work is varied and fascinating, continually reworked to cater to the separate demands of his markets at home, in France and in the English-speaking world. *Time* magazine called him one of the world's hundred most influential people and many in Senegal see him as a potential future presidential candidate.

Alsaama Day (Jololi). N'Dour's best album of recent years, released in Senegal in 2007, is the first in a long while with entirely new, original songs. Hit song "Borom Gaal" is a salsa-esque inspirational piece about emigration to Europe, sung with members of Orchestra Baobab.

Egypt (Nonesuch). Recorded with Cairo's Fathy Salama Orchestra, the result is an innovative collection of griot praise and Arabesque devotional songs, supported by flowing flutes and violins against *kora* and *balafon*.

Etoile de Dakar vols 1–4 (Stern's). The collected works of one of Senegal's seminal bands, featuring Youssou N'Dour. Near essential.

Immigrés (Earthworks). An homage to Senegalese migrant workers, this mid-period cassette, lovingly remastered for CD, has great warmth and an unusually open-ended feel.

The Guide (Sony/Columbia). Probably Youssou's most successful attempt at big-budget *mbalax*, and containing many moods, not all of them very certain. Some cringed from "7 Seconds" (with Neneh Cherry), but the single certainly found an audience.

Baaba Maal

One of the biggest stars of Senegalese music, **Baaba Maal** sings in the Tukulor dialect of Fula, accompanied by guitarist Mansour Seck and electric band Dande Lenol (whose name means "Voice of the People"). His last album was *Missing You* (2001), but a new one is on the way.

Baayo (Mango). Maal's first major international release was a breakthrough for traditional Senegalese music abroad, and features Maal's haunting cries over pulsating acoustic rhythms.

Djam Leelii (Palm Pictures). Playing acoustic guitar and singing with childhood friend Mansour Seck, Baaba Maal interprets the traditional tunes and themes of his Senegal River region homeland. Music to be transported by.

Firin' in Fouta (Mango). An exciting slab of Afro-modernism. British producer Simon Emmerson got a Grammy nomination for this meeting of Celtic resonances, salsa horn-men and Wolof ragga-merchants.

Lam Toro (Mango). One of the most personal of all Maal's albums, dedicated to his mother who died young but who remains the guiding spirit in all his art.

Missing You (Mi Yeewnii) (Palm Pictures). Recorded at one of Maal's homes, this richly atmospheric album adds influences from Mali and southern Senegal to his usual style.

Daby Baldé

A Fula from Kolda, in the Haute Casamance region of Fouladou, Daby Baldé has the potential to follow in Baaba Maal's footsteps.

Introducing Daby Baldé (World Music Network). Finely arranged, lilting songs, supported by flute, fiddle, *kora* and accordion, from a musician celebrated locally but still little-known further afield.

Orchestra Baobab

Formed in 1971 by saxophonist Issi Cissokho and vocalist Laye M'Boup,

Baobab were one of the first groups to use Wolof and Mandinka songs as the basis for electric music. The band broke up in 1982 but returned triumphantly twenty years later. They still perform regularly in Dakar – most often at the club *Just 4U*. If you find any old Baobab tapes, buy them; you won't be disappointed.

Made in Dakar (World Circuit). Their latest album, recorded at Youssou N'Dour's *Xippi* studios. Superb production of songs new and old.

A Night at Club Baobab (Oriki/Discovery). Wonderful 1970s dance set reissued in 2006, with a variety of Afro-Cuban numbers.

Pirate's Choice (World Circuit). Blissfully good, 1982 set from the best Senegalese band of the 1970s. The *On Verra Ça* collection (also World Circuit) is almost as hot.

Specialist in All Styles (World Circuit, UK; Nonesuch, US). Old hits are reinvented and new songs introduced on Baobab's inspirational comeback album, featuring guest vocals from co-producer Youssou N'Dour.

Super Diamono de Dakar

The "people's band" of Dakar's proletarian suburbs, **Super Diamono** mixed reggae militancy, jazz cool and hardcore traditional grooves into the *mbalax* stew. Their influential early incarnations await some enterprising archivist: try to hear the early album, *Ndaxona*, which features the wailing vocals of Omar Pene.

Fari (Stern's). Two cassettes of material on one CD from the early 1990s when main man Pene had reformed the band with top Dakar session men. A bit smooth for some tastes, but the overall feel is deeply Senegalese.

Cheikh Lô

A member of the Baye Fall (the dreadlocked guardians of Touba) and a sometime drummer with the band Xalam, Lô had to wait years before finally emerging from Youssou's local studio.

Lamp Fall (World Circuit). Released in 2005, this rich, layered album is filled with rhythmic tension, a strong jazz and funk feel, and a variety of influences from Congo, Guinea and Brazil. Produced by Nick Gold, who recorded *Buena Vista Social Club*.

Ne la Thiass (World Circuit, UK). Strong songs and a warm organic feel with real international appeal. Deservedly a huge hit.

Ismael Lô

Harmonica-player and guitarist, **Ismael Lô** was an early member of Super Diamono in the late 1970s. "The manager asked if I wanted to join them on tour and I stayed with them for four years. My pay was a packet of cigarettes a day, and if you wanted something like shoes, you asked the boss."

Sénégal (Wrasse). Released in 2006 after a five-year wait, this runs from ballad to *mbalax*, and many of the songs – heavy with sweeping strings – tackle pressing social issues. The moody "Le Jola" is a reggae lament about the ferry disaster.

Thione Seck

A former member of Star Band Dakar and Orchestra Baobab, **Thione Seck** is a griot son and was an early innovator of *mbalax* in the 1970s. He has recorded more than two dozen albums, and while his music is less well known beyond Senegal, he remains a cultural icon at home.

Orientation (Stern's). One of the most innovative African albums in years, Seck co-recorded these remarkable songs with forty musicians from India and Egypt, and the result is a beautiful blend of meditative, Eastern dirges and forceful West African percussion. Above it all, Seck's haunting, operatic Wolof voice rings out boldly and beautifully.

Africando

This African–Cuban studio group was founded after a meeting between some of Senegal's best singers and Cuba's most renowned salsa musicians.

Ketukuba (Stern's). Africando's seventh and latest album is filled with Afro-Atlantic rhythms and tones featuring the gorgeous voices of two new, young singers: Pascal Dieng and Basse Sarr. Prepare to move your body.

Vol 1: Trovador (Stern's). Featuring Senegalese singers Medoune Diallo and Pape Seck, this is a great introduction to the band's lively sound, with swinging salsa standards and West African originals belted out in Spanish and Wolof.

Cinema

The most established of Senegal's film-makers, **Ousmane Sembène** and **Djibril Diop Mambéty**, are both now dead, but their legacy survives in a film industry based more on themes and memories than on actual output, which is these days very limited.

Ousmane Sembène

Ousmane Sembène, who died in 2007, remains the revered "papa" of West African cinema. A Marxist, whose films are explicitly political, his career spanned more than forty years, and resulted in more than a dozen films, several of them classics of African cinema.

Besides *Borom Sarret* ("Cart-driver", 1963) and *Mandabi* ("The Money Order", 1968), Sembène's most famous works are *Xala* (1974) – a dark satire about a corrupt Dakar bureaucrat who loses touch with the people and becomes impotent – and the less accessible *Ceddo* (1977), which deals with the three-way conflict in the nineteenth century between Muslim reformers, traditionalists and the French.

The title character of his 1993 film *Guelwaar* is a deceased political activist and Catholic who, through a bureaucratic mix-up, is buried in a Muslim cemetery. Sembène uses the community's attempts to rectify the situation to expose the petty jealousies and divisive religious dogmatism of contemporary politics. Like many of Sembène's works, the film was banned in Senegal when it was released and remains difficult to see abroad.

Sembène returned to the screen in 2000 with the deceptively light domestic drama *Faat Kine*, a masterful tribute to what he described as the "everyday heroism of African women". His final, award-winning film, *Moolaadé*, made in 2004, is set in a small African village in Burkina Faso and explores the controversial subject of female genital mutilation.

Djibril Diop Mambéty

The director **Djibril Diop Mambéty**, who died in 1998, made a small number of highly acclaimed films. An actor and something of a rebel, his first feature, *Touki Bouki* ("Journey of the Hyena", 1973) won the International Critics' Award at Cannes for its portrayal of alienation and the yearning for Europe, using a fresh and idiosyncratic technique that emphasized clashes and dissonance. His only other feature film, *Hyènes* ("Hyenas", 1992), is a retelling of Swiss dramatist Friedrich Dürrenmatt's 1956 play *The Visit*. Through Mambéty's lens the piece becomes a disturbing parable of African innocence exchanged for European-style affluence.

Moussa Sene Absa

Senegalese film-makers were highly visible throughout the 1990s and into the new millennium. One of the most entertaining films of the past few years was by **Moussa Sene Absa**, whose coming-of-age film, *Ça twiste à Poponguine* (1993), is a breezy but insightful look at identity, dreams and the way cultures overlap. His *Tableau Ferraille* (1997) is more in the tradition of Sembène's *Xala* in its view of the corrosive effects of modernization on traditional culture, while *Ainsi Meurent les Anges* (2001) combines the lyricism of his first film with the acerbic social critique of his second.

Other directors

Other well-known members of the new generation are **Amadou Seck** – whose *Saaraba* (1988), an indictment of a corrupt older generation, is something of a classic in the neorealist tradition – and **Joseph Gaï Ramaka**, director of *Karmen Gaï* (2001), a colourful reworking of the Carmen story in contemporary Senegal.

Safi Faye was the first female African director to make a feature-length film, when she released *Kaddu Beykat* ("Letter from my Village") in 1975. More recently, she made *Mossane* (1996), about a teenage girl besieged by suits from admirers at home and in France.

Books

There are several **books** by Senegalese writers in the Heinemann African writers series. Other, mostly academic, English-language works are only likely to be available in libraries or possibly over the Internet. In French, there's a very wide range of literature – by both French and Senegalese writers – and a steady output of glossy tomes to whet travellers' appetites. Also see p.35 for books covering West Africa more broadly. Books marked 🏃 are especially recommended.

Boubacar Barry *Senegambia and the Atlantic Slave Trade*. An interesting, if slightly academic account covering four hundred years of the colonial trade system.

Lucy C. Behrman *Muslim Brotherhoods and Politics in Senegal*. Fascinating, though dated, study with interesting statistical information about the marabouts at the start of the last century.

Michael Crowder *Senegal: A Study of French Assimilation Policy*. Concise, fairly readable look at how the French colonized African minds.

Donal B. Cruise O'Brien *The Murides of Senegal: the Political and Economic Organization of an Islamic Brotherhood*. The definitive text in English on the Mouride brotherhood.

Sheldon Gellar *Senegal: An African Nation between Islam and the West*. A condensed and very readable survey, though not updated since 1995.

🏃 **Trevor R. Getz** *Slavery and Reform in West Africa*. One of the best accounts of the Senegalese slave trade until emancipation, with particular attention paid to the clash between European abolitionism and African agency. It's academic, but very readable.

J.B. Henry Sevigny *Narrative of a Voyage to Senegal*. Grim and harrowing account of the shipwreck of a French frigate off the Senegalese coast in 1816, recounted by two survivors.

Khadim Mbacke *Sufism and Religious Brotherhoods in Senegal*. Explores various aspects of Islam in modern-day Senegal.

David Murphy *Sembène: Imagining Alternatives in Film and Fiction*. Attempts to clarify Sembène's radical vision as a film-maker and writer of resistance and liberation narratives.

Janet G. Vaillant *Black, French and African*. Adeptly written biography of Léopold Senghor, with equal emphasis given to his writings and to the socio-political context of his rise to power.

Biography and fiction

Mariama Bâ *So Long a Letter*. Dedicated to "all women and to men of good will", this is the story of a woman's life shattered by her husband's sudden, second marriage to a younger woman. Bâ's *The Scarlet Song*, published posthumously, eloquently traces the relationship between a French woman and a poor, Senegalese man.

Birago Diop *Tales of Amadou Koumba*. A collection of short stories, based on the tales of a griot, and rooted in Wolof tradition.

Cheikh Hamidou Kane *Ambiguous Adventure*. The autobiographical tale of a man torn between Tukulor culture, Islam and the West.

Mark Hudson *The Music in My Head*. Energetic, constantly amusing and inventive "world music" novel, incorporating glowing passages of superb descriptive prose. If you're going to Senegal – sorry, "Tekrur" – this is the one for the beach.

Reginald McKnight *He Sleeps*. A passionate, inventive book about an African-American anthropologist in Senegal forced to deal with his insecurities about race, gender, love and his own identity.

Sembène Ousmane (or Ousmane Sembène) *God's Bits of Wood*; *Xala*; *The Last of the Empire* and others. A committed, political and very immediate writer (and film-maker) who could also be very funny, as in *Xala*, the satirical tale of a wealthy Dakarois' loss of virility. The best of these, by far, is *God's Bits of Wood*, the story of the rail strike of 1947.

Léopold Senghor *Léopold Sédhar Senghor: Collected Poetry*. Works from the *négritude* era, including "Songs of Darkness" and "Nocturnes".

Language

Though only twenty percent of the population has any fluency in the colonial tongue, communication is rarely a problem if you speak **French** to some degree. (English alone won't get you far.) You'll have a far better time, however, if you know some **Wolof**. It's not an easy language, but making the effort to say even a few simple greetings will gratify people out of all proportion to your ability.

Wolof is not the whole story. Important minority vernaculars include: **Fula**, spoken by the Tukulor and Fula; **Serer**, spoken by the partly Christianized people of the same name); **Kriyol**, a Portuguese creole spoken by up to 50,000 people along the coast south of Dakar; **Jola**, spoken in various dialects in the Casamance region; the **Mande** languages (Mandinka, see p.286; Malinké, see p.589; Bamana, see p.355; and Sarakolé/Soninké), spoken in scattered communities across the south and east; and the languages of the **Tenda** group – Konyagi, Bedik, Bassari. All the minority languages are a major component of ethnic identity, especially so in the case of Jola.

Jola word list

Jola is a diverse language, comprising several dialects: the following words and phrases could be helpful in Basse Casamance, but not all may be instantly recognized.

Kassoumay?	Hello, welcome
To kassaoumay Kassoumaykep	Response (peace only)
Aow	Yes
Oolat	No
Safi	Bonjour, hello
Oukatora	Goodbye
Karessy boo?	What is your name?
Karessom…	My name is…
Oubonkatom	Please
Emitakati	Thank you
Bunu kani?	How is it/Ça va?
Iman jut	I don't understand
Ounomom	Sell me
le dadat	This is good
le diacoutte	This is not good
Katenom	Stop (leave me alone)
Joom	Stop (in a car)
Sinangas	Rice
Siwolassou	Fish
Bunuk	Palm wine
Bulago bara…?	Which way to…?
Boussana	Pirogue
Sibeurassou	Trees
Karambak	Forest
Falafou	River

Simple Serer

Serer (or Sérère) is mostly spoken in the Siné-Saloum delta region west of Kaolack.

Nafio	Hello
Miheme	I'm fine
Fambina?	Does your family live in peace?
Wamaha	Yes, they have peace
Mereta	Goodbye
Dkoka djal	Thank you
Lo	Yes
Ha a	No
Koko	Coconut
Tju	Rice

Elementary Wolof

Wolof is understood by an estimated eighty percent of Senegalese. Perhaps half of these are ethnic Wolof, the rest being mother-tongue speakers of other languages, all of which are losing ground. Wolof is growing in importance all the time and there are regular calls for it to be adopted as the official national language.

Wolof is classified as a "West Atlantic" language, in the same large basket of "class languages" as Fula and Serer, quite different from the "non-class" Mande languages like Mandinka,

Bambara and Dyula. The main criterion for this classification is the grammatical system of Wolof, which groups nouns into fairly arbitrary classes something like genders. Some contemporary Wolof words, for example most of the days of the week, have foreign, often Arabic, roots.

There's the usual confusion over **spellings** created by British and French transcribers using their own norms, but the following selection should be quite pronounceable. The letter *x* denotes a throaty "h" sound like the *ch* in "loch". A double vowel simply lengthens the same sound, while a double consonant makes it harder.

If you are interested in communicating in Wolof beyond just the basics, there is some hope. If you know French, purchase the thorough course *J'apprends le Wolof*, published by Karthala, or the more rudimentary phrasebook *Kit de Conversation Wolof*, published by Assimil and available with CD. For instruction in English, Hippocrene publishes a *Wolof-English-Wolof Dictionary and Phrasebook*, while the US Peace Corps has made their Wolof grammar (⊛tinyurl.com/398qhv) and dictionary (⊛tinyurl.com/3xsk65) available for free download.

Wolof greetings

Salaam alekum	All-purpose greeting
Alekum salaam	…and response
Nanga def?	How are you?
Mangi fii rek	I'm fine (lit. "I'm just here")
Jama ngaam?	How are you? (lit. "Do you have peace?")
Jama rek	I'm fine (lit. "Peace only", can be used as the response to any greeting)
Alhamdoulila	Thank God
Jamanga fanaan?	Good morning (lit. "Did you sleep well?")
Naka waa keur ga?	How are you all? (formal)
Ana sa wa ker?	How are your family/home/people? (very informal)
Nyung fa	They're fine
Jerejef	Thank you
Naka nga tudd?	What's your name?
Mangi tudd Dave	My name is Dave
Naka nga santa?	What is your surname?
Mangi santa Warne	My surname is Warne
Mangi dem	Goodbye (I'm off)

General practicalities

Man deguma Wolof/Faranse	I don't understand Wolof/French
Wahat ko	Please repeat
Waaw	Yes
Deedeet	No
Xey na	Perhaps
Ana…?	Where is…?
Fan nga dem nii?	Where are you going?
Yoni Dakar fan la?	Where is the road to Dakar?
Ndeyjoor	Right
Chamong	Left
Sori	Far
Ndanka	Slowly
Su la nexe	Please (lit. "If you want")
Ana sema yon	I don't mind/ I don't care
Kan?	When?
Anul sono	No problem
Djabar/sohna	Wife
Jeker	Husband

Places

Marse	Market
Deuke ko	Village
Keur	House/Family compound
Neeg	Room
Lall	Bed
Toll	Field
All	Forest/bush

Days

Tey	Today
Aseer	Saturday
Dibeer	Sunday
Altine	Monday
Telata	Tuesday
Alarba	Wednesday
Alxemes	Thursday
Ajuma	Friday

Numbers

1	bena
2	nyar
3	nyeta
4	nyenent
5	jerom
6	jerom bena
7	jerom nyar
8	jerom nyeta
9	jerom nyenent
10	fuka
11	fuka bena (etc)
20	nyar fuka/nit
21	nyar fuka bena (etc)
30	nyet fuka/fanver
40	nyenent fuka
50	jerom fuka
60	jerom bena fuka
70	jerom nyar fuka
80	jerom nyeta fuka
90	jerom nyenent fuka
100	temer
1000	june

Shopping/bargaining

Mai ma/jai ma…	Give me/sell me…
Bognaa/boguma…	I want/I don't want…
Doi na	Enough
Dolili	More, again
Tutti	A little
Yu bare	Lots of
Fes	Full
Bah na	That's all
Bi nyata le?	How much is that?
Dafa ser	It's too expensive
Dafa ser torop	It's much too expensive
Yombe na	Cheap
Ser	Expensive
Serut	Not expensive
Xalis	Money
Wanil ko (tutti)	Lower the price (a little)
Hey! Yangi ma rey!	You're killing me!
Baye ma, dama sona	Leave me alone, I'm fed up/tired
Ndimbal	Gift

Other expressions

Mai man ndox bu la nexe	Please give me some water

Dama xiif	I'm hungry
Loo buga leka?	What would you like to eat?
Dama neleew	I'm sleepy
Mangi neleew	I'm going to sleep
Mangi neleew waay!	I'm going to sleep (and leave me alone!)
Fooy dem?	Where are you going?
Ndax marse ngay dem?	Are you going to the market?
Dama feebar	I feel ill
Suma biir day metti	I've got a stomach ache
Won ma yonu post bi	Show me the way to the post office
Lan nga bugg?	What would you like?
Amuloo aspirin?	Do you have aspirin?
Ndax dingay naan sung?	Do you drink palm wine?
Amuma xalis	I don't have any money
Am naa ku may xaar	Someone's waiting for me

Emergencies

Sachee!	Thief!
Dafa feebar!	S/he's ill!
Woo wall police/ medecin gewal legi legi!	Call the police/ a doctor quickly!

Trees

Gouigi	Baobab
Bentenki	Silk-cotton (kapok)
Bari	Raffia palm
Tir	Locust bean
Jorut	Mandingo
Netetu	Kola oil
Tabu	Palm

Animals

Fas	Horse
Guelem	Camel
Bei	Goat
Mbam	Pig
Nak	Cow
Yek	Bull
Gawnde/daba	Lion
Tenev	Leopard
Golo	Monkey
Nye	Elephant

Leber	Hippopotamus	Jasik	Crocodile
Koba	Large antelope	Kakatar	Chameleon
Buki	Hyena	Mbeutt	Monitor lizard
Sav	Porcupine	Onka	Gecko
Baa	Ostrich	Jan	Snake
Jagabar	Pelican	Mbonat	Tortoise

Glossary

Arachide Groundnut plant

Bana Bana Itinerant street vendor

Baye Fall Zealous disciples of Mouridism, dressed in brilliantly coloured patchwork cloaks, often seen collecting money for their marabout

Bolon(g) Mangrove creek (Casamance)

Borom Patron, chief, owner

Boubou Long gown worn by men and women

Ceddo Traditional Wolof warrior caste

Clando Clandestine bar

Damel Pre-Islamic Wolof kings

Dara Pioneering settlements of Mouride disciples

Dibiterie Roadside butcher and barbecue chef

Djigeen Woman

Fatou Somewhat derogatory term (it's a woman's name) meaning domestic servant or "girl"

Filao Casuarina tree

La Fleuve The River – ie the Senegal

Fromager Silk-cotton tree (kapok)

Gewel Griot; praise singer, musician, storyteller

Goor Man/Male

Gue Ford, river crossing

Hajj The pilgrimage to Mecca; El Hajj refers to someone who has been on the pilgrimage

Herbe Qui Tu Cannabis

HLM "Habitations à Loyer Modérés" – council flats, housing projects

Jeu de Dames Draughts, checkers; a more competitive game than *wure*

Keur/kerr/ker Place, home

Magal Annual mass pilgrimage to Touba on the occasion of Cheikh Amadou Bamba's birthday

Maquis Cheap place to eat

Marabout Enormously powerful religious leader accredited with magical powers

Mbalax Musical style, a modern expression of traditional roots rhythms

Mouridiya One of the two most powerful Islamic orders, with its headquarters near Touba

PDS Parti Démocratique Sénégalais, the ruling party under President Wade

Planton Orderly, watchman, dogsbody (slightly pejorative)

Pdt Abbreviation of Président

PS Parti Socialiste (though it has no socialist agenda), the long-time ruling party, now in opposition

Radio Kankan Public rumour

Sandarma *Gendarme*

Sayisayi Playboy

Sopi "Change" a political slogan and adoptive name of Wade's ruling coalition

Talibe Disciple of a marabout

Teranga Hospitality, generosity; sums up the Wolof code of behaviour to strangers

Tijaniya Numerically the largest Islamic brotherhood divided into dynasties, some of which are fundamentalist in nature; headquarters at Tivaouane

Touba The holy city east of Dakar; also means "happiness"

Toubab Foreigner, usually white; from the Wolof "to convert"; you'll hear it a lot from kids

Yamba Cannabis

2.1

Dakar, Cap Vert and central Senegal

West Africa's westernmost point and one of its most westernized capital cities, **Dakar** wields a powerful influence. Its pull extends well beyond Senegal's borders, drawing in migrants from across the Sahel and expatriates from overseas – especially, still, France. The city swarms with newcomers caught up in the neocolonial whirlpool, and its attractions are tempered by all this hustle and by the sheer size of the place. But the physical setting is striking, and the city has undeniable style, epitomizing the residue of French colonialism in Africa.

Out of the city itself, the **Île de Gorée** is a major draw, while the peninsula of **Cap Vert** offers beaches and out-of-town amusements. A more sheltered coast is the **Petite Côte** to the south of the city, which, beyond the dubious tourist magnet of **Joal–Fadiout**, merges into the bird-flocked creeks and islands of the **Sine–Saloum** region, adjoining the Gambian border.

Inland, the travel options from Dakar are harsher and the attractions scarcer, the focal points being the shady rail-network hub of **Thiès**, with its superb tapestry factory, and the much more distant Islamic hothouse of **Touba**.

Dakar

A giant of a city in African terms, with more than two million inhabitants, **DAKAR** is hard work. The shock of arriving can be intense: it's incredibly dynamic, sophisticated and wretched in equal measure, and a test of will if your budget is tight. **French** influence is everywhere, especially in the downtown **Plateau** area, where the architecture and the whole feel of the place is more evocative of southern France than Africa. The results can be quite beautiful: between sprouting skyscrapers, the terracotta rooftops and shady, tree-lined avenues of the older quarters give Dakar an elegant maturity shared by few other African capitals.

Unfortunately some of the most attractive parts of the centre swarm with vendors, hustlers and hostile, hooting traffic, though this frenetic pace thankfully subsides at weekends. At this time people hang out in shady shop fronts, kids play football in the streets and even the *colons* forsake their cars and taxis for a stroll out to Sunday lunch. During the week the **Île de Gorée**, **Hann Park** and the beaches at **N'gor** and **Yoff** all provide degrees of space and seclusion, and if, rather than retreat, you'd prefer a more human participation, most of Dakar's teeming **suburbs** are a lot more open and easy-going than experiences in the city centre might lead you to imagine.

Some history

The **Île de Gorée** was first settled by European merchant-adventurers in the fifteenth century, though the fortress-like peninsula of **Dakar** – the oldest European city in West Africa – was not established until 1857. The name Dakar was first used

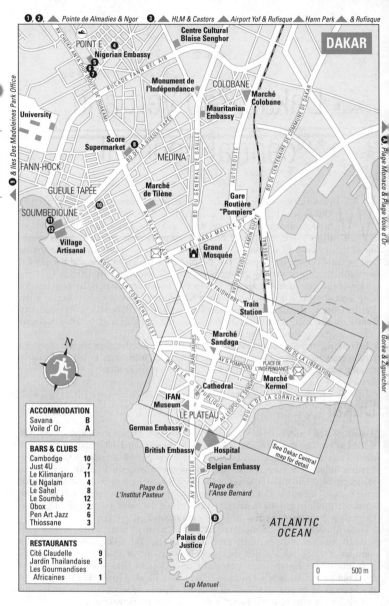

DAKAR

● **1**, ● **2**, ▲ Pointe de Almadies & Ngor   ● **3**, ▲ HLM & Castors   ▲ Airport Yof & Rufisque   ▲ Hann Park   ▲ & Rufisque

POINT E ● **4**

Centre Cultural Blaise Senghor

Nigerian Embassy

● **5**
● **6**
● **7**

Monument de l'Indépendance

COLOBANE

Marché Colobane

University

Mauritanian Embassy

Score Supermarket

● **8**

MEDINA

FANN-HOCK

GUEULE TAPÉE

Marché de Tilène

SOUMBEDIOUNE

● **10**

● **11**
● **12**

Village Artisanal

Grand Mosquée

Gare Routière "Pompiers"

Train Station

Marché Sandaga

Cathedral

Marché Kermel

PLACE DE L'INDÉPENDANCE

IFAN Museum

LE PLATEAU

German Embassy

British Embassy

Hospital

Belgian Embassy

See Dakar Central map for detail

Plage de L'Institut Pasteur

Plage de l'Anse Bernard

ATLANTIC OCEAN

● **B**

Palais du Justice

Cap Manuel

0   500 m

▲ Plage Monaco & Plage Voile d'Or
▲ Gorée & Ziguinchor

AV CHEIKH ANTA DIOP
ROUTE DE OUAKAM
ROCADE FANN BEL AIR
AV CHEIKH ANTA DIOP
BD DE LA GUEULE TAPÉE
BD DU GÉNÉRAL DE GAULLE
AV BLAISE DIAGNE
AV EL HADJ MALICK SY
ROUTE DE LA CORNICHE OUEST
AUTOROUTE
BD DE CENTENAIRE DE COMMUNE DE DAKAR
AV PRESIDENT LAMIN GUEYE
AV FAIDHERBE
AV DE L' ARSENAL
AV JEAN JAURES
BD DE LA
AV G POMPIDOU
BD DE LA LIBERATION
AV LÉOPOLD S SENGHOR
AV DE LA RÉPUBLIQUE
ROUTE DE LA CORNICHE EST
AV PASTEUR

N

ACCOMMODATION

| Savana | B |
| Voile d' Or | A |

BARS & CLUBS

Cambodge	10
Just 4U	7
Le Kilimanjaro	11
Le Ngalam	4
Le Sahel	8
Le Soumbé	12
Obox	2
Pen Art Jazz	6
Thiossane	3

RESTAURANTS

Cité Claudelle	9
Jardin Thailandaise	5
Les Gourmandises Africaines	1

in the eighteenth century and is supposed to derive either from the Wolof for tamarind tree – *daxar* – or refuge – *dekraw*.

The town's development really began towards the end of the nineteenth century, with the decline of St-Louis as a port, and the opening in 1885 of the Dakar-to-St-Louis **railway** (the first in West Africa), which gave a boost to groundnut farmers along its route. By the turn of the twentieth century the population numbered 15,000. With considerable dredging and port construction, Dakar became a **French naval base** in the early 1900s and the **capital** of Afrique Occidentale Française in 1904. It was also a calling port on the air routes to South America and West and South Africa, and throughout the century of colonial occupation, Dakar's cosmopolitan reputation as the first call on "the Coast" went before it. By the time of the opening of the Dakar–Bamako railway line in 1923, Dakar was easily the most important city in West Africa.

The original Lebu and Wolof inhabitants of the Plateau district were forced out to the new town of Medina in the early 1930s, when the Depression coincided with rent increases imposed to pay for improvements to their houses. Yet the white settlers who moved in were often poor – a rigorous colour bar prevailing over economic reality – and even today you'll see elderly French, some running small businesses, hanging onto very modest existences.

The turn of the twenty-first century saw signs that Dakar was outgrowing its peninsula-bound geography. There has been talk of a **new capital** up the coast at **Lompoul** near President Wade's birthplace, and the decision by the Organization of the Islamic Conference to hold the March 2008 **Islamic Summit** in Dakar galvanized the city into a frenzy of construction works, including a major new autoroute.

Arrival, orientation, information

While ground has been broken for Dakar's new international airport, located 40km southeast of the city in Ndiass, it is going to take years to complete. Until then, you're stuck with arrival by air into the mild confusion of **Aéroport International Dakar-Yoff-Léopold Sédar Senghor** (☏ 338 69 22 00 ⓦ www.aeroportdakar.com), 12km northwest of the city in Yoff. Track down your luggage and hang onto it: the supervision of the arrivals hall is pretty relaxed, with lots of "porters" aiming to part you from your cash. You can change money in the airport at the CBAO **bank** (daily 8am–3pm & 5–11.30pm; closed Wed), which also has a 24-hour ATM accepting Visa, MasterCard and Cirrus. There's also a left-luggage office, which charges CFA700 per bag per day. Upstairs, you'll find an expensive **restaurant** and **business centre** (daily 8am–midnight) with a bureau de change, **Internet** access (CFA2000/hr) and **telephones**. Information on flights can be had from the airport **information desk** and on **car hire** from the various agencies located opposite the exit.

For **transport from the airport**, until 9pm, you can take a blue DDD **bus** (#8), which takes you through Yoff Village and then the mishmash of Grand Dakar, past the university and right through the centre of the Plateau to the old Palais de Justice. Alternatively, **cars rapides** pass about five minutes' walk away from the airport – cross the car park and turn left. They'll take you to the **Marché Sandaga** in Central Dakar for CFA100, and from here, a taxi across downtown Dakar shouldn't cost more than CFA500. Finally, a **taxi** to the centre officially costs CFA3000 in the daytime and CFA4000 after midnight (rates are written on a sign over the taxi rank), though you'll probably still have to bargain hard and you'll be charged extra if you have large pieces of luggage.

Arriving by shared taxi or bus, you'll normally end up at the **Pompiers** *gare routière* (see "Dakar surface arrivals and departures").

From the Art-Deco **train station** in the city centre, it's just five minutes' walk (or taxi ride) south to Avenue Pompidou, though in mid-2007 the train was using the Halte de Hann, about 4km short of the terminus. The train from Bamako usually gets in after dark, so make sure you've looked at the map and know exactly where you're heading.

Orientation and information

Dakar is built on the twin-pronged **Cap Vert peninsula**. The southern spur contains the city's heart, with cliffs and coves along the ocean side and Cap Manuel, and the main port area along the sheltered eastern flank. The suburbs spread north

Dakar surface arrivals and departures

Dakar is unusual in having just one main *gare routière*, **Pompiers**, at the head of the autoroute that funnels suburban traffic into the city (a 25-minute walk from Marché Sandaga down av du Président Lamine Guèye) which makes getting in and out of the city a mostly painless affair. It's fairly organized, though not any less intimidating for that if you're not used to shouting in French at four people simultaneously while beggars pull at your clothing and the fumes from a hundred idling engines fill the air. From Pompiers, it's a two-kilometre walk to the centre: much easier to take a taxi (CFA750) or a bus.

For the past few years, the train to **Bamako** has been running a less-than-reliable service, though this is due to improve in 2008 once a new locomotive is put into operation. At the time of writing, second-class (ie very crowded) seats were selling for CFA25,500. For the latest schedule ring the Dakar station on ☏ 338 49 46 46, or for more details on service, see p.330. For transport to **Banjul**, your best option is a seven-seat (*sept-places*) Peugeot 504 from the *gare routière*.

The ferry service to **Ziguinchor** is operated by the MV *Wilis*. The boat departs from the Gorée wharf (Thurs & Sun; return trip departs Ziguinchor Tues & Fri), with fares for the overnight voyage CFA15,500 for hard seats, CFA18,500 for comfortable seats and CFA28,500 for a couchette in a four-berth cabin. If you go for a couchette, be sure to ask for the ones higher up, as the lower-level bunks soak up fumes from the nearby engine rooms. The Ziguinchor-bound trip sometimes allows you to see dolphins swimming alongside the boat in the morning.

and west towards the **airport** and the other prong of **Pointe des Almadies**, Africa's most westerly point.

Despite Dakar's size, the **city centre** is a relatively manageable two square kilometres of tightly gridded streets, with the **train station** to the north, the **museum** to the south, **Avenue Jean Jaurès** on the west, and the **Kermel market** and **PTT** to the east. In the middle of it all stands the big, sloping centrepiece of **Place de l'Indépendance**, from where **Avenue Georges Pompidou** ("Ponty" to *Dakarois*) cuts the district into a northern, heavily commercial quarter and a southern, more affluent, residential one – the **Plateau**. Most of the grand buildings of state and several important embassies are south of this central district, where the street pattern breaks into graciously radiating avenues and looping clifftop corniches. Note that while a number of Dakar **street names** have been changed in recent years – av Albert Sarraut, for example, is now officially av Hassan II – most people still use the old names, which are retained in this guide.

You may be able to glean some **tourist information** from the Ministry of Tourism on rue du Docteur Calmette, just off Boulevard de la République (BP 4049; Mon–Fri 8am–5pm; ☏ 335 37 01 98 ⓦ www.tourisme.gouv.sn), which has some leaflets and, theoretically, English-speaking staff. The free monthly **listings magazine** *Le Dakarois* can be picked up in most hotels, restaurants and travel agencies; the lesser-circulated glossies *Waaw* (free) and *221* (CFA500) are also packed with information on various city goings-on.

City transport

One of Dakar's great pluses is its reliable and efficient **bus system**, run by DDD (*Dakar Dem Dikk* – literally "Dakar to and fro"; ⓦ www.demdikk.com). The easily recognizable blue buses are numbered and carry destination signs, run fairly frequently from dawn till late evening, and charge between CFA150 and CFA250, depending on zone. You can get to most places using this service, though during rush hours the squeeze – and the heat – are sapping. Where useful, route numbers are included below.

Cars rapides – boxy Saviem or Mercedes buses that hold 24 passengers, usually sporting marabout monikers ("Touba") – are a poorer, and mostly private, version. Destinations are shouted by the fare collector (CFA50–125), and although they're more erratic than the buses and confusing to newcomers, you're guaranteed an insight into the street life of Dakar. Big white ones leave from Avenue André Peytavin, near Marché Sandaga, for the route de Ouakam, Yoff and N'gor, while slightly smaller yellow and blue ones jostle together up the nearby Avenue Emile Badiane for Grand Dakar, HLM and Colobane. These are slowly being phased out by the **Senbus**, a fleet of new and white Senegalese-built Tata vehicles, more comfortable and efficient but costing the same.

Larger than the *cars rapides* are the **Ndiaga Ndiaye** (pronounced "jag and jai") buses – big (they hold at least 42 passengers), white and sporting religious iconography and phrases – plying the major roads around and beyond the city and costing CFA100–150.

As for **taxis**, supply is ahead of demand so you can always argue about the fare. Some have meters, but nobody uses them, so agree the price up front – you can usually bargain down to about half what the driver initially suggests. Daytime journeys in the town centre should cost no more than CFA500 and trips to the suburbs roughly CFA300 per kilometre; a trip to Point E from the centre should cost about CFA1500; to N'gor beach about CFA3000. At night (from midnight to 5am) the tariff officially doubles, but more usually just increases by about twenty percent. Keep some change and small notes handy for drivers, who often deny having any. Note that some Dakar taxi drivers speak a little French, but many speak none at all, which can making communication difficult.

Accommodation

Dakar has scores of **hotels**, which are generally of a decent standard but tend to be overpriced compared with the rest of the country. It's worth **booking** around the popular Christmas, New Year and Rally period (mid-Jan; see p.203), when finding a room can be difficult.

Security in Dakar

The question of personal safety in Dakar is one you can't afford to be casual about, particularly when you first arrive. Decide quickly on an initial destination rather than wandering in hope. A few gangs of organized pickpockets operate with extraordinary dexterity and daring and, burdened with luggage, you're an easy and valuable trophy. **Place de l'Indépendance** and **Avenue Georges Pompidou** are notorious trouble-spots, especially the *place* itself during banking hours – remain alert and keep valu-ables, purses and wallets completely out of sight. Don't be deflected or distracted by anything or anyone – keep a steady pace and get where you're going. Once you've found a base you'll soon make up your own mind about the relative safety of Dakar.

As a general rule, avoid carrying anything you'd hate to lose and never keep purses or wallets in outside or back pockets. Distractions, be they words or a touch, should always be ignored or treated with suspicion, however friendly they may seem – usually it's the overly friendly people who turn out to be the crooks. One group technique is to stop you by offering a bangle, hold your legs together from behind and grab your shirt sleeves. By the time you've realized what's happening, they're off down the street with your wallet. Another common trick is for hustlers to claim that they know you from your hotel before hitting on you for a "loan".

If you lose anything of personal value (as opposed to just money or expensive items), it's worth making a visit to the **market in Colobane** (the so-called *marché aux voleurs*), 500m east of the Monument de l'Indépendance, where, if you keep asking and manage to make the right connections, you may be able to buy it back.

In the city centre, the majority of Dakar's budget options lie within a few blocks of place de l'Indépendance (though for the real bargains you're better off staying on Gorée; see p.214). Although some budget places double as informal **brothels**, they can offer reasonable value, and while the rooms can be shabby and the plumbing ropey only particularly sensitive visitors will find the seediness uncomfortable. The **mid-price** establishments can be among the city's most pleasant lodgings, their neocolonial charm far more attractive than the range of more expensive, anodyne modern blocks. Most of the **top-bracket** (⑧) hotels reviewed here charge at least CFA80,000 for a double room.

If you are planning a longer stay in Dakar, you might want to think about **renting an apartment**. The first places to look are the free adverts and listings papers *Tam-Tam* and *L'Avis*, available at hotels and restaurants; *Tam-Tam* is the more comprehensive of the two, with a large section on apartments for rent in Dakar and on the Petite Côte. Failing that, you could try a real estate firm, such as Régie Immobilier Mugnièr et Compagnie, 11 rue Mohamed V (☏338 23 43 74 or 338 23 23 76). Some hotels below offer apartments and long-term studio rentals, too, though these will be comparatively expensive. If your requirements are more modest, there are always unfurnished rooms available for around CFA20,000 a month in the Medina/Gueule Tapée quarters or CFA50,000 up in N'Gor near the beach.

All the hotels reviewed in the listings below are in **central Dakar**. Alternatives, including some more expensive options, are detailed on later pages: the region's top hotel, the *Méridien Présidentiel*, out at Pointe des Almadies (see p.216); and some pleasant options on the Île de Gorée (see p.215).

Hotels

Around Marché Kermel and east of place de l'Indépendance

Hôtel du Marché 3 rue Parent ☏338 21 57 71. An old standby (albeit something of a brothel) near Kermel market, offering high-ceilinged but grubby s/c rooms with fans. ③

Lagon 2 rte de la Corniche Est ☏338 89 25 25 ⓦwww.lagon.sn. One of the best-value high-end places in Dakar, this wonderful, eccentric hotel features a ship-like layout, with idiosyncratic rooms melding African, Continental and Doctor Who aesthetics. The rooms' balconies eavesdrop lapping waves and have views over the rocky shore towards Gorée. Guests have access to a private beach and there's an excellent restaurant. ⑧

Novotel av Abdoulaye Fadiga ☏338 23 10 90 ⓦwww.novotel.com. Bland four-star high-rise with well-endowed rooms and a large pool and tennis courts out back. ⑧

Océanic 9 rue de Thann ☏338 22 20 44 ⓦwww.hoteloceanicdakar.sn. A hit with French tourists, this *sympa*, old-style hotel has tidy a/c, s/c rooms. While they are at times a bit frayed and musty, several have small, standing balconies. There are also four-bed apartments and a small patio. The dining room does good-value meals. ⑤

Savana route de la Corniche Est ☏338 49 42 42 ⓦwww.savana.sn. Though it's no longer the cream

of the crop, this old standby won't disappoint, with deluxe four-star comfort in a fashionable setting right on the water. ⑧

Sofitel Teranga rue Colbert ☏338 89 22 00 ⓦwww.sofitel.com. Dakar's priciest hotel, with all the predictable comfort of a luxury chain. Rooms well over CFA100,000. ⑧

On and north of Avenue Pompidou

Al Baraka 35 rue El Hadj Abdoukarim Bourgi ☏338 22 55 32 ⓔhalbaraka@arc.sn. Central place offering modern, a/c rooms with palatial bathrooms. Half the rooms have street-side balconies. ⑦

Chez Vieira 23 av Pompidou, accessible through the courtyard to the right of *Ali Baba*, and up two flights of stairs ☏338 22 98 47. An excellent budget option right in the city centre, with a handful of very large rooms that are tattered and torn but perfectly adequate. A few have great balconies overlooking – and overhearing – the cacophony of Pompidou. ④

Farid 51 rue Vincens ☏338 23 61 23 ⓦwww.hotelfarid.com. Recent renovation offering decent-value modern, clean rooms, with TV, fridge, free Internet and showroom-like bathrooms and balconies. The Lebanese staff are welcoming, and there's an excellent Middle Eastern restaurant downstairs. ⑥

Indépendance place de l'Indépendance ☏338 23 10 19 ⓦwww.hotel-independance.com. Dakar's oldest four-star flagship tower-block feels like it hasn't been touched since 1974, but there are great views from many of the outmoded rooms, as there are from the terrace around the murky rooftop pool. ⑥

South of Avenue Pompidou

Al Afifa 46 rue Jules Ferry ☎338 89 90 90 ✉gmbafifa@sentoo.sn. Bland and faded but comfortable hotel, with a pleasant pool and a restaurant area, bar and nightclub. ⑦

Ganalé 38 rue El Hadj A.A. Ndoye ☎338 89 44 44 ✉hganale@sentoo.sn. Many of the spic-and-span, if smallish, rooms at this well-run, mid-level place have private balconies overlooking a quiet street. There are also some larger apartments and a popular bar/disco and restaurant, and it's a stone's throw from plenty of excellent cheap African restos. ⑦

Miramar 25–27 rue Félix Fauré ☎338 49 29 29 ⓦwww.dakar-miramar.com. More than fifty slightly aging but perfectly clean s/c, a/c rooms with satellite TV. The Afro-kitsch spaceship decor in the communal areas and the *Soninké Bar* downstairs add eccentric character. Good breakfasts. ⑥

Sokhamon bd Roosevelt and av Nelson Mandela ☎338 89 71 00 ⓦwww .hotelsokhamon.com. Dakar's newest boutique hotel is cool, sleek and minimalist all over, with inviting, superbly-styled stone and marble rooms that have every mod-con you'd need, including high-speed Internet. They have a small, pebbly beach down at the shore. ⑧

St-Louis Sun 68 rue Félix Fauré ☎338 22 25 70 ✉boubandiayecedric@yahoo.fr. A charismatic, colonial choice in colourful Louisienne style with a leafy, open patio and restaurant and tidy a/c, s/c rooms with phone. A breath of fresh air in an otherwise drab neighbourhood. ⑥

The City

Dakar is every inch a capitalist capital, with **consumption** as conspicuous and contradictory as you'd expect. Lepers, polio victims and beggars are a common sight, and you may find the contrasts repugnant. Once you've learnt to deal with the inevitable hassle, the two central markets of **Sandaga** and **Kermel** are worth a visit, and you'll find the irrepressible *commerçants* spilling out onto any traffic-free surface in the surrounding area. Also worth investigating are the superb and highly buyable offerings of the artisans at **Cour des Orfèvres**, a few minutes northwest of Sandaga.

There's more to do in Dakar than shop, from visiting the IFAN **museum** to just walking the avenues and exploring the backstreets, especially during the comfortable winter months. For a wonderful **bird's-eye view** of the city, go up to the

---

The Dakar Rally

Since the late 1970s the annual **Dakar Rally** (ⓦwww.dakar.com) has torn across the Sahara and West Africa, covering up to 10,000km in around three weeks. Originally the Paris–Dakar Rally, it used to set off from the Champs Élysées on a New Year's dawn, but the route has been chopped and changed over the years and no longer begins in Paris. The 2008 rally was cancelled after four tourists were murdered in Mauritania (see p.114) and the 2009 event was to be held in South America. Whether it will return to the Sahara remains to be seen.

The rally was once hugely popular, though this success was tempered by frequent deaths among participants and onlookers – the Vatican has publicly referred to it as "The Bloody Race of Irresponsibility" – and the questionable ethics of a multi-million-pound spectacle hurtling through the poverty-stricken Sahel. Furthermore, the loss of the event's early amateur spirit and the elimination of the central Saharan sections, where the rally earned its reputation as the world's toughest trial for bikes, cars and trucks, have removed some of the Dakar's sex appeal, though it's still followed nightly on French TV. If you're in Dakar when the rally arrives, don't expect to see much more than huge crowds and champagne-soaked desert racers parading through the place de l'Indépendance. Watch out, too, for the enormous accommodation problems the rally brings to every town on the route, Dakar especially.

ACCOMMODATION

Al Afifa	O	Ganalé	J	Océanic	C
Al Baraka	B	Indépendance	G	Provençal	E
Chez Vieira	H	Le Lagon 2	L	Sofitel Teranga	K
Continental	A	Miramar	N	Sokhamon	P
Du Marché	F	Novotel	I	St-Louis Sun	M
Farid	D				

RESTAURANTS & CAFÉS

Adonis	14	Chez Loutcha	
Ali Baba	15	Le Dagorne	
Boulangerie Sandaga	7	La Fourchette	
Caesar	31	Le Hanoi	
Café de Rome	29	L'Impérial	
Casa Créole	2	Indigo Café	

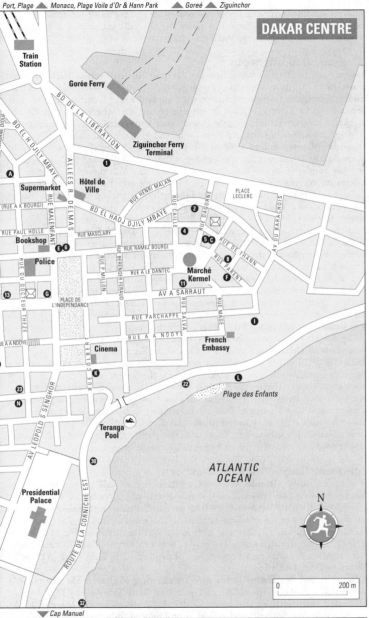

DAKAR CENTRE

Train Station

Gorée Ferry

BD DE LA LIBERATION

Ziguinchor Ferry Terminal

Hôtel de Ville

ALLEES R. DELMAS

RUE HENRI MALAN

RUE CAILLE

RUE D'AGORNE

PLACE LECLERC

AV DU BARACHOIS

Supermarket

RUE MALENFANT

BD EL HADJ DJILY MBAYE

BD EL H DJILY MBAYE

(RUE A K BOURGI)

RUE PAUL HOLLE

RUE MASCLARY

Bookshop

RUE RAMEZ BOURGI

RUE DE HANN

Police

RUE BERNGER FERAUD

RUE P MILLON

RUE A LE DANTEC

Marché Kermel

RUE PARENT

RUE DU DOCTEUR THEZE

PLACE DE L'INDEPENDANCE

AV A SARRAUT

RUE A A NDOYE

RUE PARCHAPPE

RUE SALVA

RUE MAGE

RUE A A NDOYE

French Embassy

Cinema

RUE COLBERT

Plage des Enfants

AV LEOPOLD S SENGHOR

Teranga Pool

ATLANTIC OCEAN

N

Presidential Palace

ROUTE DE LA CORNICHE EST

| 0 | 200 m |

				BARS & CLUBS			
Keur Ndeye	18	Le Plateau	9	Africa Star	25	Le Sénégalou	12
Le Lagon 1	5	Le Sarraut	22	Alexandra	11	Le Seven	4
Niani Beach	8	Restaurant le ? 2	11	Koulgraoul	10	Le Viking	26
La Palmeraie	30	Touba	19	La Siège de Gorée	32	Ozio	16
La Pizzeria	21	Toukouleur	24	Le Mex	1	Quizs	28
	6		27		17		20
	23						

seventeenth-floor swimming pool and roof terrace of the *Hôtel Indépendance* – just buy a drink to get access. From this height the old red-tiled quarters and the main avenues of dark green foliage stand out clearly.

The central markets

Down towards the port you'll find the **Marché Kermel**, rebuilt after it burned down in 1993. The smart market building houses a mass of stalls selling fish, fruit and vegetables, with flower-sellers on the surrounding pavements. To the west, around rue Le Dantec, market stands line the streets, where offerings include stacks of basketry, fashions, carvings and other **souvenirs**, plus a cornucopia of expensive produce for the old-style *colons* still living in the quarter. Beware of dastardly sales psychology – don't accept "gifts" or, if you do, insist on paying. Repeated visits improve the atmosphere as the pushers get used to your face, but it takes courage to leave without buying something. You should experience less aggressive merchandising, and far less interesting merchandise, below Kermel, along the portside **Boulevard de la Libération**, where a grubby street market has operated for some years. Don't come down here after dark though, as it's dodgy territory.

At the western end of Avenue Pompidou is the **Marché Sandaga**, Dakar's big *centreville* market, an unpretentious two-storey emporium with a tremendous variety of fruit, vegetables and dry foods, and lots of wonderful fish in the morning. Today, Sandaga has been almost completely taken over by Mouride traders. You can buy just about anything here and in the surrounding streets, from avocados to bootleg CDs and attaché cases made of beer cans. The hassle can be intense, with the politest rejection of overzealous salesmanship provoking accusations of racism; go in a patient and forgiving mood. The enormous crush also encourages pickpockets so you should take care around the fringes of the building.

The former Mauritanian silversmiths' yard, the **Cour des Orfèvres**, also known as **Keur Jean Thiam** (after an early and renowned Senegalese artisan), has long been located at 69 av Blaise Diagne, 500m downhill from Sandaga. Mauritanian artisans have been steadily returning to Dakar following the Senegal–Mauritania conflict of the early 1990s, and their superb **silver jewellery** and **wooden chests** (the latter are "authentic copies" no matter what story they spin you) are worth bargaining for; they can now also be seen all over the downtown areas, especially along rue Félix Fauré. Senegalese carved **wooden masks** and figures are also made and sold at Cour des Orfèvres – if you're serious about making a purchase, be prepared to discuss the matter over a couple of hours or, better still, a couple of visits.

Medina, Bène Tali and Castors

You can't miss the **Grande Mosquée**, a fifteen-minute walk to the northwest of Sandaga. Finished in 1964 and built after the style of the Mohamed V mosque in Casablanca, it's truly impressive, with seventy-metre minarets standing out above the low rooftops of the **Medina** quarter. Nonbelievers are strictly barred most of the time, so your only option is to peer in through the windows. The **Marché de Tilène**, a short distance north, brings you down to earth with its football-pitch-sized food market offering a massive array of **produce**. This is the place to come to absorb ordinary Dakar life.

Going a good deal further north, there's a vast array of **cloth** at the best possible prices in the market in the old African quarter of **Bène Tali** (buses #13, #20 from place de l'Indépendance), and more textiles at the less traditional **Marché HLM** in the HLM 5 neighbourhood (HLM is pronounced "ash-el-em" and stands for Habitations à Loyer Modéré, meaning "Affordable Rent Housing"). Marché HLM is in the middle-class suburbs out between Grand Dakar and the autoroute (again, buses #13 and #20).

Lastly, if you go out further to the suburb of **Castors**, there's a humdrum general market (buses #13, #18, #20) where you can wander in complete tranquillity. A place to buy food, spices, traditional remedies, cheap CDs, secondhand clothes and so on, it's somewhat cheaper than the central markets and easier to bargain.

The IFAN museum and the Plateau

In truth, Dakar's cultural showpiece, the **IFAN museum**, on place Soweto in the southwest of the centre (Tues–Sun 8.30am–12.30pm & 2–6.30pm; ☎338 21 40 15; CFA2000), does not make a great first impression. Created in 1938, the IFAN (Institut Fondamental d'Afrique Noir) was one of the first museums in the region. Today, however, the permanent collection on the ground floor basically consists of thousands of objects from all over West Africa, many of them visibly decaying, pinned to the walls, lying in glass cases or draped over clay models with little in the way of background information. You can happily spend an hour here, however, or longer if you're intrigued. The first floor, meanwhile, is given over to temporary exhibitions (CFA2000), which are a little hit and miss but sometimes feature interesting works by contemporary artists.

On the left side of the main hall as you go in, look out for the **white man mask**, obviously modelled on a moustachioed colonial officer with a wrinkly neck. Carrying on to the left, you'll come to a selection of shell-encrusted **Dogon headdresses** from Mali, now a commonplace image of West African art, and next to the central staircase some ornate **wooden doors** from Côte d'Ivoire and a lovely **balafon** from Mali. On the right side of the hall, highlights include some beautifully carved **ceremonial drums** and **chairs** from Ghana and some fine **cattle and hippo masks** from Guinea-Bissau. In the far right-hand corner, some fierce-looking **Jola masks** from Casamance are just about the only exhibits from Senegal.

Outside, an hour's wander around the Parisian quarter centred on place Soweto is enough time to see all the main state buildings of the **Plateau**. On the *place* itself, across from the museum, is the **Assemblée Nationale**; along Avenue Courbet stands the ugly **"Building Administratif"**, a mega-block of ministries crowned with scores of vultures; and then on the right, down Avenue Léopold S. Senghor, is the high-profile **Presidential Palace**, with its befezzed and unfazed presidential guards, where photos, unlike at most such addresses, are not a problem.

Second impressions at the museum

"The IFAN museum is more interesting than you imply, with the two large dioramas on the ground floor being very interesting and well done, if densely packed. The generally very good items in cases and on walls are not 'visibly decaying', although the lighting is inadequate, making it hard to appreciate them."

Bruce Kennedy, US

The corniches

Both the Corniche Est, from the end of Boulevard de la Libération to Cap Manuel, and the Corniche Ouest, from Avenue André Peytavin right up to Mermoz, are fine walks, mostly on the clifftop, with some stunning views. There are also beaches along here – on the Corniche Est, the pretty **Plage des Enfants** and the deep cove at **Anse Bernard** (crowded with local kids at weekends); on the rougher Atlantic side of Cap Manuel, the **Plage de l'Institut Pasteur**. Note, however, that walking the corniches carries some **risk**, as both have reputations for bag-snatching and various kinds of assault. Violent attacks are in fact rare, but you shouldn't carry valuables and it's better not to go alone.

The four-kilometre-long **Corniche Est** runs through dense vegetation, past the back gardens of various embassies and diplomatic residences and the front gate of the

German ambassador's bizarre house, a kind of Sudanic-Teutonic construction. It then climbs to **Cap Manuel** via Dakar's most picture-postcard viewpoints over the city and Gorée. You pass the self-consciously tropical *Hôtel Savana* – a good place for a break and a drink – and from the forbidding yellow slab of the old **Palais de Justice** nearby you can bus back into town. As you go, look out for the beautiful **Aristide Le Dantec hospital** – Sudanic architectural influences in two shades of baby pink.

The eight-kilometre-long **Corniche Ouest** has a far less intimate feel – windswept, wave-ripped and racing with traffic and joggers. City tours come out here for the **Village Artisanal** on Soumbédioune bay, but it's frankly not up to much, with high prices and loads of pressure. However, it's fun to go down on the ant's-nest-busy **beach** to watch the world go by in **Lebu** style: from mid-afternoon it's full of returning Lebu **fishermen** and women selling a diverse catch. The Lebu are related to the Wolof, from whom they broke away at the end of the eighteenth century. Most belong to the Tijaniya brotherhood rather than the Mourides, but a few are Layen, a largely Lebu fraternity. Continuing north around Soumbédioune bay and beyond, you come to the suburb of **Fann**, featuring more diplomatic and expat residences with guard dogs and iron gates, and armies of Dakarois youth working out on the skyline – the **university** is nearby, and physical fitness is a big thing these days. Any time you get tired of walking, you can ride bus #10, which follows this whole route back to the centre.

The beaches

While Dakar's beaches are hardly the finest in Senegal, several strips of sandy coastline within easy reach of the city centre make for good swimming or sunning. Closest to town are the private beaches at the *Hôtel Lagon 2* and *Savana*, or for more local colour, the beaches on the sheltered **Pointe de Bel-Air** are 3km east of the city. Here, **Plage de Monaco** is popular with Dakarois, while the adjoining **Plage de la Voile d'Or** is larger, better and a bit more touristy, stretching out to rocks at the point (modest entry charges at each). While both are clean, shaded and very safe, they border on industrial maritime and fishery grounds, and the stench can occasionally ruin a day out on the sands. Things get more promising the further north out of the centre you go: the sands are soft and clean on Île de Gorée (p.214), while those at Pointe des Almadies, N'gor and Île de N'gor are good for getting a tan and for a dip in the water. These beaches are popular with surfers on account of their good breaks – as is the small Plage du Virage and, further on, the several-kilometre-long beach at Yoff. The smaller beaches can get crowded at weekends so come early, and bring a bite to eat and also water, as even cafés and kiosks can be fairly expensive. Diving is also possible around Dakar; contact Océanium (℡338 22 24 41 ⓦwww.oceanium.org) on Route de la Corniche Est.

Hann Park

One part of the city that doesn't yet appear to suffer the security problems of the corniches – though you should be cautious nonetheless – is **Hann Park** (daily 10am–noon & 3–6.30pm; bus #12), eighty hectares of woodland and swamp with a zoo and a network of paths. It's a pleasant place for a stroll, full of joggers and keep-fit fanatics in the hour before dark, and a good complement to the beaches at Bel-Air. It's quite attractive to ornithologists, too, who can find several different habitats here. The **Parc Zoologique** (Tues–Sun 10am–noon & 3–6.30pm; CFA500), on the other hand, is not a happy place, a small collection of listless mammals and a large one of birds – not counting the vultures perched ominously on the trees outside. If you want to do it the Dakar way, go armed with sweets and groundnuts and feed all the inmates – but it's probably best avoided.

Eating

Dakar has a blaze of **restaurants** to satisfy most tastes and budgets. If you're really short of cash, you could survive on streetside snacks and fruit for under CFA1000 a day. At the top of Sandaga market you'll find a very basic food-hall selling the kind of nourishing breakfast foods sold around the suburbs of Dakar, like sour milk *thiacry* ("chagry"), with millet grains and sugar, or millet porridge *fondé*, all at about CFA50–100 a bowl. The cheapest sit-down meals are found in the **gargotes**, or for about the same price (around CFA1000) you can get a *chawarma* or other Lebanese snacks from any of the **takeaway bars** along Avenue Pompidou. Pay twice that and you'll get a tablecloth, less austere surroundings, service with a smile and a genuine choice; in the overseas-cuisine or better African **restaurants** a meal costs from around CFA3000. It's also well worth making an effort to get out of the centre to try some of the great food offerings out in Point E, Les Almadies and N'gor (see p.216).

Central Dakar

Around Marché Kermel and east of place de l'Indépendance

Casa Créole 27 bd Djily Mbaye. Dark wood and stained-glass interior is an unconventional setting for the solid (if a bit pricey) Cape Verdean meals served here, but the terrace at the back is pleasant. The *plancha créole* (CFA7500) makes a great introduction to the cuisine.

La Fourchette 4 rue Parent ☏ 338 21 88 87. Close to the *Hôtel du Marché*, this outstanding restaurant features an international, French-influenced *carte* of succulent dishes that border on *haute cuisine*.

Le Dagorne 11 rue Dagorne. Smart French restaurant that's been around for ages has a small dining room serving a great *menu*. Closed Mon.

Le Lagon 1 near *Hôtel Lagon 2*, rte de la Corniche Est. Great location, set on a small pier looking out to sea and popular with the French expat crowd. The pricey seafood dishes have lost a bit of their appeal in recent years, but it's a superb place to have an aperitif at sunset.

Le Sarraut av Albert Sarraut. Decent French restaurant popular with the expat community offering a variety of dishes such as chicken curry (CFA5900) and tournedos rossini (CFA9900). An alfresco terrace cordoned off by a thick hedge makes for a relaxing meal. The bar is also an excellent retreat from the beating sun and market touts.

On and north of Avenue Pompidou

Adonis av Pompidou. Colourful hole-in-the-wall offering Lebanese eat-in or takeaway, with great hummus and *baba ghanouj* (CFA2500). Service to the comfy, diner-style booths is fast.

Ali Baba 23 av Pompidou. A Dakar institution, where large portions of great-value Lebanese fast food is served all day here to throngs of NGO expats, backpackers and local office workers. Try the falafel-like cones of *viande hachée*. Pay at the counter first, then redeem your voucher.

Boulangerie Sandaga av du Président Lamine Guèye (open 24hrs). Excellent bread, cakes and croissants baked throughout the day.

Farid at *Hôtel Farid*, 51 rue Vincens. An excellent choice, this is Dakar's best Lebanese restaurant, with dishes from CFA4000 and daily non-Lebanese specials for a bit less.

Keur Ndeye corner of rue Sandiniéri and rue Vincens ☏ 338 21 49 73. Upmarket but well-priced Senegalese restaurant with *kora* minstrels. Any of the half-dozen *menu* specials at CFA2000 are well worth it, and be sure to try the excellent meat-filled spring rolls or *nems* (CFA1500).

La Palmeraie 20 av Pompidou. Although at the time of writing, this much-loved institution had just changed hands, the extensive list of Belgian ales and copious brasserie-style offerings of sandwiches, snacks, wonderful cakes and excellent coffee is sure to remain. A great respite from the bustling av Pompidou and with free Wi-Fi.

La Pizzeria 47 rue A.K. Bourgi ☏ 338 21 09 26 (Open 7pm–3am daily). Old-style, cavernous Franco-Italian pizza restaurant, catering mainly to expats and tourists and offering a variety of tasty pizza dishes (from CFA3500) and a good wine list.

L'Impérial (aka *Robert's Bar*) place de l'Indépendance, corner of allée R. Delmas. Pleasant restaurant/bar retreat, away from *place* hustlers, with friendly staff serving pizza and fish dishes and a good-value *menu*. The outside, covered terrace right on the *place* is a good place to watch the world go by.

South of Avenue Pompidou

Caesar bd de la République across from *Café de Rome*. Though the food isn't fast, this mostly-fried-chicken place has menus of spicy dishes from CFA2500. While you wait for your meal, smoke some *sheesha* (CFA1500) in the back with the youthful, largely Lebanese clientele.

Café de Rome bd de la République (daily until 2am). Tasty international menu with daily specials and good pastas (CFA3000–4000), served in comfortable a/c premises or out on the shaded terrace. Live music at weekends.

Chez Loutcha 101 rue Mousse Diop ☏ 338 21 03 02 (closed Sun). An exceptional Cape Verdean patio restaurant with a huge menu of typically enormous meals. Wonderful bouillabaisse, tuna salad and an insurmountable three-course *menu*, including vegetarian options. Many dishes at CFA3000.

Indigo Café 26 rue Félix Fauré (happy hour 6–7pm). Trendy bar-restaurant opposite the *Miramar* hotel, offering good breakfasts, mixed grills, desserts and cocktails. Occasional soul or salsa evenings.

Le Hanoi corner of rue Carnot and rue Joseph Gomis. A charming matron presides over the tasty and well-priced Vietnamese food – the *fondue Vietnamienne* (CFA8500), with seafood and vegetables in a hot broth, is especially good. There's a bar at the front and a shady patio at the back.

Le Plateau 56 rue Félix Fauré. Though this popular hole-in-the-wall offers zero atmosphere, the full African meals (from CFA1000) are excellent bargains.

🍴 **Le Toukouleur** 122 rue Mousse Diop ☏338 21 51 93. One of Dakar's finest restaurants, serving business types at lunch and a cosmopolitan crowd at night. The gregarious French owner presides over outstanding, meticulously-presented cuisine in a trendy, upscale interior. Try the superb *fondon du tortou* (puréed crabmeat) or the *couillé de cresson* salad. Also serves excellent fruit juices.

Niani Beach rte de la Corniche Est ☏338 22 60 71. French cuisine and beautiful views, with some tables set over the water.

🍴 **Restaurant le ? 2** ("Le Point d'Interrogation Deux") rue El Hadj A.A. Ndoye. Although the nearby original *Restaurant le ?* is no more, this remains an excellent cheapie, with long menus of quality Senegalese food at outstanding prices. Try the *yassa crevettes* (CFA2500).

Touba 95 rue Joseph Gomis. Though the interior at this busy lunchtime place is only a tad less bland than the nearby *Plateau*, the food – generous helpings of Senegalese staples – is just as good. Highly recommended *mafé* for CFA700.

Out from the centre

Cité Claudelle out past Soumbédioune, near the university. A row of five or six good-value restaurants offering specialities from various African countries. Frequented by a good mix of mostly African diners.

🍴 **Jardin Thailandais** 10 bd du Sud, just across from the *Pen'Art Jazz* club, Point E ☏338 25 58 33 (closed Sun). Regarded as the best Asian food in Senegal, this family-run spot does superb Thai dishes (try the lemongrass soup) in a great, airy atmosphere – especially in the garden at the back.

Les Gourmandises Africaines rue 3, near rue A, Point E ☏338 24 87 05. Recommended for its Senegalese and other African dishes. Eat inside or in the leafy garden.

Drinking, nightlife and entertainment

Despite the city's impeccably cosmopolitan credentials, central Dakar's **nightlife** is less exotic than you might expect. If you want a fairly unpredictable night out, most of the bars listed below will provide that, though note that most of them are pick-up joints and all are pricey. The music played is generally a cosmopolitan mix of Senegalese, Congolese, Cuban, American and European. For real action, at a price, try one of the out-of-the-centre **big discos** or **music clubs** – the hottest of which are located in Point E – which warm up around midnight (the "soirée"), but may also have an earlier session, from 7 to 11pm (the "matinée") that can be just as lively. If you're going to check out several places and move by taxi, anticipate spending at least CFA50,000 between two, and that's without many drinks – which may be as much as CFA2000–3000, though one is occasionally included in the cover of CFA2000–5000. Going in a group works out cheaper and is more fun. Take IDs but leave all valuables behind.

Another option is heading twenty minutes north of town to Les Almadies, where Dakar's coolest congregate at a number of high-class nightclubs (see p.216). Most Dakarois taxi drivers know the bigger places by name. If dancing in the sand at dawn is your thing, check out one of the many impromptu S*oirée La Plage* **beach parties** held monthly at various coastal hotels, including *Sokhamon*. Call ☏776 43 40 49 to find out when and where the next *fête* is.

For **theatre**, Théâtre Daniel Sorano (☏338 22 17 15 ✉sorano@sentoo.sn) on Boulevard de la République is the place, though shows – which sometimes feature big-name music stars – are not held nightly.

Bars

Alexandra 42 rue Wagane Diouf. With a Billie Jean–style dance floor, this bright and low-key spot is the best find on an otherwise seedy block of black-lit, mirrored brothel bars.

Cambodge corner of rue 6 and bd de la Gueule Tapée, behind the cinema in Gueule Tapée. Try the courtyard here for a cheap drink in a relaxed African bar.

Le Mex 91 bis rue Mousse Diop (Tues–Sun 10pm–dawn). Smoky, low-key karaoke spot with lots of mirrors, comfy seating and a pole-dancing corner. The clientele tends to be a mix of NGO workers, prostitutes and Senegalese hipsters.

Le Seven 25 rue Mohamed V at the corner of rue Félix Faure. A popular stop for NGOs and UN types, this modish bar tends to attract a toubab-only crowd and plays the latest European club hits. A chilled place to cool off after one of the many concerts at the nearby Institut Français.

Le Soninké Downstairs at the *Hôtel Miramar*, 25–27 rue Félix Fauré. Small and technicolour with a pool table and its share of friendly regulars.

Le Soumbé Soumbédioune, in the Village Artisanal. This breezy bar is a great place to watch the return of the fishermen in Soumbédioune bay. At weekends, the Super Cayor salsa band pulls in a slightly older crowd than *Le Kily* (see below) next door.

Le Viking av Pompidou. Cool, comfortable pub-bar whose suggestive wallpaper is a suitable backdrop for the loitering prostitutes. Still, a welcome and safe respite from the hustlers outside.

Ozio 21 rue Victor Hugo ☎338 23 87 87. This fashionable new spot works hard to pull off its zen ambience, with dim lighting, swish *chaise longues* and aloof staff. There's food as well (mains from CFA9000), but you're really paying for the cool factor.

Quiz corner of rue Carnot and rue Wagane Diouf. A mostly local, mostly male clientele visits this smoky, purple-painted corner bar to chill out after work and talk politics.

Clubs and discos

Africa Star corner of rue Raffenel and rue de Thiong. Good dance spot but very much a pick-up joint – and expensive.

Koulgraoul at Océanium, rte de la Corniche Est ☎775 05 69 69. The first Sunday of every month this diving spot puts on an immensely popular all-night dance party right on the water. Not to be missed.

La Siège de Gorée corner of allée R. Delmas and bd de la Libération, behind the Hôtel de Ville (nightly until 2am). A massive, packed, open-air dance floor with mixed European/African music and cheap beer. Free entrance, though go early – by 10pm – as it quietens down at 1am.

Le Ngalam bd de l'Est, Point E. Recorded music and expensive drinks.

Obox N'gor, next to the *Hôtel Diarama*. With lots of European music, this low-key spot caters to a fairly touristy crowd. If you're in the vicinity, well worth calling in on, otherwise the town clubs are better.

Live-music venues

Just 4U av Cheikh Anita Diop in Point E ☎338 24 32 50. Easily the best place in Dakar to hear live music, with frequent performances (usually beginning around 10pm) on the outdoor stage by Orchestra Baobab, Daara J and other Senegalese greats, as well as international stars. They also serve tasty dinners (mains from CFA4000).

Le Kilimanjaro (also known as "Le Kily"), Soumbédioune, by the Village Artisanal in Gueule Tappé ☎822 69 91. Though it's lost some of its oomph in recent years, young crowds still come to this large dance spot, owned by Thione Seck, to see various *mbalax* performers.

Le Sahel (also known as "Sunset"), corner of av Cheikh Anta Diop and bd de la Gueule Tapée. Still one of the hottest *mbalax* clubs in town, but can feel a little dodgy at times, so best visited in a group.

Pen'Art Jazz 12 bd du Sud in Point E ☎338 64 51 31 ⊛www.penartjazz.com. This low-key, intimate jazz club features a small stage and is the best place in Dakar to come hear a range of good music (not always jazz).

Stade Demba Diop SICAP Liberté, near pl de l'OUA (Jet d'Eau). If there's a concert here at Dakar's major venue, the posters all over town will be pretty obvious. Get there on time, but be prepared for several hours' delay and for pickpockets and hustlers (take no valuables and find a taxi as soon as you leave).

Thiossane SICAP rue 10 ☎338 24 60 46. Though it can get hot and the bar offerings are pretty meagre, this is probably Dakar's best-known club. Owned by Senegalese legend Youssou N'Dour, who takes the stage several times a month to put on first-class performances.

Listings

Airlines Air Algérie, 2 place de l'Indépendance ☎338 23 80 81; Air France, 47 av Albert Sarraut ☎338 20 81 21; Air Gabon, 5 av Pompidou ☎822 33 24 05; Air Guinea, 25 av Pompidou ☎338 21 44 42; Air Mali, 14 rue Sandiniéri ☎823 33 24 61; Air Mauritanie, 2 place de l'Indépendance ☎338 22 81 88; Air Sénégal, 45 av Albert Sarraut ☎338 42 41 00 or 338 23 62 29; Alitalia, 5 av Pompidou ☎338 23 31 29; Ghana Airways, 22 rue Ramez Bourgi ☎338 22 28 20; Iberia, 2 place de l'Indépendance ☎338 23 34 77; Royal Air Maroc, 1 place de l'Indépendance ☎338 49 47 47; Saudia, place de l'Indépendance, corner of rue Malenfant ☎338 23 72 42/5; SN Brussels Airlines, corner of rue Parchappe and rue Beranger Ferand ☎338 23 04 60; South African Airways, 12 av Albert Sarraut ☎338 23 27 60 or 338 23 27 62; TACV (Cape Verde Airlines), 103 rue Mousse Diop ☎338 21 39 68; TAP Air Portugal, 3 rue El Hadj A.A. Ndoye ☎338 21 01 13; Tunis Air, 24 av Léopold S. Senghor ☎338 23 14 35.

American Express The main agent is Sénégal Tours, place de l'Indépendance (☎338 23 38 38), who will sell you traveller's cheques on your Amex card (which can be cashed in all banks except Citibank).

Banks and exchange Most of the banks' head offices are on the west side of place de l'Indépendance and there are several with ATMs. There's a closed-booth ATM (seems to take most credit and debit cards), with a security guard outside, at CBAO on the south side of av Pompidou just up from the *place*.

Books, newspapers and maps The Librairie aux Quatre Vents on rue Félix Fauré, between rue Mousse Diop and rue Joseph Gomez (☎338 21 80 83; Mon–Sat 8.45am–12.30pm & 3–6.45pm), is probably the best bookshop in West Africa; they also sell a few books in English. Also try Clairafrique (☎338 22 21 69; same hours), 2 rue Sandiniéri, place de l'Indépendance, next to the Chamber of Commerce. The *Herald Tribune*, *Time* and *Newsweek* are available from newsstands along av Pompidou and the upper end of Albert Sarraut, near place de l'Indépendance. The best and cheapest large maps of Dakar and Senegal can be bought at the Direction des Travaux Géographique et Cartographique, Hann (☎338 32 11 82 ⓦwww.ausenegal.com/dtgc); head up the autoroute to the Hann exit, turn right after 1km and look for the sign for the nearby "Le Soleil". A smaller selection is available at the Librairie aux Quatre Vents.

Car rental Avis, 71 km 2.5 bd du Centenaire de la Commune de Dakar ☎338 49 77 57, airport ☎338 20 46 28; Europcar, bd de la Libération ☎338 22 06 91, airport ☎338 20 17 36; Hertz, 64 rue Félix Fauré ☎338 22 20 16, airport ☎338 20 11 74; National, av Abdoulaye Fadiga ☎338 22 33 66, airport ☎338 20 92 10. Local rental agents include Sénécartours, at 64 rue Carnot (☎338 22 42 86) and the airport (☎338 69 50 07); and the cheaper Assurcar at the Gorée wharf (☎338 23 72 50 ⓦwww.assurcar.sn), where a Peugeot 205 costs CFA69,300 per week plus CFA110 per km, and a Suzuki 4x4 costs CFA126,000 per week plus CFA200 per km; all credit cards accepted.

CDs Stacks of bootlegs are sold at stalls around Sandaga market and by street sellers in the vicinity. Beware of buying from the pavement sellers along av Pompidou. Legitimate recordings have a hologram on the box as the government supposedly cracks down on pirating. Prices for original CDs should be around CFA5000. For browsing and listening in a more controlled and relaxing atmosphere, head out to a suburban market such as Castors.

Cinemas Once cinemas were privatized in the 1990s (and once DVDs became popular), public cinema in Senegal began a slow death. There are a handful of bespoke places to catch films in town though: the Institut Français (see "Cultural centres" below) puts on regular French and African films throughout the week, while Kadjinol Station (☎338 42 86 62 ⓦwww.kadjinol-edu.com), just off av Albert Sarraut and opposite Canal Horizons TV, is a funky lounge-cum-restaurant that screens recent Hollywood and European films.

Clinics and hospitals If you need a consultation, enquire with your embassy or try one of the following: Dr F. Coulibaly (Mme), 69 rue Mousse Diop ☎822 33 19 78; Dr Y. Diallo (gynaecologist), Clinique du Cap, av Pasteur ☎338 89 02 02; Dr Djoneidi, corner of rue A and rue 1, Point E ☎338 25 75 03 (English speaker). For accidents, the Hôpital Principal is at the corner of av Nelson Mandela and av Léopold S. Senghor (☎338 39 50 50), or try SOS Médecin, the private emergencies organization (☎338 89 15 15 or 338 21 32 13).

Crafts and curios For the real thing, visit El Hadj Traoré, rue Mohamed V, between rue Carnot and rue Félix Fauré – a fine, musty collection. There are more holes-in-the-wall selling a variety of "authentic" items from all over West Africa further north on rue Mohamed V, on the left before av Pompidou. Avoid flashy "galleries" – unreasonably expensive and not special. You can find nice, inexpensive scarves and Mauritanian jewellery in various spots along the Marché Kermel.

Cultural centres The library of the American Cultural Centre has moved out to the West African Research Centre in Fann-Résidence (☎338 24 20 62 🌐www.warc-croa.org). The British Council is at rue Joseph Gomis, Amitié Zone A–B (☎338 69 27 00 🌐www.britishcouncil.org/senegal). The British–Senegalese Institute, 18 rue de 18 Juin, off av Courbet (Mon 3.30–6.30pm, Tues–Fri 9am–noon & 3.30–6.30pm, Sat 9am–noon; ☎338 22 28 70), caters to the small British community, and has a library and occasional film shows. The Centre Culturel Blaise Senghor, 6 bd Dial Diop (☎338 24 66 00 or 338 24 98 39), hosts events and concerts, shows movies and holds drumming classes. The Centre Culturel Français at 36 rue El Hadj A.A. Ndoye (☎338 23 03 20 🌐www.institutfr-dakar .org) has a French library and a relaxing, inexpensive café in the garden and puts on regular French and African films and lots of free or inexpensive open-air concerts. The Centre Culturel Français and the Alliance Franco-Sénégalaise are both part of the Institut Français. The Goëthe Institut is at 2 av Albert Sarraut (☎338 23 04 70 🌐www.goethe.de/dakar).

Embassies Burkina Faso, Lot 1, Liberté VI ☎338 27 95 09 ℻338 27 95 03; Cameroon, 157–159 rue Joseph Gomis ☎338 49 02 92 ℻338 23 33 96; Canada, 45 bd de la République ☎338 89 47 00 ℻338 89 47 20; Cape Verde, 3 av El Hadj Djily Mbaye, 13th floor ☎338 21 18 73 ℻338 21 06 97; Côte d'Ivoire, av Birago Diop, Point E ☎338 69 02 70; France, 1 rue El Hadj A.A. Ndoye ☎338 39 51 00 ℻338 39 53 59; The Gambia, 11 rue de Thiong, Plateau ☎338 21 72 30 ℻338 21 62 79; Guinea, rue 7, Point E ☎338 24 86 06 ℻338 25 59 46; Guinea-Bissau, rue 6, Point E ☎338 24 59 22; Mali, 23 rte de la Corniche Ouest, Fann ☎338 24 62 50 or 338 24 62 52 ℻338 25 94 71; Mauritania, rue 37, Colobane ☎338 22 62 38 ℻338 22 62 68; Morocco, av Cheikh Anta Diop ☎338 24 69 27; Nigeria, rue 1, Point E ☎338 24 43 97 ℻338 25 81 36; South Africa, Lot 5, École de Police, Mermoz-Sud ☎338 65 19 59 ℻338 64 23 59; UK, 20 rue du Dr Guillet ☎338 23 73 92 ℻338 23 27 66; USA, av Jean XXIII ☎338 23 42 96 ℻338 22 29 91.

Internet access Royale Boutique, corner of bd de la République & rue Victor Hugo (24hr; CFA500/hr), has a fast connection, while NTIC-Center, 77 rue Joseph Gomis (24hr; CFA500/hr), is conveniently central.

Language courses Private and group courses in French and Wolof at the Institut Français, 3 rue Parchappe (☎338 21 08 22 🌐www.institutfr-dakar .org; CFA90,000 for 50hr), or Africa Consultants International, Baobab Training Center, 509 SICAP Baobab (☎338 25 36 37 🌐www.acibaobab.org; CFA5000/hr).

Pharmacies Most central is Pharmacie Guigon, 101 av du Président Lamine Guèye at the corner of rue Pompidou (☎338 23 03 00; Mon–Sat 8am–11pm); they usually have someone who speaks some English. Pharmacie Nelson Mandela, corner of rue Joseph Gomis and av Nelson Mandela (☎338 21 21 72), is open 24hr; or look in *Le Soleil* for a listing of after-hours pharmacies.

Police Commissariat Central, corner of rue de Docteur Thèze & rue Sandiniéri ☎338 23 71 49.

Post and phones The main PTT is on bd El Hadj Djily Mbaye near the Marché Kermel (Mon–Fri 7am–7pm & Sat 8am–5pm). Poste restante costs CFA250. Large parcels can be sent from the Colis Postaux office at place d'Oran, at the junction of av El Hadj Malick Sy and av Blaise Diagne. You can also call internationally at the PTT (Mon–Fri 8am–6pm, Sat 8am–1pm). Alternatively, go to one of the numerous *télécentres* located all over town; most places in the centre charge CFA100 per unit, though if you shop around you can find cheaper.

Supermarkets The city's biggest supermarket, Score, is at the Centre Commercial Sahm out on av Cheikh Anta Diop/bd de la Gueule Tapée. More convenient are the smaller Score supermarket at 31 av Albert Sarraut, and Le Supermarché Filfili just north of place de l'Indépendance.

Swimming pools Roof terrace at *Hôtel Indépendance* (officially CFA3000, but just buy a drink); Olympic-sized and tropical at the *Savana*, Cap Manuel (CFA5000, CFA8000 Sat & Sun); chic and popular behind the *Hôtel Teranga* (CFA5000, CFA7000 Sun); huge and inexpensive at the Piscine Olympique in Point E (CFA1000).

Tailoring Good, reasonably priced tailors abound all over the centre and suburbs. The best bargains are at Marché HLM, where they will often run something up for you while you wait.

Travel agents Try Sénégal Tours, place de l'Indépendance (☎338 39 99 35 ℻338 23 26 44 ✉sngtours@sentoo.sn), or any of the following: Sandaga Voyages, 2 av Pompidou ☎338 42 50 01; SDV Voyages, 47 rue Albert Sarraut ☎338 39 00 81; Sénégambie Voyages, 27 bd de la République ☎338 21 68 31 ℻338 21 44 92 ✉sgv@sentoo .sn; or the established Nouvelles Frontières, 1 bd de la République ☎338 23 34 34 ℻338 23 65 54 ✉nouvelles-frontieres-senegal@sentoo.sn.

Wrestling *La lutte* can be seen all over the city, with regular Sat and Sun evening shows at the Stade Demba Diop attracting the big stars. Wandering around Medina and Grand Dakar at weekends you can find amateur and children's bouts; around the Monument de l'Indépendance seems a popular venue, as do a number of places down the Petite Côte (see p.219). Wrestling is also on TV every Sat afternoon.

Île de Gorée and Iles des Madeleines

Just twenty minutes by *chaloupe* from Dakar lies the tiny **Île de Gorée**, a mere 900m end to end and 300m across at its widest point. Its **slave-trading** history – which some historians now believe to have been exaggerated – has made it more or less a required visit and undoubtedly helped it win UNESCO World Heritage Site status, but it's a compelling retreat in any case, bristling with pastel-coloured old buildings and draped with bougainvillea. It's particularly beautiful in the early morning, when you may be the only visitor. Within similarly easy reach of the mainland are the **Iles des Madeleines**, which have been designated a national park and hold plenty of interest, particularly for naturalists.

Gorée

The first Europeans on Gorée were the **Portuguese**, who used the island as a trading base in the mid-fifteenth century. **Dutch** adventurers captured it in 1588 – naming it "Goede reede" (good roadstead) – but the Portuguese regained control before again losing the island, this time to the **French**, in 1678. This date marked the beginning of the golden age of the **signares** of Gorée; these daughters of white colonists and slave women wielded extraordinary power in a largely matriarchal, slave-worked society. Gorée was fought over by the French and the **English**, who repeatedly captured and recaptured Gorée from each other – the score for the eighteenth century being France 5, England 4. The island prospered despite the changes of ownership: by the 1850s there was a population of 6000 – six times what it is today. The first fortifications of Dakar in 1857 signalled the start of Gorée's slow, graceful demise.

Chaloupe to Dakar

ILE DE GORÉE

Fort d'Estrées
(IFAN Historical
Museum)

ACCOMMODATION
Asao   A
Hostellerie du
  Chevalier de
  Boufflers   B
Keur Beer
  Auberge   C

Maritime
Museum

Beach

Police
Station

Maison des
Esclaves

Jardin
Publique

OLD
TOWN

Eglise
St. Charles

Musée de
la Femme

PLACE DU
GOUVERNEMENT

N

Castle

RESTAURANTS
Restaurant
  St. Germaine   1
Tramina Eric   2

0   100 m

The **Maison des Esclaves** (House of Slaves; Tues–Sun 10.30am–noon & 2.30–6pm; CFA500) is the sole survivor of a number of buildings reputedly used to store "pieces of ebony" before they were shipped to the New World. A visit could prove anticlimactic, though – especially if you've ever seen film of weeping African-Americans here – as there is little interpretive material on hand. Still, the walls, dark chambers and slit windows more or less speak for themselves.

Although Gorée is now thought to have been too small and impractical to have been a major holding area for slaves, the building stands as a mournful and numbing symbol of the first major phase in the European exploitation of Africa. Scarcely believable though it seems, the slave traders lived in some style above the warehouse, where there are well-proportioned rooms, a balcony and a tiny reconstructed eighteenth-century Dutch kitchen.

Opposite, the **Musée de la Femme Sénégalaise** (Tues–Sat 10am–5pm; CFA500) was opened in 1994 as a celebration of Senegalese women's role in the material and spiritual well-being of the family. Exhibits include textiles, baskets, kitchenware, jewellery and traditional dress, and some of the information is in English.

The cleverly designed **IFAN Historical Museum** (Tues–Sat 10am–1pm & 2.30–6pm; CFA200), at the northern end of the island in the horseshoe-shaped Fort d'Estrées, takes you on an instructive tour through Senegal's history to the present day. A few minutes' walk south, the **Musée de la Mer** (in theory Tues–Sun 10am–5; CFA500) makes a more singular contribution, being in large part devoted to the life cycle of the dogfish – note the human foot in a preserved fish stomach. In both museums, explanations are in French only.

In the town, dozens of flaking **houses** are virtually concealed from the street behind high walls and wrought iron, including a presidential villa. There's a cluster of fine and more easily viewed Gorée houses at the northern end. Gorée's oldest building is the seventeenth-century **police station**, believed to be built on the site of a Portuguese church dating from 1482. Apart from these, the island boasts the old **church** of St Charles Barromée and, at the southern end, a **castle** topping a warren of bunkers and underground passages from where there are superb views over the island and across to Dakar. The sheltered harbour **beach**, backed by a row of low-key **restaurants** and bars, is a draw in itself, but the real pleasure of the island is just wandering the quiet, sandy lanes and soaking the place up.

Practicalities

The *chaloupe* makes up to a dozen journeys daily from Dakar's Embarcadère de Gorée, off Boulevard de la Libération, between 6.15am (7am on Sundays) and 1am every one to two hours; a return ticket, valid for as long as you want to stay, costs CFA5000. With few exceptions, the return journeys from Gorée are thirty minutes later than departures from Dakar. For a day-trip from Dakar, it's best to take an early *chaloupe* to beat the crowds, and you should try to avoid weekends, especially in the high season; Mondays are quiet, but the museums are closed. Perhaps inevitably, pushy "guides" have found their way onto the island – their services are barely necessary, but if you do decide you want to be shown round, you're better off hiring an **official guide** from the island's *syndicat d'initiative* (daily 9am–1pm & 2.30–5pm; ☎338 22 91 77) near the Maison des Esclaves.

There are two high-quality **accommodation** options on Gorée, usually heavily booked. The *Hostellerie du Chevalier de Boufflers* is the more established (☎/℉338 22 53 64 ✉goreeboufflers@arc.sn ❺), featuring classy rooms with fan and breakfast and a good but expensive seafood menu, while the modern *Keur Beer Auberge* (☎/℉338 21 38 01 ⊕www.keurbeer.xdir.fr ❺) offers cool, comfortable rooms with fridge. A good alternative to the hotels is the *Asao* guesthouse (☎338 21 81 95 ❹), above the crafts shop Galerie 3A, with four newly-renovated **private rooms** set around a leafy courtyard. You should be able to find more private rooms by asking around town or at the many restaurants facing the jetty – the friendly *Tramina Eric* (☎338 21 19 31 ✉erictgoree@hotmail.com ❹) has three available – or by accepting one of the many offers of assistance you'll receive from the moment you step off the ferry.

The **restaurants** are all pleasant, alfresco affairs with meals from around CFA3000. *Restaurant St Germaine*, just opposite the port, offers a particularly warm welcome, a *menu* from CFA6000 and several twin rooms (☎338 42 42 55 ❸).

Iles des Madeleines

Twenty minutes by motor pirogue from the mainland, the uninhabited **Îles des Madeleines** are home to a number of interesting **plants** – including a dwarf baobab and American wild coffee – and many species of indigenous and migratory **birds**: the tropic bird (*Phaeton aethereus*), recognizable by its bright red bill and immensely long pointed tail, is found nowhere else in Senegal. There's little in the way of coral to be found in the surrounding seas, but the clear waters harbour a rich variety of **fish**.

The island of **Sarpan** – the size of Gorée, and the only one at which a boat can anchor – is best visited between September and November, when the seas are not too rough and the anchoring point in the cove is generally accessible. The **park office** (☎338 21 81 82; daily 7.30am–5pm) is just north of Soumbédioune bay on the Route de la Corniche Ouest, past the Terrou-Bi casino complex on the left. Here you can buy the obligatory park permit (CFA1000) and arrange for a **pirogue** to take you over (CFA3000 return for 1–3 people, less per person for bigger groups). You can stay on Sarpan all day – just tell the *piroguier* when you want to be picked up – so take food and drink as well as binoculars, and a snorkel and mask if possible.

The island slopes from thirty-metre cliffs at its northern end to a gentler southern shore where the boats moor. Although no-one lives here (you'll almost certainly have the island to yourselves), it hasn't always been completely deserted, as occasional finds of **stone tools** indicate. More recently, however, it's acquired a malevolent reputation, and "L'îlot Sarpan" (named after a French soldier banished here) was soon corrupted to "L'île aux Serpents" – of which it has none. The Lebu traditionally believe that sea spirits live on the island; their own efforts to settle on it several centuries ago were met with odd weather and violent seismic effects and they chose Gorée instead.

North and east of Dakar

An easy and much-hyped trip out of town is to the beaches of **Pointe des Almadies**, **N'gor** and **Yoff**. From Dakar, white *cars rapides* leave from near Marché Sandaga to take you up to N'gor past the rounded hills of **Mermoz and Les Mamelles** and the turnoff to **Pointe des Almadies**, which manages not to be totally smothered by its *Club Med* holiday complex. From N'gor, the *cars rapides* continue on to Yoff; if you want to bypass N'gor, bus #8 heads direct to Yoff up the autoroute.

Public transport to **Lac Retba** and the monastery of **Keur Moussa** can be unpredictable, and in truth neither place need come high on your list. At the bottom of the list is **Kayar**, further up the coast; once a fishing village, it's now a tourist trap of the most oppressive kind, where groups are brought to see the fishermen coming in. You can see the same thing, less intrusively, all along the West African coast.

The Route de N'gor and Pointe des Almadies
A taxi to **N'gor/Les Almadies** from central Dakar should cost no more than CFA3000. The *Hôtel Méridien Présidentiel* here is the most expensive hotel in the country (☎338 69 69 69 ⓦwww.lemeridien.com ⑧) and is one of Africa's most important conference centres, with impressive facilities and standards. For superb, *gastronomique* eating at surprisingly affordable prices, look no further than ⚒ *Mogador* (☎338 20 04 02 ⓔtoukouleur@sentoo.sn), just down the road, an opulent five-star restaurant serving outstanding French cuisine. For a late-night snack, try *La Brioche*, a 24-hour patisserie serving superb cakes and coffee; they operate a half-dozen locations on and off the main Route de N'gor. Several nightspots along the same road are where the action happens for wealthy Dakarois: the newest is the sleek and polished club *Duplex* (☎338 20 00 30), while a few minutes' walk south is the Indian-themed *Le Patio* (☎338 20 58 23). Both are open daily from 7pm until dawn.

Unfortunately the westernmost tip of the Cap Vert peninsula – the **Pointe des Almadies** itself – currently lies within the private grounds of the local *Club Mediterranée*, and access, either along the shore, or through *Club Med*'s front gate, is restricted to guests.

N'gor
N'GOR itself has lost much of the charm it once had, with the hideous *Hôtel Ngor Diarama* invading the skyline (☎338 20 27 24 ⓦwww.hotels-ngordiarama.com ⑧),

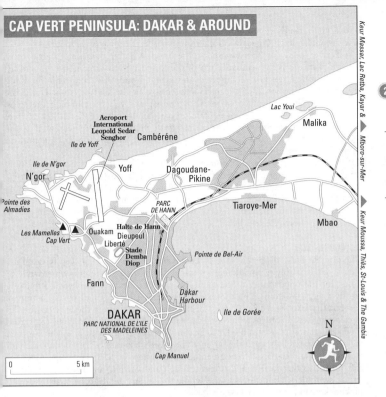

CAP VERT PENINSULA: DAKAR & AROUND

Keur Massar, Lac Retba, Kayar & ▲

Mboro-sur-Mer ▲

Keur Moussa, Thiès, St-Louis & The Gambia ▲

and a rash of beach clubs, restaurants and sporting facilities between here and Yoff airport. For a good eating spot, try *La Cabane des Pêcheurs* at plage de N'gor (☎338 20 76 75 ⓦwww.atlantic-evasion.com), which has a number of beachfront tables – great for catching the Dakar sunset. They also have small apartments (CFA30,000) and hire out fishing boats for the day (CFA80,000).

There can be a fair bit of hassle around here, but an easy escape is to take a pirogue (CFA500 return) out to the **Île du N'gor**, which is perhaps the best reason to come to this coast. The island is mostly divided into small plots for private beach houses – pretty enough retreats between the casuarina trees, but hardly idyllic. An old military assault course adds nothing to the clifftops on the island's northern side. There's a couple of small beaches on the landward shore, but not much space when the tide comes in. **Accommodation** is sparse, though there are a few rooms with balcony at *Chez Carla* (☎338 20 15 86 ❹), and at the friendly, but less atmospheric *Chez Seck* (☎776 34 57 18 or 776 47 81 66 ❷), overlooking the larger of the two beaches.

Yoff

The village of **YOFF** – a maze of houses, boats on the beach, children everywhere – has a sense of community that N'gor has lost. The beach is the start of a continuous strand that reaches north to the mouth of the Senegal River. There's also a tiny island – the **Île de Yoff** – just offshore, given over mostly to goats but yours for the exploring: a pirogue will take you over, though at low tide you can almost wade across. The recently renovated *Campement Touristique Le Poulagou* (☎338 20 23 47 ⓦwww.poulagou.ch ❸), right on the fishing beach, is a great place to stay.

Yoff is a focus for the **Layen** brotherhood, a Lebu fraternity whose most venerated shrine is the **mausoleum** of the founder Saidi Limamou Laye and his son Mandione Laye. For members of the brotherhood, this temple-like building is the holiest of sites, and it attracts vast crowds at the end of Ramadan; if the festoon of vultures perched on its roof doesn't put you off climbing the steps, respect should. A nearby grotto containing perfumed sands is believed to be where Muhammad's spirit dwelt for a thousand years before being reincarnated as the sect's founder. As the town is essentially run by the brotherhood, you'll find no alcohol in the neighbourhood.

If you want to participate in something unusual (though you won't be the only tourist on the scene) come to Yoff to watch a **spirit possession dance** (*ndeup*). The dances are performed by traditional healers to treat the mentally ill, who come with their relatives from all over Senegal. There is an annual week-long ceremony in April or May, but the dances occur whenever the family of a mentally ill person asks, and pays for, a healer's help.

Lac Retba

The popular Dakarois picnic spot of **Lac Retba** – also known as Lac Rose, "Pink Lake" – is certainly a remarkable spectacle, but a trip out here is worthwhile as much for the opportunity to get right out of Dakar and see the beach, stretching all the way to St-Louis. The pinkness of the soda lake is caused by the action of bacteria that excrete red iron oxide; for maximum effect, watch the water as the sun goes down, when it turns from coral to mauve and violet. Women collect salt from the lake – almost as salty as the Dead Sea and just as hard to swim in – which is then packed into sacks by men at the far end. The shore is a beach of bleached shells, with banana plots and casuarina trees greening up an otherwise harsh landscape. Over the soft **dunes** to the north is the Atlantic, rough and swirling and definitely only for strong swimmers. Unfortunately the whole tourist area tends to be swarming with pickpockets and troublemakers.

To get to the lake, about 40km from Dakar, take a **bush taxi** to **Keur Massar** (not to be confused with Keur Moussa; see below) and then another to **Niaga**. The *campement* here – the *Keur Kanni* – has concrete, thatched, s/c huts and a nice atmosphere (☎338 36 24 66 ⓦwww.keursalim.com ❺). It's a twenty-minute walk to the lakeside and several more *campements*.

Keur Moussa

The Benedictine monastery of **Keur Moussa**, up in the hills off the Thiès road 50km from Dakar, has acquired a reputation for its touristy *messes africaines* (African Masses) with *koras*, *balafons* and *tam-tams*, and plenty of produce for sale afterwards, including rather good goat's cheese. Sunday-morning Mass at 10am is the best. Without your own car, you'll need early transport towards Thiès and a drop-off at the junction 5km past **SEBHIKOTANE**, from where it's another 5km to the monastery.

South of Dakar

Beyond the city centre, on the busy **coast road** heading southeast, there's still forty or more kilometres before the edges of the capital finally give way to open, baobab-dotted countryside. Road and railway go through the agglomeration of **DAGOUDANE-PIKINE/GUEDIYAWE**, a huge spillover of city workers and refugees from the interior: already larger in area than the rest of greater Dakar, the sprawl is fast encroaching on the shifting dunes of the north Cap Vert coast.

RUFISQUE – the Portuguese fifteenth-century **Rio Fresco** – is the last Dakar suburb, and already provincial in feel as you head away from the city. A scruffy seafront town with a couple of hotels, it's more human in scale than anything closer to the city (you'll see *calèches* here, for example). If you enter or exit Dakar by road, you'll almost certainly get caught in bumper-to-bumper **traffic** here, during which time you'll be able to observe the wholesalers of **exotic birds** lining the road – middlemen between the poverty-stricken peasants and a market in the West which will pay the equivalent of a year's labour for a parrot.

If you're beach-hunting, there's little difficulty in travelling along here by bush taxi, and it's one area where you might successfully hitchhike. It's worth making the slight extra effort to get to **Palmarin**'s near-deserted shore – especially if **Fadiout** to the north leaves a sour taste in your mouth. Before reaching **Mbour**, check out the "Serer pyramids" – burial mounds – in the **Bandia Reserve**, 63km from Dakar just off the main highway south towards Kaolack.

The Petite Côte

At the small resort of **BARGNY**, an hour or so from Dakar, the **Petite Côte** begins, and both road and railway turn inland to the junction for Thiès, Touba and St-Louis. You'll notice a Portuguese influence in some of the region's architecture, and a strong Catholic presence, not unlike parts of the Casamance. Private taxis around most of the towns in the area cost CFA500 a hop.

Turning southeast onto the N1, 12km beyond Bargny, you pass several minor roads leading to **resort beaches** along the sandy, palm-fringed coastline. A new international **airport** scheduled to open sometime in the next decade, is under construction east of here at **NDIASS** to bring yet more visitors to the already heavily touristed coast. Two of the nicest resorts on the Petite Côte are **TOUBAB DIALAO** and, just to the south, **POPENGUINE**, both around 10km off the N1 and reachable by bush taxi or hitching. The former, popular with Peace Corps volunteers, is a fine place to chill out on the beach as you ponder how to carry home all the inexpensive, hassle-free handicrafts sold here. It also maintains a few low-key places to stay, such as the eccentric *Espace Sobo-Badê* with ocean-side rooms and a pricey restaurant (T 338 36 03 56 ❶–❸). In Popenguine, the *Campement Ker Cupaam* (T 339 56 49 51 ❺) has adequate doubles as well as cheaper dorms and runs local nature excursions. Otherwise, *Chez Ginette* is right on the beach and has a couple of roughly built rooms sleeping up to ten (T 339 57 71 10; CFA10,000 per room), with a choice between self-catering or home cooking. There's a fine restaurant, *L'Écho Côtier* (T 339 57 71 72 ✉ contact@echo-cotier.com), at the southern end of the beach, which offers dishes à la carte for around CFA5000 and can arrange rooms locally (❺–❻). The town is known for its lively, annual pilgrimage (W www .sanctuaire-poponguine.sn), which usually happens in mid-May.

Toubab Dialao

"Good place to chill on a great beach, an operating pecheur village and you see a lot of Senegalese art and handicrafts with little hassle."

Angus Neil, UK

Back on the N1, at the village of **NGUEKOKH**, a road leads southwest to the sea and the resorts of **Somone** and **Ngaparou**. A little further on, **SALY-PORTUDAL** (usually known simply as Saly) was once a tiny fishing outpost but is now a buzzing Mediterranean-style resort village with extravagant lodgings, restaurants, bars and watersports. You can stay relatively inexpensively at the plush *Royam* (T 339 57 20 70 ✉ royam@sentoo.sn; ❼), where the inviting rooms face a large pool, or go all out at the posher *Lamantin Beach Hôtel* (T 339 57 07 77 W www.lelamantin.com ❽), with private beach, pools, spa facilities and prices starting at well over CFA100,000. The rock-bottom options are a bit further down the coast at the more local **SALY-NIAKHNIAKHALE**, where you'll find the colourful *Auberge Khady* with modern rooms and a pool (T/F339 57 25 18 ⑤), and, a kilometre further south, the French-run *Ferme de Saly* (T776 38 47 90 Wwww.farmsaly.sn ⑥), with comfortable s/c bungalows and a pleasant bar on the beach. There are numerous **restaurant** options in the Saly-Portudal; *Habana Café*, on the beach walk, is one of the more atmospheric. The best place for a **drink** is the comfy, pier-side *Ponton de Espadon*. For all-out partying in town, the clubby **discos** at *Rolls* and *King Karaoke* vie for the pennant, while the music at *Macoumba* has a bit of an Arabic edge to it. Note that as the crow flies, Saly is only a few kilometres from Mbour, meaning you can easily stroll along the beach between the two in half an hour.

Away from the coastal swing of Saly, the scrub-and-baobab **Bandia Reserve** (T776 85 58 86 Wwww.reservedebandia.com; daily 8am–6pm; CFA7000, plus CFA3500 for obligatory guide; CFA30,000 for optional rental of a 4x4), to the east of the main highway to Kaolack (1km south of Sindia, 23km from the Thiès junction), contains an interesting archeological site: the **burial mounds** of the vanished Serer village of Tay, and a **burial baobab**, where Serer griots were once entombed. A collection of skulls and bones still lies at the baobab's small entrance. Don't miss the **replicas** of the burial huts which lie beneath the hardened earth mounds. The reserve also harbours various animals, including crocodile, ostrich and various antelope species, and there's an excellent, well-placed **restaurant**, *La Bandia*, set 2km after the park entrance, serving local dishes from CFA3500. Plan for a good three or four hours to take in all there is to see at the reserve.

Just go ape

"On the road to Mbour, opposite the Bandia Reserve, is an activity centre set up by a Frenchman called Akrobaobab. You can spend the day there whizzing about among the treetops – ziplines and cargo nets have been erected so you can get a bird's-eye view of the baobabs."

We were Bikers, UK

Mbour and Nianing

The dusty fishing town of **MBOUR**, 80km southeast of Dakar, is an obvious base for this part of the coast, though not the most attractive. Since the town depends mostly on fishing, the **beach** is littered with fishy remains and associated odours, and the sea is uninviting anyway – usually calm and tending to be full of seaweed – except in the small area opposite the *Tama Lodge*, where it's cleaned every morning by hotel staff. Mbour's *gare routière* is on the northeastern edge of the centre, and the town has a PTT, Internet cafés and a BICIS bank with ATM.

For **accommodation**, one of the greatest finds along the Petite Côte is the debonair *Tama Lodge* (T339 57 00 40 Wwww.tamalodge.com ⑦), a series of delightful, thatched, lodge-style bungalows tastefully decorated with Malian art and situated behind an excellent beach (they clean the hotel's patch of sand every morning). Superb meals are served at tables right on the sand and are well worth the price. If you double-back towards town, you reach the more reasonably-priced German-run *Petit Eden* (T339 57 44 77 Wwww.petit-eden.de ④) whose rooms with private baths are set around a green garden with a small wading pool; they also hire out bicycles. Cheapest of all is south of here along the coast just next to the *Coco Beach Hotel*: *Martine La Suisesse* consists of a few home-made rooms around a diminutive garden a few minutes from the beach (T339 57 31 09 ②). Mbour has a fair number of local bars and small **restaurants**, most of which serve good meals for around CFA2000; the convivial *Chez Paolo* (aka *The Calabash*; closed Mon) serves very good Senegalese food and is overseen by a local who ran his own eaterie in Covent Garden, London. *Le Djembe* is good for inexpensive Senegalese dishes and becomes a lively club at night. For more upscale, beach-front dining, head to the *Tama Lodge* (see above), which cooks exquisite fish dishes – the *carpe rouge* is highly recommended. Late at night, *Club Malibu* is a popular stop for a drink in town.

The road continues south towards **NIANING**, which has a cleaner beach, and more appealing **accommodation** options, though much of the coast has been bought up by Europeans who come to build their retirement abodes. The village has several excellent *campements*, of which *Les Manguiers de Warang* (℡339 57 51 74 ⓦwww.lesmanguiersdewarang.com ❸), just off the main road before you get to town, is the least expensive and one of the nicest, with clean and classy rooms set about lovely, sprawling grounds and a small pool. The *Ben'tenier* (℡339 57 14 20 ⓦwww.lebentenier.org ❸) has great food and a lovely garden where bands often play. They're great with excursions, too, and they also run dance and music classes. A few minutes' walk from here, *Le Virage* is a good little terrace pizzeria. Substantial **birdlife**, to be seen among the remains of the **Forêt de Nianing**, keeps the whole area pleasant, and the shore scene, with scattered palm trees, is certainly pretty.

Joal-Fadiout

From Nianing, the road bisects a couple of exclusive holiday villages – one for the French on the landward side and another for German packagers on the sands – on its way south to the next stop, **JOAL**, where Senegal's great statesman, Léopold Sédhar Senghor, was born in 1906. Another former Portuguese settlement, with a few old houses still standing (including the Senghors'), it is basically a simple fishing village, where the hauling-in of the fish at the end of the day is as enjoyable to watch as anywhere.

Apart from a visit to Chez Senghor and a pat delivery of its history from the *gardien*, the big draw is a wander over the long wooden bridge to **FADIOUT**, the fishing village on the island in the estuary facing Joal. By virtue of an accidental combination of attractive features – proximity to the resorts up the coast, houses built of crushed shells, granary huts on stilts like a field of mushrooms, and a fishermen's cemetery on a neighbouring island – Fadiout has long been one of the biggest tourist traps in Senegal. It is, nevertheless, a fascinating place. A "shell midden", entirely composed of the refuse from centuries of shellfish consumption, it takes about an hour to trail around the houses and Serer cemetery. Fadiout used to be one of the most aggressive hustler haunts, too, but a *syndicat d'initiative* created a few years ago has succeeded in reducing the hassle to an extent. From their small office near the bridge (daily 8am–6pm), they arrange **guided tours** (CFA4000) and **pirogue trips** (CFA6000) round the village.

For **food and accommodation**, look to Joal, where the best place in town is the central and well-signposted – if a bit dilapidated – *Relais 114* (℡339 57 61 78 ❸), run by a Guinean family and offering clean non-s/c doubles, a pleasant verandah with hammocks and hearty home-cooking – go for the lobster. Other options, just next to the bridge, include the tour-group-oriented *Hôtel le Finio* (℡/℻339 57 61 12 ❸) and the somewhat preferable *Le Sénégaulois* (℡/℻339 57 62 41 ❹); both have decent s/c rooms and pleasantly located restaurants overlooking the island. If you want to stay in Fadiout itself, you're limited to *Les Palétuviers* (℡/℻339 57 62 05 ❹ including dinner), a simple place on the water's edge at the far side of the island.

Palmarin

The **beaches** in Joal are too crowded, litter-strewn and hustly for abandonment to the sun, sea and sand: for that, you're better off continuing 20km south to **PALMARIN**. To get there, be prepared to wait a while and possibly to change vehicles at **KEUR SAMBA DIA**. Going back again is harder, but there's always space when a vehicle comes, and if rains have washed the road out completely, you'll hear of it. Eight kilometres along the road from Joal to Samba Dia, you'll pass what locals claim is the **largest baobab** in Senegal – 32m in circumference and thronged by souvenir sellers.

Palmarin – actually made up of four villages – has a couple of excellent **campements**, though few come cheap. The best budget option, a short distance from the first village you come to, Palmarin-Ngallou, is the *Campement Villageois* (Ⓣ776 69 03 65 ❸), an outpost of Casamance's system of CTRIs, offering thatched, twin-bed huts among the palms, with electricity and shared bathrooms and meals available. Up a few notches and a bit further down the road at a popular beach is the Swiss-run *Djidjack* (Ⓣ339 49 96 19 Ⓦwww.djidjack.com ❼), where you can pitch a **tent** alongside the pool for CFA2000 a night or stay in a large twenty-two-metre-wide *case à impluvium* (❼). But the cream of the crop is the *Lodge des Collines de Niassam* (Ⓣ776 69 63 43 Ⓦwww.niassam.com; ❻ including dinner), where you can rest on terra firma in a traditional, thatched stone hut, hop out to a stilted bungalow right at the water's edge or clamber up the pines to a lofted treehouse apartment.

The Saloum delta

Situated between Dakar and The Gambia, the delta of Senegal's third river – the **Saloum** – has become popular as a weekend destination from Dakar and a bird-watching and fishing district for foreign visitors. Within the delta, **Yayème**, near Ndangane and **Dionewar** and **Niodior** on the **Île de Guior** are laid-back villages, little affected by the gradual advance of tourism. Niodior, in particular, is very alluring under its coconut trees, with really welcoming people. Nearer the Gambian border and inside the **Parc National du Delta du Saloum**, the **Île aux Oiseaux** has variably interesting birdlife – early evening tends to yield better bird-watching, and Palearctic migrants swell numbers from October to March. Turtles are common, too, and you might even see a dolphin.

Practicalities

Visiting the maze of islands and mangrove creeks by pirogue from the landward side – the usual way – can work out expensive (though you shouldn't pay more than about CFA20,000 for six hours' worth of boat and crew), but there are lots of choices, including organized trips with one of the tour operators in Dakar (see p.213).

A cheaper option is to organize your own *balade*, best done from the bustling fishing village of **DJIFERE**, 15km south of Palmarin. Djifere has a couple of **campements**, of which much the nicer is the friendly *Pointe de Sangomar* (Ⓣ338 35 61 91; ❹), with simple huts set in leafy grounds. Note, however, that if you want to swim, you're better off staying in Palmarin, as Djifere's beach is filthy. From Djifere it may be possible to take a trading pirogue down to **Banjul**, which is the closest large town by boat; the voyage – 60km along the shore – involves an overnight stop on the **Île de Bétanti**. Pirogues go several times a week and cost CFA3000 per person, plus about CFA2500 for the night's accommodation on the island. Alternatively, if you're on haggling form and unwilling to wait, you could rent your own pirogue for around CFA50,000 and get down there in about six hours.

Another departure point for the delta is **FOUNDIOUGNE**, west of Kaolack, 33km from the main highway at **PASSI**, and also accessible by road from Fatick and then a ferry (daily 8am until mid-afternoon; every 2hr). Here you'll find a handful of good places to stay, including *L'Indiana Club* (Ⓣ339 48 12 13 Ⓦwww.indianaclub.net), which has several spacious bungalows (they'll pick you up from the ferry if you like); *Le Baobab sur Mer* (Ⓣ/Ⓕ339 48 12 62 ❹), a friendly and very popular Senegalese-run place; *Auberge les Bolongs* (Ⓣ339 48 11 10 Ⓦwww.lesbolongs.sn ❹, including dinner and breakfast) which offers African-style European comfort in a tranquil setting on the western outskirts of town; and, for a bit more luxury, the well-kitted-out *Hôtel Foundiougne* (Ⓣ339 48 12 12 Ⓕ339 48 12 10 ❻). There are many places to eat in town, but the dockside *La Cloche* is the best for watching the world

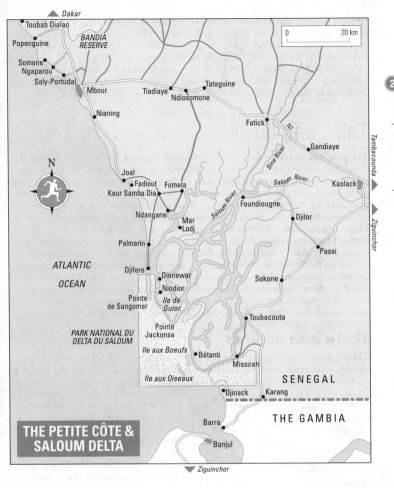

▲ *Dakar*

Toubab Dialao
Popenguine
BANDIA
RESERVE
Somone
Ngaparou
Saly-Portudal
Mbour
Tiadiaye
Tataguine
Ndiosomone
Nianing
Fatick
Gandiaye
N
Joal
Fadiout
Fumela
Keur Samba Dia
Ndangane
Mar
Lodj
Kaolack
Foundiougne
Djilor
Palmarin
Passi
ATLANTIC
OCEAN
Djifere
Dionewar
Niodior
Pointe
de Sangomar
Île de
Guior
Sokone
Toubacouta
Pointe
Jackonsa
PARK NATIONAL DU
DELTA DU SALOUM
Île aux Boeufs
Bétanti
Missirah
Île aux Oiseaux
SENEGAL
Djinack
Karang
**THE PETITE CÔTE &
SALOUM DELTA**
Barra
THE GAMBIA
Banjul
▼ *Ziguinchor*

Sine River
Saloum River
Tambacounda ►
Ziguinchor ►

go by as you tuck into a pizza. When you're moving on, it's useful to note that the first ferry from Foundiougne meets a minibus going straight to Dakar.

A convenient, but more expensive, jumping-off point is **TOUBACOUTA**, just 2km from the highway and 25km from the Gambian border. Budget **accommodation** is best at *Keur Youssou* (☎339 48 77 28 or 776 34 59 05 ❸), with charming rooms and a friendly, knowledgeable manager. Toubacouta also has two large resort camps with pools, bars, restaurants and nightclubs: *Hôtel Keur Saloum* (☎339 48 77 15 ⓦ www.keursaloum.com ❽), which is the more stylish of the two, and *Les Palétuviers* (☎339 48 77 76 ⓦ www.paletuviers.com; half-board ❽), popular with sport-fishing tours. Both organize expensive excursions, but you could try arranging cheaper ones through the souvenir stands outside the hotels. To the south of Toubacouta, at remote **MISSIRAH**, is the *Gîte Touristique du Bandiala* (☎339 48 77 35 ⓦ gite-bandiala.com ❹), a relaxing, tree-lined spot, while over the water is the exclusive *Île des Palétuviers* (run by *Les Palétuviers* ❽).

A final departure point from which to get pirogues to the delta is **NDANGANE**. There's a good range of accommodation here, but it's a bit hustly, so you're better off taking a pirogue straight to the picturesque island of **Mar-Lodj**, a little downriver on the northern side of the delta, reachable from Joal or from the main highway east of **TIADIAYE**. Mar-Lodj has a string of pleasant, low-key *campements* along the riverbank. Try *Essamaye* (☎775 55 36 67 ⓦwww.senegalia.com ④) or *La Nouvelle Vague* (☎776 34 07 29 or 339 36 39 76 ⑤), either of which has several smart little s/c huts; if you ring ahead, either lodge will send a pirogue to collect you from Ndangane, though note that there are no pirogues from Mar-Lodj itself to the delta.

Thiès and onward

The great garrison town and rail hub of colonial days, and now Senegal's second city, **THIÈS** is close enough to Dakar (70km) to be an easy visit, and also lies en route if you're travelling by train to other parts of the country. If you're interested in local crafts, the **tapestry factory** here is an essential stop; the workmanship is the very finest, and few weaving centres – if any – in West Africa match Thiès for sheer impact.

Moving north, you might visit **Tivaouane** if you're gripped by the fascination of the Islamic brotherhoods. Or, heading east, you could go to **Diourbel** and on to **Touba**, the big Mouride stronghold with the country's most impressive mosque. From Touba there's the option of following the dusty N3 highway northeast, via **Linguère** to Matam on the Senegal River. If, however, you're on the *transgambienne* highway or on the N1 to Tambacounda (see p.239), you might take time out to look at some of the Iron Age **stone circles** in the **Sine–Saloum region**. Independent transport is the best way to visit these places, though with the possible exception of the stone circles and Touba during *Magal*, you'll normally find public transport to the towns.

Thiès and around

THIÈS retains much of the character of a French town, with parks and wide shady avenues, solid brick and tiles, a remarkable old Sudanic-style cinema, and even the odd rampart from an earlier period of "pacification". Its history, even in recent times, has been punctuated by violent episodes, notably the 1947 strike by railway workers – "God's Bits of Wood" of Ousmane Sembène's novel, *Les Bouts de Bois de Dieu*.

The **Manufactures Sénégalaises des Arts Décoratifs** (Mon–Fri 8am–12.30pm & 3–6pm, Sat & Sun 8am–12.30pm; ☎339 51 11 31), focuses the output of many of Senegal's artists and has an enormous influence on younger painters. Having work painstakingly redrawn and fabricated into glowing tapestries – many for exhibition and sale abroad – is an accolade providing a rare incentive. Since its foundation in 1966, the Thiès school has produced fewer than a thousand pieces: its annual output works out at around three hundred square metres, each tapestry produced in an exclusive edition of between one and eight. Prices are accordingly high – around €775 per square metre. Common themes are village life, nature, history and myth, executed in dazzling, graphic style. Ask to see the design of the stunning *Rendezvous au Soleil* by Jacob Yacouba, a giant ten-metre version of which was purchased by Atlanta airport. It's interesting to see all the stages of work, from drawing up the original paintings to dyeing the wool and the rapid but careful process of weaving itself. However, if you turn up unannounced you will be allowed into the exhibition hall only, so it's essential to phone ahead – and even then, you stand a better chance of gaining access to the factory if you are in a group. You should be allowed to take photos in the workshops, but not in the exhibition hall.

Around the corner is the town **museum** (Mon–Sat 9am–1pm & 2–6pm, Sun by appointment; ☎951 33 15 20 or 775 88 15 31; CFA500), located in the fort that dates from 1879. It houses a number of interesting photos and a good deal of commentary on Senegalese history, as well as a fine collection of locally made muskets used against the French in the nineteenth century. Also inside the fort is a small library, a café and a very French-looking mansion in which a number of artists sell their paintings and sculptures.

Practicalities

Arriving by bus or taxi you'll almost certainly be left at the **gare routière**, 3km out of town (CFA350 to get into the centre); if you come by train, you'll be delivered straight to the *centreville*. The railway is still the pivot of much of the town's life, its rhythms adjusted to the comings and goings on the track.

The best **place to stay** is the centrally located *Hôtel Rex* (☎339 51 10 81 ⓦwww .hotelrexthies.com ❷), which offers reasonable rooms, some with air conditioning, for about as cheap as you can get in Thiès; otherwise, the *Résidence Lat-Dior* (☎339 52 07 77 ⓦwww.residencelatdior.com ❻), 2km south of town across from the stadium, has clean and modern rooms with Wi-Fi.

Thiès's numerous **restaurants** are mostly found along Avenue Léopold Senghor south of the tracks, in the town centre north of the station, or in the town's hotels. *Les Délices*, on av Léopold Senghor, has great pastries, pizza and ice cream. A good place to sit and watch the world go by is *Restaurant Le Cailcédrat* on av Général de Gaulle; meat, fish and Lebanese dishes go for around CFA3000. The centre also has several **Internet cafés**, as well as BICIS, SGBS and CBAO banks with **ATMs**.

Tivaouane and Mboro

Tivaouane, northeast of Thiès and 5km off the main N2 to St-Louis, is the seat of the **Sy** dynasty of the **Tijaniya** brotherhood, the largest in Senegal. The grand North African–style mosque is best seen during *Gamou*, the Tijani pilgrimage, or *Maulidi*, the prophet's birthday, when thousands of believers pour into the town. Accommodation, which seems pretty minimal at the best of times, is impossible to find during these periods.

Just north of Tivaouane, on the N2 highway, a road leads northwest 28km to the fishing village of **Mboro-sur-Mer** on what is known as the **Grande Côte**, a 150-kilometre unbroken sweep of sand linking St-Louis to Dakar, along which the Dakar Rally traditionally hurtles towards the capital. Despite the reforestation along this coastline, the *côte*'s exposure makes it a far less popular holiday destination than the Petite Côte south of Dakar, which may be all the reason you need to come here. *Sunuka* (☎775 84 57 75 ❹) is a basic hotel not far from the centre, offering seven agreeable rooms; if you call they'll pick you up from the centre of town.

Diourbel, Touba and on to Linguère

East of Thiès, **Diourbel**, with its beautiful, huge-domed mosque, is one of the principal saintly towns of the Mourides, and capital of the region of the same name, the heart of the groundnut basin. Fifty kilometres further east, following the

Sine valley, lies **TOUBA**, the burial place of the founder of Mouridism, **Cheikh Amadou Bamba Mbacke** (1850–1927), and thus the high holy place of the brotherhood. The extraordinary 87-metre-high mosque – built over the family tomb in 1963 and visible for miles across the flat plain – is the largest and one of the finest in West Africa, and the most important religious shrine in Senegal.

Amadou Bamba's triumphal return home in 1907, after years of detention by the French, is celebrated annually in the festival of **Magal** (see p.186 for approximate dates). At this time, around half a million pilgrims flock here from all over Senegal and The Gambia, and public transport is virtually suspended on routes to and from Touba. If you're coming for *Magal*, expect to spend the night awake with the crowd of disciples: you'll almost certainly have found companions on the journey.

Senegalese authority is minimal here: the **maraboutic militia** is responsible for law and order, which includes absolute bans on tobacco and alcohol anywhere in the town precincts. Searches – especially of *toubabs* – aren't uncommon, and you will be fined and your drugs confiscated if found. Photography, too, isn't likely to please many. Despite this, Touba can be an irresistible challenge. Be warned, though, that **accommodation** is impossible to find in Touba if you don't get invited to stay at someone's house. There's a *campement* 10km away in **MBACKE**, a kind of secular counterpoint to Touba, where the maraboutic laws don't apply. You could get stranded there for the big night anyway, as Mbacke goes into partying hyperdrive, diverting attention from the devotions at Touba and increasingly reducing *Magal* to a Christmas-style commercialism.

If you're driving into Touba, you may end up jammed in pedestrian traffic or directed to leave your vehicle in a designated zone and walk. However you manage it, don't confuse piety with honesty; a nimble army of hustlers and pickpockets filters the crowds, particularly during *Magal*. You'll also need to be aware of cultural sensitivities: shorts are not acceptable around here and heads will need to be covered if entering the mosque. You're best off adopting a local guide to help with such matters.

To Linguère

With stamina you could continue by road from Touba or Mbacke to Linguère and from there on to Ouro Sogui and Matam. This route, the N3, goes right through the heart of the Fula **Réserves Sylvo-Pastorales**, a fragmented cluster of badlands (virtually tribal reserves) glumly conceded to the pastoralists and always under threat from the expanding Mouride groundnut enterprises. With improved irrigation and increases in population, agriculture encroaches on all sides except the east, where the **Réserves de Faune du Ferlo-Nord** and **Ferlo-Sud** – areas in which no grazing is permitted – create a barrier between the cattle herds and the potentially rich Senegal river valley.

LINGUÈRE is the main town of this region. Surrounded by the reserves and no longer accessible by train, it's a bit of a dead end and rarely visited by travellers, though there is a *campement* here if you need to stay the night. If you have transport, or a dogged persistence coupled with a devotion to obscure archeological sites, you might move down the Ferlo river course from Linguère to the ruined **fortress** of Alboury Ndiaye, the last independent ruler of the Wolof kingdom of Jolof. The site is north of the road before the village of **YANG-YANG**, itself about 35km northwest of Linguère.

From Linguère, a rough track to the Senegal River near Ouro Sogui follows the normally dry upper course of the Ferlo River, between the faunal reserves. Transport is limited and vehicles depart early – you'll almost certainly be the only foreign traveller on board.

Kaolack and the Gambian border region

A big, noisy interchange town, the hub of five road routes, **KAOLACK** is not likely to be a place you'll want to linger long in. The Niasse dynasty of the Tijaniya brotherhood – based here and at one time reportedly funded by Libya – is bent on founding an Islamic republic. The **mosque** is the main sight of interest, a splendid creation paid for partly by Iraq's late secular dictator, Saddam Hussein. Kaolack also has a venerable and bustling **market** – in fact it's one of the biggest covered markets in West Africa – and there's a crafts market on the northern edge of town.

The **gare routière** for Dakar and all northern destinations is 1½ km out of town to the north; for southern destinations, including The Gambia, you need **garage Nioro**, on the southeastern corner of the town centre. The *gare routière ville* for shared taxis around town, is next to the market. **Places to stay** include the *Hôtel de Paris*, southwest of the market, whose excellent, clean rooms have everything you'll need (T339 41 10 19 @mangrove@sentoo.sn ❻); the even better value *Relais de Kaolack*, a bit further out of the centre towards the port in a pleasant riverside setting, with a pool and tennis court (T339 41 10 00 F339 41 10 02 ❻); and the bare-bones but amiable *Auberge Etoile du Sine*, on av Valdiodio Ndiaye, the main road out of town towards Tambacounda (T339 41 44 58 ❷). You may also be able to find a bed at the *Mission Catholique* (T339 41 25 26 ❷, dorms CFA2000), around the corner from the *Hôtel de Paris*.

Inexpensive **street food** is available all around the market and *gares routières*. For more varied options, including pizza, fish, meat and salads, try the restaurants at either the *Hôtel de Paris* or the *Relais de Kaolack* (count on CFA6000 for a meal). Otherwise, there is *La Terrasse* (*Chez DuDu*) on rue des Écoles, or *Le Brasero* (*Chez Anouar*), a couple of blocks north at 510 av Ndiaye – both are atmospheric and quite busy in the evenings, with main dishes from CFA3000 and *Brasero* has a good beer selection. Around the corner from *Brasero*, on av de Bugeau, is an **Internet café** and the buzzing *Blue Bird* **nightclub**, which also serves food.

Sine-Saloum stone circles

Part of the same cultural complex as the circles in The Gambia (see p.318), the **megaliths**, scattered across the plain between Nioro du Rip on the *transgambienne* N4 and Tambacounda, are vestiges of a prehistoric society about which virtually nothing is known. Including some unimpressive circles that you'd not glance at twice, they number approximately a thousand in this region. Associated with them are burial sites which have yielded a number of skeletons and a certain amount of weaponry, pots and copper ornaments. Seeming to date from before the twelfth century, they bear no sign of any Islamic impact.

Most impressive is the site known as **Djalloumbéré**, at **NGAYÈNE**, hard against the Gambian border. More than eleven hundred individual pillars here make up 52 stone circles – some of them the sites of mass burials. It's virtually impossible to get here without your own transport – turn left 9km south of **NIORO DU RIP** to **KAYMOR** (17km) on a decent track, then continue southeast another 15km via **TÈNE PEUL** and **KEUR BAKARI** to Ngayène. From here you can head straight back to the main road at **MEDINA SABAK**, 28km from Nioro. In the middle of this "circuit", 10km due south of Kaymor, is the village of **PAYOMA**, where stones from the local circles have been uprooted to support the buildings – including the mosque. Numerous other circles are visible at various points along these tracks.

Assuming you've got transport or you're using a *taxi brousse*, there are more sites along the Tambacounda highway, at **Malème Hodar** (right by the road) and **Keur Albé** and **Sali**, respectively 9km and 20km southwest of **Koungheul** on a minor road to The Gambia. This road crosses the border just north of Wassu: if you're enraptured by the circles and your documents are in order, you could cross into The Gambia for further observations and stay in Janjanbureh.

2.2

The north and east

Northern Senegal is the least populated part of the country, with few large towns and a landscape whose main interest derives from its harsh marginality. Northeast of Dakar stretches the **Sahel**, where the desert's southward advance is ever apparent. But there are two conspicuous attractions in the north: the **Senegal River**, forming the border with Mauritania and feeding a flood plain up to 30km wide; and the riveting old French colonial capital of **St-Louis**, tucked behind the bar at the mouth of the river. Two **national parks** – the Djoudj and the Langue de Barbarie – are mainly visited by keen bird-watchers.

Should you be **heading north** to Mauritania and the Atlantic route across the Sahara, St-Louis is a natural break in the journey, a few hours by *taxi brousse* from Dakar. To follow the river, however, you have to be a little more determined and transport-hop your way inland to **Richard Toll**, **Ouro Sogui/Matam** and **Bakel**. Continuing south through the hills, you'll intercept the Dakar–Bamako train at **Kidira**, on the border, where there'll be a crush to find space on board. If you're approaching in the opposite direction, into Senegal from Mali, the river course is a marginally preferable route towards the coast: the alternative, following the direct line of the railway, has very little to detain you.

The main **ethno-linguistic groups** of north Senegal are the **Wolof**, concentrated around St-Louis and along the lower reaches of the river, and the **Tukulor** higher up, who speak a dialect of Fula. In the far east, around Bakel, there are **Sarakolé** (Soninké/Serahule) speakers, while communities of semi-nomadic **Fula** live in the scorched region of Fouta Toro.

St-Louis and around

The oldest French settlement in West Africa and capital of Senegal and Mauritania until 1958, **ST-LOUIS** is something of a world apart. In later colonial times its *commune* status – shared with Gorée, Rufisque and Dakar – meant its inhabitants were considered citizens of France; today the town's crumbling eighteenth- and nineteenth-century European architecture and its white- and blue-draped Wolof and Moorish inhabitants maintain the culture clash. Like Gorée, St-Louis is a UNESCO-protected World Heritage Site. If decay, abandonment and the ghosts of slaves and fishermen attract you, then you'll enjoy this town. Several great beachside *campements* sprang up along the Langue de Barbarie during the tourism woes of the Casamance, and these days, with its warm winters, dry summers and nearby **national parks**, the St-Louis area adds up to a worthwhile few days' stay. An added attraction, if you happen to be in the area at the time, is the annual **St-Louis International Jazz Festival** (Ⓦ www.saintlouisjazz.com), which takes place over a long weekend in May or June; artists come from all around the world to perform, but finding accommodation then is nigh impossible if you don't book ahead.

Arrival, information and accommodation

St-Louis' wonderfully ornate **train station**, abandoned now that the regular service from Dakar has been suspended, is in the mainland quarter of **Sor**, close to the

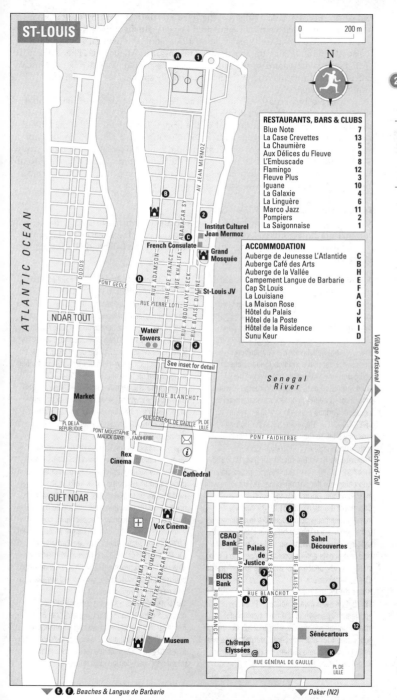

ST-LOUIS

ATLANTIC OCEAN

NDAR TOUT

GUET NDAR

Market

Senegal River

RESTAURANTS, BARS & CLUBS

Blue Note	7
La Case Crevettes	13
La Chaumière	5
Aux Délices du Fleuve	9
L'Embuscade	8
Flamingo	12
Fleuve Plus	3
Iguane	10
La Galaxie	4
La Linguère	6
Marco Jazz	11
Pompiers	2
La Saigonnaise	1

ACCOMMODATION

Auberge de Jeunesse L'Atlantide	C
Auberge Café des Arts	B
Auberge de la Vallée	H
Campement Langue de Barbarie	E
Cap St Louis	F
La Louisiane	A
La Maison Rose	G
Hôtel du Palais	J
Hôtel de la Poste	K
Hôtel de la Résidence	I
Sunu Keur	D

Institut Culturel
Jean Mermoz

French Consulate

Grand Mosquée

St-Louis JV

Water Towers

See inset for detail

RUE BLANCHOT

RUE GÉNÉRAL DE GAULLE

PL DE LILLE

PONT FAIDHERBE

PL DE LA RÉPUBLIQUE

PONT MOUSTAPHE MALICK GAYE

PONT FAIDHERBE

Rex Cinema

Cathedral

Vox Cinema

Museum

Village Artisanal ▶

Richard-Toll ▶

AV JEAN MERMOZ

AV DODDS

PONT GEOLE

RUE ADAMSON

RUE DE FRANCE

RUE KHALIFA

ABABACAR SY

RUE ABDOULAYE SECK

RUE BLAISE DIAGNE

RUE PIERRE LOTI

Inset detail

CBAO Bank

Palais de Justice

BICIS Bank

Sahel Découvertes

Sénécartours

Ch@mps Elyssées @

RUE KHALIFA ABABACAR SY

RUE ABDOULAYE SECK

RUE BLAISE DIAGNE

RUE BLANCHOT

RUE DE FRANCE

RUE GÉNÉRAL DE GAULLE

PL DE LILLE

RUE IBRAHIMA SARR

RUE BLAISE DUMONT

RUE MAITRE BABACAR SEYE

0   200 m

N

end of the iron Pont de Faidherbe; the **gare routière** is right by the tracks. It's a hectic area, thronged with stalls and child beggars. **Bush taxis** leave from here for Dakar (CFA3500; 4hr) and inland destinations along the Senegal River, including Rosso (CFA1500; 2hr), for the border crossing into Mauritania. The oldest part of St-Louis is the **island** of the same name, a ten-minute walk across the Gustave Eiffel-designed rotating bridge (which, incidentally, spanned the Danube until 1897) from the *gare routière*.

For **tourist information**, the Syndicat d'Initiative et de Tourisme (Mon–Fri 9am–1pm & 3–6.45pm, Sat 9am–12.30pm & 3–6pm; ☏339 61 24 55 ⓦwww .saintlouisdusenegal.com) at the end of the bridge, has helpful staff, some English-speaking, who can assist you with accommodation and tours (CFA5000 for a three-hour tour). There's an excellent, if outdated, bird's-eye view **sketch map** (CFA3000) of St-Louis and its environs – available from the *syndicat d'initiative*, some hotels and bookshops – which makes an informative companion for your wanderings in and around town as well as a great souvenir when you leave.

Accommodation

St-Louis offers an excellent range of **accommodation** for its size, with the old colonial-era hotels situated on the island itself, a couple of places to stay on the mainland, and *campements* strung out along the spit of the Langue de Barbarie, south of the Guet Ndar quarter.

Auberge Café des Arts rue Adamson ☏339 61 60 78. Colourful and very friendly, locally run place offering basic rooms and cheap, home-cooked meals. ❷

Auberge de Jeunesse l'Atlantide av Jean Mermoz, corner of rue Bouet ☏339 61 24 09 ⓦwww.saintlouisdusenegal.com/auberge-jeunesse. Best place in town to lodge cheaply and commune with other travellers. There are segregated dorms and twin rooms – with fans, shared ablutions and a modest breakfast included. Various *plats du jour* are on offer for CFA2000–3000, there are bikes for hire and they organize trips to the national parks. Dorm beds with breakfast CFA5700, rooms ❸.

Auberge de la Vallée rue Blaise Diagne ☏339 61 47 22 ⓕ339 64 10 92. Weathered old place with chipped paint but otherwise clean rooms with mosquito nets. Dorm beds CFA5000, rooms ❸.

Cap Saint-Louis ☏339 61 39 39 ⓦwww .hotelcapsaintlouis.com. Located a few kilometres out of town along the Langue, this sleepy resort-style option is spaciously spread out on lots of land and boasts a large pool and access to a fine, if often windy, beach. Pool available to non-guests (CFA3500) or diners. ❹

Hôtel du Palais rue Ababacar Sy ☏/ⓕ339 61 17 72 ⓦwww.hoteldupalais.net. Friendly, helpful and least expensive of the old-style hotels, offering clean s/c rooms, with a CFA2000 supplement for a/c. Adjacent café/patisserie has good croissants and coffee. Inexpensive excursions available. ❹

Hôtel de la Poste by Pont Faidherbe on the waterfront ☏339 61 11 18 ⓦwww .hotel-poste.com. The island's definitive colonial-era hotel with splendid, classic-meets-boutique rooms and ambience, and a hunter-themed bar. Ask to stay in room 219, airman Jean Mermoz's favourite while here on layovers. All the usual excursions are on offer, including day-runs down the beach to their *campement* on the Langue (see p.234). ❽

Hôtel de la Résidence rue Blaise Diagne ☏339 61 12 60 ⓦwww.hoteldelaresidence.com. One of the town's most comfortable hotels, with white stucco rooms full of colonial details, as well as a great rooftop terrace. ❻

La Louisiane at Point Nord, the northernmost tip of the island ☏339 61 42 21 ⓦwww.aubergelalouisiane.com. Excellent, underrated place on the rocks looking straight out over the water to Mauritania. Some of the simple, brightly-decorated rooms have canopied beds, and those on the top floor have super views coupled with small balconies. Also runs a great campement, *Le Robinson*, along the Langue de Barbarie. ❹

La Maison Rose av Blaise Diagne ☏339 38 22 ⓦwww.lamaisonrose.net. Spacious, boutique-style courtyard hotel with large, tiled rooms, on-site spa and nostalgic atmosphere. ❽

Sunu Keur across a sagging wooden bridge connecting the island to the Langue ☏339 61 88 00. Excellent mid-level option featuring smart wooden furnishings and rooms with balconies looking across to Ndar. Sip a cocktail on the roof terrace as the island gets ready for the night ahead. ❺

The Town

Most of the town's hotels, as well as local travel agents (see p.233) and the tourist office, offer **tours and excursions** all around St-Louis (around CFA5000 for three hours), as well as to the national parks and over the border into Mauritania; one of the best tour guides is the English-speaking Adama Sow at Agence de Voyage JV (see p.233). The *Hôtel de la Poste* offers an especially good *calèche* tour of the town and can also take you down to the beach in the morning and pick you up at the end of the day – at a price.

The **mainland** area of St-Louis, **Sor**, is on the whole an anonymous district, though there are some old buildings, and there's a lively African feel at night which the weary island can't match. The population here swells with every downward cycle of drought in the interior. On the route de Corniche at Sor's northern end is the **Village Artisanal** where you might pick up a wider and less expensive range of Senegalese and Mauritanian artefacts than those you'll be offered outside the island's better hotels.

The island

You can walk round the **island** – *ndar* in Wolof – in about an hour and a half. Shuttered windows, occasional balconies and flaking yellow paint are the abiding impressions. Some of the best houses – which, as in Gorée, tend to conceal their interiors from inquisitive strangers – are around the hotels and just to the north, especially along rue Blanchot and rue Pierre Loti. **Maurel et Prom** was a slave market, and the **Hôtel de la Poste** started as a gum-arabic warehouse. The old houses characteristically have interior courtyards, warehouses on the ground floor (mostly now converted) and first-floor, inward-facing living quarters. Don't miss the **Palais de Justice**, on rue Blanchot, with its massive, palm-shaded staircase.

At the place de Lille, named after St-Louis' twin city, you'll notice the plaque commemorating the town's most celebrated citizen, Mbarick Fall, who as **Battling Siki** became the first world professional boxing champion in 1925. Heading south round the corner from here, beneath a wonderful old silk-cotton tree, you come to **Place Faidherbe**, centering on a bust of the eponymous French governor, and surrounded by government and military buildings.

At the southern tip of the island, the **museum** is worth a look (daily 9am–noon & 3–6pm; ☎339 61 10 50; CFA500). The first floor has displays on the great marabouts and politicians of Senegal and the historic personalities of St-Louis, together with local ethnographia from Neolithic times to the arrival of the *colons*. Temporary exhibitions are held on the second floor.

Ndar Tout and Guet Ndar

Across the other arm of the river on the spit of the Langue de Barbarie, facing directly onto the ocean, the scene is much more animated. Turn right across either of the bridges and you're strolling on Avenue Dodds, main drag of the **Ndar Tout** quarter. With its tall, gracious houses rising behind the pavement palm trees, it's easy to picture this as the Champs Élysées of the local *signares* set, at a time when there were four thousand French *colons* and military based in St-Louis. At the far north end, ruination sets in – skeletal buff and red remains of French army buildings and then a marker pillar designating the **Mauritanian frontier** (it's not an official border crossing).

Massage in Wolof

If you're looking to soothe your muscles after a walk around St-Louis, visit the local hospital, a few blocks north of the museum, which offers relaxing, half-hour backrubs for CFA1000. Enter the reception area and tell them: *"Sama ganaaw, dafa meti. Bëgg naa benn massage."* ("My back aches and I'd like a massage.")

Action in Ndar Tout focuses on the **market** and sandy **Place de la République**, which gives out straight onto the Atlantic down Avenue Servatius, itself ankle deep in sand. From here you can walk south along the shore into the odoriferous fishing quarter of **Guet Ndar**, possibly the most "third-world" part of the country, down as far as the Islamic fishermen's cemetery, a net-and-stake graveyard with the familiar and disquieting vulture retinue.

Eating

St-Louis has a few reliable and economical **places to eat** around the main centre on the island. A good spot for cheap street food is around place de la République on Ndar Tout; on the island itself, the vendor on the corner of rue Blaise Diagne and rue Potin, opposite *La Maison Rose*, cooks the best *brochettes* in town (8pm–2am; CFA700). For a more refined and expensive meal, take your pick from the following independent restaurants, or any of the restaurants at the better hotels, such as the *Poste* or *Résidence*.

Restaurants

Aux Délices du Fleuve quai Roume. The best breakfasts in town – with various kinds of bread, omelettes and excellent coffee – can be had at this beloved patisserie.

Fleuve Plus rue Blaise Diagne. Popular restaurant with an extensive Senegalese menu; main courses from CFA1500 – the garlic shrimp are delicious. Also serves tasty fruit juices such as tamarind, or bring your own beer or wine from the *distributeur* around the corner.

La Case Crevettes rue Abdoulaye Seck. Cute little place done out to resemble a grass hut, specializing in prawn dishes and other tasty Senegalese fare for around CFA2500–3000.

La Galaxie rue Abdoulaye Seck. About the best deal in town: friendly service and, for once, a pleasant interior, plus dishes from CFA800.

La Linguère rue Blaise Diagne, next to *Auberge de la Vallée*. Simple, popular eatery with the best (and cheapest) *steak-frites* in town – CFA2000 for a succulent cut.

La Saigonnaise north end of av Jean Mermoz near *La Louisiane*. Elegant Vietnamese restaurant on the northern tip of the island with great views to Mauritania. The spicy Asian dishes are pricey but worth it, especially considering the upscale atmosphere.

Drinking and nightlife

Once the sun sets, St-Louis awakens from its colonial siesta to shift into a low-key nightlife mode, with a number of small bars and dance clubs that tend to pick up after midnight. For a taste of the jazz scene that St-Louis is famous for, check out *Marco Jazz*, a couple of blocks north of the *Hôtel de la Poste*, or *Blue Note* on rue Abdoulaye Seck, both of which have regular sessions. Alternatively, simply cut east across the Servatius bridge to the mainland and let your ears track down the action: community events are easily located. The Institut Culturel et Linguistique Jean Mermoz (☎339 38 26 26 ⊛www.ccfsl.net), towards the north end of av Jean Mermoz, screens movies and puts on regular music and dance performances.

Flamingo quai Roume. With the best location on the island, this riverside bar looks onto the Pont Faidherbe and is ideal for an evening beer (or meal) followed by a dip in their pool. Regular live music.

Iguane rue Abdoulaye Seck. Plan to arrive at this compact, dark Cuban bar well after midnight, when locals down bottles of Gazelle, then take to the dance floor to show off their *mbalax* and salsa moves.

La Chaumière Ndar Tout (closed Mon). Owned by the *Hôtel de la Poste*, this is Ndar Tout's sole nightspot, but what a place it is. Drink prices are reasonable, though there's usually a cover (CFA1500–3000; free to *Poste* guests).

L'Embuscade rue Blanchot. "The Ambush" is a good base of operations for many *toubabs* in town, with CFA1000 beers and live music at weekends.

Pompiers av Jean Mermoz just north of the French Consulate. Inside the fire station, this ad hoc bar serves the cheapest Flags in town (CFA400), though the draw for many seems to be the chance to make eyes at the strapping local firemen. It can turn a little rowdy later on, but is good enough for an early drink.

Listings

Banks BICIS, corner of rue de France and rue Blanchot (Mon–Thurs 7.45am–12.15pm & 1.40–3.45pm, Fri 7.45am–1pm & 2.40–3.45pm), is able to change cash and traveller's cheques. CBAO, rue Khalifa Ababacar Sy (Mon–Fri 8.15am–5.15pm), is a Western Union agent. Both banks have 24hr ATMs.

Car rental Ask at your hotel, or try Sénécartours, rue Blaise Diagne (☏ 339 61 38 12); plan ahead as vehicles are transferred from Dakar on request.

Cinemas French soft porn seems to play on a loop at the open-air Rex, on place Faidherbe. The more comfortable Vox plays lots of French-dubbed Bollywood films as well as the odd US action movie.

Internet café Ch@mps Elysées, rue Général de Gaulle (daily 8am–midnight; CFA500/hr), is the biggest and fastest Internet place in town and also serves good fruit juices.

Travel agents Try Sahel Découverte (☏ 339 61 42 63 or 339 61 56 89 ⓦ www.saheldecouverte .com) or St-Louis "JV" (☏ 339 61 51 52), both on rue Blaise Diagne.

The Langue de Barbarie National Park

The **Langue de Barbarie** – "Tongue of Barbary" – is the narrow sand bar extending south of St-Louis across the mouth of the Senegal River. As the river sweeps southwest towards the sea, the Atlantic's onshore drift from the northwest has piled sand and river deposits along the coast for some 30km south of the town. About 6km south of Guet Ndar, the thin spit is broken, and most of the Senegal's waters pour out to sea through a narrow gap. The remainder flows south, behind the Langue, to emerge at the tip of the bar

The tranquil **Parc National de la Langue de Barbarie** comprises twenty square kilometres of beautiful estuarine islands, waterways and ocean-front sand spit. South of town, you can drive (4x4 required) down the bar as far as the start of the national park (close to the river mouth), dodging the waves and hundreds of thousands of crabs as you go. With assistance from the US Peace Corps, integrated ecotourism is alive and well in the park, with fifteen percent of all profits now reinvested into community development activities managed by local villagers. There's a good chance of seeing cormorants, pelicans and turtles here, and the park also has the best swimming beaches around St-Louis.

The drive starts in Guet Ndar, passing the remains of the **Hydrobase**, the seaplane centre used as a staging post by the early airmail service between Europe and South America. The first South Atlantic crossing took off from here in 1930; the *Hôtel de la Poste* in town is full of mementos. Many of the casuarina trees planted here by Governor Faidherbe when the Langue was called La Piste des Cavaliers have since perished, and it's an often somewhat melancholy beachscape populated by a string of new *campements*.

Park practicalities

To properly **visit the park**, you need a permit. The park office (all year, daily 7am–7pm; permits CFA2000) is located 20km south of St-Louis, on the landward side of the estuary, south of the village of **GANDIOL**. You can drive here yourself, get here by bush taxi from St-Louis' Sor *autogare*, or sign up for a tour organized by one of the main hotels in town. If you're travelling independently, the park office can arrange **pirogue trips** into the park (CFA2500 per person, minimum CFA7500), plus CFA3000 for a mandatory guide.

The number of birds you see depends on an element of luck and on the time of year – from November to August the park is a breeding site for terns, gulls and egrets. Flamingos and pelicans are the most noticeable species, but rarer birds require more patience. About halfway along the road to Gandiol, you'll pass the **Réserve de Guembeul** (daily 7.30am–6.30pm; CFA2000; walking tours CFA1000), where you can see gazelles, oryx, warthogs, tortoises and a herd of deer donated by King Juan Carlos of Spain.

South of Gandiol, you can tour the fields around the village of **MOUIT** by *calèche* (CFA10,000 for a two-hour ride for up to six people), where you'll pass by the 150-year-old French fort of **Balacoste**. After a tour, relax at the park restaurant, *Le Heron Cendré*, where CFA2000 gets you a huge plate of *chep-bu-jen*, best ordered in advance.

A few minutes' walk from the park entrance is an excellent place to **stay**, *Zebrabar*, 500m from the Langue de Barbarie park office (☏776 38 18 62 ⓦcome.to /zebrabar ④). This laid-back, Swiss-run *campement* has a range of comfortable huts, good-value meals, kayaks, sailboards and a fabulous lookout rising above the palm trees. Camping is also possible (CFA2500 per person). The *Hôtel de la Poste* also runs their own comfortable, established *campement* (④) with lots of beach activities, plus pirogue and fishing excursions; they normally provide 4x4 transport.

Parc National des Oiseaux du Djoudj

Situated in the heart of the Walo delta of the Senegal River, and considerably bigger than the Langue de Barbarie park, the **Parc National des Oiseaux du Djoudj** (Nov–April daily 7am–7pm; CFA2000, cars CFA5000) is Senegal's ornithological showcase, its estimated 100,000 **flamingos** and 10,000 **white pelicans** among the world's largest concentrations. It's rated the third most important **bird reserve** in the world; if you're at all into birds and are here during the Palearctic migrants' season between October and April, you should make the effort to get in. January is probably the ideal time to visit, with the migrants in residence but the water levels already receding. Flamingos prefer the high alkalinity – and the reduced water surface tends to concentrate the birds, making them easier to spot. Crowned cranes are among the park's more ostentatious inhabitants. You should also keep a lookout on the water surface for the eyes and snouts of **crocodiles**, especially visible in the dry season.

The track into the park is signposted to the left off the St-Louis–Rosso road near the village of **NDIOL**, 25km from St-Louis. If you don't have your own transport, you can arrange a **trip to the Djoudj** with most of St-Louis' hotels for around CFA15,000 per person, which includes entrance fees, a two-hour pirogue ride and unlimited stops en route. Taxis can also be persuaded to spend the day taking you there and back, but you'll pay at least CFA20,000 per taxi (plus fuel and entrance fees) and it's hard to guarantee the length of time your driver will devote to the excursion.

Once you're in the park, restricting yourself to the tracks gives just half the picture; only by taking a pirogue across the shallow expanses can you get really close to the wildlife. You can buy tickets for **pirogue trips** at the park entrance (CFA3500 per person from the village shop next to the park office or from the hotel – see below), from where it's another few kilometres' drive to the pirogue jetty. At the park entrance, you can **stay** at the *Hôtel du Djoudj* (☏339 63 87 02 ⓦwww.djoudjhotel.com ④), which offers overpriced huts and smarter en-suite rooms grouped around a pool, on a wooded bend of the river. If you ask nicely, you may be allowed to lodge more cheaply, or camp, at the research station just inside the park gates.

Along the Senegal River

From St-Louis there is frequent transport to **Rosso** (for Mauritania) and **Richard Toll**. Vehicles from St-Louis going further east are scarcer, so you'll have to hop your way along the highway from town to town. As the heat rises noticeably inland it can be a long slog in the back of a crowded *bâche* to **Kidira**, two long days and nearly 600km from St-Louis. There's little of interest to see along this route other than glimpses of the Senegal River and rural, upcountry communities getting on with life, although you'll find the former trading outpost of **Bakel**, just north of Kidira, a charismatic stopover. If you have a little more time, however, you could make things more exciting by travelling up the river by pirogue; trading boats ply the waters between Matam, Bakel and Kayes in Mali.

Since 2006, it's also been possible to **travel by river boat** – the 52-metre, 28-cabin, fully refitted, colonial-era *Bou El Mogdad* – from St-Louis to Podor or the reverse. It's a six-day voyage in either direction, with all meals included and shore excursions along the way. Prices start from CFA310,000 per person, based on two sharing a twin or double cabin (Ⓦwww.compagniedufleuve.com).

The Lower River

Between St-Louis and Richard Toll, the scene varies sharply with the time of year: in the dry season from November to May, you'll see the oblong wicker huts of migrant Fula herders who've moved from the drier lands of the interior. Signs of human habitation include the practice of planting old car tyres in the mud to stake a land claim – common all over West Africa.

Around the turnoff to Rosso, and all along the six-kilometre causeway road to it, you see thousands of hectares of rice, along with **sugar cane**, intended not only to feed domestic sugar consumption but also, eventually, to produce fuel alcohol to offset the high cost of oil imports. In the irrigation ditches, **Nile monitor lizards** abound, growing enormous – up to two metres long – on a diet of insects, frogs and rodents.

Rosso

On the frontier with Mauritania, **ROSSO** (about 1½hr from St-Louis by minibus) is bustling with black marketeers and hustlers. As you approach the town the road curls through desperate shacks and official buildings to a tongue of land from where a barge regularly ferries vehicles across the brown flow to **Rosso–Mauritania** (see p.136). If you're **crossing the river** – and there's little point in coming up here if you're not – you'll need to get your passport stamped out of Senegal at the first flag-poled white building on the left, just after the minibus stop. You can get across the river easily enough using pirogues for about CFA300 per person, but avoid going between noon and 3pm, when both the *piroguiers* and the barge crew shut down for lunch. The border opens at 8am and closes at 6pm. Note that this can be a hustly frontier, with exit and entry charges running up to about €10 per person on each side of the river. Rosso is the furthest upriver vehicle-crossing on the Senegal until you reach the bridge at Kidira/Nayé for Mali. Other crossings into Mauritania are by pirogue and essentially for foot passengers only – though note the option of the road bridge at **Diama**, downstream from Rosso. For further information, see p.97, p.137 and p.159.

Richard Toll

The unremarkable **RICHARD TOLL** (toll is "garden" in Wolof) is named after the ambitious regional development planned by the French planter Claude Richard in the 1820s, which encouraged cotton, rice and sugar plantation farming in the region. The town's only notable building is Baron Jacques Roger's **colonial mansion**, built on an island in the Taouey River – which flows into the Senegal on the east side of town. It's surrounded by the remains of his ornamental park – now a dusty and overgrown jungle and nothing special.

For **accommodation** you've two options: directly north of the *gare routière* is the *Gîte d'Etape* (Ⓣ/Ⓕ339 63 32 40 ⑥), a great spot to rest up if you've had a tiring few days, with its lovely riverside setting, restaurant and swimming pool (CFA2500 for non-residents). Otherwise, there's the overpriced, riverside *Hôtel La Taouey* (Ⓣ339 63 34 31 ④), a few hundred metres west behind the first of two Shell stations. Along the town's long main drag you'll spot plenty of **street-food** snack bars, Internet cafés and CBAO and BICIS **banks** with an ATM. If you're moving on east and there's nothing remotely full in the *gare routière*, you might prefer to take a *calèche* the couple of kilometres to the edge of town (CFA150), and wait there for a passing vehicle.

Lac de Guiers

Protected from the Senegal River's brackish contamination by a dam in the Taouey River at Richard Toll, the **Lac de Guiers** supplies much of Dakar's drinking water, which is purified at **GNIT** on the western shore and piped 300km to the capital. The lake, some 30km southwest of Richard Toll, is a wild area, swarming with most of the birds present in the Djoudj, with the exception of flamingos. Warthogs are common and if you find a way to get out on the water you might even see **manatees** – strange, aquatic mammals which hold on to a precarious existence here. **People** of the area include Tukulor and Black Moor fishermen, and Fula herders at certain times of year.

You can't get right round the lake – it's best seen from the village of **MBANE**, on the eastern shore. The reedy western shore is accessible only from the St-Louis–Dakar road or a track which leads off south from the N2, 10km west of the Rosso junction – both unsignposted. If you don't have your own transport, you can arrange **tours** to the lake with most of the St-Louis hotels. The *Gîte* in Richard Toll would probably fix you up as well.

The Middle River

Beyond Richard Toll, the road rises out of the valley, bypassing the town of **DAGANA** – an old gum-arabic entrepôt on the Senegal, with colonial buildings and a semi-intact nineteenth-century fort. Just east of town you get a tempting flash of the river (a good spot for lunch, but stay out of the water) and from here you leave traditional Wolof country. East of here most of the people you'll see are **Tukulor** or **Fula**, and the atmosphere is more laid-back, with commerce no longer quite such a feature.

Moving upriver you pass various villages – some traditional mud-and-grass affairs, others agglomerations of concrete blocks. At the spartan settlement of **TREJI** you can change into a clapped-out Peugeot 504 for the 24-kilometre run north (CFA375) to **PODOR**, Senegal's northernmost town, right by the river. The town's name comes from its past as a centre of the gold (*or*) trade, though today the place is probably best known for being the home town of singer **Baaba Maal**. Have a peek at the remains of Podor's 1854 French fort – it was restored in 2006 and now holds a small museum and artisans' gallery. Maal owns the basic *Gîte d'Etape Keur Ninon* (℡339 65 16 42 ❸), located near the entrance of town, with six simple rooms and a rather good restaurant. Otherwise, the *Foyer des Femmes*, at the end of the main road, has two a/c rooms (℡339 65 11 16 ❷). Baaba Maal set up an annual music and cultural festival in 2006, **Les Blues du Fleuve**, using the French fort as one of the venues. It was repeated in 2007 and looks like becoming an annual event (🌐www .festivallesbluesdufleuve.com; see p.169).

Podor is situated on the western tip of the **Île à Morfil** (Island of Ivory), a long slug of floodlands (120km by 10km) between the main course of the river and the meandering Doué. The Île à Morfil lay at the heart of the **state of Tekrur** (whence "Tukulor" and the misleading French spelling "Toucouleur"), which was at its most powerful in the eleventh century, when it became a major sub-Saharan trading partner with the Almoravid Arabs of North Africa. The Tukulor claim, as a result, that they were the first West Africans to adopt Islam, and went on to evangelize, among others, the Fula – with whom they share a common language and much else. Their own state was annexed by ancient Ghana, with its power base to the east at Koumbi Saleh, in present-day Mauritania. When the Almoravids attacked Ghana, Tekrur helped the invaders, only to fall shortly afterwards to the Mali Empire.

At one time the island had a large population of **elephants**, supported by the covering of dense, silt-fed woodland. It's still a good wildlife district, with monkeys, crocodiles and a proliferation of birdlife, but elephants haven't been regularly seen since the 1960s and it's doubtful if any survive. There's a fair number of villages with Sudanic-style **mosques** scattered along the island's one main track as far as **SALDE**, the furthest east, where you can get a ferry back to the main road 90km short of Matam. If you can find transport the length of the island, it might be a preferable alternative to following the main N2 highway, which is unremittingly dull.

The Upper River

Further inland, the next town of note is **Ouro Sogui**, the biggest settlement along the *haute fleuve* and around 200km (and a hot and dusty six hours) by minibus from Treji, or shorter if you can catch a Peugeot 504. If you're coming from St-Louis you'll need to make a dawn start as there are several necessary vehicle changes. Along the way various routes to the river give access **into Mauritania** at Kaédi; branching north at **THILOGNE**, 50km west of Ouro Sogui, is the best bet. From Kaédi, there's regular transport around southeast Mauritania, and up to Nouakchott. Note that there are no ferries capable of carrying motor vehicles across the Senegal anywhere upriver of Rosso: your crossing options are limited to large motor pirogues.

Travellers frequently mistake the large highway town of Ouro Sogui for the former Tukulor slave-trading station of **MATAM**, a fading river-bank town 10km northeast of the highway, still featured as the larger settlement on most maps.

Ouro Sogui

At **OURO SOGUI**, turning south at the roundabout by the Shell and Total petrol stations leads 1km along the main street to the town centre and market, passing two cheap eating places on the left, *Restaurant Teddungal* and the adjacent *Dibiterie Islam*. A few hundred metres further on, keep an eye out for the two-storey *Auberge Sogui* on the right, the town's best-value **accommodation**, with large fan or a/c rooms, some s/c, and good *plats* in the restaurant next door from CFA1500 (☏339 66 11 98 ❸). There's also a rooftop terrace – nice to sit here when the *harmattan* isn't tearing in from Mauritania. Back on the main road, just west of the roundabout, are two new, bigger and smarter options: the *Hôtel Oasis du Fouta* (☏339 66 12 94 ⓦhotel-oasis-du-fouta .ifrance.com ❹), which has a good bar, and the posher but somewhat anonymous *Hôtel Auberge Sogui* (☏339 66 15 36 ⓦwww.hotelsogui.sn ❹). There's a BICIS **bank** beneath the *Auberge Sogui* and a CBAO next door at the Shell station. The **gare routière** is a couple of hundred metres north of the roundabout; you'll want to get there early in the day for the run on to Bakel and Kidira.

Bakel

Southeast of Ouro Sogui, the roads are much improved, and you can expect a fairly smooth ride. Tucked in a bend in the river among a knot of hills, **BAKEL**'s narrow streets and colonial architectural relics make it perhaps the only place to linger a day or two in the northeast. The hills around evoke a sense of isolation similar to the dunes surrounding Timbuktu – indeed René Caillié stayed here and later took the post as prefect of Bakel on his return from the legendary city. Another old French **fort** overlooks the river, where *piroguiers* ply for fish, onto an uncharacteristically verdant corner of Mauritania. As home to the town *préfecture*, the fort is officially closed to visitors, but if you ask politely at the gate, you'll probably be allowed to look round and climb up to the covered terrace for some good views over to Mauritania.

Bakel's **gare routière** is a few minutes' walk from the town centre, where the cheapest **place to stay** is the rather shabby but very friendly *Hôtel d'Islam* (☏339 37 90 29 ❸), with several a/c rooms (the ones without a/c have no fans either, and are stiflingly hot), plus mat space on the roof terrace. There's a **restaurant** here, too, serving big helpings of tasty dishes for about CFA400; otherwise you could try the various fast-food places along the main street. For a bit more comfort, check out the a/c rooms in the *Hôtel Ma Coumba* (☏339 83 52 80 ❸), on the riverbank a little north of town.

In common with a number of other settlements in the area, Bakel is twinned with a French town (Apt, in Provence), and the whole district is surprisingly full of émigré money: many of the Soninké villagers from here live in France, remitting savings which are put towards impressive houses. The villages of **GOLMY**, **KONGANY** and **BALLOR** are all to the north, most easily visited with your own transport. You can also get a pirogue across the river to **GOURAY** in Mauritania, or to **GUTHURBÉ** in Mali. Most of the Soninké villages organize *journées culturelles* every year or two, during which traditional Soninké ways are dusted off and presented to the community – occasions well worth planning around if you get to hear of one.

Kidira and Nayé

From Bakel's *gare routière*, bush taxis and a Mouride bus leave daily for the sixty-kilometre run to **KIDIRA** (1hr) and on to Tambacounda (see opposite; 4–5hr). On arrival in Kidira, you'll be delivered to the *sûreté* at the west end of town, where you should get stamped out of Senegal if you're heading for Mali. Unfortunately the town has little to offer apart from some street food by the Kidira railway crossing, but the Falémé River (follow the tracks 1km east) is a good place to pass the time and maybe catch up on your washing. In fact, with the slow demise of the railway, Kidira itself has been sidelined by the new paved road-bridge across the Falémé at **NAYÉ**, and it's here where you can most easily find a place to stay and a decent variety of street food. The road on into Mali is also now paved and passes through light baobab woodland to **Kayes**, just over 100km to the east. **Bamako**, a little over 500km further, is also paved all the way, and taxis do the journey in a day.

2.3

Niokolo-Koba and the southeast

Senegal's number-one **national park** and the flag-bearer for the country's conservation policies, **Niokolo-Koba** is an undulating wilderness, straddling the Gambia River and two major tributaries in the gentle uplands of **Sénégal Oriental**. Aside from the park, which itself is only visited by around two thousand people a year, **southeast Senegal** is little affected by tourism. You'll find strongly traditional ways enduring, although hunting as a livelihood took a severe blow when the park opened, displacing a large, scattered population of Mandinka, Bassari and Fula. Tourist excursions to **Bassari country**, beyond the park, have been running in a small way from the regional centre of **Tambacounda** for some years and more recently from **Kédougou**, but to reap the high rewards of this part of the country, you must be prepared to hike, bike or make your own arrangements by 4x4.

Tambacounda

Getting to Niokolo-Koba can be difficult: it's feasible without your own transport only if you're prepared to put in considerable time waiting for a ride, probably at **TAMBACOUNDA**, 80km from the park entrance. The town is eastern Senegal's major transport hub, once the big station on the Dakar–Bamako railway after Kayes in Mali, now a major road hub. Situated in the flat, dreary scrub, 180km from the Malian border and 460km from Dakar, the town has little of interest, but if you're using public transport you'll almost inevitably have to spend a night here.

Practicalities

The centre of Tamba is bunched around the station, where (if it's running) the Dakar–Mali train passes through two or three times a month in each direction. Trains are usually packed by the time they reach Tamba, whichever way they're going, so don't expect a seat or bearable toilets.

If you do want to get on the train here, you should book ahead, as there are only a handful of seats reserved for passengers embarking in Tamba. The train is supposed to take seventeen hours to Dakar and twenty-nine hours to Bamako, but you can take serious delays almost for granted.

The main **gare routière** – for services to Dakar, Kédougou, Ziguinchor, Guinea and Guinea-Bissau – is located in the town's southwestern corner. There is also a daily Mouride bus to Dakar, which leaves early from near the train station. A second *gare routière* – for services to Mali and northeast Senegal – is located about 1km along Boulevard Kandioura Noba. The **airport** is a little way south of town but doesn't see much traffic.

If you're heading for the park, stock up on **supplies** in Tamba, as there's really nothing but a handful of basic restaurants in the park itself. In addition to a couple of well-stocked *épiceries* along Avenue Léopold Senghor, the main street, there is an ATM in town at the SGBS **bank** (Mon–Thurs 7.45am–noon & 1.30–3.45pm, Fri 7.45am–noon & 2.45–4.15pm), which also offers Visa and MasterCard cash advances. Next door is a cybercafé. The **PTT**, a pharmacy and a **market** are grouped around Boulevard Demba Diop, near the station. At the **national park office**, 1km out of town on the Mali road (daily 7.30am–5pm; ☎/℻ 339 81 10 97), you can buy entry permits for Niokolo-Koba in advance and rent 4x4 vehicles.

ACCOMMODATION

Chez Dessert	F
Complexe Leggaal Pont	C
Keur Khoudia	A
Hôtel Asta Kebé	E
Hôtel Niji	D
Oasis Oriental	B

RESTAURANTS

Chez Francis	3
Hortensia	1
Le Relais du Ris	2

TAMBACOUNDA

Airport, Kolda and Basse Casamance, Niokolo Koba National Park, The Gambia & Guinea

Accommodation and restaurants

Tamba has a range of local **accommodation** options for all budgets, some of which also serve decent meals.

Asta Kebé 200m down the road from the *Niji* ☎ 339 81 10 28 ⓦ www.tatom.org/AstaKebe. Leafy, Italian-built hotel that dates from the 1970s and looks it, with porticos, arches and other design features that probably seemed a good idea at the time. The seventy-odd rooms are kitted out with either fans or a/c and TV, and there's an excellent pool. ❺

Chez Dessert next to the carpenters and opposite the *Hôtel Asta Kebé* sign ☎ 775 59 97 79. Charmingly off-the-wall place with quiet beds or floor spaces with fans. Given advance notice, they can also do meals. ❷

Complexe Touristique Leggaal Pont bd Demba Diop, 1km out of town on the Mali road ☎ 339 81 17 56 ⓕ 339 81 17 52. Tired and worn *campement* with a bar, restaurant and nightclub. ❸

Keur Khoudia bd Demba Diop, past the Mobil fuel station a few hundred metres on the way out of town ☎/ⓕ 339 81 11 02. Clean cabins that are a backpackers' favourite. It's part of the same setup as the *Simenti* in Niokolo-Koba (see opposite), and they have plenty of information about the park. ❹

Niji av Léopold Senghor, east of the main *gare routière* ☎ 339 81 12 50 ⓔ nijihotel@sentoo.sn. Once-modern option offering an array of fan, a/c and s/c rooms in varying sizes. They also organize *soirées folkloriques* (CFA50,000 for five minimum) and pirogue *balades* along the Gambia River (CFA60,000). ❹

Oasis Oriental ☎ 339 81 18 24 ⓦ www .oasisoriental.com. One of the best places in this part of the country, a resort-style hotel featuring two dozen, well-fitted individual bungalows set around a large pool. They also serve tasty Franco-Senegalese menus from CFA4500 and run a range of tours. ❻

You can **eat** cheaply at several African restaurants on Boulevard Demba Diop, on either side of the train station – *Le Relais du Rais* is one of the best – as well as at the nearby *Hortensia*. *Chez Francis*, on Avenue Léopold Senghor, has a great terrace and serves a good steak and chips for CFA2500. The *Niji* does an agreeable *menu* for CFA4500, though the food tends to be better at the *Asta Kebé* (*menu* CFA5500). The *Complexe Leggaal Pont* is a popular local dance spot, open well into the wee hours.

Routes into Guinea

Travellers heading for Guinea by **public transport** should try hard in Tambacounda to find something going the whole way rather than setting off on a series of bush-taxi hops – transport via Niokolo-Koba into Guinea is fairly hit and miss. Keep an eye out for anything going through to **Mali** (aka Mali-ville), a small town in northern Guinea, 120km south of Kédougou.

The **main route** from Tambacounda into **Guinea** splits from the Tambacounda–Ziguinchor road where it scrapes the Gambian border. From here the route goes via **Medina-Gounas** (a devout community of the Tijaniya brotherhood, where the women are veiled) to the Senegalese post at **Boundou**, from where an extremely rough *piste* leads 55km to Koundara on the Guinean side.

The first of two possible **minor routes** starts west of **Kédougou**, and heads up into the Fouta Djalon highlands, a ride you won't forget in a hurry and from which even experienced 4x4 drivers have turned back. Eventually after passing through Maliville, this ends up at the major town of **Labé**, as does the alternative route that starts a few kilometres east of Kédougou, and winds through the hills for more than 200km via Madina-Salambandé. You might be lucky with transport on the first route, which is also by far the most scenic. On the second, the Gambia River crossing in Guinea is particularly uncertain. Both have Guinean entrance formalities on the border itself, but expect to have to check in again at Maliville or Labé. With your own vehicle, you might prefer the less arduous crossing to the Guinean town of **Youkounkoun**, 100km west of Kédougou. For more route details, see p.621.

Niokolo-Koba National Park

The **Parc National de Niokolo-Koba**, covering an area of more than 9000 square kilometres – not much smaller than the total area of The Gambia – of savannah, forest and swamp, is one of West Africa's biggest and longest established faunal reserves, a UNESCO World Heritage Site since 1981, and on the list of Heritage in Danger since 2007, due to poaching and the threat posed by a planned dam on the upper Gambia River. Ecologically, it's a surprisingly diverse region, far removed from the flat scrub you might expect, the gently undulating **savannah** interspersed with river courses and **gallery forest**, **bamboo** stands and **marshes**.

The park is officially open between mid-December and late April, during the dry season, when animals gather along the watercourses, though in fact you can visit at any time of the year. Among the commoner large species here are buffalo, hartebeest (*bubale*; uniquely ugly with their long faces and hooked horns), shaggy Defassa waterbuck (*cobe defassa*), timid and fast-moving bushbuck (*antilope harnaché* or *guib*; beautifully white-marked on russet coat), warthog (*phacochère*) and, of course, crocodiles in the rivers. **Hippos** are sometimes visible from the authorized halts along the Gambia River, and you can see them in many areas where the water is deep enough all year round. Look out also for the large, maned **roan antelope** (*hippotrague*) and especially for the huge and very uncommon **western giant eland**, which stands a couple of metres at the shoulder. Baboons and other monkeys, notably vervet and red patas, are also common. The park's **chimpanzees** are exceedingly rare, but can occasionally be seen east of Assirik, probably the most northerly chimpanzee outpost in Africa.

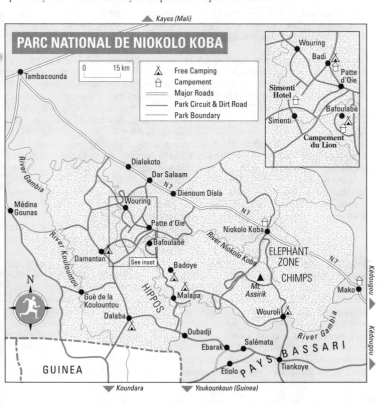

Sighting **lions** is also rare; with patience, though, you might see them in pockets of deep shade at the base of trees, or in hollows, especially around the confluence of tracks known as Patte d'Oie − "Crow's foot". **Elephants** are said to gather in a broad zone around Mont Assirik, and in the months before the rains (March–May) are sometimes found in the south of this area − a drive between Bangaré ford and Worouli could be successful. **Leopards**, like lions, can range outside the park's confines and are probably Africa's most under-counted large predator; very rarely seen, they are most likely to be spotted high in a tree.

Practicalities

The easiest way of visiting the park is to take an **organized excursion** with one of the Tambacounda hotels, though cost is a major drawback. The cheapest chauffeured 4x4 safari with the *Hôtel Niji* is CFA80,000 between five people, which includes fuel and entrance fees. The *Hôtel Asta Kebé* charges CFA80,000 each for two or three people. It's worth paying a bit more to spend at least one night in the park. One possibility for a free lift to the park from Tamba is to hang around by the pool at the *Asta Kebé* or at the *Niji* bar, where there's often a contingent of tourists about to make their way there.

Travelling independently, you can get to the park **entrance** at **Dar Salam** in a Kédougou-bound **taxi brousse** from Tamba, though you'll almost certainly have to pay the full Kédougou fare (CFA3500) and you may find it hard to continue into the park from there. Four people simply sharing a taxi from Tamba all the way to the park **headquarters** at Simenti can expect to pay around CFA5000 each. Alternatively, you can always find a **taxi** driver who's willing to spend the day − possibly even longer − driving you round. The advantage is the price − negotiable down to realistic levels of CFA25,000–30,000 per taxi per day (excluding fuel, entrance fees and guide hire). But be sure the driver knows what he's about, that the vehicle is sound and has spares, and that you pay for fuel separately, otherwise your game-viewing is going to be limited indeed. Note that the park's tracks are pretty rough, and that you'll definitely need a 4x4 if it's wet or if you're planning a trip to Mont Assirik; on the plus side, good signposting ensures you won't have much trouble finding your way around. Note that driving isn't allowed after dark.

Your chances of seeing wildlife will be greatly improved if you **hire a guide** (CFA6000 per day), either at the park entrance or at Simenti; all the guides speak French, but are unlikely to speak English. The park **fee** per day is CFA2000 per person, plus CFA5000 per car. At the park entrance you can buy entry permits and booklets with maps for CFA5000, and there's also a reasonable *campement*, the *Dar Salam* (☎339 81 25 75; ❷; tents CFA3500), which also does basic meals.

Accommodation within the park at the main centres of **Simenti** and **Niokolo-Koba** is slicker, the *campements* almost indistinguishable from hotels, with restaurants, swimming pools (non-guests can pay a fee for a swim) and fuel supplies. Set a good ninety minutes into the park, *Hôtel Simenti* (☎339 82 36 50 ⊛www.simenti.com ❹) is the most popular, with simple huts and more comfortable, en-suite rooms, plus an excellent location above the Gambia River and a good game-viewing **hide**; meals are available for CFA5000, half-day game drives for CFA6500 per person and transfers from Dar Salam for CFA15,000. Eight kilometres east of Simenti is *Campement du Lion* (℡339 85 44 00 ⓦwww .africa-safari-fr.com ❷), a well-run, fairly basic setup in one of the park's most tranquil spots, also overlooking the river. Meals are CFA3500. There is a small, thatched *campement* (❷) at Badi, and but you can **camp** for free at Malapa, Damantan, Badoye, Dalaba, Wouroli and Bafoulabé. For up-to-date information contact the **national park office** in Tambacounda (see p.239).

If you want to call it a day before arriving at the park, try the *Campement Hôtel de Wassadou* (℡339 82 36 02 ⓦwww.niokolo.com ❺), about 50km from Tambacounda on the way to the park, whose simple, clean huts with private baths are set in lush surroundings. They offer a variety of excursions into the park.

Kédougou and the Pays Bassari

Set in Senegal's verdant and rarely visited southeastern corner, the **Pays Bassari** is an area of low hills watered by the runoff from the Fouta Djalon highlands to the south and the perennial Gambia River. This is the least known part of the country, ethnically diverse and very different from the Wolof-Franco Senegal to the north and west. Living in hill villages at the foot of the Fouta Djalon mountains, the ancient Bassari people have stood against the tide of Islam that over the centuries has swept around them on the plains. Matrilineal and divided into age groups, they traditionally subsist on farming and hunting (though some still pan for gold). Major initiation ceremonies are held every year, and there's an annual **festival** before the rains in April or May, notably at the village of **Etiolo**, a few kilometres from the Guinean frontier.

KÉDOUGOU is the only major settlement, once a bit of a dead end to all but the very few pushing on to Guinea or Mali but now more easily accessible – and a viable alternative base for the Niokolo-Koba park – thanks to the good-quality surfaced road from Tambacounda, which takes about four hours (CFA3500 by minibus). The town's *campements* offer a range of **excursions** to Bassari, Beduk and Fula villages in the region, along with the spectacular **waterfall** near Dindefelo and traditional gold mines, plus tours to Niokolo-Koba (though these are no cheaper than in Tamba).

If you've just turned up from Mali or Guinea, get your passport stamped at the **police** post, 500m up the Tamba road just past the phone box. Kédougou has a **post office**, **pharmacies**, **fuel** and **Internet** access, as well as several **accommodation** options, but no bank, and no obvious place to withdraw cash. The best-value stays are *Chez Diao*, a tidy little *campement* with both a/c and fan rooms, 100m east of the *gare routière* in the town centre (℡339 37 96 07 or 339 85 11 24 ❷), and *Chez Moise*, north of the *gare routière* (℡339 85 11 39 Ⓕ339 85 12 68 ❸); both offer comfortable huts with showers. For a bit more comfort try *Le Relais de Kédougou* (℡339 85 10 62 ⓦwww.relais-kedougou.com ❸), perched high above the Gambia (Gambie) River at the west end of town and sporting a pool, which you can also use if you eat there; or the smarter *Le Bedik* (℡339 85 10 00 ⓦwww.relaishorizons.net ❺), next to the post office, whose two dozen rooms have a/c and TV. The *campements* are the best places for **food** – *Le Bedik's* restaurant has superb river views – the only other options being the fast-food restaurants at the *gare routière*. Around the *gare routière* you can also rent bikes, motorbikes and mopeds, though the mopeds in particular are unlikely to be in good enough condition to tackle the rough tracks in the surrounding countryside.

From Kédougou, Land Rovers serve **SARAYA**, 60km to the northeast, and occasionally continue another 70km along a maze of minor bush tracks to **Kéniéba** in **Mali** (a rough half-day to two days' drive). This is not a regular route and is dependent on demand as well as the depth of the Falémé River which denotes the unmanned frontier – it's usually fordable from January until the rains come. Expect to pay at least CFA6000 a seat, if the car is full, for this unusual and rarely-used back route into Mali. You can also cross into **Guinea** near Kédougou (CFA15,000 to Labé; 1–2 days), though note that public transport is best found in Tambacounda; see p.240 for routes and transport details.

Into Casamance: Kolda and westwards

Heading from Tamba by public transport for the full-day's ride (CFA7500) to Ziguinchor (see p.247) you want to be sure you catch a pre-8am minibus or you'll be waiting till noon. Few people slow down on their southwesterly way through the **Haute** and **Moyenne Casamance**, and to be honest the small town of **VELINGARA** has little to offer other than a dirt-cheap *campement*.

A better place to break the journey is the regional centre of **KOLDA**. Here you'll find the best **accommodation** at the *Hôtel Hobbe*, a hunting lodge located near the *gare routière*, with upscale rooms, a pool and Internet access (☎339 96 11 70 ⓦwww .hobbe-kolda.com ⑤). A few blocks north of here (about 400m south of the bridge and Total station) is the weathered *Hôtel Moya* (☎339 96 11 75 🄵339 96 13 57 ④), an acceptable nest of en-suite chalets with huge beds. For something to **eat**, the hotel restaurants serve food for CFA6000, though there's a cheaper alternative: two blocks west of the *Moya*, the *Restaurant Moussa Molo* does a heap of *chep-bu-jen* for CFA750 at lunchtime, and meat in the evenings for CFA1250. The **bar** at the *Moya* seems to be the evening social centre.

From Kolda a daily minibus takes a minor *piste* to Bafatá in **Guinea-Bissau**, a four-hour journey which includes border formalities – expect to have your baggage turned inside out by the Guinea-Bissau Customs – and a walk across a rickety bridge spanning the Rio Gêba. There's also a more direct bush-taxi option to Bissau (via Farim) from **TANAF**, 70km west of Kolda. At Tanaf you can also take a ferry from **SANDENIÈR**, 10km northwest of town, across the Casamance River to **SÉDHIOU** (*campement*) in the Moyenne Casamance region.

2.4

Basse Casamance

Basse Casamance – the lower reaches of the Casamance River – is the most seductive part of Senegal. Wonderfully tropical, with dense forest, winding creeks, rice fields and quiet back roads shaded by massive silk-cottons, the region seems to have little in common with the Senegal of Islamic brotherhoods, groundnuts, cattle and dust.

For centuries the mostly **Jola**-speaking population of Basse Casamance resisted the push of Islam (most successfully on the south bank of the river), while the Portuguese maintained a typically torpid presence. The ceding of the region to the French in 1886 didn't precipitate any great social shifts. Changes are under way, despite an isolation in which villages and language groups are cut off even from each other, but there's a vague sense of resolve to maintain some degree of self-determination. Since independence, the **Casamance question** and the apparent threat to Wolof-speaking, French-abetted metropolitan Senegal has been a prickly one. The charge that Casamance continues to be ignored because it produces less groundnuts than the north and can't muster heavyweight marabouts – the region is substantially non-Muslim – is not baseless. The Casamançais resent the snub, because it is Casamance rice that goes a substantial way towards feeding the country. Furthermore, without the Casamance's full participation in national affairs, the issue of *rapprochement* with The Gambia – an even more troublesome thorn in Senegal's side – will never be resolved.

Despite the ongoing **separatist conflict** (see the box on p.246 for coverage of the security issues, and the box on p.180 for the historical background), now is in some ways a good time to travel to Basse Casamance: for one thing, **prices** are incredibly low, and the local people – especially in the most run-down villages – are all the more welcoming and appreciative of anyone who makes the effort to visit.

The Jola

The people of Basse Casamance are predominantly **Jola** (or Diola; no relation to the Diola/Dyula of Côte d'Ivoire) – broadly divided by the river into Buluf and Fonyi on the north bank and Huluf (or Fulup) on the south bank. From around the sixteenth century they gradually displaced earlier Casamance inhabitants called the Banyun, who used to be great traders and still live among them. Nobody seems to know where the Jola came from, but their dialects are closely related to the Manjak spoken in Guinea-Bissau, and indeed the Jola themselves generally claim to come from the south. They never developed a unified state, and their fragmentation has resulted in some **Jola dialects** being mutually unintelligible. In fact the idea of a Jola "tribe" is mostly a colonial one: only their contact with outsiders has given the term any meaning for the people themselves. The word is supposed to derive from the Manding *jor la* – "he who avenges himself".

A distinctive style of **wet-rice farming** has been practised for at least six hundred years in the reclaimed land between the creeks. **Dykes** are built around new fields so that the rains will flood them and leach out the sea salt, which runs away through hollow tree trunks in the dykes while the fields lie fallow. Once the field is flooded, the drains are blocked and the rice plants brought out from the nurseries and planted, one by one, in the mud. After three or four months of weeding and dyke care by the men, the women gather the **harvest** in November or December. For the first half of the year, though, there's little work in the rice fields and increasingly this is a time when young people drift away to Ziguinchor, The Gambia or Dakar. Many don't return for the next season. Later in the year, you'll see villagers walking to the fields early in the morning with the amazingly long, iron-tipped hoes called **kayendos**.

Traditionally, rice was never sold. Having huge numbers of granaries full of it, often for years, brought the kind of **prestige** every Jola man wanted. Consequently, conflicts over **land rights** have always been close to the surface and still occasionally erupt.

As for the question of religion, **Islam** has made little headway among the Jola, but an erosion of traditional values has been brought about by the introduction of **groundnuts**. First planted in the region in the early nineteenth century, the crop provided a commercial alternative to rice that could earn ready money, with relatively little labour, on land that had hitherto been unplanted bush. Now grown on raised ground in many parts of Casamance, the groundnut crop has resulted in deforestation, soil degradation and reliance on imported food. "He who wears a *boubou* can't work in the rice fields" goes the Jola saying, ironically excusing the way things increasingly are in terms of Islam.

For some Jola **words and phrases**, see p.193.

Security in Basse Casamance

The bulk of the civil unrest in the Basse Casamance between Senegalese government forces and various disunified factions of the MFDC separatist movement (see p.180) had largely died down in 2004 once the peace treaty was signed with the rebels. By late 2007, however, sporadic conflict had escalated in the region following the 2007 Senegalese elections, and there have been occasional reports of highway banditry along the region's borders.

Much of Casamance's dangerous reputation has come from these intermittent **road ambushes** by rebels turned bandits: a Red Cross worker was killed in 2006 when her vehicle struck a mine on an unpaved road in Tandine, northeast of Ziguinchor; four people were killed in early 2007 when their bus was attacked after being stopped at a rebel roadblock; and in May 2007 there were reports of shootings along the Gambian border. Such incidents have rarely involved tourists, but the British Foreign Office and the US State Department still advise visitors against travel to the region, and whose advice may invalidate any travel-insurance policy you have in place while you are there.

In practice, while some remote parts of Basse Casamance are still **no-go zones** because of rebel activity and/or land mines – notably the forests south of the Kolda–Ziguinchor–Cap Skiring road, including the Basse Casamance National Park, and a couple of stretches along the Gambian border – other areas have not seen any armed conflict in years, if ever. As of early 2008, the main regional roads were considered to be quite safe during the day, thanks to army roadblocks and police checkpoints. Once within the precincts of Ziguinchor, Cap Skiring, Kafountine or any of the villages traditionally popular with tourists, the security risks are seen as negligible – certainly no greater than being mugged in Dakar, for example.

Most people in other parts of Senegal will be full of dire warnings about Casamance, but unless you meet someone who has been there recently, it may be hard to discern objective truth in what you hear. Certainly you should scour the news for the latest information and check the blogs and forums, but you can also get a fairly reliable account of the situation from the **bush-taxi drivers** who travel to Ziguinchor every day, or by calling one of the Ziguinchor hotels, especially *Le Flamboyant* or *Le Kadiandoumagne*.

Getting to and around Basse Casamance

There are three **main roads** to Basse Casamance: from **Banjul** and The Gambia's coastal resorts via Brikama; from **Dakar** via Kaolack and the *transgambienne* route; and from far-off **Tambacounda** in the east. Several minibuses and Peugeots depart daily from Tambacounda for Ziguinchor, most leaving early; a late start will probably mean changing in **Kolda**, making a full day on the road. A final and seductive alternative is the twice-weekly overnight **passenger ferry** from Dakar to Ziguinchor.

Getting around Basse Casamance is generally simple. **Ziguinchor** is the main transport hub, with daily transport to most sites of interest. You can **rent bicycles** in Ziguinchor, Oussouye and Cap Skiring, making cycling around the popular southern part of Basse Casamance a practical option. Unless you have lots of time, it's perhaps best to rent in Oussouye, where there's an excellent bike shop, or Cap Skiring, rather than Ziguinchor, as in that case you'll probably spend your first day cycling straight to Oussouye anyway – not the most exciting bike ride in the area. If you're going anywhere on your own, you should always consult first with locals, who will take care not to let you get close to any trouble. If you're unhappy about travelling by road, note that you can reach pretty much anywhere you want in the region by **pirogue**. Hiring a **guide** to show you round for a few days is cheap and also worth considering.

Because Basse Casamance is so affected by **tides**, no two **maps** of it ever look the same: much of what appears to be virtually underwater on some maps is actually firm ground except during exceptional high tides.

Ziguinchor

Something of **ZIGUINCHOR**'s appeal comes through in its exotic name, pronounced "Sigichor" by most Jola. There's a luxuriant sense of repose here, found in no other sizeable Senegalese town, and life here is a good deal cheaper than in Dakar or The Gambia. Surprisingly, you need reminding that Ziguinchor is on the river: its colonial trading houses don't stand out, and the river port isn't likely to figure prominently in your meanderings. It's a town of trees and avenues, roosting birds, orchestral crickets and fluttering bats at dusk, with a strong flavour of Guinea to the south. Less pleasant is the attention lavished by local mosquitoes from March to October – and sporadically by highly persistent hustlers, vendors and hangers-on.

Arrival, information and accommodation

The old part of town is an easy-to-get-to-grips-with half-square-kilometre grid of streets extending south of the river to **Avenue du Docteur Gabriel Carvalho** on which the **Rond Point** (the main town roundabout) is situated. Within this area you'll find the banks, post office, main hotels and other services as well as the small portside **market**, good for fresh fruit, vegetables and early-morning fish. South of the *rond-point*, Avenue Ibou Diallo leads past the **Cathedral** a kilometre or two to the more animated quarter of town around the **Marché St-Maur**.

Boats from Dakar (see p.200) arrive up the river at the **ferry terminal** right in the heart of the town and just a few minutes from the main hotels. Arriving by road from the north or from Tambacounda, you'll be dropped at the **gare routière**, 1km

Ziguinchor travel details

There are daily **Air Sénégal** (☎339 91 10 81) flights from Ziguinchor (usually starting in Cap Skiring) to **Dakar** (the cheapest flights start at CFA61,100 return).

The ferry to Dakar, the MV *Wilis*, departs Ziguinchor twice weekly (Thurs & Sun) for a voyage that takes 15–17 hours (departs Dakar Tues & Fri). Prices are CFA15,500 for a hard seat, CFA18,500 for a comfy one and CFA28,500 for a couchette in a four-berth cabin. The SOMAT ticket booth (☎338 89 80 09) is down at the ferry terminal. The trip to Dakar gives you often beautiful views of the sun setting over the River Casamance.

A regular **pirogue** service for **Affiniam** leaves from the jetty by *Le Perroquet* (Mon, Tues, Wed & Fri at 3.30pm; CFA400). Sporadically regular services also run to Carabane, Itou, Nioumane and Pointe St-Georges; a boat ride to many places down river at low tide will often give you the chance to see dolphins. You can try to reach an agreement with the *piroguiers* on the waterfront, though you're likely to pay upwards of CFA20,000. A hired pirogue to Cap Skiring will cost around CFA100,000. As an alternative to taxiing straight out of Ziguinchor, however, this is a good way of starting a tour round the north-bank region of **Buluf**. Note that the local pirogues have no shelter from the sun, while some of the tourist vessels have a canvas awning – it does make a big difference.

As for road transport, from the *gare routière*, there are frequent **bush taxis** to **Oussouye** and **Cap Skiring** and at least one **minibus** a day to many smaller villages, including **Enampore** and **Elinkine**.

For **Guinea-Bissau**, the Senegalese border post is at **Mpak** (18km) and the corresponding Guinea-Bissau post is at **São Domingos** (25km). Plan for an early start. If you already have a visa, you can take a *taxi brousse* straight from Ziguinchor through to Bissau for CFA6000.

You can get Guinea-Bissau **visas** from the consulate next to the *Hôtel du Tourisme* (Mon–Fri 8am–2pm). All visas are processed on the spot; a one-month double-entry visa costs CFA10,000.

east of town, just south of the bridge. If you've come up from Guinea-Bissau, you may be dropped off on the wide, sealed road, just east of the Marché St-Maur and close to a few cheap accommodation options. If you arrive by air you'll find the airport is a kilometre further south of the Marché St-Maur; taking an inexpensive taxi into town is a wise idea if you have some baggage.

As the **regional tourist office** on Avenue Édouard Diatta is essentially useless (Mon–Fri 8am–1pm & 3–4pm; ☎339 91 12 68), you're best off asking for advice

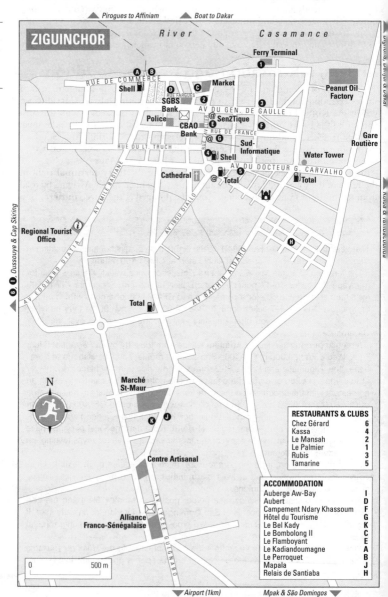

RESTAURANTS & CLUBS

Chez Gérard	6
Kassa	4
Le Mansah	2
Le Palmier	1
Rubis	3
Tamarine	5

ACCOMMODATION

Auberge Aw-Bay	I
Aubert	D
Campement Ndary Khassoum	F
Hôtel du Tourisme	G
Le Bel Kady	K
Le Bombolong II	C
Le Flamboyant	E
Le Kadiandoumagne	A
Le Perroquet	B
Mapala	J
Relais de Santiaba	H

from your hotel or visiting the excellent local website Ⓦwww.casamance.net, run by the owner of *Le Flamboyant* (see below).

Accommodation

Ziguinchor offers an excellent and inexpensive range of **accommodation** – basic, central rooms, *campement*-style setups, and a few plusher alternatives at knock-down prices. This last category suffered from the drop in tourist numbers in the early 1990s, but the better establishments remain very popular with French visitors, and as things *touristique* have started to pick up again, it's not uncommon find them at full occupancy, so booking ahead is a wise plan.

Old Ziguinchor

Aubert rue Fargues Ⓣ339 38 80 20 Ⓕ339 91 54 54. A "luxury" hotel that has long outlived its heyday. Musty rooms have adequate facilities and there's free use of the pool at the next-door sports complex, but the whole place feels a bit past its sell-by. ❺

Le Bombolong II rue Fargues ⓉError! 339 38 80 01. Owned by the *Kadiandoumagne*, this mid-range hotel offers good-value s/c, a/c rooms, but little in the way of ambience. It houses both the relaxing *Bar Américaine* and one of Ziguinchor's best nightclubs (free to guests). ❷

Campement Ndary Khassoum rue de France ⓉError! 339 36 80 20. Centrally located and with a shady courtyard, but the rooms – all with huge bathrooms and some with their own toilets – are a bit dingy. ❷

Hôtel du Tourisme rue de France ⓉError! 339 91 22 23 Ⓕ339 91 22 22. A somewhat neglected colonial-era favourite owned by the *Flamboyant* just opposite still offers reasonable s/c rooms and a good restaurant. ❸

🏃 **Le Flamboyant** rue de France ⓉError! 339 91 22 23 Ⓦwww.flamboyant.info. With nearly fifty spotless, comfortable rooms at superb prices, this well-run hotel is one of the best deals in the country. All have a/c, satellite TV and Wi-Fi, and there's also a sparkling pool and super-knowledgeable staff (the owner is the French honorary consul). ❹

🏃 **Le Kadiandoumagne** rue de Commerce ⓉError! 339 38 80 00 Ⓦwww.hotel-kadiandoumagne.com. Despite rather bland a/c rooms that occasionally disappoint, the superb views and unbeatable location mean this otherwise refined, colonial-style riverfront hotel takes home the prize for Zig's hotels. There's a pool, a beautiful grassy garden, a fine restaurant and free Wi-Fi, as well as day-trips on offer. ❺

Le Perroquet rue de Commerce ⓉError! 339 91 23 29 Ⓦwww.casamance.net/perroquet. Dashes of colour spruce up the small s/c, fan rooms at this riverside French-run establishment. The garden could use a gardener, but it's hard to beat perching at a bar stool, sipping on a beer and gazing out to the yachts bobbing on the river. ❸

Out from the centre

Auberge Aw-Bay signposted 2.5km down the Oussouye road ⓉError! 339 36 80 76 Ⓦwww.aubergeawbay.fr.fm. Clean rooms and a pleasant, shady courtyard – a reasonable option if you have your own transport. Pirogue excursions around CFA12,000. ❷

Le Bel Kady just south of Marché St-Maur ⓉError! 339 91 11 22. Popular budget option run by a friendly bunch of youths. Faintly bordello-ish with non-s/c rooms and dubious ablutions, but a good-value restaurant (mains from CFA1500). ❶

Mapala opposite *Bel Kady* ⓉError! 339 91 26 27. Basic, s/c doubles with fan, plus a cheap restaurant and bar. ❶

Relais de Santiaba quartier Santiaba ⓉError! 339 91 11 99. Decent-value *campement* that has recently seen a good renovation. Rooms are extremely basic, but clean, and there is a good bar-resto. ❷

The town and around

There's not a great deal to keep you in Ziguinchor, but just hanging out is pleasure enough. In the old quarter of the town centre, there's a string of public gardens, heavily shaded, with park benches and – sign of a non-Muslim region – rootling piglets. Pelicans and storks congregate in the trees, however, making this a somewhat noisy and unpredictable place to relax.

Both the **Marché St-Maur-des-Fossés** (named after the southeast Paris suburb with which Ziguinchor is twinned) and the **Centre Artisanal**, just to the south, are relatively hassle-free and well worth visiting. The municipal St-Maur, divided into merchandise zones, heaves with activity, while the *artisanal*, where the stall holders really are working at their crafts, is a relaxing place to get all your souvenirs in one go and offers real bargains for hardened hagglers.

Excursions

As a day-trip, or less, you can take a pirogue via the Île aux Oiseaux to **Dilapao** on the north side of the river and continue up the serpentine Marigot de Bignona to Affiniam (see p.262). At Dilapao, there's a two-storey mud-brick house owned by a local artist and decorated with sculptures (CFA500 to look round), while Affiniam's large *case à impluvium* (see p.253) is one of the oldest and nicest *campements* in the rural *intégré* circuit. Most Ziguinchor hotels and the *Mansah* restaurant offer this popular day-trip; prices start around CFA12,500 each for a motor pirogue for two people, usually less per person with a group, but can vary wildly from place to place. Ask around at the cheaper *campements* or hotels, or phone direct to one of the local guides, Dia, on ☏775 70 45 57. Alternatively, take the much cheaper, daily afternoon public boat, spend the night in Affiniam and return the next morning. To **hire a car** with a driver for exploring Basse Casamance, ring Ousmane Diallo (☏775 28 50 78), an amicable and knowledge-able young Jola who knows the region well. Depending on how far you go, he charges around CFA 20,000 per day, excluding petrol.

Restaurants

With a few exceptions noted below, food in Ziguinchor is unremarkable. **Street food** is generally limited to fruit and nuts (cashews make an inexpensive treat) or port area bread and coffee stalls. You'll find numerous nondescript **restaurants**, offering a low-priced daily *plat*, on the way to Marché St-Maur along Avenue Lycée Guignabo, south of the Total station; there's more sophisticated eating in town, especially at the hotels. The *Hôtel du Tourisme*'s high-ceilinged dining room offers excellent Franco-Senegalese three-course seafood and continental menus for CFA4500 and pricier à la carte options, while the pick of Zig's places to eat is probably the *Kadiandoumagne*, with top-quality seafood in their restaurant on the jetty overlooking the river for around CFA10,000 a head. *Le Perroquet* also has a great location, and does much cheaper Franco-Senegalese meals (around CFA2500 per plat), but bring some mosquito spray.

Chez Gérard 5km west of Ziguinchor in Djibelor at the entrance to the crocodile farm (see p.252) ☏339 91 17 01 or 776 36 08 39. This roadside patio restaurant, owned by a convivial Frenchman, serves tasty croc dishes from CFA6000. And yes, they come from the farm next door. Arrive by 8:30pm or call to reserve.

Le Mansah rue de Capitaine Javelier. Right in the town centre and well worth a visit for great-value Senegalese dishes – the *plat du jour* is CFA1500 – and delicious *brochettes*. Check out the huge carved masks up on the walls too – they're the real thing.

Le Palmier rue de Commerce (open 24hr, in theory). Cheap and cheerful, if musty, place down by the port, serving tasty regional fare for around CFA1300 a plate.

Drinking and nightlife

After dark, Ziguinchor smoulders. For a drink at sunset, there's no better place than the riverfront deck at *Le Kadiandoumagne*. A bit later on (well, after midnight), *Tamarine* fills with local *gazelles*; *La Kassa* draws an older crowd with its regular live music shows; and *Bar Américaine* (inside the *Hôtel Le Bombolong II*) remains calm, cool and collected, with beach chairs splayed out on a stone patio. For the full-on Casamance club experience, *Le Bombolong* and the riverside *Le Rubis* reign as some of the hottest spots in the country, and both repay the entrance fees of a mere CFA1500 with hot music – lots of *zouk and salsa* – and as many chance encounters as you want. *Le Bombolong* is more exclusive (and pricier) and scores highly with the French community, as well as passing *toubabs*, while *Rubis* has a greater head of steam and a largely local crowd; the patio behind is a vital cooling-off area.

Listings

Banks Of the six banks in town, the CBAO (Mon–Thurs 7.45am–3.45pm, Fri 7.45am–1pm & 2.45–3.45pm) and the SGBS (Mon–Thurs 7.45am–noon & 2.15–3.45pm, Fri 7.45am–noon & 2.45–4.15pm) are your only options for ATMs, foreign exchange, getting cash advances on Visa or MasterCard and changing traveller's cheques.

Bike rental Several spots in town have mountain bikes for around CFA5000 per day, and one-speeds for CFA2500. Try the shed just opposite the pirogue launch.

Bookshop Librairie de l'Escale, rue Javelier (Mon–Fri 9am–1pm & 3.30–6.30pm, Sat 9am–1pm) gets *The Herald Tribune*, but it's usually several days old.

Clinic/Medical treatment Dr Simon Tendeng, 50m east of the Rond Point down av du Docteur Gabriel Carvalho on the left, charges CFA5000 for an initial consultation (by appointment only: Mon–Fri 8.30am–2.30pm & 6–8pm, Sat 8.30am–2.30pm; ☏ 339 91 13 85; emergencies ☏ 339 91 17 75).

Cultural centre The Alliance Franco-Sénégalaise, south of the Centre Artisanal, puts on exhibitions and concerts, but it's worth visiting simply for its beautifully ornate building – a modern variation on a *case à impluvium* – and shady garden. There's a cheap café here, too (Mon–Sat 9.15am–noon & 3–7.15pm).

Internet access Try Cyber (Mon–Thurs, Sat & Sun 8am–11pm, Fri 8am–1pm & 3–11pm; CFA1000/hr) or Sud-Informatique (Mon–Sat 8am–7pm; CFA500/hr), both on rue Javelier near the CBAO bank.

Pharmacy Pharmacie du Rond Point at the Rond Point; Mon–Sat 8am–9pm. They usually have someone who speaks a little English. A list is posted detailing which pharmacy is on duty after hours.

Police ☏ 339 91 10 13 or ☏ 17 in an emergency.

Pool Complexe Sportive Aubert across from the *Hôtel Aubert* ☏ 339 38 80 20. Daily 11am–1pm & 3–6.30pm; CFA1000.

Travel agency Casamance Voyage Tourisme, 131 rue Javelin ☏ 339 91 43 62.

The southern Basse Casamance

Between Ziguinchor and the coast lies the heart of the **southern Basse Casamance**, a district of tall hardwood forest and rice fields cut by three major creeks and their fringes of mangrove flats. As the longest distance between significant places is just 34km, this is an ideal district for **cycling**, though the problems

"Rurally integrated" campements

Casamance's network of **campements touristiques rurals integrés** (CTRIs) was introduced by the Ministry of Tourism in the 1970s to cater for people with small budgets wanting a change from mainstream accommodation. Built by villagers with loans from central funds, often in a traditional architectural style, the *campements* theoretically bring tourist money into parts of the rural economy that don't usually benefit.

Facilities at the CTRIs – also known as *campements villageois* – are basic but include running water, kerosene lighting, three-course meals, and cold drinks from a gas fridge. They provide mosquito nets and foam mattresses and sheets. For the same price you can always camp outside using your own equipment. **Prices** are the same at all CTRIs and you can pay for accommodation only, or as many meals as you want: full board costs CFA9300; bed-only CFA2500; breakfast CFA1800; lunch or dinner CFA2500.

Many CTRIs took a severe beating from the drop in tourism caused by the Casamance conflict, but an infusion of French and some German aid money has enabled the rebuilding of five separate sites. These five locations – Affiniam, Baïla, Enampore, Koubalan and Oussouye – are now fully operational and some even have electricity, fridges and mosquito nets. In the event that you come upon a *campement* that isn't open, it will usually be no problem to find a room somewhere in the village. For more information, visit ⓦ www.ausenegal.com/campements-villageois or to book a room, contact the *campements* directly.

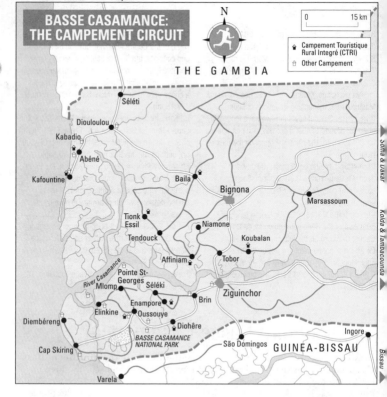

of the last decade have meant that certain areas, such as the forest paths along the Gambian border, are now off-limits (see p.246). You can rent bikes at **Oussouye** or **Cap Skiring** – or mopeds at the latter, which is Senegal's foremost holiday resort. Apart from needing a water bottle and devising a way to carry your gear, there are no special practical problems in cycling around.

Ziguinchor to Enampore and Oussouye

Climbing the gentle valley out of Ziguinchor, the road passes through the remains of the **forest** that once covered the entire area. The magnificent thirty- to forty-metre trees, strung with vines, are inhabited by large numbers of birds and small animals – though you'll only see monkeys where the trees are close enough together to form arboreal highways. About 5km out of town, you'll come to **DJIBELOR**, where the signposted **crocodile farm and orchard** (Mon–Sun 8.30am–6pm; ☎339 91 17 01; CFA1000) is well worth a visit. The orchard comprises several hectares of fruit trees – you can buy the fruit at the entrance – and flowers, among which fenced enclosures and sheds house about a thousand Nile crocodiles of various sizes.

BRIN, 6km further, has its own small, basic *Campement Filao* (☎339 92 01 20 ❶), a quiet place otherwise livened up by several local musicians who hang around here. It's right by the Enampore track, where the *taxi brousse* will drop you off.

Enampore and Séléki

It's a thirteen-kilometre, four-hour walk to **ENAMPORE**, best done in the cool of the early morning – at this time there is also a chance of getting a lift with some village-bound transport – passing Essil after 6km. The 🦌 *CTRI campement* at Enampore (☏339 93 00 38) is a beautiful, large *case à impluvium,* wonderfully constructed and a pleasure just to be in, especially during the hot hours of the day. However familiar you become with the region's *impluvium* architecture, the calm simplicity of Enampore is memorable. It's possible to rent a pirogue in Enampore to take you to the superb *Campement Les Bolongs* (CFA7500 per person; see p.255) just to the east of Oussouye.

Attempts to revive the campement at **SÉLÉKI**, three kilometres beyond Enampore, have thus far proven unsuccessful – largely on account of the lack of drinking water, a problem for many Casamance campements. As a result, your only option is to continue across the dykes and rice fields to Etama and then – if you've plenty of time – on to Bandial (a 15km round trip from Enampore). There's interesting architecture en route, and as they don't get many foreign visitors out on the mud flats, they'll be pleased to see you.

To Oussouye

Back at Brin, the road from Ziguinchor turns south, looping away from the river to cross the **Kamobeul Bolong** creek on a new bridge, from where you can catch a cheap pirogue to access several small outlying islands, good areas for walking. Oussouye, the next major focus, is 34km from Ziguinchor, across scrub, open mangrove flats, a lagoon and more scrub – good for birds west of the bridge, otherwise unenthralling. The rurally integrated *campement* at **Diohère**, signposted 14km from Brin, is rarely visited and currently not open. For mountain-bikers, the eastward route back to Ziguinchor from Diohère through farms and forest to the Ziguinchor-to-Guinea-Bissau road is idyllic, but has been closed for several years because of possible land mines.

Cases à impluvium and fetish shrines

The traditional Jola **case à impluvium** translates as "rain reservoir hut", a somewhat demeaning term that tells only half the story. The design is doughnut-shaped, with entrances into a shared, circular courtyard and internal doors into private rooms that are built as individual units. There's a stunning quality to the light reflected off the clean-swept courtyard floor to illuminate the living space. The thatched, saddleback roof circling above the living quarters is built like a funnel to allow rain to run into a central reservoir, from where it drains outside through a channel.

In the past the *impluvium* was good insurance, guaranteeing adequate supplies of water in times of war or drought, but since pure water wells have been dug all over, few *impluvium* houses are being built these days. Yet they make wonderful homes, and undoubtedly more Jola families would build new *cases à impluvium* if they could afford to – but the increasing nuclearization of families means that few can find the necessary money or labour.

Although it's often written that the only other examples of *impluvium* architecture are found in New Guinea, similar houses were traditional in Guinea-Bissau and parts of southwest Côte d'Ivoire, and also in parts of southern Nigeria, where they were square in plan.

In the bush around, you'll also come across isolated miniature huts in the briefest of clearings. Often just a forked stick under a thatched roof, these are **fetish shrines**, the earthly visiting rooms of spirits that hold power over rain, fertility and illnesses. They are consulted less frequently than in the past, but there are still matters about which many Jola feel the traditional spirits know more than modern science or medicine. You should be careful not to disturb them or take photos.

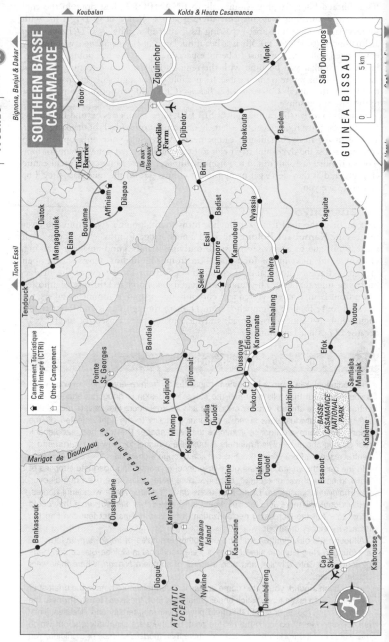

SOUTHERN BASSE CASAMANCE

■ Campement Touristique Rural Integré (CTRI)
⌂ Other Campement

Koubalan

Kolda & Haute Casamance

GUINEA BISSAU

0   5 km

Ziguinchor

São Domingos

Mpak

Tobor

Tidal Barrier

Diatok

Mangagoulak

Elana

Boutème

Affiniam

Dilapao

Crocodile Farm

Djibelor

Ile aux Oiseaux

Brin

Badem

Toubakouta

Tendouck

Tionk Essil

Bandial

Sèleki

Essil

Enampore

Kamoubeul

Badiat

Nyassia

Diohère

Kaguite

Youtou

Edioungou

Karounate

Niambalang

Efok

Pointe St. Georges

Kadjinol

Djiromait

Oussouye

Oukout

Bouktimgo

Santiaba Manjak

BASSE CASAMANCE NATIONAL PARK

Mlomp

Loudia Ouolof

Kahème

Bankassouk

Oussinguène

Kagnout

Elinkine

Diakène Ouolof

Essaout

Marigot de Diouloulou

River Casamance

Diogué

Karabane

Karabane Island

Kachouane

Diembèreng

Cap Skiring

Kabrousse

Nyikine

ATLANTIC OCEAN

N

Another 10km down the main road to Oussouye you come to *Chez Balousa* (**❶**), a quaint *case à impluvium* reached by turning left just after the roadside café at **NIAMBALANG**; go 400m along the track and it's just after the well. A *case à impluvium* built in 1980, it has a lived-in feel and is a lot livelier than most *campements*. The family charge less than the going rate for the two rooms offered, although they'll need advance warning if you want a meal. Just before Oussouye you'll pass the small village of **EDIOUNGOU**, with a winding, vaguely confusing track (stick to the right until you see arrowed signs) that leads to its pleasant *Campement Les Bolongs* (☎339 93 10 01 or 336 37 46 75 ⊛patclement.free.fr/william **❸**), a pillared and columned motel-looking structure with a terrace bar adorned with hammocks for lazing about. They offer excellent, creek-side views and pirogue and fishing excursions. Ask for one of the newer rooms at the back. The only other reason to stop here is to visit the local **crafts centre**, Le Métissage – formerly located in Oussouye – where a couple of artisans make and sell wooden figurines and statuettes, though the prices are the same if not better at the artisan market in Ziguinchor. To reach the centre, make a left about 50m after turning off the main road for *Les Bolongs*.

Oussouye

Another kilometre brings you to **OUSSOUYE**, the seat of a line of Jola **priest-kings**, and occupying the largest patch of dry land around. Royalty is not as much in evidence as it used to be, but the town is still an important and growing place, though even the market offers little of interest to the passing visitor. Behind the post office is Casamance VTT (☎/☎339 93 10 04 ⊛casavtt.free.fr), which is the best place in the region to **rent bikes** (CFA4000 for a half-day trip) and **kayaks**; they also organize recommended guided excursions into the surrounding countryside.

A track from the roundabout in the middle of town leads to three **campements**, the first of which is the small and exceptionally friendly *Auberge de Routard* (☎339 93 10 25 **❷**), with small, sculpted stone huts overseen by Gouho Diatta – his wife prepares great food and a vat of palm wine is passed around afterwards. Just behind the *Routard* is the newer *Campement Emanaye* (☎339 93 10 04 or 775 73 63 34; ⊛emanaye.free.fr **❷**), which offers clean s/c rooms, a thatched bar and restaurant and bike and canoe excursions. They also run an **Internet** café in Oussouye (Sun–Fri 4–9pm). Continuing another 600m up the track you may see men hanging beneath the crowns of the palm trees tapping the wine for the day. The pick of the town's *campements* is further up on the left. Run by its ever-gregarious *patron*, Oussouye's unusual two-storey, stone ⚓ *Campement CTRI* (☎339 93 00 15 ⊛campement .oussouye.org; prices slightly higher than normal CTRI rates) was just renovated and now offers airy and cool rooms that are a pleasure to be in, even at midday.

The road leading from the roundabout back towards Ziguinchor has a couple of inexpensive restaurants, most notably the shaded *Le Kassa* and the mural-covered *Le Passager*, with mains for around CFA1000, though there is good food at a small, newly-opened Spanish-run roadside café set just alongside the massive silk-cotton (*fromager*) tree on the road leading out of town to the west; they dish up super tortillas.

Moving on from Oussouye, there are a few bush taxis a day to Mlomp and Elinkine, while vehicles bound for Cap Skiring and Ziguinchor pass through town more frequently.

Mlomp and Pointe St-Georges

From Oussouye, the road swoops through the forest to **MLOMP**, notable for its pair of two-storey *banco* **cottages** with their amazing grove of silk-cotton trees. Two-storey buildings are uncommon in traditional African architecture, and nobody knows why Mlomp should have them; they're reminiscent of Asante houses from Ghana and it's possible that the earlier Banyun traders of Casamance brought the innovation back from their travels. The family who live there will show you round one of them (CFA500 donation), and a postcard from your home is much appreciated: many already adorn the walls.

From the village a sandy footpath leads directly north to **Pointe St-Georges,** the Casamance River's last elbow before it reaches the sea. There's not much to the place – it's just a flat, densely wooded stretch of land – but the Pointe does have its own *campement*, built after the upmarket *Village-Hôtel* was burned down by the MFDC in 1992. Access remains a problem, however, as the only driveable track (and 4x4 at that) starts from the village of **KAGNOUT**, 5km west of Mlomp.

Elinkine and Karabane island

Beyond Kagnout, the turning to Pointe St-Georges, several stands of huge silk-cottons give way to monotonous, open country as a flat, straight route leads to the fishing village of **ELINKINE**, 10km from Mlomp (also reachable more quickly from Oussouye). Little more than a tiny naval base and a collection of creek-side buildings, Elinkine makes an enjoyable stopover, with its rebuilt *Campement Le Fromager* (T775 25 64 01 ②) right in the town centre. This small but animated *case à impluvium* has energetic hosts who style their place as the village's *centre nautique*, with canoes for rent, pirogue trips to Karabane, fishing, and so forth; they can also take you by boat to Kachouane (see p.259) for CFA15,000 or all the way to Cap Skiring for around CFA25,000 if you don't fancy the circuitous road trip via Oussouye.

Île de Karabane

At Elinkine the done thing is to take a trip to the history-rich island of **Karabane** in the river mouth. A public pirogue leaves every day at 3pm (CFA1000 one way) for the thirty-minute voyage. Going the other way, the boat leaves Karabane at 10am, so you're going to be staying the night. If you hire your own pirogue, expect to pay around CFA7000 and then you could return the same day.

Karabane, or rather its headland, was an early offshore trading base with the interior, and the first French toehold in the Kasa Mansa – the kingdom of the Kasa, one of the ancestral Jola peoples. It once served as a collection centre for slaves, and ivory, gum and hides were also exported from here, paid for with cloth, alcohol and iron bars. There's a large Breton-style **church**, partly in ruins, dating back to the earliest days of the Holy Ghost Fathers, and a number of crumbling merchant houses. The beach is beautiful, with a ten-kilometre expanse of salty Casamance River in front and coconuts behind, but in truth, on a short visit, the whole place can feel slack with isolation and irrelevance. However, once everyone else has left and you can walk along the beach in peace, Karabane quickly becomes a place that's hard to leave. The *campements* of *Le Barracuda*, nearest the jetty and with great meals (℡776 59 60 01 ❷), and the more atmospheric *Chez Badji-Kunda*, a few hundred metres along the beach splayed out with hammocks and owned by a painter (℡775 53 10 54 or 339 91 14 08 ⓦwww.badjikunda.com ❷), are both preferable to the *Hôtel Carabane* between the two (℡775 69 02 84 ⓔhotelcarabane@yahoo.fr ❸), which is pleasant enough but lacking in real charm.

Cap Skiring and around

In many ways, **CAP SKIRING** feels worlds away from the rest of Casamance, offering travellers a hedonistic reprieve from the bush, with most of the tourist facilities you'd expect of a big holiday resort including lots of souvenir shops, restaurants, bars and nightclubs – as well as a *Club Med*, whose enormous, fenced-off grounds harbour a **golf course**. While there are fears that Cap Skiring is on its way to becoming the Saly of Casamance, for the moment, this coastal idyll succeeds in retaining the charms that first cemented its popularity with tourists in the 1980s. Though the village itself has little of interest, the sands are undeniably pretty – spectacular, even, along the more deserted stretches – and the sea is warm and safe, with a cool breeze during the day. Bronzing and bathing are the main activities, though you can also rent jet skis and sailboards from the more expensive hotels.

Arrival and information

From the T-junction at the western end of the Oussouye road, Cap Skiring village ("Cap" to most locals) is 1km to the north, and the cheaper accommodation opportunities are a few hundred metres to the south; *La Paillote* hotel is directly ahead here. If you're arriving **by air**, you fly practically into the heart of the village. The **gare routière** is centrally located; frequent bush taxis leave from here for Ziguinchor throughout the day, and now that the new paved road has been completed, the trip takes just 45 minutes. Cap has an **ATM** and a good **Internet** café.

Accommodation

Accommodation options are plentiful, and you won't be faced with gleaming white high-rises, either; the luxury model here is a modest construction, blending with the landscape, while budget lodgings are low-key affairs, most of them variations on the CTRI theme.

Auberge de la Paix just south of the T-junction ℡339 93 51 45. This excellent spot is the destination of choice for regional NGO workers who come to kick back on the beach for a few days. It offers the same great views and sand as its neighbours, plus good food and a choice of plain rooms, some s/c. ❶

🏃 **La Maison Bleue** ℡/℉339 93 51 61 ⓦwww.lamaisonbleue.org. Cap's newest luxury hotel offering, with eleven stunning, sumptuous rooms (three right on the beach), a pool, restaurant and views to die for. They also run

a handful of interesting excursions to Guinea-Bissau's Bijagós Islands. ❽

Le Falafu ℡775 13 31 85 or 775 68 36 17 ⓦwww.lefalafu.com. Colourful, Swiss-run *campement* with a pleasant bar and flower-filled garden. The garden-facing rooms are nothing special but the two spacious, en-suite rooms that face the sea, each with a balcony, are easily the best-value mid-range rooms in Cap Skiring. Most of the mattresses are brand new and very comfortable. ❷

Le Mussuwam ☏ 339 93 51 84 or 775 22 63 07. Established *campement* that feels a bit more ramshackle than the others, but with a good range of a/c, s/c rooms, it manages to remain popular with backpackers. ❸

Oudja Boucotte beach, 5km north of Cap Skiring centre ☏ 339 91 27 81 or 775 17 58 95. Lovely hotel, set on large plot just in from the beach. It's not easily accessible by ordinary car, so unless you have a 4x4, you'll need to park and walk down – or walk up from the beach. ❸

La Paillote opposite the Oussouye road junction ☏ 339 93 51 ⓦ www.paillote.sn. This professionally-run spot offers luxurious beachside huts set in the sands, plus a fine restaurant, an upscale souvenir shop and a wide range of excursions. ❻

Le Paradise ☏ 339 93 51 29 ⓦ pecheparadise .chez-alice.fr. While a paradise it is not, this is still one of the nicest *campements* in Cap, featuring a *case à impluvium* and excellent views from the restaurant. ❷

Savana Cap some 2.5km north of Cap Skiring village ☏ 339 93 51 52/86 ⓦ www.senegalhotel .sn/savana.htm. Cap's beautifully landscaped five-star jewel offers it all – at a price. ❽

Restaurants

For **food**, the obvious place to start is the hotels and *campements*, but a few places in town and along the beach make equally-palatable alternatives. After hours, the town is the place to be and it won't be rocket science to figure out where things are going down: just follow your ear.

🏃 La Case Bamboo just east of the town roundabout, next to an excellent disco (free entry to diners). Pleasant French bistro with simple but generous dishes – a good spot to wait for the often-delayed Dakar-bound plane, as the airport is just a few minutes' walk away.

Kassoumay in the centre of Cap. Kicking dance club that's packed to the brim with Senegalese locals and *toubabs* at weekends.

Le Kaye Fii on the beach just behind *Le Mussuwam*, this small shack prepares candlelit fish dinners to eat right on the sand.

La Paillote opposite the Oussouye road junction. Lodge-style spot for lunch in the hotel of the same name, serving expensive *brochettes* (CFA5000).

Les Palétuviers town centre. A decent town option for night-time dancing, primarily frequented by French package tourists.

🏃 La Pirogue at the road junction just as you arrive in Cap. A leafy courtyard and low prices makes this restaurant a high-quality alternative to hotel and *campement* meals.

Excursions from Cap Skiring

To get out from Cap Skiring, you'll find a couple of places in the village renting out **4x4s** (from around CFA25,000 per day), quad bikes, mopeds and kayaks – try Casamance Loisirs (☏ 339 93 53 93 ⓔ clpassions@sentoo.sn) at the roundabout in Cap – but you'll probably get more value out of renting a **mountain bike** at the nearby Casamance VTT (☏ 339 93 10 04; CFA7500 per day).

Day-trips to **Karabane island**, arranged by most hotels and *campements* in Cap Skiring, leave from the creek behind the village and cost between CFA10,000 and CFA15,000 per person (try *Le Mussuwam* or *Le Paradise* for the most competitive prices). Trips normally take in Elinkine, Karabane, the Île des Féticheurs, and an Île aux Oiseaux or two. That's a lot of messing around on the river among low mangroves, which cast little shade, so make sure you wear a hat. It's not a bad way, incidentally, of getting to Elinkine. Enquire at Sénégal Tours in town (☏ 776 32 70 56) for information on other possible trips.

Diembéreng and beyond

An ideal excursion from Cap Skiring, **DIEMBÉRENG** lies deep behind the dunes, 8.5km north. By bike you can easily get up to Diembéreng in an hour or two along the beach at low tide when the sand is firm; the main motorable track through the bush is a sandy 8km (allow at least an hour). You may get the odd dirty look weaving through the sunbeds in front of the *Club Med* and *Savana Cap* hotels, but the beach is a public right-of-way. If you don't want to walk or cycle, you could use the daily minibus from Ziguinchor, that comes through Cap Skiring about 7.30am each morning (CFA400) on its way to Diembéreng, and returns to Cap Skiring and Ziguinchor (CFA1250) every afternoon, leaving Diembéreng about 3pm.

Past the *Savana Cap*, there's one last jumble of low rocks to negotiate before a magnificent sweep of sand. Shortly after this point there's what looks like an open-air mosque built into the cliffside. Diembéreng is a traditional village, its economy based on fishing and livestock, and by no means dependent on tourism. The most striking thing about the place is the hill that rises from its centre, a steep and ancient dune crowned and stabilized by a grove of venerable silk-cotton trees. It's no more than 30m high, but in Basse Casamance it looks like a mountain, and there's no escaping the strong and mysterious sense of place.

Activity in the village has died down somewhat over the past several years, but there are three decent places to stay, each with their own charm. On your left as you come into town along the *piste* from Cap Skiring is the *Campement Asseb* (T 339 93 31 06 or 775 41 34 72 E sembesene@yahoo.fr ❸), with *palétuvier*-cooled rooms that are nothing special but with a superb cook dishing up great local dishes. Just on the other side of the massive, mother-of-all *fromagers* is the brand-new *Le P'tit Maxime* (T 776 61 09 75; ❸), quaint and French-run with a handful of small rooms. If you want to stay near the water, inquire at *Maxime* about the status of the Spanish-run beachside *campement*; at the time of writing, its future was uncertain.

If you crave true isolation, you could walk or cycle – again, preferably at low tide – north to **NYIKINE**, a village at the very mouth of the Casamance. It's a place of coconuts and seclusion, possibly worth visiting in the company of some of the youngsters hanging around in Diembéreng.

Another option is to head 7km northeast to **KACHOUANE**, a highly picturesque village set on a palm-fringed channel of the Casamance opposite Karabane island. There's the most basic of *campements* here, *Sounka* (T 776 45 37 07 ❶), as well as an excellent **restaurant**, *Chez Paul Bocuse* (warn the chef you're coming on T 775 34 93 15), popular with tour groups from Cap Skiring.

Kabrousse and around

South of Cap Skiring, the road turns through the village of **KABROUSSE**, a scattered community of farmers. There are a few tourist hotels and *campements* here, including *L'Ibiscus* (T 339 93 51 36 ❶). Kabrousse is famous as the birthplace of **Alinsitoé**, a Jola visionary who led a major anticolonial rebellion during World War II. Aged only 20, she spearheaded a revolt provoked by the tax burden placed on the Jola peasantry by the French Vichy government. After a vicious battle at Efok, near the present-day Basse Casamance National Park, Alinsitoé was arrested and exiled to St-Louis, then to Timbuktu, where she died. Her name is evoked whenever the question is raised of Casamance secession from northern Senegal.

From Kabrousse, it used to be possible to follow a magically peaceful forest path for 22km east to the Basse Casamance National Park, but at the time of writing this was unsafe because of land mines and rebel activity in the area. **SANTIABA MANJAK** was the largest village you passed through before the park gate; 2km further, a right turning leads off to the Alinsitoé battle village of **EFOK** (5km) and equally isolated **YOUTOU** (10km).

Parc National de Basse Casamance

The **Parc National de Basse Casamance** has been closed since 1993. As a result it's impossible to say which animals survive in the park, a forty-square-kilometre area of streams, marshy savannah, and partly untouched primary forest. Large mammals such as forest buffalo, leopard, hippo and bushbuck were rarely seen here anyway, but there used to be wonderful **monkey-spotting** from several of the paths and from the lookout towers known as *miradors*, there were **crocs** in the creeks, and deep in the forest, several species of **birds and insects** that couldn't be found anywhere else in Senegal. If by any chance the park reopens during the lifetime of this edition, a visit is best if you base yourself in Oussouye and arrive well into the dry season, when, even in this relatively moist part of the country, waterholes dry up and sources become good spots to watch animals. It's a highly recommended area – when safe.

Northern Basse Casamance

Coming over the border **from The Gambia** at **Séléti** is a straightforward business – many tourists visiting The Gambia take the plunge into Casamance for a few days and are rewarded by a more leisurely pace of life, reasonable transport, and some idyllic and inexpensive lodgings. It's a short taxi ride from Séléti to **DIOULOULOU**, the first Senegalese town, where you swap vehicles to head for the as-yet-unspoilt resorts of Abéné and Kafountine. Diouloulou has a good *campement* in the shape of *Auberge Myriam* (☎339 36 95 91 ❷), a short way north of the main roundabout on the Gambia road, with helpful management and well-cooked meals from CFA2500.

Kabadio & Niafarang ▲   Diouloulou ▲

Bandjikaki

Abéné

0   1 km

Diana

ACCOMMODATION

À La Nature	I
Centre Culturel O'Dunbeye Land	D
Karone	J
Kunja	G
La Belle Danielle	C
Le Fouta-Djalon	F
Le Kossey	B
Le Paradise	H
L'Esperanto	E
Village Hôtel Kalissai	A

N

Market

Kafountine

Sitokoto
CTRI

Fishing beach

RESTAURANTS

Café Couleur	2
Chez Vero	1
Le Baobab	3

ABÉNÉ & KAFOUNTINE

The potholed N5 road continues southeast across the tidal mud flats to Ziguinchor 80km away, passing through the underwhelming regional centre of **BIGNONA**, a two-kilometre string of roadside stalls at which point the N5 joins the *transgambienne* N4. In this area, various tracks lead southwest into the often-overlooked **Buluf** district of the northern Basse Casamance, formerly served by a couple of CTRI *campements* whose status is now uncertain. Still less visited is the **Yassine** region to the east, sandwiched between the Soungrougrou and Casamance rivers.

Abéné and Kafountine

Southwest of Diouloulou a road heads seaward to unbroken beaches running down to the spit of the **Presqu'île aux Oiseaux**, at which point the coastline breaks up into mangrove inlets and the north-side mouth of the Casamance. The paved road passes the village of **KABADIO**, near which a couple of good *campements* have sprung up, and shortly afterwards a turnoff to the village of **Abéné** (18km) before continuing south to the small town of **Kafountine** (24km). Waiting at the roundabout in Diouloulou for transport may take an hour or two, perhaps less in the high season.

From the main road a track leads 2km to **ABÉNÉ**, a sandy-laned village situated 2km from the sea with a charmingly isolated and relaxed feel, a lively **folklore festival** (in late Dec; ⓦwww.alnaniking.co.uk), and a number of accommodation options. The best place to stay in the village itself is *La Belle Danielle* (☎339 36 95 42/24 ❷), right in the centre of town, which offers simple rooms, an inexpensive restaurant, good excursions and bike rental; it's a couple of hundred metres down a side track leading to the nearby village of **DIANA**. Continuing down the main track to the sea, you'll find a cluster of *campements*. Turn right at the defunct *Samaba CTRI* to reach the delightful *Le Kossey*, a superior, dune-bound *campement* offering s/c huts set in a lovely garden and with half-board or full-board options (☎339 94 86 09 ❸) – this is the place to head if you're looking for beachside seclusion rather than company. At the other end of the noise-level spectrum, the Dutch-Senegalese-run *O'Dunbeye Land* (☎775 24 96 00 ⓦwww.odunbeyeland.com ❷) offers simple rooms on the beach, though you'll be forced to reckon with (or join in on) the African dancing and drumming classes taught here. Up the coast, 2km from Abéné village, the altogether different *Village Hôtel Kalissai* (☎339 94 86 00 ⓦwww.kalissai.com ❻) is beautifully sited right by the beach with a landscaped mangrove creek and sprawling lawns. Even at the price, this beats much of what's on offer in the fast lane at Cap Skiring, but it's not exactly *intégré*. There are a few places to **eat** in the village – *Chez Vero* is one of the better options – but most people opt for full board at one of the *campements*.

Kafountine

Continuing south down the sealed road another 6km brings you to the alluring fishing village of **KAFOUNTINE**, more animated than sleepy Abéné and a place which in recent years has garnered a reputation as a hip alternative to Cap Skiring's more middle-of-the-road offerings. Served by daily minibuses from Ziguinchor via Diouloulou, the village has a decent range of accommodation, a **market**, **shops**, **bike**, **moped** and **car rental** outfits and several **restaurants**: just north of the market, *Café Couleur* and, opposite, *Le Baobab*, offer inexpensive and wholesome Senegalese dishes; *Baobab* is also a great place for a beer later on. For the best eating in town, try the great seafood at the beachside *Le Paradise campement* (see below). Like Abéné, Kafountine hosts a colourful **festival** of music, dance and local culture, every February.

Most **accommodation** is ranged up and down the coast, about 1km west of the little town centre, with the newest, mostly unremarkable, developments set around a track to the south of the fishing port.

À la Nature just outside the fishing village ☎339 94 85 24 ⓦwww.casamance .net/alanature. An excellent choice for its unique bohemian vibe, with twenty clean rooms with shared toilets. No a/c or fans, but hammocks are hung around the leafy grounds and the meals (CFA3000) are first-class. Occasional drumming and dancing classes. ❸

L'Esperanto some 500m north of the *Fouta-Djalon* ☎773 05 67 56 or 776 35 02 80. In a fine location, with a beautifully designed bar-restaurant overlooking a seasonal lake. ❺

🏃 **Le Fouta-Djalon** ☎339 36 94 94 or 775 03 99 22 ⓦwww.casamance .net/foutadjalon. About 3km north of town along the coast road, this is the best of all Kafountine's *campements*. Near the beach, it features elegant, comfortable brick bungalows at very reasonable prices with a spacious, airy bar. There's live music around the campfire in the evenings, and the likable French owner organizes a variety of tours. ❹

Le Karone 2km south of the port ☎339 94 85 25 ⓦwww.lekarone.net. Once the town's most luxurious address, this hotel has fallen off a bit over the past few years. Secluded, a/c huts are set about landscaped grounds, and there's a pleasant pool, plush bar-restaurant and lots of sporting activities and excursions. Recommended for fishing. ❻

Le Kunja ☎339 94 85 23 ⓦwww.kunja .de/campement. A few hundred metres before the *Le Sitokoto*, this privately run *campement* is a top budget choice, with simple rooms and good home-cooking. ❷

🏃 **Le Paradise** on the road north towards the coast ☎339 36 94 92. The infusion of a nice chilled vibe with the recent arrival of young, French owners, make this likeable *campement* a favourite for Ibiza and Goa fans. ❸

Le Sitokoto CTRI on the beach ☎339 94 85 12. One of the best-maintained CTRI *campements* in the network. Rooms are basic, and toilets are shared, but the tranquil, beachside location is hard to top. ❷

Affiniam and Koubalan

Southeast of Diouloulou, the potholed road continues across a *marigot* or two to the village of **BAÏLA** with its welcoming CTRI *campement* (☎339 94 77 11 or 776 18 77 30 ❷), set in a grove of mango trees at the village's northern end. Between Baïla and Bignona several tracks lead southwest into the **Buluf district**, a wooded region of mango groves, orange orchards, palm trees and rice fields. Passable tracks, as well as several minor, cycle-able routes, lead to all the villages, with a dilapidated, non-functioning CTRI *campement* at the southern end of the laid-back settlement of **TIONK ESSIL**.

Southeast of Tionk, along a rough track, the peaceful village of **AFFINIAM** is regularly visited by pirogue excursions from Ziguinchor; there are also regular departures for Ziguinchor every day except Thursday and Sunday at 9.30am (1¼hr; CFA400). Spread out among the silk-cotton trees among webs of sandy tracks, the village has a strong Catholic presence and boasts one of the most appealing CTRI *campements* in the network (☎339 36 96 19 ❷). Situated south of the village, this large-diameter, galvanized *case à impluvium* is one of the best spots in the region to rest up for a few days.

Ten kilometres south of Bignona and 3km north of Tobor on the N5, a large sign marks the track leading to the CTRI *campement* at **KOUBALAN** (☎339 36 94 73 or 775 78 20 91 ⓔbadianepape@hotmail.com ❷). While not situated in an especially scenic spot – it overlooks a cleared mangrove swamp – the *campement*'s decorated, cave-like interior is cool, the welcome warm and the food excellent. South of Tobor the woodlands end as the N5 crosses the dreary tidal expanse of the Casamance to the river itself and the bridge leading into Ziguinchor.

The Gambia

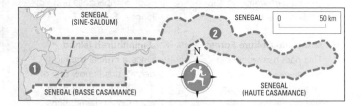

Highlights 264
Introduction and Basics 265

3.1 Banjul and around 288
3.2 Upriver Gambia 313

Gambia highlights

✳ **Tanbi Wetlands** Best explored by small boat, the mangrove-lined salt-water creeks at the mouth of the Gambia River offer superb bird-watching and angling. See p.305

✳ **Makasutu Culture Forest** This park has woodland and creeks to explore on foot and by pirogue, and also features The Gambia's most luxurious bush lodge. See p.308

✳ **The southwestern beaches** Broad, empty and palm-fringed, the best beaches in The Gambia are south of the tourist resorts, between Brufut and Kartong. See p.309

✳ **River Gambia National Park** The park's lush, jungle-covered islands are a highlight of trips upriver, offering the chance to spot chimpanzees and hippos. See p.317

✳ **Janjanbureh Island** Once a crucial trading centre, this is now one of The Gambia's emerging ecotourism destinations, and a great base for river trips. See p.317

✳ **Wassu stone circles** Mysterious relics of ancient Senegambian culture, these stones are the most impressive of The Gambia's pre-historic sites. See p.318

▲ Donkey cart, Soma

Introduction and Basics

You could dismiss The Gambia as an inconsequential little tourist trap, but this would be to overlook one of West Africa's most welcoming nations. A tiny, frail country, eking out its existence along the banks of the Gambia River, it relies heavily on the October-to-April influx of European visitors taking a step beyond Spain and the Canary Islands. Out of season, most of the beach resort hotels go to sleep or close down, and Gambians turn their attentions inland to the peanut harvest. The feeling of nothing much happening can be acute, and if you've already travelled widely in West Africa, The Gambia is hardly going to knock your socks off. It's extremely accessible, however, and most visitors quickly warm to the country.

The Gambia is an easy access point for embarking on more extensive African wanderings, with the flight from Europe taking less than six hours. Equally, after a major overland trip, it's a congenial enough place to rest up. If you want to stay put, you can spend a week or two here in package-holiday style for less than what you'd pay in many European resorts – and of course you can do it in midwinter. The beaches are good – though they get a lot better the further you go from the hotels – and the sea is usually warm. With its wonderful bird-watching and the river itself, The Gambia is also becoming an important draw for ornithologists and ecotourists.

People

Although The Gambia's population is less than two million, there's a wide diversity of tribal and linguistic backgrounds here. The majority ethnic group is the **Mandinka**, who are traditionally farmers. In the coastal region, however, especially in Banjul and Serrekunda, the Mandinka are outnumbered by the historically powerful, caste-structured **Wolof**. The Wolof language, with its strong links with Wolof-dominated Senegal, is spreading all the time, leading to a process of "Wolofization" (analagous to Americanization) of other ethnic groups. Other Gambian tribes include the **Fula**, **Manjago**, **Serahule**, **Serer** and **Jola** – President Jammeh's tribe.

Other important groups include the **Aku** (mostly in coastal and urban areas and partly of freed-slave and European descent) who have long been important in business and administration, and the **Moors** (with roots in Mauritania) and **Lebanese**, both of which groups are important traders and entrepreneurs.

Fact file

The country is officially designated *The* Gambia, a device that has a certain cachet but only tends to emphasize the fact that the Gambia River is all there is to it. The Gambia's **population**, more than 1.5 million and rising steadily, lives in a strip of only 11,300 square kilometres of riverbank, making it one of the smallest and most densely populated countries in Africa. From independence in 1965 until 1994, the country's leader was Sir Dawda Jawara – the Mandinka head of the ruling People's Progressive Party and president of a nominally multiparty democracy (there were regular elections, but no other party had ever held power). In 1994 a coup brought in a military government led by Yahya Jammeh, who went on to become the country's second elected president in 1996. Jammeh and his party have been in power ever since, and won another victory in the 2006 elections.

The Gambia's **national debt** is approximately £325 million ($650 million – a tiny figure in global terms that wouldn't pay for one day of US defence spending), equivalent to five times the value of its annual exports.

In terms of religious adherence, again, there's a great mix of faiths and expression. While ninety percent of the population are nominally **Muslim**, and the other ten percent **Christian**, traditional spiritual and animistic beliefs are widespread and often inter-mingled with the world religions.

Even the largest settlements have an overgrown-village atmosphere (smallness is part of the country's intrinsic appeal), and there's a rapidly acquired feeling of knowing everyone. Pomp and exclusivity are hard to maintain and you can find yourself in conversation with senior govern-ment officials at the hotel bar without even realizing it.

Where to go

While a surprising drabness characterizes the capital **Banjul**, and some organized excursions can seem a little superficial, West Africa does reveal itself if you make an effort to leave the crowds and visit the interior. Dominated by the daily cycle of tides and the annual swing of flood and drought, the **Gambia River** has a compelling life of its own. Once you get beyond **Brikama**, the upcountry villages and main centres of **Soma**, **Farafenni**, **Janjanbureh**, and **Basse** are little affected by the coast's tourism. Mammal and birdlife is diverse and exotic (ornithologists will recognize many wintering migrants from Europe); there are coconut trees, rice fields and mangrove swamps, and creeks plied by dugout canoes. The north bank, although still linked to the south bank only by ferry, is no longer remote and inaccessible, and is opening up now that a decent, paved road has been completed.

When to go

Deciding when to go is governed, for most people, by the **rainy season**. If you're going on a package you'll quickly see that

Photography

Be sure to ask before photographing anyone. Around the tourist areas you may be asked to pay for the privilege. Video cameras can arouse hostility as people feel they are perhaps being exploited for commercial purposes. The "security" angle is rarely played up by police – though, as usual, you should avoid photographing them without their permission, or snapping anything to do with "the state". Upcountry attitudes vary from clear hostility to enthusiasm.

RIVER GAMBIA NATIONAL PARK

Kudang Wassu
Jarreng Tenda Kuntaur
Baboon Islands Janjanbureh
Sapu
Pakaliba
Sankulay Kanda
Bansang FULADU
Sofaniama Bolon

SENEGAL

WULI

Sutukoba

Fatoto

Basse Santa Su
Sabi

SENEGAL
(HAUTE CASAMANCE) Vélingara Medina Gounas

GAMBIA

0   25 km

N

Tambacounda ▶ Niokolo Koba Nat. Park & ▶ Guinea

Kolda & Ziguinchor ▼   Kolda & Ziguinchor (Highway) ▼

there's a much reduced choice of hotels from May to October, the period when The Gambia gets up to 1300mm of rain – equivalent to around one and a half times Britain's annual average. However, there is a degree of regional variation. On the coast the rains don't begin in earnest much before July, but inland they can start in May; upriver they may finish by the end of August, down at Banjul often not until October. August is usually the wettest month, making some roads impassable for days on end.

The period from March to May is normally rainless, but dust and wind from across the Sahara can be a torment, and the haze can even block out the sun. Although year-round tourism has been promoted since the early 1990s, and going in the low season can feel less touristy, the ideal period for a visit is December or January, when you can expect dry, hot days and mild – even cool – nights.

Getting there from the rest of Africa

Despite The Gambia's tourist popularity, it is not well connected to other countries in the region, and the lack of a bridge across the river slows down overland connections with its only immediate neighbour, Senegal.

Flights

To fly into The Gambia from elsewhere in Africa, you will usually need to fly to Dakar (which is served by direct flights from most West and North African capitals) and pick up an onward flight or switch to overland transport.

There are daily flights to Banjul from Dakar with Air Sénégal International, and twice-weekly flights from Lagos and Freetown with Bellview Airlines of Nigeria.

Average temperatures and rainfall

Banjul

	Jan	Feb	Mar	Apr	May	June	July	Aug	Sept	Oct	Nov	Dec
Temperatures °C												
Min (night)	15	16	17	18	19	23	23	23	23	22	18	16
Max (day)	31	32	34	33	32	32	30	29	31	32	32	31
Rainfall mm	3	3	0	0	10	58	282	500	310	109	18	3
Days with rainfall	0	0	0	0	1	5	16	19	19	8	1	0

For details on **getting to The Gambia from outside Africa**, plus important practical information applying to all West African countries, covering health, transport, cultural hints and more, see Basics, pp.19–28.

Overland from Senegal

Whichever way you travel overland, you'll arrive first in **Senegal**. From **Dakar**, there are bush taxis from the main *gare routière* to take you to the border post at Karang, where you change for another vehicle – cab, shared taxi or motorcycle taxi – for the 1.5km hop to the Gambian border post at Amdallai. Here you have to change again for onward transport to Barra, where you can catch the ferry to Banjul. Expect routine baggage searches by customs at both border posts. From **Ziguinchor**, a batch of Peugeot 504 bush taxis runs every morning to **Serrekunda** (outside Banjul), and the border is less of a hassle.

Overland from Mali

From **Mali**, the direct route **from Bamako**, entering The Gambia at its eastern end, is more enjoyable than the dreary highway through Senegal to Dakar, though there's little to choose between them in terms of journey time or cost. On the direct route, break your journey at **Tambacounda**, then make your way to **Velingara** and pick up a bush taxi to **Basse** via the Gambian border post at **Sabi**.

Red tape and visas

Most Commonwealth and European Community passport-holders don't require a **visa**. French, Swiss, US and Japanese nationals are among those who do – in theory. In practice, if nationals of these countries fly in without a visa, they're routinely given a visitor's pass at the airport, but they may then be required to obtain a visa from the Immigration Office in Banjul. If you're simply traversing the country, from northern to southern Senegal or vice versa, visas aren't required of any nationality.

All visitors require a full passport, valid at least six months beyond your stay. You will only be asked for a yellow fever vaccination certificate if you're visiting other countries in the region.

On arrival, you'll normally be given permission to stay for up to 15 days. If you want to stay longer, ask for the maximum of 28 days; extensions cost D250 per month (for up to three months, after which you'll need to get a residence permit) from the Immigration Office in Banjul.

Visas for onward travel

For **onward travel** from The Gambia, you can obtain visas in Banjul for Mauritania, Senegal, Ghana, Guinea-Bissau and Guinea. Visas for Nigeria may be available too, if harder to obtain. Full details are given on p.304. There's no French embassy, only a French honorary consul, who can't issue visas for Francophone countries in the region.

Info, websites, maps

It's worth visiting a **Gambia National Tourist Office** before you leave, though there are not many around the world. The London office (at the High Commission; see address in Basics, p.29) is friendly enough, but only has basic information on packages, flights and the rest. In The Gambia, there are no official tourist offices, though hotel-based resort reps can be good sources of information.

Websites

There are quite a few **websites** focusing on the Gambia that are worth a look. Among

The Rough Guide to The Gambia

For a much more detailed source of information for the country, get hold of *The Rough Guide to the Gambia* (⊛theroughguidetothegambia.blogspot.com). The authors' picks from that guide's accommodation and restaurant addresses are all included in this chapter.

these, **Gambia Tourist Support** (ⓦwww .gambiatouristsupport.com) is a good place to start, with excellent general information on the country from a committed charitable organization, while the ⓦwww .asset-gambia.com, run by The Gambia's **Association of Small Scale Enterprises in Tourism (Asset)**, carries information on responsible tourism, including coverage of non-mainstream hotels. Gambian news and advertising sites come and go. Try the following:

ⓦ**www.visitthegambia.gm** Official "smiling coast" website, professionally maintained.
ⓦ**www.thepoint.gm** Outspoken independent news service and sometime newspaper.
ⓦ**www.gambiatouristsupport.com** GTS works for sustainable visitor–local relations.
ⓦ**www.gambianow.com** Substantial news and info portal.
ⓦ**www.wow.gm** News, listings, ads.

Maps

Maps can be bought in hotel shops: the best general maps are Macmillan's *Gambia Travellers' Map* (1:400,000) and Reise Know-How's *Senegal & Gambia* (1:550,000), both published in 2004. Both are reasonably good and the latter is printed on plastic paper but ongoing road improvements mean they are both somewhat out of date. If you're looking for anything more detailed, there is a 1:50,000 series dating to 1982, but you're not likely to find copies except on the odd park-office wall.

The media

Gambian **newspapers** are a little hard to track down, but include the government-sponsored *Daily Observer*, the independent *The Point* and the leftish sheet *Foroyaa*. Surprisingly, perhaps, The Gambia has one of the most repressive media cultures in Africa, with journalists routinely harassed, imprisoned, disappeared or occasionally murdered. British papers are available in several resort area supermarkets and from vendors at tourist hotels. *Time* and *Newsweek* magazines are also obtainable.

The state-owned **Radio Gambia**, part of Gambia Radio and Television Services (GRTS), broadcasts in English and the main national languages on 648 AM and 91.4 FM. It offers news, announcements and endless request shows – it sometimes seems there can be very few Gambians who haven't said hello to everyone who knows them. **Radio 1 FM** (101.2 FM), based in Fajara and flourishing, is one of the most popular stations, with an excellent selection of reggae and ragga, the favourite music of young Gambians. **West Coast** on 95.3 FM blasts out of many local bars and hangouts, playing mostly reggae, soul and R&B, plus chat shows.

Gambia TV, also part of GRTS, covers Gambian news (with plenty of coverage of presidential goings-on), as well as relaying CNN, various sports programmes and British comedy series.

Health

The Gambia poses no special health risks beyond the usual ones applying to the region (see p.37). Many doctors will recommend nothing more than antimalaria tablets, though you should certainly consider a hepatitis jab if your travels are likely to take you off the beaten track.

Given the prevalence of chloroquine-resistant malaria in the region (see p.40 for more on the subject), you should take **antimalaria tablets** even if you're holidaying for a week. That said, while Banjul and the river are mosquito-prone all year round, the hotel areas on the Atlantic coast are mostly free by the middle of the season (Christmas), and the mosquitoes aren't often a persistent menace.

As for health care, treatment costs are minimal, but hospital facilities are limited and overstretched. The Gambia's principal **hospital** is the Royal Victoria Hospital in Banjul, and there are also hospitals upcountry in Bwiam, Farafenni and Bansang. If you're seriously ill, ask your hotel to arrange a visit from a private doctor or, upriver, the nearest dispensary or foreign-aid worker. Emergency services are rudimentary. Of a range of **private clinics**, the Lamtoro Clinic (see p.304) is conveniently close to the *Senegambia Hotel* area and good if an overnight stay looks necessary (though more expensive than the other options). Otherwise, the Momodou Musa Memorial Clinics in Banjul and Serrekunda are recommended.

Water in The Gambia is considered safe when it comes from taps or pumps. You needn't hesitate to drink tap water in your hotel, but plastic bottled water is very widely available.

Costs, money, banks

The Gambia's currency is the **dalasi** (D), divided into 100 **bututs** (approximate rates of exchange are: £1 = D44, €1 = D33, US$1 = D22). Notes come in denominations of D5, D10, D25, D50 and D100, with coins of D1, and 5, 10, 25 and 50 bututs. Bear in mind that Gambian dalasis aren't officially convertible abroad, so go easy and only change what you think you'll need as you won't easily be able to change them back.

Costs tend to be somewhat lower than in northern Senegal, and overall rather higher than in the Basse Casamance region of southern Senegal. But the two countries aren't really comparable: away from Banjul and the coast there simply isn't much to spend your cash on in The Gambia. Ordinary market produce and grocery-store fare isn't going to break the bank. If you're staying on the coast, you'll soon discover which hotels charge D60 for a beer and where you can find one for less than half that. Beer and soft drinks get pricey upriver and away from main centres.

There is normally no commission for currency exchange at banks or foreign exchange bureaux. There are **banks** in Banjul, Bakau, Serrekunda, Kololi, Brikama,

Farafenni and Basse. Some of the **forex bureaux** in the tourist areas will cash personal cheques on British bank accounts with a cheque guarantee card, sometimes charging a commission. Avoid changing money at the hotels, which do a brisk trade at poor rates with their captive clients.

Debit cards are a handy back-up source of funds and can be used in **ATMs** (if you can find one that works) or in payment for tourist services such as major hotels, tours, car rental and flights. **Credit cards** (notably Visa) are handy if you're staying in one of the main beach hotels and are prepared to pay a commission of around ten percent, but most other Gambian businesses don't accept them; nor can they be used to obtain cash advances from Gambian banks.

Getting around

The Gambia has no rail routes or scheduled domestic flights and no longer has a national bus service, the former state-run GPTC bus company having been wound up as the roads destroyed the buses one by one. Nor is the river a significant means of transport: there are no bridges, so essential ferry services convey people from one side to the other, but there's no A-to-B river transport system. The principal **car ferry crossings** are Banjul to Barra and Yelitenda to Bambatenda (the trans-Gambian highway crossing between Soma and Farafenni). Both these crossings are fairly reliable (for details see the Guide). Further east, there are vehicle ferries at Basse, Fatoto and Janjanbureh. Other small ferries are for passengers only.

As for **roads**, along the **south bank,** there's one main, theoretically paved, road from Banjul to Basse. It's in reasonable condition only as far as Brikama, deteriorating soon after this and becoming really appalling as far as Soma. East of Soma the road is quieter, and the surface not too bad. At the time of writing, the worst stretches of the south-bank highway were being resurfaced, but progress

---

Fuel prices

Fuel costs start at around D30/litre for diesel and 35/litre for super, and rising. Upcountry supplies can be sporadic, so carry all you can and fill up when possible.

Organized trips

Many visitors to the resort area explore the countryside on **organized excursions**, including bush safaris, village visits, and trips to upcountry bush lodges; details are available from hotel reps. Local tour operators (see p.305) will help plan itineraries and provide transport with a driver and an expert guide. You can also make more ad hoc arrangements for local visits and longer trips with the uniformed and badged Official Tourist Guides who work in the resort area.

Particularly enjoyable are the river trips which take you through the mangrove creeks near the mouth of the Gambia River, or, upcountry, through the River Gambia National Park. It's also possible to arrange tours and **flights** (for example, to Tendaba or Janjanbureh) departing from the small light-aircraft base at Banjul International Airport.

is slow. The main road along the **north bank** from Barra to Janjanbureh is, by contrast, newly surfaced with good tarmac. The main roads from the airport to the resort area, and south down the Atlantic coast to Kartong are also excellent. Elsewhere in the country, the roads are made entirely of laterite, mud, sand or rock and you should assume you'll need a 4x4 to use them – though in the dry season you can often get around reasonably well in an ordinary car.

Bush taxis

Privately operated **bush taxis** known as "cars", *gelle-gelles* or *tanka-tankas* (mostly Japanese vans, pick-ups, a few saloons and goods trucks), run long-distance services covering the entire country. You'll find them at "garages" – the equivalent of *gares routières* in the Francophone countries. Bush taxis also operate locally (in which case they're yellow saloons with green stripes, or minibuses), running along set routes and cramming in as many passengers as they can at D5–10 per person per hop. Alternatively, the yellow cars can be privately chartered for a "town trip" direct to your destination (from D50 for a short hop). Another option around the touristy parts are **tourist taxis** (see p.288).

Car and bike rental

Car rental is undeveloped, with only a couple of recommended local operators and one international agency represented – and it's usual to rent out cars with drivers. Self-drive deals are generally only available in the Banjul/resorts area (see p.304), and start from around £20/€30/$40 per day all-in, in the low season.

Motorbikes (of variable quality) can be rented in the coastal hotel area, as can **bicycles**. The Gambia is quiet, safe and offers very flat terrain for a first try at cycling in Africa, with ample opportunity for leisurely sidetracking to the river. In the dry season, a complete circuit of the country (inland on the south bank, back to Banjul on the north) would take a couple of weeks, assuming about 75km a day.

Accommodation

The majority of visitors have hotels pre-booked for the duration of their stays, which works out relatively cheaply. Some of the tourist hotels are block-booked by tour operators, but the others are worth considering if you arrive independently and feel the urge to

Tipping

It's a bit of a problem in the resorts to know when and how much you should give in recognition of services: you somehow have to reconcile what you give a waiter or tour guide with the fact that many staff will only be paid a monthly wage of D1000 or less (say £1–2/$1.50–3) per day, while those in business for themselves, such as taxi drivers (no tipping required), might make ten times as much. D20 is a decent tip, while D50 would be very generous. Holiday reps are always good at suggesting how much you should give hotel staff at the end of a stay.

Accommodation price codes

Accommodation prices in this chapter are coded according to the following scale, whose equivalent in pounds sterling/US dollars is used throughout the book. Prices refer to the rate you can expect to pay for a room with two beds. Single rooms, or single occupancy, will normally cost at least two-thirds of the twin-occupancy rate. Gambian resort hotels have en-suite rooms, with breakfast included, and they usually have two rates – high season roughly from the end of October to Easter, and low season roughly from Easter to October. Where seasonal rates are indicated, you can expect the low-season rate to give a more accurate reflection of facilities. For further details see Basics, p.55.

① Under D250 (under £5/$10)
② D250–500 (£5–10/$10–20)
③ D500–750 (£10–15/$20–30)
④ D7500–1000 (£15–20/$30–40)

⑤ D1000–1500 (£20–30/$40–60)
⑥ D1500–2000 (£30–40/$60–80)
⑦ D2000–2500 (£40–50/$80–100)
⑧ Over D2500 (over £50/$100)

splurge (or even just the need for some decent comfort, which is all that most of them offer). The outlay is likely to be in the order of £30–60/$60–120/€45–90 for a twin room with breakfast in package hotels (⑥–⑧). The hotels ignored by the tour operators are of course cheaper, though down on the coast, options at the budget end (①–③) are limited to simple guesthouses at least 1km from the beach. The same price range covers all but a handful of upcountry places to stay, most of which (and there are very few) are extremely basic.

Camping is possible: there are virtually no campsites as such, but, away from the coastal resorts, pitching a tent is unproblematic if you have your own transport to enable you to get well off the main road.

Eating and drinking

International-style **restaurants** abound in the coastal resort area. Elsewhere, you'll find virtually no restaurants as you understand the term except at the handful of thinly scattered tourist lodges. Most population centres and trading markets have at least one or two simple **chop houses** where you can get a basic meal, usually based around Europeanized staples like roast chicken, omelettes and chips.

As for **Gambian dishes**, the quintessential Gambian meal out is *afra* – simply barbecued meat – which is easy to find in the urban areas near the coast and is the standard late-night party or post-dance food. The tourist hotels' Gambian "standard" is **yassa chicken**, delicious when prepared well, but often just casseroled fowl with a searing sauce of lemon, chilli and onions. The Mandinka dish **domodah** is invariably good (if you like groundnuts – peanuts), usually made with chicken, sometimes beef, and always served with rice. **Mafe** is the Wolof equivalent. The best feature on the coast is the good variety of fresh seafood: shrimps, ladyfish (like sole), barracuda if you're in luck, and excellent chowders and bisques in a few places. **Jollof rice** is usually served with beef (or sometimes fish), tomato purée and vegetables – sweet peppers, aubergine, carrots and squash. *Benachin* is like the *chep-bu-jen* (or *tiéboudienne*) you get in Senegal, essentially a mix of stewed fish and rice, sometimes with vegetables. **Plasas** (short for "palava sauce") is an okra and palm-oil sauce with dried fish and sometimes meat.

You'll find quite good French-style **bread** (chewy *tapalapa* and the lighter *senfour*) all over. **Pies** – resembling Britain's Cornish pasties but fried like samosas – seem to be a leftover of colonial influence; found in meat and fish varieties, they are often surprisingly tasty. **Fruit** you can get just about everywhere – bananas and papayas at any time (though the latter aren't often sold and you'll have to ask), and mangoes, guavas, avocados, watermelons and oranges in season.

Drinking

For **drinking**, you'll have to get used to Gambia's **lager** – JulBrew – which is fairly strong but not one of West Africa's better-tasting beers, and **softs** – fizzy drinks – from the same enterprise. Imported beers are increasingly common in the resorts. Bottled Guinness is a colonial relic, sold quite widely, but rarely cold and perhaps verging on the medicinal in the eyes of most Gambians.

Palm wine – which of course you'll be told is a Gambian speciality – is pretty well universal; the speciality lies in getting the tourists plastered on it during "bush and beach" excursions. As everywhere, it varies considerably in taste and strength depending on when it was tapped and what it's been stored in. As usual, too, it's tolerated but not strictly legal.

Tap water is generally safe and attacks of "Banjul belly" that affect so many are more easily attributed to the assaults of heat and unusual food – or sometimes to incautious freezing and reheating in hotel kitchens. Plastic-bottled "spring" or "mineral" water is widely available, but it can be a pricey way of avoiding contamination (D20–100 for a 1.5-litre bottle). Get it in bulk from one of the supermarkets at a fraction of the hotel price.

If you're drinking tap water, try the very cheap home-made plastic-bag **juices**, or ices, which are on sale all over. Tasty but sticky sweet, they come in three main varieties – brown, white or red – made from ginger, baobab fruit (*bwi*), or hibiscus-like *wonjo* sorrel pods.

Breakfast-time **instant coffee** from roadside stalls isn't as common as in the French-speaking countries. Brewing up green tea – **attaya** – is fairly widespread at any time of day or night, especially in Fula areas upriver.

Communications

Keeping in contact with home is relatively easy. **Internet** cafés have sprung up around the coastal area. Charges are reasonable (from under D50/hr) but vary a great deal from place to place, as does the quality of the hardware and the speed of connections. It's much harder to find public Internet access upcountry.

> The Gambia's **IDD** country code is ☎220.

Aerograms are the cheapest way of writing, if the Banjul GPO has any, and ordinary post isn't expensive, though if you plan on posting souvenirs home, it's worth knowing that there is no surface mail from The Gambia and airmailing large items can be very expensive. Poste restante in Banjul is not especially efficient compared with, say, Dakar, and there's a small charge.

Phoning home is good value, especially to the UK. You can dial from Gamtel offices and private telecentres and pay in cash afterwards, or buy a **phonecard** (the most cost-effective option, available from Gamtel or supermarkets) which gives you an access code for making calls from any landline. The **international access code** is ☎00 (except for Senegal, for which you dial ☎01 and then the number with no country code). Reverse charge (collect) calls can be made by dialling ☎0044 for the UK and asking for the operator, or ☎00111 for the US. Note that Gambian phone numbers do not have area codes.

Mobile phones are essential accessories for urban Gambians, and cell-phone coverage is generally excellent in most Gambian towns, though the signal can drop off sharply to zero on the fringes of urban areas. Gambian SIM cards (around D250) and pay-as-you-go scratch cards can be bought from either Gamcel or Africell, the country's two rival networks. You'll automatically have the benefit of voicemail that's retrievable from any Gambian landline – useful when you're out of mobile range.

All Gamtel offices around the coastal district have public **fax** machines, also very cheap to use. You can receive faxes at these public machines for a nominal fee.

Opening hours, public holidays and festivals

Government offices are open Monday to Thursday from 8am–3pm or 4pm (with a break for lunch), and Friday and Saturday from 8am–12.30pm. Most **shops and businesses**, including **banks** are open Monday to Thursday from 8am–5.30pm (sometimes later, and sometimes with a break for lunch) and Friday and Saturday from 8–11am or noon (banks are usually closed on Sat). **Post offices** are generally open Monday to Friday, 8am–noon and 2–4pm, plus Saturday morning. **Supermarkets** keep longer hours, and a few on the coast are open almost 24/7. Daily **markets** are generally open from 8am to dusk. Gamtel offices and private telecentres are usually open daily 8am–10pm.

The Gambia is predominantly Muslim and, with the exception of tourist services, everything comes to a halt on **Muslim holidays** (see p.63). Christmas and Easter are also observed, with banks, offices and most shops closed around Banjul and the coast and a few other places. Otherwise, the principal annual days off are January 1, February 18 (Independence Day), May 1 (Labour Day), July 22 (Revolution Day commemorating the 1994 coup) and August 15 (Feast of the Assumption).

The biggest popular-culture event is the **International Roots Festival**, held every even-numbered year in June in various locations around the country (ⓦwww .rootsgambia.gm). The joint themes are Gambian development and the African diaspora and the festival is usually particularly well celebrated in the presidential home town of **Kanilai**, on the south bank. In odd-numbered years, a festival also happens in Kanilai at the end of May, coinciding with the president's birthday.

Crafts and shopping

The Gambian **crafts** tradition isn't spectacular but there is plenty to browse if you're keen. Banjul, the Kombo district and Brikama are the main areas where you're likely to find worthwhile items (Brikama is a major carvers' centre). Carvings of "ebony" and "mahogany" rarely are, but in any case the hardwood trade encourages deforestation and some carvers are becoming more sensitive to the concerns of eco-aware tourists – and more aware of Gambian environmental issues. At crafts markets (**bengdula**), it's best to go for cheaper softwood carvings, gaudy cloth (including batik clothing), jewellery, leather and basketwork. A few shops in Serrekunda and Banjul sell **"antiquities"**, which are largely pre-aged crafts from across West Africa, but no less interesting and worthwhile for not being original ritual items. This kind of shop often sells drums and other **musical instruments**. It's also worth looking out for the beautiful **stationery and gift items** made from recycled materials and sold by several shops and hotels.

Crime and safety

The Banjul and coastal resort area is very **safe** on the whole, but occasionally there are muggings at night, and incidents of pickpocketing and bag-slashing take place in the markets. Avoid dark alleys and hold on tightly to your possessions, and you should be fine (as usual, try not to carry around unnecessary valuable items).

The most trouble you're likely to encounter is with **"bumsters"**, professional Gambian tourist hustlers, whom you might fail to shake off and who will later expect payment for the services you didn't want. Tell them you're not going to pay at the very beginning and they'll soon give up.

Trouble with the **police** is unusual, though overlanders with vehicles occasionally report problems over vehicle import duty, which strictly speaking you're not liable to pay. It's advisable to stay well clear of all drugs, but if you're going to smoke grass (*djamba*), be extremely discreet as hefty fines and prison sentences are regularly dished out.

Emergencies

Police ☎17; **Ambulance** ☎16; **Fire service** ☎18.

Gender issues and sexual attitudes

Sexual hassles for female travellers in the resort areas are generally not a problem, though you may find the frank scrutiny of Gambian men unnerving. Sexual interest is by no means exclusively one-sided – you will see plenty of women accompanied by local boyfriends – which can make things more difficult if you are not in search of adventures. If you find the **bumsters** a real pain, one strategy is actually to give in to one, being ruthless about your intentions – or lack of. He'll act as your chaperone and, if you occasionally offer modest payments, may become a real friend for the duration. It is hard, however, to avoid giving the impression that you might allow the rules of engagement to change: every bumster merely scratches a living while waiting for the one tourist in a thousand who wants to start a new life with him in Europe.

While **topless bathing** is fine by hotel pools and on their beaches, women should not appear elsewhere less than well-covered; unlike in many predominantly Muslim countries, uncovered shoulders are acceptable, but showing your thighs is considered very provocative. Long baggy shorts are fine in coastal urban areas but short, tight ones are only appropriate within hotel grounds. Upcountry, foreign women travelling alone are a rare sight and can arouse enormous curiosity; here, women should wear longer dresses, skirts or trousers. Disappointingly, your contacts with Gambian women may not prove any more fruitful if you're travelling alone than if you were to travel in male company.

Since even the straightest Gambian men customarily dance together and walk hand in hand, **gay men** may feel quite at home. Although there's nothing in the way of a gay scene as such (and The Gambia's laws on homosexuality are the fossilized edicts inherited from the British at independence in 1965) there's a broad acceptance of gay

male visitors and several very low-key haunts in the resort area. Lesbian women won't find the same.

Entertainment and sports

While entertainment for the majority of visitors means the hotel formula-mix of "folkloric dance troupes" and home-style discos, it's easy enough to escape the dross and find real Gambian musical entertainment. To be fair, the hotels do sometimes host worthwhile **gigs** – the country's *kora* players have all played to tourist audiences. The best time to be in the Banjul area for live music is the end of the month, when people can afford tickets for the bands that occasionally visit, usually from Senegal. There are normally two or three gigs – the first a more expensive **"dance"** (D200 or more, starting around 11pm and going on until 3 or 4am) and the next night a more proletarian **"show"** (tickets from D50) – all at the big Bakau stadium. Arrive early to get a seat or you'll never see the musicians.

If you're into the idea of musical **participation**, rather than merely being part of the audience, you can spend time with a *jali* or griot – a traditional musician – learning the *kora*, *balafon* or drums (such as the *djembe*), or singing and dancing. Maali's Music School in Nema Kunku, between Serrekunda and Sukuta, offers *kora* lessons to visitors and the music school itself is a ground-breaking project enabling the children of local non-*jali* families to learn music. For further contacts, see the Banjul area listings on p.305. Otherwise, for *kora* lessons especially, take a short ride to Brikama (see p.308), home to

The Gambian women's movement

The Women's Bureau, located in Marina Offshore near Arch 22 in Banjul (℡422 8730), is the main organ of the Gambian **women's movement**. It's concerned primarily with establishing financial stability for women and developing nontraditional income sources, especially crafts co-operatives. Emancipation is a long way off, with polygamy still the norm and six children commonly planned (even in middle-class marriages). **Contraception** is free and campaigning for family planning quite extensive, but few people take notice. Clitoridectomies are common.

many talented *jalis*, and make enquiries; you may be able to stay in your teacher's family compound.

Sport

The Gambia has no film industry and theatre is nonexistent, so **spectator sports** are the other principal entertainment in the country. **Football**, although very popular, has produced few national triumphs and only a handful of international players.

Officially, **wrestling** is The Gambia's national sport, but it's been gradually fading over the last decade or so with the universal spread of football fever. President Jammeh is keen to keep wrestling alive, and the large arena at Kanilai (see p.314 for details and for a discussion of the rules) is one of the few places where major bouts are still held, albeit irregularly.

Wildlife and national parks

The Gambia is wonderful for **bird-watchers**: around 560 bird species have been recorded here, and the country contains a remarkable variety of habitats within its small area, many easily accessible on foot. It's not a destination for anyone hoping for **big game**; the faunal heritage has been diminishing for many years. But monkeys and baboons are common enough; there are a few hippos upriver and small crocs in the

streams; bush pig (warthog) are common but over-hunted; hyenas are present in good numbers; while aardvarks and leopards, both nocturnal, are rarely seen, and their status is uncertain. Many southern Senegalese animals occasionally range towards the river, including various species of antelope.

The tiny **Abuko Nature Reserve**, 8km from Serrekunda, is the premier reserve, with great bird-watching and monkey-viewing opportunities. **Bijilo Forest Park**, very near the resort hotels, is a good place to see monkeys, and there is an excellent variety of bird habitats at the **Tanji River Karinti Bird Reserve**, which includes The Gambia's only offshore islands, the Bijol Islands, a breeding colony for sea birds.

At the upcountry **Kiang West National Park**, you can witness a completely different habitat with wild baboons and bush pig, and across the river from here is **Bao Bolon Wetland Reserve**, a large and isolated area of salt marshes and mangrove creeks. Some of the country's most beautiful riverine forest is found further upcountry in the **River Gambia National Park (Baboon Islands)**, part of which is a rehabilitation centre for chimpanzees which is closed to the public but can be passed by boat for distant views of the chimps. On the north bank of the river near Banjul is **Jinack Island**, part of the **Niumi National Park** and noted for its untouched stands of mangrove. For further information on these reserves, contact the Department of Parks and Wildlife Management at Abuko (☏447 2888 ©wildlife@gamtel.gm).

A brief history of The Gambia

The earliest people of **the Gambia valley** may have been the Jola, who traditionally keep very limited oral history. By the fifteenth century, most of the valley was under the control of small Mandinka kingdoms founded by immigrants from the Mali empire. The first European settlers of the late fifteenth and sixteenth centuries were mostly Portuguese and tended to set themselves up in partnership with headmen of the locality, marrying their daughters and trading cloth for slaves. The descendants of mixed unions became important go-betweens in the slave trade.

From the mid-seventeenth century, English, Dutch, French and Baltic merchant adventurers shared and fought over trading rights from the restricted, neighbouring bases of Fort James Island and Albreda. The British won lasting influence after the Napoleonic wars, declaring a Protectorate along the river in the 1820s and, in 1888, establishing a **Crown Colony** that comprised Banjul Island, the district of Kombo St Mary and MacCarthy Island. In the same year, the territory ceased to be governed from Freetown (Sierra Leone) and was given its own government.

Colony and protectorate

In the second half of the nineteenth century, while the British hesitated and focused their attentions elsewhere, the French were battling their way deep into the Soudan – the inland areas of West Africa – actively engaged in a mission to conquer (see the Senegal chapter). From 1850 to 1890 the whole of the Gambia region was in a state of social chaos as the **"Soninké–Marabout Wars"** repeatedly flared up eventually forcing the British to consolidate in the region or risk losing it to France.

The Gambia's acquisition by Britain, which was formally agreed at the Paris conference of 1889, stemmed less from commercial ambitions than **imperial strategy**. The intention was later to pawn the country off in exchange for some better French territory; Gabon was one chunk favoured by the British – they'd already turned down the offer of the Ivory Coast coastal forts. But the temporary expedient of holding the Gambia River became permanent when, having failed to agree on an exchange, the British succeeded merely in delimiting a narrow strip of land on each side of The Gambia, into the heart of French territory. Britain wasn't really reconciled to its responsibilities along the Gambia River until after World War I – thus The Gambia's era of effective colonialism lasted less than fifty years.

The imposition of **British hegemony** wasn't impressive. Beyond the limits of the colony, the country's headmen and chiefs, some of whom were appointed by the Crown, were allowed to rule their people little disturbed by the two "travelling commissioners" to whom they were answerable. Two or three African representatives from Bathurst (the future Banjul) were nominated to the Legislative Council after 1915, but there was no representation of the 85 percent of the population who lived in the Protectorate, the upcountry areas outside the Crown Colony.

Two-thirds of the Gambia's revenue was accounted for in the salaries of the colonial administration. The remainder was insufficient to develop the country's infrastructure, education or health systems. "Benign neglect" is about the best that can be said of the administration's performance. It started to improve only after World War II, though the government was gravely embarrassed by the financially disastrous **Yundum egg scheme**, which parasites made an unredeemable fiasco costing £500,000. **Groundnuts** (peanuts) have been the country's main export crop since the middle of the nineteenth century – The Gambia is a classic monoculture – and until the 1970s it was also self-sufficient in food. There were minor advances in education and medical services: by 1961 for example, the country had five doctors and there were 37 upcountry primary schools.

Financial pressures on the Colonial Office in the 1950s and mounting international demands for decolonization were as much instrumental in **the push to independence** as Gambian nationalism. Britain was at least as anxious to rid itself of the financial liability as the country's own senior figures (they were barely yet leaders) were to take power. From Britain's point of view, there was no reason to delay the country's return to independence – except, perhaps, a measure of concern over the fate of such a small and unprotected nation. Colonial civil servants were in broad agreement that The Gambia would be forced to merge with Senegal, but chose to defer the move.

The road to independence

The progression to independence was not a heroic one. In a manner similar to that of many other countries in West Africa, the men who led The Gambia into the neocolonial era were not so much nationalists as pragmatic and ambitious politicians.

Although the **Bathurst Trade Union** had been founded in 1928 and struck successfully for workers' rights, the first **political party** wasn't formed until shortly before the Legislative Council elections of 1951. Through most of the 1950s, the Gambian parties were reactive,

personality-led interest groups rather than campaigning, policy-making, issue-led organizations. The Reverend John Fye founded the **Democratic Party** as a vehicle for the civic ambitions of his Bathurst coterie; I.M. Garba-Jahumpa founded the **Muslim Congress Party** in an attempt to align religious consensus behind a political movement; and P.S. N'Jie founded his largely Catholic **United Party**, which maintained close relations with upcountry chiefs. All these early-1950s parties were Wolof- and Colony-based and highly sectional. The Gambia had to wait until 1960 before a party with a genuine grassroots programme emerged. This was the Protectorate People's Party, quickly relabelled **People's Progressive Party (PPP)**, led by a Mandinka-speaking ex-veterinary officer from the MacCarthy Island Division, **David Jawara**. The PPP looked to the Protectorate for support, but was distinctly anti-chief. It spoke for rural Mandinka in their resentment against corrupt chiefdoms, and for disenfranchised and younger Wolof subjects of the Colony.

Meanwhile, the administration had presented a new constitution in 1954, giving real representation to the Protectorate peoples, but sharpening demands for a greater Gambian role in the government. The new constitution also put great power in the hands of the chiefs, who were mostly supporters of the colonial status quo. To avoid a crisis, another constitution was formulated in 1959 which abolished the Legislative Council and provided for a parliament – the House of Representatives.

In the run-up to the **1960 elections**, the Democratic and Muslim Congress parties merged as the **Democratic Congress Alliance (DCA)**, but couldn't shake off the popular impression that their nominees were all puppets of the administration. As a result the DCA took only three seats, while the United Party of P.S. N'Jie (with whom the governor had recently fallen out) and David Jawara's PPP took eight seats each. The governor, in a move to placate the Protectorate chiefs, offered the post of prime minister to N'Jie, to the consternation of Jawara, who became education minister. But the 1959 constitution was bound to give rise to further indecisive election results. More talks resulted in yet another constitution, providing for a 36-seat House of Representatives with 32 elected seats and just four chiefs nominated by the Chiefs' Assembly.

The balance of power now shifted against the United Party. Jawara and the Democratic Congress Alliance found room for cooperation and, in the **1962 elections** – which were to determine the political configuration for full self-government – the two parties contested seats in concert to squeeze out the UP. The results of this electoral alliance were highly successful for the PPP, who won 17 out of the 25 Protectorate seats and one of the 7 Colony seats. The DCA, however, managed to gain only one seat in the Colony, and couldn't shift the UP from its urban power base. As a result, with the support of the DCA's two elected members, Jawara had an absolute majority in parliament and his party remained in control until the coup of 1994.

Subsequently, Jawara entered into a coalition with the experienced P.S. N'Jie to form the first fully independent government. Independence Day came on February 18, 1965, with **The Gambia** admitted to the Commonwealth as a constitutional monarchy, with the Queen as titular Head of State.

Independent Gambia

In 1966 N'Jie took his United Party out of government to lead the opposition. Four years later, on April 24, The Gambia became a **republic** and prime minister Dawda Jawara (now using his Muslim name), became president. At every election, the PPP continued to win the vast majority of seats, and at every election P.S. N'Jie claimed the vote was rigged. The PPP, however, despite its roots in the Mandinka

villages, managed to establish credible support across the country.

The first fifteen years of independence were peaceful, and the groundnut economy fared better than expected thanks to high prices on the world markets. But by 1976 prospects for the government were less favourable. Two new opposition parties had formed: the somewhat Mandinka-chauvinist **National Convention Party (NCP)**, led by dismissed vice-president Sherif Mustapha Dibba, and the more left-wing **National Liberation Party** of Pap Cheyassin Secka. And as groundnut prices fell in the late 1970s, The Gambia experienced a string of disastrous harvests.

The economic recession that ensued, and political opposition to the government – which was perceived increasingly as incompetent and corrupt – partly account for the conditions that led to the formation in 1980 of two new **Marxist groupings** and an **attempted coup**. Senegalese troops were flown in under a defence agreement and the leaders of the **Gambia Socialist Revolutionary Party** and the transnational **Movement for Justice in Africa-Gambia** (**MOJA-G**) were arrested and their organizations banned.

A far more **serious coup attempt**, in 1981 (while Jawara was in London), prompted the arrival of a force of 3000 Senegalese troops along with a group of SAS soldiers from Britain, to put down disorder around Banjul and sporadic, bloody fighting. The trouble lasted a week and cost up to a thousand lives. **Kukoi Samba Sanyang**, the self-styled revolutionary who led the plot ("We do not believe in elections, we wanted a radical transformation of the entire socio-economic system.") escaped to Guinea-Bissau and thence to Libya.

The Senegambia Confederation

The insurrection shook the government and immediate steps were taken to maintain Senegal's support. The **Senegambia Confederation** was ratified on December 29, 1981, assuring The Gambia of Senegal's protection while ostensibly assuring Senegal of The Gambia's commitment to political union. **Treason trials** in the wake of the attempted coup led to long terms of imprisonment but, with the increasingly important tourist industry to consider, there were no executions.

A popular **presidential election** in 1982 gave Jawara a personal vote of 137,000 – more than double that of Sherif Mustapha Dibba, who was in detention at the time. With Dibba released, the NCP mounted a serious challenge at the 1987 general and presidential elections. However, it was a new opposition grouping, the **Gambia People's Party** (**GPP**), led by the respected former vice-president **Hassan Musa Camara**, that made the most impact on the government. Though Jawara's party's share of the vote was also reduced, the PPP still managed to win 31 of the 36 elected seats in the House, with the NCP holding the remaining five. Supporters of the GPP, particularly in its Fula- and Serahule-speaking strongholds upriver, were left frustrated, as were supporters of the new socialist party, the **People's Democratic Organization for Independence and Socialism**, a party with close ties to the banned MOJA-G.

In the mid-1980s, the country started an **Economic Recovery Programme** to encourage aid and investment. The groundnut trade was liberalized and state hotel assets were sold off, which encouraged tour operators. But another **coup plot** – really a long-running, conspiratorial rumble – was uncovered in 1988, involving both Gambian leftists and Casamance separatists from Senegal. Senegal, facing conflict with Mauritania as well as trouble in Casamance, withdrew its troops from The Gambia, which quickly led to the formal breakdown of the Senegambia Confederation.

The confederation had been the number one national controversy for a decade, supported by the mostly urban Wolof but generally mistrusted by the Mandinka, whose dominant position in the country was always threatened by a powerful Senegal. For The Gambia's opposition parties and minorities of all ethnic groupings, the prospect of a greater Senegambia was always a provocative one which left many doors open. Those doors were now closed.

Attention was focused in 1990 on **Liberia**, with some Liberian refugees making their way to The Gambia, and Jawara sending a small detachment of Gambian troops to support the West African ECOMOG forces trying to maintain the peace in Liberia. Administrative failures resulted in the soldiers not being paid and a dangerous confrontation was narrowly averted when they returned to Banjul. The chief of the armed forces resigned, admitting he'd lost the confidence of his men, and was replaced by a Nigerian officer. It was a warning of changes to come.

President Jawara was re-elected for a sixth term in April 1992, polling 58 percent of the vote against his nearest rival Mustapha Dibba on 22 percent. Jawara softened his stance against MOJA-G and the Gambian Socialist Revolutionary Party, announcing an amnesty for all members of the previously proscribed organizations. He also began again to make noises about **corruption** in public life.

Military rule

In April 1994 there were protests in Brikama – the country's third largest town, close to the coast but not benefitting from tourism – over the unaffordable cost of public utilities. Then, on July 22, after returning ECOMOG soldiers had been offended by Nigerian commanding officers at Banjul airport, their widespread anger and demands for unpaid salaries coalesced into a successful **coup** led by **Lt Yahya Jammeh**, a Jola from Kanilai in the Foni district of the south bank, with the support of a hastily assembled **Armed Forces Provisional Ruling Council (AFPRC)**. Jawara and some of his cabinet fled to the sanctuary of an American ship, coincidentally docked at Banjul, and received asylum in Senegal. Others were arrested.

Jammeh, a young and uncharismatic figure in regulation dark glasses, made a poor impression on the international community. Casual observers had long harboured the illusion that Jawara's Gambia was one of the few admirable political cultures in West Africa. Indeed, it appeared hard at first to find an altruistic justification for a coup in The Gambia. Though the country's human rights record was not unblemished, the fundamental fairness of its multiparty system had not seemed open to question. Opposition parties were consistently frustrated at elections but the evidence for vote-rigging was limited: Jawara won because he commanded a popular following, albeit also a largely Mandinka one.

However, the AFPRC managed to convince sceptics that, fair or not, the political system was shoring up a Gambian state riddled with **corruption** from bottom to top: President Jawara himself was said to have spent the equivalent of the annual health-care budget on a six-day shopping trip to Switzerland just weeks before the coup. Jammeh insisted his administration, which included some civilian members, would seek the return of stolen state property.

However, Jammeh's announcement that the AFPRC would not step down to an elected civilian government until 1998 was greeted with disbelief. After an unsuccessful counter-coup, in which several soldiers were killed, and a reported threat by Jammeh to the safety of citizens of any countries that might be planning the forcible reinstatement of Jawara, the British government warned tourists the country was unsafe to visit. Nearly all the tour operators and charter airlines pulled out and **tourism plummeted** to twenty percent of normal levels, precipitating a genuine crisis. The response was pragmatic: Jammeh brought the date of transition forward to July 1996, which led to the withdrawal of the British Foreign Office's travel advisory notice and the tour operators' resumption of bookings for the winter 1995–96 season.

Jammeh's first few months in office convinced him he had considerable grassroots support: most Gambians noticed no downswing in their fortunes since his coup, and the country at large anticipated some results from the AFPRC's efforts to return looted Gambian funds. They were to be disappointed: rumours circulated that the AFPRC itself was not squeaky clean, ministers previously sacked by Jawara for corruption were given posts by Jammeh, and the story quickly spread that Jammeh had engineered the counter-revolt himself in order to eliminate potential rivals. Throughout 1995, there was a rash of accusations and counter-accusations of corruption and theft from the public purse on a grand scale. The finance minister died in suspicious circumstances; the death penalty was reinstated; and a new secret police service, the National Intelligence Agency, was created, with sweeping powers of arrest and interrogation.

The Second Republic

Jammeh's first real test came in 1996. With the electorate beginning to realize that an elected government would almost certainly be headed by Jammeh himself, in civilian clothing, a **constitutional review commission** was established to hear the views of Gambians and to usher in a new republic. It was manipulated by the AFPRC to give Jammeh and his coterie every advantage over all opposition elements: the age for presidential candidates was set at 30–65, thus making the youthful Jammeh eligible and ruling out many senior politicians of the Jawara era; political parties which had been active in the Jawara era were all banned from competing; and the timing of the elections was set such that Jammeh's opponents had virtually no opportunity to campaign, while the AFPRC had effectively been on the campaign trail throughout the country since soon after coming to power.

The **presidential election**, which eventually took place in September 1996 was flawed in every respect. Jammeh's 22 July Movement, which was to be dissolved, was replaced by a new party, the aptly acronymic **Alliance for Patriotic Reorientation and Construction** (**APRC**) – the AFPRC out of uniform. The Gambia's new TV station almost entirely neglected the opposition while the military breathed down the necks of the minor parties. Jammeh took 55 percent of the vote, Ousainou Darboe of the **United Democratic Party** 35 percent. In the **legislative elections**, which took place in January 1997, the severely limited resources of most of the opposition meant they could only field candidates in a proportion of the country's 45 constituencies. Jammeh's party took 33 seats, five of them unopposed, while the opposition was lucky to secure twelve seats spread among three parties and two independent MPs.

Early parliamentary sessions in the **Second Republic** were undignified affairs, with opposition members prevented from asking difficult questions by the Jammeh-appointed speaker of the house, and repeated complaints that the president seemed unable to abide by the country's new constitution in his dealings with parliament. **Unrest** rose to the surface in 2000 when twelve people were shot dead during student demonstrations in protest at the alleged torture and murder of a student by police the previous month. A few weeks later, opposition leader Ousainou Darboe and twenty of his supporters were charged with the murder of an APRC activist; they were released on bail. The arrests continued: shortly after this, nine people, including several soldiers, were charged with treason in connection with an alleged plot to overthrow the government, just one of a series of **conspiracies and attempted coups**.

Jammeh's second term

In October 2001, Jammeh won a second five-year presidential term, with a landslide victory over Ousainou Darboe. Despite rising tension beforehand, the actual polls were given a clean bill of health by foreign observers. However, the opposition boycotted the parliamentary elections in January 2002, claiming that presidential elections had been fraudulent and marred by APRC harassment of UDP candidates. Amid widespread voter apathy, the APRC scooped a victory. Ousainou Darboe and **Yankuba Touray**, tourism minister, APRC mobilizer, and one of Jammeh's right-hand men since the 1994 coup, continued to lock horns, and in November 2002 new amendments to the Criminal Procedure Code were drafted, denying bail to anyone on a murder charge, and allowing Darboe to be re-arrested. Later, Touray himself – one of Jammeh's few close associates to remain in power since the 1994 coup – was dismissed from office and arrested for embezzlement, one of a series of showy attempts to stamp out corruption and the abuse of office.

By 2003, spiralling inflation was plunging more and more Gambian families into poverty. Jammeh, while rewarding his fellow Jolas with positions in the government, tried to connect with the Mandinka farming majority in the upcountry divisions by setting off on "Meet the People" tours during which his primary message was that Gambians should "get back to the land". In an attempt to promote the interests of native workers over immigrants, he introduced an alien-registration scheme which required all foreign residents to pay a hefty annual registration fee, but the ensuing exodus of a large section of the workforce left some local industries on the brink of collapse.

Jammeh's habit of attacking the media began to increase: radio stations were forced to close and newspaper staff were regularly arrested. A turning point came in December 2004 with the murder of a respected journalist, editor of *The Point*, **Deyda Hydara**, just two days after he had criticized new laws drastically curtailing the freedom of the press. Nobody in Jammeh's close circle was directly implicated, but the campaign group Reporters Without Borders found evidence that Hydara had been receiving threats from APRC activists. Most Gambians concluded that Hydara had been murdered for his views.

Early 2006 was marked by a series of sackings of high-profile political and army figures and the quashing of an attempted military coup by close Jammeh associate Colonel Ndure Cham. In the aftermath of this coup attempt, five suspects being transported to Janjanbureh prison "escaped" after their vehicle careered off the road. They have not been seen since.

Meanwhile the entire Kombo region was being spruced up for an African Union summit, hosted by Jammeh in July at a cost of $24 million – an enormous expense, especially in view of the limited results of the poorly attended summit.

In advance of the **2006 presidential elections**, as part of Jammeh's pre-election manouevres, hundreds of journalists, lawyers, MPs and army officers were arrested, and civil servants sacked. Even the head of the independent electoral commission was removed from office. When the votes were in, the result – another landslide victory for Jammeh – took nobody by surprise.

The Gambia's future

While Jammeh continues to press for development, reform and foreign investment – his government's long-term economic policy, headlined **Vision 2020**, is supposedly geared towards securing middle-income status for The Gambia by the year 2020 – the international community has lost confidence in his leadership. In 2006, the US Millennium Challenge Corporation cancelled The Gambia's access to development funds, citing a "disturbing pattern of deteriorating conditions". And yet there is not enough at stake in The Gambia for any but its nearest neighbours – Senegal and Guinea-Bissau – to show great concern. Relations with both countries are strained (Jammeh is widely believed to support one of the two MFDC guerilla groups in Casamance and a Jola rebel group opposed to the government in Bissau) and many West African heads of state expressed their general disapproval of Jammeh by spurning the 2006 AU summit.

But nothing seems to dent Jammeh's ego: on state-owned TV and radio, in the pages of those papers not banned, and in every sphere of public life, he is almost the only visible figure. Few "cabinet" ministers have high public profiles, such is the turnover of those in Jammeh's diminishing inner circle. In a long-running publicity stunt, 2007 saw the president claiming the power to cure HIV and AIDS with traditional medicine, visiting patients with herbs and bananas and blustering against alarmed medical experts. The leader's behaviour prompted questions about his state of mind. Yet, on the opposition side, neither Ousainou Darboe of the UDP/NRP nor Halifah Sallah of the National Alliance for Democracy and Development seem likely to step aside for the other to lead a united front against Jammeh.

Meanwhile the anger and bitterness levelled at the president has plumbed new depths. Formal cabinet structure for government has been largely abandoned in favour of rule by presidential prerogative, with cash inducements and lightly veiled threats in common use. Unexplained arrests and disappearances continue. More than ever, the "Smiling Coast" looks like a country in serious financial and political trouble, propped up by tourism.

Music

Gambian music is largely indistinguishable from (and overlaps with) that of Senegal, and to some extent Mali and Guinea. Traditionally, improvisation around familiar themes is important, since a great deal of Senegambian music is based on well-known ancient songs, tunes and rhythms passed down by the *jalis*, the hereditary caste of musicians and storytellers, known in French as griots, whose music accompanies traditional dances.

Despite the common themes, however, The Gambia's musical heritage is as rich as its ethnic make-up, and each tribe has a distinctive set of traditional instruments: the Mandinkas' melodious **kora**, the flutes and rasping **riti** fiddles of the Fula, the pounding **boucarabou** drums of the Jola, and the thunderous **sabar** and rippling **tama** drums of the Wolof. Arguably the country's most distinctive music is the traditional repertoire of the Mandinka *jalis*, sung solo to tunes on the *kora*, but the music you're most likely to hear on the radio or on CD, blaring out of workshops, bars and bush taxis everywhere, is **mbalax and ndagga** dance music from Senegal and a separate creative range that encompasses **reggae, ragga, hip-hop** and **R&B**.

While The Gambia is best known for its Mandinka-speaking **kora** musicians, the most famous of these are as likely to be playing in a British folk festival or with American musicians, as in a compound in Brikama or at a wedding in Serrekunda.

Most other Gambian artists and groups – those playing "modern" music – gravitate inevitably to Dakar, if not Europe, as soon as they reap a measure of success. And it's usually from Dakar that the biggest musical attractions come, in the shape of Thione Seck, or Youssou N'Dour, for example, who quite frequently play gigs in The Gambia. Meanwhile, local stars of **ndagga** (a mellower variation on *mbalax*), such as Maudo Sey, Mam Tamsir Njai and Mass Lowe, play at the Bakau stadium when they're not performing internationally.

Discography

Various *The Rough Guide to the Music of Senegal & Gambia* (World Music Network, UK). Excellent introduction to the best of the region's music, including tracks from Mass Lowe, Ifang Bondi and Tata Dindin.

Tata Dindin *Salam – New Kora Music* (Network Medien, Germany). While this talented *jali* is known for his innovative compositions and technique, this recording finds him in traditional, meditative mode.

Pa Bobo Jobarteh & Kairo Trio *Kaira Naata* (Real World, UK). Evocative *kora* from a young Gambian *jali*, recorded on the beach and in other outdoor locations: plaintive melodies, with birdsong and ocean sounds between tracks.

Ifang Bondi *Gis Gis* (Warner Basart, Netherlands). Slick production values for a band who have been a presence on the Gambian music scene since the 1960s (when they were known as the Super Eagles), though based in Holland. Here they combine Fula, Mandinka, Jola and Wolof influences.

Yan Kuba Saho *Yan Kuba: Kora Music from The Gambia* (Latitudes, USA). Spirited and atmospheric recording made in Serrekunda with vocals and *konkondiro* (percussive tapping on the body of the *kora*) from Saho's wife Bintu Suso.

Jali Nyama Suso *Gambie: L'Art de la Kora* (Ocora, France). Classic 1970s recording from the late *kora* master who, in his prime, was one of the country's most influential artists.

Books

The choice of general books on The Gambia and fiction by Gambian writers is very limited (and several titles reviewed below are likely to be out of print). For good, general West African titles, including some with a strong Gambian connection, see p.35. If you're after a more detailed guide to the country, get hold of **The Rough Guide to The Gambia**.

Mark Hudson *Our Grandmothers' Drums*. Rich, absorbing story of Hudson's stay in the village of "Dulaba" (Keneba) in the Kiang National Park area.

Arnold Hughes and David Perfect *A Political History of The Gambia, 1816–1994*. The most up-to-date history of the country.

Rosemary Long *Under the Baobab Tree* and *Together Under the Baobab Tree*. Chatty autobiographical accounts of a Scottish writer's new life, married to a Gambian.

Berkeley Rice *Enter Gambia: the Birth of an Improbable Nation*. A digestible work, but marred by an unpleasantly derisory tone.

Patience Sonko-Godwin *Ethnic Groups of the Senegambia*. A brief and graspable social history of the region, available locally.

Fiction

William Conton *The African*. A classic rags-to-premiership story by a writer from the colonial era, heavily influenced by his Sierra Leonean upbringing.

Ebou Dibba *Chaff in the Wind*. Describes lives and loves in the 1930s. *Fafa* tells of goings-on at a remote trading post on the Gambia River.

Alex Haley *Roots*. A reasonably entertaining American saga to read on the beach, though only the first few chapters are set in Kunta Kinte's semi-mythical Gambian homeland.

Bamba Suso et al *Sunjata*. In Mande culture "Sunjata" is the big one, the legend of the founder of the Mali empire. This new Penguin edition presents two strikingly different Gambian versions of the epic.

Natural history

Clive Barlow et al *Field Guide to the Birds of The Gambia and Senegal*. Excellent, authoritative work, the bird bible for the region.

Stella Brewer *The Forest Dwellers*. The story of Brewer's chimpanzee rehabilitation project, within the River Gambia National Park.

Rod Ward *A Birdwatchers' Guide to The Gambia*. Detailed information on some of the country's prime ornithological sites, accessibly presented.

Language

The Gambia's official language is **English**, fairly widely spoken in Banjul and the resorts, but often not understood outside the metropolitan areas or upriver. **Krio**, a creole still spoken by the descendants of the **Aku**, the freed slaves who moved from Freetown, is heard less and less. The African language you'll most often hear around Banjul is **Wolof** (see p.193 for some words and phrases), but the language with the strongest claim to be the country's traditional tongue is the Mande language, **Mandinka**, which is very widespread upriver, especially on the south bank.

There's a large **Fula**-speaking contingent also, particularly on the north bank. Other languages you will come across include **Jola** towards the Casamance in the south; **Serahule**, originally from far to the northeast; **Serer**, spoken by fishermen along the coast on the north bank; and **Manjago**, the language of the palm-wine tappers, mainly in the Kombos area. Around the Bakau and Fajara resort areas many young people are Senegalese and speak **French**, while in the tourist resorts, young men may speak a smattering of German, Swedish and Dutch.

Mandinka

The Mandinka of The Gambia is a fairly mainstream dialect of the large **Mande** language group. As usual in languages of Islamic peoples, it includes a scattering of Arabic. Mandinka is not difficult to get your tongue round. A characteristic of spoken Mandinka is the omitted final vowel, lending a "clipped" quality to the language. A double vowel spelling, however, lengthens the sound. The "kh" sound is the "ch" of loch.

Greetings and useful phrases

Khaira be?	How are you? (do you have peace?)
Al be khaira to?	How are you all?
Khaira dorong	I'm well (I've peace)
Suu molu ley?	How is everyone in the compound?
Ibi jay	They're well
Kortanante?	All okay? (general, further greeting)
Tanante	All okay
Ih nimbara? (pl. Al nim baraa?)	How's the work? (if you're passing by)
Nimbara, nimbara	The work's okay
Abaraka	Thank you
Musa ley?	Is Musa at home?
Naam	Yes (I'm here)
Ito ndi?	What's your name?
Nto mu kaba leti	My name is Kaba
I bota min to ley?	Where do you come from?
Si jang	Sit down
Toubab	White person
Moo fingho	Black person
Ih kata min?	Where are you going?
Nkata Basse	I'm going to Basse
Ali nghata	Let's go
I si kontong/ Al si kontong	Goodbye (sing./pl.)
A cha!	Clear off! (to cheeky children)
Mbe bute la!	I'll beat you! (beware!)
Banano san nye	I want some bananas
Dalasi lulu	Five dalasis
Alkoleata!/ Ada jaweata!	Too much!
Atalat!/A jaweata!	Lower the price!

Numbers

1	kiling
2	fula
3	saba
4	nani
5	lulu
6	woro
7	worowula
8	sei
9	kononto

10	tang	teo	groundnut (peanut)
11	tang ning kiling	degee	groundnut paste
20	moang	dulino	groundnut oil
35	tang saba ning lulu	tulusay	palm oil
100	keme	jaboo	onion
		patansay	aubergine

Food and drink

		lemuno	orange
mburo	bread	sarro	watermelon
maano	rice	jio	water
suboo	meat	wonjo	hibiscus cordial
afra	barbecued meat	attaya	green tea
nye	fish	lemnato	soft drink
nyo	millet (grain)	tendolo	palm wine
		doloo	alcohol

THE GAMBIA | Basics

③

Glossary

This list includes Wolof and Mandinka terms and a number of suffixes used in place names.

APRC Alliance for Patriotic Reorientation and Construction
Alkalo Village elder
Ba Big, as in *tenda-ba* (big wharf)
Bantaba Men's communal siesta platform in every village and in many compounds
Banto faro River floodlands
Bengdula Craft market
Bitiko Small shop
Bolon Creek
Bumster Beach boy, hustler
Car Minibus
Duma Lower
Fode Teacher/marabout

Garage Bush-taxi park
Ghetto Unofficial palm-wine bar
Kafoo Traditional "youth club"
Kankurang Mandinka masquerade dancer
Kerr/Keur Place or compound
Koriteh Eid (the end of Ramadan)
Koto Old
Kunda Place
Kuta New
Lumo Weekly (or regular) rural market
Nding Small
Santo Upper
Su Home
Tenda Port, wharf

3.1

Banjul and around

anjul and the Kombo districts (Banjul's hinterland), fronted by 50km of beaches, are all that most visitors to The Gambia ever see, and virtually all the country's hotels are located here. A large and increasing proportion of the population of The Gambia lives in this district, but Banjul itself, sited on a flat island jutting into the mouth of the **Gambia River**, is sleepy and unfocused, and increasingly a daytime city only. At dusk, workers by the minibus-load pour back over Denton Bridge and down the highway to the relative metropolis of **Serrekunda** and the leafier districts around Bakau, behind the hotels. Banjul is not attractive in the conventional sense, and apart from a few noteworthy attractions such as the National Museum, an excellent market, and an interesting architectural heritage, there's little here that could hold you longer than a day.

The **beaches** are the big attraction, although some stretches in the resort centres at **Bakau**, **Fajara**, **Kotu** and **Kololi** suffer periodically from natural tidal erosion that strips away sand and topples palm trees. As you head south, however, you can still find some spectacular strands. Inland, in Kombo North, Kombo South and Kombo Central districts, there are dozens of small, backcountry villages set in the random patchwork of forest, savannah and farmland, all accessible on foot, or by bicycle or rented car or bush taxi.

For **naturalists**, and especially ornithologists, the region is a rewarding one. The **Tanbi Wetlands** – the maze of mangrove-festooned **creeks** behind Banjul – and the justly popular **Abuko Nature Reserve** have great appeal, and even walks in the bush near the hotels can yield delightful discoveries – monkeys, parrots, chameleons and tortoises. There is more wilderness to explore beyond the bustling, musical town of Brikama, at **Makasutu Culture Forest** and the ecotourism camp at **Tumani Tenda**.

One of the most popular (but not necessarily the most rewarding) excursion destinations is the area around **Juffureh** on the north bank, made famous by Alex Haley's novel *Roots*, and accessible either by river cruise from Banjul, or by crossing by ferry to the north-bank town of **Barra** and continuing overland. Also on the north bank and less than an hour away from Barra is **Jinack Island**, the coastal strip of Niumi National Park, a quiet area that's excellent for bird-watching.

For **transport** between Banjul, Serrekunda and the resorts, you've got the choice of **tourist taxis** or **bush taxis**. A clutch of tourist taxis – dark green with a white diamond on their bodywork – can usually be found outside every hotel, or group of hotels, with fixed **fares** to various local points displayed (as an indication, expect to pay D400 from the airport to Kololi, D200 from Fajara to Bakau and D300 from Fajara to the *Senegambia Hotel*). Note that a tourist-taxi trip costs around three times as much as the equivalent "town trip" in a bush taxi, and that tourist-taxi drivers pay a premium to be allowed to work in the tourist areas – confrontations may result if you persuade a bush taxi to carry you to or from a tourist-taxi zone. At the same time, it's worth noting that competition among the tourist-taxi drivers, especially in the high season, means that some may be prepared to offer you better prices than the fixed rates displayed.

Banjul

At no time of year is little **BANJUL** a prepossessing place. Its tarmac streets seem to pump out heat in the dry season, and its alleys become a chaos of red mud and puddles during the rains. The dilapidated assemblage of corrugated iron and peeling paint, and a lattice of open drains deep in the backstreets, with no slopes to drain them, complete a somewhat melancholy picture.

As a national capital, Banjul (or Bathurst as it was known to the colonial British) was doomed to failure by its site. It was acquired by Britain in 1816 to defend the river from slavers and to control trade with the interior, but its size was restricted to the area of land that could be kept free of flooding from the creeks and swamps behind. Kankujeri Road (formerly Bund Road) dykes the city on its present small patch, and further expansion is impossible. Hot, confined and seething with mosquitoes, Banjul is not a town where many choose to live. The exodus after business hours is understandable, and nightlife all but nonexistent.

If you have to be here, compensations are scant. To be won over by Banjul you need a little patience, and perhaps a special interest in West African history or architecture: more than any other Gambian town, the capital conveys a strong sense of the country's colonial past. However, with a population of barely 50,000 and shrinking, Banjul is too small to offer any of the ordinary facilities and diversions of a capital – though at least whatever you need to accomplish can usually be done in reasonable safety, and on foot. Walking gets you anywhere and the paranoia of some West African capitals is absent.

Arrival, orientation, information

The modern terminal building at **Banjul International Airport** is 24km south of Banjul and 18km from the resorts (for flight arrival and departures, call ☎ 447 3000. There's a **Trust Bank** exchange counter here (Mon–Fri 9am–5pm, Sat 9am–1pm), but no ATM. There's also a **post office** (Mon–Sat 8am–4pm or until after the last flight), public telephones and an outlet for mobile-phone SIM cards and scratch cards. Other facilities in the main hall of the terminal include a **Gambia Tourism Authority** office which offers sketchy tourist information.

Orientation and city transport

If you're arriving on a package deal you'll be driven straight to your hotel by complimentary shuttle (it's often possible to get a lift even if you're not a guest). Fixed **taxi** fares from the airport are posted on a board outside the arrivals area – D400–500 is the rate for either Banjul or the resorts with a green tourist taxi

---

Banjul surface arrivals and departures

The **Banjul–Barra ferry** across the mouth of the Gambia River is scheduled to depart Banjul or Barra daily from 7am to 11pm, at least once an hour in each direction (vehicles D145, foot passengers D5). You can contact the Port Authority on ☎ 422 8205 for the latest information, though note that the ferry is subject to frequent delays. There are usually two vessels in operation, and timings depend on the vessel, the load, the wind and the state of the tide. Large pirogues cover the same route, but they have an unsafe reputation – and they don't carry cars.

Banjul itself isn't much of a transport hub. **Serrekunda** sees most of the action for upcountry south-bank destinations (as well as routes to Ziguinchor and the rest of Casamance), and **Barra** is the base for getting anywhere on the north bank. From Barra, on the north bank, estate-car **bush taxis** leave the bush-taxi garage (next to the ferry terminal) for Amdillai (direction Dakar) when they are full. See the Senegal chapter's section on "Overland from The Gambia", p.160.

– but you might be able to negotiate a lower rate with a yellow local taxi. Otherwise it's a 3km walk to the main road where, during the day, you can pick up a bush taxi, either straight into Banjul or just as far as Serrekunda, from where you can get another to the beach resorts.

If you're coming from northern Senegal, you'll arrive on the north bank of the Gambia River, at the small port of **Barra** (see p.311). From here the regular ferry brings you straight to the **wharf** in Banjul town centre. Banjul has two **bush-taxi**

Banjul and around

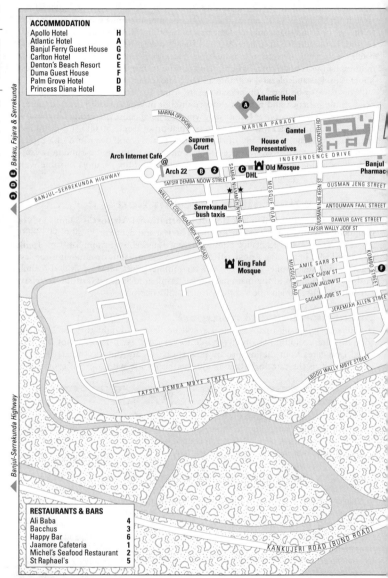

ACCOMMODATION

Apollo Hotel	H
Atlantic Hotel	A
Banjul Ferry Guest House	G
Carlton Hotel	C
Denton's Beach Resort	E
Duma Guest House	F
Palm Grove Hotel	D
Princess Diana Hotel	B

RESTAURANTS & BARS

Ali Baba	4
Bacchus	3
Happy Bar	6
Jaamore Cafeteria	1
Michel's Seafood Restaurant	2
St Raphael's	5

turnarounds: vehicles arriving from the Westfield Junction and Serrekunda use the area around Mosque Road; Bakau minibuses use the area outside the National Museum.

Despite its compactness, Banjul's layout can initially be confusing as all the streets look much the same. To add to the confusion, most of the street names in Banjul were changed in the late 1990s, in a move to further divorce the city from its colonial past, but local people and businesses still occasionally use the old names. Most of your

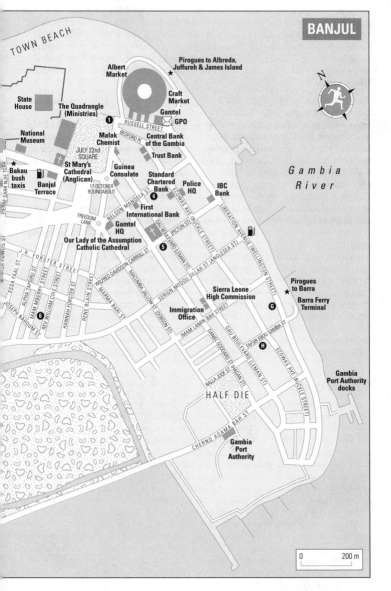

movements are likely to be centred around **July 22nd Square** – once known as Mac-Carthy Square but renamed to commemorate Jammeh's takeover – and down by the **waterfront** on Liberation Avenue (formerly Wellington Street), where you'll find **Albert Market**, the post office and banks. Traffic into and out of town uses the **Banjul–Serrekunda Highway** northwest of the centre.

Accommodation

The Gambia's capital city has only two tourist-class **hotels**, both very well known: the *Atlantic*, which is also one of The Gambia's best business hotels, on the beach near the town centre, and the *Palm Grove*, a beach hotel out of town on the Banjul–Serrekunda Highway. There's also a clutch of fairly down-at-heel hotels and **guesthouses** in the centre of Banjul, catering mainly for local business travellers. The best of these are a little shabby, while the worst rent out rooms by the hour, but for a low-cost experience of Banjul they're worth investigating.

Apollo Tafsou Ebou Samba St ☎ 422 8184. A characterless place, but a reasonable choice if you're looking for something vaguely resembling an international-style en-suite room, on a budget; however, the *Carlton* offers more atmosphere for very similar prices. ❸

Atlantic Marina Parade ☎ 422 8601 ⓦ www.corinthiahotels.com. Large and comfortable establishment. The grandly proportioned bar and restaurant areas are popular with local movers and shakers. Most rooms have views of the pool, the ocean, the flower gardens, or the jungly bird garden. ❽

Banjul Ferry Guest House Liberation Ave ☎ 422 2028. The best choice in this price range, near the Barra ferry terminal, with a communal balcony that's great for watching the incessant activity in the street below. It looks unpromising from the outside, but the rooms (some en suite with a/c) are well-kept and a good size. ❷

Carlton Independence Drive ☎ 422 8670. Old-fashioned hotel with decently furnished en-suite rooms, with optional a/c. Some just about have views of Arch 22. ❸

Denton's Beach Resort Denton Bridge ☎ 777 3777 ⓦ www.fishthegambia.com. This British-run boating base has bright, airy, cool rooms to rent. Among the many facilities is a small pool. ❺

Duma Guest House Jallow Jallow St ☎ 422 8381. Friendly guesthouse in a residential quarter; the rooms (some en suite) have seen better days but are good value. ❶

Palm Grove Mile 2, Banjul–Serrekunda Highway ☎ 420 1620 ⓦ www.palmgrovehotel-gambia.com. Tourist hotel in a pleasant location with a lagoon in front and a quiet stretch of beach 500m further. You have to rely on tourist taxis to get around from here – it's difficult to flag down bush taxis on the road outside. It's an attractive place to spend time, though, with decor that includes the work of local artists. ❻

Princess Diana Independence Drive ☎ 422 8715. Small hotel with plain, en-suite rooms with fans or a/c. Clean and adequate, but a little soulless. ❷

The Town

The **National Museum** on Independence Drive (Mon–Thurs 8am–4pm, Fri & Sat 8am–1pm; D50) though small, poky and badly lit, contains some gems: you just have to be patient to find them. A great deal of mouldering ethnographia – mostly the remains of private collections and not all of it Gambian – and a lot of old anthropological photos are the main displays. Kids who are used to interactive displays will be yawning within minutes at the yellowing notices against the exhibits; they might pause at the traditional musical instrument collection, but just for long enough to discover that you're not allowed to touch anything, unlike at the Tanje Village Museum (see p.310), where playing the instruments is positively encouraged. But if you take time to peer into some of the dark corners, you can come across excellent *warri* boards, fascinating maps and documents, and generally informative stuff about the wars and migrations of the Senegambia region. There's an impressive array of palm-wine tapping and drinking equipment too, an early Iron Age wood drill with its modern-looking bit, and a natural-resources display interesting to those unfamiliar with the flora and fauna of the region.

Less than ten minutes' walk to the east, **Albert Market** (Mon–Sat), a relatively laid-back and rather sanitized version of what you find everywhere in West Africa, is one of Banjul's big pluses. The highly enjoyable **tourist market** is deep inside the general market – take a pocketful of dalasis and argue your head off. While you're busy bargaining for D5 bangles you can eye up the better merchandise and come back later if it appeals. There are some great bargains, especially in cloth and clothing, with Chinese-made garments especially inexpensive. If you're not into parting with money at all, then you're likely to feel uneasy – and free gifts of the very thing you didn't want to buy are all part of the wearing-down process. Go in a bright mood. For more on craft shopping in the locality, see the listings on p.304.

West of the National Museum, Independence Drive is graced with the impressive, boat-shaped **Court House**. The road is spanned at its far end by **Arch 22** (daily 8am–4pm; D50), a cream-coloured monstrosity that greets you as you enter the capital. Designed by Senegalese architect Pierre Goudiaby, and built to commemorate the coup of July 22, 1994, the arch was completed in 1996 at a cost of $1.15 million, but was a technical disappointment – one of its lift shafts is unusable due to the twisting of the structure as it settled into the soft ground. However, the arch does house a **museum** of traditional textiles and tools where, incongruously, you can view the seat Yahya Jammeh was sitting on when he announced his takeover, and, halfway up, a **restaurant** and **bar**, where you can eat your snacks in a breeze while watching the Banjul traffic. The best views of the town, however, are afforded from the **balcony** right at the top.

To the north, Marina Parade is one of Banjul's pleasanter and shadier streets, fringed with somnolent government buildings and terminating, after the *Atlantic Hotel* and the hospital, at the guarded gates of **State House**.

Eating, drinking and nightlife

Banjul suffers from a serious shortage of **restaurants**, particularly in the evenings, but there is first-class simple food to be had from local eating places and fast-food joints in the daytime. For rice and sauce, there's some choice among the stalls in the Albert Market, where all the traders eat, and you'll find itinerant food-sellers everywhere – especially around July 22nd Square – with fruit, fritters, frozen juices and peanut brittle. Banjul doesn't have much **nightlife** in the conventional sense: presently the only real venue is the plush air-conditioned disco at the *Atlantic Hotel* (nightly till 3am). For the most happening clubs, you'll have to travel out to the tourist resort areas and Serrekunda.

Restaurants and bars

Ali Baba Nelson Mandela St (Mon–Sat 9am–5pm). Lebanese fast food place that's popular and highly recommended, even though it's nothing much to look at. It serves decent snacks, sandwiches and main meals, including first-class falafel and juicy burgers, plus mango and guava juice and fresh fruit smoothies.

Bacchus Beach Bar Mile 7, Banjul–Serrekunda Highway ⊤ 422 7948. Situated on the lagoon behind what used to be the *Wadner Beach Hotel* (now derelict), this popular but slightly overpriced bar-restaurant serves tourist standards like steak and barracuda.

Banjul Terrace 72 Gloucester St ⊤ 422 7826 (daily till 8pm). With a grand-looking streetside

terrace, this place is relatively smart but the menu of seafood and grills is unexceptional.

Happy Bar Rev William Cole St. A tiny hole-in-the-wall drinking place with a very local atmosphere, on a quiet street where kids play table football just outside.

Jaamore Cafeteria corner of July 22nd Square, near Albert Market (daily till 8pm). Giving a new lease of life to a lovingly preserved 1930s drinking fountain, this pleasant outdoor café does excellent meat pies and hot and cold drinks. You can order simple meals, too, if you have time for them to go and buy the ingredients and cook them for you. Patronized mostly by tourists, but not touristy.

Michel's Seafood Independence Drive, opposite the Court House ⊤ 422 3108 (daily

8am–late). Banjul's only relatively formal restaurant outside the hotels is an old-fashioned, brightly lit place with whirring fans – functional, rather than romantic – serving a good choice of fish and a different West African dish every day, at very reasonable prices. Specialities include tiger prawns, lobster and fresh local juices.

St Raphael's Wilfred Davidson Carroll St, opposite the Catholic cathedral. Low-key place that feels rather like a Catholic family drawing room. *Benachin*, *domodah*, and other West African dishes such as *chew-kong* (catfish) and *fufu* with soup are all good value.

The resorts and Serrekunda

The Gambia's principal **tourist strip**, which accommodates virtually all the country's package holidaymakers, covers just over 10km of the Atlantic coast west of Banjul. It's an appealing area to unwind, with its easy-going restaurants, low-key nightspots, and clusters of cliff-top and beachside hotels, and yet **tourism** has utterly transformed the area. It's remarkable that the Gambians who live here have retained such an equable regard for visitors who generally pay them such scant attention. As always, where the poor world meets the holidaying rich, the stories of locals who made good by marrying abroad fuel hopes and dampen the inevitable resentment. More positively, there's considerable enthusiasm for having a good time and it's not impossible for you to meet local people in the bars and discos or on the beach without the question of patronage creeping in.

There are four main **resorts**. **BAKAU**, the most significant coastal community after Banjul itself, is the longest-established. Bakau "old town", east of Sait Matty Road, is a swarming village of dirt streets and noisy compounds, home to many of the hotel staff, while the "new town", west of Sait Matty Road, is more affluent. Bakau's northern limit, at Cape Point, is nowadays part tourist village, part well-to-do neighbourhood. Along the coast to the southwest, Bakau merges with the more affluent **FAJARA**, and beyond Fajara's golf course is **KOTU**, with a clump of established hotels, at the debouchment of the small Kotu stream. Finally, further south, there's **KOLOLI** and the adjacent villages of **BIJILO**, **KERR SERIGN** and **MANJAI KUNDA**, a very mixed area where some of the most upmarket hotels, some of the most bohemian guesthouses and some of the trashiest tourist traps in the country are to be found.

If you're interested in staying close to the heart of Gambian life, **SERREKUNDA**, the country's largest town, just a couple of kilometres inland from the resorts, is a good place to be. The Gambia's energy is concentrated here and it can give you (even if you're travelling nowhere else) a strong flavour of modern, urban West Africa – a choking racket of diesel engines, half-collapsed wooden trolleys, bricolaged stalls selling a riot of dust-covered imports, and music blaring from the hundreds of stereos and radios. The focus of all this is the town's central garage and market. It's a lot of fun, and not at all unsafe, to wander round here, though avoid dangling your valuables and keep your bag under your arm. Serrekunda's residential neighbourhoods and suburbs, such as Kanifing, Latrikunda and Sukuta, see few tourists.

Street names in Bakau and Fajara

As in Banjul, a number of roads in the resort area carry the burden of more than one name. Atlantic Road, Atlantic Avenue and Atlantic Boulevard are one and the same street; Garba Jahumpa Road is still called New Town Road; Kairaba Avenue used to be known as Pipeline Road, and often still is. The main road from Kairaba Avenue to Kotu and Kololi, sometimes referred to as Hotel Road or Badala Park Way, has been officially renamed Bertil Harding Highway; beyond Bijilo it becomes the Kombo coastal highway.

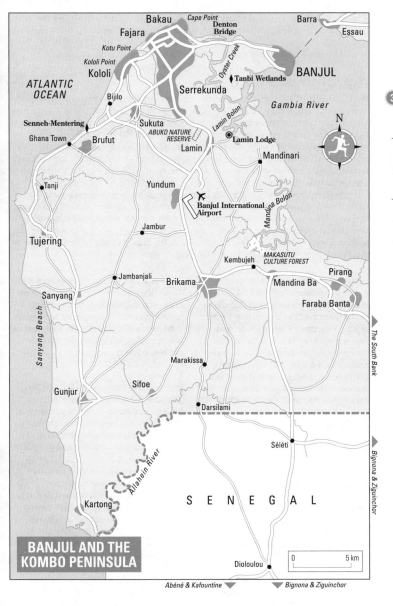

BANJUL AND THE KOMBO PENINSULA

If you choose to **stay in Serrekunda**, you can get to the beach resorts in ten minutes and get the best of both worlds – the beach bars and restaurants on the coast, and the chop houses and local dives in Serrekunda. The town is the hub for both local and upcountry transport services: there are several taxi garages serving different routes. The main **taxi stand** for local services to the beach resorts of Kotu and Kololi is at "London Corner", a five-minute walk west of the market.

The thoroughfare that links Serrekunda, Bakau and Fajara is **Kairaba Avenue**, which, only a couple of decades ago, was a rutted track running through fields and orchards. Today, Kairaba's three-kilometre length is lined with shops, bars, restaurants and offices, and commands the highest rents in the country.

Accommodation

By international standards, most of the **tourist hotels** along the coastal strip are quite basic, though they all have pools. While many are built on the beach, or very close to it, sea views are by no means guaranteed. In season, the Kotu–Kololi stretch becomes the heartbeat of the tourist industry, while Bakau and Fajara hotels are somewhat quieter. If you're travelling independently and looking for somewhere reasonably cheap to flop out for a few days, you'll find several friendly, non-package establishments a short distance away from the coast. The price codes below, unless otherwise indicated, are for self-contained, en-suite rooms, with breakfast included.

If you're interested in staying as a house guest in a Gambian compound (something which many in Bakau and Serrekunda are happy to offer as they can charge the equivalent of a week's wages per night), then just ask around and take pot luck; you should expect to be asked anything from D300 to D500 per person per day, with meals included, depending on the season. It's usually easiest to find this kind of arrangement by staying first in a cheap hotel.

Bakau and Cape Point

African Village Atlantic Rd ☎ 449 5384 ✉ europrop@qanet.gm. Conveniently located in the heart of Bakau, this 73-room tourist hotel perched on Bakau's low cliffs is a little scruffy, but good value and recommended for its warm, Gambian atmosphere. Accommodation with fans is in round-houses, crammed tightly into a leafy compound, or in blocks, some with sea views. There's a very reasonable restaurant with great Atlantic views. ❺

Cape Point Kofi Annan St, Cape Point ☎ 449 5005 ✉ capepointhotel@qanet.gm. A little faded, this 35-room tourist hotel is close to good beaches and there's a tiny pool. Some rooms have a/c, and all are spotless. ❻

Jabo Guest House Old Cape Rd ☎ 449 4906. Down-to-earth, reasonably priced place which feels more like a family compound than a guesthouse, with six simple, en-suite rooms with fridge, and the use of a well-equipped kitchen. The beach at Cape Point is within walking distance. ❸

Ocean Bay Kofi Annan St, Cape Point ☎ 449 4265 ⓦ www.oceanbayhotel.com. Impressive resort hotel with groomed, palm-shaded lawns and comfortable rooms. ❽

Roc Heights Sambu Breku Rd, Cape Point ☎ 449 4528 ⓦ www.rocheightslodge.com. Upmarket but untouristy, with large, comfortably equipped suites and mini-apartments, and a leafy garden. ❻–❽

Romana Atlantic Rd ☎ 449 5127. Unpromising exterior, but a good, basic town hotel inside. The eleven rooms have fans, and the easy-going bar and restaurant are very reasonable. ❷

Sunbeach Kofi Annan St, Cape Point ☎ 449 7190 ✉ sunbeach@gamtel.gm. This is one of the better tourist hotels, with nearly 200 a/c rooms with satellite TV, on one of the best beaches in the resort area. A good choice for young families, with an excellent pool and play area and a restaurant serving European meals. ❽

Fajara

Croc John's off Atlantic Rd ☎ 449 6068. Clean, good-sized, self-catering apartments with fans and good beds with mosquito nets, in a compound that feels homely, secure and un-touristy. Popular with volunteers and long-term visitors as well as independent travellers who don't need the facilities of a tourist hotel. ❻

Fajara Golf Apartments off Kairaba Ave ☎/℻ 449 5800 ⓦ www.fajaragolf-apartments.nl. In a pair of compounds enlivened by the work of a local artist, these eight self-catering apartments are spotless, spacious and very well-equipped, with useful extras like CD and cassette players and free bike rental. Recommended. ❹

Fajara Guesthouse Signposted off Kairaba Ave, near the golf club ☎ 449 6122. A peaceful haven offering small, simple, clean rooms with fans, around a bright white-pillared courtyard. ❸

Leybato Guesthouse off Atlantic Rd ☎ 449 7186 ⓦ www.leybato.abc.gm. Known and loved for its beach bar and hammocks, *Leybato's* has a few basic guest rooms – good if you want to be on the beach, but there are better-value places elsewhere. ❹

Ngala Lodge Atlantic Rd ☏ 449 4045 Ⓦ www.ngalalodge.com. A former ambassador's residence, converted into a hotel with luxurious suites, plus a small pool and a superb restaurant. Likely to appeal to anyone with a sense of the unusual, looking for somewhere secluded and serene. If that's you, it's worth every penny. Bookings through The Gambia Experience (see p.23). ⑧

Safari Garden off Atlantic Rd, near the golf club ☏ 449 5887 Ⓦ www.safarigarden.com. Very good value and thoroughly recommended, this un-touristy, eco-friendly independent is a gem. Besides a dozen simple rooms around a colourful garden courtyard, it boasts a small but excellent pool, a good restaurant, and extremely friendly staff and management. Pleasantly situated in a quiet neighbourhood of sandy residential streets, within walking distance of the beach. ⑤

Kotu

Badala Park Kotu Stream Rd ☏ 446 0400 Ⓦ www.badalaparkhotel.gm. Popular with independent travellers and bird-watchers, this is one of the cheapest package hotels. Some of the 200-plus rooms, with optional a/c, are shabbily furnished – the ones furthest from reception are quieter. There's a path to a pleasant beach a short walk away. ④

Bakotu Kotu Stream Rd ☏ 446 5555 Ⓦ www.bakotuhotel.com. An attractive, though rather cramped, tourist hotel, a couple of minutes' walk from the beach, with a small pool. The best rooms are upstairs, away from the road, and have balconies. The hotel also has eight small self-catering apartments – a little tired, but with private balconies offering fabulous views over Kotu Stream, excellent for bird- and monkey-watching. Rooms ⑥, apartments ⑦.

Bungalow Beach Kotu Stream Rd ☏ 446 5288 Ⓦ www.bbhotel.gm. Self-catering tourist hotel, right on a decent beach, with friendly staff and a loyal clientele, mostly of retired Europeans and younger families. The 110 mini-apartments are well-equipped, with optional a/c, but they're a little on the small side; better-value options exist elsewhere. ⑦

Kombo Beach Kotu Stream Rd ☏ 446 5466 Ⓦ www.kombobeach.com. Popular with young European package tourists, this is a lively mass-market hotel with plenty of activities, set on a reasonable stretch of beach. There's block after block of rooms (250 in all) designed to a familiar international formula, and huge crowds congregate in the bar to watch football on satellite TV. ⑦

Palm Beach Kotu Stream Rd ☏ 446 2111 Ⓦ www.palmbeachhotel.gm. Sister hotel to the *Badala Park*, with a similar atmosphere – much more Gambian than other places in Kotu – but more upmarket. Rooms (with TV and a/c) are in villas packed into jungly gardens, close to a good stretch of beach. ⑥

Sunset Beach Kotu Stream Rd ☏ 449 6397 Ⓦ www.sunsetbeachhotel.gm. Tidy tourist hotel in a good location on a well-kept stretch of beach, relatively secluded for Kotu. Most of the rooms are in utilitarian bungalows in regimented rows, but the place is clean and well-furnished. ⑥

Kololi: around the Palma Rima and Senegambia hotels

Dutch Whale Palma Rima Rd ☏ 778 9704 or 994 2361. One of the very few budget options close to the beach, with accommodation in simple huts and a friendly bar-restaurant. ③

Kairaba ☏ 446 2940 Ⓦ www.kairabahotel.com. The Gambia's top, large hotel – and prime honeymoon territory – with wide-ranging facilities, including a choice of good restaurants. The pleasant rooms, 140 in all, have direct-dial phones, excellent bathrooms, safes, TV – the lot. Loyal customers return again and again. ⑧

Kololi Beach Club ☏ 446 4897 Ⓦ www.kololi.com. Started life as a timeshare, but now operates as a hotel, with accommodation in self-catering villas in well-tended grounds, including a small golf course, and a pleasant pool edged by low palms. Expensive. ⑧

Luigi's Apartments Palma Rima Rd ☏ 446 0280 Ⓦ www.luigis.gm. Well-furnished rooms and apartments with self-catering facilities and access to a pretty garden, fifty metres from the beach. ⑤

Palma Rima Hotel Bertil Harding Highway ☏ 446 3380 or 446 3381 ℮ info@palmarima.com. A brash, mega-touristy resort hotel, famous for its huge pool, set a short distance back from the beach. Packed entertainment programme, a choice of restaurants and bars, and a tame but busy club (the *Moonlight Disco*) cranking out Europop every night. ⑧

Paradise Suites ☏ 446 3429 Ⓦ www.paradisesuites.gm. North of the main Senegambia area, and set in small but beautifully planted gardens, this self-catering accommodation is comfortable and well-furnished. Attractive options range from small apartments to large villas. ⑥

Senegambia Beach ☏ 446 2717 Ⓦ www.senegambiahotel.com. Gigantic tourist hotel, recommended for its good service and impressive tropical gardens (great for bird-watching but dusty between Feb and when the rains break). Some rooms are rather tired but all are cool and clean. ⑧

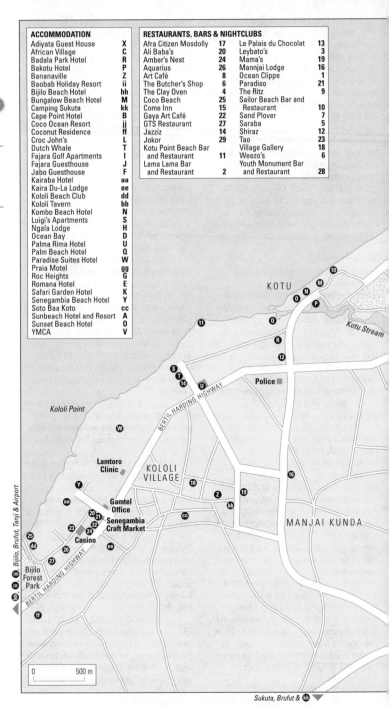

ACCOMMODATION	
Adiyata Guest House	X
African Village	C
Badala Park Hotel	R
Bakotu Hotel	P
Bananaville	Z
Baobab Holiday Resort	ii
Bijilo Beach Hotel	hh
Bungalow Beach Hotel	M
Camping Sukuta	kk
Cape Point Hotel	B
Coco Ocean Resort	jj
Coconut Residence	ff
Croc John's	L
Dutch Whale	T
Fajara Golf Apartments	I
Fajara Guesthouse	J
Jabo Guesthouse	F
Kairaba Hotel	aa
Kaira Du-La Lodge	ee
Kololi Beach Club	dd
Kololi Tavern	bb
Kombo Beach Hotel	N
Luigi's Apartments	S
Ngala Lodge	H
Ocean Bay	D
Palma Rima Hotel	U
Palm Beach Hotel	Q
Paradise Suites Hotel	W
Praia Motel	gg
Roc Heights	G
Romana Hotel	E
Safari Garden Hotel	K
Senegambia Beach Hotel	Y
Soto Baa Koto	cc
Sunbeach Hotel and Resort	A
Sunset Beach Hotel	O
YMCA	V

RESTAURANTS, BARS & NIGHTCLUBS	
Afra Citizen Mosdolly	17
Ali Baba's	20
Amber's Nest	24
Aquarius	26
Art Café	8
The Butcher's Shop	6
The Clay Oven	4
Coco Beach	25
Come Inn	15
Gaya Art Café	22
GTS Restaurant	27
Jazziz	14
Jokor	29
Kotu Point Beach Bar and Restaurant	11
Lama Lama Bar and Restaurant	2
Le Palais du Chocolat	13
Leybato's	3
Mama's	19
Mannjai Lodge	16
Ocean Clippe	1
Paradiso	21
The Ritz	9
Sailor Beach Bar and Restaurant	10
Sand Plover	7
Saraba	5
Shiraz	12
Tao	23
Village Gallery	18
Weezo's	6
Youth Monument Bar and Restaurant	28

3 3.1 GAMBIA

298

0   500 m

KOTU

Kotu Stream

Kololi Point

BERTIL HARDING HIGHWAY

Police

Lamtoro Clinic

KOLOLI VILLAGE

Gamtel Office

Senegambia Craft Market

Casino

Bijilo Forest Park

BERTIL HARDING HIGHWAY

MANJAI KUNDA

Bijilo, Brufut, Tanji & Airport

Sukuta, Brufut &

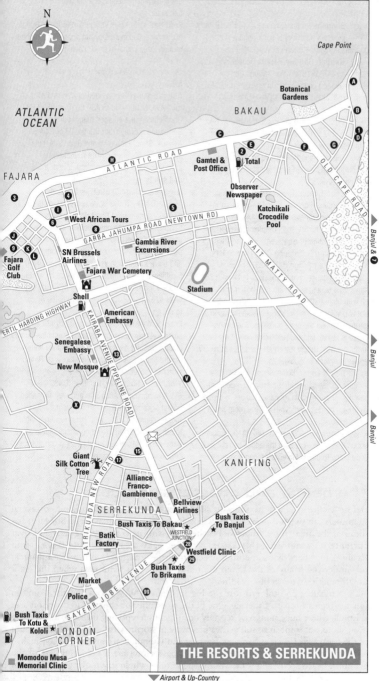

N

Cape Point

ATLANTIC
OCEAN

Botanical
Gardens

BAKAU

Ⓐ

Ⓑ

①
Ⓓ

ⒸⒺ

Ⓕ

Ⓖ

OLD CAPE ROAD

ATLANTIC ROAD

Gamtel &
Post Office

Ⓗ

Total

Observer
Newspaper

Katchikali
Crocodile
Pool

SAIT MATTY ROAD

Banjul & ⑦

FAJARA

❸

Ⓙ

Ⓛ

Ⓗ

❹

Ⓙ

❺

West African Tours

GARBA JAHUMPA ROAD (NEWTOWN RD)

❻

❽

Gambia River
Excursions

❾

SN Brussels
Airlines

Stadium

Ⓚ

Fajara
Golf
Club

Fajara War Cemetery

Banjul ▶

Shell

ERTIL HARDING HIGHWAY

American
Embassy

KAIRABA AVENUE

Senegalese
Embassy

⑬

New Mosque

Ⓥ

Banjul ▶

Ⓧ

PIPELINE ROAD

⑮

KANIFING

Giant
Silk Cotton
Tree

⑰

LATRIKUNDA NEW ROAD

Alliance
Franco-
Gambienne

Bellview
Airlines

Bush Taxis
To Banjul

SERREKUNDA

Bush Taxis To Bakau

WESTFIELD
JUNCTION

Batik
Factory

㉘

Westfield Clinic

㉙

Bush Taxis
To Brikama

Market

SAYERR JOBE AVENUE

99

Police

Bush Taxis
To Kotu &
Kololi

LONDON
CORNER

Momodou Musa
Memorial Clinic

THE RESORTS & SERREKUNDA

Airport & Up-Country

Kololi Village, Kerr Serign and Bijilo

🏃 **Bananaville** Kololi Village ☎ 444 3716. Very pleasant apartments set around a shady garden courtyard – excellent value. ❸

🏃 **Baobab Holiday Resort** Badala Highway ☎ 446 5518 ⓦ www.baobab.gm. Well-managed place catering mostly for locals, with large, clean rooms with self-catering facilities. ❺

🏃 **Bijilo Beach** Bertil Harding Highway, Bijilo ☎ 442 6706 ⓦ www.bijilobeachhotel.com. A modest, new, tourist hotel with fabulous Atlantic views. The mini-apartments and rooms are small but bright and finished to a high standard in European style. ❺

🏃 **Coco Ocean Resort and Spa** Bertil Harding Highway, Kerr Serign (information from *Coconut Residence*) ☎ 446 3377. The Gambia's first luxury spa complex promises an impressive range of treatments and facilities. ❽

🏃 **Coconut Residence** Bertil Harding Highway, Kerr Serign ☎ 446 3377 ⓦ www .coconutresidence.com. A luxurious hotel with 36 handsome suites, some with four-poster beds and all with huge bathrooms. For total seclusion there are two villas with private pools tucked away in gardens behind the main buildings. The atmosphere is suave, and the restaurant one of the best in the country. Hardly the "real" Gambia, but a very appealing place to indulge. ❽

Kaira-Du-La Lodge Kololi Village ☎ 446 0529 ⓔ kaira.du.la@qanet.gm. Smartly equipped self-catering apartments in roundhouses set in a small, well-kept garden, each with a living room and a small patio. ❹

Kololi Tavern Kololi Village ☎ 446 3410. Budget option that's frayed around the edges but still a good place to unwind in cool, African surroundings;

the garden compound has a bar and barbecue. ❸

Soto Baa Koto Kololi Village ☎ 446 0399. Budget accommodation in shabby but appealing thatched roundhouses with a shared cooking area. ❸

Serrekunda, Kanifing and Sukuta

Adiyata Guest House well-signposted off Kairaba Ave, Latrikunda ☎ 439 5510 or 992 5537. Good choice in a villagey neighbourhood of Serrekunda, away from the bustle of Kairaba Avenue. Simple rooms with large beds, nets and fans in six characterful roundhouses around a small courtyard planted with trees and shrubs. ❸

🏃 **Camping Sukuta** Bijilo Rd, Sukuta ☎ 491 7786 ⓦ www.campingsukuta.de. Well-signposted from Bertil Harding Highway and Serrekunda, this camping site and lodge is very popular with overlanders. There's plenty of shade to park and camp, accommodation is in simple huts, and there's a good shared kitchen and washing facilities. If you've crossed the Sahara by vehicle and are thinking of selling up and flying off, or just want to exchange information, this is the place to be. ❶

Praia 3 Mam Youth St, Serrekunda ☎ 439 4887. A somewhat run-down but adequate Gambian-owned place in a quiet backstreet of Serrekunda with secure parking. Rooms are en suite, with TV and either fan or a/c. ❷

YMCA off Kairaba Ave, Kanifing ☎ 439 2647 ⓦ www.ymca.gm. Adequate and well-managed hostel accommodation with single and double rooms, some en suite, with fans. Features table-tennis, a restaurant providing cheap meals (daily 9am–midnight), and a neighbouring computer centre with Internet access. ❶

The beach and coastal attractions

Before venturing into the **sea** you should make sure your patch is safe – several swimmers are swept out every year. Cape Point (also known as Cape St Mary) has some of the area's most attractive beaches, but with its cross–cutting tidal and river currents, it's a notorious blackspot, as is the rocky area by *Leybato Beach Bar* in Fajara. The rollers that sometimes sweep in further south can also bring a dangerous undertow. Many of the hotels use red flags to warn swimmers when the sea is unsafe, and it's wise to observe them.

Unfortunately, **coastal erosion** is a big problem in West Africa and the Gambian beaches regularly take a battering. One of the worst affected stretches in the resort area is Kololi, where huge sums have recently been spent on replacing the sand, and keeping it on shore, but some areas still get washed away in stormy weather. The beaches south of the tourist area, such as Sanyang, Tujering and Gunjur, don't suffer quite so much.

Beach bar-restaurants (BBR in the listings below) are a colourful part of the Gambian beach scene, and some visitors spend their whole stay moving happily from one to the next, or just setting up camp at one for the duration. They provide a laid-back alternative to the inland tourist restaurants and bars, with reggae on the sound system and local live music from time to time; many also serve excellent fresh food, notably prawns, grills, and fish baked in foil. Gambian beaches are simply too hot to lie out on for long periods, so beach bars provide a shady haven. You have to allow time to enjoy the experience, as food tends to be prepared to order. Opening times can be unpredictable, although some stay open at night and during the rainy season. Apart from the bars, all along the beach you'll also find **fruit stalls**, and **juice–pressers' stands** where you can buy freshly squeezed juices, which few bars sell.

Lebanese citizens

"It's worth knowing that the majority of Lebanese are themselves Gambians – the descendants of grandparents or even great-grandparents who came to The Gambia from the 1920s onwards."

David Somers, UK

Coastal attractions

There's a lot you can do with wheels of your own (see p.304 for details of car and bike rental): trundle down the coast in search of better beaches, explore the back-country between the coast and the airport, visit Serrekunda for the shopping – even get across to the north bank of The Gambia.

The small **botanical garden** in Bakau (D50) is a rather beautiful, though neglected, hideaway just off the main road, greenest and most impressive after the rains. Note the fairy-tale teak tree and the specimens of ancient cycads. The **crocodile pool** of Katchikali is just a ten-minute walk from here in the heart of Bakau, a path leading almost straight to it from the junction of Atlantic and Old Cape roads. Local children will show you the way. There's usually a small payment to visit the poolside to see the crocodiles – none too big and strangely white among the dense covering of lilies. No one fears these crocs: you can approach quite close even when they're out of the water and they are believed to have a magical effect on the pool, ensuring pregnancy for women who wash in it – not that there's very often much water. Every few seasons it's necessary to call a work party together to dig a little deeper, and sometimes to introduce new crocodiles.

Bijilo Forest (daily 8am–6pm; D30) is a half-square-kilometre reserve at the south end of Kololi beach, accessible from opposite the *Kololi Beach Club*. Containing one of the country's last remaining stands of striking **rhun palms**, it's managed by the Gambian-German Forestry Project. Within the reserve there are good chances of seeing red colobus and vervet monkeys, squirrels, large monitor lizards and a galaxy of birds. Trails are marked clearly, with a choice between long and short circuits of the park.

Eating, drinking and nightlife

In addition to the **bars** and **restaurants** of the main hotels (some of the best of which are found at the *Coconut Residence*, *Kairaba*, *Ngala Lodge* and *Safari Garden* hotels, all open to non-residents), there are plenty of independent, international-style places aimed at tourists and expats, many around the hotel zones, others distributed through the urban areas. For local **chop houses** and *afra* places, you need to head for the backstreets of Bakau and the market area of Serrekunda. A number of bar-restaurants have happy hours, and then become nightclubs in the evening. In season, the after-dark action can be lively along the tourist strip, with hotel nightclubs pumping out international chart music, but don't be afraid of trying strictly Gambian nightspots. For night-time mobility, unless you have your own vehicle, you'll need to rely on **taxis**. You could get a group together and rent one for the whole evening, and you might even get a taxi driver who's willing to be a guide, sharing his local knowledge and the fun. Taxi drivers and local guides often know about live-music events which aren't advertised elsewhere. If you want to hold your own party, there's usually **palm wine** for sale by the grove of tall palm trees on the landward side of Fajara golf course. **BBR** indicates a Beach Bar-Restaurant.

Bakau and Cape Point

Italian Connection Kofi Annan St, Cape Point ☎ 982 8695 (daily from 4pm). A cheerful, Italian-owned place, serving up authentic-tasting pizza and pasta.

Lama Lama off Atlantic Rd (daily 8.30am–12.30am). Live music nightly, with a busy local vibe.

Ocean Clipper *Ocean Bay Hotel*, Kofi Annan St, Cape Point ☎ 449 4265. Airy and upmarket Asian/European restaurant overlooking the beach.

Sand Plover BBR off Old Cape Rd, Cape Point ☎ 990 0231 (daily 10am–7pm). Rickety but characterful timber-built beach bar serving good, simple lunches, if you're prepared to wait a while.

Saraba off Newtown Rd (nightly 7pm–3am). A low-key place, tucked away in a quiet neighbourhood, serving top-notch *afra* to in-the-know locals, with fresh *tapalapa* from the next-door bakery.

Fajara and Kairaba Avenue

Art Café African Living Art Centre, 9 Garba Jahumpa Rod ☎ 449 5131. Tiny, elegant gallery-café serving impeccably presented tea and pastries.

The Butcher's Shop 130 Kairaba Ave ☎ 449 5069 (Mon–Sat 8am–late). This superb deli has an equally good restaurant on the decking at the front: chic by day and romantic by night, with above-average prices, but excellent-value juices.

The Clay Oven near VSO and MRC, signposted off Atlantic Rd ☎ 449 6600 (daily noon–3pm and 7pm–late). The Gambia's best Indian restaurant takes itself extremely seriously and has a loyal local following. Above-average prices.

Come Inn 17 Kairaba Ave. Town-side beer garden with an African twist, popular with a mixed crowd of Gambian and tourist regulars, this place serves steaks, fish, pizza and German fare, plus probably the best draught Julbrew in the country.

Leybato's BBR off Atlantic Rd. Long-established beach bar, with hammocks strung over the sand. It's a great place to catch the sunset, or sample home-style African cooking or tourist standards. Not a place to choose if you're in a hurry.

Le Palais du Chocolat Kairaba Ave (Tues–Sat 8am–9pm, Sun 8am–1pm & 5–9pm). Authentic French-style café with excellent coffee; the pastries are good and the calorific cakes are well worth a splurge.

The Ritz near *Safari Garden Hotel*, off Atlantic Rd ☎ 992 4205 (daily 10am–late). A friendly, casual place in a small courtyard, catering for tourists wanting a change from more formal hotel restaurants, and best known for steaks.

Weezo's Kairaba Ave ☎ 449 6918 (restaurant Tues–Sun 11.30am–3pm & 7–11pm; bar open till late; closed Mon). Casual but upmarket, Fajara's most stylish restaurant serves contemporary European dishes at lunchtime; by night it's part cocktail bar, part Mexican restaurant, part gourmet restaurant. Expensive but outstanding.

Kotu

Al Baba Kotu Stream Rd. Impressive eastern-Mediterranean restaurant with a slick, urban feel.

Sailor BBR Kotu Beach, next to Fajara Craft Market (daily 10am–11.30pm; live music every evening except Thurs). One of the better beachside restaurants, but not expensive, and good for fish and freshly squeezed juice.

Kololi: around the Palma Rima Hotel

Dutch Whale Palma Rima Rd ☎ 446 4804. Laid-back, Dutch-run bar-restaurant serving simple international favourites and cheap beer.

Jazziz Palma Rima Rd ☎ 446 2175. Ground-floor bar-restaurant and live-music venue beneath *Calabash* nightclub, with jazz, blues, Afro-beat and highlife on Fri, and salsa and reggae on Sat.

Kotu Point BBR Kotu Point, near the *Palma Rima* (daily 9am–late, happy hour Sun 5–7pm followed by a barbecue with live drum show). One of the best beach bars in the resort area, and one of the simplest, on a quiet stretch of good sand. The fresh fish, beer, soft drinks and palm wine are all good value.

Shiraz Palma Rima Road ☎ 991 0990. One of The Gambia's finest eastern-Mediterranean restaurants, with excellent *meze* and an interesting bar list.

Kololi: around the Senegambia Hotel

Ali Baba's corner of Senegambia Rd (daily till 1am; band 9pm–11.30pm). The Lebanese-run terrace bar and restaurant is a perennially popular hangout, though the cooking's not great – the garden restaurant behind (entrance round the corner) is a much better option, with a good house band.

Amber's Nest Bertil Harding Highway ☎ 446 4181. Gambian-owned, Anglo-Mediterranean restaurant, very popular with local professionals.

Aquarius near the casino ☎ 446 0247 (daily till 3am). Sleekly international cocktail bar and disco, just about big enough to dance in, popular with tourists and smart young Gambian Lebanese.

Coco Beach *Kololi Beach Club*. A cut above most beach restaurants, with light, European-style options for lunch and a more elaborate and expensive evening menu. Recommended.

Gaya Art Café Bertil Harding Highway ☎ 446 4022. Stylish though rather pricey café-bar serving healthy food and freshly ground coffee in an interesting gallery shop.

GTS Restaurant Senegambia Rd. On the edge of the Senegambia action but definitely worth seeking out, this characterful restaurant has a relaxed atmosphere and good simple food (African and European) at extremely reasonable prices.

Paradiso Senegambia Rd. This ordinary-looking place on the tourist strip serves fantastic pizza.

Tao Senegambia Rd ☎ 446 1191 (daily 7.30–10.30pm). The Gambia's only Thai restaurant, with pan-Asian influences. It's very popular with tourists, but the staff can be brusque.

Kololi Village and Manjai Kunda

Mama's Kololi Village. An excellent local restaurant with a cheerful, shaded roadside terrace, serving simple food (omelettes, *yassa* chicken, great breakfasts and buffets) at low prices.

Mannjai Lodge Manjai Kunda ☎ 446 3414. The courtyard bar at this hotel is occasionally the venue for live-music sessions featuring big names from the Senegambian music scene. The sound system isn't great, but there's a mellow, appreciative atmosphere in the place.

Village Gallery Kololi Village. The garden courtyard outside this interesting art gallery is a restaurant, serving simple and good-value daily specials such as grilled chicken or fish.

Serrekunda

Afra Citizen Mosdolly Mosque Rd (daily, evenings only till late). Cavelike *afra* shop run by Mauritanians; the setting may look medieval but their barbecued lamb is as good as it gets.

Jokor Westfield Junction ☎ 992 2555 (nightly till late). The best club and live-music venue in the area, primarily a hangout for fast-living Gambians, but friendly and relaxed – visitors rarely feel out of place. The mood is different every night, depending on the music they're playing, and you dance under the stars in a garden with trees laced with fairy lights.

Youth Monument Bar and Restaurant Westfield Junction (open all day). Unlikely location, at one of The Gambia's busiest road junctions – but this casual, low-key place is excellent for a beer, a simple cheap meal (good kebabs and grills) or a coffee. Busy as a pre-club venue for *Jokor*, nearby.

Cash not in hand

"Neither Maestro/Switch nor MasterCard are currently viable in Kololi. The ATMs only accept Visa or Visa Electron."

Judy Struys, UK

Banjul and area listings

Airlines Main airlines include: Air Sénégal International, 10 ECOWAS Ave, Banjul ☎ 420 2117 ⓦ www.air-senegal-international.com; Bellview Airlines, 16 Kairaba Ave, Kanifing ☎ 437 0594 ⓦ www.flybellviewair.com; SN Brussels Airlines, Bertil Harding Highway ☎ 449 6385 ⓦ www .brusselsairlines.com.

Airport For details of flight arrivals and departures, call ☎ 447 3000.

American Express Gamtours, Kanifing Industrial Estate, Serrekunda ☎ 439 2259 (Mon–Fri 9am–5pm).

Banks and exchange There are forex bureaux in all the resort areas. Main banks include: Standard Chartered (ATMs at most branches): 8 ECOWAS Ave,

Banjul ☏ 422 8681, ⓦ www.standardchartered.com; Senegambia area, Kololi ☏ 446 3277; Kairaba Ave, Serrekunda ☏ 439 7475; Atlantic Rd, Bakau ☏ 439 5046; IBC Bank: Liberation Ave, Banjul ☏ 422 8145; Atlantic Rd, Bakau ☏ 449 5120; Sayerr Jobe Ave, Serrekunda ☏ 439 2572; Trust Bank: 3–4 ECOWAS Ave, Banjul ☏ 422 5777; Sait Matty Rd, Bakau ☏ 449 5486; Banjul International Airport ☏ 447 2915; Sayerr Jobe Ave, Serrekunda ☏ 439 8038.

Bike rental You can rent bikes at around D150/half-day or D200/day from stands in each hotel zone. You can also buy them in town, for around D1500–4000. You can forgo the benefits of exercise under a hot sun by renting a quad bike: Quest Quad Trekking, on Palma Rima Road (between *Abi's Restaurant* and *Churchill's Pub* ☏ 446 4146) offers self-drive or bush and beach safaris with a qualified instructor on 125cc Yamaha Breezes.

Bird-watching Bird guides sometimes meet and wait for clients on the Kotu Stream Bridge, Kotu; another common meeting place is the Education Centre at Abuko Nature Reserve (see p.306). The Gambia Birding Group (ⓦ www.gambiabirding .org) is a good source of information and advice on guides and other ornithological matters. Birds of The Gambia (☏ 993 6122 ⓦ www.birdsofthegambia .com), run by the renowned ornithologist Clive Barlow, author of the region's most authoritative field guide, offers private bird-watching safaris for specialists and keen beginners. The following are all highly experienced guides: Mass Cham (☏ 992 4763), Wally Faal (☏ 437 2103) and Solomon Jallow (☏ 990 7694 ⓔ habitatafrica@hotmail.com).

Books Timbooktoo on Garba Jahumpa Rd is the most useful general bookshop. There are small selections of books for sale at supermarkets and hotel shops.

Car rental AB Rent a Car (☏ 446 0926 ⓦ www .abrent-gambia.comab.gm; Mon–Fri 8am–6pm, Sat 8am–12.30pm) is the most reputable of the independent agencies, with an office near the *Senegambia Hotel*; rates are reasonable, with reductions for longer periods. West African Tours (☏ 449 5258 ⓦ www.westafricantours.com) rent out Land Rovers with drivers and guides. In the Senegambia area, D 'n' D Bikes & Buggys (☏ 771 9756) hire out motorbikes and beach buggies, and M&M (☏ 702 3700) hires out mopeds.

Couriers DHL, Independence Drive Banjul (☏ 422 8414); Fedex, c/o Saga Express, Kanifing (☏ 447 2405); UPS, 42 Antouman Faal St, Banjul (☏ 422 4422).

Crafts and souvenirs Good *bengdulas* include the one on Atlantic Road, where you can watch craftsmen at work, and the one on the corner of Bertil Harding Highway, Kololi, which is good for bespoke leather items. Also along Atlantic Road are tourist-oriented clothing shops and stalls selling West African–style dresses, trousers and skirts, and batik hangings. For more batik and tie-dye, there's Serrekunda's famous "batik factory" – Musu Kebba Drammeh's place in Dippa Kunda, signposted off Mosque Rd. There are crafts, curios and textiles from all over West Africa at the highly recommended African Living Art Centre, Garba Jahumpa Rd, Bakau; the African Heritage Gallery, Cape Point; and, close together on Sayerr Jobe Ave in Serrekunda, Bamboo, Samory, and the African Art Collection. The Village Gallery, Kololi Village, sells contemporary West African art. Finally, there's a drum factory in Manjai Kunda where craftsmen make drums; prices start at under D500 and can go up to D5000 for something very special.

Cultural centres The Alliance Franco-Gambienne, Kairaba Avenue (☏ 437 5418). French cultural-exchange centre with live-music sessions, art exhibitions, a library (daily 10.30am–6.30pm), a recording studio, French language classes, and English and French film nights.

Dentist Swedent, signposted off Bertil Harding Highway on the opposite side from *Palma Rima Hotel* ☏ 446 1212 (Mon–Fri 9am–6pm, Sat 10am–1pm).

Embassies and consulates France, École Française, Atlantic Rd, Kairaba Ave end ☏ 449 5487; Germany, Independence Drive, Banjul ☏ 422 7783; Ghana, 18 Mosque Rd, Latrikunda ☏ 439 1599; Guinea, 78 Daniel Goddard St, Banjul ☏ 422 6862; Guinea-Bissau, Atlantic Rd, Bakau, near the Standard Chartered bank ☏ 449 4854; Netherlands, c/o Shell Company, Macoumba Jallow St, Banjul ☏ 422 7437; Nigeria, 52 Garba Jahumpa Rd, Bakau ☏ 449 5803; Senegal, off Kairaba Ave, Fajara ☏ 437 3752; Sierra Leone, OAU Blvd, Banjul ☏ 422 8206; UK, 48 Atlantic Rd, Fajara ☏ 449 5133; USA, Kairaba Ave, Fajara ☏ 439 2856.

Emergencies Banjul police station ☏ 422 3146; Bakau police station ☏ 449 5739; Kotu police station ☏ 446 3351; fire service ☏ 18. For medical emergencies, see "Hospitals" below.

Hospitals and clinics The Lamtoro Clinic (☏ 446 0934), near the *Senegambia Beach Hotel*, is highly rated but pricey. Westfield Clinic, Westfield Rd, Serrekunda (☏ 439 2213) and the Momodou Musa Memorial Clinic (Banjul ☏ 422 4320, Serrekunda ☏ 437 1683) are recommended for malaria treatment. The Medical Research Council, Fajara (☏ 449 5442), has a British nurse on duty. The British High Commission nurse, Sheelagh Fowler (☏ 449 5133, mobile ☏ 999 4785), runs a clinic.

Internet access There are plenty of Internet cafés in the resort area, with new ones springing up all the time.

Music lessons The following contacts, all based in or near the resorts, can provide lessons, or put you in touch with musicians. Alagi M'Bye, Maali's Music School in Nema Kunku, between Serrekunda and Sukuta (☎ 995 0030), offers *kora* lessons. The *Safari Garden Hotel* (see p.297) can recommend good *djembé* and dance teachers in Fajara and has weekly Gambian dance-aerobics sessions; drum lessons can also be arranged at the drum factory in Manjai Kunda.

Pharmacies Banjul Pharmacy at: Independence Drive (☎ 422 7470), Liberation Ave (☎ 422 7648), Sayerr Jobe Rd, London Corner, Serrekunda (☎ 439 1053), Kairaba Ave (☎ 439 0189); Malak Chemist at Atlantic Road, Bakau (☎ 449 6661); or Stop Step at Kairaba Ave (☎ 437 1344), Senegambia (☎ 446 5298), or Westfield (☎ 439 8437).

Post offices and telephones The GPO, Russell St, Banjul (Mon–Thurs 8.30am–12.15pm & 2–4pm, Fri 8.30am–12.15pm & 2.30–4.30pm, Sat 8.30am–noon), is the country's main post office and the best place to have mail sent to you poste restante. There are other post offices on Atlantic Rd, Bakau, and off Kairaba Ave, Serrekunda. There are Gamtel offices on Russell St, Banjul; Atlantic Rd, Bakau (opposite the *African Village Hotel*); at the bottom of Kairaba Ave, Serrekunda; and near the *Senegambia Hotel*. Private telecentres are also widely scattered around the urban area.

Sports and outdoor activities The Fajara Club has an 18-hole golf course (daily 7am–7.30pm; ☎ 449 5456). Greens fees are D200 per player per day, plus clubs and caddies if required. Temporary membership (D210/day, D840/week) gives access to their clubhouse, pool, tennis courts and other facilities. The Gambia Watersports Centre at *Denton's Beach Resort*, Denton Bridge, Banjul (☎ 777 3777), offers jet-ski hire, parascending, water-skiing and various boat rides. Lama Barry (☎ 777 6689) can arrange horseriding along the Kombo beaches for D500/hr.

Supermarkets The resort area has plenty of supermarkets and minimarkets (selling imported food, toiletries, wine and spirits, household goods and newspapers – mostly with a UK slant), along Kairaba Ave, at Cape Point, and in Bakau, Kotu and the Senegambia area, Kololi. Most are open Mon–Sat 8.30am–7.30pm, Sun 10am–2pm; some close later or are even open more or less 24/7, especially in the hotel zones. Many petrol stations also have minimarkets. Banjul has a couple of small grocery stores but no supermarkets as such.

Tour operators There are plenty of Gambian tours available: ever-popular options include Abuko Nature Reserve, Makasutu Culture Forest, "Bush and Beach" (the coast southwest of Kololi) and "Roots" (Juffureh). To book yourself on an organized trip, contact the very long established and reliable West African Tours, off Garba Jahumpa Rd, Fajara (☎ 449 5258 ✆ www.westafricantours.com), who are an ideal first port of call for tailor-made trips, as well as many popular excursions in Kombo district and upcountry. Alternatively, contact: African Adventure Tours (☎ 449 7313 ✆ www.africanadventuretours .com) who include an unusual "Roots by Land" trip in their itineraries; Discovery Tours (☎ 449 5551 ✆ www.discoverytours.gm); Faces and Places (☎ 446 2057), who organize cultural tours; Gambia River Excursions (☎ 449 4360), who specialize in boat trips; Gambia Tours (☎ 446 2601 ✆ www .gambiatours.gm); Gambia Tourist Support (☎ 446 2476), who run bespoke grassroots tours with an informal feel; Paradise Tours (☎ 449 4088 ✆ www .paradiseisland-gambia.com), who arrange pirogue visits to *Madiyana Lodge* on Jinack Island; or RM Tours (☎ 446 2226, ✆ www.rmtours.gm).

Travel agents The Gambia Experience at the *Senegambia Hotel*, Kololi (☎ 446 3867), act as agents for flights to the UK. For other flight bookings and general flight information, try Banjul Travel Agency, ECOWAS Ave, Banjul (☎ 422 8813); IPC Travel, 16 Kairaba Ave (☎ 437 5677 ✆ ipctravel @qanet.gm); or Continental Travels, 70b Daniel Goddard St, Banjul (☎ 422 4058).

Visa extensions Immigration office, 21 OAU Boulevard, Banjul ☎ 422 8611.

Around Banjul and the resorts

While many hotel guests end up on organized excursions to the places detailed in this section (see above for some recommended operators), it's easy enough to take off on your own explorations in the coastal region.

The Tanbi Wetlands

Southwest of Banjul, the **mangroves** of the **Tanbi Wetlands** are beautiful, eerie and surprisingly tall – up to 20m – and their birdlife is prolific and sometimes spectacular.

Fiddler **crabs** beckon maniacally on every mud bank, gathering in silent, jostling droves as the boat approaches. The quicksilver, dun-coloured hopping things are **mud-skippers** – fish seemingly intent on becoming terrestrial – which always seem to have gone by the time you've noticed them. Occasional, and odder, inhabitants of the mangrove creeks are **monkeys**, bounding through the foliage, presumably taking refuge from persecutors on the farm plots inland. Look out, too, for large **Nile monitor lizards**, metre-long dinosaurs of the undergrowth, sometimes seen basking on a horizontal branch, in wait for frogs, fish or birds. Hippos, incidentally, don't circulate this far downstream because of over-hunting in the past.

Lamin Lodge, reached up the snaking Lamin *bolon* – a tributary of the Gambia River – is the usual destination for boat trips to the wetlands. It's a large, triple-storey wooden pile built over the water at the creek head, which does food and refreshments for visitors – though if you arrive unexpectedly this may take some time to prepare. *Lamin Lodge* is a fine place to come by road, too, early in the morning, when you can watch the comings and goings of bird and human life in the *bolon*, and perhaps rent a pirogue by the hour to nose round the waterways. Besides the lodge, another, more distant, destination is the village of **MANDINARI**, situated near rice fields and seasonally lush jungle foliage, jewelled with a mass of birdlife that makes the creek look dead in comparison. Mandinari has one or two small shops where you can get soft drinks and something to eat.

Practicalities

In the high season half-day **boat trips** in the Tanbi Wetlands can be arranged in just about any hotel lobby for around D1000–1500 per person. The cheapest way of arranging the trip is to get a group together and fix up boat rental yourself with the fishermen on the shore close to the **Barra ferry terminal** in Banjul, or with the boat owners at **Denton Bridge**, the span that carries the Banjul–Serrekunda Highway across Oyster Creek, connecting Banjul to the mainland. Prices depend on demand and what the boatmen reckon they could earn from a day with the nets, but don't expect much of an outing for less than D500 per person, maybe substantially more in the high season. While it's always useful to have a guide acting as intermediary, try to establish exactly what is going to be provided and make sure the crew know what they're about. Being stranded up a dead-end *bolon* at low tide, miles from anywhere, in the middle of the day – or worse, with the sun going down – may give you more of the mangrove experience than you want. Take plenty of water and food, clothes and hats to cover up with, and binoculars.

By road, *Lamin Lodge* is signposted down a two-kilometre dirt track off the main airport–Banjul road at the village of **LAMIN**, close to Abuko Nature Reserve. Bush taxis run from Banjul to Mandinari, which is about 10km from Lamin and the main road.

Abuko Nature Reserve

Certainly one of The Gambia's best bits, the celebrated **Abuko Nature Reserve** (daily 8am–6.30pm; D31.50) is less than two square kilometres in extent, but within its carefully protected confines it preserves one of the last surviving examples of tropical riverine forest (also known as gallery forest) in the country. Whether you're an overlander or a Gambia holidaymaker, it's a must, and it's easily explored on foot.

Lamin stream (the tip of Lamin *bolon*) and its stunning necklace of forest was noticed in 1967 by Eddie Brewer, father of The Gambia's conservation movement, and was fenced the following year. The barrier is there to keep domestic animals, hunters and woodcutters out, rather than anything in – Abuko's three-hundred-odd bird species and dozens of varieties of small mammals and reptiles need no encouragement to stay.

Apart from pond-dredging, path-clearing and hide-building, the reserve as you'll visit it is more or less as it was found. While it includes small glades of savannah, the strongest impression is created by the magnificent **gallery forest trees**, spiralling up from the webbed fingers of their buttress roots through a canopy of intertwined trailing creepers and epiphytes to create dark cathedrals of evergreen vegetation.

The park

The whole walk around the marked trail through the reserve takes a couple of hours, but it could easily turn into half a day depending on your interest in the various bird species (more often heard than seen) and your curiosity about the more bizarre life forms on the forest floor. Early morning and late afternoon tend to yield the most wildlife sightings, as creatures take refuge from the midday heat.

You can expect to see **patas**, **vervet** and **western red colobus monkeys**, as well as plenty of – harmless – **monitor lizards** which dart across the paths and claw their way through the undergrowth. Most are small, but they can grow as long as two metres. With patience, it's normally also possible to spot **crocodiles** at the **Bambo pool** from the lookout at the **Darwin Field Station**. Watch for two distinct species: the larger, pale Nile crocodile, and the small, darker dwarf crocodile, which is critically endangered. **Snakes** are infrequently observed: the reserve boasts green mamba, puff adder, royal and African rock python, forest and spitting cobras, among others, but you'd be lucky (or unfortunate) to actually see one, especially a large python, and unless you start plunging through the jungle, they pose no threat.

At the top of the circuit is the unprepossessing **Animal Orphanage**, a rehabilitation centre set up by the Department of Parks and Wildlife Management in 1997. Primates and parrots form the majority of animals taken in, and those unsuitable for release are on display to the public alongside the orphanage's other permanent "pet" residents – one or two imported lions, plus hyenas and baboons.

Practicalities

The excursions organized by tour operators, sometimes more than thirty people at a time, are to be avoided if you're keen to get the most from your visit: shouting guides and chattering crowds shatter the tranquility of the place. The reserve is situated right by the main road from Serrekunda to Brikama, and it's easy enough to cycle down here, or take a **bush taxi** from Banjul or Serrekunda bound for Abuko, Lamin or Brikama and be dropped at the reserve's front gate. The **office** by the front gate has some good booklets and leaflets about the trees and wildlife, and you can leave bags or bicycles safely. Take something to eat and drink; alternatively, the café near the Animal Orphanage serves snacks and soft drinks. Bring mosquito repellent with you, especially during the rains.

Abuko birdlife

Well over **three hundred species of birds** are the chief faunal delight of Abuko. This is the closest patch of tropical forest to Europe, and each winter it attracts thousands of bird-watchers and hosts of **Palearctic migrants** (willow warblers, chiffchaffs, black caps, melodious warblers) to swell the numbers of its native species. Most obvious are the water birds – a couple of photo hides overlooking the stream and pools are usually occupied by murmuring birders. Look out for **kingfishers** (blue-breasted, Senegal, malachite and pied), the "umbrella fishing" **black heron** and two great bird-watcher's sights – the **painted snipe** (the male incubates the eggs) and the stunning **red-bellied paradise flycatcher**, with its thirty-centimetre-long tail feathers. You can generally see **hammerkops** around the pool at the start of the trail; in flight, their swept-back crest of feathers and pointed beaks make them look exactly like miniature pterodactyls, and their huge nests, courtship displays and trumpet calls are remarkable. In the clearings, wait to see **Fanti rough-winged swallows** and the occasional **shikra** darting through the light and, above the forest canopy, **hooded vultures**, **black kites**, swooping **bee-eaters** and **rollers**, and maybe **palm nut vultures**.

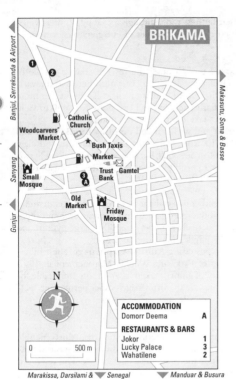

BRIKAMA

Catholic Church

Woodcarvers' Market

★ Bush Taxis

Market

Small Mosque

Trust Bank   Gamtel

Old Market

Friday Mosque

N

ACCOMMODATION
Domorr Deema   A

RESTAURANTS & BARS
Jokor   1
Lucky Palace   3
Wahatilene   2

0   500 m

Marakissa, Darsilami & ▼ *Senegal*   ▼ *Manduar & Busura*

Brikama

If you leave the Serrekunda conurbation on the south-bank road into the interior, the first town you hit is The Gambia's third largest, **BRIKAMA**, a divisional capital and a gateway to the upcountry provinces. It's famous for its rich musical heritage – many Gambian traditional musicians come from here – and its woodcarvers' market, a routine stop on tourist excursions to the area. It also has a low-key club and gig scene focused around *Jokor*, sister venue of the legendary Serrekunda club.

The only regular lodgings in Brikama are at the *Domorr Deema Mini Hotel* on Mosque Road (☎990 3302 ❷). A simple place with a local feel, it has four very small rooms with fan and shared shower; it's clean but can be noisy. There's also a small restaurant where you can sit at the streetside table and eat omelettes, chicken, steak, or rice and sauce at low prices, but for simple food you're better off heading for the fast-food places and chop houses scattered around the main road and market. One of the best is *Lucky Palace* on Mosque Road (not to be confused with the slot-machine joint opposite) which is great for omelettes, chicken, rice and *tapalapa* bread. *Wahatilene*, on the main road into town from Serrekunda, is also worth a try for drinks and plates of *domodah*. Nearby, *Jokor* occasionally hosts bands and local DJs, the best of which pull in crowds from all over Kombo district.

Further south, there's a fifteen-kilometre track from Brikama down to the Senegalese **border** at Darsilami, while the main road to Senegal branches off right at Mandinaba, a small place distinguished by a large, four-towered mosque.

Makasutu Culture Forest

Five kilometres east of Brikama (turn left at the totem pole after the Botrop School and follow the roads around to the right until you find it), **Makasutu Culture Forest** is a private forest park (daily 8am–4.30pm; D500 half-day, D700 per day if arriving independently). Run by a couple of English entrepreneurs, Makasutu is The Gambia's best-known ecotourism project. The forest edges a beautiful *bolon*, and groups of tourists visit for the day for organized bird-watching, canoe trips and forest walks, with a break in the middle of the day for lunch in an impressively designed restaurant area, while local Jola women put on a spirited show of drumming and dancing. Day-trips from the resort hotels, including transport, entrance and a visit to Brikama, typically cost around D1750. There's also a weekly Evening Extravaganza with a barbecue and entertainment by firelight.

There's a sizeable new luxury bush lodge, ⚑ *Mandina Lodge* (ⓦwww.makasutu .com; book through ⓦwww.gambia.co.uk ❽), on the far side of the site. Stunningly situated and designed, this is without a doubt The Gambia's most attractive place to stay, with a gorgeous, curvy swimming pool and accommodation in lodges built on the edge of the forest, on stilts over the *bolon*, or floating like anchored houseboats on the water.

Tumani Tenda

Around 20km east of Brikama, **TUMANI TENDA**, a Jola hamlet next to Kafuta *bolon*, has an enterprising community-run ecotourism project based on the *campement* system in Senegal. A stay at 🕈 *Kachokorr Camp* (☎984 5823 or 990 3662 🌐www .tumanitenda.co.uk ❷) is a great experience if you're seriously interested in immersing yourself in village life. The clean and very simple accommodation is outside the village, near the creek, in thatched huts. Some visitors come here just to enjoy the complete peace – the camp itself has no electricity or phones and vehicles seldom come anywhere near here. There are plenty of activities to choose from, though (D350 per group per activity), including guided tours of the school, plantations and vegetable gardens, on foot or by cart; walking in the community forest, where medicinal plants are gathered; exploring the mangrove creeks by dugout canoe; oyster gathering; batik-making and tie-dyeing. In the evening, the villagers can arrange a night of traditional Jola drumming and dancing, including the re-enactment of tribal ceremonies, for D850 a head. Meals are provided using locally sourced ingredients.

The coast from Brufut to Kartong

The Gambia's best beaches are south of the resort area. Given transport, preferably 4x4, you could get to virtually any part of **the coast** between Cape Point and the mouth of the Allahein (or San Pedro) River, where The Gambia finishes and French-speaking Senegal takes over. And if you're equipped for a few days' self-sufficiency, it's perfectly possible to walk the entire length of the Gambian coastline – less than 50km from Fajara to **Kartong**, The Gambia's southernmost village. All the beaches are within 3km of the road and a growing number of simple and pleasant lodges and beach bars, a number of them satisfyingly eco-friendly, are springing up along the coast and near the inland villages. A new paved road, the southern extension of the Bertil Harding Highway, runs all the way from the resorts to Kartong, making the whole area quickly accessible by bicycle, taxi, rented car, or a series of bush-taxi rides.

Brufut, Ghana Town and Tanji

The area south of Kololi is something of a development hotspot, with European-style housing estates and a swish new resort hotel dominating the landscape. Traces of the old ways remain, however: at **Brufut** beach, 7km south of Kololi, you'll see brightly-painted fishing pirogues bobbing offshore, or being rolled up the sand. Next to Brufut village is **Ghana Town**, a community of Ghanaian fish-driers and -smokers, not an uncommon coastal phenomenon in many parts of West Africa. If you're curious, you can stoop inside the long, low huts where the racks of blackening fish cure over smouldering wood. The finished product – *bonga* fish (basically kippers, and often good) – can be seen all over the district. Above the beach, and accessed by a steep path is the holy site of **Senneh-Mentering,** a meditative spot around a craggy old baobab tree on the cliff top, the air wafting with incense burned by the incumbent marabout. Local people come here for cures, consultations and peace, and it's a good place to visit at sundown. It used to be wonderfully isolated, but it's now somewhat overshadowed by the 🕈 *Sheraton Gambia Hotel, Resort and Spa* (☎441 0889 🌐www .starwoodhotels.com ❻), an upmarket place with the look and feel of a luxury safari lodge. As a low-key luxury alternative, there's 🕈 *Hibiscus House*, in Brufut village (☎995 8774, 🌐www.hibiscushousegambia.com ❽), an attractive and imaginative guesthouse that offers spa treatments.

Just north of the busy fishing beach at **TANJI** (also spelt Tanje), 12km southwest of Kololi, is the **Tanji River Karinti Bird Reserve** (daily 8am–dusk; D31.50), the country's only gazetted bird reserve, with a rich combination of habitats including mangrove, woodland and lagoon. The reserve includes the Bijol Islands, the country's only offshore islands and a breeding site for sea birds, which can be visited by arrangement with the Department of Parks and Wildlife Management at Abuko (Oct–March only; ☏437 5888). Highly recommended is a visit to the **Tanje Village Museum** (daily 9am–5pm; D100), by the highway south of Tanji village and fishing centre, which gives interesting insights into traditional Gambian village life and the workings of the family in an authentic traditional compound, along with displays of traditional foods, dyes and pesticides, and a nature trail. The museum also has a few basic roundhouses (☏437 1007 ❸) for those interested in participating in the goings-on at the museum, which include traditional music, weaving and metalworking sessions. Also in Tanji village is the area's most comfortable bush lodge, the *Paradise Inn* (ⓦwww.tanji.nl.paradise ☏800 0209 ⓦwww .paradiseinngarden.com ❹), which has roundhouses scattered in woodland next to the Tanji River, and is very popular with bird-watchers. Alternatively, deeper in the backstreets of Tanji village, is the *Kairoh Garden Guest House* (☏990 3526 ⓦwww .kairohgarden.com ❹), a peaceful retreat with simple rooms (some en suite), about 5km from Tanji beach. *Nyanya Safari Lodge* (☏779 7251 or 983 2934 ❷), on the beach and overlooking the mouth of the Tanji River, has a few basic rooms and is a scenic place to enjoy big platefuls of Gambian stews.

Tujering, Sanyang and Gunjur

TUJERING, about 7km south of Tanji and 4km inland, is a pleasant old village that owes nothing of its character to tourism or colonialism: whitewashed houses and a central crossroads with meeting place, mosque and market.

The long beach nearest the village of Sanyang, 12km from Tanji, is one of the best in the area – a broad, smooth sweep of firm sand backed by coconut palms, with a few mellow beach bars. It's sometimes called Paradise Beach. 🍴 *Osprey Beach Bar* is a popular option for food, on a gorgeous stretch of quiet sand. South of here, the brightest enterprise is the 🍴 *Rainbow Beach Bar*, which serves excellent fish, has a beach shower, and sometimes lights a campfire in the evening. It also has a few guest rooms (☏982 7790 ❸).

Continuing south, you approach the biggest focus of Kombo South District, Gunjur beach – a messy, active seafront where fish are more important than tourists and you'll probably be ignored. On the point north of the fishing boats is 🍴 *Sankule Beach* (☏448 6098 ❹), a relaxing, though slightly eccentric, bar-restaurant and guesthouse with a beautiful beachside garden that's noted for impromptu drumming sessions. To the south is another drummers' hangout, 🍴 *Kaira Kunda Bar and Restaurant* (☏998 5819), a friendly shack-type beach bar serving cheap drinks and couscous or barbecued fish, with a nonstop reggae soundtrack, and 🍴 *Gunjur Beach Lodge* (☏448 6065, ⓦwww.gunjurbeach.com ❹), an upbeat, welcoming guesthouse, close to a pleasant stretch of shore. Deep in the bush between Gunjur village and the sea is one of the area's most innovative lodges, 🍴 *Footsteps* (☏779 4855 ⓦwww .natureswaygambia.com ❽), which has set new standards for eco-friendliness in The Gambia and, though pricey for the area, has loads of appeal.

Kartong

Right on a glorious stretch of beach 2km north of the village of **KARTONG** is 🍴 *Boboi Beach Lodge* (☏777 6736 ⓦwww.gambia-adventure.com ❸), with a few very basic roundhouses and room to camp in a small palm-shaded compound. Opened in 2007, on another beautiful beach south of here is 🍴 *Sandele Eco-Retreat* (enquiries c/o *Safari Garden* ☏449 5887 ⓦwww.safarigarden.com ❽), an extremely promising hotel and learning centre with a beautiful, Indian-inspired design incorporating a wealth of ecologically sound features. Nearby, in the bush on the east side of the highway, the **Gambian reptile farm** (Ⓦwww.gambianreptiles.bizhosting.com; D50) is run as a small education and research centre – you get a good representation of Gambian snakes and lizards here. Overlooking the sand dunes near the village is ⚡ *Lemonfish Art Gallery*, well worth a visit for its colourful displays of West African paintings; it also has simple but spotless guest rooms (Ⓣ439 4586 Ⓦwww.lemonfish.gm ❸).

The attractions of the village itself include a **crocodile pool**, similar to the Katchikali pool at Bakau, though a good deal more atmospheric and sacred-looking (there's no money to pay for a start), set in a deep, shady grove. There are reputed to be a fair number of crocs, though why they stay in this lily-choked pond is hard to imagine. Women from both Kartong's communities – Muslim Mandinka and Christian Karoninka (Karoninka is a Mandinka dialect) – visit to pray and ask favours on Monday and Friday mornings.

The woodland and dunes on this side of the village are great for **bird-watching**; to find a local guide, ask at the KART (Kartong Association for Responsible Tourism) office in the village. They can also fill you in on the details of events such as the annual **Kartong Festival**, held in March.

If you have your own transport, you'll be able to drive **south of Kartong** to the last extremity of Gambian territory, a police checkpoint near the mouth of the Allahein River. A short drive from the checkpoint, you can turn right towards Kartong's isolated fishing beach, and left towards the riverside smokehouses where shark meat is laid out to dry.

Barra, Albreda, Juffureh and James Island

The visit to **Juffureh** used to be an inevitable business, when the *Roots* industry was at its peak and thousands of African-Americans made the pilgrimage to see the village they believed **Alex Haley** had been describing in his book. So convincing was the hype that the author himself seems to have believed the same thing – pictures of Haley with an elderly Kinte descendant are part of the myth of modern Gambia, used to boost the small country's respectability on the world stage. As an excuse for a trip to the **north bank**, the visit to the supposed birthplace of Kunta Kinte is still an enjoyable day out, but unless you do one of the organized *Roots* tours you'll find **transport** long-winded. Cycling is a possibility, but the seventy-odd kilometres there and back can be hard work, despite the flat earth roads, and well-nigh impossible if the roads are wet (if you rent a car, be sure it's 4x4 if there's any chance it's going to rain). There are only a few bush taxis a day from Barra to Juffureh (D20).

If you're travelling under your own steam, your initial target is an early morning **ferry** from Banjul to Barra (see box, p.289), a wonderful crossing at this time of day, with dolphins often plunging in the bow-wave. **BARRA**, the old capital of the Mandinka kingdom of the same name, no longer has much of interest except for the squat hulk of **Fort Bullen**, neglected on the grassy shore. There's only one hotel hereabouts, the grubby and unappetizing *Barra* by the ferry dock (Ⓣ779 5134 ❶).

Albreda and Juffureh

ALBREDA, also known as Albadarr, is down on the shore, and still has its old trading house with dangerously leaning walls and an immovable cannon pointing fiercely out over the river. **JUFFUREH**, a short walk away from the river and Albreda's immediate neighbour, isn't distinguished by any such monuments and, apart from a very basic sign, looks much like any other Mandinka village – a gathering of thatched, mud-brick cottages, *bantabas* and goat pens. It's hard to understand why this particular Juffureh (a widespread place name) or the local Kintes (a common Mandinka family name) should have been chosen by Haley as his roots. According to the book, the griot he met here told the same story as the one passed down through his family – but it was a simple and familiar history. It seems Haley had already written his Africa passages when he came here, and his account of Juffureh appears to be unrelated to the location of today's village. In the book, Kunta Kinte is surprised by a slave-raiding party, yet Juffureh is only a few hundred metres from the Gambia River and close by the sites of the trading stations of Albreda and Fort James, which would have been there throughout his childhood. On the other hand, villages can move, and ten generations or so have passed since the young Kunta Kinte went out to collect firewood and never came back. You can't be sure who is taking whom for a ride – the story has been a winner for both Haley and the Juffureh griots – but it is worthwhile participating in the pretence if you've read, and were moved by, the novel.

Most visitors to Juffureh come on an organized tour, on which they are escorted across the village and introduced to members of the Kinte family, believed by Alex Haley to be his distant cousins. If you arrive independently, people will assume you want the same, so make clear right away if you don't. First you pay a few dalasis to the guardian of the Juffureh maintenance fund and make a visit to the *alkalo*. Accompanied by a gang of children, you then proceed on a brief tour, winding up at the **Kintes' compound** to meet whoever's in, usually various Kinte sons, daughters and grandchildren. Photos are allowed, but you pay for the right to take them, and to do just about anything in this village. The **Exhibition of the Slave Trade** at the local museum (Mon–Thurs & Sat 10am–5pm, Fri 10am–1pm; D50, or D100 including James Island) is probably the most interesting part of the visit. It mostly consists of display boards, with lots of reading to do, but you'll come away with a good insight into what slavery was all about in this part of the world. There's simple **accommodation** next to the museum at the *Juffureh Rest House* (☏ 995 5736 or 770 1715 ❷), which is sometimes used as a base for Gambian music workshops organized by the French-run Kunta Kinte Association; the other place to stay is *Kunta Kinte Roots Camp* on the other side of the village (☏ 991 4508 ❷); it's slightly more comfortable but seems to receive few guests.

James Island

Less questionable history is out mid-river on **James Island**, though the very ruined ruins of **Fort James** are probably only for enthusiasts; the pirogue ride there and back should cost no more than D500 for up to six people. Originally constructed in 1651 by agents of the Duke of Courland (now Latvia and Lithuania), Fort James rode the usual roller-coaster of occupations, routings, sackings, desertions and rebuildings. It was seized by the English in 1661 when, in Britain's first imperial exploit in Africa, the Royal Adventurers Of England Trading Into Africa bundled out the Baltic occupants and set themselves up under the Royal Patent of Charles II, buying gold, ivory, peppers, hides and, of course, **slaves**. In one mercantile guise or another, the British and the **French** fought over the fort for more than a century. France held the trading "factory" of Albreda on the shore and continued slaving long after the British had opted for a new role as anti-slavers at the end of the eighteenth century. After 1779 James Island was rarely inhabited, and today the remains of the old walls and the strewn cannon are dominated by a grove of large baobabs.

Jinack Island

North of Barra, **Jinack Island** is part of The Gambia's Niumi National Park, which in turn adjoins the Parc National du Delta du Saloum in Senegal. Together, the parks protect one of the last remaining untouched stands of mangroves in West Africa and, inland, an area of dry woodland and grassland savannah. The shallow offshore waters provide excellent feeding for terns, gulls and other fish-eating birds, and the park is the stopping-off point and feeding site for seventeen species of warbler. Other wildlife in the park includes the elusive West African manatee, dolphins, green turtles, hyenas, endangered clawless otters and even leopards.

Occasional bush taxis serve Jinack from Barra (D20), dropping you a short pirogue ride away from the village of **JINACK KAJATA**, on the opposite side of the island from ✈ *Madiyana Safari Lodge*, the best place **to stay** on Jinack (book through Paradise Tours; see p.305 ❸). On the seaward side of the island, the lodge is a comfortable and relaxing beach hideaway with fine food and good nature-watching opportunities nearby. The easiest way to get there is to make arrangements with the owners to take you, usually by boat from Banjul: it takes about an hour to cross the estuary and sail up the coast by motorized pirogue. On the south side of the village, *Coconut Lodge* has bright, clean, colourful rooms (☎994 9067 or 995 48149 ❸), solar electricity, and hammocks slung under the gingerbread-plum trees.

3.2
Upriver Gambia

To travel **upcountry** is to travel upriver: the **Gambia River** is the country's very definition. With its headwaters 500km from Banjul in the Fouta Djalon highlands of Guinea, it snakes down in typically West African fashion, heading any direction but seawards most of the way.

The river's course is paralleled by the **Senegalese frontier**, which was drawn by compass at a cannon-shot's distance from the river bank. Inland, this extraordinary artificiality is madly apparent. Senegal, never more than 10km from the south-bank or north-bank highways – the only tarred road going upcountry – breathes all around The Gambia, creating an increasing osmosis of Francophone language, customs, food and music. At one point the Dakar–Ziguinchor highway cuts clean across the country, a traverse that, but for border formalities, would take only twenty minutes. Whether the Gambians like it or not, Senegal's influence looks set to increase. Nevertheless, while you might expect a frontier feel along the length of the country, there are plenty of short side-tracks off the main road, quickly getting you into districts of creeks, bushland and villages where traditional customs are preserved, more or less intact.

The principal towns of **Soma**, **Bansang** and **Basse** are all on the **south bank**. **Janjanbureh** (previously known as Georgetown) is on Janjanbureh Island, mid-river. The **north bank** has altogether more of a bush feeling, and for decades has lagged behind the south bank in terms of development, with little transport or electricity, and only a couple of important small towns at **Kerewan** and **Farafenni**. The north–south balance is changing, however, with the recent completion of the north-bank paved highway linking Barra with Janjanbureh, which is currently the best continuous stretch of paved highway in the country. The site most often visited on the north bank is **Wassu**, with its strange **stone circles**, reached easily from Janjanbureh.

If you've time to explore, upriver Gambia is interesting territory, with much to be discovered, not least for naturalists the **Bao Bolon Wetlands Reserve** and the tantalizing possibility of visiting the chimp-rehabilitation centre at **Baboon Islands**.

Travel practicalities
Unless you're heading for Tambacounda and the Niokolo-Koba National Park in Senegal, or else down into eastern Guinea, the interior of The Gambia is a bit of a cul-de-sac. Still, it's a relatively easy – and easy-going – district, and if you're just starting your travels in West Africa, not a daunting introduction to the region.

Road travel up the newly tarred route along the north bank, from Barra to Lamin Koto (opposite Janjanbureh), is the most straightforward way to explore. On the south bank, the road east of Kanilai is in a decrepit state and exhausting; only the hardiest bush taxis brave the potholes these days. Renting a car for a few days is an option, though you'll need 4x4 for the south bank or to get off the highway during the wet season. Otherwise, unless you cycle or walk, to do any sort of diversion you have to hope for an occasional bush taxi. As for **river transport**, while the steamers of colonial times are long gone, a few Gambian tour companies (see p.305) offer short cruises in large, rustic but comfortable pirogues, but these are not really a means of getting from A to B.

Cycling in the Gambia

"If you go cycling you will be a great attraction to all the kids you meet. Don't be surprised if you are asked for your bike, your drinking bottles, your glasses and more or less everything else you have. However the further east you go the more relaxed the people become. And the Gambian way of greeting – How's the morning? Fine, fine – is just fun."

Lukas Jonkers, Netherlands

Central Gambia – south bank

As you move eastwards from Banjul and the Kombo peninsula, the large concrete-block and corrugated-iron houses that set the scene on the coast are increasingly replaced with more attractive straw thatch and mud-brick compounds. Tripod water pumps – supplied by Saudi Arabia over German bore-holes – become a familiar sight in every village too. In the wet season or after the rains, brilliant emerald **rice fields** mark the shallow wooded valleys inland, and at the end of the growing season in August and September, anti-monkey watchtowers are dotted among the rows of groundnuts and bush on the ridges between the valleys.

The ruins at **Brefet**, mentioned in some tourist literature, are all but obscured by vegetation much of the year, and there's nothing to see of the "long-abandoned European trading post" which supposedly exists. Local people know of the site, but they'll be pretty surprised if you make the six-kilometre effort down the sandy track (turn off about 30km from Brikama) to look for it. More ruins at **BINTANG** (turn off about 45km from Brikama) are equally invisible, although you can stay overnight, if you don't mind forgoing some comforts. ⚓ *Bintang Bolon Lodge* (☎992 9362 or 448 8035 ❹) has attractive creekside rooms and a large *bantaba* restaurant, operating somewhat informally. Given a little notice, the staff will prepare a meal from whatever's available locally (fish is, of course, abundant) and they can also make arrangements for you to explore Bintang Bolon by canoe. Getting to Bintang can mean a five-kilometre walk from the highway with little chance of a lift, unless you have your own transport or catch one of the two bush taxis that leave Brikama in the early afternoon.

Kanilai

The Jola village of **KANILAI**, 95km east of Serrekunda and 6km from the south-bank highway, is the birthplace of President Yahya Jammeh. It's mysteriously hard to find on pre-1994 maps of The Gambia, but since Jammeh took control of the country in that year, Kanilai's fortunes have changed radically. What was once an obscure upcountry village with little to distinguish it now has a good access road, a luxury lodge, a large wrestling arena, a game park stocked with imported wildlife, a fire station, good healthcare facilities, electricity – and a vast presidential palace. The **Game Park and Zoo** (daily 7–10am & 5–7pm; D250), visitable only by vehicle, won't detain you long – the few remaining (imported) animals are not easy to spot in the long grass and the whole place reeks of presidential vainglory – but the village is well worth visiting at festival times or during wrestling championships, and is the venue for two days of exuberant celebrations and tribal rituals during The Gambia's biennial International Roots Festival and Kanilai's own biennial Cultural Festival (see p.274).

There's an attractive and upmarket place to **stay** on the edge of the village, *Sindola Safari Lodge* (☎448 3415 ⓔsindola@gamtel.gm or c/o *Kairaba Hotel*, Kololi, see p.297; ⑤), with landscaped gardens, nice pool and a good restaurant; this is an ideal place for peaceful relaxation, or to use as a base for trips. The lodge can organize fishing and bird-watching excursions, and local village visits.

Kiang West National Park

The south-bank road turns north over the head of Bintang Bolon, passing the **Kiang West National Park** (daily 8am–6.30pm; D31.50) to the west. This is one of the wildest, least-explored regions in the country, 110 square kilometres mainly comprised of dry deciduous woodland and Guinea savannah, but also containing mangrove creeks and tidal flats. Bounded to the north by the Gambia River and dissected into three areas by the Jarin, Jali and Nganinkoi *bolons*, the park is one of the most important reservoirs of wildlife in The Gambia, harbouring representatives of most of the remaining mammal species, including sitatunga, bushbuck and duiker, clawless otter, warthog and spotted hyena. West African manatees and dolphins are occasionally seen at Jarin *bolon*. The area also possesses an impressive range of more than 300 bird species, including the threatened brown-necked parrot, 21 birds of prey, all ten species of Gambian kingfisher and the booming ground hornbill.

Wrestling

Watching traditional **wrestling** (*lutte traditionelle* in Francophone countries), which goes back to the thirteenth century, is a favourite pastime of the Jola in general, and of President Jammeh in particular. Wrestling teams usually comprise members of a single tribe, and the Jola are renowned for winning most of the time – for some years the Gambian champion was a native of Kanilai – and for losing with good grace, a sure sign of a true sportsman in Gambian society.

Before a contest, drumming and whistling teams keep up steady competitive rhythms as the action builds slowly, the first few wrestlers pacing around the court flexing their muscles and psyching themselves up. The referee starts whistling the men into order and gradually the opponents pair off to start their bouts. The **object** is to land the opponent on his back as cleanly as possible. Dust flying, bodies bound with *gris-gris* – powerful amulets – and slicked with sweat and charmed potions to weaken the opponent's grip, this usually takes a few seconds. Bouts can last for several minutes, however, as contestants bluff and threaten, facing each other with backs bent and hands trailing in the dust to make for a good grip. Contestants are evenly matched, it being unusual for small wrestlers to be permitted to take on bigger men, however much the crowd roars its approval. The winner of each bout takes a triumphal turn around the edge of the arena, accompanied by his drum team, and counting on collecting a few tips as he goes (take a pocketful of small change).

Visitors are welcome at wrestling matches, which comprise dozens of bouts in the course of an afternoon; there's usually a small entrance fee. If you want to take **photos** there's no problem – it's expected – but you'll need a telephoto lens and fast settings to capture the excitement as the contest develops and the sun goes down.

The park's headquarters are at **Dumbuto**, where there is guest accommodation in plain, comfortable en-suite bungalows (for enquiries and to arrange to be picked up by vehicle, if there's one available, contact the Department of Parks and Wildlife office at Abuko on ☎447 2888 or the Kiang West warden on ☎986 0925 (❶). The most established base for visits to the park, however, is the village of **TENDABA** to the east.

🏃 *Tendaba Camp* (☎554 1024 or 991 1088 ❸) was the first tourist camp to open upcountry, in the 1970s, and still provides basic but adequately maintained en-suite chalets with mosquito netting (essential in these parts), a simple restaurant and bar, and a pool. Standard excursions from the camp are the enjoyable jeep safaris into Kiang West, and trips in a pirogue across the River Gambia to the creeks of **Bao Bolon Wetland Reserve**, a Ramsar-designated wetland, and excellent for bird-watching.

Getting to Tendaba without your own wheels, you could call the camp for a lift, or walk the 5km from **KWINELLA** on the main road, or possibly arrange to be taken in a local donkey cart. If you have to hang around at Kwinella for a while, look out for the group of silk-cotton trees in the village, the habitual roost and nesting site of hundreds of **pelicans** – cacophonous, and an extraordinary sight at close quarters.

Soma and Farafenni

A wretchedly bumpy couple of hours east of Tendaba, you're hit by the trashy, sprawling contrast of **SOMA**, about 160km from Brikama, where there's the opportunity to turn either left over the river into northern Senegal for Kaolack and Dakar, or south into the Casamance district. You can also turn south further upriver, but Soma is the furthest point at which you can easily turn north into Senegal. Soma is just a bustling truck stop, a charmless string of fuel stations, one or two inexpensive restaurants and bars and a few shops where you can get all sorts of Senegalese imports. Bush taxis whirl up the dust, collecting passengers for the 10km ride to the ferry crossing for the north bank and Farafenni. **Mansa Konko** ("King's Hill"), a couple of kilometres away to the northeast, is Soma's administrative quarter, quiet and uncommercial in exact proportion to central Soma's racket.

The best **accommodation** in central Soma is at the headquarters of the Soma Scout Group: the *Kaira Konko Lodge* (☎553 1453 ❶), on the Serrekunda road, with five breezy rooms, secure and reasonably well-kept, though unfortunately there's no generator. The other option in town, the *Moses Motel* on the Serrekunda/Trans-Gambian highway junction (☎553 1462 ❶), is a run-down Rasta place attracting a mixture of Gambians and shoestring travellers. If you've got transport though, at **PAKALI NDING**, the hamlet 3km north on the way to the river, the recommended 🏃 *TransGambia Highway Lodge* (☎553 1402 ❶) is quiet and a favourite of locally-based NGOs. The large compound provides secure parking, simple food can be provided on request, and there's a generator. Central Soma is a busy transport stop so there are plenty of chop shops and coffee stands in town.

The river is crossed by a simple drive-on-drive-off **ferry** that makes the crossing from the dock at Yelitenda to the tarmac at Bambatenda in ten minutes. Five minutes' drive north is **FARAFENNI**, whose big day is Sunday, when the *lumo* is held. *Eddy's Hotel* is the best-known place to sleep here (☎773 5225 ❷), with a courtyard that's a pleasant place for a drink, and decent-sized rooms (en suite, some with a/c), though the place badly needs an overhaul. An alternative that's more basic but in better condition is the unpretentious *Ballanghar Motel* (☎773 5431 ❶). There are a few chop houses on the main street (🏃 *Sunn Yai* does great chicken and chips) and the best bar is the unmarked *Assane's*, near the post office, serving Gambian Guinness and cold Senegalese Gazelle beer. You can buy fuel in Farafenni, and there's also a **bank** (but no ATM) and an **Internet** bureau.

Eastern Gambia

The condition of the south-bank road improves dramatically east of Soma, from potholed oyster-shell mix to hot, black macadam, as it passes through a fairly wild stretch of bush where baboons and other monkeys can be seen. If you're on the water, you can start looking out for **hippos** from this point on, as the estuarine part of the river ceases and the mangroves peter out, allowing the hippos to come ashore at night to graze. The no longer appropriately named Elephant Island, in mid-stream, appears to be the hippos' lowest grazing ground.

The village of **BUIBA** is the site of a long-established traditional curing centre for the mentally ill, but the first real punctuation in the new upriver scene is **PAKALI BA**, 50km from Soma, a village by the Sofaniama *bolon*. It's an attractive place, marked by a ridge of small rocky hills that are surprising in the undulating savannah. Pakali Ba is the source of a fable about a crocodile hunter called Bambo Bojang, who learned to control the Sofaniama crocodiles after being attacked by them; he's now the patron saint of the crocodile (*bambo* in Mandinka), and his descendants live in the area.

As the road heads on through mostly flat and open grasslands, the only place you might want to stop off is at **JARRENG**, 12km further on, where people make an impressive – and very cheap – range of palm beds, chairs and other furniture. The wharf at nearby **KUDANG TENDA**, 3km down a sidetrack, is the end-point of the popular boat trips which sail downstream from Janjanbureh, passing the River Gambia National Park on the way.

There's a convenient and particularly comfortable place to stay in this area – the National Agricultural Research Institute (NARI) **resthouse** (☎5678073 ❸) at **SAPU**, on the riverbank some 110km from Soma and 3km down the slope which lies 2km east of the road village of **BRIKAMA BA**. With air conditioning, fans, a kitchen and only seven rooms in the three houses, it often gets booked up.

A few kilometres downstream from here is the **River Gambia National Park**, also known as **Baboon Islands**. Three of the islands are home to rescued chimpanzees which have been reintroduced to the wild by The Gambia's Chimpanzee Rehabilitation Trust (🌐www.chimprehab.com), and are now breeding successfully. Landing on the islands is not permitted, but if you're passing by boat, you may see some of the chimps in the dense foliage at the water's edge. For close-up views of the chimps, make an advance booking at the project's 🏕 *Visitor Camp* (☎994 7430 ✉badimoyo@yahoo.com ❸) which has accommodation in safari tents with superb river views, and is by far The Gambia's most interesting upcountry retreat. As a guest, you can watch the chimps being fed from a boat, and then explore the river at a leisurely pace with a guide; you can also learn about the history of the project from its founder, Stella Marsden, if she's in residence.

Janjanbureh Island

The small town of **JANJANBUREH**, known in its colonial days and up until recently as Georgetown, is located mid-stream on Janjanbureh Island (previously MacCarthy Island). During the steamboat era, Georgetown was The Gambia's second town, a relatively thriving administrative outpost and a major upriver trading centre. The prestigious Armitage High School is still in business, but dismiss any notions of nostalgic, tropical languor conjured up by the colonial names: backwaters don't come much further back than this, and indeed Janjanbureh town remains the site of the country's main prison. On the north side of the island, there's a whole quarter of the town that's like an open museum of the old trading days, with tiled floors and ornate plasterwork disintegrating behind an onslaught of tropical vegetation. The big roofless barn usually labelled a "slave house" was probably no such thing, more likely a warehouse for perishable goods.

Much of Georgetown's significance was lost in the 1970s after the completion of the main south-bank highway and its fate was sealed by the closure of the riverboat

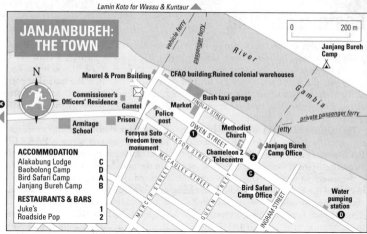

Lamin Koto for Wassu & Kuntaur

JANJANBUREH: THE TOWN

N

0   200 m

Janjang Bureh Camp

River

Gambia

Maurel & Prom Building   CFAO building:Ruined colonial warehouses

Commissioner's   Bush taxi garage
Officers' Residence   Gamtel
Armitage   Prison   Market   private passenger ferry
School   Police   FINDLAY STREET   jetty
    post   Methodist
Foroyaa Soto   OWEN STREET   Church   Janjang Bureh
freedom tree   JACKSON STREET   Chameleon 2   Camp Office
monument   MCCAULEY STREET   Telecentre

ACCOMMODATION
Alakabung Lodge   C
Baobolong Camp   D   Bird Safari   Water
Bird Safari Camp   A   Camp Office   pumping
Janjang Bureh Camp   B   station

RESTAURANTS & BARS
Juke's   1
Roadside Pop   2

MERCER STREET   QUEEN STREET   INGRAM STREET

Vehicle ferry to Sankulay Kunda for south bank highway

service. Judging by the closed shops and clubs, it's obvious that the islanders are continuing to leave. The main reason to visit is not for the town, but for the river environment – it's a peaceful place, rich in birds and good for river fishing, and it's fast becoming one of The Gambia's foremost **ecotourism** destinations. It's also a good base for visits to the Wassu stone circles.

Practicalities

The southern arm of the river, barely 100m wide, is crossed by a hand-hauled ferry from the south bank, and there's a corresponding ferry from the town, on the north side of the island, to the north-bank mainland. Janjanbureh's useful mix of **accommodation**, all either on or very close to the river, makes it a viable and laid-back place to unwind. *Janjang Bureh Camp* (☎567 6182 ❸; or book through Gambia River Excursions, see p.305) is a simple but charming and friendly lodge built in a beautiful grove of trees at Lamin Koto on the north bank of the river facing the island, and has excellent bird-watching opportunities. Boat trips are available and the camp's motor launch shuttles guests to and from the island for free. In secluded woodland at the westernmost tip of the island, away from the town, *Bird Safari Camp* has safari tents on the riverbank (☎567 6108 ⓦwww.bsc.gm ❹), plus rooms in huts, and is the only place on Janjanbureh with a pool.

Lodgings in the town itself include: the *Divisional Forestry HQ Resthouse* (☎567 6198 ❶), with attractive self-catering accommodation in a lush, wild garden by the river, intended for visiting researchers, but open to others when there's room; *Baobolong Camp* (☎567 6133 ❷), a quiet lodge with spotless rooms; and *Alakabung Lodge* (☎567 6123 ❷) on the main street, a basic but decent budget option.

Guests at *Janjang Bureh Camp* and *Bird Safari Camp* invariably make their lodgings their base for **eating and drinking**, and non-residents may visit these camps for meals, but there are also a few local-style options in town. *Juke's Bar and Bistro* serves cold JulBrew, soft drinks, some spirits and Gambian food. Also open late for decent Gambian meals and drinks is *Roadside Pop*, near *Alakabung Lodge*. There's also a clutch of simple eating and drinking places around the *badala* (wharf area) where the passenger ferries land and the bush taxis wait.

Wassu stone circles

WASSU (daily 8am–sunset; D50), a village 20km northwest of Janjanbureh, is the country's prehistory lesson, but it's no Stonehenge, so adjust your expectations accordingly. The hardened laterite pillars here, clustered in loose rings, vary from mere stumps to veritable menhirs weighing several tonnes and standing three metres high. They were apparently levered into place and then jammed upright with packed earth, hence their tendency to fall out of the circle. The burial places of senior personages, they have obscure cultural origins. Carbon dating has pinpointed some of them to 750 AD, but recent research indicates that the burials had taken place long before the circles were erected, suggesting the sites themselves were sacred. You're not likely to illuminate the mystery by asking local people – the migration of the local Mandinka clans into this area postdates the stones, and their oral history contains no clues. It's considered good form to leave rocks on top of the pillars, though again, no one knows why.

The white huts at Wassu are a small museum, with models and illustrations of how the circles and graves were made. If you're captivated by the antiquity of Wassu, you may want to go on to explore **other stone circle sites** on the north bank. There are stones on each side of the road at **Niani Maru**, the largest stones (up to ten tonnes) at **Njai Kunda**, and nine circles of pillars, including a bizarre V-shaped one, at **Kerr Batch**. And you could also pursue the quest for the stones into the Sine–Saloum region of Senegal (see p.227).

The easiest approach to the Wassu stone circles is from **LAMIN KOTO**, opposite the island on the north bank, and connected to Janjanbureh town by the vehicle ferry and the hand-paddled boats that take foot passengers across. From the north-bank landing, bush taxis to **KAU-UR** or Farafenni will drop you in Wassu a few hundred metres from the stones (this route is busiest on Mondays, the day of Wassu's *lumo*); alternatively arrange your own taxi for around D500 round trip. If you're heading to Wassu by riverboat, disembark at **KUNTAUR**, just a few kilometres away, from where you can reach the stone circles by bush taxi or on foot.

The eastern bends: Bansang and Basse

Before getting into the eastern tail end of The Gambia, you pass **BANSANG**, best known for its hospital, which was the only one in upcountry Gambia prior to the opening of new hospitals at Bwiam and Farafenni. The main highway bypasses the town, which is located on a magnificent river bend, with easily accessible low hills behind the town providing excellent views. If you're staying the night here, your best bet is the *Bansang Youth Centre* at the Basse end of town (☎991 0666 ②), with decent en-suite rooms. The alternative is the friendly *Carew's Bar*, offering basic accommodation in a few thatched huts in the middle of town (☎567 4290 ①). Bansang's **silversmiths** have a good reputation for making pieces to order – worth checking out if you're in the market for some jewellery and know what to look for.

Basse

BASSE – Basse Santa Su, in full – is The Gambia's last town, only 20km from the Senegalese town of Vélingara across the border. The town is a surprisingly animated centre that gets its energy from its proximity to Senegal: its shops tend to be full, and there are banks, bars and hotels, and a produce market that's particularly lively and colourful during the harvest (Jan–June).

Most **accommodation** choices in Basse are simple or run-down, or both, but have character nonetheless. *Traditions*, a crafts centre-cum-café housed in the 1906 trading post on the river (daily 8am–6pm), next to the vehicle ferry, sells West African arts, crafts and traditional textiles and has a couple of large but basic guest rooms (☎566 8760 ②). *Basse Guest House* (☎566 8283; ①) is perhaps the best of the cheap options, with a central location and a balcony overlooking the busy street below, but the shared washing facilities tend to be grubby. About 1km south of town in the administrative suburb of **Mansajang**, the *Government Rest House* is roomy, with an old-fashioned atmosphere (☎566 8262 ②). *Jem Hotel* (☎984 3658 ②), on the southeast side of town, has large but near-bare rooms off a pretty courtyard that would be quiet without the generator going. Basse's upmarket option is, in theory, *Fulladu Camp* (☎990 6791 ❸); it's in a great riverside location, on the north bank (there's a boat to shuttle guests across), and quite pretty, but water supplies are intermittent except when there's a big group staying and the pump is running.

The possibilities for **eating and drinking** include *Traditions* and *Fulladu Camp* plus ⅄ *Aminata's* and ⅄ *Aunty Flo's*, both in Mansajang, and both serving tasty Sierra Leonean specialities. As a busy transport hub, Basse is great for chop, street food and *afra*, one of the best chop houses being *Ebrima Ceesay International Coffee Maker*, in the centre of town.

Beyond Basse, it's just dirt track to **FATOTO**, with its derelict trading station on the higher-than-usual riverbank. There's a passenger **ferry** to the north-bank road, though connections back to Lamin Koto to rejoin the tarmac are sporadic.

Mali

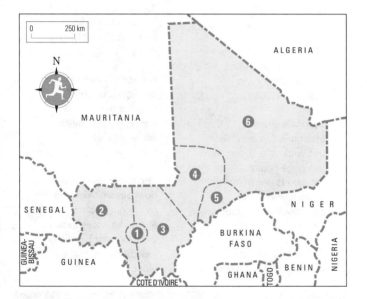

Highlights 322

Introduction and Basics 323

4.1 Bamako 358

4.2 Kayes and the west 369

4.3 Ségou and around 374

4.4 Mopti and the delta region 383

4.5 The Dogon country 404

4.6 Northeastern Mali 420

Mali highlights

✳ **The Bamako music scene** The home of international stars such as Salif Keita and Toumani Diabaté still provides great live-music opportunities at weekends. See p.367

✳ **Mopti** Mali's biggest river-port teems with trading activity and colour. See p.383

✳ **Djenné's Grande Mosquée** A masterpiece of Soudanic architecture, this huge Friday mosque is dominated by its towers and characteristic protruding beams. See p.394

✳ **Trekking in Dogon country** The best time for this is early morning, when the sandstone cliffs glow in the sun and echo to a peaceful symphony of birdsong, cocks crowing, and locals greeting each other on the footpaths. See p.407

✳ **Hombori** Mali's highest elevations consist of sheer mesas and unfeasibly needlelike spikes of rock. See p.421

✳ **The Niger River** Travel downstream from Gao by pirogue, inches above the water surface, brushing past bird-filled reed beds and herds of hippos. See p.429

▲ Togu-na (elders' meeting house), Dogon country

Introduction and Basics

Historically, geographically and from the point of view of the traveller, **Mali** is West Africa's centrepiece. Long a bridge between the north and the south – the Sahara and the forest – the area outlined by the butterfly shape of the modern country formed the meat of three great empires, the oldest of which was ancient Ghana, which flourished as early as the third century. The region's location on the main caravan routes and the banks of the Niger River later fuelled the rise of the powerful Mali and Songhai states, which lasted until the sixteenth-century invasion by Morocco. The political stability and unity of previous centuries was never recovered again.

Reminders of Mali's great past are remarkably intact. Camel caravans still make their way from salt mines in the Sahara to **Timbuktu**, where you can visit a fourteenth-century mosque built when the town was one of the world's most prestigious centres of learning and culture. Wooden *pinasses* continue to carry their cargo along the river from here to **Djenné** – a great commercial town that spawned numerous technical innovations including the Sudanic style of architecture now common throughout the region. Boats also ply the river to the Sahelian town of **Gao** – formerly the capital of the Songhai Empire and final resting place of the **Askia** kings.

Tempering the romance of the country's opulent past is the more immediate spectre of **poverty**, widely evident even in **Bamako**. Apart from a little gold, Mali lacks substantial mineral resources and is almost wholly dependent on its animal and agricultural production (especially its important cotton crop), rendering its **droughts** all the more devastating. In the early 1980s harvests failed almost entirely, and as much as three-quarters of the livestock was lost. People moved from the countryside to already crowded towns and, having lost everything, nomads were forced into a sedentary lifestyle and a cruelly inadequate wage economy. There has been reasonable economic growth in recent years, limited as ever by the vagaries of the international market for the country's main crop, **cotton**.

The country's reputation and prospects for development have been boosted by the largely successful Tuareg peace deal (see p.344), the establishment of real, if imperfect, democracy and the minor triumph of hosting the African Cup of Nations in 2002, which brought thousands of football fans to the country and saw roads and hotels upgraded or built from scratch. It's now easier than ever before to get around Mali and find somewhere reasonable to stay.

Fact file

The largest country in West Africa, the **Republic of Mali** spreads across nearly 1,240,000 square kilometres, an area five times the size of the UK and three times as big as California, with a **population** of around twelve million. The country was known as **Soudan Français** – the French Sudan – during the colonial period; the name Mali was chosen for its historical resonance for the Mande-speaking peoples of the region.

The country's **president** is Amadou Toumani Touré ("ATT"), elected in 2002 and re-elected in 2007 in elections judged fair by international observers. A military man, he leads the Alliance pour le Démocratie et le Progrès.

In 2007, Mali's crippling **foreign debt** stood at in excess of US$3.2 billion – more than eight times the value of its annual exports of goods and services (though not much more than a single day's expenditure for the US defence budget). **Cotton** production, **livestock** rearing and **gold** mining are the three largest areas of economic activity.

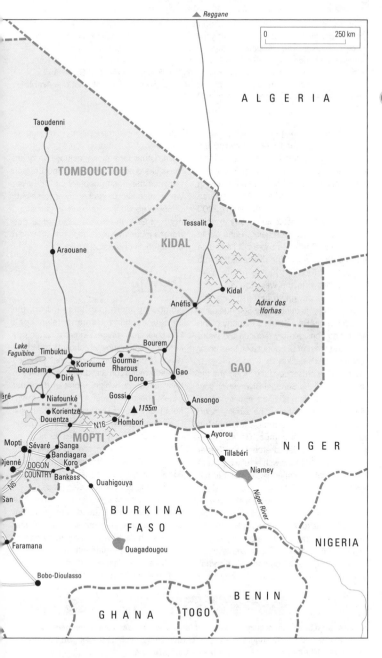

The same **names** crop up all the time and it doesn't mean everyone is related; these are great clan branches incorporating many strands, and complex class and caste-like hierarchies. The classic **Manding names** include Diabaté/Jobarteh and Traoré (which are historically related); Keïta (with its royal associations); Kanté/Konté/Kondé; and Kouyaté. **Fula names** include Bari/Barry, Diallo/Jalo, Sidibé and Cissé; and typical **Songhai names** are Maïga and Touré. Many people have at least one **Arabic name**, for example Fatima, Moussa or Ali.

The outstanding geographical feature of Mali is the **Niger River**. Known to the Greeks and Romans (who called it Nigris, a conflation of *niger* – "black" – and a Berber expression, *gher nigheren*, meaning "river of rivers"), the Niger long fascinated Europeans. But it took them nearly 2000 years – until the nineteenth-century exploits of Mungo Park, Gordon Laing, René Caillié and Heinrich Barth – to figure out its source and the place where the river emptied into the ocean. Today, 1300km of the river, from Koulikoro in the west to Gao in the northeast, is navigable at least for a few weeks of the year (though the Sélingué dam, upstream from Bamako on a tributary of the Niger, has considerably reduced the water level), and most of the population lives on or near the Niger's banks.

Despite the presence of the Niger, and the headwaters of the **Senegal River** which flow through the western tip of the country, much of Mali lies in the **Sahara**. The extreme north is desert, empty except for a few isolated oases and Tuareg camps. Between the desert and the river stretches the **Sahel zone**, mostly flat plains with scruffy bush and thin trees that are especially resistant to the arid climate.

Only a few ripples interrupt the overall impression of flatness across the country. West of Bamako, the **Manding Highlands** provide a rare hilly spectacle as they rise to heights of 500–1000m above sea level. In the southeast, the Dogon country's **Bandiagara escarpment**, which winds across the landscape for some 200km, is striking for the sheer cliffs that drop some 300m to the plain. Other formations include the gaunt mesa-like outcrops of the **Hombori region** between the Dogon country and the river, where dramatic pinnacles tower to heights of 600m above the surrounding plains and north of Gao, the inaccessible **Adrar des Iforhas** mountains astride the trans-Saharan chariot route of classical times.

People

Numbering more than three million, the Mande-speaking **Bamana** (also spelt Bambara) are the largest linguistic community in Mali. Though they're concentrated in the region of Bamako and Ségou, their influence spreads much further, due in large part to their language, which is one of the most widely spoken in West Africa. To the west, from the Manding Highlands to the Senegal River, the **Malinké** share a similar language and customs. They trace their roots to the **Mali empire** of the thirteenth and fourteenth centuries. Many Malinké have retained traditional religions, despite Islam's early penetration in the region and repeated jihads.

Several peoples live in the north. The **Songhai** are concentrated in the region of Gao to which they migrated in waves after the seventh century, probably from northern Benin. During the fifteenth and sixteenth centuries, they created one of West Africa's most powerful regional empires.

Photo permits are not required in Mali but, as elsewhere, **discretion** and good sense should be used before snapping away. In certain areas, such as the **Dogon country**, there are still many taboos associated with taking pictures.

The **Fula** – after the Bamana, one of the most populous groups in Mali – are spread across the country but are concentrated in the delta region between the Niger and the northwestern border with Mauritania – a historical region known as **Masina** (Massina is the contemporary town).

The **Tuareg**, of Berber origin, were pushed southward into present-day Mali after the Arabs spread into North Africa from the Arabia peninsula. The Tuareg mixed with sub-Saharan peoples and formed numerous independent, and often warring, clans. They still cling to their nomadic traditions, though droughts and conflict with central governments in the 1980s and early 1990s (not just in Mali, but also in Niger and southern Algeria) have forced many Tuareg to settle. They speak Tamashek, as do their former slaves, the **Bella**.

Also with strong northern ties, is the sizeable population of **Moors** (Maures), localized in between Timbuktu and Nioro. They too are of Berber origin, but adopted the Hassaniya Arabic language through their contact with Moroccans.

The **Senoufo** live near the Côte d'Ivoire border in the region of Sikasso in the south. In the sixteenth century, they formed small kingdoms at Kong, Korhogo and Odienné (now in Côte d'Ivoire), and when the Songhai Empire collapsed they began expanding northward. Their social structure is strongly influenced by the *poro* – an initiation cycle that lasts 21 years, during which time the men learn the secrets of Senoufo religion and philosophy.

The **Dogon**, who speak a Voltaic language related to Senoufo, occupy the Bandiagara

Guides

In Mali, far more than in most West African countries, it is common for young men to work full time as **tourist guides**. A guide who's touting for work will do his best to convince you that it's essential to be accompanied when travelling in Mali. With the exception of the Dogon country, this is certainly not the case, but a good guide can smooth your path and open your eyes to a lot of things you would otherwise miss. The usual rules apply: don't immediately hire the first guide to approach you, try to get personal recommendations, trust your instincts, ask searching questions, and bargain hard. Expect to pay around CFA3000–5000 per day for a guide around town, and about the same – but reckoned for each person in your group – for trekking guides. Additionally, you could negotiate over the guide's language skills (good cultural information will add immeasurably to the experience) or for an extra-long or particularly short day. It's also good to offer the incentive of CFA1000 extra if you're particularly happy with the day.

Local tourist offices have lists of qualified guides with official **ID cards**. These card-holders were given official competence tests in 2005 (blue cards for regional guides, yellow signifying competence and language abilities to guide anywhere in Mali). There is a plan for them to be reissued or for guides to be re-tested. Local tourist offices, too, may soon issue their own cards, partly because of forgery of the blue and yellow IDs.

When taking on a guide for more than a day, make sure it's clearly understood for what length of time you will need them, where you want to go during this time, and who will be responsible for expenses, including entrance fees, transport, food and drink, and sleeping arrangements. (In practice, many guides now quote a set daily per-person fee – somewhere between CFA15,000 and CFA25,000 to cover everything.)

Then, ideally, draw up a **contract** in writing and if possible have it approved and signed at a local tourist office. As a rule of thumb, the further your guide is from home, the less likely they are to know much about a place, so if you're planning extensive travels it's well worth considering employing a series of guides as you go along.

Finally, it's wise to agree a payment for your trip before setting out; pay part before leaving and the rest when you return.

escarpment east of Mopti. There is evidence to suggest that the ancestors of the Dogon may have come from the Nile Valley to their remote cliffs near the Burkina Faso border in the twelfth century. Here, they were largely impervious to the Islamicization taking place on the plains and, thanks to their tight social and religious organization, have maintained many of their ancient traditions.

Where to go

Mali breathes the very essence of West Africa, and has more good reasons to visit than any other country in the region. Remarkable visual and cultural contrasts in close proximity are Mali's hallmark. The **Niger River** is magnificent (unforgettably so at dawn) and offers the chance to make the last great river journey in West Africa, while the old cities – notably **Djenné** and **Timbuktu** – carry their ragged history with immense grace. Hiking through the fractured **Dogon country** – where traditional, non-Islamic culture has survived to a remarkable degree – is a goal of most travellers. If you approach it carefully, it's possible to get right inside this fascinating district and experience one of West Africa's most interesting civilizations.

Mali's **musical traditions** – and its music festivals as well as its international stars – are enough on their own to draw music lovers.

Mali is also the country best placed for onward travel to virtually anywhere in the region – by rail or road to Dakar, by road to the south-facing coastal states or northwest to Mauritania and Morocco.

When to go

It's tempting to sum up Mali's climate in two words – gaspingly hot. But this doesn't take into account regional, seasonal and daily variations. In the southwest, around Bamako, the rains generally last from June to September. In the northeast, from Timbuktu to Gao, they may arrive at any time during that period, either for a prolonged wet season or in a few unpredictable cloudbursts. The dry season takes over for the rest of the year. Between October and February the *harmattan* can blow for days at a time and it can be chilly in the couple of hours before dawn. Climate-wise, this is probably the best time to plan a trip, and it's also the period when the Niger is most easily navigable.

Getting there from the rest of Africa

Mali is positioned at the heart of West Africa, and its links with other countries in the region are improving. Apart from various flights to Bamako, there's a weekly rail service from Dakar in Senegal, several decent new highways from Burkina Faso, and a good

Average temperatures and rainfall

Bamako

	Jan	Feb	Mar	Apr	May	June	July	Aug	Sept	Oct	Nov	Dec
Temperatures °C												
Min (night)	16	19	22	24	24	23	22	22	22	22	18	17
Max (day)	33	36	39	39	39	34	31	30	32	34	34	33
Rainfall mm	0	0	3	15	74	137	279	348	206	43	15	0
Days with rainfall	0	0	1	2	5	10	16	17	12	6	1	0

Timbuktu

	Jan	Feb	Mar	Apr	May	June	July	Aug	Sept	Oct	Nov	Dec
Temperatures °C												
Min (night)	13	14	19	22	26	27	25	24	24	23	18	13
Max (day)	31	34	38	42	43	43	39	36	39	40	37	32
Rainfall mm	0	0	3	0	5	23	79	81	38	3	0	0
Days with rainfall	0	0	1	0	2	5	9	9	5	2	0	0

road from Côte d'Ivoire. Land connections with Mauritania, Algeria and Niger remain rough and unpredictable.

Flights

Flights into **Bamako** from other African cities are handled by a number of different West African airlines, with quite a few services routed via **Abidjan**, from where there are at least daily services. There are also plenty of flights from **Ouagadougou** (Air Burkina, five times a week; Air Algérie and Afriqiyah Airways, weekly) and from **Dakar** (Air Sénégal, daily). Other links are from: **Conakry** (Air Guinée, Tues, Wed and Fri); **Lagos** (Air Guinée, Wed and Fri); **Nouakchott** (Air Mauritanie, Wed); **Douala** (Air Cameroon, Sat); **Cotonou** (Trans Air Benin, weekly); and **Niamey** (Air Sénégal, Mon and Fri; Air Algérie, Tues).

As for flights to Bamako from other parts of Africa, these include: **Casablanca** (Royal Air Maroc, daily) **Algiers** (Air Algérie, four flights a week), **Addis Ababa** (Ethiopian Airlines, two flights a week); **Kinshasa** (Air Guinée, Wed); **Tripoli** (Afriqiyah, twice a week); **Nairobi** (Kenya Airways, four flights a week); and **Johannesburg** (South African Airways; twice weekly, changing in Abidjan).

Overland from Algeria

The **Tanezrouft route** from **southern Algeria** enters Mali at Borj Moktar/Tessalit and ends in Gao on the Niger River, from where a paved road leads to Bamako. See p.25 for more on trans-Saharan journeys, in particular on the **security issues** affecting travel through Algeria.

Overland from Niger

From **Niamey**, the main route to Mali follows the Niger River for much of the way to Gao. Niger's SNTV plus one or two Malian transport and freight companies provide bus and truck services between Niamey and Gao. Border formalities on both sides (Yassane in Niger, Labézanga in Mali) are less protracted than they used to be, but between Ayorou and Ansongo this is still a rough route, particularly in the rainy season when the *piste* can be washed away.

The simplest land connection between Niamey and Bamako is the route through

> For details on **getting to Mali from outside Africa**, plus important practical information applying to all West African countries, covering health, transport, cultural hints and more, see Basics, pp.19–28.

Burkina Faso, via Fada-Ngourma and Ouagadougou. All on tarmac, this is a long haul, but relatively comfortable and reliable.

Overland from Mauritania

The main overland route from Mauritania to Bamako starts at **Ayoun el Atrous**, with a good new road south to **Nioro du Sahel**, from where you can continue to Bamako on a road that is improved earth or paved most of the way to the capital. Another option is to get down to **Sélibabi**, just 60km from the Malian border, from where you can make your way to Kayes.

Overland from Burkina Faso

The quickest routes linking Burkina and Mali (bus and taxi details in the Burkina chapter, p.768) originate in **Bobo-Dioulasso**. From here, you can travel either via the border crossing at **Koloko** to **Sikasso** on the recently paved road (and thence to **Bamako** via the Ségou route or the less-utilized Bougouni route) or via the border crossing at **Faramana** to **San** (for **Mopti**) or **Koutiala** – again, all on surfaced roads. Direct transport also leaves from Bobo-Dioulasso to **Mopti** via **San**.

A rewarding way to enter Mali's **Dogon country** is by using the new, partially surfaced route there from Burkina – setting out from **Ouahigouya** and passing through **Koro** on the way to **Bankass**.

Some Burkinabe border posts close at dusk, but the main **Faramana crossing** north of Bobo-Dioulasso is usually open 24 hours.

Overland from Côte d'Ivoire

The main point of entry from Côte d'Ivoire is along the road from **Ferkessédougou** to **Sikasso**, linked by daily buses. The stretch of sealed highway from the Pogo/Zégoua border to Sikasso has been resurfaced and is in good condition. Traffic between **Odienné** and **Bougouni** (from where a good paved road continues to Bamako) is far less frequent.

Overland from Guinea

Most travellers cross from Guinea to Mali by bush taxi via the border crossings at **Kourémalé** or **Yanfolila**. Malian formalities are less of a hassle than Guinean.

The barge service that used to operate between **Kankan** and Bamako in the high-water season was suspended in the early 1990s, but the odd barge still comes down from Siguiri.

Overland from Senegal and The Gambia

Most overland travellers used to arrive from Senegal on the **train from Dakar**. But the service has been allowed to deteriorate by both countries to the point where a run three to four times each month is about the best current estimate of the service, with departures on no scheduled day and 44–48 hours being the normal duration of the 1200-km trip. There's more detail in the Dakar (p.200) and Bamako (p.360) surface-travel information boxes.

The latest fares are CFA25,480 2nd class, CFA34,320 1st class and CFA53,145 sleeper (wagon lit). Second class is not very dissimilar from first, and it's worth paying the difference only if you want more legroom and fewer companions. Once you're on the train, it's possible to upgrade to **sleeper** class assuming there are berths available (double cabins only), but the protracted border formalities take place during the night and you have to disembark, so you don't get much sleep in any case. Don't count on any facilities, food or water: you can buy street food from station vendors around the clock. Thieving is rife: keep an eye on your bags at all times.

The main reason for the decline of the railway is the huge improvement in the **road from Dakar to Bamako**, which is now paved through to Kayes, and paved or graded and maintained earth from Kayes through Diéma and Kolokani to Bamako.

Red tape and visas

Most nationalities need a **visa** for Mali; for addresses of Malian embassies outside Africa, see pp.29–31. The cost varies from around €28 to as much as US$80. You may need to show your yellow fever certificate when applying. If you're flying in from Paris on the French charter airline Point-Afrique, note that the airline routinely obtains visas for its passengers for a fee of €16 per visa (see p.22).

If you're arriving **overland**, it's advisable to pick up your visa en route from a Malian embassy in a neighbouring country, as they are usually issued with less fuss and sometimes less expensively than outside Africa. If you arrive without a visa you're likely to be refused entry: you might be permitted to obtain one at the nearest *préfecture* (this most likely means Sikasso, Kayes or Bamako) but there is no guarantee. **Drivers** will need Malian insurance and a "tourist visa" (carnet or *laissez-passer*) for their vehicle, and will need to get this extended at customs in Bamako unless driving straight through the country.

Immigration officials at some borders (Nayé, on the Senegal–Mali border for example) demand **passport photos** which are attached to the entry form.

Mali was once notorious for its red tape, and tourists were subject to the scrutiny and control of the dramatically named SMERT tourist organization – now defunct. Official hassles such as photography permits and tourist cards have since been abolished, and you no longer need to report to the police and get your passport stamped in towns north and east of Mopti (the **zone securité** designated during the Tuareg rebellion). However, very occasionally the police can still give you a hard time if you don't have such a stamp; to counteract this, local tourist offices stamp passports free of charge. This is especially recommended in tourist zones such as Mopti and Timbuktu (and it is, after all, nice to have a Timbuktu stamp in your passport). The government office of tourism and hotels (OMATHO) is adamant that any police irregularity should be reported to them, in line with their ambitious plans to boost tourism.

Costs, money, banks

Mali is part of the **CFA zone** (rates of exchange roughly £1=CFA880, $1=CFA450). The country is one of the region's more expensive destinations for travellers, especially if you choose to stay in comfort and eat at the better restaurants.

Costs

You'll manage most cheaply on the main highways, and especially in Bamako and around, where you can easily get by on CFA20,000 per day (CFA30,000 for two travelling together), but locations where goods have to be transported by 4x4 or portered in, for example parts of the Dogon country and the north, can see some prices doubling. In these areas, you should budget an extra CFA10,000 per person per day for guiding fees and supplementary transport costs. Conversely, these areas often have very inexpensive, basic accommodation.

Banks and cards

There are **banks** in most large towns throughout the country – and many different ones at that – but not all change foreign currency, and many that do will only process foreign-exchange transactions before noon. Almost all banks change euros, and most branches of the BDM and BNDA change dollars, though at a significantly inferior rate. The bank rate for euros and dollars is generally the same as on the **street**, the street being a lot faster and friendlier – though be sure to conduct the transaction itself in a shop or office where you can carefully count the CFA before handing over your money.

Using this parallel market, you may also be able to change **traveller's cheques**, which is worth considering as commission and charges on these can be outrageous and the whole process of cashing them fraught with delays and hassle. You can also change

money and sometimes traveller's cheques at **major hotels** – and indeed in certain shops and travel agents. Hotels usually add a commission similar to that at the banks, but often offer lower rates. Changing money informally, in shops or other businesses, may get you the best deal overall.

Thanks largely to the efforts of the BICIM in Bamako, **ATMs** are slowly being installed, both at their branches and in some of the larger hotels. Currently, most of these machines accept Visa only. Most large branches of BDM, BNDA and BIM give cash advances on Visa cards for a fee of CFA5000. Unfortunately this process depends on the phone system, which in some remoter towns can be unreliable, and it may take a couple of days before you get your cash. Don't be fooled by the presence of Visa stickers everywhere, as these often represent wishful thinking rather than real facilities. Besides cash advances, Visa cards are accepted by some of the larger hotels: MasterCard and Amex are not.

Health

The only vaccination certificate normally required to enter Mali is for **yellow fever**. Outbreaks of **cholera** occur from time to time, in which case this certificate may be necessary too. Chloroquine-resistant **malaria** is a serious problem – see p.40.

Bilharzia is another disease that remains all too common, especially in rural areas with slow streams and brackish water. Don't swim in such areas, especially if they're bordered by grass. Even stretches of the Niger can be dubious, notably in the dry season when the low waters become stagnant in many places. Elsewhere, swimming in the river is generally safe – you'll see people bathing, doing their washing and bringing their animals to drink. But if you come to a place where the locals aren't going into the water, it pays to do likewise.

Fuel prices

Fuel costs in Mali – CFA600 per litre for super, CFA510 for diesel – are average for the region, but you can expect to pay somewhat more if you need to buy from *bidons* out in the rural areas.

Tap **water** is heavily chlorinated and drinkable in Bamako and other big towns. In distant villages, wells and river water are commonly used for drinking and the purity may be suspect. Bottled water is available very widely, even in remote places like the Dogon country. Expect to pay CFA500 (in a shop) to CFA1000 (in a restaurant) for a 1.5-litre bottle. Iodine tincture, purifying tablets or filters used with local water are obviously a cheaper alternative.

Hospitals tend to be underequipped and overcrowded. For a serious problem, your best bet is either the Hôpital du Point G (☎222.50.02 or 222.50.03) or the Hôpital Gabriel Touré (☎223.99.86), both in Bamako.

Info, websites, maps

There are no Malian tourist offices abroad. In Bamako, the most useful function of the **Office Malien du Tourisme et de l'Hôtellerie** (OMATHO; ⓦwww.le-mali.com /omatho; see p.359) seems to be the policing of local guides and the establishment of tourist offices and guide associations around the country. So far offices have opened in Kayes, Ségou, Djenné, Mopti, Timbuktu, Sikasso and Gao (the most useful), and recognized guide associations exist in Ségou, Timbuktu, Gao, Bandiagara and Sanga.

The number of **independent travel agencies** has also increased significantly in recent years, mainly in Bamako and Mopti; many of these firms have websites and can usually provide leaflets. They're principally concerned with offering excursions along the Niger River, into the Manding Highlands northwest of the capital and out to the country's primary tourist attractions – the Dogon country and Timbuktu.

Recommended websites

ⓦ**www.afribone.com** General information and

The blog for this guide

For **travel updates**, news links and general information, check out ⓦtheroughguidetowestafrica .blogspot.com.

news from Mali – with many useful links, mostly in French.

ⓦ**www.maliweb.net** News, views, links and listings. In French.

ⓦ**www.friendsofmali-uk.org** Lively London-based organization.

ⓦ**www.visitgaomali.com** It may be only the Gao tourist office, but this is perhaps the most comprehensive English-language online resource for travellers to Mali, focusing on a lot more than Gao.

Maps

Probably the most useful map of the country (at least, as far north as the Niger bend) is the Reise Know-How **West Africa: Coastal Countries 1:2,200,000**, newly published in 2007. For the far northern desert part of Mali, you'll need their *West Africa: Sahel Countries* (same scale). The **IGN**'s *Mali* at 1:2,000,000 is at a slightly larger scale but dates from the early 1990s. The International Travel Maps' 1:2,400,000 map of *Mali*, published in Canada, is an alternative, but is often misleading. More detailed information is available from the IGN **1:200,000** maps, which are difficult to get hold of but indispensable when travelling in the desert. The **1:1,000,000** IGN series are good for general topography but, now forty years old, no longer useful for roads and towns.

The media

The Malian **press** is improving and is now considered amongst the best and freest in Africa (with occasional hiccups when the pride of big men is judged more important), with more than forty privately owned newspapers in circulation. There's a rash of daily French-language tabloids, of which *L'Essor* is the main state-owned paper. Other widely-read titles include the daily *L'Indépendant*, *L'Aurore*, *Le Republicain* and *Les Echos*. You will also come across several dozen magazines, any of which is worth checking out to get a feel for what's going on in the country.

As with the press, **television** and **radio** stations have mushroomed in recent years, to the extent that there are now more than fifty private radio and TV channels. **National TV** (ORTM) is broadcast from about 6pm to midnight on weekdays and from 10am to midnight on Friday and Saturday. In addition, international **satellite TV** is becoming increasingly common, especially in hotels. Government-controlled **radio** goes out in nine languages (though not in English). The big development, as everywhere in the region, is a plethora of small **FM music stations** operating from various quartiers in Bamako and other towns; Radio France Internationale (98.5FM), BBC Bamako (88.9FM; a 24-hour relay of the BBC African Service) and Africa No. 1 (the Libreville-based station, 102FM) are also available.

Getting around

The longest navigable stretch of the Niger flows through Mali and, for a short season each year, it's possible to travel by boat virtually from one end of the country to the other, stopping along the way at historic towns like Ségou, Mopti, Timbuktu and Gao. The regular boat service is almost unique in West Africa and is an exciting – if at times tiring and uncomfortable – way to see the country. Otherwise, there is a limited train service from Bamako to Kayes, plus flights linking the main towns and, of course, buses and bush taxis. Car rental is available from a few outlets, but is very costly.

Bush taxis and buses

Most Malians rely on **bâchés** (over short distances), **taxis brousse** and **minibuses** (short to medium distances) and **buses** (long distances) to get around the country. *Bâchés* are furnished with tightly packed rows of hard wooden benches filled to the brim with passengers, goods, and anything else that needs transporting, and are extremely uncomfortable for protracted journeys – which is probably why they generally only do short trips. Bush taxis and minibuses are more comfortable, though not quite as plush as in some neighbouring countries, and fares, usually fixed, are relatively high: CFA1600 from Sévaré to Bandiagara for example, a sixty-kilometre journey. In addition, drivers tend to charge quite steeply for baggage and you'll have to bargain hard.

Mali's privately run **bus network** provides a reasonably comfortable and practical means of travelling between major towns. Most companies run a one-person, one-seat system (often including an extra row sitting on stools down the aisle) and it's always a good idea to buy tickets in advance, and to claim a seat as soon as possible. The fare should cover one piece of luggage in the hold. Bani, Bittar and Binke all run decent services, while Somatra's older vehicles have a poorer reputation. Gana is reasonable for the west of the country.

As a general indication of **prices**, distances and journey times, fares tend to work out around CFA15/km and CFA1000/hour (eg the fare for the 200km, 3-hour trip to Ségou is CFA3000). All the bus companies seem to charge the same fares.

Trains

Apart from the **"Express" train** to Dakar, described on p.360, there are even slower **"Autorail" trains** – stopping at every station – between Bamako and Kayes. **Student reductions** apply on train fares at the beginning and end of term. Note that the railway line from Bamako to **Koulikoro**, the upper terminus of the Niger River boats, is currently served only by freight trains.

River boats

It's possible to travel over 1300km along the Niger River, between Koulikoro (50km downstream from Bamako) and Gao. The trip can only be made, however, in the period during and just after the rains, when the water level is high enough for the steamers – roughly from August to November between Koulikoro and Mopti, and from August to January or early February between Mopti and Gao. The exact dates vary each year with the timing and volume of the rains. Aim for months in the middle if you want to be sure of travelling by boat.

Boat schedules

The entire journey takes six days downriver from **Koulikoro** to **Gao**, and seven days back again. However, the official schedule applies only if at least two out of the three vessels are operable, which is often not the case. According to the schedule, one boat leaves weekly from Koulikoro on Tuesday at 10pm. Every third departure (ie the *Kankou Moussa*) sails only as far as Timbuktu, returning upriver from there on Sunday at 2pm. The other departures go all the way down to Gao, returning on Monday at 8pm. En route, sailings from **Mopti** to **Korioumé** (the actual port for the now high-and-dry port town of **Kabara**, and Timbuktu's nearest port) should depart on Thursday evening and arrive Saturday morning. In the other direction, boats should leave Korioumé Wednesday evening and reach Mopti Friday afternoon. In practice, the only fairly predictable elements of the service are the **approximate journey times** between ports, assuming no delays.

Fares and facilities

There are five **classes** of accommodation: **luxe**, a single or double cabin with (sometimes nonfunctioning) extras like a fridge, a/c and hot showers; **first class**, a double cabin with WC located just outside the cabin; **second class**, four people to a cabin with two bunks and shared washing facilities; **third class**, cramped no-frills cabins for eight to twelve people, depending on the boat (some cabins have fans and third-class passengers generally have access to the second-class showers and toilets); and a basic **fourth class** which provides no accommodation, just access to the lower deck.

From Bamako (Koulikoro), first-class **fares** are around CFA57,000 to Mopti, CFA101,000 to Timbuktu and CFA129,000 to Gao; from Mopti, expect to pay CFA46,000 to Timbuktu. Third-class fares are about forty percent of these prices, while travelling fourth class costs only about a tenth of the corresponding first-class fare. If you're on a tight budget, third class is probably the best option.

Food is served three times a day in separate dining rooms for each class, and the price is included in luxe, first, second and third class. Each boat has a bar. Only in the luxe, first- and second-class dining rooms can you get **bottled water**.

Pirogues and pinasses

Anywhere along the Niger, and virtually year-round, you can find local **pirogues** to get you from A to B; details are given throughout the chapter. These canoe-like vessels are rowed – or poled much of the time – and sometimes venture quite long distances with large consignments of rock salt or other goods. As for fares, after protracted negotiations you can expect to pay CFA3000–5000 per person per day (50–100km) with shared food. They provide the most rewarding, if basic, means of seeing the Niger – from a few inches above its surface.

Along certain stretches of the river, it's also possible to get **pinasses**, large handmade motorized boats covered with a woven-mat awning. They can be privately rented for longer journeys (from Mopti to Timbuktu, for example, you'd expect to pay CFA400,000–500,000 for a boat carrying from six up to twenty people) with mattresses for you to sleep on board, and food provided. Alternatively, you can pay for a seat in a public *pinasse* that primarily carries goods; it will be moored every night and you sleep on the riverbank nearby. Costs (including a share of the communal rice bowl) are CFA15,000 or so for Mopti–Timbuktu or Timbuktu–Gao. These seem to be the set prices for tourists; note, however, that locals will pay about a third of that for the same trip.

Despite the **basic conditions**, *pinasse* travel has been operating for centuries along the Niger and retains a nostalgic attraction. The experience can turn out to be either very worthwhile or gruelling and never to be repeated, depending on the vessel, the route, the goods on board and the crew. Be prepared for frequent **delays**: your journey can take twice as long as expected if the *pinasse* is heavily laden and if water levels are so low that the boat runs aground. This often happens towards the end of the dry season when the options for transporting freight begin to close down for another nine months. It's not unknown for boats to sink, too: **accidents**, and even drownings, are not infrequent.

You'll need snacks, water-purifying tablets, plenty of absorbing reading matter and infinite patience.

Car rental and driving

There are several **car rental agencies**, with offices usually located in the smarter hotels; details can be found in the relevant sections. It's also possible to rent vehicles more informally by asking around. A 4x4 vehicle is essential for reaching places not served by public transport, or with infrequent connections. Rental companies will assume that you will want a **driver** with your vehicle and will often insist. In any case, it's a wise precaution: given the sometimes awful state of the country's roads and the hair-raising traffic of the towns, driving yourself can be stressful. Prices start at around CFA50,000 per day.

Domestic flights

With the demise of the country's national carrier, Air Mali, in 2003, the domestic air schedule has been skeletal for some time. However, two new companies have recently been established which go a long way to fill the gaps. **Mali Air Express** (**MAE**) currently operate flights out of Bamako to **Timbuktu**, **Mopti**, **Kayes**, **Yélimané** and **Nioro**. They have two planes and are regarded as the more reliable company. The other airline, **Compagnie Aerienne du Mali** (**CAM**) operate only one plane and one service (**Timbuktu** via **Mopti**), so if that breaks down you can get stuck. There are regular complaints about overbooking and cancelled flights. One-way **fares** are similar on both airlines: approximately CFA60,000 for Bamako–Mopti, and CFA65,500 for Mopti–Timbuktu.

Accommodation

Smaller towns have at least one **hotel** of some description with hot water, air conditioning and a TV lounge, while larger towns usually have at least one luxury address. If you're on a tight budget, you'll also find a good range of options in between, including simple *campements*, sleeping on the roof in hotels

or *auberges*, or, in many cases, the option of putting up your own tent. Note that the **"rail" hotels** in railway towns tend to be operated on a half-board basis, and they automatically include dinner and breakfast in the rate. Also, look out for a clutch of new **designer hotels** – in Mopti, Djenné and Timbuktu.

In budget accommodation (price codes ❶–❸), you'll generally find dorm beds, some provision for camping on site or sleeping on the roof (mattress and sometimes mosquito net provided), and basic rooms, sometimes s/c. Rooms in mid-range establishments (❹–❻) are s/c, with fan or air conditioning and sometimes a TV and, at the upper end of the range they are quite comfortable, often have their own restaurant and sometimes even a pool. The expensive hotels (❼ and ❽) have most of the mod-cons and luxuries you'd expect.

Eating and drinking

Mali's main staple is **rice**, often eaten with a thin beef broth mixed with tomatoes – *riz gras*. There are numerous regional variations on this common stand-by. In the Dogon country, **millet** (*petit mil*) provides the basis of nearly every meal and is prepared in hundreds of ways. Most commonly, it's served in a boiled mush called **tô**, and eaten with sauce, often made from local onions. For breakfast it's fried in small round patties known as *beignets de mil*. The Senoufo consume rice and millet dishes less than other peoples, and tend more towards tubers (**yam** and **cassava**).

Food in Djenné has retained a strong Moroccan flavour. A type of **couscous** is eaten here, as is a noodle-like dish known as

---

Accommodation price codes

All accommodation prices in this chapter are coded according to the following scale, whose equivalent in pounds sterling/US dollars is used throughout the book. Prices refer to the rate you can expect to pay for a room with two beds, including Mali's CFA500 tourist tax. Single rooms, or single occupancy, will normally cost at least two-thirds of the twin-occupancy rate. For further details, see p.55.

❶ Under CFA5000 (under £5/$10)
❷ CFA5000–10,000 (£5–10/$10–20)
❸ CFA10,000–15,000 (£10–15/$20–30)
❹ CFA15,000–20,000 (£15–20/$30–40)

❺ CFA20,000–30,000 (£20–30/$40–60)
❻ CFA30,000–40,000 (£30–40/$60–80)
❼ CFA40,000–50,000 (£40–50/$80–100)
❽ Over CFA50,000 (over £50/$100)

kata, which is accompanied by meat. **Nempti** is a type of *beignet* mixed with hot peppers, while **fitati** is a kind of thin pancake. During special celebrations people make a pastry called **tsnein-achra** from rice flour and honey. The Tuareg make a variant of couscous from a wild grain known as *fonio* or "hungry rice".

All along the river, of course, people eat **fish** – one of the most common varieties is *capitaine* (Nile perch), in these parts usually a boney little creature that's quite good when deep-fried in oil or grilled over coals. In the northern regions the Fula herders, **beef**, **mutton** and **goat** outsell fish, although for many people red meat is still a luxury. Just about everywhere in Mali, *gargotes* and street-food sellers charcoal-grill marinated meat **brochettes** (kebabs), served with French bread and a piquant sauce.

Drinking

Beer is expensive relative to other countries in the region, at CFA900 for a large bottle (Castel is the main Malian brand) or CFA500 for a small one, rising to CFA1500 for a large beer in the remoter north and east, including parts of the Dogon country (where soft drinks, called **sucreries**, can also be relatively pricey at around CFA750 a bottle). **Home-brewed beer**, made from corn or millet, is common to many different peoples – especially non-Muslims like the majority of Dogon and Senoufo – and is known variously as *konjo*, *dolo* or *chapalo*. Lastly, sweet, green China **tea** is drunk all over the country, but with particular devotion in the north, and above all by the Tuareg.

Communications

If it were not for the mushrooming of Internet cafés across the country, contact with Europe and the rest of the world would be slow, even out of Bamako. Though inexpensive to send, **letters** usually take their time arriving: estimate two weeks from the capital, and as much as a month from the provinces.

You can make IDD calls from private, metered booths in **télécentres**, which are reasonably common in any small town; you pay afterwards for the units used. It takes a while to get through, though, and it's often easier (if more expensive) to call from the big hotels. Alternatively you can use one of the many card phones spread across the country. Sotelma, the Malian telecom company, sells cards of fifty units, which can be used for both national and international calls. Note that Malian phone numbers do not have area codes.

Mobile phones are as popular in Mali as they are elsewhere in Africa. The domestic operator Malitel, the French network Ikatel, and the global company Orange are the three main network providers, and together they cover all the main towns and cities, though away from the population centres coverage can be patchy.

Prices for **Internet access** vary enormously, from CFA500 per hour at some places in Bamako to CFA1500 where there's only one outlet in town. Connection speeds also vary; they're usually best at Internet cafés operated by Sotelma or CLIC (Centres Local d'Information et de Communication). Note also that many premises with computers advertise Internet access – even when they don't yet have it.

Opening hours, public holidays and festivals

Businesses, including banks, tend to open from Monday to Thursday between 8am and noon, and then from 2pm to 5pm, while on Friday they're open between 8am and noon. Many business are also open on Saturday afternoons. **Government offices** are open from Monday to Thursday between 7am and noon and between 2pm and 4.30pm; on Friday they open from 7am to noon.

Muslim holidays are celebrated with fervour in Mali, and during the month of Ramadan many businesses close down during the daytime – though night-time feasts redress the balance. See p.63 for approximate dates. Christian celebrations – Christmas Day and Easter – are also public holidays, as are New Year's Day and Labour Day (May 1). During Christmas and New Year

Mali's **IDD** country code is ☎223.

it's on the nights of *la veille* (Dec 24) and *le trente-et-un* (Dec 31) that Malians really let their hair down. Secular holidays include the Fête de l'Armée (Jan 20), the Fête de Martyrs (March 26), Africa Day (May 25) and National Day (Sept 22).

The **Festival au Désert**, a unique Tuareg music event, has taken place early each January since 2001, north of Timbuktu, while in Ségou, the **Festival sur le Niger**, in early February, has also become established, and more regional centres are likely to follow suit with their own festivals in the first quarter of the year. For more on the Mali music scene, see p.347.

Crafts and shopping

There's no shortage of **souvenirs** to spend your money on in Mali. A good place to begin looking is the Centre Artisanal in Bamako (see p.364), which has a wide selection of items on sale from all over the country. While it may not be the cheapest place, it does give you a good idea of what's out there. Regional specialities include silver and nickel **Tuareg jewellery** and the **leatherwork** of Timbuktu and Gao. **Pottery** is popular in Ségou, while in the Dogon region you'll find indigo-dyed **blankets** and **cloths**, as well as some extraordinary wooden carved **fetishes** and **masks**. Note, however, that these latter items may be a) very heavy and b) antique, which leaves you open to the charge of pillaging indigenous cultures. Think carefully about the repercussions before buying, as customs officials are increasingly sensitive to the issue. Otherwise, **bogolan** (striking, mud-dyed cloth) can be picked up cheaply all over, while collectors of **musical instruments** are well served, with *djembes* and *balafons* inexpensive. Similarly, **hat** collectors will delight at the three-tassled cloth affairs of the Dogon and the huge conical leather numbers of Fula farmers.

Crime and safety

Many travellers are pleasantly surprised at just how safe Mali is. True, there are certain areas of **downtown Bamako** – square Lumumba, the railway station, the bridges – that are best avoided after dark, especially if you're carrying valuables – but this is to be expected. The official encouragement of tourism in recent years means that **tourist offices** in large towns are ready and able to help if you get into any difficulties, while the **police**, having been notoriously difficult in the past, keep a generally low profile.

In terms of broader **security issues**, it's considered safe to travel throughout the country, with the possible exception of the far north where there is still discontent among some sections of the Tuareg community and roadside **banditry** remains a problem. If you have any plans to head into the Sahara north of the Timbuktu–Gao road (for example to Araouane, Kidal or Tessalit), you should speak to someone who has recently travelled there and check with the police first.

Emergencies

Police ☏017, fire ☏018.

Gender issues and sexual attitudes

Women travellers don't find Mali a special hassle. In the West African context, there's a good deal of proud, feminine freedom in the country, coupled paradoxically with the highest incidence of initiatory genital mutilation, including the brutal practice of infibulation. As many as ninety percent of women are affected, and although health-care organizations, such as Plan International, run community education projects to increase awareness, progress is slow. Other statistics are equally depressing: a third of deaths among Malian women of child-bearing age are pregnancy-related, and one in ten women die during childbirth or as a result of an unsafe abortion. Mali has the second highest birth rate in the world (surpassed only by neighbouring Niger), and the eighth highest infant-mortality rate. Only 25 percent of girls receive more than four years of schooling and it's normal for them to be married by the age of 16, with ninety percent married before 20.

Gay life in Mali is slightly less constricted than in most other countries in the region: there are no laws against gay sexual relations, on the other hand there are no proper anti-discrimination laws either. Gay men may notice a low-key acceptance in the larger towns, but nothing like a gay scene.

Entertainment and sports

Mali is world famous for its **music**. The singer Salif Keita and late, great guitarist Ali Farka Touré stand out, but other musicians such as Oumou Sangaré and Habib Koité also enjoy international recognition. There's a wealth of live music and dance on offer in Bamako; elsewhere, your best chance of hearing traditional music is to happen to be around for a festival (See "Opening hours, public holidays and festivals", above).

Two towns which are particularly famous for their Manding musical traditions are **Kita** and **Kela**, both of which have an unusually high population of *jelis* (or griots) who may be willing to give lessons or private performances.

Cinema

Malian **cinema** thrives: two of the most famous names are Souleymane Cissé, who made his international name with the memorable *Yeelen* (1986), and Cheik Oumar Sissoko, who has served as minister of culture. For more on Malian film, see p.352.

Sports

Since Mali hosted the African Cup of Nations in 2002, and won West Africa's **Amilcar Cabral Cup** in 2007, **football** has assumed an increasingly high profile in the country, and most towns have regular games. Bamako's Djoliba AC, Stade Malien and Cercle Olympique are the big teams to watch out for. Overseas, star players like Frédéric Kanouté (West Ham, Spurs and most recently Sevilla) and Mahamadou Diarra (Real Madrid) showcase Mali's growing pool of talent.

Traditional **wrestling** (*la lutte*) is still popular in Mali but, with football on the ascendant, traditional bouts no longer command the crowds and excitement of even a decade ago.

Wildlife and national parks

Mali's vast expanses of **bush and swamp** used to provide a major sanctuary for West African wildlife, with the large predators – **lions**, **leopards**, **cheetahs**, **hyenas** – and many of the large prey mammals – from buffalo and warthog to hartebeest and reedbuck – present in significant numbers. Habitat destruction and massive over-hunting has seen the numbers seriously decline and the viability of surviving populations of many species in real jeopardy. **Hippos** are, however, still relatively common all along the course of the Niger, and Mali's **elephants** also appear to be surviving and even increasing in numbers. There are herds in the region of the Parc Nationale de la Boucle du Baoulé and a separate population of 600 or more range seasonally across the dry lands between northeast Burkina and the Gourma district around Gossi, west of Gao. These latter "desert elephants" are protected in part by the presence of the Tuareg, who traditionally don't hunt them. Their migration cycle is regular and, if you have time, it's not difficult to find them, though you need a 4x4 vehicle to do so.

Mali's main national park, the **Parc National de la Boucle du Baoulé**, suffers from inaccessibility and a lack of infrastructure and is not much visited. It's believed a small population of chimpanzees is still resident here. **Bafing**, Mali's other national park, is even more remote and unvisited.

A brief history of Mali

The outstanding features of Mali's history are the old empires. Much of the modern country was part of the old Mali or Manding empire (see p.628) at the time of its maximum expansion, from Kita to Djenné and Timbuktu, in the thirteenth and fourteenth centuries. When the Moroccans crushed the Askia dynasty of the **Songhai Empire** in 1591 (see p.424), they left the region in a political vacuum, partially filled from time to time by the rapid rise and fall of mini-empires. The first was the kingdom of **Ségou** (written "Segu" in many histories; see p.375), founded in the seventeenth century and ultimately eclipsed by the Fula jihad that spread from Masina (Macina) in the 1820s, led by Cheikou Ahmadou Hammadi Lobbo – a religious zealot inspired by Uthman Dan Fodio's religious war that had spread from Sokoto in present-day Nigeria. And from Senegal, the Tukulor marabout **El Hadj Omar Tall** launched his own holy war, setting out in 1852 to conquer animist Mandinka districts to the east of his realm and then moving on to conquer and absorb Masina in its turn.

Arrival of the French

El Hadj Omar Tall's Tukulor cavalry spread across the Niger belt with lightning speed, carving out an empire headquartered at Ségou that extended from Masina to Bandiagara. Increasingly, it came to be seen as a threatening obstacle to the designs of French colonials in St-Louis, Senegal, bent on commercial and military penetration into the Soudanese interior.

The governor of Senegal, **General Louis Faidherbe**, opted in the first instance for a diplomatic response to Tukulor expansion and sent an expeditionary mission to Ségou. Arriving in 1868, the French signed a treaty with the new ruler **Ahmadou**, son of El Hadj Omar who had been killed in battle in 1864. By 1880, the French were back to renew the treaty, but, although Ahmadou was increasingly suspicious of their motives and this time had the emissary locked up, it was too little too late. **French forces** had now advanced as far east as Kita and brought with them the parts of an armed gunboat which they assembled and launched at Koulikoro. They thus managed to control the river as far down as Mopti. But the Tukulor Empire based at Ségou refused to cede. Finally, the capital fell in 1890 and the

other towns in the interior toppled like dominos in their turn – Djenné and Bandiagara in 1893, and, after fierce Tuareg resistance, Timbuktu in 1894.

Tieba and Samory

Meanwhile, resistance was growing in the Senoufo country around Sikasso. The Malinké chief **Samory Touré** had been carving out his own small empire since 1861 and had taken the Senoufo strongholds of Kong, Korhogo and Ferkessédougou. He ran into conflict with **Tieba**, king of Sikasso. Samory attacked Sikasso in 1887 and besieged it for fifteen months, but the town resisted. The French, under Lieutenant Binger, watched the rivalry with close attention and eventually allied themselves with Tieba, helping him reinforce his regional power.

Tieba died in battle in 1893 and was replaced by his son **Ba Bemba**. The new king, however, mistrusted the French and refused to follow through on the kingdom's commitment to help the colonials destroy Samory's influence. In May 1898 the French attacked and took Sikasso. The king committed suicide, escaping the fate of Samory, who was captured in September as he dashed southwest towards Liberia, hoping to get more weapons from the British. The same year, El Hadj Omar's son Ahmadou died in exile in Sokoto. France was now the sole power in the region.

The French Soudan

Confident of eventual victory, the French had already declared the **Soudan** an autonomous colony in 1890. Later it was incorporated into the colony of **Haut Sénégal–Niger**, of which **Bamako** was made the capital in 1908. The railway had been extended from Dakar to Koulikoro in 1904 and, with the creation of the Office du Niger – a national agricultural agency based in Ségou – the French hoped to turn Mali into the breadbasket of West Africa and even make the colony turn a profit through the production of cash crops like groundnuts and cotton. *Pistes* were traced through the interior to facilitate the transportation of crops and, in 1932, a dam was built near Ségou in the hope of turning hundreds of thousands of square kilometres into irrigable land.

From the beginning, however, these ambitious designs were frustrated. In the first place, the colonial authorities soon ran into a shortage of labour which they solved by forcibly recruiting volunteers from neighbouring countries, notably the region of the Upper Volta (Burkina Faso). In addition, much of the soil in the Soudan turned out to be too poor to support cotton plants and rice was substituted. Finally, the Office du Niger had restrictive financial limitations. As a result, only a small fraction of the territory destined to become an agricultural miracle was ever exploited. Not that it made much difference to Malians at the time, since the production was almost exclusively destined for export to France.

World Wars I and II

Of all the colonies in the **AOF** (Afrique Occidentale Française), Mali paid the highest price with the outbreak of World War I. The Bamana, especially, were recruited in large numbers to fill the ranks of the famous **Tirailleurs Sénégalais**. These infantry soldiers experienced European war as early as 1908 when they had been used by France to "pacify" Morocco. After 1914, tens of thousands of Africans were sent to Verdun, where one in three died in the muddy war of attrition. Back in the Soudan, uprisings to protest the draft of native soldiers for a foreign war were brutally suppressed by the French authorities.

As if the price wasn't high enough, when the war was over, the new colonial authorities began mobilizing civilians in the Soudan to develop agricultural production and the regional infrastructure. It was a move he deemed necessary to make the colony profitable after the stagnant period during the war.

Parallel to this, the French made minimal concessions to give Africans an extended role in the **politics** of their countries. By 1925, Africans could be elected to sit on the governors' advisory councils, although this gave them no direct political power. From the 1930s, laws were made to facilitate access to **French nationality** – a status considered by the government to be a great honour despite the sacrifices Africans had made during the war. But by 1937 only some 70,000 people in the entire AOF had been granted French citizenship and the vast majority of these were Senegalese.

Postwar political developments

Though World War II had the effect of nipping political and social development in the bud, it also acted as a catalyst that gave rise to a new political consciousness in Africa and a determination to achieve political rights. Independence was still only envisaged by a very few, and de Gaulle himself ruled out this possibility at the 1944 **Brazzaville Conference**, although he did say France was willing to make concessions, including greater African involvement in the respective governments.

In the aftermath of Brazzaville, three **political parties** were formed in

Mali: the Parti Soudanais du Progrès (PSP), headed by **Fily Dabo Cissoko**; a Soudanese affiliate of the Section Française de l'Internationale Ouvrière (SFIO) with **Mamadou Konaté** at the helm; and the Parti Démocratique du Soudan (PDS), founded by French Communists living in Mali. Though Cissoko came out ahead in elections to a constituent assembly in 1945, the first year of government was characterized by infighting among the parties – notably the PSP and the SFIO.

In 1946, Bamako hosted the **Rassemblement Démocratique Africain (RDA)** – a vast political convention that brought together more than eight hundred delegates from Senegal, Côte d'Ivoire, Guinea, Benin, Togo, Cameroon, Chad and Mali. For the Soudan to have a single voice within the RDA, the three political parties agreed to form a single Union Soudanaise within the RDA (USRDA) – to the surprise of everyone. But within a couple of days, Cissoko announced that a bloc with what he called "unrepentant communists" was impossible and he reformed the PSP.

The Soudan swings left

The next decade saw an intense **rivalry** between the PSP and the USRDA but, by 1957, the latter had clearly won the upper hand. This was in large part because the USRDA had more effectively distanced itself from Paris and had better grass-roots organization in Mali. After the elections of 1959, in which the PSP fared badly, they were constrained to join forces with the USRDA. On the eve of independence, there was no effective opposition to this party.

Changes had occurred within the USRDA when Konaté died in 1956. A moderate voice on the left, Konaté had advocated union of all the peoples of Mali. The void he left in the party ranks was quickly filled by more radical elements headed by **Modibo Keita**.

In the same year, the **Loi Cadre** drafted in Paris had opened the door to semi-autonomous governments in each of the territories of the AOF. This

led to divisions in the formerly united RDA between leaders like Sekou Touré of Guinea and Léopold Senghor of Senegal – who advocated the maintenance of a federal government in Dakar – and those such as Houphouët-Boigny of Côte d'Ivoire, who advocated the maximum autonomy for each of the territories.

Federalists and federation

Modibo Keita stood firmly in the camp of the Federalists, mainly because, as a poor country, the Soudan had a lot to gain from uniting itself with other territories (many of the country's colonial projects had been financed by AOF funds that originated outside Mali). Senghor's motives were more ideological, and he pleaded for a politically united West Africa that would maintain good relations with France. It became more pressing to decide on the pros and cons of a federation after the **1958 referendum** in which AOF nations voted to continue self-government within the French Union.

Sekou Touré was the only African leader who, for better or worse, had the courage to storm out of the French Union. Guinea was thereby excluded from any West African federation as well. Côte d'Ivoire was also out, since Houphouët-Boigny had stated loud and clear that he wouldn't have his country become the "milk cow" to feed the mouths of hungry neighbours.

In January 1959, the four remaining members of the former AOF – Soudan, Senegal, Upper Volta and Dahomey – met in Dakar and drew up the constitution for a **federation** of their territories. Under pressure from Côte d'Ivoire, Upper Volta eventually backed out of its commitment and Dahomey followed suit. Hopes for a broad-based political union in the region had been pared down to two nations, but it was still an important step for pan-African ideals. The **Mali Federation** of Mali and Senegal was born.

Unhappy union with Senegal

From the beginning, the alliance was uneasy. Modibo Keita was eager that Mali be granted independence. Senghor was more methodical and less hurried. De Gaulle himself helped sort out this problem by recognizing in 1959 that it was possible for the federation to be granted **independence** while staying in the French Community. The Mali Federation did, in fact, become independent – on April 4, 1960 – but the honeymoon between Senghor and Keita lasted barely two months.

Although numerous social and economic inequalities existed between the two former territories (which without doubt had an adverse effect on the union), the most glaring divergences were political, symbolized by the **clash of personalities** of the two leaders. Keita championed a Marxist approach to "African socialism". He was a man of often admirable principles who liked decisive action and who was unused to compromise. Senghor's approach was more measured and tended to favour dialogue and diplomatic action. He was especially cautious and pragmatic in his attitude to France which he hoped to keep as a friend and ally.

The stand-off between the two men – and as a consequence the territories they presided over – came to a head during the 1960 elections for President of the Federation, a powerful office that the Soudanese were wary of Senghor occupying. Senegal ruled out any alternative nominee and the brief federal arrangement collapsed.

Birth of the Mali Republic

After the failure of the federation, Keita set about creating the basis of the independent Malian state – a task of Promethean proportions at such short notice. He was helped, however, by the wave of **nationalist pride** and unity that swept the country, now destined

to stand alone. Even Keita's former opponent, Fily Dabo Cissoko, threw his support behind the USRDA in the cause of national unity. In September 1960, a special congress of the USRDA announced the implementation of a **planned socialist economy**. Shortly afterwards, Keita closed French military bases in Mali. He then set up state enterprises, starting with SOMIEX, which had a monopoly on all imports and exports of primary products – an advantage French companies operating in the country hardly appreciated. In 1962, Keita pushed his country further into **isolation** by taking it out of the CFA franc zone and creating a new national currency, the *franc malien*. In the same year, a **Tuareg revolt** in the Adrar des Iforhas mountains northeast of Gao was savagely repressed by the army.

It was a difficult start, made even worse by the fact that Senegal stopped trains to Bamako for three years after the rupture of the federation and closed its borders with Mali. As Keita continued down his radical path he distanced himself from other African nations. The West, too, turned an icy shoulder as, in the middle of the Cold War, he chose to ally Mali with the Soviet Union. Opposition mounted grimly at home as the business community saw their economic privileges being eroded into state assets.

By the **mid-1960s**, Keita had created a heavy state machinery that dragged mercilessly on the nation's fragile economy. The situation was characterized by numerous national enterprises (almost all of them running a deficit), a plethora of civil servants clogging the administrative machinery, a soaring balance-of-trade deficit and foreign debt, and a rapid weakening of the currency. Inflation soared and wages were frozen – a combination that wasn't calculated to enthuse Malians. By 1967, taking his cue from Peking, Keita was engaged in a **"cultural revolution"** to purge the nation of enemies within. He was supported in this by radical students, some of the unions, and by some lower grades in the civil service who resented the corruption of senior officials and business profiteers. But in the same year, Keita was obliged to devalue the Malian franc by fifty percent. The public outcry was immediate; the government's entire direction came under attack from all sides.

Keita seemed to believe the monumental role he'd played in his country's development absolved him from criticism by a public faced with a deepening economic crisis. He was apparently surprised and aggrieved when a group of young military officers staged a **bloodless coup** in 1968.

The Traoré years

A **Comité Militaire de Libération Nationale (CMLN)** was quickly formed, headed by a 32-year-old lieutenant, **Moussa Traoré**. Keita and senior members of his government were arrested and the former president died in prison ten years later.

The military recognized the need to correct some of the mistakes of the previous regime, bringing new discipline to the management of the economy and boosting production. However, the first years of military rule brought little relief: immediate revival of the economy was impracticable, and the military didn't challenge the nation's socialist orientation or the reliance on Soviet and Chinese technical aid.

The **drought** that ravaged Mali in 1973 and 1974 had a disastrous effect on agriculture. Industrial development didn't fare much better, and the 1974 **border war** with Burkina Faso put an extra drain on human and financial resources. Despite discouraging signs in the political and economic spheres, the military drew up a new constitution in 1974 that was approved in a plebiscite by what the government claimed was 99.7 percent of the population.

The new constitution, however, didn't go into effect until 1979, when a single party, the **Union Démocratique du Peuple Malien (UDPM)**, was charged with running the country. Traoré

remained at the head of government. This symbolic transformation to civilian rule was accompanied by a softening of the rigid socialist philosophy. The trend was accelerated after a second drought devastated the country from 1983 to 1985. In an effort to assure continued foreign aid, Traoré worked hard to improve relations with the West, notably with France. Most state companies were privatized in an effort to heat up the economy. Additionally Traoré brought Mali into the CFA fold in 1985, a move which encouraged investment.

Democracy and the Third Republic

Traoré thought he could bring his country out of a quarter century of political and economic isolation. But he also opened Mali to the calls for **democratic reforms** that were sweeping Africa by 1990 and to which a suitably upbeat official response was increasingly a condition of foreign aid.

At first, Traoré tried to contain the pressure within the party framework. Opposition leaders from the Alliance pour la Démocratie au Mali (**Adema**) wanted more, and published an article in one of the new newspapers, *Les Echos*, calling for a national conference to draft a new constitution and lead the transition to multiparty politics. Soon after, a series of independent parties came into being, including the Comité National d'Initiative Démocratique (CNID) and the Union Soudanaise–Rassemblement Démocratique Africain (US-RDA), the re-formed pre-independence party.

By December 1990, dissent was on the streets: the government tried to evict street vendors from downtown Bamako, provoking a **mass demonstration** that coincided with the anniversary of the Universal Declaration of Human Rights. On New Year's Eve, a pro-democracy demonstration attracted 15,000 marchers and, on January 8, 1991, a **general strike** for better wages was called – the first in Mali since independence. **Student protestors** jumped into the fray, organizing a demonstration that was savagely suppressed by the police and resulted in a number of deaths.

The government wasted no time in demanding that political parties and student organizations cease all activity. It closed the country's schools, and deployed heavy weapons on the streets of Bamako. In the **mass arrests** which followed, Amnesty International reported widespread torture in the prisons, sometimes on schoolchildren as young as 12.

Malians barely had time to recover from these incidents when a more concerted round of **rioting** broke out in March. In three days of intense fighting, police and gendarmes killed some 150 people and injured nearly a thousand. Wave after wave of protestors continued to swell through the city, however. In the face of a failed policy of violent suppression, coupled with international disapproval and complete disruption of the economy, Traoré promised elections but made plans to flee.

The new era

The military responded by arresting Traoré. The **coup** leader, Lt-Col Amadou Toumani Touré dissolved the government, suspended the constitution and abolished the UDPM. Within days, a multiparty committee had been formed to oversee the democratization of Mali. **Soumana Sacko**, a former finance minister sacked by Traoré when he tried to crack down on corruption a little too diligently, was appointed interim prime minister. More arrests followed, with ex-government ministers charged with corruption and murder. An unsuccessful **counter-coup** mounted by officers loyal to the ex-president was easily quashed, a jubilant crowd swarming through the streets of Bamako when it was learned the putsch had failed.

The Tuareg rebellion

The roots of the Tuareg rebellion were put in place after France's abortive attempt to form a Tuareg state – **"Azaouad"** – in 1958, on the eve of independence. The revolt began in 1990 with an attack on a military post at Ménaka, 300km east of Gao, followed up by a much bigger attack in September on Bouressa, which left at least 300 dead on both sides. The rebellion coincided with the return from Algeria of **drought refugees** who were unhappy with their reception in Mali, and was framed in terms of overthrowing Moussa Traoré and improving development aid to their regions. But as the democracy movement in Bamako took hold and Traoré was deposed, the Tuareg rebellion made more specific demands for, at the very least, greater autonomy for the desert regions. Ultimately the issues boiled down to one: race. The Tuareg viewed themselves, and were viewed as, "whites" and former lords (or oppressors), while the sedentary population considered themselves "blacks", newly enfranchised by democratic reforms.

A ceasefire agreement was signed in Tamanrasset in Algeria in January 1991. The rebels' signatory was **Iyad Ag Galli**, leader of the Azaouad Popular Movement (MPA), whose agenda listed a better deal for the Tuareg above greater autonomy and specifically excluded the ideal of independence for a Tuareg state.

The accord was rejected by other Tuareg militia, who continued a campaign of armed attacks, usually by small groups of rebels, on police stations and government sites. These attacks were invariably followed by brutal military reprisals on the most obvious Tuareg target in the district. Tens of thousands of refugees, mostly Tuareg, fled the affected areas to southern Algeria and Mauritania.

A second peace agreement – the **national pact** – was signed in April 1992, with a new umbrella organization of the Tuareg in Mali, the Unified Movements and Fronts of the Azaouad (MFUA). During the course of the year, 600 ex-rebels were integrated into the Malian army, 300 were given civil service posts, and joint Tuareg–army patrols were instituted.

The people seemed less enthusiastic at voting time, however. The hero of the democratic revolution, **Amadou Toumani Touré**, or "ATT" to his millions of admirers, did not seek a permanent role in power and, in the first free municipal and presidential elections in 1992, barely a fifth of eligible Malians bothered to vote. The Adema party secured a large majority, however, and their man, the academic **Alpha Oumar Konaré**, was sworn in as president of the Third Republic on June 8, 1992.

In 1993, Traoré and several members of his disgraced government were convicted of murder. They were subsequently sentenced to death, later commuted to life imprisonment (Mali has had no judicial executions since 1980).

Konaré was not an instinctive politician, and although his self-effacement earned him broad respect, it also made his first term in office somewhat difficult and unproductive. It was only in 1994 that he established a proper working relationship with the brusque, though effective, **Ibrahim Boubacar Keita**, who was his prime minister until February 2000. Meanwhile, the students, not surprisingly, quickly switched from backing the democrats to opposing the government that was formed, and the new order provoked rather than satisfied their demands. There were violent protests in Bamako in 1994 over the devaluation of the CFA franc, a policy popularly interpreted as neocolonial. Konaré's government was condemned by Amnesty for its frequently heavy-handed response to ordinary criticism from leading lights in the opposition – ad hoc imprisonment, harassment and detention were regular occurrences – and for not doing enough to eradicate the use of torture in prisons.

But the MFUA began to disintegrate, with factions at war with each other. As for the MPA, with its demands for full Tuareg integration into Malian national life, it was accused of a sell-out. Additionally, there were clashes between regular soldiers of the Malian army and "integrated" Tuareg troops.

Resentment at the Tuaregs' comparative success at achieving their aims through violence led to the formation of various ethnic vigilante groups. The most menacing was a Songhai resistance militia, **Ganda Koi** ("Owners of the Land"), which launched vicious attacks on Tuareg camps. Despite the widespread violence, the Bamako government remained committed to a peaceful solution and, encouraged by positive talks in January 1995 between the Tuareg and Ganda Koi representatives in Bourem, a series of community meetings was launched, followed by a lengthy tour of northern Mali and of Tuareg refugee camps in Algeria and Mauritania. The government's programme to reinstall civilian local government and to improve education and health-care provision in the conflict areas gave the predominantly young Tuareg fighters reasons to engage in civilian life, and rapidly led to the disarmament of rebel fighters.

A **repatriation scheme** to bring back tens of thousands of Tuareg refugees from Algeria, Mauritania, Burkina and Niger was launched in October 1995, and a final **peace agreement** was signed in 1996. There was a burning of weapons in Timbuktu in March 1996, which marked the end of the six-year rebellion, since when the Tuareg have reintegrated with Malian society. Many former Tuareg fighters have joined Mali's armed forces, and prospects for the Tuareg in Mali appear significantly better than for their kin in Algeria and Niger.

There is still unrest among some Tuareg, expressed as often through **banditry** as through political acts of violence – though there is resentment of American troops and advisors stationed in northern Mali. In late 2006 weapons were looted by rebels during a raid in Kidal. An Algerian-brokered peace deal agreed between the parties later that year, however, seems to have allayed fears of further fighting, at least for the time being.

In the country's **second elections**, which rolled for several tedious months through the rainy season of 1997, President Konaré got nearly 96 percent of the vote in the presidential election, while his Adema party took 130 seats out of parliament's total of 147 in the national assembly elections. In both cases, however, there was a widespread opposition boycott and a very low turnout (twenty percent across the country, and as little as twelve percent in Bamako). The opposition did more than accuse Adema of cheating; they accused the electoral commission itself of malpractice and demanded the entire electoral process be rescheduled. In the event both elections were simply rerun. To the dismay of many in his Adema party, Konaré's response to the landslide result was typically conciliatory, and he offered concessions to the opposition, including a fairer distribution of public money to opposition campaign funds.

Mali at the turn of the century

As the twentieth century came to an end, Mali's political life was dominated by the issue of the Adema party's firm grip on power. The Adema leadership was more willing to drive democracy forward than many of its rank-and-file supporters, and was frequently cited as being in the vanguard of democratic reform in Africa. But behind the steady turmoil of Bamako party politics, the legacy of the old order continued to haunt the new Mali. The country's first success in recovering **looted public money** came in 1997, when several Swiss banks agreed to repay to Konaré's government more than £1.5million/ US$2.4million of state funds stolen by the former head of the national tobacco and match company. The economic crimes committed by Traoré and his cronies were not brought before the courts until 1998 when, to the disgust of many Malians, the sums he was accused of embezzling amounted to only fifteen percent of his estimated total scoop. He

received another death sentence, which Konaré commuted to life imprisonment in 1999.

The biggest single issue faced by Konaré's government in the 1990s was the **Tuareg rebellion** (see box, p.344). At the conflict's peak, an estimated 160,000 people had fled to refugee camps in Algeria, Mauritania and Burkina Faso. Two-thirds of the country – everywhere north and east of the Bamako–Mopti road – was too dangerous to travel through, and the region's towns were transformed into besieged garrisons in the wilderness. The Tuareg fighters pursuing the war probably numbered no more than several hundred. But every new atrocity dug each side into a deeper hatred of the other. The fact that Konaré's government and the Tuareg faction leaders resolved this bitter and bloody dispute with little third-party assistance is one of the better chapters in post-colonial African history.

ATT back in power

Konaré, having failed to convince his people or international observers of his determination to crack corruption, appeared to have set himself on a course to improve his reputation after retiring. Recognizing the splits within his Adema party, he gave tacit support in the 2002 presidential elections to Mali's éminence grise, the charismatic **Amadou Toumani Touré** ("**ATT**"). ATT's campaign aimed to build links to all the parties – though allying with none – as well as civil rights groups. Twenty-four candidates stood for the election, but his two main opponents were Soumaïla Cissé (economy and finance minister under Konaré and official Adema candidate) and the prime minister until 2000, Ibrahim Boubacar Keita (IBK). Keita ultimately joined forces with ATT, whose resulting victory, on a very low turnout, came as no surprise. The election result signalled the end of Adema, which had been beset by internal strife for years.

ATT's nonpartisan "anti-politics" ticket, stressing reconciliation and economic probity, brought him plaudits at home and internationally (he has good contacts at the UN and in the US).

The presidential elections in April 2007 returned ATT and his Alliance pour la Démocratie et le Progrès (ADP) to power for a second and final five-year term, once again seeing off the challenge of Keita – president of the National Assembly and leader of the RPM, the Rally for Mali Party.

It's an uncertain time in Mali. ATT faces considerable opposition at home. And with volatile **Côte d'Ivoire** to the south (tens of thousands of emigré workers who fled home added to Mali's economic difficulties), **Algeria**'s civil conflict still making life difficult on the northern border and **Niger**'s unresolved Tuareg rebellion in the east, Mali's relationships with its neighbours are delicate.

Relations with the USA are under scrutiny, too, both on the economic front, where America's subsidized cotton farmers are seen as selfishly holding back Mali's development (and the introduction to Mali of genetically modified cotton, funded by USAID, is regarded as a potential disaster rather than a benefit), and politically, with the presence in the north of US troops and military advisors, there on the pretext of offering training to elite forces, but also sending a clear and provocative message to Sahara-based Islamists roaming the region.

It's clear that ATT's second term will be no easier than the first, with the issues of **poverty**, **job creation** and **public services** (particularly health care and education) all demanding urgent action. His willingness to toe the **IMF**'s "structural adjustment" line with continued reform of the economy, causes considerable hardship. And yet, despite the country's difficulties, the prospects for inward **investment** and for the economy overall are probably better now than they have been since independence, and better here than in most of Mali's neighbours. And the country's growing **democratic culture** receives widespread support and nurturing.

Music

Mali's **music** is steeped in tradition. The musical roots run deep even in the country's modern popular music, some of which features wide-ranging international influences. The music of the **Bamana** and **Malinké**, the **Fula**, the **Songhai** and the **Dogon** have all helped to give today's Malian music its flavour and colour. As everywhere, **hip-hop** has made inroads in Mali, especially among the young, with groups like **Tata Pound** and **Les Escrocs** stretching the tradition of *jeli* as social critic to the limit.

Manding music: the jeli tradition

Largely untouched by Western influences, "Manding" music is about sweet melodies and hypnotic rhythms, a style to which you can either dance or daydream. You'll find this broad genre from The Gambia to Mali and down through Guinea, in an area roughly corresponding to the spread of the Mande languages – in Mali the region west of Bamako.

Manding musicians are easy enough to track down. The members of certain families – notably Konté, Kouyaté /Kuyateh and Diabaté/Jobarteh – carry the title of **jeli** (**griot** in French), hereditary musician. The *jelis* have been around since at least the thirteenth-century origins of the Mali empire, based in the northeast of what is now Guinea, under Emperor **Sundiata Keita**. Traditionally, most instruments, including the **kora** − West Africa's distinctive harplute − are restricted to them.

A *jeli*'s reputation is built upon humility and correct behaviour as well as his (or her) knowledge of history and family genealogies − originally, the role was to do with the preservation of oral history. Mostly, this meant singing the praises of the noble and wealthy (no occasion − a wedding or child-naming ceremony for example − would be complete without a *jeli*), but now they're just as likely to have business patrons. *Jelis* moreover are personalities who have the ears of the people and any corrupt politician or civil servant has to reckon with them.

Jelis call on a great **repertoire of songs**. If you have the chance to hear a number of artists, however, you'll start to recognize lyrical variations on common melodic themes. Old classics like "Sundiata Faso", "Tutu Jara", "Lambang", "Koulanjan", "Duga", "Tara" and "Sori" are heard time and again, interspersed with songs from the modern era, often with a regional flavour, such as "Kaira". A griot's skill lies in the improvised flourishes and ornamentation − the *birimintingo* − that he brings to the recurrent theme or core melody, called the *donkili*.

In Mande-speaking society **men** always play the instruments. **Women artists** are considered the better singers and often receive extraordinary gifts −

even planes and houses aren't unknown. Even at ordinary live performances, people in the audience, moved by a particular song, shed jewellery and cash on performers there and then.

The Rough Guide to the Music of Mali & Guinea (World Music Network). Excellent introduction to the music of the region, with artists including Toumani Diabaté, Salif Keita, Afel Bocoum and Ali Farka Touré.

Toumani Diabaté

A brilliant *kora* virtuoso, **Toumani Diabaté** is also an ambitious and highly creative artist. He owns the *Hogon* club in Bamako.

Kaira (Hannibal). Solo *kora* music at its finest.

New Ancient Strings (Hannibal). Extraordinary artistry is evident on this collaboration with cousin and fellow *kora* master Ballaké Sissoko.

Bassekou Kouyaté

Mali's finest *ngoni* (lute)-playing jeli has been heard on numerous other artists' albums. The *ngoni* is simpler and much older than the *kora*, and Kouyaté now champions it superbly.

Segu Blue (Out Here). Accompanied by his backing band, Ngoni Ba, Kouyaté's virtuoso playing on the ancestor of the banjo has a mesmeric, bluesy quality.

Manding instruments

Kora 21- to 25-stringed harp-lute made with a large decorated half-gourd covered with a skin. The strings − which used to be twisted leather, but tend now to be various gauges of fishing line − are attached with leather thongs to a rosewood pole put through the gourd. The top of the body has a large sound-hole that doubles as a collection point for money from the audience.

Ngoni 4-stringed, lute-like instrument, the precursor of the banjo.

Bala (or *balafon*). Rosewood xylophone with between 17 and 20 keys, known to have been made since the fourteenth century.

Kontingo Small, five-stringed oval lute.

Bolom (or *bolombato*). Lute with three or four strings and an arched neck that used to be played for warriors going into battle. It's now an instrument played by men who are not of a *jeli* family.

Kandia Kouyaté

"La dangereuse" has a stunning stage presence and has been Mali's top female *jeli* singer for the past two decades. Her forceful voice and choral arrangements and her working of traditional social and court music has earned her huge wealth and a status unequalled by any other female artist.

Kita Kan (Stern's). Kandia's first international release. The *kora*, *ngoni*, guitars and *balafon* just keep on rolling and there are enough lush studio effects – and even full orchestral backing – to qualify *Kita Kan* for any number of radio playlists.

Kasse Mady Diabaté

Arguably the best contemporary Mande voice, Kasse Mady Diabaté rivals Salif Keita for beauty and lyricism, while being rooted in the *jeli* tradition.

Kela Tradition (Stern's). Kela is a Malinké village in western Mali, almost entirely inhabited by *jelis* of the Diabaté family. This is an almost entirely acoustic studio-produced album, featuring *ngoni* and *balafon* as well as guitars and Jean-Philippe Rykiel on keyboards. Includes expansive and gorgeous versions of Mande classics like "Koulandjan" and "Kaira".

Contemporary Manding sounds

After **independence**, there was a renaissance of popular music in Mali. The bands, who had for many years been playing Latin styles, became aware that people wanted to hear music from their own cultures. The government supported this search for roots and a number of groups received state sponsorship. Orchestras were at last able to afford modern instruments.

One of the most famous venues in Mali is the *Buffet Hôtel de la Gare* in Bamako, a venue which emerged from the hotel's quest for financial salvation. The director of Mali's state railway in the 1960s, **Djibril Diallo** was a big music fan and decided to create a station orchestra. The **Rail Band**, as they became known, mixed plaintive vocal styles over traditional Manding rhythms played with electric instruments. Showcased at the *Hôtel Buffet de la Gare*, the band rapidly acquired legendary status, and the venue became the hottest spot in Bamako. Over the years the Rail Band provided a launch pad for many musicians, including **Salif Keita** and **Mory Kanté**.

Salif Keita

An albino, **Salif Keita** started out singing in bars for loose change, evidently to the disgrace of his family. In 1970 he joined the Rail Band, which gave him an opportunity to modernize traditional songs. After being ousted from the *Buffet Hôtel* by the then *balafon* (xylophone) player Mory Kanté, Salif joined Les Ambassadeurs – who had immediate success with hits like "Primpin" – and recorded three albums. In 1978 he moved to Abidjan and, with Kanté Manfila, formed Ambassadeurs Internationaux, who recorded the wonderful song "Mandjou" – dedicated, ironically, to the despotic ruler of Guinea, Sekou Touré. Then he left for Paris and international stardom.

Soro (Stern's/Mango). Released in 1987, this became one of the biggest selling African recordings ever. Seamless hi-tech arrangements of Manding music with contributions from guitarist Ousmane Kouyaté and French keyboard wizard Jean-Philippe Rykiel form the perfect backdrop to some extraordinary vocals.

The Mansa of Mali (Mango). Includes highlights from his three Mango releases, plus the all-time 1978 hit with Les Ambassadeurs, "Mandjou".

Moffou (Universal). An assertion of Salif Keita's position as a truly inspired musician and songwriter, *Moffou* reflects his own roots, swaying between melancholy and bursts of energy.

Habib Koité and Bamada

A popular singer-songwriter, the *jeli* **Habib Koité** goes well beyond Bamana praise songs to include traditions from across Mali, social commentary and words of wisdom for the modern age.

Muso Ko (Contre Jour). Koité's first album was a sensation, winning him the prestigious Radio France International African Discovery award for his anti-smoking "Cigarette Abana".

Ma Ya (Putumayo). Koité's acoustic guitar is to the fore here, rounding off a subtle, highly melodic album.

Afriki (Cumbancha). Koité's rippling acoustic guitar is used to delightful effect alongside *ngoni* and hunters' horns in his latest CD, the backing as ever served up by his band Bamada.

Amadou et Mariam

Both blind, **Amadou et Mariam** are acclaimed as one of the best modern acts in Mali. Amadou Bagayoko formerly played together with Manfila Kanté and Salif Keita in the legendary Ambassadeurs, while Mariam Doumbia started playing with him in Côte d'Ivoire where they made their first five albums between 1988 and 1993.

Sete Djon Ye (Sonodisc). Their first album made back in Mali, an eclectic affair with influences from reggae and salsa.

Dimanche à Bamako (Radio Bemba). The couple's 2004 breakthrough album is stamped clearly with the marks of master producer Manu Chao, and all the finer for it. It won Best Album in the 2006 BBC World Music Awards.

Rokia Traoré

Born in 1973, **Rokia Traoré** is the voice of young women in Mali. While her roots are firmly grounded in the *jeli* and *kora* tradition her songs raise questions about women's place in society. Her soft voice, accompanied by electric guitars, *ngoni* and *bala* (see p.348), creates a mesmerizing impact.

Wanita (Indigo). More assertive than her debut *Mouneissa*, though as subtle and enchanting as ever.

Ali Farka Touré

A charismatic artist who never fitted anywhere, and not from one of the traditional families of hereditary musicians, **Ali Farka Touré** started playing purely for his own pleasure and did so in a style which resonates with American blues affinities – although he had never heard the blues until he was already firmly established. He died in 2006, the same year *In the Heart of the Moon* won Best Traditional World Music Album at the Grammies. The posthumously released *Savane* garnered similar critical acclaim, winning the **BBC World Music Awards** Album of the Year.

Radio Mali (World Circuit). Beautifully produced compilation of radio recordings made in 1970–78, a decade or more before he achieved international recognition.

Niafunké (World Circuit). A determined return to roots in every sense, allowing the world to hear Touré doing his wonderful stuff almost literally in his own backyard.

In the Heart of the Moon (World Circuit). Proving that he could do mellow as well, this album sees a more laidback side as Touré combines beautifully with the *kora* of Toumani Diabaté.

Savane (World Circuit). Toure's last solo work, recorded in Bamako with a specially assembled *ngoni* group. Touré himself thought this, his most obviously blues-influenced work, was his finest album, and few would disagree.

Wassoulou – modern Fula sounds

There are Fula communities all over Mali – their herders dominate the flat floodlands of the inland delta region for example – but it's the **Wassoulou** region of southwest Mali that has been musically the most important for Fula artists over the last two decades. The griots of Wassoulou are a less exclusive caste than the Manding *jelis* – anyone is free to make music, traditionally based on ancient hunters' songs, with pentatonic (five-note) melodies. The Wassoulou sound used to be viewed as teenage music in Mali, and only a few decades ago such songs were regarded as slightly subversive.

The Wassoulou Sound: Women of Mali and **The Wassoulou Sound: Vol. 2** (Stern's). Excellent compilations featuring a range of female voices and Wassoulou styles, including the pioneers of "Wassoulou electric", Kagbe Sidibé and Coumba Sidibé. Buy the CDs as a set – the notes were written for both.

Oumou Sangaré

Oumou Sangaré is the best-known exponent of the Wassoulou sound: her passionate style ("I sing of love, not praises") shook up the musical status quo in Mali, a country previously dominated by fat-cat *jelis* and the Paris-based elite.

Ko Sira (World Circuit). A breath of fresh air from a young woman whose impact on traditional musical culture could hardly have been greater, wielding her voice like a weapon, and deploring, as she put it, the male-dominated status quo. Beautifully produced, Wassoulou music at its best.

Worotan (World Circuit). Sangaré defies tradition with her lyrics ("Marry you? Why?!"), custom with her musical arrangements (Pee Wee Ellis and others adding funky horn grooves), and stereotyping with her range.

Tuareg music

Although Tuareg men and women both make music, they traditionally have separate forms and styles. Women's songs include **tinde nomnas** (praise songs), **tinde nguma** (songs of exorcism) and **ezele** (dance songs). The **tinde**, used to accompany women's songs, is a drum made from a goatskin stretched over a mortar. Other instruments used by women include the **assakhalebo** water drum, made from a half-gourd floating upside down in a bowl of water, and the **tabl** – a kettledrum (traditionally a battle drum) with a broad camel-skin top. There's also an end-blown flute, called the **sarewa**, constructed from a sorghum stem in which four holes are made, with leather thongs tied round its body for ornamentation and protection.

The men's songs, or **tichiwe**, are, in striking contrast to the women's, essentially lyrical. They sing about the beauty of the women they love or celebrate some happy event. The songs are performed by soloists – whose virtuosity lies as ever in improvisation – either with or without an accompaniment. This is usually provided by a single-stringed fiddle, the **inzad**, which consists of a half-gourd, goatskin-covered resonator and a horsehair string stretched over a bridge in the form of a small wooden cross.

Tinariwen

Tinariwen were formed in a Tuareg refugee camp in southern Libya in the 1980s and claim the influence of Dylan and Bob Marley on a ragged, repetitive sound which they initially used to promote the goal of Tuareg independence (getting them banned from the tape shops in Mali). Several members saw action during the Tuareg rebellion before the 1996 peace accord.

The Radio Tisdas Sessions (Wayward). Rough-and-ready first international release, recorded in a radio station in remote Kidal. A gutsy display in which every track breathes a harsh desert spirit.

Aman Iman: Water is Life (independiente). Powerful new release with great production

Cinema

Mali has one of the most thriving **film cultures** in West Africa: two of cinema's most famous African directors hail from here: Souleymane Cissé, who made his international name with the memorable *Yeelen* (1986), and cineaste turned minister of culture, Cheik Oumar Sissoko. Not that the films shot here create much income or employment: there's no sign of a "Maliwood" yet.

Souleymane Cissé

Souleymane Cissé, like the late Ousmane Sembène of Senegal (see p.190), was trained at the famous Moscow film school. Since the early 1970s, he has been as prolific as Sembène and has made a number of films which have gone on to commercial and critical success in Africa and Europe. Unlike Sembène, however, his craft always leads his message, not the other way round.

In addition to well-known early works like *Cinqs jours d'une vie* (1972) and *Baara* ("The Porter"; 1977) – a full-length look at the relationship between the workers and the boss in a textile factory – he has made perhaps the two best films to come from Africa. In the first, the Bamana-language *Finyé* ("The Wind"; 1982), about the overweening pressures of seniority on youth, the wind symbolizes a new generation of post-independence youth, struggling against the repression of the military government. It was an international success, shown at Cannes, Carthage and FESPACO, where it won first prize. The second, *Yeelen* ("Brightness"; 1986), gave him recognition as a major film-maker, winning the Grand Prix du Jury at Cannes in 1987. Through the conflict between the main character, Nianan-koro – an initiate possessed of magical powers – and his father, the film looks at the conflict of the generations in Africa and gives non-African moviegoers a spine-tingling insight into traditional values. With its deft visual impact and atemporality, the metaphysical world of the old West Africa comes alive and is as real as any drought or slave trader. For this lyricism – which made the film

an art-house hit in the West – Cissé inevitably ran into criticism from those who would prefer a more realist cinema talking about exploitation, colonialism and repression.

Cissé's last film, *Waati* (1994), is the epic story of Nandi, a South African girl growing up under apartheid. In her quest for freedom, she leaves her homeland and travels to Namibia, Mali and Côte d'Ivoire, finding a continent in search of an identity, as she discovers her own.

Other cineastes

Apart from Souleymane Cissé, two other early Malian film-makers also received their training in the USSR – **Djibral Kouyaté** and **Kalifa Dienta**. Kouyaté was the first Malian to make a fiction film, *Le Retour de Tiéman* (1970) – the story of a young agriculturalist who runs into the resistance of traditionalists when he tries to implement modern methods. Dienta is best known for his feature *A Banna* (1980), in which the main character, Yadji, takes his new bride from Bamako to meet his family in the village. The clash between urban and rural values comes into focus as Yadji's wife has to contend with everything from the authority of the griot to old-fashioned divisions between men and women.

Alkaly Kaba was another pioneer, best known for films portraying the conflict between Western and African worlds. Early films in this vein from the 1970s include *Wallanda* and *Wamba*.

Sega Coulibaly comes from a new generation of film-makers whose experiences are rooted in post-independence society. Born in 1950, he briefly studied film in Paris before returning to Mali where he helped Kaba shoot *Wamba*. Coulibaly's first feature, *Moko Dakan* (1976), follows a city teacher stationed in a village, whose success with women backfires when one of them gets pregnant. His second film, *Kasso Den* (1980), is all action, a prisoner wrongly jailed seeking vengeance on the men who framed him.

Issa Falaba Traoré gained recognition for *An Be Nodo* ("We Are All Guilty", 1980), the story of a promising student. Too poor to continue her studies, she brings shame on her family when she drops out of school and becomes pregnant.

Another name to emerge in recent years is **Draba Adama**, whose *Taafe Fanga* ("Skirt Power"; 1997) used a Dogon folk tale as a vehicle to poke fun at gender roles while making a serious comment about the status of African women.

Alongside Souleymane Cissé, Mali's other great director and supporter of the cinema has been **Cheik Oumar Sissoko**. Sissoko emerged in the late 1980s as a new film-maker in the social realist tradition. An early documentary, *Rural Exodus* (1984), considered the plight of peasants displaced by drought, while *Nyamanton* ("Garbage Boys", 1986) focused on the condition of urban children. Sissoko gained international recognition for *Finzan* (1989), a fictional piece that used the theme of genital excision to address wider social issues of women's rights and the struggle for freedom. Sissoko won the Best Picture award at the 1995 FESPACO for *Guimba*, the tale of a chief whose obsession with power drives him to make a pact with the devil – an allegory about the downfall of President Moussa Traoré. His 1999 movie, *La Genèse* ("Genesis"), is a visually stunning retelling of the biblical story of the house of Abraham, in which Salif Keita plays the lead role of Esau. His last feature was *Battu* (2000), filmed in Dakar and revolving around the relationship between government and beggars in African cities. More recently, Sissoko has served as minister of culture.

The Mauritanian-born, Moscow-trained director **Abderrahmane Sissako** won the top award at FESPACO in 2003 with *Heremakono*, about a Malian youth in Mauritania hoping to emigrate to Europe. And his rousing *Bamako* received rapturous praise in 2006 for its flaying of the international order that keeps the rich rich and the poor poor in an acted-documentary trial in a local compound, taking place against a background of daily life.

Books

There's not a great deal of accessible writing in English from, or about, Mali. **Malian literature** in French – a couple of recommendations are listed – repays the effort, though a few titles are sporadically translated into English. For good, general West African titles, including some with a strong Malian connection, see p.35. Titles marked 🎋 are especially recommended.

Ibn Battuta *Travels in Asia and Africa.* Selections from the writings of the great fourteenth-century wanderer, including his travels along the Niger.

Walter E.A. van Beek and Stephanie Hollyman *Dogon: Africa's*

People of the Cliffs. A photographic collection showing Dogon society engaged in daily work and sacred ritual.

Banning Eyre *In Griot Time: An American Guitarist in Mali.* Musician, writer and broadcaster, Eyre brilliantly captures the flavour of modern Mali through its music, in this account of a sojourn spent studying Malian guitar styles under Djelimady Tounkara.

Tom Fremantle *The Road to Timbuktu*. In which the author, using various modes of transport including dugout canoe, ox, and a donkey called Che, follows on the trail of Mungo Park up the Niger to Timbuktu and beyond, finally finishing up, like Park himself, in Nigeria (though this time the author escapes with his life).

Jean Marie Gibbal *Genii of the River Niger*. The French author's personal account of travels by pirogue through eastern Mali. Some of the more interesting passages depict healing ceremonies, which revolve around the river.

Mark Jenkins *To Timbuktu: A Journey down the Niger*. By turns macho and self-deprecating, Jenkins' account of his 1970s journey, and 1990s return (with kayaks) is a readable, if sometimes fanciful, travelogue, interwoven with the stories of the nineteenth-century explorers.

Seydou Keïta *Seydou Keïta: African Photographs*. An extraordinary collection of black-and-white studio photos of Bamako people from the 1950s to the 1970s – a testament to the richness of African urban culture.

Mamadou Kouyaté (translated by G.D. Pickett) *Sundiata: An Epic of Old Mali*. Slim and fascinating transcription of a griot's history of Mali.

Frank T. Kryza *The Race for Timbuktu: In Search of Africa's City of Gold*. Detailed account of Alexander Gordon Laing's expedition to Timbuktu and his great rivalry with the lesser-known Hugh Clapperton.

James Morris & Suzanne Preston Blier *Butabu: Adobe Architecture of West Africa*. Superbly photographed exploration of *banco* architecture – wonderful inspiration for your itinerary – with a fascinating commentary.

Anthony Sattin *The Gates of Africa: Death, Discovery and the Search for Timbuktu*. The rough outlines of the explorers' tales are familiar, but it's the detail Sattin weaves in that makes this compelling.

William Seabrook *The White Monk of Timbuctoo*. First published in the 1930s, this is the biography of Père Yakouba, a white priest who married a Timbuktu woman and changed his vocation.

Bettina Selby *Frail Dream of Timbuktu*. Selby's account of her bicycle journey from Niamey to Bamako is beautifully written and covers much more than just the journey – with interest-filled deviations and asides.

Fa-Diga Sissoko (translated by John William Johnson) *The Epic of Son-Jara*. A recent translation – and a new spelling for Sundiata/Sunjata – of the 800-year-old story of the Mali empire's founder.

Fiction

Seydou Badian *Caught in the Storm*. A tale of culture clash, set within a rural family during French colonial rule.

Maryse Condé *Segu*. An epic historical novel – already a Francophone classic before its translation into English – by a Guadeloupan author of Bamana descent, that paints a mesmerizing and unsettlingly graphic portrait of the Ségou empire from 1797 to the middle of the nineteenth century.

Amadou Hampate Ba *Fortunes of Wangrin*. Hampate Ba, born in Bandiagara, was a Fula academic and transcriber of oral literature (he died in 1991). In this novel, an administrative interpreter tells of the colonial period from 1900 to 1945, and his successful collusion with it.

Chukwuemeka Ike *The Naked Gods*. A comical tale of the clash between conservatives and progressives at a fictitious Malian university, by a Nigerian author.

Bokar N'Diaye *La Mort des Fétiches de Sénédougou*. Traumas from changes to the traditional way of life during the colonial era.

Yambo Ouologuem *Bound to Violence*. By the only Malian writer to have achieved international recognition, this exploration of brutality and deceit in an invented African empire, Nakem, screams for a new, rehumanizing look at black history, insisting that African society rests on foundations as bloody and self-destructive as any other.

Mamby Sidibé *Contes Populaires du Mali*. Captivating stories and legends from the oral tradition of different Malian ethnic groups.

Languages

French is the official language in Mali and the one you'll have to deal with for all administrative matters, though only a small percentage of people speak it fluently. The most widely spoken language is **Bamana** (often spelt **Bambara**), a member of the Mande group of languages, similar to Malinké and Mandinka, and used throughout the country, especially in the region around Bamako. Other languages include **Pulaar** (Fula), **Senoufo**, **Songhai**, **Tamashek** and **Dogon**.

Basic Bamana

Compare the words and phrases below with those in the Mandinka section in the Gambia chapter, p.286.

Greetings

N-bifo/A ni tié	Hello
Ani sogoma	Good morning
M-ba	Man's response
Oun sé	Woman's response
Ani woula	Good afternoon
Ani sou	Good evening
Somo go bédi?	How's the family?
Toro té	They're fine
I ka kènè wa?/ Hèrè bé?	How's it going?
Toro si té	Everything's fine
Ka an bé sogoma/ Kanbé	See you later

Numbers

1	kèlèn
2	fila
3	saaba
4	naani
5	douru
6	wooro
7	wolonwula
8	seguin
9	kononton
10	tan
20	mugan
25	mugan ni douru
30	bi sabi
40	bi nani
50	bi douru
100	kèmè
120	kèmè ni mugan
150	kèmè ni bi dourou
200	kèmè fila
5 franc piece	dorem
10 francs	dormè fila
25 francs	dormè dourou
50 francs	dormè ta
75 francs	dormè tan ne dourou
100 francs	dormè muga
200 francs	dormè bi nani
300 francs	dormè bi woro
400 francs	dormè bi segui
500 francs	dormè kèmè
700 francs	dormè kèmè ni bi nani
1000 francs	dormè kèmè fila
2000 francs	dormè kèmè nani

Useful expressions

Joli?	How much?
A kaï	It's lovely
A di yan	I'll take it (give it to me)
A songo ka guèlè	It's too expensive
I bi resitoran da duman don wa?	Do you know of a cheap restaurant?
Bank bé voro djimé?	Where's the bank?
Sila jira kan na	Show me the way
I bi taa min?	Where are you going?
N'ta lou	I don't know
N'ma fahamuya	I don't understand
Ya fan ma	Excuse me/Sorry
Aw kodi	What did you say? (please repeat)
Awo	Yes
Aï	No
A ni tié (kosèbè)	Thank you (very)

A few words of Dogon

The words and phrases below are intended as a guide but there are sometimes quite major differences in dialect between villages.

Standard greetings

Dogon people often run through the entire sequence.

Po	Hello/how's the work going?
Poiye	Good morning (as above but addressing a group)
Agapoyeh/Ey wahna	Good morning/evening (north village)
Agayamwe/ Eli waleh	Good morning/evening (south village)
Seyoma?	How are you?
Ginna seyom?	How's the family?
Deh seyom?	How's your father?
Na seyom?	How's your mother?
Ulumo seyom?	How are the children?
Seyo	Fine
Awa/Popo	Everything's okay/ Thanks
Yemeh ehso/ Bolanee jeh/ Pinan segeramo	See you later
Aha	Yes
Eye-ee	No
Gana	Thank you
Emiru/ Amiru	Village chief
Emeri ana	Chief's wife
Ah	Boy
Ñe	Girl
Amma	God
ti	1
loy	2
tahnu	3
nay	4
noonay	5
kuray	6
so	7
sira	8
tuwa	9
peo	10

And, of course, millet beer: konjo.

Glossary

ADP Alliance pour la Démocratie et le Progrès, ATT's political group.

ATT Amadou Toumani Touré, the president.

Azalaï Desert caravans that formerly dominated Saharan trade. They continue today in small numbers, notably between the salt mines of Taoudenni and Timbuktu.

Banco Clay or mud-brick.

Bogolan Literally "mud cloth", cotton strips with a batik print.

Cadeauter Transformation of the French word *cadeau*, meaning "gift", into a verb. Sometimes used by children in the expression "Il faut me cadeauter", meaning "Give me something".

Dourou-dourouni *Camion bâché*, pick-up or bush taxi.

FDR Front pour la Démocratie et la République, the main opposition party.

Ghana In the historical context, usually

refers to ancient Ghana, the earliest Mande-speaking kingdom (precursor of Mali). Mali's ruined capital, Koumbi Saleh, is located in southeast Mauritania. The name "Ghana" was the title used by its Soninké rulers.

Hogon Dogon priests who live in isolation. These elderly men represent the highest spiritual authority in the Dogon country.

IBK Ibrahim Boubacar Keita, presidential rival.

Mali An old empire (based southwest of Bamako) as well as the modern state, "Mali" is synonymous with "Manding", just as the language Malinké is basically the same one as Mandinka. *Mali* means "hippo" in Malinké.

Masina Historically, the Fula empire centred on the town of Massina or Macina, northeast of Ségou.

OMATHO Office Malien du Tourisme et de l'Hôtellerie, the tourist-office service run by the Ministry of Crafts and Tourism.

Oued Pronounced "wed"; French version of the Arabic word *wadi*, designating a river bed, dry except in the rainy season.

Pinasse Large wooden boat originally invented in Djenné to carry cargo. Though the basic covered design hasn't changed over the centuries, motors are the norm today.

RPM Rassemblement pour le Mali, the Rally for Mali, IBK's opposition party.

S(o)udan Former colonial name for the territory encompassing Senegal, Mali and Burkina Faso. The term is sometimes used today to refer to this same basic area. Sudanic architecture refers to the style that originated in Djenné and has nothing to do with the state of Sudan.

4.1

Bamako

Although **BAMAKO** has grown quickly since independence, evidence of modernization is only slowly penetrating the dusty city centre. Here, the mix of day-long crowds, hostile traffic and sludge-filled sewers adds up to an oppressive combination for visitors just in from the *brousse*, although arrivals from Dakar welcome the fact that Bamako's hustlers are less aggressive – perhaps debilitated by the perennial heat. At sundown, the dust settles like a pink fog as the city centre's torrid activity dissipates into the suburbs, where the conspicuous aid community shelters in air-conditioned comfort.

Architecturally ostentatious modern developments like the Saudi-built **Pont du Roi Fahd** and nearby, the neo-Sudanic **Tour BCEAO** – the city's stunning showpiece – emerge from amid the medieval sanitation and dreary Soviet-funded blocks of the early 1960s. Compared with Mali's undeniable rural attractions, the capital is just too hot, dirty and crowded to be immediately appealing, and for most visitors the few days taken to obtain the next visa, go to the supermarket, send a few emails or wait for transport connections will be long enough. However, while you're here, don't miss out on the great nightlife and the music scene.

Some history

As rock paintings attest (notably those at the **Point G caves**), Bamako is the site of ancient settlements, peopled from Paleolithic (Old Stone Age) times. Oral history traces the roots of the present city back to **Seribadian Niaré**, who sought refuge in the Bamana empire after being chased from the region of Nioro du Sahel in the seventeenth century. Upon arrival in the capital town of **Ségou**, Niaré married the sister of the king, **Soumba Coulibaly**. The couple had a son, **Diamoussadian Niaré**, and moved to the region around the present capital. A hunter of heroic dimensions, the son eventually killed a giant crocodile which had long terrorized the people of the area, thus fulfilling a prophecy and laying the basis for the establishment of a dynasty (also prophesied) that would grow up on the site. The Niarés thereby became rulers of the chiefdom at Bama-ko (crocodile-river). An alternative tale recounts how a hunter from Kong in Côte d'Ivoire, Bamba Sanogo, killed an elephant here on the north bank of the Niger and received permission from the local lord to found a town, which he named Bamba-Kong after himself and his city of origin. As he left no heirs on his death, the post of town chieftain went to Diamoussadian Niaré.

Whichever its origin, Bamako grew to be a prosperous trading centre. By the time the Scots explorer **Mungo Park** arrived in the early nineteenth century, the population had grown to about 6000 – pretty considerable for the time. By 1883 the French had built a fort here and soon afterwards colonized the region. In 1904 the Dakar railway line was pushed through from Kayes and in 1908 the town was made capital of the colony of **Haut Sénégal-Niger**. When independence was returned to the country in 1960, Bamako was the obvious capital. At the time, the city's population was some 160,000, but in the following decades of rapid growth that figure has risen nearly tenfold.

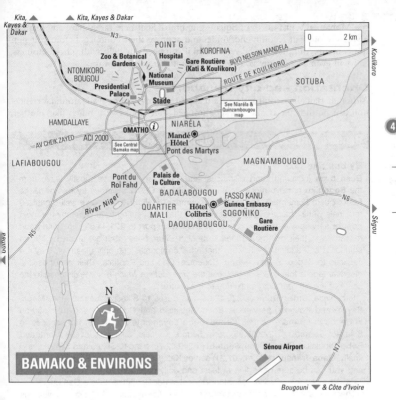

Bougouni ▼ & Côte d'Ivoire

Arrival, orientation, information

Arriving by **international airline**, or on one of Mali's small domestic carriers, all planes use Bamako's one airport (☎220.27.01), on the other side of the Niger River at **Sénou**, 15km south of the city. There are limited amenities and sporadic exchange facilities. If you have a booking with one of the city's top hotels, there will normally be a minibus waiting to take you straight there. Otherwise you'll have to catch a taxi into town, as there's no bus service; the cost shouldn't exceed CFA5000–6000 in the daytime and CFA6500 at night.

If you arrive in Bamako by **bush taxi or bus**, chances are you'll be let off at or near the **gare routière de Sogoniko**, again on the south side of the river, about 7km from the centre. From here you can take a taxi, catch a bus for a fraction of the cost, or hop on a Peugeot *bâché*. Whichever way you choose, you'll cross the overworked **Pont des Martyrs** spanning the Niger.

Arriving **by train from Kayes and Dakar**, you'll find the **station** is within walking distance of a few good accommodation options.

If you're arriving in the area by **river boat** from Mopti or further down-river, you will only get as far as Bamako's port at **Koulikoro**, 60km northeast of the city, as rapids prevent large craft from reaching Bamako itself. Koulikoro is linked to the capital by buses and bush taxis heading to Route de Koulikoro and Point G north of the centre.

For **tourist information**, the Office Malien du Tourisme et de l'Hôtellerie (OMATHO; Mon–Sat 7.30am–4pm; ☎222.56.73 ⓦwww.tourisme.gov.ml) is on rue Mohamed V, just north of Square Lumumba. Staff here rarely have any maps to give away but can recommend guides and approve their contracts before you sign someone up. And they can be very useful if you need any help with official business, and will even accompany you to the police if you need them to.

Orientation and city transport

Although Bamako's compact centre makes it an easy city to walk around, orientation can be difficult as one market-thronged street looks very much like another,

Bamako surface arrivals and departures

By bus and taxi

Bush taxis (covering short distances) and long-distance buses mostly leave from the **Sogoniko gare routière**, south of the river (a CFA125-journey by bus or *bâché* from Square Lumumba). The larger bus companies all have their own well-organized terminals within the *gare routière* itself or on the road leading to it. Currently the most popular service with travellers is run by **Bani Transport** (⊤221.44.83), and with good reason. With their own gated station, behind Bittar, buses that are smart by Malian standards and a level of efficiency that other companies can only dream of, they run services to Ségou, Sévaré, Mopti, Douentza, Gao and Koutiala. Their only possible disadvantage is that in Ségou they use the *gare routière* which is some distance to the south of the city, entailing a taxi ride to the centre.

Otherwise, **Bittar Trans** (⊤220.12.05) has buses to Sikasso, Ségou, Gao, Mopti, Sévaré and Koutiala, as well as Bobo-Dioulasso and Cotonou – and their station in Ségou is far more central; **Kénédougou Voyages** (⊤262.07.19) run services to Sikasso; **Somatra** (⊤222.38.96) go to Ségou, Koutiala, Sikasso, Sévaré, Mopti and Bobo-Dioulasso (Tues–Thurs); **Somatri** (⊤249.02.76) head to Ségou and Sikasso; and finally, **Gana Transport** (⊤243.07.21) serves Kati, Ségou, Bla, San, Sévaré and Mopti and you can be sure of finding at least one daily departure to the main towns. For Timbuktu, change at Ségou, Mopti or Douentza (for Douentza, take a Gao bus).

There are also **two smaller autogares** in Bamako: one, serving Nara and Nioro, is behind the Grande Mosquée; the other, below Point G, is used by bush taxis to Kati and Koulikoro.

By train

The **train to Dakar** is scheduled to leave Bamako approximately once a week. It's wise to make enquiries and book as soon as possible and to be there at 7am on the day of departure, to ensure your reserved seats aren't assigned to someone else. For more on the Bamako–Dakar trains, see p.330.

The same international trains also stop in **Kati**, **Diamou** and **Kayes**. These towns are also serviced by a twice-weekly domestic "Autorail" service that stops at every station, leaving Bamako at 9.15am on Sun and 7.30pm on Mon and Fri. Total journey time varies from 16 to 24 hours. Fares for couchette places are CFA11,730 to Kita and CFA18,775 to Kayes, with 1st- and 2nd-class seats much cheaper.

By boat

The Niger River ferries operate from **Koulikoro** when the rains swell the river to a suitable level, roughly from late July or early August until November for Gao and as late as February for Mopti and Korioumé – Timbuktu's port (for further details, see p.333). To reach Koulikoro catch a bus or a bush taxi from Point G – the hill in the north of the city – or from the Route de Koulikoro. For reservations (get them early, especially for second and third class) and up-to-date information on departures, contact the office of the Compagnie Malienne de Navigation (COMANAV; ⊤222.38.02; Mon–Fri 8am–4pm), just south of the train station on rue Archinard. You could also try calling the head office in Koulikoro on ⊤226.20.95.

especially at night. To get your bearings, the prominent **Sofitel l'Amitié** hotel and bat-eared **Tour BCEAO** serve as useful reference points, both of them by the river and either side of the main thoroughfare leading from the **Pont des Martyrs** to **Square Lumumba**, with the large French embassy and a couple of airline offices alongside. The **Avenue du Fleuve** (or **Avenue Modibo Keita**), leading north from this square to the **Place de la Liberté**, is one of the city's main streets, lined with banks, restaurants and shops. If you follow this street all the way to the end, you'll reach the junction with **rue Baba Diarra**, which runs parallel to the railway tracks. Turning right along this street, you'll pass the **train station** and American embassy before arriving at the **Boulevard du Peuple**, where another right turn takes you past the **Centre Artisanal** and the **Grande Mosquée**, then back down to Square Lumumba. These three streets form a triangle within which you'll find Bamako's commercial centre, including one of the city's principal (if incidental) attractions, the **street market**. As in many Francophone African cities, many business addresses are located by **immeuble** (multistorey building, commonly written as *Imm*).

There's an efficient, private **bus service** in Bamako, run by Tababus. They run on fixed routes with fixed stops and fares (usually CFA150 per hop). The alternative is to take one of the little green minivans or *Somatras*, which usually charge around CFA200.

Accommodation

Unless you're prepared to put up with something very basic, **accommodation** is likely to carve a large chunk out of your budget during your stay in Bamako. Although many options are centrally located, most of the better-quality hotels are located in the relatively prosperous **Niaréla district**, 3km east of the centre.

Central Bamako

L'Amitié Bamako av de la Marne ☎221.43.21 ⓕ222.36.37. Ugly Soviet-built landmark built to celebrate the friendship between Mali and Libya, and now part of the *Sofitel* chain, the swish interior and smart rooms leave a better impression than its charmless facade. Facilities include a pool, golf course, very good restaurant, one of the capital's few ATMs – and rooms that *start* at CFA98,000. ❽

Les Cèdres (aka *Chez Georges*) Route de Darsalam, a 15min walk from the train station ☎/ⓕ222.79.72 ⓦhotellerie.net/lescedres. Good-value if slightly faded hotel in a quiet administrative quarter of Bamako. Rooms are all s/c and some have a/c. Some Fri nights there are live bands in the front courtyard bar-restaurant. Rooms with fan ❸ or a/c ❺.

🏃 **Centre d'Accueil Catholique des Soeurs Blanches** corner of rue 130 (El Hadj Ousmane Bagayoko) and rue 133 ☎/ⓕ222.77.61. Bamako's safest and tidiest budget option. The nuns here accept travellers if there is space (being a lone woman helps) and offer commendably clean s/c rooms (though some are a little dark and cave-like) with mosquito nets, peace and quiet. There is also a laundry service

and kitchen facilities, and it's also one of the safest places in Bamako, with residents required to take a key to the front gate (key deposit CFA5000). New arrivals need to turn up between 7am and 1pm, or 4–10pm; at busy times you may only be allowed to stay for a couple of nights, and there's always a limit of four nights. Dorm beds CFA4000, otherwise ❶.

Chez Fanta close to the *Centre d'Accueil des Soeurs Blanches*. Surviving largely on the overspill from the Catholic Mission, this place is unsign-posted but it's the only two-storey building on the street; and besides, everybody in the area know Fanta's friendly family home, where there are two basic and rather dingy dorms. Bathroom and toilets are in the courtyard. Dorm beds CFA4000.

El Farouk near the Pont des Martyrs ☎222.30.30 ⓔkempinski-elfarouk@cefib.com. As smart and salubrious as other *Kempinski* hotels around the world, with all the facilities and furnishings you'd expect from a five-star establishment, and with fine views across the Niger from some of the upper rooms to boot. ❽

🏃 **Graine de Baobab** Porte 39, rue 402, Dravéla-Bolibana, west of the centre (head west from the hippopotamus roundabout, turning off opposite the SNF petrol station) ☎920.47.98

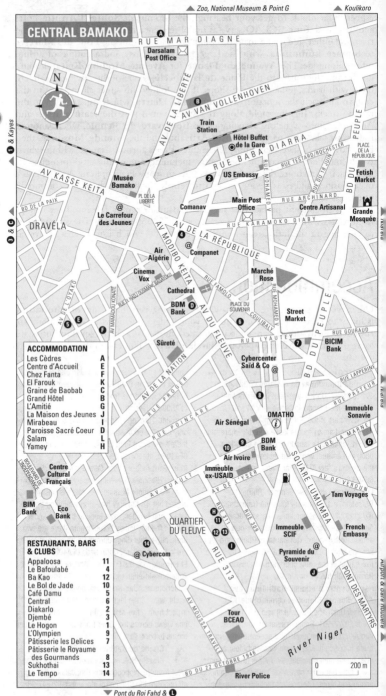

CENTRAL BAMAKO

RUE MAR DIAGNE

Darsalam Post Office

AV DE LA LIBERTÉ

AV VAN VOLLENHOVEN

Train Station

Hôtel Buffet de la Gare

RUE BABA DIARRA

RUE TESTARD/ROCHESTER

PLACE DE LA RÉPUBLIQUE

BD DU PEUPLE

AV KASSE KEITA

Musée Bamako

US Embassy

RUE MOHAMED

RUE DU 18 JUIN

Fetish Market

BD DE LA PAIX

PL DE LA LIBERTÉ

Comanav

Main Post Office

RUE ARCHINARD

Centre Artisanal

Grande Mosquée

DRAVÉLA

Le Carrefour des Jeunes

AV MODIBO KEITA

AV DE LA RÉPUBLIQUE

RUE KARAMOKO DIABY

Air Algérie

Compagnet

Cinema Vox

RUE EL HADJ OUSMANE BAGAYOKO

RUE FAMOLO

Marché Rose

RUE MOHAMED V

BD DU PEUPLE

AV DE L'OTOKO

AV MAMADOU KONATE

Cathedral

BDM Bank

PLACE DU SOUVENIR

Street Market

RUE GOURAUD

BICIM Bank

Sûreté

RUE LYAUTEY

AV DE LA NATION

Cybercenter Saïd & Co

RUE LAPPERINE

RUE PASTEUR

RUE PROGER

Immeuble Sonavie

RUE POINCARE

Air Sénégal

OMATHO

AV DE LA MARNE

Air Ivoire

BDM Bank

Immeuble ex-USAID

SQUARE LUMUMBA

AV RUAULT

AV DE L'YSER

AV DE VERDUN

Tam Voyages

Centre Cultural Français

BOULEVARD DE L'INDÉPENDANCE

QUARTIER DU FLEUVE

RUE 311

RUE 309

Immeuble SCIF

French Embassy

BIM Bank

Eco Bank

Cybercom

Pyramide du Souvenir

PONT DES MARTYRS

RUE 313

Tour BCEAO

River Niger

AV MOUSSA TRAVELE

BD DU 22 OCTOBRE 1946

River Police

0   200 m

ACCOMMODATION

Les Cèdres	A
Centre d'Accueil	E F
Chez Fanta	F K
El Farouk	K
Graine de Baobab	C
Grand Hôtel	G
L'Amitié	B
La Maison des Jeunes	J I D
Mirabeau	D
Paroisse Sacré Coeur	L H
Salam	H
Yamey	

RESTAURANTS, BARS & CLUBS

Appaloosa	11
Le Bafoulabé	4
Ba Kao	12
Le Bol de Jade	10
Café Damu	5
Central	6
Diakarlo	2
Djembé	3
Le Hogon	1
L'Olympien	9
Pâtisserie les Delices	7
Pâtisserie le Royaume des Gourmands	8
Sukhothai	13
Le Tempo	14

ⓦgrainedebaobab.bleublog.ch. If it wasn't for
its slightly obscure location, clean, friendly, spacious and airy *La Graine* would undoubtedly be
the first choice of budget travellers for its good
6-bed dorms (CFA3500), roof-terrace mattresses
(CFA2000) or choice of fan-cooled or a/c doubles
– all highly recommended. ❸

Grand Hôtel av Van Vollenhoven ⓣ222.24.92
ⓦwww.azalaihotels.com. International-class
establishment, with two pools, tennis courts,
business centre, one of the city's best bookshops
and a top-end restaurant. That said, the *Grand* is
looking tired and is steadily being eclipsed by the
Hôtel Salam, also in the *Azalaï* chain, if only for the
latter's superior location by the Niger. ❼

La Maison des Jeunes three-storey complex
near the Pont des Martyrs ⓣ222.23.20. It may be
grimy and shabby, and without mosquito nets, but
the *Maison des Jeunes* boasts the lowest rates in
central Bamako and is a very good place to meet
people. Friendly enough, but security is far from
guaranteed – the compound is not locked at any
time, and muggings have occurred in the vicinity
(so avoid unlit shortcuts at night). Choose between
dorms of six to ten beds or basic single, twin or
triple rooms, some of which have a/c. Some of
the communal bathrooms are more bearable than
others. Camping is possible in the yard (CFA1500)
and there's a fine live-music venue opposite. Dorm
beds CFA2500, otherwise ❷.

🏃 **Mirabeau** rue 311 ⓣ223.53.18
ⓦmirabeau.50webs.com. With flowers
climbing the walls and spilling over from the
balconies, the *Mirabeau* is without doubt the
prettiest of rue 311's establishments catering
largely to Bamako's tourists. The facilities are
noteworthy too: it has one of the city's few ATMs
and even Wi-Fi in the rooms, which range from
simple but decent *chambres* with shared bathroom,
to suites with private bathroom. ❼

Paroisse Sacré Coeur just south of and opposite
the cathedral ⓣ222.58.42. A very central two-
storey colonial building with single rooms and one
double, plus a five-bed dorm, all on the upper floor.
Breakfast is included (except Sun). Dorm beds
CFA5000, otherwise ❷.

Hotel Salam a little out of the centre at the junction of a couple of busy thoroughfares ⓣ222.12.00
ⓦwww.azalaihotels.com. Newest, largest and
swankiest of the *Azalaï* chain, the *Salam* boasts
more than 100 rooms, restaurants, bars, pools, a
gym – indeed, everything a business traveller could
ask for. Its location is not ideal but you can forgive
it for its views across the Niger. ❽

Yamey 211, rue 311 ⓣ223.86.88. A welcome
addition to the growing list of tourist places on this

unassuming street, the *Yamey*'s bright, smart front
terrace makes promises that its somewhat gloomy
rooms fail to keep. Nevertheless, rooms are a/c,
s/c and fair-value, the place is friendly, and it's also
a stone's throw from some of the capital's most
popular restaurants. ❺

South of the river

Colibris south of the river, 3km from the centre
on av de l'OUA near the Sogoniko *gare routière*
ⓣ222.66.37 ⓦwww.hotelcolibris.com. Good-value
hotel with swimming pool, 55 quiet s/c rooms with
a/c and TV. There's also a popular bar-restaurant
and Internet access. ❺

Niaréla, Cité du Niger and Quinzambougou

🏃 **Djenné** Missira 1, rue 08, Porte 1039, off rte
de Koulikoro, to the west of the Hippodrome
ⓣ221.30.82 ⓔ djenneart@afribone.net.ml. An
unusual Sudanic-style hotel, jam-packed with
Malian artefacts, making it just about the prettiest
and most stylish hotel in the city. Small well-kept
s/c rooms all with a/c and TV (and similarly
attractive restaurant, the *San Toro*). ❺

🏃 **Jamana** off rte de Sotuba, Niaréla
ⓣ221.34.56. Recently revamped, the *Jamana*
is one of Niaréla's more established places and, like
just about everywhere round here, all rooms are s/c
and come with a/c and TV. Breakfast is included. ❺

Le Loft 687 rue Achkabad ⓣ221.66.90 ⓔleloft
@arc.net.ml. Though you'd never think it looking
at the exterior, this hotel is one of Bamako's most
pleasant places to stay. Smart, comfortable rooms
– all s/c and with a/c, TV and even Wi-Fi access
– hide behind the tatty facade. ❻

🏃 **Le Mandé** Cité du Niger, on the north bank
of the river 2km east of Pont des Martyrs
ⓣ221.19.93 ⓦwww.mandehotel.com. Beautiful
riverside hotel offering accommodation in round
houses, a pristine pool and a recommended restaurant, *Les Pilotis*, built out over the river. ❼

Le Rabelais rte de Sotuba, Niaréla, 3km east of
the station ⓣ221.52.98 ⓕ221.21.51. Popular
French-run hotel with comfortable, tastefully decorated a/c rooms and a relaxing pool/bar area. Best
choice in its category though the hotel does feel
rather cramped, as if shoehorned into a plot of land
too small for it. Rate includes breakfast. ❻

Tamana off rte Dafaka, east of the Hippodrome
ⓣ221.37.15 ⓦwww.hoteltamana.com. A stone's
throw from some of the capital's liveliest nightspots,
this is a friendly family-run hotel set in the shade of
some beautiful old trees, with smallish, very clean
a/c rooms, some s/c. Food is prepared on demand
and served in the communal dining area. ❺

The City

Bamako's bustle, filth and especially its heat make it a tiring place to enjoy at a leisurely walking pace unless, of course, you happen to thrive in sub-Saharan urban settings. In that case the **street market** around the new **Marché Rose** is the place for you. North of the **Centre Artisanal** along the Boulevard du Peuple, you'll find a good selection of **fetish stalls** with an impressive array of decomposing animal parts. And to the north of the railway tracks, the other main north–south avenue – Avenue de la Liberté – leads through the diplomatic district past the **Musée National**: if you do nothing else in Bamako, be sure to spend some time here.

The Centre Artisanal and Grande Mosquée

Built by the French in the 1930s in the Sudanic style, the **Centre Artisanal** or **Maison des Artisans** (at the corner of Boulevard du Peuple and rue Karamoko Diaby) was designed to promote traditional Malian art. Today it houses an abundance of shops and stalls selling **crafts and curios** of variable quality – leatherwork, fabric, silverware, masks, carvings, bronze figurines and musical instruments – as well as artisans' **workshops** where you can watch woodcarvers, silversmiths, drum makers and other craftspeople at work. Prices are reasonable.

A little to the east of the crafts market, the **Grande Mosquée** was a gift to Bamako from Saudi Arabia. It's not one they can have been too enthralled by – an imposing twin-minareted construction lacking the grace of the country's indigenous Sudanic architecture.

The museums

North of the centre, at the junction of Boulevard Nelson Mandela and Avenue de la Liberté, Bamako's **Musée National** (Tues–Sun 9am–6pm; CFA2500; guides available) is housed in a low-rise building inspired by the smooth lines of Djenné's architecture and contains some remarkable masterpieces of African art. Coming from place de la Liberté, the museum lies just after the flyover. Something of a pioneering institution, the museum is engaged in efforts to repatriate some of the vast treasure-store of artefacts taken abroad in colonial times, as well as in periodically rounding up materials from different parts of the country.

Inside, the **displays** are beautifully presented, with photographs discreetly lining the walls, putting the exhibits in a broader context. Lighting is subtle and the museum comfortably air-conditioned – in short, it's a good deal more than you might expect. All the labels are in French, but some of the well-informed guides speak English and they do some excellent tours (expect to pay an extra CFA3000 or so).

Part of the museum concentrates on domestic objects, including those used in **forging** – and a large, particularly strong, section is dedicated to the techniques involved in making some of the many types of **cloth** for which the region has a wide reputation. A separate section displays religious objects from Mali's various ethnic groups. Highlights include the stylized antelope **tyiwara** (*chiwara*) masks of the Bamana; various examples of **Senoufo statuary**; and, of course, the world-renowned antique **Dogon sculptures and masks**. The museum extends across the road into a series of caves with copies of prehistoric relics and an exhibition about evolution, evidently intended for children.

Away to the northeast of the city is the small but interesting **Musée Muso Kunda**, or **Musée de la Femme**, in Quartier Korofina (officially Tues–Sun 9am–6pm, though call T224.06.21 to check as these times aren't followed strictly). The museum is devoted to the traditional customs and dress of women from Mali's various ethnic groups, with displays on clothing, jewellery, hairstyles and marriage trousseaux. There are also some artisans' workshops with quality *bogolans* and crafts for sale, and a good restaurant.

Bamako's regional museum, the **Musée Bamako**, on place de la Liberté (Tues–Sun 9am–6pm; 500CFA), occupies a new building in grounds dotted with crude fibreglass sculptures of animals from the region. On the ground floor, one room contains a jumble of items, from an ostrich egg to a full-size pirogue – none of which have any direct bearing on Bamako's past – and a second is filled with photos from the city's colonial era. On the second floor, there's a selection of art of dubious quality. If you're in the area and seeking a cool escape from the noise, you will in all likelihood have the place to yourself, and the café in the *paillote* next door has comfy chairs and cold beers. But this is not worth going out of your way to visit.

The zoo and botanical gardens

Bamako's **zoo** was a good idea whose time has passed. In theory, the cages and enclosures are designed to resemble closely the animals' natural habitats, but it's run-down and neglected, and the range of animals on show is limited. While gazelles are kept in a quite large open space, monkeys, lions, birds and others are not so lucky. The surrounding **botanical gardens** are vast and, with a little attention, could provide a beautiful retreat from the city. The **Boucle du Baoulé park office** is located here and can offer some information about visiting (Opération Parc National de la Boucle du Baoulé; ☎222.24.98 @ conservationature@datatech.net.ml).

From the National Museum and zoo, you can walk up to the **north of the city** and to the hill known as **Point G**, the location of the main hospital. There are wonderful views from here, and some abandoned cliff dwellings featuring old **rock paintings**.

Eating, drinking and nightlife

Bamako has most of the country's best **restaurants**. If you've made your way here from the northeast, you'll be pleasantly surprised at the range of French, Italian, Lebanese, Chinese and fancy Malian fare on offer, while if you've arrived from Dakar, it's the affordability of eating out that impresses. **Street food** is abundant in central Bamako, and it's worth noting the locations of the better roadside stalls or *cafémen*, who serve Nescafé and baguette-omelette breakfasts as well as meat-based snacks during the day. A popular area to check out is the square off Avenue Modibo Keita next to Cinema Vox, but pretty much every neighbourhood has its own collection of stalls.

Bamako has first-rate nightlife, though the action only really gets going late. **rue Dafaka**, near the Hippodrome east of the centre, is abuzz with life throughout the weekend, and worth seeking out; it's known locally as place Pigalle (after the notorious Parisian red-light district), and lined with bars and restaurants.

Restaurants, cafés and snack bars

As well as the following listings, most of the city's better **restaurants** – almost all French – are in the hotels. The restaurants at the *Rabelais*, *Mandé* and *Grand* have good reputations, as do *l'Amitié*'s three restaurants. It's worth booking a table whenever possible.

Central Bamako

Appaloosa rue 311, off av de l'Yser ☎222.15.14. Tex-Mex place – a real expat favourite – with steak- and burger-type dishes and decor and cowboy-hatted waiters so convincing that you almost forget where you are. *Plats du jour* are around CFA5000, the *menu complet* CFA12,000.

Le Bafoulabé off av Modibo Keita at place de la Liberté. Cheap and friendly Senegalese restaurant on a quiet first-floor terrace, serving *riz gras* and other regional dishes at fair prices. The grass walls don't quite block out the noise from the *Somatra* stop below, but it's an escape from the hubbub nevertheless.

Le Bol de Jade av Ruault, just west of Square Lumumba ☎222.63.03. Well-established restaurant offering Chinese and Vietnamese dishes, and a good-value set menu.

Café Damu rue 133, opposite the Catholic hostel. Friendly little shack whose affable owner offers good breakfasts and *riz gras* at very reasonable prices.

Central rue Loveran. Well-established formica-and-vinyl place serving French, African and Lebanese food, with a small terrace outside. The nearest thing to a tourist restaurant in this part of the city, though not the best value in town.

Diakarlo across from the train station (24-hr take-away). Inexpensive pizza place. Not the greatest food but a quiet retreat in an otherwise hectic neighbourhood.

L'Olympien av Ruault, next to *Bol de Jade* ☎223.87.23. A popular pizzeria, this one is a lot pricier than the rest, serving a few select French dishes as well. Also does takeaway.

Pâtisserie Les Délices rue Famolo Coulibaly ☎223.35.02 (Mon–Fri 6.30am–midnight, Sat 6.30am–1am, closed Sun). Welcoming, inexpensive patisserie/restaurant with an irresistible display of cakes and pastries, plus ice cream, drinks and a long menu of light meals including omelettes, pizzas, burgers and salads. Internet café.

Pâtisserie le Royaume des Gourmands av Modibo Keita (☎277.56.58). An air-conditioned haven in the bustle of the city centre, this is one of the best places to get breakfast before heading out into the hurly burly, with reasonable croissants and omelettes from CFA1300–1800.

Sukhothai rue 311, off av de l'Yser ☎222.24.48 (closed Sat lunchtimes & Sun). The best and most authentic Thai cooking – indeed, possibly the best foreign cuisine – in the whole of West Africa, this is the place to come

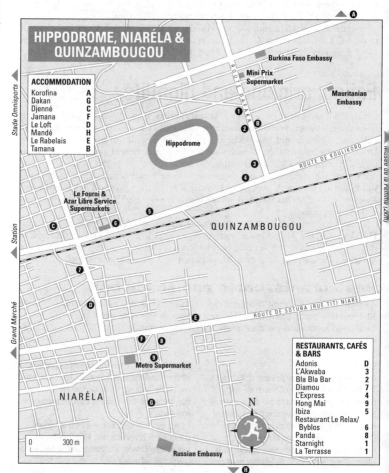

HIPPODROME, NIARÉLA & QUINZAMBOUGOU

ACCOMMODATION

Korofina	A
Dakan	G
Djenné	C
Jamana	F
Le Loft	D
Mandé	H
Le Rabelais	E
Tamana	B

Burkina Faso Embassy
Mini Prix Supermarket
Mauritanian Embassy
ROUTE DAKAKA
Hippodrome
ROUTE DE KOULIKORO
Le Fourni & Azar Libre Service Supermarkets
QUINZAMBOUGOU
ROUTE DE SOTUBA (RUE TITI NIARÉ)
Metro Supermarket
NIARÉLA
N
Russian Embassy

Stade Omnisports
Station
Grand Marché

Musée de la Femme (2km)

RESTAURANTS, CAFÉS & BARS

Adonis	D
L'Akwaba	3
Bla Bla Bar	2
Diamou	7
L'Express	4
Hong Mai	9
Ibiza	5
Restaurant Le Relax/ Byblos	6
Panda	8
Starnight	1
La Terrasse	1

0   300 m

for such fiery favourites as Thai green curry (CFA5500–7000) as well as a delicious version of that Siamese standard, *pad thai* (CFA6500).

Hippodrome, Niaréla and Quinzambougou

Adonis rue Achkabad, under *Le Loft*. Whilst it will never win any awards for culinary creativity, *Adonis* is cheap, clean and affably run, with a menu consisting of burgers, kebabs and falafel, mostly served with chips.

L'Akwaba rte Dafaka, Hippodrome ☎221.06.45 ⓦ mali.viky.net/akwaba/. Reliably good French and African food, with live music at weekends.

Diamou Boulangerie Pâtisserie rue Achkabad. Probably the best patisserie in Bamako, *Diamou* sells a huge range of treats including exquisite ice cream, pizzas, chocolates and, of course, some delicious bread and cakes.

L'Express rte de Koulikoro, near the Hippodrome (daily until late). Upmarket French and Lebanese snacks.

Hong Mai off rte de Sotuba ☎221.70.85. Just down from the *Panda*, this discreet restaurant is a firm favourite with the expat crowd and rightly so thanks to its no-nonsense, fairly priced Vietnamese menu.

Panda off rte de Sotuba, near *Hôtel Jamana*, Niaréla. Good-value Chinese food served indoors in a/c premises, or out on the porch or garden terrace.

Le Relax rte de Koulikoro ☎222.79.18. Airy patisserie/restaurant with a bright terrace, popular with the expat community. Fresh croissants and juice for breakfast, snacks and specialities such as *Capitaine la Bamakoise* (Nile perch with plantain) at any time of day.

San Toro rte de Koulikoro ☎221.30.82 (no alcohol). Refined Malian cuisine from the owners of the nearby *Djenné Hôtel*. The interior is decorated with authentic Malian artefacts and there's a pleasant garden where musicians often play.

Nightlife

The now rather grubby *Buffet Hôtel de la Gare* used to be the city's most famous nightspot, a showcase for the **Rail Band** (see p.349), who still play here on the odd Saturday. New clubs, including some quite sophisticated establishments, spring up regularly.

Bars, clubs and music venues

Bla Bla Bar rue Dafaka, Hippodrome. Still one of the hottest haunts in the city, with a busy terrace bar and dancing until the early hours.

Boa Kao rue 313, north of the Tour BCEAO, close to Malivision in the city centre. Cocktail bar and music venue, with an eclectic mix of bands (Fri & Sat) playing everything from hardcore reggae to gentle jazz noodling. French-run and a little over-priced, it's a pleasant enough spot and convenient for *La Maison des Jeunes*.

Byblos rte de Koulikoro, Quinzambougou. Next to *Le Relax* restaurant, long established and still going strong. Always draws a large crowd at the weekend.

Carrefour des Jeunes av Kasse Keita, city centre, off pl de la Liberté. You're more or less guaranteed live music every weekend at this community youth centre; there's an upstairs terrace bar where you can enjoy a beer under the stars while listening to Malian blues, Afro-Cuban dance music or reggae.

Club Ibiza rte de Koulikoro, Quinzambougou. The new kid in town – huge, garish and tacky, but popular thanks to an eclectic mix of music.

Djembé Lafiabougou, west of the city centre. Open nightly (though at its best and busiest at the weekends), the *Djembé* is an intimate affair with griot music most nights of the week.

Le Hogon Ntomikorobougou, northwest of the city centre off the Kati and Kita road (☎223.07.60). One of Bamako's smartest clubs, built in the style of a Dogon village, owned by *kora* maestro Toumani Diabaté and occasional venue for his Symmetric Orchestra.

Savana Korofina Nord, northeast of the city centre (☎671.08.24). An eclectic mix of music, including everything from reggae to Bamana and, occasionally, local troubadours in a more traditional style, attracts Bamako's trendies.

Starnight rte Dafaka. Occupying a prime position on this nightlife street. A bit too sweaty and glitzy inside – but after midnight, who's complaining?

Le Tempo av Moussa Travélé (☎222.88.00). Salubrious and expensive, with a garden bar and an indoor dance-floor and bar/restaurant. Like everywhere else, it's busiest on Fri & Sat, but the music is different every night of the week: regular sessions include a good choice of Senegalese, Cuban and Malian music.

Listings

Airlines Afriqiyah Airways (☎229.77.63), Air Burkina (☎221.01.78), Air Guinée (☎229.24.86), Royal Air Maroc (☎22167.03) and Tunisair (☎221.86.42) are all in Imm Sonavie, in the grounds of *Sofitel l'Amitié*; Air France (☎222.22.12), Air Mauritanie (☎222.87.38) and Ethiopian Airlines (☎222.60.36) are all in Imm SCIF, Square Lumumba; Air Algérie, corner of av Modibo Keita and rue 324 ☎222.31.59; Air Ivoire, between av de l'Yser and av Ruault ☎223.95.58; Air Sénégal, 555 av Modibo Keita ☎223.98.11; Cameroon Airlines, av Kasse Keita ☎223.20.05; Compagnie Aerienne du Mali, Imm TOMATA, av Cheik Zayed, Hamdallaye ☎222.24.24 ⓦwww.camaero.com/cam; Kenya Airways, Atlas GSA, Imm La Babemba, av Kasse Keita ☎222.12.35; Mali Air Express, av de la Nation ☎223.14.65 ⓦwww.malipages.com/mae; Point-Afrique, Imm ex-USAID, av de l'Yser ☎223.54.70.

Airport ☎220.27.01.

American Express The Amex representative in Bamako is ATS Agence de Voyages (☎222.78.92) in the Cameroon Airlines office, av Kasse Keita.

Banks The capital now boasts several ATMs that accept Visa cards. BICIM currently leads the field in this respect, with cashpoints in the *Sofitel l'Amitié* and the *Mirabeau*, as well as in its branches, the most convenient of which is on the bd du Peuple ☎223.33.70. The ATMs of BDM, opposite the cathedral on av du Fleuve (☎223.18.72) and on pl de la Nation (☎222.50.89), do not as yet take foreign cards though you can get Visa advances in the branches, change € or $ cash and arrange Western Union money transfers. To change any other currency, your best bet is Bank of Africa, just east of the *Sofitel L'Amitié*.

Bookshops There's a decent stock of English-language fiction and travel guides, as well as French-language newspapers and magazines at the *Grand Hôtel*.

Car rental Malienne de l'Automobile (Hertz representative), rte de Koulikoro, Korofina/Diélibougou ☎224.67.68 or 224.28.56.

Cinemas The most comfortable cinema is the Babemba, at the western end of av Kasse Keita; tickets are CFA1500–2000.

Cultural centres The Centre Cultural Français, bd de l'Indépendance, has a café-bar and a good library with French newspapers and magazines. They also organize exhibitions, film screenings and concerts. Similar activities are arranged at USIS, the American Cultural Centre on the south bank, Badalabougou Est. They have American mags and papers plus a few good books about Mali.

Embassies and consulates Algeria, 349 av de l'OUA, Daoudabougou ☎220.51.76 ⓕ222.93.74 ⓔambalg.bko@datatech.toolnet.org; Australia, c/o Canada (see below); Burkina Faso, Quartier ACI 2000 ☎229.31.71; Canada, Imm Séméga, rte de Koulikoro ☎221.22.36 ⓦtinyurl.com/24z53a; Côte d'Ivoire, rue 220 ☎221.22.89; France, Square Lumumba ☎221.31.41 or 221.29.51, ⓕ222.31.36; Germany, av OAU, Badalabougou Est ☎222.32.99 ⓕ222.96.50; Ghana, Hamdallaye/ACI 2000 ☎229.09.38; Guinea on the south side of the river, behind the *Hôtel Colibris* on rte de Magnambougou, quartier Fasso Kanu ☎220.20.36; Mauritania, off rte de Koulikoro ☎221.48.15; Niger, av Mamadou Konaté, near *Hôtel Chez Fanta* ☎221.99.25; Nigeria, south of the Pont des Martyrs, Badalabougou Est ☎222.57.71 ⓕ222.52.84; Senegal, 341 rue 287, off av Nelson Mandela, Hippodrome ☎221.82.74; UK, c/o Canada (see above) ☎277.46.37 ⓔbelo@ikaso.net; USA, 297 rue 243, ACI 2000 ☎216.270.23.00 ⓦmali.usembassy.gov.

Internet access You're not going to have any trouble finding Internet cafés in Bamako, though finding a reliable one outside of the bigger hotels (who charge the most) is trickier. Many of the bigger hotels – and indeed some of the medium-budget hotels too, such as *Le Loft* in Niaréla and *Hôtel Mirabeau* now have Wi-Fi in all rooms. The reliability of Internet cafés changes frequently, though. The Ecotel in the Pyramide du Souvenir, near the Pont des Martyrs, is popular, but Compucafé at the Carrefour des Jeunes youth centre is cheaper (CFA250/hr) and usually faster too.

Maps The Direction Nationale de Cartographie, off av de l'OUA, Badalabougou Est, is the place to go for 1:200,000 survey maps. They also have a few country maps and city plans.

Post and telephones The poste centrale (Mon–Fri 7.30am–5.30pm, Sat 8am–noon) is on rue Karamoko Diaby, not far from the market. Scattered around the city are payphones which take phone cards (Sotelma's cards are cheapest: CFA5000 for 50 minutes of local calls), sold on the street at most junctions. Alternatively, calls can be made (at higher rates) from any of the *télécentres* – there are plenty in the area around the main post office.

Supermarkets The eastern end of the city, where most of the expat community live, is a good place to find these. Metro is next to the Shell station on rte de Sotuba, in Niaréla, and Fourni and Azar Libre Service are a similar distance from the centre near *Le Relax* restaurant on rte de Koulikoro. On the other side of the Hippodrome, Mini Prix is on route Dafaka, not far from *Hôtel Tamana*.

Swimming pools The pools at the *Grand* are small, but okay for cooling off (CFA2500); *Le Rabelais* (CFA3000) has a popular poolside bar. **Travel agents** It can be useful to talk to a travel agent if you're looking to rent a 4x4 vehicle and driver, or to join an organized tour. Among the better firms are: the Tuareg-run Azawad Voyages, specializing in the Gao and Timbuktu region ☎221.98.69 ✉azawadvoy@hotmail.com; the resourceful TAM Voyages, Square Lumumba ☎222.05.47 or 221.56.93 ⓦtamvoyages @cefib.com; Saga Tours, 659 rue 802 ☎220.27.08 ⓦwww.sagatours.com; and the helpful West African Air Services, 27 rue 283, Hippodrome ☎228.81.57 ⓦwww.africa-ata.org/mali.htm. **Visa extensions** At the Sûreté Nationale, av de la Nation (Mon–Thurs 8am–2pm, Fri & Sat 7.30am–12.30pm).

4.2
Kayes and the west

Often ignored by travellers because of its poor transport connections, rough roads and inaccessibility during the rainy season, **western Mali** contains some of the country's most beautiful scenery and easily rewards travellers with their own robust vehicles, or footloose adventurers with time and patience on their hands. Fortunately, roads in this region are in the process of being upgraded and, on a good day, it's possible to travel by car between Bamako and **Kayes**, the regional capital, in less than twelve hours. It's a region of rivers, remote villages and wooded escarpments, where the Baoulé, Bakoye and Bafing rivers rush from the **Manding Highlands** through the hilly landscapes of the **Malinké country** before joining forces to form the **Senegal River**. It's also the best place to encounter some of Mali's **wildlife**: warthogs, baboons and iridescent blue kingfishers prosper in these isolated districts, and there are even small numbers of lions in the vicinity of Kéniéba. The region is also historically significant, for it was this region that was the heartland of the thirteenth-century **Mali kingdom** which expanded into a vast empire incorporating Djenné, Timbuktu and distant Gao.

The Senegal/Bafing flows through the realm of the Fula-speaking **Tukulor** people, which extends west from Kayes, a commercial centre of more than 100,000 people serving the region's mining ventures. South of Kayes, **Kéniéba** is a remote outpost serving local gold-mining activities, and a dead end unless you plan to undertake backcountry border-crossings into Guinea or Senegal.

Kayes and south to Kéniéba

An agreeable riverside town (and the first major town if you've come by road from Dakar), **KAYES** was once the capital of the Haut Sénégal-Niger colony, until the seat was transferred to Bamako early last century, when the train line pushed through from Dakar. Kayes is historically an important transport hub, with three trains a week to Bamako still slowly crossing the scenic west Manding Highlands (two of them partly in daylight). It is also the best place to seek out transport into parts of the region not served by the train, and a viable (if adventurous) departure point, for northern Guinea and southeast Senegal. Kayes also has the dubious honour of being Africa's hottest town, with afternoon temperatures between March and May crackling into the high forties Celsius.

If you're stuck here for a few days, the **French Fort** in MÉDINE, 12km southeast of Kayes on the Senegal River, is easily reached and a good side-trip. Built by the French in 1855 to protect their commercial interests in the area, it withstood a siege by the Tukolor jihadist El Hadj Omar in 1857 and became a base for French troops in 1878. The most scenic way of getting here is by pirogue – you can rent one near the new bridge in Kayes. It's a peaceful picnic and camping spot, and guides can easily be found in Kayes and Médine.

Practicalities

The **train station** is about 1km southeast of the town centre and taxis greet the arriving trains. The *gare routière* is on the north side of the river in Kayes Ndi. The town has a post office, airstrip, several pharmacies and a number of banks including BDM, near the post office on the road along the river's south bank, where you can get a Visa cash advance. The BNDA changes both cash and traveller's cheques. Note that changing on the black market (in the central market) gives you a worse rate than the banks. A reliable **Internet** place is Sotelma, next to the post office and open daily (CFA1000/hour).

Accommodation

Kayes has few accommodation options. The *Khasso* offers the best rooms, though the *Médine*, with its small restaurant, is also very popular. If you're on a tight budget, the *Centre d'Accueil* is the cheapest.

Centre d'Accueil de la Jeunesse just 300m from the station (head towards town and take the first left after *Hôtel du Rail*) ☎ 252.12.54. Described by one traveller as the worst night's sleep in West Africa, this cheapie was refurbished for the African Nations Cup in 2002 but is still extremely basic; nevertheless, if your bus makes a compulsory stop in Kayes overnight, this is probably where you'll end up. ❷

Le Khasso near the waterfront on av Macdeoura ☎ 253.16.66. The fourteen small, tidy chalets with a/c and hot water are the best in town and it's sometimes full. The bar-restaurant and terrace overlooking the Senegal/Bafing River make it a popular venue. ❺

Le Logo Across the road from the *Khasso* ☎ 252.13.81. A few fairly priced a/c rooms with bath, and a bar-restaurant serving reasonable food. ❸

Médine near the bridge on rue Magdeburg, qtr Khasso ☎ 253.11.09. Likely overnight if you're on a long-distance bus to Senegal. Modern, but not special, the a/c rooms are marginally cleaner and more comfortable than those with fan. Small but decent restaurant. Rooms with fan or a/c ❸.

Hôtel du Rail directly opposite the station ☎ 252.12.33. Long past its colonial-era heyday, this still offers a certain faded splendour with spacious s/c rooms and suites. There's a decent enough bar-restaurant and another bar set in the peaceful garden at the front. ❺

Eating and nightlife

Budget **restaurants** are thin on the ground in Kayes. The best value is provided by *Pâtisserie Eclosion*, at rue du 22 Septembre, which does good breakfasts and main meals. The alternative is **street food** at the large market or train station. Otherwise the hotels all have restaurants – *Hôtel Médine*'s is widely reckoned to be the best. **Nightlife** in Kayes isn't exactly hectic, though *Le Khasso* has an excellent garden and is always lively at weekends, with regular live music.

To Kéniéba and beyond

South of Kayes, a corrugated *piste* follows the **Falaise de Tambaoura** for 240km to the small town of **Kéniéba**, caught in a suntrap by a bend in the Tambaoura's picturesque, towering cliffs. This is the start of a possible (but arduous) route from western Mali to **Labé**, in Guinea's highland Fouta Djalon region. It also provides

Moving on from Kayes

The most obvious – if no longer the easiest – form of transport out of Kayes is the **train**. The "Autorail" domestic service is scheduled to depart Kayes at 12.15pm on Tues and Sat and 8.15pm on Sun, arriving in Bamako about 18 hours later, having stopped at every station en route. Fares are CFA11,670 in 1st-class and CFA18,775 for a couchette sleeping berth (only available on limited services). In theory you can also use the so-called "Express" Dakar–Bamako service, in either direction (slightly more expensive fares to Bamako than the "Autorail"), but note that its scheduled weekly arrivals into Kayes in each direction have gone off the scale of unpredictability at the time of writing (see p.360 for more information).

Heading to **Senegal**, you'll find that road improvements on both sides of the border make going by road much easier than trying to use the train. You can get a bus from Kayes all the way to Dakar (Wed & Sat at 5pm; CFA15,000), a relatively painless trip of fifteen hours. Bush taxis to the border town of **Diboli** leave constantly (CFA3000; 2hr), passing through light baobab woodland en route to the border, where a road bridge spans the Faléme River and leads straight into the flyblown Senegalese town of **Kidira**.

For **Bamako**, there's a reasonably reliable and comfortable daily truck-bus operated by Sangue Voyage (8am; 12hr) via **Diéma** and **Didiéni**. Buy tickets the day before at the *gare routière* in Kayes Ndi on the north side of the river.

If **Mauritania** is your destination, ask around in Kayes Ndi for vehicles heading for **Sélibabi**, 160km to the northwest, or **Kiffa** on the Nouakchott highway.

In theory at least, five weekly MAE **flights** (℡252.15.82) do the Kayes–Bamako run, flying daily Mon–Thurs as well as on Sat mornings. CAM (℡601.19.43) supplements this with a further flight per week to Bamako. The offices are close together, between the train station and the town centre.

an interesting, if time-consuming, entry point to the extreme southeastern corner of Senegal.

Transport to Kéniéba leaves Kayes from Avenue du 22 Septembre around the *Eclosion* patisserie, in the town centre. Trucks and minibuses leave in the late afternoon or early evening and take up to twelve hours (CFA7000); 4x4 vehicles leave early morning and take eight hours (CFA9000). An alternative is to ask around in Kayes for trucks making the bumpy, eight-hour journey every day. You'll have to pay, but if you get a front seat, you'll enjoy some fine views on the way down.

The road is straightforward only as far as **SADIOLA** (a third of the way to Kéniéba), a stretch maintained by the mining companies. The women in the Sadiola district have collected **gold** from the bush for centuries – local legends tell of their ostensibly destitute husbands having amassed several kilos of the metal each during a lifetime. These days, Sadiola has West Africa's most important gold mine, complete with South African technicians.

Kéniéba and on to Guinea and Senegal

The frontier-town isolation of **KÉNIÉBA**, and its proximity to the Senegalese and Guinean borders, make it something of a smuggling entrepôt for cigarettes and alcohol coming in from Guinea, just a few kilometres away. You can **stay** at the basic, very cheap, but none too clean *Casa Ronde* (●) with an okay restaurant. Down here you'll find a post office, some stores and a small **market**. The town also has a regional hospital and a couple of petrol stations.

If you're looking for transport to **Guinea**, ask around in town; trucks are said to leave regularly from the *centre transportique* opposite the post office for some illicit trading at **KALI** on the Guinea border. If you head this way expect the unexpected on the Guinean side and have money, *cadeaux* and time to spare. Alternatively you can rent a **motorbike** to Kali (CFA7500, including driver; ask for the mechanics near the market) and catch a vehicle on from there.

Rides to **Kédougou in Senegal** are dependent on there being enough passengers to fill up a Land Rover, and on the depth of the **Falémé River** (usually crossable from January until the rains resume), which marks the unstaffed frontier. If nothing turns up after a couple of days' wait, again renting a motorbike is the alternative (CFA15,000). Although twice the price of a shared 4x4, it's a memorable, no less uncomfortable six-hour ride along winding bush tracks into Senegal's **Pays Bassari** region.

From Kayes to Bamako

There is now **paved road or graded earth** for much of the way **from Kayes to Bamako** via Sandaré and Diéma (running well to the south of Nioro du Sahel), then via Kolokani, skirting the northeast side of the Boucle du Baoulé national park. As for the **old road**, further south, following the railway line **from Kayes via Bafoulabé and Kita**, early sections of it are in a terrible state, but maintenance, and some improvement, is ongoing.

Kayes to Bamako via Diéma

Between Kayes and Nioro lies a great region for exploration in your own (suitably equipped) vehicle. The whole district is beautiful, roamed by **Fula herders** and with impressive **baobabs**. But away from the new highway, the rough bush tracks are mostly in a state of advanced disrepair and any kind of transport and facilities almost nonexistent.

In recent years, there has been an emerald rush in the **Sandaré** district, 140km east of Kayes, with hundreds of miners flocking in hope to the area of **ANGOULÁ**, living in improvised camps near the mines. You are certain to be offered emeralds for sale here. The most worthwhile diversion, however, is to **YÉLIMANÉ**, turning left off the main road about 80km east of Kayes, and driving some 70km north. Ten kilometres or so before Yélimané, there's a marshy area called **Goumbogo**, highly recommended if you're interested in wildlife, especially noted for its migratory birds. West of Yélimané, you can also make a 45-kilometre trip to the **Mare de Toya**, a spectacular geological rift and lake forming part of the Mauritanian frontier. If you want to reach civilization quickly there are morning Bamako–Yélimané–Bamako flights (Mon & Thurs), with MAE (Yélimané agency ℡252.22.62).

If you're driving to Bamako, you bypass Nioro completely, forking east at Sandaré for **Diéma**, on the new route to the capital. Twenty kilometres after Diéma, the *piste* passes through the **Vallée du Serpent**, named for the **Baoulé River**'s tortuous course as it snakes down from the Manding Highlands.

Nioro du Sahel and beyond

NIORO DU SAHEL is a seventeenth-century town – one of the old royal capitals of the Bamana kingdom of Kaarta – built on a plateau and famed for its **mosque**, which is one of the most important in Mali. There's a police and customs post here, petrol stations, a bank, a pharmacy, a hospital and an airstrip but **accommodation** is limited to two frugal *campements* (CFA2000 per person). The one in the administrative quarter is a little more bearable than the one by the war memorial statue, and has a restaurant with simple food and cold beer.

Nioro is a common departure point for **Mauritania**, with a new paved road linking it to **Ayoun el Atrous**, making the 167km journey feasible in about three hours, plus border-crossing time. Check for lifts around the marketplace.

Boucle du Baoulé National Park

The route of the Baoulé River forms the northern borders of the **Parc National de la Boucle du Baoulé** – 3300 square kilometres of wooded savannah and forest, which once harboured a significant animal population, including elephant, antelope, buffalo, warthog, giraffe and even lion. Today, practically all the wildlife has been hunted out of the park and the best reason to visit (assuming you have a 4x4 vehicle) is for its many **archeological remains**: there are more than two hundred sites of rock paintings, ancient tombs and burial grounds. The park's infrastructure is extremely limited, but there are three *campements* in the southern district, the main one being at the village of Baoulé itself, at the southeast entrance to the park, north of **NÉGALA** some 60km west of Bamako on the road to Kita. You can get the latest information at the park's headquarters, inside the botanical gardens in Bamako (see p.365).

Kayes to Bamako via Kita

The Kayes–Bamako railway line passes through a scenic area of hills and wooded escarpments, a welcome change from bleak plains if you've arrived from Senegal. The west-flowing **Bakoye** and **Senegal rivers** run parallel to the tracks for a good part of the journey, thrashing into rough rapids at several points along their courses, the lowest of which are the **Chutes de Félou**, just 10km east of Kayes. There's a pleasant swimming and picnic spot at the more spectacular **Chutes de Gouina**, 65km further upstream towards Bamako, but it can be hard to get to even with a 4x4.

If you're trying to drive this route, or use local transport, you're likely to find the road in a terrible state – it can take all day just to reach **BAFOULABÉ**, where the Bafing and Bakoye rivers converge to form the Senegal about 130km southeast of Kayes. There's a good chance of seeing hippos here. The town, 3km north of the railway station at **MAHINA**, also has a small market. Heading out of Bafoulabé towards Bamako, adventurous drivers share the long rail bridge across the Bafing River and continue 200km east to Kita on an often very difficult road. Just east of Bafoulabé are the **Chutes de Kale**, followed in turn by the **Chutes de Billy**, 270km short of Bamako. None of these rapids is visible from the train, and you do need your own transport to get off the road that crisscrosses the railway line to get near them. If you're travelling by rail, you'll welcome the food stop at **TOUKOTO**, 67km west of Kita, where plenty of cooked and fresh food is brought to the train.

If you're driving from Bafoulabé to Kita, or going by bus or taxi, the easier route now deviates from the railway line, going south via Manantali, on an earth road that is usually in good condition. **MANANTALI** is perched on the Bafing, just below a dam and huge hydroelectric plant. The vast, scenic dam lake is favoured by development workers as a place to swim and hippo-watch, and you can still see the remains of submerged trees and buildings beneath the surface. There's good food and accommodation in well-kept a/c cabins available at *La Cité des Cadres* (☏940.63.23 ❷), run by the dam company; the guard will help you to get the keys from the head office.

Kita

Roughly two-thirds of the way from Kayes to Bamako, **KITA** is one of the former capitals of Sundiata Keita's medieval Mali empire, and if you're into Malian **music** it's a good place to stop over a night or two, as many traditional griots hail from around here. **Mont Kita Kourou**, with caves decorated with rock paintings, rises impressively to the west of the town. There are several **places to stay** in town. *Hôtel Dieudonné* (❷), on the Manantali road about 1.5km from town, has rooms with fans, decent food and cold beer, and is the place to find lifts for Manantali. A cheaper alternative is the *Relais Touristique* (☏257.40.02 ❸), 200m down the road from the railway station, which is a basic dive. For good inexpensive **food** try *l'Oasis* (*Chez Issa*), in the centre, which offers basic meals on the terrace, or *Restaurant Appia*, on the station road, a seedy late-night brothel-type place, which does serve excellent rice and sauce.

Trains pass through Kita three or four times each week in each direction, taking up to ten hours to Kayes (and on one service continuing to Dakar) and up to eight hours to Bamako, but even these crumbling services are in decline as the road network improves (for more details, see "Moving on from Kayes", p.371).

The **road from Kita to Bamako** is usually in reasonable condition.

Bafing National Park

For the adventurous and independently mobile, a deteriorating track leads 140km southwest of Kita to the rarely visited **Parc National du Bafing**, close to the Guinean border. Wildlife is scarce here, due to intensive hunting, with few monkeys and very few chimpanzees (not seen for a long time), and today the park is mainly visited for its flora. The park can also be reached from Manantali via **MAKINDOUGOU**, where you can find the reserve office and get permission to visit and camp. They'll also help with a much-needed guide (even to find the reserve itself).

4.3

Ségou and around

etween Bamako and the delta region lies a broad expanse of territory where numerous kingdoms rose to power after the demise of the Songhai Empire. Most important were the **Bamana Empire of Ségou** and the **Kénédougou Empire** in the **Senoufo country**, with **Sikasso** its capital. Although they were eclipsed almost as quickly as they sprang up, these towns have remained important commercially thanks to their positions on well-travelled routes, and all are interlinked with daily bus or bush-taxi services.

Ségou and around

The third largest town in Mali, **SÉGOU**, 240km northeast of Bamako, makes a very pleasant stopover between Bamako and Mopti and is fast becoming a worthwhile destination in its own right. Reminders of the colonial period still stand out in graceful administrative buildings in the neo-Sudanic style, especially at the west end of town. Traditional Bamana **architecture** is still mostly successful in holding its own against modern cement buildings, and today whole quarters of this quiet tree-lined town are filled with rust-coloured *banco* houses. In the Quartier Somono, just east of the *Auberge* hotel, thirty houses were recently restored in traditional style by a French group from Ségou's twin city, Angoulême. Away from the busy **market** (the main day is Monday), much of the modern activity focuses on the banks of the **Niger**, with its pirogues and crowds. The town also has a thriving community of artisans, including cotton weavers, *bogolan* artists, rug makers and potters, and is starting to assert itself as Mali's **cultural capital**, with its crafts galleries and annual festival.

The history of Ségou

The **kingdom of Ségou** had its roots in the seventeenth century, when a Bamana chief, Kaladjan Coulibaly, brought his people to settle in the area. In 1620 his son established the village of Ségou-Koro (old Ségou, also known by the Bamana name of Sékoro), about 10km from the present town. In 1712 the able if despotic **Biton Mamary Coulibaly**, widely considered the true founder of the kingdom, became *fama* (king). The army he formed carved out a huge kingdom stretching from Timbuktu to the banks of the Senegal River, and the enemy soldiers captured during his conquests were marched to the coastal forts in Senegambia and the Gold Coast where they were traded with slavers for firearms. Along with the Songhai to the north, the Bamana Empire of Ségou was one of the earliest in the Sahara to obtain guns, which were used effectively to subdue rival powers.

The Bamana rulers developed a **nationalist policy** in which all rights were accorded to loyal Bamana subjects but conquered peoples were excluded from the system altogether. It was a tenuous arrangement based purely on force of arms, and when the Fula empire of Masina arose in the northeast, disgruntled elements in the Bamana country rallied to it, assuring the demise of Ségou as a political entity.

In 1861, **El Hadj Omar** conquered Ségou and forced the inhabitants – who had remained one of the few non-Muslim groups in the Sahel – to convert to Islam. After the French took the city in 1892, Ségou became an important French outpost and headquarters of the Office du Niger. For a captivating description of this period, read the classic historical novel *Segu* by Maryse Condé (see p.354).

Practicalities

Compared with the relative hustle of Bamako or Mopti, Ségou is an easy place in practical terms, with a good number of **accommodation** options and several decent **places to eat** including one or two great-value rice-and-sauce places – plus a good Lebanese **supermarket**, *Chez Tony*. The town is centred on the area immediately south of the ferry port, though the *gare routière* lies an inconvenient three kilometres out of town on the main road to Mopti. Nearer the centre, **Somatra** has a terminal behind the water tower here, while Bittar Transport has a depot just north of the Muslim cemetery. *Bâchés* and donkey carts are the main options for transport around town.

The most reliable place to **get online** is Sotelma (Mon–Fri 8am–8pm, Sat & Sun 9am–8pm), on the Bamako road opposite the Commissariat (CFA1000/hr). The only **bank** that changes money is the BDM, near the hospital on the Ségou–Koro road; they're slow, but do Visa cash advances.

Ségou is as good a place as any if you want to find a **guide for the Dogon country**. The scene here is less hectic than in Mopti and Bamako, and the guides (ask to see their badges or a *carte de Guide* before agreeing to anything) are members of a new association who, besides covering the Dogon country, can arrange excellent trips around the Ségou area, in addition to renting out bikes, motos and cars. There is an office of the Guides Association (☎692.16.76) facing the river next to COMANAV (daily 8am–5pm, closed Mon), although you can usually find one of the members hanging out near one of the major hotels. Alternatively, *L'Auberge* has a notice board on its verandah, with the official rates for guides and vehicle hire.

There's a recently opened **tourist information centre** on the waterfront Quai des Arts (9am–noon, 3–5.30pm ☎232 32 06 ⓦwww.tourisme-segou.com).

Le Festival sur le Niger

Ségou's **Festival sur le Niger** (Festival on the River) – launched and supported by local hoteliers and a slew of Malian and international sponsors – takes place annually on the first weekend of February. With its purpose partly to focus on environmental threats to the Niger and the livelihoods of people living on the river, as well as on culture and partying, the festival has a lively programme of concerts by Mali's top

Catholic Mass

Attending the bilingual Bamana–French mass at Ségou's **Église de Notre Dame de l'Immaculée Conception**, is highly recommended, regardless of your faith, or lack of. The vibrant atmosphere of the service, created by the combination of drumming and the choir belting out lively and stunningly harmonious numbers, makes for an unforgettable experience. If you're going, be sure to dress appropriately – which means conservative-to-dressy – and be aware of the gender divide, with women generally sitting on the left side and men on the right. Mass is held on Sunday mornings at 6.30am and 8.30am.

musicians, films, theatre and dance performances. Particularly entertaining are the marionette shows, featuring life-sized crocodile puppets in the river. While it hasn't yet attracted the international attention of Timbuktu's Festival au Désert, it's going that way. Check out ⓦ www.festivalsegou.org for details: the price for the three-day festival is CFA65,000, under-13s free.

Crafts shops and galleries

Ségou has an enviable reputation as a thriving centre of arts-and-crafts cottage industries, particularly in the shape of *bogolan* (mud-cloth) workers' associations. All of them are worth visiting – and obviously buying from if you're so inclined – and several offer interesting tours.

Atelier Ndomo just past the *Hôtel de l'Indépendance* on the main road to Mopti. Ségou's biggest *bogolan* tourist attraction, this men's association offers CFA500 tours of the traditional-style mud buildings, during which you learn about the *bogolan* manufacturing process, and even get to paint your own small piece of cloth.

Badjidala down the street towards the river from Sininyesigi. French-owned museum-cum-artisan workshop, displaying a wide range of masks and marionettes.

Nialeni Quartier Médine across from the Médine grand marché. One of Ségou's oldest artisan associations, created in 1982, this women's co-operative specializes in wool rugs and carpets. They're happy for visitors to watch the work – stand here long enough and they'll even teach you how it's done.

Sininyesigi on the way out to Bamako, in Quartier Segoucoura. Women's association boasting one of the best *bogolan* boutiques in town, selling a variety of stuffed animal toys, dolls and bags.

Soroble on the riverbank across from the post office. Housed in a traditional red-mud building, this *bogolan* (mud-cloth) association (small fee to tour the whole place) is a recommended visit. The boutique is full of beautiful artefacts, from tapestries to dolls.

Excursions

Bozo fishermen live in permanent camps on both sides of the Niger near Ségou, and have done so since the seventh century, long before the town was founded. It's possible to take a guided trip by pirogue or *pinasse* to visit their **riverbank villages**.

The Ségou area is also renowned for its pottery: **KALABOUGOU**, forty minutes upstream by pirogue, is a picturesque potters' village where you can see the women at work. Renting a pirogue to Kalabougou costs CFA17,500 for the three-hour trip, with one hour at the village. Although you can arrange a visit any day of the week, it's best to shoot for a Saturday or Sunday when they fire their pots – quite a sight to behold as the giant bonfires lick the sky – and try to take some kola nuts, as gifts for the potters.

It's also possible to cruise upriver to **SÉGOU-KORO** – old Ségou – on the south bank of the river about 10km out of town, off the Bamako road. Sights in Ségou-Koro include the village's four mosques – including the delicate **mosque of Ba Sounou Sacko**, mother of King Biton Mamary Coulibaly – and the **tomb of Coulibaly** himself, recently restored. Look out too for the **ancient tree** that was the focal point of the royal palace and under which the council of elders sat.

Going to Ségou-Koro by pirogue will cost around CFA20,000 for the day, while a motorized *pinasse* will cost at least CFA25,000. It's cheaper, however, to visit this village by car or *mobylette*. The scale of Ségou-Koro – it's small enough to explore on foot in well under an hour – gives you little sense of the fact that this was once the seat of a powerful kingdom, but the ancient mud-brick and *banco* buildings have an unmistakable grace. It's best to hire a guide in Ségou town to show you round the village. If you can hire one with a motorbike and don't mind riding pillion, it will be cheaper than taking a taxi; expect to pay around CFA6000–7000 for transport and a tour, with a diversion to see the millet-beer makers – if your guide's thirsty enough – in Ségou's Catholic quarter on the return.

Accommodation

Ségou has a good range of places to stay, though several are away from the town centre.

L'Auberge just up from the *Djoliba* ☎232.01.45 ⓦwww.promali.org/aub-ind. Very central, almost by the river, and offering very pleasant s/c, a/c or fan-cooled rooms with satellite TV, fridges and Internet access. Lebanese-owned and popular with expats, it has a pricey restaurant with well-stocked

bar and a shady garden with a pool. Rooms with fan ④ or a/c ⑤.
Delta southwards off the Bamako road behind the Office du Niger, at the western end of town, 3km from the bus terminals ☎232.02.72. Nothing special, but reasonable-value rooms, secure

SÉGOU

Niger River

ACCOMMODATION

L'Auberge	A
Delta	E
Djoliba	C
L'Esplanade	B
Hôtel de l'Indépendance	H
Mission Catholique	D
Mivera	G
Savane	F

Ferry Port

Guides Association

QUARTIER SOMONO

COMANAV

Market

Pottery Market

Bozo Camp

Soroble Boutique

SOKALAKONO

Police

BIM Bank

Water Tower

Hospital

Somatra Bus Station

BDM Bank

Bittar Trans

Muslim Cemetery

Sotelma

Cinema

Town Hall

QUARTIER ADMINISTRATIF

MEDINE

DAR SALAM

N

RESTAURANTS, BARS & CLUBS

L'Ariane	5
Djeli Bazoumanaba	4
Fast Food Café	6
Le Golfe	2
Lavazza	7
Mobasso	3
Le Soleil de Minuit & Chez Tony supermarket	1

0   300 m

Gare Routière, Atelier Ndomo, ⓖ & ⓗ

parking, a spacious camping area (CFA3000), and peace and quiet. Rooms with fan ❷ or a/c ❸.

Djoliba on the junction with the road leading to the ferry port ☎232.15.72 🌐 www.segou-hotel-djoliba .com. Immaculate, smartly equipped, German-run establishment, with Wi-Fi. Rooms with fan ❹ or a/c ❺.

L'Esplanade on the riverfront west of the port ☎232.01.27 ✉ hotel.esplanade@hotmail.com. It takes a special sort of logic to construct a hotel on the banks of the River Niger, only then to build most of the rooms facing inwards towards a small courtyard. That grumble aside, this is a friendly and comfortable place, a little less touristy than others around here, with a good range of rooms, and the bonus of a pool. Rooms with fan ❸ or apartments with a/c ❺.

Hôtel de l'Indépendance some 5km east of the centre, along the Mopti road ☎232.17.33 🌐 www .promali.org/aub-ind. Bizarre-looking place owned by the same owners as *L'Auberge*, gaudily painted

and with a life-sized giraffe standing sentry outside. Good-sized rooms with TV. Rooms with fan ❸ or a/c ❻.

Mission Catholique in the Quartier Mission, between the tourist centre and the Quartier Administratif ☎232.04.17. Now the cheapest place in town with pleasant dorms (CFA2000) and a few private singles and doubles with fan, mosquito net and private bathroom. Good value, although it is about a 15min walk from the centre. ❷

Mivera around 5km east of the centre near the *Indépendance* ☎232.03.31 ✉ sosafi-ol@hotmail .com. Free parking, s/c rooms with TV and fan or a/c – but no more charm than motels worldwide. Rooms with fan ❸ or a/c ❹.

Savane about 200m south of *Hôtel Delta* ☎232.09.74 🌐 www.motelsavane.com. A peaceful place with a range of well-kept s/c rooms with fan and some more expensive a/c rooms and bungalows, all with TV, owned by one of the founders of the Festival sur le Niger. Rooms with fan ❸ or a/c ❹.

Eating, drinking and nightlife

The first place to go for an **evening meal** in Ségou is 🍴 *Le Soleil de Minuit*, with some great local dishes, really high standards of service and hygiene and prices not as expensive as the wonderful food would suggest (ask for their Senegalese-style *poulet-yassa*, a dish that has to be ordered a day in advance). Across the road, the *Djoliba*'s bar-restaurant is slightly more expensive though it does good **pizzas** on Saturdays. Boasting the best location, *L'Esplanade*'s restaurant, the *Kamalen Beau*, serves wonderful, Italian-influenced food (unsurprisingly, given the nationality of the owner); pity about the two crocodiles in the tiny cage by the terrace, which rather spoils the place. Moving down the price scale, the food at *Le Golfe* isn't outstanding, but it's popular nonetheless, particularly with locals, with inexpensive sandwiches and basic Malian fare. *Djeli Bazoumanaba*, opposite the BIM Bank, is a reliable rice-and-sauce spot, where you can fill yourself for about CFA200. *L'Ariane*,

Moving on from Ségou

Somatra (☎232.02.66) has a daily 5am departure for **Bamako**, and services at 9am and 12.30pm for **Mopti**, via San, Koutiala and Sévaré. Somatra also runs a service to Sikasso at 9am. Bittar Transport operates nine buses per day to Bamako, and four daily to Mopti. There is also a Somatra bus to Bobo-Dioulasso in **Burkina Faso** (daily at 11.30am; CFA6000); an alternative route is to take a bus to San or Koutiala and pick up a connection there. For **Côte d'Ivoire**, make for Sikasso where, if the border is open, you can change for onward transport south.

Binke Transport, as well as regular departures to Mopti and Bamako, has services to **Gao** (daily at 8am, 11am and noon; CFA13,000) via Douentza and Hombori. You may be lucky enough to find something going directly to Djenné – try the *gare routière* or the area around the water tower – particularly on Sun or Mon mornings (Mon is market day in Djenné), but more than likely you'll have to catch a bus to the junction with a Mopti-bound bus and find transport from there.

In the rainy season, you can also travel **by river boat** to **Koulikoro** (for Bamako) or all the way down to **Gao**. The COMANAV ferry office (☎232.02.04) overlooks the jetty in Ségou. For more information on the river boats, see p.333.

down a dusty side-street between the BDM Bank and the *Djoliba* junction, is a little overpriced though the courtyard is a pleasant place to wolf down their huge portions of largely Malian staples, while lizards scuttle under your chair. A little to the southeast, at the Bittar Trans depot, there's a fast-food café that's okay if you're waiting for a bus out of town.

If you fancy some **millet beer**, just walk around the Mission Catholique until you stumble across a brewer and you'll immediately be invited to join in. As for proper **nightlife**, the *Mobasso*, east of *Le Golfe*, is Ségou's one true nightclub, a lively garden bar and grill that frequently has live music at the weekend. *Lavazza* is a little out of the way, but has great live music every Friday and Saturday. It's also worth checking out *l'Esplanade* which has in the past had a regular club nights, too.

Zinzana, Bla, San and Koutiala

If you're travelling southeast from Ségou in your own vehicle, you might want to stop overnight some 40km from the town at **ZINZANA**, where the excellent *campement* at the agricultural research station (④) is a haven of peace and tranquillity, with spotless sheets, a vine-shaded terrace, cold beer and good food. Southeast of Zinzana, the main road divides at the junction town of **BLA**, with the N6 continuing northeast to San and Mopti and the N12 heading south to Koutiala and Sikasso. Drivers often make a stop at Bla to eat at one of the roadside *gargotes*.

SAN is an important commercial crossroads, and a major departure point for Burkina and Côte d'Ivoire. The town **market**, best on Monday, is the largest in the region, trading in everything from livestock to imported goods. There's no real reason to spend time here on any other day, but if you need to **stay**, try the rooms at the *Campement Teriya* (☎237.21.07; rooms with fan ❷ or a/c ❹), which is better known for its good restaurant. Basic **food** can also be had at the *Bon Coin*, just outside town on the road to Ségou.

The cotton-growing town of **KOUTIALA** is, like San, an exit point for travellers to Burkina, and also a staging post between Sikasso and Ségou or Mopti. There's a bank here, and if you overnight it, you can stay comfortably at *Motel La Chaumière*, which has good-value s/c rooms, all with TV (☎264.02.20; rooms with fan ❷ or a/c ❹).

Across the delta to Timbuktu

During the dry season, it's possible to zigzag from Ségou all the way across the Niger delta to **Timbuktu** by a network of tracks. Although this involves tackling long stretches of tortuous *piste* and occasional muddy river-crossings, it allows you to take in fascinating scenery along a little-travelled route. The following details assume you'll be using your own 4x4 vehicle, though given time you could achieve this with available local transport.

From Ségou, take the northern road towards **Niono**, cross the Niger and then turn east to **MASSINA**, around 150km from Ségou. The tarmac goes as far as the old city of **SANSANDING**, "the great marketplace of the Western Sudan" according to the nineteenth-century scholar, Heinrich Barth. From Massina, you can make an interesting side-trip, 44km to **DIAFARABÉ**, a village located on one of the narrowest points of the Niger (see box for details of the annual cattle-crossing here). Diafarabé has an interesting old quarter between the market and the river, with an attractive, modern, Sudanic-style mosque. There's a small ferry here, and you can stay at the basic *campement* (CFA2500 per person).

From Massina, tracks lead north towards **NAMPALA**, also accessible directly from Ségou via Niono, passing lush green fields of irrigated rice. It's 80km from Nampala to **LÉRÉ**, a small village with a Friday **livestock market** that unites herders from all over the region – and another 136km across mud-cracked lagoons to the town of **NIAFOUNKÉ**, whose most famous resident, virtuoso musician Ali Farka Touré, who died in 2005, owned the town's hotel. A ferry crosses the river here, making

In December, **Fula herders** descend en masse on the village of **Diafarabé**, on the north bank of the Niger 60km northwest of Djenné and 190km northeast of Ségou. Here, and at several other crossing points in the vicinity, they lead their cattle from the northern Sahel grazing ground to the southern banks of the river to await the return of the rains in May or June. The spectacle of thousands of **cattle** crashing into the water and swimming to the other side as herders prod them along is a memorable one if you're lucky enough to witness it. Music and festivities accompany the event, but there's no set date. Ask around in Ségou if you think you might be there around the right time.

it possible to connect with the road leading to **KORIENZÉ** and back south to Mopti. Alternatively, you can continue 90km northeast to the Songhai town of **GOUNDAM**, an important agricultural centre in the middle of a region considered to be the breadbasket of Mali. Rice, millet, corn and – remarkably – wheat, are all grown in the area. Situated on the mostly dry **Lac Télé** (part of the once sizeable Lac Faguibine), Goundam has a *campement* (❷) and is linked to the Niger River by a 34-kilometre road to **DIRÉ**, a sizeable port on the Niger, 100km upstream from Timbuktu. From Goundam, an increasingly sandy track leads over the remaining 90km to the dunes surrounding **Timbuktu** (see p.395).

Sikasso and around

Mali's southernmost and second-largest town, **SIKASSO** is an evergreen place, with a humid tropical languor in which tea, cotton and market-garden produce flourish. The town grew to become a colonial outpost, as the decaying administrative buildings from that era attest, and its gentle, welcoming atmosphere and verdant surroundings give it an appeal unique in Mali.

The people of the area are traditionally largely **Senoufo** – an agricultural people whose language and culture is steadily disappearing as Bamana takes over across Mali. You'll notice the distinctively scarified cheeks of older Senoufo – three slashes on each side – especially if you visit any village markets in the district, held on an old-style, five-day cycle.

Sikasso still gravitates around the **Mamelon**, a thirty-metre hillock which was once believed to host a spirit protecting the town (now it houses a water tower and an antenna); and the **market**, impressive on any day of the week but enormous on Sundays, and outstanding for its fruit and vegetables. The Mamelon is an easy climb, offering the best views, but apart from that and the market, Sikasso has few obvious sights, though you can still see remnants of the fortifications – known as **tata** – that, despite their impressive size, couldn't hold out against the onslaught of the French. One other place worth a visit is the **Galerie Kéné Arts**, an artisans' co-operative selling jewellery, fabrics, leatherwork, masks and carvings, located behind the Bank of Africa.

History of Sikasso

Sikasso was the last capital of the **Kénédougou Empire**, a kingdom founded by Dioula traders in the seventeenth century. A warrior named **Tieba** became ruler of the mini-empire in 1876, and he transformed Sikasso – his mother's birthplace – from a tiny agricultural village, based around the sacred Mamelon hill, into a fortified capital, expanding his empire and developing trade. On the top of the hill, **Tieba** had a two-storey house built to receive royal guests. During the same period, however, the Malinké warlord **Samory Touré** was expanding his influence in the region, and came into conflict with the Senoufo, destroying the town of Kong, as well as Senoufo strongholds like Korhogo and Ferkessédougou, in present-day Côte d'Ivoire. Samory laid siege to Sikasso in 1887 but fifteen months later the city had not fallen and, soon after, Tieba received support from a new invasion force, the French, under Binger. Tieba died in battle in 1893, leaving his son, Babemba, as ruler. But Babemba fell out with the French and they attacked and routed Sikasso in 1898, symbolically planting the tricolor flag on top of the Mamelon. Babemba committed suicide; his erstwhile enemy, Samory Touré, was captured by the French and sent into captivity in Gabon, where he died.

Practicalities

From the roundabout by the Mamelon, a road heads south across the Lotio River to the **autogare**. In fact, there is no single *autogare*, but more a huddle of different bus depots – representing all the major bus companies – some 1500m south of the town centre on the road to Côte d'Ivoire. Near the Mamelon roundabout you'll find a **post office** and five **banks** – Bank of Africa, BNDA, BIM, BDM and an enormous branch of BCEAO; BIM and BDM change traveller's cheques, the latter does Visa cash advances, and most of them change euros cash, but if you're coming from Bamako or Bobo, you're better off changing your money before you arrive. To the north of this roundabout, past the hospital and police station, is the *gouvernorat*, on the grounds of which you'll find the **tourist office**. As they have done so successfully in Gao and Djenné, the US Peace Corps are in the process of working with the office to make it more tourist-friendly. Sikasso has several **Internet cafés**, including the reliable Sikanet, by the ⚘ *Pâtisserie-Restaurant Kénédougou Palace* (daily until 9.30pm), and the Sotelma Internet café by the post office (both CFA1000/hr). There is 24-hour **fuel** at the Total garage on the Bamako road.

Accommodation

Sikasso has a number of places to stay, though tourist traffic here is minimal: with the civil war in Côte d'Ivoire, the hotels have for several years been busy putting up journalists and Malian returnees. As such, the standards are not particularly high and value for money is low.

Lotio on the Bamako road near the centre ☏262.10.01. A grubby, slightly seedy bar, but friendly enough; rooms come with fans and shared facilities. ❷
Le Mamelon close to the market ☏262.00.44. Plain, identical s/c, a/c rooms with TV. ❹
Motel Le Wassoulou on the new Koutiala road, north of town ☏262.04.24. The best hotel in Sikasso, well known for its restaurant. Rooms are in chalets with a/c and TV, and you can also pitch your tent in the peaceful garden. ❹
Saoudiata off the Bamako road next to the Marché Médine, west of the centre ☏262.19.48. A simple, friendly, relaxed place with good-sized s/c rooms with fan or a/c, secure parking and a good restaurant. Rooms with fan ❷ or a/c ❸.

Tata west of the town centre, near the *Saoudiata* ☏262.04.11. Slightly smarter than its neighbour, though still with unexceptional rooms in a variety of conditions, plus a basic restaurant. Rooms with fan ❷ or a/c ❸.
Le Touban on the north side of town on the old Koutiala road ☏262.05.34 ✉panierkone@cefib.com. Reasonable-value, secure, comfortable s/c rooms with a/c & TV. Breakfast is included in the rate, and the place is right next to a well-stocked supermarket, too. Rooms with fan ❸ or a/c ❹.
Zanga near the *autogare* ☏262.04.31. Conveniently situated and thinks itself Sikasso's best, with a few non-s/c rooms with fan (but no mosquito nets), and overpriced s/c, a/c rooms at negotiable prices. The pool, never Sikasso's greatest attraction, has been drained. Rooms with fan ❸ or a/c ❺.

Eating and nightlife

A good choice for **breakfast or lunch** is *Pâtisserie-Restaurant Kénédougou Palace*. Situated right in the centre of town by the roundabout at the foot of the Mamelon, the emphasis is definitely on the *pâtisserie* though it does serve the occasional burger

Moving on from Sikasso

Buses to **Bamako** are operated by various bus companies and leave throughout the day (and sometimes night). The local firm Kénédougou Voyages (☎260.07.19) has many daily buses to Bamako via Bougouni (5–6hr), as do Somatri (☎262.01.39) and Somatra (☎262.17.05); expect to pay CFA3500–4000 for the trip. For **Mopti** (Sévaré), you can also take the Bani Transport departure to **Gao** (Thurs & Sun 4pm); on other days, you'll have to go with the slightly less safe and salubrious Kénédougou Voyages or YT (☎262.08.27; CFA6000; daily 6pm; 9hr). Nearly all the bus companies go to **Ségou** via Koutiala and Bla, and have a daily 9am or 10am departure (CFA3500). It shouldn't take more than five hours but there are often delays, especially with Kénédougou.

For **Bobo-Dioulasso** (4–8hr depending on border formalities; CFA4500) or **Ouaga-dougou** (9–13hr; CFA11,000), there are services with Kénédougou, Bani Transport and YT, which each have at least a daily departure. Bani Transport also have services to Lomé (CFA22,500), Niamey (CFA22,500) and Cotonou (CFA25,000). If the problems in Côte d'Ivoire settle down, Kénédougou are the company most likely to resume services to **Abidjan**.

or pizza, plus *capitaine* and *chawarma* dishes. For French and Malian **food** served in a pleasant garden, full of nesting weaver birds, the restaurant at *Le Wassoulou*, on the new Koutiala road, is highly recommended: arrange a return taxi if you plan on making the trip out from the centre (CFA400 each way). Round the other side of the Mamelon, opposite the towering BCEAO bank, *Restaurant Chez Les Amis* is also a good bet, a quiet place with a friendly boss, serving excellent staples such as couscous, *capitaine*, and *poulet kedjenou* (an Ivoirian speciality). *La Vieille Marmite*, on the Bamako road near *Hôtel Lotio*, is also a good place to go for local dishes. There are several basic eating places near the *autogares* and on the Bamako road, while the best **supermarket** is attached to *Le Touban* hotel, clearly signposted from the town centre. **Nightlife** is not a big thrill in Sikasso, but you could try *Éspace Culturel Handara*; take the road north towards the *gouvernorat*, turning right at the elephant roundabout, then first right again.

Around Sikasso

About 12km southwest of Sikasso, inside a cathedral-like limestone outcrop jutting from the plain, are the **Grottes de Missirikoro**, also known as *Faramissiri* – "Stone Mosque" in Bamana. The sacred grotto is said to be inhabited by guardian spirits who Kénédougou kings once consulted before an expedition. Today, it's home to colonies of bats, some tribal relics, and a few latter-day cave-dwellers and is still used as a place of worship and sacrifice by animists, Muslims and Christians alike, each using one of the three different natural entrances. You can clamber up the outcrop itself by means of ladders and chains for a 360-degree view of the surrounding wooded plains. A taxi to the caves and back should cost around CFA6000 including waiting time. Take a torch to illuminate the gloomy recesses, and some kola nuts to offer to the caves' residents.

The **Chutes de Farako**, 30km east of Sikasso (on the road to the Burkina border), are particularly impressive in the rainy season and can be visited in a day. There are smaller but equally picturesque waterfalls some 15km south of town, which are a favourite retreat of Sikasso's Peace Corps volunteers; the pool here is deep enough to swim in.

4.4

Mopti and the delta region

The Niger's extraordinary **inland delta** is one of the most compelling parts of West Africa, and bound to leave a lasting impression. As the Niger and its major tributary, the Bani, meander out across the plain into hundreds of channels and lagoons, they pass near the medieval towns of **Djenné** and **Timbuktu** – once renowned as centres of commercial prosperity and Islamic piety, and still worthy magnets for travellers. Although the allure of Timbuktu's fabled reputation is undeniable, Djenné is undoubtedly the more impressive destination and much easier to reach. Today, the economic importance of both towns has been overshadowed by **Mopti** and its satellite town, **Sévaré**, together the joint hub of Mali's tourist industry and the country's major route intersection.

A rewarding, if by no means luxurious, way to travel through the region is by **river boat**. When you travel along the river, the ports become your *gares routières*, and your arrival at any port will be amid a rush of activity as the traders on board scramble to buy whatever goods are available before the boat pulls out and continues its ponderous journey. The boats operate only after the rains, though for the seven or so months that the river boats are out of commission, it's possible to explore the river routes – or simply travel from A to B – by chartered pirogue or *pinasse*. For more on the general practicalities of boat travel on the Niger, see p.333.

Dotting the riverbank are small towns and villages, consisting mostly of ground-hugging mud-brick buildings towered over by traditional **Sudanic-style mosques**, such as the impressive one at **QUADDAGA**, about 20km downstream from Mopti, or the two large mosques at **KOA**, 100km upstream.

Although Fula and Tuareg nomads still lead their flocks and herds through the region, vegetation is relatively sparse and the landscapes often flat and barren. Occasionally, fields of rice and other cereals can be seen – evidence of government attempts to irrigate parts of the delta before they are claimed by the advancing Sahara.

Mopti and Sévaré

Built on three islands connected by dykes, the riverside town of **Mopti**, with its reputation for hustlers, isn't immediately attractive to every visitor. The old town lacks aesthetic harmony, the new town isn't particularly modern, and the whole place, hemmed in on three sides by the waterways at the confluence of the Niger and the Bani (the "Venice of Africa" is a common sobriquet) can feel a little crowded and oppressive, especially down on the busy and odoriferous shores of the port. If you're arriving direct from Europe on Point Afrique's winter charter flight, or even by bus straight in from the bush, you can experience a strong dose of culture shock. Don't be scared off wandering around, though: as your face becomes known, and especially if you have a guide to look after you, the port and the busy canals begin to work their magic. Mopti pulls together all the peoples of Mali – Bamana, Songhai, Fula, Tuareg, Moor, Bozo and Dogon – and its buoyant pace and mix of cultures add to the charm. If you can arrange it, aim to be here on market day, Thursday.

Mopti offers little choice in accommodation, and only one realistic option at the budget end (though it is a good one). In many ways, **Sévaré**, 12km southeast on the main Bamako–Gao road, is a preferable base, used increasingly by overnighting tourists. A blander and more functional place, Sévaré is a main pick-up point for onward travel and the location of Mopti's **airport**, and it's easy to make short trips down the causeway to Mopti itself – *bâchés* ply between the two towns from around 7am to 7pm (15min; CFA250).

Mopti Town

Originally a cluster of islands inhabited by **Bozo** fishing people, **MOPTI** became an important site early in the nineteenth century when, with the jihad proclaimed by the Fula scholar and ascetic **Cheikou Ahmadou Lobbo**, it gained strategic significance as an outpost of his Masina Empire, centred on Djenné and the surrounding Fula pasturelands. Mopti was later captured by the Tukulor warmonger **El Hadj Omar**, who turned the settlement into his principal military base, from where he launched attacks against his Fula rivals. A small town grew up around the site, but Mopti remained largely overshadowed by Djenné.

Economic development was largely due to the French, who exploited Mopti's position at the confluence of the Bani and the Niger and its accessibility from the main overland routes, but it was only at the beginning of the twentieth century that the town found commercial importance – at first with the export of white egret feathers to the *belle époque* couturiers of Paris. When the Dakar–Bamako railway line was built, Mopti became the largest river port in the French Soudan. Its population has grown steadily and today, with more than 100,000 people, it rivals Sikasso as Mali's second town – though combined with Sévaré there's no competition.

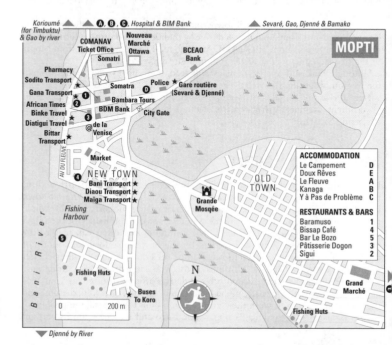

The harbour

Most of the sights in Mopti, built on three islands connected by dykes, centre around Mopti's *raison d'être*, the **harbour**, built by the French in the early part of the last century. Large, traditional *pinasses* with their canvas awnings and colourful flags tie up regularly to unload cargo and passengers, while pirogues taxi people back and forth from different points on the islands that make up the town. The terrace at *Bar Le Bozo*, a restaurant right on the riverfront, provides an excellent and breezy vantage point from which to take in all the activity in the harbour, and watch the invariably beautiful sunset.

A **fish market** occupies the southern edge of the port near *Bar Le Bozo*. Behind it is a large open-air workshop where craftsmen build the *pinasses* from large planks imported from the south. On the northern shore of the harbour, Moorish traders mill around stacks of marble-like **salt slabs**, brought by camel caravan from the desert to Timbuktu and then transported by boat to Mopti. Formerly one of the desert's great riches, salt is still a precious commodity for herders who need it for their livestock.

The harbour is the place to get boats to see the Bozo and Tuareg communities nearby. These trips are ultimately rather voyeuristic and artificial experiences, but the boat ride is enjoyable and gives an interesting perspective of the town. The **Bozo** are fishing people who, during the rainy season when the catch is most prolific, build circular thatched huts around Mopti, clustered in small *campements*. If you take a pirogue to one of these, you'll see them repairing their boats and nets. The **Tuareg** "camp" is nothing more than a few huts where women sell **crafts** – bracelets, necklaces and leather goods – at elevated prices, but beyond this there's a "beach" where you can swim during the dry season. Kids in Mopti will find you and propose the trip (just hang around the *Bar Le Bozo*); their brothers or uncles are inevitably **boatmen** who will give you a "special rate" – the going rate is around CFA1200 an hour per boat, though the first price may be several times this.

> ### Dissenting voice
>
> "Bar Bozo should be avoided. While the food is good (and you'll run into just about every traveler who comes through Mopti), it is also crawling with every bad guide and scam artist in town. While there is security to keep out most sales people, the ones who make it in are the ones to be most aware of."
>
> Ben Guerard, USA

The new town

North of the harbour in the new town, the **nouveau marché Ottawa**, a Canadian-sponsored building, is a good place to find food, plus various household items like **pottery** or **calabash** utensils. Nearby, the **Hall des Artisans** is the best place for **crafts**. **Blankets** are a regional speciality and Mopti has a wide selection at relatively low prices – costs vary according to the quality of the wool or cotton used. Here you'll find weaves of local peoples including Dogon, Fula and Songhai. Each of these peoples also has characteristic jewellery handcrafted in gold, silver (or nickel), copper and bronze. Also worth a visit is the **cloth** market on the outer limits of the Hall des Artisans.

The old town

From the harbour, the **Grande Mosquée** is easily visible to the east. As you cross over the dyke leading to it, you enter the old town with its narrow traffic-free alleys and grey *banco* houses. The mosque itself is a relatively recent construction, though faithful to the regional style that originated in nearby Djenné. Unfortunately, the interior is off-limits to non-Muslims. To the southeast in the Komuguel district is the **grand marché**, which has a small handicrafts section.

Arrival and practicalities

Pick-ups to Sévaré use the *gare routière* near the *Campement* hotel. For details of other **bus depots** in Mopti, and onward transport, see the box on p.391. The tourist office (Mon–Thurs 7.30am–4pm, Fri 7.30am–12.30pm, 2.30–5.30pm; ☏243.05.06 ⓔmoptitourisme@hotmail.com), on Avenue du Fleuve past *Hôtel Kanaga* isn't usually much help; however, they do have a list of qualified guides, if you decide you need one for Mopti or elsewhere. They also have up-to-date details of local flights out of Mopti (see p.390).

There are three main **banks** in Mopti: BCEAO, by the *gare routière*; BIM, on the road to the *Hôtel Kanaga*; and BDM, west of the city gate. BIM changes cash and is a Western Union representative, and BDM advances cash on Visa cards. To get **online**, head to Cybercafé Librairie Papeterie de la Venise, opposite *Pâtisserie Dogon* (CFA1500/hr).

There are several **travel agents** in Mopti's new town near the BDM bank, all offering tours of the main tourist circuits, including Dogon-country treks and excursions to Timbuktu, and they can usually also arrange 4x4 rental. Firms include the recommended Diatigui Travel (☏243.02.73), African Times (☏222.55.60 ⓔafrican-times@african-times.com) opposite the BDM and the nearby Bambara African Tours (☏243.00.80 ⓦwww.bambara.com).

Accommodation

Good accommodation has been slow to arrive in Mopti, but the excellent new *Y à Pas de Problème Hôtel* has woken the town up. *La Maison Rouge* (ⓦwww .lesmaisonsdumali.com; ⑥), the work of a Parisian architect that also looks set to give the *Kanaga* a run for its money at the luxury end of the market, opened shortly before this book went to press

Le Campement near the police headquarters and the *gare routière* ☏243.12.61. Smallish but tidy s/c, a/c rooms in a new building, and large s/c rooms with fans in the old colonial-style edifice. Not exactly the most atmospheric of places, but convenient for the *gare routière* and services to Timbuktu, and there's an Internet café and a backyard where you can pitch your tent (CFA2000 per person). Overnight parking CFA1000. Rooms with fan or a/c ❸.

Doux Rêves southeast of the old town on rue 540, next to the football stadium ☏243.04.90. With a variety of clean s/c rooms, a bar and the occasional band, this French-run place remains great value. It's a bit out of town but shared taxi rides from the new town run about

CFA150 or less – or walk it (the route takes you through some of Mopti's friendlier parts). Dorm beds CFA5000, mattress on the roof CFA4000, rooms with fan ❸ or a/c ❺.

Le Fleuve behind the *Kanaga* ☏&ⓕ243.11.67. Two pink buildings with good-sized s/c rooms, most with a/c. Not a great choice, and not very atmospheric, but it works as an overspill for *Y à Pas de Problème*, or perhaps if you'd prefer to be away from other tourists. Rooms with fan ❸ or a/c ❺.

Kanaga near the waterfront on the north side of the new town ☏243.05.00 ⓔkanaga@bambara .com. Formerly Mopti's best hotel (Michael Palin and Bob Geldof both stayed here when filming) though challenged by the new places, and service

---

Hiring a guide for the Dogon country

One of the biggest potential pitfalls facing a traveller in Mali is finding an adequate **guide** for the *pays Dogon*. This is likely to be the highlight of your visit so it's important to choose one carefully; one who not only knows the area well, but is also sympathetic to your requirements. You can certainly sign up with a **travel agency** in Mopti or Sévaré: at least then you know you'll be getting a guide of a reasonable quality and if something goes wrong, you have an office to complain to. However, by hiring a guide yourself you will pay only a fraction of the cost of going via an agency, for potentially the same service. A **personal recommendation** from a fellow traveller is perhaps the surest way of getting a good guide. For more information on guides, see p.327.

can be surly. Still, there are comfortable s/c, a/c rooms, satellite TV, a nice little pool and a *paillote* bar, with live music every weekend. ❽

Y à Pas de Problème back from the water-front to the south of the *Kanaga* ☎243.10.41 or 601.07.92 ⓦwww.yapasdeprobleme.com. Run by an energetic Frenchman, this new place caters for a variety of budgets and tastes, from a/c family rooms to fan-cooled dorms (CFA4500) or roof space (CFA3500). A pool and reasonably priced rooftop restaurant are two key attractions. Rooms with fan ❸ or a/c ❺.

Eating

Out on the south side of the harbour, the finely sited *Bar Le Bozo* is a famous haunt for a sundowner and it's good value, and a great place to watch the **water-front traffic and commerce**. It's also a hangout for tourist touts, but there's usually a security man on duty so a laid-back atmosphere tends to prevail, though not always. On the other side of the port, and lacking nothing except perhaps enough customers, the 🍴 *Bissap Café* is an anomaly in the chaos of the market, a very smart place with a good menu of Western food (including pizzas and milkshakes) and local dishes; it's Mopti's smartest restaurant by quite some distance but not overpriced (pizzas around CFA4000–5000). *Sigui*, on the waterfront Avenue du Fleuve, *is* overpriced and a little run-down, though its upstairs terrace remains a good place for a drink – if only they'd stop the guides from coming in. For African fare, 🍴 *Baramuso* is a cheap, unpretentious place serving local dishes. To find it, take the road running inland from Gana Transport. **Street food** is plentiful around Mopti, especially around the harbour and the transport parks, and stalls are open mornings and evenings for omelettes and bread. *Pâtisserie Dogon*, next to BDM bank, gets plenty of custom for its cakes and sandwiches.

Sévaré

SÉVARÉ hasn't got Mopti's atmosphere, but its location, on the highway between Bamako and Gao, makes it unavoidable if you're travelling by road. Boasting plenty of decent hotels and restaurants, it's also a convenient base for exploring the Dogon country and the rest of the region.

The town **centre** is the big crossroads where the Mopti–Bandiagara road crosses the Bamako–Gao highway. The **gare routière** is on the Bandiagara road 1km east of the crossroads; all buses in or out of Mopti stop there. The **airport** is 2km southeast of the town centre. *Bâchés* for Mopti depart from the roadside near the post office, five minutes' walk west of the big crossroads.

An interesting souvenir shop, selling leatherwork and traditional jewellery, with a little bead museum upstairs, is the Farafina Tigne gift shop/gallery, known as **Musée Bijoux**, on the Bamako road, 1km south of the crossroads (ⓦwww.farafina-tigne .com). The shop sells their items all over the world yet a visit and "tour" of the museum is refreshingly free of any hard sell. The owner, known universally as Peace Corps Baba, is also a bit of a Mr Fix-it and can arrange guides and 4x4 rentals. On the other (north) side of the crossroads is Sotelma, the best place for an **Internet** connection anywhere in Sévaré or Mopti (CFA1000/hr). The best-stocked **super-market** is the small Mini Prix, opposite the **post office** on the Mopti road; it's run by another of the town fixers, who will willingly change money. A bit further along, the BNDA **bank** changes traveller's cheques. There are also a couple of decent **travel agencies** in Sévaré, including a branch of the efficient and recommended 🍴 Malikow Tours (call before visiting; ☎242.10.44 ⓦwww.malikowtours.com), about 500m north of the airport turning just west of the Bamako road. Nearer the centre is Teriya Voyages (☎242.07.68 ⓔteriya-voyage@yahoo.fr), on the Bamako road opposite the *Motel Sévaré*.

Accommodation

Sévaré has, surprisingly perhaps, some of the best-value and nicest **accommodation** in Mali, and it can be hard to choose between the best two – *Mac's Refuge* and *Maison*

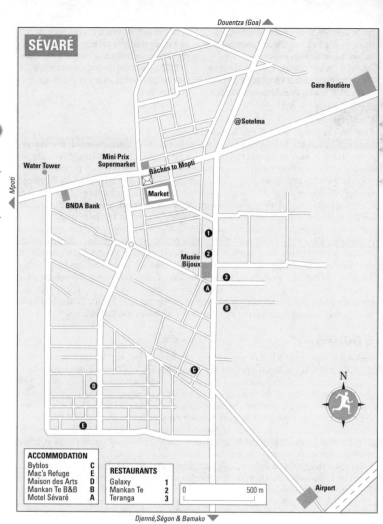

SÉVARÉ

Douentza (Goa) ▲

Gare Routière

@Sotelma

Water Tower

Mini Prix
Supermarket

Bâchés to Mopti

Mopti ◀

BNDA Bank

Market

❶

❷

Musée
Bijoux

❸

Ⓐ

Ⓑ

Ⓒ

Ⓓ

Ⓔ

N

ACCOMMODATION

Byblos	C
Mac's Refuge	E
Maison des Arts	D
Mankan Te B&B	B
Motel Sévaré	A

RESTAURANTS

Galaxy	1
Mankan Te	2
Teranga	3

| 0 | | 500 m |

Airport

Djenné, Ségon & Bamako ▼

des Arts, with the former being slightly more popular and shabbier, the latter smarter but still laid-back and extremely friendly. In high season it's worth contacting them in advance to reserve rooms, as they're often full.

Byblos signposted off the Bamako road ☎660.23.76 ⊛www.hotelbyblos-sevare.fr.st. Lebanese-owned place, a little tired now but with good facilities (including hot water in the winter months and a kindly lady in charge). A pleasant garden, too. ❺

Mac's Refuge signposted 500m west of the Bamako road ☎242.06.21 ⊛tinyurl .com/28k3jm. Owned by a Malian-American former missionary (son of the Reverend McKinney – see

p.415) who runs a helpful and hospitable, if slightly regimented hotel, *Mac's* is renowned for superb meals and delightful staff. The dining room has a refectory table where a banquet (CFA5000) is served each evening, while Mac regales guests with his stories. There's a good selection of French- and English-language videos, a book exchange and, most surprising of all, a small pool. Camp out with your own gear CFA4500, or theirs CFA6000, or take a room with fan ❸ or a/c ❺.

🏃 **Maison des Arts** around 200m north of *Mac's* ☎ 242.08.53. Now providing serious competition to *Mac's*, this part-*banco* establishment is a wonderful home-from-home for weary travellers. A wide range of smart fan-cooled rooms (each decorated with local crafts), comfy beds (with nets) and a pleasant courtyard combined with welcoming Anglo-Malian hosts make this many people's favourite place in Mali. The food is pretty tasty too. Highly recommended. ❺

🏃 **Mankan Te B&B** signposted off the Bamako road ☎ 242.01.93 ⓦ www.mankan-te.de.

Relaxed and homely, this very pleasant, small bed-and-breakfast hotel is run by a sociable German woman. Housed in two adjoining well-maintained villas, it has comfortable a/c rooms, some with shared facilities. ❹

Motel Sévaré on the Bamako road ☎ 242.00.82. Forty good-sized s/c rooms, some with fans, the rest with a/c and TV, around a huge courtyard. Government-run and a bit soulless, it's okay if other options are full or you've got a big group to house. The restaurant serves a varied menu. ❹

Eating and nightlife

Street **food** is easy to come by in Sévaré. If you'd rather sit down and eat, and yet still prefer to eat on a budget, the 🍴 *Galaxy Restaurant* is a comfortable Senegalese place serving huge portions of local food at rock-bottom prices; there are only a couple of dishes on offer each day (with *brochettes* usually served in the evening). You'll find it just down a side road by the petrol station opposite *Motel Sévaré*. On the Bamako road you'll find plenty of breakfast spots and grilled-meat stalls, and nearby, set in a beautiful flowery garden, restaurant *Mankan Te* (owned by the hotel), which does tasty *brochettes de capitaine* as well as a decent vegetarian selection. The *Teranga* restaurant is another Senegalese place off the Bamako road serving a good selection of steaks and Western dishes; budget for around CFA5000 for a meal here.

Djenné and around

DJENNÉ, on a meander in the Bani River, is unquestionably the most beautiful town in the Sahel and, despite the incessant attention of guides, a uniquely memorable place to visit. Marooned by the rising waters of the Niger Delta for several months each year, its buildings are shaped in the smooth lines of the Sudanic style, moulded from the grey clay of the surrounding flood plains. In the main square, the famous **Grande Mosquée** dominates the town with a silhouette recognized by UNESCO, which accorded world heritage status to Djenné in 1988. Every Monday, people from across the region gather in town for the festive market – it's the best day to plan a trip if you can only stay one day (transport to or from Djenné on other days can be difficult). If you can ignore the multitude of foreign visitors doing the same, it's almost possible to imagine what life in the Sahel must have been like a hundred years ago.

Djenné's history

Originally a **Bozo settlement**, Djenné was founded around 800AD, according to the *Tarikh es-Soudain* – one of the earliest written records of the Sahel. The original site was at a place called Djoboro, but it may have moved to the present location as early as the eleventh century (other sources put the date two centuries later). In the thirteenth century, during the reign of the Soninké king **Koï Kounboro**, the rulers of Djenné converted to Islam and the king himself dutifully razed his palace to make room for the town's first mosque. Djenné became a way station for gold, ivory, lead, wool, kola nuts and other precious items from the south. Merchants had their main depots here, and sold their wares from outlets they operated throughout the region, notably in Timbuktu. They developed a large flotilla of boats – some up to 20m long – capable of transporting tens of tonnes of these goods to Timbuktu, from where they made their way to North Africa and Europe.

In 1325, Djenné was incorporated into the **Mali Empire** under which it enjoyed a period of stability and prosperity until, in 1473, it was conquered

Nearly all transport in and out of Mopti and Sévaré stops in both towns (though some long-distance transport on the Bamako–Gao route doesn't make the trip right down to Mopti).

Flights

From the airstrip in Sévaré (Mopti airport), in the high season (Sept–April) MAE operate **flights** on Tuesday and Saturday to Timbuktu (Sat-only in low season) and Wednesday and Sunday to Bamako (Sun-only in low season). Schedules tend to change quite a lot, so contact the airport (☏242.01.08) or the MAE office in Mopti (☏679.47.79) for current details. CAM (☏631.74.01), based in the *campement* in Mopti, operate flights to Bamako on Sunday, Timbuktu on Satuday and Wednesday. From September–May there are weekly flights to Marseilles and Paris with Point-Afrique (☏242.07.89).

River boats

From August–January/February (depending on the rains), you can travel down the Niger to **Gao**. During this period, boats also provide the quickest link to **Korioumé**, the port of call for **Timbuktu**. Upriver, to **Koulikoro** (for **Bamako**), the boats usually stop running in mid-November due to the low waters. Mopti–Timbuktu fares are CFA5021 in 4th class (no meals), CFA20,539 3rd class, CFA34,802 2nd class, CFA49,810 1st class and CFA90,915 *luxe*; for Koulikoro, the fares are CFA6124 4th–class, CFA25,659 3rd–class, CFA43,475 2nd class, CFA62,165 1st class and CFA114,380 *luxe*; while for Gao, the prices are CFA9322 in 4th class, CFA39,910 in 3rd class, CFA67,919 in 2nd class, CFA95,952 in 1st class, and CFA179,290 in *luxe*. Tickets and schedules are available from COMANAV, near the port (☏243.00.06).

Pirogues and pinasses

For a general picture of the practicalities of travel by *pinasse* and pirogue, see p.333. From Mopti, a seat on a non-motorized goods *pinasse* or pirogue to **Korioumé** costs around CFA10,000 but even these don't operate much after February. The journey varies from spellbinding (when you push off at dawn) to alarmingly uncomfortable (early afternoon out on the river), and the romance can wear thin given the restricted space and potential for delays: the trip should take three to five days, but voyages of up to ten days aren't unheard of, on an overloaded *pinasse* repeatedly running aground on sandbanks. In retrospect at least, it's a wonderful adventure, birdlife is prolific and hippos are easily seen. Alternatively, you might prefer to charter a *pinasse* to yourself, for around CFA400,000–500,000, put quite a few travellers on board and still have room.

Besides being the major port of call on the Niger, Mopti is the most convenient springboard for trips up the Bani River to **Djenné**. *Pinasses* are most likely to leave on Sunday (around CFA3000–4000) to arrive in the morning in time for Djenné's Mon market, but ask at the port for other possible departures. Chartering a motor *pinasse* for your group, count on about CFA100,000 for a day-trip, using a boat with *two* engines (an important point, if you're not going to end up spending the night on

by the **Songhai Empire**. The intellectual and commercial exchanges with Timbuktu were reinforced during this period. Then in 1591 Djenné fell to the Moroccans, under whose dominion it remained until the nineteenth century. The town went into a slow decline that successive invasions were powerless to stop. **Cheikou Ahmadou**, a religious zealot from Masina, ousted the Moroccans in 1810, and destroyed Djenné's famous mosque. In 1862, the **Tukulor Empire** briefly swallowed up the town, but held it only until 1893 when **French troops** arrived and took control.

board). Non-motorized charters go for as little as CFA40,000, but it can take up to three days to pole and paddle to Djenné.

Road transport from Mopti

Bush taxis to **Djenné** leave from Mopti's *gare routière* via Sévaré, and normally take about three hours for the 130-km trip (CFA2500 plus CFA500 for baggage). Your best chance of finding taxis is on Sunday and early morning on Monday (Djenné's market day). At other times there is usually one per day at around 7am; otherwise, there may be nothing at all, or transport only as far as the Djenné turnoff, where you'll have to find another bush taxi for the remaining 35km – a matter of luck and patience. During the rains the overland route may be out altogether.

The main bus companies for **Bamako**, **San** and **Ségou** can be found in Mopti along the waterfront or just behind it. If you're starting from Sévaré, it's a good idea to find out which company has the next departure (depending on when they arrive from Mopti or Gao) before you buy your ticket. Bittar Transport (☏678.10.42) has three departures daily to Bamako at 6.30am, 9.30am and 3.30pm (CFA8500); Binke (☏243.09.55) has buses at 7am and 5pm (CFA7500); Gana (☏243.07.21) has one bus at 3.30pm (CFA8000); and Sodito (☏672.09.68) has one bus at 3.30pm (CFA7000). Bus offices can all be found along the waterfront just south of the *Kanaga* in Mopti.

From just north of the port, Bani Transport (☏242.01.85) has departures daily at 7am and 3pm to **Bamako** (CFA8000), while Diaou and Maïga both have a 4pm depature (CFA8000).

For **Sikasso**, Bani Transport has a departure on Tues and Fri (CFA7000). Transport to **Bobo-Dioulasso** (Burkina Faso) leaves daily, early in the evening from behind *Bar Le Bozo* (CFA6500), arriving the following morning.

For **Gao**, Bani Transport has two departures every evening except Sunday, and Binke has one departure every other day (CFA6000). Both companies stop early evening at **Douentza**, from where you can usually catch transport on to **Timbuktu** the following day. Additionally, you can make the journey from Mopti to Timbuktu by 4x4 (at least 14hr); vehicles depart from the Timbuktu *gare routière* behind the Palais de Justice in Mopti, at the place du Syndicat, also known as the place de Tombouctou. Expect to pay CFA15,000 (more for the front seats) and note that vehicles will not make the trip unless there are at least seven passengers (failing which you may want to pay extra for the remaining places).

Road transport from Sévaré

For the **Dogon country**, *bâchés* and bush taxis to Bandiagara (around CFA1400) and Bankass (around CFA2500) leave from just outside the *gare routière* in Sévaré.

Getting to **Burkina** from Sévaré, you should be at the *gare routière* by 7am to catch the truck to Koro (CFA2500; 4hr). From there a bus is supposed to leave at 2pm for Ouahigouya but, if not, shared taxis also make the trip (CFA2500). From the border, there's an 8pm bus to Ouagadougou (CFA2000).

practicalities

At the turnoff from the main highway you will be asked to pay a CFA1000 **tourist tax** as a contribution to help maintaining Djenné's fragile buildings. The small **gare routière** – in the corner of the market square in front of the Grande Mosquée – is used by all road transport. The new **tourist office**, near the mosque, has some literature, can recommend hotels and guides, and is up for handling complaints, should you have any. **Guides** aren't necessary to get around town, but CFA1000–2000 will give you a companion with some knowledge for a few hours, allow you to

Djenné-Djeno, Route Nationale for Mopti & Bamako

Mopti (by river)

Roundessirou

Senissa

DJENNÉ

ACCOMMODATION
Chez Baba   C
Djenné Djenno   D
Hôtel Campement   A
Kita Kourou   B
Le Maafir   E

N

250 m

0

Bani River

Mission Culturelle

SANKORÉ

BIMSA Bank

OMATHO

Palais de Justice

Police

Covered Market

Grand Marché

Gare Routière

Grande Mosquée

YOBOUKAINA

Tombeau de Tapama Djenero

KANAFA

Radio Jamana

CLIC Pinal

Area subject to flooding

explore unhesitatingly and – most useful of all – keep the others away. If you need to **change money** in Djenné, you're best off doing so at a hotel – the only bank is the recently opened branch of BIMSA which didn't offer exchange facilities at the time of writing. There's a central post and telephones office, across from the Palais de Justice, and, for the **Internet**, out near the hospital next to Radio Jamana (look for the tall communications mast) is CLIC Pinal, which has a decent enough service (CFA1500/hr).

In terms of **food**, all the hotels serve more or less similar dishes, with couscous, chicken and spaghetti on all menus and fish available if you're lucky. The *Hôtel Campement's* dishes are widely criticized by tourists, while the food at the *Kita-Kourou* – particularly the delicious and inexpensive traditional local speciality *thion-thion*, made with ground, dried onions and fish sauce – can be superb.

Accommodation

There are several **accommodation** options in Djenné, though they can be full in the high season, so it's wise to make reservations. Children or guides will also offer to put you up on their family roof terraces, but you can end up paying more than for sleeping on a hotel's roof, and possibly with less comfort and security.

Hôtel Campement to the side of the post office ☏242.05.37 or 242.04.97 ✉campdjenne @afribone.net.ml. The dominant force in Djenné's accommodation scene, this large place has reasonable rooms and, in a nearby annexe, cheaper dorm accommodation (CFA5000). Rooms with fan ❸ or a/c ❺.

Chez Baba on a side street off the market place ☏614.33.96 or 242.05.96. A ramshackle place offering dorms with mattresses on the floor and fan (CFA3500) or spaces on the terrace with mattress and mosquito net (CFA3000). The owner is a friendly soul, but the place seems to be coming apart at the seams.

Djenné Djenno before reaching the bridge into town, turn left, and it's about 100m past the École Franco-Arabe ☏660.01.17 ⓦwww.hoteldjennedjenno.com. Djenné finally gets a designer hotel: run by a Swedish artist-cum-interior designer, this new place is the town's most sophisticated address, with a large garden, stylish a/c or fan-cooled rooms draped in *bogolan* cloth, and a bar serving cocktails and chilled millet beer. Excellent-value rooms with fan ❷ or a/c ❺.

Kita Kourou on the other side of the post office from the *Campement* ☏618.18.11. An intimate and very inexpensive place whose best feature by far is the kind owner. The hotel itself, though small, resembles an Escher drawing with its steps and corridors, but it's perfectly okay and the restaurant is the best in town. Dorm beds CAF2500 or rooms with fan ❶–❷.

Le Maafir 700m behind the mosque ☏242.05.41. One of the smarter hotels in town, owned and designed by a former tourist minister. It has fourteen agreeable s/c rooms with a/c and mosquito nets, arranged around a courtyard. The hotel's restaurant has a set menu and doesn't serve alcohol. Rate includes breakfast. ❺

Moving on from Djenné

Road transport to and from Djenné uses the **ferry** across the Bani, 6km southeast of town.

Taxis and **minibuses** run to **Sévaré** and **Mopti** (CFA2000) on afternoons when Djenné's market closes, and there's often one first thing in the morning on other days. There are buses for **Bamako** (CFA7000) via **Ségou** (CFA500) every Monday and Thursday at 8am and 11am and an additional Thursday service to Ségou. There's also a bus to **Sikasso** (CFA7000) on Mon at 4pm.

An alternative exit from Djenné when the Bani River is high enough is by motorized **pinasse**; these leave Djenné early Tuesday morning and arrive in Mopti on Tues evening (CFA4500), transporting goods in time for Mopti's Thursday market. Any child in town can take you to the ferry dock: the location moves with the river level, though most of the year they use the ferry landing stage.

The town and around

Arriving by road along the causeway leading to the town, you'll see Djenné's **Grande Mosquée** from some distance. This architectural masterpiece dates only from 1905, but was built in the style of the original mosque constructed in the reign of Koï Kounboro. The rounded lines of the facade are dominated by three towers, each eleven metres high and topped with an ostrich egg. Protruding from the edifice, the beams serve more than an aesthetic function; like scaffolding, they are essential for the upkeep of the building. Each year rains wash away the mosque's smooth *banco* outer layer and the townspeople work to restore it in the dry season. Inside is a forest of pillars connected by sturdy arches. The mosque is said to hold up to five thousand worshippers – not bad when you consider that Djenné's total population is barely double that number.

Unfortunately, after fashion photographers used the mosque as a location, causing local outrage, the fascinating **interior and rooftop** are now formally off-limits to non-Muslims, though you can sometimes get a special dispensation if you are patient and courteous and prepared to pay; and you can get a fairly good exterior view from the roof of the house opposite for CFA200 or so (ask kids to show you the way). Two hundred metres behind the mosque is the **Tombeau de Tapama Djenepo,** the grave of a Bozo girl who, according to oral tradition, was sacrificed by the founders of Djenné to protect its buildings from collapse. Once you've exhausted these sites, just wandering the alleys of Djenné is fascinating and worthwhile: there are small mosques, many still in use, all over town.

Djenné's weekly **market** is a fascinating experience, and it's worth making every effort to time your trip for a Monday when traders from throughout the delta region make a commercial pilgrimage to town. They spread their wares on the main square in front of the mosque in much the same way that French explorer **René Caillié** described in the nineteenth century in his *Travels through Central Africa to Timbuktu.* There are few (if any) markets as animated, as colourful and as *rich* – those colossal swaying earrings are solid gold – as Djenné's on a Monday morning. After you've finished at the market it's satisfying to leave the crowds and wander through the dusty streets on your own, taking in the architecture and the way of life.

Djenné-Djeno

In 1977, a team of American archeologists discovered an ancient village 2km southeast of the town of Djenné at a spot now called **Djenné-Djeno** (old Djenné), just off the road to the highway. The foundations of buildings they uncovered here, along with terracotta statues, utensils and jewellery, date back as far as the third century BC and prick holes in a blanket of ignorance about archaic Africa – a highly developed, commercial society (like modern Djenné, the town counted more than 10,000 inhabitants) that existed long before the arrival of Islam. For reasons still unclear, Djenné-Djeno went into decline in the early Middle Ages and was abandoned by the fourteenth century.

Before visiting Djenné-Djeno, go to the **Mission Culturelle** just before the bridge into town on the north side of the road. They recommend making a small donation and taking a guide. There's a guardian at the site protecting it from antiquity thieves and looking out for unaccompanied visitors. When you arrive, keep your eyes on the ground and you'll see old pottery sherds everywhere, but beware of removing any, which can get you into serious trouble.

Villages around Djenné

There are several **villages** around Djenné, built on small elevations in the flood plains. One of the most interesting is **SENNISSA** – peopled mainly by Fula and just 4km from Djenné as the crow flies (take a guide). The village boasts two beautiful **mosques** and an abundance of artisans working along the small streets, lined with single-storey *banco* homes. You're likely to see women here wearing the huge gold heirloom earrings that were once common in the region. The biggest ones may be the size of a rugby ball and hang down to the woman's breasts; some are so heavy they have to be strung from a cord that passes over the head.

Further afield lies **KOUAKOUROU**, a Bozo village about 45km north of Djenné on the banks of the Niger. Its original architectural style, known as *saou*, is unique to the Djenné region. Of special interest are the dwellings for unmarried men whose walls are decorated with geometric forms. Market day here is Saturday and you can get here by *pinasse*, or overland in the dry season.

Timbuktu (Tombouctou) and around

"If I told you why it is mysterious then it would not be mysterious."
Former Minister of Sports, Art and Culture

"Is that it?"
Bob Geldof, after looking around during his Live Aid visit

Long associated with mysterious beauty, learning and, above all, wealth, **TIMBUKTU**, "the forbidden city", has always fascinated outsiders. From the time of the crusades, it was one of the main entrepôts for the West African **gold** which European finance relied on. From the fourteenth century, when Mansa Musa, Emperor of Mali, passed through Cairo on his way to Mecca (stunning the city with his fabulous entourage and selling so much gold that its price slumped for decades), to the sixteenth century, when Leo Africanus from Granada in Spain visited and described Timbuktu's opulent royal court, to as late as the nineteenth century when a lemming-like explorers' rush broke out to settle the enigma of the city roofed with gold, Timbuktu has achieved a near-legendary reputation. "Going to Timbuctoo" is still synonymous with going to the ends of the earth – or to hell – and only in the last few years has a more prosaic recognition forced itself into popular awareness.

Of course the town couldn't live up to the myths which disguised it for so long and any illusions of grandeur you still harbour are bound to be frustrated. As long ago as 1828, René Caillié wrote:

"I found it neither as big nor as populated as I had expected. Commerce was much less active than it was famed to be... Everything was enveloped in a great sadness. I was amazed by the lack of energy, by the inertia that hung over the town... a jumble of badly built houses... ruled over by a heavy silence."

This frank assessment rings true today. Though the entire town was formally declared a UNESCO World Heritage Site in 1988, as you walk the sandy streets, lined with pale grey stucco-covered mud-brick houses, you're more likely to be struck by the poverty than by historical monuments evoking a prouder past. Happily, apart from its been-there-done-that status, there is now another reason to visit Timbuktu, for the **Festival in the Desert**, an annual celebration of Tuareg and Malian music and culture (see p.403).

Some history

Towards the end of the eleventh century, a group of **Tuareg** who came to the Niger to graze their herds discovered a small oasis on the north bank where they set up a permanent camp. When they went off to pasture their animals, they left the settlement in the care of an old woman named Tomboutou – "the woman with the large belly button". Other tales have it that Tin or Tim Buktu was the well belonging to a woman named Buktu, while it's also possible that Buktu or *bouctou* may derive from the Arabic for "dune", while *tim* in Berber signifies "place of".

Whatever the origins of its name, the camp quickly developed into an important commercial centre where merchants from Djenné set up as middlemen between the salt caravans coming down from the north (and general dealers from the other side of the Sahara) and the river traffic bringing goods downriver from the grasslands and forests of the south. Although the Tuareg herders didn't live permanently in the town, they continued to control it, levying heavy and arbitrary taxes from the increasingly wealthy traders. Eventually, in response, the inhabitants invited the great Mali ruler **Mansa Musa** to liberate the town from Tuareg domination and he annexed it in 1330. To commemorate the occasion, the king visited Timbuktu and built a palace and the **Djinguereber mosque**.

Under the hegemony of the **Mali Empire**, Timbuktu enjoyed a period of stability and prosperity, but as the kingdom declined in the fifteenth century, the town again slipped into Tuareg control. Extortions began again, and in 1468 the merchants turned for help to the Songhai emperor **Sonni Ali Ber**, of Gao, who chased the Tuaregs west to the desert post of Oualata, in present-day Mauritania. Sonni Ali laid the foundations of the **Songhai Empire** which grew under the impetus of **Askia Mohammed**. Timbuktu reached its zenith at this point and became one of the Sahel's principal centres of commerce and learning. Reports of unimaginable wealth trickled back to Europe. The **Moroccan invasion** of 1591, however, when firearms were used in the Sahel for the first time, was a catastrophe for Timbuktu. The expedition's Andalucian leader, Djouder Pasha, had a number of senior scholars executed, exiled most of the others to Fez, and caravanned out the bulk of the city's wealth. Under the descendants of marriages between the invaders, who included conscripted Scots, Irish and Spanish soldiers and Songhai women (a group who came to be known as the **Arma**, after their guns) Timbuktu went into a steady decline that lasted throughout the seventeenth and eighteenth centuries. At different times it was attacked by the Mossi, the Fula, the Tukulor and, inevitably, the Tuareg. Subjected to pillage and oppression, the townspeople retreated behind the heavy, metal-studded wooden doors characteristic of Timbuktu houses. These were one of the few symbols of the city's former wealth that endured until the final arrival of the Europeans in the nineteenth century.

The European explorers

On the strength of a few translated books and a skein of rumours, **Europeans** set about uncovering Timbuktu's fabled riches. Between the late sixteenth century (by which time the city was already half-destitute, although they did not know it) and 1853, at least 43 travellers attempted to reach Timbuktu, of whom just four succeeded. The race really began in 1824, when the Geographical Society of Paris offered a prize of 10,000 francs for the first explorer to return with a verifiable account of the city. The earliest firsthand account by a non-Muslim, however, had already been given, not by an explorer, but by an illiterate American sailor, **Robert Adams**, who had been sold into slavery after his ship was wrecked off Mauritania, and who almost certainly spent several months in Timbuktu in 1811. But the story he related to the British consul in Morocco in 1813 wasn't given much credibility, as Adams wasn't aware of the mystique surrounding the city and his dreary description was too flat to be believed – except by Moroccan Muslims who themselves had been there. Whether or not Adams did get to Timbuktu is still a matter of some argument.

The first explorer to succeed conclusively – a prudish Scot named **Gordon Laing** – reached Timbuktu on August 13, 1826, after a hazardous desert crossing from Tripoli in which he was slashed almost to death by Tuareg robbers. The squalid slaving town was a bitter disappointment, but Laing was apparently greeted warmly by the sheikh of Timbuktu and by the townspeople. On hearing of the arrival of a Christian, however, the Fula sultan who claimed authority over the town at the time ordered Laing to get out on pain of death. Worried for his guest's safety, the sheikh sent Laing off towards Ségou (he was hoping to reach Sierra Leone) with an armed guide. Unfortunately, the latter turned out to be in the service of the sultan, and Laing and most of his servants were killed one night, 50km out of Timbuktu. One trailed back to Tripoli with Laing's notes and letters, two years later.

The first European to return from Timbuktu to write about the adventure himself was a Frenchman named **René Caillié**, whose fantastic journey started on the west coast on the Rio Nunez (now in northwest Guinea). Prior to taking off for Timbuktu, Caillié had lived in a Moorish village further north, learning Arabic and immersing himself in Muslim culture. Amazingly, he was sponsored by no government or association, and set off alone to the unexplored interior, disguised as an Egyptian. After making his way through the Fouta Djalon hills, he reached the Niger at Kouroussa, then continued to Tiémé (Côte d'Ivoire), where he fell gravely ill. After recovering, he pushed on to Tangréla and then to the devoutly Muslim town of Djenné where he made a deep and favourable impression on the sheikh – who would instantly have had him executed had his disguise been discovered. Caillié arrived in Timbuktu on April 20, 1828, and was received by a rich and pious

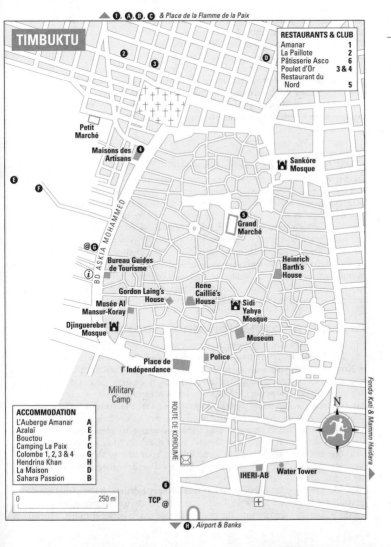

TIMBUKTU

▲ **①**, **Ⓐ**,**Ⓑ**, **Ⓒ** & Place de la Flamme de la Paix

RESTAURANTS & CLUB	
Amanar	1
La Paillote	2
Pâtisserie Asco	6
Poulet d'Or	3 & 4
Restaurant du Nord	5

②

Ⓓ

③

Petit Marché

Maisons des Artisans **④**

Ⓔ

Ⓕ

Sankóre Mosque

BD ASKIA MOHAMMED

⑤ Grand Marché

@**Ⓖ**

ⓘ Bureau Guides de Tourisme

Heinrich Barth's House

Gordon Laing's House

Rene Caillié's House

Sidi Yahya Mosque

Musée Al Mansur-Koray

Djinguereber Mosque

Museum

Place de l'Indépendance

Police

Military Camp

ROUTE DE KORIOUME

N

Fonda Kati & Mamma Haidara ▶

ACCOMMODATION	
L'Auberge Amanar	A
Azalaï	E
Bouctou	F
Camping La Paix	C
Colombe 1, 2, 3 & 4	G
Hendrina Khan	H
La Maison	D
Sahara Passion	B

0 ——— 250 m

⑥

TCP @

IHERI-AB

Water Tower

▼ **Ⓗ** , Airport & Banks

merchant, Sidi Abdallahi Chebir. Two weeks later, the adventurer joined a camel caravan and headed across the Sahara to Tangiers. In eighteen months, he had crossed 4500km, alone.

Caillié's book wasn't considered the last word on Timbuktu, however, and in Britain, especially, it was initially judged to be bogus. The person who finally convinced the world was the German polyglot and explorer **Heinrich Barth**, who left Tripoli in 1850 on an expedition financed by the British government. He survived the desert crossing to Agadez, in present-day Niger, then worked his way down to the Hausa country, his two companions dying en route. With delays and long residences in various towns, including diversions into Dogon country, he finally made it into Timbuktu on September 7, 1853. Like Caillié, he originally disguised himself as an Arab, but it didn't take long for the townspeople to discover he was Christian, after which his life was in danger. Barth, phlegmatic and undeterred, stayed eight months under the protection of Sheikh El Backay and collected the most detailed information known at the time. El Backay was virtually beseiged by his Fula overlords and only after long negotiations was Barth at last able to escape, following the river back east to Gao before continuing to Sokoto, Kano and on to Lake Chad. From here, he again set out across the Sahara, arriving in Tripoli in 1855. His explorations had lasted nearly six years and had taken him over 16,000km; the five-volume book he published at last overturned some of the myths.

Apart from a lucky young German, **Oskar Lenz**, who skipped through Timbuktu in 1880 and apparently had a wonderful time, the next European visitors were French: they came through the 1890s, little doubting success, to conquer and colonize.

Recent times

In the 1990s, Timbuktu yet again suffered the traditional depredations of the Tuareg who, threatened by the continuing suppression of their nomadic lifestyle, and increasingly supportive of a movement to create their own state from parts of Mali, Niger and Algeria, rebelled against the agents of Bamako. At one point history repeated itself as the Tuareg held the town in a state of virtual siege; it was their disruption which contributed to the dictator Moussa Traoré's fall and to subsequent reforms. Peace was finally cemented in March 1996 with the burning of three thousand Tuareg and government small arms in a ceremonial pyre commemorated by the **Flamme de la Paix** monument in the northern part of town. Since then troubles have mainly been limited to incidents of banditry in the area north of Gao, and Timbuktu is once again a safe and intriguing travel destination. In 2007 it was twinned with another town of literary repute, Hay-on-Wye in England.

Arrival, information and transport

Timbuktu's inaccessibility comes as no surprise, but unless you arrive by road, you'll still need transport to get to the town itself. Niger **river transport** docks at **Korioumé**, 19km south of town and connected to Timbuktu by a fast, paved road (CFA500–1000 by *bâché*). The **airport** is 5km south of town, off the Route de Korioumé (a jaw-dropping CFA10,000 each way by taxi).

If you want a Timbuktu stamp in your passport, the **tourist office** near the Djinguereber mosque (Mon–Thurs 8am–2pm, Fri 8am–12.30pm; ☏292.20.86) is happy to oblige, free of charge. Whilst there you might ask about **guides** (see p.327 for general advice on hiring one); as with most towns in Mali, you don't necessarily need one but good ones may add something to your tour of the town, and they do prevent other guides from approaching. The local guides office is virtually opposite the tourist office.

Just like town guides, offers to take you on **desert excursions** by camel are almost unavoidable once you arrive in Timbuktu. Everybody has a brother, an uncle or a cousin willing to take you into the desert at a rate much better than his competitors'

If you weren't impressed by Timbuktu's isolation during your stay, you will be when you try to leave. Given all the hassle of getting out of Timbuktu, it's worth trying to make arrangements for your departure as soon as you arrive. Unless you're travelling with your own vehicle, the options for **onward travel** in the rainy season (June–Oct) are pretty much limited to the river or planes, and even in the dry season there are only a few alternative overland options – and then of course you can only travel by river in small, slow pirogues.

By river

The **river journey** to Gao from Korioumé port, 19km from Timbuktu, is beautiful – the Niger snaking beneath high yellow dunes – and hippos are often seen along the way. In theory there should be two weekly boats leaving Korioumé – one upstream towards Mopti and Koulikoro (Aug–Nov), one downstream to Gao (Aug–Jan/Feb) – but regular departures on schedule are seldom the case, and your best bet is to enquire at the COMANAV booking office (☏292.12.06) for the latest information.

River travel can also be done by **pinasse**. A seat in a freight *pinasse* to Gao, for example, will cost you anything from CFA12,000 upwards – including basic food – for a journey of a minimum of two days. Call Harber (☏503.83.76) for details of imminent *pinasse* departures, though note that tough bargaining will be required. If you want more comfort and the possibility of stopping along the way, you can hire the entire *pinasse* for CFA400,000-500,000 depending on the size of the vessel and the time of year. They come with room for about 12 people.

Flights

The current **flight schedule** consists, on paper, of a Wednesday (April–Sept only) and Sunday flight to Mopti (Sévaré) and Bamako, with a further, direct flight to Bamako on Wednesday between those months. CAM can be contacted on ☏642.10.41, MAE on ☏292.11.21.

The pistes to Mopti, Douentza and Gao

In the dry season there is supposed to be a daily public 4x4 service to **Mopti** – a journey of some ten hours (though often much more). The head of the local transport syndicate (☏618.71.58) is the man to contact for this service. The fare is CFA12,500, or CFA15,000 for the more spacious front seats. Book in advance and they'll come and pick your luggage up the night before, then call in at your hotel to pick you up early the next morning. It has become just about the most reliable transport service serving Timbuktu.

In the dry season 4x4s follow the upgraded *piste* from Timbuktu to **Douentza** (CFA10,000 from Timbuktu) via Bambara-Maoundé. The 250km trip from the ferry landing opposite the port of Korioumé to Douentza takes around four to six hours. In theory, once in Douentza you can catch a ride with one of the bus companies plying the road between Bamako, Sévaré and Gao. In practice buses are often already full and you may have to wait for a vehicle with a spare seat: be prepared to spend the night in Douentza (see p.417).

If you're heading to **Gao**, truck-driving traders going via Bamba and Bourem will take passengers who are willing to sit on top of the load, exposed to the sun, heat, cold and wind, for a negotiable fee of around CFA20,000. It's a one- to two-day journey, with few stops, on a demanding, 425-km *piste*.

Lastly, in the dry season converted bus-trucks ply the road to **Bamako** via Goundam, Léré and Niono to Ségou, a two-day journey stopping overnight in Léré on the way north, and Niono on the way south. Note that the state of the road varies enormously from season to season, and cancellations and long delays are common.

prices. The tourist office and guide association should, in principle, minimize the risk of anything going wrong and ensure that you get what you pay for. Potential guides are given training – in first aid and cookery, among other things – before being awarded an official tourist guide photo ID. Trips into the desert, usually ranging from two hours to a couple of days, are magical and unforgettable. Prices vary but half a day should cost around CFA7500 and an overnight trip starting mid-afternoon around CFA15,000; this includes camel and guide and relevant meals. Part of the trip normally includes a visit to a Tuareg settlement for tea and a rest: if you choose to take photos of people, don't forget to leave a small *cadeau*. It's also possible to visit the desert by 4x4, with prices starting at CFA50,000 a day, excluding fuel, driver, and whatever food and drink you want to take. The tourist office can supply agency contacts with relatively reliable vehicles. Whichever way you choose to take an excursion out of Timbuktu, the prices quoted will initially be at least double what you should aim to agree on.

Timbuktu's **post office** and **banks** (as usual the BNDA is the one to use for changing cash dollars and euros, while BDM occasionally offers cash advances on Visa cards) are located several hundred metres down the Route de Korioumé. There are two places offering **Internet** access (CFA1000/hr), one of which, at *Hôtel Colombe 3* on Boulevard Askia Mohammed, has English keyboards (as opposed to the standard French *claviers*) but a painfully slow connection so most people prefer the other place, by *Pâtisserie Asco*. If you need to phone, there are **télécentres** scattered around town.

Accommodation

Reasonably priced **accommodation** in Timbuktu has long been a problem. Cheaper alternatives are slowly appearing, but if you can afford it, you might relax your budget here for a night or two. Alternatively, most hotels with suitable roofs will allow you to sleep on them.

Azalaï on a low rise on the western edge of town ☏/℻ 292.21.06. Overlooking a permanently dry wadi, this used to be the best option in town, with reasonable a/c rooms (with power from the hotel's own generator if necessary). Unfortunately, the complete lack of anything approaching an atmosphere puts off many. ⑤

Bouctou western edge of town just off the main drag ☏ 292.10.12. A traditional Moroccan-style building with good views of the dunes, the *Bouctou* has rooms with mosquito nets and a/c or fan, either in the main building or the nearby annexe. You can camp or sleep on the roof (CFA6500). Popular with tour groups – and, possibly as a result, with local guides too, who hang about outside. Breakfast is included. Non-s/c rooms with fan ④ or s/c, a/c rooms ⑤.

Camping La Paix On the north side of town, near the *Sahara Passion* ☏ 614.19.07 ℯ bell_ciss @yahoo.fr. Occupying what used to be *Sahara Passion*'s home, the basic *La Paix* is run by the affable Belle Cisse and features a variety of different rooms as well as a pleasant shady terrace. A worthy rival. Dorms and camping CFA4000. ②

Colombe 1, 2, 3 & 4 bd Askia Mohammed ☏ 292.21.32. Ever-expanding and bidding hard for the mainstream tourist market, the *Colombe*

now boasts no less than four different hotels in the same small neighbourhood. The s/c, a/c rooms are smart (especially in the newer units) and there's a pool in *Colombe 4*. Prices are identical in each. ⑤

Hendrina Khan turn off the main road opposite the BDM ☏ 292.16.81 ⓦ www.tomboctou.com. Another tourist-class outpost that's been put in the shade by the arrival of *La Maison*. The a/c rooms here are fine and it's hard to find fault with the place itself; unfortunately, the same cannot be said of the unsmiling staff. ⑤

La Maison about 500m northeast of the cemetery ☏ 292.21.79 ⓦ www .lesmaisonsdumali.com. The perfect antidote to those disappointed by Timbuktu's lack of romance and exoticism, this beautiful hotel is the town's best by miles. With s/c, a/c designer rooms, a Moroccan-style terrace, and excellent cooking from the owner's mother, the traces of any hardships you've suffered in getting to Timbuktu are likely to vanish if you treat yourself to a night here. ⑥

Restaurant Poulet d'Or The branch behind the cemetery (☏ 605.09.64) has some very basic, dingy rooms. Airless, windowless – truly miserable in fact – but the cheapest in town by far at CFA2500 a bed.

West African food plants

West Africa has a huge variety of fruits, vegetables, cereals and root crops. Some are native (like sorghum, yams and kola), others some came from South America (such as maize, cassava and groundnuts) and some originated in the Middle East and Asia (including mango, banana and citrus). Trying new flavours adds a special dimension to travel, especially as you move from one cultivation zone, say rice, or yams to another, like cassava or millet. But as you travel around, it's often hard to be sure what's growing in the fields and clearings at the roadside: this feature should help. There's more about fruit and vegetables in the "Eating and drinking" section of Basics.

Cereals

Millet (*gero* in Hausa). This looks like bullrushes with a maize-like stalk. It's grown mostly in the Sahel and is used for porridge, gruel and making beer.

Sorghum (*sorgho* in French). Tall, two- to four-metre-high plant, similar to maize but with feathery, white- or red-grained flower heads. Also known as "guinea corn" and "giant millet", sorghum is grown mainly in the savannah zone, and is made into porridge or sorghum beer – known as *bilibili, burukutu* and *pito*.

Rice (*riz* in French). Anything grass-like growing in bunches in shallow water is likely to be rice but it can also be grown on dry land.

► Millet

Kola nuts

Giving and receiving **kola nuts** is a traditional exchange of friendship. Kola nuts are the caffeine-containing, chestnut-sized fruit from the pods of a tree, cultivated widely all over the forest belt and traded on a grand scale throughout West Africa. Before the

arrival of tobacco, cannabis, tea and coffee, kola was the main nonalcoholic drug of the region, an appetite depressant and a mild stimulant (and used in the original Coca Cola recipe). It comes in dark red, pink and yellow varieties – yellow are the best and more expensive. Kola should be fresh and crisp, not old and rubbery, and you break off small pieces and chew – don't swallow – for the bitter juice. Buy a handful for long journeys, as much to share among fellow passengers as to stay awake.

Roots and tubers

Cassava

Cassava (*manioc* in French). Spindly two-metre shrub from South America, with hand-like leaves, seen growing all over. The tubers, which tend to have a bitter taste, are large and coarse and have to be peeled, soaked, boiled and then usually pounded in a mortar to reduce them to an edible glob of sticky starch (*fufu/foufou/eba*). Cassava leaves, finely shredded and used like spinach, taste much nicer and are full of vitamins. *Gari* is cassava flour (from which tapioca is made), but the word gets used for various types of flour.

Yams growing

Yam (*ignames* in French). Massive tubers that grow singly beneath a climbing, vine-like plant with spade-shaped leaves, commonly seen in southern parts of the region, especially in Nigeria. They come in white and yellow varieties (the former is preferred) and are used like cassava to make pounded yam *fufu*, but they have a better flavour. Cocoyams are tastier than yams and grown mostly in wet forest regions. The plants have huge, heart-shaped, edible leaves and the tubers are rounded and commonly known as "koko", "mankani", "taro", "eddo" or "dasheen".

Groundnuts

Groundnut (peanuts; *arachide* or *cacahouètes* in French). Groundnuts are grown widely as a cash crop and for use in sauces. You'll see little dollops of peanut butter for sale in markets everywhere.

Tiger nuts

Tiger nuts (*chufa*). Tiny coconut-flavoured tubers like shrivelled beans, boiled and eaten as a snack. They were a major crop in ancient Egypt and reached West Africa on the Arab trade routes.

See the "Eating and drinking" section of Basics for more about vegetables, including sweet potatoes, ladies' fingers, garden eggs and cowpeas.

Fruit and nuts

Banana If you spend long in West Africa, you may never be able to face a banana again. But local varieties are often wonderfully flavoured. Look out for very thin-skinned dwarf bananas in huge bunches, and for very fat, squat varieties with pale orange flesh and sometimes red skins.

Plantain These mega-bananas used for cooking, are found all over the rainier southern part of West Africa. When hard, they're boiled and sometimes pounded to a tasty *fufu*; when ripe they can be fried or roasted.

Papaya Also known as "pawpaws", non-seasonal papayas aren't usually regarded as worth selling and they tend to grow as giant weeds, left for the children. If you don't see them for sale, approach any compound where they're growing and ask to buy one. The seeds are also edible and, like the flesh, are considered to have a multitude of healthy properties.

Oranges and mandarins Often bright green, even when perfectly ripe, these are the main juice-fruits of West Africa. Oranges are always available for loose change from girls and women with trays piled high and sharp knives. The peel is shaved off, leaving the orange in its pith, then the top is lopped off and you squeeze the juice into your mouth and discard the emptied orange. There's no real season.

Cashew Not just a nut, the cashew also has a fruit attached, which grows and ripens behind the nut – an arrangement that's hard to believe when you first see it. You can eat the cashew apple, though the fibrous flesh can be bitter. In some parts the delicious, light juice is made into a potent hooch. Don't be tempted to feast off people's cashew trees – they only have a small number of valuable nuts each and owners get very upset.

See the "Eating and drinking" section of Basics for more about fruit, including mangoes, pineapples, dates and custard apples.

The Town

There are no obvious starting points to a sightseeing trip round Timbuktu, but most people will find themselves down on the Route de Korioumé fairly soon after arrival, and there's a good opportunity for a grand view of the town from the top of the **water tower** (*château d'eau*) near here. For another good view of Timbuktu – in silhouette – climb one of the town's **dunes** at dawn to watch the sun rising above the town. The easiest dunes to reach are a short walk north of the Flamme de la Paix monument.

There are two main **markets** in Timbuktu – the **grand marché**, a disappointing, atmosphere-free multistorey site in the heart of the old town, and the **petit marché**, which is busier, more evocative and, despite its name, larger. Close to the petit marché you'll find the **Maison des Artisans**, where you can watch artisans at work and browse a good variety of crafts. With a bit of effort you'll get good prices on nicely worked knives, leatherwork, and Tuareg silver (or nickel) crosses, bracelets and rings. Look out for delicately fashioned Neolithic arrowheads and stone axes, knives and scrapers from the Sahara's relatively recent past: these can still be found in the dunes in more remote districts of the desert.

Mosques and museums

The key sites in Timbuktu are the three ancient mosques – even though you'll have to content yourself with views of their exteriors, non-Muslims now being forbidden to enter any of them. The oldest and most famous is the Friday **Djinguereber mosque** on Boulevard Askia Mohammed. It was first built in 1327 by El Saheli – an Andalucian architect and poet whom Mansa Musa met in Cairo during his pilgrimage to Mecca – who is credited with the invention of mud bricks. Before this innovation, all building had been done using mud and straw, slapped on a wooden framework.

From Djinguereber you can continue east along the paved lane into the heart of the old town, past several tourist attractions including the rather dreary **Musée Al Mansur Korey** (8am–6pm, Fri to 2pm; CFA1500) and a couple of houses of the early explorers (see below). Eventually, the route arrives at a junction, opposite which is Timbuktu's second mosque, the **Sidi Yahya**. This mosque was first constructed in 1400 by a marabout named El-Moktar Hamalla, and was intended to serve a saint whose imminent arrival had been prophesied. Four decades later, Sherif Sidi Yahya crossed the desert and asked for the keys to the mosque. He was declared imam, and is today one of the most revered of Timbuktu's 333 saints.

Behind the Sidi Yahya is the town's **Ethnographic Museum** (daily 8am–4pm; CFA2500). With its centrepiece, the **Bouctou well** that, according to one version, the town grew up around, the museum focuses on the lifestyles and customs of the main ethnic groups in the area. Musical instruments and games as well as personal decorations of the Tuareg, Songhai and Bella are exhibited in simple and well-composed displays, though unfortunately with very little labelling. A bonus is a section devoted to the ancient rock carvings at **Tin-Techoun**.

Timbuktu's third great mosque, the **Sankoré,** lies to the north of the market on the edge of the old town. It dates from the fifteenth century and doubled as a **university** during Timbuktu's golden era, specializing in law and theology. It was renowned throughout the Muslim world – up to 25,000 students were studying here in the sixteenth century.

Timbuktu's houses

Though Timbuktu's mosques and museum are the main sights, it's also rewarding to spend some time walking through the confusion of narrow streets to take in Timbuktu's unique **architecture**. The finest homes – usually owned by Moorish merchants – are made of carved limestone brought from desert quarries. Again, the basic design of these homes may date, like that of the Djinguereber, to El Saheli; the columns of square pilasters that decorate the facades are reminiscent of those in Egyptian temples, an element he may have picked up in Cairo. The small shuttered windows and heavy wooden doors with geometric ironwork designs also bear an Arabic stamp, though they seem to hark back to the Moroccan invasion of the late sixteenth century.

Plaques still mark the homes where **Laing**, **Caillié** and **Barth** stayed during their exploits in Timbuktu. The first two are near neighbours in the Djinguereber district and any kid can point them out to you. Heavy rains occasionally reduce one or other of the houses to rubble, but they're regularly repaired again for the sake of Timbuktu's precarious tourist industry – building in mud guarantees an authentic, weathered, historical look. Barth's old house, now a private home that doubles as a small museum assembled in his honour, is the only one you can go inside (daily 8am–6pm; CFA1000). More modest houses are made of *banco* in the Djenné style. Along the streets you'll also notice dome-shaped **clay ovens** where women bake round loaves of bread, a speciality of the town traditionally made from wheat grown near Lake Faguibine and easily recognized by the crunchy, sandy crust.

Timbuktu's libraries and manuscripts

One of the greatest remaining legacies of Timbuktu's former glory is the wealth of Islamic literature that was produced here. Traditionally, families wrote their histories in **chronicles** known as *tarikh* – one of the most important of which was the *Tarikh es-Soudan*, written by El Sadi in the seventeenth century. These and other related writings have provided invaluable information about scientific, legal and social practices throughout the region, and indeed across the entire Muslim world. In addition, they've helped trace Mali's history back to the empire of ancient Ghana. Countless volumes remain in private family collections, where, exposed to damp, dust and insects, the works (some of which date back to the thirteenth century) risk being lost forever. In recognition of its status, in 2007 Timbuktu was twinned with another literary town, Hay-on-Wye in England.

Timbuktu's **Institut des Hautes Études et de Recherches Islamiques – Ahmed Baba** (IHERI-AB, formerly known as the Centre des Recherches Ahmed Baba, or CEDRAB; ⊛tinyurl.com/2hg4hz) is persuading, sometimes reluctant, families to part with their priceless documents, at least long enough for them to be restored and digitized. With South African money and academic assistance, to date more than 30,000 manuscripts have been collected, about eighty percent of them written in Arabic and most of the rest in Songhai. The centre is near the water tower on the south side of town, down the airport road and left after the post office. It's very much worth a visit but it's a good idea to make an appointment first, even to visit during their normal hours (Mon–Fri 9am–noon). An entry fee of CFA1000 is typically charged. Ask the staff to show you some of the older, handwritten documents, the most beautiful of which contain geometric artwork and gold lettering. Buying and exporting manuscripts is illegal but you can sometimes obtain souvenir copies of the originals. A new $7million home for the institute, including a modern museum and facilities for visiting academics, will be opening to the public in 2008.

Just a little further east, the private **Mama Haidara Memorial Library** was opened by one of the CEDRAB's former employee-researchers, and is also worth visiting. Its displays are more accessible than IHERI-AB's, and possibly a better bet if you're interested in the content of the manuscripts. Again, CFA1000 is elicited from visitors. A couple of blocks further on again, **Fondo Kati** (⊛www.fundacionmahmudkati.org;

CFA1500) is another worthwhile collection, open 8am–6pm daily, and there are as many as twenty other libraries in the town.

The outskirts

Around most of the outskirts of Timbuktu are scattered clusters of circular straw huts, the homesteads of Tuareg, Bella and Fula nomads; walk out to the Monument de la Paix to see them. On the northern outskirts of town is the **Abaradio district** where the *azalaï* or camel caravans formerly arrived in great numbers (even when the first European explorers arrived, as many as sixty thousand camels a year unloaded their goods here). Apart from goods from North Africa and the Mediterranean, the Sahara's biggest prize was rock salt from the ultra-remote oasis of **Taoudenni**, 700km due north of Timbuktu. Taoudenni is famous for its salt mines – and was until 1989 a Malian Siberia where political undesirables were banished and the former president Modibo Keita was detained until his death. Caravans of salt slabs still come down to Timbuktu from Taoudenni.

Eating

Eating options in Timbuktu have opened up in recent years – though they are still somewhat thin on the ground. The market itself doesn't offer a great deal, making self-catering a difficult option, though there are a couple of restaurants on the roof of the multistorey grand marché that are nice places for a cold drink if nothing else. In addition to the listings below, don't forget to try some of the street food in the evenings, particularly on the broad road leading east from the cemetery: the sausages are some of the tastiest – and greasiest – you'll encounter anywhere. Then there are the hotel restaurants: meals at *La Maison*, for example (around CFA7500 for dinner), are the best in town – unless you're lucky enough to be invited to a feast in a private home.

Amanar on the north side of town, facing the Flamme de la Paix monument. A rarity in Timbuktu – a restaurant that's easy to recommend, with good food and friendly staff. The European and local dishes are reasonably priced and there's a very popular pavement bar.

Al Hayat bd Askia Mohamed. Not spectacular, with just the usual local rice-based dishes on offer, though it does occasionally show football on the TV and it is just about the most central place to eat in town.

Pâtisserie Asco rte de Korioumé. Good Western and local dishes, but their pastries aren't great.

La Paillote to the north of the main cemetery, just west of *Poulet d'Or*. More a nightclub than a restaurant, though it does serve a few basic dishes.

Poulet d'Or to the north of the main cemetery. Standard Western dishes, with a second branch in La Maison des Artisans being friendlier and with better food.

Essakane: le Festival au Désert

Since 2001, Mali has hosted an annual **Festival in the Desert** in early January – a celebration of Tuareg and Malian music and culture, grafted onto a traditional Tuareg gathering and coordinated and publicized by Efès and Aïtma, two Tuareg associations, and by committed individuals in Belgium, Britain, France and the USA. Since 2003 the location has been **ESSAKANE**, a remote oasis 65km northwest of Timbuktu, and future events are likely to take place in the same area. On the bill in 2008 were the guitar band Tamikrest and a number of other Tuareg and Songhai groups, plus reggae star Tiken Jah Fakoly from Côte d'Ivoire and numerous other artists from Mali and overseas.

Essakane has just a couple of hundred inhabitants and virtually no supplies or facilities, so everything – from generators to stage equipment and all food and supplies – has to be trucked in. Although you may be able to pick up information locally and make your own arrangements to attend, you're recommended to get details in advance at Ⓦ www.festival-au-desert.org. The basic ticket price for tourists is €149 – quite expensive but this is, after all, the most remote festival in the world.

Along the Niger to Gao

A demanding *piste* (4x4 essential) follows the Niger's north bank some 425km to Mali's easternmost city, **Gao** (see p.424). You – or your driver – will have to negotiate ruts of deep sand on a thorn-strewn track that winds through acacia bush. It's 195km to **BAMBA**, one of the first major villages along the route – a difficult stretch with deep soft sand, along which it's easy to lose your way if you're driving. Bamba, sandwiched between the *piste* and the river, is an oasis said to have been founded by the Moroccan invaders of the 1590s. It was particularly vulnerable in the Tuareg conflict of the 1990s. Another 135km brings you to **BOUREM** on the Niger River, a Songhai village with characteristic *banco* homes and a large market – and also the southern terminus of the trans-Saharan Tanezrouft route from Algeria. From here, the road continues along the river to Gao, 95km away.

It's worth noting that a feasible route also exists from **GOURMA-RHAROUS** (about 110km east of Timbuktu on the south bank), to **Gossi** (see p.422) on the Gao–Mopti road. There's a basic car ferry across the river at Gourma-Rharous, though if you're not driving you won't need to worry much about the crossing, as pirogues cross on demand.

4.5

The Dogon country

U ntil the end of the colonial era, the **Dogon** were one of the African peoples who had most successfully retained their culture and traditional way of life, remaining largely non-Muslim. This was in large part due to the isolation of their territory in the remarkable and picturesque cliffside villages they built along the **Bandiagara escarpment** south and east of Mopti – a 200-kilometre-long wedge of sandstone, pushed up by movements of the earth's plates in prehistoric times and running from Ouo in the southwest to the Hombori Mountains in the northeast. Dogon villages are scattered over three distinct areas: the plateau, the escarpment itself (the cliff or **falaise**), and the sandy Gondo-Seno Plain which stretches out from the foot of the cliffs towards the southeast and Burkina.

The Dogon remain dogged defenders of their customs, religion and art, but in more recent years they have become the object of a fairly intense **tourist industry**. Although much of the Dogon country (**pays Dogon**) can only be visited on foot or at best with a donkey- or ox-cart (a **charette**), some of the more accessible villages on the paved roads or 4x4 routes can seem very busy with tourists, especially over Christmas.

With patience and plenty of time, you can still manage to get more or less off the beaten track, but don't be disappointed not to be the first to have done so. Leaving that aside, this is an opportunity to see **spectacular architecture** and **village environments**, to witness **traditional culture** at work, and to meet local people in a relatively unchanged context, where you share local food, sleep on the roofs of their houses and use the same **bush pathways** and tricky **cliffside alleys** that they have navigated for hundreds of years.

It can't be overemphasized that as a visitor to the *pays Dogon*, you are a **guest** in a fragile community. As long as tourists continue to respect the Dogon people's culture and environment, and their right to privacy, there is no reason for relations to become strained. Try to behave conservatively and be careful to avoid widening the generation gap between the more cosmopolitan young and their exclusively Dogon-speaking elders. It's worth carrying a supply of **kola nuts**, which are much appreciated by village elders – offering this traditional gift, especially when you arrive in a village, can help inordinately when it comes to asking permission to take photos. Remember that many older Dogon speak little or no French, so a few words in the **Dogon language** (see p.356) are bound to smooth relations – and your efforts will often make people laugh.

The Dogon are rightly celebrated for their **artistic heritage** and the whole *pays Dogon* is a UNESCO World Heritage Site. Tragically, much of their art and furniture has been sold overseas – their richly symbolic carved doors, windows and meeting-house pillars in particular. Resist buying any **artefacts** that look remotely old; there are plenty of items for sale that have been made expressly as souvenirs and the quality of workmanship is often extremely good.

Dogon history

Archeological research has uncovered caves dating to around the third century BC dug into the cliffs around the Dogon town of **Sanga**. The Dutch scientists who discovered these caves called the people who made them the **Toloy**, but there seems to be a rather large gap between this culture and the next known inhabitants of the escarpment, the **Tellem**, who arrived in the eleventh century. The Tellem were small people, often said to have been "pygmies", although they probably weren't related to the contemporary people of small stature from central Africa. They built distinctive, cellular houses in sheltered crevices and beneath overhangs on the cliffside – places where sun and rain were least able to penetrate. Their architecture is still visible today, strikingly similar to that of the ancient cliff dwellings of the southwestern USA. It is generally thought that the Tellem shared the escarpment for a couple of centuries with the **Dogon**, who arrived in the fifteenth century. Some time around the seventeenth century, the Tellem were pushed out of the Dogon country and migrated to the area that is now Burkina Faso.

The Dogon may originally have come from the region of the Nile, but before moving to the Bandiagara escarpment they lived in the Mandé country to the west. Determined to preserve their traditional religion in the face of Muslim expansionism and religious jihads, they migrated to the safety of the *falaise* in the fifteenth century. Even with this natural shelter as a homeland, they had to fight off numerous aggressors over the centuries. In the 1470s the country was invaded by the **Songhai**, and in the early eighteenth century it was attacked by the **Ségou kingdom**. Much later, in 1830, the Fula from **Massina** marched on the region and, in 1860, the Tukulor ruler **El Hadj Omar** brought his holy war to the escarpment, making Bandiagara his capital; he died in nearby Déguemberé. The **French** occupied the region of Sanga in 1893, but it wasn't until the battle of Tabi in 1920 that the colonial army finally "pacified" the Dogon people.

In the 1930s an American missionary, Reverend **Francis McKinney**, established the first Christian mission in Sanga. Several years later **Marcel Griaule**, a French anthropologist, came to the same town to study traditional Dogon religion and customs. He spent a quarter of a century living in Dogon country, helping them set up dams for irrigation and introducing the onion crop that's now one of the only exports of the region to the rest of Mali and Burkina. Respected by the Dogon, he also helped open the eyes of the world to the complexity and integrity of a civilization that had long been regarded by Muslim and Christian invaders as merely primitive.

Sex, speech and weaving: a Dogon cosmology

The Dogon believe in a single god, **Amma**, who created the sun, moon and stars. According to Dogon legend, he then created the earth by throwing a ball of clay into space. The ball spread to the four points of the horizon and took on the shape of a woman with an anthole for her vagina and a termite mound for her clitoris. Alone in the universe, Amma attempted to have sex with the earth, but the termite mound blocked his path and he tore it out. Because of this violence, the earth could not bear the twins that would have resulted from a happy union and instead gave birth to a jackal.

Amma again had intercourse with the earth, and a pair of twins resulted, known as **nommo**. They were born of divine semen, the precious water found in everything in the universe. Green in colour, their upper bodies were human and their lower bodies like snakes. Living in the heavens with their father, the *nommo* looked down on their mother and, seeing her naked, made a **skirt** into which they wove the first **language**. Thus the earth was the first to possess speech.

Meanwhile, the jackal was running loose. His mother was the only woman, and he raped her. The earth bled and became impure in Amma's eyes. For this reason, men-struating women are still considered impure in Dogon society (as they are in nearly all African cultures). When he forced himself upon the earth, the jackal also touched her skirt and thus stole language.

Having turned from his wife, Amma decided to create a human couple from clay. The couple had elements of both sexes – the foreskin being the feminine part of the man, and the clitoris the masculine part of the woman. Foreseeing that prob-lems would arise from this ambiguity, the *nommo* circumcised the male and later an invisible hand removed the clitoris from the woman (circumcision of men and clitoridectomy of women is still an important step into adulthood for the Dogon). The couple was thus free to procreate and produced eight children, the original **Dogon ancestors**. After creating eight descendants of their own, the ancestors were purified and transformed into *nommo*, and then went to join Amma in the sky. But before his ascension, the seventh ancestor was charged with giving the **second language** to humans. Using his mouth as a loom, he spat out a cotton strip from which the new speech was transmitted to humanity.

The eight ancestors didn't get along with Amma and the *nommo* and were even-tually sent back to earth. On the way, the eighth ancestor came down before the seventh, who was angry as a result. He turned himself into a snake and set about disturbing the work of the other ancestors. They told the people to kill the snake – which they did. But this seventh ancestor – whose name was Lebe – held the **third language**, needed for mankind, since the second wasn't adequate. The old-est of the eight original descendants thus had to be sacrificed and was buried with the head of Lebe the snake. Humans then received the third language in the form of a drum.

To this day, Dogon **dances** symbolize this creation story. **Masks** are an important element of the dances and the Dogon use more than eighty different varieties accord-ing to the celebration. The biggest ceremony is the **Sigui**, celebrated every sixty years (the next should be in 2027) to commemorate the passing of a generation. The frequency of Sigui is calculated by the periodicity of an invisible moon of Sirius, a sat-ellite which remained unknown to western astronomers long after it was mentioned to Marcel Griaule, the first westerner to study Dogon culture. Sirius itself appears brightly between mountain peaks exactly when expected, suggesting a level of astronomical knowledge which has long baffled outsiders. The Sigui serves to venerate the Big Mask, made in the shape of a serpent in reference to **Lebe**, who is credited with lead-ing the Dogon to the Bandiagara escarpment as well as bringing them speech and, simultaneously, death.

practicalities

The main bases for organizing your Dogon adventure are Mopti–Sévaré, Douentza, Bankass or, actually within Dogon country itself, Bandiagara and Sanga. **Bandiagara** offers the most trekking options, the quickest access to **Sanga** and the most popular treks; **Bankass**, convenient if you're arriving from Burkina Faso, takes you straight to the southern *pays Dogon* and **Douentza** to the northern districts. All over Dogon country there are rewarding sights and experiences at any time of year, but it's fair to say that the Sanga area is the most heavily developed for tourism, with lots of small hotels and *auberges* and swarms of visitors over Christmas and holiday periods, while the northern and southern ends of the escarpment are more remote and undeveloped.

A trip to the Dogon country can involve hours of **trekking** in the sweltering sun, and usually entails climbing up and down the three-hundred-metre escarpment and walking over a great deal of rocky terrain. Depending on your inclinations and those of your guide, you're likely to pass through about three villages a day in this manner. You'll want to travel light; ideally you should leave all but the essentials behind before making the trip. Most of the better lodgings and hotels will guard your luggage for a small fee while you're away, or, if you're not returning, you can always have the bulk of your luggage carried by porter or *charette*.

Much of Dogon country is rough, and while it's true that special **footwear** is not essential, a good pair of walking shoes is a big asset, especially if you're going to be walking for several days and plan to move up and down between the plain and the plateau – which, unless you suffer from vertigo, or really can't manage the occasional scramble over rocks, is really the whole point. If you aren't going to climb, it is possible to stay on the plain, and you'll still get some stunning views of the cliffs. It's worth noting that the precise **locations of villages** can be confusing, as most "villages" consist of between two and five separate hamlets, usually scattered from the plateau to the cliff edge, then down to a midway point on the escarpment and then out onto the plain.

The heat can be intense, and you will certainly need a light and comfortable **hat**. Bring a **water bottle** or canteen for the long stretches between villages, most of which have no running water. You'll be drinking water from local wells or pumps (or buying bottled water, which is widely available). It's not essential to filter the water, but it is a good idea to purify it. If you're here in the middle of the hot season, **rehydration salts** are also not a bad idea. You may also want to take some fruit or snacks with you to supplement the generally basic food you'll be eating in the villages.

It's normal practice to start **walking** as early as possible, say 6.30 or 7am, and to stop by 11am for lunch and a long rest during the hottest part of the day, leaving again no earlier than 3pm. Note that not all Dogon villages have **electricity**, and where there is a supply, it's likely to come from a small solar panel or, in wealthier places, a generator (a *groupe*). Taking a **torch** is a good idea: it will come in handy when you're scrambling around on a rooftop in the middle of the night or looking for the toilet.

Instead of purely relying on your legs, for greater flexibility and a speedier pace, you could travel by **mobylette** (moped), **moto** (motorbike), or **4x4**, though you should bear in mind that once you're off the paved road the routes can be extremely challenging even with the toughest vehicles. Travelling by *mobylette* or *moto* is an invigorating way to discover the region, but few rented bikes go really well even in the best conditions. Around here you'll spend all your time fixing your bike, and then, when you return it to the owner, arguing about who should pay for the necessary replacement parts. Finally, if you're travelling in your own vehicle and it's not a 4x4, you're best off leaving it at a secure *parking* in one of the towns.

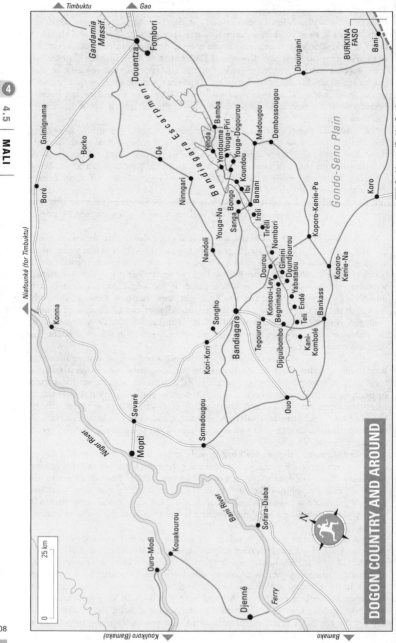

DOGON COUNTRY AND AROUND

Guides and costs

Whatever your experiences have been in Mali's other towns, **guides** are essential in Dogon country, and you'll be expected to have a local escort in every community you visit. Guides are useful for locating villages and the quickest or most rewarding footpaths between them, for figuring out market days (every five days in most villages) and harvest festivals (many around early December and also an interesting batch in April), and making arrangements for sleeping and eating in isolated places. Moreover, without a guide, you'll have real problems just communicating: many older people don't speak French and, even more so than elsewhere in Mali, the manner in which people greet each other is elaborate, and a very important element of any social exchange. There are also a number of taboos, often specific to certain villages, and without the assistance of a clued-up guide you risk making cultural faux pas at every turn. Finally, a good guide should also be able to fill you in on the history and rich culture of the places you visit, and the significance of the various elements that make up the buildings in each village.

As a rough indication of **trekking costs**, you should expect your guide to charge a basic CFA4000–5000 per day per person. On top of that you generally pay, per person, CFA3500–5000 per day for three meals (sometimes prepared by the guide, sometimes bought by him on your behalf) and CFA1500 per night (invariably sleeping on the roof, accessed by a tricky, notched tree-trunk staircase, at a basic village *campement* or *auberge*, or camping in your own tent if you prefer), which includes use of shower and toilet facilities. If you want a porter to take your bags, that will add around CFA4000 per day, which covers the bags of two people and their guide (and pro rata for a larger group). In addition, there's a visitor fee for every night you stay in a village, usually CFA1000. Worked out like this, daily costs per person, excluding drinks, should be in the range of CFA10,000–15,000.

Transport to the start of the hike, and back again, is a variable cost. If you go with your guide by public transport, the cost will be minimal. On the other hand, a 4x4 vehicle and driver (which will also enable you to get well into hiking country without a lot of foot-slogging) will generally cost CFA75,000–80,000 per day plus fuel charges of around CFA100/km. Remember you'll have to pay for the fuel for

Pays Dogon market days

It's not only useful in itself to know when markets are taking place, but it's also handy because the days often determine the availability of local transport – usually heading towards the market in the morning, and back again mid-afternoon.

7-day-week market days

Monday: Bandiagara (Dogon market), Madougou
Tuesday: Bankass
Wednesday: Djiguibombo
Thursday: Kani-Kombolé
Friday: Bandiagara (Tukulor market)
Saturday: Bamba, Koro
Sunday: Douentza, Endé

5-day-week market days

Day 1: Dourou, Ibi, Tirelli
Day 2: Nombori
Day 3: Yendouma-Sogol
Day 4: Sanga, Banani
Day 5: Ireli

the vehicle to get back again. If there are just one or two of you, plus the guide, then renting *mobylettes* to get to the relevant trailhead is perfectly feasible, and will save you at least half the cost of a 4x4. But accidents are very common: ride slowly.

It is standard practice for your guide to work out a complete price for the trip from start to finish and take a down payment, followed by instalments, with the last part paid before you part company. However, it is also increasingly common for guides to quote an **all-inclusive daily price** per person for their standard routes. This ranges around CFA15,000–30,000, depending on transport costs to be included.

A word of warning: an unfortunate by-product of the Dogon country's popularity as a tourist destination is the problem of inexperienced and unreliable **rogue guides**. It isn't essential for your guide to be Dogon (there are some excellent guides, personally known all over the region, who are not), but it is often a good start. Ideally you should choose a guide through one of the Ministry of Tourism-endorsed guide associations (ask for their guide association membership card) and better still by personal recommendation. If this isn't possible, make sure you quiz your guide carefully before agreeing to an itinerary. As ever, it's a good idea to draw up a contract before you go, stating your itinerary and a list of all your expenses and even, if there's a large group of you, having it stamped at a police station.

Bandiagara and southern pays Dogon

Although commercial tours are convenient if you want a perfunctory overview of Dogon territory, you may prefer less organization and the flexibility of following your own plans and pace. In that case it's usually best to head directly to **BANDIAGARA**, on the banks of the Yamé River, a 63-kilometre taxi ride on a fine paved road from Sévaré and 25km from the closest escarpment-edge trailheads at Djigui-bombo or Dourou (the biggest entirely Dogon village, Sanga, is 45km away). A flat, dusty, sizeable administrative town, Bandiagara is nothing like more traditional villages in the region, although the population is sixty percent Dogon. There's a good deal of commerce by Dogon standards, with a lively market on Mondays and Fridays, plus a hospital, mission and police headquarters. It's a convenient point of entry to the Dogon region, and a pleasant enough town, but in high season brace yourself for hopeful guides swarming around you and offering their services, from the minute you arrive.

Bandiagara practicalities

The notice boards of most of the hotels in town, including the *Kambary* and *Falaise*, give details of how much you should be charged for your trek. As a rough guide, all-inclusive prices (including everything except drinks and souvenirs) start at about CFA15,000 per day, rising to around CFA30,000: while there's some room for negotiation depending on the size of your group, the real difference lies in whether you use a vehicle, and what kind of vehicle (full information is given on p.407). The Mission Culturelle off the Sévaré road behind *Le Village* hotel is also recommended for advice on guides. The mission was set up to ensure the Dogon's precious cultural artefacts don't leave the region and to encourage villages to establish museums instead, an initiative that has already been very successful.

There's a good CLIC **Internet** place, down near the (often dry) river near the *Auberge Kansaye* (Mon–Fri 9am–1pm, 3.30–7pm, Sat 9am–noon; CFA1500/hr).

Accommodation and eating

There are now a few reasonable **accommodation** options catering for every budget. The **food** situation has improved massively over the past couple of years, too. Not only do the hotels now have decent restaurants that are starting to produce some reasonable dishes, but *Restaurant de la Fraternité*, very near the *Hôtel de la*

Falaise, serves some great steaks, spaghetti, *riz* and couscous – given time. Otherwise, inexpensive basic food and cold drinks are available at *Restaurant le Petit Coin*, still a popular hangout for guides despite a rather obscure location past the Palais Agibou Tall and the main mosque.

Hotels

Auberge Kansaye near the bridge over the river ☎ 549.61.34. A basic place that's still popular with travellers, despite the ever-burgeoning popularity of *La Falaise*. The shady garden restaurant is as lovely as the rooms are dark. CFA3000 to sleep on the roof. ❷

La Falaise about 100m from the bus station, across the roundabout ☎ 244.21.28. The new kid on the block and already the most popular, with a wide range of clean and well-maintained rooms catering to every budget and a lively bar and restaurant. Dorms CFA4000, terrace/camping CFA1500. Rooms with fan ❹ or a/c ❺.

Kambary well signposted off the Sévaré road ☎ 244.23.88 www.kambary.com.

Bandiagara's most upmarket, an atmospheric complex with dome-shaped *Star Wars*-like stone buildings, a pool and mini-golf course. Worth visiting even if only for a drink or meal. Rooms with fan ❹ or a/c ❻.

Toguna about 4km north of town on the Sévaré road ☎ 242.01.59. Friendly management, a very pleasant campsite and a few simple rooms, some s/c. CFA2500 to camp. ❷

Le Village near the Mission Culturelle, on the Sévaré road ☎ 244.23.31. Decent, clean rooms with shared facilities, a peaceful garden of neem trees – and cool beer. Slightly scruffy but fine otherwise. CFA2000 to camp, otherwise non-s/c rooms ❶.

The southern pays Dogon

Once you've reached Bandiagara, you can choose between making the town your base while you do short trips to visit other villages (Songho, Sanga, Dourou and Djiguibombo can each be visited in a half-day round trip by car, *moto* or *mobylette* from Bandiagara), or setting off on a longer trek, staying the night in villages as you go. Walking from the southern end of the escarpment to Sanga could feasibly be done in four days, though it's much better spread over six or seven. The route sticks largely to the plain, cutting up the escarpment to visit the interesting cliff villages of Begnimato and Dourou, and climbing again at the end of the trip to Sanga. As such it is mostly flat walking, though with two climbs which, while taxing, should not be too exhausting.

Songho

Located north of Bandiagara, the plateau village of **SONGHO** is spectacularly situated on the plateau, some distance from the *falaise*, between two craggy rock formations, and can easily be seen in a couple of hours (a guide can be found at the *campement* on the way into the village). To get there from Bandiagara, take the five-kilometre sandy track that turns off to the north side of the Sévaré road, about 10km outside Bandiagara. Although Songho is a Muslim village, the villagers keep their animist traditions very much alive, as testified by the freshness of the cave paintings at the village **circumcision site** – a large ledge 100m up the crag. Your guide will point out the rocks where the participants sit for the ceremony, and the painted targets, which are the winning posts for the running race which takes place immediately after the ceremony. The newly circumcised young men complete a three-kilometre circuit and the winner is presented with a sack of millet – and the wife of his choice. You may also be shown the vertiginous platform where dances take place, and the cave in which ceremonial musical instruments are stored.

From Bandiagara to Djiguibombo

A 25-kilometre stretch of semi-paved road separates Bandiagara from Djiguibombo at the edge of the *falaise*. This relatively flat road over the plateau passes through a sparse vegetation of bush savannah with the occasional baobab rising up to dominate the rocky landscape. After about 12km you pass the village of **TEGOUROU**, near

Dogon villages are frequently divided into **twin parts** – as in Sanga, which incorporates Ogol-du-haut and Ogol-du-bas – signifying the original twin ancestors. Many villages are further divided into distinct **quartiers** according to the religion of the inhabitants. The Christian quarter may include a simple church, while the usually larger Muslim quarter is marked by its mosque (Kani-Kombolé's is particularly impressive). Muslim practices are still generally grafted onto animist practices rather than adopted to the exclusion of traditional rites. In the animist *quartier*, the external walls of houses contain niches for fetishes that allude to primitive ancestors, and you will see small rocks, mounds or clay pilasters serving as altars.

Village walls and buildings are collectively built, using **dry stones or sun-dried mud bricks** plastered with *banco*. Walls often have graceful geometric patterns pressed into them. The roofs of the granaries and the elders' meeting place are thatched with millet stalks and waterproofed with *banco* mixed with *karité* oil. Everything has to be rebuilt, or at least repaired, at the end of each rainy season.

A Dogon village is in theory laid out according to a symbolic anatomical plan in which different areas represent different parts of the **body**, with the iron forge and the *togu-na*, or elders' meeting place, at the head (the northernmost point); the house of the *ginna bana* – the head of a *ginna*, that is, an extended family or lineage – in the chest area (the centre); one or two *maisons des règles*, where women stay during menstruation, representing the hands (at east and/or west); and sacrificial altars at the feet (south). In reality this pattern isn't always strictly followed, but there is nonetheless a symbolic purpose in the positioning and layout of every structure in every village:

Togu-na or case à palabres

This open-sided construction is the meeting place where village elders (strictly men only) gather to discuss village affairs, or to socialize and swap stories. The Dogon have an extremely rich oral tradition, so the village *togu-na* is effectively a cultural treasure-house. The *togu-na* is built according to strict rules. The roof is supported by eight wooden pillars, which represent the eight Dogon ancestors and are often decorated with carvings; there are beautiful examples at the villages of Dombossougou and Madougou. The roof is low, both to give maximum shade and also to help defuse any arguments before they get out of hand, the idea being that if people can't stand up, they can't come to blows.

House of the ginna bana

A *ginna bana*'s house tends to be more impressive than an average dwelling, and contains an altar where the founders of the village are honoured. On the outside of the front wall of the house there may be ten rows of eight niches representing the eight Dogon ancestors.

Family compounds

A compound is shared by a family unit made up of adults and young children: at 7–9 years old, children leave home to live communally in a *maison des jeunes*. The family compound consists of a courtyard, rooms and granaries, linked by stone walls. Rooms are normally square with flat roofs on which millet and other produce is left out to dry. Inside, houses are constructed according to a standard layout, symbolizing a seated man. There are specific guidelines as to which domestic duties take place where in the interior, and traditionally even rules about where and in what position a couple should make love.

Granaries

The pepperpot-shaped granaries give Dogon villages their distinctive fairy-tale quality. Tall and thin, they stand on stone legs to protect them from vermin. The interior of each granary is divided into compartments according to a pattern that represents the cosmos. They are used to store grain, but women also use their private granaries to store valuables.

Maison des règles

While they are menstruating, women are excused domestic duties, and are isolated together in a round hut, overseen by an older woman who offers them natural remedies for any ailments. The Dogon are renowned for their medical skills and their practices have recently become the subject of Western medical research.

Sanctuaire du binou

This temple-like building, decorated with *boummon* (ritual painting) in animal blood and *bouillie de mil* (millet porridge), is a place where the *hogon* (spiritual leader of the village) conducts sacred ceremonies dedicated to the *binou*, an ancestral spirit. It's often a rectangular house with rounded corners and towers and a low door blocked by rocks. Over the door is a forked iron hook which symbolizes the mythical ram's horns on which clouds are caught to bring rain. Only the *hogon* knows the meaning of the symbols and totemic objects inside the sanctuary.

Altars

Sacrificial altars are sometimes no more than small earth mounds or pilasters marked with traces of animal blood and *bouillie de mil*. It is thought that when the rain washes the blood and *bouillie* away, the *nyama* (vital power) that these carry is transferred to the fields to restore the equilibrium of the earth and ensure a good harvest. Chickens and goats are the usual sacrificial victims but special occasions may call for the sacrifice of a cow.

Tellem houses

The Tellem built cave-like dwellings high up in the cliff face. It's a mystery how these diminutive people managed to scale the *falaise* but it's thought that they did so either by weaving rope ladders out of baobab bark or other vegetation, or by climbing the large trees that used to grow right up to the foot of the cliff until the Dogon cleared the plain to grow millet. Some Tellem houses still contain ritual objects. Many are now used by the Dogon to keep livestock, store belongings, or inter their dead.

Hogon house

The isolated dwelling near the village ritual sites is where the *hogon* lives, either temporarily or permanently, guarding the village's sacred bones and relics. The walls of this dwelling are painted in totemic symbols in the ritual colours of red, black and white: red for sacrificial blood (a sign of peace) and the blood of the *hogon*; white for purity of heart and for the light of day; black for the skin of the *hogon* and for the night.

Ritual sites

The most important ritual sites of a Dogon village are often outside the village itself; in the *falaise* villages they are generally situated on an isolated platform or ledge high up on the cliff face. It is here that circumcision ceremonies take place once every three years. The act of circumcision is performed on a designated blood-blackened rock, and the walls of the site are decorated with paintings in red, black and white. Each initiate adds his own personal symbol to those of his predecessors, and while older symbols follow traditional stylized patterns, more recent additions may reflect modern interests (a car, a plane). The cave paintings at Songho are particularly fine. The walls of some ritual sites (notably at Teli and Yabatalou) are hung with monkey skulls, totems in the Dogon farmers' war against the pests that steal their crops.

which are a dammed stream and the terraced fields of the Dogon's famous onions. Before continuing the trip down the escarpment, most guides will stop at **DJIGUI-BOMBO**, a charming and friendly place in an extremely rocky area near the cliff; a stone wall surrounds it and many of the houses use stone in their construction. A Swiss expatriate has set up a *campement* here – and also helped to build the impressive school at the end of the village.

From Kani-Kombolé to Teli: along the plain

A couple of kilometres south of Djiguibombo, you finally arrive at the edge of the plateau, from where there's a sweeping vista over the plains below. If you're on foot, although the cliff appears vertiginous, your guide will lead you down walkable paths, and the 300-metre descent poses no special problems. On the plain, **KANI-KOMBOLÉ** – with its beautiful mosque, a Thursday market, a reasonable little restaurant and somewhere to stay if you need it – isn't too far off. This is where the new paved road ends and becomes a *piste*, leading to Bankass.

Following the foot of the cliffs eastwards four kilometres over a flat, sandy stretch bordered by millet fields, you come next to **TELI**. If you don't manage to get to Sanga, Teli is a satisfying, less-visited substitute. It has some of the most spectacular **cliffside houses** (now all abandoned) along this part of the escarpment. In the rainy season there are also **waterfalls** nearby. There used to be a problem gaining permission to climb up to the ruined houses, though it's a rare group that isn't allowed up these days. Teli's present inhabitants all live on the plain below.

From Teli to Dourou via Endé and Begnimato

From Teli, you could either return to Bandiagara by retracing the route described above, or continue east across the plain to **ENDÉ**. Endé is perhaps the most touristy of these southern villages, with several *campements* and where seemingly every other building has something to sell, be it Dogon masks or indigo blankets. That said, it remains a pretty place. There's a market every Sunday, and in the rainy season you can swim in the waterfall pool near the village.

After Endé, the dirt road continues east through a number of villages. One of the more picturesque is **DOUNDJOUROU**, known for its spectacular homes carved in the cliff. After this village, you can climb back up the *falaise*. After struggling through the sand of the low plains, you'll find it much easier bounding on the rocky, unyielding surface of the escarpment. At the top of the climb – towards the end of which you come to a sort of hidden Eden, a fertile grove hidden from the outside world – you come to **BEGNIMATO**, spectacularly situated under castle-like rock formations up on the plateau. The part you come to first is actually the animist and Christian quarter; further on, hidden among the rocks to the north, is the Muslim quarter. Ask to be shown the hunter's house, the exterior of which is decorated with monkey skulls. A few kilometres further on, **KONSOU-LEY** is another pretty village teetering on the edge of the escarpment, where the rocky formations that surround it serve to increase the feeling of isolation. There is just one *campement* here.

Continuing your walk along the edge of the plateau, eventually you come to **DOUROU**, a very large village which has one of the most important **markets** so close to the escarpment edge, and is also on a motorable road to Bandiagara. Every five days, vehicles arrive here from Bandiagara and Sévaré bringing traders and goods to the heart of Dogon country. In addition to the ubiquitous Dogon onions, grown nearby and sold in large quantities, you'll find cereals, Fula milk and rough cotton weaves of indigo-dyed cloth, a common element in Dogon dress. If you time your visit to coincide with market day, you can hope to get a ride back to Bandiagara, 25km to the north. Towards the northern end of the village, *Campement Teriya* has double rooms (❶, or you can sleep on the roof) as well as a restaurant serving the usual spaghetti stew and cold beer, though as in most villages this is just one *campement* among several.

This stretch contains some of the most spectacular villages in the Dogon country. Dropping back down to the plains via a narrow cleft in the rocks a kilometre or two east of Dourou, one of the first villages you come to is lovely **NOMBORI**, with its thriving weekly market and, on one side of the market square, its own **Dogon museum** (CFA500). Stretching away up the escarpment, the village has numerous *campements*, with *Campement Baobab* (❶), attractively located up the hill overlooking much of the village.

A succession of smaller villages are passed after Nombori including **IDJELI**, with its red-shuttered church and prominent *ama* sacrificial stone, and Komokan, home to two *campements*. The next major village en route is **TIRELLI**, which bakes in the heat at the foot of the escarpment. After this, you come to **AMANI**, a village remarkable for its **sacred crocodile pool**. While not the monster crocs you might be hoping to see, they're big enough to dissuade you from taking a dip, no matter how hot the day. Even more impressive than Amani's reptiles, however, is **IRELI**, built among the boulders and shattered rock of the escarpment, and another tourist favourite thanks to the colourful designs of its *togu-na*. Perhaps the most photogenic village in the southern Dogon region, it's worth spending at least an hour or two exploring the village's twisting alleyways and sunbaked squares.

From Ireli, the path continues across the plain, snaking through the baobabs – nearly all of which have had their lower trunks stripped of bark to make rope – to **Banani** (see p.419), and from the top of Banani, via a steep twenty-minute climb, to the lower quarters of **Sanga**.

Doing good in the pays Dogon

"It appeared to me that tourist exploitation was actually protecting the Dogon country; it has led them to protect their culture and keep their villages traditional and clean. By all accounts in the villages it has also had the effect of stopping depopulation and bringing back people to the area."

Angus Neil, UK

Sanga and the central pays Dogon

Much has been written about **SANGA**, a striking example of a classic Dogon village with traditional homes and granaries, sited on the plateau above the escarpment. Now more a small town than a village, or at least a conglomeration of hamlets interspersed by litter-strewn wasteland, this is where the American missionary, Reverend McKinney, set up the first Protestant mission in the Dogon country in 1931 and where, soon after, Marcel Griaule lived and studied. Overflowing down the cliffs of the escarpment, the town was too picturesque to go unnoticed for long and some of the best and most popular **walking tours** through Dogon country start and finish here. As a consequence, in the high season it sometimes feels as if tourists outnumber locals by about two to one: be prepared for a slightly more hustly atmosphere than elsewhere. Sanga is nevertheless a good place to find a **guide** if you've arrived without one – the Sanga Association des Guides (☎244.20.13) is in the *Gîte de la Femme Dogon*, or the people at the *La Guina* will advise.

In Sanga's most important hamlet, **Ogol-du-haut**, you'll find the gendarmerie and tourist **accommodation** in the shape of *Campement Hôtel La Guina* on the former site of Griaule's home and somewhat overpriced (☎244.20.28; rooms with fan ❹ or a/c ❺). A much better value option is *Kastor* (☎244.20.04 ✉grandcastordogon@yahoo.fr; overpriced roof space CFA3000 and dorm beds CFA7000, but good-value twins ❸), a delightful plant-shaded haven with a good bar and a great chef, and one of the first places you come to when walking up from the escarpment. If *Kastor* is full, then across the wasteland from *La Guina* are the basic but clean rooms at the *Gîte de la Femme Dogon* (CFA2500 for roof space, rooms ❷), which also offers reasonable food.

Tours around Sanga

Three different **day-trips** are commonly offered from Sanga, ranging from seven to fifteen kilometres in length. The first includes a tour of Sanga and a seven-kilometre round-trip trek to **GOGOLI**. The ten-kilometre tour continues from Gogoli to **Banani** (see p.419), located partly on the *falaise* near Sanga and partly on the plain below. All along the escarpment, you'll see caves – originally used by the Tellem as granaries or for defence in case of attack – cut into the rocky face. The fifteen-kilometre tour extends the loop to include **TIRELLI**, another particularly pretty village stretching from the cliff to the plain. These treks last roughly between three and ten hours, and you can also arrange longer walking trips that last anything up to a week. Don't forget, also, that visitors are increasingly opting for a non-circular walk, including a trek to Kani-Kombolé at the southern end of the *pays Dogon* (see p.414).

Dogon country from the south

One alternative to the normal route from the north into Dogon country bypasses Bandiagara altogether, entering the Dogon region via **BANKASS**, reached from the road that passes through Somadougou, south of Mopti. From this direction you start the trek from down on the plains, approaching the escarpment from below. Bankass is a small market town with a mixed population, and makes for a less busy departure point, although organized trips from Burkina Faso, via Bankass, are on the increase. Hiking access to the foot of the *falaise*, where the villages of Kani-Kombolé, Teli and Endé are located, is a fifteen-kilometre slog across the plain, but you can find transport by 4x4 or *mobylette* in the dry season, and by donkey- or ox-cart all year round.

Accommodation in Bankass covers a range of budgets. *Hotel et Campement Le Hogon* offers rooms equipped with fans and mosquito nets (❷). *Hôtel Les Arbres* behind the Centre des Impôts, offers overpriced a/c rooms with mosquito nets, and cheaper, very basic rooms (℡228.66.42; camping CFA2500, roof space CFA3500, rooms ❸).

Bankass is also the commonest entry point for the *pays Dogon* if you're arriving from Burkina Faso on the paved road from **KORO**. Koro has a large Saturday **market** and a beautiful **mosque**, but it's a little too far from the heart of the Dogon country to be an immediate springboard for a trek. That said, more than

---

Moving on from Bankass and Koro

Transport to the **Burkinabe border** is no problem. There are few direct departures from Bankass to Burkina but there are many daily departures to Koro (1hr; CFA2500), from where minibuses leave constantly for the border town of Tiou. There's also a late-afternoon SOGEBAF service from Koro to Ouahigouya.

There are two routes from Bankass to **Bandiagara** – one via Ouo, which is mostly good paved road but follows a very roundabout route; and one via Kani-Kombolé which, as far as that village, is a dirt road that can be difficult, especially during the rains. There is little scheduled transport from Bankass to Kani-Kombolé (best bet is on a Thurs, Kani-Kombolé's market day). From Kani-Kombolé, a good paved road climbs the *falaise* and runs north to Bandiagara, with frequent minibus departures.

one traveller has recommended Koro's tourism bureau chief (☎635.17.71), whose English is impeccable and who can help arrange treks at very reasonable rates. In Koro, stay at *L'Aventure* (**2**), which does good meals.

Douentza and the northern pays Dogon

DOUENTZA, stretched out beneath the towering cliffs of the **Gandamia massif**, 167km east of Sévaré on the main highway to Gao, has a good Sunday **market** and an impressive mosque, and because it's a good base for visiting the northern Dogon country is becoming an increasingly important local tourism hub. Although access to the *pays Dogon* takes a little longer from here, this is repaid by friendly villages with a less commercial atmosphere than those around Sanga. The town is strung out uneventfully along the highway, with an older quarter to the south of the road. There's **Internet** access down the street opposite *Auberge Gourma*, where the local radio station, Daande Duwansa, has a small room at the back of their plot with half a dozen computers and a good connection (CFA1500/hr).

Accommodation basically consists of a series of *campements* lining the main highway, with rooms of variable quality and the reliable low-budget standby of taking roof space for around CFA2500. The only hotel worth the name, *La Falaise* (☎245.20.95; rooms with fan **2** or a/c **3**) at the western end of town, declines with every passing year and is now firmly in the doldrums. Still, it's safe and the staff, while not the most smiling bunch, are helpful enough. More lively are the neighbouring *Dogon Aventures* (☎245.20.94; rooms with fan **2** or a/c **3**) and *Auberge Gourma* (☎245.20.54; rooms with fan **2** or a/c **3**), both of which offer similar accommodation: a little dark, a little basic, but okay for a night. The latter is also the best place to come for organizing trips into the Dogon country. Finally, past the Internet place to the south of town is *Hogon Campement* (☎943.31.04; rooms with fan **3** or without **1**), possibly the smartest and most clued-up of all the *campements* in Douentza.

Food-wise, you're limited either to the restaurant in your *campement*, or to the *Restaurant Express* on the main highway where the buses stop. You can also buy hunks of mutton on the highway, which are fine as a baguette filling. *Bar Tango Tango* across from *Dogon Adventures*, is the best place for a late-night **drink**.

The northern pays Dogon

The northern districts of Dogon country are on the whole less affected by tourism than the centre and south. You can see the evidence of that in the carved doors and windows and traditional *togu-na* pillars that are still happily to be seen in many villages, where elsewhere they have been sold to overseas collectors and dealers – check the fancy furnishing stores in New York and Paris. There are various options for **Dogon trekking** out of Douentza. The most straightforward, and pricey, option is to rent a 4x4 vehicle and driver to get you down to Bamba, about two hours' drive south, and then trek from here to Sanga over three or four days. On Bamba's market day, Saturday, you can also get to Bamba by *bâché*. If you're thinking of **driving** this route yourself in your own 4x4, the track you want is signposted to Koro off the main highway, just east of Douentza. But drivers beware: the track is very difficult (with taxing stretches of soft sand and boulders) and it's hard to follow its endless branches across the plain. Lastly, if you are planning on trying to get **lifts** to some of the villages below, note that infrequent vehicles link them on market days.

Borko

An alternative to heading straight down to Bamba is to explore some of the plateau Dogon region southwest of Douentza. Here, the most alluring destination is the extraordinary crocodile village of **BORKO**, an exceptionally beautiful and verdant

Moving on from Douentza

The family who run the *Restaurant Express* run what they happily describe as a "mafia" on bus tickets out of Douentza. Their commission ranges from CFA1000–3000 (depending on your negotiating skills and the price of the seat) and, though you may hate the setup, they do offer the best chance of getting out of town quickly. The only way to avoid them is to book with the SONEF office (☎503.69.50) next door. However, SONEF buses are often late – all having travelled long distances before reaching Douentza – and, if you book with them, you run the risk of hanging about for hours while mafia-touted buses from other companies come and go.

For **Gao**, the Bani Transport bus comes through Douentza late evening, every day except Sun; Binke Transport make the run every day as do SONEF, their buses calling in at Douentza at around 7pm. All three companies stop at **Hombori** and **Gossi**. Bani and Binke also make the journey in the opposite direction, to **Sévaré**, **Mopti**, **Ségou** and **Bamako**, usually pulling into Douentza sometime between mid-morning and early evening.

South of Douentza towards **Dogon country** and Burkina, the main "road" is a difficult track to follow (and can be treacherous in the rainy season) and there's no scheduled transport, though one or two bush taxis normally go on market days to **Bamba** (Sat) and **Madougou** via Bamba (Mon).

For **Timbuktu**, a fast, newly graded gravel road heads north from Douentza as far as the desolate outpost of **Bambara-Maoundé**, roughly halfway there, to be succeeded by a difficult sandy track winding through thorn scrub that's strictly 4x4 territory and can be very arduous in the rains. Normally, you can reach Bambara-Maoundé in under two hours, but the total journey time for the 220-odd-km trip, assuming there are no delays, is around six hours. There's no regular transport from Douentza, but put your intentions about (the *Restaurant Express* mafia will help) and you're likely to find someone heading up to Timbuktu early the next morning – so long as there are enough passengers. Most drivers will want CFA60,000–100,000 for the trip, depending on the size of their vehicle – assume CFA15,000 per person.

Dogon community that's well worth a half-day trip out of Douentza, or a serious side-track if you have your own 4x4 vehicle.

Borko is a tough 22-kilometre drive by 4x4 south of the Douentza–Sévaré road, accessed most directly from Douentza by turning left at an unmarked track by the name-board for the highway village of **Gnimignama** (also spelt Nimignama), 46km west of Douentza. Allow an hour and a half to get to Borko and bring somebody who knows the way, or else be prepared to stop frequently to ask anyone you see on the track. You'll know you're almost there when you cross a ford and reach a village checkpoint (*comptoir routier*) and the track begins to climb steeply. The village lies at the head of a valley, at the very end of a five-kilometre oasis of greenery wedged into a continuation of the Gandamia massif. Verdant fields of onions and garlic, irrigated by a network of ditches (*marigots*), and dotted with groves of mangos and doum palms, create a vivid carpet of green, even in the dry season. The centre of the village is a shady area with the local government office and meeting house and a distinguished **mosque** nearby. Soft drinks are usually available, but there are no services as such.

Borko's inhabitants have an old respect for, and relationship with, the small **crocodiles** that live in the ditches and ponds all around the village and surrounding fields. There are certainly dozens – people say hundreds – of crocodiles in this well-watered neighbourhood, and they come, almost scampering, at the first sight of a crowd of people, which signals tourists and goat meat. If you're not accompanied by a guide when you arrive in Borko, you'll need to spend some time introducing yourself, finding the old butcher responsible for feeding the crocs – the *maître des caïmans* – and negotiating a price for a few kilos of goat scraps and offal (you won't get away with less than CFA5000). The spectacle of crocodiles, some a couple of metres long, advancing from all directions on your group, is one that sticks in the mind – as does the pestering of the *caïmans* by the village children (a number of crocs have lost eyes). Accidents are said to be unheard of, but you should be extremely careful nevertheless.

Bamba and the trek to Sanga

To go trekking from Douentza, there are several options: you can walk to **FOMBORI**, 3km south of Douentza, with its Tellem cemetery and little Dogon **museum** (run like a pawnshop for Dogon artefacts); and then to **EWERLE/ EVERI**, on a high mesa (4km further).

Alternatively, if you start off by vehicle, your most likely first-night stop will be **BAMBA**, about two hours from Douentza by 4x4 and a good place to start walking, as most of the soft sand is behind you by then. Crouched at the foot of the escarpment and spilling onto the plain, Bamba's numerous hamlets add up to a thriving small commercial centre, with a highly recommended Saturday market that draws in head-loaded columns of traders, clapped-out bush taxis and donkey- and ox-carts from miles around. If you stay for the market, note that it really doesn't get going till midday. There are one or two little *auberges* in Bamba (❶).

Some 14km west of Bamba, after a twisting route across the plain via **YENDA**, you come to **YENDOUMA**, a clutch of five hamlets, dotted up the cliffs. Hike up to **Yendouma-Atô**, the prettiest of the quintet, a twenty- to thirty-minute walk from the plain, to pay a visit to a locally famous artist, **Alaye Atô**. Alaye, who lost his left hand in a shooting accident at a funeral, will sell you his book *Alaye Atô – Dessinateur Dogon* (Eds Adeiao, Paris, 1999), full of phantasmagorical Dogon imagery, mostly executed in felt pens donated by visitors. His work is on show at *Y à Pas de Problème* in Mopti. Down at **Yendouma-Sogol**, Yendouma's *chef-lieu* and the location of the school, dispensary and market, the obvious place to stay is the lively *Auberge Guina Dogon/Chez Youssouf Nango* (❶).

From Yendouma, you can follow the track southwards, directly to Koundou, or, more interestingly, strike out east towards the Youga plateau, a separate chunk of escarpment that rises over the plain. An hour of soft sand (make an early start) sees you to the foot of the cliffs and a fine climb up over boulders and beneath baobabs, to the first of the **YOUGA** villages, the cliff hamlet of **Youga-Piri**, with weavers at work and close-up views of Tellem houses. Above Youga-Piri, you reach the plateau itself, a lunar landscape of black rock, cut through by crevasses bridged by makeshift wooden spans, or simply stepped across, cautiously. Descending again from the plateau, you pass a *hogon's* burial site and a small trekker's café, and more fabulous Tellem architecture, and then reach **Youga-Dogourou** (sometimes spelt Dourou), the village where the **Sigui** (see p.406) originated. If you've seen film of this spectacular, masked dance, you'll recognize the boulder-bounded sandy square.

Finally, down on the plain, the main Youga village of **Youga-Na**, whose people decamped here in 1992 from the abandoned houses you can see a little further up, has places to stay, crafts for sale and, usually, other tourists. *Chez Akougnon Doumbo* is a pleasant midday or night stop, patrolled by its helpful, wheelchair-bound owner (❶). Or you can continue to **KOUNDOU**, a largely non-Muslim village just 4km further south along a reasonable track, and stay at *Auberge Koundou/Chez Assama Dara* (❶) or the larger and fancier *Campement Amitié* (❷).

Koundou is barely 10km from Sanga as the crow flies, and you can get there easily enough along the track. But it's much more rewarding to climb up onto the main plateau again, passing through pretty areas of grassland, huge baobabs and broken rocky scenery, including a dramatic rock arch, to descend again towards **IBI**, a straggling large village on the plain with several simple *auberges*, just an hour's walk short of Banani at the foot of the escarpment beneath Sanga.

BANANI, with its busy market area, small shops and crafts booths – and a surprising amount of gentle hustling to buy or at least inspect the wares – signals your imminent return from the wilds to something like metropolitan Mali. *Campement Hogon* has dispensed with tree-trunk staircases and provides built-in concrete ones, real showers and toilets (though the primitive versions in the remoter villages are invariably cleaner and nicer to use than these) and multiple options for sleeping in rooms (❷) or on rooftops. Banani also has a paved road snaking up the escarpment to Sanga, but a much preferable walking route takes you high above Banani and up through a steep cleft – almost a tunnel – carved in the rock, to emerge on the flat plateau a half-hour from **Sanga** (see p.415). You can continue the route southwest by following the coverage on pp.411–415 in reverse.

4.6

Northeastern Mali

Arid and inhospitable, northeastern Mali would not be habitable but for the Niger River, along which life in the area concentrates (the exception being the Tuareg nomads, who thrive in the desert). The riverside town of **Gao**, the largest in the northeast, was formerly the capital of a great kingdom, and is now the administrative and commercial centre of Mali's Seventh Region, and easily accessible by a decent paved road from Mopti (allow a full day) and Bamako (allow two days). The Mopti–Gao stretch runs through the dramatic, towering landscapes of the **Gandamia massif** and **Hombori**, encompassing Mali's highest elevations. From Gao you can strike out to **Kidal** in Mali's remote Eighth Region, or follow the river south to **Niamey** (in Niger) along a difficult but scenic *piste* leading through small fishing villages. Alternatively **the river** itself can serve as your highway, certainly a more memorable way to travel – providing you time your travels to coincide with the immediate aftermath of the rains, when the water levels are high enough for the river boats to make a few weekly voyages downstream to Gao.

From Mopti to Gao

Initially, the journey from Mopti (Sévaré) to Gao is uneventful. Around 55km from Sévaré, you reach **KONNA**, a market town close to the river, at the turning for the difficult road traversing the Niger inland delta to Timbuktu via Niafounké (requiring a ferry crossing at Niafounké and impassable during the rains). The next settlement of note, **BORÉ** (50km beyond Konna), boasts an exceptionally large and beautiful **mosque** for such a small place. Some 20km further, if you have 4x4, you can turn off the road at Gnimignama and follow a somewhat elusive track to the crocodile village of **Borko** (see p.417).

Hombori and around

East of **Douentza** (see p.417), the scenery along the highway shifts from neutral into top gear, with more than twenty huge sandstone mesas and needle-like rock formations rearing up from the plains to the north and south. Tourist offices like to refer to the whole area as *Le Monument Valley de Mali*, and the comparison has some justification. The pinnacles culminate in the spectacular shape of **La Main de Fatima**, also known as Gami Tondo – or the *Aiguilles de Gami* (Needles of Gami) – which is said to resemble the hand of the prophet Muhammad's daughter, with outstretched thumb and finger (Fatima's Hand is a protective symbol in Islamic tradition).

The small, strikingly situated town of **HOMBORI** (market on Tues) is 11km east of the Main de Fatima, straddling the highway. The newer districts lie to the north of the road, while the old stone town on the south side straggles up over the rocky apron of **Hombori Tondo** – a massive flat-topped mesa rising to 1155m – the highest point in Mali. The unusual architecture of Old Hombori makes for a highly recommended afternoon stroll: most of the houses are built of rock, and the narrow alleys between become tunnels beneath second storeys in several places. You'll certainly be tailed by a gaggle of children, but choose a couple of older boys to accompany you and the rest will leave you in peace (don't forget to tip your guides). You can return back to the main road via a series of palm-tree-shaded wells at the foot of the village.

For **accommodation** you can choose between the sweetly informal, relaxing and inexpensive rooftop, rooms and huts at *Chez Lélélé* (❶), on the north side of the road near where the buses stop, and the less welcoming, though better equipped, *Campement Mangou Bagni*, a few minutes' walk further east along the road, which offers rooms at the back with mosquito nets (❷). *Mangou Bagni* has a fridge and electricity, cold beer, a menu of sorts, and an occasionally busy roadside bar-restaurant.

Climbing and hiking at Hombori

Even non-climbers can see the massive appeal of the awesome stone spires and walls around Hombori. With accessible sheer faces rising between 100m and 600m from the rocky plain, this is one of Africa's premier technical **rock-climbing** areas, and draws experienced climbers from around the world, especially in the winter. There is, however, virtually no infrastructure for climbers and, beyond guides and some ropes (ask at the *campements*), you'll find little help, so keen climbers are advised to bring their own gear. Local guides charge around CFA5000 per day per person. The district's climbing possibilities and mesas are all sketch-mapped at ⓦtinyurl.com/2b2ecy. If you want to visit the Main de Fatima, informal *mobylette* rental is available in Hombori for around CFA7500 per day: ask at the *campements*. Apart from the two needles (the smaller is **Kaga Pamari** and the larger **Kaga Tondo**), the rest of the sacred massif is largely off-limits to outsiders.

If you aren't suitably equipped, resist the temptation to free-climb any part of the Hombori rock faces: needless to say, there are no emergency services here. Instead, pursue the wealth of hiking opportunities, the most obvious of which are the lower reaches of **Hombori Tondo** and its neighbour, the pyramid-shaped **Clef de Hombori** (Key of Hombori, pronounced "clé") rising up behind the town. It takes roughly ninety minutes, half of it jumping from boulder to boulder, to reach the col between the Clef and the main mesa, where a superb tennis-court-sized rock platform gives you a panoramic view over the yawning plain to the south and the empty wastelands of northern Burkina. Directly below you lies the village of **TONDOUROU**. From the col, you can scramble to the summit of the steep, rocky spine of the Clef – another forty minutes to an hour – but it's not for the faint-hearted. A few hundred metres to the east, the sheer walls of the western end of Hombori Tondo rise like some lost world, completely unscalable without ropes. This hike requires around four to five hours away from Hombori town, and, although the sun rises behind Hombori Tondo, so you'll be in shade most of the morning if you make an early start, you'll still need several litres of water per person.

There are a number of other good hikes you can do further west, towards the domes of **Kissim** and **Fada Tondo**, and the whale-shaped mesas of **Barkoussou** and **Ouari** which rise (in that order from east to west) southwest of the town. The main footpath to this area runs from the old quarters of Hombori between the loaf-like Fada Tondo and the broad mesa of Barkoussou, and as you climb closer you'll see the spike of **Aiguille de Xoussi** between them.

In contrast to boulders and climbing, the formation of steep **red dunes** that rises to the northeast of Hombori town, about forty minutes' walk away, is a wonderful area to visit before sunset. For a spot of dune-skiing, *Campement Mangou Bagni* rents out skis and toboggans, which go reasonably well.

Gossi and Doro

GOSSI is the next small town along the road, a largely Songhai and Bella settlement, about 85km northeast of Hombori. It's located a kilometre north of the highway, on the shore of a muddy lake, the Mare de Gossi, and is the site of a sizeable reforestation and agricultural project headed by a Norwegian church fund. It also has **elephants**: as the vegetation from the summer rains begins to diminish towards the end of the year, a herd of some six hundred – known as the elephants of Gourma – migrate from northern Burkina through Mali's **Réserve du Gourma**, and they can quite often be seen at waterholes north of the road between Hombori and Gossi, and especially near the Mare de Gossi itself. In February or March they begin to trek west through the **Réserve de Douentza** and then south again, usually crossing the road to the west of Hombori. The elephants' numbers may be increasing as the traditional Tuareg resistance to hunting them offers partial protection. But many Tuareg are making the uneasy transition to a sedentary lifestyle in this area, and their crops are threatened by the *elouan*. If the herd isn't near Gossi, you can make a 4x4 trip to see them, driving more or less cross-country, but 4x4 availability is a bit thin on the ground in this area and the elephants can be elusive, so you might end up paying quite a lot for many hours of bumpy trail-bashing, to little avail. Neither reserve has any visitor infrastructure, nor any formal system of entry fees. The usual target is the Tuareg village of **I-N-ADIATTAFENE**, 80km west of Gossi, well out in the bush.

Gossi has sandy streets, a few small shops and a couple of places to stay: *Le Campement* has utterly basic rooms (❶), while *Bohanta* (❶) is mainly a restaurant though it has a few mattresses scattered on a concrete floor. Nevertheless, the town is a pleasant place to stop off for a lukewarm drink and a bite to eat. Reasonably priced grilled meat is sold in large quantities at the market. Monday is the highlight, with the largest **cattle market** in the district.

The later stages of the Mopti road are dull, thorny country, with long stretches of monotonous Sahelian landscape. Some 62km from Gossi you arrive at **DORO**, a small settlement in a region where lions are said to exist. If the reports are true, you'd have to follow tracks a good 40km south of town to have any hope of seeing them. Ask in Doro if any have been spotted recently and enquire about the possibility of taking someone along as a guide.

Plastic wilderness

"On the environmental front, it would be good if the government could get people to re-cycle plastic carrier bags – Mali must have looked much better when all the rubbish was organic and rotted down."

Laura Stevens, UK

Gao

In the repertoire of trans-Saharan campfire talk, **GAO** was always one of the most romantic cities. As you arrived from Algeria and the void of the Sahara, Gao seemed like a miracle of civilization emerging from the wasteland. Once you'd passed the last stretch of soft sand thrown up by the desert around the town, and entered its dusty tree-lined avenues of mud-brick shops and houses, thronging with crowds, the physical sensations of admission into a new world were powerful and enchanting. Traditionally, desert-crossers would celebrate their arrival in West Africa by heading straight to the *Hôtel Atlantide* – a tatty colonial pile that might as well have been the *Ritz* out here – and downing a few cold beers. Behind the hotel (which these days is rather run-down) lies the source of all the vigour, the **Niger River**, tangibly and magically connecting Gao with the whole of West Africa.

If you've flown in from Paris, the early morning arrival can still be pretty exhilarating as you sweep low over glinting expanses of river. But if you've come up from Mopti on the main road, you may have rather different first impressions of Gao. The river, which from this direction is neither new nor unusual, is unlikely to stir special excitement, while the town itself resembles any other Sahelian town, bigger than most, but neither beautiful nor unusually dynamic.

Some history

The original founders of Gao, known in its early days as Kawkaw, were **Sorko fishermen** who migrated from the area of present-day Benin between the sixth and eleventh centuries. They mingled with the rural Gabili peoples living along the banks of the Niger, and eventually this mixture evolved into a people known as **Songhai**. The first Songhai monarch at Gao was Kanda, who founded the Za (or Dia) dynasty in the seventh century. He quickly opened the town to trans-Saharan trade and to Berbers who wanted to settle there for commercial reasons.

A later king of Songhai, Za Kossoi, converted to **Islam** in 1009. The town prospered to the point where it rivalled all the great regional trading centres in power and wealth, even surpassing the capitals of ancient Ghana and later Mali. Rulers of the Mali Empire coveted Gao's success and potential and annexed the town in 1325, although the Songhai princes managed to flee from their clutches. One of them, **Ali Golon**, went on to found the **Sonni dynasty**, still based at Gao. The greatest of the Sonni rulers was the despotic **Sonni Ali Ber**, or Ali the Great. It was he who, towards the end of the fifteenth century, expanded the kingdom at Gao to the dimensions of an empire (see box, overleaf). The capital continued to flourish under the reign of the **askias**, founders of a new dynasty that lasted throughout the sixteenth century. At the time, Gao had 70,000 inhabitants and in the busy harbour were crowded more than a thousand war boats from the *askias'* flotilla, four hundred barges and thousands of pirogues.

With the **Moroccan invasion** of Songhai in 1591, the empire collapsed and Gao was virtually razed. The town never recovered and when the German explorer **Heinrich Barth** arrived in 1854, he described the once ostentatious city as "a desolate abode with a small and miserable population". Much of the town's present look dates to the beginning of the twentieth century. The **French** built up the port, traced new streets (which explains the rather uniform grid layout) and established an administrative district with characteristic colonial buildings still used by the present government. With a population of some 65,000, Gao still hasn't returned to its former grandeur and, in its current economic and political predicament, with the troubles in Niger and Algeria limiting trade, it is struggling.

The Town

In physical terms, Gao has few reminders of its glorious past. To orientate yourself, it's best to think of Gao as a rough square, with each of the four sides demarcated by paved roads (*goudrons*) – of which there are only five in Gao. The **Grande Mosquée** in the centre of town near the police station lies on the western edge of this grid, Boulevard des Askias. The mosque was initially built by Kankan Moussa after he annexed the town in the fourteenth century but it's unimpressive compared even with those in Timbuktu and certainly in comparison with the mosque at Djenné.

By the second half of the fifteenth century, the influence and power of the Mali Empire had diminished greatly and the stage was set for **Sonni Ali Ber** – nineteenth ruler in the Sonni dynasty and the effective founder of Songhai as an empire (emperor from 1464 to 1492) – to embark on his great conquests. A shrewd administrator, Ali was also a brilliant and ruthless strategist, and it is said he never lost a battle. A half-hearted Muslim, he quickly set about terrorizing the Fula and Tuareg nomads, his bitter enemies in the region. His expansionist designs were greatly facilitated in 1468 when he was invited by the governor of **Timbuktu** to liberate that town from Tuareg domination.

Historians of the period reported that Ali's conquest of Timbuktu was brutal, and many townspeople who had longed for the Songhai "liberation" fled west to Oualata for fear of persecution. After an initial period of purging religious leaders who stood in his path, however, Ali brought stability to the town which once again prospered under his rule. At the same time, he managed to neutralize the **religious influence** of Timbuktu's powerful marabouts, who exercised considerable political power over the entire region.

Ali next turned his sights on **Djenné**, which proved a harder target. The Sonnis are said to have besieged the town for seven years, seven months and seven days before it finally fell in 1473. Rather than wreaking vengeance on the ruling class as he had in Timbuktu, Ali married his fortunes with those of Djenné by taking the queen mother to be his wife. **Massina** was his next objective, and he conquered this Fula stronghold shortly afterwards.

All the chief strategic points of the Niger and the delta region were now under Songhai control. The nation's military strength was founded in its **navy** and Ali depended so heavily on his flotilla that, at one point, he envisaged digging a canal from the port town of Râs el Mâ on Lake Faguibine to the desert oasis of Oualata, in order to attack the Tuareg there. Although work started, the plan was eventually abandoned as Ali extended his control south and east to the villages of Bandiagara, Bariba and Gourma.

After he died, Sonni Ali was succeeded by his son Bakari, but the new king followed his father's example of keeping a distance from the faith and thus incited religious disapproval. He was overthrown by Mohammed Torodo, the governor of Hombori, who formed a new dynasty known as the **askia** or "usurper". Though he had no hereditary claim to the throne, Askia Mohammed legitimized his rule through religious channels, soliciting the backing of powerful marabouts. He received the ultimate benediction after making the pilgrimage to Mecca with 500 horsemen and 1000 foot soldiers in 1493. There he was granted the title of khalif for the entire Soudan. Returning to Mali, he set about expanding his empire into Mossi country, in present-day Burkina, then pushed eastward to Hausa-land (present-day Nigeria) and into the Aïr (in what is now Niger) as far as Agadez.

While away on a campaign in 1528, Mohammed was forced out of power. Internal intrigue followed and a number of *askias* succeeded one another until the reign of **Ishak I** who ruled from 1539 to 1549 – a decade which marked the Songhai Empire's apogee. The empire now extended from Senegal to the Aïr Mountains and from the Taghaza salt mines in the Sahara to Hausa-land.

Meanwhile **Morocco** far to the north was in a period of crisis. Ejected from Andalucia and hemmed in to the east by the Turks, the Moroccan sultan turned his sights on the south, where he sought to gain control of the salt and gold trades. In 1591 he sent an army to wrest the Soudan from Songhai control. Thanks to a combination of Moroccan firearms and the disarray of the *askia* rulers, the sultan's army won a decisive battle at **Tondibi**, 60km north of Gao, and Gao, Djenné and Timbuktu all fell soon afterwards.

El Sadi, writing in the *Tarikh es-Soudan*, described the invasion in these terms: "Everything changed after the Moroccan conquest. It signalled the beginning of anarchy, theft, pillage and general disorganization." And indeed the entire Sahelian region suffered a blow to its prestige and independence from which it never recovered.

Following Boulevard des Askias north brings you to the Place des Martyrs. Turn right here along Avenue des Dia and the next roundabout features the **Meridian Monument**, the *Obélisque du Méridien 0°*, erected for the millennium on the Greenwich meridian line, and now a Gao landmark.

Follow Boulevard des Askias to the north for fifteen minutes and you come to the UNESCO World Heritage Site of the **Askia Tomb** – the *Tombeau d'Askia Mohamed* or *Tombeau des Askias*. You can visit the fascinating labyrinth of vaults and passages inside this mosque – a smaller women's side, used only on Fridays, and a large men's side – and climb the odd-shaped, fifteenth-century *banco* mausoleum (CFA1500, plus CFA2500 to use a camera) with wild wooden crossbeams sticking out porcupine-style from the facade. From the top, you get a good view of the town and the river. The tomb was built in 1495 by the first *askia*, in the style of a pyramid, after his return from Mecca to perform the hajj. He died in 1539 and is interred inside. Every two years the pyramid has to be resurfaced, the workmen climbing up the beams – the oldest of which are said to have been brought back from Mecca. Outside, in the graveyard within the precincts of the mosque, are buried ten of his descendants.

Considering the centuries of history through which Gao has played a leading role, the **Musée du Sahel** (Tues–Fri & Sun 8am–12.30pm & 3–6pm; CFA1000) on the east side of town, a few streets behind the hospital, is disappointingly small. It's dedicated to the different **peoples of the Sahel**, with displays of their art and domestic implements. You'll see farming and fishing tools (some rather impressive harpoons), musical instruments, and household items used by the **Tuareg**, **Fula**, **Chamba** and **Arma** (the last of these being the descendants of Moroccan–Songhai marriages). Guided tours are included in the entrance fee – extra donations are not declined – and the guides are extremely enthusiastic. Boards explain the exhibits in French and English, so you can easily visit alone.

In the town centre, Gao boasts two good **markets**. The *grand marché*, just opposite the *Hôtel Atlantide*, has long had an entire section devoted to **crafts**, for which the region is well known. The commonest items are Tuareg **leather boxes**, knives and swords; also on sale are numerous examples of **Sahelian sandals** – flat and wide to facilitate walking on the sands. Some pairs incorporate intricate weaving and green- or red-dyed leather in the design. Fula and Tuareg **jewellery** can also be a good buy here, but vendors generally set astronomically high starting prices: bargaining tends to be more of a headache than the good-humoured exchange you're perhaps used to (a more laid-back place to buy crafts, jewellery and other souvenirs is the **Maison des Artisans** in Château district, on the south of the city just beneath the water tower). Behind the crafts section, women bunch around desert produce – spices, dollops of peanut butter, sour milk, fish and meat, pyramids of miniature tomatoes, onions, peppers and lettuces carefully washed (in the river) – and, in season the full range of tropical fruits and vegetables.

The **petit marché**, or Marché Washington, near the police station, specializes in **cloth**. Dozens of tailors – all men of course – treadle their ancient sewing machines and will take orders if you want to have loose-fitting Sahelian clothes made to measure.

After dark, check out the small **Marché de Nuit**, or night market, with its good street-food selection, just east of the Meridian Monument.

Excursions

Gao's very go-ahead tourist office acts as liaison for an increasing number of out-of-Gao excursions and activities. A long-established tourist trip is a visit to the **Dune Rose**, visible from the top of the Askia Tomb, a picturesque sand dune that glows pink and orange at dawn and dusk. Askia Mohammed was born in a village near the dune and, after he was deposed, lived there until he died. It's a three-hour pirogue trip away (CFA7000 there and back).

A likely two- or three-day trip is a visit to **Tchintchinomé** – the Peulh (Fula) quarter of the village of **TACHARANE**, on the river, 20km south of Gao. The village's atmosphere and setting make it a beautiful place to visit and it's an unusual – and very affordable – opportunity to witness local development in a hands-on fashion. You're hosted by the village association, Zankai Aljanna, in *banco* huts on a full-board basis (CFA6000 per person per day). Apart from the usual activities of pirogue trips, camel rides and hikes (all extra but good value) they aim to show tourists around their conservation and farming projects, which include **experimental gardens** culturing spirulina, a mineral-rich, high-protein nutritional supplement grown in ponds, which they sell, among other products, at the Zankai Aljanna boutique on rte de l'Aéroport in Gao. You need to organize the visit with the tourist office (see below) a day or two in advance so they can get supplies in for you.

Practicalities

The occasional flight into Gao (often just the weekly winter charter from Paris and Marseilles with Point-Afrique) lands at the rudimentary **airport** 8km southeast of town near the Niamey road. Formalities are usually very swift and customs informal. A ride into town along Route de l'Aéroport (there are usually several *taxi brousse*

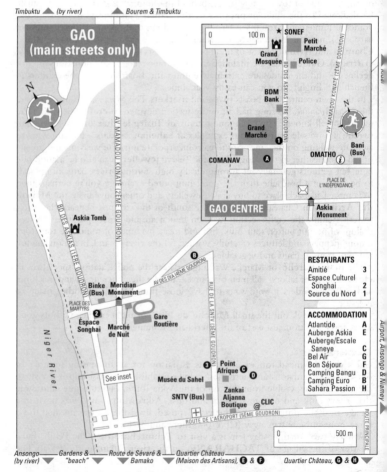

Timbuktu (by river)   Bourem & Timbuktu

**GAO
(main streets only)**

GAO CENTRE

RESTAURANTS
Amitié	3
Espace Culturel Songhai	2
Source du Nord	1

ACCOMMODATION
Atlantide	A
Auberge Askia	E
Auberge/Escale Saneye	C
Bel Air	G
Bon Séjour	F
Camping Bangu	D
Camping Euro	B
Sahara Passion	H

Niger River

See inset

Ansongo (by river) — Gardens & "beach" — Route de Sévaré & Bamako — Quartier Château (Maison des Artisans), **E** & **F**   Quartier Château, **G** & **H**

drivers on the prowl for customers) costs CFA1500 per person, though you might be able to tag along for free with a tour-operator's minibus.

The **gare routière** in Gao lies behind the stadium to the south of Avenue des Dia, the east–west running road that delimits the northern edge of the town centre. However, unless you're looking for buses to Niamey other than those operated by SNTV, it's doubtful you'll have much to do with this place, for each of the major companies has its own terminus. Amongst the other companies, Bani Transport (☏282.04.24) is on the place de l'Indépendance, SONEF has a *gare* just north of the Grand Mosquée in the town centre, and a larger depot a few hundred metres to the south on the way out of town towards the Route de Sévaré, while Binke Transport (☏282.05.58) lies to the north of town on Avenue des Dia.

Gao's **tourist office** is a recommended visit (Mon–Fri 7.30am–5pm, Sat & Sun by appointment; ☏657.62.09). With Peace Corps input, the office has extensive details on accommodation and transport, and runs the best English-language website in the country (🌐www.visitgaomali.com).

The BDM **bank** (Mon–Fri 8am–noon for exchange), halfway between *Hôtel Atlantide* and Marché Washington, changes cash and, if you're lucky, provides advances against Visa cards. International **phone calls** can be made from Sotelma or nearby at the **post office** (Mon–Fri 8am–12.30pm & 2–3.30pm, Fri 8am–12.30pm & 2.30–5pm). There's also a good **Internet** centre in Gao: CLIC (Mon–Thurs & Sat 8–11am & 4–9pm, Fri 6–9pm, Sun 8–11am) on the way to the airport, just past the turnoff for *Sahara Passion* (CFA1000/hr).

Since peace between Tuareg and government forces was cemented with the symbolic burning of arms in Timbuktu in 1996, travelling in the Gao region is no longer considered dangerous, and you don't need to register with the **police** on arrival. However, a few police officers have been slow to catch on, so to avoid the risk of them ruining your day, you may want to visit their station on Boulevard des Askias. And if you're leaving Mali for Niger, they can also put an exit stamp in your passport, which is a free service and may save hassle at the border.

Accommodation

Most of the best-value accommodation options in town are located outside of the town centre, with several in **Quartier Château** (location of the water tower), to the south of the Route de l'Aéroport. If you want to stay at one of these you'll find that it's a thirty-minute walk from the central *gare routière*. Thankfully, a couple of alternatives have opened up that, while not exactly central, are just about within walking distance of the *gare routière* and the Binke Transport terminus.

Atlantide across from the *grand marché* ☏282.01.30. Gao's most famous and most central hotel, the *Atlantide* is a colonial pile languishing in the doldrums. Despite the worst efforts of the miserable staff, the old-world charm of the place is still an attraction, and with the market heaving out front and the Niger drifting behind, its location is unbeatable. Room prices are too high, but you can sleep on the roof for CFA3000. Rooms with fan ❸ or a/c ❹.

Auberge Askia Quartier Château ☏605.64.19. An easy-going place consisting of a large converted family house with a range of rooms – some s/c with a/c – and a small dorm and traditional Songhai tents in the garden. CFA4000 to camp, otherwise ❷.

Auberge/Escale Saneye a few hundred metres from *Camping Bangu* ☏282.09.76. Dorms with fans, rooftop camping and two small Songhai round houses. At weekends, this place fills up for traditional live music and dancing. CFA3000 camping on the roof or ❸.

Bel Air Quartier Château, 1km south of the rte de l'Aéroport ☏282.05.40. One of Gao's smarter options – though it's all relative – *Le Bel Air* has a mishmash of small rooms with fans, some s/c. One block east, *Bel Air*'s annexe has large rooms (same price), a roof for camping (CFA2000) and a bar with a small stage for sporadic gigs. Rooms with fan ❸ or a/c ❺.

Bon Séjour Quartier Château, secteur 1 ☏282.03.38. A decent option set amongst a sea of Tuareg tents in the shadow of the water tower. Has a bar and menu and a range of accommodation, including sleeping on the terrace (CFA2500). Rooms with fan ❸ or a/c ❹.

🏃 **Camping Bangu** Septième Quartier, signposted off the rte de l'Aéroport. Probably Gao's cheapest option, *Bangu* boasts basic rooms with shared facilities in a *banco* building with a flat roof – excellent to sleep on – or, for the same price, an exotic Songhai tent in the courtyard. The energetic proprietress also prepares excellent meals. CFA2000 per person to sleep in a room or on the roof. Rooms with fan ❷.

🏃 **Camping Euro** off av des Dia; turn north opposite the SONEF petrol station; it's 100m further ☎608.78.27. One of the newer *campements* and already garnering praise from travellers, this Nigerian-run place – where English is spoken, and shown on the TV too – has small rooms which, if the management followed the tourist office's recommended tariff, would be overpriced. Thankfully, the charming manager is happy to discuss prices. By the standards of Gao, this is a fairly central spot – and recommended. Rooms with fan ❷.

Sahara Passion Quartier Château, secteur IV, clearly signposted 1.5km off the rte de l'Aéroport ☎282.01.87 🌐www.sahara-passion.com. Now rather in decline following the departure of the Swiss half of the partnership that ran this place, though their travel agency is still operating and organizes trips in the desert. Camping CFA5000, rooms with fan ❸ or a/c ❺.

Eating

Gao doesn't boast very classy **restaurants**, but has a few friendly and unpretentious places not to miss. The very central and inexpensive 🍴 *Source du Nord*, in front of *Hôtel Atlantide*, is the best and most popular place with locals and tourists alike. The

---

Moving on from Gao

Gao used to be a lynchpin in West African travel itineraries, the southern "port" for the legendary Tanezrouft route across the Sahara from Reggane in Algeria. These days the route **north across the Sahara**, is still pretty much off-limits to tourists. it's generally considered safe as far as **Kidal** (you will find trucks going here at the *marché de nuit* and occasional buses with Bani Transport and Binke Transport), but consult the authorities in Kidal for the latest news about travelling further north. Kidal has an excellent website at 🌐www.kidal.info.

By plane

The only flights operating from Gao's simple international airport are the high season (Dec–Mar) Point–Afrique flights on Mon to Marseilles and Paris (contact Sidi Haidara on ☎603.17.96 🌐www.point-afrique.com), and the year-round CAM flights to Bamako (CFA115,000) via Timbuktu (CFA45,000) and Mopti (CFA81,000) on Sunday (contact Idrissa Haidara on ☎605.25.55).

By river

During and after the rains, you can take advantage of the river boats that service one of the most interesting stretches of the Niger between Gao (their terminus) and Mopti. COMANAV have their offices near the *Hôtel Atlantide* (☎282.04.66). Their boat runs August–November, supposedly leaving Monday at 8pm (except the third Mon of every month) and taking three days to get to **Timbuktu**, five to **Mopti** and six to **Ségou**. Outside this period, for most of the year it's possible to use smaller river craft for transport. Upstream, poled pirogues set off for **Bourem** (all day and half the next), **Bamba** (3–4 days), **Gourma-Rharous** (4–5 days) and Korioumé for **Timbuktu** (a week). Downstream, pirogues rarely go much beyond **Gargouna** (one day away; Tues market) or **Ansongo** (two days away; Thurs market). The price of travel by pirogue or *pinasse* has increased greatly in recent years but a place on board shouldn't cost you more than CFA10,000 per day, including communal rice and fish. To arrange a trip by pirogue call Mohamed Touré (☎605.18.00), while for *pinasse* trips contact Ibrahim Maïga (☎901.85.47).

menu offers European and African dishes and they cook a delicious beef *brochette*, which they can serve with mashed potato. *Amitié*, on rue de la SNTV, serves very cheap local food, with the menu painted on the door. *Espace Culturel Songhai*, while not as fancy as its name suggests, has a pleasant garden setting and serves a decent *poulet*. And be sure to sample Gao's delicious, long, spicy sausages (*luttre*) – always a reliable evening street-food fallback, most regularly found in the area of the *grand marché* and also up at the *Marché de Nuit*.

South to Niamey

The journey **from Gao to Niamey** can be hard, especially in the rainy season, as the unpaved sections are full of sandy-to-muddy pitfalls and fringed by thorn trees whose spines work their way through hot rubber. Allow at least a full day to cover the 440-odd kilometres.

For much of the way, the road hugs the banks of the **Niger** through memorable scenery, with palms, river views and dunes. If you don't have your own transport, starting this journey by river (see "Moving on from Gao") is an excellent plan: pirogues and *pinasses* to **Ansongo** crush through deep reed beds harbouring a wealth of **birdlife**, and then break onto open water where they regularly pass several herds of snorting **hippos**.

By road

Getting from **Gao to Bamako** is easy on the fast paved road (a new bridge now crosses the Niger 12km south of Gao). Regular buses leave Gao for **Mopti** and **Bamako** from the central *gare routière*. Of the established companies, Bani (☏282.04.24), to the north of the Place de l'Indépendance, has at least one service daily for Bamako (16hr; CFA16,000) via Sévaré (7hr; CFA7000), leaving on Monday at 1pm, Tuesday–Friday at 5am, and Saturday and Sunday at 5am and 1pm. Binke (☏282.05.58), further north to the east of the Meridian Monument, has a twice-daily service to Bamako, at 4am and 1.30pm. Bani also runs a service to **Sikasso** on Tuesday and Wednesday.

Travelling overland in any other direction can be a trying experience and requires lots of time. The Nigérien SNTV bus (☏282.03.95), based near the Musée du Sahel, leaves Gao for **Niamey** (CFA8600) on Wednesday and Saturday at 5.30am. You're allowed onto the bus (actually, more of a truck) in the order you book, so it's wise to book several days in advance, as you want to avoid the bumpy back seats behind the rear axle at all costs. If things go according to plan, the bus gets into Niamey early evening on the same day, but processing all the passengers at the border can slow things down, punctures and breakdowns are common, and during the rainy season there are further delays. Other companies, including Bahiya and Askia Transport, also make the trip (though their "buses" are even shoddier than SNTV's), so there is usually at least one early-morning service every day. For the non-SNTV services, ask at the *gare routière* behind the *marché de nuit*.

To track down the exceedingly rare vehicles heading direct to **Timbuktu**, check at hotels, with guides, and at the *gare routière* behind the *marché de nuit*. In theory, Binke runs a twice-weekly service (Tues and Fri at 1.30pm) from their *gare*, west of the Meridian Monument, though the future of this service is in doubt. If you get fed up waiting, take a vehicle to Bourem (from the same *gare routière*) and try waiting there: some traffic crosses the desert as far as Bourem and turns west to Timbuktu (see p.399 for route details). It's more straightforward, however, to take a Bamako or Mopti bus as far as **Douentza**, where with a little luck you can find a 4x4 heading to Timbuktu the next morning.

By road, the initial 95-kilometre paved stretch to Ansongo presents few problems. **ANSONGO** itself has a splendid Thursday **market,** is essentially Songhai, but you'll also see numerous Fula and Tuareg.

South of Ansongo, road construction is ongoing, but despite the travel difficulties, this is a beautiful stretch officially classified as a protected natural area. Several species of **gazelle** can occasionally be seen, and a small herd of **giraffe** also roam through the region, though you're unlikely to spot them from the *piste*.

The road continues tortuously until you arrive at Labézanga, 191km from Gao, the Mali **border post** where you'll usually be subjected to minimal formalities. Procedures are a little more protracted at Yassane, the border post for Niger a few kilometres further on. From there it's another 44km to **AYOROU**, a large market town where you pass through Niger customs and immigration and the surfaced road begins, then a further 200km to Niamey via **Tillabéri**.

5

Cape Verde

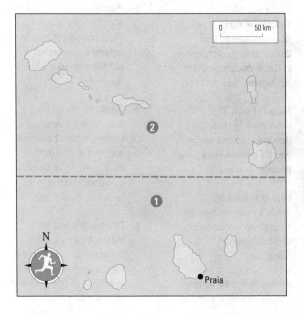

0   50 km

N

❷

❶

● Praia

Highlights 432
Introduction and Basics 433

5.1 The Sotaventos 462
5.2 The Barlaventos 483

Cape Verde highlights

* **Cape Verde's music**
Deliciously, impossibly
sad; its echo will remain
with you, long after you've
left the islands. See p.457

* **Cidade Velha** Picture-
postcard streets and
world-heritage architecture
in Cape Verde's oldest
settlement. See p.471

* **Mount Fogo** The
otherworldly beauty of
this volcano will leave
you as breathless as the
ascent. See p.477

* **Fajã d'Agua** Cape
Verde's most stunningly
located and horizontally
laid-back village.
See p.481

* **Hiking in Santo Antão**
There's scenery to make

your head spin – and
grogue-heavy hospital-
ity to make it spin even
more. See p.495

* **Pedra da Lume, Sal** The
atmosphere of a Wild
West movie set and the
cinematic sweep of a
hidden salt lake.
See p.501

* **Santa Maria Beach,
Sal** Cape Verde boasts
many glorious beaches,
and this is one of the
best, with azure seas and
excellent watersports
facilities. See p.502

* **Driving around Boa
Vista** Check your 4x4
is sound and preferably
take a guide for an off-
road tour of beaches and
dunes. See p.509

▲ Shipwreck at Mindelo

The Cape Verde Islands

From a traveller's viewpoint, and indeed a West African one, the **Cape Verde Islands** were barely on the map as recently as five years ago. If you ever heard of them, it was usually as an offshore supplement to the grim process of desertification on the African mainland, 450km away. An Atlantic world apart, the archipelago falls in more neatly with the Azores, or even the Canary Islands. But now that European **tour operators and property developers** have caught on to the islands' potential as a holiday destination, Cape Verde is beginning to change, with hotels and apartment complexes springing up on the beaches and new airports being built to service a growing schedule of direct flights from European cities.

The Cape Verdes consist of nine main islands in two groups, the **Barlaventos** (Windwards) and the **Sotaventos** (Leewards). Six of them – **Santiago**, **Fogo**, **Brava**, **São Nicolau**, **São Vicente** and **Santo Antão** – are volcanic and inspiringly scenic, while the three to the east – **Maio**, **Boa Vista** and **Sal** – are flat and sandy. Although the islands are isolated, they're not difficult to get around, with a reasonably reliable internal air service supplemented by ferries and catamarans. Even outside the main towns and resorts, there's usually somewhere to stay, a small hotel or *pensão*, and prices are reasonable. Now that the Cape Verdes are cheaper and easier to get to than ever before, the islands are emphatically worth a trip.

The **feel** of the Cape Verdes is hard to place – not quite African, scarcely European, but Portuguese-mannered and Kriolu-speaking (an African/Portuguese creole). While attractive in many ways, the islands are no tropical paradise, so banish any Caribbean associations. The most recent major **drought**, which lasted from the early 1970s to 1985, brought malnutrition and hardships which only worsened the country's economic plight in the first decade of independence. But some good rainy seasons have seen the islands increasingly green – especially on their northern windward slopes and several have interiors resembling anything but deserts, with towering, cloud-drenched peaks and ravines choked with vegetation.

Facts and figures

The islands' name, **Cabo Verde** in Portuguese, derives from their position off Cap Vert, the Dakar peninsula of Senegal. Their total **land area**, just 4000 square kilometres, is about the same size as Kent or a little larger than Rhode Island. Just over 400,000 Cape Verdeans (less than half the total population) now live on the islands, with the remainder living or working abroad.

In January 1991, Cape Verde was one of the first countries in West Africa to see democratic elections, with a peaceful transition from the PAICV single-party regime to the Movimento para a Democracia (MPD). Although the PAICV has since regained power, the multiparty system remains. Cape Verde's **foreign debt** is a severe test of its resources; at about £230 million ($460 million) in 2007, it's nearly half its annual gross domestic product of about £500 million ($1 billion), and yet the G8 do not consider Cape Verde indebted enough to qualify for debt cancellation. The country depends heavily on money sent home by Cape Verdean overseas workers, and on foreign economic aid.

Maize is the islands' staple crop, and cultivation of coffee, cassava, sugar cane, potatoes, bananas and papayas is also important, though viable agricultural land is in such short supply that a significant amount of food is imported. Tourism is the fastest-growing sector of the economy.

The **coasts** vary from white sands against metallic, azure blue to full-tempered Atlantic seas on black cliffs. Inland, the **roads** are for the most part steep, winding and cobbled, harking back to pre-motor days; typical **trees** include baobab, silk-cotton breadfruit, coconut and date palm.

People distil *grogue* from sugar cane, fish for huge tuna, and strum out mournful *mornas* on the right occasions. Rip-offs and hustle seem almost unknown. In the few small, colonial-style **towns**, each clustered around a central square – the *praça* – you'll find restless teenagers perched on mopeds,

widows in black going to Mass and potted plants on the window ledges. The towns on most of the islands are referred to simply as *povoação* – "the town". Except on Santiago island, which has several towns, there could be no confusion.

People

The Cape Verdes were uninhabited until first colonized in 1462. The Portuguese immigrants, who in the sixteenth century, made the islands an Atlantic victualling

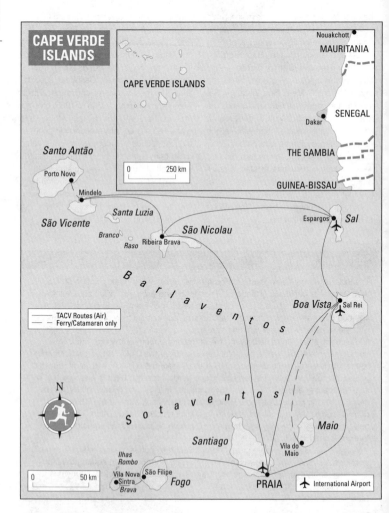

Photography is generally easy on the islands. When taking pictures of Cape Verdeans, ordinary courtesy is your only restraint: you'll rarely be asked for payment.

station and entrepôt for the trade in African produce and **slaves**, were a mixed population of landless peasants, banished malefactors, adventurers and exiles. The islands were soon being cultivated by the slaves and freed slaves who rapidly made up the bulk of the population. But while the mixed race population that emerged was considered "assimilated" – accepted as Portuguese by Lisbon – the islanders suffered in various degrees from oppressive and racist policies. In Cape Verdean society there was great emphasis on skin colour, the criterion by which "real Portugueseness" was measured.

Commercial planting was mostly of cotton, woven into *panos* – lengths of distinctive, banded blue-and-white cloth prized along the Guinea coastlands. But catastrophic **droughts** brought despair and neglect; for nearly the whole of their colonial period the islands remained a largely ignored backwater of the Portuguese empire. Over the last 150 years, tens of thousands of Cape Verdeans have left the islands for São Tomé, Guinea-Bissau, Senegal, Europe and the USA. The **New England connection** is especially strong, with *americanos* remitting much of the hard currency needed by island families.

In matters of **religion**, Cape Verdeans are mostly Catholic, although American Protestant churches have made some headway since independence. There's probably quite a lot to be learned about the arrival of Islam in West Africa from the fact that it is completely unknown in the Cape Verdes.

Where to go

Where to go in Cape Verde is a fairly simple matter – in a few weeks you can get to most of the islands and see a good deal of each one. Try, if you can, to allow for unplanned delays. Some islands – **Santiago** for its size, **Santo Antão** and **Fogo** for their stunning

scenery, **Maio** and **Boa Vista** for their beaches – may hold you longer than others, but they're all small enough to be quickly graspable.

On the islands, Cape Verde is called **Cabo Verde** (Cáu Berde in Kriolu), the people **Cauberdianos**. It's not uncommon on Santiago, however, to hear people referring to "Cabo Verde" when they mean Santiago, as if it was the mainland, while referring somewhat dismissively to the other Cape Verdes as *as Ilhas* – "the islands". There's a good deal of rivalry between the islands, with competition between the people of the Barlaventos – who see themselves as more urbane and metropolitan – and the Sotaventos where, in Santiago particularly, a larger proportion of the population are descended from slaves.

Many towns and villages are called Ribeira something, which just means River – understandable where fresh water is so important. Tarrafal is another common name; every island seems to have its Tarrafal – which makes it useful to know which one's being referred to.

There are subtle **cultural variations** from island to island, with differences in the local dialect of Kriolu. Look out too, as you travel, for the characteristic women's **headscarf style** – tied differently on each island.

When to go

The best time to visit Cape Verde is probably **October and November**, when the results of a successful rainy season are truly verdant, the islands' name suddenly no longer ironic. The first five months of the year before the anticipated July to October summer rains are not ideal because of the dry, dusty conditions. From April to June, the higher reaches of the mountainous islands are often blanketed in chilly fog. If the rains come, splendid thunderstorms and torrents of water across the roads are the norm,

Average temperatures and rainfall

Praia

Temperatures °C	Jan	Feb	Mar	Apr	May	June	July	Aug	Sept	Oct	Nov	Dec
Min (night)	20	19	19	20	21	22	23	23	24	23	22	20
Max (day)	27	28	29	29	30	30	30	30	31	31	30	27
Rainfall mm	2	0	0	0	0	1	8	76	102	30	10	2

though they shouldn't hinder your travels if you're visiting during this season. Between December and March it can be unpleasantly windy, especially in the northeast part of the archipelago, as *harmattan* winds blow across from the Sahara.

Exceptions to the above guidelines would be special visits to São Vicente, either for the annual Mindelo *Carnaval*, a riot of Rio-style floats, costumes and small-scale street entertainment which takes over the town every February, or for the August music festival.

If you're basically visiting for a **beach holiday**, then "high season" is usually considered to be July and August, the European summer, with another peak over Christmas and New Year, and sometimes Easter. These are the periods when prices are likely to be somewhat higher – notably on Sal, the main resort island – and pressure on rooms the most intense. **Sea temperatures** peak in October at about 25°C and drop to around 20°C in March.

Getting there from mainland Africa

With no ferry services running from the African mainland, **flying** to the islands is the only way of reaching them – unless you have an ocean-going yacht. Most flights from the African mainland are to the capital, Praia,

For details on **getting to Cape Verde from outside Africa**, plus important practical information applying to all West African countries, covering health, transport, cultural hints and more, see Basics, pp.19-28.

on Santiago island. Flights from **Dakar to Praia**, operated by Air Sénégal (twice a week) and TACV (five times a week), are usually full and routinely overbooked. Make a reservation as soon as you can and be sure to reconfirm your seat a couple of days before. Both airlines offer promotional fares from time to time.

Red tape and visas

All nationalities require **visas** to visit Cape Verde – see p.29 for addresses of some of the few consulates.

If you're flying to the islands from the UK or Europe with a tour operator they will invariably offer to arrange your visa for you. For US citizens applying to the embassy in Washington DC, the visa fee is $40. In West Africa the only consulate is in Dakar in Senegal (see p.213).

Once you've found a consulate, visas are no problem. In Dakar, with three passport photos, you should be able to get one in a matter of hours. Be sure to check when you're supposed to come back, as the office may keep slightly irregular hours. If you arrive on the islands without a visa, experience suggests you won't be turned away. At Sal, the visa fee is currently €45, but you may have to queue at the immigration desk for some time as your application is processed. Should your onward travel within Cape Verde require a really tight connection, it's best to try to get a visa in advance.

Visas can be granted for stays of up to 90 days. If you're planning on staying longer, you'll have to get your **visa renewed** at either the Direcção de Imigração e Fronteira in Praia (see p.471 for contact details) or any local police station.

On **duty-free allowances** of alcohol and tobacco, there's a simple rule: none. But the principle is not adhered to and, in practice, reasonable personal quantities are fine. There's rarely much of a customs check anyway.

Info, websites, maps

Cape Verde has no tourist offices abroad and the few embassies and consulates have either nothing or the most limited leaflets.

Websites

With so many Cape Verdeans away from home, social networking and online forums are an increasingly important way to stay in touch. Try the following sites for a good range of information and links:

Ⓦ **www.capeverdeinlondon.co.uk** UK portal primarily for the London-based Cape Verdean community, with useful news and message board.

Ⓦ **www.umassd.edu/specialprograms /caboverde** Plenty of useful links to Cape Verde–related information at this excellent (if not always up-to-date) site hosted by the University of Massachusetts at Dartmouth.

Ⓦ **www.caboverde.com** An Italian tourist-oriented site, partly in English; not bad for pictures of places to stay around the islands.

Ⓦ **www.caboverde24.com** A decent portal and search engine, great for up-to-the-minute news, weather and Web links.

Ⓦ **www.cvmusicworld.com** Slick, US-produced site dedicated to the islands' musical history and supporting current artists.

Ⓦ **www.caboverdeonline.com** Features some insightful articles written by ordinary Cape Verdeans and useful introductions to the island's history, politics and demographics.

Ⓦ **www.asemana.cv** Local news and listings in English, French and Portuguese.

Ⓦ **www.ecaboverde.com** Photo forum with albums on every island, a great way to take a virtual tour.

The blog for this guide

For **travel updates**, news links and general information, check out Ⓦ theroughguidetowestafrica .blogspot.com.

Maps

There's an increasing range of reasonably priced good-quality **maps** coming onto the market from Germany. Reise Know-How's 1:135,000 map is printed on durable Polyart, up-to-date and just about large-scale enough to hike with (1cm:1.35km). A series of superior 1:50,000 (1cm:500m) hiking and mountain-biking maps covering Santo Antão, São Nicolau, Boa Vista–Sal–Maio, Santiago and Fogo–Brava, complete with suggested routes, is produced by Goldstadt Wanderkarte.

The media

Radio and TV are important in Cape Verdean culture, with the national Rádio Televisão de Cabo Verde handling both. The TV arm (TNCV) broadcasts an eclectic mix of Brazilian soap operas, European football and right-on documentaries while the radio (RNCV) broadcasts on FM (in Portuguese and Kriolu) with an enlightened playlist. Other local radio stations include the government-run Voz de São Vicente and a growing number of private commercial outfits. The Portuguese-run cable-TV channel RTP Africa is ubiquitous.

The **press** consists of one state-run daily newspaper, *Jornal Horizonte*, and a few privately owned weeklies and monthlies, the most popular of which, *A Semana*, includes Cape Verdeian news stories in English on its website (Ⓦ www.asemana .cv). Other local news weeklies include *Expresso das Ilhas* and the Mindelo-based *O Cidadão*. There's also a decent arts and culture publication, *Artiletra*. Portuguese is easier to read than to speak, which is just as well, as foreign papers are virtually unobtainable.

Health

Arriving direct from outside Africa, you don't need any inoculations and on the whole there are few **health issues** to worry about. If you're coming from the African mainland, yellow fever (and, very rarely, cholera) certificates may be demanded.

One of the health successes of Cape Verde has been the virtual elimination of **malaria**. Until the nineteenth century a posting to the islands from Portugal was viewed as one step short of a death sentence. Now, all planes arriving from Africa get insect-sprayed before any passengers are allowed off and all visitors are issued with a health card asking them to report any fever they get on the islands. Only parts of Santiago have a malaria risk and few people use anti-malaria pills. If you're on Cape Verde for a short time only, however, and planning to return to the mainland, you shouldn't break your course.

Water from the tap is almost always safe but water shortages mean that you'll sometimes be drinking water that's been stored or sold, so beware (there was an outbreak of **cholera** in Mindelo in 1995). And be sparing too: islanders pay for tap water, which is metered, and big price increases are common during droughts. Bottled brands are widely available.

Health care on the islands isn't bad and while infant mortality is still high, life expectancy, at 71, is very impressive. Surprisingly few people **smoke** – though it's a habit enjoyed in pipes by elderly ladies in rural Santiago. Litter bins and enjoinments to social responsibility are features of urban life and Praia is a refreshingly clean capital.

There are **hospitals** in Praia and Mindelo with adequate facilities for ordinary problems. Dispensaries, cottage hospitals and pharmacies (*farmácias*) exist in most towns or, failing these, *postos venda medicamentos* (health posts) should fulfill basic needs.

Finally, if on your travels in West Africa you have the misfortune to get seriously ill, Cape Verde is a good place to **convalesce**. Low humidity, sea breezes and clear skies are the norm.

Costs, money, banks

Cape Verde's **currency** is the Cape Verdean **escudo** (CV$ or CVE). On the islands, it's usual to put the dollar sign after the number of escudos – thus 500$00 means 500 escudos; centavos account for the zeros. You'll encounter notes of 5000, 2000, 1000, 500 and 200 escudos, and coins of 100, 50, 20 and 10 escudos (with the occasional 200 escudo coin). A **conto** is the colloquial term for 1000 escudos.

Cape Verde is not a cheap destination, though your **outlay** will very much depend on how much travelling you do between the islands, and your mode of transport. Since inter-island flights cost from €50 per leg with a TACV Cabo Verde Air Pass (only available to those flying into Cape Verde with TACV; see p.22) and considerably more without, travel costs can quickly break into even fairly generous budgets. The new inter-island catamarans are more reasonably priced; ferry crossings, though cheaper, can be very slow and rough. Road travel is inexpensive but the cost of exploring those islands which don't have much public transport can soon mount up. A basic room in the very cheapest type of *pensão* will cost upwards of £8/€12/$16 and while you can buy a plate of *cachupa* for £1.50/€2.25/$3, a straightforward three-course meal goes from about £5/€7.50/$10, with individual dishes in fancier establishments costing about the same.

Visiting half a dozen islands in three weeks, keeping flights to a minimum, staying in the cheapest *pensões* and restricting yourself to one restaurant meal a day, you'd likely spend £40/€60/$80 a day, and perhaps somewhat less if you're sharing rooms (much less if you spend any time hiking and sleeping out).

Prices are much lower outside the few main towns, but noticeably higher where there are international connections or a whiff of tourism (Sal, Praia, São Vicente, Fogo, Boa Vista). Save for any dealings with the ubiquitous Senegalese traders, you won't save much by **bargaining** either. This is hard to accept at first, if you've

Fuel costs

Fuel costs are fixed at CV$124/litre for petrol (gasoline) and CV$85/litre for diesel fuel.

grown accustomed to West Africa's noisy exchanges of mock outrage, but it makes life more relaxed and seems entirely appropriate in Cape Verde's almost hassle-free environment.

On Sal, room rates in the "high-season" periods of June to September and Christmas/New Year tend to be higher.

Cape Verdean **sales tax** (called IVA) of 6 percent on room rates and restaurant bills and 15 percent on consumer purchases is usually included in the prices quoted by hotels, restaurants and shops, but it's always advisable to double-check.

Banks and exchange

The escudo is fairly stable at £1=CV$165/ €1=CV$111/$1=CV$82. Escudos are not convertible outside Cape Verde, so buy currency upon arrival. Many businesses, particularly in the tourist areas, accept euros, but in doing so they often round the exchange rate down to about CV$100 = €1. There are banks with **ATMs** at Sal and Praia airports.

The **Banco Comercial do Atlântico** and **Banco Caboverdiano de Negocios (BCN)** are the most useful banks, with branches in most towns and all island capitals. They take traveller's cheques in all major currencies but tend to give better rates for euros than for US dollars or pounds sterling. Larger hotels also accept traveller's cheques. Commission charges tend to be rather high and start at a minimum of around CV$500. The limited **black market** isn't worth bothering with; at most you'll add one or two percent to your spending power. Western Union money transfers are handled by branches of Caixa Económica.

Credit and debit cards

Credit cards don't help much on the islands. The big tourist hotels in Santa Maria (on Sal) usually take Amex, Visa and MasterCard, but they're about the only establishments that will. You'll be routinely charged around CV$500 for most transactions. Banks will issue cash against credit or debit cards if you're prepared to queue and pay at least CV$1000 in commission per transaction. The cheapest way to obtain cash is from an ATM, with a debit card.

Getting around

The most important inter-island connections are by **plane**, with high-speed **catamarans** and **ferries** providing good alternatives. Except on Santiago, **road transport** on the islands is fairly limited.

Domestic flights

All the inhabited islands are linked by **internal flights** run by Transportes Aereos de Cabo Verde (TACV); details for each island are given later in this chapter. Fares range from CV$6600–12,400 one way (£40–75/€60–112/$80–150). It's worth considering a **Cabo Verde Air Pass**, which must be purchased abroad in conjunction with a TACV ticket to the islands. The pass is valid for 22 days and comprises anything from two flight coupons (£115/€170/$230) to ten flight coupons (£320/€473/$640), with child (67 percent) and infant (10 percent) rates.

Unfortunately TACV have a patchy reputation, with flights cancelled or overbooked on a fairly regular basis and poor customer communication. It's important to reserve seats as far ahead as possible and to reconfirm 72 hours before flying. It's often possible, even when there's no direct flight, to get where you want to on the same day with a little island-hopping. Note however that international arrivals delayed into Sal airport can sometimes knock the whole domestic service out of joint, as domestic planes may be delayed for connecting passengers. The upside is that TACV staff are used to fixing up passengers who have been delayed overnight with complimentary hotel accommodation, with minimal fuss.

Catamarans

Cape Verde's inter-island public transport recently received a much-needed boost with the launch of new express **catamaran** services (☎ 260.30.97 ⓦ www.moura company.net), making some crossings four times faster than before.

One ("Auto Jet") catamaran links São Vicente with Santo Antão and São Nicolau, another ("Jet Caribe") runs from Praia to Fogo, Brava, Maio, Sal and Boa Vista and a third is due to link Praia and São Vicente (5hr; CV$4870). Prices are higher than the ferries, but still reasonable. **Fares** are for single (each-way) journeys and the same price in either direction.

Auto Jet timetable:

Mindelo–Porto Novo 7.20am, daily except Thurs (30min), CV$800;

Porto Novo–Mindelo 8.50am, daily except Thurs

Mindelo–Porto Novo 2.20pm, Mon, Tues, Fri & Sat

Porto Novo–Mindelo 3.50pm, Mon, Tues, Fri & Sat

Mindelo–São Nicolau 10.20am, Wed & Sun (2hr), CV$1800

São Nicolau–Mindelo 1.50pm, Wed & Sun

Jet Caribe weekday timetable:

Praia–Fogo 7am, daily except Thurs & Sun, CV$3220

Fogo–Praia 10.55am, Tues, Fri & Sun; 4.40pm Mon, Wed & Sat

Fogo–Brava 10.55am, Mon, Wed & Sat, CV$1050

Brava–Fogo 1.30pm, Mon, Wed & Sat

Praia–Maio 2.20pm, Tues & Fri, CV$1550

Maio–Praia 6.40pm, Tues & Fri

Other fares: Praia–Brava CV$3220

Jet Caribe Sunday timetable:

Praia–Maio 7.30am, CV$1550

Maio–Boa Vista 9am, CV$3220

Boa Vista–Sal 12.30pm, CV$1600

Sal–Boa Vista 3.05pm

Boa Vista–Maio 5.10pm

Maio–Praia 8.40pm.

Other fares: Praia–Boa Vista CV$3600; Praia–Sal CV$3870; Maio–Sal CV$3600

Ferries

Meanwhile, the islands' **ferries** continue to run fairly regular services, though schedules are variable and difficult to pin down precisely. The route most commonly taken by visitors is from Mindelo (São Vicente) to Porto Novo (Santo Antão), a reliable twice-daily crossing taking 60–90 minutes, operated by the Canarian ferry company **Naviera Armas**. The ferries leave Mindelo at 8am and 3pm, and return from Porto Novo at 10.30am and 5.30pm. Tickets, which officially cost CV$700 one way for tourists (although in practice everyone seems to be charged the local rate of CV$400) can

be purchased from the harbour offices in Mindelo and Porto Novo.

It's possible, in theory, to travel by ferry from Mindelo to Praia (Mon 6pm, Thurs noon; CV$3900), from Mindelo to São Nicolau (Thurs noon; CV$1300) and from São Nicolau to Praia (Thurs 8pm; CV$2600). There are also irregular services linking Mindelo to Palmeira (Sal) and Palmeira to Boa Vista. However, services linking the smaller islands, such as the ferries between Praia, Maio and Boa Vista, and between Praia, Fogo and Brava, only run when they have sufficient cargo and the weather is favourable – in other words, highly irregularly. If you take one, you may find yourself sharing a cramped, uncomfortable deck with goats, donkeys and seasick locals; for more comfort, it's worth paying extra for a cabin. It's also advisable to bring your own provisions as onboard catering is basic.

If you want to plan ahead, the following ferry companies can advise you, but even they may not know the precise schedule more than a couple of weeks in advance:

Agenamar: Fogo ☏ 281.10.12.

Agência Nacional de Viagens (ANAV) Praia ☏ 260.31.02; Mindelo ☏ 232.11.15; Sal ☏ 241.13.59; São Nicolau ☏ 236.11.70; Boa Vista ☏ 251.12.07; Brava ☏ 285.12.70; Santo Antão ☏ 222.18.87; ⓦ www.anv.cv.

Companhia Nacional de Navegação Arca Verde (CNNAV) Praia ☏ 261.54.97; Mindelo ☏ 232.13.49.

Buses, taxis and hitching

Compared with getting between them, **getting around each island** is relatively straightforward: the longest land journey is less than 100km, on Santiago, and in practice most trips take less than an hour. On some islands, however, transport to and from outlying villages is infrequent.

Minibuses, called **carrinhos** (but usually known simply as "Hiace" after the popular Toyota vehicles), and trucks with bench seating in the back (occasionally with a tarpaulin over them but usually open to the elements) have replaced nearly all the large buses that used to cover the islands. These vehicles operate wherever there's sufficient demand and usually carry a sign in red marked **aluguer** – "for hire". They're very inexpensive (rarely more than CV$200 per hop) although you'll normally have to wait until the vehicle is full before the journey begins; in practice this rarely takes more than half an hour.

Carrinhos are also available for private hire which is much more expensive – reckon on CV$40 per kilometre, the rate rising to CV$50 at night. Unsurprisingly, many drivers are keen on this arrangement, especially when dealing with tourists. In more rural areas in particular, they'll try to tell you the public services have finished for the day. While this may be true, don't take their word for it. Tell them explicitly you want a **coletivo** ("public bus") and be prepared to walk away or hang around for a bit in the hope that they change their tune.

A ride in a **taxi particular** (a "private" taxi) or car costs about the same as hiring a *carrinho* privately. For an extended charter, however (often referred to as a **deslocação**), expect to pay CV$3000–4000 per half-day; this can be a viable option for inaccessible places on the smaller islands.

Hitchhiking, when there are any vehicles, is easy and drivers *simpatico* – though habitually reckless. The lack of traffic gives some drivers a vivid sense of immortality, but the combination of tortuous bends and precipices with cobbled roads is perilous. Be confident in saying *Devagar!* ("Slow down!"). It's normal to pay for lifts when hitching, though it won't always be expected – agree in advance.

Car rental and cycling

Car rental in Cape Verde is small, but growing in line with tourism. This is especially noticeable on Sal, where international companies like Hertz and Avis have moved in. Outside of Sal, the largest choice of outlets is in Praia and Mindelo; the small, local operations on the more outlying islands are not very impressive, but at least they're not overpriced (from CV$4500/day). Deposits are normally around the CV$10,000 mark but occasionally as much as CV$30,000 (in cash). Credit card guarantees aren't required. **Fuel costs** are standardized at CV$124/litre for petrol (gasoline) and CV$85/litre for diesel fuel.

Cape Verde is wonderful **cycling** territory for the fit and fanatical and, in view of the gradients, not to mention the cobblestone roads, obviously suited to mountain bikes. You'll need your own bike: there are few if any opportunities to rent.

Accommodation

Putting your head down for the night is a simple business. You will usually find a Portuguese-style *pensão* (plural *pensões*) or *residencial* (plural *residencias*) offering clean, down-to-earth accommodation – often with a fan, though bathrooms are usually shared – for around CV$1200–1500 (❷) for a room. Ask to see several rooms and perhaps ask *Tem um quarto mais barato?* ("Do you have a cheaper room?"). Cheaper places don't always offer hot water routinely, or provide breakfast except as a supplement.

Full-scale hotels – with hot water, private bath, air conditioning and restaurants – are increasingly common, with rooms starting from around CV$2500 (❹) and rising to CV$8000 or more (❼–❽) in a few establishments. Santa Maria, on Sal, has ninety percent of them: **seasonal rates** apply

---

Accommodation price codes

All accommodation prices in this chapter are coded according to the following scale, whose equivalent in pounds sterling/US dollars is used throughout the book. Prices refer to the rate you can expect to pay for a room with two beds, including Cape Verde's 6 percent tourism tax. Single rooms, or single occupancy, will normally cost at least two-thirds of the twin-occupancy rate. For further details, see p.55.

❶ Under CV$825 (under £5/$10)
❷ CV$825–1650 (£5–10/$10–20)
❸ CV$1650–2500 (£10–15/$20–30)
❹ CV$2500–3300 (£15–20/$30–40)

❺ CV$3300–5000 (£20–30/$40–60)
❻ CV$5000–6600 (£30–40/$60–80)
❼ CV$6600–8250 (£40–50/$80–100)
❽ Over CV$8250 (over £50/$100)

in some, peaking during European holiday periods. Breakfast is usually included in more expensive places.

It is often assumed that you'll know about the twelve o'clock **checkout** rule, sometimes applied quite ruthlessly. Hotels (more rarely *pensões*) will try hard to make you pay an extra half-day or whole day if you haven't vacated on time. That said, many people will allow you to leave your bags behind the desk for a few hours if your onward travel is later in the day.

In smaller towns you may have to ask to locate your accommodation: everyone knows where the lodgings are, and signposting is often absent. This may apply particularly in the case of the local *pousada municipal* – the town resthouse – where you may need to track down the landlord for the key. Such places are usually very basic and cheap.

Cape Verde has no youth hostels or campsites. Surprisingly perhaps, truly wild country suitable for camping – as opposed to marginal agricultural land – isn't plentiful. Still, as an eccentric foreigner you'll be happily tolerated if you camp in the neighbourhood. You're likely, anyway, to have an opportunity to ask permission when you collect water.

Eating and drinking

It would be surprising if Cape Verde had an extensive and flourishing **cuisine**: with severe malnutrition and famines that killed tens of thousands in living memory, the question of food has tended to concentrate on the number of calories – and in respect of variety, mainland West Africa can usually do a lot better than the islands. Still, the dishes on offer are a wholesome and always filling selection, little changed since the sixteenth century.

Apart from the big hotels on Sal and in Praia and Mindelo, and a handful of restaurants where you'll get a decent variety of unremarkable international fare as well as local dishes, the choice is always strictly limited. In smaller towns the *pensões* usually serve meals somewhere in the building, but a **casa de pasto** (dining room/diner) is the

standard, and often unmarked, place to eat. You eat what they have, the *prato do dia* (dish of the day), which as often as not will be *cachupa* (see box opposite), the national dish, the name of which is believed to derive from the same African term that resulted in ketchup or catsup.

Staples include rice, potatoes (Irish as well as sweet), beans, maize, squash, pork and – inevitably – tuna. Meals often start with a solid vegetable broth and finish with fruit, occasionally *pudim* (crème caramel).

Unfortunately, **vegetarians** will have to make do with omelette and chips most of the time. On the plus side, eggs are wholly free-range and usually delicious, as are the home-made fries. As an alternative, you can risk the *cachupa*; just ask if it contains any meat. Also, in large towns like Mindelo and Praia you can vary your diet with some quality pizza.

Drinking

When it comes to drinking, Cape Verdeans usually think first of **grogue** or *canna* (sugar cane distillates known collectively with other spirits as *aguardente*), which get consumed – and apparently made at home – in large quantities. A cautious approach is recommended when trying a *copa* (glass): the liquor often comes from anonymous bottles and sacking-wrapped jars and you're never quite sure what the effect will be. There are "new" (*novo*) and "old" (*velho*) varieties and different degrees of smoothness. It's usually clean, but even so can be quite deadly, gasping stuff. "Punch" (*ponche*, *panche*) – a concoction of dark rum, honey and lemonade – is, like *aguardente*, often on sale over the counter in rural shops. It's not an ideal midday thirst-quencher.

Beer (*cerveja*) is still largely imported from Portugal – Sagres, and to a lesser extent, Superbock – but Praia has a brewery (Ceris) and bottles of very malty Coral are now available in the bars and cafés. Some establishments serve the above beers on draught but they are often slightly flat – ask for a *cleps* (a glass of beer). Ceris also makes soft drinks. For juices ask for **sumo** – *de laranja*, *limão*, and so on.

Wine has some potential on the islands as a significant industry, but the remarkably

Essential food vocabulary

Feijões	Beans
Pão	Bread
Bolho	Bread roll
Manteiga	Butter
Queijo	Cheese (usually goat's cheese)
Café	Coffee
Ovos	Eggs
Peixe	Fish
Comida	Food
Marmelade	Jam/marmalade
Milho	Maize/corn
Carne	Meat
Ementa	Menu
Leite	Milk
Carne de porco	Pork
Batatas	Potatoes
Arroz	Rice
Sal	Salt
Mariscos	Shellfish
Sopa	Soup/broth
Abóbora	Squash
Açúcar	Sugar
Chá	Tea
Atum	Tuna
Legumes	Vegetables
Agua	Water
Inhames	Yams

Dishes

Cachupa	A mash of beans and maize, sometimes with bacon and sausage, eaten primarily at breakfast
Cachupinha	Similar to cachupa, with green bits
Caldeirada de peixe	Fish stew

Carne de vaca	Beef
Coelho	Rabbit
Espadarte	Swordfish
Feijoada/ Feijão Congo	Beans and salt pork
Frango	Chicken
Langosta	"Lobster"; strictly crayfish
Lapas	Tiny mussels, usually in a spicy sauce
Licuda/linguiça	Sausage
Linguado	Sole
Polvo	Octopus
Prato do dia	Dish of the day
Tubarão	Shark

Cooking terms

Assado	Roasted
Bife as in Bife de Atum	Steak or cutlet,
Cozido	Boiled
Frito	Fried
Molho	Sauce
Piri piri	Hot sauce

Fruit

Banana	Banana
Frutapão	Breadfruit
Tāmaras	Dates
Toranja	Grapefruit
Goyaba	Guava
Manga	Mango
Melão	Melon
Laranja	Orange
Papaya	Pawpaw
Melancia	Watermelon

Snacks and desserts

Doce	Dessert/sweet
Croquetes	Fish cakes
Gelado	Ice cream
Pasteles	Pies
Iorgurte/Yaourt	Yoghurt

heavy, spicy, red product of Fogo's volcanic slopes doesn't inspire much enthusiasm just yet. Reasonably inexpensive **imports** of Portugal's favourites can be found in most bars and groceries.

Coffee is usually of a fair standard and sometimes freshly brewed. At breakfast it's usually served with a pitcher of hot milk but beware of the awful concoctions served in some of the cheapest *pensões*. Angola once supplied a lot, but Fogo's own more recent contribution isn't that great; it's often stale or mixed with chicory. Santo Antão, meanwhile, produces some wonderfully mellow beans which you can purchase direct from the villages.

Communications

Post in Cape Verde is run by the **CTT**, or simply Correio, while telecommunications are handled by **Cabo Verde Telecom**. There's at least one **correio** (post office) on each island, usually open Monday to Friday 8am to noon and 2.30pm to 5.30pm. **Post**, both outgoing and incoming, is generally efficient and honest, though not especially swift. For poste restante have your mail marked "Lista da Correios".

If you have **urgent mail** for home to post from one of the more isolated islands, apply the appropriate postage and try taking it to the local airstrip for the next flight to Sal, or even ask at the local TACV office if someone could give it to the pilot – people are usually understanding.

You'll find solar-powered **telephone boxes** (which take phonecards, not coins) in most towns and villages. To make an international call, dial ☏00 then the country code. Phones are often out of order, however, while some booths (in Sal Rei on Boa Vista, for example) have had the phones removed completely. **Phonecards** are available from CV Telecom offices (there is one in every large town; Mon–Fri 8am–noon & 2.30–5.30pm) as well as post offices, Shell garages and certain shops, bars and restaurants in values of CV\$500 and CV\$1500.

A convenient alternative is to use the public phones available in most post offices. You pay the clerk after finishing the call but be aware that costs are fairly high, and you can't normally make reverse charge/collect calls.

Mobile phones are as popular in Cape Verde as they are elsewhere, and the operator CVMovel has many roaming partners. Local SIM cards can be bought from outlets at the airports and most of the larger towns.

Online services are relatively abundant in Cape Verde with at least one Internet café in every large town and two or three in places like Praia and Mindelo. The cost is usually CV\$200–300 per hour although some places prefer you to pre-pay for 15- or 30-minute periods.

Cape Verde's **IDD** country code is ☏238.

Opening hours, public holidays and festivals

Most shops and businesses are open from about 8am to noon and again from 3pm to 7pm or 8pm, Monday to Friday; on Saturday they close at noon for the weekend. Lunch hours are long and lazy and *everything* closes, even – curiously and frustratingly – many bars and cafés.

Cape Verde follows the main **Catholic holidays** with some local additions:
Circumcision of Our Lord Jan 1
National Heroes' Day Jan 20
Labour Day May 1
Independence Day July 5
Assumption Aug 15
All Saints' Day Nov 1
Immaculate Conception Dec 8

There's a whole host of other days off – including any number of saints' days and a major **Carnaval** every February in Mindelo, emulated in the same month by Praia.

In addition, **annual island festivals** with horse and mule races, discos, bands and more than the usual level of *grogue* consumption, take place on many islands. Generally lasting about a week, they include:
Boa Vista June 24
Brava June 24
Fogo April 20
Maio early May
Sal Sept 15
Santo Antão early June
São Vicente May 3, June 13 and August (the last of these is a three-day music festival; see p.490).

Crafts and shopping

Most of the **crafts** you're offered in the Cape Verdes are touted by Senegalese traders proffering the sort of wooden carvings and little souvenirs you'd be pestered with in Dakar. Locally made crafts are harder to find, and limited mostly to **lava carvings** (Chã das Caldeiras, Fogo), small **pottery** items and **basket ware** (São Domingos on Santiago) and, if you're lucky, locally woven **cloth**. Mindelo also has some **galleries**.

Crime and safety

It's hard to imagine getting into any **trouble** in Cape Verde, where etiquette has grown out of the combination of Latin manners and West African social convention that you'd expect. You are also unlikely to be a victim of **crime**. While theft is not unknown, the islands are one of the safest places in the world for absent-minded travellers. Even long-term expatriates agree on this, which must say something – though they tend to single out Praia as an exception.

Though Cape Verde is a largely tolerant country, **drug use** carries a strong stigma in the close-knit island communities and doesn't go unnoticed. While quite a few youngish men smoke home-grown weed, you could expect a barrel-load of trouble if seen doing so by the wrong people. **Nudity** and **topless bathing** are pretty well out of the question and particularly ill-advised for unaccompanied women.

Emergencies

Police ☎ 132; ambulance ☎ 130; there is no general fire-service number.

Gender issues and sexual attitudes

Women travellers will find the Cape Verde Islands relaxed after mainland West Africa. While **sexual attitudes** do contain an element of machismo, it's normally expressed as nothing much stronger than winks, whistles, stares and strong expectations that you *will* dance. It can also come across as almost absurdly innocent: heavy sexual pestering is unusual. Younger women, travelling without men, may find that their "unmarried condition" gives them almost adolescent social status, which can be frustrating. But, with the possible exception of Praia, the towns are too small for problems to last long.

As for the lives of **Cape Verdean women**, little seems to have changed despite the government's commitments to reducing sex discrimination and promoting their rights and welfare. Yet there are good reasons why change is needed: the continued emigration involves mostly men; there are 105 females for every 100 males, and in many rural households, women are the de facto heads. The Organizão das Mulheres de Cabo Verde (Rua Unidade Guiné-Cabo Verde, Praia; ☎ 261.24.55) is quite active and the main contact-making body.

Tampons are usually available from larger general stores, but not easily obtained outside the main towns.

Contraceptives: you can get condoms (*preservativas* or, more colourfully, *camisas de vênus*) from most pharmacies and *postos venda medicamentos*.

Although the social climate for **gay people** in Cape Verde isn't particularly helpful – patriarchal, somewhat macho and occasionally very small-town – since 2004 the law itself guarantees equal rights for men and women of any sexual orientation over the age of 16. There's a low-key **gay scene** in Mindelo, Praia and Santa Maria, largely driven by tourists and newly arrived European residents.

Entertainment and sport

Cape Verde has little in the way of an organized leisure industry and the commonest entertainments are home-spun – births, baptisms, confirmations, marriages and funerals all providing occasions for gathering together. In the evenings it's common for young people to meet in the town square (*praça*) with a guitar or two. Otherwise, there's barely a handful of cinemas in Praia and Mindelo, no local film industry and no theatre to speak of. Happily, the Portuguese never established bullfighting. The African game of *orzil* or *oril* (see p.69) is popular everywhere, as is draughts or chequers.

Cape Verdean **music** (see p.457) is becoming better known abroad, with an increasing number of CDs available generally – notably those by **Cesaria Evora**. The islands have a number of nightclubs (*boites*), a clutch of which are regular venues for live music (*musica ao vivo*), as are certain restaurants. More often than not, however, you'll stumble spontaneously upon the best music in the most unlikely and out-of-the-way places. Most towns also have a decent **record shop**; CDs are priced in the CV$1500–2500 range.

Sports

The big spectator sport on the islands has always been **football**, and Cape Verde is now beginning to assert itself as the home of some players of international class, playing in European clubs. The national team are known as Tubarões Azuis (the Blue Sharks).

In terms of participatory sports, Cape Verde is creating a name for itself as a prime **water-sports** venue, with world-class surfing, windsurfing and diving opportunities on several islands, notably Sal and Boa Vista.

Wildlife and national parks

Cape Verde's **native fauna** is a meagre show, with no large mammals and few outstanding birds. There are introduced African **vervet monkeys** on Santiago and Brava. Herpetologists are excited by *Tarentola giganta* (the **giant gecko**) and the probably extinct **Cape Verde Island skink** (another relative giant) – there are in fact endemic island species of gecko and skink on most of the islands – but disappointed at the total absence of snakes. Bird-watchers might want to go out of their way to spot the rare endemic **Razo skylark**, though non-specialists will find it fairly uninteresting. Much more exciting are the aptly named **red-billed tropic bird** and **magnificent frigatebird** – a rapacious fish and bird-hunter with a 2.5-metre wingspan – which you have a good chance of seeing in flight over the sea. The seas themselves are also rewarding, with good chances of seeing **dolphins**, **whales**, **turtles** and amazing **flying fish**.

There are no fully-fledged **national parks** on the islands, but gazetted *parques naturales* offer some protection to the **crater of Fogo** and to the peaks of the **Serra Malagueta** and **Serra do Pico do Santo António** ranges on Santiago. **Marine parks** have also been gazetted, on the north coasts of Santiago and Maio, on the north, west and southeast coasts of São Vicente and along the southwest coast of Sal, but it's not clear how much environmental protection they offer.

A brief history of Cape Verde

The Cape Verde Islands blew out of the Atlantic in a series of volcanic eruptions during the Miocene period some 60 million years ago – though Maio, Sal and Boa Vista may be a geological extension of the African mainland. The islands were uninhabited (so far as is known) until 1462, making the country unique in West Africa. In the gloriously clumsy eloquence of Adriano Moreira, Portugal's Overseas Minister from 1961–62, the Cape Verdes were "islands asleep since the eve of time, waiting to be able to be Portugal". After five centuries of such paternalism, the turn of recent events has been remarkably peaceful.

Discovery and colonization

Although African sailors may have visited the islands in earlier centuries, it was a Genoese navigator, **Antonio da Noli**, working for Prince Henry of Portugal, who discovered and first documented Santiago (which he called São Tiago – St James) and four other islands, some 500km off Africa's Cap Vert, in 1455. Three more in the northwest (Santo Antão, São Nicolau and São Vicente) were reached by Diogo Afonso in 1461. Santiago, by far the biggest prize, was split between the two navigators, who were granted a captaincy each: da Noli set himself up at **Ribeira Grande** in the south and Afonso made his headquarters in the northwest. Slaves were brought from the African mainland to work the parcels of land allotted the handful of immigrants, and in the capital, Ribeira Grande, work began on a cathedral. The Portuguese crown viewed the new extension of empire – 2500km from Lisbon – with some indifference: the archipelago could serve as a stepping stone to exotic riches, and it would certainly do as a penal colony.

Fogo was settled in the 1480s and its western region was singled out as one of the most likely productive areas on the islands – rolling, partly wooded country, with substantial rainfall in most years. But Fogo islanders were forbidden to trade with foreign ships – a right reserved by Santiago – and the island was considered a hardship post for the Portuguese officials sent there. By the end of the sixteenth century its population had barely reached two thousand and there were appeals to Lisbon for more settlers – petitions which were met with the arrival of convicts and political undesirables (*degredados*) from Portugal and the internal banishment, from nearby Santiago, of certain offenders.

The tiny volcanic pimple of **Brava** attracted its first colonists in the early 1540s. They kept much to themselves: climatically the island was one of the easiest to survive on, yet it was very remote. It was only when large numbers of families escaped here from Fogo in 1680, after volcanic eruptions and an earthquake, that Brava became heavily populated. It has had the densest population of the islands ever since.

The big island of the far northwest, **Santo Antão**, got its first inhabitants in 1548 but its large size, with remote and rugged interior valleys and craters, and its distance from the main shipping lanes, kept it very isolated and little known for at least two hundred years. Among its settlers were Jewish families fleeing the Portuguese Inquisition and subsequent European persecutions. The village of Sinagoga is a reminder.

São Nicolau offered fewer opportunities to adventurous migrants and only

As the New World opened across the Atlantic in the sixteenth century, the **trade in slaves** gathered momentum and the Cape Verde Islands – by then important stepping stones to Brazil and the Caribbean – became an emporium for their **trans-shipment** and taxation.

Although they were more expensive, slaves at **Ribeira Grande** on Santiago (the main entrepôt; now called Cidade Velha – see p.471) were better value than those bought directly on the Guinea coast: they tended to be healthier, as the sick had already perished; they spoke some Portuguese and some had even been baptized (the Portuguese were keen on finding religious justifications for their slave-trading, safeguarding the captives from purgatory). And for the slave ships, buying at Ribeira Grande was a much safer option than sailing directly into the creeks of Guinea to barter for slaves.

Between 1600 and 1760 (the peak years), anything from a few dozen to several thousand slaves were sold annually through Ribeira Grande, most of them exported to the Spanish West Indies and Colombia. Large numbers were shipped off in years of bad drought on Santiago, when planters would sell their farm slaves to traders when they couldn't afford to feed them. This was prohibited in law: the only slaves supposed to be exported from Cape Verde were those just imported from the coast under licence.

From the earliest years of the colony, Lisbon had passed a succession of laws governing trade in slaves and other products. This was to ensure that as much of the profit and tariffs as possible accrued to the Crown, even if that meant relegating much business to the status of smuggling – from which the Crown received nothing. Besides ruling that the resale of slaves and foreign trade partnerships were illegal, Portugal obliged contract holders in the trade to buy the limited range of goods for resale and barter offered by the state supply monopoly. Between 1512 and 1519, crushing (though unenforceable) edicts were issued outlawing the much-in-demand Indian and Dutch cloth from the islands, banning the commissioning of *lançado* adventurers to trade on the mainland, and ruling that all legally contracted slave ships bound for the Americas should first detour to Lisbon – because Ribeira Grande could not be trusted to extract duty honestly.

Successive **governors** of the islands, who generally viewed their appointments with misgivings if not actual horror, succumbed to the inevitability of corruption (if they survived malaria and other diseases long enough to care). Some succumbed too enthusiastically for the likes of the islands' clergy, aldermen, court and treasury officials – whose own commercial interests they threatened – but most governors managed to amass reasonable wealth while leaving space for smaller operators to do business.

Lançados, tangomaus, grumetes and ladinos

As well as bona-fide licensed contractors waving charters from Lisbon or Madrid, the people involved in the complex mesh of buying, selling and bartering for slaves and other goods included:

• *Tangomaus* (dragomans): Cosmopolitan Africans, familiar with Portuguese ways, who traded in the Guinea interior and did much of the initial negotiating for slaves.

• *Lançados* ("sent outs") Originally white or part-white Cape Verdeans who had familiarized themselves with African ways on the mainland and had settled in African communities to trade and transport goods along the coast. They eventually became indistinguishable from *tangomaus*. The bane of Lisbon, the *lançados* eventually became totally estranged from Portugal and even at times from Santiago. Once fully acculturated in Guinea, and unable to return to Portugal (on pain of death), they had no need to worry about the trade rules and could deal with the Dutch, English and French boats which sailed around the Atlantic in growing numbers. In this way they kept a good selection of merchandise for purchasing slaves and other African goods.

• *Grumetes* African or mixed-race deckhands and carriers working for the traders.

• *Ladinos* Slaves or other Africans who could speak Portuguese or Kriolu.

its northwest valleys made colonization viable in the middle of the sixteenth century, and even these had uncertain rainfall. The town of Ribeira Brava became an important literary and ecclesiastical centre and was the seat of the Cape Verdean bishopric from the end of the eighteenth century until the beginning of the twentieth.

São Vicente, one of the driest islands, was virtually uninhabited until the start of the nineteenth century, when the sheltered bay at Porto Grande (the best harbour in the islands) was chosen as the site of a British coal-bunkering station for steamships on the Brazil and East Indies runs.

The "flat islands" of **Boa Vista**, **Maio** and **Sal** were also late in being fully colonized. Maio and Boa Vista had small numbers of herders and poor farmers, most of them freed or escaped slaves, and Maio eventually became the virtual private fiefdom of a freed slave family, the Evoras.

Trade development

An early plan, conceived by Genoese merchant adventurers, was to create a major **sugar** industry on Santiago, following its success in Madeira. With the conquest and colonization of tropical lands, Europe could begin to grow the crop for itself instead of relying on expensive imports. But the Cape Verdean climate proved unsuitably dry and, although the **rum** which normally came as a by-product of sugar production was found to be useful for **slave trading** along the Guinea coast, the sugar plantations at Ribeira Grande never really took off. By the late sixteenth century their output was already eclipsed by the vast quantities being produced in Brazil.

Instead, the Cape Verde Islands found themselves in the middle of a growing network of **trade routes** – between Europe and India, between West Africa and the Spanish American colonies and between Portugal and Brazil. They took on the function of **victualling stations**

for the trading vessels, supplying fresh water, fruit, salted and dried meat, and carrying on a trade of their own in commercial goods – salt, hides, cotton *pagnes* and slaves.

With the break-up of the union between Portugal and Spain in 1640, business went into the doldrums for a number of years. Several governors were denounced to Lisbon after they monopolized what trade there was or even started applying the rule of law in order to confiscate and penalize foreign trading ships for their own gain. The islands were at a severe disadvantage because international demand for slaves had saturated the Guinea coastlands with **iron bars**, the principal currency, causing huge increases in the price of slaves. Portugal, which produced very little iron and forbade its export, was unable to compete.

Cotton, though, had become Cape Verde's main commercial crop, grown especially on the estates of Fogo. Slave women spun it; men wove it into strip cloth, dyed it with cultivated indigo and native *orchilla*, and sewed the strips together into *pagnes*. Some of the material found its way to Brazil but most was traded – generally for more slaves – on the Guinea coast. From the sixteenth century to the eighteenth, Cape Verdean cotton **panos**, in a multiplicity of inventive designs, were the prized dress material of the West African coast. They were traded as far east as Accra (until slave trading began to be threatened by abolitionists) and were as valuable as iron bars in many districts. The value of Cape Verde cloth became so universal in the region that it was also the usual currency of the archipelago: administrative officials were commonly paid with it and accumulated vast hoards of the stuff.

The Crown Monopolies

In the second half of the seventeenth century, after the split with Spain, the private contracts system fell out of use. Portugal's African territory and trade routes were seriously depleted and for some years, only the most recklessly optimistic merchants had been willing to purchase the expensive rights on slaving in those parts. With wily Cape Verdeans stealing the trade from under their noses and the price of slaves going up all the time, it was difficult to make contracts pay.

Instead, in 1675, the first of the **Crown Monopolies** – the Companhia de Cacheu – was set up, reserving for itself sole rights to trade in foreign goods with the coast and outlawing (again) the transshipment of slaves through Santiago. Cape Verdeans were only allowed to export their own produce, a state which aroused bitter feelings in Santiago.

When a new company, the Company of the Islands of Cape Verde and Guinea, was formed, and bought a fat contract to supply four thousand slaves a year to the Spanish West Indies, the governor of the islands was placed on the company payroll. With their governor now effectively playing for the opposition, the islanders were more disgruntled than usual. And true to form, the new company did nothing for their prosperity, stockpiling goods to inflate prices, undersupplying vital commodities and levying high freight charges for their meagre exports. However, with the **War of the Spanish Succession** (1701–13), into which Portugal was pulled against Spain and France, the company's valuable slaving contract was lost and in 1712, Ribeira Grande itself was comprehensively sacked and plundered by a French force. The **cathedral**, a century and a half in the building, had only been completed nineteen years earlier. About this time, serious attention began to be given to creating a new and better fortified capital at Praia. Ribeira Grande was in steep decline from the middle of the eighteenth century and **Praia** was eventually dedicated as the seat of island government in 1774.

The eighteenth century

The first half of the eighteenth century had witnessed a great **relaxation** of **trade embargoes**. But Lisbon's neurotic attempts to prevent the transshipment of slaves and the sale to non-Portuguese of Cape Verdean cloth mystified foreign traders, especially English and Americans, who broke the laws with no qualms at all. Apart from its triumphant (but peaking) textiles industry, the archipelago was in a state of **economic ruin**.

With the foundation in 1757 of the **Companhia de Grão Para e Maranhão**, which had the sole purpose of providing slave labour to the states of the new Brazilian empire, a twenty-year era of unparalleled cruelty and hardship began for the islands. The annexation of political control which had begun with the last company was taken to its logical conclusion, so that the Company now effectively *owned* the islands; while in Lisbon, a clique of English gentlemen maintained discreet but weighty capital interest in its enterprises.

Apart from the utter destitution which the enforced bypassing of trade brought to the archipelago, a severe **drought** struck from 1772 to 1775. By this point in the islands' history the population had grown too big to be able to survive such disasters on whatever came to hand – as they had during the famine of 1689 in Santiago when they ate horses and dogs. In the face of **starvation** throughout the islands, the Company was implacable – it held back food supplies, pushed up prices and milked the islanders of every last resource. In return for food, hundreds were abducted abroad and forced into slavery by English and French traders. Smuggling, of course, had never been so essential nor so profitable. The famine left an estimated 22,000 dead – out of a total population of 60,000. By the time the rains returned in 1777, the Company's charter had expired and it went into merciful liquidation.

The nineteenth century

At the beginning of the **nineteenth century** the Cape Verdes faced a quite different future. The harsh Company regime had battered the textile industry with enforced low prices, while drought had extinguished the cotton crop as well as many of the field slaves and textile workers. The emergence of the newly independent **USA** as a major economic power began to be more important than the distant historical links which tied the islands to Portugal. Lisbon, in any case, was too distracted by Napoleonic strife at home, and tail-and-dog upsets with Brazil about who ruled who, to be much concerned with the insignificant islands and their irrepressible flouting of trade laws. Moreover, Angola and Mozambique held far more promise.

New England whalers began calling at the Cape Verdes from the end of the eighteenth century, to take on supplies and crew and to do a little trading. Goatskins were a profitable sideline back in the States and, once the practice had become established, the Americans arrived each year with holds full of merchandise. Brava, Fogo and São Vicente were the main islands of contact and from these a steady trickle of impoverished Cape Verdeans escaped to New England through the closing decades of the nineteenth century.

Slavery in the nineteenth century was contained by the British and (ironically) by the American presence. While the trade in slaves from the Guinea coast was forbidden from 1815, slaves were still sold well into the 1840s. Only with the end of the American Civil War and with pressure from Britain (to whom Portugal owed a debt going back to the Napoleonic era) was an abolition process set up on the islands. Slaves were not formally emancipated until 1869 and even then they had to work for their ex-owners as indentured labourers for a further ten years.

Famine and emigration

A series of disastrous **famines** hit the islands during the nineteenth century. In the first of these, from 1830–33, an estimated 30,000 people died. No relief of any kind came from Lisbon, but America, on this and several other occasions, sent large consignments of relief aid, though towards the end of the century it was generally wealthy émigré Cape Verdeans who organized it.

While the dispossessed of the Sotaventos moved to Praia or tried to emigrate, the poor of the Barlaventos headed to the new "city" of **Porto Grande** (Mindelo) on São Vicente to find work at the British-run **coaling station** or in the shops, bars and bordellos.

At the peak of its importance at the end of the nineteenth century the port of Mindelo was servicing over 1300 ships every year – and tens of thousands of sailors. The latter industry had a far-reaching effect on the culture of the islands, introducing even more of a racial mixture and enriching Kriolu with words like *ariope* (hurry up), *fulope* (full up) and *troba* (trouble).

Meanwhile, Portugal's first efforts at "humanitarian relief" took place during the drought of 1863–65 (with a death toll of some 30,000). It seemed an ideal time to profit from the availability of labour eager for food by engaging the people in civil engineering projects. The islands' first **cobbled roads** date from this famine, when peasants were rounded up to work for starvation wages.

A more sinister method of dealing with famine was **enforced migration** to the "Cacao Islands" of São Tomé and Principe. The abolition of slavery here led to serious labour shortages. In the Cape Verdes the shortages were of land. Offered apparently huge bonuses by the recruiting agencies when (and if) they returned, thousands of poverty-stricken Cape Verdeans were persuaded to "go south" over the next ninety years to a system of equatorial plantation labour that was little better than ordinary chattel slavery. Like the monopoly companies of a century before, Portugal's **cocoa industry** found drought on the Cape Verdes was easily turned to its advantage.

The twentieth century

The trickle of emigrants to New England became a flood between 1910 and 1930, when an estimated 34,000 people left the islands. This exodus became highly significant after World War II, when the emigrants were able to send back substantial **remittances** to the islands.

Drought continued to be the single most important factor shaping the lives of Cape Verdeans in the twentieth century, with big crises in 1902–04 (15,000 dead), 1920–22 (17,000), 1940–43 (25,000) and 1947–48 (21,000 lives lost). The drought of World War II was probably the worst catastrophe in Cape Verde's history. Brava and Fogo suffered appallingly when they had to cope with a surge of re-emigrants returning from the American depression, the "rainy" years of the 1930s having lulled islanders into a false sense of security. And during the war years remittances from American relatives dried up completely. Only following the drought of 1959–61 were genuinely compassionate measures taken to alleviate the suffering, and these seem likely to have been initiated mostly by international outrage at the colonial labour-migration policies.

Agitation for independence

A small number of Cape Verdeans emigrated to **Guinea-Bissau** – not out of destitution, but with ambitions. Following the opening of *liceus* (the colleges of São Nicolau in 1866 and São Vicente in 1917), about two-thirds of mainland Portuguese Guinea's teachers and civil servants had been Cape Verdeans. It was principally from their ranks that organized **resistance to Portuguese rule** first germinated. In response to what they described as a "wall of silence" around the islands, a group of mostly Cape Verdean intellectuals led by **Amílcar Cabral** – and including Luiz Cabral and **Aristides Pereira** – met secretly in Bissau in 1956

to form the **PAIGC** (Partido Africana para Independência da Guiné e Cabo Verde).

When peaceful representations to the colonial government were met with indifference and more repression, culminating in a massacre of striking dockers in Bissau, the PAIGC began planning for a **guerilla war** on the mainland, with the declared aim of liberating both Guinea-Bissau and Cape Verde. After four years of preparation and frequent efforts to negotiate a peaceful alternative, war began in 1963. The Cape Verdes became a massive Portuguese military base, swarming with Portuguese troops drafted to the front in Guinea-Bissau – and in Angola and Mozambique, where wars of independence had also begun.

On the Cape Verdes themselves, the question of a violent uprising was purely academic. The small, barren and isolated islands are unpromising ground for guerilla warfare. Yet the island government and police force (with help from the military and the PIDE secret police) were acutely sensitive to the possibility of open revolt: every subversive indication was examined and squashed, and activists sent to Tarrafal on Santiago, or worse places in Angola. On Santiago, a *badiu* religious cult movement, known as the **rebelados**, was labelled communist for criticizing the corrupt, state-run Catholic Church, advocating the hands-together system of community help (the *juntamão*) and resisting outside interference, especially the antimalaria campaign, which tried to spray members' homes. The movement virtually deified Amílcar Cabral. Its leaders were brutally interrogated and deported to other islands, though their threat was no more politically coordinated or potentially subversive than that posed by the **Nazarene Church**, whose American-led, Puritan-inspired clergy were also subject to repression for their denunciations of the Salazarist Church.

Cultural opposition was the only kind available and cultural repression the inevitable response. **Kriolu**, virtually

Cape Verdean society

The slave estates had varied in size from small landholdings run on paternalistic lines, where landlord and slave led similar lives, to extensive plantations (especially on Santiago) where wealth differences were extreme. The traditional **morgadio** system of land tenure, in which inheritance was strictly by primogeniture (inheritance by the eldest son), produced a growing population of landless aristocrats and tenant farmers on marginal land. Under the system, land could not be bought or sold. The estate slaves were often tied closely to the landlord's family, occasionally by blood. Over the centuries, intermarriage blurred the distinction between slaves and share-cropping peasants, the only practical difference being that the sharecroppers were always in debt to the landlords, a life in many ways as arduous as slavery. Freedom for slaves – an act of "charity" periodically undertaken by some landlords, or else an economic necessity when food supplies were exhausted in a famine – was no release from the cycle. If they ran into debt as sharecroppers, freed slaves lived on the sufferance of the landlord.

This, together with the fact that the islands are too small to offer much refuge, meant that slave rebellions were rare and provoked only by the most savage treatment. Among the landed families there were real fears, principally because they themselves were divided (the *morgadio* system created bitter feuds) and sometimes engaged in fierce vendettas with their rivals. At one time many slaves were armed by their masters, and gangs of pistol-toting slaves are known to have clashed on occasions, even in Praia. There was a certain insecurity about what might happen if the arms were turned against the elite. In the Santiago interior there was a large underclass of freed and escaped slaves, the *badius*, partly independent of the estates. And on Santiago, relations were less paternalistic and the estates often owned by absentee landlords. A group of slaves did organize a stand against their particularly oppressive landlord in 1822 and there was an aborted general slave revolt in Santiago in 1835 (given passive encouragement by the administration's ragged armed forces). But that was about the extent of resistance, and it was largely brought about by anticipation in the run-up to the abolition of slavery.

As for political resistance which might eventually culminate in an independence movement, there isn't a great deal of early evidence for that either. Conditions on the estates in the twentieth century became worse. With the old *morgadio* system discredited and abandoned, and the landlords themselves in debt to the National Overseas Bank, much of the land was bought up by a new class of absentee landlords, often returned United States emigrants. Coaling labourers mounted strikes for increased pay at Mindelo in 1910, and again in 1911, but they were defeated.

Opportunities for dissent on the islands in the fascist "New State" of Portugal's prime minister Salazar (1932–68) were limited to the private publication and distribution, among a small intellectual circle, of poetry and subtly nationalistic Kriolu literature. Organized demonstrations of opposition were impossible, and even further ruled out by the chronic plight of the islands during the famine years of World War II and the labour migrations of the early Fifties. Debtor peasants were treated as criminals and could claim nothing from the state until their debts had been repaid. Political dissidents found themselves imprisoned in the notorious detention centre at **Tarrafal**, alongside victims ejected from Portugal, and interrogated by the Gestapo-modelled PIDE political police.

To make the possibility of grassroots resistance even less likely, Cape Verde has an **alcoholism** problem going back to the earliest years of the sugar industry. Never viable as a major export, cane was still grown in large quantities for distilling *grogue*, on land that could otherwise have provided food crops. The national addiction to *grogue* was such that, in the drought years of the 1960s, sugar was imported to satisfy demand.

unintelligible to ordinary Portuguese-speakers, was considered subversive in itself and its use banned from state property.

On the mainland, the war was drawn-out but successful. Only the **assassination of Amílcar Cabral** at his headquarters in Conakry on January 20, 1973 (partly inspired by jealousy of the Cape Verdean role in Guinea-Bissau's revolution), deflected it from a well-planned and predictable course. In September 1973, with most of Portuguese Guinea controlled by the PAIGC, the party proclaimed de facto independence. Portugal **withdrew from Bissau** the following year after the overthrow of the dictatorship in Lisbon on April 25, 1974.

Independence

On the islands, the pre-coup government continued in office, though in less than a week, the clandestine fragments of Cape Verde's own PAIGC cells had coalesced, and a **public meeting** was held in Praia on May 1, 1974. The Tarrafal detainees were released and the PAIGC took its message around the islands, agitating semi-legally for the independence that was almost at hand. The "wall of silence" had caved in. Other parties, hatched and nurtured by the administration, tried to promote the idea of some kind of "shared independence" between the islands and Portugal, but none of them convinced many islanders.

Lisbon sent a new governor in August 1974, charged with asserting **Portuguese continuity** in Cape Verde. He was shouted out of Praia and back to Lisbon within a month. Another arrived with a heavier hand, his troops shooting into a demonstration in Mindelo in September. But with Guinea-Bissau already independent, the **demonstrations** only grew larger. By October, with "continuity" sounding increasingly hollow, the Portuguese were negotiating with PAIGC leaders. In December, a meeting in Lisbon agreed on a transitional government consisting of three PAIGC members and two Portuguese representatives. The Portuguese conceded a general election the following June. With a landslide of votes, **Aristides Pereira**, took office on **July 5, 1975**, as president of the new Republic of Cape Verde. The PAIGC party also monopolized power in Guinea-Bissau, and while that territory retained a separate constitution from the islands, the long-term aim was to unify the two into one country.

The split with Guinea-Bissau

Amílcar Cabral had been obsessive about the importance of **Cape Verde–Guinea unity** and Aristides Pereira continued to emphasize it. But the most significant political event in the first twenty years of Cape Verdean independence was the 1980 coup in Bissau which overthrew **President Luiz Cabral**, Amílcar's half-brother, and led to the formal separation of the two countries.

After the liberation war there had been lingering unease within the PAIGC in Guinea-Bissau. Luiz Cabral, though a close friend of party leader Aristides Pereira, was not a statesman of the same rank, and he became an increasingly isolated figure, mistrustful of his own ministers. Suspicions grew that policy in Guinea-Bissau was being constructed by the two presidents in secret and that Cape Verde, which had achieved independence relatively painlessly – though at the cost of Guinean lives – was seeking to dominate the union. Furthermore, while Cape Verdeans had been instrumental in starting the independence movement, they had also formed a large proportion of the colonial civil service in Guinea-Bissau, most of whom had passively collaborated with the Portuguese. The charge of **neocolonialism** didn't have to be made explicit.

Against Pereira's advice, Cabral modified Guinea-Bissau's constitution to give himself more power and his prime minister **Nino Vieira** less. It was Vieira who subsequently led the coup in 1980, putting himself in the Bissau presidency, a move condemned by Pereira. On January 20, 1981 (the eighth anniversary of the assassination of Amílcar Cabral), the Cape Verdean arm of the party renamed itself the **PAICV** and ratified the divorce.

The PAICV era

After 1981, with the union of the two countries a fast-fading dream, Cape Verde at least had a chance to address purely **national problems**. The question of the very habitability of the islands was raised, but the **economy** was made viable, a result of careful and sensitive development and a remarkable absence of corruption.

The PAICV government answered OAU demands that it apply the sanctions policy on South Africa, and refuse refuelling rights to South African Airways on Sal, with the response that it could not afford to commit suicide by solidarity. It also increased the level of **aid** coming into the country and used it on local projects of direct utility. Non-governmental aid, channelled through the National Development Fund, matched foreign interests to Cape Verdean requirements. By leaving the door open for *americanos* to return, it encouraged **private investment** and maintained goodwill among the vast majority of the Cape Verdean diaspora, whose remittances continued to be the number-one economic pillar.

One hundred percent **adult literacy** as well as free and compulsory **primary education** were goals that the PAICV pretty well achieved. **Agrarian reform** was patient, seeking to avoid alienating landlords and always to avoid damaging the country's overseas image of independence and openness. The worst effects of **drought** and flash floods were combated with tree-planting programmes on all the islands, dyke-building and better terracing.

Health was a priority for the PAICV government, which reckoned to spend three times as much per person as the average developing country. High-profile

Mother and Child Protection and Family Planning programmes were run at a community level, with theatre shows and public demonstrations organized to mobilize people on issues that included breast-feeding, contraception and nutrition. The off-loading of unwanted First World drugs, so common in under-developed countries, was avoided by setting up a national pharmaceuticals industry.

Even under one-party rule, the **legal system** in Cape Verde was one of the most progressive in Africa. There were no political prisoners – indeed there are still few prisoners of any kind – and there is no death sentence.

Despite the successes, there remained several lurking problems which would not fade away. **Alcoholism**, especially in the rural areas, has been an ongoing problem for centuries. At root a strictly male issue, it is triply destructive where it not only wastes productive land on sugar cane but hard earnings as well, and reduces the workforce.

A more pointed issue in the late 1980s was the battle between church and state over the issue of **abortion** on demand, which the PAICV supported. Although the majority of children are brought up in mother-only families, the position of **women** in Cape Verdean society has never had as much attention focused on it as the male-formulated charter of the Organization of Cape Verdean Women – OMCV – would suggest. The division of views was by no means straightforward: there were OMCV members among those taking part in the anti-abortion campaign.

Good **rainy seasons** in the late 1980s broke a drought that had persisted on some islands virtually throughout the years of independence. But the PAICV was not equipped to ride out the inevitable wave of rising expectations that came with better harvests and the end of the Cold War. It never properly examined its own renewal mechanisms, thus allowing the former activists of the party to grow old and stagnant together.

At the PAICV party congress in 1988, there were discussions led by younger members about ending its status as the country's sole political party. The new **Movimento para a Democracia (MPD)**, led by lawyer Carlos Veiga, held its first meeting in June 1990, and demands were made for sweeping reforms to Cape Verde's "revolutionary" constitution and the established political culture in which the PAICV held such sway.

Under a tide of mounting pressure, especially from the Church, the prime minister Pedro Pires took over as PAICV party secretary from Aristides Pereira (who saw himself as state president, outside politics), in preparation for the introduction of a **multiparty system**. In January 1991, the MPD swept to power in Portuguese-speaking Africa's first ever multiparty legislative elections, taking more than two-thirds of National Assembly seats. **Carlos Veiga** was subsequently elected prime minister and former supreme-court judge **António Mascarenhas** won the presidential election, soundly defeating Pereira. The MPD also won most of the seats in local council elections held later in the year, with PAICV wins only on the home islands of PAICV dignitaries.

Economically, the MPD government put great efforts into making the country **investor-friendly**, with emphasis on its tourism and fishing potential. The scrapping of the PAICV's last major initiative, the agrarian reform laws, was popular at home, and was judged to have signalled the right messages to overseas investors. The civil service payroll was reduced by half and embezzlement of state funds by former PAICV officials was investigated.

Yet despite the peaceful transition to multiparty politics, there remained widespread **dissatisfaction** with lack of progress and the slow rate of economic improvement on the islands. The MPD was subsequently torn by splits, resignations and defections. One ex-MPD official, Eurico Monteiro, formed a new party, the Partido da Convergência Democrática, and gained a seat in the 1995 elections.

Further internal disputes led to the sacking of two government ministers and the Secretary of State for Decentralization in one fell swoop in late 1999, while the MPD performed poorly in municipal elections in early 2000. Veiga himself was to resign later that summer with the intention of standing for the presidency.

The early twenty-first century

The PAICV emerged anew and went on to secure a narrow majority in the legislative elections of 2001 and 2006. Led by prime minister **Jose Maria Neves** and president **Pedro Verona Pires**, the PAICV have set about improving the precarious financial situation they inherited, committing themselves to a healthy economic policy and prudent fiscal management. While they've succeeded in balancing the budget and reducing inflation, the IMF has obliged them to go further and implement the kind of conservative policies, including privatization, which they wouldn't have dreamed of twenty or thirty years earlier. In addition to this burden, their relatively slim majority in the national assembly has put a brake on their ability to effect change. Despite a measure of success in tackling joblessness – within five years, unemployment has dropped from 25–18 percent – life is still desperately hard for those families not in receipt of overseas remittances.

On a brighter note, **tourism** is expanding rapidly. The opening of new international airports on Santiago, Boa Vista and São Vicente and the stepping up of airport services on Sal have led to dramatic increase in direct flights from European cities, and new complexes of investor-friendly hotels, villas and apartments are springing up on the islands concerned. Partnerships between the state and the private sector are successfully financing some of these projects. The more far-sighted of the developments should benefit local communities through the provision of much-needed housing and services.

Inevitably, however, some are concerned about the **social consequences** of change; petty theft and drug-related crime, once practically unknown, are beginning to crop up in the tourist areas – in 2007 there was even a double murder of two Italian expats who became involved with a local tour guide on Sal, which deeply shocked the island community.

Foreign investors are being seen as key to the establishment of light manufacturing industry geared towards export;

a number of duty-free zones have been set up, and at the time of writing Cape Verde was engaged in negotiating a special trading partnership with the European Union. In tandem with this, more and more retired emigrants are returning to the islands to invest in their homeland.

Prospects for Cape Verde look reasonably healthy – at least in West African terms – assuming the occasional good rainy season and continued foreign investment. The danger for the government is that expectations in the poor, rural heartlands of the most heavily populated islands of Santiago, Santo Antão and Fogo will outstrip its ability to deliver.

Music

The most widely known Cape Verdean forms are guitar and fiddle songs – the **morna**, a mournful lament reminiscent of Portuguese fado, and the more upbeat and very danceable **coladeira**, music with a wonderful muscular rhythm. Many songs are love songs – addressed to the islands – and powerfully sentimental. **Cesaria Evora**, the "barefoot diva", has released a number of superb CDs and is the foremost musical emissary of the isles, now based in Paris. Working hardest for the cause of Cape Verdean music inside Cape Verde itself are **Simentera**, an ensemble dedicated to preserving and rekindling interest in the islands' various musical traditions.

In the past, in smaller towns and rural areas, you might have heard someone playing the **cimbó** or the **berimbau**, old one-stringed instruments of African origin producing plangent, ancient sounds – either with a bow on the former, or plucked and resonating in a sound box, or the mouth, with the latter. Both have virtually fallen into the realm of folklore, though in parts of Santiago you might still be lucky.

To whet your appetite, the following brief list recommend some CDs, most of which are available outside the islands. Cape Verde's musical legacy is rich, however, and there are always new

discoveries to be made. There's currently great enthusiasm for *batuko*, the traditional, bottom-twitching, African dance rhythm of rural Santiago, either performed community-style, traditionally, or used as a springboard for musical creativity. And hip-hop is colonizing the islands, too, with mixed results. Check out ⓦwww .cvmusicword.com for the latest news.

Têtê Alhino *De-Cor-a-som* (available locally). The pick of the Simentera singer's solo albums, this has a wonderfully sensual, Brazilian flavour.

Mayra Andrade *Navega* (Record company). Slickly produced, Brazil-flavoured

457

songs from a rising star with a sweetly inflected voice, who sings in Kriolu, Portuguese and French.

Bau *Cape Verdean Melancholy* (Doçura/ Lusafrica). A choice selection culled from this master guitarist and violinist's four instrumental albums.

Raíz di Djarfogo *Traditions of the Fogo Island* (Ocora). Beguiling roots music from perhaps Cape Verde's most beguiling island. Full of vibrant *coladeiras*, composed in Fogo's tradition of strident social criticism.

Cesaria Evora *Café Atlântico* (BMG). Her best album, an irresistible combination of windswept *mornas* and Cuban instrumentation. Alternatively, go for the obvious *Best of Cesaria Evora* (BMG), or her most recent release, *Rogamar* (BMG).

Simentera *Cabo Verde en Serenata* (Piranha). Simentera have both an uncannily intuitive feel for tradition and the vision to take the music forward. Includes the powerful "Dor Di Amor".

Tchéka *Nu Monda* (Lusafrica). Another Andrade – Manuel Lopes, stage name

Tchéka – bases his sound on *batuko*, transposing it to guitar. His first solo outing is a cool and confident set, showing off his superb voice on his own compositions.

Various artists

Cape Verde: Anthology 1959–1992 (Buda Musique). If you want to educate yourself properly, this is the place to start. Includes extensive sleeve notes and photos.

Evocação de Amílcar Cabral No Folclore Cabo-Verdiano (A. Rui Machado/Sons D'Africa). Beautifully packaged tribute to national icon Amílcar Cabral, with incredible 1970s recordings from the likes of Tony Lima and Nhô Balta.

The Rough Guide to the Music of Cape Verde (World Music Network). Another good entry point for the beginner, with the emphasis on modern releases.

The Soul of Cape Verde (Lusafrica). Another outstanding collection featuring hauntingly atmospheric 1960s tracks from Humbertona & Piuna, Bana and Voz de Cabo Verde alongside newer material. A peerless introduction.

Books

Cape Verde is one of the least documented countries in the world. Sources of information in English are few, and most are technical, research-based studies that you'll find only in university libraries. For good general titles, including some with Cape Verdean coverage, see p.35. Books marked 🏃 are especially recommended.

Charles Darwin *The Voyage of the "Beagle"*. The first chapter of the Victorian scientist's journal of his round-the-world voyage is entitled "St Jago – Cape de Verd Islands" and recounts in engrossing detail his natural history observations on Santiago.

Basil Davidson *The Fortunate Isles – a Study in African Transformation*. A

positive, kid-glove survey, mixing impression with historical accounts.

🏃 **A.B. Ellis** *West African Islands*. First published in 1885, this covers adventures from Madeira to Ascension, with a couple of lively chapters on "St Vincent" and "San Antonio". Entertaining stuff.

Marilyn Halter *Between Race and Ethnicity, Cape Verdean American Immigrants 1860–1965.* An exhaustive study of a fascinating subject, one that cuts to the heart of the unique relationship between the land and its people.

Richard Lobban *The Historical Dictionary of the Republic of Cape Verde.* Great for dipping into, with a wealth of useful information on Cape Verde's roots, as well as sections on ethnomusicology, linguistics and more. The same author's *Crioulo Colony to Independent Nation* is a comprehensive overview of Cape Verde's 500-year history, with the emphasis on modern politics and economic development.

Archibald Lyall *Black and White Make Brown: An Account of a Journey to the Cape Verde Islands and Portuguese Guinea.* Worth trying to find for its vivid account of Cape Verde prior to the disastrous drought during World War II.

Joe Würfel *Cabo Verde West of Africa.* A fascinating and original collection of contemporary monochrome photography documenting the diversity of Cape Verde's people.

Language

The day-to-day language of Cape Verde is **Kriolu** (Creole), quite distinct in structure and in much of its vocabulary from the official language, Portuguese: the two are not really mutually intelligible. Kriolu contains many elements of Fula and Mandinka and a wide range of adopted vocabulary from archaic seafaring Portuguese and other European languages, including English. It also varies across the archipelago, and principally between the Barlavento and Sotavento islands.

If you speak **Portuguese** – and it's one of the easiest languages to pick up, particularly if you're familiar with Spanish or Italian – you'll find you can get by easily everywhere. Even in rural areas everyone speaks some: papers, signs and radio are all in Portuguese and education is largely conducted in it. Learning Kriolu is another matter: Cape Verdeans tend to slip in and out of Kriolu and Portuguese, and Kriolu takes some time to tune into.

While a little Portuguese goes a long way, if you don't have any you may just be able to get by in **French,** which a surprising number of Cape Verdeans speak relatively well and which – even more surprisingly perhaps – they seem to enjoy doing. **English** is a different matter; many people seem somewhat shy of speaking the little English they know. In most places, though, you'll run into younger people who've learned both languages at school, as well as returnee emigrants from Europe, Senegal and especially the USA, who speak them fluently.

Kriolu for beginners

Basic terms and phrases

Bon dia	Hello
Kuma ño sta?	How are you?
N sta ben	I'm fine
Kali e bo nómi?	What's your name? [or more formally]
Kal e nómi di ño/ di ña?	What is your (masculine/feminine) name?
Ña nómi é Caroline	My name is Caroline
Ño ten…?	Do you have…?/ Is there any…?
Bon dia/te lóg	Goodbye

459

Te lóg/te dipos di mañan	See you soon/ sometime
Deus ta kunpaño-lo	God go with you
Pur fabor	Please
Brigod	Thank you
Oshi	Today
Mañan	Tomorrow
Ónti	Yesterday
Ántis	Before
Dipos	After
Pértu	Near
Lonzi	Far
Li	Here
La	There

Travelling

N kre agu	I'd like some water
Kma n pode bai pa Tarrafal?	How do I get to Tarrafal?
Undi e paraza di otukaru pa Tarrafal?	Is this the bus stop for Tarrafal?
Ki óra avion ta sai/tchga?	What time does the plane leave/arrive?
Undi ño/ña tabai?	Where are you (masculine/feminine) going?
Nu ta bai pa Praia	We're going to Praia
Kal e presu?	How much is it?
Troco	Change (money)
Ten penson li pértu?	Is there a cheap hotel near here?
N kreba kuartu pa un psoa/ dos psoa	I'd like a room for one person/two people
Ten kasa di bañu li?	Is there a toilet-bathroom here?
Kuse e es?	What is this?
N ka sabe	I don't know
Nu ka ta papia kriolu	We don't speak Kriolu
Abert	Open
Fetchod	Closed
Undi?	Where?

Numbers and days

un	1
dos	2
tres	3
kuatu	4
sinku	5
sais	6
séti	7
oitu	8
nóvi	9
dés	10
ónzi	11
dozi	12
trezi	13
katorzi	14
kinzi	15
dizasais	16
dizaséti	17
dizóitu	18
dizanóvi	19
vinti	20
vinti y un	21
trinta	30
korenta	40
sinkuenta	50
sasenta	60
satenta	70
oitenta	80
novénta	90
sén	100
sén-t y un	101
duzéntus	200
kiñéntus	500
mil	1000
segunda-feira (2ªF)	Monday
terça-feira (3ªF)	Tuesday
quarta-feira (4ªF)	Wednesday
quinta-feira (5ªF)	Thursday
sexta-feira (6ªF)	Friday
sábado (S)	Saturday
domingo (D)	Sunday

Glossary

Achada Volcanic plateau, usually formed by lava meeting the sea

Aluguer Shared taxi-van or pick-up truck (the public transport of the islands)

Americano Cape Verdean living in America

Badiu Peasant from rural Santiago descended, according to tradition, from runaway slaves

Bairro Suburb, outskirts of town

Boite Nightclub

Branco White – or wealthy – person

Camâra Town hall

Chã Plain, plateau

Cidade City, town

Conto One thousand escudos

Criança Child

Crise Drought, community crisis

Deslocação Private taxi trip

Festa Feast, festival, party

Funco Round, stone, thatched house

Grog, Grogo, Grogue Sugar-cane firewater, *aguardente*

Igreja Church

Lenço Traditional headscarf worn differently by women of each island

Liceu Secondary school

Mercado Market

Morabeza Kindness, gentleness, considered to be a peculiarly Cape Verdean quality

Morna The heavy-hearted music of the islands, sweet-sounding, nostalgic and very characteristic

MPD Movement for Democracy

PAICV African Party for the Independence of Cape Verde

Pano Cloth, *pagne*

Paragem Bus stop

Pelourinho Pillory, the slave auction post

Povoação "Town", the local town

Praça Square, place

Praia Beach

Quinta Estate, owned by a landlord; rare today

Quintal Courtyard of a house

Ribeira Stream, river or rivercourse

Seca Drought

Sobrado A Portuguese-style house of two or more floors, particularly opulent examples of which were built in Fogo's capital, São Filipe

Sodade A defining term of Cape Verdean identity, signifying yearning for homeland

Tabanka Musical form based around call-and-response singing. The same word also signifies village or community and is identified with *tabanka* festivals on Santiago and Fogo, with their origins in freed slave communities.

Vila Town

5.1

The Sotaventos

Santiago, Fogo, Brava and Maio make up the **Sotaventos**, the leeward group of islands, with two-thirds of the population, more of the rainfall (which arrives from the south) and a good deal of the wealth.

If you're coming from Dakar, your first port of call on the islands may well be **Praia** on **Santiago island**, Cape Verde's capital and the nation's largest town. It's a pleasant enough place but there are no gripping reasons to spend time here: if you're stuck for a few days, your time is better spent enjoying one of the easy and satisfying short trips out of town. The rest of Santiago offers more enticing attractions in the mountainous **central region** and the beaches in the northwest, though Santiago's scenery doesn't compare with that of the Barlavento islands of São Nicolau and, outstandingly, Santo Antão.

Fogo island is a vast, semi-active volcano, rising to nearly 3000m above sea level, whose last eruption was in 1995. There's a magnificent road tracking along the lava-covered eastern slopes, fine walking country in the gentler western parts, and fascinating and very feasible hiking up in the old crater itself, now a domain of citrus orchards and vineyards. The hike to the peak itself is a tough morning's work, but well worth it.

The smallest of the inhabited islands is **Brava**. Cape Verdeans often rate it the most beautiful island and it's still somewhat hard to visit as there are no scheduled flights and the sea journey is rough and unpredictable. Brava is certainly the most cultivated island, with a relatively benign climate – and it's long been a sanctuary for those families who could afford to flee the droughts on other islands.

Maio, one of the *ilhas rasas* or "flat islands", is duller and drier. Locally famous for its cattle, which provide the country's limited milk supply, it has some remote, desert island–style beaches and incipient water-sports tourism. Attempts to drum up interest in it seem a little desperate, however. As one Portuguese brochure once put it: "The desolation of its landscape contrasts with the warm welcome of its people and the fine flavour of its fresh lobsters." So there you have it.

Santiago

With half the cultivable land and half the population, **Santiago** is the **agricultural backbone** of Cape Verde. Unusually among the islands, it's large enough that it takes a few hours to get from one end to the other, switchbacking through the mountains or along the jagged eastern coast.

Santiago's main focus is the capital, **Praia**, at the southern tip. From Praia, one main road snakes through the interior, with secondary roads branching off down to the coast; another forks off it to the northeast to link up the east-coast fishing villages before meeting with the main route again at **Tarrafal** in the northwest – site of the best beaches. The village of **Ribeira Grande** (Cidade Velha), west of Praia, was the first settlement on the islands and remained the effective administrative centre until early in the eighteenth century when Praia took over the role of capital. Today, Cidade Velha is one of Santiago's principal tourist attractions, with its handful of picturesque streets, indomitable hilltop fort (now a museum) and assorted ruins in various stages of restoration.

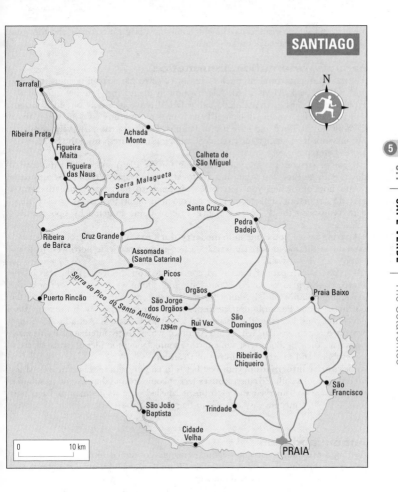

There are dozens of hamlets and villages scattered across the island, and any number of hidden coves and *ribeiras*. A few of the travel possibilities are covered in the next few pages, but Santiago, in common with all the islands, is still little explored by outsiders. Most of your discoveries will be very much your own.

Praia and around

Cape Verdeans – and foreign residents too – tend to complain that **PRAIA** is soulless, thinks of nothing but money and has no *joie de vivre*. If you're already tuned to Cape Verde's gentle sensibilities this may be relatively true. But if you fly in from Europe or particularly Dakar, it all comes as the nicest possible culture shock. The presence of a couple of power-generating windmills rotating on the brown hills across the *ribeira*, the layout of the little town on its small proud plateau, indeed everything about Cape Verde, you can see, is going to be quite different. Though Praia has almost little to offer in terms of sights or entertainment, it is a capital where just being here is enjoyable: the streets are friendly; the *praça* has benches and a bandstand where visiting naval bands sometimes play on Sundays; and there are good views from the edge of the plateau.

Arrivals, orientation, information

The new **international airport** northeast of town has a small terminal building with a BCN bank, ATMs, a little café/bar (usually open 24hr), Internet café and Wi-Fi, Hertz and Avis car rental desks and a TACV office (the only one in Santiago). The manageable muddle of central Praia is only ten minutes away by taxi – about CV$400 to the Platô and CV$500 to Prainha. The taxi drivers are very laid-back, but may not have change for large-denomination notes fresh from the ATM, so it's worth being prepared.

If you're arriving by day, you're heading for the Platô and are not too loaded down with luggage you might just ask for the main *praça* – **Praça Alberquerque** – and hop out when you get there – it tends to be cheaper than naming a specific destination. This tactic is best avoided at night, though, as unwary after-dark visitors to the Platô run a small risk of being targeted by opportunistic thieves.

Arriving by sea, you come in to the **ferry dock** east of the Platô, roughly beneath the end of the old airport runway. It's a five-minute taxi ride northwest to town, barely 2km if you walk.

The downtown part of Praia is all concentrated on the fortress-like slab of the **Platô**, a neat grid of streets 800m long and 300m wide, which overlooks the expanding suburbs and is simplicity itself to get around. Off the Platô to the northwest is the **Fazenda** district; to the southwest is **Várzea**, with the impressive new ministries' building, the Palácio do Governo; beyond is **Achada do Santo António** (often written Achada Sto António) where many international organiza-tions have their headquarters; while further south, facing the islet of Santa-Maria, is the embassy and smart hotels district of **Prainha**.

For **tourist information**, your best bet is to enquire at a travel agency: Praia has no official tourist office. Transcor **buses** ferry people around the city and its suburbs; the stops are well-marked and each bus is labelled with its destination. Fares start from CV$70. **Cabs** are easy enough to flag down; a short hop is likely to set you back CV$200.

Accommodation

Although the budget accommodation – mainly consigned to the Platô (see map, p.467) – is limited, there's a decent range of mid-range and upmarket options, and you're unlikely to get stuck without a bed.

Praia arrivals and departures

TACV (office at the airport ☏260.88.88) operates flights to Boa Vista (Sun; 40min), Fogo (daily; 30min), Maio (Mon, Wed & Fri; 20min), Sal (at least 2 daily; 50min), São Nicolau (Mon, Wed & Fri; 50min) and São Vicente (at least 2 daily; 50min). For airport information, call ☏263.10.10.

Private **Hiace minibuses** run to out-of-town destinations from the depot next to the main Sucupira market, though *aluguers* to Cidade Velha go from a parking area in Terra Branca, southwest of the Platô.

For details of **ferry and catamaran** sailings, see p.440. Moura Company catamaran tickets are sold by Agência Sol Atlântico (Praça Albuquerque, Platô ☏261.66.92) and in the port. Ferry tickets are available from Polar at 141 Rua Serpa Pinto, Platô (☏261.52.23), or Companhia Nacional de Navegação Arca Verde at 153 Rua 5 de Julho in Platô (☏261.54.97), though you can also try the Agência Nacional de Viagens on Rua Serpa Pinto, Platô (☏260.31.02 ⊛www.anv.cv).

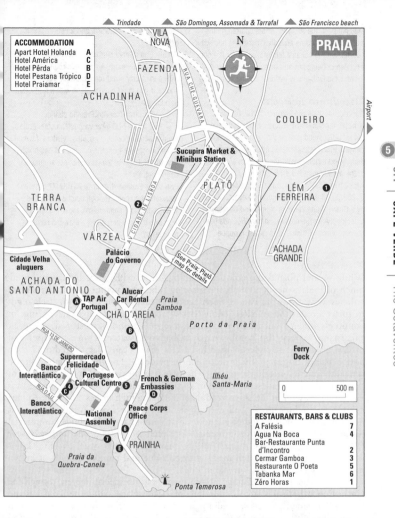

ACCOMMODATION

Apart Hotel Holanda	A
Hotel América	C
Hotel Pérda	B
Hotel Pestana Trópico	D
Hotel Praiamar	E

Trindade ▲   ▲ *São Domingos, Assomada & Tarrafal*   ▲ *São Francisco beach*

VILA NOVA

FAZENDA

ACHADINHA

TERRA BRANCA

VÁRZEA

Cidade Velha aluguers

ACHADA DO SANTO ANTONIO

PALÁCIO do Governo

Alucar Car Rental

TAP Air Portugal

CHÃ D'AREIA

RUA 13 DE JANEIRO

Supermercado Felicidade

Banco Interatlântico

Portugese Cultural Centre

French & German Embassies

Banco Interatlântico

National Assembly

Peace Corps Office

PRAINHA

Praia da Quebra-Canela

Ponta Temerosa

PLATÔ

Sucupira Market & Minibus Station

See Praia: Platô map for details

LÉM FERREIRA

COQUEIRO

ACHADA GRANDE

Airport ▶

PRAIA

N

Praia Gamboa

Porto da Praia

Ilhéu Santa-Maria

Ferry Dock

0   500 m

RESTAURANTS, BARS & CLUBS

A Falésia	7
Agua Na Boca	4
Bar-Restaurante Punta d'Incontro	2
Cermar Gamboa	3
Restaurante O Poeta	5
Tabanka Mar	6
Zéro Horas	1

Platô

Felicidade Rua Andrade Corvo ☏ 261.55.85 ✉ felicidade@cvtelecom.cv. This mid-range hotel and restaurant aims primarily at local business travellers. All rooms come with TV, fridge, a/c and spotless bathrooms, although some rooms are windowless. ⑥

Residencial Paraiso Rua Serpa Pinto ☏ 261.35.39. Clean if slightly cramped rooms set around an open courtyard. Somewhat overpriced, although the balcony rooms (#3 & #9) offer better value. ⑤

Residencial Praiamaria Rua 5 de Julho ☏ 261.85.80 ✉ res.praiamaria@cvtelecom.cv. An oasis of calm from the heat and bustle below with

smart, freshly furnished en-suite rooms, all with a/c, satellite TV, fridge and safe. ⑥

Residencial Rosymar 32 Rua Tenente Valadim ☏ 261.63.45. Down a narrow side-street at the northern end of the plateau, this has bright and quiet, if slightly musty, en-suite rooms with hot water. ④

Residencial Santa Maria 35 Rua Serpa Pinto ☏ 261.43.37 ✉ res.praiamaria@cvtelecom.cv. Owned by the same company as the *Praiamaria*, this has similarly smart rooms, some with balconies. ⑥

Residencial Sol Atlântico unmarked entrance on Praça Albuquerque at 24 Av Amílcar Cabral ☏ 261.28.72. The oldest place in town, and one of the cheapest, the *Atlântico* offers spartan rooms with character, some en suite. There's no hot water but the lived-in colonial feel makes up for it. Room #1, despite being hot and noisy, is recommended for its window/balcony overlooking the square. ❸

Elsewhere in Praia

América Achada Sto António ☏ 262.14.31 ℮ hotel_america@cvtelecom.cv. Located opposite the EU offices and next to the *Agua Na Boca* restaurant, this friendly hotel is fitted out in beautiful dark-wood furniture with the requisite a/c, TV and fridge. Recommended. B&B ❻

Apart Hotel Holanda Achada Sto António ☏ 262.39.73 ℮ hotelholanda@cvtelecom.cv. Run by a Dutch–Cape Verdean couple and boasting a decidedly orange colour-scheme, *Holanda* has decent rooms with shared facilities, grouped around an open courtyard, and an atmospheric old bar. ❸

Pérola Chã d'Areia district ☏ 260.14.40 ℮ perola@cvtelecom. A modern, urban *residencial* with generously sized rooms, this is a comfortable choice if you don't need a place with a restaurant or pool. ❽

🏃 **Pestana Trópico** Prainha district ☏ 261.42.00 ⓦ www.pestana.com. Praia's most expensive hotel, a business-visitors' favourite, looks prison-like from the outside but has luxurious, tasteful and spacious rooms set around a large pool. ❽

Praiamar Prainha district ☏ 261.37.77 ⓦ www .oasisatlantico.com. Though outclassed by the *Trópico*, this is a comfortable, top-end choice with swish decor and an airy, elevated seafront position. ❽

The Town

While several dilapidated colonial buildings on the Platô are being renovated, much of Praia is new and drab, the scrawny suburbs crawling up boulder-strewn gulches away from the centre. Such action as there is on the Platô itself tends to focus around the **market** (Mon–Sat) which, despite its small size, brings in country women from all over Santiago and, in a good harvest year, can pack surprising variety and colour: papayas, bananas, watermelons, potatoes and cassava, goat cheeses, piglets trussed in baskets, dried beans, slabs of red tuna, even potted palms. **Sugar** products are much in evidence. For the Portuguese in the sixteenth and seventeenth centuries, the islands were strategic in their efforts to dominate Atlantic trade routes: rum in particular – distilled from cane sugar – was enormously useful in the **slave trade**, commanding high prices along the Guinea coast. Cane, which grew well enough in lusher valleys on several islands, was never produced in the kind of quantities that would have led to huge commercial success. But Cape Verdeans continue to distil plenty of *grogue*, *canna* and *aguardente* (all variants on the same theme), and to make irresistible sweets. Various kinds of slightly sickly fudge, often made with coconut, and cuplike moulds of brown molasses crystal, are always on sale in Praia.

The few large public buildings around town hold no special interest, though the **Catholic Cathedral** is quite an imposing block of a place with its potted plants and figurines. Formerly, if you wanted a glimpse of the interior courtyard and gardens of the then Office of the Prime Minister, now the **Praia Municipal Council headquarters**, you needed the excuse of visiting to see if they were holding any unwanted seats on flights. With the advent of democracy, you can nowadays walk freely around the council building's pretty grounds and the perimeter of the presidential palace itself, the **Palácio da República**, which overlooks the beach. The **statue of Diogo Gomes**, the Portuguese explorer who was one of the first to visit the islands, stands here.

There are a couple of **museums** worth a look, though note that labelling is in Portuguese. In a nicely restored colonial building with a poorly marked entrance at the north end of the plateau, the **Museu Etnográfico da Praia** on Rua 5 Julho (Mon, Wed & Fri 10am–noon & 3–6pm, Tues 10am–1pm; CV$100) has a deliciously cool interior housing displays of traditional domestic artefacts and blue-and-white *pano* weaving. In the basement you'll find coins, vases, cannonballs and other items salvaged from shipwrecks. Another fascinating collection is on show at the **Centro de Restauração e Museologia** on Rua Alfândega, Chã d'Areia (Mon–Fri 9am–noon & 3–6pm), which has coins, guns, ivory and other artefacts

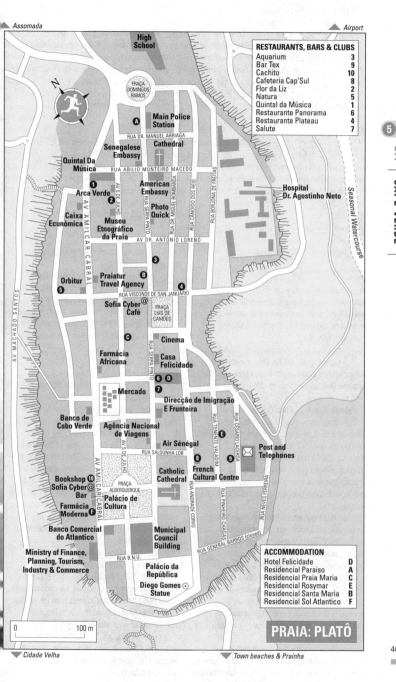

High School

PRAÇA DOMINGOS RAMOS

RESTAURANTS, BARS & CLUBS

Aquarium	3
Bar Tex	9
Cachito	10
Cafeteria Cap'Sul	8
Flor da Liz	2
Natura	5
Quintal da Música	1
Restaurante Panorama	6
Restaurante Plateau	4
Salute	7

A Main Police Station

RUA DR. MANUEL ARRIAGA

Senegalese Embassy

Cathedral

Quintal Da Música

RUA ABILIO MONTEIRO MACEDO

1 Arca Verde
2

American Embassy

Hospital Dr. Agostinho Neto

Caixa Económica

Museu Etnográfico da Praia

Photo Quick

AV DR. ANTONIO LORENO

Orbitur
5

3

Praiatur Travel Agency **B**

4

RUA VISCONDE DE SAN JANUARIO

Sofia Cyber@ Café

PRAÇA LUIS DE CAMÕES

C

Cinema

Farmácia Africana

Casa Felicidade

6 D

7

Mercado

Direcção de Imigração E Frunteira

Banco de Cabo Verde

Agência Nacional de Viagens

Air Sénégal

E

Post and Telephones

RUA SALDUNHA LOB

8

9

Bookshop 10

Sofia Cyber@ Bar

PRAÇA ALBERQUERQUE

Catholic Cathedral

French Cultural Centre

Farmácia Moderna F

Palácio de Cultura

Banco Comercial do Atlantico

Municipal Council Building

Ministry of Finance, Planning, Tourism, Industry & Commerce

RUA B.N.U.

RUA GENERAL BARROS (closed)

Palácio da República

Diego Gomes Statue

ACCOMMODATION

Hotel Felicidade	D
Residencial Paraiso	A
Residencial Praia Maria	C
Residencial Rosymar	E
Residencial Santa Maria	B
Residencial Sol Atlantico	F

0   100 m

PRAIA: PLATÔ

Seasonal Watercourse

AV AMILCAR CABRAL

AV MACHADO SANTOS

AV 5 DE JULHO

RUA SERPA PINTO

RUA CANDIDO DOS REIS

RUA BORJONA DE FRETAS

RUA DR. MIGUEL BOMBARDA

RUA TENENTE VALADIM

RUA CÉSARIO LACERDA

RUA PINHEIRO CHAGAS

RUA NEVES FERREIRA

RUA ANDRADE CORVO

salvaged by Portuguese firm Arqueonautus Worldwide (ⓦ www.arq.de describes their work) from shipwrecks littering the seabed around Cape Verde.

Despite the name Praia (meaning **beach**), all the town's coves are filthy and unappealing. The grey strip beneath where the road snakes off the end of the Platô – **Praia Gamboa** – is the site of a music festival in May (worth checking out if you're in Praia at the right time), but is more commonly used by exercising soldiers, and the pair of small crescents on either side of the *Hotel Praiamar*'s peninsula are nothing special. You'll do much better, if you can find transport, going out to São Francisco, 13km east of Praia (see p.470).

Eating

Praia has a decent variety of **restaurants** ranging from workaday eating-house *casas de pasto* (CV$400–600) to more upmarket places (from CV$1000). The cheapest places are mostly away from the Platô area. Note that many establishments close on Sunday. If you want to save money, use the market or one of the **supermarkets** and put together your own picnics: the Supermercado Felicidade in Achada Sto António is the biggest shop in Cape Verde, and there's a small branch next to the *Hotel Felicidade* on the plateau. The friendly Parisienne bakery at the northern end of the plateau is a good place to stock up on cakes.

Restaurants and cafés

Platô

Aquarium Rua Serpa Pinto ☎ 261.32.38. Pleasant and lively place to eat and drink, with a daily set menu for CV$300 and inexpensive sandwiches, omelettes and *cachupa*. The decor includes, of course, a fish tank.

Cachito Praça Albuquerque, Av Amílcar Cabral ☎ 261.92.78. Chic, friendly and funky little café with great, freshly brewed coffee, draught beer, and a range of cakes and savoury snacks.

Cafeteria Cap'Sul Centro Cultural Francês, Rua Andrade Corvo (Mon 2.30–7pm, Tues–Fri 9am–noon & 2.30–7pm, Sat 10am–1pm). Pleasant outdoor retreat.

Flor da Liz 43 Rua 5 de Julho ☎ 261.25.98. An unassuming place, serving large helpings of freshly prepared food from a limited menu. Good value, with main courses in the CV$600–700 range.

Natura Rua Visconde de San Januário. Snug and bright little pine-furnished café connected to the health-food shop of the same name and serving tasty snacks.

Panorama Rua Serpa Pinto, on the *Hotel Felicidade* rooftop ☎ 261.41.00 (daily except Sun 11am–3pm & 7pm–12.30am). Though its lofty position is perhaps the main attraction, this rather upmarket place does the most delicious omelettes in Cape Verde, cooked to perfection and beautifully presented.

Plateau Rua Cândido dos Reis ☎ 261.32.54. Small, smart eating place that's a popular venue for business lunches, with daily Cape Verdean specials

such as *feijoada* and *cachupa* at surprisingly reasonable prices.

Quintal da Música Av Amílcar Cabral ☎ 261.72.82. This unmissable venue is a performance venue, restaurant, bar, arts centre and recording studio rolled into one – it serves lunch and is the best place in the capital to catch live Cape Verdean music in the evenings (from 8pm Tues–Sat).

Elsewhere in Praia

Agua Na Boca Rua Union Europa, Achada Sto António ☎ 262.60.28. Up next to the *Hotel América*, this pleasant, pastel-shaded restaurant offers a very respectable range of pasta dishes alongside the usual fish and meat choices.

Bar-Restaurante A Falésia Rua 19 de Maio, Prainha district ☎ 261.77.76. The best reason to visit this friendly clifftop restaurant is to take a table on the terrace, which has great sea views.

Bar-Restaurante Punta d'Incontro Av Cidade de Lisboa, west of the Platô ☎ 261.70.90 (evenings from 7pm). Popular with hip locals, this Italian establishment does quality pizza and exquisite Catalan-style desserts, and there's a pleasant thatched-roof terrace on which to enjoy them.

Cermar Gamboa Chã d'Areia district ☎ 991.21.24 (daily noon–5pm & 7pm till late). Award-winning restaurant, very popular with well-heeled families and tourists from the nearby hotels. Expensive, but worth it, with Brazilian specialities at weekends.

Restaurante O Poeta Achada Sto António ☎ 261.38.00. Bland, upmarket establishment with reasonable international-style food. The sea views are undeniably good.

Drinking and nightlife

At nights the Platô is all but deserted by about 10pm, when even the kiosks in the *praça* are stacking up their chairs and battening down their hatches, and only the wonderful **Quintal da Música** (see above) keeps the flag flying. The *praça* is a little livelier earlier in the evening, especially on Sunday evenings when the brass band occasionally fires up.

The **nightclub** scene is limited: none have opened in the restrictive streets of the Platô, though there are a number of friendly **bars** here. Clubs are mostly scattered across the suburbs and never get going until around midnight. Music is generally a sweaty mixture of chart-topping European and American sounds and Cape Verdean *coladeira* and *funana* dance styles. Weekend admission charges are pretty uniform at CV$500.

Bars

Apart Hotel Holanda Achado Sto António. The vintage bar here, frequented by expats and worldly locals, has long played host to up-and-coming local musicians.

Aquárium Rua Serpa Pinto, Platô (Mon–Sat 7am–11pm). Friendly atmosphere, beer on tap and English-speaking boss.

Bar Tex unmarked entrance on Rua Cesário Lacerda, Platô, opposite the post office (nightly except Sun). Great little subterranean bolt-hole where local musicians often take to the tiny stage.

Restaurante O Poeta Achada Sto António ☎261.38.00. A better place to drink than eat, with a pleasant bar with sea views.

Salute Rua Serpa Pinto (Mon–Fri 8.30am–12.30pm & 3–7pm, Sat 9am–1pm). Pleasant wine bar with an old-fashioned, Mediterranean atmosphere, and distinctly odd hours.

Clubs

Bomba H On the road to Cidade Velha, about 1km from the intersection where the Cidade Velha *aluguers* ply their trade. The hippest place in Praia, with a playlist geared towards younger clubbers.

Tabanka Mar Prainha district. Funky terrace cocktail bar with sea views. Gets steamy at night when there's live music from local bands and visiting *fado* singers.

Zero Horas Achada Grande, between the port and the airport. An open-air affair with perhaps the most cosmopolitan musical mix of any of Praia's big clubs.

Listings

Airlines TACV, airport ☎260.88.88; Air Sénégal, Av Amílcar Cabral, Platô ☎261.75.29; TAP Air Portugal, airport ☎261.58.26.

Banks Branches of Banco Comercial do Atlântico, the national Banco de Cabo Verde and BCN (Banco Caboverdiano de Negócios) are all situated on Av Amílcar Cabral. Banco Interatlântico have a couple of branches on either side of *Hotel América* up in Achada Sto António.

Bookshop The best – nearly the only – one is the Instituto da Biblioteca Nacional on Av Amílcar Cabral, Platô, under the *Sofia Cyber Bar* (together, they make up the *Palácio da Cultura*) which has a limited stock of books in Portuguese. There are a few imported publications but nothing in English.

Car rental Alucar, Chã d'Areia, south of the plateau (☎261.45.20), is the largest local firm; Hertz operate from the airport (☎261.28.58 ✉hertz-praia@cvtelecom.cv), as do Avis (☎993.83.24). All offer reasonable Japanese saloons for between CV$4000 and CV$7000 per day, inclusive of 80–100km travel. Taxis can be rented by the hour for around CV$1000.

CDs Head for the Instituto da Biblioteca Nacional (see above) where you'll find a good stock of Cape Verdean sounds as well as a decent Brazilian selection.

Cultural centres The Centro Cultural Francês is at Rua Andrade Corvo, Platô (Mon 2.30–7pm, Tues–Fri 9am–7pm, Sat 10am–1pm; ☎261.11.96 ✉www.ccfpraia.com). They have a French-language library and run a programme of film nights, exhibitions and concerts. Next to the Portuguese embassy, the Portuguese Cultural Centre at Achada Sto António (Mon–Fri 9am–noon & 2–6pm; ☎262.30.30 ✉cult.portugues@cvtelecom.cv) also has a library and screens Portuguese films.

Embassies and consulates Several consuls, including the UK Honorary Consul, are based in Mindelo (see p.489). In Praia, the French (☎261.55.91) and German (☎262.31.00) embassies are located together in Prainha (Mon–Fri 8.15–11am & 2.30–3.15pm); the French embassy issues visas for Burkina, Côte d'Ivoire, Mauritania and Togo. The American embassy is at 6 Rua Abilio Monteiro Macedo, Platô (Mon–Sat 8am–5pm; ☎261.56.16), and is generally helpful to Anglophone travellers. Senegal also has an embassy at Rua Abilio Monteiro Macedo, Platô (Mon–Fri 8.30am–12.30pm & 2.30–4.30pm; ☎261.56.21).

Hospitals The Agostinho Neto Hospital at the northern edge of the plateau (☎261.24.62) is adequately equipped.

Internet access The arty *Sofia Cyber Bar*, above the Instituto da Biblioteca Nacional on Av Amílcar Cabral, and their stylish branch on Rua Serpa Pinto have a good number of computers with Internet access for CV$180 per hour; both places also serve a range of drinks. There's also an Internet café and Wi-Fi hotspot in the airport terminal.

Pharmacies Farmácia Moderna and Farmácia Africana, on Av Amílcar Cabral, Platô, are both well-stocked.

Post and telephones The post office on Rua Cesário Lacerda, Platô (Mon–Fri 8am–noon & 2–5.30pm; ☎61.10.49), has an express service if you need to rush a letter back home, with collections on Mon, Wed and Fri. Poste restante is available and there's also a public telephone service in the same building.

Travel agents Travel agents such as Cabetur, 4 Rua Serpa Pinto, Platô (☎261.55.11), Orbitur, 9 Rua Candido Reis, Platô (☎261.57.37), and Praiatur, Av Amílcar Cabral, Platô (☎261.57.46), tend to specialize in Brazilian package holidays for local residents, although they can organize flights, accommodation and excursions around Santiago for foreign visitors.

Visa extensions Direcção de Imigração e Fronteira on Rua Serpa Pinto (☎261.18.45).

Around Praia

All the following trips from Praia are feasible within a day, or even half a day if you're pressed for time. The **São Francisco** area of beaches northeast of Praia has been earmarked as a tourism development zone. West of Praia, **Cidade Velha** is just about Cape Verde's only historical site and, while the ruins are interesting in their own right, the old village streets are among the prettiest in Cape Verde.

São Domingos

There's no great reason to visit **SÃO DOMINGOS**, about 20km north of Praia, but it's worth it for the pretty **journey** – only half an hour from Praia by Hiace – which takes you rapidly from the trashy outskirts of the capital into the heartland of rural Santiago. The minibus plunges into deep valleys where straight-backed women grind corn with a boulder against a flat rock (a *pilão*), pigs root at the roadside, and children toting satchels walk to school. São Domingos itself is one of the earliest settlements on the island, over 450 years old; its church has a famous boat-shaped pulpit. Drake ventured this far inland in 1585 and, finding the settlement abandoned, thought better of continuing into the wild interior. On the way into town from Praia, there's a craft sales co-operative on the right, with a limited selection of pottery, weaving and ornaments, at sensible prices. There's also a *pensão*, *El Dourado*, which has a couple of simple guest rooms (☎268.18.65 ●) and a restaurant using homegrown produce.

São Francisco beaches

The string of coves at **SÃO FRANCISCO**, about 13km northeast of Praia, is worth the effort required to get there, to escape the unsavoury pollution and occasional hassles at the town beaches. There's no scheduled transport, but hiring a taxi from Praia, allowing you two hours at the beach before returning, will cost around CV$3000. Otherwise, head in the direction of the old airport, turn left just over the bridge, walk through the *bairro* and try hitching – which is most likely to be successful on a Saturday or Sunday morning. The track from Praia has been scraped across the island's steep and rocky southern corner, and tips you out onto a flat sandy plain by the sea, where there are several **beaches** to choose from. The first you reach on the track is the biggest, dotted with palms and a couple of villas built further back, but the furthest to the south is the best, with steps for the arthritic ex-President Pereira to climb down for his swims. There's clean sand and good waves, though take food and drink, as there's nothing at the beach.

Cidade Velha

Heading west out of town for 10km in the opposite direction brings you to the old capital of the islands – **Ribeira Grande** – now known simply as **CIDADE VELHA**, "Old City". After the hot, dry moors on the way from Praia, you round the last bend and the village is down below. The setting is everything – a living, moving sea, awash with foam, thundering against the black crags.

Nowadays Cidade Velha is a village of fishing people and farmers living among the ruins of sixteenth- and seventeenth-century Portugal. As one bit of local tourist literature pointed out a few years back: "One can find valuable patrimonial witnesses still in ruins, thus deserving restoration, good keeping and consolidation." Fortunately, it looks as if this sage advice is finally being heeded. The ruins of the cathedral are now home to archeologists and restorers – as well as the occasional tourist – while Cidade Velha itself is about to be designated a UNESCO World Heritage site.

Down in the town *praça* stands Cidade Velha's most famous relic, the **pelourinho** or pillory, where captives were shackled on display. The most notable building is the **cathedral**, finished in 1693, a century and a half after the foundation of the diocese; it's located on the hillside to the right as you arrive from Praia. The large fleet of red fishing boats on the beach indicates more activity than you'd at first think, though many young people have moved to Praia. Today the village is increasingly popular with both Cape Verdean and foreign tourists, most of whom seem to retire to the thatch-roofed beach bar after a hard day's sightseeing. Should you wander into the tiny "tourist office" cum craft shop off the main square in fruitless search of glossy brochures, you may well find yourself pleasantly waylaid with a game of *ouril* and a few glasses of *grogue*.

It's worth going down to the *ribeira* west of town and up the other side, through cane and corn and under mango trees, to further, less explored ruins – the church of **Nossa Senhora do Rosário** which served as a cathedral in miniature when the diocese was first created, and the Capuchin **Monastery of São Francisco** higher up the valley, neither of which should take more than twenty minutes to reach on foot. Once up there, you can admire the palm-filled valley and muse on what five

---

The rise and fall of Ribeira Grande

Ribeira Grande was the site of the **first Portuguese base** in Africa, founded to create a slave-trading entrepôt, selling labour to the Spanish West Indies. With a relatively good anchorage (there was nothing any safer in Madeira or the Azores), Ribeira Grande rapidly became the main mid-Atlantic victualling point for European merchant vessels in the sixteenth century. The *ribeira* almost never dried up and was dammed at its mouth to provide a permanent pool of **fresh water**. The town became a "city" in 1533 when a papal bull made it the seat of a diocese extending along half the West African coast.

In Atlantic trading circles Ribeira Grande's reputation soon spread. The English sea dog **Sir Francis Drake** caught the scent in 1585 and attacked the settlement with a force of a thousand. The well-planned assault was more than just piracy – the union of Spain and Portugal meant that Cape Verde was considered enemy territory by the English. Drake landed at Praia to sneak overland and attack Ribeira Grande from behind, only to find the town deserted: the inhabitants had sensibly fled inland. Drake's crew stayed a fortnight, plundering what little there was and foraying into the interior without reward. One of the attacking force was killed and mutilated by African slaves and Drake torched Ribeira Grande in reprisal, sparing only the hospital – the Casa Misericorde – whose ruins are still visible to the right as you descend into the centre of the present-day village.

Ribeira Grande's eventual defeat by a French force in 1712 led to a rethink on the part of the Portuguese and the more considered development of the new capital of Praia. The cathedral was already falling apart by 1735 and, when a new bishop was appointed in 1754, he quickly left Santiago and spent the rest of his life on Santo Antão.

centuries of Portuguese rule have brought, and taken from, the islands. When the first buildings were put up the treeless scene must have had much the barren cast of a tropical Iona: all the trees have been established since that time. Today, you're likely to come across sugar-cane presses and *grogue* stills as you climb through the jungly allotments – the aroma is unmissable.

Alternatively, hike back up the road into town from Praia and cut back to the left, to look over the extensive remains of the **Fortaleza Real de São Filipe** (CV$200), which dominates the whole of Cidade Velha from on high. The fort has weathered the years incredibly well and offers stunning views of the *ribeira* and, behind, of the Serra do Pico do Santo António.

Practicalities
Aluguers from Praia leave regularly from Sucupira (Praia's main general-purpose market place) and from the parking area in Terra Branca, southwest of the Platô. Getting back to Praia can be a little problematic, though you can easily pass the time waiting for the next *aluguer* by drinking *grogue* with the elders down in one of the village stores. If you want to **stay** the night, there are a couple of rather overpriced B&B rooms for rent in one of the old thatched cottages on Rua Banana. Ask in the craft shop or just ask around for the owner, Abel Borges (☎267.13.74 ✆actal7 @hotmail.com ➍). An attractive alternative, on the rocky coast just west of town, is *Por do Sol* (☎267.16.22 ✆axa@cvtelecom.cv ➎), a guesthouse with a pool.

North and east Santiago
The main reason to go north is to visit **Tarrafal**, a beautiful fishing village that makes an ideal spot to rest up for a few days. It's at the opposite end of Santiago from Praia, and there are two different minibus routes that go there – one over the rugged spine of the island, the other along the indented east coast. The journey can make a very satisfying round trip.

The mountain route
The mountain route goes straight across an unexpectedly fairy-tale interior – peaks and rocky needles, soaring valleys, narrow terraces and ridges – a fine journey, especially during or after the rains. There are steep climbs and some great views before Assomada, then higher passes in the Malagueta range, rising to over 1300m. High in the hills near **São Domingos** in the hamlet of **RUI VAZ** there's **a great place to stay**, ⚎ Quinta da Montanha (☎268.50.02 ✆quintamontanha @cvtelecom.cv ➎), a comfortable rural *pousada* close to some thrilling hiking trails.

The highest point of the island, the 1394-metre Pico do Santo António – with some of the few monkeys in Cape Verde on its slopes – rises above the town of **São Jorge dos Orgãos**, a few kilometres south of the main road.

Shortly before you reach Assomada from the south, you come to the small town of **PICOS** perched on a crag on the right, next to a huge basaltic outcrop looking out over a wide, deep valley. In season, blooms of jacaranda and frangipani bubble around the small *praça* and church. The town is the site of the INIDA, the National Institute of Agrarian Research and Development, which has a *miradouro* (panoramic viewpoint) overlooking the plantations, and a flourishing botanical garden where you can see Cape Verdean flora and birdlife.

Assomada
ASSOMADA, also known as Vila de Santa Catarina, is the second largest town on the island. This is a lively place by Cape Verdean standards, with interesting old architecture, a large market, a small museum – the **Museu da Tabanka** (Mon–Sat 10am–7pm; ⓦwww.ic.cv/museu-tabanca.html) – and its famous *tabanka* carnival each May. On market days (Wed & Sat) Assomada can be very hot and hectic, not the kind of place you want to be carrying heavy or bulky baggage around between bus rides.

If you have only an hour or two, take a short walk north out of town and a turning right, then a steep path down into the *ribeira* to see what must be a contender for the biggest **silk-cotton tree** in the world (though it's always referred to locally as a "baobab"); ask for **BOA ENTRADA**, the neighbouring village, tucked in the *ribeira*. You can't fail to see the tree standing on the slope across the valley: it's a monster. The trunk – more than thirty metres round at the base – is a maze of contorted buttresses, and it would stand out anywhere, but in Cape Verde, land of limited leafiness, it's a fantastic sight. The tree must be as old as the first generation of settlers. In 1855, according to a Reverend Thomas, chaplain to the African Squadron of the US Navy, it was "forty feet in circumference" and had been "standing where it now stands when the island was first discovered".

There's no shortage of **accommodation** options in Assomada. The obvious choice, and good value, is the smart, modern and central *Hotel Avenida* on Avenida de Libertade (℡265.34.62 Ⓔhotelavenida@hotmail.com ⓸), but if you're on a budget it's worth trying *Asabranca* (℡265.23.72 ⓷). For snacks, *Café Central* off the main square is a cool retreat offering quality coffee, ice cream and cakes. Internet access – and quite possibly Cape Verde's biggest pool table – is available at the improbably named *Ciber Buggs Bilhar*, five minutes' walk from the main square on the main road out of town.

The east coast route

Heading north by the **east coast route**, you follow the same road out of Praia as for the mountain route, then cut right at the Ribeirão Chiqueiro junction, with the village of **PRAIA BAIXO** 7km away on the coast. There is direct transport to Praia Baixo from Praia's Sucupira depot, but you're only likely to be the only visitor if you come outside the weekend. The village is reached down a long, low *ribeira* of partially deserted smallholdings, the road to it passing over concrete flood-crossings. The beach is safe, in a deep, sheltered bay, with beach shades on the sands, one or two holiday villas behind, and at least one functioning beach-bar. Men do some fishing by boat, but it's very quiet and it all has a rather depressing air.

The first village you come to on the main road is **PEDRA BADEJO**, with a magnificent **coconut** grove marking the entrance to the settlement and gigantic bananas on sale – if you're lucky. You can see *pedreiros* making cobbles here, each mason shaded under a banana leaf on the clifftop. The atmosphere is rather run-down, but there are good beaches and caves nearby, and a few places to stay including *Tiara* (℡269.18.19 ⓸), a strange, almost apocalyptic-looking concrete block looking out to sea at the edge of town, with reasonable, pine-furnished rooms, a restaurant and even a disco. The most popular spot for a drink is the crumbling but well-located *Falucho*, a terrace bar built over the sea wall. Out of town, there's an interesting coastal hideaway with good eco-credentials at **ACHADA FAZENDO**, 4km from Pedra Badejo – *Pousada Mariberto* (℡269.19.00 Ⓦwww.hotelmariberto.com ⓺). This place offers simple but comfortable rooms, with French cuisine to order, and the owners are building a seawater swimming pool.

CALHETA DE SÃO MIGUEL, the next stop, has a big old church on the hilltop. The dependence on rainfall in the Cape Verdes comes home to you as the road repeatedly drops to cross stony *ribeiras* where women wash clothes in the narrow streams: when water is about, the flanks of the gulches are dense with crops – banana, papaya, cane and cassava – and heavy rains can also bring floods that smash the cobbles in many places.

Tarrafal

TARRAFAL doesn't look much at first. You have to go right through the small town to discover the wonderful, clean white **beach** below its gentle cliffs. Once the site of the country's main political prison under the Portuguese, Tarrafal's claim to fame nowadays is this beach. The town has an attractive hibiscus-filled *praça* with church and marketplace set around. There are palms and discreet beach houses to one side and a working, fishing-beach atmosphere on the other. Once installed in Tarrafal it's easy to pass a few days – or even much longer – swimming and lounging, drinking cold beers, eating slabs of fresh tuna and watching the fishing boats coming in and the children playing. Except at weekends, when Cape Verdean tourists and expatriate beach-hunters target it, Tarrafal is fairly peaceful, and with the mountainous interior of the island looming behind, the place can seem incredibly isolated. Yet a boy shooting down the cobbled hill on his shiny new American mountain bike is a reminder of close and important ties with the outside world.

If you fancy something more active than sunbathing, try the dive centre, Blue Adventure (☎266.18.80), right on the beach. Walk south and you come to **further beaches** – of black sand – and more coconuts. Head north and a fine **coastal path** leads up over the cliffs above the crashing surf for as far as you like, with terrific views. There are some tiny coves along here, with great, natural swimming pools.

In stark contrast is the former prison camp just outside town. Now a **museum** (daily 7am–6pm; CV\$100), this intimidating place was used to incarcerate Portuguese communists during the 1940s, and was reopened by the Portuguese authorities in the 1960s to house prisoners from the wars of independence in the various African colonies. Nowadays the only inmates are a few wandering goats, although the ruined barracks and solitary-confinement tanks retain an oppressive atmosphere. A chalet has been built outside the perimeter walls to house a fascinating collection of documents and photographs (including a great shot of the prisoners rushing ecstatically towards their families on the day of the camp's liberation). To reach the museum, head out of town on the Assomada road for about 2km and you'll see the white-stone entry portal on your right.

Practicalities

The town's pleasant *praça* has a church and marketplace, together with a branch of the Banco Comercial do Atlântico and a **post office**. **Accommodation** is easily arranged. Sleepy but appealing *Baía Verde* has well-equipped, palm-shaded chalets right on the beach (☎266.11.28 ✉baiaverde@cvtelecom.cv ❺) while the nearby *Hotel Tarrafal* (☎266.17.85 ✉htltarrafal@cvtelecom.cv ❼) is more upmarket, and the only place with a pool. The *Solmarina* (☎266.12.19 ❹) overlooks the fishing boats on the shore; it's the cheapest option close to the beach, but it has seen better days. In town itself, among a number of *pensões*, your best bet is the bright and clean *Tátá* (☎266.11.25 ❸).

At the market, the *Casa de Pasto Sopa de Pedra* and *Graciosa* are cheap, basic places to **eat**. For a leisurely lunch or dinner, you might want to try the pleasant but pricey *Baía Verde*, a terrace restaurant overlooking the beach and the hotel of the same name.

Fogo

The first impression of **Fogo** is of its tremendous mass – a brooding volcanic cone rising forbiddingly nearly 3000m out of the sea, its steep peaks soaring above the clouds. Flying from Praia, sit on the right of the plane for the best views. The arrival at the capital **São Filipe**, on the west coast, involves the plane dipping low over the rough ground to touch the runway, perched high on the dunnish cliffs. Below the airport, a striking beach of baking black sand drops straight into an ultramarine sea. If you arrive by ferry, you dock at the tiny port of **Vale dos Cavaleiros**, 3km north of São Filipe.

Although all the islands have their own personalities, it's Fogo which stands out as the great character of the Cape Verdes – it's impossible to forget you're on a **volcano** here. Fogo – which means "fire" – last had an eruption in 1995, when deluges of molten lava streamed into the main caldera, and four thousand people were evacuated. On the west side of the island, the land is gentler, with better soil,

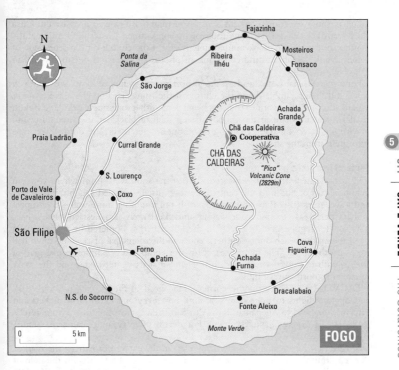

low trees, farms and plantations. The ancient volcanic base in this district is undisturbed by fresh eruptions and after rain it's often cloaked beneath a pastoral blanket of wild flowers.

Transport on Fogo depends on *aluguers* and the odd private vehicle; the southern road between São Filipe and Mosteiros in the northeast is the only one on which there's any real traffic. People on Fogo are often startlingly kind, accommodating hikers, showing you directions miles out of their way and doing everything possible to help.

São Filipe and around

SÃO FILIPE has an orderly civility which sits oddly with its steeply sloping clifftop location, high above the black beach. The streets link a number of small squares and gardens and a promenade along the cliffs, while a number of the town's pretty *sobrados* (colonial houses) have been exquisitely restored to their former glory. Others lie in various states of disrepair but the architecture is never less than captivating, making São Filipe one of Cape Verde's most attractive towns.

Although it has an unhurried bustle during the day, after dark it can be very quiet. All in all, however, it's a significant improvement on the 1930s when an English visitor, Archibald Lyall, reported a community in the grip of diabolical poverty, isolated from Praia, let alone Lisbon, and totally without electricity or transport – small, shaggy horses were the only way to get about.

The town and around

There's little to do around town, but strolling through the cobbled streets has its own quiet satisfaction: there are several small *praças* to sit in, while the tiny **market**, with

475

an all-purpose selection, is worth a visit. You might also care to drop by the **Casa da Memória** (Wed–Fri 10am–noon or by appointment), a restored nineteenth-century house on the block immediately north of the church on the south side of town; it holds an interesting collection of photos and artefacts documenting Saõ Filipe's history.

For a recreational walk, head up the airport road a couple of kilometres south of town and then scramble down the cliffs, past the ruins of a tiny church to a *ribeira*, where you can join a path to the beach and some fish-processing works. The **beach** itself is great if you're in the mood: a steep shelf of black sand – ferociously hot – with big waves breaking, seemingly without any fetch, directly onto it. You dive into them from the shore.

Practicalities

The town's small **airport** is located 2km to the southwest, from where you can get an *aluguer* or taxi into the centre. The town itself – divided roughly into upper and lower parts (Bila Riba and Bila Baxo) by an imposing stone wall – is compact and it's fairly easy to find your way around the largely nameless cobbled streets. The small, irregular grid of streets in the lower part is bordered by a promenade overlooking the beach on its southern end, and the municipal market and town hall on its northern side. The upper part of town is composed of a more regular grid of streets, with the town's main park (the *pracinha*) at its western edge and the main square at its northeastern tip.

TACV have an office on the corner at the head of the *pracinha* (℡281.17.01), and operate flights to Praia (daily; 30min). For **ferry** and **catamaran** tickets and information, head to Agenamar, Rua Alto São Pedro, across the square from TACV (℡281.10.12 ✉peres@cvtelecom.cv). For details of ferry and catamaran sailings, see p.440.

Aluguers use a small, mercifully shady *praça* in the centre of town, by the market. For **car rental**, try Discount Auto Rent-a-Car (℡281.14.80) or enlist the help of Qualitur, Fogo's friendly and efficient tourist agency (Rua do Hospital; ℡281.10.89 ⟳www.qualitur.cv), who also arrange volcano trips, outdoor-activity excursions and the like.

There's a branch of Banco Comercial do Atlântico on Rua do Hospital (Mon–Fri 8am–3pm). The **post office** on the main square keeps similar hours to the bank. For **Internet** access, try Eduteca Alf (Mon–Fri 8am–8.30pm, Sat 8am–2pm) on the same block as TACV, or Megabyte (Mon–Fri 8am–10.30pm), across the square from the post office.

Accommodation

São Filipe has a decent range of rooms and restaurants, most of them modestly priced.

Casa Renate opposite the cathedral on Baixo da Igreja ℡281.25.18 ✉renatefogo@hotmail.com. Two beautiful one-bedroom apartments let out by a friendly German woman, Renate. Both are en suite, tasteful and modern with a communal terrace, while the larger one has a small kitchen – great value for money. You can normally get hold of Renate in *O Bistro* (see below), which she also owns. ❹ & ❺

Pensão Fatima Rua São Filipe, near the cathedral ℡281.13.59. Decent place with en-suite rooms and a rooftop terrace. ❹

Pensão Las Vegas Achada Pato ℡281.12.23. Pleasant, light and airy, with a roof terrace, restaurant and ice-cream parlour. The en-suite rooms come with a/c, TV and fridge. ❹

Pensão Open Sky off the main square ℡281.27.26 ✉majortelo@yahoo.com. Popular place with decent, well-equipped rooms, a roof terrace and a restaurant. ❹

Pousada Bela Vista Achada Pato, near the TACV office ℡281.17.34. This offers good value for money with clean, very pleasant en-suite rooms in a graceful, atmospheric *sobrado* (colonial building) on a quiet square. ❹

Xaguate on the northwestern edge of town on the way out to the port ℡281.12.22 ✉hotelxaguate@yahoo.com.

Once the crumbling, sole hotel in São Filipe, a thorough renovation has completely transformed the *Xaguate* into a smart modern four-star commanding the best location in town, with fantastic views across to Brava. Although the rooms feel a little cramped and the restaurant gets mixed reports, it's a stylish option with a great pool terrace. ⑧

Eating, drinking and nightlife

Katen Tádju Achada Pato, across from the *Pensão Las Vegas* ☏ 281.21.75. The *boite* (club) kicks in on Fri & Sat nights and special occasions, while the rooftop bar/café is open daily 7am–11pm for beers, wine, *grogue* and a small range of snacks.

O Bistro in the centre of town ☏ 281.25.18 (daily until late, breakfast from 7am and dinner from 5pm). Brightly painted, slightly arty little German-run restaurant (co-owned with *Casa Renate*), with a great terrace. As well as meat and fish dishes there are simple but tasty options for vegetarians who've overdosed on omelettes – the soups are especially recommended (try the pumpkin).

Restaurante Seafood on the lower side of town ☏ 281.26.24. Located in a prime position above the beach, this is a popular place with good lobster at a decent price and a fine terrace.

Tropical Club near the *Pensão Las Vegas* ☏ 281.21.61. A bar-restaurant rather than a club, popular as an evening meeting place where people gather to enjoy beautifully cooked local fish or beer and cocktails in the leafy courtyard garden. There's live music on Fri.

Exploring the volcano

The **volcano** is a dominant and potentially time-filling lure. At the caldera rim you may be lucky and have the whole eight-kilometre-wide bowl of the Chã das Caldeiras ("Field of Boilers") – the huge **collapsed crater** that was created by the island's formative eruption – spread clearly before you, or it may be blotted out by thick cloud. It's an extraordinary, unearthly, black-lava landscape and nothing can quite prepare you for the strange thrill of witnessing it for the first time, even if the scanty vineyards and other cultivation soften it a little. There are in fact a number of families on the upper reaches of the road to the crater who brew their own **wine**, and who will be only too glad to offer a tasting.

The cobbled road winds through the crater like a causeway. The small, oblong houses are built of lava stone and crouch low against the ground. It's hard to imagine what keeps people here, or how they make ends meet in this inhospitable environment, but you'll see a variety of livestock, and the vineyards are relatively successful. Many families in this district trace their descent from a **Duc de Montrond** who is said to have fled France in the nineteenth century after a duel – and thoughtfully brought some vines with him. You may well find the people of the crater among the friendliest and kindest in Cape Verde, in stark contrast with the harshness of the landscape and despite their obvious grinding poverty.

The Pico de Fogo

The moonscape of lava and scattered mini-craters is dramatically surmounted by the main cone, the **Pico de Fogo**, which rises in a cindery, pyramid-shaped heap on the east side, about a thousand metres above the caldera floor. This cone has been dormant since the eighteenth century, but volcanic activity continues in a big way deep below the surface and, once every few decades, as in 1995, new "mini-cones" are blown up within the caldera. You may be reassured to know that vulcanologists monitor the activity and local people now get good warning of impending eruptions.

To **climb** the 2829-metre-high Pico, you should aim to make an early start. If you set off much after 7am, you'll find you're still out there in the midday sun, instead of back down in the village having a celebratory drink. It's an exhausting three-to-four hour scramble to the summit, up a two-steps-forward-one-step-back slope of fine volcanic scree. There are several guides in the village who will happily accompany you for around CV$2500 – without one of them you won't easily find the best route, which changes sporadically. Companions are a good idea, anyway, as a fall in a remote place like this can be dangerous. When you reach the top, don't be tempted to try to ascend to the very highest point – it's an unstable and tricky little climb which has resulted in accidents in the past. There are routes down into the deep, red and yellow, egg-cup-shaped crater of the peak itself. But few people feel like tackling them at this stage in the day – it's much more tempting just to sit and absorb the views, especially down towards the eastern side of the island. Here, tens of thousands of years ago, during a heightened period of seismic activity, a cataclysmic landslide removed a huge part of the eastern side of the island, taking the original crater edge with it into the Atlantic and leaving the crater exposed on its eastern flank.

Coming down, in contrast to the climb, is like a free fairground ride, as you simply gallop down through the scree of the forty-degree slope in big bounds, and reach the floor of the caldera in little over an hour.

Caldera practicalities

It can be hard to reach the caldera if you try to set off at the wrong time of day. You can take a vehicle from São Filipe to the village of **CHÃ DAS CALDEIRAS**. There are **aluguers** most mornings (2hr; about CV$500) but they are not super-abundant. If you ask taxi drivers about hiring a *particular* you'll usually get quoted at least CV$4000 and as much as CV$6000 for the one-hour-plus drive straight there. If you've got the time, an alternative plan would be simply to set off with water and supplies and **walk up**. The main staging post in this case is the straggling village of **ACHADA FURNA** on the south side of the caldera, about 15km from São Filipe. From here, the caldera rim is about 6km as the crow flies, but it's a steep climb and a good three-hour hike up the road that twists for 9km up the mountainside. Before you set off from São Filipe, make sure you have adequate snacks and drinking water. And if you plan to climb the peak itself, it's best to have hiking boots.

When arriving in Chã das Caldeiras, arrange to be dropped at the house of a guide in the first part of the village; most *aluguer* and taxi drivers will do this anyway. The only formal **accommodation** in the village is 🏠 *Pousada Pedra Brabo* (☎282.15.21 ✉pedrabrabo@cvtelecom.cv ❹), a basic guesthouse run by a hospitable Frenchman and tastefully constructed, partly from local materials. You could quite easily spend a few days here, sunning yourself in the courtyard and marvelling at the Pico looming up behind the walls. Delicious meals are also available and breakfast is included in the price. Alternatively, you can go local and opt for dinner, bed and breakfast in a private house; the going rate is CV$1500 and you can fix this up at the Cooperativa (see below). While facilities are basic, you'll be made very welcome; more importantly, you'll be contributing towards a much-needed source of income for the villagers. You could also pick a spot anywhere on the black cinders and camp, but you should count on bringing your **food** requirements with you – there are no real shops in the caldera.

Even if you aren't organizing a homestay, at some point during your visit you should pop into the **Cooperativa**, the community's principal social venue, where you can buy bottles of the fearsomely robust local red, plus mouthwateringly fresh goat's cheese and basic provisions. You'll also be able to buy the ubiquitous model houses which the locals fashion from volcanic rock, matchsticks and straw; they make great presents. It's surprising how often the Cooperativa **band** sets up for a Cape Verdean jam – guitar, violin, *cavaquinho*, keyboard, scraper – around the bar. If you are lucky enough to hear music up here, it will be the rawest, most visceral and emotional you'll hear anywhere in Cape Verde. The gas storm-lamps (there's no mains electricity) only add to the atmosphere, but take care if you've been indulging in the wine: the lack of any street lighting whatsoever can mean a potentially hazardous stagger home as you negotiate the low lava-brick walls.

It's hard to get **public transport** back to São Filipe after finishing the climb or indeed if you've merely overslept. Most vehicles leave before 6am, so you're likely to have to stay in Chã das Caldeiras a second night. If you have to get back for a flight, you're at the mercy of whatever a vehicle-owner wants to charge you. Alternatively, you could hike out down to Achada Furna (14km), where you should have more luck with transport, or hitching.

If you aren't pressed for time, an alternative descent that is rewardingly beautiful, either on foot or in a vehicle if you can find one, is from Chã das Caldeiras down the exposed northeastern side of the volcanic massif to Mosteiros.

Mosteiros to São Filipe

From **MOSTEIROS** ("Monastery"), transport clockwise round the island to São Filipe shouldn't be too much of a problem, although, as usual, most *aluguers* leave early in the morning. Otherwise, you'll probably have to walk a couple of kilometres to **VILA IGREJA** ("Church"), which is the nearest thing to a town centre in this part of the island, with a handful of *pensões*: *Christine & Irmãos* (☎283.10.45 ❹), *Pirâmide* (☎283.13.95 ✉fatinhacv@yahoo.com ❹) and *Tchon de Café* (☎283.16.10 ❹). The ordinary *aluguer* fare to São Filipe shouldn't be more than CV$1000, but a *particular* could cost ten times as much.

Anticlockwise from Mosteiros to São Filipe
Heading **anticlockwise** out of Mosteiros, there's a breathtaking road up to the hamlet of **RIBEIRA ILHEU**, terrifyingly steep if you're in a vehicle. Scarcity of lifts aside, this is really worth the walk – allow a day to climb the 15km – which rewards you with stunning views, sheltered and overgrown little valleys, and a village where your arrival will cause a minor sensation. Once committed, you'll probably have to continue on foot, covering the worst portion of the round-island road, another 10km or so, as far as **SÃO JORGE**, where you should find transport on to São Filipe, some 17km further south. There's a good beach at Ponta da Salina, a short walk from São Jorge.

Clockwise from Mosteiros to São Filipe
Travelling clockwise, you climb quickly from Mosteiros and skirt beneath the crater walls over a battlefield of strewn lava. The road runs high in places and, with a fast driver, it's not a journey you'll ever forget: the cobbled highway traverses the cinder slopes in an unnerving series of undefended loops hundreds of metres above the waves. Eastwards, below the horizon and the distant shape of Santiago, clouds scud over the sea. The isolated **settlements** of lava-block houses on this side of the island have a temporary, desperate look about them – there's a menacing slag-heap darkness here. It's high up on this eastern side that most of Fogo's famous **coffee** is grown.

Once the road curves round to the **west**, the countryside opens out to more relaxing dimensions; southern Fogo is a mellow, rolling landscape of maize and agave and there's a surprising amount of tree cover, mostly acacias. In the pockets of fertile volcanic soil that haven't been rainwashed away, there are beans growing around the maize stalks, with squash, sweet potatoes and cucumbers between.

Brava

Brava, the smallest inhabited island, has always been the most isolated of the Cape Verdes, only properly settled at the end of the seventeenth century after a major eruption on Fogo, in 1675. Its capital, **Vila Nova de Sintra** (Vila) – named after the royal resort of Sintra outside Lisbon – is one of the archipelago's loveliest towns, sedately arranged in a long-extinct crater high above the coast. The island's stone walls overflow with lobelia and vines, and clouds drift through even when the rest of the archipelago is parched with drought. Although its name means "wild", the island has long enjoyed a remarkable degree of domestication, with virtually all the

land under neatly tended cultivation, supporting the archipelago's highest population density. Bravans have a long seafaring tradition: the American **whalers** called at this island more than any other, and the largest contingent of *americanos* comes from Brava. Sadly, much of Brava's infrastructure was destroyed in 1982 by Hurricane Beryl, and not all has been rebuilt.

Small enough to walk all over, but precipitous too, Brava is worth the few days' visit you'll have to devote to it between ferry or plane connections. There haven't been any flights from Praia for a good few years now (the airstrip on the west coast is so short, and usually so windy, that pilots were having to return to Praia without having landed) and the situation doesn't look like changing any time soon.

Although there should be about two **ferry** crossings a week between Fogo and Brava, in practice connections are inconvenient and irregular. The channel between Fogo and Brava is notoriously rough: you may well need seasickness pills and the voyage, even in "normal" conditions, can be quite frightening; there are moments when you seriously have to hang on. On many trips, everyone and everything gets drenched, so be sure to waterproof any delicate belongings. The new Moura Company **catamaran** service promises more convenience (tickets from Agenamar in São Filipe or Barros & Barros in Vila; Ⓦwww.mouracompany. net). For details of ferry and catamaran sailings, see p.440. Vessels dock at the tiny port of **FURNA**, five winding kilometres below Vila.

Vila Nova de Sintra

VILA is tiny – a five-minute walk from one side to the other. There's little to do in town: the market has nothing to offer, and there's no real sightseeing or shopping to do (the late-opening Shell station shop on the east side of town probably has the best selection of groceries). Music lovers, however, are better served, Vila Sintra being another excellent place to catch some authentic local sounds.

There's a Banco Comercial do Atlântico on the road north of the square and a post office on the square's east side. **Accommodation** is a straightforward matter: stay at the clean and quiet little state-run *Pousada Municipal* (☎285.16.97 ❸); if there's nobody about, ask for keys in the Camara Municipal). Alternatively, check out the *Pensão Paulo Sena* (☎285.13.12 ❸), which has a good reputation; the owner's effusive welcome and the large survey map of Brava on the wall are two other reasons you might call in, and Paulo also does good food to order, with his restaurant/front room pretty busy most nights.

The *Por Sul* bar/restaurant on the main *praça* is dedicated to showcasing what it calls *tocatina*, basic but captivating acoustic music played on guitar, *cavaquinho* and occasionally violin. You might be lucky enough to hear a spontaneous warm-up in the tiny bar (where the barman speaks English with a New Jersey accent) but failing that, a full band plays in the restaurant on weekend evenings. Even if you haven't ordered one of the generous portions of seafood (from CV$500), you can go through and watch the band. Also in Vila, a nightclub, *Kananga*, fires up at weekends.

Around the island

Fajã d'Agua, on the west coast, is one of the most idyllic villages in Cape Verde, worth at least a day of your no doubt limited time in Brava. As for the rest of the island, it's small enough to explore simply by **walking**: there are fine hikes and strolls everywhere, and even from coast to coast won't take more than a day. Be aware, however, that distances on the winding roads are always longer than they look on the map. There's a superb three- to four-kilometre walk from Vila Nova de Sintra down to **SANTA BARBARA** and the fountain at **VINAGRE**, and another beautiful short walk from **NOSSA SENHORA DO MONTE** to nearby **COVA JOANA**. From Cova you can ask directions for the steep path down to Fajã; it's a bit hairy in places and will take a few hours, but the vistas are wonderful. Your view of Fajã is obscured until the very end; to emerge from the tangle of greenery at the bottom of the *ribeira* and suddenly be confronted with the stunningly situated village is one of the highlights of Cape Verde. There's also a good one-hour trail from **CAMPO BAIXO** down to the beach at **TANTUM**, 2km south of Portete; and a fine, easy walk from Vila Nova to the impressively sited village of **MATO GRANDE**, perched out on a promontory high above the east coast.

Fajã d'Agua and Portete

From Vila, you can walk to **FAJÃ D'AGUA**, two hours down an incredible switchback of a road, or take an *aluguer* (one or two drivers make the trip regularly enough) for CV$200 in a *coletivo* (locals pay only CV$50: a rare example of tourist profiteering) or CV$800 if you charter the vehicle. Fajã's setting is unforgettable, a pretty hamlet strung out along the shoreline, dotted with palm trees, hemmed in by imposing, sun-baked mountains and backed by a steep, lush *ribeira*. People here are very friendly and you'll quickly feel part of its tight-knit community. It has possibly the best budget **hotel** in Cape Verde, *Burgo's Pensão* (☎285.13.21 ❷), or, to give it its full name, *Ocean Front Motel and Sunset Bar Restaurant*. Three pretty en-suite double rooms, with a shared balcony, perch above the family's own accommodation and the little bar/restaurant below. Alternatively, if you manage to track down Danny Pereira (☎285.14.18), you may be able to rent his sister Julia's house (❸). With two bedrooms, a living room, kitchen and bathroom, it offers great value, but its best feature is a perfectly positioned balcony where you can watch the moon shimmer over the bay. More upmarket and undeniably appealing but rather overpriced is *Sol*

Tavares, writer of mornas

A native of Brava, **Eugénio Tavares** (1867–1930) is a romanticized figure in Cape Verdean lore. A journalist and civil servant for most of his life, he was the country's best-known writer of the **morna** song form, the distinctive Cape Verdean music. Like Portugal's *fado*, the *morna* has a minor-key melody and both may have originated in the Portuguese slave islands of São Tomé. But the heart of a *morna* is its lyric. *Mornas* evoke an unmistakeably Cape Verdean feeling of *sodade* – yearning, longing, homesickness – and the classic examples are all by Tavares, who achieved his huge popularity through his use of the Kriolu language rather than Portuguese.

Tavares' *mornas* deal with the pain of love and loss. One of his best known is "O Mar Eterno", inspired by his affair with an American woman visiting Brava by yacht. Her disapproving father set sail one night and the two never met again. Another famous composition, "Hora di Bai" ("The Hour of Leaving"), was traditionally sung on the dock at Furna as relatives boarded America-bound ships. You can hear a set of his songs on a CD entitled *Saozinha Canta Eugénio Tavares*, by the singer Saozinha, on the American MB Records label.

Na Baia (☎285.20.70 ⓔpensao_sol_na_baia@hotmail.com ➐), with bright, beautifully furnished rooms, a dining room with French cuisine and a lovely garden.

The locals spend the days drinking *grogue* and drifting from group to group along Fajã's single street, a round of ceaseless but harmonious socializing which you'll soon find yourself drawn into. It's utterly peaceful but you can always work up an appetite for the hearty meals (courtesy of *Bar Coqueiro*, where you can also play bingo under the thatched awning) by hiking up the terraced *ribeira* or out to the wind-whipped, deserted airstrip, a couple of kilometres to the south. On Saturday nights, the tiny sweatbox of a club splutters into haphazard life and continues until everyone's finally had enough (usually Sunday afternoon). You may also be treated to the highly entertaining sight of local lads shimmying up vertigo-inducing palm trees in sixty seconds flat. If the coconuts are ripe you won't taste anything sweeter in Cape Verde.

If you want to swim, go beyond the airport to the neat little black-sand beach at **Porteto**, about an hour's walk in total from Fajã. You should take a companion from Fajã the first time you go, to get on the right path. At Porteto you'll meet the odd fisherman, and sometimes a couple of children, but it's otherwise deserted.

Maio

Maio was first sighted on May 1, 1460 – hence its name – but there's really nothing very spring-like about it. Early on, slaves were taken there to look after the livestock surplus of landowners on Santiago, but historically, Maio was important as a **salt collecting** island: vast quantities of evaporated sea salt – "huge heaps like drifts of snow" by Francis Drake's account – were available for the cost of the labour needed to load it on board ship. As that was often paid in old clothes or other unwanted items, the trade was a lucrative one. The English were largely in control of it and for a period Maio was, by Portuguese default, in English hands.

Today, Maio is a godforsaken place, poor in agriculture and a neglected neighbour of weighty Santiago, where most of its young people soon migrate. Surprisingly, more than a few people on the little plane are likely to be tourists these days, although the place is hardly geared up for them. If you do take the **flight** from Praia (Mon, Wed, Fri; 20min) or arrive by **ferry or catamaran**, you'll find a place with a very distinct flavour. It's perhaps the least European of the Cape Verdes, with a relatively wooded, savannah-esque interior and long, white, desolate beaches. For details of ferry and catamaran sailings, see p.440.

Once you've explored the main town, **VILA DO MAIO** (the pretty white nineteenth-century colonial church overlooking the main square is practically the only "sight" of real interest), you can take a stroll along the desert island-style beach where there's nothing but the occasional fisherman, impossibly blue water and blinding white sand as far as the eye can see.

The **airport** is situated 3km north of Vila do Maio. Ferries dock centrally at the town pier. It's surprising to find that at least one of the limited **accommodation** options is so good: *Hotel Marilú*, on Rua 24 Setembro northeast of the main square (T255.11.98 F255.13.47 ❹; discounts in low season), has very pleasant rooms in a rustic kind of way and a good **restaurant** with excellent breakfasts. On the west side of the square, the rooms at *Hotel Bom Sossego* aren't too bad (T255.13.65 F255.13.27 ❺), and there's a restaurant downstairs. If you fancy a cold **beer**, the owner of the little shop on the corner of the square will set a couple of battered stools on the cobbles for you. As for facilities, there's a branch of Banco Comercial do Atlântico on the square, a **post office** up on the hill, a TACV office (T255.12.56) and limited **Internet** access (Mon–Fri 9.30am–1.30pm) at the *Casa de Juventud* off the main road into town.

To see the rest of Maio, rent one of the bicycles from Agemoto (CV\$600 per day,) and set off up either flank of the island. Taking the western route, there's an extended salt pan reaching more than halfway up the coast to **MORRO**, site of another paradisiacal beach, where *Villas Bela Vista* (T256.13.88 Wwww .terra.es/personal/hawaii ❻) has a number of lovely, semi-detached stone chalets to rent. They also offer tennis, a pool and car rental, and run Jeep **safari tours** around the island.

5.2

The Barlaventos

nternationally – at least in the English-speaking world – it's the **Barlaventos** that have drawn most attention to the Cape Verde Islands. Among them, **São Vicente** stands out, the location of a British coal-supply depot for more than a hundred years. Its capital, **Mindelo**, is now the travel hub of the Barlaventos and focus of much of what's happening culturally in the Cape Verdes. While the interior of the island is relentlessly barren, the town has a self-contained appeal that draws a good deal on its evident cosmopolitanism, and its rivalry with Praia for civic pre-eminence.

To see the Cape Verde Islands at their most naturally glorious, hop across the channel from Mindelo to **Santo Antão**, the most northerly isle, for restorative **hiking** among the magnificent canyons (*ribeiras*). Santo Antão is a splendid massif, comparable to Fogo but no longer volcanically active, with an awesomely rugged interior.

São Nicolau is like a poor relation of Antão. Its four hundred years of human habitation seem to have been a dirge of destitution and fruitless toil, and yet its town has the oldest educational and literary tradition in the country. It also offers breathtaking scenery, as well as opportunities similar to Santo Antão's for determined walkers.

Sal, the aptly named "Salt" Island, is Cape Verde's tourist hub, with its main international airport and a glut of hotels strung along one glorious beach, Santa Maria. The last of the windward islands is **Boa Vista**, a large and flat island in the east of the archipelago that's beginning to vie with Sal as a target for watersports and beach enthusiasts. It also has exhilarating desert-travel opportunities.

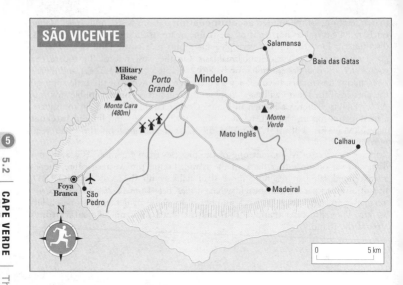

São Vicente

It's hard to avoid identifying **São Vicente** with its main town and, indeed, there's not a lot on the island that matters outside **Mindelo**. The music festival at Baia das Gatas every August is a major event (see p.490), but unless your visit coincides with this or the February carnival, the one or two unexceptional things to do are best achieved by striking out from the town – there are no other significant centres of population on this small hunk of moonscape.

The **British**, as the operators of the **coaling station** at Mindelo, had a long and influential connection with the town. From 1838 until the 1950s, Mindelo – or rather Porto Grande as the town was then called – grew from nothing to a major supply depot on the East Indies and South America shipping runs. With the opening of the Suez Canal in 1869, the eastbound shipping diminished and diesel eventually took over from coal. But by the end of World War II, the hundred years of British presence had made some impact on the cultural life of the island. A number of English words were adopted into São Vicente Kriolu, including *blaqyefela* (blackfellow), *trôsa* (trousers), *ovacôte* (overcoat), *boi* (boy), *ariup* (hurry up), *djob* (job), *ovataime* (overtime) and, under American influence, *sanababiche*. British influence is still discernible in the architecture of some of the larger mansions. The English also introduced **cricket**, and though the game no longer figures very prominently, a team still plays occasionally.

Mindelo

A sense of identity has never been a problem for **MINDELO**. "Taken as a whole," thought Major A.B. Ellis of the First West India Regiment in 1873, "it is, perhaps, the most wretched and immoral town that I have ever seen." He stayed in the *Hotel Brasiliero* where a notice over the door proclaimed "Ici on parl Frances, Man spreucht Deutsch, Man spiks Ingleesh, Aqui se habla Español, Sabe American"; and where his room was invaded by a French farce of characters during the night. By the second half of the nineteenth century, Mindelo's importance as a coaling and victualling station was at its peak, and less-reputable ancillary industries were in top gear.

Today, while only the faintest traces of the bawdiness remain, this is the liveliest town in the Cape Verdes – and no longer especially wretched. Relatively well-provided with hotels, restaurants and bars, it buzzes contentedly after dark, its *praça* a noisy hang-out zone, its streets cheerfully animated. Although it's a small town, don't be surprised to find the atmosphere here tainted with hustle around the edges: yachts and cruise ships are intermittent and not infrequent callers (even the *QE2* makes a stop once or twice a year) and the boys on the waterfront are still making escudos out of naive travellers in time-honoured ways – and occasionally just mugging them.

Arrivals, transport and information

The **airstrip** is 11km from town on a bleak flat at São Pedro. For around CV$800, a taxi gets you to Mindelo (*aluguers* are hard to come by at the airport, though on your way back you can take one from Mindelo to São Pedro and get them to drop you off) past brave acres of **reafforestation** where windswept acacias struggle for a foothold. With a strong ambience of desert desolation, Mindelo initially gives rise to fairly bleak impressions. Yet these soon recede as you get into the town with its Portuguese buildings, restored pink governor's residence and palm-tree-lined esplanade. Arriving **by boat**, it's a ten-minute walk south along the seafront to the town centre.

The main **taxi** ranks are in the obvious centre of town near the church (*igreja*). Short cab journeys within town cost CV$120–150.

A very limited array of **tourist information**, including maps of other islands and Mindelo itself, is available from the small kiosk on the far corner of Praça Aurélio Gonçalves. There's **Internet** access at several places (see "Listings", p.490).

Accommodation

In keeping with its cosmopolitan image, Mindelo boasts a good range of accommodation. Budget travellers are adequately catered for, but the best-value options are the mid-range establishments.

Aparthotel Avenida Av 5 de Julho ☎232.11.76. Old, fairly stylish apartment-style hotel with a/c and TV. Some rooms have balconies and views of the bay. Also acts as an agent for local apartment lets. ❻

Mindelo arrivals and departures

TACV has an office on Avenida 5 de Julho (☎232.15.24 ☏232.37.19). Flights go to Praia (at least 2 daily; 1hr), Sal (2 daily; 55min) and São Nicolau (Mon, Wed & Fri; 30min). Availability on flights to Sal and Praia, notably those connecting with international departures, is often very tight.

For details of **ferry and catamaran** sailings, see p.440. The Moura Company catamaran office is opposite the football ground. For ferry tickets and information, visit Naviera Armas at the ferry terminal (☎231.16.42; Mon–Sat 7am–noon & 2–6.30pm, Sun 7–8am), which runs the daily ferry to Santo Antão (Porto Novo). If you're not using the catamaran, the best ferry is reckoned to be the *Mar d'Canal* and, for comfort's sake at least, on this rough crossing, you're strongly advised to use it.

Ferry information can also be had from Polar on Rua da Moeda (☎231.56.41) and Arca Verde, 12 Rua Senador Vera Cruz (☎232.13.49 ☏232.35.16). The travel agency Agência Nacional de Viagens, Avenida da República (☎232.13.56 ☒www.anv.cv), can also advise on shipping and flight schedules.

As for transport on São Vicente itself, **aluguers** to São Pedro, Baia das Gatas and Calhau (all around CV$100 a seat) leave from the far end of Praça Estrela. It's also worth just flagging down a lift with anything available, which often works.

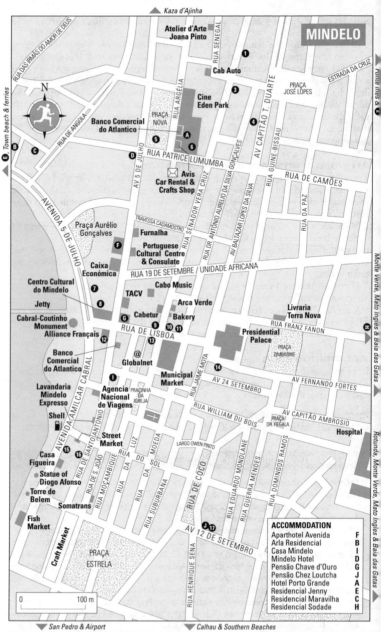

MINDELO

5.2 | CAPE VERDE

ACCOMMODATION

Aparthotel Avenida	F
Arla Residencial	B
Casa Mindelo	I
Mindelo Hotel	D
Pensão Chave d'Ouro	G
Pensão Chez Loutcha	J
Hotel Porto Grande	A
Residencial Jenny	E
Residencial Maravilha	C
Residencial Sodade	H

RESTAURANTS, BARS & CLUBS

Café Estrela	14	Chez Loutcha	17	La Pergola	12	Quiosque Praça Nova	5
Café Lisboa	13	Club Nautico	7	La Pizza	8	Restaurante Escale	3
Café Mindelo	I	Disco Galxia	1	Nella's	13	Syrius	6
Café Musique	10	Discoteca Hi-Step	2	Pastelaria Algarve	11	Tradisson e Morabeza	15
Café Portugal	9	Jazzy Bird	4	Pica Pau	16		

Arla Residencial off Rua de Angola, Alto São Nicolau ☎ 232.86.88 🌐 www.arlaresidencial .com. Modern, en-suite rooms arranged around a communal living room, some with balconies overlooking the bay. Good value. ❹

Casa Mindelo 6 Rua Governador Calheiros ☎ 231.87.31 🌐 www.casacafemindelo .com. Above the coolest café in town are the coolest guestrooms. They're simple (bathrooms and a kitchen are shared) but have an airy, arty, boutique-hotel atmosphere. Perfect if you can manage without a pool. ❻

Hotel Porto Grande Praça Nova ☎ 232.31.90 🖷 232.31.93 🌐 www.oasisatlantico.com. Its rooms may be a little tired, but this dignified place is still the best address in town. It's also the only Mindelo hotel with a decent swimming pool and even a gym. It's right on the *praça*, which can be lively on weekends. ❽

Mindelo Hotel Av 5 de Julho ☎ 232.88.81 📧 mihotel@cvtelelcom.cv. A modern block with a corporate feel, smallish rooms and a tiny rooftop pool. Delicious pizza, pasta and *calzone* are served in the busy downstairs restaurant, which is frequented by well-dressed locals as well as guests. ❽

Pensão Chave d'Ouro Av 5 de Julho ☎ 232.70.50. The "Golden Key" is a Mindelo institution and a long-established budget focus. It's undoubtedly a bit run-down, but its colonial charm and the quaint officiousness of the staff (all dressed in sober black and white) make for a memorable stay. There are tiny, inexpensive but hot, top-floor attic-style rooms and big airy rooms on the first floor, all with shared facilities. ❸

Pensão Chez Loutcha Rua do Coco ☎ 232.16.36. While the rooms are a bit hit-and-miss (some are dark and musty; the better ones have balconies), *Chez Loutcha* has a popular restaurant and regular live music. ❺

Residencial Jenny off Rua Angola, Alto São Nicolau ☎ 232.89.69. In a commanding position overlooking the port, this guesthouse has well-kept en-suite rooms, some with balconies. ❻

Residencial Maravilha off Rua Angola, Alto São Nicolau ☎ 232.22.03 📧 gabs@mail.cvtelecom.cv. With beautiful, tastefully fitted rooms and an interior decorated with rustic materials such as *panos*, this is good value, and a bargain in low season. ❻

Residencial Sodade 38 Rua Franz Fanon ☎ 230.32.00 📧 residencialsodade@hotmail.com. Friendly place with English-speaking staff. The cheapest rooms (a bit dark) are on the bottom floor with more expensive lodging upstairs, with a/c and TV. The big selling point is the great view from the rooftop restaurant. ❹

The Town

Mindelo is the town that Cape Verdeans resident abroad always go on about – perhaps because so many Cape Verde expatriates come from here – and compared with Praia it does have a more animated, less official feel. Helped along by the bay with its twin headlands, its esplanade and its clutter of backstreets, Mindelo feels like a holiday. The **carnaval** in February tends to infect the town for the entire year, so it never entirely stops partying.

Exploring it for yourself is the main daytime pursuit and the seafront provides an obvious anchor point. The unusual eagle-topped **monument** near the old jetty (soon to be incorporated into a new marina) commemorates the first Lisbon–Rio air crossing, in 1922, by aviators Cabral and Coutinho, who spent a number of days recuperating in Mindelo after their 80mph leg from the Canaries in the flying boat *Lusitania*. There's another monument to the courageous duo near the ferry port. Away to the south, the curious, ornate little castle is the **Torre de Belem**, a copy of the tower of the same name outside Lisbon; the latter was built in the early sixteenth century, the Cape Verdean replica in the 1920s. For many years the Torre at Mindelo was the seat of the Portuguese administrator of São Vicente, but even before independence it had been abandoned. For decades, the shored-up and rat-infested structure looked as if it had been deliberately ignored; people say it is about to be restored, but they've been saying that for years. Back in town a short way, the old **Presidential Palace** has been well looked after and was restored in pale pink some years back. Now the headquarters of São Vicente island council, it's clearly the object of considerable civic pride.

Mindelo's **beach**, the Praia da Lajinha, is a kilometre out of town on the north side. Backed by a rumbling industrial area, the dark yellow sands are clean, nonetheless, the sea is warm and clear, and there are a couple of beach bars on the other side of the road. Continuing northwards in the same direction, you can walk or drive up to the **Fortim del Rei**, a deserted hilltop fortification – one-time prison – overlooking the city and the bay.

If you're drawn to **crafts and paintings**, you should pay a visit to a couple of Mindelo's workshops and galleries. Colourful woven wall hangings are a speciality, though they don't come cheap; you can see some fine examples, and works in progress, at **Joana Pinto's studio** on Rua Senegal, north of Praça Nova. **Kaza d'Ajinha** on Avenida 5 de Julho, a cultural project founded by a local painter, shows art in convivial surroundings, with a café serving home-made food (daily from 3pm). **Casa Figueira**, near the Torre de Belem, is a private gallery of canvases by a father-and-son team.

For more routine shopping, Mindelo is at least as well-provided as Praia. There's a scattering of small **supermarkets**, a lively **fish market**, and a fine **municipal market**, running to two floors, bang in the centre of town, which contains a good number of small retail enterprises. There's also a little *azulejo*-tiled **market village** on the far side of Praça Estrela with stalls staffed by both West Africans and Cape Verdeans. Some of the back walls depict sculpted scenes of toil from Mindelo's past.

Eating and drinking

There are more than a few decent restaurants and snack bars – though it's well to remember that many of them close once a week, usually on a Sunday, and few take orders after 9.30pm. Ironically, many of them also close over lunch at the weekend.

Café Estrela Av Fernando Fortes, by the palace. Limited range of top-value meals and snacks.

Café Lisboa and **Café Portugal** facing each other on Rua de Lisboa. Established downtown cafés – unfussy, fast places where locals of every strand congregate, business types read *A Semana*, and much coffee, beer and *aguardente* are consumed.

Café Mindelo 6 Rua Governador Calheiros ☎ 231.87.31 ⊛ www.casacafemindelo .com (Mon–Fri 8am–midnight, Sat 8am–2pm, Sun closed). Effortlessly cool café-restaurant in a restored colonial building close to the site of the new marina, serving grills, pasta, pastries, fresh juice and local beer to a soundtrack of contemporary jazz.

Chave d'Ouro Av 5 de Julho ☎ 232.70.50 (open for lunch from noon–3pm and dinner from 7–11pm). Upstairs in the *pensão* of the same name, this huge, antique dining room serves good food to a loyal local clientele. Breakfasts are served from 8am in the equally atmospheric little bar along the corridor.

Chez Loutcha Rua do Coco ☎ 232.16.36 (closed Mon). Popular with locals and visitors, this place has a huge international menu, including Senegalese fare, and great live-music sessions.

Escale Rua Senador Vera Cruz ☎ 232.44.34 (closed Sun). In a former consulate building on the smart side of town, this is a spacious, upmarket eating place. The fish is delicious and the *pudím* is possibly the best on the islands.

La Pergola Alliance Française, Rua de Santo António (Mon–Fri 8am–7pm, Sat 8am–1pm).

Simple but good French food at low prices make this spotless little courtyard restaurant a handy stop for a quick lunch.

La Pizza Av 5 de Julho sandwiched between *Club Náutico* and the Centro Cultural. Great seafront kiosk for feasting on cheap, tasty pizza and watching the sunset over the bay.

Nella's Restaurant/Bar Rua de Lisboa, above *Café Lisboa* ☎ 231.43.20. Trendy bistro serving French-influenced Cape Verdean cuisine with the menu chalked up on a blackboard. Main courses start at around CV$600.

O Guloso 10 Rua Angola ☎ 231.70.66. Engagingly eccentric place where you definitely need to reserve ahead to get any food at all. English-speaking owner guarantees to provide food fit for the "gourmand" of her establishment's name.

Pastelaria Algarve Rua de Lisboa. Snacks and cakes, with a bar and a leafy streetside terrace.

Pica Pau 42 Rua de Santo António ☎ 232.82.07 (evenings only, reserve ahead: it's usually full). The "Woodpecker" is a Mindelo institution, a tiny restaurant, largely unchanged for twenty years, though now festooned with the multilingual testimonials of happy eaters. There's great-value seafood, especially the piping hot and tasty *arroz mariscos* or lobster, with wine and beer from the even tinier bar to wash it down.

Tradisson e Morabeza Av Amílcar Cabral ☎ 232.48.41 (closed Sun). Large, upbeat restaurant with a jaunty tropical-island theme and a stage for live bands.

Nightlife

After dark, social gravity sooner or later draws most people down to Praça Nova, where there's always some excitement and a lot of rather Mediterranean courting and flirting going on, accompanied by huge volumes of noise. Although the town's youth are steadily deserting Mindelo for Praia and further, it still holds a racy and sophisticated reputation for the young people of the Barlavento country hamlets. Sitting in the square really is fun: you'll quickly find yourself in some kind of conversation, tuning in to the evening grapevine. There's also a cinema here showing Hollywood features, and they sometimes screen big international football games.

Mindelo has a number of **boites** (down-to-earth nightclubs), generally discos rather than live-music venues. Apart from Cape Verdean *morna*, *coladeira* and *funana*, you're most likely to come across variants of Antillean *zouk*, often with Senegalese influences. Not surprisingly, successful singers and bands don't wait long before flying out to Lisbon, Paris, Holland or the USA, where Cape Verdean audiences (and certainly the market for CDs) can be larger than in Mindelo itself.

Clubs and bars

Argentina Av 5 de Julho, beneath the *Chave d'Ouro*. Earthy watering-hole.

Café Musique Rua de Lisboa. Stylish bar and live venue rolled into one. European tourists and male yachting types flock to this place, both to witness the abundance of local musical talent and to congregate on the balcony and shout to the girls below.

Club Náutico Av 5 de Julho. Touristy bar with a maritime theme, an open courtyard and views of the port. There's food too, but the service is painfully slow.

Disco Galaxia Rua Senador Vera Cruz. Always hot and crowded, although at present it's only open during the summer months. CV$300 entry charge.

Discoteca Hi-Step Fonte Inés, just off Estrada da Cruz, east of the town centre. A good midweek bet; busy on a Thurs when you'll pay CV$200 (CV$300 at the weekend).

Jazzy Bird Rua Patrice Lumumba. Brilliantly named little backstreet bar with good sounds but no live music.

Pub-Dancing A Cave Alto São Nicolau district, opposite the *Residencial Maravilha*. Long-established subterranean club with a dedicated older crowd. Admission is CV$500 (with one free drink). Starts to swing around 1.30am.

Quiosque Praça Nova Praça Nova (closed Mon). Essential open-air drinks-stop in Mindelo's most sociable square.

Syrius Situated below the *Porte Grande* (weekends and every night in summer). The most desirable disco in town, a great place to discover that Cape Verdean men and women dance *together*, even if the soundtrack happens to be hip-hop. CV$300 cover.

Listings

Banks Branches of Banco Comercial do Atlântico in the old building on Rua de Santo António, south of Rua de Lisboa and in front of the *Hotel Porto Grande*. There's a branch of BCN at 8 Rua Libertadores d'Africa.

Bookshops You could try the Livraria Terra Nova on Rua 19 de Setembro, but it rarely has anything but a limited range of foreign-language dictionaries and evangelical tracts in Portuguese. Otherwise try the Centro Cultural do Mindelo (see below) or *Furnalha* (see "Internet access"), which have a limited stock.

Car rental São Vicente is a good island to explore for a few hours by car. Half-daily or daily rates are around CV$2000 or CV$4000. One of the best is Cab Auto, CP 117 Largo Medina Boé, behind the *Hotel Porto Grande* (℡ & ℻ 232.28.12). A CV$10,000 deposit is required. More expensive is Avis (℡ 232.71.71), in front of the *Hotel Porto Grande*.

CDs Cabo Music, in the arcade behind Av de 5 Julho, is a decent music shop.

Cultural centres Alliance Française, Rua de Lisboa (Mon–Fri 10am–12.30pm & 3–7pm, Sat 10am–12.30pm; ℡ 232.11.49), is worth visiting for books, mags, movies and Internet access. The Centro Cultural Portugués do Mindelo is at Av 5 de Julho (℡ 231.30.40 ℮ ccpmindelo@cvtelecom.cv), next door to the Portuguese embassy. Also worth a visit is the Centro Cultural do Mindelo, opposite the *Chave D'Ouro* (℡ 32.58.40), a long-established locally run institute promoting Cape Verdean culture, with a good Portuguese-language bookshop, a gallery and a lively theatre that's always in use.

Consulates The British honorary consul is Mr Antônio Canuto (℡ 232.28.30, assistant

☏ 232.35.12 ✉ antonio.a.canuto@scv.sims.com).
Internet access *Furnalha* is a café and shop on
Av 5 de Julho (daily 9am–midnight) where online
services are in fact the main attraction. Also worth
trying are Globalnet (daily 7.30am–11pm) or *Café
del Mar* on Rua Argela,.
Laundry Lavandaria Mindelo Expresso, 24 Rua de
Sto António (Mon–Fri 8.30am–7.30pm, Sat & Sun
8.30am–1.30pm), is cheap, friendly and efficient.
You pay by weight.

Post and telephones CV Telecom on Rua Patrice
Lumumba (Mon–Fri 8am–noon & 2.30–5pm).
You can also make international calls and buy
phonecards here.
Travel agents Barracuda Tours, Av Baltasar
Lopes de Silva ☏ 232.55.92; Cabetur, 57 Rua
Senador Vera Cruz ☏ 232.38.47; Agência Nacional
de Viagens, Av da República ☏ 232.13.56
🌐 www.anv.cv; Tropictour, off Praça Nova
☏ 232.41.88.

Around São Vicente

If you don't venture beyond Mindelo you'll not be in a minority. Away from
Mindelo, the rest of the island is desperately arid, for the most part treeless, and
largely uninhabited – all but a couple of thousand of the island's 50,000 inhabitants
live in the *povoação*.

Baia das Gatas and Monte Verde

For a break, and really quite a nice beach, the twenty-minute drive to **Baia das
Gatas** is a good trip. Baia, as it's commonly known (*gata* means nurse shark,
a harmless, small species), is protected by a concrete mole and black boulders
to break the thrashing surf. In the **lagoon**, the water is calm and delightfully
transparent, though even with a mask there's not a lot to see. Beyond the lagoon's
confines, the sea is more challenging and the urchin-covered rocks should be
enough to put you off. At the time of writing, this quiet little resort was about to
change radically with the construction of a sizeable new luxury accommodation
complex and golf course.

The road to Baia climbs steeply past the junction for **Monte Verde**, the dark
mass commonly wreathed in clouds that rears up behind Mindelo, and the island's
highest point. This too is worth an outing but you'll have to rent a car or take
a cab (CV$1000-plus) and you'll need to set aside a full morning or afternoon.
The last section on the Mato Ingles branch gets right to the summit. It is, truly, a
"green mountain", covered in the once commercially important *orchil* lichen, used

---

Live at the Bay of Sharks

The **Baia das Gatas Music Festival** has become Cape Verde's major summer attraction, with thirty thousand people attending for the three days in August. People camp
out (it never rains in August), sleep in cars on the dunes, or occupy the weekend
chalets around the bay. Cape Verdean emigrants time their summer vacations on the
islands to coincide with the festival, and the crowd is full of reunited families and long-
unseen friends bumping into each other. Inter-island flights are all heavily booked at
this time and hotel rooms in Mindelo hard to find, while public transport between town
and bay may involve some waiting — and inflated prices.

The event is now in its third decade, and national radio and TV cover it nonstop.
Cesaria Evora has headlined in the past, though the quality of the music varies from
year to year and indifferent overseas groups are sometimes booked for local youth
appeal, while top local acts can be disappointingly absent.

In 2007, the festival moved from late to early August to encourage overseas
visitors, especially from the USA, and despite technical and programming problems and lengthy delays, there was a return to form on the bill, which included
Bau, Paulino Vieira, Titina and Mayra Andrade. For further information, visit 🌐 www
.mindelo.info/gal_baia.php.

to produce brilliant scarlet and purple dyes. The views down over Mindelo and Baia can be stunning, but they're not to be counted on, as the summit area is often wreathed in cloud.

A walk on São Vicente

"A nice walk goes from Baia das Gatas via Salamansa to Mindelo. The beach in Salamansa is polluted with plastic and glass, but there are nice sand dunes. Follow them to the interior, and you will find a path leading to Mindelo."

Igor Fabjan, Slovenia

Southern beaches

A difficult road leads southeast from Monte Verde to **CALHAU** (the direct route from Mindelo is easier), a deliciously tranquil (at least during the week) village full of empty holiday homes where there's a good beach and a couple of restaurants: *Hamburg*, open daily year-round, is a colourfully painted, slightly eccentric place where you can lounge in the courtyard all afternoon without seeing a soul, while *Chez Loutcha* (a branch of the Mindelo hotel-restaurant) is open Sundays only, when townies head for the seaside. Another road heads south to **MADEIRAL** and the island's most dramatic and isolated region, a fifteen-kilometre ridge (altitude 500–700m) paralleling the southern coast at a distance of just two or three kilometres, from which *ribeiras* plunge down to the sea.

Another worthwhile beach, somewhat easier to get to, lies in the other direction, just beyond the airport at **Praia de São Pedro**. This is the location of a resort hotel, *Foya Branca* (☎230.74.00 ✉foyabranca@cvtelecom.cv ❽), a rather bland but upmarket complex of rooms with three pools, close to the beach but under the local flight path. Across the bay, the scruffy, but colourful, little village of **SÃO PEDRO** has a certain charm but offers nothing beyond an excuse for a walk along the shore.

Santo Antão

Santo Antão, the second largest of the Cape Verdes, is rugged and exciting – a tortoise shape cut into deep **ribeiras**, with the savage grandeur of a much bigger land mass. The island is also the last to suffer whenever a prolonged drought ravages the archipelago, the northern slopes and valleys retaining a perennial verdure which is hard to believe after the desolation of Sal or São Vicente. In times not so long past, Mindelo got almost all its drinking water from Santo Antão – a lucrative trade that dried up with the withering of the coaling industry on São Vicente and the opening there of a water-desalination plant.

Getting here today, you travel by ferry or catamaran across the deep, shark-infested channel from Mindelo to **Porto Novo**, on the opposite side of the island from the island capital, **Ribeira Grande**. A single **highway** snakes up over the barren south-facing slopes on the island's eastern tip, then edges between the peaks and abysses to Ribeira Grande on the north coast. Plans are afoot to build a fast new coastal route. In the past, however, communications were even more difficult. The story goes that Bishop Jacinto Valente visited Santo Antão from Santiago in 1755 (see box "The rise and fall of Ribeira Grande", p.471), and set off to cross the island on foot. Having been hauled up several precipices dangling from a rope, he eventually lost his nerve and had to stay put between a cliff and a chasm. The islanders went on ahead, sent him back a tent and supplies, and began to construct a road for his rescue. Even as late as 1869, three hundred years after it was first colonized, the Portuguese minister of colonies remarked that Santo Antão had "the appearance of an island that had only been discovered months ago".

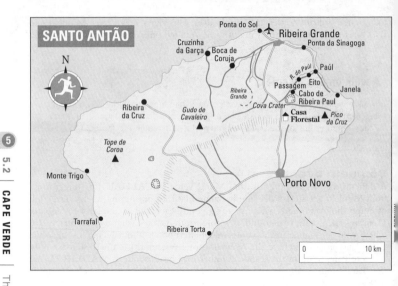

Porto Novo

Porto Novo itself used to be an uneventful place subsisting on the daily contact with Mindelo across the channel, but in recent years, development funds have seen considerable growth. A crowd is always down on the quay to welcome the ferry, and the terminal has a small **tourist information booth** as well as a ferry office (☎231.81.87; Mon–Sat 8am–noon & 3–6pm, Sun 9–10am & 3–6pm). For **catamaran** tickets and further transport information, visit Agência Nacional de Viagens on Alto de Peixinho (☎222.18.87 ⓦwww.anv.cv). For details of ferry and catamaran sailings, see p.440.

A fleet of **minibuses** meets the ferry, usually tailing back way up the hill. Most of them head over the island's spine to Ribeira Grande (1hr–1½hr; CV$300). You should try to get a front seat on the right for the most heart-stopping views.

If you need **rooms** in Porto Novo, the best place is the very pleasant, and great-value *Residencial Antilhas* in Alto Peixno (☎222.11.93 ⓔresidencialantilhas @hotmail.com ❸), just above the port, with en-suite rooms, hot water and a separately run bar-restaurant on the ground floor. Many rooms also have balconies overlooking the channel to Mindelo. It's right on the edge of town and, if you want to stretch your legs, you can hike eastwards along the coast until the path peters out and you're faced with nothing but baking brown rock, wind and sea. Less attractive, more expensive and less conveniently located, a couple of minutes' walk inland from the clifftop is the *Girassol*, also in Alto Peixno (☎222.13.83 ❹), where the rooms are not en-suite, but breakfast is included in the rate. *Residencial Pôr do Sol*, a huge blue-and-yellow edifice a minute's walk off to the right of the main street, past the bank, at Fundo de Lombo Branco (☎222.21.79 ⓔpordosolpn@cvtelecom.cv ❻), is a newish mid-range place located down in the main part of town, with sleek, spotless, good-value en-suite rooms with a/c and TV.

You can **eat** quite well, and catch up with European football on the TV, at the *Sereia*, a bar perched on the clifftop whose terrace fills up quickly after the ferry has docked. Alternatively, the *Pôr do Sol* has a sunny rooftop **restaurant** (main dishes from CV$600; try the delicious *pudím do queijo*) with fine views to São Vicente.

The road to Ribeira Grande

As you head north out of Porto Novo, the haul up the **south slope of the island** presents a bleak picture to begin with, the road snaking steeply through a lifeless mountain desert of tumbled volcanic rocks, bleached pale in the sun. Temperatures drop and views over Porto Novo become dramatic as the vehicle climbs; if it's a clear day, you can see São Vicente – a black mountain sitting, strangely, below the horizon.

But save your enthusiasm and your camera batteries for the descent down the northern side of the island. As you approach the crest, the road's contours relax as groves of coniferous trees and low herbage make an appearance. The **Casa Florestal** (forest station) is a sort of halfway house, a convenient place to hop out, where people will try to sell you large quantities of goat's cheese. Continuing by minibus to the *povoação*, you sweep over the island's twisted spine and skirt the magnificent circumference of **Cova crater**. Clouds drift below the altitude of the road, and above the houses and sugar-cane plots patched into the crater's colossal scoop. From this point on, the bus repeatedly veers past steep terraced slopes and chasms of hundreds of sheer metres. Bishop Valente's vertigo was understandable: even Cape Verdeans gaze down – and cross themselves – at the hairpins. Glimpsing the sea through the crags, it seems impossible the road can get down to Ribeira Grande in such a short distance.

Ribeira Grande and northeast Santo Antão

With fortress-like cliffs and narrow streets, **RIBEIRA GRANDE** feels like a mountain town lost in a huge range, its slightly forbidding, singular atmosphere compelling and not quickly forgotten. The town, a cluster of closely bunched and shady houses, perches at the mouth of the *ribeira* and is hemmed in by cliffs rising behind and by the dark sea lashing a shingle beach in front. A broad *praça* sets off the **Igreja de Nossa Senhora do Rosário**, the formidable church intended, at one time in the eighteenth century, to be the cathedral of Cape Verde.

The town provides the basics – a **petrol station**, a **post office**, a **bank**, some **stores** and a clutch of Chinese shops selling cheap imports – but little else. Finding a **place to stay** is simple enough, even if none of the trio of inexpensive *pensões* is particularly inviting. The options are the unremarkable *Residencial 5 de Julho* (near the church; ☎221.13.45 ③), the tidy but old-fashioned *Residencial Aliança* (☎221.24.88 ②) and *Residencial Biby* (☎221.11.49 ②), down an alley opposite the *5 de Julho*, which has good-value, carefully looked-after rooms. There's also a solitary mid-range place, *Residencial Tropical* (☎221.11.29 ④), situated a minute's walk from the *Biby* and offering immaculate, if slightly dark, rooms with TV, a/c, hot water and an attached **Internet** café.

Ribeira Grande has little to offer in the **food** line. The *Tropical* is your best bet for a **meal** with a nice little patio dining area, attentive service and main dishes in the CV$600 region. The *5 de Julho* serves breakfast and basic meals like *feijoada* and *cachupa* (CV$500) in an unattractive little dining room, while the *Aliança*'s menu sometimes includes pizza. But that's about the limit of the town's offerings.

In fact, by far the best accommodation and eating option in the area, and indeed on the whole island, is some 8km out of town in the hamlet of **BOCA DE CORUJA**, reached by taking the road leading southwest. ⚶ *Hotel Pedracin Village* (☎224.20.20 Ⓔpedracin@cvtelecom.cv ⑥) is a small cluster of comfortable but appealingly rustic-looking stone-built cottages clinging to the slopes of a stunning valley, with a decent restaurant, a small, bright pool and fabulous views of green peaks.

Ponta do Sol

As an appealing alternative to Ribeira Grande, you could take an *aluguer* ten minutes up the coast to **PONTA DO SOL**, a more spacious little town of cobbled streets and colourful houses, with a leafy *praça,* a picturesque little shorefront and a good choice of simple but pleasant places to stay, eat and drink. Now that its tiny airport, the only one on the island, is closed indefinitely, it's pleasantly quiet and practically traffic-free. In comparison with Ribeira Grande's claustrophobic feel and chronic lack of facilities, this is a pretty, laid-back place to visit.

If you're heading in by road, you'll pass *Pensão Chez Louisette* (☏225.10.48 ✉chezlouisette@cvtelecom.cv ④), which has clean, graceful en-suite rooms and breakfast included. The larger *Residencial Ponta do Sol* (☏225.12.38 ✉residencialpsol @cvtelecom.cv ⑤) is a minute further on, on the right – a bright hotel with a bar-restaurant and sparkling en-suite rooms, some with balconies

Down in the main part of town, the relatively upmarket *Hotel Blue Bell* (☏225.12.15 ✉bluebell@telecom.cv.com ⑤) boasts a friendly English-speaking owner, smart rooms, some with sea-view balconies, and an airy ground-level restaurant. Directly opposite, *Residencial-Bar-Restaurante Lela Leite* (☏225.10.56 ③) offers local dishes and cold drinks (call two hours ahead to order a meal) and basic, cheap rooms. The popular, family-run *Dedei Residencial* (☏225.10.37 ③), in a green-painted house in the street behind *Blue Bell*, offers reasonable B&B rooms, some with hot water.

Much more interesting is the fresh and arty, French-owned 🍴 *Por de Sol Arte* down on the harbour (☏225.11.21 ✉porsolarte@yahoo.fr ③). With a handful of pastel-shaded rooms upstairs (complete with log beds) and a craft shop and café down below, this is a vibrant and memorable place to stay. Nearby is another appealing place to eat, the 🍴 *Restaurante Por d'Sol*, with a cool downstairs bar hung with contemporary photography and art and an upstairs terrace restaurant with sea views, serving Senegalese classics such as *poulet yassa* and *tiéboudienne*. The *Esplanada Nova Aurora* on the *praça*, near the church, is the smartest place in town, with a good restaurant, a funky bar and mountain views.

Hiking around the island

The most compelling activity on Santo Antão is **hiking**, with routes all over the island. It's very helpful to have a decent **map**; the Goldstadt Wanderkarte hiking map (see p.437) is perfect (also worth looking out for is the huge, though somewhat out of date, 1:25,000 map of the island on the wall of a small, nameless bar on the south side of Ribeira Grande's main street). With several days to spare, you would have the chance to explore the three big **ribeiras** of eastern Santo Antão, Grande, Paúl and Janela – "Great", "Swamp" and "Window".

To explore by bike, get in touch with local bike-hire and tour company Cabo Verde Bikes (⊛www.cabo-verde-bikes.com). A worthwhile target either by mountain bike or cab is the stunningly picturesque and precariously sited hamlet of **FONTAINHAS**, reached by the winding coastal track which clings to the vertiginous cliffs west of Ponta do Sol. One option for a short hike – a particularly dramatic route in its later stages and just about viable for confident cyclists by mountain bike – is to continue from Fontainhas on to the tiny fishing village of **CRUZINHA DA GARÇA** via a cliff-face footpath that is at times barely half a metre wide, with nothing but rocks and dust and crashing ocean waves for company.

It's also possible to hike and take *aluguers* east along the coast from Ribeira Grande, via the verdant mouths of the *ribeiras*, about 20km to **PONTINHA DA JANELA**, where you can enjoy superb panoramic ocean views.

Hiking Ribeira Grande

The hike up the **Ribeira Grande**, a solid morning's work, requires an early start and a good supply of drinking water. You may be lucky and see the *ribeira* cloaked in green, especially in September or October, but unfortunately it can't be guaranteed. You might want to make arrangements with a driver and vehicle in town to take you part way up the *ribeira*, to get you over the less interesting lower stretch, and possibly to pick you up again at the top and return you to Ribeira Grande or Porto Novo. If you get a *particular* to meet you at the head of the *ribeira*, expect to pay upwards of CV\$3000 (alternatively, you can take a chance on hitching a lift). You might also want to hire a guide for the day – CV\$2000 is a fair price.

Hiking Ribeira do Paúl

Ribeira do Paúl is the most beautiful and densely planted of the three canyons. Get there by *aluguer*, 10km along the coast road – a busy enough route (CV$70). Your starting point is the village of **VILA DAS POMBAS**, basically one long street lashed by Atlantic waves and watched over by a Rio de Janeiro–style statue of St Anthony. It's peopled by a memorable array of characters and prone to spontaneous outbursts of music-making, so keep your eyes and ears peeled. There's a solitary accommodation option on the main road, the basic *Residencial Vale do Paúl* (☎223.13.19 ❷), which has a reasonably priced restaurant with amazing views; get your order in a few hours beforehand. The other place to eat is *Restaurant Morabeza* (☎223.17.90), which serves local dishes and looks out over sugar-cane fields.

A steep kilometre or so inland, through the first tresses of deep, sugar-plantation verdure, you come to the hamlet of **EITO**, where the *Casa Familial Sabine* (☎223.15.44 ⒺSabine@caboverdemail.com ❷), situated 50m south of the road from the two-storey orange house (turn left if walking inland), offers slightly eccentric, beautifully located accommodation. The cobbled road up the *ribeira* (there's not much transport along here) climbs far inland, snaking through a fantastic riot of vegetation and at one point skirting an almost vertical wall of rock that is dizzying in its immensity. Equally dizzying is the local *grogue*, sold in the little shops and bars along the way and produced by sweaty, soot-blackened men at *trapiches* (stills) along the route; they'll normally let you look round and take photos. A couple of kilometres off the main road at **LOMBO COMPRIDO** (a 15-min climb) is *Casa das Ilhas* (☎223.18.32 Ⓔcasadasilhas@yahoo.fr ❸), a pretty seven-room guesthouse with good views and home cooking. Some 4km from Paúl, at **PASSAGEM**, the path fetches up at a kind of tropical garden with a neglected swimming pool and café. At times the landscape, with its robustly constructed stone path and vertiginous, neatly ordered terracing is reminiscent of Inca Peru.

In the upper reaches of the valley is the hamlet of **CABO DE RIBEIRA PAÚL**, where you can stay at *Chez Simon*, with two very basic but wonderfully situated rooms (☎23.10.39 ❶); Simon is available for hire as a guide if needed, and can prepare traditional food given notice. The village is also home to Sandr'Arte, a little craft shop selling various permutations of *grogue* and *ponche* (which you may well be invited to sample) as well as coffee beans from the surrounding hills.

As a fine and arguably even more scenically spectacular alternative to hiking up, you can walk *down* the Ribeira do Paúl by getting dropped off on the main trans-island road above the Cova crater (CV$1700 if you're hiring privately, a fraction of that if you leave early on one of the morning runs from either Porto Novo or Ribeira Grande). Ask your driver to point out the initial stretch and you can't go far wrong.

Paúl

"The quaint little town of Paúl takes a bit long to get to, but is truly a beautiful place to walk around. The valley is full of sugarcane fields, and banana and breadfruit trees in this most green area in all of Cape Verde. I'm a US Peace Corps volunteer and helped set up a website for the area, www.paulbelezanatural.com"

Kayo Shiraishi, USA

Tarrafal

If you really want to get away from it all, you might want to strike out for the remote west-coast settlement of **TARRAFAL.** You should be able to find an *aluguer* headed there among the throng on Porto Novo's pier. The journey is a long one by Cape Verdean standards and the road isn't the best, but when you arrive there's wonderfully peaceful, friendly accommodation to be had at the idyllic *Mar Tranquilidade* (☎227.60.12 ⊛www.martranquilidade.com ❹), courtesy of a German–American couple, with a series of stone-walled, thatch-roofed cottages right on the beach. The little town is sheltered by mountains from the winds which buffet many parts of Cape Verde and there are miles of secluded, black-sand beaches to escape to. A few rooms are also available from José Almeida Delgado (☎222.31.05 ❶), who can provide breakfast and dinner at extra cost.

❺ Santa Luzia, Ilhéu Branco, Ilhéu Razo

Three desert islands line up in the lee of São Vicente. The biggest, **Santa Luzia**, had a bit of a population towards the end of the eighteenth century – mostly destitute farmers from São Nicolau – but successive droughts and an impossibly harsh terrain expelled them. A more recent inhabitant was the "Governor of Santa Luzia", Francisco António da Cruz, who fled there from his wife and eighteen offspring and lived as a hermit for a number of years. It's now deserted again and, unless you make special efforts by boat, out of reach. Charles Darwin called here in the *Beagle* and herpetologists know Santa Luzia as the only habitat of a large, herbivorous lizard – the Cape Verde giant skink, *Macroscincus coctei* – though it seems likely that it's now extinct.

Ilhéu Branco is more of a rock than an island, white (hence the name) from the guano deposits of generations of sea birds, and rising sheer from the sea in a shape supposed to resemble a ship at anchor. Ships stay well clear of its dangerous approaches. If you're sailing between Mindelo and São Nicolau, you're likely to get a good view of the **dolphins** which frequent this leg. **Flying fish** are common too – skittering things the size of a seagull which streak above the surface.

By the time you reach **Ilhéu Razo**, you can see the jagged, cloud-protected silhouette of São Nicolau. Razo is famous – among ornithologists and conservationists – for the **Razo lark**, a dun, ordinary-looking lark noted for its confiding nature, that nests only on this barren slab, making it an exceedingly rare species. The Razo lark has an extra-strong beak for digging up the drought-resistant grubs it feeds on. It should survive until population pressure and a solution to the problem of drought bring the first human colonists to the island.

São Nicolau

Like the peaks of a submerged mountain, **São Nicolau** rises from the ocean between São Vicente and Sal. There's no doubt about its **beauty** – an elegant, hatchet-shaped trio of ridges meeting in spectacular summits above the hidden capital of **Ribeira Brava**. But the cruelly desolate slopes (this is the driest of the "agricultural" islands) testify to a history of extraordinary hardship – eternal isolation, migration and desertion. The problem, as ever, is water, or chronic lack of it. Over the last decade, efforts have been made to tap the deep underground water-table – notably with the help of French *cooperants* aid workers – but the legacy of centuries of neglect lives on, and the drift away from the island is continuous. However there have been a few good rainy seasons in the last couple of decades; maize, planted every year, actually grows to maturity some seasons, and water has flowed again from village pumps.

Arriving **by ship** at **Tarrafal**, the island's main port, you should aim to get the first transport up to Ribeira Brava. Shared *carrinhos* charge about CV$400, chartered taxis about CV$3000, and the journey time is about an hour. The **airstrip** is just 4km from Ribeira Brava (midway between the town and the minor port of

PREGUIÇA), and you're likely to be able to find a taxi into town (CV$250). For details of ferry and catamaran sailings, see p.440.

São Nicolau is a good place to have **transport** of your own. If, as is likely enough, you haven't – and don't have unlimited time on the island either – you should make efforts to fix something up straight away as there's very little public transport. One of the few available Land Rovers is sometimes rented out (with owner) for around CV$5000 per day: it's almost worth the expense for the pleasure of being able to offer lifts to dozens of foot-weary Nicolauans as you go.

Tarrafal and the west

At **TARRAFAL**, straggling along the southwest coast, none of the island's meld of destitution and scenic splendour is immediately obvious. The shallow bay gives on to the largest district of relatively gentle terrain on São Nicolau, from where the spectacle of the interior isn't apparent.

Tarrafal's main activity is **tuna fishing**, supplying an important canning plant. While you can see the great beasts being hauled up on many a Cape Verdean beach, at Tarrafal the evening business seems to yield some particularly spectacular specimens, many as big as a person, and people are quite happy to have you watching as the fish are wheeled into the factory on wagons. You can also join the kids on the **swimming beach**, the hot, grey sands of which are said to be good for rheumatism. A few kilometres further north, however, towards **BARRIL**, there are much better beaches, safe and good for snorkelling, among them the little white-sand cove of Praia das Francêses.

If you get stuck at Tarrafal, you'll soon locate the good *casa de pasto* at *Pensão Alice* (☎236.11.87 ❷), along the shore to the north, which offers basic rooms and a warm welcome. The sparkling white *Residencial Natur* (☎236.11.78 ❸), located in the same general direction, is another good option, with breakfast CV$250 extra. There's also limited accommodation at the more upmarket *Pensão Aquário* (☎236.10.99 ✉kusterscabverd@cvtelecom.cv ❺), where tuna is the culinary speciality. A couple of decent bars and restaurants complete the picture; *Patchê* has main courses around the CV600 mark.

Over the island's spine

The 26 kilometres of nearly deserted cobblestone between Tarrafal and Ribeira Brava is another of Cape Verde's scenically outstanding routes. After a steady and satisfying pull away from the broad, southwest bay and up to around 800m, the road takes a sudden and breathtaking swing to the west and within seconds is skating above the fractured bowl of the island's north side. Going by foot from here is a good plan: there's a steep track down to the town, an hour or two's knee-wobbling on foot or, with the day before you, take the gentler descent along the main road, incised into the cliff, with the soaring needle peaks of **Monte Gordo** dominating the skyline to the southwest. During the late summer months this valley, **the Fajãs**, can be fabulously beautiful, spilling with green from the concerted efforts of farmers and hydrologists, dashed with colour from briefly flowering plants, spiked with the strange shapes of drought-resistant **dragon trees**. The enchanting road, about 15km from the peaks down to the town, winds down past the hamlets and farm plots via a swerving series of deep rents along the north coast.

Ribeira Brava and the east

RIBEIRA BRAVA, facing out to sea on the north side, is firmly Portuguese in feel. A delightfully pretty mesh of narrow streets and whitewash, nestled deep between towering crags, it was established in the seventeenth century, about as far inland as possible, in order to resist the attacks of pirates. The attractions are all rather obscure perhaps, but they're central to the town's appeal: Ribeira Brava, once the flourishing centre of academic and literary life in Cape Verde, quickly establishes its remote, insular identity and is a rewarding place to stay for a few days.

The big, sky-blue **parish church** here, the Igreja Matriz, was the Cape Verdean see until the twentieth century. It's supposed to hold a small museum of religious bits and pieces, among them a valuable and unusual sixteenth-century golden chalice, but it rarely seems to be open. Prospects are better at the **seminary**, a little way up the *ribeira*, which once provided a classical education for students from all over the islands. Here there's a library and reliquary attached to the chapel, and you should be able to persuade the priest to let you in. Back in town there's a fine *praça* and a town hall with neatly tended gardens in front, the site of the birthplace in 1872 of José Lopes da Silva, a leading Cape Verdean poet. Down on the bank of the *ribeira* a shady, second *praça* hides a café and tables for serious draughts playing and *grogue* imbibing.

Practicalities

The town musters a **TACV office** (☎235.11.61), **bank**, **post office**, a small **mercado** and two or three basic **general stores**. You may even stumble across a **workshop** manufacturing cups and utensils – both functional and miniature – out of bamboo: a tiny part of a tiny souvenir industry. It's not enough to keep many younger people here and the drift to Mindelo, Praia and overseas is unceasing.

For **accommodation**, if you're counting the escudos, check out the large but rather scruffy *Pensão da Cruz* (☎235.12.82 ❷) or the basic but good-value *Residencial Jumbo* (☎235.13.15 ❷). The third option, if you want a simple, clean, comfortable room, is the beautifully located *Pensão Residencial Jardim* (☎235.11.17 ❹). Rooms #201 and #202 have the best views, while the compact little restaurant (order a few hours beforehand) offers reasonably priced traditional fare (including *modje*, a hearty local stew of meat, potatoes, onions and maize) and incredible vistas over the town below. Just inland from the main square is the *Pensão Santo António* (☎235.22.00 ❺), a strikingly pretty, renovated colonial townhouse with lovely en-suite rooms, TV and a/c.

Ribeira Brava has several small **casas de pasto**. Chief among these is the *Bela Sombra Dalila* (☎235.18.30) – try the tasty tuna steaks, though as ever it's as well to order in advance. Another decent place is *Bar Restaurant Sila* (☎235.11.88) where you'll find good, filling fare and an old, but still functioning, pool table.

TACV flights are scheduled to leave the airstrip on Mondays, Wednesdays and Fridays for São Vicente, Praia and Sal but in practice these are among the most-cancelled routes in the network.

Out of Ribeira Brava

Out of town, a very pleasant day is to be had **hiking** up the *ribeira*, where you'll meet an array of colourful locals and the odd donkey buckling under a load of water or firewood. Look out too, for the discarded dragons and other papier-mâché monsters from the carnival (the biggest outside Mindelo) which often turn up in the strangest of places. There's a *grogue* distillery about halfway up on the left-hand side; they may let you look around if you ask politely. A little church is perched at the very top, keeping a sentinel-like watch over the valley below.

Looking **east**, the long axis of the island stretches for 30km, narrowing at one point to less than 3km across. There are two principal tracks – a "ridgeway" and a north-coast path – which meet high above the harbour of **CARRIÇAL** to the east. You'll need to be fit and determined to hike out here – supplies are very few and far between.

Sal

Sal, the "island of salt" – a piece of Sahara in the middle of the ocean, relentlessly windy and mostly barren and flat – is the least inviting of the archipelago, ironically so, since it's the most touristy. It was one of the last islands to be colonized, early in the nineteenth century, when the Portuguese began to exploit its **salt** ponds properly and introduced purification techniques. In earlier centuries, vast heaps of salt could be loaded onto ships for the cost of the labour alone, though since it was full of donkey dung it was considered low-grade even then. Sal's salt was picked up by trawlers from England on their way to North Atlantic fishing grounds, and exported to the Newfoundland fishing towns, and later to Brazil for beef preservation.

Despite its natural shortcomings, Sal receives more tourists than any other Cape Verdian island. Its international airport is well-established, its southern resort town, **Santa Maria**, is growing steadily, and much of its remaining beachfront has been parcelled up into development sites for more new hotels, villas and apartments.

Even if you haven't planned to stay here, there's a high chance you'll sample Sal sooner or later, whether you fly in from Europe or pass through on a boat or plane connection. Attractions are simple to list – one beautiful, though windswept, white **beach** and burgeoning associated watersports, which you're recommended to aim for without delay. Save for the magnificent **salt pans** at **Pedra de Lume**, there's almost nothing else worth a pause. **Espargos**, the capital, is the business end of things, with a

SAL

Monte Grande
▲ 403m

300m
▲

Palmeira

Pedra Lume

Espargos

International Airport ✈

Baía de Murdeira

Murdeira

N

ACCOMMODATION
Belorizonte/
Novorizonte   **B**
ClubHotel Riu
Funana-Garopa   **A**
Dunas do Sal   **C**

Ⓐ   ● Santa Maria
Ⓒ Ⓑ

0   5 km

Sal airline and transport information

Airlines
Cabo Verde Express ☎991.28.13 (a local air-charter company)
South African Airlines ☎241.36.95
TAAG Angolan Airlines ☎242.10.51
TAP Air Portugal ☎241.12.55
TACV ☎241.13.05

Car rental agents
Avis ☎241.30.30
Hertz ☎241.37.02
Rental Auto ☎241.35.19

TACV flights from Sal
Boa Vista: daily (30min)
Praia: at least 2 daily (50min)
São Nicolau: Mon, Wed, Fri (40min)
São Vicente: 2 daily (50min)

smattering of budget accommodation but nothing to see. On a positive note, if Sal is your first stop in Cape Verde, you can at least be sure that everywhere else you go will be more interesting.

Arrivals and information
Surprisingly modern as the airport is, it only bursts into life when an international flight is in. If you've arrived without a **visa**, you'll have to report to the immigration office to pay the standard fee (€25 at the time of writing, but subject to change); there may be a lengthy queue. Check-in for **domestic flights** is adjacent to international arrivals and departures; if you're arriving from outside Cape Verde and catching a connecting flight you'll need to collect your baggage, clear customs and check in again.

Inside the small terminal building are a forex bureau, BCN and BCA banks, ATMs, a mobile-phone outlet and a couple of cafés. There's an efficient and helpful baggage store where you can leave bulky items (CV$100/24hr), if you want to spend a few hours unencumbered down at Santa Maria.

Espargos is less than 2km north up the road from the airport – you could probably walk there in twenty minutes – while Santa Maria is 17km south (a 15–20min drive). **Taxis** to Espargos charge CV$200, with a thirty percent surcharge at night; the tariff is CV$700–1000 *deslocação* to get to Santa Maria, though you might well get a free lift or grab a place in an *aluguer* (CV$100) if you walk out to the Espargos–Santa Maria road.

Arriving **by sea**, you enter a drab grey bay – **Palmeira harbour** – 4km from Espargos, and will have to wait for a lift, which shouldn't be too long in coming. For catamaran and ferry tickets and information, ask at the Polar office on Rua da Moeda (☎241.42.45). For details of ferry and catamaran sailings, see p.440.

Espargos and the north
Little **ESPARGOS** may be uninspiring but it's always buzzing with activity. You can make a jaunt out of town quickly (and perhaps illicitly, so don't stop to ask anyone) by climbing to the summit of the **telecommunications hill** just five minutes' walk from the main square. From up there behind the dishes you have a good view of the entire, drab island; to the north a number of old volcanic hills; southwards the bleak brown wastelands fading away to the fringe of white beach

at Santa Maria. On the east coast of the island, about 6km from Espargos, lies a peculiar highlight of Cape Verde (and perhaps Sal's saving grace), the salt pans at **Pedra da Lume**.

Espargos itself has a **post office**, a branch of the BCA **bank**, **Internet** access (Com Cyber Space in the street behind *Paz e Bem*), a few bars and a *praça* which, on occasional Saturday nights, the entire population seems to squeeze into. The **aluguer** park is at the southern end of town.

If you're travelling on a budget, or have the briefest of stopovers between flights, it's worth taking advantage of Espargos' **accommodation**, which is cheaper than that in Santa Maria. Your best bet is *Residencial Santos* on Murro Curral near the post office (T241.19.00 Eresidencialsantos@hotmail.com ⑤), which has a rooftop restaurant and bright rooms with a/c and fridges, or the plain and simple en-suite rooms at *Casa Angela*, 20 Rua Abel Djassy (T241.13.27 ④), or *Residencial-Restaurante Violão*, on Ribeira Funda (T241.14.16 Ebarviolao@cvtelecom.cv ④). Other decent budget options are the antiquated-feeling but spotless *Residencial Central* on Rua 5 de Julho, off the main square T241.13.66 ④), and the more modern *Pensão Paz e Bem* on Rua Jorge Barbosa, the side-street off the northeastern corner of the square (T241.17.82 Epensaopazbem@cvtelecom.cv ④). Opposite the *aluguer* park on Rua Amílcar Cabral, the relatively upmarket *Hotel Atlântico* (T241.12.10 Ehotelatlantico @cvtelecom.cv ⑤) is a large place with ho-hum three-star facilities.

For **eating**, options are a bit more limited; if you've gone down to Santa Maria for the day, you're probably best advised to have dinner before returning. Worth a try are the dining room at *Violão* (which hosts live bands at weekends), the rooftop bar and grill at *Residencial Santos* or the amiable, Portuguese-run *Restaurant Salinas* halfway along Rua 5 de Julho (T241.17.99), all of which serve reasonably priced fish and meat dishes. *Esplanada Bom Dia* (opposite the *Atlântico*) is good for snacks.

Cycling on Sal

"Renting a bicycle is a good option – only in Santa Maria, from €10 per day, or €3 per hour. Strong wind might be a problem, but the roads to the only real tourist sight, Pedra da Lume, are paved and flat. From Santa Maria it takes 2–3 hours. It is easier to get back – because of the constant wind."

Igor Fabjan, Slovenia

Pedra da Lume

Aluguers heading to the old salt-mining station of **PEDRA DA LUME** are few and far between, although it's a pleasant enough – if windy – walk. The village itself is a desolate, haunting place comprising a row of old miners' cottages, a lonely white church, a picturesque if tiny harbour too shallow for any but the smallest vessels, and an ancient, towering set of wooden pulleys and loading equipment. There's also a (barely functional) ship repair yard, while the harbour has a bizarre slipway used to haul out small boats for loading.

Follow the creaking overhead pulley system uphill for a kilometre and you come to a tunnel gouged through the hillside. Aim for the shaft of light at the end and you suddenly emerge blinking onto the rim of a gigantic, shallow crater. On its floor is a patchwork of salt pans, squared off by paths and channels, and tinted various shades of the spectrum by dissolved minerals. People will tell you it's all still in use, but it certainly doesn't look that way. A neat row of white plastic sun-loungers at the far end adds an utterly incongruous and rather surreal touch, a reminder that large tour groups frequent the place to wallow in the pans en masse. Also incongruous is the restaurant, *Ca'da Mosto* (T242.22.10), on the beach front, a place which caters to the tour groups and serves undeniably fine, good-value pizza (around the CV$500 mark).

Santa Maria

SANTA MARIA DAS DORES (St Mary of Sorrows) was practically a ghost town only a few years ago. Ruined timber buildings in ornate style were scattered across the flats, linked by the twisted remains of narrow-gauge rail track which once shifted tuna for the Portuguese and ran out to the end of a thoroughly unsafe jetty. Now it is the engine room of Cape Verdean tourism, helping to power the archipelago's economy. Its simple draw is a stunning flex of white sand dipping into blue-green waves of scintillatingly clear water, and the heady shade of the hotels by the beach. The old town, still slightly ragged around the edges, is rapidly taking on the mantle of a bona fide holiday resort, with a main drag, various restaurants with different themes, and enough small-time property investors and vacationing Europeans – a hard core of them globetrotting windsurfers – to give the place a gentle buzz.

In terms of sightseeing or town-based activities, there's next to nothing, but part of Santa Maria's appeal is the complete lack of pressure – including no pressure to see sights. Half an hour's wander will give you a good feel for the town. Down on the beach, you'll see the rickety **jetty**, poking out 100m over the azure waters, already an archetypal image of Cape Verde. Behind it stands the **White House**, part of the old salt-export infrastructure of the early twentieth century, now converted for various businesses.

Orientation and transport

The short trip from the airport or Espargos down to the south coast is a journey through a real desert. Goats are about the only animals you'll see: their introduction in the seventeenth century, before any significant human settlement, began a process of **soil destruction** which is now virtually complete. Nothing really grows, wild or cultivated – in fact the whole landscape looks as if it was scoured by bulldozers earlier in the day.

The long, narrow grid of Santa Maria runs in an east–west direction parallel to the beach with its main street, Rua Amílcar Cabral, merging with the Espargos road. The other principal streets are Rua 1 de Junho, one block south towards the sea, which gives on to the main Square Marcelo Leitão halfway along. The street closest to the beach is Rua 15 de Agosto, one block south again. At the western edge of town, a new road runs out parallel to the busy beach for a few kilometres, along which are bunched most of the upmarket resort hotels, the most distant of which are a good half-hour's walk from town. A cobbled pedestrian **promenade** also runs out in the same direction, just behind the beach: this is the main route for resort guests to head into the town centre.

For out-of-town trips, **aluguers** gather at the western end of town on the corner opposite the bank; **taxis** also ply their trade from this area. While they run between Espargos and Santa Maria all day, *aluguers* can be thin on the ground at night, so be prepared for a wait if you're travelling after dark.

Accommodation

There's a huge range of **places to stay** for such a small, compact town, from the affordable to the super-expensive, although genuine budget accommodation is sorely lacking. One thing to consider is how far you're prepared to be from town: Santa Maria's newest developments are 2–3km from the town centre's bars and restaurants.

The satellite resort of **MURDEIRA**, 10km north of town and midway between Santa Maria and the airport, is particularly isolated, but it has one of the island's few large self-catering complexes, *Murdeira Village* (℡241.16.04 ⓔmurdeira.village @cvtelecom.cv ⓐ). This quiet option for families, but pricey compared to the privately owned and rented **apartments and villas** advertised on the islands' Web portals from time to time. However, the swimming here is good, and more

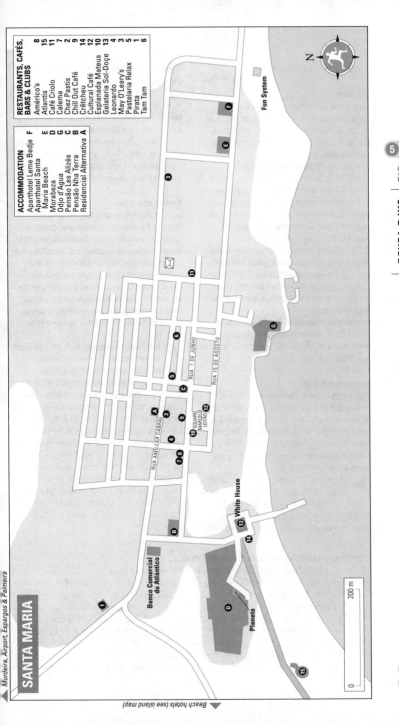

SANTA MARIA

▲ Murdeira, Airport, Espargos & Palmeira

▼ Beach hotels (see island map)

ACCOMMODATION
Aparthotel Leme Bedje	F
Aparthotel Santa	E
Maria Beach	
Morabeza	D
Odio d'Agua	G
Pensão Les Alizés	C
Pensão Nha Terra	B
Residencial Alternativa	A

RESTAURANTS, CAFÉS, BARS & CLUBS
Américo's	8
Atlantis	15
Café Criolo	11
Calema	7
Chez Pastis	2
Chill Out Café	9
Crêtcheu	14
Cultural Café	12
Esplanada Mateus	10
Gelateria Sol-Doçe	13
Leonardo	4
May O'Leary's	3
Pastelaria Relax	5
Pirata	1
Tam Tam	6

RUA AMÍLCAR CABRAL

RUA 1 DE JUNHO

RUA 15 DE AGOSTO

SQUARE MARCELO LEITÃO

Banco Comercial do Atlântico

White House

Planeta

Fun System

N

0   200 m

sheltered than Santa Maria, with two small coves: the southern one has good snorkelling.

Hotels and resorts

The Town

Aparthotel Santa Maria Beach out on the eastern stretch of Rua 15 de Agosto ☎242.14.50 ✉stmaria-beach@cvtelecom.cv. Cape Verdean–owned, with simple, pleasant, airy rooms, some with balconies. ❺

Pensão Les Alizés off Rua Amílcar Cabral ☎242.14.46 ✉lesalizes@cvtelecom.cv. Run by a French father-and-daughter team and housed in a traditional *sobrado* with very bright, tasteful and comfortable rooms with timber shutters and verandahs, and an exquisite roof terrace. ❻

Pensão Nha Terra Rua 1 de Junho ☎242.11.09 ✉nhaterra@hotmail.com. Sunny, clean and good-value rooms within striking distance of the beach and the action in the centre of town. Downstairs, there's a tiny pool and a neighbourhood-style restaurant which serves good seafood. ❺

Residencial Alternativa Rua Amílcar Cabral ☎442.12.16. One of the cheapest places to bed down in central Santa Maria, and modest, but clean and homely. ❻

Central beach area

Aparthotel Leme Bedje far-eastern edge of town, a stone's throw from the beach ☎242.11.46 ⓦwww.lemebedje.com. Rooms, bungalows and apartments fitted out in upmarket but rustic style using local art and materials. Besides offering reasonable value and a quiet location, they also rent out mountain bikes. ❼

🏃 **Morabeza** at the start of the beach promenade ☎242.10.20 ⓦwww.hotelmorabeza .com. A fine resort that's been in business since the 1970s, and is widely praised for its atmosphere, location and service. There's a good beach restaurant, diving centre and popular after-dark entertainment. ❽

🏃 **Odjo d'Agua** off Rua 15 de Agosto, near the municipal market at the eastern end of town ☎242.14.00 ⓦwww.odjodagua.net. Undeniably attractive and charmingly sited hotel, on a tiny private beach. The open-sided restaurant is a little pricey but worth it for its glorious sea views. The pool is small but pretty, and the foyer has some great old black-and-white photos of Cape Verde. ❽

Western beach area

Belorizonte/Novorizonte the first of the big hotels on the west-bound beach road ☎242.10.45 ⓦwww.oasisatlantico.com. Considering the price, this place – used by European tour operators – has a disappointing holiday-camp atmosphere and mediocre catering. It comprises two parts, both with pools and buffet restaurants: the *Belorizonte*, with standard international-style rooms, and the *Novorizonte*, which has wooden cabins with space for two adults and two children. Seasonal rates apply. ❽

🏃 **Dunas de Sal** set back from the westbound road ☎242.90.50 ⓦwww.hoteldunasdesal .com. Not on the beach, but within easy walking distance, this is the first place in Santa Maria to opt for a sleek, urban look with contemporary extras such as a small spa. The service can be patchy but the stylish ambience makes up for it. ❽

ClubHotel Riu Funana-Garopa at the far west end of the resort ☎242.90.60 ⓦwww.riu.com. This vast upmarket beach-resort complex, styled like a Disneyfied Sudanic palace, receives mixed reports – families who buy into the all-inclusive concept enjoy the abundant facilities, but it's far too contrived and impersonal for some. The beach, though beautiful, is often too windy and rough for swimming. ❽

Eating, drinking and nightlife

Many of the hotels have their own **restaurants**, the best of which have been mentioned in the reviews. These, together with the places listed below, provide Sal with possibly the most varied and cosmopolitan range of food you're likely to encounter anywhere in Cape Verde. Most of the restaurants serve lunch from noon until three, are closed in late afternoon and begin serving dinner in the early evening. With most hotels laying on all kinds of entertainment to keep their clients on the premises at night, the centre of Santa Maria can be disappointingly quiet. There's nevertheless a scattering of bars and at least one nightclub. Many of the restaurants have regular live music, though some of it can be of the tacky cabaret variety.

Américo's Rua 1 de Junho ⊤ 242.10.11. Near Praça Marcelo Leitão, this long-established seafood restaurant often has live Cape Verdean music towards the end of the evening.

Atlantis on the beach between the *Belorizonte* and the *Morabeza* ⊤ 242.18.79 (open daily 10am–10pm). This large, open, beach restaurant is popular with windsurfers and is good for a relaxed lunch or a jug of *grogue*-laced sangría.

Café Criolo between Rua Amílcar Cabral and Rua 1 de Junho ⊤ 242.17.74. Small, atmospheric bar with more local flavour than most and constantly busy with islanders and tourists. Tapas-style snacks.

Calema Rua 1 de Junho. Cool bar that's long been a fixture of Santa Maria's nightlife, particularly with the surfing and windsurfing crowd.

Chez Pastis Rua Amílcar Cabral ⊤ 984.36.96 (evenings only, closed Sun). A real find – this tiny, tucked-away Franco-Italian restaurant in a pretty courtyard serves delicious smoked fish, Mediterranean-style pasta dishes and expertly prepared grills such as lobster and octopus.

Chill Out Café Rua 1 Junho. A mellow café-bar with a streetside terrace made for people-watching.

Crêtcheu Restaurante Pizzeria at the start of the beach promenade on the western edge of town ⊤ 242.12.66 (closed Tues). Quality seafood, pasta and pizza cooked by an Italian chef, with main dishes from around CV$700.

Cultural Café Square Marcelo Leitão. With patio tables (each carved in the shape of one of the islands), this place draws flocks of tourists for drinks at dusk. Foodwise, the emphasis is on traditional, locally sourced fare.

Esplanada Mateus Rua 1 Junho ⊤ 242.13.13. With a prime location on Santa Maria's town square, this is an attractive, though touristy, place with a good choice of seafood dishes and entertainment from local musicians.

Gelateria Sol-Doçe on the beach near the jetty ⊤ 994.65.62. Part of the historic White House now houses this unpretentious café, where you can tuck into ice cream, crépes and caipirinhas under a shady tree.

Leonardo off Rua 1 Junho. One of the more upmarket Italian restaurants in town, this is an attractive little place with a stone-walled courtyard, and a tourist favourite.

May O'Leary's east end of town. With bright, brash decor, loud music and rowdy conversation, this bar makes no attempt to blend into its surroundings, but is popular with Santa Maria's growing contingent of Irish residents and visitors.

Pastelaria Relax Rua Amílcar Cabral ⊤ 242.11.83. A favourite with tourists and locals alike, serving delicious cakes, yoghurt, fruit, sandwiches and pizza.

Pirata on the Espargos road. This perennially popular, pirate-themed club gets going in the early hours.

Tam Tam Rua Amílcar Cabral (Mon–Sat 8am–12.30am). A popular hub of local gossip for English-speaking expats and holidaymakers, this Irish-owned bar is packed in the evenings, particularly when there's a major football match on the box.

Listings

Bank Banco Comercial do Atlántico (Mon–Fri 8am–3pm) is on the corner at the western end of Rua Amílcar Cabral.

Car rental Hertz ⊤ 242.16.62; Alucar ⊤ 242.11.87; Europcar ⊤ 242.17.00. Local operators like Hifacar (⊤ 242.16.51) have 4x4 vehicles for around the CV$5500/day mark.

CDs The Oficina de Arte at the eastern end of Rua 1 de Junho has a well-chosen couple of shelves (as well as a large stock of good-quality, tourist-oriented souvenirs; Visa cards accepted), although your best bet is the shop in the airport.

Diving Sal is a major diving centre, with several hotel-based centres offering a variety of training courses and trips by rigid inflatable boat. PADI-recommended outfits include Cabo Verde Diving at the *Hotel Djadsal* on the beach past the *Novorizonte* (⊤ 997.88.24 ⊛ www.caboverdediving .net) and Scuba Caribe at the *Riu Funana-Garopa* (⊤ 242.90.60 ⊛ www.scubacaribe.com). If you're qualified, diving and equipment hire costs around €55 for a single dive or €240 for six dives.

Fishing It could be you landing one of the whoppers on the pier: Max Dias is the man to sort you out (⊤ 294.29.22), whether you're after tuna, wahoo or marlin, big game or bottom fishing. Expect to pay CV$27,500 per half-day for a group of four or five with a boat and skipper provided.

Internet access Santa Maria has a handful of Internet cafés which charge CV$200–400/hr.

Police Espargos ⊤ 241.11.32; Santa Maria ⊤ 242.11.32.

Post office Towards the northeast end of town (Mon–Fri 8am–noon & 2–5pm).

Travel agents Barracuda Tours at the airport (⊤ 241.24.52) or in Santa Maria (⊤ 242.20.33 ⊛ www.barracudatours.com) is experienced in planning group tours and can also put together tailor-made inter-island itineraries for individuals. Oceanis (☏ 242.13.17) organizes Jeep safaris around Sal, quad-bike rental, shark-watching trips and tours to other islands; as does Planeta (☏ 242.17.27 ℮ info@planeta-caboverde.com), based near the *Aparthotel Leme Bedje*.

Windsurfing/kitesurfing Sal being the windsurfing capital of Cape Verde, there are very good facilities: Surf Zone at the *Hotel Morabeza* (☏ 997.88.04 ⓦ www.surfcaboverde.com) is a friendly outfit, offering equipment rental for CV$1650 per hour or CV$4400 per day, and private windsurfing lessons for CV$3850 per hour, 3hr introduction to kitesurfing CV$9350; 10hr course CV$30,800. Club Nathalie Simon near *Restaurante Atlantis* (☏ 996.77.06 ⓦ www .windcaboverde.com) charges a little more. Club Mistral near the *Hotel Belorizonte* (☏ 993.47.99 ⓦ www.club-mistral.com) is also very good, though mainly geared towards people on pre-booked windsurfing/kitesurfing holidays. Finally, Fun System (ⓦ www.fun-system.com) has a small but friendly operation on the beach at the eastern end of town.

Boa Vista

"Boa Vista is said to have been productive at one time; at present it is almost a desert. Its people, of whom there are four thousand, are almost always hungry, and the lean cattle, with sad faces and tears in their eyes, walk solemnly in cudless rumination over grassless fields. In the valleys there is some vegetation. Fishing, salt-making and going to funerals are the chief amusements and employments of the people."

Reverend Charles Thomas, writing in the 1850s

Life was not easy on **Boa Vista** in the nineteenth century, but things have improved a little, at least for the cattle. Drought continues to plague this hillocky pancake of an island, though, and it still retains large areas of spectacular shifting **sand dunes**, notably in the west. The island has a captivatingly desolate interior, and a necklace of spectacular white **beaches** all around, most of them entirely free of development (and, for that matter, of shade-giving trees). The one at Santa Monica is particularly long and beautiful. It's a great island to explore in a rented 4x4, with a clear enough route right round the island: *aluguers* tend to be very scarce. If you make the effort to get into the parched and peaceful countryside, you'll find the few people (well under 4000 people live on the island, all but 800 of them in Sal Rei) graciously welcoming, with a high proportion of English-speakers who've spent years at sea. The traditional *morna* folk songs of the island are rated the most cheerful and upbeat in Cape Verde.

The island's struggling economy long depended on **salt**, but that industry has died out, and date farming – there are large palm groves in the northwest – supplemented by fishing and some livestock-grazing provided the main alternatives to emigration. These days, tourism is turning the island's fortunes around; Boa Vista has a new international airport terminal and the first of a growing number of beach hotels and holiday complexes have already opened. Italian visitors are by far the most prominent but German and British tourists are beginning to join them. Boavistans themselves seem to have made best use of the island's famous **shipwrecks**; vessels frequently came to grief in the treacherous rocky shallows on the north and northeast coasts – and still occasionally do, since navigation charts for the seas around Boa Vista are inaccurate, in some cases by several hundred metres. There are judged to be about a hundred wrecks, some of them quite old, and most have provided an unexpected bounty for needy islanders.

Turtles were grist to the Boavistan mill as well, and unfortunately still are – there are precious egg-laying sites on many beaches. **Humpback whales** are also regularly seen in the waters around Boa Vista, specifically in the bay southwest of Sal Rei. This is the most important breeding site for this small population only now recovering from centuries of hunting. Unfortunately, their future recovery cannot be taken for granted, with ongoing tourist developments posing a threat. While the whales are often visible from the beach, you may be able to persuade local fishermen to take you out for a closer look.

Arrivals and information

Flights arrive at the **airport**, 5km south of Boa Vista's capital, **Sal Rei**, near the old village of **RABIL**. The fare into town depends on the number of passengers and the mood of the driver; you'll often be quoted a price of CV\$600–700 but it's possible to bargain them down. On your return journey, it may be difficult to find any vehicle, never mind an inexpensive one, so if you haven't made an advance booking, start looking for one on the square well before your check-in time.

Ferries come close to the port, in the heart of the little town, and passengers come ashore by lighter. For details of ferry and catamaran sailings, see p.440.

To **get around** the island under your own steam, any of the main hotels will arrange for a Japanese 4x4 to be parked outside ready for you first thing (CV\$6500 for 24hr; CV\$10,000–30,000 deposit). To rent a vehicle independently, head to the Morena travel agency on the north side of the square (☎251.14.45), which also runs half-day or full-day excursions to the island's villages, oases and beaches for CV\$2500–3000, including guide and insurance. Alternatively, you can rent **mountain bikes** at Hotel *Dunas* (see overleaf; expect to pay about CV\$1500 a day).

Sal Rei and around

SAL REI has a gentle buzz: there are always people knocking around the central square, usually boisterous teenagers, while the row of African market stalls beyond the square's northern edge are suitably animated. The town beach is at its liveliest on weekends, and if your visit coincides with a football match at the Sal Rei "stadium" you'll see most of the male population in one go. If you can find a boat, a trip out to the **Ilhéu de Sal Rei**, an islet opposite the town, is interesting: it holds the ruins of an old **fort** (Fortaleza Duque de Braganza) and the waters are good for snorkelling. Around the month of August you may even see turtles here.

If you want to be active, Sal Rei can offer a number of diversions, including **mountain biking**, **diving** and, of course, **windsurfing**. There are currently a couple of places you can get your sea wings: Happy Surf (in conjunction with *Hotel Dunas*) offers an hour's rental for around CV\$1800; a full eight-hour beginners' course is CV\$6000 and they also hire kitesurfing equipment. The smaller, friendlier Boavista Wind Club (☎251.10.36 ⊛www.boavistawindclub.com) charges €220 for six days' equipment hire and boasts a small, shaded wooden terrace with hammocks – a great place to chill and play chess after a hard day on the waves. **Diving** is another popular diversion; the Submarine Dive Centre (☎992.48.65 ⓔatilros @hotmail.com) can provide equipment and lessons from beginner to advanced – its Brazilian owner is a certified PADI instructor. All of the above firms are to be found next to one another on the beach at the southern edge of town.

Mountain biking is more fun than it might at first appear. Head south out of town, and turn immediately left opposite the Enacal petrol station to join the cobbles of the old road, the **Via Pittoresca**, down to the airport and **Rabil** village; the route undulates through a veritable forest of palm trees for several pretty kilometres before rejoining the main road. Considerably more taxing is the Boa Vista **Ultramarathon**, a gruelling annual desert race over 75km or 150km (the latter in two stages; for more info, see ⓦ www.boavistaultramarathon.com).

With a 4x4 vehicle, it's possible to get close to the wreck of the **Cabo de Santa Maria**, 8km northeast of Sal Rei. The Spanish freighter has been rusting off the beach since 1968, when its cargo of car parts, garlic, rosemary and pornographic magazines was seized and rapidly traded across the island. From Sal Rei, drive out towards the *Marine Club*, then leave the road before the hotel entrance and head across country to the east, following the tracks for a few hundred metres until you reach a little church in a large, white-walled plot. From here, continue generally uphill and over the crests until you emerge above the island's northern coast with a clear view of the wreck a couple of kilometres away. A driveable track goes down to the beach and tyre marks lead you the whole way there.

Sun and heat

"I went to Cape Verde in August, and that isn't the best time to go. It's too hot, even at night. It's better to go in the winter, then it cools off at night. Also important is a good sun protection lotion. The sun can be very burning on the islands."

Johan Schepkens, Belgium

Practicalities

The town is simplicity itself to navigate, with a huge, rather bare central square fringed by acacia trees and flanked by two main streets, Avenida Amílcar Cabral and Rua Dos Emigrantes, running roughly north–south. There's a branch of the BCA **bank** on the square, while both the **post office** and **TACV** (☏251.11.86) are up the slope of Rua Dos Emigrantes. The latter operate flights to Praia (Sun; 40min) and Sal (daily; 30min). For **catamaran** and **ferry** enquiries, visit Anavmar in the port area (☏251.17.30). For details of ferry and catamaran sailings, see p.440.

For **Internet** access, try the Centro Informático Municipal, in the middle of the square (daily 10am–1pm & 4–9pm).

Aside from the hotels, there are few places to eat, drink or shop in Sal Rei. The best (and busiest, so book ahead) restaurant by a mile is *Riba D'Olte* (☏251.15.63; 6–10pm daily, closed Wed) which serves pasta good enough to attract lots of Italian visitors. *Bar Naida* on the main square (☏255.11.73) has a good reputation for local fare, while *Bar Restaurante Tambrera*, just off the square (☏251.11.45), serves simple meals in bright surroundings and *Restaurante Maresias*, near the wharf (☏251.14.30), is worth trying for fish and seafood. You might also make arrangements to head out of town to eat in Rabil, at the *Sodade di Nha Terra* (☏251.10.48) – a prepared-to-order-only Cape Verdean restaurant run by an excellent cook.

Hotels and pensões

Aparthotel Ca'Nicola Estoril beach, south of town ☏251.17.93 ⓦ www.canicola.com. Rather pricey but undeniably stylish, this Italian-run, beachside place has self-catering accommodation with plenty of space to spread out. ⑧

Dunas on the seafront ☏251.12.25 ⓔ dunas @bwscv.com. Pleasantly informal and welcoming establishment with fine, bright rooms, some of which offer incredible vistas across the bay. ⑧

Estoril Beach Resort Estoril beach, south of town ☏251.10.78 ⓦ www.estorilbeachresort.com.

Italian-run, this sizeable, stone-clad beach hotel offers brightly decorated rooms and suites. There's a nice upstairs restaurant serving quality Italian fare. ⑦

Migrante Guesthouse Sal Rei ☏251.11.43 ⓦ www.migrante-guesthouse .com. This beautifully restored *sobrado*, decorated in a wonderfully relaxed, ethno-chic style by its Italian owners, is the best choice in town. ⑦

Parque das Dunas Praia de Chaves ☏251.12.88 ⓦ www.parquedasdunas.com. Pleasantly informal collection of bright, well-spaced bungalow-style rooms 5km south of town, on a wide and beautiful beach. The focus is a very pleasant pool with good sea views. **8**

Pensão Santa Isabel on the square ☏ 251.12.52. Central, with en-suite rooms, this is arguably the best-value budget option. **4**

Residencial A Paz off the square's southern end ☏ 251.16.43 ⊛ www.a-paz.com. Good value, with

small, bright en-suite rooms fitted out with lots of natural fabrics, and a wonderful roof terrace. You're assured of a hearty welcome from the Italian owner. **5**

Residencial Boa Esperança Rua Tavares Almeida, one block east of the south side of the square ☏ 251.11.70. With simple rooms above a basic restaurant, this is one of Sal Rei's cheapest options. **3**

Driving round the island

A highly recommended day can be spent **circumnavigating Boa Vista** with your own transport, though ensure you have sufficient drinking water and a good spare. And don't go alone either: either take a companion or hire a guide. If you have an accident out here (and Suzukis have been prone to roll), you may have a long wait for the first *aluguer* to come by.

The road south of Sal Rei goes through wiry little **Rabil**, then descends to a seasonal watercourse to cross through palm trees; take the left fork and you'll find yourself on a desolate open road heading across the central and northern part of the island. After 45 minutes you reach **JOÃO GALEGO**, the first of three tiny hamlets comprising the small, inhabited district known as "Norte" (pretty much the only populated part of the island apart from Sal Rei and Rabil and a small town in the southwest, Povoação Velha). A couple of kilometres further is **FUNDO DE FIGUEIRAS**, with a little surrounding farmland, whence a six-kilometre off-road diversion down a gentle shelving valley takes you to the splendidly wild and remote beach of **Baia das Gatas**. You'll find turtle bones and even the occasional dolphin skeleton here. Back at the "main road", the southernmost Norte settlement is **CABEÇA DE TARAFES**, and at this point the cobbled surface ceases abruptly and the real adventure begins. The track (easy to follow even though you're now unlikely to see another human being for a couple of hours) scales the gentle, brown rocky slopes of the depopulated eastern part of the island, crawling across the little ravines of seasonal watercourses, and speeding up over the hilltops. As you finally descend to reach the **southern coast**, near a deserted palm-tree oasis, and turn right to follow the shore, you'll need that four-wheel-drive as the track meets soft sand and, at certain times of year, even mud. You can drive straight down to a marvellously empty strand from here.

Curral Velho, an abandoned settlement at Boa Vista's southern extremity, is 28km beyond Cabeça (about 2hr). Don't try to continue direct to Praia de Santa Monica from Curral Velho – the rough track deteriorates as you leave the old settlement behind and rapidly becomes impassable, with boulders blocking uncertain wheel marks. Instead, as you arrive in Curral Velho from the east, turn right at the first large wall leading off inland and start to follow it north, and you can pick up a clear track which leads across the great, bare back of the island, more or less north or northwest, to rejoin the Norte road after about an hour. This track is mostly firm going, with some soft sand: keep the distinctive cone of Monte Santo António in view to your left and you can't really go wrong.

Guinea-Bissau

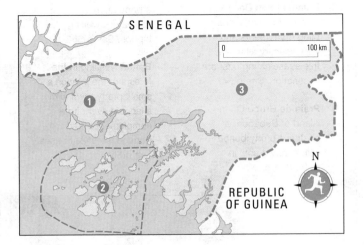

Highlights	512	6.2 The Bijagós islands	545	511
Introduction and Basics	513	6.3 The south and east	554	
6.1 Bissau and the northwest	537			

Guinea-Bissau highlights

* **Varela** A beach to rival Senegal's Cap Skiring coast just across the border. See p.544

* **Bolama town** Decaying colonial buildings, crumbling monuments and leafy scenery all make this a fascinating offshore destination. See p.547

* **Praia da Bruce** On the island of Bubaque, a postcard-pretty beach with hardly a soul in sight. See p.551

* **Orango** This Bijagós island not only features pristine tropical beaches but is home to unusual wildlife too – a population of saltwater-dwelling hippos. See p.553

* **Bafatá** Nestling in the forests of the interior, a small, pretty town with a languid river and a complement of red Portuguese-style houses. See p.555

▲ Bijagós children

Introduction and Basics

One of the smallest and least-known countries in West Africa, **Guinea-Bissau** isn't on the region's tourist trails. But if you're driven by a taste for adventure and discovery, you will spend an unforgettable time here – the opportunities to explore little-visited districts are always available.

Guinea-Bissau only gained its independence from Portugal in 1974 after a long and painful **war of liberation**, which contributed to the overthrow of the dictatorship in Portugal and turned the nation into a highly charged symbol of colonial repression. Until the end of the 1970s, the country's struggle for national survival inspired progressive movements in Europe and North America, as Nicaragua did in the 1980s. But political rigidity set in with economic failure, and enthusiasm for the revolution waned both in Guinea-Bissau and overseas. A military takeover in 1980 and subsequent lurch into a flawed democratic system brought little improvement. Long-standing rifts within the armed forces, fuelled by economic desperation, were the cause of the 1998/99 **military uprising** which ousted the elected government. The country has yet to fully recover from the civil war which ensued, and is, sadly, still characterized by political instability and crippling poverty.

The **Guinea-Bissauans** are renowned for being very laid-back company, and the country is refreshingly free of hassle. The sense of personal security which travellers experienced prior to the fighting has returned, but it's important to keep tabs on the situation when planning a trip in this unpredictable country.

In 2007 the country had no mains **electricity grid** (a situation that had remained unchanged for the previous four years), the lack of which leaves Bissau pitch black at night, except for the candles of traders and for establishments with their own generator – which means most hotels and guesthouses, some restaurants, and ministries and embassies. However, generators get rarer and nights darker the further upcountry you venture.

People

For its small size, Guinea-Bissau features a great diversity of ethnic groups. Most numerous are the **Balante**, mainly concentrated in the southern coastal creeks and forests. Much of the area under rice cultivation has been cleared by them over the centuries. In the northwest, the smaller population of **Fulup** (part of the Jola group concentrated in southern Senegal) are also great rice-farmers. **Pepel** and **Manjak** farmers from the Bissau region are heavily dependent on the city as a market, and operate a more diverse economy.

In contrast, the **Bijagó** people, who inhabit the Bijagós islands, are mostly self-sufficient (principally through fishing and palm-nut gathering), though men increasingly find work on the mainland or abroad. Numbering fewer than 40,000, the Bijagó have been under little pressure to change over the last two hundred years. They've resisted Islam and Christianity, and remain attached to traditional ways – as indeed is roughly sixty percent of the country's population as a whole. It's interesting to note that women have relatively greater economic power than is usually the case, as traditionally they are the owners of houses.

Most of the **Mandinka** live in the north, along the Senegalese border. The **Fula** inhabit the northeast and, as ever, they are powerful players in local politics: their conservative, feudal roots can't be ignored by whoever governs the country.

A large proportion of Guinea-Bissauans are mixed-race **Kriolu**-speakers, the majority of whom are Cape Verdean by descent, though some are descendants of the small number of Portuguese settlers and traders. There still exists a fragmented Portuguese settler community who arrived in colonial times, and a growing population of French expatriate workers.

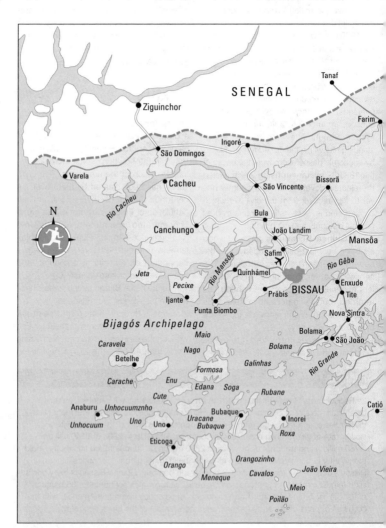

Where to go

The country is spread across a region of low-lying jungle and grassland, mangrove swamp, estuarine flats and meandering rivers. The most worthwhile destination is the **Bijagós archipelago**, a scattering of largely immaculate and admirably languid islands. Thanks to their distance from the mainland, these islands have preserved a unique culture, and have escaped the worst consequences of the unrest that has troubled the country in recent years.

The islands are a short boat ride from the city of **Bissau**, which is strangely – and pleasantly – low-key for a capital city. Most visitors merely pass through Bissau on the way to the islands, though the city is an excellent place to relax and admire Portuguese-influenced colonial architecture.

With its abundance of greenery and a handful of gorgeous beaches, the country's **mainland** has some appeal, but travel there

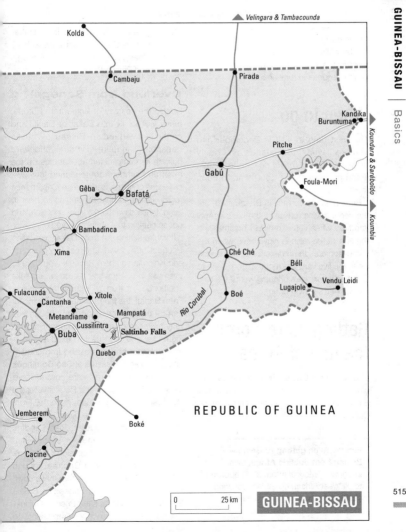

Officialdom is fairly suspicious of **cameras**. In Bissau, avoid the port, presidential palace and most other places with your camera and don't take pictures of people, unless you've asked permission. During *carnaval* you may be asked to pay for "permission" if you're wielding a camera (see "Crime and safety"). In country areas, people aren't much concerned and may even ask you to take pictures of them – they call them "postales". Photography on the islands is relaxed – and the soft lighting can make for some good shots, particularly at dawn and dusk. Video, and photography in general, is much easier if you're connected to an aid project, rather than a tourist.

requires patience (most journeys require at least one ferry ride), and you should be prepared for the stark poverty and inadequate facilities – for example, infrequent electricity and lack of running water – that you'll encounter in rural areas.

When to go

The best time to visit is December and January, when the islands are really pleasant. The *carnaval* season in Bissau (February/March) is a good time to be in the capital.

Bad times, particularly in Bissau itself, are the nerve-fraying run-up to the rains in April and May when you can hardly breathe, and the end of the rains in November, when the sun evaporates the moisture into the leaden air. In the five very wet months, from June to October, the air feels dripping wet all the time – whether it's raining or not.

Getting there from the rest of Africa

Most visitors to Guinea-Bissau either fly in or cross the border from Senegal, though a few European yachts make it down here from the Canaries.

For details on **getting to Guinea-Bissau from outside Africa**, plus important practical information applying to all West African countries, covering health, transport, cultural hints and more, see Basics, pp.19–28.

Flights

The only regular **flights** are from **Dakar** (sometimes via Banjul or Conakry) with Air Sénégal (daily), Lisbon with TAP Portugal (weekly) and Praia with TACV.

Overland from Senegal

Due to the scarcity of flights from Europe, many visitors fly into Dakar or Banjul and continue **overland to Bissau** by public transport. The journey is straightforward despite its complicated appearance on the map; and although the enduring low-level civil conflict in the Senegalese Casamance region (see p.246) is something to bear in mind, these days the risks are negligible and not something that should put you off.

If you're setting out **from Dakar**, you'll find Peugeot 504s heading direct to Ziguinchor and Kolda in southern Senegal. You have to overnight in one town or the other, and take another bush taxi on to Bissau in the morning. From **Banjul**, the trip to Bissau via Ziguinchor can be made in one long day, though you may prefer to plan for an overnight stop in Ziguinchor and continue the next day.

The closest border crossing from Ziguinchor into Guinea-Bissau is at **São Domingos** (daily 8am–6pm), from where onward travel to Bissau is via Ingoré and Bula, involving a short ferry crossing at São Vincente. From Bula, bush taxis follow the direct, southward route across the bridge at João Landim, taking only thirty minutes or so to reach Bissau. There's also an occasional **ferry link from São Domingos to Cacheu**, though using this route to Bissau is rare these days.

In the event of disturbances in Basse Casamance, it can be safer to enter Guinea-Bissau east of Ziguinchor. It's possible to travel from **Kolda**, 188km east of Ziguin-chor, to **Bafatá** in central Guinea-Bissau via Cambaju (2hr) and from **Velingara** in south-eastern Senegal to **Gabú via Pirada** (4hr). Both Bafatá and Gabú have several daily connections to Bissau.

Overland from Guinea

Driving **from Guinea** in your own vehicle, you have a choice between two main routes. The first takes the tarmac road to **Labé** via Mamou, battles on north to **Koundara** (a stretch that can be reason-able during the dry season), then crosses the border at **Kandika**, and follows the difficult bush track to **Gabú**, from where it's smooth tarmac all the way to Bissau. This is normally a two-day trip.

The second route goes from Conakry north to Boké, through **Koumbia** and **Foula-Mori**, then takes the ferry crossing at the border and joins the main road to Bissau at Pitche. Normal driving time between the capitals in the dry season is not much less than 22 hours on this route. With a dawn start from Conakry in a 4x4 you might just make it to the border in time to catch the ferryman at dusk, and thus arrive in Gabú or Bafatá late at night, but planning on a two-day journey is much more realistic.

There's **public transport** on both the above routes. Count on around eleven hours from Labé to Gabú and six hours from Koumbia to Gabú. You can also find taxis going direct from Conakry to Gabú, usually via Koumbia.

The third, more obvious-looking route **following the coast** is an arduous trek, not recommended unless you have bags of time. From **Boké** it goes to Buba, from where it's a relatively straightforward taxi ride to Bissau. A more adventurous alternative upon reaching Buba would be to travel to Enxude

and catch a pirogue from there to Bissau. Whichever option you choose, hardly anyone travels this route and, until you reach Buba, public transport is extremely light.

Red tape and visas

Visas, generally easy to obtain, are required by nearly all nationalities apart from West Africans. If you're flying into Bissau from one of the many countries with no Guinea-Bissau embassy or consulate, you can usually get a visa at the airport in Bissau.

At the consulates in Banjul, Ziguinchor and Conakry, visas are cheap and normally issued while you wait. The embassies in Dakar and Abidjan are more formal. The consulate in Ziguinchor, Senegal, issues multiple-entry visas for up to six months on the spot for CFA10,000. Shorter, single-entry visas cost the same, and since you'll be given what you ask for, it's a good idea to overestimate the duration of your stay and number of entries required.

Extending your visa, once in the country, isn't difficult, but allowing it to expire and overstaying can lead to serious problems if detected.

Visas for onward travel

For **onward travel**, don't count on getting many stamps in Bissau, as many embassies that closed during the civil war haven't returned. At the time of writing, Nigeria, Senegal, The Gambia, Mauritania and Guinea were the only West African states with diplomatic missions (details on p.543), though the French consulate can issue visas for certain countries. The following types of visa are issued for neighbouring countries: Senegal, 30-day double-entry for CFA5000; Guinea, 30-day double-entry for CFA30,000;

Average temperatures and rainfall											

Bissau

	Jan	Feb	Mar	Apr	May	June	July	Aug	Sept	Oct	Nov	Dec
Temperatures °C												
Min (night)	18	19	20	21	22	23	23	23	23	23	22	19
Max (day)	32	33	34	34	33	31	30	29	30	31	32	30
Rainfall mm	2	2	7	1	45	200	850	900	390	180	40	5

The Gambia, 3-month single-entry for CFA15,000. In all cases, visas are normally issued on the same day.

Info, websites, maps

Tourist information on Guinea-Bissau in English is almost nonexistent. There are no official tourist offices, nor much of an organized government department dealing with this minor industry. If you want to exhaust all possibilities, you could pay a direct visit to the Ministério do Turismo e do Ordenamento do Territorio, on Estrada de Santa Luzia in Bissau (☎20 60 62).

The 1:500,000, 3615 series IGN **map** of the country, updated in 1993, is reasonable (and the only one available) but, if anything, more optimistic in terms of road conditions than is now warranted.

Websites

There is very little about Guinea-Bissau on the Web, especially in English. One of the best portal sites is ⓦwww-sul.stanford.edu/ africa/guin-bis.html, where you'll find links to a variety of Guinea-Bissau-related sites. For French-speakers, ⓦwww.guinee-bissau.net has detailed tourist information and a good picture gallery.

The media

Radio is the most important form of broadcast media. Programmes are generally in Portuguese, although Radio Mavegro (100 FM) transmits the BBC World Service news in English at most hours. Mavegro is one of several private stations, the other main ones being Radio Bombolon and Radio Pidjiguiti.

As for **television**, the national station RTGB broadcasts every evening from 7pm. In Bissau, the Portuguese channel RTP International is

widely available, though reception gets harder the further inland you go, and there are very few TV sets outside of Bissau.

Looking to **the press** for news, there's the state-run *Nô Pintcha*, as well as the privately owned *Diário Bissau* and *Gazeta de Notícias*. Guinea-Bissau's international standing on **press freedom** is relatively good, with one of the best recent records in West Africa, according to Reporters Without Borders.

English-language foreign papers are notoriously hard to obtain.

Health

Healthcare in the country is very basic. Unsurprisingly, the main **hospital** in Bissau is the best equipped, and Bafatá, Canchungo, Bolama, Bubaque and Gabú have some limited medical services, but pharmacies are few and far between, and out on the remote islands and in the south, your health problems are largely your own to deal with.

Always keep your **yellow fever** certificate in your passport while travelling, in the unlikely event that you're asked for it. **Bilharzia** is a menace on sluggish inland waters, but the rivers are tidal far into the interior (the Rio Gêba as far upstream as Bafatá, the Cacheu past Farim and the Corubal as far as the Saltinho falls) and the schistosome worms can't survive in brackish water. There are also occasional **cholera** outbreaks, so keep up to date on local health advisories.

Costs, money, banks

Guinea-Bissau is part of the **CFA zone** (rates of exchange roughly £1=CFA880, $1=CFA450, €1=CFA656). Though public transport is inexpensive, petrol is fairly costly, a factor to be taken into account even if you're not using your own vehicle. This also has an impact on accommodation prices, since hotels run their own generators. There are virtually no budget places to stay in the capital, where the majority of hotels charge at least £15/$30 a night for a twin room. Outside Bissau, there's very little to spend your money on, and accommodation is cheaper, except in a smattering of resorts on the islands.

Banks and exchange

Thanks largely to the recent opening of the efficient Ecobank in Bissau, changing money in **banks** is a marginally quicker and smoother process than before – even so, go early in the day, and don't be surprised if it takes an hour or so. Ecobank changes cash without commission and traveller's cheques at 2 percent commission. Elsewhere, unlicensed moneychangers at the Central Market and one or two shops selling imported goods will change euros and dollars at slightly lower than the bank rate. You should change enough money in Bissau to see you through your travels inland or out to the islands; there is a bank in Gabú, but no guarantee that it will change money.

At the time of writing, Ecobank were planning to introduce cash advances on credit cards. However, on the whole, plastic is virtually useless in Guinea-Bissau. There are **no ATMs**, and don't count on even Bissau's top hotels accepting cards. All of this means you should arrive with sufficient cash, though you can have funds transferred to Guinea-Bissau via Western Union should you run out.

Getting around

Domestic air travel in Guinea-Bissau is limited to the occasional private charter flight out to the Bijagós islands. In this compact country, however, getting around by **road** is usually manageable.

Boat travel

Most travel in Guinea-Bissau is ruled by the **tides**: on the coast there's a tidal range of five metres, more than twice the world average. Several communities are cut off except at high tide when boats can reach them. Passenger services to the Bijagós islands aim to leave with the tide, so always check the departure time the day before.

In the past, a number of basic inshore ferry services have operated, using small tug-like vessels. Of the few services that are still operational, the short crossing at São Vincente (on the journey between São Domingos and Bissau) is the one most likely to be used by travellers. Getting out to the Bijagós islands is done by **pirogue**, a vessel which, in Guinea-Bissau terms, means a large, motorized plank boat, some 20m in length, and capable of carrying several dozen people, and perhaps a tonne or two of goods. Smaller versions of these types of pirogue do the shorter trips, such as those between Bissau and Enxude, and São Domingos and Cacheu.

In addition, there are dozens of small hand-hauled ferry bridges and **canoa** (non-motorized pirogue) services around the country. As a rule of thumb, it's not recommended to use the pirogues or to hitch a ride in one of the local fishing boats, as these vessels aren't well maintained or equipped for emergencies. That said, we've mentioned pirogues in the text where there is little alternative to using them.

Road transport

The **bush taxi** network has been augmented by a large number of modern **minibuses** (referred to as *toko toko*) imported since the end of the war and providing reasonable links to the east and north of the country. In the south, getting to the main towns is generally unproblematic, although when travelling to the smaller settlements you might occasionally find yourself getting a ride in one of the **banana wagons** which transport the fruit to market; negotiate a fare with the driver.

You generally have to be out and about first thing in the morning to get anywhere, as taxis and buses tend to leave around dawn. Later departures can take forever to fill up. As an indication of fares, expect to pay CFA2200 from Bissau to Bafatá, a 150km journey of about three hours.

Hitching might seem a hopeless task, but it's fairly safe and you might find it preferable to waiting in the *paragem* (taxi park) of some distant village. Guinea-Bissau's main routes enjoy a regular traffic flow, but as soon as you venture off the beaten track, transport becomes a problem. Passing vehicles carrying NGO workers and volunteers will often oblige, and it's always worth asking fellow guests at your hotel if they happen to be heading in your direction.

Car and bicycle rental

There are no **car rental** firms in Guinea-Bissau. Some of the hotels in the capital or Bubaque can either rent you a vehicle directly or help you to make private arrangements: expect to pay at least US$60 a day, plus **fuel**. Fuel is a lot more widely available than it used to be – every major town now has a petrol station – though super is relatively expensive for West Africa.

Cycling through Guinea-Bissau, so long as you choose your season, is an attractive option. The five-hundred-odd kilometres of paved road are pleasantly quiet and flat or gently undulating, and often flanked by dense foliage and grass pouring over the road. With a week or two to spare you could explore the south and east quite extensively this way. Renting a bike privately in Bissau isn't too difficult. You could also try to do this if you're visiting the islands as, with the exception of Bubaque (where it's easy to rent bikes), transport on them is hard to come by.

Accommodation

There are few hotels in Guinea-Bissau, and inexpensive rooms (*pousadas* or *hostes*) aren't plentiful, even in rural areas. Such **budget** places as exist (often in the ❷

bracket) are usually very basic affairs, though better value is on offer at a few upcountry establishments and in Bubaque, which, outside of the capital, has the country's best choice of accommodation.

Staying in Bissau itself is expensive and almost all of the hotels are in the **mid-range** category (❹–❻) – some are hardly better than the cheap hotels, while a few do actually offer a decent level of comfort. The capital is also where you'll find a very few international-class establishments (❼ & ❽). During *carnaval* in February or March you may even have trouble finding a room in Bissau. Most hotels include breakfast in their rates.

An alternative to regular hotels is the **pensão** (plural *pensões*) – a family-run establishment along Portuguese lines – although these are not necessarily less expensive than the hotels. In most of the older, Portuguese-built towns – Bafatá and Gabú for example – you'll find a couple of adequate accommodation options, but in more out-of-the-way places basic, sleazy, bar-restaurant establishments with a few rooms are the norm. All but the cheapest hotels and guesthouses have their own **generators**, which tend to be turned on from early evening until late – but often not for the whole night (and sometimes not at all if there's no fuel – or no spare money).

Camping is tolerated, and a tent is particularly helpful on the islands. There are no campsites, however. Food and water supplies may be a problem if you're camping far from any village or town. The Mavegro supermarket in Bissau sells a wide range of camping supplies.

It's not uncommon for travellers to find **private lodging** with Guineans they have met on their travels. This can be

---

All accommodation prices in this chapter are coded according to the following scale, whose equivalent in pounds sterling/US dollars is used throughout the book. Prices refer to the rate you can expect to pay for a room with two beds. Single rooms, or single occupancy, will normally cost at least two-thirds of the twin-occupancy rate. For further details, see p.55.

❶ Under CFA5000 (under £5/$10)
❷ CFA5000–10,000 (£5–10/$10–20)
❸ CFA10,000–15,000 (£10–15/$20–30)
❹ CFA15,000–20,000 (£15–20/$30–40)
❺ CFA20,000–30,000 (£20–30/$40–60)
❻ CFA30,000–40,000 (£30–40/$60–80)
❼ CFA40,000–50,000 (£40–50/$80–100)
❽ Over CFA50,000 (over £50/$100)

a rewarding experience, but given the incidence of poverty, most people appreciate a contribution in cash or in kind towards the evening meal.

Eating and drinking

In a small country as poor and battered as this, it's no surprise to find little attention paid to gastronomy. **White rice** is the staple diet of nearly everyone and, for the majority, something to accompany it once or twice a week is the best they can expect.

This is unlikely to be your diet, at least not in Bissau itself. Restaurants in the capital make the most of **seafood** and whatever else is available, and hotel dining rooms usually manage to produce enormous four-course meals in rustic **Portuguese style**. Rice soup, fish, chicken, tough beef or pork and potatoes are standard fare with, invariably, a banana to finish.

If you're used to eating **bananas** all day, then Guinea-Bissau will be less of a shock to your system. Together with oranges, cashew nuts and small loaves, they're obtainable just about everywhere. Although small supermarkets and corner shops exist, they carry less of a range of produce than you'd find in, say, Ziguinchor or Conakry, and you'll turn to the markets for basic food requirements.

There are few Guinea-Bissauan **specialities** but some dishes to try are: *kalde de manjara*, a peanut stew; *kalde de chebeng*, crushed palm-nut stew; *kalde branco*, fish in white sauce; and *galinha cafriella*, a chicken dish. *Cachupa*, a beans, corn and pork dish characteristic of the Cape Verde Islands, is a meal for special occasions. **Monkey meat** (*carne de mono*) is common everywhere except in the Muslim North, though monkey-hunting poses a threat to many species and eating the meat can be a threat to your health. If you find yourself offered it, be certain it's well cooked to avoid the possibility of catching a dangerous virus. Seafood is good in Bissau. Delicious **gambas** – king prawns – are the stock in trade of the European-style restaurants. **Oysters** and other shellfish are often on Bissau menus too.

Cashews are very widespread (Guinea-

Bissau is one of the world's largest cashew exporters). Together with the magnificent mangoes, they help to make the end of the dry season bearable. If you're given unshelled cashew nuts, beware of trying to crack them open with your teeth: the shell contains an intense irritant that will inflame your mouth for days.

Drinks

Locally made **palm and cashew wine** are the national brews. Both are usually tasty and sweet, but beware that their alcohol content can be anything from virtually zero to highly potent. And make sure you don't ask for the cashew liquor, **cana**, by mistake – it's a lethal brew made from cashew apples.

Grape wine, mostly imported from Portugal, is also easy to find, cheap (from CFA1000 per bottle) and often quite good. There are a few imported **beers** – including Sagres from Portugal – and soft drinks are available. Local juices (lime, lemon and the wonderful **cashew juice**) can all be found for about CFA50–100 a bottle.

Bitter-sweet **green gunpowder tea**, taken in tiny glasses, is the habitual drink of the Muslim areas in the northeast.

Communications

Guinea-Bissau's **mail** service isn't particularly efficient or reliable. Sending or receiving parcels is best not attempted, as many get tampered with or simply don't arrive. The main post office is in Bissau, and **poste restante** letters should be marked Lista da Correios, CTT, Bissau. There are functioning branch post offices in provincial towns, but you should be prepared for considerable delays if you send letters from them.

The telephone system is generally reliable, though calls are pricey (except to Portugal). Telecentres have sprung up in recent years, mainly concentrated in the capital, and these are the most convenient places to make calls. Alternatively, phonecards are sold for CFA1500, CFA3750 or CFA7500 to be used

Guinea-Bissau's **IDD country code is** ☏245.

in the few public phone boxes dotted around the country. You can phone Guinea-Bissau direct from abroad, and IDD calls aren't difficult. Note that reverse-charge (collect) calls can be made to Portugal only. Guinea-Bissauan phone numbers don't have area codes.

As elsewhere in West Africa, **mobile phone** use has gained in popularity, with newly constructed antennae giving wireless access to previously out-of-touch places such as Bolama and Bubaque. Mobile numbers typically have seven digits.

Getting online is becoming steadily easier, though be prepared for very slow connections. Internet cafés were mainly confined to the capital at the time of writing.

Opening hours, festivals and public holidays

Guinea-Bissau has very little consistency in **opening hours**. A long lunch break is common, however, usually from 11.30am or noon to 3pm.

The following **public holidays** are observed: New Year's Day, Heroes' Day (Jan 20, marking the assassination of Amilcar Cabral), International Women's Day (March 8), Labour Day (May 1), Pidjiguiti Day (Aug 3, commemorating the Pidjiguiti Massacre), National Day (Sept 24, commemorating the proclamation of the republic in the liberated zone of Boé in 1973), Redemption Day of the Republic (Nov 14, marking the 1980 coup that brought the PAIGC to power), Christmas Day and December 26 (a family occasion in Bissau).

The **Islamic calendar** is observed throughout the northeast, where a few closures and Muslim holidays aren't likely to have much noticeable effect on your travels.

The weekend before Shrove Tuesday (Feb or March) is when Bissau celebrates **carnaval** (see p.540), a low-key event as far as worldwide carnivals go, but still the highlight of the Bissau social calendar. Festivities begin on the Friday, continue through the weekend and peak for the Tuesday parade, only subsiding on the Wednesday morning.

Crafts and shopping

A couple of spots in Bissau sell **wood carvings**: the main one, the Centro Artistico Juvenil (see p.540), is rather good. Most vendors take a fairly relaxed approach, and you can mull over a fair range of items without being hassled. Apart from these centres, **Senegalese** crafts traders are often the ones with the most gear. Around the rest of the country, tourism is a novelty to most people and, except on Bubaque, few Guinea-Bissauans devote much effort to souvenir-making or the like. People do make their own tools, utensils, furniture, strip cloth and other items, however – and in some communities masks and other ritual paraphernalia – and these can be picked up all over at relatively low prices, and make good souvenirs.

Crime and safety

Guinea-Bissau is currently calm and largely **trouble-free**. It's safe to stay out late at night, particularly in the company of local people. Crime isn't a particular problem, though it pays to be discreet about carrying valuables, as pickpockets and muggers aren't unheard of. The only checkpoints are in border areas and on the main road out of Bissau.

If you're asked by police or any other officials to pay for **"permission"** or a *propina* (for example to take photos) it's normal to ask for a receipt. Sometimes, a semi-official scam operates during carnival, fleecing photographers of up to CFA15,000.

The laws on **drug possession** are very tough: possession of a few joints normally leads to deportation, quite often after a spell in jail. The maximum sentence for this offence is 25 years. As the country has recently been in the news as a cocaine-trafficker's channel to Europe, you'd be wise to stay very clear indeed of any involvement.

If you're out on the street at 8am or 6pm, when the official **flagraising and lowering** takes place, accompanied by a bugle, you are required to stand still in silence. The same rule applies when VIP convoys pass you on the road, or when a funeral procession goes by.

In terms of its civil war aftermath, Guinea-Bissau still has some **mined areas** and parts where other unexploded ordnance still poses a potential danger. All the roads are quite safe in this respect, as are the islands, but don't use footpaths on the mainland unless you see other people doing so or you're accompanied by a competent local guide.

Gender issues and sexual attitudes

For **female travellers**, Guinea-Bissau is one of the most relaxed countries in West Africa, one where men and women can mix freely without their association carrying sexual connotations. Guinean women fought in the war of independence, and their presence in the ranks of the revolutionary cadres made a lasting impression in the traditionally conservative and Islamic parts of the country. The women's movement, the União Democrática de Mulheres (UDEMU) still has a lot of work to do, however, with the literacy rate among women running at less than half of that for men.

Gay equality is a long way off, and there's little public respect for the low-key gay community. The laws on homosexuality date back to Portugal's 1886 penal code, making gay sex illegal, punishable by imprisonment or hard labour.

Entertainment and sports

The main cultural event of the year is the *carnaval* in February or March (see p.540).

Guinea-Bissau's **cinema** output revolves around one major figure, **Flora Gomes**, whose films span three decades. In his most recent film, the deeply symbolic musical comedy *Nha Fala* ("My Voice", 2002), the central character emigrates to Paris while bearing the family curse that kills all who sing. Gomes's vibrant work (*Nha Fala* was shortlisted at FESPACO 2003) is constrained by conditions at home and, unsurprisingly, no other film-makers have matched his career. The **music** scene (see p.533) shows much more promise, and the capital's nightclubs are in full swing, despite power cuts.

Football

The big sport is **football**, encouraged by the cultural ties with soccer-mad Portugal and Brazil. There are even two women's teams. Village football is often played at dusk, but the most exciting games take place at the impressive stadium outside Bissau. The country has never competed in the African Nations Cup but competes, instead, in the **Amílcar Cabral Cup** for West African nations, held every odd-numbered year usually in November. It was hosted by Guinea-Bissau in 2007. Guinea-Bissau has also twice won the Five Nations Cup of African Lusophone countries.

Wildlife and national parks

Much of Guinea-Bissau's indigenous **wildlife** was hunted out during the war years in the 1960s and early 1970s, or lost its habitat to defoliants or subsequent land clearance. Still, for such a small country, the fauna can be rewarding. The best areas to look are the hilly southeast, parts of the forested centre, and the outer islands.

Guinea-Bissau has a number of protected areas, notably the **Tarrafes do Rio Cacheu** and **Lagoas de Cufada** natural parks on the mainland, and the **Orango** and **João Vieira-Poilão** national parks in the Bijagós archipelago. Though the large terrestrial mammals are seldom found, the many species of **primate** (including chimpanzees), some forest antelopes and some unusual coast-dwellers – manatees, and saltwater-dwelling hippos and large sea turtles in the Bijagós islands – compensate for this, and reptile life is prolific. The Instituto da Biodiversidade das Areas Protegidas (IBAP), Rua São Tomé, Bissau (℡20 71 06), manages Guinea-Bissau's protected areas.

The abundant waters in the Bijagós archipelago are a favourite destination for sports fishermen, with species such as barracuda, tarpon, crevalle jack and grouper all up for grabs.

A brief history of Guinea-Bissau

From the thirteenth to the fifteenth centuries, large areas of West Africa, including much of what is now Guinea-Bissau, were under the control of the **Mali empire**, established by the legendary Mande leader Sundiata Keita. When Mali began to decline in the mid-fifteenth century, the Guinea-Bissau states joined together to become the empire of Kaabu (Gabú). By the early sixteenth century, this had coalesced into an important regional power.

The Kaabu Empire

Ruled from heavily fortified trading capitals – first **Kassang**, on the north bank of the Gambia (near Kuntaur) and later **Kansala** (a site between the present-day towns of Farim and Gabú), the Mandinka empire of Kaabu became one of the most powerful states in West Africa, dominating the whole of the Guinea-Bissau region except for the immediate costal hinterland, for more than three centuries, from around 1540 to 1868.

Although historical sources are scanty, we know that Kaabu was Mande-speaking, and ruled by a privileged warrior class of men and women, usually with the family names Sané or Mané. These were the **Nyancho** – praised by their *kora*-playing *jeli* as half human–half-spirit – who thrived on trade between the gold-, kola- and slave-exporting far interior and the rivers of the west coast where the European ships waited. The fiercely non-Muslim Nyancho soon became important partners of the Portuguese and Cape Verdean traders.

Kaabu flourished until the mid-nineteenth century, when war broke out between Mandinka-led Kaabu and the neighbouring Fula empire of Fouta Djalon, at the end of which, in 1868, Kaabu's last ruler Janke Wali was defeated by Fula horsemen at Kansala.

Kriolu society

Guinea-Bissau was first visited by **Europeans** in 1447 when Nuno Tristão, the Portuguese explorer, was killed by Bijagó warriors. In 1456, Cadamosto, an Italian navigator working for the Portuguese Crown, sailed as far as the Rio Mansôa and the Bijagós islands looking for the gold which figured so hugely in the trans-Saharan trade. Other sailors settled on the uninhabited Cape Verde Islands over the following decades. By 1500, these communities had sprouted subcolonies on the Guinean mainland: groups of Portuguese or mixed-race immigrants, partly absorbed into African society, trading with the interior and looking to the ocean. More about this early history of European contact is detailed in the Cape Verde chapter.

While the export of gold was significant during the first half of the sixteenth century, subsequently much of what is now Guinea-Bissau was drawn into the **slave trade** linking West Africa with Europe, the Caribbean and the Americas via Cape Verde. **Cacheu** was the headquarters: by 1600 it had as many as a thousand Kriolu (mixed-race) slave traders and employees. Portugal established a military garrison in 1616 in order to guarantee the maximum revenue to the Crown, charging duty on exported slaves and sending cargos on to the Cape Verdes where they paid further duty. Other towns were established at Farim, Ziguinchor and, later, Bissau and Bolama. But despite Portugal's efforts, the benefits of trade tended to bypass Lisbon; French and English ships could offer better trade goods and more choice. Repeated efforts by the Portuguese government to enforce

trading monopolies in their area of influence simply pushed traders into illegal commerce.

The local **slaves** tended to come from the least-stratified ethnic groups of farmers, fishers and hunters: Fulup and Jola, Manjak and Pepel. The main **slavers** were Mandinka and, later, Fula. The Bijagó were notorious slave-hunters too, launching lethal canoe raids against the mainland. Yet who was slave and who slaver depended much more on economic strength or vulnerability and on family contacts and position, than on tribal identity. It wasn't unusual for a king or headman to sell off people under his own rule, such was the attraction of cloth and other imported goods. **Firearms** were available from the early eighteenth century to those who could afford them.

With the general **abolition of slavery** in the early nineteenth century, the slave trade from Guinea continued illicitly, given new life by the needs of Cuba's plantations. Domestic slavery (which was not abolished) was commonly used as a cover. The last big shipments from Guinea crossed the Atlantic in the 1840s.

Meanwhile, the local use of labour rather than the sale of labourers became significant with the introduction of **groundnuts**, first grown along the Gambia River at the end of the eighteenth century. Phillip Beaver's attempt to start an English colony of groundnut planters on Bolama had been a disaster (see box, p.548), but local Kriolu landowners had more success. Agreements were made with Bijagó elders on Galinhas and Bolama, from where the crop was spread to the shores of the Rio Grande on the mainland. On the islands, the plantations used slaves; on the shores of the Rio Grande they called them contract labourers, with tools, transport, food, clothes and accommodation charged to the plantation workers out of their share of the crop, usually leaving nothing for wages. Portugal, however, benefited little from the exploitation of its colonies. As much as eighty percent of the crop was sold to French trading concerns.

In 1879, Portugal's Guinean territory was separated from Cape Verde administration. The French had occupied Ziguinchor and, following a brief British occupation, **Bolama** became the **first capital** of "Portuguese Guinea".

The Portuguese province

The **partition of Africa** after 1885 left Portugal with a scattering of territories, of which Guinea-Bissau was perhaps the least promising. Portugal did not make any great effort to develop its colonies. Portuguese settlers were fearful of the climate, and there appeared to be no attractive natural resources. Then, Fula-led jihads against non-Muslim plantation workers and raids on the foreign-run *feitoria* groundnut stations along the Rio Grande led to a slump in the only viable export. With the region now formally annexed to Portugal, only Bolama and the fort towns of Bissau, Cacheu, Farim and Gêba were in any sense under colonial rule.

Military campaigns of "pacification" took fifty years to subdue the state of general **revolt** that ensued in the 1890s. In that time there was precious little attention paid in Lisbon to the administration of the African territories. The republican government in Portugal, wracked as it was by one military intervention after another, and by the costly involvement in World War I, virtually ignored Guinea-Bissau.

Hut taxes were imposed and labour conscripted to help maintain the colony with as little support from Portugal as possible. Almost the entire African population was classified as **indígena** – disenfranchised, second-class non-citizens. Opportunities for education were very limited, and in practice most urbanites with prospects were Cape Verdeans, or the descendants of Cape Verdean marriages. They, together with Kriolus and a tiny proportion of **assimilado** mainlanders, formed the bulk of the civil service as government agents and tax collectors.

It was from this small middle class that the first calls for political reform were heard. Before World War I, a political group called the **Liga Guineense** campaigned for the interests of small traders and landowners, highlighting the abuse of power by government agents and calling for a change in the laws favouring the big commercial enterprises. The Liga was outlawed in 1915 without making much impact, but it provided a background – the only indigenous political example – for the radical demands of the PAIGC that emerged forty years later.

The **groundnut trade** began to pick up after about 1910, though it crashed again in 1918 when a law came into force prohibiting peasant farmers from trading their crop to foreign buyers. The law was repealed, and by the 1920s, the central parts of the country, particularly the region around Bafatá, had become the groundnut heartland.

Despite the heavy exploitation and inequalities, there was a looseness in governing the overseas territories that failed to suppress freedom of expression completely. The paternalistic idea of **"colonial trusteeship"** was taken seriously by some: Portuguese culture allowed a vague and distant respect for Africans stemming partly from its own infusion of African culture during the medieval Moorish occupation. But these sentiments were smothered after 1926.

Guinea under the Portuguese "New State"

In 1926, a military takeover turned Portugal into a violent dictatorship that was to last until 1974, holding the country back and crippling its overseas territories. **António de Salazar**, a monetarist economics professor, was prime minister from 1932 until 1968. He promulgated the Estado Novo, or **"New State"**, and ran Portugal on strictly authoritarian lines. The "Province of Guinea", along with the other parts of "Overseas Portugal" were brought to heel. The last pockets of resistance to the colonial invasion were finally "pacified" in 1936 and any chinks of progressive light from republican days were blacked out by the quasi-fascist curtain now drawn across the country.

Guinea was forced to become one giant groundnut and oil-palm plantation with **compulsory planting** and purchases. Small traders were banned from dealing in cloth and alcohol, while Portuguese commercial agents tried vainly to interest the people in Portuguese wine and cotton clothing.

Economic repression, passbook laws and a continuation of forced labour came with an unwieldy and over-staffed **bureaucracy**. All potential sources of opposition were organized into officially sanctioned associations, from within which their members could be scrutinized by the PIDE, Salazar's political police. For more than four decades, there was an almost total suspension of political life.

In the 1950s, **Amílcar Cabral**, an agronomist of mixed Cape Verdean and Guinean parentage, was working in the colonial service, conducting agricultural censuses across the country. He analyzed his remarkably detailed land-use surveys in Marxist terms of modes of production. His conclusions convinced him that mechanization, collectivization, a rejection of the groundnut monoculture and a return to mixed farming could transform Guinean society and set the country on a path to socialism. His reputation as a subversive assured, he quit the service and left the country.

The war of liberation

A small coterie of African tradesmen and Lisbon-educated civil servants resident in Bissau (capital since 1941) began gently to agitate for independence from Portugal. On September 12, 1956, Cabral, briefly back from work in Angola, and five others met secretly and formed the Partido Africano para Independência da Guiné e Cabo Verde

(**PAIGC**). With painstaking discretion and patience, they recruited people to their ranks. Within three years they had about fifty members.

The spark for armed conflict came with a **dockworkers' strike** for a living wage. On August 3, 1959, police confronted the strikers on the **Pidji-guiti** waterfront in Bissau. When they refused to go back to work the police opened fire at point-blank range, killing fifty men and wounding more than a hundred. The massacre and subsequent police interrogations convinced Cabral and the party leadership that peaceful attempts to bring about independence would be fruitless. Cabral, his half-brother Luiz, and Aristides Pereira went to Conakry (the capital of the Republic of Guinea, newly independent from France) to set up a party headquarters and training school. In Guinea-Bissau, others began to prepare clandestinely for **social revolution** and a **war of liberation** against the Portuguese.

Other nationalist groups were forming at the time, both inside Bissau and in Senegal. Their ideologies tended to be less well honed than the PAIGC's. They were prepared to accept a transfer of political power without a transformation in the economy, and they didn't work on behalf of the Cape Verde Islands. Nor did they approve of the Cape Verdean intellectuals who characterized PAIGC's executive. These other groups coalesced into the Front for the Liberation and Independence of Portuguese Guinea (**FLING**), based in Dakar under Léopold Senghor's sponsorship.

There had been scattered attacks by the PAIGC from 1961, but military action began in earnest in January 1963. Senghor and Secou Touré reluctantly allowed the guerillas to launch operations from Senegal and the Republic of Guinea. In Europe, the Scandinavian countries voiced their solidarity. Internally, the most enthusiastic insurgents were the brutally exploited, rice-planting **Balante** of the southwest, though coordination of their sabotage attacks with PAIGC strategy was often tenuous. At the other extreme, many **Fula** communities in the north and east, long established in a feudal framework which had Islamic sanction, and positively supported by the Portuguese, resisted subversion, or tried to prevent their peasants from being politicized.

As large stretches of bush and countryside, and then the first few towns, were liberated, the guerillas of the PAIGC became consolidated into an effective, mobile army, clearing the way for a network of "people's stores", new schools, medical services and political institutions. Portugal attacked their bases with weaponry purchased from **NATO**. Napalm was used by Portugal, and the fighting was at times as intense as in Vietnam. In retaliation, the PAIGC's guerilla army – the People's Revolutionary Armed Forces (**FARP**) – persuaded the Soviet Union to deliver arms on a regular basis.

While the war continued with steady success for the liberationists, the first **internal cracks** were being felt in their upper ranks. All PAIGC decisions were now being taken in Conakry by the Cape Verdean leadership. The need to coordinate a national policy came increasingly into conflict with democratic imperatives. Although Cabral enjoyed enormous support and trust, his growing stature as a world leader physically distanced him from his half-million followers and in many liberated areas, there were very few democratically elected representatives between the top leadership and the people.

Cabral was conscious of these difficulties. In 1970, the war could have been won in a few months, as heavy armaments had just been delivered from Eastern Europe. But Cabral decided to hold off the final assault on Bissau because only Soviet-trained Cape Verdeans knew how to use the weapons, and he did not want such a display to reinforce the unpopular high profile of the Cape Verdean elite. After seven years of fighting, however, all the indications were that the mass of the people were fed up with the war and popularity would have been more likely to follow a swift end to it.

External factors intervened. In November 1970, an invasion force of Portuguese troops and African collaborators set off from Soga island in the Bijagós archipelago to attack Conakry, with the intention of assassinating President Sekou Touré and Amílcar Cabral. They failed, and retreated in chaos. Two years later, however, a more carefully planned action in Conakry, involving PAIGC defectors who sought a deal with the Portuguese dictatorship, led to the **assassination of Amílcar Cabral** on January 20, 1973.

Portugal's plan to install a puppet "liberation government" in Guinea-Bissau had no chance of success. The PAIGC, nurtured for so long by one of Africa's most radical and humane political thinkers, did not disintegrate. Nonetheless, the damage to morale was serious and the leadership vacuum plain to see. Aristides Pereira took over as party chief and Luiz Cabral as president-in-waiting.

The FARP deployed major weaponry straight after the assassination; one aircraft after another was shot down by heat-seeking missiles. The Portuguese, based in military camps across the country, were increasingly besieged by a confident People's Army under the general command of **João "Nino" Vieira** (later to succeed Luiz Cabral as president). In four months, through the end of the dry season of 1973, the Portuguese lost the war. With their air force demoralized and growing discontent among their conscripted troops, rumbles of revolution began in Portugal itself.

On September 24, 1973, in the liberated village of Lugajole in the southeast, the People's National Assembly declared the **independence** of Guinea-Bissau. It only remained to kick out the enemy. Around the world, dozens of countries recognized the new republic and the United Nations passed a resolution demanding Portugal's withdrawal. The **military coup in Lisbon** on April 25, 1974, made

withdrawal inevitable. Portugal and the PAIGC signed a treaty on September 10, and the last Portuguese troops were gone within a month. **Luiz Cabral** became the new head of state, while the party leader and senior ideologue, Aristides Pereira, became president of the new sister republic of Cape Verde.

The early years of independence

The colonial bequest to the newly independent country was dismal. Guinea-Bissau had only a handful of graduates and doctors, and not more than two percent of its population were literate. Its industrial base consisted of one brewery – there was no other manufacturing plant – and there was almost no energy production. Earnings from exports barely covered a tenth of the cost of imports, and the Portuguese had left a colossal national debt.

The PAIGC took over a centralized and autocratic administration. Far from Amílcar Cabral's optimistic ideas of a decentralized state, **Bissau**, by far the largest and most developed town in the country – and to this day the only city – became the main centre of government. The urgency of the takeover, the shortage of material and human resources, and the refugee problem in the capital all led to government by crisis management. The peasants of the liberated zones, who had supported the party and the war for so long and at such cost, were hardly consulted: nor were the minor-ranking party cadres who now expected to receive the fruits of independence.

Apart from national reconstruction, there was **political work** to do in Bissau. Compared with the peasants of the liberated zones, some of whom had lived under PAIGC government for ten years, Bissau's inhabitants were more cosmopolitan, the best educated and the most cynical. Now that the PAIGC was in control, they had to come to terms with it, but did not necessarily support it down the line.

There were national **"elections"** in 1976, with voting consisting of a "for" or "against" to candidates nominated to the regional councils (who themselves elected the members of the National Assembly). There were no alternative candidates. Results showed the widest dissent in the traditionally anti-PAIGC northern and eastern regions, a fifteen percent opposition in Bissau, but over ninety percent support everywhere else.

The broad approval seems surprising in light of the **difficulties** the party was having in delivering on its independence promises to build a new society. Bissau city, for example, received over half the country's resources – justified by Luiz Cabral in terms of attracting investors and foreign-aid agencies, who poured funds into the country between 1976 and 1979. **Drought** damaged the prospects of new agricultural projects and efforts to become self-sufficient in food made no progress. A joint fisheries enterprise with Algeria was a flop. The ludicrous N'Haye car-assembly plant was a grotesque waste of money, as was the massive and never-finished agricultural processing plant at Cumeré near Bissau. Salaries in the state sector were eating away (in fact exceeded) the national budget. The currency was kept overvalued, and inflation soared, while in real terms agricultural production and exports declined. In a remarkable echo of the fascist "New State" policy, the government tried to control the marketing of produce, setting prices at levels too low to be worth selling at and thus encouraging a black-market economy. People in the rural areas could no longer afford basic imported goods like soap and matches.

The persistent street rumour was that all this was the fault of the Cape Verdeans who, in many cases, had kept civil-service positions since Portuguese times. Many of the "people's stores" were run by them, too, and often corruptly. But it was their visibility, as part of the self-interested and irrepressible middle class, that made them popular scapegoats for a **failing economy**.

In November 1980, an extraordinary session of the National Assembly discussed the unification of Guinea-Bissau and Cape Verde. Luiz Cabral, having increasingly isolated himself, refused to temper his support for the idea. Four days later came the largely bloodless **coup of November 14**, which toppled his government. The Commissioner for the Armed Forces, **Nino Vieira**, revoked the constitution and took control of the country. Luiz Cabral was detained on Bubaque, then allowed to fly to Cuba.

The 1980s

Despite popular anti-Cape Verdean sentiment, the new "Provisional Government", formed in 1981, looked much like a rearranged version of Luiz Cabral's. Several of Cabral's Cape Verdean ministers had fled, but Vieira was adamant in his speeches that Cape Verdeans were welcome in Guinea-Bissau, and that the two countries' destinies remained linked.

One of the first announcements of the new government was the disclosure of a series of **mass graves**, containing up to five hundred bodies, in the Oio region northeast of Bissau. The story was taken up by the foreign press. Vieira's intention was to point out the summary justice meted out by his predecessor's government to dissidents and those who had collaborated with the Portuguese. But there were counter-claims from a furious **Aristides Pereira** (the president of Cape Verde), who believed Vieira had sabotaged any chance of unification, that Vieira had known about the murders and was even implicated. Cape Verde set up its own party, and broke relations.

Coup attempts, allegations of plans for coup attempts and widespread repression characterized the early 1980s. In 1984, however, there was a shift to a freer climate with new elections, a rewritten constitution and a return to civilian government, though the country was still a one-party state and Vieira remained president. Still, the plots continued. An attempted coup in 1985 led to the execution of Vice-President **Paulo Correia** and five co-accused in July 1986. Six more of those accused of involvement were said to have died in prison.

None of this, of course, helped the government to run the country effectively. Although the IMF and the World Bank had given loans, the **austerity measures** on which they were conditional were hardly followed through and, despite debt rescheduling, the country's economic plight continued to worsen.

In August 1986 the government finally agreed to the **abolition of trade laws** that had reserved all import and export licences for state monopolies. The peso was massively devalued, knocking the life out of the black market and encouraging potential investors. Support for Vieira's government was suddenly stronger as exports rose impressively and the economy began to revive. Within a year, Guinea-Bissau was entering into long-term agreements with the IMF and World Bank to **restructure the economy**, prune the state payroll, reduce fuel subsidies and boost agriculture, fisheries and technical training. Although the countryside still lagged behind Bissau, the economic future began to look a little brighter. **Cashew nuts** continued to be the most valuable export, and many farmers were paid for their cashew harvest in rice. The negative side-effect of this policy was a serious alcohol problem from the widespread distillation of cashew juice from the fruits, which have no other use.

The advent of multiparty politics

In the late 1980s and into the early 1990s, political opposition to the one-party state increased. The banned **Movimento Bafatá**, with offices abroad, upped the pressure in 1990 with demands that the PAIGC should hold talks with it or face unspecified consequences. At the same time, and in common with other African partners of the World Bank and IMF, Guinea-Bissau was asked to reform its political institutions as a condition of further aid.

By the beginning of 1991, Vieira had set a schedule for **multiparty elections**. He also cut the link between the PAIGC and the **military**, which had supported the party in its early years. The army had long felt betrayed by the years of independence from which it had received so little benefit, but this event marked the start of the slow crisis of relations between the government and the military. Increasingly, soldiers turned to making a living from regional cannabis smuggling and arms trading to the rebels in Senegalese Casamance.

Over a dozen small **political parties** were formed and recognized between 1991 and 1994. Among the most important were the Partido para a Renovação Social (**PRS**), headed by former teacher Dr Kumba Yala, and the Resistência da Guiné-Bissau-Movimento Bah-Fatah (**RGB-MB**), formed from the previously outlawed Bafatá movement. In addition, **FLING**, the old Frente da Luta para a Libertação da Guiné (banned for thirty years and exiled in Senegal until 1992) made a comeback. Safeguards in the registration process ensured that none of the new parties had an entirely ethnic or regional basis, though the PRS, for example, was dominated by the Balante, while the RGB-MB began as a movement of business interests with Mandinka and Fula support, opposed to the Marxist rhetoric of the PAIGC in the 1980s. However, once the PAIGC had shed every vestige of socialism from its agenda, it was hard to see how it differed from the RGB-MB except in the ethnic constituents of its membership.

The brief election campaigns mounted by the parties were mostly personality-led and ignored the big issues facing the country. At least Kumba Yala's PRS campaigned for the restoration of state property held in private hands – an open threat to the PAIGC elite. The **elections**, when they were finally held in July

1994, were surprisingly trouble-free, and the results widely judged to reflect a fair poll. The PAIGC won just under half the votes for seats in the National Assembly (which, however, gave it 64 of the 100 seats), while Nino Vieira, the incumbent president and leader of the PAIGC, won a similar proportion of votes for president. To win, Vieira needed an outright majority, which he obtained a month later in a run-off against his closest rival, **Kumba Yala**.

Yala, Guinea-Bissau's most charismatic and trenchantly outspoken politician, complained, not unreasonably, that the PAIGC had been able to use the resources of the state, particularly in the remotest areas, to weigh the dice in Vieira's favour. Tactics included heavy-handed campaigning among largely illiterate communities and the denial of seats to Yala's poll-observers on the only helicopter flying to outlying islands. Nevertheless, Yala's acceptance of his defeat seemed to bode well for the future stability of the country.

Guinea-Bissau's **economy** was in decline again, however. The PAIGC government seemed powerless to halt the slide (and was, in the view of many observers, complicit in it) and appeared immune, too, to the scathing reproaches of the opposition and the majority of the electorate, whose only viable course of action was mass protest. Dropping the peso and entering the **CFA franc zone**, in April 1997, added further to the miserable lot of most Guineans, as inflation spiralled.

The civil war

But it was the deteriorating situation in Senegal's Casamance region (see p.180) on Guinea-Bissau's northern border which finally tipped the country into civil war. A Casamance-bound arms cache was discovered at a military barracks and the chief of staff, Brigadier **Ansumane Manè** (a Jola, born and raised in The Gambia, and with close connections to the Casamançais), was sacked and went into the bush with his supporters.

When news emerged in June 1998 that Vieira was planning to halve the army to ten thousand men, a group of **rebel troops**, led by Manè, seized strategic locations around the capital, including the airport, and demanded Vieira's resignation and immediate elections. Dakar and Conakry sent troop reinforcements to shore up the Vieira regime, and **war** broke out in and around Bissau. Diplomats and expats were evacuated, a quarter of a million residents fled the capital for the countryside and towards the Senegalese border, which was promptly closed. Virtually the entire army joined Manè's forces. Efforts by President Jammeh of The Gambia to bring the sides together came to nothing, as his partiality in the conflict was widely suspected.

Cape Verde eventually brokered talks between the government and Manè's side, and a grudging **stalemate** was reached in December 1998, when Manè and Vieira agreed to a power-sharing arrangement. The Senegalese troops withdrew in early 1999, while the contingent from Guinea and smaller forces from other West African nations sustained serious losses before also pulling out.

There was an **international dimension** to the Bissau conflict: since Guinea-Bissau's adoption of the CFA franc, it had been clear that Vieira was aiming for closer cooperation with Francophone West Africa and Paris. These trends were viewed with great unease by the Portuguese, as well as by Kumba Yala and many others in the opposition, who traditionally looked for support from the Casamance and The Gambia, and who received sympathetic coverage in the Portuguese media.

A fragile peace

Finally, in May 1999, remaining loyalist troops surrendered to Ansumane Manè after fierce fighting in Bissau, and Vieira was granted political asylum by Portugal. Ansumane (now General) Manè installed the former leader of the national assembly, **Malam Bacai**

Sanhá, as acting president. Elections followed in January 2000, in which **Kumba Yala** gained an overwhelming victory, winning more than seventy percent of the vote. In November of that year, General Ansumane Manè rejected President Yala's senior army appointments as ethnically biased, and attempted to declare himself head of the army. A few days later he was killed in a shoot-out with government troops. His removal from the scene simplified regional politics: Manè and Yala had been allied to opposing factions of the rebel movement in the Casamance, and Manè had also enjoyed support from President Jammeh of The Gambia.

Kumba Yala's presidency hardly brought the democratic wind of change that the country needed. He regularly dismissed members of the government and other figures in authority who voiced doubts about his policies, and he fell out with his partners, the RGB-MB, who pulled out of the coalition government. Judges and journalists were arrested and the sacking of "rebellious" ministers continued into 2002. Later that year, Yala dissolved parliament and replaced the entire cabinet. All ministries were sealed off and for several days the country was effectively without a functioning government.

During 2003, proposed elections were postponed three times, prompting a bloodless coup led by **General Verissimo Correia Seabre** on 14 September 2003. Yala was overthrown and placed under house arrest while the military appointed **Henrique Pereira Rosa** as interim president. The coup was condemned by some African countries, but received wide support within Guinea-Bissau.

Presidential elections eventually took place in June 2005. Former presidents **Nino Vieira**, **Malam Bacai Sanhá** and **Yala** himself were allowed to stand, with Sanhá winning the first round but Vieira prevailing in the run-off the following month. A new government was formed in November 2005, with **Aristide Gomes** as prime minister.

Although the elections, which were generally considered to be fair,

should have returned a degree of political stability to Guinea-Bissau, the reverse has been the case. Gomes was seen as too close an ally of Vieira and a coalition of opposition parties – to which many of the president's own supporters had defected by early 2007 – passed a no-confidence motion in the prime minister. Gomes offered his resignation, but Vieira only accepted it after hundreds took part in street demonstrations. In April 2007, Vieira appointed the coalition's choice of PAIGC leader **Martinho Ndafa Kabi** as prime minister, thus averting another crisis, but doing little to relax the tensions between the political parties that remain an ongoing threat to the country's precarious stability.

Economically, Guinea-Bissau is in reverse gear, with 2006's cashew crop finding few buyers for high fixed government prices, so that farmers ended up selling for next to nothing in order to realize any income at all.

Meanwhile, mounting evidence that Guinea-Bissau is not just an occasional trans-shipment point for drugs from South America but the key West African entrepôt in the **narcotics trade** from Colombia to Europe, shone an unwelcome spotlight on the country in 2007, and particularly on its army and navy, elements of which are colluding in the trade. Several huge shipments of cocaine were seized, and then mislaid, while several Colombians were arrested, and then released.

The scandal threatens to frighten off island tourism investment and to undermine legitimate efforts to develop Bissau and the hinterland beyond a cashew-nut economy. It is also bound to infuriate the **USA**: in March 2007, Condoleezza Rice signed a Memorandum of Understanding with Brazil and Guinea-Bissau in a welcome new move to consolidate democratic advances and harness a tiny and impoverished nation to the relative success story of Brazil. Such efforts will be for nothing if the country is overwhelmed by drugs money.

Music

Guinea-Bissau's special music is **gumbe**. Always sung in Kriolu, it's a creative amalgamation of local musical traditions with contemporary sounds – a true expression of Guinea-Bissau's Kriolu culture. It has a slight Latin feel to it, and has been compared to samba, though it's much more polyrhythmic. In Bissau you may also encounter youngsters entertaining themselves by playing *gumbe* beats on spoons, empty plastic containers and calabash drums (*tina*).

The many musical styles that echo in popular *gumbe* all continue their independent existences: each of the country's ethnic groups has its own musical tradition, and especially in the non-Muslim regions, there are plenty of opportunities to see local groups perform during ceremonies or for their own enjoyment.

An absolute treat is the *broxa* dancing of the Balante people, which is frequently accompanied by the gentle plucking of the *kussunde* (a lute). Other regional traditions include the wild acrobatics and haunting flute tunes of the Fula, the Mandinka *kora* (which has its origin in the area), and the drumming and masked dances of the Bijagó.

For some outrageously sexy dancing, you should try to see the performance of a **kuduru** troupe. *Kuduru*, originating in Angola, sounds like a slightly crazed African form of house coupled with ragga, soca and other Latin beats.

Guinea-Bissau has brought forth some fantastic singers, and though many in the current crop have left to take up residence in Portugal (or, more rarely, France), few have made much of an impact on the international stage. Their music is generally smooth as honey, blending *gumbe*, *zouk* and a wagonload of other influences (from Arabic to ragga) into a sugary concoction.

Local **hip-hop** hasn't taken off in Bissau in quite the same way as neighbouring countries, though you'll hear snatches of American, European, Senegalese and Guinean rapping often enough.

José Carlos Schwartz

This soulful singer, who died in the 1970s, is regarded as the "father" of modern Bissau music. His outspoken lyrics gave a powerful voice to the people in colonial days and since, and have made him a national hero.

Flema Di Corçon (available in Guinea-Bissau). Subdued, moving, guitar-based material, containing plenty of evergreen songs that today's musicians are reworking.

Dulce Neves

Virtually the only female professional singer in the country, Neves is outspoken about women's rights. She apparently divorced four times, unable to find a husband who would tolerate her career.

Balur di Mindjer (Maxi Music). Produced by Manecas Costa, this is probably the best of her albums to date, a well-executed, accessible blend of *gumbe* and *zouk*.

Kaba Mané

Born into a Beafada family – a Mande people –Mané is one of the few Guinea-Bissauan musicians whose albums you might find in the West, though he's not much of a figure at home. A master of a variety of styles, he learned the *kora* when young and plays his guitar in a *kora* style.

Best of Kaba Mané (Mélodie). Tasty compilation of the best material from two earlier albums.

Manecas Costa

Having for years carved out a career for himself at home, Manecas Costa has an international deal with a BBC label.

Paraiso di Gumbe (Late Junction). A masterpiece of semi-acoustic Guinean music, letting his exceptional guitar skills truly shine and subtly interweaving a number of local styles, such as *broxa*.

Zé Manel

A long-established artist, formerly with Mama Djombo, Manel has maintained a highly politicized stance throughout his career.

Maron di Mar (Mélodie). An enjoyable album that reworks some of his biggest hits with jazz-tinged arrangements.

Super Mama Djombo

Mama Djombo, who put *gumbe* music on the map, were favourites of the first independent government, but soon fell out with them. Their 1980s recordings still sound remarkably fresh.

Super Mama Djombo (Cobiana). A great retrospective of a key Bissau band, including tracks from five albums recorded in Lisbon in 1980 at the height of their popularity.

Gumbezarte

One of the best bands to emerge in Bissau in the 1990s, Gumbezarte was led by the witty, inventive Maio Coopé, with members from Cobiana Jazz and Mama Djombo.

Gumbezarte Camba Mar (Balkon Zuid, Guinea-Bissau; Lusafrica, France). Gumbe is in the title and in some of the songs, but this is really an electrifying tour of lesser-known musical styles. Recommended.

Bidinte

Guitarist and singer-songwriter Jorge da Silva Bidinte was born in Bolama, and began composing music for singer Maio Coopé when he moved to Bissau to attend secondary school. He later emigrated to Spain.

Kumura (Nubenegra). Subtle and distinctive music reflecting a multiplicity of influences, from David Byrne (who was present through most of the recording) to flamenco, with a melting blend of guitar and Kriolu lyrics.

Justino Delgado

Active in several bands, including Docolma, where he made three records with fellow Bijagós islander, Bidinte, Delgado is known for his narrative songs which touch on everything from politics to marriage.

Toroco (Sonovox). One of Delgado's stand-out albums, bristling with sarcastic and entertaining lyrics.

Tabanka Jazz

Bissau's one-time bestsellers, the group started in the mid-1980s in the Tabanka restaurant. They've gone on to success as far afield as the USA.

Sintimento (Sonovox). Highly danceable, with excellent bass riffs, neat use of synthesizers and the essential ingredient of Micas Cabral's compelling voice.

Books

Works in English specifically about Guinea-Bissau are extremely sparse, and there's no Guinea-Bissauan literature in translation. For good general titles, see p.35. Books likely to be out of print are marked o/p below; those marked 🏃 are especially recommended.

George E. Brooks *Landlords and Strangers: Ecology, Society and Trade in Western Africa, 1000–1630*. Largely concentrating on the history of the Guinea-Bissau region, drawing on Portuguese records.

Amílcar Cabral *Unity and Struggle* (o/p). Speeches and writings from the father of the revolution – and he did speak and write well.

Patrick Chabal *Amílcar Cabral: Revolutionary Leadership and People's War.* The biography if you're a committed student, and Chabal does a good job of contextualizing Cabral's thinking.

Basil Davidson *No Fist is Big Enough to Hide the Sky: The Liberation of Guiné and Cape Verde*. Enthusiastic, quirky account of the war of liberation and its aftermath. The late Davidson's close and sympathetic involvement with the liberation fighters, particularly Amílcar Cabral himself, gives a rosy picture, tarnished by subsequent events.

🏃 **Toby Green** *Meeting the Invisible Man* (McArthur & Co). Story of a surreal journey with a Senegalese photographer – much of it through Guinea-Bissau – in search of magic powers. Green's descriptive writing is elegant and sparse and his transliteration of dialogue impeccable, as he leads the reader through a universe that flips unnervingly between dusty banality and a parallel world of magic and spells.

Henrik Vigh *Navigating Terrains of War: Youth and Soldiering in Guinea-Bissau*. Written in an academic yet engaging style, this is a study of the *Arguentas*, a youth militia group recruited during the 1998–99 civil war.

🏃 **Walter Rodney** *A History of the Upper Guinea Coast 1545–1800* (Monthly Review). An Afrocentric history covering the region from the Casamance to Sierra Leone, dealing in depth with the area the Portuguese moved into and providing a mass of fascinating material on its social complexity.

Language

Although the official language of Guinea-Bissau is **Portuguese**, the widely used, street-friendly vernacular is **Kriolu** (or Crioulo). An old amalgam of seafarers' Portuguese with various African languages, Kriolu becomes semi-intelligible if you speak Portuguese, and is very similar to Cape Verdean Kriolu (see p.459). Just about every Guinea-Bissauan speaks Kriolu, often next to one or two other local languages. Among the most common tongues are **Mandinka** (see p.286), **Fula** (see p.589), **Balante**, **Manjak**, **Pepel**, and **Bijagó**, spoken on the islands of the same name. The surrounding Francophone influence means that Guinea-Bissauans often have some basic knowledge of French, but seldom of English.

Useful Bijagó

Bijagó dialects don't vary much. The phrases below, some of them recognizably Kriolu in derivation, are from Orango. Accented letters are stressed syllables.

Ména?	How are you?
Ñekagobo	I am fine
Eséyta	Thank you/expression of agreement
Eng	Yes
Ñidóku	No
Amenáwe?	What is your name?
Aynáme John	My name is John
Ororá	White person
Utúngko	Black person
Mindánewe?	Where are you going?
Ñibóy	See you later
Omán	Rice
Ngokáto	Fish
Ño	Water
Ngoséney	Good, beautiful
Odéyney	Bad, ugly
1	Mudíge
2	Asóge
3	Oñyóko
4	Ngoyagáne
5	Modevokóko
6	Modevokóko na mudíge
7	Modevokóko na asóge
8	Modevokóko na oñyóko
9	Modevokóko na ngoyagáne
10 (with a handclap)	Muranáko

Numbers after 10 are expressed with a combination of claps and the numbers 1 to 9.

Glossary

Assimilado In colonial times, an indigenous Guinean who, through education and connections, had achieved the status of Portuguese citizen.

Bairro Suburb.

Cana Cashew alcohol.

Canoa Pirogue.

Feitoria "Factory", in the historical sense of a trading post.

Fermanza Local name for the dry, dusty *harmattan* wind from the north.

Kirintim A fence of woven brushwood (like wattle) often surrounding and identifying a bar.

Navetanes Seasonal migrant workers.

Paragem Taxi park or, more generally, transport stop.

Ponta Small land concession or trading post in Portuguese Guinea.

Praça Square.

Tabanka Rural village.

Toko toko Public minibus.

6.1

Bissau and the northwest

The majority of overland travellers approach the relaxed capital, **Bissau**, from the north, using one of several overland routes from southern Senegal to travel for a day or so through **northwest Guinea-Bissau**. The northwestern region has little to offer apart from the vast beach along the coast at **Varela** – one of the best reasons to come to the country.

Bissau

Although its narrow nineteenth-century houses with their wrought-iron balustrades provide some architectural interest, **BISSAU** itself isn't a sightseeing city. Instead, its most engaging feature is the absence of tension and clamour – the compact city centre has little traffic and is a pleasant place to explore on foot – which will come as a relaxing surprise if you've just arrived from one of the adjacent Francophone countries. Legacies of the civil war remain, however: war damage is still evident, notably at the ruined presidential palace, and at night, it can be hard to find your way around due to the lack of electricity. Though still one of the most impoverished West African capitals, Bissau is on the move again, a fact particularly apparent along the main road out of town towards the airport, where a number of smart buildings, including a brand-new five-star hotel, have recently appeared.

Arrivals, orientation and information

Osvaldo Vieira International **airport** at Bissalanca is 9km from the centre of Bissau. The limited facilities include a post office, but nowhere to change money. Private charter taxis meet all flights, but you can also get shared transport into the centre (CFA100) on the main Safim–Bissau road; wait by the Total service station opposite the airport terminal. You'll be dropped behind the National Assembly building, leaving you a ten-minute walk along Avenida Francisco Mendes into the centre. There's one main road into the capital, and if you arrive by bush taxi from other destinations in Guinea-Bissau, you'll be dropped at the *paragem* roughly halfway between the city centre and the airport, from where a charter taxi into the centre costs around CFA500.

City transport and information

The best way to get around the compact centre of Bissau is on foot: distances are short and there is none of the gridlock common in so many other West African capitals. For longer distances use a **shared taxi**. These blue-and-white cabs follow a fixed route: simply hail a taxi that is heading in your direction, and you'll be dropped off at the front door. Expect to pay around CFA300 for a short ride, twice that if you're going across town. For zipping up and down Avenida 14 de Novembro, blue-and-yellow **toko toko** minibuses charge a flat fare of CFA100.

For **tourist information**, visit the Ministério do Turismo e do Ordenamento do Território (Mon–Fri 8am–4.30pm ☏20 60 62) on Estrada de Santa Luzia, near

BISSAU

ACCOMMODATION
24 de Setembro	A
Bissau Palace	C
Caracol	E
Libya	B
Tambarina	D
Terrassos Ruby	F

RESTAURANTS, BARS & CLUBS
Asa Branca	6
Bamboo 2000	1
Mansa Flema	3
Papu Louca	4
Santa Rosa	5
Stop	2

0   250 m

N

Most road transport leaves from the **paragem**, the main motor park or *gare routière*, which is about six kilometres out of town on the way to the airport. The busiest route is the one to **Bafatá** (3hr, CFA2200) and **Gabú** (4hr, CFA3000). There's also regular transport to most major towns on the mainland, including **Buba** (3hr, CFA3600), **Catió** (5hr, CFA4400) and **Canchungo** (1½hr, CFA1125). Bissau is also the departure point for travel to the **Bijagós islands** (see box, p.546).

To get to southwest Guinea-Bissau, and as an alternative, and considerably slower route to Bolama, you can take a pirogue across the Rio Gêba to **Enxude** from **Limpar** port east of Bissau's centre (Mon–Fri at 7am, 1½hr, CFA1500). Once at Enxude, catch a bush taxi bound for Buba. If you're going to Bolama, get off at the junction at **Nova Sintra** to hitch (or possibly walk) the final 14km to **São João**, from where pirogues ply the 2km journey across the channel to Bolama. There's a basic motel at Nova Sintra (❶) if you want to break the journey.

For **international destinations**, you can usually find a few bush taxis every morning travelling direct to **Ziguinchor** (4hr, CFA2200), although it's just as easy to get a taxi to São Domingos (3hr, CFA1500), from where you'll find onward transport. For **Kolda** and **Tambacounda**, you're better off first travelling to either Bafatá or Gabú and catching a Senegal-bound taxi from there. Likewise, for destinations in **Guinea** you'll first have to get to Gabú, from where there's transport to Koundara, Boké and Conakry.

the presidential palace. Ask to see the Secretaria de Estado do Turismo (Secretary of State for Tourism), who may be helpful, but don't expect any brochures or useful documentation.

Accommodation

The choice of accommodation in Bissau offers little of good value, and if you're travelling around West Africa on a budget, you'll find you spend more on lodgings here than you're accustomed to. *Hotel Caracol* (❷) and *Hotel Tambarina* (❸) are two miserable budget options northwest of the centre and best avoided; if there is no room at the excellent *Pensão Creola* (see p.540), you might be able to get a cheap room at the officially defunct *Grande Hotel* (❸). The two state-run hotels, *24 de Setembro* and *Hotti Bissau* (the rebels' headquarters during the civil war, and now renamed *Libya Hotel*) have both been sold and were in the transition phase at the time of writing. See the map on p.541 for locations of central establishments.

Lock your room

"Special attention in cheap hotels. It is normal to hear customers complain about small objects stolen from their rooms if they leave them open for a few seconds. Thieves walk freely around the hotels as most of them have no security guards."

Cláudio Vítor Vaz, Portugal

Bissau Palace av 14 de Novembro ☎664 30 00 ⓦwww.bissaupalacehotel.com. New luxury business hotel with comfortable, albeit rather bare, rooms, swimming pool, health centre, bar and restaurant. ❽

Jordani av Pansau Na Isna ☎20 17 19. Slightly run-down mid-range option, not great value. Includes breakfast. ❻

Lobato av Pansau Na Isna ☎21 35 48 ⓕ20 24 05 ⓔaparthotellobato@mail.gtelecom.gw. Large s/c and a/c rooms with TV and fridge, but indifferent service. Includes breakfast. ❽

Pensão Centrale av Amílcar Cabral ☎20 12 32. Still a popular place for travellers and the younger NGO crowd, though rates for its basic, s/c rooms with fans aren't especially competitive these days

– and it has a reputation for things going missing. Includes breakfast. ⑤

Pensão Creola av Domingos Ramos ☎663 30 31 @marcelkuehne@yahoo.com. By far the best option for travellers, with comfortable accommodation in either a four-bed dorm or s/c private rooms. Electricity, running water, communal kitchen, laundry service and a convivial atmosphere created by the well-travelled Swiss host and his family. Recommended – and often full. Dorm beds ②, private rooms ⑤.

Residencial Coimbra av Amílcar Cabral ☎21 34 67. Pleasant s/c rooms with a/c, fridge, safe and TV (free DVD library), and the rooftop terrace is a nice place to unwind. One of the best of the expensive hotels. ⑧

Residencial Tropicana av Pansau Na Isna ☎662 05 25. Spartan but spacious s/c rooms with either fan or a/c. One of the cheaper places in town, with breakfast included. ④

Solmar rua Victorino Costa ☎20 60 04 ☏20 60 05 @solmar@mail.gtelecom.gw. Comfortable, modern rooms or suites with a/c, satellite TV and safe. ⑦

Terrassos Ruby rua Vitorino Costa ☎664 49 17 @osvaldinagomesadao@yahoo.com .br. A famous local actress has turned her luxurious mansion into the city's most comfortable place to stay. The s/c rooms feature a/c, huge beds, flat-screen satellite TV and tasteful African decor, all of which make it very good value. Includes breakfast. ⑦

The City

There is little specifically worth going out of your way to see in Bissau. The old ruined **presidential palace** at the Praça dos Heróis Nacionais is worth a look, with a substantial monument in front dedicated to the heroes of the independence struggle. The covered **central market** is another obvious attraction, but its range of produce and other goods isn't huge and prices are usually higher than in neighbouring countries. The out-of-centre **Mercado Bandim** is much bigger.

Down by the port, you won't miss the stark black, weatherworn **Pidjiguiti Memorial** to the striking dockers massacred here on August 3, 1959 (see p.527). A couple of hundred metres east of the memorial the narrow streets of **Old Bissau** contain some attractive, sometimes quite dilapidated examples of Portuguese colonial architecture. Regrettably, the imposing **Fortaleza d'Amura** that marks the eastern boundary of Old Bissau is still a military barracks and there's no way you'll get in to look around. The **mausoleum** of Amílcar Cabral is located inside, but even Guineans only get to pay their respects on rare occasions, such as September 24.

Carnaval – and exhibitions

If you're in Bissau at **carnaval time** – February or March – you'll get a lopsided view of the city's entertainment value, as an endless stream of floats and elaborate papier-mâché masks is paraded through the streets on **Shrove Tuesday** (Mardi Gras), especially along Avenida Amílcar Cabral. You can see the best creations (there's usually a theme, and winners) from past years at the **Museu Ethnográfico Nacional** at the Amílcar Cabral University on Avenida 14 de Novembro (Mon–Fri 9am–3pm; CFA1000). The floats occupy the entire first floor of the country's main museum – and is the clear highlight of a tiny collection that also features some intriguing Bijagó fetishes and a wonderful Nalù drum. The **French Cultural Centre** also occasionally has temporary exhibitions.

Crafts

There's been an enormous resurgence of **strip-woven cloth** (*pamo de pinte*) in recent years, produced mainly by Pepel and Manjak people. You'll find a decent selection at the **Mercado Bandim**, with prices for a single *pamo* at around CFA6000, perhaps twice as much for heavier weaves. Popular patterns include *kassave* (a check) and *volta de Bissau* (bands).

You'll usually find a spread of **carvings** and similar souvenirs opposite the bank by the *Pensão Centrale*, and there are always one or two crafts stalls at the central market. However the recommended place to browse is the **Centro Artistico Juvenil** (also known as the Centro Padre Batista; irregular times), located 3km from the centre

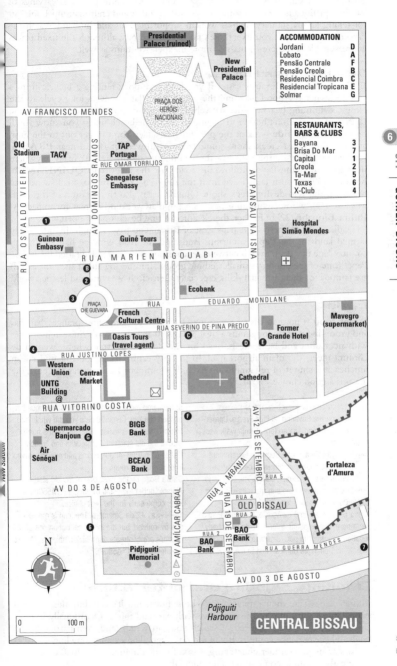

ACCOMMODATION

Jordani	D
Lobato	A
Pensão Centrale	F
Pensão Creola	B
Residencial Coimbra	C
Residencial Tropicana	E
Solmar	G

RESTAURANTS, BARS & CLUBS

Bayana	3
Brisa Do Mar	7
Capital	1
Creola	2
Ta-Mar	5
Texas	6
X-Club	4

Presidential Palace (ruined)

New Presidential Palace

PRAÇA DOS HERÓIS NACIONAIS

AV FRANCISCO MENDES

Old Stadium

TACV

TAP Portugal

RUA OMAR TORRIJOS

Senegalese Embassy

RUA OSVALDO VIEIRA

AV DOMINGOS RAMOS

AV PANSAU NA ISNA

Hospital Simão Mendes

Guinean Embassy

Guiné Tours

RUA MARIEN NGOUABI

Ecobank

PRAÇA CHE GUEVARA

French Cultural Centre

RUA

EDUARDO MONDLANE

RUA SEVERINO DE PINA PREDIO

Former Grande Hotel

Mavegro (supermarket)

Oasis Tours (travel agent)

RUA JUSTINO LOPES

Western Union

Central Market

UNTG Building @

Cathedral

RUA VITORINO COSTA

Supermercado Banjoun

BIGB Bank

Air Sénégal

BCEAO Bank

AV 12 DE SETEMBRO

Fortaleza d'Amura

AV DO 3 DE AGOSTO

RUA A. MBANA

RUA 5

RUA 4

OLD BISSAU

RUA 3

BAO Bank

RUA GUERRA MENDES

N

Pidjiguiti Memorial

AV AMÍLCAR CABRAL

RUA 19 DE SETEMBRO

RUA 2

BAO Bank

AV DO 3 DE AGOSTO

Pidjiguiti Harbour

CENTRAL BISSAU

0   100 m

Max Stadium

on the north side of Avenida 14 de Novembro. The centre produces carvings of varying quality, among them some pieces with real flair and craftsmanship. Look out for telling family statuary such as woman supporting kids and husband. Watch the carvers for as long as you like: there's no pressure to buy, although the fixed prices are reasonable and there's a mass of more inexpensive items as well.

Beaches around Bissau

Exploring beyond Bissau is easier if you have transport; renting a bicycle from a private owner is a good plan and the countryside flat, but it's a long cycle to the closest swimming beaches. Alternatively, rent a car or motorbike or negotiate the charter of a taxi. Don't bother struggling to get to the beach unless you know you'll be there at **high tide** – ask at the port for tide tables. You can get out to the bush and the Rio Gêba creek shore some 18km southwest of Bissau near **PRÁBIS**, reached by following the road past the stadium, though there isn't really anywhere near here to swim. If you follow the road past the airport to **QUINHÁMEL**, however (39km; bush taxis leave from the *paragem*), you'll find a small swimming beach on the Rio de Tor creek shore. Quinhámel is also the location of the *Hotel Marazul* (⑥), whose swimming pool is a popular weekend retreat for expats. At **Punta Biombo**, 22km further, there's a nice, if tiny, beach on the open sea.

Heading out on these short trips west of Bissau, you pass through the intensively farmed lands of the **Pepel**, a curious landscape, the road winding like an English country lane in a deep trough between fenced and carefully-tended raised fields. The Pepel (one of the country's smaller ethnic groups, numbering about sixty thousand) are famous for their artisanal skills, especially their cloth-weaving and leather work.

Eating

Street food is poor in Bissau, pretty much limited to ubiquitous oranges, bananas and groundnuts, with doughnuts a treat at CFA50 apiece. If you're in search of cafés with no names and basic meals, head for the Bandim quarter, where Avenida de Cintura meets the main airport road. In the city centre itself, you can find cheap lunches at a cluster of restaurants on Avenida Domingos Ramos near the port; the *Texas* is a good choice.

Restaurants and cafés

Asa Branca rua Severino de Pina Predio. Upmarket Portuguese and African fare, 10min walk west of the centre.

Bayana praça Che Guevara. Government ministers are sometimes to be found here, sipping early-morning coffee. The terrace is great for people-watching and the meals (around CFA2500) aren't bad value.

Brisa Do Mar av do 3 de Agosto. More bar than restaurant, this pleasant, informal café in a shady location opposite the port, caters to thirsty dockers.

Creola av Domingos Ramos. Next to the *pensão* of the same name and specializing in delicious barbecued chicken. CFA3500 gets you the whole bird.

Papa Louca av Francisco Mendes, on the north side of the old stadium. Portuguese and French dishes (CFA3000–4000), pizzas and snacks, served in a cosy dining room.

Santa Rosa on the west side of the old stadium. Reliable buffet food sold by weight (CFA5500 per kilo); come early for the best choice.

Ta-Mar av 12 de Setembro. The food is mediocre and overpriced, but the tables set out on one of Old Bissau's pretty streets don't lack ambience. There's a buffet on Sat (CFA5000).

Drinking, nightlife and entertainment

Guineans describe their capital as a 24-hour fiesta, and it's certainly the case that from Thursday to Sunday, Bissau is alive with bars and music. Occasionally, impressive street parties are organized, at which you can watch (and even participate in) *zouk* and *gumbe* dance contests. If you intend to spend an evening trawling the city's clubs, you might consider **chartering a taxi** for the duration (CFA4000 or so), best done early as cabs become scarce after midnight.

There are several **nightclubs** with reasonable admission (around CFA2000). Cape Verdean, Guinea-Bissau and Antillean *zouk* is the music that dominates all of Bissau's dance floors. It's slower and easier to learn than salsa, and arguably sexier too – don't hesitate to plunge right in. Popular, unpretentious discos favoured by locals include *Bambu 2000*, a couple of kilometres from the centre on Avenida 14 de Novembro, and *Stop*, on Avenida de Cintura in the lively district of Cupelon de Cima. Rather more stylish is the *Capital*, one of the more expensive places with a wide selection of music. The *X-Club* on Rua Osvaldo Vieira is a plush club with costly drinks, Latin music, and an almost entirely Portuguese clientele.

The best place to hear **live music** is the enduring though slightly scruffy *Mansa Flema* bar in Cupelon de Cima. DJs spin local music from around 9pm and live gigs (usually Fri, Sat & Sun) tend to start around midnight. Another venue known for hosting live acts is *Lennox*, opposite the Amílcar Cabral University on Avenida 14 de Novembro, a bustling entertainment complex with several snack bars, an Internet café and a big screen showing music videos. The French Cultural Centre on Praça Che Guevara also organizes music and dance performances, as well as showing French **films** every Tuesday.

Listings

Airlines Air Sénégal, av Osvaldo Vieira ☏ 20 52 11; TACV, av Omar Torrijos ☏ 20 68 20; TAP Portugal, 14 Praça dos Heróis Nacionais ☏ 20 13 59.

Banks and exchange Ecobank on av Amílcar Cabral is the best place to change cash (no commission) and traveller's cheques (2 percent commission). The other banks – BAO on rua Guerra Mendes and BIGB on av Amílcar Cabral – change cash, but may be reluctant to accept traveller's cheques. You can also approach the street moneychangers outside the main post office or at the central market, or try the Mavegro supermarket (see below). There are as yet no ATMs in Bissau.

Bike rental Finding bikes is a matter of asking around; the *Pensão Creola* will probably be able to point you in the right direction.

Car rental Try the *Bissau Palace* hotel, or talk to Guiné Tours on rua Marien Ngouabi or Oasis Tours on rua Severino de Pina Predio, either of which may be able to help you find a private car with driver.

CDs The music stalls on the corner of av Domingos Ramos and rua Vitorino Costa sell a wide range of cassettes and CDs of Guinea-Bissau music.

Cultural centre The French Cultural Centre on Praça Che Guevara (Mon–Fri 9am–1pm & 3–7pm; ☏ 20 68 17) has a cinema, theatre and café. There's also an a/c library (Mon 3–6pm, Tues–Fri 9am–1pm & 3–6pm, Sat 9am–1pm) with French newspapers and magazines.

Embassies and consulates France, av 14 de Novembro, opposite the National Assembly ☏ 20 13 12 ⓕ 20 50 94 (issues visas for various Francophone countries); The Gambia, rua Vitorino Costa ☏ 20 50 85; Guinea, rua Marien Ngouabi ☏ 20 12 31; Mauritania, rua Eduardo Mondlane ☏ 20 36 96; Nigeria, av 14 de Novembro

☏ 21 18 76; Portugal, 6 Av Cidade de Lisboa ☏ 21 12 61 ⓕ 20 12 69; Senegal, rua Omar Torrijos ☏ 21 29 44; UK Honorary Consul, Jan van Maanen, Mavegro ☏ 20 12 24 or 20 12 16 ⓔ mavegro@hotmail.com; US liaison office, 1 Rua Ulysses S Grant, Bairro de Penha ☏ 24 22 73.

Hospital Hospital Simão Mendes, av Pansau Na Isna, just north of the *Grande Hotel*.

Internet access One of the most central places to get online is at the STA Cibercafé on rua Vitorino Costa, near the central market; the quickest and most reliable connections, however, are at the *Lennox* entertainment complex on Av 14 de Novembro.

Pharmacy Rama, rua Vitorino Costa (Mon–Fri 8am–1pm & 3–7.30pm, Sat 8am–1pm).

Post office The main post office (Mon–Fri 8am–6pm) is on the corner of av Amílcar Cabral and rua Vitorino Costa.

Supermarkets Supermercado Bonjour, on rua Vitorina Costa, has a wide variety of imported foods and other goods; Mavegro, rua Eduardo Mondlane, also has food and other supplies, including camping equipment.

Travel agents Oasis Tours, rua Severino de Pina Predio (☏ 20 68 67), organize excursions to the Bijagós islands. Other agencies include Guiné Tours, rua Marien Ngouabi (☏ 720 88 97); Surire Tours, rua Angola (☏ 21 41 66); and Agencia de Viagens Sagres, av de República (☏ 21 37 09).

Visa extensions The immigration office (Mon–Fri 8am–3pm) is on av 14 de Novembro near the Mercado Bandim; visa extensions are usually quick and hassle-free.

Western Union They have a representative on rua Justino Lopez (Mon–Thurs 8am–6pm, Fri 8am–5pm; ☏ 20 45 55), as well as at Ecobank.

The northwest

With the exception of the beautiful beach at **Varela**, the northwest of the country is little visited except by travellers passing through on their way to or from Senegal; **São Domingos** is the country's principal entry point from its northern neighbour. With only an infrequent pirogue crossing the river from São Domingos to **Cacheu**, the old route south to Bissau – via **Canchungo** – is rarely used; most travellers instead take the tarred road via Ingoré and Bula.

Canchungo and Cacheu

CANCHUNGO is a sleepy place, enlivened on weekends by a couple of night-clubs. You can get here by hopping on a direct *toko toko* from Bissau, or you could change at **BULA**. The fine avenue of trees running into town gives a favourable first impression, and the central *praça* market area with sellers of boiled starch and oranges, is alive with people waiting for transport. Just off the square are a few places where beer, meals and rooms (❷) are available.

CACHEU, 100km from Bissau, has nothing much to offer in itself, though you may want to visit the nearby **Parque Natural dos "Tarrafes" do Rio Cacheu**, established to protect the area's extensive mangrove swamps. There's also varied birdlife, including pelicans, and some difficult-to-spot hippos. Rather than bank on there being staff to guide you, it's better to contact IBAP before venturing out (see p.529). You'll get a decent look at the park if you're coming to Cacheu on the daily pirogue from São Domingos (1½hr, CFA1500), the departure time depending on the tides – usually between noon and 4pm. As for Cacheu, it is the site of a sixteenth-century **fort**, the whitewashed substance of which (only 20m square) is still in place, along with its guns, and more ruins to the right, down on the shore. Notice the unusual material used on the roads in Cacheu: broken oil-palm-kernel pits which are very hard-wearing, like vegetable gravel. Cacheu has little in the way of shops or food, and just one hotel, closed at the time of writing, though you should have no problems finding locals willing to put you up for a small fee. Alternatively, IBAP has six basic rooms (❷) intended for people visiting the park, but open to all. A traditional "fair" or market is held every eight days.

São Domingos and Varela

For most travellers, **SÃO DOMINGOS** is a transit point to the beach at **Varela**, 50km to the west. Few people overnight in São Domingos, but if it can't be helped there's a surprisingly comfortable hotel, *Chez Octavio*, fifty metres south of the roundabout, with pretty s/c rooms (❸), some with a/c, and good food.

The beach at **VARELA** is stunning, arguably outdoing Cap Skiring across the Senegalese border, with gorgeous swimming, pine trees and low cliffs. **Accommodation** is available at the well-established and pleasant *Chez Helene* (❸) – the only option until the *Jordani Hotel* reopens after renovations. You can also camp on the beach. As a place to come for the weekend, it's a favourite with affluent locals and Guinea-Bissau's small expat community. Despite this, it's relatively quiet, thanks to the extremely rough road – which gets very muddy after rain – from São

Pigs

Some of the scrawniest, most long-legged and hirsute **hogs** you'll ever see live in Guinea-Bissau: many of them look like dogs. It's possible the breed is a survival of the ancient **pig culture** of north and west Africa that has mostly been obliterated by the spread of Islam. Widespread outside Muslim regions, the pigs wander freely, performing the useful street-cleaning functions normally associated with goats.

Domingos. It's easy enough to get a bush taxi to São Domingos from the *paragem* in Bissau (3hr, CFA1500), but only one or two vehicles a day do the journey from São Domingos to Varela (2½hr, CFA1000). You may well see hunters en route with monkey carcasses slung over their shoulders.

6.2

The Bijagós islands

T he largest island group along the West African coast, the **Bijagós archipelago** is made up of more than forty islands, only some of which are inhabited or used for fishing. Not all the islands are accessible, but if you rent a speedboat and have at least a week to spend here, you should be able to see **Bubaque**, the principal island, **Bolama**, **Galinhas**, **Rubane** and maybe even **Orango**. At the moment, the islands are pretty much devoid of tourists, competitive anglers accounting for the majority of the hotel guests.

Now declared a UNESCO Biosphere Reserve, the islands are mostly covered in dense forest, with large stands of oil palm and cashew groves, patches of garden cultivation and necklaces of white sand or mangroves along the seashore. The waters of the archipelago are warm and shallow, and it's not uncommon for pirogues to run aground in mid-channel, or to see flamingos sunning themselves on sandbars. These shallow, reef-free waters mean that large fishing vessels cannot trawl their nets in the archipelago. The nutrient-rich water spilling out from five rivers further sustains the sea life, making the Bijagós islands extremely popular among sports fishermen. The islanders themselves, predominantly Bijagó-speakers who've lived surrounded by these calm waters for centuries, are remarkably autonomous. Quite a few communities remain matriarchal societies, and you'll still see women in traditional short palm-fibre skirts (*saiya*). Many of the more remote islands felt little impact from the centuries of Portuguese presence in the region (several were never, officially, "pacified" at the end of the nineteenth century when the rest of the country was being shot into line). And several still have only the most tenuous of links with whoever happens to be in government in Bissau, or with the outside world.

In consequence, you should be prepared for an almost complete lack of facilities away from the two small towns of Bubaque and Bolama, and even those two had no banks at the time of writing, so bring sufficient funds to cover your stay. Bubaque is the only island equipped with a choice of hotels and restaurants and it's the best base from which to organize other trips.

One disquieting feature of the Bijagós that has emerged in recent years is their use as a **narcotics** staging-post in the smuggling of cocaine between South America and Europe. Guinea-Bissau officials appear to be in on the traffic, but you are strongly advised to look the other way if you see any evidence.

Bolama

A warped sliver of jungle and farm plots, 22km long and mostly just a couple of kilometres wide, pressed in on most sides by dense mangroves, **Bolama** is the island closest to the mainland. In the past it exercised the imaginations of the British as well as the Portuguese, and was the subject of a protracted colonial dispute in the nineteenth century. Today, the town of Bolama makes for an interesting historical and architectural excursion, and if you're equipped with a bicycle, it's straightforward to head off to the island's most beautiful beaches, on the southern coast.

Curiously, the first colonial adventure attempted on Bolama was conducted by the **British** in 1792 (see box, p.548) and they tried again in 1814. But the agreements with local Bijagó elders on which these incursions were based were no more binding than the treaties the Bijagó had also signed with the **Portuguese**. And it was the latter – particularly the mixed-race Cape Verde islanders – who survived both Bolama's fevers and the Bijagó warriors long enough to establish a real community. Throughout the nineteenth century the British returned periodically to claim sovereignty by pulling up the Portuguese flagpoles, shouting at the settlers and shipping their domestic slaves off to liberation in the colony of Sierra Leone. But they made no serious efforts to settle permanently, or to take charge of the island, until 1860, when Bolama was annexed to Sierra Leone, hundreds of miles to the south. The Portuguese, desperate to preserve their stake in the slave trade which the British were busy trying to abolish, had formally lodged their own claim in 1830 and, by the time the British annexed the island, there were seven hundred loyal Portuguese subjects living there. The dispute wasn't settled until 1870, when a commission headed by United States President Ulysses S. Grant found in favour of Portugal. Grant's efforts were rewarded with a statue in the town square, pulled down some years ago.

Getting to and around the Bijagós islands

Getting to the islands is limited by the scarcity of ferry services and a more or less complete absence of air links. Most of the Bijagós-bound motorized pirogues leave from the Pidjiguiti harbour in Bissau, but even visiting the main islands usually requires a good deal of time. You can usually find boats to **Bolama** on Tuesday, Friday and Sunday, returning to Bissau on Wednesday, Friday and Sunday (3hr, CFA2000). An alternative route to Bolama, feasible every weekday, is via Enxude (see box, p.539).

For **Bubaque**, pirogues carrying passengers leave Pidjiguiti harbour on Tuesday and Friday, returning to Bissau on Wednesday and Sunday (5hr, CFA2500). You might also be able to find pirogues going to the islands of Formosa, Galinhas and Orango, but probably no more than once a week.

As a rule of thumb, departure times vary from day to day depending on the tides. Enquire a day in advance about when your boat is meant to leave at the blue building on the right-hand side of the Pidjiguiti harbour entrance.

More basic vessels known as *canoas* leave sporadically for the islands from the Porto de Canoa southwest of Bissau centre. These boats are usually old, overloaded and not recommended as a safe way to travel.

Unfortunately, real **island-hopping** is difficult without your own boat. Bubaque is the only island where you'll find services to other destinations in the archipelago: these basically amount to **Rubane** and **Soga** – both short hops from Bubaque – and the islands of **Uno** and **Orango**, which are served by a weekly pirogue that leaves Bubaque on Sat and returns on Tuesday (CFA1500 to either island).

The alternative to public transport is to arrange through one of the hotels in Bissau or Bubaque for a **speedboat** to take you to the islands: count on Bissau–Bubaque costing around CFA25,000 one way, CFA50,000 return, or CFA250,000 for the whole boat. Several Bubaque hotels also organize angling excursions around the islands (about CFA40,000 per person, plus fuel).

Finally, Bubaque has a rudimentary airstrip and **charter flights** from Dakar, Ziguinchor and Cap Skiring can be arranged through *Kasa Afrikana* in Bubaque (see p.550) or Oasis Tours in Bissau (see p.543).

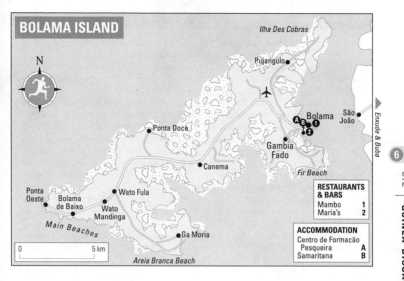

RESTAURANTS & BARS
Mambo	1
Maria's	2

ACCOMMODATION
Centro de Formacão Pesqueira	A
Samaritana	B

Bolama town

The town of **BOLAMA** is on the landward side of the island, facing the mainland barely 2km away. With a slight feeling of dereliction, it echoes with the past grandeurs of the Portuguese empire. Solid mansions attest to a century of trading in ivory and forest products and the opening up of the West African groundnut industry, but ever since the capital of Portuguese Guinea was transferred to Bissau in 1941, Bolama has been steadily crumbling away. The town is still the seat of government of Bolama Region, which includes most of the islands and a little chunk of mainland, and it has its own regional president, a hospital and a teacher training college, but this is a forgotten place, and jungle vegetation sprouts between the scattered buildings.

Walking around the town will take you all of forty minutes. Down by the port you'll not miss the ugly **sculpture** bestowed on the island by Mussolini after an Italian seaplane crashed here in 1931 (Bolama used to be a "hydrobase" on the Rome-to-Rio seaplane route). Behind the monument, the **Governor's Palace** remains one of the island's grandest buildings. A couple of hundred metres from here is the overgrown main *praça*, the colonnaded **Town Hall** and dilapidated **church**, its roof gone but with bell and altar still intact, are other noteworthy architectural relics. The only reminder of Britain's ephemeral presence on Bolama is 300m down to the left behind the church: the reddish two-storey ruin flanked by mango trees is the **Casa Inglesa**, a monstrous edifice built entirely of corrugated iron. Architecturally, at any rate, the Portuguese deserved to win the island.

There's a pleasant evening **stroll** out of town – set off from the main *praça* by taking the road beside the church – past the secondary school and down an attractive, sandy avenue of trees, with compounds set back on both sides – surely a colonial conception, but one that's endured. Out this way too, at the start of the avenue on the left, there's a rather Gothic graveyard which is worth a look: a curious assembly of souls, including a number of Middle Europeans and even one or two Britons.

Practicalities

Facilities for visitors on Bolama are very limited. A couple of places close to the jetty offer **accommodation**: the friendly *Samaritana* (☎724 24 76) has basic rooms with bucket showers and a noisy generator (❷), while the Centro de Formacão

Beaver's colony

If the **British expedition to Bolama** had resulted in a successful colony, the map of West Africa might today be radically different. **Phillip Beaver**, 26, set sail from Gravesend in England on April 4, 1792, with 274 prospective settlers, intending, with government backing, to start an African colony. Included among the party were a ready-made Legislative Council and Governor, chosen in the *Globe Tavern*, London.

The first deaths occurred through **smallpox** before they had reached the Isle of Wight, and by the time the two ships, *Hankey* and *Calypso*, were nosing through the Bijagós islands six weeks later, half the passengers had **malarial fever**. Bolama, at first, seemed perfect and uninhabited, and those colonists who were well enough went ashore to chase elephants and butterflies, lie in the sun and collect oysters. Beaver was irritated at their lack of industry. They saw a Bijagó war canoe, but Beaver insisted "the inhabitants were thought to be of peaceable disposition, well-inclined towards the English culture". A week later the warriors attacked, surprisingly well armed with muskets and Solingen swords, killing and wounding a dozen people and kidnapping several women and children. The settlers' cannons had never even been unpacked.

The **colony** looked doomed from then on. Although the captives were released when Bolama was "bought" for £77 worth of iron bars from a pair of local headmen, over half the emigrants chose to continue to Sierra Leone in the *Calypso* in July. As the rains set in, the remaining 91 died of malaria at a remarkably even rate, until by the end of the year there were only thirteen survivors. A typically laconic entry in Beaver's journal reads:

"Sun 2nd Dec. Killed a bullock for the colony. Died and was buried Mr. Webster. Thermometer 92. Three men well."

Beaver and five others survived the rains of the following year and he and a companion sailed back to England in May 1794. "An ill-contrived and badly executed, though well intended expedition," he mused. The timing, arriving at the start of the rains, could not have been worse. His book was entitled *African Memoranda: Relative to an Attempt to Establish a British Settlement on the Island of Bulama on the Western Coast of Africa in the year 1792, with a Brief Notice of the Neighbouring Tribes, Soils, Productions Etc., and some Observations on the Facility of Colonising that part of Africa with a View to Cultivation; and the Introduction of Letters and Religion to its Inhabitants but more particularly as the means of gradually Abolishing Slavery*. Published in 1805, it's hugely readable and worth scanning the antiquarian bookshops for.

Pesqueira – formerly PRODEPA – (☎724 20 08 or 720 70 73) offers smarter a/c rooms with shared bathroom (❸), as well as meals. A local woman named Maria runs a **restaurant** in her house 200m up from the jetty to the left; it's fish and rice most days, which you'll have to order in advance. There's a limited market (in a large, walled marketplace) where a small selection of fruit and vegetables, fish, peanut butter and bread is usually available. Bring with you what you can from Bissau and what you don't use will find eager recipients. For a **drink**, try the *Mambo* bar next to the jetty, which has tables looking out across the water to the mainland.

The Centro de Formacão Pesqueira **rents boats** for CFA50,000–75,000 per day and conducts dolphin-watching excursions (CFA3000 per person) during the season (around July to October). Exploring the island otherwise means a lot of footwork, and it's a good idea to bring a **bicycle** with you from Bissau. Bike rental is difficult in Bolama and there's no more than a handful of vehicles on the island.

Walks and rides near Bolama town

Fork right off the main road out of the town and you soon find yourself on a delightful narrow lane twisting through cashew groves. There are no beaches down here, but you do pass a **cashew jam factory** which is open a few days every year – they make potent cashew wine rather than jam (out of the fruits, not the nuts) – and a cloth manufacturing plant that evidently hasn't been open from the day the looms were delivered. Passing the abandoned airstrip and the hamlet of **PUJANGULO**, the path becomes a muddy track through the mangroves at low tide, at which time it joins the main island to the uninhabited **Ilha das Cobras**. It's exciting stuff, but watch out for snakes on the other side and don't get stranded by the tide. The walk or ride is about 15km there and back.

There are other, shorter walks you can do in the peninsula immediately south of Bolama town. The most obvious one is to **Fir Beach**, a pleasant and predictably quiet stretch hemmed in by mangrove swamps 4km from the town. If you want to swim, make sure you come at high tide. To get there, follow the road to the right of the Town Hall for about a kilometre until you reach the village of **GAMBIA FADO**. Turn left at the village and continue along the bush track for another thirty minutes. There are two forks in this track: first take the left, then the right; you are going in the correct direction if you can see the old electricity pylons poking through the trees.

Travelling across Bolama island

The main interest, however, lies further **south across the island** where, unless you're prepared to set off early with food and water sufficient for a couple of days, you're really going to need transport. The dirt road cuts through pretty forest, farm and plantation lands, following the central ridge of the island (maximum elevation just 26m), never far from the sea. The people you'll meet are mostly Bijagó and for these rural people, tourists are a sensational novelty: you'll still occasionally find children for whom such a meeting is a first.

Hamlets and clusters of compounds are, in many cases, named after ethnic groups. Some 17km from Bolama you turn left at **WATO FULA** and plunge into a tunnel of cashews. **Areia Branca beach** is a further 7km down here, a narrow lip of white sand dipping beneath the coconuts into a milky blue sea. There are other beaches along the southern coast, but this is said to be the best spot, and you're unlikely to find it anything but deserted. This corner of the island is very sparsely populated and you can nose around for hours completely alone. Remember, however, if you're tempted to knock off a few coconuts for their milk and flesh, that all the trees are individually owned.

Trust the boatman

"Although they seem to have a dangerous reputation, boats in the Bijagós islands aren't any more dangerous than anywhere in West Africa, with lack of life vests and overloading the norm. You do put your trust in the boatman but that's more a question of trusting he won't run aground in the extremely shallow waters in these parts – which, again, is no real cause for concern. Indeed, this happened to me on my way to Bolama and everyone just kicked back and drank palm wine until the tides lifted us off the sand and we were on our way again."

Ross Velton, Canada

Bubaque

In Guinea-Bissau, the tourist industry begins and ends in **BUBAQUE**. In colonial days the island was a Portuguese favourite, and after independence Swedish aid provided a hotel and a tarmac road to the beach. Trips were arranged here from The Gambia in the 1970s, later to be replaced by regular visits from French tourists, flying in for the renowned game-fishing in the waters of the archipelago. The country's civil war reduced tourism in the Bijagós islands, and although Bubaque has yet to regain its pre-war popularity, sea-anglers still come here in considerable numbers, joined by a small but steady stream of curious travellers. For details on how to get to Bubaque, see box, p.546.

On the outward voyage from Bissau, until you have cleared the island of **Galinhas**, a sea as flat as a millpond is the normal vista in the dry season. But as you approach the isle of Rubane, the mood improves. The intense tropicality of the green, horizontal islands leaves a strong sense of place, reinforced as you enter the channel between Bubaque and Rubane (see p.552) and see the red tin roofs and high pier of Bubaque. The scene – the verdant foliage of the two islands tumbling to the water, the soft lighting, the tranquillity after the racket and diesel fumes of relatively bustling Bissau – is magic.

Accommodation

In contrast to Bissau, Bubaque has a wide range of **accommodation** for all budgets. There is usually electricity from 7pm to 7am, although most hotels have their own generators.

Bella Vista directly opposite the port ☏ 724 84 37. Cramped rooms with shared bathrooms.

Cadjoco ten minutes' walk from the port ☏ 724 84 08. In a peaceful location, with a relaxing garden, but slightly overpriced rooms with shared bathrooms. ❸

Calypso ☏ 724 84 09. One of the more expensive options, although the s/c rooms are a bit tatty and the swimming pool very murky. ❹

🏃 **Casa Dora** ☏ 724 84 50. Also known as *Aparthotel Canoa*, this Portuguese-run place has attractive s/c bungalows set in a flower-strewn garden and offers good value. ❸

Chez Raoul near the port ☏ 725 06 90. Friendly and popular budget accommodation. ❷

🏃 **Chez Titi** ☏ 725 41 62. The two sea-facing rooms at this Senegalese-run place are the best budget bases on the island. ❷

Cruz Pointes I & II ☏ 82 11 35 or 724 84 30. *Cruz Pointes I* is the cheapest accommodation in Bubaque, with small, dark rooms (❶) and bucket showers; *Cruz Pointes II* has larger, brighter rooms (❸) with breakfast included.

🏃 **Kasa Afrikana** ☏ 724 33 05 ⓦ www .kasa-afrikana.com. You won't find better accommodation than this anywhere in the country. Friendly staff, lovely sea views, attractive pool, great food and creature comforts including a/c, satellite TV and drinkable tap water. Pricey, but worth it. ❽

Les Dauphins ☏ 82 11 56 ⓦ www.lesdauphins .com. Dedicated to anglers and usually full of people on package holidays from France. ❽

Bubaque town

Bubaque town lacks the architectural interest of Bolama, but is a pleasant place for walking, particularly early morning and late afternoon when the island is bathed in gorgeously subdued sunlight. Immensely picturesque seascapes flicker through the mango boughs: oil palms in massive stands are covered in the nit-like nests of weaver birds, and resound with their chatter; lizards and butterflies dart everywhere; and mambas are occasionally seen. A **produce market** sets up every morning next to the jetty and a growing number of **shops** selling souvenirs line the road leading up from the harbour. There's also a reasonable **beach** on the northern tip of the island by the airstrip, thirty minutes' walk from the harbour. The sand is expansive at low tide and it's a good place for camping.

Renting **bicycles** in Bubaque is straightforward: several hotels, including *Casa Dora*, *Chez Titi* and *Cadjoco*, have them and charge CFA5000 per day; check the condition of your wheels carefully. The *Calypso* rents **cars** for CFA30,000 per day; and *Kasa Afrikana* can arrange boat rental and fishing expeditions.

Eating, drinking and nightlife

The **restaurant** at *Kasa Afrikana* serves the best food on the island, but it's expensive. If you're on a tighter budget, you might try *Chez Raoul* for excellent Senegalese

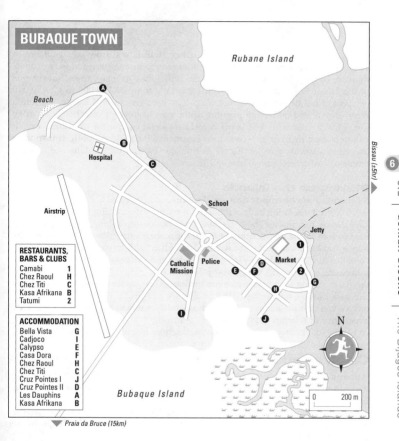

BUBAQUE TOWN

Rubane Island

Beach

Ⓐ

Hospital Ⓑ

Ⓒ

Airstrip

School

Jetty

RESTAURANTS, BARS & CLUBS

Camabi	1
Chez Raoul	H
Chez Titi	C
Kasa Afrikana	B
Tatumi	2

ACCOMMODATION

Bella Vista	G
Cadjoco	I
Calypso	E
Casa Dora	F
Chez Raoul	H
Chez Titi	C
Cruz Pointes I	J
Cruz Pointes II	D
Les Dauphins	A
Kasa Afrikana	B

Catholic Mission   Police   Market Ⓞ

Ⓔ Ⓕ Ⓓ

Ⓗ

Ⓘ

Ⓙ

Ⓖ

Bubaque Island

Bissau (±5hr)

N

0   200 m

▼ *Praia da Bruce (15km)*

cooking or *Chez Titi*, whose table overlooking the sea makes a wonderfully romantic setting for a meal. The *Camabi*, built under the rusty scaffolding of a ruined palm-oil factory, is the local bar, where you can get drunk on cheap palm wine and *cana*. **Nightlife** in Bubaque is pretty much restricted to the *Tatumi*, which has a surprisingly good sound system and plays the usual mix of Guinean and Cape Verdean music for locals and tourists, and *Chez Raoul*, which sometimes has music and dancing on Saturday nights.

Praia da Bruce

Don't miss out on a trip to **Praia da Bruce**, 15km away on the south coast. It's very appealing: the beach offers shady cashew trees, as much clean sand as you could wish for, and an isolation that's palpable – though one or two fishermen may come by, stationing themselves in the waves to catch a garnish for the evening rice. There are no facilities here, so you'll have to bring your own food and water.

Most of the Bubaque hotels can arrange a trip to Praia da Bruce. Alternatively, you could rent a bike and venture out on a beautiful ride along Bubaque's straight, flat road, which is lined by thick forest and passes by the occasional village. Make sure you leave early in the morning, as the heat becomes unbearable around midday. Try to get to the beach when the tide is high, and bring drinking water – lots of it.

Other islands

If you think Bubaque is beautiful, the **other islands** will truly take your breath away. Getting to them may be hard without your own transport, and living conditions are rough, but it's worth it. Bubaque is the place to rent a **speedboat** at one of the bigger hotels. Be prepared to pay anything from CFA20,000 to CFA50,000 per person per day, excluding fuel, for a four-passenger boat. You may also find a reasonably-priced motorized **pirogue** at the port or through your hotel, but make sure it's in a good state. The larger hotels have radio equipment you can take with you to contact them in the event of an emergency. Inter-island **public transport** is limited to a weekly pirogue that leaves Bubaque on Saturday for Uno and Orango, returning to Bubaque the following Tuesday.

Staying on the islands

Recognized **accommodation** on **Rubane** consists of two French-run *campements* (a third was being built at the time of writing) specializing in fishing holidays, *Club Tarpon* and *Tubaron* (both ⑥), but if you're not into fishing, you might find it hard to join in the conversations. On **Orango**, there's the *Orango Parque Hotel* (⑥), which had been sold at time of writing with plans for it to continue to function as an eco-resort; and on **João Vieira** the *Titeline* and *Carangue* (both ⑥) also cater to fishermen. Since both Orango and João Vieira are national parks, there's also the option of staying at the basic accommodation (②) set up for ecotourists, researchers and park officials, but contact IBAP in advance (see p.523). Apart from these possibilities, you're at the mercy of **Bijagó hospitality** – usually profound. There is little experience of tourism out here and any generosity you respond with is unlikely to be exploited. The Bijagó have very severe sanctions in cases of stealing.

Central and northern isles

Rubane and **Soga** (the latter being the island from which the 1970 Portuguese invasion of the Republic of Guinea was launched) are close to Bubaque and not hard to get to.

There are occasional pirogue services from Bissau's Pidjiguiti harbour to the relatively populated and forested **Formosa** island; ask to be dropped at **Nago** in the creek between **Maio** island and Formosa.

On the archipelago's northwest periphery the string of stunning beaches and crystal-clear water surrounding **Caravela** are the jewel in the Bijagós' crown: the island is a traditional stop-off point for luxury cruises such as those operated by the 17-cabin yacht *Africa Queen* (Ⓦwww.africa-queen.com).

If you wish to visit **Roxa** (also known as **Canhabaque**), the most traditional of the islands, it's best to take a guide from Bubaque with you – any hotel should be able to put you in touch with one. A guide is essential, above all, to indicate sacred sites that should not be walked upon. On arrival you'll be taken to meet the local chief, whom you present with rum and other gifts in exchange for permission to visit the island.

Southern and western isles

The wilder, and perhaps most beautiful islands are on the archipelago's ocean-facing, southwestern edge and require a concerted effort to reach, with the probability of several days' wait for a return passage. All of them make Bubaque look cosmopolitan by comparison and offer tremendous rewards if you're adventurous and flexible – and preferably have your own tent. You'll find no shops, police or *pensões*, almost no motor vehicles and negligible outside influence. The tenuous **missionary presence** has succeeded only superficially in subduing the islanders' traditional values: clandestine **initiation ceremonies** incorporating the use of *irãn* (fetishes) combine freely with Christian beliefs and practices. You're almost certain to witness the rich cultural life of the islanders, expressed through drumming and dancing.

The marine and terrestrial **wildlife** on these remoter islands is extraordinarily prolific, much of it found within two protected areas, **Orango National Park** and **João Vieira-Poilão National Park**. Exploratory walks through the bush will reveal hornbills, monkeys and green mambas, while sharks and stingrays patrol the shallows. While the mamba's bite has no remedy (just don't get bitten), a ray's excruciating sting is soothed by the islanders with a slice of fresh papaya and a few cow-hornfuls of *cana*.

Orango

Orango has an unusual population of saltwater-dwelling **hippos** in the creek south of **ETICOGA**, the island's principal settlement. The hippos are able to swim between the islands, and are held in some fear by the islanders owing to their penchant for ruining crops and exhibiting menacing behaviour in defence of their young. It's a ninety-minute pirogue ride from Eticoga to the creek, and the hippos are best seen in the late afternoon from December to March. At the time of writing, IBAP (see p.523) were building new accommodation (❷) close to the hippo creek. Orango is the ancient seat of the Bijagó queen, **Pampa**, whose life is celebrated in legend, and artefacts dating back centuries have been found on the island.

João Vieira

Further to the east, the pint-sized island of **João Vieira** is famous for its marine turtles, which attract researchers and conservationists. It costs CFA20,000 per person per day to see the turtles and involves spending the night on the remote islet of **Poilão**. Green turtles are the most common species and the season runs from July to October. For more information, contact IBAP.

Uracane and Unhocuum

The islands of **Uracane** (with its colony of flamingos outnumbering the residents a hundredfold) and **Unhocuum** take some getting to. On the outside of the furthest island, Unhocuum, the seas become rough Atlantic swell, traversed by the sea route to the main settlement, **ANABURU**.

Uno

Between Uracane and Unhocuum, the island of **Uno** is a feasible destination thanks to the weekly pirogue service from Bubaque, and on arrival you can camp in the schoolyard at **UNO** port. But you can still expect to be the source of much curiosity and you should rehearse a plausible answer to the big question on local lips: "Why have you come here?"

6.3

The south and east

The **interior of Guinea-Bissau** – a patchwork of low ridges, divided by the country's creeks and rivers – is of less obvious appeal than the islands. However, for nature-lovers with plenty of time and energy, or if you're interested in the country's Muslim influences, this area has its rewards. From the travel perspective, the rest of the country divides into two: the **south**, a relatively inaccessible and little-known region, fronting up against the Republic of Guinea; and the **east**, hardly explored by travellers either, though Guinea-Bissau's main road runs out this way, with a couple of large towns along the line of travel.

The south

The south – with its impressive areas of rainforest – has seen steady improvements in both roads and public transport, but it still takes a lot of effort to get to the more interesting places. The traditional gateway to the region is **ENXUDE**, across the Rio Gêba from Bissau and accessible from the capital by pirogue (see box, p.539). From Enxude, there are always bush taxis waiting to take you on to **TITE**, **FULACUNDA** and **Buba**. Alternatively, you can easily get to Buba without the pirogue crossing (and on a road that's paved the whole way) via **Bambadinca**. Banana wagons are a popular form of transport around the southwest.

Buba and local beauty spots

The main town and transport hub of the south, **BUBA**, partly surrounded by water, on a fork on the Rio Grande de Buba, is easily reached from Bissau by pirogue (via Enxude) and bush taxi (total 3hr, CFA3600). It has a few small places to stay, of which *Pousada Bela Vista* (☎664 70 11 ❸) is the most popular.

Approaching the south of the country from the Bissau to Bafatá highway, rather than starting with a pirogue to Enxude, you turn off the highway, south, at Bambadinca, 117km east of Bissau and 32km west of Bafatá. Some 60km south of here, on a paved road, at the only bridge across the Rio Corubal, you're in the vicinity of a swimming beach with warm, clear water and waterfalls near the graceful arches of the **Ponte do Saltinho**, the only crossing point between north and south Guinea-Bissau. You should know that the falls and water level are much less impressive in the dry season. The closest place to stay is the Portuguese-run *Pousada Saltinho* (❻), on the right 100m before the bridge when coming from Bambadinca. **Cussilintra**, a dozen kilometres downstream and closer to the town of **XITOLE**, was a colonial beauty spot, like Saltinho, and is still a popular weekend excursion with good swimming nearby – again, in the right season.

East of Buba, along a track which skims the Guinean border, the town of **BOÉ** is famous as the first place to be liberated from the Portuguese by the PAIGC back in 1967. Its reputation is undeserved, though, as the first town to be liberated was in fact in Boé *district*, a place called **Lugajole** in the deep southeast; a small plaque and hut there commemorate the occasion. Strange, hilly landscapes around Lugajole – the outliers of the Fouta Djalon – make a change from the maze of mangroves and mud nearer the coast.

The Matas de Canthanhez

To the south of Buba, the little crossroads village of **JEMBEREM** is part of the **Matas de Cantanhez**, an area of fairly unspoilt tropical rainforest that has been slated for future national-park status (for updated information, contact IBAP – see p.523). Currently, however, there is virtually no infrastructure and access is difficult, although there is the chance of spotting chimpanzees, rare forest elephants and other wildlife, especially monkeys, which are often seen in the trees near the village. A local NGO called AD offers very basic accommodation (❶).

To get to the *matas* (forest in Portuguese) from Bissau, take a bush taxi as far as **CATIÓ** (5hr, CFA4400), then hitchhike for whatever transport is around. Alternatively, banana wagons can take you directly there (ask at the banana-wagon station near the Catió airstrip).

The east

While animist beliefs predominate along the coast, the further east you travel, the more apparent the country's Islamic culture becomes. This is most evident in the two main towns of the interior, **Bafatá** and **Gabú**, both located along Guinea-Bissau's one main highway. You'll find **transport** fairly easily along here, with several daily *toko toko* and taxi departures connecting both towns with each other and Bissau.

Mansôa

The highway east from Bissau is a good road most of the way (with just a few potholes on the approach from the west to Bafatá) lined by unremarkable scenery of tall grass and charcoal-burning villages. Before Mansôa, the road forks: right for the east, and left (north) over the Rio Mansôa for the town.

At the centre of fighting in 1998, **MANSÔA** is home to a Balante community, and if you happen to be here during the season of their initiation ceremonies, you might encounter one of the brilliant Balante **broxa** dance troupes moving from village to village. With their warrior-like dress – fantastic head-shaving patterns, sea-shell adornments strapped on arms and legs, metal chains draped around their necks, and other accoutrements including turtle shells, body paint and sometimes army helmets and red berets – the *broxa* dancers are an impressive sight. If you get to watch a show, hold on to your things, as some groups specialize in comedic thieving routines, and you'll have to buy back the small items they take off you during their dance.

If you want to **stay here**, *Hotel Rural de Uaque*, some 3km west of Mansôa and signposted on the south side of the road (☎670 64 85 ⓦwww.hotelruraldeuaque .com ❺), has comfortable a/c bungalows geared mainly to a foreign hunting clientele, and gets popular at weekends when people from Bissau come here for lunch and to use the swimming pool.

The road north from Mansôa, on to **FARIM** and the Senegalese border town of **TANAF** is decent enough, with several bush taxis making the journey each day from both Bafatá and Bissau.

Bafatá and Gêba

On the south bank of the old trading river, the Rio Gêba, **BAMBADINCA** marks the start of the road to the south but isn't especially worth a stay. Some 30km northeast of here, **BAFATÁ** is definitely worth a couple of days. Perched on a low rise, above an elbow of the Rio Gêba, at the confluence of a smaller tributary, it's an orderly, appealing town, dominated by – and as placid as – the river that winds

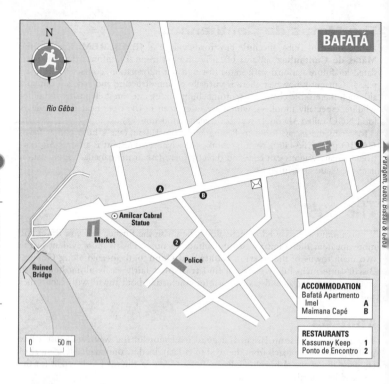

gracefully below. Come down to the riverbank at sunset and the peace and tranquillity are palpable. Bafatá's centre is made up of tiled Portuguese-style houses and a pretty covered market, in front of which stands a statue of Amílcar Cabral, who was born here.

Bush taxis will drop you at the *paragem*, 3km east of the centre. You'll find good **accommodation** at the pleasant and comfortable *Maimana Capé* (T664 13 73 ⑤), right in the centre of town. A few metres down the road towards the river, the cheaper but perfectly acceptable *Bafatá Apartamento Imel* (②) has s/c rooms with fans and bucket showers. The Cape Verdean owner of the *Maimana Capé* organizes hunting trips as well as wildlife tours around Bafatá. If you prefer to be close to the antelopes and monkeys that inhabit the surrounding forest, the *Campement Capé* is a great place to stay (⑥), sharing management with the *Maimana Capé* (enquire here; they'll drive you out to the *campement*) and offering bonuses such as a swimming pool and good views. For **food**, try the Portuguese restaurant *Ponto de Encontro*, serving decent portions of chicken and chips for around CFA3000. The best place for a **drink** (with simple meals also available) is the open-air *Kassumay Keep*, in a peaceful setting surrounded by trees.

The most thriving upcountry trading post of the Portuguese province of Guinea in the late nineteenth century was **GÊBA**, 12km west of Bafatá down a side road off the highway on the Bissau side of town. Gêba is now virtually a ghost town, and the overgrown **ruins** are worth a look if you're drawn to such places. You can charter a taxi in Bafatá for the trip.

North of Bafatá, there's a well-maintained dirt road to the **Senegalese border** at **CAMBAJU** (1hr, CFA1500), from where it's easy to find onward transport to **Kolda** (1hr, CFA1000) on the Ziguinchor–Tambacounda road. From Bafatá to Gabú (1hr, CFA650–800), unusual tall stands of **bamboo** flank the road.

Gabú

Vying with similarly-sized Bafatá as the country's most significant eastern town, **GABÚ** is also the country's Fula and Muslim capital. If you are familiar with the Fouta Djalon – the Fula heartland of the Republic of Guinea – you'll instantly recognize the cultural similarities between both regions, which have strong historical ties. Until the nineteenth century, Gabú lay at the heart of the Kaabu empire and was home to a mixed population of animist Mandinka, from whom the rulers of the empire were drawn, and Muslim Fula, who represented a substantial minority. When religious and ethnic conflicts mounted, the Fula called upon the neighbouring Fouta Djalon empire for support. The Fula army occupied the land, overthrowing the Mandinka ruler Janke Wali, and worked towards the Islamization of the region.

Today, Gabú is an animated commercial centre, prospering from trade with Senegal and Guinea, and bearing little evidence of the battles fought in the district in the past. Though not of great architectural interest, the town is worth strolling around in the early evening when the seemingly endless street-market really comes to life, featuring an abundance of merchandise from bread and oranges to CDs and colourful cloth.

The *paragem* is at the eastern end of the market, from where it's an easy walk to most of Gabú's decent, and reasonably priced, **hotels**. A couple of hundred metres north of the *paragem* in the Bairro 14 de Novembro quarter, *Hotel Visiom* (☎722 19 19 ②) is a popular, safe and comfortable place featuring s/c rooms (some with a/c), running water, electricity and a bar/restaurant that gets busy at weekends. *Residencial Djarama* (☎672 94 45; ③) offers rooms eccentrically decorated with pots of fake flowers and crucifixes, with fans and shared bathroom and, although it's a little overpriced, the owner is willing to haggle. The *Medina Boé* (☎666 28 33 ②), about twenty minutes' walk from the centre, is also worth considering for its nicely decorated huts scattered around a large, tree-lined garden area; facilities include a nightclub, restaurant and video lounge.

Some of the best and cheapest **food** in town can be had in the numerous street cafés, serving large bowls of rice, plus sandwiches and coffee. Chicken and beef dishes for CFA1500–2500 are available at the *Visiom*'s restaurant, where you can

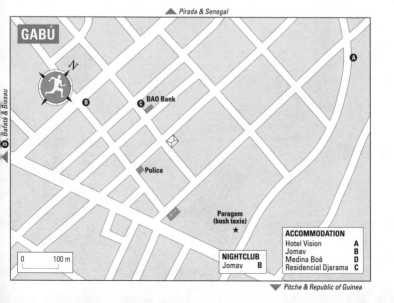

GABÚ

▲ Pirada & Senegal

B

C BAO Bank

A

◄ ◎, Bafatá & Bissau

Police

Paragem
(bush taxis)
★

NIGHTCLUB
Jomav   B

0   100 m

ACCOMMODATION
Hotel Vision   A
Jomav   B
Medina Boé   D
Residencial Djarama   C

▼ Pitche & Republic of Guinea

eat in a pretty garden, or at *Po Di Terra*, another restaurant with a pleasant outdoor dining area. For **nightlife**, Gabú has the surprisingly slick club *Jomav*, featuring one of Guinea-Bissau's most powerful sound systems and a good selection of music. (There are also small, clean and good-value rooms here in the ➋ bracket, but noise from the disco rules out sleep at the weekends.) Given the town's location, the ubiquitous *zouk* mixes here with Senegalese and Guinean beats, plus a wide selection of global sounds. Late on Saturday night is best, when the club gets packed out.

Gabú to Senegal

Gabú is a crossroads for travel to or from Senegal and Guinea, and the town has good **transport** connections to both of these countries, as well as to all points along the road to Bissau. For Senegal, the route out of Gabú to Pirada (2hr, CFA1500) is a reasonable, maintained track. From Pirada, bush taxis will take you to the Senegalese town of **Kounkané** (1½hr, CFA1200), where you'll find plenty of Tambacounda-bound taxis travelling along the paved highway. For onward travel to Guinea, see below.

Gabú to Guinea

The route east from Gabú to the Guinean border is in a terrible state, especially between Gabú and **PITCHE**. From Pitche to the Guinea-Bissau border town of **BURUNTUMA** the road improves slightly, but still expect a rough earth track winding and bumping its way through the bush – chokingly dusty in the dry season, barely passable in the rains. There are regular bush taxis from Gabú to Buruntuma (2–3hr, CFA2000), from where you'll be able to find transport to the Guinean towns of **Saréboïdo** (FG5000) and **Koundara** (FG15,000) – Saréboïdo's Sunday market generates increased commercial traffic. There are also occasionally direct taxis from Gabú to Labé (11hr, CFA11,000). Most drivers bound for Conakry prefer to take the route **south into Guinea** via **Foula-Mori** and **Koumbia** (further details on p.565), an exciting journey that involves an unsurfaced road through woodland, use of a hand-hauled ferry over a small river and the traversal of sandy troughs. Taxis leave almost daily from Gabú, charging CFA5000 to Koumbia and CFA14,000 to Conakry.

Guinea

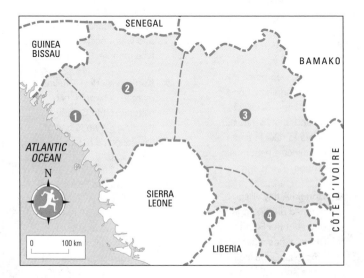

Highlights	560		7.2 The Fouta Djalon	610	559
Introduction and Basics	561		7.3 Haute Guinée	623	
7.1 Conakry and around	591		7.4 Guinée Forestière	631	

Guinea highlights

* **The Îles de Los** A short boat ride off the coast from Conakry, this attractive cluster of islands offers some of Guinea's best and most accessible beach destinations. See p.565

* **Conakry nightlife** Conakry's nightlife is one of its saving graces, with an astoundingly good club scene as well as a handful of live-music spots to take in some of Guinea's best music groups. See p.604

* **Doucki** A tiny village perched on the edge of one of the Fouta Djalon's most spectacular drop-offs, Doucki offers views and hiking to rival anything else in West Africa. See p.617

* **Pita to Télimélé** One of the finest 4x4 and hiking trails in the country, this route offers a great range of magnificent scenery and warm encounters with local people. See p.617

* **Kankan Market** The vast *marché central* in this historic Haute Guinée university town is one of the country's best. See p.626

* **Monts Nimba** Rising from the lush forests of the south, Guinea's tallest peak affords excellent views into Côte d'Ivoire and opportunities to track wild chimpanzees. See p.638

▲ Fula meeting house, Dalaba

Introduction and Basics

Between 1958, when it reclaimed its independence and effectively cut itself off from France, and the death of dictator Sekou Touré in 1984, the **Republic of Guinea** was an isolated and secretive country. Only in the late 1980s did it begin, hesitantly, to open its borders to tourists.

Despite immense cultural and natural riches Guinea is one of the **poorest countries** in West Africa. Although it holds the world's third-largest reserves of bauxite and is potentially rich in agriculture, fisheries and forest products, its infrastructure problems and corruption mean that its wealth doesn't trickle down very far. For visitors, there is hardly any semblance of a functioning tourist industry, and travel around the country is as rough as it is exciting.

Guinea holds great appeal as a place to **travel**, sprawling in a great arc of mountains and plains from the creeks and mud banks of the mangrove coast to the forests on the border with Côte d'Ivoire. The great rivers of West Africa – the Gambia, the Senegal and the Niger – all rise in Guinea, while the Michelin map shows more green-bordered scenic routes in Guinea than any other country – always a promising indication.

At the time of writing, however, Guinea is existing in a permanent state of suspense. Although the conflicts in Liberia, Sierra Leone and Côte d'Ivoire have largely abated, Guinea has recently been beset by its own political uprisings and there are still fears that the country will plunge into turmoil once the ailing president Lansana Conté dies. You should check the **security situation** as carefully as you can before visiting.

People

Guinea's people display a wide cultural diversity. No single language predominates and there's considerable regional variation. **Susu**, spoken mainly in the coastal region, is the language of Conakry, as well as that of most of Lansana Conté's government. Most of the coastal **Baga** people are now assimilated into Susu culture. An easy-to-learn Mande tongue, Susu is related to **Kouranko** and **Malinké**, the languages of Haute Guinée, to the trading lingua franca known as **Dyula**, and more distantly to the minority languages of the highland forests – **Guerzé** and **Loma**.

Thanks to the business activities of the **Fula**, markets all over Guinea tend to resound with the musical tones of their language, otherwise primarily spoken in the Fouta Djalon region.

In terms of **religion**, Guinea is mixed. As usual, the pig is a fair indication of the boundaries of Islam. You won't see many between the jungles of the northwest and the hilly forests in the southeast. Islam continues to consolidate and displace the indigenous religions, and its international dimension is increasingly important in shaping Guinean society. The vast majority of practising Muslims (more than three-quarters of the population) are members of the Tijaniya brotherhood, though the Wahabiya school is increasingly gaining

Photography

Although Guinea's notorious photography permit has been abolished, that doesn't give you carte blanche. Apart from the usual provisions about not taking photos of police and military installations, or anything remotely official or strategic, many ordinary people are averse to having their photos taken by strangers, and you're likely to cause a scene if you get your camera out and start snapping away. Children, on the other hand, are usually thrilled, and will throw themselves in front of your camera with abandon.

ground. Christianity is a minority religion, only significant locally around Conakry and in Guinée Forestière.

Where to go

On the plains of **Haute Guinée** to the east, towards the Mali border, you feel the cultural echoes of the Niger valley's old kingdoms – this was the heartland of the Mali Empire. The Niger and its big tributaries the Tinkisso and the Milo meander across a rolling savannah region traditionally rich in big game. Although much of the wildlife has disappeared, the region's mango-shaded old towns – Dinguiraye, Kankan, Kouroussa, Siguiri – still hold plenty of allure and the cultural heritage is strong.

Guinea's best-known attraction is probably the **Fouta Djalon** highlands. In the centre-north of the country, this plateau region is dramatically dissected into countless hills and valleys and spouts waterfalls like a colossal

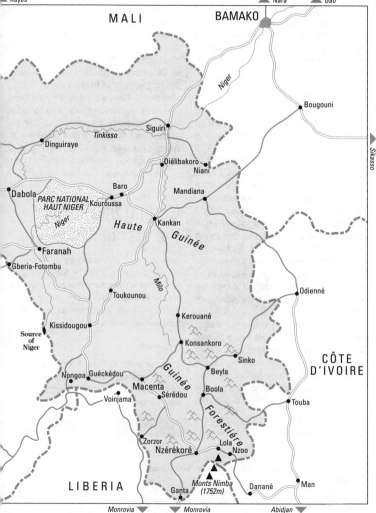

rock garden. In these high sandstone hills, where the valleys tend to be clogged with jungle and the flat, grassy peaks are too infertile for anything much but cattle pasture, the Fula inhabitants lived, in the eighteenth and nineteenth centuries, under a local **Muslim theocracy**, whose influence spread far and wide in West Africa. That history makes the region culturally very distinctive to this day. **Hiking** is a good activity in the Fouta Djalon: it's mostly fairly adventurous, independent stuff, though one or two one-man businesses

have started offering guided tours, exploring the ravishing landscapes.

To the south lies another of West Africa's great upland regions, **Guinée Forestière**, comprising a zone of wet forest and remote peoples, where liana bridges cross the rivers and pre-Islamic traditions survive. Here, as in Haute Guinée with its waning wildlife, the forest cover is threatened by loggers and farmers and diminishes every year, but if you want to experience rain-forest travel, this is one part of West Africa where you can still do it.

It's sometimes hard to be positive about Guinea's capital, **Conakry**, but its treasure islands – the **Îles de Los** – and nightlife are good compensations for aggressive vendors, police roadblocks and pollution.

When to go

When you visit Guinea and where you go is likely to be determined largely by the **seasons**. Overall, the easiest time to travel in Guinea is from late November to March. Away from the country's limited network of surfaced highways, much of the remote countryside is isolated during **the rains**, which are mainly concentrated between June and October, during which period flooding can leave many minor routes completely impassable for days or weeks, and you should be prepared for plans to go awry. You may find, though, the spectacular storms, gushing waterfalls and abundance of greenery are more than adequate compensation.

The weeks following the rainy season are the best time to visit the **Fouta Djalon**, which has a very agreeable climate all year round. While temperatures are high in the middle of the day, they can plummet at night: you'll need warm clothes and possibly a sleeping bag if you're going to hike. As the

dry season progresses, travel in the Fouta Djalon and especially in the Malinké plains of **Haute Guinée** becomes increasingly dusty and hot. The *harmattan* winds from the north can bring dry haze and dust as early as December, and by April you'll find travel around the region of **Kankan** almost impossibly stifling. **Conakry** has an insupportable climate at the best of times, with humidity rarely below eighty percent and July delivers the heaviest month's rainfall anywhere in West Africa apart from Cameroon – many parts of Europe and North America don't receive 700mm in a whole year.

Getting there from the rest of Africa

Guinea is well connected **by air** to neighbouring countries. If you're not planning to fly in, there are **overland routes** into Guinea from all its neighbours, though the only route that is in any way straightforward is the road from Bamako in Mali.

Flights

There are flights to Conakry from most **West African capitals**. Air Guinée has suspended its domestic and international routes; check with Conakry travel agents (see p.608) to

Average temperatures and rainfall

Conakry (coast)

	Jan	Feb	Mar	Apr	May	June	July	Aug	Sept	Oct	Nov	Dec
Temperatures °C												
Min (night)	22	23	23	23	24	23	22	22	23	23	24	23
Max (day)	31	31	32	32	32	30	28	28	29	31	31	31
Rainfall mm	3	3	10	23	158	559	1298	1054	683	371	122	10
Days with rainfall	0	0	1	2	11	22	29	27	24	19	8	1

Kouroussa (Haute Guinée)

	Jan	Feb	Mar	Apr	May	June	July	Aug	Sept	Oct	Nov	Dec
Temperatures °C												
Min (night)	14	17	22	23	23	22	21	21	21	21	19	15
Max (day)	33	36	37	37	35	32	30	30	31	32	33	33
Rainfall mm	10	8	22	7	135	246	297	345	340	168	33	10

Mamou (Fouta Djalon)

	Jan	Feb	Mar	Apr	May	June	July	Aug	Sept	Oct	Nov	Dec
Temperatures °C												
Min (night)	13	15	18	19	20	18	19	19	19	18	17	13
Max (day)	33	34	35	34	31	29	27	25	28	29	30	31
Rainfall mm	8	10	46	127	203	257	335	401	340	203	6	8

The **République de Guinée** is often called Guinea-Conakry, to distinguish it from other Guineas around the world. The population is just under ten million, some 1.5–2 million of whom live in Conakry. Guinea's land area (246,000 square kilometres) is about the same as that of the UK or Oregon. Guinea has a huge foreign debt, estimated to be more than £1.5 billion ($3.2 billion), or roughly ten times the value of its meagre annual export earnings, yet equivalent to less than a month's expenditure by the British Ministry of Defence (or little more than a day of the USA's defence budget). As of early 2008, the ruling party was still the Parti de l'Unité et du Progrès (PUP) of the ailing President Lansana Conté (in power since 1984). It currently holds 71 of the 114 seats in the National Assembly. There are around a dozen other significant political parties.

find out whether service has been reinstated. Alternatively, Air Ivoire provides the widest range of services, with nonstop flights from **Abidjan** (four times weekly) and **Bamako**, **Douala**, **Libreville**, **Dakar** and **Cotonou** (weekly), although the most regular and reliable connection to Dakar is provided by Air Sénégal (six weekly). TACV flies from **Cape Verde** to Conakry, while Ghana Airways has twice-weekly flights from both **Accra** – one via **Abidjan** and **Freetown**, the other via Abidjan only – and from Dakar via **Banjul**. West Coast Airlines flies in twice a week from **Freetown**. Air France has several services weekly to Conakry from **Nouakchott**, while SN Air Brussels has two weekly flights from **Dakar**. Royal Air Maroc has two weekly flights from **Casablanca** and **Freetown**, and Slok Air operates several flights weekly from **Abidjan**, **Banjul**, **Bamako** and **Dakar**.

Overland from Mali

From **Bamako**, there are regular bush taxis to both Siguiri and Kankan. Thanks to a recently-paved road and new bridges over the Niger River, the journey between Bamako and Kankan can take as little as six hours (though even with an early start you'd be unlikely to connect through to Conakry on the same day). The border closes at midnight, and vehicles arriving late have to wait till morning.

Overland from Guinea-Bissau

Despite their proximity, **Bissau to Conakry** is one of West Africa's toughest international journeys, liable to be cut by floods and mud

pools during the rains. Most travellers make part or all of this journey by **private 4x4** (hitching a lift or arranging one in advance) as public transport along the various sections of the route, especially in the border districts, can be tenuous.

First, forget about the seemingly most direct – coastal – route to Conakry, across the creeks from **Buba to Boké**. It's a barely viable option in your own vehicle and barely feasible with the limited public transport available, unless you really have no time constraints at all.

The usual route follows the reasonable paved road inland through Guinea-Bissau via **Gabú** and **Pitche** to the end of the surfaced road, where you cross into Guinea at **Buruntuma/Kandika**, then continue to **Koundara** and eventually get back onto a paved road at **Labé**. On this route, bush taxis for Koundara leave Gabú two or three times a week, and the Sunday market in the Guinean town of **Saréboido** (17km east of the border and 25km west of Koundara) generates some local traffic too. From Koundara there are daily departures for Labé, through the beautiful northern Fouta Djalon. Note that officials at Koundara will try to persuade you to change money with them, but their rates are poor. Change a note or two only.

For details on **getting to Guinea from outside Africa**, plus important practical information applying to all West African countries, covering health, transport, cultural hints and more, see Basics, pp.19–28.

You can also cross the border into Guinea from **Pitche to Foula-Mori**, connected in the dry season by a passable, though rough, 30-kilometre track and a hand-hauled ferry over the Koliba River. Transport on this route can be limited except on Mondays, Pitche's market day. You go through Guinea-Bissau formalities at the ferry and Guinea formalities at the friendly Foula-Mori post (where you can see folk hero Alfa Yaya's birth hut; see p.621). **Koumbia**, 80km further on, is the first town of any size and from here there's regular transport to the coast or up into the Fouta Djalon. If you're heading to Conakry, it's a rocky, dusty journey to Boké, from where a paved road leads all the way to Conakry.

Driving yourself, in good conditions you can do the trip from Koumbia to Conakry in under twelve hours; public transport can take up to two days. Travel times invariably depend on the ferry crossing over the Fatala River at Boffa. The ferry usually closes around 9pm, and late arrivers are obliged to spend a night in mosquito-ridden Boffa.

Overland from The Gambia and Senegal

The choice is between two main routes. Firstly, there's the fairly straightforward bush-taxi route to **Koundara**. Taxis go from **Basse** in The Gambia or **Diaobé** in Senegal via the border posts at Dialadiang (Senegal) and Missira (Guinea). The journey from Diaobé to Koundara takes roughly six hours. Secondly, there are a couple of more scenic but rough routes from **Kédougou** in Senegal up into the highest parts of the Fouta Djalon and on to **Labé** (for route details, see p.621). The western route, via **Maliville** near the Fouta's highest point, is more commonly used.

Overland from Sierra Leone

At the time of writing, there were no buses running along the relatively busy – and fairly well-paved – main route from **Freetown** via Kambia and Pamelap to **Conakry**, though buses have operated on this route in the past. It is a day's journey if things go well, though frequent checkpoints and lengthy searches and interrogations of passengers on the Guinean side of the border can extend the journey up to two days. These days the only means of transport is a regular **bush taxi**, even though you'll have to change either at the ruined border town of Pamelap in Sierra Leone or in pretty Forécariah on the Guinean side.

All other routes between Guinea and Sierra Leone are less travelled, more uncomfortable and riskier in terms of general hassle. A second route leads from the former rebel centre of **Koindu** in Sierra Leone's eastern highlands to **Guéckédou**, a town that has been completely destroyed in the years of conflict. A third route, with occasional transport, runs from northern Sierra Leone via **Kabala** to **Faranah**. A fourth possibility is to find transport heading north from **Kamakwie** to **Madina-Woula**, and from there get to Kindia or Mamou.

The **ferry service** which formerly ran from **Freetown** to Conakry has re-started operations.

Overland from Liberia

There's a range of border crossings along the watershed frontier between Liberia and Guinea, but given the amount of smuggling that goes on here and the two countries' longstanding mutual distrust (not to mention the more recent refugee problem resulting from the Liberian civil war), it's no surprise that these borders can be troublesome to negotiate – always seek local advice. The **main frontiers** are at Foya–Guéckédou, Voinjama–Macenta, Ganta–Diécké and Yekepa–Yalézou/Bossou (for Nzérékoré).

The **ferry service from Monrovia** to Conakry is currently suspended.

Overland from Côte d'Ivoire

The following assumes that a permanent peace agreement has been established – not the case at the time of writing. There are three main routes from Côte d'Ivoire to Guinea. The first, from **Odienné to Kankan**, is better than it looks on most maps, but it's still an extremely tough drive and customs checks at the border are rigorous. The second route is from **Odienné to Sinko** and then Beyla. There's a huge market in Sinko (Guinea) on Friday, for which vehicles leave Odienné early Thursday morning.

The third main route is the lovely forest road from **Danané to Nzérékoré**. You'll sometimes find taxis along here, and there's always transport on a Tuesday for Nzérékoré's big weekly market. The road is normally passable throughout the year, but it can be surprisingly difficult to find transport to **Gbapleu** – where Ivoirian formalities are conducted – and from there on to the Guinean frontier near **Nzo**.

Red tape and visas

Visas are required by everyone entering Guinea except West Africans. Once notoriously difficult to obtain, they are now obtainable in a number of African cities, and officials in Guinea are generally welcoming to tourists.

Depending on where you apply for a visa, you may simply be required to present your passport with a photocopy of the ID pages, photos and a fee of a cool CFA85,000. The embassies at **Accra**, **Banjul**, **Bissau**, **Bamako**, **Dakar** and **Freetown** normally issue visas within 48 hours; there are also embassies in **Monrovia** and **Lagos**. Alternatively, some travel agents in Conakry are able to organize visas ahead of your arrival for around FG120,000 (approximately £15, €21 or $30, transferable via Western Union). You email them a scanned copy of your passport photo page, after which they take care of the formalities and email you back a temporary transit visa. A representative then meets you on arrival at Conakry airport to ensure the transit visa is stamped as a permanent visa into your passport by immigration officials. Three-month single-entry visas are the norm, but you can get an extension for FG85,000 (approximately £11, €15 or $21) at the Direction Nationale Police Aire et Frontières in the district of Coléah in Conakry. If you want to stay for longer than six months, you may be required to apply for a very expensive *carte de séjour*, though this is not always a necessity.

It's possible to pick up **visas for onward travel** in Conakry for all neighbouring countries, plus Ghana, Morocco, Nigeria, Togo and Cape Verde. See p.607 for a full list of addresses.

The only **health certificate** formally required is yellow fever – though in practice this is rarely demanded at the airport or borders, and only occasionally at Guinea's checkpoints. You no longer need a **photography permit**, but you should still be very discreet with your camera.

Checkpoints

Since most of Guinea's **checkpoints** were dismantled in 2003, travel around the country has become much less irksome. However, Conakry's main roads still get blocked off after midnight, and the notorious checkpoint at **Km36** outside the capital is as onerous as ever. Checkpoints are staffed by a mix of military, police, anti-gang units, customs and gendarmerie. They exist for the sole purpose of maintaining the officials who operate them, and some will try anything to find a fault with your passport, visa or, if nothing works, your vaccination papers.

Put on a stony and patient face, don't accept their phony claims (for example that passports aren't valid after midnight), and you won't have to pay. If nothing helps, a few thousand Guinean francs is a sufficient bribe. You're not advised to venture out alone in Conakry at night, and definitely not to argue with drunken military. Always carry your passport and vaccination certificate with you.

Costs, money, banks

Guinea uses its own currency, the **franc guinéen** (FG). The currency has been steadily falling in value for two decades, and by late 2007 the **official exchange rates** stood at $1=FG4200, £1=FG8400 and 1€=FG5900. These rates are likely to continue to decline until Guinea's political and economic climate stabilizes, so expect to see $1=FG5000 or more within the lifetime of this edition.

At the time of writing, no banks were accepting **traveller's cheques**. Guinea is essentially a cash economy, and you'll need to make sure you've got enough cash on you before travelling upcountry, since if you run out, you'll have to rely on an expensive Western Union transfer or return to Conakry.

The **Banque Internationale pour le Commerce et l'Industrie de la Guinée (BICIGUI)** is the country's main bank, with (generally efficient) branches in Conakry, Boké, Fria, Kankan, Kamsar, Kissidougou, Labé, Macenta and Nzérékoré. All these should change euros and dollars and, with less certainty, pounds sterling cash, though only the Conakry and Nzérékoré branches have ATMs.

The lack of banks may force you to change money unofficially. In most towns, the **black market** generally flourishes around markets and the *gare voiture*. You'll get a somewhat better rate than at the banks, but you're advised to go with a local friend, if possible, to avoid getting ripped off or robbed.

Credit cards can only be used in a few of the larger hotels, and to pay for car rental and air tickets.

Costs

Prices fluctuate widely, but Guinea is currently one of the cheapest countries in the region. Cheap **hotels** outside Conakry generally charge FG20,000–50,000 a room. Rice and sauce are usually around FG2000–3000, and you can get several pieces of most kinds of fruit for FG500–1000. **Conakry** is much more expensive than the provinces, particularly for accommodation – and you'll be lucky to get a basic room for under FG60,000, and it will most likely be in a brothel at that.

Transport costs can also be high, especially if you're renting a car or travelling in your own vehicle. Seat prices in taxis are fixed on the main routes, however, and work out fairly cheap (for example FG55,000 from Conakry to Labé, or FG120,000 from Conakry to Nzérékoré), but you'll be squeezed into a heavily overloaded vehicle. If you want some comfort, you can always pay the double rate and enjoy the luxury of having the front seat all to yourself.

Fuel prices

In 2007 a litre of petrol or diesel cost around FG4300, or a little over $1.

Health

Guinea provides some of West Africa's roughest travelling and it's this – the possibility of accidents far from help, or of falling ill in a remote district – rather than any intrinsic unhealthiness, which can lead to problems. Out in the wilds, the basic health infrastructure is too limited to be a safety net.

Guinea is largely hilly, and **temperatures** drop quickly after dark in the higher parts. Travelling by public transport, it makes good sense to keep something warm close at hand: your vehicle may roll for hours into the night with your luggage stowed in some inaccessible corner.

Water, as usual, is a major consideration. You may be offered water originating from pumped boreholes, which is usually safe, though not as safe as using bottled water or using purifying tablets (bottled Coyah water is widely available in the provinces). Try to avoid wading through slow-flowing waters and dry-season pools, since there's a high incidence of **bilharzia**.

Malaria is a major health risk throughout the entire country, and you are strongly advised to maintain your course of antimalarials. **Yellow fever** has become an increasing problem, and large vaccination missions are undertaken to combat the disease.

Info, websites, maps

It's a good idea to get reliable advice before heading into the country's interior. In Conakry, the **Office de Tourisme** (see p.593) is surprisingly helpful and can suggest itineraries and even recommend tourist guides.

In the regions, it's always worth trying the local **radios rurales** (see "The Media"), which are generally well-informed about local attractions and culture.

Recommended websites

There are several **online resources** worth checking out:

Ⓦ **www.aminata.com** First port of call for news and comment.

Ⓦ **friendsofguinea.org** US Peace Corps–related site with good links and info.

ⓦ**www.radio-kankan.com** Best of the local radio services, with a lively website (news, links, music news) and live streaming.

Maps

As for **maps**, the 1cm=10km IGN map of Guinea (published 1992) is definitely worth obtaining before you go, and vital if you intend doing any hiking, though it is very out of date and roads are easier to read on the Michelin or Reise Know-How maps of West Africa. For long stays in Conakry, the IGN map of the capital (published in 1982) is worth getting hold of, if you can, but Conakry has of course changed enormously in 25 years.

The media

Guinean **TV and radio** is state-controlled, though in 2006 the government agreed – in theory at least – to allow private radio stations. TV programmes remain full of government propaganda, while radio is dominated by Guinean music, though the music of other African countries and Cuba also gets a look in (thankfully, for a change, unlike European and American music). Radiodiffusion-Télévision Guinéenne (RTG) broadcasts radio shows in French, Susu, Malinké and Fula and puts out evening TV in French with news in six Guinean languages. Cultural programming is a priority, and the **radios rurales** in Kankan, Kindia, Labé, Nzérékoré, Mamou and Faranah broadcast mainly traditional music. The BBC has recently begun 24hr programming in French on 93.9FM, which is available in many regions.

The national **press** used to consist only of *Horoya*, a weekly rag of almost inspired awfulness, carrying limited African news. These days there's a host of other newspapers, and you'll find the press is far more critical of the state and the government than radio or TV. The main independent papers are *L'Observateur*, *La Lance*, *L'Enqueteur*, *L'Indépendant* and *Le Lynx* – the last is a satirical weekly that is equally scornful of the government and the opposition. If you're famished for overseas news, a number of foreign (especially French) papers and magazines are available in Conakry. Try the large supermarkets, street vendors in town or bookshops.

Getting around

Most travellers find Guinea the toughest country to get around in West Africa. Given the lack of domestic air services, there's no alternative to travelling by road (the railway line you'll see on some maps is completely defunct). Journeys are frequently long and often follow tedious waits while seats are being filled.

Bush taxis, trucks and taxi-motos

Transport on Guinea's main routes is largely by **bush taxi**, usually aging and crammed-full Peugeot 504s and 505s – the front passenger seat always shared by at least two people (avoid the space above the gearshift, unless you feel like getting very close to the driver). On more remote byways, you might find all sorts of vehicles, anything from relatively new minibuses to converted goods vehicles and lorries.

Beware of climbing on the back of a **truck** (*gros camion*), as they regularly break down or overturn, and are notorious for their dodgy brakes.

Before you step into any vehicle, have a look to see what sort of condition it's in and make sure it has a spare tyre. If you have a choice, opt for the vehicle least likely to break down or kill you (cars get driven until they fall to pieces).

The **fare** is usually payable before the trip. On regular routes, you can generally rely on the price given, and you'll be handed a ticket. Travel by bush taxi is relatively cheap: FG80,000 (£10/€14/$20) will get you from Conakry to Kankan, for example, though prepare for much higher prices, pro rata, if you're travelling between small villages, as you'll often have to rent the whole car. Unless you are travelling with huge amounts of luggage, you shouldn't have to pay for baggage on bush taxis, though touts banking on your ignorance may ask for it anyhow.

Expect long waits for bush taxis along any of the unpaved roads between the country's smaller towns: the more remote your destination, the less frequent transport will be. Your best (sometimes your only) chance of finding a taxi in small villages is on the local **market day**; ask locally for information.

In recent years, with rising fuel prices and a flood of cheap Chinese motorbikes, **taxi-motos** have become a popular means of transport in the main towns. Rides are cheap, generally costing no more than FG2000, but drivers don't provide passengers with a helmet, so choose your *taxi-moto* carefully.

Routes and road conditions

The road from **Conakry to Mamou** is the busiest in the country, with bush taxis departing until early afternoon. The trip to Mamou takes five hours along a smooth, well-surfaced road. **Mamou to Labé** (3hr) is also busy, and the road is in good condition. **Mamou to Faranah** is fairly quiet, with few local vehicles. The road from **Mamou to Kankan** is riddled with potholes as far as **Kouroussa**, where a brand-new, perfectly straight and flat road takes you the rest of the way.

Don't travel from **Kankan** to **Nzérékoré** via **Kérouané** unless you have a sturdy 4x4 and exceptionally good off-road driving skills. Going by taxi, breakdowns are almost unavoidable on this route, and you might wait days for help to arrive.

Domestic flights

Guinea's **domestic air service** is in a sad state. Over the past decade or so, Guinea has seen the birth and demise of a series of small private airlines, but regular flights have not been in operation for several years now. Air Guinée once flew several times weekly to all the country's major domestic airports: Sambailo (Koundara), Boké, Labé, Kankan, Siguiri, Nzérékoré and Kissidougou. At the time of writing, the last domestic carrier, Paramount, had just gone out of business,

but it would be worth checking with Conakry travel agents to see if any others have sprung up to fill the void.

Car rental

Car rental rates are high. You should expect to pay upwards of FG400,000 per day for a 4x4 (or around £50/€70/$100), the high cost reflecting the damage wrought by Guinea's road system. There are some Hertz and Avis outlets in Conakry Ville, at the airport and at the *Novotel* (see p.594), but none upcountry. There are always people in town along av de la République offering private car-and-driver rental deals, while the Centre Culturel Franco-Guinéen (see p.607) may also be able to help. You always have to hire a driver along with the car.

Other forms of transport

Guinea is wonderful territory for **hiking**, **cycling** and **motorbiking**. Reliable guides for hiking trips around the Fouta Djalon can be found at the *Tangama* hotel in Dalaba or the *Tata* hotel in Labé. It's also worth contacting the Office de Tourisme or Mondial Tours in Conakry (see p.608). You'll need to be self-sufficient and well-equipped, with a tent, cooking equipment, water bottles, spares if you're cycling, and as much time as possible.

Guinea also has several **canoeing** rivers – the upper Niger (see p.625) is probably the best. Again, you'll need to be entirely self-sufficient.

Accommodation

The **hotel** business in Conakry is booming, with sparkling new establishments going up in several areas, while facilities in the provinces are also slowly being improved. The Fouta Djalon has the best hotels outside Conakry. In the remotest parts of the country, you'll have to content yourself with fairly basic lodgings. There are no hostels or campsites to speak of.

The **cheapest places** (❶) are usually primitive in terms of their facilities: electricity is sporadic and water generally comes in buckets (though it may sometimes be warmed for you) but even places costing

Accommodation price codes

Accommodation prices in this chapter are coded according to the following scale, whose equivalent in pounds sterling/US dollars is used throughout the book. The prices refer to the rate you can expect to pay for a room with two beds, or, in the cheapest places, a room with one double bed. Single occupancy, will normally cost at least two-thirds of the twin-occupancy rate. For further details see Basics, p.55.

❶ Under FG42,000 (under £5/$10)
❷ FG42,000–84,000 (£5–10/$10–20)
❸ FG84,000–126,000 (£10–15/$20–30)
❹ FG126,000–168,000 (£15–20/$30–40)
❺ FG168,000–252,000 (£20–30/$40–60)
❻ FG252,000–336,000 (£30–40/$60–80)
❼ FG336,000–420,000 (£40–50/$80–100)
❽ Over FG420,000 (over £50/$100)

less than FG50,000 can vary significantly in atmosphere and cleanliness: by comparison with neighbouring countries, some upcountry hotels are remarkably cheap. In smaller towns and villages you can always ask to see the *sous-préfet* (district officer) with a view to spending a night at the **villa** (accommodation for visiting government employees).

Cheaper mid-range places (❷–❸) are usually modest hotels, normally with en-suite, self-contained (s/c) rooms and a choice of fan or air conditioning (a/c). Moving up the price scale there are also some reasonable business and tourist-class hotels (❹–❺) with s/c, a/c rooms and restaurants. At the **top end** of the scale (❻–❽), there are a few relatively luxurious establishments with pool and other features, including perhaps Internet connections, though nearly all of these are in Conakry.

As for **private accommodation**, Guineans are very hospitable, and once it's understood that you need a roof, you'll often be offered a place to stay in people's compounds. Don't forget to pay for, or contribute to, meals.

Camping, in the bush, shouldn't be a problem. Doing so near large towns is bound to cause suspicion, and you might end up having to bribe someone to avoid hassle.

Electricity, water and other essentials

Guinea's **electricity supplies** are very erratic and are very much tied to the season. During the rainy season and shortly after, when reservoirs are full and hydroelectric stations running properly, you might occasionally be treated to 24 hours of electricity. In the dry season (Dec–March), electricity is usually only supplied at night, and 24-hour cuts can occur. Decent hotels have their own generators, while smaller guesthouses are more likely to rely on state provision, or only switch on their generators at night. Remote villages aren't connected to any electricity services. It's wise to have a torch and a few candles handy.

Don't expect to find **running water** outside established hotels. Many cheap places, especially in the interior, only have bucket water drawn from a well. Just like electricity, water supplies dwindle with the dry season. If you're staying with locals, be aware that each bucket of water you use may be precious.

Toilet paper is often hard to obtain away from the few major towns, so stock up when you can.

Eating and drinking

Guinean food is based on three main ingredients – rice, leaves and groundnuts – but there's a surprising and welcome variety of delicious flavours. Hotel restaurants all over the country serve **European food** and you can nearly always rely on them for chicken and chips if all else fails.

Street food is a serious business, with big pots of rice, sauces, chipped yams, potatoes and bananas available in key sites around most towns, in large villages, and at important road junctions and transport parks. If you're not alone, order for one person at a time and share – servings are on the gigantic side. And keep a careful eye on hygiene, ensuring you always buy from busy and efficient-looking cooks.

Every region has its own **local specialities**. Fish and spicy food are most common in Conakry and near the coast. The Fouta Djalon's classic meals are sauce with **fonio** (millet couscous) and **lacciri e kosan** (Fula for "sweetened or salted maize couscous served with sour milk"). **Tori**, a steamed cassava stodge, and **yams** are a staple of the diet in Haute Guinée, while Guinée Forestière has the best **aloko** (plantains) and **atiéké**, a grated cassava dish that originated in Côte d'Ivoire.

The consistently delicious – and usually meatless – **sauce de feuilles** is best made with the finely chopped leaves of young cassava, sweet potato or aubergine. **Bouillon** is usually a beef or mutton stew made with offal. **Mafé** is the standard term for rich, usually meaty, groundnut sauce, and fish or meat **brochettes** (little kebabs) are common everywhere. **Maganyi** is rice doused with meat or prawn sauce, sometimes known by its Senegalese name, *thié-bou-gap*. **Bush meat** of various kinds is mostly found in Guinée Forestière: of the various kinds, bush rat is probably the tastiest and most reliable; if it's monkey meat, make sure it's been very well cooked or you risk being poisoned (not to mention the conservationist's argument that you shouldn't be eating any primates).

There's an abundance of delicious **fruits** all year round. **Bananas** in various shapes and sizes are sold everywhere, but are particularly good around Nzérékoré. Kindia is **mango** heaven from April to May, though heavy mango trees line streets all over the country at the end of the dry season. **Papayas** reach gigantic sizes, are very sweet and are available most of the year. **Oranges** are the biggest fruit crop; in the Fouta Djalon they're abundant from November to April and cheap enough to buy all day as a drink. The Fouta is also the place to come for huge **avocados**.

Beer drinkers can choose between locally brewed Skol (around FG3500 for a half-litre) and Guiluxe, Guinea's "national beer". **Palm wine** is common in non-Muslim areas such as Guinée Forestière and some coastal regions. The most popular **spirits** are pastis, whiskey and gin. Guinea being a predominantly Muslim country, bars are usually hidden behind grimy plastic curtains and generally only visited by men and prostitutes.

Aside from all the usual bottled **soft drinks**, white **coffee** (Nescafé/*café au lait*) is served as a rule with *pain beurre*, not drunk on its own. For black coffee order a **petit café noir**, and you'll usually get a strong espresso made from ground coffee beans rather than instant powder. Guinea's *kenkeliba* herbal tea is healthy and worth a try. **Sour milk**, laced with sugar, is more of a meal (see *lacciri e kosan*, above) than a drink.

Communications

Guinea's **telecommunications** network is disastrous: most land lines in the country rarely work, you're never guaranteed a line beyond Conakry, while phoning the capital from the provinces can take days. As a result, the country has gone almost entirely mobile in just a few short years. Several operators compete for **mobile phone** business – Areeba and Orange are the best – but coverage around the country is spotty and as neither provider is particularly reliable, many people have several numbers to increase their chances of getting through. It may well be worth your while picking up a mobile SIM card (*puce* in French).

Phone numbers in Guinea were overhauled in 2006. Numbers beginning with 30 are generally landlines, while those prefixed with a number in the 60s are mobiles. In all cases, you must add the prefix to call. Calls to Europe cost FG1000–1500 per minute from reputable *télécentres* or Internet cafés, while local calls are cheapest at the ubiquitous ramshackle corrugated kiosks on street corners all over the country.

The **postal service** is no better than the phones. DHL and FedEx operate in Guinea, but incoming parcels often end up detained at the airport indefinitely by Customs, and a sizable "*cadeau*" is often required to get the package. It's better to have packages sent to your embassy or consulate. Post office opening hours vary (Mon–Sat 8am–5pm in Conakry, 7.30 or 8am–4pm in Kankan and Nzérékoré). There are other main post offices at Boké, Kindia, Labé and Faranah and you

Guinea's **IDD** country code is ☏224.

can phone or fax abroad (theoretically at least) from any of these offices.

Internet access has spread like wildfire throughout Conakry, but the rest of the country is still fairly poorly provisioned. Rates rarely exceed FG5000/hr.

Opening hours, public holidays and festivals

Guinea's **opening hours** are somewhat less formalized than those of other countries in the region: outside of Conakry there are simply not many formal, public-facing shops and businesses. But in general they follow the 7.30am-start–4pm-close that's common in West Africa (this applies to banks), with some places closing for a long lunch break and reopening from late afternoon until nightfall. Fridays are sometimes a half day, but most businesses work Saturday mornings.

Public holidays

As for **public holidays**, aside from New Year's Day and the usual shifting Islamic calendar (and Christian holidays which are observed more haphazardly), the principal **Guinean holidays** are as follows, including commemorations of various significant moments in Guinea's history where political considerations sometimes decide whether they are celebrated or not:

March 8 International Women's Day
April 3 2nd republic day, anniversary of the 1984 coup
May 1 Labour Day
May 14 Anniversary of the founding of the PDG party
May 25 Africa day
August 27 Anniversary of the day in 1977 when the market women revolted and forced Sekou Touré to change tack
September 28 Anniversary of the "No" vote against de Gaulle
October 2 Independence Day

Traditional festivals

Regional and **local non-Islamic festivals** were attacked as sectarian and unproductive during the Touré dictatorship, and in many cases the generation-long repression destroyed their

viability. You might still come across one if you're well-placed and well-timed – January to March is the most propitious season. And one annual festival you can be sure of is the mad fishing festival that takes place near any receding body of water at the end of the dry season (usually May) across Haute Guinée, known as the Fête de Mare (see p.623).

Crafts and shopping

Guinea's **crafts tradition** would be more developed if there was some economic backbone to support it – tourism always helps. As it is, the country does include some of the big **mask-making cultures** of West Africa, including the Baga on the coast and the Toma in Guinée Forestière, and you'll find a few examples of their work, together with much more from Côte d'Ivoire, where the tourist-crafts tradition is well-established.

There are good **artisanal shopping** opportunities in most parts of the country, and with the local currency so weak, there are real bargains to be had. Look out for excellent **cloth** and **sandals** in Labé, general **leatherwork** and **jewellery** in Nzérékoré and **mudcloth** manufacture in many parts of Haute Guinée and Guinée Forestière.

Traditional **musical instruments** are a good bet in many areas, too, with *koras*, *djembes* and *balafons* fairly easy to get, though if you want something you can play as well as admire, be sure to start negotiations over a real instrument and not a wooden-sounding replica.

Also in the music field, Guinea's street and market vendors offer the best music deal in West Africa – about FG10,000 for **pirate CDs**. You might resist buying them when no money goes to the artist. But you'll be hard-pressed to find a shop in the country selling authentic originals – and the sellers can do with the cash.

Crime and safety

Guineans aren't used to tourists and the expat community is fairly small, so the notion that visitors might involuntarily provide a source of supplementary income isn't widespread. A general mood of self-reliance, little begging and a degree of real pride in their nation all add up to a fairly **low threat of muggings and theft**.

Unfortunately, the **men in uniform** manage to compensate for that. Guinea is essentially a military state, and though you're unlikely to have any serious problems, you should be aware of the potential for trouble. If you're confronted with trumped-up accusations, you will usually have to resolve them with a "voluntary donation". This is more likely to happen if you're driving in your own vehicle, and you will experience repeated efforts at extortion from the police and military, ranging from mildly humorous or irritating to contemptible. Treat the police with caution, try to squeeze out some humour, defuse them with cigarettes. Never argue with them – they'll happily keep you hanging around for hours.

Emergencies

There are no nationwide police, fire or ambulance emergency numbers. Conakry's ambulance service is ☎30.41.15.00.

Gender issues and sexual attitudes

Women travellers have a reasonably easy time in Guinea, sheltered from some of the hassles of Mali, Senegal or Côte d'Ivoire by the lack of tourists. So long as your French is adequate, you'll find quick access to people's lives and homes wherever you go.

Be prepared for **low-key sexual harassment**, and respond to roadside hassles firmly and unambiguously, and you'll be left in peace. You might prefer to describe yourself as something other than a tourist, which can carry slightly pejorative connotations.

Sexual attitudes in Guinea are still quite conservative and in 2007 there was a brief backlash in the capital against bare midriffs and provocative dance styles from Côte d'Ivoire, when groups of men attacked local girls out clubbing. Remember you're in a Muslim country, so don't wear shorts or tiny tops in the street. Polygamy remains common, prostitution is widespread and **homosexuality** is frowned upon and illegal on the statute book.

Entertainment and sports

The best place to check up on the latest **cultural events** is the Centre Culturel Franco-Guinéen in Conakry (see p.607). They have regular exhibitions, concerts and films, and are generally well-informed about events in and around Conakry. **Theatre** is getting some encouragement, and there are several young groups that do great stuff, though they suffer from a lack of decent venues. Try to catch one of the regular rehearsals (actual perform-ances are rare) of the historical ballet troupe **Ballets Africains**, founded by Fodeba Keita in the early 1960s, and still one of the most renowned dance troupes of West Africa. Equally enticing are the shows of the young **Circus Baobab**, West Africa's first aerial circus (Ⓦ www.circusbaobab.org), which merges traditional dancing and drumming with hip-hop and experimental perform-ance, and the **Ensemble Instrumental**, one of the country's famous traditional music ensembles. The groups all rehearse regularly at various places and times in Conakry; to find out where and when, drop by the Agence Guinéenne des Spectacles, just inside the museum, and ask for Isto Keyra.

For more on **Guinean music** and **cinema**, see pp.583–587.

Football

The absence of good stadiums and slow media development has held **football** back in Guinea. There are, nevertheless, strong connections with French football, and while the country has produced no international stars, the national squad is invariably a decent team that usually reaches the quarter-final stage of the African Nations Cup. At home, look out for former league champions Satellite FC and Horoya AC, as well as past cup-winners AS Kaloum Stars and Hafia FC (all from Conakry).

Wildlife and national parks

Guinea is one of the few West African countries that has preserved a diverse indigenous fauna. Most large species – including chimpanzee, hippo, lion and buffalo (though apparently no longer elephant) – survive, unprotected and rarely seen. There have been few surveys in recent years and the current position is hazy, but hunting appears to pose as much of a threat as environmental destruction.

Guinea has two national parks: the **Parc National du Haut Niger** (see p.626), near Kouroussa, and the **Parc National Niokolo-Badiar** (see p.622) along the Guinea-Bissau border at Koundara. There is negligible infrastructure for tourists, however. There are also various **forêts classées**, designed to help preserve the environment rather than strictly as faunal reserves. Of these, the most important is **Monts Nimba**, an iron-ore-rich range straddling the Guinea Liberia border, and home to rare wildlife, including chimpanzee.

Outside the parks and *forêts classées*, the best **wildlife districts** are the hilly acacia savannah in the northeast, between the Tinkisso River and the Malian border; the undulating bush and grassland between Mamou and Faranah where the Fouta Djalon slopes down to Sierra Leone; and the southeast highlands, particularly east of the Macenta–Nzérékoré road.

A brief history of Guinea

Some of West Africa's most influential **old empires** stretched across the area covered by present-day Guinea. It was on Guinean soil in the early thirteenth century that the sorcerer-king Soumaoro Kanté was defeated by **Sundiata Keita**. Sundiata subsequently established the Mali Empire (see p.628), which stretched at its height from the Atlantic coast to east of the Niger bend. Its capital was at Niani, today an insignificant little town in Haute Guinée (see p.630).

In 1725, horse-riding Muslim **Fula** fought the first of many West African jihads, establishing a flourishing Muslim theocracy in the Fouta Djalon (see box, p.618), which survived until the late nineteenth century, when infighting between the Muslim leaders prevented them putting up any unified resistance against the French.

The French occupation

The first French expedition into the hinterland of the Guinea coast set off from Boké, a creek-head settlement whose population had been in contact with Europeans – mostly Portuguese – since the fifteenth century. Guinea's northwest coast – in particular coastal towns such as Boffa and Kamsar – played a key logistical role in the holding and transport of slaves to the Americas; a departure from Guinea was considered to be the quickest route to the Antilles. Following the expansion initiated by Colonel Faidherbe across the Sahel, and to prevent the British linking The Gambia with Sierra Leone, the French commanders in "the rivers of the south" (as the Guinea region was known) forced protection treaties with dozens of small rulers through the middle of the nineteenth century. In the 1880s they came up against the first serious resistance in the shape of the guerilla army of **Almamy Samory Touré**. Once Samory had been deported to Gabon in 1898, there was only relatively minor resistance to the French. The forest communities put up a fight, and were aided by the hilly jungle in which the French couldn't use cavalry, but their political organization was weak and the villages submitted one after another in the years leading up to World War I.

In the early colonial days, wild **rubber** was Guinea's main crop. By 1905 the commerce was supporting a 700-strong Lebanese community in Conakry. But the export declined after 1913 as plantation markets opened in Southeast Asia. By 1914, the French had driven a **railway** over 600km through mountain terrain to the river port of Kankan, linking Conakry with Bamako by rail and river. This, however, was a strategic railway rather than a commercial one. Apart from limited gold and diamonds, Haute Guinée didn't appear to offer much return. Better prospects lay in the forest regions to the south, where coffee and other tropical crops were developed on French-owned plantations, and near the coast and southern foothills of the Fouta Djalon, where bananas flourished. The French largely neglected Guinea's biggest prize, however: **bauxite** (aluminium ore). The country still possesses a third of the world's reserves, but it wasn't until the 1950s that the French began to exploit these systematically.

French **rule** in Guinea followed standard patterns except that, more so than elsewhere, the opportunities to become a privileged *evolué* were desperately few: until 1935 there was no secondary **education** in Guinea and, on the eve of independence, only 1.3 percent of Guinean children were receiving even primary schooling. With one singular exception, almost all the prominent Guineans before independence came from wealthy families who had sent them to the École Normale William Ponty near Dakar.

The rise of nationalism

Ahmed Sekou Touré, a Malinké-speaker from Faranah, first came to attention as a disruptive and perspicacious schoolboy in the late 1930s, and then as founder of Guinea's first labour union, the Post and Telecommunications Workers' Unions, in 1946. In 1947, Touré and others formed the Guinean section of the Rassemblement Démocratique Africain (RDA; a broad alliance of French West African political groupings) and named it the **Parti Démocratique de Guinée** (PDG).

Guinea made huge strides after World War II, with major investment in the bauxite industry and a rapidly urbanizing workforce. Touré, meanwhile, was making his name as a politician and unionist. He was a delegate to the 1947 Communist French Trade Unions Congress in Dakar and, with support from the French Communist party, he backed several **strikes** in the early 1950s and produced the labour newspaper *L'Ouvrier*. The most trenchant strike was the ten-week action in 1953 over the demand for a twenty-percent wage rise to accompany a reform in the labour laws. The industrial action made a lasting impression on the Guinean public and across French West Africa.

Sekou Touré's rise to power

By the time of the strike, Sekou Touré was the territorial assembly member for Beyla. From this platform, he and other trade unionists began a campaign to disaffiliate and Africanize the Guinean sections from the parent French unions.

In 1955, at the age of 33, Touré became **mayor of Conakry**. A year later, he also became first secretary of the **African Federation of Labour Unions** (UGTAN), created after the break of the Guinean unions from the French. Uniquely in West Africa, Touré now succeeded in marrying the PDG party with the labour federation. In 1957, he became vice-president of the new **Territorial Council of Government**,

a post that made him effectively prime minister of Guinea under the low-profile Governor Jean Ramadier. Touré firmly advocated an independent West African federation of states and denounced Senghor of Senegal and Houphouët-Boigny of Côte d'Ivoire as puppets for wanting to consolidate the French connection.

One of Touré's first major acts was the **abolition of chiefs** and their replacement by party cadres. The move was particularly resented in the Fouta Djalon, where chiefdoms had some traditional legitimacy. It was accompanied by some bloody settling of scores: the groundwork for the Guinean state security network was being prepared. With **de Gaulle's return to power** in France, Sekou Touré was soon given the chance to wield full power. The new constitution of the French Fifth Republic was unacceptable to him, and the idea of a free federation of completely independent states wasn't acceptable to de Gaulle – who insisted on their giving up some of their sovereignty to the federal government.

De Gaulle's visit to Conakry to put his case was a waste of time. He would "raise no obstacles" in Guinea's path if the country chose to "secede" from the community of French states, but he would "draw conclusions". Sekou Touré replied, "We prefer poverty in freedom to riches in slavery," and the two leaders snubbed each other at every opportunity for the rest of the visit. "Good luck to Guinea," sneered de Gaulle on his departure.

Guinea under Sekou Touré

While other Francophone leaders thought he was bluffing, Sekou Touré prepared his country to go it alone. On September 28, 1958, there was a 95 percent "No" vote to the referendum on staying in the French community. On October 2, **independence** was declared.

The example of Ghana under Nkrumah was an inspiration, while the swift reaction of the French in Guinea

– flight with the booty, sabotage of the infrastructure, burning of files and cancellation of all cooperation and investment – was made to seem like good riddance by the party, though the severity of the withdrawal was a vindictive blow. The country had virtually no technical expertise and a total of six graduates. It started work from scratch, with aid from Czechoslovakia, the Soviet Union and seven other communist countries, and solid support from the European and Third World left. Morale was high and the PDG organization initially effective.

France excluded Guinea from the CFA franc zone of the newly independent Francophone nations. Guinea adopted its own franc (and later the syli) which isolated it still further from neighbouring states, and hindered what little (non-French) trade remained, but at least stemmed the drain of capital to France. Despite NATO fears that Guinea might become a West African Cuba, US President Eisenhower waited six months before even sending an ambassador to Conakry, for fear of offending de Gaulle. In 1962, a substantial American **aid package** was finally worked out and the US Peace Corps went in. Revolution aside, American aid and investment, particularly in the profitable bauxite industry, has been firm ever since.

Poverty in slavery

As the first few years of independence unrolled, Sekou Touré, the Pan-African ideologue and coauthor of the OAU charter, began to be seen in a less glamorous light as his extreme policies started to bite and the popular enthusiasm of 1959–60 sloughed away. A planned economy without planners was taking shape (or rather not); state enterprises were extended; private business was curtailed; and a small middle class was reaping illicit benefits from mismanagement and fraud.

The results of the first **three-year plan** weren't encouraging. Critics in the PDG complained the party was out of its depth in trying to control the market economy, and mistaken in extending power to the illiterate masses. Sekou Touré scolded them in a twelve-hour speech designed to weed out the party faithful from the conspirators. He wrote later: "Everything became rotten, the elite enjoyed riding in cars and building villas."

There was a massive **market crackdown** in November 1964, with widespread harassment of traders and confiscation of assets. Limits were set on the number of traders allowed outside the state sphere, and arrests, interrogations and arbitrary punishments grew in frequency. The party was moulded in Touré's image and political life stagnated. The very freedoms that lay at the heart of party policy, on paper, were savagely suppressed. Thousands fled the country.

In 1965 a group of opposition exiles, the **Front pour la Libération de Guinée** (FLING), began to organize outside the country with tacit support from Senegal and Côte d'Ivoire and less discreet help from France. The discovery in 1966 of the **"traders' plot"** – an apparent attempt to install a liberal government with capitalist leanings – resulted in a complete rupture of diplomatic relations with Paris.

The Terror

Guinea now entered a dark period of isolationism and widespread terror. At the end of 1967 the eighth party congress had radicalization of the revolution at the top of the agenda. To shore up its bankrupt ideology, the party formally adopted a path of **"Socialism"**. Local revolutionary authorities were set up in every village – ostensibly to allow power to flow from the base up; in reality to extend the security blanket to every corner of the country. And as China was promulgating its bloody Cultural Revolution, Guinea, one of China's biggest African aid recipients, started its own campaign against "degenerate intellectuals".

The elaborate and cruel security apparatus continued to grow. The army was kept under constant surveillance by a network of junior officers. Early in 1969 came the first big **purge** of figures close to the party leadership – Fodeba Keita, Minister of Justice (former teacher and founder of Les Ballets Africains), met his death in Camp Boiro, the notorious prison camp he himself had helped construct. There was an assassination attempt on Touré and more arrests in Labé the following year.

The invasion and after

Although Sekou Touré had been predicting an "aggression" with more than his usual conviction, the country was unprepared for the **invasion** of November 22, 1970. Four hundred troops landed from ships at night and attacked Conakry and the peninsula. This was supposed to trigger a general uprising of Guinean dissidents and the overthrow of Sekou Touré. But although three hundred defenders were killed, and a number of prisoners released by the attackers, none of the key targets (the presidential palace, radio station or airport) was taken. When the invaders' ships moved away 48 hours later, they left behind large numbers of stranded troops who were rounded up and subjected to people's justice.

Reactions to the invasion proved a crucial test of party loyalty and provided the military victory over the "forces of imperialism" that Sekou Touré had always craved. It was, he wrote, "one of those sublime moments of exaltation and patriotism: the affirmation of collective dignity". A United Nations fact-finding mission ascertained that most of the force had been composed of Guinean exiles of FLING and loyalist African soldiers from Portuguese Guinea, commanded by Portuguese officers from the Caetano fascist regime, with West German logistical support. The real aim of the invasion was to destroy the base in Guinea of the **PAIGC guerillas** fighting for independence from Portugal. It was to the lasting humiliation of the Guinea-Conakry opposition that their alliance with Caetano's fascist forces failed.

The purge which followed was predictably brutal. Ninety-one people were sentenced to death and hundreds of others imprisoned and tortured. The hundred-strong German technical mission was expelled and dozens of Europeans spent time in jail in the aftermath.

But the popular rage whipped up by the party against imperialist aggression obscured the **mass violations of human rights** – torture, disappearances, summary executions and detention without trial – that ravaged Guinea through the early 1970s. Tens of thousands of Guineans, particularly Fula-speakers, continued to flee the country every year. As the internal and external pressures against his regime mounted, Sekou Touré resorted to increasingly desperate measures. As there was nothing to encourage farmers, **food shortages** became increasingly common. Obstinately, Touré authorized the local revolutionary authorities to handle all the production and marketing of commodities.

Early in 1975, came the **banning of all private trade** and, at the same time, the setting up of agricultural production brigades. The borders were closed and Touré declared a "holy war" against smugglers, who were shot if caught. In the north of the country, the Sahel drought added to deteriorating prospects.

Guinea struggled for two and a half years, going through another purge in 1976 in response to the **"Fula Plot"** (see box, p.580). Meanwhile, the exodus from Guinea continued: by the end of the 1970s, as many as a million Guineans were believed to be living abroad.

The turnaround

In August 1977, **market women** in Conakry and other towns spontaneously rose up against the intolerable trade situation, which made it impossible for them to afford the produce of their own harvests. It was a turning point. Riots flared across the country

The permanent plot

The idea that there was a permanent, **anti-Guinea plot** obsessed the party hierarchy. The first plots had been exposed even before independence, but the climate of conspiracy thickened until virtually any action could be read as suspicious. At the height of Guinea's isolation, "citizen" and "suspect" became virtually synonymous.

For the first decade of independence, most of the "plots" originated outside the country and the party skilfully manipulated them to maintain control, timing announcements to coordinate with national events. Internal dissent was simply annihilated wherever it first breathed, usually before any chance of genuine conspiracy. In 1969, however, the focus was shifted squarely to **internal opposition**, and the Fula came under increasingly harsh attack. Touré was convinced that the densely populated Fouta Djalon was trying to secede, with the help of Senegal. Army units at Labé were purged and, after the Portuguese invasion of 1970, it was the Fula who bore the brunt of his revenge.

In 1973, Sekou Touré announced the discovery of a "fifth column active in all walks of life". Again, the Fula came under concerted attack with waves of arrests, executions and disappearances. This ethnic repression culminated in 1976 with the announcement of the **"Fula Plot"** and Touré's declaration that the Fula-speaking peoples were "racist" and "enemies of socialism". Diallo Telli, a Fula, and the first OAU secretary general, was accused of leading a CIA-backed conspiracy. He was arrested and starved to death. If there was any real "permanent plot" during Sekou Touré's tyrannical rule, it would appear to have been his own genocidal one against the Fula.

and several provincial governors were killed. Sekou Touré's resolve collapsed. He began a slow process of **economic liberalization**, as well as adopting a more pragmatic approach to government, reducing revolutionary rhetoric and making cosmetic improvements in democratic practices and human rights.

In his last few years, Touré left the running of the party and state more and more to a leading clique of ministers while devoting himself to the cultivation of an image as the grand old man of Pan-Africanism – 1982 saw the grotesque spectacle of Touré in Washington being hailed by President Reagan as "a champion of human rights".

Touré forged close links with **King Hassan** of Morocco (whose side he took in the dispute over Western Sahara), and other bastions of the rigid right. Hassan provided the money desperately needed by Touré to tide him over after the collapse of IMF negotiations in 1983, and arranged with conservative Arab states for Guinea to be the largest recipient of **petro-dollar aid** in sub-Saharan Africa.

In January and February 1984, groups of soldiers were arrested near the Senegalese border and accused of plotting against the government. At the time of **Sekou Touré's death** on March 26, 1984, in a private clinic in Cleveland, it appears that sections of the army had indeed been planning a coup d'état.

The new regime

Colonels **Lansana Conté** (president) and **Diara Traoré** (prime minister) waited several days after the lavish funeral before announcing, after an almost peaceful takeover, the dissolution of the constitution and the party, the freeing of political prisoners, the unbanning of trade unions and the reopening of Guinea to private investment. Judicial reforms began and French was reintroduced as the official language of education. Most of the old party structures swiftly disintegrated. Asked why the military hadn't acted years earlier, Conté said: "The spirit of the Guinean was such that he would not think. Some Guineans behaved like imbeciles. They were remote-controlled."

The **Comité Militaire de Redressement National** was given an enthusiastic welcome and ministers went on foreign tours to introduce the new Guinea and cultivate aid donors. But apart from a general liberalization, it was hard to pinpoint the direction of the new government. There was soon a split with prime minister Traoré, and his post was abolished. Predictably, perhaps, Traoré and fellow Malinké officers attempted a coup against Conté in July 1985. Two years later, it was announced that those involved, together with a number of detainees from Sekou Touré's government – sixty people in all – had been given secret trials and were to be executed. It was widely presumed, however, that most of them had died extra-judicially long before and Conté was merely setting the record straight.

On the **economic front**, Conakry was soon full of French technical advisors and business people. One of the IMF's structural adjustment programmes was put in operation which, coupled with general austerity, state sector job losses, and widespread civil service corruption and ostentation, was not warmly received. Conakry boiled over in January 1988 with **street riots** over price rises – which, yet again, had outstripped wage increases. The riots forced the government to back down, and commodity prices were reduced.

The 1990s

The initiative Conté had lost after abolishing the post of prime minister and the subsequent coup attempt was recovered when he increased **civilian representation** in the government, though some of his rivals were banished from Conakry in the process.

Malinké-speakers have been particularly under-represented since the demise of the old regime and they, together with the Fula, are regarded as the unofficial opposition to Conté's predominantly Susu leadership.

By the end of 1990, serious protests were emerging from schools and the university in Conakry against conditions, educational standards, and the slowness with which democratic reforms were being instituted. A number of students were killed by police or army gunfire during demonstrations. Conté maintained his slow pace, setting up a **Comité Transitoire de Redressement National** (CTRN), which he ensured had some recently departed members of his own cabinet sitting in it. Meanwhile, demonstrations and strikes continued.

In 1991, **Alpha Condé**, long-exiled Malinké opposition leader and secretary general of the Rassemblement du Peuple Guinéen (RPG), briefly returned home, but fled soon after when the security forces fired on a crowd of his supporters. Despite this setback, the RPG was formally registered in April 1992, with Condé returning once more to Guinea.

Lansana Conté himself formed a puppet party as a front for the CTRN. Called the **Parti de l'Unité et du Progrès** (PUP), it focused on the parts of the country where the CTRN was providing development funds. Despite intimidating the opposition and operating with state support and government money, Conté's PUP was insufficiently confident of its electoral strengths to stick to the election dates scheduled for the end of 1992. The CTRN deferred the presidential and legislative elections for another year,

Achievements

In retrospect, the first quarter-century of independence was a tragic waste. Yet there were one or two significant achievements which can't be overlooked. Touré's radical anti-colonial stance has meant that many Guineans have a freedom of political thought that isn't found in the same way in other countries of Francophone West Africa, and there's a genuine national pride among people that has so far succeeded in uniting the country's distinct ethnic groups and prevented serious rifts between individual peoples. Sekou Touré also encouraged artistic expression in Guinea and nurtured the creation of a modern musical tradition that inspired many surrounding countries.

during which Guinea saw some of the most savage political violence of the post-Touré era.

In the **presidential election**, finally held in December 1993, Conté polled just over 51 percent, while the votes from two massively anti-Conté (and pro-Condé) prefectures, Kankan and Siguiri, were disallowed for reasons of the RPG's "malpractice". As it became clear that the opposition had been cheated, there were chaotic scenes at polling stations. Several Guinean embassies, acting as polling stations for Guinean émigrés in other parts of West Africa, were ransacked.

As "democratic" presidential elections in West Africa go, Guinea's first effort was impressively dishonest. In its wake, Condé's RPG and the Parti pour le Renouveau et le Progrès (PRP), led by a former journalist on *Jeune Afrique* magazine, **Siradiou Diallo**, formed an alliance to contest the legislative elections. In response to this and other signs of opposition, the government disenfranchised Guineans overseas, thus excluding some three million potential voters. Meanwhile, there were rumours of a coup attempt, and arrests in May 1994.

The **multiparty general elections** to the legislative assembly were finally held in June, 1995. In the run-up, opposition rallies throughout Guinea were disrupted by the security forces. Condé and Diallo, having earlier said they would not boycott the elections despite the PUP's flagrant rigging, ultimately pulled out on the day. Although the coalition won about a quarter of the seats (28 out of 114 seats to the PUP's 71) they boycotted the national assembly.

Late pay was the provocation that led part of the army to **mutiny** in February 1996. The incident – when various units seized the airport and radio and TV stations, and shelled the city centre – came close to toppling Conté, but was defused when the president, banged up in his palace, offered an immediate 100 percent pay increase and no prosecutions, in exchange for his freedom. True to form, he reneged on the deal soon afterwards and a ragged

series of trials and hearings ran on for the next two years.

In the (once again, openly rigged) **elections of December 1998**, Conté's PUP scored 56 percent against a divided opposition. Alfa Condé, the country's most high-profile opposition leader, had bided his time in exile in Paris – his personal safety in Guinea always in doubt – until days before the election, arriving finally to a hero's welcome in Conakry. Soon after his arrival, he was arrested and accused of being a threat to state security.

Guinea today

Since the late 1990s, Guinea has been on a downward political and economic spiral. In addition to internal problems of state oppression, poverty and corruption, the country has become increasingly embroiled in the conflicts raging in neighbouring countries. Between September 2000 and March 2001 there were repeated attacks by **Liberian** and **Sierra Leonean rebels** at the frontiers, while in the same period **Guinean rebel groups** appeared on the scene, some believed to be soldiers who quit the army at the time of the 1996 mutiny. Some 1500 Guinean civilians are said to have died in the confrontations that left the town of **Guéckédou** completely ruined. The conflicts in Liberia and Sierra Leone have also seen huge numbers of refugees seeking sanctuary in Guinea, with up to half a million displaced people in the country at the peak of the crisis in early 2001.

In November 2001, President Conté staged a referendum on constitutional changes to allow him to stand for another term as president, while increasing the length of term from five to seven years and abolishing the age limit of 70. Not surprisingly, this move created strong opposition, and marches from Kankan and Labé to Conakry were blocked by the military, and all opposition leaders temporarily arrested. A united opposition alliance, **CODEM**, called for a boycott of the referendum – which produced the inevitable governmental success. In December 2003, the aged and ailing president was re-elected in polls that were dismissed as fraudulent by both opposition parties and international observers.

In January, 2007, Guinea's workers' unions declared a nationwide **general strike** in response to the rampant inflation and rising cost of living that had beset the country for years. Guinea ground to a virtual halt as, for eighteen days, tens of thousands marched in protest in towns throughout the country demanding Conté's resignation. The strike was suspended when the president agreed to name a new prime minister, but his choice, political ally Eugene Camara, merely inflamed the situation further. The following week saw some of the bloodiest rioting in Guinea's history as mobs destroyed and looted administrative buildings, shops and petrol stations in most major towns. At least 140 people were killed and 2000 injured as demonstrators clashed with marauding soldiers. Martial law was declared and a curfew enforced.

In February, 2007, Conté named popular diplomat **Lansana Kouyaté** as the new prime minister, thus satisfying both the Guinean people and the trade unions. At the time of writing, early 2008, Conté is still in power, though his health has been extremely poor for years and he has no clear successor. Meanwhile, Lansana Kouyaté is struggling to hold the line against a population increasingly agitated and resentful of rising prices for basic commodities (particularly rice and bread), which went up from FG1200 to FG2000 a loaf in August 2007. Anti-government **demonstrations** in September 2007 saw police once again using tear gas on the streets of Conakry.

With almost limitless agricultural potential, plus its bauxite, iron and other mineral reserves – not to mention the stunning landscapes and cultural assets on which tourism could be based – Guinea has the potential to become the most prosperous state in West Africa and the region's dominant Francophone nation. But there are big hurdles to jump.

While Guineans can appear surprisingly optimistic about their political future, the country remains tense. Lingering discontent, along with unresolved economic problems, could well lead to further serious unrest at any time in the future. Until Lansana Conté is gone and a credible new president has been elected by popular mandate, Guineans won't be able to concentrate on improving their lives and building the country.

Music

Guinea was once West Africa's most influential musical nation. With independence in 1958 and Sekou Touré's *authenticité* campaign, the government encouraged the creation of a modern sound that married the country's traditional roots with the electric tones, jazz, Cuban and Congolese influences of the big bands. They sponsored regional bands across the country – musicians on the state payroll hired to please the masses.

The revolutionary style created during that time still resounds in the latest Guinean releases, and has influenced the music of most neighbouring countries. But Guinea's musical roots run much deeper than the modern era.

Guinean folk music

Guinea's four geographical regions correspond roughly to four population zones, which all have their own forms of **traditional music**. In the lowland coastal area of the west, the **Mande**-related music of the Susu

583

dominates with the sound of the *bongo* lamellaphone (thumb piano) and the **balafon** (xylophone). The latter originated in Susu culture but has become an essential element of Mande music all over West Africa.

Public performances are more difficult to find in the strongly Islamic, **Fula**-inhabited Fouta Djalon highlands, though weddings, baptisms and other community celebrations give visitors the chance to enjoy the breakneck acrobatics and passionate flute-playing and drumming of the hugely entertaining *nyamakala* performers.

The eastern savannah of Haute Guinée is mainly occupied by the **Malinké**, whose cultural domain spreads into western Mali. The Mande griots are the leaders of the Guinean music scene, stunning audiences with their refined vocal and instrumental skills and historical knowledge. Guinea's most typical sound – the intricate polyrhythms of **djembe** drumming ensembles – also comes from Haute Guinée.

In the southeast highland forest region, the **Kissi**, **Toma**, **Guerzé** and **Kono** have nurtured musical traditions which have more in common with the music of Central Africa than the rest of West Africa, dominated by polyphonic cow-horn ensembles, single- and double-headed drums, slit-drums and xylophone-drums. Mask dances are also more common here than elsewhere in Guinea, a legacy of the region's strong animist traditions.

Modern Guinean music

The post-independence era's most famous band was the mighty **Bembeya Jazz**, but there were several other similar orchestras, including **Les Amazones**, the all-female army orchestra, who released an amazing comeback album (Wamato, Sterns) in 2008; Tele-Jazz de Télimélé, from the Fouta Djalon; Balla et ses Balladins; Keletigui et ses Tambourins; and the forest band Orchestre Nimba Jazz. Their recordings were originally released on the state-owned Syliphone label of the Touré era, and have now been largely re-released by the Paris-based Syllart label.

During the post-Touré years of the mid-1980s, Guinean popular music became increasingly influenced by Antillean *zouk*, which retains a powerful hold over Guinean pop to this day. In addition, younger musicians have gradually merged in reggae, techno and hip-hop with Guinean sounds inherited from their elders. Some of the biggest artists, based most of the time overseas, include the unrivalled **Sekouba Bambino Diabaté**, the charming **Oumou Dioubaté** and her daughter **Missia Saran**, and the awesomely accomplished "techno griot" **Mory Kanté**.

And just as Mory Kanté has been turning to his acoustic roots, so the roots-rocking quartet **Ba Cissoko** have been reminding Guineans why they still love the *kora* and the *jeli* tradition.

In common with most of its neighbours, Guinea has a new generation of musicians who want to put Guinea on the global stage, many of them with the help of **hip-hop and R&B**. The biggest names of the past decade have been the US-influenced early-adopters **Kill Point** and the more interesting and recent solo rapper **Bill de Sam**.

Compilations

The Rough Guide to Mali & Guinea (World Music Network). A fine selection of Guinean tracks from Balla et ses Balladins, Sekouba Bambino, Bembeya Jazz, Jali Musa Jawara and the late Momo Wandel Soumah.

Ba Cissoko

Fouta Djalon foursome led by *kora* wizard Ba Cissoko, bent on modernizing the traditional repertoire.

Electric Griot Land (Totolo). With its title playing deliberately on Hendrix's *Electric Ladyland*, and collaborators including Somali rapper K'naan and Ivoirian reggae star Tiken Jah Fakoly, a lively set – partly of reinvented Mande classics – for powered-up *kora*, guitar, bass and calabash.

Les Ballets Africains

West Africa's foremost musical ensemble, created in 1952, have made many international tours and put on spectacular, if rare, live performances.

Héritage (Buda). Recorded in Germany in 1995, this production ranges across the country's cultural heritage – from the mythical origin of the *balafon* to family totems – creating a richly woven sound tapestry.

Bembeya Jazz

Formed in 1961, Guinea's greatest band of the post-independence era mixes Malinké praise songs with Congolese musical threads, and Cuban styles with Islamic tradition. The death in 1973 of their celebrated lead singer Aboubacar Demba Camera robbed Africa of one of its greatest vocalists. The band is now led by lead guitarist, Sekou "Diamond Fingers" Diabaté, and is currently enjoying a revival in its fortunes after a period of near-complete silence.

The Syliphone Years: Hits and Rare Recordings (Sterns, UK). Glorious, 2007 double-CD compilation of 1960s and 70s hits. Excellent booklet.

Live – 10 Ans de Succès (Bolibana, France). Atmospheric recording from 1971 of Guinea's most famous band at their finest. Wild solos from Diabaté alternate with Camera's unforgettable voice.

Bembeya Jazz National (Sonodisc/ Esperance, France). Bembeya in the mid-1980s with their classic recording of "Lanaya", featuring the romantic voice of Sekouba Bambino.

Balla et ses Balladins

One of Guinea's best-ever bands, who have superbly modernized classic Malinké songs.

Reminiscin' in tempo with Balla et ses Balladins (Popular African Music).

Compilation of greats with the classic Guinea-rumba sound of the 1960s and 1970s, including two stunning versions of one of the greatest Mande love songs, "Sara".

Bill de Sam

Using traditional Mande musical threads to confront Guinea's political and social impasse in a way no *jeli* would ever do, Bill de Sam's head-on rapping has achieved a major following among the Guinean diaspora in Europe and with clued-up fans in Guinea.

Simiti (Tour d'Ivoire, France). Bill de Sam's latest release from 2004 proclaims "Things Must Change" and "Guinean Rappers United For Change" with songs rapped in French, Susu and Malinké. In a gently melodic musical culture, this is strong meat.

Sekouba Bambino Diabaté

Once Bembeya Jazz's youngest lead singer, Bambino is now Guinea's best-loved solo artist, gifted both with an ethereal voice and an uncanny instinct for heart-rending melodies, as well as a taste for the experimental.

Kassa (Syllart). A daring album featuring the beautiful ballad "Damanseya".

Sinikan (Sonodisc). African music that isn't afraid to look forward, this is Bambino's most fully realized album to date and sees him experimenting with a wide range of styles, all perfectly executed.

Kade Diawara

Guinea's finest female singer in the Mande tradition.

L'Archange du Manding and **L'Eternelle Kade Diawara**. Wonderful old ballads and love songs from a superb voice.

Oumou Dioubaté

A griotte of the dance floor from Kankan, and one of the country's most successful artists, based in Paris since the 1980s, Dioubaté earned the soubriquet "La Femme Chic-Shoc" for her style and confrontational approach.

Wambara (Stern's, UK). Stunning melodies, irrepressible beats and great guitar backing mark a set of fine songs from a real individual.

Kaloum Star Felenko

Founded in 1969 by Maître Barry, Kaloum Star from Conakry were the last state-run band to be set up during the rule of Sekou Touré.

Felenko (Buda). Fine, well-developed songs: the title track carries a strong flavour of Fela Kuti's Afro-Beat.

Jali Musa Jawara

Mory Kanté's *kora*-playing half-brother leads an excellent acoustic ensemble.

Yasimika (Hannibal, UK). A classic of Mande acoustic music from 1983, never since matched by him, with Jawara's soaring vocals and luscious choruses from Djanka Diabaté and Djenne Doumbia over guitar, *kora* and *balafon*.

Mory Kanté

Mory Kanté started playing music at the age of seven, later joining the Rail Band in Bamako before embarking on a hugely successful solo career playing what he described as "kora-funk". Although his earlier solo career attracted scorn from purists, the music had an infectious global-village feel that brought him stardom on the world stage. And his recent return to an acoustic sound shows he's more than a one-trick pony.

Akwaba Beach (Barclay). Kanté's breakthrough album, with his world-wide hit conversion of the traditional "Yeke yeke" – high-tech *kora* music for the dance floor.

Tatebola (Arcade/Missliin). Still driven by techno rhythms but in slightly more mellow mode, with a lovely version of the classic kora song "Alla l'aa ke".

Sabou (World Music Network). With this 2004 release, the multi-instrumentalist Mory Kanté returned delightfully to acoustic music, with a superb set, backed by stunning female chorus.

Famoudou Konaté

A master of the *djembe*, the ever-popular, egg-timer-shaped drum of western West Africa, who formerly toured with the Ballets Africains. He now fronts his own Ensemble Hamana Dan Ba.

Guinée: Percussions et Chants Malinké (Buda). A series of immaculate set-piece renditions of traditional songs.

Kanté Manfila

The guitar wizard of the Ambassadeurs, Kanté Manfila (aka Manfila Kanté) is one of Africa's most innovative guitarists.

Tradition (Celluloid). Gorgeous, rolling acoustic melodies from Kankan with guitars and *balafon*, and *kora* accompaniment by cousin Mory Kanté.

Diniya (Celluloid). Some fine melodies buried underneath a full-blown, high-tech production.

Kankan Blues (Popular African Music). Probably the best of the acoustic offerings on PAM.

Momo Wandel Soumah

Momo Wandel Soumah was a conservatoire-trained saxophonist who studied jazz and performed with the Orchestre Keletigui during the Sekou Touré era. He died in 2003.

Guinea: "Matchowe" (Buda). A rich voice to complement a strongly flavoured union of jazz and Guinean music.

Cinema

A lack of resources has meant that **cinema** has never been a major cultural force in Guinea. Even so, some fine films have come out of the country, notably *Naitou* (1982) by **Diakité Moussa Kemoko**. Featuring the Ballet National de Guinée, the film recounts an African folk tale exclusively through music and dance – a radical attempt to deal with the issue of finding the best language for African cinema.

Among the newer film-makers, **Mohammed Camara**, who trained as an actor, made an impressive entry at the 1993 FESPACO with the short film *Denko*. Camara tackles his difficult subject with sensitivity: a mother commits incest to restore sight to her blind son and reveals the hypocrisy of society through her transgression. Diving deeper into controversy, Camara's *Dakan* (1997) was the first film in sub-Saharan Africa to treat the subject of male homosexuality; filming was often interrupted by protests.

Director **David Achkar** also created a stir with his 1991 experimental documentary *Allah Tantou* – the story of his father, Marof Achkar, who was Guinea's ambassador to the United Nations until his imprisonment and death in Sekou Touré's infamous Camp Boiro.

In a totally different vein, film historian and critic **Manthia Diawara**'s documentary *Rouch in Reverse* (1995) is an interesting analysis of one of the most influential ethnographic film-makers ever, and provides a rare look at European anthropological studies from an African perspective.

Cheick Doukouré's first feature – *Paris Selon Moussa* – won the Human Rights prize at the 2003 FESPACO for its touching tale of a farmer sent to Paris to buy a water pump for his farming co-op.

Check out the Centre Culturel Franco-Guinéen (see p.607) for films by the French film-maker **Laurent Chevalier**. His documentary of *djembé*-player Mammadi Keita and his cinematic realization of Camara Laye's *L'Enfant Noir* are both worth watching. The Centre can also direct you to films by Guinea's new generation of young directors, among whose recent productions include **Cheick Fantamady Camara**'s *Be Kunko* (2005) and **Gahité Fofana**'s tragic story of teenage aeroplane stowaways, *Un Matin Bonne Heure* (2006).

Books

There's little published in English, though a hunt through libraries may turn up some of the following. For good general West African titles, including some with a Guinean connection, see p.35. Titles marked 🏃 are especially recommended.

Manthia Diawara *In Search of Africa*. Diawara, best known for his books on film, returns to Guinea to shoot a documentary on Sekou Touré, and pens a moving analysis of the state of Africa forty years after the independence movement.

Alioum Fantouré *Tropical Circle*. A novel about Guinea between the end of World War II and the reign of terror.

🏃 **Mamadou Kouyaté** *Sundiata: an Epic of Old Mali*. Transcribed into French and annotated by Djibril Tamsir Niané and translated into English by G.D. Pickett, this is the slim but fascinating griot's history of the Mali Empire, the epicentre of which was near Siguiri, in Guinea.

Camara Laye *The African Child*. One of the best-known books by an African writer, these sweet-scented memoirs of a privileged rural childhood are a homage to the author's parents. Other translations of works by Laye include *The Radiance of the King*, *A Dream of Africa* and *The Guardian of the Word*.

Various *Politique Africaine, Guinée: L'après Sekou Touré*. A collection of articles about political and economic changes in Guinea since the death of Sekou Touré in 1984.

Language

French is Guinea's official language, and is spoken to some degree of fluency by most people who've had a school education (English is rarely spoken except by refugees from Sierra Leone or Liberia). The most important Guinean languages are **Susu** (mainly spoken in the capital), **Fula** (spoken in the Fouta Djalon), and **Malinké** (spoken in Haute Guinée).

Simple Susu

Susu, the main language in Conakry, is more straightforward in many respects than Fula and relatively easy to learn. It is related to Mandinka (see p.286), Bamana (see p.355) and Malinké (see below).

Greetings

Inwali	Hello (to one person)
Wo inwali	(two or more people)
Wo mamabé	Good day
Tana mokhi?	Good morning (literally, "Did nothing bad happen in the night?")
Tana mogegné	Good afternoon/ evening
Tana modinbayama?	How's the family?
Won je segué	See you later/ goodbye

Numbers

keren	1
firin	2
sakhan	3
nani	4
suli	5
senné	6
soloferé	7
solomasakham	8
solomanani	9
fu	10
mokhein	20
mokhein nu suli	25
tongosakhan	30
tongonani	40
tongosuli	50
tongosenné	60
kémé	100
kémé firin	200

Useful expressions

Yéri?	How much?
A sun nyi	I'll take it (give it to me)
Asaré khorokho	It's too expensive
Kira ma sembé	Show me the way
M'ma kolon	I don't know
M'ma fahamukhi	I don't understand
Diyema	Excuse me
Nakhadi	Please repeat it
Banque na mindé?	Where's the bank?

Minimal Malinké

Malinké, spoken in Haute Guinée, is a member of the same language family as Mandinka (Senegal and The Gambia), Bamana or Bambara (Mali) and Diola or Dyula (Côte d'Ivoire). Although the grammar and vocabulary are relatively simple, each word can have several meanings, making it tricky to grasp even the most basic of phrases.

Greetings

Iniké	Hello
Tana ma télé	Good day
Tana si te	Response:
Ine soma	Good morning
Inu wura	Good evening
Tana te denbaya la?	How's the family?
Tana si te	Response:
Ambay kofé	See you later
Oh-oo-oh	Goodbye

Numbers

kelen	1
fila	2
saba	3
nani	4
lolu	5
woro	6
woronfila	7
seyin	8
konondo	9
taan	10
mwan	20
mwan ni lolu	25
bisaba	30
binani	40
bilolu	50
biworo	60
kémé	100
kémé fila	200
waa kelen	1000
waa fila	2000

Useful expressions

Jéli?	How much?
A di n'ma	I'll take it (give it to me)
Iniké huh	Thank you

A ka gbelen	It's too expensive
N'ma lon	I don't know
N'ma men	I don't understand
Bank ye mi?	Where's the bank?
Konko ye n'na	I'm hungry
N wa tô Kankan	I'm going to Kankan
I tô di?	What's your name?
N tô le Sara	My name is Sara

Fundamental Fula

The Fula or Pulaar language (properly called Fulfulde) is one of the most difficult West African languages: it has an immensely rich vocabulary, an unusual and complex grammatical structure, and guttural tones that are hard to pronounce – and there's little instructional material in English. Note that the following is based on the Fula of Fouta Djalon; the Fula spoken in other parts of West Africa – Senegal, Mali, Nigeria and Cameroon – differs markedly.

Greetings

On djaarama	How are you?
Tana alaa ton?	Are you fine?
Djam tun	[response: fine]
Bengure no edjam?	How's the family?
Bengure no edjam	[response: fine]
Gollere nden?	How's the work?
No marsude or No jokka	[response: fine]
Achanee lan hakke	Sorry
Hakke alaa	Never mind

Conversation

A wawi Pulaar? or A nani Pulaar?	Do you speak Fula?
Hi-hi	Yes
O-o	No
Mi andaa	I don't know
Mi famaali	I don't understand
Kohundun wi'idha?	What did you say?
Ko tooli!	Welcome!
Mi weltikke fii ma	Nice to meet you
Ko hundun inettedha? or Inde ma?	What's your name?
Ko Michael me wi'ete	My name is Michael

| Ko huntu djeedha? or Ko huntu iwurudha? | Where are you from? |
| Ko Angleterre mi iwri | I'm from England |

Travel

Ko huntu yahataa?	Where are you going?
Ko huntu woni Dalaba?	Where is Dalaba?
No yeeso	Straight ahead
Sengo nyaamo	Right
Sengo nano	Left
No woddhi	Far away
Fulawaa	Village
No njandi	Big
No fandi	Small
Fello	Hill
Djurnde	Waterfall
Julirde	Mosque

Shopping and food

No satti!	It's too expensive
Duytanan seedha, fii Allah	Please reduce a little.
A duytantaalan seedha?	Won't you reduce it?
Ko huntu bank woni?	Where's the bank?

Ko jelu?	How much?
Nyaamete	Food
Maaro	Rice
Pute	Potatoes
Tewu	Meat
Bira	Milk
Kosan	Sour milk
Ndiyan	Water
Dute	Tea
No moyy'i!	It's excellent (food)!
Mi haari (tef)	I'm full

Numbers

goo	1
dhidhi	2
tati	3
nay	4
jowi	5
jeego	6
jeedhidhi	7
jeetati	8
jeenay	9
sappo	10
sappo e goo	11
nogay	20
nogay e jowi	25
teemedere	100
teemede dhidhi	200

Glossary

Alfa King (Fula)

Bowe Eroded Fouta Djalon hill (pl **bowal**)

CTRN Transitional Committee for National Redress

Dougou/Dugu Place (Mande languages)

Foté, Porto White person (corruption of "Portuguese"; Susu); pl **portobhe**

Gara Indigo (and indigo cloth)

Koro Old (as in Dabolakoro – old Dabola)

Lumo Market held weekly (or sometimes every four or five days)

PDG Democatic Party of Guinea, the party of the old regime

PUP Unity and Progress Party, the ruling party of Lansana Conté

Sofa Malinké soldier (nineteenth century)

Syli Elephant (and defunct Guinean currency)

Villa Administration guesthouse, often usable by travellers

Woro Kola (Mande languages)

7.1

Conakry and around

C **ONAKRY**, once known as "the Paris of Africa", is these days a city of few graces. A continuous sprawl of urbanization claws its way off the peninsula and up into the hills behind the city centre. This elongated conurbation is animated but morbidly dirty; heavy with the raw noise and choking exhaust fumes of lines of jammed vehicles trying to get from one end of town to another. Although downtown Conakry is gradually becoming a more pleasant place to visit, with lively restaurants and cafés, it's relatively expensive and too full of shady street vendors and stifled by pollution to allow for a peaceful stay. You may spend much of your time here planning your escape to the fabled hills and grasslands of the interior.

That being said, it would be unfair not to acknowledge the city's charms. For one, it's absolutely worth visiting Conakry's markets, especially the vast **Marché de Madina** and the slightly smaller **Marché du Niger**: both are bountiful, constantly expanding, and have become much safer over the past several years. The city also boasts a first-rate **nightlife** – one whose DJ club scene at times rivals Dakar's – while the strikingly pretty **Îles de Los** offer an easily accessible retreat a few kilometres out to sea. A handful of day-trips to spots around the region's Atlantic coastline – **Dubréka**, **Coyah**, **Boffa**, **Kamsar** and **Boké** – are also within reach of the capital, all easily accessible by bush taxi.

Some history

Conakry was originally an island – as you can still see from the narrow causeway between the Palais du Peuple and the motorway bridge. For many years known as **Tumbo**, the island provided safe haven for slavers and merchant vessels trading along the Guinea coasts. The Portuguese adventurer Pedro da Sintra first set foot here around 1460 and named it Cap de Sagres, after Prince Henry the Navigator's residence in Portugal. At this time the inhabitants of what is now Conakry were idol-worshipping, skin-wearing farmers, cultivating indigenous African dry-land rice and millet. By the sixteenth century, the Portuguese had began to use the deep waters on the southeast side of the island as an anchorage, and over the succeeding centuries they and the Dutch, English and French all took turns to occupy the site and trade in slaves, transforming the **Îles de Los** into an entrepôt for the transfer of slaves from smaller coastal vessels to ocean-going merchant ships.

Yet by the time Britain ceded rights over the fledgling colony to France in 1887, Tumbo island still only had four tiny settlements – Bulbinay and Konakiri and the non-native African toeholds of Krootown and Tumbo – with just a few hundred inhabitants. A road into the interior was started and the channel between Tumbo and the Kaloum peninsula on the mainland was filled in to create a causeway. By the time Britain handed over the Los islands in 1904, Conakry – the new capital of Guinée Française – had acquired its present grid pattern and a population of ten thousand. The **railway** to Kankan was completed in 1914 and bananas from Kindia became the country's biggest export. Major developments came in the postwar colonial period, and concentrated on improving the port for the shipping of newly discovered iron ore and bauxite. The last twenty years have seen massive growth: the city, whose population is rapidly approaching two million, now covers the entire peninsula.

Although people may tell you that Conakry is a den of thieves, in comparison with, say, Dakar, it's relatively peaceful, though you should always be on guard for pickpockets. Depending on the political climate, the police may be given to hassling visitors in a variety of ways, and it's wise to carry your passport and vaccination certificates at all times.

Arrival, information and city transport

Conakry's open-plan Gbessia **airport** is fairly well organized, with the only hassles these days coming from money-thirsty porters who will insist on carrying your bag or from customs officers who may want to sift through your bag in search of contraband. It's still best to be met by a friend or hotel staff in order to avoid lengthy price debates with taxi drivers. A **taxi** into central Conakry (La Ville) should cost around FG50,000 for the *déplacement* (private hire). Alternatively, walk to the so-called autoroute outside the airport entrance and wave down a taxi (around FG3500 depending on the distance travelled; you may be charged extra for luggage). If your flight arrives early enough in the day, you may be able to leave Conakry and head upcountry immediately. In that case, take a taxi towards the *gare voiture* in Matam which should cost you half the full fare to the centre.

Arriving overland in Conakry, most taxis will drop you along the main autoroutes and may not physically terminate at either of Conakry's main *gares voitures*. Of the two main *gares*, the busiest is in the **Matam** quarter, 8km from the city centre, with a less chaotic one further out in **Bambeto**.

Orientation and street names

Conakry is built twenty kilometres out to sea on a promontory. Much of what you'll want in the way of banks, embassies and other services is right at the end, in the two square kilometres of the city centre, usually called simply **Ville**, arranged on an easy-to-follow grid plan. The northern *quartiers* of this downtown area – **Cité de Chemin de Fer**, **Almamya** and **Kaloum** – are the focus of business and bureaucracy, while the southern districts – **Manquepas**, **Boulbinet**, **Sandervalia** – are mostly made up of tight-packed, single-storey city compounds and still have a village-like atmosphere of brush-swept yards, open-fire cooking and kids playing in the streets. Conakry's port operations all take place on the north side of the Ville district: a thousand-metre long groin, the **Épi Nord**, stretches out to sea, with a popular hotel-restaurant halfway along.

Landwards, past the huge **Palais du Peuple** and over the strategically narrow causeway onto the mainland, you hit the **Autoroute** (not a motorway or freeway in the usual sense, since all vehicles and pedestrians use it) and pass under the bridge at **Place du 8 Novembre**. The **Grande Mosquée**, Hôpital Donka and **Camp Boiro** (the main Touré-era prison camp) are over on the left, to the north, while stretching along the north coast of the peninsula, you hit the rapidly expanding and more affluent districts of **Rogbané**, **Taouyah**, **Ratoma**, **Kipé**, **Kaporo**, **Nongo** and **Taady**, where many of Conakry's best hotels, clubs and restaurants can be found.

Apart from a few main roads, Conakry's streets are numbered, rather than named, and matters are complicated by the fact that the locals themselves are rarely aware of road numbers, and locations are usually only identified by the nearest well-known landmark. In the downtown **Ville district**, avenues run from east to west and boulevards from north to south; 1ère av ("1st Avenue") and 4ème bd ("4th Boulevard") are the common local abbreviations. Note that 10ème av is also known as **av de** la Gare (the defunct railway station); 8ème av is av Tubman; 6ème av is av de la République (which leads into Route du Niger and the Autoroute); 6ème bd is bd Telly Diallo; and 3ème bd is bd du Commerce. There are also two important *bis* ("repeat") avenues: 9ème av bis and 7ème av bis, not to be confused with 9ème av and 7ème av, which run next to them.

On top of all this, all downtown street names have officially been altered to KA numbers (after Kaloum) – the old boulevards becoming odd-numbered KA numbers (with "1ère bd" changing to "KA 001", for example) and the old avenues becoming even-numbered KA numbers (so that "1ère av" changes to "KA 004"). The map of Central Conakry on pp.596–597 shows both the old and new street names. Streets on the peninsula follow a similar system of numbering, according to district – Ratoma streets are prefixed RA, for example, with even-numbered streets following the peninsula and odd numbers crossing it.

Lastly, remember when looking for office addresses, most offices are located by reference to their building, or *immeuble* in French, abbreviated to Imm.

Information

The Office du Tourisme, on av de la République, next to Ecobank (☎30.55.73.63 ⊛www.mirinet.com/ont or ⊛www.ontguinee.org; neither site working properly on last check), can give you general information, and has country maps and some old guidebooks for sale. They can also recommend a tourist guide to accompany you, though be sure to agree firmly on a price beforehand. Mondial Tours (see p.608) is often very helpful with advice on getting around Conakry and the region. The free listings magazines, *Djeli* and *Tam Tam* are published irregularly. Copies of the latest editions are usually available at the Centre Culturel Franco-Guinéen on Place Sory Kandia Kouyaté (see p.607) and at various bookstalls and supermarkets.

City transport

There are four forms of public transport in Conakry: crammed minibuses or *magbanas* and a small number of regular buses, plus battered yellow taxis and an increasing large fleet of *taxi-motos* – single-passenger motorcycle taxis. The cabs and *motos* are really the only useful options for visitors, as the buses and minibuses are too irregular and shambolic. Shared cabs run strictly along four main routes: "Route Donka" (north side of the peninsula), "Autoroute" (Autoroute bridge to the airport), "Route du Niger" (joining with "Autoroute") and "Route du Madina". To hail a taxi, follow the example of others by the road until you've mastered the local hand signals indicating your destination and have learned to

Conakry surface arrivals and departures

Getting into, or away from, Conakry may appear chaotic, but the options are limited: all **upcountry road transport** arrives at and leaves from one or other of the two *gares voitures*, either Matam or Bambeto. As neither private buses nor SOGETRAG buses are running any longer, travelling to other parts of the country requires a seat in a bush taxi; the standard Peugeot 504s link Conakry direct with all major Guinean towns, though few taxis make regular through-runs to neighbouring capitals – Freetown and Bamako are occasionally available. You stand the best chance of finding a taxi about to leave at the busier Matam *gare*, but get there as early as possible, and not after 8am; later departures fill up more slowly, and vehicles never leave until every seat is sold.

Driving out of Conakry, the smog-laden road to Coyah heads up through the oily squalor of the city immigrants' highway-side *ateliers*, manufacturing every conceivable kind of item, before reaching the tedious **checkpoint** at Km36 that marks the official exit of Conakry – an outlandish and somewhat intimidating scene of strutting and loafing khaki-clad officials where delays are commonplace.

read drivers' responses. **Fares** in shared taxis work according to a zone system, with a fixed fare of FG800 per leg (or FG1500 along the Autoroute). *Moto* hops are negotiable, around FG1000 for the equivalent of a single leg by cab. Rip-offs on any form of transport are very rare.

If you're not up for the sardine-can mode of travel – or if you want to go somewhere off the main shared-taxi routes – it's possible to hire a taxi for your own exclusive use: a so-called **déplacement**. Simply hail any empty taxi and negotiate a price, though be aware that you'll have to bargain ruthlessly – from La Ville to Kipé and other nearby suburbs shouldn't cost more than FG15,000.

Accommodation

Accommodation options in Conakry are very limited if you're on a tight budget: there are no **hostels**, and anything under FG50,000, even for a single room, is likely to serve as an informal brothel, and be quite grungy and unreliable in terms of electricity and water. Conakry does, however, have an increasing number of mid-range and expensive **hotels**; don't be afraid to negotiate the price at any of these places. If you don't mind getting into the city by boat, you could in theory stay on the Îles de Los (see p.599).

City centre (La Ville)
The following places are marked on the map on p.596.

Centrale next to the *Patisserie Centrale*, off av de la République ☎63.35.18.88 or 64.21.62.60. Fairly clean and comfortable French-run hotel in a very central location with large, fully equipped rooms, some of which have balconies. Good value for money. ❺

Galaxie 5ème av, near l'UGAR ☎60.21.22.33 ✉hotelgalaxie.gn@yahoo.fr. Well-furnished, efficiently-run spot with clean and airy rooms with a/c and satellite TV and a good restaurant just next door – all in a central location and for a comparatively low price. ❹

Hôtel du Niger 6th blvd ☎30.41.41.30. Just paces from the Marché de Niger, you couldn't be any more in the thick of chaotic Conakry. The frequent visitors at this *hôtel de passage* mean the rooms are quite weathered, but they are clean enough for a night's stay. ❷

🏃 **Le Rocher** Sandervalia ☎30.41.37.04 or 64.43.55.55 ✉hotel_rocher@yahoo .fr. This sparkling *luxe* hotel near the city museum easily holds its own against the *Novotel*: it's much smaller, less of an anonymous business hub, the service is impeccable and the dozen-odd a/c rooms are always very clean. There's an excellent bar and restaurant, and Internet connections in every room. ❼

Maison d'Accueil rte de Niger ☎30.34.36.55. For that authentic bordello-ish feel, without being in a red-light establishment, check out this large Christian mission, a run-down place offering some of the cheapest rooms in the

centre. Ask for private facilities at all possible. ❸

🏃 **Novotel Grand Hôtel de l'Indépendance** Boulbinet ☎30.41.50.21 or 30.41.50.22 ⓦwww.novotel.com. Though quite dated in decor and more frayed than the other upmarket options, this still reigns as Conakry's top hotel, with more than 200 rooms, suites and apartments. Located a bit out of the way at the peninsula's south-western tip, it's well insulated from Conakry's fickle utility cuts and has superb views out to the islands, plus Wi-Fi, two restaurants, a pool, souvenir shop and an Avis outlet. All credit cards accepted. ❽

Petit Bateau Épi Nord, Port de Plaisance ☎63.40.61.06 or 63.40.62.75 ⓦwww .hotelpetitbateau.net. Clean, well-equipped hotel out on the groin, and famous for its superb seafood restaurant and yacht club. Can be a bit of a pain to reach if you don't have your own transport. Visa accepted. ❺

Riviera Royale on the north side of the causeway, on the way into the Ville district from the peninsula ☎64.22.33.04 or 30.43.24.15 ⓦwww.rivieraroyalhotel.com. Lebanese-owned luxury establishment featuring mostly plain, well-appointed rooms with all you need, including Wi-Fi. There's an airy terrace bar, tennis courts, pool and sauna, plus a popular nightclub. ❼

Sacha 5th av, Manquepas ☎30.43.22.49 or 60.48.48.48. Brand-new hotel with a mirrored facade and stylish, if slightly stuffy, rooms, some of which have balconies (but not much of a view). Ask for one of the larger suites, which only cost a few euros more. ❻

Out of the centre

The following places are marked on the map on p.602.

Camayenne Camayenne ☎64.31.30.31 🌐www
.camayenne.net. Set right by the sea, the hundred or so darkish rooms here are clean and some have spacious balconies with good views. There is every facility you'd expect, including pool, bar, gym and tennis courts, though the restaurant doesn't compare to those at the other high-end hotels. Car and private pirogue rental available. All cards accepted. ❼

César Taouyah ☎30.22.10.67 or 60.22.10.67 ✉hotel_cesar@yahoo.fr. Small and cheap Italian-run hotel with comfy rooms and a friendly atmosphere. ❸

Kaporo Beach Kaporo ☎30.52.79.78. Located on a fine site at the water's edge (though with sadly no "beach" to speak of), the rooms here are clean and the restaurant food not bad. ❹

Kipé Tourisme Kipé ☎60.22.08.99 or 60.37.20.50 ✉ktourismeh@yahoo.fr. A few minutes from the airport, this residence is surprisingly clean and well-organized for the area. A two-storey affair set about a tiled courtyard, it tends to attract overseas workers who sign on for long-term stays, but there are almost always a few rooms available. ❸

🏃 **L'Eau Vive** just off the main road in Nongo (turn left after the gendarmerie) ☎60.54.73.41. See "Restaurants: out of the centre", p.604. ❺

Mariador Palace Ratoma ☎60.23.47.28 or 60.26.02.32 🌐www.leshotelsmariador.com. The nicest and largest of the *Mariador* properties, down on the rocky shore and decorated with local artisan crafts. Rooms are clean, with fridge, satellite TV and views, either onto the ocean or across the bay. There are also tennis facilities, a pool and a pretty terrace, but give the restaurant a miss. Power cuts are not uncommon, even at this price. All cards accepted. ❻

Mariador Park Taouyah, off the Carrefour Transit ☎30.22.97.40 or 60.26.06.20 🌐www
.leshotelsmariador.com. This mid-level hotel is slightly more basic than the other two *Mariador* properties, but also a little cheaper and still comfortable enough. ❺

Mixte Kipé ☎64.31.22.51. Mixed it certainly is, a dingy flophouse but adequate in a pinch.

If you're lucky, electricity might make a rare appearance. ❹

Océan Ratoma ☎30.22.66.85 or 62.66.32.38 🌐www.galion-conakry.com. While the building feels a bit forgotten, the spacious stucco rooms with fan or a/c are clean, the lobby is airy and the excellent Cameroonian garden restaurant and pool look right onto the ocean. ❹

🏃 **Pension Ghussein** Ratoma ☎60.59.38.03 or 64.29.44.84. A homey, kitschy old guesthouse run by a charming lady from Avignon. Rooms can get musty, but they're very clean and well-maintained, and there is a pretty terrace looking straight out to sea. Breakfast included. ❺

Pension La Maison Blanche Kipé, signposted off rte de Donka ☎64.61.66.74. Quiet, well-priced place off the main road with acceptable, if worn, rooms without a/c that are only occasionally sold by the hour. ❷

Pension Les Palmiers Ratoma ☎30.42.11.03. Quiet place right on the water with very friendly service and great views. The s/c rooms have TV. ❸

Plein Sud Corniche Sud, Matam ☎60.20.35.35 ✉pleinsudguinee@yahoo.fr. See "Restaurants: out of the centre", p.604. ❹

President Motel route de Donka in ☎60.45.87.86. Possibly the cheapest place to stay in Conakry comes with a catch: it's a 24-hour open house for local military, police and big men and their female companions. Overnighters must check in after 11pm and leave by 8am. Reception is frosty, but at €6 a night it's hard to complain. Restaurant serves cheap *brochettes*. ❶

🏃 **Résidence Fleurie** Coléah ☎64.40.17.15. Excellent choice that is quite well located near several good restaurants and a block from the city's main park. This low-priced guesthouse has a country-house feel to it with several cushioned sitting rooms crammed with statues, flowers and portraits – the late owner was a prominent Guinean diplomat. ❹

Taady Club Tady, on the road to Lambaye ☎60.55.71.69 or 60.21.31.69 🌐www
.hoteltaadyclub.com. Nearly 20km from the town centre, this one-time booming sports and leisure centre is long past its heyday. Rooms are mostly quite clean, well furnished and come in various sizes, but the swimming pool, restaurant and bar are rather sad sights. ❻

The City

Conakry doesn't have much to offer in terms of sightseeing, and despite being surrounded by ocean, most of the shore is inaccessible. The only stretch of coast with any pretensions at being a **beach** is at **Rogbané**, about 10km up the peninsula

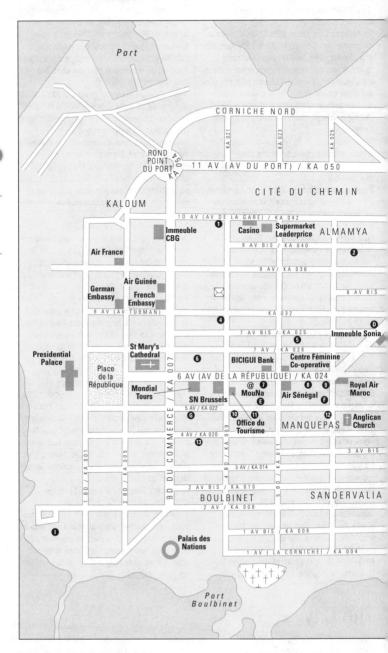

CENTRAL CONAKRY LA VILLE

0   200 m

9 BD

10 BD

11 BD

12 AV

ROUTE DU NIGER / KA 080

BD TELLI DIALLO

Ⓒ

10 BD

10 BD BIS

11 BD

BICIGUI Bank

Marché du Niger

■ **Total**

KA 036

❸

Sogel

KA 031

9 BD / KA 033

8 BD

KA 033

Hospital Ignace Deen

⓮

Ⓗ

CORNICHE SUD

National Museum

⓯

N

ACCOMMODATION	
Centrale	F
Galaxie	G
Hôtel du Niger	D
Le Rocher	H
Maison d'Accueil	C
Novotel	I
Petit Bateau	A
Riviera Royale	B
Sacha	E

RESTAURANTS, CAFÉS, CLUBS & BARS	
Africana	14
Bembeya Jazz	4
Chelsea	8
Fourchette Magique	12
Gentilhommière	2
Joy	11
L'Atlantis	B
La Gondole	7
Le Cédre	5
Le Conakry	13
Le Damier	3
Le Mondial	6
Le Soft	10
Patisserie Centrale	9
Petit Bateau	A
Point Zero	1
Timis	15

from the city centre, which has been cleared by local youths to provide an area for beach football – though the sand isn't very clean and some stretches are obstructed by jagged rocks. Nevertheless, it's a good place to people-watch and enjoy the sunset (beach entry FG2000) and there's a pleasant terrace bar-restaurant. For the area's best beaches, head out to the Îles de Los (see opposite) or up to Bel Air, north of Boffa (see p.609).

You could spend an unexceptional half-hour or so at the city's **National Museum** (Tues–Sun 9am–5.30pm; FG5000; ☏30.41.50.60), in the Sandervalia quarter off the Corniche Sud. The single-roomed permanent collection consists of masks and other carvings, musical instruments, a few weapons and a small traditional pirogue. The "temporary collection" hasn't manifested itself in over a decade. In the yard, you can admire a few colonial statues and monuments and a reconstruction of the hut of explorer Olivier de Sanderval, who once lived in some of the museum buildings. Several museum annexe rooms display assorted costumes, masks and jewellery, though how much this part of the museum is a public collection and how much a showroom can be gauged by how readily items are offered to you for sale. There is also a small, openly commercial workshop next door which produces leather chests and Tuareg silver and jewellery.

Other activities in the town centre include a visit to the lovely **Cathédrale Ste-Marie**, located just next to the current **Palais Présidentiel**, and a gawk at the once-grand **Palais des Nations**, further south towards the *Novotel*, where the president was pinned down for a while in 1996 until it was shelled by soldiers demanding pay increases and he negotiated his release. Outside of the Ville district, traverse the causeway to make like the locals and enjoy a stroll through the lush **Jardin 2 Octobre**, accessible via either Corniche Nord or Corniche Sud just before the entrance to town. Further northeast, past the **Pont du 8 Novembre** (also known as Pont des Martires on account of the revolutionaries hanged from the bridge in 1990), have a walk around (and delicately enquire about entrance to) the elephantine, Saudi-financed **Grand Mosquée**, located along the Autoroute in Camayenne; Sekou Touré's mausoleum is in the grounds. Finally, spend an hour or two relaxing in the breeze in the **Botanical Gardens**, located a few minutes' walk south of the mosque on the Route de Donka.

Shopping and markets

Conakry is a great place for **shopping**. If your haggling is up to snuff, you can get some very good deals on African artifacts – much cheaper than in Dakar or Bamako. Don't fail to rise to the challenge of a stroll around the infamous, chaotic and almost unbearably crowded **Marché de Madina**, some 4km up the peninsula from the causeway, where you can buy anything from fine African fabrics to CDs, carvings, clothes and food. The market is a vast maze of narrow alleyways lined by makeshift market stalls, always full of people and ringing with the noise of beeping cars, shouting drivers, screaming vendors and dickering customers. Madina used to be almost a no-go area due to its high crime rate, and while the police stationed everywhere have made it a bit safer, thieves still filter the area. Be sure to keep money and possessions secure, don't bring any big bags and be cautious of bogus street vendors aiming to distract and rob you; ideally, visit the market with a local. To get to Madina, catch a shared taxi on the "Autoroute" route.

Just across the peninsula from Marché de Madina, in Camayenne, several stalls opposite the *Hôtel Camayenne* offer a good selection of **masks** and carvings; there is a smaller but equally representative collection at a few kiosks located up along the Autoroute just before you reach Kipé. For **drums** and other musical instruments you can try the drum maker on the main road in Coléah, near Camayenne, or contact the Centre Culturel Franco-Guinéen (see p.607) for advice.

In La Ville, you'll find several trendy **boutiques** selling Western clothes and shoes at high prices, and a few **arts and crafts** stalls. For CDs and DVDs, La Ville's

Marché du Niger is less frenetic than Madina, but still a very in-your-face experience where a robust attitude and reasonably good French are essential. You can buy almost anything here, from every kind of local product and standard import, to fancy foreign foods, mobile phones and crafts.

Lastly, for colourful **batik cloth**, check out what's on offer at the **Centre d'Appui à l'Autopromotion Féminine** cooperative, behind the bank at av de la République and 5ème bd. It's all good, though prices here tend to be fixed.

The Îles de Los

Just a few kilometres offshore from Conakry, the **Îles de Los** are well worth a visit and have become quite a magnet, especially at weekends, when half the expat community of Conakry seems to head out to Île Roume to kick back in weekend homes and sprawl out on the beach.

The islands have a colourful past: they were inhabited from the earliest times by idol-worshipping farmers, which earned them the Portuguese map label "*Idolos*", transmuted by the French into Îles de Los. Roume itself – a lavishly picturesque pair of jungle-swathed hillocks joined by a sandy-shored isthmus – was once a slaving base, the site of the execution in 1850 of the notorious slaver Crawford, whose name the island carried until the end of the nineteenth century. Tales of Crawford's buried loot are supposed to have inspired Robert Louis Stevenson's *Treasure Island*.

There are various ways of **getting to the islands**. The easiest and most hassle-free method is to hire pirogues through Conakry's major hotels, including the *Novotel* or *Camayenne*, though these run pricey: the latter does a comfy trip to Soro and Roume for FG200,000, including a seafood lunch. Somewhat cheaper are the tourist agencies in town,

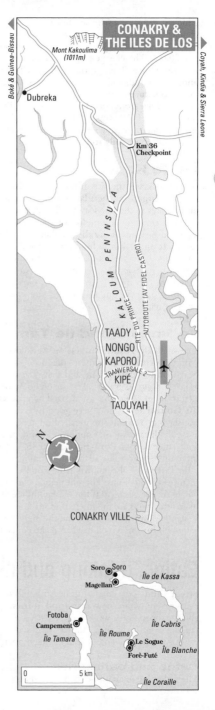

which organize trips for around FG150,000. Cheaper still is to charter a pirogue yourself, at Port Boulbinet, not far from the *Novotel*. The price will depend greatly on your negotiating skills, but you should be able to get a boat for a full day for FG100,000. The cheapest option of all is to use the **public pirogue** services from Port Boulbinet, although travel by these is usually slower, since services don't leave until they're full, while massive overcrowding and absence of safety measures make for a sometimes uncomfortable and potentially dangerous little voyage. Public pirogues leave from Port Boulbinet and the *Petit Bateau* port to Soro village on Île de Kassa (about FG1500 per person), and to Île Roume (FG2000). On Sundays there are also usually pirogue services to Soro beach (FG2000) on Île de Kassa. There's also at least one boat daily to Fotoba on Île Tamara (FG2000).

Île de Kassa

Île de Kassa is the site of the sandy, palm-fringed **Soro beach** (FG1000 access fee), the largest on the islands, though its popularity means that it gets crowded on Sundays in the dry season – beware of thieves scouring the beach. Spending a few days on eight-kilometre-long Kassa gives you the opportunity to explore the secluded beaches along the west shore, and the settlements which dot its lovely forests. It only takes an hour or so to walk to **Kassa village** from Soro beach and you're likely to see monkeys and birds along the way. There are also a couple of **hotels** here: *Soro* (❷; open dry season only) and, a little further away, the swanky *Magellan*, run by the owners of *L'Océan* in Conakry (☎30.42.20.22 ⓦ www .galion-conakry.com ❺), where you can kick back by the pool and arrange pirogue trips.

Île Roume and Île Tamara

The small **Île Roume** is best on weekdays, when it's very quiet. A favoured spot with the expat community, it's the most expensive island to visit, with a long, public beach on the north shore and pricey accommodation on the south shore at the *Hôtel le Sogue* (☎60.21.59.59 or 66.66.38.68 ⓦ www.lesogue.com ❹; open early Oct to June), which has good-sized bungalows, its own, sheltered and private **Plage du Gouverneur** and a very good fish restaurant (Fri–Sun; reserve ahead if you're not staying). You can also usually find inexpensive accommodation in private homes – ask the locals. Another option is joining one of the short-term classes at the drum and dance school **Forè-Foté** (☎30.45.12.55 ⓦ www.fore-fote.com) where they often offer good-value ad-hoc accommodation in their ten-room villa.

Île Tamara – also known as Île Fotoba – used to be a penal colony and was for many years off-limits. The old penitentiary near Fotoba village is worth visiting if you're on the island, as is the old lighthouse, but as on Roume and Île de Kassa, the main attractions are the forests and seashore. There's no hotel on Tamara but there is a *campement* if you want to spend the night, and private house rentals are possible too – though for this, you'll need to make contact with an expat in town.

Eating, drinking and nightlife

Street food – the likes of grilled fish, plantains and huge plates of rice – is served everywhere, while new **fast-food joints**, specializing in *chawarma*, burgers and chicken, open every week. Conakry has a good selection of proper **restaurants**, too, ranging from fairly cheap, simple meat-and-rice *gargotes* to others which serve quite extensive European and African menus, though some of these can be very overpriced.

Cafés and patisseries

The following establishments are keyed on the maps on p.596 and p.602.

Café Folle's at MouNa at the MouNainternet café, av de la République, La Ville. This hangout serves pricey pizzas, ice cream and sodas, and is one of the town's most popular pick-up spots for local students.

Chelsea av de la République. Down the road from *MouNa*, this new café has uninspiring minimalist decor, but delicious, if pricey, offerings, including smoothies, good coffee, various sandwiches, buttery ice cream and tasty breakfast omelettes.

Domino Boulangerie Domino, Coléah. Excellent fresh bread, pastries and cakes served 24/7.

🏃 Le Damier opposite Marché Niger ⓦwww .damier-conakry.com (daytime only).

French-run patisserie specializing in rich homemade pastries, chocolates and natural juices. Sat mornings, the sumptuous FG95,000 brunch is a huge buffet spread, including suckling pig, paella and salads.

Le Mondial behind av de la République, La Ville. Patisserie-restaurant serving snacks, cakes and light meals all day. A good place to duck in and take a break from the action.

Pâtisserie Centrale av de la République, city centre. Something of a Conakry landmark and a cult address with expats, this serves great butter croissants and a good selection of snacks, cakes and ice cream, as well as tasty pizza.

Restaurants

City-centre

The following places are marked on the map on pp.596–597.

🏃 Africana off 7ème bd, behind the Anglican church. Quiet, friendly, inexpensive and unassuming place that serves the best *poulet yassa* in town, plus other excellent African specials including *thié-bou-gap* and *maganyi*. If you come around lunchtime, you may be treated to live *kora* music. Daily specials around FG12,000.

Le Cédre 7ème av bis, Almamya. Small, intimate Lebanese restaurant, popular with expats at lunchtime, with excellent steak dishes – the *Chateaubriand* and mushroom cream are two of the best.

Le Conakry 4ème av, by the Ministry of Finance (closed Sun). Venerable, Guinean business-class restaurant, with a French chef at lunchtime, house menu (FG8000), and à la carte (dishes FG6000-plus).

🏃 Gentilhommière 9ème av bis, Almamya. Classy, cheap and tasty African food with good service – a popular stop for extended business lunches, but casual enough for travellers and NGOs.

Joy 5ème av, Manquepas. Korean-run, Chinese restaurant featuring steak, chicken and vegetable dishes at lunch and dinner (from FG20,000). A little grubby but adequate.

La Gondole av de la République. Very expensive patisserie, with the best ice cream in town, shakes and freshly brewed coffee. There's also a pizza and *chawarma* place attached.

Le Soft 5ème av, Manquepas. Popular *gargote* serving two or three tasty African main dishes each day, including *poulet yassa* and *djem bojan*.

🏃 Petit Bateau at the *Petit Bateau* hotel, Port de Plaisance. Expensive restaurant overlooking the sea, popular with well-to-do

Guineans. Great salads, marinated steaks, grilled lobster and shrimp, off the *carte* (mains from FG15,000).

Point Zéro 10ème av, just south of the Rond Point du Port. Casual spot with a front patio for sinking a few beers and a small menu of Guinean food – fish dishes and *brochettes*. The food could be better, but it couldn't be any cheaper. Popular with local harbour employees.

Out of the centre

Al Forno Camayenne. Crêpes and very good pizzas. Meals from FG10,000 to FG30,000.

Belvédère Dixinn, near the Rond Point Bellevue (Sun–Fri 2pm–1am, Sat 2pm–3.30am). This large, landmark Middle Eastern restaurant is a big hit with Tunisian wedding receptions. Set right near the coast, it features plastic tables set under a breezy, covered bandstand, though the food – basic meat and pizza dishes for around FG30,000 – isn't as flashy as the surroundings. Occasional live music.

Casa Bella in Taouyah. Those who manage to locate this hard-to-find Lebanese *meze* spot are rewarded with an excellent breezy setting right at the water. The food includes Middle Eastern staples such as hummus and dolma, as well as a number of surprisingly good Mexican dishes. It's also a great place to smoke sheesha – water pipe.

Chez Mame Diarra Bousso Taouyah. One of the cheapest and best Senegalese *gargotes* in town, with gigantic plates of *riz gras* or *yassa poulet* for FG4000. Also serves delicious home-made *bissap* sorrel juice. Highly recommended.

🏃 Hanoi Corniche du Sud in Coléah. Much cheaper than the similar *Indochine*, this great-value place serves super Vietnamese vegetarian and meat dishes from FG30,000. Be sure to try the *nems*, mouthwatering fried spring rolls.

GREATER CONAKRY

0   2 km

RESTAURANTS, CAFÉS, BARS & CLUBS

3615	20
Al Forno	19
Albatros	15
Belvédère	16
Calebasse Plus	9
Casa Bella	14
Chez Mame Diarra Bousso	8
Crisber	2
Domino Boulangerie	22
Hanoi	26
Indochine	13
Jardins de Guinée	24
KSK	5
L'Oxygène	6
La Paillote	23
Le Cheval	7
Le Loft	17
L'Eau Vive	C
Le Waffou	1
Les Copains d'Abord	11 & 21
Nelson	3
Petit Paris	25
Plein Sud	N
Rogbané Plage	12
Taj Mahal	18
Tally	10
Wakili Guinée	4
Wil Planète	27

ACCOMMODATION

Camayenne	O
César	M
Kaporo Beach	B
Kipé Tourisme	E
L'Eau Vive	C
Les Palmiers	I
Mariador Palace	K
Mariador Park	L
Mixte	D
Motel Président	G
Océan	H
Pension Ghussein	J
Pension La Maision Blanche	F
Plein Sud	N
Résidence Fleurie	P
Taady Club	A

N

ATLANTIC OCEAN

Guinea-Bissau Embassy
ROND POINT BELLEVUE

Sierra Leone Embassy

BD. BELLEVUE

CARREFOUR DIXINN

DIXINN

RTE DONKA

Stade Dixinn

CAMAYENNE

AUTOROU

Marché Madina

MADINA

CORNICHE SUD

RTE NATIONALE

DONKA

DONKA

Hôpital Donka

CORNICHE NORD

O
17
18

Grande Mosque   Cyber Domino

19   Jardin Botanique

COLÉAH

@ 20 21
22

DOMINO

23

25 P 24

PONT DU 8 NOVEMBRE

27   26

ROND POINT 2000

Palais du Peuple

Jardin 2 Octobre

British Embassy

Centre Culturel Franco-Guinéen

◄ Ville (city centre)

7

7.1 | GUINEA

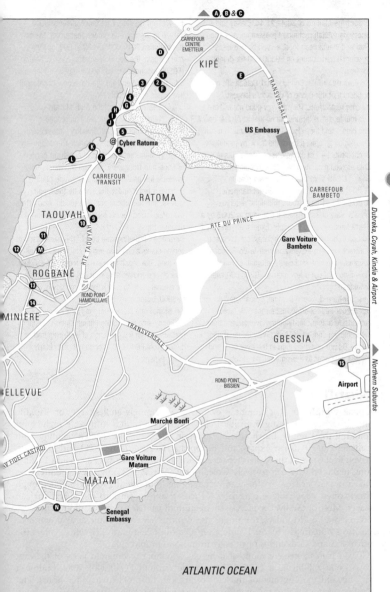

KIPÉ

Ⓓ

① ②
Ⓕ

③

④
⑥

Ⓗ
Ⓙ

⑤

@ **Cyber Ratoma**

Ⓚ

Ⓛ

⑦

CARREFOUR TRANSIT

RATOMA

Ⓔ

TRANSVERSALE 2

US Embassy

CARREFOUR BAMBETO

⑧

TAOUYAH

⑩ ⑨

⑪

⑫ Ⓜ

ROGBANÉ

⑬

⑭

MINIÈRE

ROND POINT HAMDALLLAYE

RTE TAOUYAH

RTE DU PRINCE

Gare Voiture Bambeto

TRANSVERSALE 1

GBESSIA

ROND POINT BISSIEN

⑮

Airport

ELLEVUE

AV FIDEL CASTRO)

Marché Bonfi

Gare Voiture Matam

MATAM

Ⓝ

Senegal Embassy

ATLANTIC OCEAN

Indochine Minière ☎ 30.42.21.44. Classy and pricey pan-Asian restaurant presenting very good Thai and Vietnamese food, served by Guineans in oriental garb. Count on FG300,000 for dinner for two.

Jardins de Guinée Corniche Sud, Coléah. It's no accident that this is one of Conakry's longest-running restaurants. They do very good meals here – favourite dishes include the Roquefort *filet de boeuf* and crab – and they also bake great pizzas. You can dine out on an open patio at the back, by moonlight or candlelight – just as well, since power cuts in this area are common. Also has a late-opening bar.

L'Eau Vive just off the main road in Nongo (turn left after the gendarmerie) ☎ 60.54.73.41 (last orders midnight, reserve ahead). Very classy restaurant opened in 2007 by a Sierra Leonean–Dutch couple. Exquisitely-prepared European dishes – *gambas grillées*, bouillabaisse – attract Western expats and well-to-do Guinean couples. Excellent, and partly affordable, wine list. They also rent out a few rooms (FG240,000 with breakfast).

Les Copines d'Abord Domino, Coléah, next to *3615*. Low-key roadside restaurant with tables both inside and out for lingering over super-cheap fried chicken and fish dishes. Lively Guinean and salsa CDs are piped through in the evenings, and it's just next door to a simmering nightclub.

Le Waffou rte Kipé. Excellent Ivoirian seafood served in the open-air garden restaurant. Mains run between FG10,000 and FG30,000, or try a real bargain, the house speciality, *poisson Waffou* (FG8000), a grilled catch-of-the-day with fries and a tasty mustard and vinaigrette sauce. Occasional live music on Fri nights.

Plein Sud Corniche Sud, Matam (☎ 60.20.35.35 ✉ pleinsudguinee @yahoo.fr). One of outer Conakry's most alluring sites for a restaurant, this French-run, lodge-style establishment set about an ocean-front garden of cacti and frangipani. Though the meals tend towards the basic, it's also just a nice place to have a drink under the stars by the lapping waves, and has occasional live music. Also offers five good-sized rooms (FG65,000), and runs pirogue trips.

Rogbané Plage Rogbané beach. The bar-restaurant serves drinks along with fish or chicken plates all day long. The beach here is a bit rocky, but it's clean enough and always alive with lots of locals. Makes for a great place to watch the sun go down. Beers FG5000, beach entry FG2000.

Taj Mahal one block from the *Hôtel Camayenne* in Camayenne (closed Mon lunch). Indo-Pakistani restaurant with a wide range of well-prepared dishes from FG40,000, though not particularly spicy. Expensive drinks.

Nightlife

Conakry **nightlife** is as vibrant as ever, with a seemingly endless array of drinking and dance joints ranging from local clubs with local sounds to upscale night spots spinning the latest in hip-hop and Euro-pop, the latter places often teeming with Lebanese and Russian expats, and European and American NGO and UN staff. If you're staying in the Ville, there are plenty of downtown bars and clubs to fill a long night, while a trip to lively Coléah or Camayenne is only a few minutes' taxi ride away. Cover fees for clubs can vary, ranging from nothing to FG15,000, though this is often negotiable – especially for *fotés* trying to get into the purely African places. Most of the livelier places stay open until 6am at weekends, though they are often closed on Mondays. You might also want to have a go at the city's downtown **casino** (☎ 30.43.53.35), on 10ème av, in Cité du Chemin de Fer, which offers the usual slots and cards and is open daily from noon to midnight.

If you plan to make a night of it by club-hopping to different parts of the city, you're best off hiring a car for the evening (around FG50,000), since finding a taxi beyond the confines of the city centre can be problematic after hours. The roadblocks put up after midnight only occasionally become a frustration; keep a few FG1000 bills on hand to facilitate your passage through them and make sure you have your passport or other ID on hand.

Bars and clubs

The following **clubs and bars** are keyed on the maps on p.596 and p.602. Thursday to Sunday nights are invariably livelier than Monday to Wednesday. The atmosphere is usually genial, but occasionally quite boisterous – with a lot of very upfront solic-iting by strikingly decked-out prostitutes. **Live music performances** can happen almost anywhere, but there's more guarantee at the specific venues listed under "Live-music venues", below.

3615 (trente-six quinze) Domino, Coléah. The central dance floor at this *bar de passage* is surrounded by comfy red-leather couches, and popular with bling-happy Lebanese *commerçants* and their young Guinean arm-candy. Generally only fills up after 3am, when the DJs cue up the West African dance hits. Cover FG20,000.

Albatros Route Nationale, by the airport in Gbessia. Upmarket club, catering to a slightly older generation moving gently to salsa or Guinean rhythms – ministers, businessmen and the like tend to come here with their girlfriends (or, more rarely, their wives).

Calebasse Plus east of the *rond-point* in Taouyah. Lively, dimly-lit nightspot with leather divans and a terrace at the back. Features performances by local musicians several times a week.

Crisber Kipé. Until recently known as *Climax*, this is still one of Conakry's most popular venues. The large dance floor attracts fashionable Conakrois of all ages, with its hip-hop, ragga and *zouk*. Cover FG10,000.

KSK Ratoma. This large disco and decent restaurant was opened in 2007 by a group of Liberians and has rapidly become *the* spot for late-night partying. The DJs spin up-and-coming Guinean music and attract a good mix of customers while the plush VIP room upstairs attracts anyone who can afford the overpriced bottles of third-rate fizz. Cover FG30,000 or FG10,000 for women on weeknights.

La Paillote near Pont du 8 Novembre, Coléah. This was one of Guinea's most vibrant venues during the Sekou Touré era, and it now exudes nostalgia, with members of former star orchestras hanging out during the week in the early evening. Concerts are rare, but you can be sure of meeting old band members telling stories over a beer. Weekend nights, it reinvents itself as a happening club with a FG10,000 cover.

L'Atlantis at the *Riviera Royale* hotel, on the north side of the causeway, on the way into the Ville

district from the peninsula. Expensive and classy place with a good sound system, often patronized almost exclusively by wealthy Lebanese. Large dance floor.

Le Cheval at the Carrefour Transit in Taouyah. One of several clubs near this junction. Specializes in techno and hip-hop.

Le Loft Camayenne. Smallish, intimate bar with two small dance floors for locals strutting their stuff to Arab and Spanish hits as they gawk at the coterie of prostitutes checking themselves out in the mirrors. Beers FG10,000.

L'Oxygène Ratoma. Tiny but vibrant dancing place that's always packed at weekends. Live musicians occasionally play at the weekend.

Nelson Kipé. Large, established disco that now rivals the nearby *Crisber* in popularity, with a good atmosphere and a great mix of reggae, US and African music. Largely frequented by an older crowd.

Petit Paris Coléah. Crowded, sweaty, local – a wonderful *boîte* that gets packed with svelte Guinean twenty-somethings and the occasional *foté*. A seat in the central VIP circle gets you a good vantage point of the dance floor and videography behind it. Hosts occasional live-music events and also serves solid local-fish lunches from noon to 3pm. Cover usually FG25,000.

Tally Taouyah. Across the road from *Calebasse Plus*, this large dance spot plays mixed music for an almost exclusively African clientele. Cover around FG15,000.

Timis on the corner of Corniche Sud and 9th bd behind the museum in La Ville. Black lights, disco lights, Christmas lights – this place is well lit after midnight, when it becomes a last-ditch destination for men looking to score before sunrise.

Wil Planète Pont du 8 Novembre. This cosy nightclub, located across from the Franco-Guinean cultural centre, looks a bit ragged but remains quite popular with Conakry's younger set. Sofa-lined alcoves run around the small dance floor.

Live-music venues

While Guinea may be famous for its music, Conakry still suffers from a lack of decent **live-performance venues**, and you might get the sense that Guinean bands exist only to rehearse endlessly without actually performing. But if you have patience (and time), you'll find Conakry does offer some rare concert and club performances by some of the country's best groups. Most of the better spots are concentrated out in **Taouyah, Ratoma and Kipé**, where live shows generally get going around midnight, and they can last well into the early morning (see listings, above). To find out where the famous Ballets Africains are currently practising – their open rehearsals of drumming and dancing are legendary – contact Isto Keyra at the **Agence Guinéenne des Spectacles**, just inside the museum. Conakry is also home to dozens of percussion and dancing schools, called **maisons de jeunes**, dotted around in various locations – for information about these, contact Saido Dioubaté at the **Ministère de la Jeunesse**, Corniche Nord (on the north side of La Ville, by the start of the Épi Nord breakwater). And on many Friday evenings after 9pm, **local groups** perform on the small square across from the BICIGUI bank on av de la République in downtown Ville.

Bembeya Jazz on the corner of av Tubman and 4ème bd, Ville. Long-established mirrored club with a central raised stage which still hosts regular performances by traditional Guinean bands. The crowd is usually a mix of tourists, expats and prostitutes, as well as many local musicians. Cover FG25,000.

Centre Culturel Franco-Guinéen pl Sory Kandia Kouyaté, just north of the city centre near Pont du 8 Novembre. One of the city's most interesting places for live music, this lively meeting-point was completely renovated, expanded and modernized in 2007. Weekly concerts attract crowds of young people to see Guinean and foreign artists.

Fourchette Magique 5ème bd, Ville (closed Mon & Tues). Downtown dinner-time resto-bar best known for its Guinean weekend house band. The sister club out in Taouyah is larger and tends to be a bit livelier, and also serves lunch at the weekend.

Les Copains d'Abord Taouyah. Spacious open-air bar-restaurant (good pizzas) with loud, and often trashy, live music at weekends, headlined by their traditional bands. Busy with expats and tourist-hunting prostitutes.

Palais du Peuple just north of the city centre on the causeway. This huge, Chinese-built edifice is Conakry's most famous and prestigious special-event venue. Though it's a rather soulless affair, all Guinea's main music events, including perform-ances by the country's biggest stars – plus any major festivals – tend to be put on here. Check the radio and posters around town for announcements.

Stade Dixinn Camayenne/Dixinn. The capital's major sporting venue hosts occasional big concerts and festivals. Check *Djeli* magazine, posters and the radio for announcements, or inquire with the tourist office.

Wakili Guinée Ratoma. This local cultural centre features folk music, drumming groups and theatre performances, and has a small dance club.

Conakry live

"I spent my six days in Conakry out dancing every night, and by the time I left the music had inspired me to stay for another week of a drumming and dancing class out on the Îles. Live music in the capital isn't easy to find, but don't be shy of talking to DJs or musicians you see at clubs or bars – they're super open to talking to anyone, and no one will know better where things are going down."

Sadie Rose Mank, USA

Listings

Airlines Unless otherwise noted, the following are all clustered along av de la République in La Ville: Air France, 2ème bd and 9ème av ☏30.43.10.46; Air Guinée ☏30.43.14.53; Air Ivoire ☏64.21.87.17; Air Sénégal, Imm Sonia, rte du Niger ☏64.31.48.31; Bellview ☏30.43.33.40; Gambia Airways, opposite Imm CBG, bd du Commerce ☏30.44.30.00; Ghana Airways ☏30.45.48.13; Nigeria Airways ☏30.44.40.82; Royal Air Maroc, Imm Sonia, rte du Niger ☏30.43.11.10; Slok-Air ☏64.53.72.66; Brussels Airlines ☏30.45.10.61; West Coast Airlines ☏30.45.38.01.

American Express No representative. The *Novotel* may help.

Banks and money-changing The reason-ably efficient BICIGUI, on av de la République (Mon–Thurs 8.30am–12.30pm & 2.30–4.30pm, Fri 8.30am–12pm; ☏30.41.45.15), is the main bank for foreign exchange, and the only one with an ATM (maximum withdrawal FG400,000). They no longer accept traveller's cheques. Ecobank, just across the street, has similar hours but is also open Sat. You'll get a somewhat better rate on the black market at Madina or Niger markets or along av de la République – moneychangers will approach you constantly in all these places, but shop around at a few spots to make sure you're getting the best rate.

Book and map shops The best selection of French books is at Maison des Livres, just east of Pont du 8 Novembre in Coléah. L'Harmattan, 7ème av and 5ème bd, La Ville, has French-language African history, politics and sociology titles, while Soguidip, 4ème av, La Ville, has some books and magazines in French and a few in English. Papeterie Centrale, 8ème av, sells stationery supplies and maps. All are open Mon 9am–5pm or 6pm. Harmattan is also open Sat 9.30am–3pm.

Car rental Expect to pay around a minimum of FG300,000 for a standard car, and FG400,000 per day for a 4x4, including driver but excluding fuel. You can rent vehicles at the Hertz outlet on av de la République (☏30.43.07.45 ✉sashertz_conakry @yahoo.fr) and at Avis at the *Novotel* (☏30.41.15.15 ✉avisg@sotelgui.net.gn), or at *À Tout Service* at the *Hôtel Camayenne* (☏64.31.30.31 ✉mail atout@afribone.net.gn). Alternatively, you can always rent informally with drivers waiting along av de la République, but you won't get a much better deal. You always have to hire a driver along with the car – perhaps just as well, given the state of the roads.

CDs Guinea is West Africa's pirate CD capital, though you'll want to listen before purchasing anything to make sure you're getting what you want (and what the label says). The Marché du Niger is the best spot to pick up CDs of the most popular Guinean and other African groups, along with pirated DVDs of Hollywood movies. The vendor at Taouyah junction also has a good variety of music on offer, while most of the stalls in town specialize in pirated CDs of the latest R&B and hip-hop. Pirated CDs should cost around FG10,000, while original versions – much harder to find – can be picked up for FG15,000 and up.

Cinemas Cinema-going was never anything big in Guinea, and it's nearly nonexistent as a cultural activity today. Your best bet is the Centre Culturel Franco-Guinéen, pl Sory Kandia Kouyaté, for showings of European (particularly French) and African films. The Cinéma Mimou, near the Marché Bonfi in Matam, and Cinéma Rogbané, near Taouyah junction, both screen Bollywood and Hollywood films, though the latter is often closed. Entrance at both is FG5000.

Crafts and curios The city's top-end hotels usually have a selection, but they're always more expensive than you can find if you hunt around a bit. In addition to the markets, check out 4ème bd between av de la République and av de la Gare, near the post office as well as the craft stall in Camayenne. Also see "Shopping and markets", p.598.

Cultural centres The newly-renovated Centre Culturel Franco-Guinéen, pl Sory Kandia Kouyaté (☏64.29.50.53 ✇www.ccfg-conakry.org), just north of the city centre, hosts exhibitions, theatrical and music events, and also has Internet access and serves coffee, sandwiches and soft drinks during the day.

Embassies and consulates Cape Verde, Minière ☏30.44.42.75; Côte d'Ivoire, bd du Commerce, La Ville ☏30.45.10.82; France, bd du Commerce, entry on 8ème av, La Ville ☏30.47.10.00 ✇www .ambafrance-gn.org (also issues visas for Burkina and Mauritania); Germany, 2ème bd, La Ville ☏30.41.15.06 ✇www.conakry.diplo.de; Ghana, Matam ☏30.40.95.60; Guinea-Bissau, rte de Donka ☏30.41.21.36; Mali, Matam, between the Autoroute and rte de Niger, after the Total station ☏30.42.32.32; Morocco, Villa 12, Cité des Nations, La Ville ☏30.41.36.86; Nigeria, Corniche Sud, Coléah ☏30.41.16.81; Senegal, Corniche Sud, Coléah ☏30.41.44.13; Sierra Leone, Bellevue ☏30.44.50.99; Togo, Matam ☏30.46.47.72; UK, Corniche Sud, by the Pont du 8 Novembre ☏63.35.53.29 ✉britcon.oury@biasy .net; USA, Transversale 2, Ratoma, near the *gare voiture* Bambeto ☏30.42.08.61 or 30.42.08.62 ✇conakry.usembassy.gov.

Internet access Internet cafés have sprung up all over town, and connections are now reasonably fast in most places. In the centre, the best spot is undoubtedly MouNainternet, av de la République, with scores of super-fast PCs (FG5000/hr), printers, CD burners, photo-card readers, international phone lines, fax service, a photocopier and a small café and restaurant. It's open 24 hours, and prices drop by half after 11pm. Outside of town, particularly recommended are Cyber Ratoma, on the Route de Donka in Ratoma (Mon–Fri 9am–10pm, Sat 11.30am–10pm, Sun 12.30am–10pm; FG6000/hr) and Cyber Domino at the Marché Domino, Coléah (daily 10am–10pm; FG4000/hr).

Medical treatment Conakry's ambulance service is on ☏30.41.15.00 but in an emergency you're probably best off making your own way straight to: Hôpital Ambrose Paré in Dixinn (☏30.21.13.20); Hôpital Ignace Deen in La Ville (☏30.41.20.34, 30.44.20.53, 30.41.43.36 or 30.44.20.78); or the public Hôpital Donka, in Donka (☏30.44.19.33). Clinique Pasteur, 5ème bd at 5ème av (☏30.74.75.76), has a good reputation. For the most up-to-date information on doctors and medical services in the city, contact either the French or US embassy.

Pharmacies Parts of Conakry seem to have a pharmacy on nearly every block, though you won't easily find an English-speaking pharmacist. In theory, all pharmacies post a list outside of the *pharmacies de garde* (the out-of-hours pharmacy rota).

Photography Digital photos can be downloaded and burned at MouNainternet (see above). There are photo labs all over town for developing print film; try the central one on av de la République, which also repairs cameras.

Post The main PTT (Mon–Thurs 9am–5pm, Fri 9am–2pm) is just off the av de la République in La Ville. Poste restante is neither very secure nor organized, so avoid having anything of value sent to you by post. DHL (ⓣ64.40.00.20) is centrally located at av de la République and 4ème bd. For Federal Express, contact Saga Express (ⓣ30.29.74.22), 4ème bd and 9ème bis av, La Ville.

Supermarkets The big ones are Superbobo, rte de Donka, Camayenne (which sells English-language newspapers and magazines); A-Z Supermarket, Bellevue, next to the Sierra Leone embassy; and Leaderprice, on 5ème bd in Almamya in La Ville. While all of these carry most Western goods, they are patronized by expats and can be quite pricey. You can find similar items at better prices in local Guinean kiosks.

Telephones The cheapest places to make domestic calls are the tin *télécentre* kiosks on street corners all around the city. These charge FG500–700 to call a Conakry number, depending on the network. For international calls, try MouNainternet (FG1000–1500/min to Europe or the US).

Travel agents Airline offices (see p.607) often also act as general travel agents. One of the most reliable and best-organized travel agents is Mondial Tours, on av de la République in La Ville (ⓣ30.43.35.50 or 60.21.35.58 ⓦwww.mondialtours.net), who book tickets, organize car rental, and run interesting tours into the interior. Other agents worth trying include Karou Voyages, av de la République, La Ville (ⓣ30.41.50.21 ⓔkarouvoyagegn2003 @yahoo.com), who specialize in flight bookings; Dunia Voyages, av de la République, La Ville (ⓣ30.45.48.48 ⓔduniavoyages@yahoo.fr), who operate some tours inland; and Guinée Voyages (ⓣ30.45.19.92 or 30.45.24.35).

Visa extensions FG85,000 for three months; available from the Direction Nationale Police Aire et Frontières (ⓣ30.41.13.39) near the Marché Domino in Coléah.

Around Conakry

A new road out of Conakry, on the north side of the peninsula, avoiding the often congested road up to the city-limits checkpoint at **Km36**, now facilitates visits to Guinea's Atlantic coast, known locally as **Guinée Maritime**.

Dubréka and the Cascades de la Soumba

The closest separate town to Conakry is **DUBRÉKA**, home town of President Conté; you could even avoid Conakry entirely and head here straight from the airport. The town is surrounded by mangrove swamps, which you can visit on motorized pirogues, available for hire (FG200,000) at the port – though you'll have to bargain hard. You can also negotiate pirogue rental to visit the **Baie de la Sangareah**, which has dolphins, crocodiles, migrating birds and a few good beaches. The cheapest overnights in Dubréka are the cramped rooms at *Chez Eva* (ⓣ64.42.57.88 ❷), with fans but rarely any electricity.

Dubréka's most famous attraction is the **Cascades de la Soumba** (FG7500; ⓣ63.35.20.24), a pretty waterfall that you can bathe in, except at the end of the dry season. There are a handful of well-kitted-out bungalows located just before the falls (ⓣ60.26.71.14; B&B ❹) as well as a restaurant with Lebanese and African dishes and a bar. The falls are around 10km from Dubréka, off the road to Boffa. For **hiking** excursions, there's **Mont Kakoulima** (1011m), the closest large mountain to Conakry, and locals will point out the rock formation **Bondabon**, more readily known as **Le Chien Qui Fume** (the smoking dog), though it's really not as impressive as it's sometimes made out to be.

Coyah

Coyah, 18km beyond the Boffa turning at Km36, is surrounded by dense green forest and plantations and is best known for producing the spring water that is bottled and sold all over Guinea. **South of Coyah**, pale, dramatic cliffs rise from a broken plain of bush and palms, forming isolated tablelands crowned with greenery, and apparently uninhabited on top. If you're interested in hiking up onto the tablelands, stop at the village of **TABILI** and follow the left bank of the Badi River upstream between the cliffs, as it runs off the plateau.

Boffa

Further north along the coast, and now connected by bridge to the Conakry road, **BOFFA** and the nearby towns of **FARENGHIA** and **DOMINGHIA**, formed a transit hub for the slave trade, and many local residents retain European surnames that indicate their mixed ancestry. There has been talk about building a slave museum in Boffa for well over a decade now, but until that happens, the town will continue to be known mainly for its mosquito swarms. At present, it doesn't have much to offer apart from a slightly depressing choice of guesthouses, including the *Nyara Beli* (T30.41.27.66), a small spot with a reliable restaurant whose clean rooms have fans.

Most non-Guineans who pass through Boffa do so only on their way along the paved road to **BEL AIR**, a seaside haven, with lengthy stretches of silver-white sand, gentle breezes and luxuriant vegetation, located at Cap Verga about 40km further north. This is one of Guinea's most beautiful beaches and has become a popular weekend escape for wealthy Lebanese, foreign aid workers and well-to-do locals. Dominating the shore is the luxury hotel built by President Conté, the *Hôtel Bel Air* (T30.43.48.40 or 60.27.75.20 ⑥). Set right on the beach, it has a hundred-odd small rooms (ask for one closest to the sands) and roomier suites, plus a great pool and a private beach. The restaurant, however, is dire, and you're advised to bring your own food from Conakry, like many other visitors. There is also in fact a decent restaurant (count on FG30,000 for a meal) a few kilometres east of Bel Air at **SOBANÉ**, where the *Complexe Village Touristique* (T30.54.51.29 or 60.27.75.20) has a fine collection of thatched huts, some with a/c (❸), spread beneath the *palmiers*. This makes for a more low-key place to spend the night, but be aware that their power is frequently off.

Kamsar

Lying at the mouth of the Rio Nunez river and 135km northwest of Boffa, **KAMSAR**'s sole *raison d'être* is to receive aluminum ore from Boké by rail and transfer it to cargo ships waiting offshore. There isn't much going on in town – the port itself is inaccessible to visitors – and its most remarkable feature is a 2km-long bauxite conveyor belt jutting out into the sea. Nonetheless, it is a pretty place to spend some time (and it has a **bank**), and northwest off the coast bordering Guinea-Bissau are the lovely **Îles Tristao** and **Îles Alcatraz**, sandy estuaries with extensive mangrove forests that are great for bird-watching – flamingo, spoonbill and brown booby are the most common – though you'll need to locate a decent boat to make it out there. There is reasonable accommodation on the road into town at *Océan Hotel* (T30.26.64.62 ❷), which features a small restaurant and disco and whose rooms offer a/c and TV – though electricity only operates at night.

Boké

Overlooking a bend of the Rio Nunez, 55km northeast of Kamsar, **BOKÉ** first made its name as a major assembly point for slaves, and later in the mid-nineteenth century as a French protectorate from which Faidherbe organized his incursions into Senegal, consolidating coastal rule. The centrally-located fort, the **Fortin de Boké**, built in 1878, functioned as a barracks and administrative centre for Faidherbe's office, and served more notoriously as an interrogation centre for the Tirailleurs sénégalais, the corps of locally-recruited militiamen who fought for the French Army up until World War II. The **museum** (no regular hours; free) which now occupies the grounds holds an assortment of ethnographic items, including masks, statues, drums and a collection of *guinzé*, the stubby, hammered iron rods that were the currency of slave-trading forest states in this part of West Africa (known as Kissi pennies in Sierra Leone; see p.703). Downstairs, you can visit the grim interrogation chambers and holding cells, used for "interviewing" potential recruits. If the museum is locked, address yourself to any of the men hanging around outside; offer a *cadeau* and a key will quickly appear.

The UK music and travel company, Batafon Arts (Ⓦwww.batafonarts.co.uk), has a *campement* just outside Boké and runs regular trips here – a link that often results in local **live music** performances. The town has a petrol station, BICIGUI **bank** and a well-stocked **market** for picking up provisions – useful if you're heading north towards Guinea-Bissau. Located at the eastern entrance to town, *Hotel Filao* (Ⓣ30.31.02.02; ❸) offers small rooms with a/c and TV and a pleasant courtyard, but again, as you'd expect, with electricity only on some of the time.

7.2

The Fouta Djalon

Covering the greater part of the western interior, the **Fouta Djalon highlands** are Guinea's major attraction. Cut into innumerable, chocolate-bar plateaux, the sandstone massif is the source of hundreds of rivers, including the Gambia and Senegal, major tributaries of the Niger and a lattice of streams running down to the Guinea coast – after the rains, waterfalls spume everywhere. Populated by **Fula** herders and the remnants of the indigenous agricultural groups in whose territory they settled hundreds of years ago, the region has a fascinating ethnic history, as well as an extraordinary variety of **landscapes**. Lushly cultivated or jungle-filled valleys rise – sometimes with sheer cliffs – to scrubby high ground, bare and rocky wastelands or lightly wooded plateaux. Wherever the contours are gentle enough to retain the soil, swaths of grassland roll in the wind. It's fabulous country and needs only time, and average determination, to explore.

Kindia

The gateway town to the Fouta Djalon, **KINDIA** (135km from Conakry) developed following the construction of the railway line in the early 1900s and is now a bustling, workaday place dramatically located beneath the hulk of Mont Gangan and shaded by innumerable mango trees (Kindia is a wonderful place for mangoes in season, boasting many different varieties: *chocolat*, *fini pas*, and so on). The railway has long since stopped being used and there aren't any obvious attractions in town apart from the huge market – a large section of which is devoted to local **cloth** – the *marché aux tissus* – one of the best places in Guinea to find cloth and an animated spot where the vendors shout to be heard over the whirring of sewing machines. A pair of batik *pagnes* (two-metre lengths of printed cloth) here should go for FG40,000–50,000, indigo dyed cloth (*gara*) for not much more, and beaten damask (*lepi*) for around FG80,000 a pair. Various beads and leatherwork items are sold across the street. You could also visit the woodworkers near the old station.

Hiking, biking and related practicalities

The Fouta Djalon is one of the best regions in West Africa for serious **off-the-beaten-track travel**. There are hundreds of kilometres of sometimes optimistically labelled "motorable tracks" and footpaths throughout the region. For serious **hiking**, it's best to get hold of the IGN map of the country (the Michelin 741 isn't sufficient). **Mountain bikes** are ideal, and on the main routes you'll have little trouble loading them onto vehicles whenever your enthusiasm for pedalling wanes. **Motorbikes**, preferably trail bikes, are also fine. **Cars and off-road vehicles** however – even 4x4 ones – will run into repeated difficulties on steep, rugged terrain and narrow footpaths, and you'd need the most agile and powerful machine to negotiate less-travelled minor routes. If you're cycling or on a motorbike, take obsessive care: roads which seem relatively good can turn a bend and disappear without warning into a river, or lose themselves in a jumble of rocks and gullies. Have purifying tablets for water – which often comes straight from the local stream – and carry some back-up rations for emergencies.

This is the most densely populated part of the country and there's a growing population of English-speaking refugees from the wars in Liberia and Sierra Leone. The **people** of the Fouta Djalon are, in general, wonderfully kind and show a disinterested concern for the welfare of wayward *portobhe* (white people). People will nearly always get water for you when you need it. The highlands, moreover, are a major citrus-growing area and during the early dry season you'll be able to rely on oranges in their hundreds as a cheap source of fluid. Remember, of course, to stock up on **essentials** like toilet paper and batteries, which don't grow on trees, and also bear in mind that temperatures at night can drop below 10°C, so you'll need something warm.

Kindia has a **post office**, but no bank. Mondial Tours in Conakry (see p.608) runs short package tours to Kindia and to the nearby Kilissi falls.

Practicalities

Kindia is a three-hour (FG15,000) *taxi-brousse* ride from Conakry. It offers a good choice of **accommodation**, though the most exciting place to stay is without doubt the *campement* at the Voile de la Mariée falls, 18km further east (see p.613). There are a few budget spots in the centre of town, while a small cluster of semi-stylish hotels lies a short drive along a dirt road from the edge of town to the west.

Kindia's best **eating** options are primarily spread about its hotels, though you can always get a quick plate of *atiéké* on the street, served with fish. In town you could also try the *Café de l'Amitié*, a friendly spot to come for a coffee or tea either indoors or on the small terrace. Another excellent option is eating at the falls in Kilissi, though you have to reserve in advance (T30.52.96.29).

In town, come the evening, several bars and clubs draw in locals, travellers and NGO staff. The disco at *Bungalow* is Kindia's top nightclub; *Linsan* is nearly as popular, with a powerful sound system and renowned musical selection (and rooms ❷) that attract clubbers from Conakry every weekend; *King Kindy's* is a good place for a pint of Skol in the garden, but turns a tad shady later on in the evening as it becomes a last-ditch pick-up joint; and *Soli* is a new club outside of town with a large garden, two separate dance floors and, again, a few rooms (❷).

Accommodation

3 Avril a block south of the market in the town centre. Bare-bones hotel with a couple of grubby and dirt-cheap rooms, but it does its best to retain whatever charm it may have once had. Has a shady nightclub to boot. ❶

Buffet de la Gare on the road out towards Mamou T60.33.04.03. The town's oldest hotel doesn't try to hide its age. There are fifteen shabby but just about inhabitable rooms, a restaurant doing chicken, fish and steak dishes, and a nightclub that

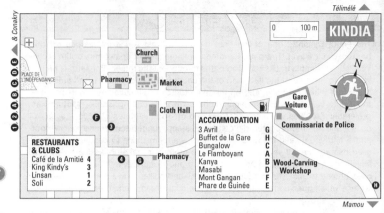

0   100 m

Télimélé

Conakry & Conakry

1 2 A B C D E

PLACE DE L'INDÉPENDANCE

Church

Pharmacy

Market

Cloth Hall

Gare Voiture

Commissariat de Police

ACCOMMODATION

3 Avril	G
Buffet de la Gare	H
Bungalow	C
Le Flamboyant	A
Kanya	B
Masabi	D
Mont Gangan	F
Phare de Guinée	E

Wood-Carving Workshop

RESTAURANTS & CLUBS

Café de la Amitié	4
King Kindy's	3
Linsan	1
Soli	2

Pharmacy

Mamou

---

means you won't get much sleep if you stay here at the weekend. **①**

Bungalow west of town centre ☎60.29.84.49 or 60.29.40.59. Built in a stand of mango trees just outside town, this is one of Kindia's best places to stay, and it's little surprise that it quickly fills up with in-the-know foreign aid workers. Guests are housed in good-value, modern a/c huts with TV that give onto a leafy garden. It also has one of Kindia's best nightclubs. Reserve ahead if at all possible. **②**

Kanya adjacent to the *Bungalow* ☎60.29.29.81 or 60.55.65.85. A much-loved place with simple, spacious, spotless rooms and a nice terrace. But no generator means the a/c goes off after midnight – so bring lots of mosquito repellent or your own mosquito net. **③**

Le Flamboyant ½km out of town on the Conakry road ☎60.26.36.57 and 60.33.23.38

€ basory@hotmail.com. Though not what it used to be, this once-elegant French-owned hotel has a pool, plus TV and a/c in all rooms. **③**

Masabi at the entrance to town 500m before the Total station on the Conakry road ☎60.29.42.63 or 60.59.81.42 € sencerydiallo@ yahoo.fr. Vies for the best stay in town, with twelve nicely decorated rooms, hot showers, a/c, TV and breakfast included. **②**

Mont Gangan This bare-bones youth hostel lies a short distance from the town centre. The restaurant serves African dishes and a surprisingly extensive French menu. **①**

Phare de Guinée town centre immediately west of the place de l'Indépendance ☎60.52.91.66 or 60.36.28.57. Aiming to keep the dirt out of dirt cheap, these 22 decent, courtyard rooms vary in size and have either fan or a/c. Also has a nightclub. **②**

Around Kindia

There are several worthwhile day-trips in the Kindia area: **Mont Gangan**, rising above the town 5km to the northwest; **Pastoria**, the birthplace of TB immunization; and the **Voile de la Mariée falls**, where you might even be tempted to stay a few days.

Moving on from Kindia

The main road out of Kindia heads southeast out of town and then northeast to **Mamou**. Plenty of taxis leave the *gare voiture* in Kindia for Mamou first thing every morning. A minor route winds north out of Kindia to **Télimélé**, from where you could continue to **Pita** and the far north of the Fouta Djalon. There's a handful of vehicles each day and the road condition is kept up fairly well. For travellers heading for **Sierra Leone**, Kindia has occasional bush-taxi departures for **Madina-Woula**, from where it's possible to reach the area around the Outamba–Kilimi National Park and Kamakwie.

Mont Gangan

The massif of **Mont Gangan** is one of the highest peaks (1117m) in the southern Fouta Djalon and is relatively easy to climb. The big plateau halfway up offers brilliant views over Kindia, especially after the rains. You can arrange hiking tours at the *Flamboyant* in Kindia (see opposite), or venture out on your own, but be careful not to stroll through the military camp on the way.

Pastoria

Three kilometres up the road to Télimélé from Kindia is **Pastoria**, the "Institut Pasteur". The institute was founded in 1925 as a primate research centre, principally with the aim of developing various vaccines for human use – we have their consumptive chimps to thank for the BCG (Bacillus Calmette-Guerin) antituberculosis jab. The Institut Pasteur in Paris later charged Pastoria with the collection of snake venom for antivenin preparations. They used to have a large collection of primates and reptiles, of which only a few snakes and a couple of unhappy crocodiles have survived. The institute is still open for visitors, but doesn't hold much attraction beyond the architectural layout of the place itself. If you want to visit, you'll have to *déplace* a taxi or walk.

Les Chutes de la Voile de la Mariée

The best known of Kindia's local excursions is to **Les Chutes de la Voile de la Mariée**, the "Bridal Veil" falls, a five-kilometre diversion off the road to Mamou, 13km from Kindia. Here, the Santa River leaps from a black and yellow cliff in two streams to crash against the rock face and break into a broad fan – a total drop of some 60m. It's a year-round phenomenon, but most impressive during and shortly after the rains. The area is looked after by a hotelier who manages fifteen spacious concrete huts (built by order of Sekou Touré for his weekly visits), now converted into a pleasant **campement**, set amid the jungle, with camping space and self-contained twin rooms in huts (☎41.50.21 ❸). Meals are available if ordered in advance. If you stay several days, the manager will be pleased to escort you into the nearby hills for a jungle trek and bird's-eye views of the district. If you just visit for the day out of Kindia, you'll pay an entrance fee of FG2000, a FG5000 parking fee and whatever you agree with your taxi driver (FG25,000 round trip is about right). Alternatively, take a *taxi brousse* as far as **SEGUEYA** (FG2000), then walk the final couple of kilometres to the falls.

Mamou

From Kindia, the steep, hairpinning 130-kilometre climb up to Mamou offers a sweeping panorama back over the broad tributary basins of the Kolente (or Great Scarcies) River, which marks the border with Sierra Leone. If you're coming by taxi from Conakry, you're likely to take a short break in the village of **LINSAN**, some 50km before Mamou – a lively market town where you can find a cheap plate of rice, *brochettes*, and calabashes full of sweetened sour milk (*kosan*). Some 25km before Mamou, a 5km detour leads to the village and falls of **KONKOURÉ**. There's an old sacred grove here, containing remnants of the ancient forest that once covered large parts of the Fouta Djalon between the hill tops.

MAMOU, piled up on the hillside, strikes a surprisingly low-key note. Before the building of the railway, the religious and political centre of the Fouta Djalon was **Timbo** – now just a village 50km northeast of Mamou. Despite considerable local opposition, the French decided to bypass Timbo and set up a new railway halt and fuel depot at the hamlet of Mamou. The Fula chieftaincy was transferred and, until the end of World War II, Mamou served as the chief administrative centre for much of the highlands. Today, the old railway station offers an overgrown reminder of Mamou's former glory, though it's now better known for its agricultural college and meat-processing industry.

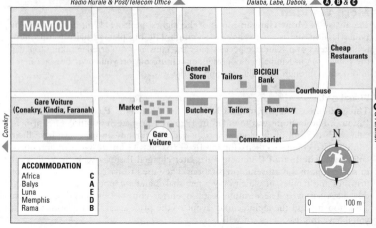

MAMOU

Cheap
Restaurants

General
Store   Tailors   BICIGUI
Bank

Courthouse

Gare Voiture
(Conakry, Kindia, Faranah)   Market   Butchery   Tailors   Pharmacy   **Ⓔ**

Gare
Voiture   Commissariat

N

ACCOMMODATION

Africa	**C**
Balys	**A**
Luna	**E**
Memphis	**D**
Rama	**B**

0   100 m

Conakry

U & Faranah

Accommodation has improved in recent years, with the opening of a number of new hotels. *Hôtel Luna* (☏64.64.72.15 **①**) is the most central place to stay, though also the most dilapidated, with thirty s/c rooms overlooking a large courtyard. The *Hôtel Memphis* (☏60.35.57.54 **①**), 1km down the Faranah road, is more comfortable and cleaner and has a pleasant front terrace. The rest of the hotels are all grouped around the road out of town towards Labé. The *Rama* (☏30.68.04.30 **①**) offers basic rooms, a restaurant and a popular disco, while the nearby ⌂ *Hôtel Africa* (☏30.68.01.43 **①**) is clean and spacious. About 3km further out, the *Balys* (☏60.20.59.06 **③**) is one of the country's best mid-range hotels, with clean, brand-new rooms and good service. A new underground nightclub has made *Balys* into one of Mamou's liveliest party spots.

Mamou has plenty of **street food**, grimy **bars** hidden behind dirty plastic curtains, and a few good **restaurants** – try the *Pergola* for large plates of African or European food, the *Luna* for more basic meals, or any of the unnamed eateries around the centre of town.

Mamou is such a major transport hub that **moving on** is rarely a problem. The town's three taxi *gares* are hives of activity from dawn to dusk. The two in the town centre handle the **Conakry–Faranah** route, and the one on the road out of town towards Labé handles **Fouta Djalon** traffic, and the less busy routes to **Timbo**, **Dabola** and **Dinguiraye**.

Mamou to Faranah

Southeast of town, the rough road from **Mamou to Faranah** (see p.624) drops down from the highlands through forest and hilly bush before reaching the plains below, where the road runs through monotonous elephant grass and bush savannah for the rest of the journey to Faranah. At times the road is within a dozen kilometres of the Sierra Leone border – this area is one of the richest districts for fauna in Guinea, and your chances of seeing large wild animals are quite high.

Timbo

The surfaced road from **Mamou to Dabola** (see p.623) cuts through impressive scenery, with sheer rocky outcrops and forest populated by chimpanzees and monkeys. Cradled between forest-covered mountains 50km along the road, **TIMBO** is the old capital of the Fula *almamys*, or religious leaders, and a worthwhile day's excursion from Mamou (taxis leave every morning from Mamou's *gare voiture*). You can pay tribute at the **tombs** of two former Islamic leaders, have a look at the restored eighteenth-century **mosque** (though only from the outside) and soak up the village's unusual air of religious devotion. You'll also come across traditional Fouta Djalon **houses**: fine conical beehive structures, with solid tiers of thatching to exclude the cold.

The central Fouta Djalon

The central Fouta Djalon – including the ancient settlements of **Dalaba**, **Pita** and **Télimélé** – offers some of Guinea's most beautiful countryside. About 15km out of Mamou, the eastward-flowing stream you cross is the Bafing, the first headwater of the Senegal; its source is in the hills a few kilometres off the road to the west. The road steepens after **BOULIWEL** (which has a Saturday market), then drops to enter Dalaba, hidden in a conifer-carpeted valley.

Dalaba and around

DALABA has a beautiful setting in the hills at 1200m, and the town's agreeable climate (though with very cool nights during the dry season) and pretty green scenery make it ideal for extended walks. The French considered the site so therapeutic that they built a sixty-room sanatorium, now in ruins. The South African jazz singer Miriam Makeba spent time in Dalaba during her period of political exile from the USA in the 1970s, and you can still visit her large white house near the ruined sanatorium.

Dalaba's layout is easy to grasp. The town centre is comprised of a couple of streets around the limited **market** – greatly enlarged on Sundays, when it hosts the district *lumo* (market). There's a row of cheap eating and drinking places on the street along the bottom of the market. Market produce includes, from the end of December to March, locally cultivated strawberries – a colonial bequest.

Practicalities

There's a **post office** but no bank in Dalaba. Staff at the *Tangama* hotel (see below) can put you in touch with the local **tourist office**, where the well-informed Daymou Diallo (☎60.26.93.48 ⓔdaymou_diallo@yahoo.fr) arranges motorbike hire (FG50,000 per day) and organizes sightseeing excursions around Dalaba and as far away as Pita. A ten- to fifteen-minute walk west across the valley from the *gare routière* is the administrative quarter of **Etaconval** – rural in feel, and spread among the woods – where you'll find some of Dalaba's nicest **restaurants** and the only three **places to stay** it currently has to offer. The formerly luxurious *SIB Hotel du Fouta* (☎60.41.10.56 ❷) now smells a little mouldy, but it's still well worth enjoying a meal or drink on its terrace, from where there's a stunning panoramic view of the surrounding hills. It's more pleasant however to stay at the small ⚑ *Hôtel Tangama* (☎60.32.95.26 ❶) – a clean, cosy place with hot water, a fireplace in the lounge and an excellent restaurant. ⚑ *L'Auberge (Chez Kofi*; ❶) offers four tidy rooms and a restaurant with a wide selection of African and European food. For good Senegalese **food**, try the unnamed but easy to find Senegalese family place near the junction leading to the *Tangama* hotel (order in advance). At weekends, Dalaba's youth usually gathers in the popular *Le Kouratier* **nightclub**.

Moving on **from Dalaba to Pita** by public transport is an easy affair, with *six-place* taxis leaving regularly from just outside Dalaba's *gare voiture*.

Around Dalaba

A walk of several kilometres through the forest from the *Hôtel Tangama* (ask at the hotel for directions) takes you to the old colonial Villa Jeannine and the **Case de Palabre**, a former assembly hut for Fula chiefs built in the 1930s and boasting an inscribed floor, elaborate ceiling decorations and exceptional carving on its interior walls. A guard is usually on-duty to show visitors around the villa and the *case*, though be prepared for grumbling unless your tips are generous. Two other worthwhile walks offering good views (though you'll need a guide), go to **Pont Tangama** and **Mont Diaguissa**. Five kilometres outside Dalaba on the right, a steep road leads to Tinka and **Le Jardin de Professeur Chevalier**, an ornamental garden constructed in 1908 as a botanical experiment designed to prove that European plants could grow in West Africa; the startling groves of pine trees around Dalaba and Pita were all part of the same venture. The garden is still just about kept up, and is worth a visit. From November to May, you can also visit the **Jardin de Fraises** in **DOUNKIMANIA**, where strawberries are grown; a small basket costs FG4000. If you're interested in local **arts and crafts**, Daymou Diallo can take you to the villages of **POUKÉ** and **SEBHORY**, where local women have established a collective that manufactures the woven wall hangings (*beddo*) and baskets typical of the Fouta Djalon region – prices are cheap, and you can watch the women at work. Overnight stays in Pouké can also be arranged through Daymou for travellers keen to experience village life first-hand.

There are two impressive **waterfalls** off the main road from Dalaba to Pita. The **Pont de Dieu**, around 10km outside Dalaba, is a pretty little waterway that snakes its way over and under rocks resembling a natural bridge. Some 30km further towards Pita are the famous **Chutes de Ditinn**, an eighty-metre-high cascade, dropping from a perfectly vertical cliff. It's an impressive sight when there's sufficient water (usually best Oct–Dec), and you can also swim in the plunge pool. Other falls are more easily seen from a distance than reached, such as the **Bomboli** falls, about 15km south of Pita, which are very difficult to get to, though clearly visible, several kilometres over on the right.

Pita and around

PITA isn't as restful as Dalaba, but has a lively and appealing atmosphere. Market day is Thursday, when locals visit the town to buy sticks of delicious white **bread** – the town is home to some of Guinea's best bakeries. Dalaba makes a better overnight base for excursions in the area, but if you are obliged to sleep in Pita, the *Hôtel Kinkon* (❶) does have a handful of basic, dingy rooms. You may also be able to find accommodation in some of the neighbourhood bars, such as the *Forêt Sacrée* near the hotel, but the rooms are likely to be equally dire. Pita boasts a popular **nightclub**, *Le Koubi*, a short walk or drive from town, and you can catch daily showings of American and Bollywood movies at the former Cinéma Rex – now essentially a video club.

The pretty and well-known **Chutes de Kinkon** are 8km from Pita, an easy cycle ride or a more taxing walk. Before setting off you have to get permission to visit the falls in the shape of a *laissez-passer* issued by the *commissariat* on the north side of town – this is issued on the spot and costs FG3000. To reach the falls, go past the checkpoint at the exit from town on the road to Labé and take a left at the sign to the falls. After a mostly downhill 7km you arrive at a control post where you hand in your *laissez-passer*. From here, it's 500m down to the right if you want to inspect the unimpressive hydroelectric dam across the lake (the reason for the *laissez-passer*) and about a kilometre to the left for the main falls. You can stand directly on the **rock platform** above the falls which – before the dam was built – would have surged with water. There's evidence of colonial safety measures in the broken stumps of cliff-edge railings, but nothing to stop present-day visitors plunging dramatically to their deaths – take care, as the flow is powerful. Behind, on the cliffs, is a scrappy but just about legible list of various heads of state, with the dates of their visits.

Far more impressive, though only reachable after a very strenuous walk or hard mountain-bike ride, are the gigantic **Chutes de Kambadaga**, which gush down over two steep rock terraces. It's best to take a local guide to visit these falls, in order not to get lost in the wilderness surrounding Pita. If your thirst for waterfalls still isn't satisfied you could visit the small but pretty **Mitty** waterfalls near the village of

MACI, a few kilometres outside Pita on the road to Dalaba. The turning to Maci is indicated by a sign; the falls are a short walk off the main road from there.

Pita to Télimélé

Exceptionally beautiful in parts, the **Pita–Télimélé road** is a relatively straightforward drive and ideal for **motorbikes** or **4x4s** (count on eight hours-plus from Pita to Télimélé), **mountain bikes** (two days) or **hiking** (four to six days). The Paris–Dakar rally came this way in January 1995, but it's still little used by public transport. The route in reverse is considerably less attractive as the rewards are mostly westwards (eastbound you face a continuous thirty-kilometre climb from Léi-Mîro to Dongol-Touma). If you're cycling or hiking, you may want to deviate from the road to take short cuts in the company of local people. One walking route follows, roughly, the course of the Fétoré River, which flows westwards, a few kilometres to the north of the road. Alternatively, you might try to get a lift as far as the village of **Dongol-Touma**, where the thrills begin, and walk or ride from there on. There's transport from Pita to Dongol-Touma at least once daily, though you'll probably have less of a wait if you go to the junction 3km north of Pita, where vehicles from Labé, as well as Pita and Mamou, turn off westwards towards Télimélé.

The people of the area, who live in immaculate mud-moulded compounds, are happy to bring visitors water from their wells or the local stream, and will just as soon give you handfuls of oranges and bananas as sell them to you.

Over the bowe — and exploring the Doucki canyons

A signpost 3km up the Pita–Labé road marks the turnoff to Télimélé, which at first brings you to a confusion of tracks. Bear right where another sign points left to the Chutes de Kinkon (see above; given an early start, you could easily visit the falls as part of the journey). The correct track soon starts bucking and twisting unmistakably, with many descents to narrow streams and many wearing climbs to short, level ridges. There are usually a fair number of Fula people about, invariably surprised to see any strangers, let alone foreign travellers. The track heads northwest, southwest, east and south before establishing a more or less westerly course along a barren hogsback of rocky land discernible on the IGN map. This part of the journey, across the **bowe** – the Fula name for these high, sere plateaux – isn't scenically enthralling. In December smoke from burning grass obscures any views and the hazy dust brought by the *harmattan* wind normally fogs the horizon between January and April.

The path runs over unrelenting bare rock in places, then begins to descend gently, with occasional wooded intervals. The village of **TIMBI-TOUNI** has an enormous mosque, while an hour's walk further west brings you to **COMBOUROH**, location of a remarkable country market every Tuesday during which hundreds of Fula women converge to share news, sell and shop – their assortment of hairstyles and print patterns is superb, and typical. Some 46km from the Pita junction, and 9km east of Dongol-Touma, is the village of **DOUCKI**, which unassumingly offers some of the best hiking in West Africa. Perched on the edge of a spectacular gorge, Doucki has not just stunning scenery but a host of interesting ways to explore it. Local tour guide Hassan Ba (℡60.39.36.42) has been leading visitors on his signature hikes for nearly a decade. Each excursion has an apt title ("Chutes and Ladders", "Indiana Jones World") and they range from easy to exhausting. If you're suitably adventurous, you can climb liana ladders, wend your way between fantastic rock formations and swim beneath any of the myriad small waterfalls in the area – this is basically **canyoning** *à la Guinéen*. Hassan will put you up in basic but comfortable huts, and his fee of around FG75,000 per day covers lodging, home-cooked meals and all the hiking you can handle.

At the end of the *bowe*, you reach the strung-out village of **DONGOL-TOUMA**, 55km from the Pita junction, and site of a Wednesday *lumo*. If you see the *sous-préfet* you'll likely be able to **stay the night** in Dongol's *villa*, superbly sited on a high bluff with a 270-degree panoramic view.

The rise of the jihad state

The original inhabitants of the highlands were Jalonke, Baga and Nalo – all of whom coexisted in relative harmony, herding on the hills and farming the valleys. The region was known then as **Jallonkadugu**, after its dominant inhabitants. The first **Fula immigrants** arrived in the fifteenth century from Tekrur on the Senegal River and Djenné on the Niger River in search of pasture for their herds of cattle. Their numbers increased when **Koli Tengela** and his followers settled in the north of the Fouta, looking to establish an area free of Muslim influence. This relatively peaceful state of affairs began to change when the first Muslim Fula arrived in the late seventeenth century from Macina in Mali and Fouta Toro in Senegal. They began spreading Islam, and in 1725 started West Africa's first jihad under the leadership of **Karamoko Alfa Barry**, who won a breakthrough military victory against the animist populations at Talansan in 1730.

The **Muslim Theocracy of Fouta Djalon** emerged as a result of this victory, with Karamoko Alfa Barry as its leader, or *almamy*, and its capital at **Timbo**. Karamoko's nephew, Ibrahima Sory, took power when his uncle went insane in 1767 and the kingdom was divided into nine provinces, one of which, **Labé**, became a noted centre of learning. There were **conversions** among the animists, but many fled. Throughout the nineteenth century, Labé drew apart from Timbo, and by the 1890s its territory extended over most of northwest Guinea, making Labé as powerful a state as the Timbo-based kingdom of Fouta Djalon itself. With the arrival of the French, separate treaties were entered into with both realms. Today, both **Alfa Yaya**, the great-grandson of Karamoko Alfa Barry and the last ruler of Labé, and **Bokar Biro**, the last ruler of Timbo, are considered folk heroes.

Downhill to the Kakrima River

The road snakes out of Dongol-Touma and starts a **steep descent**, with inspiring sweeps of Fouta Djalon horizons visible through the trees. If you're cycling or motorbiking, the only effort you'll need to make for 26km is to keep the brakes on. Driving a car or truck, exercise extreme caution: parts of the route here are likely to have succumbed to erosion and you could turn a bend and run into a jumble of boulders and bedrock. When you're not watching the surface ahead, however, this is a breathtaking ride, zigzagging down a long spine, with striking views of the bush country to the south, the fortress-like hills rising in a ridge to the west, and plunging valleys below. Streams, flecked with butterflies and patrolled by parrots and hornbills, cut across the road, while giant leaves litter the ground and lianas tangle overhead. Occasionally a hunter or a woodcutter emerges – usually to stand still, nonplussed, on seeing you. Monkeys, the hunters' main targets, are common.

At last the gradients relax and the road unwinds, through more cultivated country, towards the Kakrima River. The village of **DJOUNKOUN** leaves little impression, but **LÉI-MÎRO**, 4km east of the river, is the second large settlement along the route. You'll find rice and other street food if you turn up early enough, or bread and sandwich ingredients if not. Léi-Mîro's *lumo* takes place every Thursday.

The winch-ferry across the **Kakrima River** has an engine, but it's not far across (either hauling the ferry's line or renting a pirogue) in the event of breakdown. **KOUSSI** is just beyond, where people know a good short cut, useful if you're walking to Télimélé. The main route beyond Koussi is hard work on a bicycle, mostly flat – and sandy in parts – with tall elephant grass blocking any view. Sixty-one kilometres beyond Dongol-Touma the route hits the broad, red sweep of the Kindia–Télimélé road, where you should find a lift easily enough. The final gruelling 15km to Télimélé up the soaring flank of **Mont Louba** are noted for gut-churning accidents on the hairpins.

Télimélé

A pleasing, well-kept town, perched as if to admire its grand views, **TÉLIMÉLÉ** sees very few visitors. Nearby lies **Gueme Sangan**, the ruined fortress of the fifteenth-century Fula warlord Koli Tengela (see opposite). Télimélé is a town of pine trees, citrus orchards and fresh air, surrounded by imposing mountain flanks and trench-like valleys. There are two adequate **hotels**: the *Petit Palais* (●) and, across the street, *Larry's Hotel* (●), where the cook serves up a mean chicken.

When you're ready to leave Télimélé there are usually daily taxis to **Gaoual**, 130km away along a beautiful route to the north. The road down to **Kindia** isn't too bad and transport is reasonably frequent, but it's worth investing a little extra for a place in a Peugeot rather than one of the minibuses. Look out, during the last half-hour before Kindia, for some outstanding tabular mesas, rearing like lost worlds across the valley.

Labé and the northern Fouta Djalon

Heading north from Pita, the **road to Labé**, 38km away, loops across a mellow, pastoral landscape of undulating grass, scattered with boulders and copses of oak-like *koura* trees, and fringed with lines of forest along the watercourses. The district, one of the highest in the Fouta Djalon, is a watershed between the streams that flow west and the Gambia and Senegal tributaries pouring off northwards.

Labé

Strategically situated in the middle of the highlands lies **LABÉ**, the historic stronghold of the Fula and capital of the Fouta Djalon. It's now the largest town in the region, and a good place to check your emails, make phone calls, and enjoy the nearest thing this part of Guinea has to a real city. Labé's appeal arises from its status as the Fouta Djalon's largest market town and the area's main artisanal centre. **Tata** district, a kilometre or so to the left as you head out to the airport, is home to the workshop yards of a couple of **weaving** guilds. You might do well to enlist someone to guide you to the weavers (*tisserands*) if you're interested in seeing them at work. Also on the way to the airport, you pass the National Apiculture Centre, with local potted **honey** for sale.

For something a little more substantial in the way of food, the **market** in the town centre – huge, vibrant and teeming – is one of Labé's strong points, though a tight squeeze to walk around. There's a remarkable variety of groundnut pastes on

offer, and all the usual Fouta Djalon profusion of produce. Look out for exquisite **gara** cloth, made from Czech damask, tie-dyed with local indigo and beaten with clubs to make it shine; it's sold, as usual, in pairs of *pagnes*. Inside the market, you can also watch **shoemakers** at work manufacturing the colourfully ornamented leather sandals the region is famous for; a pair will cost around FG10,000–15,000 depending on your negotiating skills. Labé also has a pretty little **museum** in a bright new building slightly away from the town centre; exhibits include various historical items, examples of traditional arts and crafts, and musical instruments.

Practicalities

Labé boasts the only **bank** in the Fouta Djalon, a branch of the BICIGUI (Mon–Fri 8.15am–12.30pm & 2.30–4:30pm), as well as a **post office** (Mon–Thurs 8am–6pm; Fri 8am–1pm) and an **Internet** café, next to the *Hôtel de l'Indépendance*.

The town offers an ever-expanding list of **hotel** options. Those in the centre can be somewhat pricey, but if you have transport, you might prefer to stay in one of the better-value hotels on the south side of town. The market offers a wealth of food, and the town's **restaurants** are equally well-stocked. Being at the centre of Guinea's potato-cultivating region, Labé's *restos* do a brisk trade in home-made fries and potato salad. Besides the *Restaurant Tata* and *La Campagne*, try any one of the host of small restaurants around the *Hôtel de l'Indépendance* for snacks and drinks. The sociable *Petit Dakar* serves drinks and sandwiches, and is the main meeting spot for Labé's youth in the evenings. The best informal dining is to be had at night, when local women come out to sell delicious *atiéké*, salad and grilled fish. These roadside stands can be great places to eat, drink and meet the locals; try the area in front of the *Hôtel de Tourisme*, or ask around downtown and people will be happy to direct you to the nearest *atiéké* lady.

Discos in town include the popular *Faningo*, which gets massively crowded at weekends, and *Le Parrain*, which attracts a mixed crowd. Labé has several **live-music** venues: you could try the seedy *Sansuna*, which has a local dance band at weekends, but watch out for the drunks and prostitutes and be prepared to find yourself the constant centre of attention. Labé's **radio rurale** (☎60.51.03.05) is a useful source of information on music events, and also carries information on upcoming traditional concerts or other special events.

Accommodation

There's a growing number of places to stay in Labé and the nearby countryside, but the following are tried and tested.

Hôtel de l'Indépendance at the lower end of the *gare voiture*. This rambling old building is very central, though the cavernous rooms get noisy and could use some upkeep. ❶

Hôtel de Tourisme west side of the town centre. This once-grand establishment, conceived in a vaguely Swiss-chalet style, was under renovation at the time of writing, but both the hotel and the lively *Tinkisso* nightclub downstairs were due to reopen.

La Campagne near the *Tata* on the south side of town ☎30.51.23.70. A new hotel near *Tata* offering similarly comfortable rooms at a slightly lower price, along with a pizza restaurant that holds its own against its better-known neighbour. ❷

Provincial a little out of town to the west ☎60.31.77.40. This friendly hotel is best known as the home of one of Labé's more stylish nightclubs

but also offers an attractive courtyard, a small restaurant and nice rooms with TV. ❷

Saala 2km west of the town centre ☎60.31.74.22. This pretty place has spacious rooms and a very good restaurant, and its club, the *Saala Plus*, is one of the most popular in Labé. ❷

Safatou about 6km west of town ☎60.57.01.89. Labé's most reputable place for a night's sleep, with large rooms equipped with TV and a/c. Its nightclub is considered *the* place to be seen. ❷

🏃 **Salaam** town centre. One of the cheapest options in town, with basic but clean rooms in a leafy courtyard. ❶

🏃 **Tata** on the south side of town ☎60.54.08.86. Run by an Italian/Guinean couple, this is the favoured gathering place for local expats and US Peace Corps volunteers. It also serves some of the best pizzas in Guinea in its signature restaurant. ❸

Day-trips out of Labé

Labé is a good base for excursions into the surrounding countryside – indeed, if you hire a taxi for yourself by *déplacement* and get an early start, you could get all the way to **Maliville** (see below) and back in a day. The *Hôtel Tata* has a couple of knowledgeable guides, who will take you on **hiking trips** around the district (fees negotiable); alternatively, you could always venture out on your own.

One of the Fouta's most impressive waterfalls, the **Chutes de la Saala**, lies 40km north of Labé. Follow the road to Koundara, then turn off near the road to **LÉLOUMA** and follow the unpaved road until you reach the falls. A day's taxi hire at Labé's *gare routière* should cost no more than FG200,000 plus petrol. Take stout shoes so you can climb around the falls (there are good views of the multiple cascades from all sides) and swimming gear to bathe in the plunge pool, plus some food for a picnic. And be careful on the cliff edges.

The northern Fouta Djalon

If you've come up to Labé from the south, the most obvious onward option is to continue, on dirt *piste* and rocky roads, to the towns of **Maliville** (known locally simply as Mali) and **Koundara**, from where it's possible to continue to Senegal. Taxis make the hair-raising run between Maliville and **Kédougou** in Senegal most mornings, and most days there are also vehicles from Koundara into Senegal. If you tackle these routes in your own 4x4, be prepared for one-in-four gradients, some dangerous hairpins and several skeletal bridges.

Gaoual and north to Guinea-Bissau

The route from Labé to **Gaoual** is an option if you're heading for Guinea-Bissau and Senegal's Basse Casamance region. On this route you're almost certain to have to take a Koundara vehicle and change at **KOUNSITEL**, from where local vehicles head to Gaoual, Koumbia and north to Guinea-Bissau. **GAOUAL** itself is a friendly little town, with a wide avenue of trees and an old colonial PTT, though it gets extremely hot here in the dry season.

Right on the border with Guinea-Bissau, the town of **FOULA-MORI** is home to the birth hut of legendary Fula leader **Alfa Yaya** (see box, p.618). The impressively

Jungle-hiking

"I recommend hiking to Mont Lansa. It drops steeply off the Fouta Djalon plateau in a stunning cliff face, and the summit offers views into Senegal. You can climb around to the base of the cliff face to see some of the baboons that live in the dense jungle there."

Matt Brown, USA

well-kept hut is maintained by Alfa Yaya's descendants, who will show you around for a small tip; exhibits include the shards of Alfa Yaya's war drum, his bed and a few other items. Officials at the friendly border post can put you in touch with locals who can provide lodgings for a night or two.

North to Maliville and on into Senegal

The 110-kilometre route from Labé to the small town of Maliville switchbacks through the loftiest sections of the Fouta Djalon, with a number of fair-size villages on the way. Some 14km north of Labé, **TOUNTOUROUN** still has beautiful Fula houses, while just a kilometre or so further the road crosses a small stream running east – this is the **Gambia River** (here known as the Gambie), whose source is just up on the heights to the west of the road. Further villages include **SARÉKALI** at 35km; the pretty hamlet of **PELLAL** off to the left at 65km; and **YEMBÉRING**, the largest, at 74km.

At 1460m, the town of **MALIVILLE** is the highest settlement in the Fouta Djalon, renowned for its low temperatures (down to 3°C) and magnificent views. It's a growing highlands centre, with a good **covered market**, three blocks north of the *gare voiture*. On market day, Sunday, hundreds of villagers come to town to sell their produce. For good cheap **meals**, several shops near the *gare* sell rice and sauce. A surprising asset is the town library, the *bibliothèque de Maliville*, up on the hill west of the town centre, which has good resources (in French) on Guinean and Fula history and knowledgeable, welcoming staff. There are two main **places to stay**: the small and primitive *La Dame de Mali* (1) and the slightly better *Auberge Indigo* (1). If you're looking to buy things, there's a local women's collective that sells high-quality artisanal goods from their boutique.

Try to give yourself a couple of days in this area, as there are some excellent hikes with extraordinary views. These are particularly good from Mont Lansa, 12km west of town, and from the summit of **Mont Loura** (1538m), the highest peak in the Fouta Djalon, which lies 7km northeast of town. On its eastern flank you can spot the **Dame de Mali**, a cliff eroded into a feminine profile. If you have your own tent you can camp on the mountain, or stay the night in one of the very basic huts facing the *Dame* in the village of **TINSERA** (1).

You can hike down off the highlands from Maliville north into Senegal, but it's easiest to do so with a local guide or companions headed in the same direction to take advantage of short cuts not available to motor vehicles. It's more than 50km from Maliville to **GADALOUGUÉ** (the Guinean border post), and a further 12km to the Senegalese post at **SÉGOU**, which has supplies and a simple *campement* (1), and from where you can pick up regular daily transport to the town of Kédougou.

Koundara and the Parc National Niokolo-Badiar

KOUNDARA, 50km from the Senegalese border, is the jumping-off point for excursions to the **Parc National Niokolo–Badiar** (closed during the rainy season), which lies on the border adjoining Senegal's Parc National Niokolo-Koba. Visitors stand a good chance of seeing monkeys, baboons and hippos, but most of the bigger game has been over-hunted and sightings of lions, leopards and antelopes are increasingly rare. Facilities for visitors are still basic, but the staff in the park office are helpful and can arrange car hire, which is the only way to get around the park without your own 4x4. If you want to stay in Koundara, try the reasonable *Hôtel du Gangan* or the *Mamadou Boiro* (both 1). There are no facilities in the park.

7.3

Haute Guinée

he great plains of the east, known as **Haute Guinée**, stretch immensely vast and flat over more than a hundred thousand square kilometres. In this huge expanse, the few towns – **Kankan**, **Kouroussa**, **Faranah** and **Siguiri** – seem lost amid yellow grass, thorn trees and termite spires. In contrast to the Fouta Djalon to the west and the rainforest-covered highlands further south, the population is sparse: most people live along the meandering **tributaries of the Niger** which pull together in a fan in the most populous part of the region around Kankan and Kouroussa.

Without your own **transport** you're mostly restricted to the clutch of main routes (a mix of surfaced roads and dirt tracks) which traverse the region. Away from the main routes, distances between settlements are often too far for comfortable walking or cycling – indeed even on the main roads you can go miles without seeing a soul. In addition, Haute Guinée gets blisteringly hot and painfully dry during the dry season.

Dabola and around

DABOLA grew up after 1910 as a staging post, and it retains a slightly Wild West feel, hemmed in by gaunt plateaux rising directly behind the town and making a living by keeping those passing through well fed and entertained. It's not an unattractive place, with neat compounds surrounding the small commercial centre, and there are two very decent **hotels**. The upmarket *Hôtel Tinkisso* (☎60.32.24.42 ❷), set in large grounds, has comfortable s/c rooms with showers and a large bar-restaurant with satellite TV. Equally comfortable, but slightly cheaper, is the more intimate *Hôtel Mont Sincery* (☎60.36.22.48 ❷), whose cute outdoor lobby doubles as a TV lounge bar.

Just outside town, the **Tinkisso falls** are worth a short detour. A gentle six-kilometre climb along the road to Mamou brings you to a track on your left, which drops over the old railway line through a teak plantation and, forking right, to the top of the **dam** and a mass of birdlife (an alternative route follows the power

---

The Fête de Mare

If you visit Haute Guinée around the end of the dry season, you might be lucky enough to witness one of the region's most festive traditions. The **Fête de Mare** ("pond celebration") takes place every May once the lakes and ponds of the savannah have shrunk to mere puddles and the fish inside have nowhere to hide. Thousands of people gather around the pond on the appointed day and, upon signal from the village elders, rush in en masse to trap, spear and grab as many fish as they can in a joyful riot of plenty before the lean season sets in. The *fête* is held across dozens of villages around Kankan and Siguiri. The largest and most famous is in **Baro**, an otherwise unremarkable hamlet 8km off the Kouroussa–Kankan road, where people from across the country converge each year to dance, fish and celebrate the season.

Moving on from Dabola

Dabola has daily transport connections to Mamou, Faranah, Kouroussa and Kankan. The 110-kilometre earth road to **Faranah**, which descends gradually from Dabola before running past irrigated rice fields and along the stripling Niger valley into Faranah, is in rough condition. The road to Kankan is paved, though the stretch between Dabola and Kouroussa is so peppered with potholes that the journey is bound to test your patience.

lines from town straight to the falls). The **falls** themselves – which must have been impressive indeed before the dam was built – cascade over rocky shelves (except at the end of the dry season, when there's no water). Determined hikers might want to extend the walk into a circular trek by following the path from the falls which descends steeply to the power station. Continue on the same footpath downstream and you reach an immaculate Fula village and, eventually, the Dabola–Faranah road. The circular walk makes a good day's excursion for the landscape and birdlife, whether or not the falls are in spate.

Dinguiraye

From Dabola, you can also arrange transport to **DINGUIRAYE**, a tough 100-kilometre drive further north, which is home to Guinea's most famous **mosque**, a huge and well-maintained construction dedicated to the legendary **Al Haj Omar Tall**, a Fula religious leader who made mass conversions throughout West Africa in the nineteenth century. The *Hôtel de l'Amitié* (●) has reasonable rooms for the low price, but a better option is the guesthouse run by the American NGO Africare (●) where you may even be treated to running water and electricity.

Kouroussa

KOUROUSSA is in a beautiful area, but there's little more to it from the travel point of view than a place to spend the night if you can't make it all the way from Dabola to Kankan in a day – and the road from Kouroussa to Kankan is in excellent shape. Kouroussa, on a strategic bend of the Niger – a traditional ferry and fording point and now the site of an important bridge – was the birthplace of Guinea's best-known author, **Camara Laye**: the Laye family house is near the old railway station and easily found if you want to pay homage. The town is pleasant and leafy, though its **accommodation** options are sparse. The only half-decent hotel is the *Le Segona* (●) along the road to Conakry, but you can also try any of the bars at the market, such as *La Baobab* and the *Chateau d'Eau* near the *gare voiture* for information on rooms. You can get food at the friendly *Café Savane*, near the market.

Faranah and around

Until independence in 1958, **FARANAH** was an unimportant village on the old road from Dabola to Kissidougou. **Sekou Touré** pumped money into his native village, building a large mosque, as well as the Cité du Niger conference centre in 1981 and a massive block of a villa for himself, which served as a hotel for a while but unfortunately is now closed. If he hadn't died, Touré would undoubtedly have set about, in true dictatorial fashion, turning Faranah into Guinea's capital. Today, the town is slipping back to its original state as a sleepy village, its selection of restaurants and hotels diminishing year by year and its general infrastructure decrepit. It's a town you're still likely to pass through, though, and it's adequate for most practical needs. If you're visiting the Parc National du Haut Niger, you can get information at their office in town (☎60.81.04.82).

Accommodation is very limited. Try the relatively decent *Hôtel Bati* (**1**) or ask in the popular *Bantou* bar next door for a bed in one of Faranah's informal guesthouses. In the town centre, cheap **eateries** compete at one end of the main *gare voiture*, serving high-quality street food all day, and in some cases at night too.

When you're ready to move on from Faranah, you'll find vehicles bound for **Mamou** and **Kissidougou** cluster at the main *gare voiture* below the market. It's easy to reach Conakry, Labé, Kankan or Nzérékoré in a day, though it's worth noting that the highway from Faranah to Kissidougou is in bad shape. The *gare voiture* for **Dabola** and **Kouroussa** is at the opposite end of town, its only landmark being a blue house.

Some 15km west of Faranah, a big sign on the left saying "Direction Sierra Leone" points the way across the border to **Kabala**. Since the civil war in Sierra Leone, bush taxis rarely take this route, and you'd get to Freetown faster using the main route via Pamalap on the road between Conakry and Freetown. But if you have your own 4x4, or the time to walk and hitch lifts, going from Faranah to Kabala, via **Hérèmakono** and **Gberia-Fotombu**, takes you through beautiful backwoods hill country.

Canoeing down the Niger

If you're looking for adventure, and have a full life-support system (GPS, tent and cooking equipment essential), Faranah is a good place to acquire a boat and **canoe down the Niger**, either as far as Kouroussa, or all the way to Bamako in Mali. A four-metre plank boat, adequate for one, can be made to order for about FG250,000, a job that can be done in a matter of days. A six- or seven-metre boat, big enough for two, will cost up to FG600,000, and can also be finished in less than a week (alternatively, you might be able to buy a sound boat that's already in use). The wood is the main expense, and while a plank boat is slightly more expensive than a dugout, it is lighter, faster and more manoeuvrable. You don't need to be an experienced canoeist for the trip, but you will need to take sufficient **food** (rice and canned food) to last the whole journey, as you cannot rely on the occasional fishing camps having food for sale (there are no villages between Faranah and Kouroussa). Money and precious items need to be protected in waterproof bags, as you're almost certain to capsize sooner or later.

The 350-kilometre trip from **Faranah to Kouroussa** should take between ten and fourteen days. The river, which widens from 30m to more than 100m in the course of this stretch, winds through **forest** which looms out from the banks, and there are several sections of **rapids** along the way, though only two difficult sections – any local fisherman will give you advice. **Wildlife** is abundant and interesting: you'll see beautiful birds, monkeys and baboons, antelope, warthogs, snakes, small crocodiles and several groups of hippos. Because they are hunted, hippos tend to stay well clear of boats but you should give them a wide berth anyway, as they can be dangerous. There are some larger crocodiles (up to four metres) but you are very unlikely to see them, and you're safe in a boat. Bilharzia is not a problem and the swimming, hippos permitting, is fine nearly everywhere. **Downstream from Kouroussa**, the riverscape opens out, running through farmland and savannah, and the channel is dotted with islands and well over a kilometre wide in places. There are plenty of villages to restock your supplies along this stretch, but the journey is less interesting, with no rapids, no crocs and few hippos. Kouroussa to Bamako is roughly a two-week trip of about 400km.

The **best time** to do this trip is after the rains (they usually finish in Oct) and before the end of the dry season (March–April). At the end of the dry season, parts of the river are very shallow, making progress slow, and the rainy season is a bad time because the water level fluctuates and camping on the banks is unsafe.

The Upper Niger National Park

The **Parc National du Haut Niger** is the second national park to open in Guinea in recent years. The park's headquarters are in the village of **SIDAKORO**, 45km from Faranah, where you can also spend the night in the very basic *campement* (●). There's no public transport to Sidakoro, so you'll need your own vehicle to get to and around the park (you can rent a vehicle and driver for a day-trip at Sidakoro for around FG200,000), and you may be able to spot buffalo and waterbuck among other wildlife (including rare chimpanzees), though the animals tend to scatter after the rains. An alternative tour of the park can be had from the waters of the **Niger River**: hiring a pirogue and guide for the day will cost around FG50–100,000 – unless you fancy having a boat made to order – see the box on p.625.

Kankan

The name alone is alluring: **KANKAN** may be mostly very ordinary, but there's a sense of place here and a depth of history that knocks spots off every other place in the country. The spell it casts arises largely from the fact that Kankan is one of the oldest and biggest Malinké towns anywhere in West Africa – the town is actually made up of a loose federation of villages which have grown into each other over time, a fact which goes some way to explaining its very laid-back and open atmosphere. At the height of the dry season, however, Kankan is so unbearably hot that you may decide to abandon visiting the region altogether. Conversely, if you're in Kankan in the **mango** season (March–April) you're in for a real treat – the town is full of mango trees.

It was Muslim warrior-traders, the **Soninké**, who are credited with the foundation of a mini-empire centred on Kankan. They arrived at the end of the seventeenth century and set themselves up in a dozen villages stretched out along the banks of the Milo River, including the embryonic – and at that time non-Muslim – Kankan. This trading empire was known as **Baté** (the village of Baté Nafadj, 40km north of Kankan, is a reminder). Kankan grew to become its capital, and by 1850 had grown to a considerable size and acquired protective walls, while its fleets of pirogues plied the Milo and Niger rivers as far as Gao in Mali. Caravans arrived from the Sahel and the desert, while from the highland forests in the south, which it largely controlled, came kola nuts, palm oil and slaves. Another reason for Kankan's ascendancy was gold, from the Buré goldfields, which extended from north of Siguiri to far up the Milo. Kankan's apogee did not last long: Samory Touré (see p.576) smashed the hegemony of the city in 1879 after a ten-month siege, and twelve years later the French were in occupation.

The Town

Kankan has a beguiling ambience, with a spacious layout and long, mango-shaded avenues; a woman on a bicycle is a rare sight in most of West Africa, common enough here. There's a university and *lycées* and lots of students (this is where many of Guinea's student unrests have started), two hospitals and a considerable, scholarly, Islamic presence. The vast **markets** are well worth a visit. The covered

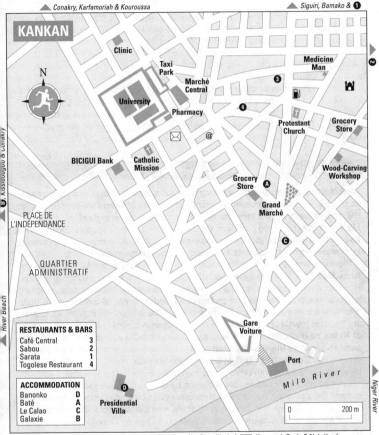

Conakry, Karfamoriah & Kouroussa

Siguiri, Bamako & ❶

KANKAN

Clinic

Taxi Park

Marché Central

Medicine Man

❸

University

Pharmacy

❹

Protestant Church

Grocery Store

BICIGUI Bank

Catholic Mission

Grocery Store Ⓐ

Grand Marché

Wood-Carving Workshop

PLACE DE L'INDÉPENDANCE

Ⓒ

QUARTIER ADMINISTRATIF

Gare Voiture

Port

RESTAURANTS & BARS

Café Central	3
Sabou	2
Sarata	1
Togolese Restaurant	4

ACCOMMODATION

Banonko	D
Baté	A
Le Calao	C
Galaxie	B

Ⓓ

Presidential Villa

Milo River

0   200 m

Mandiana (for Côte d'Ivoire), ▼ Kerouané, Beyla & Nzérékoré

River beach

Kissidougou & Guinéa

7.3 | GUINEA | Haute Guinée

Niger River

Marché Central sells mostly clothes: a lot of trashy imports, but also brilliantly coloured local confections that look great (but would require lots of guts to wear), plus myriad selections of *pagnes* and items imported from Mali and Niger, mostly rugs and blankets. There are also a couple of stalls specializing in old bits of carving, *gris-gris*, amulets and mystical substances. If you're interested in receiving some supernatural aid, then Kankan is the place to ask: **marabouts** here are considered some of the most powerful in West Africa and inscriptions and potions can be obtained easily, for a fee – you don't have to be a Muslim.

Practicalities

The main **gare voiture** is a shady patch of dust down by the river at the edge of town, but you may well find yourself dropped off at one of the minor taxi parks near the town's access roads. The main budget **accommodation** is the *Hôtel Galaxie* (☎60.30.72.53 ❶), in a quiet neighbourhood near the *briquetterie*, which has passable s/c rooms though it's a long walk to the town centre. *Hôtel Bate* (☎30.71.23.68 or 64.36.62.55 ❷) has a good restaurant, a bar and comfortable a/c rooms. An equally good and even cheaper option is the *Hôtel Le Calao* (☎30.71.27.97 ❷) right next to the market, which has spotless carpeted rooms

627

with TV and fridge, set around a surprisingly quiet courtyard. Kankan's most upmarket option is the new *Banonko Hôtel* (☎60.36.47.61 ④), locally known as *Villa Syli* – a sprawling complex of round buildings that used to be Sekou Touré's presidential palace. Rooms include breakfast, a/c and cable TV, though the quality doesn't quite justify the price. There is also a popular restaurant and bar on the grounds.

There's a host of little **cafés** and **bars** around the centre of Kankan – try the delicious 🍴 Togolese food served up in a courtyard near the Marché Central, or the fresh potato salad at the *Café Central*. The best place for a cold drink is the balcony of the 🍴 *Hôtel Baté*, where you can watch the seething activity of the market from your perch in peaceful anonymity. The most popular nightclubs are the *Sarata*, which

Sundiata, Niani and the Mali Empire

West African **gold** helped to fuel the trading networks of the Mediterranean basin as early as 500 BC. By the late eleventh century AD, the empire of **Ghana** (no connection with the modern country of the same name), with its capital at **Koumbi Saleh** in present-day Mauritania, was supplying gold, from the **Bambuk** goldfields of the upper Senegal River and the **Buré** goldfields around the present-day town of Siguiri, to trans-Saharan traders, from whose North African towns it circulated throughout the medieval world.

There are very few documentary sources for the origins of the Mali Empire – the name **Mali** itself seems to have been either an Arabic or a Fula corruption of **Mande**. However, the oral traditions of every ethnic group speaking a Mande language recount a similar tale of a charmed and charismatic founding prince, **Sundiata** of the Keita clan, who revolted against the region's oppressive **Susu** overlords in 1235 AD, defeating **Soumangourou** of the Kanté clan who had been in control of Ghana, at the **Battle of Kirina**, near Koulikoro. The Keitas captured Koumbi Saleh and then relocated the empire's capital to **Niani**, on the west bank of the Sankarani, a tributary of the Niger in present-day Guinea. (The Susu, in defeat, migrated west, moving to the Fouta Djalon highlands in the fourteenth century, and then to the coast by the fifteenth.)

Sundiata Keita consolidated his territories by declaring himself **mansa** (ruler) of all *mansas*, incorporating Aoudaghost (in present-day Mauritania), into his empire. His "control" over Djenné and Timbuktu, however, was limited, and it was not until the era of Mansa Musa I, nearly a century later, that Djenné, Timbuktu and Gao were formally annexed.

The Mali Empire was first noticed in Europe in the 1330s, when rumour spread of a **Rex Melly** ("King Melly"), an immensely rich, powerful and indulgent sovereign from the land of the black people. This story arose directly from the *hajj* pilgrimage that the seventh *mansa*, **Mansa Musa I**, made to Mecca in 1324–25, with a huge caravan of retainers and courtiers. Musa's largesse with ostentatious gifts, and the general spending-spree of his party, especially in Cairo, caused the price of gold to drop on the Egyptian market for a decade.

In a period of energetic expansion from 1325 to 1330, Musa I incorporated Djenné and Timbuktu, annexing both cities and repelling their Tuareg "protectors", marking the new era with the commissioning of huge mosques designed by the Andalucian architect **El Saheli** (whom Musa had met in Cairo) and the Sankoré university in Timbuktu. With security and unity, the trading networks and cultural exchanges flourished as never before, as people from Mali visited the great cities of North Africa, and Arab scholars based themselves in Djenné and Timbuktu.

In the religious sphere, the rulers of old Mali had been **Muslims** since the time of Sundiata, who is believed to have converted, along with his family and court. Islam, however, was closely linked with the Saharan trade, and was at least as much about oiling the wheels with incoming merchants as a personal set of beliefs. In the empire's lower ranks, the farmers, fishers, hunters, crafts people, traders and slaves were less touched by the religion of the Arabs, and remained enthusiastic adherents of their

is always packed on weekends, and the *Sabou*, a large disco with several dance floors. Kankan has a couple of thinly stocked supermarkets where you can splash out on luxuries like marmalade and soft toilet paper and the town also has an important PTT and a BICIGUI **bank**.

Moving on from Kankan is straightforward: the beautifully paved Kouroussa–Kankan road makes the trip from Kankan to **Conakry** possible in a single, long day, and the new, Chinese-built road between Kankan and **Bamako** has transformed one of the most arduous journeys in Guinea into one of the easiest. If you don't get held up at the Malian border, the trip can take as little as six hours. The best way to enter the southern forest region is via **Kissidougou**, though there is an alternative route, to the east, via Kerouané, outlined below.

traditional belief systems. As described by the Moroccan traveller **Ibn Battuta**, who visited in 1352, masked dances and recitations were part of daily life. Although richer people wore clothes, this was more a mark of status than custom, and poorer families, and most women and children, went naked, especially in the countryside.

At the time of the empire's greatest extent in the middle of the fourteenth century, the array of West African states under the control of the Keita dynasty at Niani was the largest pre-colonial political entity that ever existed in West Africa – a broad **federation** that spread from the Atlantic coast in the west to east of the Niger bend and from the Sahara in the north to the highlands of what is now Guinée Forestière in the south. Despite its size, the empire was controlled with a surprisingly light touch, through a careful hierarchical system that preserved optimum autonomy at every level, while ensuring rulers from village chiefs up always owed more allegiance to a greater authority than to each other.

Although the town of **Niani** never functioned in the centralized way that the capital of a modern state does, and other settlements were also prominent in the empire's affairs, the town was ideally positioned to control and tax the gold trade from both **goldfields**, as well as being a major salt-trading hub, jealously guarding its rights over **salt mines** deep in the Sahara. From Niani, the empire's **cavalry** and **naval fleet** could access most parts of its territory in a matter of weeks. As well as thousands of horsemen, the empire also had a **standing army** of as many as 100,000 foot soldiers, carrying spears and poison-tipped arrows for their bows.

By the late fourteenth century, Mali's **economy** had become highly sophisticated, especially with the introduction of portable cowrie shells as a new form of currency, permitting more complex forms of transaction and taxation to take place and standard exchange rates to be adopted for different commodities. Agriculturally, the empire was largely dependent on **millet**, **sorghum**, **rice** and **beans**. The American food crops – including groundnuts, cassava, maize, potatoes, tomatoes and papaya – were unheard of.

More than twenty *mansas* came and went after Sundiata, the most successful of them being Mansa Musa I, but his fourteenth-to sixteenth-century successors were largely unable to hold back the changes taking place around the empire, including the impact of **Moroccan troops** with firearms and of **European visitors** on the coast. One by one, Mali's vassal states moved out of the control of the *mansas*.

In 1545, Niani was raided by forces from the empire of Songhai, based at Gao – by now much more powerful than Mali. The Mali capital moved to **Kangaba**, downstream on the Niger River, and the "empire" was reduced to the relatively small, original Mande heartland, the **Mande Kurufa**. Over the next century it became increasingly divided and inward-looking and while remaining nominally independent of Songhai, was a spent political force. What has endured, uniquely, to the present day, is the powerful oral tradition of **epic literature and music**, linking Sundiata Keita with his distant descendants through the tales of the Mande *jelis*, or griots. Sundiata has no equal in any other West African cultural tradition.

Siguiri and Niani

North of Kankan at **SIGUIRI** lie the remains of the **French post**, established in 1888 on the hilltop over the Niger River, at the height of the campaign against Samory Touré. At independence, parts of the original defences were still standing around the administrative district of the town. Apart from that, Siguiri is known for its goldsmith industry, based on the Buré goldfields north of the town, and for being the birthplace of Ballets Africains founder Fodeba Keita and superstar singer Sekouba Bambino Diabaté. There is one budget **place to stay**: the *Niani* (①) off the Bamako road. The popular *Hôtel Tamtam* (②–③) and the *Hôtel de la Paix* (②–③) are more comfortable and reputable options. The more luxurious *Hôtel Djoma* (☎60.58.27.68 Ⓦhotelpetitbateau .net) was ransacked during the 2007 general strike, but there are plans to rebuild and its nearby club, *Acropolis*, is still the place to be on a Saturday night.

Some 80km on a very rough track southeast of Siguiri lies **NIANI**, a village on the Sankarani River (which forms the border with Mali). Nowadays, Niani doesn't look any different from your average north-Guinean town, but it was here that **Sundiata Keita** (also known as Mari-Diata; 1205–1255), the legendary founding king of the **Mali Empire**, installed his capital (see p.628). Mande griots have transmitted the legends of his reign for generations, though only excavations among the baobabs, with the uncovering of the sites of foundries and cemeteries dotted around the town, have convinced Western historians of the truthfulness of their claims.

Kérouané and Beyla

South of Kankan, the direct route to Guinée Forestière runs alongside the gaunt whaleback of the **Chaîne du Going** ridge to the town of Kérouané and then up into the remote and rugged region beyond Beyla. This is a richly historical route. On the way down to Kérouané you pass **Bissandougou**, the recruiting point and eventual capital of **Almamy Samory Touré**'s first empire; travelling by public transport, people in your vehicle will point it out to you. Whether the small cemetery with its *banco* wall surround is still there, is hard to tell, but the nineteenth-century fort has definitely returned to the soil.

Samory signed a treaty with the French at Bissandougou in 1887, hoping to keep them confined to the left bank of the Niger, but new French commanders swept the agreements aside and moved on Kankan and Bissandougou in 1890. Samory adopted scorched-earth tactics and retreated south, burning villages in his path. At Kérouané he had a fort constructed on the hilltop and from here his forces harassed the French while the warrior planned his next move (for more on Samory, see p.576).

Today, the small prefecture of **KÉROUANÉ** barely hints at its place in history. The remains (and very little remains) of the **Tata de Samory fortress** on a low hill are now the site of the "Villa" – the administrative quarter. Archeologically the interest is thin: a huge block of laterite bricks – part of the massive old wall of the fort which measured 170m across – and what looks like a gate house: a hollow hut like a honey pot near the entrance. Inside, you're supposedly able to see the stone-enshrined profile of a pregnant woman whom Samory enclosed in the wall before his withdrawal. Alongside, on the new wall, there's a faded portrait of Samory.

Moving on from Siguiri

From Siguiri it's only about an hour's drive on the new road to the **Malian border** and there's a constant flow of vehicles heading for Bamako in the morning. When the river is high enough, for the first couple of months after the rains, there are also occasional **barges** between Siguiri and Bamako.

With table-top hills rising around and the steep, bluish ridge of **Going** soaring to over 1300m, it's a fine setting. Kérouané is surprisingly lively and, although the attractions are hard to pinpoint, it does have a certain appeal. Because of the transport situation, you may well end up **staying the night** here in *chambres de passage* – very basic rooms without electricity or running water. For **meals and food**, there's a large market and some good rice and sauce in the street leading away from the police station. Nice *café fort* and *thé vert* can be had at a couple of licensed cafés up here on the left, with pleasant patios to loaf around and meet people. From here during the dry season you can watch the progress of bushfires on Mont Going – a sombre spectacle on December and January nights as giant orange tongues leap from its flanks.

South of Kerouané

There's normally a truck or two and the occasional *taxi brousse* out of Kérouané to **Nzérékoré** early each morning, though you only undertake this journey if you're willing to spend an entire day in a vehicle trying to negotiate one of the country's toughest routes, and be prepared for any eventuality – such as spending several days in the bush while the driver tries to get his vehicle out of a ditch, waits for help, and eventually abandons all efforts in favour of finding a wife in a nearby village.

From **KONSANKORO**, south of Kérouané, there's a highly rated but extremely rough hundred-kilometre track over the ranges to **Macenta**, through rarely visited **diamond-mining** country. The road is beautiful, though you may be too busy praying for safe arrival and long life to enjoy the sight of massive granite sugarloaf mountains and mesas pushing up from the bush.

Beyla

South of Kérouané lies **BEYLA**, founded in the thirteenth century by Mande-speaking kola traders, and favoured by the French in colonial times as a tobacco-growing area. If you've a tough vehicle of your own, the Beyla region is unquestionably one of Guinea's most worthwhile – a number of tracks run through the Kourandou mountains, just northeast of town. For **accommodation**, the grubby *Hôtel Simadou* (❶) is your only option.

7.4

Guinée Forestière

P iled up in the fractured border region where Guinea meets Sierra Leone, Liberia and Côte d'Ivoire, the highland chains of the southeast – commonly known as **Guinée Forestière** – provide inducements to match or surpass the Fouta Djalon. Although the region lacks the Fouta Djalon's towering cliffs and waterfalls, the highlands of Guinée Forestière weigh in with rainforest-covered ridges, challenging routes and a largely non-Islamic cultural scene. While the **environment** is under immense pressure, and huge swathes of forest have been felled by loggers and subsistence farmers, the remaining stands still harbour significant numbers of **wild animals**, including leopards, forest elephants and buffalos, and hippos and crocs in the

The Kissi – and their stone figures

The **Kissi** are a long-established indigenous people who live across the wide swath of territory from the Niger headwaters to the foothills of the southeast highlands. Adroit farmers (it's their swamp rice which you'll see along the Kissidougou–Guéckédou road), they traditionally worship their ancestors, on whose benevolence they believe they depend for the success of their crops, and maintain strong beliefs in witchcraft. Until recently, nearly all Kissi villages had their own witch-hunters (the *wulumo*), whose skills were called upon to divine the evil-minded whenever misfortune struck.

Kissi people still venerate small stone figures, each imbued with the spirit of an ancestor. These sculptures, usually in soapstone and called **pomdo** ("the dead"), can be dug up in the fields, or found in the forest, but are no longer carved today. The Kissi traditionally believe the sculptures are the physical essence of their ancestors, but their origin is an enigma. Like the *nomoli* of Sierra Leone (see p.678), they were certainly carved by an ancient culture, probably before the fifteenth century, though it's not certain that they were produced by the direct ancestors of the people who now revere them.

rivers. Chimpanzees are still hanging on, but the troops are now split into increasingly small territories of safe forest.

Climatically this is perhaps the most appealing part of the country, even if travel can be stubbornly difficult between April and November. Altitude and clouds keep it mild or warm most of the year, and while the rains are torrential, storms are accompanied by impressive electrical phenomena. There also tends to be a drier spell in the rainy season, between the end of April and mid-June.

Ethnically, the southeast is singular territory. The region's predominant **Kissi**, **Toma** and **Guerzé** inhabitants are linguistically diverse and resolutely independent. Ancestor worship, totemism and *forêts sacrés* ("sacred forests": usually a clearing within the forest where rituals are performed) are all important cultural elements. Islamic influences are far less pronounced than elsewhere and the impacts of colonialism have been light. Colonial subjugation – a gruelling village-by-village war of invasion – wasn't complete until 1920, having persisted bloodily since Samory's demise in 1898. Most of the **towns** in the forest region are recent creations, dating back no further than the first French post located at a suitable source of food, water and labour. Once victorious, the French maintained a thin and rather miserable presence. During the reign of Sekou Touré, many Guineans sought refuge in the relatively unpoliticized highlands, and tens of thousands more fled the country from here, especially to Côte d'Ivoire.

Sadly, this is not only Guinea's most beautiful, but also its most troubled region. In 2000 and 2001, the **civil wars** of Liberia and Sierra Leone spilled over into the region, and severe clashes between rebel troops and the Guinean army left some places, such as Guéckédou, in ruins. During the crisis years, Guinée Forestière also had to cope with large numbers of Sierra Leonean refugees, who returned home only to be replaced by new truckloads of people escaping the fighting in Côte d'Ivoire in 2002 and 2003. Guinea's three war-torn neighbours were all at peace at the time of writing, but it would be wise to keep an eye on political events in the area and check with your embassy or consulate before travelling into the forest. The region's recurring troubles have also meant that the **roads** are in poor condition, and travelling around the area is harder than in any other part of the country.

Kissidougou

The gateway to Guinée Forestière, **KISSIDOUGOU**, comprises three no-longer-easily-distinguishable villages. **Kenéma Pompo** is the oldest, a Kissi village which goes back to the eighteenth century, when it was tucked in its sacred forest.

The second, **Hérèmakono** (which means roughly "Home Sweet Home"), is the administrative and commercial district built away from the forest. The third, **Dioulabou** (the "Dyula town"), lies on the east side and was established by Samory's vanquished lieutenants in 1893. Kissi Kaba Keita, the ruler of the town at the time of French penetration, put up a notional resistance. Today, Kissidougou borders the largest zone of **forest** in West Africa and the sense of transition is apparent in the patches of tropical woodland around the town. The town is also notable as the centre of Guinea's main coffee-growing area.

Spacious and unusually flat, Kissidougou doesn't seem such a bad place after one of Haute Guinée's arduous taxi rides. A tiny **museum** (free), opposite the Commissariat de Police Centrale, contains two or three dozen local objects of interest, including various bits of Kissi and Kouranko ethnographia and some contemporary domestic items. Fading black-and-white photos show scenes from French colonial days. The **covered market**, in the quarter behind the central *fromager* (silk-cotton tree), is worth exploring on any day, though it is considerably more lively on Tuesdays. You'll find a fair selection, at fair prices, of the kind of imported stuff (Sierra Leone country cloth, Malian blankets, printed *pagnes*) that's found in greater quantities at the international markets of Nzérékoré and Kankan. Goods from Mali for example, often inflated in markets there, are offered at knockdown prices.

An interesting trip leads out to Kissidougou's **pont artisanal**, a liana bridge about 2km east of the town centre off the road to Kankan. Take the second turning on the right after the roundabout and keep walking towards the water supply building.

Practicalities

Kissidougou has a surprising selection of places to stay. A very decent option is the slightly distant *Hôtel Savannah* (℡60.43.97.54 ❷), with well-appointed a/c rooms and others with fan. It's the only hotel that provides reliable electricity, and also houses a good restaurant and nightclub. In town, the comfortable *Mantise Résidence* (℡60.46.75.80 ❷) is the most popular haunt of well-heeled travellers, while the once-luxurious *Mantise Palace* (❷) is technically functional but mostly deserted. The staff at the basic *Hôtel Béléfé* (℡60.63.89.00 ❶) are friendly and obliging, though rooms are dark and set around a noisy bar. Two quieter budget options are the *Doussou Condé* (℡60.49.80.52 ❶) near the market, or the pleasant and shady 🏃 *Hôtel Nelson Mandela* (❶), which offers enormous rooms and a reliable restaurant.

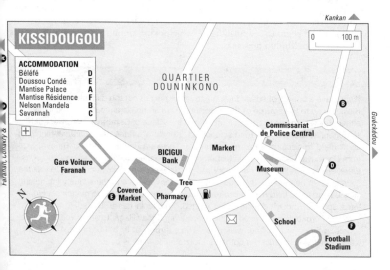

The Faranah road has the largest selection of **street food**, including huge servings of delicious fried plantain and *atiéké*. There are few proper **restaurants** in town but plenty of enjoyable, mostly unnamed bars along the roadside. Kissidougou has both a **post office** and BICIGUI **bank**, which face each other across the curve of the main street, as well as a hospital.

Moving on from Kissidougou, the road surface to **Faranah** has been improved, reducing the journey time to a couple of hours. The road to **Kankan** is slower: minibuses ply the route daily, but the best day to find a more comfortable vehicle is Thursday, when Kankan traders return from the Guéckédou market. A scenic place to stop en route to Kankan is **TOKOUNO**, crowded beneath a mountain escarpment. There's a hotel here, eating places and a *balafon* workshop, where you can buy the instruments and watch them being made.

Kissidougou to Nzérékoré

The road from Kissidougou into the deeper regions of Guinée Forestière leads via Guéckédou to Macenta and Nzérékoré. **GUÉCKÉDOU** used to be a flourishing centre, attracting a vibrant mix of Sierra Leonean, Ivoirian, Liberian, Guinean and Malian traders to its lively market. Unfortunately, much of the fighting between the Guinean army and rebels from Sierra Leone and Liberia in 2000–01 was concentrated here, killing hundreds of townspeople and leaving the town completely in ruins. While scars of the conflict still linger in the form of wrecked houses and a visible military presence, the town's residents have been busy rebuilding and Guéckédou is once again bustling with traffic and trade. It even boasts a few decent hotels, including the *Terminus* (**①**) along the road to Kissidougou, and the more upscale *Tomandou* (**②**), near the hospital.

The route southeast from Guéckédou has been vastly improved in recent years, reducing total transport time between Kissidougou and Nzérékoré to as little as six hours.

Macenta and around

Once out of Guéckédou, the serious forest starts with the climb on the road from the bridge over the Makona, just beyond **BOFOSSOU** – a large village and military post dating back to 1905. It's a steep haul up what's known, somewhat mysteriously, as the *descente des cochons*. Whether pigs or nefarious humans are being referred to, you do indeed begin to see small hairy swine poking around at the roadside – signs of a strong non-Muslim presence.

The source of the Niger

If you have a couple of spare days, an adventurous but not too difficult trip leads from Kissidougou to the **source of the Niger** (there are no hotels en route, so you'll have to either stay with locals or camp). First base is the village of **Bambaya**, northwest of Kissidougou, accessible up a road signposted "Kobikoro" off the Kissi–Faranah highway; you'll need to *déplace* a taxi to reach here. There's a Friday market at **Baleya**, 3km from Bambaya. Second base is **Kobikoro**, 12km further on, where the *chef* and *sous-préfet* are both welcoming – in theory you need the *sous-préfet*'s permission to visit the source. From here on up, the route gets tough for walkers and the scenery interesting as you head up to third base, **Forokonia**, 20km further on. There are magnificent forest trees up here, though they're being logged. Forokonia has a Thursday market. On reaching Forokonia you'll need a guide (ask around the village) to show you the actual source, a three- or four-hour walk away. The **source** – at 9° 5' 00" north, 10° 47' 14" west – itself isn't impressive, but the surrounding scenery is beautiful.

The oldest inhabitants of the Macenta district, the **Toma**, earned respect from the French "pacification" troops for their resilience despite raid after raid on their isolated villages. Of all the highland peoples, it was the Toma who most harried the French invaders. Their last stronghold, the fortified village of Boussedou, was attacked by two French expeditions and numerous cannon before it finally succumbed in 1907.

Once battered into submission, the Toma found favour with the French for being good scouts and solid soldiers, utterly at home in the forest. They're fairly small people and they may have distant "pygmy" ancestors: oral history in the forest regions recounts stories of ancient inhabitants of small stature who were decimated by the taller invaders from the north. What's certain is that the Toma lost ground to the Malinké and ultimately mixed with Dyula Malinké to form the Toma–Manian. Today, their language – **Loma** – is a Mande tongue, related to Malinké.

You should look out for highly impressive **dancing** while you're in the Toma region, but you'll be lucky indeed to have the opportunity to witness one of the major life-cycle **celebrations**. Traditionally at circumcisions, marriages, births and funerals, "bird men" – the *onilégagi* – danced, dressed in feathers and painted with kaolin; *lanebogué* pranced and hopped on their stilts; and *akorogi* swirled and bounded in their raffia-leaf costumes and haunted masks. Similar dances take place in Côte d'Ivoire (at least in times of peace), but generally with your attendance and money in mind.

Around 44km from Guéckédou the route passes through **NIAGÉZAZOU**, tucked in the forest near a liana bridge over the Makona. Then, some 5km beyond the road bridge over the Makona River, you might check out the village of **NIOGBOZOU** up a side track shortly after the old mission centre of Balouma. Built on a rocky platform and apparently encircled with lianas, Niogbozou used to have a famous troupe of acrobats, dancers and stilt walkers who toured Europe several times before independence.

Passing from Kissi country into the lands of the Toma you arrive in **MACENTA**. This used to be the most important town in the highlands, chosen for its central position as a supply base for the "pacification columns" sent to the remote areas. Free Liberian troops attacked Macenta in 1906 but were fended off, and it was only in 1908 that the limits of the two territories were set. The French tried to grow tea in Macenta, but not with much success. They had much more luck with **coffee**, which remains important, though much of the crop is smuggled out of the country. The biggest indigenous cash crop is **kola**.

Today, Macenta is a pleasing, moderate-sized town set amid a tumble of hills with fine views all around, and still composed of hundreds of thatched, round-house compounds. It's unusual in having a **bank**. If you find yourself **staying** in town, you have the choice between the pretty *Palm Hôtel* (℡60.42.02.40 ●) in the centre and the very basic *Hôtel Magnetic* (●), practically in the *gare voiture*. There are also two nicer hotels several kilometres from town along the Nzérékoré road: the friendly *Badala* (℡60.58.52.23 ●) and the slightly more upmarket *Hôtel Rougni* (℡64.44.77.42 ●). Out of Macenta through the Malinké quarter, there's the wild **route to Kérouané** (see box, p.631) and, ultimately, Kankan.

Sérédou to Nzérékoré

As you burrow through the jungle and over the ridges, there's a string of minor but interesting stopoffs if you have your own transport. One place where trucks and Peugeots often stop to stock up on palm wine or food is **SÉRÉDOU**. At 800m it straddles a col through the moist, jungly **Ziama hills** and most vehicles need the rest by the time they've got here. Church bells are heard ringing here: it's an old mission and quinine research station. The roadside cafés serve delicious bush-rat stew to passing drivers and daring tourists.

The Guerzé

The people of the Nzérékoré district and eastwards are **Guerzé**. In Liberia, the same people call themselve **Kpelle** and are the largest ethnic group. Part of the Mande-speaking peoples who trace their ultimate origins back to the Mali Empire, they are related closely to the Mende of Sierra Leone and by language and some cultural elements to the Toma of Macenta. By tradition, they are profoundly animist and quite resistant to Islamic influence; their mythic ancestor descended from the sky, married a local woman and settled east of Nzérékoré. Tradition relates that a man called **Yegu**, with a number of followers, populated the Nzérékoré district late in the nineteenth century, and these headmen were the ones in power at the time of the French arrival. It's hard to unravel the veracity of stories like these – they can easily be read as apologetics for subsequent French actions – but it seems more likely that the Guerzé had been around for rather longer than the French wanted to believe, and that colonial chiefs were not often pre-invasion notables.

There's no doubt about the **Guerzé revolt** in 1911, abetted by free Kpelle forces from Liberia, which was put down by a Captain Hecquet. His life was abruptly ended during the campaign by a poisoned arrow.

The stretch of road from Sérédou to **IRIÉ** is renowned for its *lepidoptera*, including the giant swallowtail *Papillio antimachus*, Africa's largest **butterfly**, with a wingspan of up to 23cm. The males are occasionally seen around the treetops and, very rarely, sipping moisture at muddy puddles; female giant swallowtails, however, are extremely elusive.

NZÉBÉLA is a traditional music centre, though whether you will have much chance of hearing *divogi* drums and *pouvogi* trumpets is hard to tell. Shortly after the village of **SAMOÉ**, a path leads left to a small hamlet where a group of **sacred tortoises** are kept by the community. Different groups of people throughout the forest region identify with a range of animals; the tortoise is popular totem. If you can't find them, you could try asking the White Fathers in Samoé.

Nzérékoré

With a very large Wednesday market and an atmosphere of thriving commerce, **NZÉRÉKORÉ** is the emerging city of Guinée Forestière. Set amid the forest and traced through by tributary streams which feed the Mani River border with Liberia, the town's shack-lined dirt streets straggle stylelessly over hillocky ground for several kilometres in each direction. Yet for a backwoods agglomeration with not much of a discernible centre, so far from anywhere (it's closer to Monrovia and even Abidjan than to Conakry), Nzérékoré is really rather an enjoyable place to be.

In the 1990s, when the flood of refugees began pouring in from wars in neighbouring countries, the UN and NGO presence in Nzérékoré mushroomed until white Land cruisers became nearly as numerous as yellow taxis. However, at the time of writing, the last refugee camp in the area was about to close, so the town may soon be returned largely to its inhabitants.

Nzérékoré just has to be visited on **market day**, Wednesday. From the permanent market, stalls overflow onto the main street and the activity stretches from the hospital to the roundabout. Liberians and Ivoirians are prominent; women show off their best wraps and the atmosphere vibrates with the racket of trade – everything from palm oil in all its various grades and qualities to a riot of local produce to clothes (some cotton-shirt bargains), Liberian plastic trinkets, prints and indigo *gara*. By no means unique to Nzérékoré, but unmissable if you've not seen them before, are the traditional **pharmacists** who set up on market day with a festoon of graphic boards, illustrating

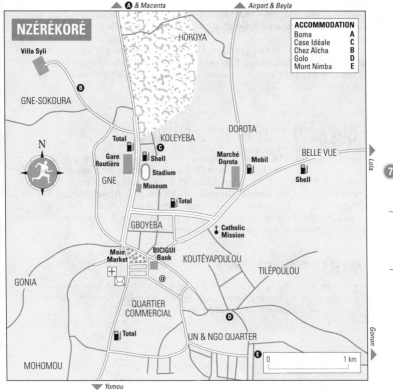

NZÉRÉKORÉ

HOROYA

Villa Syli

GNE-SOKOURA

KOLEYEBA

DOROTA

BELLE VUE

Total
Gare
Routière

Shell

Stadium

Museum

Marché
Dorota

Mobil

Shell

GNE

Total

GBOYEBA

Catholic
Mission

Main
Market

BICIGUI
Bank

KOUTÉYAPOULOU

TILÉPOULOU

GONIA

@

QUARTIER
COMMERCIAL

Total

UN & NGO QUARTER

MOHOMOU

Yomou

ACCOMMODATION	
Boma	A
Case Idéale	C
Chez Aïcha	B
Golo	D
Mont Nimba	E

their range of treatments for complaints ranging from worms to impotence. Crafts, unless you count fabrics, are fewer, but there are good lines in sandals, wallets and some beautifully worked and relatively inexpensive silver. A better bet for crafts are the stalls dotted among the trees in the forest to the west of town, where you can see women creating traditional orange-and-black **mud cloth**.

As for **moving on from Nzérékoré**, the town is a bit of a cul-de-sac, as Liberia isn't yet a destination high on most people's itineraries while Côte d'Ivoire, and particularly the western region across the border from Guinée Forestière, remains unpredictable in the aftermath of the Ivoirian civil war. The Monts Nimba range, 40km to the southeast, is worth a visit, however.

Practicalities

There's a BICIGUI **bank** by the market (Mon–Fri 8.00am–12.30pm & 2.30–4:30pm) with an occasionally-functional ATM (the only one outside of Conakry). **Internet** access is available just south of here. The **post office** (Mon–Sat 8am–4pm) is a couple of minutes' walk south of the market.

As for **accommodation**, there's a decent selection of places to stay around town.

Boma 3km from town in the northern Boma *quartier* ☎60.36.57.05. Tidy rooms scattered around a pleasantly landscaped garden. ➊
Case Idéale town centre ☎30.80.11.08. This tidy place has the advantage of being close to the *gare*

voiture, though its noisy nightclub will keep you awake at weekends. ➊

Chez Aïcha northwest of the town centre ☎64.36.27.63. Run by an effusive Senegalese woman and offering a handful of immaculate rooms behind an excellent courtyard restaurant. Often full, so try to reserve ahead. ❶

Golo down a dirt road in the eastern part of town ☎64.37.61.66. Comfortable rooms with fan and TV, though the restaurant may not have much of a choice. ❸

Mont Nimba out beyond the NGO *quartier* in the southeast of town ☎64.67.70.15. Owned by President Lansana Conté, with all mod-cons including a/c, satellite TV, a casino, swimming pool and a fabulous nightclub – all quite some surprise in the rainforest so far from Conakry. ❹

Lola and the Monts Nimba

East of Nzérékoré, the scenery along the way is nothing special as you go through the sizeable town of **LOLA**, 37km from Nzérékoré (excellent Tuesday market) and then reach **NZOO**, 28km further, from where you start to get good views of the dramatic ridge of the **Monts Nimba** – with their peak Mont Richard Molard at 1752m, Guinea's highest point – running into Liberia. On the way to the Côte d'Ivoire border, the road tunnels through impressive thickets of **giant bamboo** and tracks over precarious wooden bridges in the forest.

Ask the female shopkeepers

"As a rule it is safer to ask women or those who are fixed in boutiques for directions. Why? Because women don't generally hassle you and those who have to tend a boutique will not insist on accompanying you."

Ezra Simon, USA

The Monts Nimba Reserve

The main road to the UNESCO Biosphere Reserve of **Monts Nimba Reserve**, which begins at the village of **GBAKORÉ**, 15km southeast of Lola on the way to Nzoo, has been closed to tourists "due to mining activities in the mountains". The peaks are still accessible (and it seems the southern part of the range in Guinea is being conserved, un-mined), but trekkers have to approach them via a different route, not off the route to the Ivoirian border, but via the village of **BOSSOU**, due south of Lola and easily reachable by taxi along a 20km track.

The forest-covered hills of **Mont Gban** rising immediately behind Bossou are home to a troupe of tool-using **chimpanzees**, held sacred as totems by the local **Manon** people and the subject of research by Guinean and Japanese primatologists –one of only six long-term chimp research projects in Africa. Their **Green Corridor** tree-planting project (⊛tinyurl.com/3cztzh) aims to reconnect the Bossou hills chimp habitat with the much bigger Monts Nimba biosphere reserve, providing a corridor of woodland along which chimpanzees can move freely. It's an ambitious project but one that is entirely realizable with the support of the Manon.

Staff at the **Bossou Environmental Research Institute** will give you an update on the project and on trail conditions and may be able to take you up into the forest to see the chimps – sightings are almost guaranteed – but you need an early start as the trip takes several hours. Be sure to hire a knowledgeable guide to tackle the peaks – the path is rough and it's easy to get lost. The best plan is to stay the night at the guest house in the village of **SÉRINGBARA**, at the end of the tree-planting corridor, 5km from Bossou, and make an early start from there: it's a stiff six-hour hike to the top of the ridge. The best time to go is during the dry season; otherwise, you risk having your views obscured by thick cloud cover.

Sierra Leone

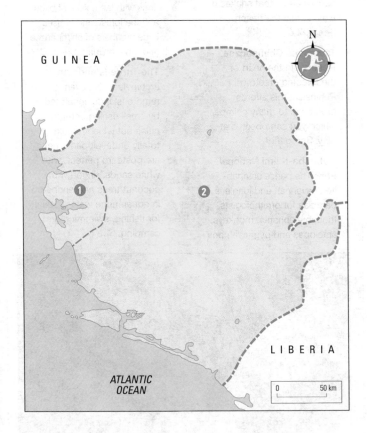

GUINEA

N

1

2

LIBERIA

ATLANTIC
OCEAN

0   50 km

Highlights 640
Introduction and Basics 641
8.1 Freetown and around 670
8.2 The interior 689

Sierra Leone highlights

✳ **River No. 2 Beach** Among the irresistible beaches of the Freetown Peninsula, River No. 2 offers crocodile-spotting excursions up the narrow creek that snakes its way across the beach. See p.686

✳ **Tacugama Chimpanzee Reserve** In the heart of the forested Freetown Peninsula, this affords protection to many chimps, which you can observe at play. See p.688

✳ **Outamba-Kilimi National Park** The park's uninhabited savannah and jungle is paradise for ornithologists, though elephants, monkeys, antelopes and pygmy hippos may also be spotted. See p.691

✳ **Tiwai Island** This small island in the Moa River is covered in colourful tropical scenery, rings with the noises of birds and the forest, and houses large numbers of chimpanzee and other animals. See p.697

✳ **The Turtle Islands** An archipelago of seven remote islands, inhabited by small fishing communities but which remain totally undeveloped. They are postcard perfect, with white sands, ringed with coconut trees and anchored in aquamarine waters. Ideal for fishing, swimming and camping. See p.700

▲ Moa River, Tiwai Island

Introduction and Basics

Having emerged from a ten-year war imported from neighbouring Liberia, which devastated the entire country and forced more than a third of the population into exile, **Sierra Leone** is now enjoying some stability and economic development. The dramatic transformation in the country's fortunes owes much to the fortitude of a war-weary population and an economy buoyed by exports of rutile, bauxite and diamonds. The departure of **UN troops** in December 2005 was the clearest sign yet of the country's successful rehabilitation. Britain continues to play a significant role with Sierra Leone receiving the highest level of British foreign aid per capita in Africa. As Côte d'Ivoire and Liberia follow Sierra Leone's lead in national reconciliation and peace-building, any jitters felt in Freetown these days tend to come from the fragile political situation in neighbouring Guinea.

With foreign investment coming in and the country's infrastructure being rebuilt, Sierra Leone is peaceful, safe, and starting to reclaim its place as one of West Africa's most attractive destinations. With long stretches of white, sandy beaches, lush forests and significant nature reserves, the country has an intrinsic appeal that surpasses that of many other West African nations.

People

Sierra Leone's **ethnic configuration** is unusual. Two language groups dominate: the **Temne**, who speak one of the idiosyncratic West Atlantic languages, are concentrated in the central north, inland from Freetown; the **Mende**, whose language is distantly related to the rest of the large Mande group, are dominant more to the southeast, especially around Bo and Kenema. The Mende are a many-sided group, incorporating the Komende, the Gbamende (which just means "different Mende") and the Sewa. In addition, both Temne and Mende have culturally absorbed many of the less populous groups around, often through the powerful influence of their flourishing **secret societies**. Along the coast, for example, the **Bullom** and **Sherbro**, who once spoke the same language (Bullom), now tend to speak Temne north of Freetown and Mende to the south.

Smaller inland groups like the **Loko** (around Port Loko) and the Limba have moved into close association with the Temne, while in the east and southeast, the **Kono** and **Kissi** have moved towards Mende culture.

In the far north, the **Susu** (northwest), **Koranko** and **Yalunka** (northeast) have remained closer to their Mande roots. In the north and east there's also a fair scattering of **Fula** communities – many of them exiles from Guinea.

What is remarkable about Sierra Leonean society is the influence of the **Krios** (Creoles) – ex-slaves of diverse origin who were settled here for several decades from the end of the eighteenth century and who were established in positions of power before the interior was carved onto Britain's plate a century later. Numerically, Krios have always been a small group, confined mostly to the Freetown Peninsula. With the invasion and "protection" of the interior, they lost their influence with the colonial government to British-appointed tribal chiefs, whose descendants have mostly run the country since independence.

If you travel widely in Sierra Leone you're likely to meet quite a few **chiefs**. These men – and women – will often be your introduction to a small town or village. Local government in the three provinces (Northern, Southern and Eastern) is organized around the 169 paramount chiefdoms, which have the status of local councils. They are not structured according to strict ethnic divisions, though most of them have a dominant group. Beneath the paramount chiefs come section chiefs and village chiefs.

In the same way that the **Krio language**, partly derived from archaic English, has made a lasting and widespread imprint on

Sierra Leone's **area**, about 72,000 square kilometres, is a little smaller than Scotland or Maine. The country has a relatively high **population** density, with just over six million people.

Sierra Leone's foreign debt was estimated at a manageable US$110 million in 2007 following the landmark cancellation of debts worth US$994 million under the World Bank's heavily indebted poor countries (HIPC) initiative. At the time, the World Bank hailed the post-conflict recovery as the most successful in Africa after the government effected key reforms to the economy, government, administration, health and education.

After two terms as president, Ahmed Tejan Kabbah of the SLPP stepped down after presidential elections in August 2007 to the APC's **Ernest Bai Koroma**.

Suggestions as to the derivation of the **name** "Sierra Leone" (Salone in Krio) include the first Portuguese visitors supposedly referring to the peninsula as *serra leão*, or "lion-like mountain". The possibility that the area swarmed with lions in the fifteenth century seems the most likely.

Sierra Leonean society, so Krio influence has given a broadly **Christian** colouration to the whole country, especially the south and west, but most deeply ingrained in and around Freetown. You'll see more **mosques** around the northern and eastern fringes of the country. **Indigenous religion** is deep-rooted and widely practised, with the powerful **secret societies** (see p.698) playing a major role in keeping it alive.

Where to go

Geographically, Sierra Leone is diverse. A steep indented coast at the capital, **Freetown**, and shallow sand-banks and mangrove swamps elsewhere along the Atlantic coast are backed by tidal creeks that penetrate far inland and make a mess of the road system in the south and west. Further upcountry, the land rises through dense forest (most of it now cleared) to rolling savannah hills, rocky outcrops and mountains. The remaining patches of **rainforest**, mostly in the far southeast, beyond the Moa River, are nowadays islands in a sea of secondary growth and shifting agriculture. Most of central Sierra Leone is covered by dry open plains (*bolylands*). In colonial days, these lands used to be intensively cultivated, but these days, they are farmed on a household or community basis, though cultivation suffers from lack of tools, seeds and labour.

Swamp rice still covers large parts of the lowlands.

Freetown has experienced a massive boom in the construction of hotels and guesthouses, with rooms in the capital now exceeding demand. During the week, the peninsula's beaches are largely deserted, while weekends see a scattering of NGO workers and resident expats heading particularly to Lakka and River No. 2 Beach. The small tourist industry that had been established along the coast by the British and French in the 1980s is only slowly recovering. While most visitors tend not to look beyond the obvious appeal of the peninsula, travel out of Freetown into the provinces and right up to the borders with Guinea and Liberia is safe and highly recommended: **Outamba-Kilimi National Park** in the north, **Tiwai Island Nature Reserve** and the **Gola Forest** in the south and some unusually high hills and mountains in the east (including the spectacular **Mount Bintumani**) are all worthy goals. With peace restored, the greatest danger – and not an unusual one in West Africa – probably comes from using the roads.

When to go

From **May to November**, most of the country gets drenched in heavy and prolonged **monsoon rain** (an average of more than an inch a day – 30mm – throughout July & Aug).

Freetown itself has a tough attitude to cameras, and you're advised to be careful. There's no permit necessary, however, and so long as you avoid getting uniforms, banks and government buildings in the viewfinder and apply due respect, you'll find that most of the country is easier than usual for photography. Often enough, people will line up enthusiastically for group portraits ("Mek yu snap wi").

Plugs and power

Electricity is rationed in Freetown, with only a quarter of the city receiving power at any one time. Upcountry the situation can be even more unreliable, and small towns may not have any mains supply at all, in which case it's down to who has a generator and fuel.

Only in the extreme south, around Sulima, is there a short break in the rains during July or August. While temperatures aren't extremely high, humidity is usually excessive, above all along the coast.

The country has an unusual statistic: the **lowest night-time temperature** ever recorded in Freetown (19°C) is actually the *highest* record minimum for any African country (every other country has recorded a cooler night) – an indication of Freetown's altogether very uncomfortable climate much of the year.

The "risk" of visiting either at the start of the rains or when they've nearly finished – in other words the months of May or November – is often repaid with brilliant green landscapes, wonderful skies and tolerable road conditions; but between these months, travel away from the hard-surfaced routes varies from slow and gruelling to literally impossible.

In the **dry season**, a *harmattan* wind from the northeast can bring slightly cooler, dusty weather even to the coast. It's very difficult to predict clear blue skies and good visibility between December and April.

Getting there from the rest of Africa

Geographically, Sierra Leone is isolated, with just two neighbours, neither of them well

Average temperatures and rainfall

	Jan	Feb	Mar	Apr	May	June	July	Aug	Sept	Oct	Nov	Dec
Freetown												
Temperatures °C												
Min (night)	24	24	25	25	25	24	23	23	23	23	24	24
Max (day)	29	30	30	31	30	30	32	31	32	29	29	29
Rainfall mm	13	3	13	56	160	302	894	902	610	310	132	41
Days with rainfall	1	1	2	6	15	23	27	28	25	23	12	4
Bo												
Temperatures °C												
Min (night)	20	21	21	22	22	21	21	21	21	21	21	20
Max (day)	32	34	35	34	32	31	28	28	30	31	31	31
Rainfall mm	8	16	76	130	252	368	406	436	419	325	170	38
Koidu-Sefadu												
Temperatures °C												
Min (night)	14	17	19	20	21	20	20	20	20	20	19	17
Max (day)	32	34	35	34	33	31	29	29	31	32	31	31
Rainfall mm	10	20	96	160	228	282	269	411	401	292	145	41

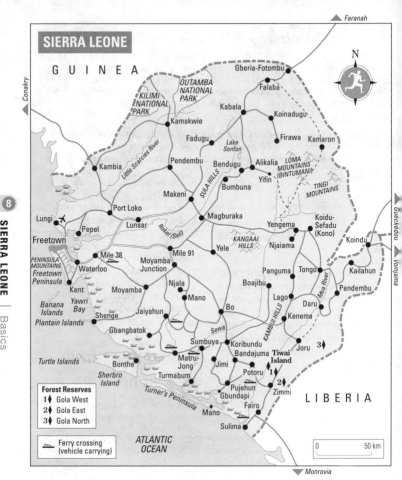

Forest Reserves
1♦ Gola West
2♦ Gola East
3♦ Gola North

🚢 Ferry crossing
(vehicle carrying)

0   50 km

connected themselves. Nearly all visitors arrive in Sierra Leone by air.

Flights within Africa

International flights arrive at Sierra Leone's main Lungi international airport, across the Sierra Leone River estuary from Freetown. From **Banjul**, there are flights operated by

For details on **getting to Sierra Leone from outside Africa**, plus important practical information applying to all West African countries, covering health, transport, cultural hints and more, see Basics, pp.19–28.

Bellview (twice weekly) and SLOK (three times a week). Bellview also connects **Lagos** with Freetown four times a week. From **Conakry**, there are flights with Paramount twice a week. Bellview operates once a week from **Accra** while Kenya Airways and SLOK each have three flights a week from Accra. Brussels Airlines and Bellview have weekly flights from **Abidjan**. SLOK flies in from **Monrovia** three times a week and from **Dakar** twice a week. Dakar also has a weekly flight with Bellview.

Check with your travel agent about **airport tax**, usually included in the price of the ticket on flights to Europe, but sometimes payable on departure for regional African flights.

Overland from Liberia

With **Liberia** at peace again, there's regular traffic between the two countries, the journey from Monrovia to the border at Bo (Liberia) by the bridge over the Mano River taking about two hours and the onward trip to Bo (Sierra Leone), using a small ferry over the Moa River, another three hours.

Overland from Guinea

From **Guinea**, the principal **Conakry–Freetown** route is via Pamelap and Kambia. By private vehicle or bush taxi, assuming no border delays, this route, mostly on tarred road, is about a seven-hour drive. By bus, usually involving a change of vehicle on the Guinean side of the border as well as tiresome waits at Guinea's numerous military checkpoints, the journey takes a full day – at least.

Less-trodden routes into Sierra Leone include the track off the Conakry–Mamou road east of Kindia, to **Madina-Woula** for access to the Outamba-Kilimi National Park and Kamakwie (an extremely tough route, even with your own 4x4); and the very little used route from Faranah to Falaba in the northeast, on which there's a good chance you'll have to walk the 10km of no-man's-land in the middle.

There is also significant passenger traffic on large, motorized canoes, known as *pampas*, between Guinea and Sierra Leone. Take advice and use your common sense before buying a passage as they are frequently overloaded: dozens drowned when a boat sank in August 2007. The latest **passenger ferry** on the Conakry run is the 350-seater *Thanasis*, commissioned in October 2007.

Red tape and visas

Visas are required by all nationalities except for ECOWAS (Economic Community of West African States) nationals. They range from three months' validity from the date of issue for a single-entry visa, to six months or one year (multiple-entry). Stays granted depend on your circumstances, but you can always extend your stay (within the limits of your visa) at the immigration office on Rawdon Street in Freetown.

In West Africa, Sierra Leone has embassies, high commissions or other representatives in Dakar, Banjul, Conakry, Monrovia, Accra, Abuja and Lagos. In countries with no Sierra Leonean representation, British embassies and consulates are a good starting-point for enquiries.

Once in Sierra Leone, you can obtain visas in Freetown for The Gambia, Ghana, Guinea, Liberia, Mali, Nigeria and Senegal.

Info, websites, maps

The best place to get tourist information is the **National Tourist Board** in Freetown (see p.671 for addresses). They have leaflets, maps (including the Shell map – see below) and up-to-date information on travel and accommodation. They carry their own *Visitor's Guide to Sierra Leone*, plus hotel flyers and potential excursion itineraries from fledgling tour-operators. Otherwise, you can also rely on the British High Commission to have up-to-date information for travellers. If you're intending to travel upcountry to visit the nature reserves, it's really worthwhile contacting the **Conservation Society** in Freetown (see p.682).

Maps

Up-to-date **maps** of Sierra Leone are rare – about the best you'll find is the 1:560,000 map published by International Travel Maps. Shell Sierra Leone also publish a dated tourist map of the country at 1:396,000, with a fanciful rash of tarmac roads, and Freetown street plans on the reverse. You can get it from the Tourist Board or from vendors outside the Post Office on Siaka Stevens Street.

If you're looking for **regional mapping**, try the Department of Lands and Surveys in the New England neighbourhood, where, if they're in stock, you can buy somewhat old but useful 1:50,000 maps from a mapped grid of the whole country. The UNDP office at 13 Bath St is a much better bet and holds an extensive map collection, including recent satellite imagery, showing detailed topography and vegetation cover. You make your selection from a catalogue and the maps are printed in A1 size for a fee of about £2.60/$5.00 each.

For **travel updates**, news links and general information, check out Ⓦtheroughguidetowestafrica .blogspot.com.

Websites

Sierra Leone is still chasing a full online presence, but the following can be very useful:

Sierra Leone High Commission UK Ⓦwww.slhc-uk.org.uk. Useful starting-place.
Sierra Leone Encyclopedia Ⓦwww.daco-sl.org /encyclopedia. Impressive raft of materials, annually updated, funded by the UN Development Programme.
Visit Sierra Leone Ⓦwww.visitsierraleone.org. Regularly updated, this is the main portal for up-to-date info, nicely straddling the tourist–local divide. Useful discussion board.
Sierra Leone Web Ⓦwww.sierra-leone.org. No longer has news but you can still access a mass of archived news and cultural articles, including some fascinating old documents, plus an email directory.
Patriotic Vanguard Ⓦwww.thepatrioticvanguard .com. User-friendly news and opinion site.
Cocorico Ⓦtinyurl.com/ypawub. Interesting online newspaper.

The media

There are perhaps a dozen **papers**, mostly in English and mostly published at best once a week in Freetown. *Standard Times* (Ⓦtinyurl .com/2ajuox), *Concord Times* (Ⓦwww .concordtimessl.com) and *Awareness Times* (Ⓦtinyurl.com/yq97ax) are the most high-profile. Overseas news mags are also available, including *Africa Week* (usually on sale in Freetown the week after its Friday publication in the UK), the monthly *Africa Business* and the quarterly *BBC Focus on Africa*.

The state TV station **SLTV** broadcasts news, movies, local football and cheap imported docu-fillers. A new TV station **ABC Television-Africa** was launched in 2005.

Radio, apart from the Sierra Leone Broadcasting System (**SLBS**) on 99.9FM, includes FM stations FM98.1, **VOH FM 96.2, SLAJ** and Kiss FM104, airing a mix of music and chat. **BBC World Service** can be heard in

Freetown on 94.3FM, in Bo on 94.5FM and in Kenema on 95.3FM. **Kalleone**, 105.7FM, owned by footballer Mohamed Kallon, is the best for sports news while **Capital** 104.9 FM (Ⓦwww.capitalradio.sl; Freetown and Bo), is the pick for music and reliable weather and travel info, with a fresh, western play-list and loquacious British presenters.

Health

Schistosomiasis (bilharzia) and **river blindness** are both common in the countryside. But apart from a high incidence of **malaria** (for more on prophylaxis and treatment, see p.40), Sierra Leone's main health problems for travellers revolve around water supplies. The lack of clean water is especially acute towards the end of the dry season in the north; even piped water may come straight from an open tank. Freetown's water supplies come from a huge dam up in the hills of the Freetown Peninsula, and, although it is equipped with a purification system, it is old and occasionally breaks down. It's best to drink bottled water or use water-purifying tablets.

Medical treatment in Sierra Leone is best avoided, but in an emergency, contact one of the hospitals in Freetown listed on p.683. There are pharmacies in Freetown and larger regional towns.

Costs, money, banks

Sierra Leone's currency is the **leone** (£1=Le5800; $1=Le2950; €1=4300). Notes of Le500, Le1000, Le5000 and Le10,000 are in circulation and larger denominations should appear before 2010. Coins of Le50, Le100 and Le500 are also in use. Potentially confusing for travellers going upcountry is the northern habit of referring to "**pounds**" rather than leones, a pound being Le2 (when leones were introduced in 1964, they were valued at UK£1=Le2).

As for **costs**, Freetown is expensive (despite the boom in hotel building coinciding with the departure of the UN contingent and many NGOs), with the price of keeping generators running through the night to

Sierra Leone's official fuel costs hover around Le14,500/gallon or Le2900/litre, for petrol or diesel, but if you want some you may have to pay the black-market price, which is more like Le20,000/gallon (Le4500/litre).

Units of measurement

Most measurements in Sierra Leone are still given in old Imperial units – yards, feet and inches, pounds and ounces, gallons (100 fluid ounces) and pints (20 fluid ounces). Where distances are given on signposts, they are usually in miles. To convert from miles to kilometres, multiply by eight and divide by five: 5 miles is about 8km.

supply air conditioning a major factor. Up-country costs are reduced by the limited range of options for spending money, including no hotels or restaurants of real standing. Basic chop-house meals can be had for around Le3000, though Western-style restaurants tend to charge Western-style prices.

Cash advances on **credit cards** and exchange of traveller's **cheques** are both offered by the Rokel Bank on Siaka Stevens Street in Freetown, though it is still easiest to travel with a large bag of Le5000 notes. You can change foreign cash either at the main banks or in one of the **exchange bureaux** around Freetown's Siaka Stevens Street or on Lumley Beach Road, which usually have a better rate. There's also a significant parallel ("black") market in pounds, dollars and euros centred on Siaka Stevens Street, where higher-denomination notes tend to get better exchange rates. Be sure to count notes carefully before handing over your hard currency.

Getting around

There are no scheduled internal flights in Sierra Leone, although Eagle Air offers **charter services** to the provinces and Paramount, UTair and Helog Aviation charter helicopters to anywhere, though naturally this doesn't come cheap.

Even with the road network being rebuilt with EU funding, heading upcountry by road requires a lot of patience. There's no large bus service in Sierra Leone, but **bush taxis** and **poda podas** (minibuses) connect Freetown with major towns in the interior, including Port Loko, Bo, Makeni,

Kenema, Pamelap and Kabala, with at least daily services, though as ever it pays to arrive early at the garage. It's much harder to explore smaller villages upcountry, and once you leave the main arteries, long waits may be required to find transport. (Note that the railway lines and abandoned stations you'll see in several towns speak of a rail network that went defunct in the 1970s.)

If you aim to spend much time in the interior you may want to **rent a vehicle** in Freetown (see p.682 for firms to contact). If you're chartering a 4x4 jeep from outside *Bintumani* or *Cape Sierra* hotels expect to pay up to $150 per day to travel upcountry, or $80 to get around the peninsula. The driver's pay is included in the rate, though petrol (around £2.40/$5 per gallon, or 5 litres), is not. If you want to rent from a rental firm like Motorcare, be prepared to pay $250 a day, $1000 a week or $2700 a month.

Hitchhiking is pretty easy in and around Freetown, and not too difficult elsewhere; private drivers are usually sympathetic. Most of the time you'll be expected to pay.

Accommodation

Freetown and the Freetown Peninsula have a growing number of relatively pricey **places to stay**, though few inexpensive lodgings. Bo, Makeni, Kenema and Koidu all have a good number of basic boarding-houses, and after the huge UN and NGO presence, an increasing number of reasonably comfortable motels, but nothing luxurious. At the moment, accommodation beyond the larger towns is scarce, and completely unavailable in many smaller towns.

If you happen to arrive at dusk in a strange village, it's best to ask to see the **chief** and explain to him your "mission" and your needs. Custom dictates that you should be accommodated somewhere, but since the war destroyed entire communities, many people are still living in overcrowded and impoverished conditions and may not be able to put you up. **Camping** is not recommended (people aren't accustomed to the practice and nerves are still fragile, especially after dark), unless you are heading out to nature reserves and are able to link up with conservation staff on-site. If you camp, you'll need to be entirely self-sufficient.

Modest Freetown hotels charge £20–50/$40–100 for a twin room, though you can only expect something decent at the upper end of this price scale. A twin room in one of the more established international-style hotels costs from £75/$150. Upcountry, the cheapest lodgings will cost you at least Le30,000 (nearly £5/$10) for a rudimentary room with a couple of beds and somewhere to wash.

Eating and drinking

Freetown has an excellent selection of **restaurants** serving (mainly European) food at prices comparable to what you'd pay in the West. There are also inexpensive **chop houses** serving variations of rice and palm-oil-based meals during lunchtime, and rarely having anything left by the afternoon, where you can eat for Le5000 or even less. For quick snacks, fried-chicken places are the most popular option – you can't fail to spot their colourful frontages.

Freetown, and, to some extent upcountry towns, boast a good range of **street food**, including rice *akara* (rice cake), fried dough (doughnuts), roast meat, egg sandwiches, boiled cassava, yams, plantains and sandwiches. A popular snack is the "steak sandwich" – slivers of kebab with palm oil in bread, known as *rosbif* in Krio. Be sure your sandwich really is steak, unless you like grilled tripe: at night, it can be hard to see what's cooking.

The generic term for **sauce** is *plasas* ("palava sauce"), and in Sierra Leone this is usually made with finely shredded leaves of sweet potato or cassava, okra, dried fish and hot pepper, all cooked in palm oil. There are numerous varieties of *plasas* – a version based on groundnuts is most common in the north – and it's often served with meat or chicken. You may also get *egusi* sauces or soups, based on crushed squash seeds. Along the coast, fish stew is very common.

Whatever sauce you have, you'll eat it with a **starchy staple** – most commonly rice, the national staple food. Stay long in Sierra Leone and you'll begin to appreciate significant differences in taste and texture between the **rice** of different regions. Upland "hill rice" is the more traditional short-grain variety; the red-speckled Mende kind is the best and can be delicious. **Plantains** are commonly used as a staple in place of rice. **Fufu** (fermented, mashed cassava stodge) and **agidi** (heavy, maize-meal stodge) are also eaten as the main meal, though not often prepared in chop houses.

If you're far off the beaten track, you won't find chop for sale. In these areas, it's quite acceptable – and quite the custom – to carry rice, palm oil, Maggi stock cubes and other ingredients around with you and to ask local people to cook meals for you, in exchange for some of the food (the family meal is usually prepared late afternoon), or perhaps for a small cash payment.

Yebe is a good and popular breakfast dish, a kind of stew made of potato, cassava or mangoes when in season. You buy it by the ladle in markets and truck parks between dawn and 8am. **Pap**, a sweet rice broth, is also nice for chilly, early starts upcountry.

Sweet bread (sugar-laden) and ordinary bread (a basic, non-sweet, white bread) are sold almost everywhere; specify which kind you want, otherwise the seller will probably give you the sweet kind.

Of the wide variety of **fruit** you'd expect, oranges are probably the cheapest; in the

Krio food and drink terms

agidi	corn stodge	kabej	cabbage
airish petete	potato	kasada	cassava
akara	rice and banana cake	kek	cake
		kenda	seasoning
aweful	variety of fish	kohn	corn (maize)
behni	sesame seeds	kondo	basic chop
bia	beer	krain-krain	slimy leaf sauce
bif	meat, any edible animal	letu	lettuce
		lemon	mandarin/ clementine
binch	beans, peas		
biskit	biscuit	lif	leaf
bita	bitter leaf for sauces	magi	Maggi stock cube
		mampama	palm wine
bolgoh	bulgar wheat	okroh	okra
bonga	dried fish	omole	liquor, hooch
bota	butter, margarine	orinch	orange
brefos	breakfast	oriri	seasoning
brefrut	breadfruit	pamai	red, banga nut oil
buli	jug for palm wine	panapul	pineapple
bush bif	game meat	pap	porridge
chak	drunk	petete	sweet potato
egusi	squash seeds used in sauces	pia	pear (avocado)
		plantan	plantain
fis	fish	plasas	(palava) sauce
fohl	chicken	plet	plate
fud/chop/yit	all terms for food	pongki	pumpkin
fresh	new palm wine	popoh	pawpaw (papaya)
frut	fruit	rehs	rice
funde	millet	sawa-sawa	plasas made of sour leaves
gari	cassava flour		
golik	garlic	sof	soft drink
granat	groundnut (peanut)	sol	salt
grepfrut	grapefruit	stek	beef
grin	greens, used in plasas	stu	stew
		suga	sugar
jibloks/kobokobo	aubergine (eggplant)	sup	soup
jolof	rice in tomato paste served with stew of beef, goat or fish	tamatis	tomato, tomato purée
		ti	tea
		yabas	onion
		yams	yam

north, in season, they'll cost you a penny each. Mandarins, misleadingly, are called lemons in Krio.

Drinks

As for drinking, it all comes down to Star **beer**, one of West Africa's best and also reasonably priced. Imported beer costs about twice the price of Star and there is a reasonable choice in Freetown. **Palm wine** is socially and commercially very important, and a pleasant way to while away a lazy afternoon. Sierra Leonean liquor from Freetown distilleries, on the other hand, is a more self-destructive commodity; Pegapak, Daddy Kool gin and Man Pikin rum are names to be wary of. Nonalcoholic, home-made ginger beer is popular in Freetown and normally sold in small plastic bottles.

Lastly, while Sierra Leone is more or less outside West Africa's "green-tea culture" zone, **coffee**, which is quite often freshly ground (and invariably served with Peak evaporated milk), can be a pleasant surprise.

Communications

The Sierra Leone **postal system** (run by Salpost) usually takes seven days between Sierra Leone and the UK, and ten days to the USA. Aerograms are fastest and safest. Upcountry, the mail – incoming as well as outgoing – is unreliable. Freetown has one or two courier/air-freighting agencies (see p.682).

Phones and mobiles

Sierra Leone's **landline** network isn't complete, and only works fairly reliably in the Western Region and Freetown Peninsula areas. With so many **mobile-phone** companies competing for your business, however, most tourists and expats use mobiles, as do the majority of Sierra Leoneans who need to make a phone call.

Of the four **mobile-phone** providers, Africell, Celtel, Comium and Tigo, Celtel has the widest coverage, Comium and Africell

offer cheaper rates and are improving their coverage, and Tigo offers Internet access.

You can usually buy **SIM** packs on arrival at the airport or in most supermarkets in town (Africell, for example, offers a SIM plus 3 minutes of international talk for Le5000). Should you be tempted to simply keep your overseas SIM in the phone, most networks also support roaming, though at exorbitant prices.

Internet access

Internet access is relatively fast and inexpensive in the Freetown area, with Internet cafés sprouting all over the capital. There is, however, only limited online access up-country.

Opening hours, public holidays and festivals

Most offices, banks and embassies are open Monday to Friday (sometimes Sat morning, too) 8am–5pm, though some close for an hour at lunch. Shops usually close by 5pm, but are open Saturday morning. Many restaurants and other establishments are closed all day Sunday. Most supermarkets on the other hand remain open seven days a week, including public holidays.

The somewhat unpredictable secular **holidays** include **Republic Day** (April 19) and **Independence Day** (April 27). The Islamic calendar only affects business and office openings at the end of Ramadan (Korite).

If you are in the North, don't miss the New Year's Day "outing" in Kabala (see p.691). And if you're in the Freetown area over Christmas and New Year, go to Lumley Beach, Goderich Beach, Kent Beach or River No. 2 Beach on Boxing Day or New Year's Day, when literally thousands of people come to dance, swim and party.

Crafts and shopping

Sierra Leone's best buys are **cloth** (indigo tie-dyed *gara*, rusty red and black block-printed *ronko*, soft and heavy strip-woven country

Sierra Leone's **IDD** country code is ☏232.

cloth – single-weave *barri* and double-weave *kpokpoi* – and batik); **leather** goods (especially slot-together neck bags and purses); **masks** connected with the secret societies (but the made-for-tourist ones are overpriced and often crude, while the real thing is seriously expensive and requires the museum's permission to export); and **nomoli** soapstone figurines (see p.678; strictly speaking these cannot be exported if they're authentic). Freetown and the peninsula are the only areas where you'll regularly come across crafts and souvenirs for sale to tourists and expats.

Crime and safety

While Sierra Leone is once again amongst the safest countries in West Africa to travel in – granted the occasional mugging or pickpocketing incident – it is still worth **registering** with your embassy on arrival. Freetown and the peninsula present no special danger, though it's advisable to avoid the East End of Freetown after dark. Areas that used to be risky – bordering Liberia, the Moa River and Gola Forest – are now readily accessible and trouble-free. Visitors to Kono or diamond-mining areas, however, are still likely to arouse suspicion at checkpoints or from people who think their tourism may just be a cover for buying or smuggling diamonds.

As for **drugs**, grass (*dhambi*, *yamba*) is widely smoked, but not in public. You're advised to stay clear.

Gender issues and sexual attitudes

With the exception of Lumley Beach on the Freetown Peninsula, where beach boys of all descriptions gather, Sierra Leone is one of the friendliest, least hassle-prone countries for **female travellers**. Women in shorts and T-shirts don't raise too many eyebrows. Settle somewhere to stay, or work, though, and you're bound to be persistently irritated by inflamed egos. "When can we meet to do some loving?" is the kind of question that Sierra Leonean

women have to field all the time, though the perceived cultural gap and your potential as a source of funds, too, make you more vulnerable. It's possibly unfair in individual cases, but broadly true, to expect more posturing in the North and less arrogant attitudes in the South.

In the wider field of **sexual attitudes**, public displays of affection are more acceptable in Sierra Leone than in many other countries in the region, though in certain Krio quarters of Freetown, conservative "Victorian values" are still prevalent. Female genital mutilation is widely practised within the framework of the traditional women's sande society (see p.698). Power for women in the provinces tends to be determined by ethnic affiliation. While there are a number of women paramount chiefs in the Mende and Sherbro chiefdoms, a Temne female paramount chief would be unheard of.

As for attitudes to **gay relations**, they too range from relatively accepting in the more cosmopolitan corners of the peninsula, to rigidly anti in conservative, rural areas. Fannyann Eddy, the campaigning founder of the **Sierra Leonean Lesbian and Gay Association** was raped and murdered when her office was broken into in 2004. On the statute book, gay sexual relations are still illegal (based on English law's Offences Against the Person Act, 1861), so discretion is advised.

Entertainment and sport

Sierra Leone has a rich variety of **music** and the influence of Freetown over the last 200 years has been large. Today, Sierra Leone's music industry is going through something of a revival with new songs being released on an almost weekly basis. There's a short account, with recommended CDs, on p.665.

Cinema and theatre

Cinema is, no surprise, dormant if not extinct; imported movies and videos are all you'll see. That said, there is a growing "movie night" trend in the capital where newly-released Western movies are shown in upmarket venues like the *Country Lodge*, *Mamba Point* and the *Sports Bar*. Yet film could perhaps be great in Sierra Leone, if the country's record in the field of **drama** is any indication – Freetown has a remarkable tradition of popular theatre. Quite a few theatrical groups are currently functioning, and all of them write their own plays or translate scripts for local productions.

The 1979 banning of *Poyotong Wahala*, about high-level corruption, led to routine censorship of plays. In their attempts to outwit the censors, playwrights moved increasingly from the concert party – a sort of musical variety show – to exuberant farce and satire. Shows are uproarious, even rowdy, and there's a strong blend of comedy and social comment in these Krio plays. Some of the main professional groups are the **Freetong Players**, **Kailondo Theatre** and the **Wan Pot Soja Comedy Group** – the latter the most popular at the time of writing with adaptations made for local TV and radio making household names of characters such as Van Boi and Rosalie.

More **conventional international-style theatre** tends to be put on at the British Council Library in Freetown. Forthcoming events are usually well advertised; look out for banners, especially around Freetown's Cotton Tree and Law Courts.

Sport

Football is popular all over the country, but most of the big action is concentrated around Freetown, where Mighty Blackpool, East End Lions and FC Kallon are some of the clubs you might watch. Even if you never get round to watching FC Kallon, you'll soon enough hear of the proprietor, **Mohamed Kallon** – the country's most famous footballer. Kallon, whose career has taken him to the likes of Inter Milan and AS Monaco, is also the owner of a nightclub and a radio station and is in the process of building a swanky beach hotel. Most promising Sierra Leonean players end up in Europe, and often in English league football.

Wildlife and national parks

Sierra Leone's **fauna** still includes elephant (in the Outamba-Kilimi National Park and the Gola Forest), chimpanzee (a high concentration in the Loma Mountains and widely if thinly dispersed across the whole country) and pygmy hippo, which are so solitary and secretive that it's hard to know what their status is.

There are several important faunal reserves. The big one is the **Outamba-Kilimi National Park** in the north. It was nearly becoming a fully operational park with visitor facilities and an active research programme when the US Peace Corps workers based there left the country. At the time of writing, it's in the process of being rehabilitated. The other park is the **Tiwai Island Nature Reserve**, a jungle-covered island in the Moa River near the Liberian border. Its population of chimps and endangered monkey species has made an astonishing recovery since the end of the war and the camp has new and comfortable facilities.

The December 2007 announcement that Sierra Leone would make its 750-square-kilometre **Gola Forest reserves** (east of Tiwai) into a unified rainforest national park met with widespread approval at the Bali climate-change talks. The area is expected to have tourist facilities before 2010.

If you're a wildlife enthusiast, you'll want to visit the **Conservation Society of Sierra Leone** in Freetown (see p.682). They can advise on travel routes, accommodation, worthwhile destinations and security concerns, and may be able to find you a reliable guide. If you're planning a trip to Tiwai Island contact the **Environmental Foundation for Africa** (Ⓦ www.efasl.org .uk; see p.697), who can advise on costs and travel plans.

A brief history of Sierra Leone

Sierra Leone has one of the longest "modern histories" of any West African nation. It was in the 1560s that, in effect, Sir John Hawkins started the American slave trade, at the watering station by the present site of the King Jimmy Market in Freetown. Inland, at Port Loko, Afro-Portuguese *lançado* traders settled and flourished through the seventeenth century. Early British colonists gravitated to the slaving "factory" of Bunce Island (downriver from Port Loko) and the coasts of Sherbro and the other islands further south. Here, the more adventurous married into local royalty and seeded new, Creole dynasties. At the end of the eighteenth century, the first free black settlers arrived to establish themselves on the Freetown Peninsula.

The Province of Freedom

There were tens of thousands of **freed slaves** in the English cities of Bristol, Liverpool and London in the late eighteenth century. After the outbreak of the American War of Independence in 1775, many slaves deserted to the British side from their Southern plantation owners, and later made their way to London. And as early as 1772, a legal test case had ruled that, once freed, a slave could not be returned to captivity.

In 1787, the first settlers arrived in Sierra Leone from Britain. They were a group of 411 people, mostly "black poor" immigrants but including some sixty deported white women – "wives" for the freed slaves – transported for prostitution and other offences. Their patron, Granville Sharp, declared the mountainous shore of the peninsula "The Province of Freedom". The expedition was nearly a disaster. Sierra Leone had been chosen on the recommendation of a botanist, Henry Smeathman, who'd lived there for some years and whose private intention had been to set up plantations – using slave labour. He died before the expedition set off, but many of the putative settlers had second thoughts at the last minute and backed out. The expedition was badly managed and much delayed, so that the ships finally arrived just before

the onset of the rains. The colonists had tents, and built makeshift huts, but within three months of living through the rainy season on the sodden hillside, a third of them were dead, of malaria or other diseases.

They bought the area of what is now Freetown from King Tom, a Temne headman and tributary of King Naimbama. But Naimbama hadn't been consulted and the area had to be bought again from him (the treaty can be seen at the Public Archives in Fourah Bay College). Tom was succeeded by King Jimmy, who resented and harassed the Bunce Island slave-trading operation that was still going on. A British naval vessel, which had by coincidence arrived with new supplies for the flagging colony, torched one of Jimmy's towns – with the approval of the settlers, who had also been in dispute with him.

And there ended the "Province of Freedom". King Jimmy **evicted the settlers** from their homes and burnt their little colony to the ground. Those who remained (it was now 1790) were absorbed into surrounding Temne villages.

Nova Scotians and Maroons

A new consortium, the **Sierra Leone Company**, was formed to take over the assets of the defunct Province of

Freedom and make a second attempt to establish a colony. Its members were Granville Sharp (the driving force), the liberal lord William Wilberforce, and a young radical, Thomas Clarkson.

They soon found a new group of colonists – some twelve hundred **"Nova Scotians"** – for their philanthropic experiment. These were freed-slave refugees from the United States whom the British had fobbed off with a dead-end resettlement scheme in the Canadian colony. One of them went to London, where Sierra Leone was suggested to him as an alternative. The small hill farms the new settlers were allocated were not much of an improvement on Canada, but the Nova Scotians formed a viable community. They brought strong churches, and some of them became Company administrators. French Revolutionary forces caught the ill-defended British off-guard in 1794 and ransacked Freetown. But the Nova Scotians rebuilt and the **colony of Sierra Leone** (as it became in 1808) was to owe its existence to them.

In 1795, five hundred escaped Asante slaves – the **Maroons** – who had set up an independent state in the mountains of Jamaica, were tricked into negotiations, leading to their capture and deportation, once again to Nova Scotia, and then eventually to Sierra Leone. The Maroon settlers arrived at Freetown in 1800, just as a group of Nova Scotians, in an attempt to form their own government, were in the middle of Sierra Leone's first rebellion. The Maroons, and a detachment of soldiers accompanying them, came to Governor Thomas Ludlam's rescue. The Nova Scotian rebels were captured; two were hanged and the rest banished. From the beginning of the nineteenth century, the settlers were given no voice in the government of Sierra Leone, Britain ruling directly.

Temne defeat

Pushing home their new strength, the Sierra Leone Company refused to countenance claims by members of the Temne ethnic group that a new treaty be negotiated whenever there was a new Temne king as landlord. For the governor, the treaty of 1788 was good in perpetuity. To make the point, the British garrison built a stone fort, now part of State House. The Temne, led by a new King Tom and encouraged by a partisan Nova Scotian named Wansey, attacked it in November 1801 and were quickly repulsed. In a counter offensive, the British ousted the Temne and their Bullom relatives from most of the peninsula and carried out savage punitive raids on many villages in King Tom's dominion.

While the Temne prepared a new plan, a Susu ally of theirs arrived with his retinue to settle in Freetown. This sell-out turned the tide against the Temne, who gave up the peninsula.

The Crown Colony and the recaptives

On January 1, 1808, the Sierra Leone Company, by now deeply in debt, handed over the running of the settlement to the British government, and Sierra Leone became a **Crown Colony**. In the same year, Westminster passed the **Abolition Act** and the anti-slavery movement at last had some teeth, although the last slave ships weren't intercepted until 1864. Bunce Island ceased slave trading and the Temne country inland turned to timber (another nonrenewable resource) to maintain its economic strength.

Freetown had a naval base, charged with intercepting slave ships and "recapturing" the slaves. It soon became clear that few of them could be returned to their original homes, and they were simply released at Freetown to found new villages. Between 1808 and 1864, some 70,000 **"recaptives"** were resettled in the Sierra Leone colony. Leicester was founded by Wolof and Bambara people, Kissy by freed slaves from the Scarcies River district and Congo Town by Congolese recaptives. In the 1820s, in war-torn Yorubaland

(Nigeria), thousands of slaves of war were shipped west, in Cuban, Brazilian or American vessels, many of them to be quickly recaptured by the Freetown frigates. The "Aku", as they were called, formed the first significant Muslim community in the colony. Slave trading also continued along the southern coasts of the Sierra Leone region. Many of the recaptives here, far from being complete strangers to the region, had roots in the territory which later became the republic of Sierra Leone.

After peace was achieved with the French in 1815, many of the **African soldiers** who had served in British regiments were pensioned off to the colony, where they founded villages with pugnacious names like Waterloo, Hastings and Wellington. From the interior came determined Fula and Mandinka traders who settled in Foulah Town. And much of the town's heavy labour was done by the Kru (or Kroo), who came to the coast on long residences from their homes in southeast Liberia.

In this melting pot of people, many of them traumatized by their experiences, the **Church Missionary Society** made headway through the early decades of the nineteenth century. Many who felt that the Bible had saved them from slavery were converted to Christianity. The Nova Scotians were an example: African and yet European in their ways, they were prosperous, literate, worldly and Christian. Many recaptives adopted European names and, with intermarriage and the inevitable breakdown of many ethnic barriers, there was the gradual moulding of a new configuration – the Creoles, or **Krios**.

In the **interior**, the British paid kings and headmen annual stipends to try to guarantee peace between peoples whose economies had been damaged by the termination of the slave trade. Centuries of dependence upon it had left many Temne families, and whole districts, in disarray; while the farming peoples, like the Limba and the Loko, whom the Temne had exploited for so long, were now attacked and harassed by them. By

the 1820s, the Temne had emerged as the dominant language group northeast of Freetown.

On the **peninsula**, recaptives began moving to Freetown from their villages. Captured cargos of European goods for slave-trading were auctioned off and a number of recaptive traders took advantage, selling inland, even setting themselves up in business in the interior, under the patronage of village headmen, who called them "white men". The timber trade declined with the introduction of iron steamships and a more easily undertaken trade in wild-collected **palm nuts**, for the burgeoning industries of Europe and the USA, spread across the country.

Further afield, the first **recaptive missionaries** began to follow the traders, not just inland from Freetown, but along the coast, and especially to Nigeria. From the 1850s onwards, the advent of steamships made Freetown the hub of the whole West African coast. With the return of peace in Yorubaland, large numbers of Krios headed back there and went on to colonize the coast of Cameroon.

Expansion and consolidation

Expansion of the Freetown colony in the 1860s took in parts of Sherbro Island and the southern coast. Treaties were signed by local chiefs, who were forced to choose the lesser evil of British overlordship, when French traders made clear their designs on the region. Inland from the peninsula, a minor incident was used to force the "leasing" (in reality annexation) of the low-lying Koya Temne farming district around Songo – about as far inland as present-day Mile 38. Loko and Mende mercenary allies of the British helped clear the area of recalcitrant Temne.

The end of the slave trade in 1864 was in fact just the cessation of **transatlantic shipments**. Slaves continued to be traded in the interior of the country, for domestic work and for labour on export crops. As the pace of trade and competition increased, the British in Freetown made no effort to control slavery beyond the border of the Freetown colony, if anything recognizing its usefulness and the danger of upsetting the chiefs who profited from it.

Alongside these developments, missionaries, in particular those of the American United Baptist Church, aimed to create conditions in the interior that would result in the gradual dismantling of traditional ways. They spread the gospels, of course, and set a lot of store in conversions. But more significantly, they taught new economic practices in their boys' schools and offered credit to their graduates to set them up as traders. As more and more traders left the colony to trade outside the British customs area, so Freetown Krios, complaining of unfair competition and price wars, demanded an extension of British control to annex the whole coast. London, however, explicitly prohibited any further annexations. Indeed a parliamentary committee of 1865 had already laid out a general principle of eventual withdrawal and self-government for the West African colonies.

In 1882, the borders of separate spheres of influence with Liberia and France were settled along the coast, and Britain found itself operating a **customs area** that extended from the Great Scarcies in the north to the Mano River in the south. The purely exploitative nature of this arrangement, in which no responsibility for internal affairs was taken by the British, led to the beginning of a draining of Krio confidence in the colonial government. One incident that incensed them was the execution of William Caulker in 1888 for the murder of his half-brother, the disputed king of Shenge (the coast between Freetown and Sherbro). Although the king had the government's support for his succession, his enthronement had been unpopular. Krio opinion had it that such affairs could be avoided if Britain were to annex and administer the whole country, rather than simply extract duty.

The creation of the new customs area also coincided with a general recession in trade in the 1880s and repeated confrontations and battles between the trading chiefdoms along the coast and in the interior. A number of statelets, which managed to stay on the right side of the British, emerged supremely powerful in Mende country – among them Senehun, under Madam (Mammy) Yoko; Panguma, under Nyagua; Pujehun, run jointly by Momo Ja and Momo Kai Kai; and, in the east, Kailahun, a new Mende–Kissi confederation under Kai Lundu.

Partition

With the recognition of Freetown's importance as a coaling station for British shipping, and a sense of urgency in Europe's attitude to Africa, a new pragmatism overcame the colonial government in the closing years of the nineteenth century. The French were chasing Samory Touré's giant *sofa* army (which was supplied with weapons from Freetown) across territory in the British zone of influence. A war between Britain and France in the region couldn't be discounted.

Hastily, the British began formulating exclusive friendship treaties with as many chiefs as would entertain them, hoping to set up a buffer zone of allies between the French and Freetown. Boundary agreements were signed with the French in 1895, a partition that forced the British to accept the **Protectorate of Sierra Leone**. The domineering governor Frederic Cardew initiated a system of **indirect rule** through local chiefs under European District Commissioners – a system that was later followed in northern Nigeria. All kings and queens became **paramount chiefs** (under Queen Victoria) and their sovereignty over their peoples strictly limited to whatever their district commissioner considered appropriate. The "treaties of friendship" they'd signed were reinterpreted as surrenders of power in the new Protectorate.

Cardew's decision to build a **railway**, based on the need to encourage trade, and the requirement that the Protectorate's administration should not be paid for by the colony, led unavoidably to the invention of ways of paying for it. It was the first ever built and run by the British government: all previous lines had been private. Trading licences were introduced and a tax imposed of five shillings per year on every house in the Protectorate. Payments had to be forced out of people. The undisciplined **Frontier Police** (initially mainly Krio, later largely upcountry men) smashed their way across the country, effectively robbing the people to pay for the administration they had never asked for. People of the Protectorate regarded the white man's **"hut tax"** as an inversion of the proper order of things, which should have had them extracting payment from the newcomers. They assumed they were being charged rent on their houses, which had been stolen from them.

The Hut Tax War and the Mende Revolt

In the north, the Loko chief **Bai Burreh** resisted demands for the hut tax and fought a protracted guerilla war against better-equipped but untrained Caribbean troops. There was support for Bai Burreh's action from the Krio, whose views about taxes concurred with his and who detested Governor Cardew's arrogance.

At the beginning of the rainy season in 1898, there was a massive organized **uprising**, planned through secret society meetings. Hut tax and trading licences were the main grudges, but decades of resentment were released in unprecedented violence directed against "every man in trousers and every woman in a dress". Hundreds of administrators, traders and missionaries were hacked and bludgeoned to death. Atrocities were widespread and few escaped; the Krio traders in the Protectorate suffered most. Although there was panic in Freetown, the colony was not invaded.

Pro-British chiefs helped the government resume control in the Protectorate,

although there were fierce skirmishes in several districts. Over 200 arrests were made and 96 people were hanged. Many others, including, eventually, Bai Burreh, were deported to the Gold Coast. A new West African regiment having replaced the West Indians, Cardew followed the crushing of the resistance with a military victory tour around the country. The Krio community was sickened. The hut tax was not repealed.

A new authoritarianism

The beginning of the twentieth century saw a new, more complex Sierra Leone. The Krios were demoralized, being ignored by the government and mistrusted by the people of the Protectorate. The Protectorate people had been defeated by the government and now found themselves paying allegiance (and corruptly inflated taxes in many cases) to increasingly alienated chiefs in the pay of the British. At least the Frontier force was disbanded. Chiefdom "court messengers" were given the job of policing the Protectorate.

British policy in general moved right away from the benevolence of a century earlier. In concordance with the new authoritarian order, **racial discrimination** became policy. Blacks – whether "natives" or "creoles" – were kept in subordinate positions no matter how highly qualified. Social mixing between the races became rare and, with the discovery that mosquitoes transmitted malaria, a new whites-only suburb was created on the high ground above Freetown – Hill Station, served by its own railway. Once malaria became less of a deterrent, more and more European companies came to trade in Sierra Leone, buying out the less prosperous Krio traders and bringing venture capital with them.

But it was the arrival of **Lebanese traders** in the 1890s (many, it's said, brought by unscrupulous ships' captains who told them West Africa was America) which really did for the Krio traders at the smaller end of business. World

War I and the influenza epidemic, and the food shortages that followed, stalled the political advances that might otherwise have taken place. Predictably, perhaps, the Lebanese (who never seemed to go short) were accused of hoarding and profiteering. Anti-Lebanese demonstrations took place and their shops were looted.

Railway workers went on strike in 1919 and again in 1926, but their demands for improved pay and conditions were not met. Although an increased quota of Africans was nominated to the Sierra Leone Legislative Council, only three were elected, and then only by restricted suffrage for the literate and propertied. The voices of Africans were timid and restrained. The **abolition of slavery** as an institution came only in 1927, when the outrage from abroad became impossible to ignore. Slave-owners lost little, as most slaves preferred to stay with them as employees.

Apart from an isolated Islamic resistance movement led by a marabout, Idara (who was killed near Kambia in 1931), there wasn't much motion on the political scene. But the radical propaganda of **I.T.A. Wallace-Johnson** represented a break from conservative reformism. Organizing a mass-consciousness nationalist movement in the Gold Coast and Sierra Leone, he formed the West African Youth League and outspokenly denounced the government of Sir Douglas Jardine. Wallace-Johnson's use of Krio, a language more widely understood than English, was especially provocative. He was imprisoned on a charge of criminal libel, followed by years of detention through World War II, on the spurious pretext of his threat to security.

The road to independence

Only World War II broke the numbing spell of repression which had settled on the country since partition. By the time peace was declared in Asia and the African veterans of the Burma campaign and RAF were coming home to Sierra Leone, it was clear that profound changes could not be held off much longer.

To begin with, the colour bar was removed, opening senior civil-service posts to Africans. And there was a major change in budgetary policy too, with British taxpayers now funding colonial development. Independence at some point in the future was explicitly stated to be the goal. The **new constitution** of 1947 gave the Protectorate fourteen seats on the Legislative Council, and the Colony just seven, which was still a gross under-representation of Protectorate interests, despite Krio complaints that the Colony should have held a majority of seats. Wallace-Johnson bitterly opposed the new order and reminded the government of the 1865 proposals to allow for self-government in the Colony, now being swept aside.

Surprised at the vehemence of the Krio attacks, the government stalled in implementing the new constitution. In the Protectorate, meanwhile, the **Sierra Leone People's Party** (**SLPP**) was being formed, the country's first. It was led by **Milton Margai**, a doctor (the first Protectorate man to receive a medical qualification) from a Bonthe business family, related to the powerful and pro-British Banta Mende chiefdom. His brother, **Albert Margai** (the first lawyer from the Protectorate), and **Siaka Stevens**, a Vai-Limba man with a trades-union background, were also founder members. The SLPP insisted on the introduction of the new constitution. Elections held in 1951 gave them a huge majority over the **National Council of Sierra Leone**, the Krio-based party.

The People's Party gradually took over power from colonial appointees. Margai became Chief Minister in 1954, but was in no hurry to form a government to run the country independently. "It will come," he said, "but we are not ready yet. We have not got the men to run it. We want our friends to go on helping us for some time to come."

Throughout the 1950s prosperity and confidence grew. The **diamond fields** in the east were opened to private licensees and there was considerable investment in health and education, as well as general infrastructure. There were also signals of rumbling discontent at the way political reforms lagged behind growth. In 1955, price riots in Freetown and anti-chief demonstrations throughout the north drew little response from Margai, whose conservative and parochial leanings were becoming increasingly apparent.

The creation of a House of Representatives (the Sierra Leonean parliament) in 1956 replaced the Legislative Council. There was a **general election**, in which all tax-paying men were eligible to vote, in 1957, which returned the SLPP to power with a slightly reduced majority.

Independence

Albert Margai and Siaka Stevens, unhappy with Margai's record, left his cabinet to form opposition parties. Although a brief, ritualistic, all-party unity was on show in the United Front for the **independence talks** held in London in 1960, there was a rapid fission of interests in the final, faster-than-expected lead-up to independence. Stevens formed the **All-Peoples' Congress** (APC); Sir Milton Margai, now the prime minister, refused his demands for a general election before independence and went further by detaining Stevens and several others for over a month, throughout the transition, on the pretext that they posed a risk to the country's stability. Sierra Leone's **Independence Day** came on April 27, 1961. A general election held the following year, under **universal suffrage** for the first time, reaffirmed SLPP dominance, but also confirmed mass opposition support for the APC.

Dissatisfaction with the SLPP was spreading, but the death of Sir Milton Margai in 1964, and the return to the fold of his brother Albert quickened popular resentment of the government, especially in the north. The party appeared to be squandering

the foreign funds that were pouring into the country, still showed scant concern to reform the corrupt and antiquated system of local government by chiefs, and was much too interested in its own, **Mende**, power base. In Freetown, however, important developments were under way. Siaka Stevens was elected **mayor** from 1964 to 1965 and he built up solid support among the disenchanted Krios, for whom independence had so far been disappointing.

The coups and Siaka Stevens

The **general election** in 1967 was a turning point. As soon as Siaka Stevens (elected leader of the victorious APC) had been sworn in as prime minister, a chauvinistic army brigadier, David Lansana – an eastern Mende whom Albert Margai had been grooming in a push for regional dominance – attempted a coup to retain Margai. The following day, Lansana's own officers usurped him and seized power, eventually succeeding in nominating **Andrew Juxson-Smith** to chair their army-and-police National Redemption Council (NRC).

Stevens went into exile in Guinea, with his senior supporters. At first, they had to restrain him from launching an armed invasion of Sierra Leone, with the help of Guinea's president Sekou Touré. He waited a year in exile, while the NRC's popular promises to restore the flagging economy, clean up corruption and return the country to civilian rule came to nothing. In April 1968 a mutiny in the lower ranks led to the arrest of the members of the NRC and Stevens' return to power.

Stevens in power

Stone wey dey botam wata, no no say wen rain de cam.

A stone under the water doesn't know when it's raining.

– Krio proverb

Siaka Stevens' first decade in power was characterized by a growing alienation from his political roots and the jettisoning of virtually all objectives apart from "national unity". Publicly, he quickly ceased to be the champion of Freetown's interests. His former outward adherence to socialist principles was ploughed under by the need to retain his power base. At the same time, he was careful to shed those of his supporters who became dangerously close. He avoided clear ethnic affiliation, using his mixed background to adopt a succession of tribal identities. And all the time, he continued to accumulate a massive personal fortune.

Early after the return to civilian rule, senior ministers in Stevens' government – Mohammed Forna and Ibrahim Bash-Taqi – resigned to form the **United Democratic Party** (the UDP, banned in 1973). A coup attempt by the army commander, John Bangura, and two assassination attempts on Stevens, all led to executions and to the arrival of detachments of Guinean troops to protect Stevens from his own military. Repeatedly, too, states of emergency were imposed. Sierra Leone became a **republic** in 1971, with Stevens, now president, replacing Queen Elizabeth as head of state.

Such was the political climate by 1972 that there was no further effective opposition for nearly five years. The House of Representatives became a discussion forum for APC members, in which the pronouncements of Pa Siaka (old man Siaka) were aired and approved. A bomb explosion in April 1974 at the home of the finance minister gave Stevens an opportunity to smash home his dominance. Eight opponents of the regime, including the ex-APC members Forna (see "Books", p.666) and Bash-Taqi, were hanged in public and their bodies desecrated.

The general election of 1977 came in the wake of student-led demonstrations across the country, amid mounting economic disarray. Despite vote-rigging, and violence that resulted in more than a hundred deaths, the SLPP gained fifteen seats at the expense of Siaka's supporters and, for a short period, the opposition was bolstered with new confidence. This lapsed again with Siaka's announcement that he was "obliged" to hold a referendum on the question of a **one-party state**, to save Sierra Leone from tribalist chaos. The results of this poll (officially, more than 97 percent in favour) led to the absorption of the SLPP into the ranks of the APC and the formalization of one-party rule.

To seal his control, Siaka was lavish with his political patronage. But his appointment of the chief of the armed forces, **Major General Joseph Momoh** (from the minority northern Limba-speaking group), to the House of Representatives and the Cabinet itself as president-in-waiting was a strategic bequest to the country. His two vice-presidents, Francis Minah and Sorie Koroma, were ignored.

The hosting of the 1980 **OAU conference**, which cost an estimated US$100 million, marked the end of the era of stagnation and corruption. Food shortages, price rises and nonpayment of salaries led to huge and general discontent in the towns, while in the rural areas production was depressed by the low prices paid to producers. The black economy was tolerated, and even thrived under the bankrupt official system. By 1985 Sierra Leone's economy was on the verge of total collapse – where it was to teeter for four years.

Momoh in power

Siaka Stevens retired in November 1985. (He died, in his mansion overlooking Freetown, on May 29, 1988, after a long and painful illness.) The transfer of power to Major General Joseph Momoh was peaceful, the new man welcomed with enthusiasm after seventeen years of Siaka's hollow rhetoric. Elections in 1986 saw many of the old guard lose their seats and some 150 new APC members installed in the House of

Representatives. A number of political prisoners were released, including twelve convicted after the bomb attack of April 1974.

Momoh's economic strategy was to cut back on public spending, in line with IMF-imposed financial conditions. Fearful of the results of austerity measures in the already hard-pressed towns, however, he declined to follow through with a full implementation that might have satisfied the IMF. In **agriculture**, a "Green Revolution" was promulgated but, from lack of consultation with subsistence farmers, it never had much chance of success. Farmers were deserting their plots for diamond and gold prospects in the east. And, despite an economy dominated, in human terms, by rice farms, self-sufficiency in rice was far from being achieved.

The causes of growing public disillusion with the new government were easy to fathom. While the "New Order" tag was lauded, there was no clean sweep; a number of Stevens' old cabinet cronies were retained in senior positions. Corruption blazed in all corners of society. The government's economic measures bit deep, yet apparently had little effect, as Momoh still fell out with the IMF for refusing a comprehensive currency devaluation and insisting on retaining the petrol subsidy. Sierra Leone was working itself into a deep mire.

By the end of 1987, all other problems were overshadowed by the treasury's predicament in finding itself unable to pay the salaries of government employees, due to the hoarding of money and a consequent severe shortage of currency in the banks. Declaring a state of **economic emergency**, Momoh beefed up border controls, announced severe measures against diamond and foreign-currency smugglers, slapped limits on the amounts of Sierra Leonean currency that could be privately held, and gave Sierra Leoneans a deadline to deposit their cash in the banks.

In March 1991, a serious threat to national security emerged from the east of the country. Here the forces of the then Liberian warlord, **Charles Taylor** (who subsequently became Liberian president), and the Revolutionary United Front (RUF) – a Sierra Leonean rebel army under the leadership of an ex-army corporal, **Foday Sankoh** (supported by Taylor and his own backer, President Blaise Compaoré of Burkina Faso) – began taking control of the diamond areas. They proved to be too strong a force to be submerged by the undersupplied and underpaid army. It was this trigger that led to the **military overthrow** of Momoh's government a few months later.

The NPRC

The coup of April 29, 1992, was not unexpected – and it was certainly not unwelcome. A group of exasperated young officers led by Captain Valentine Strasser, 26, stormed into the president's office to claim back-pay and demand more support for the war. Momoh then broadcast messages intended to be reassuring from the SLBS station, while Strasser, speaking on 99.9 FM, claimed he was in charge of the country and, to a backing of "Ain't No Stopping Us Now!" made a string of pronouncements about the price of food, unpaid company taxes and the cancelling of diamond-export licences. Strasser's **National Provisional Ruling Council (NPRC)** took control, and the whole country seemed to be cheering while Momoh went into exile in Guinea.

The honeymoon for the coup leaders was relatively brief. Sober behaviour soon gave way to high living and excess, and popular cynicism set in just as quickly. As the ebb and flow of the war in the provinces gradually turned more and more against the government troops, now led by Strasser, Foday Sankoh's RUF rather than Liberian rebels were identified as the main enemy. But the war fronts became increasingly complex, as the anti-Taylor **ULIMO** forces in Liberia and a new rebel group, the National Front for the Restoration of Democracy (**NAFORD**) who fought to reinstate Joseph Momoh, entered the conflict. Rebel forces, the *kamajors* (members of the traditional hunter societies who generally supported the army), **"sobels"** (soldiers turned rebels) and the national army supported by the West African nations' **ECOWAS Military Observer Group (ECOMOG)**, clashed in an increasingly tangled war primarily fuelled by the desire to control the nation's extensive diamond fields, and largely fought by teenage, even child, soldiers.

The rebel war

In January 1996, the Strasser government was overthrown in another military coup led by **General Julius Maada Bio**. Elections held the following month resulted in a clear victory for **Ahmed Tejan Kabbah**, leader of the SLPP. But the RUF did not participate in the elections and the conflict continued. On May 25, 1997, the government was ousted in yet another coup perpetrated by junior soldiers and RUF units who formed a ruling junta called the **Armed Forces Revolutionary Council (AFRC)** under the leadership of Major General **Johnny Paul Koroma**. President Kabbah went into exile in Guinea, and Sierra Leone descended deeper into a chaotic, brutal, guerilla war. Sierra Leone was suspended from the Commonwealth, and an oil and arms embargo was put in place, secured by **ECOMOG** troops. By 1998, the war had engulfed almost the entire country. Thousands of people had been mutilated or killed, and even more forced into exile.

In February, the Nigerian-led ECOMOG forces (almost a quarter of the entire Nigerian army was deployed in Sierra Leone at the time) launched a military attack that led to the collapse of the junta. ECOMOG was supported by imports of arms funnelled through a British company, **Sandline**, technically breaking the UN embargo and causing severe embarrassment to the British Foreign Office – who either hadn't known, or had chosen to look the other way. Large numbers of rebel forces fled the capital, only to regroup in less accessible parts of the country. ECOMOG managed to consolidate control over Freetown and, in March 1998, President Kabbah made a triumphant return to Freetown. The UN withdrew the oil and arms embargo, yet stability could not be secured. The rebel alliance once again took territory in the interior, eventually gaining control over more than half the country. In December 1998 the RUF and its allies began a brutal offensive to retake Freetown, which culminated in **"Operation No Living Thing"**, a carefully planned assault, supported by South African mercenaries, in which over six thousand lost their lives. All UN personnel were evacuated and much of Freetown's East End was left ruined. Though ECOMOG troops retook the capital later that month, it became clear that dialogue with the RUF would have to be sought in order to bring the enduring war to an end. The RUF had become an organization of killers and mutilators, kidnapping and co-opting children into its ranks, forcing families to execute each other, and routinely hacking off the limbs of those not murdered.

Negotiations between government and rebel units began in May 1999, and on July 7 the unhappy **Lomé agreement** was signed, which gave the RUF leader Foday Sankoh the powers of a vice-president and control over diamond production. It was never put into practice.

With the agreement, the UN Security Council authorized the formation of a much larger UN mission to Sierra Leone – the **United Nations Mission in Sierra Leone (UNAMSIL** – eventually numbering 17,500 troops, making it the largest peacekeeping mission in the UN's history. However, clashes between army and rebels continued, and UN forces were increasingly drawn into the hostilities.

In April 2000, another crisis – the abduction of three hundred UN troops – tipped the balance of power. They were released the following month when Foday Sankoh was finally captured, and his rebel troops forced onto the defensive by a vigorous assault of unilaterally deployed **British forces**, operating under the protection of the UN contingent. Following this success, the British brought in military trainers to strengthen the Sierra Leone army, a police inspector to run the civil police force, and numerous other specialists to work alongside the faltering Sierra Leonean civil service. There were even calls from some quarters in Sierra Leone for the country to become a British trusteeship – not a serious option for the Blair government, but a stark reminder of how low the country had sunk.

The aftermath of war

In August 2000, the UN agreed to pursue the rebels through an **international tribunal**, and efforts to put a Special Court in place, composed of Sierra Leonean and international representatives, began in July 2001. Sporadic clashes with rebel forces were finally halted in February 2002 with the disarming of remaining troops by UN forces. The war was officially declared over.

Peaceful **elections** followed in May 2002. **Ahmed Tejan Kabbah** won the presidency convincingly for the SLPP, and with the RUF as a political party garnering little support, there was cautious optimism for a new era of stability.

In August 2003, President Kabbah controversially told the **Truth and Reconciliation Committee** that he had no say in the activities of the pro-government *kamajor* militias during the war, thereby distancing himself from the prosecution by the **Special Court of Sierra Leone** of his one-time ally and head of the Civil Defence Force, **Chief Sam Hinga Norman**. Hinga

Norman's death in custody during a medical visit to Senegal was a further blow to the work of the Special Court. **Foday Sankoh** died of natural causes in 2003 and his chief lieutenant, **Sam Bokari**, was killed in Liberia in 2004. **Johnny Paul Koroma** is still on the run. And of the eight remaining defendants, only one – **Issah Sesay** – is a prominent figure. That it was Sesay who was ultimately responsible for suing for peace with the government only added further to the debate over the usefulness of a court that will have cost $150 million by the time it finishes its work.

In February 2004, the UN officially announced the end of the disarmament and rehabilitation of more than 70,000 **former combatants**. And by September of that year, security in the capital was handed back to Sierra Leonean forces.

The official withdrawal of UN forces in December 2005 marked a turning point in the country's international credibility. The armoured trucks and helicopter gunships of UNAMSIL were replaced by the United Nations Integrated Office in Sierra Leone (**UNIOSIL**), a peace-building mission.

The 2007 elections

With talk of forthcoming presidential elections dominating the political landscape, 2006 proved to be a fraught year for the ruling SLPP. The minister for internal affairs, lawyer **Charles Margai** (son of Albert Margai and nephew of Milton), was snubbed by President Kabbah as the party's presidential candidate in favour of vice-president **Solomon Berewa**. Margai abandoned the SLPP to form his own party, the southern-based People's Movement for Democratic Change (**PMDC**) in October 2006.

While a fractured SLPP leadership was expected to assist its traditional rival, the northern-based **All People's Congress (APC)** under the Christian, northern businessman **Ernest Bai Koroma**, the

PMDC under Margai failed to get the momentum to mount a serious bid for the presidency.

The non-populist approach of Berewa (SLPP) and his close association with an outgoing president – Kabbah – widely seen to have failed to grasp the peace dividend for the benefit of the poor, made Berewa, and his somewhat elderly party, a dim prospect for the young.

In the event, in the **first round of the elections** (which were held at the height of the rainy season, a timing widely seen as aiding the incumbent SLPP), the APC's Koroma achieved 44 percent, and the SLPP's Berewa 38 percent with the PMDC's Margai, who received 14 percent, set to determine the second round outcome. The **second round**, although marred by violence (quelled by police firing tear-gas rounds), was clearly, if not entirely fairly, won by Koroma, who got 54 percent of the vote. The US observer team, having declared the first round "transparent, credible and largely peaceful", had little positive to say about the highly flawed run-off, but didn't undermine its overall credibility.

Prospects

Britain's continued support for Sierra Leone was endorsed by visits in 2006 by Prince Charles and in 2007 by the outgoing Tony Blair. The British **IMATT** training team running Sierra Leone's armed forces will be in place until at least 2010, and there is British naval presence on close standby off Freetown.

At the time of writing, Sierra Leone appears to be holding its peace, though concerns are frequently raised as **Guinea** teeters on the precipice of huge internal strife. Should its neighbour collapse, the relative proximity of Freetown to Conakry could spark off a massive humanitarian crisis that would stretch Sierra Leone's recovering resources and infrastructure to breaking point.

Sierra Leoneans joke that when God created the world, he endowed the country with such a wealth of natural resources that the angels protested it was unfair on other countries. "Don't worry", God replied, " just look at the people I've put there!" The country does have exceptional **natural resources**: diamonds and gold are the most obvious, but iron ore, titanium ("rutile"), chrome, coffee and cocoa, palm oil and rice could all create the conditions for a country as prosperous as any in West Africa.

With the war behind it, with **UN and British support**, with a functioning democracy, and with international controls over conflict diamonds at last stemming that traffic, there has to be a better chance now for Sierra Leone than for decades. The dramatic **north–south split** highlighted by the 2007 elections is the biggest political issue facing President Koroma. But the new government's management of the **economy** – and in particular its ability to deliver electricity (a massive issue in a country of generators) is the real litmus test of Sierra Leone's prospects. One of its first, surprise moves was to confirm the **ban on timber exports**, which scared Chinese loggers. But what happens beyond its borders and out of its control – in **Guinea and Liberia** – may ultimately decide the future.

Music

Sierra Leone has a rich variety of **music** and the influence of Freetown over the last 200 years has been large. Today, Sierra Leone's music industry is going through something of a revival with new songs beings released on an almost weekly basis. The experience of collective tragedy during the war has also led to a new wave of socially engaged Sierra Leonean music.

The **new wave** has been led by the likes of **Emerson** with such album hits as *Borbor Bele* and *2 Foot Arata*. Emerson's large following owes much to lyrics like those in his seminal song, "Borbor Pain", speaking of the hardship on the streets and the institutional corruption of the state.

Other popular musicians include the godfather of modern Sierra Leonean music, **Jimmy B**; and **K-Man**, **Daddy Saj** and the groups **Dry Eye Crew** and **Ngoh Gbetuwai**. Sierra Leonean popular music on the whole is a rich mix of local-style house and R&B, mixing Krio with English.

Various

Sierra Leone Music (Zensor). Compilation of Krio and upcountry tracks, recorded for the radio in Freetown in the 1950s and 1960s. Including tracks by the Krio singer Ebenezer Calender, who played guitar and trumpet and wrote all his own songs, this is a real collector's item with an excellent accompanying booklet.

Afro-Nationals

The Afro-Nationals were by far the most popular Sierra Leonean band of the 1970s.

CD Classics 1 & 2 (H&R Enterprises, US). These unmistakable cuts feature the sweet lead guitar, trademark brass and live percussion that epitomized the Afro-Nationals' era.

Patrice Bart-Williams

German–Sierra Leonean singer-songwriter, whose work is a hybrid of folk, reggae and blues (Ⓦwww .patrice.net).

Ancestor Spirit This critically acclaimed first album from 2000 has been followed up with the albums *How Do You Call It?* and *Nile*, which included a collaboration with Youssou N'Dour.

Vicky Fornah

In a country with strong Christian traditions, the doyenne of Sierra Leone gospel music is Vicky Fornah – Sierra Leone's top diva.

Hold My Hand The hit album that won her the best recording artist in Sierra Leone in 2002, *Sweet Mother Land Sierra Leone*, featured warm lyrics with African, *zouk* and reggae roots. *My Wedding Day* was released in December 2007.

Refugee All Stars

The six men who fled to Guinea from war-torn Sierra Leone and formed a folk-reggae group have become international stars.

Living Like a Refugee A surprise hit – or perhaps it should be no surprise – widely acclaimed for its raw inspiration. A documentary of the group's odyssey claimed the Grand Jury Prize at the AFI Festival in Los Angeles in 2005. As their name suggests, this is music born of suffering and exile.

S.E. Rogie

Doyen of Sierra Leonean musical entertainers who developed an effortlessly sensual style of palm-wine guitar playing and had hits in the 1960s all along the West African coast. He emigrated to the US and died in the UK in 1994.

Palm Wine Guitar Music: the 60s Sound (Cooking Vinyl). Fabulous collection of some of the late Rogie's most famous songs, including "My Lovely Elizabeth" and the nostalgically sexy "Please Go Easy With Me".

⑧ Books

While Sierra Leone may not have in the past received as much literary or scholarly attention as Ghana or Nigeria, the tragedy of the war led to a surge of publishing. For good general titles about West Africa, including some with a strong Sierra Leone connection, see p.35. Titles marked 🐿 are especially recommended.

Phil Ashby *Unscathed: Escape from Sierra Leone.* Story about the daring escape of a captured British major from behind enemy lines.

Ishmael Beah *A Long Way Gone – Memoirs of a Child Soldier.* Compelling – if troubling – autobiographical account of the horrors perpetrated (and endured) by child soldiers at the height of the rebel war.

🐿 **Daniel Bergner** *Soldiers of Light.* One of the best books on the civil war, this clever narrative subtly explores the obsession with supernatural beliefs held by fighters on both sides. Bergner skilfully juxtaposes the hopes of an American missionary family arriving in Sierra Leone in the early 1980s against the despair of a country imploding.

Sylvia Ardyn Boone *Radiance from the Waters: Ideals of Feminine Beauty in Mende Art.* Circumspect account of the Mende women's Sande society by an art historian who promised not to reveal all.

Greg Campbell *Blood Diamonds.* To understand the impulses behind Sierra Leone's descent into anarchy, you have to get to the diamond trade – the economic driver that financed the conflicts in neighbouring countries, and still helps prop up Al-Qaida. Campbell traces a sticky web of corruption and brutalization that links impoverished diamond-collectors with the arms trade and the ring on your finger.

Syl Cheney-Coker *The Last Harmattan of Alusine Dunbar.* An American-educated professor's first novel – a black comedy of life in a neocolonial state.

Gerald Durrell *Catch Me a Colobus.* Includes a lengthy account of the naturalist's 1965 visit to Sierra Leone, collecting endangered species for the Durrell Wildlife Conservation Trust and filming with the BBC.

Mariane C. Ferme *The Underneath of Things.* A sensitive and thoughtful ethnography of the Mende. Subtitled *Violence, History and the Everyday in Sierra Leone*, it shows how the secret societies have served both to foster the country's bloody chaos and provide a means of coping with it.

🐿 **Aminatta Forna** *The Devil that Danced on Water.* Subtitled

A Daughter's Quest, Forna's deeply affecting account of her return to the Sierra Leone she lived in until the age of 10, and where her politician father was hanged for treason, is tender and excruciatingly painful, as she assesses the war and its roots in the 1960s. Forna's 2006 debut novel, *Ancestor Stones*, also set in Sierra Leone, charts the lives of four women over the last century's history.

William Fowler *Operation Barras*. One of two books on the remarkable SAS rescue mission in Sierra Leone, which goes some way to documenting how Britain got involved in ultimately bringing peace to the country.

Lansana Gberie *A Dirty War in West Africa: The RUF and the Destruction of Sierra Leone*. A rare work by a Sierra Leonean journalist, Gberie's book traces the pivotal role played by the diamond trade in the country's history – revelatory because of his first-hand knowledge of most of the protagonists in the conflict and his background as an international diamond-market researcher.

Graham Greene *The Heart of the Matter*. Set in Freetown during World War II and touching on the racism and repression then present in the colony, Greene's novel uses the town as a seedy web in which his protagonists struggle. Greene's atmospheric *Journey without Maps*, narrating his walk through Sierra Leone and Liberia in 1935, is also still worth reading.

Gail Haddock *What for Chop Today?* Recollections of a young volunteer doctor in Sierra Leone in the early 1990s, mostly delivered through warm and witty dialogue. Good, light preparatory reading – with dark undertones.

Eugene Harkins *Where Witch Birds Fly*. Enjoyable work of fiction, based on a journey of self-discovery which goes some way to making sense of

the political and economic forces that fostered the imbroglio in Sierra Leone.

Tim Hetherington *Dem Ol Bod Ose* (published by the British Council). Collection of exceptional images documenting the dilapidated beauty of Freetown's creole architectural heritage.

Michael Jackson *In Sierra Leone*. Beautifully written reflections on Sierra Leonean history and ethnography by an anthropologist who returned in 2002 to the country in which he had worked in the early 1970s.

Emily Joy *Green Oranges in Lion Mountain: the Accidental Optimist*. An upbeat portrayal of the everyday trials and tribulations faced by NGO workers and medical volunteers in war-torn Sierra Leone – a humbling narrative which demands the reader put the values of Western society into perspective.

Damien Lewis *Operation Certain Death*. Another lively, blow-by-blow account of the SAS's mission to liberate British hostages held by the so-called Westside Boys.

Yulisa Amadu Maddy *No Past, No Present, No Future*. Three Sierra Leonean boys in Europe make up for, and make the most of, their different backgrounds.

Robert Young Pelton *Three Worlds Gone Mad*. Wry look at the insanity of the war in Sierra Leone (one of three extended essays also covering Chechnya and Bougainville), by the gonzo-travel-writing author of *The World's Most Dangerous Places*.

People's Educational Association *Fishing in Rivers of Sierra Leone*. A major collection of oral literature – stories and songs – from thirteen Sierra Leonean language groups, with hundreds of photos of the performers in action.

Paul Richards *Fighting for the Rainforest*. Written during the war by an author married to a Sierra Leonean. Richards' study initially offers solid analysis of the schism between politics in Freetown and the interior before erroneously flirting with the idea that the RUF were a group of "marginalized intellectuals".

Teun Voeten *How de Body?* Dutch photojournalist Voeten visited Sierra Leone in 1998 on assignment to photograph child soldiers. The result is harrowing and occasionally funny, though perhaps not as illuminating as you might hope.

Language

The most useful thing you can do to keep in touch with events around you in Sierra Leone is learn some **Krio**. Unless you have lessons, however, this isn't as easy as it might appear: Krio isn't a pidgin, so you can't guess it. Krio is written phonetically. Although many words look familiar (and numbers are the same as in English), it's a different matter to get them right in speech, and to structure your sentences correctly. Remember, too, that even with reasonable Krio, you'll still be speaking a foreign language to the nine people out of ten who are more likely to speak Mende or Temne.

Krio

Aw di bohdi?	How are you?
No bad, bohdi fine	Not bad, fine
Mohnin-o!	Good morning!
Ivinin-o!	Good evening!
Kushe-o!	Hello
A no sabi tok Krio	I don't speak Krio
Usai yu kohmot?	Where are you from?
A kohmot …	I'm from …
Wi go si bak	Goodbye/see you again
Dehn geht hotel na dis tohn	Is there a hotel in this town?
A ebul slip naya?	Can I sleep here?
Dehn get chop os naya?	Is there a chop house here?
Wetin na yu nem?	What's your name?
A nem …	My name is …
Usai yu de go?	Where are you going?
A de go na…	I'm going to…
Wan naya!/ Lef me naya	Let me off!/ Drop me here
Tap!	Stop!
A wan wata/ Gi mi wata	Can I have some water
Ohmos foh di panapul?	How much is the pineapple?
(Duya) lehs mi smohl	(Please) lower your price a little
Ustehm wi de go?	When are we leaving?
Wi de go jisnoh	We're going now
Bai gohd in powa	By the grace of god/Insh'allah
Aw foh du?	What can a person do? (rhetorical)
Nafoh bia nomoh	Just bear it, nothing can be done

Mende

Mende, one of the Mande languages, is related to Susu and Mandinka. It's somewhat "tonal", so that meaning varies with the pitch of voice.

Buae! (sing.)/ Wuae! (pl.)	Hello there! (response the same)
Bisye! (sing.)/ Wusye! (pl.)	Thanks, greetings (said as you pass through the village)
O bi gahui?	How are you? (lit. "Your bones?")
Kaye Ngewo ma	Response ("God can't be blamed")
Ngi ya le	I am leaving

Mm, ta mia, ma lo-o	Yes, okay, see you again	Yila	1
Bi lei?	What's your name?	Fele	2
Nya la a...	My name is...	Sawa	3
Pelei ji a li mi?	Where does this road go? -	Nani	4
		Lolu	5
A li...	It goes to...	Woita	6
Sao	No	Wofela	7
Li lele!	Go slowly!	Wayakpa	8
Gbe jongo lo a ji?	How much is this?	Talu	9
Na bagbango, ba mayeilo?	It's too much, can you lessen it?	Pu	10
		Pu mahu lolu	15
Kulungoi	All right	Nu yila gboyongo	20

(lit. "one man finished"; ie ten fingers and ten toes)

Glossary

Alagba Bigwig, personage

Ambohg "Humbug"; to bother or pester someone

APC All People's Congress party, opposition party voted into power in 2007 (colour: red)

Bafa Shelter made of thatch or leaves

Bohboh Small boy

Bruk To wash clothes

Bundu Generic term for secret societies

Cora Lebanese or Syrian, after the coral they used to sell

Gara Indigo; usually refers to dyed cloth

IMATT International Military Advisory and Training Team, the British team training the SLAF

Johnks Used clothes, "deadmen's clothes" from Western charities

Kola Can mean a tip or inducement, not always of kola nuts

Lorry Often a minibus or converted pick-up

Pampa Large dug-out canoe equipped with outboard motor

Pikin Child

PMDC People's Movement for Democratic Change, second party of opposition, having split with the SLPP (colour: orange)

Poda poda Minibus

Porto European, white person (from Portuguese)

Pumwe European (Mende)

Salone Sierra Leone

Siraman Lebanese, or other white

SLPP Sierra Leone People's Party, establishment party (colour: green)

SLAF Sierra Leone Armed Forces

Titi Small girl

Turntable Roundabout, traffic circle

Wetman "White man"; can apply to anyone with a European lifestyle

8.1

Freetown and around

n aged and crumbling tumble of sagging streets, clapboard and cement-block buildings, with a population now approaching a million, **FREETOWN** fills the level areas and spreads up the steep hillsides of the otherwise vegetation-flanked Freetown Peninsula. Immediately after the war, the city made for a poignant collage of listless abandon – rot and collapse ubiquitous among the many palm and mango trees. Today, it could be said that the Sierra Leonean capital is shedding its skin: the signs of urban decay and the scars of war are fast vanishing under fresh coats of paint while the rubbish that regularly built up on street corners is being swallowed by the city's new fleet of garbage disposal trucks.

The eerie feeling of driving after-hours through a city centre shrouded in darkness, seemingly abandoned to the Cotton Tree's bats, is no more. Now, the darkness is penetrated by the glow of street-lights which, like the hopes of Freetown's inhabitants, had been extinguished for decades. The garish billboards of rival mobile-phone operators and the posters of newly released music all offer signs of a population fast rediscovering its voice and swagger. Notwithstanding the construction and renovation boom, there are still haunting edifices, like the burnt-out **City Hall** and the derelict **City Hotel**, where Graham Green penned *The Heart of the Matter*, both of which still stand as sombre reminders of the country's past. Yet, if you're arriving from almost anywhere else in West Africa, Freetown's overall effect is still enchanting. The town (and it feels like a town, not a city) gurgles with twice as much atmosphere as any other West African capital. The hilly relief gives constantly changing points of view and there are photogenic street prospects in every direction.

Architecture and a real depth of history have much to do with it. Pastel-painted creole houses, with rusty-red tin roofs, often propped up on posts against steeply scaling streets, are preserved even in the town centre. The anonymous apartment blocks and broad thoroughfares of many cities are largely absent from Freetown. After dark you catch domestic glimpses, through the burglar bars and tatty curtains, of murky interiors lit by dim light-bulbs – or kerosene lamps. Freetown's electricity supply is far from stable, and is distributed under a rotation system, with only about a quarter of the town receiving electricity at any one time.

Walking or driving through the town in the heat of the day is best avoided: you'll find yourself surrounded by maddening chaos, or spending hours in unmoving traffic jams, which usually don't dissolve until long after dark. There's a fair choice of places to stay and eat, though, and the business and embassy districts are compact and central. Uniquely in West Africa, Freetown has some exceptionally beautiful beaches close to the city: they're all nearby on the **Freetown Peninsula** – far enough away to ensure clean sea and tranquillity, but still an inexpensive taxi-ride from the town.

Arrival, orientation, information

Sierra Leone's **international airport** at Lungi is cut off from the capital by the mouth of the Sierra Leone River. The airlines run connecting **helicopter** services (£30/$60; 10min) to the *Mammy Yoko* and WFP (World Food Programme) landing sites behind Lumley Beach. Alternatively, speedboat hires are available, operating from

| SIERRA LEONE | Freetown and around

Mahera Beach and arriving into Man O'War Bay (£40/$80), which is the preferred option when you've missed your helicopter or **hovercraft** shuttle, or when either mode of transport is out of action (as they both were at the time of writing). The journey by ferry is much slower and cheaper, ferries crossing from **Tagrin Point Ferry Terminal**, 16km from Lungi, to the old **Kissy Ferry Terminal** about 4km east of the town centre (Le5000). To get from the airport to the ferry terminal, either charter a whole taxi (Le35,000) or jump into a shared taxi (Le3000). This journey from the airport to the town centre takes a minimum of 1½ hours and can easily stretch to three or four hours depending on the state of the ferry and traffic conditions on the east side of town. There is also the simple option of going by road the whole way, which is likely to take as long as your international flight – allow six hours.

Orientation and information

Freetown's hilly layout is sprawling and confusing, and its north-facing aspect curiously disorientating. The town begins in the east at **Wellington**, and stretches into the poor residential areas of **Kissy**, **Cline Town**, **Fourah Bay**, **Kossoh Town** and **Foulah Town** (together known as **East End**).

The half square kilometre of the main **commercial** and **business district** roughly coincides with the historical centre. The oldest and most established blocks are roughly within a triangle formed by **Siaka Stevens Street** (the town's major thoroughfare), Pademba Road and Waterloo Street. This triangle, its apex the famous, huge **Cotton Tree**, was home to the freed-slave Nova Scotians and the Maroons from Jamaica. Down by the shore near the centre, **Kroo Town** is an area still largely inhabited by Kru fishing-people from Liberia. The unfortunate English immigrants of 1787 settled a few hundred metres to the north of here on the peninsula of **Kingtom**.

West of the centre – the **West End** – through a mix-up of ridges, ravines, streams and sprawling shanties, stretch the more residential, less commercial areas of **Congo Town**, **Murray Town**, **Wilberforce** and other nineteenth-century freed-slave settlements. **Wilkinson Road** – the town's main shopping street – and **Aberdeen Road** cut west out of the centre. Aberdeen Road runs down the steep hillside to the sea and over a bridge to the **Aberdeen Peninsula**, on the far side of which lies the five-kilometre sweep of **Lumley Beach** and the head of the road that runs south along the peninsula shore. The West End is where most NGOs have their premises, and the employees their homes. This is also the area where most of Freetown's reasonable guesthouses and hotels are located.

There are ongoing **street-name changes** in Freetown, though in common with other West African cities, it can take years for them to stick. In the centre, Percival Street is now Peters Street; Charlotte Street has become Sengbeh Pieh Street; and Waterloo Street has been renamed Olaudah Equiano Street. Out west, Aberdeen Road is now officially Sir Samuel Lewis Road.

For **tourist info**, contact the **National Tourist Board**, whose main office is at the *Cape Sierra Hotel*, Aberdeen Hill (☏022/23.66.20 ⓦwww.welcometosierraleone.org). They have a less-useful branch off Lumley Beach.

Freetown surface arrivals and departures

There's only one main road into Freetown, from the east. Most taxis, *poda podas* and lorries have drop-off and pick-up points in the centre or east of town. The main location for those serving the north of the country (Makeni and Kabala) is **Ashoebi Corner**, on Blackhall Road at the Upgun turntable (roundabout), a taxi ride from the centre. Vehicles for Bo (4hr) and Kenema use the **Dan Street bus park** (just off Kissy Rd to the west of Upgun turntable). Upcountry vehicles also use the Shell petrol station in Kissy on the road to Waterloo. Conakry vehicles park in **Free Street**, a couple of hundred metres west and uphill from the PZ turntable, at the eastern end of the town centre.

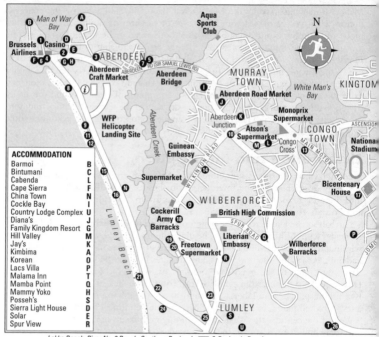

ACCOMMODATION

Barmoi	B
Bintumani	C
Cabenda	L
Cape Sierra	F
China Town	N
Cockle Bay	I
Country Lodge Complex	U
Diana's	J
Family Kingdom Resort	G
Hill Valley	M
Jay's	K
Kimbima	A
Korean	O
Lacs Villa	P
Malama Inn	T
Mamba Point	Q
Mammy Yoko	H
Posseh's	S
Sierra Light House	D
Solar	E
Spur View	R

Lakka Beach, River No. 2 Beach, Southern Peninsula ▼ & Peninsula Beaches

City transport

There's no regulated bus service in town although you won't find it hard to come by passing **poda podas**. Generally you can walk between most points in the centre – indeed the permanent traffic jams in the heart of town may convince you to do so. For slightly longer trips, wave down one of the shared *poda podas* or **route taxis** (unmetered, with yellow licence plates) going in your direction. These vehicles run on agreed routes, dropping off and picking up anywhere (expect to pay less than Le1000 for short hops). You can always charter a taxi if you can find an empty cab; a trip from the centre of town to Lumley Beach shouldn't cost more than Le15,000, though you might end up paying double if you don't bargain effectively. In fact, it can be handy to charter the taxi for an hour or two if you have a few places to visit (this should cost no more than Le15,000/hr). Alternatively, try hitching a ride, especially if you're heading out to the beaches, as many drivers will oblige. You can offer to pay (reckon on twice the shared-taxi fare), but you'll often get free lifts. Siaka Stevens Street at the Cotton Tree roundabout is a likely spot.

Accommodation

Inexpensive lodgings are hard to find in Freetown. The cheapest places are in the East End of town, but it really isn't a great idea to stay in this poor, crime-ridden area until the country has truly settled down. Practically all the accommodation reviewed below is **west of the centre**. There are also a couple of places to stay on the southern beaches, reviewed on pp.685–687. Many hotels, especially the

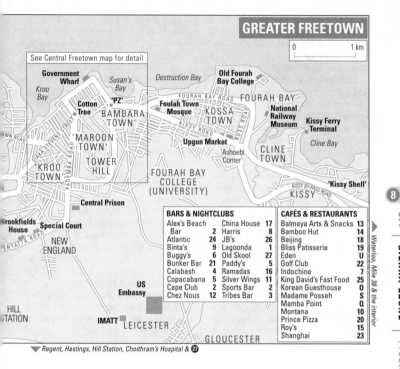

See Central Freetown map for detail

GREATER FREETOWN

0   1 km

Government Wharf

Kroo Bay

Susan's Bay

Destruction Bay

Old Fourah Bay College

FOURAH BAY ROAD   FOURAH BAY

Cotton Tree

'PZ'

Foulah Town Mosque

KOSSA TOWN

National Railway Museum

Kissy Ferry Terminal

'BAMBARA TOWN'

KISSY ROAD

'MAROON TOWN'

Upgun Market

Cline Bay

'Ashoebi Corner'

CLINE TOWN

'KROO TOWN'

TOWER HILL

FOURAH BAY COLLEGE (UNIVERSITY)

KISSY BY-PASS ROAD

'Kissy Shell'

KISSY

Central Prison

rookfields House

Special Court

NEW ENGLAND

ENYATTA ROAD

US Embassy

HILL STATION

IMATT   LEICESTER

GLOUCESTER

BARS & NIGHTCLUBS			
Alex's Beach Bar	2	China House	17
Atlantic	24	Harris	8
Binta's	9	JB's	26
Buggy's	6	Lagoonda	1
Bunker Bar	21	Old Skool	27
Calabash	4	Paddy's	5
Copacabana	5	Ramadas	16
Cape Club	2	Silver Wings	11
Chez Nous	12	Sports Bar	2
		Tribes Bar	3

CAFÉS & RESTAURANTS	
Balmaya Arts & Snacks	13
Bamboo Hut	14
Beijing	18
Bliss Patisserie	19
Eden	U
Golf Club	22
Indochine	7
King David's Fast Food	25
Korean Guesthouse	O
Madame Posseh	S
Mamba Point	Q
Montana	10
Prince Pizza	20
Roy's	15
Shanghai	23

Waterloo, Mile 38 & the interior

▼ *Regent, Hastings, Hill Station, Choithram's Hospital &* ㉗

more expensive ones, now have 24/7 electricity, while some of the mid-range places might have power overnight. With cheaper lodgings there is no guarantee.

Barmoi (ex-Cape Guest House) 75C Cape Rd, Aberdeen ☏076/91.87.71 ☏022/23. 67. 02. Popular, well-run hotel with a homely feel and enthusiastic staff, now expanded into a fully-fledged hotel with 24hr electricity, a/c rooms, satellite TV and two pools, one of which directly overlooks Cape Sierra Point. ⑧

Bintumani Lumley Beach Rd ☏022/23.39.96 ✉keafa456@yahoo.com.cn. Once Freetown's top hotel, this was used as the RUF rebel HQ during the war, and was completely destroyed in fighting. Rebuilt by Chinese investors, it is once again a stylish luxury complex with all the facilities you'd expect, plus Chinese decor, bilingual signs and menu. ⑧

Cabenda 14A Signal Hill Rd ☏022/23.05.44 ⓦwww.hotelcabenda.com. One of Freetown's up-and-coming new hotels, this is a charming place with easy access to central Freetown, a pool and Wi-Fi. ⑧

Cape Sierra Lumley Beach ☏ 022/23.03.21 ✉capecater@hotmail.com. Comfortable, if slightly sterile international establishment, with pool, business centre, beautician. Chalets available for longer stays. ⑧

China Town Lumley Beach Rd ☏076/62.52.39. A small hotel with just 7 rooms bang in the middle of Lumley Beach. Simple, clean and comfortable. ⑦

Cockle Bay Aberdeen Rd. Basic, s/c rooms – at outrageous rates. ⑥

Country Lodge Complex Hill Station ☏022/23.55.89 ✉countrylodgecomplex@ yahoo.com. Freetown's top hotel, with a hilly location and cooler climate than the rest of Freetown. Luxury rooms, gym and pool, which all have great views, as do the bars and restaurant. ⑧

Diana's 19 Mudge Farm, off Aberdeen Rd ☏022/23.33.91. Trying-to-be-English B&B, and quite reasonable, though a little scruffy. ⑤

Family Kingdom Resort Lumley Beach Rd ☏022/23.11.36 ✉fkingdomresort@yahoo.com. With its playgrounds, child-friendly shallow pool, open-air stage and mini-zoo, this looks more like a theme park than a hotel. Comfortable a/c rooms. ⑧

Hill Valley 34 Signal Hill Rd ☏022/23.55.82 ✉hilvalleyft@yahoo.com. Looks like an apartment block, with no character – and a loud generator. But the clean, a/c en-suite rooms, with TV and, in some cases, good views, compensate. ⑦

Jay's 1A Sir Samuel Lewis Rd (Aberdeen Rd), at the junction with Wilkinson Rd ☎076/62.21.80. Simple and modestly priced rooms with a large terrace and bar. ④

Kimbima Bintumani Drive, off Cape Rd, Aberdeen ☎022/23.66.10/11 ⓦwww.hotelkimbima.com. New hotel, popular with the business crowd. Good pool overlooking Man O'War Bay and very helpful staff. ⑧

Korean Guesthouse 34 Quarry Lower Pipe Lane, off Wilkinson Rd ☎076/64.79.59. Spacious, a/c rooms, tiled floors, pretty decor and an outstanding Korean restaurant at one of Freetown's best-value options. Electricity every night. ⑥

Lacs Villa 3A–9C Cantonment Rd ☎022/24.07.14 ⓔlacs@sierratel.sl. From the carpets to the breakfast menu, a very English B&B hidden in a quiet, leafy courtyard. There's a good restaurant too. ⑧

Malama Inn Regent Rd ☎03376.61.38. Basic hotel in busy Lumley residential district. ⑥

🏃 **Mamba Point** Wilberforce ☎022/23.28.72 ⓔmamba_point@yahoo.com. One of Freetown's most popular lodgings with clean a/c rooms and a lively bar. ⑥

Mammy Yoko Aberdeen Rd ☎022/29.56.14. Formerly one of Freetown's top hotels, the *Mammy Yoko* was taken over as the UN peacekeepers' headquarters. The UN presence has significantly reduced but the hotel is still in transition, the rooms grubby and the pool not yet in use. ⑧

The Place 42 Rawdon St ☎022/22.92.41. Very good budget hotel, with clean rooms and all-night electricity. ③

🏃 **Posseh's** Babadorie, Lumley ☎022/23.06.64 ⓔpossehres2004@yahoo .com. Situated in a residential district, this has bags of character (like an English B&B) and an excellent restaurant. ⑦

Sierra Lighthouse Man O'War Bay ☎022/23.66.74 ⓔinfo@sierralighthouse.com. Unattractive and block-like from the outside but with clean rooms and good service, and a beautiful outdoor terrace and restaurant serving excellent Lebanese specialities. ⑧

Solar 66 Cape Rd, Man O'War Bay, Aberdeen ☎030/21.68.46. Simple studio-style rooms and chalets, ideal for longer-term visits. There's also a good bar, restaurant and pool. ⑥

Spur View 26C Spur Rd ☎022/23.33.91. Sharing management with, and of a similar standard to, *Diana's*. ⑤

YMCA 32 Fort St, in the town centre ☎022/22.36.08 ⓦwww.ymca-sl.org. Once a crucial standby for volunteers and low-budget travellers, the *YMCA* is these days, sadly, little more than a dingy dive, and only recommended to the hardy. ③

The Town

Wandering around Freetown is generally easy, though it can be murderously uncomfortable outside the cooler season, and you may not delay long before migrating out to the beaches. The town's decrepitude conceals a few sights, including a **museum** and, remarkably, nearly one hundred established **churches and mosques**.

An obvious place to start a walking tour, and Freetown's most famous landmark, is the **Cotton Tree**, a magnificent silk-cotton older than the town itself and as tall as any of its buildings. Beneath the tree's younger branches, slaves were once sold and, in 1787 in the same place, the first colonists from England are supposed to have gathered – a group of "black poor" immigrants and sixty white women who had been deported to Sierra Leone. Notice the large **fruit bats** hanging in the Cotton Tree and other trees in the town centre, sleeping or squabbling above the town traffic: every evening at sunset, they launch off, in dramatic fashion, for their feeding sites in the interior of the peninsula. The statuesque 1920s **law courts** nearby were built on the spot where the trials and adjudications of captured slave-ship captains and crew took place after the British parliament had banned the slave trade in 1808.

Down by the **waterfront**, there's a meagre pair of historical monuments. At the west end of Wallace Johnson Road, the entrance to what is now the lower dispensary of Connaught Hospital is formed by the **"Slave Gate"**. Slaves liberated from slave ships were detained behind it in the "King's Yards" while arrangements were made for their resettlement. It was through this gate that they walked to an unknown future in "Free Town". The sanctimonious inscription still reads:

Royal Hospital and Asylum for Africans
Freed from Slavery by British Valour and Philanthropy
A.D. 1817

The **Portuguese Steps**, below Wallace Johnson Street, were built the same year by Governor Charles McCarthy. They're a handsome flight, certainly, but nowadays utterly neglected and unnoticed.

Fourah Bay College

Freetown's most famous institution is **Fourah Bay College**, the oldest university in West Africa. The modern (though atrophied) university is located up at Mount Aureol, south of the town centre, and is worth a visit itself, partly for the stunning view. But it's interesting to go and see the **original Fourah Bay building**, founded in 1827 by the Church Missionary Society, and now a half-ruined Magistrate's Court. It makes a good excuse for an exploration of one of the town's poorer, older and much-bypassed East End quarters. The old four-storey building at the end of College Road in Cline Town dates from 1845, and is made of red laterite bricks and decorated with iron fretwork. Samuel Adjai Crowther, the college's first student, later became the first home-grown Bishop of West Africa.

Churches and mosques

Like no other country in Africa, Sierra Leone is a paragon of religious tolerance. While it may be unheard of to have cross-religion marriages in many communities in Africa, this is common practise in Sierra Leone and an attitude reflected in the casual mosaic of churches and mosques you'll find across the town. Former president Kabbah proudly described this phenomenon as a "noble characteristic" of his countrymen. A practising Muslim himself, Kabbah's late wife was a devout Catholic.

Sunday is the day when you can't fail to notice the importance of Freetown's churches, as thousands of people, and especially the Krio community, dress in their Sunday best – classically, men in dark suits and homburgs, women in frocks and creative hats, boys in sailor suits and girls in virginal white frills. Services are long and enthusiastic.

Of more than 150 churches and nearly forty mosques, Freetown's oldest place of worship is **St John's Maroon Church**, a diminutive white chapel on the south side of Siaka Stevens Street, two blocks west of the Cotton Tree. It was founded by the first freed-slave settlers from Jamaica in about 1820. In construction around the same time was the colonial high temple of **St George's Cathedral**, on Lightfoot Boston Street, completed in 1828 and dedicated in 1852. Memorial plaques inside commemorate British administrators and traders who didn't survive the "White Man's Grave". The **Zion Church** on Fort Street is one to check out during a service. The Catholic community, much smaller than the reforming churches, has its

The Reverend Koelle and his Polyglotta Africana

It was at Fourah Bay College, in 1852, that a young German pastor, the Rev S.W. Koelle, published an extraordinary collection of vocabularies from nearly 200 West and Central African languages, the **Polyglotta Africana**. Working with immense speed, he interviewed 205 informants – most of them freed slaves – and recorded the translations of about 300 words and phrases in their natal languages. He got some curious replies: one man apparently replied "Gud-bai" when Koelle asked him to give the phrase for "I am going". But the finished book is a remarkable achievement, far in advance of anything produced until then, still useful to linguists and interesting to look through today; there are copies in the Fourah Bay College library and recent editions available abroad. Apart from giving clues about the relatedness of different West African languages, the *Polyglotta* also offers up interesting cultural information. Less than a third of the informants, for example, could come up with words in their mother tongues for "butter" or "ink" and there were problems too with "book", "hell" and "soap". Missionaries must have found the blanks provocative.

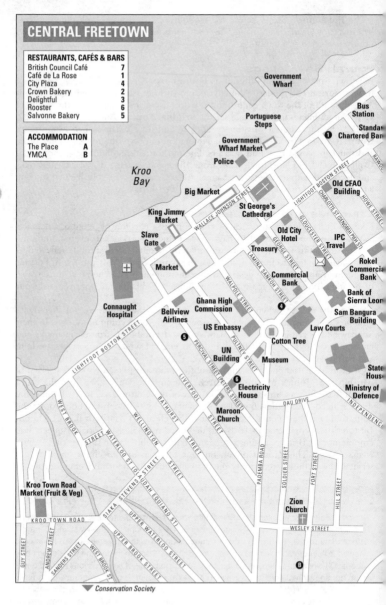

CENTRAL FREETOWN

RESTAURANTS, CAFÉS & BARS

British Council Café	7
Café de La Rose	1
City Plaza	4
Crown Bakery	2
Delightful	3
Rooster	6
Salvonne Bakery	5

ACCOMMODATION

The Place	A
YMCA	B

Kroo Bay

Government Wharf

Bus Station

Portuguese Steps

Standard Chartered Bank

Government Wharf Market

Police

Old CFAO Building

Big Market

St George's Cathedral

King Jimmy Market

Old City Hotel

IPC Travel

Slave Gate

Treasury

Rokel Commercial Bank

Market

Commercial Bank

Bank of Sierra Leone

Connaught Hospital

Ghana High Commission

Sam Bangura Building

Bellview Airlines

US Embassy

Law Courts

Cotton Tree

UN Building

Museum

State House

Electricity House

Ministry of Defence

Maroon Church

Kroo Town Road Market (Fruit & Veg)

Zion Church

Conservation Society

relatively modest **Sacred Heart Cathedral** on Siaka Stevens Street, on the corner of Howe Street.

In a country where new churches of all denominations seem to be springing up each month, the most renowned of these is **Mammy Dumbuya's Jesus is the Lord Ministry** situated by Parliament on Tower Hill. Famed across Sierra Leone for her miracle work, Mammy Dumbuya enjoys a large following. Her service is always

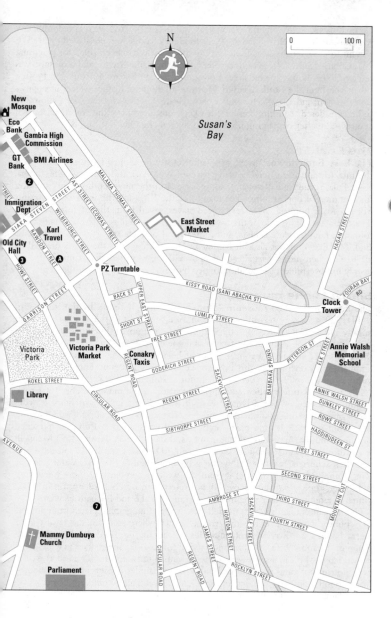

full, taking more than a thousand people each Sunday and often right through until the next morning for "all-night prayers".

The oldest mosque is **Foulah Town Mosque** on Mountain Cut, just off Kissy Road in the East End. It's surprisingly churchlike in its design, possibly in deference to the concerns of colonial and Creole ruling groups in the mid–nineteenth century – there was considerable opposition to Islam from Christian freed slaves. The freed

Yoruba slaves from Nigeria (known as "Aku" or "Oku") were predominantly Muslims. In 1832, a British lawyer, William Henry Savage, was persuaded by his Aku servant to press for the release of a group of Aku who had been jailed for practising "Muhammedanism". In gratitude, several took the name Savage, and a mosque was built near his house, in the street now called Savage Square. Encouraged by this, other Aku built the **Foulah Town Mosque** a kilometre further west. But opposition to Islam, and a low-key conflict between the Creoles and the Aku (who came to be considered "Muslim Creoles") has kept mosques out of the commercial town centre – a quarter containing no less than sixteen churches – to this day.

The East End

The **East End "towns"** were originally mostly developed by immigrants from the interior and from neighbouring parts of West Africa (Temne, Mende, Limba, Kissi, Fula, Yoruba and Bambara). Some arrived in the nineteenth century looking for commercial opportunities, but many, like the Kissi and the influxes of Muslim Yoruba from Nigeria, were recaptured slaves, saved from the Atlantic crossing. The character of this side of the town thus has a less creolized flavour. Many of its founding families were traders, and a great deal of trade still goes on in the East End. The East End was also hit hardest by the fighting after the rebels invaded in 1998/99, when most of its already dilapidated houses were left in ruins. Today, it's deeply impoverished, chaotic, and gripped by traffic jams throughout the day.

Sierra Leone museum

The newly refurbished **museum** (Mon–Fri 10am–4pm; entry by donation) was, until 1929, a railway terminus ("Cotton Tree Station") at the foot of the "Hill railway" up to Wilberforce and Hill Station. The diminutive white building then saw service as a school, a soft-drinks factory and a telephone exchange before becoming the repository of Sierra Leonean cultural heritage in 1957. The collections are emphatically worth a visit: this is Sierra Leone's only museum. There aren't many visitors and you're likely to get a guided tour of some kind.

The **Ruiter stone replica** takes pride of place in the museum. This 1664 rock graffito, scratched by bored Dutch sea-captains during a lull in a military expedition against the English, was discovered in the course of drainage work on the waterfront in 1923. It's the oldest archeological evidence of a European presence on the peninsula. A rubbing of the names and date ("M. A. Ruiter, I. C. Meppell, Vice Admiralen, Van Hollant en Westfriesland, AD 1664") was made and the stone was then reburied "six feet below the ground just above the high water mark at King Jimmy Market, to protect it from the weather". Potentially more interesting is another stone, yet to be uncovered, but referred to by Richard Burton in 1862, which is supposed to carry the initials of Francis Drake and Richard Hawkins.

The museum's main interest, though, lies in the ethnographic pieces from around the country. There's an interesting **mask** corner where some of the regalia from Sierra Leone's still lively **secret societies** is fearlessly displayed. Look out for the figure of "Mammy Wata", the transmogrifying Medusa-like sea goddess (a widespread coastal icon) who can assume serpentine or human form and act for good as well as evil. Notice too, some excellent and rather rare examples of Sierra Leonean home-made country cloth, instruments of music and war, and a fine old *warri* board.

The statue of **Bai Burreh** is dressed in the nineteenth-century Temne guerilla leader's own clothes and holds the cutlass with which he fought in the Hut Tax War of 1898. Bai Burreh was captured and taken to the Gold Coast to rot in jail, but was allowed to return in 1905 to end his years in his old kingdom. The kind of "bullet-proof" *ronko* cloth he wore can still be bought today in Kabala, in Northern Province.

Upstairs, there's an impressive photo exhibition of **Sierra Leone's chiefs**, by Vera Viditz-Ward in collaboration with the Smithsonian Institution. The large images capture the regional leaders in their traditional regalia. Other displays include minerals, prehistoric stone tools and Mende **nomoli** – small, rather arcane soapstone

Freetown markets

Freetown as a whole resembles one big, colourful, noisy market, and though most of the merchandise available comprises mundane household goods and cheap clothes, you can spend an enjoyable time just browsing. For specific purchases, try the following:

Central

King Jimmy Market (Tues & Thurs). Fruit, vegetables and fish.
Government Wharf Market (daily). General goods, from pomade to potato peelers.
Big Market ("Basket Market"; daily). A covered market for a range of crafts, tourist bric-a-brac, traditional medicines and mystical materials. There are good baskets (*shuku, blai*), some nice musical instruments and rather a lot of small animal skins, but you need to spend some time at the stalls to discover interesting bargains that you'd actually want to take home.
Victoria Park Market Can be fun, but keep your wits about you: a lot of people are after your custom. This is the best market in Freetown for Sierra Leonean "country cloth" and locally tailored dresses and shirts.
Kroo Town Road (daily). Fruit and vegetables.

East End

East Street (ECOWAS St)/Kissy Road (Sani Abacha St) Market (daily). A place of some commotion, with a good fruit and veg market, and some small stores trading in cloth and other merchandise.
Upgun/Kennedy Street Market On the left, 1500m further east down Kissy Rd from the East Street Market, immediately before the Upgun roundabout.
Bombay Street Market In Kossa Town, the old Bamana (Bambara) quarter, not far from the shore.

Beach

Lumley Beach Craft Market Situated on the turn to the WFP helicopter landing site, this market has a mixture of everything from masks, country cloth, trinkets and other carvings to hammocks and sandals.

figurines, first identified from a pair dug up on Sherbro Island in the 1880s and later found in huge numbers in farmland right across the centre of the country. The Mende don't claim any connection with them, though they traditionally revered them and believed they protected the fertility of the land. Like the *pomtan* (singular *pomdo*) of the Kissi country in eastern Sierra Leone and Guinea (see p.632), they were almost certainly carved by earlier peoples as ancestor figures. The most likely artists are thought to be the **Sherbro**. Now mostly living on the island of the same name, the Sherbro were displaced from the interior by the Mende around the fifteenth century. Early Portuguese sources suggest they were the best artisans in the region. Much larger figures – life-size heads from Mende and Kono country known as *mahen yafe* ("spirit of the chief") – have also been found. As with the *nomoli* and *pomtan*, the best ones are mostly in private collections or museums abroad.

Lumley Beach

Lumley Beach is the most outstanding example of everything that is good and bad about the Freetown construction boom. A pleasant urban beach, which once offered just a handful of bamboo-shack-style bars, is gradually being transformed into Freetown's own strip, with dozens of bars, restaurants and a long line of unfinished entertainment complexes. Enjoying the beach itself is still free, though, and on Sunday mornings, it becomes a long football pitch, when seemingly all of Freetown's aspiring stars show up to display their skills.

To **get here** from the centre, you can get a share taxi from the Cotton Tree to the junction for Lumley village/Aberdeen (5km; marked by a busy petrol station), from where there are slightly cheaper shared vehicles to Aberdeen and the beach.

At Lumley Beach's first roundabout, the **Hotel Bintumani** is up on the right. Continue west and the entrance on the right leads to the small, sheltered, north-facing beach of Man O'War Bay and some beach bars and restaurants. On the left is the **Mammy Yoko** (named after the nineteenth-century queen). A second roundabout to the right sends you up to Cape Sierra and the hotel of the same name, to the headland lighthouse, and the **Lagoonda** entertainment complex, with its lights glittering across Man-O'War Bay after sunset. In front of you starts the great sweep of Lumley Beach, dotted with the odd coconut tree, but backed mostly by scrub, grass and building sites. The beach here is pleasant, sloping gently, with little undertow and, on occasions, half-pint waves. The National Tourist Board has erected colourful watch-towers manned by lifeguards along the beach. Late in the afternoon, the beach road from the hotels down to Lumley village makes a nice walk, and an equally good run or cycle ride (it's exactly 5km from Lumley Beach north to the **Atlantic** bar and restaurant in Lumley centre). A lift back again should be easy to find. Be wary of bag snatchers at the southern extremity of the beach, by the golf club.

Eating, drinking and nightlife

Freetown is well endowed with eating places, admittedly a number of them heavily dependent on resident volunteers and aid workers. There are good Lebanese establishments and chop houses and, unsurprisingly, numerous fried-chicken places too. Many restaurants close on Sunday, and some of the more established places tend only to open in the evening. Note, also, that many of the hotels listed on p.673 have good restaurants, and there are several decent restaurants and bars out at Lumley Beach.

Snacks and fried food

Bliss Patisserie 137 Wilkinson Rd ☎076/40.68.00. New establishment trying to bring Western coffee culture into the capital. Cappuccinos, croissants and excellent pastries in an air-conditioned setting.

British Council Café Tower Hill. Snacks and light meals.

City Plaza 31 Siaka Stevens St ☎076/66.44.99. Stylish first-floor hideaway directly facing the Law Court Buildings. Comfortable sofas, excellent fresh sandwiches and smoothies.

Crown Bakery Wilberforce St ☎076/63.93.49 (open daytime only). This has long been a major meeting-place in Freetown, clean, a/c and well run, with the best pastries in town and decent food for lunch – fried chicken, sandwiches, pizza.

Delightful 16 Howe St, just off Siaka Stevens St ☎033/51.59.64. Brightly coloured fast-food venue with a good choice of snacks and rice dishes.

King David's Fast Food 34 Freetown Rd, Lumley ☎076/66.96.69. Cheap fried chicken, burgers and the like, served on a terrace bar overlooking the Wilkinson Rd/Spur Rd junction.

Prince Pizza Wilkinson Rd. A modest selection of smallish pizzas from Le10,000.

Rooster Restaurant Electricity House, Siaka Stevens St. Slightly grubby fast-food joint with great fried chicken and sandwiches.

Salvonne Bakery 28 Percival St, yards from the Cotton Tree ☎076/71.34.27. Discreet takeaway spot and probably the best bakery in town. Fresh olive and cinnamon bread, sausage rolls, banana muffins and a host of other treats.

Restaurants

Balmaya Arts & Snacks 32 Main Motor Rd, Congo Cross (☎022/23.00.55. Airy terrace restaurant, popular with NGO workers, offering

tasty, reasonably priced snacks and drinks. The attached gallery is worth a look if you're interested in buying crafts.

Bamboo Hut Wilkinson Rd ☏022/23.04.62. This small, understated place serves reliable African and European meals, at prices that are much more reasonable than most places in the area.

Beijing 112 Wilkinson Rd (☏022/23.06.95 (daily noon–11pm). One of the oldest Chinese restaurants in town. A bit run-down but does reasonable food.

Café de La Rose 2 Howe St ☏076/77.29.19. Downtown lunchtime venue which has been completely refurbished and extended over two floors. Tasty African dishes in a modern setting.

Eden Hill Station, part of the *Country Lodge Complex*. High-end restaurant, with beautiful views overlooking the pool and Lumley Beach in the distance, and no shortage of good wines and innovative food.

Golf Club Lumley Beach ☏022/27.29.56. Popular for Sunday brunch.

Indochine 64 Sir Samuel Lewis Rd, Aberdeen (opposite *Paddy's*) ☏076/67.24.80. Vietnamese–Thai food served in ornate restaurant setting. Expensive but excellent and probably the best service in town.

Korean Guesthouse 24 Lower Pipe Lane, off Wilkinson Rd. Delicious Korean food and a laid-back ambience. Dishes from Le20,000.

Madame Posseh Babadori Hills, Lumley ☏076/61.78.34. In a residential setting up a dirt road that winds round the back of Lumley, this is one of Freetown's best-kept secrets and not the easiest place to find. Intimate restaurant with plants, blowing fans and memorabilia, plus a great hostess and a broad choice of African and European dishes, all exquisitely prepared.

Mamba Point Wilberforce Junction ☏076/62.29.33. Large menu featuring everything from fish and chips to Chinese and French cuisine. Busy most days and especially good for lunch on Fri.

Montana Wilkinson Rd ☏022/27.33.47. Stylish place with a pretty terrace and fairly steep prices. Especially well known for its ice cream, though it also does very passable sandwiches and salads.

Roy's Lumley Beach ☏033/40.50.60. Newly-opened Lebanese restaurant whose outdoor space attracts a good crowd on weekends. You can also sample Arab-style *sheesha* pipes here.

Shanghai 194C Wilkinson Rd ☏076/62.56.41. Another newly-opened Chinese with authentic specialities – a favourite with Freetown's growing Chinese community.

Nightlife

After years of curfew-enforced early nights, Freetown's **nightlife** is now as vibrant as ever. The spacious, open-air entertainment complexes are famous far beyond the country's borders, and certainly worth a visit. They're very chilled about how you enjoy yourself, encouraging you to move on and off the dance-floor, hang out at the bar, play a game of snooker or simply relax in a quiet corner and watch the crowds. Francophone West Africans love Freetown's nightlife for its American-style swagger, and you'll get to hear plenty of hip-hop and R&B in addition to a cross-section of African music. **Live-music** venues, however, are rare, and good live bands even rarer. The groups you'll see performing at places like *Buggy's* or *China House* tend to be mediocre local cover-bands, though you may stumble across the occasional gem.

Though you can't call to book a taxi, you should have no problems finding a cab at night, as long as you don't leave it too late (and it's not a good idea to walk around Freetown alone at night).

Alex's Beach Bar 64 Cape Rd, Man O'War Bay, Aberdeen (☏076/67.92.72 (closed Mon). Overlooking the lagoon, this smart bar and restaurant is where you'll find many off-duty NGOs at the weekend.

Atlantic Lumley Beach Rd ☏076/66.76.77. Quiet bar/restaurant from Mon–Thurs, good for drinks and light meals. At weekends it transforms itself into an all-out bar when it is very much the place to go. Sometimes has live boxing.

Binta's Lumley Beach Rd. One of several bars and snack bars along the beach road. Delicious fried chicken.

Buggy's Lumley Beach. One of Freetown's most popular clubs – a spacious open-air place where you can move lazily between dance floor, bar, snooker corner, restaurant and the people-watching benches along the sides.

Bunker Bar Lumley Beach Rd ☏033/35.21.24. New, two-tiered, breezy, characterful bar and restaurant. The quaint wooden structure, like the service, is a bit rough round the edges but gets full points for trying to create an original ethnic feel. Reasonable food and great views of Lumley Beach.

Calabash Lumley Beach ☎076/69.93.09. Pretty beach bar with a relaxed ambience and occasional live music.

Cape Club Man O'War Bay, Aberdeen. Another beach bar – with tasty grills and fish dishes – amid the cluster of drinking spots around Man O'War Bay.

Chez Nous Lumley Beach Rd ☎033/54.38.37. Busy beach bar with Lebanese proprietor offering a full range of main courses.

China House King Harman Rd, Brookfields. Bustling town-centre bar, popular with locals. It doesn't hurt to pop by on Fri to catch the occasional dodgy live act.

Copacabana 67 Sir Samuel Lewis Rd, Aberdeen. Lively Thurs-night, upper-deck dancing spot which is yards away from *Paddy's*. Latin music and an all-participating crowd.

Harris Lumley Beach Rd ☎033/46.96.50. One of the first beach bars you come to on your way along the beach, this is popular for its long line of diminutive huts and brightly coloured hammocks.

JB's Hill Station. Bustling city club, popular mainly with local youth. The usual staple diet of hip-hop, R&B and African sounds.

🏃 Lagoonda next to the *Cape Sierra Hotel*, Lumley Beach ☎022/27.24.81. Freetown's slickest entertainment complex, housing a casino, restaurant, nightclub and the only decent cinema in town. Open day and night, it really comes to life on weekend nights.

Old Skool Hill Station. Upmarket nightclub with VIP lounge and cocktail bar. The venue bears all the hallmarks one would expect from its football-star owner, Mohamed Kallon.

🏃 Paddy's Sir Samuel Lewis Rd, Aberdeen. Quite a phenomenon – arguably one of the best bars in West Africa – this open-air, all-round entertainment complex has a good selection of Sierra Leonean music, hip-hop and R&B. Extremely popular with locals, NGO members and expats alike.

Ramadas Lumley Beach Rd. One of the better bamboo beach bars that doesn't get too over-crowded; offers the usual selection of drinks and a simple choice of fish, prawns or beef skewers.

Silver Wings Lumley Beach. Colourful and laid-back bar with limited menu and cheap drinks in a pleasant setting.

🏃 Sports Bar 64 Cape Rd, right next to *Alex's* ☎076/62.29.33. New venture – a good Sat-night venue (order food from *Alex's*). Offering comfy chairs, quiz nights and movie nights (there are big screens to keep up with all the major sporting events), a popular watering-hole with pleasant decor and bar staff.

🏃 Tribes Bar 75 Sir Samuel Lewis Rd, Aberdeen. Small, colourful, unassuming local bar, with reggae playing, especially at weekends.

Listings

Air charter Eagle Air Ltd ☎033.77.66.40.

Airlines Astraeus is represented by Karl Travel, 24 Rawdon St ☎022/22.84.05; Bellview, UMC Building, 31 Lightfoot Boston St ☎022/22.73.11; British Airways, 14 Wilberforce St ☎022/22.88.00; Brussels Airlines, 72B Cape Road, Aberdeen ☎022/23.64.45/7/9 🌐www.flysn.be; Paramount, *Mammy Yoko*, Aberdeen ☎022/27.20.06; Slok, 11 Siaka Stevens St ☎022/22.32.11.

Banks Standard Chartered, 9/11 Lightfoot Boston St ☎022/22.50.22; Sierra Leone Commercial Bank, 29/31 Siaka Stevens St ☎022/22.52.64; Rokel Commercial Bank, 25/27 Siaka Stevens St ☎022/22.23.50. Banking hours are usually 9am–3pm.

Boat rental Cape Shilling Ltd, 24 Charlotte St ☎076/87.91.06. The main operator whose fleet of speedboats cater for everything from game-fishing, excursions to the Turtle Islands and airport connections. Boats leave from Man O'War Bay.

Car rental The big international agencies aren't represented. Try Motorcare, 58C Lightfoot Boston St, off Wilkinson Rd (☎022/23.08.06 🌐www.motorcare.com). Alternatively, travel agents IPC and Yazbeck's, and established hotels such as the *Cape Sierra* and *Bintumani*, can arrange private rental for you. Cars are always rented with a driver.

Cinemas The only cinema currently worth the name is at the *Lagoonda* entertainment complex at *Cape Sierra Hotel*, Lumley Beach ☎022/27.24.81.

Conservation The Conservation Society of Sierra Leone, 2 Pike St (☎022/22.97.16 or 24.21.70 ✉cssl@sierratel.sl 🌐tinyurl.com/2lalz5) is an active focus for ecotourism and conservation efforts around the country. The Environmental Foundation for Africa works closely with Tiwai Island and has an office at 1 Beach Rd, Lakka ☎076/61.14.10, where you can get info on visiting the reserve.

Courier DHL, 15 Rawdon St ☎022/22.52.15 📠22.90.76.

Cultural centres The British Council has a massive building at Tower Hill (☎022/22.22.2 ✉info.enquiry@sl.britishcouncil.org), with a well-equipped library and theatre.

Dentists Dr Dennis Wright, 47 Percival St ℡ 022/22.25.40; Dr Rekab, Rawdon St ℡ 022/22.26.71; Dr I. Reffel-Wyse, 27 Pademba Rd ℡ 022/22.38.83.

Embassies and consulates France, consular affairs handled by the British High Commission; The Gambia, 6 Wilberforce St ℡ 022/22.51.91 ℻ 22.68.46; Ghana, 13 Walpole St ℡ 022/22.34.61 ℻ 22.70.43; Guinea, 6 Carlton-Carew Rd, off Wilkinson Rd ℡ 022/23.25.84; Ireland, Honorary Consul, 8 Rawdon St ℡ 022/22.71.01; Liberia, 10 Main Motor Rd ℡ 022/23.09.91; Mali, Honorary Consul, 40 Wilkinson Rd ℡ 022/23.17.82; Nigeria, 37 Siaka Stevens St ℡ 022/22.42.02; Senegal, Honorary Consul, 9 Upper ECOWAS St ℡ 022/22.29.48; UK, 6 Spur Rd, Wilberforce ℡ 022/23.29.61 ⓦ tinyurl.com/26x8wt; USA, Regent Rd, Leicester ℡ 022/515 000 ⓦ www .freetown.usembassy.gov.

Hospitals and doctors The main hospitals are Choithram Memorial Hospital, Hill Station ℡ 022/23.25.98; Connaught Hospital, Percival St ℡ 022/22.44.05; Marie Stopes, Adelaide St ℡ 022/24.16.07; Netland Nursing Home, College Rd, Congo Cross ℡ 23.01.35. Dr Anthony Williams has a surgery at 33 Goderich St ℡ 022/22.50.87. Others include Dr W.A. Renner, 8 Pultney St ℡ 022/22.45.55; Dr Patrick Coker ℡ 022/22.22.25; Dr I. Hyde-Foster, 4 Lightfoot Boston St, corner of Rawdon St ℡ 076/70.71.72.

Internet access There's a growing number of high-speed Internet cafés in Freetown, costing about Le5000/hr. If you're in the centre of town, try Xara Computers on 9 Malamah Thomas St; heading west from town, there's Nafai Communication Services, 28B Sir Samuel Lewis Rd; and there's also a 24hr Internet café, Lumley Beach Dot Com, on the busy Lumley roundabout.

Newspapers and magazines The British Council has some of the London dailies, as does the British High Commission. You can also buy papers outside some of the more popular lunchtime haunts like *Crown Bakery*. *Africa Week* magazine is fairly widely available and should be sold for the price printed on the cover. Copies of *Newsweek* are also readily available.

Pharmacies Imres, 18 Wilberforce St ℡ 022/22.76.29; Capital, 15 Siaka Stevens St ℡ 022/22.67.51; New Chemist, 30 Wallace Johnson St ℡ 022/22.41.45.

Police Headquarters are on George St ℡ 022/22.30.01.

Post office The main post office is on the corner of Siaka Stevens St and Gloucester St (Mon–Fri 8am–5pm).

Supermarkets With the large number of expats now in the country, supermarkets are doing good business in Freetown. Some of the main ones include Atsons, 16 Wilkinson Rd; Freetown Supermarket, 137D Wilkinson Rd; Essentials, 38 Wilkinson Rd, and Monoprix, 4C Wilkinson Rd.

Travel agents IPC Travel, 10 Siaka Stevens St (℡ 022/22.14.81 ⓔ ipctrav@sierratel.sl) the largest and best known. Karl Travel, 24 Rawdon St (℡ 022/22.84.05 ⓔ karl@hotmail.com), represents Astraeus; Karou Voyage, 11 Wilberforce St (℡ 022/22.73.42 ⓔ globaltravel@yahoo.com), particularly useful for travel to Guinea.

Visa extensions The Immigration Office is on Rawdon St ℡ 022/22.71.74 ℻ 22.47.61.

Western Union c/o Union Trust Bank, Lightfoot Boston St ℡ 022/22.69.54 or 22.27.92.

Wildlife See "Conservation".

Around Freetown

The **beaches** of the Freetown Peninsula are arguably the finest in West Africa, and certainly only those in western Côte d'Ivoire offer any competition. Single women should beware of irritating beach boys and all visitors should look out for nimble-fingered bag snatchers: bring nothing of value, and your camera only if you're going to take pictures. Ideally, go in a group. Two of Sierra Leone's handful of beach resorts are to be found here, nestling on the strands south of Lumley.

Much mentioned but less often visited than the beaches, **Bunce Island** in the Sierra Leone River is definitely worth a visit for its old slave fort. Elsewhere on the peninsula there are a handful of minor attractions, among them the **chimpanzees** of the Tacugama reserve.

The southern beaches

For committed sun-and-sand devotees, the southern reaches of the peninsula harbour some spectacular shores. The sand of every beach is a different colour, from

▲ Mahera & Lungi Airport

Bunce Island

Tasso Island

Airport transfer by hovercraft & helicopter

Tagrin Point

FREETOWN

Car ferry

Aberdeen

Kissy

Lumley Beach

Wilberforce

Leicester

Hill Station

Gloucester

Lumley

Wellington

Leicester Peak

Regent

Goderich Beach

Bathurst

Goderich

Sugar Loaf

Charlotte

Milton Margai College

Lakka

Tacugama Chimpanzee Reserve

Lakka Beach

Hamilton

Guma Dam

Hastings

Sussex Beach

Waterloo

Sussex

River No.2 Beach

Tokeh Beach

Tokeh

'Devils Island'

York

Picket Hill

Black Johnson Beach

N

Tombo

Maroon Island

Bureh Town

Mama Beach

Kent

Passenger ferry to Plantain Islands, Shenge & Bonthe

Dublin Island

Dublin

Banana Islands

Ricketts Island

Mes-Meheux Island

▲ Mile 38 & The Interior

0   5 km

FREETOWN PENINSULA

dazzling white to golden yellow. The best way to take in the beauty of the shoreline is by boat. You can arrange **speedboat hire** through Cape Shilling, who offer a one-day Banana Islands and Peninsula tour. It's also possible to get a **canoe rental** from *Pierre's Beach Resort* on Lakka (see below) or from the River No. 2 Development Association – devote a whole day, or more, to a leisurely coastal tour. Take some food and drink with you and settle down for a picnic on one of the deserted beaches. Fresh coconut juice is delicious, and easily obtained by paying a few local kids to pick some coconuts.

It's useful to have transport of your own to get around the peninsula, though you can get around using public transport, hitching or muddling along in whatever "public" transport comes your way. *Poda podas* head down this way several times a day, as far as York. You're more likely to score a lift at the roundabout in Lumley village with weekenders or expatriates. On weekdays, the sand lorries that scour some beaches for Freetown's building requirements often give lifts. Be prepared for some walking; it's a badly maintained road, but pretty for most of its length. Road signs, **distances** and directions aren't always clear: those included in the following accounts, unless indicated otherwise, are road distances from Lumley roundabout. After decades of seeing successive governments fail to rebuild the Peninsula road, work is finally underway, with the section between **WATERLOO** and Tokeh already transformed into an impressive highway and – at the time of writing – work starting on the remaining portion between Tokeh and Lumley, arguably amongst the worst stretches in the country.

If you go as far as Tombo, there may be an occasional **ferry** southwards via the Plantain Islands to Shenge, which is an attractive means of heading on down the coast.

Goderich, Lakka and Sussex beaches

Out of Lumley village, past the quaint red-brick St Mary's Church, and Siaka Stevens' distant mansion perched high above, you cross Lumley creek, then come to the somewhat cluttered **Juba Beach** (which also goes by the name of **Levuma**) and then **Goderich** (3km from Lumley and 1km off the road). This beach is a perfectly good place to see an archetypal West African event late every afternoon – the return of the fishing boats – but not one to go out of your way for otherwise. **GODERICH** village sits behind the kilometre of steeply shelving yellow sand.

From here on, the coast road steadily deteriorates. In places, the tar surface gives up completely; if you're driving, beware some dastardly potholes and virtually invisible speed-bumps. A sign (4km) for the "Milton Margai Training College" indicates one means of access to the first really wonderful beach, **Lakka**, which consists of a pair of long, gently shelving bays punctuated by a minuscule, rocky peninsula, two-thirds of the way along. At the far north end, the bay curves to face the south, beneath a riot of vegetation. Beyond the rocky promontory, the second bay crescents down towards Hamilton, with a cascade of coconut jungle behind it.

Lakka is an attractive and sheltered bay, popular with the expat crowd at weekends, and it still has the semblance of a **beach resort** in *Pierre's Bar and Resort* (T030/20.78.35 ◎). These days the "resort" is now only superficially attractive and too run-down to offer any blissful diversion. The spacious wooden bungalows aren't devoid of charm, especially the ones offering a beach view (discounts can be arranged for longer stays) where you wake up to the sound of the sea and revel in glorious sunsets from the beach bar. For food, the *Hard Rock*, truly set on a hard rock on a nearby islet, hanging over the sweeping bay, offers cold drinks, some tasty, simple food and great views of the bay.

The underrated **Hamilton Beach** (largely ignored because of its unappealing fisherman's strand) abuts Lakka to the south and is also home to the weekend haunt of *Samso's Paradise*. Nestled in a beautiful corner of the beach, you can easily walk round to reach *Samso's* (note that the food, although good, can take some time so be sure to order early). You can also overnight here, with two small rooms and a two-bathroom, a/c apartment with satellite TV accommodating up to eight guests (☎030/21.23.93 ⓦwww.samsos-paradise.com ⑧). Beyond the broken coastline of Hamilton you reach **Sussex Beach**, another inviting shoreline. Be careful if you choose to take a dip though, as the sea is deep, and depending on the tide the current here can be strong. There's a pleasant guesthouse, *Franco's*, named after its Italian owner (☎076/74.44.06 ⑥), separated from the beach by a narrow river at high tide. The open restaurant, with its stunning sea views, is a very popular weekend venue for fresh seafood, and in particular fish *carpaccio* and grilled lobster.

River No. 2 and Tokeh beaches

Most people who reach Sussex head on, close to the shore, to **River No. 2** (19km) and the much-hyped beach of the same name. This is magnificent country – dense, green jungle hills rising steeply behind a beach of brilliant white sand, through which the River No. 2 (or Guma River) slices in an ever-changing course. If you're patient and lucky, you might spot dwarf crocodiles and other animals in the clear river water or surrounding mangroves. Hiking upriver, you'll come to a small waterfall which can be stunning in the rainy season (or unimpressive when dry). Appealing though No. 2 beach is, you should be careful crossing the river-mouth that connects it with Tokeh as the current can be quite strong. If you're tempted to cross but an unsure swimmer, you can be taken across the short distance in one of the waiting dugouts for a small fee. Swimming or just floating in the clear lagoon behind the sand ridge is a fantastic way to while away an afternoon. A small **guesthouse** here has fairly inexpensive rooms (❹). On weekends in the dry season and on public holidays, the beach gets busy with "car park attendants", plus food stalls and even crafts, set up among the village houses behind.

At low tide you can get across the river to the much longer stretch of **Tokeh Beach**; but you're then stuck until the next low tide (if you fail to find a dugout) unless you walk the 3km or so to **TOKEH** village to find the track up to the main road. The beach is usually deserted and absolutely stunning, with fine white sand and a background of luscious forest. A small gateway of clear water separates Tokeh Beach from **Devil's Island**, which is reputed to be a meeting place of male *poro* society members. Unfortunately, with the once-fabulous *Africana* beach resort now in ruins, Tokeh Beach is without any accommodation or eating places.

York, Black Johnson and John Obey beaches

Four kilometres beyond Tokeh junction, you come to the village of **YORK** (31km) at the mouth of Whale River creek. There's an old fort on the other side of the village, with glorious views. The coast bends in a smooth arc, and forest-covered mountains rise steeply behind the narrow shoreline.

With the peninsula road from Tokeh right the way through to Waterloo complete, transportation is now easier to at least one half of the peninsula. Most people heading here use the dirt-track route down from Regent before joining the surfaced road towards Waterloo and back round the neck of land. If you're fairly self-sufficient, and don't expect to get back anywhere the same day, you could walk on to **Black Johnson Beach** (36km) on Whale Bay, five hilly kilometres round the creek from York. You might also find a boat to take you the relatively short distance across the creek. Palm-fringed, remote and quite undeveloped, with clear sea, Black Johnson, whose sand has the curious effect of leaving you with blackened feet, is an excellent area for swimming and forgetting about the rest of civilization.

Further south and round the intimate coves of Black Johnson, you stumble on to the golden sands of **John Obey Beach**. Here, the clarity of the water magnifies the contours of the sea bed. Swim in a little further towards the rocks which form the bay and you're bound to get great snorkelling.

Kent, Bureh and Mama beaches

At the southern extremities of the peninsula, and off the main dirt road, are **BUREH TOWN** (48km) and Kent (52km), both of which have postcard-perfect beaches several kilometres long (Kent Beach is a popular venue for Sierra Leone music bands to launch new albums). The forested **Maroon Island**, just 300m from the shore, lies between Bureh and Kent beaches. Near the village of **KENT** you'll see a series of fairly large caves, some of which were used to hold slaves before they were shipped across the Atlantic. There is now a tourist/weekender base at Kent, the peaceful *Sengbeh Pieh Holiday Resort*, which offers chalets with en-suite facilities and excursions to the Banana Islands (℡076/62.58.30 ⓦwww.sengbehpiehsl.com ⑧).

East of Kent, on the peninsula's south-facing coastline, there's a chain of coves and small bays. Heading back to Freetown or Lumley Beach from this far south, it's quicker now to use the highway to **Waterloo** (20km past the turnoff for Bureh and Kent), where you can then pick up the reasonably surfaced highway into Freetown.

Banana Islands

The main point of coming down to Kent Beach is to find a boat across to the **Banana Islands** 5km offshore (prepare yourself for some vigorous bargaining). **Dublin** and **Ricketts** islands are joined by a causeway and have villages of the same names at opposite ends connected by an 8km footpath. Dublin has a couple of small beaches (limpid water and some coral) on its northwest coast and now a fledgling community-owned and managed resort which features six basic but comfortable chalets with en-suite facilities, solar-powered lighting and a newly thatched restaurant and bar (℡076/98.99.06 ⓦwww.bananaislandguesthouse-biya.org ⑥). They run fishing and snorkelling trips and hiking, or historical tours that take in some of the islands' old churches and the remains of its slave fort.

Ricketts is steeper (233m high) and more densely forested. You can camp here, but neither island has any real facilities, so take all the supplies you might need. **Mes-Meheux**, an uninhabited island, lies just off Ricketts' southwest shore, separated from the larger island by a 40-metre-wide channel with excellent snorkelling, especially by the rocks on the Mes-Meheux side. Here, in the right season, you can occasionally hear the cries of migratory whales.

Bunce Island

"I am an American ... but today, I am something more. I am an African too. I feel my roots here in this continent"

Colin Powell, former US secretary of state

Just 500m long and 100m across, **Bunce Island** lies 30km up the mouth of the Sierra Leone River. Situated on the islet, almost buried in jungle, are the ruins of a massive **slave fort** (a proposed UNESCO World Heritage Site) built in 1670 by the British. Attacked by the Portuguese, and reclaimed by the British, the fort was rebuilt several times, and remained in use until 1807. In the course of more than a century, an estimated fifty thousand slaves were sold from this fortress. As late as the 1780s, Fort Bunce was supplying up to three thousand slaves a year from the interior to Danish traders alone, who sold them to the new American rice plantations of South Carolina. Though protected as a national historic monument, the old fort's remains haven't been adequately preserved and there are no facilities on the island. Although the ruins are almost entirely overgrown, they are still impressive, and rather eerie to wander around. Old British cannon still lie scattered around the entrance and lookouts. The two nearby cemeteries are the resting place of several British slave-traders and their local accomplices.

Slaves from the rice-growing areas of Sierra Leone who were transported to the low country of South Carolina and Georgia soon became the dominant people in that remote part of the USA and retained many of their African customs and linguistic ties. Their descendants, called the **Gullah**, are today the African-American community that has preserved more of its African cultural heritage than any other. The connection is remarkably well documented, and there were several Gullah "homecomings" to Sierra Leone in 1989 and 1997. In 2005, Thomalind Martin Polite, a 31-year-old Charleston speech therapist, was welcomed to Bunce Island as the direct seventh-generation descendant of a 10-year old slave girl named "Priscilla", brought on the slave ship *Hare* from Bunce to Charleston in 1756.

Getting to Bunce

Transport to **Bunce Island** can be arranged through Cape Shilling in Freetown (see Listings, p.682). The boat journey from Aberdeen takes you past the city centre, across Tagrin Point and up the mangrove-decked Sierra Leone River. You might also be lucky on the ferry quay at Kissy and find a motorboat willing to make the voyage. But in view of the distance – 30km – you should make sure the vessel is seaworthy and the fuel, shade and water supplies sufficient. If you're very patient and adventurous, you can try to get the regular boat from **King Jimmy Point**, west of Government Wharf in Freetown, which goes every Tuesday, Thursday and Saturday to **PEPEL**, from where Bunce lies a couple of kilometres offshore. It's easier to reach Pepel by road, via **PORT LOKO**, but that is a journey of 160km from Freetown. From Pepel, negotiate a pirogue with the local fishermen (expect to pay Le10,000–20,000), and they'll happily take you to Bunce and back. On the island, you'll probably be joined by the old employee of the National Museum who himself lives in Pepel, but nips across in a dugout when he spots the occasional visitor, to whom he can relate his anecdotes of the island's history in strongly accented Krio.

Regent Village and Chimpanzee Reserve

A short, rewarding excursion on the peninsula itself is a tour through the mountains to **REGENT** and the adjacent chimpanzee reserve. To reach the village, simply follow the road into the peninsula's interior at Hill Station. With your own transport, you can leave your vehicle before reaching the village and take a diversion to **Leicester Peak**, one of the highest points on the peninsula, from where you get a an excellent panoramic view of Freetown. Regent village itself is famous mainly for **St Charles Church**, one of the oldest in West Africa. The small, pretty church lies up a steep hill from the village centre.

The road winds its way through forest and greenery, past the villages of **GLOUCESTER** and **BATHURST**, beyond which there's a sign indicating the **Tacugama Chimpanzee Reserve**. A brief walk up a very steep hill takes you to the reserve, established as a rescue and rehabilitation centre for chimpanzees who are ill, in danger, or have been kept as pets by residents of Freetown and outgrown their welcome. Beautifully laid out on forty hectares of land, it now holds more than eighty chimps who can be observed leaping around the trees during the day. Following a security breach in 2006, visits are now by appointment only (℡076/61.12.11 ⓦwww.tacugama.com).

8.2

The interior

While Freetown and surrounding districts have experienced up to two centuries of Creole history, this influence has hardly rubbed off on the upcountry towns, chief among which are **Makeni**, **Kabala**, **Bo**, **Kenema** and **Koidu**. All of these grew from small seeds in the early part of the last century, though with the exception of the diamond centre Koidu (also known as Koidu-Sefadu or Kono), they reached some sort of zenith of development shortly after independence, subsequently increasing in size but not in stature.

The north

The Northern Province's top attraction is **Outamba-Kilimi National Park**. Pressed around the foot of the Kuru Hills, and hard up against the Guinean border, the park is the only one in this part of the country and worth the effort to visit. To the southeast, on wonderful mountainous back-roads beyond **Kabala**, there are a couple more adventurous possibilities, the beautiful **Lake Sonfon** and the trail to the top of **Mount Bintumani**.

The diversions en route from Freetown are limited, though **PORT LOKO** is a pleasant stop, split by tumbling streams and positioned on steep slopes above Port Loko creek. Once the site from which Loko slaves were shipped to await the Middle Passage crossing from Bunce Island, it was a strategic town in the eighteenth century, when there was a significant Portuguese-speaking community. For ornithologists with their own transport, the creeks and flats to the west of here offer exceptional birding.

Makeni

The provincial capital of the north, **MAKENI**, is a two-hour drive from Freetown on a surprisingly good road. The landscape is fairly flat and indistinct and takes you through the heart of the country's rice-growing fields – the "Boli-lands". In the right season, lush rice-fields flank either side of the road. The first hint you're approaching Makeni comes in the shape of the peaks of the Wusum and Mene hills (Mene being the venue of a colourful community picnic-outing on Boxing Day) which break through the suburbs of the town.

Makeni boasts a famously good **market**, though, like Sierra Leone's other provincial centres, it can make few credible touristic claims. It was once the terminus of the northern branch railway line, and quite a boomtown in the 1920s. Before the rebel war, it was still a busy trading centre, and its market continues to attract vendors and buyers from the whole region.

During the war, Makeni became a headquarters of the **RUF** rebels and the townspeople suffered horrific cruelty and hardship; today, memories seem to be fading rapidly (outwardly, at least). The town is rather let down by a maze of terrible roads squirming around an unfinished independence arc with steel rods jutting ominously towards the sky. On a positive note, if you're interested in *gara*-dyeing, you should have a wander through the dusty streets of the Manikala neighbourhood, arguably

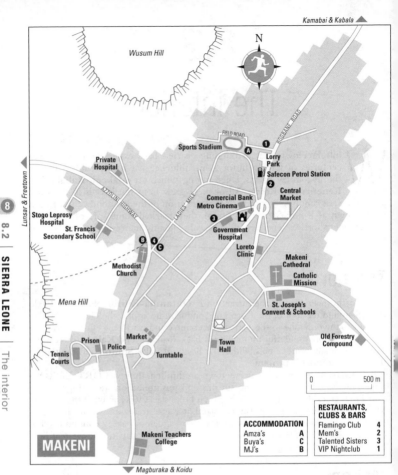

MAKENI

Kamabai & Kabala

Lunsar & Freetown

Magburaka & Koidu

ACCOMMODATION	
Amza's	A
Buya's	C
MJ's	B

RESTAURANTS, CLUBS & BARS	
Flamingo Club	4
Mem's	2
Talented Sisters	3
VIP Nightclub	1

the epicentre of Sierra Leone's tie-dyeing tradition: on any sunny day the streets and washing lines are decked out with rows of richly dyed cloth.

While a trek up the breezy Wusum or Mene peaks will offer only relative adventure, the town itself has something to look forward to in the unlikely construction of the five-star 50-room *Wusum Hotel* on Tekho Road, opposite the old Forestry compound, by business magnate Vincent Kanu, himself originally from Makeni. The hotel, worthy of a place in Freetown, looks set to invigorate a little tourist interest in the area over the next few years.

Practicalities

If you're **staying over**, you'll find several reasonable hotels and guesthouses and even a couple of nightclubs.

Amza's 7 Field Rd, right by the Wusum Sports Ground ☎076/88.83.29. Though austere-looking, this offers a reasonable range of prices and acceptable rooms with a/c or fans. ❸

Buya's Motel 25 Ladies' Mile ☎076/75.16.17. A long-established survivor, glorying in all its most rudimentary appeal. ❶–❷

The better hotels promise **Internet** connections "some time soon", but actually getting online is as yet only available in the Fatima Institute along the Azzolini Highway. As for a **bite to eat**, among the better – but very basic – local chop houses are *Mem's* at 8 Rogbane Rd, and *Talented Sisters* at 13 Mabanta Rd.

Onwards from Makeni

The route out of Makeni towards Kabala, via **BINKOLO** – the home village of late President Momoh (10km from Makeni) – offers a fine scenic interlude, with high rocky hills and massifs crowned in trees, rising dramatically on either side of the road. Northeast of Makeni, the architectural interest improves, too, with small, steeply conical houses of the Temne pattern, topped with an extra tuft of thatch and an entrance lobby at the front. Muslim praying circles are to be seen all over, though sometimes, as reserved areas, they're used for drying rice or other grain.

Outamba-Kilimi National Park

The **Outamba-Kilimi National Park (OKNP)** was set up in 1980 after the International Union for the Conservation of Nature singled the region out for urgent protection. Much of it was formerly occupied by the **Tambakha chiefdom**, named after the Tamba – "leader" – of a successful nineteenth-century slave revolt. Slave-owning Susu were massacred by their captives, who moved to this region and set up their own, very mixed, kingdom, in which Susu, the slaves' customary language, was retained. Sensitive work with the people of the Tambakha chiefdom (or at least with their paramount chief) led to agreements to cede land for the park and give up hunting rights. For over a decade, there was steady progress, with major US Peace Corps involvement and the Worldwide Fund for Nature supporting the energetic work of the people on the ground. The Peace Corps have now left and the park is vulnerable to poaching.

The park's thousand-odd square kilometres cover two great slabs of untouched, undulating **savannah and jungle**, in the basins of the Great and Little Scarcies rivers. There's a rich diversity of animal species, including elephant and most of the other large West African savannah mammals (lion and giraffe excepted), as well as a solid population of chimpanzee and twelve other primates, among them red colobus, black-and-white colobus and sooty mangabey. Largely unhunted, the monkeys tend to approach the accommodation site. In the deepest sections of forest there are rare and scattered bongo antelope – magnificent, heavily built animals – and in the overgrown water margins you may spot pygmy hippo if you're extremely lucky. More than 150 different bird species, including the rare **iris glossy starling** and thousands of watering birds make the park a particular attraction to ornithologists.

Practicalities

The nearest town to the park, **KAMAKWIE**, 15km south of the main entrance, has one guesthouse (*Sella* ❷). Although the park continues to suffer from a lack of investment, there has been some progress, in the shape of donations of boats from the Americans and funding from the UK's Department for International Development (DFID), rehabilitating visitor huts, wells and showers. OKNP, however, for all the goodwill of its staff, is still some way off being fully operational, and the occasional breakdown of the pulley-ferry on the **Kabba River** has also played its part in isolating the park.

Before heading to OKNP, try to get up-to-date information on facilities and access from the Forestry Department in Freetown (basement, Yuwi Building ℗076/68.03.62).

Despite the constraints, if you're adventurous enough and self-sufficient – equipped with sleeping bag, torch, mosquito repellent and provisions – OKNP offers good adventure. The best time to visit is at the end of the dry season when the trails have mostly been cut. As it is, some of the most accessible game-viewing comes from river trips (insist on being given a lifejacket), where in the dry season your boat will drift past hippo pools and high river-bank trees dotted with colobus monkeys. If you want to see elephants (you're more likely to see their paths or spoor) you'll have to go deep into the park (at least 15km from the headquarters) towards the **Yombo waterfall** and possibly camp the night. For birdlife ask to be taken down the **Lake Idrissa** trail.

Kabala

Ringed by a circle of hills – the Wara Wara range – the highest of which leap, bold and bare, right above town to the west, **KABALA** is an attractive highland centre with an appreciably more comfortable climate than Freetown. The capital of the Koinadougou district, it divides roughly into two: on the way in from Makeni, the town centre is dominated by the **Koranko** people; while across the stream on the northwest side of town, the district is more **Limba**. If you're not interested in buying the sacks of **local fruit** then try to buy some **ronko cloth**: made by the Koranko, this is a rusty-red country cloth, patterned in black block prints, sewn together from narrow strips. Soft yet durable, it's claimed by some to have bullet-proof powers and became emblematic dress-wear of the *kamajor* pro-government fighters during the rebel war.

The Koranko

More than most of Sierra Leone's ethnic groups, the Koranko of the northeast have maintained a fairly distinct cultural integrity. Koranko is a Mande language, very close to the most mainstream Mande tongue, the Malinké of Guinea and Mali, and only distantly related to the more peripheral Mende language of southern Sierra Leone. The Koranko are great **rice farmers**, filling the valleys with an emerald green carpet, and they grow a fair amount of cotton, too, for their famous *ronko* cloth.

The Koranko are also hunters of some repute (and have always supplied most of the troops for the Sierra Leone armed forces). Traditionally, they belonged to totemic clans, known as "houses", each called by a "surname" and symbolized by taboo animals that were never eaten (not that all these animals were commonly eaten by members of other clans). For example, the Kagbo and Sise clans' totem was the crocodile, the Fona's was the royal python, the Mensereng had the monitor lizard and the lion, the Kamara had the hippo and the chimpanzee, and the Mara's was the leopard.

Today, a growing contingent of the Koranko community is Muslim, and the old clan divisions are less significant. But the Bundu society initiations (*biriye* in Koranko) are still important for young people in rural areas, with girls in seclusion for a few weeks' instruction during the rains and boys going off in the dry season. Circumcision and clitoridectomy usually take place at the same time. Another pre-Islamic activity that's pursued with enthusiasm is the making of *kamakuli* – bamboo wine. It's not always available, but you should try to get a taste of it if you're in the territory for a few days; talk to the youth of the village rather than the big men.

Cursory Koranko

Greetings, thanks, goodbye	*N-weli*	Yes	*Ohn* (pronounced like
Greetings (plural)	*Wa-n-wali*		the French *non*)
Good morning	*Tanamase*	No	*Oh-oh*
Good day	*Tanamatale*	Thank you	*Kubaraka*
Good evening	*Inoor-agh*	Bamboo wine	*Kamakole*
		What's your name?	*Eh tu kama?*

If you're **staying over** in Kabala, there's *Gbawuria Guest House* at 28 Yangala Rd (❶) and *Pay Gay's Pub* (☎076/99 46 25 ❶), which both have reasonable rooms, or, if you're looking for somewhere a little removed from the sometimes noisy nights in town, then the *Sengbeh* is a quieter option (☎077/58 20 43 ❶). For **food**, there's good street-food, but otherwise little more than *Choice's Bar & Restaurant* at 17 Barrier Rd, where they serve great couscous and other African dishes.

Around Kabala – picnics and hikes

In 2001, there was great commotion in Kabala when a lion was shot in the nearby village of **SINKUNIYA**, 40km to the north. The male lion, reported to have migrated from Mali or Guinea and which had feasted on nearly a hundred livestock was the first lion recorded on Sierra Leonean soil in more than fifty years. The local hunter, said to have used supernatural powers to entrap the beast, was afforded an audience with the then president Kabbah.

Kabala is a friendly and easy-going town, offering some of the best opportunities for **hiking** in the country, with little danger of running into a predatory big cat. **Gbawuria Hill**, the prominent massif to the west of the town, is the site of Kabala's famous **New Year's Day Picnic**, when several thousand townspeople – and good numbers of friends, relatives and visitors – spend the day up on the gaunt inselberg, eating, drinking and dancing. It's a steep climb, but not difficult or long. Other than on New Year's Day, the heights are usually deserted. The Wara Wara Mountains which surround the town offer excellent opportunities for hiking, as do the road routes out of Kabala to **Koinadougou**, **BAFODIA** and **FALABA**, where, amid a multitude of scenic breaks you may just have to trust your judgment, leave your vehicle at a village and set out with a local guide.

Lake Sonfon

Lake Sonfon is Sierra Leone's largest inland lake, cradled in the picturesque landscape of the **Sula Mountains**, south of Kabala. It's worth the effort getting there if you're happy to spend a couple of days in perfect solitude amid stunning scenery, though it should be said that the environment has suffered a little from the gold-mining in the area, and that hunting has taken its toll on the wildlife that once inhabited the hills.

The lake is extremely difficult to reach, and the trip should only be attempted if you're travelling in a sturdy 4x4. From Kabala, head towards **MAKAKURA** on the Makeni road (9km south of Kabala), where you turn off and continue on the **Alikalia** road, reaching **ARFANYA** after 24km, where you can ask someone to show the way to the lake. If you're heading up from the south, make for **MAGBURAKA** and **BUMBUNA**, and then take the Kabala road with a guide.

Mount Bintumani

Midway between Kabala and Koidu in the east, **Mount Bintumani** in the Loma Mountains is the highest peak in Sierra Leone, and the highest mountain in West Africa west of Mount Cameroon. The mountain is best climbed at the beginning or end of the rainy season (April/May or Oct/Nov) as dry-season dust limits visibility. Whenever you go, it can get very cool at night near the 1945-metre summit and you should take some warm clothes, as well as a decent sleeping bag.

There are no tarred roads nearby, and climbing Bintumani of necessity involves some trekking from the end of the nearest motorable road. **Kabala** is probably the easiest base to start from if you're using public transport. The aim is to reach **Firawa** (51km southeast of Kabala), from where a five-day hike will get you to the top and back again. There are usually several people in **FIRAWA** who know some English and who will be more than willing to hike up the mountain with you. The small town of **KOINADOUGOU** (28km from Kabala) is the most likely destination of vehicles heading this way. Koinadougu's hill-top location and venerable silk-cotton trees make it a great place to stay. **YIRAFILAIA BADALA** (36km) is another nice village, located above a rocky bend of the Seli River. There's a sandy beach here, wonderful for swimming, fishing and washing clothes. Just beware of the current if you're here at the height of the rains. If you have your own transport or a sturdy rental car, an even better option is to head for the village of **YIFIN**, east of **ALIKALIA** and 15km from the peak, where the local chief resides. At the very end of the dry season, when the rivers and streams have dried up, it is possible to drive through to the village of **SINIKORO** (reducing your initial hike by 22km) from where, if you're energetic, you could hope to reach the summit in a day.

If you're taking a couple of weeks or more to climb Bintumani, you may even want to walk the whole way from Kabala. All the villages along the Bintumani trail are **Koranko** (for whom the mountain is Loma Mansa – King of the Lomas) and you'll find charming hospitality. Indeed, while most people tend to rush on to the summit, one of the real delights of trekking to Bintumani is in taking the time in the higher reaches to quietly explore the many hills, valleys and waterfalls that make up the Loma Mountains – where you have a good chance of seeing **wildlife**. If you want to stay in a village, ask to speak to the headman, who'll arrange overnight accommodation for you. It's important to carry some basic provisions – rice, palm oil, onions, salt and pepper – as supplies along the way can be short, especially in the "hungry season" before the rice harvest (August and September). Don't worry about cooking, as this will be fixed for you; naturally you'll be expected to share some food. Take a supply of the freshest **kola** you can find, as well. This is the traditional gift in return for hospitality, though you can give leones instead. For snacks on the move (don't forget most people only cook once a day) take fruit and groundnut cakes from Kabala.

After Firawa or Yifin, you'll need a guide to find your way along the maze of footpaths to **BANDA-KARAFAIA**, about 20km distant from both. This day's hike is where the trip becomes exciting and the scenery spectacular. At Banda-Karafaia, you have to sign the headman's register of people climbing the mountain. A cash gift is expected for this service and, while there's no fixed fee, it will be made clear if your offering is too small. About 13km further is **YALEMBE**, a small village at the foot of the mountain, where you hire a guide for the final ascent.

The south

The frustrating thing about the geography of southern Sierra Leone, as of much of West Africa's southwest-facing shores, is that the coast itself tends to be indistinct and often miles from the nearest road. The sea lies beyond vast expanses of mud, marsh and mangroves, only accessible down narrow ridges of slightly higher ground between the maze of creeks. The coast in Sierra Leone seems to be separating entirely from the mainland and, indeed, **Sherbro** (with its town of **Bonthe**) and the Turtle Islands are already adrift in the Atlantic. Southeast of Sherbro, however, the surf hits a tremendous, unbroken beach, which stretches 110km to the little port of **Sulima** on the Liberian border. Backed by small fishing villages, this is a highly recommended week-long walk.

Inland, much of the south is sticky, palm- and bush-specked grassland, which makes for uninspiring travel. But the higher forest areas are another matter. In the southeast, the hills come to within 50km of the sea and here, south of the provincial capital, **Bo**, there are opportunities for some of the country's most rewarding explorations. The trip to **Tiwai Island Nature Reserve**, blanketed in rainforest in a crook of the surging Moa River, is one of Sierra Leone's major highlights.

Bo

Long established as the most important town in the colonial "Protectorate" of upcountry Sierra Leone, **BO** or "Sweet Bo" as its residents affectionately refer to their town, is the provincial capital of the south. While it was overtaken in size some years ago by the burgeoning diamond-fed Koidu conurbation in the northeast, Bo today holds a big, spread-out population of around 100,000 people, mostly Mende,

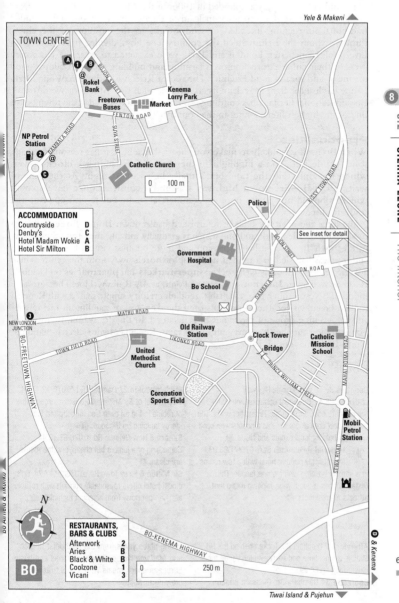

but with a heavy Krio presence still reflected in the random scattering of quaint, wooden, Krio houses across town. Though Bo did suffer during the war, it wasn't hit as badly as Freetown. Nowadays it is once again a vibrant and even pleasant trading centre, where plenty of **diamond traders** have their businesses. Don't get tempted into purchasing any stones, though, as you're likely to be cheated or run into difficulties with customs or police on leaving the country.

The town's best-known institution, the "Chief's School" (now Bo School) north of the old railway yards, was founded in 1906 for the education of chiefs' sons from the Protectorate. It was a curious amalgam of English public school and extended traditional instruction, intended to lend weight to the position of the chiefs, through whom the British ruled the country. The boys, divided into "houses" of Liverpool, Manchester, London and Paris, were expected to wear the customary dress of their fathers, learn improved farming and building methods, adopt "good manners" and speak "good English". The use of Krio was forbidden. While Sierra Leone has lost the fight to reclaim its erstwhile label as the "Athens of West Africa", Bo's educational heritage has continued to flourish, and to this day the town boasts one of the highest literacy rates in the country.

Practicalities

While Bo itself is unlikely to make your heart skip a beat, it has reasonable roads, some gentle hills, and a highlight in the shape of its landmark **clock-tower**, which not only tells the time but actually lights up at night. At the time of writing the **Bo–Freetown highway** was under construction, a development which is bound not just to improve commercial traffic but to also open up the south to discovery.

The long line of newly built or refurbished banks down **Bojon Street** reflects a town in reasonable health, and one which is gradually moving away from the shadow of Freetown. Increased urban expansion and more business visitors from the capital and overseas have led to a modest new crop of **hotels** away from the centre. There are one or two reasonably well stocked **supermarkets** and **pharmacies** on Dambala Road as well as an **Internet** café, Access Point, at 4A Railway Line. The agreeable mood in Bo owes much to a reasonably good **electricity** supply, shared with Kenema (unlike Freetown, local residents are spared the daily toil of standing in fuel queues and the evening drone of thousands of generators). In the dry season, Bo's thermal power station supplies Kenema, and in the rains, Kenema's hydro-electric station at Dodo-Panguma tops up Bo.

Hotels

Countryside 70 Bo–Kenema Highway ☏076/63.28.48. Bo's most upmarket hotel with tennis court, pool, a/c, satellite TV and hot water. The bar and pool area also serves as a popular weekend watering-hole for local expats and NGOs. **⑤**

Imperial 9 Pessimah St ☏076/71.98.93. Increasingly popular hotel with a few rooms in a homely building with a stone facade. The restaurant has a good, wide-ranging menu that attracts nonresidents. **⑤**

Madam Wokie 27 Dambala Rd ☏076/92.17.74. Sister hotel of *Sir Milton* also offers a large choice of rooms but in an even less embellished four-storey building up the road. **③**

Sahara 8 New Gerihun Rd ☏076/97.40.44. Something of a jumble but cheap, and the rooms are clean. **②**

Sir Milton 6 Kissy Town Rd ☏076/92.17.74. Bo's oldest hotel offers reasonable comfort with reliable a/c. Can get noisy from adjacent nightclub. **③**

Restaurants

Afterwork 2 Dambala Rd. Tucked behind the NP station, a lunchtime and early evening venue for cheap food and drinks.

Coolzone 34 Dambala Rd. Pleasant enough

eating place yards from the Methodist Church and *Madame Wokie*. Salonean dishes and basic European snack meals with a cool breeze blowing through.

Aries 2 Kissy Town Rd. Downtown Bo's out-and-out nightclub, playing a good mix of European and Salone hits.

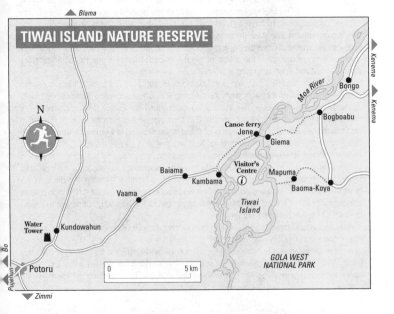
Black and White 8 Kissy Town Rd. A Bo landmark and the town's answer to *Paddy's*

in Freetown. Airy and simple first-floor nightspot which is also a popular lunchtime restaurant.
Vicani London Junction. New nightclub which gets lively on Sat nights.

Tiwai Island Nature Reserve

The **Tiwai Island Project**, which was run by Njala University College and the US Peace Corps before war engulfed the district, is now under the tutelage of the **Environment Foundation for Africa** (**EFA**; W tinyurl.com/33lf8r). Although only covering twelve square kilometres, the largely pristine, forest-cloaked island shelters an extraordinarily rich fauna, including pygmy hippos, red river hogs, crocodiles, electric fish, and the chimps and ten other primate species (it has one of the highest monkey biomasses in the world) for which it is famous.

While the reserve suffered from poaching during the war, the animals, and in particular the highly endangered **olive colobus monkey** and **chimpanzees** have made an astonishing recovery. This truly is the Africa of the imagination, the air saturated with the incessant chirrups, squawks and yelps of birds, chimps and monkeys, **tree hyraxes**, assorted insects and hundreds of other species, all doing their thing in the rainforest. Look out, too, for **giant snails**. The tiger snail, *Achatina achatina*, is the world's largest and Sierra Leone holds the record for the species: in June 1976 a tiger snail was found with a length of 273mm and weight of 0.9kg.

As you weave along paths between the giant buttress roots of the trees, Tiwai guides will track troops of **colobus** and **diana monkeys** and should know where the chimps are. The rarest and most secretive of Tiwai's denizens is the hog-sized **pygmy hippo**, which you're not likely to see unless you go jungle walking at night, when they traipse their habitual solitary paths through the undergrowth (a BBC film crew visiting Tiwai were the first to capture footage of a pygmy hippo in the wild).

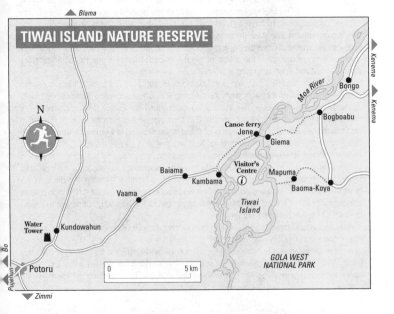

TIWAI ISLAND NATURE RESERVE

Blama

Moa River

Bongo

Bogboabu

Kenema

Canoe ferry
Jene

Giema

Baiama

Visitor's
Centre

Mapuma

Kambama (i)

Baoma-Koya

Vaama

Tiwai
Island

Water
Tower

Kundowahun

GOLA WEST
NATIONAL PARK

Bo

Potoru

0   5 km

Pujehun

Zimmi

N

Exploring **after dark** with a guide is, in fact, highly recommended – take a lamp with plenty of kerosene, and a good torch. By night, the forest is a powerful presence, with an immense, consuming vigour. Every rotten branch teems with termites, and all around, you sense the organs of detection of a million unseen creatures waving at you as you stumble over the roots.

Practicalities

To get to Tiwai, head for the island office at **KAMBAMA**, 17km northeast of the small town of **POTORU**, an hour's drive southeast of Bo, where you also will find an EFA regional office (☏076/92.27.92). With the visitors' facilities on the other side well established, the river crossing is arranged by EFA staff with a small motorboat (10min).

Although not all the forest trail grid has been re-cut since the end of the war, the comfortable **visitor centre** facilities in Tiwai have been admirably restored and are now much better than they were before the war. There's a dorm (❷) and camping platforms (Le10,000 to pitch your tent) and a well-furnished kitchen and dining area, but no electricity (kerosene lamps are available). Bring all your food supplies and cook on-site.

Sulima and the south coast

SULIMA was a trading station in the nineteenth century. The first Englishman here was John Myer Harris, a trader who arrived in 1855. Harris soon creamed off much

---

The Mende and secret societies

There is a thing passing in the sky; some thick clouds surround it; the uninitiated see nothing.

Opaque Mende proverb

The **Mende** are skilled and very long established farmers, for whom trading and hunting are low priorities. Rice, sorghum and millet, root crops, oil palm and kola are the big crops. Women fish the streams, too, with circular nets, as much for relaxation as for the meal of the day. The Mende **language** – they are the biggest language group in Sierra Leone – is supposed to have arrived from the northeast, either with people fleeing the chaotic conditions in sixteenth-century Songhai, or perhaps before the creation of the Mali empire in the thirteenth century. Ptolemy's second-century map even indicates *Purrus Campus* in roughly the place where the ancient Mende might have had a "Poro Bush" – a secret society grove.

Along classic "divide and rule" principles, the British split the Mende kingdoms into dozens of "paramount chiefdoms", introducing a new tribal identity. The Mende chiefs came to see themselves as the natural successors to the British, in competition – or association – with the powerful Temne. But the upper-class Krio families of Freetown had the same idea. The most serious of the anti-tax revolts, in Mende country in 1898, resulted in the deaths of hundreds of Krio traders and deepened a rift, never completely bridged, between the indigenous Protectorate peoples and the non-native Krios of the Colony. The Bo School for chiefs gave an incentive to Protectorate ambitions. Later, Mende politicians from a pro-British family of Bonthe – Milton Margai and his brother Albert – became the country's first and second prime ministers. Krio opponents attributed much of the second Margai's attachment to the trappings of power to membership of the secret **poro** society.

You can't spend more than a week in the country without hearing mysterious rumours about the **secret societies**, which still dominate life in Sierra Leone. They're followed in almost all communities, as secret brotherhoods and sisterhoods, cutting across the family and clan divisions, maintaining stability and marking life-cycle events. Christians don't exclude themselves from membership, and the local version of Islam, while

SIERRA LEONE

8.2

The interior

698

of the Moa River trade, which had previously been controlled by the Liberian government, thus effectively pushing the Protectorate frontier back to the Mano River. A number of the old colonial buildings are still standing and there's a fresh-water lagoon, where you can swim and wash. Sulima used to gather a community of holidaying NGO volunteers every Christmas, building *baffas* (shelters) and sitting around fires on the beach.

In theory it's possible to follow the unbroken **beach** west from Sulima (110km) in a walk that takes from five days to a week without strain. This long bar is **Turner's Peninsula**, a strip of land ceded to the British as long ago as 1825. The people are Vai, Krim and Sherbro but, increasingly, everyone speaks Mende first, Krio second and English a poor third. Most houses along the beach are made from entirely natural materials – woven palm-frond walls with thatched roofs.

Most of Turner's Peninsula is backed by low scrub, but towards the western end, coconut palms start to appear. The most attractive stretches of coast, however, are on **Sherbro Island** and the nearby **Turtle Islands**.

Sherbro Island

Though very much in ruins these days – it was attacked several times during the war – **Bonthe**, the main settlement on **Sherbro Island**, is one of Sierra Leone's most appealing towns. When the retired colonial officer, Frederick William Hugh Migeod, visited in 1924 while writing his *View of Sierra Leone*, he found "about

opposing them, makes no purist insistence. Society graduates are sworn to secrecy and the arcane details remain hidden. Among older or more traditional Mende people, enquiries get a hostile response, and the few books on the subject tend to disappear from libraries.

The general name for the societies is **bundu**, a Krio word. **Poro** is the men's society (the same name is found elsewhere in West Africa, for example among the Senoufo in Côte d'Ivoire) and is by far the most powerful; the women's is called **sande**. Poro and sande provide the framework for traditional instruction to adolescents about sex, adult behaviour and folk knowledge. Traditionally, too, the period of seclusion and endurance in the bush was when circumcision and clitoridectomy were performed. Boys of the same age group go through the school in the dry season, girls in the rains. Beyond the teenage rites of passage, membership of poro proceeds by different stages. In addition to poro and sande, there's a kind of high poro society called **wunde**, and a number of other societies, some operating as professional associations of medical, psychiatric and social-welfare specialists – including **humo**, **toma**, **njaye** – and some of entertainers and conjurers, the **njoso**.

Heavy black bundu **masks** worn by women in the sande society (the masks are called **sowo** by the Mende) are the most visible signs of the societies' active existence. Carved by men, they reveal a lot about Mende ideals of feminine beauty – high-domed foreheads, elaborately braided hair, fine-pointed features, eyes that see nothing, mouths closed. As an outsider, you should beware of "No Entry" signs in the bush, indicating a society grove, and fenced compounds outside villages. It's acceptable to witness youngsters with whitened faces, however, celebrating their new names and status.

"Animal societies" – "Baboon" (chimpanzee), "Boa" (python), "Alligator" (crocodile) and "Leopard" – were always uncommon, though sensationalized. Their members would mount attacks in the guise of wild animals, the aim being to obtain human organs for witchcraft. These societies have tended to die out along with the animals imitated. Nobody would believe a chimpanzee murder in Bo any more.

Belief in **witchcraft** is another matter.

forty Europeans there, including those on York Island, and a big gathering at tennis every evening". The atmosphere has changed somewhat in the intervening years, but Bonthe is still very pleasant. Wide sandy lanes cross the town, and some of the great old run-down buildings of the glory days are still upright. The secondary school is magnificent and the people of Bonthe are charming.

One of the prettiest, and it must be said, cleanest towns in Sierra Leone, **BONTHE** now boasts an upmarket holiday resort – the *Bonthe Holiday Village* (Satellite ☎00 882/165.425.1087 ⓦ www.bontheholidayvillage.com ⓮). Opened in December 2006, the resort's principal aim is to lure in professional **fishermen** vying for world records of "big silver", tarpon. But even if game-fishing is not your bag, this is a great location to wind down in perfect peace for a few days.

The Turtle Islands

Idyllic coconut-fringed islands with shimmering white sand drifting lazily in olive waters behind Sherbro Island, the **Turtle Islands archipelago** is an almost surreal sight. The clear waters are excellent for snorkelling and the shores harbour an incredible array of shells. As the tides recede, intricate forms and patterns emerge from long sandbanks on which you can sit and watch fishing communities go about the routines of daily life. Delicately pushing their bamboo poles into the sea, the narrow dugouts glide through shallow channels. The main islands are **Baki**, **Muti**, **Sei**, **Yele** and the diminutive **Yankai** (one of the most densely populated). With no ambient light around for miles, the nights here are perfect for star-gazing.

The journey to the Turtle Islands from Aberdeen at Freetown takes approximately three hours by speedboat, although it's also possible to catch the weekly *Pampah* from Tombo on the other side of the peninsula (Le25,000). The journey this way takes anything from five to seven hours, depending on how laden the vessel is and the number of stops en route. **Arriving** at the Turtle Islands, you initially have to put up with the curiosity of locals and you're expected to pay your respects to the local chief. There is an eco-camp (contact *Cape Shilling*) with decent camping facilities, toilets and showers on a beautiful bay on Sei Island, but you should take camping gear, plenty of water and provisions with you.

Eastern Province

The lure of **diamonds** and cross-border trade have made **Eastern Province** one of the country's most densely populated regions, and **Koidu-Sefadu** (aka **Kono**) the biggest provincial town. Kono remains a good jumping-off point if you want to access Mount Bintumani (see p.693) from the east or the Tingi Mountains and the source of the Niger (the latter just yards over the border in Guinea – see p.634). More commonly visited, however, is **Kenema**, the bustling second town of the old Protectorate, with the forested **Kambui Hills** and important **Gola Forest** reserves both nearby. Lastly, in the eastern panhandle, **Koindu** (not to be confused with Koidu), is tucked into a remote frontier region, hard up against the Guinean and Liberian borders, and really only likely to be visited if you're heading for south-eastern Guinea or northern Liberia.

Kenema

Less than an hour from Bo, **KENEMA** is the busy provincial capital of the east and gateway to the country's southern forest reserves. Its setting, nearly surrounded by the verdant if partially deforested Kambui Hills, makes it an attractive town, especially at the end of the rains, and it's the best departure point for the Liberian border and the beautiful Gola Forest reserves

Originally a Mende settlement, Kenema grew fast on the strength of its railway exports of timber, coffee and cacao, and then burst into development after the discovery of diamonds in 1931, a few kilometres to the east, and the opening up of the **Tongo diamond field** to the north. Large and vividly hand-painted signboards featuring glittering gems hang before the grilled entrances of many Lebanese diamond dealers, and testify to the trade's continued strength. If you want to see **diamond miners** at work, then ask your hotel for assistance: otherwise if you go wandering about you're bound to be hassled by security guards. For district news and background, check out Ⓦwww.kenemadistrict.org.

Practicalities

Kenema's main artery is the Blama Road–Hangha Road axis that snakes through town, punctuated by a quaint, and clock-less, clock tower. You'll find almost everything along this road, including new banks, petrol stations, Kenema's only supermarket, Choithrams, and right next door, a surprisingly modern **Internet café**, Quantum SL. Kenema enjoys a largely stable **electricity** supply, making places to stay and eat a little more reliable than most upcountry centres. Among the best eating and drinking venues (day or night) are the likeable *Re-Concile* at 1 Blama Rd, and the old favourite *Capitol* at 51 Hangha Rd, which serves Lebanese and African dishes from dawn to dusk. *Capitol* is also the location of Kenema's main nightspot, *Capitol Disco*, sometimes referred to as *Villa 1*.

Accommodation

If you're staying the night, there are various options. And if they're full or closed, you can also approach the **Catholic Mission**, situated in a beautifully tended compound, where they have been helpful to travellers in the past.

KENEMA

▲ Kono (Koidu-Setadu) & Kailahun

KOROMA STREET
SUMALA STREET
MAMBU STREET

Sierra Tel Ⓒ — Safecon Petrol Station

RESTAURANTS, CLUBS & BARS
Capitol	1
Capitol Disco (Villa 1)	1
Re-Concile	2

ACCOMMODATION
Lambayama Motel	D
Ribbi's Motel	A
Sameday Guest House	B
Sinava Guest House	C
Swarray Kunde Lodge	E

St Paul's Cathedral

Capitol Cinema

SHOWFIELD ROAD
Mobil Spot & Petrol Station

NP Petrol Station
SHOW AVENUE
Freetown & Kono Lorry Park
DEMBY STREET
WESLEY ST
SAHARA ST @ Quantum SL
SHORT ST
KOMBEMA ROAD
SUMALA STREET

Choithrams supermarket

Produce Market
General Market

Police
MAXWELL
KHEBE STREET
HANGHA ROAD
Koindu Transport Park
Fish Market
Bo Taxi Park
Clock Tower
DAMA ROAD

Texaco
BLAMA ROAD

NP Petrol Station

Holy Trinity Parish Hall
ARUNA STREET
N

SWARRAY KUNDA ST
Carefree Bridge

0 — 500 m

District Forest Office

8.2 **SIERRA LEONE** | The interior

Kombema ▶
Pastoral Centre, Tiwai Island & Liberia ▶

▼ Bo & Freetown

701

Lambayama 2 Aruna St ☎033/79.87.54. Set in a compound with an appealing outdoor area and one "luxury", a/c, round hut. Not at all bad, though standards throughout are inconsistent. ❹
Ribbi's 20 Mambu St ☎033/79.87.54. Cheap and friendly, but much further afield, so you'll probably need to be energetic or have your own transport, to want to use it. ❷
Sameday Guest House 1 Sahara St ☎033/76.65.28. While certainly cheap, this is depressingly basic. ❷

Sinava Guest House 9 Blama Rd ☎076/42.01.09. Situated above a shop, this offers the town's best in terms of facilities like a/c and hot water – but it's perhaps not really worth the price. ❺
Swarray Kunde Lodge 14 Swarray Kunda St, off Blama Rd ☎076/65.89.07. Well-maintained, clean en-suite rooms offering proper value for money. If you check in early, there's a chance of landing the one double a/c room for a small surcharge. ❹

Kambui Hills

Scenic, and festooned with tall forest – albeit much of it cleared over the last few decades – the **Kambui Hills** are worth a side trip if you can find a way into them. Unless you have your own 4x4 and ideally a guide from the **District Forest Office** on Maxwell Khobe Street in Kenema, the easiest target by any kind of public transport is the **forest school** above Bambawo. To get here, vehicles heading for **LAGO** or Kono will drop you at **NGELEHUN**, and from here **BAMBAWO** is 2km west, up in the hills. Continuing through the village a further steep and rocky two kilometres, past an abandoned chrome mine (naturalist Gerald Durrell used the mining camp here on his animal-collecting trip in 1965), you eventually reach the summit area, with magnificent scenery. Birders will want to look for local rarities such as the **white-necked rockfowl**, which nests in the area.

Gola National Park

Reputed to be among Africa's top biodiversity hotspots, the 750-square-kilometre **Gola Forest Reserves**, which include impressive swathes of primary rainforest, with the canopy reaching up to heights of more than fifty metres, stretch across the swamps and low-lying hills between the Mano and Moa rivers. Gola West and Gola East, southeast of Tiwai Island, contain the most undisturbed areas of forest; Gola North is hillier and, although larger, is more fractured by recent human incursion. The combined reserves are home to more than 270 bird species, of which fourteen are critically threatened. These include the ghostlike **rufous fishing owl**, the **Gola malimbe** and the **green-tailed bristlebill**. The reserves are also a stronghold of **pygmy hippo**, **leopard**, **forest buffalo**, **forest elephant**, **chimpanzee** and the elusive forest antelope, the **zebra duiker**.

With Sierra Leone having already lost most of its original primary rainforest cover, President Koroma used the occasion of the UN's climate-change conference in Bali in 2007 to announce the creation of the **Gola National Park**, Sierra Leone's first rainforest national park, complementing the national parks of Sapo in Liberia, Tai in Côte d'Ivoire and Kakum in Ghana, all of which fall within the Upper Guinea forest belt, seventy percent of which has been felled over the course of the last century.

The Gola plan, which relies on a $12 million EU trust fund and support from the UK's Royal Society for the Protection of Birds, is a bold community initiative aiming to provide sustainable long-term benefits to the **local communities** in seven chiefdoms, all of whom have agreed to forgo their logging rights. In return, the 100,000-odd people of the area will earn annual compensation payments, and participate in the country's nascent ecotourism industry.

Although there are no visitor facilities as yet, you should check with the Conservation Society of Sierra Leone (see p.682) about plans to set up an eco-camp for visitors, with guided walks through sections of the forest.

Koidu-Sefadu (Kono)

Koidu and Sefadu are both official names, but most locals refer to the capital of Kono District as **KONO**. More so even than Bo or Kenema, Kono is synonymous with diamonds and is at the very heart of Sierra Leone's diamond-mining industry. More than 130,000 people live in the town (out of 500,000 in the district), and this is the one place in the country where it's possible to make money without connections, hunting for **diamonds** in the alluvial deposits. The 969.8-carat Star of Sierra Leone, the largest alluvial diamond in the world, was found here in 1972.

Even the town centre is pitted with water-filled **diggings** and you see people everywhere sifting gravel. Curiously, the mining of diamonds is an exclusively male activity whereas the mining of **gold** (often from the washed diamond gravel) is the preserve of women. Since the end of the war, exports of gems have reached record figures thanks largely to the Kimberley process (which certifies the origin of stones and confirms they are conflict-free) and low government levies aimed at dissuading smuggling. Yet don't expect to see any of this wealth as you drive around town. Formerly a busy trading centre with luxury goods in the stores, street lighting and tightly guarded villas humming smugly with air conditioning, Kono is only gradually recovering from its **trashing** during the war. Ransacked by all sides, this is the one major town in Sierra Leone where travellers still get a palpable feeling of the aftermath of the rebel war. Foreign commentators have often referred to the Sierra Leonean conflict as a "battle over resources", which is rather confirmed by the number of times Kono changed hands during the conflict. Hollywood films like *Blood Diamond* and *Lord of the War*, or even Kanye West's Grammy-winning *Diamonds from Sierra Leone* song, all have particular resonance here.

Practicalities

While Kono continues to get on its feet amid heightened investment, the town has an unmistakably transient feel. There is one comfortable **motel**, the *Kono Hotel* at Mile 210 Quaquima-Kono (☎076/66.66.18 ❹) which, in tune with the mining ethos, now has its own small casino, and a bar-restaurant popular with expats – usually miners and diamond dealers. Otherwise, a couple of basic guesthouses serve the passing NGO crowd and the odd traveller – *Toby's* (❷) and *Zuzu's Inn* at 112 Main Kainkordu Rd, which has a small upstairs terrace (❷).

Around Kono

Sakanbiriwa, in the Tingi Mountains, is Sierra Leone's second highest peak (1709m) – a botanical sanctuary for its **orchids**, especially at the end of the dry season, but more remote and much less visited even than Bintumani. First step in getting there is transport to **JEGBWEMA**, 18km east of Koidu, where you turn left into the mountains. The village to head for is **KUNDUNDU** (38km from Jegbwema), along a really rough road.

Koindu

KOINDU (not to be confused with Koidu) was originally a Kissi settlement, but it's been swelling for decades with immigrants from a wide reach and was the RUF rebels' base during the war. As a tri-frontier town, Koindu is a sort of tradesman's entrance to Sierra Leone, where everything from rice and sugar to diamonds and human sacrifices is available, or rumoured to be – and most of the rumours are verifiable on a Sunday, **market day**. There's locally made cloth in the market (cotton is sown in with the local rice crop and harvested afterwards), along with excellent silversmiths who specialize in filigree earrings and pendants. And you can still buy **"Kissi pennies"** here, the regional currency of pre-Protectorate days, that continued to be used until World War II – pieces of twisted iron rod, about 30cm long, with the ends flattened into a T-shape.

Burkina Faso

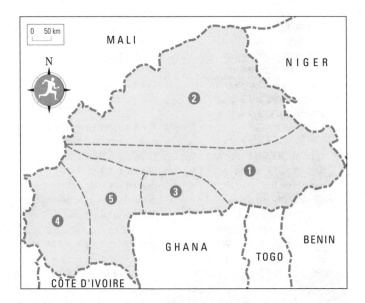

Highlights 706
Introduction and Basics 707
9.1 Central and eastern Burkina 731
9.2 Northern Burkina 750

9.3 The Gourounsi country 760
9.4 Bobo, Banfora and the southwest 765
9.5 The Lobi country 776

Burkina Faso highlights

✳ **FESPACO and SIAO** Ouaga comes alive during these vibrant, internationally renowned festivals. See p.717

✳ **Ouaga's café culture** Whether you're sipping coffee on the street or tucking into cakes at a patisserie, Ouaga's myriad cafés are a great way to get to know the city. See p.742

✳ **Gorom-Gorom** Dynamic and colourful village market on the edge of the Sahara, where turban-clad merchants ride in from the desert on camels to trade. See p.753

✳ **Tiébélé** Deep in Gourounsi country, the town of Tiébélé boasts wonderful architecture and intricately painted houses. See p.762

✳ **Balafons** Head to Bobo to hear the addictive rhythmic sounds of these West African xylophones. See p.765

✳ **Banfora's environs** The area around Banfora boasts a waterfall and lake, and the dramatic domes and craggy summits of magnificent rock formations, all reached by moped along sandy tracks. See p.774

▲ Burkinabe women near Pô

Introduction and Basics

Few countries are as unlucky as **Burkina Faso**. But for a twist of administrative fate in colonial times, it would never have existed. It is desperately,
and famously, poor, with an almost total lack of raw materials or natural
resources. And although it shares its **landlocked** predicament with Niger
and Mali, unlike them it lacks direct access to historically important trans-
Saharan trading routes. From the traveller's point of view the country also
suffers from several superficial disadvantages: it's unremittingly flat, and
offers little of the natural spectacle and traditional cultural colour of its
neighbours, while its **image problem** in the foreign press acts as a further
deterrent.

Despite all this, however, most visitors really **enjoy** Burkina. Poverty here is
no more apparent than in neighbouring
countries, and there's an increasing range
of **places to stay**. The numerous military
checkpoints that once littered Burkina are
now less evident, and the soldiers and customs agents who you do meet treat you
with respect, venturing a "Bonne arrivée,
ça va?" while verifying your passport – the
type of **friendliness** that travellers can
expect to encounter throughout Burkina.
Improvements to the country's basic **infrastructure** and the provision of services
such as medicine, water and electricity has
given the country a climate of youthful **optimism**, backed up by a vital popular culture
which has spawned a small yet dynamic
tourist industry. The downside to this is the
increasing hassle from **guides**, vendors and
the like, which has made the more popular
attractions a little less laid-back than they
once were.

People

With some sixty different **language groups**,
Burkina has the usual West African ethno-
linguistic mosaic. But most Burkinabe
(Burkinabè is also used, but not Burkinabé)
speak languages of the large **Voltaic** group,
and the country is unusual in having an
overwhelming majority of a single people,
the More-speaking **Mossi**, who live in the
central plains around Ouagadougou, and
make up over half the population. They are
related to the **Gourmantché**, who live in the
east around Fada-Ngourma, and less closely
to the Grusi or **Gourounsi** from around Pô
and Léo.

The main peoples of the north include the
Fula (who are also called Peul or Fulani),
the **Hausa** and the **Bella** (Tamashek-
speaking former slaves of the Tuareg).
Near the northwestern border with Mali
live small enclaves of **Dogon**, **Samos**
and **Pana**. In the south, different **Bobo**

Fact file

The country's **official name**, Burkina Faso, is a hybrid of a More word meaning
"dignity-nobility-integrity" and a Dioula word meaning homeland. The name, changed
in 1984 from Haute Volta (Upper Volta), and commonly abbreviated to Burkina,
thus means roughly **"Land of the Honourable"**. With an **area** of 275,000 square
kilometres, the country is slightly larger than Great Britain and slightly smaller than
Nevada. Burkina's population numbers some thirteen and a half million people, just
over a million of whom live in the capital, Ouagadougou. Since 1991 it has had a
constitutional democracy, in theory at least, if not always effectively in practice. On
the economic front, despite debt relief, Burkina's **foreign debts** total some £832
million ($1.65 billion), more than double the value of its annual exports of goods and
services – though it's still a trifling amount in international terms, less than the cost of
an aircraft carrier, for example.

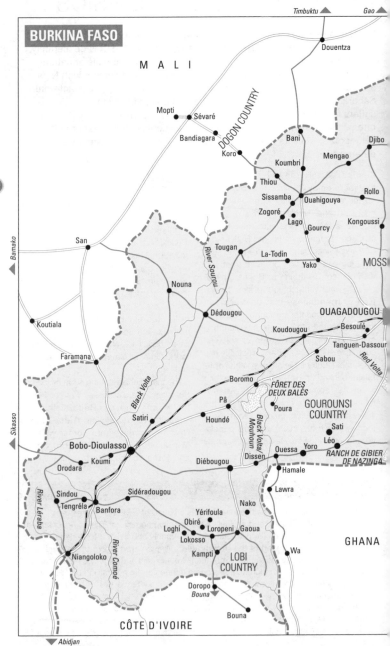

BURKINA FASO

MALI

Timbuktu ▲   *Gao* ▲

Douentza

Mopti   Sévaré

Bandiagara

Koro

DOGON COUNTRY

Bani   Djibo

Koumbri   Mengao

Thiou

Sissamba   Ouahigouya   Rollo

Zogoré

Lago   Gourcy   Kongoussi

Bamako ▲

San

Tougan   La-Todin

Yako   MOSS

River Sourou

Nouna

Dédougou

OUAGADOUGOU

Koudougou   Besoulé

Tanguen-Dassour

Koutiala

Faramana

Sabou

Red Volta

Black Volta

Boromo

FÔRET DES
DEUX BALÉS

Pâ   Poura

GOUROUNSI
COUNTRY

Satiri   Houndé

Black Volta
Mouhoun

Sati

Léo

Sikasso ▲

Bobo-Dioulasso

Koumi

Orodara

Diébougou   Ouessa   Yoro

Dissen   RANCH DE GIBIER
DE NAZINGA

Hamale

Sindou   Sidéradougou

Tengréla   Banfora

Lawra

River Léraba

Nako

Yérifoula

Obiré

Loghi   Loropeni   Gaoua

Lokosso

River Comoé

Kampti   Wa

Niangoloko

GHANA

LOBI
COUNTRY

Doropo
Bouna

CÔTE D'IVOIRE

Bouna

Abidjan ▼

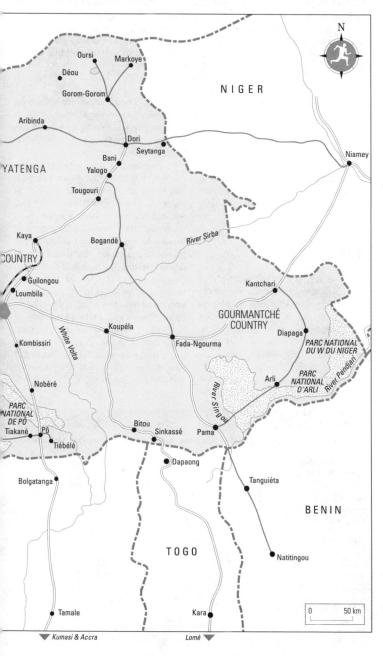

Until recently, before taking any pictures in Burkina you needed to obtain a (free) photo permit at the ONTB tourist office in Ouagadougou. However, at the time of writing these permits had been suspended, with the likelihood that they will not be reinstated. Even when they were required, permits were rarely checked for by officials.

peoples – Bwaba, Kos and Siby – populate the area around Bobo-Dioulasso. The **Senoufo** occupy the southwestern tip near Côte d'Ivoire and Mali, while the **Lobi**, towards the border with Ghana, remain one of the most isolated peoples in the country. As ever, with rapid growth and communications improvements, people from different ethnic backgrounds are found throughout Burkina.

Where to go

Burkina is largely flat, and most of the country is swathed in semi-arid grasslands. The further north you go, the drier things become, until you arrive at the denuded Sahelian landscapes of the extreme north. Only in the southern regions of Banfora and the Lobi country will you find much greenery. Although the three big rivers, the Volta Blanche (Nakambé), Volta Rouge (Nazinon) and Volta Noire (Mouhoun), all rise

in Burkina, only the Volta Noire flows in the dry season. The three meet up much further south in Ghana where they form the navigable river which the Portuguese called Rio da Volta, or "River of Return".

Specific targets for travel include the second city, **Bobo-Dioulasso** ("Bobo"), which is unquestionably one of the most attractive cities in West Africa; the hilly and prettily wooded **Banfora region** in the southwest; the mysterious stone ruins of the remote and fascinating **Lobi country** in the south; and the lively Sahelian market at **Gorom-Gorom**. The appeal of the capital, **Ouagadougou** ("Ouaga"), isn't especially strong, but you'll get more out of a visit here if you have some background knowledge of the venerable **Mossi kingdoms**, of which Ouaga was formerly one of several in the central region. Ouagadougou also has a major attraction in the **FESPACO** festival of African film, which is held every odd-numbered year (2009, 2011, 2013) in February.

Average temperatures and rainfall

	Jan	Feb	Mar	Apr	May	June	July	Aug	Sept	Oct	Nov	Dec
Ouagadougou												
Temperatures °C												
Min (night)	16	20	23	26	26	24	23	22	23	23	22	17
Max (day)	33	37	40	39	38	36	33	31	32	35	36	35
Rainfall mm	0	3	13	15	84	122	203	277	145	33	0	0
Days with rainfall	0	1	1	2	6	9	12	14	11	3	0	0
Bobo-Dioulasso												
Temperatures °C												
Min (night)	18	21	23	24	24	22	21	21	21	21	20	18
Max (day)	33	34	35	35	34	31	30	29	31	32	34	32
Rainfall mm	3	5	28	54	119	124	253	310	219	65	18	0
Gorom-Gorom												
Temperatures °C												
Min (night)	12	17	22	26	28	26	25	23	25	25	18	15
Max (day)	32	35	38	42	41	38	36	33	38	38	35	32

When to go

Burkina's climate is characterized by two main seasons. The **rains** last from June to October; violent storms gather quickly, inundate everything, then blow away, leaving clear blue skies behind. Many of the country's **pistes** are impassable during this period, and except on the main routes, you could have trouble getting around the country. The **dry season** lasts from November to May. This is when the **harmattan** blows across the country, whipping up dust and smothering everything in a dreary ochre haze. At night it can get quite chilly, especially in the north. The best period to travel is from December to February – after the rains have finished, but before the ground gets hot and temperatures reach oppressive levels.

Getting there from the rest of Africa

Burkina Faso is a great West African **travel crossroads**, with main highways converging in Ouagadougou from Niger, Benin, Togo and Ghana, and roads from Mali and Côte d'Ivoire meeting at Bobo-Dioulasso. **Road transport** along these axes is relatively good, although most border crossings are only open from 6am to 6pm.

Flights within Africa

Compared with the road links, **air links** are mostly poor. Air Burkina flies five times a week to Ouagadougou from **Bamako** and **Abidjan** (usually via Bobo-Dioulasso); four times a week from **Lomé**, **Cotonou** and **Dakar** (via Bobo); and once a week from **Niamey** (via Abidjan). Bobo-Dioulasso also has connections with all these cities, often via Ouaga on one of the three weekly flights

For details on **getting to Burkina from outside Africa**, plus important practical information applying to all West African countries, covering health, transport, cultural hints and more, see Basics, pp.19-28.

between Bobo and the capital. Antrak Air provides a twice-weekly link between **Accra** and Ouaga, while Air Ivoire flies from **Abidjan** to Ouaga three times a week, Air Sénégal flies from **Dakar** to Ouaga three times a week and Afriqiyah flies from **Tripoli** to Ouaga five times a week.

There are no direct flights to Ouagadougou from Banjul, Bissau or Conakry: in most cases Abidjan or Dakar offer the best connections. Similarly, there are no direct flights from **east and southern Africa**: again, the best connections are via Abidjan.

Overland from Niger

A 514-kilometre surfaced road links **Niamey** with Ouagadougou via Fada-Ngourma. **Bush taxis** regularly make the trip in about twelve hours; fares range from around CFA10,000–11,000, depending on the vehicle.

Overland from Mali

Buses use the main route from Mali to southwest Burkina via **Koutiala**; the busy 24-hour border crossing at **Faramana** is generally straightforward and Burkinabe formalities efficient. The best service is on the comfortable **TCV bus** (on alternate days, TCV's sister company, the equally good Malian-operated Bittar Transport, does the route), which runs daily from Bamako to Ouaga (CFA15,000) via Bobo (CFA10,000). Now that it's paved the whole way, the road from Bamako via **Sikasso** is a feasible alternative – the 168-kilometre Sikasso-to-Bobo stretch, previously very rough **piste**, now takes about three hours.

Taxis also run regularly along both the Koutiala and Sikasso routes, taking some twelve hours in good conditions. They're slightly cheaper than the buses, but far less comfortable and reliable.

It's also possible to come down through Dogon country via **Koro**. On the Malian side, south as far as Koro, you'll have to rely on **bush taxis**, but from there onwards you can pick up the daily SOGEBAF service to **Ouahigouya** (CFA5000), from where there are plenty of connections on to Ouaga. You can't rush this approach, but it gives an interesting first perspective on Burkina through Ouahigouya and northern Burkina's historic Yatenga region.

Overland from Côte d'Ivoire

The Ivoirian-run **train service** from **Abidjan** to Ouagadougou via Bobo-Dioulasso operates on Wednesdays, Fridays and Sundays. Trains leave Abidjan at 10.30am and it's supposed to take about 26 hours. However, more realistically, the train usually rolls into Ouaga at any time after midnight on the second night. An Abidjan–Ouaga 1st-class ticket costs CFA40,000 or CFA35,000 in second.

Bus and **bush taxis** are generally a little faster, and the 1224-kilometre road is in reasonable condition. STBF have a daily service from Abidjan to Ouaga (CFA35,000). Note that the routes through the Lobi country on the northeastern edge of the Ivoirian border are very lightly trafficked and transport there mostly depends on markets on five-day cycles.

Overland from Ghana

Ghana's STC buses run to Ouagadougou from **Accra** (GH¢30/CFA16,000), four times a week. The entire 977km of road between Accra and Ouagadougou is in good condition, and the journey takes sixteen to eighteen hours, assuming there are no hitches – the border closes at 6pm. The Burkinabe company SKV runs a twice-weekly bus from **Kumasi** (GH¢24/CFA13,000).

An alternative route from Ghana crosses the border at **Hamale**, though transport is scarce on both sides. From Hamale, one or two **bush taxis** leave daily (before 9am) for both Ouagadougou (GH¢16/CFA9000) and Bobo (GH¢6/CFA3500). Alternatively, Rakieta operates a daily bus between Hamale and Bobo.

From Togo

Bush taxis ply regularly between **Lomé** and Ouagadougou (around CFA12,500), taking about twenty hours of travel to cover the 970 kilometres (the border is open only from 6am to 6pm). As usual, you'll save money by changing vehicles between countries, but you'll have to spend the night in **Dapaong**, in Togo. The surfaced road is generally in good condition the whole way. If you'd rather go **by bus**, SKV, SOGEBAF, TCV and others run several services between Bobo, Ouaga and Lomé (CFA15,000–18,000).

Note that **customs and immigration** can sometimes be a hassle at the Sinkassé border, and there are several more checkpoints en route to Ouaga, which can draw out the Burkina part of the journey to a whole-day affair.

Overland from Benin

The journey from **Cotonou** to Ouaga is increasingly easy, with a good tarred road as far as Natitingou, and major improvements made on the remaining section via Tanguiéta to the border. On the Burkina side of the border, the road via Pama and Fada-Ngourma is tarred and in excellent condition. The reputable TCV, and others, run several services a week from Cotonou to Ouaga (CFA17,500–20,000), some with continuation or connections to Bobo (CFA23,500–26,000). This **border** is open 24 hours a day.

Red tape and visas

Visas for Burkina are required by everyone except nationals of ECOWAS countries. Burkina is part of the **Visa Touristique Entente** arrangement (see p.32) that includes Togo, Benin, Côte d'Ivoire and Niger.

Burkinabe embassies are few and far between, but in many countries where Burkina lacks representation, the French embassy can process the application. Burkinabe embassies in West African countries charge around CFA30,000 for a three-month multiple-entry visa, and usually demand payment in CFA.

Alternatively, **visas on arrival** can be obtained without hassle at Ouagadougou airport, and (in theory, at least) at all the country's land borders – straightforwardly at Sinkassé and Faramana, for example. You'll get a seven-day visa (two photos required) for CFA10,000, which you can then extend for up to three months at no extra charge at the immigration offices in either Ouagadougou or Bobo-Dioulasso. However, you may not be able to obtain a visa at less frequently used entry points such as Hamale, so if you plan on entering Burkina at an obscure border crossing, get a visa in advance.

Visas for onward travel

The following types of visa are issued for neighbouring countries (for embassy contact details see p.746): **Côte d'Ivoire**, 3-month single-entry for CFA33,000 (issued in 48 hours); **Ghana**, 3-month single-entry for CFA15,000 (issued in 24 hours); **Mali**, 2-month multiple-entry for CFA20,000 (issued the same day); **Niger**, 30-day double-entry for CFA20,000 (issued the same day); **Togo**, 48-hour visa issued by the French embassy in Ouaga for CFA40,000, extendable upon arrival in Togo (but note if you're travelling overland, Togolese immigration issue visas at the border at Sinkassé). Note that the French embassy also handles visas for several West and Central African countries, including Mauritania, though they don't take care of visas for Benin, Cameroon or Guinea, none of which have representation in Ouagadougou. For **Benin**, 48-hour visas are obtainable at the border (CFA10,000), and are easily extended (usually for 30 days) for CFA12,000 in Natitingou or Cotonou.

Info, websites, maps

Burkina Faso doesn't have any overseas **tourist offices**; in the country itself, there are branches of the Office National du Tourisme Burkinabe (ONTB) in Ouagadougou and Bobo-Dioulasso, although neither one is particularly well equipped or knowledgeable.

On the **Internet**, the French-language Ⓦwww.culture.gov.bf contains useful practical information relating to Burkinabe arts and culture, including festivals, museums and cinema; while the English-language Ⓦwww.ouaganet.com has general information and a public forum for Burkina-related subjects.

The best **map** of the country is the IGN **Carte Touristique** (1:1,000,000), most recently published in 1994 and available in good map shops. In Ouagadougou, the Institut Géographique du Burkina (open Mon–Fri; Ⓦwww.igb.bf) has good **regional topographic maps** – ideal for hikers and the like – while recent (2005) **city maps** of Ouaga (showing the new street names) are sold at the Trésorie Régionale du Centre (Mon–Fri).

The media

The **national press** consists of a government French-language daily, *Sidwaya* ("Truth"), and the independent dailies *Le Pays* and *L'Observateur*. The weekly *Journal du Jeudi* attempts a satirical treatment of current events and is worth a look. Another weekly that has sprung up in the "democratic" era is *L'Indépendant*, whose editor, Norbert Zongo, was infamously assassinated (see p.724).

Listening to **Radio Burkina**, the government radio (in sixteen Burkinabe languages, on 747 AM) or watching **TV** (one state-run channel, with very limited transmission and audience) aren't likely to be major leisure activities. For something a bit livelier, there are various commercial stations including Canal Arc-en-ciel (96.6FM), Savane FM (103.4FM), Horizon FM (104.4FM in Ouaga and 102.7FM in Bobo) and Radio Bobo-Dioulasso (92.0FM). The **BBC World Service** can be heard in the capital on 99.2FM.

Health

Chloroquine-resistant **malaria** is a serious problem in Burkina (see p.40), with around five thousand people dying each year of the disease. As elsewhere in West Africa, you'll need a **yellow fever** vaccination certificate (even if it's rarely asked for by officials). During outbreaks of **cholera** or **meningitis**, you may (unpredictably) need a cholera certificate or proof of immunization against meningitis; bus companies will check on this if you intend to use one of their international routes during an epidemic. **Tap water** is treated in Bobo-Dioulasso and Ouagadougou; it smells of chlorine, but is drinkable. In the bush, progress has been made on water purity, but some supplies

If you're **driving**, you'll soon discover that Burkina has some of the region's highest fuel prices, with pump prices in the main towns around CFA585/litre for diesel and CFA600/litre for super. Prices can be even higher out in the sticks.

are still dubious. If you have any doubts, use purifying tablets. The only other real worry is **bilharzia**; except around Bobo, where there are several bodies of clean water, you should be careful of swimming, especially where the water is stagnant or grassy.

Costs, money, banks

Burkina Faso is part of the **CFA zone** (rates of exchange roughly £1=CFA880, $1=CFA450). **Banks** in Ouagadougou and Bobo-Dioulasso will readily change **cash** euros, dollars and sterling and will usually change **traveller's cheques**, preferably in euros (providing you can show the original purchase receipt). In other towns, banks will usually only change euros cash – and sometimes may refuse to change even these – so plan ahead and change enough money in the major towns to see you through your travels. Bank **opening hours** vary: they're typically Monday to Friday 7.30–11.30am and 3.30–5.30pm.

Credit cards are not widely accepted, though you'll find Visa of some use to pay for expensive hotels and travel services in Ouagadougou and, to an even more limited extent, Bobo-Dioulasso. However, plastic is useful for withdrawing money from the country's increasing number of **ATMs**: several banks in Ouaga and Bobo have them, as do branches of the BIB bank in Koudougou, Fada-Ngourma, Ouahigouya, Dori and Gaoua. ATMs invariably accept Visa, but not MasterCard. Elsewhere, it's very difficult to get a cash advance on Visa, while Master-Card is even more difficult. If you get in a fix, try the major hotels.

Costs

Compared to neighbouring Francophone countries, prices in Burkina are reasonable, and even Ouagadougou isn't too expensive (although if you've come from Ghana, costs

may seem very high). **Accommodation** in budget hotels around the country costs from CFA3000 to CFA6000, rising to CFA10,000 to CFA20,000 in mid-range places, while eating street **food** you can fill up on *riz sauce* or *tô* for as little as CFA300. **Transport** costs are also reasonable, ranging from CFA10 to CFA30 per kilometre (rarely more), depending on the type of vehicle and whether the road is paved or *piste*.

Getting around

Due to Burkina's geographical location in the heart of the region, a decent **road system** crisscrosses the country, with Ouagadougou being the main crossroads. Nowadays, tarred roads connect Ouaga with Bobo-Dioulasso, Ouahigouya, Fada-Ngourma, Pô and even remoter places such as Gaoua and Dori. There are toll booths (*péages*) set up at the entrance and exit of main towns where drivers have to pay a **road tax**; Ouaga to Bobo, for example, cost CFA800 at the time of writing. The dirt roads linking other villages, including Gorom-Gorom, are generally in a reasonable condition and negotiable without much difficulty during the dry season (Nov–May). Travelling conditions get more challenging in the wet season (June–Oct), although even during this period you should be able to get almost everywhere.

Bush taxis, trucks and buses

Bush taxis are usually 504 *breaks* (estate cars/station wagons), Japanese minibuses in varying states of repair or 404 *bâchés* with boarded-up back ends. The last of these are cheaper and, given the level of comfort, rightly so. You won't see much of the countryside in them unless you pay a small supplement to sit in the cab.

Far better options are the numerous **private bus companies**, which offer competitive prices, less hassle at highway checkpoints and greater reliability and comfort (some even have a/c). Between them, STMB, SOGEBAF and Rakieta offer services to most parts of the country, while other companies such as TSR, TRANSMIF, STAF, SKV and TCV serve particular regions or ply the international routes – each company usually has its own separate bus station.

Routes, frequencies and sample fares

There's plenty of traffic along the main route nationale axis of Banfora–Bobo–Ouaga–Fada-Ngourma, and frequent enough vehicles north to Ouahigouya and Dori and south to Pô. It's only when trying to get to more remote northern towns – or to other isolated areas such as the Lobi country – that you might experience long waits for vehicles of several hours (sometimes even days).

Ouaga–Bobo (360km): CFA5000, hourly (6hr).

Ouaga–Fada-Ngourma (234km): CFA3000, 5 daily (4hr).

Ouaga–Gaoua (385km): CFA5000, 2 daily (5hr).

Ouaga–Gorom-Gorom (300km; paved as far as Dori): CFA6000, twice weekly (6hr).

Ouaga–Dori (270km) CFA3000, 2 daily (4hr).

Ouaga–Ouahigouya (182km): CFA3000, 6 daily (3hr).

Ouaga–Pô (142km): CFA2000, 4 daily (2hr 30min).

Car and bike rental

You'll find official **car rental** agencies in Ouagadougou, and you should also be able to rent a vehicle in Bobo-Dioulasso without too many problems (see the "Listings" for those towns). Prices are not excessively expensive, although check first whether or not it's mandatory to hire a chauffeur as well. It can be more economical, and potentially much more satisfying, to rent a **bicycle**, **mobylette** (moped) or **motorbike**. This is an excellent way to see several interesting sights around Bobo-Dioulasso, Banfora and Ouahigouya: you'll find people around the market places who rent out machines, and you can even transport bicycles on the roofs of bush taxis (for an extra charge) if you get bored with riding.

Trains

The Ouagadougou–Abidjan train runs three times a week (in theory at least, though services are often disrupted) via the Burkinabe stations at **Koudougou**, **Bobo-Dioulasso**, **Banfora** and **Niangoloko** – the Burkinabe border post. Details in the Ouagadougou section, p.735.

Domestic flights

Air Burkina flies on Tuesdays and Fridays from **Ouaga** to **Bobo** (en route to Abidjan), and from Bobo to Ouaga on Tuesdays, Fridays and Sundays.

Accommodation

Ouagadougou and Bobo-Dioulasso have their fair share of international-class **hotels**, which are invariably full during the big festivals (see p.734). In Ouaga, hotel rates usually carry a **tax** known as the "Contribution au Développement de la Commune": it works out at CFA500 per hotel star per night. Elsewhere around the country, accommodation tends to be more basic. In smaller towns, especially in the extreme north, **electricity** and **running water** become more sporadic.

Accommodation price codes

All accommodation prices in this chapter are coded according to the following scale, whose equivalent in pounds sterling/US dollars is used throughout the book. Prices refer to the rate you can expect to pay for a room with two beds, including taxes. Single rooms, or single occupancy, will normally cost at least two-thirds of the twin-occupancy rate. For further details, see p.55.

❶ Under CFA5000 (under £5/$10)
❷ CFA5000–10,000 (£5–10/$10–20)
❸ CFA10,000–15,000 (£10–15/$20–30)
❹ CFA15,000–20,000 (£15–20/$30–40)
❺ CFA20,000–30,000 (£20–30/$40–60)
❻ CFA30,000–40,000 (£30–40/$60–80)
❼ CFA40,000–50,000 (£40–50/$80–100)
❽ Over CFA50,000 (over £50/$100)

In terms of **room rates**, anything under around CFA5000 (**1**) is likely to be quite rudimentary – sometimes a *chambre de passage* rented to most guests by the hour and not used for sleeping. Above CFA5000 (**2**–**3**) you'll get a basic hotel with simple amenities, usually self-contained with fan (or a/c, at higher rates). Mid-range establishments (roughly CFA15,000 and upwards; **4**–**6**) are usually reasonable business- or tourist-class hotels, while above CFA40,000 (**7**–**8**) you're looking at a comfortable, first-class hotel, with good facilities.

A network of **auberges populaires** has been set up by the Ministry of the Environment and Tourism. These very basic hotels at least ensure that there's somewhere to stay in each of Burkina's thirty main towns. Off the few beaten tracks, **staying with people** is a viable and recommended option. Several hotels also allow **camping**.

Eating and drinking

Despite its drought-stricken reputation, most towns in Burkina have an array of **street food**; and throughout the country you'll find bean or banana fritters, yam chips, fried fish and, especially in the evenings, **brochettes**. The streets of every town fill with *brochette* vendors gathered around their kerosene lamps, tending their charcoal braziers, grilling sticks of beef and mutton, often nicely marinated. Note that if you want to savour the smoky flavour, you should be sure to ask for your sticks *sans piment* (without chilli sauce). Kerosene lamps also light the tables of *les cafémans* who are also out in the morning to whip up omelettes and sticky Nescafé concoctions to accompany French bread *tartines*.

The home-cooking staples in Burkina are **rice** and **millet**. After grinding, the grain is boiled and made into a mush known as **tô**, often eaten with a sauce made from **cassava** (manioc) leaves with palm oil, fresh fish and seasonings. *Gumbo* (okra) is another common sauce base.

Fresh **yoghurt** is popular; sold in small sachets, it makes a refreshing and cheap snack.

Drinking

Nationally brewed **beers** include SOBRA, Brakina and Flag. You may be offered the unopened bottle to see if it's cold enough. Different home-made drinks are enjoyed in the various regions. A national favourite is **chapalo**, locally made millet beer, also known as *dolo*. The deadly African gin, known in Burkina as **patasi** or "qui me pousse", is also widely available. Around Banfora, you'll find a lot of palm wine, **banji**, which you can order by the (beer) bottle in most small bars (*cabarets*). Sweet and frothy, it goes down easily and has the added advantage of being cheap.

Throughout the country (especially at the *gares routières* and around the markets), you'll find **lemburgui**, thirst-quenching home-made ginger beer and red bissap (hibiscus flower) juice, frozen in small plastic bags – if you want one that's still hard, ask for *bissap formé*. Lafi **mineral water** is available across the country in 1.5 litre bottles, not too expensive at around CFA500.

Communications

You can make direct-dial **international phone calls** from Burkina to the UK, North America and most of Europe. Even the smallest of towns have **telecentres** where you can make local, national and international calls. **Mobile (cell) phone** connectivity through Celtel, Telecel and Onatel is increasing rapidly and mobile-phone ownership is now widespread. Your mobile will work in Ouaga and Bobo, around several other large towns and along some main highways, though connections can be tenuous. As usual, you'll save a packet by buying a **local SIM** card and call time.

Ouagadougou's **poste restante** works well, although you should be careful to have your letters addressed with the exact name that appears in your passport – which you'll have to produce to claim your post. There's also a poste restante service in Bobo-Dioulasso.

For **Internet** access, you'll find a good selection of cybercafés in Ouaga. Bobo

Burkina Faso's IDD code is ☏226.

also has a choice of places where you can get online, although connections are much slower than in the capital. In most other significant towns, you'll usually find at least one cybercafé. Prices hover around CFA300 per hour in Ouaga and Bobo, rising to as much as CFA1500 per hour in the remoter places.

Opening hours, public holidays and festivals

Business hours are generally 8am–12.30pm and 3–6pm on weekdays; many are open Saturday mornings too. Government offices typically operate 7am–12.30pm and 3–5.30pm on weekdays only.

Public holidays include all the usual Muslim (see p.63) and Christian celebrations. Additional Christian holidays include Ascension Thursday (sixth Thurs after Easter), Pentecost (seventh Sun after Easter Sunday) and Assumption Day (Aug 15). New Year's Day is also a bank holiday. The principal national holidays are January 3 (1966 Revolution), March 8 (Women's Day), May 1 (Labour Day), August 4 (Revolution Day), August 5 (Independence Day) and December 11 (Proclamation of the Republic).

Festivals

Burkina has a growing reputation for major **arts festivals**, of which the best known is the big African film fest, **FESPACO**, held in February in odd-numbered years (2009, 2011, 2013). To balance the film jamboree, three other major arts festivals take place each even-numbered year (2008, 2010, 2012): the **Salon International de l'Artisanat**, the **Festival du Théâtre** and the **Semaine Nationale de la Culture**. It's well worth timing a trip around one of these.

FESPACO

The Festival Panafricain du Cinéma, held in Ouagadougou at the end of February, every two years since 1969 (ⓦwww.fespaco.bf), is dedicated to promoting African film-makers throughout the world. Thrusting Burkina to the forefront of African cinema, the festival now attracts tens of thousands of visitors, for whom the great attraction is the chance to rub shoulders with movie people from all over Africa and beyond. The festival is West Africa's most star-studded event, with celebrities from the African diaspora increasingly making the pilgrimage. Locals and visitors crowd the streets, stopping for drinks or browsing the countless booths for traditional crafts and FESPACO merchandise, and local bands play everywhere.

Organization is good: **schedules** are posted throughout town; a free daily festival paper lists each day's events; and free shuttles are provided from major hotels. An "Etalon Pass" **ticket** costing just CFA10,000 allows you entrance to all the myriad films showing simultaneously in the capital's cinemas. You can also purchase individual tickets at the respective cinemas (about CFA1000) – if you have the stamina, you could easily take in thirty or more African films in the course of the event.

If you're going to be in Ouaga during FESPACO, be sure to **book your hotel in advance**, as rooms go quickly; rooms in private homes help mop up the overflow (enquire at the headquarters on av Kadiogo, not far from place de la Bataille du Rail).

SIAO

Another biennial ten-day event (ⓦwww.siao.bf; Oct in even-numbered years), the **Salon International de l'Artisanat de Ouagadougou** is touted as the largest crafts festival in Africa. The SIAO attracts over 100,000 visitors, including buyers from throughout the world. The entire city centre fills with exhibitors' booths and stalls, with the focus around the **SIAO village**, a purpose-built structure on the eastern outskirts of the city. While the objective – to promote African crafts as cultural expression while stimulating the industry – is serious, the atmosphere is festive, with music, food, fashion shows, and performances of dance and theatre on every street corner.

Festival International du Théâtre et de Marionnettes

Ouagadougou's biennial **Festival du Théâtre** (late Nov in even-numbered years) hosts national troupes performing works as diverse as Greek tragedy and modern African comedies, usually at the Théâtre Populaire Désiré

Bonogo. For information, contact the Espace Culturel Gambidi (01 BP 3479, Ouagadougou ☎50.36.59.42 @gambidi@cenatrin.bf).

Semaine Nationale de la Culture

The **Semaine Nationale de la Culture** is another biennial event (ⓦ www.snc.gov.bf; Feb/March in even-numbered years), this time held in Bobo-Dioulasso. The town becomes a fair for the event, with nonstop dance and percussion performances. You can also catch demonstrations of traditional wrestling and archery, while booths everywhere display national crafts and regional cooking.

Other music festivals

The nine–day **Jazz à Ouaga** festival (ⓦ www .jazz.zcp.bf) kicks off in late April and showcases the talents of mainly African jazz musicians, with concerts, jam sessions and expositions taking place in Ouagadougou and to a lesser extent Bobo-Dioulasso. For two weeks in October, Burkina's burgeoning hip-hop scene takes centre stage during **Ouaga Hip Hop**, which also features rap artists and other styles of urban music as well as workshops. **Les Nuits Atypiques de Koudougou** is based on the idea of bringing different cultures together through the arts: the four-day festival takes place at the end of November in Koudougou, where the town's Théâtre Populaire and other venues host a diverse range of musicians and dance troupes, with plenty of other festivities going on around town.

Crafts and shopping

Crafts are an increasingly important cottage industry in Burkina, ranging from those intended for everyday use (**basketwork**, wooden **utensils**) to crafts used in ceremonies (**masks**, **statues**) or as **decorative items** or for **tourist souvenirs**. **Bronze statues**, cast using the lost-wax method, were traditionally made for the royal court, but are now widely available in Ouagadougou. **Pottery** is the most widespread craft in Burkina and pots are used everywhere. Look out for **leatherwork**, too, an offshoot of the country's large livestock industry.

Crime and safety

Burkina is a safe and easy-going country in which to travel. **Police** roadblocks are relaxed by West African standards and travel along the country's main highways is usually smooth and unproblematic. This said, incidents of roadside **banditry** have been on the increase; be particularly cautious when driving in the area east of Fada-Ngourma towards Niger and Benin, around Pô in the south, and near the Côte d'Ivoire border; and try to avoid driving anywhere after dark.

The relatively high number of tourists visiting Ouaga and Bobo has brought the **guides** and wannabe guides out in force and their tactics, though rarely threatening, sometimes blur the line between hard-sell and harassment. Try to keep a cool head and a sense of humour when dealing with them.

Following crackdowns by the police, Ouaga is now generally safe, but incidents do still happen, mainly at night. Watch out for **bag-snatching** by thieves riding on the back of *mobylettes*. Make sure you have a good grip of any bags and try to walk on the left-hand side of the road against the traffic. There have also been reports of **scams** involving a crooked taxi driver working with an accomplice, who poses as a disabled passenger needing help to shut his door, and another involving a fake diabetic man who has been robbed and needs a hefty loan to buy insulin. Such scams are rare and easily anticipated.

Emergencies

Police ☎17, fire service ☎18.

Gender issues and sexual attitudes

Travel in Burkina presents no particular problems for **women travellers**. If you're not travelling in male company, you'll receive plenty of propositions from Burkinabe men, which are generally made respectfully and are easily declined. And if your new-found popularity with the opposite sex starts to get a little wearisome, head to the Catholic mission in Ouaga (see p.734) where the maternalistic sisters who run the place have a clear policy of admitting women before men.

Burkina has relatively progressive attitudes towards **gay people**: while homosexuality is either specifically outlawed or simply not acknowledged in most other West African countries, it is not illegal here. The lively arts scenes in Ouaga and Bobo, and the large student population in Koudougou make these the most gay-friendly towns, but nowhere should you expect to find much – if anything – specifically geared to gay or lesbian travellers or anything like an established gay scene. Some hotels will charge extra if a male couple want to share a double room with one bed – the additional wear and tear on the bed rather than any intrinsic homophobia is usually the motivation behind the policy.

Entertainment and sport

Burkina Faso has a thriving, though severely underfunded, popular-culture scene. In Ouaga and Bobo, **live music** is a nightly occurrence, and even isolated villages periodically come alive with the sounds of impromptu **balafon** bands. During the major **festivals** (see p.717), Burkina's international stars can be counted on to make appearances. For more on Burkinabe music, see p.726.

Burkina is best known, however, as the capital of African **cinema**: you have a better chance of catching an African movie here than in any other country in the region, especially during the huge **FESPACO film festival** (see p.717). For more on Burkinabe cinema, see p.726.

Burkinabe **drama** has received a boost in recent years and the country now has more than a dozen drama troupes giving regular performances, whilst the major towns (Ouaga, Bobo, Koudougou) all have well-equipped theatres. You can check out what's going on by calling in at the French cultural centres in Ouaga or Bobo. If you're really keen, be sure to catch the **Festival du Théâtre** (see p.717).

The country has a thriving **football** culture, though team and player success is still a purely Burkinabe business – no World Cup qualifiers or international star players here. The team that has dominated the league since the turn of the century is Ouaga-based **Association Sportive du Faso-Yennenga** (ASFA Yennenga), who have won the league title four times since 2002.

Wildlife and national parks

Burkina's flat, overgrazed and relatively highly populated lands offer poor refuge for the country's natural **savannah fauna**. A conscientious **conservation** programme does exist (with controlled tourist hunting as part of its policy), though its best chances of success lie with the Burkinabe ethic stressing community before individual – for example, the numerous **hippo and crocodile "pools"** are recognized tourist assets. Recent initiatives such as the establishment of an **elephant corridor** between the **Ranch de Gibier de Nazinga** and the **Parc National de Pô** (see p.763) are moves in the right direction – although the tourist infrastructure in all of Burkina's wildlife parks remains very rudimentary, if not entirely absent. For information on the game reserves, contact the Direction de la Faune et de la Chasse in Ouaga – a couple of kilometres north of the *Mercure Silmandé* hotel on the road to Kaya – (☎50.35.63.14 or 50.37.69.71).

A brief history of Burkina Faso

The **Mossi empires** dominated the Volta region's politics until the French usurped the independence of their states in the 1890s. For two decades the colonials simply merged their new territory with the Colonie du Haut-Sénégal Niger, and it wasn't until 1919 that they divided this huge mass into two separate colonies – Soudan Français and **Haute Volta**. In 1932, commercial considerations (primarily a need for manual labour in neighbouring colonies) led the French to divide Upper Volta again, annexing half the colony to Côte d'Ivoire and dividing the rest between Soudan Français and Niger. It wasn't until 1947 that Haute Volta (Upper Volta) emerged once again as a permanent entity.

Independence

Maurice Yaméogo, a prominent figure in pre-independence politics, founded the **Union Démocratique Voltaïque** – the **UDV**, a local section of **Félix Houphouët-Boigny**'s Rassemblement Démocratique Africain – shortly after World War II. By 1958, Upper Volta had become an autonomous territory, and Yaméogo its prime minister. When full independence was granted on August 5, 1960, he was elected the country's first president.

Yaméogo had inherited a desperate situation – the French had done little to give Upper Volta an infrastructure capable of spurring economic development – and the new president failed to reverse the trend: outside of Ouagadougou the country had barely any roads or communications systems. As the economic situation deteriorated, Yaméogo introduced austerity measures, making him increasingly unpopular with disgruntled workers and civil servants. In the face of rising opposition, he banned political parties apart from the UDV and adopted an autocratic style. He was ousted, on January 3, 1966, in a coup led by the army chief of staff, **Sangoulé Lamizana**.

The 1970s

The army, with Lamizana at its head, ruled the country during a four-year period in which the nation was ostensibly being prepared for a **return to civilian rule**. Parties were formed and a new constitution was drafted. In 1970, a semi-civilian government was elected, with the UDV winning a majority of the seats in parliament. The UDV's leadership was split, however, with a rivalry developing between **Joseph Ouédraogo** and **Gérard Ouédraogo** (both Mossi, though unrelated). After a period of political infighting, it was agreed that Gérard would serve as prime minister and Joseph as president of the National Assembly. Lamizana remained in office as head of state and the army retained real power.

By the early 1970s, drought had struck the country and the economic outlook was bleaker than ever. As parts of the north were faced with the prospect of starvation, a scandal erupted with the discovery of **food-aid embezzlement** by members of the government distribution committee – confirming rumours of widespread administrative corruption. The government suffered a further crisis in 1973, when conflict developed between civilian leaders and the militant teachers' union, and a **general strike** swept through the public sector. As the situation deteriorated, the National Assembly refused to pass further legislation until the prime minister stepped down. Gérard Ouédraogo refused to do so, and on February 8, 1974, the army took control of the country again, dissolving the assembly and suspending the 1970 constitution.

A new crisis hit Upper Volta in 1975, when **war** broke out with Mali over the Agacher Strip. Their rival claims to this 150-kilometre-wide border strip in the desolate northern regions of the Sahel – believed to be rich in mineral deposits – were based on legal documents dating back to when Haute Volta had been divided and redivided between Côte d'Ivoire, Soudan Français (Mali) and Niger. Before the dispute was settled with OAU mediation, a new generation of popular military heroes had arisen, including a young officer, **Thomas Sankara**.

The rise of Sankara

Under pressure from the labour unions, elections were once again held in 1978, and on May 28 of that year, the **Third Republic** was proclaimed. Lamizana was elected president, but his UDV party didn't have an overall majority in parliament and his tenure was challenged by the students and trade unions (at the time, an unusually powerful force, since half of all wage earners belonged to one of the four national unions). He was overthrown in a quiet palace coup on November 25, 1980, by **Colonel Saye Zerbo**, who became head of the new "Military Committee for Recovery and National Progress" (**CMRPN**).

The coup was initially supported by the unions, but they quickly became disgruntled after the CMRPN's **banning of political activity**. Relations deteriorated utterly when the Military Committee withdrew the right to strike in 1981. Serious cleavages appeared in the Military Committee, and in 1982 Thomas Sankara – whose popular appeal was growing – was removed from his influential position in the Ministry of Information.

Unrest quickened, and a **coup d'état** followed. On November 7, 1982, a group of military officers forced out Zerbo and set up the "Provisional People's Salvation Council" (CSP) with an army doctor, **Jean-Baptiste Ouédraogo**, at its head. The new regime denounced Zerbo's corrupt, repressive government and took a radical pro-union position, championing the right to strike. In January 1983, Sankara was named prime minister.

By early 1983, it was clear that the new government was divided between **traditionalists** – led by the army chief of staff, Colonel Gabriel Somé – and **radicals**, headed by Sankara. The two factions came into open conflict when Sankara invited Colonel Gaddafi to Upper Volta in May 1983. The day after the Libyan leader's departure, Ouédraogo ordered Sankara's arrest on the grounds that he had dangerously threatened national unity.

The arrest of the prime minister triggered a rebellion in Sankara's commando unit at Pô, a town near the Ghanaian border. The commandos, led by **Captain Blaise Compaoré**, believed the move to have been instigated by Somé and encouraged by France. They took control of Pô and refused orders from the capital until Sankara was unconditionally released. But Ouédraogo refused to dismiss Somé and gradually the rebellion spread to other commando units in the country. On the eve of the 23rd anniversary of independence – August 4, 1983 – Sankara seized power. Ouédraogo had lasted less than a year as head of state.

The Sankara reforms

Sankara settled in as president of the new governing body, the Conseil National de la Révolution (**CNR**), and as head of state; Compaoré was nominated minister of state to the president; and the country was renamed **Burkina Faso**. The CNR quickly set about reorganizing the administrative regions of the country and ousting traditional rulers from their positions of power and influence. Revolutionary **"people's courts"** were established to try former public officials charged with political crimes and corruption. One of the first to be tried was Lamizana, who was acquitted. But several former ministers were convicted and sentenced to prison, as were ex-president Zerbo (who was also ordered to repay US$200,000 in public funds) and Gérard Ouédraogo, former UDV leader.

Only 34 years old when he came to power, Sankara symbolized a new generation of leaders with innovative ideas, but his popularity went beyond his eloquent denunciations of capitalism and imperialism or his ability to compose revolutionary music on his guitar. Sankara may have had a penchant for facile rhetoric, but he could also transform words into action. He waged war on desertification, women's inequality and children's diseases (creating a "vaccination-commando"). When foreign investors refused to finance a railway line to magnesium deposits in the north of the country, he launched the *bataille du rail* – encouraging peasants to build the tracks themselves (although critics said his recruitment methods were uncomfortably reminiscent of French *travaux forcés*). But perhaps his greatest achievement was the virtual elimination of **corruption** and government waste, proving his commitment to the cause by having himself chauffeured around in the back of a Renault 4, rather than the customary black Mercedes. In another popular move, Sankara announced **free housing** for all Burkinabe and called a moratorium on rents (an incautious decision which he later retracted). But even as the young president proved himself a capable, if unpredictable leader, he was gaining a long list of enemies.

Detractors – at home and abroad

By early 1984, there was growing **opposition** to Sankara's radical style, and in May of that year a plot to overthrow the government was uncovered. The leaders were hastily arrested and tried. Unlike the people's courts, these proceedings took place in secrecy and the penalties were severe. Seven of the alleged plotters were executed and five others sentenced to hard labour.

In light of these events, **relations with France** soured, and Sankara accused the French government of supporting exiled political rivals. Other Western nations also viewed the new regime with scepticism, though the fact that Sankara made efforts to distance his government from Libya and the Soviet Union was interpreted as an encouraging sign. Gradually, the "revolution" came to be identified less with Marxist ideology and was seen more as a means of unifying a wide cross-section of society. The success of the CNR and the genuine popularity of the movement hinged primarily on the dynamic personality of its founder.

In 1985 **war with Mali** flared up again and more than fifty people were killed. In 1986, the International Court of Justice in The Hague divided the disputed Agacher Strip between the two countries and peace was restored. But relations were also deteriorating with other West African neighbours – especially **Côte d'Ivoire** and **Togo**. Close ties between Sankara and Jerry Rawlings of **Ghana** were regarded suspiciously by these conservative nations – especially after 1986 when the two socialist neighbours decided to work towards political integration. Relations with Togo were nearly broken off after an attempted coup in Lomé shook President Eyadéma's regime in September 1986. Both Ghana and Burkina were accused of involvement and of harbouring Togolese dissidents. And, despite a 1987 visit to Ouagadougou by François Mitterrand, France continued to treat Burkina with reserve – a wait-and-see attitude generally shared by Western powers.

At home, Sankara was frequently criticized by **intellectuals**, **labour unions** and **business leaders**, though he had a charismatic knack for diffusing enmity from all these groups. Even salary cuts for civil servants and the military were accepted on the grounds that they were necessary to raise the level of social services among the poor. In the absence of serious opposition from traditional political forces, it was a growing lack of consensus within the governing CNR and resulting rifts that ultimately proved Sankara's downfall.

On October 15, 1987, Thomas Sankara was killed in a botched and bloody **coup**. It was precipitated by a group of soldiers loyal to **Blaise Compaoré** (Sankara's companion-in-arms and partner in the government), who opened fire on Sankara after arresting him. The precise nature of the overthrow is still shrouded in mystery. It did not, at any rate, take a planned course and it doesn't seem likely that Compaoré intended to come out of it looking like a murderer. He later said "Thomas confiscated the revolution and brought untold suffering to the people", and it's clear at least that Sankara had allowed himself to become fatally isolated. But Compaoré's image as a West African leader with the blood of a brother on his hands has never been erased.

The new regime

Sankara's death sent shock waves through the region and chilled progressive movements round the world. For even if his methods were often open to question (something he never denied), he had proved himself a sincere and credible friend of the people. Most importantly he had managed to instil **national pride** and create a realistic sense of hope in one of West Africa's most impoverished countries. Most West African, and not a few Western governments, seemed relieved with the change, but the Burkinabe people's response varied from mournful to muted – not a good sign for the new president.

The basis of the revolutionary system Sankara set in place remained intact, although Compaoré quickly announced that "rectification" would be made, signalling a willingness to conform to the inevitable pressure of World Bank and IMF loan negotiations. The early years of the new regime were characterized by the almost continuous rumble of rumour and incident within the Front

Populaire (high-level **disagreements**, **coup attempts** and a number of subsequent **executions**). Though by 1990 the party had been purged, by death or desertion, of all members of the original 1983 revolution, events suggested considerable latent support for Sankara and serious threats to the survival of the new leadership. In response, Compaoré sought to bring disenfranchised political groupings into the fold and to achieve peace with the powerful unions.

Towards this end, a new constitution was drafted in 1990, which called for a multiparty **electoral system**. Political parties mushroomed, and a transitional government was set up with Compaoré as head of a council of ministers that contained a smattering of opposition leaders. But conflict arose quickly at a conference to discuss the constitution's implementation. The new parties decried the fact that their input was merely consultative and there was to be no sovereign national conference such as those taking place elsewhere in West Africa. Soon after, opposition leaders resigned their government posts to protest Compaoré's intransigence on the issue.

The Fourth Republic

As the presidential elections approached, opposition parties united under the banner of the **Coordination des Forces Démocratiques** (**CFD**) and collectively pushed for a sovereign national council. Popular demonstrations in support of opposition demands occurred throughout the second half of 1991, and, as the outcomes tended increasingly towards violence, the government banned political rallies. By the end of the year, it was clear there would be no council and no opposition: "opposition" candidates withdrew from the presidential race and called for an election boycott. Compaoré was left as the only candidate and, naturally enough, won the election, although three out of four voters stayed away from the polls. He was sworn in as president of the **"Fourth Republic"** on December 24, 1991, but was probably no closer to having obtained wide public support than he was after the unpopular coup of 1987.

Even as the president called for **national reconciliation** following the elections, he became increasingly mistrusted when opposition leaders were attacked. One, Clément Oumarou Ouédraogo, was assassinated just outside the Hôtel Indépendance as he left a CFD meeting. Although Compaoré condemned the murder, there was general public cynicism, and angry crowds stoned the minister of defence when he showed up at Ouédraogo's funeral. Still, with some deft political manoeuvring, the president managed to persuade much of the opposition to participate in the upcoming **legislative elections**. By the polling date in May 1992, almost half of the nation's 62 political parties had decided to contest.

Although Compaoré's party, the Organisation pour la Démocratie Populaire Mouvement du Travail (**ODP-MT**) won a majority of the parliamentary seats, the president's image suffered as a result of the popular belief that the elections had been rigged. In keeping with the theme of reconciliation, the new cabinet contained some opposition leaders – though mostly relegated to the least important posts.

In the early years of the Fourth Republic, Burkina Faso was most often in the headlines as a **sponsor of various rebel forces** in West Africa and as a mediator of regional conflicts. Compaoré actively supported Charles Taylor in the civil war in **Liberia**, supplying arms and troops to Liberian forces and to rebel militias in Sierra Leone, as well as being implicated by the UN in the notorious "blood diamond" trade.

More positively, Compaoré also played a key role in negotiating a settlement of the **Tuareg crisis** that gripped Mali and Niger – partly because Burkina was one of the countries most affected, with 50,000 refugees sheltering there at the height of the conflict. Burkina's relationship with France grew warmer following the election of Jacques Chirac in 1995.

At home, Burkina's economy experienced the fastest growth of any country in West Africa at the end of the 1990s – a performance that bolstered Compaoré's chances of keeping his seat as his first term drew to a close. More importantly, there was no real alternative to his candidacy. As the **1998 elections** neared, the main opposition parties again called for a boycott, but this time voters seemed weary of complaints about the electoral process, and the boycott gathered only a lacklustre following. More than fifty percent of voters participated in the elections and gave Compaoré a resounding victory, making him the first president since independence to survive a first term and be re-elected.

The Zongo scandal

Compaoré barely had time to bask in the glow of his victory, however, when a scandal erupted that had far-reaching political implications. In December 1998, four charred bodies were found in a vehicle that had apparently crashed near the village of Sapouy, south of Ouagadougou. One of the victims was **Norbert Zongo**, editor of the *L'Indépendant* newspaper and president of the Private Press Association in Burkina. Zongo had been investigating the business dealings of Compaoré's younger brother François, as well as the suspicious circumstances surrounding the death of François' chauffeur, whom Zongo alleged had been tortured to death by the Régiment de Sécurité Présidentielle, the president's own security forces. **Demonstrations** in Ouagadougou called for an investigation into Zongo's death, which the public widely believed to be murder, and Compaoré set up an independent commission to look into the matter.

The commission's report, returned in May 1999, was damning to the presidency: "Norbert Zongo was assassinated for purely political motives because he practiced investigative journalism. He defended a democratic ideal and had chosen to become involved, with his newspaper, in the struggle for the respect of human rights and justice, and against the poor management of the public sector and impunity."

Protestors flooded the streets of Ouagadougou, setting up barricades and burning tyres as they marched to the Ministry of Justice. Security forces met them with tear gas and, as unrest spread to the university, police raided dormitories and arrested students. The rest of the country was not spared from the violence. In Koudougou – the birthplace of Zongo – rioters burned private residences and attacked public buildings. The key opposition leader and MP, Herman Yaméogo, was accused of inciting the rioters, and arrested.

Although Compaoré denounced the commission's findings, the damage was already done. It was a huge blow to his attempts to reinvent himself as a legitimately elected democratic leader and it reignited the opposition. At the same time, the president lost a friend and political ally in the region when Niger's head of state, **Ibrahim Mainassara**, was assassinated in Niamey. At the start of 2002, Compaoré's standing was shaken again when Amnesty International claimed there had been more than a hundred extra-judicial **executions** since the launch of an anti-banditry campaign in November. The incidence of armed robbery and rural violence grew, along with other signs of internal unrest, culminating in October 2003 with the arrest of sixteen people accused of conspiring to overthrow Compaoré in a military coup.

Burkina Faso today

Undeterred by criticism of Compaoré's undemocratic ways, his party – renamed the Congrès pour la Démocratie et le Progrès (**CDP**) – argued successfully that a constitutional amendment in 2000 limiting the president to two five-year terms could not be applied retroactively. Buoyed by the ruling, Compaoré sought a third term in **presidential elections** held in November 2005. The country's fragmented opposition proved no match for him, and the incumbent president won just over eighty percent of the vote.

Despite his clear win, and the fact that in terms of basic infrastructure and communications, Burkina works better than some of its neighbours, serious doubts remain over Compaoré's **authoritarian style of leadership**. Sankara's political legacy is still a powerful force in Burkinabe politics, and although none of the eleven other candidates who ran against Compaoré in the 2005 elections won more than five percent of the vote, several of them portrayed themselves as guardians of Sankara's ideology.

Continuing economic problems, exacerbated by a steep **fall in world cotton prices**, and tensions in the fractured neighbouring state of Côte d'Ivoire, where there are around 3.5 million **Burkinabe migrants**, mainly working on cocoa plantations, are major issues for Compaoré's third term. However, in a country that the UN ranks as the third poorest in the world, and where 81 percent of the population live on less than $2 per day, relieving its stark poverty remains the main challenge.

Music

Despite the variety of local music on offer in Burkina, with *balafons* (xylophones) and complex drumming particularly characteristic, very few artists have reached a wide African or international audience, apart from a few traditional groups, who have made tours of Europe. Dance is an important part of their acts, so they tend to get booked at outdoor festivals.

The best-known artists outside the country are the brilliantly watchable percussion group **Farafina** and the very exciting **Les Frères Coulibaly**. Other national artists rising to prominence include the singer **Bil Aka Kora**, whose catchy pop is grounded in the traditional rhythms of his Gourounsi people, and **Tim Winsé**, who is on a one-man crusade to promote the *lolo* fiddle of his Samo people from the northwest. They all tend to be based, when at home, in Bobo-Dioulasso, the town to head for if you want the best of Burkinabe music. The big Semaine National de la Culture festival held each even-numbered year in February or March offers a tremendous spectacle for dance and percussion enthusiasts, and is attracting increasing interest from drummers around West Africa.

As you'd expect, it's **R&B** and **hip-hop** that have really grabbed attention in the towns in recent years, with names popping up and fading just as fast. Listen out, however, for the foursome **Yeleen**, **Faso Kombat** and the rising teenage star **Madson Junior** who, at the age of ten, won "Most Promising African Artist" at the 2004 Kora Music Awards.

Farafina

The musicians of Farafina have been touring Europe and America since the mid-1980s, getting audiences on their feet and collaborating and recording with the likes of Brian Eno, Jon Hassell, Malcolm Braff, and even the Stones, on their *Steel Wheels* album.

Faso Denou (1993, Real World). Feel the percussive power of the two *balafons*, *bara* calabash, *doumdou'ba* tall drums and voluble *djembe*.

Kanou (2001, L'Empreinte Digitale). Features the enchanting voice of Fatoumata Dembele, the first female addition to the band.

Les Frères Coulibaly

The Coulibaly griot family are Bwaba, from northwest Burkina. Originally started by twins Lassina and Ousséni, the group now numbers eight and forms a standard percussion orchestra with *djembe*, *bara*, *tama* and *kenkeni* drums, *barafile* rattle, *balafon* and *kamele ngoni* harp-lute.

Séniwè (2000, Trace). Plenty of ferocious *djembe* and *dundun* action, *balafon* and tight call-and-response vocals, and even digital beats on a couple of tracks.

Various

Gang Rebel du Faso (2005, Vent d'Échange/Mosaic). Featuring thirteen Burkinabe groups, mostly playing in the reggae tradition with a political slant to many of the lyrics. Away from the ska-like beats, listen out for the excellent Soeurs Doga, playing a purely traditional style.

Haute Volta (Agence de Coopération Culturelle et Technique). Good compilation of Mossi, Fula, Bamana, Lobi and Gan music.

The Art of the Balafon (Arion). Various artists, with a sound similar to Farafina, featuring music from six ethnic groups including the Lobi, Gan and Dagara.

The Balafons of Bobo-Dioulasso – Sababougnouma (Playasound). Powerful *balafon* and *djembe* ensemble, featuring mainly Djola and Senoufo rhythms, and using the pentatonic, as opposed to the heptatonic, *balafon*.

Cinema

The government of Burkina Faso has long been active in promoting **cinema** in West Africa. The country nationalized movie theatres in 1979 (although less than a dozen are still operational around the country) and is internationally renowned for the FESPACO film festival. In its early days, the national film company helped finance mainly educational films, as well as producing *Le Sang de Parias* (1973) by **Mamadou Djim Kola**, the first national feature. Kola, who also made the award-winning *Étrangers*, died in 2004.

In 1981, a private businessman, Martial Ouédraogo, invested in **Cinafric** – a production company with 16mm and 35mm cameras. The only private film company of its kind in Africa, Cinafric has been criticized as "Hollywood on the Volta", yet despite its commercial intent, it has helped free local film-makers from dependence on their government, or on overseas help. Within a year, Cinafric produced its first feature, *Paweogo* (1981), and thus launched one of the country's most prolific film-makers, **Sanou Kollo**.

Burkina was given further publicity by **Gaston Kaboré**, who won a French César in 1985 for *Wend Kuuni* – a rural tale which demonstrates how traditional values can heal a modern African state. A prominent African cineaste (he is currently director of the Pan-African Federation of Film-makers – FEPACI), Kaboré went on to make several features, including *Zan Boko* (1988) about urbanization, and *Rabi* (1991), a gentle parable about tradition and the environment. *Buud Yam* (1996), a sequel to *Wend Kuuni*, won the grand prize at the 1997 FESPACO.

Idrissa Ouédraogo is probably Burkina's best known film-maker, with an enthusiastic international following for his gentle, concentrated work. *Yaaba* (1988), *Tilai* (1990) – Cannes Jury Prize, FESPACO Best Film, 1991 – and *Samba Traoré* (1992) are strongly rooted in the African rural experience. *Kini et Adams* (1997) was a Zimbabwe co-production – a cross-continental collaboration that is increasingly common. *La Colère des Dieux* (2003) concerns the bloody power struggles of a royal family while his latest, *Kato Kato* (2006), is a modern tale of a middle-class teacher's struggle against conflicting pressures.

Burkina's government continues to be supportive to film-making, and new film-makers continue to emerge. **Drissa Touré** was widely acclaimed for his first feature *Laada* (1991), while **Pierre Yaméogo**'s *Wendemi* (1992) was well received at the 1993 FESPACO, after which he went on to direct *Silmande* ("Whirlwind", 1998), *Moi et Mon Blanc* ("Me and My White Friend", 2002) – which was shortlisted at FESPACO 2003 – and *Delwende* ("Get Up and Walk", 2005).

The son of a griot, **Dani Kouyaté** wove together the traditional epic of Soundiata with the present-day education of a young boy in *Keita* ("The Heritage of the Griot", 1995), while *Sya, Le Rêve du Python* (2000) won the jury prize at FESPACO 2001. His latest film, *Ouaga Saga* (2004), is an urban comedy set in one of Ouaga's poorer neighbourhoods.

Women film-makers are also beginning to emerge. At FESPACO 2001, **Fanta Regina Nacro** won first prize for best short film with *Bintou*, exploring the survival of a downtrodden housewife against the odds – while her first feature, *La Nuit de la Verité* (2004), received a screenplay award at FESPACO 2005.

Books

There's next to nothing published in English on **Burkina** – and nothing very digestible in French either. A handful of locally published French-language novels are available in Burkina. For good general titles on West Africa, see p.35.

Lars Engberg-Pedersen *Endangering Development: Politics, Projects and Environment in Burkina Faso*. From a development perspective, the Danish author critically examines NGOs' development practice in Burkina.

Pierre Englebert *La Révolution Burkinabè*. Thorough look at the country's modern history by a political scientist.

Ben O. Nnaji *Blaise Compaoré: The Architect of the Burkina Faso Revolution*. Unashamedly propagandist offering, with some general information on the country.

Thomas Sankara *Thomas Sankara Speaks*. Collection of the revolutionary's speeches – worth dipping into to see where the revolution was supposed to be going.

Robin Sharp *Burkina Faso: New Life for the Sahel*. Published by Oxfam and showing the depth of the country's difficulties without being patronizing.

Malidoma Patrice Some *Of Water and the Spirit*. The autobiography of a Dagari man, born in southern Haute Volta in the late 1950s, who fell into the hands of Jesuit missionaries when he was four and didn't return to his roots until adulthood. Some's descriptions of his initiation and, to put it mildly, unusual experiences back in the Dagari community are recounted with a lucidity and persuasiveness that invite comparison with Carlos Castaneda – and inevitably risk the same criticism of exaggeration. Malidoma Some (Ⓦwww.malidoma.com) is now a cult speaker on the US men's-movement circuit.

Languages

French is the official language of Burkina, although it's estimated that only fifteen percent of the population actually speak it with any degree of fluency – that percentage is noticeably higher in the large towns. The most widely spoken African language is **More**, mother tongue of the Mossi and spoken by over half the population. Other widely spoken languages are **Pulaar**, spoken by the Fula herders of the north (see p.589), and **Dioula** (Dyula), which has become the major commercial lingua franca spanning most of the borders in this part of West Africa. The samples of **Gourounsi**, spoken in southern Burkina, come from "Kassem", the main dialect of Gourounsi, spoken by the Kassena. **Lobi** is restricted to a small area of the southwest on the Côte d'Ivoire border.

A little More

Greetings

Neyibeogo	Good morning (early)
Yibeoog soab yeaala	Response
Naaba	Further response (men)
Eyn	Further response (women)
Neywindaga	Good day
Windg soab yeaala	Response

Neywungo	Good evening
Yung soab	Response
Yaa laafi?/	How are you?
Laafi beeme?/	
Laafi bala?	
Laafi bala	Response
Wend na tasse	Goodbye
Wend na kodnin daare	See you later
Wend na kodbeogo	See you tomorrow
Wend na kodbeogo/Ammi	Response

Daily needs

Ysugri	Excuse me
Ykabre	Sorry
Barka	Thank you
Nye	Yes
Ayo	No
Wanwana?	How much?
Ligidi kabay	I have no money
Koom	Water

Days

Dunna	Today
Beoogo	Tomorrow
Zaame	Yesterday
Zaabre	This evening
Fene	Monday
Falato	Tuesday
Arba	Wednesday
Lamusa	Thursday
Arzuma	Friday
Sibri	Saturday
Hado	Sunday

Numbers

Aye	1
Ayiibu	2
Ataabo	3
Anaase	4
Anu	5
Ayoobe	6
Yopoe	7
Anii	8
Awe	9
Piiga	10
Koabga	100
Tusri	1000

Minimal Gourounsi

Greetings

Din le	General greeting/ Thank you
Tim paga	Good morning
Tim dadan	Good evening

Numbers

Kalo	1
Inle	2
Nto	3
Nna	4
Unu	5
Trodo	6
Tirpai	7
Nana	8
Nogo	9
Fuga	10
Finle	20
Finnu	50
Bi	100
Bi yennu	500
Moro	1000

Limited Lobi

Greetings

Me foaré	Hello
Monicho?	How are you?
Michor	Fine thanks
Ferehina foaré	Thank you

Food

ñyoñi	water
yolo	chicken
pala	egg yolk
nuni	meat
wologyo	maize
gyo/di	millet
puri	yam

Times

ni	today
kyo	tomorrow
gye ale	day after tomorrow
daoule	yesterday

Numbers

Biel	1
Yenyo	2
Yetter	3
Yena	4
Yamoi	5
Maado	6
Makonyo	7
Makotter	8
Nuor biri pero	9
Nuor	10
Kpuele	20
Kpalanyo nuor	50
Tama	100
Bulani	1000

Glossary

Américain General term for a missionary, regardless of nationality or religious affiliation. Early missionaries in the region were anglophone Protestants.

Brousse Common West African term for bush or countryside, but to the Mossi it means anywhere outside the Mossi country, especially outside the purlieu of Ouagadougou. Thus someone who has gone to study in Côte d'Ivoire or France is said to be *en brousse*.

Burkinabe (or Burkinabè). A person from Burkina Faso; there is no masculine or feminine form.

Cabaret A rural bar (especially in Lobi country).

CDR (Comités pour la Défense de la Révolution). First established by Sankara to implement government policy and organize local affairs on a regional level.

Ghanéenne A popular term for a prostitute, equally insulting to Ghanaian women and to barmaids (most of whom are Ghanaian). Many of the prostitutes in Ouaga, however, do indeed hail from Ghana.

Koure Mossi funeral ceremony.

Kwara Gourounsi chief's sacred insignia, equivalent of a staff of office.

Marabout Muslim holy man who may use his spiritual powers for divination.

Mogho Naba Also spelled Moro Naba; traditional leader of the Mossi people who resides in Ouagadougou. Mogho signifies the traditional cultural realm of Ouagadougou.

Naba King of a Mossi state, and also village chief.

Nassara Common appellation for white people and other foreigners (from "Nazarene").

Ouédraogo The most common surname in Burkina, it's derived from the More *ouefo* (horse) and *raogo* (male). It is the Mogho Naba's name and that of other important political and cultural leaders.

Zaka Round house in the countryside with *banco* walls and thatched conical roof. The plural is *zaksé*.

9.1

Central and eastern Burkina

Lying plumb in the centre of Burkina, **Ouagadougou** is an inevitable stop-off point for visitors to the country and a pleasant place to rest up for a few days before heading off to more isolated outposts. Though relatively small for a capital city, it offers a satisfying amount of commercial and cultural activity.

Main roads head from Ouaga to all major destinations. West of the capital, the route to **Bobo-Dioulasso** is lined with small Mossi towns and villages such as **Sabou**, famed for its sacred crocodile pond, while a branch road leads off to **Koudougou** – the nation's third-largest town and a centre of Burkina's textile industry. The eastern route to Niamey in Niger passes through the **Gourmantché country** and the important market town of **Fada-Ngourma**. Another busy junction along this route is **Koupéla**, where the highway to Dapaong in neighbouring Togo starts its southern course.

Ouagadougou

On the surface, **OUAGADOUGOU** – pronounced "Wagadougou", and routinely abbreviated to **Ouaga** – has little to offer. Capital of one of the world's poorest countries, it seems more like a shambling provincial town than the centrepiece of a nation. Yet despite its unpromising appearance, Ouaga is exceptionally animated. Over the last twenty years or so, drastic measures have been taken to try to improve the city's image: the ambitious, and ongoing, **Projet Zaca** (see box, p.742), for example, involves literally demolishing a large chunk of the city centre and building it again from scratch; and the swanky, modern **Ouaga 2000** district south of the centre is where you'll find the luxurious homes of politicians and businessmen.

Ouaga is the traditional capital of the **Mossi empire**, but all the country's major ethnic groups, religions and languages coexist here with remarkable harmony. A good number of international organizations, and the nation's largest university, are also based in Ouaga. Life moves at a surprisingly brisk pace, and as a visitor you'll find that contact with the people is as immediate as in any West African city.

Some history

Mossi oral literature traces the beginning of the **Mogho** or **Moro** (the Mossi empire: *Mogho* literally means "the world") to the thirteenth century and a chief named Gbewa or Nédéga who ruled over Pusiga in present-day Ghana. In the course of a battle, Gbewa's daughter, a horsewoman named **Yennenga**, was separated from the clan when her horse took fright and fled into the Bitou woods. She chanced upon the forest's one inhabitant, an elephant hunter named **Rialé** (a corruption of the More words *ri*, "to eat", and *yaré*, "anything", since bush-dwellers ate anything they found). The couple eventually returned to Gambaga and had a baby, which they named **Ouédraogo**, after Yennenga's steed – from *ouefo*, "horse", and *raogo*, "male".

But according to folk history, the territory of Pusiga became overpopulated and Ouédraogo set off with a company of his father's cavalry to conquer the northern territories. He established a kingdom at **Na Ten Kudugo** (Tenkodogo). Later,

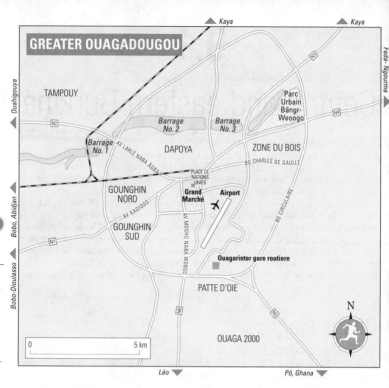

GREATER OUAGADOUGOU

Kaya

Kaya

TAMPOUY

Ouahigouya

Fada-Ngourma

Parc
Urbain
Bângr-
Weoogo

N4

Barrage
No. 2

Barrage
No. 3

N2

Barrage
No. 1

AV LARLÉ NABA AGBA

DAPOYA

ZONE DU BOIS

BD CHARLES DE GAULLE

PLACE DE
NATIONS
UNIES

Bobo, Abidjan

GOUNGHIN
NORD

Grand
Marché

Airport

AV KADIOGO

BD CIRCULAIRE

N1

GOUNGHIN
SUD

AV MOGHO NABA WOBGO

Ouagarinter gare routiere

Bobo-Dioulasso

PATTE D'OIE

N5

OUAGA 2000

0   5 km

N

Léo

Pô, Ghana

Ouédraogo's grandson **Oubri** sought to conquer new territories and founded the statelet of **Oubritenga**, later known as Wogodogo. A grandson of Oubri broke off to form another small state, **Yatenga**, with Ouahigouya as its capital.

The autonomous Mossi states or kingdoms remained remarkably stable for more than four centuries, but by the end of the nineteenth century, the French, Germans and British were pressing in on the region. In 1898, the French occupied Wogodogo (which they spelled Ouagadougou), and within a short time subjugated the surrounding kingdoms, which they integrated into their colony of **Haut-Sénégal Niger**. Today, there are still four Mossi kings, whose authority is applied in parallel with that of the Burkinabe state in the kingdoms over which they hold sway.

Arrival, orientation, information

The **international airport** is only a couple of kilometres southeast of the central commercial district. Collecting your baggage and going through **customs and immigration** is normally an untraumatic experience, but you'll be asked your place of residence; if you don't have a reservation, just put the *RAN Hôtel* or any other that comes to mind. There's a small **bureau de change** at the airport which changes euros, dollars and pounds at reasonable rates (Mon–Sat 8am–12.30 & 3.30pm until the last flight arrives).

The only regular domestic flights are the 50-minute **flights to Bobo-Dioulasso** on Air Burkina (Tues & Fri; 50min; CFA42,500; ☎50.49.23.45 ⊛www.air-burkina.com). For more airline information, see "Listings", p.745.

To **get into town from the airport**, it's a twenty-minute walk to the market; turn left out of the terminal building and right up Avenue Yennenga. A quick zip up

Avenue Yennenga in a shared taxi costs CFA200 (CFA1000 if you hire the vehicle as a *déplacement*).

Arriving **by train** is straightforward – the **station** is just a stone's throw from Avenue de la Nation and the *zone commerciale* in the heart of the city. There are several hotels within walking distance of the station, though taxis aren't expensive

Road transport either stops at Ouagarinter or at the bus company's own city terminal (see box). Some are more centrally located than others – which can be a factor to consider when choosing which company to use.

The **Office National du Tourisme Burkinabe** (ONTB) is on Avenue Sangoulé Lamizana (Mon–Fri 7am–12.30pm & 3–5.30pm; ☏50.31.19.59 ⓦwww.ontb.bf). They have a few dated brochures, but are really not that helpful as a resource for visitors.

Orientation and city transport

Ouagadougou spreads across a considerable area, though the centre is fairly compact. The city is officially divided into thirty *secteurs* (like the *arrondissements* of Paris), though you're likely to spend time only in the few at the centre.

All major roads in Ouaga seem to start from the **Place des Nations Unies**, with its ironwork globe sculpture. To the east, **Avenue de l'Indépendance** leads through the **administrative quarter** down to the *style-coloniale* former **Palais Présidentiel**. **Avenue Sankara Thomas Isidore** leads off to the northeast, becoming **Avenue Kumda Yôore** as it passes the **hospital** and continues on towards the **Zone du Bois** (formerly the Bois de Boulogne). This road then joins the main route to Niamey. West of the place des Nations Unies, Avenue de la Nation passes through the **zone commerciale** and continues to the semi-modern **Maison du Peuple** and the expansive **Place de la Nation** where political gatherings take place. To the south, **Avenue Kwame Nkrumah** provides a foretaste of what Ouaga's new skyline (see box, p.742) might look like: the street is lined with some of the city's grandest buildings adorned with neon signs, and is an exciting place after dark. Another main artery, **Avenue Yennenga**, runs parallel to Kwame Nkrumah past the **Grande Mosquée** and **central market** before ending near the **airport**.

The town also has distinctive *quartiers* within each *secteur*, each with its own flavour. North of the train station, **Cité An III** is the traditional Muslim neighbourhood, home to Ouaga's grand imam and its first mosque. Further north, **Niogsin** is a residential area known for its metalworkers, many of whom still work here in small *ateliers*. East of here, the **Paspanga** *secteur* reputedly has the city's best *dolotières* (women who make *dolo* or millet beer) and bars and small *cabarets* are common. In the centre, Avenue Yennenga passes through **Tiendpalogo** and **Peuloghin** – the latter is a Fula neighbourhood with Muslim-style homes and Koranic schools. **Zangouetin**, at the eastern end of Avenue Houari Boumédienne, is a Hausa neighbourhood with a similar feel to Peuloghin.

City transport

The city centre is compact enough to walk around. Alternatively, shared **taxis** – usually battered green Mercedes saloons or Renault 4Ls – can be flagged down on the street. If the other passengers on board are headed the same way, the driver will pick you up. The normal daytime fare is CFA200 to anywhere along the taxi's route. Prices at night are more flexible: CFA300–500 depending on the number of customers around at the time. Green Sotraco **buses** also serve fixed routes throughout the city for a flat fare of CFA150. However, these routes are difficult to decipher and it's usually simpler to take a shared taxi. One useful Sotraco bus is the #1, which travels along Boulevard Charles de Gaulle and passes the national museum and Sankara's grave before terminating at the SIAO site.

Bus companies – depots and domestic and West African routes

For **arrivals by road**, the main *gare routière*, commonly known as **Ouagarinter** (or Patte d'Oie), is some 4km south of the city centre on the Route de Pô. You'll have no problem finding a shared taxi (CFA200) to take you into the centre. Most **long-distance buses** arrive at their various company terminals dotted around the city (see map, p.732).

When planning to **leave Ouagadougou**, it's hard to know which companies are the most reputable, but if you have any choice with your destination, then STMB is rated highly, and TCV also has a solid reputation for reliability and comfort.

KZA av Kadiogo ☎70.17.52.66. Koudougou (7 buses daily; CFA2000).

Rakieta ☎50.31.40.56, to Pô, from rue Damiba Emile, one block south of the cemetery (4 buses daily; CFA2000); to Fada N'Gourma from rue du Commerce in the city centre (4 daily; CFA3000).

Rayi's rue Mogho Naba Koom I ☎76.61.83.64. Koudougou (every 2 hours from 6am–6pm; CFA2000).

SKV av du Mogho, across from the Théâtre Populaire in Bilbalogho Secteur ☎50.39.81.45. Lomé (CFA16,000), Cotonou (CFA15,000), Bamako (CFA16,000), Kumasi (CFA13,000).

SOGEBAF av Kadiogo, at bd Naaba Zombre ☎50.34.42.55. Bobo-Dioulasso (8 buses daily; CFA5000), Banfora (8 daily; CFA6000), Ouahigouya (6 daily; CFA3000), Sinkassé (2 daily; CFA5000). From a separate station between av de la Liberté and rue Kiendrebeogo Nobila Didier to Dori (2 daily; CFA4000), Gorom-Gorom (2 weekly departing Wed & Sun; CFA6000).

STAF rue Mogho Naba Koom I ☎50.30.19.21. Ouahigouya (5 buses daily; CFA2500), Djibo (1 daily; CFA4000).

STBF av Larlé Naba Âgba ☎76.54.12.93. Bobo (1 bus daily; CFA6000), Bamako (1 daily; CFA15,000), Mopti (2 daily; CFA15,000), Abidjan (1 daily; CFA35,000).

STC Ouagarinter *gare routière* ☎76.64.44.42 (must book in advance). Accra (8.30am Mon, Wed & Fri; CFA16,000) via Bolgatanga, Tamale and Kumasi (all three CFA13,000).

STKF rue de la Femme, across from *Auberge Rose des Sables* ☎50.33.57.50. Kumasi (daily except Sat; CFA10,000).

Accommodation

Ouagadougou has a wide range of **places to stay**, from dormitories to four-star hotels. Beware, however, of arriving in town without a reservation during the biennial FESPACO film festival (Feb 2009, Feb 2011, Feb 2013; see p.717), as everywhere will be full. Accommodation options in the city centre are marked on the Central Ouaga map, p.741; others are marked on the map, pp.736–737.

Budget

City centre

Delwendé rue Patrice Lumumba, half a block west of the Grande Marché ☎50.30.87.57 ⓔhoteldelwende@yahoo.fr. Decent s/c rooms, some a/c – ask for one facing the street with a balcony from where you can take in the busy life around the market. The balcony restaurant is a popular place for salads and grilled meat. ❸

Fondation Charles Dufour rue du Grand Marché ☎50 30.38.89. Two rooms (non-s/c) and a fourteen-bed dorm, plus the use of a communal kitchen. An appealing small courtyard makes for a relaxed atmosphere, and profits go to a good cause. Dorm beds CFA3000; rooms ❷.

Les Lauriers in the gardens of the Catholic cathedral ☎50.30.64.90 ⓕ50.31.65.90. Very popular with tourists, especially women, seeking

STMB between rue Kiendrebeogo Nobila Didier and rue Tapsoba Tenga Dominique ☏50.31.13.63. Bobo (8 buses daily, of which 2 a/c; CFA5000–6000), Ouahigouya (3 daily; CFA3000), Dori (2 daily; CFA4000), Pô (4 daily; CFA2000), Fada (5 daily; CFA3000).

TCV av de la Grande Mosquée ☏50.39.87.77. Bobo (5 daily; CFA6000), Bamako (1 daily; CFA15,000), Lagos (1 weekly, Sun; CFA32,500) via Cotonou (CFA17,500).

TSR av Kadiogo ☏50.34.25.24. Léo (4 buses daily; CFA2500), Diébougou (2 daily; CFA4000), Gaoua (2 daily; CFA6000), Dori (1 daily; CFA4000).

Official taxi-brousse stations

Taxis from the **Ouagarinter gare routière** leave for Niamey (CFA10,000) and towns in Ghana such as Bolgatanga (CFA4000) and Kumasi (CFA12,000). You can also get to eastern destinations like Fada and Niamey from the **Gare de l'Est**, about 6km northeast of the centre. Note that the bus companies normally stop at either of these two stations after leaving their respective depots, although the buses will likely be full and you may not get a seat. The **Tampouy gare secondaire** on Avenue Larlé Naba Âgba, just north of the railway tracks, has taxis to Bobo and Ouahigouya.

Unofficial taxi-brousse stations

There are also several **unofficial stations** in town, which are subject to closure by the police (not that the vehicles themselves are in any way illegal). There's a fairly well established station at the **Total station** near the Zaka Cultural Centre, southwest of place des Nations Unies. Taxis collect fares here for Lomé (CFA12,500), Cotonou (CFA17,500), Niamey (CFA11,000) and to the eastern towns on the road to Fada (CFA3500).

If you're heading southwest – to Bobo, Diébougou, Gaoua and Léo – it's worth checking the station on **Avenue Kadiogo**, at Avenue du Conseil de l'Entente (across from the Shell station).

Trains

The Ivoirian-run company Sitarail (☏50.31.74.74) runs trains to **Abidjan** (CFA35,000) via Koudougou, Bobo and Banfora. Services depart 7.30am Tues, Thurs & Sat, arriving (very approximately) in Bobo at 4pm (2nd class CFA5000) and Banfora at 6.30pm (2nd class CFA8000), returning to Burkina from Abidjan on Wednesday, Friday & Sunday.

refuge from the hassles of town (prospective male guests are sometimes turned away), this place offers spotless twin rooms with fans, starched sheets, mosquito nets and showers, plus excellent-value breakfasts and dinners. Reserve ahead. ❷

Yennenga av Yennenga ☏50.30.73.37. Long-standing hotel next to the Grande Mosquée (the early-morning *adhan* is quite audible), whose range of rooms with a/c or fan has long been good value. ❷

🏃 Zaaka av Yennenga, two blocks south of the Grande Mosquée ☏50.39.87.32. One of the best budget options, this newer version of sister hotel *Yennenga* offers a central location and comfortable beds in bright rooms, all with shower and fans and some with a/c. ❷

Out of the centre

Auberge Rose des Sables rue de la Femme, Saint Leon ☏50.31.30.14 @ la.rose.des.sables@fasonet .bf. Very clean rooms, with fan or a/c, next to a leafy garden bar and restaurant. Rates are negotiable. ❸

L'Entente Niogsin one block east of av de l'Armée ☏50.30.27.75. Set in an interesting neighbourhood of bronze-workers, with clean – if slightly shabby – s/c rooms with fan (a/c also available, but check first that it's working). ❷

Oubri av de la Mosquée, near the airport ☏50.30.64.83. Clean, but cramped and overpriced rooms, some with fan and shared bathroom, others s/c and a/c with TV. Also a nice airy terrace. ❷

🏃 Pavillon Vert av de la Liberté ☏50.31.06.11 @ pavillonvert@liptinfor.bf. Popular place with a wonderful garden and a range of options, from non-s/c rooms to attractive s/c a/c

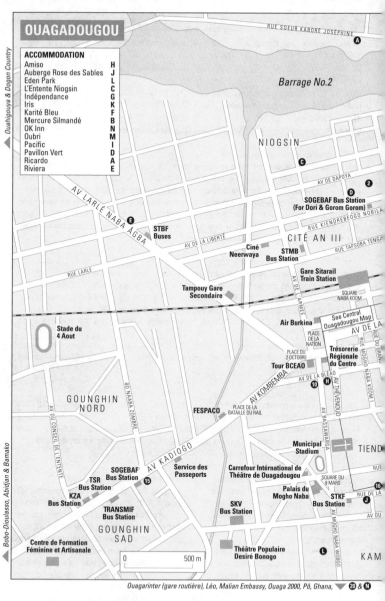

OUAGADOUGOU

ACCOMMODATION

Amiso	H
Auberge Rose des Sables	J
Eden Park	L
L'Entente Niogsin	C
Indépendance	G
Iris	K
Karité Bleu	F
Mercure Silmandé	B
OK Inn	N
Oubri	M
Pacific	I
Pavillon Vert	D
Ricardo	A
Riviera	E

RUE SOEUR KABORÉ JOSÉPHINE Ⓐ

Barrage No.2

NIOGSIN Ⓒ

AV DE DAPOYA ❷

Ⓓ

SOGEBAF Bus Station
(For Dori & Gorom Gorom)

RUE KIENDREBEOGO NOBILA

CITÉ AN III

RUE TAPSOBA TENGA

AV LARLÉ NABA ÂGBA Ⓔ

STBF Buses

AV DE LA LIBERTÉ

Ciné Neerwaya

STMB Bus Station

RUE LARLE

Gare Sitarail Train Station

SQUARE NABA KOOM

Tampouy Gare Secondaire

See Central Ouagadougou Map

Air Burkina

AV DE LA

Stade du 4 Aout

PLACE DE LA NATION

PLACE DU 2 OCTOBRE

Trésorerie Régionale du Centre

Tour BCEAO

AV DE LA BLÉAO ❿ Ⓗ

GOUNGHIN NORD

FESPACO

PLACE DE LA BATAILLE DU RAIL

Municipal Stadium

TIEND

SOGEBAF Bus Station

TSR Bus Station

KZA Bus Station

Service des Passeports ❶❺

Carrefour Intérnational de Théâtre de Ouagadougou

SQUARE DU 8 MARS

Palais du Mogho Naba

STKF Bus Station ❶❻ Ⓙ

TRANSMIF Bus Station

GOUNGHIN SAD

SKV Bus Station

AV DU

Centre de Formation Féminine et Artisanale

Théâtre Populaire Desiré Bonogo Ⓛ

KAM

0   500 m

Ouagarinter (gare routière), Léo, Malian Embassy, Ouaga 2000, Pô, Ghana, ▼ ❷⓿ & Ⓝ

---

apartments. The congenial atmosphere and setting make up for the distance from the centre. ❷

Riviera av Larlé Naba Âgba, near the STBF bus station ☏50.30.65.59, Ⓕ50.30.66.81. Attractive round huts (good-value singles with fan or a/c; pricier doubles only with a/c), a pleasant courtyard and nice management. Basic meals available. ❷–❹

Mid-range and expensive

City centre

Belle Vue rue du Commerce, at av Kwame Nkrumah ☏50.31.10.32 Ⓕ50.30.00.37 @hbv.hotel-belle-vue2000@caramail.com. Lively and centrally located hotel with slightly dated s/c,

Ouahigouya & Dogon Country

Bobo-Dioulasso, Abidjan & Bamako

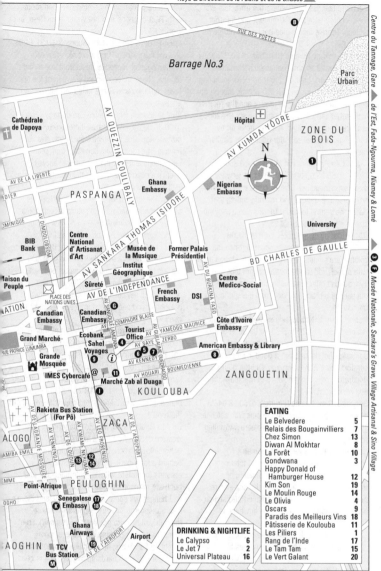

Kaya & Direction de la Faune et de la Chasse ▲

RUE DES POÈTES

Barrage No.3

Parc Urbain

Cathédrale de Dapoya

Hôpital

ZONE DU BOIS

AV QUEZZIN COULIBALY

AV KUMDA YÓORE

N

AV DE LA LIBERTÉ

Ghana Embassy

Nigerian Embassy

PASPANGA

Centre National d'Artisanat d'Art

Musée de la Musique

Former Palais Présidentiel

University

BIB Bank

AV SANKARA THOMAS ISIDORE

Institut Géographique

BD CHARLES DE GAULLE

Maison du Peuple

Sûreté

AV DE L'INDEPENDANCE

French Embassy

DSI

Centre Medico-Social

Canadian Embassy

PLACE DES NATIONS UNIES

AV SANKARA LAMIZANA

G

AV COMPAORÉ BLAISE

Canadian Embassy

Ecobank

Tourist Office

AV YAMEOGO MAURICE

Côte d'Ivoire Embassy

Grand Marché

Sahel Voyages

AV SAYE ZERBO

American Embassy & Library

Grande Mosquée

AV KENNEDY

8

IMES Cybercafé

AV HOUARI BOUMEDIENNE

ZANGOUETIN

Marché Zab al Duaga

KOULOUBA

Rakieta Bus Station (For Pô)

ZACA

AV DE L'AÉROPORT

EATING

Le Belvedere	5
Relais des Bougainvilliers	7
Chez Simon	13
Diwan Al Mokhtar	8
La Forêt	10
Gondwana	3
Happy Donald of Hamburger House	12
Kim Son	19
Le Moulin Rouge	14
Le Olivia	4
Oscars	9
Paradis des Meilleurs Vins	18
Pâtisserie de Koulouba	11
Les Piliers	1
Rang de l'Inde	17
Le Tam Tam	15
Le Vert Galant	20

ALOGO

AMIBA EMILE

AV YENNENGA

AV DE LOUDUN

AV KWAME NKRUMAH

AV LÉO FROBENIUS

Point-Afrique

PEULOGHIN

Senegalese Embassy

Ghana Airways

Airport

TCV Bus Station

AOGHIN

DRINKING & NIGHTLIFE

Le Calypso	6
Le Jet 7	2
Universal Plateau	16

a/c rooms with TV. Also has a rooftop terrace from where you can look over central Ouaga. ⑤

Central av de Lyon ☎50.30.89.24 ⓔh.central @fasonet.bf. Great location in the heart of the town and a range of comfortable a/c rooms, though some are on the scruffy side. The popular bar-restaurant (great pizzas and cocktails) is always busy. ⑥

Continental av de Loudun ☎50.30.86.36 ⓔhotelcontinental1@yahoo.fr. The rooms upstairs are dingy and bare, although many have balconies overlooking the bustling commercial centre. Also has a popular restaurant. ④

Pacific av Léo Frobenius ☎50.31.32.42 ⓦwww.pacific-hotel.bf. Friendly and modern business hotel where the attractive s/c rooms come with a/c, TV, minibar and Internet access. There's also a nice pool area with palm trees. ⑦

Palm Beach av Kwame Nkrumah ☎ 50.31.09.91 or 50.31.68.29 Ⓔ hotel.palmbeach@liptinfor .bf. Rooms here have all the mod-cons, including a/c, satellite TV, fridge and IDD phone, though the overall atmosphere's a bit dreary and the rooms look rather tatty. The pool (non-guests CFA2000) is murky and uninviting. A sister hotel on av Yennenga, also called *Palm Beach*, has similar facilities. ⑦

🏃 **Les Palmiers** rue Mogho Naba Koom I ☎ 50.33.33.30 Ⓕ 50.39.91.91 ⓦ www .hotellespalmiers.net. Stylish rooms with a/c and hot water in a tranquil and relaxing setting that belies the central location. There's also a pool the size of a large bathtub. ⑥

RAN Hôtel av de la Nation ☎ 50.30.61.06 Ⓕ 50.30.28.32 Ⓔ hotran@fasonet.bf. Once the colonial era's finest, this renovated old station hotel with a pool, and rooms featuring bath tubs and TVs, doesn't offer great value these days, even if the service remains excellent and the staff are very friendly. ⑦

Relax av de la Nation, across from Maison du Peuple ☎ 50.31.32.31 Ⓕ 50.30.89.08 ⓦ www .groupe-soyaf.com. One of the better-value upmarket hotels, offering a good level of comfort, even if the rooms are a little dourly decorated, plus a nightclub, slot machines, bar and restaurant. ⑦

Soritel 370 av Kwame Nkrumah ☎ 50.33.04.78 Ⓔ soritel@liptinfor.bf. Modern rooms with satellite TV, a/c and hot water, plus a mediocre swimming pool. ⑧

Splendid 1108 av Kwame Nkrumah ☎ 50.31.24.54 ⓦ www.le-splendidhotel.com. The best located of Ouaga's sprinkling of four-stars, right in the heart of the bar-and-restaurant strip, offering well-equipped and stylish accommodation. The pool area, however, is a little austere. ⑧

🏃 **Yibi** rue Dr Koné Moussa ☎ 50.30.73.23 Ⓔ yibi.hotel@fasonet.bf. Across the road from the *Palm Beach*, this large yet intimate hotel has immaculate rooms (though the decor's dated) and a pretty pool in a lovely courtyard setting. Avoid the noisy rooms at the front. ⑥

Out of the centre

Amiso 198 av Thevenoud ☎ 50.30.86.74 Ⓕ 50.30.86.78 Ⓔ amiso@fasonet.bf.

Ultra-smart hotel, with comfortable tiled rooms with TV, a/c, phone and hot water – spotless, but sterile. ⑦

Eden Park av Mogho Naba Wobgo ☎ 50.31.14.91 ⓦ www.edenpark.bf. Upmarket high-rise with swimming pool, nightclub, restaurant and a roof terrace. There are some good views from the upper floors, but the rooms have dated furnishings and are overpriced. ⑧

Indépendance av Sangoulé Lamizana ☎ 50.30.60.63 ⓦ www.azalaihotels.com /azalai_indp. One of Ouaga's top hotels and very popular. The rooms have benefited from recent renovations and now feature Internet access. There's a popular bar next to the excellent pool, as well as tennis courts. ⑦

Iris av Yennenga ☎ 50.33.00.53. Smartish and comfortable a/c rooms with spacious bathrooms – most with balconies. ⑤

🏃 **Karité Bleu** 214 bd de l'Onatel, off bd Charles de Gaulle, Zone du Bois ☎ 50.36.90.46 Ⓔ karite.bleu@yahoo.fr. Stylish s/c, a/c rooms decorated with masks and batiks, all with TV and mosquito nets. The inclusion of breakfast, the quiet garden in a residential neighbourhood and free Internet access make this good value. ⑤

Mercure Silmandé 3km northeast of the centre, near the reservoir ☎ 50.35.60.05 Ⓔ H1325@accor.com. One of the few high-rises in town, the *Silmandé* is Ouaga's luxury base, with total comfort and lots of facilities – tennis courts, pool, Wi-Fi – at prices to match. Great views and photo opportunities from the roof. ⑧

OK Inn Route de Pô, next to Ouagarinter *gare routière* ☎ 50.37.00.20 Ⓕ 50.37.00.23 Ⓔ hotelok-inn@cenatrin.bf. Inauspicious setting behind a lorry park, although the spacious grounds (complete with 12-hole mini-golf and pool) are relaxing enough. The attractive rooms and bungalows come with a/c and TV, and there's free transport to the city centre and airport (though you have to get back by yourself). Free camping/vehicle parking, with use of pool, toilets and showers, on condition you eat one meal per day – no hardship, as the food is good. Otherwise ⑥.

🏃 **Ricardo** 3km north of the city centre ☎ 50.30.70.72 ⓦ ricardotel.ifrance .com/ricardotel. A bit out on a limb, but the tastefully decorated s/c rooms, friendly reception and waterfront setting are worth the effort of getting here. Good restaurant and pool, and a disco with pricey drinks. ⑥

The City

Ouaga has few sights, and in this period of reconstruction (see box, p.742) much of the city centre is a bit of a wasteland. The city's two modest **museums** won't take up much of your time, but the shopping possibilities at numerous **crafts markets** are endless. A satisfying way to get to know Ouaga is to settle at a *café terrasse* (or make a habit of going for breakfast at one of the city's excellent *pâtisseries* – see p.742) and simply observe life as it passes by your table. Once you become known you'll find it easy to make contact with other *habitués*, who always have time for a chat.

Museums

A group of yellow buildings occupying a desolate compound 3.5km along Boulevard Charles de Gaulle house Ouaga's disappointing **Musée Nationale** (Tues–Sat 7am–noon & 3–5.30pm; CFA1000; ⓣ50.39.19.34). The exhibits are confined to just two of the buildings and change every three to six months. One building showcases the lifestyle, customs and traditions of a particular Burkinabe tribe (which also changes sporadically), giving a rather haphazard tribal-society resumé through clothes, musical instruments, clay pots and the like, and touching on birth and death rituals, initiation rites and marriage ceremonies. The other building contains a much more interesting collection of **masks** showing different regional styles: abstract and geometric in the north; exaggerated animal shapes in the Senoufo country; cylindrical helmets used by the Mossi; and horizontally shaped *masques papillon* ("butterfly masks") common among the Bobo-Bwa. The macabre group of antelope-, hyena- and monkey-masks hang eerily against a backdrop of whitewashed walls, infusing the museum with some much-needed atmosphere. Before leaving, check out the gift shop, which seems to have a better selection of collectibles than the museum itself. Sotraco bus #1 stops in front of the museum.

Ouaga's other main museum, the **Musée de la Musique**, is back in the centre on Avenue Sankara Thomas Isidore (Tues–Sat 9am–12.30pm & 3–6pm; CFA1000, including guided tour in French; ⓣ50.32.40.60 ⓦwww.museedelamusique.gov.bf), and will appeal if you have more than a passing interest in African instruments. Exhaustive descriptions (in French) of several categories of instrument – membranophone, aerophone, idiophone, chordophone – explain the history, workings and traditional uses of the *balafon*, *kora* and plenty of less familiar instruments. The highlight for groups of visiting school children is the music room, where they get a chance to bang on drums and xylophones while singing and dancing – an amusing spectacle.

The small **natural history museum** in the grounds of the Parc Urbain Bãngr-Weoogo (see p.740/below; CFA200) in Zone du Bois contains a few stuffed animals and is only worth a brief glance when visiting the park.

Sankara's grave

After Sankara's assassination (see p.723), his body was relegated to an **unmarked grave** outside the centre. Martyrdom made the leader an international symbol of hope, and people from throughout Africa still make the pilgrimage to his burial site. The route to the grave (which is also the route of Sotraco bus #1) follows much the same path the body took – from the former presidential palace, head east along Boulevard Charles de Gaulle for 3.5km, turn right at the Musée Nationale and head straight on along Boulevard de la Jeunesse until you reach the Maison de la Femme. Continue on for another 200m and turn right at rue 29.150, following the path for 300m into the rubbish-strewn cemetery. To your left you'll see a row of whitewashed tombs, bearing only the name and rank of those killed in the 1987 coup – among them, Thomas Sankara. Despite the site's isolation, it's not uncommon to find mourners paying their respects, or leaving scribbled notes on the grave.

The Nabayius Gou

Ouagadougou's answer to Buckingham Palace's Changing of the Guard, the **Nabayius Gou** is a re-enactment, every Friday at 7am by the western side of the Mogho Naba's palace, of events that took place in the early eighteenth century, in the reign of Ouarga, the twentieth **Mogho Naba**. During this period, the kingdom's frontiers were under threat by raids from Yako. The Mogho Naba's favourite wife had obtained his permission to visit her family, but she hadn't returned on the agreed date. Heartbroken, he prepared to set out and find her, but his courtiers, fearing war, begged him to stay. With a heavy heart, the king agreed that his duty to his subjects came before personal concerns and, dismounting from his horse, he returned to his palace.

The Nabayius Gou reaffirms the Mogho Naba's commitment to his people. The present-day Mogho Naba comes out of his palace, dressed in red for war. His courtiers surround him, begging him to stay, and eventually he heeds their pleas and returns to the palace, to re-emerge in white. This rather solemn affair isn't a spectacle put on for tourists, and needs to be approached with some respect. Nonetheless, it's a fascinating ceremony, for which it's well worth getting up early. The taking of photographs is not allowed and the palace itself is not open to the public.

Parks

The **Parc Urbain Bãngr-Weoogo** in Zone du Bois (daily 6am–6pm; CFA100) offers plenty of wooded acres for pleasant strolling, plus a zoo and small museum (see p.739/above). The park, whose name is a More word meaning "where knowledge is acquired", has numerous well-maintained tracks and shady benches, and is sprawling enough to really escape the city's dust and fumes. The main entrance is along the road to Fada-Ngourma, about 800m east of the bridge leading to the *Mercure Silmandé* hotel.

The Grand Marché and crafts markets

Sankara razed the old market in 1985, and its replacement, the **Nouveau Grand Marché "Rood Woko"**, was the most modern marketplace in West Africa until it was gutted by fire in May 2003. Much to the consternation of city traders, it's still not clear what the plans for its future are. The hulking structure continues to be a focal point in the heart of the city, but all trading activity these days takes place in the streets surrounding it. This has turned central Ouaga into one large marketplace, with goods and produce sold on virtually every street corner. Just to the east of the centre, between avenues de l'UEMOA and Sangoulé Lamizana, **Marché Zabré Daaga** is a scaled-down version of the Grand Marché – a few stalls grouped together selling **fruit and vegetables**, household items, clothes and mobile phones.

A good place to start shopping for **crafts** is at the state-operated **Centre National d'Artisinat d'Art**, 3 av Dimdolobsom, near the main BIB Bank on the north side of the city centre (Mon–Fri 8am–noon & 3–6pm, Sat 9–noon & 3–6pm). The quality of the bronze castings, carvings and weavings is quite good, and prices are fixed, while Burkinabe artists have arguably mastered the exotic **batik** form better than any others in West Africa, mixing beautiful colours with striking village scenes. Come to get an idea of how much items should be before heading off to bargain at the **Vitrine du Bronze**, whose operators sell from a specially constructed centre on Avenue de la Nation, opposite the French Cultural Centre. Despite signs to the contrary, they don't deal in antiques, but do offer one of the widest selection of **bronzes** in town in addition to other crafts. **Masks**, imported from Côte d'Ivoire and Mali, may be treated in workshops in Laglin or Dapoya to give them an ancient look, which is often aesthetically effective if nothing else. Other wooden objects include **Senoufo chairs** and **Dogon carvings**. You'll also find **jewellery** – desert crosses and terracotta beads from Niger for example, and the ubiquitous old glass trade beads.

On the eastern outskirts of town next to the SIAO site, some 5km from the centre, the **Village Artisanal** is open daily and has a wide selection of crafts on sale in a hassle-free atmosphere. The boutique at the front offers a taste of the quality, at fixed, but very high, prices – far more interesting are the craftsmen working in their shops in the main part of the building. You can get here on Sotraco bus #1, which terminates at SIAO.

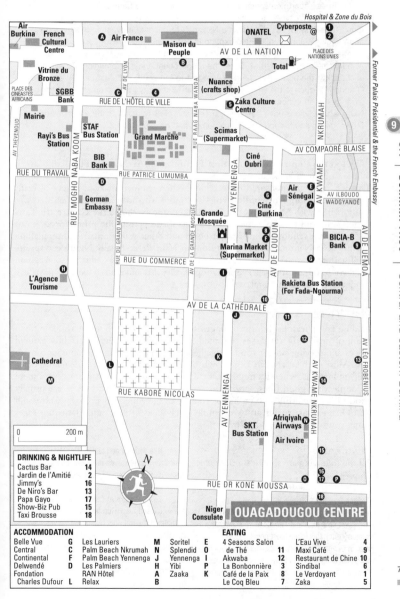

Hospital & Zone du Bois

Former Palais Présidentiel & the French Embassy

DRINKING & NIGHTLIFE

Cactus Bar	14
Jardin de l'Amitié	2
Jimmy's	16
De Niro's Bar	13
Papa Gayo	17
Show-Biz Pub	15
Taxi Brousse	18

OUAGADOUGOU CENTRE

ACCOMMODATION								**EATING**			
Belle Vue	**G**	Les Lauriers	**M**	Soritel	**E**	4 Seasons Salon		L'Eau Vive	**4**
Central	**C**	Palm Beach Nkrumah	**N**	Splendid	**O**	de Thé	11	Maxi Café	**9**
Continental	**F**	Palm Beach Yennenga	**J**	Yennenga	**I**	Akwaba	12	Restaurant de Chine	10
Delwendé	**D**	Les Palmiers	**H**	Yibi	**P**	La Bonbonnière	3	Sindibal	**6**
Fondation		RAN Hôtel	**A**	Zaaka	**K**	Café de la Paix	8	Le Verdoyant	**1**
Charles Dufour	**L**	Relax	**B**			Le Coq Bleu	7	Zaka	**5**

Projet Zaca

The idea of giving Ouaga's centre a complete facelift first cropped up in 1985, when town planners decided that the modern architectural style used to build the new *grand marché* (see p.740) should be accompanied by an equally attractive **zone commerciale** surrounding it. At the same time, posh new three-storey buildings, boutiques and high-rise apartments were constructed along the southern part of Avenue Kwame Nkrumah to give visitors arriving at the nearby airport a good first impression. It didn't take long for Avenue Kwame Nkrumah to become a dynamic business district, encouraging planners in 1990 to expand the improvements intended for the *zone commerciale* around the market to a larger area called the Zone d'Activités Commerciales et Administratives, or **Projet Zaca**, the rough boundary lines of which are Avenue de la Nation to the north, Avenue de l'Aéroport to the south and east, and Avenue de la Grande Mosquée to the west. Projet Zaca will take many years to complete, and so far work has been concentrated in the area around the southern part of Avenue Kwame Nkrumah. Buildings have been demolished and plots remain vacant until investors are found, giving south-central Ouaga a surreal and desolate look.

Try, too, the **Centre de Formation Féminine et Artisanale** at the exit of town off the Bobo road in Gounghin Sud Secteur (Mon–Fri 7.30am–12.30pm & 3–6pm). This is a religious-sponsored organization, where women make a variety of crafts such as Tuareg-inspired **woollen rugs** and more workaday tablecloths and napkins embroidered with African motifs. For **leather goods**, there's the **Centre du Tannage**, 4km from the city centre on the Fada road opposite the prison; or look out for the Tuareg vendors selling leather boxes and other wares, usually roaming along Avenue de la Nation, particularly in front of *Hôtel Relax*. Finally, **Nuance**, opposite the Total station on Avenue Yennenga, just north of the Zaka Cultural Centre, is an excellent boutique and gallery selling top-quality arts and crafts, especially jewellery, handbags and batiks, in a relaxed atmosphere.

Eating

Finding good, reasonably priced **places to eat** is no problem in Ouaga. The town is full of small **café terrasses** separated from the dusty streets by brightly painted fences and serving similar food – spaghetti, rice and meat sauce, couscous, potato stew. Most of them also do large bowls of home-made **yoghurt** – delicious, especially at breakfast when it's freshly made. The more upmarket restaurants – and there are some very good ones, serving a range of international cuisines – are usually good value; you'll find several in the vicinity of the American Embassy. And you'll find Ouaga's **pâtisseries** are wonderfully lively places to sit eating fattening cakes while you watch the world go by.

City centre

All the following are shown on the map on p.741.

Budget

La Bonbonnière av de la Nation. Along with the excellent *Pâtisserie de Koulouba* (see opposite), this is the most popular pastry shop in Ouaga. The flakey croissants and delicious meat pies and cakes just have the edge over the *Koulouba*'s, although the a/c dining area is smaller and slightly less appealing.

Café de la Paix av de Loudun. The *Hôtel Continental* restaurant serves mostly African food, with baked chicken a speciality. There's also a nice verandah.

Les Lauriers At *Les Lauriers* hostel (closed Sun). Run by the sisters of the Catholic cathedral, this restaurant serves daily set meals of filling, home-style food with soup, veg, meat and dessert (CFA1800; servings at noon and 7pm). Book ninety minutes in advance and turn up punctually. A great place to meet fellow travellers.

Maxi Café av de l'UEMOA. Buy *brochettes* from street vendors next to this informal café and eat them with some *frites*, rice or *attieke*.

Sindibal av de Loudun. The dining area is a little cramped, but this is a great spot for snacks like burgers, *chawarmas* and other Middle Eastern fast food.

Moderate to expensive

4 Saisons Salon de Thé av de la Cathédrale. You pay for the clean, comfortable dining room at this café geared to expats. Burgers, pizzas and *chawarmas* from CFA2500.

Akwaba av Kwame Nkrumah ☎50.31.23.76 (closed Sun). Excellent and original African dishes, such as agouti with groundnut sauce, prepared by Ivoirian cooks; a bit on the pricey side (CFA3500–5500), but worth it.

Le Coq Bleu av Kwame Nkrumah ☎50.30.01.93. One of the best places in town, this chic restaurant serves excellent French cuisine. Mains CFA4000–6000.

L'Eau Vive rue de l'Hôtel de Ville ☎50.30.63.03 (closed Sun). The most famous restaurant in Ouaga, this is an enjoyable place where the waitresses (who are also nuns) pause daily at 9.30pm to belt out *Ave Maria*. More international than French, the menu features African, European and American dishes in the CFA3000–6000 range. There's an attractive shop attached selling clothes and handicrafts; proceeds help fund an orphanage.

Restaurant de Chine av de la Cathédrale ☎50.31.18.60 (closed Tues). Excellent but expensive Chinese restaurant with a/c and attractive decor (mains around CFA4000).

Le Verdoyant av Dimdolobsom ☎50.31.54.07 (closed Wed). Justifiably popular restaurant serving fantastic pizza, pasta and ice cream in a stylish open-air setting. Prices are moderate (from CFA2700) and the food is excellent value. Be sure to reserve at weekends.

Zaka at Zaka Cultural Centre, av Yennenga. A good place to sample African dishes such as *poulet Kedjenou* in an attractive garden accompanied by nightly live traditional music. Mains CFA2500–4000.

Out of the centre

The following are all indicated on the map on pp.736–737.

Budget

Chez Simon av Kwame Nkrumah. Popular spot for a variety of snacks (great *chawarmas*, pizzas and

burgers), pastries and ice cream.

Happy Donald of Hamburger House av Kwame Nkrumah, opposite *Chez Simon*; daily until 3 or 4am. Serves up reliably tasty and cheap snacks – pizzas, omelettes, sandwiches, burgers and chips.

Oscars av de l'UEMOA. Popular with both expats and locals, serving the best ice cream in town – although not much else.

Pâtisserie de Koulouba av Sangoulé Lamizana. Along with *La Bonbonnière* (see opposite) this is Ouaga's other outstanding *pâtisserie*. A great breakfast address with its bustling dining room, tasty omelettes and generous selection of cakes and pastries.

La Rose des Sables at the *Auberge Rose des Sables*, St Leon. Popular restaurant serving good and inexpensive European food in a sheltered courtyard.

Moderate to expensive

Le Belvedere av Saye Zerbo ☎50.33.64.21 (evenings only; closed Tues). One of Ouaga's fancier restaurants, with a shaded terrace, a/c dining room and a well-established reputation for pizza and other Italian food, plus African and Lebanese dishes.

Diwan al Mokhtar av du Burkina Faso ☎50.33.57.75. Delicious Lebanese dishes (around CFA3000) plus a range of European offerings served by attentive staff.

La Forêt av Bassawarga, down a small drive opposite the Groupe Hage building ☎50.30.72.96. This is a place where well-heeled Ouagalais head for lunch, with good African food – try the *yassa poulet* – served in a secluded wooded courtyard with a swimming pool (CFA1000 for non-diners).

Gondwana off bd Charles de Gaulle, Zone du Bois ☎50.36.11.24. Ouaga's most original restaurant has three dining rooms re-creating, quite wonderfully, Gourounsi, Mauritanian and Tuareg dwellings, complete with sandy floors and eye-catching artefacts (all of which are for sale). The pricey food, from tapas to T-bone steaks, is more cosmopolitan than the decor would suggest.

Kim Son av Kwame Nkrumah ☎50.30.88.31 (closed Mon). Small, informal Vietnamese restaurant with a sound reputation, popular with expats. Mains from CFA3500.

Le Moulin Rouge av Kwame Nkrumah. Bordered by red lanterns, this is the most attractive – and one of the most popular – street terraces on av Kwame Nkrumah; the good pizzas stand out on the mid-priced menu.

Le Olivia av Yaméogo Maurice ☎50.33.58.71 (closed Sat lunch, Sun dinner, Mon). Classy, pretentious and very expensive (mains from CFA6000) restaurant serving impeccably prepared French cuisine that you can watch being cooked.

🏃 **Paradis des Meilleurs Vins** av Kwame Nkrumah. Order a bottle of wine (from CFA2000) and drink it with a plate of cheese or grilled meat (CFA2000–3000) at this enjoyable European-style eatery with a strong local following.

Rang de l'Inde av Kwame Nkrumah. Reputedly the only Indian restaurant in Ouaga, offering well-spiced dishes (mains CFA2500–3500), including plenty of veggie options.

Relais des Bougainvilliers av John Kennedy ☎50.31.48.81. Stylish wining and dining with great pizza and pasta in a pleasant indoor restaurant or attractive outdoor terrace. Meals from CFA4000.

Le Tam Tam av Kadioga next to the SOGEBAF station ☎50.34.71.03. Dishes up a range of Austrian specialities – sauerkraut, sausages, breaded veal – you never dreamed of seeing in Burkina, all well prepared and not overly pricey (from CFA2500).

Le Vert Galant Ouaga 2000 ☎50.30.69.80. This expensive and hugely popular French restaurant features fish and meat dishes accompanied by salads and soups, crêpes and sorbets, plus a small wine list. Mains from around CFA5000.

Nightlife

One of the few Sahelian towns that's predominantly non-Muslim, Ouagadougou's **nightlife** has a rewarding mix of trendy clubs, lively bars and a good range of cinemas and music venues. Avenue Kwame Nkrumah, throbbing with packed **clubs** and **bars**, is popular with expats looking for company. Cover charges for clubs are never more than CFA4000, but pricey drinks can make for an expensive night out. For **live music** in the centre, head to the Zaka Cultural Centre on Avenue Yennenga, where bands play nightly (schedule posted on the noticeboard outside).

As a direct result of FESPACO, Ouaga is full of cinephiles and boasts some great movie theatres, showing some of the very best in new African **cinema**. For **theatre**, it's worth checking out the Théâtre Populaire Désiré Bonogo off Avenue du Mogho in the southwest of town (☎50.30.23.44), which also hosts a biennial theatre **festival** in late November (see p.717), or the Carrefour International de Théâtre de Ouagadougou, next to the Municipal Stadium, also in the southwest of town (☎50.30.45.48), whose eclectic programme includes everything from Molière to Amadou Hampate Ba. You might also catch a show at the French Cultural Centre (see opposite).

Clubs and bars

Cactus Bar av Kwame Nkrumah. Plush a/c bar with Western music, numerous pool tables, pinball, cocktails and burgers.

Le Calypso av Kennedy, near the American Embassy. A good alternative to the expat-friendly clubs along av Kwame Nkrumah, this one has an indoor disco and courtyard tables outside.

De Niro's Bar av Léo Frobenius, opposite *Pacific Hôtel*. Intimate bar with two pool tables and a small covered outdoor seating area. Perfect for a quiet drink.

Jardin de l'Amitié av Dimdolobsom, near place des Nations Unies. Very popular garden bar, with live music nightly and traditional drumming Wed & Sun. A bit on the touristy side, however.

🏃 **Le Jet 7** Dapoya Secteur, rue Henri Guissou, north of av de la Liberté, Cité An III. Happening local hangout with outside courtyard, occasional concerts and nightly disco sounds. No cover.

Jimmy's av Kwame Nkrumah (open from 10pm). One of the best established and most popular discos in Ouaga, usually packed out on weekends. CFA3500 cover at weekends and pricey drinks thereafter.

Papa Gayo av Kwame Nkrumah, in the same building as *Jimmy's*. Similar to *Jimmy's*, but aimed at an older clientele (one cover charge gives access to both clubs).

Show-Biz Pub av Kwame Nkrumah. Smart a/c bar with red leather decor and a range of spirits, cocktails and fast food.

Taxi Brousse av Kwame Nkrumah. Kick off your evening at the large street terrace of this bar which gets going earlier than the clubs.

Universal Plateau Secteur Tiendpalogo, near the *Auberge Rose des Sables*, St Leon. Local drinking bar with a friendly atmosphere that picks up at night. Simple, cheap meals also available.

Cinemas

Ciné Burkina rue du Liptako Gourma. Modern a/c theatre with an outdoor bar and newest releases.
Ciné Neerwaya Cité An III, off av de l'Armée. The city's newest a/c theatre, with a big screen, showing some African films.
Ciné Oubri av Ilboudo Waogyandé. Outdoor theatre, low prices and generally older films.

TC's TCs

"It is very difficult to cash traveller's cheques in Burkina. We had to trek to every bank in Ouaga to get Thomas Cook cheques accepted – we did eventually after an interview with the bank manager."

Phil Twomey, Ireland

Listings

Airlines Afriqiyah Airways, av Kwame Nkrumah ☎50.30.16.52; Air Algérie, av Kwame Nkrumah ☎50.31.23.01 or 50.31.23.02; Air Burkina, av de la Nation ☎50.49.23.45; Air France, 493 av de la Nation ☎50.30.63.65; Air Ivoire, av Kwame Nkrumah ☎50.30.04.50; Air Sénégal, av Loudun ☎50.31.39.05; Antrak Air, c/o Faso Services, av Kwame Nkrumah ☎50.30.41.46; Point-Afrique, Immeuble Nouria Holding, rue de l'Hôtel de Ville ☎50.33.16.20; Royal Air Maroc, av Kwame Nkrumah ☎50.30.50.82.

American Express No official representation, though the BICIA-B Bank on av Kwame Nkrumah will replace lost or stolen cheques if you present receipts – as should all other banks that sell Amex traveller's cheques. You'll need a police report, and the whole process could take a week or longer.

Banks and exchange The fastest service tends to be at the BIB's upstairs exchange counter on av Dimdolobsom off place des Nations Unies, which offers good exchange rates, but you'll have to show receipts for traveller's cheques. The recommended Ecobank (open Mon–Fri 8am–4.30pm with no break for lunch and Sat 8am–noon) changes cash with no commission. ATM machines are widespread, with Visa the preferred card. If you want to change cash when the banks are closed, and are willing to accept a lower rate, try the counter at the Marina Market supermarket on av Yennenga (US$ and € only) or the bureau de change at the *Hôtel Indépendance*. Try to get the smallest denominations possible when changing money, as change is always a problem.

Bicycles and mobylettes A new Yamaha bike costs about CFA425,000; around half that second hand. You can rent, too – rates are open to negotiation, but range between CFA3000 (*mobylette*) and CFA6000 (motorbike) per day. For buying or renting, try Ekaf Motos, rue de l'Hôtel de Ville, on the northeast side of the Grand Marché, or the mechanics shops on rue du Grand Marché next to the cemetery.

Books and magazines The premier place for books is the Diacfa Librairie on rue de l'Hôtel de Ville, at rue Raag Naba Wanda. They have a large selection of French titles and a good sampling of foreign magazines, plus some maps and travel guides. Also check out the bookshop at *Hôtel Indépendance*.

Car and taxi rental In Ouaga, typical rates for a small car are CFA40,000/day, generally including insurance and 200km (count on about CFA170/km after that). Chauffeurs are usually obligatory when renting a 4x4 vehicle (CFA5000/day in town, CFA8000 around country, CFA12,000 outside country); check first whether the driver's meals and lodgings are also your responsibility. The main rental agencies are located opposite the airport car park on av de l'Aéroport: Avis (☎50.32.81.00); Europcar (☎50.30.09.09); National (☎50.31.65.80). Alternatively, taxis can be rented in town for about CFA20,000 per eight-hour shift.

Cultural centres The French Cultural Centre (Centre Culturel George Méliès) is on av de la Nation (Tues–Sat 9am–noon & 3–5.30pm; ☎50.30.60.97 ©ccf@fasonet.bf). With a vast library (see "Libraries"), exhibition space, open-air theatre, indoor cinema and shaded café featuring French TV and occasional live music, this is the most active cultural centre in Ouaga and an excellent source of information. You can pick up their monthly schedule of events at the big hotels and at Marina Market supermarket. The Zaka Cultural Centre, av Yennenga (☎50.31.53.12 ©espace-zaka@yahoo.fr), has live music nightly, and both open-air and indoor restaurants, plus a bar.

Embassies and consulates Canada (handles the affairs of Australian nationals in Burkina), 586 av Compaoré Blaise ☎ 50.31.18.94 ℱ 50.31.19.00; Côte d'Ivoire, av Saye Zerbo ☎ 50.31.82.28; France (issues visas for Togo and Mauritania), bd de l'Indépendance ☎ 50.49.66.66 ⓦ www .ambafrance-bf.org; Ghana, av Sankara Thomas Isidore ☎ 50.30.17.01 or 50.30.76.35; Mali, av Mogho Naba Wobgo ☎ 50.38.19.22 or 50.38.19.23; Niger, av Yennenga ☎ 50.30.53.59; Nigeria, av Kumda Yõore ☎ 50.30.66.67; Senegal, av Yennenga ☎ 50.30.12.06; UK, Honorary Consulate, ICI, 330 Impasse Thévenoud ☎ 50.30.73.23 ⓦ tinyurl.com/35zj5x; USA, av Saye Zerbo ☎ 50.30.67.23 ⓦ ouagadougou.usembassy.gov.

Horse riding The French-owned Cheval Mandingue on the Bobo road on the right just before the police barrier (☎ 50.43.60.76 ⓦ chevalmandingue .free.fr) can arrange riding in the countryside and horseback trips in the Dogon country in Mali.

Hospital and clinics Hôpital Yalgado Ouédraogo, av Kumda Yõore ☎ 50.31.16.55 ℱ 50.31.18.48. The best place for a consultation is the Centre Medico-Social de l'Ambassade de France off av du Burkina Faso, open Mon–Fri 8am–noon & 3–5.30pm, Sat 9am–noon; ☎ 50.30.66.07 or 70.20.00.00 in emergencies ℮ cms.fr@fasonet.bf.

Internet access One of the best places in town is DSI (Direction des Services Informatiques), 876 bd du Burkina Faso (CFA400/hr). More central options include Cyberposte at the main post office (CFA500/ hr) and IMES Cybercafé, av de l'UEMOA (CFA300/hr).

Libraries There's a good English-language library run by the American Embassy on av Kennedy (Mon–Thurs 9am–5pm). French-speakers should head to the library at the French Cultural Centre (Tues & Thurs–Sat 9am–noon & 3–6.30pm, Wed 3–6.30pm).

Maps Recent (2005) maps of Ouaga, complete with new street names, are sold at the Trésorie Régionale du Centre, next to the Mairie at 70 rue de l'Hôtel de Ville, for CFA1500. The Institut Géographique du Burkina (☎ 50.32.48.23 ⓦ www .igb.bf), 651 av de l'Indépendance – with a kiosk at the airport – also sells these maps for nearly twice the price, along with a decent national map dating from 2000 (CFA4000) and detailed regional topographic maps (around CFA3000), useful if you're heading off the beaten track.

Pharmacies Two central pharmacies are Pharmacie de la Cathédrale, opposite the cathedral (☎ 50.33.08.91), and Pharmacie du Kadiogo, av Kwame Nkrumah (☎ 50.31.87.88).

Photography For film, try Photo Luxe, av Ilboudo Waogyandé, opposite Ciné Oubri; they also do ID photos for visa applications. Alternatively, there's a photo booth on av Loudun, across from Sindibal restaurant (CFA2000 for six photos).

Post office The main PTT is on av de la Nation, just west of place des Nations Unies (Mon–Fri 7.30am–noon & 3–5pm, Sat 8am–11.30am).

Supermarkets Marina Market (open daily until at least 9pm) and Scimas, both on av Yennenga, are two of Ouaga's best-stocked supermarkets.

Swimming pools Many hotel and restaurant pools are open to non-guests or non-diners. One of the cheapest is at La Forêt restaurant on av Bassawarga (CFA1000). Although it's quite a trek, the Ricardo has an excellent and relaxing pool and terrace (CFA2000), while the Mercure Silmandé has one of the larger – and more expensive – pools (CFA2500). Pick of the bunch, however, is the pretty pool at the Yibi, which is free to use provided you buy a drink.

Telephones There are télécentres all over the city where you can make domestic and international calls.

Travel agents Besides excursions to regions like the Lobi country, the Sahel and the wildlife reserves, larger operators arrange trips to the Dogon country and Timbuktu, Togo, Ghana and Benin. Some of the major ones are: Vacances OK Raids, av Kwame Nkrumah ☎ 50.30.03.52 ⓦ www.okraid.com; L'Agence Tourisme, at Hôtel Les Palmiers ☎ 50.31.84.43 ⓦ www .agence-tourisme.com; Sahel Voyages, 608 av Sangoulé Lamizana ☎ 50.31.53.45 ℱ 50.33.04.71; and Meycom Voyages ☎ 50.33.09.83 ⓦ www.faso-ong.org/meycom.

Visa extensions The Service des Passeports at the Direction de Contrôle et de l'Immigration on the road to Bobo (Mon–Fri 7am–12.30pm & 3–5.30pm; ☎ 50.34.26.43) will extend the CFA10,000, seven-day visas issued at the airport and land borders to ninety days at no additional cost.

Western Union Money transfers can be made at the main PTT on av de la Nation and at most major banks in town.

From Ouaga west to Koudougou

Just west of Ouaga, the road to Koudougou passes through the small town of **Tanguen-Dassouri**, which has a lively market every three days. From here a *piste* leads 6km north to **BESOULÉ**, a friendly village renowned for its sacred crocodiles. You'll be expected to pay CFA1000 plus the cost of a chicken. In return, you'll be shown where the crocodiles (*caïmans*) live: the chicken is used to lure them out of the water, and the prospect of food apparently keeps them from taking bites out of visiting tourists. After sacrificing the chicken, you can touch and photograph the reptiles. There's no public transport from Tanguen-Dassouri to Besoulé, and the place is much less visited than **SABOU** – about 90km further down the main road towards Bobo – whose **crocodile pool** is a staple destination for tour operators. Sabou has become a ghastly tourist trap, although at least it's in a pleasant setting and has a modest *campement* (❶).

West of Sabou, you may see **elephants** – your chances are greatly increased if you come during the dry season (Nov–May) and have your own transport and time to turn off the main highway. The elephants are to be found in the vicinity of the **Parc National des Deux Balés**, named after the Petit Balé and Grand Balé rivers. The best opportunities are around **Poura**, reached down a dirt road leading south off the highway about 25km east of the small town of **BOROMO** (itself 90km west of Sabou). At the Poura junction there's a small huddle of roadside stalls and businesses where you may well find a guide. Alternatively, ask in Boromo itself, where you can stay at the *Relais Touristique* (☎20.53.80.84 ❸), which has rooms with fan or a/c. If you have your own transport, the nicely located *Campement Touristique Le Kaïcedra* (☎76.63.97.29 or 76.62.17.78 ❹), 7km away, is a better option. There's a chance that you'll see elephants here drinking in the nearby river, and the *campement* can organize sightseeing trips around the park.

Any bus travelling between Ouaga and Bobo can drop you at Sabou or Boromo.

Koudougou

Before reaching Sabou, the main road to Bobo branches in the direction of **KOUDOUGOU**, Burkina Faso's third-largest town. It's a quiet place with wide tree-lined avenues, though a certain degree of liveliness is assured by the presence of the country's largest textile factory, **Faso Fani**, and no less than three secondary schools (*collèges*). Koudougou was also the hometown of the first president of Upper Volta, Maurice Yaméogo.

The new covered **market** is especially good for its fruit – mangoes, pineapples, avocados, bananas – as well as vegetables and cereals. There's also a reasonable selection of **handicrafts**: woven goods (hats and baskets), leather (handbags, wallets and shoes) and pottery (jugs and bowls of all sizes). You'll also find ready-to-wear outfits made from locally hand-woven and embroidered cloth. There's a superb **bronze-maker** in Koudougou – Gandema Mamadou and his sons have a shop called Espace Art Culture Fabrique, 200m up from the train station opposite the Gendarmarie Nationale, where you'll find sculptures of birds, camels and tribespeople in traditional dress.

Practicalities

Many of Koudougou's **places to stay** – including some of the best ones – have been requisitioned by the town's schools to provide student accommodation. Of the central options that remain, the smartest is the renovated *Toulourou*, down a dirt track across from the church (☎50.44.01.70 ❹), which has comfortable s/c rooms, some with a/c, plus a European-style restaurant serving good, reasonably priced African and international meals. Also centrally located, 200m east of the old mosque, *La Bache Bleu* (☎50.44.46.19 ❷) offers bright, pleasant s/c rooms with fan and mosquito net, although the adjoining bar can be noisy. You could also try the run-down *Relais de la Gare*, 100m from the train station (☎50.44.48.56 ❶), even if the dusty s/c rooms with fan or a/c look like they haven't seen a guest in years. A little out of the centre on the eastern edge of town by the junction with the road to Ouaga, *Photo-Luxe* (☎50.44.00.88 ❷) has seen better days, but still has clean s/c or non-s/c rooms, a good bar, restaurant and nightclub. Another 500m or so further east in a residential area, *Hôtel Denver*, signposted off the road to Ouaga (☏50.44.18.83 ➋), is the best value in town, with fresh and attractive s/c rooms in a quiet setting. Finally, a kilometre out on the other side of town – follow the Dégoudou road and turn left 100m after the Palais de Justice – an organization called DREBACO (☏70.11.08.23 ➊) has several basic and cheap rooms dotted around its spacious compound.

Apart from the hotel restaurants, there's plenty of **street food** near the market or at the train station. A Koudougou speciality is *pintade* (guinea fowl) which you see being grilled on roadside braziers in the evening. For more formal dining, the smart *Nayā Abrendu*, next to the train station, offers a range of chicken, beef and fish dishes for around CFA3000; and *Chez Coco*, on the Ouaga road between the old mosque and *La Bache Bleu*, sells fresh croissants and other baked items.

For evening entertainment, you could catch a Hollywood or Bollywood film at the **Ciné Sibiri** opposite the mosque. The town also boasts an impressive **théâtre populaire** a kilometre west of the centre behind the Palais de Justice. Koudougou has its own troupe that puts on periodic performances (mostly in More) at the theatre – worth seeing if you're in town at the right moment – and the town hosts the **Nuits Atypiques de Koudougou** music and culture festival at the end of November every year. Good **discos** in town include the popular *Challenge Plus* on the Ouaga road just before *Hôtel Photo-Luxe*; and the equally lively and colourfully painted *La Joie du Peuple*, set around a courtyard in the north of town between the water tower and the Ouaga road. *La Bache Bleu* is good for a daytime or evening drink.

Changing money is far easier in Bobo or Ouaga. The Koudougou BICIA-B, near the mosque, changes cash (euros only), and both they and the BIB, just up from the train station, have ATMs that accept Visa. The **post office** is just west of the market and there are several **Internet** cafés around town – try Cybercafé Coconut on the Ouaga road between *La Bache Bleu* and *Hôtel Photo-Luxe*.

Moving on, a **train** leaves Koudougou on Tuesdays, Thursdays and Saturdays for Bobo and on Wednesdays, Fridays and Sundays for Ouaga. **Bush taxis** for Ouaga and other destinations leave from south of the market opposite the Total station, although for Ouaga it's better to take one of the frequent **buses** operated by Rayi's and KZA, both departing from stations east of the market near the mosque (1½hr; CFA2000); Rayi's also have a service to Bobo twice a day (6hr; CFA5000).

From Ouaga east to Fada-Ngourma

The route to Niamey runs from Ouagadougou through the **Gourmantché country**. The first town of any size on this road is lively **KOUPÉLA**, on the main road to Togo. The town has a large daily **market** renowned for its pottery (which is concentrated around the southern end) and better-value **accommodation** than Fada-Ngourma a little further to the east – something to bear in mind if you're going to Niger or Togo and want to break the journey somewhere. On the main Ouaga road in the town centre, the pleasant *Campement Hôtel Kourita* (☏40.70.01.33 ➊) has a bar, restaurant and basic rooms, some with their own bathrooms and a/c. Next door, the *Calypso* (☏40.70.03.50 ➋) is okay if you can stand the noise from the adjoining bar, with its clean, slightly overpriced rooms (two men sharing pay more than a mixed couple) with showers and immaculate communal toilets. Other options include the excellent-value *Wend Wogo* on the Togo road near the BICIA-B bank (☏40.70.01.64 ➊), and the less appealing *Hôtel de la Gare*, opposite the *gare routière* (☏76.19.50.40 ➊). If you want to escape the constant activity and noise of Koupéla, the best option is the *Mission Catholique* in the Centre Zacharie Nikiema behind the church, 200m back from the junction of the Ouaga and Togo roads (☏40.70.05.05 ➋), which has spotless doubles with showers (some with a/c).

Food is no problem. Countless vendors line the streets waiting for taxis and buses to roll in. Buy a grilled *pintade*, take it to the *Amicale Bar* on the eastern edge of the market (which also serves couscous, *brochettes*, and chicken and chips) and wash it down with a cold Brakina, or buy good grilled fish from just outside the *Campement Hôtel Kourita* and eat it in the bar there (which also offers simple meals itself).

There's a BICIA-B **bank** at the junction of the Ouaga and Togo roads with an ATM that accepts Visa, though there's no guarantee that they'll change traveller's cheques. For **Internet** access, head to the Foyer des Éleves in front of the church opposite the turnoff for Togo.

Koupéla's **gare routière** is 300m down the Togo road on the right. You can find taxis here for Sinkassé (aka Cinkassé; 2hr; CFA3000), from where you can get onward transport to Dapoang in northern Togo (a further 1hr; CFA1000).

Fada-Ngourma and beyond

Midway between Niamey and Ouagadougou, **Fada-Ngourma** is another of Burkina's junction towns – you can join the road to Benin here. The town was founded by Diaba Lompo, who is variously claimed to be the son, maternal uncle or cousin of Ouédraogo, grandfather of the founder of Ouagadougou. Fada is an unremarkable place, but does host a colourful **market** with a wealth of goods from across the Sahel region. The beautifully woven **blankets** and **rugs** on sale are invariably better buys here than in Ouagadougou. The town was originally called Bingo, meaning a slave settlement, and Fada-Ngourma is a Hausa appellation, mysteriously meaning "The place where you don't pay tax". It happens to be twinned with Epernay, France's Champagne capital – a more unlikely match would be hard to imagine.

Practicalities

The best **places to stay** are located a little outside the centre. Of the central options, *Auberge Yemmamma*, conveniently positioned 100m to the right of the STMB bus station (℡40.77.00.39 ❷), has plain and slightly overpriced rooms with fan or a/c, plus a good restaurant in a shaded garden serving the likes of grilled chicken and chips. *Auberge Liberté*, roughly 400m south of the *Yemmamma* between the two paved roads (℡70.41.03.81 ❶), offers cheap, grubby and smelly rooms with bucket showers – an unappealing yet safe last resort if everywhere else is full. Out on the road to Niamey, around a kilometre from the turn-off for Benin, the *L'Avenir* offers clean and comfortable s/c rooms and a courtyard bar (℡40.77.04.09; ❷). On the same road, 300m back towards town, you'll find *Panache* (℡40.77.03.73 ⓦpanachehotel.com ❸), whose modern a/c rooms with TV, phone and hot water are easily the smartest in town; there are also cheaper rooms with fan arranged around the attractive pool area. On the other side of town, a kilometre along the Ouaga road, the recommended *Auberge La Belle Étoile* (℡40.77.08.09 ❷) has small but stylish rooms with fan and mosquito net.

For **eating and drinking**, *Caraïbes*, in front of the *Panache*, is a popular and lively drinking spot, serving simple dishes such as spaghetti and couscous. The best place in town is the *Restaurant de l'Est*, some 200m from here as you walk towards town, set inside a refined and relaxing walled courtyard and serving European dishes for around CFA2000. If you're in the mood for **dancing**, try *Océan Pacifique*, near the *L'Avenir* (Fri & Sat; entrance CFA1000).

Moving on from Fada

You'll find the small **autogare** on the main road next to the Total station and near the modern cathedral with its strange corrugated-iron pyramids. There are frequent departures direct to **Niamey** (4hr; CFA6000) and Ouaga, and less regular vehicles for **Pama** (2hr; CFA1500). STMB buses (℡40.77.06.94) leave for **Ouaga** (six buses daily; 4hr; CFA3000) and for **Kantchari** (2½hr; CFA2500) and **Diapaga** (4hr; CFA4000) on Mon, Wed and Fri; Rakieta (℡40.77.10.09) have four daily services to Ouaga.

The BIB **bank** will change euros cash and has an ATM accepting Visa, but the BICIA-B does not change money.

From Fada to Benin and the Parc National d'Arli

From Fada, a decent road heads to the Benin border past the worthwhile **Parc National d'Arli** (hunting season Dec–May; open year-round for tourism; CFA5000), home to a variety of large mammal species including lions, hippos, buffalos, baboons and elephants. The park has virtually no infrastructure and is difficult to access without your own (preferrably 4x4) vehicle. You can **stay**, in the village of **PAMA**, at the central and characterful *Campement Bonazza* – aka *Safari Bonazza* – (T70.14.36.82 ❷), an ex-Italian colonial setup where the house is adorned with impressive hunting memorabilia, including black-and-white photos of the ex-proprietor's prize lion kills. The rooms are spotless and good value, and you can also camp here. Some 15km west of Pama in the town of Kompienga, *La Kompienga* (T40.77.65.03 Wwww.agence-tourisme.com/p-kompienga ❹) is an upmarket option with its own pool and tennis courts. An attractive alternative is the *campement* at Tagou, about 14km west of Pama (open mid-Dec–mid-May; T70.12.91.79 ❽), with great lake views, a pool and all meals included at the restaurant.

The SKV and TCV **buses** from Ouaga to Cotonou (see box, p.734) stop at Pama, and these services are also your best bet for onward transport south from the village, since traffic along this route is extremely sporadic. If you're **driving** – and there's really no other way of exploring the park – you might do better to continue on the Ouaga–Niamey road to **Kantchari** and then skirt south along a dirt road through **Diapaga** – where there's a hunting lodge (*La Palmeraie*; ❸) – to **ARLI** village 75km further south, where you'll find accommodation at the *Eden d'Arli* (T40.79.15.78; ❸), which is also the main national-park office and the base for game-viewing trips around the park.

9.2

Northern Burkina

A drier, more distinctively **Sahelian landscape** typifies northern Burkina. You'll see plenty of camels, nomadic tribespeople and hazy desert scenes in the atmospheric market town of **Gorom-Gorom**, near the point where Burkina, Mali and Niger meet, an easy day's travelling from Ouaga. The alternative route across northern Burkina passes through the old Yatenga state to the historic town of **Ouahigouya** – an obvious overnight stop if you're heading for the Dogon country in Mali.

The Burkinabe Sahel

Until recently, the 300-odd kilometres of dirt roads and tracks separating Ouaga from the remote outpost of **Gorom-Gorom** in the **Sahel** took a considerable time to cover, even in the dry season. Now the road is paved as far as **Dori**, making it a relatively easy journey from the capital. Along the way you'll notice a change in the peoples as More-speakers give way to northerners – principally Fula, Tuareg and Bella – and the Muslim influence becomes more predominant. The vast majority of the people of the north are farmers and herders, whose livelihoods are especially sensitive to the drought conditions that continue to threaten the country.

From Ouagadougou to Kaya

The route to Kaya passes a couple of villages which have important roles in Mossi tradition. Whenever the Mogho Naba dies, a **blacksmith** is sent to the Muslim fief of **LOUMBILA** and confined there for three years in order to cast a bronze effigy of the deceased ruler. Since the death of Ouédraogo, thirty-six sets of five statues (each representing the Mogho Naba, one of his wives, a servant and two musicians) have been cast, and are carefully guarded in the chief's compound. The other village, nearby **GUILONGOU**, marks the spot where, according to Mossi legend, pottery was first invented. It's still an important industry here.

Kaya

KAYA, 98km from Ouaga, is the last major Mossi town on the road north. The flourishing **market** here sells many of the **crafts** for which the region is known. There are weavers and tanners in town, and more pour in from neighbouring villages to sell their wares: this is *the* place to buy leatherwork. STMB, TSR and SOGEBAF **buses** stop here en route to and from Dori.

From Kaya to Dori and Djibo

Sixty-eight kilometres beyond Kaya, the town of **Tougouri** marks the northern limits of the Mossi country. A short distance further on is **Yalogo**, a Fula village with a large Tuesday **market**. Another 60km brings you to the Islamic stronghold of **Bani**, whose solid, large mud-brick mosque stands out among the numerous other minarets that push against the side of a hill; there's also an important regional market here every Tuesday.

Dori

Despite its small size, **DORI** is an important administrative centre. The town's **market day** is Friday and, just as reported by the German explorer Heinrich Barth – who passed through in July 1853 – it's really good for blankets. They have a variety of styles and prices, those woven from camel hair being the most expensive. Also worth a visit is the Artisanal Groupement Féminin, 200m back towards the town centre from *Sahel Hébergement* (see p.752) – a huge array of napkins, tablecloths, aprons and bags, which are sold as far afield as France. Dori receives its fare share of tourists en route to nearby Gorom-Gorom, and hassle from **guides** can be a problem, especially in the day or two preceding Gorom's popular Thursday market. If overbearing guides get on your nerves, consider

Moving on from Dori

Dori's *gare routière* is next to the market in the town centre. STMB (℡40.46.03.32), SOGEBAF (℡40.46.01.10) and TSR (℡76.65.80.13) all have either one or two **buses** daily to **Ouaga** (4hr; CFA3000). SOGEBAF and TSR have services arriving from Ouaga on Wednesday that continue on to **Gorom-Gorom** (2hr; CFA1500), while TSR also goes to Oursi on Saturday (3hr; CFA2500). Niger-bound travellers can find 4x4 bush taxis at the *gare routière* going to **Seytanga** (2hr; CFA2000), from where you can get onward transport to **Téra** in Niger (1hr; CFA2000).

arriving in Dori (and Gorom-Gorom, for that matter) before the bulk of other visitors.

Dori has plenty of **accommodation** options. The newest is the *Liptako*, opposite the Total station in the centre of town (℡40.46.01.70 ❷), offering fan-equipped rooms with shared showers and TV room, or s/c rooms with a/c and TV. Another central option is the *Auberge Populaire*, 200m north of the *gare routière* (℡40.46.05.55; ❶), which has spacious huts with or without fan in an orderly compound frequented by vultures (same-sex couples pay slightly more than mixed couples). A kilometre along the road heading east from the *Liptako*, the popular *Sahel Hébergement* (℡40.46.07.04; ❶) has a range of rooms with or without bath or a/c; the s/c rooms at their nearby annexe (❷) all have a/c, but are rather bare and not worth the extra money. Roughly 500m further east from here is the more upmarket *Oasis du Sahel* (℡40.46.03.29 ✉jamel@fasonet.bf; ❷), originally built to house Italian workers constructing the road from Ouaga; the "villas" in the older part of the hotel resemble portacabins, but do all have a/c and hot water, while the pricier rooms in the newer section (❹) are extremely spacious and come with TV. Finally, if you want to stay out of town, the Fomtugol Association, opposite the *Auberge Populaire*, can help arrange homestays with Peul families (CFA7500) and camel excursions to nearby villages (CFA25,000). If you time it right, you might also catch a rehearsal by **Fomtugol**, an internationally acclaimed dance and theatre troupe.

Most of the hotels also do **food**, the most enticing menu being the one at *Oasis du Sahel*, where you can get a filling three-course meal for CFA3900. Another place worth trying is the *Regal*, opposite *Sahel Hébergement*, whose chips are particularly good.

The BIB **bank** opposite the *gare routière* changes euros and traveller's cheques and has an ATM; Ecobank were also due to open a branch at the time of writing. There are a few **Internet** cafés clustered around the bank, La Colombe being the most reliable.

Djibo – and Kongoussi

From Dori, a rough but pretty route runs across a barren landscape to **DJIBO**, about 180km west (there's no public transport along this road; hitching is possible, although traffic is light). Founded in the sixteenth century, the town became capital of the Peul (Fula) kingdom of Djilgodji, then, in the nineteenth century, came under the control of the Muslim state of Masina, in present-day Mali. Little evidence of this past remains, however, outside the handed-down memories of a few old men and women. Djibo today is a **livestock market**, at the mercy of the encroaching desert. Tourists rarely come here and the persistent guides who can make Dori and Gorom-Gorom hard work are relatively inconspicuous, giving Djibo an agreeably laid-back feel.

The town's limited **accommodation** includes the *Auberge Populaire*, 1km out of town on the Ouaga road (℡40.56.02.27 ❶), where the bare rooms in a large scruffy compound have fans and occasionally mosquito nets; and the overpriced *Hôtel Massa* in the centre of town (℡70.39.95.08 ❷), which has basic doubles with shared facilities or s/c rooms with a/c.

Both of the hotels also serve simple **meals** – *riz gras*, *riz sauce*, *brochettes* – as does *La Causette*, a soup-kitchen-style restaurant about 200m down the road past *Hôtel Massa* and the OTAM service station. *Mimi-Laiterie Kosam*, near *La Causette*, sells good, fresh yoghurt; while in the same area there are several other eateries serving cheap street-food.

STMB (⊕40.56.00.88) has a twice-daily **bus** service linking Djibo with Ouahigouya (3hr; CFA2000), although, unlike the majority of STMB's fleet, the buses plying this route are in a terrible condition and breakdowns are common. You can connect in Ouahigouya for Ouaga, or take STAF's daily service from Djibo to Ouaga via Kongoussi (4hr; CFA4000).

If you want to break the journey in **KONGOUSSI**, the central *Ambiance* (❶) has basic rooms with shared bathroom; while the nicer *Hôtel du Lac*, a five-minute walk from the centre near the lake, has rooms with fan or a/c (❷) and the liveliest bar-restaurant in town.

Gorom-Gorom

Fifty-three kilometres of lousy earth road separate Dori from **GOROM-GOROM**, a large Sahelian village with a **market** – one of the biggest in the north – that draws a vast array of northern peoples. Tuareg, Fula and Bella nomads trek into the mostly Songhai-run market on Wednesday evening and Thursday, the main trading day. In addition to foodstuffs, you'll find a variety of leather goods, jewellery and textiles, all produced locally. A short distance away, camels, goats, sheep and donkeys are bought and sold at the **animal market**. The village itself retains its picturesque blend of *banco* houses and narrow dusty streets dotted with numerous mosques.

Practicalities

Upon arrival in Gorom-Gorom you should, in theory, visit the police station (on the road to Dori near the *Kawar* restaurant) to register and pay the local **tax touristique** (CFA1000 per person per day). Some visitors adhere to this system; others don't, and appear to suffer no problems as a result.

One of the best and cheapest **places to stay** is *Campement Tondikara*, not far from the market and most easily found by looking for the red water-tower around which it is built (⊕70.31.57.68 ❶). The rooms have showers (though there's often no water), fan or a/c, mosquito nets and individual terraces for gazing at the stars; there's also a shared kitchen. The nearby *Campement Hôtel de Gorom-Gorom* (formerly *Point Mulhouse*) is located right next to a rock known as Tondikara and has modern s/c rooms with fan and mosquito net (❷) or tiny fold-out beds in a rather spartan dorm (CFA2500). Two other establishments can be found on the road to Dori. Closest to the centre, the *Auberge Populaire* (⊕40.46.94.18 ❷) has cleanish accommodation (no fans or mosquito nets) set around a busy courtyard where locals eat, drink and watch TV, especially on the eve of market day. At the entrance to town, *Hôtel de l'Amitié* (⊕40.46.94.40 ⓔamitie@fasonet.bf ❷) is Gorom's swankiest hotel with a constant water supply and a good selection of s/c rooms with either fan or a/c.

The *Amitié's* restaurant offers the best choice of meals, although prices are on the steep side for what you get. *Le Kawar* is a recommended locals' restaurant opposite the old cinema, serving tasty and inexpensive fare like macaroni and *riz gras*. Likewise, the friendly *Kiosk de la Paix*, opposite *Campement Tondikara*, dishes up well-prepared couscous and spaghetti for less than CFA1500.

SOGEBAF **buses** leave from the *gare routière* near the market for Ouaga via Dori and Kaya on Thursday at noon and Monday at 2.30pm (6hr; CFA6000). Heading in the other direction, the SOGEBAF bus from Ouaga continues on to Markoye on Sunday and Wednesday. Finding bush taxis from Gorom-Gorom to Dori is easy on either of these towns' market days; on other days there is usually only one taxi a day, which has usually left Gorom by 8am (2hr; CFA2000).

Excursions from Gorom-Gorom

Numerous self-appointed "guides" in Gorom-Gorom will try to convince you to take a **camel trek** to the surrounding villages, with a night's camping out in the sands. It's an enjoyable experience, although one that can be expensive. The starting price is CFA20,000 per person including food, plus a guiding fee of CFA15,000 for the group.

Alternatively you can do a shorter, three-hour camel trip to the village of **MENEGOU**, some 12km from Gorom-Gorom (CFA8000 per person plus CFA12000 guiding fee per group). Fees are highly negotiable unless you opt to go with a guide belonging to the Association des Guides de l'Oudalan (☏70.42.26.85), which has a price list of services and generally reliable guides.

If you've got your own 4x4 transport, it's worth driving to the sand dunes at **OURSI**, a two-hour drive from Gorom – or you could rent a 4x4 vehicle and driver for the day (CFA47,500 including a guide, but excluding fuel). The **Mare d'Oursi**, near the dunes, is a vast watering hole which attracts herders and livestock from throughout the region – an amazing sight in such a dry and barren region. The dunes themselves offer a picturesque foretaste of the Sahara. Ask any of the small kids from Oursi village for directions.

Finally, if you find Gorom's market a bit on the touristy side, the much less visited Monday extravaganza at **MARKOYE**, 37km northeast of Gorom-Gorom, is equally exotic and colourful.

Ouahigouya and the Yatenga state

Bone dry but historically important, **Ouahigouya** (pronounced "Weegooya"), 182km northwest of Ouagadougou along a good paved road, is the main town of northern Burkina. It was founded in the eighteenth century as capital of **Yatenga**, the northernmost Mossi kingdom, which had broken away from Ouagadougou some three hundred years before. It's a relaxed and pleasant place to mooch around, perhaps dallying in its large market, or taking in some of the 37 picturesque mosques. Most of the sights of Yatenga, however, lie outside Ouahigouya in the villages: the kingdom's former capitals at **La** and **Gourcy** in the south; the burial sites of many of its *nabas* at **Somniaga**; and the region's most impressive mosques at **Ramatoulaye** to the west, and **Yako** to the south. All these places are worth a look, but you'll be back in Ouahigouya by sunset if you value cold beer and music.

The **Yatenga region** is an arid, undulating plateau, barren for most of the year. The rains in May cover the earth in a green carpet that lasts until October, during which time millet and sorghum, maize, cotton, groundnuts and indigo are sown and harvested. Outside the farming season, Yatenga reverts to a scrubby savannah of thornbush dotted with trees, including shea nut, carob (*neré*), false mahogany, tamarind and types of plum (*nobega*) and fig (*kankanga*).

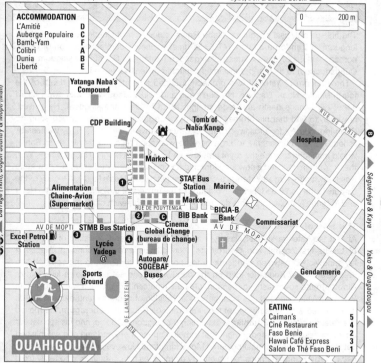

Ouahigouya

OUAHIGOUYA's wide streets and low buildings impart a lazy feeling of space, especially after the dust and shimmering heat of the day. The market sprawls, the *autogare* sprawls, the main square sprawls: you can't rush about here. The town's lack of specific sights belies its significant **history** – most important buildings were destroyed in the nineteenth-century Yatenga civil wars. Ouahigouya, the last of Yatenga's capitals, founded in 1757, marked the northern limit of the state's expansion. The king **Naba Kango**'s summons to the chiefs of Yatenga to pay him homage gave the town its name (from *Waka yuguya!* – "Come and greet!"). Unfortunately, the great palace where this took place was destroyed in 1825 during one of the struggles for the throne, in which the city was razed to the ground.

Kango may originally have built Ouahigouya as a salt depot; he certainly had his eye on trans-Saharan commodities (gold and kola for example), and hoped to make money by channelling more of their trade through Yatenga. Another motive in building the town could have been to escape from the power of the Mossi aristocracy which had always resented his rule and may well have been responsible for usurping him in the first place. At any rate, Kango populated the new city with slaves and ethnic minorities, from whose number he chose many of his officials.

As well as the dynastic struggles of the 1820s and 1830s, Ouahigouya suffered serious damage in the later wars between the "Sons of Sagha" and the "Sons of Tougouri" (see box, pp.756–757). By the time the French managed to secure their stooge Boulli on the throne at the end of 1896, it was half in ruins again, but

The first great Mossi conqueror, **Naba Rawa**, eldest son of Ouédraogo, founded the kingdom of **Zandoma** around 1470. His great nephew Ouemtanango, son of Oubri, perhaps jealous of Rawa's success, expanded his father's Oubritenga kingdom (later Ouagadougou) to the north, moving its capital from Tenkodogo to **La**.

The kingdom of Yatenga was probably founded around 1540 on the death of the fourth Mogho Naba, **Nasbire**. Nasbire's son and heir, **Yadega**, who was away, heard about his father's death and rode straight to La to claim the kingdom. He arrived, however, to find that his brother **Kumdumye** had taken power and moved south to Ouagadougou. Yadega followed, but found Kumdumye's authority already well established. He returned angrily to La, where he was soon followed by his sister Pabre, who'd managed to seize the **royal amulets** embodying the Mogho Naba's power. With these, Yadega declared a new kingdom and had himself enthroned at La. His new state was known after him as **Yatenga** (from *Yadega tenga*, "Yadega's land"). A legacy of the dispute is the continued mutual avoidance of the holders of the offices of Mogho Naba and Yatenga Naba, who to this day refuse to set eyes on each other.

The rise of Yatenga

At first the Yatenga statelet was the runt of the Mossi litter. Consisting of the towns of **La**, its first capital, and **Gourcy**, its second, plus a few surrounding villages, it lay sandwiched between Zandoma to the north and Oubritenga to the south. When Yadega's brother Kouda jumped on the bandwagon and set up his own kingdom of Risiam, to the southeast (independent until the nineteenth century), it was bigger than Yatenga. What changed this balance was a tradition of conquest and expansion that commenced with the activities of the ninth Yatenga Naba, **Vanteberegum**. He moved the Yatenga capital to **Somniaga**, extending the kingdom to do so, and his son set out on a campaign of aggrandisement that gobbled up most of Zandoma and established Yatenga as the second most powerful Mossi kingdom. However, it was the twenty-fifth *naba*, **Naba Kango**, famous for his cruelty as much as his conquests, who really fixed Yatenga in the oral histories.

Deposed almost as soon as he took power in 1754, Naba Kango returned after three years, aided by the formidable advantage of **firearms**, to retake power with an army of mercenaries. He then built a new capital and an enormous palace at **Ouahigouya** and summoned all Yatenga's chiefs (including the *naba* of Zandoma) to pay homage to him there. Those who failed to do so received a visit from his soldiers, who then went on to invade neighbouring territories, leading to a vast expansion of Kango's kingdom. Within it, he maintained an impressive unity, largely by burning down any villages that defied his authority. He had criminals publicly burnt to death and even massacred his own Bamana troops when they misbehaved. He was succeeded in 1787 by his nephew, **Naba Sagha**, but the large kingdom was growing unwieldy, and within forty years Yatenga had plunged into the series of civil wars that were to destroy it.

they needed a base for eastward conquest and "pacification" of Yatenga, and so constructed a fort and rebuilt the town as the regional capital.

Accommodation

Ouahigouya's **hotels** are mainly basic, although there are a couple of more luxurious options.

L'Amitié av de Mopti, 500m from the centre ☎40.55.05.21 or 40.55.05.22 ✉amitie @fasonet.bf. Long-established hotel with a range of rooms to suit every budget. The older block (*Amitié I*) has the cheaper options, including large and bare rooms with fan (❷). The upmarket extension opposite (*Amitié II*) offers classy s/c rooms (❻) with hot water, fridge, satellite TV and IDD phone, plus a pool. Both blocks have their own restaurants.

Civil war and dissolution

The wars concerned the succession of Sagha's 133 sons, the first of whom, **Tougouri**, managed to succeed him in 1806. Following his death in 1825, war broke out between those of Sagha's sons who were next in line. Only after 1834 was there a lull in the strife. On the death of Naba Yende, in 1877, however, the dynastic conflicts flared up once more. This time the dispute was between Sagha's grandsons. The sons of his first-born and successor, Tougouri, claimed that they alone were entitled to rule. The sons of Tougouri's brothers and successors disagreed, pointing out that the intended *naba*'s mother had been a concubine, and that in any case, each branch of Sagha's family should take a turn. The two groups formed opposing parties called **Sons of Tougouri** and **Sons of Sagha**.

When two Sons of Sagha were successively enthroned as *nabas*, the Sons of Tougouri went to war against them. Baogo, the incumbent *naba*, turned to the **French** – who, although new on the scene, had just taken Bandiagara (in Mali), and were hovering on Yatenga's borders. **Desteneves**, the leader of the French expeditionary force, offered only to mediate. Undeterred, Baogo went into battle against the Sons of Tougouri in 1894 and was killed.

All other eligible branches of Sagha's family having had their turn, the kingdom now returned to Tougouri's family. His senior son, Naba Boulli, took the throne but predictably the Sons of Sagha refused to accept him and set up a rival *naba* in **Sissamba**. Boulli turned to the French, who this time seized the opportunity and, on May 18, 1895, declared Yatenga a protectorate, thus usurping its independence.

The French sacked Sissamba, but the Sons of Sagha successfully recaptured Ouahigouya as soon as they had left. The French bailed out Boulli and put him back on the throne twice more, by which time half of Ouahigouya was in ruins. The rebellion of the Sons of Sagha wasn't put down until 1902, and violent incidents in connection with it continued until as late as 1911.

Modern Yatenga

French military occupation ended in 1909, when Yatenga passed to civilian colonial rule, and the region was generally quiet during the 1916 anti-conscription rebellion. With the 1932 division of Upper Volta, Yatenga became part of the French Sudan until the re-creation of Upper Volta in 1947. The 1930s and 1940s saw the rise of **Hammalism**, a reformist and anti-colonial Muslim cult. The movement was largely responsible for the spread of Islam in Yatenga (hitherto strongly resisted because of its association with hostile empires, especially the Songhai to the north). This in turn became the base for opposition to the traditionalist, chief-led Union Voltaïque in the region. A UV breakaway, the MDV (Mouvement Démocratique Voltaïque), carried Yatenga in the 1957 election with a base of Muslim support. Since independence, Yatenga has been a province of Burkina, divided into eleven *départements*.

Auberge Populaire av de Mopti, next to the cinema ☎40.55.06.40. Simple and dirty rooms with fan, shower and grubby walls. Can be very noisy due to the attached bar and adjacent road. ❶

Bamb-Yam 1km south of the centre ☎40.55.00.88. Clean, simple s/c rooms with fan or a/c in a pleasant courtyard. Just about worth the effort of getting there. ❷

🏃 **Colibri** 1km northeast of the centre, just off av de Chambery ☎40.55.07.87. Relaxing place with spacious s/c rooms with fan or a/c and mosquito net. The best-value budget accommodation in town. ❷

🏃 **Dunia** rue de Paris, 1.5km east of the centre ☎40.55.05.95 ✉mbachoarf@yahoo.fr. Boasts a great atmosphere, a pool and luxury a/c rooms (❺), plus cheaper rooms with fans (❸). Comfortable yet unpretentious – like staying in someone's house.

Liberté 100m off av de Mopti, follow the signs ☎40.55.05.72. Quiet location, with small rooms, some with private bathroom, a/c and TV. Also has beds in eight- or three-bed dorms (CFA3000–4000). ❷

The main ethnic group in Yatenga is the **Mossi**, who had settled here by the end of the 1330s, when they sacked Timbuktu. It's probable that the Mossi took power in the region in the second half of the fifteenth century, though some claim that this happened several centuries earlier. The Dogon, then living in the north of the region, fled up to the Bandiagara escarpment in Mali, while the Samos, based in the east, stayed on and have now more or less assimilated with the Mossi.

The principal state was run by the **Kurumba**, or Fulse, who claim to have come from the region of Say and Niamey some two hundred years before the Mossi to establish the Kingdom of Lurum, whose last capital was at Mengao, now in Djibo district. Just as the Dogon hadn't resisted the Kurumba invasion, so the Kurumba hardly opposed the Mossi, and the two communities merged into the dual sociopolitical system, still largely operational today, in which the **Mossi** hold political power (as "masters of the sky") while the Kurumba have authority over agriculture and the land (the "masters of the earth"). Each village has a Kurumba "earth chief", whose functions complement those of the Mossi *naba*. Within this same system are the **slaves or captives** (*yemse*). Descendants of prisoners of war, and loyal to the Yatenga *naba*, they live in their own section of town called the *bingo* and were not traditionally considered outright chattels: society gave them opportunities for independence, status enhancement and property rights. Ouahigouya's *bingo* consists of half the city and captives form more than half its population. Village chiefs and court dignitaries are often descendants of captives.

Within this system, there are well-defined occupational roles, including that of **blacksmiths** (*saaba*), who never marry out of the community, usually live in their own wards (*zaka*) inside Mossi villages (though they have one or two villages of their own, like **Séguénéga**), and have special ceremonial duties such as performing circumcisions.

The **Peul** (Fula) are the Yatenga region's other main ethno-linguistic group. Although based in Djibo and outside the Mossi–Kurumba system, they've often played a major role in Yatenga's history. The **Silmi-Mossi**, descendants of unions between Fula and Mossi (which were once considered somewhat disreputable), live in their own villages, mainly isolated in the south and southeast of the region. Lastly, members of three Islamic trading nations, the **Songhai**, **Bamana** and Mande-speaking **Yarse**, also live in Yatenga. The Mossi themselves, despite having resisted the advances of Islam for so long, are nowadays mostly Muslim too.

The Town

Ouahigouya lends itself to gentle meanderings. The only sight as such is **Naba Kango's tomb**, an imposing circular space enclosed by a low white wall between the Mairie and the present *naba*'s compound. According to popular legend, anyone who walks all the way round it will die soon after. The **Yatenga Naba's compound** lies on the old site of Kango's palace. With luck, you may even get to meet the *naba*, who's said to be an expert on Yatenga history – as well he would need to be to justify his position. On the way back towards the centre, the bustling open-air **market** is always worth a wander. Ouahigouya also boasts no less than 37 **mosques**, built in a pretty and distinctive style. Not to be overlooked either is the attractive lake formed by the **barrage** (dam) 1km west of town – the best place for an early-evening stroll. To reach the *barrage*, take the track on the left just before *Hôtel L'Amitié* and then the second turning on the right.

Eating and other practicalities

Hotel food in Ouahigouya is good: *L'Amitié* serves up satisfying meals in two restaurants – one offering European-style three-course menus from CFA4000, the other with simpler local meals for around CFA1750; and the *Dunia's* excellent French–Middle Eastern food makes it the first choice among expats (meals from CFA3000; order in advance). Smaller places, where you pay for the food – rice, yam, pasta, soup, chicken, liver, beans and salad – rather than the service, include the *Faso Benie* next to the STMB bus station – which is not to be confused with *Salon de Thé Faso Beni* on rue de la Suisse opposite the market, where you'll find a small selection of delicious pastries. Another great spot for breakfast (omelettes and coffee) and fresh yoghurt is the *Hawai Café Express* on Avenue de Mopti. If you're near *L'Amitié*, *Caiman's* is popular with locals, offering the likes of *steak-frites* and *pintade* in an attractive open-air setting. For **picnic supplies**, the best place is *Alimentation Chaine-Avion* opposite the Lycée Yadega on Avenue de Mopti.

In the evenings, there's a pleasant atmosphere with fires burning and food being prepared along the roadside. The **cinema** occasionally shows African films, while for **drinking** there's cold beer at the *Auberge Populaire*. The main weekend **nightspot** in Ouahigouya is *Dancing de L'Amitié*, next to the hotel of the same name (Fri & Sat only; CFA1000–2000).

The BICIA-B **bank** changes euros cash; the BIB bank changes nothing, but does have an ATM accepting Visa. Global Change on Avenue de Mopti is a bureau de change with decent rates for cash euros and dollars. **Internet** access is available at the Lycée Yadega or the main **post office** opposite the Mairie. If you want to explore some of the sights around Ouahigouya, **renting a bicycle or mobylette** makes good sense; head to the section of the market near the STAF bus station to make enquiries and expect to pay around CFA500/day for a bicycle or CFA3000/day for a *mobylette*.

Around the Yatenga district

Most of Yatenga's sites of interest are spread around the villages in the vicinity of Ouahigouya. Its first capital, and the Mossi capital before Yatenga's secession, was La, now called **LA-TODIN**, beyond the borders of modern Yatenga, 22km west of Yako. The fourth Yatenga Naba, Guéda, moved his capital north to **GOURCY**, where you can see the **sacred hill** on which his successors are still enthroned. Here, too, are the royal amulets stolen by Pabre on behalf of her brother Yadega. In the civil wars of the 1890s, the Sons of Sagha kidnapped the amulets, thus preventing the French from crowning Naba Boulli until they were returned at the end of 1897. Gourcy is on the main Ouagadougou–Ouahigouya road, 42km south of Ouahigouya.

The kingdom's third and penultimate capital, **SOMNIAGA** was seized from the kingdom of Zandoma by Naba Vanteberegum as part of his campaign to enlarge Yatenga. Seven kilometres south of Ouahigouya on the Ouaga road, it makes a good walk first thing in the morning (but don't forget to carry a few litres of water), or you can rent your own wheels in Ouahigouya. Most of Yatenga's *nabas* are buried here in the **royal cemetery** (*nayaado*) and looked after by the Yaogo Naba, the man to find if you want to see it. One quaint Yatenga burial custom was the interment of the *nabas*' court jesters – alive – with their dead king.

Moving on from Ouahigouya

There are plenty of **buses** every day running along the good paved road to **Ouaga** (3hr; CFA3000), including SOGEBAF (eight buses daily; ☎40.55.07.31); STMB (four buses; ☎40.55.00.59); and STAF (five buses; ☎40.55.30.75). For **Djibo**, STMB runs twice daily (11am & 5pm; 3hr; CFA2000), while for **Bobo-Dioulasso**, try SOGEBAF (eight buses) or STMB (three buses) via Ouaga. If you're heading to **Mali**, transport is scarcer; you'll have to take the daily SOGEBAF bus leaving at 10am to **Koro** (2½hr; CFA2500) and change there.

Of the capitals of neighbouring traditional states, **YAKO** is the easiest to visit, lying some 70km south of Ouahigouya on the Ouaga road. The most striking first impression is of its **mosque**, but its main claim to local fame goes further. Capital of a kingdom founded by Naba Yelkone – son of the same Kumdumye who split with Yadega over the question of the Mossi throne – it was a perpetual object of Yatenga–Ouagadougou rivalry, generally a fief of the latter. Naba Kango managed to force it into submission. The French also found Yako a tough nut to crack. More recently, **Thomas Sankara** was born here; with some discretion, you may be able to get someone to show you exactly where.

ZANDOMA, the region's very first Mossi capital, is now a tiny village some 40km southwest of Ouahigouya, northwest of Gourcy. The chief still claims descent from **Naba Rawa**, whose tomb can be seen close to his compound.

Other places of interest in and around Yatenga include: **RAMATOULAYE**, 25km east of Ouahigouya on the road to Rollo, with another impressive **mosque**, a major centre of Hammalism (see p.757) in colonial days; **LAGO**, some 30km south of Ouahigouya (reached via Zogoré), **burial site** of the first Yatenga *nabas*; **SIS-SAMBA**, 11km southwest of Ouahigouya and en route to Lago, where the Sons of Sagha installed their pretender to the throne on Naba Boulli's accession in 1894 and which the French sacked the following year; and **MENGAO**, 82km northeast of Ouahigouya on the road to Djibo (27km further), which was the last capital of the kingdom of Lurum and is still the home of the Kurumba paramount "earth chief", the counterpart of the Yatenga Naba, who himself is the Mossi paramount sky chief.

9.3

The Gourounsi country

The area around Pô on the Ghanaian border **south of Ouagadougou** is dominated by the **Gourounsi**, or Grusi (an ethnic group who are usually said to include the Kassena, the Nouna and the Sissala from around Léo), whose distinctive architecture provides the region's main attraction. Gourounsi country also boasts a couple of national parks – difficult to get to without your own transport – and some interesting archeological remains near Léo.

The Gourounsi traditionally build their **houses** from mud in smooth, sand-castle shapes, often painted with striking diamond patterns. Larger compounds may consist of whole labyrinths of submerged rooms and doorways through which people weave and duck. Buildings are not expected to last more than a few seasons and new houses are built around the foundations of older dwellings, resulting in a characteristic organic appearance to compounds and villages. Also typical are the forked and notched logs, leant against the walls, which are used as ladders to the flat roofs where grain is commonly dried, out of the reach of goats. Women gather here to chat and smoke during the day, the whole family sleeps here, and all sorts of stuff is stored on these roofs. You can often tell the status of a family from the height of its walls and village chiefs usually have the largest and most impressive compounds – though not necessarily the prettiest.

How long the people known as **Gourounsi** (originally a Mossi term of denigration) have lived in the region isn't clear, but Mossi tradition claims they were pushed back across the Red Volta River by the thirteenth Mogho Naba, Nakiem, at the end of the seventeenth century. Never united, the various strands of Gourounsi-speakers have long existed in a state of near-permanent village war. Their lack of central government has always made them vulnerable to attack from more organized groups, especially the Mossi, who often made raids into the area for slaves. Conversely, many Mossi dissidents set themselves up as chiefs in Gourounsi-land, and their families continue to live here. Gourounsi chiefs possess sacred objects called *kwara* – insignia of office – which are handed down from generation to generation.

At the end of the nineteenth century, the Gourounsi were the targets of Djerma Muslim zealots from the Niamey region, who stormed down on horseback and engaged in heavy **slave-raiding** under the pretext of a jihad. They converted the son of the chief of **Satí** and set up shop there, almost decimating the lands of the Sissala, Nouna and Kassena, before being defeated by a Gourounsi–French alliance in 1895.

If you learn no other **words of Gourounsi**, at least learn to say *Din le*, the all-purpose greeting, which means "Thank you". There's a little more vocabulary on p.729.

Travelling from Ouagadougou to **Pô**, the region's main town, you pass through **KOMBISSIRI**, 40km south of the capital. This town became a Muslim centre following the settlement here of a community of **Yarse** (Mande-speaking traders) in the eighteenth century. Its religious status was developed by the pro-Muslim 25th Mogho Naba, Sawadogho, who ruled from 1825 to 1842 and had the mosque built. The mosque is 4km east of the town: follow the *piste* from the police checkpoint at the northern end of Kombissiri.

Pô

PÔ lacks traditional architecture, but has plenty of fountains with revolutionary names – "Nelson Mandela", "Enver Hoxha", "Les Trois Luttes". Coming from Ghana, Pô is a gentle introduction to some of French Africa's more tiresome aspects – higher prices and an obsession with *papiers*. The Pô police are fond of asking for these and you can expect a fair number of spot checks, but like most of the townspeople they're friendly enough and there's no big hassle. The legions of goods-carrying lorries plying the road between Accra and Ouagadougou are also not immune from these checks, resulting in frequent bottlenecks on the main road through town, where the choking exhaust fumes can be quite oppressive. Pô is also a garrison town with a chequered history – though the soldiers don't obtrude.

Some history

According to legend, Pô was founded around 1500, by a Mossi man, **Nablogo**, son of Mogho Naba Oubri. He started cultivating a field (*pô*) but got into a land-rights dispute with Kassena neighbours. About this time, a certain **Gonkwora** from Kasana near Léo turned up here, having left his village after being disinherited of his rightful chiefship. He brought three magic bracelets with him (still looked after by his descendants in Pô) and fell in with Nablogo, who helped him, and in whose dispute with the Kassena he interceded. Gonkwora's brother – the ancestor of Pô's present chief – then arrived from their home village with the village *kwara*. Gonkwora meanwhile married Nablogo's daughter and they all lived happily ever after. Gonkwora's tomb is supposed to be under a sacred baobab in the Kasno quarter of town.

More recent and less halcyon history has also been made in Pô. In 1976, **Thomas Sankara** set up the Centre Nationale d'Entrainement here, taken over by Blaise Compaoré in 1982. The following year the Ouédraogo regime arrested Sankara and fellow officers. Pô became a radical focus for students, young workers and academics, who came to join the commandos. In August 1983, the coup that toppled Ouédraogo, fired the revolution and put Sankara in power was launched here. And it was from Pô that Compaoré planned a second takeover in 1987, which led to Sankara's untimely death and put Compaoré in power.

Practicalities

Accommodation in Pô is pretty basic, but as a frontier town, there is at least some choice. All of the hotels are located on the Ouagadougou (north) side of town. The friendly and brightly painted *Auberge Agoabem* on the main road (℡50.40.31.42 ❶) has running water, clean rooms (some s/c), and a decent restaurant and bar on site. A good alternative is the nearby *Hôtel Mantora*, 100m off the main road behind the *cité* (housing development) (℡50.40.30.25 ❶); the 24 aid-workers' houses here, built by Sankara, have fans (some with showers) and are set around an attractive courtyard. Just north of here, 300m off the main road, *Hôtel Lido* (℡50.40.32.41 ❷) has comfortable s/c rooms with fan and a reasonable restaurant, but is overpriced and not particularly friendly. A little further north, 500m off the main road near the water tower and cattle stables, *Esperance Tiandora* (℡50.40.34.39 ❷) offers pleasant rooms with tiled floors in a quiet rural setting.

For street **food**, try near the market and around the cinema. Every evening, there's good fried fish from the Black Volta, *brochettes*, guinea fowl, roast mutton and plenty more. There's a handful of sit-down places, too, dishing up all of the above, plus couscous, omelettes, rice, spaghetti and *tô*: try *Resto Café de la Cité*, around the corner from the *Mantora*, with its relaxing open-air eating and **drinking** area, or *La Pyramide*, opposite *Auberge Agoabem*, whose road-facing terrace is ideal for watching the world go by. Pô's main **nightlife** venue is *Le Matignon*, just down the road from the *Lido*, where there's dancing on Friday, Saturday and Sunday nights (CFA500–1000).

The banks in Pô don't **change money**, but money-changers milling around the departure point for taxis to Ghana will exchange Ghanaian cedis, euros, dollars and (if you're lucky) sterling for CFA francs, albeit at bad rates. You'll find **Internet** access at G Ati Cyber Café on the main road on the Ouaga side of town.

Around Pô

The best of the Gourounsi country is to be found outside Pô and in the smaller villages along the roads parallel with the frontier both to the east and west of the town. The Gourounsi traditional capital, **Tiébélé**, has the finest architecture, and the highest volume of visitors. The rudimentary **Parc National de Pô** traverses the Ouaga–Pô road and, south of **Nobéré**, you may see representatives of the district's elephant herds – one of the few places in West Africa where "Elephants on Road" is a delightful possibility. Finally, if you can find transport from Pô (tricky except on Sun, which is Léo's market day), you could make the 126-kilometre trip to the Djerma-Gourounsi ruins near Léo.

Tiébélé

TIÉBÉLÉ, the traditional Gourounsi capital, 31km east of Pô, is something of a tourist attraction, and worth a visit. The chief here is the most important *chef de canton* in Gourounsi country and his **compound** – a magnificent maze of mud-pie huts – is the town's main attraction. Coming into town from Pô, you'll pass the excellent *Restaurant Titanic*, soon after which the road bends to the left. Follow the track to the right here for about 400m, past the football field, to reach the chief's

Moving on from Pô

Travelling to **Ouagadougou** (2½hr; CFA2000), you're less likely to be held up at police checkpoints if you use one of the main bus companies: **Rakieta** (☎50.40.30.42) go to Ouaga four times a day; **STMB** do the route three times daily (note the Rakieta terminus in Ouaga is in the city centre, within easy walking distance of many of the capital's hotels). Bush taxis also leave for Ouaga from Pô's *autogare* next to the police station.

Heading south into **Ghana**, taxis congregate on the eastern side of the main road 200m south of the *autogare* and go to Paga (30min; CFA500) and Bolgatanga (1hr; CFA1500), especially on Fri (market day in Bolga). Alternatively, you could hitch from the customs post just south of town. The STC Ouaga–Accra bus also halts in Pô and is scheduled to roll into town four times a week – though you may struggle to get a seat.

Transport to **Tiébélé** and **Léo** is much easier to find on market days (held every third day in Tiébélé, and on Sun in Léo). On other days, you'll usually find vehicles to Tiébélé (1hr; CFA500) leaving from opposite the Rakieta station – but come before 8am. To other destinations such as the wildlife reserves, you may have to make private arrangements with taxi drivers or car or moped owners, though taxis are expensive if you want to do a *déplacement* (around CFA30,000/day). To **rent mopeds** (around CFA4000/day), enquire at *Hôtel Mantora*.

compound. You're bound to be met by one of the guides from the Association pour le Développement de Tiébélé (☎76.59.93.02), who will ask you to sign the visitor's book and pay CFA1500 to visit the compound. The interesting tour lasts some thirty minutes – ask to scale the refuse heap by the entrance, which has excellent views of the compound and the town. For those wishing to stay the night, there are one or two basic *campements* (●).

Tiakané

The houses at **TIAKANÉ**, 7km west of Pô, aren't as striking as Tiébélé's and consequently the village is less visited. This is especially true since the collapse of the **Cave du Binger** in the chief's compound. This mini-underground labyrinth was where the villagers hid the nineteenth-century French explorer Binger from a party of Mossi fighters who were out to kill him. Poking around underground – previously the highlight of any visit is now impossible. Binger went on to become governor of Côte d'Ivoire; and more recently, his family sent funds from France to build a school for the village. Tiakané does, however, make a nice early-morning walk from Pô, especially after rain.

The Ranch de Gibier de Nazinga and Parc National de Pô

There are two **reserves** near Pô, but you'll need your own transport or hired vehicle to reach them. The **Ranch de Gibier de Nazinga** (hunting season Dec–June; open year-round for tourism; CFA8500; camera CFA1000; guide CFA2000), of which the northern boundary runs along the south side of the Léo road, is easily reached and offers good chances of spotting wildlife. If you're setting out from Pô, count on spending CFA40,000–60,000 for a day in a rented vehicle.

Set up by Canadians to study wildlife resource management, the park is relatively bursting at the seams with elephants, and also harbours several species of monkeys, baboons, antelopes, gazelles, warthogs and, rather surprisingly, lions. There's **accommodation** at the *Camp Touristique de Nazinga* (☎50.41.36.17 ●), which offers basic bungalows with electricity and fans or dorm rooms (CFA5000 per person). There's also a **restaurant** serving meals from CFA1000. A ranger will accompany you around the reserve; if you don't have your own transport, you can hire vehicles at the reception (CFA15,000 per trip), although the two on offer are regularly booked up. It's even possible to do an unofficial tour on foot, though you do so at your own risk. There's an observation area in the *campement* grounds, from which you can often spot a fair amount of wildlife.

The **Parc National de Pô** (hunting season Dec–June; open year-round for tourism) has been in severe decline, although recent initiatives such as the 2006 programme to establish corridors allowing elephants to move, unobstructed by human settlements, between Nazinga, the Parc National de Pô and the forests of northern Ghana, may have a positive effect on the park's dwindling wildlife. However, the infrastructure remains nonexistent, with no organized park-viewing trips, and the few *pistes* are in poor shape. You can check to see if the situation has improved at the park office, 50m past the post office in Pô on the road to Tiébélé (T50.40.32.29). The park's main gate is 31km north of Pô, 5km south of the bridge over the Red Volta; baboon and antelope are the most obvious inhabitants, but the park also shelters elephant, buffalo and warthog, though they're more difficult to spot. About 11km south of the entrance, on the west side of the road, you'll see the **tomb of Kaboré Tambi**, a park ranger shot in this spot by poachers in 1987. The park's other name is Parc National Kaboré Tambi.

Léo and the Djerma-Gourounsi ruins

A small border town with a smattering of places to stay and eat, **LÉO**'s main attraction is the nearby **ruins** in the villages of Satí and Yoro. They date from the period of the **Djerma invasions** at the end of the nineteenth century, when the Djerma made alliances with Gourounsi Muslim chiefs. Satí became the capital of a Djerma mini-state and Yoro was fortified as a holding place for slaves and booty acquired in raids on the local "infidel" Gourounsi. Later, the Gourounsi Muslim leaders had a change of mind about their Djerma business partners and revolted – a resistance which eventually involved collusion with a Djerma renegade called Hamaria, who successfully enlisted French support to defeat the Djerma. French involvement led, as everywhere, to a colonial sell-out and the formal "protection" of the Gourounsi.

SATÍ, 22km northwest of Léo, has patchy remains of fortifications and battlements, especially on the eastern side, while a kilometre to the south, the chief's personal mosque and compound is still visible. Seven kilometres back down the road to Léo are the ruins of more fortifications – including triangular loopholes and a well, used by the Djerma while besieging Satí. **YORO**, 32km west of Léo on the way to Diébougou, still preserves a long stretch of wall, part of the Djerma treasure house. Admittedly, none of these remains are very impressive, but the search for the ruins makes a good excuse to poke around the area. If you have your own transport, Léo is a reasonable night-stop en route from Gourounsi to **Lobi country** (see p.776); for accommodation try *Auberge de la Sissili* (T50.1.32.32 ①) or the noisier *Bar Cosmopolis* (T50.31.30.19 ①).

9.4

Bobo, Banfora and the southwest

Fed by the **Comoé** and other lesser rivers, the southwest is the hilliest and most densely forested region in Burkina, and a pleasant change from the relentless grasslands which cover most of the country. Rich vegetation camouflages a wealth of natural sites, ranging from **waterfalls** and **lakes** to striking **cliff formations**. The southwest also contains important urban centres – **Bobo-Dioulasso** and **Banfora** – that grew up on the Abidjan railway line in this productive agricultural region.

> ### By bus from Ouaga to Bobo
>
> "For the first-time visitor the hours shoot by with picture-book traditional villages in a landscape changing from arid to the greener savannah of the west. Bring bottles of water, and maybe a scarf to counteract the dust/sun streaming through curtain-less windows."
>
> John Falkner, UK

Bobo-Dioulasso and around

Burkina's second city, with around 350,000 inhabitants, **BOBO-DIOULASSO** ("Home of the Bobo and the Dioula") was long the country's economic capital, a position which has only in recent decades been usurped by Ouagadougou. Yet life moves at a slow pace here, and Bobo has style and a great atmosphere. Sweeping avenues roofed by the foliage of cool mango trees, colonial buildings in the *style soudanais* and a rich mixture of peoples give it a unique character that makes it one of the most inviting places to unwind anywhere in West Africa. It's also a traditional music centre, with *balafon* orchestras and electric bands adding night-time action to the town's many bars. As Burkina's principal tourist destination, Bobo's only drawback is the hassle of dealing with countless guides and vendors constantly touting for business. Unfortunately, despite efforts by the authorities to control the situation, the aggravation is steadily getting worse. Guides hang around the hotels and bars, the market and main attractions, and the tedious business of fending them off can compromise Bobo's relaxed vibe.

Some history

Bobo was founded in the fifteenth century, when it was known as **Sya**, or "island". According to tradition, a man named Molo Oumarou came here and, after founding villages in Timina and Sakabi, built a house in a clearing of the woods by a stream called the Houët. A village of Bobo-Fing and Bobo-Dioula people grew up around this original home. The French arrived in the late nineteenth century, setting up

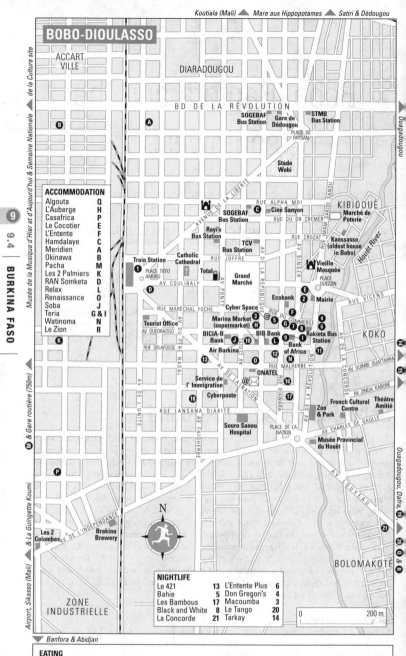

BOBO-DIOULASSO

Koutiala (Mali) ▲ Mare aux Hippopotames ▲ Satiri & Dédougou

ACCART VILLE

DIARADOUGOU

BD DE LA RÉVOLUTION

SOGEBAF Bus Station
Gare de Dédougou
STMB Bus Station
PLACE DE PAYSAN

Stade Wobi

RUE ALPHA MOI
KIBIDOUÉ
Marché de Poterie
SOGEBAF Bus Station
Ciné Sanyon
RUE DU DR CREMER
Kanssasso (oldest house in Bobo)
Rayi's Bus Station
TCV Bus Station
RUE CROZAT
Vieille Mosquée
Train Station
Catholic Cathedral
RUE JOFFRE
Total
Grand Marché
PLACE OUEZZIN
PLACE TIÉFO AMORO
RUE COULIBALY
Ecobank
Mairie
RUE VICENS
KOKO
RUE MARÉCHAL FOCHE
Cyber Space
Tourist Office
Marina Market (supermarket)
BICIA-B Bank
BIB Bank
Rakieta Bus Station
Air Burkina
Bank of Africa
RUE DELAFOSSE
Service de l'Immigration
ONATEL
Cyberposte
RUE MALHERBE
AV GUIMBI OUATTARRA
AV ZINDA KABORÉ
RUE LANSANA DIAKITÉ
Souro Sanou Hospital
PLACE DE LA NATION
Zoo & Park
French Cultural Centre
Théâtre Amitié
Musée Provincial du Houët
AV CHARLES DE GAULLE
BOLOMAKOTÉ
Les 2 Colombes
Brakina Brewery
AV DE L'INDÉPENDANCE
N
ZONE INDUSTRIELLE
0   200 m

ACCOMMODATION

Algouta	Q
L'Auberge	H
Casafrica	P
Le Cocotier	E
L'Entente	F
Hamdalaye	C
Meridien	A
Okinawa	B
Pacha	M
Les 2 Palmiers	K
RAN Somketa	D
Relax	L
Renaissance	O
Soba	J
Teria	G & I
Watinoma	N
Le Zion	R

NIGHTLIFE

Le 421	13	L'Entente Plus	6
Bahie	5	Don Gregori's	4
Les Bambous	17	Macoumba	3
Black and White	8	Le Tango	20
La Concorde	21	Tarkay	14

EATING

Amina Yaourt	18	L'Eau Vive	12	La Nouvelle Canne d'Or	15	Sidwaya	1
La Bonne Miche	7	L'Escale	19	Restaurant L'Entente	10	La Sorbetière	2
Delwende	9	Glacier Les Oscarines	16	Mandé	11		

Banfora & Abidjan

9.4 BURKINA FASO

Musée de la Musique d'Hier et d'Aujourd'hui & Semaine Nationale

de la Culture site

Ouagadougou

Ouagadougou, Dafra,

Airport, Sikasso (Mali)

& La Guinguette Koumi

M & Gare routière (750m)

their first administrative headquarters here in 1897. In 1928, Pépin Malherbe broadened the town limits as Bobo awaited the arrival of the **railway line** from Abidjan. The RAN pushed through in 1934, two decades before the line was extended to Ouaga, and a large colonial town grew up around the station, a short distance from the original settlement (the graceful, Sudan-inspired architecture of the *gare routière*, market and Palais de Justice dates from this period). Bobo thus gained a large economic headstart on Ouaga, which helps to explain its commercial importance today. On the main routes to Mali and Côte d'Ivoire, the town has also acquired an international flavour, with numerous foreign workers and students, plus a constant stream of overland travellers.

Information and accommodation

For **tourist information**, contact the Office National du Tourisme Burkinabe (ONTB) on Avenue de l'Unité just south of the train station (Mon–Fri 7am–12.30pm & 3–5.30pm; ☏ 20.97.19.86 ⊛ www.ontb.bf). The staff can answer questions about nearby excursions, provide some very dated brochures and a more up-to-date list of approved **guides**. For airline and flight information, see "Listings", p.770.

Accommodation

Bobo has a good range of **accommodation** to suit all budgets, much of it conveniently located right in the centre of town.

Budget

🏃 **Algouta** Secteur 5, off av Louveau, 2km from the centre ☏ 20.98.07.92. Cosy little place in a quiet residential area. Tastefully decorated rooms with large bathrooms, or there's the possibility of camping (CFA2000) in the shady grounds in the company of two resident tortoises. Also has a noteworthy terrace restaurant (see review, p.769). ❷

Casafrica off av de l'Indépendance near the Brakina Brewery ☏ 20.98.01.57 ⊛ www.casaafrica .free.fr. Popular place (booking in advance recommended) with clean rooms arranged around a quiet, shady courtyard (where you can also camp for CFA1500). Good value, but indifferent service. ❶

🏃 **Le Cocotier** place Ouezzin, opposite the Mairie ☏ 20.98.47.10. The best budget option in town, with a good choice of fan-equipped rooms with or without bathroom, a wonderful roof terrace overlooking Bobo's main square, a restaurant and attentive staff. ❷

Hamdalaye rue Alpha Moi, near Sogebaf ☏ 20.98.22.87. Nice management and very clean, s/c rooms with fan. Tranquil place in a busy part of town. ❷

Meridien av de l'Unité ☏ 20.98.03.42. Offering several categories of sensibly-priced rooms, some s/c with fan or a/c. ❷

Okinawa Accart Ville district, Secteur 9, on the way to the stadium ☏ 20.97.05.97. Well-maintained and welcoming hotel with simple rooms (some s/c) with fan and an adjoining bar. A bit far out, but very good value. ❶

Pacha rue Malherbe, 500m west of the railway tracks ☏ 20.98.09.54. Swiss/French-owned hotel with spotless, albeit a little overpriced, rooms with fan or a/c. Camping (CFA2000) in the attractive gardens is an appealing alternative. The on-site restaurant offers excellent, though expensive, dishes from CFA3000. ❸

Renaissance av de la République ☏ 20.97.86.24. Ordinary rooms with mosquito net and fan or a/c grouped around a nondescript courtyard. A new building has been added, but the rooms don't differ much. ❷

Teria 2129 av Diawara ☏ 20.97.19.72 ⓔ hotelteria@yahoo.fr. Comfortable and calm place with an ideal location near the market, a very nice, leafy courtyard, and friendly staff. There's another branch of the hotel, with similar rooms, in the building of the former *Oasis* hotel on av Ouédraogo. ❸

Le Zion Kunima district, Secteur 6, 5km southeast of the centre ☏ 78.86.27.25 ⓔ cbodelet@voila.fr. Basic but satisfactory rooms (with or without bathroom) in a quiet setting, with the possibility of various cultural events organized by the management. There's an on-site restaurant serving a good selection of food. Popular despite its distance from the centre, so book ahead. ❶

Moderate to expensive

Les 2 Palmiers 200m west of the railway tracks ☏ 20.97.27.59 ⓕ 20.97.76.45 ⓔ hotelles2palmiers @fasonet.bf. Seven cheerful s/c rooms with a/c and

Bobo surface arrivals and departures

In addition to domestic destinations, Bobo is a springboard for **Mali** (Sikasso, Mopti, Bamako) and **Côte d'Ivoire**. You can get details on buses and flights from Bobo's travel agents: try Tropic Voyages at *L'Auberge* hotel (T20.97.67.63). To reach Gaoua in the Lobi country, it's better to take the paved route via Pâ and Diébougou than travel via Banfora.

Trains

Ouagadougou–Abidjan trains operate three times a week, departing Bobo at 4pm on Tuesday, Thursday and Saturday, and offer one possible means of reaching **Banfora** (2½hr). The train returns Wednesday, Friday and Sunday, departing Bobo for Ouaga at 3pm (7hr). For more information, contact Sitarail (T20.98.15.71) or check at the station – and buy your tickets in advance. Trains often run late and departure times are only rough estimates.

Bush taxis and buses

The main *gare routière* for bush taxis is on the west side of Bobo, about 1km beyond the railway tracks. However, unless you're going to Sikasso in **Mali** (4hr; CFA4000; road now paved the whole way) or various places in northern **Côte d'Ivoire**, you won't really need to use the *gare routière*, since all other destinations are served by private bus companies, whose depots are conveniently located in the city centre.

Rakieta T20.97.18.91. Ouaga (1 bus daily; CFA5000), Banfora (10 daily; CFA1000), Gaoua (2 daily; CFA4000), Hamale (1 daily).

SOGEBAF off rue Alpha Moi, near the *Hamdalaye* hotel (T20.97.15.37). Ouaga (every 2 hours; CFA5000) and Banfora (every hour; CFA1000); destinations in Côte d'Ivoire and Mali from their main station on bd de la Révolution.

STMB T20.97.08.78. Banfora (2 buses daily; CFA1000), Ouaga (6 daily; CFA5000–6000).

TCV rue Crozat T20.97.76.76. Ouaga (5 buses daily), Banfora (5 daily), Bamako (1 daily; CFA10,000), Cotonou and Lagos (1 weekly, Sat).

TV in a quiet location within easy walking distance of the centre. ⑥

🏃 **L'Auberge** 685 av Ouédraogo
T20.97.17.67 F20.97.21.37 Ehoberge @fasonet.bf. Central, colonial-style upmarket hotel with attractive, quite luxurious rooms with hot water, satellite TV, fridge and a/c. There's a fantastic pool with a terrace that's a popular place for drinks, and billiards in the bar. Try to get a room with a balcony. The restaurant, serving French cuisine, can be rather hit and miss, however. ⑥

L'Entente rue du Commerce, at av Binger T20.97.12.05. Good s/c rooms with fan or a/c and mosquito nets, right in the thick of the action. ⑥

RAN Somketa av Coulibaly, opposite the train station T20.97.09.00 F20.97.09.12 Ehotran@fasonet .bf. Three-star hotel with bright, well-equipped rooms with all mod-cons and a pool, though the place lacks

atmosphere and is beginning to look a little dated. Not really worth the high prices. ⑦

🏃 **Relax** rue Diawara T20.97.22.27 or
20.97.00.96 F20.97.13.07. The s/c rooms here have benefited greatly from extensive renovations and are now among Bobo's most comfortable, with superb beds, satellite TV and a/c. There's also a pool. ⑥

Soba av Clozel T20.97.10.12. Colonial-style place, with spacious rooms, some with a/c and TV, and a pleasant patio garden. Same owners – and prices – as *L'Entente*. ⑧

Watinoma rue Malherbe, at av Binger T20.97.20.82 F20.97.57.30. Adequate though small s/c rooms with a/c, hot water and satellite TV. The restaurant serves European dishes (from CFA3000) and speciality pizzas (around CFA4000). ④

The Town

Situated in the heart of Bobo, the **Grand Marché** is the town's bustling centrepiece, with traders selling all manner of goods. Despite the constant hassle of would-be guides in the streets around the market, few will pester you once you're inside the covered area, and the atmosphere is generally relaxed. The **Vieille Mosquée** (sometimes referred to as the Grande Mosquée) – a *banco* construction originally built in 1880 – is located in Bobo's **old town** in the **Kibidoué** district. You're not allowed in the mosque, but you can take photos from outside. Here, you'll be asked to buy a ticket (CFA1000) and you'll be assigned a **guide** to show you around the historic core of town (there's nothing to stop you wandering through the old town by yourself, although you'll be badgered by guides who rarely take no for an answer). First on the list of worthy sites is the "Kanssasso", the **oldest house** in Bobo, said to date from the fifteenth century. As you follow the guide through the narrow streets of the ancient neighbourhoods, he'll point out **traditional artisans** – mostly blacksmiths and weavers – and finish the tour with a stop at the **sacred fish pond**: the murky backwaters of the Houët stream where huge catfish peer up for food. There's no telling what makes them sacred: fishy totems are a Bobo speciality.

In the midst of your meanderings, don't miss the **Marché de Poterie**, two blocks north of the mosque, where demand is still high for earthenware vessels from remote villages like Dalgan, Tcheriba and Sikiana. Pots vary in size and shape depending on their function, but they're all quite reasonably priced, and there are striking examples of unusual water jugs painted in bright colours and bold designs.

Lastly, it's worth making time to see Bobo's two decent museums. The **Musée Provincial du Houët** on place de la Nation (Tues–Sat 8am–noon & 3–6pm, Sun 8am–noon; CFA500) boasts an interesting collection of **ethnographic artefacts** such as Bobo wooden statues and Senoufo funeral masks, as well as regional clothing worn by the Fula, Senoufo and other peoples. Outside, in the grounds of the museum, you can stroll through beautifully decorated and furnished, full-scale examples of Bobo and Fula houses.

The **Musée de la Musique d'Hier et d'Aujourd'hui** (Tues–Sun 8.30am–6pm; CFA1000; ℡20.98.15.02 ⊛www.aspac.ifrance.com) on Boulevard de la Révolution opposite the site of the Semaine Nationale de la Culture – see p.718 – is run along similar lines to its equivalent in Ouaga (see p.739), although here you'll find more individual examples of different types of instrument (there are over a hundred), all put nicely into context by good descriptions of their cultural significance (in French). You can also watch a short film about African music and listen to CDs.

Bobo's **zoo**, on Avenue de la Révolution (daily 7.30am–6pm; free), which seems to comprise three monkeys, is very missable; the adjacent **park**, however, is the ideal place to escape the guides for a while, and becomes a favoured reading spot for students towards the end of the day.

Eating

Quite apart from its consistently good hotel restaurants, Bobo has plenty of fine **places to eat**, many of them serving up the especially delicious local **beef**. A tempting alternative is the city's excellent **street food**, the clear highlight of which are the delicious and filling chickens cooked in a bag with vegetables and spices over an open fire (CFA1500). The best proponents of this local culinary masterpiece can be found on rue du Commerce opposite *Hôtel L'Entente*.

Les 2 Colombes av de l'Indépendance, opposite the airport roundabout ℡20.97.76.30 (closed Tues). Upmarket restaurant specializing in French cuisine such as *canard aux olives*. Sophisticated atmosphere and meals from CFA4000.

Algouta at the *Algouta* hotel. One of Bobo's most original restaurants, serving the likes of antelope, gazelle, porcupine and other game meat, from CFA2500.

Amina Yaourt av Faidherbe. The best yoghurt in town – and popular with a young, hip crowd.

La Bonne Miche av Binger, at av Ouédraogo. Popular bakery serving good bread and *pain aux raisins*. The dining area is an obvious place for breakfast, even if it's a little dark and uninviting.

Delwende (aka *Chez Tanti Abi*) rue Diawara, opposite the *Relax Hôtel*. Friendly and informal

Bobo, Banfora and the southwest

eaterie serving very cheap local dishes with great fish soup, *riz sauce* and salads.

L'Eau Vive rue Delafosse ☎20.97.20.26 (closed Sun). Sister restaurant to *L'Eau Vive* in Ouaga (see p.743), with similar French and international specialities (steak *tartare*, rabbit *à la niçoise*), waitressing nuns and themed nights with food from around the world. Meals for around CFA4000.

L'Éscale Secteur 5 cité CNSS, off av Charles de Gaulle, 2km from the centre ☎20.97.44.15. One of the classiest places in town, with tables in a pleasant courtyard set around a great pool (CFA1500) where you can order anything from *crêpes* to shrimps (meals from CFA3500).

Glacier Les Oscarines rue Diawara. Sister café to *Oscars* in Ouaga, and with a similar selection of delicious ice creams and other snacks.

Mandé av de la Révolution ☎20.98.28.42. Popular, mid-range restaurant with pleasant outdoor seating serving European dishes for around CFA2000.

La Nouvelle Canne d'Or av Zinda Kaboré, 500m from the French Cultural Centre ☎20.98.15.96 (dinner only; closed Wed). Beautifully decorated with local art and craft works and serving classic French cuisine, excellent seafood and fantastic deserts. Most mains CFA2500–4000.

Restaurant L'Entente rue Delafosse ☎20.97.03.96. Attractive terrace restaurant (not to be confused with *L'Entente* hotel) where you'll find a large menu of African and European meals for less than CFA2000. The attached courtyard bar gets lively from 9.30pm, with loud music and dancing.

Sidwaya place Tiéfo Amoro, next to the train station. One of several bar-restaurants set in their own large gardens around the train station, this one serves a wide range of African dishes from *riz gras* to *yassa poulet* for CFA500–1500.

La Sorbetière av Binger. Just beats *La Bonne Miche* as the town's best bakery, with slightly better pastries and a more cheerful dining area that makes a great place for breakfast.

Nightlife

Like the Ouagalais, the people of Bobo are great night-timers. The percussionist **Frères Coulibaly** and **Mahama Konaté**, the founder of Farafina, are from Bobo and regularly play the town clubs when home from Europe. Some restaurants are worth a visit, notably *Restaurant L'Entente* (see above). There's also a wealth of **traditional music** in the Bolomakoté district just south of the city centre – including *balafons* and calabash drums at *dolo* bars – by far the cheapest entertainment in town.

Le 421 In the *Hôtel Sobur-Tours*, rue Malherbe, at av Faidherbe. Dark indoors club – very frenetic and usually full at weekends.

Bahia rue Diawara. Happening club across from *Hôtel Teria*; busy at weekends. Also serves mediocre food.

Les Bambous av Binger, 200m from place de la Nation ☎78.81.58.12. Named after the resident pet monkey, this French-owned restaurant and music venue is set in attractive gardens and hosts live music every night from 9pm, regularly featuring top-class musicians (CFA600 entrance). Popular with tourists, so expect some hassle from hustlers.

Black and White av Binger, at rue du Commerce. The restaurant is bad (limited menu, dreadful service), but the nightly disco is fine, with good music and plenty of sweaty bodies.

La Concorde av Louveau, Bolomakoté. A favourite local haunt with an upbeat atmosphere in a lively district. A limited selection of meals is also available.

Don Gregori's av de la Révolution. Plush interior reminiscent of a gentleman's club, with African and European music nightly.

Macoumba av de la République. Central and popular club with music every night, although the best atmosphere is definitely at weekends.

Le Tango rue 435, off av Charles de Gaulle, Zone des Écoles. Out of the centre, but well known by taxi drivers. Energetic local drinking spot, with seating under *paillotes*.

Tarkay av Guimbi Ouattara, 1km from the French Cultural Centre. Lively bar and dancing, popular with older Ouagalais. Open, and often busy, all day.

Listings

Airlines and flights Air Burkina is on av Clozel next to *Hôtel Soba* ☎20.97.13.48. They have flights on Tues, Fri & Sun from Bobo to Ouaga (50min; CFA42,500) and flights to Abidjan (Tues & Fri; 1¼hr; CFA116,500).

Banks BIB on av de la République, BICIA-B on

av Ouédraogo and Ecobank on rue Diawara all change cash and traveller's cheques; Ecobank don't charge commission when changing cash. Bank of Africa on av Ouédraogo changes cash € and $ only. BIB and BICIA-B both have ATMs accepting Visa cards.

Bicycle/mobylette rental Easy to find around the Grand Marché, especially at the west end towards the train station; CFA2500–6000/day.

Books, newspapers and maps International press, mostly French, is available at the French Cultural Centre or *L'Auberge* hotel. Bookshops in the market area include Diafca, where you might also be able to buy (dated) city maps.

Car rental The tourist office has a list of guides who also rent cars. Alternatively, you can rent 4x4 vehicles at *L'Entente* hotel (CFA50,000/day for a vehicle seating ten).

Cinemas The comfortable, a/c Ciné Sanyon (closed for renovation at the time of writing) is on av de la République across from the stadium.

Cultural centres French Cultural Centre, av de la Concorde, at av Charles de Gaulle ☏ 20.97.39.79 ⓦ www.ccfhenrimatisse.com. The centre has a good library (Tues & Sat 8.30am–noon & 3–6pm, Wed & Fri 3–6pm, Thurs 8.30am–noon & 3–6.30pm) and outdoor reading area, with French-language magazines and newspapers. African, European and American films on Tues & Sat (CFA800), plus occasional concerts.

Hospital Hôpital Souro Sanou, rue Lansana Diakité ☏ 20.97.00.44.

Internet Try the a/c Cyberposte at the main post office or Cyber Space opposite *Macoumba* (both CFA300/hour).

Post office av de la Nation, at av de la République (Mon–Fri 7.30am–12.15pm & 3–5.30pm, Sat 8–11.30am). Poste restante service available.

Supermarkets Marina Market on av de la République is the best in the centre of town.

Swimming pools Non-guests can use the pools at the *Relax* (CFA2000) and the *RAN Somketa* (CFA1500); another option is the pretty pool at *L'Éscale* restaurant (CFA1500).

Telephones There are *télécentres* all over the city where you can make domestic and international calls.

Theatre Check the schedule at the Théâtre Amitié on av Charles de Gaulle. Also pick up the monthly programme of events at the French Cultural Centre, which usually includes live music and dance performances.

Visa extensions The Service de l'Immigration on av Ponty near the intersection with av de la Nation (Mon–Fri 7am–noon & 3–5.30pm; ☏ 20.97.21.74) will extend the CFA10,000, seven-day visas issued at land borders to ninety days at no additional cost. Bring two photos.

Western Union There are branches at almost every bank in Bobo.

Around Bobo

There are some rewarding side-trips within easy distance of Bobo. If you haven't got a car, the recommended way to see them is by renting a bicycle or moped (see "Listings", above). The best of these excursions used to be to a swimming hole called **La Guinguette**, 18km west of town in the **Kou Forest**, where you could splash around in bilharzia-free waters. However, the site has been officially closed since an Italian film-maker was caught making a porn movie there. If it has reopened (check with the tourist office in Bobo), you can get there by taking the road to Sikasso as far as **Koumi**, interesting in itself, with characteristic pseudo-fortified Bobo architecture (guided visit CFA1000). In the village you'll see a sign to the Guinguette pointing right; follow this path, passing through two villages to reach a fork, then turn right and go straight ahead till you reach the entrance gate (CFA1000).

DAFRA, 8km southeast of Bobo, boasts a **pool of sacred fish** in beautiful surroundings, much more interesting than the underwhelming mud-hole in Bobo. Chickens are sacrificed to the enormous catfish, which are the symbol of the Bobo and reproduced on the wall of the Mairie (town hall) in town. **To get to Dafra** from Bobo, you can either take a taxi most of the way or walk along the path from the junction of Boulevard Charles de Gaulle and Avenue du Gouverneur Général Eboué, right on the eastern edge of town – it's tricky to follow, however, and you'll probably need a guide (kids en route will no doubt oblige for the customary *cadeau*) but it's worth it for the scenery. Set off early and take water. It's a quiet area and muggings are not unheard of, so don't take any valuables. Remember, too, not to wear anything red – it's prohibited at this sacred place, as is taking photos.

Another popular attraction, the **hippo lake** (*mare aux hippopotames*), is located some 60km from Bobo, near Satiri on the road to Dédougou and Ouahigouya. It's a little far to do on a moped, so take a Dédougou-bound taxi from the *gare* de Dédougou, on Boulevard de la Révolution opposite the Shell station near place de Paysan, as far as Satiri (1hr; CFA1000). The taxi stops in small villages along the way, many of them featuring picturesque **Sahelian-style mosques**. To get to the lake from Satiri (another 20km or so), you could try to catch a lift with passing tourists at weekends; alternatively, you could probably find someone to take you on the back of a bike. Fishermen at the lakeside will take you out by pirogue for as close an inspection of the hippos as you're likely to want. Agree a fee in advance – they appreciate aspirins and cigarettes as a tip. If you're extremely lucky, they say you may even spot elephants.

Banfora and around

Although the town of **Banfora** lacks the spark of Ouaga and Bobo, it lies in a beautiful region of cliffs and forests – you'll notice the vegetation getting denser as you approach from Bobo, with the sight of streams and waterfalls from the roadside. Today, the region's economic importance springs from the vast **sugar-cane** projects that have made Burkina a net exporter of refined sugar.

Banfora

With a population of some 50,000, **BANFORA** is Burkina's fifth largest town, developed during colonial times due to its position on the railway line. There are few distractions in town and wandering about won't turn up much apart from the **traditional drinking places** scattered about the backstreets, where you can guzzle *banji* (palm wine) and *chapalo*. To kill an hour or two in the afternoon, a ten-minute walk along the Sindou road takes you across the tracks to the **palm-wine sellers**. Join the old men and women under the mango trees for a calabash or two. In the **evening**, you could head to one of the many open-air nightclubs with garden seating and large dance areas.

The BICIA-B **bank** only changes euros cash, but does have an ATM that takes Visa cards. There's **Internet** access at *Restaurant Calypso*, which is fast but pricey (CFA430/10mins); a cheaper alternative is the cybercafé at the main post office.

Accommodation

Since the area around Banfora has become a major attraction in Burkinabe terms, enterprising young people have started **renting rooms** in their homes (you may be approached and offered rooms upon arrival). A bed and bucket shower at these places usually costs less than CFA2000. There are a few reasonable official places too, including a couple of quite luxurious options.

Market days in western Burkina

Market days west of Bobo follow a predictable weekly pattern which can be useful in itself and for ensuring you don't get stranded somewhere remote without transport: most small villages only have taxi connections with main towns on market days.

Monday Koloko, Kotoura, Samorogouah, Sindou, Soukouraba
Thursday Mahon
Friday Kangala
Saturday Oroda
Sunday Banfora, Gaoua

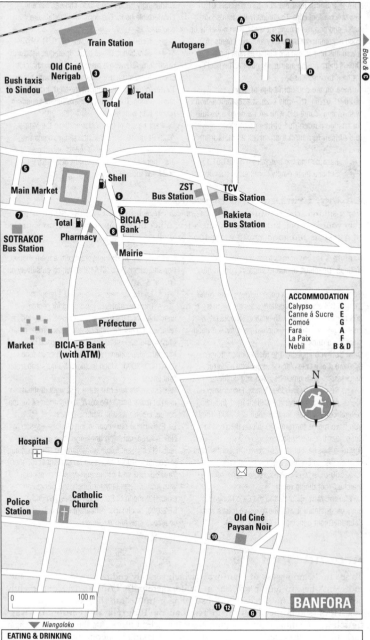

Chutes de Karfiguéla & Domes de Febedougou

Bobo & C

Train Station

Autogare

SKI

Old Ciné
Nerigab ❸

Bush taxis
to Sindou ❹

Total

Total

D

E

❷

Sindou, Lac de Tengrela & Les Pics de Sindou

❺

Main Market

Shell

ZST
Bus Station

TCV
Bus Station

❻

Rakieta
Bus Station

❼

Total

BICIA-B
Bank

Café Colbyco ❽

SOTRAKOF
Bus Station

Pharmacy

F

Mairie

ACCOMMODATION

Calypso	**C**
Canne á Sucre	**E**
Comoé	**G**
Fara	**A**
La Paix	**F**
Nebil	**B & D**

N

Market

Préfecture

BICIA-B Bank
(with ATM)

Hospital ❾

@

Police
Station

Catholic
Church

Old Ciné
Paysan Noir

❿

⓫ ⓬

G

BANFORA

0   100 m

▽ Niangoloko

EATING & DRINKING

Banfora Kossam	**3**	Djiguiya	**1**	McDonald	**6**
Baobab	**12**	Le Flamboyant	**4**	Pâtisserie de la Fraternité	**7**
Calypso	**11**	La Fontaine du Roi	**5**	La Provincial	**10**
Café Colbyco	**8**	La Gaieté	**9**	Yankadi	**2**

Canne à Sucre near the *autogare* ☎ 20.91.01.07
ⓦ www.banfora.com. Traditionally Banfora's top
hotel, and popular amongst expats, with a variety of
good accommodation: luxury a/c apartments (❻),
a/c rooms and stylish s/c thatched huts (both ❹).
Unless there are no apartment guests, the pool is
for their exclusive use.

Comoé on the southern edge of town
☎ 20.91.01.51. No-frills budget accommodation
with rooms (some s/c with a/c) around a beautiful shaded garden (full of mango trees
and African furniture) that serves as restaurant
and bar. ❷

 Fara behind the *autogare* ☎ 20.91.01.17.
Set in a huge empty compound, but with

surprisingly good rooms with shower, fan and
comfortable beds. The communal toilets are
spotless. ❷

Nebil near the *autogare* ☎ 20.91.19.19
ⓔ nebilhotel@yahoo.fr. Upmarket establishment complete with a restaurant, bar and a nice
pool, whose attractive s/c rooms (❺) with a/c and
TV are in round huts with white-tiled floors and
high ceilings. The nearby annexe has cheaper s/c
rooms (❹) with fan.

La Paix centre of town, just north of the Mairie
☎ 20.91.00.16. Six basic and dingy rooms with
mosquito nets, and shared toilets and showers. There's a decent restaurant attached. Basic
breakfast included. ❷

Eating, drinking and nightlife

For a splurge, the **restaurant** at the *Canne à Sucre* hotel (CFA3000–4000) is probably your best bet, but there are quite a few other options in town, and no shortage
of snackbars and good, cheap street-food as well.

Banfora Kossam across from the old Ciné
Nerigab. Delicious milk and yoghurt served all
day.

Baobab at the southern edge of town, near *Hôtel
Comoé*. Chicken and *brochettes* served up in a
laid-back atmosphere with seating indoors or
outside under roadside thatched *paillotes* – a good
place for a drink.

Café Colbyco opposite the Mairie (open from
6.30am). Cosy little place – especially good for
breakfasts – with omelettes, tea and coffee.

Calypso near *Hôtel Comoé*. French-owned
restaurant serving excellent food, including
several curry dishes, for less than CFA3000. They
also have rooms for rent (❶) out on the road to
Bobo near the fire station.

Djiguiya just east of the *autogare*. Decent fish and
chicken dishes such as *capitaine* and *yassa poulet*
(CFA2500-plus), and *crêpes*, served up in an airy
thatched-roof dining room.

Le Flamboyant opposite the old Ciné Nerigab.
Busy bar-restaurant with inexpensive meals and
Saturday-night dancing (CFA500).

La Fontaine du Roi just west of the main market.
Bar and dance floor (CFA1000) which gets lively on
Fri, Sat & Sun nights.

La Gaieté near the hospital. Cheap and
friendly café, well positioned for people-
watching along the town's main paved road, and
reliable for omelettes, salads and other simple meals.

McDonald opposite *Hôtel La Paix* (closed Wed pm).
Popular independent restaurant with good food
(CFA1000–2000) which includes burgers and fresh
fruit juices.

Pâtisserie de la Fraternité just west of the main
market (daily 6am–10pm). A useful address for tea,
coffee, croissants and other pastries.

La Provincial next door to the old Ciné Paysan
Noir. A large, rambling drinking venue (meals on
request only), set in pleasant gardens. The spacious
indoor dance-floor opens up on Sat nights (CFA500).

Yankadi just east of the *autogare*. Very popular
with locals, especially for lunch, this serves an
extensive menu of European dishes (around
CFA2000) or cheaper African meals such as
couscous *gras* and *riz sauce*.

Around Banfora

To see the region **west of Banfora** – which is richly endowed with scenic beauty
spots – it's best to rent a *mobylette* in Banfora (around CFA3000/day), or a slightly
faster moped (CFA6000/day, both excluding petrol) – the shop opposite the ZST
bus station should be able to help. The **Lac de Tengréla** and **Chutes de Karfiguéla** can be difficult to find (numerous tracks lead through a tall growth of sugar
cane most of the year), so you might consider taking someone from town along
with you. Enquire at the hotels or look around the market area for guides – who are
not hard to find.

The Abidjan-bound **train** is scheduled to pass through Banfora at 6.30pm on Tues, Thurs and Sat, returning en route to Bobo and Ouaga on Wed, Fri and Sun. Rakieta (☎20.91.03.81) and TCV (☎70.31.89.20) run regular **buses** to **Bobo** (1½hr; CFA1000); Rakieta also travel the dirt road to **Gaoua** (one bus daily; 4hr; CFA3500); TCV go to **Ouaga** (five buses; 6hr; CFA6500–7000). For destinations in northern **Côte d'Ivoire**, try ZST (☎76.47.44.87). The *autogare* is by the main road on the northern side of town. Taxis depart when full to **Niangoloko** (1hr; CFA800), **Bobo** (1½hr; CFA1000) and **Gaoua** (4hr; CFA4000). You'll have a better chance of leaving promptly if you're there early in the morning.

Lac de Tengréla

Some 7km from Banfora, the **Lac de Tengréla** makes a great excursion. Take the Banfora–Sindou road west out of town; after about 6km, a sign points left to the lake, along a track which runs for 1km to the hamlet of **TENGRÉLA**. Just beyond the village, you can stop and refresh yourself with a cool drink at the *Campement Farafina*, near the lake (☎70.24.46.21 ⊛farafinaclub.free.fr ❶), which has food and basic accommodation in round thatched huts with mosquito nets and bucket showers; you can also camp here. The owner, Souleymane, leads a traditional dance and drumming school, and if you stay here you will probably be treated to an energetic live performance.

At the lake itself, you'll have to pay an entrance fee of CFA1000, or CFA2000 including a pirogue ride. It's occasionally possible to spot the **hippos** that live in the waters here – especially during the dry season (Nov–May). At the edge of the lake, an abandoned cement house provides an ideal place for **camping** if you've got your own tent, although mosquitoes are a problem.

Chutes de Karfiguéla

The **Chutes de Karfiguéla** waterfalls, located in a beautiful, verdant setting, are about 12km from Lac de Tengréla, though the route there is difficult to find (ask the fishermen or people in the vicinity to point you to the *chutes* or *cascades*). They are probably easier to reach direct from Banfora, as the route is signposted most of the way – make sure you turn left at the barrier, along the side of the rice fields, and then make another ninety-degree left turn shortly afterwards. Note that the river has been dammed, and in the dry season (Nov–May) the falls are a disappointing trickle. During the rains, however, they swell to thunder impressively over the solid rock formations. From the car park and entrance, where you pay CFA1000 plus a nominal parking fee, you approach the falls by means of a narrow path bordered with huge mango trees. If you're tempted to swim, be aware that bilharzia is a risk here. You can continue upstream from the falls to reach a number of less spectacular but still attractive falls. About halfway between Banfora and the Chutes, the *Baobab Campement* (☎76.01.28.18 ❷) is a good place to rest up en route and has drink and food (European and African) as well as accommodation in attractive round huts, or you can camp.

Around 3km from the falls are the **Domes de Febedougou** (entrance CFA1000), an oddly shaped cluster of rock formations created by water erosion. Climbing to the top is relatively easy and gives you a great view over the far-stretching fields of sugar cane. Bring plenty of water. The Domes are relatively easy to find from the falls – return to the main track and turn left alongside the cane fields. At the crossroads turn left and follow the signs.

Sindou

SINDOU, 51km west of Banfora, derives its fame from **Les Pics de Sindou**, a three-kilometre-long chain of sculpted crags which form a dramatic backdrop to the village, particularly at sunset. The sandstone has been eroded by the elements into spectacular pancake towers and 50-metre-high needles, often topped with precarious rocky crowns. It's an excellent place to spend a day or two exploring or rock climbing. There's an entrance fee of CFA1000, payable at the roadside by Les Pics, where you'll also be assigned a mandatory guide, although the post is frequently unstaffed – in which case just ask someone in Sindou to show you the easiest route to scramble up to the top of the rocks. Despite the area's natural beauty, Sindou remains little visited. Mango trees line the main street of conically thatched *banco* houses, yet to be replaced by corrugated-iron shacks.

If you opt not to rent a *mobylette* or bike in Banfora you can still **get to Sindou** by public transport, especially on Sindou's market day (Mon). Taxis leave when full from just west of the defunct Ciné Nerigab (2½hr; CFA1250). Once in Sindou, **supplies** are limited to street food and a couple of tiny restaurants. There is some relief, however, with tepid beer at the **bar** which also has ultra-basic *chambres de passage* (❶), but if you have your own equipment, it's much better to camp out among *les pics*.

If you get stranded in Sindou, you can try hitching a ride with the enormous Sofitex cotton trucks that occasionally depart for Banfora.

9.5

The Lobi country

Nestling between the Ghanaian and Ivoirian frontiers, the hilly, tree-scattered savannah of the green and pleasant **Lobi country** is a favourite travellers' destination and an interesting diversion en route from Bobo and southwest Burkina into Ghana. Although the lively town of **Gaoua** and the strange ruins of **Loropeni** are the region's only real tourist draws, the welcoming Lobi themselves, with their well-preserved traditions and *cabaret* drinking bars, make their corner of the country one of the best to visit, especially now that good, tarred roads connect Ouagadougou with Gaoua via Pâ and Diébougou.

Gaoua and around

Although the **ruins** and bustling **market** at **Loropeni** make for an interesting excursion, the principal reason for coming to Lobi country is to soak up the atmosphere of the region's main town, **Gaoua**, which is absolutely shaking with *cabarets* and is the obvious base during your stay in the area.

Gaoua

GAOUA is almost certainly the best place to get acquainted both with *chapalo* and traditional roots music, though obviously the sounds in Bobo-Dioulasso are more refined. The main draw in town, apart from the *cabarets*, is the magnificent Sunday **market**, a maelstrom of colour and activity. Look out for the leatherworkers just north of the market, spread out under a tree west of the mosque. You could also visit the town's sacred grove, **Bafuogi**, which is easily identified by the masses of plucked feathers from sacrificed chickens. The grove is about 1km south of town on the edge of a small hill – head south up the hill towards the hospital office; you'll spot the large water tower on top from a distance. There are great views across town from the grove, too. You're supposed to have a guide, who will tell you spine-tingling tales about the pythons living in the caves.

Up another hill in the administrative quarter, the **Musée de Poni** (Tues–Sun 8am–12.30pm & 3–6pm; CFA2000 including tour) is set in an old colonial-style house and has exhibits of traditional art, the Lobi lifestyle and homes typical of Lobi and other local ethnic groups, together with interesting photographs from the colonial period.

Practicalities

Gaoua has limited **accommodation**. The basic *Hôtel de Poni*, on the southern side of the market (⌁20.90.02.00 ❶), has reasonably clean rooms with fan, although the shared toilets are very grubby – choose an odd-numbered room away from the noisy bar. Even

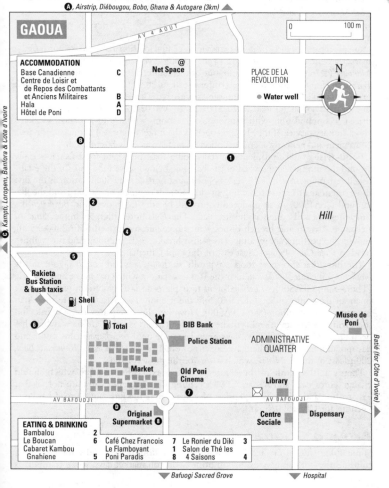

GAOUA

Ⓐ, Airstrip, Diébougou, Bobo, Ghana & Autogare (3km)

AV 4 AOUT

0   100 m

Ⓞ, Kampti, Loropeni, Banfora & Côte d'Ivoire

ACCOMMODATION
Base Canadienne	C
Centre de Loisir et de Repos des Combattants et Anciens Militaires	B
Hala	A
Hôtel de Poni	D

Net Space @

PLACE DE LA RÉVOLUTION

● Water well

N

Hill

Rakieta Bus Station & bush taxis

Shell

Total

Musée de Poni

Batié (for Côte d'Ivoire)

BIB Bank

Police Station

ADMINISTRATIVE QUARTER

Market

Old Poni Cinema

Library

AV BAFOUDJI

AV BAFOUDJI

Original Supermarket Ⓓ ❽

Centre Sociale

Dispensary

EATING & DRINKING
Bambalou	2	Café Chez Francois	7	Le Ronier du Diki	3
Le Boucan	6	Le Flamboyant	1	Salon de Thé les	
Cabaret Kambou Gnahiene	5	Poni Paradis	8	4 Saisons	4

▼ Bafuogi Sacred Grove   ▼ Hospital

Lobi traditions

The Lobi believe in maintaining their **traditions**. Lobi men, for example, still hunt with a bow for hare, guinea fowl and gazelle, and it's common to see men carrying their weapons – arrows traditionally tipped with poison – as they walk along the road. Some customs, however, are disappearing: few Lobi women nowadays wear the disc plugs through their lips which used to be so admired; and the all-in-one method of house building is giving way to easier mud-brick construction.

The traditions the Lobi maintain best are the ones with widest appeal – booze and music. No Lobi town or village would be complete without its **cabarets** – not night-clubs, but places where *chapalo* and *qui-me-pousse* or *patasi* (home-brewed firewater) are consumed in serious quantities and **traditional music** is often played. Many *cabarets* brew their own *chapalo*, and it's so much cheaper than bottled beer that you could afford to shout the whole place a drink for the same price as a bottle of Brakina in a bar. *Cabarets* often keep a drum and a *balafon* handy in case anyone feels like playing, which they often do. Even in the unlikely event you don't acquire a taste for *chapalo* and Lobi music, *cabarets* are the best places to mix with the locals – who are always very welcoming.

more primitive, but dirt cheap and enjoying a central location a few blocks north of the market, are the fanless rooms at the *Centre de Loisir et de Repos des Combattants et Anciens Militaires* (☏76.67.52.39 ❶). A little out of the centre, the spacious compound of the *Base Canadienne*, 1km along the Banfora road (☏20.90.02.11 ❷), is scattered with excellent-value two-room s/c bungalows with a/c. The *Hala*, a pleasant 1.5km walk out on the Diébougou road (☏20.90.01.21 ⓕ20.90.02.66 ❹), offers somewhat over-priced accommodation, with comfortable s/c rooms with a/c or fan and TV; there's also a laundry service. If they have re-opened, the motel rooms (❷) at the *autogare* are a convenient and perfectly adequate option if you have an early bus to catch.

Food-wise you'll find plenty of stalls doing roast meat and fried fish, especially around the mosque, and several of the bars (see below) serve food too. Of the established restaurants, *Salon de Thé Les 4 Saisons*, just north of the Shell station, is the one most orientated to tourists, serving sit-down meals of chicken, spaghetti and the like (around CFA1500) in an enclosed courtyard. Nearby, the more basic *Bambalou* has omelettes, tea and coffee at the streetside. The *Hala* hotel offers a limited range of Lebanese, African and French dishes – mediocre and overpriced (CFA2000–2500), though the portions are gigantic – as well as breakfasts (CFA2000). And for yoghurt, head to *Café Chez François*, just east of the Poni Cinema.

The **bars** that also serve food – typically *riz sauce*, yam and potato ragout, salads, *brochettes* – include: *Le Boucan* near the Rakieta station, which has music and dancing (Thurs–Sun; CFA500); *Le Flamboyant* near place de la Révolution, with its large open-air dance-floor (Sat; CFA500); and the friendly *Poni Paradis*, where there's an indoor a/c dance-floor (Sat; CFA500). However, the best places for a **drink** and socializing are the town's *cabarets*: the venerable *Cabaret Kambou Gnahiene*, which has been around since the 1950s, stays open late – or until the *chapalo* runs out – and has sporadic live music. There are dozens of other places, such as *Le Ronier du Diki*, 200m east of the *Bambalou*, which is one of the most convivial.

There's a BIB **bank** in the centre of town next to the mosque which should change euros cash and has an ATM accepting Visa. **Internet** cafés are not all that easy to find and relatively expensive: Net Space near the Diébougou road has connections for CFA1500/hour.

Around Gaoua

Some 40km west of Gaoua, **Loropeni** has a colourful market and some intriguing ruins nearby – it's an easy excursion from Gaoua on market days, when transport is guaranteed, although you can get there on other days too, using the Rakieta bus to Banfora (to return to Gaoua, you can get aboard when it comes through Loropeni on its return leg from Banfora at around 5.30–6pm).

Loropeni

LOROPENI's **market**, held every five days, is a bustling throng of colour. You can buy fruit, hot food, chillies, multicoloured ground spices and peanut paste, and watch flip-flops being made out of old tyres, and enamel bowls being re-bottomed with bits of vegetable-oil tins ("furnished by the people of the USA"). You might meet Ghanaians selling worming tablets (armed with lurid photographic displays), or Gan women from the west, often wearing brown string mourning bands on their heads, arms, necks and ankles.

If you're looking for **accommodation**, take the road out to Kampti for about a kilometre and ask at the bar on your right, just before the mosque, for directions to a very basic *Maison de Passage* (❶) with no electricity and bucket showers. Across the road from here, the Italian-funded *Foyer Amelioré* (❶) has accommodation in round huts with corrugated-iron roofs, although again there's no electricity. Apart from the *riz-sauce* **restaurant** in the middle of Loropeni's market, there are plenty of vendors along the main road selling grilled meat and soup. *Club Yemsafa* has cheap servings of rice and cold drinks – you'll see a sign to it as you walk to the *Foyer Amelioré*. Drinks are also available at the *buvette* behind the *autogare*.

The ruins

To get to Loropeni's enigmatic **ruins** (entrance 1500CFA), head out of town on the Banfora road. After 3.5km you'll come to a small hill, at the top of which a sign-posted track leads off to the right. Follow it for 500m to the ruins. Though not massively impressive, the Loropeni ruins are among West Africa's very few stone remains, rising up out of the scrub like some lost temple in a Hollywood movie. Unlike the great stone ruins of East Africa and Zimbabwe, they don't get many visitors, and since their origin and the identity of the people who built them are still mysteries, your ideas about them are probably as good as anyone else's. The ruins are more or less rectangular, around 50m long by 40m wide, and would originally have stood 6–7m high. They lack any doors or windows. Inside, the ruins are divided into two enclosures, one large and one small, connected by a door, and each subdivided into further chambers.

Moving on from Gaoua

The best day for transport into or out of Gaoua is Sun (market day). **Bush taxis** and Rakieta buses depart from next to the Shell station just west of the market. To reach **Loropeni** (1hr; CFA1000), it's easiest to catch the 7.30am Rakieta bus to Banfora (a second bus leaves at 2pm) and get off at Loropeni; irregular bush taxis also head out that way. This service is also the surest way to get to **Banfora** (4hr; CFA3500); if you can't find a bush taxi going direct to Banfora, consider first going to **Kampti** (45min; CFA1000), where you should find onward transport. There's usually something to **Doropo** in Côte d'Ivoire, especially on its market day, Thurs, where you'll probably have to change for other Ivoirian destinations.

All the **bus** companies except Rakieta leave from the new *autogare* 3km out of Gaoua on the road to Diébougou (a shared taxi from the centre costs CFA300). Transmif (☎70.22.99.64) and SOGEBAF (☎78.86.27.05) both have a daily service departing at 7.30am to **Ouaga** (5hr; CFA5000–6500), while TSR (☎70.14.87.20) make the same journey twice daily (7.30am and 3pm). All Ouaga buses travel via **Diébougou** (1hr; CFA1000) – the road is tarred all the way to the capital, with occasional rough patches and road repairs slowing things down just a little. TSR also have a twice-daily service to **Bobo** via Diébougou and Pâ (4hr; CFA4000) departing at 8am and 3.15pm.

If you don't have transport, you can usually persuade somebody to let you hire their *mobylette* or bicycle to visit the ruins, as well as the Gan village of **OBIRÉ**, 8km northwest of Loropeni, which is remarkable for its round thatched huts (a thatching style very different from Lobi houses) and for its life-size **mud statues** of ancestral kings (entrance CFA1500). If you prefer, a local will also happily guide you there for a *cadeau*.

The **Gan country** a few kilometres north and west of Loropeni harbours more archeological oddities if you can organize transport. There are ruins near **Yérifoula**, others near **Oyono** and **Lokosso**, and some large relics at **Loghi**.

Diébougou and Hamale

Lying outside the Lobi country proper, **DIÉBOUGOU**'s people are mostly Lobi-Gan and Dagara (Dagarti). There's not a lot to see here, but it's a friendly place, surrounded by more greenery than you'd normally find in a Burkinabe town, and the intricate system of underground defence tunnels nearby – known as **La Grotte** – add some interest. The tunnels were commissioned by the French in 1900 and built using local labour. They are an easy fifteen-minute walk out of town along the Bobo road in Diébougou forest; get directions at the *Relais La Bougouriba* and take a torch.

During the wet season (June–Oct) **crocodiles** collect in the swampy area at the eastern end of town – they're best observed around dawn.

Practicalities

There are a few **accommodation** options in town, the most convenient of which is *Hôtel St Paul* in the compound of the *gare routière* (T70.45.34.74 ❷) where, despite the dirty exterior, there are some surprisingly pleasant rooms with fan and mosquito net. At the other end of town next to the Bobo road, *Campement l'Hôtel* (T20.90.51.60; ❶), which also serves as a bar and pick-up joint, has very dark, basic rooms with fans, and grimey, communal showers and toilets. The nearby *Relais La Bougouriba* (T20.90.52.80 ❹) is smarter and cleaner, with a shower and fan in every room, but very overpriced. The best option is *L'Auberge*, 500m west of *Campement l'Hôtel* (T20.90.52.62 ❷), which occupies a rambling complex with an out-in-the-country feel and has rooms with fans and mosquito nets, clean communal bathrooms, and plenty of peace and quiet.

For **eating and drinking**, *La Bougouriba* has a bar and restaurant offering rice, chicken and *capitaine* fish, while the small eatery inside the *gare routière* and the nearby *Denvers* both do simple meals. For breakfasts of omelettes, yoghurt, tea and coffee, try the friendly *Maison Blanche de la Paix* across from *Campement l'Hôtel*. In addition, there's a run of food stalls around the market and lots of *cabarets* to slake your thirst. **Nightlife** revolves around *Le Point Final* nightclub, which has drinking, an indoor dance-floor and a few streetside tables that make a good place for watching the town's movers and shakers come and go. The BIB **bank** changes euros cash only.

TSR and TRANSMIF **buses** coming from Gaoua stop in Diébougou en route to Ouaga (4hr; CFA4000), usually arriving at 8.30 or 9am. The same companies return to Gaoua (1hr; CFA1000) daily between noon and 1pm from the *gare routière*. Traffic along the road to Léo (paved as far as Dissen, then a reasonable dirt track) is very light; your best chance of finding a bush taxi to Léo (4hr; CFA5000) is on Tuesdays and Saturdays.

Hamale and into Ghana

A busy border town and the main crossing point into Ghana from Bobo-Dioulasso (there's a daily Rakieta bus from Bobo), **HAMALE** has little to offer. If you're looking for a place to drink and sleep, *Mandou* (❶) has basic but reasonably clean rooms; better value than those on the Ghanaian side. Cedis are available at the ordinary (poor) border rate, which is beaten just about everywhere else in Ghana. Almost all **transport on the Ghanaian side** goes to Lawra and Wa, although be prepared for a long wait as traffic is very infrequent along this rough *piste*. From Wa, there are onward connections to Tamali, Kumasi and Accra.

Ghana

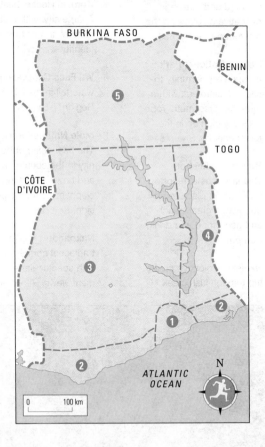

Highlights 784

Introduction and Basics 785

10.1 Accra and around 815

10.2 The coast 831

10.3 Kumasi and central Ghana 852

10.4 The southeast:
       Akosombo, Ho and Hohoe 864

10.5 Northern Ghana 871

Ghana highlights

* **Cape Coast Castle** Among the most impressive of the forts along the coast, sympathetically restored and housing evocative displays on the slave trade. See p.838

* **Kakum National Park** A superb opportunity to see the rainforest, with a three-hundred-metre rope walkway high up in the forest canopy. See p.840

* **Busua** The best of Ghana's coastal resorts, a wonderful place to chill out, with a great beach and good food and drink. See p.849

* **Nzulezo** A glorious canoe trip through lush creek jungle takes you to this community of stilt-house-dwellers. See p.851

* **Kumasi** Hectic, bustling Asante city, with a strong cultural and historical identity. See p.852

* **Wli Falls** Captivating waterfall in the hilly Volta Region. See p.870

* **Mole National Park** The best safari opportunity in the country: relax and unwind spotting elephants from the poolside. See p.874

* **Nakpanduri** An isolated, traditional northern village with spectacular escarpment views. See p.882

▲ Kakum National Park

Introduction and Basics

From a traveller's point of view, **Ghana** has a lot to commend it. Compared with the other Anglophone countries in West Africa, it offers a transport and accommodation infrastructure that's second to none; a cultural mix that's every bit as rewarding as Nigeria's (without that country's immense size or intimidating reputation); and better beaches than The Gambia. Moreover, the Ghanaian government has an enthusiastic commitment to tourism with a number of regional tourist offices set up and plenty to engage visitors.

Ghana was the first modern African country to retrieve its **independence**, in 1957. At the time it was one of the richest nations on the continent – the world's leading **cocoa** exporter and producer of a tenth of the world's **gold**. But after Kwame Nkrumah's optimistic start it suffered a hornet's nest of setbacks. For years, coups, food shortages and sapping corruption combined to make Ghana a place to be avoided.

However, since the near economic collapse of 1979, conditions have improved almost out of recognition and the country is back on its feet. Ghanaians still complain, justifiably, about continued inefficiency and corruption, but politically Ghana is increasingly viewed as a good example of an African **democracy**.

The country has a distinctive personality and perhaps more claim to a **national character** than any other in the region. Formal education has had a major impact, going back four generations now, and there's an inventiveness with language – both written, on signs and in the press, and spoken, in repartee – that hints at a creativity as yet barely unleashed in Africa. Ghanaians are hospitable and generous to a fault, and there's more warmth to be experienced in Ghana than in either of its coastal neighbours.

As regards the **terrain**, Ghana has few highland regions, with the exception of the striking **scarp system** curving through the country – from the Gambaga escarpment in the northeast round to the Wenchi scarp west of Lake Volta, and southeast as the Mampong scarp through the forest. There are some attractive rolling green landscapes and, in the central regions, away from the **cocoa** plantations and the **goldfields**, several large districts of dense **rainforest** with giant hardwoods and palms vying for space. In the eastern Volta region, between Lake Volta and the Togolese border, the hills of the **Akwapim range** roll across the landscape to

GHANA | Basics

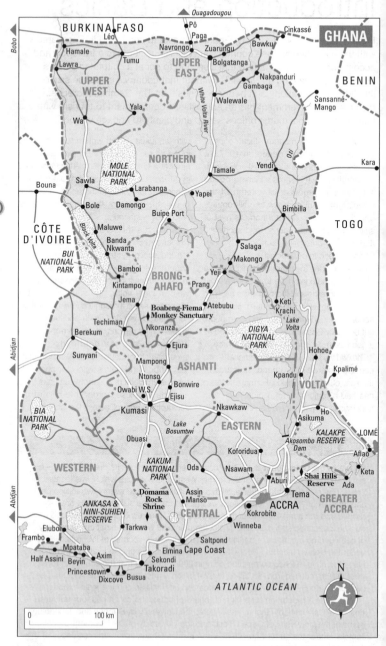

ATLANTIC OCEAN

0   100 km

N

create a district of verdant green valleys and gentle peaks. The biggest impact, however, is made by **Lake Volta**, an enormous artificial lake created in the wooded savannah in 1966, to supply the Akosombo dam with a source of hydroelectricity, which has totally changed the anatomy of the country – not to mention the lives of the thousands of rural dwellers its waters displaced.

The **Accra district** and much of the surrounding bushy, **coastal plain** is surprisingly dry – almost desolate in places, partly the result of an unusual local subclimate – but the coastal road to the west runs within striking distance of the shore for much of its length, and the beaches themselves are alluring. The coast has a special dimension, too, in its European **forts and castles**, some dating from the fifteenth century, which were built as trading posts for gold, ivory and, later, slaves. The beaches of the far southwest are backed by lowland forest and patchy jungle agriculture.

People

Of the myriad ethnic groups who people Ghana, the **Akan** – including the **Fante** and **Asante** (also spelled Ashanti) – predominate. The Asante occupy the central forest, and in pre-colonial days their empire stretched much further west and east, into the regions of present-day Côte d'Ivoire and Togo. The **Ga-Adangme** and **Ewe**, who probably came from Yorubaland in Nigeria, settled mainly in the east and south of the country. The major peoples of the north are all speakers of Voltaic languages and have much in common, culturally, with the Burkinabe over the border in Burkina Faso. They include the southern Mossi kingdoms of **Mamprusi** and **Dagomba** in the northeast, the **Wala** and **Dagarti** in the northwest, and the **Gonja** and other Grusi

peoples – **Kassena**, **Frafra**, **Sissala**, **Builsa** and **Talensi** – near the Burkinabe border.

Islam is widespread among the northerners, some of whom migrated south from Muslim communities in Mali. **Christianity** spread with European involvement in the Gold Coast, but pantheistic beliefs and ancestor veneration remain the most widely practised religions in the country.

Where to go

After decades of neglect, **Accra** looks the part of a capital once again. Unless you're drawn to the nightlife, and your visit coincides with some weekend live shows, you'll only want to spend a few days here before getting out along the coast or into the interior, but however long you're here, it's manageable and friendly enough. The **west coast** is exceptional, and the **castles**, most of which can be visited, provide excellent focuses for beach-hopping. Slightly inland, the protected rainforest of the **Kakum National Park** is one of the country's major natural attractions. To the east, the lush hills and waterfalls of the **Volta Region** are also currently generating great interest among travellers. **Kumasi**, in the centre of the country, has a strong sense of identity, and the forest region around it is scenically and culturally Ghana's most appealing area. The **north** is quite different, both in landscape and people,

Gold

Away from the big goldfields southwest of Kumasi you'd be hard pressed to find much sign of the precious metal, except during major festivals, notably the Ogua Fetu Afahye in Cape Coast. The Ashanti Goldfields Company in Obuasi is the best set up facility to receive visitors (see p.861).

Average temperatures and rainfall

Accra

	Jan	Feb	Mar	Apr	May	June	July	Aug	Sept	Oct	Nov	Dec
Temperatures °C												
Min (night)	23	24	24	24	24	23	23	22	23	23	24	24
Max (day)	31	31	31	31	31	29	27	27	27	29	31	31
Rainfall mm	15	33	56	81	142	178	46	15	36	64	36	23
Days with rainfall	1	2	4	6	9	10	4	3	4	6	3	2

Tamale

	Jan	Feb	Mar	Apr	May	June	July	Aug	Sept	Oct	Nov	Dec
Temperatures °C												
Min (night)	21	23	24	24	24	22	22	22	22	22	22	20
Max (day)	36	37	37	36	33	31	29	29	30	32	34	35
Rainfall mm	3	3	53	69	104	142	135	196	226	99	10	5
Days with rainfall	1	1	1	6	10	12	14	16	19	13	1	1

but its climate is more tolerable and, if there's not a lot that demands to be seen as you pass through – apart from **Mole National Park** – there's plenty of interest in its ethnographic history if you have more time in the area.

When to go

Ghana has a lot more climatic variation than most of West Africa. **Central and southern Ghana** – south of Tamale – is unusual in having two distinct rainy seasons, the first lasting roughly from March to June and the second from September to October. The **far southwest** gets heavy rains, but in **Accra** the rains tend to be light, and it's uncommon to experience day after day of torrential downpour. The **central rainforest** regions tend to be wetter and slightly cooler – although you wouldn't know it because of the high humidity. **The north** is basically hot and dry most of the year, with a climate much like that of Ouagadougou in Burkina, and a single rainy period from June to October.

Getting there from the rest of Africa

Ghana is one of the most popular countries for independent travel in West Africa, its central location making it an excellent starting point for longer travels.

Flights within Africa

All international flights arrive into Accra. From the coastal capitals, Slok Air International operates flights from **Monrovia**, **Freetown**, **Dakar** and **Banjul**. Air Ivoire operates several flights a week from **Abidjan**, **Lomé** and **Cotonou**. Afriqiyah Airways links Accra with **Abidjan**, **Lomé** and its hub of **Tripoli**. Virgin Nigeria operates nonstop flights from **Lagos** (daily) and Chanchangi Airlines operates flights from **Lagos** and **Abuja**.

Ouagadougou is linked with Accra by twice-weekly flights on Antrak Air. Flights from other cities in West Africa require a change of plane, and you'll find it well nigh impossible to get a convenient connection from Nouakchott, Bissau, the Cape Verde Islands or Niamey.

From South Africa, South African Airlines fly four times a week from **Johannesburg**. Ethiopian provides a link from East Africa with a flight from **Addis Ababa** three times a week, while Kenya Airways serves Accra from **Nairobi** five times a week. EgyptAir has flights from **Cairo** to Accra twice a week.

> For details on **getting to Ghana from outside Africa**, plus important practical information applying to all West African countries, covering health, transport, cultural hints and more, see Basics, pp.19–28.

Overland from Burkina

Coming **from Ouagadougou**, you can either take a **bush taxi** or **bus** to the border at Paga, or get transport through to Navrongo, Bolgatanga or Accra. You'll make better time on the road by bush taxi, but the buses are more comfortable and generally get through the border and various checkpoints more quickly. If you're lucky with connections, it can sometimes work out cheapest and fastest to change transport at the border, which is generally an amicable process – though note that it closes at 6pm. The direct STC bus leaves Ouaga for Accra four times a week, and is by far the most comfortable of all the options (around GH¢30 or CFA16,000).

Other crossings include the one between Léo and Tumu and the one at Hamale. Transport is patchy on both sides of the border, and there's no direct through-transport to speak of in either case – your prospects are best by far on market days.

The **fast route to Accra** goes via Tamale, Kintampo and Kumasi; the more easterly route, involving a Lake Volta ferry or canoe crossing between Makongo and Yeji, is rougher and slower.

Overland from Togo

The **border** at Aflao–Lomé is open daily from 6am to 10pm. Watch out for hassles and scams on both sides.

The **Lomé–Accra road** is surfaced, but is tortuously slow in places. Be warned: if you're driving, there are active speed cameras on the few fast stretches.

The quickest way between the two capitals is by **bush taxi** but you'll save the hassle of sitting through vehicle searches if you first get to the border on the western outskirts of Lomé, cross on foot to Aflao in Ghana, and then continue by bush taxi or bus – a total journey of about three hours. You can also take one of the Intercity STC buses which depart Aflao three times a day to Accra (GH¢2.20), and which are more comfortable than bush taxis, but take slightly longer.

Other possible crossing points are: northwest of Kpalimé (Klouto or Wli, both near **Hohoe**) or southwest of Kpalimé (to **Ho**); **Badoudjindji**, a few kilometres west of Badou; northwest of Bassar (hassle-free formalities at Natchamba near **Yendi**); and Pulimakum in

the far northwest corner of Togo, about 30km from **Bawku** (Togolese border formalities take place in Sinkassé as there is no official Togolese exit post at Pulimakum; you go to the officials at the Togo–Burkina crossing in Sinkassé to be officially stamped out of Togo, before entering Ghana at Pulimakum, several kilometres west of Sinkassé). All these routes involve rough travel and delays due to a lack of transport, which is much easier to find on relevant market days (see relevant Guide pages for those).

Overland from Côte d'Ivoire

The coastal stretch of road between Abidjan and Accra is in good condition, and intercity STC and STIF **buses** – not to mention fleets of **bush taxis** – connect the two capitals in around fourteen hours. Buses leave from the Treichville *gare routière* in Abidjan. There's also a fast route direct to Kumasi via Abengourou – also a day's journey – from Abidjan's Adjamé *gare routière*.

Red tape and visas

Visas are required by most non-ECOWAS nationals visiting Ghana. Single-entry (£30 in the UK, $50 in the USA) and multiple-entry visas (£40/$80) are available, though note that upon entering the country, you will be stamped with a sixty-day limit of stay. Extensions are, in practice, only available in Accra and are painfully slow to obtain (see p.829).

If you're carrying more than $5000 or the equivalent in foreign currency into the country, you'll need to make a currency declaration upon arrival.

Info, websites, maps

The **Ghana Tourist Board** has offices in Accra and all the regional capitals throughout the country (Cape Coast, Takoradi, Kumasi, Tamale, Wa, Bolgatanga, Ho, Koforidua, Sunyani). Services are uneven across regions, with little communication between them; they're most useful in tourist areas such as Cape Coast. Their website (Ⓦwww .ghanatourism.gov.gh) has wide-ranging if not always up-to-date information on destinations, tour operators and accommodation.

You can get a feel for Ghanaian **current events and culture** through the very detailed Ⓦ www.ghanaweb.com, which has links to major national newspapers as well as a directory and classified section. More **news**-based coverage is provided by Ⓦ ghanareview.com. A couple of other websites worth a look are: Ⓦ www.ghana .co.uk, containing a miscellany of news, music reviews, recipes and other Ghana information; and Ⓦ www.noworriesghana .com, where the North American Women's Association provides practical information on life in Accra. For basic information about Ghana's **museums**, check out Ⓦ ghana .icom.museum.

The monthly free lifestyle magazine, **Enjoy Accra**, is available in restaurants, shops and hotels in Accra, and **Discover Ghana**, a quarterly magazine providing information about travel, culture and history, costs GH¢2 and is available from the Accra Visitors Centre.

Maps

There is still no really accurate and up-to-date **map of Ghana**. The ITMB (International Travel Maps) 1:500,000 (2005) map is full of roads and villages, but tends to be very schematic and is often misleading. A reasonable map, if you can find a well-printed copy, is the Accra map by Surf Publications (2003), which has a country map on the reverse. Otherwise, the Michelin or Reise-Know-How maps of West Africa (see p.34), though at much smaller scales, will probably serve you better, though they aren't without their foibles, being better on the Francophone countries.

In Accra, the best place to find maps is at the Accra Visitors Centre on Ring Road. They sell **town maps** for a number of places outside the capital, as well as an **Accra city map**.

The media

Ghana has an established and respected press, with an enthusiastic readership. Press freedom is a fact of everyday life and there are dozens of weekly papers and periodicals.

Main **newspapers** include the state-owned dailies Daily Graphic (Ⓦ www.graphicghana .com), and the Ghanaian Times and privately owned Ghanaian Chronicle. Other papers include the Daily Guide, New Nation, the Accra Daily Mail and the Mirror. Most are unsophisticated in their layout and tend more towards editorializing than hard journalism, but they offer real cultural insights.

As for the **foreign press**, there's normally a reasonable selection of British and American papers available at the airport and the more expensive Accra hotels, as well as in expatriate areas, such as along the main Cantonments Road in Osu. Magazines such as The New African and Africa Week are always on sale.

TV comprises three channels: the state-owned GTV, which transmits CNN, Al-Jazeera and BBC World at certain times; Metro TV, partly state-owned, and the private TV 3. These are all competitive and constantly improving in their programming. DSTV, a satellite subscriber service, is increasingly available in mid-range and top hotels, and includes M-Net, a channel featuring international programming.

Ghana also has several **radio** stations, the most popular of which are music stations, including Gold FM (90.5), Choice FM (102.3), Atlantic FM (the only jazz station), Vibe FM (91.9) and Groove FM (106.3). The state-owned GAR FM (95.7) covers news and the social scene and plays current pop. Joy FM (99.7) is the most highly respected, carrying a mix of music and news, including the BBC's Focus on Africa at 3pm daily. The BBC World Service itself is available in Accra on 101.3 FM. Radio Canada and Radio France and Voice of America are also available on FM all day in some areas.

Health

Yellow fever jabs are in theory required for entry, but vaccination certificates are rarely checked at the airport, more so at land borders. Outbreaks of **cholera** occasionally occur, especially in isolated regions with limited sources of clean water, but there's nothing you can do to protect yourself apart from avoiding the area. **Bilharzia** is another concern – Lake Volta is a notorious risk; in general, stay away from stagnant ponds or slow-running streams, especially in savannah areas. Chloroquine-resistant **malaria** is also a serious issue (see p.40).

In large towns, **tap water** is usually drinkable. In smaller places, and villages, the well or stored rainwater isn't always the purest and you may want to try some combination of boiling (not always practical), filtering or purifying tablets. Except in the remotest areas, bottled water is available at around GH¢1 for a 1.5-litre bottle.

The main **hospitals** are in Accra and Kumasi. Smaller hospitals and clinics can be found in towns throughout the country, but for a major medical problem you may prefer a private clinic. Your embassy may be able to recommend a suitable practice.

Ghana has a surging **AIDS** problem, as much as any other country in the region, with thousands of new cases reported each month and hundreds of thousands of HIV carriers. Fortunately, there is a growing acknowledgement of the problem, as demonstrated by radio and TV broadcasts and several recent awareness campaigns.

Costs, money, banks

Ghana's currency is the **cedi** (¢; pronounced "CD"). In July 2007, the low-value and almost unusable old notes were withdrawn and the currency was "re-denominated" by a factor of 10,000, so that 20,000 old cedis (¢20,000) is now equivalent to 2 new Ghanaian cedis (written GH¢2). At the same time, coins known as pesewas (Gp) were re-introduced,

with 100 new pesewas (Gp100) to the cedi. There are notes of GH¢1, 5, 10, 20 and 50 and coins of Gp1, 5, 10, 20, 50 and 1. As this book went to press, the new Ghanaian cedi was valued at approximately GH¢1=$1, or GH¢2=£1.

Costs

Accommodation in Ghana is reasonable: a basic hotel can cost less than GH¢10 (£5/$10) a night for a double room, and can be cheaper still upcountry. **Transport** is also cheaper in Ghana than surrounding countries – roughly half the cost of travel in Burkina Faso or Côte d'Ivoire – especially if you travel by intercity State Transport Corporation (STC) buses. Although Ghanaians find even street **food** expensive on their wages, it will seem cheap enough to you, as you can usually eat heartily for less than a cedi (£0.50/$1), while dining at a decent restaurant will typically set you back no more than GH¢6 (£3/$6) for a main course.

Businesses which rely heavily on customers wielding foreign currency (which of course includes the more expensive hotels and restaurants, imported-goods outlets and so on) tend to keep a close eye on the exchange rate and adjust their prices accordingly. Often they actually quote prices in dollars, though they'll often accept payment in sterling or euros, with the exchange rate skewed in their favour, or in cedis. Note that a 12.5 percent **value added tax** is always added to your bill at hotels and restaurants; check the prices quoted to see if it's already included.

With an **ISIC card** (the only recognized student card), you will get a discount (typically fifty percent) on admission at most of Ghana's tourist attractions. **Volunteers** with NGOs are also eligible for discounts at many attractions, though you may have to produce a staff card or other proof of your status to claim the reduced rate.

Fuel prices

Ghana's fuel prices average around GH¢1.02 per litre for diesel and about GH¢0.95 per litre for premium petrol, significantly cheaper than in neighbouring countries. If you're driving through West Africa, fill up here. Note that fuel is usually sold by the Imperial gallon (4.54 litres).

Changing money

You'll find **foreign exchange (forex) bureaux** in Accra, Kumasi and other major towns. You may want to shop around, but the variation in the exchange rate is rarely more than 1–2 percent. Forex bureaux offer slightly better rates for cash than the banks, but note that they don't always change traveller's cheques.

For changing **traveller's cheques**, banks are a better option, and this is generally more straightforward than in Ghana's francophone neighbours. Barclays and Standard Chartered have branches in all the main towns, and offer the best rates. Other banks which may be able to help include the Ghana Commercial Bank, Ecobank and SG-SSB (Société Générale Social Security Bank). **Banking hours** are Monday–Friday 8.30am–3pm.

Credit cards and wiring money

Credit cards are accepted in major hotels in Accra and Kumasi and at some travel agencies. Outside the main cities they won't get you far. Barclays handles Visa cash advances at a reasonable exchange rate, but subject to a two percent fee. With Master-Card, you can obtain cash through **ATM**s at most branches of Barclays and Standard Chartered Banks.

You can have **money wired** to you easily enough at the Bank of Ghana, High Street, Accra (PO Box 2674; ☎021/669362). In the UK you can do this through the Ghana International Bank, 69 Cheapside, London EC2P 2BB (☎020/7248 2384 ⓦwww .ghanabank.co.uk). You can also transfer money using **Western Union**, who dispatch funds to branches of the Agricultural Development Bank throughout the country.

Getting around

Kufuor's government has made real improvements to the **transport infrastructure**, resurfacing roads and expanding the country's bus service. Buses are, in fact, the most convenient means of travelling around the country and you'll find them a real luxury after the battered bush taxis you may have grown accustomed to using elsewhere. There are good surfaced roads in most parts of the country and traffic outside the cities is fairly light.

Buses

Buses operated by **STC** provide probably the cheapest way to get around the country, with a minimum of waiting at roadside checkpoints – though their mechanical reliability isn't what it was. The buses run on fixed, though rather variable, schedules to all towns of any size and are reasonably comfortable. However, they do get very booked up, so it's always a good idea to book seats in advance, especially if you're heading for popular destinations like Accra, Kumasi or Tamale and particularly at holiday times. You will need to get your luggage weighed and paid for too, if you want to get your gear into the hold.

In some parts of the country you'll also find OA Travel and Tours, M Plaza Travel and Tours, Kingdom Transport Services and GPRTU, some of which have reputations that score over STC.

Sample bus fares

Accra–Cape Coast/Takoradi GH¢6.50 (3–4hr)
Accra–Kumasi GH¢7.50 (4–5hr)
Accra–Tamale GH¢18 (12hr)
Accra–Bolgatanga GH¢25 (15hr)
Tamale–Bolgatanga GH¢7 (3hr)

Shared taxis and tro-tros

Tro-tros (minibuses) and **shared taxis** (which have a characteristic orange stripe) are less comfortable than the coaches, but they leave more frequently and are marginally cheaper – and you can ask to be let off (ask for a "drop") at any point you choose. They're notoriously overloaded, though, and if you're out to enjoy the ride, should be used only if you're not going far or can't get on a bus. Worse than the shared taxis are **lorries**, or mammy wagons, which you'll only want to consider as a last resort. These squeeze as many people as can possibly fit onto wooden planks in a boarded-up truck. You'll see nothing on the way and collect lots of bruises to boot. Fortunately, perhaps, few are still running these days – you'll come across the odd one on remote routes.

Transport **within cities and towns** generally involves *tro-tros* or shared taxis running on set routes, though things may appear chaotic if you've just arrived. Fares shouldn't exceed GH¢0.30 for a short hop.

You can **charter a taxi** for private use (see "Driving and cycling", below).

Trains

Ghana railways have virtually collapsed, with only local Accra commuter services still functioning to Nsawams and Tema. Of the three main lines, the only useful route for travellers is the sleeper-train service, linking **Kumasi with Takoradi** (12hr), which may have been revived when you read this.

Domestic flights

Flights within Ghana are run by **Antrak Air** (☎021/782814/17 ⓦwww.antrakair.com), which flies between Accra and Kumasi (twice daily; 40min; $84) and Accra and Tamale (4 weekly; 1hr 20min; $146) and Citylink (☎021/785725 ⓦwww.citylink .com.gh), which flies between Accra and Kumasi (twice daily Mon–Fri, one service on Sat; $75), Accra and Tamale (3 weekly; $125), and Accra and Sunyani (daily Mon–Fri; $100).

Volta ferries

You can cover part of the country by boat, as a weekly Lake Volta **ferry service** links the southern town of Akosombo (100km north of Accra) with Yeji, via Kpandu and Kete Krachi. Apart from this "scheduled" passenger service, vessels also ply this route and venture further north – as far as Buipe, southwest of Tamale (except at the end of the dry season), a voyage which can take up to three days, depending on stops en route. The scenery is not as exciting as you might expect – long stretches of dead tree trunks sticking up through flooded landscapes, but it is a peaceful alternative to *tro-tro* travel. For more details, see the box on p.866.

Driving and cycling

Renting a car might seem an expensive way to get around, but with limited time it's the best way to see a lot of the country. Outlets for car rental are limited, though Accra has a number of possibilities, including some licensed outlets representing the big international agencies. Most large hotels can also arrange car rental. Note that car rental in Ghana normally means paying for a **vehicle and driver**, starting at about $120 per day for a decent 4x4 vehicle (negotiable down to perhaps $100 a day for longer periods of, say, a week or more). Of this, around $20 is the "driver allowance", from which the driver finds his own accommodation and meals – though if you stop for drinks or lunch it's usual for you to pay for the driver. On longer trips you'll be expected to "dash" your driver at the end as well – $5 a day on top of the agreed rate would be considered an excellent tip.

If you make **informal arrangements**, rather than going through an agency or hotel, you can expect to pay at least GH¢5 per hour, possibly a little more in tourist areas, and around GH¢50 per day, excluding fuel. Be sure to agree the price before setting off. You might also need to pay the driver a little extra if your journey involves any rough dirt roads.

Outside of Accra, Ghana is a good country for **cycling**, being of a manageable area (two to three weeks from north to south) and offering immense scenic variety. You don't need to be super-fit as the hilly zones are fairly restricted. But aim to avoid the busiest routes, especially Accra–Kumasi.

Accommodation

Major Ghanaian towns have a good range of accommodation options and in all except the most expensive places you can often negotiate down from the first price quoted. There are plenty of **budget** hotels (❶–❸), basic and tolerable at the lower end of the scale where rooms won't always have self-contained (s/c) bathrooms, but surprisingly comfortable at the pricier end, with TV, hot water and air conditioning (a/c) often available. **Mid-range** hotels (❹–❻) offer excellent value, including all mod-cons, slick decor and a good level of comfort. Expensive hotels (❼ & ❽) are found mainly in the cities and in a few resorts, and feature international standards of comfort and service.

Running water and air conditioning can be had in most places, and should be reliable in Accra and Kumasi, though they may prove sporadic elsewhere. Special mention should also be made of the handful of coastal **forts**, sections of which have been converted into basic resthouses (see p.834).

Ghanaians are generally curious to meet travellers, and if you're on your own, you may be surprised how many offers you get to **stay with people**. It can be rewarding, but you should be extremely conscious, when accepting such offers, of the expense your stay imposes; even for salaried government employees a bottle of beer may be a rare luxury representing many hours of work. Be as generous as your host; pay when you go out together, and, if you go to the market, pay for the food. Ghana's cost of living is incredibly high relative to local wages and most people are barely scraping by, and generally doing so outside the official economy.

Community-based ecotourism projects and tour operators sometimes offer homestay accommodation (see p.25).

Camping

Camping is feasible in the bush. In practice it's most pleasant in the north, beyond the damp forest zone. If you arrive in a village, always ask to see the chief to find out if and where you can spend the night, and he'll make the arrangements. Camping **gas** is very hard to find in Ghana; stock up in neighbouring Francophone countries where it's more readily available.

Eating and drinking

Plantains are used a lot in Ghanaian cooking and, together with **beans**, **groundnuts**, **rice**, fresh and dried **fish**, **guinea fowl** (especially in the north) and **grasscutter** (the large, tasty rodent, also known as bush rat, hunted mainly in the south), supply the basis of one of West Africa's best national cuisines. If you're adventurous, there are other flavours, including clay-baked **lizard** (in Dagomba country; the skin comes off with the clay) and giant forest **snails** – even bat, rat, cat and dog in various parts of the country.

In southern Ghana, the most common staple is **kenkey** – fermented maize-flour balls, steamed and wrapped in maize leaves. You'll see it in markets everywhere. The sour taste takes a while to acquire, and you don't often get much sauce to help it down – just a splash of ground tomatoes, onions, peppers and deep-fried fish. But it does, eventually, taste good. In the north, **tozafi** (or TZ) takes over – a mush made from millet (occasionally maize) flour, and commonly eaten with palm nut or okra soup.

As for **foreign cuisine**, in Accra and Kumasi you'll find restaurants serving Chinese, Lebanese, Indian, Italian or other European fare, and some American-style fast-food places. Further afield, the most common alternative to local staples is Chinese-style dishes, invariably sweet-and-sour or black-bean-sauce stir-fries, and fried rice.

Bread, as you would expect, reflects the taste and style of the British former rulers and is usually soft, white and plastic bagged, available in "tea", "sugar", or "brown" varieties. Baguette-style bread sticks and wholemeal loaves are becoming more widely available.

The country's outstanding fruit is the **pineapple** (notably along the coast), cheaper in Ghana than anywhere else in West Africa. **Coconuts**, too, are incredibly cheap.

Ghana has a lot of good **chocolate**, available everywhere and not expensive for tourists. Kingsbite chocolate is the most popular and is available across the country, sometimes in lemon, orange and coffee flavours.

Finally, Accra-made **Fan** ice cream and frozen yoghurt products, including Fan-ice, Fan-yogo and Fan-choco, have become something of a phenomenon, and can be found in neighbouring countries as well. Sold by young men with ice-boxes on a bike or on their heads, the frozen sachets are very inexpensive and the ice cream in particular is delicious.

Drinking

Ghana was the first West African country to possess a brewery and now has a wide range of **beers**. The most popular are Star and Club, with Gulder, Stone and ABC also on sale – all come in 750ml bottles or smaller "mini" bottles. Bottled Guinness is also very popular. Voltic mineral water is widely available, as is "pure water" – sachets of filtered water. **Minerals**, as fizzy soft drinks are referred to locally, include the usual

Ghanaian food terms and dishes

Abenkwan	Palm nut soup (Akan)	Khosay	Bean cakes (north)
Aduane	Food (Akan)	Klaklo	Ripe plantain dough, deep-fried
Akawadu	Banana (Akan)		
Akokoh	Chicken (Akan)	Koko	Corn or millet porridge with milk and sugar
Amadaa	Fried, ripe plantain (Ga)		
		Kokonte	Cassava meal (Akan)
Ampesi	Plantain and yam	Kontumbre	Cocoyam leaves
Banku	Corndough, good with groundnut soup	Kyinkyinga	Beef with vegetable sauce (Hausa)
Bodie (kokoo)	(Ripe) plantain (Akan)	Momone	Sun-dried fish (Akan)
Boflot	Doughnut (north)	Nsuomnam	Fish (Akan)
Borodo/Panu	Bread (Akan)	Nuhuu	Cocoyam porridge (Akan)
Ekwei bemi	Boiled, sweetened corn kernels		
		Ode	Yam (Akan)
Enam	Meat (Akan)	Omo tuo	Mashed rice balls with soup or stew, usually served Sundays only (also written Emo or Amo tuo)
Fufu	Pounded yam, cassava or plantain		
Gari	Cassava, grated and dried		
		Palava sauce	Spinach- or leaf-based sauce
Gari foto	Gari dish, mixed with palm oil and other ingredients		
		Red Red	Spicy bean stew normally served with fried plantain
Groundnut soup	Spicy groundnut (ie peanut) stew with meat or fish		
		Rice water	Rice pudding, often for breakfast
Jollof rice	Spicy rice with chicken or meat cooked into it	Shito	Hot pepper and shrimp or fish sauce (Ga)
		Suya	Small spicy kebab
Kelewele	Spicy, fried ripe plantain	Tatale	Ripe plantain, pounded and fried
Kenkey	Steamed, fermented corn-flour balls	TZ (Tozafi)	Millet mush (north)
		Waachi	Rice and red beans

Coke and Fanta varieties, as well as Malta Guinness, dark and sugary with a burnt caramel flavour.

Home-made drinks include **taka beer**, a ginger drink; and **ice kenkey**, sweetened, fermented maize flour in water, a taste you may not acquire. **Pito** is the millet-based beer commonly drunk, from shared bowls, in the north; it varies greatly but is quite likeable. In the south, the favourite local brews are naturally fermented **palm wine** (known in Akan as *ntunkum* when it's fresh and low in alcohol, and *nsa* when it's winey) and **akpeteshie**, a potent firewater distilled from palm wine, also called "Kill-me-quick" and similar names.

Communications

Ghana's **postal services** are inexpensive and relatively efficient to Europe and North America. Letters take a week to ten days to reach the UK, slightly longer to North America. Accra's poste restante is free and reliable.

Telephones are improving all the time and card-operated public phones in the major towns provide international direct dialling. Phonecards can be bought from petrol stations and roadside kiosks. AT&T's World Traveler service can be accessed on ☎0191. **Reverse-charge calls** are expensive from a hotel or a telecentre (called a "communication centre" locally). Note that some communication centres allow **"reception"** – basically, you make a quick call to let your family or friends know where you are, then they call you back at the telecentre, for which you pay a small fee based on the duration of this call.

Mobile phones can be used in all major towns through the main networks Tigo, Areeba and Onetouch. Coverage extends to towns in the far north such as Bolgatanga and Wa, and includes a wide radius of Accra. Sim cards are easy to get hold of and cost about GH¢10.

Internet access is easily available in the major cities and towns, and connections

are improving all the time. Expect to pay GH¢0.60 or so for half an hour.

Opening hours, public holidays and festivals

Government offices are open Monday to Friday from 8am to 12.30pm and from 1.30pm to 5pm. Most **businesses** operate Monday to Friday from 8am or 9am until noon and again between 2pm and 5.30pm. Many shops open also on Saturday, from around 8am to 1pm. Shops are closed on public holidays, without exception – it's the law.

The main Christian and Muslim **holidays** are celebrated in Ghana, the impact of Islam being strongest in the northwest. Shops and businesses also close down for Fourth Republic Day (Jan 7), Independence Day (March 6), Revolution Day (June 4), Republic Day (July 1) and Farmers' Day (first Fri in Dec).

Though not a public holiday, **Emancipation Day** (Aug 1), commemorating slavery and its legacy, is observed with much ceremony in Accra, Cape Coast and Assin Manso (on the Cape Coast–Kumasi road). On July 31 wreaths are laid in Accra at the DuBois Center, the George Padmore Library and the Nkrumah Memorial Park. That evening a candlelight procession walks the streets of Cape Coast to the castle, ready to welcome the dawn. On August 1 itself a procession (*grand-durbur*) gathers in Assin Manso, to lay wreaths at the graves of slaves from Jamaica and the USA, whose remains were repatriated to Ghana when Emancipation Day was first marked here in 1998.

In odd-numbered years at the end of July/beginning of August, the major cultural festival, **Panafest** (ⓦwww.panafest.org), hits Cape Coast, Elmina and Accra in a celebration of African unity, featuring films, music, theatre and processions.

In addition to the official public holidays, many **regional celebrations** or outdoor festivals (*afahye* in Twi) animate the country throughout the year. In some cases the local name of the occasion just means "festival". The selective listing below covers most of the country but there are very many more.

Ghana's IDD country code is ☎233.

Precise dates vary around the country and from year to year, often depending on weather and crops (yam festivals range from Aug to Jan). Note that traditional festivals sometimes coincide with Islamic holidays, especially in the north, which can lead to a great binge of merrymaking, music and dancing.

Islamic calendar

Konyuri Northern Ghana. Corresponds to Eid ul-Fitr, the festival at the end of Ramadan.

Chimisi Northern Ghana. Corresponding to the Muslim festival of Eid ul-Adha, two months after Eid ul-Fitr, this is also known as Tabaski or the Sheep Festival.

Sallah Northern Ghana. Muslim New Year festival held three weeks after Eid ul-Fitr.

Damba Northern Ghana. Muslim festival, also known as Mouloud or Maulidi, celebrating the birth of the Prophet Muhammad. Depending on when this date falls (two months after the Muslim New Year), and particularly further south, it can also be combined with harvest festivities.

January

Adae Kese Kumasi (variable dates). Major Asante festival reinforcing the unity of the Asante nation and the Asantehene's traditional authority over his confederation, culminating in the purification of the ancestral stools.

Edina Bronya Elmina (first Thurs). Fante Christmas festival celebrating the bond between the locals and historic Dutch visitors, with much drinking, eating and Asafo company competitiveness.

March

Golgu Bolgatanga (around Easter). Sacrifices to ensure good harvests.

April

Dzimbenti, Jintigi or **Bugum** A fire festival held throughout Upper West and Upper East and much of Northern Region. Linked in devoutly Muslim areas with Noah's survival of the flood (an event marked on 10th Muharram, just after the Islamic New Year), the festival is now more commonly tied to the Gregorian calendar and the agricultural cycle. Everyone gathers after dark in a procession with lighted sticks or bundles of straw.

Godigbeza Aflao. Celebrations commemorating migration from the tyranny of the Ewe ancestral lands at Notse (Togo) include drumming, dancing and ceremonial costumes.

Aboakyer Winneba, Central Region (late April/early May). The famous "deer-hunting" festival involves two teams of hunters competing to be first to bring back a live antelope to the chief and elders and be proclaimed champions.

July

Bakatue Elmina (early July). Competitions and processions, celebrating the end of the annual ban on fishing in the lagoon.

August

Asafotu/Asafotifiam Ada, east of Accra (first Sat). Festival of remembrance for those lost in battle.

Bontungu Anomabu, near Saltpond, west of Accra. Five days of drumming and dancing in which villagers clear all superfluous objects from their homes, and ask God for good health and prosperity in the coming year.

Homowo Accra, Prampram and surrounding districts (Aug/Sept). Important traditional thanksgiving and harvest festival of the Ga people including street processions of twins, suspension of behavioral sanctions and offerings of ceremonial kpekpele or kpokpoi – kenkey with palm soup and smoked fish – to the gods.

September

Odwira Kumasi and Asante country (some time in Sept depending on local calendar). Major purification, thanksgiving and harvest festival (marking an end to a Lenten period of quiet living and reflection), with music and dancing, military re-enactments and chiefs' durbars.

Yam Festival Volta Region (second half). Before the feasting starts, cooked yam is offered to the traditional shrines, and durbars take place in which chiefs and local dignitaries are on show in public places.

Oguaa Fetu Cape Coast (first Sat). A big, dressy occasion lasting several days, in part marking the arrival of Europeans on the coast.

Yam Festival Effiduasi, Asante Region (last week Sept or early Oct).

October

Kobina Lawra, Upper West (late Oct). Harvest festival with dancing contests, drawing crowds from throughout northern Ghana.

November

Yam Festival Ejura, northeast of Kumasi.

Hotbetsotso Anloga (first Sat of Nov), on the coast southwest of Keta. Like the Godigbeza in Aflao in

April, commemoration of the Anlos' migration from a tyrannical kingdom to their homeland.

December

Fao Navrongo, Upper East. Harvest festival.
Kwafie Berekum (over the New Year). Purification festival, culminating in a big bonfire.

Crafts and shopping

Ghana has a huge variety of **arts and crafts**, still widely made for local consumption.

The **Asante region** is a prolific producer of **textiles** and well known for its **kente** and **adinkra** cloths. These can be bought in villages around Kumasi or at the town's cultural centre. The region is also famed for its carvings – especially of stools made in Ahwiaa.

The north specializes more in **leather** goods, rough **cotton** weaves (look out for the traditional indigo and off-white *fugu* tunics and trousers made from Gonja strip cloth), mat-weaving and basketry, all of which can be found in the markets at Tamale and Bolgatanga.

Perhaps the best selection is in **Accra** where arts from all over the country – and from throughout West Africa – comes together at the crafts market. Accra also has one or two good galleries and is the headquarters for a thriving mail-order company specializing in African crafts – Ⓦ www.eshopafrica.com – which is well worth checking out (they even sell Ga coffins).

If you buy **antiques** you may have to obtain an export permit – declaring that the item has no historical value – from the Ghana Museum and Monuments Board. Take your purchases to their office in the Centre for National Culture or the National Museum and they'll sell you a certificate on the spot.

Crime and safety

Muggings aren't too much of a problem in Ghana, not even in Accra – though there have been reports of muggings in Black Star Square and neighbourhoods frequented by tourists and expats. The worst place for

ordinary pickpocketing is probably Kumasi market, while theft is a problem on the Accra beaches. Police sometimes stop travellers (and Ghanaians) and feign anger about a minor offence (such as jaywalking, which is illegal at certain places including Kwame Nkrumah Circle in Accra) and customs and immigration officers have been known to employ similar tactics. They're almost certainly angling for "dash" (a small present or bribe), and you may have to pay up, though politeness and smiles will help to alleviate the situation.

As for genuine infringements of the law, **drug use** is a possible area of concern. *Wee* (marijuana/cannabis) is illegal, though widely available, its main areas of commercial production around Ejura in the Asante region and Nsawam north of Accra. Its use is generally looked upon more as a bad habit than a dangerous practice, though extreme discretion is strongly advised.

Emergencies

Police ☏ 191, fire service ☏ 192.

Gender issues and sexual attitudes

There are few special problems for **women travellers** – indeed, many rate Ghana one of the most hassle-free countries in West Africa.

Ghana more actively encourages women to become more involved in business and other areas of public life than most other African countries, and many **women's organizations** have sprung up in recent years. The 31 December Women's Movement (DWM), for example, led by the former First Lady, Nana Konadu Agyemang, has made considerable advances – such as providing day-care centres for children throughout the country. If you're interested in making contact with women's groups, check out Ⓦ www.obaahema.com or PeaceWomen at Ⓦ tinyurl.com/2pdv6f. Interestingly, the **matrilineal** system of inheritance (in which men inherit from their maternal uncles rather than their fathers) practised by the Akan-speaking people has, if anything, had a negative impact on women's status. There is firm government pressure against this form of inheritance.

Gay travellers will find that popular attitudes are a little more liberal than in most neighbouring countries. Although laws against same-sex relationships are still on the statute books, they are rarely enforced and a very low-key gay scene does exist in Accra and one or two other places. However, greater awareness of the issues, and some coverage in local press, can also mean that traditional hackles are raised more easily. As ever, discretion and sensitivity are the watchwords.

Entertainment and sports

Ghana has a satisfying **cultural life**, with theatre, cinema and especially music richly developed and accessible. Every odd-numbered year, some time between the end of July and early August, you will find the **Panafest music and arts festival** in progress (Ⓦ www.panafest.org), with some events tied in to **Emancipation Day** (see p.796).

Theatre

Accra's fine, Chinese-built **National Theatre** and the **Greater Accra Centre for National Culture** are the capital's two main theatre venues. The **School of Performing Arts** at Legon University also stages occasional productions in Accra. In the country as a whole, **"concert party"**, a traditional, lightly satirical musical-comedy-drama, is the theatrical form you're most likely to come across. A high degree of audience participation is the norm, with *akpeteshie* the accompanying drink, and the "party" typically goes on all night. For more information have a look at the book *Ghana's Concert Party Theatre* by Catherine Cole, and its accompanying documentary.

Cinema

Ghanaian **cinema** has a wealth of unexplored potential, with plenty of acting talent and production ambition in the wings, held back by financial constraints, but you're still more likely to get a helping of Bond or Stallone (usually on video) than something from top Ghanaian director **Kwaw Ansah**. There's more on Ghanaian film on p.811.

Music

While Ghana is famous for the urban goodtime dance sounds of **highlife**, the country has an active tradition of **rural music and dance** and you should listen out for folkloric gigs and events, often linked to the traditional festivals listed above. Roots music continues to influence urban musicians, including the latest **hip-life** artists.

Although "big-band highlife" declined in the 1970s with the frequency of coups, curfews and power cuts, these technical problems didn't much affect guitar highlife, which can still be heard all over. Concert parties and **gospel highlife** took off in the 1970s and are still thriving, and even secular musicians record gospel albums to appeal to this expanding market. There's a more detailed exploration of Ghana's musical culture on pp.808–810.

For **concert dates** in Accra, get hold of a copy of the listings mag *Enjoy Accra* and see the *Daily Graphic*'s "Entertainments" page every Saturday.

The **AAMA cultural centre** at Kokrobite, near Accra (see p.833), is a good place to immerse yourself in drums and music, especially if you want to participate.

Sport

Football is by far the country's most popular sport. In the 2006 World Cup, Ghana reached the second round, losing creditably to Brazil, and with the country having played host to the 2008 African Nations Cup, football fever is set to become even more frenzied. Ghana's healthy, relatively clean football culture nurtures some of the best players on the continent and is only held back by lack of investment, leading many players to take up lucrative overseas contracts, among them **Michael Essien** (Chelsea), **Stephan Appiah** (Fenerbahce, Turkey), and the awesomely talented midfielder **Sulley Ali Muntari** (Udinese, Italy). They have all followed in the footsteps of the great **Abédi Pelé**, who played a key role in the success of several overseas teams in the 1980s and 90s. At home, the Ghanaian premiership is dominated by two teams – Kumasi's **Asante Kotoko** and **Accra Hearts of Oak**.

Wildlife and national parks

Investment in the protection of Ghana's native flora and fauna has increased significantly over the past few years and **ecotourism projects** are increasingly being established across the country, designed to maximize the benefits of tourism for local communities. On the downside, much of the rainforest was felled decades ago and it won't be returning soon, if ever.

The Wildlife Division of the government's Forestry Commission (W www.fcghana.com) has opened up several parks to visitors. However, while the largest and longest-established park, **Mole National Park**, has the full complement of bush-savannah mammals, some of the newer parks don't yet provide facilities and not all tracks are maintained. This means you are limited to what you can see on foot, though the park rangers are typically very enthusiastic and helpful in organizing excursions.

Apart from Mole, **Kakum National Park**, just 35km from Cape Coast, with its famous aerial walkway, is easily accessible and has been a popular target for visitors for some years.

In the Western region, the twin reserves of **Ankasa** and **Nini-Suhien**, near the Ivoirian border, now have some tourist facilities including limited accommodation.

In the Volta region, **Shai Hills Reserve**, home to more than 160 bird species, several species of monkey and a colony of tomb bats, is a popular day-excursion from Accra.

Listen on the travellers' grapevine to find out if there have been any developments at **Digya National Park**. Bordering the western edge of Lake Volta, this is one of Ghana's larger parks, harbouring elephants, various antelopes, hippo, waterbuck and a wide range of other species, but you need to be completely self-sufficient.

It's also worth checking the latest developments at **Bia National Park** in the rainforests of the west near the Côte d'Ivoire border. Facilities for visitors here have improved, with several camps and trails established.

Further north, the **Bui National Park** straddles tributaries of the Black Volta in a protected woodland district, with plentiful hippos. There's very basic chalet accommodation and camping facilities.

Other parks and reserves with no facilities at the time of writing, include: the **Kalakpe Resource Reserve**, 15km southwest of Ho, which has a proliferation of birdlife, along with buffalo, antelope and several species of monkey; and the small but scenic **Kyabobo National Park**, near Nkwanta in Volta Region (not to be confused with Nkwanta in Western Region), which shares a common border with the Parc National Fazao-Malfakassa in Togo and may open to the public during the lifetime of this edition (it's said to harbour several large mammal species, including elephant, lion, leopard and buffalo).

The **Nature Conservation and Research Centre** website (W www.ncrc-ghana.org) is useful. Ghana **Friends of the Earth** is an active group (W www.foeghana.org) – one of the few such in Africa. And the Ghana Wildlife Society is worth checking out (W www.ghanawildlifesociety.org).

A brief history of Ghana

The **earliest humans** in Ghana, as everywhere in West Africa, were hunter-gatherers whose descendants have been gradually displaced by farmers and herders. The earliest, reasonably clear movements of present-day peoples in Ghana took place around the eleventh century, when the Ntafo, early ancestors of the Akan-speaking peoples, moved south to the parkland west of Gonja, in northern Ghana. By the 14th century, successive generations spread further south, in three waves, consisting of the Guan, Asante and Fante peoples.

Early **trading relations** existed with much of the rest of West Africa, particularly with the western Soudan (the region which is now Mali). Gold and kola nuts were important products which poured out of the region, across the Sahara and into North Africa. And Mande peoples from the Niger bend greatly influenced the economy and culture of northern Ghana as they established numerous trading centres alongside existing towns.

European arrival

European involvement in the region provoked a shift in the emphasis of trade away from the northern routes to the southern ports. Searching out new trade routes and a way to obtain the gold of the trans-Saharan caravans closer to source, the first **Portuguese** ships came to Ghana in 1471. By 1482 they had returned to build a fort at **El Mina** ("the mine"), using a mixture of persuasion and threats to gain the consent of the local ruler. The region turned out to be rich in gold, ivory, timber and skins, and other Europeans followed the Portuguese. Over the next four hundred years, sea powers, principally the Dutch and British, competed heavily for the trade. With the European colonization of America, this expanded to include **slaves** (see box, p.840), in exchange for which the Europeans brought hard liquor and manufactured goods like **cloth** and **weapons**. Guns eventually helped the **Asante** – the principal suppliers of slaves to the foreigners – to expand their influence over the region's interior and to apply pressure to the **Fante** middlemen of the coast through whom they'd been dealing with the British since the 1600s.

The British colony

By the early nineteenth century the Gold Coast interior had developed a complicated network of northern states – **Gonja**, **Dagomba**, **Mamprusi** and **Nanumba** – and, in the south, smaller confederations (the Akan-speaking **Fante** for example) and statelets like the **Ga**, **Ewe** and **Nzima**. In the central region, the Akan-speaking **Asante** confederation was rapidly mushrooming. Given time, the Asante empire might have conquered and assimilated most of the smaller political units in the surrounding territories which were later to come under French rule.

Such a scenario, however, was thwarted by the colonial experience. By the early nineteenth century, the British, based at Cape Coast Castle and a string of minor forts, had emerged as the strongest foreign power on the **Gold Coast**. In 1807, they abolished the slave trade in the region and began looking for other exploitable resources. Over the next hundred years, palm oil, cocoa, rubber, gold and timber were developed as exports. These products drew the British – hitherto content to remain in their coastal forts – increasingly into the hinterland.

The stage was set for the outright **conquest** of the interior when the Asante invaded the Fante confederation in 1806. The Fante had long been able to resist the attempts of their powerful northern neighbours to dominate them, thanks in large part to their role as preferential trading partners with the Europeans. Now the British rallied to the aid of their Fante allies, even offering them protection when the fort at Anomabu was attacked.

Hostilities flared and **tenuous treaties** were reached between the two Akan factions throughout the first half of the century. But, as competition increased for the control of trade, the British decided there could be only one victor. They ultimately found the excuse they needed to invade the interior when war again broke out between the Fante and Asante in the 1870s. In 1874, the British sacked the Asante capital, Kumasi. Subsequent **Asante wars** followed in 1896 and 1900, when the ruling Asantehene was finally exiled (see box, p.857).

By this time Germany, France and Britain had already agreed on borders for the areas they would control in Africa. The British introduced elements of **indirect rule** in their new colony, even allowing the Asante confederation to be re-established under the "Ashanti Confederacy Council" – a government agency – in 1935. After World War I, part of German Togoland was integrated into the British colony.

The rise of nationalism

Nationalist movements were created early in the colonial period, with one – the **Aborigines' Rights Protection Society** – dating as far back as 1897. Other parties sprang up during the 1920s and 30s and by 1946 concessions to African demands for representation had led to an African majority in Ghana's Legislative Council, although the executive branch – and effective rule – was still in the hands of the British Governor.

In 1947, **J.B. Danquah** formed the United Gold Coast Convention (UGCC), a party which favoured the principle of a gradual shift to self-government and independence. In the same year, the party invited **Kwame Nkrumah** to join its ranks as party secretary in an effort to broaden a base that consisted mainly of the educated elite – civil servants, lawyers, businessmen and doctors.

In the aftermath of the 1948 **Accra riots** (see p.815) Nkrumah lost patience with conservatives in the UGCC and split from it to form his own party, the Convention People's Party (**CPP**), under the campaign slogan "Self-government now". He gained prominence among the masses as a result and the British detained him when he called for a national strike in 1950. The CPP, meanwhile, won the Legislative Assembly election of 1951, and the governor, Sir Charles Arden-Clarke, prudently released Nkrumah and invited him to help form a government. Thus, in 1952, Nkrumah became the first African prime minister in the Commonwealth. He went on to win the elections of 1954 and 1956 – a period during which his CPP party shared power with the British. On August 3, 1956, the Legislative Assembly passed a unanimous motion calling for complete independence.

Independence: Ghana under Nkrumah

When **independence** was ultimately realized on March 6, 1957, the future looked bright for the first African country to break colonial bonds. Ghana was then the world's leading cocoa exporter and produced a tenth of the world's gold. Other valuable resources included bauxite, manganese, diamonds and timber. Perhaps Ghana's greatest asset was a high percentage of educated citizens who seemed well qualified to run the new nation (a quarter of the population was literate, compared, for example, to an estimated one percent in Portugal's colonies).

Nkrumah became a larger-than-life figure, respected throughout Africa and the African diaspora and highly regarded in the West. He was an eloquent advocate of **pan-Africanism** and the **nonaligned movement**. His economic principles looked sound, too, as he sought to create an industrial base that would reduce dependence on foreign powers while improving social services throughout the country (hospitals and clinics, universities and schools were part of his legacy). The port city of **Tema**, with its smelting and other industrial plants, was constructed at this time as was the ambitious **Akosombo Dam**, built to supply hydroelectric power.

Nkrumah's economic strategy was, however, extremely costly, and with hindsight it seems painfully clear that his biggest mistake was to emphasize **prestige projects** at the expense of a solid agricultural base. Accra's showy conference centre – designed to be the headquarters of the Organization of African Unity, which instead based itself in Addis Ababa – and symbolic monuments like Black Star Square and the vainglorious State House, were the dizzy results of a belief in the invincible rightness of Nkrumah's ideals. Foreign currency reserves dwindled rapidly and the country accumulated a debt running to hundreds of millions of pounds.

As the economic situation turned bleak, political discontent rose. Government suppression of a 1961 workers' strike had already seriously alienated Nkrumah from the working class, and the educated elite had become disillusioned with his expensive brand of scientific socialism. When the world price of cocoa plummeted in the mid-1960s, Ghana's hopes for economic self-sufficiency – and long-term stability – were dashed.

By 1964, Ghana was legally a **one-party state**. As the CPP tried measures to stamp out opposition, the government increasingly arrested those it feared under the Preventive Detention Act which allowed for "enemies" of the regime to be held for up to five years without trial. Public gatherings were strictly controlled, press censorship became commonplace and an extensive network of informants was developed by the party central committee. Such measures were effective in crushing opposition, or at least in driving it deeply underground, but Nkrumah still had to contend with the **military**.

Suspicious of the army's loyalty, he lost his nerve and made policy decisions that were bound to antagonize officers – placing limits on recruitment and hedging military procurement procedures with elaborate safeguards. Isolating himself still further from army support, he formed an independent **presidential guard**, accountable only to himself.

In the light of such developments, Western nations increasingly criticized government corruption and the personality cult surrounding Nkrumah, who was forced to abandon his nonalignment and turn to the Soviet Union and its allies for support. By then he had totally lost the backing of the military and almost every other element of society. Only a blind sense of impunity could have allowed him to travel abroad. On February 24, 1966, while on a visit to China, he was **overthrown** in a bloodless coup by British-trained officers. He died in exile in Conakry in 1972.

Coups and "kleptocrats"

Following Nkrumah's departure, Lieutenant-General **Joseph Ankrah** was appointed head of the National Liberation Council (**NLC**) that ruled until 1969. The conservative junta went on a witch-hunt, arresting left-wing ideologues, banning the CPP and harassing its leaders. The junta's **economic direction** seemed promising to the West, however, as they privatized many state enterprises and broke off relations with the Soviet Union. But for all the promises made to better the economy, life for most people without special connections grew steadily worse.

From its inception, the NLC viewed itself as a provisional government and much of its period of rule was spent preparing for a return to civilian democracy. A bill of rights was drawn up, and safeguards were implemented to ensure the independence of the judiciary and prevent the reconstitution of an autocratic one-party state. In May 1969, political parties were legalized.

The **Progress Party**, headed by Dr Kofi Busia – an Asante who represented the traditional middle-class, right-of-centre opposition to Nkrumah's rule – was counterbalanced by the **National Alliance of Liberals** led by Komla Gbedemah, an Ewe and one-time associate of Nkrumah who had broken with the leader and gone into exile.

In September 1969, Ghanaians gave democracy another try, and elected **Busia** prime minister. But the new leader struggled to wade through the economic mess. Cocoa prices dropped again in 1971, sparking a new crisis and, at the same time, mismanagement and racketeering led to shortages in food production, supplies and foreign exchange. Under mounting pressure, Busia took the politically dangerous steps of expelling up to half a million Nigerians and **devaluing the cedi**. Massive price increases followed and the public enthusiasm that had ushered in the new regime faded almost immediately. Busia was overthrown on January 13, 1972.

Kleptocracy

From 1972 to 1979, Ghana was led by a military junta with extraordinarily **corrupt generals** at the helm. The first, and the most flagrant offender, was **General Ignatius Acheampong**, who headed the National Redemption Council (**NRC**) from 1972 to 1975 and then the Supreme Military Council until 1978. During his period in office, Ghanaians coined the term "kleptocracy" – rule by thieves – as the official economy moved closer and closer to complete collapse. The **black market** thrived, meanwhile, as basic goods like bread and eggs became unattainable for the poor. Production declined even further and the few agricultural goods produced were smuggled abroad to Togo and Côte d'Ivoire, where they fetched higher, hard-currency prices. The educated elite – doctors, teachers, lawyers – led a brain drain to Nigeria and overseas where they had some chance of supporting themselves.

The basis of Acheampong's economic policy was **"self-reliance"**, symbolized by programmes such as "Operation Feed Yourself", launched in 1972. Moderate successes were achieved in the early years of the NRC, but by the mid-1970s the economic outlook was so grim that the professional middle class, and especially the Ghana Bar Association, demanded a return to party politics. Acheampong sought a compromise by proposing a **"union government"** where power would be shared between civilians, the armed forces and – radically – the police. The opposition viewed this as a mechanism to keep the military in power and reacted cynically when Acheampong pushed his idea through on the back of a trumped-up referendum held in 1978.

As criticism grew, so did **repression**, and hundreds of opposition leaders were jailed without trial. Viewed increasingly as a tyrant, Acheampong withdrew into isolation. He was quietly deposed in a coup led by **General William Akuffo** on July 5, 1978. Akuffo established the "Supreme Military Council II" and eventually set a date for elections in June 1979, but little else changed and widespread discontent in the country now spread to the ranks of the military.

Rawlings Mark I

On May 15, 1979, there was a bungled uprising of junior ranks in the army, led by a 32-year-old flight lieutenant of mixed Scottish–Ghanaian parentage – **Jerry Rawlings**. He was captured and imprisoned but freed by fellow soldiers and they made a second, successful, attempt to take power on **June 4, 1979**.

Rawlings made it clear that his coup would be different, that he was out to eliminate corruption and restore national pride to an economic order neglected in fifteen years of waste. The title of his governing **Armed Forces Revolutionary Council** (**AFRC**) set the tone – Rawlings envisaged a "moral revolution" based implicitly on socialist principles of an economy for need rather than profit. He took a hard line, sending high-ranking officers to the firing squad (including Acheampong and Akuffo) and approving a purge of public figures under suspicion of fraud. At the same time he pledged that the AFRC would work quickly to restore order and return the reins of power to a civilian government.

The world community noted little more than another coup d'état in Ghana, but, in a remarkably speedy departure (no African military ruler had ever voluntarily relinquished power before), the promise was kept. Following elections held on June 18, 1979, the newly elected president, **Dr Hilla Limann**, took office in September and the soldiers returned to their barracks barely three months after leaving them.

Limann rode in on a wave of popularity at home and in the West, where his conservative politics won respect. But despite his best intentions, the economy continued to slide – production dropped further, the cedi remained overvalued (fearing unpopularity, the president refused to devalue the currency and thereby cost his country a major IMF loan) and the country's infrastructure became hopelessly eroded. And despite the moral high ground captured by the Rawlings clique, and Rawlings' own shadowy behind-the-scenes presence, **corrupt practices** had been re-established by the end of 1980 in virtually every sphere of public life.

Rawlings' second coming

On December 31, 1981, Rawlings led a **second successful coup**, toppling the Limann government, abolishing the entire "democratic" framework, and placing the government in the hands of a **Provisional National Defence Council** (**PNDC**). As before, he justified the action by the urgent need to halt corruption and put Ghana's wrecked and abused economy in order.

This time, however, no plans were made to restore the country to civilian rule. Rather, the PNDC decided to put into practice the leftist populist principles of the original coup. Early moves were made to democratize the decision-making process and to decentralize political power. This was done through **People's Defence Committees** (**PDCs**), which replaced district councils and were intended to increase local participation in the revolution while raising political consciousness at the grassroots level.

Rawlings initially enjoyed huge popularity among the masses fed up with government lies and excesses. With his battle cry of "accountability", he proved sincere in the **war against corruption** and, although the economy continued to slide during his first years, he soon managed to produce a turnaround (by 1984, the economy was showing a five percent growth rate, the first upswing in ten years). Despite Rawlings' penchant for revolutionary rhetoric, his early friendship with Libya's leader Colonel Gaddafi and his ties with Cuba and Eastern Europe, his pragmatic economic approach – including taking the risky political step of drastically devaluing the cedi – earned him high marks with the IMF, which started once again to provide sizeable loans to the country.

Relations with **Thomas Sankara**, the charismatic revolutionary leader of Burkina Faso, were warm. Predictably, more conservative regimes were less receptive to Rawlings' style of government. Relations with **Britain**, **Côte d'Ivoire**, and especially **Togo** were, at best, cool. By the end of the 1980s, Rawlings had made much of what seemed a hopeless situation. But he had not had an easy time straddling diverse elements in Ghana. Although most rural dwellers and many wage earners remained loyal, he had suffered scrapes with the ambitious middle class, who loathed his socialist rhetoric and raised the banner of **human rights**, accusing the regime of imprisoning, torturing and murdering political dissidents. Many students and academics also charged him with selling out to the **IMF**, saying he presided over a neocolonialist state. Still, the performance of the economy (Ghana recorded the highest consistent rates of economic growth in Africa throughout much of the 1980s) seemed to shield the president from pressure to liberalize, whether it came from disgruntled nationals or Western donors.

The 1990s

Ghana entered the 1990s against the background rumble of the **Quarshigah Affair** – Major Courage Quarshigah and six other officers were sentenced for their connection with an alleged plot to murder Rawlings and overthrow the PNDC. Ghanaians rallied around the affair, demanding the abolition of a number of laws, particularly those relating to detention, and an end to the ban on political parties. Foreign pressure to democratize also increased.

Rather than entrenching, Rawlings surprised many when, in July 1990, he formed a **National Commission for Democracy** to review decentralization and consider Ghana's political future, which by 1991 was recommending a new constitution and presidential and legislative elections – recommendations approved by the PNDC which, contrary to all expectations, endorsed the restoration of a **multiparty system**. In addition to the completion of the new constitution and the unbanning of political parties, the following year saw the emergence of a **free press** and three new human-rights organizations, plus the release of remaining political detainees.

As the November **presidential election** drew near, opposition parties were confident of success, yet Rawlings' newly formed National Democratic Congress took 58 percent of the vote. As the stunned opposition claimed, some **voting irregularities** undoubtedly did take place, though the margin of victory was large enough to have ensured Rawlings' win even under fair conditions. In the eyes of many Ghanaians, however, Rawlings had held onto power without a clear popular mandate. The subsequent **opposition boycott** of the ensuing legislative elections assured victory to the NDC and its affiliates, the NCP and the EGLE party, and denied the new **Fourth Republic** (based on the constitution devised by the National Commission for Democracy) the legitimacy it might otherwise have had. As a result, the post-democracy government looked oddly like the military dictatorship that had preceded it, and rather than usher in a new era of optimism, the elections poisoned the political atmosphere which had seemed so promising at the beginning of the 1990s.

But there were encouraging signals. In his first address to parliament, Rawlings offered an olive branch to opposition parties, inviting them to dialogue with the legislature from which they had excluded themselves. Also encouraging was the role of the **press** in providing an opposition platform. Despite acerbic anti-Rawlings headlines, journalists were mostly allowed to work freely.

Opposition to Rawlings

Important as political issues were, success or failure for Rawlings' government was dependent ultimately on the **economy**, as it tried to juggle policies that maintained foreign approval while not further alienating Ghanaians at home. The IMF talked about Ghana in glowing terms, and recommended an Asian-style growth strategy.

Despite the rapid expansion of the country's new **stock market** and populist programmes including rural electrification and road building, lower wage-earners and the poor paid a heavy price for economic reform. Equally troublesome was the fact that much of the expansion had been fuelled by a boom in gold mining rather than new economic initiatives.

The first signs that the population at large had reached breaking point came in May 1995, when parliament introduced **Value Added Tax** at a rate of 17 percent. With a rallying cry of *kume preko* ("You may as well kill me now"), tens of thousands of protestors demonstrated on the streets of Accra. Five people died in the melee, including at least two killed by unidentified gunmen. It was the most serious display of popular opposition to date and was seized upon by detractors – many in exile – who deplored Ghana's human rights record.

With **elections** on the horizon in 1996, the government was forced to rescind the tax. Against its defensive posturing, a group of opposition parties found room for agreement. The NPP, PCP (People's Convention Party) and NDM (New Democratic Movement) formed the **Alliance for Change**, with NPP member **John Kufuor** – a Danquah-Busiaist lawyer from Kumasi – as its candidate. Rawlings nevertheless on personal charisma or party organization. Rawlings won 57 percent of the vote at the December elections.

Renewed from his election victory, Rawlings once again was hailed in the West as a champion of constitutional democracy with a wise free-trade policy. Economic prospects seemed less fortuitous from within the country itself, where the years right after the election were characterized by budget deficits, debt servicing burdens and slow aid disbursements. The same period saw the world price of gold plummet, and with it much of Ghana's foreign earnings.

The Kufuor era

By the end of the 1990s, the depressing economic outlook had been coupled with accusations against the NDC leadership of mismanagement, corruption and intimidation. This reputation gained credibility at the grass roots and even within the NDC itself. Rawlings, having served two terms (the maximum allowed by the constitution), thrust **John Atta Mills** forward as the NDC's presidential candidate.

The elections of late 2000 were closely fought, with a result emerging on the second round of voting: in a peaceful transfer of power, the career politician **John Kufuor** of the NPP was sworn in as president. Kufuor, though considered to lack the common touch and oratorical skills of his predecessor, had the backing of many people who simply wanted a clean break from the past. He established a **National Reconciliation Commission** to look at human rights violations under Rawlings and set about transforming Ghana's international reputation. Kufuor was re-elected in December 2004 with 53 percent of the vote. A the time of writing, it looks like John Atta Mills will run against the NPP again in the December 2008 elections.

Politically and economically, Ghana has moved a long way in the last decade. In 2002, the country was granted **debt relief** under the Heavily Indebted Poor Countries (HIPC) programme and it completed a three-year IMF poverty reduction strategy in 2006, reducing the country's debt by half. But although Kufuor succeeded in stabilizing the economy, power supply remains a problem, especially when Lake Akosombo recedes each year before the rains break causing a drop in hydroelectric production. Meanwhile, water and electricity prices have soared.

Against this background, Ghana's patient population witnessed the 2007 celebrations for the **50th anniversary of independence** with mixed feelings: President Kufuor was accused of wasting money on the 2008 African Nations Cup, while health and education were neglected. New **oil finds** off the coast in 2007 should do much to make life easier for his successor –and, if well managed, for the country as a whole. Keeping up with the aspirations of increasingly urbanized and cosmopolitan Ghanaians is the biggest challenge.

Music

Ghana's **urban music** is well known abroad, but the country also has a strong living tradition of rural music, which continues to influence urban sounds. **Gospel** has boomed in recent years, with artists such as the Tagoe Sisters, Cindy Thompson and the Daughters of Glorious Jesus benefiting from the trend. Many artists, like reggae singer Kojo Antwi, and Nana Acheampong and Charles Kwadwo Fosu (Daddy Lumba), who sometimes perform together as the Lumba Brothers – have focused on their solo careers, often abroad. Increasingly, the music of Ghana has an international **hip-hop** flavour, defined by video and commercial success, with sponsors latching onto whatever works.

Traditional music

The main types of music are **court music** played for chiefs, **ceremonial music** and work songs – and of course music for its own sake. In northeastern Ghana, you'll find mostly fiddles, lutes and wonderful hourglass **talking-drum** ensembles. It's customary for musicians to perform frequently for the local chief – in the Dagomba country each Monday and Friday. In Tamale and Yendi professional musicians, although attached to chiefs, regularly perform for the general public. Dagomba **drummers** are always a great spectacle, their flowing tunics fanning out as, hands flying, they dance the **takai**.

10

GHANA | Basics

808

Ghanaian instruments

Northeast
Gonge One-stringed fiddle
Kologo Two-stringed lute
Donno Ensemble talking drums

Ewe
Sogo and **kidi** Drums
Atsimewu Master drum
Axatse Rattles
Gankogui Double bells

Asante
Atumpane Set of twin drums
Ntahera Ensemble of ivory horns
Premprensua Giant hand piano, sat on by the player
Seperewa Harp-lute, a bit like a kora

In the northwest, the main instrument of the **Lobi**, **Wala**, **Dagarti** and **Sissala** is the **xylophone** – either played alone or with a small group of drums and percussion instruments. Finger bells and ankle bells are often worn by the dancers.

The music of the **Ewe** of eastern Ghana is closer to the traditions of Togo and Benin than to that of other Ghanaian peoples, and with their enthusiasm for music associations and dance clubs they've developed many different kinds of recreational music.

In southern central Ghana the Akan peoples, notably the **Asante** and **Fante**, have an elaborate court music using large **drum ensembles** and groups of **horns**. Another great spectacle is that of the huge log xylophones played in **asonko**, a form of recreational music.

Musicians playing traditional African music on the world stage include the great **Mustapha Tetteh Addy** who, with his **Obunu drummers**, incorporates African drums and xylophones into his music (you can see him at his music centre at Kokrobite; see p.833), and **Nana Danso Abiam** and **Dela Botri** and their **Pan African Orchestra**.

Palm-wine music

"**Palm-wine**" is the generic name for the popular music of the Asante. Primarily solo, good-time guitar music, it originated in the palm-wine "bars" – usually a spot under a big tree. A musician would turn up with his guitar and play for as long as people wanted to buy him drinks. Such palm-wineists tend to be comedians and parodists of the local scene. Palm-wine music is dying out, partly because musicians are being enticed into guitar bands. In any town someone will be able to point you in the direction of a palm-wine player but you may have to find an instrument for him to play on. Buy the man a drink and you may well find your name included in the current song.

Koo Nimo

A guitarist who has done as much as anyone to enrich and preserve Ghana's traditional guitar music, Koo Nimo (Daniel Amponsah) commands huge respect among Ghanaians at home and abroad. After a spell teaching in the US, he still performs regularly at concerts and festivals around Kumasi with his all-acoustic Adadam Agofomma band.

Tete Wobi Ka (Human Songs, US). Palm-wine highlife of the first order, including box guitar, the seperewa harp-lute and the giant premprensua hand-piano thumping out the bass line.

Highlife

Highlife originated in Ghana and Sierra Leone and has proved to be one of the most popular and enduring African styles. Originally a fusion of traditional percussion and melodies, with European influences like brass bands, sea shanties and hymns, it started in the early 1920s with the growth of major ports along the West African coast. The term itself is no more than a reference to the kind of European-derived evening of dressing up and dancing (the "highlife") to which new immigrants to the towns of West Africa between the wars were quite unaccustomed – but which they soon made their own.

The first 78rpm records were released in the 1930s and highlife's international reputation started to grow. There are about a dozen different styles of highlife but the two main ones are the guitar-band and dance-band styles. **Guitar-band highlife** is basically a more organized form of palm-wine music, and became known as **concert party** when exponents added other elements – dance routines and comic turns. **Dance-band highlife**, in its extreme form, was all top hats and tails and as much brass as possible. There's a wonderful highlife variation in "gospel highlife" – do everything possible to hear something recorded by the **Genesis Gospel Singers**.

Various artists

The Rough Guide to Highlife (World Music Network). A wonderful mix of Nigerian and Ghanaian numbers from the 1960s and 70s, including Ghanaians E.T. Mensah, Alex Konadu, George Darko, Jerry Hanson and the Ramblers, and Nana Ampadu and the African Brothers.

The Rough Guide West African Gold (World Music Network). Fantastic collection of classics from the late 1950s to the early 80s, including highlife tracks from Ghanaians E.T. Mensah, the Sweet Talks and Eric Agyeman.

I've Found My Love (Original Music). Guitar-band highlife from the 1950s and 60s. Relaxed shuffles based on the prototype highlife tune, "Yaa Amponsah".

E.T. Mensah

The "King of Highlife", E.T. Mensah (1919–96) had a musical childhood and, during World War II came into contact with British and American styles like calypso, swing and cha-cha. In 1948 he formed the Tempos, the first professional dance band in Ghana. After a string of hits, the group went international with frequent tours of West Africa – a golden age of highlife. Soon there were hundreds of bands imitating their style.

All for You (RetroAfric). All the classics from the 1950s, including the wacky "Inflation Calypso", "Sunday Mirror" and the title track. Never mind the crackles, everyone likes it.

King Bruce & the Black Beats

King Bruce (1922–97) was a major figure of the classic highlife era, a trumpeter who formed the Black Beats, the first of a string of successful Accra dance bands in the early 1950s.

Golden Highlife Classics from the 1950s and 1960s (RetroAfric). Superb introduction to the sound of Ghana nearly half a century ago – all laid-back grooves and claves and slightly pear-shaped horns.

A.B. Crentsil's Sweet Talks

One of Ghana's most successful 1970s bands, the group gained national popularity after a string of hit albums.

Hollywood Highlife Party (Popular African Music). An out-and-out classic, recorded in the USA in 1978, here re-issued with bonus tracks.

Osibisaba

Taking their name from osibisaba, a proto-highlife rhythm, the band were formed in London by Teddy Osei, Mac Tontoh and Sol Amarfino. Three of their Afro-rock singles, "Dance the Body Music", "Sunshine Day" and "Coffee Song", rose to the UK Top 10.

Fire – Hot Flashback Vol. 1 (Red Steel). All the hits are here: if you're too young to remember what all the fuss was about, move heaven and earth for this collection.

Hip-life

In 1992 **hip-life** – a hybrid of US hip-hop and Ghanaian highlife – exploded onto Ghana's music scene. Now the biggest selling genre in Ghana, it's played in clubs and bars across the country, and particularly in Accra. Hip-life artists to listen out for include Sidney, Obrafour, Batman Samini, Okeame Quame Obour, Kwabena Kwabena, Abrewa Nana, Castro Destroyer and especially the godfather of the genre, the strongly US-influenced **Reggie Rockstone**, familiar across the country for his Guinness endorsements.

Reggie Rockstone

Pioneer of hip-life, whose time in the US has given him a perceived edge over competitors. His wry lyrics speak well to his local audience.

Last Show (OM/Kassa). Raps in Twi and English, over digital disco-funk, minor-key highlife and R&B beats. Rockstone also features on **The Rough Guide to African Rap** (World Music Network).

Cinema

The wave of productivity that swept the Francophone countries generally bypassed the English-speaking states, only two of which – **Ghana** and Nigeria – have gone beyond government-sponsored documentaries to create anything like an independent cinema. In Ghana, independent film-makers began producing features that combined comedy and melodrama.

The documentary style of the former state-run Ghana Film Industry Corporation influenced directors such as **Sam Aryete** (*No Tears for Ananse*, 1968), **King Ampaw** (*They Call It Love*, 1972; *Kukurantumi*, 1983; *Juju*, 1986), **Kwate Nee Owo** (*You Hide Me*, 1971; *Struggle for Zimbabwe*, 1974; *Angela Davis*, 1976), and **Kwaw Ansah** (*Love Brewed in the African Pot*, 1981; *Heritage Africa*, 1989).

By the late 1990s film-making invariably meant **video production** and it's now estimated that more than 100 feature videos a year are produced in this way with local actors and even amateurs. The subject matter is always relationships, and tends to revolve around love and death, jealousy and illness, morality and honesty, polygamy and Christian monogamy, and often incorporates ghosts and the power of the ancestors – beliefs woven deep into the fabric of all Ghanaian communities. Popular hits of recent years have included *Divine Love* and *Injustice Cell 17*.

A new **film festival**, the Ananse International Film Festival (Ⓦ www.anansefilmfestival.com), was launched in March 2007.

Books

Ghana has an established literary tradition, with a number of widely available works. For good general titles, including some with a strong Ghanaian connection, see p.35. Out-of-print titles below are denoted o/p and especially recommended books are marked 🏃.

Peter Adler, Nicholas Barnard & Ian Skelton *Asafo!: African Flags of the Fante*. Striking visual introduction to the colourfully competitive symbolism of coastal culture.

Maya Angelou *All God's Children Need Traveling Shoes*. The story of American black activist Angelou's emigration to newly independent Ghana and her growing sense of disillusion, picked out in dialogue.

F.K. Buah *History of Ghana*. A basic text, with a fair amount of illustration.

Gracia Clark *Onions Are My Husband: Survival and Accumulation by West African Market Women*. Insightful portrait of Kumasi market traders.

Ekow Eshun *Black Gold of the Sun*. British Ghanaian writer and broadcaster travels through Ghana in search of his roots. The book was nominated for the Orwell Prize for political writing 2006.

🏃 **John Miller Chernoff** *Hustling Is Not Stealing* and *Exchange Is Not Robbery*. Unique, funny, and in places almost unbearably poignant reportage – the verbatim stories of a bar girl, related to Chernoff in the late 1970s and rendered with breathtaking skill and honesty.

🏃 **Max Milligan and Lesley Lokko** *Ghana: A Portrait*. Coffee-table book released in time for Ghana's

811

50th anniversary celebrations paints a stunning photographic portrait of the country.

Paul Nugent *Big Men, Small Boys and Politics in Ghana.* Subtitled *Power, Ideology and the Burden of History*, this is the best account of the Rawlings years, simultaneously academic in approach and accessible.

Thierry Secretan *Going into Darkness: Fantastic Coffins from Africa.* Coffee-table coffin portraits – the extraordinary lifestyle-in-death caskets (sardine for fisherman, Merc for businessman) of the Ga in Accra.

William St Clair *The Grand Slave Emporium: Cape Coast Castle and the British Slave Trade.* A highly readable new study illuminating the history of Cape Coast Castle and the British role in the slave trade.

David Wedd *The Sunshine Land.* A young British army officer's experiences during the changeover to independence.

Fiction

Ama Ata Aidoo *The Dilemma of a Ghost* and *Anowa.* In the former, Aidoo, one of Africa's relatively few female writers, deals with the unusual theme of an African-American girl married into a Ghanaian family; in the latter, a play published in 1970, the subject is a Ghanaian legend about a girl who refuses her parents' chosen suitors. Also available is the short-story collection *No Sweetness Here*, most of whose tales handle the theme of conflict between traditional and urban life in Ghana.

Ayi Kwei Armah *The Beautyful Ones Are Not Yet Born.* Politics, greed and corruption in newly independent Africa, seen through the life of a railway clerk. Armah beautifully

captures the sense of frustration and crisis that befell Ghana after the fall of Nkrumah. More recently, a compelling historical novel, *The Healers*, is set in the Asante empire at the time of its demise. His most recent book, *KMT: in the House of Life* tells the story of a translator of secret hieroglyphic texts.

Akosua Busia *The Seasons of Beento Blackbird.* The author, the daughter of a former Ghanaian prime minister, created quite a stir with this debut. Here she deals with the condition of the African diaspora through the story of one man, loved by three women (one from the Caribbean, one from America and one from Africa), exploring the contrasting emotional, sexual and cultural forces they embody.

Joseph Casely-Hayford *Ethiopia Unbound.* Generally considered the first West African novel (it appeared in 1911), this treats a theme that later became familiar in African literature: the student who goes to study in London, and returns home to find he's a stranger.

Amma Darko *Beyond the Horizon.* Provocative story of a Ghanaian woman's prostitution in Germany. *The Housemaid*, a later work, addresses gender politics in modern Ghana.

Manu Herbstein *Ama: A Story of the Atlantic Slave Trade.* Winner of the 2002 Commonwealth Writers Prize first book award, South African Herbstein's novel recounts the story of a young Dagomba woman's experiences of the transatlantic slave trade.

Benjamin Kwame Kwakye *The Sun by Night.* Won the Commonwealth Writers Prize in 2006 for best book from the African Region. This is a thriller that takes place around the death of an Accra prostitute.

Francis Selormey *The Narrow Path.* A novel of growing up in Keta in the 1930s.

Languages

Ghana's official language is English, which you can use without much trouble throughout the country, although you'll likely need a period of adjustment before completely understanding the broader **pidgin** accents.

The two main language "families" into which Ghanaian languages fall are Kwa in the south and Voltaic in the north. The great **Twi group** of Kwa languages and dialects includes the **Akan languages** like **Asante–Twi**, spoken by the Asante and Fante; **Ewe** and its associate dialects (spoken in the southeast – see p.905), and **Ga**, or Ga-Adangme, the traditional language of the Accra region. Important **Voltaic languages** include the large **More** (or Mole) cluster – among them **Dagomba** and **Mamprusi** – and various **Grusi** tongues, such as **Frafra** and **Nunumba**.

A number of Ghanaian languages have long been written with unfamiliar **orthography** and you'll see satisfyingly exotic-looking spellings used in many hand-painted signs, including:

ɔ – pronounced "o" as in cost;
ε – pronounced "e" as in men;
ŋ – pronounced "ng" as in sing;
ɣ – pronounced as a very soft "h".

Twi

Twi, pronounced somewhere between "Twee" and "Tree", is the name commonly given to the language of the Asante and Fante people. It's a difficult tongue to master, with a complex tonal system, but a few words and phrases in Twi always go down well. Note that it's usually written with the somewhat impenetrable orthography mentioned above, but we've opted for a simple transliteration that should sound okay.

Greetings

Akwaaba	Hello/Welcome
Yaa	Response
Mma ache	Good morning
Mma aha	Good afternoon
Mma adjo	Good evening
Ye muu	Response
Obi wo fie?	Anyone home?

Basic conversation

Wo hu te sen?	How are you?
Me ho ye	I'm fine
Bra	Come here (children)
Koh	Go away (children)
Aan	Yes
Dabe	No
Me pawocheo	Please ("I beg you")
Ye ferew sen?	What's your name?
Ye fere me …	My name is …
Wo fri he?	Where do you come from?
Me fri …	I come from …
Meda ase	Thank you
Mme enna ase	Response (you're welcome)
Wote Borofo anna?	Do you speak English (lit. "white language")?
Mnta se	I don't understand
Ma ware	I'm married
Ma me nsuo	(Please) give me water
Me pe …	I want/like …
Me nti apoh	I'm not well
E komdeme	I'm hungry

Travel

Me ko	I'm going
Ye ko	We're going
Enne	Today
Echina	Tomorrow
Enrah	Yesterday
Annajoh	Tonight
Lore	Lorry
Bossoji inabea	Bus stop

Numbers

biako	1
abieng	2
abiesa	3

anang	4	oha	100
anum	5	ahannu	200
asia	6	ahasa	300
asong	7	ahannang	400
awotwe	8	ahannum	500
akrong	9	ahansia	600
du	10	ahansong	700
dubiako	11	ahangwotwe	800
aduonu	20	ahangkron	900
aduasa	30	apem	1000
aduanang	40		

Glossary

Adinkra Cotton funeral cloth with printed black symbols worn by mourners (Akan peoples).

Afahye Outdoor festival (Akan peoples).

Agbada Large embroidered robe, usually white, worn on special occasions.

Akan The language that includes dialects spoken by the Fante and the Asante.

Asafo Military-style "company" of the Fante.

Asante Standard spelling of the Kumasi-based ethnic group.

Ashanti Popular European spelling and name of the administrative region.

Burglar Means rip-off artist in general, including con-merchant.

Chop Food, or "to eat".

Colo Ingratiating, "colonial" behaviour.

Concert party Popular entertainment that started in the villages. When people couldn't afford to go to clubs, they began "concert parties", a theatrical performance – usually humorous – accompanied by highlife music.

Dash From Portuguese for "to give", meaning a gift or bribe. Can also function as a verb, as in "How much you dash me?"

Drop In the context of public transport, can mean either "to disembark" (as in "Where do you want to drop?") or "chartered" (as in the phrase "dropping taxi").

Durbar Term introduced by the British from the Hindi, but unlike the horse rally of northern Nigeria, this is the occasion that climaxes traditional festivals, when chiefs receive distinguished guests.

Highlife "Big Band Highlife" is Ghana's best-known dance-music form, but Ghanaians use the term to refer to a much broader range of music which is no more homogenous than, say, rock.

How be? Common greeting meaning "How are you?"

Kalabule Corruption and palm greasing.

Kente Multicoloured, woven strip fabric, sometimes silk, made by the Akan and Ewe.

Kotoko Porcupine, symbol of the Asante. The animal's countless sharp quills stand for boundless Asante bravery, reflected in the saying *Kotoko wokum apem, apem beba* ("Kill a thousand porcupines and a thousand more will come").

Obruni wawu Imported second-hand clothes (lit. "a white man has died").

Obruni/Bruni Akan word for white man, often chanted by children.

Oware The game of pebbles and holes (see p.69).

Paa "Very"; for example "It's expensive, paa", ie very expensive.

Posuban Shrines made by Asafo companies.

Silly Pejorative term implying an insult to one's intelligence – stronger term than in US or Britain.

Stool The royal throne of Akan-speaking peoples. "Stooling" means enthronement.

Wee Marijuana.

Weeding/Weeding-off Collective grave-tending ceremony that takes place some time after a funeral.

10.1

Accra and around

lat, sprawling and for the most part nondescript, the cityscape of **ACCRA** is still blighted by heavy concrete stacks harking back to the Soviet-inspired early years of independence. Belying first impressions, though, Accra is an exciting city making a rapid comeback. Soulless concrete blocks are offset by some attractive tree-lined avenues and glitzy, modern hotels, the vibrancy of which is matched by the energy of the people, including a good number of foreigners attracted to one West African capital that can look ahead with some confidence.

With a population of 2.2 million (unofficial estimates put the figure much higher), Accra is one of Africa's biggest cities, and though its trees make it exceptionally green, it hasn't been spared from traffic, noise or overcrowding. Rush hours are dynamic, the streets thronged with a racket of vehicles and people, while after dark, Accra's club scene is one of the liveliest in West Africa.

Some history

Accra's **Ga founders** arrived in the region some time before 1500, setting up their capital at Ayawaso ("Great Accra") some 15km inland, and building a "Small Accra" on the coast for trade with the **Portuguese**, who put up a fort here in the sixteenth century. Trade – of slaves, gold and palm oil for guns – increased over the next hundred years with the building of the Dutch **Fort Ussher**, the Danish **Christiansborg** and the English **Fort James**.

Accra originally consisted of **seven quarters** – the Ga quarters of Asere, Abola, Gbese, Sempe and Akunmadzei; Otublohu, the Akwamu quarter; and Alata, which later became the core of the British-protected area of Jamestown. Other quarters placed themselves under Dutch protection and became Usshertown. Much later, in 1840, the chief of Abola was chosen as the military leader (Ga Mantse) for the whole city, and treated by the British as the Ga king; nowadays he is considered the Ga paramount chief.

Akwamu expansion from the north led to victory over the Ga in 1660 – Chief Okai Koi, defeated by treachery, put a curse on Accra that it should remain disunited against its enemies ever after – and to the destruction of Ayawaso, now just a tiny village. But the Ga regained much of their independence in 1730, when Akwamu fell to the Akim state of Akwapim, which now took over control of the **"notes"** (documents issued by African rulers giving Europeans the right to trade) for the Accra forts. These "notes" later passed to the Asante, who gained control of the area at the beginning of the nineteenth century, but gradually lost it in a series of wars with the British. Battle was averted in 1863 when British and Asante armies were both struck by dysentery and too ill to fight, but a decisive victory in 1874 led to the British taking over and setting up the Gold Coast Colony with its capital at Accra from 1877.

Since then the city has expanded considerably, despite serious earthquakes in 1862 and 1939. After the introduction of **cocoa**, Accra became a major export port, also shipping out gold, palm oil and rubber and, from 1933, boasting West Africa's first brewery (Club). The municipality, set up in 1896, was expanded east to include Christiansborg and, in 1943, to encompass the ancient, walled, farming and salt-producing village of Labadi. On February 28, 1948, major **anticolonial riots** in the city centre followed British police shootings at a demonstration at the junction of

ACCRA

KOKOMLEMLE

Accra North P & T

Tro-tro Station

KWAME NKRUMAH CIRCLE

Barclays Bank

Shell

The Loom Gallery

ASYLUM DOWN

Busy Internet

KUSTA STREET

OROKO STREET

STAR AVENUE

ROYALT CASTLE ROAD

RING ROAD CENTRAL

KING TACKLE / KANDA HIGHWAY

Standard Chartered Bank

Accra Visitors Centre

Chocolate Avenue

Burkina Embassy

Mawuli

German Embassy

FARRAR AVENUE

ADABRAKA

Trust Towers

Speedway Travel

CASTLE ROAD

Niger Embassy

National Museum

JONES ROAD

KOJO THOMPSON ROAD

KWAME NKRUMAH AVENUE

Ghana Tourist Board

Ridge Hospital

Valco Trust House

INDEPENDENCE AVENUE

AFRICAN LIBERATION SQUARE

British Council

National Theatre

LIBERIA ROAD

BARNES ROAD

International Conference Centre

GRAPHIC ROAD

Cocoa House

Railway Station

Tudu Station

TUDU CRES

Makola Market

STC Bus Park (East)

KINBU ROAD

Tema Station

Mali Embassy

Ministry of Interior

Stadium

DERBY ROAD

Supreme Court

Parliament

28TH FEBRUARY ROAD

Shell

USSHER TOWN

Standard Chartered Bank

Bank of Ghana & Ghana Commercial Bank

Arts Centre

Kwame Nkrumah Memorial Park

INDEPENDENCE SQUARE

Barclays Bank

JAMESTOWN

HIGH STREET

Ghana Telecom

Department of Wildlife

Ussher Fort

ATLANTIC OCEAN

STC Bus Station-North, West & Central Ghana (1km), Kaneshie Motor Park & Cape Coast

RESTAURANTS, BARS & CLUBS

Abusua	12	Champs Sports Bar	I	Haveli	27
Adonis	29	Chez Lien	25	Home Touch	3
Asanka Local	32	Choo's Eatery	10	Ivy Coffee Shop	6
Asassepa	4	Country Kitchen	14	Jazz Tone	2
Banana Leaf	18	Cuppa Cappuccino	1	La Tawala Spot	34
Buku	16	Don's Place	28	Le Magellan	21
The Caribbean	22	Dynasty	24	Le Tandem	G
Celsbridge	30	Frankies	T	Little India Sunshine Salad Bar	15

Macumba	17	The Office	
Mamma Mia's	19	Orangery Crepe & Salad Bar	
Maquis Tante Marie	11	Osu Food Court	
Monsoon	23	Papaye	
Monte Carlo	13	Pit Stop & 4Q Bar	
Next Door	33	Savannah	
Nourish Lab Smoothies	26	Venus Cocktail Bar	
		Vienna City/Waikik	

816

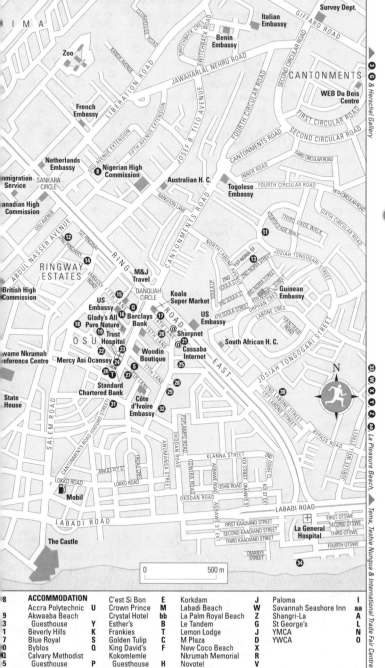

Survey Dept.

Italian
Embassy

GIFFARD ROAD

Benin
Embassy

CLUBHOUSE ROAD

SWITCHBACK CRES

SWITCHBACK ROAD

KANDA AVENUE

KANDA LANE

LIBERATION ROAD

JAWAHARLAL NEHRU ROAD

SECOND CIRCULAR ROAD

CANTONMENTS

WEB Du Bois
Centre

FIRST CIRCULAR ROAD

SECOND CIRCULAR ROAD

Zoo

FIFTH AVENUE EXTENSION

JOSEF B. TITO AVENUE

FOURTH CIRCULAR ROAD

French
Embassy

OSU AVENUE EXTENSION

CANTONMENTS ROAD

THIRD CIRCULAR ROAD

INNER ROAD

Netherlands
Embassy

❾ Nigerian High
Commission

Australian H. C.

FOURTH CIRCULAR ROAD

Togolese
Embassy

FIFTH CIRCULAR ROAD

Immigration
Service

SANKARA
CIRCLE

RANGOON LANE

CANTONMENTS ROAD

SIXTH CIRCULAR ROAD

Canadian High
Commission

OSU AVENUE

ABDUL NASSER AVENUE

1ST RINGWAY

RING ROAD

NORTH LABONE AVENUE

❶❶

THIRD DADE WALK

FOURTH DADE WALK

1ST NORLA ST

SECOND CIRCULAR ROAD

JOSIAH TONGOGARI STREET

❶❷

RINGWAY
ESTATES

❶❹

M&J
Travel

❶❸

2ND
SOULA ST

3RD SOULA ST

3RD NORLA STREET

2ND NORLA STREET

4TH NORLA STREET

British High
Commission

EMBASSY ROAD

❶❺

DANQUAH
CIRCLE

Koala
Super Market

SOULA ST

3RD SOULA ST

Guinean
Embassy

US
Embassy

❶❻

Barclays
Bank

4TH SOULA STREET

ORPHAN CRES

LABONE CRES

VANTRAB

US
Embassy

Gladys All
Pure Nature

❶❼

RING ROAD

FOURTH LANE

Sharpnet

South African H. C.

VANTRAB ST

❶❽

Trust

OSU Hospital

❶❾

❷❶

Cassaba
Internet

Woodin
Boutique

❷⓪

JOSIAH TONGOGARI STREET

Kwame Nkrumah
Conference Centre

Mercy Asi Oansey

❷❷

❷❸

Ⓢ

❷❺

2ND LABONE STREET

EAST

1ST LABONE STREET

❷❻

❷❹

Ⓣ

17TH LANE

❷❽

❸⓪

N

State
House

Standard
Chartered Bank

❸❶

Côte
d'Ivoire
Embassy

❷❼

❷❾

❸❷

BYPASS ROAD

SALEM ROAD

CANTONMENTS ROAD (OXFORD STREET)

TRIAS CRES

AWULEY ST

OKODAN ROAD

ANIMANSA STREET

POPLAMPU ROAD

KLANNA STREET

2ND KOI STREET

KOI STREET EXT

KOI STREET

OSHIE CL

JUBILEE WELL STREET

LOKKO ROAD

Mobil

LOKKO ROAD

OKODAN ROAD

AGBAWE ROAD

OSHIE ROAD

DMANYE ST

OSWIR ROAD

LABADI ROAD

The Castle

LABADI ROAD

FIRST KAADIANO STREET

SECOND KAADIANO STREET

THIRD KAADIANO STREET

AGBAWE ST EX

La General
Hospital

FIRST OTSWE

SECOND OTSWE

THIRD OTSWE

FOURTH OTSWE

OMANYE
STREET

❸❹

0   500 m

ACCOMMODATION		C'est Si Bon	E	Korkdam	J	Paloma	I
Accra Polytechnic	U	Crown Prince	M	Labadi Beach	W	Savannah Seashore Inn	aa
Akwaaba Beach		Crystal Hotel	bb	La Palm Royal Beach	Z	Shangri-La	A
Guesthouse	Y	Esther's	B	Le Tandem	G	St George's	L
Beverly Hills	K	Frankies	T	Lemon Lodge	J	YMCA	N
Blue Royal	S	Golden Tulip	C	M Plaza	D	YWCA	O
Byblos	Q	King David's	F	New Coco Beach	X		
Calvary Methodist		Kokomlemle		Nkrumah Memorial	R		
Guesthouse	P	Guesthouse	H	Novotel	V		

Rowe, Castle and Christiansborg roads. Twenty-nine protestors died and 237 were wounded in an outburst that caused £2 million worth of damage.

After an optimistic start to **independence** in 1957, the city's infrastructure declined as fast as its population grew as a succession of repressive, mostly military governments used Accra as a base from which to milk Ghana's resources. By 1980, conditions had bottomed out, with few functioning services and no investment. The governments of Rawlings and Kufuor have since brought Accra back from the brink, and the city is now recognized as one of West Africa's best capitals in which to live and work, with a dynamic economy and a thriving cultural life.

Arrival and orientation

At **Kotoka International Airport** there's generally a crowd of KIA porters in boilersuits (inscribed "Porter", with a number) trying to handle your luggage for a fee of GH¢2. Keep cool and nominate one, or make it clear you'll do it yourself. Customs and immigration procedures are pretty straightforward. You can **change money** at the forex bureau in the arrivals hall, which stays open for all but the late-night flights, and their rates are not too bad in comparison with the city. The airport has little in the way of **facilities**, however, if you have to spend any time there.

Most large hotels organize shuttles, but there's no airport bus into town and **taxi drivers** converge on you as soon as you leave the terminal building. They can be quite pushy and stories circulate about menacing demands; stay cool and do nothing until someone calms down enough for you to go with them. The fare into the city centre should be clearly agreed before you go, and although it's easy to be pressurized into paying GH¢10 or more, the fare to virtually anywhere should be no more than GH¢5, even at night. The city centre is about 8km away – a twenty-minute taxi ride depending on traffic (it can take much longer in the daytime). Alternatively, you can walk out of the airport zone to the main road, and pick up a **shared taxi** for around GH¢1.50 to Kwame Nkrumah Circle, or other points around the Ring Road.

For **flight bookings** for internal flights to Kumasi or Tamale on Citylink (☎021/785725 ⓦwww.flycitylink.com) and Antrak (☎021/765337 ⓦwww.antrakair.com) either go direct through the airlines or use M&J Travels and Tours (☎021/773498 or 706081).

City layout

Despite the urban sprawl, downtown Accra is neatly contained by the **Ring Road**. The core of Accra stretches from the banking district of **High Street** near the waterfront to the **Makola market** – a colourful hive of activity that overflows into the surrounding streets. In between, the ample proportions of the stately colonial **Old Parliament House** and **Supreme Court** give an idea of the importance the British placed on their Gold Coast Colony.

Lined by shops and commercial and business premises, two main thoroughfares – Nkrumah Avenue and Kojo Thompson Road – run through the city centre south to north from the old districts of **Usshertown** and **Jamestown** to **Kwame Nkrumah Circle** (known simply as "Circle"). Shady **Independence Avenue**, sprinkled with embassies and business headquarters, also leads north, past East Ridge and North Ridge and Ringway Estate to **Sankara Circle** in the northeast and on out to the airport. **Oxford Street** (formerly **Cantonments Road**) runs from the coast near **The Castle** (the seat of government) northeast through the frenzied district of **Osu**, seething with fast-food restaurants, hotels and supermarkets, to **Danquah Circle**, and then on through the Cantonments district to the airport. Cutting east to west through the city centre are the main arteries of Castle Road, Liberia Road and

STC buses for the **west and north** depart from the STC station (℡021/221414). **Kumasi**-bound STC buses (some of which are a/c) leave roughly hourly, from dawn until 6pm or so, taking up to five hours (GH¢7.50). Air-conditioned STC buses also run direct to **Abidjan** three times a week, and to **Ouagadougou** twice a week (GH¢30) – but be prepared to spend the night at the Bolga bus station since you arrive slightly after the Burkina border closes at 6pm. Alternative routes to Ouaga are either to change in Kumasi and spend the night there, or to take an STC bus to Bolga (3 weekly; 15hr; GH¢25) or Paga (2 weekly; 15 hr) and find a taxi heading across the border. STC also runs a direct service to **Wa** (2 weekly; 14–16hr).

STC buses for the **east** go from the transport park along Kinbu Road, between Tudu Crescent and Barnes Road, serving **Ho** and **Hohoe**, as well as **Aflao** on the Togolese border.

Buses operated by **other firms** follow roughly the same division, with north- and westbound buses operating out of a transport park just to the west of Nkrumah Circle and eastbound buses departing from Kinbu Road.

Tro-tros pretty much follow the bus pattern – with less organization. Greater Accra and the coast are the main areas of operation. For the northern and eastern suburbs including Tema and Aburi, get a seat at the Tema Station. For Ada Foah, Keta and towns in eastern Ghana go to Tudu Station near Makola market. For the western suburbs and towns north of Accra, including Kumasi, go to Nkrumah Circle. Finally, for the western coast, at least as far as Takoradi (though you really have to want to save money to go so far by tro-tro), go to Kaneshie.

Kinbu Road. The **beaches** lie not far from town: the nearest is **La Pleasure beach**, 5km east of the city centre.

If you're **arriving by road**, entering Accra can be a confusing business, with little in the way of landmarks to indicate where you are and a generally chaotic cityscape of dust (or mud) on the outskirts. The main STC **bus station**, handling arrivals from the north and west, is on the Ring Road between Nkrumah and Lamptey circles. STC arrivals from the east, including Ho, Hohoe and Aflao, use a separate station on **Kinbu Road** near Makola market.

Tro-tros use a number of stations. *Tro-tros* (and shared taxis) arriving from Western Ghana head to the **Kaneshie station** near the market of the same name, about 2km west of Nkrumah Circle. From eastern towns, *tro-tros* arrive in **Tudu station** near Makola market, while *tro-tros* from northern centres such as Kumasi use the station just west of Nkrumah Circle. *Tro-tros* from Aburi and Tema arrive at Tema Station between Kinbu Road and 28th February Road.

Public transport

Shared **line taxis** (around GH¢0.20–0.30 per hop) roll along fixed routes, often from one traffic circle to another, servicing virtually the whole city. For these, flag down a taxi and state your destination; tourists are generally assumed to be chartering, so make it clear if you're not. If you do want to charter a taxi for a specific journey, expect to pay GH¢1.50–2.50 in town and GH¢5–8 for the outskirts, depending on the distance. Confirm the price before setting off, and note that fares may increase at night and during the rain. **Tro-tros** are slower and cost about thirty percent less than line taxis. The *tro-tro* driver works with his "mate", a conductor of sorts, who leans out of the door shouting the destination.

Tro-tro drivers and some taxi drivers use a circling motion of the finger to mean the vehicle is headed to Kwame Nkrumah Circle. The word "Accra" is shorthand for downtown Accra, with Tema Station as the final destination, and is often signalled by a finger pointing in the air.

Information

You can visit the **Ghana Tourist Board** on Barnes Road (Mon–Fri 8am–noon & 1–4.30pm ☎021/231817 ✉gtb@africaonline.com.gh) and pick up their directory of hotels, restaurants, travel and car-rental agencies. The **Accra Visitors Centre** (Mon–Sat 8am–6pm ☎021/252186) is better and can provide maps of Accra and further afield as well as travel and tour information. If you'll be spending a lot of time venturing into national parks, you may want to drop by the **Wildlife Division**, near Independence Square (☎021/666351), although they provide limited information and maps. If you're planning to spend some time in the capital, the third edition of the excellent *No More Worries – The Indispensable Insider's Guide to Accra*, is a useful directory of businesses and services, available at GH₵22.50 from the ATAG shop in the Trade Fair Centre (see p.824) and from some supermarkets and hotels. Handy listings can also be found in the monthly *Enjoy Accra* booklet, available free from many hotels and restaurants.

Hotel prices

"Prices of hotel rooms in Ghana were always negotiable and we usually managed to reduce the rack rate by about 20 percent."

Allan and Margaret Rickman, UK

Accommodation

Accommodation in Accra is relatively cheap compared with other regional capitals and varies from absolutely basic dorm space, if you're counting every penny, to luxury rooms.

Hostels and student rooms

Dorm beds at the hostels go in the range of GH₵2–2.50 a night. The nearest **campsite** is at Coco Beach, about 10km east of the centre on the Tema road (around GH₵2 per person), but beware of theft in the area.

Accra Polytechnic opposite the *Novotel*, on Barnes Rd ☎021/662939. Basic and very inexpensive accommodation outside school time (ie around Christmas and Easter, and also over the northern hemisphere summer). Dorm beds ❶.

YMCA Castle Rd ☎021/226246 ✉ymca@ghana.com. Basic, unventilated dorm rooms, but central,

and some of the cheapest accommodation in town. Good place to meet Ghanaians. Dorm beds ❶.

YWCA Castle Rd, near the intersection with Kojo Thompson Rd ☎021/220567 ✉ywca@ghana.com. Cleaner and more pleasant than the men's version, with dorm beds and one excellent-value s/c room with a kitchenette. Dorm beds ❷.

Hotels and guesthouses

The majority of the city's **inexpensive hotels** are to be found within a two-kilometre belt stretching from Adabraka, just north of the centre, through Asylum Down and up to Kokomlemle north of the Ring Road.

Inexpensive lodgings

At this level, quality varies greatly, both between establishments and sometimes at a particular hotel.

Beverly Hills Farrar Ave ☎021/224042. Decent mid-range place with clean, old-fashioned rooms (although they're a little on the small side) and

a terrace restaurant serving tasty Ghanaian food. ❸

Calvary Methodist Guesthouse opposite the National Museum, Barnes Rd, Adabraka ☎021/234507. Some of the best-value accommodation in central Accra with excellent, spacious, modern s/c rooms, and balconies with attractive views. ❷

C'est Si Bon Royal Castle Rd ☎021/229004. The singles and doubles, with fan or a/c and private bath, are in reasonable condition, but the whole place is gloomy. ❷

Crown Prince Kojo Thompson Rd, ☎021/225381. Good-value, spotless a/c s/c rooms, a homely feel and a great courtyard bar and restaurant. Unfortunately there's a lot of noise from the busy road. ❶

🏃 **Crystal** 27 Akorlu Close, Dar Kuman Main Rd ☎021/304634 🌐www.crystalhotel .com. Although a little far from the centre (you need to get a *tro-tro* into town), this has comfortable and excellent-value singles and doubles with fan as well as dorms (all s/c) and space for pitching tents. There's Internet access, a leafy garden and roof terrace with comfy chairs for lounging. The hosts make a real effort to make their guests feel welcome and will whip up delicious meals given advance notice. First-class budget traveller's focus. Dorm beds ❶, rooms ❸.

Kokomlemle Guesthouse Oroko St, Kokomlemle ☎021/224581. If you're heading there by taxi, tell the driver it's near the ATTC (Accra Technical Training College). Popular with visiting NGO workers and travellers for its cleanish s/c rooms, friendly staff and a relaxed atmosphere. However, the rooms are small and the courtyard bar and restaurant disheveled. ❷

Korkdam 18, 2nd Crescent Rd, off Mango Tree Ave, Asylum Down ☎021/226797 🌐www .korkdamhotel.com. Range of rooms in a sinfully ugly concrete block from s/c singles with hot water and fridges to well-equipped "executive suites" (phones, TV, a/c). ❸

Lemon Lodge 2nd Crescent Rd, off Mango Tree Ave, Asylum Down ☎021/227857. This once good-value and popular place has gone downhill of late. Rooms are cheap and spacious but could be cleaner and the whole place feels run down. ❷

Nkrumah Memorial Kojo Thompson Rd, Adabraka ☎021/254688. Walls are thin, but the place is kept clean and the location is very convenient. ❷

Savannah Seashore Inn Lagoon Rd, Teshie/Nungua ☎0243/523363 ✉bethbrehmer@hotmail.com. Just west of Coco Beach, this is bang on the beach and a great place to get away from the noise of the city centre. Simple mud, wood and thatch rooms with shared bath, beautiful sea views and a great bar with vegetarian options. ❷

St George's Amusudai Rd, opposite the Methodist School, Adabraka ☎021/224699. In an excellent location near the museum, this restored colonial home has charming, clean, comfortable s/c, a/c rooms, with fridge, phone and TV. ❸

Mid-range hotels

There are some excellent places to stay if you're prepared to spend $50-plus a night for a double room. Most of the following include breakfast and some take major cards.

🏃 **Akwaaba Beach Guesthouse** 28 Beach Rd, Teshie-Nungua Estates ☎021/717742 🌐www.akwaaba-beach.de. Beautiful, Spanish-style villa right on the ocean. There's plenty of space for relaxing including a guest lounge, a roof terrace, a large palm-shaded garden, and a private stretch of pristine beach. Individually designed rooms include a gorgeous glass-fronted penthouse studio with stunning views out over the gardens to the sea. Camping is also possible. ❺

Blue Royal 18th Lane, Osu ☎021/783075 ✉blueroyalghana@yahoo.com. Fantastically located just off Oxford St, this has large, clean a/c rooms with bamboo furniture, plants and African art on the walls. Some have small balconies with views over the town. ❻

Byblos 11th Lane/Embassy Rd, next to *Venus Cocktail Bar*, Osu ☎021/782250. Ideal location if you're drawn to the 24-hour energy of Osu, with stylish rooms equipped with TV, fridge, a/c and phone line, and a ground-floor restaurant serving a well-prepared Middle Eastern and European menu. ❻

🏃 **Esther's** 4 Volta St, Airport Residential Area ☎021/772368 or 765750 🌐www. esthers-hotel.com. Housed in a chalet-style building, *Esther's* is one of the nicest places in Accra, with clean and elegantly decorated wood-floored rooms – either doubles or huge, airy apartments with kitchenette, separate sitting room and balcony – a shady, terraced restaurant and a serene, flower-filled back garden. The welcome is extremely warm and a delicious (and huge) German breakfast is served every morning. ❺

Frankies Oxford St, Osu ☎021/773567 🌐www.frankies-ghana.com. Reliable and well located, if a little soulless, the extremely clean, tiled rooms come decked out in shades of blue and pine with mini fridges, a/c and Wi-Fi. Good breakfasts included and a fine restaurant of the same name downstairs. ❼

King David's near Nkrumah Circle, Kokomlemle ☎021/225280 🅕665960. Small, very clean hotel with friendly staff and large rooms. Good restaurant too. ❺

Paloma C137/2 Ring Road Central ☎021/228700. Comfortable rooms, including stylish new chalets, in a good central position, with every comfort and facility, including Wi-Fi. ❻

Le Tandem 6 Mankralo St, East Cantonments ☎ 021/762959. You can't miss the shockingly bright red building, and the theme continues inside, with orange hallways adorned with vivid paintings by local artists, many of which are for sale. It all seems to work though, and there are five extremely comfortable rooms with huge wooden beds, Moroccan lamps, glass-brick showers and balconies. It's also very friendly and has a good French restaurant. ⑥

Expensive hotels

Hotels in this bracket start at around $90 for a double room, though most are over $200. All of them accept major cards. Pools are available for non-guests for around GH¢2–5 per day.

Golden Tulip Liberation Rd, ☎ 021/213161. One of Accra's most popular business hotels, this place has rather bland (although very well-equipped) rooms and more stylish chalets set among the gardens behind the pool. The café/bar area surrounding the swimming pool is a popular meeting place and there are live bands daily. ⑥

Labadi Beach next to *La Palm* ☎ 021/772501 ⓦ www.labadibeach.com. Comfortable rooms and modern amenities, including a gym and a pool set in lush grounds leading directly to the beach. The breakfast buffet is particularly good. ⑧

La Palm Royal Beach La Pleasure Beach, 5km east of the centre ☎ 021/771700 ⓦ www.gbhghana.com. With basic doubles at $250, this is Ghana's most expensive hotel – a wonderful place to spend a few days if you have the money, but quite divorced

from city life. Lavishly appointed, it has huge grounds, superb pool complex, health club, conference centre and some excellent restaurants (the Polynesian *Bali Hai* rates particularly highly). ⑧

M Plaza Roman Rd, Roman Ridge ☎ 021/763417. Architecturally over the top, with its monumental pillars and gleaming chandelier-festooned lobby, the atmosphere is impersonal, but the rooms are good quality and it has every necessary facility, including a large pool, gym, sauna, travel agent and business centre. ⑧

New Coco Beach 10km east of the city in the suburb of Nungua, near Coco Beach ☎ 021/717235 ⓔ newcocobeach@yahoo.com. An increasingly popular option, much more affordable than most other hotels in this bracket, and good value, although rather lacking in character. Local bands play reggae and highlife every weekend on the poolside stage. ⑦

Novotel Barnes Rd, north of Kinbu Rd ☎ 021/667546 ⓕ 667533 ⓦ www.novotel.com. Accra's first international establishment. Free airport shuttle for guests; non-guests are welcome at the sumptuous buffet breakfast. Large pool and gym. ⑧

Shangri-La 1500m from the airport ☎ 021/777500 ⓕ 774873 ⓔ shangri@ncs.com.gh. Very handy for the airport (free shuttle), and friendlier, more intimate and much less expensive than most others in this bracket. The rooms though, arranged village-style in the grounds, are shabby, with clunky a/c and tatty bathrooms, the once lively restaurant and garden lack atmosphere and the food isn't up to much – though they do have an excellent Chinese restaurant. Tennis courts and a nice pool compensate. ⑧

The City

Accra doesn't especially lend itself to scenic walks and, by day, there's not much in the way of things to see. The main diversion is simply absorbing the energy of an African urban centre. Even the coast and lagoons aren't shown off to any real advantage and, from most places in town, you're barely aware that Accra lies right on the seafront – Jamestown is an exception. A visit to the interesting **National Museum** is recommended, as is a quick trip to the **W.E.B. DuBois Memorial Centre**. With the gradual restoration of a number of buildings in **Ga Mashie** ("Old Accra"), the city is at last beginning to make more of its attractions. The Old Accra Community Guides association trains young people in local history and tourism. Home Tours (☎024/3216187 ⓔ toursathome@yahoo.com) run interesting **tours of Old Accra** with an excellent local historian, Sam Baddoo.

The National Museum of Ghana

The **National Museum of Ghana**, on Barnes Road near the junction with Castle Road (☎021/221633; daily 9am–6pm; closed Monday; GH¢4.50 and GH¢0.50 for cameras), houses one of West Africa's best ethnographic, historical and art collections, with exhibits from Ghana and across the continent. At the time of writing the museum was undergoing some renovation and reorganization of the exhibits.

The museum is dedicated in large measure to still-thriving **local crafts**. There are numerous examples of clay water-coolers, bowls and lamps, calabash drums, iron clappers and wooden zithers, ornamental brass pots and implements, while complementary exhibits show various cottage-industry **technologies**. You can see displays showing how iron is forged (still common in the north), how brass weights, once used for weighing gold, are cast, and how glass beads are manufactured.

Interesting, too, are the **ceremonial objects** so common among the Akan and other peoples of the country. Gilded umbrella tops, carved royal stools, metal swords of state and intricate *kente* cloth are charged with a social and religious significance illuminated by the displays. Upstairs, dusty **archeological relics** trace the country's history back to the late Stone Age.

There's also a permanent and excellent exhibition on the **slave trade** which includes fascinating maps of the slave route from West Africa to the Americas as well as examples of iron shackles and weapons of the trade.

The **National Theatre**, on the corner of Liberia Road and Independence Avenue, is a striking construction, designed and funded by the Chinese. The lobby houses four huge drums and two evocative carvings, specially commissioned for this site; the drums are played only on auspicious occasions, which included the transfer of government in 2000. To arrange your obligatory guided tour (GH¢1), visit the PR Unit in room 310 on the second floor. If you can catch a **performance** here – anything from hip-life gigs to comedy shows and beauty contests – so much the better, but this is only likely at the weekend.

Old Accra and other central sights

Jamestown, a bustling centre of small commerce at the heart of the colonial town, is worth a wander, though not **Fort James** itself – it's a prison. **Ussher Fort**, however, has been restored for public visits, and has a small museum of slavery (GH¢3) and good views over the cliffs. You can also visit the nearby colonial-era **lighthouse** for scenic town views. Nearby, the newly opened **Brazil House** (GH¢5) records the fascinating story of nineteenth-century Brazilian freed-slave returnees – the Tabom community (after the Portuguese greeting "Ta bom?").

East of here, opposite the Parliament building on High Street, the **Kwame Nkrumah Memorial Park** (daily 10am–6pm; GH¢3 plus GH¢2 for cameras) pays homage to the pan-African pioneer and nation builder who became Ghana's first president; it was here, formerly the site of a polo ground, that Nkrumah first declared Ghana's independence. Built in the 1990s, the monument is a throwback to 1960s triumphalism, but the surrounding gardens provide a peaceful refuge from the mayhem of the city. The grounds contain a small **museum** dedicated to Nkrumah's life.

To the east again, **Independence Square** (also known as Black Star Square) is worth a wander, but be aware of possible muggings and theft at night. The **Triumphal Arch** here, an Nkrumah-era monument of heroic dimensions built to herald African liberation, looms west of **Osu Castle** (no photos allowed), the former Danish Christiansborg, today the seat of government and referred to simply as "The Castle". All surrounding streets are barricaded, so you can't get too near to this historical curiosity. Independence Square itself is a giant parade ground, site of the Eternal Flame of African Liberation, lit by Nkrumah. Nearby are the ministries and **National Stadium**, north of which is the impressive **International Conference Centre**, built in record time to house the 1991 conference of nonaligned nations. A few hundred metres to the northeast of the square stands the first president's proudest legacy, the monumental **State House** and adjoining **Kwame Nkrumah Conference Centre**, built in 1965 to serve as headquarters of the Organization of African Unity.

The W.E.B. DuBois Memorial Centre

In the northeast of the city, the house where **W.E.B. DuBois**, the African-American champion of pan-Africanism, died in 1963 and is buried has been turned into the

W.E.B. DuBois **Memorial Centre for Pan-African Culture** (Mon–Fri 8.30am–4.30pm, Sat 11am–4pm; tour GH¢2, camera GH¢0.50, video GH¢1). Located on 1st Circular Road (off Giffard Road, opposite the Midwives Association), it's a highly informative and inspiring monument to pan-Africanism and its vanguard, and features a research library and gallery full of manuscripts and other DuBois memorabilia. On auspicious occasions, the commemorative wreaths from devotees – including reggae dancehall greats Shabba Ranks and Buju Banton – are brought out of storage and once again laid at his tomb.

A lively artists' and creative group called the **Foundation for Contemporary Art** (www.ikando.org/fca.html) is based at the Dubois Centre – they are a good way to tune into the Ghanaian arts scene.

Markets, crafts, galleries and shops

The vast **Makola market**, along Kojo Thompson Road, is where you feel the retail pulse of the city centre most strongly. Makola is a massive and wonderful market, friendly and not overly intimidating, and it's best to wander without any particular goal (though mindful, obviously, of potential pickpockets). If you're buying anything, you may end up parting with a little more than a local, but not much – it's rarely a rip-off. Traders and hawkers spread their wares over any available flat surface and, along the alleys, you're accosted (together with everyone else) by touts scouting for prey, brandishing a small pair of pants, or a single shoe, as examples of wares from their main bases somewhere in the interior. From right across the food and domestic lines – from yams to garden shears, from cheap glass beads to metal suitcases, from buckets to mobile phones, from great blocks of soap to mini-tins of liniment – just about everything is here.

Kaneshie market, by the motor park of the same name on Weija Road, is also huge and an excellent place for rummaging. It's less frenetic and more clearly laid-out than Makola, with food on the ground floor, household goods on the second, and cloth and tailoring on the third.

Crafts

Spreading out around the Centre for National Culture on 28th February Rd is the **"Arts Centre"**, a huge outlet for craft works from throughout West Africa (in fact the formally titled Centre for National Culture consists now *only* of this crafts market). On the whole, buying here isn't as satisfying or cheap as searching out the crafts in the regions where they're made, but if you've got no time or just like one-stop shopping, this is the place. Beware that much of it is quite removed from any cultural roots and for every beautifully worked carving, you'll find a shoddy bit of amateurism. But you will find everything here from **Asante sandals** and **kente cloth** to **leatherwork** from the north, woven cotton fabric and glass beads, any of which can easily be bought elsewhere, and more cheaply. The wooden crafts – **masks**, **musical instruments**, **carvings** and **boxes** – and the **brass work** are somewhat harder to find. Expect heavy pressure to buy; bargaining tends to be a battle of wits here and not a great deal of fun.

A more relaxed place to buy is from the craftsmen selling in stalls set up around the **International Trade Fair Centre** just north of the *Labadi Beach Hotel* at La Pleasure Beach. It's less overwhelming if you're not up to speed with your bargaining skills, and there are plenty of good-quality items on offer. The permanent **ATAG Crafts Shop** (Mon–Fri 8am–6pm, Sat 10am–4pm; ☎021/771325 www.ataggh .com). ATAG (Aid to Artisans Ghana), offers practical assistance to Ghanaian crafts-people and markets and sells their wares, which is also located here.

Galleries – and coffins

For artwork, the **Loom Gallery** at 117 Kwame Nkrumah Ave (☎021/224746) sells pricey canvases and sculptures by local artists. The **Herschel Galley** (Mon–Sat

9.30–5pm; ☎0243/380668) on Mankrolo Street, just down the road from the arty *Tandem* hotel, has a good selection of canvases and sculpture as well as an upstairs craft shop selling *kente* cloth, leather goods and other high-quality souvenirs. The huge new **Artists Allianz Gallery** in La is a fine space, with some superb work on show.

The tendency for bereaved Ga (the main people of the Accra area) to send their loved ones off in elaborately designed **coffins** (see "Books", p.828) has brought international renown to one or two casket-makers in the capital. Out by the main road in **Teshie**, the beach suburb 10km east of the city centre on the way to Tema, you'll see the evidence in all its sumptuous, intricately detailed and glossily painted glory. Paa Joe's is the biggest coffin-maker here – for around GH¢300 and up, he'll send you off in any make of car, in a lobster, in a mobile phone (brand of your choosing) or in a bottle of beer inscribed with your sell-by date. Smaller collectibles are also available for the non-deceased – they make superb souvenirs.

Shops

See "Listings" on p.828 for bookshops and supermarkets. The following addresses are aimed more at those seeking souvenirs and luxuries or just in need of retail therapy.

Chocolate Avenue on North Ridge opposite the Ghana Broadcasting Corporation (☎0242/557766). Everything cocoa related, with a vast array of excellent Ghanaian chocolate and choc-flavoured products including cakes, chocolate drinks and cocoa-butter cosmetics.
Glady's All Pure Nature 10th Lane, Osu (Mon–Sat 8.30am–8pm). Accra's answer to Body Shop, with a good range of beautifully packaged hand made soaps, lip balms and lotions, all manufactured from local raw materials.
Mawuli Water Rd, north of the German embassy (☎021/225813 ⓦwww.mkogh.com; Mon–Sat 9am–7pm). For clothing that's a mixture of stylish/modern and traditional, a hugely popular boutique owned by fashion designer Mawuli Kofi Okudzeto.

Mercy Asi Ocansey and Sons Dyeing Enterprise 4th Lane, off Cantonments Road, Osu, next to *Frankies* and opposite the police hospital (☎021/777835). Batik designs of superb quality.
Sun Trade SOS Children's Village, Mango Tree Ave, Asylum Down (☎021/235982; Mon–Fri 10am–6pm, Sat 10am–5pm). Ghana handicrafts outlet, specializing in beads. Visit ⓦwww .eshopafrica to see their wares.
Wild Gecko off Tetteh Quarshie Circle, near Unique Ceramics (☎021/508500; Tues–Sat 10am–6pm). A fine selection of Ghanaian crafts and items from across Africa. Again, ⓦwww.eshopafrica displays most of what they sell.
Woodin Boutique Oxford St. Extremely popular fabric and clothing shop with branches around the country. Greater variety than Mercy.

Beaches

The best area for sea swimming in Accra is **La Pleasure Beach** (also known as Labadi; GH¢2 entrance fee), directly below the International Trade Fair site. Unusually for Ghana, there are lifeguards stationed here, occasionally called upon to rescue swimmers swept out by the strong undertow. This is *the* place to see and be seen, especially at weekends when Accra's young crowd turn out for beach parties. Several bars and restaurants line the beach, and you may be plagued by hangers-on trying to sell something or play you music for a "dash". Taxis and *tro-tros* run here from Nkrumah Circle. To relax in a more serene environment, **Coco Beach**, a fifteen-minute drive further east, is a better bet. If you just want to swim in comfort and safety, pay a few cedis to indulge at the pool of one of the big hotels.

Eating, drinking and nightlife

Meals in Accra are usually good, and often excellent, and the city's reputation for independent restaurants offering fresh, well-prepared food is growing all the time. In addition to the places listed below, cheap **street eats** are available in the motor parks and markets and in certain districts – Adabraka, for example. If you're staying in one of the neighbourhood's inexpensive hotels, you'll find numerous *kenkey* and fish vendors in the backstreets.

Inexpensive

In most of the following establishments you can eat a hearty one-course meal for GH¢2–4. Most offer standard international fast food, with healthier alternatives, salads and some Ghanaian dishes also featuring.

Asassepa Ring Road central, next to the Accra Visitors' Centre ☏021/761936 (daily 9am–9pm). Small health–food café serving veggie spring rolls, samosas, tofu kebabs and the like as well as a selection of extraordinarily pungent herbal drinks.

Choo's Eatery 1st floor, Trust Towers, Farrar Ave (daily 7am–11pm). Nice balcony space overlooking the street, and African and Caribbean specials such as coconut chicken curry for around GH¢2.50. There's a GH¢3.50 buffet every Fri lunchtime.

Cuppa Cappuccino 3rd Close, Airport Residential Area, opposite *Jazz Tone*. Funky little coffee bar with a great range of freshly brewed coffees as well as smoothies, salads, sandwiches and light meals.

Nourish Lab Smoothies 3rd Lane, Osu ☏024/4607862. Tiny café with limited outdoor seating serving delicious natural fruit smoothies as well as milkshakes, iced cappuccinos and healthy salads and snacks.

Osu Food Court Oxford St, Osu. Food court with large patio overlooking Oxford St. There's a patisserie, pizza, fried chicken and *Nando's* copy, *Galitos*.

Papaye Oxford St, Osu (daily 9am–midnight). Another fine example of Accra's growing fast-food culture, with excellent charcoal-grilled chicken (around GH¢3) and fish which you can eat out on the breezy first-floor balcony or indoors in the a/c area. Try to catch the cultural dance performance on the forecourt every Sat night.

Moderate and expensive

Mid-priced restaurants (GH¢3–6 for a main course) offer a varied cuisine, with a good variety of Asian restaurants and several high-quality Middle Eastern and European-style establishments, as well as a number of very classy African places. Prices at the most expensive eating houses, which include hotel restaurants open to non-guests, run to about GH¢8–12 per main course.

African

Abusua 43 Ringway Estate, Osu ☏021/769168 or ☏0244/522766. Friendly place serving Ghanaian and Senegalese food with a dash of French. Nice courtyard area outside and a smaller, more intimate-ochre-walled inside dining room. First-rate tilapia and snails.

Asanka Local Adzoatse St, Osu ☏021/502715 (daily 11am–11pm). Very popular local restaurant (won the coveted "Chop Bar of the Year" in 2004) in a huge, open-plan outdoor space. Excellent Ghanaian dishes including groundnut and palm nut soup, *omo tuo* and grilled snails.

Buku 10th Lane, Osu. Tasty West African dishes (the grills are particularly good) served in a stylish open air, first-floor dining area with views over Accra. Service can be rather surly, though.

Country Kitchen 2nd Ringway Estate, Osu ☏021/229107. Laid-back restaurant with a nice leafy courtyard setting serving very high-quality Ghanaian cuisine.

Maquis Tante Marie 5th Norla Link, Labone ☏021/778914 ⊛www .maquistantemarie.com (daily 11.30am–late). One

of Accra's nicest restaurants, serving superb West African food in an open-air setting, with a spread-out garden dining area and a breezy wood-and-thatch upstairs bar/dining room. Service is friendly and the food – which includes grilled tilapia with home-made pepper sauce and Senegalese chicken *yassa* – delicious. Excellent home-made fruit juices, including *bissap*.

Asian, Lebanese & Caribbean

Adonis Adzoatse St, Osu ☏027/6880880. Excellent, lively Lebanese restaurant with tasty food, host to regular live music and belly-dancing nights.

Banana Leafz House No. C-713/1, Salem Rd, Osu ☏021/780790 (Mon–Fri noon–3pm & 6.30–11.30pm). Indonesian and Indian, the place for excellent satays, sambal and beef rendang.

The Caribbean 5th Lane, Osu ☏024/3437352 (Wed–Sun noon–10pm). Friendly, relaxed place serving delectable jerk chicken, coconut fried shrimp, candied yams, rum punch and other Caribbean delights.

Chez Lien Dadebu Rd, Osu ☏021/775356 (daily noon–3pm & 6.30–11pm). The small, dimly lit dining room of this Vietnamese place gives it an intimate feel and there's a pretty 1st-floor balcony for al fresco dining lit up with fairy lights and lanterns. The cooking is superb, with plenty of chillies, garlic and lemongrass as well as the odd French dish thrown in.

Dynasty Oxford St, Osu ⊕021/775496. Accra's most established (and some would say best) Chinese restaurant with fresh well-prepared food served in fancy surroundings. The fish and lobster dishes are particularly good. Dim sum is served every Sun afternoon.

Frankies Oxford St, Osu ⊕021/773567 (daily 7am–11pm). Family-owned complex includes a ground-floor *boulangerie* (fresh baguettes, pastries, Italian ice cream) and a terrace overlooking the busy street. There's also a fast-food takeaway (burgers, chicken, Lebanese *chawarmas*) and a sit-down 1st-floor restaurant, popular with tourists and middle-class Ghanaians (excellent mezes, grills, kebabs and pancakes). Mains about GH¢6–7.

Haveli Colorama Photo Lab Compound, Osu ⊕021/774714 (daily noon–3pm & 7–10.30pm). Popular Indian restaurant with a large variety of tandoori, rice, vegetable and curry dishes.

Little India Sunshine Salad Bar 11th Lane, Osu (Mon–Sat 9am–5pm). Excellent lunchtime place with an interesting range of Asian-influenced salads and sandwiches (eg lamb kofta sandwich and chicken satay salad) as well as more substantial curries. Food is served on a planted patio overlooking the street. Takeaway sandwich/salad bar next door.

European

Ivy Coffee Shop Ring Rd Central, between the Lufthansa and Alitalia offices ⊕021/228449. Pricey café with great sandwiches and salads, an unusually good range of French cheeses, and a choice of magazines and papers laid on.

Le Magellan Ring Rd East ⊕021/777629. Popular French restaurant with an excellent wine list and top-notch cooking. The seafood dishes (for example king prawns in whisky and lobster gratin) are particularly good.

Le Tandem 6 Mankralo St, East Cantonments ⊕021/762959. In the hotel of the same name, this is an elegant place decorated in shades of yellow and orange with bold art on the walls. The menu is written up daily and specials include sea bass with truffle butter, grilled lobster and lamb *navarin*.

Mamma Mia's 7th Lane, Osu ⊕021/264151. Italian restaurant set in a sunny courtyard complete with red-checked tablecloths and wood-burning pizza oven. Pizzas and pastas are the name of the game but the place also does a nice line in gargantuan seafood platters.

Monsoon 41 Oxford St, Osu, above the food court ⊕021/782307 ⓔsteve@bar-monsoon .com. Hugely popular place with a large terrace, a cigar bar serving mojitos and other cocktails, separate sushi and tepenyaki bars and an elegant dining room specializing in grilled steaks, game meat and seafood. The tempting menu doesn't quite deliver on taste but it's a lively and fun place to be.

Orangery Crepe and Salad Bar Farrar Ave, Adabraka ⊕021/232988. Outdoor balcony restaurant decorated with fishing nets and fish-inspired ornaments. Good place for breakfast with great home-made muffins, freshly squeezed juice, waffles and omelettes on offer. There are also heavier French-influenced meals on the menu for later in the day as well as wonderfully indulgent desserts.

Pit Stop and 4Q Bar Asylum Down ⊕021/222944 (daily 8.30am–midnight, Sat until 4pm). Unusual set-up, attached to a garage and, for those in the know, a popular spot for full English breakfasts, fish and chips, and delicious steak sandwiches.

Nightlife

Nightlife in Accra is an ever-evolving scene, one of the hottest in West Africa. Many of the venues below serve food and some even present themselves as restaurants some of the time, just as certain restaurants sometimes offer live music – anything to get the punters in. The big nights out are Thursday to Sunday; from Monday to Wednesday the action – if it happens at all – starts late (Mon are pretty much dead), though there are one or two "ladies' nights", usually Wednesday, when women get free admission. Wednesday is also when the La Pleasure Beach party (GH¢1.50) takes place, drawing Accra's youth to drink and dance the night away under the stars. At weekends you can party most of the daytime, too, in some venues. Cover charges are reasonable by international standards – GH¢5 is about the most you'll pay.

Celsbridge 2nd Labone St. Laid-back bar and café with really cold Star, popular with journalists and other media types.

Champs Sports Bar Ring Rd Central, set within the *Paloma Hotel* complex. Canadian-owned sports bar, with screens showing big fixtures, regular karaoke nights, and pricey Tex-Mex food and cocktails.

Don's Place 30 Ajoatse St, Osu. Small bar attracting an older crowd for the jazz soundtrack, regular live music and big-screen premiership football.

Home Touch Giffard Rd ☎ 021/776662 (daily 8am–midnight). Huge bar and restaurant with plenty of outdoor seating, chilled beer on tap and a lively atmosphere.

Jazz Tone 3rd Close, Airport Residential Area ☎ 021/761082 (live music Fri & Sat). Tiny jazz bar with a great atmosphere owned by an African-American jazz singer who also performs. Southern-style food and cocktails and a stack of old *Ebony* magazines for browsing.

La Tawala Spot Simple, friendly beachside bar and café. A great place to chat to the locals with a beer and a cheap plate of *jollof* rice.

Macumba Ring Rd East, near Danquah Circle. ☎ 021/732531. The oldest and best-known club in town, a notorious meat market.

Monte Carlo 1st Norla St, Labone. Casino, nightclub, restaurant and bar attracting a glamorous crowd to quaff champagne and dance on marble floors.

Next Door in Teshie-Nungua on the road to Tema ☎ 021/713947. Open-air weekend hot spot for quality live African music in a cliffside setting by the sea, with great views. Highly recommended.

The Office Osu Avenue, Cantonments. ☎ 021/762867. This popular place attracts Accra's most stylish and beautiful to drink cocktails and dance in a small, chic space. The box files on the walls are a nod to the TV show.

Savannah (formerly Chester's) 14th Lane, Nyaniba Estate, Osu, signposted from Ring Rd, clockwise past Danquah Circle ☎ 021/777503 (live bands Wed, Fri & Sat from 9pm). Friendly and recommended straight nightclub at the front and members-only gay backroom.

Venus Cocktail Bar 11th Lane, Osu. Bamboo terrace bar attached to the *Byblos Hotel*, serving good cocktails but rather less impressive food. Very popular with backpackers.

Vienna City/Waikiki Kwame Nkrumah Ave ☎ 021/258551. Formerly the *Piccadilly*, a huge nightclub, bar, restaurant and pool hall with regular live music. Not for the faint-hearted.

Listings

Airlines Afriqiyah Airways, c/o al-Anisa Travel, 433/1 3rd Lane, off Oxford St ☎ 021/912732; Air Ivoire, Cocoa House, Kwame Nkrumah Ave ☎ 021/674456; American Airlines, Valco Trust House ☎ 021/688804; Alitalia, Ring Road Central ☎ 021/239315; Astraeus, Pyramid House, Ring Road Central, Nima ☎ 021/257581; British Airways, Horizon Plaza, 60 Liberation Rd, Airport Area ☎ 021/214996; Delta Airlines, Silver Star Tower, Airport City ☎ 021/213111; EgyptAir, Ring Road East, just south of Danquah Circle, Osu ☎ 021/773537/8; Ethiopian Airlines, Cocoa House, Kwame Nkrumah Ave ☎ 021/664856/7/8; Ghana International Airlines, Silver Star Tower, Airport City ☎ 021/213555; KLM, 86 North Ridge, Ring Road ☎ 021/214747; Lufthansa, Meridien House, Ring Road Central ☎ 021/243893/4; North American Airlines, opposite Nestlé Ghana, Dzorwulu ☎ 021/911086; South African Airlines, Millennium Heights Building, Airport Commercial Area ☎ 021/783676; Slok Air International, No. 3 Aviation Rd ☎ 0243/166206; Virgin Nigeria, 60 Liberation Rd, Airport Area ☎ 021/701266.

American Express Represented by Stanbic Bank, Silver Star Tower, Airport City ☎ 021/687670.

Banks and exchange The head branches of the major commercial banks are on High Street near the intersection of Bank Lane and include Barclays Bank ☎ 021/664901; Ghana Commercial Bank ☎ 021/664911; SG-SSB ☎ 021/223375; and Standard Chartered Bank ☎ 021/664591. There are branches of Standard Chartered, Barclays and Ecobank on Oxford St in Osu and a Stanbic Bank at Silver Star Tower near the airport. Forex bureaux are widespread, with several on Kojo Thompson Rd.

Books and newspapers Riya's Bookstore, near the Côte d'Ivoire Embassy off Cantonments Road (☎ 021/781005) has an excellent selection of new books, as does Arabisco Enterprise Payless Books in Naktan House on Ring Road East (☎ 021/760975), opposite the US Embassy Chancery Section. There's a good selection of second-hand books at Books For Less, 11th Lane, Osu (☎ 021/770770). Overseas newspapers, mostly British, can be bought at most upmarket hotels. Alternatively, you can read them at the British Council's library (see "Cultural Centres", below). The bookshop at the University of Ghana (see "Legon", p.830) is the best place for Ghanaian history, politics and culture, and has a good range of children's books and lots of second-hand English-language novels.

Car rental Avis, 199 Soula Loop, North Labone ☎ 021/761751; Hertz, Hertz International House, Nima Maamobi Highway ☎ 021/230773; Vanef Car Rental, 37 Dzorwulu Rd ☎ 021/222374. The big hotels can usually help arrange car rental as well

– the *Shangri-La* is particularly helpful and will deal with phone enquiries.

Cinemas The best places to see Ghanaian and other African films are Executive Filmhouse and Ghana Films Theatre, near Sankara Circle. For the latest European and US releases on DVD, try Busy Internet on Ring Rd Central on weekend evenings (GH¢2), or *Champs* on Sun nights (no cover).

Couriers DHL, near KLM on North Ridge Crescent (ⓣ021/221647, ⓦ www.dhl.com/gh. EWALD, 34 North Ridge (ⓣ021/228883 ⓦ www.ewaldghana .com), are reliable agents.

Cultural centres The British Council, Liberia Rd, just off Independence Ave (Mon–Fri 10am–8pm, Sat 10am–6pm; ⓣ021/683068 ⓦ www.britishcouncil .org/ghana) has an excellent library with British newspapers, and sometimes hosts music and theatre events. The Alliance Française, Liberation Link Rd, Airport Residential Area (ⓣ021/760278 ⓦ www .alliancefrancaiseghana.com), does the same in French. The German Goethe-Institut on Kakramadu Rd, East Cantonments (ⓣ021/776764 ⓦ tinyurl .com/2v6pcg), also runs active programmes.

Embassies and consulates Australia, 2 2nd Rangoon Close ⓣ021/777080; Benin, 3 Switchback Lane, Cantonments ⓣ021/774860; Burkina Faso, 772/3 Asylum Down, off Mango Tree Ave ⓣ021/221988; Canada, 42 Independence Ave ⓣ021/228555 or 211521; Côte d'Ivoire, 9 18th Lane, off Oxford St, Osu ⓣ021/774611; France, 12th Rd, off Liberation Rd ⓣ021/774480; Germany, 6 Ridge St, North Ridge ⓣ021/221000; Guinea, 161A 4th Norla St, Labone ⓣ021/214550; Italy, Switchback Lane, off Jawaharlal Nehru Rd ⓣ021/755621; Mali, Liberia Rd near the junction with Kinbu Rd ⓣ021/663276 or 775160; Netherlands, 89 Liberation Rd, Sankara Circle ⓣ021/214350; New Zealand, c/o British High Commission; Niger, E 104/3 Independence Ave ⓣ021/224962; Nigeria, 5 Josef B Tito Ave ⓣ021/776158/9; South Africa, Plot 10, Klottey Crescent, North Labone ⓣ021/762380; Togo, Cantonments Circle ⓣ021/777950; UK, 1 Osu Link, off Abdul Nasser Ave ⓣ021/221665; USA, 6th and 10th Lanes, Osu ⓣ021/776601/2.

Hospitals The best medical facility in town is the Nyaho Clinic, a small hospital in Airport Residential Area (ⓣ021/775341). The Trust Hospital in Osu (ⓣ021/776787), next to *Dynasty* restaurant, is open 24hr and does fast laboratory tests.

Internet access Busy Internet on Ring Road Central has fast connections (ⓣ021/258800; GH¢1.20/hr). Sharpnet on Ring Rd East and Cassaba Internet in Osu are the two Cyberia Internet cafés in Osu, both reasonably fast and charging GH¢1.20/hr and GH¢1/hr respectively.

Photos If you want decent-quality passport photos, the best place is Photo Me at the end of Oxford St, where the process takes a matter of minutes; expect to pay around GH¢5. Or there's a photo booth on the lower ground floor of Busy Internet.

Post & telephones Post restante is available free of charge at the GPO in Usshertown (Mon–Fri 8am–4.30pm). As for phone calls, there's no shortage of communication centres and phone booths.

Supermarkets Many supermarkets have sprung up in the heart of Osu, to the south and west of Danquah Circle. Koala is expat heaven, with fresh cheese, meat and French bread. Others nearby include Quick Pick and Afridom. Max Mart (ⓣ021/783750) near the *Golden Tulip* hotel has a similar selection; next door, the Bacchus Wine Shop has an excellent selection of wine. Petrol-station shops are popular for bottled water, bread, cheese and ice cream.

Swimming pools The best pool for the money is the one at the *Shangri-La*, which non-guests can use for GH¢2. There are also good pools at the *Golden Tulip*, *Labadi Beach* and *La Royal Palm*.

Travel agents Speedway Travel and Tours, 5 Tackie Tawia St, near Trust Towers in Adabraka (ⓣ021/227744 or 228799), is very helpful for a range of organized tours in Ghana. M&J Travels and Tours, Embassy Rd, Osu (ⓣ021/773498 or 706081 ⓦ tinyurl.com/2g7q3c), and Sunseekers (ⓣ021/775524 ⓦ www.sunseekerstours.com), at the *Novotel*, are also reputable.

Visa extensions The Immigration Office is on Independence Ave, near Sankara Circle (Mon–Fri 8am–1pm). They expect two photos and proof of an air ticket home to extend a visa, and will usually retain your passport for around two weeks while this is done – very inconvenient.

Western Union At branches of Agricultural Development Bank, the most central of which is in Adabraka on Kojo Thompson Road.

Inland from Accra

Getting out of the city for a while, especially at the hottest and most humid times of the year, from January to June, can be a relief. **Legon**, 14km north of Accra, is the headquarters of the **University of Ghana**, described by the Ghana Tourist Board as "a showpiece of Japanese architecture". There's a very good bookshop here but less opportunity to meet students than you might wish. **Aburi**, a former hill station whose large gardens are still well maintained, offers the best escape from the heat. Slightly further inland, there are wildlife-spotting and bush-walking opportunities at the **Shai Hills Reserve**.

Aburi and around

You can visit the botanical garden in the university grounds at Legon, but there are older, more interesting and extensive gardens at **ABURI**, on Akwapim Ridge, 23km further north, with potentially magnificent views north over the forest and south to the city when the air is clear. Aburi, several hundred metres above the plain, was a colonial hill station and the site of a sanatorium, now a hotel. The **Aburi Botanical Gardens** (GH¢2) still bear the hallmarks of landscaped colonial taste, with hundreds of impressive tree specimens from all over the tropical and subtropical regions. You'll find a community of **craft sellers and woodcarvers** at Aburi – it's a good place to be based if you want access to various kinds of wood – and there are some good bargains to be had, certainly in comparison with the Arts Centre in Accra, but be sure to visit the town of Aburi itself as well as the carvers setting out their wares in the botanical gardens.

If you want to stay over, there's somewhat dismal **accommodation** at the *ABG Guesthouse* (☏0876/22022; room with three beds ❷, private bungalow ❷) though the rooms are spacious and well kept. An excellent alternative is the *Olyander Hotel* (☏0876/22058 ❶), which has very homely carpeted rooms. *Sweet Africa Guest House* (☏0876/22069 ❶) has clean, non-s/c rooms, while the upmarket choice is the *Little Acre* (☏0876/22103 ❸), out of town on the road to Accra, which has attractively furnished, tiled rooms with TV and fridge, and an expensive restaurant. There are three **restaurants** in the gardens: *Roses Plot* is a simple place with a nice verandah and basic fare next to the *ABG Guesthouse*; the *Royal Gardens Restaurant* is smarter with fantastic views, and a much fancier menu – lobster, filet stroganoff; and finally, the tiny *Club House Canteen* has the cheapest fare on offer, with filling plates of *banku*, *fufu* and tilapia.

A final point of interest in town is the impressive structure near *Sweet Africa* with the Lions of Judah at the gates – this is in fact a top-notch **recording studio** established by Rita Marley, wife of the reggae legend.

The forest around Aburi has **cycle routes** which you can explore by renting a bike from Aburi Bike and Hike Tours, by the south gate of the Botanical Gardens (Mon & Thurs–Sun 9am–6pm; ☏024/267303/90 ✉aburibike@email.com; GH¢5 per day). A good target lies about 15km out of Aburi towards Nsawam (and a couple of kilometres north of the road) – the **Ahyiresu Naturalist Centre** (☏024/3505535), a 20-hectare "campaigning botanical garden" where they aim to conserve and propagate as many species of Ghanaian tree as possible to counter the sometimes reckless use that wood carvers and others make of trees without thinking of replanting. Check out the **nkontombre** with its large, edible leaves; the **holahena** favoured by Aburi carvers and another carvers' favourite, the **sese**, with its white wood; the **lemon citrus**, used for grafting other citrus trees; and the **izora**, with its red flowers used in cosmetics. Ahyiresu is linked with *Roses Plot* in Aburi, where you can make enquiries.

Tro-tros from Tema station run frequently to Legon, taking half an hour or so, and **buses** from the same station take about an hour to Aburi (the last one back to Accra leaves at about 6.30pm, not at 6pm as taxi drivers may tell you). If you're driving to Aburi, you continue past the airport to Tetteh Quarshie Circle, then take the Akosombo road until it forks right; take the left-hand fork and start climbing.

Shai Hills

Some 60km to the northeast of Accra is the **Shai Hills Reserve** (GH¢2.50). The main gate to the reserve is on the Akosombo road, and the reserve's location makes it a better staging post than Aburi if you're en route to Akosombo or Ho.

Troops of **baboons** and flocks of **parrots** are the most likely sights here, though hefty **kob antelope** and **ground hornbills** can also be seen. There are also some extensive bat-populated **caves** which can be visited. These were used as sites of worship by the Shai people until they were moved out by the British in colonial times; nowadays the Shai return annually to perform ceremonies.

The easiest way to get here by public transport from Accra is by changing in the junction town of **ASHAIMAN**, served by *tro-tros* from the Tema station in Accra. If you want to stay over, the *Midway Spot*, opposite the reserve gates, has uninviting, fanless cell-like rooms (➊). Nearby, the rooms at the *Shai Hills Resort Hotel* (☏022/250114 or ☏0244/836883 ➌) on the Tema–Akosombo Highway, 300 metres before the reserve, are large and comfortable, and there's a pool and restaurant, but the place is often empty so standards vary. A possibly better alternative nearby is *Stone Lodge* (☏0244/549124 ⓦwww.stonelodge.biz ➌–➎), 5km off the main Accra–Akosombo highway on the Asutsuare Road, which has lovely, simple stone and thatch chalets and a farm on site from which much of the restaurant's delicious food is sourced.

10.2

The coast

The scenic coastline stretching **west from Accra** to the Côte d'Ivoire border is one of the most obvious tourist targets in West Africa. The unique attraction is the densest concentration of European **forts and castles** anywhere on the continent – 29 of them, some over 500 years old – and innumerable Fante **fishing villages** tucked between links of sandy, coconut-backed beaches. Despite the development going on and the frequent use of the beach as a toilet, the castles-and-coast combination is irresistible, and you won't be alone in discovering it. You have to come on a weekday or out of season to have much hope of finding your own isolated paradise. Nevertheless, few places are ever more than quietly humming with tourist business. Away from the coast proper, **Kakum National Park** is an essential highlight of any visit to the region.

East of Accra: Ada and Keta

The small, pleasantly faded riverside town of **ADA FOAH**, 120km from Accra, attracts tourists drawn by the scenic attractions – river beaches, ocean beaches – around the Volta river mouth. To reach Ada from Accra, take a bush taxi from the Tudu station (GH¢1) direct to the village, or change at the junction town of Ada Kasseh on the highway for a ride to Ada Foah, located on a narrow promontory formed by the river on one side and the ocean on the other, close to the river mouth itself. (Big Ada is a workaday settlement between the two.) Ada has an unofficial **tourist office** – basically a travel agent – on the main road (daily 9am–6pm), where you can book yourself onto an excursion or, when public services are running, a ferry ride across the Volta.

The most popular **accommodation** at Ada Foah is the *Cocoloko Beach Camp Resort*, a collection of basic but comfortable reed-and-concrete huts built on the sands near the ocean beach, about 3km west of Ada Foah town centre (☎024/416 0409 ⓦmitglied .lycos.de/cocoloko ❷). The *Garden Club Annex* near the market offers just about acceptable rooms with fan (☎0968/22262 ❶). The upmarket choice in the area, with jet skis, sailing dinghies, windsurfing and a beautiful pool, is the *Manet Resort* (☎021/768531 ⓔmanet@ghana.com ❼), superbly located at the eastern end of Ada Foah, on the sheltered north side of the peninsula, and just five minutes' walk from the ocean beach on the other side. If you're not **eating** at your lodgings, you might try, for local Ghanaian dishes (GH¢2) in a cheerful garden setting, *Brightest Spot*, off the main road.

The serene golden sands and unbelievably blue ocean at **KETA**, out on the far eastern edge of the Volta delta, 175km from Accra (served by *tro-tros* from Tudu station, in Accra), were once among the nicest in Ghana. Unfortunately, a lot of the village, built on a sand spit, has been swept away by the sea – leaving a ghost-town feel – and a recent multi-million-dollar sea defence project has not improved its appeal. At least the causeway and landfill project has fixed Keta's transport problem, allowing rapid-enough connections with Accra and Aflao. And the fishing village is still inviting, with a welcoming local community.

If you're looking for **accommodation**, then off the main road, the rooms at the *Keta Beach Hotel* (☎0966/42288 ⓦwww.ketabeachhotel.com ❷) need an overhaul, but it has a good garden restaurant. *Agblor Lodge* (☎0966/42379 ❶) is also still popular for the price, though the staff can be miserable, while the plusher *Lorneh Lodge* (☎0966/42160 ❸), down in the village of **TEGBI** (7km southeast of Keta along the beach road), offers bland, good-value rooms and a small pool, and hosts the odd live band.

You can hop on any passing *tro-tro* to the northeast end of town, for a brief visit to **Fort Prinzenstein** (a GH¢1 tip to the caretaker who walk you around is appreciated). There was a plan to develop this eighteenth-century Danish-built slave castle, but that seems to have fallen into abeyance while Keta waits for the tourists to return.

Some visitors to the area have never been deterred: both Ada and Keta offer first-class **bird-watching** and **turtle-spotting** in the "Keta Lagoon Complex" Ramsar Convention–designated wetlands area. The Forestry Commission's Wildlife Division have managed to get local people on side to curb the killing of sea birds for sport and food – especially the very rare and now protected **roseate tern**, which migrates to these shores every winter from northern Europe. And the area is an important one for **turtle nesting**, with olive ridley, green, and huge leatherback turtles all coming ashore to lay eggs.

To reach the **Togolese border** from Keta, take a *tro-tro* from the Keta lorry station (GH¢1; 1hr). Since the hard-surfaced causeway was finished, reaching the firm ground on the northeast side of the delta is straightforward, and the road then ploughs right along the beach, in reasonable condition, straight to **DENU/AFLAO**. There are however, plenty of palms and sand to encourage you to break your journey at one of the small villages along the way.

West: from Accra to Cape Coast

West of Accra, the highway at first stays well inland, running through hot and unyielding scrubby bush and farming country. Down between the road and the coast is a significant Ramsar-Convention wetlands site, the delta of the **River Densu**, harbouring turtle-nesting beaches and important overwintering areas for European migrant birds.

Kokrobite and westwards

Just 30km west of Accra is the first break, at the beach resort of **KOKROBITE**. You can reach the village directly from Accra by *tro-tro* from Dansoman station in the

Kaneshie motor park (GH¢0.50; 1hr). If you're coming from the west, disembark at the junction for Kokrobite at the police barrier, and either charter a taxi for around GH¢2.50 or wait for a passing *tro-tro*.

Dance and music lessons are offered at Kokrobite by the Academy of African Music and Arts Ltd (look out for the "AAMAL" sign on the main road; ☎021/665987). The internationally renowned Ga master drummer Mustapha Tettey Addy is the leader of the group and joint owner of the establishment, which doubles as the *Kokrobite Beach Resort & Bar*. There are wonderfully dynamic drumming and dance displays on weekend afternoons between 2pm and 6pm (non-guests GH¢1) but the accommodation (**②**) needs refreshing and is no longer good value for money. The **restaurant** is excellent however, providing a foretaste of the grilled seafood that abounds further along the coast.

Without question the best **place to stay** here is *Big Milly's Backyard*, aka *Wendy's Place* (☎0244/607998 ⊛www.bigmilly.com; double rooms **②** or dorm beds GH¢4), an incredibly successful set-up that just gets more and more popular every year, with a variety of huts – ranging from the basic with shared bucket showers to a swish Moroccan-style self-contained suite – in a pretty compound on the beach. You can also camp. There's a 24-hour bar-restaurant (plentiful vegetarian options) which is very lively at weekends with cultural groups and live music. East of *Big Milly's*, *Andy's Akwaaba Lodge* (☎024/277261 **②**) offers simple, concrete-floored rooms in a spacious grassy compound, with German specialities in the restaurant, and there's even cheaper accommodation away from the beach in a small compound called the *Black Stone Guesthouse*. Excellent pizza and pasta is to be had at the Italian-run restaurant *Kokrobite Gardens* nearby, and the *Root Love Bar & Café*, west along the beach from *Big Milly's*, is also worth a look.

The village of **GOMOA FETTEH**, or just Fetteh, 15km west of Kokrobite, is the site of two attractive resorts and an increasingly popular destination on this stretch of coast. *Tills No. 1 Hotel* has neat and comfortable rooms and an appealing location looking down onto a stretch of clean, private beach (☎027/550480 ⓔtillsbeach@yahoo.com; rooms **⑥**, camping GH¢7). The excellent 🏄 *White Sands Beach Club* (☎027/550707 ⊛www.whitesandsbc.com **⑧**) has a unique set-up where guests have to use a motor boat to travel from the reception area and stunning "mainland" restaurant out to the hotel's beach (GH¢5 non-guests) and funky *Barefoot Bar*. The accommodation, in a separate location five minutes' drive away, is in charming, luxurious villas.

The first **fort** along this stretch is **SENYA BERAKU**, 5km west of Gomoa Fetteh. To get here from Accra, take a bush taxi to Awutu junction (not Senya junction, from where you won't easily get onward transport). From there, you can get another taxi down to the coastal village, 10km away. The village is dull, but the setting is scenic, and the trip interesting mainly for the fishing activities of the Fante inhabitants (note, however, that the Fante don't fish on Tuesdays). You get sweeping panoramic seascapes from the looming **Fort Good Hope**, now converted into a simple resthouse, where you can **stay** the night (**①**) and have a delicious plate of chicken and chips prepared on request.

Winneba and Apam

The main town in these parts, **WINNEBA**, is perched on raised ground between the Muni and Oyibi lagoons. It's easily reached from Accra: transport leaves from Kaneshie station for Swedru junction (aka Winneba junction), 6km away on the main coast highway, from where shared taxis continue to Winneba. Although it is beginning to acquire a reputation for its **pottery**, Winneba is most famous in Ghana as the site of the Aboakyer or **"deer-hunting festival"** which takes place at the end of April or early May (see p.797). At other times of year, there's little to do around town apart from watch the **drag fishing**, with music and singing, and fifty men hauling the net rope, observe the catch being prepared and smoked, and enjoy the clamour and bustle of dusk.

Soon after the Portuguese worked out the maritime routes to the Gulf of Guinea in the fifteenth century, they began setting up trading posts. Rumours of the vast wealth of the region filtered back to Europe and it wasn't long before other nations established themselves on the coast, negotiating **leases** with Fante headmen to be allowed to build sturdy **fortresses** to protect their interests in the trade of gold, ivory and, later, slaves. By the end of the eighteenth century, 37 such forts dotted the coastline, 29 of which are still standing.

After independence several forts started taking in travellers and it's possible to stay at the **resthouses** (indicated below) in at least four of them. They offer accommodation that is exceptionally cheap and, if generously interpreted, characterful – in basic rooms with shared facilities and sometimes a fan. The tourist office in Cape Coast may be able to help with bookings, recommended in high season as they don't have many rooms.

Some of the **restoration work** undertaken in recent years, including the whitewashing of slave cells, and the setting up of limited catering facilties, has upset some African-American visitors, who complain that the Ministry of Tourism is trampling over their history for profits. They argue they have a right to a say in how such historical relics are to be preserved. It's a conversation that will continue to be aired, and possibly amplified, as the true nature of the relationship between Africans and African-Americans is better understood.

Along the coast from east to west, sites with **major forts and castles** (eleven of which form a UNESCO World Heritage Site) include:

• **Accra** Christiansborg (now "The Castle") was built by the Danes in 1659. Earlier a Swedish fortress, which at one time had probably belonged to the Portuguese, stood on the same spot. Ussher Fort was built by the Dutch in 1642. Ten years later it was taken by the French and named "Fort Crêvecoeur", then passed through the hands of the Dutch and finally the British, who rebuilt it in 1868. James Fort was built by the Portuguese in the mid-sixteenth century, taken by the English, and rebuilt in 1673. "The Castle" and Fort James are not open to visits, but Fort Ussher is being restored for public visits.

• **Senya Beraku** The last fort built by the Dutch, Fort Good Hope (resthouse; UNESCO), was constructed in 1702 and extended in 1715.

• **Apam** Fort Leydsaemheyt (resthouse; UNESCO) was built in 1698 by the Dutch. Occupied by the British (who named it Fort Patience) in 1782 and retaken by the Dutch three years later, it was abandoned around 1800.

• **Abanze** west of Saltpond. Fort Amsterdam (UNESCO), near Komatin/Kormantse was finished by the English in 1638 and captured by the Dutch in 1665. It was

---

The best **accommodation** in town is the friendly 🍴 *Lagoon Lodge* (☎0432/22435 Ⓦwww.lagoon-lodge-winneba.com ❷), down a sandy track near the lagoon, with spotless s/c doubles with fans and tiled floors, great views, and a courtyard restaurant serving up wonderfully fresh barbecued fish and huge mugs of fresh juices. More upmarket options can be found 3km from the centre off the Winneba–Agona Junction road at *Hunter's Lodge* (☎0432/22318 ❸), which has a mix of budget rooms and stylish doubles with satellite TV, fridge and hot water.

For **meals**, *Hut d'Eric* off the Accra road near Swedru junction, serves a few European and Ghanaian dishes for around GH¢4, including excellent Chinese-style spring rolls. In the town centre, *Halo Halo* is the best bar. For **Internet** access, try Wills Internet or Teddy Annette Internet in the town centre.

Some 20km west of Winneba is **APAM**, where you can stay at the resthouse in the impressively sited **Fort Patience**. Getting here from Accra requires taking a taxi or *tro-tro*

abandoned after an attack by the people of Anomabo in 1811 and left in ruins for 140 years.

• **Anomabo** A Dutch lodge was founded here in about 1640 and taken by the English in 1665. Fort Charles was built on its site in 1674. In 1753, work started on Fort William, built expressly as a slave fort. It served as Britain's second-biggest slaving base after Cape Coast.

• **Mouri (Moree)** Fort Nassau was built by the Dutch in 1598. It went back and forth between the British and Dutch until it was finally abandoned in 1815. It is now in ruins.

• **Cape Coast** The original castle (UNESCO) was founded by the Swedes, then taken by the Danes and passed to the hands of the Dutch before finally being taken by the English in 1664. It remained the English, later British, Gold Coast headquarters until 1876.

• **Elmina** St George's Castle (UNESCO), the oldest European monument in sub-Saharan Africa, was built by the Portuguese in 1482 with dressed stones brought from Europe. The original castle was expanded by the Dutch in 1637 and remained their Gold Coast headquarters until it was sold to the British in 1872. Fort St Jago (UNESCO) which faces St George's, was built by the Dutch in 1666.

• **Komenda** Fort English (UNESCO) was founded in 1663. Fort Vredenburg was built by the Dutch in 1688, taken by the British in 1782 and abandoned three years later. Both forts are now in ruins.

• **Shama** Fort Sebastian (UNESCO) was founded by the Portuguese around 1560 and occupied by the Dutch in 1640.

• **Sekondi** Fort Orange was built by the Dutch in 1640; it became British after 1872.

• **Dixcove** Fort Metal Cross (UNESCO) was built by the English in 1692, and occupied by the Dutch from 1868 to 1872.

• **Butre** Fort Batenstein (UNESCO) was built by the Swedes in 1656, and subsequently saw service under Dutch and British rule as a supply station.

• **Princestown** Grossfriedrichsburg (resthouse) was built in 1683 by the German Brandenburgers and taken by the Dutch and later British. In ruins at independence, the fort has since been restored.

• **Axim** Fort Santa Antonia (Fort St Anthony; UNESCO), built in the fifteenth century, was the second Portuguese fort on the coast. Taken by the Dutch in 1642, it was rebuilt on several occasions.

• **Beyin** Fort Apollonia (resthouse) was built by the English Committee of Merchants in 1756.

to the Apam junction and changing. It's about 8km down to Apam – too far to walk in the heat of the day. At the entrance to town is an imposing *posuban* shrine, a three-storey affair topped by a white Jesus and decorated with colourful statues of Africans mounted on horseback. Fort Patience is beautifully located on an outcrop above the town and has spartan rooms and well water for washing (❶). A more comfortable, if less atmospheric place to stay is the *Lynnbah Guesthouse* (☎021/307208 ❶), a homely establishment set around an attractive, planted courtyard, with a wide verandah full of comfy chairs for lounging . Eating here is an option if you order in advance; otherwise food in town is limited pretty much to the market.

Saltpond, Anomabo and Biriwa

The next town to the west is **SALTPOND**, 42km west of Apam junction, which offers precious little reason to call in, particularly as a bypass skirts the town. En

The Asafo companies and posubans

Like other Akan states, the Fante maintain a highly formalized military institution known as **Asafo** (from *sa*, "war", and *fo*, "people"). The original function of the Asafo was the defence of the Fante state. Although that role largely disappeared after the colonial invasion, Asafo companies still thrive, and they exercise considerable political influence locally. They enstool chiefs – and can destool them in certain instances – and act as royal advisors.

The companies put on at least one major festival each year and also provide community entertainment in the form of singing, dancing and drumming.

A Fante town typically has between two and twelve Asafo companies, each identified in a military fashion by number, name and location (for example No. 5 Company, Brofumba, Cape Coast), with members in ranks, easily identifiable as general, senior commander, divisional captain and so on. Asafo membership is patrilineal (in contrast to the chieftaincy, which is matrilineal, passing to the next man through the line of his maternal uncle).

As well as their military-ceremonial duties, the Asafo are active in the arts. In every Fante town there are painted cement **Asafo shrines**, known as **posuban**, for each of the town's companies. Rich with symbolism, each *posuban* evokes proverbs proclaiming one company's superiority over its rivals. The shrine of No. 3 Company, Anomabo, for example, is guarded by two life-sized cement lions, recalling the saying "A dead lion is greater than a live leopard". The rival No. 6 Company boasts a warship-shaped shrine, symbolic of its military prowess.

Similar symbolism carries over into the vibrantly coloured, appliqué **Asafo flags** made and paraded by each company. These can be seen flying over shrines or, more often, displayed throughout a company's area during town festivities. They have recently acquired serious value in European and American galleries and private collections – a phenomenon that, more than anything else, threatens to unravel the social fabric of the Asafo companies.

route, you may have to change buses at Mankessim, 35km west of Apam junction. If you fetch up at Saltpond for the night, try the gently decaying *Palm Beach* (☎031/46683 ②). And if you're wondering about Mankessim, it's one of those towns that shows no sign of its immense historical significance: it was the capital of the Fante people after they split from the Asante in the thirteenth century.

A better plan is to go another 6km west of Saltpond to **ANOMABO**, which has some decent accommodation options and a very fine beach. On the western side of town, the *Anomabo Beach Resort* offers comfortable, if characterless accommodation in two separate compounds set just back from the beach (☎042/91562 ⓦanomabo2 .digitafrica.com; non–s/c rooms with fans ❸ or s/c a/c rooms ❹). The open-air restaurant is raised above the sands, with a nice breeze, and is good for seafood. *Weda Lodge* (☎020/8140435 ❹) is unmissable: formerly a private residence, perched on a hilltop nearby, it offers five spacious, stylish rooms with balconies and wonderful views. At the other end of town, *Mariesabelle* (☎042/33734 ❶) is recommended for its clean rooms, while *Ebenezer Rest Stop* (☎042/33673; ②) is of a similar standard.

Anomabo's fort, **Fort William**, recently stopped serving as a prison, so visits are allowed. But do look out for the *posuban* shrines dotted around town – Dontsin No. 3 shrine, near *Ebenezer's*, is particularly intricate.

The last place of note on this stretch is the idyllic crescent of sand and coconuts at **BIRIWA**, 3km west of Anomabo, a safe swimming and body-surfing beach. It's right beneath the main highway, which makes it both accessible and a little too popular at weekends. Time was it sheltered various semi-resident hippies in wooden shacks at the village end of the beach, but those days passed in the early 1980s and there's now a fair-sized crowd on the beach at weekends, most of them drawn by the magnet of the German-owned *Biriwa Beach Hotel* (☎244/446277 ⓦwww.africannaturetours.com;

a/c rooms ⑤, sea view rooms ⑥), a simple place high on the slopes behind the beach. In truth, it's a bit past its best – the line of musty rooms sport breeze-block bathrooms, clunky air-con units and peeling walls – though the location and value for money are hard to beat (room 101 at the end has the best views). Where it scores highly is in its shaded, modestly priced, open-air terrace restaurant, with views of distant breakers and fishing boats, and terrific lobster – at GH¢8.50 the most expensive item on the menu. If staying here is outside your price bracket, you can normally camp for a small charge. Supplies are available in the village above the rocky bluff.

Cape Coast

British capital of the Gold Coast until 1876, **CAPE COAST** is a relatively large town with a solid infrastructure, the site of the nation's first secondary school and some important secondary schools. Your major focus of interest is bound to be the seventeenth-century **Cape Coast Castle** and its extraordinary **museum** devoted to the history of the slave trade.

Arrival and information

Coastal traffic doesn't go through the town, but round its north side on a **bypass**. Transport to and from Takoradi, Anomabo and Kakum uses Kotokuraba **tro–tro station**, near the market of the same name. Accra transport has its own station, from where you can also get transport to Kumasi. **STC** (located west of the Pedu junction at the Goil station) runs four daily services to Accra and two to Kumasi (fewer services on Sun); for Takoradi you can join one of the numerous buses passing through from Accra every day; and for the north, the service leaves between 8am and 9am on Monday, Wednesday and Friday, calling at Tamale, then Bolgatanga. Shared taxis heading for Elmina (GH¢0.40) – along the nicest stretch of the coastal highway, where it runs directly above the beach through endless swaying coconut

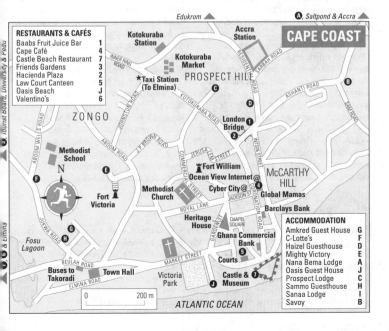

RESTAURANTS & CAFÉS

Baabs Fruit Juice Bar	1
Cape Café	4
Castle Beach Restaurant	7
Friends Gardens	3
Hacienda Plaza	2
Law Court Canteen	5
Oasis Beach	J
Valentino's	6

CAPE COAST

Edukrom — Accra Station — Ⓐ, Saltpond & Accra

Kotokuraba Station
Accra Station
Kotokuraba Market
★ Taxi Station (To Elmina)
PROSPECT HILL
ZONGO
Methodist School
London Bridge
Fort William
Ocean View Internet
Cyber City
Methodist Church
Fort Victoria
McCARTHY HILL
Global Mamas
Barclays Bank
Heritage House
Ghana Commercial Bank
Courts
Fosu Lagoon
Buses to Takoradi
Town Hall
Victoria Park
Castle & Museum
ATLANTIC OCEAN

Tourist Board, University & Pedu
Saltpond & Elmina

0   200 m

ACCOMMODATION

Amkred Guest House	G
C-Lotte's	F
Haizel Guesthouse	D
Mighty Victory	E
Nana Bema Lodge	A
Oasis Guest House	J
Prospect Lodge	C
Sammo Guesthouse	H
Sanaa Lodge	I
Savoy	B

trees – leave from both the junction of Jackson and Commercial streets in town, and from a small transport station just off the Inner Ring Road.

The **Cape Coast Tourist Office** is located in Heritage House (formerly the governor's house) in the centre of town, as is the **Ghana Wildlife Society**, which has information on ecotourism sites in the region (℡042/36350). The headquarters for **Kakum National Park** (℡042/30265) is on the second floor and can help you book guided tours around the park. The organizers of **Panafest** (☜www.panafest.org), the biennial arts and culture festival that takes place in odd-numbered years at the end of July and the beginning of August, have an office on the ground floor, and they also organize celebrations for Emancipation Day.

If you need **money**, Barclays and SG-SSB are centrally located, with ATMs outside and similar exchange rates. Barclays also give cash advances on Visa and MasterCard. The 24-hour cybercafé, Ocean View **Internet**, on Commercial Road, one block south of the Crab monument, has excellent high-speed connections.

Accommodation

Cape Coast has a decent range of hotels, though most are fairly basic. If you're on a tight budget, however, it's also worth trying the town's university hostels (GH¢2.50 per person). Adehye Hall, at the entrance to the main campus on the western side of town, is your best bet.

Amkred Guest House behind *Sammo Guest House* ℡042/32868. Decent place, with a range of s/c rooms with hot water and fan or a/c, and secure parking. Meals available on request. ❶

C-Lotte's Aquarium Junction, corner of Jukwa Rd and Aboom Wells Rd ℡042/36393. Simple and good-value pink-walled rooms, friendly staff and a good restaurant. ❷

Haizel Guesthouse Residential Rd, south of the Accra lorry station ℡042/32044. Despite the hideous three-storey exterior, this is a good, clean, no-frills central option. ❶

Mighty Victory Aboom Rd, close to Fort Victoria ℡042/30135. Run by American–Ghanaians, in a convenient location, this has spotless, comfortable rooms with TV, hot water and great towels. ❷

Nana Bema Lodge Sam's Hill, off Sarbah Rd ℡042/32822. Comfortable hotel in an elevated position – fabulous 360-degree view of Cape Coast – with a variety of rooms. ❶–❹

Oasis Guest House ℡042/35958. Recently established, with dorm beds or doubles in grass-roofed rondavels set along the beach, plus a good

restaurant and lively bar and club offering live music. Double rooms ❷ or dorm beds GH¢12.

Prospect Lodge at the top of the steep Prospect Hill, off Commercial St ℡042/31506. Three-storey pale yellow building with clean and comfortable rooms. Great views over the town and a nice terrace bar and restaurant to sit and watch life go by – marred (or enhanced, depending on your taste) by the very loud music. ❹

Sammo Guesthouse ℡042/33242. Well maintained and deservedly popular, with a ground-floor restaurant serving Ghanaian cuisine, and a rooftop bar with excellent views and limited European fare. ❶

Sanaa Lodge off the Elmina Rd ℡042/32570 ℻ 32898. 2km out of the centre, this is still the town's best, if now frayed around the edges. There's a pool, however, and the place does work. Reasonable a/c, s/c rooms with minibar. ❼

Savoy Ashanti Rd ℡042/32805. Centrally located near the beachfront on the east side of Cape Coast, this is the best-value budget accommodation and often full. The restaurant serves middling food. Clean rooms with fan ❶.

The Town

A UNESCO World Heritage Site since 1979, **Cape Coast Castle** perches on a rocky ledge jutting out over the ocean. Originally a Swedish and then a Danish fort (but named after the Portuguese "Cabo Corso", or Short Cape) it was taken in 1664 by the English, and was the British Gold Coast headquarters until 1876, by which time it had been enlarged to its present dimensions (after a French bombardment in 1757, it was entirely reconstructed in 1760 when it lost its original design). A guided tour (GH¢6.50; half-price for self-guided tours; cameras GH¢0.50, videos GH¢1;

The Oguaa Fetu harvest festival

Of many harvest festivals held in Central Region, one of the biggest is Cape Coast's **Oguaa Fetu Afahye**, which takes place on the first Sat in September, when traditional chiefs from the surrounding districts, bedecked with gold crowns and medallions, parade in sumptuous *kente*-cloth togas. The most important rulers are carried in canoe-like stretchers balanced on the heads of four manservants and shaded by huge parasols. They're accompanied by the queen mothers, wearing bracelets, necklaces and rings of solid gold, with more gold ornaments in their beehive coiffures. Fetish priests dance through the procession dispensing good fortune and collecting payment and, no surprise, the palm wine flows freely. The parade lasts most of the day, terminating in **Victoria Park** for speeches by the chiefs and government representatives. Later, the streets fill up again and the party continues through the night with brass bands, music and dancing. This carnival atmosphere reigns for a couple of days and is really worth a special visit, but book a hotel in advance – most are crammed solid for the duration – and try to arrive early.

student discounts available; 9am–4.30pm daily) takes you through the dungeons of the damp, suffocating prison – what the British traders upstairs called the **"slave hole"** – where captives were held before being herded through the "door of no return" and shipped across the Atlantic. Some visitors may be moved to the point of tears: the experience can create deep, personal connections.

The **castle museum** contains a well-made and thought-provoking exhibition documenting Ghana's history, exploring the conditions endured by slaves and the legacy of slavery, including its impact on the lives of African-Americans. Castle **guides** are usually very good, and more even-handed than you might expect, given the history: you'll hear plenty, for example, about how the institution of slavery was endemic long before the arrival of the Europeans.

Other sites of interest in Cape Coast are scattered around the town: neither of the small subsidiary forts, **Fort William** or **Fort Victoria**, can be entered, but both are worth the short hikes up for different views of the town.

The Centre for National Culture near the university is worth seeking out – it houses a **Gramophone Records Museum** that's a must for serious devotees of highlife music and students of early West African recordings (daily 9am–5pm; Ⓦghana.icom.museum; GH¢2). The collection includes 15,000–20,000 recordings representing 700 artists dating back to 1900.

Also worth a visit is **Global Mamas** (Ⓦwww.globalmamas.org), a shop selling batik clothing and other products handmade by Ghanaian women. Dedicated to the education and development of women in the area, the centre runs a batik vocational training school, and profits from the shop go directly to the women themselves.

The **crab statue** at London Bridge doesn't appear to have any special significance beyond the role of the crab as a symbol of Cape Coast fishing traditions.

Eating and drinking

One central and unusual place to grab a bite is the Law Court's canteen by the castle, which is open to all (Mon–Sat 7am–7pm). *Cape Café*, next to Global Mamas (daily 8am–8pm) slowly serves fast-food staples such as fried chicken and burgers. *Oasis Beach* and *Castle Beach Restaurant*, unsurprisingly, both have attractive coastal settings and offer good and varied food for GH¢5 or less. *Oasis* also has a musical or cultural performance every Saturday night. The central *Hacienda Plaza* on Kotokuraba Road is a buzzy evening hangout with a good selection of snacks and grilled fish. Another lively spot for a drink, with a small indoor restaurant, is *Friends Gardens*, up the Jukwa road. Heading out of town across Fosu Lagoon, you can't miss *Valentino's*, offering grilled food and cheap beer to the accompaniment of loud music, until the early hours. Lastly, by London Bridge you'll find 🎍 *Baabs Fruit Juice Bar* (Mon–Fri

10am–9pm; Sat & Sun 4–8pm), a hole in the wall with a couple of plastic chairs outside serving delicious fresh juices and smoothies as well as veggie snacks such as wholewheat kebabs, tofu sandwiches and yam rolls.

Kakum National Park and around

The superb **KAKUM NATIONAL PARK**, 35km north of Cape Coast, protects one of the last areas of intact lowland rainforest in Ghana. Consisting of 360 square

The Gold Coast slave trade

The earliest **Portuguese** traders on the coast were seeking to outflank Europe's traditional suppliers of gold from the region, the trans-Saharan caravans. There was also a ready supply of human captives available for trade. Although by the middle of the sixteenth century, the market for slaves was waning in Europe, it was booming in Portugal's new island colonies off the African coast – the Cape Verdes and São Tomé – and in **Brazil**, which by 1600 was a major slave importer. The pace of colonization in the Caribbean and the Americas soon became so fast, and the demand for slaves to work the plantations so great, that **Dutch** and **English**, together with a few French, Danish, Swedish and even Prussian traders, soon came to fulfill a trans-Atlantic demand that the Portuguese alone were unable to meet. The Gold Coast slave trade was one segment, perhaps a tenth, of an African trade that also featured Senegambia, Sierra Leone, the "Windward Coast" (present-day Liberia), the "Slave Coast" (present-day Porto Novo to Lagos), the Niger Delta and Cameroons, the Congo and Angola.

In 1700, the **population** of what is now Ghana is estimated to have been about one million. During the course of the eighteenth century, the numbers of slaves from the Gold Coast forts sold into the **Middle Passage** (the central leg of the Europe–Africa–Americas–Europe trading triangle), rose from around 2000 a year to perhaps 10,000, with up to two out of three being men and boys aged between 8 and 20. The majority of Gold Coast slaves were deported to the **Caribbean**, where they worked for the rest of their lives on British, Dutch, French or Spanish sugar plantations. Until the middle of the eighteenth century, there were relatively few slaves in the North American colonies. But by 1750, **Charleston** and other ports were starting to buy African slaves from Caribbean traders. By the end of the eighteenth century, the USA was importing slaves directly, to work the cotton and tobacco fields supplying European factories.

It is estimated that for every 100 slaves who survived the crossing, another 50 to 100 died, perishing during capture, while on the overland trek to the coast, while awaiting shipment in the dungeons, or at sea. The impact of removing so many of the fittest and most able young people – perhaps averaging ten percent each year from affected communities – was devastating, akin to a **pandemic**: every family suffered direct consequences as husbands, brothers and sons, as well as wives, sisters and daughters, were captured or disappeared. The population in the Gold Coast, which had been increasing by forty percent each century, hardly changed for more than a hundred years. The best available estimate is that around one **million slaves** were transported from the Gold Coast to the Americas between 1600 and the mid-nineteenth century, when the (by then illegal) trade finally dried up.

Some slaves were **convicts**, others were **kidnapped** deliberately, but the majority of slaves were taken from communities destroyed in **wars** or ruined in the **aftermath of conflict** – for example during famines when families often **pawned** children they were unable to care for to richer communities. The period of the **Asante empire**'s greatest military expansion, 1699–1800, coincided with a period of rapid growth in the **American colonies** and the start of the **industrial revolution** around 1770 (and the same period saw the deportation of an estimated 700,000 slaves). During this time,

kilometres of forest, the park (☎042/33278; daily 8am–5pm; GH¢2) harbours hundreds of species of birds and butterflies, as well as several species of monkey and antelope. There are many other small mammals, and elephants are also said to inhabit Kakum, but you're very unlikely to see them according to the rangers – who apparently haven't seen any themselves. To get here by **public transport**, *tro-tros* are fairly frequent from the Kotokuraba station in Cape Coast to the **visitors' centre** near Abrafo – most of them going on to Twif Praso.

Park **facilities** have greatly improved over the past few years, and there's an attractive restaurant, the *Rainforest Café* (daily 7.30am–3.30pm) and a small **museum**

the Asante enslaved hundreds of thousands of enemy combatants, refugees and civilians – especially from truculent vassal states in the Northern, Upper West and Upper East regions of present-day Ghana, as well as from further afield in present-day Côte d'Ivoire, Burkina and Togo – and sold them to **Fante** middlemen who passed them on to the **fort-based traders**, receiving payment largely in **firearms**, in a spiralling cycle of aggressive expansionism (see p.856). The few dozen Fante-speaking Europeans based on the coast virtually never engaged directly in slave capture, only rarely venturing inland and remaining in the forts to manage their import-export businesses.

How much the slave trade *drove* the Asante military machine, and how much it was driven by it, is hard to say, but the trade itself was certainly driven as much by the **African demand** for European goods – cloth, liquor, metal tools, straight cash and especially firearms and gunpowder – as by the insatiable demand from the Americas for slaves and by the unquenchable appetite of the European cash economies for **sugar and cotton**.

Down on the coast, captives were canoed through the surf, then herded onto slave ships anchored offshore, where they sometimes waited months for them to fill. Or they spent long periods in overcrowded dungeons and holding pens in the forts – or "factories" as the early English traders called them – run mostly by British or Dutch chartered trading companies, with a mixture of paid and enslaved local labour. Once embarked on the Middle Passage, a voyage of five to seven weeks, **conditions for slave deportees** were grim and terrifying. On their backs, bent forwards, or paired together to save space, they were shackled in irons, in claustrophobic confinement, for hours on end. Captains concerned for their cargo's health – or for reduced losses – brought the slaves onto the main deck during the day, but in rough weather they were confined between decks for days at a time. In Britain, the Regulated Slave Trade Act of 1788 stipulated a space allowance of 6ft by 1ft 4in (1.8m by 0.4m) for each adult man. But such legal niceties carried little weight and paled in relation to the reality: washing was rarely possible; excrement accumulated in the waste tubs; disease spread rapidly; bodies were disposed of overboard; and punishment beatings and forced feeding were not uncommon.

Although there was undoubtedly **public consternation** about the slave trade, the business peaked at a time when the legal rights of Europeans themselves were embryonic in comparison with today: in Britain, transportation to Australia (effectively as slave labour) was a routine punishment and burning at the stake still practised. From the 1760s, reformists lobbied for a ban, but it was the **slave revolt on Haiti** (1792–1804) that triggered moves toward an end to the trade. The trading nations, partly sensitized by the **French revolution** and the newly **independent United States of America**, partly terrified of what the future might bring if more slave revolts should occur, steadily turned against the trade. The first Europeans to outlaw the slave trade were the Danish, in 1804, followed by the British in 1807. Other trading nations followed suit, but it wasn't until the British **abolition** of the institution of slavery itself, in 1833, that the trade began to decline rapidly, to be replaced by a burgeoning trade in ivory, hides and, later in the nineteenth century, **palm oil** for the soap and chemical industries. In the Gold Coast, palm oil was produced mostly on Asante and Fante palm plantations – worked partly with slave labour.

near the visitors' centre. The famous highlight of Kakum is the hugely popular 350-metre **aerial walkway** through the rainforest canopy, 30–50m above the forest floor, located close to the entrance and park HQ. Although it costs a steep GH¢9 to walk it (students and NGO volunteers GH¢5), and can be crowded, it's still a must, just to mingle with the birds, butterflies, squirrels and monkeys among the towering trees. Get there early morning or late afternoon to avoid the rush, and try to avoid weekends, which also tend to be very busy. Don't go up in the heat of the day, as the light is bad for photos and the animals are wisely hiding from the sun. To make the most of the viewing opportunities the walkway offers, make arrangements the night before to start a guided tour with a ranger at 5.30am. This costs a little extra (GH¢2 per person on top of regular hourly hike fees), but is highly recommended.

Back down on the forest floor, **trail hikes** to see the plants, insects and larger animals cost GH¢4 per hour with a mandatory guide. Again, very early morning or late afternoon are the best times. As well as identifying the fauna, guides will point out "mushroom-style" termite mounds and a wide range of plants and trees, explaining their various medicinal and domestic uses – ask them about "rainforest Viagra", the bark from the mahogany tree.

If you're **staying the night** at Kakum, it's possible to camp at a campsite fifteen minute's walk from the visitors' centre, where you sleep on roofed platforms, with toilet and shower facilities (GH¢9 per person with your own equipment, GH¢18 if you use the park's equipment of bedding and mosquito net). As the restaurant closes at 3.30pm, you should bring your own food for the night. Alternatively you can spend the night on the atmospheric *Masomagor Tree Platform*, ten metres up in the forest canopy, a 1½-hour walk from Masomagor village, right over on the northeast side of the park. You need to book in advance (GH¢9), and bring your own food and equipment. For more comforts, another place to consider is the oddly named *Hans Cottage Botel* (☎042/33621 ⓦwww .hansbotel.com ❷), 23km south of the park on the Cape Coast–Kakum road, which boasts a terrace restaurant on stilts over a crocodile pool. The crocs are usually difficult to see except at feeding time, but the bird-watching is good. It's a great place for a late breakfast after an early-morning park trip, or for a late-night drink in the double-decker thatched bar-restaurant overlooking the pond. There's a variety of rooms to suit most budgets, or you can camp, and they have Internet access and a small swimming pool. On your way in and out, you're saluted smartly by the gateman – decked out with a 1960s-style English policeman's helmet and dress uniform.

Overrated?

"Kakum National Park was overrated in my opinion, but I wouldn't have missed Hans Cottage Botel for anything."

Kathy Bright, USA

Wassa Domama Rock Shrine

Some 26km further northwest of Kakum, an eerie array of giant boulders, known as **Bosom Kese**, or the "Great God", at **WASSA DOMAMA**, is becoming an increasingly popular tourist destination, largely through the efforts of a community-based ecotourism project. Although the spiritual importance of the shrine seems to have waned somewhat and the rocks are not spectacular in themselves, the site is set incongruously in dense jungle and still makes for a good excursion, the walk to reach the rocks being a highlight in itself. A visit to the shrine, 7km from the village of **Wassa Domama** (where you pay the GH¢2 admission fee and are assigned a guide) is along a rough dirt track, usually followed by a 45-minute canoe tour of the Pra River (GH¢1.50), though the latter isn't permitted on Wednesdays when activity on the river is taboo. Occasional direct **tro-tros** leave for Domama from

Kotokuraba station in Cape Coast (market days, Tuesdays and Fridays, are your best bet), or you can take a Twifo Praso–bound vehicle and get off at the junction at Ankaako – either way you may be in for a long wait. You may be able to find a taxi to charter, though expect to pay a phenomenal rate. There's a very basic **guest-house** with no electricity or running water in Domama (**①**), and simple Ghanaian food can be prepared on request.

Elmina and around

A small, active fishing town, appropriately twinned with Macon, Georgia, in the heart of cotton country, **ELMINA** was one of the first European toe-holds on the West African coast (*el mina* means "the mine" in Portuguese, after the supposed gold mine in the interior). The principal attractions remain the **Portuguese castle and fort**, and the relaxed pace of life makes Elmina a rewarding place to absorb the rhythms of a coastal town. But it's not all calm – when the fishing boats come in at high tide, Elmina can be spectacularly vibrant – and the town's unusual layout is arresting, counterposing the ocean against the lagoon and the two castles against each other. It's an interesting place to walk around, and is slowly being restored with Dutch and EU funds (**W**www.elminaheritage.com), so there are a number of colonial buildings and facades to admire. And with four outstanding **posuban** shrines to boot (see box, p.836), this is one of the most rewarding places for photographers along the coast. Just be aware that the hectic and colourful **fish market** is off limits for casual photography, and minor hassles from would-be **guides** and sponsorship-seekers are beginning to impinge on your freedom to wander completely at peace. On the other hand, if you can find a guide you like, and agree a sensible fee, then the hassles disappear.

Call by the **tourist office** and pick up the good fold-out map of Elmina (GH¢4) showing an hour-long **heritage walk** around the *posuban* shrines, restored buildings

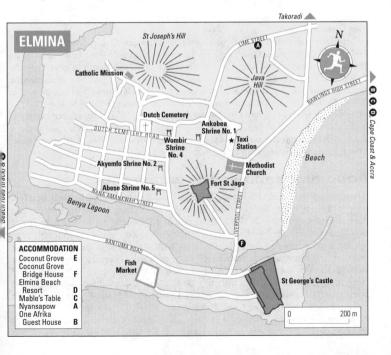

ELMINA

Takoradi

St Joseph's Hill

Catholic Mission

LIME STREET

Java Hill

RAWLINGS HIGH STREET

N

Dutch Cemetery

DUTCH CEMETERY ROAD

Wombir Shrine No. 4

Ankobea Shrine No. 1

★ Taxi Station

Akyemfo Shrine No. 2

Abese Shrine No. 5

NANA AMANKWAH STREET

Methodist Church

Fort St Jago

Beach

Benya Lagoon

LIVERPOOL STREET

BANTUMA ROAD

ACCOMMODATION
Coconut Grove   E
Coconut Grove
   Bridge House   F
Elmina Beach
   Resort   D
Mable's Table   C
Nyansapow   A
One Afrika
   Guest House   B

Fish Market

St George's Castle

0   200 m

Cape Coast & Accra

and Dutch cemetery: they now offer several **guided walking tours**. The tourist office can also arrange boat trips around the lagoon (GH¢40) or you could charter a fishing boat more informally (aim for around GH¢7 for an hour or so – ask around the bridge and be prepared to haggle).

Elmina Castle and Fort St Jago

The oldest European building in Africa, and now part of Ghana's Forts and Castles UNESCO World Heritage Site, the large and imposing **Castle of St George El Mina** (GH¢6.50 plus GH¢0.50 for cameras and GH¢1 for videos; student discounts available) was built by the Portuguese in 1482 – ten years before Columbus discovered America – although the original stockade was barely half the size of the present structure. It served as the **Portuguese headquarters** in West Africa for over 150 years until it was captured by soldiers of the Dutch West Indies Company in 1637. By that time, St George had grown roughly to its present size and the Dutch used it with dedication to exploit the valuable trade in human lives that dominated the coast through the eighteenth century, always conscious of the British in competition just a few kilometres to the east at Cape Coast. Finally, it was the British who, in 1872, bought the castle, along with the other Dutch possessions on the Gold Coast.

Given its age, St George has held up well, though more restoration work is needed. Extremely good, free **tours** of the castle run daily from 9am till 5pm, every hour on the hour. Alternatively you can simply walk around on your own, communing with a past that at times can feel overwhelmingly close, especially on a quiet day. The oppressive holding cells, or **dungeons**, are chillingly unpleasant to visit and it's not difficult to forget the twenty-first century buzzing around in the town beyond the walls.

In the courtyard, you'll notice a **Catholic church** built by the Portuguese. The Protestant Dutch transformed this place of worship into a mess hall and **slave market** – an onerous image that poignantly drives home the barbarity of the trade. Today the church houses a fascinating exhibition documenting Elmina's history, people and culture.

Facing the castle atop a steep, partly artificial hill, **Fort St Jago** (daily 9am–5pm; GH¢1) was built by the Dutch in 1666 to protect the castle from future attacks. Its Portuguese name comes from the hill on which it stands. Briefly a guesthouse in the 1970s, which is still the eventual plan, the fort has little in the way of displays or information – just superb views of the ocean and sprawling town and lagoon below.

A **walk around the backstreets** of Elmina is rewarding, but call in at the tourist office before setting off, as restoration work is ongoing, and newly restored buildings and shrines are likely to feature during the course of this edition. Wherever you go, don't miss the huge and surreal *posuban* of **Asafo Company No. 4**, Wombir, along Dutch Cemetery Street, with its life-sized biblical figures.

Accommodation and restaurants

There are several decent mid-range **hotels** in and around Elmina, but at the budget end of the scale the choice is still limited. The *Nyansapow* has very basic, and very cheap, rooms (☎042/33955; ❶). Located opposite St George's Castle is the ⚓ *Coconut Grove Bridge House* (☎042/40045 ⓦwww.coconutgrovehotels.com .gh ❺), a stone mansion dating back to the 1830s. Rooms here are s/c and have all mod-cons, and several have fantastic views of the castle. There's a simple restaurant (try the chicken with palaver sauce) and a few tables outside, right by bridge and river, though this is possibly a little too close to the all-pervading smell of fish and open gutters for total comfort. Alternatively, try *Bridge House*'s sister resort, right on the beach, the *Coconut Grove Beach Resort* (☎042/33648 ❽), 3km from the centre on the western outskirts of Elmina, where modern s/c chalets, ranging from standard doubles to oceanfront two-bedroom suites with kitchen, sit in manicured grounds around a fine swimming pool. The sound of crashing waves accompanies meals at the poolside, sea-view restaurant. Competing with the *Coconuts* for top-end status, but really not keeping up, is the older *Elmina Beach Resort* on the eastern side of town (☎042/40010 ⓦwww.gbhghana.com ❼), which offers variable standards in the rooms, but a decent pool, tennis and the only squash court in the region. Further afield, about 3km from town on the road to Cape Coast, a couple of options are signposted on the right: *One Afrika Guest House* offers six delightful thatch bungalows with sea views (☎ & ⓕ042/33710 ❸), and almost next door, *Mabel's Table* has accommodation of a similar style and standard (☎042/33598 ❸). All of these places except *Nyansapow* have reasonable **restaurants** attached, but there are several basic chop houses and fast-food eateries in town.

Brenu-Akyinim and Ampenyi

Ten kilometres west of Elmina, accessible by foot along the coastal track (3hr), **BRENU-AKYINIM** has one of the most spectacularly perfect beaches on the Ghanaian coast, a long strip of palm-laden white sand with swimmable breakers, though beware the strong current. The unpretentious *Brenu Beach Resort* occupies part of the beach (☎042/36620 ⓦbrenubeachresort.com), where the sand is kept clean and changing facilities are available (admission GH¢1). They also have a simple guesthouse (❶) and reputable restaurant. Weekdays can be delightfully quiet, while most Saturdays see "beach parties". In the village itself, built like Elmina between the sea and the lagoon, there are basic, clean rooms to be had at the *Celiaman's* (❶). Coming from Elmina on public transport, ask to be dropped at Ayensudo junction, from where your quickest option is to take a taxi the remaining 4km down to the *Brenu* and the beach (GH¢1).

Alternatively, the next turning on your left, 200m further along the Takoradi road, leads you to **AMPENYI** (5km), home of the eco-friendly 🍴 *Ko-Sa Cultural Centre and Guesthouse* (☎0244/375432 ⓦwww.ko-sa.com ❹). Striving to emulate traditional styles, they have an exquisite garden compound dotted with thatched clay bungalows (or you can camp very cheaply), while meals, often vegetarian, are taken communally in the small open-air restaurant. The natural sea-pool here guarantees unusually safe and relaxing swimming. Poles apart in style, *Alberta's Palace Beach Resort* just along the beach (☎024 387937 ⓦwww.albertaspalace.com ❼) provides all your creature comforts in modern, luxury-style accommodation.

En route to Takoradi, **KOMENDA** and **SHAMA** are small coastal settlements off the highway with visitable European forts of real antiquity (see p.835). Neither offers much in the way of accommodation, however, and the beaches aren't worth a special detour.

Takoradi

By no stretch of the imagination is **TAKORADI** – colloquially "Tadi" – another scenic coastal stop. Primarily an industrial centre, it has few redeeming features, though as Ghana's second **port**, it does have a certain vitality. The country's first commercial port opened here in 1928 and, though later superseded by Tema, it still accounts for much of Ghana's container traffic, including a significant transit trade to landlocked Mali and Burkina Faso. The teeming central market provides a decent focus for a visit, but in truth it's better seen as a convenient springboard for places as far afield as Abidjan, or as near as the beaches at Busua and Dixcove.

Takoradi has a minor natural attraction in **Monkey Hill**, a small patch of woodland on the northeast side of town, that has in recent years been home to white-nosed and colobus monkeys. It's not formally a nature reserve, so there's no guarantee how long the primates will stay, but it's worth an early-morning or late-afternoon visit if you're interested.

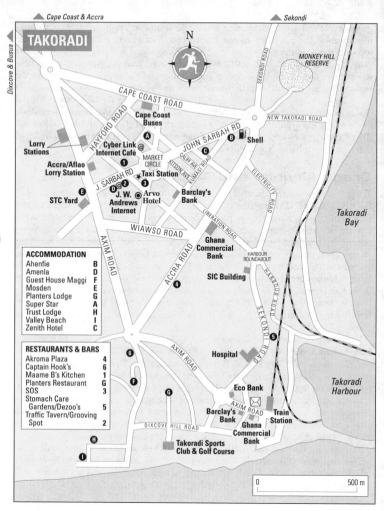

Takoradi is often referred to as Sekondi-Takoradi, **SEKONDI** being the naval base 10km to the east which existed before Takoradi's harbour was built – in many ways, the more interesting part of the city, dating back to the Dutch era and still retaining its fort, **Fort Orange**, and some faded British colonial buildings.

Practicalities

The **main market**, completely encircled by an enormous roundabout, is Takoradi's nerve centre. Liberation Road leads from Market Circle south towards Takoradi harbour, where the **GPO** and hospital are located; shared taxis ply the route. **STC** buses (info on ☎031/23351, 23352 or 23353) use the station on Axim Road, from where there are services to Accra (10 daily), Bolgatanga, via Tamale (Mon, Wed, Fri at 8am) and Kumasi (daily at 4.30am, 10am and 4pm). Three **lorry stations** line the Axim Road north of the STC yard. Accra and Aflao have their own depot; the remaining two stations are slightly further north, with Axim and Tema transport leaving from the more easterly station near Hayford Road, and vehicles to Abidjan, Beyin and Kumasi leaving from the depot on the northern side of Axim Road. Cape Coast transport leaves from a separate yard off the Cape Coast road. To get to Busua, you can take *tro-tros* from Takoradi to Agona junction (40min), then pick up a shared taxi to Busua – or if you don't want to wait, charter a taxi for around GH¢5. Shared **town taxis** operate from a station on John Sarbah Road.

All the major **banks** are represented on Liberation Road, and there are **forex bureaux** on John Sarbah Road on either side of the market. The **Tourist Board** (Mon–Fri 8am–5pm; ☎031/22357 ℱ23601) can be found on the third floor of the SIC building near the harbour roundabout. It's a bit far to walk, however, and they don't have a lot of information to offer. A centrally located **travel agent**, Esam Travel and Tours, across from *Amenla Hotel* on John Sarbah Road, organize regional and national tours (☎031/24540 ℱ24117). Practically next door to the hotel, JW Andrews offers a fairly fast **Internet** service (daily 8am–9pm) as does the Cyberlink Internet Café, near Market Circle.

Accommodation

There are several convenient **places to stay** around the triangular town centre, but for the nicer (and more expensive) places you have to head out to the harbour.

Ahenfie corner of John Sarbah and Kumasi roads ☎031/22966 ℮info@ahenfiehotel.com. Well-established mid-range option with a popular restaurant and disco (Fri & Sat night; GH¢2), plus an Internet café. S/c rooms ❸.

Amenla John Sarbah Rd ☎031/22543. Reasonable hotel in the heart of Takoradi, with cleanish, non-s/c and s/c rooms with fans or a/c grouped round a leafy pink courtyard. The four s/c rooms fill up fast. ❶

Guest House Maggi off Axim Rd ☎031/22575 ℱ30183. Peaceful location, a range of tasteful rooms all with TV, a/c, hot water and fridge, some with attractive balconies. Breakfast included. ❷

Mosden on the first floor of the Mankessim White House Building, 77A/10 Axim Rd ☎031/22266 or 22872. On the roadside and adjacent to the STC station, therefore convenient while noisy. The rooms, though slightly drab s/c affairs, are good value, mostly with TV and fridge. ❷

Planter's Lodge Dixcove Hill Rd ☎031/22233 ℱ22230 ℮planters @africaonline.com. The nicest place to stay in Takoradi, Takoradi's former Services Mess Club has six spacious chalets each containing two tasteful one-bedroom suites with separate sitting rooms,

huge mahogany beds, proper linen and tea-making facilities. The small pool lies in a lovely garden bowl below the rooms, where shaded seating and an a/c restaurant serve excellent pan-European food. ❻

Super Star Kitson Ave, near Market Circle ☎031/23105. This three-storey building has a very gloomy reception and corridors but the rooms, decked out with shiny satin bedcovers and deep pile carpeting, are fine and it's well located. The restaurant is best avoided though. ❸

Trust Lodge N16 the Circle Ridge, off Beach Rd ☎031/23923. Housed In a lovely old colonial house, this lodge has seven comfortable rooms with balconies and spacious bathrooms, a shady bougainvillea-filled garden at the back and very friendly service. ❺

Valley Beach 181 Beach Rd ☎031/26900. Swanky business-class hotel with large plush rooms with oriental rugs and really comfortable orthopedic mattresses. They also have a gym. ❻

Zenith Califf Ave ☎031/22359. If the *Amenla* is full, try the not-quite-so-spruce selection of budget rooms here, which are spacious and s/c, with TV and fridge. ❶

Eating, drinking and entertainment

If you fancy combining some **food** with a spot of physical activity, try the crumbling 1920s relic, the Takoradi Sports Club, opposite *Planter's Lodge*, a pleasant setting for a very cheap beer overlooking the brown golf course and the ocean. In theory there's a GH¢1.50 guest fee, but normally only if you want to have round (caddies are available); in practice, just stroll in. Otherwise, there are several decent **dining options** in Takoradi. For groceries, there's a **Max Mart supermarket** on Liberation Road.

For a **drink**, try the ever-popular *Stomach Care Gardens*, the bar at *Dezoos Ocean View Restaurant*, which has views of the container port and an attached disco (GH¢1 entrance). Also worth considering are the *Traffic Tavern* and *Grooving Spot*, two adjacent street-side bars on John Sarbah Road across from the taxi station, which offer a great atmosphere for a beer.

Restaurants

Akroma Plaza Accra Rd. Good and popular place with a very long menu, including Indian, Chinese, fast food and Ghanaian, with most dishes in the GH¢3–5 bracket.

Captain Hook's just off the Axim Rd roundabout ☏031/27085 (restaurant daily from 5pm, beer garden daily except Mon from 11am). German-owned and highly recommended for its huge variety of tantalizing dishes, from grilled fish to steaks, pizzas to seafood pasta. The food is excellent, if expensive – dishes range from GH¢12–20 for fish, grilled lobster, *fritto misto* and the like. The attractive outdoor beer garden is a pleasant spot where you can relax in wicker chairs.

Maame B's Kitchen 22/5A Collins Ave, across from *Grooving Spot* ☏031/30540. The menu is a little brief, but the portions of local and European dishes are generous and prepared to a high standard. Daily 9.30am–midnight.

🏃 **Planters** at *Planters Lodge*, Dixcove Hill Rd ☏031/22233 (daily noon–3pm & 7–10.30pm). Although on the pricey side, with mains around GH¢10 and up, this is perhaps the nicest place to eat in town. Service is friendly and efficient, and the dishes – try sea bass with lemon butter, grilled king prawns or herb-marinated pork – are delicious. Australian Shiraz and real Italian coffee (they proudly boast the only cafetieres in Takoradi) are a fine bonus.

SOS corner of Market Circle and Ashanti Rd ☏031/25064. Fast-food outlet serving burgers, kebabs and fried rice to eat in or take away for around GH¢2. The balcony has great views of the market.

Dixcove, Busua and around

Sheltering behind Ghana's southernmost headland, Cape Three Points, the twin villages of **Dixcove** and **Busua** have long been a favourite overlanders' hideaway. There are two principal attractions: first the cute, whitewashed hilltop **Fort Metal Cross** at Dixcove, overlooking the exceptionally animated fishing village and its deep, forest-bound, circular bay; and second, the long strand of **Busua beach**, with its host of backpacker-friendly lodgings. Dixcove and Busua are no longer isolated retreats, as the highway between Ghana and Côte d'Ivoire makes it easy to visit them as a small diversion en route, and the area draws people from Abidjan as well as Accra.

If Busua does get a little crowded at weekends (particularly in season, Dec–Feb), it doesn't detract much from the area's intrinsic appeal – the quintessential Ghana **beach scene**. More disappointing is the dying coconut forest all around, attacked by a morbid blight that has reduced it to a miserable cemetery – there are plans, however, to replace the trees with resistant varieties at some stage. A multitude of short **walks** are possible in the area, either west to Cape Three Points, 5km beyond Dixcove, or east along Busua Beach, cutting over the headland and down to **Butre**, just a kilometre beyond the beach, which used to have a fort of its own – Fort Batenstein – now completely in ruins.

If you're on public transport, alight at the Agona junction on the main Takoradi highway and either charter a taxi (GH¢2) or wait for a shared taxi. With your own transport, after turning south towards the coast at the Agona junction, you'll come to a fork 6km down the road, where you head left for Busua or right for Dixcove: the two are connected by a twenty-minute walk through the coastal bush.

Dixcove and Akwidaa

DIXCOVE is home to **Fort Metal Cross**, built by the English between 1692 and 1698. The fort's otherwise idyllic site is marred by a monolithic block of flats of surpassing ugliness – ironically the Chief's Palace – right in front of it. A fee of GH¢1 allows you entry to the fort and a brief tour.

Arts and crafts

A huge range of crafts are made in West Africa, from baskets to strip cloth, from silver jewellery to leather ware, from pottery to bronze figurines and from children's toys to musical instruments.

No matter where you are travelling, you can pick up beautiful work and have fun bargaining. Be sure to avoid ivory and restricted items – some governments are rightly clamping down on exports of national heritage.

Wooden carvings

Traditionally, West African woodcarvers produced two main types of items – doors and furniture, and masks for ceremonial use. Masked dances are commonest among peoples of the forest, and often take place after dark, or during initiation ceremonies bringing children into adulthood. The masks themselves are usually handed down from generation to generation, and these days only rarely fashioned anew for ceremonial use. The smaller offerings designed to hang on your wall and sold at crafts stalls are generally much less impressive, though some centres, like Ouagadougou for example, have excellent selections of purely decorative masks. Be prepared for serious bargaining and very high initial prices. Avoid buying anything that is of genuine antique value – a trade which has led people to sell their own doors and furniture, with these sometimes ending up in New York apartments.

▲ Buyng cloth, The Gambia

Basket-making

Basket-making is a popular cottage industry all over the region: using natural materials it's almost impossible to mechanize, which makes it a useful bulwark against the imported factory substitutes for so many other local manufactures. Most countries have districts and towns where basket-making is a thriving local business, and the resulting containers can range from delicate purses to huge, theatrical jobs you could hide a person in. Old-style baskets may include unusual fibres such as baobab bark, while newer baskets, with roadside sales and exports in mind, often incorporate coloured string, leather or plastic beads. Light, and affordable, they all make wonderful souvenirs.

Pepsi can attaché case

There's a huge inventiveness in West African crafts manufacture. Wooden attaché cases decorated with soft-drink cans beaten flat and lined with French comics were all the rage a few years back in Dakar. The rug behind this example is from Niger and features the Tuareg cross motif.

Potting

Like basketry, potting has its inherited culture and practitioners, and its regional centres. Well-made, unglazed pots were the traditional way to keep water cool, through evaporation. A good supply of clay mud is a prerequisite, and potting is invariably tied to local rivers and wetland sources, with the length of the Niger basin a highly productive area. Unlike basket-making, the results are easily replicated in a Chinese plastics factory: buy pots when you see them.

Bronze-casting

The lost-wax (or *cire perdue*) method of bronze-casting is used widely. Cameroon and Côte d'Ivoire produce a lot of small, sometimes comic or obscene statuary by this method, which involves making a basic form in clay, modelling the detail on top of that with wax, repeatedly dressing the delicate sculpture with clay "wash" and allowing it to dry, and then finally covering the whole thing with solid clay and firing it. The wax melts out, and into the channel is poured the molten alloy. When that cools, the cast is broken and the work is done.

◄ Bronze statue, Togo

Textiles

Textiles are perhaps the most pervasive craft in West Africa: cotton is widely cultivated and is used, along with wool and imported threads, to produce a great variety of fabric. Weaving is a male craft, and you can often find young boys learning the skill, their hands flying to send the shuttle across the loom, weaving narrow strips a couple of metres in length, which are then sewn together to form a sarong-type wrapper (*lapa* in pidgin English; *pagne* in French). Locally manufactured cloth is often dyed or painted with leaf dyes, indigo or mud, which hold their colour extremely well – Mali's bogolan cloth is the classic example (see overleaf). Look out for dramatically hued, geometrically patterned blankets and rugs, especially from Niger (see opposite); for appliqué work from Ghana; and also for finely woven, high-status Ghanaian *kente* cloth.

◄ Weaving kente cloth

▲ Arrow heads, Mauritania

Other crafts and souvenirs

In the markets of the Sahel towns such as Timbuktu and Agadez, look out for **leather** and **silver**, or **nickel-silver** ware. You can get wonderful inlaid chests and superb camel-whips. Here, too, you'll find piles of Neolithic **arrow heads**, stone knives and scrapers collected from the dunes of the Sahara where they have lain since being abandoned by their makers and users in the last few hundred years. Small and beautifully worked, you can buy a pocketful for a few dollars. Also in the market stalls, you'll find **glass trading beads**, some old and Venetian, some of recent, local manufacture. In parts of Guinea, Sierra Leone and Liberia, you can still find **currency** predating the era of notes and coins, usually in the form of slender iron rods – called "Kissi pennies" in Sierra Leone.

▲ Trading beads, Nigeria

Many of the best souvenirs from African travels are the items made for the local market rather than for tourists. **Toy cars** and trucks made of old food cans are hugely popular with local children. If you have time to get one made to order, rather than from the tourist market, so much the better.

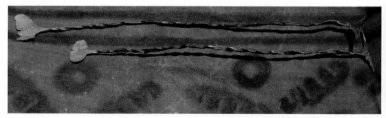

▲ Kissi pennies, Sierra Leone (on Sierra Leonean ronko cloth, similar to Mali's bogolan)

There's nowhere to stay in Dixcove, but there are a couple of excellent options some 10km along the beach road, west of the town, near the village of Akwidaa. From Takoradi, Agona junction or Dixcove transport park, *tro-tros* or taxis will drop you at either of the following, respectively 2km and 1km east of Akwidaa Old Town.

The first, an excellent ecofriendly beach resort, is the ⚲ *Safari Beach Lodge* (☎0246/651329 ⊛www.safaribeachlodge.com). Rather more glamorous, quieter and more expensive than the neighbouring *Green Turtle* (see below), its decor gives it the feel of an old-fashioned safari camp, and its s/c suites, with fantastic outdoor stone showers and views down to the water, are seriously comfortable (❸–❺). The food (including such delights as lobster, game meat and flambé deserts) tastes as stunning as it looks and there's a good selection of wines to match. Their art gallery and a range of trips on offer, from canoeing in the mangroves to hiking, are real pluses.

With a more youthful vibe, ⚲ *Green Turtle Lodge* (☎0244/893566 ⊛www .greenturtlelodge.com), set on a stunning, pristine beach, is an eco-lodge owned by a young English couple and built from local materials, run entirely on solar power and with self-composting toilets. Options include non-s/c doubles (❷) or s/c huts with bamboo four-posters and small verandahs looking out towards the ocean (❸). You can also camp (GH¢2.50). The menu changes daily and the food is fresh and delicious and includes grilled fish. Breakfasts tend to feature big fat omelettes or French toast with bananas and local honey. The owners can arrange a variety of trips in the area (from canoeing to biking) and during turtle-nesting season (Oct–March) there are regular night-time turtle walks.

Busua and around

You can walk to **BUSUA** from Dixcove via the bush-farm footpath that leads northeast from behind Fort Metal Cross. Once you climb the rise, you can practically see Busua. There's a small tidal river as you descend the hill, which you may have to wade through to reach Busua village. Though a very pleasant walk, several muggings have been reported, and it's best to be accompanied by a guide. The beautiful sands and clean waters of Busua are enticing, but watch out for the strong offshore current.

For a modest village, Busua is full of **accommodation** choices, none of them far from the junction where taxis drop you. The oldest hotel in the area, and the most expensive, *Busua Beach Resort* (☎031/21210 ⊛www.gbhghana.com ❻) is rivalled by the *African Rainbow* (☎031/32149 ⓔafricanrainbowresort@yahoo.ca ❺), a three-storey block with large, comfy rooms with balconies and a rooftop restaurant serving some of the best food in town (the only downside here is the lack of direct beach access). The new and friendly, French-owned *Busua Inn* (☎0243/087354 ⊛www.busuainn.com ❷–❹) is a recommended alternative, directly on the beach, with four s/c rooms with sea view and a beachfront terrace restaurant serving very good French and West African food. For budget-priced stays, the *Alaska Beach Club* is a popular option with a collection of huts – from basic thatched-roof affairs with shared bathroom to more comfortable s/c brick bungalows (⊛www .alaskabeachclub.com ❶–❷), a lively bar and restaurant and an excellent beach-front location. Also reasonably priced is *Dadson's Lodge* (❶), where the rooms are comfortable and airy, and some are s/c; they have a nice little restaurant off the courtyard. Finally, *Bliss Joy Lodge* has four neat rooms, all s/c, some with TV (☎031/22823 ❶).

All of Busua's lodgings serve **food**. Alternatively, the village is full of itinerant food vendors: the "pancake man" now has a restaurant behind the local school, with a range of reasonably priced meals and excellent pancakes, and you're bound to meet the "lobster man" and the "juice man" too. A visit to *Black Mamba Corner*, where tasty pizzas are the speciality, is highly recommended – you'll see the entrance on the Dixcove side of Busua.

Butre

A half-hour walk east along the beach from Busua, by the fishing village of **BUTRE**, is the idyllic 🕊 *Hideout Lodge* – aka *Ellis Hideout* – which offers sunny yellow bungalows set on a beautiful beach among the palms, two dorm rooms, plenty of space for camping and a small restaurant and bar (☎0207/369258 Ⓦwww.ellishideout.com; camping GH¢2.50, dorm beds GH¢5, bungalows ❸). Reminiscent of an old-style Ko Samui beach haunt, this is an unusually friendly, well-run set-up, with plentiful activities on offer, including wildlife-spotting river trips (GH¢5) and visits to the skulking, but largely intact ruins of **Fort Batenstein** on a hilltop at the mouth of the Butre river.

Princestown and the far southwest

The principal attractions on the westernmost stretch of Ghana's coast are **Princestown** and **Axim**, the latter served by most buses along the main road towards Côte d'Ivoire. Both have fine castles, magnificent views and great stretches of beach. Inland from **Beyin**, which lies on the coast 45km west of Axim, you'll also find the traditional stilt village of **Nzulezo**.

Princestown

In 1681, Prince Friedrich Wilhelm of Brandenburg (the district around Berlin) sent an expedition to the area of what is now **PRINCESTOWN** (also written "Prince's Town") in an effort to break the Portuguese, English and Dutch hold over West African trade at the time. This led to the founding of **Fort Grossfriedrichsburg**, within whose walls the Brandenburgers soon fell victim to malaria and repeated attacks by the Dutch and English. They abandoned the citadel in 1708, turning it over to the Ahanta-Pokoso chief **Johnny Konny**, who earned the dubious title "Last Prussian Negro Prince". The Dutch stormed the fort in 1748 and renamed it Hollandia and then, around 1800, it was finally abandoned.

Direct transport to Princestown from Takoradi or Agona Junction is possible, but slow to fill, even on market days. It may be quicker to drop at the junction for Princestown on the main highway, some 15km west of Agona Junction, though you still may have a wait for onward transport down the rough eighteen-kilometre track to the village. The fort, classically sited on a jutting headland with the village, lagoon and ocean all around, has been restored and offers spectacular **views** (daily 6am–6pm; GH¢1). You can spend the night in one of the very basic rooms in the Fort's resthouse (❶); the caretaker is very helpful. The nearby beaches are beautiful, and for real isolation you can take a canoe trip across the Kpani river.

Axim and west along the coast

Now in the small town of **AXIM**, **Fort San Antonio** was built by the Portuguese, probably at the end of the fifteenth century, and taken by the Dutch in 1642. Until recently the fort housed government offices, but it has now been taken over by Ghana Museum and Monuments Board, who have plans to renovate. You can still visit the fort (daily 8am–6pm; GH¢1) which is very run down but offers excellent views.

Arriving by road transport, you'll be dropped at the **station** just east of the castle. The only decent place to stay in the town itself is the *Frankfaus Hotel*, on the road into the centre (☎0342/22291 ❶), with clean rooms, running water and an excellent restaurant. Another upmarket option near Axim is the *Axim Beach Hotel* (☎0342/22260 Ⓦwww.aximbeach.com ❹), perched on a hilltop on the eastern side of town and thus offering fantastic views of golden sand from its chalet rooms. Bikes, boogie boards and fishing gear are available to rent.

A very appealing new place in the Axim area is *Lou Moon Lodge* (☎0244/424497 Ⓦwww.loumoonlodge.com ❺–❻) at **AGYAM** (Egyambra), 6km southeast along the coast towards Princestown, with a selection of stilt-raised, s/c bungalows with terraces overlooking the sea. It's an idyllic, unspoilt part of the coast.

Ankobra

Some 5km west of Axim and 800m off the main coastal highway, the *Ankobra Beach Resort* (☎0342/22400 Ⓦwww.ankobrabeachresort.com) is also a cultural centre, hosting African music, dance, and craft workshops and performances. There are wooden chalets set back from the beach in the workers' compound (❶), or you can camp, but more interesting is the accommodation modelled on the round huts of northern Ghana, featuring stone interiors and a more substantial price-tag (❸). If you can't afford to stay here, it is worth visiting just for a drink on the spectacular palm-fringed beach, though watch out for the rocks. *Ankobra* arranges transport to a variety of nearby villages, including **Nzulezo** and to the **Ankasa and Nini-Suhien reserves** (see below).

Into Côte d'Ivoire

Onward travel **into Côte d'Ivoire** is simple from Axim. There are daily buses through to the border a little way inland at **ELUBO**. You may prefer to get through the same day as the main place to stay, *Hotel Cocoville* (☎0345/22041; ❶), near the motor park, is on its last legs. You can change money at the Ghana Commercial Bank in **Half Assini**, though this entails a detour on the coastal road west of Beyin.

Beyin and Nzulezo

By the village of **BEYIN**, **Fort Apollonia** (daily 7am–5pm; GH¢1) is the western-most of the forts along the Ghana coastline, and the last to be built, by the British, in 1756. Today, it has rudimentary accommodation (❶), although renovations are planned which will turn the entire fort into a museum. Alternative lodgings can be found right on the beach near the fort, with Robinson Crusoe–style bamboo huts built on stilts (❶). Unless you charter a taxi, transport to Beyin from Axim is painfully slow, and you may have to change vehicles at Esiama, west of Axim. Arriving from Elubo, you proceed via **Mpataba** and **Tikobo I** village before heading east along the coast to Beyin.

Beyin is the departure point for the stilt village of **NZULEZO** on the **Amansuri lagoon**. Tradition has it that the inhabitants of the village originally came from Mali and moved to the lagoon for protection from enemies, led by a snail to their current place. You can arrange to visit Nzulezo by canoe at the Ghana Wildlife Society Visitors' Centre on the western edge of Beyin; the outing (GH¢4, students GH¢2, camera GH¢0.80, video GH¢5) takes two to four hours depending on the season. The canoe trip is a highlight in itself, nosing along the jungle-fringed banks of the lagoon before arriving at Nzulezo, where you show your receipt and sign the visitors' book. Your reception at the stilt village may be frosty, however: local people need reassurance that wealthy visitors are actually bringing them some benefit. The office in Beyin can also arrange **homestays** in very basic, fanless rooms in the stilt village (❶).

Ankasa and Nini-Suhien reserves

Near the border town of **Elubo**, the adjoining rainforest **reserves** of **Ankasa and Nini-Suhien**, run as one park, have a visitors' centre at the park gates, and basic, rough-and-ready accommodation – or you can pitch your tent or park your vehicle. *Nkwanta Camp*, 7km from the park entrance, and *Elubo Camp*, are the most developed, with outside toilet and shower and basic cooking facilities (❶), but you will need to bring all your food requirements with you. With forest elephants, a small population of chimpanzees, monkeys, leopards, an abundance of birds and butterflies, and some unique plant species, the area boasts a rich biodiversity which arguably surpasses that at Kakum.

To get to the park gates, some 6km north of the main coastal highway on a rough dirt road, your best bet is to take a *tro-tro* from Axim to **AIYANASI**, the nearest town to the park, and then charter a taxi from there to the main gates. Alternatively you could ask to be dropped at the Ankasa junction (signposted) and walk the remaining 6km – bring plenty of water. After paying the park entrance (GH¢4) fees you can take informative guided walking tours of the forest along well-marked trails (GH¢1.50 per hour).

10.3

Kumasi and central Ghana

The **central part of Ghana** is one of the country's most attractive regions. The road from Accra, skirting past the northeast fringe of the old **Asante heartland**, is scenic and hilly. Around the great hub of **Kumasi** itself, a clutch of different routes radiate through steep scarp and forest country. Much of this has long been under cultivation – especially **cocoa**, which brings a dark, gloomy silence to the woods – but enough is still jungle-swathed, stacked with impressive, buttress-rooted forest giants, and scattered with hillside villages, to deliver a strong and characteristic sense of tropical Africa. The settlements, misty grey-green in the chilly mornings, sticky and brilliantly coloured in the afternoons, are the key elements in an area to savour. Travel is easy, and the cultural heritage as rich as anywhere.

Kumasi

KUMASI still oozes with the traditions and customs of the **Asante**, one of the most powerful nations in West Africa in the middle of the nineteenth century. Additionally, the town has remnants of colonial architecture, a reminder of half a century of British domination. The combination of the old order and hectic modernity makes this extremely active commercial centre one of Ghana's most satisfying cities. Kumasi is also a good place to base yourself for trips into the surrounding countryside (see p.860). Within easy reach are a handful of natural attractions, including three **national parks**; several villages known for their **crafts**; and other potential excursions – including the **gold mines** of Obuasi.

Arrivals, transport and information

Even in its early days, Kumasi was an imposing capital. Today it spreads widely over the hills, and is home to 1.5 million people. The heart of the downtown district is marked roughly by **Kejetia Circle**, and nearby, the **central market** – the largest in Ghana and one of the very biggest in Africa – spills over the disused railway tracks to fill a hollow in the city centre. Just west of the market, the **Adum district** is the commercial centre where you'll find major banks, supermarkets, department stores, the post office and most forex bureaux. Uphill, northwest of Adum, **Bantama district**, site of the expansive **Ghana National Cultural Centre**, takes over.

The **airport** is 4km east of town, from where taxis charge around GH¢2 to the centre. Antrak and Citylink have regular **flights** to Accra.

There are several major **lorry parks**, used by bush taxi and *tro-tros*; these include **New Tafo park**, in the north, used by vehicles to and from Tamale, Bolgatanga, Navrongo and Yendi; **Asafo park**, by the Asafo market, for Lake Bosumtwe, Koforidua, Accra, Cape Coast and Takoradi as well as plush M Plaza air-conditioned coaches for Accra; and **Kejetia park** for Mampong, Sunyani, Berekum, Wenchi and Abidjan.

STC buses use the station on Prempeh I Street, around the corner from the *Presbyterian Guest House*. There are services to Accra (4–5hr), Takoradi (5hr), Cape Coast (3–4hr), Tamale (8hr) and Bolgatanga (10hr). Most of these destinations have twice-daily services, though runs are sometimes cancelled at the last minute. Less frequent are buses to Ouagadougou (twice weekly) and Abidjan. Buses to and from Wa use the **Alaba station**, east of the central market. The **Ghana Tourist Board** (☎ & ⓕ051/26243), adjacent to the museum in the Ghana National Cultural Centre, has friendly and enthusiastic staff, and guides to hotels, restaurants and sights in the Asante Region, plus large-scale Kumasi city maps.

For **Internet** access, try the central Unic Internet on Bank Road (☎051/27972), 24-hour Supanet on Nsene Road near the Methodist Cathedral, Bee Buzy Internet Café on Asomfo Road, just down from *City View Restaurant* or Internet Ghana Internet Café above the Shell garage on Harper Road (☎051/21563). The **British Council** has premises on Bank Road (Mon–Fri 9am–6pm, Sat 10am–4pm; ☎051/23462 ⓦwww.britishcouncil.org/ghana-kumasi.htm).

Kumasi post office

"We gave Kumasi post office our Best in Ghana award – for outside phone boxes mostly working, helpful staff who point you to the correct post box, postcards available in a shop right next door, and the fact that they arrived in the UK four days later!"

Ken Shaw and Carolyn Spice, UK

Accommodation

Although Kumasi lacks any really luxurious **accommodation**, inexpensive lodgings abound, and get better-value the further you move from the centre. Outside term time, the university halls of residence 7km from the centre are often open to visitors; the pleasant **Unity Hall**, for example, has gardens and no lack of company.

Budget

Guestline Lodge just around the corner from the STC station, Adum ☎051/23351 ⓔmahash161us@yahoo.com. Owned by the Baboos (of *Vic Baboo's Café* fame) and popular with budget travellers, this has overtaken the *Presby* as the budget traveller's abode, with its nice courtyard garden at the back. However, rooms could be cleaner and it's not the friendliest place. Car rental with driver available at GH¢55/day. Dorm beds GH¢5.50, non-s/c rooms ❷, s/c rooms ❸.

Montana Adum ☎051/32389. Slightly run-down place located within easy walking distance of points of interest downtown. The non-s/c rooms are dimly lit and have fans. ❶

Nurom Annexe 2 Nsene Rd, Adum ☎051/24000. Besides an excellent location, this has clean, spacious (especially on the top floor) non-s/c rooms and pleasant communal areas, and it's extremely cheap. ❶

Presbyterian Guest House Mission Rd, near the STC station and British Council ☎051/23879. The imposing colonial "Presby" used to offer

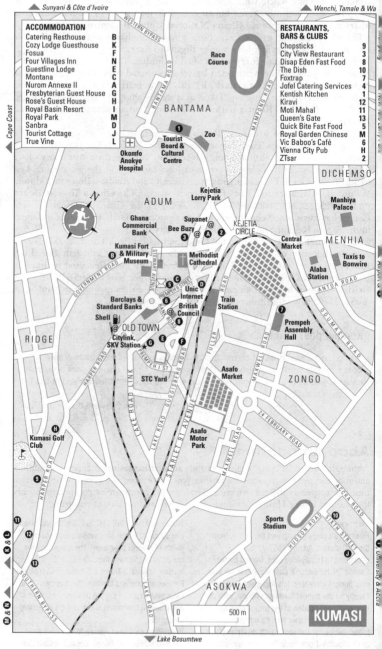

ACCOMMODATION

Catering Resthouse	B
Cozy Lodge Guesthouse	K
Fosua	F
Four Villages Inn	N
Guestline Lodge	E
Montana	C
Nurom Annexe II	A
Presbyterian Guest House	G
Rose's Guest House	H
Royal Basin Resort	I
Royal Park	M
Sanbra	D
Tourist Cottage	J
True Vine	L

RESTAURANTS,
BARS & CLUBS

Chopsticks	9
City View Restaurant	3
Disap Eden Fast Food	8
The Dish	10
Foxtrap	7
Jofel Catering Services	4
Kentish Kitchen	1
Kiravi	12
Moti Mahal	11
Queen's Gate	13
Quick Bite Fast Food	5
Royal Garden Chinese	M
Vic Baboo's Café	6
Vienna City Pub	H
ZTsar	2

Sunyani & Côte d'Ivoire

Wenchi, Tamale & Wa

WESTERN BYPASS

Race Course

BANTAMA

Cape Coast

Tourist Board & Cultural Centre

Okomfo Anokye Hospital

Zoo

DICHEMSO

ADUM

Kejetia Lorry Park

Manhiya Palace

Ghana Commercial Bank

Supanet

KEJETIA CIRCLE

MENHIA

Bee Buzy

Kumasi Fort & Military Museum

Methodist Cathedral

Central Market

Taxis to Bonwire

Alaba Station

ANTOA ROAD

Unic Internet

Train Station

Barclays & Standard Banks

British Council

Prempeh Assembly Hall

Shell

OLD TOWN

Citylink, SKV Station

RIDGE

STC Yard

Asafo Market

ZONGO

24 FEBRUARY ROAD

Kumasi Golf Club

Asafo Motor Park

Sports Stadium

ACCRA ROAD

ASOKWA

SOUTHERN BYPASS

0   500 m

KUMASI

University & Accra

Lake Bosumtwe

comfortable twin rooms and was an excellent place to meet fellow budget travellers, but it's long past its sell-by date and hard to recommend any more. You can camp here if they're full – which is a bit unlikely. ①

Tourist Cottage in Asokwa, not far from the stadium ☎051/25219. A bit hidden away, but worth the search. Pleasant good-value rooms in a quiet setting. Recommended. ①

Mid-range

Catering Resthouse just off Government Rd ☎051/26506 ⑤23656. Despite being so close to the centre, this is very tranquil, with pretty gardens. More expensive rooms, huge with massive bathrooms and verandahs where you can be served dinner, are better value. ③–⑤

Cozy Lodge Guesthouse Mango Tree Lane, Nhyiaeso, 3km from the centre ☎051/20164 ⑥cozygardens01@yahoo.com. Stylish rooms in a quiet, leafy setting, with a 24hr fast-food restaurant, jazz club and a bar on the grounds. ⑤

Fosua Aseda House, Odum St ☎051/37382 ⑥www.fosuahotel.com. Decent mid-range hotel on the top floor of an office building. Rooms are clean and well equipped but a bit on the small side. ⑤

Rose's Guest House 4 Old Bekwai Rd ☎051/24072 ⑥oasis@ghana.com. An intimate place with art-adorned corridors and very comfortable, tidy s/c, a/c rooms, complete with satellite TV, in a nice garden setting. There's a bar with pool table, serving burgers and sandwiches (adjoining rooms can be noisy). ④

Sanbra Paul Sagoe Lane, Adum ☎051/31257 ⑥sanbra@yahoo.com. Classy establishment right in the heart of town. Clean and simple s/c rooms with hot water, a/c, satellite TV and fridge, some

with balcony. Ask for a room overlooking the courtyard rather than the main road If you want some peace and quiet. ③

Expensive

🏃 **Four Villages Inn** Old Bekwai Rd, around 5km from downtown ☎051/22682 ⑥www.fourvillages.com. Warm and friendly B&B in suburban Kumasi, run by an amiable and very helpful Canadian–Ghanaian couple. Essential to book ahead as there are only four s/c, a/c rooms, each individually decorated with traditional crafts and featuring big beds, satellite TV and access to their DVD library. There's a cosy communal lounge, great breakfasts included – eggs, fresh fruit, home-made sausages, real coffee – and superb Ghanaian dinners available on request (GH¢15, wine and beer available). Tours are offered (especially of Kumasi market with a member of staff). Easily the nicest place to stay in Kumasi. ⑦

Royal Basin Resort 10km from the centre, off the Accra Rd ☎051/60144 or 60169 ⑥www.royalbasinresort.com. Kumasi's fanciest hotel, and perhaps rather overpriced, though with a jazz bar with live music (Thurs–Sun), car rental, consistently good restaurant, Internet access, and a (disappointingly small) pool. ⑦

Royal Park Old Bekwai Rd, just beyond the Southern Bypass ☎051/39353 ⑤25584. Chinese-run, unpretentious establishment with an excellent restaurant. Rooms are stylish and have all mod-cons. ⑦

True Vine off the Southern Bypass, Nhyiaeso (take the road opposite the turning to *Moti Mahal*) ☎051/21024. Friendly little place with large, cool rooms with huge raised tubs in the bathrooms and Wi-Fi Internet access. ⑤

The Town

Kumasi is one of the rare West African towns where you can go **sightseeing** in the accepted sense. In addition to the **museums**, other historic points of interest, like the **palace** of the Asante king, dot the cityscape, and you could easily spend a few days just checking them out. The enormous **central market** alone merits a couple of trips to search hidden corners for unusual finds. The main attraction at the large **University of Science and Technology** off the Accra road is its Olympic-sized swimming pool, open to the public. Avoid at all costs the terrible "**zoo**", north of Kejetia Circle and note that on **Sundays** more shops and services than usual seem to be closed.

Kejetia market

Despite the tumbledown appearance of rambling, rusty, corrugated-iron-clad stalls, the central **Kejetia market** is a fantastic place to explore, and the largest market (certainly in terms of area) in West Africa. The traders come from all the surrounding countries, and beyond, to buy and sell here, and while the atmosphere is bustling and sometimes intense and overwhelming, it's not at all intimidating. Few people mind if you want to take photographs (it's polite to ask first) though you might be asked for a dash.

The Asante

The Asante trace their **origins** to the northern regions of the savannah belt. Along with other Akan peoples, they came to this region around the eleventh century and settled in the area of **Lake Bosumtwe**, carving farms from the wild rainforest. These districts contained rich goldfields and trade in the metal gradually developed, at first to the north, supplying the Saharan caravans. By the fifteenth century, however, the Akan also had commercial links with the Portuguese at Elmina and, by the seventeenth century, they were organized into dozens of small states, each vying for control of the mines and the slave-supplying districts in the northern interior where European merchants hadn't ventured.

The founding of the Asante nation
In the 1690s, **Osei Tutu** – the first great **Asante king**, or Asantehene – brought together a loose confederation of states into a single nation under his rule. **Kumasi** was chosen as the site of the new capital on the advice of Osei Tutu's most trusted adviser, **Okomfo Anokye**, an extremely powerful fetish priest. Okomfo planted the seeds of two *kum* trees in separate locations, one of which sprouted, indicating where the Asante seat was to be established (*kum asi* means "under the *kum* tree"). Having received this sign, the priest evoked the **Golden Stool** from the heavens. This "throne" descended from the clouds to alight upon Osei Tutu, and thereby became the single most important symbol of national unity and the authority of the king. The Asante nation was born.

Expansion and consolidation
Osei Tutu set about expanding his empire. One of his most important early victories was against the Denkyira king, **Ntim Gyakar**, under whom the Asante had traditionally lived as vassals (the Denkyira were based to the southwest of Kumasi). Ntim Gyakar was captured, tried and killed in 1699. Other rival powers fell to the Asante in their turn, each conquered state left intact, but owing allegiance and taxes in goods and labour to the Asante and creating fertile conditions for the supply of the coastal **slave trade** from refugees and destroyed communities (see p.841). Gradually the Asante kingdom grew to include most of present-day Ghana and the eastern part of Côte d'Ivoire, with only the **Fante** states of the coast putting up realistic resistance, using their European allies to their advantage.

The increasing size of the Asante kingdom spawned a royal **bureaucracy** and **judicial system**; administrative functions were transferred from the hereditary nobility to a new class of appointed functionaries controlled by the king. Even **commoners** could fill lower court offices, such as linguists and commissioners or governors sent to oversee vassal states. In the matrilineal system, the Asantehene himself was chosen from the king's brothers or his sisters' offspring by the queen mother, who consulted with advisers before making her decision. Though his power was nearly absolute, an unworthy Asantehene could be "destooled" – removed from the throne – by the royal family.

More clearly demarcated than Accra's Makola, Kejetia market is split into various **"zones"** – for food, clothes and every kind of Asante craft – and though you're bound to get lost without a guide you'll eventually get your bearings, especially if you gain some height at one of the peripheral buildings or walkways, when the whole teeming market-opolis is laid out before you. There are endless fascinating corners and quarters, from the sweatshop rooms of fast-fingered tailors sewing school uniforms to the stalls selling all manner of recycled items (including sandals made from old tyres and tools from scrap metal). Beads, leather goods, domestic utensils, dried foodstuffs, pottery and cloth all have their separate alleys and areas, while in the noisome fish and meat section you can browse the fly-ridden stalls for bush meat (antelope, grasscutter), smoked and fresh fish, giant snails and glistening

War with the British

The Asante empire had reached its apogee by 1800, when **Osei Bonsu** was enstooled. The borders of the country now extended well beyond the present-day borders of Ghana, and Kumasi was a capital with a population of 700,000. In the vast market in the heart of town, trade was so healthy that the king's servants periodically sifted the sand to collect loose gold dust. Despite the prosperity, **rebellion** was simmering among Asante refugees who took shelter in the Fante confederation of the coast. In 1806, Osei Bonsu launched a full-scale attack against the Fante and invaded their lands. The attack marked the beginning of the last phase of the great conquests.

The coastal **Fante** had traditionally traded directly with the British, and Osei Bonsu's invasion thus led to direct conflict between the British and the Asante. In 1824, on the death of Osei Bonsu, the British were anxious to squash this main obstacle to the control of Gold Coast trade. Hostilities, which were to simmer throughout the nineteenth century, erupted in the **First Anglo–Asante War**. War broke out again in 1826 when the Asante were heavily defeated and Britain assumed the role of "Protector" along the coast and for up to three days' march inland. A third war, in 1863, was inconclusive, though Asante history relates it as a victory, with a strong force from Kumasi sweeping south over the Pra river and holding the British back for a few years. After some preparation, the British marched on Kumasi in the **Fourth Anglo–Asante War** (1874), but found the palace empty since the Asantehene and his retinue had fled to the forest. The British troops took whatever treasure they could find in the palace (most of which was later auctioned in London) and then blew it up. The rest of the city was razed to the ground. The Asante nation never recovered.

Downfall

By the end of the nineteenth century, the British, fearful of French and German aims in the aftermath of the Berlin conference over the partitioning of Africa, were close to controlling the Asante country as part of their Gold Coast colony. When the young Asantehene, **Agyeman Prempeh**, challenged the British, rejecting their protection and aiming to reconsolidate his kingdom, the British sought to humiliate and demoralize the Asante by publicly arresting him, and exiling him to the Seychelles. In 1900 the demand of the new colonial governor, Sir Frederick Hodgson, to be given the **Golden Stool** to sit on, provoked a military uprising from the Asante. (Royal court members had made a fake golden stool and concealed the real one, which was only discovered by accident much later, in the 1920s.) The queen mother, **Yaa Asantewaa**, led a siege of British officials holed up in Kumasi and Asante troops inflicted heavy losses on British units in the bush. But these Asante military successes were short-lived: British Maxim machine guns finally subdued the Asante army at the **Battle of Aboaso**, northwest of Kumasi, in 1902, and the formal annexation of the Asante nation was declared. The rest of the Asante royal family were arrested and sent to join Prempeh in exile.

mounds of groundnut paste (peanut butter). Meanwhile, along the railway line, the fetish stalls offer monkey skulls, crocodile heads, dried lizards, skins and pelts, while away from the market in the north of the city is a separate, vast district called Magazine which is entirely devoted to vehicle spare parts.

This is probably the best place in Ghana to buy **kente cloth** and it's worth paying a child to take you to the row of stalls where it's actually stored – a dedicated lane in the northwest of the market, near Kejetia lorry park – as they're easily missed otherwise. Prices are high and depend on whether you're buying single- or more expensive double-weave *kente*. To add a further complication, there's *kente* woven from imported rayon and real silk. For less than a cedi you can sometimes buy just a small piece, or even a souvenir strip.

Prempeh II Jubilee Museum and the National Cultural Centre

West of the zoo, in the grounds of the **Ghana National Cultural Centre**, the small **Prempeh II Jubilee Museum** (Tues–Sun 9am–5pm; GH¢2) holds a rich collection of Asante artefacts. They're housed in a reproduction of a traditional Asante regalia house, few examples of which remain since the nineteenth-century wars with the British. Such buildings served both as palaces and **shrines** – note the characteristic mural decorations on the lower walls. The designs, like those found on the **adinkra cloth** for which the region is famous, symbolize proverbs commenting on Akan moral and social values.

Among the many historical articles inside the museum is the **silver-plated stool** that the Denkyira chief Nana Ntim Gyakar was supposedly sitting on when captured in a surprise attack by the Asante in 1699. This victory marked the start of the expansion of the Asante empire and the stool, with its intricate carving and design, became an important symbol of liberation and power. Also on display is the fake **golden stool**, designed in the nineteenth century to deceive the British, who demanded that the most sacred of all Asante symbols be handed over to them. The real one remains guarded in the Asantehene's palace east of the central market, and is only brought out for special occasions. Note, too, a **treasure bag** on display that was presented to the Agona king by the fetish priest Okomfo Anokye. No one knows what the leather sack contains, for according to tradition to open it would bring about the downfall of the Asante nation. Other articles include examples of traditional dress, jewellery, furniture and musical instruments.

In addition to the museum, the grounds of the cultural centre contain a model Asante village, a cocoa farm, a palm-wine "factory", performance facilities for music and dance, and a **crafts centre** where you can see how **kente** and **adinkra fabrics**, traditional sandals, brass weights and pottery are produced. Prices are fixed and seem fair. Don't miss the centre's small **library** with numerous works dedicated to Asante civilization.

The Okomfo Anokye sword

Just up the hill from the National Cultural Centre, the **Okomfo Anokye Teaching Hospital** contains another sacred Asante symbol in its grounds (Mon–Sat 9am–5pm, Sun 11am–2pm; GH¢1). The symbol in question is the Okomfo Anokye **sword** that Osei Tutu's fetish priest planted on the spot shortly after choosing Kumasi as the Asante capital in around 1700. According to the legend, the day this sword is pulled from the ground, the Asante nation will collapse. The deteriorating state of the heavy metal blade seems an ominous portent, but locals swear that bulldozers have tried and failed to budge it (they don't explain why). At the hospital's main entrance take the small door in the wall on the right-hand side – in the courtyard behind you'll spot the building housing the sword by the *adinkra* symbols on its walls.

Fort Kumasi and the Armed Forces Museum

West of the central market, the collections of the **Armed Forces Museum** in Fort Kumasi (Tues–Sat 8am–5pm; GH¢1) have a heavy emphasis on modern **weaponry** captured by Ghanaian troops in World War II's East Africa and Asia campaigns. Far more interesting, but less extensive, are the exhibits documenting the **Anglo–Asante wars**, with period photographs and mementos.

Fort Kumasi itself – a bright red British-built edifice dating from around 1900 – is an intriguing structure where, as part of the obligatory guided tour, you'll be locked in a dark dungeon, to experience briefly the manner in which the British dealt with rabble-rousers. Those who went in rarely came out alive, and a few seconds is plenty to impart a sense of the terror the condemned must have felt.

The Manhyia Palace Museum

The **palace** of the present Asantehene, **Otumfuo Nana Osei Tutu II**, a direct descendant of Osei Tutu, the founder of the Asante empire, is glaringly modern, and security will see you off before you get close enough for a proper look. Just behind is the former palace, opened as a **museum** in 1995 (daily 9am–noon & 1–5pm; GH¢2). There are obligatory guided tours (45min) with no fixed fee but a "dash" is gratefully received. The former palace was built by the British in 1925 to serve as the residence of Nana Prempeh I when he returned from exile. It was then home to two subsequent kings until the late Otumfuo Opoku Ware II moved to his new palace next door in 1972. The tour of the former royal home gives insights into the curiously colonial lifestyle of the Asantehene, typified by his desk, gramophone, coffee table and dresser. Even more eerie are the life-sized effigies made at Madame Tussauds, London, of the kings and their queen mothers.

Adae festivals

Roughly every six weeks and usually on a Sunday, the Asantehene receives visitors, and particularly chiefs to pay homage, in an event called **Adae**. Foreign tourists and expats are welcome to join the crowd – a recommended experience to coincide with if you can. It's a spectacular event, with tumultuous drumming and singing and lots of dancing, everyone in their finest *kente* cloth, and the chiefs shaded by umbrellas carried by burly retainers. Check when the next Adae takes place with the tourist office in the National Cultural Centre – it's based on the Akan calendar of nine 42-day months (with one month omitted every three years to synchronize with the Gregorian calendar). Assuming the Asantehene is in residence and nothing clashes, the Adae normally happens on a Sunday morning, and you can arrive at any time – just join in the throng and look around, no one minds.

Eating and drinking

Kumasi is a fine place for **street food**, which you'll find throughout town, notably in the motor parks and markets where numerous **chop bars** serve rice dishes, *fufu* or plantains with sauce. At breakfast time, streetside coffee-men whip up two-egg omelettes with Nescafé and sweet Ghana bread.

As for **drinking**, besides the bars at some of the **restaurants** below, there are numerous other drinking spots. Popular places include the lively open-air *Timber Gardens*, 6km south of town, and the slick *Moves Pub*, near *Chopsticks*, for the smarter Kumasi set. *BB Spot*, across from Asafo market, serves cheap beer and is popular at the weekends.

Restaurants

Chopsticks Harper Rd, near the golf club ☎051/34176. Chinese restaurant which also happens to do excellent pizzas. Relatively high prices reflect its popularity.

City View Restaurant 3rd floor of Wesley House on Asomfo Rd ☎051/829982/3. Doesn't look like much from the outside but has a calm, elegant dining room with Chinese and Ghanaian dishes (around GH¢4.50) served in the smart indoor restaurant or out on the balcony overlooking the town.

Disap Eden Fast Food just off Bank Rd. Inexpensive, cosy restaurant serving mainly Ghanaian dishes, plus burgers and chicken.

The Dish 6th St, off Hudson Rd ☎051/30355. Subdued place serving mainly Chinese dishes, and some Ghanaian fare, for around GH¢2.50 a dish. The adjoining bar is a lively spot and has pool tables.

🏃 **Jofel Catering Services** Airport Rd, Asokwa, 6km from the centre ☎051/21213 (Mon–Fri 8am–10pm, Sat & Sun 8am–midnight). Reliable establishment serving a variety of Ghanaian, Chinese and European dishes. There's also an attractive bar outside, underneath the trees, and a 1st-floor terrace bar. The food's fine, but it can take an age to arrive.

Kentish Kitchen at the National Cultural Centre (closed eves). Tasty, moderately priced Ghanaian dishes.

🏃 **Moti Mahal** Up a dirt track off the southern bypass, Nhyiaeso district ☎051/29698. Upmarket Indian restaurant (GH¢6–9 for a main), with an excellent selection of vegetarian dishes and sublime, fresh Indian food. There's a good wine selection and excellent, friendly service. One of the best Indian restaurants in the country.

Queen's Gate opposite the Alliance Française. Serves up good *jollof* rice and groundnut soup in a nice outdoor patio setting. There's a buffet every Sun.

Quick Bite Fast Food Prempeh II Rd, Adum. Small, low-key restaurant in the heart of town, with healthy portions from a limited menu, including great chicken and chips. Popular with locals and often full at lunchtime.

Royal Garden Chinese at the *Royal Park Hotel* ☎051/39353. Arguably the best Chinese in Kumasi, with the opportunity to sample frog's legs. More refined, though no more expensive, than *Chopsticks*.

🏃 **Vic Baboo's Café** corner of Bank Rd and Prempeh II Rd, Adum ☎051/27657. Vast menu of tasty pizzas at around GH¢5 (including banana and chocolate), Indian dishes (GH¢5–6),

and burgers. There's also fresh-brewed coffee, milkshakes and a huge cocktail menu featuring more than 150 recipes, including avocado daiquiri and melon halves soaked in vodka, all in a/c comfort. Extremely popular with travellers.

Vienna City Pub Old Bekwai Rd ☎051/24072. Sharing premises with *Rose's Guest House*, the bar here is somewhat seedy, but there's also a pleasant restaurant serving excellent European meals for around GH¢5.

Nightlife and entertainment

Keep your eyes and ears open for live music in Kumasi; shows take place irregularly at the main hotels. The National Cultural Centre hosts programmes of music, dance, poetry and drama, as well as occasional live concerts – often of highlife – and less recreational choral evenings with church choirs. Also watch out for live jazz at the weekends at the *Royal Basin* and *Cozy Lodge*.

Good places in the evening include *Jofel Catering Services* for its outdoor setting and regular live music and *Vic Baboo's Café* for a drink in the company of backpackers and volunteers. Among the **clubs**, *Tsar* near Kejetia Circle has a cocktail bar and pool tables, and plays hip-life and R&B. Other popular nightspots include *Kiravi*, a spacious disco in Nhyiaeso district, and *Foxtrap* in Bompata, which has pool tables, a big screen and dancing.

On Sunday afternoons it's worth checking if there's a **football match** at the Sports Stadium; tickets are very inexpensive. The home team, Asante Kotoko (meaning porcupine, the Asante symbol), is one of the county's best.

Around Kumasi

In the rainforest hills around Kumasi, numerous villages offer a less urbanized glimpse of Asante lifestyles. Many of these settlements – **Bonwire** to the northeast, and **Pankronu**, **Ahwiaa** and **Ntonso** along the road to Mampong – are known for the **traditional crafts** industries for which the entire region is famous, and best treated as day-trips. You may want to spend a night in the resthouse at the **Boabeng-Fiema Monkey Sanctuary**, 100km or so to the north of Kumasi. **Lake Bosumtwe**, too, offers a variety of accommodation and makes a good retreat. If you have your own transport, even a bicycle, **the road past Mampong** to the shore of Lake Volta – once the main route through Ghana, but now very much a back road – offers some exciting travel.

Kumasi is also the obvious base for visiting the Bia, Bui and Digya **national parks**. **Bia**, west of Kumasi on the border of Côte d'Ivoire, is primarily a primate reserve, containing large areas of forest. Elephants are certainly here, and so too is said to be a small population of the large and rare forest antelope, the bongo. There are trails and one or two camps (❶–❷) but conditions are basic: check with the Wildlife Department in Accra (⌖021/664654) for the latest on the infrastructure and to make bookings. From Kumasi, it's a day-long *tro-tro* ride to the park headquarters at New Debiso, via Bibiani.

Bui, spanning the Black Volta River and adjacent to the Ivoirian border, is notable for its large population of hippos. To get there, head to **Wenchi**, 35km northwest of Kumasi, from where a daily *tro-tro* makes for the village of Bui, passing the ranger base. There's a rudimentary cabin (❶) but willing rangers to organize hippo walks and river trips.

Digya National Park, east of Kumasi and bordering Lake Volta, is one of the country's largest parks, with elephants, antelopes and hippos, though there are no facilities for travellers, so be prepared to camp totally self-sufficiently if you visit the area.

Owabi Wildlife Sanctuary

An easier, and immediately rewarding destination, is the small **OWABI WILDLIFE SANCTUARY** (entrance and obligatory guide GH¢5), a mere 4km across, surrounding a lake, and just twenty minutes northwest of the city off the Sunyani road. More than 160 birds have been identified at Owabi, which is Ghana's only inland protected Ramsar Convention–designated wetlands site. You're bound to see at least mona monkeys here, too, if not anything more unusual.

Obuasi

Another straightforward excursion is to the gold mines at **OBUASI**, 50km southwest of Kumasi, a relatively easy trip (*tro-tros* head there from Kejetia motor park). The Obuasi district is an interesting – though hardly a scenic – place to visit: the whole area is scarred into a lunar landscape by the open mining pits. The Ashanti Goldfields Company has established a visitors' centre to organize underground and surface tours (GH¢15; book in advance on ⌖0582/404309). If you want to stay over, there are several hotels here; the most comfortable is *Miners Lodge* (⌖0582/40550 ⓦwww .coconutgrovehotels.com.gh ❺), and they also arrange mine tours.

Along the Accra road

The **Nana Yaa Asantewaa Museum** in **EJISU**, twenty-five minutes' drive from Kumasi, was opened in 2000 and burned to the ground in an accidental blaze in 2004. UNESCO has promised to fund the reconstruction of this dedication to the "heroine of Asante resistance", the queen mother who was born here and who led the revolt against the British in 1900, but as of late 2007, there had been no progress. The Kumasi tourist office will know if it's reopened. The original museum was a beautiful reminder of traditional architecture, made of striking orange clay and adorned with huge black wooden *adinkra* symbols. To get to Ejisu from Kumasi, you can charter a taxi for about GH¢3 or take a *tro-tro* from Asafo motor park.

Just a couple of kilometres further on towards Accra in **BESEASE** is the **Besease Shrine** (Tues–Sun 8am–5pm; GH¢1), a fine example of Asante heritage, built in 1850, used by Yaa Asantewaa herself, and renovated with help, once again, from UNESCO. To get here, take the last turning on your right before the speed bumps which signal that you're leaving Besease.

The **BOBIRI RESERVE** (GH¢1) lies about another 12km along the Accra road, an idyllic tract of forest that is home to 350 species of butterfly. With a small arboretum to visit and a charming guesthouse (❶) as well, it makes an ideal retreat if you're prepared to make the effort to get here. From Kumasi, take a *tro-tro* from Asafo lorry park heading for **Konongo** and alight at Kubease. Transport can drop you at the large archway marked "Akwaaba" – head through it and remain on the path for at least a kilometre, then take the branch to your right. Continue straight on for another two kilometres and you'll arrive at the guesthouse. Alternatively, charter a taxi direct from Kumasi (GH¢7) or take a *tro-tro* to Ejisu and charter a taxi from there.

Lake Bosumtwe

Some 35km south of Kumasi, **LAKE BOSUMTWE** is the largest natural lake in Ghana, filling a crater 8km in diameter. Surrounded by steep hills rising nearly 400m above sea level, the lake lies in the midst of lush greenery, a superbly relaxing area to unwind. Traditional boats are still used to fish the lake, propelled by fishermen with calabashes cupped in their hands to serve as paddles. Formerly, the spirit of the lake forbade other forms of transport but, as one villager commented, "People used to be scared, but we don't believe in that nowadays" – clearly not, with expats and rich kids from Kumasi coming to water-ski and motorboats buzzing over the lake. Government-run one-hour boat trips cost a pricey GH¢25, or you may be able to find some locals to take you out on a motorboat for less. Swimming is fine – the waters are free of bilharzia.

You can get here from Kumasi by taking a Benz **bus** or **tro-tro** from the Asafo lorry park to the town of **KUNTANASE** (a half-hour drive that costs almost nothing); from there you can either catch another vehicle (ask for the "Abono/Lake" car, though expect a long wait) or walk the remaining 5km to the village of **Abono** on the lakeshore. There are a few places to **stay** in the vicinity. In Kuntanase, *Lake Bosumtwe Tourist Lodge* (Ⓔbosomtwilake@yahoo.com ❶) is set in quiet, attractive grounds. Down on the lake shore, *Lake Bosumtwe Paradise Resort* is the upmarket choice, set in a fine location, with twenty stylish s/c, a/c rooms, satellite TV and fridge (☎051/20164 Ⓔfrontdesk @lakebosomtweresort.com ❺) and very helpful and friendly staff. ⚡ *Lake Point Guesthouse* (☎243/452922 Ⓦwww.ghana-hotel.com ❷–❸) has bright, breezy chalets set amongst landscaped tropical gardens, good food (including excellent Austrian coffee and cakes) and a range of spa treatments on offer. *Rainbow Garden Village Guesthouse* (☎243/230288 Ⓦwww.rainbowgardenvillage.com; double rooms ❷, dorm beds GH¢6, camping GH¢3) is a budget lodge, popular with backpackers. Spruce dorms and doubles are housed in stone huts dotted around a sloping hill with views down to the lake. There's a resident tour company organizing boat trips, walks and cultural tours.

Bonwire and Adanwomase

A frequent target for tourists, **BONWIRE** is a traditional Asante village. It's also the principal home of **kente cloth**, which dates back to the early days of the Asante empire and still is the usual dress of Asante people on special occasions. Along the

---

Kente cloth

The dazzling **patterns** of *kente* are intended to enhance their owners' status as kings, queens and nobles. Court designs took the name of the clan or individuals by which they were commissioned: a common pattern known as *mamponhema*, for example, derives its name from the Queen of Mampong, while *asasia* designates a pattern and type of cloth worn only by the Asantehene.

Like most African cloth, *kente* is woven in narrow strips, later sewn together. The highest-quality pieces are made entirely of silk threads. In former times these were unavailable to the Asante, so to satisfy the demands of royalty, craftsmen unravelled imported silk fabric and rewove the threads into *kente* patterns. In addition to the name denoting their owner, the most valuable cloths bore another name – *adweneasa* – a technical term indicating that the already complicated pattern contained an additional inlaid design. The word means "my skill is exhausted", indicating that the weaver had made his supreme effort.

streets in town you can still see weavers working hand-operated looms to turn out the long strips of intricately patterned material. Because of its importance and its complex design, *kente* remains very expensive – especially here.

Just northwest of Bonwire, the smaller centre of **ADANWOMASE** is recommended if you find Bonwire and other *kente*-weaving centres too hustly: here they've deliberately gone out of their way to lay off the high-pressure sales techniques for a "hassle-free cultural tourism experience" and to ensure that revenues from tourism are shared as equitably as possible. The village runs a fascinating tour that takes in the whole process of *kente*-weaving, and you can have a go yourself – not that easy. Of course sales are important, but the approach remains low-key and prices seem fair. Simple homestays are also possible (●).

Bonwire is just over 20km northeast of Kumasi, while Adanwomase lies between Bonwire and Ntonso (on the Mampong road). **Taxis** go to Bonwire and Adanwomase regularly from Kumasi's Kejetia motor park.

Boabeng-Fiema Monkey Sanctuary

An increasingly popular target, about 100km north of Kumasi, the **Boabeng-Fiema Monkey Sanctuary** (entrance GH₵4) is a remarkably successful experiment in community conservation. The villagers of Boabeng and Fiema have a traditional veneration for the large numbers of monkeys living in the small patch of forest nearby. This sacred grove, just 4.5 square kilometres in size, complete with a monkey cemetery, has been set aside under their guardianship. The forest has one of the highest densities of monkeys of any forest in West Africa, the inhabitants including Lowe's mona monkey and the strikingly beautiful black-and-white colobus; they're best seen in the early morning or late afternoon and you need be accompanied by a guide only on your first walk.

You can reach Boabeng by taking a bush taxi from Kumasi to **TECHIMAN**, a shared taxi from there to **NKORANSA**, and finally another shared taxi from Nkoransa for the remaining 12km to **BOABENG**. There are also *tro-tros* from the race-course lorry park near Kejetia Circle in Kumasi (it's the same station as for Techiman taxis) direct to Nkoransa. The villagers run the friendly but basic **guesthouse** at the sanctuary itself, and they can prepare simple meals (●).

The Mampong road

Within a short distance of Kumasi, the small towns along the Mampong road have developed reputations for artwork and handicrafts; it's feasible to charter a taxi and visit all three within the same day, though you may find the expectation to buy and the general level of hassle spoils the experience. The first you'll come to is **PANKRONU**, just 5km from Kumasi, a village known for its **pottery**, which is traditionally produced by the women; they'll do a demonstration for a small donation.

The next stop along the road is the town of **AHWIAA**, which specializes in decoratively carved wooden tables, statues and games, but the **carved stools** you'll see being sculpted stand out among the wares. Commonly, the first gift a father would give to his child was a stool, which his soul was believed to occupy until death. To this day, stools still represent one of the most important elements of a chief's regalia and symbolize his office. When he dies, a good chief's stool is blackened with ash and smeared with the yolk of an egg, and this **black stool** is preserved in a special house in memory of the late owner. The stools carved in Ahwiaa today are mostly made with an eye for tourism – note the lacquers and shoe-polish dyes that give them a tawdry finish – though they do contain many intricate traditional symbols. They're expensive, reflecting high tourist demand and the fact that they take an age to make. It's worth avoiding the more expensive hardwoods – not just for the sake of the forests, but because softer wood is lighter, cheaper and more authentic.

Further down the Mampong road, **NTONSO** is the famed home of **adinkra cloth**. Not quite as prestigious as *kente*, it's made of cotton material – often a deep red colour

– covered with black patterns which are produced with stamps carved from bits of calabash and dipped in a tree-bark dye. Some stamps have geometric patterns, others are stylized representations of plants or animals, but most use symbols reflecting an Asante saying. A cloth incorporating all such symbols in its pattern was known as the **adinkrahene** and was reserved for the Asante king; equally a ruler may have worn a cloth marked by a single symbol that reflected a specific message he wanted to convey to the people. These cloths are still worn by the Asante today, notably at funerals.

Mampong and northeast to Lake Volta

MAMPONG is surprisingly large and busy, perched on the lip of the impressive **Mampong escarpment**. A good place to stay is the *Video City Hotel*, a welcoming establishment in the town centre with s/c rooms (❷). North of Mampong, the road north curls down through formidable forest to the deep valley of the Afram River and then steeply, in a series of hairpins, up the other side to **EJURA**. The scenic beauty of this road is matched by the pleasure of being relatively off the beaten track. **ATEBUBU**, the next settlement, is a small, smoky town at the savannah's edge. Beyond, there's only the villages of **PRANG** – which, with a resurfaced road, no longer has an appropriate name – and then **YEJI**, on the hot, bleak shore of **Lake Volta**, where small boats irregularly make the crossing to **MAKONGO**, 150km short of Tamale.

10.4

The southeast: Akosombo, Ho and Hohoe

Formerly part of German Togoland, **southeastern Ghana** has periodically been a bone of contention between the governments of Ghana and Togo and those who favour the reunification of the **Ewe** people, who live here and in Togo. Traditionally engaged in agriculture and fishing, the Ewe primarily grow maize and yams. The administrative capital of the region is **Ho**, a large town in the middle of an agricultural area rich with cocoa plantations. The mountains add to the beauty of the fertile landscape, but the outstanding geographical feature of these parts is artificial – the vast body of **Lake Volta**, created when the dam and hydroelectric plant were built at **Akosombo** in the mid-1960s.

This region provides an interesting alternative **route to northern Ghana**, either through the remote eastern border region via **Hohoe** or straight across the great lake to **Yeji** by ferry. The forest and hills – Ghana's highest – are rapidly becoming a major draw for travellers, and transport and facilities are steadily improving, at least as far as Hohoe.

Akosombo

Nkrumah's pet hydroelectric project – the giant **Akosombo Dam** – once provided electricity for the greater part of Ghana, with some left over for export to neighbouring countries, but Ghana's economy has grown beyond its capacity. Indeed, in recent years the diminishing level of **Lake Volta** – the largest artificial lake in the world – has prompted power rationing throughout the country. Amid the landscape of hills and water, the general interest of the once insignificant village of **Akosombo** lies more in the **scenic beauty** than in the traditional lifestyle of the employees here, who come from all over Ghana.

Note that both the Akosombo Dam and the Atimpoku Bridge are considered strategic installations and it's therefore technically illegal to photograph them. But with tours available of the site, so many people have done so that few officials seem concerned any more.

Atimpoku district

Five kilometres south of Akosombo on the main Accra road, the bustling district of **Atimpoku** runs parallel to the river, in the shadow of the large bridge spanning the Volta River. Taxis run regularly from here to the lower part of Akosombo town proper. Atimpoku has most of the **cheap accommodation** in the area. Right by the noisy central roundabout, the *Adomi* offers rather bare rooms with decent toilets and showers (❸), but it doesn't compete with the *Benkum*, 300m south of the roundabout, which looks very basic from the outside, but has good-value, comfortable rooms at the back (❷), and certainly not, just north of the roundabout, with the ⚜ *Aylos Bay Garden Lodge* (☎0251/20901 ⓦwww .aylosbay.com ❹) with its beautiful setting among the palm trees, five comfortable, stylish chalets overlooking the water and good food – Sunday lunch at GH¢5 is a steal.

THE VOLTA

Bimbilla
River Oti
N
TOGO
Nkwanta
Borae No 2
Dambai
Yeji
Kete Krachi
Badoudjindji
Badou
Apesokubi
Atakpamé
Jasikan
Lake Volta
Wli
Hohoe
Mt Afadjato
Wegbe
Liate
Wote
Golodkuati
Kpandu
Kpalimé
Tokor
Biakpa
Amedzofe
Tafi Atome
Dodi Is.
Ho
Kpetoe
Mount Adaklu
Akosombo
Aburi, Shai Hills
Accra
Aflao
0   50 km

Crossing Lake Volta

Transport on Lake Volta has been erratic and timetables unreliable for years, a fact which deters many travellers, but the trip is a highly enjoyable one. If you're setting out from Akosombo, there'll usually be some kind of vessel in a day or two.

The official **ferry** is the *Yapei Queen*, which plies between **Akosombo** and **Yeji** once a week. Departures from Akosombo have in recent years been Monday afternoons (around 4pm), stopping at **Kete Krachi** around twelve hours later before finally arriving in Yeji at around 6pm on Tuesday; meals are available on board. Ferries return from Yeji to Akosombo on Wednesday at 4am, again calling in at Kete Krachi before arriving at noon on Thursday. If you're after first-class tickets (about GH¢10), make sure you book well in advance as there are only three cabins available. Both second class (GH¢4.50) and third class (GH¢3) provide a limited number of benches on which to spend the journey. Midweek, the vessel is supposed to run a shuttle between Kete Krachi and **Kpandu**, though this often doesn't operate. Note that the ferry dock in Kete Krachi is a ten- to fifteen-minute walk from the centre of this isolated town: there is nothing at the dock itself by way of services or food. If you must spend a night or two in Kete Krachi awaiting the ferry, you can stay at the well-hidden *Administration Guesthouse* overlooking the lake (①), but you'll need to find a vehicle to take you there.

When the passenger ferry isn't running, **cargo barges** – the *Volta Queen* and *Buipe Queen* – also make the trip, but rarely run on fixed schedules. They sometimes go as far upriver as **Buipe**, on the course of the Black Volta, usually stopping en route at **Kpandu**, Kete Krachi and Yeji. The voyage to Buipe takes between one and two days (and nights) and you sleep on the deck. You should stock up on **food** for the trip: water and cooking facilities are provided.

At weekends and bank holidays, the leisure cruiser *Dodi Princess* goes out to **Dodi Island** (see "Akosombo town" for details).

For more details of shipping services, enquire at the Volta Lake Transport Company at Akosombo port (☎0251/20686 ✉akoport@ghana.com) or in Accra (☎021/665300).

Street food abounds in Atimpoku: oyster kebabs and smoked shrimp to go with *abolo*, the slightly sugary, but not unpleasant, dumpling commonly eaten in the region. For more formal meals, try *Aylos Bay* for excellent European dishes.

Akosombo town

Shared taxis and *tro-tros* run between Atimpoku and **AKOSOMBO** during daylight hours. Akosombo consists of two communities, both of which emerged in the 1960s when workers flooded here to fill demand for labour. The first settlement perches on a hillside, commanding a magnificent view of Lake Volta and the mountains around. The spot was too scenic for developers to resist putting in luxurious expat and executive villas, a yacht club and the swish *Volta Hotel* (☎0251/20731 or 662639 ⓦwww.voltahotel.net ❸), with a bird's-eye view of the lake and dam, modern, comfortable a/c rooms, tennis courts, swimming pool and golf facilities. At least have a drink in the terrace **restaurant** overlooking the lake – the views are terrific. The second community, in the valley below, is a neighbourhood for employees of the Volta Power Authority. There's a **lorry station** here (though note that it's easier to get onward transport from Atimpoku), a Ghana Commercial Bank and several bars. On a lane behind the lorry station, the *Zito Guesthouse* (☎0251/20474 ❷) is pleasant and quiet and serves decent food.

To visit the **dam** itself, contact the Visitors' Reception Centre (☎0251/20550) by the Ghana Commercial Bank to book one of the hourly **tours** (Mon–Sun 9am–3pm; GH¢2). For a fun, if touristy take on Lake Volta, you can take a noisy pleasure **cruise** on the *Dodi Princess* (no connection) out to the attractive Dodi Island on the lake (every Sat, Sun and public holidays at 10.30am, returning at 4pm; GH¢20). There's a plunge pool for children and sometimes live music on board – it can be a bit of a non-stop party, depending on the other passengers.

Ho and around

Despite its prestigious designation as the Volta Region's capital, **HO**, 50km northeast of Akosombo, remains a quiet, rural community, and is an excellent base for exploring the Volta region. Set in a green valley dominated by **Mount Adaklu**, the town is graced with a tidy tracing of narrow paved roads winding through the trees, and the interesting **Volta Regional Museum** (daily 8am–5pm; GH¢1) – some surprise in a rather remote corner like this. Well presented and little frequented, the museum is worth a visit to see exhibits of ceremonial objects (Akan

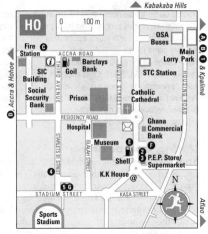

▲ Kabakaba Hills

ACCOMMODATION		RESTAURANTS, BARS & CLUBS	
Alinda Guesthouse	G		
Chances	D	Ka Nea Wape	2
Dorllah Guest House	C	Let Them Say Spot	5
Fiave Lodge	B	Phil's	1
Freedom	A	Pleasure Garden	4
Malisel	E	The White House	3
Tarso	F		

"linguist" or "spokesman" **staffs** and **swords**), traditional **musical instruments**, and carved **stools** from various regions. **Colonial relics** complement the ethnic displays, including some dating to the district's German Togoland period.

Practicalities

The road leading up from the south, from Aflao, on the coastal border with Togo, constitutes the main street in town. It heads from the Shell garage at the south end of Ho, past the Ghana Commercial Bank and up to the **STC station**, from where there's an early-morning bus to Accra. Shared taxis and *tro-tros* to a variety of destinations, including Accra, Hohoe and Amedzofe, leave from the **lorry park** in the northeast of town. Opposite here is a station used by OSA buses to Kumasi and the capital. There's a branch of Barclays Bank along the Accra road, and a **post office** near the large roundabout on the Aflao road.

The **Ghana Tourist Board** is on the third floor of the SIC Building, on the Accra road (Mon–Fri 8am–5pm; ☎091/26560 ✉gtb@africaonline.com.gh), and offers helpful information for the entire Volta region. For **Internet** access, try Link Sat Café in KK House, on the roundabout south of the *White House* restaurant at GH¢0.80/hr; alternatively, the post office offers a few terminals.

Accommodation

Ho has a good choice of inexpensive **accommodation**, and one hotel to tempt you upmarket.

Alinda Guesthouse off Starlets 91 St. Basic inexpensive accommodation, with a pleasant courtyard, but a bit run down. ❶

Chances 4km out on the Accra Rd ☎091/28344 ☏27083 ✉chanceshotel @hotmail.com. Ho's most upmarket hotel, with

stylish chalets as well as newer rooms in two 3-storey blocks. Set in lovely landscaped gardens with the Kabakaba hills as a backdrop, the hotel also has a small pool, Internet facilities and a good restaurant. ❺

Dorllah Guest House Across from the SIC Building ☎091/26141. Homely budget option (the name is pronounced "dollar") with rooms and facilities that feel well-cared-for. ❶

Fiave Lodge off the Kpalimé Rd, 800m from the lorry park ☎091/26412. Clean and quiet, an intimate retreat with friendly management. ❶

Freedom on the Kpalimé Rd ☎091/28151 ⓦwww.freedomhotel-gh.com. Well-established hotel with good facilities, though the restaurant is merely average. Something of a social focus, with regular music and comedy nights, so often noisy, but clean and well located. ❹

Malisel next to the stadium ☎091/26161 or 020/8969622. Four-room building with simple singles and doubles, and friendly management. ❷

Tarso up the main street from the Ghana Commercial Bank ☎091/26732. Pleasant place with s/c rooms. ❶

Eating and drinking

Street food is readily available near the main lorry park: a traditional Ewe dish is cat, often advertised rather graphically. The *White House* restaurant attracts a lot of travellers, serving decent foreign and local dishes with cheap beer. *Ka Nea Wape* bar next door does similar fare. *Let Them Say Spot* is a good option for cheap and tasty food and a convivial atmosphere that often lasts late into the night. On the Kpalimé road, the 24-hour *Phil's* prepares generous portions of mainly Ghanaian food. For drinking, the *Pleasure Garden*, on Starlets 91 Street, is a popular **bar** in an attractive setting and you can get a huge plate of *fufu* and soup for GH¢1.50.

Around Ho

About 15km southwest of Ho at **ABUTIA KLOE**, the **Kalakpa Resource Reserve** has an abundance of birdlife, monkeys and antelope. The Wildlife Office in Abutia Kloe will point you in the direction of the reserve, where the rangers will – for a dash – give you a tour of the park.

Some 12km due south of Ho, you'll find the village of **HELEKPE** at the foot of **Mount Adaklu** – it's a challenging two- to three-hour guided hike to the summit (GH¢2). There's a range of simple accommodation: a room in the guesthouse (GH¢2), a homestay in the village, or you could camp if you've got the gear.

For an isolated retreat on the banks of Lake Volta, head out to 🦋 *Xofa Eco-village*, near **ASIKUMA**, southwest of Ho. The staff can arrange a range of activities including canoe trips on the lake, bird-watching and nature hikes, and drumming and dance workshops. Accommodation is in thatched, stone huts with camp beds and mosquito nets (☎021/514989 ⓦwww.xofa.org ❷), or you can camp for GH¢5 per person, and the staff can arrange activities including trips on the lake. To reach the village, take a *tro-tro* to Asikuma Junction, and then a taxi to Dodi Asantekrom, from where you can walk or rent a canoe to take you the last stretch to the village.

North of Ho

In addition to the verdant slopes of some of Ghana's highest hills, the road **north** towards Hohoe passes traditional Ewe cemeteries shaded by groves of white, pink and yellow frangipani. However, opportunities to explore off the main road are limited if you don't have your own transport.

Relatively easy to get to by public transport from Ho (although virtually impossible from Hohoe) is the village of **AMEDZOFE**, 30km north of Ho and just east of the road at the base of **Mount Gemi**. At the community-run **visitors' centre** (☎0931/22037) you pay the fee – GH¢2 for the village's namesake waterfall, GH¢1 for Mount Gemi – and are assigned a guide. A guide is very helpful when seeking out the **waterfall**, as it's difficult to find on your own and is accessed by a steep leaf-strewn path, but is much less so when walking the straightforward path up Mount Gemi. At the summit you'll find a tall iron cross erected as a transmitter by German missionaries in the 1930s, but more striking are the vistas stretching in every direction. From up here, the Volta stands out shimmering beyond the Biakpa hills.

In **BIAKPA**, the ⚡**Mountain Paradise Lodge** (℡024/4166226 or 020/8137086 ⓦwww.mountainparadise-biakpa.com; double rooms ② or camping GH¢5 per person per night), a former government resthouse, a couple of kilometers from Amedzofe, is a great little place up in the hills with wonderful views over the surrounding countryside. The rooms are basic but clean and there are great porches around the lodge from which to appreciate the surrounding countryside, a little library with books on loan and excellent **food and drink**, including cold Stars, fresh squeezed juice and coffee. Staff can arrange bikes (GH¢3), and abseiling and hiking – like Ghanaian canyoning – to a nearby waterfall (GH¢3 for a half-day).

From the main road, you could branch westward, 25km north of Ho, towards the **Monkey Sanctuary and Cultural Village** at **TAFI ATOME**, a town famous as a refuge for various species of **monkey**. Early in the morning, they romp unhindered through the streets and courtyards looking for scraps. Later in the day, they retreat to the surrounding bush and you'll have to rely on a guide to find them. With the help of US Peace Corps volunteers, the villagers set up a visitors' centre, from where you can arrange **guided tours** to see the monkeys in the jungle (GH¢5) and either a **homestay** with a local family (mosquito nets included, meals upon request; ②) or a room in the guesthouse (②). Evenings can be lively, with drumming, dancing and story-telling sessions.

Hohoe and around

A town of no sights of specific interest, **HOHOE** ("ho-hoy") is both restful and convenient as a base for treks to nearby waterfalls, or as a stopping point on the eastern route to the north. The main **motor park** is south of the centre on the Ho road. Vehicles leave here for points north (including Nkwanta and Bimbilla) as well as for **Ho** and **Accra**. Bush taxis also go direct to Kpalimé in **Togo**. There are two daily STC buses for **Accra** from the main intersection in town, near the post office.

Barclays Bank, a couple of minutes' walk from the centre on the road to Wli, changes both cash and traveller's cheques, and there's also a **forex bureau** near the post office. You can get **online** at Photocopy Internet Café just down the road from *Taste Lodge*. For **information**, check out ⓦwww.hohoetourism.com.

Hohoe has a reasonable choice of places to **stay**, reviewed below. For a sit-down **meal**, the hotel restaurants are your best bet – *Taste Lodge*, *Geduld* and the *Grand* all serve reliably good food at reasonable prices. For cheap eating, the area around the post office abounds with street stalls. Across the road from *Hotel de Mork*, *Kitcut* serves mainly Ghanaian food and has a pleasant seating area outside for **drinking**. An alternative place for a beer is the *Tanoa Gardens*, a small relaxed place with comfy chairs and a TV, off the main road near Ghana Commercial Bank.

Accommodation

Hotel De Mork 2km out on the main Accra road in Kpoeta ℡0935/22082. Clean rooms at this hotel make up for the concrete bunker of an exterior and the inconvenient location. Good value. ❶

Evergreen Lodge off the Jasikan road, past the *Matvin* ℡0935/22254. Clean rooms, with nice little touches like *kente* bedcovers, but lacks atmosphere. Deluxe rooms in a separate annexe are very spacious and better value, with large lounges. ❸

Geduld Near the *Pacific Guesthouse*, south of the centre, where lack of taxis means a hike to

the town centre ℡0935/2177. Good-value s/c rooms, some with TV and a/c, set in an attractive courtyard. ②

Grand on the main street opposite the Bank of Ghana ℡0935/22053. Bright rooms and a courtyard bar and restaurant serving good food. ❶

Matvin signposted off the Jasikan road, a 15min walk north from the post office ℡0935/22134. A range of accommodation is on offer here, from a/c chalets with fridge and TV to non-s/c rooms with fan. Though the pricier rooms don't offer great value and the whole place is in need of a lick of paint, it does have a reasonable restaurant and bar, and some fine views over the Danyi River. **①**

Pacific Guest House signposted off the Helu road beyond *Taste Lodge*, 600m south of the post office ☎0935/22146. Quiet and clean with a communal lounge/TV area. **①**

Taste Lodge Complex off a dirt track on the Helu road ☎0935/22023. Small, but very clean rooms with fridge, TV, a/c and private porch, in a relatively quiet courtyard setting. Excellent restaurant with reasonable prices. **②**

Wli Falls and on to Togo

The most obvious target for sightseeing around Hohoe are the **Wli Falls**, 20km to the east, in the **Agumatsa Wildlife Sanctuary**. Relatively frequent *tro-tros* from the Hohoe motor park head out to the village of **WLI** (pronounced "vlee"), nestling at the foot of the hills forming the Togolese border. You'll be shown to the Game & Wildlife Office to pay a GH¢7 fee for entry and be assigned a largely unnecessary guide. The hour-long path to the lower falls crosses and re-crosses a winding brook over eight sturdy log bridges. The cascade itself, set in a cool and sheltered combe where thousands of bats nest, plunges 30m into a pool just deep enough for swimming. With your own gear you can **camp** by the falls, where the tranquillity is disturbed only by kids shooting the bats with home-made flintlocks and locally manufactured shot. They'll gladly sell you their catch, should you be interested in sampling it, and even cook it up for you. If you're feeling fit, you can also undertake the **two-hour hike** to the top of the lower falls (there are upper falls which are barely visible from the base), for which a guide is essential (GH¢2). The walk up is extremely steep and at times a little dangerous, and thus only permitted in the dry season – bring plenty of water. If you don't want to camp, there are clean, good-value rooms available at the German-owned *Waterfall Lodge* near the Wildlife Office (☎0209/370448 ⓦwww.ghanacamping.com; double rooms **②** or tents **①**) or at the equally good, locally-owned *Water Heights Hotel* (☎0208/373163 **②**).

En route to **Togo**, Ghanaian border formalities are casually carried out at the eastern end of Wli. From there, you must walk the half-kilometre to **Yipa-Dafo** for the Togo crossing. Transport onwards from here heads either to Dzobégan or Kpalimé, both routes tracing the scenic curves of the Danyi plateau.

Liati Wote, Mount Afadjato and around

Southeast of Hohoe, the village of **LIATI WOTE** is near the base of Ghana's highest peak, **Mount Afadjato** (968m). *Tro-tros* head to the village from Fodome station in Hohoe, near the post office. On arrival, seek out the guesthouse (see below) where they can arrange guided tours to either the **Tagbo Falls** (GH¢2) or the summit (GH¢1) – or both (GH¢2.50). It's an easy one-hour walk, through dense bush full of bright flowers and butterflies, and plantations of cocoa and coffee. The falls appear without warning as they flow off an almost circular cliff formation covered with moss and ferns, into a pool beneath. Equally satisfying are the views from Afadjato, across the border to the Togolese hills; it's a manageable one-hour trek to the top. The **guesthouse** in Liati Wote, adjacent to the visitors' centre, has basic rooms with mosquito nets (**①**) or you can camp, and inexpensive food can be prepared on request; plus there's the possibility of a warm beer at *Stella's Inn*.

West and north of Hohoe

Around 10km west of Hohoe, off the Kpandu road, the "seven-stepped cascade" **Tsatsudo Falls** provide another opportunity for exploration. Stop at the village of **ALAVANYO ABEHENEASE** to visit the chief for permission (GH¢3) and pick up a guide.

Heading north, cultivation declines as you follow the **alternative route to northern Ghana** (the main route being from Kumasi). The best road along the east side of Lake Volta is the fast highway that skirts the lakeshore from Kpandu to Dambai, skirting the eastern shore of Lake Volta. At **DAMBAI** you can catch a fifteen-minute ferry or canoe across the lake (boats leave several times daily) or continue north over the flat, open landscapes that lead directly to Bimbilla. En route is the **Kyabobo National Park**, adjoining Togo's **Parc National de Fazao–Malfakassa** and home to several large mammal species, including leopard and elephant and possibly lion, but as yet barely developed.

The important transport crossroads of **BIMBILLA** provides a convenient place to break up the long trip from the Ho/Hohoe region to Tamale. There's basic **accommodation** (●) and various **chop bars and street food** around the old market. From Bimbilla, buses leave for **Kete Krachi** (Mon, Wed & Fri between noon and 3pm; change here for Akosombo ferries). Daily buses to **Tamale** leave between 5am and 6am via Yendi, or you can try to grab a seat on the Wulensi bus, which passes through Bimbilla around 9am. The daily bus to **Accra** via Hohoe leaves at 11am and arrives in the late evening.

10.5

Northern Ghana

Coming either from Kumasi, or up the country's eastern fringe, you'll be struck by the changing landscape, as the central forests give way to arid, low-lying **grasslands**. Due to the harsher, less predictable climate and the legacy of the Asante empire and the slave trade, the region remains relatively sparsely populated, characterized by traditional **compound agriculture**. The few urban centres like **Tamale** or **Bolgatanga** seem more subdued than their counterparts to the south.

The main peoples of the Upper West, Upper East and Northern regions include the More-speaking **Dagomba**, with their capital at Yendi, and the **Mamprusi** people, based around Nalerigu. The **Gonja**, with their capital at Damongo, are formed partly of the remnants of sixteenth- and seventeenth-century Mande-speaking migrant invaders from Songhai in the north, and partly of local Voltaic-speaking peoples. As a result, the Gonja, who are mostly Muslim, speak different languages according to their class – the nobles using a dialect of Akan known as Guang, the commoners speaking Wagala. **Sudanic influences** have been important in this region, reflected in architecture, customs and dress – *boubous* (body-length, embroidered gowns) or *fugus* (long, woven tunics or smocks) for the men and long veils for women, draped over their heads. In short, the north is a completely different world and – with the exception of the popular **Mole National Park**, which is easily visited and well set up for relatively inexpensive stays – remains a region where you're unlikely to run into throngs of fellow travellers.

It's worth noting that in the northeast, **ethnic conflict and local chieftaincy disputes** have led to outbreaks of violence in recent years, and that it's possible you will encounter curfews or transport disruption. The biggest recent outbreak was in Yendi, in 2002, when a militant group beheaded the powerful king of the Dagombas, Ya-Na Yakubu Andani, and killed 25 of his supporters. A surge of violence followed between rival factions and curfews were imposed in Yendi and Tamale. The area was calm as this book went to print, but the prevailing mood was described as "hot peace" by local officials, so keep your ear to the ground.

Tamale

Capital of the **Northern Region**, **TAMALE** is a large commercial town, at the junction of the main roads from Burkina Faso in the north, Togo in the east and Accra and Kumasi in the south. It has a laid-back feel, with wide, dusty streets and a comparative lack of vehicles – although there are plenty of bicycles and quite a few motorbikes. The town underwent a regeneration in advance of the 2008 African Nations Cup. Although there are few specific sights, if you're stopping over en route to other destinations, you'll find a reasonable number of hotels and diversions. Note that **water** is a constant problem in Tamale, with the taps often dry.

Arrivals, transport and information

The centre of Tamale wraps around the **motor park** – used by taxis and *tro-tros* – and the **STC bus station**, easily recognized by the towering telephone transmitter which juts up next to it and can be seen from almost anywhere in town. The **central market** (good for locally woven cloth) and major **banks** with ATMs are an easy walk away. If you arrive at the airport, some 20km north on the Bolgatanga road, you can charter a taxi into town (around GH¢8).

The **Ghana Tourist Board** has an office in the Regional Coordinating Office (RCO) on the eastern fringes of town (Mon–Fri 8am–5pm; ☎071/24835). In addition they run an office in the Goil garage, opposite the STC station in the town centre. Both are relatively helpful, offering advice on regional attractions. For the **Internet**, the best option in the centre is the Fosumel Internet café and the Fosumel Annex near the main mosque.

Moving on from Tamale

As the north's major city, Tamale is the springboard for **Burkina Faso** via Bolgatanga, and the road north is in excellent shape. **Heading south or west**, the highway is

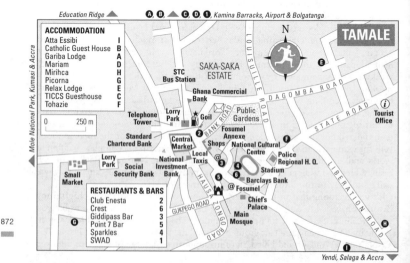

ACCOMMODATION

Atta Essibi	I
Catholic Guest House	B
Gariba Lodge	A
Mariam	D
Mirihca	H
Picorna	G
Relax Lodge	E
TICCS Guesthouse	C
Tohazie	F

RESTAURANTS & BARS

Club Enesta	2
Crest	6
Giddipass Bar	3
Point 7 Bar	5
Sparkles	4
SWAD	1

Education Ridge — **A**, **B**, — **C**, **D**, **I**, Kamina Barracks, Airport & Bolgatanga

TAMALE

N

Mole National Park, Kumasi & Accra

Yendi, Salaga & Accra

good to Kumasi and Accra, and passes through Yapei, with a bridge across Lake Volta. On the west side of the lake, a road for Sawla in western Ghana, via Damongo (for the Mole National Park) splits off from the Accra highway.

STC buses head out in all these directions, as do *tro-tros* and taxis. There is also one daily bus at 11am from Tamale to Yendi and Bimbilla, where you can continue to Accra via eastern Ghana, using roads now mostly in good condition. The nearest ferry link with Akosombo and the south is at Buipe port (*tro-tros* head there from Tamale's motor park), where cargo vessels sporadically take passengers. Full ferry details are given on p.866.

There are several weekly Antrak and Citylink **flights** to Accra, bookable through the *Gariba Lodge*.

Accommodation

There's an increasing range of accommodation in Tamale, a few more upmarket hotels having opened in recent years. Most of the places reviewed here are outside the centre, but all are easily reached by shared taxi from the central local-taxi station.

Atta Essibi St Charles Rd ☏071/22569. Clean, comfortable rooms with fans, some s/c, on the southern side of town. ①

Catholic Guest House Gumbihini Rd, off the Bolgatanga road, 1km north of the centre ☏071/22265. Slightly shabby but clean s/c rooms, a nice shady bar area and a chilled-out atmosphere. A good place to meet other travellers and often full. Rooms with fan ① or a/c ②.

Gariba Lodge 4km from town on the Bolgatanga road ☏071/23041–3 ✉gariba@africaonline.com.gh. Tamale's most expensive rooms are rather sterile but have all the facilities – a/c, IDD phone, satellite TV. The slightly dull restaurant serves European food. ⑥

Mariam Gumbihini Link Rd ☏071/23548/23948/25497. Out of town a bit, but the nicest place to stay in Tamale with clean, modern doubles with larger than average bathrooms, peaceful gardens and a good restaurant. Very popular with NGOs. ⑥

Mirihca off Liberation Rd ☏071/22935. Ten well-cared-for rooms with satellite TV, set in a pleasant leafy courtyard, with attractive tiled floors in the pricier rooms. ①

Picorna Kaladan Park ☏071/22672 ✉picornaho-telgh@yahoo.com. The cramped s/c, a/c rooms are looking rather run down these days but the central location is good. There's a bar and restaurant, and large outdoor cinema screen and stage area in the grounds, which mean it can get very noisy at weekends. Service and facilities have become increasingly unreliable – not a first choice. ②

Relax Lodge northeast of town off Dagomba road ☏071/24981. Gloomy and overpriced – everything from the peeling walls and rusty bathrooms to the clashing 1970s-style decor feels hopelessly out of date. There's an okay restaurant attached and they accept Visa and MasterCard. ④–⑥

TICCS Guesthouse Gumbihini Link Rd ☏071/22914 ⊛www.ticcs.com/res.htm. When not being used by groups, the Tamale Institute of Cross Cultural Studies offers airy, good-value s/c doubles with a/c or fan, opening onto a green, shady courtyard. It also has the lively *Jungle Bar*. ②

Tohazie State Rd, close to the town centre ☏071/24174/76. Former government resthouse undergoing renovations at the time of research. The renovated bungalow rooms, with clean tiled floors, a/c, sparkling bathrooms and small verandahs are excellent value. ②–④

The Town

Tamale has few sights worth a pause. The **central market** is really good, to be fair, with quite an impressive **leather tanner's** section and busy **weavers**. Otherwise, the **National Cultural Centre**, near the central market off the Salaga road, is in a horrific state of repair, but holds sporadic performances of **regional music and dance**; in the afternoons, you can sometimes catch a rehearsal. You can also watch some excellent **football** on Sunday afternoons, when major Ghanaian teams play at the main stadium.

A paved road leading out from the west of the market heads down past the Social Security Bank and a small market before arriving at a large **classified forest** – a rather unusual thing to find in the middle of an important administrative town. The shade of the teak trees makes for an excellent place to retreat from the afternoon heat, which reaches oppressive levels on the exposed avenues downtown.

It's possible to rent a **bicycle** in town (hotels can help) and ride up to Education Ridge, off the northwesterly road out of town. There's a fine ride commencing behind the polytechnic and running for about 8km through lovely villages, coming back the same way. If you need to cool down afterwards, check out the **swimming pool** at Kamina barracks (℡071/22707; GH¢1), about 5km out of town on the Bolgatanga road.

Eating, drinking and nightlife

There are plenty of **places to eat** in Tamale, including the hotel restaurants. All around the Goil garage after about 6pm there's a mass of street food on offer, especially guinea fowl. The restaurant at the Goil garage itself is popular with locals, serving fantastic chicken and chips. *Sparkles Restaurant* in the National Cultural Centre does decent sandwiches and salads during the day, while the *Crest Restaurant* does good-value, no-frills Ghanaian and Chinese dishes for under GH¢2.50. The *Giddipass Bar*, southeast of the STC bus station, is a perennial favourite, with a similar menu to the *Crest* at nearly double the price, though you do get the option of dining on the terrace or in the rooftop bar. Out past the *Catholic Guest House*, *SWAD* has a more sophisticated menu of seafood, pizzas and some Indian dishes.

Nightlife in Tamale is sometimes affected by a 10pm curfew, though local establishments take this in their stride. Across the street from the *Giddipass*, the *Point 7* **bar** is a long-standing favourite for cold beers, or try the dingy but cheerful *Club Enesta* down the road, which livens up on weekend nights. The *Jungle Bar* at TICCS – the Tamale Institute for Cross Cultural Studies, on Gumbihini Link off the Bolgatanga road, 1km north of the centre, is an excellent place to relax and unwind in comfy chairs on the breezy terrace, and also does American-style burgers and hot dogs. Southwest of the centre, *Picorna Hotel's* disco can be lively on Saturday nights, and they serve up good kebabs, or you can sometimes catch an evening film there (Fri–Mon 8.30pm).

Mole National Park

Set in the savannah country west of Tamale, the 5000-square-kilometre **MOLE NATIONAL PARK** (pronounced "moh-lay"; GH¢4, students GH¢2.50, vehicle GH¢4.50, camera GH¢0.20, video GH¢2.20) is Ghana's most important reserve and protects a wide variety of fauna – including elephant, buffalo and numerous species of antelope, monkey and bird, plus the occasional lion or leopard – in an environment which varies little but for the Konkori escarpment, which runs northeast to southwest. Around Christmas is the best – though also busiest – time to visit, when animals are most visible and the mosquitoes least oppressive (at other times it's vital to have repellent).

Park practicalities

Although the concentration of animals isn't as high as in some other West African parks, Mole's striking advantage, if you don't have your own transport, is **ease of access**. An OSA bus leaves daily from the transport yard in **Tamale** (officially at 3pm but frequently late – check at the station to be sure; 5–7hr; GH¢2.50) and takes passengers all the way into the park, dropping them off at the *Mole Motel* (the last stop). Alternatively you can catch the 6am OSA bus from Tamale to Wa, and disembark in **Larabanga** (see opposite) to make your own way into the park on foot or by bicycle. Be sure to purchase tickets early to ensure a space, as the bus is always crowded. Reservations for the return bus to Tamale must be made the night before departure at the motel. Approaching from any other direction – most obviously Bouna in Côte d'Ivoire or Wa – you can connect with one of these buses at **Damongo** (any other transport is extremely rare), where they stop before continuing into the reserve, although be warned that they are very often full. Driver and bus stay the night in the reserve, and depart again for Tamale at 5 or 6am, so you will really need to stay at least two nights in the park in order to see any animals.

A network of **tracks** crisscross the park; in the dry season, you can cover a lot of ground in an ordinary car. The only mode of transport that can be easily rented at the park are the rangers' **bicycles** (GH¢2 per day).

Accommodation

At the park's entrance, **accommodation** at the *Mole Motel* – which is the only option – ranges from rooms in a dorm to spacious twin-bed chalets with large bathrooms and screened verandahs overlooking the water holes (℡071/22045 **②–③** or dorm beds GH¢4.50; electricity blackout 1–6am). You can **camp** near the hotel buildings in your own tent (GH¢1 per person) or in one of the hotel's tents (GH¢2.50 per person), using the washing facilities for the dorms.

The motel perches on a bit of a hill dominating two artificial water holes where animals gather to drink in the dry season. Electricity and water are fairly reliable and there's also a wonderful **swimming pool** and **restaurant**. In many ways it's a little oasis, but the decor needs an update, and it would be much improved if the hotel staff were more pleasant.

Unless the hotel is busy, you're best advised to order **meals** in advance. And if you're arriving by bus in the evening, eat before leaving Tamale and bring your own food: you won't get anything much here until next morning's breakfast. Note that the **park ranger's canteen** does food and drinks for about half the price of the hotel.

In addition to the motel, three **camps** are in operation (no provisions, so bring your own bedding and food): **Nyanga** right in the centre of the park on the Mole River; **Lovi**, 30km from the *Mole Motel*; and **Brugbani** (9km). It's feasible to walk to Brugbani, but you'll need your own vehicle to reach the other two sites.

In the dry season – especially during weekends or holidays – you should **reserve** in advance (direct with the hotel or via their Accra office on ℡021/765810), as accommodation is often fully booked. During the rains, this doesn't seem to be much of a problem.

Around the park

When you check in at the motel, book a place on one of the **walking safaris** (6.30am & 3.30pm). The official hourly fee of GH¢7.50 is well worth it as the guides are generally quite helpful and know where to find the animals. Your chances of seeing **elephant**, **antelope** and **buffalo** at dawn near the motel water-holes are relatively good. In fact, you're unlikely to miss one or two of the elephants whose familiarity with the hotel is beginning to pose a danger to guests – watch out. To have any real chance of seeing other large animals, however, such as lions, you'll need a **vehicle** –hirable when available, for about GH¢40 an hour. In the absence of other transport, you might try your luck with other park visitors. Even with your own transport, for safety reasons you're obliged to take a ranger to help in the quest for wildlife.

Larabanga

Only 4km from the park gates, **LARABANGA** was once merely a village which tourists speedily passed through en route to Mole. Thanks to the efforts of a **community-based tourism project** (⊛www.larabanga.netfirms.com), with US Peace Corps and Slovenian sponsorship, it has become a regional attraction in its own right. The principal point of interest is the mud-and-stick Sudanic-style **mosque**, reputedly the oldest in Ghana, dated to somewhere between the fifteenth and seventeenth centuries. You pay a fee for a tour of the village (GH¢1, plus a GH¢0.50 obligatory donation to the imam), a visit to the **mosque** (though note that the interior is off limits to non-Muslims) and the **mystic stone** – a large boulder on the outskirts of the village – where you receive an explanation of the role it played in the origins of Larabanga. A simple **guesthouse** here, run by the Salia brothers, founders of the project, has five rooms, some of which have fans; alternatively you cam sleep up on the roof beneath the stars (❶). They also have **bikes** (GH¢1.50) and binoculars (GH¢1.50) for Mole available to rent. The OSA bus stops right outside the guesthouse on both its inward and outward journeys. Beware of touts and mischief connected with tourism in Larabanga – a number of travellers have been conned into ad hoc arrangements with unofficial chancers, and thefts and robberies at knife-point have been reported.

The ubiquitous machete

"Machetes are everywhere, from the one-eyed oldster with three missing fingers changing a lorry tyre to the ones carried by toddlers no bigger than their sharpish blades. They're used for practically everything, from chopping firewood and opening coconuts to bicycle repairs. Brilliant."

Ken Shaw and Carolyn Spice, UK

Wa and Upper West Region

Capital of the Upper West Region, **WA** is predominantly Muslim as the many **mosques** dotting the townscape attest. Although it's noticeably poorer than towns in the south, shortages of food and other goods no longer pose the problems they did twenty years ago. Though a number of office workers have come from outside to work in local administrative posts, Wa feels very remote from Accra and Tamale seems positively metropolitan in comparison.

Wa is the home of the **Wala** people who migrated from Mali and, upon arrival in Ghana, chased the resident Lobi population to the west and converted the Dagarti inhabitants to Islam. The **traditional chief**, the Wa-Na, formerly lived in a large white **palace** built in the Sudanic style. However, since the death of the last Wa-Na in 1998, a chieftaincy dispute between four rival factions has not been resolved, and the palace has remained unoccupied since. You can visit the palace (located behind the government transport yard), although you're not officially allowed inside as the building is considered unsafe. The small Wa **museum** would be worth visiting if there was anything in it, but it's just a shell.

Practicalities

The small **STC bus station** is on the town's central roundabout, and is also used by City Express buses. The main **lorry park** 400m west of here is used by *tro-tros* and shared taxis for surrounding towns such as Lawra, Hamale and Wechiau, as well as OSA buses. STC buses leave for Accra via Kumasi, departing at 2pm on Sundays, Tuesdays and Thursdays. For Bolga, City Express have a daily service (10am; GH¢4.50), and for Tamale and Sunyani, OSA provide daily services. For all other destinations, including GPRTU buses to Kumasi, go to the main lorry park.

Located in block B of the town's administration buildings (known locally as "Ministries"), the **Ghana Tourist Board** (☏0756/22431) can offer information on nearby sites. The *Kunateh Lodge* (☏0756/22102 ❶), a ten-minute walk from the lorry park, has the best-value **accommodation** in town, with clean comfortable rooms and an upbeat atmosphere, but get there early since it fills up fast. A fall-back budget option is the clean *Hotel du Pond* west of the lorry park (☏0756/20018 ❶). The local Catholic diocese's *Tiegber* (meaning "stretch your leg") *Guest House* (☏0756/22375 ❶) is 3km

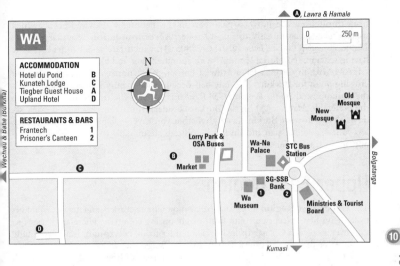

from the centre of town, but has extremely clean rooms, a garden bar, and a good restaurant run by the friendly nuns. The upmarket option in Wa is the *Upland Hotel* west of the centre (☏0756/22180 ❷), also with a garden bar and restaurant.

The **restaurant** at the *Tiegber* is probably the best choice for Ghanaian and Western dishes, while slightly more expensive and with a wider range of European fare is the restaurant at the *Upland*. For budget meals, *Frantech*, behind the SG-SSB Bank, serves up simple meals. Otherwise meals are pretty much limited to the usual **chop bars** located around the market and transport park. Cold beers can be had at the *Prisoner's Canteen*, a popular weekend spot for volunteers in the area.

Around Wa

On the Kumasi road south of Wa, there are interesting mosques at **Sawla**, **Maluwe**, and especially at **Bole** and **Banda Nkwanta** (one of the oldest in the district). They all date from the sixteenth-century Gonja conquest.

Wechiau Hippo Sanctuary

Wechiau Community Hippo Sanctuary, west of Wa on the Burkinabe border, offers a good opportunity to see hippos in the wild – September to May is the best time of year. Wechiau is around 40km from Wa, and the sanctuary, along a stretch of the Black Volta River, begins some 20km beyond **WECHIAU** village. There are two basic lodges for accommodation. The admission fee of GH¢9 per person includes land and river guides as well as lodging, so the trip is good value, but you'll need to bring your own food. Alternatively you could spend the night in Wechiau village in a homestay (GH¢3–4) and see the Wechiau-Na's palace. You can get the morning *tro-tro* from Wa to Wechiau but you'll need to get to the motor park early, as you'll have to charter a taxi if you miss it (GH¢20–30, depending on your bargaining skills). From Wechiau, you can rent bikes to do the final leg to the sanctuary – it's a hard cycle down a rough track, or again you can try to charter a taxi, though some drivers may refuse to attempt the rough track.

Lawra and Hamale

LAWRA, 80km north of Wa on the road to Hamale, is well known locally for its **musical instruments**, notably *balafons*, and also hosts the culmination of the important northern harvest festival of **Kobine**. Dancing and percussion teams come from throughout the north to take part in this nationally televised event, which usually takes place in early to mid-October. **Accommodation** is available at the *District Assembly Guest House* (☎0756/22805 ❶), which rarely sees tourists despite having spacious, comfortable rooms with running water and electricity.

HAMALE, in Ghana's far northwest corner, 35km north of Lawra, is a regular crossing point for Burkina. The only half-decent place to **stay** is near the lorry park, the unsignposted *By the Power of God Resthouse* (❶) and you might instead go on to the preferable *Mandou* (❶) on the Burkinabe side. Hamale's market is held every six days. It's easy to visit Burkina briefly, whether you have your passport or not (much less your visa): Ghanaian and Burkinabe officials are unlikely to mind if you want to pop across the border for a few hours.

Upper East Region

The **Upper East Region** is one of Ghana's most remote corners, and not many visitors make it up here except en route from neighbouring countries. There are reasons to stop over, however: Ghana's main Burkina border town, **Navrongo**, is a relaxed little centre, while the regional capital, **Bolgatanga**, or Bolga as it's widely known, is a bit of a boomtown, relatively speaking, with a good feel. And east of Bolga, in the hilly savannah towards the Togolese border, lies a clutch of interesting, low-key historical sites.

The Upper East is the traditional domain of the **More-speaking peoples** whose history goes back to a thirteenth-century chief, Gbewa, who founded a kingdom at **Pusiga**, east of Bawku on the Togolese border (where his tomb can still be seen). Gbewa's sons fought over their inheritance and founded a number of mini-states in the region which grew from the fourteenth century and remained essentially intact until the nineteenth, including **Mamprusi**, founded at Gambaga, and **Dagomba**, and the other "Mossi" kingdoms mentioned in the Burkina Faso chapter. These mini-states are now the names of distinct ethnic groups speaking dialects of More.

Navrongo and around

NAVRONGO is the first Ghanaian town south of Ouagadougou on the main highway, peopled mostly by **Kassena** farmers. In the middle of a vast but undeveloped **agricultural region** (where crops include rice, millet and yams), it's the second town of the Upper East Region, Bolgatanga being the first. Market day is the day after Bolga's.

Navrongo enjoys a reputation in the north as a centre of education because of its large secondary school. It was also one of the first towns in the region to have a church. Built in 1906 by priests from the Basle mission in Ouagadougou, incorporating a Lourdes-like grotto in the grounds since 1934, and now the **Our Lady of Seven Sorrows Cathedral**, it was constructed in the traditional mud-and-wood style, and the interior decor reflects regional art and cultural values. Today it's the only "sight" in town and definitely worth a visit, especially on a Sunday. There's a small museum opposite (GH¢1.50). The museum and original cathedral are both now overshadowed by the concrete **modern cathedral**.

Practicalities

Your most likely point of arrival is the **lorry park** in the heart of Navrongo. Shared cars and *tro-tros* leave regularly, either north to Paga, from where you can continue on to Ouagadougou, or east to Bolgatanga. Heading west to Wa, the daily 6am City Express bus from Bolgatanga stops at Navrongo but is often full.

Navrongo has very limited facilities, which make it less convenient as a stopping point than Bolgatanga, though the lively *Catholic Social Centre* (☎0742/22161 ❶), just across from the cathedral, does have good, clean s/c **rooms** and prepares food on request.

Hotel Mayaga, a large building set back from the road to Wa (☎0742/22327 ❶), offers a variety of tired rooms, some with a/c. The only other choice is the *St Lucien Guesthouse* (☎0742/22707 ❶) inside the lorry park, with reasonably neat rooms. They also have a pleasant **restaurant** serving simple inexpensive dishes – fried rice, fish and *banku*; or else try the numerous **chop houses** and bars crowded around the market and the motor park, on either side of the Bolga road. *Pito* bars are also plentiful. In the evenings you have a choice of several **video theatres** or – if you've timed it right – the monthly disco at *St Lucien*.

Around Navrongo

Some 6km from Navrongo (GH¢3 in a shared taxi), down a turning off the Tumu road, are the Irrigation Company of the Upper East Region's residences and *Guesthouse* (☎0742/22629 ❷), built within comfortable walking distance of **Tono Lake**. Sometimes referred to as the "Akosombo of the Upper Region", the lake resulted from an over-ambitious 1970s dam designed to create a massive irrigation project for sugar, rice and tomato production. Though the guesthouse has seen better days, the lake is still a scenic spot for bike rides, bird-watching or a picnic.

Twenty kilometres further west, beyond **Chuchiliga**, are the **Chiana-Katiu caves**, 1km out of **CHIANA** village. They feature natural rock formations that appear, eerily, to be of human construction – though no one seems to know much about them. Any *tro-tro* on the Tumu road can drop you in Chiana.

Five kilometres north of Navrongo on the Burkina border, the **sacred crocodile pools** at **PAGA** have been developed into an ecotourism project. After you pay the fee of GH¢3, which includes the cost of a live chicken, the crocs are lured onto land by throwing the chicken into the shallows and general splashes in the water. You pose for snaps holding their tails or squatting lightly on their backs, until finally the chicken is fed to them. The Chiefs' Crocodile Pond is the most regularly visited, on the northern side of the village and within sight of the border post. You can also visit the **Paga Pio's Palace** (GH¢1.20), in which case it pays to have kola nuts on hand if you are introduced to the chief.

Bolgatanga

Capital of the Upper East Region and of the Grusi-speaking **Frafra** people, **BOLGATANGA** (aka Bolga) is much larger and busier than Navrongo. If you're entering the country from Burkina Faso, it's a good place – far better than Navrongo – to take care of business, change money or find decent accommodation. The large town **market** has some good local **handicrafts**, especially leather, and there are several interesting sites to explore in the vicinity.

Arrival and information

From Bolgatanga's central intersection, the **Navrongo road** runs approximately northwards, the **Zuarangu road** eastwards, and the **Tamale road** southwestwards. Most of the town's places to stay and other facilities lie northeast of the central intersection. Some 500m away is the **STC bus station** on the Tamale road. **OSA buses** use a station on the south side of the market. The main **lorry park**, used by shared taxis and *tro-tros* as well as by City Express buses, is 250m north of the southern end of Bazaar Road. STC (☎072/24669), OSA (☎072/22372) and City Express all have daily mid-afternoon services to Accra via Tamale and Kumasi. Additionally, STC depart for Ouaga (Sun 6am) and Bawku (daily 6.30am); OSA leave for Hamale (Mon & Fri 7am); and City Express for Wa via Tumu (daily except Sun 6am). Shared taxis and *tro-tros* serve the surrounding towns plus destinations further afield such as Ouaga, Tamale, Kumasi and Accra. The main **taxi station** for town transport is on the north side of the Zuarangu road, a couple of minutes' walk east of the central intersection.

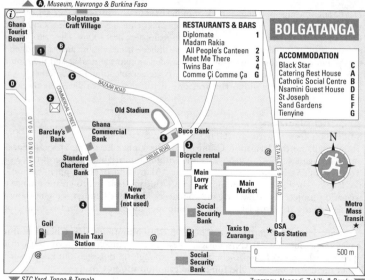

ⓘ Ghana Tourist Board

Bolgatanga Craft Village

RESTAURANTS & BARS
Diplomate	1
Madam Rakia	
All People's Canteen	2
Meet Me There	3
Twins Bar	4
Comme Çi Comme Ça	G

BOLGATANGA

ACCOMMODATION
Black Star	C
Catering Rest House	A
Catholic Social Centre	B
Nsamini Guest House	D
St Joseph	E
Sand Gardens	F
Tienyine	G

BAZAAR ROAD

COMMERCIAL STREET

Old Stadium

NAVRONGO ROAD

Barclay's Bank

Ghana Commercial Bank

Buco Bank

ABILBA ROAD

Standard Chartered Bank

Bicycle rental

Main Lorry Park

STARLETS 91 ROAD

N

New Market (not used)

Main Market

Goil

Social Security Bank

Metro Mass Transit ★

Main Taxi Station

Taxis to Zuarangu

OSA Bus Station ★

Ⓖ **Ⓕ**

Social Security Bank

0 — 500 m

The **Ghana Tourist Board** has a helpful regional office (Mon–Fri 9–5pm; ☏072/23416) on a small road which leads west off the Navrongo road 1500m north of the central intersection. The area between Bolga and Bawku, the **Red Volta Valley**, has been identified as a prime location for ecotourist projects; it may be worth asking at the tourist office about canoe trips and wildlife treks in the area.

You can change both cash and traveller's cheques at the **Standard Chartered Bank** on Commercial Street, 500m north of the Zuarangu road. The bank is located at the intersection with Abilba Road, which runs east here along the north side of the market. There's a **bike rental** outlet on the corner of Abilba Road.

Accommodation

There's plenty of accommodation to choose from in Bolga, most of it at the budget end of the scale – some of the cheapest town hotels in Ghana.

Black Star Bazaar Rd, just east of where it meets Commercial St ☏072/22346 or 23042, @ghandaa@yahoo.com. A reasonable standby – the rooms are unimpressive for the price and due for renovation, but the shared bathrooms are surprisingly clean. Decent restaurant attached. ❷

Catering Rest House off the Navrongo Rd, 3km north of the centre ☏072/22399. Ugly concrete blocks with TV, fridge and a/c. Feels very dated. ❷

Catholic Social Centre off the Bazaar Rd ☏072/23216. Clean, non-s/c rooms or dorm accommodation. A bit on the scruffy side but very cheap and with a simple restaurant attached. ❶

Nsamini Guest House off the Navrongo road ☏072/23403. Friendly atmosphere and six spotless, non-s/c rooms, all with fan, set around a welcoming courtyard – a good deal. ❶

Sand Gardens up a lane leading north from the OSA bus depot ☏072/22355. An increasingly popular choice – consider reserving – with a wide range of good-value rooms, some s/c. TV, a/c and fridge available in some rooms. ❷

St Joseph on a dirt track behind the National Investment Bank, 700m from the southern end of Bazaar Rd ☏072/23214. A hideous exterior and a mix of middling accommodation, with s/c rooms, some with a/c, TV and fridge. ❶

Tienyine Starlets 91 Rd, north off Zuarangu Rd about 1200m east of the central intersection ☏072/22355. Attached to the well-established *Comme Çi Comme Ça Restaurant* in a quiet location. Very clean a/c rooms with TV, phone and fridge, arranged around a nice courtyard. Best accommodation in town. ❸

The Town

The main feature of downtown Bolga would be the renovated **central market** except that it is stillnot being used. Many crafts goods, including leather items, superb basketwork and clothes, are still made by hand and can be browsed at the crafts village, off the Navrongo road, on the north side of town. There are beautiful examples of handmade *fugu* tunics, sewn from locally woven material and commonly worn by men throughout the region. The main market day is on a three-day cycle so you have a good chance of coinciding. If you can't find **baskets** in the main market, head past the main banks to the corner of Commercial Street and Bazaar Road – it can be rather a high-pressure sell, but you'll pay a much better price than in Accra.

Bolgatanga has a **museum** (daily 8am–5pm; GH¢1), in the administrative block behind the library off the Navrongo road; to find it, take the road leading east off the Navrongo road about 300m beyond the northern end of Bazaar Road. Housed in the two small rooms is a permanent exhibition on the region's cultural, historic and ethnographic heritage, with displays of stools, pots and musical instruments, and there some more ephemeral exhibits on issues of contemporary interest. Though not a big draw, it's an interesting way to spend an hour or two.

Eating and nightlife

Both the *Sand Gardens* and *Tienyine Hotel* have recommended restaurants, with a wide selection of dishes for less than GH¢3 – the *Comme Çi Comme Ça* at the *Tienyine* is particularly good. More centrally, the *Diplomate* (inside SSNIT House) is a pleasant enough place with European and local cuisine; it's open from 7.30am for breakfasts too. *Madam Rakia All Peoples' Canteen*, on Commercial Street, has *banku*, plantain and *jollof* rice. In the evening, omelette and chop stands are scattered along Commercial Street and among the houses behind the *Black Star Hotel*. The favourite local dish is TZ, often eaten with *kino* sauce made from bitter green leaves. A more specialized Bolga taste is hot **dog**, available as very spicy kebabs from stalls at the lorry park.

Meet Me There on Bazaar Road and *Twins* – local aliases for two adjacent bars, *Midway* and *Street View* on Commercial Street – both guarantee a jolly **drinking** atmosphere. On Saturdays, try *Old Timer's* at the *Black Star Hotel* – a popular **disco** (GH¢1.50) that draws a mixed crowd.

Around Bolgatanga and Upper East Region

SAMBRUNGO, 8km out of town on the Navrongo road, has a **night market**, offering an atmospheric – romantic even – stroll through the lanterns in the cool, evening air. Some 15km north of Bolga, the village of **BONGO** is the starting point for hikes through the attractive Bongo Hills. Notable here is **Bongo Rock** which, when thumped, makes an appropriately resounding boom that can be heard all over the district. *Tro-tros* leave regularly for Bongo from Bolga's main lorry park.

Eastwards to Bawku

The road **east from Bolga** takes you through the villages of **NANGODI** (20km away), with sacred fish and a gold mine (though only small-scale mining continues today); **ZEBILLA** (40km from Bolga), with beautifully decorated houses (people are supremely hospitable if you're invited in); and on to the market town of **BAWKU**, right on the Burkinabe border and only 30km from Togo. Apart from smuggling, now on the wane, Bawku is a centre for the manufacture of *fugu* shirts, the north's characteristic costume. The hospital **guesthouse** offers four very comfortable rooms (℡0734/22345 ❶). Across the street from the Mobil garage, regular *tro-tros* leave for Bolga (up to 2hr) and an STC bus departs daily for Accra (4pm). Alternatively you could head east into Togo, or to Burkina, both via Sinkassé (Cinkassé).

Tongo and around

Southeast of Bolga, the hills around the Talensi village of **TONGO** make for an interesting and scenic day-trip. The best time to visit the area would be for the **Sowing Festival** around Easter or the **Harvest Festival**, usually in September or October. Both reflect a curious blend of old and new – iron-bangled dancers shaking radios, tennis racquets and rubber dolls. However, the principal attraction in the area is the **Tengzug shrine**, a famous religious site in a rocky cavern. The British destroyed it in 1911 and again in 1915, but couldn't prevent people from going there. Now the subject of a local community tourism initiative, the shrine is a twenty-minute walk from the village of Tengzug, a steep climb concluding with a mountain of feathers – the by-product of sacrificial offerings – at the shrine entrance. There are good views over the village and the surrounding area. It costs GH¢3 to enter the village and another GH¢2 to see the shrine; note that both sexes are required to enter the holy site topless and bare footed.

Tro-tros run sporadically to Tongo every day from Bolga's main lorry park, though the journey is easiest on market day (the market here follows the same cycle as Bolga's). With your own means of transport, head 9km down the Tamale road, then take the clearly signposted turning off to your left to Tongo; from here it's another 4–5km up a winding track to Tengzug. Several kilometres north of Tongo, the village of **Bare** features a sacred **bat tree**, making for a change from crocodile pools and holy fish ponds.

The road from Walewale to Nakpanduri

South of Bolgatanga en route to Tamale, you leave Upper East Region and enter Northern. The first town, **WALEWALE**, is the site of a venerable mosque, the Nakora. **GAMBAGA**, 50km northeast of here, is famous for its scarp, stretching out towards the Togolese border and up to 300m high in places. Gambaga is also the ancient **Mamprusi** capital and the site of current excavations investigating the origins of the Mamprusi kingdom. The modern Mamprusi capital is **NALERIGU**, 8km east of Gambaga, home of a highly regarded mission hospital. Here you can see the palace of the Mamprusi kings, as well as remains of the defensive walls built around the town when it was founded in the seventeenth century. At **BAGALE**, in the remote country south of Gambaga, stands the Dagomba kings' **mausoleum**. The house built over the mausoleum is the abode of the spirits of all departed Ya Nas.

NAKPANDURI, 30km further east, is an unspoilt village situated high on the scarp. The **government resthouse** here (❶) is superbly sited, with a magnificent view north and some inspiring hikes nearby through rocky outcrops. Eating options in town are severely limited to the odd chop bar, but you may use the resthouse kitchen. Vehicles run here from Bawku (early departures from the market around 6am), and though traffic is slow outside the market day (a three-day cycle), the relaxed and scenic atmosphere makes it worth a detour.

Togo

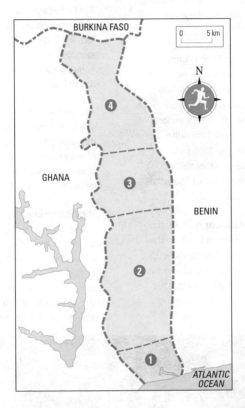

BURKINA FASO

0   5 km

N

GHANA

BENIN

4

3

2

1

ATLANTIC
OCEAN

Highlights 884
Introduction and Basics 885
11.1 Lomé and the coast 907

11.2 The plateau region 925
11.3 Sokodé and the north 933
11.4 Kara and the far north 939

Togo highlights

* **Lomé** The friendly capital still has a genuine appeal and is an attractive place to hang out and enjoy an exceptional range of bars and restaurants. See p.907

* **Agbodrafo and Lac Togo** Set on the southern shore of idyllic Lac Togo, the relaxing village of Agbodrafo offers various watersports, as well as pirogue trips over the lake to the historic voodoo town of Togoville. See p.921

* **Mont Klouto** A dramatic, winding road leads to the village of Kouma-Konda, from where you can climb Mont Klouto for fabulous views and go hiking in the surrounding jungle-strewn hills, which boast an amazing abundance of beautiful butterflies. See p.928

* **Akloa Falls** A fantastic walk through dense forest brings you to this stunning waterfall, where you can swim in the pool at the base. See p.932

* **Aledjo** Near the dramatic site of the Faille d'Aledjo, this welcoming village offers impressive views across a barren landscape. See p.937

* **Tamberma country** Living in fortress-like houses in the far north of the country, the isolated Tamberma continue to preserve their fascinating and unique architecture and customs. See p.944

▲ Voodoo dolls, Akodessewa fetish market

Introduction and Basics

Togo – French-speaking West Africa's smallest nation – is still comparatively little known outside the region, and has been through heavy political weather in the last two decades. In the post-independence years of the 1960s and 1970s it attracted investors, expats and trans-Saharan tourists, while in 1975 it hosted the Lomé Convention, forever linking the country's capital with co-operation in development. If it wasn't democratic – well, nor were many other countries in West Africa.

The country's reputation for stability and prosperity carried it into the 1980s, when opposition to long-time President **Gnassingbé Eyadéma**'s one-party regime began to mount. The government's political repression repelled visitors through most of the 1990s, and Togo's fortunes plummeted. Further political upheavals in 2005 following Eyadéma's death and the appointment by the military of his son, Faure Gnassingbé, as the new president. The violence left hundreds dead and saw 30,000 political refugees fleeing the country.

Under President **Faure Gnassingbé**, the economy continues to struggle and infrastructure is in decline. People are usually jumpy when the conversation turns to politics – which it rarely does, and almost never in public places – but Gnassingbé's government has made some progress towards democratic reform.

On the plus side, the Togolese themselves remain welcoming and friendly. The country has a wonderful **climate** and good **food** and packs a satisfyingly diverse range of **scenery** into its small area, ranging from the forest and rolling hills of the cocoa triangle in the southeast to the savannah and barren landscapes of the north. It also boasts a vigorous **cultural diversity**, with more than a dozen linguistic and ethnic groups.

People

The big groups in Togo are the **Ewe** (pronounced midway between "Ehveh" and "Eyway") in the south, and the Kabyé in the north. The Ewe, divided into a multiplicity of local and district communities, have linguistic and cultural affinities with other **Twi-speaking peoples** like the Akposo in central Togo, the Asante and Fante in Ghana, and the Fon in eastern Togo and Benin. The Ewe diaspora – especially in France, Benin and Ghana – is a source of firm opposition, while the Ghanaian border, which splits the Ewe traditional homeland into two regions, is the butt of considerable frustration. The Togolese Ewe, particularly the **Mina** group, are the producers of much of Togo's export earnings, through coffee and cocoa.

The **Kabyé** and related **Tamberma** peoples are mostly poor subsistence farmers who have tended to unite behind the ruling (Kabyé) dynasty's regional development

---

Fact file

The **République Togolaise** is a strip of a country with a 56-kilometre coastline and an area of only 57,000 square kilometres – less than half the size of England or New York State. The name Togo comes from *togodo*, meaning "behind the lake" in Ewe. The **population** is estimated at around 5.4 million, with some 700,000 living in the capital, Lomé, although hundreds of thousands of refugees have fled to Ghana and Benin since the early 1990s. Togo has a **foreign debt** of about $2 billion (£1.1 billion), a relatively small sum even by modest West African standards, yet still amounting to more than twice the annual value of its exports. The country is under theoretically democratic **government**: in practice one father-and-son dynasty (the Gnassingbés) have dominated Togo since 1963.

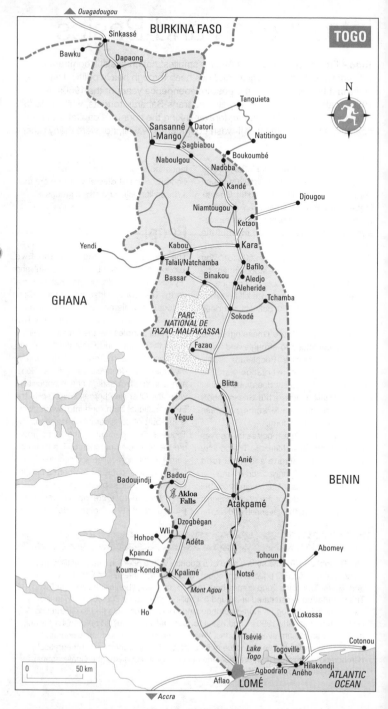

plans. Most of the top military and governmental jobs are also held by Kabyé-speakers. Since Eyadéma first seized power in 1963, this ethnic discrimination has been a major cause of political conflict. Other Voltaic-speaking northerners include the **Tchamba** and **Bassari**, and the **Kotokoli**, one of Togo's most populous groups, whose people are also influential traders.

Where to go

The country's small size makes getting around relatively easy. The main **Route Nationale**, which shows off the country's cultural and geographical variety, runs from Lomé north to Dapaong, near the Burkina Faso border, and even the most isolated villages lie within 100km of its route.

The capital, **Lomé**, feels like a large provincial town, tuned to the shuffling pace of crowded narrow streets, where goats and chickens share space with clapped-out taxis, over loaded cars and swarms of motorcycles. During the worst periods of the military madness, tens of thousands of people fled the city, leaving it like a ghost town. Many refugees have returned, and although the heyday of the late 1980s – when Lomé was one of the places to be in West Africa – is over, the capital is still a friendly place to relax and enjoy some creature comforts before or after a trip to the rural areas.

The coast is also worth savouring, not just for the palmy villages rustling between the lagoons and the Atlantic, but also for **voodoo**. The fetishes, shrines and festivals of Togoville, Aného and Glidji reveal a lot about a religion no less bizarre than the Catholicism with which it is strikingly interwoven. Followers are usually open about *vaudau* and willing to discuss it with interested travellers – surprising in view of the secrecy under which traditional religions are usually shrouded.

Northwest of Lomé stretches the mountainous and fertile **plateau region**. Although the peaks of this area never exceed 1000m, they feel higher, especially when you're climbing the twisting roads to Badou, Kpalimé or Atakpamé. These three towns delineate the coffee and cocoa triangle – the richest agricultural district in the country, characterized by thick woodland studded with fruit orchards and palm plantations.

In the **mid-northern region**, Sokodé and Bafilo are Muslim strongholds, while Bassar has retained predominantly traditional religious beliefs.

In the **far north**, the president's home town, **Kara**, is also less Muslim in flavour, and has benefited from a number of industrial and development projects that have catapulted it into "second city" status. The **Tamberma country** should not be missed if you're in this region, as it eclipses all other attractions in the north. Mango and Dapaong, located in the semiarid savannah region of the extreme far north, already evoke the Sahel, though Dapaong is a cheerful enough arrival point from Burkina Faso.

As for **wildlife-viewing**, there is relatively little left to see, most of the large mammals having been poached to virtual extinction during the troubles of the past two decades. However, the **Parc National de Fazao-Malfakassa**, west of Sokodé – offers good hiking and cycling opportunities.

When to go

Except in small villages off the paved roads, the **weather** in Togo won't greatly hamper your travels. Indeed, the country's pleasant climate has always been a factor in its popularity with visitors, and the rainy seasons, which vary from north to south, need not be an overriding factor in deciding when to go.

Southern Togo gets a "long rainy season" from March to June and a period of short

Photography

No photography permit is required in Togo, though the usual restrictions apply to taking pictures of military installations and strategic points. People tend to be generally less camera-shy here than in other parts of West Africa.

Lomé

Temperatures °C	Jan	Feb	Mar	Apr	May	June	July	Aug	Sept	Oct	Nov	Dec
Min (night)	23	24	25	24	24	23	23	22	23	23	23	23
Max (day)	31	31	32	31	31	29	27	27	28	30	31	31
Rainfall mm	15	24	52	118	145	224	71	8	35	61	28	10
Days with rainfall	1	2	4	8	9	12	5	1	5	9	2	1

rains some time between September and November. Note, though, that there's not a lot of rain, even in the south (the baobab, that archetypal dry-country tree, grows right down to within 10km of the coast) and the table given here for Lomé is an average of wet and dry years.

Northern Togo gets a single, and less predictable, rainy season between April and September.

In the winter, the **harmattan wind** which blows down from the Sahara in January and February keeps temperatures down and mosquitoes at bay, especially in the north, but brings desert dust which can cloud visibility.

Getting there from the rest of Africa

If you can't fly direct to Lomé, use Accra, Ghana, or Cotonou in Benin as arrival points, with onward air or land connections.

Flights within Africa

There are daily flights from **Abidjan** to Lomé on Air Ivoire and Air Sénégal. Royal Air Maroc, Benin Golf Air, Antrak Air and Air Burkina fly most days from **Cotonou**. Ethiopian Airways, Afriqiyah Airways and Antrak Air have flights from **Accra**, while Air Burkina and Antrak Air fly two or three times

For details on **getting to Togo from outside Africa**, plus important practical information applying to all West African countries, covering health, transport, cultural hints and more, see Basics, pp.19–28.

a week from **Ouagadougou**. Air Burkina also offer twice-weekly flights from **Bamako** and **Dakar** via Ouaga while Air Ivoire flies to Lomé from **Libreville**.

From East Africa, Kenya Airways flies direct from **Nairobi** to Lomé and South African Airways flies from **Jo'burg** to Accra. Ethiopian Airlines flies from **Addis Ababa** to Lomé twice a week.

Overland from Burkina

The road from **Ouagadougou** is sealed most of the way to Lomé, apart from a rough stretch between Koupéla and the border on the Burkinabe side. The border is open from 6am to 6pm, and formalities are straightforward. Coming from Ouaga by taxi, you can save money by going as far as Sinkassé or Dapaong and changing vehicles there. By bus, SOGEBAF provide a weekly service from Bobo to Lomé (CFA18,000) via Ouaga (CFA15,000), while SKV has air-conditioned services (CFA18,000) twice a week. On these buses you can get off anywhere along the Route Nationale but you will still have to pay the price of a ticket to Lomé.

Overland from Ghana

The chaotic main border crossing with Ghana is at **Aflao**, 2km west of Lomé city centre and is open from 6am to 10pm. Taxis from Ghana going all the way to Lomé's Grand Marché *autogare* charge a big premium for the few hundred metres. It's cheapest to get transport to Aflao, then cross on foot and take a taxi or *mobylette* for the final 2km to the centre, though you'll have to contend with the border's aggressive moneychangers and hustling drivers (don't pay more than CFA1000). You may prefer to walk a few hundred metres from the border to escape these hassles, have a beer at the *Bronco Bar* while you get your bearings and then flag down transport.

There are more relaxed border crossings on the following, less frequented routes. Not all of them have Togolese immigration officers who can give you a seven-day visa if you don't already have one (see "Red tape and visas" below) and in that case they will normally direct you to the nearest town to finish formalities – don't take that as a sign that it's not important. Routes include: from **Ho**, Ghana, to **Kpalimé**, Togo; from **Kpandu**, Ghana, to **Kouma-Konda**, Togo; from **Wli**, Ghana (east of Hohoe), from where there's a short walk to **Yipa-Dafo**, Togo, then on to Adéta; from **Badoudjindji**, Ghana (north of Jasikan), to **Badou**, Togo; from **Talali**, Ghana (east of Yendi), to **Natchamba**, Togo, near **Kara**; and from Pulimakum, near Bawku to **Sinkassé** in the extreme far north of Togo. There's no official post on the Togolese side at the Pulimakum crossing, so you'll have to go to Sinkassé to be formally stamped in.

Overland from Benin

The main border crossing between Togo and Benin is at **Hilakondji**. The post is open 24 hours a day and is relatively hassle-free. Regular taxis and a once-daily STIF bus ply the *route internationale* between Cotonou and Lomé, which is in good condition. Less frequented border crossings can be found at **Tohoun**, west of Abomey (be warned, the *piste* to the main *route nationale* at Notsé is pretty rough); at **Tchetti**, west of Savalou; at **Ouaké/Kemerida**, west of Djougou; and at **Bouukombé/Nadoba** in the Tamberma country, where you cross from Natitingou. If there's nobody awake at this latter crossing to process your entry: get your passport stamped in Kandé.

Red tape and visas

Visas for Togo are required by everyone except nationals of ECOWAS countries. Where Togo has no diplomatic representation, you can usually get one at the French consulate. Visas are also issued at the country's major border crossings: Aflao, Sinkassé and Hilakondji (CFA15,000). These are valid for one week only but can be extended in Lomé (see

---

The blog for this guide

For travel updates, news links and general information, check out ⓦtheroughguidetowestafrica .blogspot.com.

p.921). The **Visa Touristique Entente** (see p.32) covers Togo as well as Benin, Burkina Faso, Côte d'Ivoire and Niger.

Whether you enter by air or overland, customs and immigration officials usually give you little hassle. You may sometimes be asked how much money you're carrying, but the amount is rarely verified. The only other piece of paper you'll theoretically need is a **yellow fever certificate**.

For **visas for onward travel**, Lomé has only a limited number of West African embassies and consulates (see p.920). Visas for some Francophone countries, including Burkina Faso, are issued from the French consulate but you're generally better off getting them at the border. Benin now has an embassy in Lomé which issues visas for up to 3 months in 24 hours (CFA10,000). The 48-hour visas issued at the Hilakondji border (also CFA10,000) can be extended in Cotonou. Ghana's embassy will issue single-entry visas (CFA10,000) with minimal fuss, but Nigerian visas are issued to residents of Togo only. The Niger consulate issues one-month visas in 24 hours (CFA22,500) and can also issue a Visa Touristique Entente (CFA25,000), which covers you for one entry into Burkina Faso, Benin, Niger and Côte d'Ivoire.

Info, websites, maps

North Americans can get tourist information from the Togo Tourist Information Office at the Togolese embassy in Washington, DC. In Europe, you can try contacting the Togolese embassy in Paris (see p.30). The best Togo website is ⓦwww.republicoftogo .com, which mainly covers the latest political and economic news, but also has a range of country information.

The best map of Togo is the large 1cm:5km sheet produced by the French

11

TOGO | Basics

IGN, although it's somewhat out of date (the last edition was published in 1995). In Lomé, the Togolese survey office, the Direction de la Cartographie Nationale, is responsible for large-scale (1:200,000 and 1:50,000) mapping. Whether they will sell you any sheets is another matter.

The media

The country's most readily available **newspaper** is the state-owned *Togo Presse*, published daily in French; its international coverage is sketchy, but local news items can be interesting. After years of intimidation, a more **independent press** has recently re-emerged to offer an alternative slant on events, with titles including *Liberté*, *Le Canard* and *Le Crocodile*. Togo's ranking in the Reporters Sans Frontières' index has improved since the death of Eyadéma to borderline respectability, but the reality is that to avoid being shut down by the government, most of the press is self-censoring.

You'll find international **English-language** papers and magazines like the *Herald Tribune*, *Time* and *Newsweek* (as well as French and German magazines and papers) at the airport and the big hotels.

Radio is the most important medium of mass communication. Radio Togo, the national station, broadcasts news in French, Ewe, Kabyé and English (endless reports of the president's activities followed by a wrap-up of West African events). Radio France Inter (91.5FM), broadcast from Lomé and Kara, is better, with more comprehensive international news coverage.

There are also numerous so-called **private stations** (Zephyr, Metropolys and Nana FM are the most popular), although many are effectively controlled by the government so their news coverage is not of a very high standard and they are careful to avoid courting controversy.

The national TV company, **Télévision Togolaise**, broadcasts every evening – news in French and local languages plus music videos and old movies. The pay-per-view Media Plus channel broadcasts various foreign programmes.

Health

In common with most of West Africa, a **yellow fever** vaccination certificate is compulsory, though rarely checked. **Malaria tablets** are essential (see p.40).

As for medical facilities, towns and large villages have either a hospital or, more likely, a dispensary, but except in Lomé, these are often overcrowded and may lack adequate supplies (there is a very good Baptist hospital in Adéta, between Kpalimé and Atakpamé). Having said that, **pharmacies** should be your first port of call if you get sick; they offer good advice, on-the-spot tests and appropriate drugs for most ailments, including malaria, and every town will have a rota of duty pharamacies open through the night (*pharmacies du garde*). A course of malaria treatment will cost about CFA3000.

If you get seriously ill, it's best to contact your embassy. They'll be able to refer you to a specialist or decide if you would be safer flying home to get the help you need (see "Clinics", p.920).

Costs, money, banks

Togo is part of the **CFA zone** (rates of exchange roughly £1=CFA880, $1=CFA450).

Costs

The **cost of living** in Togo is substantially lower than that in West Africa's other Francophone countries, though if you plan on living and eating *à l'européen*, you'll pay dearly for imported goods that would be cheap at home. Budget **hotel rooms** start from around CFA3500 in the countryside (slightly more in Lomé), while mid-range hotels start at around CFA8000. Ready-cooked **street food** and market produce is very cheap, especially in the productive southwest. **Restaurants** serving European food generally do meals from about CFA2000, although more expensive eateries abound in Lomé where you can easily pay more than CFA5000 for a main course – still very good value. **Beer and soft drinks** are very inexpensive and cost about the same price in local bars countrywide (CFA600 for a large beer, CFA450 for large soft drinks), although big hotels and tourist hangouts knock prices up, as you'd expect.

Money and cards

If you're **arriving overland**, you're likely to have some CFA. Arriving by air, there's a **24-hour ATM** at the airport but it's a good idea to bring some euros, especially if you're getting a visa on arrival.

Euros are the easiest currency to change once you're in the country. In smaller towns, banks will only change euros.

Changing most **major international currencies** is no problem in Lomé, Kpalimé, Kara and Sokodé, though traveller's cheques are always time-consuming to change.

If you need money **wired** to you in Togo, you can have it sent to one of the many Western Union agencies.

Banking hours are short and inconvenient (usually Mon–Fri 7.30–11.30am & 2.30–4.30pm). Outside of Lomé, banks are closed on Mondays but open on Saturday mornings from 7am to 1pm instead.

Credit cards are accepted only in major hotels, with Visa the most useful. In Lomé, you can get Visa cash advances at most banks. BTCI banks in Lomé and Kara have Visa ATMs. Travellers report difficulties using other credit cards, especially Amex which is not recognized anywhere in Togo.

The black market

Lomé has the biggest **currency black market** in West Africa, most visible around the BIA bank and along the aptly named rue du Commerce – and also near the old Cotonou taxi station and Grand Marché. The quarter is notorious throughout the region, and the black market operates here quite openly. You can buy Nigerian naira and Ghanaian cedis here, as well as CFA (useful if you get caught short when the banks are closed) and international currencies. Though you're not breaking any Togolese law by changing money here, bear in mind the fact that cedis and naira may not legally be exported or imported.

Streetwise **moneychangers** are very adept at sleight-of-hand tricks. It's best to go with a friend, only carry the money you want to change, get the correct exchange rate in

advance and pay attention. You should try to avoid the sharks on the street who'll perform magic before your eyes, and deal with one of the bigger bosses at a shop, doing the actual exchange inside. Ask for a seat, take your time and don't hand anything over until you've checked the money you've been given note by note.

Getting around

Getting around Togo is now only possible by road, since the railway service in the south has been discontinued and there's no domestic air service. Which is not really a problem: the main roads are generally well-maintained, while Lomé is linked by tarmac highways to Accra and Cotonou.

Given the lack of alternatives, you're likely to do most of your travelling in Togo by **shared taxi**. These are traditionally Peugeot 504s, though every year Japanese minibuses – Nissans and Hiaces – gain ground. You'll sometimes be asked to pay extra for your **luggage**; this should never be more than CFA100–300, according to the length of the journey and the size of your bag.

The Rakieta **bus** company runs very efficient daily services between Lomé and Kara; for destinations north of Kara, catch one of the several Burkina-bound buses from Lomé and get off along the way (although you'll probably have to pay the full fare).

In Lomé and all other towns, **zemidjans** or *zemis* (moped taxis) are common, cheap and convenient, if a little dangerous, since no helmets are provided. Avoid boy-racer types and make sure you agree the fare before you set off. Lomé has a few car-rental agencies, but prices are prohibitive.

Routine **police checks** along the roads are more prevalent in Togo than in neighbouring countries but they generally wave bush taxis straight through. Negotiating them in your own vehicle may sometimes take a little longer, but turning the conversation to Togo's qualifying for the 2006 World Cup should help smooth the way for years to come.

Accommodation

Except in Lomé, Togo has little in the way of luxury **accommodation**, although it does have an adequate number of more modest lodgings, either privately owned or government run. Most places have nets at the windows, though you should check for holes before assuming you'll have a mosquito-free night. Accommodation is usually good value compared with neighbouring Francophone countries, although amenities like TV and phones are less common. Air conditioning (a/c) isn't always worth paying extra for: not all hotels have control over their electricity supply, and some that do are running expensive generators that are sometimes turned off.

Basic budget hotels (①–②) start at around CFA3000 in the rural areas and range from rudimentary *chambres de passage* to decent self-contained rooms. At the top of this range some even have a/c. **Mid-range** business- or tourist-class hotels (③–⑤) typically offer self-contained (s/c) rooms with a/c and often amenities like TV and phone, and a restaurant, but some have cheaper rooms that you shouldn't hesitate to ask for. Top-end hotels (⑥–⑧) are found more or less only in Lomé.

Togo has no youth hostels and little in the way of mission accommodation, though the *Affaires Sociales* government resthouses will always put you up cheaply if they have a room free.

There's a handful of organized **camping sites** east of Lomé and a very limited number of other sites throughout the country. Some hotels allow campers to pitch a tent on their grounds for CFA1000–3000 a night. If you have your own transport and are out in the bush, you can pull off the road discreetly, but it's advisable – not to mention polite – to let local people know you are there. Officially, staying with people is frowned upon unless you have made a declaration at the town *préfecture*. However, Lomé is big enough for you to be able to skip this formality, and it seems that, even outside the capital, the authorities don't worry too much about it nowadays.

Eating and drinking

Togo has a deserved reputation for some of the best **cooking** in West Africa, and small restaurants and street stands as far afield as Niamey, Bamako and Abidjan are often run by Togolese women. The secret of their success lies in their sauces, which tend to be less oily than usual and contain more vegetables. Not that you'll necessarily love Togolese food; some of it may seem unappealing at first (not everyone is a fan of slimy gumbo, or okra) and all of it is heavily laced with hot peppers.

Staples vary across the country. In the south, **cassava** (manioc) predominates, along with **palm oil** and **maize**. Cassava is often grated and steamed and known as *atiéké*. In the plateau region, the diet

---

Accommodation price codes

All accommodation prices in this chapter are coded according to the following scale, whose equivalent in pounds sterling/US dollars is used throughout the book. Prices refer to the rate you can expect to pay for a room with two beds, including taxes. Single rooms, or single occupancy, will normally cost at least two-thirds of the twin-occupancy rate but you will often have to haggle hard. For further details, see p.55.

① Under CFA5000 (under £5/$10)
② CFA5000–10,000 (£5–10/$10–20)
③ CFA10,000–15,000 (£10–15/$20–30)
④ CFA15,000–20,000 (£15–20/$30–40)
⑤ CFA20,000–30,000 (£20–30/$40–60)
⑥ CFA30,000–40,000 (£30–40/$60–80)
⑦ CFA40,000–50,000 (£40–50/$80–100)
⑧ Over CFA50,000 (over £50/$100)

contains more tubers – **yam**, **cocoyam** and **sweet potato** – boiled, grilled, steamed or fried. **Plantain** is another favourite staple, commonly pounded into *fufu* (which can also be made with cassava or yam). In the north, **sheanut oil** is more commonly used than palm oil. Likewise, **rice**, **millet** and **sorghum** (any of them can be ground, boiled and served as a staple mash, accompanied by a sauce) are eaten more frequently in the north than towards the coast. **Pâte** – also found in Benin – is the generic term for any pounded starch derived from cassava, yam or sweet potato.

Vegetables include **tomatoes**, **gumbo**, **aubergines** (small and yellowish), **squash** and **beans**. These are used in sauces with cassava, baobab or taro leaves and mixed with fish, shellfish, meat or poultry. Common **spices** include ginger, peppers, anis, garlic, basil and mustard. The south and plateau region have the most **fruit**, though even in the extreme north you'll find a good variety. Pineapples, mangos, papayas, all the citrus fruits, avocados and guava are plentiful in the markets (depending of course on the season) and especially cheap in the south.

Supplements to the basics include **"agouti"** (the large and tasty herbivorous rodent known in Ghana and Nigeria as "bush rat" or "grasscutter"), **pintade** (guinea fowl) and **koliko** (deep-fried yam chips). In the north, look out for **wagashi** — fried cheese served with a spicy sauce.

Togo's best-known dishes are **moutsella** (a spicy fish and vegetable dish), **adokouin** (shellfish with a prawn sauce known as *azidessi*), **djekoumé** (chilli chicken), and **gboma** (a spinach and seafood based dish). You're most likely to sample these at an important private gathering, or as part of a *cuisine togolaise* menu in one of the more expensive restaurants.

Togo has great **street food** and, even in the smaller village markets, women sell exotic as well as fairly familiar food by the portion, from basins. The variety is huge and it's very cheap – CFA150 will get you a good-sized bowl. In addition, all large towns have restaurants serving European food, mainly French dishes, though these tend to be comparatively expensive. In Lomé, you'll also find a limited range of Chinese, Lebanese, Italian and German restaurants.

Finally, you'll find boys on bicycles selling delicious and inexpensive **Fan Milk** ice creams and frozen yoghurt in most large towns.

Drinking

Togo has its share of local drinks, similar to the other common intoxicants of West Africa. **Palm wine** is big in the south: the juice that flows from the trunks is already fermented and ready to drink, its frothiness indicating its freshness (if it's flat it will be high in alcohol). A hard liquor can be produced by distilling it. Though illegal, this highly potent "African gin", or *sodabi*, flows freely in the coastal region. Northern Togo specializes in *choucoutou* — millet beer known locally as *chouc* — a taste reminiscent of dry cider. Filtering it produces *chacbalo*, which is clear and slightly sweeter than *choucoutou*.

Togo's **beer** is excellent and cheap. Bière du Bénin (referred to as BB, pronounced "Bé-Bé") produces both "Lager" and "Pils", along with Castel, the slightly more expensive Flag and the more potent Eku. Guinness is also available. There's a wide range of soft drinks, including good Lion Killer lemonade, soda water, tonic, sugar-free "Sport Actif" and the splendidly fruity, carbonated "Cocktail de Fruits". These come in large and small bottles and are all refreshingly inexpensive.

Bottled water is readily available from any shop or supermarket (CFA350). Better value are the 500ml bags sold on the streets for CFA25. Ask for *essi* or "poorwata", often sold by young Ghanaians: it's purified, sealed and branded, and not to be confused with the unmarked plastic bags tied in a knot.

Communications

Mail isn't too expensive: letters cost CFA650 to Europe and CFA700 to the US. Postcards are slightly cheaper. Parcels can only be sent air mail and are very expensive. If you want to call home, reverse-charge (collect) calls are possible but very expensive for the person paying the bill. Roadside phone booths are found throughout the country and offer cheap rates to land and mobile lines nationally and internationally. Phoning mobile numbers is usually the cheapest option with international rates about CFA300 per minute.

Mobile phones can be used in Togo on various networks and coverage is relatively good. Togolese SIM cards and top-ups are readily available and affordable. If you're expecting to use SMS messaging, you'll be able to send texts abroad, but not receive them.

Internet access is available in most towns, although connections can be slow. Costs are around CFA400 per hour.

⑪

TOGO | Basics

Opening hours, public holidays and festivals

Offices and most **businesses** are open from 7.30am to noon and from 2.30pm to 4.30 or 5.30pm Mon–Fri and 9am–noon on Sat. Banking hours vary slightly from one institution to the next, but are roughly 7.30–11.30am and 2.30–4.30pm. Note that in Lomé, these hours apply Monday to Friday, but outside of Lomé, banks are closed on Mondays and often open on Saturday mornings instead. The more modern *journée continue* hours (roughly 7.30am–2pm or later, with no closure) are increasingly common.

Muslim holidays (see p.63) are widely observed, especially in Sokodé and the north. Roughly two months after Tabaski, the Kotokoli around Sokodé celebrate the Gadao-Adossa or knife festival, when men give thanks to their ancestors for the coming harvest and perform a dangerous-looking knife dance, protected by a potion from a marabout.

Christian holidays – including Catholic festivals like Pentecost, Ascension and Assumption (the former two are variable; the latter is on Aug 15) – are also celebrated widely in Togo, especially in the south, along with New Year's Day everywhere.

National holidays are: January 13 (National Liberation Day); April 27 (Independence Day); May 1 (Labour Day); June 21 (Martyrs' Day); and November 1 (All Saints' Day). There are also a few days in July on the occasion of Evala which, with so many Kabyé employees granted leave, is increasingly considered a public holiday.

Traditional festivals take place in the regions, many with ancient ethnic roots and corresponding celebrations in Ghana and Benin. The following are the most notable.

July

Evala Initiation celebration in the Kabyé country with wrestling matches (*lutte traditionelle*). The tournaments in villages around Kara are now televised nationally.

Akpema Kabyé young-women's initiation ceremony.

August

Kpessosso Harvest festival of the Gun (an Ewe group), celebrated in the region of Aného and marked by traditional dances (*Adjogbo* and *Gbékon*).

Dzawuwu Ewe harvest festival celebrated on the first Sat of the month around Kpalimé.

Ayize Bean-harvest festival celebrated by the Ewe, particularly in the region of Tsevié.

September

Agbogbozan Festival of the Ewe diaspora celebrated on the first Thurs in Sept and especially colourful in Notsé.

Yékéyéké or Yakamiakin Week-long festival starting on the Thurs before the second Sun in Sept, in Glidji near Aného.

Dipontre Yam festival celebrated around the first week of Sept in Bassam.

December

Kamaka The best and most venerated farmer is carried on a hammock through the streets of Bafilo on the second Sat of the month.

Crafts and shopping

There are numerous places throughout the country where **crafts** are plentiful. The principal market in Lomé is the rue des Sculpteurs, an alley by the *Hôtel du Golfe* where vendors sell **sculptures**, **bronzes**, **jewellery** and **textiles** from across West Africa. The nearby Village Artisanal sells crafts made on site.

In Kpalimé, the Centre d'Enseignement Artistique et Artisanal gives traditional forms of **pottery**, **batik**, **calabash** decoration and **woodcarving** a modern, more commercial flavour. Kpalimé is also a good place to buy *kente* cloth (see p.862), which is woven in the town's streets.

Traditional **cloth** is also woven in Bafilo and Dapaong and can be purchased directly from the Groupement Essovale Dégbembia, the weaver's co-operative in Bafilo town centre, and from the Coopérative Tissage in Dapaong. Niamtougou has a very good co-operative selling a range of crafts made by disabled residents.

An unwelcome footnote is the presence of **ivory** in Lomé's craft shops and a flourishing ancillary trade in fake ivory bangles.

Crime and safety

Togo is generally pretty safe for tourists but the usual rules still apply: keep your wits about you and if you're carrying **valuables** make sure they are well hidden and close to you at all times. Only take out what you need; keep passport, cards and money in your hotel's safe. If you're out for a night on the tiles, beware of opportunistic **bag/purse snatchers**, especially if you're going to have a few beers. Street hawkers are the prime suspects.

There are lethal **undertows** all along Togo's coastline so take extreme care when swimming and don't be tempted to go out of your depth. Also on the **beaches**, the ones around Lomé are renowned for muggings after dark, sometimes at knife- or machete-point. Muggings have also been reported on the backstreets near the Ghanaian border.

If you have any contact with the **police**, treat them with politeness and patience. Mentioning the marvels of the Togolese football team may help to oil the wheels.

Emergencies

Police ☎171 or 117, fire service ☎118.

Gender issues and sexual attitudes

Tradition, in rural areas especially, dictates a strict sexual division of labour. Women do have considerable economic clout, particularly in the south where the well-organized women traders – known as the **Nanas Benz** after their favourite cars – are a political force. However, while the government recognizes the Union Nationale des Femmes Togolaises and women have access to all professions and are equal to men under the law, the reality is that education, though in theory compulsory for all children, is less likely to be given to girls than boys, and there are few women in high-level positions in government or business.

Traditional customs often supersede the legal system with the usual results; female genital mutilation is practiced on about 12 percent of girls and women have no maintenance or inheritance rights after divorce or on the death of a husband. Many marriages are polygamous and the law does not specifically prohibit domestic violence. As in Benin, trafficking of women and children, locally and overseas, is an ongoing problem.

With its western orientation and history of welcoming European tourists, you're not likely to experience a high degree of gender- or sexuality-related **harassment** in Togo. Having said that, if you're **gay**, be very discreet, as the country shares the punitive laws of most of Africa – gay sex is illegal and can result in jail terms.

Entertainment and sports

Togo's **music** scene isn't especially vivacious, partly because over the years the country's nightlife has been repeatedly curtailed by violence and curfews. There's a short account of Togolese music on p.903. Once the troubles settled down, clubs lowered their prices to attract business and many are once again in full swing.

No **film** industry has developed in Togo, and in the current conservative media climate, there's little incentive.

Sports

The **football** scene is increasingly dynamic. Dozens of players are based in overseas teams, including striker **Emmanuel Adebayor** at Arsenal, who was instrumental in securing the famous 3–2 victory of national squad Les Eperviers (the "Sparrowhawks") over Congo that qualified them for the 2006 World Cup. On the domestic side, there's particularly fierce competition between **Semassi**, the team from Sokodé, and **Gomido**, from Kpalimé.

Traditional **wrestling** – *la lutte* – is huge in Togo, and receives official patronage from Gnassingbé's government (see "Festivals", above, and p.894).

Wildlife and national parks

Most of Togo's former game reserves and national parks have been closed down, and the largest park, **Parc National de la Kéran**, has reverted to farmland, as most of the game has been killed off. The only park which is still functioning is the **Parc National de Fazao-Malfakassa**, west of the main north–south highway near Sokodé. Closed for rehabilitation for many years after much of its wildlife was poached or frightened off, it has been taken over by the Fondation Franz-Weber and is open to visitors. Although the chances of seeing larger mammals are extremely slim, it's set in stunning scenery and offers good odds of seeing monkeys and a variety of birdlife.

A brief history of Togo

For centuries, **Togo** has been on the fringes of several empires – Mali, Asante, Benin, Mossi – but the centre of none. The country, which formed part of what was once called the Slave Coast, came into contact with Europeans in the fifteenth century as the **Portuguese** made their sweep of the African seaboard. Porto Seguro (Agbodrafo) and Petit Popo (Aného) grew to become important trading posts where slaves were exchanged for European goods. By the end of the nineteenth century, trade had shifted to "legitimate" products – principally palm oil, used in soap manufacture in Europe. French and German companies competed along the coast in their dealings with the **Mina** people.

The colonial period

In 1884, **Gustav Nachtigal** sailed into Togo and signed a treaty with a village chief that made the country a **German protectorate**. In the following years, **Togoland** developed into the Reich's "model colony" as the Germans tried to force the country to produce economic miracles. Railways and roads were laid, and forests cleared for coffee and cocoa plantations. A direct radio link with Berlin was established and wharves were built.

The beginnings of an ill-defined educational system tried to create Christians and wage labourers out of reluctant farmers and fishermen. It took the Germans until 1902 to "pacify" the people of Togo, relying on forced labour and other repressive measures to push through their demands.

Despite the colony's economic importance, Germany's military presence in Togoland was weak. When World War I broke out, the British and French easily overran the territory, forcing the Kaiser's soldiers to capitulate at **Kamina** on August 26, 1914. The tiny village was thus the site of the Entente Powers' very first victory. After the war, a **League of Nations mandate** placed a third of the territory under British administration and two-thirds (corresponding to the present country's borders) in the hands of the French.

Towards independence

Both **France and Britain** showed only half-hearted interest in their new acquisitions, which technically were not colonies. The British quickly attached western Togo to the Gold Coast (it is now the Volta Region of Ghana), but the French took over the administration of eastern Togo as an entity separate from their other territories in West Africa. Thus several of Togo's peoples – especially the **Ewe** – suddenly found their communities divided by a border. Reunification was an early political theme, but the European powers viewed it unfavourably. A "pan-Ewe" vision, championed by early nationalist leaders like **Sylvanus Olympio**, was dealt a blow in 1956 when the people of West Togo voted in a referendum to amalgamate with the Gold Coast, then preparing for independence.

At the same time, the French were grooming eastern Togo for independence. In 1956, following a plebiscite, Togo became an autonomous republic with the pro-northern **Nicolas Grunitzky** appointed as prime minister. Two years later, UN-sanctioned elections saw Grunitzky ousted in favour of Sylvanus Olympio's Togolese National Unity Party and, when Togo became fully independent on April 27, 1960, Olympio was elected the nation's first president.

Sylvanus Olympio

Olympio aspired to the ideals of early African nationalists such as Ghana's Nkrumah, Guinea's Touré and Senegal's Senghor, although he never achieved their stature. In any case, even as he ushered in a new era, the stage was set for his own demise. In a scenario all too common in the former colonies, the Germans, and later French, had groomed a class of coastal peoples to be an **educated elite** of civil servants. After independence, these peoples inherited political power and, as a consequence, economic advantages. It was a formula guaranteed to result in ethnic tension in countries where unity should have been of primary importance.

Olympio, an Ewe from Aného, was openly contemptuous of the northern Togolese, whom he called *petits nordistes*. Increasing repression, fiscal austerity and disregard for the poor north didn't help to broaden his already narrow political base. In 1963, returning **Togolese soldiers** who had fought for France in the Algerian war of independence, were prevented by Olympio from joining Togo's national army, since in his eyes they had betrayed the African liberation movement. For these troops, mainly Kabyé men from the north, it was a humiliating snub and seeming proof that Olympio was determined to exclude northerners from participation in the new nation.

On January 13, 1963, a group of these disenfranchised soldiers, including a young Kabyé sergeant named **Etienne Eyadéma**, staged the first coup in independent Africa. They stormed the president's home and, according to the official version, shot and killed Olympio while he was trying to escape by scrambling up the wall from his residence and into the grounds of the American embassy where he had hoped to seek refuge. The soldiers set up a civilian government and placed Grunitzky, who had returned from exile, at its head. The new president lasted four ineffectual years and, as the country's increasing problems outstripped his competence to deal with them, he was replaced in a **bloodless coup** by Eyadéma – staged (in a symbolic style that became his hallmark) on January 13, 1967, four years to the day after Olympio's assassination.

Eyadéma's early years

After his second coup, Eyadéma suspended the constitution, dissolved political opposition and set about protecting his political future through the powerful mechanism of the single party he himself controlled – the Rassemblement du Peuple Togolais (RPT). By 1972, he was secure enough to hold a referendum on his future as president, which he won by a purported 99 percent of the votes.

Two years later, the president profited from a bizarre series of events that seemed to give supernatural backing to the demonstration of popular support. It started in 1974 with what has gone down in Togolese political legend as the **"Three Glorious Days"**. On **January 10**, Eyadéma announced that a 51 percent share of the French-operated phosphate mines (one of the country's principal resources) would be nationalized. Exactly two weeks later, on **January 24**, the president's private plane crashed over **Sarakawa**, but Eyadéma walked away from the wreck virtually untouched. An international plot was suspected, and, without any real proof, the world was led to believe this was a classic case of capitalist meddling – an assassination attempt on the man who had dared to liberate his country's economy from foreign control. After recovering, the president made a drawn-out journey from Kara to Lomé, and throngs of people came to look at the man who had become a myth. On **February 2**, Eyadéma made his **triumphal return** to the capital and announced that the phosphate industry was henceforth one hundred percent in Togolese hands.

The incident turned into a political windfall that made Togo look like the mouse who roared. Eyadéma's **anti-imperialist record** was enshrined in myth. He began an **"authen-ticity"** campaign, modelled closely on Mobutu's in Congo (then Zaire), abolishing French names (and renaming himself Gnassingbé) and introducing

Kabyé and – with a little shrewdness – Ewe into the schools as languages of instruction. Phosphate money helped construct a few modern buildings in Lomé and Kara along with ambitious projects like an oil refinery, steel plant (both now closed) and cement factory near Lomé. But rather than creating jobs, these simply lost money, forcing the country to bend to IMF pressure to denationalize as the economy slumped badly in the 1980s.

International affairs

Despite economic decline, Eyadéma managed to keep a high diplomatic profile and created a new larger-than-life image for himself as **West African peacemaker**. At one point he served as an intermediary between combatants in the Chadian civil war and helped smooth over relations between Nigeria and the Francophone countries that had backed Biafra. He also provided an African platform for **Israel**, with which Togo opened diplomatic relations in 1987.

On an economic level, Eyadéma championed ECOWAS (the West African common market, known in French-speaking countries as the CEDEAO), established in 1975 when fifteen countries signed the Treaty of Lagos. But his proudest achievement was hosting the meeting that resulted in the signing of the first **Lomé Convention** in 1975, giving countries in Africa, the Caribbean and the Pacific preferential treatment from the European Community and linking the name of Lomé with cooperation in development policy.

Cross-border relations

Relations with **Ghana** have traditionally been rocky, partly as a result of the pan-Ewe movement, which dates from the colonial era and continues in a more subtle form today. The ideological opposition of Gerry Rawlings' and Eyadéma's regimes also led to serious tensions between the two neighbours.

During Thomas Sankara's period in power in **Burkina Faso**, Togolese relations with Burkina also chilled, but improved rapidly after Blaise Compaoré took power in 1987. Eyadéma was the first African head of state to recognize the new Burkinabe government, just hours after Sankara was killed, and the two countries continue to have a close relationship.

Ideology has also been a source of conflict with **Benin** – a country charged by Togo, along with Ghana, with giving refuge to political exiles, particularly following the troubles of 2005.

Opposition mounts

Eyadéma was always careful to nip **opposition** in the bud. Active underground dissent has long existed, and it rose to the surface in periodic eruptions of violence.

In 1984, when the Pope's visit focused international attention on Togo, a series of **bombings** rocked Lomé. A **coup attempt** occurred in a 1986 shoot-out with armed rebels who got perilously close to the presidential residence. The attempted takeover was blamed on the exiled Gilchrist Olympio (son of the late president) who was subsequently sentenced to death *in absentia*.

In 1990, the government was again shaken when members of the **Convention Démocratique des Peuples Africains du Togo (CDPA-T)**, an opposition group which had been based in Côte d'Ivoire until ousted by Houphouët-Boigny in 1989, were arrested for distributing anti-government literature. The ensuing trial led to massive demonstrations in Lomé which left many dead or injured.

Subsequent protests forced Eyadéma to **legalize political parties**, but unrest again erupted in April 1991. Fatalities were reported in Lomé when security forces dispersed demonstrators demanding Eyadéma's resignation. Afterwards, mutilated bodies began surfacing in Lomé's brackish Bé district lagoons. Twenty corpses were discovered, and the opposition blamed the brutality on the military. A **general strike** was called, more protests followed, and in June 1991 the government was forced to agree on the mandate for a **national conference**, similar to the one that had brought sweeping reforms to Benin.

In July 1991, delegates of newly legal political parties and the government convened, the conference proclaimed itself sovereign and suspended the constitution. By August, Eyadéma had been stripped of most of his power and the RPT had been outlawed. In an act of defiance, the president suddenly changed course and suspended the conference.

Opposition leaders refused to disband and proclaimed a **provisional government** under the leadership of **Joseph Kokou Koffigoh**, a lawyer and leader of the Ligue Togolaise des Droits de l'Homme. Eyadéma consented to recognize Koffigoh but within weeks of being instated, the new prime minister woke up to find soldiers had seized his house, captured the radio and television stations, and surrounded his office with tanks. Troops returned to the barracks on Eyadéma's orders, but in the following months, repeated popular protests led to bloody clashes with security forces. In November, the army **arrested Koffigoh** and demanded the transitional government be disbanded.

In prison, Koffigoh "reconsidered" his stance and consented to Eyadéma's euphemistically titled **"government of national unity"** which paved the way for the RPT's re-entry into the political scene. Although he spared the transitional government and allowed Koffigoh to remain as head, Eyadéma padded the council of ministers with close associates.

1992 was marked by repeated delays in the transitional process and by resulting violent protests. The sham of democratization was highlighted when security forces stormed the parliament and held forty MPs hostage until the speaker pushed through a bill returning frozen funds to the RPT. In November, another **general strike** was called as opposition parties and union members demanded the creation of a politically neutral security force, a new government, and free and fair elections.

The promised elections still hadn't materialized by January 1993 and the strike dragged on. A French and German delegation arrived in Lomé to help mediate the crisis, but their efforts were thwarted when security forces fired on a crowd of opposition supporters, killing at least twenty. After two security officers were found murdered on January 30, the army went on a retaliatory **shooting and looting spree** which left hundreds dead.

The new wave of violence led to a **mass exodus**, and forty thousand refugees streamed over the borders to Ghana and Benin, straining Togo's already dismal international relations. While both Ghana and Benin mobilized troops along their borders to protect the refugees, the United States, France, Germany and the EU suspended aid to Togo.

New elections and more of the same

Against the troubling backdrop, Eyadéma announced that **presidential elections** would be held in August but denied the candidature of Gilchrist Olympio on the grounds that his medical examination was invalid.

The team of international observers monitoring the elections denounced the polls as undemocratic, and US and German observers withdrew from the process. Candidates **Edem Kodjo** (Union Togolaise pour la Démocratie, UTD) and **Yao Agboyibo** (Comité d'Action pour le Renouveau, CAR) pulled out of the race in protest and called for a **national boycott**. On a turnout of only 36 percent, Eyadéma garnered 96 percent of the vote and proclaimed himself victorious. The following day, fifteen CAR members, who had been arrested for allegedly tampering with electoral material, died in prison. On January 5, 1994, gunfire once again erupted near Lomé's Tokoin military base where President Eyadéma normally slept. Simultaneous **rocket fire** blasted a presidential motorcade. The government issued a communiqué saying that the city was under a **commando attack**, but that the president and prime minister, who were in a private meeting far away from the motorcade at the time of the incident, were unscathed.

Fighting continued for four days as Loméans remained locked in their homes. When the dust had settled, Eyadéma announced that government forces had defeated the insurgents which he claimed had infiltrated the capital from Ghana. Official reports put the death toll at 69, mostly members of the commando forces. Some estimates, however, ran as high as 300–500 victims, including many civilians.

The nation was shocked and demoralized as **legislative elections** were held in February. In a tight race, Agboyibo's CAR won 36 seats in the 81-member parliament, while Kodjo's UTD won 7 and the RPT 37. Though the RPT thus formed the minority in parliament, Eyadéma gained leverage by appointing Kodjo to the premiership – a move that gave the appearance of benevolence to the opposition, while effectively dividing it, since Agboyibo naturally felt he had claims to the post. Despite their majority in parliament, the opposition couldn't get a grip on governance, and Kodjo complained that he was increasingly left out of the decision-making process. Angered at the fact that the president refused to live up to his earlier promises and appoint an international monitoring committee to oversee **by-elections** in 1996, CAR refused to participate. The RPT and allied parties gained enough seats to have a majority and Kodjo was swiftly replaced by **Kwassi Klutse**, a more conciliatory technocrat and former minister. The opposition was left out of the cabinet completely.

The continuing slide from democracy

In 1997, as he celebrated thirty years as head of state – and his survival through six years of political upheaval and the economic ruin of his country – Eyadéma was firmly back in control. The EU, especially Germany (one of whose embassy staff was shot dead at a roadblock in 1996), remained highly critical of the regime and refused to renew much-needed financial aid.

Reports of **human rights abuses** were legion by 1997, and the president's security forces were charged with extra-judicial killings, beatings and arbitrary arrests that the government neither investigated nor punished. Intimidation restricted freedom of speech and the press. In January 1998, a **student strike** to protest against the non-payment of study grants ended abruptly when gendarmes raided Lomé's Université du Bénin. In the ensuing mêlée, the president of the Union Nationale des Étudiants Togolais – who had refused to sign a government communiqué ordering students to return to classes – "fell" from a second-storey window, fracturing his spine. Eleven other students were arrested.

Trade unions fared no better. The Union Nationale des Syndicats Indépendants (UNSI) could do little to improve working conditions, complaining that it operated under "extreme difficulty". The government promised reprisals for even modest strike action; in 1998, the deputy secretary of the UNSI was assassinated in his Lomé home. Nobody was charged in connection with the killing.

The mood was thus sombre as the **presidential elections of 1998** took place. Olympio and Agboyibo, along with four other opposition candidates, courageously contested the elections. The establishment of a **National Election Commission** (NEC) to oversee the voting was a positive sign, but members were packed with supporters of the RPT and refused to act on the recommendations of international observers. The government ban on political rallies, conveniently ignored by the RPT, was widely viewed as an attempt to limit the opposition's ability to recruit supporters. And the state-owned radio and television gave little coverage to opposition candidates, despite constitutional guarantees of equal access.

Voting in June 1998 proceeded amid allegations of intimidation, violence and electoral fraud and, unsurprisingly, Eyadéma was declared the winner, having received 52 percent of the vote. From Ghana, Olympio, who received 34 percent by official accounts, claimed that he had been robbed of the victory and many international observers believed he was right. Days of protests and strikes followed the elections, but the government would not budge on the results, which the Supreme Court duly ratified.

Completely demoralized, and with no hope of a better outcome for the **legislative elections** planned to follow in July 1999, the opposition called for a **boycott** of them. Klutse resigned in May and the Eyadéma-friendly Kodjo was reinstated as PM. As the crowning achievement of Eyadéma's return to absolute supremacy, the RPT took all but one of the seats in the assembly.

Having silenced critics at home, Eyadéma decided in May 1999 to take on his international detractors, and hired a French lawyer to sue Amnesty International over allegations that large numbers of people were killed by security forces before the presidential elections of 1998. More than a hundred bodies had been washed ashore in Benin's coastal villages, many of them found handcuffed. French president Jacques Chirac's visit in July 1999 coincided with confirmation from the Benin League for the Defence of Human Rights that **mass executions** of hundreds of people had taken place and their bodies dumped at sea. However, Chirac's surprise visit seemed to pay dividends when he gained assurances that Eyadéma would step down before the 2003 elections – which he was constitutionally obliged to do in any case, having served the maximum two terms.

Eyadéma ... again

Despite the agreement with Chirac, further tampering with the democratic system soon followed. The legislative elections of 2002 were a repeat performance of 1999 – they were boycotted by the main opposition parties and the RTP were voted in with a healthy majority. Two months later, the National Assembly pushed through an amendment to the 1993 constitution abolishing the restriction that allowed presidents to serve only two terms, thus allowing Eyadéma to stand once more. The amendment also stated that all presidential candidates had to be resident in the country for twelve months prior to the elections, meaning Eyadéma's main rival, the exiled Gilchrist Olympio, could not stand. The **2003 presidential election** followed in a similar vein to that of 1998, with the same results. The EU decided not even to bother sending international observers.

Dozens were killed and wounded in clashes between opposition and government supporters. Eyadéma received 57 percent of the vote, whilst his nearest challenger, **Bob Akitani**, behind whom Olympio had thrown his support, received 34 percent. By the time the results were officially declared, the government was hailing the result "a victory for democracy in Togo", while Akitani was forced into hiding out of fears for his safety. After three decades in power, Eyadéma had managed to cling on once again. Togo's economy continued to slide and the gaping pockets of resentment in Togolese society continued to deepen. With the world's attention focused on fears of terrorism and rogue states, Eyadéma seemed to be correct in assuming the world would take little notice of another minor African dictatorship, while his personal friendship with French president Jacques Chirac offered another example of France's often unhelpful involvement in West African affairs.

The new order

In February 2005, at the age of 69, and having been in power uninterrupted for 38 years, Eyadéma died of a heart attack. There was little time for celebration, however, for the military moved swiftly to install his son, **Faure Gnassingbé**, as president. International condemnation of this coup led to Gnassingbé stepping down and calling an election. Gilchrist Olympio was barred from standing and Gnassingbé won with a 60 percent majority. The opposition refused to concede defeat and widespread violence once again erupted, leaving hundreds dead and 30,000 political refugees fleeing to Ghana and Benin.

Gnassingbé has since made some positive progress. He replaced Edem Kodjo as prime minister with Yao Agboyibo, the leader of the CAR, who has been working solidly towards improving relations with the EU. In 2004 the EU had agreed to resume financial aid if Togo met 22 specific criteria addressing issues such as electoral reform and repeal of the controversial press laws. Most of these criteria have so far been met, including the readmittance of Olympio's UFC party into the government, and a pledge that the armed forces will stay out of politics.

The final EU aid qualification was to hold **free and fair legislative elections**, which – something of a landmark for Togo – took place peacefully in October 2007, opening the doors to the resumption of EU assistance for the first time in fourteen years.

At the time of writing, there was finally cause for cautious optimism about Togo's future; however, there remains widespread scepticism amongst the southern based opposition, many of whom still regard Togo as being run as a profligate northern based family business. As with many other African countries, Togo is now welcoming **Chinese** aid and investment, but the long-term benefits of this new "friendship" for the Togolese people are highly questionable.

Meanwhile, Gnassingbé's decision to drop action against suspects in the violence which followed the 2005 elections has merely sharpened the hunger for revenge on the dynasty for the many atrocities perpetrated by it since the early 1990s. This simmering resentment is probably the greatest threat to Togo's future.

Music

Traditional music splits into two broad regions: **Kabyé** in the north and Ewe/Mina in the south. The Kabyé have a rich musical culture, with some of the most interesting instruments used only for special celebrations, like the *picancala*, a xylophone-like instrument made of stones, and the unusual water flutes. There's also music played on horns, flutes and whistles and even a trumpet – the *xokudu* – made from the fruit of the baobab tree.

Modern music in Togo has not thrown up any international stars and most performers derive their material from foreign styles. Togo's urban music was greatly influenced by Congolese styles in the 1960s and 1970s and reggae, soul, highlife and Latin music have all dominated the local scene at some time or other. **Bella Bellow** was the leading singer in the late 1960s and dominated the music scene until her death in 1973. More recent Togolese stars who have gained fame throughout West Africa include **Nimon-Toki Lala**, **Fifi**

Rafiatou, **Afia Mala**, **King Mensah** and **Jimi Hope**. Hope is one of Togo's biggest stars, a rock and blues musician with a huge following among the older crowd. **Ali Jezz** and **Wézépé** are currently the hottest names on the hip-hop scene: the annual AfricaRap festival in Lomé is a major platform (see p.918).

Various artists

Togo: Music from West Africa (Rounder Records, 1992). Excellent selection with a good mixture of traditional and modern styles, and some nice acoustic-guitar songs from Ali Bawa.

King Mensah

Mensah Ayaovi Papavi, born in 1971, has performed on stage since he was nine. A singer with Les Dauphins de la Capitale, he is also a storyteller, worked with the Ki-Yi M'Bock Theatre in Abidjan, and is today one of the most popular musicians in Togo.

Madjo (Bolibana). Driven by powerful percussion deeply rooted in African traditions, Mensah's music moves from Afrobeat to reggae, with strong jazz influences.

Ammy Coco

Zombie (Thoreco AM). Latest release from the Togolese-born singer based in the UK (sadly not likely to be seen in Lomé), who fuses R&B with a variety of African styles – she calls it soca-ragga – often backed by a big, pan-African group.

Books

Very little devoted to Togo has ever been published in English. For good general titles on West Africa, see p.35. Books marked 🏃 are especially recommended.

David Ananou *Le Fils du Fétiche*. Intended to combat the racism of its time by a portrayal of a typical Togolese family, the effort is confounded by Ananou's rejection of traditional beliefs for the "lofty" tenets of Christianity.

🏃 **John Miller Chernoff** *Hustling Is Not Stealing: Stories of an African Bar Girl*. Vibrant tales. See Ghana, p.811.

Yves-Emmanuel Dogbé *La Victime*. A treatment of the interracial theme in West Africa: a white girl's parents come to recognize the error of their prejudice, but too late.

🏃 **Fauziya Kassindja** *Do They Hear You When You Cry?* This powerful work describes Kassindja's own experiences, first fleeing Togo at the age of 17 to escape an FGM ceremony and forced marriage, then her years in US prisons while her landmark political asylum case was being fought.

Tete Michel Kpomassie *An African in Greenland*. The narrative of a Togolese explorer on a whimsical journey among the Inuit. Never quite gets past the sheer oddity of its theme, but entertaining nonetheless.

George Packer *The Village of Waiting*. Informative, wide-ranging and all too relevant account of the experiences of a Peace Corps volunteer (now journalist and novelist) near Notsé in the early 1980s.

Comi M. Toulabor *Le Togo sous Eyadéma*. A solid discussion of the 1980s – and about the only one to appear.

Languages

The official language of Togo is **French**, which is widely spoken. Due to commerce with Ghana and Nigeria, some traders also speak rudimentary **English**, especially in the area around Lomé.

There are some fifty African languages and dialects in Togo, the most widely spoken being **Mina** and **Ewe**. Mina is spoken by thirty percent of the population in the coastal region. **Kotokoli** – the language of Sokodé and environs (see p.906) – is also prevalent, whilst **Kabyé** (also known as Kabré or Kauré), President Gnassingbé's mother tongue, is widely spoken in the region around Kara. Other languages include **Bassari**, in the area around the town of Bassar, **Tchamba** in the east, and **Moba** around Dapaong. There are also scattered communities of speakers of **Hausa**, **Fula** and **Mossi** in the extreme north.

Minimal Mina, essential Ewe

Mina is spoken by about a third of the population in Togo, making it the most common language in the country. You'll run into it mostly along the coast, as well as in parts of Ghana and Benin. Unlike **Ewe**, to which it's closely related, Mina is not written. Both languages are tonal, so that meaning varies (as in Chinese for example) with the pitch of the voice ("ò", for example, denotes a descending tone). They're therefore rather hard languages for speakers of European tongues to come to grips with. The following words and expressions are only a very rough guide to pronunciation.

Mina greetings and basics

Sobaydo	Good day
Dosso	Reply
O foihn?	How are you?
aaaaa (as in cat)	Reply ("fine")
Akpay	Thank you
Akpaykaka (kaka)	Thank you very (very) much
Nkekay anenyo	Have a nice day
Aaaaa	Yes
Ow	No
Va	Come here (to a child)
Sodé or Sodaylo	See you later
Mia dogou/ mia dogoulo	Until we meet again
Ayee'soh	See you tomorrow

Mina numbers

Dekaa	1
Amevé	2
Ametòn (low tone)	3
Amené	4
Ametón (high tone)	5
Amadé	6
Ameadrreh	7
Ameni	8
Amesidiké	9
Amewo	10

Ewe greetings and basics

Woezon	Welcome (general greeting)
Nngdi	Good morning
Nngdo	Good afternoon
Fie	Good evening
Do agbe	Good night
Woe zo	Welcome
E foa?/ Ale nyuie?	How are you?
Mefo/Meli nyuie	I'm fine
Edzo dzi nam be medo go wo	Pleased to meet you
Nye mese egome o	I don't understand
Hede nyuie	Goodbye
Amedzro menye	I'm a stranger
Taflatse	Please
Nko wode?	What is your name?
Nngkonyee nye ...	My name is ...
Mele Evegbe srom	I am leaving Ewe land

Ewe numbers

Deka	1
Uhve	2
Etoh	3

Enah	4
Atoh	5
Adee	6
Aderen	7
Enyee	8
Asiekee	9
Ewo	10
Wedekee	11
Weuhve, etc	12
Blave	20
Blatòh (low tone)	30
Blana	40
Blatóh (high tone)	50
Bladee, etc	60
Alohfa deka	100

A little Kotokoli

The Voltaic **Kotokoli** language is spoken by the largely Muslim people of the same name in the mid–north region, especially around Sokodé and Bafilo.

Nodé	Welcome
Nyavinakozo	Good morning (5–8am)
(pl. Mivinekozo)	
Nawsé	Good day (8am–4pm)
(pl. Minawose)	
Neda nana	Good evening (4–7pm)
(pl. Minadananga)	
Esofesi	Good night ("May God wake you well")
Blabtcheri/blabtesi	See you tomorrow/ later
Eesobodi	Thank you for your gift
Natimaré	Thank you for your help
Mmm	Yes
Ay	No
Alafyaweh?	How are you? ("Are you in health?")
Mumumum	Fine ("fit")
Kokani	Fine ("The work is fine?")
Ngyinidé?	How much?
Lidé	Money
Byé	Five
Byefu	Ten
Tchente	Twenty-five
Alfa	One hundred
Alfa nolé	Two hundred
Milé	One thousand

Glossary

Anasara In the northern parts, a white, derived from Nazarene, or Christian.

Authenticité Programme initiated by Eyadéma to instil pride in "authentic" roots, requiring French names to be exchanged for African, and proficiency in Ewe, Mina or Kabyé for all school children.

Auto-suffisance alimentaire Food self-sufficiency – which, in non-drought years, Togo had nearly obtained before the unrest of the early 1990s.

Evala The annual wrestling matches in the president's home-town of Kara.

Soukala A compound of round huts connected by a wall, found in the north.

Tata Fortress-like house of the Tamberma people, properly known as a *takienta*.

Vaudau/Vodu Generic names for the spirit children of God – Mawu-Lisa in Ewe.

Yovo White person (Mina).

11.1

Lomé and the coast

omé's mix of urban sophistication and rural informality once combined to make it West Africa's most enticing capital: for overlanders a popular respite from the rigours of travel in the bush; for the large expat community working in finance, development or as volunteers, an important centre of operations. The violence of the 1990s and following the death of Eyadéma in 2005 hit Lomé badly, but the city's spark is gradually returning. The pace of Lomé falls far short of the frenzied tempo of several of West Africa's other big cities, with most of its activity centred around the bustling market and surrounding commercial district – a pleasantly archaic area laid out by the French.

Ghana starts on Lomé's western city limits, while east of the city, a mere fifty kilometres of coastline runs up to the Benin border. The surf is notoriously rough, even dangerous at times, yet the whole **Atlantic shorefront** is picture-postcard perfect, with its coconut groves, white-sand beaches and fishing villages – none of them more than an hour's journey from the capital. The towns of **Togoville**, **Aného** and **Glidji**, with their fetishes, shrines and festivals, offer interesting insights into local voodoo customs. These towns also served as the spearhead for the German colonial invasion which began in 1884 – the year when Gustav Nachtigal landed in Togoville and signed a treaty placing the chief under the Kaiser's "protection". Soon after, Aného became the capital of German Togoland. Today, the coastal villages are full of colonial vestiges, in varying states of dilapidation, standing in sharp contrast to the dominant voodoo culture all around.

Lomé

Although **LOMÉ** spreads widely, the city's population of around 700,000 is hardly enough to push it into the major metropolis category. The heart of the downtown district sweeps around the crowded old **Grand Marché**. In the immediate vicinity, throngs of **shoppers and street vendors** press through a maze of narrow avenues and sandy streets lined with two-storey colonial buildings – the domain of Lebanese shopkeepers and small import-export businesses, most of them Chinese. The whole area is dominated by the **beach** and pervaded by ocean breezes. Only along **Boulevard 13 Janvier** (still frequently referred to by its old name, Boulevard Circulaire) do you encounter the broad streets and high-rises that attest to Lomé's former status as West Africa's financial capital. The city's few remaining **industrial plants** are out of sight, about ten kilometres east, beyond the port.

Some history

Lomé was founded in the eighteenth century by Ewe people fleeing a tyrant ruler in their homeland of Notsé. By the end of the nineteenth century, the Germans had moved the **capital** of their newly declared colony from Aného to Lomé. Reminders of their rule – like the **neo-Gothic cathedral** and the **old wharf** near the Grand Marché – are still visible. Lomé remained the capital of the French protectorate

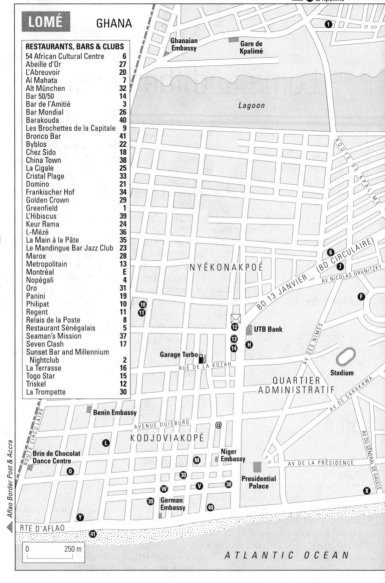

LOMÉ GHANA

RESTAURANTS, BARS & CLUBS

54 African Cultural Centre	6
Abeille d'Or	27
L'Abreuvoir	20
Al Mahata	7
Alt München	32
Bar 50/50	14
Bar de l'Amitié	3
Bar Mondial	26
Barakouda	40
Les Brochettes de la Capitale	9
Bronco Bar	41
Byblos	22
Chez Sido	18
China Town	38
La Cigale	25
Cristal Plage	33
Domino	21
Frankischer Hof	34
Golden Crown	29
Greenfield	1
L'Hibiscus	39
Keur Rama	24
L-Mézé	36
La Main à la Pâte	35
Le Mandingue Bar Jazz Club	23
Marox	28
Metropolitain	13
Montréal	E
Nopégali	4
Oro	31
Panini	19
Philipat	10
Regent	11
Relais de la Poste	8
Restaurant Sénégalais	5
Seaman's Mission	37
Seven Clash	17
Sunset Bar and Millennium Nightclub	2
La Terrasse	16
Togo Star	15
Triskel	12
La Trompette	30

Ghanaian Embassy

Gare de Kpalimé

Lagoon

ROUTE DE KPALIMÉ

(BD CIRCULAIRE)

BD 13 JANVIER

AV NICOLAS GRUNITZKY

NYÉKONAKPOÉ

UTB Bank

Garage Turbo

RUE DE LA KOZAH

AV DES NIMES

QUARTIER ADMINISTRATIF

AV DE SARAKAWA

Stadium

Benin Embassy

AVENUE DUISBURG

KODJOVIAKOPÉ

Niger Embassy

Brin de Chocolat Dance Centre

AV DE LA PRÉSIDENCE

AV DU GENERAL DE GAULLE

Presidential Palace

German Embassy

RTE D'AFLAO

0   250 m

ATLANTIC OCEAN

Aflao Border Post & Accra

after World War I, but Togo had lost its former importance, and development was minimal compared with other colonies.

Much of the infrastructure of the old part of town dates from the colonial period and has proved inadequate in coping with rapid growth. **Development** has been concentrated elsewhere. The first part of the city to be modernized was the **administrative centre** west of the Grand Marché. Wide tree-lined avenues

ACCOMMODATION

Aristos	I	Copacabana	J	Hôtel du Golfe	N	Montréal	E
Aurore	P	Corinthia Hôtel du 2 Février	F	Ibis Lomé Centre	X	My Diana	M
Belle-Vue	W	Digbawa	G	L'Arbre du Voyageur	A	Napoléon Lagune	B
Chez Lien	L	Equateur	Q	Le Cedre	O	Palm Beach	U
City	K	Folyana Guest House	H	Le Galion	V	Tano	Y
Coco Beach	T	Hôtel du Boulevard	C	Mawuli	D	Veronica Guest House	S
				Mercure Lomé Sarakawa	R		

were laid out here, and the capital's first skyscraper – the **Hôtel du 2 Février** (or *Corinthia Hôtel du 2 Février*, as it's now officially named) – was constructed. This 37-storey marble-and-glass tower, complete with 52 presidential suites, was part of Eyadéma's bid to have the Organization of African Unity's headquarters transferred to Lomé. The plan failed and, despite government PR, the hotel – one of the most luxurious in Africa – was for many years virtually empty. Further expensive symbols

909

were built to promulgate the glory of Eyadéma and Togo – the **Palais de Congrès** (formerly the convention hall of the RPT), the **ECOWAS** building and the various **ministries** with their gold-tinted glass.

Development of the city's **northern and eastern fringes** came to a standstill when the troubles started. The Avenue Jean Paul II and the Boulevard Gnassingbé Eyadéma lead to neighbourhoods that may still have an economic future – if Lomé ever regains its regional status. For the moment, however, the **Nouveau Marché**, the **Lomé 2000 conference centre** and the *gares routière* at **Agbalépédo** and **Akodessewa** still feel isolated from the city centre.

Arrival, city transport and information

Lomé's **airport** is about 6km northeast of the centre and relatively hassle-free (customs and immigration are thorough, but not intimidating). You can get your visa on arrival for CFA10,000 or €15; make sure you have the exact money. Once you've passed through customs and immigration, there's a **bureau de change** (daily 8.30am–8pm) plus a branch of the Union Togolaise de Banque (closed Sun), which changes cash (not traveller's cheques) at slightly poorer rates, and a 24-hour ATM.

Lomé surface arrivals and departures

From the east: coming in by *taxi brousse*, from **Benin** or **Nigeria**, you're most likely to be deposited at the *nouvel autogare* at **Akodessewa**, near the fetish market, about 4km east of the city centre. From here, you can take a shared or private taxi into town, most easily to the **Grand Marché autogare** (sometimes known as "Holando Gare"), in the heart of the city, from where you're within walking distance of a number of hotels. This old downtown *gare routière* is where vehicles from Aflao and Aného terminate, and some international vehicles linking Lomé with **Accra**, **Cotonou** and **Lagos** also still use it.

From the north: most vehicles to and from **Ouagadougou** and **northern Togo** (including Atakpamé, Sokodé, Kara and Dapaong), use the *gare* in the **Agbalépédo** neighbourhood, a good 10km north of downtown Lomé. To get to the city centre from Agbalépédo (or vice versa), either hire a private cab (around CFA2500) or pile into one of the collective taxis (CFA500) which ply between the Agbalépédo *gare routière* and the Grand Marché *gare*.

From Kpalimé: you'll arrive (unless your driver continues to the centre) at the large **gare de Kpalimé** just off the route de Kpalimé, about 5km northwest of the city centre in the Kondomé neighbourhood. Again, there are collective taxis waiting to take you into town.

Departing for the north: Rakieta buses (☏251.16.56) to **Kara** (CFA5000) via **Atakpamé** (CFA2500) and **Sokodé** (CFA 3500) leave from a depot in **Klikamé** opposite the high school, 3km north of the centre, daily at 7.30am. Buy your ticket in advance or arrive very early.

Going to Benin, Ghana and Côte d'Ivoire: a private taxi from the border to **Accra** will cost about CFA20,000 and takes about 4 hours. Good daily bus services to **Cotonou** (CFA3000; 8.30am), **Accra** (CFA4000; 4pm) and **Abidjan** (CFA17,000; 4pm) are provided by STIF (☏221.38.48), which has a *gare* at the eastern end of Boulevard de la République, about 400m west of the junction with Boulevard 13 Janvier.

Heading for Burkina and Mali: the Burkinabe company SOGEBAF uses the same *gare* as STIF (above), and has a once-weekly bus to **Bamako** (CFA26,000) via **Ouagadougou** (CFA13,000) and **Bobo-Dioulasso** (CFA18,000). A little further east by the Mobil petrol station is the STMB bus station (☏993.76.53) where buses depart Tuesday and Friday at 6pm for Bamako (CFA27,000) via Ouaga (CFA12,500). If you buy your ticket in advance, make sure there are no festivals or holidays in Burkina when you are travelling; buses are sometimes cancelled at short notice.

The information desk is open whenever flights are arriving or departing. There's also a branch of **Union Tours** (☏226.42.28 ✉uniontour@infrance.fr) who, among other services, arrange car rental. There's no airport bus service, so you'll have to rely on taxis; fares to various destinations are posted up outside in the car park – allow around CFA3000 to the town centre. It's slightly cheaper to flag down private cabs (CFA2000) on the main road outside the airport a few hundred metres from the arrivals hall.

At peak holiday times **Air France** frequently overbooks its flights to Paris and it's common to get bumped. Avoid this by checking in your bags between 10am and noon on the day of the evening flight. If you do get bumped, there's some comfort in the standard compensation of €600 cash and a night in a swanky hotel.

Orientation

Getting around Lomé isn't difficult if you think of the Grand Marché as the hub from which all the major roads shoot out like spokes. The city's residential areas and commercial centres fan out from here in concentric semicircles, the first of which is hemmed in by the **Boulevard 13 Janvier** or **Boulevard Circulaire** as it's more commonly known. Beyond the **Quartier Administratif** and west of this artery, the **Kodjoviakopé** neighbourhood was hardly more than a fishing village thirty years ago and still moves to a slower rhythm than the city centre. Many travellers opt to stay in this area. To the northeast, the **Amoutivé** neighbourhood – the home of the traditional chief of Lomé, a descendant of the city's founder – is presently one of the busiest quarters in town. Streets here are more crowded at night than in other neighbourhoods and the area throbs with commerce.

Bé-Apéyémé, to the east, is another lively neighbourhood that was formerly a village in its own right. Although it's still a stronghold of **voodooism**, the external signs of the religion are increasingly rare. Flagpoles bearing a white banner in certain homes in the area indicate the presence of a fetish priest. North of **the lagoon**, another semicircle unfolds. Important institutions such as the CHU hospital, the Université du Bénin and the new US embassy are situated beyond this natural barrier and are accessible both via the Atakpamé and the Kpalimé roads.

The **locations** of most hotels, restaurants, banks and shops are known by their relationship to key landmarks like the *Ibis* or *Sarakawa* hotels, or office buildings like the **Immeuble TABA** at 2 rue du Commerce.

Note that Lomé has its fair share of **street names** surplus to requirements. Among the more important, the Boulevard 13 Janvier is almost always known as the Boulevard Circulaire; the route d'Amoutivé is also known as Avenue Mama N'Danida; and the main seafront avenue goes by the names Boulevard de la République, Boulevard de la Marina, route d'Aflao, route d'Aného and *route internationale*.

Information and city transport

The **Direction de la Promotion Touristique** (Mon–Fri 7am–noon & 2.30–5.30pm; ☏221.43.13 or 221.56.62), in a small courtyard off rue du Lac Togo, just east of *Marox*, has a few rather out-of-date leaflets on offer, the most helpful being a small booklet featuring tourist highlights across the country.

In the absence of a bus system, public transport in Lomé is in **taxis**, either *taxis collectives* (about CFA200 per short hop), or chartered for a specific journey (about CFA600 for the average hop around town), or **zemidjans** ("moped taxis"), which will take you right to your destination for around CFA150, more at night. These are especially useful at night, when they're easier to find than taxis, though not all the moped drivers are very good, and you won't be protected by a helmet. Anybody on a motorbike will pick you up; older men with wing mirrors tend to be the safest bet. Terminals for *collectives* are scattered around the vicinity of the Grand Marché: those for Kodjoviakopé, Tokoin and Agbalépédo are located west of the market; those for Amoutivé and Lomé 2000 are to the north on Avenue Mama N'Danida;

Crime rates in Lomé rose sharply during the 1990s, and during the troubles of 2005. Muggings, some at knifepoint, are not infrequent along the beach and around bd de la République, whilst the area around the Grand Marché should also be avoided after dark. Walking anywhere at night with valuables is inadvisable.

those for Bé-Apéyémé and Ablogamé are to the east. *Collectives* run on fairly fixed routes – for example up and down the main radial thoroughfares from the Grand Marché to Boulevard Circulaire, or clockwise around Boulevard 13 Janvier to Bé and back again.

Accommodation

Lomé has dozens of hotels, many of which are getting very run-down. **Kodjoviakopé** has the best-value hotels in town, from cheap flophouses on the beachfront to chic rooms with all mod-cons in more sedate establishments on the sleepy streets to the north. The **camping sites**, beyond the port to the east of the centre, all have rooms and/or bungalows, as well as tent pitches.

Budget hotels

Hôtel du Boulevard bd 13 Janvier, just west of av Mama N'Danida ☎221.15.91. Very run-down, but friendly. Rooms are basic but clean, and there are great views from the roof. A/c rooms a little pricier. ❷

Le Cedre Kodjoviakopé ☎901.98.93. Rambling place recently taken over by a charming Lebanese family who exude hospitality. Wide range of rooms and a great bar/restaurant serving traditional Lebanese fare and good pizzas, on the balcony overlooking the ocean. Great-value rooms with fan, or a range with a/c. ❷–❸

Chez Lien Kodjoviakopé ☎220.35.85 or 910.11.78 ⓔchezlien@ighmail.com. Vietnamese-run with decent rooms and a good restaurant. A favourite with Peace Corps volunteers. Rooms with fan ❷ or a/c ❸.

Copacabana 65 rue Litimé ☎221.64.57. Rooms are good value for this part of town and better than you might expect from the grim facade. Friendly staff and rooftop bar are bonuses, but the adjoining nightclub won't suit light sleepers. Rooms with fan ❷ or a/c ❹.

🏃 **Le Galion** rue des Camomilles, off route d'Aflao, Kodjoviakopé ☎222.00.30 ⓦwww.hotel-galion.com. One of the city's best budget places, with delightful staff, laundry service and spacious, often immaculate rooms in a refurbished home with a landscaped courtyard. The newer building has the more expensive rooms – if you're counting the pennies go for the older part. Rooms with fan ❷ or a/c ❸.

Mawuli 21 rue Maoussas, northeast of the main post office ☎222.12.75. Amongst the cheapest

you'll find, a bright, pink building, with simple but well-maintained rooms (no fans or nets) and a friendly, homely atmosphere within the small courtyard. ❶

Montréal 211 bd 13 Janvier near *Brochettes de la Capitale* ☎221.39.50 or 901.18.81. Good-value rooms in the thick of the bustling nightlife, but it can be noisy. Handy for the pink pool table in the bar below. Laundry service. Rooms with fan ❷ or a/c ❸.

🏃 **My Diana** rue des Jonquilles ☎222.16.62 or 935.63.49. Simple, spotless rooms with fans on a quiet street. Periodic electricity problems can be a pain. ❷

Tano route d'Aflao ☎220.29.41 ⓔtanohotel @yahoo.com. Jolly hotel on the beach just a few hundred metres from the Ghanaian border. Cheap, clean rooms and a very lively bar. Rooms with fan ❷ or a/c ❸.

Moderate hotels

🏃 **L'Arbre du Voyageur** off route de Kpalimé, 3km from the centre behind the Atikoumé market next to the IAEC (international business school) ☎933.62.64 ⓔlpennaneach@yahoo.fr. A real find – a guesthouse rather than a hotel, with large, comfortable rooms, English-speaking owners and very good dinner for CFA2500. They also organize tours. Phoning or emailing in advance is essential. Rooms with fan and a/c ❹.

Belle-Vue Kodjoviakopé, behind the German embassy ☎220.22.40 or 946.13.27 ⓔhotel-bellevue.lome@hotmail.fr. Set on a quiet road near the beach, with fine views from the balcony, this chic, German-run hotel offers excellent-value rooms with a/c, TV, fridge and plentiful hot water. Very good bar and restaurant, and even a tiny pool. ❹

City bd 13 Janvier ☎220.96.48 or 999.99.09. Rather overpriced and lacking in character, but all rooms are immaculate and come with a/c, phone and TV. ❺

🏃 **Coco Beach** route de Cotonou, 10km east of the city past the port ☎271.49.37 ⓦwww.cocobeach.tg. This French-run beachside complex has immaculate, stylish rooms and bungalows all with a/c, satellite TV and hot water, and offers better value for money than the more expensive top-end hotels in the city. There's also a very classy restaurant, and the sheltered beach is one of the safest on a dangerous coast. Rooms ❺ or bungalows ❻.

Digbawa rue de Paris ☎221.14.88. A little shabby but centrally located. Quiet rooms with a decent bar and friendly staff. Rooms with fan ❸ or a/c ❹.

Equateur 102 rue Litimé, off bd 13 Janvier ☎221.99.92. A gem of a place, with tasteful decor, a peaceful atmosphere and an attractive first-floor bar/restaurant. Rooms come with a/c, TV and hot water. ❹

Folyana Guest House bd 13 Janvier. ☎221.02.22 or ☎911.58.28 ⓔfolyana@aol.com. Clean and spacious rooms in a good location with bar, restaurant, pool and outdoor cinema screening decent French, English and American films Fri, Sat & Sun at 7pm. A/c rooms range from ❹–❺.

Hôtel du Golfe rue du Commerce ☎221.02.78 ⓕ221.49.03. Set in an extremely central location, this older establishment has seen better days but still has some charm. The more expensive rooms have a/c and phones (and some have TV) ❹, and there's a cheaper block with rooms with fan ❷.

Napoléon Lagune 3km northeast of the centre, off bd de l'Oti ☎227.56.66 ⓦwww.woezon .com/napotogo. Set on the banks of the lagoon, the rooms here are stylish, clean and excellent value for money, and there's a small pool. ❺

Expensive

Aristos rue Aniko Palako ☎222.97.20 ⓔhotelaristos@yahoo.fr. Quiet, despite the central location, and with modern, attractive rooms – good value for creature comforts without chain-hotel sterility. ❼

Corinthia Hôtel du 2 Février Place de l'Indépendance ☎221.00.03 ⓦwww .corinthiahotels.com. This glitzy, self-important landmark skyscraper offers dated but comfortable rooms, plus a pool, tennis courts, several restaurants and a nightclub. The bar on the 35th floor makes up with fantastic views what it lacks in style. However, it faces east, so don't go there for sunset. Rooms from CFA70,000. ❽

Ibis Lomé Centre on the seafront, corner of av du Général de Gaulle ☎221.19.63 or 944.00.00 ⓦwww.ibishotel.com. After extensive renovations, this (formerly the *Hôtel-École Le Bénin*) is now somewhat corporate but offers good-value international standards in a great location. Decent, well-equipped rooms, pleasant pool but mediocre restaurant. Car hire and various tours on offer. ❼

Palm Beach 1 bd de la République, corner of rue Koumore ☎221.85.11 ⓦwww.palmbeachtogo .com. High-rise hotel overlooking the beach. The swanky, comfortable rooms have everything, and there's also a nightclub, casino and rooftop pool (open to non-residents: CFA2000). The restaurant isn't recommended, but good coffee is served in the lobby bar. ❼

Mercure Lomé Sarakawa 4km east of the centre ☎227.65.90 ⓦwww.accorhotels.com. Arguably the best of the top-end hotels, set in 25 hectares of tropical gardens, with a 50m pool (the largest in West Africa; non-guests CFA3000), three tennis courts and horse-riding facilities. Rooms are luxurious and come with IDD phones, satellite TV, and hot water. Reasonable restaurant and popular basement club; business centre and ATM in the lobby. Overpriced, however, with rooms from CFA94,000. ❽

Veronica Guest House bd du Mono, just off route de Aného ☎222.69.07 or 222.96.98 ⓔveronicagh@bibway.com. An international-standard hotel, with the rooms beautifully decorated, and including phone, fridge, hot water and a/c. Tiny and very popular – so best to book in advance. ❻

Camping

There are two beaches near Lomé where you can camp; **rates** are around CFA1000 per person at both, and they also have rooms. Unfortunately, the immediate vicinities of the beach camping sites are now notorious for **robberies**. Take precautions if you're carrying valuables and be especially careful after dark. If you don't have your own transport, collective taxis can get you out to the campsites for about CFA300.

Chez Alice 12km east of central Lomé near the village of Baguida, 300m from a dirty beach ☎ 227.91.72 ⊛ www.hartmann-design.com /chezalice/chezalice.html. Something of a roadside holiday camp, with rooms of varying standards, as well as tent pitches. The good restaurant and bar make this a favourite overlanders' haunt, and the live music every Wed (8pm) is a big added draw. Rooms with fan ❶.

Robinson Plage 10km east of the centre, next to *Coco Beach* ☎ 947.00.17. Somewhat run-down these days, but still a good option if funds are tight. Tent pitches plus self-contained rooms and a reasonable seafood restaurant, though some people are less than impressed by the service and the mini-zoo attached to the site. Rooms with fan ❶.

The City

Lomé has few specific sights, but there's plenty to take in as you wander through town. At some stage in your stay, try to have a look at the **Hôtel du 2 Février**, built to commemorate Eyadéma's miraculous escape and "Triumphal Return" after his plane crashed near Sarakawa. On clear days, you get a splendid panoramic view of Lomé, Ghana and the coastline from the top-floor restaurant and bar, though even a small drink costs a packet.

Beaches

If you're looking for a **beach** in the downtown area, you're limited to the stretch of shore in front of the *Ibis* hotel, although it's dirty and prone to crime, while the sea has a strong undertow and is very polluted. Out of town past the port, *Robinson Plage* draws a weekend crowd, and the fact that it's a private beach means it's safer, although again the sand and sea are not particularly inviting.

The best place to try is *Cristal Plage* (☎ 930.30.00; see "Eating"), about 1km past the *Sarakawa* – go through the port entrance and then follow the signs. The private beach here offers the best swimming, and there are lifeguards on hand, so it's the safest bet. Sun loungers (CFA2500) and *paillotes* (CFA4000) can be rented for the day and riding is also available at CFA4000 per hour. If you're not eating, entry to the beach is CFA1000. On Sundays the place is packed with expats so be sure to book.

The Grand Marché

The focal point of the city, the **Grand Marché** takes up a full city block near the ocean. Business here has picked up considerably after the strikes of the early 1990s, and though the market is not the regional draw it once was, there's a vast range of goods and it's therefore about the only place you need to go for provisions, presents, or purchases of any kind whilst in the city. Commerce spills over into all the surrounding streets as traders (mostly girls and women between the ages of 3 and 103) zigzag through the crowd to hawk everything from rat poison to greeting cards.

The **ground floor** of the unattractive market building is filled with a mish-mash of cosmetics, bags, clothes and food – canned food, fruit and vegetables, meat, poultry, fish and staples like yams, rice, cassava and pasta, spices and peanut butter. Sellers have a flair for display, and fruit and vegetables are invariably arranged in eye-catching pyramids. Quality is generally high, though if you're cooking it's best to buy meat first thing in the morning, for obvious reasons. Up on the **first floor**, the celebrated, and extravagantly proportioned, **"Nanas Benz"** (which, roughly translated, means "Mercedes Mamas", a reference to the cars they often drive) lounge around fanning themselves in a decadent style befitting their reputation as some of the richest and most adept businesspeople in Africa. They monopolize the sale of **cloth** and travel to Europe and the Gulf to assure a stock that attracts buyers from the whole region. "Made in Holland" Dutch wax prints are their most expensive and prestigious wares, but most textiles now come from Indonesia or China which means they're cheap but low-quality. You'll also find some English and African prints, hand-woven *kente* cloth from Ghana, Ewe strip cloth, naturally dyed indigo wraps from Guinea and Mali, and rough cotton weaves from the Sahel.

Generally you'll have to buy in relatively large **quantities** here (the rue du Commerce is the best place for single cloths or *pagnes*), though after recent lean years the mamas have begun to make exceptions. Material is traditionally sold by *la pièce*, *une pièce* being six *pagnes*, and a *pagne* roughly equal to an arms' spread – or about 1.8m, the length of a wrap. The smallest length you can traditionally buy in the market is a *demi-pièce* or three *pagnes'* worth, the cost of which varies according to the method and place of manufacture. Prices are marked and, although you may be able to get the vendor to come down slightly, bargaining never gets you very far.

The **second floor** at the top of the market is a hodgepodge emporium of goods – everything from bicycle tyres to wigs, envelopes and Chinese enamel basins to plastic dolls (white as well as black). Mountains of cosmetics – lotions, shampoos, make-up – swamp an entire section.

Handicraft markets and shopping

Crafts from all over West Africa filter into Lomé and there are several locations in town to look for them. The main venue is the **rue des Sculpteurs**, also known by the local English-speaking community as "Rip-off Row", an alley next to the *Hôtel du Golfe*, where you'll find a large selection of carvings, batiks, sculpture and other handicrafts. The majority come from Nigeria, Cameroon, Ghana and even Kenya; there's little in the way of typically Togolese art. Beware of "antiques", which almost never are. Prices are steep, but the unwelcoming urgency of the vendors gradually gives way to something more bearable and friendly if you hang on for a few minutes and engage in some good-natured haggling, especially if you make a purchase, even of something small.

You can pick up comfortable and sturdy handmade **sandals** on the streetside near the cathedral on Avenue de la Libération. The kind with the cushioned soles and toe loop go for about CFA3000 and are worth every franc. On the same street, you'll also find **cloth**; you can easily buy short lengths of one or two *pagnes* here. A decent piece of Dutch wax print will cost about CFA6000.

Look out for the brilliantly patterned **blankets** – mainly from Mali and Niger, sold on rue Koumaré, just north of Imm.TABA. These are handmade and expensive, but patient bargaining gets results. Something big enough to cover a double bed or look huge and striking on a wall should ultimately cost somewhere between CFA20,000 and CFA30,000, though price is determined to some extent by the state of the market, the time of year and the number of punters in town.

The friendly and hassle-free **Village Artisanal** (Mon–Sat, 7am–5.30pm), on Avenue de la Nouvelle Marché, 400m north of Ramco Supermarket, is well worth a visit. You can watch local craftsmen creating batik, wood sculptures, pottery, jewellery, sandals and baskets – you could even have an outfit made to order. Work is of a high standard, and prices are reasonable.

Shops and produce stalls

Biloko next to *Bar Mondial*, av de la Présidence. Chic bags and jewellery designed by the French owner and made locally. The gallery next door sells good-quality antiques.

Fruit and vegetable stalls rue du Lac Togo. The best fruit and vegetables are to be had from the market stalls at the eastern end of the street, much of it grown on carefully tended plots less than a mile away.

Galerie le Loft 15 rue du Commerce ☎ 221.15.11. Interesting antique and repro furniture and arte-facts with negotiable prices.

Supermarkets The best-stocked supermarkets are Leader Price on rue du Commerce, and Ramco, on rue de Koumaré just past *Hôtel Palm Beach* – you'll find everything you'd expect of a medium-sized European store, including electricals, alcohol and tobacco, picnic equipment and camping gas. Champion, on rue de Lac Togo, is also good. Unless you're confident enough to buy fish as it's landed on the beach, the *supermarchés* are the most reliable places to buy seafood – and meat. Marox supermarket next to the *Marox* restaurant has good, fresh, well-cut meat, as do both Ramco supermarkets.

Woodin rue du Commerce. If you can't face the mayhem of the Grand Marché, shop for fabrics in a/c comfort and also have garments made up. Expect to pay about CFA10,000 for a two-piece outfit.

The Musée National

The **Musée National** (Mon–Fri 8am–noon & 2.30–5.30pm, Sat 9am–3pm; CFA1000) has been relegated to a small room in the Palais de Congrès, formerly the party headquarters, for more than a decade, and the pickings are decidedly slim. **Musical instruments** and **religious objects** – statues, masks and ceremonial costumes – give the merest glimpse into the material cultures of various ethnic groups, including the Kabyé, Mina and Ewe, but it's still worth a visit. The basement room is dedicated to the colonial period, tracing it from Nachtigal's landing in 1884, through the division of Togoland between the French and British in 1914, and ploddingly on to independence, with a succession of pictures of moustachioed governors puffing out their bemedalled chests.

Akodessewa fetish market

The **Marché des Féticheurs** at Akodessewa is a popular draw for visitors and Loméans alike, despite being more than 4km from the city centre. West Africa's largest fetish market, it has myriad stalls displaying animal skulls, rotting bird carcasses, statues, bells, powders and all the imaginable and unimaginable ingredients of **traditional medicine and religion**. Though fetishers won't hesitate to make a quick sell, at times giving the feeling of a fleecing operation, it's a serious profession, still handed down jealously from generation to generation. The reputation of the Togolese for their spiritual gifts is widespread and the powers of the *féticheurs* are sought after by all classes, while the reputation of Akodessewa attracts people from throughout West Africa, and from as far away as Gabon and Congo. In Togo, the overwhelming majority of people still practise traditional ("animist") religions, and even the Christian and Muslim minorities commonly incorporate animist practices into their beliefs. You'll find disarmingly inexpensive talismans to ensure safe travel or success in love, as well as more ghoulish items like scorpions and dead snakes, which are used to make potions for ailments such as arthritis and rheumatism. A little time spent here listening to tales of supernatural healing and therapy will sow seeds of doubt in the most rational mind.

Guides will pounce on you the moment you approach and demand very expensive entrance fees – CFA15,000 for a tour with your video camera for example, or CFA10,000 for a still camera and CFA5000 just to visit the market, with a guide to accompany you and answer your questions. It's a public area, however, and if you're prepared to be pleasantly robust, you should be able to knock the price down considerably. CFA1500 per visitor is ample for a guide for an hour or so, while you'll find photography easier if you simply engage your subjects by actually buying the odd item.

There are two ways of **getting to the market**. The first is to head out on the Nouvelle rue de Bé or the rue Notre Dame des Apôtres, beyond the Boulevard Circulaire. These two avenues converge, after just over a kilometre, by the old **Forêt Sacré** ("Sacred Forest", on the left) and pass the former site of the fetish market at Bé. The forest is a remarkable little jungle, surrounded by buildings, but out of bounds to nonbelievers. Continue past the forest, 3km further east, on Boulevard Houphouët-Boigny, and you'll arrive at the market. Alternatively, you can go the more boring way, by taking the route d'Aného along the coast, past the *Hôtel Sarakawa*. At the *rond-point du port*, 6km from central Lomé, turn left and follow the road for 1.5km. If you're getting to Akodessewa by private taxi, expect to pay about CFA1500. A *zemidjan* all the way there shouldn't cost you more than CFA400–500.

Eating

Lomé has an excellent variety of **restaurants**, including a particular abundance of French establishments and all the big hotels serve French cuisine at elevated prices. There's also a decent selection of more reasonable places, while cheap **street food** is easy to find, mainly around the different markets in town. At the Grand Marché, women serve delicious salads from stands directly opposite the taxi park. They'll throw anything that strikes your fancy onto a bed of lettuce – tomatoes, macaroni, avocados, even grilled chicken or Guinea fowl – and top it off with a tangy vinegar sauce. It's an excellent meal, so long as your system is fully adjusted. If you're delicate, go for a boiled-egg sandwich. Behind these stalls, women sell *fufu* or *akoumé* (fermented white-corn mash) with different sauces and beef, goat or chicken. At **breakfast**, keep your eye out for *les cafémans*, scattered about town, who serve cheap omelettes with Nescafé and bread at their outdoor benches and tables.

Phone numbers are given in the following listings where reservations are advisable.

Budget (under CFA1000)

Al Mahata bd 13 Janvier. Not to be missed, this Lebanese bakery and rough-and-ready restaurant serves the best flatbread and hummus in the city. Cheap and very cheerful; no alcohol.

Bar de l'Amitié off bd 13 Janvier near *Sunset*. Local, inexpensive, unpretentious food – choose from four or five gigantic pots of sauce with fish or meat and rice. Very popular at lunchtimes.

Bar 50/50 (known as "fifty-fifty" not "cinquante-cinquante") bd 13 Janvier. Cheap grilled meat and salads, served at pavement tables. A popular choice, not too touristy, and a good place to kick the evening off.

Metropolitain bd 13 Janvier, next to the *50/50*. Looks like a bar-cum-kiosk from the road, but behind there's a small outdoor seating area where you can tuck into inexpensive dishes like rice and sauce or spaghetti.

Nopégali 229 bd 13 Janvier. Delicious, fresh African cuisine served in a relaxed and friendly atmosphere.

Restaurant Sénégalais rue du Commerce. This basic restaurant with blaring TV serves up healthy portions of spaghetti, couscous and salad with a few Senegalese specialities.

Seaman's Mission (Foyer des Marins) route d'Aného opposite the port entrance. If you're staying to the east of the centre, this is handy for good cakes in the mornings and cheap beer late at night. There's also a small swimming pool.

La Terrasse bd 13 Janvier (9am–midnight). Very good and cheap Lebanese food at this great bar. Pool tables and fruit machines inside.

La Trompette Kodjoviakopé. Low-key bar with great pizzas, cheap beers and a pool table.

Moderate (up to CFA4000)

Abeille d'Or av Georges Pompidou (7am–11pm). Top-notch Lebanese food (snacks from CFA2000; meals from CFA4000) in cool a/c surroundings. Great for breakfast pastries with *illy* coffee – the best in Lomé.

Les Brochettes de la Capitale bd 13 Janvier. A local institution, this place has huge barbecues which turn out an endless supply of juicy meat kebabs in crusty baguettes. You can eat at tables on the sand under the stars, though you may have to wait for a seat at weekends.

Frankischer Hof off route d'Aného, 11km from the centre. Almost impossible to find – head out of town, the turnoff is to the right after the Total garage but before Texaco, immediately after the concrete monument with the Pharmacie Baguida sign. Then take the first left and it's 50m on your left. The German owner has been here since 1983 and imports beer from home to serve alongside vast plates of roast meat and excellent black bread. Well worth the journey if you're looking for a surreal twist. From CFA3500.

Le Galion at *Hôtel Le Galion*, off bd de la République. Great food at moderate prices, including pasta, fish and some good Vietnamese specialities, and live music on the terrace every Fri evening. Swiss-run, and frequented by various expats, it's a good place to catch up on local gossip.

L-Mézé rue d'Aného, opposite and slightly to the east of the *Sarakawa* ☏ 227.77.00 or 925.59.11. Brilliant Lebanese food, great atmosphere and a delightful manager – their meze plate (CFA10,000) is huge and particularly recommended.

Marox 24 rue du Lac Togo ☏ 222.41.38. German-run place which does a big trade in sausages and meat dishes with fries and salads (from around CFA2500). There's always a crowd in – mainly expats and flashy Togolese.

Montréal 211 bd 13 Janvier (daily from 6pm). Flash new bar-restaurant with three TVs, great for snacks, salads, burgers and sandwiches, all for under CFA2400 – and reasonable draught beer.

Relais de la Poste av de la Libération. Despite the dismal decor, this long-established place has a friendly atmosphere and serves decent French food at reasonable prices – their chocolate mousse is something else.

Expensive
(mostly more than CFA4000)

Alt München route d'Aného, 2km out of town past the *Sarakawa* ☎ 227.63.21. Dine in the lovely garden on big portions of hearty Bavarian fodder or lighter, French-style dishes. Good German beers, too. From CFA3500.

🏃 **Barakouda** route d'Aflao ☎ 220.17.54 or 930.32.82 (evenings only; closed Sun). Swanky restaurant and bar on the seafront specializing in excellent fish dishes (CFA3500–7000). The French owners have a boat and take tourists deep-sea fishing or whale watching (see "Listings").

China Town bd 13 Janvier, near bd de la République ☎ 222.30.06. Friendly and unpretentious Chinese restaurant – though not the smartest place in town. Mains with rice from CFA4500.

La Cigale bd 13 Janvier, 250m north of bd de la République ☎ 221.99.30. Lavish setup with European dishes from CFA4000 to CFA10,000, plus pizzas. They also do takeaways.

Coco Beach 10km east of the centre ☎ 271.49.35. Well worth the trip out of town for excellent seafood and French dishes served right on the beach. A small pool is on hand as well as loungers to rent on the beach, which is one of the safest in Togo. Highly recommended.

Cristal Plage 4km east of the centre; go through the entrance to the port then follow the signs ☎ 930.30.00. Lebanese-owned operation on the best beach in Lomé with a classy Mediterranean feel – crisp napkins, spotless glassware and fantastic seafood in the restaurant, or first-rate sandwiches and beer on the beach.

Golden Crown bd du Mono, near the corner of bd 13 Janvier and route d'Aného. First-class Chinese–Vietnamese restaurant with wonderful dishes. Mains from CFA4000.

Greenfield rue Akati, just east of the route de Kpalimé ☎ 222.21.55 (closed Mon). Set in a leafy courtyard, with eccentric decor, where the chef slaps pizzas together and the overworked waitresses try to cope with hordes of customers. Special nights include DVDs on Tues, candlelit meals on Fri, and occasional live jazz at weekends.

L'Hibiscus Kodjoviakopé, behind the German embassy ☎ 222.74.99. Set in an extension of the owner's beautiful home, this new, small French restaurant already has a solid reputation for excellent food and service.

Keur Rama bd 13 Janvier ☎ 221.54.62. Authentic West African dishes cooked and served with passion and great charm. More familiar French classics are available for the less adventurous. Main dishes from CFA4000; *menu dégustation* CFA6500.

La Main à la Pâte rue de Litimé ☎ 221.63.62 (closed Mon). French-owned a/c restaurant serving good pizzas and classic French dishes from CFA4500 with decent wine.

🏃 **Philipat** Kodjoviakopé, opposite the *lycée française* ☎ 904.06.42 (daily from 5.30pm; closed Mon). French-owned restaurant set in a charming garden with some of the best pizzas in Lomé, plus good pasta and fish dishes from CFA4500.

Triskel bd 13 Janvier, next to the post office (closed Sun lunch & Mon) ☎ 220.95.57. Under new ownership, this offers tip-top, if pricey, Breton cuisine and a brilliant bartender in a tropical garden complete with birds, tortoises and a children's play area. Perfect for a treat. Mains from CFA5000.

Sister food

"Don't be afraid of street food. It is delicious and *so* cheap. The stalls are almost always run by women so they're good places to do sisterly bonding."

Kate Hawkings, UK

Nightlife

Nightlife has picked up considerably since the early 1990s, when people tended to keep indoors after dark, but sections of town are still considered dangerous when the sun goes down, notably anywhere along the beach road or around the Grand Marché. There's a range of **discos**, running the gamut from popular spots where you pay no entrance and drinks are hardly more expensive than in daytime bars, to flashy joints with complicated light shows and DJs.

If you're after **live music**, *Chez Alice* (see p.914) hosts African music and dance on Wednesdays from 8pm, and *54 African Cultural Centre* (see below) is also good. Lomé's **AfricaRap festival** (Nov/Dec) is a major annual platform for new and emerging hip-hop talent (see p.904).

Bars, clubs and discos

The area at the northern end of rue de la Gare is often referred to as the **Bermuda Triangle** (locals say once you enter the area you'll quickly be led astray) marked by three of Lomé's most notorious night haunts – *Domino*, *Mini-Brasserie* and *L'Abreuvoir*. At the weekend, the bars on the eastern sweep of Boulevard 13 Janvier have tables on the pavement and are all rocking: hawkers work them selling cigarettes, tissues, condoms and Viagra – it's that kind of vibe. Good fun, but watch your belongings.

54 African Cultural Centre bd 13 Janvier. Simple, cheap food and live music Thurs, Fri, Sat & Sun. Free entry.

L'Abreuvoir rue de la Gare. Lively bar, popular with travellers, with European and African music.

Bronco Bar route d'Aflao. The best beach bar in Lomé. Hang out under the palm trees, but watch your stuff if you're here after dark.

Byblos bd 13 Janvier, next to *Panini*. Playing mainly modern African music, this club is about as bling as it gets; it has a good atmosphere and is popular with hip-hop stars and wealthy Togolese, though entrance is expensive (CFA5000) and drinks similarly pricey.

Chez Sido 42 rue de la Gare, above *L'Abreuvoir*. Longstanding and popular European-style bar, with slot machines, red leather stools and many willing ladies of the night. Watch your wallet.

Domino rue de la Gare, opposite *L'Abreuvoir*. Popular, dimly lit and very seedy nightspot which hots up after 11pm. Expensive drinks.

🏃 **Le Mandingue Bar Jazz Club** 8 rue Koketi, just off rue de la Gare. Top-quality live music (Wed–Sat from 9pm, Sun from 7pm). Mostly jazz, but with good blues and rock as well. No cover, but pricey drinks (Wed is happy hour all night).

Bar Mondial av de la Présidence. A great place to retreat after the rigours of the Grand Marché. Sit upstairs with cold beer and delicious pastries and watch the world go by below.

Montréal 211 bd 13 Janvier near *Brochettes de la Capitale*. Friendly bar with famous pink pool table.

Oro rue de Litimé, east of bd 13 Janvier (Wed–Mon from 10pm; closed Tues). French-owned club playing a variety of African and European music. CFA3500 cover.

🏃 **Panini** bd 13 Janvier. Get down and dirty at this perennially popular pick-up joint with great waitresses and plenty of life to watch. Avoid the toilets.

Privilège At the *Hôtel Palm Beach*. The biggest club in Lomé. No longer the place to be seen, but still popular on Fri and Sat nights with the younger crowd. Entry CFA4000.

Regent opposite the *lycée française*, Kodjoviakopé. Funky bar with eccentric decor. Popular with Peace Corps and other expats.

Seven Clash bd 13 Janvier. Hardcore bar with banging music and occasionally an Evangelical Christian warm-up. Bizarre, but has a certain charm.

🏃 **Sunset Bar and Millennium Nightclub** bd 13 Janvier, corner of route de Kpalimé. Great buzzy atmosphere in the outdoor bar where you can eat cheap *brochettes* and play table footy, pool and slots. The adjoining tacky club is a giggle, too.

Togo Star bd 13 Janvier. Everybody will be your friend here; the girls are hot and the beers are cold.

Lomé Listings

Airlines Most airline offices and tour operators are found in the TABA Building (Immeuble TABA) at 2 rue du Commerce, behind the *Hôtel Palm Beach*. Afriqiyah Airways, 25 rue de la Gare ☎ 221.76.94; Air Burkina, rue de la Gare ☎ 220.00.83; Air France, Imm. TABA ☎ 223.23.23; Air Gabon, Imm. TABA ☎ 221.05.73; Alitalia, c/o Equinox Holiday Club, rue du Grand Marché ☎ 222.01.08; Benin Golf Air, at the airport ☎ 221.41.21; Ethiopian Airlines, Imm. TABA ☎ 221.56.91; Ghana International Airlines, Imm. TABA ☎ 221.56.91.

Air freight Air France will fly cargo to Paris and can than transfer to other destinations. 42kg to JFK, for example, will cost CFA170,000. Go to the AF office in Imm. TABA for more information.

Banks Ecobank, 20 rue du Commerce (Mon–Fri 7.45am–4pm, Sat 9am–2pm), change cash and traveller's cheques with no commission; UTB, bd 13 Janvier, change cash and TCs, but service is very slow; BTCI, bd 13 Janvier, is the biggest bank in town, with a 24/7 ATM and Visa cash advances. The BTCI branch at rue du Commerce and the Banque Atlantique at av Georges Pompidou also have ATMs.

Books and magazines You'll sometimes find *Time* and *Newsweek* hawked around town. Librairie Bon Pasteur, on the corner of rue du Commerce and av de la Libération, has a wide selection of French papers and mags, plus fiction, reference books and good maps. For second-hand books in English, try the hawkers along the rue du Commerce.

Car rental Union Tours, at the airport (☎ 226.42.28 @ uniontour@infrnace.fr), charge around CFA35,000 for a day's car rental including driver, for driving just in the Lomé area. Alternatively try Europcar, 3824 bd 13 Janvier (☎ 221.44.79 @ www.europcartogo.com), or Avis, 252 bd 13 Janvier (☎ 221.05.82 @ www.avis.co.uk/carhire/africa/togo). Both companies can arrange to have a car waiting for you at the airport. A driver will cost around CFA15,000 per day. The larger hotels also arrange car rental with or without a driver.

Church services The Catholic cathedral offers mass in English on Wed at 6pm as well as services in French and Ewe. The newly-refurbished church opposite the *Hôtel Palm Beach* caters for other denominations.

Cinemas The Centre Culturel Français (CCF; see "Cultural centres") is your best for art-house French and European films; *Greenfield* restaurant shows French and Hollywood movies with English subtitles every Tues. For Hollywood films with sub-titles head for Cinéma Concorde at *Hôtel 2 Février* (☎ 221.00.03), Cinéma Opéra on rue du Commerce (☎ 221.85.12), Cinéma Elysées in Imm. TABA or *Folyana Guest House* on bd 13 Janvier.

Cultural centres and libraries The Centre Culturel Français (CCF) on av 24 Janvier ☎ 223.07.60 (closed Mon), is the most active cultural centre with a bar/restaurant, exhibitions, theatre, film, dance, music, a library and videos. The American Cultural Centre, at the US embassy, offer the usual stateside-style comforts and resources and regular movies and events. The German equivalent, the Goëthe Institut, just up from the Grand Marché, runs language courses but little in the way of events. The bar-resto *54 African Cultural Centre* at bd 13 Janvier, runs African music classes and has some interesting books.

Dance Brin de Chocolat, rue Pétunias, Kodjoviakopé (☎ 220.06.59 or 904.32.86 @ www .brindechocolat.org), is an inspirational dance centre supporting young Togolese dancers and running classes in African and Tahitian dance, tae kwon do, and yoga. They also put on some excellent music and dance performances.

Dentists Dr Akouvi on av de Calais in the Tokoin district (☎ 221.22.93) speaks English and will see you right.

Embassies and consulates Benin, 61 rue des Rossignocs ☎ 220.98.80; Congo DR, 325 bd 13 Janvier ☎ 221.42.33; France, 13 av du Golfe ☎ 223.46.00; Gabon, Tokoin Super-Taco

☎ 226.75.63; Germany, bd de la République ☎ 221.23.70; Ghana, Tokoin-Kondomé, just north of the lagoon ☎ 221.31.94; Niger, rue de Dahlias, Kodjoviakopé ☎ 222.43.31; Nigeria, bd Eyadéma, ☎ 221.34.55; UK, Concession OTAM, Zone Por-tuaire, Porte de Peche ☎ 227.11.41 @ tom @netcomg.tg (commercial office only; consular services at the British High Commission in Accra); USA, bd Eyadéma ☎ 261.54.70 @ 261.55.01 @ lome.usembassy.gov.

Flowers Fresh flowers are sold daily at the end of rue du Commerce opposite *Hôtel Palm Beach*.

Golf There is a surprisingly lush 18-hole golf course 3km out of town on route d'Atakpamé. The *Sarakawa* and *2 Février* hotels have mini-golf courses.

Gym Power Star Gym, bd 13 Janvier (☎ 905.69.30), has a good range of equipment and charges CFA2500 per day membership.

Horse riding Head to *Cristal Plage* near the port (☎ 930.30.00; see "Eating") and gallop along the beach for CFA4000 per hour.

Hospitals and clinics Lomé's main hospital is the Centre Hospitalier Universitaire (☎ 225.47.39), in the north of town past *Greenfield* in Tokoin. Alternatively, try the Clinique de l'Union in Nyékonakpoé in the west of the city. The Clinique de St Hélène just off bd 13 Janvier behind *Hôtel du Boulevard*, is open 24 hours a day (☎ 221.65.39). Dr Bruce speaks English and can arrange medical evacuation if necessary.

Internet access You're never far from an Internet place in Lomé. Cyber Montréal, bd 13 Janvier, next to *Brochettes de la Capitale* (Mon–Sat noon–1am), has fast service in a quiet environment, whilst across the road is Siloe Intercom (closed Sun). Both places charge CFA500 per hour. The Internet café in Kodjoviakopé is open till 11pm every day, charges CFA400 per hour and also has reliable connections.

Maps Visit the Direction de la Cartographie Nationale, in the Ministère des Travaux Publiques (☎ 221.03.57) or Librairie Bon Pasteur. In theory, survey maps of the whole country, at 1:50,000 and 1:200,000, are available.

Mechanics Garage Turbo on the north side of rue de la Kozah, two blocks in from bd 13 Janvier, Kodjoviakopé (☎ 222.16.02), offers a professional and reliable service. Rue Aniko Palako is the place to find spare parts, tools and other hardware, with plenty of workshops where mechanics can fix most things.

Opticians Togoptic, next to the Relais de la Poste on av de la Libération (☎ 222.01.31; Mon–Fri 8am–12.15pm & 3–6.30pm, Sat 8am–12.15pm), is recommended.

Pharmacies Pharmacie les Étoiles on av de la Nouvelle Marché is probably the best and even takes Visa cards. Each district has a night-rota pharmacy (*pharmacie de garde*). For information call ☎242.

Phones There's a telephone and fax service behind the PTT. Calls can also be made from major hotels but the cheapest are the many phone kiosks found on the streets. Note that it is usually cheaper to call mobile numbers – with a Togolese SIM card – than land lines.

Photography For passport/identity photos, Photoland in Imm. TABA charges CFA1500 for a one-hour service, or ask one of the many camera-wielders hanging out on the street here. Magic Photo, rue du Commerce, offers more expensive one-hour development and on-the-spot passport photos. Cristal Photo Lab on av de la Nouvelle Marché is also good.

Post The main PTT (Mon–Fri 7am–5.30pm, Sat 8am–noon) is on av de la Libération. Stamps can be bought from the stalls selling postcards and newspapers outside the PTT. Poste restante is helpful and reliable. There is a post box at the airport which offers the fastest delivery for air mail post, but it closes at 5pm.

Sports clubs English-speakers who want to make friends could head for the pool at the British School of Lomé (BSL)'s Club in *La Caisse*, an expat enclave opposite the Université de Bénin, about 4km up

bd Eyadéma, which also has several restaurants, tennis courts and a supermarket.

Swimming pools The best pools are at certain hotels: the *Sarakawa* (CFA3000 for non-guests) or the *Ibis* (CFA2500) are the best, the *2 Février* (CFA5000) is less good. The rooftop pool at the *Palm Beach* is a reasonable downtown option (CFA2000), as is the small but pleasant pool at *Hôtel du Golfe* (CFA1000). Or try the BSL club (see "Sports clubs").

Tennis The *Sarakawa*, *2 Février*, *Ibis* and *Palm Beach* hotels have tennis courts, as does the BSL Club (see "Sports clubs").

Travel agents Among the more reliable operators are Odyssée Voyages (☎221.80.26; English spoken) and Satguru (☎220.64.87 ⓦwww .satgurutravel.com), both in the Imm. TABA; Togo Voyages, 13 rue du Grand Marché (☎221.12.77), who mainly deal with flights; and Union Tours, based at the airport (☎226.42.28 ⓔuniontour @infrance.fr), who arrange both flights and tours.

Visa extensions The Service des Étrangers et Passports (7.30am–noon & 2.30–6pm; ☎250.78.56) is based at the Ministère de la Défense Nationale, some 10km north of the centre and adjacent to the enormous Imm. GTA (the GTA building; most taxi drivers know this landmark). Extensions are free (apart from a CFA500 fee for the form) but take at least 24 hours to process. You'll need three passport photos.

East of Lomé

The short drive from Lomé to the Benin border passes along the coastal highway, with alternating views of the Atlantic and **Lac Togo**, a large, bilharzia-free lake which provides a scenic retreat from the city and has become a popular weekend destination thanks to its sandy shores and clean water for swimming and water-sports. The villages along this stretch are peopled by Mina and Gun (or Guin), who migrated from Ghana at the beginning of the nineteenth century. Today, they make their living principally from fishing, coconut planting and small-scale cultivation.

On the lake's south shore, the village of **Agbodrafo** has an excellent range of hotels and is where you're most likely to stay. It's also the departure point for pirogues to the town of **Togoville** on the northern bank of the lake, interesting both for its history and voodoo shrines. Further east along the coastal highway is the crumbling former colonial capital of **Aného**, whilst the nearby village of **Glidji** has a variety of interesting fetish shrines and hosts the annual Yékéyéké festival.

Shared taxis will take you from Lomé to Aného for CFA700.

Agbodrafo

Only 30km from Lomé, **AGBODRAFO** was formerly known by its Portuguese name, Porto Seguro, and was the site of a small coastal fort similar to those in Ghana. It's now ruled by one **Apeto Eneke Assiakoley V**, who keeps the royal sceptres, thrones and weapons that have symbolized his family's authority in the region for 170 years.

There are several **accommodation** options in the village, although little choice if you're on a tight budget. Right on the lakeshore, the *Hôtel Le Lac* is the most expensive and luxurious, with comfortable a/c rooms with satellite TV (☎331.60.19 or 936.28.58 ➐), as well as a pool (CFA2500 for non-guests), and pedalos and jet skis for hire on the private beach. Not far away and next to the main jetty for pirogue rides, the *Hôtel Swiss Castel* (☎904.15.08 ➋) is shabbier and not the best choice. A hidden gem is the Swiss-owned *Hôtel Safari* set a kilometre from the lake and only 300m from the sea with excellent-value, stylish rooms built around a beautiful courtyard, with a good restaurant as well (☎902.65.13; rooms with fans ➋ a/c ➌). Just around the corner, you can't miss the grandiose *Maison Blanche*, which offers ten stylish, comfortable s/c, a/c rooms with hot water and an enormous American-themed restaurant (☎331.60.14 ➎). Finally, about 3km west, along the road to Lomé, a track to the right leads to the *Auberge du Lac*, which offers thatched, self-contained bungalows in idyllic surroundings on the sandy lakeshore, with windsurfers and sailing dinghies for hire (☎904.72.29 ✉auberge-du-lac@hotmail.com; rooms with fans or a/c ➋ or camping CFA2000/tent).

Pirogues ply regularly between Agbodrafo and **Togoville**, leaving from a lagoon landing about 100m from the highway near the *Hôtel Swiss Castel*. You can rent a pirogue by negotiating a fare for the round trip (aim for about CFA2000 per person) and arranging to be picked up in Togoville at a specified time. Alternatively, you can simply wait for the boat to fill up with market women, though you'll have a hard time convincing the *piroguier* to take you for the normal collective fare, and you may have a lot of hanging around to do on both shores. The simplest option is to visit the *Hôtel Le Lac*, who can organize a pirogue for around CFA1500 per person for the return trip – which is a good deal.

If you don't fancy the pirogue ride, or want to avoid the would-be guides who wait at Togoville jetty, you can also reach Togoville by **taxi** from Aného, a 30-minute drive along a dirt road. Note, however, that if you're planning to take a pirogue back to Agbodrafo, be warned that you may be quoted extortionate prices for the one-way trip. Haggle if you need to and pay no more than CFA1000.

Collectives from Agbodrafo to Aného charge CFA300.

Togoville and Vogan

Despite its historic importance, **TOGOVILLE** is almost catatonically laid-back and is more sleepy village than buzzy tourist hotspot. Pirogues pull up on the sandy beach where bored locals may offer to be your guide but there is no obligation. Although it's easy to walk around alone, hiring a guide will somehow make you feel less intrusive and will hardly break the bank – CFA1500 should cover it.

It was in Togoville that the treaty was agreed which made the Germans protectors of the region (at which time the town was known simply as Togo). The contract signed by **Mlapa**, the chief of this tiny community, was the basis on which the colonial government laid claim to all of present-day Togo and part of Ghana. In the past it was necessary to visit the chief, who was thought to be a direct descendant of Mlapa, although the last chief of Togoville, Mlapa V, was de-stooled in 2001 due to a political disagreement with the government and now lives in exile in Europe. For the present, you're free to visit at will.

The **Maison Royale** is normally the first call, where you'll be shown memorabilia, including old photographs and copies of the famous document signed with the Germans. You'll also be asked to sign the scruffy notebook labelled "Livre d'Or", and a small gift is expected at this point. Wandering around town, you'll easily spot the imposing **Catholic cathedral**, near the lakeside, which was built in 1910 by the Germans. Notice the interior murals of African martyrs being burned at the stake, and a shrine to the Virgin, who was allegedly seen walking on the lake in the early 1970s. This miracle inspired the 1985 visit of Pope Jean Paul II to Togoville – he stayed in the *Hôtel Le Lac* before arriving by pirogue at a specially constructed jetty in town. Celebrations are still held every year on November 7 to commemorate the Virgin's appearance. Despite the work of the Catholic Church, Togoville remains essentially animist. Walking through the narrow backstreets, you'll be shown several fetishes, including two **fertility shrines** – one of Mama Fiokpo, a well-rounded woman with spikes protruding from her body, and the other of her feebly endowed male counterpart lurking around the corner. Photographs are permitted provided you leave a small offering. Beyond the small market, on the north side of town, a modern **statue** marks the centenary of the Germano-Togolese treaty, celebrated in 1984. Lastly, the **Centre Adanu Co-operative d'Art et d'Artisanat**, set under a thatched roof between the main jetty and the cathedral, has a limited choice of wood carvings and other crafts for sale.

Although there's hardly enough to warrant an overnight stay, there's excellent **accommodation** at the *Hôtel Nachtigal*, near the market, which offers spotless, tiled rooms and has a pool, tennis court and a decent restaurant (☎333.70.76; rooms with fans ❷ or a/c ❸). The only other option in town is the ultra-basic setup with bucket showers at the *Auberge QG* (☎905.25.30 ❶).

The Friday market at **Vogan**, a few kilometres northeast of Togoville, is well worth a visit for all your voodoo requirements. Take a bush taxi from Lomé or, more atmospherically, get a pirogue to Togoville in the morning and negotiate a taxi or *zemidjan* to take you to the market and back again. Expect to pay about CFA1000 each way.

Aného and Glidji

Of all Togo's towns, the colonial presence is most strongly and most eerily felt in **ANÉHO**, 10km from Agbodrafo and only 2km from the border with Benin. The Portuguese were the first to come to the spot – a pleasing natural setting with sea and lagoon vistas – which soon developed as a major slave market. Current African family names like de Souza and the light skin of the people are surprising reminders of this "Brazilian" period, further reflected in the history and culture of Ouidah in Benin (see p.983).

Many buildings bear witness to the days when "Anecho" was the capital of Kaiser Wilhelm's prized African possession, among them the **Peter and Paul Church** (1898), close to being washed away by the ocean, the thick-walled **préfecture** near the bridge, the interesting **German cemetery**, and the finely restored **Protestant church** (1895) on the route de Lomé. Other buildings offer a reminder of the French presence, including a number of fine villas used by colonial administrators when Aného was capital of the protectorate.

Despite the architecture, residents are too trapped in their daily routines of farming, fishing and trade to have any illusions of grandeur – or much opportunity to bring the old town to life. Overshadowed by Lomé, it has been in a slow decline for decades, and most young people move to the capital. They leave it a satisfyingly moody place to visit, though with a slightly malevolent aura, too: the town has long been an opposition stronghold, and in the dark days following the death of Eyadéma in 2005, many government opponents disappeared and scores of bodies were washed ashore here, many bearing the marks of torture.

Voodoo culture

In contrast to the crumbling reminders of European occupation, Aného's **voodoo culture** thrives, though you'll see few outward signs of it other than on Tuesdays, main market day, when the fetish selection features monkey heads, crabs and various skulls. Fetish priests are highly respected members of the community and are often more trusted than medical doctors. Sacrifices are offered to shrines guarding many of the homes, and regular festivals are dedicated to the cult. For some background on "voodooism" and the *vodu*, see the box on p.984 in the Benin chapter. If you're interested, a good place for further voodoo immersion is **Glidji** (see below), reached most easily by *zemidjan* (around CFA500).

Practicalities

It isn't hard to find your way around Aného since virtually the whole of the town stretches along the **route de Lomé/Cotonou**. The market, post office, bank, *préfecture* and most shops can be found along this street between the Protestant church and the bridge. Across the bridge in the east of town lies a more residential neighbourhood with the *autogare* and some of the town's **hotels**.

The cheapest place to stay is the friendly and reasonably comfortable *Auberge Elmina* on the seafront about 80m east of the Peter and Paul Church (☎335.03.53 ❷). Sandwiched between the lagoon and the main road, just east of the bridge, is *L'Oasis*, which has somewhat dated s/c rooms with fans, and the best views of the sea and lagoon in town (☎331.01.25 ✉oasisaneh@hotmail.com ❸). Even if you don't stay, have a drink at the terrace restaurant and watch the fishermen cast their nets in the shallow waters. *Le Becca*, on the route de Lomé/Cotonou west of the market, is a newer establishment with spotless rooms (☎331.05.13; rooms with fans ❷ or a/c ❸). The town's fanciest accommodation is at the *First Hotel-Nightclub*, on the western edge of town on the route de Lomé/Cotonou, which has excellent a/c rooms with hot water, phone, satellite TV and tiled floor, as well as some cheaper – though poor value – rooms with fan(☎331.10.04; rooms with fans ❸ or a/c ❺). There's also a good pool (CFA500 for non-guests), tennis facilities, and the best **nightclub** in town (Sat only; CFA3000).

The market is the place for cheap **eating**, or try *Anastasia* just opposite, a lively café serving up omelettes, sandwiches and light meals. *Café Délice*, on a road behind *Le Becca*, is a great breakfast joint for tea, coffee and omelettes, whilst across the *autogare*, *Pago Pago* is a lively bar which also serves spaghetti, couscous and other basic meals. Otherwise, try one of the hotels. For **drinking**, check out the *Bar Amité de la Gare*, opposite the SGGG supermarket and near the market, which has a shady *paillote*, and *brochettes* in the evenings, or *Bar Marigot* just before the bridge, where you can sit by the lagoon and absorb the curious atmosphere.

Glidji – and the Yékéyéké

On the surface, **GLIDJI**, 4km north of Aného, looks just like any other Mina village. You'll notice the same *banco* huts with thatched roofs and the same narrow sandy streets found all along the coast. Yet the town is symbolically important, since the present chief is a direct descendant of **Foli-Bebe** – the first ruler of the region and the man responsible for the political organization of the Gun and Mina into independent chiefdoms after these peoples migrated from the Accra area in the early seventeenth century. Before starting off through town, you should pay a **visit to the chief**. To do so, you have to fill out a request at the royal secretariat. If the chief is around, and not otherwise occupied, he will receive you.

Glidji is also important from a religious perspective, since all the major sanctuaries to the principal **voodoo deities** are found in this town. You won't have trouble finding a boy to take you around to visit the different fetish shrines and voodoo meeting places. Ask to see the **temple of Egou**, the deity who is the traditional protector of the Mina people.

Moving on from Aného

The main *autogare* in Aného is across the lagoon in the east of town towards the Benin border at Hilakondji. **Bush taxis** run direct from here to Cotonou and Lomé. It's also possible to flag down taxis to Lomé if you stand on the main road near the market. There are less frequent taxis to Togoville; if you don't want to wait for the car to fill, you could charter the whole vehicle for around CFA3500 one way.

Because of its historical and religious pre-eminence, Glidji is the site of the **Yékéyéké** festival, celebrated annually on the Thursday before the second Sunday in September and coming hot on the heals of the **Kpessosso** harvest festival in August. Delegations arrive from all the major Mina and Gun centres to make offerings to the deities and to be blessed by the priests. Animals are sacrificed, but the climax of the ceremonies occurs when the colour of the sacred stone is revealed, predicting the fortune of the coming year. A blue stone, for example, indicates abundant rain.

If your stay in the area coincides with the festival, these are four days of celebrating not to be missed, but note that room availability is very tight. In fact, your only option for **accommodation** in Glidji itself is the *Auberge Alpha & Omega* in the Adamage neighbourhood, which has six slightly grubby and overpriced s/c rooms (☎331.05.40 ②).

11.2

The plateau region

Some of Togo's most beautiful and fertile rural backcountry districts are located in the **plateau region** in the southwest corner of the country along the Ghanaian border. This is Togo's most agriculturally significant area, with lush plantations of coffee, cocoa and fruit crops, but it also contains wilder parts, especially around Badou, with mountain vistas, vine-strewn forests and streams leaping in cascades from ragged clifftops – just how you always imagined the jungle should look, especially if you've been brought up on Tarzan-type images.

Given that it's just a few hours from Lomé, the whole area is wonderfully accessible too, as well as being ethnically diverse and full of hiking opportunities. The **coffee and cocoa** triangle, hemmed in by the towns of **Kpalimé**, **Badou** and **Atakpamé**, is home to several ethnic groups who came here from Ghana and the coast. Kpalimé and the surrounding villages retain essentially Ewe populations, but Badou and Atakpamé are melting pots of agricultural peoples.

Kpalimé and around

Capital of the *pays cacao* – the **cocoa country** – and of the entire fruit-growing region, **KPALIMÉ**'s unusually busy market is the first hint of its economic importance. Early in their brief rule, the Germans recognized the agricultural potential of this mild and attractive district. Once the plantations were established, they wasted no time in driving a railway through the forested hills to the town, and since that time Kpalimé (pronounced "Pal-ee-may" with a silent *k*) has never been long out of the news. It was a stronghold of Olympio support in the early days after independence, and today continues to harbour much anti-government sentiment.

There's enough to see and do around Kpalimé to keep you busy for a couple of days – and longer if you're into **trekking** in the nearby mountains. But the town is small and, if you have less time, you can still get a good feel of the place in a day.

Note that if you're here in **August**, the **Dzawuwu harvest festival** is celebrated around Kpalimé on the first Saturday of the month.

Arrival and orientation

The **gare routière**, where **bush taxis** arrive, is on the eastern side of town. There are two **banks** just north of the market (UTB is better than BTCI for changing money; neither have ATMs), whilst **shops** and cheap **restaurants** line the streets that box in the market area. The **post office** is on the main road in town, across from the Shell garage. If you've just arrived from (or are heading to) Ghana, **moneychangers**, who hang around the *gare routière*, convert cedis to CFA and vice versa – get an idea of the correct street rate in advance (you're looking for at least GH¢2 [Ghana's new currency] or more for CFA1000).

Accommodation

Kpalimé has a good choice of hotels, and you can also find accommodation amidst the beautiful scenery around the pretty nearby town of **Kouma–Konda** on the route to **Mont Klouto** (see p.928), though you're likely to feel stranded there if you don't have your own car. The evenings can get chilly in Kpalimé and its environs, so you will rarely need a/c, and cheaper places don't offer it.

(see p.928)

Auberge Bafana Bafana 100m west of the post office, near the church ☎940.21.69. A great budget option, in a convenient location, with cheap drinks at the terrace-bar and simple rooms – they're spartan, and lacking nets, but comfortable and quiet – set around a pleasant courtyard at the back. ❶

Auberge Mandela on the north side of town, behind the *Gomido* bar ☎441.12.40. In a quiet neighbourhood with a front patio for people-watching and fresh bread across the street. S/c rooms with fans ❶.

Chez Fanny 2 km south of town on the road to Lomé ☎441.00.99 or 905.28.52, Ⓔhotelchezfanny@yahoo.fr. Homely place with six spotless and well-furnished s/c, a/c rooms with TV. There's also an excellent restaurant serving up European dishes including great pizzas, sandwiches, a range of desserts and French cheeses. ❸

Cristal 100m northwest off the Atakpamé road ☎441.05.79. Large, new hotel with a range of rooms – not particularly stylish, but most come with a/c, TV, fridge and hot water. The cheaper rooms are very cramped. There is also a very kitsch pool: CFA1500 for non-guests. Rooms with fans or a/c ❸.

Domino close to the centre, just off the Texaco roundabout ☎441.01.87. Old favourite in a great location offering basic accommodation and the bonus of an attractive garden at the back. Rooms with fans ❶ or a/c ❷.

Le Geyser on the road to Kouma-Konda, 2km from the town centre ☎441.04.67 Ⓔhotelle geyser@hotmail.com. Attractive, quiet place with a pool (CFA1000 for non-guests) and spacious, clean rooms. Rooms with fans ❷ or a/c ❸.

Royal 2.5km from the centre on the road to Kouma-Konda ☎449.15.52 or 936.97.56 Ⓔhotelroyal@gmx.net. A calm retreat from the town with large a/c rooms with TV and a good restaurant. Tours and guides can be organized, too. ❹

Ewe names

As in the Asante country in Ghana, Ewe people usually take at least one name after the day of the week on which they were born.

	Girls' names	Boys' names
Monday	Adzo	Kodjo
Tuesday	Abla	Komla
Wednesday	Aku	Kokou
Thursday	Ayawa	Yao
Friday	Afi	Koffi
Saturday	Ami	Komi
Sunday	Kosiwa or Essi	Kossi

The Town

Kpalimé's **market** (Tues & Sat) is the town's most compelling attraction, and one of the region's best produce markets. Among the citrus you'll find beautiful oranges, grapefruit and mandarins, all green-skinned, juicy and sweet – street vendors squeeze them into plastic mugs to make a delicious juice for next to nothing (make sure to tell them not to add water if you don't want it). Avocados as big as boats sell for a few pennies, and bananas, pineapples and lesser-known fruits are all available in abundance. You'll also find woven *kente* cloth and other fabric for sale. Kpalimé is known for its weavers and the quality of the material is very good. It was also in Kpalimé that, on August 30, 1971, Eyadéma announced the founding of what was then the nation's only political party, the RPT. A giant statue of Eyadéma was erected to commemorate the event just south of the market, but was toppled in the riots that followed the 1991 coup attempt. Thousands of refugees passed through the border here into Ghana during the upheaval of the early 1990s and again during the troubles of 2005. Just off the market square, the **train station** (now disused) stands on a hilltop, giving views of mountains rising in all directions around you. To the east, a TV tower marks the summit of **Mont Agou** (986m), Togo's highest peak.

ACCOMMODATION		RESTAURANTS & CAFÉS	
Auberge Bafana Bafana	F	Amical Bon Café	4
Chez Fanny	G	Cafeteria BelAir	5
Cristal	A	Chez Lazare	3
Domino	E	Gomido Bar	B
Le Geyser	C	Maquis 2000	6
Mandela	B	Restaurant Le Fermier	1
Royal	D	Restaurant Macumba	2

On the eastern side of town, the towering steeple of the **Église Catholique** dominates the skyline. Built by the Germans in 1913, the church looks like it's jumped straight out of the Bavarian countryside, and exudes an incongruous beauty and calm.

Down near the stadium, **weavers** work foot-operated looms in a shack by the roadside and are happy to chat, though without ever breaking the rhythm of their movements during conversation. It's not hard to appreciate the time involved in making cloth and why it's so expensive. You can order directly from the weavers, but you'll have to wait several days (or even weeks) for bespoke products. There's further local craftsmanship on display at the **Centre d'Enseignement Artistique et Artisanal** (Mon–Sat 8am–6.30pm) on the route de Klouto, a couple of kilometres from the town centre. This state-run crafts school has two boutiques where all items manufactured at the school – batiks, clothes, bags, ceramics and wooden carvings – are for sale. Prices are slightly higher than on the street, but can be haggled down and considering there's an excellent range to choose from and the quality is high, it's a relaxed environment to shop in. Visitors are welcome to watch the students and teachers at work, but ask permission at the office first. Various crafts courses are available and there's also an Internet café.

Out on the road to Kouma-Konda, **ADETOP** (Association Découverte Togo Profond ☎441.08.07 ⓦwww.adetop-togo.org) is a nonprofit organization working on environmental, education and ecotourism projects. They offer a range of tours to sites in the vicinity, including **Mont Agou**, **Mont Klouto**, the monastery at **Dzogbégan** and various waterfalls, some across the border in Ghana (no visa required for a quick visit). If you prefer to go under your own steam, they'll also give you up-to-date information on the area.

Eating and drinking

There are lots of good cheap **food stalls** in the market. For **drinking and nightlife**, try *Maquis 2000*, an outdoor bar set in a scruffy courtyard on the main road just south of the post office; or the trendy *Imperial Nightclub* at the *Hôtel Cristal* (open Fri & Sat from 10pm; cover CFA3000, free for guests).

Amical Bon Café Long-standing, tiny café serving up a good range of dishes including chicken and chips, omelettes, couscous and *riz gras* at inflated prices.

Cafeteria BelAir Dilapidated shack south of the Texaco roundabout open 24 hours. Decent omelettes with baguettes, coffee and tea – a good place for breakfast or a late-night snack.

Chez Lazare 1km on the road to Kouma-Konda. Great omelettes and sandwiches as well as ice cream and cold beer.

Gomido Bar on the north side of town, in front of *Auberge Mandela*. Reliable and good-value daytime snacks and meals.

Restaurant Le Fermier 1km northwest of the centre, just off the road to Kouma-Konda. A good range of European dishes, as well as good ice cream, which you can eat either in the café (which has the added attraction of table football) or in the a/c restaurant.

Restaurant Macumba 2km northwest of the centre, just off the road to Kouma-Konda. The best place in town, with friendly service – it's a pain to find, but well worth the effort for the delicious meals including steaks, chicken and fish dishes for around CFA2000 – outstanding value for money.

Mont Klouto and Mont Agou

Some 12km northwest of Kpalimé stands **Mont Klouto**, a highland district of vertiginous jungle-swathed slopes and site of an old **German hospital** built before World War I. The views from the summit are stunning, and the area around boasts a huge variety of **butterflies** and offers good opportunities for hiking, with dense forest, streams and waterfalls in season. The road up here from Kpalimé is also spectacular: carved out by the Germans, it snakes up steep slopes through cocoa plantations and burrows through the dense **Missahohé Forest**, where tree branches form a tunnel over the road in certain areas.

A few kilometres before Mont Klouto you'll see the entrance to the **Chateau Viale** – a medieval-looking stone fortress built during World War II by a French lawyer, François-Raymond Viale. It became state property in 1971 and is now used by the president. ADETOP can arrange tours if you plan ahead.

Overcrowded collective **taxis** (CFA250–300) run fairly regularly from the Kpalimé *gare routière* to **KOUMA-KONDA**, the local centre. If you don't want to wait for a taxi to fill up (your best chances are on market days, Tues & Sat), it costs around CFA2000 to charter a taxi one way. A *zemidjan* will cost CFA300. You'll be dropped in Kouma-Konda village just 1km short of Mont Klouto. Here, you can find **accommodation** at the *Auberge Papillons* (@prosnyanu@yahoo.fr; no phone ❶), run by

---

Moving on from Kpalimé

Taxis run from Kpalimé's *gare routière* to **Lomé** (2hr) and **Atakpamé** (2hr) via a pretty route skirting the Danyi plateau. They also go to **Dzogbégan** (2hr), **Sokodé** (5hr), **Kara** (7hr) and **Dapaong** (12hr) in the north, and along a rough road to **Ho** (1hr 30min) in Ghana. Shared taxis for **Mont Agou** and **Kouma-Konda** leave from a tiny station next to the stadium, just south of the market.

local celebrity lepidopterist Prosper, who offers simple, fanless rooms (no running water) set in fledgling jungle, arranged round a *paillote*. Prosper organizes guided bushwalks and *safaris papillon* ("butterfly safaris") in the surrounding area, visiting small waterfalls, explaining the uses of local plants and trees and observing butterflies – there are more than five hundred different species in the area, most easily seen from September to February. Prices are CFA6000 per person for the day (lunch included), or CFA3000 for a two-hour trek. Just outside Kouma-Konda, *Auberge Nectar* has six basic, clean double rooms (☎335.61.58 ❷). Less rudimentary lodgings can be found near the summit of Mont Klouto, at the *Campement de Klouto* (no phone ❷), which provides a rustic retreat with pretty views in every direction. Even if you don't sleep here, it's worth stopping at the large *paillote* for something to eat or drink. From the *campement*, a path bordered by huge mango trees leads to the top of **Mont Klouto** (741m). Before you set off on the twenty-minute hike, you'll be asked to pay a CFA500 fee by the guides at the *campement*, who keep the paths clear. From the mountain, you can see across into Ghana and may even be able to make out the shining, artificial expanse of the dammed **Lake Volta**, 35km away to the west. Guides at the *campement* will offer to take you on other hikes through the forest – they're all young men trained by Prosper and really know their stuff.

On market days, it's also possible to catch taxis from Kpalimé to various villages on **Mont Agou** and hike around its 1000-metre peaks. Taxis in Kpalimé leave from a small station next to the stadium and you may need to ask for Pic Agou to be understood. You'll have to set off at dawn and return early, or you risk missing the last taxi back to Kpalimé. If you have your own vehicle, a good road leads all the way to Mont Agou's 986-metre summit, the highest point in Togo. ADETOP (see p.927) can arrange accommodation with meals with a local family for CFA15,000 per person per day, including a hiking guide.

From Kpalimé to Atakpamé: the Danyi plateau

The road from Kpalimé to Atakpamé runs along the base of the sheer cliffs of the **Danyi plateau**, rising up to the west. About 10km out of Kpalimé in the village of Kpimé-Seva you can see the **Kpimé falls** on the left, signposted from the roadside (passengers will point them out if you're in a taxi). It's an easy 1km walk along a good path to the entrance of the falls, where you'll have to pay the CFA500 entrance fee. The results of the hydroelectric dam built in the late 1970s haven't done much for the site's aesthetic appeal and in the dry season the falls are little more than a trickle, but during or after the rains, they tumble rewardingly a hundred metres down the cliffside. It's possible to walk to the top of the falls and visit the dam, a 90-minute walk from the falls' base.

It's a picturesque drive onwards to Atakpamé, passing through **Adéta** and numerous other Akposso villages where you could easily stop and have a look around if you have your own transport. A kilometre outside the village of **DZOGBÉGAN** (turn off the road at Adéta, 30km from Kpalimé, from where it's a further 20km), the **Benedictine monastery** features an unusual chapel built entirely of local materials – teak, *iroko*, mahogany, bamboo. The real interest here is gastronomic, however: the monks run an orchard and produce jams from the exotic fruit, as well as coffee, honey and other goodies not so often found in these regions. The *soeurs bénédictines*, who run

---

Travel in comfort

"Taxis don't leave until all the seats are sold, so you may have a long wait. Sometimes we would buy the empty seats to speed up departure, which gave us more space, and it also tended to endear us to fellow passengers."

Kate Hawkings, UK

a convent closer to the village, sell some of the same stuff. It's possible to **stay** at the monastery and the convent in simple rooms with shared facilities (ⓔabdzog@cafe.tg; full board ❶). Be warned that silence is expected after 8.45pm and the power goes off at 9pm. Don't be tempted to roll back drunk from the village.

Atakpamé and around

Situated in the mountains, **ATAKPAMÉ** has historically been a place of refuge. The **Ewe** were the first to arrive, from Notsé, in the seventeenth century. They were followed by the **Ana** – a people related to the Yoruba who came from the east in the nineteenth century – and then by the Akposso, who came down from the surrounding mountains in the early part of this century to farm the fertile plains. Today, Atakpamé's roads linking it with Lomé, Badou and Kpalimé and the industry in the area – like the new hydroelectric power station and a sugar refinery 20km to the north in Anié – have all helped it maintain its status as a regional hub and ethnic melting pot.

Hippos can sometimes be spotted at the **Barrage de Nangbéto** 36km east of Atakpamé. Take a bush taxi from the Lomé *autogare* (CFA900) early in the morning. If you don't charter a vehicle for your sole use, which will cost at least CFA10,000, you'll have to flag down a taxi back to town when you're done, which could take a long time, so take provisions. There is nowhere to stay near the *barrage*.

Arrival and orientation

The most scenic approach to Atakpamé is from Kpalimé via Hihéatro, a couple of kilometres west of the town. After this village, vehicles wind their way up one last steep hill and, before you're aware the town is anywhere nearby, you turn a bend to pull into the *autogare* near the main market. If you're coming by bush taxi from

Lomé or towns in the north, you'll arrive at the *gare routière* on route de Lomé, some 3km southeast of the centre; Rakieta buses from Lomé and Kara stop on the route nationale near *Hôtel Sahélien*.

The town's hilly topography and scattered environs are confusing. The town centre is 3km northwest of the route nationale. The major thoroughfare, the Avenue de la Libération, runs northwest–southeast and turns into the route de Lomé to meet the route nationale. The PTT and most hotels are along this street, whilst **banks** (BIA, UTB and BTCI, none with an ATM) and **shops** cluster around the **market** on the west side of the centre; on Friday – market day – the commotion is sensational. For **Internet** access, head to CIB (daily 8am–10pm; ☎ 440.12.73) on the route de Lomé near the Shell garage, which has fast connections (CFA400/hr).

Accommodation

Most of the **places to stay** listed below are on the route de Lomé, between the centre and the route nationale.

Hôtel de l'Amitié Agbonou, set back 100m from the route nationale, a few minutes' walk north of the main junction ☎ 440.06.25. Located well out of the town centre, this lovely, quiet place has a family feel and clean rooms, plus a bar and a good restaurant. Rooms with fans ❶ or a/c ❷.

Délice des Retraites (formerly the *Hôtel Miva*) route de Lomé near the route nationale junction, 3km from the centre ☎ 440.04.37. Friendly place offering some of the cheapest accommodation in town, with clean but very basic, cell-like rooms, all with fan and shared facilities. ❶

Foyer des Affaires Sociales route de Lomé near the Shell garage ☎ 440.06.53. Clean, spartan rooms and dorm beds. ❶

Relais des Plateaux route de Lomé by the Commissariat de Police ☎ 335.82.30. Not too far from the centre, this well-maintained place has clean and comfortable s/c rooms, with good views across town from the balconies. Rooms with fans ❶ or a/c ❷.

Roc up a steep drive near the Shell garage, off the route de Lomé ☎ 440.02.37. Government-run place that is the town's most expensive, though increasingly dated and tatty and unfortunately reminiscent of the *Overlook Hotel* in *The Shining*. The s/c, a/c rooms are still comfortable though, and the views are great. Rooms with fans or a/c ❸.

Le Sahélien route nationale, 500m north of the main junction ☎ 440.12.44. Very inconveniently located and right on the busy route nationale, but the s/c, a/c rooms with TV are excellent value for money, and there's a great rooftop bar/restaurant. Probably the liveliest place in town. ❷

Eating, drinking and nightlife

Atakpamé's **bars** and **restaurants** are mostly workaday places, but there's a decent number to choose from. If you're after something more swish, head to one of the hotel restaurants – the rooftop setting at *Le Sahélien* is probably the best choice for food, whilst *Hôtel Roc* offers great views from their terrace but the food is pretty dire.

Best of Best route de Lomé near *Hôtel Delices des Retraites*. Throbbing bar and nightclub open very late at weekends.

Bar Château southeast of the centre off rue du Grand Marché. Lively drinking spot with great views where dancing takes over on Fri and Sat nights.

Moving on from Atakpamé

Taxis for **Badou** (2hr) and **Kpalimé** (2hr) leave from the *autogare* in the town centre, just south of the market. For **Sokodé** (3–4hr; CFA2550), **Kara** (5–6hr; CFA3500) and other northern towns the *gare routière* is on the rte de Lomé some 1km north of the junction with the route nationale. For **Lomé** (2hr 30min CFA2300), most vehicles go from the Lomé *autogare*, just south of the junction. Rakieta buses to Lomé, Sokodé and Kara leave from the Rakieta *gare* on the route nationale near *Hôtel Sahélien*.

Fan Milk rue Atakpah. Usual good ice cream and yogs.

Kfête rue du Grand Marché, near the Église Évangélique (open 24hr). Decent range of European and Togolese snacks and meals.

Caféteriat Muset route nationale near Hôtel Sahélien (open 24hr). The best of many *maquis* along this stretch of road.

Maquis Oncle Sam route de Lomé just east of the route nationale junction. Lively bar/restaurant with good, cheap food and loud music.

Bar St Louis rue de Grand Marché. Basic but very friendly and serves decent food on the balcony overlooking the street.

Wadjo Nightclub rue du Grand Marché, opposite the BTD Bank. The small, quiet restaurant upstairs serves decent European dishes for around CFA2000. The music downstairs gets going on Sat nights (CFA1000 cover), with a selection of mainly modern Togolese tunes.

Badou and around

Located 79km west of Atakpamé, and less than 10km from the Ghanaian border, the pretty village of **BADOU** is the smallest, most isolated and most distinctly rural of the three towns of the coffee-and-cocoa triangle. Most of its people are cash-crop farmers and, despite the small size of the average farm, and fluctuating world prices, cocoa and coffee have brought a measure of prosperity to the people of the region, which offers some of Togo's most attractive jungle walks. Badou is most easily reached from Atakpamé, a spectacular drive around hairpin bends through the hilly peaks.

Practicalities

Arriving from Atakpamé, you'll be dropped at one of two *gares*: either **Tomegbé Gare**, at the entrance of town by the junction of the Atakpamé and Tomegbé roads, or **Dayconta Gare**, nearer the centre. At the latter, you'll find the first **accommodation** option in town, *La Cascade Plus*, which has good-value, clean s/c rooms with standing fans, as well as the liveliest **bar** in town (☏443.00.71 ❶). To get to the **market** from here, turn right down the road that leads to Ghana, across a small bridge. Further along this same thoroughfare, you'll come to a road junction marked by the *Carrefour 2000*, another lively place at night, which also offers basic, bare rooms with shared facilities (☏926.39.09 ❶). Turning left at this junction, you pass the **post office** en route to the government-run *Hôtel Abuta*, Badou's fanciest accommodation (☏443.00.16 or 993.85.25 ❷). You can also **camp** in the grounds here for CFA1500 per person and the friendly staff can organize trips to nearby waterfalls and hiking spots.

Young boys like to earn a few francs by showing visitors round their town and its surrounds. Although Badou itself is too small to need a guide, you might want someone to take you to nearby hamlets. They'll sometimes even offer lodgings *en famille*, which can be a cheaper and more enjoyable option than staying in town. In practical terms, Badou's offerings are limited – there's a **pharmacy** just behind the *Hôtel Abuta*, but nowhere in town to change money – but it's a pleasant place to hang out.

Around Badou

One of the main attractions in the Badou area is the spectacular **Akloa Falls**, 11km south of the town. To reach the falls, you first need to take a taxi from the Tomegbé *gare* to the village of **Akloa** (Akrowa on some maps). Shared taxis and pick-ups can take a while to fill – if you're short of time you can charter a vehicle for about CFA2000. At the entrance to the village, you'll see a hand-painted sign advertising the falls. This is the official starting point for the hike to the falls, and the place where you pay CFA500 for a ticket and can hire a guide if you want one.

The **climb** to the falls is fairly strenuous, but requires determination rather than fitness. In any case, there's no rush; it's hard to resist dawdling through the cool, dark underbrush of the forest. After some thirty minutes of hiking through the dense vegetation, you arrive at the falls – a drop of over thirty metres from the granite cliff. You can swim in the pool at their base and it's said the waters are therapeutic. Ask the guide to tell you about **Mamy Wada** – the spirit that guards the water – or about the numerous other supernatural forces in the forest. Two generations ago this whole area was sacred and off-limits to the uninitiated.

There are also good waterfalls at **Adomi Abra**, 57km southeast of Badou. You can stay at the tiny guesthouse in nearby **Agbo Kopé** where Monsieur Momo can organize a tour to the falls.

11.3

Sokodé and the north

I n the semi-daze of a long and comfortless taxi ride, you could miss the many signs indicating the shifts in peoples and lifestyles as you move from the balmy south of Togo to the central and northern regions. Gradually, however, you take in the change from the traditional square buildings of the south to the round, thatch-roofed **banco huts** of the interior. Around these are fixed silos of baked earth, used to store millet and corn. North of the coffee-and-cocoa zone, **subsistence farming** is the major economic activity, and along the roadside the earth is pushed up into small mounds planted with yams, groundnuts and cassava. Traditional **African religions** retain a tight hold on the inhabitants of **Bassar** and **Tchamba**, two major towns in the region. The place of the Church in southern Togo, however, is increasingly taken by **Islam** as you head north. And by the time you reach **Sokodé**, a long day's travel from Lomé, the whole environment – natural, cultural, social – has changed.

The predominant ethnic group of this mid-northern region is the **Kotokoli**, a people who migrated south from Mali in the late eighteenth or early nineteenth century. They brought Islam with them and Sokodé is now the most devoutly Muslim town in the country. Numerous **mosques**, in faded pastel colours and crowned with the star and crescent moon, attest to their adherence. So, too, does **dress style**, especially the flowing *boubous* (embroidered gowns) and skullcaps commonly worn by men. Women don't wear veils, but they do drape a long, transparent scarf over their heads, wrapping it around their necks and letting it fall over their backs to flap on the ground when they walk. For a few Kotokoli words, see the "Language" section on p.906.

Sokodé

In terms of population, **SOKODÉ** is easily Togo's second largest town, with around 100,000 inhabitants, but it has a far sleepier pace than third-placed Kara, a little

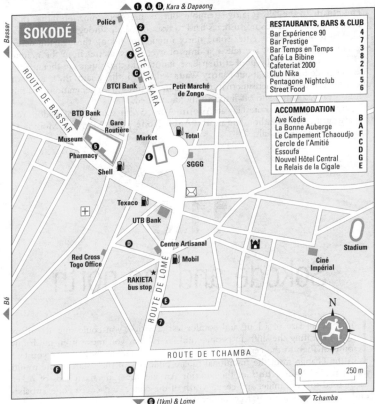

Within the map:

SOKODÉ

Bassar

Route de Bassar

Police

Route de Kara

BTCI Bank

BTD Bank

Gare Routière

Museum

Pharmacy

Petit Marché de Zongo

Market

Total

Shell

SGGG

Texaco

UTB Bank

Centre Artisanal

Mobil

Red Cross Togo Office

RAKIETA bus stop

Route de Lomé

Stadium

Ciné Impérial

Route de Tchamba

0   250 m

N

Bé

● ▲ ⑱ Kara & Dapaong

● (1km) & Lome   Tchamba

RESTAURANTS, BARS & CLUB

Bar Expérience 90	4
Bar Prestige	7
Bar Temps en Temps	3
Café La Bibine	8
Cafeteriat 2000	2
Club Nika	1
Pentagone Nightclub	5
Street Food	6

ACCOMMODATION

Ave Kedia	B
La Bonne Auberge	A
Le Campement Tchaoudjo	F
Cercle de l'Amitié	C
Essoufa	D
Nouvel Hôtel Central	G
Le Relais de la Cigale	E

further north and is certainly less significant on the national scene. In fact, there is not a great deal to see or do here, but it makes a pleasant enough place to spend a night or two and things hot up on market days (Mon & Thurs). If you're here at the right time of year, local **festivals** do bring the town alive (see opposite).

Development has been slow in coming to Sokodé, but several roads are now paved, including the Lomé–Dapaong route nationale and the road to Bassar, both of which run through the centre. Sokodé's position at the crossroads of these routes assures it a certain vitality, despite the government's obvious lack of interest in stimulating the local economy. A good number of homes in the heart of town are still made of *banco* and thatch, and most people are involved in trade and subsistence farming.

Arriving in Sokodé, most vehicles will drop you at the *gare routière* in the centre, just south of the market. The Rakieta bus will drop you near the Mobil petrol station.

Accommodation

Sokodé has a number of **places to stay**, but note that rooms can fill up quickly during the town's festivals.

Ave Kedia signposted off the route de Kara 2km from the centre, then 100m up a dirt track ☎550.05.34. Inconveniently located, but very quiet and with well-furnished rooms, a bar and a

small but well-stocked shop. Rooms with fans ① or a/c ③.

La Bonne Auberge about 2km from the centre on the route de Kara ☎550.02.35. Good-value accommodation in spacious rooms (fan or a/c) with comfy beds and tiled floors, but ask for a room at the back to avoid the noise from the main road. There's also a good restaurant and an attractive bar under a thatched roof. Rooms with fans or a/c ❶.

Le Campement Tchaoudjo off route de Lomé, near the *préfet*'s residence ☏ 550.15.57. Set in an old colonial building on a wooded hill overlooking the town, this place hasn't been well kept up, but the modest rooms with standing fans are amongst the cheapest in town, and you can also camp on the grounds. Rooms with fans ❶ or camping CFA1500.

Central 1.5km south of the centre on route de Lomé ☏ 550.07.06 ✉ bawacentral@yahoo.fr. Something of a misnomer, but this friendly hotel, set in attractive, leafy grounds, has comfortably dated, s/c rooms or round bungalows with wacky 70s furniture, private balconies and hot water. There's also a pleasant restaurant and bar, tennis facilities and helpful staff who can give you reli-able information about festivals. Rooms with a/c or bungalows ❸.

Cercle de l'Amitié route de Kara, next to the BTCI bank ☏ 550.09.06. Relatively funky hotel and restaurant with an African theme and cheap, clean and comfortable rooms, though it's set right on the main road, so can be noisy. ❶

🏃 **Essoufa** on a side-road off the route de Lomé, ☏ 550.09.89. This popular place has a variety of options, ranging from rooms with fan and shared facilities to a carpeted a/c room with satellite TV. All are spotless and good value, and there's also a bar and restaurant. Rooms with fans ❶ or a/c ❷.

Le Relais de la Cigale route de Lomé ☏ 550.00.19. Set back from the road, the rooms here are scruffy but clean and brightly decorated. The restaurant has a good choice of European dishes and the bar tables set under the trees offer the best spot in town to while away a hot afternoon. ❶.

The Town

The route internationale running through Sokodé – known as the **route de Lomé** on the south side and the **route de Kara** on the north – is the town's main street. Numerous bars and restaurants jostle for custom along this two-kilometre thoroughfare, while in the middle of it all, Sokodé's centre of gravity is defined by a major roundabout and the large, two-storey **market building**. On the same roundabout is the filling station where every taxi passing through stops to refuel. Passengers with five minutes to spare mill around the market buying presents and provisions, and there's an incessant barking from hawkers desperate to sell their gear before the driver pays the filling station *pompiste*, yells his passengers

Festivals in Sokodé

Sokodé is well known for its **festivals**, most of which revolve around Muslim religious holidays, when the town breaks from its normal slow pace to become surprisingly animated. One of the most important festivals is that marking the **end of Ramadan** (see p.63 for dates), when the town's entire male population – decked out in embroidered *boubous* – gathers at the stadium for collective prayers, before returning to town for feasting and dancing.

The **Fête du Tabaski** – celebrating Abraham's sacrificing the lamb in place of his son – takes place two months later. Several days prior to this festival, the streets in town begin filling with sheep and goats, which are slaughtered en masse on the day of Tabaski, then roasted and shared out among the community. The **Knife Festival**, or **Gadao-Adossa** (about three months after Tabaski), mixes Muslim elements with a custom which pre-dates the introduction of Islam into Kotokoli society and has many parallels in other West African societies. On this occasion – marking Muhammad's birthday, but also giving thanks to ancestors for the expected coming harvest – the men drink a potion specially prepared by a marabout which supposedly renders their skin impenetrable. In public dances, they then proceed to cut one another with knives. It's even said that babies who have been administered the potion are rolled over broken bottles with no harm coming to them.

back into the sweat-box and hits the road again. Northeast of the central market, the **Petit Marché de Zongo** is more traditional in flavour, with narrow streets full of thatched stalls selling everything from charcoal and yams to used shoes and clothing. There is a small **Centre Artisinal** opposite the Mobil petrol station which sells some good batik.

One block south of the roundabout, the route de Lomé intersects with the route de Bassar, Sokodé's other important street. The UTB **bank** and the **PTT** (with a poste restante that works, incidentally) face each other at this junction. Turning to the west up the route de Bassar, the paved road leads to the Tchaoundja neighbourhood and passes by the hospital, *Les Affaires Sociales* and the modern-looking BTD bank (no foreign exchange). The tiny **museum** opposite the BTD offers dusty artefacts of some interest; somebody will find the key if you ask around. Turning east, the dirt road leads down to the town's main **mosques**, the **cinema** and the **stadium**. If you happen to be in town during a football match, be sure to get a ticket: **Semassi**, the home team, is one of the nation's best and, even if soccer isn't your bag, the enthusiasm of the crowd would give anyone a buzz.

Near the stadium is the site of Sokodé's new **Grande Mosquée**. The old Grande Mosquée, located a couple of streets southwest of the post office, is beautiful for its simplicity, and completely devoid of ornamentation – you could walk right by and not even notice it – but the humble architecture has a tolerant and undogmatic appeal.

Eating, drinking and nightlife

For **food**, budget travellers head for the market. **Local specialities** include *watche* (rice and beans boiled together with onions and hot peppers), *kadadia* (mash made from finely ground cassava mixed with millet or corn) and *wagashi* (locally made cheese either served plain or deep-fried). In the evening you can get lamb kebabs. For snacking, be sure to try *kosse* (bean batter deep-fried in peanut oil) or *koliko* (yam chips), both local favourites.

Besides the hotel restaurants, of which *La Bonne Auberge* and *Essoufa* are particularly good, there's little choice. Your best bet is the friendly *Cafeteriat 2000* on the route de Kara, a 24-hour café which serves up generous portions of the usual staples including chicken and chips, spaghetti and couscous but no alcohol. *Café La Bibine*, on the route de Lomé, is another 24-hour option serving similar food, whilst just up the road *Bar Prestige* has more limited options of rice, spaghetti or couscous with sauce, but serves cheap, large beers.

The town has a few lively **bars and clubs** which stay open until the early hours. Two to start the evening off are *Bar Temps en Temps* – great for *brochettes* and people-watching – and *Bar Experience 90*, which are both very close to each other on the route de Kara. *Club Nika* (cover CFA1000), 2km from the centre on the route de Kara, gets going at weekends, playing a variety of Togolese, American and European music. The only other option for dancing till late is the *Pentagone Nightclub* (cover CFA1500), on the route de Bassar.

Moving on from Sokodé

Taxis brousse from Sokodé head in all directions from the *gare routière* in the town centre, including Bassar (2hr), Lomé (7–8hr), Kpalimé (5–6hr) and Kara (1–2hr). There are no direct taxis to **Ouagadougou**, and vehicles coming up from Lomé are already full. You'll have to take a taxi to Sinkassé (7–8hr) on the border, or alternatively go to Dapaong (6–7hr) and stop there for the night before picking up an onward connection. The Rakieta bus running between Lomé and Kara stops by the Mobil petrol station.

Around Sokodé

The highland landscapes and good roads around Sokodé provide opportunities for some easy excursions. Southwest of Sokodé, the **Parc National de Fazao-Malfakassa** is set in stunning mountainous scenery and offers some wildlife-viewing opportunities. North of Sokodé, the route nationale passes near the **Barrage d'Aleheride**, an old reservoir which allegedly houses a few crocodiles, before winding between the dramatic rocks of the **Faille d'Aledjo**. Not far from here, the friendly village of **Aledjo** offers spectacular views.

Parc National de Fazao-Malfakassa

The **Parc National de Fazao-Malfakassa** has now reopened under the management of the Fondation Franz-Weber (🌐 www.ffw.ch; though very little information is available at present), which is working to repopulate the park, most, if not all its lions and elephants having been poached during the troubles. Currently there is little wildlife to see other than some monkeys and a variety of birds. The best way to visit the park is to stay overnight at **Sotouboua**, 50km south of Sokodé – there is an *auberge* where you can also camp – then leave very early the next morning and enter the park at **Fazao**. There is no longer any accommodation in the park itself. **Entrance fees** are CFA10,000 per vehicle, plus CFA3000 per person. If you don't have your own transport, you may be able to rent a car and driver in **Sotouboua.**

North of Sokodé

The road to **Bafilo** runs through striking scenery, though the old dam at the crocodile village of **Aleheride** no longer has enough *caïmans* – or at least visible ones – to be worth the visit.

Following the route nationale, the scenery becomes more dramatic as you continue north to the famous **Faille d'Aledjo** – a dramatic chasm, dynamited out of the cliff, through which the highway passes. Pictures of it help keep the Togolese postcard industry alive. Skull-and-crossbones warning signs line the twisting and looping road as it works its way over the mountains: if you're driving, the wrecked vehicles strewn in the valleys below are evidence they should be taken seriously. If you're a bush-taxi passenger, tell the driver *allez doucement!*

At the top of the pass, about one kilometre north of the Faille d'Aledjo, you'll come to **Kpéwa** village, where a dirt track on the right leads 6km to the village of **ALEDJO**. Set high on a ridge which runs parallel to the route nationale, the village offers panoramic views in every direction. It's best to ask the chief for permission to visit – his compound is on the left as you enter the village, past the hospital – and he'll probably send a boy with you to show you around. You'll be taken to see the derelict *campement* at the far end of the village, built on a rocky summit from where there are stunning views, then to the other side of the village and the rocky outcrop known as the **Rocher de la Morte** – the views are again fantastic, and the sheer cliff face dauntingly high. Local boys will tell you how evil sorcerers were once thrown off the cliff, and will probably also show you the tree to which the executioner was tied in order to prevent him being pulled off as well.

Bafilo and around

Surrounded by mountains, **BAFILO** is the second largest town of the Kotokoli, and famous for its hand-weaving industry. It's also another Muslim fief – you'll see the town's large white **mosque** some time before you arrive. Bigger than any of the mosques in Sokodé, it was paid for by a single **alhadji** (one who's been to Mecca), a wealthy merchant and native son.

The town's main dirt road leads from the *gare routière* down to the mosque. About 100m before the mosque, a small road to the right leads up to the **weavers' co-operative** known as the Groupement Artisanal Tisserands (Mon–Fri 7am–5pm). Look for the single-storey cream building – you can hear the knocking of their looms as you approach. If you can't find them, ask someone to take you *chez les tisserands*. The quality of their work has earned them national fame, but prices, depending on your bargaining skills, are as low here as anywhere. They sell either strips of woven cloth, complete *pagnes* or ready-made clothes direct from their boutique next door, and you can wander into the main workshop to see the sixteen or so looms packed into the room. You'll be asked to sign the visitors' book and offer a small donation. Bafilo has just one **hotel**, the friendly *Maza Esso* ("I thank God"), on the route de Kara. Although it looks attractive from the outside, the rooms are increasingly run-down, particularly the cheaper rooms with fan and shared facilities; the a/c rooms are better value (rooms with fan ❶ or a/c ❷). There's also a good bar and restaurant – but make sure you order well in advance.

Bafilo Falls

The **Bafilo Falls**, some 5km from town, are the main local attraction. Before you set off, it's best to visit the chief of Bafilo to ask permission, especially since he has a key which you'll need if you want to visit the higher falls – his compound is on the right as you leave Bafilo heading towards the waterfall. To reach the falls, continue down the main road past the mosque for about 2km, then turn right along a footpath through the fields of corn, groundnuts and beans and head for the mountains. There are usually villagers around to offer directions; ask for *les cascades*, which you should soon be able to see in the distance. Alternatively, you can take a *zemidjan* the whole way for about CFA1500, although the last 2km along the footpath is very bumpy. A concrete staircase leads to a gate (which you unlock using the key) at the top of the falls, which are slightly disappointing in the dry season, especially now that swimming isn't allowed in the small dam. Nevertheless, the walk to the falls is worth doing in itself, and the whole trip makes for a pleasant excursion. There are a couple of **other waterfalls** located a bit further from town, several kilometres further on from Bafilo Falls; the hotel can give you directions, or ask someone in town.

Bassar

Culturally, the **Bassari** (no relation to the people of southeast Senegal) are worlds apart from the Kotokoli – and linguistically they belong to another cluster of Voltaic languages, **Gurma**, while the Kotokoli speak a **Tem** language. Unlike the Muslim Kotokoli, the Basssari maintain traditional religious beliefs, and they are known for their many festivals and powerful fetishes. Traditionally the Bassari were the iron smelters for the region – in Africa, indication enough of their special status – and traces of their smelting furnaces can still be seen in some of the villages neighbouring the town of **BASSAR**. The Bassari **fire dance** is still celebrated in the town and surrounding villages, but dates are hard to determine.

Unless you are turned on by remains of iron furnaces, there is little to hold your interest here for long. To visit the furnaces, get a *zemidjan* for about CFA1500 round trip, but go carefully as the road has many twists and lots of soft sand.

Practicalities

The paved road coming up from Sokodé runs right into the town **marketplace**. A dirt road runs in a ring round the market and functions as the town's high street. Note that there is no bank in town.

Bassar's best **accommodation** option is the *Hôtel de Bassar*, and it's nicely sited on the hilltop overlooking the town, with comfortable enough s/c, a/c rooms (T 663.00.81 ❶). The cheapest option is the *Campement de Bassar*, off the paved road in the Kebedipou neighbourhood, near the *préfecture*, with its grubby and unappealing fanless cells (❶). For cheap **eating**, the market provides the best sources of tasty food, while two nearby **bars** – *Le Palmier*, 100m down the dirt road that runs left out from the market as you enter from the Sokodé direction, and the quieter *Tchin Tchin* (aka *Centre Culturel de Bassar*) by the *gare routière* – usually run spirited discos with a small entrance charge.

11.4

Kara and the far north

R elatively harsh geography and climate make the **far north** Togo's poorest region, and one where you're unlikely to spend a great deal of time. Much of the area is open savannah, where the ochre grass of the dry season suggests the drought conditions of the Sahel, just a few hours' travel to the north. During the rains, however, green shoots quickly cover the hilly countryside, briefly lending a lush appearance to the region.

The region's **people**, mainly small farmers of the Voltaic language group, including Tamberma, Lamba, More and Kabyé, grow staple crops of millet, yams and corn. Cotton is grown around Dapaong but currently the industry is in disarray with farmers forced to buy seeds and fertilizers on credit from the government-controlled central agency who then fail to pay them for their cotton. Farmers are turning to food crops using fertilizers intended for cotton, with dangerous results for the land and the safety of the crops.

The only town of any size north of Sokodé is **Kara**, which is gradually becoming the nation's administrative centre. The **Kabyé country** is the homeland of former President Eyadéma and his son, the current head of state, Gnassingbé – who, not unexpectedly, have made great efforts to develop the district and transform the humble town into the capital of the north. The Kabyé country spreads over a rocky, mountainous area centred around Mont Kabyé, some 20km north of Kara; its people have acquired a reputation as skilled agriculturalists, despite the hostile setting.

Despite its problems, the north offers a number of interesting places to visit. The principal attraction is the **Tamberma country**, in the valleys east of **Kandé**, a district famous for its architecture, each home being built like a small fortress. This region remained quite isolated until recently, and as a result the traditional folklore, festivals and customs of the Tamberma people have changed little over time. Of the region's other notable spots, **Niamtougou**, 28km north of Kara, hosts a lively Sunday market and is home to a co-operative of disabled artisans who produce good-quality crafts; whilst in the far north, **Dapaong** is a worthy stopoff en route to Burkina.

Kara

KARA has come a long way since its days as a rural village called Lama-Kara in the 1960s, and it's now routinely referred to as "Togo's second city", even though its population is a good deal smaller than that of Sokodé. Crucial political considerations – it was the nearest village of any size to Eyadéma's birthplace, and home town of his most ardent supporters – led to Kara acquiring favoured status, and in the space of a few years it became the nation's second most important centre for administration and manufacturing industries. Now incontestably the main town of the north, Kara has been boosted by the arrival of new regional industries, including the Brasserie du Bénin brewery, which have been the driving force behind the city's expansion. Some of the institutions here are worthy of a city of international pretensions, including the four-star *Hôtel Kara*, the imposing Banque Centrale, the sophisticated radio station and, especially, the grandiose **Maison du RPT** – the party headquarters. The town also boasts more paved roads than anywhere outside Lomé.

Kara also has a lot going on, with plenty of accommodation, eating and drinking possibilities. Every July, the **Evala** initiation celebrations and **wrestling contests** take over the surrounding villages. Traditionally a strictly Kabyé affair, *Evala* is now a national event, televised across the country, and of huge importance to the town's economy (*Akpema* is the equivalent girls' initiation). Competitions start as neighbourhood bouts on the second Saturday in July, then move on to competitions

▲ *Dapaong & Ouagadougou*   ▲ *Dapaong & Ouagadougou*

KARA

0 ——— 500 m

UTB Bank
BTCI Bank
AV EYADEMA
RUE DU COLLÈGE CHAMINADE

Banque Centrale
Palais de Justice
Stadium
Lufthansa Complex
AV EYADEMA
BTD Bank
RUE DU L'HOTEL KARA
Mairie
AV DU 23 SEPTEMBRE
Shell
Grand Marché & Gare du Marchée
RAKIETA bus depot
AV DU 13 JANVIER
Craft Shop
Total
SGGG
BTA Bank
Fan Milk Depot

AV MAMA N DANIDA

► *Kéïao*

Kara River

ROUTE NATIONALE

ACCOMMODATION

Auberge de la Détente	I
La Concorde	G
La Fayette	H
Hôtel de l'Union	E
Idéal	D
Le Jardin	F
Kara	C
Marie Antoinette	J
La Providence	B
Le Relais	A

N

Gare Routière

RESTAURANTS, BARS & CLUB

Bar Cascade	5
Bar La Détente	11
Bar Fiestadora	2
Bar Jet Set	10
La Bodega	3
Café Muset	6
Café Muset 2	4
Catholic Sisters	12
Le Château	7
Chez Navi	9
La Colombe	8
Marox	1

▼ *J, Sokodé & Lomé*

within villages, and finally competitions between villages. Champions from the first, second and third year of initiation face each other for the supreme bouts. Greased with sheanut butter (to prevent their opponent getting a firm grip), each wrestler tries to grab his opponent's arms or legs to topple him over and pin him in the dust. Bouts rarely last longer than a minute or two but the atmosphere among the rival supporters is feverish.

Arrival and information

The centre of Kara is occupied by the **Grand Marché** and the adjoining **Gare du Marché**. Most of the town's shops and bars are near here, and there's an SGGG supermarket on the corner of the market on Avenue du 13 Janvier. The main **gare routière** is some 2km to the south of town on the route nationale, next to the Total station. This is where you're most likely to arrive, and there are plenty of taxis and *zemidjans* waiting to take you into the centre.

Your best bet for changing money and traveller's cheques is the UTB **bank** on Avenue Eyadéma, 2km north of the centre. The BIA bank next to the SGGG changes cash euros only, whilst the BTCI bank near the UTB has an ATM, but doesn't change cash. At weekends, you may be able to change money at the *Hôtel Kara*'s reception desk. There's good, cheap **Internet** access at CIB on av Mama N'Danida or at the Catholic Sisters' bakery nearby. A small **craft shop** opposite *Le Château* sells reasonably-priced jewellery from Togo, Mali and Burkina.

Accommodation

There's a good range of **places to stay**, though they fill up quickly in July for the *Evala* festival.

Auberge de la Détente one block south of av du 13 Janvier ☎660.14.22. Good location in the centre of town, with clean, secure rooms with fan or a/c. The rooms in the new block are cleaner and better value. ❶

La Concorde off av du 13 Janvier, near the post office ☎660.19.00 ✉rokpatcha @voila.fr. Friendly place in a good position, with the best pillows in Togo and with a range of very clean rooms, from cheap and basic to swanky a/c rooms with satellite TV, fridge and phone. Rooms with fans ❶ or a/c ❸.

La Fayette av du 13 Janvier, east of the market ☎660.00.69. New accommodation in a central location, with great views across town from the rooftop bar. Rooms are comfortable and excellent value, and come with a/c, TV and phone. Rooms with a/c from ❷.

Idéal av 23 Septembre ☎601.25.58. Basic but perfectly acceptable, and extremely cheap, non-s/c rooms, with fans. There's a reasonable bar, too – a good budget option. ❶

Le Jardin just off rue de l'Hôtel Kara, opposite the BTD bank ☎660.01.34 ✉le.jardin@bibway.com. Best known for its very pretty French-style garden restaurant, but also has four comfortable a/c rooms at the back. Very peaceful. ❷

Kara rue de l'Hôtel Kara ☎660.05.18 or 900.11.44 ✆660.62.42. Rather a dated concrete eyesore

but worth knowing about its small pool (CFA1000 non-guests) – a good way to beat the heat. Rooms all have a/c, satellite TV, phone and hot water, and there are also some pricier, more stylish bungalows. ❺–❼

Marie-Antoinette 3km south on the route nationale ☎660.16.07 ✉hotel-marie-antoinette @gmx.net. Great if you want to stay away from town, this has a touch of the French Riviera about it: good, clean rooms with TV. If you want to hang out with expats and sleazy businessmen, eat outside in the charming restaurant which caters well to European tastes. Rooms with fans ❶ or a/c ❷, or camping for CFA1400.

La Providence off av Mama N'Danida, east of the centre ☎660.17.42. A bit far from the centre, but with clean rooms in a pleasant garden and meals available. Rooms with fans ❶ or a/c ❷.

Le Relais off av Mama N'Danida ☎660.01.88. A 2km trek from the centre and slightly difficult to find, but set in a quiet courtyard with *paillotes* and exotic plants. The spacious s/c rooms, with fan or a/c, are tiled and spotless, and there's a pleasant bar as well, but, contrary to what the sign says, no camping. Rooms with fans ❶ or a/c ❸.

Hôtel de l'Union av 23 Septembre ☎660.14.88. Somewhat up-market, if dull, this offers comfortable a/c rooms in the middle of town and a boring restaurant. ❸

Eating

Despite Kara's rapid modernization, the town still has many traditional features like the old **streetside restaurants**, which can be found around the Gare du Marché and the market. At the northern end of the market, stalls under corrugated-iron roofs have been set aside as *fufu* bars – this is where you'll get the best calorie-to-money ratio in town, though if you want something a bit more exciting, women nearby sell rice, beans, macaroni and so on, while *choucoutou* is served in calabashes by women at the Gare du Marché. Also look out for tasty *wagashi*. Fan Milk carts are found all over town.

La Bodega route nationale just north of the main roundabout. Run by an ex–Peace Corps volunteer, offering wood-fired pizzas and the coldest beers in town.

Catholic Sisters off av Mama N'Danida. Great bakery and a good Internet café to boot.

Le Château near the market. Co-owned with *Marox*, with an identical menu (if smaller portions and inferior food) and meals served on a terrace overlooking the town's liveliest street. The games room, with darts and pool (free if you eat), is popular with Peace Corps volunteers on R&R.

Bar Fiestador av Eyadéma. Cheap and cheerful outdoor restaurant serving good Togolese and European dishes. The bar gets lively late at night.

Le Jardin just off rue de l'Hôtel Kara, opposite the BTD bank. The best of the hotel restaurants, with excellent French and Chinese specialities. Even if you don't eat here, it's worth a visit for a drink on the garden terrace.

Marox (officially *Centre Grill*) av Eyadéma. Popular, German-owned place with a vast selection of pizzas (CFA1000–3000), salads, pastas and American specialities. It's also home to the town's best-stocked supermarket, and has tennis courts and a children's playground attached.

Café Muset route Nationale opp Shell petrol station. rue de l'Hôtel Kara. Open 24 hours, this place does excellent cheap breakfasts and cheap meals like couscous, spaghetti and chips, and the bar is great late at night. Its sister, *Muset 2*, on rue de l'Hôtel Kara, offers very similar fare.

Chez Navi opposite the market. The best place in town for inexpensive, tasty Togolese cuisine, with rice or *pâte* served with spicy sauces from huge pots, and very good *wagashi*.

Drinking and nightlife

After dark, there's a limited number of good **bars** to choose from. *Bar Cascade*, next to *Café Muset 2*, is a popular choice, while *Bar Idéal*, across the road, has cheap beer and a few slot machines. *Bar la Détente*, just off Avenue du 13 Janvier and near *Fan Milk*, is another lively place with cheap beer. More expensive entertainment can be found at the *Lafeve Nightclub* (Sat only; cover charge CFA1000) at the *Hôtel Kara*. The glitzy *Nondwou Discothèque Kara* (CFA1000 entrance) at the *Hôtel de l'Union* is popular on Friday and Saturday nights with a younger crowd, but *La Colombe*, next to *Hôtel La Fayette*, is currently the hottest place in town (CFA2000 entrance). *Bar Jet Set*, around the corner, is open 24 hours.

Moving on from Kara

Kara's *gare routière* is the largest in the north and has departures to every point between **Lomé** (7–8hr) and **Dapaong** (4hr), including **Kandé** (1hr 30min). Taxis to Dapaong can take an age to fill up – you may well be better off catching an unofficial vehicle from the Shell petrol station. The Rakieta bus is by far the most comfortable and reliable way to Sokodé (CFA1500), Atakpamé (CFA3500) and Lomé (CFA5300). It leaves at 7.30am every day from their depot, but be sure to book your ticket the day before departure. If you're heading to **Bassar** (2hr), there are direct taxis from the Gare du Marché which travel along a good *piste*, saving you the trouble of changing in Sokodé. The road to **Benin** is good as far as Kétao and the border, but deteriorates after that until you arrive in **Djougou** (regular taxis from Kara), from where it's paved all the way to Parakou. The road to **Ghana** is also good on the Togo side.

North of Kara

The route north from Kara leads through the **Kabyé country**, dotted with charac-teristic *soukala* – round *banco* houses covered with conical thatched roofs, called *tatas* by the French. The picturesque road, with its striking mountain vistas, goes through **Niamtougou** before reaching **Kandé**, the departure point for travel in the **Tamberma country** to the northeast of the town. After Kandé, it passes through the farmland that was formerly the **Kéran National Park** and the village of **Naboulgou**, once the site of the reserve's lodgings, now abandoned. On the other side of Kéran it runs through **Sansanné-Mango** before finally reaching **Dapaong**, the last major town before Burkina Faso.

In the dry season, if you have your own vehicle and fancy a trip into Benin, it's possible to do a circuit from **Nadoba** to **Datori** via the Béninois towns of **Boukoumbé**, **Natitingou** and **Tanguiéta** without worrying about visas (though it wouldn't do any harm to have a Benin or Entente Cordiale visa). Just keep driving, it's well worth the time. Nadoba is on the Béninois border northeast of Kandé, while Datori is on the Béninois border north of Naboulgou about 30km from Togo's route nationale (the junction is at Sagbiabou, 25km northwest of Naboulgou).

Just north of Kara, a deviation in the road takes you around **Pya** – Eyadéma's birthplace. Look out for an odd building on a distant hilltop, with monumental dimensions that might lead you to mistake it for a modern cathedral – it's the general's humble abode.

Niamtougou

North of Kara, the first town of any size is **NIAMTOUGOU**, home to the Co-opérative des Handicapés de Niamtougou (CODHANI), at the southern entrance to the town on the route nationale. The co-op produces a variety of clothes and crafts and you can wander around the workshops and watch batik being made. Items made here can be bought at the co-op's shop – prices are high, but the quality is good and profits go back to this worthwhile cause. They also have pleasant **accommodation** in well-furnished, thatched huts with fans (℡665.00.30 ❶).

Kandé

If you're heading for **Tamberma** country by public transport you'll have to spend a night at **KANDÉ** (also spelled Kanté), 55km north of Kara. It may look like a sleepy, one-horse town straggling along the route nationale but it is in fact the capital of the *préfecture* and has enough going for it to make for a very agreeable overnight stay. There's an unofficial *gare routière* at the Oando garage by the *douane* in the middle of town on the route nationale.

By far the best **place to stay** is ⚑ *Auberge la Cloche* near the water tower (℡916.78.02 ❶) – take a *zemidjan* from the main road for CFA150. Its rooftop bar is the perfect place for sundowners with awesome views. Some 800m north of the *gare routière*, off a dirt track just west of the main road, the modest *campement* has **accommodation** in spartan rooms with fans, although you're likely to be the only guest (℡667.00.73 ❶). The nearby *Bar Elino* also has a small shop, and next door is the CIB Internet café. Street food by the Oando garage is good, or

---

Moving on from Kandé

Vehicles heading north and south, and those going to **Nadoba**, can be picked up by the Ouando garage on the route nationale. If you have your own vehicle, the border crossing between **Nodoba** and **Boukoumbé** in Benin is one of the easiest in the coun-try. Get your passport stamped in **Kandé** and then again in **Natitingou**.

try *Buvette l'Olympic* behind the truck stop. *Bar Oasis* near the market is another good watering hole.

The Tamberma country

The region to the east of Kandé was settled by the **Tamberma** (closely related to the Somba across the border in Benin) in the seventeenth century, as they sought refuge from the king of Abomey in present-day Benin, who raided far and wide in his quest for slaves to trade with the Portuguese. This explains the amazing fortress-like construction of Tamberma houses – called *tata* by the French but properly known as *takienta* – and their deep-rooted suspicion of outsiders. Because they lived in isolation for more than three hundred years, Tamberma customs have remained largely unadulterated by outside influences, and if you get the chance to visit one of the villages, it can be a fascinating experience.

The **homes** are indeed remarkable settlements, both aesthetically and function-ally, each self-sufficient and built some distance from the others, with millet and groundnut fields planted around each one. The large central entrances were origi-nally designed to protect animals in case of attack, while grain was stockpiled in the towers and everything necessary for preparing and cooking food kept inside the house. The roof doubled as a lookout post, with rooms for sleeping built into those towers not being used as silos. With **fetishes** and shrines devoted to ancestor worship dotted around the house and built into the walls, the Tamberma had every-thing necessary in their homes to allow them to withstand long sieges. While the threat that led to the creation of such fortresses no longer exists, their architectural style has remained unchanged and *takientas* are still built by young men when they get married and leave home.

The Tamberma cultural landscape was named a UNESCO World Heritage Site in 2004 and has long figured on the route of tour buses driving up from Lomé. This has given the community an appetite for tourist money and can lead to misunder-standings between local people and visitors. Tours tend to stop at **BASSAMBA**, the first village you come to, about 16km from Kanté, which has a reputation for hassles and rip-offs. You may be invited into a Tamberma home here, only to find as soon as you enter, the women pulling off their tops, inserting stones through their lips, lighting up pipes and grinding millet. Meanwhile the men are rounding up bows and arrows, clay pipes, carvings and anything else that looks like something a tourist might buy. It's all about as spontaneous as a circus performance, and probably not as traditional. You can certainly take pictures – as long as you pay.

Nadoba

NADOBA, 10km further along the dusty road beyond Bassamba, and just 5km short of the border with Benin, is a much better target. On arrival, check out the AJVDC (Association des Jeunes Volontaires pour le Développement Communau-taire), who are building a cultural centre to protect and preserve the area's heritage and promote sustainable tourism (℡924.61.74 @ ajvdckante@yahoo.fr). They rent bikes for CFA1000 per day – a great way to see this extraordinary part of the world. Alternatively, seek out ⚒ Jacques at the little shop on the right at the entrance to the village (℡996.20.29), and ask him to organize a tour of the area for you. Expect to pay CFA500–1000 per person for a guide, plus about the same again to the owner of the *takienta*.

If you want to **stay the night**, the AJVDC have a few very cheap rooms (❶), as does *Bar Mandarin*, next to Jacques' shop (❶) and the *Tata Bar* in the centre of the village (℡667.20.10 ❶), but you should call ahead if you would like them to prepare a **meal**. There's not enough of a demand for street food in Nadoba except on Wednesdays (market day) when you can also sample some of the best *tchoukoutou* in Togo. The whole town seems to be hammered on the stuff by mid-afternoon.

Transport into Tamberma country

Unless you have your own vehicle, **getting to the Tamberma country** can be mighty difficult. You can charter a **taxi** in Kandé, but drivers will charge as much as they can get away with and are unlikely to take you at all for much under CFA10,000. Much cheaper are the collective taxis (CFA800) which run on market day (Wed) to **Nadoba**, 26km from Kandé. It's also possible to take a *zemidjan*, for about CFA3000, but be prepared for a long, dusty ride.

With your own vehicle, follow the *piste* from Kandé, which leads east off the main road just before the *gare routière* and heads all the way to **Natitingou** in Benin. Although at times it's hard to tell if you're still on the road or in the middle of a millet field, locals will always put you right, and if you see people walking your way, don't hesitate to stop and give them a lift. It could lead to a friendship with someone who'll invite you to their village, but you should always assume a payment will be expected.

Note, too, that all tourists have to pay a **tourist tax** (CFA1500) at the police hut 1km outside Kandé.

Air Kanté

"I'm flying south in 'Air Kanté', the greatest bush taxi in all of Togo, when an old man on a bicycle floats across the street. Luckily for him, the chauffeur is highly skilled in dodging – safety is Air Kanté's number one priority. But he is not happy. He swerves to the side and pulls down a whip hanging from the rearview mirror. As we drive past at 20kph, his co-pilot hangs out the window and whips the old man on the bike. Stunned, I struggle to look back to see if the old man is still pedalling. Slowly but surely the old man pedals. For the next hour, conversation does not stray from the man on the bike. The last word on the subject: 'That man is lucky to be alive.'

Jon Lascher, togototogo.blogspot.com

Sansanné-Mango

About 75km north of Kandé, **SANSANNÉ-MANGO**, or Mango as it's often called, has little of specific interest but it's large enough to sustain an overnight stopover if you're **hippo-spotting**. Hippos can sometimes be seen at the dam, 6km northeast of the town, usually at dawn or dusk – a *zemidjan* will take you there and back for about CFA2000. You can stay in town at the *Campement de Mango* (❶) north of the main roundabout. Alternatively, the convent at **Sadori**, 5km to the west on the road to Nandoti, is a wonderful retreat where you can be housed and fed by the nuns (❶).

Dapaong

Togo's last town in the north, **DAPAONG** (also spelled Dapaongo and Dapango) is home to a mixture of peoples, of whom the **Gourma**, immigrants from Burkina Faso, are the most numerous. This is a hilly, farming district, with cotton and millet the most important crops, while cattle ranching is also prevalent, owing to the presence of a sizeable Fula (Peulh) population, who came down from the Mossi country in Burkina in the mid-nineteenth century. Not many travellers show up in these parts, but Dapaong is a very pleasant and friendly town, and a reasonable enough place to stop over on a journey north or south.

Arrival and orientation

The route nationale bypasses the centre, curving in a semicircle to the east. The main **gare routière** and *douane* are at the southern entrance to Dapaong some

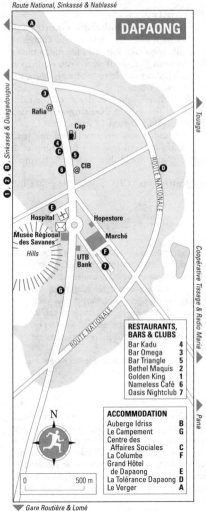

Route National, Sinkassé & Nablassé

DAPAONG

Ⓐ

B. Sinkassé & Ouagadougou

①, ②,

Ⓑ

❸

Rafia @

Cap

❹

Ⓒ

❺

❻

@ CIB

Ⓔ

Ⓓ

ROUTE NATIONALE

Touaga

Hospital ✚

Hopestore

✉

Musée Regional
des Savanes

Marché

Hills

Ⓕ

UTB
Bank

❼

Coopérative Tissage & Radio Maria

Ⓖ

ROUTE NATIONALE

**RESTAURANTS,
BARS & CLUBS**
Bar Kadu	4
Bar Omega	3
Bar Triangle	5
Bethel Maquis	2
Golden King	1
Nameless Café	6
Oasis Nightclub	7

Pana

N

ACCOMMODATION
Auberge Idriss	B
Le Campement	G
Centre des
Affaires Sociales	C
La Columbe	F
Grand Hôtel
de Dapaong	E
La Tolérance Dapaong	D
Le Verger	A

0	500 m

▼ *Gare Routière & Lomé*

2km south of the centre. Smaller vehicles are allowed into town and will drop you by the roundabout in the town centre near the Pharmacie de Soleil, with the Hôtel de Ville and hospital off to the west. From here, it's an easy walk to many of the town's hotels. If you do get dropped at the *gare routière*, get a *zemidjan* to the centre.

The **market** (main market days Wed & Sat) is down the dirt road opposite the Hôtel de Ville. Besides the usual bric-a-brac, you'll find handmade farm tools, pottery and cheap woven gear, including the broad-rimmed hats that are so common in the region – and there's no shortage of *choucoutou* bars where you can pause. Around the market square are several small shops while most of the best **eating places** are on the route nationale north of the centre. There is Internet at CIB near the Affaires Sociales building or, better, at RAFIA (CFA300/hr). The **post office** is by the central roundabout in town. The nearby **Musée Régional des Savanes** (Tues–Fri 9am–12.30pm & 3–6.30pm; CFA500) isn't particularly interesting, but is worth a look if you've got time to kill. The UTB **bank** (closed Mon) on the hill behind the market is the only place in town to change money. Hopestore on rue de Stade is the town's supermarket and sells some European treats.

The Coopérative Tissage by Radio Maria, 2km east of the centre (CFA150 by *zemidjan*), is worth a visit. Good-quality woven *pagnes* are made here by local women who keep a profit of about CFA4000 on a *pagne* that costs CFA12,000 and takes two weeks to weave – your money is well spent. There is also a soap-making workshop.

Worth an excursion is the extraordinary sustainable agriculture and ecotourism project at **TOUAGA**, 5km east of Dapaong (CFA1000 by *zemidjan*). Ingenious irrigation devices have been used to establish a productive market garden and fish farm, and young men from neighbouring villages are taught techniques at the education centre here, which offers real hope for the area's fragile economy. Contact Paul Sinandja, who speaks English, for details (☏905.57.56 or 27.35.14 ✉aspadwm@yahoo.fr).

Accommodation

There is nowhere luxurious to stay in Dapaong, but several pleasant and inexpensive hotels compete for custom.

Heading south: You can get taxis to Kara (5hr), Sokodé (6–7hr), Atakpamé (9–10hr) and Lomé (12–13hr) from the *gare routière*. Note that if you want to get off before Kara (for example in Sansanné-Mango, Kandé or Niamtougou), you'll probably have to pay the full fare to Kara.

Heading for Burkina Faso: Many people up from Lomé change taxis in Dapaong because it's cheaper than going direct to Ouagadougou (you'll save about a third on your fare). But you'll almost certainly wait several hours for a Ouaga-bound vehicle – if not a day or two – which can cancel out any saving. Alternatively, take a taxi to Sinkassé and pick up a Ouaga-bound vehicle there.

Auberge Idriss 1.5km out of town towards Sinkassé ☎770.83.49. Sleepy but very pleasant, with a nice garden and a restaurant serving Togolese and Western dishes. Rooms with fan or a/c ❸.

Le Campement 500m south of the market on the main road into town ☎770.80.55. The best and most expensive accommodation in Dapaong, set in a colonial-style building with well-furnished, attractive rooms. The courtyard bar and restaurant, with giant carved elephants and a small craft shop, is a pleasant place to while away the time and serves decent French food. Rooms with fan ❷ or a/c ❸.

Centre des Affaires Sociales off the route de Burkina, 1km north of the market. Typical of *Affaires Sociales* throughout the country, with clean dorm beds and self-contained rooms, some with a/c. It's all a bit grubby, but very cheap. ❶

La Columbe (formerly *Le Sahélien*) on the main market street ☎770.81.84. An old favourite in the heart of town, but not too noisy and with good-value s/c rooms with probably the only toilet brushes you'll see in Togo. Charming staff and reasonable food. ❶

Grand Hôtel de Dapaong off the route nationale ☎770.86.70. Hardly grand, but has clean, cheerful a/c rooms in a central location. ❷

La Tolérance Dapaong off the route nationale east of the centre ☎770.89.48. On the outskirts of town, with reasonably comfortable rooms set around a small courtyard, and a rooftop restaurant. Convenient if you're driving, but not very busy. Rooms with fan ❶ or a/c ❷.

Le Verger off the route nationale, 2km north of the centre ☎770.81.39. Set around a leafy courtyard with well-maintained, good-value rooms with fan – don't be put off by the run-down exterior. ❶

Eating, drinking and nightlife

There's plenty of the usual **street food** around the market, including coffee and omelettes in the morning, but a dearth of more sophisticated places to eat and drink. There is a great *maquis* and bar at the Cap garage on the route nationale, and *Bar Omega*, by the *carrefour* Sinkassé, has tables under the trees, pretty good food and very friendly staff. *Bar Kadu* does brilliant couscous for CFA800 and runs a lively bar. The nameless café opposite *Bar Triangle* serves the best spaghetti and *lait caillé* (similar to yoghurt) while *Bethel Maquis*, near *Auberge Idriss*, serves good European food in pretty surroundings. If you want a change from Togolese beer, look out for Castle Milk Stout imported from Ghana and very popular in Dapaong. For **nightlife** head to the *Golden King* near *Bethel Maquis* which rocks at weekends and also serves excellent food – try the *pintade* (guinea fowl). A classier alternative is the *Oasis Nightclub*, 50m behind *Hôtel La Columbe*.

Sinkassé and around

A better alternative to waiting in Dapaong for transport over the border is to take a taxi to the border town of **SINKASSÉ**, nominally in Burkina (though much of it spreads into Togo), from where you have a better chance of finding transport to Ouagadougou. Shared taxis leave for Sinkassé from the station in Dapaong's Zongo quarter, although they are not frequent except on Sinkassé's market day (Sun). If you're in a hurry, try to cross the border on foot to avoid the long queue of vehicles waiting to get through customs, and pick up onward transport on the far side. If you get stuck, there's basic accommodation in the Togo side of town at the *Relais du Prince* (☎716.00.87 ❶) in the main *gare*. Whatever option you take, be sure to leave early for Burkina, as the stretch to Ouaga is notorious for checkpoints (for more details, see p.712). Moussa Agouda (☎920.41.67 ✉maribmou@yahoo.fr) acts as an unofficial travel agent and ticket booker in Sinkassé. He doesn't speak English but is helpful with travel arrangements (CFA1000 fee), and, if you're here for a day or two, he can also arrange hiking in the surrounding hills.

From Sinkassé, it's also possible to cross the border into **Ghana**, heading for the town of **Bawku**, some 30km to the west (for more details, see p.789). If you're in this neck of the woods and have time to spare, there are interesting fortress buildings in the pocket of Togolese land around **BOADÉ** west of Sinkassé, as well as crocodiles in the river.

12

Benin

Highlights 950
Introduction and Basics 951
12.1 Cotonou and the coast 971

12.2 Central Benin 992
12.3 The northern uplands and parks 997

Benin highlights

* **Ouidah** Former slave town and now centre of voodoo, where you can retrace the Route des Esclaves, leading down to the beach and the Door of No Return. See p.983

* **Grand Popo** An ideal spot for relaxing on the sands, with several good resorts nearby. See p.988

* **Porto Novo** Benin's official capital retains crumbling colonial buildings in shades of orange and brown, dominated by a beautiful multicoloured mosque. See p.989

* **Abomey** Explore the history of the Dan-Homey kingdom through its palaces, now partially restored and vividly evoking its past grandeur and cruelty. See p.993

* **Parc National du "W" du Niger** Newly accessible park offering some of the best wildlife-viewing in West Africa. See p.1001

* **Tatas-Somba** The fascinating, fortress-like homes of the Somba tribe; there's a particular concentration near the remote village of Boukoumbé. See p.1002

* **Natitingou to Kandé** Superb, rough route over the Atakora range from Benin to Togo, with impressive views and local culture. See p.1004

▲ Ganvié

Introduction and Basics

The world's lack of awareness of **Benin** – the Gulf of Guinea's least-known nation – is partly the result of two reclusive decades of struggle through one of West Africa's least successful and most repressive revolutions. Then, in 1991, the revolutionary rhetoric was thrown out, and Benin adopted a multiparty democracy and a liberal economic system. The government's long wariness of tourism changed rapidly, and Benin is now a popular and straightforward enough place to travel, with a steadily improving tourist infrastructure.

Benin's years of seclusion have left it an intriguing country, considerably more open than you might suspect and with several key factors distinguishing it. First, a number of sophisticated indigenous states developed here, the largest and most urbane of which was the Fon kingdom of **Dan-Homey**, whose capital, in the heartlands of the southern savannah, was **Abomey**. Second, this well-organized and prosperous kingdom was one of Africa's biggest centres of the slave trade from the sixteenth to the nineteenth centuries. The trade wasn't finally ended until 1885, when the last Portuguese slave cargo steamed out of Ouidah, bound for Brazil. By then, a considerable amount of imported wealth had been amassed in the country. Lastly, it was in the French colony of Dahomey – as Benin was known – that Catholic **mission schools** were most influential in the old empire of Afrique Occidentale Française. Thousands of highly qualified students graduated from its secondary schools and taught all over West Africa, giving the country a dynamic intellectual reputation that has coloured its personality deeply.

People

The ancestors of the **Béninois** of today come from many different areas and arrived in the territory of what is now Benin after several centuries of migrations, a fact that explains the wide variation in social organization and cultural practices. Most Béninois adhere to traditional African **religious beliefs**. Along the coast, **voodooism** is common, particularly among the Ewe-speakers. In many ways, the practices of the Ewe are similar to those of the Yoruba and Fon: all believe in a single supreme god who created the universe (Mawu in Fon). On earth, lesser divinities are charged with power over thunder (Xebioso or Shango), iron and war (Ogun or Gu), land and disease (Sakpata or Cankpana), and so on. They possess or "mount" the bodies of their devotees and their help can be solicited through the work of fetish priests. See the box on p.984 for more details.

Islam was brought from the north by Arab, Hausa and Songhai-Dendi traders. It extended as far south as Djougou, and even into the Yoruba country. Perhaps as much as

Fact file

Known as **Dahomey** during the colonial period (after the Fon kingdom, Dan-Homey), the **République du Bénin** adopted the name of the old West African kingdom (located in present-day southern Nigeria) after the 1972 coup led by northerner Mathieu Kérékou. Kérékou's dictatorship collapsed in 1990 and the nation began converting to a **multiparty democracy**. In 2006, political newcomer Thomas Boni Yayi became the country's latest president.

The **population** is nearly 9 million, a good tenth of whom live in Cotonou, the de facto capital. The **official capital** remains Porto Novo, a much smaller coastal town that served as the colonial administrative centre. Benin's area is 113,000 square kilometres, approximately the size of Louisiana, or slightly smaller than England. Benin's national **debt** stood at around £750 million ($1.5 billion), but in 2005, the G8 Summit agreed to cancel some 63 percent of money owed.

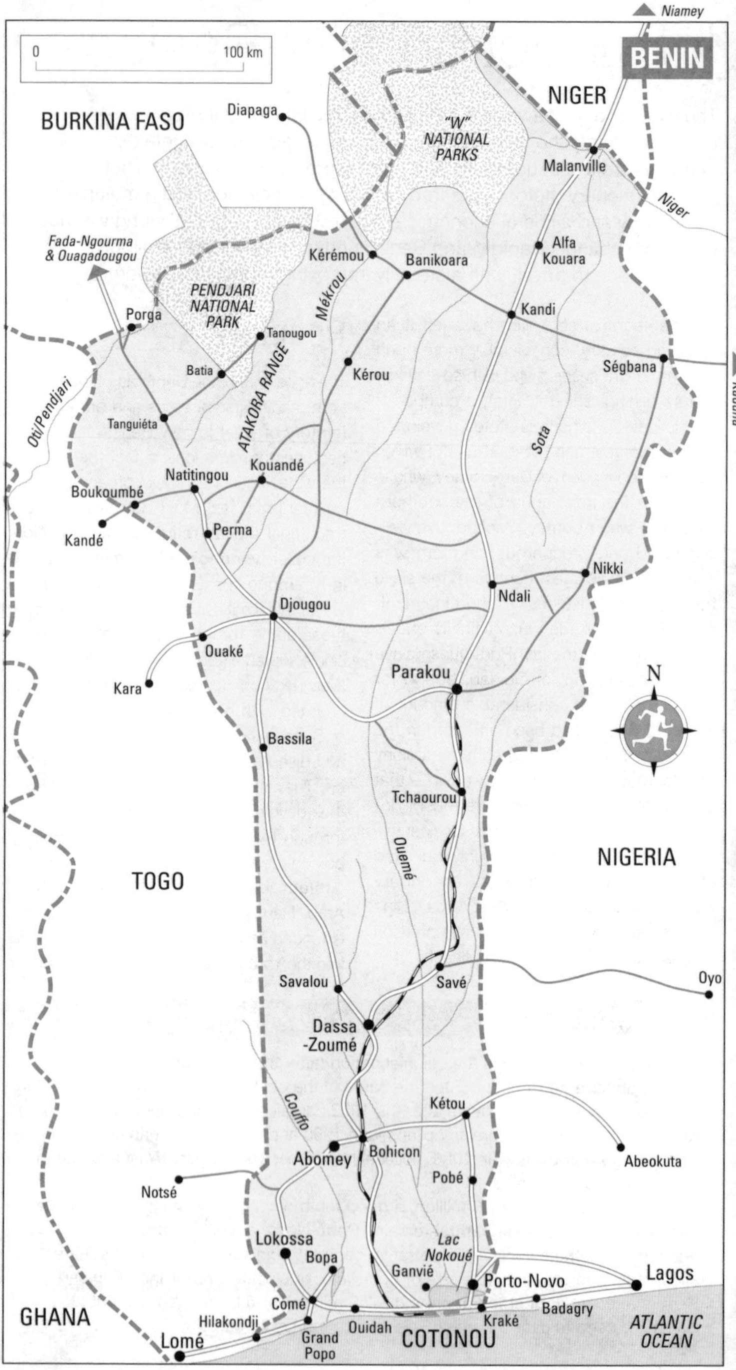
0
100 km
BENIN
Niamey
BURKINA FASO
Diapaga
"W" NATIONAL PARKS
NIGER
Malanville
Niger
Fada-Ngourma & Ouagadougou
Kérémou
Banikoara
Alfa Kouara
PENDJARI NATIONAL PARK
Mékrou
Kandi
Porga
Tanougou
ATAKORA RANGE
Ségbana
Batia
Kérou
Oti/Pendjari
Tanguiéta
Sota
Kouandé
Natitingou
Boukoumbé
Perma
Kandé
Nikki
Ndali
Djougou
Ouaké
Parakou
Kara
N
Bassila
Tchaourou
Ouemé
NIGERIA
TOGO
Savalou
Savé
Oyo
Dassa -Zoumé
Kétou
Couffo
Abomey
Bohicon
Abeokuta
Pobé
Notsé
Lokossa
Lac Nokoué
Bopa
Ganvié
Porto-Novo
Lagos
Comé
Badagry
GHANA
Hilakondji
Kraké
ATLANTIC OCEAN
Lomé
Grand Popo
Ouidah
COTONOU

fifteen percent of the population are Muslim. **Christianity** came with the Europeans and spread principally along the coast – where it was soon integrated into voodoo – and north over the central plateau.

Where to go

Benin is mostly thinly wooded savannah, part of the **open country** known as the "Dahomey Gap" that penetrates south more or less to the coast between the rainforests of Nigeria and Ghana, and which partly accounts for the different shifts of history that have taken place here – easier travel and trade, more successful armies and faster conquests.

A flat sandy plain runs the whole length of the **coast**, broken up by a string of picturesque **lakes and lagoons**. The coast offers little enticement in the sea (rough and terrifyingly dangerous) but the **old towns** – including **Porto Novo**, Benin's crumbling capital, and the old Brazilian quarters of **Ouidah** – have a certain flaked-out appeal, and are full of interest in their museums and markets. The over-exploited stilt village of **Ganvié** is the coastal site of which you're most likely to catch a (tourist's-eye) glimpse, while grubby, post-revolutionary **Cotonou**, the country's only city, makes a rather poor first impression but isn't a bad base when you get to know it.

Inland, the improvement is rapid, as a gentle **plateau** slopes gradually north to spread over the entire centre of the country in a rich patchwork of agriculture. Coffee, cotton and oil-palm **plantations** collide with small fields of **subsistence crops** – maize, millet, rice, yams and cassava. The most interesting town is **Abomey** – capital of the Dan-Homey kingdom and site of its surviving royal palaces and museum.

In the northwest, the sheer cliffs and abundant greenery of the **Atakora Mountains** rear up in a long, dramatic ridge that stands in impressive contrast to the plains and provides a striking backdrop for one of the country's most interesting and inaccessible cultures – that of the **Somba**, who lived in relative isolation until the 1970s.

On the border with Burkina Faso, the **Parc National de la Pendjari** is rated one of West Africa's most interesting faunal reserves; while in the extreme north, the Gourma plains roll up in sweeping grasslands to the **Parc National du "W" du Niger** – not at all easy to get to without your own transport – which spreads across the borders into Niger and the southeast tip of Burkina.

When to go

Although roads are improving, the weather can have a very adverse effect on travel, particularly if you intend to travel off the main highways. It's best to avoid the rainy seasons, which can be prolonged and oppressive. **In the south**, there are two **rainy seasons** (a long one from April–July and a short one in Oct & Nov) and two **dry seasons** (a short one, Aug & Sept, and a long one from Dec–March). Temperatures fluctuate little throughout the year.

In the north, the year divides simply into the rainy season, which lasts from late May to October, and the dry season, which lasts from November to early May. In parts of the Atakora region – Natitingou, for example – the rain falls almost every day from April to November. Temperatures vary more

Average temperatures and rainfall

Cotonou

Temperatures °C	Jan	Feb	Mar	Apr	May	June	July	Aug	Sept	Oct	Nov	Dec
Min (night)	23	25	26	26	24	23	23	23	23	24	24	24
Max (day)	27	28	28	28	27	26	26	25	26	27	28	27
Rainfall mm	33	33	117	125	254	366	89	38	66	135	58	13
Days with rainfall	2	2	5	7	11	13	7	3	6	9	6	1

dramatically than in the south, and when the northerly *harmattan* wind blows in December, nights can be quite cool.

Getting there from the rest of Africa

All flights from outside Benin operate to **Cotonou**, the country's only international airport. There are few convenient connections to Cotonou from Accra, Lagos, Conakry, Banjul, Bamako or Bissau.

Flights within Africa

Air Ivoire and Air Sénégal fly from **Abidjan** to Cotonou three times a week, with additional flights on this route operated by Air Mauritanie. Air Ivoire and Air Burkina offer flights from **Lomé**. From **Ouaga-dougou** to Cotonou, Air Burkina provides a service three times weekly, and there are also three flights a week from **Douala**, with Air Ivoire. Air Sénégal fly four times a week from **Dakar**.

From **Johannesburg**, you may be able to fly to Cotonou on Cameroon Airlines via Douala. Otherwise Kenya Airways, hubbing at **Nairobi**, also flies to Cotonou.

Overland from Nigeria

The commonest point of entry has traditionally been via the **Badagri** coastal road from Lagos to **Kraké** on the Benin side. This border crossing is always crowded

For details on **getting to Benin from outside Africa**, plus important practical information applying to all West African countries, covering health, transport, cultural hints and more, see Basics, pp.19–28.

and it may take some time to get through the formalities. Your bags will be given a perfunctory search, but it's not likely your Nigerian currency declaration form will even be checked. On occasions when the Badagri route has sometimes been closed, travellers have used the border crossings between **Idiroko** in Nigeria and **Igolo** in Benin, a little way north of Porto Novo, or between **Meko** and **Kétou**, even further north, which avoids Lagos and connects you with the less chaotic Nigerian city of Abeokuta. Roads on these routes are surfaced and in reasonable shape.

Overland from Niger

The road is tarred the entire way from **Niamey** to Cotonou, around 1030km. By public transport, a limited number of bus services operate the complete route, taking around 24 hours, but it's usually more straightforward to change at Gaya on the border.

Overland from Burkina

The road from **Fada-Ngourma** in Burkina Faso is tarred to the border on the Burkina side, from where there's a stretch of decent *piste* down to Natitingou where the hard surface starts again. There's a TCV bus once a week from **Ouagadougou** to Cotonou, and a daily service from Ouagadougou to Pama, from where infrequent transport runs to the border at Porga, where you can change for Tanguiéta or Natitingou.

Overland from Togo

Taxis speed along the coastal highway from **Lomé** to Cotonou all day long. Although there's no Béninois embassy in Togo, visas are issued on the spot at the border post of **Hilakondji**.

From the north of Togo, a paved road leads from Kara to the border post at **Kétao**. The *piste* leading on to Djougou in Benin is well maintained, if a bit slippery when wet.

Alternatively, if you have your own vehicle, you could take a very minor *piste* that branches off the main road at **Kandé** and heads through the **Tamberma country** to the border crossing **between Nadoba and Boukoumbé**. This is a beautiful, but tough route, with little traffic and it can be impassable in the rainy season. You're not likely to be aware that you've crossed the border until you get to the main road to Natitingou. You need to get an exit stamp at Kandé, and again when you get into Natitingou.

Red tape and visas

Béninois **customs and immigration** rarely present any special problems, but at most border posts you must state where you plan to stay. All border posts now operate around the clock and can issue 48-hour **transit visas**.

All nationalities, apart from those from ECOWAS member states, need a **visa** to enter Benin. Single- and multiple-entry visas can be obtained from Benin's embassies. If you're flying in on a charter with Point-Afrique, note that they routinely obtain visas for their passengers (see p.22).

All **border checkpoints** issue 48-hour transit visas, requiring no photos and costing CFA10,000. Visa extensions (CFA12,000 for one month) are easily obtained both in Cotonou at the immigration office and in Natitingou at the Police Nationale Commissariat. For details of embassies in Benin, see p.981.

Info, websites, maps

Benin has no overseas tourist offices. In Cotonou, the **Direction du Tourisme et de l'Hôtellerie** has limited material, but check out ⓦ www.benintourism.com. Otherwise, ⓦ www.ambassade-benin.org has general information in French on Benin's culture, arts and government, as well as facts on accommodation and transport for visitors to the country. For news and current affairs, see "The media", below.

The best **map** of Benin, at 1:600,000, published by IGN (ⓦ www.ign.fr), includes detailed *pistes* and topographical material, and is especially useful in the confusing lagoon areas along the coast. The Institut National de Cartographie in Cotonou (see p.981) has reasonable maps – their *Cotonou* map is excellent.

The media

Although perhaps not as visible as the press in other countries, Benin's press is rated as the freest in Africa and there are two daily **newspapers** – *Le Matinal* (ⓦ www.everytic .com/lematinal) and the government-owned *La Nation*. There are also dozens of small weekly or monthly sheets but none has a big circulation. Foreign newspapers and magazines can sometimes be found at newsstands in Cotonou and at major hotels.

The state-run Office de Radiodiffusion et de Télévision du Bénin (**ORTB**) broadcasts **radio** in French, English and eighteen national languages, and several hours of **television** in the afternoon and evening. There are many privately owned radio stations, and a commercial TV channel, LC2. The **BBC World Service** can be heard in Cotonou on 101.7 FM.

Health

Yellow fever is currently the only vaccination required for travel to Benin. **Malaria** is widespread and, as in neighbouring countries, increasingly resistant to chloroquine-based drugs (see p.40).

Except in Cotonou, some sort of **water purification** is highly recommended unless you're sticking to the widely available mineral water Possotomè, from the southern lakeside village of the same name.

The blog for this guide

For **travel updates**, news links and general information, check out ⓦ theroughguidetowestafrica .blogspot.com.

You should **avoid swimming** in streams and lakes in the lagoon regions of coastal Benin, and don't walk barefoot in the grass surrounding them. These areas are almost invariably infested by schistosome parasites which transmit **bilharzia**. Throughout the country **hospital facilities** are meagre, with drugs and equipment in short supply. Cotonou has more reliable places, while Tanguiéta has the best hospital in the north. Major towns have a sprinkling of **pharmacies**.

Costs, money, banks

Benin is part of the **CFA zone** (rates of exchange roughly £1=CFA880, $1=CFA450). You can get by on £10/$20 a day if you're staying in inexpensive hotels and eating street food; reckon on at least £20/$40 if you want to stay in mid-range places and enjoy one decent restaurant meal a day.

The major **banks**, including Ecobank, Financial Bank, Bank of Africa and the Banque Internationale du Bénin (BIB), have branches in most towns. Bank opening hours are usually Monday to Friday 8am–12.30pm and 3–6pm, with the exception of Ecobank which conveniently stays open from 8am to 5.30pm with no break, and is open Saturday mornings. The Financial Bank usually offers the best service and good exchange rates, and they also give cash advances on **Visa cards** and (far less often) **MasterCard**. Most banks in major towns have **ATM machines** that accept foreign Visa cards, but you'll have a lot more difficulty with MasterCard or Maestro. **Euros** are by far the best currency to bring; dollars and sterling can only be changed in the major towns. As for **changing traveller's cheques**, all the banks will insist on seeing receipts and your passport before any transaction.

Getting around

Benin's **road network** has improved dramatically since the early 1990s with main connections now hard-surfaced. The **railways**, on the other hand, are down to one line between Parakou and Cotonou, which suspended operations in 2007. There are no fully-functioning scheduled **domestic airlines**, though you could enquire if Bénin Golf Air or Trans Air Benin (contacts in Cotonou listings, p.982) are operating any services.

Road transport

The main **national highway** runs for 742km from Cotonou to Malanville and is paved the entire distance. The other main road runs 114km along the coast from the Nigerian border in the east to the Togolese border in the west. The road from Parakou to Natitingou is now in excellent condition, and major engineering is currently under way to improve the road through to the Burkina border via Tanguiéta. Police checks are these days refreshingly infrequent.

The Béninois have remained faithful to the **taxi brousse**, Peugeot 504 *familiales* which can be found at the *gare routière* (also known as the *autogare*) in every town and are by far the easiest way to navigate the country. These nine-seater estate cars are the common mode of transport for most people, or there are faster, five-seater cars which are usually slightly more expensive (prices quoted in the chapter are for the cheapest possible). Cross-country taxi journeys generally cost around CFA15 per kilometre per place.

There are a couple of privately-run **bus companies**, which are more comfortable but less convenient than bush taxis. The best of these Is Confort Lines which has regular services to Natitingou (10hr; CFA9000) and Parakou (7hr; CFA7000) as well as further afield to Malanville and Tanguiéta for the

Fuel prices

If you're **driving yourself**, you'll find fuel noticeably cheaper than in Benin's Francophone neighbours — though much more expensive than in Nigeria — at around CFA410 per litre for diesel and CFA415 per litre for super.

national parks. The buses stop in most towns en route – contact their head office in Cotonou for more information and to book seats in advance (☎21.32.58.15).

Public transport in large towns is the preserve of **shared taxis** and **zemidjans**. The latter (pronounced "zemi-john"), usually known as a *zem* or *zemi*, are *mobylette* or moped drivers, usually identifiable by a coloured shirt, who rent out the back of their scooter seats to passengers. They're a cheap (and negotiable) means of transport, but you won't be protected by a helmet. Rush hour in Cotonou is a sight to behold, with thousands of *zemis* dodging cars and each other, and accidents are common. Always carry a handful of CFA100 coins as drivers will swear they can't change a bill and most journeys are CFA200–300.

Trains

The national **railway** company, **OCBN**, (l'Organisation Commune Bénin-Niger des Chemins de fer et Transports), operates the only railway line, from **Cotonou to Parakou**. In theory, there's a service three times a week in each direction departing Cotonou and Parakou at around 8.30am. However, the service was suspended in 2007 and a revival looks unlikely.

Accommodation

Typical **budget** accommodation (**①**–**③**) offers quite pleasant rooms, almost always with electricity, fans and running water, sometimes with a private bathroom. Increasingly, and especially in well-travelled towns

like Ouidah, Abomey and Natitingou, a few good **mid-range hotels** (**④**–**⑥**) are opening, with self-contained (s/c) rooms with air conditioning (a/c). International-class establishments (**⑦**–**⑧**) are limited to Cotonou; the only place upcountry approaching this standard (and actually featuring much cheaper rates) is Natitingou's hotel in the *Accor* chain.

Look out for the French-run chain of **"auberges"** (ⓦ www.hotels-benin.com). All called "*Auberge de...*" followed by the name of the town, they offer clean rooms, some with air conditioning, and are usually a safe bet for comfort and value for money, with the additional bonus of good restaurants attached.

Béninois people are hospitable and may invite travellers for meals or to stay the night – activities which were forbidden until the advent of democracy. **Camping sauvage** (pitching your tent in the bush, or on the beach) has been legalized beyond city limits, but use your discretion and don't leave your tent unattended.

Eating and drinking

Food in Benin largely resembles that of neighbouring Togo: for background and details on local staples and popular dishes, refer to the food section in that previous chapter. Cotonou has no particular gastronomic reputation in West Africa, but there is a good range of restaurants serving French, Lebanese and Chinese food. Outside of Cotonou, most cuisine is Béninois or French.

Many hotels, even less expensive ones, have their own restaurant. In the provinces, eating houses are usually small *buvettes* specializing in rice, **pâte** (the generic term for pounded starch based on cassava, yam or sweet potato), **moyo** (like wheat semolina) or **macaroni** served with sauce.

Street food is very inexpensive, and you can easily eat your fill for less than CFA1000. Mid-range restaurants charge between CFA1000 and CFA3000 for a main course – although in Cotonou there's little at the lower end of this scale.

One of Benin's leading industries is the Société Nationale des Boissons which produces the national beer, **La Béninoise**, and a variety of carbonated soft drinks. The mineral water Possotomè is widely available in 1.5-litre bottles. Along the coast, **palm wine** is plentiful, as is the lethal African firewater known as **sodabi**. In the north, **home-made beer** made from millet, known as *chapalo* or *tchacpalo*, is more common.

Communications

Cotonou is the only reliable place to receive **post**. The main PTT here is fairly efficient and the poste restante service good. Parcels can only be sent airmail, which is very expensive.

International phone calls can be made either from PTTs in most towns or from any other telecentre. Expect to pay CFA1500 per minute to France, CFA1800 elsewhere in Europe, CFA1600 to the USA and CFA2500 to Australia.

Cellphones are increasingly popular in Benin, especially due to the poor landline system. You can use your mobile in the major towns and in a wide radius of Cotonou through the Areeba, Telecel or Bell Benin networks, although connections can be sporadic. Local SIM cards with Areeba – one of the best networks – cost CFA6000.

Internet access is available in the major towns. Connections are relatively good and cost anything from CFA500 to CFA1000 per hour.

Benin's IDD code is ☎229.

Opening hours, public holidays and festivals

Most **businesses** are open from Monday to Friday between 8am and 12.30pm, and again from 3.30pm until 5.30pm or later; government offices open and close half an hour earlier in the afternoons.

Christian holidays and New Year's Day are **public holidays**. Muslim celebrations are less formally observed, though in the north most businesses tend to shut down for them. In addition the following public holidays are observed: Martyrs' Day (Jan 16), Labour Day (May 1), Independence Day (Aug 1), Assumption (Aug 15), Armed Forces' Day (Oct 26), All Saints' Day (Nov 1), National Day (Nov 30) and Harvest Day (Dec 31). An annual festival centred around Ouidah is held on January 10, celebrating the importance of the voodoo religion in Benin. Since 1996 this has been designated a national public holiday, known as Vodoun or Traditional Day, and is celebrated throughout the country.

The Festival International Gospel et Racines (**Roots and Gospel Festival**), bringing together local and international musicians to celebrate the unity of the African diaspora, takes place every year for a week in November or December, in Cotonou, Porto-Novo and Ouidah.

Crafts and shopping

Items to look out for in Benin include **leather** goods and **wooden sculpture** – stools, wooden figures and masks are all common and widely available in tourist areas. You'll also find a great selection of **fabrics**: in Abomey you'll see vibrant patchwork tapestries depicting traditional folkloric symbols, especially those relating to the old kings of Dan-Homey. Excellent cloth, renowned for its quality and bright colours, can also be found in the north near Natitingou. **Cotonou** is overall the best place in the country for shopping, however. Head for the Centre de Promotion de l'Artisanat in Cotonou for arts and crafts, or the mammoth Dantokpa Market where you'll find everything from western-style clothes to fetishes.

Crime and safety

Benin is, for the most part, a very safe country to travel in. However, in recent years there have been a number of **armed robberies** after dark on the northern highways, and local people say it is inadvisable to travel in the north at night. The Malanville—Kandi road has occasionally been closed at night for extended periods.

Cotonou presents the usually urban risk of **muggings** and the beach is best avoided.

A special natural risk on the coast is very strong **currents** and a steep drop-off.

Emergencies

Police ☎17, fire service ☎18.

Gender issues and sexual attitudes

The **position of women** in Benin has been little improved by the revolutionary 1970s and 1980s, or by democratization. In fact it appears they have even less involvement in politics and decision-making than elsewhere in West Africa.

People-trafficking from Benin – especially women and children – is a serious problem, though not one you're likely to come into direct contact with.

From the traveller's point of view, there's relatively little **sexual harassment**. If you're **gay**, it's worth bearing in mind that homosexual acts are still illegal and in theory can result in prison sentences of up to three years. There's no visible gay or lesbian scene, but if you're discreet, you shouldn't have any problems.

Entertainment and sports

Musical culture is well developed, but global sounds continue to exert a strong influence on local musicians. For a short account of musicians and CDs, see p.968.

Theatre has never been a significant part of cultural life, and **cinema** has long been in the doldrums (though Djimon Hounsou, the Oscar-winning movie actor, was born and spent his childhood here). Béninois and French cinéastes recently tried to jump-start the industry with an annual (January) film festival in Ouidah – **Quintessence** – with support from one of the country's best-known directors, Jean Odoutan, whose first and most successful feature film, the darkly comic *Barbecue-Pejo* (2000), recounts the disastrous purchase of a European's Peugeot car by an impoverished farmer. *Africa Paradis*, a film by Béninois director Sylvestre Amoussou, was shortlisted at FESPACO 2007.

Sports

In **sports**, the lacklustre performance of the national football team, Les Écureuils (the "Squirrels") has for many years suppressed the game's profile in Benin. Key local teams to look out for are Mogas 90 and Dragons de l'Ouémé (both from Porto-Novo) and Requins de l'Atlantique from Cotonou.

Wildlife and national parks

Benin's **northern regions**, although densely farmed and populated in their southern parts, spread into a broad zone of thinly populated savannah and uplands, making this one of West Africa's best game-viewing areas.

There are significant concentrations of wildlife, especially in the **Pendjari** and **"W" du Niger** national parks, including several hundred – possibly a thousand – elephants. Now that the Parc W is finally being opened up to visitors, with drivable dirt roads and basic infrastructure, it's likely that the richness of this park will become increasingly apparent.

A brief history of Benin

The earliest history of the territory that is now Benin is obscure. The far north was partly controlled by the Niger River's Songhai empire by the end of the fifteenth century. Meanwhile, in the south, having built the first slave fort at Elmina in Ghana in 1482, the **Portuguese** continued along the coast and began trading with local rulers from the 1520s. Porto Novo and Ouidah developed through the sixteenth and seventeenth centuries into important commercial centres where slaves were traded for European cloth and guns.

The British, Dutch and French, seeking labour for their American colonies, soon joined the Portuguese in the **slave trade**, establishing their own coastal forts and commercial depots during the seventeenth century. By the 1690s, as many as ten thousand slaves were being shipped annually out of Ouidah and lesser ports along this coast.

The Slave Coast

By the beginning of the eighteenth century, the **Dan-Homey kingdom** (a vassal of the great Yoruba Oyo empire to the east, in present-day Nigeria) dominated the politics of the region. One of Dan-Homey's rulers, **Agadja** (in power 1708–40), subjugated the districts south of his capital Abomey, and finally took Ouidah itself. With access to the coast, his empire was now poised to control international trade – primarily in slaves. But he had exceeded the terms of his licence with Oyo and a protracted conflict ensued which resulted in Oyo's definitive conquest of Dan-Homey. There followed a period of desperate slave-hunting as the Dan-Homey king **Tegbesu** (1740–74) tried to rebuild his country's war-shattered economy (see p.995).

After the French Revolution, a wave of **antislavery sentiment** began to sweep Europe. In France, the *Decret du 16 pluviôise an II* of February 4, 1794, outlawed the trade, though it was later reinstated by Napoleon. In 1802, Denmark became the first European nation to abolish the slave trade permanently. Britain followed in 1807 and from 1819 to 1867, British ships patrolled the coast, arresting slave ships and resettling the captives in Freetown, Sierra Leone. France definitively outlawed the trade in 1818.

These moves coincided with a severe shortage of slaves in the region, in large part because of excessive human sacrifices in Abomey. A Brazilian mulatto, **Francisco Felix de Souza**, entered into a blood pact with the young **King Ghezo** of Dan-Homey (1818–58) and supplied the guns for him to overthrow the incumbent of the stool (throne) in Abomey in 1818, in return for which he was granted a monopoly over the slave trade (and became the "Viceroy of Ouidah"; see p.969).

By the 1830s, however, the nature of most commerce in the region had fundamentally changed and **palm oil** became the primary export. The French soon gained the upper hand in the regional trade when representatives from Marseille soap-making companies arrived in Ouidah in 1843 and travelled to Abomey, where they signed a contract with King Ghezo, granting them trading rights at Ouidah.

In 1861, Lagos became a British colony. **King Toffa** of Porto Novo had claims on the town of Badagary which the British now controlled. Worried that their influence would spread westward, Toffa called on the French for support and, in 1863, Porto Novo became a **French protectorate**. In 1868, King Ghezo's son, the new **King Glele** of Abomey (1858–89), ceded rights to Cotonou to the French, who had by now established themselves as the most prominent European power along Benin's coast.

French conquest

Good relations between France and the Dan-Homey kingdom had soured by the end of the century. In December 1889, a new king, **Behanzin** (1889–94) was enstooled. He adopted a more combative attitude to the French, who were beginning to look less like trading partners and more like a force of occupation. Behanzin refused to recognize French rights over Cotonou and was angered that the foreigners had allied themselves with Toffa, one of his bitterest enemies. After funeral ceremonies for his father Glele, Behanzin ordered an **attack on Cotonou**. On March 4, 1890, some five to six thousand Dan-Homey warriors marched on the city and withdrew only after inflicting numerous casualties. A month later, the army surrounded Porto Novo and clashed with the French at Atchoukpa on the northern outskirts of the city.

Other skirmishes followed and in April 1892, Behanzin sent the following message to French authorities: "I warn you that if one of our villages is touched by the fire of your cannons, I will march directly to crush Porto Novo and all the villages belonging to Porto Novo. I would like to know how many independent French villages have been overtaken by me, King of Dan-Homey. I request you to keep calm and do your business in Porto Novo. That way, we can remain in peace as it was before. But if you want war, I am ready. I will not finish it. It will last a hundred years and will kill 20,000 of my men."

The threat was taken seriously by the French, who knew that Behanzin possessed more than 5000 modern firearms and was still being supplied by the Germans and the British. The government in Paris sent a distinguished commander to handle the situation, **Colonel Dodds**, a mulatto from St-Louis in Senegal. In August 1892, Dodds began his northern march to conquer Abomey. Accompanied by Senegalese and Hausa infantry, the French went to the Oueme River and followed its course. Although the army was sporadically engaged by Dan-Homey troops, including divisions of so-called **"Amazons"** – skilled female warriors specially trained to use the new Martini-Henry rifles – it was the Dan-Homey on whom the heaviest casualties were inflicted. By November 1892, when the French arrived at Cana – the traditional burial village of Dan-Homey kings – Behanzin's army had lost 4000 dead and twice as many wounded.

King Behanzin prepared himself for a **last stand**. He recruited every warrior capable of carrying a gun, including the massed ranks of his Amazons, and got the nation's slaves to join the battle, promising them freedom in return. But the effort was in vain; the army was defeated and Behanzin was forced to retreat with meagre reserves. On November 16, 1892, Dodds marched on Abomey to find the city already in flames, torched by the retreating army. It took another two years for the French to track down and capture Behanzin (betrayed by the newly French-enstooled Fon king) and he was transported to exile in Martinique.

The colonial era

With their main rival in the region at last conquered, the French went on to subdue the north of the country, which they now called **Dahomey**. Colonial frontiers were drawn up in agreement with Britain to the east and Germany (which held Togo) to the west. In 1901, the present borders were fixed and, in 1904, Dahomey became part of Afrique Occidentale Française or AOF (French West Africa).

French policy in Dahomey was partly shaped by the influence of Catholic missions, which sent large numbers of envoys into the territory in the 1920s and 1930s. Catholic seeds had been sown from a very early period, with the arrival in the eighteenth century of influential Brazilian families and Christian **freed slaves**. Moreover, the climate, open country and dominant voodoo religion of the south were not strongly antithetical to missionary activity. The result was that early in the colonial period, Dahomey acquired a reputation for mission-educated academics and administrators. By the 1950s, many middle-ranking posts in the French colonial service right across West and Central Africa were occupied by Dahomeyans, most of whom were Fon or Yoruba from the relatively prosperous south.

With few mineral resources (no gold or other precious metals), Dahomey's economy depended very heavily on its **oil–palm plantations**. In addition, there were close commercial relations with Nigeria, both legal trading and illicit smuggling.

Independence and instability

No single, national leader rose to pre-eminence during the fifteen-year period after World War II on the road to independence. Instead, an ethnic and regional competition developed in which three prominent figures jockeyed for position. They were **Hubert Maga**, representing the north, **Migan Apithy** of the southeast, and **Justin Ahoma-degbe** from the southwest. On the eve of independence, the three managed to form a coalition, the Parti Progressiste Dahoméen, but the unity was superficial. Each commanded the loyalties of about one-third of the country's population and distrusted the others. After some seventy years of French rule, the **Republic of Dahomey** became independent on August 1, 1960, and later that year Maga became president.

But dissatisfaction prevailed in the south where supporters of Apithy and Ahomadegbe accused Maga of tribalism, and by 1963, unrest led to **political riots**, as students and workers took to the streets of Cotonou.

Maga was deposed in a peaceful **military coup** led by **Colonel Christophe Soglo**, who immediately set about restoring civilian rule. A new constitution was adopted and, in January 1964, blatantly undemocratic **"elections"** took place.

With Maga in jail, it was now the turn of **Apithy** as president and **Ahomadegbe** as prime minister. Under the guise of unity, the two men worked against one another, each trying to consolidate his own position. The **exclusion of the north** from the political process led to riots in Parakou, further political detentions and finally paralysis in the government, with the head of state and his PM at loggerheads. The military again intervened, Soglo forcing Apithy and Ahomadegbe to step down.

A provisional government freed Maga and set about writing a new constitution with the joint consultation of all three leaders but Maga and Apithy allied themselves against Ahomadegbe in a move which triggered trade-union protest and a third intervention by Soglo, on this occasion assuming power himself as the head of a **military regime**. Maga, Apithy and Ahomadegbe went into exile in Paris.

Soglo remained in charge for two years, but his military government was rife with **corruption**. Protest strikes were followed by a ban on union activity and, just as predictably, another **coup**, led by **Major Maurice Kouandété**, and supported by junior officers including one Captain Mathieu Kérékou.

The new military government had a strongly northern cast. Kouandété drew up another constitution and scheduled new elections for May 1968. Many politicians were banned from participating, however, including the three elder statesmen. The trio, reunited in their exclusion, called for a boycott, and on the day of the elections, only 26 percent of eligible voters turned out, the elections were annulled, and the military conferred the presidency on the low-profile former foreign minister, **Emil Derlin Zinsou**. In December 1969, sixteen months into his term,

Zinsou was overthrown by the man who had put him in power, Kouandété. There were no justifying factors and it was the first time force had been used. Zinsou's car was sprayed with bullets in downtown Cotonou, but the president escaped with his life.

Fellow officers prevented Kouandété taking power himself. Instead, a **Military Directorate** was established with Lt-Colonel **Paul Emile de Souza** in charge. Once more, elections were set and this time the three old-guard politicians were allowed to participate. Maga was set to win in his loyal Atakora region, but not to receive a majority over Apithy and Ahomadegbe combined. De Souza cancelled the Atakora poll. Declaring that the north would secede if the Military Directorate refused to accept his presidency, Maga pushed the country to the brink of civil war. Apithy upped the stakes still further by stating his southeast region would attach itself to Nigeria if Maga was instated. In a last-ditch compromise to save Dahomey from self-destruction, a **Presidential Council** was formed in which the three men would rotate power every two years. Maga was the first to serve as president, replaced in 1972 by Ahomadegbe.

The system seemed to be working when, in 1972, internal army rivalries triggered two mutinies at the Ouidah military camp. Though these were put down, twenty high-ranking officers were arrested, six of them – including Kouandété – sentenced to death. That move prompted one last coup, led by a man who, like Kouandété, was a northerner from Natitingou – **Major Mathieu Kérékou**, a soldier who had served with the French army.

Kérékou's revolution

At the time of Kérékou's takeover on **October 26, 1972**, Dahomey had suffered nine changes of government in twelve years. Administration had grown used to the notion of government by crisis control and the country had struggled with no clear lead and almost continual uncertainty.

Although remarkable stability marked the next phase in the country's history, it seemed at first that the pattern of biennial coups might continue. In **1975** former president Zinsou was sentenced to death *in absentia* (he had been living in Paris where he headed the outlawed Parti Démocratique Dahoméen) for allegedly planning to assassinate Kérékou. And in the same year, Captain Michel Aikpe, the Minister of the Interior, was shot dead by a Kérékou bodyguard when the president allegedly caught him in flagrante delicto with Mme Kérékou. In **1977** a group of **mercenaries** landed at Cotonou airport and, after trying to shell the presidential mansion, were forced to retreat (events on which some of Frederick Forsyth's thriller *The Dogs of War* is supposedly based). Most of the mercenaries, led by the notorious thug Bob Denard, were French and, afterwards, already dismal Franco-Dahomeyan relations sank to a new low. A personal experience of the events is described by Bruce Chatwin in "A Coup" (*Granta 10: Travel Writing*; Ⓦ www.granta.com).

Kérékou weathered all the storms. Two years after his coup, the new leader announced that Dahomey would engage in a **popular revolution**, based on Marxism-Leninism. The country established relations with the People's Republic of China, Libya and North Korea, and received the blessing of Sekou Touré of Guinea. Benin also moved closer to the Soviet Union.

Also in 1975, Kérékou changed the country's name from Dahomey to the **République Populaire du Bénin** (after the old city-state in neighbouring Nigeria) and launched the single political party, the Parti de la Révolution Populaire du Bénin (PRPB). The new course instigated significant changes. Schools were nationalized, the legal system was reorganized and committees were established round the country to stimulate participation in local government. In 1977, a *Loi*

Fondamentale established new political structures including the 336-member Assemblée Nationale Révolutionnaire. In 1979 the party selected Kérékou as the sole presidential candidate and the assembly unanimously elected him.

Kérékou was never a convincing Marxist. His was a late conversion which only became clear long after he took power. However, while the **centralized economy** hardly produced miracles, the revolutionary stance was a major contributing factor in maintaining stability through the 1970s. It significantly reduced the regional disputes that continuously brought down early governments, by shifting political argument from ethnic loyalties to issues of social and economic ideology and it helped to appease Benin's radical intelligentsia. For a long time, Benin's dissatisfied intellectual elite (the French called the country the "West African Latin Quarter") were unable to find work in the stagnant economy. Many of them had worked in other French colonies in the 1950s, and their calls for radical reforms in the early days of independence were popular with unions and student groups and helped to topple more than one president.

Liberalization

While rhetorically supporting the revolution, Kérékou began gradually to embark on a path of **liberalization**. By 1982 the government was busy selling off or reforming its unproductive and corrupt state-run companies. Under IMF and World Bank pressure, Cotonou also began retraining officials and adopting measures to encourage private investment. In 1985, the government asked the IMF for assistance – a policy, it said, designed to "exploit the positive factors of capitalism".

The former leaders Maga, Apithy and Ahomadegbe had been released in 1981 and many other political prisoners were pardoned (though those implicated in the bitterly resented "mercenaries invasion" of 1977 remained behind bars). The country also began fostering **relations with the West**. The relationship with France improved after the French Socialists came to power in 1981, especially following President Mitterrand's official visit to Benin in 1983. Three years later, Kérékou made a series of trips to Western Europe urgently seeking more aid and better debt terms. He also moved closer to conservative African nations, repairing old rifts with Togo, Côte d'Ivoire, Cameroon and Gabon.

Most of the policy reforms of the early 1980s were prompted by the deteriorating state of the economy and a scramble to find new sources of foreign aid. **Oil**, discovered off the coast, began to be exploited in 1982. It provided some relief to the government as the country was able to produce enough to export small quantities. Bright prospects, however, turned gloomy as the world price of oil dropped and ambitious plans for increased exploration and drilling were scrapped. With few other viable resources, the economy was still heavily reliant on the agricultural sector – especially palm oil and cotton.

Economic woes had already forced the government to devise extreme austerity measures, announcing in 1985 that it would no longer guarantee **jobs to graduates**. That decision sparked bloody rioting and widespread arrests. Kérékou quickly removed the minister of education, who was a Fon, thereby isolating himself from that ethnic community. When the border with Nigeria closed that year and relations with Benin's powerful neighbour deteriorated, resentment also grew among the Yoruba-speaking communities in the southeast, diminishing still further Kérékou's political stock. His resignation from the army seemed to impress nobody.

The democratic era

There were **demonstrations in 1989**, calling for Kérékou's resignation, the adoption of a multiparty system and a complete purging of entrenched economic corruption. Students and civil servants hadn't received allowances or pay for months, absenteeism had reached epidemic proportions and the country was in a state of muddle, discontent and stagnation not witnessed since the 1960s. Because of the **fear of coups**, most of the armed forces were no longer armed and, for several days in December 1989, anti-riot police stood by in Porto Novo and Cotonou as tens of thousands of protesters roared for Kérékou's downfall. In the middle of all this, Kérékou decided to go on a walkabout in the poor quarters of Cotonou. He got a mixed response, state radio reporting his progress at one stage as taking place "amid ovations and stone-throwing".

The events were inevitably compared to similar scenes being played out in **Eastern Europe** as the Iron Curtain came down, and certainly most Béninois were encouraged by the limited news that filtered through. But it had been obvious for years that Benin's inefficient command economy was not working and that some of the best-trained **administrators and teachers** in West Africa were being wasted in the top-heavy bureaucracy.

After the events of December 1989 – which coincided with an agreement by the IMF and World Bank to bale out Kérékou one more time – the Marxist-Leninist ideology was dropped: this was a condition of French economic support. In March 1990, a **national conference**, at which fifty-two different political groups were represented, was held to establish a framework for the country's future – and to decide on Kérékou's role. The conference declared itself sovereign, reduced Kérékou to a figurehead and appointed a new cabinet headed by **Nicéphore Soglo**, a former World Bank official.

So wide-reaching were the reforms and so effective was the transitional government in replacing members of the military regime with civilian administrators, that Benin was quickly dubbed the first country in West Africa to experience a "civilian coup".

Independent newspapers sprang up; Amnesty International commended Benin for releasing all its political prisoners; a giddy sense of renaissance swept the country. With the referendum of August 1990 overwhelmingly supporting the conference's draft multiparty constitution, the way forward seemed optimistic and when Soglo soundly beat Kérékou in the **presidential elections** of 1991, the nation's mood was ecstatic.

Despite the new lines of credit, Western-imposed structural adjustment hit wage-earners especially hard, reducing Soglo's popularity. Labour unrest continued through the early years of his administration with strikes and demonstrations causing occasional havoc in Cotonou, and several coup attempts were reported in the early 1990s. Approval for Soglo had already begun to drop in 1994, after he accepted a regional agreement for the devaluation of the CFA, a move widely interpreted as bending to Western insistence on painful **economic remedies**.

Soglo, never a man of the people, was accused of nepotism for transforming the government into a family affair: his wife Rosine was a member of parliament; his brother-in-law Desiré Vieyra was minister of defence; and his son Liadi was in charge of military affairs at the presidency. But more troublesome to most were the rising prices and high levels of unemployment at a time when aid was arriving. There was a feeling that money was being squandered, and Soglo was blamed.

In the run-up to legislative elections in March 1995, Soglo formed the **Parti de la Renaissance du Bénin (RB)**, which soon merged with another new party, the Pan-African Union for Democracy and Solidarity. At the elections, 31 parties fielded over 5000 candidates for just 83 deputies' seats. The majority went to the opposition alliance, with the Front de l'Action pour le Renouveau et le Développement (FARD) capturing a commanding 18 seats. Though FARD was led by a barrister and long-time political activist from Porto Novo, **Adrien Houng-bédji**, the job of speaker of the assembly went to the head of a smaller opposition party, **Bruno Amousso**, who was voted to the position with the help of ministers loyal to Soglo, apparently in an attempt to diminish Houngbédji's influence.

Return of "the Chameleon"

At the same time, **Kérékou**'s star was beginning to rise again. By now known as "the Chameleon", he had managed to appear genuinely dignified in the way he accepted the results of the elections in 1991, and human in the way he conceded the failures of his rule. His post-leadership conversion to Catholicism was accompanied by speeches defending the poor and displaced. When he announced that he would run for the presidency in 1996, conventional wisdom held that he was the candidate Soglo needed to beat. When both Houngbédji and Assoum threw their party support behind Kérékou, it was enough to give the former president 52 percent of the vote.

Calling for national unity, Kérékou created the position of **prime minister** – the post was not stipulated in the new constitution – to repay Houngbédji for his support. The fact that the two men had come together at all surprised many – in 1975, Kérékou had sentenced his new ally to death for plotting against the revolution. It was a measure of how much things had changed. Still remembered as a Marxist-Leninist, Kérékou included privatization as part of his economic revival plan and continued the **austerity measures** that Soglo had initiated.

International relations had improved in the aftermath of democratization, particularly with the US and France, and the goodwill continued following Kérékou's return to power. Cooperation also improved with neighbouring **Nigeria** as negotiations took place over the demarcation of their common border and measures to curb smuggling. In 1998, Kérékou was elected chair of the Conseil de l'Entente, and worked to consolidate relations among countries in the group, including Benin, Côte d'Ivoire, Togo, Burkina Faso and Niger.

As he got deeper into his term, Kérékou, like Soglo before him, began to feel the pull between the agencies that set up austerity programmes and the people who felt their sting. Some aspects of economic reforms were palatable, such as Kérékou's early **crackdown on corruption**. In 1997, he took his own cabinet to task for the mismanagement of funds allocated for development projects; later that year the bosses of four large state-owned companies were sacked on charges of fraud. But the unveiling of the 1998 budget led to a series of **strikes** by civil servants who called for the scrapping of VAT and demanded an end to privatization and unpaid bonuses. As the strikes continued, Houngbédji resigned from his post as prime minister and withdrew the FARD's remaining ministers from the governing coalition.

That departure proved decisive in the legislative **elections of 1999**, when Houngbédji switched allegiance and aligned his Parti du Renouveau Démocratique (PRD) with those parties opposing Kérékou, including Soglo's RB. Once again providing the swing vote, Houngbédji gave a one- seat majority to the opposition and was elected president of the national assembly.

To the present

These same three key figures – Houngbédji, Soglo and Kérékou – faced each other in the **2001** presidential elections with Kérékou retaining the presidency.

The elections of March **2006**, however, by which time both Soglo and Kérékou were over 70 and thus constitutionally too old to stand, saw a political newcomer from near Parakou, **Thomas Boni Yayi**, a former head of the West African Development Bank with much overseas experience, sworn in as the country's new president. Yayi got 74 percent of the popular vote, on a ticket that emphasized his safe hands, his anti-corruption stance and his ambition to modernize and liberalize Benin's economy.

In 2005 the G8 Summit had agreed to a package of **debt relief** for Benin which would reduce its foreign debt by some 60 percent. Although Benin has seen growth and **investment** over the past decade it remains one of the world's poorest countries. Thousands of Togolese refugees flooded into the country in 2005 and still compete for jobs and the CFA in people's pockets with local Béninois.

The **parliamentary elections** of March 2007 were convincingly won by Yayi's coalition, the **Forces Cauris pour un Bénin Émergent** (**FCBE**). Only two weeks earlier, however, the president's campaign convoy was attacked by gunmen on the highway near Ouèssè, south of Parakou. Presumed at first to be an **assassination attempt** (a violent response to his anti-corruption drive, claimed Yayi), it may in fact have been an attempted armed robbery on a convoy of expensive vehicles.

Meanwhile, the struggle continues to sell **cotton** (the country's biggest export-earner) on the world market against subsidized competitors, notably the USA's cotton farmers. Two out of three Béninois depend on cotton for a living. If anyone in Cotonou can articulate Africa's needs in this area, it is President Yayi.

Yayi also seems set to reappraise the somewhat cosy relationship that Kérékou and his crowd eventually enjoyed with the French political establishment – **"françafrique"** as it came to be known – especially in light of the angry response in the media and on the streets to the visit of the much vilified French interior minister (now president) Nicolas Sarkozy, in 2006.

Music

Benin has diverse **musical traditions**. The music of the Fon played a crucial ceremonial role in the court at Abomey, capital of the country's major pre-colonial state, Dan-Homey. The Gun people use a wide variety of instruments including a huge double-log xylophone, percussion pots and raft zithers. During the **1970s** Benin's popular-music scene was constrained by government curfews, but orchestras carried on somehow, the most successful being **Orchestre Poly-Rythmo** and **Black Santiago** (led by horn player Ignacio de Souza). As everywhere, **hip-hop** has really arrived in Benin, with the Diamant Noir crew and Skykoon – who raps in English – having the highest profiles.

Angélique Kidjo

A singer of extraordinary power and grace, Kidjo is the first female African musician since Miriam Makeba to achieve real international stardom. Brought up in an artistic household in Ouidah by parents who provided unusual support for her stage-struck ideas, she is an irrepressible figure who spurns artistic ghettoization.

Ayé (Island). Some of this powerful album was recorded at Prince's Paisley Park studio in Minneapolis. It includes the huge hit "Agolo", a dance floor killer.

Black Ivory Soul (Sony). Featuring international musicians from Africa, Brazil and the USA, this album explores the musical and cultural kinship between Benin and Brazil.

Fifa (Island). In 1995, Angélique and her husband, bass player Jean Hébrail, travelled through Benin recording traditional songs that inspired the songs on this album.

Oremi (Island). A remarkable journey round the African musical diaspora – especially R&B. Kidjo covers Hendrix's "Voodoo Child", employs jazz saxophonist Branford Marsalis, and generally funks things up big-time.

Oyaya (Sony). This, the final part of Kidjo's transatlantic trilogy, explores Caribbean styles from bolero to ska. Stylish and tremendously fun.

Stan Tohon

With his wild stage act, Stan has led his Tchink System to popularity all over West Africa since the late 1970s.

Tchink Attack (Donna Wana). This may lack some of the spontaneous power of the band's stage performances, but it's a vibrant disc, nonetheless, with some very interesting rhythms on the hit song "Dévaluation".

Books

A limited range of literature is available on Benin, which includes work from Bruce Chatwin, who also contributed a memorable piece to *The Best of Granta Travel* on the coup that installed Kérékou. For good general titles on West Africa, see p.35. Books marked 🏃 are especially recommended.

Stanley B. Alpern *Amazons of Black Sparta: the Women Warriors of Dahomey*. Alpern's fascinating book has rekindled interest in the all-female regiments of the Dahomey Amazons. It makes for a good read – not overwhelmingly technical, despite the thorough discussion of the methods of training and the tactics of battle.

Suzanne Preston Blier *African Vodun: Art, Psychology, and Power* (University of Chicago Press). Detailed academic study of the voodoo art of Benin and Togo – and related Haitian and New Orleans traditions.

🏃 **Annie Caulfield** *Show Me the Magic: Travels around Benin by Taxi*. Amusing and revealing account of a hectic trip around the country from the back of a battered Peugeot taxi, with a control-freak driver, Isidore.

🏃 **Bruce Chatwin** *The Viceroy of Ouidah*. Without a doubt the first book to read on Benin – gripping, in Chatwin's inimitable style, from the prologue on, in its fictionalized account of the life of the Brazilian slave-trader Francisco Felix de Souza (see p.983).

Christophe Henning and Hans Oberlander *Voodoo: Secret Power*

in Africa (Taschen). A sumptuous coffee-table book of strong images, with anecdote-based text from the author/photographers who travelled the country.

Patrick Manning *Slavery, Colonialism and Economic Growth in Dahomey 1640–1960*. Heavy scholarship, but well done, showing how Dahomey's economy continued to prosper through the slave trade until the eve of colonialism.

Francesca Pique, Leslie H. Rainer *Palace Sculptures of Abomey: History Told on Walls*. Exploring Fon culture, history and the kingship system, and the role of the royal palaces in Abomey, this also gives a fascinating insight into the significance of the bas-reliefs on the palace walls.

Fiction

Olympe Bhêly-Quénum *Snares Without End*. An intriguing novel of village life, by the only Béninois writer to have been translated into English.

Paul Hazoumé *Doguicimi*. The essence of the Dan-Homey kingdom is captured in this carefully documented work of realist-romantic fiction.

Languages

Benin's official language is **French**, which is widely spoken. The fifty or so Béninois ethnic communities speak about as many different languages or distinct dialects, though some languages have become regional lingua francas. In the south, **Adja** and **Fon** – closely related to Ewe and Mina under the "Ewe group" umbrella – are widely spoken and probably the most useful if you want to learn a few phrases (see p.905 for some Mina). In the centre and east, **Yoruba** (see p.1114) takes over.

Bariba, a Voltaic tongue, is the common language of Parakou and the northeast, while the old Songhaic language, **Dendi**, is spoken in the extreme north near the banks of the Niger. **Hausa** and **Fula** are also widely used in the north.

Because of the proximity and influence of Nigeria and the importance of commerce, some Béninois speak a kind of trading **English**, though English is not likely to get you very far, even in Cotonou.

Glossary

Amazon The name given to female Fon soldiers by visiting Europeans. In Greek mythology, it referred to a race of Scythian female warriors who supposedly underwent mastectomies to facilitate use of their longbows; the word probably derives from the Greek for "without a breast"; see p.995.

FCBE Forces Cauris pour un Bénin Émergent ("Cowrie Forces for an Emergent Benin"), the cryptically named governing coalition, whose cowrie-shell name and logo refer to the traditional exchange token and symbol of prosperity.

Féticheur Traditional religious leader.

Tata Fortress-like houses built by the Somba in the region of Natitingou.

Vaudou/Vodu "Divinity" or "Other" (Fon). The belief system of the coast based around these divinities, spread from these parts to Haiti with the slave trade.

Yovo/yobo "White" or "European" (Fon).

Zemidjan/zemi *Mobylette* driver, usually identifiable by a coloured shirt, who operates an informal taxi service using his scooter.

12.1

Cotonou and the coast

On the basis of physical appearances, **COTONOU** is one of West Africa's least enticing cities. Though the population isn't much more than a million, the city spreads over a great reach of monotonously flat landscape, dotted with lakes and clogged with residential, commercial and administrative *quartiers* that run chaotically into one another. At rush hour, the cratered, grubby grid of streets becomes a seemingly endless tide of rattling *mobylettes* kicking up clouds of dust and exhaust fumes. You might expect the **waterfront** to add a picturesque backdrop to this environment, but the harbour view is unfortunately blocked by the **modern port** – located right in the heart of the city and redolent of export produce that's waited too long in the sun. To cap it all, with not a hill or geographical landmark in the whole of Cotonou, it's difficult to get your bearings on first arriving in the smoggy clamour.

But the city is something of an African melting pot, with a still-intact intellectual reputation that has only grown more visible with the government's liberalization since the early 1990s. Commercially, it has gained considerable importance due to the frequent closures of Lomé's duty-free port and the eclipse of Abidjan, and most hotels here are more geared to regional traders than to tourists. Cotonou's saving grace is its fantastic **markets** and, for want of other things to do by day, you could spend a good deal of your time in town shopping and browsing. Cotonou **nights** are thoroughly enjoyable by any standards, buzzing with people out to enjoy the cool air, and vendors crowding through the streets.

Three of the country's best-known attractions are each less than an hour out of the city. The stilt village of **Ganvié** is something of a rip-off – though no less striking for that – but the official capital of Benin, **Porto Novo**, has a proud gravity that no amount of superficial exploitation could conceal, and **Ouidah** has an intrinsic appeal beyond its over-baked "fetish tourism". If you're heading west to Lomé, or arriving from the Togo direction, you might stop a night at the virtually derelict old trading town of **Grand Popo**, whose magnificently picturesque lagoons and coconut groves provide the backdrop for a lethargic day or two sunning on the beach.

Ethnically, the coast is dominated by various Ewe-speaking peoples including the **Adja**, one of the earliest groups to arrive and formerly a community of renowned warriors who settled near the Togolese border town of Tado. Over time, the group fragmented and dispersed to form the **Xwala** and the **Xuéda** (Ouidah) along the coast, and the **Gun** a little inland around Porto Novo.

Cotonou

The diamond-shaped **centre** of Cotonou is defined by three main thoroughfares – **Boulevard Saint Michel** in the northwest, **Boulevard Steinmetz** in the northeast and **Avenue Clozel** to the southeast. The **port** forms a natural barrier to the southwest, marking the centre's fourth boundary. Many of the hotels and restaurants listed below are within the confines of these streets, as are the major **businesses**, the **post office** and the **banks**.

East of the centre, Boulevard Saint Michel extends to the **Pont Martin Luther King** (formerly the Nouveau Pont), and crosses the **lagoon** that cuts Cotonou in

two, linking the downtown districts with the **Akpakpa district** on the east side of the city. At the bridge's western foot spreads the vast **Dantokpa Market**, one of the largest along the West African coast. About 1500m down the lagoon towards the ocean, Avenue Clozel extends over the **Ancien Pont** and continues east to join the road to Porto Novo. A newly built road bridge – the new **Nouveau Pont** – close to the Ancien Pont, now links the city centre with the eastern shore of the lagoon.

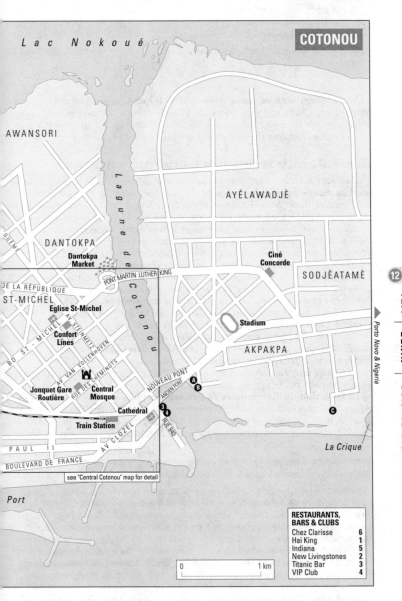

COTONOU

Lac Nokoué

AWANSORI

DANTOKPA

Dantokpa Market

Lagune de Cotonou

AYÉLAWADJÈ

Ciné Concorde

SODJÈATAMÈ

Pont Martin Luther King

JE DE LA RÉPUBLIQUE

ST-MICHEL

Eglise St-Michel

Confort Lines

BD ST - MICHEL

AV STEINMETZ

AV VAN VOLLENHOVEN

RUE DES CHEMINOTS

Jonquet Gare Routière

Central Mosque

Cathedral

Train Station

AV CLOZEL

PAUL II

BOULEVARD DE FRANCE

see "Central Cotonou" map for detail

Port

Stadium

AKPAKPA

Nouveau Pont

Ancien Pont

RUE 840

La Crique

Porto Novo & Nigeria

RESTAURANTS, BARS & CLUBS

Chez Clarisse	6
Hai King	1
Indiana	5
New Livingstones	2
Titanic Bar	3
VIP Club	4

0   1 km

West of the centre, Boulevard de France becomes Boulevard de la Marina and follows the coast. Running parallel, Avenue Pape Jean Paul II leads to the high-rent **Cocotiers** and **Haie Vive** districts near the airport, where the international hotels are located. Along the way, it passes near the French and American embassies and the imposing Presidential Palace, or **Présidence**, a modern pile protected by a seriously large fence with security cameras peering from every corner.

Flying out of Cotonou, the departure tax is CFA2500, usually included in the ticket price.

On the **north side of town**, Avenue de la République leads west from Pont Martin Luther King up to the **Place de l'Etoile Rouge** – a monumental square (complete with torch–bearing cast-iron statue rising up from the giant red star at its centre) commemorating the country's now lapsed revolution.

Arrival, city transport and information

The **airport** is located 5km west of the centre along route de l'Aéroport. It has a small **exchange bureau** that opens for the day's few incoming flights, a branch of the Financial Bank (Mon–Fri 8am–10pm) that changes cash and some traveller's cheques, and a Hertz car-rental office. You'll need to take a taxi to get into town; there's an official list of prices in the arrivals section, with various fares for day and night journeys (CFA3500–7000). If you don't have much luggage, you could consider one of the **zemidjans** waiting in front of the airport who will take you to the centre for around CFA500, though be prepared to bargain strenuously.

Arriving by bus or bush taxi, you're most likely to be let off in the city centre. Domestic destinations have their own *gares routières* or *autogares*, conveniently situated around one of the three main streets marking the centre (see box). You're unlikely to arrive by rail, but the **train station** is also centrally located, just off Avenue Clozel. **Confort Lines** buses use a *gare* near the Marché St Michel.

Within the city centre, **taxis** are shared and cost CFA250–350 for most destinations, though they are not as widely available as **zemidjans** – by far the most frequent form of transport in the centre. These should only cost you CFA150–300, even for quite long rides in town, but make sure to agree a price before setting off. There's no town bus service.

The **Direction du Tourisme et de l'Hôtellerie** (℡21.32.68.24, ℻21.32.68.23, ⓦwww.benintourisme.com), 2.5km out of town off the Place de l'Etoile Rouge, is happy to hand out a slew of brochures and maps, but they can't really do much for you. To find out about renting a car or joining an organized excursion to somewhere

Cotonou surface arrivals and departures

The main international *gare routière* for travel along the coast on the Lomé–Cotonou axis is the **Gare de Jonquet** right in the heart of the downtown district, just off rue des Cheminots. Vehicles depart regularly from here for Ouidah, Grand Popo, Porto Novo, Lagos and Lomé. The **Gare d'Itajara** just southeast of Jonquet is the place to get vehicles for Parakou and the north. For Porto Novo and Lagos, head to the **Gare de l'Ancien Pont**. Vehicles for Lagos also leave from the **Gare de Dantokpa**, as do vehicles to Porto Novo and Abomey-Calavi (for Ganvié). **Abomey-Bohicon** transport has its own *autogare* located on rue de Dahomey, between Boulevard Steinmetz and the lagoon.

Confort Lines buses to Parakou and Natitingou depart from their *autogare* on Boulevard St Michel. It's best to book tickets in advance as services fill up quickly; see p.956 for details.

Intercity STC buses head for Abidjan via Accra three times a week from an *autogare* near the Bank of Africa.

SNTV runs air-conditioned buses three times a week to Niamey, departing 5am for the 16hr journey. The *gare* is at carrefour de Cadjehoun.

like Ganvié or the Pendjari National Park, you're better off going to a travel agent (see "Listings", p.982).

In terms of **security**, Cotonou is probably no worse than any other big city, but its recent emergence as one of the major ports along the West African coast has brought its fair share of extra pressures, the occasional mugging and the usual pick-pocketing and snatchings. In particular, don't venture alone or with valuables onto public beaches in the immediate city environs.

Accommodation

From dirt-cheap *chambres de passage* to luxury money-temples, Cotonou has **accommodation** for everyone except campers – there's nowhere to pitch a tent or park your vehicle overnight (forget the beach). Unless you're really counting the pennies, avoid the low-budget places where levels of hygiene are about as low as the prices. There are some very decent mid-range lodgings which aren't too pricey. Most of the less-expensive hotels are near the centre, while the more upmarket places are found east across the Ancien Pont, in Akpakpa, or west towards Cocotiers, with the odd, more central, exception.

Central Cotonou hotels

Ayihoué bd Steinmetz ☏ 21.31.80.81 ⓕ21.31.80.82. A new and well-regarded choice. The clean, white rooms are appealing and good value, with a/c, phone, fridge and TV; an attractive restaurant and bar are attached. ❹

Babo rue Agbeto Amadore ☏ 21.31.25.02 ⓕ21.31.46.07. A towering building visible from bd St Michel. Basic, tolerable, non-s/c rooms on the fourth and fifth floors, some with balconies; the rooms on the top floor are slightly more appealing. ❶

Bénin Vickenfel off bd Steinmetz ☏ 21.31.38.14 ⓔvkfhotel@intnet.bj. The rooms are fairly small but comfortable and good value, with a/c, satellite TV and big bathrooms. Excellent location and the bonus of an Internet café. ❺

Concorde bd Steinmetz ☏ 21.31.55.70 ⓕ21.31.13.68. Carpeted a/c rooms with hot water and private bathrooms, or spacious s/c rooms with fan and cold water. A decent, central option if you're on a budget, the chief drawback being the noise from the busy main road. ❶

Le Crillon off bd Steinmetz ☏ 21.31.51.58. Just down the road from the *Vickinfel*, this place has bare, gloomy s/c rooms with fan or a/c. On the plus side, it's very central. ❷

Crystal bd Steinmetz, above *Carnival des Glaces* ☏ 21.31.22.08. First-floor hotel reached by a spiral staircase. Exceptionally clean rooms with attractive wooden panelling and fan or a/c, and relatively quiet for the location on the busy main street. ❸

🏃 **Hôtel de la Plage** near the main post office ☏ 21.31.25.61 or 21.31.34.67, ⓕ21.31.25.60. Central, colonial-style place, nicely furnished and boasting a good deal of old-time charm, with a pool and private beach. All rooms have a/c and rates include breakfast. ❺

Pension de l'Amitié off av Proche ☏ 21.31.42.01. This has long been a popular budget option, but is looking a bit the worse for wear with dirty, spartan rooms. ❷

Pension de Famille av Proche ☏ 21.31.51.25. This central place has friendly staff and simple, clean rooms, with fan. Noise can be a problem though, as it's bang on the main road. ❶

🏃 **Riviera** rue Dako Donou, off bd Steinmetz ☏ 21.31.26.20 ⓕ21.31.41.88. New upmarket hotel, right in the centre of town, with spacious, stylish rooms with huge beds and swanky bathrooms, some with views of the lagoon. There's also an excellent restaurant. ❺

Hotels outside the centre

Alédjo On the east side of town, 3km from the centre ☏ 21.33.05.61/2 ⓕ213.15.74. Dull and decaying, in a large tropical park, the *Alédjo* trades on its place in history as the venue of the 1990 democracy conference. There's a pool (CFA2000 to non-guests), and the hotel is right next to a sheltered ocean bay ("La Crique") but the rooms aren't great value for a "luxury" hotel. ❻

Benin Marina bd de la Marina, 4km from the centre near the airport ☏ 21.30.01.00/30.12.56 ⓦwww.benin-marina.com. Two hundred luxury rooms and bungalows (some with hazy ocean views), all fitted out with satellite TV, video and phone. The hotel is on the beach with a popular poolside bar (pool use CFA3500 to non-guests) and a flourish of restaurants, including one with first-class breakfast buffets. There's also a disco, sauna, crafts shop, travel agency and bank. Busy, but generically international and sterile. ❽

Croix du Sud off route de l'Aéroport ☏ 21.30.09.54/55. Rooms are divided between a main block and a complex of more attractive thatched bungalows clustered round a 25-metre pool. Everything, though, is in need of a lick of paint. ⑥

🏃 **Hôtel du Lac** Akpakpa, near the Ancien Pont ☎ 21.33.19.19 ⓦ www .hoteldulac-benin.com. This is a great-value place, with huge, comfortable rooms or luxurious bungalows at the water's edge and an excellent pool (CFA2500 to non-guests), bar and restaurant with fabulous views over the lagoon. ⑥

Hôtel du Port bd de France ☎ 21.31.44.43/44 ⓔ hotelduportcotonou@yahoo.fr. Not in the most attractive part of town but hugely popular for its spacious, a/c rooms, bungalows and apartments. Rooms around the courtyard come with balconies overlooking the attractive 25m pool (CFA2500 to non-guests). ⑦

Maison de Passage Allemagne Haie Vive, 200m east of *New Livingstones* bar ☎ 21.30.45.76.

Priority at this well-kept house is given to German development workers, but spare rooms are let to visitors (although the maximum stay is four nights). It's a bargain, considering you have use of a well-equipped kitchen and communal lounge/dining area. ②

Novotel Orisha bd de la Marina, near the Nigerian embassy ☎ 21.30.41.77 ⓕ 21.30.41.88, ⓦ www .novotel.com. A large, international-standard hotel with all the facilities you'd expect, including a great pool surrounded by lush gardens (CFA3000 for non-residents) and a top-notch French restaurant. ⑧

Pacific av Clozel, on the east side of the Ancien Pont ☎ 213.22.35. Looks dire from the outside, but things improve once you're through the door, with rooms of various standards, most quite spacious (avoid the noisy ones facing the road) and some with lagoon views. ②

The City

By way of **sights**, Cotonou is unexciting. On the western approach to the city, a striking example of revolutionary architecture, the Chinese-built **Stade de l'Amitié** ("Friendship Stadium"), dominates the district and flaunts an atypical **pagoda** at the entrance. In the city centre, there's a **cathedral** built in the Italian neo-Renaissance style. Making a special effort to see these buildings, however – or for that matter, the **central mosque** over by the Gare de Jonquet – seems like scraping the bottom of a very small barrel. In the end, it's really only the **markets** that will leave a lasting impression, and Cotonou boasts some very good ones.

Beaches

There may seem to be **beaches** all round, but the undertow means you can't safely swim at any of them, and few are any good for relaxed sunbathing. The only town beaches you'd want to go on are the private one at the *Hôtel du Port* (right next to the pirogue harbour so not especially clean – nobody swims) and the beach near the *Alédjo*, the sheltered cove known as La Crique. If you head a kilometre or two west of the airport, there are some beach cafés which get customers at weekends. Or, if you have transport, try further west at Jacquot Plage, a 9km drive. Don't take valuables onto any beach and always check with the hotel or beach-café staff before putting a foot in the sea.

The Dantokpa Market

Every day, a steady stream of people can be seen skirting down the Boulevard Saint Michel or over the Pont Martin Luther King (still known as the "Nouveau Pont") towards the **Dantokpa Market**. From the bridge, you can sense the energy of commerce as you look down on the confusion of taxis, traders, stalls and merchandise spreading out in a thousand directions near the banks of the lagoon. In the middle of it all stands the heavy cement shoe-box structure of the **market building**, inside which are the cloth boutiques and stands of merchants.

The ground level of the market building is the food hall, devoted to everything from locally grown tubers and grain to boxes of Milo and Nescafé. Other floors have their own ranges of goods. One large section is filled with Nigerian-made cosmetics – skin lotion, shampoos and hair softeners. Piles of Savon de Marseille crush against Chinese enamel bowls and Nigerian plastics. **Cloth** is an especially important item; colourful Parakou prints are quite reasonable, though less prestigious than the expensive Dutch wax designs. **Clothes** and **shoes** – plastic sandals, Bata-style loafers and imitation Italian dress shoes – also have their own specialist domains and dealers.

The Dantokpa **Fetish Market** is worth investigating, with the usual wide assortment of animal body parts and whole dried specimens, and the usual excessive demands for cash if you want to take photos. It's north of the main market building, up along the lagoon shore beyond the pole market, the wicker market and the empty-bottle market.

Marché St Michel, the Centre de Promotion de l'Artisanat and Marché Ganhi

The **Marché St Michel**, on Avenue de la Republic west of Gare de Dantokpa, is a small, pleasant area, on the edge of which you'll find people selling books – in English as well as French. To the southwest, the **Centre de Promotion de l'Artisanat** (crafts market) on Boulevard St Michel provides the best location in town to shop for Béninois handicrafts. A series of hut-like shops contain familiar specimens of traditional national art – for example, the colourful **patchwork cloths** originating from Abomey that were once used as the banners of that city's kings. Wooden carvings and **masks** from the various regions are also common, as are different varieties of drum – though the ones sold here are mainly decorative. The good collection of jewellery makes for easily portable gifts.

Marché Ganhi is a small produce and consumer goods market down near the port, essentially these days aimed at and used by expats and wealthy Béninois. There's a general selection of produce here, but it's also a good place to buy cheap CDs of the latest sounds.

Zemi tips

"Always carry a stock of CFA100 coins, as the drivers swear that they have no change. And *always* agree the price before you sit on the motorbike. Get the driver to state the agreed price and nod your head in acknowledgement. In many cases, street names mean nothing to drivers, so mention a useful landmark like a restaurant."

James McCarthy, Ireland

Eating and drinking

There are several good French **restaurants** in Cotonou, as well as a handful of decent Asian choices. Local food is pretty good, and the Béninois have a flair for tasty sauces made with plenty of vegetables and seafood or meat.

For **street food**, try around the markets and *gares*, and also beside the rail tracks just off av Clozel, around the corner from the *Gerbe d'Or* (see below). Also look out for sandwich stalls, where you can pick up a fresh baguette crammed full of ham, steak *haché*, fish and other such delights for around CFA400. In the following listings, phone numbers are given where reservations are advisable.

Central Cotonou

Inexpensive (up to CFA3000)

Awa Seck av Proche, corner of rue des Cheminots. Senegalese-run establishment with *poulet yassa*

and other filling dishes (there's more choice if you order in advance) in a small, pleasant setting. Around CFA1000 a meal.

Chala-Ogoi av St Jean, just north of the intersection with bd St Michel. One of the city's

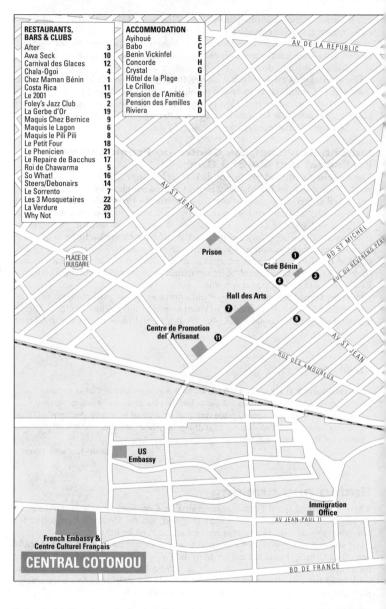

RESTAURANTS, BARS & CLUBS

After	3
Awa Seck	10
Carnival des Glaces	12
Chala-Ogoi	4
Chez Maman Bénin	1
Costa Rica	11
Le 2001	15
Foley's Jazz Club	2
La Gerbe d'Or	19
Maquis Chez Bernice	9
Maquis le Lagon	6
Maquis le Pili Pili	8
Le Petit Four	18
Le Phenicien	21
Le Repaire de Bacchus	17
Roi de Chawarma	5
So What!	16
Steers/Debonairs	14
Le Sorrento	7
Les 3 Mosquetaires	22
La Verdure	20
Why Not	13

ACCOMMODATION

Ayihoué	E
Babo	C
Benin Vickinfel	F
Concorde	H
Crystal	G
Hôtel de la Plage	I
Le Crillon	F
Pension de l'Amitié	B
Pension des Familles	A
Riviera	D

PLACE DE BULGARIE

Prison

Ciné Bénin

BD ST MICHEL

RUE DU RÉVÉREND PÈRE

AV ST JEAN

Hall des Arts

Centre de Promotion del' Artisanat

AV ST JEAN

RUE DES AMOUREUX

US Embassy

Immigration Office

AV JEAN-PAUL II

French Embassy & Centre Culturel Français

CENTRAL COTONOU

AV DE LA REPUBLIC

BD DE FRANCE

---

best open-air restaurants, serving home cooking in cauldron-like pots; try the *purée d'igname* with *pied de boeuf*. Good salads too.

Chez Maman Bénin near Ciné Bénin. A great selection of fish, chicken, beef and an array of tasty sauces are on offer at this well-established, popular haunt. The upstairs restaurant

is more upmarket, with prices to match. Mon–Sat 9am–midnight.

Maquis le Lagon bd Steinmetz, corner of rue des Cheminots (evenings only). Excellent grilled chicken and chips, served at tables on the pavement – a lively atmosphere is guaranteed. Around CFA2000 per person.

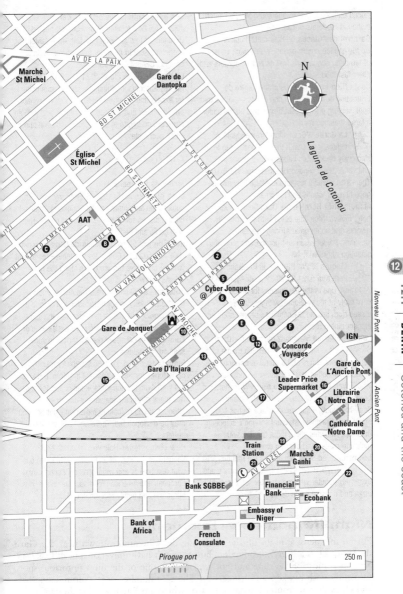

Marché
St Michel

AV DE LA PAIX

Gare de
Dantopka

BD ST MICHEL

Église
St Michel

BD STEINMETZ

AV DE L'ORME

Lagune de Cotonou

N

AAT

RUE D'ABOMEY

RUE AGBETO AMADJOKO

RUE D'ABOMEY

C

B A

AV VAN VOLLENHOVEN

RUE DU DAHOMEY

RUE DURAND

2

5

RUE GRANGE

Cyber Jonquet

@ 6

@

RUE 511

D

Gare de Jonquet

AV PROCHE

10

RUE DES CHEMINOTS

E

9

F

G

12

H

Concorde
Voyages

IGN

Nouveau Pont

Gare D'Itajara

13

RUE DAKO DONOU

14

Leader Price
Supermarket

16

Gare de
L'Ancien Pont

Librairie
Notre Dame

Ancien Pont

15

17

18

Cathédrale
Notre Dame

Train
Station

19

AV CLOZEL

21

Marché
Ganhi

20

22

Bank SGBBE

Financial
Bank

RUE BBB

Ecobank

Bank of
Africa

Embassy of
Niger

I

French
Consulate

Pirogue port

0   250 m

Roi de Chawarma bd Steinmetz, corner of rue
des Cheminots. Popular lunchtime destination
for the office crowd with great *chawarmas*
(CFA2000–2500), kebabs and sandwiches, and
tasty stews and couscous.
Steers/Debonairs bd Steinmetz, near the
cathedral. One of the few fast-food places in town,

this branch of the South African chain has the
usual burgers, chicken and pizzas.

Moderate (up to CFA5000) and expensive
After bd St Michel, 50m east of Ciné Bénin.
Upstairs restaurant, red velvet upholstery and a
pleasant terrace, serving tasty and reasonably

priced European, African and some Middle Eastern dishes at moderate prices.

Carnival des Glaces bd Steinmetz. Popular *salon de thé* and ice-cream parlour with a wide variety of tempting sundaes as well as pizzas, burgers and other fast food.

Costa Rica in the grounds of the Centre de Promotion de l'Artisanat. Long a very popular expat spot, serving pricey pasta dishes and pizzas under a large thatched roof.

La Gerbe d'Or av Clozel (closed Mon). A deli/patisserie with the best pastries in town since way back – rum babas, eclairs, croissants and wholewheat sandwiches from around CFA1000. There's an upstairs restaurant, where they also do good burgers, salads and ice cream.

Maquis Chez Bernice rue Dako Donou, near the hotel *Riviera*. Nice little place with very friendly owners and some great African specialities including *poulet yassa* and *gombo*, and a great selection of grilled fish.

Maquis le Pili Pili rue du Révérend Père Kitti ☎21.31.29.32 (noon–4pm and 7–11pm). One of the best places for African food, very lively at the weekend, with a selection of dishes from around the continent served up in an elegant dining room.

Le Petit Four bd Steinmetz (daily 7am–10pm). Swanky coffee shop with an Art-Deco theme, comfy leather chairs and a menu of delicious patisseries, coffee, pasta dishes and fantastic wood-oven-baked pizzas. It's also a Wi-Fi hot spot.

Le Phénicien av Clozel, near the PTT (daily 6am–midnight). A surprising refuge on this busy street, an attractive restaurant serving a selection of European dishes throughout the day, with tempting crêpes and beer on draught.

Le Sorrento bd St Michel behind the Hall des Arts ☎21.30.37.79. Benin's best Italian restaurant, and extremely popular with the smarter set. Excellent pizza and unusual pasta dishes.

Les 3 Mousquetaires off av Clozel ☎21.31.61.22 (closed Sun). For well-heeled Béninois or tourists with CFA to burn – tantalizing French cuisine in an attractive setting. Main courses CFA6500–15,000.

La Verdure off av Clozel ☎21.31.32.17. Casual bar-restaurant (something of a social focus point for expats and moneyed youth) serving reasonably priced lobster and seafood specialities, and with an attractive courtyard at the back, plus pinball and a small pool table.

Out from the centre

Moderate to expensive

Chez Clarisse next to the US Embassy. Popular choice with an intimate dining room and excellent French dishes such as *sole meunière* or escargots with garlic and herbs.

Hai King just off the Carrefour de Cadjehoun near Haie Vive ☎21.30.60.08. Great Chinese restaurant with an attractive terrace overlooking the busy streets below.

Hôtel du Lac Akpakpa, near the Ancien Pont ☎21.33.19.19. A great terrace for a drink and a meal, looking out across the lagoon as the sun goes down. Delicious cuisine covering a range of European and Lebanese dishes, including some seafood specialities.

Indiana Haie Vive ☎21.30.03.20. A rare opportunity for an Indian meal in Benin. Decked out with over-the-top knick-knacks and fabrics, this place offers a wide variety of curries, although if you're looking for a really hot one you may be disappointed. There are regular weekend buffets.

New Livingstones Haie Vive ☎21.30.27.58. Vaguely reminiscent of an English pub, kitted out with dart boards and wide-screen TV sport. Great European and American food such as steaks, ribs, burgers – and highly recommended pizzas.

Nightlife and entertainment

For an inexpensive night on the town, rue des Cheminots, down near the **Gare de Jonquet**, is a lively introduction, but it doesn't have universal appeal. The *Playboy*, open most of the time and not expensive, is one of the most notorious spots, swarming with hookers and hangers-on. There's a number of less intimidating bars and clubs dotted around town, the best of which are listed below, although names and owners tend to change rapidly.

Le 2001 rue des Cheminots (nightly from 11pm). Extremely popular despite the relatively high price of drinks and the cover charge (CFA3500–4500). Attracts a younger crowd looking for music and encounters – it can get rather sleazy.

Foley's Jazz Club rue du Dahomey, off bd Steinmetz (nightly from 8pm). Tiny place with a laid-back atmosphere, good drink specials and live bands most nights.

Le Repaire de Bacchus rue Immeuble Natalys, off the southern end of av Proche (daily happy hour 6–7pm, live music Thurs–Sun, open to 11pm weeknights, 2am Fri & Sat). Popular though pricey restaurant and jazz bar with a Western feel, beer on tap, and a long wine list and cocktail selection.

 So What! off bd Steinmetz, above Librairie Buffalo (closed Mon; ☎ 21.31.06.66). One of the most popular, consistently good live-music venues, playing host to musicians from Benin, Togo and Nigeria, and an extraordinary range of styles. Drumming lessons can also be arranged here. CFA3000–4000 cover on big concert nights (Fri & Sat), no entry charge for jam sessions (Tues–Thurs).

Titanic Bar rue 840, part of a complex near the Ancien Pont and the Lagune de Cotonou (nightly 7pm till late). On the roof of a massive yellow and green building right by the water – a great location for a drink and panoramic views across the city – with live bands on Fri and Sat nights.

VIP Club rue 840, next door to the *Titanic*. As the name suggests, a rather upmarket nightspot for clientele who can afford the CFA7000 cover charge (Fri & Sat), which includes a spirit of your choice.

Why Not av Proche (Mon–Sat from 11pm, Sun 8pm). Basement club drawing quite a crowd. Dance till you drop to African and European music. Cover CFA4000, drinks same price.

Listings

Airlines Air France, route de l'Aéroport ☎ 21.30.18.15; Air Ivoire, bd Steinmetz ☎ 31.31.86.14; Point-Afrique, Lot H, av Jean-Paul II, Cocotiers ☎ 21.30.98.62 🖳 cotonou@point-afrique.com.

Banks There's an ATM at the SGBBE on av Clozel (☎ 21.31.83.00); Bank of Africa on av Jean Paul II (☎ 21.31.32.28) has reasonable exchange rates. The Financial Bank, one block south of av Clozel (☎ 21.31.31.00), also has acceptable rates.

Books and magazines SONAEC, almost next door to the *Gerbe d'Or* patisserie on av Clozel (☎ 21.31.22.42), has all the local papers as well as the best international selection, along with books in French – African and French literature, travel guides and so forth, and even a few novels in English. Alternatively, try the well-equipped Librairie Notre Dame, near the BSS supermarket on av Clozel, beside the cathedral; or the Librairie Buffalo off bd Steinmetz, beneath the *So What!* club.

Car rental Hertz has a branch at the airport which only opens up for incoming flights. They are also represented in Akpakpa (☎ 21.33.96.81 📠 21.31.96.82). The *Benin Marina* hotel operates its own car-rental service (☎ 21.30.01.00). Also see "Travel agents", below.

Cinemas It's generally hard to see a decent film except on a small video screen or at the American or French cultural centres. Ciné Bénin shows a range of films (two or three a night), mostly action movies in French, as does the Ciné Concorde in Akpakpa.

Cultural centres and libraries The dynamic Centre Culturel Français is on route de l'Aéroport (☎ 21.30.08.56 📠 21.30.11.51), near the French embassy. Besides a library (Tues, Fri & Sat 9.30am–noon & 3–7pm, Wed 9.30am–7pm,

Thurs 3–7pm) and a café, they have regular art exhibitions and theatrical performances by local artists: pick up a schedule of events. The American Cultural Centre, off the bd de la Marina (☎ 21.30.03.12), is also pretty lively and regularly shows movies.

Embassies and consulates France, route de l'Aéroport, Cocotiers ☎ 21.31.26.38 📠 21.30.15.47, with a consulate on av du Général de Gaulle, near the Niger embassy ☎ 21.31.26.80 or 21.31.26.38 (Mon–Fri 8–11am); Ghana, route de l'Aéroport ☎ 21.30.07.46 (Mon–Fri 8am–2pm); Niger, one block behind the main PTT ☎ 21.31.56.65 (can issue the Visa Touristique Entente, allowing entry to Togo, Burkina and Côte d'Ivoire, as well as Niger and Benin); Nigeria, bd de la Marina ☎ 21.30.11.42 (visas usually only issued to Benin residents); UK, Mrs P. Collins (British community liaison officer; no embassy or consulate), British School of Cotonou, Haie Vive ☎ 21.30.32.65 or 95.85.38.73 (emergencies only); USA, rue Caporal Anani Bernard ☎ 21.30.06.50, 🖳 cotonou.usembassy.gov.

Hospitals and clinics The privately run Polyclinique les Cocotiers (general consultations Mon–Fri 8am–12.30pm & 4–7pm; ☎ 21.30.14.20) has the best reputation, though the most obvious place to head for treatment is the Centre National Hospitalier et Universitaire in the Patte d'Oie district (☎ 21.30.01.55). For an ambulance, call ☎ 21.30.06.56.

Internet access Across from the *Hôtel Ayihoué* there's a cybercafé offering a cheap but slow service (CFA600/hr). Cyber Jonquet, near the bus station of the same name, charges CFA550/hr. *Le Petit Four* (see "Eating and drinking") is a Wi-Fi access point.

Maps The Institut Géographique National (IGN), opposite Cash Supermarché next to the Nouveau

Pont (☎21.31.24.41) has reasonable survey maps of the country in 1:50,000 and 1:200,000 series.

Pharmacies Pharmacie Jonquet, rue des Cheminots ☎21.31.20.80 (24hr); Pharmacie Notre Dame, av Clozel (☎21.31.23.14); Pharmacie Camp Ghezo, bd St Michel (☎21.31.55.52).

Photography Royal Photo, next to SONAEC on av Clozel, has an express passport-photo service for CFA2500.

Post and phones The main PTT is off av Clozel, near the port. International calls can be made easily from the telephone office on av Clozel (collect calls can be made only to France).

Supermarkets The three largest are all near the intersection of av Clozel and bd Steinmetz. La Pointe and Codiprix (both owned by the same people; daily 9am–1pm & 4–8pm, Sun am only) are the best for imported European products. Leader Price on bd Steinmetz offers more of the same.

Swimming pools The cheapest and most central pool is at the *Hôtel du Port*, which non-guests can use for CFA2500. Though much nicer, the *Benin Marina*'s pool costs a steep CFA3500 and it's circular, so no good for length-swimming. The *Alédjo* has a smaller and cheaper alternative (CFA2000). The 25-metre pool at *Hôtel du Lac* is better value at CFA2500, and has several diving boards.

Travel agents One of the best organized is Agence Africaine de Tourisme (AAT), in the quartier St Michel (☎21.30.21.88 ⓦwww.aat-voyages .com), which runs trips to national attractions like Ganvié and Pendjari as well as selling plane tickets. Also reputable are Concorde Voyages, off bd Steinmetz (☎21.31.34.13). CBM Voyages, bd de France (☎21.31.49.02 ⓕ21.31.05.28), by the *Hôtel du Port*, has English-speaking staff and is extremely helpful; and finally, Benin Gulf Tours (☎021.30.04.04) in the grounds of the Centre de Promotion de l'Artisanat is also a good option.

Visa extensions From the Immigration Office, av Jean-Paul II (Mon–Fri 8–11am & 3–5pm; ☎21.31.42.13). Extensions for a month cost CFA12,000. One photo is required and the process takes about 48hr; visas can only be collected during the afternoon session.

Ganvié

GANVIÉ, said to be Africa's largest **lake village**, is an extraordinary sight. The entire settlement spreads across the shallow, grey-green waters on the northwest side of **Lac Nokoué**, behind Cotonou, with wood and thatch houses built on tall stilts rising above the rippling surface. The village is only accessible by boat; even the market is held on the water, women selling wares from their canoes. The lake is "grooved", as the tourist leaflet puts it, "not by gondolas like in Venice but by graceful pirogues or heavy boats loaded to the boards". Not altogether surprisingly, Ganvié is at times overrun with tourists whose presence has encouraged a commercial free-for-all in the little town, destroying the initial impressions of a tranquil aquatic idyll. If you have a low tolerance for this sort of thing, it's best to avoid it altogether and make your way to the less-commercialized places around Porto Novo (see p.992).

Some history

As the **slave trade** expanded after the Portuguese arrival on the coast in the sixteenth century, armies of the Dan-Homey king swept the surrounding countryside, rounding up people to be traded with the Europeans for exotic goods such as cloth, gin and guns. Insecurity led to the widespread migration of weaker communities, and thus the ancestors of the **Tofinu people**, who now inhabit Ganvié, came to settle in the area around Lake Nokoué, where they found sufficient space for grazing and farming. They were safe from invasion since the Dan-Homey were forbidden for religious reasons to extend their attacks over water. The name Ganvié probably derives from the Tofinu words *gan*, meaning "we are saved", and *vié*, "community". Today the stilt village is home to more than twenty thousand people who make their living primarily from **fishing**, planting branches in the shallow waters to form a network of underwater fences or fish traps known as *akadja*. If you fly over the area you can see hundreds of old fish traps. Fish trapped in this way can be eaten, sold or kept for breeding.

Practicalities

The departure point for Ganvié is **Abomey-Calavi** (often shortened to Calavi), 18km northwest of Cotonou. From the Gare de Dantokpa in Cotonou, take one of the frequent shared **taxis** (around CFA400), which will drop you at the station in Calavi. From here it's a ten-minute walk (or CFA100 on a *zemidjan*) to the jetty where there's an official price-list for the tour of Ganvié. If you're on your own, it's an expensive CFA6050 for a two-hour pirogue ride or CFA7050 for a faster, motorized pirogue. The price decreases for groups: for an ordinary pirogue it's CFA4050 per person for groups of two to four, CFA3050 for larger groups, with a surcharge of CFA1000 or so if you want a motorized vessel. If, instead of stopping at Abomey-Calavi, you continue 5km up the northern highway to **Akassato**, you can approach Ganvié from behind and at slightly less cost, avoiding the worst tourist excesses. Pirogues punt you south 4km or so through the creeks and marshes to the edge of the lake and the stilt village. Whichever way you arrive, be aware that **taking photos** can be an uncomfortable experience, with many locals preferring to hide their faces or disappear.

You can **stay** the night at the brightly painted *Expotel Ganvié* (aka *Chez Raphael*) which offers cold drinks and four basic rooms with bucket showers (☎21.49.75.99 ❷) – you can't miss the shocking red structure as you approach the village from Calavi. A step up, and worth the extra cost, ⚞ *Auberge Carrefour Ganvié* (aka *Chez M*) has comfortable and recently renovated s/c doubles with mosquito nets and a good restaurant (☎21.42.04.68 ❷) and they also offer complimentary transport back to Calavi.

Ouidah

Hauntingly quiet after centuries of dynamic history, **OUIDAH**, 40km west of Cotonou, works a wonderful spell. This is a **voodoo** stronghold and the religion's influence penetrates as deeply as the salt air blowing off the ocean, its power outliving that of the **Portuguese fort** (now a museum). There are streets of French **colonial architecture** – all cracked facades and sagging wooden porches and shutters, and now dwelt in by poor families. The **python temple** adds a kitsch touch, but the use of snakes is part of authentic fetish practice – never mind the fact that they get rather more of a workout than they did in the days before tourism. There are plenty of other altars and temples scattered about the town, keeping the faith alive without the touristy overtones.

Back in the days when the shore of the Gulf of Benin was known as the **Slave Coast**, some of the largest trading posts and slave markets were sited here. Grand Popo, Porto Novo and Ouidah were synonymous with the trade. Ouidah was captured by the "Amazon" warriors of King Agadja of Abomey in the early eighteenth century (see p.995) and, in the following years, the town grew into one of the foremost trading posts between Europe and the Dan-Homey empire. The **Portuguese**, who arrived at the spot, then known as Ajuda ("Help"), in 1580, waited over a century to build the fort of **São João Batista**. Part of their story is told in Bruce Chatwin's *The Viceroy of Ouidah* (see "Books" on p.969) and another version in Werner Herzog's quirky 1987 film *Cobra Verde*. Nearby, the **Danes**, **English** and **French** also built forts as they tried to gain their share of the growing trade with Africa. The last Portuguese slave ship left for Brazil in 1885. The Danish and English bastions today house businesses, while the Place du Fort Français now features a small outdoor theatre. Ouidah remained an important coastal city while under French dominion, but in the early twentieth century the colonists built a new and larger port at Cotonou. From then on, the old town went into a slow decline.

The Town

The **Museum of History** (Mon–Fri 8am–noon & 3–6pm, weekends 9am–6pm; CFA1000), just east of the market and on rue du General Dodds, is housed in the **Portuguese fort of São João Batista**, built in 1721. Remarkably enough, a Portuguese flag waved symbolically over the building until the eve of Dahomey's independence in 1960, although the rest of the town was in French hands. The present museum traces the history of European exploration and exploitation of the Slave Coast region, and follows the dispersal of its people to the Caribbean and Brazil. The documentation includes displays of enlarged maps juxtaposed with period photographs and engravings. Many of the exhibits concentrate on the spread of the **voodoo religion** to Haiti, Cuba and Brazil, with examples of religious fetishes and pictures of rituals.

The **Maison du Brésil** (daily 7am–6pm; CFA1000), on the western side of town on Avenue de France, is a noteworthy Afro-Brazilian building from the turn of the last century. The main building holds an exhibition on Women in Africa, and features a series of interesting sculptures, handicrafts, photographs and other information illustrating the role of women across the continent. In an adjacent house is an exhibition of contemporary art that incorporates voodoo symbols into modern forms of expression. Sculptures made from the transformed carcasses of rusty *mobylettes* are the highlight of a collection that also includes less-memorable paintings and collages, though some of the old photos on the upper floor are remarkable. Many of the

Voodoo

"**Voodoo**", also spelt *vodu*, *vodun*, *voudou* or *vudu*, is a confusing term. It does not signify a religion, at least not in Africa, but is a word used by the peoples of Togo and Benin for a spirit, demigod or intermediary. *Vodu* "priests", male and female, are individuals who are particularly susceptible to *vodu* influence, easily "possessed" or "mounted" by the *vodu*, who can thus display its emotions through a human channel. A **fetish** is an ordinary object imbued with some of this sacred power – a *vodu* charm available at any market.

The **Ewe** and other people of the coast – as well as the Fon around Abomey in Benin – believe in a supreme god, **Mawu**. Their religious stories link him (in some societies, Mawu is a woman, or even a couple, Mawu-Lisa) with creation. Shrines are rarely built for Mawu, however, but for the *vodu*, many of whom are associated with **natural forces** or with **ancestors**. The benevolence of *vodu* is sought by offerings; communities often pay homage to a specific *vodu* who becomes their main spiritual protector. In Ouidah, for example, **Dangbe** has a special place. Represented by the snake and sometimes by rainbows, curling smoke, running water or waving grass, Dangbe is associated with life and movement. In Abomey, he is known as **Da** and is shown on the bas-reliefs of the royal palace as a snake swallowing its tail – a symbol of eternity.

Throughout Togo and Benin, people honor **Buku** – a *vodu* associated with the sky. At Dassa Zoumé in Benin, townspeople dedicate one of their oldest temples to her. Renowned as an oracle, Buku's name is evoked in proverbs, blessings and curses, and people travel long distances to her shrines to pray, give offerings or make sacrifices. **So** (Hebiosso in Fon) is the *vodu* of thunder, with the power to strike down the impious. He is depicted at the Abomey palace as a red ram with lightning shooting from his mouth and two axes at his side. **Gu**, the guardian of smithing and war, also has associations with the sky.

Sapata is more closely identified with the earth and shrines dedicated to this *vodu* are usually seen outside villages near the fields. Linked to disease, he is respected and feared. Priests devoted to Sapata are known for their ability to treat illness and for their understanding of medicinal plants. **Hu** is connected with the ocean and water. His works pay tribute to Africans in the diaspora in recognizing the cultural connection between Africa and the Americas.

Ouidah's **basilica**, in the centre, is a formidable monument that was upgraded to its present status during the 1989 visit of Pope John Paul II, who also consecrated the new altar. Dating from the start of the twentieth century, it's recently been restored and fitted with new stained-glass windows.

The cathedral, however, attracts nowhere near as many visitors as the nearby **python temple** (CFA1000; photography fee CFA2000; video fee CFA5000), which guards the secrets of Ouidah's snake cult. Visitors get a brief tour of the temple and various fetishes before being asked to make an offering at a shrine, and seeing and posing with the tame pythons – wrap-around snakes believed to give vitality and protection over your person. The whole performance is rather graceless, and on days when the reptiles are, understandably, tired, you may get no more than a peek into the room where they're kept.

An interesting walk through residential streets to the northeast of the centre leads to the **Kpasse Sacred Forest** (daily 9am–6pm; CFA1000), just off rue de la Roncière. Tradition holds this site to be where Kpasse, a fourteenth-century chief, transformed himself into a tree in order to hide from his enemies. The ancient *iroko* tree still marks the spot and believers leave offerings by its roots. Modernist bronze statues depicting voodoo divinities are scattered about the woods and are explained during a guided tour – photography is permitted. While not an extraordinary adventure, a visit here is a pleasant pretext for a tramp through some pretty woods.

daughter, **Avlekete**, is honoured at the port of Cotonou and in nearby villages. **Legba**, the trickster, whose image is distinguished by an exaggerated phallus, contains elements of good and evil. Though Legba can bring bad luck on a house, he can also chase it away. His shrines can be seen everywhere – guarding the entrance to a community or compound, in a market, in fields, or at a crossroads.

Countless other *vodu* exist, and many occupy natural niches. **Iroko** trees, for example, are often believed to be inhabited by *vodu*. They are associated with fertility or new life, and you will often see sacrifices lying among their roots. The creation stories of some societies in the region tell of men and women descending to earth from the branches of an *iroko*.

There are many parallels between the *vodu* and the *orisa* of Yoruba religion in Nigeria, and also between *vodu* and elements of Akan religion further to the west in Ghana and Côte d'Ivoire – all the result of migrations and the wax and wane of empires. A further complexity was introduced by the return of Brazilians between the seventeenth and nineteenth centuries to the land of their (partial) ancestry. They reintroduced elements of Yoruba custom when they settled on this part of the coast.

Slaves sold across the Atlantic took their religious systems to North and South **America** and the Caribbean. Even metropolitan areas carry reminders: Legba statuaries made in the last fifty years can be found in New York City and Miami. But West African religions are more often identified with Brazil, Cuba and **Haiti**. Many Haitian slaves came from the Dahomey (Benin) coast and to this day Haitian names for numerous *vodu* are virtually unchanged: Legba is known as Papa Legba, Sapata as Sabata, Avlekete as Aizan-Velekete. The *iroko* tree, known as *loko* in Fon, became Papa Loko. Only the supreme god Mawu was given a completely new, French, name – Bondieu.

In the Americas, **Catholicism** and the *vodu* system were soon melded together. But even in West Africa, many elements of Catholic teaching found fertile soil in the local belief system: the pantheon of a supreme god, the Virgin Mary and saints who could be called upon for help was a similar enough structure to Mawa and the *vodu*. St Patrick, not surprisingly, was identified with the snake *vodu* Dangbe, while St Peter was considered to be the Catholic incarnation of Legba.

A final, popular excursion is along the **Route des Esclaves**, the four-kilometre sandy track walked by slaves from their holding points in town to the beach. Starting in the Place Chacha (La Place des Enchères), the route runs down rue Don Francisco de Souza, past the old railway station, before continuing through attractive, lush scenery. Dotted along the route are vivid green statues, the royal emblems of the various chiefs of Abomey, including Ghezo and Behanzin (see p.995). Various other monuments line the route, reminders of the scale and savagery of the slave trade. You pass a statue marking the tree of forgetfulness, which slaves were forced to walk around to forget their previous life, religion and culture, "to become a people with no will to react or rebel". Further along, just before the village of Zoungbodji, the **Monument of Repentance** is a colourful memorial, with bas-relief art depicting scenes of slavery. Continuing past other monuments, you eventually reach the beach and the **Door of No Return**, a vast and imposing arch also decorated with bas-relief images and metal sculptures of slaves in shackles. If you're short on time, you can easily find a guide (and are likely to be approached by a few) to take you through the slave route by *zemi*, explaining the sights and monuments along the way, for around CFA4000. This will take about 1½ hours.

French exchanges

"It's really important to be able to speak at least a minimum level of French to get on. People really don't speak English. Also, you need euros to change. In some places in Benin and Togo you can even pay for things in euros. The top exchange place in Ouidah turned out to be the chemist."

Sarah Brown, UK

Practicalities

Ouidah is easy to get to, with regular bush taxis heading here from the Gare de Jonquet in Cotonou. Ouidah's **gare routière** is in the centre of town, but vehicles passing through drop passengers on the main highway, by the *Hôtel Gbena*, from where it's easy to catch a *zemidjan* for a ten-minute ride to the centre. The *gare routière* has irregular transport for Cotonou only; for Grand Popo and the west it's better to go to the main route of Lomé, where you can pick up (frequent) transport from opposite the *Hôtel Gbena*. There's reliable **Internet** access at FIC on rue Olivier de Montaguerre (CFA350/hr), open 7am to 10pm.

Accommodation

🏃 **Casa del Papa** Ouidah plage, 7km past the Door of No Return ☎21.34.12.15 ℗21.34.12.03. This is the fanciest accommodation in the Ouidah area, with airy and comfortable rooms set in bungalows amongst the palm trees, a swimming pool, and canoe and kayak tours on offer. There's a good restaurant and great views out to the waters beyond. ⑥

Hôtel DK route de Lomé, 1500m northeast of the centre ☎21.34.11.97. The rooms here are fine, with a/c and satellite TV, but the place feels rather clinical and the noise from the main road can be a problem. There's a swimming pool, terrace and an okay restaurant but it has definitely seen better days. ④

Hôtel Gbena route de Lomé, 2km northwest of the centre ☎21.34.12.15 ℗21.34.12.03. For a long time the only place to stay in town, but the now

dated decor reinforces the soulless atmosphere. Rooms have decent amenities, but ask for one away from the noisy main road. The restaurant serves okay food. ④

Le Jardin Brésilien (aka *Auberge de la Diaspora*) 4km south of the centre and 200m east of the Door of No Return ☎21.34.11.10 ℮dyasporah @yahoo.fr. Attractive thatched bungalows set among the palm trees by the beach, or less appealing budget accommodation behind. There's also a good restaurant. Rooms ② or camping CFA3000/tent.

🏃 **Oasis** across from the *gare routière* in the town centre ☎21.34.10.91. Good value for money, with simple, clean rooms with a/c and fan and a rooftop terrace with great views out over Ouidah. The friendly manager is also a good chef and can rustle up tasty meals given advance notice. ③

OUIDAH

ACCOMMODATION
Casa del Papa	G
Gbena	A
DK	C
Le Jardin Brésilien	F
Motel Oriki	D
Oasis	E
PAMFF	B

RESTAURANTS, BARS & CLUBS
Buvette au Bel Air	3
Café/Bar Equinox	4
Café/Bar la Pacha	2
Cafétéria Tour de Musée	5
Doigts Bleus	7
L'Escale des Arts	8
La Préférence	6
Le Soleil de Minuit	1

250 m

Ficisan (Internet café), FIC (250m), **A** (500m) & **B** (2km)

Lomé (Ouidah bypass)

Cotonou

Cotonou **G** (200m)

Kpasse Sacred Forest

WOMÉ

TOVÉ

GBÉTO

ABATA

CAMP MILITAIRE

Église Catholique

Église Protestante

Basilica

Site of English Fort

Catholic Mission

Python Temple

Market

Portugese Fort & Museum of History

Site of old French Fort

Centre Culturel

Gare Routière

Old Train Station

Maison du Brésil

Tribunal

Stadium

PLACE CHACHA

RUE DE LOMÉ
ROUTE DE LOMÉ
RUE DU GÉNÉRAL DODD
RUE DU ROI KPASSE
RUE DE LA RONCIÈRE
RUE DU ROI GUÉZO
RUE DU GOUVERNEUR BONFILS
RUE STEINMETZ
RUE PIERRE BONNAUD
RUE OLIVIER DE MONTAGUÈRE
RUE DES FRÈRES BÉRAUD
RUE D'ORDRE
RUE COLOMBANI
RUE ST. LOUIS
RUE VAN VOLLENHOVEN
ANCIENNE ROUTE TOGO-NIGERIA
RUE MILITIS LA CROIX
RUE DU RPG KITI
RUE DON FRANCISCO DE SOUZA
RUE DOUBLET DE HONFLEUR
ANCIENNE ROUTE TOGO-NIGERIA
AVENUE DE FRANCE
RUE DES PALMISTES
DANGBÉHOU

Total

N

G (4km), Beaches, Route des Esclaves, Door of No Return (4km) & **G** (11km)

Lomé

12

Motel Oriki rue des Palmistes ☎21.34.10.04.
Very presentable, s/c rooms set in a quiet area.
Clean and spacious, but overpriced considering
there's no a/c. ❸

PAMFF 2.5km northwest of the centre,
signposted off the route de Lomé ☎21.34.10.30
Ⓕ21.34.10.81. Popular 26-room hotel with clean,
comfy rooms arranged around a courtyard, and an
attractive restaurant. ❷

Eating and drinking

For **food**, the friendly *Caféteria Tour de Musée* or the *Café/Bar Equinox* are good
places for a coffee or a snack. *Café/Bar la Pacha* has a large outdoor space and does
good lunches. For something slightly more formal, the thatched roof tables and
shady garden at *L'Escale des Arts* in the Village Artisanal de Ouidah serves limited
filling meals. Otherwise, *La Préférence* opposite the Total filling station, *Doigts Bleus*
by the town's mosque and *Buvette au Bel Air* are all good for a **drink**; while *Le
Soleil de Minuit* on rue du Roi Guezo is the best **club** in town, if slightly sleazy,
with glitzy mirrors.

Grand Popo and around

At the height of the slave trade, **GRAND POPO**, some 70km west of Cotonou,
rivalled Porto Novo, Ouidah and Aného (in Togo) as a major port. With the demise
of the trade, however, its importance declined more dramatically than the other
towns and today even vestiges of the more recent colonial past have literally been
washed away by the advancing ocean. Locals remember the large church, commercial depots, administrative buildings and colonial mansions that disappeared into the
water as recently as the 1960s, and though a few **antiquated buildings** still dot the
road that leads to the old village from the main highway, most of the old quarter is
entirely submerged.

As a result, Grand Popo looks very much like any of the other small fishing villages
that stretch between Lomé and Cotonou, tucked between the lagoon and the ocean
and lost in a sea of coconut trees. Though **voodoo** thrives here, few visitors even
notice the snake pit, fetishes or temples, and most confine themselves to the idyllic
beach. If you do manage to drag yourself from the sands, look out for the *Villa
Karo* (☎21.43.03.58 ⓦwww.villa-karo.org), a Finnish–African cultural centre which
hosts weekly film nights, regular free concerts, dance classes and language lessons,
and features a museum exhibiting art from all over West Africa and a library with
hundreds of books about Africa.

Lac Ahémè provides the possibility for excursions (small boys will try to recruit
you the moment you arrive), and fishermen are happy to supplement their incomes
by ferrying visitors in pirogues. The most popular destination is the **Bouche du
Roy** – a vast expanse of water where the Mono River empties into the ocean. Along
the way, you pass through scenic island villages.

> ### "Yovo!"
>
> "Children shout the word *Yovo* ad nauseum. It means white person and is not
> done maliciously. It's an amicable term."
>
> James McCarthy, Ireland

Practicalities

Taxis from Cotonou depart from the Gare de Jonquet, and as with transport from
Lomé, let you off at the junction on the main highway. It's 4km down the sandy
track, through the old village to the town's most exclusive **accommodation**, the
French-run *Auberge de Grand-Popo* (☎21.43.00.47 ⓦwww.hotels-benin.com ❹).

Housed in refurbished colonial buildings, the lodgings offer a refreshing combination of nostalgia and comfort; all rooms have private baths and fans, or you can camp for CFA2000 per head near the uninviting pool. The hotel's **restaurant** terrace sits right on the waterfront – spectacular scenery for European dishes (around CFA5000 for a meal). Back at the junction, *Hôtel Etoile de Mer* (T21.43.04.83 ➋) is conveniently located on the main road, and has spotless rooms, some with a/c; camping is allowed for CFA2500 per tent, though the highlight is the attractive restaurant set in a garden. On the western side of town, 2km from the junction near **Ewé Condji**, the excellent ⚑ *Awalé Plage* (T21.43.01.17 ✉awaleplage@yahoo.fr ➍) has homely s/c chalets set in a large attractive compound. Camping is possible (CFA4700 per tent) down on the golden beach, and there's a rustic bar serving cold beers and juices. The entertainment here is excellent and they regularly book big-name bands. Try to time your stay with their extravagant fortnightly full-moon and "black-moon" (new-moon) beach parties. There are a couple of cheaper places to stay out on the road to the *Auberge*, namely *Plage Coin des Amis* (T21.43.03.98 ➋) and *Doue Plage* (T21.43.02.42 ➋), virtually next door, both offering basic, fan-less rooms with mosquito nets; the latter place is more established and comfortable. They both also allow camping for CFA1500 per person.

Among several **eating** options, *Farafina*, some 400m east of the *Auberge*, is popular with tourists and serves European cuisine for around CFA3000 a meal, plus a selection of cocktails; *Pizzeria Chez Marcel* just down the road is a cheaper alternative.

Lac Ahémè

A highly picturesque area to visit, **Lac Ahémè** is the lagoon that extends 30km inland from Grand Popo. There's a pleasant **hotel–restaurant** on the west shore, *Village-Club Ahémè* (T21.43.00.29 F21.43.02.23 ➍) – a place for lazing away a few days, with plain, comfortable s/c, a/c rooms and optional excursions on the lake and around the district. **Possotomè**, 87km from Cotonou, is the nearest village and source of the eponymous bottled water. To reach the area, either charter a taxi and head north from Comè on a bad dirt road direct to Possotomè, or alternatively from Comè or Cotonou, take a shared taxi to Zoungbonou and then a *zemidjan* to Bopa or Possotomè on the lagoon itself.

Porto Novo and around

Official capital of Benin, **PORTO NOVO** has two attributes that Cotonou lacks – a **geographical setting** of some presence and a place in **history**. Sprawling over the hills surrounding the sizeable lagoon of Lac Nokoué, the town was formerly the centre of a large kingdom of the Gun people, whose **palace** has now been restored. More recently it served as capital of the French colony of Dahomey – the **colonial buildings** are reminders of this period – and the town was, and remains, the centre of the country's intellectual life and something of a barometer of political opinion in Benin.

Despite a population of around 230,000, Porto Novo seems much smaller. Perhaps this is because of its coherent layout, but the narrow streets and absence of modern structures also add to the provincial, passed-by feeling: most of the architecture in town harks back to the colonial and pre-colonial periods. For visitors, it's one of Benin's most interesting towns, with a strikingly good ethnographic museum, and is easily accessible, only 30km northeast of Cotonou, to which it's connected by good roads.

The Town

Porto Novo consists of four main parts. The **old town** in the centre is characterized by narrow dirt roads and *banco*-built houses and runs into the **commercial centre** along Avenue Vicot Ballot, with the **Grand Marché** and surrounding businesses stretching down to the lagoon on the southwestern flanks of the town. To the east, the **administrative district** is the location of the Présidence – the former **Governor's Palace** – and a couple of ministries and office buildings. Scattered around the margins, the zone of new **residential quarters** is inhabited by people who have moved to the city in recent years. Your most likely arrival point is at the *gare routière* on the northern side of the bridge, from where you can walk to most of the town's hotels, or easily take one of the waiting *zemidjans*.

Porto Novo's superb **museum of ethnography** on Avenue no. 6 (Mon–Fri 8.30am–6pm, Sat & Sun 9am–6pm; ☎20.21.25.54; CFA1000) contains artefacts from all Benin's peoples, each item accompanied by explanations and background. The visit kicks off at the entrance with a pair of beautifully **carved doors** from the palace of the king of Kétou, 100km north of Porto Novo. Impressive murals adorn the walls of the courtyard inside and on the ground floor of the museum you'll find a selection of voodoo masks, each with their own meaning and significance. There's also a small collection of musical instruments on display. Upstairs the exhibition explores "Birth, life and death in Benin". The guided tour, in French and English, and included in the entrance fee, really brings the exhibits alive.

The **Musée da Silva** (daily 9am–5pm; CFA2000, inclusive of obligatory guide) is a privately owned museum opposite the Bank of Africa, housed in a beautiful old Afro-Brazilian house dating back to the nineteenth century. The eclectic collection includes information on Benin's tribal culture and history, an exhibition on slavery and the African Diaspora, and a collection of classic cars and motorbikes. The house also offers some rooms to rent (see "Accommodation") and has a restaurant.

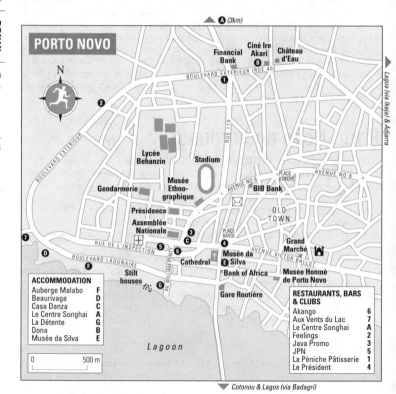

PORTO NOVO

N

ACCOMMODATION
Auberge Malabo	F
Beaurivage	D
Casa Danza	C
Le Centre Songhai	A
La Détente	G
Dona	B
Musée da Silva	E

RESTAURANTS, BARS & CLUBS
Akango	6
Aux Vents du Lac	7
Le Centre Songhai	A
Feelings	2
Java Promo	3
JPN	5
La Péniche Pâtisserie	1
Le Président	4

0   500 m

Lagoon

▲ **A** *(3km)*

Financial Bank

Ciné Ire Akari

Château d'Eau

BOULEVARD EXTÉRIEUR (RUE 40)

Lagos (via Ikeja) & Adjarra

Lycée Behanzin

Stadium

Musée Ethno-graphique

Gendarmerie

PLACE KOKOYE

AVENUE NO 6

BIB Bank

OLD TOWN

Présidence

Assemblée Nationale

RUE DE L'INSPECTION

PLACE BAYOL

Grand Marché

Musée da Silva

AVENUE VICTOR BALLOT

BOULEVARD LAGUNAIRE

Cathedral

Bank of Africa

Musée Honmè de Porto Novo

Stilt houses

Gare Routière

BOULEVARD EXTÉRIEUR

RUE 110

AVENUE NO 8

AV. WILLIAM PONTY

▼ *Cotonou & Lagos (via Badagri)*

Porto Novo's **Grand Marché** is on Avenue Victor Ballot. Held every four days in keeping with the traditional calendar, the market is a colourful affair that spreads over a large central square, with stalls selling agricultural goods from the surrounding countryside and fish from the nearby lagoon. The curious Brazilian-style building painted in muted pastel colours was constructed in the nineteenth century as a church, but is today the **central mosque**, dominating the scene.

Just southwest of the market, the **Musée Honmè de Porto Novo** (daily 9am–6pm; ☏20.21.35.66) has been restored and costs CFA1000 for the obligatory guided tour. It's an impressive maze of baked mud and thatch divided between the private residences of **King Toffa** and his entourage and the public assembly halls, but rather empty, except for a scant few mementos of the local kings. You have to rely on your imagination to bring to life the guide's detailed explanations of local history and court life.

Practicalities

Although Porto Novo is Benin's official capital, Cotonou is the centre of business and government; Porto Novo doesn't even benefit greatly from Lagos traffic and trade, as it's off the main coastal highway. There is a **post office**, a **hospital** (☏20.21.35.90) and some pharmacies, but for banking (the three banks in town will only change cash euros) and just about every other facility, you'll find Porto Novo very limited indeed. **Internet** access is available at the Centre Songhai on the route de Pobè to the north of town (CFA500/hr; 9am–10pm). For an evening film, head to Ciné Ire Akari (☏20.22.48.73) next to *Hôtel Dona*. There's also an outdoor **cinema** in the courtyard of the Musée da Silva which sometimes shows French films or puts on small concerts. Taxis and minibuses run to both Cotonou and Lagos from the **gare routière** near the bridge.

Accommodation

Porto Novo has a limited range of hotels for a town of its size.

Auberge Malabo bd Lagunaire ☏20.21.34.04. Friendly atmosphere and clean, spacious s/c rooms with good views across the lagoon, but rather seedy, thanks to its lively bar-restaurant. ❷

Beaurivage bd Lagunaire ☏20.21.23.99. Venerable, well-maintained hotel with a nicely planted terrace overlooking the lagoon. Comfortable s/c, a/c rooms, but the staff and food are variable. ❹

Casa Danza Near the Assemblée Nationale ☏20.21.48.12. Porto Novo's most central accommodation, the once-popular restaurant now offers mediocre food. Rooms are s/c and come with choice of fan or a/c; some also have attractive tiled floors or balconies. ❷

🏃 **Le Centre Songhai** 3km north of town on the road to Pobè ☏20.22.50.92 ⓦwww .songhai.org. In a vast, beautifully wooded site, this voluntary organization, established by a US/Nigerian academic, hosts students of varied subjects, including fishing, agriculture and "sustainable socio-economic entrepreneurship". There's spotless accommodation (a/c or fan) with shared facilities – an excellent deal. ❷

La Détente off bd Lagunaire ☏20.21.44.69. Well located, offering a panorama of the lagoon and nearby stilt village, and within walking distance of the palace and market. Rooms are homely enough, with comfortable furniture. ❷

Dona bd Extérieur, near Ciné Ire Akari ☏20.21.30.52 ⒻF20.21.25.25. Modern hotel housed in a pink building on a busy main road with 20 nicely furnished s/c, a/c rooms, a bar-restaurant and a nightclub. It gets pretty noisy. ❹

Musée da Silva opposite the Bank of Africa ☏20.21.50.71. In an annexe next to the museum are a few dusty and run-down rooms. The larger ones have *salons* – meaning a couple of tatty-looking chairs separated from the bedroom by a curtain. ❷

Eating and nightlife

In addition to the **street food** in the markets and around the *gare routière*, and the pricey hotel restaurants at the *Dona* and *Beaurivage*, Porto Novo has quite a number of places to eat. For **European** fare specifically, the moderately priced restaurant under a pleasant *paillote* at the JPN (across from the Assemblée Nationale) is popular at breakfast and lunchtimes. For **pastries and cakes**, *La Péniche Pâtisserie* (on bd Extérieur) has excellent *pain au chocolat*, croissants and yoghurt. There's also the stylish *Akango* on rue de l'Inspection and the bustling *Java Promo* on av Victor Ballot. Moving **upmarket**, *Le Président* in place Bayol (☎20.21.44.21), is the most stylish of Porto Novo's restaurants, with a decent wine list. If you have transport or are staying out there, the *Centre Songhai* has an excellent restaurant serving wonderfully fresh fruit juices, salads and sandwiches as well as more substantial meals, and also serves wine by the carafe.

Finally, in the evenings, *Aux Vents du Lac*, off bd Lagunaire a little north of the *Beaurivage*, has a limited menu of European and local dishes, but boasts a fine little courtyard at the back. *Feelings Night Club*, 500m beyond *Hôtel Beaurivage*, is where the well-to-do of the town **dance** the night away to African, *zouk* and American music (Wed & Fri–Sun 10pm till late; CFA3000 cover).

Around Porto Novo

Just 8km northeast of Porto Novo is the lively market centre of **ADJARRA**, where an important market takes place every fourth day. This small village has a reputation for its **drum-makers** and attracts many buyers from Nigeria drawn by the more than fifty kinds of *tam-tam* on offer, varying in construction, material (wood or clay) and colour. Alongside fruit and vegetables, the market also sells a selection of useful fetishes, medicinal herbs and *gris-gris* (lucky charms), as well as locally made pottery and hand-woven cloth. Frequent taxis, especially on market day, leave from the *gare routière* in Porto Novo, or alternatively, hire a *zemidjan* for the journey.

The stilt villages

The lagoon around Porto Novo has a number of stilt villages not unlike Ganvié, but until recently travellers seldom ventured to them. Apart from the very small cluster of stilt houses near the *Détente* hotel in town, the closest and easiest to reach is **Aguégué**, 12km through the creeks west of Porto Novo (about 4hr by pirogue). There's no accommodation in the village, but just gliding through and having a look makes for an interesting excursion. You may be asked to pay if you want to take pictures. *Piroguiers* near the bridge in Porto Novo can easily be found to take you there; alternatively, enquire after Hilaire, a very helpful tour guide who lives in the stilt houses near the *Détente* – his agency Iroko Tours offers visits to Aguégué and other stilt villages at competitive prices (CFA7000 per person by pirogue, CFA20,000 for a group in a motorboat). The *Hôtel Beaurivage* in Porto Novo also organizes trips to the villages (CFA12,000 for two people by pirogue; CFA20,000 for a larger group by motorboat).

12.2

Central Benin

B enin's interior is a relatively homogeneous series of **plains** dominated by low, sloping hills. This was the site of early kingdoms, most notably that of the **Fon** founded at **Abomey**. The Fon were formed by the arrival and intermarriage of the Ajda from the coast with local inhabitants, and today are one of Benin's biggest ethnic groups. The **Yoruba**, who share some cultural affinities with the Fon, also established a number of chiefdoms in the area. They came in a series of vague movements, setting out on family and community migrations from Oyo and Ife in present-day Nigeria in the twelfth century, and often ended up dominating the commercial activities of the interior. Further north, the **Bariba** carved out a small territory – the **Borgou country** – in the region of **Parakou**. These are still the main peoples of central Benin, an area of intensive agricultural production and small industries. The road **north from Cotonou** to Abomey passes through the **Lama depression**, a low-lying swampy region of clay soils, patches of rainforest and a designated forest reserve, the **Forêt de Ko (Lama)**.

Abomey and Bohicon

Capital of one of the great West African kingdoms in pre-colonial times, **ABOMEY** boasts a fascinating history and counts as one of Benin's greatest attractions. Commercially the town is overshadowed by **BOHICON**, 9km to the east, of which Abomey is essentially the ancient precursor, and which has benefited from its position on the rail line and main north–south highway (the French deliberately laid the railway to the east of Abomey to reduce the commercial power of the Abomey royal dynasties). Despite Bohicon's immense **market**, however, the town is a chaotic sprawl

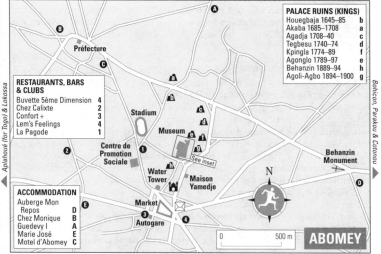

PALACE RUINS (KINGS)

Houegbaja 1645–85		b
Akaba 1685–1708		a
Agadja 1708–40		c
Tegbesu 1740–74		d
Kpingla 1774–89		f
Agonglo 1789–97		e
Behanzin 1889–94		h
Agoli-Agbo 1894–1900		g

RESTAURANTS, BARS & CLUBS

Buvette 5ème Dimension	4
Chez Calixte	2
Confort +	3
Lem's Feelings	4
La Pagode	1

ACCOMMODATION

Auberge Mon Repos	D
Chez Monique	B
Guedevy I	A
Marie José	E
Motel d'Abomey	C

Préfecture

Stadium

Museum

Centre de Promotion Sociale

Water Tower

Maison Yamedje

Market

Autogare

Behanzin Monument

See inset

N

0   500 m

ABOMEY

Aplahoué (for Togo) & Lokossa

Adanjeho Soldiers' oathing temple		1
Ahosihoue Queens' courtyard		2
Ajalala Main palace reception hall		3
Boho Spirit hut		4
Doho Tomb		5
Hounnouwa Entrance lobby and main access to a palace		6
Jalalahennou Interior courtyard – the king's private quarters		7
Jeho Temple		8
Jonnonho Reception hall for receiving visitors		9
Kpodoji Exterior courtyard – a waiting and meeting area		10
Logodo Entrance lobby to the jalalahennou where audience-seekers would wait		11
Singbo Two-storied hounnouwa		12
Zinkpoho Throne room		13

0   50 m

Ghezo's Palace (1818-58)

Glele's Palace (1858-89)

with little that could tempt you to stay, and most people skip Bohicon altogether and head straight out to Abomey, which is more manageable and, with the **royal palace and museum**, infinitely more interesting. Regular taxis connect the two towns, or by *zemidjan* it's a fifteen-minute ride for around CFA500.

If you want to **stay in Bohicon**, try the friendly *Hôtel Relais Sinoutin* (aka *3 Paillotes*), on the main road at the southern end of town (℡22.51.00.88 ➋), with clean s/c rooms and a decent restaurant. You'll also need to visit Bohicon if you need to **change money**; the Bank of Africa in the centre changes both cash and traveller's cheques. From the **train station** right in the centre of Bohicon (℡21.51.02.10), there are thrice-weekly services to Cotonou (at least 3hr) and Parakou (6hr).

Abomey

Abomey is fascinating to wander through, any path off the main roads leading through twisted alleyways with *banco* houses and colourfully painted **fetish temples**. Between the **royal palace** and the *préfecture*, overgrown plots with weather-worn mud ruins are vestiges of former royal palaces. It's also an excellent place to shop for local **crafts**.

The royal palace and museum

In the three hundred years of the Dan-Homey empire, the kings gradually constructed a magnificent **palace** in the centre of Abomey. In fact, it was a vast complex of many palaces, since the sovereign never occupied the residence of his predecessor, but built a new one next to the old. By the time the French attacked the city in 1892, there was thus a honeycomb of twelve **adjoining palaces**, ten of which were soon destroyed by the combined efforts of the fleeing Fon and the invading French.

Today, only two palaces – those belonging to Ghezo (1818–58) and his son and successor Glele (1858–89) – remain intact and house the **Musée Historique d'Abomey** (daily 9am–6pm; ⓦepa-prema.net/abomey; CFA2500 with compulsory guided tour; English guides available). But even these royal buildings have suffered badly from the effects of the climate, ultimately no less severe than war damage. Ongoing work has taken place with the help of funds from UNESCO among others, and several buildings have had their corrugated-iron roofs replaced with traditional thatch. In addition, Japan paid for the restoration of the walls circling the Palace of Behanzin. However, plans to rebuild the other nine ruined palaces, which would require decades of work, have been ruled out. Nevertheless, the palaces magnificently recall the pomp and grandeur of the royal court, and have been designated a UNESCO World Heritage Site.

The numerous artefacts on display in the museum are frequently changed and moved, but look out for the **throne** and banner of King Ghezo. The throne is built on top of four human skulls, symbolizing the king's conquests and domination over weaker peoples. The banners, which are known as the **royal tapestries**, are remarkable, vivid patchworks, woven with symbols and emblems relating the qualities of the various kings. The Palace of King Ghezo houses a display on the daily routine within the palace.

The massive walls of the complex are clad in brilliantly coloured bas-reliefs (the designs were re-created by American specialists and some of the originals are now stored inside) and as you walk round, the history of this powerful, energetic and brutal society comes alive. The **House of Pearls** is an animist temple, built by Glele so that his father's spirit could rest here after he was killed in battle with the Oyo kingdom. The walls incorporate the blood of 41 Oyo slaves (41 being a sacred number) and animal sacrifices are still performed here. After removing your shoes, you can also visit the **tomb of King Glele**, and the neighbouring tomb of the 41 wives selected to be buried with him (out of his supposed three thousand spouses), in addition to much of his treasure.

The Dan-Homey kingdom

From as early as the sixteenth century, much of the present territory of Benin was coalescing into small, socially stratified **states** – a string of them along the coast (including Grand Popo and Ouidah) and a cluster of less clearly defined smaller states inland. A more powerful (though still very small) city-state had developed around the town of **Allada**, just 40km from the coast, which was renowned for its slave trading. At the end of the sixteenth century, three princes were in dispute over the rule of this little empire. The first, Meidji, eventually wrested power from his father. Of his two brothers, Zozerigbe headed south to Porto Novo where he founded the **Hogbonou** kingdom, while Do Aklin went north, where he founded the kingdom at **Abomey** in the early seventeenth century.

In 1654, one of the descendants of Do Aklin, **Houegbaja**, killed the sovereign of Abomey, a king named **Dan**. Houegbaja then built his palace over the body of the deceased monarch and his kingdom came to be known as **Dan-Homey**, meaning "from the belly of Dan". In the succession of kings, one of the greatest was **Agadja**, who ruled from 1708 to 1740. He conquered the surrounding mini-states of Allada, Savi and Ouidah and, in expanding his empire to the coast, earned the title Dé Houito, or "man of the sea". Having gained a gateway to the Atlantic, the empire embarked on a period of direct trade with Europe, a trade dependent above all on slaves. Meanwhile, however, the powerful Yoruba state of **Oyo** (to the east, in present-day Nigeria) was increasingly bent on retaining as much as possible of the trade for its own benefit. Through the middle of the eighteenth century, it repeatedly intimidated and attacked Dan-Homey, which, after 1748, formally became a vassal state of Oyo.

The Dan-Homey state became a dictatorship under the reign of **Ghezo**, who overthrew **Adandozan** (1797–1818) and ruled bloodily for forty years. He ceded his monopoly rights in the slave trade to his right-hand man in Ouidah – the Brazilian **Francisco Felix de Souza** (the "viceroy" depicted in Bruce Chatwin's biographical novella and by Klaus Kinski in Werner Herzog's movie *Cobra Verde*) – and increasingly preyed on his own subject peoples. His autonomy was only limited by the duty he owed to Oyo. He reorganized the army into a powerful unit comprising 10,000 soldiers and 6000 female **"Amazon"** warriors, who were better armed than their male counterparts. Trained to use rifles as well as bows, they were reputed to cut off one of their breasts if it impaired their ability to shoot – an apocryphal story that probably sprang from the reactions of European visitors to the sight of well-drilled female soldiers.

The Dan-Homey kings amassed a stockpile of weapons through trade with the Europeans. By the end of the nineteenth century, the royal arsenal was full of modern weaponry and the stage was set for an intense conflict as the French started out in conquest of the interior. Hostilities were intense and fighting had already broken out between the French and the Fon when **King Behanzin** led an attack against the forces of **Colonel Dodds** as they advanced on Abomey. Behanzin lost the battle, and the capital of the Dan-Homey kingdom fell to the French on November 16, 1892. Abomey was already in flames as the colonial army marched into the city.

Crafts outlets

Attached to the palace, the **centre artisanal** is an effort to keep alive the craftsmanship that was the pride of the Abomey kings. The artisans were formerly constrained to produce their works for the royal court only. Crafts that were popular with the kings – brightly decorated tapestries, bronze statues made by the *cire perdue* (lost wax) method and jewellery – are still churned out, although the quality required by tourists is rather less than that demanded by royalty. This centre is the most obvious place to shop for crafts – although it may seem expensive, prices are wide open to negotiation.

Along the road running in front of the museum, the house with the lion and inscription on the front is the residence of the **Yamedje family** – the traditional embroiderers for the king. Members of the family still weave the tapestries, their works strewn over the ground, all for sale. Near to *Motel d'Abomey* there's a small but well-stocked craft outlet, the Black Hand, where weavers sell reasonably priced cloth.

Practicalities

Arriving in Abomey, you'll be let off somewhere around the market square or in the small **autogare**. Most of the hotels are a little too far away to walk, but there are plenty of *zemidjans* around. The *autogare* has vehicles to surrounding villages, while bush taxis for Cotonou fill up around the market. For road transport to most other destinations, it's faster to take a *zemidjan* or taxi to Bohicon for onward connections. Despite its importance as a tourist centre, Abomey has few services beyond the town's **post office**, which offers fast Internet connections.

Accommodation

Auberge Mon Repos on the road to Bohicon ℡ 22.50.17.66. Good budget choice with small but spotless s/c rooms with fan, a good restaurant and very friendly staff. Food can be prepared with advance warning. ❷

🏃 **Chez Monique** on a dirt side-street, 200m west of the *préfecture* ℡ 22.50.01.68. Immensely popular with overlanders, *Monique*'s is an exotic spread, with pet monkeys, crocodiles and antelopes in the sprawling yard. The simple, clean s/c rooms have fans and insect screens and are quite comfortable, or you can camp for CFA3000 per person. Food is also available if ordered in advance. ❷

Guedevy 1 some 2km north of the centre ℡ 22.50.03.04 🅕 22.50.08.42. A vast complex – a main block with mock bas-reliefs on the entrance walls, and newer, more attractive thatched bungalows behind. Rooms are all s/c with fan or a/c, and there's a plain, inexpensive restaurant. ❷

🏃 **Marie José** just off the Lokossa road west of the market ℡ 22.50.02.89. Homely, welcoming setup in a shady, flower-filled garden with lots of room for relaxing, and a range of spotless s/c rooms – an excellent retreat. ❷

Motel d'Abomey 200m south of the *préfecture* ℡ 20.50.00.75 🅕 20.50.00.93. The town's best hotel, with well-furnished private rondavels with TV, video and phone, plus s/c, a/c rooms, although everything is a little frayed around the edges. As a bonus, the restaurant is one of the town's best, and the *Prestige Nightclub* (CFA2000 entrance) is an added draw. From ❸.

Eating and drinking

Apart from the hotel restaurants, there's a surprising dearth of formal places to eat in town. Inexpensive **street food** is available around the market, or for a broader range of West African dishes, try *Chez Calixte* to the west of town. Just south of the stadium, the tiny, tidy *La Pagode* is a good place for a breakfast of omelette with coffee, or a lunch of rice and fish. Near the market, the *Buvette 5ème Dimension* is not only the liveliest **bar** in town but also offers simple **European meals** for around CFA1500. Another busy bar is the *Confort+* near the *autogare*. *Lem's Feelings Nightclub*, next door to *5ème Dimension* (with which it shares management), is the town's best **club**, with European and African music pumping out at the weekends (CFA2500 entrance).

Dassa and rough routes in the west

The most straightforward way north from Cotonou is via the **trans–Benin highway** to Parakou. Alternatively you could fork left at Dassa to follow the western *piste* leading directly to **Djougou** (see p.1002), though public transport is slow and irregular. **The west** is an agricultural region hemmed in by the forests of Mont Kouffé and Mont Agoua, and was the location of an early **Yoruba** kingdom, conquered in the eighteenth century by the **Maxi** (related to the Fon). These are still the main peoples of the area, although numerous smaller groups result in a variety of regional building styles and customs. Despite the relative difficulties of travel along this stretch it can be rewarding to get off the beaten track, and you're likely to find contacts with people warm and immediate.

DASSA (or Dassa-Zoumé), 77km from Bohicon and 203km north of Cotonou, is a village tucked into a stunning landscape of heavy boulder formations. Aside from its aesthetic appeal, there's nothing of essential interest, with the possible exception of **La Grotte Marial Notre Dame d'Arigbo** – a cave in which the Virgin Mary is said to have appeared, and which has become a pilgrimage site for Christians from across Africa and even Europe, who congregate for the **15 August** Feast of the Assumption of the Virgin Mary (l'Assomption de la Vierge Marie). An impressive **basilica** has been constructed in front of the cave, from where you can see the small statue of Mary and the shrine built into the rock face. Behind, a path marks the *marchez à genoux*, leading you past thirteen shrines. If you want to explore more of the surrounding countryside, you can **stay** at the *Auberge de Dassa-Zoumé*, just by the main roundabout on the highway (℡22.53.00.98 ⓦwww.hotels-benin .com ❸). It's overpriced and feels frayed around the edges, but the rooms with fan or a/c are the best in town, and there's excellent food in the restaurant – and antelope, monkeys and a few ostriches lurking in the gardens. In town, there's the *Auberge St Augustin*, a friendly, family-run place with comfortable s/c doubles (❷). Finally, *Auberge Le Cachette* on the road to the hospital offers good-value, no-frills rooms and has an attractive bar/restaurant – worth the trip for a drink even if you don't stay here (℡22.53.02.11 ❶).

The western route beyond **SAVALOU**, 30km north of Dassa, is little travelled, and involves longer waits for transport, but the road has been resurfaced. Beyond Savalou itself, which has a decent hotel in the *Auberge* chain (*Auberge de Savalou* ℡22.54.05.24 ⓦwww.hotels-benin.com ❸), **BASSILA**, 173km from Dassa and hard against the Togolese border, is the first town along the way where you'll find **accommodation** and, perhaps more importantly, a *buvette* with the possibility of cold drinks. There's a small *chambres de passage* (❶) next to the filling station, run by a very friendly family.

12.3

The northern uplands and parks

Parakou is the northernmost large town on the main road. Beyond it, in the **northeast**, the only important centres of activity are **Kandi** and **Malanville**, small towns bolstered by agriculture and trade. The **northwest**, though harder to travel through, is a region of striking natural beauty dominated by the country's only serious highlands, the **Atakora range**, and populated by a relatively ancient people, the **Somba**. Two towns of some size, **Natitingou** and **Djougou**, are the bases for discovering this outback region.

Northern Benin has some of West Africa's best faunal areas in the **Pendjari National Park** and, in the extreme north, the **"W" du Niger National Park**, which spreads across the frontiers of Niger and Burkina Faso. Access to Pendjari is relatively straightforward and there are several places to stay, but the Benin sector of the "W" park is less accessible (the most promising access is via Kandi) and has abundant wildlife – probably as a result.

Parakou

Formerly a station on the caravan routes to the coast, **PARAKOU**, with a population of nearly 200,000, is now the undisputed commercial centre of the interior. Its importance still derives from its position on the major roads and on the **railway** which terminates its snail-like trail here. The brewery and peanut-oil mill have brought about rapid growth in the last couple of decades, but Parakou is a town of little enduring interest, though abuzz with the activity of hundreds of small businesses, bars and passing traders.

Practicalities

Coming by bush taxi, you'll arrive in Parakou at the busy **gare routière**, located next to the main market and across from the post office. Confort Lines buses stop at the Gare Kuandé to the north of the centre or outside the Financial Bank. The **train station** is on the western side of town. With the burgeoning business activity, there are branches of all the major **banks**; Ecobank gives the best rates for cash and Bank of Africa has an ATM. You can get **online** at Par@k Cyber-Café on route de Transa, near *Le Miel* (see "Eating"), which has plenty of workstations and fast connections for CFA450/hr.

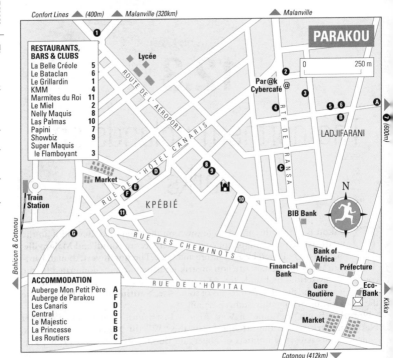

RESTAURANTS,
BARS & CLUBS
La Belle Créole   5
Le Bataclan   6
Le Grillardin   1
KMM   4
Marmites du Roi   11
Le Miel   2
Nelly Maquis   8
Las Palmas   10
Papini   7
Showbiz   9
Super Maquis
  le Flamboyant   3

ACCOMMODATION
Auberge Mon Petit Père   A
Auberge de Parakou   F
Les Canaris   D
Central   G
Le Majestic   E
La Princesse   B
Les Routiers   C

PARAKOU

Accommodation

Parakou has nothing in the way of world–class **accommodation**, but there are plenty of small, comfortable hotels, and one or two cheaper alternatives.

Auberge Mon Petit Père 200m past *La Princesse* ☎23.61.10.57. Offering a relaxed feel and large, non-s/c rooms with mosquito nets, which are looking a bit the worse for wear, this is a popular backpacker abode. The garden contains a colourful outdoor bar/restaurant and the friendly owner loves to chat and make his guests feel at home. ❶

Auberge de Parakou rue de l'Hôtel les Canaris ☎23.61.03.50 🕸www.hotels-benin.com. A member of the French-run chain, this is a good setup with seven attractively furnished rooms with minimalist decor, some with a/c, a lovely garden and a peaceful terrace restaurant serving up tasty French dishes. ❸

Les Canaris rue de l'Hôtel les Canaris ☎23.61.11.69. Two shady courtyards provide a pleasant backdrop for various rooms ranging from non-s/c, low-comfort quarters (among the cheapest in town) to fully furnished a/c, s/c accommodation with private bath. There's also a good restaurant with nice views of the town. ❷

Central rue de l'Hôtel les Canaris ☎23.61.01.24 ⓕ23.61.38.51. West of the centre, in an imposing building hidden behind a walled garden, where you'll find their bar and restaurant. Slightly dated s/c rooms have a/c, TV and phone; some rooms have hot water. ❹

Le Majestic rue de l'Hôtel les Canaris ☎23.61.34.85 🕸www.lemajestichotel.com. One of the nicest places to stay in Parakou, this place has a range of rooms, from small and basic with fan, to luxurious affairs complete with massive bathrooms, satellite TV and flowery balconies overlooking the lawn. ❹–❺

La Princesse qtr Ladjifarani, off route de Transa ☎23.61.01.32. Set around a courtyard, the comfortable rooms offer phone, TV and video, and the town's best nightclub is attached. French and African food served in the *Nafi* restaurant, snacks in the *Plantation* bar. ❺

Les Routiers route de Transa ☎ 23.61.04.01. Centrally located, swish (and slightly overpriced) accommodation, popular with expats. The rather bland a/c rooms have satellite TV, plus there's a garden and small pool at the back. ❺

Eating and nightlife

Despite Parakou's status as second city, **nights** are low-key; kerosene lamps light the darkness, indicating the stands of hundreds of vendors. It's safe and satisfying to wander around the route de l'Aéroport, stopping for **street food** or a drink at one of the many *buvettes* – *Nelly Maquis*, *Showbiz* and *Las Palmas* are all recommended.

For **nightlife**, the hottest club in town is *Le Bataclan* opposite (and linked to) *Hôtel La Princesse*, which plays African and European music (Thurs–Sun from 10pm). *KMM* is a cheaper, less pretentious alternative, which draws a large crowd to its disco and lively outdoor *buvette*, tucked in a clump of teak trees on route de Transa. The prospects for good **eating** are actually better than the town's initial impression suggests, and you'll find a wide range of good African and European cuisine.

La Belle Créole qtr Ladjifarani, near *La Princesse*. One of the best restos in town, with an extensive menu of French, Italian and other European cuisine at moderate prices. Tables under a *paillote* with unmistakable lion statues at the garden entrance.

Le Grillardin next to *Auberge New Cigale* ☎23.61.27.81. Tatty accommodation in the *auberge*, but their restaurant is plush, under a beautiful thatched roof, and offers a range of French cuisine.

Marmites du Roi off the rue de l'Hôtel Canaris ☎23.61.25.07. Highly recommended for upmarket African food, with excellent *yassa* chicken and peanut soup.

Le Miel (aka *Pâtisserie La Borgoise*) route de Transa. Patisserie serving fantastic pastries, sandwiches, salads and ice cream, or a more filling *menu du jour*. Eat in the laid-back *salon de thé* upstairs.

Papini 600m beyond *Auberge Mon Petit Père* ☎23.61.04.26. Another hotel restaurant, quite an upmarket affair set around a tranquil courtyard, and serving pizzas cooked at an open oven and excellent steaks. If you can't find a *zemidjan*, it's actually a pleasant walk back to town.

Super Maquis Le Flamboyant qtr Ladjifarani, near *Hôtel la Princesse*. The usual rice with fish, or couscous with chicken, plus Ivoirian specials, including chicken *kedjenou*. Attractive gardens and friendly service.

The northeast

The **northeast** is characterized by woodland and savannah scenery, broken by a series of small rivers (the Mékrou, Alibori and Sota) that descend gradually to join the Niger. It's the least densely populated region of the country, and ethnically very diverse. The **Dendi**, for example, are migrants from Mali's Songhai empire, who migrated south from the Niger River in the sixteenth century to the savannah districts around Kandi, Malanville and Djougou. **Fula** cattle-herders crossed the Niger River at around the same time and still make up a sizeable proportion of the northern population. The **Bariba**, whose ethnic and linguistic affiliations are obscure, arrived before the fifteenth century from somewhere in present-day northwest Nigeria. They first settled around Nikki, but population pressure soon spread their communities to the west and north. Here they came to dominate predecessors like the **Bussa**, speakers of another obscure language (probably a Mande relict), who had also migrated west from northern Nigeria.

Despite the important highway running through the region, linking Cotonou with Niamey, the **Niger Basin district** in the far northeast remains economically undeveloped. Cotton is a big cash crop, but industrialization hasn't penetrated much beyond a cotton-seed plant in Kandi and a rice-husking factory in Malanville.

Kandi and around

Like Parakou, **KANDI** was formerly a stopping point on the caravan routes and grew to become a sizeable chiefdom – a vassal state of Bariba rulers in Nikki, to the southeast. Located 213km north of Parakou, it's a small town, and relies heavily on farming, an occupation with which young people are becoming increasingly disenchanted. They have been deserting the countryside in large numbers, and heading east to Nigeria, which is linked to Kandi by a well-travelled *piste* that heads through Ségbana. You may question the attractions of a place from which even the townspeople are engaged in a mass exodus and, true enough, there's not a lot of note. Still, it's a convenient highway stopover and, with its dusty mango-shaded streets, not completely without charm.

In the dry season, you can make arrangements in Kandi or at **Alfa Kouara**, about 40km north of Kandi, to walk to a nearby **waterhole** near the edge of the "W" National Park, where **wildlife** gathers; with luck, you'll even see elephants there.

Practicalities

As district headquarters, Kandi has a **PTT** and a **bank** – though note that the latter is not open full business hours. There are several good options for **accommodation** in town. *Auberge de Kandi* (☏23.63.02.43 ⓦwww.hotels-benin.com ❷), some 1500m from town on the road to Malanville, has an attractive, spacious courtyard, well-kept rooms and a pricey restaurant. If you want to book accommodation at the *Chutes de Koudou* in the Park National du "W" (see opposite), you can do so here. As you head in to town from here you'll pass the *Motel de Kandi* on the left (☏23.63.03.03 ❷), where there are good-value, tidy s/c rooms, though the compound is quite scruffy. More centrally located near the *autogare*, the *Auberge La Rencontre* (☏23.63.01.76 ❷) has a friendlier feel, with spotless s/c doubles with fan, some with a/c, and a great rooftop bar-restaurant.

Cheap *buvettes* for **eating and drinking** are scattered around the marketplace. More formal meals can be had at *Restaurant La Gargoterie*, which serves up the usual rice and sauce dishes. *Tropicana Nightclub* next to the cotton factory is a popular haunt with locals (Fri–Sun from 11.30pm; CFA2000).

If you're heading to the Parc National du "W", the **Centre Nationale de Gestion des Reserves de Faune** or **CENAGREF** (☏23.63.00.80), on the southern entrance to Kandi from Parakou, will provide a compulsory guide and can help you find 4x4 transport and book accommodation in the park. They'll also give you the lowdown on the Alfa Kouara waterhole and viewing platform (CFA5000 per person).

Malanville

Tucked in the northeast corner near the borders of Nigeria and Niger and 733km from Cotonou, **MALANVILLE** is a trading town *par excellence* where you can run into people from all over West Africa. The **market**, held from Friday to Sunday morning, is Benin's largest after Cotonou, and large-scale regional rice-planting attracts wage-hungry labourers from as far afield as Mali. The presence of many foreigners, mixed with the Fula- and Songhai-speaking **Dendi** locals who form the majority of the town, makes for an upbeat atmosphere, and the lorries that line the main street add to the border-town feel. However, unless you time your visit with the huge market, the lack of notable sights means you're not likely to want to make an extended stay.

Practicalities

Numerous bush taxis wait for passengers in the central *autogare*, mainly heading south to Kandi or Parakou and Confort Lines have daily services to Cotonou via Parakou. If you're heading north to **Niamey**, it's quicker and cheaper to catch a taxi (CFA1000 a seat) to Gaya in Niger, on the other side of the river, and find another vehicle there.

If you're **staying the night** in Malanville, a variety of rooms are available at the French-run *Rose des Sables* (T23.67.01.25 ❷), on the southern edge of town, about 1500m from the *autogare*, with comfy but slightly overpriced s/c bungalows, or simpler rooms in a small "tower block" – there's also a restaurant attached with meals from CFA3000. About 500m further south, on the banks of the Sota (the tributary of the Niger that parallels the road), are the best rooms in the district, at the new *Le Sota Hôtel* (T97.64.97.48 Wwww.lemajestichotel.com ❹), sister establishment of the *Majestic* in Parakou, with cool comforts and a pool. A little closer to the centre of Malanville itself, 1500m west of the *autogare*, *Motel Issifou* is clean enough and has a nice roof area; the restaurant serves basic fare such as chicken and chips. Numerous **street-food stands** line the paved road near the *autogare*, and you'll find a host of *buvettes* with cold drinks.

Parc National du "W" du Niger

The **"W" du Niger National Park** (open daily 6.30am–7pm mid-Dec to mid-June depending on rains and road conditions; CFA10,000 per person; CFA2000 per vehicle; CFA5000 daily guide fee) spreads over 10,000 square kilometres of wild bush in Niger, Burkina Faso and Benin – an area virtually without human habitation. The part of the park that borders the Kandi-to-Malanville highway is a "zone cynégétique" or hunting block. The waterhole of Alfa Kouara is located on the edge of this district, close to the road. The "W" (pronounced *double-vé* in French) refers to the double U-bend in the course of the Niger River at the point where the three countries meet. Though nearly half the park is in Benin, most of the viewing trails and facilities are in Burkina and Niger (see p.1043).

Most of the big plains mammals are found in the park. Although the **buffalo** herds are thinning out, **elephants** can still be spotted in the Béninois sector – notably in the Mékrou valley – while in the Mékrou's waters, unmistakable herds of snorting **hippo** are fairly plentiful. All the cats are found in the "W" – **serval**, **caracal**, **leopard**, **cheetah** and **lion** – but you can visit repeatedly and never see a single specimen. Most commonly encountered are a good number of **antelope** species – bushbuck (*guibs harnachés* in French), cobs or waterbucks (*cob de buffon, cob defassa*), reedbuck (*redunca*) and the red-fronted gazelle – and, of course, **warthog** (*phacochères*) and **baboon** (*babouins*). Aardvark (*oryctéropes*) are around, too, but their nocturnal habits ensure they're rarely spotted.

Practicalities

You need a 4x4 vehicle to visit the park - there's no public transport and no entrance allowed on foot – and the most common access is from Kandi to **Banikoara** (69km from Kandi), a small town where you'll find very basic **accommodation** (a small *campement* ❶) before entering the reserve. From here, it's a short, 17-kilometre drive to **Kérémou** – one of the main gateways to the park in Benin.

The main **overnight** option on the Benin side is the *Campement des Chutes de Koudou*, bookable in Kandi through the *Auberge de Kandi* (see p.1000) or CENAGREF (☎23.63.00.80), which has several safari tents complete with comfortable beds and bathrooms, and views over the Koudou falls and the river Mékrou. There's a good restaurant, and walks in the surrounding area can be arranged.

The area that's most frequently visited (though you won't be jostling with too many other visitors) is the 400-square-kilometre triangle formed by the Kéré-mou–Diapaga (Burkina) road, the Mékrou River (which the road crosses) and the Benin–Burkina border. There's a *piste* along the left (west) bank of the Mékrou that leads up to the **Koudou falls (Chutes de Koudou)** on the Burkina border. The new bridge here allows you to continue north along the right bank to a point called **Point Triple**, where the borders of Benin, Niger and Burkina meet. A plan is rolling out to continue this *piste* all the way along the right bank of the Mékrou, through the Gorges de la Mékrou and down to **Pékinga**, at the confluence of the Niger, upstream from Malanville.

Northwest Benin: Somba country

The **northwest** is home to some of the oldest **civilizations** to migrate to Benin – a number of which lived for long periods with virtually no interaction. The best known are the **Somba** (more accurately the Otammari, or Betammaribe), famous for their fortress-like houses known as **Tatas–Somba** that they built to protect themselves from the slave raids of Dan-Homey warriors. They still live in largely isolated villages scattered along the base of the **Atakora Mountains**, though the young people are increasingly inclined to migrate to urban centres such as **Natitingou**, the Atakora provincial capital. Further south, Somba give way to the Yowa, part of the same cluster of Voltaic-speaking peoples, and the Songhai-speaking Dendi who live in the region of **Djougou**, a large commercial town on the main road to Togo.

Djougou

With a population of some 170,000, **DJOUGOU** is a large and busy town, locat-ed 134km from Parakou and easily accessible by paved road. Its importance as a major regional market has been assured by its position on the main roads linking Natitingou to Savalou, and Parakou to the Togolese border and through to Kara.

Djougou's large **autogare** adjoins the market and you shouldn't have any problem finding transport to Natitingou and Parakou. Many vehicles also head to **Kara** in Togo, via the border post at Kétao. Confort Lines buses stop in front of the Maison des Jeunes in the centre of town.

Accommodation options are surprisingly limited. The *Motel du Djougou* on the road to Parakou (☎23.80.00.69 ❷) is reliable, with attractive thatched bungalows in a large compound, some with a/c. *Motel du Lac* (☎23.80.15.48 ❸), 3km out of town on the road to Savalou, on the lakeshore, has large s/c rooms with satellite TV and balconies and a top-notch French restaurant. Opposite the *Motel du Djougou*, *Le Quasar* is a smart dining option under a thatched roof, with a diverse range of local and foreign dishes for around CFA2000. To while away the night, try *New Jack's Night Club* out on the road to Savalou (Fri & Sat; CFA2000), or Ciné Sabari, not far from the *autogare*.

Natitingou

Home town of former President Mathieu Kérékou, **NATITINGOU** has never received the level of patronage extended to Yamoussoukro in Côte d'Ivoire or Kara in Togo by those countries' respective former presidents. Though only a small centre, Natitingou has the beginnings of an industrial base with the siting here of a SON-AFEL juice factory and peanut-husking factories. You're more likely to notice other manifestations of Kérékou's munificence in the town's modern Financial Bank on the main street and the beautiful luxury hotel. But despite these surprise perks, the real draw of the town lies in the countryside that surrounds it, a magnificent region of hills dotted with the Tata-Somba homes that have become as famous as anything in Benin. The **Musée Régionale de Natitingou**, near *Hôtel Bourgogne*, is worth a brief visit (CFA1000) to explore the music, clothing, housing and history of the region.

Practicalities

If you've entered the country from Burkina Faso and only have the 48-hour visa issued on the border, visit the Police Nationale Commissariat (on the left as you approach from Tanguiéta) for your visa extension. For **cash**, there's an ATM at Financial Bank. **Internet access** is available at Cyber Centre du Boulevard near the centre of town.

Accommodation

Natitingou has a good range of accommodation, from budget to business-class, and you can often bargain rates down.

Auberge la Montagne ☎23.82.11.16. Up a dirt track beside Ciné Atacora. A homely setup with spacious, spotless s/c rooms. Good value. ❷

Auberge le Vieux Cavalier Signposted up a track beside Ciné Atacora, 300m after *La Montagne* ☎23.82.13.24. The cheapest in town and excellent value. Rooms with fan or a/c are set around a leafy courtyard, dotted with traditional-style bas-relief sculptures. They also have 4x4 vehicles for rent. ❷

Bellevue signposted up a dirt track about 200m north of Ciné Atacora ☎23.82.13.36 ⓦwww .natitingou.org/bellevue. Good hilltop location, with a very helpful manager, though the s/c rooms, some with a/c, are a little overpriced. There's a good three-course *menu* at CFA6000. ❸

Bourgogne On the main road across from *Le Gourmet* ☎23.82.22.40 ⓕ23.82.24.40. A step above the budget hotels – simple, clean and comfortable accommodation, all a/c, in a convenient location. ❹

Kantaborifa Off the route de Djougou on a dirt track just before *Auberge Tanekas* ☎23.82.11.66. Friendly place, with very presentable rooms, some with a/c, ranged around an attractive *paillote*. ❷

Nekima near the town's stadium in the quartier Winké ☎23.82.10.46. Good if you're on a budget, with a selection of single and double rooms with fan or a/c. The best rooms are in the recently renovated bungalows. There's a cyber café opposite. ❶–❷

Tata Somba 1km west of the centre ☎23.82.11.24 or 23.82.20.99. Natitingou's best, a classy hotel in the *Groupe Accor* chain, with a swimming pool (CFA1500 for non-guests), tennis court, the town's swankiest restaurant, and comfortable a/c rooms. The same chain manages the *campements* in the Pendjari National Park, so this is the best place for info on accommodation and vehicle rental if you're heading there. ❺

Eating and nightlife

In addition to the hotel **restaurants** and the market, *Le Gourmet* opposite *Hôtel Bourgogne* offers simple but tasty meals at reasonable prices. It's also a place to meet people from the region and possibly arrange to visit some of the Somba countryside. Another possibility is *Chez Antony*, on the route de Tanguiéta, a popular local drinking spot where they serve up well-prepared and relatively inexpensive African dishes or the likes of chicken and chips. *Le Basilic*, located 200m further up the same track as *Hôtel Kantaborifa*, has a diverse menu including pizzas, and highly recommended home-made ice cream.

Bush taxis leave sporadically for Boukoumbé, Tanguiéta (for Pendjari), Djougou and Parakou from the **gare routière** in the centre of town. Just across the street, Confort Lines buses depart daily for Cotonou at 7am (CFA7000) from just outside the *Hôtel Kantaborifa*. If you're heading for Burkina Faso, bush taxis usually stop at the border where you may have a long wait for onward transport. By preference, take the Afrolines bus that runs three times a week between Natitingou and Fada N'Gourma in Burkina.

You'll find a couple of **discos** in town, including the open-air *Le Village*, located to the west of town out on the road to *Hôtel Tata Somba* – it's not too expensive and very local in flavour. Ciné Atacora, on the left if you're heading out of town towards Djougou, has nightly showings of fairly recent American and French films.

Around Natitingou

The **Betammaribe** were one of the first peoples to arrive in Benin, settling near the Atakora range at an unknown date a thousand years or more ago. Living in relative isolation, these people, commonly known as the **Somba**, resisted changes inflicted by the spread of Islam and the French invasion. Until quite recently, they lived in the seclusion of their fortified *tatas* and farmed their lands, wearing no more than the traditional *cache sexe* (pubic covering) of their ancestors. Although their subsistence way of life had been ignored for centuries, in the 1970s they were exposed to the raw glare of the French press – delighted to have located a rare example of "real Africa". Stung by the sensational reports of naked tribesmen, Kérékou's government ran a campaign to force the Somba to wear clothes. As a result of this humiliation and other insensitivities, the Somba remain a very private, reserved people, and outside of the main towns, such as Natitingou – where traditional ways are fast breaking down – it's difficult, and perhaps from no one's point of view very desirable, to penetrate their tight-knit communities.

Rather than forming large communities, the Somba built their homes about 500m apart from one another – the distance a man could throw a spear, you'll be told, which would surprise the holder of the world javelin record (under 100m). Whatever the brawn of their throwing arms (it seems more likely that 500m is the maximum dangerous range of an eighteenth-century musket), this defensive safeguard was adopted during slave-raiding days and the custom has carried over. Houses are still built like fortresses with round turrets for grain storage and internal animal pens. During slave raids, families could hole up in these houses for days on end until the marauding Dan–Homey armies went off in search of easier prey (see the section in the Togo chapter on the **Tamberma**, a people closely related to the Somba, for more information about this regional architecture; p.944). With your own vehicle, you could cross the nearby border and drive the *piste* that leads through the region of the Tamberma, arriving at **Kandé** in Togo (see "Boukoumbé", below). Though difficult, it's one of the most beautiful drives in this part of West Africa.

The **Tatas-Somba** still dot the countryside around the Atakora region and it's worth a trip through these parts to take in the unusual architecture. The more accessible communities are generally friendly and not too camera-shy, provided you ask permission. Coming in by bush taxi from Djougou, you'll see some of the architecture from the roadside, notably along the stretch between Perma (56km from Djougou) and Natitingou.

One of the highest concentrations of Tatas-Somba is found further west, however, along the road from Natitingou to **BOUKOUMBÉ**, 43km west of Natitingou, near the Togolese border. It's easiest to reach on market day – a four-day cycle – which is always the day before Natitingou's, but you should be able to get there by *zemidjan* most days (CFA5000 for the somewhat exhausting return journey).

There are a couple of simple but decent **hotels**, including *Auberge Dinaba* (aka *Auberge Villageoise de Tourisme* ❶) – ask around for directions in the vicinity of the Catholic mission, where you can have food prepared. Alternatively, *Chez Pascaline*, in the Zongo district not far from the roundabout at the northwest exit of town, serves up couscous, rice and sauce.

Parc National de la Pendjari

The **Pendjari National Park** (open daily 6.30am–7pm mid-Dec to mid-June, depending on rains and road conditions; CFA10,000 per person, CFA3000 per vehicle; optional guide fee CFA5000 per day) is one of the best game reserves in West Africa. It spreads over 2750 square kilometres of woody savannah north of the Atakora range, up against the Pendjari River, which runs along the Burkina border. Like the "W" National Park, the more accessible southern margins of the park are designated "zones cynégétiques", or hunting zones, catering to trophy hunters, while the further reaches of the interior on the Burkina border, are a true sanctuary. Unlike the "W" National Park, access to Pendjari is relatively straightforward.

From Natitingou, the usual route winds through the Atakora Mountains for 45km to **TANGUIÉTA**, a village at the edge of the reserve, with a lively market on Mondays. There are several options for **accommodation**. The friendly and central *APP Bar-Dancing* (☎23.83.01.73 ❶) has grubby rooms with mosquito nets and fans, and there are video nights on Fridays and noisy dancing on Saturdays. *Le Baobab* (☎23.83.02.25 ❷), about 2km northwest of town on the route de Porga, has comfortable s/c rooms and an attractive garden. Tanguiéta has an office of CENA-GREF (☎23.83.00.65) the national park organization, which can provide practical advice on travelling to the park. The town is also the location of northern Benin's best **hospital**, the Hôpital Saint Jean de Dieu.

There are two **waterfalls** in the area, the first – the **cascade de Tanguiéta** – about 1500m south on the road to Natitingou, and the second, larger, **cascades de Tanougou** near the village of the same name, 33km northeast of Tanguiéta on the road to Batia. Swimming at the latter, with the falls pounding your back, is a memorable experience. *Le Relais de Tanougou* (❷), by the waterfall, has six rooms you can book through the *Hôtel Tata Somba* in Natitingou.

At Tanguiéta, the road divides. You can aim northeast to **Batia**, where there's a park entrance, though no accommodation. However, most people continue northwest to the town of **PORGA**, 61km from Tanguiéta on the Burkina border, which has **lodgings** and the main park entrance gate. The *Hôtel Campement de Porga* (☎23.82.20.39 ❹) has bungalows and rooms, some air-conditioned: it most caters to hunters. If you've made it this far without your own transport, you might hope to tag along with tourists heading into the park at Porga, though your chances would be just as good if you looked for a lift at the *Hôtel Tata Somba* in Natitingou. The south and northeast of the park are called **zones cynégétiques** – hunting blocks which can be traversed even when the park is closed.

Lions still stalk these parts and your chances of seeing them are relatively good. Other large mammals you have a good chance of spotting include **elephants** (notably in the south of the park) and **buffalo**, which roam in large herds. **Hippos** and **crocodiles** (*caïmans* in colloquial French) are widespread in the Pendjari River, while the same species of **antelope** as are found in the "W" park, plus **warthogs** and several species of **monkey**, are pretty sure bets. As usual, however, all the animals are most easily and abundantly seen at the end of the dry season, when their movements are restricted by the need to stay close to water.

Park practicalities

Permits to visit can be obtained from the *postes forestières* in Porga, Batia and Banikoara, but for complete information, contact the Direction du Tourisme et de l'Hôtellerie in Cotonou (see p.974) or the *Hôtel Tata Somba* in Natitingou. If you don't have your own vehicle, you can rent a car and driver in Natitingou or Tanguièta (4x4 isn't necessary except after rain), but negotiating a fair deal with a competent driver in a reliable vehicle equipped with spares is up to you.

Inside the park, **accommodation** can be found at the remote *Hôtel Campement de la Pendjari* (☎23.82.11.24 ➌), located in the north of the park near the Burkina border and the Pendjari River, which must be booked in advance through the *Hôtel Tata Somba* in Natitingou (see p.1003). They have smart bungalows and twin rooms, plus a restaurant, bar and, miraculously, a swimming pool. If the *hôtel campement* is fully booked, it's possible to **camp** for CFA3000 per person. Camping, under the supervision of rangers, is also permitted at the **Mare Yangouali** and the **Pont d'Arli**, where you can cross the Pendjari River into Burkina Faso and the Pendjari's extension there – **Arli National Park**.

Niger

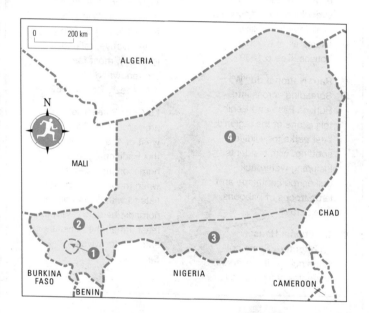

Highlights	1008	13.2 Southwest Niger	1044
Introduction and Basics	1009	13.3 Southern Niger	1049
13.1 Niamey	1033	13.4 The Nigérien Sahara	1056

Niger highlights

* **Musée National, Niamey**
One of West Africa's finest museums, home to a zoo, crafts centre and exhibition halls featuring everything from dinosaur skeletons to full-size examples of Nigérien houses. See p.1039

* **Parc National du "W"**
Spreading across into Burkina Faso and Benin, this is one of the region's best parks for wildlife spotting, with residents including waterbuck, duiker, roan antelope and large troops of baboons. See p.1047

* **Traditional Hausa architecture** Some outstandingly well-preserved examples can be found in the southern town of Zinder. See p.1053

* **Tuareg jewellery** The Tuareg silversmiths of Agadez are celebrated throughout West Africa for fashioning a variety of innovative, refined jewellery, most famously the renowned "Croix d'Agadez". See p.1062

* **La Cure Salée** The area around In-Gall, west of Agadez, hosts this traditional yearly homecoming celebration, when the area's large salt flats fill with water and the nomadic herders return to feast, fatten their animals and look for wives. See p.1064

▲ Gerewol festival, In-Gall

Introduction and Basics

Even by West African standards, **Niger** is a tantalizingly remote and little-visited destination. Most of the country consists of vast expanses of largely uninhabited **Sahel and desert**, with the only areas of significant population concentrated in a small ribbon of cultivated land in the southwest along the Niger River. Although the country formerly saw a steady trickle of trans-Saharan travellers arriving from the north, the troubles in **Algeria** effectively closed that route to Westerners and have left Niger more isolated than ever.

Niger is afflicted by **drought** and desperately poor (currently ranked 177th out of the 177 countries on UNDP's human development index) but there's little obvious sense of destitution. The country generally exudes a feeling of orderliness and composure, and was experiencing a new-found sense of optimism following the return to democracy after a period of military rule and the resolution of the **Tuareg conflict** which threw much of Niger into turmoil during the 1990s. Renewed hostilities in 2007 put the brakes on again, but, assuming the MNJ rebellion is a temporary glitch, and tensions drop once again, there's plenty to go back for. The **Sahel landscapes** of the north are among West Africa's most remarkable, while in **Agadez** the country has a desert city to rival – or even surpass – Timbuktu. Niger is also one of West Africa's most hassle-free countries, while well-maintained roads and good buses make getting around unusually straightforward.

People

Nearly half the population of Niger are **Hausa**-speaking. Engaged principally in agriculture and commerce, the Hausa have been long settled in the south, where they established large urban centres such as Maradi and Zinder. The overwhelming majority of Hausa are Muslim, but small splinter groups have retained traditional religious beliefs, notably in the Birnin-Konni district. If you don't have a chance to get further south to the original Hausa city-states in Nigeria, you can still see the brilliant **durbar festivals** – cavalry charges, clashing costumes and all – in Zinder, which retains its sultanate and beautiful quarters of traditional architecture.

Fact file

The **République du Niger** has a confusing name for English-speakers. Pronouncing it like an unfinished "Nigeria" means nothing to Nigériens – the people of the country – who pronounce it "Nee-zjé". It's a vast country on the map, spreading over 1,270,000 square kilometres – twice the size of Texas and five times as big as Britain. In reality, however, the Sahara covers most of the northern region, making a large part of the country uninhabitable except to hardy nomads. A population of some **12.5 million people** is concentrated at fairly high density, mainly along the borders with Nigeria, Benin and Burkina Faso. More than a million live in Niamey.

Although the country has had democratic reforms, there is serious discontent and in 2007 **President Mamadou Tandja** was struggling with a resurgence of the **Tuareg rebellion** in the north.

Niger has a **foreign debt** amounting to £900 million ($1.8 billion) – a trifling figure in global terms (the USA spends more than that on its defence budget every two days) – but with annual exports of only about £125 million ($250 million) it's perhaps no surprise that the country is, by UN figures, the poorest in the world. Some 98 percent of the population is employed in agriculture, livestock and informal trade; and mining and manufacturing continue to struggle due to the unstable price of Niger's principal export resource – **uranium**.

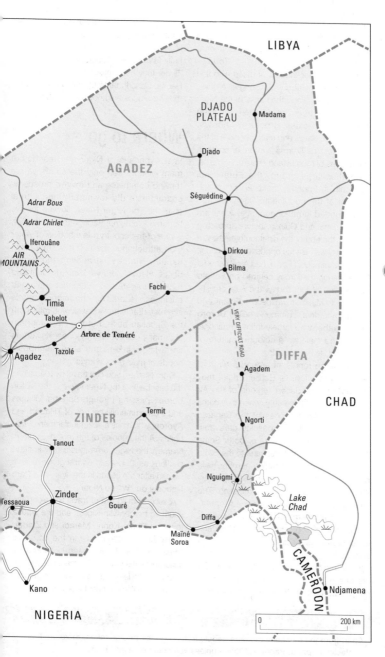

The **Djerma** and **Songhai** speak the same language and probably have common origins. Numbering about one and a half million, they're the second largest group in Niger and have been politically dominant in the country for generations. Today's Songhai are descendants of those who fled the collapse of Gao's great Songhai empire, and live mostly along the banks of the Niger as far downstream as Tillabéri, retaining the essential class structure – nobles, commoners, slaves and craftspeople – of the old empire. The Djerma live further south in the regions of Niamey and Dosso.

Another large group, the **Fula** (Peul or Peulh in French), make up some ten percent of the population. Centuries ago they founded large kingdoms in what are now Senegal and Guinea, before spreading east. By the end of the nineteenth century, a group of town Fula (as opposed to nomads), led by Uthman Dan Fodio, had established a huge Islamic theocracy centred on Sokoto in Nigeria. In Niger today, the Fula are still divided into Muslim townspeople (**Fulani**) and nomadic herders, commonly called **Bororo** or **Wodaabé**, who largely follow traditional beliefs and maintain a colourful culture of dance and life-cycle rituals.

The **Tuareg** represent around a tenth of Niger's population. Of Berber origin, they migrated to the desert regions of the Aïr around the seventh century, when they came to control long stretches of the Saharan routes, either pillaging passing caravans, offering protection to them, or both. Some Tuareg still take camel caravans to the Bilma salt mines, but an increasing number have been forced to seek jobs in the towns by the recent droughts and the rebellion. The Tuareg have a rather exaggerated reputation as sharp operators: they often work as guides and also produce some of Niger's finest crafts – especially leather ware and silverwork.

In the region of Lake Chad, the **Kanouri** are one of Niger's smaller groups. These people are part of the legacy of the great neighbouring empires of **Kanem** and **Bornu**, which reached a peak in the sixteenth century. With the advent of colonialism, their territory was divided between Chad, Nigeria, Niger and Cameroon. Today, they're principally farmers and fishers, and in towns like Zinder they have mixed significantly with the Hausa. Descendants of marriages between the two groups are known as **Beriberi**.

Where to go

Vast expanses of Niger are desert, but many visitors see only the south, where thriving commerce and relative prosperity characterize the towns and agricultural districts. The **Niger River**, flowing for five hundred kilometres through the southwest, is one of the country's few bodies of water – an attraction in itself. The cosmopolitan capital, **Niamey**, straddling the banks of "Le Fleuve", draws a mix of local and regional traders and international aid and business visitors. Air-conditioned hotels and restaurants provide welcome relief from the Sahelian bush, but the city's modern high-rises coexist slightly uneasily with its sprawling markets and slum neighbourhoods of mud-brick homes.

From Niamey, you can travel by road along the east bank of the Niger towards the Malian border, passing through Songhai villages and the commercial centres of **Tillabéri** and **Ayorou**, which has a spectacular market that unites all the peoples of the region. South of Niamey, the Niger is navigable only in short sections as it closes in on the game reserve named after the bends in the river – the **Parc National du "W" du Niger**.

A second main line of travel lies along the southern border with Nigeria and the **Hausa** towns of **Birnin-Konni**, **Maradi** and **Zinder**. These historic centres lie in the country's "green" belt and have been bolstered by agriculture – the region's dominant feature. The road from Zinder is paved as far as **Nguigmi**, a Kanouri settlement near **Lake Chad**.

Photography

Apart from the reticence of some people to having their photos taken, there are few obstacles to photography in Niger – unless you count dust and heat.

	Jan	Feb	Mar	Apr	May	June	July	Aug	Sept	Oct	Nov	Dec
Niamey												
Temperatures °C												
Min (night)	14	18	22	26	27	25	24	22	23	23	19	15
Max (day)	34	37	41	42	41	38	34	32	34	38	38	34
Rainfall mm	0	0	5	8	33	81	132	188	94	13	0	0
Days with rainfall	0	0	0	1	4	6	9	12	7	1	0	0
Agadez												
Temperatures °C												
Min (night)	10	13	17	21	25	24	24	23	23	20	15	12
Max (day)	29	33	38	41	44	43	41	38	40	39	35	32
Bilma												
Temperatures °C												
Min (night)	6	8	13	17	31	22	23	24	21	16	11	8
Max (day)	26	29	35	40	43	44	42	40	41	39	33	28

The remote desert regions of the **north** were beginning to open up to visitors again following the general ceasefire at the end of the Tuareg rebellion. By mid-2007, however, a series of attacks and widespread insecurity had effectively closed all the area north of the Niamey–Zinder axis. Coverage in the Guide should be read with the assumption that peace has returned once again. Assuming that's the case, the attractions are manifold: the region's main town, **Agadez**, is an ancient desert metropolis and seat of a powerful sultanate, and one of the most important centres in the southern Sahara. For determined travellers, it is the starting point for visits to isolated oases in the **Ténéré** and **Bilma** regions and to the historic villages of the less remote **Aïr mountain region**, such as Timia, Iferouâne and Assodé. Getting to any of these places requires specialized preparations for desert travel, and whether you sign up for some kind of tour or take a guide in your own vehicle, the whole expedition is likely to cost a small fortune.

When to go

Most of Niger is scorching hot all year round, though the heat is least oppressive from November to March. If you're travelling on the rough overland route from Gao to Niamey – or for that matter anywhere in the south

off the main roads – it's also worth trying to avoid the **rainy season**, which falls roughly between July and September, when heavy storms can knock out the *pistes* for days. In contrast, when the **harmattan** wind blows down from the north in November, it can kick up blinding clouds of dust and sometimes cause morning temperatures to tumble near to freezing point, especially around Agadez, and in the Aïr Mountains.

Getting there from the rest of Africa

Niger was formerly West Africa's main **overland** entry point (from Algeria across the Sahara), but the security situation in Algeria over the past few decades has placed Niger on the extreme fringe of West African travel routes. **Air connections** with the rest of Africa remain poor, and with the demise of Air Niger are only getting worse.

Flights

Within **West Africa**, direct flights to Niamey are nearly all from **Abidjan**, with Air Ivoire flying the route twice weekly. Air Sénégal flies from **Dakar** via **Bamako**, also twice weekly (Mon & Fri). Toumai Air Chad flies in from **Ndjamena**. And Afriqiyah flies direct from **Bamako** (Fri) and **Cotonou** (Sun) on its return leg to Tripoli.

13

NIGER | Basics

There are no direct flights from Accra, Banjul, Bissau, Lagos or Nouakchott. Air Ivoire can get you to Niamey from Bamako, Conakry, Cotonou, Dakar, Douala, Lomé and Ouagadougou, though all involve sometimes lengthy connections in Abidjan.

From **the rest of Africa** (apart from Afriqiyah, which flies twice weekly from Tripoli) Abidjan is again the obvious hub, with some sort of connection most days from East, Central or Southern Africa using Ethiopian Airlines or South African Airways.

Overland from Algeria

Once the classic trans-Saharan overland route, the Hoggar route from Tamanrasset via Assamakka to Arlit was closed through the 1990s due to the Algerian civil war and the Tuareg rebellion in Niger. Since 2000, it had begun to open up again with overland vehicles and local trucks making the crossing in increasing numbers. In 2007, however, there were several armed robberies in northern Niger, and then a concerted campaign by the Tuareg MNJ group led to the closure by the Nigérien army of all travel in northern Niger except under armed escort. This means that, at the time of writing, you can travel south through Algeria (and indeed much of the route is paved) but, assuming you are allowed entry to Niger at Assamakka, you may be forced to wait for – and possibly pay for – an armed escort out of the danger zone.

Overland from Mali

The route follows the Niger River from **Gao to Niamey**. It can be a difficult stretch for drivers, particularly in the rainy season when the *piste* section between Ansongo and Ayorou can be un-drivable for days. Frustrations are more than compensated by Sahelian scenery at its best, with numerous fishing villages along the bank and dust-shrouded sunsets over the broad river. SNTV

in Niger, and various local companies in Mali provide bus services between Niamey and Gao. Alternatively, bush taxis are available as far as the respective border posts – Labézanga in Mali and Yassane in Niger.

Overland from Burkina

The 500-kilometre paved road linking **Ouagadougou** with Niamey is a relatively busy and straightforward route. The border is now open 24 hours a day and formalities are pretty routine. SNTV run a daily service from Ouagadougou to Niamey and there are frequent bush-taxi services from Ouaga and Fada-Ngourma.

Overland from Benin

The 1030-kilometre road **from Benin** is paved all the way from Cotonou. The offices on both sides of the border at Malanville are open 24 hours and present no special problems. Again, SNTV run a daily service.

Overland from Nigeria

Numerous paved roads feed into Niger **from Nigeria**, retaining a Hausa-land commercial unity despite the frontier. The main entry routes are from Sokoto to Birnin-Konni, Katsina to Maradi, and Kano to Zinder. From the south, the best route is direct to Sokoto, then to the border at Birnin-Konni. If you're setting off from Kaduna or Kano, the best surfaced route is via Katsina to Maradi. Border crossings provide no unusual problems though you will need a Nigerian visa before you arrive at the border, and these have long been hard to obtain in Niger.

Red tape and visas

Visas for Niger are required by all visitors except citizens of ECOWAS countries. They are not issued at the border, and are most easily obtained in neighbouring West African countries: Benin, Côte d'Ivoire, Ghana, Mali and Nigeria (Lagos and Kano). Visas cost around €60. Niger is part of the **Visa Touristique Entente** arrangement (see p.32) that includes Benin, Burkina, Côte d'Ivoire and Togo. Note that French embassies don't handle visas for Niger, but some Ivoirian embassies do.

If you apply for a visa outside Africa, Nigérien embassies may ask for a return air ticket or, at the very least, the registration details of the vehicle you'll be travelling with.

To enter Niger from another African country you need a **yellow fever certificate**.

Visas for onward travel

In Niamey, you can get visas for most West African countries with little problem. Benin, Mali and Guinea have diplomatic representation in Niamey and issue visas relatively painlessly. Burkina Faso, Côte d'Ivoire and Togo have no direct representation, but the French consulate handles their visas. Visas for Nigeria are, in principle, only granted to residents of Niger, but if you make a good case for yourself, exceptions can be made.

Vehicle red tape and guides

If you're driving, you'll need a **carnet**. Alternatively, if you don't have one, the police will issue you with a Temporary Importation Document. You'll also be issued with a *laissez-passer*, like a visa for your vehicle, with the same details as your Vehicle Registration Document (V5) or *carte grise*, to be surrendered on exit. There should be no charge.

Third-party **insurance** is compulsory, and the police like to check you have it. It's not available at frontier posts, so the police allow travel without insurance to the nearest town where you buy it. The large and efficient Société Nigérienne d'Assurances et de Réassurances, av de la Mairie, Niamey (☎20.73.73.36), has branches throughout the country and charges about CFA2000 a day for the average vehicle.

If you want to drive north of Agadez or Nguigmi, you're required to have a **feuille de route** (official itinerary), which can only be issued by a licensed Nigérien travel agency. You're also required by law to take a **licensed guide** if you're driving in these regions. In theory, you need a *feuille* if you're driving anywhere in the country off a paved road, but in practice this wouldn't apply to short journeys on unpaved stretches in the South or Southwest.

Even assuming peace prevails in the north, if your itinerary includes the Djado in the far north, near the Algerian and Libyan borders,

The blog for this guide

For **travel updates**, news links and general information, check out
ⓦ theroughguidetowestafrica .blogspot.com.

it's unlikely to be authorized. The *pistes* linking Iferouâne and Djanet with Algeria are permanently closed to tourists.

Info, websites, maps

Tourist **information** on Niger is virtually nonexistent outside the country and not much better when you get there: there are no tourist offices abroad and not many useful **websites**.

Recommended websites

ⓦ **www.friendsofniger.org** Site of current and former Peace Corps volunteers (PCVs) with info and links.
ⓦ **www.joelmayer.com/niger** Run by a returned PCV, lots of useful links.
ⓦ **www.temoust.org** French-based website of the Temoust: Tuareg Survival organization, covering culture and news.
ⓦ **www.planeteafrique.com/Liberation** Website of *Libération-Niger*, a reputable, weekly French-language independent news and opinion magazine.

Maps

There are few good **maps** of Niger. The French *IGN Niger* at 1:2,000,000 is usefully detailed, but dates from 1993, while the Canadian *ITMB Niger* (same scale; 2004) flags its reliability by placing Niamey on the wrong side of the river. In Niamey, the tourist office has a good, up-to-date plan of the capital, with many of the city's restaurants and hotels marked. The IGN also publishes some regional maps, but they're not widely available.

The media

There are few newspapers in Niger: *Le Sahel*, a government-owned news-sheet, is published daily in Niamey, but has a very small circulation and holds little of any

13

NIGER | Basics

interest. There are various independent news magazines, including *La Hache Nouvelle*, *Libération-Niger*, *Le Républicain*, *L'Enquêteur*, *L'Evènement* and the satirical *Le Canard Déchaîné*, all of which operate under the eyes of the government: press freedom laws are in the offing, but have not been enacted. You can find French papers and news mags in some of the bigger Niamey hotels and one or two newsstands and bookstores, but little or nothing in English.

Nigérien government **radio**, La Voix du Sahel, is the sole nationwide station and broadcasts in French, Hausa, Songhai-Djerma, Kanouri, Fulfuldé (Fula), Tamashek, Toubou, Gourmantché and Arabic. Private FM radio stations have also started to flourish in Niamey; R&M (aka REM: Radio et Musique) was the original private radio station, but these days Ténéré and Anfani are the most popular music stations and have a social conscience too, promoting health and education. As for **TV**, the state-run Télé-Sahel comes on air each evening for a few hours, showing news and old movies dubbed into French. It has since been joined by the private Ténéré TV. Many hotels and restaurants now also have **satellite TV**, generally subscribing to French-language channels.

Health

In Niamey and other large towns, **tap water** is usually safe to drink; the borehole water of Arlit and Agadez is noted for its purity. **Cholera** outbreaks, however, occur frequently along the Niger, and in the bush you should use purifying tablets or boil water. In case of an epidemic, even town water is suspect.

Health-care facilities are very limited. For minor ailments you can be treated at Niamey's **hospital**. If you have a medical problem, embassies will always recommend a **private clinic**. For anything serious – surgery for example – they're sure to suggest repatriation.

Costs, money, banks

Niger is part of the **CFA zone** (rates of exchange roughly £1=CFA880, $1=CFA450, €1=CFA656). There are, as yet, no **ATMs** in Niger and it's essential, arriving either by air or from Nigeria, to have **euros** in cash (or, less usefully, US dollars) to tide you over until you reach a bank. Note that money in Niger is frequently counted in multiples of CFA5 (called a *dela*) – see p.1032.

Changing money is an expensive business. All the main **banks** – BIA, Ecobank, BOA and SONI – charge a flat fee of CFA10,000 *plus* a percentage commission of between 2 percent and 3 percent, on traveller's cheques or credit card cash advances. The one exception to this rule is a Visa cash advance with Western Union in Niamey (see p.1042), which does not charge the CFA10,000. Changing cash is cheaper and relatively straightforward, either in banks or hotels or private businesses, some of whom will also give you CFA for your traveller's cheques.

Credit cards can only really be used in Niamey, and even then only for major expenses such as car rental, luxury hotels and a handful of upmarket restaurants. Visa is by some distance, the most accepted.

Costs

As far as **costs** are concerned, Niger is **expensive** relative to other CFA countries, though still fairly cheap in real terms. You can always find cheap street food and a basic room for the night, even if the choice is often limited. If your budget is less restricted, the biggest expenses are likely to be hotels and car rental, both of which can eat deeply into your pocket.

Getting around

Niger has a decent bus service, and it's possible to hitchhike at some checkpoints. Three main **surfaced routes** cover the

---

Fuel prices

Fuel costs in Niger are around CFA630 per litre for petrol (*super*), CFA575 for diesel (*gasoil*). If you're arriving from Nigeria, fill up there, as it's much cheaper.

western parts of Niger: Niamey to Gaya, Niamey to Nguigmi and Birnin-Konni to Agadez and Arlit (the latter portion of which is nicknamed the Route de l'Uranium).

Buses, taxis, trucks and motorbikes

The former state-run Société Nationale des Transports Voyageurs (SNTV) operates a scheduled **bus network** between major towns. Because of the popularity of the service, it's imperative to book a seat in advance at the local SNTV office. The main competitor, EHGM (El Hadji Garba Maissagé), runs reliable services between Niamey and Zinder, Agadez and Diffa that are about ten percent cheaper than SNTV. Two other companies with fairly extensive networks are Aïr Transport and Rimbo Transport, though the latter have an unsafe reputation. **Fares** work out at just over CFA1000 per estimated hour's travel (so, for example, the 12-hour journey from Niamey to Agadez runs CFA12,500–14,000).

Cheap but always overcrowded **taxis brousse** soak up the excess passengers. **Trucks** also run between certain centres and often take travellers for a fee – a useful backup in remote areas where transport is scarce.

Certain cities – Maradi and Zinder particularly – have begun to see the sprouting of that quintessentially West African form of public-transport-for-one, the **motorcycle taxi**. Known in Niger as *kabo-kabos*, you'll pay around CFA100–200 for a five-minute ride on the back of one. Helmets and insurance aren't supplied, so take care who you climb on with.

Driving your own vehicle

Driving on the main paved roads is fast and straightforward: visibility is excellent and bends and hazards are clearly marked. Official **road tolls** are in force on all paved roads (the barriers are on the exit of towns), though the fees are low, in the order of CFA1000/1000km.

Driving **off the paved roads** is still subject to police jurisdiction. By 2006, they were becoming less interested in trying to control off-road tourism, though that relaxation evaporated in the north with the advent of

the 2007 rebellion. For details of the red tape – and guide requirements – that drivers need to bear in mind, see p.1015.

Vehicle **fuel supplies** are generally plentiful, but filling stations can be far apart. Fuel can also be bought from roadside entrepreneurs with half a dozen fifty-gallon drums. Along the Nigerian border between Birnin-Konni and Zinder there's a thriving black market in cheap Nigerian petrol. North of Zinder, engine oil and transmission fluids can be hard to come by.

Hitchhiking

Roadblocks and police checks at the entrance to every large town help to make **hitching** a possible and reasonably safe alternative to public transport. Cars are obliged to stop at these controls and while the gendarmes are checking the papers you can ask drivers if they're headed your way. The police may even help. Foreign aid workers often take hitchers for free; Nigérien drivers will invariably expect payment, in which case it's useful to have an idea of the corresponding bush-taxi fare. Hitching is fast: on the three main highways you can expect a vehicle going to one of the big towns or a neighbouring country at least once an hour, and most vehicles will stop. Truck drivers sometimes make detours en route, so check the final destination and any detours to be made. A lift in a truck usually means standing in the back for several hours under the blazing sun; plenty of drinking water and a hat or *cheche* are essential.

Boats

Large steamers don't ply the Niger below Gao, in Mali, but motorized **pirogues** venture along limited stretches of the river between Ayorou (near the Malian border) and Gaya (near the Benin border). However, they operate only during and after the rainy season when the water level is high enough. Deals have to be struck on your own in the river towns. Between March and September, it may also be possible to canoe-hop downstream from Gaya into Nigeria, but rapids and artificial barriers block the way at numerous points and prevent a continuous journey in the same vessel.

Domestic flights

There are no scheduled domestic **flights**. To fly, your only recourse is to charter a plane in Niamey (see p.1042).

Accommodation

Hotels tend to be relatively expensive in Niger, but at least you'll find comfortable places with toilets and air conditioning in all the major towns. Budget accommodation seems especially bad value: you'll often have to pay CFA10,000 or more, even for a room with just a fan and shared facilities.

Camping sites are an idea that's caught on in Niger and you'll find them scattered lightly throughout the country, usually on the edge of towns. They usually cost around CFA2500–3500 per person, plus a fee for each vehicle. There's no law against camping in the wild (officially you're supposed to camp at least 20km from the closest village – which is hard to check) and **staying with people** or presumably camping on their land with permission, is now officially permitted.

Eating and drinking

Niger may have concentrated heavily on improving its agriculture, but food shortages still occur in years of bad harvests or drought. Staples tend to be less varied than in countries to the south, meals being usually based around **millet**, **rice** or **niebé** – a type of bean that has become an important crop. Along the river, these are usually eaten with sauces and fresh or smoked fish. Millet-based **foura**, eaten throughout the country, is one of Niger's commonest dishes, consisting of small balls of ground and slightly fermented millet, crushed in a calabash with milk, sugar and spices. Songhai people often make a cornmeal stodge, or **pâte** (from the French for pasta), which is eaten with a baobab-leaf sauce perked up with fish or meat.

Beef and mutton are common in the Hausa country and the nomadic regions of the north. As a fast-food snack, kebab-like beef or mutton **brochettes** are sold everywhere on the streets: stuffed into a *demi-baguette* and doused with a bit of Maggi sauce, they make a quick, satisfying meal. Other **street food** includes omelettes, salads, *riz gras* and a variety of other cheap meals.

Niamey has a reasonable selection of **foreign restaurants**, but outside the capital, eating places tend to be much more modest, the selection of dishes usually being limited to the likes of grilled chicken or *steak-frites*.

Drinking

Niger's great beverage – in common with other Sahel countries – is green China **tea**, drunk on every possible occasion, especially on the road whenever a little time is available to fix up a fire to boil a brew. You'll also find **beer** in most towns, though it's rather expensive.

Communications

Niamey's **PTT** is quite modern and efficient, though seems to be suffering from the increasing popularity of the Internet, to the point where post offices are usually deserted and it may take a few minutes

---

Accommodation price codes

All accommodation prices in this chapter are coded according to the following scale, whose equivalent in pounds sterling/US dollars is used throughout the book. Prices refer to the rate you can expect to pay for a room with two beds. Single rooms, or single occupancy, will normally cost at least two-thirds of the twin-occupancy rate. For further details, see p.55.

❶ Under CFA5000 (under £5/$10)
❷ CFA5000–10,000 (£5–10/$10–20)
❸ CFA10,000–15,000 (£10–15/$20–30)
❹ CFA15,000–20,000 (£15–20/$30–40)
❺ CFA20,000–30,000 (£20–30/$40–60)
❻ CFA30,000–40,000 (£30–40/$60–80)
❼ CFA40,000–50,000 (£40–50/$80–100)
❽ Over CFA50,000 (over £50/$100)

to find someone to serve you. Making IDD **international phone calls** is straightforward from *télécentres*, found in all major towns. If you want to make a reverse-charge (collect) call, dialling ☎16 from a payphone puts you through to the foreign operator, who should be able to connect you to anywhere. Persistence may be needed.

Mobile phone coverage in Niger has come on in leaps and bounds, to the extent that most towns now have some sort of reception, though coverage is patchy along the roads. The two main providers are Celtel (⊛tinyurl.com/ysvuhf) and Telecel (⊛www .telecelniger.com).

Internet cafés haven't made much progress yet, and are only found in Niamey and a few bigger towns. Connections are often brain-numbingly slow, particularly in Maradi. Rates range from CFA500 to CFA1600/hr, but there's no guarantee that connections will be better at more expensive places.

Opening hours, public holidays and festivals

Due to the heat, businesses start work early in the morning and generally close down for at least three hours in the early afternoon. Banking hours vary from one institution to the next, but they're usually roughly Mon–Fri, 7.30–11.30am and 3.30–5.30pm. Government offices are open Mon–Fri 7.30am–12.30pm and 3.30–6.30pm. Most other businesses are open Mon–Fri, 8am–12.30pm and 3–6.30pm, plus Saturday mornings.

As some 85 percent of Nigériens are Muslim, Islamic holidays (see p.63) are of great importance. The best place to be during Muslim festivities is Zinder. Other **national holidays** are: New Year's Day (Jan 1), Concorde Day April 24 (commemorating the 1995 Tuareg peace agreement), Aug 3 (Independence Day) and Dec 18 (Republic Day). Christmas and Easter are also office holidays.

As well as Muslim festivals, local traditional **festivals** happen all over the country, but the best known events are the **Gerewol**, or male beauty contests, that take place during the **Cure Salée**, a traditional gathering of nomads and their herds that takes place in the In-Gall region at the end of the rains (see p.1064).

Crafts and shopping

Niger has a wealth of mostly inexpensive and portable **crafts**. Agadez is well known for its silversmiths, who turn out some fine jewellery: popular items are the pendants known as "desert crosses", particularly the Croix d'Agadez. The Hausa towns, notably Zinder, specialize in leather goods, including sandals, bags and boxes. Fula weavers (*tisserands* in French) are noted for their geometrically patterned blankets. To get a good overview of the nation's crafts, the National Museum in Niamey shows a wide range of the country's output. The best buys are in local markets, though for guaranteed quality and variety it's also worth checking out the official *centres artisanales* in Niamey.

Crime and safety

Crime against tourists, particularly violent crime, is thankfully rare in Niger, though pickpocketing and petty theft are prevalent in markets, bus stations and busy areas. The volatile situation in **the north** had effectively shut down the tourist industry in that region at the time of writing, early–2008, and you're advised to closely watch the latest developments. See box on p.1057.

Emergencies

There are no national police, fire or ambulance phone numbers.

Gender issues and sexual attitudes

Although Niger is a largely Muslim country, **women** don't wear the veil and their presence is strongly felt in public. Nevertheless, Niger

13

NIGER | Basics

has not ratified the Maputo protocol, which seeks to give African women equality under the law, and it is one of the few countries in Africa where little progress has been made on **female genital mutilation** – which is still widespread.

Women travellers generally have few problems, however, and **female volunteers** usually feel comfortable making trips across the country unaccompanied. Advances from men tend to be frequent but harmless and easily rebuffed.

For **gay** Nigériens, the law can impose lengthy jail terms for what it describes as "public indecency" – ambiguous in a country where the public and the private blend so easily. Indiscreet gay travellers may find themselves subject to the same laws. There is no visible gay scene at all.

Entertainment and sports

Traditional **wrestling** (*la lutte*) and one-armed **boxing** (with a fist wrapped in cloth) attract big crowds but, unusually for Africa, **football** has yet to find a true place in the nation's heart, with the national team ranked in 134th position by FIFA.

On the **arts** side, there's not a great deal going on in terms of national culture – no theatre except the odd event in Niamey, and a **music scene** that hasn't yet set the world alight (see p.1029). The **film** tradition, brief as it is, shows more promise (see p.1029).

Wildlife and national parks

Niger's harsh climate and terrain have preserved some rare species from the usual habitat destruction and hunting (which was outlawed in 1964). Even in the south, **hippos** can nearly always be seen in the Niger River, and the last large herds of giraffe in West Africa live in the vicinity of Tillabéri, Baleyara and Dosso where they can sometimes be seen from the road. The **Parc National du "W" du Niger** (which crosses borders into Burkina and Benin) has a good cross-section of savannah fauna, including several hundred elephants. Niger's portion of the park has the best visitor facilities.

A brief history of Niger

After the demise of the **Songhai empire** (see p.424), whose territory spread into western Niger, two spheres of influence predominated in the region. In the twelfth century, the **Tuareg** settled in the north around Agadez, and soon controlled regional trade. The **Hausa** spread from the original seven city-states founded in Nigeria in the tenth century (see p.1186) to settle in southern towns like Zinder and Maradi. Unlike the western Sudan, where the trans-Saharan trade focused mainly on gold, the mainstay of the eastern routes, and the basis of local economies, was the **slave trade** with North Africa.

Explorers on the river

For centuries, rumours about Timbuktu on the Niger River had circulated in Europe, but although the Portuguese had been trading along the coast since the fifteenth century, no Western power had penetrated the interior. It wasn't until the late eighteenth century that expeditions were launched into a region notorious for its hostility to Christians. The Scottish explorer **Mungo Park** reached the Niger River in 1796 and described its eastward flow. But it was another thirty years before the Europeans saw Timbuktu and not until 1850 that the first European set foot on the sands of present-day Niger, when the German explorer **Heinrich Barth** led an expedition from Tripoli that took him south through Agadez, Zinder and across the Hausa country as far as Kano.

Colonial conquest

The information gleaned by the expeditions opened the doors to colonial conquests. France, anxious to link colonial settlements in West and Central Africa, was the most ambitious usurper of Sahelian territories. In 1854, General Louis Faidherbe became governor of Senegal and plotted the eastward expansion of France's West African empire. He sent troops up the Senegal River and east to the Niger. Following its course, they broke the resistance of such formidable adversaries as **Samory Touré** and **El Hadj Omar Tall**, who had founded the Tukulor empire of Ségou. By the end of the nineteenth century, the French had established a military presence at **Niamey**, which they quickly turned into the most important army post east of Bamako.

In 1898, spheres of influence were established between France and Britain, the principal powers vying for control of the Niger. The following year, the French sent an expedition to Lake Chad to demarcate borders between Niger and Nigeria. Led by two generals, **Voulet** and **Chanoine**, it was to be one of the bloodiest of the colonial missions. As the two soldiers pushed east with troops of Senegalese infantry, they embarked on a series of massacres, torching villages in their path and slaughtering the people. Birnin-Konni was virtually razed to the ground. Reports of the atrocities reached France and the government sent an expedition led by Colonel Klobb to investigate. Infuriated that their tactics should be questioned, the generals went even further, murdering Klobb, breaking with France and apparently setting about conquering the territories for themselves. The madness was only stopped when Voulet and Chanoine were killed by their own infantrymen. Replacements were sent out and the French finally reached Lake Chad in 1900.

French rule

With the territory's southern borders established, Niger became part of French West Africa in 1901. But the nature of this territory differed from that of its West African neighbours: officially, it was an **autonomous military territory**, and its importance was strategic, rather than commercial. Outside the army, the French presence was minimal: there was no French settlement and the idea of economic development was barely considered.

"Pacification" was a difficult process in Niger, as resistance sprouted in pockets across the country. One of the most serious **uprisings** was that of the **Kel Gress Tuareg**, who occupied Agadez from 1916 to 1917 and controlled most of the Aïr highlands. And in 1919, a rebellion broke out in the region of Tahoua, which was only quelled in 1921, the same year that Niger was finally upgraded to the status of a **colony**.

World War II was a turning point in West African politics, and following the Brazzaville Conference of 1944, reforms were enacted which provided African representation in the national assembly, the senate and the assembly of the French Union. In 1956, the famous **Loi Cadre** was passed, establishing local government for the French colonies.

In the wake of these reforms, two political movements developed in Niger, the more radical of which was embodied in the Union Nigérienne Démocratique – also known as **Sawaba** – which dominated political life in the 1950s. Led by **Djibo Bakary**, the party fought vigorously against close ties with France and de Gaulle's proposed constitution, the main provision of which was for a Franco-African Community with limited autonomy for individual colonies, but continued economic dependence on Paris. For a while, it seemed probable that Niger would join Guinea in saying "no" to de Gaulle's proposal and in opting for immediate independence.

In the event, the new constitution was approved in the landmark **1958 referendum** – a victory for the Parti Progressiste Nigérien (**PPN**) of **Hamani Diori**, who had advocated the alternative of close links with France, though it's generally believed the results were falsified. Despite its wide support, the Sawaba party was banned in 1959,

and Bakary forced into exile. With the implicit backing of the French, the PPN was thus poised to dominate post-independence politics and Diori was assured the presidency of the new nation, formed in 1960.

Niger under Diori

Conservative politics prevailed in the days after independence, as Diori aligned his country with France and developed close ties with moderate neighbours, notably Côte d'Ivoire. Diori ruled with a small Council of Ministers, carefully selected to maintain the status quo. The Sawaba party tried to operate from abroad, with backing from Algeria, Ghana and China, but internal opposition to government policies was rigorously suppressed. Various plots to overthrow Diori's regime in the early 1960s led to mass arrests and violence. When the Sawaba opposition was accused of leading a series of guerilla attacks near the Nigerian border in 1964, seven of the alleged assailants were publicly executed in Niamey.

By the late 1960s, the PPN – by then the only political party – was in a state of disarray and despite Diori's tight control over the political reins, he began to lose his grip on power as the economic situation deteriorated. He got a political reprieve when the mining of **uranium**, discovered in 1968, gave new financial hope to a country that had previously earned most of its foreign exchange from groundnut exports. Eager to take advantage of the new source of revenue, Diori accepted a minimal seventeen percent share for the national mining company, Société des Mines de l'Aïr (SOMAÏR), which was controlled by the French Atomic Energy Commission. However, 1968 also saw the start of the first great **Sahel drought**. Lasting until 1974, the natural catastrophe brought Niger to its knees.

By the early 1970s, more than a million head of livestock (nearly two-thirds of the national herd) had died, and the pasturelands of the northern nomads had disappeared. International organizations helped establish emergency refugee camps and sent food supplies, but rumours began circulating that government officials were hoarding food and selling it off, rather than distributing it to those facing starvation. These were quickly confirmed by the discovery of **emergency food aid** stockpiled in the homes of several of Diori's ministers.

Kountché's coup

Disillusion with the government turned to anger. When Lieutenant-Colonel **Seyni Kountché** overthrew Diori in April 1974, there was widespread support, and even the French conceded they could do business with the new order. Kountché established a Conseil Militaire Suprême (**CMS**), which made a priority of dealing with corruption and reinvesting the government with credibility. In a conciliatory move, hundreds of political prisoners were released and Djibo Bakary returned home from exile.

In 1975, Kountché managed to renegotiate the terms under which uranium was mined, raising SOMAÏR's share to 33 percent and making the national company the biggest single partner. Fuelled by uranium revenues (prices for which soared following the oil crisis of the 1970s) and aided by the end of the drought, the economy began to pick up. Government workers received wage increases, roads were improved and prestigious building projects undertaken in Niamey. Even the agricultural sector improved dramatically. Niger, one of the countries hardest hit by the drought, was also one of the quickest to recover, and by the end of the decade, it could boast self-sufficiency in food production – no mean feat.

Niger had become something of an **economic oasis** in the middle of a poverty-stricken region, and that alone was enough to lend stability to Kountché's military regime. But policy and personality conflicts within the CMS threatened his authority, and he repeatedly reshuffled the ruling council

and expelled critics. Following a new outbreak of political activity, Bakary was rearrested in 1975. A coup attempt the following year led to the execution of its alleged protagonists.

Even as he tightened the screws, however, Kountché made a number of goodwill gestures. In 1980, Diori and Bakary were granted a degree of freedom, along with many of their supporters. And by 1982, the president appeared to be making plans for a return to a constitutional government.

Setbacks in the 1980s

A Conseil National de Développement was established in 1983 as a means of granting greater participation on a local level. But the CND had barely started functioning when another coup attempt, this time led by some of Kountché's closest aides, nearly toppled the government while he was abroad.

Reforms thereafter proceeded at a slower pace, though the president eventually announced that a **National Charter**, or draft constitution, would be drawn up and submitted to a referendum. The charter was submitted to voters in May 1987 – the first time elections had been held in the country since independence – and received overwhelming approval.

But even as Kountché was setting about reorganizing the government, the **economy** took a new dive. Already in 1980, a combination of the world recession and cuts in nuclear-power programmes had led to a drop in the price of uranium. Hopes that Niger would become one of the world's leading uranium producers faded rapidly. And as revenues dwindled and the national debt grew, another **drought** struck the country in the early 1980s. By 1984, the number of livestock had dropped by a half and, as cereal shortages climbed, the country again found itself importing vast quantities of food, much of it from the USA.

The downswing was accompanied by tensions with Niger's northern neighbour, **Libya**, which claims some 300 square kilometres of territory in northern Niger, an area with certified uranium deposits. After the Libyan army occupied northern Chad in 1980, Kountché's government had become wary of possible destabilization – with some justification after Gaddafi told reporters "We consider Niger second in line." Many observers suspected Gaddafi of behind-the-scenes support for the 1983 coup attempt. Gaddafi accused the Niger government of persecuting its **Tuareg** population – an issue about which Niamey is acutely sensitive – and may have encouraged dissent among the nomads, who have generally been sold short since independence.

Colonel Ali Saïbou

Kountché died during a visit to France in November 1987. His chosen successor as head of state, **Colonel Ali Saïbou**, the military chief of staff and a longtime supporter, followed the same conservative orientation as Kountché. Saïbou announced the creation of a one-party state and, in 1989, the first congress was held of the military council's **National Movement for a Society of Development** (MNSD), a supra-political organization which promised great things, but was elitist and urban-based. The government's fear of ethnic divisions in the country was so great that even acknowledging plurality was seen as dangerous.

The IMF-managed economy forced in austerity measures which hit poor urbanites hard. Students also felt the full impact of rising prices and reductions in already strapped services. In 1990 the university in Niamey was the scene of large-scale **student demonstrations** that ended in a violent clash with security forces, and this was followed by a mass protest rally in Niamey.

Niger was put under the international spotlight in June 1990, after *Le Monde* reported a **massacre** of about two hundred Tuareg civilians in reprisal for a Tuareg raid on Tchin-Tabaradene, near

Tahoua. Amnesty International reported other atrocities near Tchin-Tabaradene and at In-Gall in which dozens of people were summarily executed.

"Democracy" and Tuareg rebellion

As the national crisis deepened, and with democracy breaking out in many parts of the world following the fall of the Berlin Wall, Saïbou was compelled to speed up reforms. By the end of 1990, he had legalized opposition parties and formed a **national conference** to plot the country's future. Within a year, conference delegates had reduced the president's role to a ceremonial level and voted to suspend austerity measures imposed by the IMF and World Bank – the SAP or structural adjustment programme – which effectively made the country an outcast from the international financial community.

Despite two mutinies among the military over late pay, plans for **elections** pressed on. A majority of seats in the national assembly was ultimately won by a new group of opposition parties – the Alliance des Forces du Changement (**AFC**) – whose candidate for president, **Mahamane Ousmane**, won the title in the presidential elections in March 1993. A Muslim and the first **Hausa head of state** in a traditionally **Djerma political culture**, the new civilian leader of "democratic" Niger pledged to address the country's economic and social crises. He appointed another presidential contender, **Mahamadou Issoufou**, as his prime minister.

But student and labour unrest continued through 1992–93, and **Tuareg resistance** in the wake of Tchin-Tabaradene grew into a full-blown rebellion headed by the Front de Libération de l'Aïr et l'Azaouad (**FLAA**). Martial law was imposed across the entire north as security forces launched a major offensive against the rebels. Secret negotiations in France in 1993 led to a precarious truce whereby the north was to be demilitarized and talks were to open on the principal **Tuareg demands**: greater political autonomy, assistance for the return of refugees from Algeria and a commitment to regional development. Though the truce held into 1994, the FLAA began to splinter into more militant groups that refused to support any agreement that didn't specifically address demands for a federal system of government.

Meanwhile, President Mahamane tried to rekindle talks with Western creditors in the hopes of securing new loans and much-needed debt relief. During a 1993 visit to France, he received emergency financial assistance which allowed him to settle some pay arrears to public-sector employees, but when he conceded the government could not afford the back pay accumulated under the transitional administration, new **strikes and mutinies** broke out in Maradi, Agadez, Tahoua and Zinder. By mid-1994, the country was in a state of continual upheaval. A campaign of civil disobedience seeking proportional representation was mounted by key opposition leader **Mamadou Tandja**, of the National Movement for the Society of Development–Nassara (**MNSD– Nassara**) which had been the sole party between 1988 and 1990. Meanwhile, Prime Minister Issoufou resigned and his successor was quickly voted out of office on a no-confidence ballot. Instead of nominating a third prime minister, President Mahamane announced the dissolution of the national assembly and called a general election.

The election, held in January 1995, gave a majority to the opposition parties grouped under the banner of the MNSD, whose candidate for prime minister was **Hama Amadou**. Hama's cabinet was chosen entirely from the ranks of the opposition. Two women were among them – a first in Niger – but no associates of President Mahamane. The political climate had come full circle.

The country seemed ready for **reconciliation**. The new government came to a back-pay agreement with the unions, and repealed anti-strike legislation. And

in Ouagadougou the new government and the Tuareg rebels signed what was billed as a definitive and lasting peace accord – with Algerian, Burkinabe and French mediation.

After a brief period of goodwill, however, political cohabitation in Niger turned sour. Frequent disputes arose between Mahamane and Hama, who wrangled over everything. The rift wasn't helped by the fact that Mahamane was a Hausa and Hama a Djerma and both were in different parties. Mahamane frequently refused to convene the Council of Ministers or to sign legislation and the wheels of government were just barely turning by the end of 1995. In the midst of the deadlock, the unions once again invoked strikes to demand payment of arrears to civil servants. They were soon joined by miners and students, who formed a campaign of disobedience.

The Maïnassara coup

In January 1996, the military intervened through a **coup d'état** led by **Ibrahim Baré Maïnassara**. He formed a ruling military body, the Conseil de Salut National (**CSN**), suspended the constitution, placed Hama and Mahamane under house arrest and declared a state of emergency. Western nations viewed it as an assault to democracy, and the IMF broke off loan negotiations. Maïnassara, however, seemed sincere in his desire to turn power back to the people, and within a few months scheduled fresh elections and set up a committee to draft a new constitution. Apparently being in charge agreed with him, however, since he also announced his intention to run for the presidency as a civilian.

Mahamane, Hama and the last elected head of the assembly, Issoufou, all threw their hats in the ring. The poll took place, but candidates outside the CSN were not reassured when the electoral commission overseeing the voting was dissolved before the polls had closed, nor by the fact that the government put them all under house arrest on election day. Under these dubious circumstances, in a first-past-the-post race, Maïnassara won, with 52 percent of the vote.

The Fourth Republic

In his inaugural address as first president of the **Fourth Republic**, Maïnassara called for national unity as a means of creating social and economic stability. But in its outrage against the manipulation of the elections, the opposition was hardly in the mood to be charitable. As elections for the legislative assembly approached, major opposition parties grouped to form the Front pour la Restauration et la Défense de la Démocratie (**FRDD**), which demanded the presidential election results be annulled and an unbiased election committee be re-established. There was no chance of either happening and, thus cornered into boycotting the elections, the pro-Maïnassara parties swept the seats in the national assembly.

Future attempts to form a government of "national unity" met with equal resistance, so Maïnassara set out to further exclude and silence the opposition. **Human rights** organizations bemoaned the worsening situation, citing increased arrests and internal exile to northern towns and the intimidation of journalists. On the anniversary of the coup, the FRDD organized a demonstration in Niamey, which degenerated into violence. Among those arrested (yet again) were Mahamane, Hama and Issoufou. It was only a precursor of protests that would continue throughout 1997–98, most notably in the politically sensitive Hausa strongholds of Maradi and Zinder.

The government enjoyed more co-operation from the unions, but the privatization programme Maïnassara had committed the country to seemed to put him on a collision course with state workers too. Faced with a very narrow political base, Maïnassara based his presidency on the support of the military. In regional and municipal elections in 1999, the opposition swept the polls throughout the country

– excluding the government strongholds of Dosso and Agadez – but the results were annulled in their most powerful pockets of support, including Tillabéri, Tahoua, Maradi, Zinder and Diffa. Once again, the democratic process had been railroaded and the threat of unrest seemed imminent. And there were rumblings that Maïnassara planned to reshuffle the military to tighten still further his diminishing circle of support.

Before he got the chance, however, Maïnassara was **gunned down**, in April 1999, as he prepared to board the presidential helicopter. Although he was nearly sliced in two by the blast of gunfire that came from his own presidential guard, the military played down the incident as "an unfortunate accident". Junior officers seized power and quickly formed the Conseil de Reconciliation Nationale (**CRN**), headed by Major **Daouda Malam Wanké**, which dissolved the assembly and the supreme court and sacked all senior members of the army and the police. On a more positive note, Wanké immediately held closed-door meetings with the leaders of Niger's five largest political parties to set up guidelines for an interim government and a calendar for the restoration of democracy.

Although the country remained calm following the putsch, **international opinion** came down hard on the new regime. West African leaders condemned the assassination. The EU suspended aid to the country, followed by the Organisation de la Francophonie, the international community of Francophone nations, whose thirtieth-year anniversary was scheduled to be marked in Niamey in 1999.

The turn of the millennium

In October and November 1999 the promised legislative and presidential elections took place. The presidency was won by **Mamadou Tandja**, a retired lieutenant-colonel who had been unsuccessful in the elections of 1993 and 1996. The MNSD, the party he stood for, won the majority of seats in the parliament. Tandja retained former Tuareg rebel leader **Mohammed Anako** as a special advisor and minister without portfolio in the government, a gesture widely seen as a move to appease Tuaregs, who remained frustrated throughout the Maïnassara era at the slow pace of their reintegration into Niger society following the peace accords. Other Tuareg gained posts in the government, too, among them **Rhissa Ag Boula**, who served as minister of tourism for several years.

Early on, President Tandja committed to upholding the structural adjustment that his predecessor had worked out with the IMF and World Bank. But economically, Niger remains a classic case of a country overdependent on a **single resource** – uranium – and thus hostage to commodity-price fluctuations.

Improving agriculture is critical, as only three percent of the land is arable. In 2005 the World Food Programme warned that three million people were in danger from an impending drought, and there were further alarms in 2006, with the World Food Programme claiming that they were feeding 1.5 million people. To try to resolve these issues, vast **irrigation projects** have been undertaken in the regions around Tillabéri, Birnin-Konni and Dosso, and there has also been a trend towards smaller-scale projects involving co-operatives.

Whilst feeding its population remains the biggest problem facing Niger, it's not the only one. Condemnation of the country's tradition of **slavery** – only officially banned in 2003, and still in effect widely practised through institutionalized vassal-lord relationships – has meant that the supply of international aid has occasionally been interrupted. The issue has sometimes been conflated with trans-Saharan **people-trafficking** (truckloads of desperate chancers heading north to Libya and, they hope, Europe) which is, in fact, a separate and serious problem – though since Algeria and Libya deported thousands of Nigériens in 2005 and 2006, dumping them across the border in the desert, the message may

have been received in Agadez and Bilma that spending hard-earned cash on a ride north is a waste of money and potentially a fatal mistake.

In 2006, relations with an important part of the community were soured when the government tried to expel up to 150,000 **Mahamid Arabs** back to Chad. The Arabs, some of whom have lived in Niger for more then three decades since moving across the border to escape drought in the 1970s, are concentrated around Diffa in the southeast (birthplace of President Tandja) where their herds compete for scarce water and grazing with the local population. Some members of the Arab community have risen to senior positions in government and the military, however, and the plan eventually fizzled out after a few thousand Arabs had been expelled.

Looking across its borders, Niger's relations with neighbours have often been troubled. A **dispute with Benin** over the ownership of sixteen small islands in the Niger (believed to be rich in oil and iron) was finally settled in the International Court of Justice in 2005, with Niger awarded ownership of the main island, Lété, and six others. The ruling did little to improve relations, and Niger still depends, uneasily, on Cotonou for its exports of uranium.

The new rebellion

But the most serious development of recent years was the resumption of the **Tuareg rebellion** in 2007. The new group of rebels fight under the name Mouvement des Nigériens pour la Justice (**MNJ**) and may have some support from Libya and the USA's new "war-on-terror" ally, Colonel Gaddafi himself. They have been responsible for the deaths of dozens of Forces Armées Nigériennes (**FAN**) soldiers. Dismissed by President Tandja, who refuses to negotiate with them, as "bandits and drug traffickers", the MNJ is a grouping of Tuareg fighters and activists who don't believe that the promises of the 1995 peace accord are being fulfilled. Their specific grievance is over the revenues from uranium mining in their territory, which they claim line the pockets of the Niamey elite but bring no development to the north, where salt and tourism are the only other – mercurial – sources of income. As long as the rebellion continues, the north can forget about tourism (tourists were banned from the region at the time of writing).

Tandja continues to hope the FAN will achieve military success without alienating civilians in the north. The MNJ, for their part, have been scoring notable successes against the FAN and trying to present themselves as an organized military force, bound by the rules of the Geneva Convention. They called on the Red Cross to evacuate injured government troops – though they kept FAN hostages too.

At the time of writing, early 2008, all the towns of the north were subject to night curfews and effectively under a state of siege. The FAN were rounding up anyone found outside the towns, accusing them of supporting the MNJ, while the MNJ were warning people to leave the towns or risk coming under fire.

There have been **defections** on both sides, but there appears to be little grass-roots support for the MNJ, even among many Tuareg. Mohammed Anako, a key signatory of the 1995 peace accords, is not supporting them and some senior Tuareg have been outspoken: "Beware," said the opposition MP Sanoussi Jackou, "Democracy is not on your side like in the 1990s: the context has changed."

Although people point to the genuine democratic reforms that the country experienced in the first years of the new century, the Nigérien **media** is once again under severe pressure to conform and to support Tandja's line. The local FM relay of Radio France International (the Francophone equivalent of the BBC World Service) was suspended for broadcasting "false information" about the conflict.

With **journalists** barred from the northern region, and the government saying little about an increasingly perilous situation, the media initiative seems to be in the hands of the MNJ, with their busy blog and willingness to be interviewed for the foreign press by satellite phone.

The most critical developments revolve around the status of **Areva**, the largely French government-owned nuclear energy conglomerate, that runs the uranium mining operation in the Aïr Mountains. While the MNJ has severely criticized Areva, and the company's poor environmental record is a scandal in France, there are also strong suggestions that the company has had discussions with the rebels and some reports suggest it has been financing them: the French chief of operations was barred from returning to Niger in July 2007 for unspecified reasons. In Niamey, there is a historical mistrust of France, long suspected of promoting Tuareg nationalist ideals with the aim of creating a Francophile state – Azawad – in the Sahara. But in the end, the row was mostly about the **price paid for uranium**, which Niger managed to get increased, at the same time as it extended prospecting licences to Canadian and Chinese companies.

Meanwhile, the USA's **Pan-Sahel Initiative** which has seen hundreds of American troops and advisors deployed in small teams across the southern Saharan countries to face off a possible threat from Islamic fundamentalists in the region, adds a further unstable element to an already explosive cocktail (in Washington, Niger is associated principally with the infamous claim in the run-up to the Iraq war that Sadam Hussein had tried to buy uranium from Niger).

Although the MNJ has no religious agenda, there is a clear danger that this particular Tuareg rebellion will be dragged onto the same US radar screen as the Al-Qaida Maghreb organization, based across the border in Algeria. It looks like things are going to get a lot more complicated in Niger before peace is restored. Development and progress will be on hold in the meantime.

Music

Not much is heard in Europe about **music from Niger**. A few records of traditional music are available, but little of the modern music travels far.

In Niamey, listen out for performances of the national music and dance troupe **Karaka**. For a taste of Nigérien music, the Agence de Cooperation Culturelle et Technique has put out two volumes of a record entitled *Festival de la Jeunesse Nigérienne*.

Pop artists you may well hear include Hausa singers **Mahaman Garba** and **Yan Ouwa** and the reggae of **Amadou Hamza**. In Niamey, listen out for the female singer, **Madelle Iddari**, as well as **Saadou Bori** and **Moussa Poussy**. Bori's and Poussy's collaborative CD, *Niamey Twice* (Stern's), which helped put Niger on the musical map, features six original compositions from each singer which swing happily along. Bori's music is perhaps the most exciting, thanks to its rare presentation of Hausa influences, and on the more offbeat tracks, like "Dango" and "Bori", the polyrhythms bubble through frenetically.

Inspired by Fula, Hausa, Songhai and Djerma traditional music, **Mamar Kassey** was the first group from Niger to take their music to an international audience and they can now compete with the best from Mali. Their album *Denké-Denké* (Daqui) features flute, lute, percussion, electric guitars and vocals.

As with Mali's Tinariwen, Niger has produced its own desert-rock variants, in the shape of **Tidawt**, whose lolloping acoustic guitars have been a big hit on tour in the US, and **Etran Finatawa**, who combine the music cultures of the Tuareg and the Wodaabé (Fula). *Introducing Etran Finatawa* (World Music Network) is a set of hypnotic, muscular songs, blending traditional instruments and Wodaabé polyphony with electric guitars.

Lastly, hip-hop, which has, of course, taken off in a big way in Niger, especially in Niamey and the southwest, with youthful rappers venting their views in a range of Nigérien languages, French and snatches of English. Artists to listen out for include the **Metaphore** crew, **Kamikaz** and **Rass Idris**.

Cinema

Nigérien **cinema** has been dominated by three film-makers: Oumarou Ganda, Moustapha Alassane and Djingareye Maïga. Unfortunately, its heyday was in the first decades after independence and recent years have seen a cinematic drought.

Oumarou Ganda began his career as an actor in Jean Rouch's *Moi, un Noir*, after he was discovered by the noted French cinéaste on the docks in Abidjan. After appearing in other Rouch films, notably *La Pyramide Humaine*, he went on to become a film-maker in his own right and one of the great cultural archivists of African cinema, with works such as the autobiographical *Wazzou Polygame*, which won the Étalon de Yennenga (first prize) at the first-ever FESPACO in 1972; *Saitane*, which looks critically at the authority of the Muslim marabouts; and *L'Exilé*. He died in a road accident in 1981, at the age of 46, while filming *Gani*

Kouré, Le Vainqueur de Gourma. Reflecting a distribution problem faced by most contemporary African film-makers, you're more likely to see his films abroad, or possibly at Niamey's Franco-Nigérien Cultural Centre, than in any of the few Nigérien cinemas.

Jean Rouch also inspired another relatively well known film-maker, **Moustapha Alassane**. After studying at the Institut Nigérien de Recherche en Sciences Humaines, Alassane made a number of shorts in the 1960s, including *Aouré* and *La Bague du Roi Koda*. One of his most best-loved films was *Femme, Villa, Voiture, Argent* (1972), a popular comedy dealing with the issue of cultural identity.

The third director to gain international acclaim was **Djingareye Maïga**, producer of *L'Etoile Noire*, in which he also starred. Like many early African film-makers, Maïga's movies deal with the clash between Western values and traditional wisdom. His last feature, in 1986, was *Le Médecin de Gafire*.

Books

Published material in English on Niger is really limited: if you want more than the handful of volumes devoted to the country, you'll need to read French. The late **Boubou Hama** was one of Niger's most prolific writers, publishing historical works on the empires of Gao and Songhai. A former president of the National Assembly, he also wrote works on politics, philosophy and folklore. For good general titles, including some with a strong Niger connection, see p.35.

Carol Beckwith and Marion Van Offelen *Nomads of Niger.* Superbly illustrated essay on the Wodaabé Bororo and the Cure Salée.

Robert B. Charlick *Niger: Personal Rule and Survival in the Sahel* (o/p). Profile of the nation.

Peter Chilson *Riding the Demon: On the Road in West Africa.* Account of a year spent crisscrossing Niger by *taxi brousse*, getting inside the lives of drivers and passengers – recommended preparatory reading for serious budget travellers.

Jeremy Keenan *Sahara Man: Travelling with the Tuareg.* Political scientist Keenan lived with the Kel Ahaggar Tuareg in southern Algeria in the 1960s and returned to Tamanrasset in 1999 to find old friends.

Paul Stoller *Fusion of the Worlds: an Ethnography of Possession among the Songhay of Niger,* and **Paul Stoller and Cheryl Olkes** *In Sorcery's Shadow: a Memoir of Apprenticeship among the Songhay.* Stoller is a kind of Nigérien answer to Carlos Castaneda – apprenticed to a sorcerer, taking drugs. All interesting stuff.

Fiction

Kathlin Hill *Still Water in Niger.* In this novel, the unnamed narrator returns to Zinder after seventeen years.

Ibrahim Issa *Grandes Eaux Noires.* The first Nigérien novel to be published (before independence), this humorously manages to describe the travails of second-century BC Mediterranean explorers south of the Sahara.

Language

Surpassing even French and English, **Hausa** is the most international language in West Africa, estimated to be spoken by between 25 million and 100 million people. In terms of the area over which it's spoken, Hausa is today second only to Swahili in sub-Saharan Africa. The language developed into a regional lingua franca in the fifteenth century, when Hausa traders led caravans to North Africa, and it was through such commercial liaisons that Hausa became a trade language throughout northwest Africa.

Hausa

Though there are many dialects of Hausa, the two most important are **Kano** and **Sokoto**. Differences are primarily phonetic and discrepancies don't prevent speakers of different dialects from understanding each other. The following words and phrases are based on the Kano dialect, which is generally considered to be "classical" Hausa.

Greetings

If the following list seems long and trivial, it barely gives a taste of the extended formal exchange that's so important in Hausa, as in most African languages.

Salamu alaikum	All-purpose greeting (men)
Alaika salamu	(Response)
Sanu	Greetings
Yauwa, sanu kadai	(Response)
Kazo lafiya?	Are you in good health?
Lafiya lau	(Response)
Ina gida?	How's the household/ your family?
Ina kwana?	Good morning (lit. How was the night?)
Yaya yara?	How are your children?
Lafiya lau	Fine (general response)
Ina gajiya?	Are you tired? (lit. How's the tiredness?)
Ba gajiya	No, I'm not tired
Ina labari?	What's the news?
Labari sai alheri	Everything's fine
Barka da yamma	Good afternoon
Barka kadai	(Response)
Sai gobe	See you tomorrow
To, sai gobe	Okay, see you tomorrow
Sai an juma	See you later
To, sai an juma	Okay, see you later

Shopping

Nawa nawa ne?	How much?
Akwai lemo?	Do you have oranges?
I, akwai/ ah ah babu	Yes, I have/ no I don't have
Lemo, nawa nawa ne?	How much are your oranges?
Kai, suna da tsada!	They're expensive!
Zan biya ka dela ashirin	I'll give you CFA100
Albarka	No deal (seller refusing)
Kawo kudi	Give the money (offer accepted)

Numbers

daya	1
biyu	2
uku	3
hudu	4
biyar	5
shida	6
bakwai	7
takwas	8
tara	9
goma	10
goma sha daya	11
goma sha biyu	12
ashirin	20
ashirin da biyar	25
talatin	30
arba'in	40
hamsin	50
sittin	60
saba'in	70
saba'in da biyar	75

tamanin	80
casa'in	90
(or tamanin da goma)	
dari	100
dari biyu	200
dari biyu da hamsin	250
dubu	1000

The dela

In Niger, money is commonly counted in multiples of CFA5 (*dela*) – which can be difficult to calculate even if you're thinking in English.

CFA100	dela ashirin
CFA150	dela talatin
CFA200	dela arba'in
CFA450	dela tamanin da goma
CFA500	dela dar
CFA1000	jikai

Glossary

(13)

NIGER | Basics

Azalaï Camel caravan.
Baba Old man; a term of respect.
Birni Hausa word meaning a formerly fortified town and referring specifically to the walls, hence the (misspelled) town name Birnin-Konni.
Boro Bi Black person or people.
Canaris Large clay pots for storing water.
Dela CFA5, used as a basic unit for enumerating prices; thus CFA100 is expressed as twenty delas.
Djoliba Malinké name for the Niger. Literally "River of Blood", since the body of water was as vital to life as blood flowing in the veins.

Erg Shifting sand dunes common in the Ténéré.
Fech-fech Soft sand hidden beneath a hard crust.
Gravures rupestres Rock paintings, common in the Aïr and Djado regions.
Kaya-kaya Wandering salesmen.
Kori Seasonal river course, or wadi (Hausa).
Razzia Slave raid.
Reg Stony wastes.
Wonki-wonki Launderers, common along the banks of the Niger in Niamey.
Zongo Section of a town or village where newly arrived strangers live.

13.1

Niamey

As uranium money showered on Niger in the 1970s, **NIAMEY** changed rapidly. Many of its dusty roads were paved, and a Voie Triomphale was traced through town, its bright streetlights blotting the Sahelian nights from memory. Avant-garde buildings such as the Palais des Congrès and, fittingly, the Office National de Recherches Minières were built, to be joined by a scattering of futuristic hotels, banks and offices. This development, however, was nowhere near as dramatic as in Abidjan or Lagos, and the juxtaposition of modernity and tradition remains less jarring. Although it's rarer than it used to be to see camels being led over Kennedy Bridge, Niamey is not part of some metropolitan sprawl but a city planted in the bush, as the spectacle of Fula and Djerma traders gathering at the Petit Marché in the shadow of the office blocks attests.

Two decades ago Niamey was one of the key stopovers for trans-Saharan overland tourists. But the combination of the civil conflict in Algeria and Tuareg rebellions in Niger and Mali put an end to the steady flow of travellers, and Niamey's tourist industry almost ground to a halt. In the early 2000s, visitors began slowly trickling back, but the 2007 Tuareg rebellion halted the process again. Until a general all-clear is sounded in the northern regions of Niger traditionally popular with overlanders, the lack of tourists visiting the capital makes for an agreeably low-key atmosphere, while the city also offers a fairly good (by the standards of this part of the world) museum, good markets and some pleasant excursions within a short drive of the centre.

Some history

Before the colonial era, Niamey was no more than a small village whose origins probably didn't predate the eighteenth century. When French troops swarmed into the desert in the 1890s, they recognized the strategic importance of this spot on the river and dug in their heels. By 1902, Niamey had grown into one of the most important military and administrative posts east of Bamako. When Niger officially became a colony, the larger urban centre at Zinder was chosen as the new capital, but the French administrators preferred Niamey's climate and, in 1926, transferred the capital back again.

Throughout the colonial era, Niamey never developed much beyond the **European quarter** built in the plateau district. The population in the 1930s was under two thousand, though by independence it had increased to around thirty thousand. Real growth only occurred in the 1970s, with the population surging to a quarter of a million by 1980. A great deal of the influx was caused by the **drought** of the mid-1970s, which sparked a rural exodus of biblical proportions. Niamey, fattened on uranium income, flourished as immigrants from the devastated provinces poured into the city to find work. Further periodic droughts have brought new waves of immigrants and today it's estimated that the best part of a million people live in Niamey, representing every ethnic group in the country.

Arrival, orientation and information

Niamey's **Diori Hamani airport** (☎20.73.47.25) is 10km southeast of the city centre on the Boulevard de l'Amitié (which becomes the Boulevard du 15 Avril).

GREATER NIAMEY

ACCOMMODATION
Camping Touristique ... A
Chez Tatayi ... C
Hôtel du Sahel ... E
Ténéré ... D
Village Chinois ... B

RESTAURANTS, BARS & CLUBS
Bada ... 6
Le Byblos ... 4
Chez Chin ... 3
Les Délices ... 2
Le Djimkoumé ... 5
Diamangou ... 8
Guiguinya ... 7
Ize-Gani ... 9
Le Tinga ... 1

13.1 NIGER

1034

There are no buses from here into the centre, so you'll have to take a cab (around CFA5000 day or night). You can often get good deals on **flights to Europe**, notably with Air Algérie, Royal Air Maroc and Point-Afrique. For up-to-date information, contact the airlines direct. There are no scheduled **domestic flights** in Niger, though you could charter an aircraft from Nigeravia (see p.1042).

Niamey spreads along 10km of the Niger's left (north) bank, and has now expanded to the other side of the river. The size of the city makes it difficult to get an immediate grip on its layout – a problem compounded by the French-style planning, with a radiating street grid and numerous roundabouts.

You'll spend virtually your whole time on the left bank. To define a centre, use the **Pont Kennedy** as a landmark. To the north of the bridge, rue de Gaweye leads straight up to the **Grand Marché**, bordered by Boulevard de la Liberté. The entire **commercial centre** lies between this new market and the river, and this is where you'll come to shop, eat, change money and visit sights such as the **Musée National**. A bank and a number of airline offices are located in two important commercial buildings along rue de Gaweye: **Immeuble Sonara II** and **Immeuble El Nasr**. Northeast of the Grand Marché, rue du Sénégal leads to the residential neighbourhoods of **Abidjan** and **Kalleye**, and to Niamey's **Grande Mosquée**.

To the **northwest of Pont Kennedy**, Avenue Mitterrand runs past the impressive *Hôtel Gaweye* as it heads towards the tree-lined avenues of the **Plateau district**. This

Niamey surface arrivals and departures

Arriving by *taxi brousse*, you're most likely to be dropped off at the **Wadata gare routière** – also known as Ecogare Wadata – in the east Niamey district of the same name, about 4km from the centre. Wadata is the main *gare* for Peugeot 504s and Japanese minibuses to: Tillabéri; Dosso and Gaya; Birnin-Konni, Maradi and Zinder; and Tahoua and Agadez.

EHGM

The big buses of **EHGM** (aka Maissagé, short for El Hadji Garba Maissagé; ☎20.74.37.16) stop at the EHGM terminal 500m south of Wadata with services to: Zinder via Maradi; Arlit via Tahoua and Agadez; and nonstop to Diffa. The same *autogare* serves most **international destinations**, including Kano, Cotonou and Lomé.

Burkina transport

Taxis to Burkina leave from the Rive Droite – across the Pont Kennedy from the city centre, near the customs (*douanes*). This is also where you can catch a *taxi brousse* to Say (and possibly on to Tamou for the Parc National du "W"). To leave quickly, it's best to break up the trip, paying for a seat in anything heading in the direction of Kantchari, the Burkinabe border town. From here, you can catch another bush taxi or bus for Ouagadougou. Arrive early in the morning as traffic on this stretch is sparse – after midday, you could wait hours for a vehicle.

SNTV

SNTV buses are the obvious choice for international travel, and have their own **gare SNTV** on avenue de Gamkalé, southeast of the city centre. There are daily SNTV services to **Ouagadougou** (CAF10,000; departs 6am); **Cotonou** and **Lomé** (departs 3.30am); **Arlit** and **Agadez** (departs 3.30am); and **Zinder** (departs 5am). SNTV services to **Gao** run on Monday and Thursday. On other days you might want to consider using Askia Transport or Bahiya (you'll find their ticket offices next to the Grand Marché).

You'll need to buy **SNTV tickets** in advance to be sure of a seat. If you can't get to their *gare* in Gamkalé, you can always visit one of their city-centre agents, such as Boukoki, behind the Garage Mairie, next to the Station Azawak on Boulevard Mali Béro (the road with Ecogare Wadata on it).

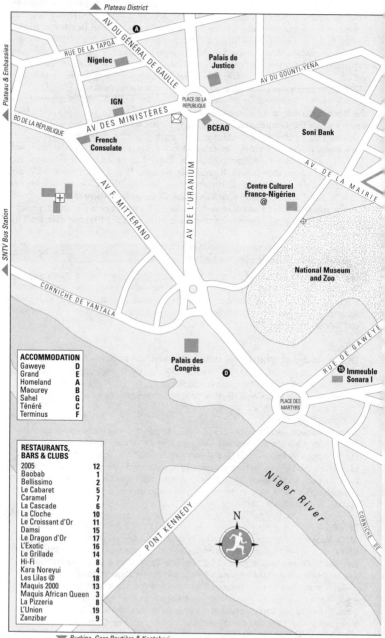

Plateau District

AV DU GÉNÉRAL DE GAULLE

RUE DE LA TAPOA

Nigelec

Plateau & Embassies

IGN

BD DE LA RÉPUBLIQUE

AV DES MINISTÈRES

French
Consulate

AV F MITTERAND

SNTV Bus Station

CORNICHE DE YANTALA

Palais de
Justice

AV DU GOUNTI-YENA

PLACE DE LA
RÉPUBLIQUE

BCEAO

AV DE L'URANIUM

Soni Bank

AV DE LA MAIRIE

Centre Culturel
Franco-Nigérien
@

National Museum
and Zoo

RUE DE GAWEYE

Palais des
Congrès

D

Immeuble
Sonara I

PLACE DES
MARTYRS

Niger River

CORNICHE DE

N

PONT KENNEDY

ACCOMMODATION

Gaweye	D
Grand	E
Homeland	A
Maourey	B
Sahel	G
Ténéré	C
Terminus	F

**RESTAURANTS,
BARS & CLUBS**

2005	12
Baobab	1
Bellissimo	2
Le Cabaret	5
Caramel	7
La Cascade	6
La Cloche	10
Le Croissant d'Or	11
Damsi	15
Le Dragon d'Or	17
L'Exotic	16
Le Grillade	14
Hi-Fi	8
Kara Noreyui	4
Les Lilas @	18
Maquis 2000	13
Maquis African Queen	3
La Pizzeria	8
L'Union	19
Zanzibar	9

Burkina, Gare Routière & Kantchari

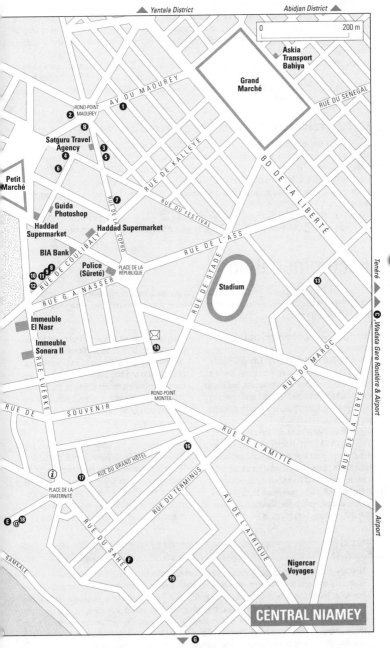

0   200 m

Askia
Transport
Bahiya

Grand
Marché

RUE DU SENEGAL

AV DU MAOUREY

ROND-POINT
MAOUREY ❷ ❶

BD DE LA LIBERTÉ

Satguru Travel
Agency ❽

❸
❹ ❺

❻

RUE DE KALLEYE

Petit
Marché

❼

RUE DE LA COPRO

RUE DU FESTIVAL

Guida
Photoshop

Haddad
Supermarket

Haddad Supermarket

RUE DE L'ASS

BIA Bank

RUE DE COULIBALY

Police
(Sûreté)

PLACE DE LA
RÉPUBLIQUE

RUE DE STADE

Stadium

❿ ❾❽
⓬

❶❸

RUE G.A. NASSER

Immeuble
El Nasr

Immeuble
Sonara II

RUE LIEBKE

✉
⓮

RUE DE SOUVENIR

ROND-POINT
MONTEIL

RUE DU MAROC

RUE DE L'AMITIÉ

RUE DE LA LIBYE

⓰

ⓘ
⓱

RUE DU GRAND HÔTEL

PLACE DE LA
FRATERNITÉ

Ⓔ @⓲

GAMKALE

RUE DU SAHEL

Ⓕ

RUE DU TERMINUS

AV DE L'AFRIQUE

Nigercar
Voyages

⓳

CENTRAL NIAMEY

Ⓖ

colonial neighbourhood is where most government ministries are located, along with the Palais du Président and many of the embassies. Continuing west, you come to the bustling **Yantala districts** (Yantala Haut is south of bd de l'Indépendance, while Yantala Bas is to the north), which you'll become familiar with if you stay at the *Camping Touristique* overlanders' place near the entrance to town on the Tillabéri road.

Southeast of Pont Kennedy, the rue du Sahel leads to the comfortably shaded residential streets of **Niamey Bas** district, where you'll find a good number of hotels and restaurants. Further east, Niamey Bas gives onto the **Gamkalé district** and then to the capital's **industrial zone**.

City transport and information

It's easy to get a taxi into town from the Wadata *gare routière* and other road-transport arrival points: seats in **collective taxis** cost around CFA200 and around twice that after midnight. If you hire the whole cab as a *location* it will cost around CFA1000 per short trip. **City buses** (daylight hours only) work out a little cheaper than shared taxis but there are no printed schedules or map routes and they're very infrequent.

Staff at the **tourist office**, on rue Luebke at place de la Fraternité (Mon–Fri 8am–noon & 3.30–6pm; ☏20.73.24.47), aren't much help with anything practical.

Accommodation

Although Niamey has a number of mid-range and expensive **hotels**, there are few budget options, though some relief is provided by the **camping site** out of town and the ever-popular *Chez Tatayi*.

Budget accommodation and camping

Camping Touristique route de Tillabéri, Yantala (CFA200 by shared taxi from the centre). Set in a spacious site with two bar-restaurants, this is now somewhat run down and only just about hanging on while the overland trade is subdued. CFA3500 per person.

Chez Tatayi route de l'Entente ☏20.74.12.81. Niamey's backpacker centre, this is a truly great little spot with cleanish rooms, a kitchen and dining area available for guests to use, a whole bookcase of books and magazines (some in English) and a fairly convenient location within walking distance of Ecogare Wadata. Dorm beds CFA5000 or rooms with fan ❸ or a/c ❹.

Village Chinois bd du Zarmaganda, next to the new stadium ☏20.72.33.98. Fair-value basic accommodation. The functional and clean rooms all come with one single and one double bed and each pair of rooms shares one toilet and shower. There's also safe parking, a cheap restaurant and a pleasant outdoor bar doing grilled fish. Rooms with fan or a/c ❷.

Mid-range to top-end hotels

Maourey Rond-Point Maourey ☏20.73.28.50 ✉hotmaou@yahoo.ne. Set in a good location midway between the Grand Marché and the Petit Marché, this is quite a friendly little place, at the bottom end of this category, but with decent and reasonably priced self-contained a/c rooms. ❺

Security

Niamey has gone through a rough period in recent years, and the increase in crime is mainly the result of Niger's dismal economy. The principal area to avoid is the **river bank** on the north side, especially the stretch along the corniches. The area around the **Petit Marché** can also seem tense, though given the volume of people, the greatest danger here – and also in front of the **banks** – is posed by pickpockets. Apart from these areas, the town still feels quite safe, even at night, and by taking precautions (like leaving all bags at your hotel) you're unlikely to feel, or be, threatened.

Hôtel du Sahel rue du Sahel ☎20.73.24.31
@hotel_sahel2006@yahoo.fr. Well-maintained
and comfortable place, with 35 a/c rooms (some
facing the river) and a selection of bungalows in
the grounds. Restaurant with pizzeria, cybercafé
and *Fofo* disco. ❺

Ténéré bd de la Liberté ☎20.73.20.20
ⓦwww.hoteltenere.com. West of the
centre, popular with local businessmen, friendly
and with a refreshing lack of formality, with
spacious a/c rooms, a restaurant and a popular
poolside bar. ❻
Terminus rue du Sahel ☎20.73.26.92/93 @hotermi
@intnet.ne. Thirty-eight good-value a/c bungalows
and 14 rooms, set around a well-kept garden, plus a
swimming pool, gym, bar and restaurant. ❼

Luxury hotels
Gaweye place Kennedy, near the Palais des
Congrès and the river ☎20.72.27.10 @gaweye@
intnet.ne. Once Niamey's most luxurious hotel and
still the number one place for expense-account
travellers, the *Gaweye* is a bit impersonal but
is little different in this respect from others in
this category. The fully equipped rooms come
with either river or museum view, and facilities
include a pool, tennis courts, restaurants, bars and
nightclubs. ❽

Grand place de la Fraternité ☎20.73.26.41
ⓦwww.grandhotelniger.com. With its more
informal atmosphere, this hotel holds its own
against the more modern competitors on either
side and is once again leading the field as Niamey's smartest hotel. Choose between comfortable
rooms or slightly bigger bungalows (same price).
There's also a great pool and restaurant. ❽
Homeland rue de la Tapoa ☎20.72.32.82
@homeland@intnet.ne. Three-star place in a quiet,
leafy location near the Centre Culturel Américain.
Pleasant pool, kind staff, comfy rooms, but rather
overpriced – though good low-season discounts
are available. ❽

The City

Niamey isn't exactly brimming with pleasures and pastimes, but it's not difficult to
find ways of passing the day. The obvious place to start is the **National Museum**
complex, which, apart from exhibits on culture and peoples, incorporates extensive
gardens, a zoo and various shops. Niamey also boasts a couple of innovative cultural
centres, regularly featuring exhibitions, films, and theatre and dance performances.
The **markets**, too, each with its own character, provide active diversions – the
Grand Marché is one of the biggest in the Sahel.

The Musée National

Opened in 1959, the **Musée National** (closed Mon; Nov–March 9am–noon &
3.30–5.30pm; April–Oct 9am–noon & 4–6pm; museum grounds 8am–6.30pm;
CFA1000, camera CFA5000) was a radical breakthrough at the time and is still out
on its own among West African museums. Contained within the extensive grounds
are the exhibition halls, a zoo, a working crafts centre and samples of Nigérien
housing styles. The place feels alive and, especially at weekends, is crowded with an
eclectic mix of young and old, foreign and local, scholarly and illiterate.

The main entrance to the grounds is from a side-street off the Avenue de la Mairie.
Before heading into one of the pavilions housing the exhibition spaces, take a stroll
around the **zoo** – especially popular with young kids from town. A big draw are
the hippos in their artificial pond, but cages scattered around the grounds display
other fauna of Niger – lions, hyenas, various monkeys, crocodiles and tortoises, all in
a reasonable state of health, though in depressingly cramped cages. Aviaries contain
vultures and a variety of more colourful birds.

Each of the museum pavilions – constructed in a stylized Hausa architectural
design – is dedicated to a particular theme, such as costumes and jewellery,
weapons, handicrafts and musical instruments. The paleontology and botany
pavilion contains **dinosaur skeletons** from Gadoufaoua, in the Agadez region.
Discovered accidentally by geologists prospecting for uranium, these skeletons are
around 100 million years old, and the remote district is today one of the world's
most renowned dinosaur sites. You won't miss the fearsome, reconstructed skeleton

of *Suchomimus*, an 11-metre long "crocodile mimic" whose head rocks gently. Outside the same pavilion, set in concrete, are two dry branches of the famous **Arbre du Ténéré**, a tree that once stood alone in the Ténéré Desert and became a famous overlanders' landmark until it was knocked over by a truck driver. Formerly the only living thing for hundreds of miles around – and still marked on the Michelin map – the tree was transported to the museum and a sturdy steel replacement erected in the desert.

One section of the park is home to various examples of traditional Nigérien housing – a good opportunity to compare Fula thatched cones, Hausa mud-brick and plaster, Tuareg tents and other styles. The park also houses a *buvette* (bar) serving cold drinks and tasty *brochettes*. In addition, be sure to check out the **Centre Artisanale**. Goods sold here are usually more expensive than on the streets (in certain cases, substantially so), but part of the profits subsidizes the museum. Quality is controlled, so your silver jewellery won't turn green hours after you buy it or the camel-hide bag smell suspiciously of goat when it gets wet.

Cultural centres

Across from the museum's main entrance, the **Centre Culturel Franco-Nigérien** (℡20.73.48.34 Ⓦwww.ccfn.ne) has a busy schedule that includes exhibits by local artists and craftsmen, dance and theatre performances, and regular outdoor film screenings. You can stop by and pick up their events programme, or check the pages of *Le Sahel*. There's also a library and **Internet café** here.

Right across on the other side of town on Boulevard Mali Béro, near the Grande Mosquée, is the **Centre Culturel Oumarou-Ganda**, named after the late, great Nigérien film-maker. The centre's open-air amphitheatre hosts performances of traditional music, ballet and theatre, and there's also an open-air cinema. Check the local papers for details of upcoming events.

The **Centre Culturel Américain** (Mon 9am–noon & 3–6pm, Wed, Fri & Sat 9am–noon ℡20.73.31.69) also sponsors events and screens American news and movies (Wed & Fri 4.30pm; free). It's located off av du Général de Gaulle near Nigelec, the state electricity supplier; ask a taxi to drop you there, and then follow the dirt side-street behind the petrol station.

The markets

Niamey's **Grand Marché** (daily until sunset) – also called the Nouveau Marché – makes a decidedly modern statement, with monumental entrance gates and a couple of fountains for show (neither are usually working), although the smooth lines and earth tones respect the more traditional styles of the Sahel. Inside, paved alleys lead through a maze of stalls grouped according to wares – clothing and fabrics; soaps, cosmetics and pharmaceuticals; hardware; ironmongery and utensils; and so forth. Along with the main market in Ouagadougou, this is one of West Africa's finest.

Ten minutes' walk southwest, in the **Zongo district**, where rue du Président Luebke and avenue de la Mairie intersect, the **Petit Marché** has a more casual flavour. Traders who can't secure a space in one of the Grand Marché stalls simply clear space on the ground and set up shop here. It's primarily a **food** market, and you'll find a good selection of fruits and vegetables, meat, fish and grains. People from all over the country converge here to buy and sell – a wide mixture of Fula, Djerma, Tuareg and Hausa. Nearby streets give way to **crafts** stands – reasonable places to pick up jewellery, leather goods or blankets, though dealers tend to be aggressive and bargaining can turn into a battle.

There's another small market, devoted entirely to **pottery**, across from the tall Soni Bank down av de la Mairie – look out for the beautiful hand-painted water pots produced in the village of Tondibia, just outside Niamey.

Eating and drinking

Niamey's **street vendors** are widespread and in the mornings there's a *caféman* on every busy corner, while evening stalls sell *fufu*, rice, macaroni or *tô* (cornmeal dough). The city also has some good, upmarket **restaurants**.

Inexpensive

During the day, you can get really cheap food at the Petit or Grand Marché or the *gare routière*. For street food after dark – notably beef *brochettes* or omelettes with onions, tomatoes and Maggi sauce – head for the places around rue de Kabekoira. If you're staying at *Chez Tatayi* you'll also find several decent street vendors on avenue de L'Entente. The Nigerian "stew man" on the corner of Boulevard Mali Béro serves delicious meat stew with bread for CFA550, and is extremely popular with the locals. You can eat at all the places listed below for under CFA1500.

Baobab av du Maourey near the Grand Marché. Excellent Senegalese place, perfect for a quick and filling cheap meal, with rice or spaghetti stews (CFA700) and, unusually, bottles of *bissap* juice (CFA150). Gets packed with local business types at lunchtimes.

Caramel (Chez Michel) rue de la Copro. Pastry shop with decent, affordable croissants, brioches and sandwiches on home-made bread.

Les Délices bd de l'Indépendance, next to *Le Tinga*. One of Niamey's oldest and best bakeries and patisseries, a great place to reacquaint yourself with croissants and coffee.

Le Grillade south of the PTT and sharing the same plot. Popular fast-food restaurant with pleasant outdoor seating.

Guiguinya av de L'Entente. Largely a local bar and pick-up joint, this place deserves a mention as the nearest "restaurant" to *Chez Tatayi*, and because of its tasty and very cheap food (rice with vegetable sauce for CFA300 for example). But ask for the price of everything and count your change.

Kara Noreyui rue du Festival. Another cheap and cheerful Senegalese place, lacking the atmosphere (and the *bissap*) of the *Baobab* but pleasant enough and fine value.

Les Lilas rue de Grand Hôtel. One of the town's smartest and best-stocked patisseries, as befits its location by the entrance to the *Grand Hôtel*.

Maquis African Queen rue de la Copro. Despite the extravagant claims on its signboard about serving food from all over West Africa, this is mainly a drinking den for the owner and his mates. Nevertheless, it's cheap, does *riz sauce* and other basics, and tends to be open longer hours than the nearby *Baobab* and *Kara Noreyui*.

Snack Bar La Cloche Near the corner of rue Luebke and rue du Coulibaly. Expat haunt serving salads, sandwiches and *chawarma*.

L'Union Behind *Hôtel Le Terminus*. A friendly, colourful place serving inexpensive, well-made food and cool beer in a small courtyard.

Moderate

From Italian pizza to Ivoirian *poisson braisé*, it's possible to treat yourself to something a little out of the ordinary without spending much more than CFA4000.

Bellissimo Rond Point Maourey. Beauty salon and café rolled into one, with a terrace overlooking the busy junction. Standard African dishes (*brochettes* and the like) with a good alcohol selection and occasional live music at weekends.

Le Croissant d'Or rue de Coulibaly. Patisserie patronized by French expats – a good sign if you crave something sweet.

Damsi ground floor of Imm Sonara I. Excellent French, African and Asian food served on the terrace.

Diamangou corniche de Gamkalé ☎20.73.51.43 (take a cab there and back). French and African dishes (try the *brochettes*

de capitaine), and served aboard a boat docked on the Niger – one of the town's more romantic venues, and often completely full. A fantastic spot for a sundowner over one of their great aperitifs.

Le Djinkoumé behind the German embassy in Plateau (closed Mon). A popular place serving mouthwatering Togolese and Nigérien dishes.

L'Exotic rue de Grand Hôtel. Not as exotic as its name suggests, this is nevertheless a fun pizzeria-cum-ice-cream restaurant with pleasant outdoor seating and live music most weekends.

Maquis 2000 behind the old stadium. Slightly upmarket Ivoirian food, featuring shellfish and *grillades* served on a pleasant terrace.

La Pizzeria rue du Coulibaly, next to *Hi-Fi*.
Niamey's best pizza, using real mozzarella
and fresh vegetables, as well as many other well-
prepared Italian dishes.

Le Tinga bd de l'Indépendance, near the *Délices
Pâtisserie*. Not the most authentic Chinese restaurant
you'll ever come across but good value and set in an
atmospheric garden illuminated by red lanterns.

Expensive

Niamey has a surprisingly good selection of upmarket places to eat, with the raw
ingredients usually imported direct from France. You'll pay up to CFA10,000
or more.

Bada av du Général de Gaulle ☏ 20.72.59.29.
Excellent Asian restaurant, specializing in Japanese
and Korean dishes.

Le Byblos bd de l'Indépendance, Plateau.
Classy Lebanese restaurant and perhaps the
most authentic Middle Eastern food in West Africa.
Choose between outdoor seating in a relaxing
compound garden, or eating inside in what looks
like a large sitting-room.

La Cascade near the Petit Marché ☏ 20.73.28.32.
Still one of the best restaurants in town, with
Lebanese/French dishes and a flair with fish.

Chez Chin bd de l'Indépendance, Plateau
☏ 20.72.25.28. Popular Chinese restaurant with
seating in an air-conditioned interior and on a
pleasant outdoor terrace.

Le Dragon d'Or rue du Grand Hôtel
☏ 20.73.41.23. Very popular place serving a wide
variety of Chinese food.

Nightlife

At first glance, **Niamey nights** seem very low-key, but if you persevere there's a lot
of fun to be had. The bigger hotels have **discos** – the *El Raï* at the *Gaweye* and the
Fofo at the *Sahel* for example (the latter can be fun at weekends) – with high covers
and expensive drinks. Downtown clubs include:

2005 near *La Cloche*. One of the best clubs in the
centre, drawing an enthusiastic crowd (Thurs is
ladies' night). Mainly Western music.

Le Cabaret near the *Hôtel Maourey*. This
outdoor bar is a good place for a less Eurocentric
evening out – if you're lucky, there'll be a
spontaneous outbreak of dancing (most likely
Fri or Sat).

La Cloche rue du Coulibaly. European-style place
(and full of hookers after dark), though if this
doesn't put you off, it's actually quite fun, with
a pool table and pinball machines, plus a great

selection of Lebanese snacks. They even have
nargileh (hubble-bubble pipes).

Hi-Fi rue du Coulibaly. Energetic – at weekends
anyway – and with a good mix of African and
Western music and occasional Senegalese nights.

Ize-Gani corniche de Gamkalé (take a cab there
and back). Glitzy and exotic place, popular with
expats and always crowded at weekends, when
you can dance under the stars until the wee hours.

Zanzibar rue du Coulibaly, by *Hi-Fi*. European-
owned and one of the more laid-back bars in this
area, with a fine alcohol selection.

Listings

Airlines Air Algérie ☏ 20.73.32.14, Royal
Air Maroc ☏ 20.73.28.85, Toumai Air Tchad
☏ 20.33.04.05, all in Imm El Nasr; Air Burkina
☏ 20.73.31.21, Air France (responsible for Air
Ivoire and Air Sénégal) ☏ 20.73.31.21, in Imm
Sonara I; Point-Afrique (known locally as Point Air
Niger), opposite *Hôtel Terminus* ☏ 20.73.40.26;
Sahel Airlines/Afriqiyah Airways/Sudan Airways
☏ 20.73.65.71, rue de Rivoli.

Air Charter Nigeravia, opposite the tourist office,
rue Luebke ☏ 20.73.30.64. You're looking at
a minimum of CFA500,000/hr for a six-seater
plane.

Banks and cash advances Most banks are on,
or near, av de la Mairie; the most convenient are
the BIA, BOA and SONI Bank. All charge a flat fee of
CFA10,000 for cash advances. The one exception
to this rule appears to be the Western Union office,

at the back of the main BOA building, which was not charging the CFA10,000 when last visited.

Books, newspapers and magazines Guida Photoshop, around the corner from Haddad Supermarket on av de la Mairie, is well stocked with French newspapers, international magazines (mostly French), coffee-table books, Michelin maps and a wide selection of travel guides. For browsing, there's also the library at the American Cultural Centre (see "Cultural centres", p.1040).

Car rental The country's Avis representative, CFAO Niger (T 20.74.01.58), has its office on route de l'Aéroport. Nigercar Voyages, av de l'Afrique (T 20.73.23.31 E nicarvoy@intnet.ne W tinyurl .com/38vuhy), is the most professional outfit in town, with a wide range of vehicles available. The tourist office (see p.1038) may also be able to set you up with less formal rental agencies.

Cinemas Check out what's on at the two cultural centres (see p.1040).

Embassies and consulates Algeria, off av de l'Imazer, Plateau T 20.72.35.83; Benin, Plateau T 20.72.32.19; Canada, off bd Mali Béro near the junction to av des Zarmakoye T 20.75.36.86; Chad, av du Général de Gaulle, Plateau T 20.75.34.64; France (consulate) place Nelson Mandela T 20.72.27.22 (issues visas for many Francophone African countries, including Burkina Faso, Côte d'Ivoire, Senegal and Togo); Germany, av du Général de Gaulle T 20.72.35.10 E amb-all-ny@web.de; Guinea (Honorary Consulate) T 20.73.89.17; Mali, just off bd des Sy et Mamar T 20.75.42.90; Mauritania, off bd Mali Béro, Yantala T 20.72.38.43; Morocco, rue Luebke T 20.73.40.84; Nigeria, bd des Ambassades, 400m west of the US embassy T 20.73.24.10; UK, Mrs Susan Jarrett (British Honorary Consul) T 20.72.38.60 or 96.87.81.30; USA, bd des Ambassades, Yantala T 20.73.31.69 W niamey .usembassy.gov.

Internet access You won't have any trouble finding Internet cafés in Niamey. Cyberspace (Tues–Sat 9am–12.30pm & 3.30–6.30pm; CFA500/hr), at the Centre Culturel Franco-Nigérien, across from the National Museum, has pretty good connections most of the time and is one of the more comfortable places to surf the Net. Pl@net is handy for those staying near the *gare* Wadata and is reasonably priced (CFA500/hr), if a little cramped

and clammy. *Pâtisserie Les Lilas* has an Internet café branch by the entrance to the *Grand Hôtel*. Telstar Niger, 17 rue Taiwo, is supposed to have a Wi-Fi spot.

Pharmacies Almost every *quartier* has a small neighbourhood pharmacy. Two of the most central and best stocked are Pharmacie Kaocen, on the rue du Coulibaly (T 20.73.54.54), and Pharmacie El Nasr, on the ground floor of Imm El Nasr.

Post and phones There's a PTT on rue de Kabekoira, down from the Sûreté National, and another at place de la République.

Supermarkets The best of the European-style supermarkets are the two branches of Haddad on av de la Mairie and rue de Coulibaly. They're air-conditioned carbon copies of a Parisian *supermarché* – from the shopping trolleys down to the boxed Camembert. Veg and fruit are flown in directly from France – for which you'll pay prices two to three times higher than at source. They also have very good wine selections.

Swimming pools Non-guests can use the pools at the three major hotels – the *Terminus*, *Grand* and *Gaweye* – for CFA2000–2500. The last is the nicest, most central and priciest. Less expensive than any of the above is the Piscine Olympique on rue du Sahel, near the *Hôtel du Sahel*, and most days you'll have the whole place to yourself.

Travel agents The IATA-registered Satguru Travel Agency, next to *Hôtel Maourey* on rue de la Copro (T 20.73.69.31 E stts-nim@intnet.ne), is a general ticket agency and can make bookings for all the airlines flying out of Niamey. Nigercar Voyages, av de l'Afrique (T 20.73.23.31 E nicarvoy@intnet .ne W tinyurl.com/38vuhy), is reliable and offers a comprehensive roster of trips through Niger – they specialize in the Parc National du "W" du Niger (see p.1047) – and neighbouring countries. Other travel agents tend to go in and out of business unpredictably.

Visa extensions You can get your visa extended at the Sûreté National, on the corner of rue Nasser and av de la Mairie.

Wrestling Just down from the Centre Culturel Oumarou-Ganda, on bd Mali Béro, the Arène des Jeux Traditionels is a good place to check out some bouts of *lutte traditionelle* – African-style wrestling – at which Niger excels. Check local papers for announcements.

13.2

Southwest Niger

outhwest Niger is the greenest and most densely populated part of the country. As well as being an important crossroads for travel between Nigeria, Benin and Burkina Faso, there are some worthwhile destinations in the region, just a few hours' travel out of Niamey, including superb markets to the northeast, and pleasant riverside excursion areas just north of the city.

North of Niamey, the scenic road to Gao in Mali, via **Tillabéri** and **Ayorou** (at the end of the paved section), hugs the river most of the way. A paved road runs the whole way **south** to the Niger–Nigeria–Benin border at **Gaya**, but it's less interesting scenically than the route north of Niamey. A second southbound route traces the west bank of the river, paved as far as **Say**, before reverting to *piste* en route to Niger's only game reserve, the **Parc National du "W" du Niger**.

Northeast of Niamey

For a change of pace and a taste of Nigérien rural life, make a trip a few hours out of the city to the northeast. Taxis head daily from Niamey along the scenic route to **Filingué**, passing through the market towns of **Baleyara** – itself worth a day-trip from the capital – and **Bonkoukou**. There's considerable regional commerce here in crop and livestock production, and the paved road runs along a water-worn valley – a vestige of a river that once flowed south from the Sahara into the Niger. It's inspiring scenery, with rugged cliffs and hills for the whole 179km to Filingué. If you're heading for **Tahoua** and **Agadez**, this route also provides an alternative to the main highway via **Birnin-Konni**.

Baleyara

Although the name of **BALEYARA** (96km from Niamey) roughly translates as "where Bellah come together", it is primarily a Djerma settlement, and one where Tuareg, Hausa and Fula people congregate to trade at the gigantic **Sunday market**. The Bella of the town's name are the traditional vassal-herders of the Tuareg and the animal market is well known throughout western Niger. For days beforehand, caravans can be seen wending their way towards the village. This is also one of the best places to find hand-woven Fula and Djerma blankets, leather goods, and intricately carved calabashes. There's really nowhere to stay in Baleyara, but there are several bars and no shortage of street food. A share-taxi is CFA2000–CFA2500 from Niamey's Ecogare Wadata, or it's CFA1650 by minivan (with the option to pay more for a front seat). For the return, curiously, it's always CFA1500 regardless of what transport you take.

Bonkoukou and Filingué

Beyond Baleyara, the road southwards follows the **Dallol Bosso** – a rich valley cut out centuries ago by run-off waters from the Aïr Mountains and feeding, when in spate, into the Niger River. To the north, this depression is known as the **Dallol Boboy**, and extends past **BONKOUKOU** – a town of semi-sedentary Tuareg which is home to an impressive Saturday market. Although it's big, unlike at Baleyara you have to work hard to find crafts at Bonkoukou, but they are here if you look.

A Hausa settlement and administrative town, with characteristic architecture (note the *chef du canton's* house), **FILINGUÉ** boasts another important regional market, though it's a notch down from the two described above. On Sundays, the town snaps into life as traders make their way from the countryside and converge on the market square. Herds of livestock file in and are sold beside millet and other regional produce; you'll also find good buys of crafts ranging from pottery to woven blankets and mats. Filingué is the only town along the route with **accommodation** – *Cases de Passage Korfey* (T20.77.10.88; rooms with fan ❶ or a/c ❸). There's a filling station in town, and a pharmacy, though little else in terms of services apart from a couple of small stores selling canned goods.

Transport to **Tahoua**, 225km beyond Filingué, depends on the demand created by local market days; you may have to wait several hours – or sometimes even days. The main route – which can get washed out during the rains – passes through **TALCHO** (where the tarred surface ends) then veers eastward through an agricultural region dotted with Hausa villages, the largest of which are **SANAM** (market on Tuesday), **CHÉGUÉNARON** and **TÉBARAM**.

Northwest of Niamey

A small village on the banks of the Niger, **BOUBON** has become a popular weekend rural getaway for Niamey's expatriates. The town is some 25km northwest of the capital, approached by a small *piste* leading southwest from the highway; **taxis from Niamey** leave from in front of the Petit Marché. The village is especially known for its **pottery**, sold at its Wednesday market and in vast quantities in the markets of the capital. It's also very good for **bird-watching**. There's a *campement* (T20.68.02.82; ❹) on **Boubon Island**, reached by pirogue from the mainland, with eight beautifully renovated, a/c, thatched chalets, a good restaurant and a pool.

Midway between Niamey and Tillabéri, the town of **FARIÉ** used to be an important crossroads, as the only point between Gao and Gaya where cars could cross the river. A **ferry** still links the Niger's banks, and at the end of the dry season there's usually a passable ford, but the Kennedy Bridge in Niamey has removed the crossing's importance. Although there's nothing of specific interest here, Farié makes a reasonable base for scenic riverside meanderings.

The route to Burkina: Gothèye and Téra

A viable, if slow, alternative to the direct Niamey–Ouagadougou route is to cross the river at Farié and continue 10km north towards **GOTHÈYE**, which has basic food supplies and a bar-restaurant, but no fuel. The Sunday market boosts the otherwise limited traffic. Here, the road – paved all the way to Téra – veers "inland", away from the river towards northern Burkina Faso. The route passes through occasional villages among the millet stubble and acacia, with larger trees and more intensive cultivation taking over as the road climbs away from the river. Some 40km further, **DARGOL** only comes to life for the Friday market. The next stop along the route, **BANDIO**, has a small Saturday market, but otherwise no facilities.

The largest town in the region, **TÉRA** is backed by an earth dam that forms a reservoir after the rains (July–Dec). Built in the early 1980s to irrigate rice and bean fields, the reservoir and the pools below are now the focus of village life. Minibuses leave Niamey for Téra from the Wadata *gare routière*. If you're heading to Burkina Faso, leave your passport at the police checkpoint over the bridge on the way into Téra. They'll hold it until you leave, and stamp you out of Niger, as this doubles as the border control. The *gare routière* and two filling stations are near the market on the opposite side of town to the *campement*.

A walk along the Niger

If you've missed out on seeing riverside village life from a pirogue, a viable – albeit arduous – alternative is to make the four-hour **hike from Farié to Gothèye**. The path takes you close to the Niger through a series of small villages surrounded by vegetable gardens and mango orchards. After the rains, rice is grown in the shallows, but a short distance inland, the verdure soon gives way to Sahelian savannah with cattle and goats foraging for meagre nourishment from the gleanings of the harvest. Occasional water-holes provide some good **bird-watching** opportunities: golden orioles are common.

The Djerma-speakers who inhabit the villages are unused to tourists, especially those on foot, and are keen to talk – even if *Ça va?* is about the limit of the conversation. The general greeting in Djerma, *Fofo* (literally "Thank you"), will help break the ice.

There are plenty of opportunities to **camp** along the riverbank, but you'll need to bring everything with you. Supplies in the whole region are sparse. From the Niamey–Tillabéri road, it's 2km down to the vehicle ferry at Farié, which crosses every hour during the day (10min). A **path** then leads upstream from the tiny market on the far side, running roughly parallel to the road.

Tillabéri

A Djerma town, and an important agricultural centre surrounded by fields of rice and millet, **TILLABÉRI** was never very lively even in the days when it saw a steady stream of overlanders grateful for the paved road after enduring hundreds of miles of thundering desert *piste*. Moreover, since the drought of the 1980s, the **giraffe herds** that once roamed the wooded savannahs and provided a tourist attraction have migrated further south, and there's little to do in town besides take in the **market** – notably on the big trading days, Sunday and Wednesday. Tillabéri is a good place for a roadside stop, however, as it has a number of small **restaurants** and **bars**, some with fridges.

Ayorou

AYOROU, 88km north of Tillabéri, is a quiet Songhai fishing village on weekdays. But on Sundays the population is swelled by a swirling mix of Sahel peoples who, having crossed the river by pirogue or the savannah by mule, camel or on foot, converge for the weekly **market**. Famous throughout West Africa, it's an event well worth catching. An important element is the **animal market**, the main draw for nomads – Fula-cattle-herders, Tuareg with their camels, and Bella with mules. Songhai, Djerma and Sorko people bring fruits and vegetables, various grains, fish, goats and chickens, while Moorish merchants from Mauritania, in distinctive light blue robes and white headscarves, run their typical general stores. Traders also sell traditional medicine and a variety of **regional crafts**, especially jewellery and leatherwork.

Though most of Ayorou crouches along the eastern bank of the river, the oldest part of town, with traditional *banco* houses, spreads over the island of **Ayorou Goungou**. You can rent a pirogue to visit the island, or one of the surrounding islands, at the mooring point near the market square. Your chances of seeing **hippos** along this stretch of the river are good, and exotic **birds** are common, especially near the island of **Firgoun**, 12km north of town. If you have time for a jaunt downstream, you could take a pirogue from Ayorou to **Tillabéri** after the market closes – a one-day voyage, setting off Sunday evening or Monday morning. The trip involves plenty of weaving between the rapids and manoeuvring down narrow channels; there are some particularly exciting rapids just before you enter Tillabéri. There's no fixed price. During or shortly after the rainy season – when the river is high enough – you may even be able to rent a pirogue to take you as far as Niamey.

Ayorou's sole **hotel** is the once four-star *Hôtel Amenokal* (☎20.72.36.00 ❹), which serves primarily as a hunters' hangout; it tends to close and reopen quite frequently; ring in advance to check the latest situation.

South of Niamey

South of Niamey, towards the Benin border, the main road and river separate, joining up again only at Gaya. Near the town of **Kouré**, 60km down the road from the capital, the **giraffe herds** that were once the pride of Tillabéri have found refuge from drought and poaching in the surrounding countryside. A day's giraffe-spotting here is easily arranged from Niamey. From Niamey's Ecogare Wadata you can catch a minibus to **KOURÉ** (CFA1200) where you'll be asked to pay a CFA4000 entry fee. A guide is compulsory, currently costing CFA5000 per group. The final expense, depending on the season, is for a 4x4 taxi to take you from the road to the giraffes (the prices varies from a few hundred francs to several thousand per person, depending on how far the giraffes are from the road: you may have to travel no more than a couple of kilometres before spotting these extraordinary animals sailing by in their slow-motion canter; however, often much greater distances are involved). The experience is well worth it, even more so given that these are some of the last giraffes in West Africa.

Further south, the road passes through the important crossroads trading town of **DOSSO**. The *gare routière* here is frenetic, and there's a large market (though no bank). Dosso still has its traditional Djerma chief who lives in the *Djermakoye* – a compound built in the Sudanic style. With his permission you should be able to have a look inside.

There's a limited range of **accommodation**. The motel-like *Hôtel Djerma* (☎20.65.02.06; ❸), near the *gare routière*, has spacious self-contained a/c rooms and a good, inexpensive bar-restaurant, though the pool has clearly not seen water in a while. The more basic *Auberge du Carrefour* (☎20.65.00.55; ❶–❷) on the Route de Niamey, a good fifteen-minute walk from the *gare routière*, has simple rooms (a/c or fan) with private showers but shared toilets. The town teems with **places to eat and drink**: best is the *Restaurant des Arts*, at the new Complex Artisanal de Dosso, though it's open during the high season only.

GAYA is the last town in Niger before crossing the river into Benin, the border open 24 hours. There are one or two places to stay here, the best being *Hôtel Hamdallah* (☎20.68.04.68 ❸), off the main road; *Hôtel Dendi* (☎20.68.03.40 ❷) is cheaper but an inconvenient 15-minute walk south of the *gare routière*. You may also notice people in your taxi heading to a house near the *gare routière*, where they get mats to sleep on the earth floor inside. People pay next to nothing for this privilege and there's no reason not to join them, though you'll elicit some embarrassed laughter.

Parc National du "W" du Niger

Part of the vast reserve that spreads across into Burkina Faso and Benin, the **Parc National du "W" du Niger** (pronounced *double-vé* and named after the double U-bend in the Niger River; ☎20.78.41.12) covers 2200 square kilometres in Niger alone. It's one of West Africa's better game parks and relatively good for animal-watching, with herds of **elephant** concentrated in the Tapoa valley and **buffalo** (*buffle*) on the wooded savannah. Reports still come in of **lions** and **leopards** roaming the park, but they stay very well hidden. Easier to spot are antelope – especially **waterbuck** (*cob de buffon* or *cob defassa*) and **duiker**, as well as the big **roan antelope** (*hippotrague*) and **hartebeest** (*bubale*) – and large troops of **baboons** (*babouins*) scampering through the bush, often near the camp. **Warthogs** (*phacochères*) and **hippos** are also quite common. The park counts some 300 species of **bird**, with

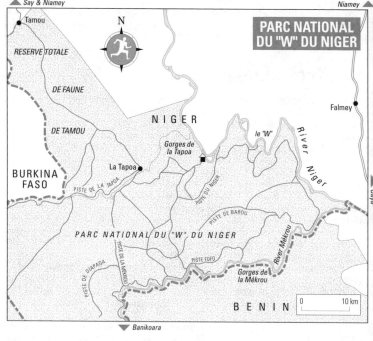

good showings of stork, heron and ibis. When the rainy season begins in June the park closes down, and doesn't usually reopen until early December, after the 400-odd kilometres of *piste* have been groomed.

The park entrance is 150km south of Niamey, via **Say** and **Tamou**. For the last 40 kilometres, after turning south at Tamou, the route runs through the **Réserve Totale de Faune de Tamou**, a salient of the main park. A visit is hard to arrange if you're not driving or on an organized tour: public transport from Niamey will get you as far as Say, where you may have to change to continue to Tamou. You're not likely to get down to La Tapoa without a lift from a park administration vehicle or from fellow travellers.

At the park entrance you pay for a visitor's permit valid for the duration of your stay (CFA3500 per person per day plus CFA2500 if you want to stay inside the park overnight). You can also pick up a quite detailed and useful road map, though you're obliged to visit with a **guide**. The main park **accommodation** is at the 🏨 *Hôtel de la Tapoa* (☎20.74.25.22; rooms with fan ❹ or a/c ❺, including breakfast). Reservations can be made in Niamey at the tourist office, or through any travel agent. The hotel is situated in the village of **LA TAPOA** on the edge of the reserve and has comfortable bungalows and a/c rooms grouped around a swimming pool (though that's currently empty). Nigercar Voyages (see p.1043) have set up an excellent tented camp on the banks of the Niger, about 20km east of *Hôtel de la Tapoa* (half-board ❹ or full board ❺; camping with own equipment also permitted).

13.3

Southern Niger

S outhern Niger is the nation's richest agricultural zone, and also contains the bulk of the country's population and is home to its biggest ethnic group, the **Hausa**. Renowned traders and leatherworkers, with a long history of regional statehood, the Hausa are energetically commercial, the vigour of their towns enhanced today by the region's proximity to Nigeria.

Note that parts of this section – 13.3: Southern Niger – may be affected by the serious trouble that was brewing in the north at the time of writing. Read the background on p.1057 and keep your ear to the ground, especially if you're travelling to the far east.

From Dogondoutchi to Birnin-Konni

Some 230km east of Niamey, **DOGONDOUTCHI** (commonly shortened to "Doutchi") is a small town surrounded by sculpted red cliffs like something from a Western. It's inhabited by the **Maouri**, a people of Hausa origin who consistently refused to adopt Islam, even in the nineteenth century, when the Sokoto jihad led to the conversion of almost the entire region. Islam has made some inroads in recent years, but this is still a stronghold of traditional beliefs, and local fetishers – notably the old chief of the nearby village of **Baoura Bawa** – are respected and feared, and are even said to have control over the elements.

Doutchi's only **place to stay**, *Hôtel Magama* (☎20.81.43.51 **①**–**②**), is signposted about 200m from the bus park and has a number of comfortable self-contained a/c bungalows, as well as some very cheap and basic rooms with shared facilities. The hotel's bar-restaurant is also the town's best place to eat; otherwise, the alternatives include *Horizon 2000*, near the *autogare*, which does filling, stodgy meals for next to nothing, and the glitzy new *Sarradounia Mangou*, in the centre of town on the main road, which offers sandwiches and a standard chicken-and-chips menu at fair prices.

Birnin-Konni

BIRNIN-KONNI is a lively town with traditional *banco* houses and characteristic dome-shaped granaries in the older neighbourhoods around the market. The town owes its prosperity to its position on the border: some neighbourhoods actually spill over into Nigeria, and a paved road pushes through the town to the relative metropolis of Sokoto in Nigeria, only 93km south. There's a lot of **trafficking** going on in these parts – most notably of cheap Nigerian fuel, which you can usually buy from *bidons* on the streets for a fraction of the price you pay at the pumps. Birnin-Konni also lies in one of the country's most fertile regions – the main streets are shaded by towering trees planted during the colonial period, and the **market** has a range of goods and produce that are expensive and scarce further north (Wed is the main trading day). The rows of moneychangers at the *autogare* surrounded by piles of Nigerian naira and CFA francs attest to the amount of cross-border trade. In fact, the *autogare* is the only place where you can **change money** – and, of course, it's cash only. **Bush taxis** to Sokoto leave constantly from a corner of the *autogare*, but you'll have to bargain hard.

Accommodation

Birnin-Konni has a couple of comfortable and reasonably affordable **places to stay**. The ⚓ *Relais Touristique* (❷), off the Doutchi road on the outskirts of town, has a handful of excellent self-contained rooms and spacious bungalows, plus camping facilities (CFA1500 per person to camp, plus CFA1000 per vehicle). The bar and restaurant here are also pretty good, and they sometimes pull the TV onto the terrace in the evenings – a chance to see Niger's tiny TV station (Télé-Sahel) at work. The more central *Kado Hôtel* (☎20.64.03.64 ❷) has some basic self-contained rooms with fan on the ground floor, and some better and more expensive a/c rooms upstairs with a good streetside view, although they are getting a little tatty. If you're broke, head for the super-cheap *Hôtel Wadata* (❶), on the main road about 500m north of the *autogare*, which looks like an old caravanserai and is just as basic.

Maradi

Sometimes dubbed Niger's "groundnut capital", as over half the country's peanut crop is grown in the surrounding region, **MARADI** – Niger's third largest town – in fact now lies in a nascent industrial region. Maradi was formerly a province of Katsina, one of the original seven Hausa city-states, which lies over the Nigerian border. After the nineteenth-century Sokoto jihad, Hausa refugees fled to Maradi and eventually overthrew the Fula here. Sokoto and Maradi remained at odds for years afterwards. The town is still strongly influenced by the teachings of Islam, so that nightlife is subdued and beer sales mostly confined to the fancier restaurants.

Maradi has lost much of its traditional flavour (an anonymous-looking grid of streets was laid out in the 1950s), but it isn't entirely devoid of interest. Foremost among the sights is the **place Dan Kasswa**, bordered by the **Grande Mosquée** and the **Chief's Palace** – a colourful and typically Hausa confection. The **market place** is also impressive, spreading over a couple of blocks along the main Katsina road. You'll find a vast array of produce grown in the region or imported from Nigeria at prices much lower than in Niamey (Mon and Fri are the main days). Over by the Hôtel de Ville there's a shady public garden, with gazebo-like bar at one side and the Catholic church nearby.

Practicalities

Maradi has three **banks**: the BIA, across from the Sûreté; the Bank of Africa (BOA), on the Katsina road next to the market; and SONI Bank, across from the market. Zenith Cybercafé, just down from the *Hôtel Jangorzo*, has a very slow (a complaint that can be levelled against all cybercafés in Maradi) but cheap Internet service (CFA600/hr). The **post office** is also on the Katsina road, near the Palais de Justice. For **medical** needs, head to the Pharmacie Populaire, on place Dan Kasswa, or to the **hospital**, in the south of town.

Cheap **accommodation** options include the fine ⚓ *Hôtel Larewa* (☎96.87.01.44), which is a twenty-minute walk away from the centre, near the EHGM/Maïssagé bus terminal, but is good, clean, safe and inexpensive, with basic self-contained rooms (fan ❷ or a/c ❸) and a number of cheaper rooms with shared facilities. Nearer the centre, the *Hôtel Jangorzo* (☏20.41.01.40), on the Route de l'Aéroport, about 3km from town next to the water tower, has slightly run-down rooms (small non-s/c rooms with fan ❷, s/c rooms with a/c ❹), as well as a nightclub and one of the town's better restaurants (though don't be surprised to find yourself dining alone in their cavernous hall – it can be a bit quiet here sometimes). But the outstanding accommodation in Maradi is supplied by the ⚓*Maradi Guest House* (☏20.41.07.54), a real expat refuge, with six fully-equipped and luxuriously furnished a/c rooms (❻–❼; another thirty less expensive rooms are planned), a tiny swimming pool – more like a paddling pool – and an excellent restaurant doing European-style food. To find it, follow the signs on the east side of the Katsina road, then turn right at the water tower.

The area around the market is the place to look for inexpensive Nigérien **food**. *Martaba*, northeast of the *gare routière*, is a relaxing garden restaurant where, not uncommonly for this part of Africa, they tell you what they have cooking, rather than you telling them what you want. It's a bit rough and ready, but the garden setting is very pleasant. Reliable basic meals can also be had in the imaginatively named *Restaurant African Food*, nearby. In the evenings the Jardin Publique is a popular spot for grilled chicken cooked and served at outdoor stands or at the bar. The Mairey is the only

MARADI

Ⓐ, EHGM Terminal, Niamey & Zinder

Cinema
Dan Kasswa

❷ ❶

Gare
Routière

MOKOYO

SONI Bank

Cinéma Vox

Police Sûreté

Market
Place

❸

Chief's
Palace

BIA Bank

Pharmacy
Populaire

BOA
Bank

Gare
SNTV

PLACE
DAN KASSWA

DAN GOULBI

❹ Jardin
Publique

@
Sareli Internet

Pharmacie
Populaire

Catholic
Church

⚓ Dan Kasswa
Mosque

Mairie

N

Air Transport
(bus)

BAMBARA

Palais de
Justice

Gendarmerie

RESTAURANTS, BARS & CLUBS	
African Food	1
Club Privé	5
Jardin Publique	4
Mairey	3
Martaba	2

ACCOMMODATION	
Jangorzo	B
Larewa	A
Maradi Guesthouse	C

0   200 m

❺

Airport, Rimbo Transport (Bus), Zenith II (Internet) & Ⓑ   Customs,   Katsina, Kano & Ⓒ

Maradi's main **gare routière** is right next to the market on the Katsina road, a short hop from the centre by *kabo-kabo*. Vehicles head off from here to all points. There are daily **buses** with all the main companies (SNTV, Aïr, Rimbo, EHGM/Maissagé) for Niamey and Zinder. Note that you won't get into Nigeria without a visa and there are no issuing facilities at any of the border posts. **Taxis** generally stop at the border town of **Dan-Issa**, where you change vehicles for onward travel into Nigeria.

bakery in town, and does good cakes and breads. The *Club Privé* at the southern edge of town, has various facilities including a swimming pool, tennis courts, gym and video room, which you can use for CFA5000 per day, plus a reasonably priced bar-restaurant serving European dishes like crispy salads and freshly made burgers.

Zinder

Formerly the largest town in Niger and briefly capital of the French colony, the influence of sleepy **ZINDER** has waned in recent decades. It's still Niger's second city, but much of the commerce with Nigeria – long the main source of its wealth – now passes through Maradi on the faster Kano-Niamey highway. But even in decline, Zinder remains a centre of trade, as a quick stroll through the impressive Grand Marché confirms. Nor has the town lost all its former glories, retaining some of the finest **traditional Hausa architecture** anywhere, and the old town quarter of **Birni** is much better preserved than its Nigerian counterparts in Kano, Zaria and Katsina.

Some history

The sultanate of Zinder was founded by the **Kanouri**, descendants of the Kanem Bornu empire of the Lake Chad region. The Kanouri settled here after being chased out from northern territories by Tuareg invaders, and mixed with the Hausa population, which itself had fled the region of Sokoto under pressure from the Fulani. In the eighteenth and nineteenth centuries, the Kanouri and Hausa joined forces to found the powerful **Damagaram state**, of which Zinder was capital.

Zinder reached its apogee in the mid-nineteenth century under the reign of **Tamimoum**, who greatly enlarged the boundaries of Damagaram, introduced new crops and developed trade. Under his rule, a vast wall or *birni* was erected around the town. Originally ten metres high and fourteen wide, this wall has long since crumbled, though its remains can still be seen around the old town. According to legend, the structure's invincibility was ensured by incorporating into the walls a number of Korans and several virgins. Under subsequent rulers, however, Zinder's fortunes were tied more to those of the slave trade than to magic. By the mid-nineteenth century, one of the Sahel region's biggest **slave markets** was regularly held here. To support his empire, the sultan led frequent raids, known as *razzias*, on vassal villages. Captives were sold in town, some to be taken to Kano and then force-marched down to the coast (by this era often the Portuguese forts supplying Brazil), others to be taken north across the Sahara to be sold in Tripoli. The **French** captured Zinder in 1899. With a population well in excess of 20,000, it was by far the region's biggest metropolis at the time and remained the effective capital of Niger until 1926.

The Town

Zinder comprises three separate districts, so distinct they're almost individual towns. To the north, **Zengou** was the original Hausa settlement, formerly a stopping point for camel caravans. **Birni** – the old fortified town and site of the sultan's palace and Grande Mosquée – lies about a kilometre to the southeast. Between the two is the **new town**, with administrative buildings laid out in characteristic French-colonial style.

The most obvious attraction is the old quarter of **Birni**, reached from the new town by following Avenue de la République south beyond the old French fort, which is still used by the Nigérien military. This will take you past the **Grande Mosquée**, the front of which gives onto a large public square facing the **Sultan's Palace**, a two-storey *banco* building set apart by its size. There are tombs of the former sultans in the grounds, which you should be able to visit with authorization from one of the guides lingering outside. Another noteworthy residence is that of the Fulani chief, just east of the mosque; the facade is decorated with colourful raised motifs, a common feature of Hausa architecture. All of Birni's buildings have been left in the traditional style, and walking through the narrow streets you get a real sense of what life was like in Zinder's heyday 120 years ago.

Although **Zengou** has its fair share of modern cement buildings and corrugated-iron roofs – elements that are completely absent in Birni – the **traditional flavour** is still strong. The oldest house in Zinder is in this quarter, and some of the town's showiest examples of Hausa architecture have been built here by the wealthier merchants. The pride in this style of decoration is by no means dead, and new, quite innovative, examples are commissioned all the time.

Zinder's **Grand Marché**, one of the country's biggest, has long been an important way-station between the Sahel and the regions to the south. Thursday is the main

▲ **ⓐ**, *Rimbo Transport & Agadez*

ZINDER

ZENGOU

RUE DE LA LIBERTÉ

Catholic Mission

Supermarket

Gare Routière

Petit Marché

Grand Marché

ⓐ Police Sûreté

EHGM Terminal

Cybercafé **ⓑ** Kandarga

Air Transport (bus)

SNTV SONI Bank

Assembly of God Church

Pharmacie Populaire

PLACE DE LA POSTE

Centre Culturel Franco-Nigérien

BIA Bank

NEW TOWN

Fort

Customs

AV DU MARADI

Arene des Jeux

⓶

Old Town Wall

Trésor

Grand Mosque

Sultan's Palace

BIRNI

Fulani Chief's Palace

AV DE LA RÉPUBLIQUE

BD DE L'INDÉPENDANCE

AV SAHARA

AV DES BANQUES

BD DE L'HIPPODROME

N

ⓔ, *Club Privé, Niamey & Kano*

ACCOMMODATION	
Amadou-Kourandaga	E
Auberge Mourna	B
Central	D
Damagaram	C
Malam Kalka Damou	A
RESTAURANTS	
Damsi	1
El Ali	2

0   250 m

▼ *Nguigmi*

1053

trading day. Salt pillars brought down from the Ténéré are sold next to the **animal market**, with its Tuareg, Fulani and Bousou traders. Hausa and other peoples from the south sell a variety of local and imported goods in and around the arcaded market building, which dates from the colonial period. This is perhaps the best place in the country to get low-price, good-quality **leather**, for which the Hausa have a long-standing reputation: sandals, bags, pouffes and pouches are sold around the market or by wandering traders. Craftsmen also sell their wares direct from a number of workshops in the district.

Practicalities

Services are concentrated in the **new town**. They include the hotels and better restaurants, two **banks** (BIA and SONI), the **post office** and a couple of small **supermarkets**.

For such a large town, Zinder doesn't have an overabundance of **places to stay**. The most popular choice amongst travellers – and indeed, the only hotel that really caters for foreign visitors, is the central ⚶ *Auberge Mourna*. Smart, clean, friendly, and with the town's best restaurant, this is the place to stay if you can afford to (a/c rooms ⑤). If you can't, then for **budget accommodation**, about twenty minutes' walk past the *Central* in the direction of Agadez lies *Hôtel Malam Kalka Damou* (☏20.51.05.68; ①–②), the best of the cheapies, with fanned rooms and shared facilities in a friendly family compound. Back in the centre, the *Mourna*'s two main rivals are both located off the central Place de la Poste. The slightly dingy, colonial-style *Hôtel Central* (☏20.51.20.47; s/c rooms with fan ② or noisy a/c ③) is the cheaper option and if you have the means, it's also possible to camp on the rubble parking lot behind the hotel (CFA4000). The *Central*'s outdoor bar is a popular, low-key evening hangout. Across the street, the *Hôtel Damagaram* (☏20.51.00.69) is bigger, nicer and correspondingly more expensive, with s/c, a/c rooms (④–⑤). The hotel's restaurant is fair and the lively outdoor bar is still going strong.

Heading out of the centre towards Maradi, the Kano road leads past the customs building (where, if you're driving, you may or may not be stopped), on to the *Hôtel Amadou Kourandaga* (☏20.51.07.42; ④), with spacious a/c rooms surrounding a courtyard and hot water on tap. There are also a couple of cheaper rooms with fan. This is a popular expat hangout, and the favoured place for Zinder's salaried citizens to go for a quiet drink, so you might end up having a beer with the chief of police or the mayor. The hotel also has a well-stocked souvenir shop and safe parking.

For **food**, the *Mourna*'s restaurant is deservedly popular, with good pizzas, though like the hotel it's not particularly cheap. For something more affordable, **street food** is easy to find in town, especially in the place de la Poste, across from the *Hôtel Central*, or in the small night market, just south of Malam Kalka Damou. Further south, across the main Indépendance roundabout, *Le Damsi* is a curious place,

---

Moving on from Zinder

SNTV buses (☏20.51.04.68) have departures daily from Zinder to **Niamey** via Maradi, Birnin-Konni, Dogondoutchi and Dosso (departing at dawn on Mon, Tues & Fri), **Nguigmi** via Diffa (Mon & Fri) and **Agadez** (Mon & Thurs). The *gare* SNTV is on av de la République, a 10min walk (or 2min *kabo-kabo*; CFA100) from the *Hôtel Damagaram*. **EHGM/Maïssagé** buses (☏20.51.04.49) have four weekly 6am departures to Niamey (Mon, Tues, Thurs & Sat) from their terminal near the cinema. Unfortunately, their Niamey-to-Diffa buses don't stop in Zinder, so you'll have to return to Maradi to make that connection. **Private buses** and **bush taxis** leave from the **gare routière**, near the Petit Marché, and connect with all major towns. **Taxis** also head regularly to Kano in Nigeria along a good road, though it works out a little cheaper to take a vehicle to the border, where you can easily find a taxi on to Kano.

reached by a small alley between buildings, with a good balcony view over the street. Despite the menu flourished by the waiter, there's usually only one thing available (often fish and chips), but it's fairly tasty and reasonably priced. Towards Birni, *El Ali*, behind Nigelec, serves good chicken and *steak-frites* (but not alcohol) in their small garden. Watch the hygiene everywhere: Zinder's **water** is considered suspect and usually needs purifying.

Nightlife is confined largely to the hotel bars: both the *Damagaram* and the *Central* have one. If you're feeling homesick or decadent, try the *Club Privé*, which has a pool, sports facilities and a classy bar (open until 2am on weekdays, and all night at weekends). Officially, you need to be introduced by a member, so some smooth talking may be called for. For **live music**, check out what's on offer at the *Centre Culturel Franco-Nigérien*; they also have a decent, though pricey, bar-restaurant.

Zinder to Agadez

The journey north **from Zinder to Agadez** (see p.1058) can be accomplished comfortably in a day. This, despite the fact that a huge section of the road is currently undergoing upgrading, and thus for much of the journey your vehicle is forced to travel through the sand on a rough old *piste*, while the sparkling new road taunts you from nearby. That said, if you're driving, it's worth taking your time on this stretch, as it's a relatively narrow band of the Sahel, with sights you won't get elsewhere. The **Kel Gress Tuareg** live in the region in their huts of fibre matting. There are tall Sodom apple trees, as well as many smaller, sometimes colourful plants, and you might see an ostrich or two. Be careful walking in what appear to be tufts of grass – the seeds have a spiky casing that can draw blood.

The small town of **TANOUT**, 140km north of Zinder, is a good stopping point for a cold drink or some dry Fulani cheese, and they sometimes have fuel here. Several wells beyond Tanout contain water – though you'll need a forty-metre rope. At the little village of **ADERBISSINAT**, there's sometimes a cursory police check, and foreigners stopping here are regarded with interest and curiosity by traders in the market (leather, sweets and basic food). The road then passes near the **Falaise de Tiguidit**, an escarpment with a wonderful view back across the plain.

On to Lake Chad

This infrequently travelled route heads through a region that was part of the Kanem Bornu empire until the nineteenth century, and is now peopled by Hausa, Kanouri, Dangara and Manga. The road is paved all the way, albeit with numerous potholes, particularly around Gouré, occasional sand-drifts around Maïné-Soroa and the usual hazards of animals and large birds in your path. Just 22km east of Zinder you arrive at **MIRIA**, the first oasis in these arid parts. The gardens here harbour date palms and groves of mango and guava. Sunday is the main **market day**; look out for the local pottery on sale.

A further 144km brings you to the small *sous-préfecture* of **GOURÉ**; then it's another 330km to **MAÏNÉ-SOROA**, the next place of any size, where the people make a living drawing salt from the earth. The desert looms close to the east of town, and you can see large dunes from the roadside. **DIFFA**, an administrative town on a seasonal meander of the **Komadougou River** – which in theory sometimes flows into Lake Chad – is 75km further on and has the last reliable filling station for eastbound drivers. The *Hôtel Le Tal* (☎20.54.03.32; rooms with fan ❷ or a/c ❸) behind the filling station, is the only accommodation in Diffa, with cleanish self-contained rooms and a reasonable bar-resto.

At the end of the road, **NGUIGMI** is nearly 600km from Zinder and a full 1500km from Niamey. If you're heading **into Chad**, Nguigmi is where you take your official leave of Niger and drive, or find a ride, east, then south, around the lake to Ndjamena. Nguigmi is devoid of even basic facilities (including hotels, restaurants and petrol stations), so stock up in Diffa. An SNTV bus leaves for Zinder (Wed & Sun); depending on the state of the road, you might end up spending the night under the stars.

Nguigmi, an important town during the days of the Kanem Bornu empire, when it was home to the semi-nomadic Kanouri princes, became wealthy from its position on the trade routes to the **Kaourar oasis** (whence salt was brought by caravans) and as a fishing port from its site on the erstwhile shores of **Lake Chad**. Today, access to the lakeshore is difficult: the permanent lake, never more than a few metres deep, has shrunk deep into Chad and northern Cameroon and only after a good rainy season do the waters spread across the plains into Niger, an hour or two of rough *piste*-driving east of the town.

An arduous *piste* leads north of Nguigmi towards **Bilma** (see p.1067), a trip that takes two to three days. The actual *piste* only goes as far as **N'GOURTI** (145km north of Nguigmi), after which you've got a 450-kilometre desert transit ahead of you, with more than a hundred sand dunes to cross. A guide for this expedition is a must, and that's assuming the security situation makes such travel feasible: but if you're contemplating this trip, you won't need advice from a Rough Guide.

13.4

The Nigérien Sahara

To travel through the north of Niger takes some determination. It's a region with an extreme climate, great expanses of emptiness and very little water. From Niamey, a paved road leads up to the uranium-mining town of **Arlit** – the northernmost major settlement – passing through the commercial centre of **Tahoua** and the historic Tuareg stronghold of **Agadez**. Other interesting sites are difficult to reach and require preparation and a good guide. The effort and expense is worth it, however, as you'll be rewarded by beautiful **desert oases**, many of whose inhabitants still eke out a living from the **salt trade**, using camel caravans to cross the region. Trips through the volcanic moonscapes of the **Aïr Mountains** or the awesome dunes of the **Ténéré Desert** also provide opportunities to visit a wealth of **prehistoric sites** – including the rock paintings near **Iferouâne** – and a number of **springs and waterfalls**.

Tahoua

Niger's fifth largest town, **TAHOUA** is a major stopping point on the main road between Niamey and Agadez. Despite a population of more than 60,000 and a wide mix of peoples, the town hasn't really warmed up to travellers – indeed it was expressly closed to them until the mid-1980s. There's little to detain you here, and even the pretty rosy dunes that have settled permanently on the edge of town have now been turned into a motorcross circuit and are only worth a special detour if you're into sand-dune racing. That said, the mountainous area east of Tahoua around the town of **BOUZA** is dotted with tiny, picturesque villages and offers some interesting hiking opportunities.

Tahoua is primarily a commercial centre and boasts an animated **market** – the building is itself an attractive example of Sahel-inspired architecture. It's one of those places where everyone in Niger – Djerma, Hausa, Bororo, Fula, Tuareg, the odd tourist – comes together, notably on Sunday, the main trading day. The nomads bring salt pillars, dates, livestock and leather, which they sell to regional farmers who provide grain, cotton, spices, peanuts, tobacco and locally-made indigo fabrics. Look out for the intermediaries called *dillali*, who bring together traders, help them strike a deal and even serve as translators. You could also check out the **Centre Artisanal**, at the northwestern edge of town, whose workshops are busy with Tuareg craftsmen making jewellery and leatherware. Bargain hard if you want to buy anything.

Practicalities

Tahoua has a branch of the BIA (which changes traveller's cheques as well as cash). **Accommodation** in Tahoua is limited. If you're on a budget, head for *Hôtel les Bungalows* (℡20.61.05.53 ②), across from the town hall and a short walk from the *gare routière*, which is surrounded by pleasant gardens and has a few bungalows, the cheaper ones with fan only, the more expensive and comfortable ones with a/c. More expensive is the a/c *Hôtel de l'Amitié* (℡20.61.01.53; rooms with a/c ③), about 1km from the centre on the Birnin-Konni road (look for the model giraffes outside) which is also home to a popular bar, a good restaurant, and a large car park where overland trucks used to park in days gone by, and which the overland crowd are beginning to find again.

The town's best **restaurant** is *Le Milanais*, just up from the Centre Artisanal, a reasonably authentic Italian which offers big food at small prices, including dishes

---

Armed conflict in the north

The tempting travel opportunities of the Nigérien Sahara assume that the region's **security** difficulties can be overcome. At the time of writing (early 2008) the **conflict** between a splinter Tuareg group, the **MNJ** (the Mouvement des Nigériens pour la Justice) and the **FAN** (the Forces Armées Nigériennes, in other words the Nigérien army) was spreading, with the entire northern region, and especially the Aïr, steadily separating into besieged FAN-held towns and garrisons, and the ostensibly MNJ-controlled desert and bush. What little public transport was running went in convoys, with FAN escorts, and tourists were banned from the region. Curfews were in place in several towns, with all civilians expected to be back in the town centre by dusk. The MNJ accused the FAN of laying mines along remote *pistes* and in the bush, and the government said the same about the MNJ. Ordinary Nigériens – not to mention expats, NGOs and travellers – were increasingly caught between the two sides, and sometimes accused by one side of supporting the other. And while the violence in 2007 was almost entirely between the opposing armed forces, incidents of carjacking and kidnapping were perpetrated on tourists by armed Tuareg groups in the run-up to open conflict, and are likely to be a problem in the future.

The mood of Nigériens in the Aïr region, including many Tuareg who had been happy to rebuild the tourist industry, was gloomy and frustrated, as they saw years of post-rebellion confidence-building being blown away by an impatient minority.

The following sections, therefore, to the end of the Niger chapter, assume the resumption of the **status quo ante** during the life of this edition: an essentially safe region, with public transport running without armed escorts, tour operators offering 4x4 trips into remote districts, and tourists who have the right paperwork allowed to explore in their own vehicles. At the time of writing the Nigérien Sahara was closed: be sure to check before assuming it's safe again.

like *gnocchi*. The Jardin Publique houses the open-air *Restaurant Les Délices*, with African and European dishes. Tahoua's only **nightclub**, *Galaxy* (Fri & Sat only), is next to the *Hôtel de l'Amitié*.

Agadez

AGADEZ has been a major stopping point on the trans-Saharan routes for hundreds of years. You can read its history through buildings like the **Grande Mosquée** – a monument known throughout West Africa – or the **camel market**, which has drawn the peoples of the Sahel for generations. Following the uprisings of the early 1990s and the troubles in Algeria, once-common visitors – who formerly included everyone from Bilma salt caravans to trans-Sahara tour groups and film crews – tapered off, while even the discovery of uranium to the north and the construction of new roads to Niamey and Zinder failed to lift the town out of its dusty isolation. Then, with the **Tuareg peace settlement** in 1995 (and the subsequent appointment of a Tuareg rebel leader as the minister of tourism), tourists gradually started returning, and, with flights from Europe during the winter, new hotels and restaurants opening up and dozens of travel agents offering desert tours, Agadez was booming again, until the conflict of 2007 once again halted business.

Some history

In the fourteenth century, Agadez was a small but flourishing commercial centre where Arabs from Tripoli traded with Hausa from Nigeria and Songhai from Gao. By the fifteenth century it was on its way to becoming the **capital of the Tuareg** – in so far as the nomads had such a thing – and in 1449, a **sultanate** was established under the leadership of **Ilissaouane**. Fifty years later, the town came to be controlled by the Songhai, and throughout the sixteenth century, Agadez marked the northernmost point of their great empire, with a huge population, for the time, of perhaps 30,000.

After the Songhai were defeated by the Moroccans, the Tuareg regained control of the town, but like other trading posts in the region it was already entering a period of long decline. Agadez fared better than most, however, thanks in large measure to its location near the salt mines of Bilma; trade continued, especially with Hausaland to the south. Nonetheless, by the time the German explorer **Heinrich Barth** arrived in 1850, the population had dwindled to about 7000, and many of the old buildings were in ruins.

Early in the twentieth century, Agadez was incorporated into French territory, though not without resistance. One of the most serious threats to colonial rule was led by the Tuareg reformer **Kaocen Ag Mohammed**, who swooped down from Djanet to take Agadez in 1916, aiming to reunite all Muslims of the region and to terminate foreign domination. Supported in his efforts by the Germans and the Turks, Kaocen held the town for three months before being ousted by the French, who sent up emergency reinforcements from Zinder. The rebellion having been quelled, the French killed more than 300 suspected conspirators and guillotined many of the town's marabouts.

Since independence, the population of Agadez has rapidly increased, in part because of the discovery of **uranium** in Arlit, which provided an economic boost to the entire north, and partly due to the **droughts** of the 1970s and 1980s, which resulted in tens of thousands of Tuareg and Wodaabé herders converging on the town for food and water. The Tuareg rebellion also drove displaced people into the supposed safety of the town. Meanwhile, there are many others who use Agadez as a chance to escape Niger entirely, either through tourist friendships, or by more radical means: you may well see trucks getting ready to cross the desert to Libya, packed with potential migrants into Europe.

ACCOMMODATION

Agreboun	B
Auberge d'Azel	I
Auberge La Tendé	A
Hôtel de l'Aïr	F
Hôtel de la Paix	H
Pension Tellit	E
Tchintoulous	G
Telwa Bungalow	C
Tidène	D

N

Tahoua, Niamey, In-Gall & Assamakka

Ⓐ, Arlit & Maissage Transport (Bus)   Old Arlit Road

Air Transport
(Bus)

Gare Routière
& SNTV Station

Palais de
Justice

Rimbo Transport
(Bus)

Customs

Camel
Market

Village
Artisanal

Grande
Mosquée

Mobil

Marché de
Nuit

Police

Grand
Marché

Bank of Africa
BIA Bank

Vieux
Marché

Mission

Barth's
House

**RESTAURANTS, BARS
& CLUBS**

Bistrot	5
Le Gourmet	1
Le Palmier	2
Pâtisserie Madara Rahama	4
Le Pilier	3
Tamgak	6

0   200 m

RTE DE L'AÉROPORT

RTE DE BILMA

Airport   **Ⓗ, Ⓘ, Ⓢ, Ⓖ** & Bilma, Zinder, Kano & Internet

13

13.4 | NIGER | The Nigérien Sahara

Arrival and information

As the main administrative town in the north, Agadez has plenty of facilities: **service stations**, a **hospital** and a small international **airport**, plus a **PTT** (Mon–Fri 7.30am–12.30pm & 3–5.30pm). The Bank of Africa and BIA are both just off the Grand Marché; the latter is your best bet for changing euros cash and traveller's cheques. For **Internet** access, you have two options. The quickest is Cybercafé Desert Télécom at the *Hôtel de la Paix* (CFA1000/hr), though this is rather inconvenient for most travellers. Nearer to the town centre, the Internet café next to the service station at the junction of route de Bilma and route de l'Aéroport is slower but still okay.

The **tourist office** (Mon–Fri 7.30am–12.30pm & 3–6pm; no phone) is in an out-of-the-way location in the heart of the old town, just to the east of Place de Tamallakoye; though as, like all Niger tourist offices, they're pretty useless, there's no real point trying to find them anyway. If you do want to find it, or indeed anything else in the old town, you may find it saves a lot of time to hire a **guide**. Guides should have a professional guide card: check it. For tours within town expect to pay about CFA7000 per person per day, although you shouldn't pay more than CFA500 just to be shown the way to Heinrich Barth's house or the Maison du Boulanger. For sights further afield, there are now almost one hundred **travel agents** in town, some of them a lot more professionally set up than others. For details on booking an adventure into the Ténéré Desert and Aïr Mountains with them, see overleaf.

First, read the **box on p.1057**, check your own country's foreign office or state department's travel advice for Niger, and whatever the political and security climate, don't plan any off-road trip without having enough time and money to do it safely. Even if you're safe from mines and bullets, the sun and the sand will get you if you're ill-prepared.

The **dunes**, **cliffs**, **mountains** and **prehistoric art** of the desert surrounding Agadez are among Niger's most popular tourist attractions. They are also some of the most difficult to visit, especially if you don't have your own transport. For this reason, agencies organizing trips into the desert are flourishing in the town (or were, until the resurgence of the Tuareg conflict in 2007). For their services, which include all permits, transport, fuel, food, camping equipment, as well as a driver and cook, you can expect to pay around CFA800,000 for a medium-range eight-day tour for four people, or around CFA25,000 each per day.

Currently the **most popular agency** with Anglophone travellers is Tinarawene Tours (T96.96.25.40). The English-speaking owner's office-cum-home is in an obscure location behind the Irish Red Cross base (*Croix Rouge Irlandais*) to the east of Agadez town centre, so it's probably easiest to give him a call and get him to come to you. Other recommended agencies include Expédition Ténéré Voyages (T20.44.01.54 Wwww.expeditionstenere.com), which is one of the most professional and established of all the agencies, with international connections; Agadez Expéditions (T20.44.01.70 Wwww.agadez-tourisme.com); Dunes Voyages (T20.44.03.72 Wwww.dunes-voyages.com); Adrar Madet Voyages (T20.44.03.37 Wwww.onlinemadet.fr); and Tidène Expéditions (T20.44.05.68 Wwww.agencetidene-expeditions.com).

Accommodation

The number of **places to stay** in Agadez has increased steadily over the past few years, as have the prices, though there are still only a couple of budget places. If money is no object, however, you'll find some of West Africa's most outstanding accommodation here.

Agreboun town centre, not far from the *gare routière* T20.44.03.07. A peaceful and inexpensive place and the backpackers' choice, with dark rooms with fans, wash basins and outside toilets. You can park inside the fenced courtyard. ❷

Auberge d'Azel route de Bilma, near the junction with route de l'Aéroport T20.40.01.70 Wwww.agadez-tourisme.com. Fabulous small hotel with nine individual and beautiful rooms with brick vaulted ceilings, all sparkling clean and with every imaginable comfort, including a well-stocked bar, a French restaurant, and a fantastic rooftop terrace with a beautiful view over downtown Agadez. The helpful French–Tuareg couple who run the place also run Agadez Expéditions (see above) and can advise on trips in the region. Often full, booking recommended. ❻

Auberge La Tendé next to the EHGM/Maïssagé bus station T20.44.00.75. Wonderfully friendly, civilized hotel with birdsong echoing through the plant-filled grounds. Rooms

are simple but cool and the whole place is infused with a welcome sense of relaxation. Rooms with fan ❸ or a/c ❹, or you can camp (CFA2000).

Hôtel de l'Aïr town centre, near the Grande Mosquée T20.44.02.77. Formerly the sultan's palace and still reasonably quiet and dignified, despite the constant presence of souvenir sellers outside. Despite the architectural grandeur, the rooms aren't fancy. Rooms with fan or a/c ❸.

Hôtel de la Paix route de Bilma T20.44.02.34. Smart hotel with pool, bars, nightclub, and the town's best cybercafé, situated about 1km east of route de l'Aéroport. Caters mainly to non-Western tourists and businessmen, and worth checking out if the *Azel* is full. ❺

Pension Tellit across from *Hôtel de l'Aïr* T20.44.02.31. Luxurious Italian-run place with a handful of attractively decorated and clean self-contained a/c rooms, and the souvenir-brandishing hordes outside kept at bay by security gates. ❹

Tchintoulous route de l'Aéroport, in front of the Grand Marché ☎ 20.44.04.59. Geared mainly towards backpackers and tour groups with a range of rooms suiting most tastes, some fully self-contained with a/c, others with fans and shared facilities. The place feels a bit like a caravanserai, maybe because of the gravel floor in all the rooms. Rooms with fan ❸ or a/c ❹.
Telwa Bungalow off the Tahoua road, northwest of the Grand Marché ☎ 20.44.02.64. Newly

renovated motel-like place, with comfortable, self-contained a/c rooms, a bar and a restaurant (with excellent pizza and pasta, as well as a few select Tuareg dishes). Friendly staff. ❸–❹
Tidène not far from the mosque by the Tamoil station on route de l'Aéroport ☎ 20.44.04.06. A *banco*-style building with a pleasant garden and clean rooms, all en-suite and with fan or a/c. The restaurant is good value, too. Rooms with fan ❹ or a/c ❺.

The Town

Agadez is a sprawling town, so taking up the offers of a young guide may be invaluable. You might find yourself invited into houses (men should avoid looking at the women within the courtyard), and you'll get to see any of the town sights you might ask about.

The Grande Mosquée and around

Spiring through the one-storey skyline to a height of 27 metres (it doesn't sound much, but all is relative), the tower of the **Grande Mosquée** is a landmark whose fame has spread beyond West Africa. Built in 1515, the mosque is a classic example of early Sudanic architecture, with the wooden support beams protruding from the minaret like quills from a porcupine. Over the years the structure has been much renovated and was completely rebuilt in 1844, following the original style. In former days, the tower doubled as a sentry post, and it's worth climbing for views of the town and surrounding countryside. Though the mosque is normally off limits to non-Muslims, there's a guardian who, in exchange for a *cadeau*, will lead you to

---

Silversmiths and saddle makers in Agadez

The refined craftsmanship of the Agadez **silversmiths** has become a byword in West Africa and even internationally. Though these artists make a variety of innovative jewellery and other objects from precious metals, they're best known for the **desert cross** pendants, especially the renowned "Croix d'Agadez". Other towns with their own unique crosses include Bilma, In-Gall, Iferouâne, Tahoua and Zinder.

The smiths still work out of small *ateliers*, which you won't have to seek out, as young boys make it a point to propose a **tour** of the workshops to every tourist passing through. They say there's no obligation to buy, but once you're in the shops, the pressure to do so is intense. If you're fairly certain you're not interested in making a purchase, it's perhaps best to decline the whole show. That said, watching the *forgerons* producing jewellery by the old **lost-wax process** is genuinely interesting. A wax shape of the intended object is used to make a clay mould, which is then baked in a charcoal fire until all the wax has trickled out of the holes made for that purpose; liquid silver is poured into the mould, which after cooling is broken to free the hardened metal. Detailed carving and polishing can then take place. The craftsmen are known not only for the quality of their work, but also for the honesty of their materials. Unlike the market vendors, they have a reputation for straight dealing – when they say something is pure silver, it usually is. If you can't be bothered with a whole tour, the **Village Artisanal d'Agadez** has various craftsmen at work among the stalls.

Other artisans specialize in the **leatherwork** for which Agadez is also famous. The workshops still produce *rahlas* (camel saddles), covering the wooden frames with treated hides that are then decorated. They also make colourful sandals, with red and green leather incorporated into the design, and Tuareg "wallets" – stylized pouches worn round the neck with compartments for money, tobacco and other necessities.

the top, providing you don't arrive at prayer time. He's recently become accustomed to hefty tips from wealthy tourists, and you may not be let in for less than several thousand francs.

The nearby *Hôtel de l'Aïr* served as the **Kaocen Palace** early in the twentieth century. It's a beautiful building, and even if you don't stay here you should stop by for a look. The large dining hall is where the sultan formerly received his audiences and, it's said, where subversives were hanged after the 1916 Tuareg uprising. You can go upstairs to the rooftop terrace bar for an interesting perspective on the mosque and town.

Also in the town centre, the massive *banco* structure of the **Sultan's Palace** is the current residence of the traditional city ruler. The Nigérien government has left the basic structure of the sultanate intact, but although he's often called upon to mediate in local disputes, the sultan has no more than modest powers at state level. Agadez's main festivals always culminate at the informal public square in front of the palace.

About ten minutes' walk east of the mosque, the **Maison du Boulanger** (CFA1000, double if you want to take photos) is a beautifully decorated baker's house, with the old oven and other tools of trade still in place, not to mention the Sudanic splendour of the building itself. Nearby (ask a kid to show you the way) through some narrow dusty alleyways, the house where explorer **Heinrich Barth** stayed when passing through Agadez in 1850 has been opened up as a small museum (CFA1000). The house itself is quite unimpressive but inside – in one of the rooms – you'll see a small collection of Barth's belongings.

The markets

Not far from the mosque, the **Grand Marché**, often called the Marché Moderne, is the town's main commercial venue. Tumbledown, corrugated iron sheds offer a variety of goods, loosely divided into food sections (expensive, as most fruit and vegetables have to be trucked in from the south), tools, fabrics and so on. Many traders sell **crafts** aimed at the tourist trade, and this is one of the cheapest places to get Tuareg and Fula **jewellery**. Quality is often wanting, however, since the shiny trinkets are often made from melted-down Algerian dinars or other alloys that quickly acquire a dull green patina. Leather goods – sandals, pouches and bags – also abound. To the west of here, on rue Bilma, is the Village Artisanal d'Agadez, where you can watch much of the stuff being made – and the quality tends to be better here too.

On the eastern side of the main north–south road that splits the town in two, the **Vieux Marché** is much less hectic, but worth visiting, since it lies in one of the town's oldest quarters. The dusty streets surrounding the market are tightly hemmed in by *banco* houses bearing the stamp of Sudanic and Hausa influence, with their smooth lines and decorated facades.

Most interesting, though, is the **camel market**, on the town's northwestern outskirts. In the mornings, camels, donkeys, sheep and goats are bought and sold in an open field bordered by stalls featuring nomadic goods – mostly salt pillars, rope, water containers and mats. If you've never sat on a camel, you can do so here by approaching one of the Tuareg traders. In exchange for a small tip, he'll help you into the saddle and let you circle the area – not exactly an adventure, but it gives you the feel.

Eating and nightlife

In addition to the hotel **restaurants**, Agadez has several small places dishing up inexpensive meals. At the cheaper end of the scale, the Marché de Nuit, opposite *Hôtel Tidène* on Route de l'Aéroport, consists of rows of stalls selling a vast range of stews and grilled meat, all freshly cooked. For **picnic supplies**, you can find European canned and dried foods, plus a selection of wine, at the Mini Prix on the Route de l'Aéroport. They sell French cheese, British biscuits, Italian pasta, Mars bars and the like – and it's not that expensive. Incidentally, the **water** in Agadez is

The **gare routière** is on the paved Arlit road (the old *piste* to Arlit is no longer used), across from the *douanes*. The easiest *taxi brousse* journey to make is to Niamey via Tahoua (900km; one long day, with luck on your side), though with patience you can also find taxis doing the scenic 450km route to Zinder via Tanout (again, feasible in a single day) and the *piste* to Assamakka on the Algerian border. It's easier to get transport to Assamakka here, than in Arlit.

SNTV **buses** leave from their terminal near the *gare routière* and can get you to Arlit (three times a week – when the bus arrives from Niamey), Zinder (daily), and Tahoua, Maradi and Niamey (daily, early am). EHGM/Maissagé are round the corner on the Arlit road, next to *Auberge La Tendé*. They too have buses to Zinder (Tues am) as well as to Niamey.

Agadez **airport** now receives regular charter flights from Marseilles and Paris during the winter months with Point-Afrique (⊕www.point-afrique.com).

perfectly drinkable straight from the tap. Note that, recently, the authorities have clamped down on **drinking** in Agadez, to the extent that the hotels seem to be the only places where you can still get a beer.

Bistrot route de Bilma, next to the *Auberge d'Azel*. Very smart new restaurant serving fine, mainly French cuisine, including a very decent dessert section. Prices run CFA5000 for two courses, CFA6200 for three.

Le Gourmet near the mosque. Copious helpings of Togolese dishes, as well as salads, stews, omelettes etc; perfect for a lunchtime break during the sightseeing.

Palmier route de l'Aéroport. Small restaurant serving some of the tastiest – and certainly best-value – dishes in Agadez, including delicious rosemary-seasoned steaks. The menu is small but wait for the Algerian owner to tell you the day's specialities. An unexpected treat.

Pâtisserie Madara Rahama route de l'Aéroport, across from the small mosque. Good cold yoghurt and fresh pastries.

Le Pilier near the Grand Mosquée ⊕ 20.44.03.31. Run by the owner of the *Pension Tellit*, with outstanding – if pricey – Italian specialities, plus traditional Sahel dishes. Meals from around CFA10,000 per head.

Tamgak route de Bilma, just past the *Bistrot*. Straightforward restaurant serving local dishes to mainly local clientele, which means the dishes are often tasty but the meat can be tough and a little fatty. Their Tuareg mutton, however, is very good.

Arlit and Assamakka

Fifty years ago there was nothing at **ARLIT**, but after the discovery of **uranium** in the mid-1960s, a town burgeoned beside the vast open-cast mining complex and it's now home to more than 70,000 people. Several hundred are expats, mostly technicians working for the French nuclear-energy conglomerate, **Areva**, which runs all the operations in Arlit and the neighbouring underground uranium-mining area of **Akouta**, through its local subsidiaries, SOMAÏR and COMINAK. Niger is still the world's sixth largest producer, and most of France's nuclear energy depends on these mines, but the market has partly collapsed with the downturn in the world price for uranium, and is currently threatened by the latest Tuareg insurgency.

Arlit is really **two towns**. The first, built entirely for the mining company and its employees, is well planned and exclusive, with villas for engineers and executives, supermarkets stocked from France, a well-equipped hospital, and the town's best restaurants. The disturbing but hardly surprising divisions between African and European workers – unequal housing, salaries and living standards – make Arlit a disquieting place, though it's only when the trans-Saharan route between Assamakka

Agadez celebrates the Muslim holidays in style, especially the end of **Ramadan**, **Tabaski** and the **Prophet's Birthday**. Festivities marking these events have minor variations and will also vary slightly depending on the time of year, but they always begin with a morning prayer led by the imam, who then kills a lamb. Families return to their homes for a feast, after which the entire town reassembles along the streets between the mosque and the sultan's palace, as drummers announce the recommencement of festivities. Men gather on horseback, among them the red-turbanned sultan's guards, ready for the **cavalcades**, the highlight of the celebrations that last until sunset and then pick up again the next day. When the signal is given, the riders race their horses at a frenzied pace, kicking up clouds of dust. Men, women and children all strain for a better look, pressing dangerously close to the horsemen, who halt their charge in front of the palace, where the sultan and dignitaries are gathered.

A week after Tabaski, the week-long **Bianou** festival is also a feast for the senses, with music, colourful costumes and a carnival atmosphere. The town is divided into two sections (east and west), competing against each other through dancing. Young musicians from each section dress up with dangling hats that look like floppy roosters' combs, which they shake back and forth while dancing and playing various instruments. It's an all-day, all-night celebration, especially lively when the two groups meet directly and try to outshine one another.

The Cure Salée

Along with the Muslim festivals, one of the more interesting celebrations of the nomadic Fula and Tuareg is the **Cure Salée**, a traditional homecoming that takes place some time at the end of the rains, or shortly after they have finished, usually in mid-September. Herders who have migrated to the far south in the dry season return to the region around **In-Gall**, west of Agadez, when the large salt flats fill with water. During this period, animals are fattened and given the "salt cure", with this traditional veterinary activity punctuated by festivities – including music, dancing, and camel and horse races. Meanwhile, more serious forums gather to discuss development and political issues. The event has become significant in the national calendar as the success or otherwise of the Cure Salée is to some extent a barometer of the national mood, and government representatives from Niamey are usually present, along with film crews, journalists, NGOs and tourists.

and Tamanrasset is busy that many foreign visitors with no nuclear-industry connections even come here, and as a casual visitor you won't easily have access to Arlit's facilities. You might prefer to avoid Arlit on health grounds: Areva has come in for heavy criticism in France for not maintaining adequate health and environmental standards, and for endangering its local employees with radiation-contaminated machinery and waste.

Alongside the mining complex, a more **traditional town** has grown up in chaotic fashion. The large **market** – a maze of tiny stalls covered by mats and corrugated iron – sells vegetables, fresh meat (cut before your eyes in the open-air abattoir), and household items like decorated calabashes, pottery and basket ware.

Practicalities

There's a BIA **bank** in town. **Accommodation** is hard to come by: you can stay at the grubby but cheap and reliable *Tamesna* (☎20.45.23.32 ❷), on the main street near the market, which has a few noisy rooms behind the bar, or you can sleep on the terrace. Alternatively, 🍴 *Hôtel L'Auberge la Caravane* (☎20.89.29.49; room with fan ❷ or a/c ❸) is slightly smarter, but a little further out of town, not far from the *gare* SNTV. The **restaurant** at the *Tamesna* does reasonable European-style meals

Gerewol festivals

During the cure, or sometimes shortly afterwards, communities of the **Wodaabé** – a nomadic Fula people known as the Bororo by Tuareg and sedentary Fula – stage remarkable ceremonies called **gerewol**. Often likened to a beauty pageant, a *gerewol* is essentially a party for unmarried men, who spend hours adorning themselves with jewellery and putting on make-up – red ochre on the face, white outlines for features like the nose and mouth, black on the lips and around the eyes. Elaborate hairpieces are also concocted using scarves, beads, braids and feathers. Having prepared themselves to emphasize Wodaabé ideals of male beauty – long slender bodies, bright white teeth and eyes, and straight hair – the bachelors line up in the festival arena to dance, roll their white eyes, flash their broad smiles and chant a droning melody. The young women, who also spend a considerable amount of time beautifying themselves, look on, and one by one come forward and take their choice of the most handsome man. According to custom, if a girl doesn't like the husband proposed for her by her parents, she can marry the man she desires, chosen at the *gerewol*. Conversely, a man who isn't happy with the partner who has chosen him at the *gerewol*, has some difficulty getting out of the social obligation to spend at least a night with her. Nevertheless, this unusual institution does result in numerous marriages.

Another Wodaabé *Cure Salée* event is the virility test known as the **soro**. In this, men stand in front of their girlfriends and allow their peers to strike them several times across the chest. To demonstrate their courage to their loved one, they're expected to smile as they're beaten.

These elaborate demonstrations of manliness are part of an extensive and complex **codified social life**, which characterizes many pastoral peoples – it's similar in many respects, for example, to that of the Maasai, Samburu and Dinka in East Africa – and which finds expression in a mesh of taboos and ritual behaviour maintaining extraordinary social cohesion and group identity.

Although the events around the *Cure Salée* have been filmed and photographed often enough to make them relatively familiar images, you have to remember that the occasion is not a tourist spectacle. That said, more and more tourists seem to make it here, and it's no longer as difficult to get to as it used to be: many of the tour operators in Agadez organize trips once the dates are set.

such as *poulet frites* with canned peas, while the **bar-nightclub** here is a popular place to hide from the heat with a cold beer or soda with ice cubes – Arlit's water is perfectly pure – and the tables spill over into the shaded interior courtyard. At night this is the centre of the town's activity. Away from the hotel, there's a good breakfast place in the shape of the patisserie by the BIA, opposite the Total petrol station, where they serve yoghurt and cakes.

As for **onward transport**, SNTV buses (℡20.45.20.13) leave for Niamey daily except Tuesday and Thursday, stopping overnight in Agadez. If you're heading north to Assamakka, there are only occasional vehicles starting from Arlit, though you may be lucky and get a place in a taxi coming up from Agadez.

From Arlit to Assamakka

The 200-kilometre drive from Arlit to **ASSAMAKKA** on the Algerian border takes three to six hours, depending on your vehicle and desert-driving experience. From Arlit, the main *piste* runs parallel to the line of *balises* (marker drums, which have in many cases been replaced with piles of tyres or rocks), within a distance of at most 3km. The Assamakka customs and immigration post closes at 6pm and entering Assamakka after dusk is prohibited. If you have to camp en route, choose a mound or a gully well off the *piste* – where you won't be hit by a night-driving smuggler's lorry.

The Aïr Mountains and Ténéré Desert

Two classic journeys from Agadez lead through the great massif of the **Aïr Mountains** and the rolling dunes of the **Ténéré Desert**. *Pistes* wend through both areas, but most of them are extremely demanding, and they often get washed away during the rainy season or obliterated from sight when winds kick up a desert sandstorm. Travel in this area requires experience, a very good guide, and reliable equipment, none of which comes cheap. It's also recommended that you drive two vehicles together in case of breakdowns or any other emergencies.

The Route de l'Aïr

The **Route de l'Aïr**, accessible from the old, unsurfaced Arlit road northeast from Agadez, is relatively good *piste* apart from the washboard surface and one or two other unexpected hazards. The road forks at **TÉLOUA** (take a left); about 15km further on you can make a diversion left to **TAFADEK**, a deep spring that's great for swimming and which is believed to possess curative properties. Back on the main *piste*, 77km out of Agadez, you branch off to the right from the Arlit road and follow the sign to **ELMÉKI**, 125km from Agadez.

Just outside Elméki, you'll notice a number of tracks leading off the main route – they head to Arlit. Follow instead the large *piste* to the village of **KREB KREB**, 72km from Elméki. (About 15km before Kreb Kreb, an alternative route leads directly north to **Assodé**, a shortcut that bypasses Timia.) Just after Kreb Kreb, the tracks lead through the beautiful **Agalak range** – difficult driving, as the route crosses dry riverbeds (*kori*) and hidden stretches of sand.

Timia to Iferouâne

Roughly 220km from Arlit and a little more from Agadez is **TIMIA**, a large Tuareg village nestled between the Agalak Mountains and a wide desert *kori*. The town itself is one of the most beautiful oases in the Aïr, with extensive gardens and palms. Away from the boxlike *banco* houses that spread over the valley, well-maintained **Fort Timia**, also known as Fort Massu, was built by the French in the 1950s. You can stay here for a small fee and enjoy the striking view of the In-Sarek *kori* and mountains. Alternatively, there are several *campements* in town where you can camp or stay in basic rooms (❶–❷). On the outskirts of town, the **Cascade de Timia** grows from a trickling waterfall into something quite spectacular during the rains.

North of Timia, the road continues some 30km to the **ruins of Assodé**. Founded as long as a thousand years ago, Assodé preceded Agadez as capital of the Tuareg and was once the most important town in the Aïr. As trans-Saharan trade declined, so did its fortunes, and Kaocen dealt the final blow when he sacked it in 1917. Today the site is a ghost town – its ruins lie east of the *piste* and you'll need sharp eyes to spot them. A maze of empty streets winds through abandoned houses and squares, though many of the larger buildings – including the **grande mosquée** – are remarkably well preserved.

Beyond Assodé, the tracks become progressively easier. After a further 90km, they lead to Niger's northernmost settlement of any size, **IFEROUÂNE**, a marvellous oasis on the fringes of the striking **Tamgak Mountains**. The *kori* running through town breathes life into some of the most beautiful **gardens** in the Aïr. When it comes to **accommodation**, the choice is limited, but happily enough, to the new *Pension Tellit* (☎20.44.02.31 ❹), run by the Italian owners of the same-named hotel in Agadez. It's a beautiful *banco* building with five comfortable, fanned rooms with shared facilities and a good, small restaurant with expensive beer.

In times of peace, Iferouâne is the venue for the **Festival de l'Aïr**, a celebration of Tuareg culture that is Niger's version of Mali's Festival in the Desert (see p.337).

Iferouâne is also the starting point for visiting the Aïr region's wealth of **prehistoric sites**. Just north of the town along the **Zeline** *kori*, Neolithic rock paintings of giraffes, cattle and antelopes can be seen on a distinctive boulder outcrop. There are more such paintings in the valley of the **Aouderer** *kori* near **TEZIREK** (aka Tazerzait), 90km from Iferouâne.

The Ténéré

The route east from Agadez to Bilma leads through what's often described as the most beautiful desert in the Sahara: the **Ténéré**. This is strictly for the well-equipped: an arduous, 620-kilometre journey, with a great deal of very soft sand and hardly any supplies or water along the way. Even in times of peace and security, you must have a guide, and usually be in convoy, before the police will let you go: markers along the route include the graves of victims of the crossing.

Leaving Agadez, the first 200-odd kilometres run through the southern Aïr, with alternating stretches of soft sand and rock-strewn *piste*. After 270km, you arrive at the site of the **Arbre du Ténéré**, formerly the only tree growing in a region the size of France. For over a century it served as a landmark for desert crossers, until it was knocked over by a truck driver in 1973. A scrap-metal sculpture now marks the spot, while the remains of the real tree are exhibited in Niamey's National Museum. There's still reasonable **drinking water** at the well here – forty metres down.

After 440km, you arrive at **FACHI**, a small Toubou and Kanouri village with a few hundred inhabitants and cool groves of date palms. In the centre, the fortified *ksar* or palace is built of salt blocks; you can also visit the **salines** (evaporation salt pits) on the eastern outskirts of town. The road covering the remaining 110km to Bilma is the one used by the *azalaï*, or camel caravans, that still ply the region. It's full of long stretches of soft sand, and can be tough going for the most able of vehicles.

Bilma

With around a thousand Kanouri, Tuareg and Toubou inhabitants, the small fortified town of **BILMA** seems nearly a miracle out here in the middle of nowhere. Set against the backdrop of the **Kaouar Cliffs** – and as picturesque and hospitable as you could wish – Bilma owes its existence to natural water sources, which support a sizeable *palmeraie* and gardens. People in Bilma often refer to themselves, distinctively, as **Beriberi** (or *Blibli*), a term which has various interpretations but usually implies Hausa-Kanouri. Many Beriberi are Hausa in all but name, and some speak Hausa as their first language.

Bilma is best known for its **salt manufacture** (for animal, rather than human, consumption) which just about maintains the viability of one of the desert's last camel caravan routes. Anything from twenty to forty caravans a year make the trek from Agadez, with up to a thousand camels in each one – although in living memory the figure was sometimes 50,000 or more. In recent years, the demand for Bilma's commodity has slackened in the traditional Hausa markets of southern Niger and Nigeria, where drought has depleted so much livestock. Meanwhile, Bilma is filled with unsold sixty-centimetre pillars of rock-hard salt, and the locals continue to make them in moulds of saline mud, piling up vast reserves for a fatter future.

If you want to stay in Bilma, there's basic **accommodation** and a **restaurant** at *Le Camping Touristique de l'AKFO* (☏20.44.04.88 ❷). They can also help with well-informed guides to the region.

Nigeria

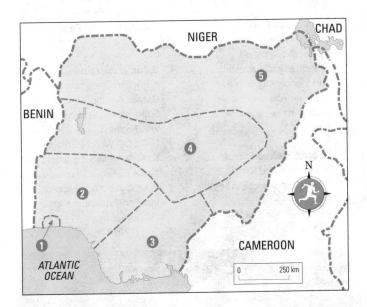

Highlights 1070
Introduction and Basics 1071
14.1 Lagos 1117
14.2 The southwest 1133

14.3 The southeast 1152
14.4 Central Nigeria 1169
14.5 The north and northeast 1185

Nigeria highlights

* **Suya** Delicious, spicy, grilled kebab street-food (usually beef or goat), available throughout Nigeria. See p.1084

* **Lagos** West Africa's biggest and wildest metropolis, a dense, vibrant, visually arresting and friendly city with a lively music scene, street life and markets galore. See p.1117

* **Osogbo Sacred Forest** A tranquil shrine to the Yoruba water-goddess Osun, now a UNESCO World Heritage Site. See p.1145

* **Wikki Warm Springs** A true West African highlight, where crystal-clear waters bubble up over silver sand in the remote confines of Yankari National Park. See p.1184

* **Sukur Mountain Kingdom** Once part of Cameroon, this remote 500-year-old settlement was Nigeria's first UNESCO World Heritage Site. Go during the annual Yawal festival and meet the King and hundreds of traditional drummers in full pageantry. See p.1214

▲ Osun grove wall, Osogbo

Introduction and Basics

Of all the countries in Africa, **Nigeria** is perhaps the hardest to introduce. Many might feel it needs no introduction – corruption, military coups and email scams being all you need to know. Perhaps not surprisingly, this is only a fraction of the truth, for Nigeria is also the land that has produced inspirational visionaries such as Wole Soyinka and Fela Kuti, and contains a wealth of cultural and scenic diversity equal to any in the region.

As the most populous country on the continent, bursting with entrepreneurial energy, Nigeria should also have Africa's largest and most dynamic **economy**, and yet it languishes behind smaller, less populous nations like Egypt and South Africa. Often decried as a country which has suffered from poor leadership, Nigeria does suffer from dire security and infrastructure issues, forcing most Nigerians into permanent survival mode, which they suffer with enormous good humour. The complexity of Nigeria's **human picture** is often reduced to the relations of three ethnic groups, the Yoruba, the Igbo and the Hausa, when in fact its peoples speak more than five hundred distinct languages.

Nigeria is in many ways **Africa in microcosm**, with the rest of the continent's landscapes and weather patterns rolled into one nation, from the Sahel and savannah landscapes of the Muslim north, to the humid forests and creeks of the largely Christian south.

In truth, this is a fascinating country, offering a lifetime of discoveries for curious travellers and expats willing to defer judgement.

Nigeria's notoriety is unduly influenced by its capital, **Lagos** – a city of incalculable population and urban distress – and even Lagos, for all that its poorer districts may be terrible to live in, can be a dynamic, exhilarating and surprisingly friendly place to visit, with a nightlife unrivalled in West Africa, and indeed most of the world. But if the unforgiving tempo of Lagos is too much, then leave the city – for **Oyo**, **Osogbo**, **Ife**, **Benin**, or even giant **Ibadan** – and Lagos soon seems an anomaly: other cities certainly have their share of blight and bluster, but none really compares. These hinterland towns, where growth has been less dizzying and local traditions not yet bulldozed into oblivion, still show you hints of the greatness of the old Yoruba and Benin kingdoms in their palaces and museums, festivals and sacred sites.

To the **east** – beyond the geographical and cultural dividing-line of the **Niger River** – the forests and plantations of the **Igbo country** stretch out behind the vast fan of the **Niger River delta**. This region has made a remarkable recovery since the civil war of the late 1960s, caused by its attempted secession.

The creek and waterfront cities – **Onitsha**, **Warri**, **Port Harcourt** – have gained a new prosperity with their oil reserves. These are mostly busy, self-interested cities where the **internal conflict** of recent years over oil money and development has deterred all but the best-protected expat and business visitors (see "Crime and safety" p.1086). One exception is the engaging old trading base of **Calabar** whose attractive setting adds to its reputation as the country's most easy-going city. There's also a conservation focus in this corner of the country, since the rediscovery in 1987 of **gorillas**, long thought to have been extinct, now protected in the wilds of the **Cross River National Park**.

Central Nigeria is a region of lower population, higher ground and some inspiring scenery, dotted with outcrops and massive stone inselbergs. This is one of the best parts of the country to travel around and its main cities, the new capital **Abuja**, and **Jos**, an old hill station, have reasonable infrastructure. Two other **national parks** – **Kainji Lake** in the northwest, and the long-established **Yankari** with its remarkable natural swimming

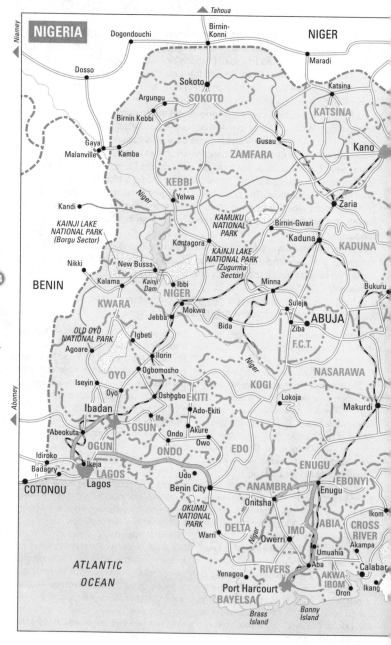

NIGERIA

pool – are located in this central region. And the **eastern highlands** are some of the most beautiful and unexplored mountains in Africa, abutting Cameroon's much better known Roumsiki region.

The north of the country is **Hausa–Fulani** territory, predominantly Islamic, like the neighbouring regions of the French-speaking Sahel. There's a more comfortable climate at these latitudes and the cities are manageable, but it's the region's history – embodied in the **walled old city** quarters of Zaria, Katsina and the big metropolis of Kano – that gives northern Nigeria a special slant. While they can't compare for flavour and historical atmosphere with the old cities of North Africa or the Middle East, these once independent emirates (the emirs are now largely ceremonial figures) have their

special character. In the afternoon crush of the **Kurmi market** in Kano, or wandering through Zaria's striking **architecture**, or witnessing any of the amazing **Sallah Durbar** festivals at the end of Ramadan, a much bigger and more rewarding view of Nigeria begins to emerge than the one you might have brought with you.

People

Geographically, Nigeria has been profoundly shaped by its two great rivers – the **Niger** and the **Benue** – which merge together in a Y-shape at the town of Lokoja. This "Middle Belt" area isn't the centre of the country, but it exactly corresponds to the meeting place of the three great cultural spheres

Fact file

The **Federal Republic of Nigeria** is the most populous country in Africa, with an estimated 140 million people; its land area of 924,000 square kilometres is nearly four times as big as Britain and bigger than Texas and New Mexico combined. **Lagos**, the largest city (with at least fifteen million inhabitants), is the country's economic and cultural hub; administration, however, has been transferred to **Abuja**, in central Nigeria, which became the country's capital in 1991. The principal exports are **oil and natural gas**, followed at some distance by cocoa, palm products, rubber, timber and tin. Despite debt relief, the national debt stands at a colossal $32 billion, or $230 for every Nigerian man, woman and child.

In 1999, Nigeria returned from years of kleptocratic **military rule** to an elected government. After two terms in office, Olusegun Obasanjo handed over to **President Umaru Yar'Adua** in 2007, the first transition from one elected leader to another in Nigeria's history.

Nigeria is a federation divided into **36 states**, plus the **Federal Capital Territory of Abuja**. Each state has its own state government and **capital** (in parentheses below). The states are commonly divided into six geopolitical zones.

South-West	South-East	North-Central
Ekiti (Ado-Ekiti)	Abia (capital Umuahia)	Benue (Makurdi)
Lagos (Ikeja)	Anambra (capital	Kaduna (Kaduna)
Ogun (Abeokuta)	Awka)	Kogi (Lokoja)
Ondo (Akure)	Ebonyi (Abakaliki)	Kwara (Ilorin)
Osun (Osogbo)	Enugu (Enugu)	Nassarawa (Lafia)
Oyo (Ibadan)	Imo (Owerri)	Niger (Minna)
		Plateau (Jos)
South-South	**North-West**	
Akwa Ibom (Uyo)	Jigawa (Dutse)	**North-East**
Bayelsa-(Yenagoa)	Kano (Kano)	Adamawa (Yola)
Cross River (Calabar)	Katsina (Katsina)	Bauchi (capital Bauchi)
Delta (Asaba)	Kebbi (Birnin Kebbi)	Borno (Maiduguri)
Edo (Benin City)	Sokoto (Sokoto)	Gombe (Gombe)
Rivers (Port Harcourt)	Zamfara (Gusau)	Taraba (Jalingo)
		Yobe (Damaturu)

which dominate Nigerian life – the southwest (**Yorubaland**), southeast (**Igboland**) and north (**Hausaland**).

The **ethnic differentiation** of these regions is a convenient way of coming to grips with exceptionally complex cultural and linguistic groupings, but it does the country's "minorities" – several of which number in the millions – a profound injustice. Nigeria in fact has no fewer than 500 ethnic groups, speaking as many languages, making it linguistically one of the world's most complex regions.

Beyond the three main groups of the Yoruba, Igbo and Hausa, other sizeable minority groups are the **Nupe** on the northern fringe of Yorubaland, the **Ijaw** in the Delta region, the **Tiv** and **Idoma** in the Middle Belt, the **Edo** in Edo State, the **Efik** and **Ibibio**, who live in and around Calabar in Cross River State, and the **Kanouri** who live in the far north east around Maiduguri. Many of the smaller ethnic groups in Nigeria are in danger of dying out, with some languages only spoken by a few hundred people. Some ethnic groups are closely related to others, such as the Itsekiri and the Nupe, both of whom speak languages grounded in Yoruba.

In the **north**, the great Hausa–Fulani configuration has tended to obscure groups such as the **Gwari**, as well as the **Bauchi-area** languages. In the northeast the picture is very fragmented and, in the many mountain districts where languages of the **Adamawa** and **Chadic groups** are spoken, who speaks what and who claims common ancestry with whom are questions still largely unanswered. Nigeria also has native speakers of Arabic – the Shua Arabs who live in the far northeast, who are closely related to the Baggara nomadic tribe in Sudan.

The Nigerian government has allowed **traditional rulers** to keep their titles and in some cases has even supported regional monarchies. Although the Yoruba *obas* have less *de jure* power than they once did, they still enjoy considerable prestige and often mediate in local disputes. In some cases, they've taken on official government functions to complement traditional roles.

When to go

There's a clear climatic division between north and south and many variations within the two major zones. The most comfortable time to be in Lagos is December and January; on the Plateau, November to February; in Kano, November and December; and in Calabar, December.

Rains in **the north** fall during a single season, roughly between May and September. Usually this amounts to no more than 500mm, most of it falling in the months of July and August. Typically the hottest months are March and April, when the *harmattan* winds have run their course and the rains not yet begun; at this time, midday temperatures often rise above 45°C (113°F) in the shade.

In the **southwest**, the long rains bucket down from March to July, with the wettest months usually May and June. There's a short lull, usually sometime in August (the "little dry"), then further heavy rain from September to October. The yearly rainfall in the southwest averages around 1800mm. In the **southeast**, the total annual rainfall can exceed 4000mm (about five times the annual average of, say, London or Minneapolis) and there is a continuous and somewhat depressing rainy season from April to October, with a brief drying-off period in the middle which is not guaranteed every year. Temperatures in the south tend to be lower than in the north despite the region's proximity to the equator, but the humidity can be really oppressive.

Getting there from the rest of Africa

Air connections from the rest of Africa have been steadily improving in the past few years, most airlines still flying into Lagos rather than Abuja, however, with onward connections north to the capital. **Land borders** are gradually getting somewhat easier to cross, too.

Flights within Africa

From other cities in **West Africa**, Virgin Nigeria (ⓦ www.virginnigeria.com) has direct

Average temperatures and rainfall

Lagos

	Jan	Feb	Mar	Apr	May	June	July	Aug	Sept	Oct	Nov	Dec
Temperatures °C												
Min (night)	23	25	26	25	24	23	23	23	23	23	24	24
Max (day)	31	32	32	32	32	29	28	28	28	29	31	31
Rainfall mm	28	46	102	150	269	460	279	64	140	206	60	25
Days with rainfall	2	3	7	10	16	20	16	10	14	16	7	2

Kano

	Jan	Feb	Mar	Apr	May	June	July	Aug	Sept	Oct	Nov	Dec
Temperatures °C												
Min (night)	13	15	19	24	24	23	22	21	21	19	16	13
Max(day)	30	33	37	38	37	34	31	29	31	34	33	31
Rainfall mm	0	0	3	10	69	117	206	310	142	13	0	0
Days with rainfall	0	0	0	1	8	8	14	19	12	1	0	0

Jos

	Jan	Feb	Mar	Apr	May	June	July	Aug	Sept	Oct	Nov	Dec
Temperatures °C												
Min (night)	11	12	15	17	17	16	16	16	16	16	13	11
Max (day)	31	33	34	34	33	30	28	28	29	31	31	31
Rainfall mm	3	3	27	85	205	226	330	292	213	41	2	3

Calabar

	Jan	Feb	Mar	Apr	May	June	July	Aug	Sept	Oct	Nov	Dec
Temperatures °C												
Min (night)	23	23	23	23	23	22	22	22	22	22	23	23
Max (day)	30	32	32	31	30	30	28	28	29	29	30	30
Rainfall mm	43	76	153	213	312	406	450	405	427	310	191	43

flights from Dakar, Accra and Douala to Lagos, while Aero Contractors (@www.acn.aero) flies to Lagos from Abidjan three times a week, from Accra up to twice a day, from Bamako every Thursday, from Libreville twice weekly, from Monrovia three times a week, from Malabo twice a week and from São Tomé every Saturday.

From **southern Africa**, South African Airways (@www.flysaa.com) flies daily from Johannesburg to Lagos, competing with the daily Virgin Nigeria flight.

Meanwhile, daily flights in from **East Africa** are covered by Kenya Airways and Emirates.

Overland from Niger

From Niger, two main routes aim for **Kano**: one from **Maradi**, which would allow you to take in the old Nigerian emirate of **Katsina**; the other from **Zinder**, a beautiful Hausa town. You can also cross from **Birnin-Konni to Sokoto**, or, further west, from **Gaya to Kamba**, from where you can connect to Sokoto. All four routes have good bush-taxi transport.

Overland from Ghana, Togo and Benin

The **coastal route** from **Accra** (476km) and **Lomé** (275km) to **Lagos** takes in some picturesque coastal scenery of palms, creeks and beaches. By private car, the trip from Accra takes about eight hours; it may take half as long again or more if you're travelling by public transport, as the vehicle is repeatedly unloaded and reloaded at the three borders, each with customs and immigration posts on both sides.

You can get taxis direct to Lagos from Accra, Lomé or Cotonou. They're relatively cheap these days, but you can further cut costs by taking the taxi only as far as the Benin frontier post at the village of **Kraké**, on the Benin–Nigeria border, and finding another

vehicle on from there. On public transport, you'll end up at the Oshodi motor park on the northern outskirts of Lagos, from where you can get onward transport without going into the city centre.

If you're intent on avoiding Lagos altogether, get yourself to **Porto Novo** in Benin, from where you can enter Nigeria 30km north at the Igolo–Idiroko frontier post, continuing from here on the A5-1 to meet the main A5 Lagos–Abeokuta road 10km north of Ikeja.

Overland from Cameroon and Chad

The main frontier crossing from Cameroon is **Mamfé to Ikom**, over the Cross River bridge. Customs and immigration for Cameroon are in **Ekok**, on the east bank of the Cross (border open 24/7), whence you walk over the bridge to **Mfum**, the Nigerian post. From Mfum, you can catch a taxi to **Ikom** and onwards to **Calabar** or **Enugu**. There's a less often used route from **Mamfé** to Calabar, turning off south (left) from the "main" Ikom road at **Eyumajok**, 48km west of Mamfé. Note that the Mamfé–Ikom road is frequently impassable on the Cameroonian side during the rainy season. There's also a twice-weekly ferry from **Limbé** to Calabar (see p.1266).

Further north, out of the Bamenda Highlands, you can cross on foot from **Dumbo to Bissaula** (see p.1294), and there are minor crossings all the way along the mountainous border, though few see much traffic. The rough route from Garoua to **Yola** is a little busier, as is the northern route from Mora to **Banki** – a village straddling the border. Customs and immigration at Banki are generally low-key, and this is considered to be the easiest border crossing between Cameroon and Nigeria. Taxis are generally no problem from here to Maiduguri.

Finally, there's the northernmost crossing from **Kousséri** to **Fotokol** (Cameroon formalities) and **Gamboru** (Nigerian post). This is your most likely way into Nigeria coming from **Ndjamena** in Chad. If you're transiting Cameroon like this and have a Nigerian visa, the Cameroon customs will issue you with a free one-day transit visa at the immigration post in Kousséri.

Red tape and visas

Visas are required by all except ECOWAS nationals. Most Nigerian embassies or high commissions will only issue visas to nationals (or long-term residents) of the country where they are located. Thus it's better to obtain a visa in your country of residence before travelling abroad: it seems to be much easier for Nigerian embassies to renew expired visas than issue new ones.

On arrival in Nigeria, you may be asked to pay **customs duty** on some of your personal belongings – it's up to you to prove as cheerfully as possible that they are your personal belongings, and not dutiable merchandise, and that you will be taking them out of the country again.

It's illegal to export **"antique works of art"**, and there's full scope for anything that looks old to be confiscated when you come to leave, unless you have obtained a **certificate of export** from the National Museum in Lagos. Barring that, anything you buy that looks like art or an "antique" is best sent home through a freighting agency.

Info, websites, maps

Tourist offices and local branches of the Ministry of Information can be found throughout the country, and are listed in the guide section of chapter. There are now local tourism boards in most states, as well as six federal tourism boards. None of these offices, however, are of much use to travellers on the ground.

Surprisingly, there is no good standalone **map of Nigeria**. In Nigeria itself, the best map is the *Nigeria Road Map* published by MDZmultimedia Ltd. The *Nigeria Road Atlas*, published by Mapit (1:700,000), is the best of its kind currently available. Another useful map is *Historical Sites of Nigeria* (published by Legacy), which lists 129 historical sites,

48 national museums and all 15 national parks.

Fairly easily obtained outside Nigeria is International Travel Maps' topographical road map, *Nigeria* (1:1,600,000), though it's so riddled with errors and typos that you're probably better off with the slightly smaller-scale but much more reliable and readable Reise Know-How *West Africa Coastal Countries* (1:2,000,000), printed on durable plastic paper.

Recommended websites

The most useful Nigeria-related **websites** are:

Nigeria Tourism Development Corporation Ⓦ www.nigeriatourism.net. Among its features is information on each of the country's national parks.

Nigerian Government Ⓦ www.nigeria.gov.ng. Includes a section on culture and tourism, a current list of Nigerian embassies abroad, and links to the websites of all the country's main daily newspapers.

NigeriaWorld Ⓦ nigeriaworld.com. The latest news from Nigeria, with headline stories and features.

Pidgin English Dictionary Ⓦ tinyurl.com/2uczqh. Babawilly's comprehensive glossary of all the *essenco* you need to *sabi* local pidgin English like a real Naija.

Nigeria Arts Ⓦ www.nigeria-arts.net. An excellent database of Nigerian arts and artists.

Lagos Live Ⓦ www.lagoslive.com. An excellent online guide for visitors to Lagos.

Nigerian Field Society Ⓦ www.nigerianfield.org. Founded in 1930, the NFS is dedicated to the human and natural history of West Africa, in particular of Nigeria. An excellent site for background and contacts.

African Legacy Ⓦ www.tinyurl.com/387m9k. Bournemouth University's School of Conservation Sciences offers a short cut to some of Nigeria's most underrated (and under-visited) archeological sites.

Niger Wives Ⓦ www.nigerwivesnigeria.com. Great resource for women, especially partners of Nigerian men.

NaijaBlog Ⓦ naijablog.blogspot.com. Stay in touch with all that matters in the fields of culture and politics with this much-read blog written by one of the updaters of this chapter.

The media

Although Nigeria has a lively **print-media** sector, standards are poor and corruption amongst journalists is rife thanks to low wages and the 'brown envelope' syndrome. The highest-selling newspaper sells well under 100,000 copies per day – an indication of the distrust with which many Nigerians regard the press (and perhaps of the level of poverty). Twelve national dailies dominate – the *Guardian*, the *Punch*, *This Day*, *Vanguard*, *Leadership*, *Nigerian Tribune*, *Daily Trust*, *The Sun*, *The Comet*, *Daily Independent* and two business papers *Financial Standard* and *Business Day*. Of these, the *Guardian* provides the most complete economic and political analysis, while the *Punch* and *This Day* are the most outspoken, but none of the papers is very strong on international news. The most widely read and influential political magazines are the weekly *Tell Magazine* and *NewsWatch*. In the past few years, various women's magazines have emerged, the two most popular being *Genevieve* and *True Love West Africa*. There are also numerous celebrity-targeting photo-based magazines, the most popular being the glossy *Ovation*. Also worth a look is the entertaining scandal sheet *City People*.

Television

The first **private TV stations** were licensed in 1993, when the government gave up its monopoly, and there are now more than thirty stations. NTA is the government-owned station, with programmes in English and the three main national languages. Rivalling NTA are private operators AIT, Channels, MiTV and Silverbird. Satellite dishes pick up the South African–owned DSTV network, where you can catch up on CNN, BBC World, Sky News and the English Premier League from the comfort of your room.

Radio

Radio is organized under the **FRCN** (Federal Radio Corporation of Nigeria), which broadcasts three short-wave programmes in English and national languages nationwide. Individual stations for the different states also broadcast their own medium-wave programmes. In Lagos particularly, a number of privately run FM stations have emerged, including Cool FM, Ray Power and Rhythm FM. Music on Nigerian radio can be extremely good, and covers a wide spectrum of African styles, as well as gospel, soul, reggae and hip-hop – both imported and home-grown.

Health

Vaccination certificates for **yellow fever** are mandatory. Immigration officials sometimes also ask for cholera vaccination certificates. **Malaria**, however, should be your main health concern (see p.40).

Water is good and drinkable from taps in most towns across the country. In isolated rural areas, it requires boiling, filtering or purification tablets. If you're travelling in rural areas in the dry season, don't be surprised if there's a certain reluctance to fill your water bottles, at least for free – water shortages are common.

Hospitals are reasonably well equipped in comparison to neighbouring countries. In Lagos, the **Eko Hospital** is one of the better places to go for treatment (see p.1132). Also recommended is the **Sacred Heart Hospital** in Abeokuta, 100km north of Lagos. In a case of serious illness, contact your embassy. All major towns have **pharmacies**, though some aren't particularly well stocked.

Costs, money, banks

Nigeria's currency is the **naira** (₦), divided into 100 **kobo**. There are coins (though you rarely see them in use), and notes of ₦5, ₦10, ₦20, ₦50, ₦100, ₦200, ₦500 and ₦1000. The naira has fluctuated substantially over the last few years; currently, the approximate **rate of exchange** is US$1 = ₦120, £1 = ₦230. Export and import of naira is prohibited.

You should generally find **costs** reasonable – outside of Lagos, even quite decent hotels can usually be found for under £20/$40 a night, and you can eat well for £12/$25 a day. Long-distance travel can be a real bargain.

If you're **wiring funds** through **Western Union**, you'll find that their main representatives in Nigeria are the First Bank of Nigeria. In principle they pay out in naira only, but money may be paid out in dollars at certain branches so long as it is wired in dollars.

14

NIGERIA | Basics

Changing money

For changing money, **banks** are very much a last resort. Some may grudgingly agree to change cash US dollars, or occasionally sterling, at a very low rate, and take all day about it. You're much better off using privately operated **forex bureaux** (bureaux de change), found in most large towns – sometimes attached to upmarket hotels – and offering much the same rate as the **parallel market** (also known as the "black market" but without the illegal connotations). If using the latter, be wary of changing on the street – go to an office or shop if possible, always count out your naira and have them in your hand before handing over your hard currency, and abort the transaction if the dealer tries to hurry or distract you; private arrangements with expats or businesspeople are best. Dollars are the preferred currency, sterling second; euros are still unfamiliar to many people, but most forex bureaux will accept them, as they will (usually) CFA francs.

Traveller's cheques are pretty much unusable in Nigeria, even though some Nigerian embassies demand them as proof of funds when you apply for a visa. If you do happen to bring them, your best bet is to go to the issuer's local representative and hope for the best. At the very least you'll need to have your purchase receipts to hand.

Credit cards aren't much use in Nigeria either: you can't use them for ATM cash advances, and only the most expensive hotels accept them. Moreover, there's a significant **fraud** risk if you do use your card.

Getting around

Nigeria has some 70,000km of **paved roads**, a remarkable figure for this part of the world. An old but still just about operational **rail network** connects the northern and southern extremities of the country. Domestic **air services** are relatively good and reasonably priced. River travel on the Niger and Benue isn't developed commercially, most boats being for the benefit of bulk goods traffic rather than passengers.

Hitchhiking in Nigeria isn't especially difficult – but you need to be confident of your abilities to tell a bad driver from a fast one, and to act decisively on your conclusion – it's much better to be stranded on the highway than spread over it. Truck drivers are your best bet, and they'll often want payment.

Flights

The domestic air travel market in Nigeria has developed significantly in the past two years. Virgin Nigeria (Ⓦ www.virginnigeria.com) and Arik Air (Ⓦ www.arikair.com) both offer several flights a day between Lagos, Kano and Abuja, as well as links between Lagos and Benin City, Calabar, Kano, Enugu, Jos, Port Harcourt, Owerri and Sokoto. Expect to pay from around ₦12,000 for a seat from Lagos to Abuja. Several airlines compete on these routes, including Aero, Bellview, Chanchangi, IRS and Overland Airways. There are some discounts available for advance booking, but in practice it's often easiest just to turn up and buy your ticket for the next available flight. Schedules and contact details for domestic airlines can be found online at Ⓦ www.lagoslive.com/airlines.

Fuel prices

Although the price has rocketed in recent years, fuel is still inexpensive in Nigeria at around ₦80 per litre. The problems of unavailability and long queues at filling stations are now largely a thing of the past, though they still occur sporadically. For the benefit of those who can't be bothered to find a filling station, fuel is still sometimes sold by the roadside. If you're driving through Africa, it's worth stocking up with as much fuel as you can transport. You won't be taxed on it at the border, and it can be twice as expensive in the CFA countries. Beware of taking large quantities of fuel into Cameroon, however: you don't want to be accused of being part of the major trade there in smuggled Nigerian petrol.

Trains

The Nigeria Railway Corporation (NRC) operate, services from **Lagos to Kano** (via Ibadan, Kaduna and Zaria), from **Port Harcourt to Kano** (via Enugu), and from **Port Harcourt to Maiduguri** (via Enugu and Bauchi). Services are extremely erratic however – all services are liable to suspension at any time – and you should check the latest situation with the NRC headquarters in Abuja (℡ 09/523 7498 or 523 1912). Even when running, and even if on time rather than hours late, trains are painfully slow. **Fares** are a little lower than on buses. Hopes are pinned on an upgrading of the rail network by Chinese and Korean infrastructure projects planned for the near future.

Motors and buses

Road transport in Nigeria is easily the fastest in West Africa – often dangerously so. Bush taxis (called **motors** in Nigeria) are quick and comfortable, though any concerns you may have about speeding are justified: be prepared to shout at the driver to slow down if you fear for your life. Fortunately, overcrowding is the exception rather than the rule. There's usually a choice between a Peugeot 504 (estate or saloon, referred to as a "wagon") or a 16-seat Japanese minibus (known graphically as a "mauler"). There's rarely a long wait in the motor parks of major cities. Full-size **buses** ("luxury buses" as the operators like to call them, though they offer few comforts – apart from a little more legroom – than you might expect) also link major cities and usually run to fixed schedules. There are innumerable small bus companies but, surprisingly, no major firms whose route networks cover the majority of the country.

As a rough indication of **fares**, the overnight Lagos–Sokoto trip costs ₦4000, only slightly more than the much shorter Lagos–Abuja journey, while the four-hour ride from Abuja to Jos costs ₦1500.

Driving and cycling

Nigeria requires a **carnet** (see p.27) if you want to enter the country in your own vehicle. Be sure to get one before arriving here as the alternative is to pay 250 percent of the value of the car in hard currency at the border and receive it back in naira when you leave. When leaving the country, be wary of giving up your carnet, as the authorities may neglect to return their copy of the document to your national motorists' association as required, thereby holding up the release of your funds from bond.

Local Nigerian **insurance** doesn't cost much at the frontier, so it seems foolhardy not to buy it. If you have already bought a *carte brune* (see p.27), note that it is valid in Nigeria.

If you have your own vehicle, be careful where you leave it. Overlanders will encounter no special problems in northern Nigeria, but in the south some take a lesson from residents who carve their licence numbers on all windows and use crook locks. Never park in an unguarded area and leave nothing of value in your car at any time.

Car rental

The cost of **car rental** has gone down in recent years, but it's still quite pricey, as you're often obliged to hire a **driver** as well. Many Lagos outlets insist on this – and it's preferable if you're new to the city; elsewhere you may be able to drive yourself. The distinction between chauffeur-driven car rental and taking a taxi is blurred; make it clear who will pay for fuel.

Roads

Most Nigerian **main roads** were superb until the early 1990s, by which time they were beginning to need more maintenance than they were getting. Since then, the neglect of the network has become an increasing problem, causing serious accidents and millions of dollars' worth of damage in a society that is now very mobile. In theory, collapsed sections of road are flagged by signs with a skull and crossbones followed at 100-metre intervals by "60", "50", "40" and "30" "Slow Down" signs. But hundreds of kilometres of road surface are now in a very bad state and the warning system is becoming redundant, so drive with caution. The worst roads are in the southeast.

Few traffic signs are posted along the roads outside the major cities, except for regular roadside **marker stones** marked with the first three letters of the name of the next and previous major towns, and the distance in kilometres.

There are few **roadblocks** in central Nigeria, but they appear with increasing frequency towards the borders. Although often privately on the make, the officials are there to maintain law and order. Usually, they'll wave you through, but it's always advisable to slow down to be sure. If stopped, remain in your vehicle until told what to do, as half the officials will want you to stay put and the other half will want you to assemble outside: it's impossible to predict which. Often they'll be after a dash (₦50 is often enough), but it's wise to wait until that is clearly hinted at before offering one. They may also be waiting for a lift, and the minor inconvenience of an extra passenger is far outweighed by the ease with which one passes through subsequent roadblocks. Sometimes they may like to have a joke at your expense (such as storming up to shout about some minor misdemeanour, only to grin and give you a hearty thump on the back when you've been adequately terrified). It is wise to accept such jokes with good grace.

Lastly, it's not unknown for enterprising traders, or even highway **bandits**, to pose as a roadblock by setting up their wares on a couple of oil drums. Their ingenious exploits are faithfully reported in all the newspapers – but the number of robberies, as a proportion of the number of journeys made, is negligible. Nigerian officials are sometimes in plain clothes, but they usually show their ID as soon as you pull up, or on request. The more you talk to locals, the more you'll hear, and the safer you'll be. Incidents are reported close to the Niger border, on long-haul routes between the north and the south, in and around cities during "go-slows" and, of course, in the delta.

Cycling

The perspective you get on the country from a **bicycle** saddle is unlike any other. Everyone you meet will think you're mad, but the rewards of cycling in Nigeria are as big as the country itself, and the supposed dangers fade to a manageable scale once you're here. You will never be ignored on the road, so the chance of being hit is diminished. Nevertheless, you should keep off the main highways as much as possible.

City transport

Every Nigerian town has countless falling-apart old **taxis** making the rounds. The usual distinction applies between vehicles driving fixed routes and piling customers in for very modest fees per sector (known as **drops**), and those working as private cabs that cost appreciably more for pre-agreed journeys. Whichever you choose, your progress in big cities may be slow during rush hours. To overcome these "go-slows" (traffic jams), a very cheap, common alternative in most cities are motorcycle taxis which you hail at the roadside – called **okadas** in the south (after a defunct airline), and **achabas** in the north. Drivers are mostly very competent, will usually find a way to take your luggage if you don't have too much, and can be hired in pairs or groups if you're not travelling alone.

Accommodation

The **hospitality** sector has been re-energized recently, with the aggressive expansion of the South African *Protea* business-hotel chain across the country, and luxury brands such as *SAS Radisson* and *Hyatt* entering the Lagos market. One important general point to note is that many hotels require a **deposit**, often equal to about 150 percent of the rate, requiring you to obtain a refund of the balance in the morning. Some of the newer hotels (such as *Protea*) allow you to pay with a credit card, but beyond Lagos and Abuja, expect to pay in cash.

These days, in towns of any size, rooms without electricity are rare, though cheap places without their own generator will be subject to power cuts. Not everywhere has running water, however, and even places with self-contained (s/c) rooms may only be able to supply water in a bucket at certain times of day.

Water and electricity problems aside, **upmarket hotels** (**7**–**8**) will have every mod-con in the rooms and quite often tennis courts and pools. Most hotels of standing have rates for residents and nonresidents, the latter being substantially higher and often payable in foreign currency (though unless nonresidents are frequent guests the higher rates may be overlooked). **Mid-range** hotels (❺ & ❻) tend to be reasonably comfortable, with conveniences like satellite TV and air conditioning as standard.

Rooms in **budget hotels** (❶–❹) range from a sunken foam-mattress bed and four bare walls to gadget-filled abodes cluttered with TV, rattling air-con units and leaking fridges. What you may want to check, though, is whether there's a working shower and constant running water – hot would be a bonus. Note that some hotels, particularly the cheapest ones, double as informal brothels.

The Evangelical Church of West Africa (**ECWA**) runs a series of **mission guesthouses** throughout the country, often in association with the Sudan Inland Mission (**SIM**). They're very inexpensive – and VSO and other volunteers get a discount. Rooms are generally spartan but tidy and can be quite well-furnished.

If you're **driving**, it's essential to find a hotel with a secure **compound**, where the gates are locked and guarded through the night. There's usually no extra charge for parking in the compound.

Camping

If you have your own transport, wild **camping** is an option – but the further off the beaten track you can get the better. You should be very wary of camping within 50km of the urban centres and it's wise to stay right away from the more congested parts of the southwest. Don't camp anywhere near busy roads with a car or other large vehicle, as the attention you'll attract spreads rapidly and isn't always welcome.

Eating and drinking

Food is perhaps not one of Nigeria's highlights, but European, Lebanese and Asian restaurants are found in large towns, and most hotels have their own restaurants for either Nigerian or "continental" (usually meaning British) meals, often with separate menus for the two cuisines. Beware: Nigerian food in the south is usually fiery hot. Many hotels serve standard "English" breakfasts of eggs, toast, marmalade, tea and juice.

In recent years, numerous **local fast-food chains** have opened, offering rice- and chicken-based food in a clean and usually reliable environment – look out for the likes of *Tantalisers*, *Mr Biggs*, *Chicken Licken*, *Chicken Republic* and *Sweet Sensation*. For more Nigerian-oriented staple fare, try the *Mama Cass* chain found nationwide.

There's a wide range of foods and dishes in **chop houses** (*buka* in Yoruba) and local restaurants. In addition, chicken and chips and omelette and chips are universally available; in cheaper places the price of an omelette includes bread and "Lipton's" (tea-bag tea).

Vegetarians have a slightly difficult time of it in restaurants, as many apparently (even explicitly) "vegetarian" items on menus should be understood as "plus a bit of meat" – usually goat. But salad vegetables are often crisp and fresh, and delicious once you overcome any worries about them having been washed in unsterilized water. Good transport helps to provide fresh fruit and vegetables even to dry regions and parts of the country where they would otherwise be out of season. Vegetarian street-food options include *ákárá* (tasty bean-cakes generally available only in the morning), *boli* (roasted plaintain usually eaten with peanuts), *dundun* (fried yam) and *mosa* (deep-fried balls of mashed plaintain and flour).

If you're travelling cheaply it's easy enough to live on the basics. Bread (sweet, brick-shaped and often coloured yellow or pink), hard-boiled eggs, portions of deep-fried fish (with or without scalding chilli sauce), bananas, oranges and salted roast peanuts make for a reasonably balanced diet that's obtainable in the remotest parts of the country.

Drinking

Nigerians are great **beer** drinkers. Every state has its own breweries and their advertising hoardings are one of the country's most pervasive symbols. The most widely available brands are **Star** and **Gulder**, both equally alcoholic, though Star has a lighter flavour than Gulder. Among the other dozen-odd brands, Rock, Harp and 33 are probably

Nigerian food

Staples

Apu	Pounded cassava, mostly eaten in the southeast
Àmàlà	Yams ground before boiling – the finished product has a brown colour of little initial appeal (mostly eaten in the southwest)
Eba	Moist ball of steamy *gari* (cassava flour), overwhelmingly the favourite national dish
Fufu	Fermented pounded cassava, most common in the southwest
Pounded yam	Boiled yam that's been pounded to a wonderful, glazey, aerated blob
Tuo	Cornflour mass, mainly eaten in the north

Main dishes

Àkàrà	Fritter made from ground black-eyed beans (also called cow peas or *ogbono*) and chilli, usually sold from street stalls
Begiri	Yoruba bean soup
Bitter leaf	Similar to spinach
Bush meat	Any kind of game meat, often porcupine or grasscutter (aka cutting-grass or bush rat)
Cowleg	Prosaic local term for shin of beef
Dodo	Fried plantains
Draw soup	Slimy soup that "draws" into threads, made from viscous, ground *ogbono* seeds
Egusi	Oily "soup" based on pounded melon seeds, usually containing stockfish or meat, and green leaves (bitter leaf or pumpkin leaf)
Eja gbigbe	Yoruba smoked fish on a stick
Ìgbín	Large, rubbery forest snails
Jollof rice	Rice cooked with palm oil, and sometimes with vegetables and meat
Moin-moin	A delicious steamed bean-cake snack with a slightly gelatinous texture, usually wrapped in a banana leaf, and found mainly in the south (*kause* are the fried variety)
Okro	Gumbo, okra, ladies' fingers
Pepper soup	A fiery-hot chilli soup with meat (often goat's head or cowleg) that will make your eyes water and your nose stream.
Soup	Any stew, often thick, fiery and palm-oil-based, with meat or smoked fish; eaten with rice or any of the starchy staples.
Stockfish	Air-dried fish, usually soaked and cooked cod (from Iceland, Norway or Portugal)
Suya	The most common street food of grilled kebabs, usually beef or goat, sold everywhere but especially in the north
Wara	Curd cheese (Yoruba)

the most popular. Be cautious with Nigerian **Guinness** – an impressive eight-percent alcohol by volume – and with cheaper brands, which tend to provoke treacherous hangovers and, some maintain, diarrhoea. A popular local drink is the nonalcoholic cocktail known as a **Chapmans**, a mixture of Fanta, Sprite, grenadine, lemon juice and angostura bitters. Don't leave Nigeria without trying it.

Western-style **wine** is often available in upmarket restaurants – be careful to taste before accepting the bottle. **Palm wine**, freshly tapped from oil palms, is consumed in the south. Pasteurized and bottled versions of palm wine are available, although their taste is a far cry from the delicious sweetness of the bush brews. Distilled, the wine becomes potent *ogogoro*, also common but usually more discreetly sold.

Tea and **coffee** are never great, but tea-bag tea, instant coffee, and chocolate drinks such as Bournvita can often be found during the morning at street breakfast stalls, which usually also rustle up bread and omelettes, sometimes even rice and beans.

Bottled **water** is widely available, as is the much cheaper "pure water" sold in plastic bags, and supposedly filtered, though not everybody trusts it. The usual international brands of fizzy **sodas** ("minerals") are sold cold from fridges – at a filling station if nowhere else – all over the country. The same outlets also usually sell nonalcoholic malt sodas, often made by beer companies, which cost about twice the price.

Communications

Mail is unpredictable: letters to and from Europe and North America can take anything from a couple of days to two weeks or more to arrive. Packages sent by post are quite likely to go astray. The postes restantes in Lagos, Kano and Kaduna still work well enough. To send mail out, the post office's EMS Speedpost is quick, inexpensive and reliable. Courier services are easily available – both DHL (Ⓦ www.dhl.com.ng) and UPS (Ⓦ www.ups.com) have offices in major cities and towns.

To **phone** abroad, you can dial directly from all cities and most towns. The access code

Nigeria's IDD country code is ☏234.

for international calls is ☏009. To make a **reverse-charge** (collect) call to an overseas number, dial the international operator on ☏191. Phone connections are usually good, but you may be cut off mid-conversation for no apparent reason. The cheapest way to call is using **VoIP** on the Internet, a service provided by most cybercafés, though the line is echoey, with a time delay, and you can't speak and listen at the same time.

Mobile (cell)phones are ubiquitous. If you're spending more than just a day or two in Nigeria, the best bet is to buy a local prepaid SIM card and insert it into your handset – all three main operators MTN, Celtel and Glo sell them for around ₦200. Phoning abroad with any of these providers is relatively inexpensive (around ₦60–100 per minute).

Internet connections are available in even the smallest towns. In big cities, you'll find cybercafés open around the clock. Connection speeds vary but are generally very slow compared to broadband speeds in Europe or North America. Prices are typically in the region of ₦200–300 per hour (some places charge by the minute). Usually you have to prepay for a specific time, getting cut off when you've used it up, but you don't have to use it all in one sitting. Don't be surprised if you see so-called "Yahoo Yahoo boys" typing out email-fraud letters (popularly known as 419 letters) around you.

Opening hours, public holidays and festivals

Banks are open from Monday to Friday between 8am and 4pm, although some close early on Friday in the north. Shops are usually open Monday to Saturday 8am to 5pm, closed Sunday.

Nigeria's official **public holidays** include the major Christian and Muslim celebrations plus New Year's Day, Labour Day (May 1) Democracy Day (May 29) and Independence – or National – Day (Oct 1). Muslim holidays, including those marking the end of Ramadan (Id al-Fitr, known locally as Sallah), Abraham's sacrificing of the sheep (Tabaski) and Muhammad's birthday (Maulidi) are based on the lunar calendar (see p.63 for dates). In the north, notably in Kano and Katsina, these occasions often climax with spectacular cavalry displays known as **durbars** – a Punjabi term imported from India by the British, referring to a traditional reception for the local ruler.

Traditional festivals

Ekpe festival (three days in Jan). Harvest festival and general thanksgiving for surviving the year; it's a ritualistic occasion celebrated among the Oboros in the area between Umuahia and Ikot Ekpene.

Fishing festival (Feb). Argungu, near Sokoto – unfortunately this has been cancelled for the last few years, though there's a smaller one in Gorgoram, which is less subject to cancellation.

Pategi Regatta (Feb & Mar). A regatta held every other year at Pategi, the big crossing-point on the Niger, 100km downstream from Jebba. This is one of the country's best-known events, and includes horse racing, swimming, dancing and music.

Egungun (usually April). A whole host of Yoruba ancestor festivals. Those at Ibadan, Badagri (near Lagos) and Okene (on the A2 between Benin City and Lokoja) draw huge crowds. There are masquerades and sporting events accompanied by exhilarating dancing and drumming.

Ikeji Izuogu (usually April). A five-day yam festival celebrated by the Arondizuogu people in parts of Imo State, for religious worship, thanksgiving, census and family reunion.

Ogun (June–Aug). Yoruba festival in honour of the god of iron, with singing, dancing and drumming. Held in numerous towns of the region.

Osun (Aug–Sept). Festival in honour of the river goddess and guardian spirit of the people of Osogbo. This festival draws hundreds of thousands of visitors, including Osun devotees from Brazil and Cuba.

Sekiapu (Oct). Masquerades, regattas and a great deal of merriment in River and Cross River states.

Igue (Dec). Procession of the Oba of Benin. The ensuing celebration lasts several days and includes traditional dancing and a lot of eating and drinking.

Ofala (Dec). Festival in Onitsha and other towns along the Niger to honour the traditional ruler, who appears before his people.

Crafts and shopping

Nigeria has a fantastic wealth of **things to buy**, both utilitarian and aesthetic. Jewellery (including the antique, multicoloured glass trading beads that are now getting expensive), leatherware, carved calabashes, bronze figures made with the lost-wax method, hand-woven cloth and woodcarvings are the most obvious. Unfortunately, you're likely to be offered ivory from time to time as well as various other animal products, including lizard-, snake- and crocodile-skin bags and belts. Possibly the best value and longest-lasting interest is to be had from musical instruments, which you'll find if you look beyond the souvenir stands at the big hotels. Talking drums – the expressive *iyaalu* tension drums which so unerringly imitate the Yoruba voice – are particularly worth looking out for.

For suggestions on where to buy **books**, see "Books", p.1109.

Crime and safety

Nigeria's dire **reputation** for trouble is exaggerated (and fuelled by the easily evaded predation of Internet fraudsters, many of whom are not, these days, Nigerian). Even so, security is not something to take lightly in Lagos and other large cities – read the "Arrivals" information on p.1118 carefully. Lagos gangs are active and well organized and the huge number of handguns and other weapons in private possession and the implication of some police in criminal activities are disturbing. Despite mandatory death sentences for armed robbery, burglaries are common and night-watchmen are often killed.

Visitors, even long-term ones, are however rarely at risk and have rarely been victims of worse crimes than the usual bag-snatchings and thefts. Though outlaws may "control" entire neighbourhoods, you're most unlikely ever to see one, or anyone out of uniform carrying a gun. Leave valuables behind when you go out, and you're likely to be fine. Be alert, not paranoid.

You're unlikely to get yourself into real trouble in Nigeria unless you cross someone with serious influence. There are a lot of **drugs** floating around Lagos, however, and if you become involved you could easily find yourself in deep water. **Marijuana** (*igbo* or "wee-wee") is cultivated in the south – especially Delta State – and commonly smoked. It became popular in the army

The police emergency number is
℗ 199, but help doesn't always come
in a hurry if you run into trouble.

during the civil war but its use is officially treated as a serious offence. Lorry drivers have long used amphetamines, but Lagos's pivotal position in the worldwide transport of **hard drugs** in the 1980s and 1990s brought heroin and cocaine, plus accompanying misery and violence, onto the streets of Nigeria's towns and cities.

In the north, **sectarian conflict** between Christians and Muslims rarely entangles foreigners, but it's worth keeping an ear to the ground to avoid finding yourself in the wrong place at the wrong time. Ethnic conflict between Tivs and Jukuns in Plateau State occasionally erupts into violence too.

The greatest danger currently posed to foreign visitors and expats is in the strife-torn **delta region** (the states of Delta, Rivers, Bayelsa and parts of Abia and Akwa Ibom – see p.1158), where hundreds of foreign workers have been abducted and ransomed in recent years. Almost without exception, they have been released unharmed after a few days (and an undisclosed payment), but the potential for a botched rescue attempt or a sudden change of attitude on the part of the rebels, the Nigerian authorities or the foreign oil company concerned could precipitate a violent climax to any incident. Anyone, anywhere, who looks as if they could raise a ransom is a potential victim, and you should for the present avoid the whole delta region and in particular keep out of the city of Port Harcourt and neighbouring oil towns unless your visit is essential.

Gender issues and sexual attitudes

Flirtatious sexual harassment may occur in clubs and at parties, but not on the street. In the north of the country, it is a good idea to **dress modestly** (covering arms and legs for example, and wearing baggy rather than tight clothing).

In a country where the change from traditional to urban-industrial values is taking place remarkably quickly, women have achieved larger real gains here than elsewhere in West Africa. But while they occupy positions in business, government and increasingly in the universities, there's still a lot of ground to cover. **Baobab** (ⓦ www.baobabwomen.org) is a Nigerian NGO campaigning for human rights for women, as does **WRAPA** (ⓦ www .wrapaifl.com), while **KIND** (ⓦ www.kind.org) promotes women's empowerment initiatives across Nigeria.

Gay life

Being gay in Nigeria is not easy. On top of the **conservative penal code** inherited from the British and little modified since the 1960s, the **Nigerian Church** has reacted strongly against the Anglican Church's stance on the ordination of gay priests, while the imposition of **sharia law** in some of the northern states has brought a new level of intolerance, which in theory includes the death penalty for homosexuals (never applied, to date). Gay and lesbian Nigerians are not invisible, but there is widespread lack of support for their rights. In practice, gay visitors in the big cities will attract little interest but, as usual, discretion about being openly gay is strongly advised, much as it might jar.

Entertainment and sport

Nigeria has a thriving and complex cultural scene. **Music**, of course, is a massive industry (see p.1103), but **cinema** is blighted by financial incapacity, despite a plethora of straight-to-video releases (see p.1108). **Theatre** is lively and inventive and now benefiting from cross-fertilization with TV. In sports, **football** and **athletics** are the big crowd-pullers.

Theatre

Nigeria has a 400-year-old theatrical tradition, with the **Yoruba language** as its outstanding vehicle. **Alarinjo Theatre**, originally the court entertainment of sixteenth-century Oyo, spread from city to city once the rulers allowed it to become a popular art form. By the nineteenth century, it was a major cultural influence, but waned with the penetration of Christianity, only to resurge again in the 1940s, when players performed biblical scenes before church congregations.

The most famous names in the travelling theatre genre were **Duro Lapido**, **Kola Ogunmola** and **Hubert Ogunde**; they gave voice to the changing social and cultural scene in southern Nigeria, right through the pre-independence era and successive federal governments since. You may be lucky and catch one of the noisy, half-improvised productions, though these days many groups are more involved with making their own films, which are popular well beyond southwest Nigeria.

English-language drama groups are mostly attached to the universities, don't attract any state or federal support and inevitably don't have a mass audience. **Wole Soyinka**, **John Pepper Clark**, **Femi Osofisan**, **Ola Rotimi** and **Bode Osanyin** are some of Nigeria's best-known playwrights. In Lagos, the **PEC Repertory Theatre** in George V Street (round the corner from the Onikan National Museum) is home to Nigeria's first full-time professional rep group, established by John Pepper Clark in 1992.

Any stay in Nigeria of more than a few days wouldn't be complete without sampling the hugely popular **comedy** scene. Top comics such as **Basket Mouth**, **Julius Agwu**, **Ali Baba** and **Tee-A** often draw in huge crowds with their often hilarious impersonations of politicians and pastors – as well as more adult-oriented material. Many Nigerian comics employ a rapid-fire, highly improvised delivery, speaking in *Wafi* pidgin English (pidgin English that originates from Warri in the delta region). *Laffs and Jams* is a long-running comedy night running in Lagos. If you're in the city, ask around and you'll soon find yourself escorted to a genuine performance treat.

Football

Nigeria's soccer skills are highly respected in Africa. The national side – nicknamed **Super Eagles** – qualified for the World Cup finals in 1998 and 2002 and won the African Cup of Nations in 1994 (they usually achieve second or third place).

One of Nigeria's top league clubs of recent years has been **Enyiba** of Aba, whose matches are often attended by enormous crowds.

A number of outstanding Nigerian players play for English clubs: tall striker **Nwankwo Kanu** and quick **John Utaka** for Portsmouth; lightning fast **Obafemi Martins** for Newcastle; promising young midfielder **Jon Obi Mikel** for Chelsea; and the powerful **Yakubu Aiyegbeni**, youthful **Victor Anichebe** and defensive hard man **Joseph Yobo** all for Everton.

Wildlife and national parks

There's still a fair bit of wildlife to be seen in Nigeria, though little in the big-game league. The northern **Yankari** and **Kainji Lake** national parks contain elephant, hippo and larger antelope (although poaching has severely depleted their populations), and there's the remote possibility of glimpsing lions. There are gorillas in the thick forests of the southeast close to the Cameroonian border, but you're most unlikely to see them. The **Gashaka-Gumpti National Park** covers a huge area with terrain that varies from savannah grassland to mountain forest. There are no elephants left here, but a variety of other wildlife, including chimpanzees. The Nigerian Conservation Foundation (NCF), PO Box 74638, Victoria Island, Lagos (Ⓦ tinyurl.com/2h42t3), is making valiant efforts to rouse Nigerians from a complacent attitude to the country's wildlife heritage, but without a flow of tourism revenue it's an uphill struggle. One positive sign is the creation – following lobbying by environmental groups – of the **Cross River National Park**, comprising rainforest and mountain forest reserves.

The **Nigerian Field Society** (Ⓦ www .nigerianfield.org) is an active organization in existence since 1930, with seven branches (including a UK branch). In Nigeria, the NFS organizes regular walking and exploration trips around the country.

A brief history of Nigeria

Nigerian history is the most complex and also one of the most ancient in West Africa. The earliest indications of the use of iron in the region come from the **Nok culture** (named after the Jos plateau village where much of the evidence was found) and date back to 300 BC. For reasons unknown, this civilization faded, and the next discoveries date from more than a millennium later. By the ninth century AD, the development of mineral wealth in the Yoruba and Igbo regions of the south, led to long-lasting and sophisticated political structures. In the north, kingdoms arose at much the same time – first the **Bornu empire** in the ninth century, then, not long afterwards, the **Hausa city-states**. These became powerful stations on the trans-Saharan caravan routes, supplying many of the exotic requirements of medieval Europe.

The **slave trade** and, much later, **colonial invasion**, wreaked havoc on these indigenous states, as well as on the weaker, stateless communities living among them. (Detailed coverage of pre-colonial history is included on a regional basis throughout the main guide section of this chapter.)

Since the end of the nineteenth century, the **colonial protectorates**, and then the **federation** of modern Nigerian states, have been the setting for a panoply of events and characters set against a background of poverty, booming population and almost continual crisis. A substantial and expanding literature exists on the history, sociology and political science of Nigeria (see p.1109); the following summary is only the simplest historical framework, picking out the most salient features of the country's history.

The arrival of Europeans

The **Portuguese** were the first Europeans to reach the Gulf of Benin, in 1472, and within a short time they had made contact with the kingdom of **Benin** in the area of present-day Benin City. Trade soon began, initially centred on pepper, ivory and other exotic goods. It was not until the second half of the seventeenth century, when the Americas had been widely colonized and plantations needed increasing

supplies of labour, that the focus shifted to slaves.

The early Europeans had few permanent forts or settlements, basing themselves instead on offshore "hulks" near the ports. By the 1660s, these permanently moored ships were highly developed, sparking off an explosion of competitive slave-trading at ports like **Lagos**, **Warri**, **Calabar** and **Bonny**. Much of the driving force behind the trade, which was exploited by local chiefs, came from the insecurity of a West African arms race for the latest European muskets and cannon. In exchange for weaponry, the French and British, who had supplanted the Portuguese and Brazilians by the eighteenth century, were scarcely interested in buying anything except slaves.

The colonial carve-up

At the beginning of the nineteenth century, things began to change, as the newly republican **French** sent warships to the southeast Nigerian coast to break up the slave trade. To French cries of *"Liberté, Egalité, Fraternité"*, the British added their own hollow "Christianity, Commerce and Civilization". In fact, slaves no longer made economic sense; instead, in the wake of the European industrial revolution, **markets** were needed for manufactured goods and there was a massive demand for supplies of raw materials – cotton, sugar and the rest.

In 1851, the British shelled Lagos, ostensibly to quicken the demise of the slave trade, in practice to impose a puppet regime and improve the newly important palm-oil trade. The slave trade went underground, and slavers hid out in the lagoons around Lagos from where they would sneak out their cargo to Brazil, which was still an importer of slaves. Meanwhile, the British seized Lagos Island in 1861 – which then became Lagos Colony, the first element of Nigeria.

After the European Powers' **Berlin Conference** of 1885, the London-based **Royal Niger Company** was granted exclusive trading rights in the Niger River basin. With the Germans expanding to the east, and the French to the north and west, the British government took over the RNC in 1899 and began pushing it in all directions.

By 1900, they'd succeeded in drawing borders around a vast region of diverse peoples, who found themselves under the ultimate authority of northern and southern protectorates. In 1914 a federation was formed – in preference to a united colony – and named **Nigeria**, a term coined by Flora Shaw, correspondent to *The Times* and wife of the British colonial commander Lord Lugard.

Indirect rule

From the beginning, Nigeria was an ill-matched association and it was clear that conflict would arise between the conservative, largely Muslim and feudal **north**, and the more outward-looking **south**, with its Christian missions and, in the southeast, lack of rigid social hierarchies. At the very least, problems would be caused by the new territory's southward-looking orientation, away from the old Saharan routes and towards the ports and European trade.

The British, however, pressed ahead with their system of **"indirect rule"**, which in the **north** worked easily enough, to the benefit of both the Hausa–Fulani emirs (who carried on much as before) and the British administration. Lord Lugard simply took over the role of regional overlord from the Sultan of Sokoto, whose functions became purely religious and ceremonial.

In the **southeast**, however, indirect rule was a disaster. Here, decisions and judicial processes were traditionally applied by consent among groups of senior men. In **Igboland**, the "Warrant Chiefs" commissioned by the British had no mandate for their authority: on the contrary, they were usually independent-minded status-seekers who had acquired a mission education.

In **Yorubaland**, another variation was imposed. Here, the British held Yoruba traditional rulers, with British "advisors", accountable for their decisions. But the British had failed to understand the fabric of Yoruba politics and perceived in their centralized **government of obas** and the traditional ceremonial-executive titles of the **alafin of Oyo** and the **oni of Ife**, simple dictatorships somewhat akin to the emirates of the north. Disregarding the fact that the Yoruba offices were posts given to selected senior men by others of high rank, Lugard tried to control the selection of compliant chiefs by men who, again, had no mandate to enforce his requirements. And he actively connived to empower those Yoruba elements who posed the least threat to white prestige, to turn the clock back, as far as possible, to his own avowedly racist vision of an Africa untainted by progress.

While British rule led to internal schisms in Yorubaland, the region benefited from the fastest input of technology and **modern infrastructure**. There was electricity in Lagos by 1898, and, by 1900, bridges between the islands and a rail link with Ibadan, all of which was to prove another source of division for north and south to deal with after independence.

The road to independence

Nigerians became involved in the political process relatively early, by the standards of other African colonies.

In 1923, the first Africans, led by **Herbert Macaulay** – whose father, born in Sierra Leone, was an *Aku* (a Yoruba descended from freed slaves) – were elected to a legislative advisory council in Lagos. But local parties really only developed after the experience of World War II, when Nigerians returned from fighting for European ideals like "self-determination" and "liberty".

In 1944, the **National Council for Nigeria and the Cameroons** was formed by Herbert Macaulay and **Dr Nnamdi Azikwe**, an Igbo. Four years later, **Chief Obafemi Awolowo**, a Yoruba, founded a second party, the **Action Group**. By the end of the decade, the northerners, with major tacit support from the British, who favoured their ascendancy, also had their own party, the **Northern People's Congress**, with **Tafawa Balewa** at its head. In fact the NPC is now widely regarded as having been a creation of the British, whose manipulation of politics in Nigeria was much more astute than they revealed at the time.

Predictably, these three parties came to represent **regional interests** – the NPC for the north, the NCNC for the east, and the AG for the west. As they jockeyed for position to rule an independent nation, the parties agreed on nothing, delaying reform in the process. In a dispute over the date for self-rule, suspicious northerners walked out of the colonial assembly in 1953, and bloody **riots in Kano** followed. Members from each region felt sure the other two were conspiring to dominate, and there was talk of dividing the country into several smaller political units in an effort to relieve the tension. The British argued such a measure would only stall independence further, an argument in which they were supported by the northern region, which had to have a friendly route to the sea.

Finally, in 1957, it was decided the nation would be formed of the three rival regions. Tafawa Balewa became the head of the new central government and Nigeria gained independence on October 1, 1960.

Independence: the early years

The early 1960s were characterized by an **uneasy coalition** between the **north** and the **southeast** against the powerful **southwest** region dominated by the Yoruba. The latter thus saw its worst fears realized and its leaders panicked when a bogus census in 1963 suggested the north had four million more inhabitants than the rest of the nation combined.

The southeast eventually slipped out of the coalition and Chief Awolowo raised angry cries against government tinkering with the country's structure. He was tried for treason and jailed. Early chaos seemed to be gaining momentum and in January 1966 the army toppled the government – killing Prime Minister Tafawa Balewa and the premier of the Northern Region, **Ahmadu Bello**, in the process – and set about trying to restore order.

Military rule

The new **military government** was headed by **General J. Aguiyi-Ironsi**, an Igbo. Northerners rioted in reaction to the radical early reforms that abolished the federation and imposed a unitary government dominated by Igbos. Fighting broke out within the army and, after only six months, Ironsi was killed in another **coup**, this time led by northern officers. As many as 7000 Igbos living in the north were massacred in the aftermath and up to half a million fled to the southeast.

But the military's new leader was different from his predecessors. **Yakubu Gowon** was a Christian northerner, a young and charismatic figure, who restored the tripartite federation and released Awolowo and other Action Group leaders of the west. But the southeast region, led by the military governor, **Lieutenant-Colonel C. Odumegwu-Ojukwu**, who rejected Gowon's leadership, pushed instead for a loose confederation.

In September 1966, elements of the northern army began the systematic **killing of Igbos** who had remained in the north. Official reports placed the deaths at 5000, though Igbos claimed that as many as 30,000 were massacred. The pogrom was a decisive blow to the shaky federation. High-ranking Igbo civil servants began returning from Lagos to the regional capital at Enugu and pressuring Ojukwu to secede.

National politics in the early part of 1967 were completely dominated by the question of the future of the federation. The Ghanaian government attempted to mediate between the sides, but meetings, guarantees and gestures of appeasement to the east achieved nothing. Fearing breakdown, Gowon announced the **division of the federation** into twelve separate states in an attempt to undermine the north and disarm his ethnic-minority critics, especially in the southeast, who had long sought greater autonomy. It was too late: Ojukwu unilaterally withdrew the Eastern Region from the federation and declared the independent **Republic of Biafra** on May 30, 1967.

The Biafran War

In July 1967, Biafran troops marched into the Western Region in an attempt to surround Lagos. Federal troops responded by blockading eastern ports and by attacking Biafra from the north and west. Despite a lack of manpower and resources, Biafra scored a number of military successes in the early days of the war, but by the end of 1967, the conflict had degenerated into a brutal **war of attrition**. Fighting was vicious and confused. Most of the major towns changed hands several times. Federal forces captured a number of coastal towns, reducing Biafra to an enclave in the Igbo heartland. Federal military atrocities, of which many were reported, further convinced the Igbos that they were engaged in an all-out war for survival.

Biafra gained considerable sympathy in the international press: for the first time, public opinion in the rich world was mobilized against Third World poverty. Yet few countries gave official recognition to Biafra, and French military and technical aid appeared self-interested. The war dragged on for two and a half years, claiming the lives of at least 100,000 soldiers, but many more Igbo civilians, of whom between half a million and two million are estimated to have perished as a result of the federal government's policy of **blockade and starvation**. Supported by British aid and Soviet arms, the federal government finally captured the last rebel-held town of Owerri and quelled the rebellion in December 1969. Much of the southeast was ravaged.

Reconstruction

The gaping wounds of the war appeared to heal with remarkable speed. Gowon, who was still in power after four years, was careful not to humiliate the defeated and bereaved easterners or exclude them from the new federation. In fact, he offered an **amnesty** to all who had fought on the Biafran side, and vowed to rebuild the east while furthering the economic development of the entire country.

Reconstruction didn't take place overnight, but it is remarkable today how little evidence of the war remains, even in cities that were virtually destroyed. Gowon was aided in the early days of reconciliation by **oil revenues** that flooded into the coffers in the early 1970s, as Nigeria became one of the world's ten largest producers. But as blatant corruption became a national issue, and Gowon began dragging his feet on promises of a return to civilian rule, devoting most of his energies to international image-building, he was ousted, after nine years in power, in a bloodless coup led by **General Murtala Muhammed** in July 1975.

Murtala Muhammed

Of all Nigeria's leaders, Murtala Muhammed has been without doubt the most popular. Even today, his name is referred to with a reverence not normally reserved for politicians. Another northerner with considerable charisma, he structured all his policies around the return of power to an elected leadership and devoted himself to wiping out corruption.

Shortly after coming to power, Muhammed instigated **"Operation Deadwoods"** – a policy of forced dismissal or retirement of public officials on a whole range of charges from corruption to "infirmity". In all, more than 10,000 civil servants – police officials, senior diplomats, university professors, even military officers – were relieved of their posts. Swift action was taken against embezzlement of public funds. Assets were confiscated. Appointees were sacked for reasons as simple as a conflict of interests. It was a breath of fresh air in a stagnating bureaucracy and brought the government huge popularity.

By the end of 1975, Muhammed had concluded the purge and announced a four-year countdown to return the country to civilian rule. He had come to be regarded as a politician who made promises and kept them, and drew attention to the future and away from the divisive tragedy of the past. Nigerians felt they were leaders in a liberalizing movement that would sweep the continent and break the cycle of totalitarianism in Africa.

It's difficult to know if posterity would have been so kind to Muhammed had he lived to see his programmes carried out. After only six months of reshaping the country he was assassinated by disgruntled members of the military, shot while his car was in a Lagos traffic jam.

The Second Republic

The counter-coup was effective only in eliminating Muhammed, for the plotters were rounded up and with the help of Major General Ibrahim Babangida, power was smoothly transferred to Muhammed's chief of staff, **Olusegun Obasanjo**, a Christian Yoruba. Obasanjo pledged to adhere to Muhammed's schedule for the return to civilian government and continued reshaping the civil service. A new constitution, based on that of the USA, was drawn up, and political parties were legalized in September 1978.

Five **political parties** were finally approved, but four were headed by familiar old names, had vague right-of-centre programmes and seemed to indicate the persistence of regional divisions. **Awolowo** and **Azikwe** (by then both in their 70s) headed parties largely representing the west and the east respectively, or at least their personal power bases in those regions – the Unity Party of Nigeria and the Greater National People's Party. The National People's Party, from which the GNPP was a breakaway group, was led by a northern businessman, **Alhaji Waziri Ibrahim**. The National Party of Nigeria, based in Kaduna and led by **Alhaji Shehu Shagari**, claimed to cut across regional loyalties but was essentially the old NPC northern party, controlled as ever by the Fulani oligarchy. Shagari, himself a Fulani from a leading northern family, had been a member of the first civilian government and had served under Gowon's military regime. Lastly, in opposition to the NPN, another northern party had also been formed – the People's Redemption Party. Led by **Alhaji Aminu Kano**, it had radical socialist leanings and was explicitly committed to the cause of inter-ethnic cooperation.

In the complicated elections that spread over six weeks in 1979, all the parties achieved some representation, but Shagari won the all-important **presidential election**. He rode out his first term in Nigeria's new "Second Republic" on a wave of genuine popularity and public relief that the long period of military rule was over. But the new president didn't survive long untarnished. **Crackdowns on the press** – which had begun reporting government corruption, and even daring to point fingers at Shagari and his Kaduna clique – clearly signalled his insecurity, and he faced serious challenges from other northern parties and eastern allies in his unstable coalition.

The **economy**, too, was slipping badly. The oil boom had peaked in 1980. In December of that year serious **riots** broke out in Kano, prompted by the popular "jihadist" teachings and calls for social justice of the preacher **Maitatsine**, who was killed by security forces during the riots.

As foreign-currency reserves dwindled and Nigeria's debt skyrocketed, the standard of living for most Nigerians rapidly declined, while government officials, cabinet ministers and President Shagari himself made fortunes, indulging in what came to be known as "squandermania". Further, serious **riots in Maiduguri**, in October 1982, were dismissed by Shagari as "religious agitation". In a diversionary response, in February 1983, some two million migrant workers – from Ghana, Cameroon, Chad and Niger – were expelled as economic scapegoats.

Despite these various obstacles, Shagari managed to get elected to a second term in October 1983, a sounder win, in fact, than his first, though achieved with less than sound methods.

Another coup: a new military regime

The inevitable happened barely three months after the 1983 elections, when another northerner – **Major-General Mohammed Buhari** – staged a bloodless takeover of power and suspended the 1979 constitution.

Buhari announced the "voluntary retirement" of high-ranking military officers and the inspector general of the police, all of whom were implicated in financial mismanagement and corrupt practices on a gigantic scale. Prominent members of Shagari's party were arrested, as was the president himself. Through such moves, Buhari sought to associate his regime with the purist popularity of Murtala Muhammed. Important elder statesmen from the martyred president's administration were brought into the new government, including former head of state Obasanjo.

The attack on graft – the **"War Against Indiscipline"** – even crossed international borders. One of the most wanted offenders was the former transport minister **Alhaji Umaru Dikko**, who was living in luxurious exile in London, from where he openly criticized the new government. In one of the more bizarre instances of abuse of diplomatic privilege, Dikko was kidnapped, drugged and bundled into a crate, ready to be shipped off as diplomatic baggage from Gatwick airport. The plot was only aborted when British customs officials queried the contents of the crate. Buhari's government quickly denied any responsibility, although the Nigerian High Commission was strongly implicated in the abduction. Diplomatic relations between the UK and Nigeria nearly broke over the incident.

Buhari, however, seemed serious in his efforts to wipe out corruption, and as a result was initially quite popular with people fed up with government abuse. But it soon became apparent that members of Shagari's Kaduna clique were not prominent among those convicted on corruption charges. In addition to the accusation of partiality, it was not long before Buhari himself was gaining a reputation as an unbending **autocrat**. As those accused of corruption were given sentences as long as 72 years, Buhari arrested many of his regime's critics and suppressed the Nigerian media in ways Shagari had not dared. On the discovery of an alleged coup plot in 1984, he swiftly executed a group of some forty soldiers. And two government decrees, reflecting the new hard line, proved extremely unpopular with the masses. The first, known as Decree 2, allowed for detention without trial of citizens regarded as a threat to the state. Decree 4 imposed press controls by insisting journalists verify the "truth" of their reporting.

Even more unpopular were **austerity measures** adopted by Buhari in 1984 as he sought to remedy the country's growing economic problems. Strong opposition to his rule grew as resultant price increases and shortages of consumer goods jolted the nation – especially its poorer citizens. Buhari tried to deflect criticism, as Shagari had done, by blaming the country's economic woes on foreign workers robbing Nigerians of jobs. **Mass expulsions of immigrants** were instigated and, in May 1985, up to a million foreigners – again many of them Ghanaian – were shipped out under chaotic conditions.

None of Buhari's drastic measures worked, partly because there was virtually no popular support for the man behind them and principally because the naira was overvalued and worthless. A new coup was orchestrated, in August 1985, by close associates of Buhari in the Supreme Military Council, led by army chief of staff **Major-General Ibrahim Babangida**, born in Minna in Niger State, but brought up in Kano.

The "period of transition": Ibrahim Babangida

Within a short time of taking office, Babangida and his new Armed Forces Ruling Council had released many of the political prisoners from Nigerian jails and a new sense of freedom began to be felt. Babangida began preparing the country once again for national elections. Such political moves went down well at home, though his economic policies were tough and unyielding. Shortly after taking power, he declared an **economic state of emergency** and, in 1985, broke off loan negotiations with the IMF – a move that met with popular nationalistic support. But enthusiasm waned when the president imposed austerity measures of his own. He devalued the naira fourfold in the hope of attracting investors, and began privatizing unprofitable public enterprises and lifting government subsidies, notably on petrol.

Periodic **demonstrations and strikes** resulted, and, although conflict tended to be sparked by economic policies, **ethnic and religious tensions** were never far away. In 1986, Babangida announced that Nigeria had joined the Organization of the Islamic Conference. Despite stressing this had been done for cultural and religious reasons – and not political ones – non-Muslim southerners feared that the government and its northern power base were trying to impose Islamic rule on the whole country. There were campus protests and a number of deaths in northern universities in 1986 and, in 1987, **religious riots** broke out between Muslims and Christians in Kaduna State, leading to the deaths of dozens of people, the arrest of more than a thousand and the banning of religious organizations at schools and universities.

Adding to the political frustration, Babangida **postponed elections** three times between 1990 and 1992, leading many to question if he ever intended to step down. In April 1990, a group of junior, Christian, officers attempted a coup, which was quickly put down but resulted in 300 deaths. Over the next two years, ethnic-religious clashes intensified. In April 1991, Muslim demonstrations erupted in Katsina, leading to violence and many deaths. In Bauchi, 130 people were killed when Christians slaughtered pigs in a market shared by Muslims. Later in the year, 300 people died in Kano, following demonstrations provoked by a touring Christian preacher.

Babangida's solution to the regional problem was to create **nine new states** in 1991, arguing they would stimulate stability and development while ensuring more equitable representation of ethnic minorities. Despite the measures, it seemed ethnic enmities remained the driving force of Nigerian politics. In February 1992, fighting broke out in Kaduna State between Hausa Muslims and Kataf Christians. In the east, a land dispute between the Tiv and Jukun peoples resulted in an estimated five thousand deaths.

The deteriorating economy put a further strain on Babangida's government. By mid-1992, the **inflation rate** stood at fifty percent and widespread rioting broke out in Lagos over a sharp increase in transport fares. There were a number of deaths as anti-government demonstrators were brutally dispersed by security forces. More protests ensued after prominent human-rights activists, including Dr Beko Ransome-Kuti (brother of musician Fela Kuti) and Chief Fani Fawehinmi were arrested for accusing the government of instigating the riots in order to delay elections. In June 1992, the Academic Staff of Nigerian Universities called a nation-wide strike in a wage dispute. Despite his stated commitment to collective bargaining, Babangida banned the union and, with it, the National Association of Nigerian Students. Most of the nation's thirty universities closed as a result.

The mood of the country was therefore downbeat as Nigerians prepared for **National Assembly elections** in July 1992. Despite the vast sums of money spent on the campaign, the election sparked little excitement among voters. Babangida had insisted on a **two-party system** and created the Social Democratic Party and the National Republican Convention in order to prevent the rise of regional, ethnic or religious interest groups. But Nigerian commentators liked to call them the "Yes" party and the "Yes Sir" party. The fact that the increasingly unpopular military regime had created, funded and written the platforms of both SDP and NRC led to widespread **voter apathy**. Despite slick, state-financed media blitzes, neither party challenged the government's handling of issues such as inflation or ethnic tension. Serious opposition seemed only to come from the nation's human-rights organizations, students and lawyers.

Although the SDP won majorities in both the House of Representatives and the Senate, the Armed Forces Ruling Council decided in mid-July that the legislature would not be inaugurated until after a new civilian president was sworn in.

Failed elections

When the **presidential elections** finally rolled around in June 1993, there were few signs of voter enthusiasm. The two candidates that emerged – **Moshood Abiola** of the SDP and **Bashir Tofa** of the NRC – stood out more for their abilities to amass huge fortunes than for any record of public service. Cynicism ran high among voters who found it hard to digest promises of prosperity in a country where annual per capita income had fallen from $1000 to $290 in the ten years preceding the elections.

The results, however, surprised observers. Abiola – a Muslim from the mainly Christian Yoruba country of the southwest – won an apparently clear victory with 58 percent of the vote. Winning in several northern states, he appeared to seal a mandate that cut across ethnic lines. Marring this triumph was a deadlock created by legal wrangling over the election results. The judiciary's partisan colouration in giving judgements on the elections created an atmosphere of suspicion between the north and south. Babangida stepped in and annulled the elections.

Human-rights organizations immediately called for a campaign of civil disobedience. Mass **pro-democracy demonstrations** led to more violence and brought Lagos and much of the southwest to a standstill. Abiola declared himself winner, stating in a national broadcast, "From now on, the struggle in Nigeria is between the people and a small clique in the military determined to cling to power." But the standoff between civilians and the military also aroused old regional divisions: southerners remained convinced the military would never accept a southern president.

Babangida, who had started his presidential career as a liberal reformer, seemed, after the elections, ominously entrenched and intolerant of dissent. As troops put down anti-government riots in Lagos, the military shut down critical newspapers and threatened the death sentence for anyone whose words or deeds might undermine "the fabric of the nation". Abiola fled the country.

Babangida steps down

In August 1993, Babangida unexpectedly stepped aside as president and commander-in-chief of the armed forces. He insisted, however, that an **interim government** backed by decree would be the most favourable alternative to military rule and appointed **Ernest Shonekan** – former chairman of the United African Company, Nigeria's largest conglomerate – to lead the country until the next elections were held.

Abiola promptly returned from abroad, where he had been trying to rally foreign support for his claims to the presidency. But within weeks of taking over as head of state, Shonekan seemed to have swung public opinion behind himself. Former presidents **Nnamdi Azikwe** and **Olusegun Obasanjo** supported the interim government and the unions called off strikes. Meanwhile, Abiola isolated himself from the masses with his calls for an "economic blockade" of Nigeria and warnings of "a bloodbath" were he not sworn in. Preferring to stay in Lagos rather than tour the country to rally support, he increasingly became associated with a Yoruba, rather than a national, cause.

But neither was Shonekan a credible figure. Ardent democrats labelled him a puppet of the military. Shonekan's ultimate downfall, however, was provoked when he tried to cut fuel subsidies in late 1993. As the price of petrol increased six-fold, rioting again broke out in Lagos and a general strike threatened economic devastation.

Military rule: the Abacha government

In November 1993, **General Sani Abacha**, who had been instrumental in the coups that toppled Shagari and Buhari, seized power – once again, the military stepped in "to save the nation from chaos". Abacha quickly set about purging the military of former Babangida loyalists, and dissolved all political parties and elected institutions. By then, politically numbed Nigerians didn't seem much worried that elected governors were replaced by military appointees and that the National Assembly ceded authority to a mainly military legislative council.

By mid-1994, Abacha was already being attacked from all sides. Civil-liberties groups, students and unions, with the support of retired generals like Olusegun Obasanjo, publicly urged him to step down. Although political parties were banned, **political organizations** were formed and began turning up the heat. Abacha could count only on northerners for support, and even there he was losing ground. The Sultan of Sokoto and other powerbrokers, from Katsina and Maiduguri, criticized the military's policy, leaving the **Emir of Kano** as Abacha's only ardent supporter.

The **Campaign for Democracy** became influential, having gained credibility by organizing many of the demonstrations that led to Babangida's downfall. Meanwhile, the **National Democratic Coalition** (Nadeco) campaigned for a return to a civilian government headed by Abiola, and grew into a broad-based movement with support in the north as well as the south. On the first anniversary of the elections, Abiola was persuaded to declare himself president. He was promptly arrested.

Abacha never fared well in terms of **international relations**; Nigeria effectively was a pariah state throughout his rule. Western nations deplored the banning of parties, arbitrary detention of opposition members and tight controls on the press. Officially, it was these policies that provoked **economic sanctions** against Nigeria, although the West was equally displeased with Abacha's resistance to IMF pressure to impose a tougher economic policy, the country's continued refusal to address the question of its massive debt and the new administration's tougher terms for drilling rights to Nigeria's oil reserves. The Commonwealth suspended Nigeria's membership, the US government "decertified" Nigeria, making the country ineligible for aid or for US support credits from the IMF, and Canada withdrew its diplomatic representation in Lagos. Some leaders – Nelson Mandela in particular – pushed for harder sanctions, including an oil blockade.

Amid the political turmoil, the economy provided no good news for Abacha. A crisis in the oil industry had been triggered by a fall in world prices, by repeated strikes and by gross corruption. Billions of dollars were stolen from the country's oil earnings between 1995 and 1998. Nigerians had few illusions about the level of **government theft**, but seemed more angered than during past regimes, when grand building projects and government spending at least had a trickle-down effect.

The **Ogoni affair** and the execution of writer and publisher **Ken Saro-Wiwa** (see box, p.1158) did not encourage foreign investors and led to EU sanctions. During Abacha's tenure, Nigeria was ranked the world's third riskiest location for business investment, after Iraq and Russia, with (to add to its unenviable human-rights record) a well-established reputation for perpetrating fraud against unwary foreign investors through the notorious so-called **"419 scams"** – named after the clause dealing with fraud in the Nigerian penal code.

Throughout Abacha's presidency, revelations of coup plots and reports of bombings near the army barracks in Abuja led to the arrest of numerous officers, including high-ranking generals whom Abacha had considered loyal. Hundreds of dissenters languished in jail – including the 24 men convicted of a supposed coup attempt in March 1995, one of whom was former head of state Olusegun Obasanjo.

In June 1995, the exiled Nobel-laureate Wole Soyinka and others announced the formation of a **National Liberation Council** (**NLC**) of seventeen prominent opposition leaders. The NLC aimed to form a government-in-exile to campaign for the removal of the Abacha regime. Like many before him, Soyinka was charged *in absentia* for treason and, more than ever, was forced to militate in exile. Shortly thereafter, **Kudirat Abiola**, the wife of the imprisoned victor of the last presidential election and an outspoken critic of the administration, was murdered by unidentified assailants. The nation saw the hand of the government behind the assault and rioting broke out, above all in Abiola's Yoruba homeland. Students were especially vociferous and the University of Ibadan was closed by government troops.

Unrest was not limited to the south. In 1996, the arrest of the local leader of Kaduna led to Muslim demonstrations that were violently quelled by the army. A year later, **Shehu Musa Yar Adua**, a respected northern politician who had been deputy head of state under Obasanjo, died mysteriously in jail, provoking thousands of supporters to riot in Katsina, calling for Abacha to step down. And in the delta region, early 1997 saw an escalation of violence between the Ijo and Itsekiri.

The country's poverty soared to its highest level since independence and disruption in petroleum production, along with gross mismanagement and the siphoning of billions of dollars into the pockets of the generals, led to a national **fuel shortage**, leading to the effective suspension of public transport throughout much of the country in 1998. To head off a deepening crisis, the world's sixth-largest oil producer was now forced to import oil.

In 1996, Abacha made some gestures at **reform**, when he announced the creation of five new parties and a calendar for the return to civil rule by

1998. But most of the country's civilian opposition was already in jail, and the parties that had been granted official status by the national electoral commission were all headed by Abacha loyalists. At the same time, the government talked of sweeping economic reforms that included the sale of state assets, even in the oil and gas sector, the elimination of the preferential exchange rate for government ministries, and a campaign against corruption. These plans, intended to impress the IMF, World Bank and foreign investors, were shot down by the military Provisional Ruling Council, who feared a short-term hike in unemployment and a long-term setback to their system of political patronage.

Just months before the scheduled elections, in June 1998, Abacha died of a **heart attack** and opponents of the regime celebrated in the streets of Lagos.

Return to civilian rule

Following Abacha's death, a transitional government under **Abdul-salaam Abubakar** took office, released hundreds of political prisoners, including Obasanjo, and promised elections the following year. But just days later, Nigerians were shocked and sceptical when Moshood Abiola died of an apparent heart attack in his jail cell after four years of solitary confinement,

---

Sharia law in the northern states

Islamic religious law – known as **sharia**, Arabic for "the way" – is based on the Koran, the sayings of Muhammad, and the interpretations put on these over the centuries by Islamic jurists. Unlike Christian canonical law, it covers all aspects of life.

In the north, Muslims have long been able to settle family and civil disputes in *sharia* courts if they so wish, though criminal law was secular. In January 2000, however, the state of **Zamfara** made every Muslim who commits an offence against Islamic law within the state liable to punishment under *sharia*. Among other things, this involves amputation for theft, flogging and imprisonment for extramarital sex, and stoning to death for adultery. Gambling and alcohol are banned, and possession of a *juju* charm is a capital offence, as is worship of any god but Allah. In theory, apostasy (renouncing Islam) is also punishable by death under *sharia*. The law was supported by most of Zamfara's population, well over ninety percent of whom are Muslim.

Seeing its popularity, other northern states were soon implementing similar laws, with Zamfara followed by Kano and Kaduna states, where demonstrations against the new law by members of the state's large Christian minority led to sectarian riots in which more than 300 people were killed. Since then, every state north of the Niger and Benue rivers, with the exception of Plateau and Abuja – twelve states in all – have introduced *sharia* penal codes. The first **amputation** was carried out in Zamfara in July 2000, and the following month two *okada* drivers were flogged for carrying female passengers – Zamfara has legislated for female-only transport, and women are not allowed to use anything else. As the state does not trust Nigeria's federal police, vigilante groups have been empowered to enforce *sharia*.

In October 2001, a woman in Sokoto was sentenced to **death by stoning** for adultery. Amid a hail of worldwide condemnation, the appeal court backed down and acquitted her on a technicality. But in March 2002, a court in Katsina sentenced the 30-year-old **Amina Lawal** to death by stoning for bearing a child out of wedlock (more than nine months since her divorce). President Obasanjo warned that carrying out such sentences would lead to Nigeria's isolation from the international community, and to date all *sharia* death sentences have been commuted or overturned on appeal. Lawal herself was freed and has remarried.

While the twelve northern states retain *sharia*, capital cases now result in a confusing standoff with the federal government, while the mortal danger to women of reporting a rape has become notoriously apparent.

and just one day before his scheduled release. Foul play was immediately suspected and news of the death led to clashes between demonstrators and police on the streets of Lagos.

Accompanying preparations for a return to **civilian rule**, Abubakar began talking about economic reforms to lift the country out of crisis. Negotiations began with the IMF for the implementation of a structural adjustment programme that included privatization and accountability – two essential ingredients for restoring the faith of creditors. In December 1998, three out of nine political parties contesting nationwide local elections – the People's Democratic Party (PDP), the Alliance for Democracy (AD) and the All People's Party (APP) – gained more than five percent of the vote in 24 states, entitling them to official status and the right to present candidates in the upcoming presidential elections.

The PDP – which had won sixty percent of the vote in the local elections – chose **Obasanjo** for its presidential candidate. Remembered for being the only military leader ever to hand power back to civilians, and for governing during a time of economic prosperity, Obasanjo was the front-runner from the start (people joked that PDP stood for "Pre-Determined President"), and enjoyed broad support throughout the country. In fact, northerners were more enthusiastic about his candidacy than his fellow Yorubas, and his choice of a northern running-mate gave him extra impetus in the region. **Chief Olu Falae**, an economist who represented a combined AD/APP ticket, struggled to keep pace with the PDP's campaign machine. Also a Yoruba with a northern running mate, Falae had less money and only patchy support outside his southwest stronghold. When polling took place in March 1999, Obasanjo captured nearly two-thirds of the votes.

The president-elect didn't squander the foreign support the elections had engendered. One of his first visits after being elected was to Sierra Leone, where President Ahmad Tejan Kabbah requested, and got, continued Nigerian backing for the peacekeeping force. In the interval before being sworn in, Obasanjo did a world tour that covered Asia, Europe, the US, and Africa from Cape Town to Kenya. Nigeria was an international player again.

Nigeria under Obasanjo

Abubakar dutifully turned power over to the **elected government** in May 1999, and in his last official act, banned Decree 2, the detention-without-trial law that had come to symbolize the tyranny and terror of successive military governments.

In his inaugural address, Obasanjo declared his determination to "make significant changes within a year". Certainly the most extreme excesses of the military regime were curbed. However, the tensions between north and south, and resentment of the foreign oil companies' activities in the delta region, have resurfaced in new forms.

In addition to the introduction of *sharia* law in the twelve northern states (see box), ethnic tensions elsewhere in the country were simmering and sometimes boiling over. June 1999 saw more than one hundred dead in clashes between Yoruba and Hausa in Shagamu near Lagos, followed in November by clashes – blamed by the government on the Yoruba-nationalist Oodua People's Congress (OPC) – that left some fifty dead in Lagos itself. In Nassarawa State, in central Nigeria, an unrelated dispute between Tiv and Hausa-speaking Jukun, left a hundred dead. When Tivs kidnapped nineteen soldiers sent to restore order following rioting in Benue State, the army retaliated by going in mob-handed and killing some two hundred Tiv.

The 9/11 attacks in the USA and the subsequent US invasion of Afghanistan predictably sparked off fresh rioting between northern Muslims and Christians. In Jos, where tension between the two communities was already high, Muslim protests against the Afghan campaign renewed intercommunal riots that had only been quelled the previous month.

The planned staging of the 2002 **Miss World** beauty pageant in Abuja caused further ructions. Various contestants pulled out in protest when a Sokoto *sharia* court passed a death sentence on a divorcee for adultery (see box), and when columnist Isioma Daniel joked in the popular daily *This Day* that the Prophet Muhammad himself would have enjoyed watching the show and would probably have chosen a wife from among its contestants, outraged young Muslims in Kaduna burnt down the paper's offices and then went on a rampage against Christians that left two hundred dead and forced the pageant to relocate to London.

There were fresh **presidential elections** in April 2003 and a number of registered political parties (far more than ever before) to contest them, most with no particular ideology or programme. On a 69-percent turnout, Obasanjo retained the presidency with 62 percent of the vote against 32 percent for his nearest rival, former military dictator Muhammad Buhari. Buhari immediately called the result "fraudulent", and certainly blatant ballot-stuffing took place, though Commonwealth observers still felt the result represented the will of the voters.

National strikes in June 2003 were called off only after planned 50-percent fuel-price increases were cut back by the government. The Independent Corrupt Practices and Related Offences Commission began looking into past misdeeds and achieved some successes, but on the streets, the police seemed powerless to deal with local ethnically-based vigilante groups who frequently engaged in bouts of mob violence against other groups.

In May 2004, officials arrested senior opposition figure **Buba Galadima** in connection with "security breaches" which some officers described as a coup plot to topple Obasanjo. The year before, Galadima had been in charge of Buhari's failed election campaign.

The same month saw violent clashes between Christians and Muslims: Christian militia attacked the largely Muslim market town of Yelwa, in the north, killing several hundred people, and soon afterwards, retaliatory attacks by Muslim Fulani on Christian Tarok resulted in eighty deaths in Plateau State. Obasanjo ordered police to "take all necessary action" and eventually declared a state of emergency, placing a retired general in charge of the region in place of its elected officials.

By September 2004, the government had signed an agreement with Virgin Atlantic, establishing a new airline in Nigeria. **Virgin Nigeria** would be majority-owned by Nigerian investors and receive special expertise and services from Richard Branson's Virgin Atlantic. But this came just a year before another airline disaster for Nigeria, when a Bellview Airlines Boeing 737-200 crashed, killing all 117 people on board.

Obasanjo had been president of Nigeria since 1999, elected initially for a four-year term, and then for another four years in 2003. By the end of 2004 some sections of the country's media had started to claim that he intended to amend the **constitution** so he could extend his tenure beyond 2007, something his spokesman was forced to deny. At the same time a tribunal was deciding on a challenge by twenty opposition parties to the 2003 election, which they claimed should be invalidated due to "corrupt practices". The tribunal eventually decided some balloting fraud had occurred and cancelled results in Obasanjo's home state of Ogun, where the votes counted exceeded the number of registered voters, but ruled that this would not have altered the final results.

By the end of 2005, trouble was reaching unmanageable proportions in the delta, with militant groups kidnapping oil-industry workers almost on a daily basis.

In January 2006 Obasanjo announced that Nigeria would have settled all its

14

debt to the Paris Club of creditors by that Spring. The Paris Club had cancelled 18 billion dollars of Nigeria's **30-billion-dollar debt** the previous year, but in return, Nigeria had been forced to pay 12 billion dollars debt-service charge. "We are determined to change the current image of Nigeria," Obasanjo said. Unfortunately changing the image of Nigeria didn't include ensuring freedom of the press. In March, police impounded 2000 copies of a book that was critical of the presidency, and arrested its publisher and author Adamu Yashim.

The same week a special parliamentary committee, set up to review the constitution, recommended adding an amendment to give Obasanjo a chance to run for a third term as president. Tensions were rising. Obasanjo had, in the past, said he wanted to complete reforms he had been working towards over eight years, but his special assistant said the president was committed to working within the democratic process, and the president had never publicly declared his third-term ambitions.

Supporters of the bid attempted to acquire the two-thirds majority in parliament necessary, but after a unanimous vote, the senate president said the bill to amend the constitution had been rejected.

Many complain that Obasanjo's legacy has left Nigeria rife with problems - its infrastructure decayed, fuel shortages and power cuts routine, and the oil-producing delta in turmoil.

The People's Democratic Party put forward Umaru Yar'Adua as their candidate for the presidency. Born in 1951 in Katsina, Yar'Adua had worked first as a lecturer at Katsina College and Kaduna Polytechnic, before moving into the corporate sector in the 1980s. He served as governor of Katsina State from 1999 until 2007.

When the elections went ahead in May 2007, they did so under the watchful eye of international election monitors; and the monitors were less than happy with what they saw. The two main opposition candidates, Mohammed Buhari of the All Nigeria People's Party (ANPP) and Atiku Abubakar (the former Vice President) of the Action Congress (AC), claimed the election had been rigged in Yar'Adua's favour.

Yar'Adua: a new era?

Since his election **President Umaru Yar'Adua** has managed, on the whole, to confound his critics. Three months after he was elected, his 39-member cabinet was sworn in. In June 2007, Yar'Adua publicly declared all his assets, becoming the first Nigerian leader to do so, reportedly against the advice of the Code of Conduct Bureau, who felt it would set a precedent and put pressure on other public officials. The release of information was said to be consistent with the president's campaign pledge to make the declaration of assets an effective weapon in the fight against corruption and abuse of office.

The **Economic and Financial Crimes Commission** had already managed to secure the conviction of former Bayelsa State governor, Diepreye Alamieyeseigha, on charges of corruption and money-laundering, and he was sentenced to two years imprisonment. In July 2007, the **EFCC** charged a further five former governors – of Abia, Plateau, Taraba, Jigawa and Enugu states – with various corruption offences.

Meanwhile, the Niger delta crisis is escalating, with a nightly curfew in force, and many feel the president still has a lot to prove. Southerners increasingly feel that Nigeria should divide into its three constituent parts, an idea generally opposed by people in the north, who have a lot less in the way of natural resources and would be left economically marooned between the coast and the desert. Some have suggested that radical **decentralization** of power to the states could ease the tensions tearing the country apart, but the fact is that, great though its problems may be, Nigeria has managed to live with them for fifty years, and can probably continue to do so for the foreseeable future.

Music

The Nigerian musical heritage extends from stately court drumming and trumpeting in the northern emirates to the fiercely anti-establishment music of the late **Fela Kuti**, and today's new wave of Christian rappers. Even if few Nigerian stars have been successful overseas, and the last international label gave up and quit the country in 1989, Nigeria has a well-developed music industry with numerous recording studios, and a huge market in pirated cassettes and CDs. And there is a large enough population to sustain artists who sing in regional languages and experiment with indigenous styles. For a quick overview, try the compilation CD *The Rough Guide to the Music of Nigeria and Ghana* (World Music Network).

Musical basics

The emirates of **Katsina** and **Kano** together with the sultanate of **Sokoto**, and to a lesser extent **Zaria** and **Bauchi**, are the major creative centres for **Hausa music**, which is surveyed on p.1200.

Southern Nigeria, however, and in particular the southwest, has by far the most musical energy, and the greatest profusion of artists and styles. Three main styles of music developed through the mid- to late twentieth century, and drew on traditional sources and outside influences – **highlife**, **juju** and **fuji**, the latter two almost entirely sung in Yoruba.

As everywhere, Nigeria has its own enthusiastic exponents of local variants of **hip-hop** and **reggae** – often the most followed music in the dancehalls and on the airwaves.

Igbo traditional music

The Igbo of southeast Nigeria have always been receptive to cultural change – an ease reflected in their music and in the incredible variety of instruments played in Igboland. No local occasion would be complete without musicians and you should find them at any event associated with the *obi* or chief. The other major occasions are seasonal festivals, wrestling matches, and visits by (or funerals of) high-ranking officials or prominent citizens.

In more traditional communities, royal music is played every day, when the **ufie** slit drum is used to wake the chief and to tell him when meals are ready. A group of musicians, known as **egwu ota**, playing drums, slit-drums and bells, performs when the *obi* is leaving the palace and again when he returns.

One of the most pleasing Igbo instruments is the **obo** – not an oboe but a thirteen-stringed raft zither, which can be heard at many a nostalgic palm-wine drinking session.

Traditional Yoruba

Yoruba instrumental traditions are mostly based on drumming. The most popular form of traditional music today is **dundun**, played on hourglass tension drums of the same name. The usual *dundun* ensemble consists of tension drums of various sizes together with small kettledrums called **gudugudu**. The leading drum of the group is the *iyaalu* ("mother of the drums"), which talks by imitating the tone patterns of Yoruba speech. It's used to play out praise poetry, proverbs and other oral texts. Another important part of Yoruba musical life is **music theatre**, which mixes traditional music with storytelling and live drama.

Juju

The **origins** of *juju* music are not very clear, but it seems to have emerged as a Lagos variant of Ghana's palm-wine music (see p.808). The word *juju* is thought to be a corruption of the Yoruba term *jo jo*, meaning "dance" – or equally it may just be a dismissive epithet coined by colonial officers and retained, defensively, by its exponents.

The first records in this style started coming out in the early 1930s but it really took off just after World War II with the introduction of amplified sound. The major stars of the prewar period were **Irewolede Denge** ("grandfather of *juju*") and **Tunde King**, while after the war **Ayinde Bakare** and the **Jolly Orchestra** were the big names.

The **1960s** saw the arrival of dozens of new *juju* singers and bands, of whom three – **I.K. Dairo**, **Ebenezer Obey** and **Sunny Ade** – came to dominate the scene. During and after the Nigerian civil war of 1967–70, *juju* thrived at home as highlife artists from the eastern region either went to Biafra or fled abroad, and highlife as a whole lost its popularity.

Juju Roots, 1930s–1950s (Rounder, US). Excellent introduction to the early *juju* years, with comprehensive sleeve notes, featuring Irewolede Denge, Tunde King and Ojoge Daniel.

I.K. Dairo

Dairo had been playing in bands for a good part of his life when he formed the Morning Star Orchestra in 1957. By 1961, he had set up the popular Blue Spots and rose to become Nigeria's best-known exponent of *juju*.

Juju Master (Original Music). A round-up of classic Decca West Africa 45s. Singer, composer and band leader, Dairo introduced the accordion to *juju*.

Ebenezer Obey

Obey formed his first group, the International Brothers, in 1964. The success of his blend of talking drums, percussion and guitar had already caught on by the time he renamed them the InterReformers, in 1970. With a vast number of albums to his credit and

now in his 60s, Obey maintains a loyal following for his infectious, danceable *juju*, though his output has slowed since the millennium.

Ju Ju Jubilation (Hemisphere/EMI). Satisfyingly bluesy, slightly offbeat *juju* compilation, from a musician whose expansive features and rather right-wing, Christian image are in contrast to rival *juju* artist Sunny Ade.

King Sunny Ade

Ade started his musical career playing with highlife bands in Lagos before making the transition to *juju*. He formed The Green Spots in 1966, changing the name of the group to the African Beats in 1974. By the end of the decade, Ade was one of the most popular musicians in the country, and in the 1980s he broke internationally, making three albums for Island Records and touring worldwide.

Juju Music (Universal). The record that launched a million passions for African sounds. Still wonderful after all these years, *Juju Music* includes many of Ade's best songs, among them the sweet "365 is My Number".

On Bobby (Sunny Alade). This Nigerian release is probably the best *juju* album of all time – Ade runs through all the classic riffs in a flowing 1983 tribute to legendary band-leader Bobby Benson.

Apala and fuji

Though never achieving the international success of *juju* and highlife, the wall-of-percussion sound of *fuji* has been popular in Nigeria since the 1970s. It has its roots in the Yoruba styles of *apala* and *sakara*, themselves products of Muslim influence on older musical forms in northern Yorubaland.

Haruna Ishola, one of Nigeria's greatest *apala* performers, helped pave the way for *fuji*. Before he died in 1983, he had produced some 25 LPs and opened his own recording studio. It's still relatively easy to find many of his later records like, *Apala Songs*.

Sikiru Ayinde – "Barrister"

The leading Yoruba *fuji* singer, Barrister started singing *were* – the songs performed for early breakfast and prayers during Ramadan – at the age of 10. After a brief army career, he turned back to music and, in the early 1970s, formed the Supreme Fuji Commander, a 25-piece outfit. They soon became one of Nigeria's top bands, firing off a battery of hit records.

New Fuji Garbage (Globestyle). A recording which is likely to define *fuji* for Western ears for years to come. Barrister's voice here is slightly mellower than usual and the band surround it with a pounding panoply of sound.

Ayinla Kollington

Fuji's "man of the people", Kollington is the source of social commentary in the Yoruba Muslim music scene. He was at one time a rival of Barrister, but the two now peacefully coexist in a market big enough for both.

Ijoba Ti Tun (KRLPS). Challenging lyrics, driving percussion and a touch of Hawaiian guitar on this Nigerian release.

Highlife

Highlife came to Nigeria from Ghana in the 1950s (see p.809 for more on Ghanaian highlife), and was quickly moulded by indigenous styles and influences from Cameroon and the Congo that give it a distinctively Nigerian flavour. Extra polish, and Western instruments – brass sections, electric keyboards and guitars – were added to home-grown rhythms and, by the 1960s, highlife was in the forefront of popular urban music. It lost its universal appeal during the civil war, when it retained mass popularity only in Igboland, quite quickly losing ground to *juju* among the Yoruba.

Old albums from the early highlife stars are rarities these days, although it is still possible to lay your hands on 1970s and 1980s material by the fabulous Oriental Brothers (and offshoots Dr Sir Warrior and Kabaka). Meanwhile a steady trickle of re-releases continues to refresh the style.

Oriental Brothers

Originally formed by three virtuoso musicians, brothers Dansatch and Godwin Opara, and the late Christogonus "Warrior" Obinna, the Orientals spawned three of the finest highlife bands ever, dominating the 1970s with hit after hit.

Heavy on the Highlife (Original Music). Wonderful burn-up of a guitar-highlife album – relentless, sexy grooves.

Prince Nico Mbarga and Rocafil Jazz

The late Prince Nico will forever *be* Igbo highlife – it's reckoned he sold some thirteen million copies of the 1976 release, "Sweet Mother", making it the biggest-selling African song of all time. Hundreds of bands copied it; radio stations played it incessantly; vinyl copies could only be had at twenty times the normal price.

Aki Special (Rounder). Includes "Sweet Mother" – which makes as good a starting point as any for a collection of Nigerian music.

Afro-beat and the Kuti dynasty

Afro-beat was almost solely the creation of one extraordinary musician, the singer and multi-instrumentalist Fela Anikulapo-Kuti (see below). The style, developed in the early 1960s, has its own distinctive beats and rhythms, fusing jazz and highlife. The characteristic rhythms were the hallmark of drummer and long-time Fela collaborator, Tony Allen. Afro-beat demanded a large group of musicians playing a wide variety of instruments. Its energy and repetitive, improvised segments, were almost hypnotic. And vocals were usually sung in a mixture of Yoruba and Pidgin.

Fela Kuti

Fela Anikulapo-Kuti (1938–97) is best known overseas as the pot-smoking Nigerian singer who married 27 women in one day and declared his house an independent state – the Kalakuta Republic. He remains one of the most influential musicians to emerge from the continent and his lifestyle was much misunderstood in the West.

Fela was born into a middle-class family in Abeokuta (also the home town of former president Olusegun Obasanjo). Fela was the son of a preacher and Nigeria's first feminist activist, the first woman to drive a car in the country. Radicalism was in his blood.

He endured countless beatings from the authorities, and was imprisoned for his outspoken views.

In 1977 Fela released the song "Zombie", comparing Obasanjo's army to robots. In retaliation, a thousand soldiers surrounded Kalakuta and began climbing the fence. They then began shooting. Fela, who was inside, managed to escape from the compound, but his mother Funmilayo was thrown from a top-storey window and later died from her injuries.

The Kalakuta was torched to the ground, but Fela's response was to move to a new building and place a coffin on its roof with a banner that read: "This is where justice was murdered." He later took the coffin and dumped it at the gates of Obasanjo's army barracks. The song "Coffin For Head of State" chronicled the events that day.

Fela's lyrics were overtly political. He chose to sing in Pidgin to avoid limiting his audience, and his eruptive performances and defiant lifestyle found him a huge following and brought him into constant conflict with the Nigerian authorities. A steady stream of hit albums included *Black President*, *Perambulator*, and *Expensive Shit*.

Especially if you're a vinyl devotee, you'll find that Barclay's Fela boxed sets of classic original vinyl discs take Afro-beat appreciation to a higher level, pulling together key releases from the 1970s, his purplest period. One of the best places to hunt for Fela CDs is Obalende market in Lagos.

69 Los Angeles Sessions (Stern's). Some vintage numbers from Black Panther days – and ten tracks all under seven minutes make it unique in the Fela oeuvre.

Shakara/Fela's London Scene (Wrasse). The first of these is an all-time classic, paired here with a very early release.

The Best Of Fela Kuti/The Black President (Barclay/Talking Loud in the UK; MCA in the US). Twin-CD compilation packed with immortal material.

Femi Kuti

Fela Kuti's son has had an independent career since the late 1980s with his group, the Positive Force. But only since his father's death in 1997 has his stock really risen.

Shoki Shoki (Barclay in the UK; MCA in the US) and **Fight to Win** (Wrasse; MCA). Femi is recognizably a Kuti, both in his voice and in the subject matter and lyrics of the songs with their muscular arrangements, but these albums are infused with a fresh dance-floor sensibility which old man Kuti's stoned diatribes never aimed to deliver.

Seun Kuti

Most Nigerians would say Seun Kuti (ⓦwww.myspace.com/seunkuti) – Fela's youngest child – is more like his father than older brother Femi. Seun still lives in the Kalakuta Republic, which was Fela's house up until his death. And since then he has fronted Egypt 80, his father's old band.

He looks like Fela, and can be seen playing regularly around Lagos.

Lágbájá (aka Bisade Ologunde)

Lágbájá (ⓦ www.lagbaja.net) is the new prince of Afro-beat, wearing a mask when he performs, on a sound base of massed percussion, to empathize with the faceless masses and remind Yoruba fans of their roots. In 2000, he released three CDs simultaneously in Nigeria, *We*, *Me* and *Abami*, and won "Artist of the Year" despite his harsh criticism of Obasanjo.

Ragga, galala and hip-hop

By 2003, after Obasanjo's re-election, a little confidence was returning to the nightlife scene in the south, though *sharia* law (see box, p.1099) had all but destroyed live music in the north. Local **ragga** is perennially popular (Tupac Shakur was a major youth icon) and the likes of Arthur Pepple, Blakky and Lt. Shotgun attract big audiences, but their songs, when recorded, are often banned from the radio.

Galala – a broadly reggae-style "healing" mix of Nigerian, Jamaican and African-American influences devised, or at least fostered, by born-again Christian toaster and owner of Lagos's Jahoha Studios, John Oboh (**Mighty Mouse**) – is currently the biggest sound in the poor quarters of the city and **Daddy Showkey** its big star.

Lastly, the hugely successful gospel-inflected hip-hop threesome of the 1990s, **The Remedies**, split up in 1999 and spawned new bands and

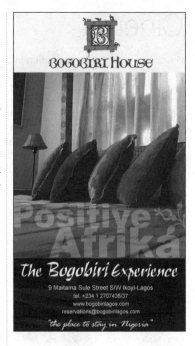

The Bogobiri Experience
9 Maitama Sule Street S/W Ikoyi-Lagos
tel. +234 1 2707436/37
www.bogobirilagos.com
reservations@bogobirilagos.com
"the place to stay in Nigeria"

recording careers, including the **Plantashun Boyz** and **Tony Tetuola**, who had a massive hit in 2002 with "My Car". This **Afro-hip-hop** is clubby, non-threatening stuff that appeals to a more upmarket fan-base than *galala* and it continues to flourish, with **TuFace Ndibia** (formerly of the Plantashun Boyz), **Rugged Man**, **Soul E**, **Styl-Plus** and **Dbanj**, amongst others, creating huge demand, with CD sales of a million or more for the top musicians. You'll have no trouble finding cassettes and CDs, invariably pirated, in any Nigerian town, but none of this music is easily available outside the country.

Cinema

Despite its vigor, the **Nigerian film industry** has a very low profile everywhere except Nigeria, where video completely dominates. In the past couple of years, however, there have been signs of change, with the arrival of the South African **NuMetro** cinema chain, opening multiplexes in Lagos and Abuja, with many more planned. The rival **Silverbird** chain plans a similar roll-out, to complement their first modern cinema at the Silverbird Galleria in Lagos. So a theatrical-release film industry may yet re-emerge, with much higher-quality production values than exist today in the video market.

Nigerian directors

The country's first feature film was *Kongi's Harvest* (1970), based on the play by Wole Soyinka and directed by **Francis Oladele**. Oladele's next film, *Bullfrog in the Sun* (1971), was adapted from Chinua Achebe's novels *Things Fall Apart* and *No Longer at Ease*, and never properly distributed in Nigeria because of its politically sensitive subject matter. Such troubles have hit other films too. **Eddie Ugbomah** had great success with *The Rise and Fall of Dr Oyenuzi* (1977), the true story of a Lagos gangster, and *The Mask* (1979), about a Nigerian spy sent to Britain to retrieve a stolen Benin mask. He even got away with *Death of a Black President* (1983), covering events leading up to the much-loved Murtala Muhammed's assassination, but his *Great Attempt* (1990) and *Ha, Yoruba* (1995) were both banned for political reasons.

One of Nigeria's most prolific film-makers is **Ola Balogun**. He was behind the first Yoruba feature film, *Ajani Ogun*, in 1976, with stage actor Ade Folayan. Balogun secured his reputation abroad with films like *Cry Freedom* (1981) and *Money Power* (1984). Other important Nigerian directors include the late **Hubert Ogunde**, whose films, such as *Aiye* (1980; with Ola Balogun) and its sequel *Jaiyesinmi* (1983), often dealt with witchcraft and the significance of tradition. Perhaps the greatest living Nigerian film director is **Tunde Kelani**, director of classics such as *Ò le Kù* (1997) and *Thunderbolt* (2001).

Video releases

In the past decade, cinemas in Nigeria have been in retreat – in Lagos most have been converted into charismatic churches. But if cinema-going has dwindled, the film industry is more prolific than ever. The reason is the shift to video **"home movies"** largely sparked off by the success of **Christian Onu**'s 1992 Igbo-language witchcraft movie, *Living in Bondage*.

As in Ghana, films shot and released on video for home-viewing are now the norm in Nigeria, and hundreds are made every year, especially in the Lagos suburb of Surulere – dubbed **Nollywood**. The majority are very low-budget and shot in Yoruba – Igbo and English releases tend to be higher-budget and aim for exportability.

Among the new breed of directors, **Chico Ejiro** is Nigeria's "Mr Prolific", with more than eighty video movies to his name, including the 2001 hit *Outkast* and its sequel *Outkast 2*, both among a slew of films that have been in hot water with Nigeria's board of censors for allegedly promoting "immorality".

A similar video market exists in the north, with Hausa-speaking actors – a genre increasingly known as **Kannywood**.

Books

There's a vast body of books on and from Nigeria in print – and more being published all the time. Nigeria's post-colonial **literature** has been the continent's most prolific and most outspoken, its writers enjoying a greater liberty than most of their African counterparts. One of the greatest impetuses to national writing was **Onitsha Market Literature**, which emerged between 1947 and 1966. At the time, Onitsha was one of Nigeria's most important commercial centres, with a long history of mission education and cosmopolitan influence. Dozens of spare-time writers – teachers, office clerks and journalists – turned out some two hundred books that were printed in the market itself. A similar body of work, based around **Kano**, has emerged in the north, although many of the works have yet to be translated from Hausa.

There's a clutch of great Nigerian writers, including US-based Nobel Prize–winner **Wole Soyinka** and the renowned and more accessible author and opinion-moulder **Chinua Achebe**, also based in the US. Since 2003, there's been something of a renaissance in Nigerian writing, with **Helon Habila, Helen Oyeyemi** and **Chimamanda Ngozi Adichie** winning international awards and gaining widespread exposure outside Nigeria. And three of the five short-listed short-story writers for the 2007 **Caine Prize for African Writing** – **Uwem Akpan, E.C. Osondu** and **Ada Udechukwu** – were Nigerian. After decades of slumber, the publishing industry in Nigeria shows signs of a reawakening, with outfits such as **New Gong**, Kachifo (**Farafina**), **Cassava Republic Press** and **Bookcraft** catering to an eager market. The publishers of titles most easily available in Nigeria are indicated below.

Several online Nigerian literature websites have emerged at the same time, notably ⓦ www.farafinamagazine .com. As elsewhere, Nigeria has staked a worthy claim on the blogosphere. Check out ⓦ www.everythinliterature.blogspot. com, which focuses on northern writing and Molara Wood's literary blog ⓦ www .wordsbody.blogspot.com. Many of the most popular Nigerian blogs are listed at ⓦ www.naijablog.blogspot.com.

The South African-owned **NuMetro** chain of Media Stores (currently in Lagos and Abuja) are the best places to pick up books, although if you're in Lagos, **Jazzhole** and **Glendora** have more varied and discerning collections. Titles marked 🎋 are especially recommended.

Country and state

Chinua Achebe *The Trouble with Nigeria*. Two decades after its first publication, this remains an immensely useful insight into the complexity of Nigerian society and politics.

Claude Ake (ed) *The Political Economy of Nigeria*. A classic work, uncompromising in its critique of political and economic conditions and the stranglehold on Nigeria of structures beyond its grasp. This book made the late Ake's reputation as one of Nigeria's most outspoken academics. With his later works, like *How Politics Underdevelops Africa* and *Democratization of Disempowerment*, he became one of the most brilliant observers of what went wrong.

William D. Graf *Nigerian State: Political Economy, State, Class and Political System in the Post-Colonial Era*. An overview analyzing political, social and economic shifts over the last 25 years.

Peter Holmes *Nigeria: Giant of Africa*. Coffee-table format with nearly two hundred photos. Detailed and interesting notes; nothing else on Nigeria of this type compares.

Samuel Johnson *The History of the Yorubas*. A detailed and vivid account of Yoruba history, published in Nigeria by CSS.

🏃 **Karl Maier** *This House Has Fallen: Nigeria in Crisis*. An incisive survey by the London *Independent*'s former Africa correspondent, of the political problems besetting modern Nigeria. Maier explains the issues thoroughly, and without ever taking sides.

Adewale Maja-Pearce *Remembering Ken Saro-Wiwa and Other Essays.* Twenty-three profound essays by the former editor of the Heinemann African Writers Series. Published in Nigeria by New Gong.

Egohosa E. Osaghae *The Crippled Giant*. A concise introduction to four decades of Nigerian political history – the pessimism in the title relates to the book's publication during the Abacha crisis.

Abraham Oshoko *June 12: The Struggle for Power in Nigeria* (Farafina). A graphic novel account of the events that led up to the annulled 1993 elections and the Abacha dictatorship.

🏃 **Andrew Rowell** *The Next Gulf.* A concise and lively account of the oil industry in Nigeria and its relation to politics and Western interests, published in 2005.

Ken Saro-Wiwa *A Month and a Day, A Detention Diary*. A living testimony from the leader of MOSOP (executed by the Abacha regime in 1995) against the atrocities meted out to the Ogoni people in Cross River State.

Wole Soyinka *The Open Sore of a Continent: A Personal Narrative of the Nigerian Crisis*. Accessible diagnosis of one of Africa's biggest wounds from one of its most admired writers.

Arts and peoples

Omofolabo S. Ajayi *Yoruba Dance: The Semiotics of Movement and Body Attitude in a Nigerian Culture*. An insightful introduction to Yoruba dance and the theme of movement as communication.

J.S. Boston *Ikenga*. Explores the symbolism of carvings among varied peoples of Nigeria.

T.J.H. Chappel *Decorated Gourds in North Eastern Nigeria*. A substantial survey of their use, decoration and symbolism.

Henry J. Drewal and John Pemberton III *Yoruba: Nine Centuries of African Art and Thought*. Sumptuous and terribly expensive – a majestic, detailed photo and essay documentary on various Yoruba states and their individual artistic traditions.

Robert Farris Thompson *Flash of the Spirit: African and Afro-American Art and Philosophy*. Classic work of art history and ethnography by one of America's leading African – and especially Yoruba – art experts.

Edward Fox *Obscure Kingdoms*. Excitingly written and brilliantly evocative accounts of journeys to the world's remoter royal corners, including a sizeable chapter on meetings in Nigeria with various *onis*, *obas* and emirs.

Berkare Gbadamosi and Ulli Beier *Not Even God Is Ripe Enough*. Full of amusing Yoruba folk tales.

Paula Girshick Ben-Amos *The Art of Benin*. Plenty of photos of bronzes and more.

Barry Hallen and J.O. Sodipo *Knowledge, Belief and Witchcraft*. A survey of Yoruba philosophical ideas.

G.I. Jones *Ibo Art*. Well-illustrated survey of arts and their role in Igbo society.

Babatunde Lawal *The Gelede Spectacle: Art, Gender and Social Harmony in African culture*. Fascinating account of one of the most powerful traditions in Yoruba culture.

🏃 **A.D. Nzemeke and E.O. Erhage** (eds) *Nigerian Peoples and Culture* (United City Press, Nigeria). Highly recommended in-depth cultural history of Nigeria's ethnic groups.

Robert S. Smith *Kingdoms of the Yoruba*. The classic historical work on pre-colonial Yoruba civilization.

Michael Veal *Fela: the Life and Times of an African Musical Icon*. A fascinating, well-researched account of Fela Kuti's life and music and the Nigeria he lived through.

Ken Wiwa *In the Shadow of a Saint*. Ken Saro-Wiwa's son Ken Wiwa's highly readable account of his complex relationship with his father.

Fiction and poetry

Chris Abani *Graceland; Becoming Abigail; The Virgin of Flames*. Chris Abani grabbed the world's attention with his startling debut novel *Graceland*, a cinematic take on life in Lagos under Abacha, with its memorable, Elvis-impersonating narrator.

Chinua Achebe *Things Fall Apart; No Longer at Ease; Arrow of God; A Man of the People; Anthills of the Savannah*. One of Africa's best-known novelists, Achebe gained international fame with his classic first novel *Things Fall Apart* (1958), which deals with the encounter, at the turn of the last century, of missionaries, colonial officers and an Igbo village. Okwonkwo, a self-made man, rises to respected seniority, then falls, inexorably and tragically. It's a brilliant, moving book – universal in what it says on pride, and on fathers and sons. With it, the three following novels form part of a loose quartet: in *No Longer at Ease*, Okwonkwo's grandson, Obi, is a corrupt Lagos civil servant, trapped in his head between home and ambition; in *Arrow of God*, set in the 1920s, there's direct confrontation between an Igbo priest and a colonial officer; and in *A Man of the People*, Achebe adopts a more satirical approach, setting up an idealist against a rogue and showing how close their paths run. Achebe's characters bend and sweat with life and develop unexpected traits just as you thought you had the measure of them. His 1995 novel, a humanist fable, *Anthills of the Savannah*, was shortlisted for the Booker Prize.

Chimamanda Ngozi Adichie *Purple Hibiscus* (2005) and *Half of a Yellow Sun* (2007). Winner of the Orange Prize for her second novel, Adichie is in the vanguard of a new generation of Nigerian writers born after the civil war. *Half of a Yellow Sun*, written with almost unbearable compassion, explores the war from the perspective of an Igbo family.

Segun Afolabi *A Life Elsewhere* and *Goodbye Lucille* (Farafina). Part of the new wave of Nigerian writers, *A Life Elsewhere* is a fine collection of short pieces. *Goodbye Lucille* is Afolabi's first novel.

Zainab Alkali *A Virtuous Woman; The Stillborn*. Alkali is unusual in being a woman writer from the conservative north. "I see myself as a typical Nigerian woman who wants to get married, raise a family and live according to the expected norms of the society… A woman can never be anything else but a woman."

T.M. Aluko *One Man, One Wife* (1959). Entertaining tale of Yoruba villagers' disillusionment with the missionaries' God and their return to traditional worship.

Sefi Atta *Everything Good Will Come* (Farafina). An emerging voice in Nigerian letters and short-listed for the Caine Prize in 2006, Sefi Atta (ⓦwww .sefiatta.com) is a writer to watch. Her second book, *Swallow*, is about a heroin mule.

Biyi Bandele *Burma Boy* (Farafina). Gripping account of a young African soldier in the Second World War.

Simi Bedford *Yoruba Girl Dancing*. A British Nigerian's depiction of early life in Nigeria and adjustment to the UK. Her latest book, *Not With Silver*, explores the issue of human trafficking.

John Pepper Clark *A Reed in the Tide*, *Casualties* and *A Decade of Tongues* are poetry collections with which Clark first gained recognition. He is now better known as a playwright: for *Ozidi*, a play based on an Ijo saga; *State of the*

Nation, a piece of social criticism; and *America, Their America*, a biting indictment of values in the United States, where he studied in the early 1960s.

Teju Cole *Every Day is for the Thief* (Cassava Republic). A poignant study of a young man's return to Lagos after years of absence, in the style of Berger and Sebald.

Jude Dibia *Walking with Shadows* (Black Sand Books). In Nigeria's first gay novel, Dibia reveals a hidden aspect of Nigerian society in this eminently readable debut. *Unbridled* is his second novel.

Iheanyichukwu Duruoha *Eaters of Dust*. As Biafra collapses, a teenage boy in its disintegrating army witnesses a war crime. Poignant, highly readable, and easily one of the best among a multitude of civil-war novels.

T. Obinkaram Echewa *I Saw the Sky Catch Fire*. Fictional accounts of the effects of war, especially as it touches the lives of women. Powerful and moving, from a Nigerian-American author best known for his novel *The Land's Lord* about a French missionary in Africa.

Cyprian Ekwensi *Jagua Nana*. Superbly captures the life and rhythm of 1950s Lagos using a style like that of a traditional storyteller. *Burning Grass* is set in the north among Fula herders.

Buchi Emecheta *Slave Girl*; *Second Class Citizen*; *In the Ditch*; *Head above Water*; *Joys of Motherhood*; *Double Yoke*; *The Bride Price*; *Destination Biafra*; *Gwendolen* and *Rape of Shavi*. Emecheta writes – with a humour that won't be submerged – about the struggle to be a woman and an independent person in Nigeria and the UK.

🏃 **Helon Habila** *Waiting for an Angel*. Much-acclaimed debut novel about the precarious life of a journalist under the Abachas regime. His second novel, *Measuring Time*, explores the life of twins growing up in the 1970s in the northeast and is destined to become a classic.

Festus Iyayi *Violence*; *Heroes*. A committed political writer, Iyayi was detained in 1988 for protesting against human-rights abuses. *Violence* is a howl of anguish at the inhumanity of urban Africa; *Heroes* is set in the dark backyard of Nigeria's soul, during the 1967–69 civil war.

(Vincent) Chukwuemeka Ike *Toads for Supper*; *The Naked Gods*; *The Chicken Chasers*; *The Children are Coming*; *The Potter's Wheel* and *Sunset at Dawn*. A series of entertaining, critical novels by a brilliant comic writer.

Eddie Iroh *Forty Eight Guns for the General*; *Toads of War*; *The Sirens in the Night*. Three thrillers that rode in on the wave of writing following the Biafran War.

Uzodinma Iweala *Beasts of No Nation*. A graphic, award-winning account of an African child-soldier written by a 22-year-old Nigerian to huge acclaim in 2005.

Toni Kan *Ballad of Rage* and *Nights of the Creaking Bed* (Cassava Republic). An emerging talent from the Lagos literary scene. *Nights of the Creaking Bed* is an absorbing set of short stories.

Karen King-Aribasala *Kicking Tongues*. A wonderful collection of perspectives shared by travel companions – who range from a prostitute to village chief who meet up at the *Eko Holiday Inn* in Lagos before embarking on a trip to Abuja.

Adewale Maja-Pearce *Loyalties*. Evocative short stories and vignettes, by a writer based in Britain, set in a Nigeria always on the brink of chaos.

Dulue Mbachu *War Games* (New Gong). A tender yet compelling coming-of-age story during the Nigerian Civil War.

🏃 **Flora Nwapa** *Efuru*. As in the later *Idu*, the late Flora Nwapa, the first African woman to publish a novel, looks at women's roles – not always in a traditional way – in a society precariously balanced between the traditional and the new.

Christopher Okigbo *Labyrinths.* An extraordinary series of interlinked poems from a poet who lost his life during the civil war.

Ben Okri *Flowers and Shadows.* Okri's first novel was published when he was only 20. The angry, hallucinatory short-story collections, *Incidents at the Shrine* and *Stars of the New Curfew*, propelled Nigerian literature into a new wider audience. Okri, based in Britain, provides razor-sharp dialogue and settings, fine evocations of character and an angular wit. With his Booker Prize–winning *The Famished Road*, he comes home to the themes of tradition and of Yoruba mythology. It was followed by a sequel, *Songs of Enchantment*, then by *Astonishing the Gods*, *Dangerous Love*, *Infinite Riches* and *In Arcadia*. His book of short essays *A Way of Being Free* is a gem of poetic and spiritual musings. His latest novel is *Starbook*.

Niyi Osundare *Moonsongs; Songs of the Season; Waiting Laughters; Midlife.* One of Africa's best-known poets, committed to poetry-performance, drumming and dancing, Osundare is a Commonwealth Prize–winner, who received the NOMA Award in 1991 for *Waiting Laughters*.

Helen Oyeyemi *The Icarus Girl; The Opposite House.* The new literary sensation of 2005, *The Icarus Girl* was written as the teenage writer was revising for her A-levels. Both novels explore the Yoruba spirit-world with a strikingly mature pen, offering a new take on magical realism.

Abidemi Sanusi *Kemi's Journal* and *Zack's Story* (Cassava Republic). Humorous chick-lit style account of a young Nigerian woman and her life-issues: faith, relationships, babies.

Ken Saro-Wiwa *Sozaboy; A Forest of Flowers; Basi & Company; The Prisoner of Jebs; Pita Dumbrok's Prison.* Saro-Wiwa, a major figure on the Nigerian literary, political and TV scenes, was executed by the Abacha regime for his campaigning work on behalf of his Ogoni people in the Niger delta. His creative fiction

is often written in Pidgin: *Sozaboy* remains a classic of its kind.

Lola Shoneyin *The Other Wives* (Cassava Republic). Shoneyin's first novel explores life in a polygamous Ibadan family ranging from childless-ness and paternity, to the tragicomic consequences of an educated woman marrying an uneducated polygamist.

Wole Soyinka *Ake*, *Isara* and other works. Known primarily as a playwright, Soyinka was the first African winner of the Nobel Prize for Literature (1986). Often mentioned in the same breath as his US-based literary compatriot Chinua Achebe, Soyinka's work is denser and less easy-going than Achebe's. He is also politically more outspoken, and during the Abacha regime, helped organize a major opposition group in exile. His early works include *The Lion and the Jewel*, *A Dance of the Forests* – an exercise in demythologizing Africa's historic idyll – and *Kongi's Harvest.* He later published poetry, sketching beautiful images in *Idanre, and Other Poems.* He has also worked substantially as a novelist with *The Interpreters* – in which a circle of intellectuals living in Lagos attempt to "interpret" their roles in Nigeria – and the luminous, dream-like *Ake*, an autobiographical account of his childhood in Abeokuta. *Isara* is a biographical account of Nigeria in the times of his father, the memorable schoolmaster "Essay" from *Ake*. The sequel to *Isara* is *Ibadan: the Penkelmes Years*, which focuses on his fight against the everyday repression of early post--independence Nigeria. *You Must Set Forth at Dawn* (Bookcraft) is the next biographical instalment.

Amos Tutuola *The Palm-Wine Drinkard.* Heavily under the spell of Yoruba oral tradition, this recounts a journey into the "Dead Towns" of the supernatural. It was followed by *My Life in the Bush of Ghosts.*

Chika Unigwe *The Phoenix* (Farafina). The first novel by an Afro-Belgian writer of Nigerian origin, from Enugu.

Language

Nigeria's official language is **English** and in the larger cities – especially those with universities – it's spoken widely and with accents you'll adapt to easily. **Pidgin English,** however, which is spoken as a lingua franca everywhere, especially in the smaller towns and rural areas, will initially throw you. Keep trying, though; ask people to repeat phrases, and before long most visitors find their own speech punctuated with Pidgin expressions.

The three most widely spoken ethnic languages are **Hausa** (see p.1031), **Yoruba** and **Igbo**. Next to these, are some five hundred separate languages representing twelve language families. The linguistic situation in central and southeast Nigeria is one of the most complicated in the world – on the islands of the Niger delta region there are villages a few kilometres apart with mutually incomprehensible tongues.

Yoruba

Yoruba is the name given to a cluster of close dialects in the **Kwa** grouping. As a tonal language, it can be difficult for foreigners to master even the basics. Because tone carries so much meaning, it's possible to communicate with little or no vocalization: talking drums were (and still are) able to transmit messages, and you don't have to listen to much of Sunny Ade's music to realize how easily this is accomplished. The diacritics in the following words and phrases are not accents but indicate the tone of the sound – either rising (´), or falling (`). **E** is pronounced "eh" or "ey" and **O** is pronounced "or" or "oh". The prefix "E" indicates a plural or formal construction: a younger person greets an older person first and uses a respectful "E" at the beginning of a greeting, which may be dropped when talking to someone of the same social standing and the same age or younger.

Greetings

E káàárò	Good morning (and response)
E káàsán	Good afternoon (and response)
E káalé	Good evening (and response)
E kúulé	On entering a house
E káàbò	Response
E kúushé	Greeting someone who is working
Shé alaáfìà ni	How are you?/ How's life?
Adúpé	Response (lit. thank you)
Ó dàbò	Goodbye

Basic chat

Mo féé	I want
Mi ò féé	I don't want
È wo?	Which one?
Eléyìí	This is the one
E gbà	Take (it)
Omi	Water
Eran	Meat
Emu	Palm wine
E sheé	Thank you (on receiving something)
Èló ní?	How much is it?
Naira mewa ni	It's ten naira
Sanwó	To pay
Owó	Money
E dín owó lori e	Please, reduce the price
E fún mi	Give me
Ó dáa	All right/Okay
E jòó	Please
E má bínú	Don't be annoyed
Kini oruko ré?	What's your name?
Dayo ni oruko mi	My name is Dayo
Pèlé	Greetings/ commiserations
Mi ò gbo	I don't understand
Rárá	No, (not) at all
Òré mi	My friend

Numbers

ookan	1
méjì	2
méta	3
merin	4
marun	5
mefa	6
meje	7
mejo	8
mesan	9
mewa	10
mokanla	11
mejila	12
metala	13
merinla	14
mèedogun	15
meridlogun	16
metadinlogun	17
mejidinlogun	18
mokondinlogun	19
ogun	20
mokan le logun	21
meji le logun	22
mèd ogbon	25
meridin logbon	26
ogbon	30
ogoji	40
adota	50
ogota	60
aadorin	70
ogorin	80
adorun	90
ogorun	100

Igbo

Igbo is also a tonal language and part of the great Kwa grouping – but it is not intelligible to Yoruba-speakers. Again, be prepared to squeeze your mouth a little to get an intelligible vowel sound.

Greetings

Kèdú/Kèdú ka í mère?	Hi/How are you?
Kèdú maka umú-àka?	How are the children?
Ó dì nma	I'm fine
Ututu òma?	Good morning?
Ka chíí fò	Good night
Nnòo	Welcome (to one who has arrived)

Jisie ike work (Well done!)	Keep up the good
Daalu/Imèela	Thank you
Ka e mesia	Good bye

Basic chat

Bìkó	Please
Ndó	Sorry (commiserations)
Kèdú àha gí?	What's your name?
Áhà m bu Theodora	My name is Theodora
E béè ka ísí?	Where are you from?
E sim Scotland	I'm from Scotland
E béè ka í na-ijè?	Where are you going?
Á na m èje Enugu	I'm going to Enugu
Á chorò m	I want
Á chorò m ije ahia	I want to go to the market
Á chorò m ego	I want to buy
Nke á	This one
Nka á bù olé?	How much is this?
Olé?/Egó olé?	How much?/ How much money?
Nyé	Give
Nyé m	Give me
Byá	Come
Jé	Go
Bhàta	Come in
Ézí	Good
Ófé tòrò èto	This soup's tasty
Ó dè úmá	It's good
Áné	Meat
Ose	Pepper
Mmírí	Water

Numbers

ótu	1
abúo	2
àtó	3
ànó	4
isé	5
isí	6
asáà	7
asáto	8
itenanì	9
irí	10
irí na ótu	11
irí na abúo	12
irí na àtó	13
irí na ànó	14
irí na isé	15
irí na isí	16
irí na asáà	17

irí na asáto	18
irí na itenani	19
irí abúo	20
irí abúo na ótu	21
irí abúo na abúo	22
irí àtó	30
irí ànó	40

irí ìsé	50
irí ìsí	60
irí asáà	70
irí asáto	80
irí itenanì	90
nari	100
puku	1000

Glossary

419 Refers to the part of the Nigerian penal code referring to fraud, and originally applied to scam letters and emails, it's now shorthand for any scam or fraud.

Abule Hamlet or small village (Yoruba)

Achada Motorcycle taxi (Hausa)

Agbada Yoruba cloak for men

Alafin Traditional Yoruba ruler (Oyo)

Alhaji One who has been to Mecca

Amingo White person (from the Portuguese)

Area Boys Local hoodlums; in Lagos they're partly organized into a banned vigilante group called the Odua People's Congress, or OPC, who assert Yoruba supremacy at every opportunity.

Ariya Enjoyment, having a good time (Yoruba)

Babanriga Long Hausa tunic

Bakassi Boys A banned, Aba-based Igbo vigilante group, the equivalent of Lagos's OPC "Area Boys", whose avowed aim is a separate southeastern state.

Batouri White person (Hausa)

Buba Yoruba shirt

Buka Chop house (Yoruba)

Chiroma Traditional title of the far northeast

Chop A verb meaning "to eat", though it can also be used to mean "food"

Dash Bribe or payment for service rendered or simply a gift (verb and noun)

Drop Can mean a shared taxi, a journey in one, or to disembark from a taxi or bus

Durbar Staged horse gallops in which senior men pay homage to an emir in the Muslim regions

FCT Federal Capital Territory (Abuja)

Galadima Traditional title of the far northeast

Go-slow Traffic jam

GRA Government Reserved Area, civil servants' housing district

Hisba Young Islamist vigilante (Hausa)

IBB General Ibrahim Badamasi Babangida

Ile Old (Yoruba), as in for example Ile-Ife

Ileto Village (Yoruba)

Ilu Alade Big town (Yoruba)

Ilu Oloja Small market town (Yoruba)

Kabu kabu Commercial transport (Hausa)

Kofar City gate (Hausa)

Lappa Casual loin cloth (men and women)

Mai Traditional Kanuri ruler

Mopol Mobile police

Moto Any car – a term you'll hear a lot if travelling by bush taxi.

Nassarawa Christian/European (Hausa)

Oba Traditional Yoruba ruler

Off To turn/switch something off

Okada Motorcycle taxi (Yoruba/Igbo)

On To turn/switch something on

Oni Traditional Yoruba ruler (Ife)

Onyeocha White person (Igbo)

Oyibo White person, or returning Nigerian (Yoruba)

RWAFF Royal West African Frontier Force, a colonial-era army raised from British colonies, disbanded on independence

Sabi To know (from the Portuguese)

Sabon Gari Also spelt Sabongari, this is Hausa for "foreigners' town", meaning the Igbo and Yoruba quarter of a northern city.

SAP Economic Structural Adjustment Programme

Sardauna Traditional ruler (Sokoto)

Shehu Chief, big man (Hausa)

Sokoto Yoruba trousers

Yandabas Hausa vigilantes, the equivalent of Lagos's Area Boys

14.1

Lagos

I f you're reading nervously, you wouldn't be the first traveller to approach **Lagos** with a feeling of despair and trepidation, convinced you're going to hate the place – should you live through it. A city with somewhere above fifteen million inhabitants, Lagos has grown too big too fast. Long ago, the city overflowed from the **islands** at its heart, and the urban sprawl on the mainland has mushroomed alarmingly. Of the infrastructure – housing, roads, public transport, water, electricity and sewerage – only the new expressways show any sign of keeping up. Pollution, squalid overcrowding, violent crime and a 24-hour din are the inevitable results of the shortfall.

But you might just be surprised. The **international airport** that was largely to blame for many travellers' terrible first impressions has been largely cleared of the touts who made life hell for newly arrived first-timers, the once-predatory customs officials have also cleaned up their act, and even the traffic isn't quite as bad as it was a few years ago. On approaching the city itself, you may find rather less chaos – and more to excite. For West Africa's foremost metropolis is, at the very least, a city of intense, voluble personality and breathtaking dynamism. Ships from around the globe berth at its **ports** of Apapa and Tin Can Island, and the **skyscrapers** that spike Lagos Island house a swarm of international firms. Whenever the commuter traffic packing the **flyovers** grinds to a halt in rush-hour "go-slow" traffic jams, the opportunity is exploited by thousands of irrepressible **street vendors** trying to sell everything from imported apples to bathroom scales, and from cellphone top-up cards to gym equipment. And beyond the nonstop, unrestrained commercialism on the streets, universities, museums, galleries and the national theatre all attest to a thriving **intellectual and cultural life**.

While it would be misleading to downplay its problems, Lagos is no more of a hell hole than any other seething, impoverished city in the developing world. The risks of mugging and pickpocketing are real, but most people get through their stays safely, and find the city a friendly rather than a dangerous place. Travel with confidence, take elementary precautions, get into the rhythm, and you will almost certainly enjoy your visit.

Some history

The swampy mangrove zone around Lagos was originally inhabited by small hunting and fishing communities, but rainforest and marshes probably prevented large-scale settlement. **Portuguese mariners** first arrived at the islands around Lagos in 1472 and named the place *Lago de Curamo*, but it wasn't until much later that the area became an important port of trade. In the sixteenth century, **Yoruba settlers** came to Iddo and later moved onto Lagos Island and beyond. The settlement was eventually incorporated into the **Benin kingdom** – which at the time extended all the way across southern Nigeria – and renamed Eko, the Benin name for camp or war camp. In the early eighteenth century, the ruling *oba* granted a trade monopoly to the Portuguese whose main export was, by then, **slaves**. A hundred years later, the French and British governments began sending warships to break up the slave trade, as Lagos was used as a hideout by profiteers who took advantage of the many creeks and rivers to conceal their human cargo. In 1851, the **British** shelled Lagos and eventually forced the *oba* to abandon the slave trade. Soon after, they captured the islands and formed Lagos Colony.

Early in the twentieth century, Lagos grew into an important commercial centre thanks to the port and the **railway line** – begun in 1896 and extended through to Kano in 1912. Lagos became the capital of the southern Nigerian protectorate and later of the entire federation, when north and south were merged. After independence, the city maintained its role as capital until 1991, when the seat of government moved to Abuja. The city is still the country's undisputed commercial, industrial and cultural centre, although more and more countries are moving their main embassies to the new capital.

Arrival, information and city transport

Lagos spreads over some 200 square kilometres and comprises myriad **neighbourhoods**. But the heart of the city, where you're likely to spend most of your time, is tucked onto **Lagos and Ikoyi islands** – now merged – and **Victoria Island**, to the south towards the ocean and the main expat focus. If your stay is going to be any longer than a day or two, it's worth getting hold of a street atlas as soon as you arrive.

However you come to Lagos, the **mainland** is your point of entry. Although there are bland neighbourhoods here (such as the administrative district of **Ikeja**), most districts are populated by the city's working class and poorer inhabitants – and these areas can feel distinctly threatening. Largely because most of the city's rich don't live in these districts, this is where many Lagos horror stories have their origins. As a temporary visitor, however, you're no more likely to run into serious, violent trouble on the mainland than anywhere else in Lagos, and perhaps, in truth, less likely.

Arrival

Flying into Lagos from abroad, you'll land at **Murtala Muhammed International Airport (MMIA)**, 8km north of Lagos Island as the crow flies. Until recently, arriving at Murtala Muhammed was a daunting prospect with the arrivals hall jammed with people. Now anyone entering needs a good reason to get past the security guards onto the slip road outside the arrivals door, and as such it's less of a scrum. Only limited numbers of official yellow **taxis** are licensed to trade at the airport (if in doubt, ask to see the driver's ID card), and there are no buses out here. Taxi fares into town are fixed (currently ₦3000 to the islands), and you should pre-pay, getting a receipt, at a desk by the exit from the arrivals hall, where you will be shown to a cab. Make sure that the driver knows the way to your destination, especially if it's after dark.

Domestic air travel has developed in recent years, with a new domestic terminal, **MMA2** (15min drive from the international terminal), looking set to transform the experience of flying in Nigeria and a slew of airlines competing on the main routes (see p.1080). Rather than trying to check travel times in advance, it's best just to turn up and buy your ticket for the next available flight. The one exception to this advice is if you're leaving Lagos for Abuja on a Sunday – when many Abuja residents return home after a weekend in Lagos – when it's highly advisable to book in advance. In any case, avoid all contact with ticket touts who will approach you before reaching the travel desks.

The best option is to arrange to be **met at the airport** – all the travel agents detailed on p.1132 offer this service, as do all but the cheapest hotels. Unfortunately there have been instances of new arrivals being scammed by bogus airport drivers copying down a name from one of the boards used by company drivers at the arrivals area, then driving the unwitting visitor to the edge of town and relieving

Jibowu Motor Park, on Ikorodu Road, serves all the main cities. The most popular and reliable companies are ABC Transport at 22 Ikorodu Rd (ⓦwww.abctransport.com) and Ground Air Travel at 45/47 Ikorodu Rd (ⓦwww.gatlimited.com), both offering luxury coach travel, with meals and entertainment. Expect to pay ₦5000 for the Lagos–Abuja journey.

Ojota Motor Park, on Ikorodu Road near the junction with the airport road in the Ojota district, is for cheap minibus transport to the east of Nigeria, including Benin City, Onitsha, Enugu and Port Harcourt, plus Ibadan and some southwestern destinations.

Ojota New Garage, on Ikorodu Road, 300m south of the main Ojota motor park, serves the southwest, including Ibadan, Osogbo, Ilorin, Ife and other towns in Yorubaland, again by minibus.

Iddo Motor Park, on Murtala Muhammed Way near the train station, is the place for minibus travel to the north, including Kaduna and Jos, Zaria, Sokoto and Kano.

Ojuelegba Motor Park, at Ojuelegba junction in Surulere district, has vehicles to Benin City, Onitsha, Enugu, Aba, Port Harcourt and Calabar.

ABC Amuwo-Odofin Terminal at Mile 2 (Plot 79, Oba Kayode Akinyemi Way) serves international destinations, including Cotonou, Lomé and Accra. The coach to Accra leaves at 8am daily.

them of their possessions. Make sure you know your driver's name, or arrange a code word with the company or person who has arranged the transfer.

Arriving by **minibus or long-distance taxi** from elsewhere in Nigeria, you'll arrive at one of several points on the mainland – Mile Two, Yaba, Ojota, Iddo, Ojuelegba or Ebute Ero. From these places, battered yellow private buses will drop you at Lagos Island or Obalende, where you can get a cheap taxi to a hotel.

Information

The Nigerian Tourism Development Corporation's **tourist office**, the Tourism Information Centre, is on the mainland on the second floor of the Hanco Plaza Building, 113 Ikorodu Rd, by the Fadeyi bus stop (Mon–Fri 8am–5pm; ☎01/493 0220). They can help with general tourist information and hiring guides. For a detailed **map** of the city, there's WABP's *Street Map of Lagos*, an up-to-date and comprehensive atlas. If you plan an extended stay, the guidebook *Lagos Easy Access*, available from Quintessence at Falomo Shopping Centre in Ikoyi (see p.1131), is chunky and expensive at ₦2500, but is an invaluable source of more detailed information. The book is packed with some three hundred pages of information (including maps). For online info, ⓦwww.lagoslive.com has useful hotel, restaurant and what's-on information.

City transport

Getting around Lagos can be a nightmare unless you have unlimited time or patience – or your own car and driver, like many expats. Lagos **taxis** are usually yellow Peugeot 504s with black stripes. You hail them by yelling out your destination. Use some discretion over where you say you're going (be prepared to get out and walk a hundred metres) as it can affect the fare, which you should discuss and agree on first. Stand in the door till you're sure the driver knows the price is agreed. Try also to have the notes ready, as change is a rare thing. Fares vary from ₦300–500 for short hops to ₦1000–3000 for cross-city journeys; be prepared to haggle. An air-conditioned car with driver costs around ₦15,000 per day.

In addition, Lagos swarms with motley, **privately owned minibuses** – either VWs or Japanese *kombis*, or local Mercedes or Bedford conversions known as *molue* (large, with aisles) or *danfo* (small, seat only). While these are cheap (maximum fares

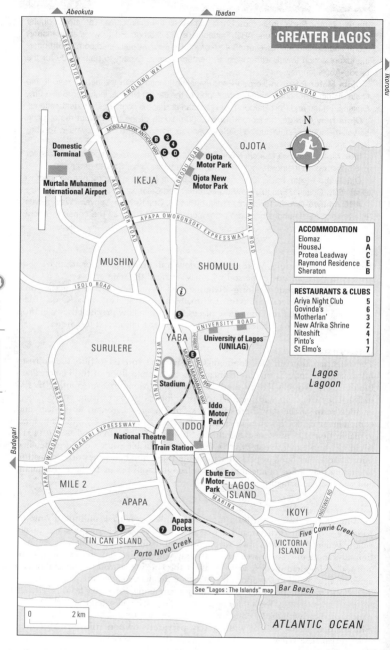

GREATER LAGOS

▲ Abeokuta

▲ Ibadan

► Ikorodu

N

AWOLOWO WAY

IKORODU ROAD

AGEGE MOTOR ROAD

MOBOLAJI BANK ANTHONY WAY

❷

❶

Ⓐ

❸ Ⓑ

❹ Ⓒ

Ⓓ

Domestic Terminal

Murtala Muhammed International Airport

IKEJA

KORODU ROAD

OJOTA

Ojota Motor Park

Ojota New Motor Park

THIRD AXIAL ROAD

APAPA OWORONSOKI EXPRESSWAY

MUSHIN

SHOMULU

ISOLO ROAD

ⓘ

❺

UNIVERSITY ROAD

SURULERE

YABA

HERBERT MACAULAY WAY

University of Lagos (UNILAG)

Lagos Lagoon

WESTERN AVENUE

Stadium

MURTALA MUHAMMED WAY

Ⓔ ❻

Iddo Motor Park

BADAGARI EXPRESSWAY

National Theatre

Train Station

IDDO

APAPA OWORONSOKI EXPRESSWAY

▲ Badagari

MILE 2

Ebute Ero Motor Park

LAGOS ISLAND

MARINA

APAPA

❻

Apapa Docks

❼

IKOYI

KINGSWAY RD

TIN CAN ISLAND

Porto Novo Creek

Five Cowrie Creek

VICTORIA ISLAND

See "Lagos : The Islands" map

Bar Beach

0   2 km

ATLANTIC OCEAN

ACCOMMODATION

Elomaz	D
HouseJ	A
Protea Leadway	C
Raymond Residence	E
Sheraton	B

RESTAURANTS & CLUBS

Ariya Night Club	5
Govinda's	6
Motherlan'	3
New Afrika Shrine	2
Niteshift	4
Pinto's	1
St Elmo's	7

are around ₦200), the discomfort and – when traffic is heavy – hair-pulling slowness of them can undermine the resolve of even the staunchest city survivor. For short journeys, especially within the islands, **okadas** (motorcycle taxis) are the easiest way to get around. The drivers have a reputation for knowing the city well, but usually balk at trips far afield. Expect to pay anything from ₦50 to ₦200, depending on the length of your journey. Just like a taxi, you should agree the price before getting your leg over. It's advisable to avoid *okadas* at night as there is a criminal element among their drivers. However, some housing developments, particularly on the Lekki Peninsula, have organized training schemes for *okadas* and provide them with helmets and high-visibility jackets. These are a safer bet.

A one-hundred-seater **ferry** runs across Lagos Harbour, from the south of Lagos Island (midway along Apongbon Street) to Apapa, then on to Mile Two using a canal west of the Apapa–Orowonsoki Expressway. Ferries also run from Victoria Island to the beaches (see p.1128).

Accommodation

There's no shortage of **hotels** in Lagos, most of them on the mainland, which is on the whole less convenient than the islands. Although parts of the mainland have a reputation as dangerous areas, those who enjoy Lagos's teeming streets and vibrant nightlife won't be intimidated – for example, most of the night clubs are in these areas.

Upmarket hotels are expensive and often priced in dollars if you're paying the nonresident tariff (which some will insist on if you're a foreigner), but mid-range places with air conditioning and satellite TV can be good value. Slowly, increased competition is providing more choice to mid-range travellers, with new entrants such as the South African *Protea* franchise opening up several hotels in Lagos in recent years. Budget travellers will find plenty of cheap hotels and hostels, although safety does remain an issue at the budget end of the market. In general, even the cheapest places have air conditioning, virtually a necessity in Lagos's sweltering climate.

Because of recent security issues, we've omitted Lagos Island addresses from this edition.

Ikoyi and Victoria Island (V.I.)

For locations, see the map on p.1126.

Bogobiri House 9 Maitama Sule St, South West Ikoyi ☎01/474 7421 ⓦwww .bogobirilagos.com. Real gem of a boutique hotel, and a far better option than the staid, predictable hotel chains. The staff are friendly, each room is tastefully decorated with contemporary Nigerian art, and wood carvings adorn the lounge. Breakfast included. ❻

Eko Hotel & Suites, V.I. ☎01/262 4600–19. The *Eko* is the obvious business-traveller option on Victoria Island, with a range of bars and restaurants, a business centre, gym, pool and tennis courts etc. Ask to stay in the newer *Eko Suites* complex. ❽

Hillside Gardens 7B Abimbola Awoliyi Close, off Saka Tinubu St, V.I. ☎01/722 2894. A classy, stylish guesthouse set in a serene environment, conveniently located in the heart of Victoria Island and managed by a professional couple with a background in UK property development. Expect dedicated and courteous service and attention to detail. Ten en-suite rooms, with satellite TV, minibar and safe. ❻

Le Chateau 292 Ajose Adeogun, V.I. ☎01/461 3739 ⓦwww.lechateaunigeria.com. One of the best guesthouses in Lagos, *Le Chateau* has sixteen private, stylishly appointed rooms, with double-sized bed, satellite TV, Internet access and a DVD player. ❻

Moorhouse Sofitel 1 Bankole Oke Rd, Ikoyi ☎01/267 0231. Don't be put off by the state of the road outside, the *Moorhouse* lives up to *Sofitel* standards, with tastefully designed rooms, an upmarket restaurant (not very veggie friendly however), free Wi-Fi in all rooms etc. The new extension should ease the near 100 percent occupancy rate (best to book ahead). The poolside area is the perfect place to kick back with friends in the evening. ❽

Protea Hotel Kuramo Waters Kuramo Waters Close, off Akin Ogunlewe St, V.I. ☎01/271 2962 ⓦ tinyurl.com/32q6n9. A newish and stylish upmarket hotel, with rooms set within individual buildings, creating an air of privacy. Situated in the Victoria Island Extension, the hotel is both quiet and yet conveniently close to Victoria Island and Ikoyi. Features an outdoor pool with bar. ⑥

Protea Hotel Victoria Island Plot 1700, Violet Yough Close, off Adetokunbo Ademola St, V.I. ☎01/461 0236 ⓦ tinyurl.com/34kcl9. Fifty-eight well-designed en-suite rooms with minibar, safe and Wi-Fi. ⑧

Travelhouse Budget Hotel Lekki Km14, Lekki–Epe Expressway ☎01/462 7423 ⓦ www .travelhousenigeria.com. A new, budget business hotel in Lagos, offering clean, comfortable, secure accommodation, if a little far from the centre. ⑦

Victoria Crown Plaza 292B Ajose Adeogun St, V.I. ☎01/271 9810 ⓦ www.vcp-hotel.com. A new entrant on the island luxury-hotel scene, with 46 well-appointed rooms with all the frills (including free Wi-Fi in all rooms). The only drawback is the tiny pool. ⑧

Victoria Lodge 5 Ologun Agbaje St, V.I. ☎01/262 0885 ⓕ01/261 3318. Very pleasant, homely and clean, with a/c bar and restaurant, and satellite TV in all rooms. ⑨

YMCA 77 Awolowo Rd, Ikoyi ☎01/773 3599. Recently rebuilt, this is one of the best budget options, with new a/c family suites, non-a/c single rooms, and men-only four-bed dorms. Nigerians and other Africans board here and can be a big help showing you around the city. It's sometimes full, so worth booking ahead; stays are limited to seven days. ③

Mainland

Elomaz 3–5 Immanuel St, off Mobolaji Bank Anthony Way, Maryland, Ikeja ☎01/496 0989 ⓔ info@elomazhotels.com. Soulless but clean business hotel close to the airport. Includes a cybercafé, bar and restaurant. ⑥

HouseJ 1 Sir Michael Otedola Crescent, off Joel Ogunnaike St, Ikeja ☎01/497 2288 ⓦ www .housej.com. Clean and quiet hotel with 14 rooms, restaurant and bar. Only 10min drive from the airport. ⑦

Protea Hotel Leadway 1 Mogambo Close, Maryland, Ikeja ☎01/279 0800 ⓦ tinyurl. com/2q3k5d. The *Protea* group's first venture on to the Lagos mainland, with 47 well-appointed rooms, fitness centre and business centre. Each room is equipped with a minibar, safe and Internet access. ⑧

Raymond Residence 13 Raymond St, Yaba ☎01/472 4303. Quiet guesthouse near the University of Lagos campus. Cable TV in each of the 9 rooms with guaranteed 24-hour power supply make it a viable alternative to staying on the islands – and it's good value. ⑤

Sheraton Lagos 30 Mobolaji Bank Anthony Way, Ikeja ☎01/497 8660 ⓦ www.sheraton .com/lagos. Smart hotel, 15min drive from the airport, catering for business people with no need to head south to the islands. All the usual five-star facilities, plus booking desks for BA and Virgin. Be warned: drinking and eating here is not cheap – an omelette and coffee in the hotel's *Crockpot* restaurant costs around ₦2500. Free Wi-Fi for residents. ⑧

The City and the beaches

The sheer effort (and expense) of **getting around** the city is the only thing that really detracts from its worthwhile sites. It can literally take hours to accomplish journeys by car that you could probably walk more quickly. Don't be afraid of venturing out on foot during the day, but be aware that some parts of town are dangerous at night, when mugging is common. In particular you should steer clear of the western half of Lagos Island and the poorer districts on the mainland after nightfall. And don't carry anything of value around with you if you can avoid it.

Lagos is almost alone among West African cities in having more than a single museum, although most are now in a somewhat dilapidated state. The **Onikan National Museum** has some interesting pieces, but the general air is of neglect and decay. The same goes for the **National Theatre**, slowly sinking into the marshes and unloved for years. **Lagos Island**, the oldest part of the city, preserves a number of ramshackle **Brazilian-style buildings** in the area around Campos Square and Campbell Street, and some colonial buildings along Broad Street.

Lagos Island

Lagos Island was the former commercial centre of Lagos and site of the towers that provide the city's striking skyline. Although Eko, as it's known to locals, has suffered a decade or more of neglect, there are signs of gentrification, especially towards the Onikan end of Lagos Island where it merges with Ikoyi. Many of the high-rises – including most of the bank headquarters and **NITEL House**, are on the south side of the island behind **Marina Street** (usually known simply as Marina), which used to run along the waterfront. Today, Marina is several hundred metres back from the water, shadowed by the zooming, split-level expressway of **Apongbon Street**. But it retains some buildings of note, including the former **State House** (former residence of the British governors); the headquarters of the famously inefficient **NEPA** (the electricity corporation), with the bronze statue of Sango the thunder god before it; Lagos's **General Post Office**; and the eighteenth-century **Anglican church**.

Broad Street, which runs parallel to Marina, is another well-known thoroughfare with more banks and markets and thousands of street-side vendors. Buildings of interest include the 1925 colonial **courthouse** on the corner of Kakawa Street, and the **tomb of Chief Daniel Conrad Taiwo**, who died in 1901 at the ripe old age of 120. The tomb stands 100m west of **Tinubu Square**, a landscaped roundabout with a perpetually defunct fountain (originally donated to the city by its Lebanese community in 1960 to celebrate Nigeria's independence), in one of the busiest parts of town. To the northwest, the **markets** of **Jankara**, **Isale Eko**, **Ebute Ero** and **Balogun** fill this part of the island with frenetic small-scale commerce.

Between the high-rises and the market stalls, and the exhaust emissions and the rains, a few Brazilian-style buildings have survived in the **Brazilian Quarter**, founded by returned former slaves. They're jealously guarded against photographers, however, and in any case falling apart: the **Palace of the Oba**, on the northern tip of the island on Upper King Street, is particularly unimpressive. Still, if you're keen on a hunt, the following, all on Lagos Island, may still be worthwhile: **Chief's House**, Ado Street; **Ebun House**, 85 Odunfa St (300m east of Tinubu Square), a great pile of a place dating from 1914; **Brazilian House**, 29 Kakawa St, off Broad Street; **Water House**, 12 Kakawa St, built in the 1860s and one of the oldest houses in Lagos; **Cuban Lodge**, 40 Odunlami St (adjacent to Kakawa Street), styled on an English cottage but with Brazilian features; **Da Silva House**, Odufege Street; and the comely **Shitta Mosque** on Martins Street, with its Brazilian tilework, built in 1894.

The eastern end of Marina is dominated by the enclosed open area called **Tafawa Balewa Square**, with its monumental equine statues rearing up at the entrance on the south side, in memory of the old racetrack that used to be here. The north side of the square was where many of the major airlines and travel agencies had their offices, though many have now relocated to Victoria Island; the south side is a bus and taxi park. A few minutes' walk away is the **Muson Centre**, home to *La Scala* restaurant and a popular events venue. Beyond the Muson Centre lies the atmospheric **Onikan** neighbourhood. Walk down Military Street and environs for more Brazilian buildings mixed with tall modernist structures. Onikan looks set to be gentrified in the next few years.

The Onikan National Museum

Just east of Tafawa Balewa Square, the **National Museum** (daily 9am–5pm; ₦100) is a huge disappointment. It appears to have suffered from a lack of funding and care, with lights flickering on and off and attendants sleeping at their desks. The only hope is that the new administration places a stronger emphasis on Nigeria's cultural treasure-trove.

In the permanent collection, the **Symbols of Power and Authority Gallery** is designed to give an overview of the regal insignia of Nigeria's diverse ethnic groups.

The display of **masquerades**, common to a range of peoples, shows off one of the oldest forms of cultural and artistic expression. In Nigeria, masquerades not only served to provide a link with the realm of the dead but were important in instigating other art forms like music, dance and drama. Other exhibits range from decorated pottery and calabashes from the different regions to shrines and household gods reflecting the importance of the supernatural in people's lives.

The **Benin Gallery** contains a selection of bronzes and ivory carvings. Unfortunately, many masterpieces of Benin art are still held abroad, despite numerous requests for their return from the Nigerian government. An additional permanent exhibition, **Nigerian Governments: Yesterday and Today**, traces the political history of the country from the slave trade to the present, though the only really impressive exhibit here is President Murtala Muhammed's bullet-holed car, which pays menacing homage to one of Nigeria's most popular leaders, assassinated in February 1976.

If you're looking to buy woodcarvings, check out the museum's **craft village**, at least for an idea of how much you can expect to pay for works in Lagos – prices here are fixed. In fact, the chances are you won't find prices any cheaper outside the big hotels, where all the gear is often laid out. Lastly, you can take a break from all the culture and have a bite to eat in the very good **Museum Kitchen**.

Right next to the National Museum is a new shopping complex – **City Hall**. The mall has a good range of outlets, with a cinema and bar on the top floor. *Café Vergnano* is one of the best places for coffee and cakes in Lagos, offering a *Starbucks*-style experience.

Ikoyi and Victoria Island

The swamps that once divided **Ikoyi** from Lagos Island have been filled in, and today the two sections of town are separated only by a tangle of motorway flyovers, though Ikoyi still retains its own flavour. Its main artery, **Awolowo Road**, links it with Victoria Island via the **Falomo Bridge**. Awolowo Road is home to chic **boutiques** (many operating out of converted private homes), high-priced **restaurants and bars** and the **Polo Club**, a reminder of the days when Ikoyi was the posh colonial neighbourhood. The **Falomo shopping centre**, at the junction with Kingsway Road, near the bridge, looks to be living on borrowed time, though it's worth checking out to visit **Quintessence** – a great place to pick up ethnic artefacts – and the **Glendora** bookshop two doors down. On the other side of the Falomo roundabout, off Bourdillon Road, lie the quiet leafy streets of the former Government Residential Area (GRA). This is a neighbourhood of $60,000 rents and many oil companies own apartment blocks here.

The centre of Ikoyi, dominated by the former **administrative district**, includes the former **State House**. Further west, **Obalende** is a vibrant working-class neighbourhood with a large market, numerous chop bars (good places for authentic pepper soup or *suya*) and watering holes where locals come to drink and dance.

The new commercial and retail centre of Lagos, **Victoria Island** (usually referred to as V.I.) is now headquarters for most of Nigeria's banks and large businesses, with upmarket restaurants and hotels taking over formerly residential plots. Near the **Independence Bridge** to Lagos Island, **Walter Carrington Crescent** (still occasionally known by its former name, Eleke Crescent) still has a number of embassies, including those of Britain and the USA. **Bar Beach**, the city's closest strand, runs along V.I.'s southern flank, and is currently being redeveloped, with a concrete boardwalk acting as a flood barrier to the turbulent Atlantic Ocean. Further along Ahmadu Bello Way, the **Galleria** is a relatively new shopping mall, with a Borders-style bookshop (The Media Store) and a multiplex cinema on the top floor.

The Lekki Peninsula

Another new mall complex is found along the **Lekki Expressway** near the first roundabout. **The Palms** mall, like the Galleria, has a large bookshop, cinema, food courts and Lagos's first western-scale supermarket – an outlet of the South African Shoprite chain. Beyond The Palms, the Lekki Peninsula has experienced rapid development in recent times, with large housing estates, hotels and businesses thronging either side of the road for twenty kilometres. Heavy traffic into Victoria Island builds from 7am in the morning on weekdays, and again in the other direction in the afternoons. Miss these peaks to avoid hours in crawling traffic. At the weekend, a trip out along the Lekki Peninsula is a good option, with the **Lekki Conservation Area** (just before Chevron on the right as you head away from V.I.; ₦100) an excellent choice if you don't have much time to get out into Nigeria's rural areas. You enter into a tranquil tropical paradise – a raised wooden boardwalk taking you on a loop around the conservation area. Expect to see monkeys swooping about, and even the odd crocodile.

The mainland

A vast reach of working-class districts, industrial zones and shanty towns heaves over the mainland for miles. Other than getting to and from the airports or motor parks, there's little reason for visitors to spend much time here, although the residential **Surulere** district, 10km from Victoria Island, is home to the **National Stadium** and has a vibrant **nightlife** quarter; and **Ebute Metta**, just short of Lagos Island, is the site of the **National Theatre** complex.

The National Theatre complex

Rising out of the low-rent district of Ebute Metta above the creeks, the **National Theatre**'s characteristic concave roof soon appears on your left-hand side if you take the Eko Bridge from Lagos Island to the mainland. Built for

Lagos markets

Wherever you fetch up in Lagos, you'll find a market close by: there are literally dozens on the mainland, notably Tejuoso in Surulere, and the market in Apapa, which is also close to a good range of ordinary shops and supermarkets.

Probably the best bet for tourists is **Lekki market** (also known as **Ola Elegushi market**) which has recently undergone renovation, is extremely safe, and has a gated car park. You can buy everything here from mud cloth and jewellery, to wood carvings and clothes. As it is a tourist market, expect to pay slightly over the odds, but it's a far less stressful bet than some of the others.

On Lagos Island, the bustling **Jankara market** is the prime site and one of the cheapest places for new and secondhand clothes, general hardware, traditional musical instruments, CDs, cassettes and DVDs, jewellery and trading beads, magical materials (*jujus*, skins, powders) and *aso-oke* – the beautiful woven cloth which is used on special occasions. Northwest of Jankara, between Adeniji Adele Road and Ebute Ero Street, **Isale Eko market** specializes in food, crockery and basket ware, and there are some ready-made clothes here too. In the same area, near the old Carter Bridge, is an *ogogoro* market where you can buy the scorching (and sometimes dangerous) local spirit.

Focusing around the street of the same name on Lagos Island, **Balogun market** is the best place for **cloth**. In the rambling maze of alleys you'll find mostly imported material, including damasks, plus a wide range of African prints. A little to the east, around Nnamdi Azikiwe Street, you can find batiks and ready-made clothes, plus CDs and cassettes.

Between Lewis and Simpson streets at the eastern end of Lagos Island, **Sandgrouse market** is the best bet for **food** – fresh fish, shrimps and huge snails, as well as more conventional provisions.

Mainland

Mainland

Mainland

THIRD MAINLAND BRIDGE

CARTER BRIDGE

EKO BRIDGE

ADENIJI ADELE ROAD

UPPER KING ST

Lagos
Lagoon

*Lagos
Lagoon*

Oba's Palace

Isale Eko
Market

Ebute Ero
Market

Jankara
Market

RING ROAD

Central
Mosque

Ita Faji
Market

Market

SAVIOUR ST

OKOPOPO MARINA STREET

OKEPOPO STREET

OYINKAN ST

OROYINTON ST

ST JD ST

Shitta
Mosque

Chief Taiyo's
Tomb

FREEMAN STREET

SIMPSON STREET

NNAMDI AZIKWE ST

DOCEMO ST

ISSA WILLIAMS ST

BALOGUN ST

MARTINS STREET

IDUMAGBO AVE

IDOLUWA ST

MASSEY ST

IGA IDUNGANRAN ST

JOSEPH ST

TINUBU ST

TOM JONES ST

BREADFRUIT ST

TAIWO ST

NEWMAN ST

KOSOKO ST

DAVIES ST

ODUNFA ST

GIWA ST

UK High Commission
(Consular Section)

BROAD STREET

MARINA ST

BAMGBOSE STREET

CSS Bookshop

KAKAWA STREET

TINUBU
SQUARE

CAMPOS
SQUARE

BAMGBOSE STREET

BRAZILIAN
QUARTER

Mandilas
(Amex)

LEWISH STREET

Sandgrouse
Market

Angelican
Church

National
Library

CATHOLIC MUSEUM ST

IGBOSERE ROAD

KING'S COLLEGE RD

KING GEORGE ROAD

RING ROAD

NEPA

BROAD STREET

CAMPBEL ST

@

1

ONIKAN

TAFAWA
BALEWA
SQUARE

MARINA ST

NITEL House
(International
telephones)

CABLE ST

AWOLOWO RD

Lagos

Harbour

Old State
House

City Mall

2

4

Muson
Centre

WALTER CORRINGTON CRESCENT

US Embassy

British High
Commission

N

Guinean
Embassy

Benin
Consulate

AHMADU BELLO WAY

Silverbird Galleria Mall

RESTAURANTS, BARS & CLUBS	
Bacchus	5
Bambuddha	21
Bangkok	15
Bonzai	22
Cactus	6
Café Vergnano	9
Casa del Habano	8
Chill Out	17
Chocolate Royal	19
Churras	7
Club Tower	13
Debonaires	20
Flamingo	11
Il Sorriso	24
Imperial Chinese	18
La Scala	4
Pat's Bar	16
Pattaya	14
Pearl Garden	25
Prince Place	1
Reeds	3
Saipan	12
Soul Lounge	10
Swe Bar	2
Yellow Chilli	23

ACCOMMODATION	
Bogobiri	B
Eko Hotel & Suites	I
Hillside Gardens	H
Le Chateau	G
Moorhouse Sofitel	A
Protea Hotel Kuramo Waters	K
Protea Hotel Victoria Island	F
Travelhouse Budget Hotel	D
Victoria Crown Plaza	E
Victoria Lodge	J
YMCA	C

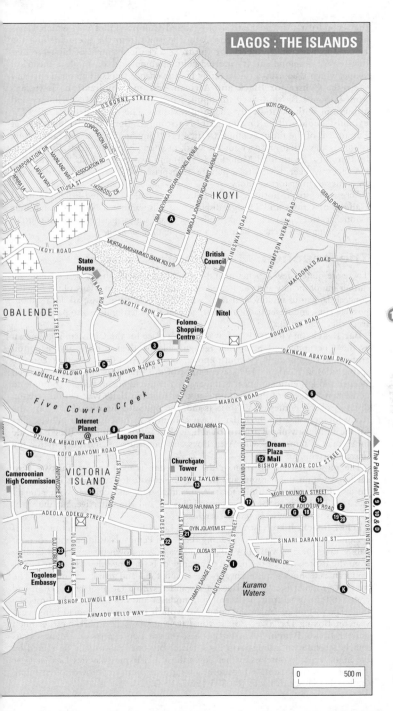

OSBORNE STREET

CORPORATION DR

CORPORATION DR

MAINLAND WAY

ASSOCIATION ST

IKORODU CR

LAFIAJI WAY

ETI-OSA ST

MBARI LA

IKOYI CRESCENT

OBA ASEYINKA OYEBAN SECOND AVENUE

MOBOLAJI JOHNSON ROAD (FIRST AVENUE)

IKOYI

KINGSWAY ROAD

GERALD ROAD

THOMPSON AVENUE ROAD

MACDONALD ROAD

A

IKOYI ROAD

MURTALAMOHAMMED (BANK RD) DR

State House

British Council

RIBADU ROAD

KEFFI STREET

OBALENDE

OKOTIE EBOH ST

Nitel

Folomo Shopping Centre

BOURDILLON ROAD

AWOLOWO ROAD

OKINKAN ABAYOMI DRIVE

3

B

5

C

ADEMOLA ST

RAYMOND NJOKU ST

Five Cowrie Creek

FOLOMO BRIDGE

MAROKO ROAD

6

Internet Planet @

7

OZUMBA MBADIWE AVENUE

8 Lagoon Plaza

KOFO ABAYOMI ROAD

BADARU ABINA ST

ADETOKUNBO ADEMOLA STREET

Dream Plaza Mall

11

VICTORIA ISLAND

ANIFOWOSHE ST

Churchgate Tower

IDOWU MARTINS ST

12 BISHOP ABOYADE COLE STREET

LIGALI AYORINDE AVENUE

Cameroonian High Commission

14

IDOWU TAYLOR

13

MURI OKUNOLA STREET

AKIN ADESOLA STREET

SANUSI FAFUNWA ST

17

15 **16**

E

ADEOLA ODEKU STREET

F

AJOSE ADEOGUN STREET

G **18**

19 **20**

OLU COUBUN CL

OYIN JOLAYEMI ST

22 **21**

SINARI DARANIJO ST

KARIMU KOTUN ST

23

IDEJO ST

ADETOKUNBO ADEMOLA STREET

OLOSA ST

A J MARINHO DR

24

Togolese Embassy

H

25

I

TIAMIYU SAVAGE ST

J

BISHOP OLUWOLE STREET

Kuramo Waters

K

AHMADU BELLO WAY

0   500 m

the second pan-African Festival of Arts and Culture (FESTAC), which Lagos hosted in 1977 at incredible cost (other legacies from the event include the Festac Town housing project), the theatre is a classic example of high-prestige, low-reward development. It's more a cultural complex than simply a theatrical venue, which is actually a role it rarely has the chance to play. The main ancillary site is the **Centre for Black and African Arts and Civilization** (downstairs from Entrance B; Mon–Sat 8am–5pm), which contains archives, a library and a museum with periodically changing exhibits. The original FESTAC 1977 exhibits should still be on show. The **National Gallery of Modern Art**, at Entrance B of the theatre complex (Tues–Fri 10am–5pm, Sat & Sun noon–4pm; ₦100), is an exhibition space for the work of young Nigerian artists. Entrance C leads to a bar (with food Mon–Fri 1–5pm) and two cinema halls. The complex has recently been leased to a private enterprise, which may help restore the amenities to their former glory.

Across the street, northwest of the theatre complex, the red-brick **National Gallery of Crafts and Design** displays and sells traditional Nigerian handicrafts (Mon–Sat 9am–5pm). The drinks stalls nearby are a great place to hang out in the early evening with a cheap beer and a meat pie or *moin-moin*.

The beaches

There are quite a few beaches in and around Lagos, although the best of them are further out of the city and you'll need transport to reach them. Many of the beaches conceal dangerous undersea currents which regularly claim lives; ask locals about possible risks, and never bathe alone. In general, the safest option is to paddle in the sea, rather than swim.

Bar Beach, on Victoria Island, is a meeting place for the Christian sect known as the Cherubim and Seraphim, recognizable by their pristine white cotton attire), and the unemployed youth known locally as Area Boys. Since exceptional spring tides in 1990 and 1994 swept most of the sand away, the beach has been steeper and less enticing but it is undergoing redevelopment. People continue to come here because of the location – just off Ahmadu Bello Way, within walking distance of the homes on Victoria Island, and opposite the *Eko Hotel*. Until the redevelopment has finished, Bar Beach continues to function as a public toilet for locals. Meanwhile, **Kuramo Beach**, at the eastern end of Bar Beach, is little more than a slum, rife with Area Boys and prostitutes – and only fit for the brave-hearted.

The most attractive beach near the city centre is 6km east at **Tarkwa Bay**, sheltered within the harbour and the only beach safe for swimming in the state. Locals offer food and drinks for sale, including *suya* and chicken with plantain and rice. **Lighthouse Beach** is beyond Tarkwa, and also attractive, but the sea is dangerous here because of strong currents.

Lekki Beach, 10km east of town, off the Lekki Expressway (a continuation of Ozumba Mbadiwe Avenue) and along the Lekki Peninsula, is lined with coconut palms. Take a taxi to **GBARA** village and walk 2km down the sand road leading from the expressway to the beach, or arrange to be dropped directly at the beach. You can ride horses quite cheaply here, and food and drink are on sale. The **market** at Lekki is a good place for a wander, with a range of beads, cloth and crafts, and the usual fruit, herbs and commodities, and Lekki Beach also hosts the Nigerian version of Jamaica's famous **Sunsplash** music festival, held here every year on Boxing Day (Dec 26). If you have your own transport, try the much quieter **Eleko Beach**, 50km further east on the Epe expressway. Many expats rent beach huts on a long-term basis, but empty ones can usually be rented by the hour. A few kilometres further down the Lekki Expressway lies *La Campagne Tropicana* resort, boasting a private beach far away from the crowds often filling the beaches closer to Lagos (℡0805 126 7317 ❽).

In the other direction, **BADAGRY**, 55km west of Lagos along the highway towards Benin, also has a lovely beach, stretching on for miles, but it belies a terrible history. For the estimated half a million-plus slaves between the sixteenth and eighteenth centuries who were packed here into horrific floating prisons for shipping abroad, this was the last place in Africa they ever saw. Today a **Slave Museum** has been set up in a building where captives were held awaiting transportation, and you can see the chains and shackles, whips and dungeons used to keep them under control. You can also see the port from which they embarked on a journey that many never survived, and the market at which they were bought and sold. If you want to stay in Badagry, accommodation is available in the *Whispering Palms Resort* (☏01/777 0639 ❻).

Closer in to the city, a long spit of land between the western end of the lagoon and the ocean is home to a series of privately owned beach-huts. The area is known as **Ilashe Beach**. There's one resort open to the public, offering accommodation, tennis and watersports – *Halemson Beach Resort* (Ⓦwww.halemsonbeachresort.com ❻) – and they can pick you up from V.I.

You can hire a motorboat to take you to **Tarkwa Bay** and other local beaches from Tarzan Jetty, just beyond the Mobil building on Ozumba Mbadiwe Avenue.

Eating, drinking and nightlife

Lagos has thousands of cheap eating places (known locally as *buka*), but is also geared up for splashing out: flashy restaurants, bars, clubs and discos abound, as do tackier establishments. If you think you might go out on the town late in the evening, leave all but the necessary minimum of valuables in your hotel.

Street food and cafeterias

On **Lagos Island**, the supermarkets along Marina Street on Lagos Island all have cafeterias for reasonable lunches, and there's a cheap *Luncheonette Diner* serving tasty Nigerian meals in the yard to the southwest of Tafawa Balewa Square on Broad Street. McCarthy Street, by the Ghanaian High Commission in Onikan, also has a few good chop-houses. *Prince Place*, 40 Lawson St, Onikan, is a small shack serving excellent, inexpensive barbecued fish with chips in the evenings from 6.30pm.

The **Obalende** area, on the west side of Ikoyi, is full of inexpensive restaurants and outdoor stands where you can buy fish, *suya* (kebabs), rice and so on. Don't miss the pepper soup, a speciality of this quarter, and the wonderfully flavoured chicken, charcoal-grilled to order. On **Victoria Island**, street food is available from a small side-street directly opposite the *Eko Hotel*: boiled yams, beans and rice, *fufu* with meat or fried fish. Eat here and then have a drink in the *Eko* for rapid culture contrast.

Restaurants

The restaurant scene has dramatically improved in Lagos in the past few years, with a good mix of Asian eateries expanding the quality and choice, especially on V.I. But the restaurant business in Lagos is fast-changing, so call to check your chosen eatery is still there, and reserve a table. On the **mainland** you're best off in the upmarket hotels, all of which have restaurants of a reliable standard. Prices range far and wide, but this is one of West Africa's most expensive cities, so expect to pay from around ₦1000 to ₦6000 a head.

Lagos Island
La Scala Muson House, 8/9 Marina, Lagos Island

☏01/264 6885. Upmarket restaurant specializing in Italian and French food.

Ikoyi and Victoria Island

Bambuddha 1310 Karimu Kotun St ☎01/761 4198. Swanky lounge bar with mustard walls and plum seats. Snacks in the bar or there's a separate restaurant serving Asian-influenced food. Beware: they take their "no T-shirts" dress code seriously, and will provide you with a black suit-jacket if you forget.

Bangkok 244A Muri Okunola St, V.I. ☎0803/307 7666. Excellent, tasty food, good service and friendly owners. They also deliver takeaways to the Islands.

Bonzai 1303 Akin Adesola St, V.I. ☎01/318 9000. Very good, expensive sushi and other Japanese food, and an excellent wine list. Fantastic, authentic decor and nice, atmospheric touches.

Cactus 20/24 Ozumba Mbadiwe Ave, V.I. ☎01/262 4928. Tried and tested Lebanese cuisine. There's an open area at the back which looks out on to the lagoon, for alfresco *meze*. Wi-Fi available.

Café Vergnano The Palms Shopping Mall, Lekki Peninsula (daily 8am–9pm). Lovely, spacious café offering excellent coffee, pizzas, and free Wi-Fi. Good option for Sun breakfast.

Chocolate Royal AIM Plaza Etim Inyang Crescent, V.I. ☎01/262 3055 (daily 7am–10pm). One of the best places for cakes and pastries and a good place for a coffee after checking your emails at the nearby Cool Café.

Churras 1C Ozumba Mbadiwe Ave, V.I. ☎01/262 9961. Lagos's first *churrascaria*, with typically endless helpings of roast meat carved onto your plate (₦3500–₦5000) or a vegetarian option (₦2000).

Debonaires Pizza 44A Adeola Odeku St, V.I. ☎01/792 1111. Excellent-value wood-fired pizza joint (₦750–₦1500). They do take-outs, too.

Flamingo 10 Kofo Abayomi St, V.I. ☎01/262 2225. Good-value Indian food, with a slightly tacky interior.

Il Sorrriso 27A Oju Olobun Close, V.I. ☎01/774 9382. This popular restaurant is as close as Lagos gets to *The Sopranos*. Authentic Italian food, lovingly prepared, and with a good wine list.

Imperial Chinese Plot 274 Ajose Adeogun St, V.I. ☎01/261 4255. Popular, no-nonsense Chinese restaurant.

Pattaya Upper floor, 13A Musa Yar'Adua, off Idowu Martins St, V.I. ☎01/874 3696. Excellent Thai restaurant with all the usual dishes.

Pearl Garden 10A Tiamiyu Savage St, V.I. ☎01/270 8889. Reliable though pricey Chinese restaurant.

Reeds 190 Awolowo Rd ☎01/271 5593. Excellent, well-presented but pricey Thai cuisine with a chichi interior. Good selection of vegetarian dishes.

Saipan 3rd & 4th Floors, Dream Plaza, 7 Bishop Aboyade Cole St, V.I. ☎01/461 2056 ⓦwww.saipannigeria.com. Sleek bar downstairs, and spacious Chinese restaurant upstairs, *Saipan* is a treat. Excellent food and service. Highly recommended.

Yellow Chilli 27 Oju Olobun Close, off Bishop Oluwole St, V.I. ☎01/723 2666. Stylish eatery serving Nigerian cuisine in a relaxed setting.

Apapa

Govinda's Vegetarian Restaurant 21A Badagry Rd, off Marine Rd, Apapa. An excellent-value option for vegetarians in the main Hari Krishna centre in Nigeria. All-you-can-eat Indian buffet for ₦900. They even do vegan suya.

St Elmo's 20 Warehouse Rd, Apapa (daily 9am–10pm). Reliable pizzeria above *Chicken Licken*.

Drinking and nightlife

Lagos is famous as a **music** centre, and the styles that have originated and evolved here – **highlife**, **juju**, **fuji** and **Afro-beat** – are as legendary and international as any in Africa. Check with ⓦwww.lagoslive.com for details of what's on across the city. Several restaurants morph into nightclubs as the clock turns 11pm, while other nightclubs are used purely as music venues. Gate fees are typically ₦1000–2000, with a "ladies night" offering free entry, usually on Thursdays. It is generally safe to leave places on V.I. late at night – provided your hotel is also on the islands.

Ariya Night Club 12 Ikorodu Rd, off Jibowu St, Yaba. *Juju* club belonging to maestro King Sunny Ade, who used to play here quite often, though he rarely does nowadays.

Bacchus 57 Awolowo Rd, Ikoyi. A grotto-like interior, *Bacchus* has been a popular club for the

past few years. Although it's looking slightly worn these days, the joint still rocks all night on Fri.

Casa del Habano Lagoon Plaza (opposite 1004 flats). While it's a tranquil place to enjoy a cigar by day (there's a walk-in humidor selling Cuban cigars), at weekends *Casa del Habano* becomes one of the hottest spots in town, with dancers dazzling the dance-floor with the sultriest salsa and *merengue* moves.

Chill Out (formerly Saga VIII) 35A Adetokunbo Ademola St, V.I. ℡01/270 2606. Arranged over two floors (VIP rooms upstairs), this is just about the swankiest club in Lagos. On Fri and Sat nights the place is packed with the Lagos elite at play.

Club Tower 18 Idowu Taylor St, V.I. A good option for an all-night weekend dance workout. Popular both with locals and expats.

 Motherlan' 64 Opebi Rd, Ikeja. Popular club in an outdoor amphitheatre, run by the equally popular musician Lágbájá, who plays here on the last Fri of the month.

New Afrika Shrine Pepple St, Ikeja (Thurs–Sun from late until dawn). Fela's son Femi Kuti's club. Ask to find out when Femi's playing, as he is often on tour.

Niteshift 34 Salvation Rd, off Opebi Rd, Ikeja. Former Lagos celebrity hangout, now relocated to a domelike building called the Coliseum, less than 10min drive from the *Sheraton* and *Airport* hotels.

Pat's Bar Plot 292C Ajose Adeogun St, V.I. ℡01/320 0424/5. Popular expat hangout in V.I.

Pinto's 5 Allen Ave, Ikeja (open all night at weekends). Expensive but still very popular, this is one of the best international-style clubs, with a resident jazz band accompanying different singers.

Soul Lounge The Palms Shopping Mall, Lekki Expressway. A recent addition to the Lagos scene, this joint serves up rum cocktails and is one of the hottest spots on the islands.

Swe Bar 2nd floor, City Mall, Onikan. Trendy bar which packs them in on Fri and Sat, with occasional live music.

Listings

Airlines Most airlines have their offices on Victoria Island (V.I.) and their opening hours are roughly Mon–Fri 8am–4pm: Aero, desk at the *Sheraton*, Ikeja and at MMA2 airport ℡01/764 4183; Air France, Plot 9999F Idejo Dammol St, off Adeola Adeku St, V.I. ℡01/461 0461 ✉los@airfrance.fr; Bellview, Waterfront Plaza, Plot 270 Ozumba Mbadiwe Ave, V.I. ℡/01/791 9215 ⊛www.flybellviewair.com; British Airways, C&C Towers, Plot 1684 Sanusi Fafunwa St, V.I. ℡01/261 1225, plus desk at the *Sheraton*, Ikeja; Chanchangi, at MMA2 airport ℡01/493 9744 ; EgyptAir, 22B Idowu Taylor St, V.I. ℡01/619 2332; Ethiopian Airlines, 3 Idowu Taylor St, V.I. ℡01/263 7655; Ghana Airways, 128 Awolowo Rd, Ikoyi ℡01/269 2363; IRS Airlines, 10 Wharf Rd, Apapa ℡01/773 8014; Kenya Airways & KLM, 30 Churchgate Building, Afribank St, V.I. ℡01/461 2501; Lufthansa, 150 Broad St at Martins St, Lagos Island ℡01/266 4430; Overland Airways, 17 Simbiat Abiola Rd, Ikeja ℡01/497 6599; Skyline, 28 Creek Rd, Apapa ℡01/587 4434; South African Airways, 28C Adetokunbo Ademola St, V.I. ℡01/262 0607; Virgin Atlantic, The Ark Towers, Block A, Plot 17 Ligali Ayorinde St, V.I. Annex ℡01/320 2747; Virgin Nigeria, c/o UBA, Mobolaji Bank Anthony Way, Ikeja (near MMIA) and c/o UBA, 1st floor, 19 Adeyemo Alakija St, off Sanusi Fafunwa St, V.I. ℡01/460 0505 and 271 1111 ⊛www.virginnigeria.com.

American Express Mandilas Travel Ltd, 33 Simpson St, Lagos Island ℡01/636 887.

Banks and exchange There are no ATMs and nowhere to change traveller's cheques. The *Sheraton* and *Eko* hotels have forex bureaux, or try Consolidated Bureau de Change, 94A Bode Thomas St, Surulere ℡01/585 1595. Black-market changers usually hang out around the *Bristol Hotel* on Martins St, along Broad St on both sides of Tinubu Square, on Marina outside the post office, and on Victoria Island opposite the *Federal Palace* and *Eko* hotels. There are several banks along Broad St and Marina which will change cash dollars and occasionally sterling. Western Union agents First Bank of Nigeria are at 35 Marina (℡01/266 5900).

Bookshops Lagos has the best English-language bookshops in West Africa. In Ikoyi, Quintessence and Glendora in Falomo Shopping Centre stock a good selection of books, as does Jazz Hole, at 168 Awolowo Rd – which has the best collection of novels on sale in the city – although the books are not cheap. Jazz Hole also boasts a great coffee shop which also sells fresh mango juice and delicious coconut nibbles. The South African NuMetro chain has set up store in Lagos, with the Borders-esque Media Store in the Silverbird Gallery (on Ahmadu Bello Way) and another branch at The Palms, just outside V.I. on the Lekki Expressway. On Lagos Island, there's CSS Bookshop at 50/52 Broad St – which has decayed in tandem with the rest of Lagos Island; secondhand books can be found at Affordable Books, opposite 29 Marina St.

Car rental There are many agencies in Lagos, nearly all of whom insist on supplying a driver with the vehicle: Avis is at the airport (℡01/497 4420) and c/o Holt Leasing, 25 Creek Rd, Apapa

(☎01/587 1531). Hertz is at 12 Keffi St, Obalende (☎01/269 3978–80), and at the airport. Cars can also be rented at the *Eko Hotel* (☎01/269 2194) and from Planet Rent-a-Car at the *Sheraton* (☎01/497 8600–9 ext 8049 or 8050).

Couriers DHL has offices at 32 Awolowo Rd, Ikoyi (☎01/269 2176–80); in the Lufthansa Building, 150 Broad St, Lagos Island (☎01/264 0013); and has other premises citywide. FedEx is at Okoi Arikpo House, 5 Idowu Taylor St, V.I. (☎01/261 0586 or 470 5074). UPS is at 12 Idowu Taylor St, V.I. (☎01/545 1883), and has other offices citywide.

Cultural centres and libraries Alliance Française, 2 Aromire Rd off Kingsway Rd, ☎01/269 2035; the British Council, 20 Thompson Ave, Ikoyi ☎01/269 2188–92 ⊕www.britishcouncil.org/nigeria.htm; the National Library, 4 Wesley St ☎01/265 6590 (Mon–Fri 7.30am–3.30pm; good reference library with books and periodicals).

Embassies and consulates Many have moved to Abuja, but of those still in Lagos (or with regional offices in Lagos), most are on Victoria Island (V.I.) and are open Mon–Fri. They include: Australia, 2 Ozumba Mbadiwe Ave, V.I. ☎01/261 8875 or 261 3124; Benin, 4 Abudu Smith St, V.I. ☎01/261 4385 or 261 4411; Burkina Faso, 15 Norman Williams St, Ikoyi ☎01/268 1001; Cameroon, 5 Elsie Femi Pearse St, V.I. ☎01/261 2226 or 261 4386; Canada, 4 Idowu Taylor St, V.I. ☎01/262 2516; Central African Republic, Plot 137, Ajao Estate, New Airport, Oshodi ☎01/268 2820; Chad, 2 Goriola St, V.I. ☎01/261 3116; Côte d'Ivoire, 3 Abudu Smith St, V.I. ☎01/261 0936; Equatorial Guinea, 7 Murtala Muhammed Drive, Ikoyi ☎01/268 3717 or 268 2013; France, 1 Oyinkan Abayomi Drive, Ikoyi ☎01/269 3427–30; Gabon, 8 Norman Williams St, Ikoyi ☎01/268 4566 or 268 4673; The Gambia, 162 Awolowo Rd, Ikoyi ☎01/268 2192; Ghana, 21/23 King George V St, Onikan, Lagos Island ☎01/263 0015 or 263 0493; Guinea, 8 Abudu Smith St, V.I. ☎01/261 6961; Ireland, 35 Sinari Daranijo St, V.I. ☎01/262 4820; Liberia, 3 Idejo St, off Adeola Odeku St, V.I. ☎01/261 8899 or 261 1294; Mauritania, 1A Karimu Giwa Close, SW Ikoyi ☎01/268 2971; New Zealand, c/o High Commission in London ☎+44 20 7930 8422 ⓔnzhc.consular@freeuk.com; Niger, 15 Adeola Odeku St, V.I. ☎01/261 2300 or 261 2330; Senegal, 14 Kofo Abayomi Rd, V.I. ☎01/261 1722; Sierra Leone, 31 Alhaji Waziri Ibrahim St, V.I. ☎01/261 5900; South Africa, 4 Maduike St, off Raymond Njoku St, SW Ikoyi ☎01/269 3842; Togo, 96 Awolowo Rd, Ikoyi ☎01/268 1337; UK, 11 Walter Carrington Crescent, V.I. ☎01/261 9537 ⊕www.ukinnigeria .com; USA, 2 Walter Carrington Crescent, V.I. ☎01/261 0139 or 261 0097.

Hospitals and clinics The best hospital is undoubtedly the Eko Hospital in Mobolaji Bank Anthony Way, Ikeja, near the *Sheraton* (☎01/497 8800–2). St Nicholas Hospital at 57 Campbell St (☎01/260 0070–9), near the National Library on Lagos Island, is more central, with a 24hr casualty service. Recommended general practitioners include Dr M. Semaan and Dr D. Semaan, St Francis Clinic, Keffi St, Ikoyi (☎01/269 2305); for dental treatment try Dr Bode Karunwi, Schubbs Dental Clinic, 5 Douala Rd, Apapa (☎01/545 2228).

Internet access If you're staying anywhere near V.I., by far the best cybercafé is Cool Café on Eyim Itang Crescent. Access, in a quiet work-like atmosphere, costs ₦200/hr. Cybercafés elsewhere and on the mainland are similar – crowded "business centres", often full of so-called "Yahoo boys" concocting 419 email scams.

Mail and telephones The GPO is on Marina St, Lagos Island (Mon–Fri 8am–noon & 2–4pm, Sat 8am–noon), with main branches on Awolowo Rd (at the junction with Kingsway Rd), Ikoyi, and Adeola Odeku St, V.I. Both branches are closed Sat. NITEL is on Cable St, Lagos Island (open 24/7).

Pharmacies Chyzob, 168 Awolowo Rd, Ikoyi ☎01/269 4545; Medicine Plus, 2nd floor, Mega Plaza, 14 Idowu Martins St, V.I.; Nigerian Medicine Stores Ltd, 4 Tinubu Square, Lagos Island ☎01/263 2546.

Supermarkets Choice is limited in Ikoyi to Goodies Supermarket at 195 Awolowo Rd. On V.I., the largest supermarket in Nigeria is found at The Palms Shopping Mall – Shoprite is the first branch of the South African chain in Nigeria. Another reasonably-stocked supermarket is found on the ground floor of Dream Plaza, 7, Bishop Aboyade Cole St. On the mainland in Ikeja you'll find Park 'N' Shop at 16 Mobolaji Bank Anthony Way.

Swimming pools The *Eko Hotel*'s pool is the cleanest, but is reserved for residents only. The Self Centre Alshonny Place, 1A Shonny Highway, Shonibare Estate, Ikeja (☎01/493 7553 or 270 0855), boasts a pool, gym, hair salon, steam room, massage room, bar and BBQ. It's basic, but also a quiet place to unwind.

Travel agents and tour operators Many agencies are grouped around the north side of Tafawa Balewa Square on Lagos Island. Others include: Bitts Travels & Tours, E7 Falomo Shopping Centre, V.I. (☎01/269 6095, ☎269 1337), which organizes excursions for groups to various tourist destinations; Transcap Travel, CFAO Building, 1 Davies St (between Balogun and Martins streets), Lagos Island (☎01/266 0321 or 266 5063); and Jemi-Alade Tours, 5 Olaide Tomori St, Ikeja (☎ & ☎01/496 0297), which runs upmarket slave-route tours covering southwest Nigeria and the Republic of Benin.

14.2

The southwest

The towns and rural parts of the southwest, often referred to as **Yorubaland**, have an exceptional wealth of cultural interest and natural beauty. In precolonial times, the **Yoruba** created one of the most powerful empires in West Africa – and the area is still charged with reminders. Most of the larger towns, for example, still have ruling **obas**, or kings, who wield a good deal of political clout despite limitations imposed on them by the federal government. The *obas* continue to live in **royal palaces**, many of which can be visited, like the palace at **Oyo**, former capital of the Yoruba kingdom of the same name.

Some of what is now known about the area's more distant past is the result of excavations carried out in **Ife**. The brass and terracotta statues found here drew international attention and suggest a sophisticated civilization dating back to at least the ninth century AD. According to Yoruba legend, however, Ife is even older – the first place in the world to be created. It has naturally enjoyed a position as the holiest place in the Yoruba realm, a sort of Mecca of Yoruba religion. Here and throughout the region, the living wood of the **old religion** still breathes beneath a thick layer of Christian or occasionally Islamic belief. You'll see shrines and temples in almost all the towns. At **Osogbo**, a whole **Sacred Forest** has been set aside as a reserve for worshippers, or "fetishers": the shrines here are vast and amazing and the worshippers only too eager to show visitors around. It's a major Nigerian highlight and now a UNESCO World Heritage Site.

Once you cross over into **Edo State**, it's a short distance to **Benin City**, once a formidable kingdom, though already in decline by the time the British arrived. Faced with the modern town of the same name, you may be hard-pressed to conjure up images of the former empire, but there are vestiges of the past, including the fast disappearing remains of the great wall that surrounded the city, and numerous brass and ivory **sculptures** housed in the city's renowned museum. Some traditional skills have been preserved in the numerous workshops and galleries around town, which are excellent places to buy art and crafts, particularly in brass and bronze.

Abeokuta

ABEOKUTA, 100km north of Lagos, on the old road to Ibadan (1hr by minibus from Ojota new garage), is "Ake" in Wole Soyinka's novel of the same name (the name of the royal district of the town where he grew up), and birthplace of not only Soyinka but also musician Fela Kuti and former president Olusegun Obasanjo. The capital of Ogun State, Abeokuta was founded in the early 1800s as a site for freed Yoruba slaves, some of whom were liberated by the British Royal Navy, and some of whom had made their own way back to their homeland from Freetown and elsewhere. It's an attractive town, with a spectacular, and easily climbable, outcrop of gigantic granite boulders overlooking it – Abeokuta means "under the rock". Abeokuta was originally inhabited by the Egba people who found refuge under Olumo rock during the Yoruba civil wars of the nineteenth century. The rock provided a hiding place for the people as well as a point from which to monitor the enemy's advance. Olumo rock can be visited and climbed (daily 7am–6pm; ₦200,

Adire cloth

Abeokuta is famous for its **adire cloth**. Designs are drawn on the cotton cloth in a hot wax paste made from cassava starch, the cloth is then dyed in an extremely pungent indigo and sulphur concoction, and the wax boiled off in large vats of water. The sheets of colourful material are then hung out to dry on washing lines that crisscross the spaces between houses set back from the road, and are finally sold from the market stalls. The process is undertaken almost exclusively by women. Today it is more common to find multicoloured wax-resistant cloth known as **campala**, though a few people still call this *adire*. Head to Itukun Street and ask the market traders to take you to the back, behind the rows of shacks, to where the cloth is made.

plus ₦500 to bring a camera, ₦1000 camcorder), and guides are on hand to show you the old war hideouts, and the main shrine where the chief oba makes a public sacrifice to the gods every August 5th for the peace and tranquillity of the town. In bygone times the sacrifice was human, a curfew having been declared some days before, and anyone unwittingly in breach of it (invariably a stranger in town) was arrested to be the victim. From the top of the rock you can look out over a sea of rusted tin roofs, and in the distance, lush greenery, while birds of prey circle at head height. Avoid the restaurant on the site – a branch of the *Sweet Sensation* chain.

Abeokuta boasts some beautiful, if dilapidated, colonial architecture – stone buildings with wooden shutters, beneath which people ply their trade from wooden shacks and market stalls, selling everything from *adire* cloth to pineapples, lush ripe tomatoes, and chillies in a striking array of colours. The centre of the town is dominated by the chief *oba*'s palace (Abeokuta also has four lesser *obas*) and adjacent Anglican church, the oldest church building in Nigeria. The **Oba's Palace**, on Ake Road, in the Ijemo district, is an unimpressive structure, but ask for a guide and you will be regaled with some fascinating historical stories concerning the unification of Yoruba subgroups when faced with attack from Usman Dan Fodio's jihadists in the early nineteenth century.

Practicalities

Vehicles from Lagos use the Kuto garage. The town's top **hotel** has long been the *Gateway*, on Ibrahim Babangida Boulevard, conveniently near Kuto garage (☎039/241 904–5 ☏241 716 ❹) but although it is set in lush, tropical grounds, inside it has seen better days – the smaller rooms look like student bedsits, with air-con units falling off the walls. It has satellite TV, a Chinese restaurant, a cinema, and an Olympic-size pool and, despite its dilapidation, retains a certain relaxed charm. Hang out here maybe, but sleep elsewhere. A cheaper option is the hotel's own annexe, run as a separate establishment, not far away on Ademola Road (☎039/240 004 ❸). A relaxing retreat set among slightly scruffy gardens, the annexe has a good restaurant and very helpful management. Other budget options are the *Alafia Guest House*, in Oke Ilewo district (☎039/240 788 ❸), and the *Front Line*, on Oluwo Road, Onikolobo Ibara (no phone ❷). The *Continental Suites* on IBB Boulevard (☎039 245 317 ❸) consist of basic rooms, a separate Internet café, and friendly staff.

Ibadan

The south's second city and the modern capital of Oyo State, **IBADAN** (pronounced with the stress on the first "a") is a vast metropolis that sprawls so far you think it's never going to stop. The city's horizons are marked not by the few Lagos-style high-rises but by a plethora of two-storey, corrugated-iron-roofed

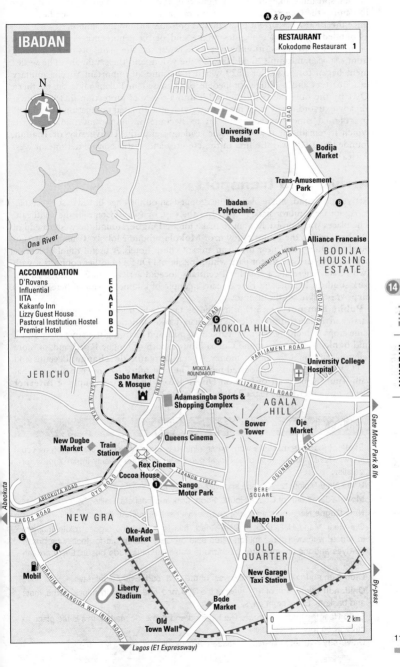

IBADAN

& Oyo

RESTAURANT
Kokodome Restaurant 1

N

Ona River

ACCOMMODATION
D'Rovans	E
Influential	C
IITA	A
Kakanfo Inn	F
Lizzy Guest House	D
Pastoral Institution Hostel	B
Premier Hotel	C

University of
Ibadan

Bodija
Market

Trans-Amusement
Park

Ibadan
Polytechnic

Alliance Francaise

BODIJA
HOUSING
ESTATE

OSHUMTOKUN AVENUE

OYO ROAD

BODIJA ROAD

MOKOLA HILL

PARLIAMENT ROAD

University College
Hospital

JERICHO

MARZINE ROAD

DUGBE ROAD

MOKOLA
ROUNDABOUT

ELIZABETH II ROAD

AGALA
HILL

Sabo Market
& Mosque

Adamasingba Sports &
Shopping Complex

Bower
Tower

Oje
Market

OGUNMOLA STREET

New Dugbe
Market

Train
Station

Queens Cinema

Rex Cinema

Cocoa House

Sango
Motor Park

LEBANON STREET

BERE
SQUARE

ABEOKUTA ROAD

OYO ROAD

Abeokuta

LAGOS ROAD

NEW GRA

Oke-Ado
Market

Mapo Hall

OLD
QUARTER

E

F

IJEBU BYPASS

Mobil

IBRAHIM BABANGIDA WAY IRING ROAD

Liberty
Stadium

New Garage
Taxi Station

Bode
Market

Old
Town Wall

0   2 km

Lagos (E1 Expressway)

Gate Motor Park & Ife

By-pass

houses, spreading like an urban fungus over the low hills. People here still assert Ibadan has the biggest population of any city in Africa, though this hasn't been true since the 1960s; the current population is probably around five million.

Founded by Yoruba renegades at the end of the eighteenth century, Ibadan occupies a strategic position between the forest and the plains, its name deriving from *eba odan*, meaning "field between the woods and the savannah". The settlement began to grow after 1829, when it became an important Yoruba military headquarters and a refuge for people dispossessed in Fulani raids on northern Oyo. By the time the British forced it into a treaty of protection in 1893, it was already extraordinarily large for its time, with an estimated population of 120,000. In colonial times, Ibadan went on to become an important trading centre, which it remains. It is also a major academic city: the **University of Ibadan**, founded in 1948, was the first in the country and is still considered one of West Africa's best.

Arrival and transport

Arriving **by road**, you're likely to be dropped off on the edge of town, at Iwo Road or Agodi Gate motor park ("Gate") in the east, or New Garage in the southeast. The places you'll probably want to make for are **Dugbe**, around the western end of Dugbe Road in the centre of town; or **Mokola**, around Mokola Roundabout 1km north of Dugbe and near the main area of cheap hotels. A useful minibus service connects Agodi Gate motor park with Mokola and Dugbe; another connects it with Iwo Road. There are a couple of centrally located arrival points – Sango motor park south of Dugbe, and Bere Square a couple of kilometres east of here. Ibadan's **airport** is 12km southeast of town.

Public transport consists of minibuses, taxis (which look exactly like ordinary cars) and *okadas* (motorcycle taxis). Shared taxis function like buses, using the same stops (which are often unmarked, so ask), and charging the same fares. You'll find **banks** in the area around Cocoa House, south of Dugbe Road, and, of more relevance if you're changing money, several **bureaux de change**. Leventis and UTC **supermarkets** are located nearby. The post office (Mon–Fri 8am–5pm, Sat 9am–1pm) is just west of here on Dugbe Road. There are a couple of **Internet** places in Center Point Plaza, Dugbe.

Ibadan area markets

Some of Ibadan's **markets** work on an eight-day cycle, which is fine as long as you know where you are in it: check local papers such as the weekly *Irohin Yoruba* for details.

Bode Near Molete bridge, and specializing in beads.

Mokola 3km north of Cocoa House. Food, pots and baskets. Daily.

New Dugbe Near the train station. A massive general market. Daily.

Oje Near Mapo Hall, east of Bere Road, this is one of the biggest cloth markets in Africa, with over three million yards sold annually (watch out for locally produced tie-dyes and the *aso-oke* strip cloth made in Iseyin), plus trade beads. Every sixteen days.

Ojoo 2km north of the university, west of the Oyo road. Every eight days.

Onidundu 14km north of IITA, west of the Oyo road, specializing in spices, herbs, mats and baskets. Every eight days.

Sabo Near the Friday mosque. The big food and domestic market; this is *the* place to get a good food pestle. Daily.

University market University of Ibadan. A souvenir market. Daily.

Accommodation

Ibadan has dozens of hotels and lodging houses, but they tend to be pricey for what you get.

D'Rovans Hotel, Chief Francis Aiyegbeni Close, Ring Rd ☎02/231 2908 ✉drovans@skannet .com.ng. Small, clean rooms and consistent power supply in a modern setting. The bar area next to the pool hosts live highlife music at the weekend. ❻

Hotel Influential On Mokola Hill ☎02/241 4894. Reasonably priced, recently renovated and clean, and in a handy location. ❹

International Institute of Tropical Agriculture (IITA) Oyo Road, 5km north of the University of Ibadan campus ☎02/241 2626 ✉hotel@cgiar.org. By far the best place in Ibadan, set in lush tropical grounds, with a private guesthouse offering accommodation in single or double rooms and one- or two-bedroom apartments with kitchens. Amenities include a pool, tennis courts, a nine-hole golf course and fishing around the lake. Advance booking essential. ❼

Kakanfo Inn 1 Nihinlola St, off Ibrahim Babangida Way, near the Mobil station on Ring Rd ☎02/231

1471–3 or 231 8600–1 ⊛www.kakanfoinn. com. Stylish 68-room (and 14 suites) hotel on the south side of town Each room has a minibar, Wi-Fi and satellite TV. The restaurant is excellent, with both Indian and Nigerian food on offer. There is a swimming pool, a small gym, and a spa offering massage. ❼

Lizzy Guest House 844 Adenle Ave, off Easy Life Rd, signposted from Oyo Rd ☎02/241 3350. Comfortable guesthouse with 14 inexpensive s/c, a/c rooms with satellite TV. ❸

Pastoral Institution (PI) Hostel Bodija Rd, near the university ☎02/810 3928. Clean s/c rooms with fans and mosquito nets, with breakfast included. Strict 10.30pm curfew. Supplement for a/c is ₦800 per room. ❷

Premier Mokola Hill ☎02/240 0340. Expensive-looking place that's not unreasonable for what it offers. You can relax in relative style here, with all the amenities, including a pool and Chinese restaurant, not to mention some of the best views in town. ❻

The City

Given Ibadan's unwieldy dimensions, it's hard to pinpoint the city's heart, though by default you'd have to say it beats around the **New Dugbe market** – one of Nigeria's largest. Should you lose your way, look for the strange **Bower Memorial Tower** on **Agala Hill** to the east, a good viewpoint to climb and a visible reference point from virtually anywhere in the city. The tower of **Cocoa House** is another guide for the disoriented. One of the few skyscrapers in town, it's evidence of the regional importance of a vital export crop and marks Ibadan's commercial centre. More good views are to be had in the **Old Quarter**, where the British established themselves on the city's highest hill. **Mapo Hall** was built on the summit of Mapo Hill in the 1920s and served as the colonial government house. Today, the stylish building is mostly used for wedding receptions, and if it hasn't been rented out, you can wander around.

On the north side of town, on Oyo Road, the campus of the **University of Ibadan** (UI) was designed for the most part by the distinguished British architect, Maxwell Fry, who also worked with Gropius and Le Corbusier. You can meet and mix with people here at the **cafeteria** or the **coffee shop** (open to all), or use the university **bookshop** (Mon–Fri 7.30am–4.30pm). The Institute of African Studies building houses a **museum** (open by special request) with bronze statues and carvings. The UI **Zoo**, near the Zoological Department, has been neglected for years, but has recently got a face lift and some new animals.

On your way to the university, you'll pass the **Transwonderland Amusement Park**, Ibadan's now very run-down attempt at a Disneyland. Many rides are closed, but it's still popular with locals. Nearby, the **Alliance Française**, 45 Oshumtokun Ave, on the corner of Bodija Road (☎02/241 4937), has a good range of French-language reading material and a full artistic and cultural programme.

Vehicles for Ife and the southeast mostly leave from **Gate motor park**. Minibuses for Gate leave from **Queens Cinema** on Dugbe Road, by the footbridge 300m north of Dugbe centre. For Oyo and points north (Abuja, Kaduna, Kano), transport mostly leaves from **Iwo Road** (accessible by bus from Gate), though a few still use Sango motor park. Vehicles for Lagos leave from **New Garage**, but there are also Lagos vehicles from Iwo Road, from Bere Square, and even direct from Dugbe.

There are **flights** to Lagos, Abuja and Ilorin with Overland Airways from Ibadan's domestic airport. A number of **travel agents** act for the international airlines; Tess Travels, F3 Centre Point Plaza, opposite AfriBank in Dugbe (℡0802/350 9261), is an excellent place to make travel arrangements in Nigeria and beyond.

Eating and drinking

For inexpensive dining, chop houses are a bit thin on the ground around Dugbe, but up on Mokola Hill, there are *bukas* serving *begiri* (traditional bean soup) and *àmàlà*.

Bisi at the *Kakanfo Inn*, 1 Nihinlola St ℡022/311 471 (daily 11am–9.30pm). One of Ibadan's best Indian restaurants, with a varied menu and friendly service. Pricey.

Golden Dragon at the *Premier Hotel* on Mokola Hill, a few minutes' walk from *Lizzy Guest House* and the *Influential Hotel* (daily noon–3pm & 7–10.30pm, closed Mon lunch). Good-quality Chinese food.

Kokodome Restaurant by Cocoa House (Mon–Sun 9am–11pm). Lebanese, European and American food, including cheeseburgers and fries. For a small supplement, you can spend the day at the pool and have food brought to your patio table. Formal sit-down eating is upstairs. Popular nightclub next door, open Fri & Sat 11pm–dawn (free entrance for diners).

Oyo and around

OYO is a relatively small town by Nigerian standards, with only a quarter of a million inhabitants, and its characteristic rust-stained roofscape looks like an Ibadan that never quite took off. On its earlier site to the north, the town was the capital of a Yoruba-speaking empire that stretched as far as present-day Togo (including such important vassal states as Dahomey; see p.995). At its apogee around 1700, Oyo was probably the most powerful state in West Africa.

Oyo was founded on the northern Yoruba savannah some time between the eleventh and thirteenth centuries, according to legend by **Oranmiyan**, the youngest of the Ife princes (sons of Oduduwa). It was strategically located in a part of the savannah relatively free from tsetse flies, and so could use **horses** for transport and war. From its old capital in **Oyo-Ile** ("Old Oyo"), buried deep in the present-day **Oyo-Ile National Park**, Oyo began to expand southwards in the sixteenth century, using both its highly efficient cavalry and its infantry to extend its power to the coast. Until the end of the eighteenth century, most of its wealth came from control of the trade routes between the coast and the north. By the late eighteenth century, however, the courts of Lisbon and Oyo were increasingly involved as partners in the slave trade. The name "Yoruba" is a corruption of "Yooba", meaning "the dialect of the Oyo people". The fact that missionaries applied the term to all the peoples of the region attests to the city's far-reaching power, but revolt by its vassals and war with the Muslim jihadists from the north spelt the end of the empire in the nineteenth century.

The present town of Oyo was founded in the 1820s, when Oyo-Ile fell to Muslim raiders. The *alafin* (the local name for the traditional ruler) attempted to re-establish the grandeur of the old capital at **Ago**, a market town south of Oyo-Ile, which he named Oyo. Although the only hint of its grand past is a sign welcoming visitors to "The City of Warriors", Oyo is an excellent place to buy crafts (carved calabashes, talking drums and so forth) and a good base for visiting Old Oyo National Park.

The Town

Although, transport-wise, your main point of reference will probably be **Owode**, where Antiba Street and Iseyin Road meet the main Ibadan–Ilorin highway, the town of Oyo really centres around **Abiodun Atiba Hall** (also called Town Hall), perched high on a hilltop. If you're walking up from the highway, you can see this monumental building from a kilometre away. When you arrive at the hall, you'll see the market spreading out before you on Palace Road.

Oyo's main point of interest is the **Alafin's Palace**, situated on Palace Road beyond the market. Townspeople will tell you that the present ruler is still head of all the *obas* of Yorubaland, although the *oni* of Ife is also considered to hold the title. In fact, a raging dispute – going back to colonial times when the practice of rotating the Chair of the Council of Obas was upset – has occupied attention for years and the two leaders are effectively at daggers drawn. The *oni* of Ife, as the descendant of Oduduwa, is more a spiritual leader, however, and in theory should not be open to challenge by earthly office-holders. Whatever disputes there may be, the *alafin* of Oyo is one of the nation's most influential traditional rulers. His residence is a curious compound – statues and carvings line the grounds, and there are numerous low buildings, some decorated with traditional symbols and all roofed in the ubiquitous rusty corrugated iron. You'll have to get a guide at the gate before visiting the grounds – money is never discussed, but at the end of the tour you're expected to dash something. Put all thoughts of seeing inside the palace out of your head.

Back at the **market**, besides the usual provisions and various household goods, you can find wonderful leatherwork and intricately carved **calabashes** – a local speciality, carved at the market in small workshops. Another speciality is "talking drums" (*dundun*), these too made and sold in market workshops. Although shops on the highway sell those wares to passing travellers (LSA at 19 Owode Commercial Rd, 200m east of Owode junction, is a good place for drums), you'll get a better deal and more choice, certainly for calabashes, in the market itself, where you can also see them being made. The Akesan Oyo Co-operative Calabash Carvers Society, just 20m on the left down the street opposite the post office, is an excellent place where you can even choose your calabash and have it carved to order.

Practicalities

Vehicles for Lagos and Ibadan arrive and leave from Owode junction. For Ilorin and the north, they leave from across the main road, 200m east. Vehicles for Osogbo leave from Awe, 2km east of Owode.

The **post office** is directly opposite the market. There are branches of First and National **banks** on Atiba Street, and moneychangers hang out by the town hall, but in view of the lack of forex bureaux, you're best advised to change money before arriving. If you're planning to visit Old Oyo National Park, contact the **park headquarters** off Iseyin Road, Isokun (☎038/240 125, ⨎240 699; Mon–Fri 8am–4pm), before leaving Oyo.

The best-known **hotel** – *La Bamba* on Ibadan Road, 3km west of Owode (☎038/240 443–4 ❷), has groovy 1970s science-fiction-style chalets in well-kept grounds. The second option if you're on a budget is *Oyo Merry Guest House* at Owode junction (☎038/230 344 ❶), with reasonably clean s/c rooms behind the New Covenant Church.

For cheap **eating** in Oyo, you can eat at the chop bars in Owode, and wash down the meal with frothy palm wine (ask around in the market – you'll soon locate a place that sells it). Don't leave town without sampling *begiri* (bean soup) and *wara* (curd cheese), which you can buy in **Akesan market**.

Around Oyo

Heading **north from Oyo** towards Jebba (see p.1170), you pass through **OGBOMOSHO**, a large and unpleasant industrial centre, and **ILORIN**, the capital of Kwara State, a workaday trading town with a strong Muslim flavour. Ogbomosho has an excellent Baptist hospital. If you're driving, note that the road between the two towns is a notorious accident blackspot. Ilorin is home to two universities: the large University of Ilorin, and Al-Hikmah University. The town was also the military headquarters of the ancient Oyo empire. The best **hotel** in Ilorin is the recently refurbished *Kwara* at 9A Ahmadu Bello Ave (☎031/221 490/3 ext 8854 ❺). It's got a busy, if slightly soulless bar, but the staff are friendly, and there's an adjoining nightclub, *Enigma*, which heaves (unenigmatically), even on a Thursday night.

Some 50km southeast of Ilorin, on the Lokoja road, turn off at the small town of **ORO** to the fascinating village of **ESIE**, where a small, well-signposted and well-kept 🏛 **museum**, established in 1945, houses more than fifteen hundred carved soapstone images of humans and animals (the largest collection in Africa) dating from as long ago as the twelfth century. Male and female statues of musicians, warriors and figures dressed in rich attire and head gear stand side by side in the open-air atrium. Don't get out your camera as **photography** is forbidden, and there are no postcards on sale (if you want to take pictures you need "permission from the headquarters of the National Commission for Museums and Monuments in Abuja" – though a little dash might help as a suitable alternative). Said to have been discovered by a local hunter in the later eighteenth century, the Esie statues remain a mystery, though some resemble findings from the Nok culture.

West of Oyo, though best reached on the new highway from Ibadan, the small town of **ISEYIN** is famous locally for its wonderful **night market** and cashew trees. It's also one of the main centres for **aso-oke** strip cloth – most weaves coming from here. If you're staying, try the *Trans-Nigeria Hotels Resthouse*, on the way into Iseyin from the south. A good day-trip from Iseyin is to the **Ikere Gorge Dam**, where you can go fishing or boating on the lake.

Between Iseyin and the border of the Republic of Benin, there's a wealth of beautiful countryside dotted with old Yoruba **hill forts**. If you've got your own transport, visit **ADO-AWAIYE**, 26km south of Iseyin, and **SHAKI** and **OGBORO**, respectively 87km and 105km to the north of Iseyin, both off the Agoare–Kaiama road that leads north through the Oyo and Kwara backcountry to Borgu Game Reserve (see p.1171).

Old Oyo National Park

North of Iseyin is **Old Oyo National Park** (Dec–April; ₦300 for "non-natives", ₦150 for each vehicle, ₦500 for each camera). The park is important not only for its mammals (including buffalo, antelope, hartebeest and duiker), but also archeologically, as the northern part is the site of the ruined city of Oyo-Ile, the original site of Oyo. The main entrance for wildlife-viewing is at **SEPETERI** (accessible by direct public transport from Iseyin; from Oyo, you'll need to take a vehicle to Shaki, then another to Sepeteri), where you'll find park rangers, guides and rudimentary chalet accommodation (❶). For the Oyo-Ile archeological site, however, the best point of entry is at **IGBETI**, also staffed by rangers and with chalet accommodation (❶). If you are heading to Oyo-Ile you must pick up a pass in Igbeti first, and can also rent a 4x4 here – a must if you plan to get through the jungle terrain in one piece. What's left of the ruins and impressive **Agbaku rock and cave** are actually located near the village of **OGUNDIRAN**, about an hour's drive from Igbeti. When we visited, only 16 people had signed the visitors' book in four months. This is surprising because although the **ruins** aren't much to look at (foundation stones from a group of houses, nestled in overgrown weeds and grass), the Agbaku rock dwelling itself is well worth the considerable trek to get there. Inside the cave is a noisy, and smelly, **bat** colony, and guides will lead you inside and up through a gap in the rock until you climb to a vantage point overlooking miles and miles of lush, verdant hills and jungle – surely one of the most incredible views in Nigeria. Overnight camping is allowed, so take a picnic – but watch out for mischievous **baboons**.

Igbeti is connected by public transport with Sepeteri and with Ogbomosho, which is the best way to get to it from Oyo. Igbeti is also notable for the huge **Yamafo Rock**, a towering, charcoal-grey mound, peppered with grassy clumps – just as impressive as Abuja's famous Aso Rock – that looms above the town.

Ife

According to Yoruba legend, **IFE** (also known as **Ile–Ife**), was the first Yoruba city, and indeed, the first city in creation. Custom says it was at this spot that the supreme God **Olodumare** threw an iron chain from the heavens into the waters below. He then instructed his son **Oduduwa** to climb down the chain, carrying with him a calabash full of sand, a chicken and an oil-palm nut. Oduduwa dumped the sand on the water and let the chicken loose. The bird began scratching in the sand, causing dry earth to appear, and meanwhile the palm nut produced a tree. The sixteen fronds of the palm tree represented the sixteen crowned rulers of Yorubaland and its sixteen cities. More prosaically, **excavations** indicate that Ife was probably founded as a Yoruba city in the ninth century. They have also revealed much about the lifestyle of the royal court: many of the brass and terracotta sculptures from the digs are today on display in the **Ife museum**.

Although Ife was already in political and economic decline by the early 1500s, the town remained a spiritual focus and is still an important symbol of Yoruba nationhood. In addition, it has had a post-independence renaissance as a modern cultural centre with Nigeria's most extensive university campus – the **Obafemi Awolowo University**. The thousands of students add energy to what would otherwise be a sleepy town and provide the opportunity for some animated conversations.

Arrival and accommodation

Coming into Ife, you'll almost certainly arrive from the west, on the Ibadan road. At the beginning of town this forks, with the Ondo road heading south toward the *oba*'s palace and museum, while Ibadan Road continues into the commercial centre, where a right turn down Aderemi Road will equally take you down to the palace and museum.

Diganga Ibadan Rd, 300m past the campus gate ☎036/233 200 or 231 791. Good-value, clean and friendly. Most rooms are s/c with a/c, fans and satellite TV, but there are some ultra-cheap non-s/c singles in the annexe. The bar-restaurant fills with students in the evening. ❸

Hilton Mayfair Rd ☎036/232 819. Not that *Hilton*, but 20 reasonable rooms with a/c, fridges and satellite TV, a restaurant and bar – a good-value option. ❷

University Guest House on campus ☎036/230 809 ☻230 705. Rooms with TV and a/c, plus and large restaurant, though the pool and tennis courts belong to the staff club and aren't available to guests. Good-value, though, and not too far from the centre of the campus (take an *okada*). ❸

The Town

The traditional ruler of Ife is the *oni* of Ife. Although you won't be able to visit his actual residence at the **oni's (or oba's) palace** in the Enuwa district of the town, it's easy enough to walk around the courtyard, with its statues and dignitaries milling about. One of the *oba*'s messengers will take you around (with a translator) to show you the **meeting hall** where local criminal cases are tried under the Yoruba penal code, and the **shrine to Ogun**, where a dog or goat is sacrificed each September.

Adjacent to the royal palace, and not to be missed, is the **National Museum** (daily 8am–6pm; ₦20). As long as a millennium ago, the *oni* of Ife wielded great political and spiritual powers. He commanded a whole army of servants, including indentured artists who made brass castings for him and his retinue – staffs, chest ornaments, and miniature pieces in abstract designs or animal shapes. The museum also contains terracotta works dating from the tenth to the thirteenth centuries and more recent wooden carvings. But the most precious treasures are the magnificent **brass and bronze heads** of the *oni* and other senior royal figures, made by the lost-wax method (some of the best examples are in the National Museum in Lagos). The sculptors of the heads worked pure copper and copper alloys of various composition – either with more tin (to make bronze) or more zinc (to make brass) – in a realistic mode of expression that is relatively uncommon in African art. They were clearly technical virtuosos of enormous skill, producing heads of rare grace, scored with the fine lines of scarification indicating royal rank. But there is an imperious remote vanity about these heads, and a sense of duty and proscribed creativity, indicating the sculptors' obsession with formal ways of doing things. In an unmarked garden not far from the museum, the **Oranmiyan Staff** – a carved and decorated stone monolith about five metres high – symbolizes the sword of the first *alafin* of Oyo.

Ife also has a small **Pottery Museum**, two floors of dusty pottery works including musical jars (like skinless drums), coolers and cooking jugs. It's located on More Road (daily 8am–6pm; free, though donations are encouraged), a couple of kilometres east of the National Museum.

The university

Obafemi Awolowo University, west of town, was established in the 1960s, and renamed after the first premier of the Western Region when he died in 1987 – a name tag that didn't meet with unanimous approval. Oduduwa Hall, opposite the students' union cafeteria, but best seen from the other side, is an amazing piece of 1960s architecture, and the scope of the grounds and facilities (this is the third largest university campus in the world) is an impressive indication of the stress laid on higher education by the governments of the early independence era.

The university has its own **Museum of Natural History** (Mon–Fri 8am–3.30pm; free) on the top floor of the agriculture faculty, 200m from the university hall. The nearby trees are full of bats, whose wheeling swarms make something of a spectacle, and nearby there's a rather unspectacular **zoo** (daily 10am–4pm; ₦100). There's also an excellent bookshop by the university hall, with a wide selection of Nigerian literature at very low prices. To get there, take one of the frequent minibuses from the town centre to "Campus", which drops you in the heart of things.

Eating and drinking

For **cheap eating**, the *Momo Ade Food Centre* at 14 Aderemi Rd (behind Prof. Ojulari's Pool Agency) is one of several basic chop-houses on Aderemi Road near the junction with Ibadan Road serving *eba* and pounded yam with soup. *Ogbe Restaurant*, on Ondo Road by the junction with Ibadan Road, also has cheap and filling Nigerian food, and cold beer. There's a host of eating places on or around the **campus**. Apart from whole areas of *bukas* doing hot food all day, the student union cafeteria offers a pretty good and inexpensive selection, with further choices in the adjoining New Buka concrete yard, two rows of largely African mini-restaurants.

Osogbo

Despite a population close on half a million and an important modern sheet-metal plant, **OSOGBO** seems somehow smaller and more traditional than either Ife or Oyo. **Traditional religion** is perhaps no more prevalent here than in other Yoruba

Aje The malevolent and destructive aspects of womanhood.

Efe Male masks.

Egungun Masks to honour family ancestors, worn during the annual festival of the secret, male society of the same name. Some *egungun* are put on just for entertainment, to mock police, prostitutes, avaricious traders, people with deformities or anyone who unsettles the community. Many come from Abeokuta, and reflect that town's links with Sierra Leone.

Ekiti masks These come from the eastern (*ekiti*) Yoruba kingdoms. Best known is the *ekiti epa* mask, a wooden helmet surmounted by a carved figure.

Eshu Messenger of the *orisha* (gods) and the divine trickster responsible for everything that goes wrong in the world. Every Yoruba marketplace has a shrine to him, often a simple pillar of sun-baked mud, over which the priests pour daily libations to preserve harmony in the market and community. Devotees of Eshu keep wooden sculptures of him in their houses.

Gelede The Gelede society is found only in some of the western Yoruba kingdoms. Its job is to appease female witches by entertaining them.

Ibeji Twins. If a twin dies, an image is carved of the dead child.

Ifa (also known as Orunmila). A powerful and respected oracle, consulted by those afflicted by disease or madness, or by anyone with a problem to solve. A series of sacred texts – poetic sayings – are interpreted by the *babalawo* or "father of secrets" using the Ifa board, and cowries, seeds or stones thrown in a pattern.

Ijebu masks The Ijebu kingdoms of southern Yoruba have imported some of the delta region's religious societies (like Ekine) from the Ijaw. Their masks tend toward the formalistic cubism of Ijaw sculpture, quite distinct from the naturalistic lines of northern Yoruba sculpture.

Iyamapo Goddess of women's crafts, including weaving and dyeing.

Nanabuku Controller of the wind.

Obatala (or Orishanla). Responsible for the creation of each individual human form, to which Olodumare gives life and destiny. Obatala's devotees wear white beads and dress in white cloth on ceremonial occasions.

Ogboni The Ogboni society, to which all Yoruba chiefs, priests and senior men belong, is the cult of the earth. It also has a judicial role, being responsible for all cases of human bloodshed – which are an offence against the earth – and a political one, in providing a forum for discussion free of outside interference. Meetings take place in a cult house, where the society's rites and discussions are kept secret from nonmembers.

Ogun God of war and iron, traditionally worshipped at times of war to seek success in battle, and by hunters seeking successful hunting. More modern devotees include all those who use iron or steel to make a living, or who drive on roads or fly planes.

Olodumare (also known as Olorun). The Yoruba supreme deity and creator god.

Orisha General name for a spirit or god.

Orisha Oko God of the farm.

Osanyin God of medicine, responsible for the magical therapeutic action of leaves, herbs and other ingredients. There's a fundamental relationship between Osanyin and all other cults: devotees use appropriate medicines in order to enter into a close relationship with their chosen *orisha* during their initiation and subsequent life in the cult.

Osun (or Oya). Goddess of the river which flows through Osogbo, the patron deity of the town and bringer of fertility to women.

Shango God of thunder and lightning, identified with one of the very earliest kings of Oyo. Has now been co-opted by NEPA, the national electricity company.

towns, but it's more obvious, especially in the **Sacred Forest**, with its sculptures and temples. Ironically, the renaissance of the religion and art of the town was in part due to an influx of European artists and philosophers who moved here in the 1950s, the most notable of whom was **Suzanne Wenger**, an Austrian painter and sculptor. In 1991, Osogbo became capital of the then newly created Osun State, a status which brought a flurry of activity and pushed up rents, but never quite translated into increased prosperity for local people.

The Town

The normal way to get around Osogbo is by shared taxi or *okada*. In town, try to visit the **oba's palace**, on the junction of Catholic Mission and Osun Shrine roads. Besides the old and new palace buildings, the grounds contain a temple to Osun (see box, above) with traditional wall paintings and sculpted wooden pillars. Elderly priestesses guard the inside of the temple and will say prayers for you in exchange for an offering. Directly across from the palace is the **market shrine**, the meeting place for elders and "King Makers", decorated with carved wooden totems and abstract paintings at the front, and with a tree growing out of the back. Flamboyant-looking **Brazilian houses** with wild ornamentation and bright colours line the whole length of Catholic Mission Street to the northwest.

King's Market spreads out opposite the palace. Besides the wide selection of fruit and vegetables, which grow easily in this fertile part of the country, you'll notice a lot of *juju*, sacred pots and other ritual articles. **Suzanne Wenger's house** is nearby on Ibokun Street and it's worth having a look at from the outside for the imaginative architecture and the ornamentation replete with traditional imagery and symbolism. If Adunni (Suzanne Wenger's Yoruba name) is in, you may be able to meet her; she has a shop with artefacts for sale, and will gladly sell you a copy of her book, *The Sacred Groves of Osogbo*. For a deeper understanding of Yoruba religion, it makes interesting reading, and the photographs are beautiful.

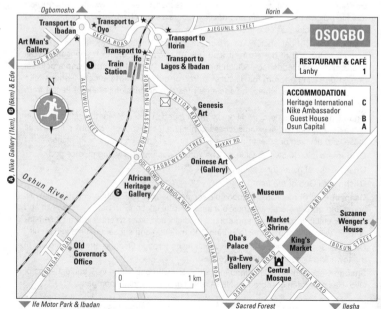

Osogbo was the site of a famous **artists' workshop**, set up as an offshoot of Ibadan's Mbari Club in the 1960s by writer **Ulli Beier** (previously married to Suzanne Wenger) and artist **Georgina Beier**. They ran it for three years, attracting a collection of locals and performers involved in the Duro Ladipo Travelling Theatre. Nigerian artists such as Twins Seven Seven, Muraina Oyelami, Jimoh Buraimoh, Rufus Ogundele, Adebisi Fabunmi and others learnt new techniques from Georgina Beier. Some of these artists are now world-famous, and rich and influential at home. Osogbo remains a major centre of artistic activity, with a large number of galleries and studios.

You can meet the artists and buy their work (and batiks, a speciality of Osogbo) at their open studios. **Twins Seven Seven (Art Man)** is a particularly entertaining, maverick character, who has determinedly made his art the most commercially successful (if you and he are talking money, talk hard). His gallery, where you can buy ceramics, metal sculptures and appliqué, is off Ede Road by the Boras filling station. **Jimoh Buraimoh** works with beaded collage, beads being traditionally a part of royal insignia on the Yoruba beaded crown, and his murals adorn public buildings all over Lagos. He and his sons run the African Heritage Gallery off Odi Olowo Road in Buraimoh Street.

Nike Davies-Okundaye (a former wife of Twins Seven Seven) runs the 🏛 **Nike Art Center** for young artists, west on Iwo Road (ask for the Dada estate and look out for the signpost). The centre is booming with creativity, and heavily into batik, painting, carving and even quilt-making (see ⓦ www.nikeart.com). Other galleries you might want to visit include **Onirese Arts**, 58 Station Rd, for rather pricey, engraved calabashes and batiks; **Genesis Art**, 138 Station Rd, for paintings and wood and brass sculptures; and **Iya-Ewe**, 7 Osun Shrine Rd, for paintings.

Ulli Beier's **museum**, at 27 Catholic Mission Rd (daily 10am–5pm; free), contains a small collection of antiquities from around Nigeria, and some from Papua New Guinea.

The Sacred Forest

Now in her 90s, Suzanne Wenger was interested in the beliefs and language of the Yoruba as inspiration for her paintings, but she soon became a follower of **Obatala** – the Yoruba god of creation – and, as local women came to appreciate her charismatic artistic power, became herself a priestess of the religion in the 1960s. She has been a prime mover in restoring Osogbo's **Sacred Forest**, which is devoted to the female water-deity **Osun**, the bringer of all things loving, sensual and fertile. With the help of Nigerian artists, Wenger set about rebuilding the broken-down shrines, places of worship and sculptures, using modern cement on frames of wood and steel, and a style that combined traditional elements with her own inspiration. The results are spectacular, mysterious and unique, though getting a little weather-beaten now.

The forest is on the outskirts of town. It's not far to walk – about 2km south of the centre – but you're better off taking a taxi there the first time you go. From the roadside, you can observe various shrines and an elaborate fence confining the retreat, before arriving at the gate. During the **Osun Festival**, usually celebrated in August, you'll find followers waiting by the road. The forest costs ₦100 to visit, plus ₦500 for a camera and ₦2500 for a camcorder. Guided tours are available, and it's best to be accompanied during your visit, since it's difficult to make any meaning out of the sites without explanation, although the artistic expression is impressive in itself.

The first place you'll be shown is the **Osun Temple** – the main place of worship and said to be the first building of the old town (Osogbo used to be on this site until Osun said she couldn't live with human beings any longer and sent them off to found the new town). If you go into the temple, you'll see shrines dripping with palm oil and might be asked to make a **sacrifice**, after which prayers will be made.

You may also be asked to kneel in front of the shrines and pray yourself: what you do at this point is up to you, though a rendering of the Lord's Prayer or any humble invocation would be quite adequate.

Next, you'll be taken down to the **river** – the sacred domain of Osun, where you may be handed a calabash full of murky river water. It makes a big impression if you drink from it and you probably won't die if you do, but you know best how your body is likely to react. Either way, you're unlikely to cause offence.

Walking through the forest, you'll be shown shrines depicting a myriad of deities (see box, p.1143), all of whom are represented by statues on the site of the market of the old town. The god of creation, **Obatala**, is portrayed riding on an elephant. Other temples in the forest include **Ohuntoto's Building**, a place of prayer to Ohuntoto, the son of Obatala. Designed by Wenger, the architecture forces you into the world of the fantastic – one of the rooms is in the shape of an ear so that those who pray will have their prayers heard.

Practicalities

The main **motor park** is Dugbe (old garage) on Okefia Road, with others nearby and spread around at the entrances to the town; for Ilesha, there's a motor park outside town on the Ilesha road. The **post office** and NITEL telephone office are both on Station Road. To get **online**, the best place is Ladatex Links, opposite the *Osun Capital Hotel* on the Iwo-Ibadan Road. For good Nigerian or European **food**, *Lanby Restaurant* at 3 Alekuwolo Rd is the best in town, and less than ₦750 for two courses plus a soft drink. Osogbo has several **hotels**:

Heritage International Gbongan/Ife Rd ☎035/241 881 or 240 228. Good-value, clean option, with an outside bar. ❸

🏃 Nike Ambassador Guest House Ede Rd, 6km west of the Nike Art Center. The best place to stay in Osogbo. Twelve rooms set in two blocks (only two rooms are en suite). You need to arrange your stay in advance by calling Nike

Davies-Okundaye in Lagos on ☎01/270 5965 or 0803/303 6969. ❽
Osun Capital Ede Rd ☎035/240 396. Slightly grimy accommodation featuring s/c single rooms with fan, and doubles with a/c, fan and TV; also has its own restaurant and bar. The water supply is sporadic. ❷

Osogbo's brand of Nike

"Nike arranged a day's tuition for us in one of the older cloth-dyeing techniques. On arrival at the workshop we were greeted enthusiastically by the several dozen students working there in dyeing, wood carving and other crafts. The art gallery itself is outstanding. The hospitality we were given was remarkable."

Piers and Shirley Miller, UK

Around Osogbo: Iragbiji

If you've made the trek as far as Osogbo, it's worth stopping off at nearby **IRAGBIJI**. It's a friendly little town, and boats one of the most vibrant and well-attended **Egungun festivals** in Yorubaland. The folklore surrounding the founding of the town suggests it was discovered by a great hunter who climbed Ori-oke – the hill dominating the town – and caught sight of his prey. The animal ran into a huge hole in the centre of the hill and the hunter climbed in after it. Eventually both emerged from a large well-like opening in front of the present Iragbiji Town Hall before the animal was eventually killed. The hole, now boarded up, is a historical monument, and the centrepiece of the annual Egungun celebrations.

Iragbiji's Egungun takes place in May. It's a seven-day festival of traditional music and dance, with masquerades representing the spirits of the dead interacting with the living. Masqueraders in colourful costumes and masks parade the streets followed by thousands of revellers.

The current Chief of Iragbiji is the artist and musician **Muraina Oyelami** who studied at the Osogbo Art School and has exhibited around the world. His **Obatala Centre for Creative Arts** runs workshops and performance classes and can arrange accommodation. If you're interested, contact him at ©murainaoyelami@yahoo.com or visit Ⓦwww.oyelami.com/iragbiji.htm.

Benin City and around

Long before Europeans arrived on the West African coast, Benin City, now the capital of Edo State, was capital of a powerful empire with a **divine king**. A direct descendant of this line, the **oba**, still reigns over his kingdom, though his duties are of course largely ceremonial nowadays. Today the city is as business-like as any in Nigeria – feverish, dirty, noisy and crowded. It has no coast, and little in the way of open spaces to escape to, yet its remarkable history, traced in the **Benin National Museum**, has made the town into something of a cultural centre.

Some history

"When you go into it you enter a great broad street, which ... seems to be seven or eight times broader than the Warmoes street in Amsterdam ... and thought to be four miles long ... The houses in this town stand in good order, one close and evenly spaced with its neighbour ... They have square rooms, sheltered by a roof that is open in the middle, where the rain, wind and light come in ... The king's court is very great ... built around many square-shaped yards ... I went into the court far enough to pass through four great yards ... and yet wherever I looked I could still see gate after gate which opened into other yards."

From *O.lfert Dapper's Description of Benin*
Recorded in 1602, published in Amsterdam in 1668

Benin is west of the Igbo country, and mainly peopled by the **Edo** or **Bini** (hence "Benin") who, according to their own oral history, migrated from the east – according to some accounts from Egypt. Whatever the case, the new Edo settlement was founded by **Ere**, a man credited with being the inventor of order and instigator of traditions. Some time in the late twelfth century, the chiefs impeached their king and for some years were governed by an elected ruler. But this system also failed and the chiefs appealed to Ife to send over a capable monarch. The Yoruba prince **Oranmiyan** arrived and married a local woman. Their son **Eweka** became the first *oba* and the royal palace was built during his reign.

From Oranmiyan's time onward, **bronze** achieved an important symbolic status: the very notion of kingship seemed to reside in this alloy of locally mined tin, and copper, which was imported at great expense. When an *oba* died, it was customary to send his head to Ife to have a portrait cast, but in the mid-fourteenth century, the Edo became bronze-workers themselves. This art form, however, was reserved strictly for the court. A smith foolish enough to waste his talent on anyone other than the *oba* was quickly executed.

The kingdom enjoyed its **golden era** between the fifteenth and the seventeenth centuries, its warrior kings conquering and ruling a huge empire reaching from Porto Novo in the West to beyond the Niger River in the east. One of the greatest rulers was **Oba Ewuare**, who ascended to the throne around 1440. He expanded the empire and brought new wealth – slaves, ivory, livestock – into the city. Ewuare also greatly enlarged the capital, adding wide avenues and nine new gates, each manned by a tax collector. When the **Portuguese** first arrived here, in 1485, they encountered a vast capital – the heart of a capable kingdom.

Other Europeans – English, Dutch, Florentines – quickly followed the Portuguese to the Bight of Benin. Their requirements were slaves, ivory, pepper, leather and handmade cloth. The *oba*, **Ozula the Conqueror**, had plenty to offer from a string of fruitful conquests but refused to sell slaves after 1516, after only a few seasons of trade. He willingly exchanged his stocks of pepper and ivory, however, for metals, silk and velvet cloth, mirrors and European horses – most of which quickly succumbed

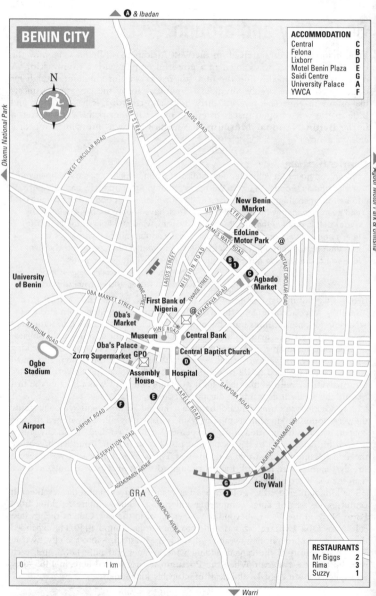

BENIN CITY

ACCOMMODATION

Central	C
Felona	B
Lixborr	D
Motel Benin Plaza	E
Saidi Centre	G
University Palace	A
YWCA	F

RESTAURANTS

Mr Biggs	2
Rima	3
Suzzy	1

Warri

0   1 km

to sleeping sickness. Ambassadors were exchanged with several European nations in the sixteenth century and the *oba*'s court acquired a Portuguese cultural veneer.

The *oba* became interested in **guns**, but the pope had forbidden traders to sell weapons to heathens. Oba Ozula sent a son to Portugal to be converted and promised to build churches in his kingdom. He never built any, but he got the guns: the Vatican looked the other way and trade flourished. Copper and copper alloys became plentiful and the *oba* could afford to commission unlimited metal plaques to line his palace walls. Heady from the booming business, the trade partners even fought side by side, as when Portuguese mercenaries aided the Edo in their war against the neighbouring kingdom of Idah to the northeast, at the end of the sixteenth century. The Portuguese did very well out of the trade, even though it was only in the eighteenth century that they succeeded in overturning the sanction against slave-trading out of Benin's dominions. Even then, the *obas* placed strict limits on the numbers sold.

By the late nineteenth century, the **British Empire** had become the Benin kingdom's principal partner, and London was increasingly determined to develop new commodity sources and expand British markets for manufactured goods. The *oba*'s council increasingly perceived the calculating Europeans as a threat, while the *oba* himself tried hard to find ways of negotiating a peaceful takeover that would allow him maximum power. But his council sabotaged his plans by ambushing and slaughtering a British negotiating team. Benin retreated behind the massive city walls to concentrate on metaphysical ways of dealing with the impending disaster of invasion.

Creating an image of savagery was in Britain's interest, since public opinion at home would accept relatively painless war and invasion as long as it was linked to a "civilizing mission". When the British Army launched a retaliatory "punitive expedition" to crush and seize Benin in 1897, they found the *oba* had apparently made one last, desperate effort to save the city in the only way he knew, and had ordered human sacrifices on a massive scale. The British reported corpses lying everywhere and the pervasive stench of death in the town. The king himself had escaped, but was captured in the forest and sent into exile. His palace was pillaged; the great art treasures were sent to England – where they remain to this day, many in the British Museum in London – while others were sold to private collections. The rest of the city was razed to the ground.

The stories of sacrifice undoubtedly had some basis in fact – the *oba*'s efforts to appease the spirits and ward off the encroaching white men were by no means extraordinary – but there was certainly sensationalist reporting too. Writing in the *Evening News* forty years after the event, Major James F. Ellison referred to a "14 hours running fight with the fleeing enemy" all around the city walls. Inside,

> "Benin ran with blood. Human sacrifices were everywhere. Some of the human beings who were in chains were still alive, speedily to be liberated. Around a huge tree in the centre of the city were erected poles on which were cross-pieces. On these were bodies, remains of those who had been sacrificed. In the Valley of the Skulls were hundreds of human heads and bones."

After the campaign, the British press referred to Benin as the "City of Blood and Crucifixions". Robert Home's *City of Blood Revisited: A New Look at the Benin Expedition of 1897*, published in 1983, reveals the fumbling mix of greed and hand-wringing behind British imperialism in West Africa.

Arrival and accommodation

Although Benin is a big city with more than a million inhabitants, it's well laid out and not especially difficult to get to grips with. Everything centres around **King's Square** (popularly known as **Ring Road**), a roundabout at the heart of town, with minibuses and shared taxis heading here from all the motor parks. The airport is 2km southwest of town, down Airport Road.

Vehicles to **Onitsha and the east** leave from the Agbor motor park on Ikpoba Slope, out at the end of Akpakpava Road to the northeast, 8km from Ring Road. To **Lagos** and the west, head to the Uselu motor park on Lagos Road. **Buses** – cheaper and slower than taxis – leave from a row of service stations on Urubi Street in the Iyaro neighbourhood. Departure times and destinations need careful advance checking.

If you're **driving** on the main road east out of the city (the A232), you'll find that the road goes to Onitsha, from where you branch either to Enugu by the expressway link, or south on the A6 to Owerri and Port Harcourt. You'll hear dire warnings about this route, as it holds something of a record for accidents in Nigeria – and that says a lot. If you're going directly to **Port Harcourt**, you might want to consider the A2 rainforest route via Sapele and **Warri**. Look for palm-wine sellers along the roadside, but don't even inhale near the stuff if you're behind the wheel.

There are normally several **flights** a day linking Benin City with Lagos and Abuja. Try Arik Air (ⓦwww.arikair.com) or Aero (ⓦwww.aero.com); buy tickets at the airport.

Just off Ring Road is the **Oba's Market**, once one of the largest and most animated in the region. **Moneychangers** hang out on the north side of Oba Market Street by Ibiwe Street, with major **banks** nearby on Ring Road. The most central **post office** and **NITEL** call office are just off Ring Road, on Akpakpava Road, but the **GPO** is just south of it on Airport Road. A number of places offer **Internet access**, among them the Presok Cybercafé at 128 Akpakpava Rd, which is open 24/7, and Vic Biz International, off Ring Road on the second floor at 7 Akpakpava Rd (daily 7am–8.30pm); both places charge ₦100/hr.

Accommodation

As you would expect in a big city, there are plenty of hotels to choose from in Benin, from basic sleazy dives to attempts at international reputation-building. Several are conveniently located near Ring Road.

Central 76 Akpakpava Rd ☎052/250 536. A little run-down, but perfectly acceptable s/c rooms with a/c, or cheaper ones with fans. Listen out for live-music performances in the popular courtyard bar. ❷

Hotel Felona 6 Dawson Rd, off Akpakpava Rd ☎052/251 194. A fairly new, very comfortable hotel with a/c rooms, satellite TV and a good restaurant. ❺

Lixborr 4 Sakpoba Rd, Idubor Arts Gallery Building ☎052/256 699. Ideally situated near the museum and King's Square. Comfortable a/c, s/c accommodation. ❸

Motel Benin Plaza 1 Reservation Rd ☎052/254 779 or 254 742 ⓦwww.motelbeninplaza.com. In a quiet neighbourhood, with chalets grouped around a pool, each with a/c and satellite TV. There's a pleasant bar and restaurant serving Nigerian and European dishes. ❺

Saidi Centre 271 Murtala Muhammed Way, near Sapele Rd junction ☎052/252 125 ⓕ250 588. Large, popular (and somewhat kitsch) hotel with a/c rooms and suites with satellite TV. Good Chinese and European restaurant, pool and bar. ❺

University Palace 4 Federal Government Girls College Rd, Ugbowo ☎052/600 361 or 602 095. The guesthouse of the University of Benin, but located outside campus, some 5km north of town. Some rooms have a/c, and there's a restaurant with assorted European and Nigerian dishes. ❸

YWCA 29 Airport Rd ☎052/252 186. Budget accommodation for women only. Central and friendly. ❷

The City

King's Square, as its name (if not its various bronze statues) would suggest, is where you'll find the **Oba's Palace**. You may have to ask someone to point it out among the various buildings along the square, because the exterior is bland. The equally modest interior of the palace can be visited by prior arrangement (addressing your letter to The Secretary to Oba, Oba's Palace, Benin City, Edo State), though you'll have to state the date you want to visit and provide a return address. The *oba* himself never makes public appearances except for festivals or important court or state occasions. By simply showing up at the palace, on the other hand, you're virtually guaranteed to find someone willing to recount the history and give a short tour of the grounds outside the palace.

The **Benin National Museum**, in the middle of Ring Road (daily 9am–4pm; N20) – when the traffic's heavy, it's a life-risking manoeuvre getting to it – contains many sacred royal treasures and some of the legendary artworks of the former empire. Most of the kingdom's treasures were stolen and taken abroad following the British invasion of 1897, so that today Benin can claim only the world's third largest collection of Benin art – after London and Berlin. It's an impressive collection nonetheless and well displayed: there are examples of the **bronze plaques** that lined the palace interior together with masks, ivory works and a series of heads exemplifying the three distinct periods of an art form that spanned five centuries.

If you're interested in the vestiges of the **old city wall** – once a complex series of ramparts amounting to hundreds of kilometres of earthworks radiating out from the city, and the world's second largest man-made structure after China's Great Wall – there's a small morsel of the inner wall on Ibiwe Street, northwest of Ring Road. **Chief Orokhiri Norie-Eson House** at 19 Ibiwe St is one of the few buildings left which survived the 1897 British onslaught; it faces a nice old colonial building across the street at no. 14. A larger chunk of city wall – or at least a mound that used to be the city wall – can be seen to the southeast on **Sakpoba Road**, and on Sapele Road, 100m past the Agil station and immediately after the Oredo Primary Health Care Centre. Here too, you can just about see the **moat**, a defensive ditch dug on its outside to supplement the wall and provide the earth to build it. Both the moat and the wall are now largely overgrown with vegetation.

The best place for buying **crafts**, naturally including brass and bronze busts, is on **Igun Street**, renamed Brass Casters Street since a UNESCO-funded project reinstated what had almost become a lost art in the city. There are further workshops and galleries on Airport Road and Mission Road.

Eating

One of the best markets for street food is **New Benin Market** northeast of the centre. You can get some of the town's best fruit here during the day and cheap finger-food (*suya* or grilled chicken, for example) at night, when this turns into a very active area and many shops and bars stay open late. A smaller market in a similar vein near Ring Road is the **Agbado Market**, on Akpakpava Road, just next to the *Central Hotel*.

For Nigerian **food**, the *Suzzy Restaurant* isn't at all bad; it's at 2 Hudson Lane, off Akpakpava Road by no. 95. Over on Murtala Muhammed Way, just off Sapele Road, you can get decent, moderately priced Chinese food at *Rima Restaurant*, which also has a snack bar. Just across the street, the *Saidi Centre* hosts the city's best restaurant, with a Chinese, Lebanese and European menu, and the energetic owner is always in the background.

Okomu National Park

The **Okomu National Park** (N200) is a patch of indigenous forest of the kind that blanketed southern Nigeria before the nineteenth-century European invasion and, as such, it's an important island of biodiversity. Some 35km west of Benin City, near the small town of **UDO**, it makes an easy day-trip. You might make it to Okomu by taxi, but most visitors drive themselves. It's possible to **stay** in the forest reserve, in one of twelve air-conditioned en-suite chalets at *Okomu Ecoresort*, in the heart of the forest (℡0808/468 0294 ⓦwww.okomuecoresort.com ⑤). Despite encroaching development, a herd of **forest elephants** is hanging on at Okomu, as well as scattered bush cows and yellow-backed duikers, plus various species of monkey including the endangered white-throated guenon, more than two hundred species of bird and seven hundred species of butterfliy, as well as the usual startling variety of reptiles and invertebrates. Two, canopy-level **observation platforms**, thirty and forty metres respectively up silk cotton trees, provide good viewing possibilities (you have to climb up enclosed ladders: it's not for the faint-hearted), and there's a river where you can swim.

14.3

The southeast

The dominant ethnic group in the southeast is **Igbo**, although numerous other peoples also live in the region. The whole southeastern area, from Enugu south to Port Harcourt, has also been called the "Taiwan of Nigeria", due in part to its heavy industry and oil riches, but mostly because of its industries, capable of fixing and copying almost any product. There are a number of thriving commercial towns in the region which might provide a useful stopover on longer journeys, though none are worth going out of your way to see. The **Niger River** passes through one such town, **Onitsha**, which was heavily damaged in the Biafran War but has quickly regained its commercial buzz. **Enugu**, to the northeast, survived the civil war largely unscathed, and is a vital economic centre, home to many multinational firms.

As the Niger River approaches the coast, it fans out into the endless meandering channels of the **Delta Region**. The major city in the area, **Port Harcourt**, is another modern conurbation that has grown quickly since independence. You'll understand why when you see the **oil flares** belching black smoke and flames on the seaward horizon: this is the heart of Nigeria's oil country, with years of corruption depriving locals of the huge wealth the black gold has created. The growing **conflict in the delta** and the frequency of **abductions** of foreign expats for ransom ("white gold" according to the local gangs) mean you should avoid the whole region, including Port Harcourt, unless your visit is really essential – a point reiterated by most countries' travel advisory services.

Further to the east, in contrast, **Calabar** is scenic and relatively relaxing, spreading over a hill overlooking the Calabar River. Once a big slave-port, the town is one of Nigeria's most enjoyable. It's the obvious base for a visit to one of Nigeria's most exciting natural-history sites, the **Cross River National Park**. As at the long-established **Obudu Cattle Ranch**, a little further north, there are **gorillas** in these protected hill forests, and basic facilities are in place for visitors to at least *try* to see them.

Igbo-speakers (the language and people were also formerly called Ibo) have played an important role in the history of Nigeria. Unlike the Yoruba of the southwest, or the city-states of the centre and north, the people of the southeast forest country have traditionally maintained much more clan-based societies with fewer social hierarchies, centred around the village and its all-male council. The lack of evolution of a central kingdom among the Igbo is partly explained by the difficulties of communication in their rainforest enviomnent.

Largely spurning slavery in their own culture, the Igbo communities fell easy prey when slavery was imposed from outside from the sixteenth to the nineteenth centuries. Later, having few cumbersome political structures to set up barriers, they quickly adapted to the new ideas of colonial society – its stress on personal achievement, on virtue earned through work and self-advancement, on business acumen and the creation of wealth. By the time World War II was over, the Igbo were clearly dominating the roles allowed to native Nigerians by the colonial government. Their success was partly responsible for the bloody trauma of **Biafra** – the still-born Igbo republic declared in 1967 – which resulted in civil war and a federal blockade that brought widespread starvation. Yet the Igbo's enforced ingenuity and technological inventiveness during the three years of isolation gave the region a boost from which it was to benefit for years afterwards. The Igbo's continued dynamism remains a source of frustration among other groups in Nigeria – in particular the Hausa and Fulani Muslims of the north. It has tended to earn southeast Nigerians a reputation as survivors – after all, they have the **oil**. But having relatively poor representation in the Federal Republic's formal political structures (and those representatives often corrupt and rarely called to account) has meant an acknowledged deficit of infrastructure and social services in the southeastern states. The Igbo's image in Nigeria is a cruelly contradictory one which has parallels with many commercially successful peoples around the world. Meanwhile, the dream of an independent Biafra is far from dead, and many Igbo believe that its eventual realization is just a matter of time.

Enugu

In sharp contrast to its neighbour to the west, Benin City, **ENUGU**, capital of Enugu State and the effective capital of Igboland, is a town without a long history. It was founded in 1909 when **coal deposits** were discovered in the area. Some time later iron ore was also found, and when the railway came through in 1916, the town's economic future was mapped out. It became capital of the Eastern Region in the 1930s (most of the large government buildings date from this era) and later was the headquarters of the secessionist republic of Biafra. Although the town was all but deserted during the civil war, it has long since rediscovered its vitality. Industry has taken off and there's even a Mercedes assembly plant, which must be some crude indicator of local prosperity. Enugu displays a certain colonial charm and has the odd, shady open space, but its main interest is as the putative capital of the Igbo region, and a good place to hang out and meet people despite the lack of obvious sights.

Some 3km north of the centre, at 58 Abakaliki Rd, the **National Museum** (daily 8am–4pm; free) houses cultural artefacts from the area, including carvings and masquerade objects, costumes and fabrics, musical instruments and weapons. It doesn't get many visitors, so you may have to wait while someone fetches the key. A number of **city parks** dot Enugu, including the Murtala Muhammed Park, west of the centre across from the bustling new market; jacarandas and other flowering trees make it a pleasant place to relax in the afternoon heat.

RESTAURANTS & BARS

Bush Bar	3
Emily	4
Palm Wine Bar	5
Raya Chinese	1
Star Restaurant	2

ACCOMMODATION

Grand Metropole	E
Lucha Guest House	F
Modotel	B
Nike Lake Resort	A
Pan Afric	C
Placia Guest House	G
Zodiac	D

Practicalities

Most vehicles arrive at **Ogbete motor park**, slap-bang in the centre of town, but you may be dropped at **Garki motor park**, on Agbani Road 3km south of town, in which case you'll probably want to take a taxi or *okada* into town. The **airport**, 5km north of town, is served by buses and taxis. The area around Okpara Avenue is

Most vehicles leave from **Ogbete motor park**. There are two main yards, with southbound vehicles for Port Harcourt, Aba and Umuahia leaving from near the Holy Ghost Cathedral, while northbound and westbound vehicles leave from Okpara Avenue opposite the prison. Others line Market Road and Okpara Avenue between the two yards. Other vehicles leave from **Garki motor park**. Arik Air (ⓦwww.arikair .com) and Aero (ⓦwww.acn.aero) between them offer a least a daily **flight** to Lagos, and Arik also flies several times a day to Abuja. Tickets can be bought most easily at the airport itself.

where you'll find most of the banks and the **post office**, with **NITEL** next door. Enugu's vast **administrative district** straggles off behind. On Ogui Road you'll find a branch post office, plus several **bureaux de change** – one cluster at the southern end, and another in the row of shops adjoining the stadium.

Accommodation

There's a decent selection of mid-range **hotels** in Enugu, though inexpensive places are thin on the ground.

Grand Metropole 19 Ogui Rd ☎042/251 971 or 252 235. Flamboyant decor, clean and comfortable a/c rooms, and a decent restaurant and bar. ❸

Lucha Guest House Nweko Lane, off Ogidi St ☎042/253 795. Budget guesthouse with friendly staff and decent s/c rooms, though the water comes in buckets, and electricity supply is sporadic. ❷

Modotel 2 Club Rd, off Garden Ave ☎042/258 780 ⓕ258 868. A sparkling international-class set-up in the heart of the administrative district, with a wide range of facilities and surprisingly reasonable prices. ❺

Nike Lake Resort by Nike Lake ☎042/557 000 ⓦwww.proteahotels.com. The takeover of *Nike Lake* by the South-African *Protea* franchise has transformed this grand old resort, set in extensive grounds. Two hundred and sixteen a/c international-standard rooms, with an excellent restaurant, cocktail bar, pool and two tennis courts. ❻

Pan Afric 24 Kingsway Rd, GRA ☎042/256 089 or 255 248. Elegant gardens and reasonably priced s/c rooms equipped with a/c and satellite TV. ❸

Placia Guest House 25 Edinburgh Rd, Ogui New Layout ☎042/255 851 or 251 565. Choice of s/c, a/c rooms with TV and telephone in this good-value, well-kept guesthouse in the older part of town. Good restaurant and bar, and exceptionally nice staff. ❸

Zodiac 5/7 Rangers Ave, Independence Layout ☎042/457 900 ⓔzodiachotels.enugu@skannet .com. Busy, well-established hotel, with a pool, excellent restaurant and s/c rooms with a/c and satellite TV. ❺

Eating and drinking

Enugu is not a terribly inspiring place gastronomically speaking, but you won't starve. Station Road has a smattering of small **chop houses**, and there are several cheap Nigerian restaurants in the stadium complex on Ogui Road, most of them on the upper floor. *Emily* at 3 Market Rd offers similar fare – rice, *eba* and so on, with a choice of two or three soups to accompany the starch. For reasonable fast-food (fried chicken, *jollof* rice and the like), try *Star Restaurant* on Ogui Road near the stadium. The *Bush Bar*, off Agbani Road by Mayor bus stop and the junction of Kenneth Road, is a chop house specializing in the likes of grasscutter, porcupine, crocodile and wild pig. *Full Time Garden* by *Modotel* on Club Road is a livelier Nigerian restaurant and bar, with open-air drinking and dining. For something more international, try the pleasant but pricey *Raya Chinese Restaurant* at 77 Ogui Rd. **Palm wine** isn't always very good, and is sometimes adulterated, but one place that does serve up a tasty mugful of the real McCoy is a bar opposite the entrance to *Placia Guest House*, which gets fresh deliveries around noon every day.

Onitsha

ONITSHA, about halfway between Benin City and Enugu, was almost completely destroyed during the Biafran conflict, and has since been rebuilt as a congested, frenetic commercial centre. Famous as the location of the earliest indigenously published literature in Nigeria (novels and tracts from 1949, under the label "Onitsha Market Literature"), it's still a highly energetic place – though your first impression might be that there's no compelling reason to stay, except for an unavoidable night stop. If you are staying, there's decent **accommodation** at the *Traveller's Palace Hotel*, conveniently located near the motor park at 8 Agbu Ogbuefi St, Woliwo Layout (☏046/211 013 or 211 025; ❷). Also worth considering are the nearby, excellent-value *People's Club Guest House*, off Owerri Road (☏046/212 717; ❷), with huge if rather tatty rooms; and the more upmarket *Bolingo Hotels and Towers*, at 74 Zik Ave, Fegge (☏046/210 948; ❸), where all rooms have air conditioning.

Umuahia

Midway along the expressway linking Enugu and Port Harcourt, **UMUAHIA**'s large central market and quiet tree-lined streets belie the days when this town served as a strategic military headquarters in the Biafran conflict. As a fitting memorial to that conflict, a **National War Museum** (Mon–Fri 9am–5.30pm, Sat & Sun 10am–5.30pm; ₦120) has been set up in the former Eastern Nigeria TV relay station from where the *Voice of Biafra* was transmitted. It's an interesting collection of memorabilia, with period photographs accompanying displays of guns, swords and uniforms. Outside you can wander among the "Red Devil" Biafran troop transporters, field guns and aircraft. Most striking among the latter is the tiny "Baby Biafran" bomber, adapted from a Swedish sports plane and utterly dwarfed by the Nigerian Air Force's Ilyushin, supplied by Egypt along with pilots, whose random bombings earned it the nickname "Genocide". Also in the grounds, a small **café** has been set up on board the NSS *Bonny*, a former naval vessel that was instrumental in the federal forces' capture of Bonny Island from the Biafrans. The museum is located on War Museum Road, which leads off the main Enugu road at the eastern end of Umuahia. Across town from the museum, you can also visit its annexe, the private **bunker** at 15A Okpara Ave, GRA, from where Biafran leader, Colonel Emeka Ojukwu, commanded his troops.

Adjoining the bunker is a **guesthouse** offering cheap accommodation in functional, government-issue rooms (no phone; ❷). Nearby, the grandiose *Hotel Royal Dangrete* off Eze Akanu Ibaru Road (☏088/221 955 or 222 102, ☞223 787; ❼) offers deluxe rooms and an independent electricity supply. In the centre of town, reasonable budget accommodation in s/c rooms, some with a/c and/or TV, or ultra-cheap non-s/c singles, can be had at *Panadim Guest House*, 28 Warri Rd (☏088/220 518; ❷). Around the corner on the same block, the *Lily Christus Standard Canteen* on Ibeku Road has good chop at very low prices.

Aba

Continuing south from Umuahia, the road bangs into the unprepossessing outskirts of **ABA**, the capital of Abia State and an ugly commercial town, with its vast **Ariara Market** spilling onto the expressway. If you choose, or are obliged, to stop here, the **Museum of Colonial History** (daily 9am–5pm; ₦20) is only a two-minute walk from the chaos of the main motor park, on the A342 Ikot Ekpene Road (leading east out of town). The small, orderly collection, housed in a wooden British administrative building, traces the history of Nigeria through informative exhibits of photos from pre-colonial times to the 1960s, but is too dark to see properly during power cuts. There's a cluster of crafts shops, chop bars and weaving huts in the museum compound.

Among the more inexpensive **hotels**, the *Ariss Plaza Hotel*, at 70B Ikot Ekpene Rd (℡082/221 731 @gincov@phca.linkserve.com; ❷), and the newer *Lekota Springs Hotel* at 49 Ikot Ekpene Rd (℡0803/341 2138; ❸), are central and fairly good value. Further from the town centre, and more upmarket, are the modern *Binez Hotel*, at 5/7 Nwogu St, Umungasi, where all rooms are s/c and a/c (℡082/440 030 ⓕ222 941; ❺); and the deluxe *Crystal Park Hotel*, Crystal Park Avenue, off Port Harcourt Road (℡082/221 588 or 221 742; ❻).

Port Harcourt and around

Capital of Rivers State, **PORT HARCOURT** ("Po-ta-ko" in Pidgin, PH to expats) promotes itself as the "**Garden City**". Given its location in the rainforest, it would be remarkable if it wasn't green, at least in parts. But it's no garden. The area first came to prominence during World War I, as a result of military operations mounted from here against German Kamerun. But Port Harcourt's modern wealth – and problems – are thanks to the **oil wells** that have sprouted throughout the region since 1956, when commercial quantities were discovered in **Oloibiri**. The first shipload of Nigerian crude was exported from Port Harcourt in 1958 and the country was launched on a new economic course that promised rapid industrial development and prosperity. Port Harcourt acquired a modern aspect, with wide avenues, flyovers and high-rise blocks easily outshooting the last of the giant forest trees left standing at the city limits.

Yet the "**Old Township**", founded in 1913, has survived the city's rapid growth and, were it not for the serious security risks of travelling in the delta, then this part of the city, down by the waterfront, could still be recommended as a small town with a good deal of charm. There are expats – some of whom have lived in Port Harcourt, or PH as many know it, for years – who phlegmatically put up with the menace and even thrive on the adrenalin, guarded by armed police and soldiers and aided by regular visits to the bars and restaurants in the new town. They know their streets and neighbourhoods and they stay closely in touch with each other. If this isn't your scene, now is not the time to go exploring what is a potentially dangerous city. If you are visiting Port Harcourt, take a good look at the expats' website ⓦwww.oyibosonline.com.

Orientation, arrival and information

The international **airport** is 40km northwest of town (a 45min ride into the centre by taxi – official cabs are dark blue with a white stripe), but all flights currently use the **airforce base** on the north side of the city centre while the international airport is being refurbished. If you're using road transport, you're likely to be dropped at either the **Abali motor park** (also known as **Leventis motor park**), located on Aba Road by the flyover, or at the **Diobu Mile 3 motor park** at Owerri Road, which is a good 5km north of the old town. Fortunately, public transport connections are good, with plenty of minibuses, drops and *okadas* connecting Abali ("Park" or "Flyover") and Mile 3 with most parts of town. A minibus service connects Abali motor park with Lagos Road bus station ("Lagos") opposite the Old Market, while another runs south, to Creek Road, then Churchill Road and Harold Wilson Drive.

Port Harcourt is divided by the **flyover** – a freeway overpass that's something of a symbol of the town's modernity – into two distinct zones, the new town to the north and the old town to the south. The **Aba Road**, also called the **Expressway**, runs clean through the new part of town, from the air-force base in the northern suburbs down to the flyover. "Expressway" is no exaggeration, since cars seem to be

More than ninety percent of Nigeria's export earnings come from **crude oil**, and two states astride the mouth of the Niger – Delta and Rivers – produce more than 85 percent of it. But the local population – most of whom belong to various **ethnic minorities** – have seen precious little of the wealth their states generate. Instead, they have seen their land and rivers polluted and health problems in their communities arising from high carbon-dioxide emissions at gas flare-offs. Billions of dollars' worth of crude oil are extracted each year, while they themselves are left in abject poverty.

The region's largest ethnic group, the **Ijaw**, contended on independence that they had never ceded their sovereignty to the British and were therefore not part of Nigeria. In the 1970s, local communities began lobbying the government for a share of oil resources to compensate for pollution and destruction of farmland and fisheries by the oil industry, to little avail.

In 1990, the well-known publisher and TV writer, **Ken Saro-Wiwa**, penned an article in the government-owned *Sunday Times*, entitled "The Coming War in the Delta", in which he accused the Shell oil company of racism towards the Delta peoples, and called on the government to give local residents a share of the oil wealth. To campaign for this on behalf of his people, the Ogoni, he set up a pressure group called the Movement for the Survival of the Ogoni People (**MOSOP**) which, thanks to Saro-Wiwa, was able to link up with environmental groups in the West and generate worldwide publicity.

The security forces began to combat opposition to the oil companies, often brutally. Faced with a demonstration by villagers from Umuechem in October 1990, Shell requested protection from the police, who broke up the protest and shot dead eighty demonstrators – a pattern subsequently repeated elsewhere. In July 1993, a more sinister tactic emerged: members of a neighbouring ethnic group, the Andonis, carried out two **massacres** of Ogonis for no apparent reason. Government sources blamed ethnic rivalry, but witnesses saw men in military uniforms directing operations. The government also began a campaign of harassment against Saro-Wiwa, banned unauthorized foreigners from visiting Ogoniland and set up a brutal **Internal Security Task Force** (subsidized by Shell).

MOSOP also had its thugs, unemployed youths who branded as traitors any Ogoni leaders inclined to conciliation. When a mob of them beat four Ogoni moderates to death, the authorities arrested Saro-Wiwa and the MOSOP leadership, convicted them of the murders and, in November 1995, hanged them, despite an international outcry.

out to break speed records as they scream down it; pedestrian overpasses are few and far between. Banks and various governmental buildings line the Aba Road, while **Azikwe Road**, south of the flyover, is effectively the city centre, where you'll see the towering state headquarters of several banks.

Moneychangers hang out in front of the *Presidential Hotel* in the new town, and in the Old Township on the four westernmost blocks of Victoria Street (parallel with Aggrey Street, a block to its south). There's also a legitimate bureau de change operated by Emerald Tours on Aba Road a short walk south of Garrison junction. The **GPO** is on Station Road, north of the Old Township, with **NITEL** directly behind it. The offices of the **Rivers State Tourism Board** are at 35/37 Aba Rd (☏084/334 901), but don't expect information or assistance. The **British High Commission** Liaison Office is at 300 Olu Obasanjo Rd (☏084/237 173 ⓔbhcliaison@phca.linkserve.com).

Accommodation

Port Harcourt's security situation being as it is, if you have to be here, you should only stay at one of the two most secure upmarket hotels. At the time of writing, the city was under a nightly curfew.

The Internal Security Task Force now started terrorizing communities other than the Ogoni, and the **violence escalated**. In 1997, a gathering of Ijaw community representatives demanded the companies suspend all operations "pending the resolution of the issue of resource ownership and control in the Ijaw area". When Ijaw youths protested in support of this in Yenagoa, security forces opened fire on them, killing dozens. This was taken as a declaration of war, and youths began sabotaging pipelines, occupying company premises and kidnapping oil workers. The oil companies started employing people from certain communities to guard installations against others, sparking off **intercommunal feuds**. This added to tensions already existing between some ethnic groups, notably between Ijaw, Itsekiris and Urhobos in Warri, which erupted in 1999 into riots resulting in the deaths of some two hundred people.

1999 saw a series of horrific incidents. In **Choba**, Rivers State, following attacks by local youths on the American pipeline-laying firm Wilbros, police and troops took over the village and raped 67 women, including girls as young as 12, atrocities that shocked the nation. Soon afterwards, a gang took over part of **Odi**, the second-biggest town in Bayelsa, and abducted and killed twelve police sent to arrest them. The government responded by **sending in troops** who razed the town completely, killing several hundred people and evicting thousands more. The massacre was followed by police and army attacks on Ijaw communities throughout Bayelsa, Delta and Rivers states. Since then, militants have repeatedly occupied oil installations and abducted expat workers to extract ransoms and drive the news agenda. Despite internal rivalries and conflicts of interest between delta leaders, an organization called the **Movement for the Emancipation of the Niger Delta (MEND)** emerged in 2005. One of its leaders, **Mujahid Dokubo-Asari** went to Abuja for talks with the federal government, and has been in detention ever since. Throughout 2006 and much of 2007, MEND rebels, based in the delta's creeks, abducted hundreds of foreign oil-workers in targeted ransom hits and acquired a huge arsenal of weaponry.

While MEND agreed a **ceasefire** to give newly elected President Yar'Adua time to address their claims, late 2007 saw a **night-time curfew** imposed across Rivers State in the wake of vicious (though less politicized) gang-fighting across Port Harcourt, involving armed robbers, oil thieves, gun traffickers and co-opted elements of the armed forces sent in to restore order.

🏃 **Le Meridien** Ogeyi Place, 45 Tombia St, GRA 2 ⊕084/461 770. Perhaps the most luxurious hotel in Nigeria, with 86 en-suite rooms, each with whirlpool bath, Internet, minibar and electronic safe. The hotel has an upmarket restaurant and a cocktail lounge. ⑥

🏃 **Protea Hotel Garden** City Evo Crescent, GRA 2 ⊕084/463 401 ⓦwww.proteahotels.com/gardencity. A luxurious new addition, this offers 106 en-suite bedrooms, with minibar, satellite TV and electronic safe. ⑥

The City

These days, Port Harcourt for most foreign visitors and expats means strictly the newer parts of the city on the northern side. The **Old Township**, down on Dockyard Creek, in the crowded southern quarter of the city is, however, the true heart of Port Harcourt and the most atmospheric and interesting part of town (if and when it becomes safe to visit again). Aggrey Road runs through the heart of the Old Township and constitutes the high street. From this district you get striking views of the distant oil flares as you take in a wide variety of stalls, restaurants and shops. On the southern side of the township, down near the creek, you'll find two of Port Harcourt's main markets – the wonderfully chaotic **Creek Road Market**, excellent for fish, and **New Layout Market**.

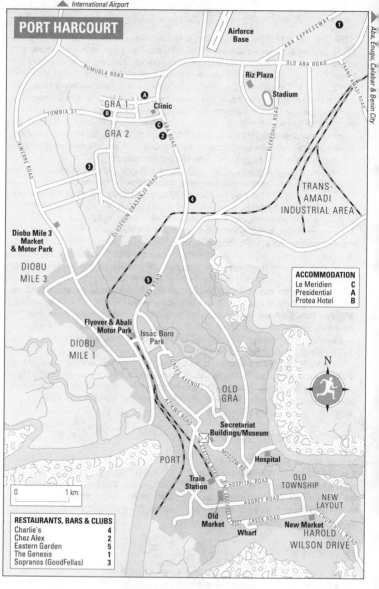

PORT HARCOURT

International Airport

Airforce Base

Aba Expressway

Old Aba Road

Trans-Amadi Road

Aba, Enugu, Calabar & Benin City

Rumuola Road

Riz Plaza

Stadium

GRA 1

Clinic

Tombia St

GRA 2

Aba Road

Elekeohia Road

Ikwerre Road

Olusegun Obasanjo Road

TRANS-AMADI INDUSTRIAL AREA

Diobu Mile 3 Market & Motor Park

DIOBU MILE 3

Aba Road

ACCOMMODATION
Le Meridien   C
Presidential   A
Protea Hotel   B

Flyover & Abali Motor Park

Isaac Boro Park

DIOBU MILE 1

Forces Avenue

OLD GRA

Azikwe Road

Secretariat Buildings/Museum

Moscow Rd

Hospital

PORT

Station Terr

Train Station

Hospital Road

Aggrey Road

OLD TOWNSHIP

NEW LAYOUT

Kaduna Street

Creek Road

Churchill Road

Old Market

Wharf

New Market

HAROLD WILSON DRIVE

N

0   1 km

RESTAURANTS, BARS & CLUBS
Charlie's   4
Chez Alex   2
Eastern Garden   5
The Genesis   1
Sopranos (GoodFellas) 3

In the northern direction, the Secretariat Complex at the bottom of Azikwe Road in the **Old GRA** district, houses the small **State Museum** (Mon–Fri 7am–4pm; free). Its examples of regional art include outstanding examples of the colourful, often bizarre local **masks**, plus a few domestic utensils from major ethnic groups in the area – Ijaw, Ikwerre, Etche, Ogoni, Ekpeye and Ogba. Just off the Aba Road, the **Kaduna Street Public Market** is a good place for produce, including the fresh fish which is so plentiful around here. Other markets are in **Diobu neighbourhood** at Mile 1 and Mile 3. Azikwe Road has a decent showing of **supermarkets**. For a good selection of **books**, and nice coffee, try Books on the Loose, Plot 19, Riz Plaza, Stadium Rd (℡084/486 947).

Eating, drinking and nightlife

People have been going out less in the evenings in recent years, as PH's security situation has worsened, especially not down to the Old Township. In the past, for inexpensive eating, expats would head to "Suya Street" – their name for Ogu Street, two blocks east of King Amachree Street – an atmospheric road lined with food stalls and glowing with the warm light of wood fires in the evening. Current favourites in the **new town** include:

Chez Alex 175B Aba Rd. Good range of well-prepared Lebanese, Chinese, Nigerian and European dishes.

Eastern Garden Chinese beneath the airline offices, 1 Ogbunabali Layout, 47 Aba Rd. Vies with *4,5,6* at the *Presidential* for the accolade of best Chinese restaurant in town.

The Genesis near 1st Artilery Junction, 198 Rumuogba Estate. Long-established and highly regarded eating-house, with a variety of menus, including Chinese, continental and Nigerian.

Hotel Presidential Aba Expressway. Hosts the excellent *Why Not* for Lebanese and European dishes, and also offers the *4,5,6*, a Chinese restaurant with excellent cooking from a Chinese chef.

Ororo at Le Meridian 45 Tombia St ℡084/571 488. The closest you'll get to "fine dining" in PH, with an ever-changing menu and great-value Sun buffet at ₦2500.

Nightlife

The **curfew** of 2007 knocked out nightlife in Port Harcourt, but the city has numerous **nightclubs**, mostly catering to expat oil-workers' tastes (or what club-owners imagine expat oil-workers want). Assuming you're allowed out, they'll be open and you should ask around to find out which are currently most popular or likely to have live music at weekends, and which have the best security. The most famous PH club, formerly a popular watering-hole and karaoke bar, is *Sopranos* – formerly *GoodFellas* – at 7 Abacha Rd, GRA 2 (℡0803/312 3878), which was the scene of a kidnapping of seven oil workers in 2006, and was in the headlines again in 2007 when the British–Nigerian owner's 3-year old daughter was briefly abducted.

Moving on from Port Harcourt

Port Harcourt has vehicles to almost everywhere – it's literally at the end of the road, or at least the Old Township is – and transport isn't hard to find. There's transport to the nearer towns (Owerri and Onitsha), and to Ibadan and the Borikiri terminal in Lagos, from **Mile 3 motor park**, though for services to Calabar, Benin City and just about everywhere else, head to **Abali park**. To get a seat on the cheapest luxury buses, you'll need to book a day in advance, or start very early.

There are plenty of flights to **Lagos** – on Virgin Nigeria, Bellview, Aero and Chanchangi, among others – plus five flights a week to **Abuja** on Overland, and international services to London (on Virgin) and Paris (on Air France). Carriers and schedules change rapidly as security varies. The rebuilding of the international airport also brought flights into the city air-force base as a temporary, but convenient, arrangement. **Airline offices** include: Bellview (℡084/230 518–9), Air France (℡084/238 106) and KLM (℡084/235 468), all of which have offices above the *Eastern Garden* restaurant at 47 Aba Rd; Aero at the airport (℡084/230 006 ⓔreservations.phc@acn.aero); British Airways at the State Tourist Hotel Corporation Building on Aba Road (℡084/238 351 or 233 011); and Swiss, represented by Panalpina, Plot 463/4, Trans-Amadi Layout (℡084/238 679–80).

Calabar and around

It's not just its position perched high on the hills overlooking the river that makes **CALABAR** such a pleasant town to visit. There's a general good ambience created by its compact size and the outgoing nature of the Efik, Ibibio and Kalabari residents. Calabar offers a fine introduction to the nicer facets of Nigerian life and, if you're heading east, it's a good place to prepare for in-your-face Cameroon and the rigours of Central Africa. The waterfront sums up its elegantly run-down, colonial feel: apart from Lagos, Calabar is the only Nigerian city near the coast, and the tension that crackles in so many other large towns is absent, as if whisked away on the ocean breeze. Calabar also has the best **culinary reputation** in the country, with lots of varied, traditional cooking. Nigerians say that if a Calabar woman cooks for you, you'll never leave the town. If you've any choice about when you visit, opt for December, with the streets full of masquerades. A large area near the centre of town becomes an open-air fair for the whole month, with stalls and restaurants creating a festive atmosphere.

Some history

The **Qua** (or Ekoi), who came from the northern woodlands and were principally hunters and farmers, were the first people to settle in the Calabar area. Later migration brought the **Efik** and **Efut** – predominantly fishers and subsistence farmers. The Portuguese arrived in the closing years of the fifteenth century and the economic orientation of the local people slowly shifted to **trading**. By the seventeenth century, the Efik were in control of the lucrative export of **slaves**. Efik settlements in the estuary of the Calabar River developed into trading **city-states** that dealt with the Portuguese, Dutch, French, German and English. Rich and powerful, the rulers took European names to emphasize their importance – the Dukes, the Jameses, the

Moving on from Calabar

Most vehicles go from the **Watt Market motor park**, from where there's regular transport west to **Port Harcourt**, north to **Ekang** (the route you need for Oban Rainforest Reserve and Cameroon) and north to **Ikom** (for Cameroon and northern Cross River State). Crosslines has its own garage in Calabar Road, north of the *Metropolitan Hotel* and runs a daily bus to **Jos** (12–14hr), plus services north to **Ekang** (via Oban village) and **Obudu** (via Ikom), and west to **Aba**. There's also a motor park for **Oban** at the junctions of Akim Qua Town Road and Ndidem Nsang Iso Road. Arik Air, Chanchangi and Virgin Nigeria **fly** daily to Lagos from Calabar's **airport**.

Into Cameroon

Details on crossing into Cameroon by **land** from Ikom are given on p.1168, but the most direct crossing into Cameroon from Calabar is 120km to the northeast, between **Ekang** and **Otu**, at the end of the Oban Division road. For **sea crossings**, there is a regular ferry service direct from Calabar to Limbé (usually twice a week) from Calcemco beach, on the river just north of town; alternatively, boats depart from Oron (see p.1166), 25km away from Calabar, to the Cameroonian town of Idenao, 48km north of Limbé. Ferries from Calabar to Oron leave from near the *Nsikak Hotel*. It's also possible to cross by boat from the seaside border-town of **Ikang** over to **Ekondo beach** and **Bula beach** in Cameroon, near the town of Mundemba, from where you can get transport through Ekondo Titi to Kumba (see p.1273).

Tourist **visas** are usually issued in Calabar with no fuss at the Cameroonian Consulate, 21 Ndidem Nsang Iso Rd (☏087/222 782). They cost CFA30,000 for single entry (CFA60,000 multiple entry), plus CFA1000 for a stamp, and require three passport photos. They normally take two working days to issue, but you may be able to get one on the same day if you come early.

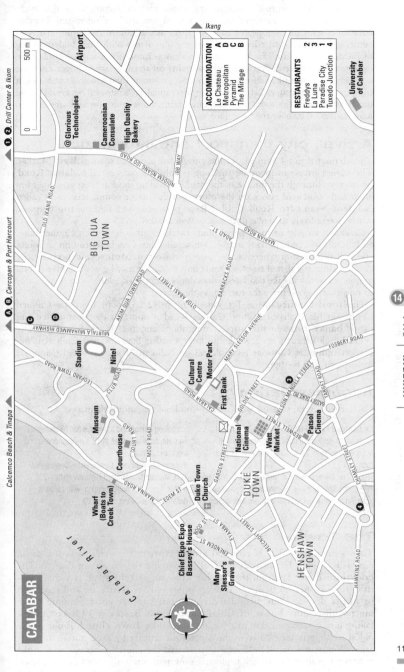

CALABAR

Calabar River

ACCOMMODATION
Le Chateau	A
Metropolitan	D
Pyramid	C
The Mirage	B

RESTAURANTS
Freddys	2
La Luna	3
Paradise City	1
Tuxedo Junction	4

◀ Ikang

Airport

@ Glorious Technologies

Cameroonian Consulate

High Quality Bakery

NOIDEM NSANG ISO ROAD

IBB WAY

BIG QUA TOWN

OLD IKANG ROAD

AKIM QUA TOWN ROAD

ADAZI ST.

MARIAN ROAD

BARRACKS ROAD

OTOP ABASI STREET

MURTALA MUHAMMED HIGHWAY

MARY SLESSOR AVENUE

FOSBERY ROAD

LEOPARD TOWN ROAD

Stadium

Nitel

CLUB ROAD

Cultural Centre

Motor Park

CALABAR ROAD

First Bank

GOLDIE STREET

NELSON MANDELA STREET

BEDWELL STREET

BASSEY DUKE RD

TARGET ROAD

Museum

COURT ROAD

MOOR ROAD

Courthouse

National Cinema

GARDEN STREET

Watt Market

Patsol Cinema

CHAMLEY STREET

Wharf (Boats to Creek Town)

MARINA ROAD

EDEM ST.

Duke Town Church

DUKE TOWN

Chief Ekpo Ekpo Bassey's House

GOLD ST.

ENENDEM ST.

EYAMBA ST.

EKAMBA STREET

BEECHCROFT STREET

HENSHAW TOWN

Mary Slessor's Grave

HAWKINS ROAD

University of Calabar

N

500 m

0

◀ Calcemco Beach & Tinapa

◀ A, B, Cercopan & Port Harcourt

◀ C, D, Drill Center & Ikom

14.3 | **NIGERIA**

14

1163

Henshaws – and welcomed **missionaries**, despite their opposition to the slave trade. Calabar thus became a centre of education and religion, and local rulers gained further advantages with the European trading partners, as the Efik forbade missionaries to come into contact with ethnic groups in the hinterland. With their understanding of European ways, the Efik made the transition as smoothly as anyone could have expected when trade shifted from slaves to **palm oil** and, later, when Nigeria became a colony and the Efik were ruled "indirectly", through their chiefs. At the end of the nineteenth century, Calabar became the capital of Southern Nigeria. During the **Biafran War**, the town was recaptured from the secessionists and served as an important naval base for the federal forces.

Arrival, city transport and information

The **airport** is just 1.5km east of the city. At the centre of town is **Watt Market**. The busiest streets in town are the long-established and central **Calabar Road**, which runs through the middle of the market, dividing foodstuffs on one side from cloth and household goods on the other, and the newer commercial street called **Ndidem Nsang Iso Road**. Calabar Road is where you'll find the **motor park**, where you're likely to arrive, northeast of Watt Market.

Calabar is an easy town to get around. **Taxis**, together with even cheaper buses and motorcycle taxis, provide nearly 24-hour mobility. City buses run on set routes and will usually stop wherever you wave them down. **Motorcycle taxis** usually cost the same as a shared taxi for a short hop, though it may be double this for long transits across town. Like taxi fares, prices double after dark, though you may be able to negotiate a good price for two up on the bike.

The **tourist office** (Mon–Fri 9am–4pm; ☏087/235 606) is in the Cultural Centre on Mary Slessor Avenue. Calabar Road is home to the **post office** and major **banks**, between the market roundabout and the *Metropolitan Hotel*. The **NITEL** call office is up towards the huge Calabar Stadium at 2 Club Rd. You can get **online** at Glorious Technologies on Ndidem Nsang Iso Road (Mon–Sat 8am–10pm, Sun 6–10pm).

Accommodation

Calabar has several pleasant, small, family-run hotels, at affordable prices.

Le Chateau Plot 56 MCC Rd ☏087/238 823/4 ⓦwww.ths-lechateau.com. Good-value, small hotel with satellite TV, a/c, and minibars in each room. ⑥

The Mirage Plot 230 Unit D, Block B, MCC Rd ☏087/236 293/4 ⓦwww.themiragecalabar .com. An award-winning hotel with two restaurants, a smoking lounge and a karaoke bar. All rooms are en suite, have a/c, satellite TV, a minibar and an electronic safe. ⑧

Pyramid Hotels and Conference Centre Plot 160, Murtala Muhammed Highway ☏087/237 642/3. A no-frills budget option, with clean, if distinctly uninspiring, rooms. ⑤

The Town

There's still a good deal of **colonial architecture** in the older parts of Calabar, especially around Henshaw Town, Duke Town and the waterfront districts. The **courthouse**, not far from the Calabar Museum and the river, is a character-istic piece of period design and many other old properties are still inhabited or in use despite their dilapidated condition. Another good example is the nineteenth-century **house of Chief Ekpo Ekpo Bassey** at 19 Boco St, now falling into extravagant disrepair. Nearby, the **Duke Town church** is one of the oldest in Nigeria, established in the nineteenth century by Presbyterian mission-aries. Continuing uphill on Eyamba Street past the church takes you to the **old cemetery** – an enchanting, if neglected, spot, with stunning views over the town and the Calabar River. The tomb of one of southern Nigeria's most influential missionaries, **Mary Slessor**, from Dundee, near Edinburgh, lies here, marked by a plaque.

Recently opened, closed and reopened, Calabar's **Tinapa Business Resort** is the brainchild of former Cross River State governor Donald Duke. Tinapa is a free-trade zone, featuring a multiplex **cinema**, a film studio, retail and wholesale spaces, and a business hotel. The jury is still out on whether Duke's dream will flourish and turn Calabar into the Dubai of West Africa, or whether it will slowly turn white and elephant-shaped.

Calabar Museum

On the hill overlooking the waterfront, **Calabar Museum** (daily 9am–6pm; ₦200) is housed in the **Old Government House**, the former residence of the colonial governor. The building, designed and built in Glasgow and shipped over in pieces, has been beautifully restored. As a museum, it has few, if any, equals in the country.

The museum concentrates on the **history** of old Calabar, rather than on ethnography or art, and the collections are clearly documented and displayed. In fact, there's almost too much to contemplate here in one visit, with a mass of details on trading, missionary activities and colonial administration. It's a remarkable collection spanning pre-colonial days, the slave and palm-oil eras, British invasion and anticolonial resistance, ending with the path to independence. The museum also contains a shop, where you can pick up a miniature Ekpe masquerade doll. In the grounds of the museum, you will come across a small stone **monolith**. This is an example of the strange stone monoliths of Ikom which lie in northern Cross River State – see p.1167.

The Drill Monkey Rehab Center

Northeast of town, off Ndidem Nsang Iso Road, the Oregon-based wildlife conservation group Pandrillus have set up the **Drill Monkey Rehab Center** (Ⓦtinyurl.com/ywfakn), where they take in orphaned drill monkeys and prepare them for release into the wild. The drill – native only to Cross River State in Nigeria, the southwest corner of Cameroon and the island of Bioko in Equatorial Guinea – is one of Africa's most endangered primates, and the biggest threat comes from poachers who hunt it for bush meat. Often, having killed a nursing mother, the poachers will sell the babies as pets – something they become increasingly unsuited for as they grow – and it is these infants, seized by the authorities or given in by members of the public, that are rehabilitated in the centre, which also takes in chimpanzees in similar circumstances. The centre can be visited (daily 9am–5pm; no charge but donations appreciated) and there's usually someone on hand to show you around. It is also possible to visit Pandrillus's other Nigerian project, the **Afi Mountain Drill Ranch** near Katabang in the north of Cross River State (see p.1168).

Cercopan

Based in Ishie Lane, on the north side of town, the **Centre for Education, Research and Conservation of Primates and Nature** (Ⓦwww.cercopan.org; daily 9am–5pm; no charge, donations appreciated) rehabilitates several species of local monkey and relocates them to its forest reserve at **RHOKO**, 120km northeast of Calabar. They welcome visits in town, or – with advance notice – to the reserve, and you can watch various species of guenon (*Cercopithecus*) and red-capped mangabey at close quarters.

Eating, drinking and nightlife

For **food**, try the nationally famous Calabar soup containing periwinkles. For outdoor street-food, Bogobiri Corner has an excellent range of *suya* vendors. *Freddy's Restaurant* at 90 Atekong Drive (Ⓣ087/232 821) is a Calabar institution, run by the popular Ellie, and a popular expat choice, with a menu of mainly continental and Lebanese dishes, and specialities like hummus, pepper steak and avocados stuffed with shrimp.

A number of zesty **clubs** enliven Calabar nights: *La Luna*, on Nelson Mandela Street, has regular live music at weekends; *Paradise City*, at 87 Atekong Drive, off Ndidem Nsang Iso Road, is flashy and always busy, with live reggae or highlife from Wednesday to Saturday; and *Tuxedo Junction*, at 39 Chamley St, loosens its necktie after midnight.

Creek Town

From Calabar's waterfront (Marina Road), you can catch a "fly boat" (motorboat) or a rowing boat to nearby **CREEK TOWN** (also spelt Greek Town: even residents seem to have lost track of the correct name), a one-hour ride up the Calabar River and through the creeks, with dense mangrove greenery reminiscent of scenes from *The African Queen*. On arrival, there's little specifically to visit, but you can wander around and absorb the intimate creekside-village atmosphere. The people here are very proud of the **Creek Town church**, which is, indeed, a fine piece of colonial architecture, one they claim to be older than the church in Duke Town. Some of the houses still have small "factories" where they produce **palm oil** using antiquated nineteenth-century mills from Britain. If you express interest, people will be happy to show you their production methods. The town has a small **market** and numerous **palm-wine bars** – look for the tell-tale phallic gourds that serve as cups, hanging in front of the bars – where you'll find the beverage much fresher, and therefore much less alcoholic and more quaffable, than in Calabar town itself. At one time it was commonly served with grilled **monkey meat**, but the killing of monkeys for bush meat is now illegal and the trade quite clandestine.

Oron

Across the mouth of the Cross River from Calabar, **ORON** is a departure point for **boats to Cameroon**. Boats ply regularly from Oron to the Cameroonian town of **Idenao**, 48km north of **Limbé** (Victoria). Motorboats are the quickest option (3–4hr) for the 150-kilometre sea voyage around the creeks and mangroves, though substantially more expensive than the fishing boats that take up to two days. The latter are commonly taken by local people, but you may be dropped on the coast almost anywhere and then run the risk of missing official entry procedures to Cameroon. Make sure your passport is stamped as soon as possible after arrival.

It's likely you'll have to spend the night in Oron in order to get an early boat to Cameroon, in which case, decent and affordable **accommodation** can be found at the *Maycom Guest House* (❷). You'll find a brilliant collection of regional artwork at Oron's **National Museum**, located right next to the ferry dock and easily visited while waiting for a boat. The Oron district is famous for its woodcarvings, especially the Ekpe figures, used in ceremonies for communication with ancestors. There are some fine examples on display in the museum which is quite extensive, despite being greatly damaged in the Biafran conflict. You can pick up a copy of the *Guide to the Oron National Museum* which is full of information about the musical instruments, bronzes, pottery and carvings on display.

Cross River National Park and around

The natural vegetation of **Cross River State** is almost entirely **rainforest**, though large reaches have been cleared for oil-palm plantations since the early twentieth century. Some of the most exciting wildlife and conservation projects in Africa are currently under development in the two districts of the **Cross River National Park**: the **Oban Division** between Calabar and Ikom, and the **Okwangwo**

Division north of Ikom – the latter with its rediscovered **gorilla** denizens. It was thought the gorilla had disappeared from most of West Africa in the nineteenth century, and from Nigeria and western Cameroon several decades ago, but the WWF has located at least four separate gorilla populations, mostly around Mbe Mountain in the Okwangwo Division. It's thought there may be around a hundred individuals in the park. The park is one of the richest reserves in rainforest plant species in the whole of Africa, and also features some 1500 species of animals, including forest elephant (about 400, all in the Oban Division), duiker, antelope and chimpanzee. Visiting is quite difficult, however, and realistically you are unlikely to see chimps, gorillas or elephants.

Oban Division

Because the main purpose of the park at present is to conserve wildlife rather than to be a tourist attraction, there is little infrastructure and few facilities, and the Oban Division can really only be visited if you have your own transport. From Calabar, you can **rent a vehicle** and obligatory driver through one of the larger hotels.

Turn off the A4-2 road to **Ekang**, near the village of **ANINGEJE** (about fifty minutes' drive north of Calabar: look for the sign indicating the Kwa Falls oil-palm plantation) and have a wander around the dramatic **Kwa Falls**. A little further north from Aningeje, just outside **OBAN** village, **accommodation** can be found at the *Jungle Club*, with simple s/c rooms (❶).

Each village between Oban and the Cameroon border at Ekang has a **Village Liaison Assistant (VLA)**, a resident employee of the Nigeria National Parks, easily tracked down by asking around on arrival. Besides providing up-to-date information on the state of the conservation project and how it affects their local communities, VLAs can also arrange **guided treks** in the forest for a reasonable fee. The forest trail at **MFAMINYEN** (the last village before the border) is the best organized.

You could also drive straight to the park's headquarters at **AKAMKPA**, an hour's drive north of Calabar along the A4 highway to **UGEP** and Ikom. Akamkpa has an **Information Centre** (☏087/222 261 or 221 694 ℱ221 695) and the nearby *Motel de Conscience* has s/c rooms and good food (❶).

Ikom and around

The border town of **IKOM** is hardly a Cross River attraction, but it's busy and bearable enough. The surrounding countryside is famous for the **Ikom Monoliths**, curious stone steles intricately carved with abstract human figures. There are some three hundred of these blocks spread throughout the area, but the easiest examples to reach are near the village of **ALOK**, just off the A4, 50km north of Ikom. You can find a guide in the village. Though initial estimates traced the monoliths to the sixteenth century, they may date as far back as 200 AD. Their origin is unknown, but a researcher and UN arts and culture ambassador, Catherine Acholonu-Olumba, has recently claimed that her deciphering of some of the text on the stones proves that the ancient sea port of **Dilmun**, dating back to 3000 BC, was in fact Calabar (and not an island in the Persian Gulf as is normally believed). It's a lively idea, but one that archeologists have stiffly chosen to ignore, for lack of any published evidence.

If you need to stay in Ikom, the *Lisbon Hotel* at 70 Calabar Rd (❶) is clean and has friendly staff and reasonable food. The town has a number of shops and the usual services. Moneychangers in the market will buy and sell Central African CFA and naira. If you're making for Cameroon, there are regular taxis during the day and early evening to the border post at **MFUM**, 26km to the east.

Okwangwo Division

Hidden in the bush between Ikom and Obudu, the **Okwangwo Division** of Cross River National Park consists of a breathtaking expanse of cloud-drenched mountain

Cross River State's main-crossing point into Cameroon is from **Mfum** to Ekok, south-east of Ikom and northeast of Ekang. Taxis from Ikom will take you to the Nigerian customs and immigration post at Mfum, where you complete border formalities before crossing the bridge into Cameroon (see p.1225). Early in the day, shared vehicles are hard to come by and you may need to charter a taxi or *okada*. **Ekok** is a lively place to stay the night, with something of a Wild West feel about it. There are four basic hotels, several bars and plenty of loud music, but no bank, though moneychangers will sell Central African CFAs for naira, and will also change dollars or euros, though not at a good rate. Naira are acceptable currency for the short journey to **Mamfé** (see p.1277), which has banks. There are also direct vehicles from Ekok to **Bamenda**.

forest, home to a number of rare primates, including gorilla, chimpanzee and drill, as well as duiker, mountain fox and porcupine. A trek along its trails (allow a couple of days at least) will see you crawling through thickets, fording streams and grabbing at branches as you slip on mossy boulders. Expect to come out bruised, battered and blistered – and to have a brilliant time. There are two forest camps at the park, with **tents for hire** and basic catering facilities, but no electricity; bring your own provisions and sleeping gear.

One camp is situated near the small town of **KANYANG**, some 45 minutes from Ikom. If you're relying on public transport, ask to be dropped at Kanyang and follow the signs to the Kanyang forest camp. You may be able to get a local guide here to take you off through the forest to places with evocative names like **Gorilla Rock** and **Swimming Pool Camp** (a large splash pool formed by a waterfall cascading into a limestone gully). You camp out along the way, and you should be prepared for dampness and cold. Don't forget provisions and something to start a fire.

Half an hour further north is **BUATONG**, where you'll find the **park headquarters** for the Okwangwo Division (4km off the main road), where there's accommodation (again, take your own provisions). There's a botanical garden here, and numerous trails for trekking, and you can take guided treks into the heart of this spectacularly beautiful area. To get to Buatong from Calabar by public transport, you'll need to start out early and change at Ikom.

The Afi Mountain Drill Ranch

About 4km south of Kanyang, a track leads 6km west to **KATABANG**, which can be reached by shared taxi and produces some excellent palm wine (visitors to the village traditionally pay a visit first to the chief and bring a courtesy gift, usually a bottle of spirits, though this is not expected if you're just passing through). Some 6km north of Katabang is the **Afi Mountain Drill Ranch**, part of the Afi Mountain Wildlife Sanctuary. Dedicated to the rehabilitation of drill monkeys, the ranch is run, like the centre in Calabar (see p.1165), by the American wildlife charity Pandrillus (W tinyurl.com/ypenpd). As well as rescued and rehabilitated drills and chimps, the area has a small and critically endangered population of Cross River gorillas, though you would be extremely lucky to see any. It also offers excellent bird-watching, with a large migratory swallow roost.

Visitors are welcome, and accommodation can be arranged through the Drill Center in Calabar (T 087/234 310 E drill@infoweb.abs.net; camping ₦1000 per person, or cabins ⑤) – but you should take your own food, and preferably drinking water, or a water purification kit. There is a small access fee to the Wildlife Sanctuary (₦500 per car), and the ranch also levies a small fee for community development (₦250) as part of its commitment to working for the benefit of local residents. If you want to explore the area, wildlife rangers are on hand to act as guides (₦1000/day).

Obudu Cattle Ranch

The best-known attraction in Cross River is **Obudu Cattle Ranch**, in the north of the state. This hill resort and cattle station is spread across the north-facing slopes of Oshie Ridge in the folds of the beautiful **Sonkwala Mountains** (1500–1900m above sea level). Obudu Ranch used to be a fashionable place for oil-industry expats to escape the rough climate of the delta oilfields, as it offers a temperate climate and exotic, fresh garden produce like strawberries and cauliflowers. Today, the 🏃 *Ranch Resort* offers chalet **accommodation** ranging from moderate singles to executive suites, or you can rent a private house (☎087/238 994 ⓦwww.crossriverstate.com/obudu.htm ❺). The ranch gets busy during holidays and **advance bookings** are always advisable. Bebi airstrip is the nearest landing strip (charter flights from Calabar), otherwise it is five hours via shuttle bus from the Cross River Tourism Bureau in Calabar. An 11km **cable-car** service – one of the world's longest – carries guests up to the ranch in spectacular fashion in this remote area (no NEPA here).

More interesting than the putting green or table tennis are the **hiking** opportunities in the district. The best time to visit is just after the rainy season, when the air is clean and fresh, the views are fantastic and the nights almost cold. A path leads from the hotel to a striking waterfall about 7km away. Also in the area is a natural spring – "the grotto" – but most interesting is the **Gorilla Camp**, a thirteen-kilometre trek through dense bush, involving some arduous climbing over hills and valleys. A guide is necessary and even though you're unlikely to see gorillas, the lush mountain scenery is reward in itself.

The easiest way up here from Calabar is to head to Ikom (take the A4 if driving, not the A4-2). There are usually direct vehicles from Ikom to **OBUDU** village (along the N40), or you can find transport from Enugu or Ikom to **OGOJA**, whence it's 66km to Obudu. In the village, you can rent a taxi or motorbike to the ranch. The road is good all the way and still improving; the final stretch – a tangle of hairpins as it snakes up to the ranch – is a wonderful climax to the trip. If you don't have your own transport, getting away depends on the vagaries of taxis returning to Obudu after dropping other guests, or lorries heading into town. From Obudu there are occasional vehicles to Ikom, Ogoja or Calabar, but you may have a long wait.

14.4

Central Nigeria

The huge area that is **"Central Nigeria"** is an artificial division, and really consists of the middle margins of the country's more natural divisions into southwest, southeast and north. However, the centre has quite a concentration of places of interest. The federal capital of **Abuja** has an increasingly sophisticated infrastructure and services, and **Jos** is one of the country's most favoured towns, on its fine, high plateau with an almost Mediterranean climate. **Bauchi** is less attractive, though pleasantly spacious, while **Yankari National Park**, not far away, is the country's best organized park and its **Wikki Warm Springs** are a pristine attraction in their own right. The **Kainji Lake National Park** is also worth striking out to, though this is quite tricky if you don't have your own transport.

Kainji Lake National Park and around

Scenically and climatically, the **Kainji Lake National Park** feels more like a part of northern Nigeria, but it's remote and far to the west, and most commonly and easily approached from the south. Open from December to June, the park is split into two sectors, **Borgu**, mainly savannah and indeed the only one equipped for wildlife spotting; and **Zugurma**, more forested and inhabited by colobus monkeys. The best time to visit is in the dry season, after the grass has been burned, when you have a better chance of seeing the animals – waterbuck, lion, leopard, baboon, green and patas monkey, crocodile, warthog and hippo. For **information** about the park and its accommodation, contact the park offices in New Bussa (☎031/670 424 or 670 315) or Abuja (☎09/530 0429).

Jebba and Zugurma

North of Ilorin (see p.1140) you leave Yorubaland and enter a drier and less monoethnic environment, populated by a mix of Nupe, Bussa, Borgu, Kamberi, Fulani and Hausa communities. After some 70km you reach **JEBBA** (off the road to the east) before crossing the Niger on a fine, low bridge. The bridge passes over an island in the river where, just to the west, a monument marks the last resting place of Scottish explorer **Mungo Park**, killed near today's Kainji Dam in 1805 by people who apparently thought he and his expedition were a party of raiding Fulani jihadists. His boat is preserved at Jebba train station. There are several reasonable **places to stay** should you decide to break your journey at Jebba. One option is the excellent-value *Nigerian Paper Mill Guest House*, with rooms with a/c, fridge and TV, a kilometre up the hillside to the west of the highway (turn off 300m south of the bridge; ☎031/400 007 ❷). On the other side of the highway, decent singles and doubles, some with a/c, are available at the very inexpensive, friendly *Goodwill Guest House and Canteen* at 2 Elder Etim St, 500m up Paper Mill Road, the main street through the centre of town (☎031/400 114 ❶).

From **MOKWA**, 38km north of Jebba (if you're heading to Kainji on public transport, ask to be dropped off here at Kainji junction), a good road sweeps off northwest to New Bussa and Kainji Lake National Park. There are few towns up here amid the wild bush and dry, patchy farmlands. **ZUGURMA** (24km from Mokwa) is a pretty halt, however, with a fine, jungly stream running past. Beyond here you're sure to see some wildlife – monkeys at least. Some 18km further up the road towards Kainji Dam, **IBBI**, the gateway to the smaller **Zugurma sector** of the national park, has spacious, cool, comfy **rooms** with a/c, TV, fridge and running water at the *Ibbi Tourist Camp* (❷). A small **museum** houses weapons and skins seized from poachers.

Kainji Dam and New Bussa

Kainji Dam is impressive, though you probably won't be allowed to go onto it – the road runs past it, below. It was just north of here, at Old Bussa, which has now been submerged by the artificial Kainji Lake, that the Scottish explorer Mungo Park was killed (see above). You can take a **cruise** on the lake, and even tour the hydroelectric complex.

The local town, **NEW BUSSA**, around 100km from Mokwa, is dull and scruffy with little of interest, but it's an excellent first base for the national park's Borgu sector, just 20km to the west. The park office 7km south of town doesn't sell tickets or arrange transport – for that you'll have to continue to Wawa (see below).

New Bussa has two good places to **stay**: *Hotel Holy Year '75* on the Wawa Road (℡031/670 709 ❷), and *Hotel Brahmatola* at 199 Ibadan Way (℡031/670 027 ❶), both with inexpensive a/c doubles and even cheaper non-a/c singles. The *White House Guest Inn* (no phone ❶), 50m from the *Holy Year '75*, also has very cheap, non-a/c rooms. A pleasant alternative, 3km out of town and popular with expats, is the *Kainji Motel* on Niger Crescent, with its chalet rooms and safari atmosphere (℡031/670 032 ❷). Run by NEPA, who also manage the dam, the a/c accommodation here has hot water and satellite TV, and there's a decent **restaurant**. Niger Crescent is at the end of Murtala Muhammed Road, where a left or a right will take you to the motel.

The Borgu sector

Though it's the only part open for wildlife viewing, the **Borgu sector** of Kainji Lake National Park (Dec–June) doesn't get a lot of visitors, and it's doubtful if it has a lot of big game – in fact it seems certain that much has been poached out. However it has no human inhabitants, and its 4000-odd square kilometres do contain plentiful numbers of various **antelope** species, monkeys and warthogs, plus several families of **hippos** in the pools of the somewhat seasonal Oli River which flows through the reserve. **Lions** may still roam the bush too, but **elephants** have not been seen for years.

The roads through Borgu are mostly well maintained. Vehicles can be rented and rangers hired as compulsory companions to your game drive; you can find them at the guard post and headquarters at Kaiama Road, in **WAWA**. This is where you pay your fees (entrance ₦400 per person; ₦400 per car; ₦2000 per camera; ₦4000 per camcorder; ₦400 per guide), and where you'll find a small **museum**, as at Zugurma, of guns and animal remains seized from poachers. **Rooms** are available here at the *Hotel Annex* (❷) or, for students only, the *Student Hostel* (₦200 per person). Alternatively, you can stay inside the park at the *Oli River Tourist Camp*, 72km from Wawa, on the banks of the Oli River, with chalets and hotel accommodation, and full catering facilities (four-person chalet ₦2000, rooms ❷).

Bida

Heading east towards Abuja from Kainji Dam, you'll pass through the old Nupe capital of **BIDA**. Nupe was an early kingdom, contemporaneous with the Hausa emirates, that lasted from around 1400 until its submission to Fulani rule after the nineteenth-century jihads. The traditional ruler is the **etsu** of Nupe, normally known as Etsu Nupe. The Nupe people (who speak a Kwa language related to Yoruba) are still renowned **crafts** experts, and Bida has a reputation as a place to buy locally made metal jewellery, as well as cylindrical coloured-glass trading beads whose style is derived from those originally manufactured in medieval Venice.

Neither of the town markets particularly reflects Bida's reputation for crafts, but a quick walk along the **Sotamaku Road** brings you to a host of **metal workshops** heralded by a glittering array of brass and aluminium plates, bowls and ornaments. Inside, school-age boys pump away at goatskin bellows while their elder brothers reshape old pans and scrap metal using gearbox housings, crankcases and steel rods as anvils. The same sweatshop approach is used in the **Masaga** area where **glass beads** are made from melted-down beer and minerals bottles, which lend an opaque lustre quite different from the trading beads found elsewhere. Steel rods are dipped into the glass and a single bead is formed as the rod is spun over a furnace. The panoply of patterned beads so formed is then strung on to necklaces or sold singly on roadside stands.

Harder to locate are the traditional Nupe **ten-legged stools** carved from a single piece of wood. Apart from their intricately patterned tops and unsurpassed stability, they're unusual because the seat is cut along the grain of the wood rather than across. The stools can still be bought in local villages, but dealers rapidly snap them up to sell in Lagos, where they fetch high prices. If you're keen to buy one, start asking around a hundred metres south of the Total petrol station, and hopefully someone can lead you to an artisan with some unclaimed stock.

Practicalities

Arriving in Bida, you're likely to be dropped at the motor park on the Abuja–Ilorin road. Most points of interest are within walking distance of here, but you may want a taxi to the **hotels**, which are mostly on the outskirts of town. The best place to stay is the *CS&S Guest House* near the *etsu's* palace (☎0803 464 0770 ❸).

Abuja

Work on the new federal capital of **ABUJA** began in 1981 and, almost overnight, the peaceful setting of this hitherto sparsely populated corner of the Niger State was transformed into Africa's biggest construction site. The federal government's decision to create a new capital dates from 1976, when the experience of the civil war made it clear that Lagos, with a seventy-five percent Yoruba population, was not conducive to relieving ethnic tensions – and besides, Lagos had already outgrown its capacities. However, the enormous cost of creating a city from scratch, especially one with such ambitious designs and such opportunities for misappropriation, led to serious economic difficulties for the civilian presidency of Shehu Shagari. After the 1983 coup which deposed him, the project came to an abrupt standstill and it wasn't until 1991 that the capital was officially transferred from Lagos. Only since the turn of the millennium has Abuja started to feel like the capital city of the most populous country on the continent, with an increasing number of hotels, restaurants and bars serving increasing numbers of visitors, as well as a rapidly growing number of Nigerians moving to the FTC (Federal Capital Territory) from elsewhere in the country. It's estimated that nearly one million people now live in Abuja.

Arrival and information

The only way into town from the **airport**, 43km distant, is by taxi; expect to pay ₦3000–3500 in an official green cab. There are numerous air links with Lagos (1hr) on various airlines, the most reliable currently being Virgin Nigeria and Arik (both of which fly from the International terminal in Abuja to the International terminal

---

Abuja surface arrivals and departures

The main **interstate bus park** is in the Utako district just outside the main ring road. Here you'll find ABC Transport (ⓦwww.abctransport.com) and Chisco Transport among others. Both ABC and Chisco operate modern, comfortable, air-conditioned buses with daily services to Lagos, as well as to northern and eastern destinations. Ground Air Travel's (ⓦwww.gatlimited.com) Abuja station is at Sabondale Shopping Complex (next to *Mr Biggs*) in the Jabi district.

If you can't find a direct vehicle to your destination, try the regular service to **Suleja**, one of the original local settlements now swamped by the FTC. It's just a few kilometres west of the main Lokoja–Kaduna A2 highway, and has an active motor park.

Something to look out for when heading to or through Suleja is **Zuma Rock**, the kilometre-long inselberg 55km west of Abuja and east of the main road between Ziba and Suleja, that is Nigeria's Ayers Rock. It can only be scaled by technical climbers, so for most people isn't worth a close-up visit in its own right, but it's an impressive landmark and highly photogenic.

in Lagos). There are also regular flights to Maiduguri (with IRS Airlines), Kano and Calabar. If you're flying to Lagos, beware the Friday evening exodus from Abuja, when seats can be hard to secure: book in advance. Airline offices are detailed in "Listings" on p.1177.

Unfortunately, the city, designed for motor transport, is too large to manage on foot, and it can be a challenge to find the rare buses and shared taxis, even *okadas*. For **tourist information**, the Nigeria Tourism Development Corporation have their headquarters at the Old Secretariat in Garki Area 1 (℡09/234 2764 ✉ntdc@metrong.com). A helpful **online resource** for leisure activities in Abuja is ⓦwww.gladng.org.

Accommodation

Really inexpensive lodging doesn't exist in Abuja, though good-value weekend deals can be found at the international hotels. Many hotels are found in **Garki**, the southern district of Abuja, with another cluster in **Wuse**, west of the market.

Chelsea Plot 389, Cadastral Zone, Central District ℡09/234 9080 ⓦwww.chelseahotelabuja.com. Good-value alternative to the larger hotels, with 75 clean, comfortable rooms, tennis courts and a decent pool. ❻

Golden Gate Plot 1994 Mombasa St, Wuse Zone 5 ℡09/523 3443 ℻523 3561. Excellent-value Chinese-owned hotel with clean and tidy rooms with minibar and satellite TV. Top-quality Chinese restaurant downstairs. ❻

🏃 **Mediterranean** 42 Justice Mamman Nasir Crescent, Asokoro ℡09/314 8048–9 ✉mail@themediterraneanasokoro.com. A gem of a boutique hotel in the affluent and leafy Asokoro neighbourhood. Twenty-five well-appointed rooms, a designer pool and outside bar and a restaurant. Great value. ❼

Nicon Luxury Plot 903 Tafawa Balewa Way, Central Area ℡09/461 9000 ⓦwww.niconluxury .com. Formerly the *Meridian*, the *Nicon Luxury* has 250 deluxe rooms and a well-designed interior. At ₦40,000 for a standard twin, it is also the most expensive hotel in town. ❽

Protea Hotel Asokoro Bola Ige Close, Mohammadu Ribadu St, off Shehu Shagari Way, Asokoro ℡09/314 6767 ⓦwww.proteahotels.com/asokoro. Right up

there with the *Nicon Luxury* in terms of facilities and prices, but also offers free Wi-Fi throughout. ❽

Rockview Plot 374/789 Central Area ℡09/413 0101 ⓦwww.rockviewhotels.com. Comfortable and clean alternative to the larger and more expensive hotels, the *Rockview* is split into two sites 100m apart. The Extension is newer, has slightly better rooms, and a good pool and tennis courts. ❽

Sheraton Ladi Kwali Way, Wuse Zone 4 ℡09/523 0225/44 ⓦwww.starwood.com/sheraton. Unusual, ziggurat-shaped hotel with more than 600 rooms. Standards can sometimes be below par for this level, however, and the restaurants are seriously overpriced. ❽

Transcorp Hilton Shehu Shagari Way, Maitama ℡09/413 1811–40 (29 lines). The de facto city-centre of Abuja, formerly the *Nicon Hilton*, this must be *the* busiest hotel in Nigeria, and is the biggest hotel in West Africa, with nearly 700 rooms on ten floors. There's a good range of restaurants and bars and a huge pool. ❽

Valencia Blantyre St, Wuse II ℡09/461 8300 ⓦvalenciahotelsabuja.com. Newish, clean and comfortable hotel with a well-designed pool area. And at $140/night for a standard twin, this sits squarely in Abuja's middle ground. ❽

The city – and around the FCT

Abuja was designed with a population of three million in mind; at the current rate of growth, the city could soon be too small. That said, don't expect to meet an "Abuja local". The indigenous **Gwari**, a semi-nomadic people, were unceremoniously evicted from their ancestral lands, and the capital is now populated by people from all parts of the country. Today, the Gwari have nearly disappeared as a distinct ethnic and linguistic (Kwa-speaking) community – with one indigenous settlement in Garki remaining.

The city has a beautiful setting, with a backdrop of stunning stone inselbergs and a good deal of greenery, thanks to numerous parks that are spread all across the city. The magnificent **Central Mosque**, with its large golden dome and

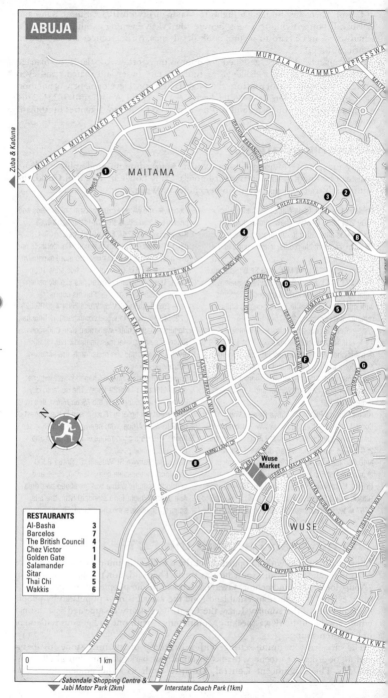

ABUJA

MAITAMA

WUSE
Wuse Market

RESTAURANTS

Al-Basha	3
Barcelos	7
The British Council	4
Chez Victor	1
Golden Gate	1
Salamander	8
Sitar	2
Thai Chi	5
Wakkis	6

14

14.4 NIGERIA

0 — 1 km

Sabondale Shopping Centre &
Jabi Motor Park (2km)

Interstate Coach Park (1km)

Zuba & Kaduna

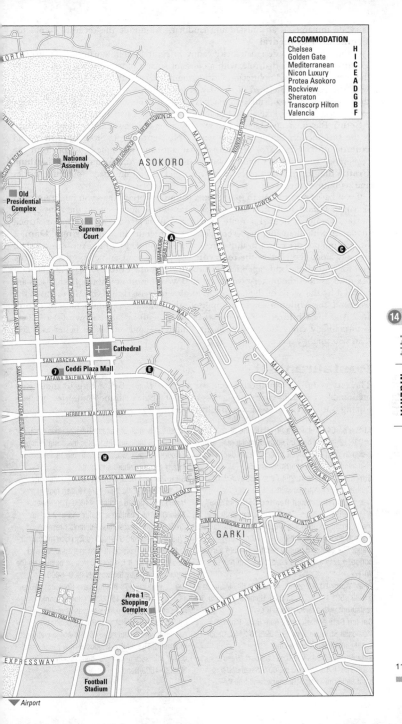

ACCOMMODATION

Chelsea	H
Golden Gate	I
Mediterranean	C
Nicon Luxury	E
Protea Asokoro	A
Rockview	D
Sheraton	G
Transcorp Hilton	B
Valencia	F

Airport

fairytale minarets, is an outstanding landmark, alongside the recently completed **Ecumenical Cathedral**.

In the absence of a designated city centre or central public square, the **Transcorp Hilton**'s lobby plays that role, with a constant stream of cars flowing in and out of the one entrance, and politicians, visiting dignitaries and their hangers-on mingling with the conference crowd of the day. If you're not normally part of that crowd, then stopping by for a drink or a snack is always fun. For an earthier, more authentic experience, however, take a taxi out to one of Abuja's **bush bars** (see below).

Ceddi Plaza, at 264 Tafawa Balewa Way, near the new Central Bank building, is the first modern shopping mall, with a NuMetro Media Store **bookshop** and **cinema** (☎09/672 3573) as well as restaurants and boutiques. Just up from the conference venue, library and exhibition spaces at the **Yar'Adua Centre** is **Abuja Craft Village** – the best place in town to pick up locally made souvenirs, fabrics and sculptures.

If you have an afternoon to spare, Abuja has more options than you might imagine. A trip to **Guara Falls** in nearby Niger State – most impressive in the rainy season – takes about an hour. En route, you pass **Zuma Rock**, a huge molar-shaped inselberg with dramatic, near-vertical sides. Closer to the city, **Usman Dam**, a twenty-minute drive, is a beautiful reservoir surrounded by hills. You can drive all the way along the edge of the **reservoir** nearest the road, and climb the hill at the end for a stunning landscape view. Nearby, the **Ushafa Pottery** village stocks local ceramics, as does the pottery workshop at **BWARI**, north of Abuja. Both places are inspired by the work of the late, great, local ceramicist Ladi Kwali. In town, at the weekend, the **Millennium Park**, opposite the *Hilton*, is a popular local recreation area. And the **Children's Zoo** (₦200, children ₦50) in the shadow of Aso Rock, is surprisingly enjoyable – especially for children – and somewhat better as a zoo than you might expect.

Restaurants

The city is full of fast-food *Tantalizers* and *Mr Biggs*. But eating in them isn't memorable. The following range across most of Abuja's cuisines and price brackets (dining out is as expensive as you might expect).

Al-Basha 643 Sassandra St, off Usuma St ☎09/413 8038. Popular Lebanese restaurant, with a slightly odd, cave-like interior. Alfresco dining is also available in the courtyard outside.

Barcelos Ceddi Plaza, 264 Tafawa Balewa Way, Central District. *Nandos*-style eatery.

British Council Rooftop Café Plot 2395, IBB Way (Mon–Sat 9am–10pm). Both a major landmark, dividing Wuse from the Maitama district, and a popular hangout and meeting place. The cool and breezy penthouse café serves coffee, pizzas and rice-based food, and has free Wi-Fi.

Chez Victor 20 Ganges St, Minister's Hill, Maitama ☎0803/591 1997 (closed Sun). Upmarket French restaurant with a decent wine list.

Golden Gate at the *Golden Gate Hotel*, Plot 1994 Mombasa St, Wuse Zone 5 ☎09/523 3443. Good-quality, affordable Chinese food.

Salamander 72 Aminu Kano Crescent, Wuse 2 ☎09/708 4518. Opened in 2007, *Salamander* is a coffee bar offering light snacks and free Wi-Fi access. A branch of Lagos's Glendora bookshop is also part of the café. Upstairs is the design shop Colours in Africa, where you can buy tasteful, locally made furniture and crafts.

Sitar Plot 664 Usuma St, off Gana St, Maitama ☎09/413 9834. Well-prepared Indian food in a tastefully designed setting. ₦4000–7000/head.

Thai Chi The Penthouse, Safire Plaza, 2 Kolda Crescent, off Adetokumbo Ademola Crescent, Wuse 2 ☎09/523 6798/09 (daily noon–midnight). Authentic Thai cuisine served in a spacious and tasteful interior. If it's not too hot, sit outside on the balcony and enjoy the view. ₦3000–6000.

Wakkis 171 Aminu Kano Crescent, Wuse 2 ☎09/413 4552/3/6 (closed Mon). After the former *Wakkis* site was demolished by former FCT Minister el-Rufai's bulldozers, residents and frequent visitors to Abuja went into mourning. Thankfully, *Wakkis* is now bigger and better, still serving simple, delicious Indian food. ₦2500–4000/head.

Drinking and nightlife

One of the most pleasant things to do in the evening in Abuja is to visit one of the many **bush bars** that dot the city. They mainly do roasted fish and purvey Star, Guinness or Gulder beer in very relaxed outdoor settings. There's a very good one near the upmarket mall, the Dunes Centre. To get there, take a taxi to the Wuse area and, on Aguiyi Ironsi Way less than five minutes' drive from the *Hilton*, you'll see a line of parked cars up on the pavement – the local bush bar is a short walk down a path by the cars. Don't go there if you're already ravenous, however, as your fish may take up to an hour to arrive.

Blakes Excellency Resort Garki. One of the most enjoyable places to spend a Fri night. Four scantily clad dancers perform to a mix of Nigerian and international music played by the local band. At midnight, it becomes a church for half an hour, with all the artistes praising Jesus, before returning to their bottom-wiggling. If you stay late enough, you'll catch the Fela impersonator who sings in his underpants.

The Dome Independence Ave in the direction of the national stadium. Fri & Sat nights see a heaving dancefloor by 1am. ₦1000 entrance fee.

Nectar downstairs at Ceddi Plaza, 264 Tafawa Balewa Way. Increasingly popular bar, with a separate champagne lounge. A good spot for a drink before adjourning to the cinema upstairs.

The Point Aminu Kano Crescent, Wuse 2, just before you get to Emab Plaza shopping centre coming from the Central Area. This bar gets very busy from around 1am on Fri & Sat nights.

Tucano 26 Maitama Sule St, Asokoro. A relaxing bar by day, *Tucano* takes on a busy, club-like vibe late on weekend nights. Be warned: the plasma screens over the bar loop soft porn in the evenings.

Listings

⑭

Airlines All the local airlines (Aero, Virgin Nigeria, Bellview, Arik and Chanchangi) have desks on the first floor of the *Transcorp Hilton*, as does British Airways (☎09 413 9608/10) and Lufthansa. KLM is found at the *Sheraton* (☎09/523 9965/6).

Banks and exchange Bureaux de change can be found at the Luzumba Commercial Complex off Moshood Abiola Rd in Garki and among the Zone 4 corner shops adjoining Addis Ababa Crescent and Lady Kwali St near the *Sheraton* in Wuse Zone 4. Moneychangers hang out near the *Sheraton* on Lady Kwali St. Among the various banks in town, Western Union's representative, First Bank of Nigeria, has its main branch at Plot 777, Muhammadu Buhari Way (☎09/234 6833–5).

Couriers DHL, Plot 609, Dambata Close, off Tafawa Balewa Way, Garki Area 7 ☎09/234 6557–8; UPS, Plot 781, Obafemi Awolowo St, Garki Area 2 ☎09/234 7979.

Cultural Centres British Council, Plot 2935, IBB Way, Maitama ☎09/413 7870–7; Alliance Française, 32 Udi St, off Aso Drive, Maitama ☎09/523 5088.

Embassies Australia, Arizona Building, opposite Maitama Hospital, Maitama ☎09/314 3778; Benin, Plot 2858A, Danube St, off IBB Way, Maitama ☎09/523 8424; Canada, 3A Bobo St, off Gana St, Maitama ☎09/413 9910–1; Chad, Plot 152, 10 Mississippi St, Maitama ☎09/413 0751; The Gambia, Plot 25, Ontario Crescent, off Mississippi St, Maitama ☎09/413 8545; Germany, 9 Lake Maracaibo Close, Maitama ☎09/413 0962; Ghana, Plot 301, Olusegun Obasanjo Way, Garki Area 10 ☎09/234 5192–3; Guinea, Plot 679, Agadez Crescent, off Amino Kano Crescent, Wuse 2; European Union (also representing several member states), Europe House, 63 Usuma St, Maitama ☎09/413 3146–8; Ireland, Plot 415, Negro Crescent, Maitama ☎09/413 1751; Mali, Plot 465, Nouakchott St, Wuse 1 ☎09/523 0494; Niger, 7 Sangha St, off Mississippi St, Maitama ☎09/413 5434–6; South Africa, Plot 676, Vaal St, off Rhine St, off IBB Way, Maitama ☎09/413 3776; Togo, Plot 664, Usuma St, Maitama ☎09/413 9833; UK, Plot 364, Dangote House, Aguiyi Ironsi Way, Wuse ☎09/413 2010/1 ⊛www.ukinnigeria.com; USA, Plot 1075 Diplomatic Drive, Central District Area ☎09/461 4000 ⊛abuja.usembassy.gov/contact.html.

Hammam/spa For women in need of a pampering treat, there's a Moroccan ladies-only spa – MB Hammam – offering a steam room and hammam room, staffed entirely by Moroccans. It's at 31B Suez Crescent, Sheraton Housing Estate, Wuse 4 ☎0805/493 2650 or 09/672 4117.

Internet access Availability is still limited. The free Wi-Fi at *Salamander Café* is a good option. Otherwise, *Cool Café* on Independence Ave is about the most reliable place. There's free Wi-Fi at the rooftop café at the British Council, although the network is often down. Other reliable cybercafés are Maitama Business Centre at Maitama Plaza, off Yedsaram St, and NIIT Express Centre, 144 Adetokunbo Ademolo Crescent.

Post office The GPO (Mon–Fri 8am–4pm) is on Moshood Abiola Rd, Garki Area 10. There's a branch office in Garki Area 1 shopping complex.

Travel agents Try Emerald Tours, Alli Akilu Crescent, off Usman dan Fodio Crescent, Asokoro, who can arrange trips to Yankari, Obudu Cattle Ranch, Kano and Katsina.

Jos and around

Set 1200m above sea level, **JOS** enjoys a mild climate that has long attracted Europeans weary of the coastal humidity or the northern heat and dust. Laid out in a beautiful, rocky landscape, the hill resort grew up around **tin mines** exploited by the British at the beginning of the twentieth century – and still partly managed by expatriates. Jos's history, though, can be traced back much further, to the **Nok culture** (named after the Jos plateau village of the same name) which spread throughout central Nigeria between 2800 and 1800 years ago. Terracotta artefacts left behind by this civilization were discovered quite accidentally in the mines and are today housed in the **Jos Museum**.

Other diversions include the **zoo** (admittedly now rather depressing) and the **Museum of Traditional Nigerian Architecture**, where life-size replica buildings from Zaria, Kano, Katsina and other cities have been constructed. Here you can visit the gems of traditional architecture which have largely fallen into disrepair or disappeared altogether in their native areas.

On the downside, in 2001 Jos experienced an echo of the intercommunal violence that tore through Kaduna in 2000, after petty tensions led to **ethnic clashes**, leaving dozens dead and parts of the town centre gutted, including the splendid market building.

Orientation, arrival and information

The **main market** used to be an unmistakable landmark, covering a large area in the middle of town – a massive modern structure with a wild, colourful design. These days, the market is a rambling, outdoor affair and stalls fill all the spaces between Bauchi Road and Ahmadu Bello Way. From the market, **Ahmadu Bello Way**, one of the town's main thoroughfares, runs down towards the **post office**.

The **airport** is 29km south of town, and served by taxis. **Beach Road** ("The Beach") and **Murtala Muhammed Way** are the city's major central thoroughfares, the latter becoming **Bauchi Road** towards the north. Arriving by road transport from the north, you'll probably be dropped at **Bauchi Road motor park**, 3km northeast of the centre. A similar distance northwest of the centre is the **Zaria Road**

Moving on from Jos

The main motor park for the **northeast** is the **Bauchi Road motor park**, serving Bauchi, Kano, Kaduna, Maiduguri, Sokoto and all points north. Daily morning bus services to Calabar and Port Harcourt are operated by Crosslines from their office on Bauchi Road by the motor park. The main motor park for the **south**, including Lagos, Ibadan and Abuja is the **Zaria Road motor park**. Overnight **luxury bus** services to Lagos and Ibadan are operated by a handful of firms with offices around the junction of Zaria By-Pass and Tafawa Balewa Street. Fast Peugeots and minibuses, pre-bookable and mostly leaving in the morning, go from **Plateau Riders motor park**, serving Abuja, Kano, Benin City and other long-distance destinations. Arik Air flies from Jos to Lagos daily Mon–Fri at 1pm.

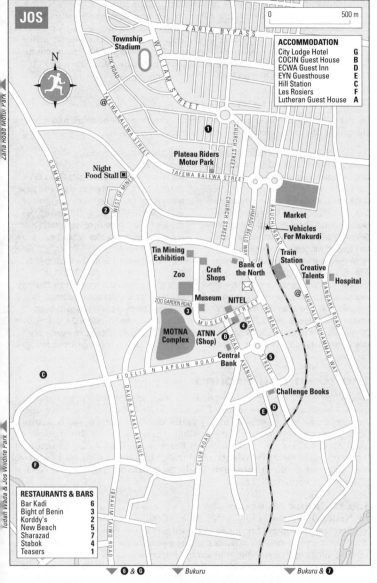

JOS

Zaria Road Motor Park ▲   Bauchi Road Motor Park, University & Ⓐ ▲

0   500 m

ACCOMMODATION

City Lodge Hotel	G
COCIN Guest House	B
ECWA Guest Inn	D
EYN Guesthouse	E
Hill Station	C
Les Rosiers	F
Lutheran Guest House	A

RESTAURANTS & BARS

Bar Kadi	6
Bight of Benin	3
Korddy's	2
New Beach	5
Sharazad	7
Stabok	4
Teasers	1

motor park, where you might well end up if arriving from the south. If you arrive by Peugeot or minibus, you'll probably be dropped at **Plateau Riders motor park**, on Tafawa Balewa Street in the centre.

Along Ahmadu Bello Road are a number of **supermarkets** and several **banks**, although the major ones are behind the post office around Bank Street. **Bureaux de change** are plentiful in Jos, with one on Museum Street, several at the southern end of Beach Road, and a good one at 15 Beach Rd, on the corner of Fidelis N. Tapgun Road, which claims to change "any currency" – they certainly take dollars, pounds, euros and CFAs. For international **phone calls** and Internet access, Afrione and Logic, both on Ahmadu Bello Way, are the cheapest and best. The **tourist office** is at 31 Yakubu Gowon Way (Mon–Fri 8am–4pm; ☎073/465 747 ✆platstate@tourism .hisen.org), and can organize vehicle rental; it also maintains information desks at the *Hill Station* and *Plateau* hotels (Mon–Sat 8am–2pm).

Accommodation

Jos has a variety of places to stay, including several excellent-value mission-type guesthouses, but surprisingly little at the top end.

City Lodge 9 City Lodge Hotel Close, off Apollo Crescent, GRA ☎073/464 100 or 464 103/4. Newish hotel getting close to international standards, with a restaurant. ❸

COCIN Guest House 5 Noad Ave, behind Central Bank ☎073/452 286. One of the town's many mission-oriented places with clean and comfortable s/c rooms and dorms; they'll put you up if they have space. Dorm beds or rooms ❶.

ECWA Guest Inn off Kano Rd behind Challenge Books ☎073/450 572. Clean, inexpensive and safe, the rooms (including dorms) come at various prices, some s/c with hot water. The restaurant serves solid meals like "Irish stew & two veg" and there's a pleasant living room with satellite TV. Dorm beds ❷.

EYN Guesthouse Opposite *ECWA Guest Inn*, off Kano Rd ☎073/452 056. Good-value budget

accommodation with cooking facilities available. ❷

Hill Station Hotel Tudun Wada Rd ☎073 455 300 or 454 817. This old pile used to be the place to stay in Jos. These days, there's a very tired air about it, in spite of the beauty of the hill-top location, and the food in the *Elysar* restaurant is basic. Rooms have a/c and satellite TV and there's a pool (nonresidents ₦300). ❹

Les Rosiers 1 Resthouse Road, opposite *Plateau Hotel* ☎0803/357 5233 or 790 1296 ✆www.lesrosiers.sampasite.com. Charming B&B homestay in a colonial garden setting. ❻

Lutheran Church of Christ in Nigeria Guest House Dogon Dutse Rd ☎073/612 810 or 0803/495 1201. The best place to stay in Jos if you're on a tight budget. Clean, with a tranquil atmosphere. ❶

The town and around

Jos's tourist attractions are concentrated in a small area around the museum, best accessed by taking Museum Street off Ahmadu Bello Way by the post office. Sightseeing aside, Jos is a good place to buy **crafts**, especially leather- and basketwork. Craft shops can be found by the Tin Mining Exhibition near the museum, on Noad Avenue and at the southern end of Beach Road. There is also an upmarket craft shop called **Creative Talents** on Murtala Muhammed Way, and a fair-trade craft shop run by the **Alternative Trade Network of Nigeria (ATNN)** at 1 Museum St, opposite NITEL.

Jos National Museum

Jos National Museum (daily 8am–5.30pm; ₦200) was created in 1952 to house **Nok terracotta figures** first found in the tin mines near Nok in the 1920s. These pieces are complemented by exhibits showing aspects of the art and culture – masks, weaving, medicine, ceremonies – of central Nigerian peoples. The collections are extremely well presented and the brief explanations are helpful. At the end of the museum (notice, as you're leaving, the massive gate taken from the ancient wall around Bauchi), an extensive **pottery collection** is displayed in a cool courtyard with ponds and trees.

The zoo and Tin Mining Exhibition

Set in a park opposite the Jos National Museum, the **zoo** (daily 8am–6pm; ₦200) has recovered from former neglect, but it is still less interesting than the wildlife park. Near the zoo, several old locomotives and carriages plus track from the

Bauchi Light Railway (which closed in 1959) are on display, along with other vehicles from the early twentieth century. Also nearby, the **Tin Mining Exhibition** (Mon–Sat 9am–4pm; ₦200) is a tiny one-room museum dedicated to the history and technology of mining in the area.

Museum of Traditional Nigerian Architecture

Probably the most unusual museum, and one well worth spending some time to discover, is the **Museum of Traditional Nigerian Architecture (MOTNA)**, which covers a vast area opposite the zoo (free, but dash expected). Full-scale reproductions of the country's most impressive monuments have been built on the site. You get a better idea of the magnitude of the **Kano Wall** here than you do in its city of origin, especially if you climb the narrow staircase leading to the top. The **Zaria Friday Mosque** with its impressive vaulting reveals the highly sophisticated technical skills of the Hausa. There are also smaller copies of the **Katsina Palace** and the **Ilorin mosque**. Entry is free, but guides show you round for a fee that goes to the upkeep of the museum.

Jos Wildlife Park

Not to be confused with the zoo, the **Jos Wildlife Park** (daily 10am–dusk; ₦100), southwest of town, off the Jos–Bukuru road (Yakubu Gowon Way), used to be a more worthwhile encounter, the drive-through park, covering an area of about eight square kilometres, containing a large variety of animals in semi-natural large enclosures. These days, however, most of the animals are in tiny enclosures and it is essentially another dismal Nigerian zoo. The best feature is the walk to the observation tower at the highest point in the park, where there's a good view of Jos and the plateau: it's a fine spot for a picnic. You can also drive up (4x4 is best), or rent a taxi in Jos for a three-hour visit, or take Bukuru-bound public transport and get out at the huge sign (the park entrance is 4km down this turning).

Jos Plateau

If you want to get into the **Jos Plateau** countryside, take a taxi or minibus out to **BUKURU** from the end of Tafawa Balewa Street, near the market. For **camping**, the **VOM** area to the southwest of Jos is pretty, with plenty of good grassy spots amid boulders and groves of gum trees. At **Assop Falls**, 64km south of Jos on the A3 Abuja Road, you can scramble across rocks and get quite close to the falls (₦200 entry), which are at their most impressive in the rainy season from July to September.

Eating

For a town of its size, Jos has one of the widest choices of eating places in Nigeria, with some good Nigerian restaurants and a couple of excellent Lebanese ones for good measure.

Bight of Benin Zoo Garden Rd, near the museum. Good cooking, in a replica of a Benin noble's house. A cool place to take a break, with a limited menu of Nigerian dishes at reasonable prices.

Elysar at the *Hill Station Hotel*, Tudan Wada Rd. Jos's only Chinese Lebanese, and not bad at all for a change from *suya* and starch – in fact probably one of the best restaurants in Jos.

Korddy's off West-of-Mines. A very popular restaurant where the specialities include goat head and fish pepper soup.

New Beach 5 Bank St. Moderately priced English and Nigerian dishes, the former including mushroom soup and curry beef.

Sharazad Yakubu Gowon Way, 2km out of the centre towards Bukuru ☎073/462 281. A range of good, well-prepared Lebanese, European and Chinese dishes at reasonable prices (although it's one of the more expensive places in town). Popular with expats.

Stabok Bank St. Toasted sandwiches and fish-and-chips-type meals complement Nigerian specialities in this popular local bar-restaurant.

Teasers 2 Niger Ave. A bar-restaurant serving good, solid Nigerian chop at very reasonable prices. The *jollof* rice is fiery, and particularly recommended.

Drinking

Nightlife options are somewhat restricted; however, for an outdoor experience, West-of-Mines is the place to head. Outdoor bars are arranged around a square here. Musicians playing Hausa music will come and serenade you, but beware of the working girls. The liveliest bar/club in town is 🏃 *Bar Kadi*, on Naraguta Avenue near *City Lodge Hotel* in the GRA area, with a modern bar, good range of food, late music, and seating under a thatched roof or in very pleasant gardens.

South from Jos

South of Jos, beyond the plateau, the topography is complex and travel delightful. Forests of gum trees spread around **PANYAM** and from here on the road drops down a breathtaking escarpment through coniferous woods and Mediterranean landscapes to **SHENDAM** and **YELWA**. It's fine driving (or cycling) country; otherwise, apart from one or two exhausting through-bus services to big cities in the southeast, travelling by public transport becomes chancy as you get into this eastern part of Central Nigeria.

Makurdi

Located in the fertile middle belt, where the forests of the south gradually turn into the savannah of the north, **Benue State** has been called "the food basket of Nigeria". **MAKURDI**, its capital, has become a major agricultural trading centre and is one of the original homelands of the farming Tiv people, and also on the fringes of Igboland. Lying roughly midway between Jos and Cameroon, on the south bank of the Benue River, Makurdi is a fair-sized town with several small and medium **hotels**: the *Dolphin* – part of a complex of cinemas, restaurants and lodgings in Secretariat Road to the north of town – is clean, welcoming and inexpensive.

Northeast from Jos: Bauchi and Yankari

Northeast from Jos, the road drops down from the plateau in a spectacular curve, turns east and then runs across featureless plains to **Bauchi**, capital of the state of the same name. Bauchi is the nearest big centre to **Yankari National Park** and if you don't have your own transport you'll very likely have to spend a night here before getting to the reserve.

Beyond Yankari, in Gombe State, the terrain between **GOMBE** and Numan (on the edge of Adamawa State) is a fine stretch of scenery: if you've got your own transport, you can attempt some superb **hikes and climbs** in the Mouri Mountains. **Tangale Hill** near **KALTUNGO** is a steep and stunning volcanic plug and a brisk three-hour climb, but you'll need permission from the emir of the little town and help from local men in guiding you up. Don't count on staying in **NUMAN**, a shabby town with two dreadful hotels, that was caught up in Muslim–Christian violence in 2003.

Bauchi

Arriving in **BAUCHI**, you get a more exotic first impression from its northern approach, down the A3 Kano–Maiduguri route, an approach which lines up a grand assembly of inselbergs known as the **Belo Hills** shortly before you arrive. After the Fulani jihad, in the 1840s, an emirate was established at Bauchi, but despite the **emir's palace**, the **old mosque**, and some remnants of its **city wall**, the town – which radiates in several directions from the roundabout by its **Central Market**

– is a large, seemingly impersonal place with little of enduring interest. If you're stuck here waiting for transport, you could spend an interesting half-hour at the **Mausoleum of Tafawa Balewa** (daily 7am–6pm; free), 300m north of the Central Market roundabout on Ran Road. Balewa was Nigeria's first prime minister, assassinated in the first coup of 1966: on weekdays you may be able to see a video of his independence speech. A tour of the complex takes you up a ramp through spaces of dark and light – symbolizing colonial repression and the hope of independence – and leads to the roofless mausoleum. The concrete and stone are austere, but the site remains a powerful monument to the fight for self-determination.

Practicalities

Bauchi's main **motor park** is on Ran Road, north of Ran Gate in the old city wall and 1km north of the Central Market. There's no airport here, the closest being at Jos. There are a dozen or more **inexpensive** hotels in Bauchi, the best being the *CFA*, 800m east of Central Market on Gombe Road, just outside Wambai Gate and conveniently located if you're planning to get an early taxi to Yankari (☏077/543 563 or 643 ❷), and the slightly run-down but inexpensive *Sogiji*, 1km north of the Central Market on Ran Road, just outside Ran Gate (☏077/543 454 ❶). Of the more **upmarket** places, the *Zaranda*, 3km west of town on the Jos Road, used to be the poshest place in town (☏077/543 814–20, ⓕ543 640 ❺), but it's gone right downhill and a far better place is the *Awalah* on the Kano Road, which has friendly service, comfy rooms and a good-sized pool (☏077/542 344 or 542 377 ❷; pool ₦150 for nonresidents). Both hotels have now been fully eclipsed by the luxury two-storey units of the *Protea Hotel Bauchi VIP Suites*, in Yakubun Bauchi Road, which seem to have everything, even flat-screen TVs and DVD players (☏077/541 424 ⓦwww.proteahotels.com/bauchi ❽).

Yankari National Park

Covering more than 2200 square kilometres of protected bush, **Yankari National Park** was the first game reserve in Nigeria and it remains the most popular (entry ₦300/person, car ₦100, camera ₦1000, camcorder ₦1500). However, despite the authorities' best efforts, poaching is still widespread and has taken its toll on the once abundant wildlife. You're likely to see herds of **gazelle** and **antelope**, and **elephants** with a little luck, but **lions**, which still hunt in the park (together with leopards), are getting increasingly shy and elusive. Other animals include warthog\, hippo, waterbuck, buffalo, several species of duiker, hartebeest, various monkeys, and crocodiles. Although the park is open all year, the best time to see animals is during the dry season (Feb–April), when they are driven closer to the lodge. In addition to the animals, ☀**Wikki Warm Springs** is reason to come to the park in itself. If you have any difficulty organizing game-viewing trips at the lodge, you probably won't be unhappy spending your time in its crystal-clear waters.

Transport

There is no regular transport from Bauchi east to *Wikki Warm Springs Lodge*, the sole focus of activity in Yankari. If you don't have a car you can take a **shared taxi** from the Gombe motor park on the east side of Bauchi. These vehicles can drop you at **DINDIMA** on the A345 highway, where the Yankari road splits off south – or they sometimes go to villages along this latter road and will let you off right in front of the park gate en route. Either way, you still have to get a lift for the rest of the journey with incoming visitors (if you inform the guards at the gate you're looking for a ride into the park, they're usually pretty good about asking drivers on their way in). Note that in the middle of the week, and on the odd quiet weekend, the park may be devoid of visitors, in which case you would be really stuck without your own transport. For that reason, avoid setting off from Bauchi after midday.

Another way of getting to the camp is to **charter a taxi** in Bauchi and arrange a price with the driver – you'll pay around ₦8000.

Park accommodation and eating

A range of accommodation is available at **Wikki Warm Springs Lodge** (☎077/543 674) which has recently been completely overhauled. Either stay in the comfortable rondavels (⑥) or camp with your own equipment (₦300 per person). There's also a cheap hostel with dorm accommodation for students (₦100). If you're visiting the park on a weekend or any major holiday, it's a good idea to make advance **reservations** as the lodge gets very full, particularly at Easter. Travel agents, and most larger hotels will happily do this. The **restaurant** near the lodge serves European meals at reasonable prices and a pleasant **outdoor bar** has views across the savannah. Alternatively, you can self-cater, although there are no cooking facilities.

Game-viewing

Morning and afternoon **game-runs** are organized at the lodge. If you don't have your own car, you can go on one of the camp vehicles – a lorry with benches in the back – for a fee of around ₦300 per person, provided they get enough customers to form a worthwhile group. If you have your own vehicle, you must take one of the rangers – which isn't a bad idea anyway, as they're most likely to know where to see animals and can direct you to other sites like the **Marshall Caves** prehistoric cave dwellings and the **Borkono Falls** (at their most spectacular in September). On any drive – assuming you go early in the morning, which is best, or late afternoon – you'll see antelope and gazelle of various species, and there's every likelihood you will see some of the park's 500-odd elephants. To see any predators at all, however, you'd need to be very lucky.

Wikki Warm Springs

Below the restaurant, a steep path leads down to **Wikki Warm Springs** (₦300/person on top of park fees, valid for the duration of stay). It's hard to think of any site in West Africa more completely satisfying from a hedonistic point of view. Twelve million litres a day of perfectly clear, clean water at a steady ideal temperature of 31°C come bubbling up from a dark hole at the bottom of a deep pool, at the base of a steep, sheltering cliff. Nothing, save perhaps the persistent hassles of monkeys and baboons, detracts from the site's beauty. From its source, the water flows out for one hundred metres or more past steep banks of overhanging foliage, over a bed of glistening sand. It's almost *too* pretty, especially at night when it's lit by flood lamps – like an elaborate bit of New-Age interior design.

The access side of the stream is concreted over, which keeps it clean, and there are areas shallow enough for toddlers to enjoy, and deeper areas for bigger swimmers. Downstream, camp staff do their laundry and bathe. A reminder: if you take food or valuables down to the springs, watch out for those monkeys.

14.5

The north and northeast

ormerly a conglomeration of disunited and often warring emirates, the **Hausa country** spreads over the arid savannah of the northern plateaus and comprises the largest geographical entity in Nigeria. In this vast region, Hausa makes sense as a linguistic rather than an ethnic grouping, since there are many different northern peoples. The religious (and in many respects political) head of all the Hausa peoples is in fact a Fulani – the **Sultan of Sokoto** – and has been for nearly two hundred years. Thanks to the common faith of **Islam** and the lingua franca of Hausa, however, a bond has been created among northerners that puts them politically at an advantage over the south. In recent years, the introduction of *sharia* law, although interpreted differently from state to state (see box, p.1099), has widened the north–south divide even further.

The area near **Lake Chad** in the northeast of the country is peopled by the **Kanuri**, who, in about the ninth century, migrated from the northern, desert regions of Kanem to form the new empire of Bornu which grew rich on **trans-Saharan trade**. In the context of the current Federal Republic, this kingdom translates roughly into the thinly populated **Yobe** and **Borno** states, the latter with its capital in **Maiduguri**, the only major town in the rather isolated northeast. Further west, the Hausa city-states (the "Seven Hausa" or *Hausa Bakwai*: Gobir, Katsina, Kano, Zaria, Daura, Rano and Biram) developed into powerful emirates from around the eleventh century, and had partially converted to Islam by 1400. Old walled cities from this era still exist in **Katsina**, **Zaria** and **Kano**. Kano today is a major metropolitan centre, with an international airport and diverse industries. Development has come more slowly to the conservative Islamic stronghold of **Sokoto**, the spiritual capital of the north, while **Kaduna** (further south and regarded by many as part of Central Nigeria) is a much more anonymous, modern town neatly laid out by the British colonials as a supposedly uncontroversial administrative capital. Unfortunately, Kaduna's halfway-house position and mixed Muslim/Christian population has seen it play an unhappy role in recurring religious riots.

This section also includes the remote eastern reaches of Nigeria – the states of **Adamawa** and **Taraba** – where the mountain forests remain poorly mapped and very little travelled. Here, there are some fine opportunities for hiking and some unusual options for travel routes into Cameroon.

The introduction of Islamic **sharia** law in the northern and northeastern states naturally has implications for travel in the region, though the impact on travellers isn't as wide-ranging as you might expect. It's true that *sharia* has led to a palpable decline in drinking and nightlife options in the cities, and the only **hotels** that serve alcohol on the premises are the priciest ones, and those with federal government or military links, or the ones located in predominantly Christian neighborhoods. It's certainly not taboo to ask if alcohol is allowed on the premises when choosing a place to stay; staff will readily suggest alternative accommodation if they can't oblige. Hotel **swimming pools** haven't escaped *sharia*: many pools in the stricter states – Sokoto, Katsina and Zamfara – have been emptied, and where pools remain in use you may find that men and women are allocated separate sessions. In Zamfara State even women-only **bush taxis** have been introduced, though in most cases foreign women will be treated as honorary men and allowed to ride in whichever taxi they wish. Ultimately, however,

The Hausa have a rich oral literature outside the influence of more recent Islamic tales. In folk history, the origin of their seven states, the *Hausa Bakwai*, is traced to **Bayajida**, son of the king of Baghdad, who fled his homeland after a bitter dispute with his father. After years of wandering, he arrived in Bornu and was recognized as a natural leader by the *mai* or king, who gave one of his daughters in marriage to the boy. Bayajida fell out with his father-in-law, and fled again, with his pregnant wife, to a place called Garun Gabas. He left his Bornu wife here, where she gave birth to a son, **Biram**, who later established the first of the *Hausa Bakwai*, named after him, in the area to the east of Kano. Meanwhile Bayajida had taken off again for the west and, in the middle of the night, fetched up at Daura, a place east of Katsina that was ruled at the time by a dynasty of queens. He stopped an old woman, Ayana, to ask for water and was told it was the wrong day of the week: the snake who owned the well only allowed people to draw water on a Friday. Nobody had been able to kill the snake. Bayajida, of course, went straight to the well, woke up the snake and chopped its head off. Then he drank his fill, pocketed the head and moved on. The next day was Friday and the queen wanted to know who had killed the snake. Ayana told her about the stranger and the queen sent messengers to catch up with the restless Bayajida, who agreed to return – and then asked her to marry him as a reward. They had a son, **Bawo**. Following the death of Bayajida, Bawo's own six sons went on to found the remaining towns of the *Hausa Bakwai* – Daura, Katsina, Kano, Rano, Gobir and Zaria.

foreigners – and indeed non-Muslims – aren't expected to know or be able to adhere to the same codes of behaviour that local people observe – it would be very unlikely, for example, for an unmarried foreign couple to be prevented from sharing accommodation. The usual, common-sense codes regarding **appropriate dress** are all you really need to bear in mind: shorts and skimpy clothes – on men or women – don't go down well with the more conservative locals (for more on appropriate clothing for women, see p.73).

Kaduna

KADUNA is usually looked on as the first town of the north. This is a slightly misleading assumption since it doesn't have much in common with the other towns in this section. It's a place, however, that on any major travels through Nigeria, you're unlikely to avoid. With no palace (the town was formerly a fief of the Zaria Emirate), no city wall and no ancient mosque, Kaduna is essentially a modern town with broad avenues and a bustling business environment. It's not the kind of place you'd want to spend weeks or even days discovering (indeed there's not much to find), but hitting upon this kind of cosmopolitan atmosphere, second only to Kano in the north, is not completely disagreeable either, especially if you've just arrived from the remote rural areas of Niger or Nigeria.

Some history

Originally conceived as the capital of the Northern Region, and, it was thought, perhaps the entire federation, Kaduna represents one of the best examples of a town created to be the seat of government. The original **northern capital** was at Zungeru, on the Kaduna River, 150km southwest of Kaduna, but when **Sir Frederick Lugard** became governor of the amalgamated colonial federation in 1912, he shifted the site to the small town of Kaduna, which had the advantage of being near a good water supply and on the line of the newly constructed railway. Within easy striking range of all the former emirates, the spot was also strategically

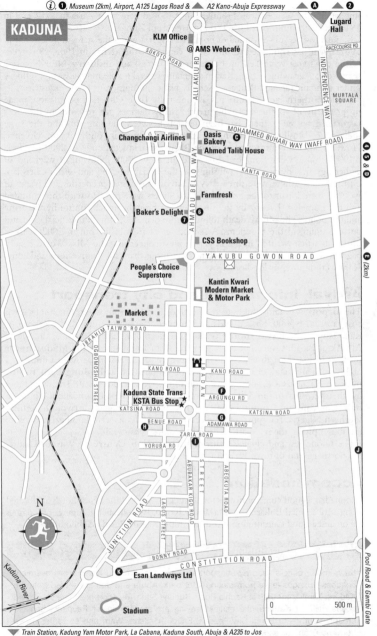

KADUNA

Lugard
Hall

RACECOURSE RD

KLM Office

SOKOTO ROAD

@ AMS Webcafé ❸

INDEPENDENCE WAY

MURTALA
SQUARE

Ⓑ

Changchangi Airlines

ALLI AKILU RD

Ⓒ Oasis
Bakery

MOHAMMED BUHARI WAY (WAFF ROAD)

Ahmed Talib House

KANTA ROAD

④⑤ & Ⓓ

Farmfresh

AHMADU BELLO WAY

Baker's Delight ❻

❼

CSS Bookshop

Ⓔ (2km)

People's Choice
Superstore

YAKUBU GOWON ROAD ✉

Kantin Kwari
Modern Market
& Motor Park

Market

IBRAHIM TAIWO ROAD

OGBOMOSHO STREET

KANO ROAD

BADAN

KANO ROAD

Kaduna State Trans
KSTA Bus Stop ★

Ⓕ
ARGUNGU RD

KATSINA ROAD

Katsina Road

Ⓖ
ADAMAWA ROAD

Ⓗ BENUE ROAD

ZARIA ROAD

Ⓙ

YORUBA RD

Ⓘ

ABUBAKAR KIGO ROAD

ABEOKUTA ROAD

STREET

LAGOS STREET

JUNCTION ROAD

BONNY ROAD

CONSTITUTION ROAD

Pool Road & Gambi Gate

N

Kaduna River

Ⓚ Esan Landways Ltd

Stadium

0   500 m

▼ Train Station, Kadung Yam Motor Park, La Cabana, Kaduna South, Abuja & A235 to Jos

ACCOMMODATION		Command Guest		Hamdala	D	RESTAURANTS & BARS	French Cafe	1
Adriel	B	House	C	Mussafir	K	Arewa Chinese	Habil Fast-Food	4
Catholic Social		Crystal Garden	E	The Pyramid	A	Restaurant	6	Kaduna Club
Centre	J	Duncan	G	Traveller's Rest	F	Byblos	7	Restaurant	5
Central Guest Inn	H	Gloria Moria	I			Food Palace	2	Sou's Place	3

important. The West African Frontier Force moved here from Zaria in 1912, and in 1917 the civil administration was transferred from Zungeru.

Kaduna lost its role as capital of northern Nigeria when the states were created in 1967, but it has continued to thrive as a centre for the **army** (in 1965, 28 percent of the city's area was taken up by the armed forces) and **industry**. Near Nigeria's main cotton-growing region, Kaduna contains several textile mills, a vast oil refinery under constant repair, a Peugeot assembly plant and numerous other industries.

For a northern city, Kaduna has an unusually large Christian population, made up primarily of southerners who arrived many decades ago to work in the city's factories. Ever since, there has been tension between the migrants and the large indigenous Muslim population, occasionally resulting in outbreaks of violence. However, after the introduction of the Islamic **sharia** legal code in 2000 (see box, p.1099) things went from bad to worse. In May 2000, following a weekend of gatherings, first by pro-*sharia* Muslims on the Friday, later by anti-*sharia* Christians on the Sunday, there were three days of **havoc**: businesses, properties and places of worship were burnt to the ground and the streets were flooded with the wounded and the homeless. Eventually the situation was brought under control by the army and the police. The official death toll was more than 400, though unofficial estimates put the figure in the thousands. A second set of riots broke out in 2002, sparked off by an article written in the Nigerian press concerning the **Miss World** beauty pageant due to be held in Abuja. This time more than 200 people died and some 1500 were injured or left homeless.

Arrival, information and city transport

The **airport** is roughly 40km to the north of Kaduna, from where a taxi into town costs around ₦3000. Shared taxis and minibuses arriving from Zaria, Sokoto or Kano stop at the **Kawo motor park** at the northern edge of town, at the top of Alli Akilu Road. Overnight buses arriving from Lagos stop at the **Mado motor park** nearby, a short distance down Western Bypass. If you're arriving from Abuja or Jos by shared taxi, chances are you'll be dropped off at **Kadung Yam motor park** on Kachia Road, about 2km south of the river. Kaduna State Transport buses use their terminal in the centre of town on the Katsina Road roundabout. The Esan travel company on Constitution Road has six-seater Peugeots arriving here from southern Nigeria. Transport into the centre from outlying arrival points is easy, with minibuses plying the main arteries nonstop; a drop costs ₦30.

The phone-less and clueless **Tourist Information Centre** on Wurno Road at the northern end of town isn't worth a visit.

Accommodation

Kaduna has a good range of **hotels** for all budgets. Most of the better hotels are located along Mohammed Buhari Way (aka WAFF Road). Two cheaper groupings of lodgings are on and around Constitution Road and in the Katsina Road neighbourhood.

Moving on from Kaduna

Kawa motor park is used by transport for **Zaria**, **Sokoto** and **Kano**, while overnight coaches to Lagos leave from Mado motor park. **Abuja** and **Jos** are served from the Kadung Yam motor park at Kachia Road. Kaduna State Transport has three scheduled buses daily to **Katsina**, the earliest leaving at 7am. Six-seater Peugeots heading broadly south – to Benin City, Ibadan, Enugu, Onitsha, Warri and so forth – leave from the Esan car park on Constitution Road; seats on these need to be booked in advance.

According to the (not altogether reliable) schedules, there are at least daily **flights** to Lagos on IRS and Chanchangi. See "Listings", p.1190, for contact details.

Adriel 4 Bank Rd, off Ahmadu Bello Way
☎062/210 456–8 ⓦwww.adrielhotelconsultants
.com. 25 clean and well-kept rooms in a quiet
neighbourhood. Each room is en suite, with minibar and electronic safe. ❺

Catholic Social Center Independence Way next to
the chapel. A large compound with three buildings
containing tidy, comfortable and clean s/c fanned
or a/c rooms. There's also a good-value restaurant
serving set meals throughout the day. ❷

Command Guest House Mohammed Buhari Way
☎062/242 918 Ⓔcommandguesthouse
@yahoo.com. The most exclusive place in town,
within an ex-military compound. Soldiers still
maintain security, which has its benefits. The
luxurious s/c, a/c rooms all come with TV and a
constant supply of hot water. There's also a classy
restaurant, snooker room, and a relaxed garden
bar doing excellent grilled fish. Tennis and squash
courts are open to nonresidents. ❼

Crystal Garden 103 Isa Kaita Rd, Ungwan Rimi
GRA ☎062/218 157–9 Ⓕ 218 160. Pleasant and
clean hotel with restaurant and bar, and Wi-Fi in
every room. ❼

Duncan 6 Katsina Rd ☎062/240 947. Friendly
and good-value hotel offering 20 s/c rooms, some

with fan, others with a/c and TV, some also with
a balcony. There's a good upstairs restaurant. No
alcohol. ❷

Gloria Moria 222 Ahmadu Bello Way ☎062/240
720. A good budget option, newly refurbished.
Rooms have a/c and satellite TV. ❸

Hamdala 20 Mohammed Buhari Way ☎062/245
440. A huge edifice of a hotel with more than
200 rooms. The s/c, a/c rooms are somewhat
run-down, but it does have a bar serving cool beer,
and an inviting, well-maintained pool (open to
nonresidents). ❺

Mussafir 15 Constitution Rd ☎062/213 578.
Clean and comfy a/c rooms all with TV. The rooms
are a bit on the small side, but the restaurant does
decent food – and there's room service. ❷

The Pyramid 13 Lafia Rd, off Independence Way
☎062/218 415–9 ⓦwww.asaa-hotels.com. A
newish entrant to the Kaduna hotel scene, with 82
well-appointed rooms, restaurant, two bars and a
pool. ❼

Traveller's Rest 19 Argungu Rd, across from the
lively *Safari Hotel* bar ☎062/217 912. Although
slightly run-down, this central hotel is still good
value, with a range of large, clean s/c rooms, some
with a/c. ❷

The Town

Kaduna's vast and purposeful layout reflects its former function as seat of government. One of the principal tree-shaded avenues, Independence Way, is lined with
administrative buildings, including, at the northern end, the monumental
Lugard Hall with its impressive dome. The **golf course** and **racecourse** are
nearby. The main commercial axis, **Ahmadu Bello Way**, runs north–south, parallel
to Independence Way. The major offices and businesses are along this street, as are
most banks and restaurants and some hotels. In the far north of town, Ahmadu Bello
Way becomes Alli Akilu Road.

Past the State House on Alli Akilu Road, the **Kaduna National Museum**
(daily 9am–5pm; ₦100) houses a small collection of masks, musical instruments, leather- and brass work and miscellaneous ethnographia. Its **Gallery of
Nigerian Prehistory** traces the country's past back to Neolithic times (the
New Stone Age ended in parts of Nigeria, as in many other parts of West Africa,
within the last two thousand years), and exhibits Nok bronzes and terracotta
work from Ife and Benin. It doesn't take very long to look round the museum,
but the exhibits are well presented and documented. Behind, a **Hausa village**
has been re-created, and **traditional crafts** – weaving, forging, leatherwork
– are carried out in the different buildings. Just north of the museum, the **Arewa
House** on Rabah Road, off Alli Akilu Road, was the residence of Sir Ahmadu
Bello, the Sardauna of Sokoto, when he served as Regional Premier of Northern
Nigeria. It now contains a well-stocked library with archives, pleasant gardens,
and a large, historic conference-hall used when northern rulers get together
for talks.

Kaduna's large **market** is off Ahmadu Bello Way, in the centre of the commercial
area. As in many northern cities, it's a good place to get leather goods and cloth,
although most of the area is dedicated to plastic ware, factory clothes and other
modern goods. There's a good food section at the back of the market with a range

of fruit and vegetables. Further south, Ahmadu Bello Way becomes Junction Road, then crosses the bridge spanning the **Kaduna River** to **Kaduna South** – the industrial side of town.

If you fancy getting out of town a little, the **riverbank** on the southeast side of Kaduna is a recommended area, though somewhat difficult to get to. Get a town taxi and ask for Malali, and get out near Malali "GTC" on Rabah Road. A walk parallel to the school, then over the hill through a housing estate, brings you down to the river. You can watch fishermen and lounge around on the rocks in relative peace and quiet; *kaduna* means crocodile in Hausa, but you're very unlikely to see one. There's a pleasant but modest restaurant, *Lesbora*, on Rabah Road on the way back. Another relaxing riverside outing is to the **small park** running alongside the river by Gambi Gate off Pool Road (the continuation of Constitution Road).

Eating and nightlife

There's good **suya** from street-food stalls, and a number of good **bakeries** are to be found on Ahmadu Bello Way; try the *Oasis Bakery* near the junction with Kanta Road, or *Farm Fresh* on Ahmadu Bello Way, both selling yoghurt, cakes and delicious pies. The *French Café* on Alli Akilu Road has a great bakery as well.

Since the riots in 2000 and 2002 people have become less inclined to go out at night, and Kaduna's already sedate nightlife has become even quieter.

Restaurants

Arewa Chinese 28 Ahmadu Bello Way ☎062/240 088. A decent Chinese in pleasant airy surroundings.

Byblos 80 Ahmadu Bello Way. Nice a/c place serving Chinese and Nigerian food.

Food Palace 1 Alkali Rd. Traditional Nigerian food, with a focus on northern cuisine.

French Café 2 Alli Akilu Rd. An excellent place serving fantastic pizzas, burgers and salads (takeaway available). The in-house bakery also turns out a huge selection of tasty bread and pastries. Just steer clear of the disappointing ice cream.

Habil Fast-Food Mohammed Buhari Way, near the *Hamdala Hotel*'s main entrance. Kaduna's best burger joint, offering an agreeable combination of fast food, a/c and music videos.

Kaduna Club Mohammed Buhari Way, opposite *Hamdala Hotel*. Popular place that, besides showing CNN, serves reasonably priced, well-prepared Nigerian and continental dishes.

Sou's Place 2 Waziri Ibrahim Crescent ☎0803/588 6404. Pleasant eatery based around open-air garden huts offering excellent pizzas and *chawarma* (and alcoholic drinks).

Listings

Airlines Chanchangi, Ahmadu Bello Way ☎062/249 949; IRS, at the *Hamdala Hotel* ☎0803/7879 316; KLM, Philips House, 4 Alli Akilu Rd ☎062/241 133. Also see "Travel agents", below.

Banks and exchange Main branches of the major banks cluster around the intersection of Ahmadu Bello Way and Yakubu Gowon Rd. For foreign exchange, try Al-Ameen Bureau de Change at the *Hamdala Hotel* (☎062/238 474).

Consulates British Deputy High Commission Liaison Office, 3 Independence Way ☎062/244 380/1 ⓔbhc.kad@patmoengr.com.

Internet access Inet, on the junction of Issa Keita Rd and Sultan Rd, and AMS Web Café, on Alli Akilu Rd, are both fast and reliable, and there are plenty of other places scattered around town.

Pharmacies The two pharmacies in front of the *Hamdala Hotel* are well stocked.

Phones The NITEL call office is on Golf Course Rd, with additional offices at Lafia Rd, GRA, and in Kaduna South.

Post office The GPO is on Yakubu Gowon Rd in the heart of the banking district. Poste restante here is reasonably reliable. Branches can be found across from the train station and at Bank Roundabout, Kaduna North.

Supermarkets There's a large People's Choice Superstore and a Baker's Delight on Ahmadu Bello Way near the intersection with Yakubu Gowon Rd, both well stocked with foreign goods.

Travel agents In addition to the usual services, the Eminence Travel Agency, Ahmed Talib House, 18/19 Ahmadu Bello Way (☎062/210 034 or 235 432), represents a number of airlines.

West of Kaduna: Kamuku National Park

About 120km west of Kaduna on the A125, the town of **BIRNIN GWARI** is where a dirt road a few kilometres south of the centre leads off northwards to a village called **DAGARA**. Head up this road and, after anything between one and three hours (depending on recent weather and the condition of the road), you'll arrive at the entrance to **Kamuku National Park** (₦200, plus ₦100 for a camera), home to a small herd of elephants and other savannah species, along with a long list of birds. You'll need a guide to trek into the reserve, something the park HQ in Birnin Gwari or people in Dagara should be able to help with. There's basic **accommodation** at *Winners Guesthouse* (①) across the road from the park HQ.

Zaria

One of the seven Hausa states, the old town of **ZARIA** has withstood the tests of time rather better than most of the other emirates. The **ancient wall**, built by Queen Amina some 950 years ago, has largely crumbled away, but some of the old gates have been restored and are very impressive. The **emir's palace** is a beautiful example of traditional architecture. Almost all the homes in old Zaria are built in the traditional style, and many display the detailed exterior decoration for which the town is famous. It's quite possible to arrive in Zaria, 80km north of Kaduna, in the morning, take a look around, and then head out before evening.

Zaria is also noted for the radical student life of **Ahmadu Bello University**, to the north of the centre, which has been the scene of some violent clashes with security forces in the past, though things calmed down after the vice chancellor, a former army major, left office. However, during the 2000 and 2002 clashes in Kaduna, Zaria experienced a resurgence of tension, and the university was once again the scene of violent disturbances. It's worth keeping your ear to the ground before deciding on a visit to Zaria, though frankly you're unlikely to encounter any problems in the town itself.

The Town

To explore the **old town**, the best plan is to rent a taxi with a clued-up driver for half a day or, failing that, to rent a taxi and find a guide at the same time. To visit the emir's palace you have to make a request at the secretary's office next door – normally granted if the emir is at home.

The main centres of activity in the old town are the **emir's palace** (*gidan sarki*) and the **market**. Scattered around the latter are the houses and stores of traders and the craftsmen's workshops (including leatherworkers, tailors and dye pits), many of which can be visited. The palace, with its elaborately decorated facade, is to the south of the market (as in other northern cities, palace and market are set well apart from one another) and is surrounded by a high-walled enclosure. The main entrance, the **kofar fada**, faces a large square where ceremonies are held, including the annual **durbar** cavalry charges.

Nearby, the **Friday mosque** was formerly one of the most magnificent in the region, though it's now enclosed by a plain-looking modern structure. It dominates one side of the square, surrounded by the offices of court counsellors and the homes of leading citizens. According to the story (tales of this ilk are common in Nigeria, told in relation to other magnificent buildings), the architect who designed it in 1834, Babban Gwani Mallam Mikaila, was later commissioned to build a mosque for the emir of Birnin Gwari. Immediately after it was completed, this emir seized him and had him put to death so he would never create a more beautiful building elsewhere. The architecture is outstanding, especially the inside

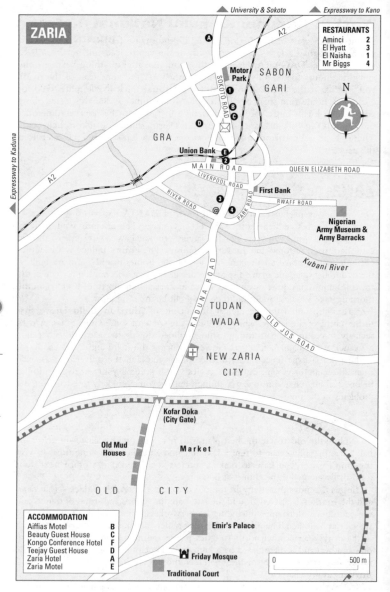

ZARIA

University & Sokoto   Expressway to Kano

SABON GARI

Motor Park

SOKOTO ROAD

GRA

Union Bank

MAIN ROAD   QUEEN ELIZABETH ROAD

LIVERPOOL ROAD

RIVER ROAD

First Bank

PARK ROAD

RWAFF ROAD

Nigerian Army Museum & Army Barracks

Kubani River

KADUNA ROAD

TUDAN WADA

OLD JOS ROAD

NEW ZARIA CITY

Kofar Doka (City Gate)

Old Mud Houses

Market

OLD   CITY

Emir's Palace

Friday Mosque

Traditional Court

0   500 m

RESTAURANTS	
Aminci	2
El Hyatt	3
El Naisha	1
Mr Biggs	4

ACCOMMODATION	
Aiffias Motel	B
Beauty Guest House	C
Kongo Conference Hotel	F
Teejay Guest House	D
Zaria Hotel	A
Zaria Motel	E

vaulting, though the replica of the mosque in Jos gives a better idea of what the building actually looks like.

The new town

After the British arrived in Zaria, a new town – **Sabon Gari** – was built some 3km north of the walled city, across the **Kubani River**, with a Government Residential

Area (GRA) with beautiful, old colonial villas west of Sokoto Road, the town's main artery that becomes Hospital Road at the junction with Main Road. It was in this part of town, now home to the main market, that Yoruba and Igbo traders settled near the rail tracks early last century. The flowery, shaded streets are perfect for a walk. Hospital Road leads south across the bridge to the **Tudan Wada** neighbourhood where most of the infrastructure is located – the hospital, schools and teacher-training colleges.

East of Hospital Road, the Chindit army barracks – Zaria's second most important employer after the University – house the **Nigerian Army Museum**, a small exhibition tracing the history of the Nigerian armed forces through displays of weaponry and other assorted memorabilia (uniforms, medals, maps and period photographs). The eras of military government are covered with a degree of comradely back-slapping, but the sections on the Biafran War and the Burma Campaign during World War II make a visit worthwhile. To get there, follow the signs along RWAFF Road, or take a motorbike from Sabon Gari (it's a long walk). You need a visitor's pass from the guards at the gate to enter the compound; a dash usually helps. ⓪

Practicalities

Arriving on public transport, you'll be dropped at the **main motor park** by the Kano expressway junction at the northern end of town, from where there are plenty of **minibuses** and **taxis** into town. **Banks** can be found in the vicinity of the market in the new town. There's an **Internet** café on Hospital Road, near *El Hyatt* restaurant. *El Hyatt* aside, there's reasonable food to be had at the town's hotel restaurants. Due to the strict interpretation of the *sharia* in Zaria, the only places you'll find beer are at a few federal government-run hotels (such as the *Zaria Motel*). Don't expect a refreshing swim either, as all the hotels' swimming pools have been emptied. ②

Accommodation

Zaria has a number of pleasant and moderately priced **hotels**.

Aiffias Motel 9 Sokoto Rd ☎069/332 033 or 335 399. Clean and comfortable with hot water and satellite TV in each room. ④

Beauty Guest House Sokoto Rd ☎069/334 038 or 331 688. Slightly unkempt but with decent s/c rooms with fan. There's also a plain little restaurant serving Nigerian food, and a very easy-going atmosphere. ②

Kongo Conference Old Jos Rd ☎069/332 872 ☎332 875. Part of the *Arewa* chain, this hotel has seen better days (in the 1970s). The 80 rooms have a/c, fridge and TV, and there's a spacious restaurant and a very dated terrace bar. Hardly one to write home about, but one of the few places in Zaria with cold beer, even during Ramadan. ④

Teejay Palace 6 Western Way Close, GRA, signposted from Sokoto Rd ☎069/333 303. A clutch of modern white blocks in a walled compound. The 50 rooms are s/c and a/c, and of a high standard. ④

Zaria Hotel Sokoto Rd ☎069/333 092 ☎zaho @yahoo.com. One of the slickest places in town, with 52 a/c rooms, a restaurant and bar serving alcohol, and a good bookshop. Nightclub Wed, Fri & Sat. Frequent minibuses to the town centre stop in front of the hotel. ⑤

Zaria Motel off Queen Elizabeth II Rd, GRA ☎069/332 451. Central and friendly government-run guesthouse set in a spacious, leafy garden with large a/c bungalows equipped with showers and TV. The bar serves cool beer and snacks. Advance booking recommended. ③

Eating

Al Naisha 4 Sokoto Rd. Good-value Nigerian food.
Aminci opposite the *Aiffias Motel* on Sokoto Rd. Cheap Nigerian fare.
🏃 **El Hayatt** Hospital Rd (Mon–Fri 8am–10pm). Large, glitzy establishment doing the

best Nigerian food in Zaria as well as snacks, good salads, and chicken and chips.
Mr Biggs Sokoto Rd. Nigerian chicken and rice fast-food.

Kano

The largest city in the north, and effectively Nigeria's second city (despite being smaller than Ibadan), the 1000-year-old Hausa metropolis of **KANO**, capital of the state of the same name, is a strange mixture of modern and traditional, with the former gaining ground and invading the latter every year. The city has a population now estimated at about 4 million, and the population continues to spread, apparently unchecked, across the dusty savannah, the growing industrialization across the region drawing people in from the countryside. Kano's vehicle pollution, especially at the close of the dry season in April or May, has to be breathed to be believed. Like Ibadan, Kano combines its commercialism with its strength as an academic centre.

The other side of Kano is its **history**. The **Gidan Makama Museum** is a beautiful effort to protect the city's heritage, housing historical exhibits of Kano and its environs in the fifteenth-century palace of Rumfa, the *makaman* Kano (or emir of Kano), restored to show off the intricacy and technical excellence of the ancient architecture – qualities which can also be admired at the **emir's palace** and the **central mosque** nearby. Other reminders of the past include the **old market** and the **dye pits** where, beside a busy multi-laned avenue, cloth is still soaked in indigo in the gloriously messy way it's been done for centuries. Yet everywhere there's a distinct feeling that much more could be done to preserve the ties with Kano's past, especially upkeep of the **old city wall**, which resisted British colonial invaders with greater success than it has the elements in recent years. Although a few of the great **gates** that once protected the emirate still stand, much of the wall has now become huge lumps of rain-smoothed mud, and people still dig away at it to make bricks for new homes.

Some history

Kano's history (its courtly history at any rate) has been preserved in the **Kano Chronicles**, which give the most detailed account of any Sudanic nation with the exception of Songhai in Mali. The chronicles, a compilation of brief histories of the region, originated in the mid-seventh century, shortly after the introduction of Arabic. The first settlement of Kano was founded on **Dala Hill**, where archeologists have uncovered furnaces and slag heaps indicating iron-working from as early as the sixth century; this settlement was later conquered by the descendants of **Bagauda** – one of the six sons of **Bawo** who founded the *Hausa Bakwai* – the seven legitimate Hausa states (see p.1186).

Kano was fortified at the beginning of the twelfth century during the reign of **Gijimasu**. Later, under **Yaji** (1359–85), it developed a powerful army that used new technology – quilted armour, iron helmets and chain mail – to overthrow its adversaries. The city became independent of its neighbours and gained control of the trans-Saharan trade in gold and salt. It thus acquired wealth and power to rival Timbuktu and Gao. Additions to the walled city were made in the fifteenth century under **Muhammed Rumfa**, who had converted to Islam and who transformed Kano from a local military chiefdom to an Islamic sultanate with close links across the Sahara and to Arabia. Rumfa's palace, built for him by his grandfather, is the Gidan Makama, or emir's palace.

Contact with Europe came in the mid-sixteenth century. **Portuguese** attempts to establish a trading centre were thwarted, but settlers from **Ragusa** (now Dubrovnik in Croatia) maintained a presence in Kano throughout the 1560s and 1570s, under the protection of the North African–based Turkish Ottoman sultan.

Over the next two centuries, Kano warred continuously with the neighbouring states of Bornu and Katsina. At the same time, European maritime powers on the coast slowly undermined the trans-Saharan routes that were the basis of Kano's power and autonomy. Although the textile and leather **industries** kept the economy going (indigo-dyed cloth and soft red leather, known as "Moroccan", were exported as far afield as Europe), the state's political structure was fragile. When the Fulani, led by Usman dan Fodio, waged their religious war, or **jihad**, Kano was unable to resist and the city fell in 1807. A new era of hostilities followed, and it was during this period that **European explorers** reached Kano – Clapperton in 1824, Barth in 1853 and Monteil in 1891. By the end of the nineteenth century, **British imperial designs** posed a direct threat to the emirate. Kano refortified its walls and prepared to resist, but in 1903 the city fell to British troops.

Kano effectively became a laboratory for testing the theories of colonial rule. The British appointed a compliant emir in order to try out a system of **indirect rule** – successful in colonial terms, but a disastrous precursor to independence. The railway was opened in 1911, the airport in 1937, and Kano's future as the dominant city of northern Nigeria, and the biggest in the Sahel, was sealed. After World War II, Kano became the centre of a renewed **Islamic nationalism** in Nigeria, intent on resisting the power of the southern regions of the country as much as, if not more than, the British, who were clearly intent on pulling out. The rift with southern Nigeria, especially with the Igbo community in the southeast, continued after independence, through the Biafran War and into recent years. In 1980, a charismatic Kano preacher, **Maitatsine**, whipped up a frenzy among landless peasants and unemployed townspeople against Nigerian armed forces in the city, in an uprising that resulted in dozens of casualties, including the preacher himself. And almost every year sees at least one major disturbance arising from ethnic tensions, usually an ordinary urban murder that leads to an ethnic riot. Seen in this light, it seems quite surprising that the introduction of *sharia* law (see box, p.1099) hasn't had the same violent repercussions here as it has in Kaduna. But not only is the *sharia* not interpreted as strictly here as it is in the neighbouring Katsina and Kaduna states, there also appears to be more tolerance of people of different religious backgrounds.

Arrival, transport and information

Kano, with its international Aminu Kano Airport, is a good place to start West African travels – reasonably lively but not so intolerably frenetic and intimidating as to put you right off – and well placed for Niger and Mali. The airport is only 8km from the central Sabon Gari quarter of Kano, an inexpensive cab ride (₦500). **Domestic flights** are with Virgin Nigeria, which flies into Kano every evening from Lagos via Abuja and makes the same flight in reverse every morning.

The Tourist Information Centre (open when flights arrive) in the arrival hall has similar materials to the Kano State tourist office in town (see p.1197). The main **motor parks** are all off the main roads leading into town. Vehicles arriving from Katsina and Niger stop at the **Kofar Ruwa motor park**, off Katsina Road north of the old city. Long-distance taxis and minibuses coming in on the Kaduna Expressway and from the east arrive at the **Nai Bawa motor park** off Zaria Road,

Kano surface arrivals and departures

Most long-distance taxis and minibuses heading south on the expressway towards Zaria and Kaduna, or east towards Jos, Bauchi, Maiduguri and Yola, leave from the **Nai Bawa motor park**. Buses and minibuses towards Katsina, the Niger border and to Niger itself (Maradi and Zinder), go from the **Kofar Ruwa motor park**. Vehicles heading, broadly, northeast – to Nguru and Gashua – leave from the **Gashua motor park** on Hadejia Road. Overnight buses to Lagos and Port Harcourt leave daily from New Road at around 5pm to reach Lagos around 12 hours later (₦2000; tickets go on sale on the day itself).

KANO

N

DALA HILL

FAGGE

OLD CITY

Kofar
Mazugai

Kofar
Wambai

Orion
Cinema

KOFAR WAMBAI ROAD

Kurmi
Market

Kofar
Mata

Cloth
Market

Dye Pits

KOFAR MATA ROAD

Festival
Stadium

RIMI MARKET ROAD

ACCOMMODATION

Baptist Guest House	F
Central	L
Criss Cross Hotel	C
ECWA Guest House	B
Hotel De France	I
Kano Tourist Camp	J
Le Mirage	A
Ni'mah Guest Palace	G
Prince Hotel	M
Royal Tropicana	K
Skyworld	D
Tahir Guest Palace	H
TYC	E

**RESTAURANTS,
BARS & CLUBS**

Arabian Sweets	7
Baker's Delight	6
Empire Peking	4
La Locanda	3
Mr Biggs	1
Smart Tandoor	4
Spice Food	5
University of Suya	2

Central
Mosque

Emir's
Palace

British Council
Library

Kofar
Nassarawa

EMIR'S PALACE ROAD

Gidan Makama
Museum

BUK ROAD

Kofar
Sabwar

Old City Wall Alignment

Kofar
Na Isa

Kofar
Dan Agundi

▼ Kaduna & Lagos

University Guest House & University

about 5km south of the centre. The smaller **Gashua motor park** off Hadejia Road in the east is used by vehicles arriving from Hadejia, Nguru and Gashua. Overnight buses arriving from Lagos and Port Harcourt stop in New Road in Sabon Gari, next to the old Eldorado cinema.

Transport within the city takes the form of taxis, minibuses and *achabas*. A shared-taxi ride into the centre, from any of the motor parks on the outskirts, costs

14

14.5 | NIGERIA | The north and northeast

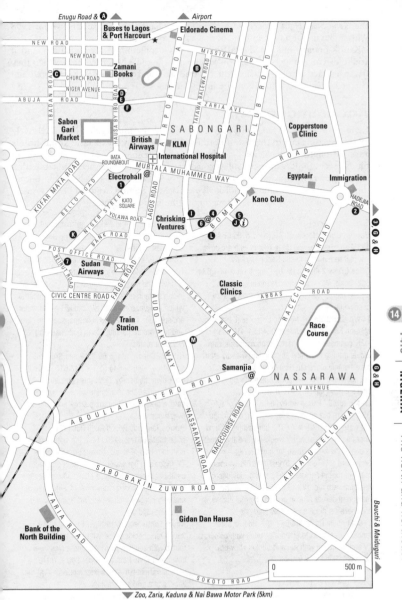

Buses to Lagos
& Port Harcourt ★   Eldorado Cinema

NEW ROAD

NEW ROAD

Zamani
Books

MISSION ROAD

Ⓑ

CHURCH ROAD Ⓒ

NIGER AVENUE

ABUJA ROAD

Ⓓ
Ⓔ
Ⓕ

ZARIA AVE.

Sabon
Gari
Market

SABONGARI

British
Airways

KLM

BATA
ROUNDABOUT

International Hospital

Copperstone
Clinic

MURTALA MUHAMMED WAY

ROAD

Electrohall ❶

KATO
SQUARE

YOLAWA ROAD

Chrisking
Ventures

❻
❾ ❹
@
Ⓛ

❺
Ⓙ ⓘ

Egyptair

Immigration

Ⓗ

Kano Club

❷

Ⓚ

BANK ROAD

POST OFFICE ROAD

❼
Sudan
Airways

CIVIC CENTRE ROAD

Train
Station

Classic
Clinics

ABBAS ROAD

Race
Course

Ⓜ

HOSPITAL ROAD

Samanjia
@

NASSARAWA

ALV AVENUE

Bank of the
North Building

Gidan Dan Hausa

SABO BAKIN ZUWO ROAD

SOKOTO ROAD

0   500 m

▼ Zoo, Zaria, Kaduna & Nai Bawa Motor Park (5km)

₦100–200. A drop in a minibus is ₦30. Travelling by *achaba* within the centre, at ₦50 a drop, is quick and easy, but to head into the centre from the outer motor parks it's best to get a taxi or minibus as the traffic is notoriously chaotic.

The Kano State **tourist office** is at the *Kano Tourist Camp*, 11A Bompai Rd (Mon–Thurs 8am–3.30pm, Fri 8am–1pm ☎064/633 105 or 631 541). They organize excursions around the city and to nearby sites, and have maps, copies of the *Kano State Hotel Guide*, and a *Kano Tourist Guide Book* – a pamphlet from 1998 with a few useful bits of information.

Kano's orange-uniformed **traffic cops** have something of a reputation, and if you're driving, sooner or later you're bound to be pulled over by them. When they try to extract a bribe, explain you have no cash and will have to be arrested and charged – call their bluff. Don't be intimidated.

Accommodation

Kano has a very wide range of places to stay, though accommodation here is relatively expensive compared to the rest of northern Nigeria. Many inexpensive **small hotels** are concentrated in the Sabon Gari district, and the business-class hotels are all within the Nassarawa GRA district. Unless you're staying at one of the better hotels with a private generator and water tank, chances are you'll be in for a spell of cold-bucket showers. You can consume alcohol at all the places in Sabon Gari listed below – many of which have their own bars – though not at mission guesthouses.

Sabon Gari

Baptist Guest House 58 Abuja Rd ☎064/648 113. Large, simple and clean rooms with a/c or fan – a real haven from hectic Sabon Gari. ①

Criss Cross 2 Ibadan Rd, by Church Rd ☎064/634 652. Basic, clean accommodation in single or double rooms with fan and bucket shower. Very good value. ①

ECWA Guest House Mission Compound, between Mission Rd and Zaria Ave ☎064/631 410. Large leafy compound with spacious rooms (some with a/c, and there are a few singles) and friendly staff. It's a homely place but be aware that smoking is not allowed on the premises. And it fills up quickly, so it's a good idea to book in advance. ①

Le Mirage 27 Enugu Rd ☎064/637 788 or 640 037. Seedy, but all rooms are s/c with a/c, fridge, hot water and satellite TV. The bar-restaurant next door has live music every weekend, and the street is one of the best in town for nightlife. ②

Skyworld 95 Niger Ave ☎064/647 622. A mishmash of rooms packed with kitsch, gaudy decor. All come with a/c, TV and bucket shower. The restaurant serves African and continental dishes, and there's a disco some weekends. ③

TYC 44 Abuja Rd ☎064/647 491. Rooms here range from singles to elaborate suites with colour TV and fridge, all with a/c and bucket showers. Good value and very friendly. ②

Elsewhere in Kano

Central Bompai Rd ☎064/630 000–9 ⓕ630 628 or 633 841. In dire need of a complete overhaul, the a/c rooms are somewhat grubby. But it does have a good location, and the bar serves cold beer. ④

Hotel de France 54 Tafawa Balewa Rd ☎064 646 416. One of the longest-established hotels in Kano, still very pleasant and breezy with cool tiled floors and a/c rooms with satellite TV.

There's a bright and welcoming restaurant serving well-prepared, reasonably priced Nigerian and European dishes. ④

Kano Tourist Camp 11A Bompai Rd ☎064 642 017. Close to lots of shops and good places to eat, and with the Kano State Tourist Board and a good Indian restaurant on site. Range of rooms, most of which are s/c, some with a/c, but NEPA and water are sporadic. There are also dorms, space to camp, and free secure parking. Dorm beds/camping ₦300, or rooms ②.

Ni'mah Guest Palace 8B Sulaiman Crescent ☎064/642 946 or 644 557 ⓕ647 616. More laidback than the nearby *Tahir*, this has comfortable rooms with all the usual mod-cons, an Internet café, a pleasant restaurant, a small pool and its own mosque. ⑥

Prince Tamandu Rd, off Audu Bako Way ☎064/200 601–2 ⓕ200 604. Top-notch place with fully equipped s/c rooms (a/c, satellite TV, fridge and hot water) as well as a pleasant patio-bar serving alcohol, a pool, and a pricey but highly recommended restaurant. All efficiently run and very popular with expats. Advance booking recommended. ⑦

Royal Tropicana 17/19 Niger St ☎064/639 350. A ramshackle place, with characterless a/c rooms with satellite TV, fridge, and a nice view of downtown Kano from the upper floors. There's a dark basement bar – with beer available – at the back, and a pricey restaurant. ⑤

Tahir Guest Palace 4 Ibrahim Natsugune Rd ☎064/646 988 🌐www.tahirguestpalace.com Substantial, marble-clad place with its own mosque, four generators and a private water tower. Apart from the usual luxuries (a/c, hot water, satellite TV), the spacious rooms come with gigantic double beds. There's also a small pool and a restaurant serving Nigerian and European food. ⑥

The Old City

Most of Kano's special appeal lies in the **old city**, down Kofar Mata Road from the modern centre. The fortified **town wall** has all but disappeared, but some of the original **city gates** (*kofar*) have been restored and are worth a look. The best-preserved gates are both on B.U.K. Road – Kofar Na Isa (literally, "I have arrived") and Kofar Dan Agundi – though other old gateways have been replaced with modern archways over the road.

As you walk round the old city, be on the lookout for examples of traditional **Hausa exterior decorations**. Particularly beautiful is the "masque" style of house facade – there's a fine example just past the dye pits, on the left as you head into the old city by the modern Kofar Mata gate. However, the Kano houses are grubbier than similar buildings in, say, Zinder in Niger, where the toll of rain, exhaust fumes and industrial pollution is that much less.

The dye pits

Inside Kofar Mata (small hillocks indicate where the wall used to be), you'll see the **dye pits** on the right. They soak cloth here in natural indigo using great basins of dye buried in the hard ground. Kano fabrics once clothed most of the people in the Sahara region and were highly valued. You can buy material or ready-made clothes from the several small stalls nearby, or even have some of your own clothes dyed. But beware: if you take a picture, you'll be asked for a dash (the demanding upturned palms are plain to see on most images of the dye pits). More spectacular than Kano's dye pits are those in **KURA**, a small town 30km south of Kano, just off the expressway to Zaria, in the heart of a major cloth-dyeing area.

The Central Mosque and emir's palace

Further along Kofar Mata Road into the Old City, the **Central Mosque** is imposing, though not the most noteworthy building architecturally. It has, however, been of enormous importance as a focus for the Islamic nationalism that has so bedevilled successive federal governments. The best time to visit is before or after

---

Id al-Fitr in Kano

In the cities of the north, the festival of **Id al-Fitr**, at the end of Ramadan (for dates, see p.63), is an important social as well as a religious occasion, allowing the emirs, their officers and their people to meet and reaffirm their mutual positions in society. Some festivals, particularly those in Kano and Katsina, draw sizeable crowds of visitors to see the annual **durbars**, or cavalry parades.

Kano's Id al-Fitr festivities begin at 7.30am, when the emir leaves his palace on foot through the compound's northeastern Fatalwa gate, and appears at the *id* ground east of the Kofar Mata, where, after a prayer, the chief imam of Kano slaughters the emir's ram, followed by other sacrifices. The emir leaves, reappearing at the palace's Kwaru Gate at around 9.30am to address the crowds.

The following day, the **Hawan Daushe Durbar** is the most dramatic, when hundreds of heavily decorated riders parade through the streets of the old city to salute the emir. The durbar sets out from Kofar Arewa at 4pm and ends when the emir returns to his palace at around 6.30pm.

The third day of Id al-Fitr dates back to colonial days when the emir used to pay homage to the resident administrator, followed by an exchange of addresses. This tradition (**Hawan Nassarawa**) is maintained, only with the colonial governor replaced by the head of the state government. On the fourth day, known as **Hawan Fanisau**, or the Dorayi Durbar, the emir treats his district, village and ward heads to lunch at his palaces of Fanisau or Dorayi.

Friday prayers when tens of thousands of worshippers turn up – an impressive sight. With proper authorization you can climb one of the mosque's two minarets for fine views over the city (enquire at the secretary's office at the entrance to the emir's palace or at the tourist office).

Behind the mosque, the **emir's palace** spreads out over a huge acreage. Its traditional architecture blends easily with the buildings of the old city, albeit on a rather larger and more stately scale. The front is far more modern and deliberately palatial. The tourist office will arrange a visit for a steep ₦1000 per person, not really worth it unless you've a fetish for palaces. The emir and his family still live in a section of the palace that you won't see, and the remainder is a collection of administrative buildings that don't have much regal atmosphere to them.

Hausa music

Hausa communities are concentrated in the cities of northern Nigeria and Niger, but the Hausa have spread right across West and Central Africa, setting up shops in the smallest towns, content to live among strangers. They have long been famous for their art and music, which has flourished since the sixteenth century and the fall of the Songhai empire, with whose music theirs has many parallels.

Hausa music splits into **urban music** of the court and state, and **rural music**. Ceremonial state music – *rokon fada* – still plays a great part (though to western ears not a very tuneful one) in Hausa traditions, while court praise-singers still play for the amusement of emirs and sultans, usually in private. The emirates of **Katsina** and **Kano**, together with the sultanate of **Sokoto**, and to a lesser extent **Zaria** and **Bauchi**, are the major creative centres.

The instruments of **ceremonial music** are largely seen as prestige symbols of authority, and ceremonial musicians tend to be chosen for their family connections rather than any musical ability. **Court musicians**, on the other hand, are always chosen for their musical skills. It's hardly surprising that the most talented players are rarely seen in public, as each is exclusively dependent on a single wealthy patron. The greatest praise-singer was **Narambad**, who lived and worked in Sokoto. He died in 1960 and it's doubtful you can still get his recordings.

The most impressive of the state **instruments** is the elongated trumpet called the *kakakai*, which was originally used by the Songhai cavalry and was taken up by the rising Hausa states as a symbol of military power. *Kakakai* are usually accompanied by *tambura*, large state drums. Lesser instruments include the *farai*, a small double-reed woodwind instrument, the *kafo*, an animal horn, and the *ganga*, a small snare drum. Ceremonial music can always be heard at the *sara*, the weekly statement of authority which takes place outside the emir's palace on a Thursday evening. The principal instruments accompanying **praise songs** are percussive – small kettledrums, called *banga* and *tabshi*, and talking drums, *jauje* and *kotso*.

Traditional **rural music** appears to be dying out in favour of modern pop, which still draws inspiration from traditional roots. Perhaps the most authentic expressions of rural music are to be found in traditional dances like the *asauwara*, for young girls, and the **bori**, the dance of the spirit possession cult, which dates back to a time before Islam became the accepted religion and continues to thrive alongside the teachings of the Koran, especially in Zaria.

The leading Hausa singer, **Muhamman Shata**, who died in 1999, was always accompanied by a troupe of virtuoso drummers playing *kalangu*, small talking drums. There's a fair number of other worthy artists such as **Dan Maraya Jos**, leading exponent on the *kontigi* one-stringed lute; **Audo Yaron Goje** who plays the *goje* or fiddle; and **Ibrahim Na Habu**, who popularized a type of small fiddle called the *kukkuma*. All such musicians are threatened by the north's widespread adoption of *sharia* law. Catch them while you still can.

Kurmi market and Dala Hill

North of the Central Mosque and emir's palace, the ancient **Kurmi market** (also known as the **city market**) forms an almost impossibly tight maze of alleys and stalls. They're pressed together to exclude the heat, but there are so many people milling about that it gets claustrophobic and sweaty anyway. The busiest and best time to visit is the afternoon, any day except Friday. The market retains a strong traditional flavour, although certain sellers with an eye on tourist bucks turn out shoddy and not very traditional junk. As always, you have to confront the question of the "authenticity" of the goods you're buying, but it's not yet too common a dilemma, and **leather**, **textiles**, **brass**, **silver** and **ironwork**, **pottery**, **calabash carving** and **beads** will continue to be made whether tourists buy them or not – and are good value. Be sure to stop at the section for local riding tack, housed in the market's oldest structure, dating from the nineteenth century.

The market swarms with petty hustlers and "**guides**". A guide can be instructive and helpful, once the two of you have got to know each other, as his presence saves you from the onslaught of other would-be assistants. Come to terms with just one, accept you'll have to pay him something and be prepared for a little transparent salesmanship at certain stalls of his acquaintance.

Dala Hill, site of the original settlement in Kano, rises up to the north of the Kurmi market, pretty well in the centre of the old city. You can walk up – it involves finding your way through narrow alleys and backstreets – and can usually find a kid to take you for a dash, but remember to agree the price first. Early morning visits are the most rewarding, the cocktail of cool air and the sun rising over Kano truly magical.

Gidan Makama National Museum

The grandiose building across the square in front of the emir's palace is the **Gidan Makama National Museum** (daily 8am–5pm; ₦100). Formerly a palace itself, the building is as interesting for its fifteenth-century Sudanic architecture (sadly beginning to show signs of disrepair) as for the exhibits inside. Fittingly, the displays in the first room explain the technological and decorative aspects of traditional Hausa building styles. Rooms two to six trace the history of Kano and the other Hausa states through drawings, photographs, documents and reconstructions spanning a thousand years – a dense and informative chronology, not for the faint-hearted. The seventh room focuses explicitly on the colonial era, while room eight is devoted to the arrival of Islam and the Muslim tenets. Finally, rooms nine and ten are dedicated to a less demanding selection of **traditional arts** – music, weaving, brass work and so on. Set aside a couple of hours to visit, as it's well worth the time. The museum courtyard is also interesting, with the replica of a Madobi hut (a woman's hut), full of the bits and bobs she needs to collect in preparation of marriage. There's also a poorly stocked craft shop and a small arena used for cultural events.

The Kano State History and Culture Bureau

The **Gidan Dan Hausa** in the old colonial residential quarter – the Nassarawa area – is another impressive Hausa structure worth visiting. Built in 1909, it was the first British colonial residence in Kano. Today it houses the Kano State History and Culture Bureau (Mon–Fri 8am–5pm; free), whose "hall of fame" photo gallery, with portraits of administrators and rulers in the history of Kano State, is curiously informative.

The New City

The intersection of Murtala Muhammed Way and Lagos/Airport Road is the centre of modern Kano, or the heart of its main commercial district, at any rate. Continuing south on Lagos Road brings you to Post Office Road and the **GPO**. Vendors on Bompai Road sell various **crafts** of reasonable quality, though the old city is a better place to shop for these.

North of Murtala Muhammed Way, the **Sabon Gari** ("New Town") neighbour-hood is home to mainly Igbo and Yoruba workers and has a distinct southern Nigerian flavour, with a large number of Kano's churches and missions, and plenty of cheap hotels and energetic bars. It's particularly animated after dark and something of a relief after the more austere "dry" areas of the old city. The recently rebuilt **Sabon Gari Market** always draws the crowds; get provisions and other odds and ends here.

Slightly out of town on the Zaria road, the **Audu Bako Zoo** is in reality more of a botanical garden, with very few animals left. It's nothing to go out of your way for, but a good excuse for a late-afternoon stroll.

Eating, drinking and nightlife

If your travels have featured Kano as a significant goal for any length of time, you won't be disappointed with the variety of **food** on offer. The whole gamut of West African food is available here, together with a full variety of imports in the shops and supermarkets. If you fancy a beer together with some southern delicacies, head for one of the many outdoor bars lining Enugu Road, in the north of Sabon Gari, where you can also try a bowl of their speciality of *isi iwu*, or goat's-head pepper soup (mind the eyeballs).

The only area of town to retain something approaching the pre-*sharia* level of **nightlife** is **Sabon Gari**, but this always was the red-light district. Down Enugu Road, you'll find a line of terraced bars where the party continues until the wee hours, as well as *Le Mirage* bar-restaurant with live music every weekend. On some weekends the conference hall at the *Skyworld* hotel becomes a disco. The rest of the city is quiet in the evening, with the notable exception of the quite animated bar at the *Central* hotel.

Restaurants and cafés

If you want to take pot luck, there are two clusters of **restaurants** to opt for – along Bompai Road near the *Tourist Camp* (various Chinese and Indian restaurants, as well as street food) and in Sabon Gari, where you will also find bars and illicit entertainment.

Arabian Sweets 4 Beirut Rd. Inexpensive Leba-nese pastry shop with deliciously sticky Middle-Eastern sweets, Italian ice cream, and a burger-bar extension at the front.

Bakers Delight 3 Bompai Rd (daily 10am–1pm). Freshly made bread and cakes, as well as meat pies and breakfasts.

Calypso at the *Prince Hotel*, Tamandu Rd ☏064/639 402. High-quality, pricey Lebanese cuisine, arguably the best in town. A popular expat hangout with a well-stocked bar.

Empire Peking 3 Bompai Rd. Popular Chinese which does mouthwatering dishes at very reason-able prices.

La Locanda 40 Sultan Rd, off Ahmadu Bello Way. Among the top places in town, where you can splash out on superb Italian food. They also do piz-zas to take out and there's a well-stocked bar.

Smart Tandoor 3 Bompai Rd ☏064/645 089 or 647 879. Superb Indian restaurant with fabulous chicken *tikka masala* and Indian sweets. Reasonable prices.

Spice Food Magasin Rumfa Rd ☏0803 450 0653. Excellent-value Indian. The owner loves to chat with his clientele and is clearly a genuine food-lover. The dishes are slow-cooked and made with love.

University of Suya *Duala Hotel* compound. *The* place in Kano to buy your *suya* street-food.

Listings

Airlines British Airways, African Alliance House, F1 Airport Rd ☎064/637 310; EgyptAir, 14C Murtala Muhammed Way ☎064/630 759; IRS, 16C Murtala Muhammed Way ☎064/637 939; KLM, 17 Sani Abacha Way ☎064/630 061; Virgin Nigeria, at the airport ☎064/947 513, 947 970 or 947 960.

Banks and exchange Most banks are located around the intersection of Lagos and Bank roads. There are good forex bureaux at the *Central hotel* parking lot (to the right of the hotel's entrance) and at the *Tourist Camp*.

Books Zamani Books, at 84 Church Rd, Sabon Gari (Mon–Fri 8am–12.30pm & 2–5.30pm, Sat 8am–2.30pm), has a broad range of books, including novels by African writers, and a *Kano Street Guide*.

Consulates Niger, 52 Sultan Rd, Nassarawa GRA ☎064/632 986; UK, honorary consul at 5 Tamandu Close, Nassarawa ☎064/631 686 ⓔbhckan@ecnx.net.

Cultural centres The British Council is sited in a lovely mud-built complex with classic Kano designs on the walls, at 10 Emir's Palace Rd (Mon–Fri 9am–6pm, Sat 9am–2pm; ☎064/646 652 or 643 489). They occasionally stage events at the small theatre behind.

Hospitals and clinics Classic Clinics on Abbas Rd, just off Hospital Rd in Nassarawa GRA is the best place for emergencies. International Hospital on the corner of Niger St and Airport Rd is open 24hr (☎064/649 533 or 643 093 ⓔinterclinic-shospital@yahoo.com). Their dentist is available daily (except Sun) 2–7pm. Otherwise try the Copperstone Hospital, 5 Court House Close, off Miller Rd (☎064/634 620).

Internet access Electrohall, Murtala Muhammed Way at the junction to Niger St; Chrisking Ventures, opposite *Central hotel* (Mon–Fri 8am–7pm, Sat 9am–6pm); Samanja, Race Course Rd, Nassarawa GRA between the two Hospital Rd roundabouts. There are many more Internet places in the Niger St/Beirut Rd area.

Pharmacies Well Care Pharmacy, Hadejia Rd, is well stocked.

Phones The new NITEL office at the end of Zoo Rd has better long-distance connections than the Lagos Rd premises (near the corner of Ibrahim Taiwa Rd). They both have fax and card-phone services. Otherwise, there are telecentres on almost every street corner.

Post The GPO is on Post Office Rd (Mon–Fri 8am–5pm & Sat 9am–1pm). The poste restante service is free and reliable.

Supermarkets Well Care supermarket and pharmacy, on Hadejia Rd, has the widest range of imports, but the row of shops in front of the *Central* hotel are also well supplied.

Travel agents Most travel agents are found in the Civic Centre, Beirut Rd, and Post Office Rd area. One of the more established is Habis Travels Ltd, 15/16B Post Office Rd ☎064/631 258.

North from Kano: Nguru and Katsina

Three hours' drive northeast of Kano is **NGURU**, the gateway to the **Hadejia-Nguru Wetlands Conservation Project**, where there are excellent opportunities for **bird-watching** if you have your own 4x4. The wetlands are unique both in their extent – encompassing eastern parts of Jigawa State and western parts of Yobe State – and in their location in a region that is otherwise attractively desert-like, with scattered camel caravans and several oases. The Nguru Wetlands Project was started in the 1980s, to manage water resources sustainably by preserving the wetlands for agricultural purposes while creating a sanctuary for migrating birds seeking refuge in Africa during the cold European winter – thousands of birds shelter here during the dry *harmattan* season. Unfortunately, the project seems to be running out of steam, and support.

At the headquarters in Nguru there's a rudimentary **guesthouse** with very basic self-help facilities (❶). Staff can help you rent a canoe to get out to the **Dagona Wildfowl Sanctuary**, situated on a small island; it's one of the best spots to view the birdlife, including ibis, duck, geese, waders and pelicans. If you're here in February, it's worth checking whether the **Gorgoram Fishing Festival**, cancelled in recent years, is taking place again. It's similar to the Argungu festival (see p.1209), where fishermen gather to compete and show their skills, but on a much smaller scale.

From this district, it's possible to spend a night under the stars on the sand **dunes** of the far north, near the border with Niger. This fascinating trip takes you past some of the most isolated villages you are likely to come across in Nigeria, as well as numerous nomadic **Fulani settlements**, before reaching the perfectly shaped, incredibly photogenic dunes of the extreme north. You'll need to rent a vehicle and driver (or a guide if you have your own transport) in **GASHUA**, 65km east of Nguru, through the North East Arid Zone Development Programme (NEAZDP; ☎076/700 044) which is based there. There's a very reasonable ⚡ guesthouse here, just 400m south of the **POTISKUM** junction, complete with a/c and generator (❸) and good meals available.

Dune alert

"From the NEADZP office we hired a vehicle and driver. He showed us abandoned villages which the migrating sand dunes had devastated, and the project's attempts to save other villages about to suffer the same fate. The dunes were bare sand – a spectacular trip. We started at 6.30 and the 7 hour trip took us to the Niger border and back, off-road almost all the way."

Piers and Shirley Miller, UK

Katsina

KATSINA is tucked away in the extreme north, floundering in the dry Sahelian badlands. During the *harmattan* season, from December to May, it's easy to appreciate the value of the traditional clothing, protecting everything except the eyes from the blowing sand. Efforts to pump some modern development into the region, notably through the installation of a steel-rolling plant in 1982, have so far brought few noticeable signs of change, other than the dual-laned highways that wrap around the outskirts of town.

Vestiges of the once-powerful **Katsina Emirate** – one of the oldest of the seven Hausa states – have hardly fared better. One or two of the original city gates still stand, in varying states of ruin, but the fortifications that once surrounded the town have been all but flattened. Reminders of the past remain in the **emir's palace** and the **Gobarau Tower** that once served as a sentry post. You can visit these, but the real pleasure of Katsina perhaps lies more in simply wandering the dusty streets, absorbing the atmosphere of a traditional Hausa city that shows few signs of modernity.

Katsina is strategically located along the highway linking Kano with Niamey, the capital of Niger. Besides the long-haul transport passing through, there's an important short-distance trade across the border, making for lively **markets** in both Katsina and nearby Nigérien neighbour, Maradi.

The Town

"Downtown" Katsina spreads along Ibrahim Babangida (IBB) Way between the **Kofar Kaura**, a recent stone gate built to replace an older mud-brick one, and the **Central Mosque** with its onion domes. Just beyond the mosque, the road veers left and continues to the **emir's palace**. The entrance to this building looks more recent than you might expect, but this is in part because it's one of the few buildings that is well maintained. Inside, the large compound is a hodgepodge of old mud-brick and new concrete buildings. To visit the palace, you'll need to enquire at the Ministry of Information building on IBB Way.

The huge **Kangiwa Square**, in front of the palace, is filled every Friday with the overspill from **Katsina Central Mosque**, just to the south. The square is the site of the annual **Sallah Durbar**, the high point of the Id al-Fitr celebrations. The celebrations begin in the early morning with prayers outside the town wall, following which horsemen, decked in their finest regalia parading through town, stage a durbar in front of the emir's palace, while women perform traditional dances.

Follow the paved road to the west to reach the **central market**, a short way from the palace. You'll find a few fruits and vegetables here, decorated calabashes and pottery with a metallic glaze, cereals and livestock, including the occasional camel. Note the Fulani women selling milk and *nono*, home-made yoghurt, from calabashes.

The **Gobarau Tower** can be made out to the north of the market. To reach the minaret, follow the unmarked street (actually Gobarau Rd) on the eastern edge of the market. Built in the seventeenth century as a lookout post, the tower later served as the muezzin's platform in pre-loudspeaker days. For a small dash a guide will take you to the top and explain the history. From the minaret, Hospital Road leads past a walled cemetery to the **Kofar Uku**. This gate "of the three doors", built in the seventeenth century according to locals, was formerly attached to **Katsina Teacher Training College**, the first institute of higher learning in the town, and the alma mater of four key figures in Nigeria's modern history: Ahmadu Bello (Northern Nigeria's first premier), Abubakar Tafawa Balewa (the country's first prime minister), Alhaji Shehu Shagari (the first president) and General Yakubu Gowon (former military head of state). Other gates of note include the **Kofar Guga** and, at the end of Nagogo Street, the **Kofar Durbi**, where you can still see part of the ancient wall called **Ganuwar Aminu**, supposed to originate from the reign of King Marabu some nine hundred years ago.

Practicalities

From the **motor park** on the outskirts of town on Kano Road, you can get a taxi or an *achaba* into the centre. IBB Way has the major **banks**, the **post office** and the big trading stores, as well as most of the central **hotels**, clustered outside the Kofar Kaura. The *Abuja Guest Inn*, off IBB Way (☏065/304 412 ❸), has s/c rooms with a/c and fan. The serenely located *Katsina Motel*, 1 Mohammed Bashir Rd has comfortable s/c, a/c rooms (☏065/430 017 ❸). For a spot of something approaching luxury, *Liyafa Palace* off IBB Way is the biggest and best in town, although some distance outside the centre on the Kano road (☏065/431 165 ℉432 690 ❺). As for **eating**, *Katsina City*, at 115 IBB Way, serves local and European dishes, but no alcohol.

Sokoto and around

Until the beginning of the nineteenth century, **SOKOTO** was a small town of little significance, surrounded by the Hausa city-states. It only gained its present status as **religious capital** of the north after Usman dan Fodio's jihad led to the creation of the **Sokoto Khalifate** in 1807. The present emir is leader of all other Hausa emirates to this day, and effective spiritual leader of Muslim Nigeria. Modernization came slowly to this region as development goals conflicted with the khalif's own ideas about what "civilization" should entail. At the wish of the khalif, the railway line that pushed northwards from Zaria as far as **KAURA NAMODA**, in the 1920s, was never extended to Sokoto. The town's isolation from corrupting outside influences was thus preserved.

Some history

The **Fulani** of Sokoto are thought to have migrated from Mali in the thirteenth century and to have settled in **Gobir**, then a powerful ancient kingdom located around the present-day Nigérien border-town of Birnin-Konni. Known as *fulani gidan* (town Fulani as opposed to pastoral nomads), they were mainly traders and highly regarded Muslims. The most learned were welcomed into the Hausa emirs' courts as advisors, where some succumbed to lives of indolence; others kept on the move and preferred a more ascetic lifestyle, teaching and speaking on behalf of the poor.

Usman dan Fodio, from Gobir, was of the latter mould, preaching energetically against the corrupt influence of high office and the lax ways of the traditional non-Muslim (or quasi-Muslim) Hausa emirs. There was much support for his

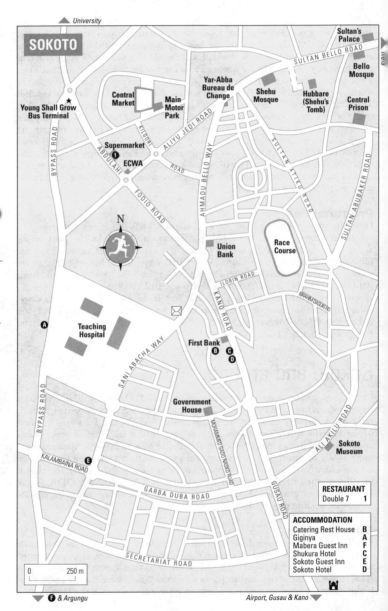

SOKOTO

▲ University

Sultan's Palace

SULTAN BELLO ROAD

Bello Mosque

Young Shall Grow Bus Terminal

Central Market

Main Motor Park

Yar-Abba Bureau de Change

Shehu Mosque

Hubbare (Shehu's Tomb)

Central Prison

Supermarket

ECWA

ABDULAHI

KIGBI ROAD

ALIYU JEDI ROAD

FODIO ROAD

AHMADU BELLO WAY

SULTAN KITTU ROAD

SULTAN ABUBAKER ROAD

BYPASS ROAD

N

Union Bank

Race Course

ILORIN ROAD

KANO ROAD

IBRAHIM DASUKI RD

Teaching Hospital

SANI ABACHA WAY

First Bank

Government House

MUHAMMED BADO NASKO ROAD

BYPASS ROAD

KALAMBAINA ROAD

GARBA DUBA ROAD

GUSAU ROAD

ALI AKILU ROAD

Sokoto Museum

SECRETARIAT ROAD

0   250 m

RESTAURANT
| Double 7 | 1 |

ACCOMMODATION
Catering Rest House	B
Giginya	A
Mabera Guest Inn	F
Shukura Hotel	C
Sokoto Guest Inn	E
Sokoto Hotel	D

▼ **F** & Argungu

▼ Airport, Gusau & Kano

stand, which called for the widely ignored or circumvented *sharia* legal code to be respected. Naturally, there was also plenty of resentment of his politicking piety from traditionalists with an interest in maintaining the status quo. By 1804, the tension had led to the birth of a radical reform movement and to civil war in Gobir, where the traditionalist emir first used arms against the reformers. Dan Fodio was a reluctant warrior and, while he agreed to be appointed Amir al-Muminin (Commander of the Faithful), the military leadership of the jihad was handled by his brother Abdullah and son Muhammadu Bello.

Weakened from centuries of warring, the Hausa emirates fell quickly and, over the space of four years, with growing popular support, dan Fodio became the uncontested ruler of the entire north. Although often characterized as a war of pious Muslim Fulani against corrupt Hausa, the reality was considerably more complicated and very much determined by people's economic position – the jihad promised a more equitable distribution of wealth and the reduction of taxes and levies. In 1809, dan Fodio's son, **Bello**, who later became the first sultan, established Sokoto as the *sarkin musulmi*, the spiritual and political capital of the empire. By the time of Bello's death in 1835, Sokoto was effectively the capital of Islam for the whole of West Africa.

The **social consequences** of the jihad were many. Dan Fodio had created, for the first time in the region, a single state with a central government controlling the entire north (with the exception of Bornu) and extending deep into present-day Cameroon and south into the Yoruba country which up to then had resisted Islam. As a result, trade was facilitated throughout the region and Arabic language and writing spread with the teachings of the Koran. When the **British** conquered Sokoto in 1903, they took advantage of the highly stratified and unified government system to implement their policy of indirect rule.

The Town

Despite Sokoto's rich history, there's little in the way of sightseeing unless you regard the city, with its calm self-esteem and well-structured pattern of wide streets, as an attraction in its own right. The city's core is the **sultan's palace**, the nearby **Masallachin Shehu** (Shehu Mosque), and Bello Mosque, on Sultan Bello Road. The mosques, with their Sudanic aura, are pleasant enough to look at, but non-Muslims aren't allowed in. As for the palace, there's not much of a Sudanic aura left as the place was completely renovated in marble and glass in the 1970s. On Thursday mornings, a group of colourfully-clad Hausa musicians play in front of the main palace gate and are worth waiting around for.

Just before the Shehu Mosque, if you take Sultan Bello Road from the palace, a dirt road leads off to the left towards **Hubbare**, the former home of Shehu Usman dan Fodio (a small signboard on the centre strip of Sultan Bello Road indicates the way). Follow it until you reach a small square, where you'll have to ask around to be pointed towards the otherwise unremarkable house. Inside it is the **Shehu's Tomb**, where dan Fodio is buried alongside eight family members including his mother, his companions and his imam. On Thursdays and Fridays, people from throughout the region still make pilgrimages to this spot to pay homage. Non-Muslims are not welcome inside, and Muslim women can only visit the house after nightfall.

The **Sokoto Museum**, now known as the **Waziri Junaidu History and Culture Bureau**, on Alli Akilu Road (Mon–Fri 9.30am–4pm; ₦200), is a surprisingly interesting museum and archive devoted to the region's history. On the ground floor, one room is dedicated to the pre-jihad Hausa state as well as the jihad period, both well documented and richly illustrated with maps, weapons and tools. A second room looks at the colonial era: letters, photos, weapons and furniture, including a wooden throne with a naked boy carved into its back given to the Sultan of Sokoto by a culturally insensitive Queen Elizabeth. The boy's head had to be removed before the Sultan could sit in it. Two other rooms contain musical instruments, Sokoto's old city gates, and various ancient farming implements, as well as a photo exhibit of the various administrations – military and civilian – that have ruled Sokoto State since independence; note the very gradual arrival of women into power. Upstairs, the archives contain original religious scripts by Usman dan Fodio and his brother Abdullah. Well-informed guides are happy to show you around and give you their take on recent politics.

You won't be disappointed by Sokoto's **central market** either, adjacent to the central motor park. It's one of the biggest and best stocked in the entire Sahel Region – an amazingly well-planned, clean, modern site with a startling abundance of flowering plants and trees. And for what seems like such an isolated city there's a remarkable variety of stuff here – produce ranges from pineapples, coconuts and mangos to millet, sorghum, a mass of vegetables and all the usual proliferation of spices and condiments. There's a large **cloth emporium** with busy tailors, and the prices, especially for cloth, are cheap when compared with elsewhere in Nigeria and mostly fixed – there's little or no haggling here. A pleasant and inexpensive **outdoor restaurant** has been set up round the large, green-and-white tower that dominates the whole area.

Practicalities

Sokoto's **airport** is 9km south of the city. The main **motor park** is north of Sokoto's centre, near the central market. If you arrive on one of the overnight buses from **Lagos** operated by Young Shall Grow, you'll end up at their terminal off Abdulahi Fodio Road, in front of *Ibro International Hotel*, not far from the main motor park. **Public transport** in Sokoto is based almost entirely on motorcycles (*kabuski* or *kabukabu*) and taxis. An average motorcycle drop is ₦30–50, while taxis cost a little more.

Sokoto's main commercial district lies along Kano Road, where you'll find the major **banks** and hotels. The **GPO** is on Sani Abacha Way, not far away. The Yar-Abba **forex bureau** is on Aliyu Jedi Road, north of the centre. **Internet cafés** are scattered about, but still fairly thin on the ground.

Accommodation and eating

Most of the **hotels** are located on and around Kano Road, near the teaching hospital, but a few good places can also be found near the main motor park. However, it's disappointing that in such a baking-hot place, all the hotel pools have been emptied, thanks to the local implementation of *sharia*.

Catering Rest House Shinkafa Rd ☏ 060/232 463. There are two entrances, one via the *Shukura Hotel* (continue right past the hotel), the other off

Shinkafa Rd. All rooms are s/c and most have a/c, though there are some spartan doubles with fan. ❶

Moving on from Sokoto

The main **motor park** in the north of the city handles transport leaving regularly for **Kano**, **Zaria**, **Kaduna** and **Illela**, the border town facing **Birnin-Konni** in Niger. Note that the quickest way from Sokoto to Katsina is to head into Niger and follow the Niamey–Kano highway from Birnin-Konni through **Maradi** and head back into Nigeria, although this requires a visa for Niger and a multi-entry visa for Nigeria. The route is used by some public transport – expect to have to change vehicles in Maradi or Birnin-Konni. Vehicles to **Argungu** (and on to the Nigeria–Niger–Benin border at Gaya/ Malanville) are less frequent, as are vehicles heading south down the A1 to **Yelwa** and **Kontagora**. Young Shall Grow overnight buses to Lagos leave from their terminal daily at 3.30pm (₦2500), arriving in Lagos in the early hours of the morning.

Virgin Nigeria flies from Sokoto to Lagos twice a week via Abuja.

Giginya Bypass Rd ☎060/231 263 or 231 466 ⓕ231 671. Sizeable business-class hotel (200 rooms) with spacious doubles equipped with a/c and satellite TV. There's a good restaurant too. ❹

Mabera Guest Inn 15 Darge Rd ☎060/232 178. Smallish s/c, a/c rooms, a 10min *kubukubu* ride from the centre. No restaurant. ❶

Shukura Kano Rd ☎060/230 006 or 230 007 ⓕ234 648. A comfortable choice, not of the same standard as the *Giginya* but quite a bit cheaper. ❸

Sokoto Kano Rd ☎060/232 126. Declining rapidly, now that the once popular bar and pool have closed. Rooms are a/c and s/c, though some have bucket showers. ❸

Sokoto Guest Inn Kalaimbaina Rd ☎060/232 672 or 233 205. Good-value accommodation with well-kept doubles and a good restaurant, with special discounts on Fri & Sat nights. ❷

Sokoto doesn't abound with **restaurants**. The Lebanese-run *Double 7* on Abdulahi Fodio Road, next to a well-stocked (for Sokoto) supermarket of the same name, serves tasty Middle-Eastern meals, including good salads. The restaurant at the Young Shall Grow bus terminal does excellent Nigerian fare at keen prices.

Argungu

Almost 100km southwest of Sokoto on good paved roads, **ARGUNGU** makes for an interesting excursion, particularly when the annual fishing festival takes place in February/March. Sadly, this well-known event has been cancelled – for various reasons – more often than it's taken place in recent years. The town also houses the **Kanta Museum** with historical relics and traditional artefacts, and a notable **emir's palace**.

Argungu has an illustrious place in the annals of West African history. The **Kingdom of Kebbi**, which had formerly been an outlying province of the **Songhai empire**, was founded near here in the early sixteenth century by **Muhammadu Kanta**, a general in the army of the Songhai emperor Askia Muhammed. When the Songhai invaded the Hausa states between 1512 and 1517, Kanta revolted against his overlords, and established himself as an independent ruler of the area between the Niger and Sokoto rivers. The capital of his kingdom was Argungu or "Birnin Lelaba Dan Badan" as it was named at that time.

Later, Argungu was one of the pockets of traditionalist resistance to Usman dan Fodio's Fulani jihad, and was never successfully conquered by Sokoto. An apocryphal account even derives the town's name from the Fulani moan *Ar sunyi gungu* ("Oh dear, they've regrouped"), since their invasions were repeatedly repulsed. Another theory has it that the original name of the town was changed to Argungu from the Kebbi saying *Ar! Mu yi gungu*, a fishing expression meaning "Let's gather in one place". The Kebbi emirate fell to the British at the beginning of the twentieth century and became part of the Northern Nigeria protectorate.

The fishing festival

Although historians date the **fishing festival** back to the era of the great Kunta in the sixteenth century, the festival as it exists today dates from 1934, when the Sultan of Sokoto made his first peaceful visit to Argungu. It normally takes place in February or March on a stretch of the **Sokoto River** (the **Rima** to people who live here) known as Matan Fada, where it braids into a multitude of channels. Here, thousands of huge *giwan ruwa* fish (some weighing as much as 100kg) are penned in a confined, shallow lake. On the chosen day, the signal is given and hundreds of fishermen plunge into the waters watched by thousands of onlookers. Using only hand-held "butterfly" or clap nets called *homa*, and hollowed calabashes with an opening at the top, they thrash around among their prey. Fishing is banned for the rest of the year in this part of the river, and rituals are performed to try to ensure the biggest possible catches.

The fishing show, however, is only the climax of a festival that spreads over three days, and includes a long list of other sporting activities and competitions (boxing, archery, camel and donkey races), punctuated with endless speeches by local leaders and sponsors. In **MALA**, downstream from Argungu, the **Kabanci displays** are another side-show, with canoe races and swimming and diving contests.

You can find out whether the festival is happening (and get dates and details) from the Kebbi State Liaison offices in the government administrative districts of state capitals throughout the country. To visit at festival time, it's imperative to make room reservations in advance; you can **stay** at the *Grand Fishing Hotel* (☎060/550 547 ❶) or at one of several guesthouses in nearby **BIRNIN KEBBI**, the modest capital of Kebbi State, 50km southwest of Argungu.

Maiduguri

The northeast's closest major town to the Cameroon border, **MAIDUGURI** is the first (or last) stop in Nigeria for many overlanders. The town is incredibly flat and hot, and has that quiet, nothing-happening feeling characteristic of so many places in the arid Sahel. If it wasn't for the **neem trees** lining the neatly laid-out avenues and providing a bit of respite from the merciless sun, you might find it unbearable. But as capital of the **Borno State**, Maiduguri has good infrastructure and makes a reasonable resting-point before embarking on further travels in the arid north.

The people of Borno are largely **Kanuri**; women, especially, are elegant dressers and hairstylists and often wear nose rings. If you spend a night here, you may come to appreciate a second level of life in Maiduguri, as experienced by the many students from all over Nigeria, who live on the **university** campus and probably feel almost as much strangers in this northwestern outpost as you do.

The Town

Thanks to its fairly modern origins, Maiduguri is a well-planned city and easy to get around. Its characteristic landmarks are the **roundabouts** which have almost come to designate neighbourhoods and are thus convenient markers for orientation. The major ones include "**West End**", with three large cast-iron fish in the middle, "**Banks**", a large spiky phallic symbol, "**Welcome**", a green-and-white concrete statue, "**Post Office**" near the GPO, "**NEPA**" near the market, "**Customs**" near the museum, and "**Eagle**", with a large eagle statue in the south of town.

Maiduguri doesn't have much in the way of sights, and any exploring, at almost any time of year, should be done in the early hours before the town gets intolerably hot. An obvious place to start would be the **shehu's palace**, but it doesn't officially allow visits, and there's nothing interesting to see anyway. Much better for a historical overview are the two **museums** (no set entry fees but small donations appreciated). The **Borno State Museum** (Mon–Thurs 8am–4pm & Fri 8am–noon), next to the open-air theatre and off Shehu Lamido Way, gives a historical introduction to the people of Borno State, and displays fishing, farming and hunting tools in one room. The other room focuses on typical Borno cooking utensils, traditional pottery, blacksmithing, weaving and a display of local jewellery, all accompanied by informative plaques. Not quite as good is the **National Museum** (Mon–Fri 8am–4pm) south of Customs Roundabout on Bama Road, where there's a similar display, plus an interesting replica of the **Dufuna canoe**, the oldest boat ever found in Africa (dating from between 8000 and 6000 BC); the original is in **DAMATURU**, Yobe State. In the courtyard there is a reproduction of a Shua hut (the Shua are a nomadic Arabic-speaking people from northern Borno and Yobe states), and a traditional mud house furnished with cooking gear and calabashes.

Maiduguri's colourful **Monday market** takes place in a covered cement building in the commercial centre of town. The **New market** is in the Gamboru district near Customs Roundabout and, apart from all the usual merchandise, is well known locally for its attractive hand-woven **mats** made of reeds from Lake Chad.

When the afternoon sun begins to drum down, head to one of the town's hotel **swimming pools** – generally in use and available to non-Muslims. The best is at the Deribe (₦200), which has crystal-clear water.

The Kanem-Bornu empire

The rise of the **Kanem-Bornu empire**, more than a thousand years ago, was a consequence of the spreading Sahara and the subsequent migration of nomadic peoples who concentrated in the **Lake Chad** basin, in districts that had been covered in lake water in earlier times. Conflicts flared between the newcomers and established communities. The **Kanuri** (a people of distinctively Saharan origins, with a language quite unrelated to Hausa, whose distant ancestors are presumed to have farmed and hunted in the era of Saharan fertility) eventually gained the upper hand in the struggles, out of which arose the **Sefawa dynasty** which ruled over **Kanem** – the grouping of ministates northeast of Lake Chad – from about 850 AD.

Oral history claims that the founder of the dynasty was **Sayf Dhi Yazam**, and that he was of Arab origin, though it is more likely that the first dynastic family had Berber connections. Whatever the truth, the authority of the *mai* (as the kings of the dynasty were known – they converted to Islam in the eleventh century) gradually spread over nomadic peoples, and the *mai* came to be accepted as a divine ruler. In Mecca, a special guesthouse was built for Kanem pilgrims and in Spain, the court of El Mansur (1190–1214) in Seville numbered renowned Kanem poets among its courtiers.

The Bornu empire functioned as a channel for trade and the **exchange of ideas** across the Sahara, connecting the three major camel-caravan routes from Tripoli, Egypt and Sudan. It was through Bornu power that Islam entered Nigeria from the twelfth century onwards, spreading peacefully across the northern Hausaland during the fourteenth century, and reaching as far as the borders of Yorubaland in the same period.

A new series of conflicts arose in the thirteenth century that incited **Mai Umar bin Idris** to emigrate west to Bornu. The new empire – now effectively Bornu, rather than Kanem – remained unstable until the end of the fifteenth century when **Mai Ali Gaji** came to power. He put an end to dynastic squabbles and established a new capital at Ngarzagamo, the first permanent residence in more than a century. A new golden era was thus launched that reached its peak under the best known of the Bornu rulers – **Idris Aloma** – who ruled until 1603. He was a zealous Muslim reformer under whose reign Islam became the basis of Bornu ideology and who also achieved military advances by importing Turkish mercenaries and military advisors to instruct his troops in the use of muskets.

Although the empire was among the most severely affected by the decline in trans-Saharan trade, Bornu was the only northern power to repulse Usman dan Fodio's invasion. The Fulani did manage to attack the capital city and sent the king into retreat, but a Bornu *malam* (teacher) named **Al-Kanemi** organized a counteroffensive that successfully drove out the enemy. Al-Kanemi took the title of *shehu* and moved the capital to **Kukawa**, near Lake Chad. In a later power struggle with the Sefawa dynasty, the *mais* were defeated and the dynasty abolished. As a result, Al-Kanemi became the Bornu ruler and his sons started a new dynasty, bringing to a close the dynasty of the Sefawa, which, with its origins in the ninth century and a final date of 1846, was one of the world's most enduring royal lines. Kukawa, on the other hand, still exists today, ruled by the *shehu* ancestors of Al-Kanemi.

Maiduguri gained its importance as a regional capital only after 1907 when the British reinstated the *shehu* in the new town where they had established a military base. It wasn't until after independence, however, that the town was linked to Kaduna by rail and thus gained a slight advantage for its beef, leather and groundnut exports.

Map labels:

RESTAURANTS
Hanna's	5
Jil	1
Lizzie	3
Mr Biggs	2
Villagers	4

MAIDUGURI

Train Station

GALADIMA

Cattle Market

BOLORI LAYOUT

GAMBORU

New Market

KASHIM IBRAHIM ROAD

SHEHURI

CUSTOMS ROUNDABOUT

WEST END ROUNDABOUT

RAMAT SQUARE

MAFONI

Race Course

Shehu's Palace

Barewa Exchange Bureau

BANKS ROUNDABOUT

BANKS ROAD

HAUSARI

N

WELCOME ROUNDABOUT

POST OFFICE ROUNDABOUT

National Museum

Monday Market

GWANGE

Zoo

SHEHU LAMIDO WAY

AHMADU BELLO WAY

NEPA ROUNDABOUT

AHMADU BELLO WAY

ACCOMMODATION
Ali Chaman Guest Inn	A
Borno State	G
Deribe	B
Dujima International	F
Lake Chad	C
Maiduguri International	D
Safari	E

Borno State Museum & Open Air Theatre

Exchange Bureau

ADAMAWA ROAD

0   500 m

LAGOS STREET

Biu, Damboa & Bauchi   GRA & Eagle Roundabout

University, Bama, Banki, Mubi, Yola Motor Park, Kawo Supermarket & Maroua (Cameroon)

Baga, Baga Motor Park, Lake Chad & Ndjamena

Dikwa, Kousséri (Cameroon), Ndjamena (Chad) & Gamburu Motor Park

Airport, Motor Parks for South and West, Kano &

Practicalities

The **airport** is 6km west of Maiduguri, a short cab ride. **Motor parks** are scattered around the outskirts, and the easiest way to get around town is by **collective taxi** to any of the roundabouts, then walk to your destination (alternatively, take an *achaba* straight there). Maiduguri's **banks** are all centred around Banks Roundabout. The city's two main **forex bureaux** are Barewa Exchange, next to the racecourse, and Exchange Bureau, across from the *Dujima* hotel; both are quick and efficient and able to change both types of CFA francs.

Accommodation

Maiduguri accommodation ranges from cheap lodgings to tourist-standard hotels. Although many of the following are run by southerners, none serves alcohol.

Ali Chaman Guest Inn Sir Kashim Ibrahim Rd ⓣ & ⓕ 076/236 939. Comfortable rooms, some with a/c and TV, all s/c with cold water (hot water supplied by the bucket on demand). There's also a restaurant serving cheap Nigerian food. ❷

Borno State 1 Talba Rd, Old GRA (turn right at Eagle roundabout on the way out of town) ⓣ 076/233 919 or 371 008. Maiduguri's most expensive hotel is overpriced for its s/c, a/c chalets. There's also a basic restaurant. ❺

Deribe Sir Kashim Ibrahim Rd ℡ 076 231 662. The best place to stay in town, with 100 clean and smart rooms with a/c and satellite TV. There's also a decent pool. ❹

Dujima International Shehu Laminu Way, opposite the open-air theatre, in the old GRA ℡ 076/232 397 or 233 231. Business-traveller hotel with large s/c singles and doubles, all with a/c and TV. The only drawback (and rather non-business-class feature) is the cold-water bucket showers. ❸

Lake Chad Sir Kashim Ibrahim Rd ℡ 076 232 400. A somewhat dilapidated affair with 60 rooms, restaurant and pool (sometimes filled). ❹

Maiduguri International Stadium Rd, turn right after the Kano motor park junction ℡ 076/235 102 or 235 871 ℻ 235 871. Huge hotel with international pretensions, opened by the state government in the late 1990s. The s/c rooms have TV, fridge, great views and usually hot water. There's also a pool, tennis courts and two restaurants. Good rates, but the drawback is the distance from the centre (₦100 by *achaba*). ❸

Eating, drinking and nightlife

Most hotels in Maiduguri have **restaurants** but they often charge outrageous prices for simple meals; better-value options are easily found around town. And you don't have to fall back on *Mr Biggs*: near the *Dujima* hotel, along Shehu Laminu Way, you'll find the shack-like *Hanna's* serving assorted African dishes as well as good salads at reasonable prices. Next door, *Villagers* serves similar good-value food. *Jil* (daily except Sun) is a popular place halfway between West End and Banks roundabouts, dishing up a wide range of European and African meals and fresh juices: they have a generator, which means light and cold drinks, and a TV showing CNN. Finally, the welcoming *Lizzie Restaurant* next to *Lake Chad* hotel (daily except Sun) does an array of well-made local and European dishes.

With the introduction of *sharia*, the already quiet Maiduguri nights have become even more tranquil. However, two places always have **beer** – both on military premises south of the centre: the *Mamy Market* at the army barracks, and the *Air Force Officers' Mess* next to NIPOST (off Shehu Lamido Way). Officially, you have to be a member to get in, but guests are usually welcome.

Moving on from Maiduguri

Shared taxis to **Kano**, **Gashua** and **Bauchi** leave from the motor park outside the town gate, along Airport Road. Departures for **Baga** set off from the motor park north of West End, past the railway tracks. Heading for **Yola**, you pick up transport at the motor park on Bama Road.

Only IRS Airlines flies (three times a week) from Maiduguri to **Abuja** with connections elsewhere. *Lake Chad Hotel* and *Maiduguri International Hotel* both have IRS ticket desks (Mon–Thurs & Sat 10am–5pm).

To Cameroon and Chad

If you're making the short crossing of Cameroon to **Ndjamena** in Chad, start by taking a vehicle from the **Gamboru motor park** on Dikwa Road, east of Customs Roundabout (you need a visa for Chad, but you won't need a Cameroon visa if you're simply passing through this narrow neck of the country en route to Chad: you'll be given a free transit visa at the border). Four- and six-seater taxis shuttle to Gamboru village. From **Fotokol** on the Cameroonian side (where you'll have to seek out the *douaniers* and *gendarmes*, 1km away, for your transit stamp) you take a much more expensive ride to **Kousséri**, 100km away. For Kousséri and onward into **Chad**, see p.1337.

The main route into Cameroon via the border town of **Banki** is on a good tarred road that leads past Bama straight to the border (minibuses from the **Bama motor park** leave continually throughout the day). Once in Banki, *achabas* will be waiting to take you to customs, but unless you're heavily laden you might as well do the short distance by foot. Border formalities are surprisingly painless. Vehicles for Mora and Maroua wait outside the Cameroon immigration office, as do moneychangers ready to swap your naira for CFA.

The far east

Although Maiduguri feels like the end of the road – and certainly most Nigerians consider the town is already in the back of beyond – it is 100km further to the borders of Niger, Chad or Cameroon. Getting to **Lake Chad** is somewhat difficult, and police are suspicious of people heading there, whether they're on public transport or driving. An additional problem is the total retreat of the lake itself from Nigerian territory over the last few years. The place to go if you want to check out the situation is **BAGA**, connected to Maiduguri by shared taxi. When you get into town, check in with the police, who won't take long anyhow to discover your arrival. There's a customs and immigration post at Baga and, if the water is high, foot passengers may be able to get a boat across into Chad: the village of Baga Sola is 76km away to the northeast, about three days by pole and paddle or a full day by outboard. If there's no water (and chances are there won't be), you can put up at the *Baga State Hotel* (**❶**).

Adamawa and Taraba states

The wedge of **Adamawa State** spreads from the Sahel near Maiduguri south along the mountainous Cameroon borderlands to Taraba State. It's a huge, little-visited region but, if you can devote the necessary time, offers some of Nigeria's best rewards in terms of landscapes and traditional rural communities. *Sharia* law is interpreted less strictly here than in other northern states and the largely endemic conflicts are more to do with competition over limited resources – between cattle-herding Fulani and settled farmers – than religion. That said, the chances that you'll witness a clash are minimal; they mostly happen in remote rural areas, at night.

If you enter the state south of **GWOZA**, the scenery starts to become spectacularly spiky and volcanic. There are terrific hikes up into the **Mandara Mountains** east of the A13 road between **MADAGLI** and **MUBI**. One route starts off from **CHAMBULA**, about 12km southwest of Madagli, and goes some 10km southeast to **MILDO MARKET**. About 5km further you reach a **school** (keep asking, young people generally speak English and there's even hope of flagging down transport, especially during the market on Tues) from where you can hope to be taken around the region.

The payoff for such meanderings in this remote region is **SUKUR**, the seat of a once powerful mountain kingdom, and now a UNESCO World Heritage Site. There's a remarkable stone causeway – product of ancient civil engineering – from the Mildo Market school up to this village. Few travellers make it this far and the people are refreshingly welcoming. However, there is now 🏕 **chalet accommodation** with five comfortable rooms boasting satellite TV and air conditioning, and even a restaurant (call ☎0803/608 0099 or 0805/327 4432 to let them know you're coming). The people in the village are more than willing to share their guinea corn and green-leaf soup and show you around their unusually constructed compounds – round huts held together with stone, mud and thatch and surrounded by a protective wall. You can also visit the **king** (the *heedi*) and if you remember to do slow-clapping when you greet him the gesture will meet with enthusiastic approval. He's remarkably hospitable, and seems eager to recount the history of Sukur, from the early slave raids to the period when this village was part of Cameroon. People round here don't expect payment, even, as yet, for staying in the guesthouse, but given the level of generosity, you should absolutely reciprocate with a gift (food offerings from your last supermarket visit will do just fine).

Further south along the A13, **KAMALE** is a village with a nearby, and amazing, **volcanic plug** – accessible from **MICHIKA**, 20km south of Chambula. This whole area has everything in common with its Cameroonian counterpart (see p.1333) and mountain people don't generally draw much of a boundary line. But, whereas the Cameroonian side is geared towards tourism (in some villages to an almost grotesque degree, with postcard sellers and potential guides throwing themselves at you) the Nigerian experience is a lot more challenging, but also much more authentic.

Yola–Jimeta

The Adamawa State capital is **YOLA**, an unexceptional, flat, spacious town near the banks of the Benue. **JIMETA**, the administrative side of Yola, is 5km north of the city centre, on the river bank, and this is where all the hotels and the main **motor park** on Galadima Aminu Way are located. There are shared-taxi departures to Maiduguri, Gombe, Bauchi, Jos, Kano and local destinations throughout the day. The **mass transit motor park** on Atiku Bubakar Way, next to Jimeta's main shopping complex, is where the slightly cheaper, long-distance buses leave from, with daily early departures to Abuja, Jos, Kano, Lagos, Kaduna and Maiduguri. Yola's **airport** is 9km from town; IRS Airlines (℡0805/496 7763) have several flights a week to Abuja. One of Jimeta's few **Internet** places is Micoh at 10 Hospital Rd, in front of Eyn Church. The **Gashaka-Gumpti National Park office** is on Mubi Road behind Micoh.

As for **places to stay**, the options aren't great, but *Jokems* on Numan Road in Jimeta (℡0805/587 7344 ③) and the *Meridien*, on Galadima Aminu Way, also in Jimeta (℡0802/644 1744), are both reasonable. Apart from the hotels, the best place to **eat and drink** is the *Pool Bar Restaurant* on Garkida Road, at the northern edge of Jimeta. They have a long menu, cold beer and a pretty garden. Also good is *Dreams* at 13 Atiku Abubakar Rd, next to the police roundabout, with burgers, chicken and chips and the like, but no alcohol.

Gashaka-Gumpti National Park

Some dramatic highland regions span Adamawa and Taraba states: to the southeast of Yola the **Atlantika Range**; to the southwest the **Shebshi Mountains** (with 2042-metre Vogel Peak); and, far to the south, in the corner of Nigeria tucked into western Cameroon, the verdant **Mambilla Plateau** with Nigeria's highest peak, the 2418m Chappel Waddi (which means "Mountain of Death"). Although these high grassland plateaus, with a pleasant climate and sparse cattle ranches and tea plantations, are similar to Obudu (see p.1169), it wasn't until recently that travellers began visiting.

An area of 6670 square kilometres of mountain forests and savannah abutting the Cameroonian border is now protected as the **Gashaka-Gumpti National Park**. This is the site of a major World Wildlife Fund project, in collaboration with the Adamawa and Taraba state governments, who are responsible for the Gumpti and Gashaka sectors respectively. The area harbours a sizeable **chimpanzee** population and, after an absence of several decades, **elephants**; it is thought that the park also protects such rare species as leopard and lion, as well as giant forest hogs and hartebeests.

Efforts to gear up the park for visitors are in progress at the park office in **SERTI**, a village on the "main" Yola-to-Gembu road, where there is simple **accommodation** (①) but no electricity or running water. The park entrance is 15km to the southeast, and rangers will gladly give you a lift if they need to venture into the park, but you can't rely on that. If you want to visit the park under your own steam and don't have your own vehicle, you may be able to rent one from the rangers, one of whom will accompany you as driver and guide (allow ₦3000–4000 per day for this kind of deal).

Gembu

In **GEMBU**, the main town of the region, 137km south of Serti and 430km south of Yola (very hard and slow travel by occasional bush taxi or land rover), there's the *Daula Hotel*, with basic rooms and sporadic electricity and water (①). An hour's trek towards Cameroon from Gembu takes you to the red-clay valley of the **Donga River**, a superb sight as it snakes through the jungle. You can cross by canoe or raft, and climb a towering rocky peak on the other side for magnificent views (two hikes or 4x4 routes lead up into Cameroon near here, but ask local people about current conditions and the viability of driving). Another excursion from Gembu takes you to the **Highland Tea Plantation**, beyond **KAKARA** (a village 30km northwest of Gembu). You'll probably be the first traveller the management here has seen in a while, and they'll not only give you a tour of the place but let you stay in the club for a small fee, watch TV and videos, feed you and ply you with beer, before sending you off with a kilo of produce.

Wukari to Cameroon – the Dumbo Trek

The bustling market town of **WUKARI**, down in the Benue Valley, has a number of hotels: try the good-value *Hospitality* on IBB Road (❶), or the central and very inexpensive *Ishaku* (❶), at the junction of the Takum and Rafia roads. To go direct to Cameroon's spectacular Ring Road region from here, head first for **TAKUM**, where the highlands ahead begin to make their presence felt (the *Dadin Kowa Guest Inn*, on the Yola road, is a reasonable place to stay; ❶). Takum is at the southern end of the paved road and beyond it, looping into the green hills, with bananas and fleshy jungle plants increasingly conspicuous, there is just an earth track, mostly in reasonable condition, passing over innumerable frog-filled streams up to the village of **BISSAULA**. You'll be able to get transport as far as Bissaula, though don't miss any vehicles that are going, as they're not numerous.

The route that snakes up from Bissaula to **Dumbo** in Cameroon consists of a rough footpath inaccessible to any vehicle. If you are keen to do some **trekking**, though, it's a winner: a moderately tough two-day hike of about 40km that takes in towering trees, squealing parrots, leaping monkeys, thatched-hut hamlets in smoky forest clearings, and lines of porters (mostly portering on their own accounts, beer, cigarettes and cloth). When you reach the top of the escarpment, about halfway through the journey, it seems half of southern Nigeria is spread out behind you.

You shouldn't set off trekking on your own as orientation here is very difficult. For about ₦4000 (CFA15,000) you can hire the services of a **porter** to walk up to Dumbo with your luggage (the Nigerian immigration post will stamp you out and write "Footing" in your passport). If you opt to carry your own bag, you should join a group for the initial stages of the trek. You walk for about two hours through lush forest and farm plots, then start climbing the steep scarp, which takes a couple of hours to the top. People generally leave Bissaula late afternoon, and either spend the night in a village at the foot of the scarp and then set off at 4am, or reach the top of the scarp after dark and spend the night in the village there. With an early start on day two you can be in Dumbo (see p.1294) by evening, but it's less exhausting to arrive mid-morning on day three. You should be aware of the fact that the Cameroonian immigration and customs post at Dumbo doesn't get many tourists and may try to extract presents from you. If you take photos on the trek, try to be discreet, this being a border area.

Cameroon

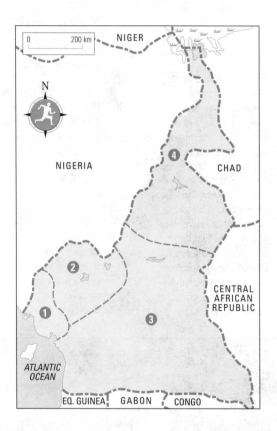

Highlights	1218	15.2 The western highlands	1279
Introduction and Basics	1219	15.3 Yaoundé and the south	1300
15.1 Douala and South West Province	1252	15.4 Northern Cameroon	1321

Cameroon highlights

✳ **Cameroonian music** One of West Africa's most varied musical feasts – from sexy urban *makossa* and *bikutsi* to the strange music and instruments of the forest-dwelling Baka. See p.1244

✳ **Mount Cameroon** West Africa's highest mountain, offering a challenging ascent and a memorable range of landscapes and views en route. See p.1269

✳ **Biking around the Ring Road** A classic Cameroonian adventure and an excellent way of experiencing the road's varied landscapes, from forest and savannah to mountains and crater lakes. See p.1290

✳ **Kribi** Relax on the beautiful white sandy beaches and enjoy delightful food. See p.1312

✳ **Hiking with the Baka** Hiking through the rainforest with "Pygmy" guides. See p.1318

✳ **Hiking in the Mandara Mountains** Explore the haunting volcanic landscapes of these peaks and get to know the staunchly independent mountain people who still live there. See p.1333

✳ **Waza National Park** Probably the best area for savannah game-viewing in West Africa, with a good chance of spotting giraffe, lions and elephants. See p.1336

▲ Bamenda, from Up Station

Introduction and Basics

The **landscapes of Cameroon** are exceptional. The country stretches from the fringes of the Sahara in the north to the borders of Congo and Gabon in the south and takes in every African variation in between: from equatorial rainforest (some of the continent's most unexploited tracts) to moist, tree-scattered savannah; from dry grassy plains to bucking volcanic ranges flecked with crater lakes; from gaunt rocky massifs to the hot basin of Lake Chad; and, to cap it all, the highest mountain on this side of the continent – the 4095 metres of Mount Cameroon – rising direct from the ocean shore to an impressive cloud-wreathed summit. For good measure, the country also has some entrancing beaches and several large wildlife parks, with rewarding numbers of large mammals, including species found nowhere else in the region. At the level of tourism, it's hard to oversell Cameroon – it's simply the most dramatic and diverse country in West Africa.

There's another side to Cameroon in its hugely stimulating cultural make-up, which exhibits some striking **ethnic distinctions**. The Muslim sultanates of the north are reminiscent of northern Nigeria, and also have strong Arab connections, but exist alongside the avowedly non-Muslim people of the mountainous Roumsiki district. In the forests of the far south, the so-called "Pygmies" – the region's original inhabitants – still attempt to live a life of hunting and gathering although the modern nation state encroaches on them. And in the mountains and pasturelands of the country's western "bulge", a remarkable complex of kingdoms has developed over the last four hundred years, speaking dozens of Bantoid languages (closely related to Bantu). This is the only country in West Africa with a large **Bantu-speaking** population (the Bantu languages, including Swahili and Zulu, are some of the most important in Africa), which gives the south much in common with the Central African region. Coupled with its natural diversity, it's a country that can claim to embody cultural elements of the entire continent.

Cameroon has a colonial past of German, French and British occupation. With the current division between Francophone and Anglophone affecting every aspect of national life, impressions of contrast and fragmentation are never far away. Recurring, and occasionally fierce, outbursts of old Anglo–Francophone tensions have led repeatedly to calls for secession in the west. But with the current growing economy, opposition in general has become a lot less vocal.

The increasing importance of **tourism** as a source of foreign exchange has led to some improvement in official attitudes to foreign visitors. The searches and controls that once dogged visitors from the moment they arrived are no longer so aggressive. There are, however, still numerous roadblocks throughout the country – little havens where police and customs officials extract "dash money" (bribes). And the tourist industry remains wed to its upmarket expectations: backpackers who sleep in cheap hotels and

Photography

Taking photographs is hedged about with restrictions. These go beyond the usual military and "national security" taboos to include anywhere the president is likely to stay when travelling, parades, festivals and anything "likely to cause a decline in morality and damage the country's reputation". The interpretation of this law is left to the person who decides to take you to task for breaking it. Taking pictures in Yaoundé and Douala is likely to lead to trouble unless you're very discreet or very charming.

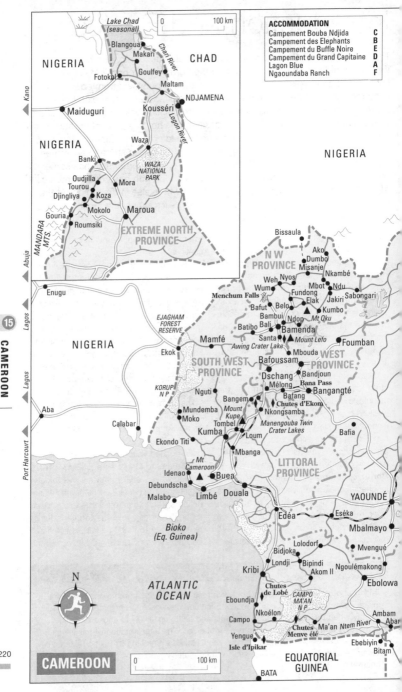

ACCOMMODATION

Campement Bouba Ndjida	C
Campement des Elephants	B
Campement du Buffle Noire	E
Campement du Grand Capitaine	D
Lagon Blue	A
Ngaoundaba Ranch	F

CAMEROON

0   100 km

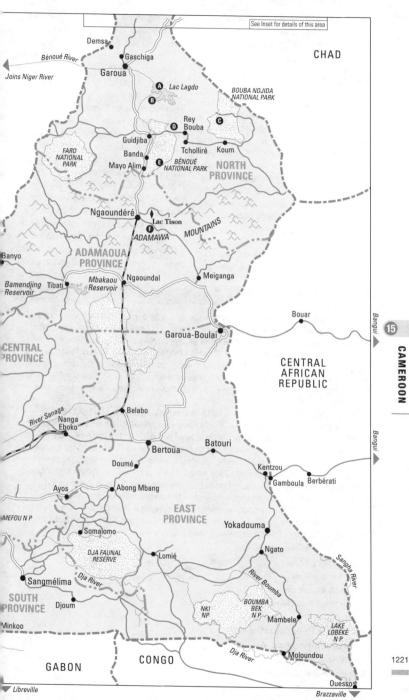

Demsa

Bénoué River

Joins Niger River

Gaschiga
Garoua

CHAD

Ⓐ Lac Lagdo
Ⓑ

BOUBA NDJIDA
NATIONAL PARK

Ⓓ Rey
Bouba   Ⓒ

Guidjiba
Banda   Tcholliré   Koum
Mayo Alim Ⓔ BÉNOUÉ
NATIONAL PARK

FARO
NATIONAL
PARK

NORTH
PROVINCE

Ngaoundéré
Lac Tison

Ⓕ
ADAMAWA

MOUNTAINS

Banyo

ADAMAOUA
PROVINCE

Bamendjing
Reservoir   Tibati   Mbakaou
Reservoir   Ngaoundal   Meiganga

Bouar

CENTRAL
PROVINCE

Garoua-Boulai

CENTRAL
AFRICAN
REPUBLIC

River Sanaga
Nanga
Eboko   Belabo

Bertoua   Batouri

Doumé   Kentzou
Ayos   Abong Mbang   Gamboula   Berbérati

MEFOU N P

Somalomo

EAST
PROVINCE

Yokadouma

Lomié   Ngato   River Boumba

DJA FAUNAL
RESERVE

Sangmélima   Dja River

SOUTH
PROVINCE   Djoum

Minkoo   NKI
NP   BOUMBA
BEK
N P   Mambele   LAKE
LOBÉKÉ
N P

Sangha River

GABON   CONGO   Dja River   Moloundou

Libreville   Brazzaville   Ouesso

Bangui

15

CAMEROON

1221

cram into bush taxis are still prone to be put down as *pauvres blancs*, and may experience the disdain of local officials.

People

The oldest group of people to have lived in Cameroon are the **"Pygmies"** of the south and southeast forests. Forced onto the defensive by the expansion of the various Bantu-speaking groups, and with their livelihood threatened by extensive logging, many have today settled in small villages. However, some still opt for the traditional independence of the few remaining impenetrable areas of the rainforest, where they continue to live by hunting and gathering.

Bantu-speaking populations have spread gradually southeast through the Cameroon region into Central Africa over the past two thousand years, migrating in strength from the Adamawa range and settling along the coast from about the fifteenth century. The first to migrate were the **Bassa** and **Bakoko**, followed by the **Duala**. In the nineteenth century, pushed out of the plateaux in the east after the Fulani Sokoto invasions in Nigeria, the **Fang**, **Ewondo**, **Eton** and **Béti** (President Paul Biya's tribe) came to settle in the central southern region around Yaoundé.

In the west of the country, waves of northern immigration between the sixteenth and nineteenth centuries saw the installation of **"Semi-Bantu"** peoples. The first to arrive were the **Tikar**, who probably came from the area near Ngaoundéré and who today live in semi-autonomous chiefdoms throughout the Grassfields region. In the eighteenth century a splinter group broke away from the Tikar country to form the powerful **Bamoun** Empire

Fact file

The **Republic of Cameroon** (or République du Cameroun to Francophones) covers 475,000 square kilometres – an area twice the size of Britain and slightly larger than California, with a population estimated at eighteen million. The name derives from *camarões*, the Portuguese for prawns, which the first European visitors found in large quantities in the Wouri River. The plural reference to **"Cameroons"** is a reminder both of the shrimps and of the legacy of the colonial division into two Cameroons – French and British – a dual heritage preserved in the official bilingualism (easily dominated by French).

The country has been ruled since 1982 by **Paul Biya**, long the head of the Rassemblement Démocratique du Peuple Camerounais (RDPC), the country's sole political party until opposition parties were legalized in 1990. The country's foreign debt was slashed significantly in 2006 with Heavily Indebted Poor Countries Initiative debt relief, to £1.8 billion ($3.6 billion), which still equates to more than $200 owed for every person in the country. Cameroon's main export earnings come from oil, timber and agriculture – mainly the extensive cocoa and rubber plantations in the south.

Cameroon is divided into ten administrative **provinces**, with governors appointed by the president. You may find their names confusing at first, especially in western Cameroon in that, for example, South West Province extends further north and west than West Province. The provinces and their capitals are:

Centre/Centre: Yaoundé
South/Sud: Ebolowa
East/Est: Bertoua
Littoral/Littoral: Douala
South West/Sud Ouest: Buéa
West/Ouest: Bafoussam
North West/Nord Ouest: Bamenda
Adamawa/Adamaoua: Ngaoundéré
North/Nord: Garoua
Extreme North/Extrême Nord: Maroua

a little to the east. The **Bamiléké** – a fusion of peoples from the north, east and southwest, whose arrival spread over three centuries – settled in the plateau region south of the Noun River. The Bamiléké, now the country's largest single ethnic group, are also numerous in Douala where they have come to control a good deal of the national economy.

The predominant group in the north is the **Fula** (also known as Fulani, Foulbé or Peul), who settled in principalities (or *lamidats*) around the early nineteenth century, bringing Islam with them.

The Mandara Mountains of the far northwest are inhabited by staunchly non-Muslim groups known collectively as **Kirdi** – which just means "infidels". Pushed to these desolate extremities by the Muslim invasions of Usman dan Fodio, an early nineteenth-century Islamic leader from Nigeria, they comprise numerous Adamawa- and Chadic-speaking peoples: the **Podoko**, **Fali**, **Kapsiki**, **Mafa** and **Bata**. Principally farmers, they grow millet and sorghum in terraced gardens on the rocky slopes of the mountains.

The northern plains near Lake Chad are home to the **Shua**, semi-nomadic peoples of Arab origin who share these open spaces with the **Kotoko** – descendants of an ancient culture called **Sao** – who live from fishing and growing a few cereals. Near the Logone River, live the **Toupouri**, **Massa** and **Mousgoum**, people of pre-Islamic beliefs who are increasingly becoming Islamicized.

In matters of **religion**, Cameroon is very mixed, with about half the population, mostly in the rural areas, following **traditional belief systems**, while around a third are Christian and a sixth Muslim. Christians divide roughly evenly into **Catholics** (especially in the Francophone provinces of the southern and western regions) and **Protestants** (largely in the Anglophone North West and South West provinces). **Muslims** are concentrated mainly in the north provinces, though the Bamoun people of West Province are also predominantly Muslim.

Where to go

Cameroon's main city, **Douala**, is a seething, sweltering metropolis that wins few accolades. Fortunately, an hour's drive from Douala, the black-sand beaches of **Limbé**, in South West Province, are a good, quick getaway. Between the strands, in the rich soil beneath Mount Cameroon, the dense vegetation pushes right to the water's edge, although it has increasingly been cleared to create plantations of tea, bananas, rubber trees and oil palms. The trek up **Mount Cameroon**, a still active volcano, is a challenging but perfectly feasible ascent. To the north of the mountain, the country drops towards the Nigerian border and the **Korup rainforest**, now a fairly easily accessible national park.

North West and **West** provinces (the former predominantly Anglophone, the latter mostly Francophone) are the most densely populated parts of Cameroon, and contain some of the country's most popular sites for visitors. Both are relatively well equipped for tourism, with a developed infrastructure and even a quite cosmopolitan feel in the larger towns. Nevertheless, the landscapes are often rugged. Together, these provinces form probably the easiest part of Cameroon in which to strike out on your own; visiting the **Bamiléké district** and **Foumban**, with its Sultan's Palace and crafts market; the **traditional chiefdoms** of the Bamoun, Tikar and others around the 400-kilometre red-earth **Ring Road**; and the beautiful **Grassfields** area through which the Ring Road circles. The whole of this upland region is renowned for its thatched architecture and animated traditional life.

The capital, **Yaoundé**, has a better climate to live and work in than Douala, and it's a more relaxed place to rest up from travels, though it remains a fairly aggressive metropolis with its share of tensions. The vast **plateau** that stretches to the southeast, covered with huge tracts of hardwood rainforest, has been severely damaged by logging during the past decade. With eighty percent of all Cameroon's indigenous forests now divided up into logging concessions, new roads and tracks are constantly being cleared and the great expanses of the **Central**, **South** and **East** provinces are no longer as impenetrable as they once were. A number of **"Pygmy"** bands, including groups of Baka, hunt and gather in the jungle, which is also the domain of **gorillas** – quite prolific in certain areas. The reserves of Campo Ma'an, Dja and Lake Lobéké are slowly becoming more accessible, and some basic tourist facilities have been developed.

North of Yaoundé, the northern sectors of Central and Eastern provinces comprise an immense, empty savannah, patched with forest. Together with the gaunt **Adamawa range**, they effectively cut the country in two and hinder north–south overland travel. Further north, you come into pre-Sahelian grasslands and dusty bush country. The upper tributaries of the Bénoué (Benue) flow through this region, where you'll find the **Bénoué** and **Bouba Ndjida** national parks, home to herds of elephant and buffalo, and lions.

In the flat plains of the far north, **Waza National Park** is Cameroon's outstanding faunal reserve, with elephants, lions, giraffe, ostriches and a host of antelope species. To the west, a few hours away, the other-worldly volcanic plugs of the **Mandara Mountains** offer a beautiful backdrop to the stony homeland of the non-Muslim Kirdi "mountain people". The northernmost tip of the country, leading up to what's left of **Lake Chad**, is usually dry, but it floods under the waters of the **Logone** and **Chari** rivers during the region's brief annual rains.

When to go

The region around Mount Cameroon and the western mountains has the dubious distinction of boasting one of the world's highest levels of **rainfall**: Debundscha, 30km west of Limbé, is the second wettest place on earth, after Cherrapungi in India. The general pattern here, and in **the south**, can be divided into three approximate seasons: a period of relatively light but persistent rains from March to June; the long rainy period from July to October; and the dry season from November to February. Travel can involve long waits during the rains, especially to towns accessible only by unsurfaced roads, such as Mamfé.

Roads around the **Grassfields** are often unmotorable during the rains, when even 4x4s can have problems. The savannahs further north choke towards the end of the dry season with fine red laterite dust, blown up by the northerly *harmattan*. Plants and crops turn rusty red, while lungs – and cameras – seize up.

North of the Adamawa Plateau, **northern Cameroon** has a different weather pattern, characterized by a long rainy season from May to October and a dry season for the rest of the year, culminating in a tinder-dry period.

Average temperatures and rainfall

Yaoundé

	Jan	Feb	Mar	Apr	May	June	July	Aug	Sept	Oct	Nov	Dec
Temperatures °C												
Min (night)	19	19	19	19	19	19	19	18	19	18	19	19
Max (day)	29	29	30	29	28	28	26	26	27	28	28	29
Rainfall mm	23	66	147	170	196	152	74	79	213	295	117	23
Days with rainfall	3	5	13	15	18	17	11	10	20	24	14	4

Douala

	Jan	Feb	Mar	Apr	May	June	July	Aug	Sept	Oct	Nov	Dec
Temperatures °C												
Min (night)	23	23	23	23	23	23	22	22	23	22	23	23
Max (day)	31	32	32	32	31	29	27	27	29	30	30	31
Rainfall mm	46	94	203	231	300	539	742	693	531	429	155	64
Days with rainfall	4	6	12	12	16	19	24	24	21	20	10	6

Kousséri

	Jan	Feb	Mar	Apr	May	June	July	Aug	Sept	Oct	Nov	Dec
Temperatures °C												
Min (night)	14	16	21	23	25	24	22	22	22	21	17	14
Max (day)	34	37	40	42	40	38	33	31	33	36	36	33
Rainfall mm	0	0	0	3	31	66	170	320	119	36	0	0
Days with rainfall	0	0	0	1	6	10	15	22	13	4	0	0

Although travel in the north doesn't present any special problem during this period, it's worth noting that visibility in many national parks is limited between May and December, due to the relatively dense vegetation. Overall, the **ideal time to visit**, taking into account the different regional patterns, is December and January.

> For details on **getting to Cameroon from outside Africa**, plus important practical information applying to all West African countries, covering health, transport, cultural hints and more, see Basics, pp.19–28.

Getting there from the rest of Africa

For years, getting to Cameroon was made easy by the extensive coverage of the excellent national carrier, Cameroon Airlines, or CAMAIR. Now, in financial dire straights, CAMAIR's network is constantly shrinking and the future is looking very bleak. Filling the gaps left by CAMAIR are a whole host of small regional airlines with ever-changing timetables and routes, making advance booking somewhat difficult. Flying in means arriving in the rather heavy city of Douala (unless you catch one of the few direct flights to Yaoundé or Garoua).

Arriving **overland**, from the east Cameroon feels like the threshold of a new region, which it is, as you leave the confines of the Central African rainforest and enter West Africa. Arriving overland from the west, Cameroon is noticeably the threshold of Central Africa.

Flights

Cameroon has **international airports** at Yaoundé and Garoua, but most foreign flights still hub in Douala. **Departure taxes** are CFA10,000 on international flights and CFA500 on domestic departures.

The flagging **Cameroon Airlines** still has six flights a week to Douala from **Dakar**, all via **Abidjan** and **Lagos** (three of them also via **Bamako** and three also via **Cotonou**).

More reliably, Virgin Nigeria flies thrice weekly to Douala from **Lagos**, while Bellview Airlines has five weekly flights from Lagos. Hewa Bora Airways has two weekly flights from **Lomé** via Lagos and there are two weekly flights from **Cotonou**. From **Abidjan**, Benin Golf Air and Air Ivoire make a total of five weekly flights via Cotonou. Kenya Airways also flies to Douala from Abidjan four times

a week, en route to Nairobi. From **Ouagadougou** and **Niamey**, the easiest connections to Douala are via Abidjan with Air Ivoire.

Cameroon has good air links with Central Africa. Cameroon Airlines has three weekly direct flights to Douala from **Bangui** and three flights a week from **Ndjamena** (one nonstop, one via Bangui and Yaoundé, and one via Garoua and Yaoundé).

Toumai Air Chad has four weekly flights to Douala from **Ndjamena** via Bangui. Afriqiyah Airways has a weekly flight from Ndjamena.

There are flights to Douala most days from **Brazzaville** (some originating in **Kinshasa**) with Cameroon Airlines, Hewa Bora, Toumai Air Chad or Trans Air Congo.

From **Libreville** to Douala, Air Service operates at least a daily direct flight. Bellview Airlines and Cameroon Airlines both have three daily flights.

Cameroon Airlines has two flights a week from **Malabo**, while Benin Golf Air also flies this route once a week.

From east and southern Africa, Kenya Airways has a daily flight from **Nairobi** to Douala (via **Yaoundé** three times a week, otherwise nonstop), while Ethiopian Airlines has four weekly nonstop flights from **Addis Ababa** to Douala. From **Johannesburg** to Douala, there is one weekly nonstop flight with Cameroon Airlines and two nonstop flights with Bellview.

Overland from Nigeria

The two main overland routes from Nigeria head for **Mamfé** in the west of Cameroon and **Mora** in the north. You'll need to have a visa already to use the Mora crossing (see p.1213). The straightforward western route involves getting a bush taxi from **Calabar to Ikom**, from where taxis leave regularly for the busy border. After completing the often protracted Nigerian customs and immigration formalities, you walk over the bridge spanning the Cross River and up the hill to the Cameroonian post at **Ekok**. Taxis from Ekok to Mamfé rattle along bumpy tracks through a beautiful but tortuous hilly region. A variation on this route involves travelling by pirogue up the Cross River to Mamfé. A second and more straightforward sea option is to take the **twice-weekly ferry** from Calabar to Limbé (see p.1162).

The main northern route to Mora (which involves less border hassle than the western route) leads from **Maiduguri** via **Bama** over a good, flat paved road to the border post at Banki. Customs and immigration formalities are dealt with swiftly and black-market money traders are ready and waiting once you're done. From here it's easy to find transport at the Banki motor park next to immigration, from where it's a bumpy two-hour journey on rough tracks across the plains (look out for antelope) to **Mora** and on to Maroua or up to Waza National Park.

Overland from Chad

There is a bridge between **Ndjamena**, in Chad, and **Kousséri**, in Cameroon. Details of this border crossing are given on p.1337. There are several other possible border crossings further south, but they're in insecure areas and rarely used.

Overland from Congo

The 400km border between Cameroon and Congo is currently closed.

Overland from Central African Republic

Western CAR is a lawless region, and the **CAR–Cameroon border area** has become very insecure in the last few years, with numerous incidents of carjackings and highway robberies on the roads in eastern Cameroon as a knock-on impact of the war in Darfur, and the refugee crisis and internal conflicts in CAR and Chad. Driving into eastern Cameroon in **your own vehicle** is definitely to be avoided, but, as with travelling **by public transport** in this region, you will already have passed through some very rough districts further east, so you should know the score.

The main Cameroonian border post is at **Béloko–Garoua-Boulai**. Once you've crossed the border, a reasonable dirt road connects Garoua-Boulai with **Meiganga**, 100km to the north, while a decent paved road runs 260km south from Garoua-Boulai to **Bertoua**.

Overland from Equatorial Guinea and Gabon

The main road from **Bata** in **Equatorial Guinea** heads far inland to **Ebebiyin**, at the point where Gabon, Cameroon and Equatorial Guinea all meet. From here, the route goes via **Ambam** to **Ebolowa** where there's the choice of heading either direct to Yaoundé on a fast paved road or taking the slower but more scenic coastal route via **Kribi**. From Bata there's also the option of travelling straight north on the *piste* to the border town of **Yengue** on the **Ntem River**, where you can pick up motorized pirogues travelling downriver to the beach a few kilometres south of **Campo**. From Campo there are shared taxis to Kribi.

You'll use Ambam if you're travelling from **Libreville**.

Red tape and visas

All passport holders (other than certain African nationals) need a visa to enter Cameroon. In theory, it is also possible to obtain visas on arrival (CFA50,000) at **Douala and Yaoundé airports** if you're coming from a country without Cameroonian diplomatic representation. It's best to contact the nearest Cameroonian embassy or Cameroon Airlines beforehand, if you want to use this option. A number of West African states – including Mali and Niger – have no Cameroonian consulate, so you need to plan ahead.

Visas cost about £60 ($120), are valid for three months and must be activated within three months of issue. You'll usually need to show a return air ticket or proof of your intended onward route – including any other relevant visas. Bank statements showing sufficient funds, and a letter of invitation from a Cameroonian resident or a hotel booking confirmation, are also usually requested. It's not hard to extend your stay in any of the provincial capitals, but it's just as pricey as getting a visa in the first place.

If you're coming from Central Africa, Cameroonian consulates can be found in **Central African Republic** (Bangui ☎61.16.87); **Chad** (Ndjamena ☎52.28.94); **Equatorial Guinea** (Malabo ☎922.63); **Congo** (Brazzaville ☎83.34.84); **Congo DR** (Kinshasa ☎12.33.166); and **Gabon** (Libreville ☎73.28.00).

When you arrive in Cameroon – especially if you arrive overland – immigration officers may well want to check that you have what they consider to be **sufficient funds** to stay in the country. A credit card usually does the trick. **Health certificates** are rarely checked at checkpoints on the roads, but may be asked for at the border. A certificate for yellow fever is obligatory, as is one for cholera when there is an outbreak in Cameroon or a neighbouring country from which you're travelling.

Information, websites and maps

When getting a visa, you may find some leaflets at the embassy, but there is very little up-to-date official information.

It's well worth getting hold of **maps** before arriving in Cameroon. The 1994 French IGN map (1cm: 15km) is detailed, but out of date – or just disingenuous – on the year-round viability of many roads. The Michelin 741 is okay, though you need Michelin 746 as well if you want coverage of the southernmost hundred kilometres of the country. Good **city maps** of Yaoundé and Douala and a few less-detailed country maps are sold on the street and in bigger bookshops in Cameroon itself.

Recommended websites

The best Cameroon-related **websites** are:
🌐**www.bcenter.fr/cameroun** The Ministry of Tourism's official French-language website, which is

---

The blog for this guide

For **travel updates**, news links and general information, check out 🌐theroughguidetowestafrica.blogspot.com.

---

supposed to be replaced by the bilingual 🌐www.tourisme.cm.

🌐**www.cameroonnews.com** Current Cameroonian news and sport updates.

🌐**www.cameroun-plus.com** French portal, with loads of practical information including hotels, banks and travel agencies.

🌐**tinyurl.com/25qkvd** WWF Cameroon page with news updates and links to their various projects throughout the country.

🌐**www.fecafootonline.com** Official website of the Cameroonian football federation with match reports, news updates and a host of results tables.

🌐**www.museumcam.org** Official site of museums at Bandjoun and Baham in West Province, and Babungo and Mankon in North West Province.

The media

Compared with its neighbours, Cameroon is a highly literate society, with eighty percent adult literacy and more than ninety percent of children receiving a primary education. It's somewhat surprising that the press is quite limited, especially in comparison to print-mad Nigeria, though the frequent harassment of journalists (Reporters Without Borders reported that "draconian laws regularly put journalists behind bars") goes far to explain it. The country's main daily **newspaper**, *The Cameroon Tribune* (🌐www.cameroon-tribune.net), is published in French and English editions and presents the (laconic) voice of the government – with so few lines to read between it's hard keeping informed. *The Herald* is the thrice-weekly Anglophone opposition-party paper, though in fact it's almost as uninformative as the *Tribune*. The Francophone, Douala-based opposition paper *Le Messager* (🌐www.lemessager.net) and the English-language *Cameroon Post* (🌐www.postnewsline.com) are the two most widely read weekly opposition papers. The new quarterly Anglophone magazine, *Summit*, has been received enthusiastically.

The Cameroon Radio and Television Centre in Yaoundé broadcasts on one **television** channel across the country. The programme quality isn't bad, and there are some English-language broadcasts, but **satellite** is becoming more and more common, with hotel bars more likely to show CNN (or TV5 in Francophone areas).

CRTV also runs a national **radio** station in English and French. Local news, often in local languages, is broadcast from its ten provincial stations between programmes of African music. There is no BBC FM relay in Cameroon, though you can pick up the BBC via local stations near the borders of Central African Republic and Nigeria.

Health

Malaria prophylaxis is essential throughout the country (see p.40).

A serious health risk in the southeast is the often fatal **Ebola fever**: this may have crossed over from Congo or Gabon, where it is widespread among chimpanzees and gorillas and transmitted through eating their meat.

Cameroon, like most countries in West Africa, has a serious **schistosomiasis** (bilharzia) problem, though it's usually safe enough to use free-flowing stream water in the highlands, especially after rain. It's not recommended you drink the **tap water** in major towns, however; you can find bottled water everywhere except in small villages, though it becomes increasingly expensive the further you get from urban centres.

Most **pharmacies** have a good stock of medicines, and **hospital care** is adequate in the cities, although the "polyclinics" in the rest of the country are generally poorly stocked and often dirty.

Costs, money, banks

Cameroon is part of the Central African grouping of the **CFA franc zone** (rates of exchange roughly £1=CFA880, $1=CFA450, €1=CFA656). Although Central African CFA are exactly equivalent in value to West African CFA, the bills for the two regions are different and cannot be used on the street.

The best way to carry your money is in **euros**, ideally in cash, though if you are going to use traveller's cheques, banks are more likely to accept them in euros, and commission fees are lower than for other currencies. Only a few banks in the major towns change **sterling** and **dollars** cash or traveller's cheques. Banks that may change sterling include Standard Chartered and the main branches of BICEC (Banque Internationale du Cameroun pour l'Épargne et le Crédit). Citibank, CBC (Commercial Bank of Cameroon) and the main branches of SCB (Société Commerciale de Banque Cameroun) will usually change dollars but not sterling.

Credit cards (strictly speaking, usually Visa) can be used in big-city hotels and some shops and restaurants. You can only use them to get **cash advances** in hotels where you're actually staying. Branches of SGBC (Société Générale de Banques au Cameroun) and BICEC in Douala, Yaoundé, Limbé, Bamenda, Bafoussam, Bertoua, Maroua and Garoua have **ATMs** which accept Visa and Plus cards. SGBC and BICEC are also linked up with **Western Union**, and it's possible to have money transferred to Cameroon at no cost to the recipient.

You can also change money on the **parallel market** – it's not really a black market as it isn't illegal – where you may be able to get up to twenty percent above the bank rate for your cash. It shouldn't be too hard to find a businessman who needs foreign currency – try asking in your hotel. A few **exchange bureaus** have opened, though offering similar rates to the banks.

Costs

Cameroon is one of the more expensive countries in West Africa. A cheap night's **accommodation** costs around CFA4000–8000 (or around CFA7000–10,000 for two people sharing a room); Douala is significantly more expensive. The country's most

---

Fuel prices

Fuel prices vary widely throughout the country depending on the distance from the source and whether it's black market fuel smuggled in from Nigeria and sold from jerry cans at the roadside (a serious fire hazard and often not clean) or fuel sold from official pumps. As a rough average regular petrol (*essence*) costs CFA540 and diesel (*gasoil*) CFA490 per litre.

expensive hotels charge CFA150,000 per night or more.

The cost of **public transport** by road varies widely, depending on the remoteness and condition of the route. As a rough guide, count on CFA1000 for an hour's travel on good roads; in the rainy season, or where the roads are bad, you'll pay more to cover the same distance.

Getting around

Cameroon's **roads** can be okay, though the good-quality paved sections are often separated by many kilometres of rough dirt *piste*. The country's **trains** only cover certain very limited routes, and it's only really the rail link between Yaoundé and Ngaoundéré that is worth considering, as it's a much faster and more comfortable option than the bumpy roads. As for **flying**, Cameroon Airlines is rapidly deteriorating and its network shrinking. Things might change if and when a long-sought European partner has been found and the once outstanding domestic network covering most of the larger towns is revived, but expect tickets to come at a price.

By road

Although 50,000km of roads crisscross Cameroon, only a fraction (roughly 5000km) of this network is paved, and even this is often in disrepair, with sections washed out by floods or pitted with potholes. Less-used dirt roads in particular can be blocked for days by overturned vehicles or collapsed bridges.

That said, the roads around and between **Douala** and **Yaoundé** are always reliable, as are those from Douala and Yaoundé to **Bamenda** and **Foumban** via Bafoussam (though not via **Mamfé**, which some maps show as the main road).

Western Cameroon has a reasonable road network, while the north is well served by the highway between **Ngaoundéré** and **Kousséri**.

The entire **centre** of the country, however, lacks a good system, the **Adamawa Plateau** providing a formidable obstacle. Between **Yaoundé** and **Ngaoundéré**,

where the dirt roads are appalling, you'd be wiser taking the train. In the east of the country, the dense forest is another barrier to overland travel, though there is a good road linking Yaoundé and Abong Mbang, and another linking Bertoua with Meiganga in the centre. **South of Yaoundé** there are good paved roads to Ambam and the border of Gabon and Equatorial Guinea via Ebolowa, Sangmélima and Kribi. The rest of the south is held together by dirt roads and forest tracks.

There are **tollgates** (*péages*) on the outskirts of most large towns, where a standard CFA500 toll is extracted by local authorities from each vehicle passing through. Travelling by public transport, tolls are covered by the driver. Tollgates are always lively with traders, and are reliable spots to pick up supplies for the trip.

There are a few problems and potential dangers peculiar to road travel in Cameroon. Firstly, the speeds at which many drivers travel on the country's few smooth highways can be hair-raising, and horrendous **accidents** aren't uncommon. Be extra vigilant when driving on these fast roads, especially at night, and expect the unexpected from oncoming traffic. Secondly, the law that forbids motorists involved in an accident to move their cars until the police have inspected the site – meaning that all traffic may be held up for a couple of hours – is responsible for frequent **delays** on busy roads. And thirdly, Cameroonian **hitch-hikers**, who often attempt to stop cars by standing in the middle of the road with both arms outstretched, can be unnerving for the uninitiated driver. People of all ages routinely hitch lifts, and stopping is an implicit offer of a ride, so hitchers tend to wait on blind corners where you're forced to screech to a halt to avoid killing them.

Recent years have also seen an increase in **carjackings**, especially in Adamawa Province and further north near the Chadian border. Bandits, who tend to go for expensive 4x4s, operate in large gangs, are often armed and can turn nasty if they encounter resistance.

Taxis and buses

Most Cameroonians rely on **share taxis**, **clandos** or **agences de voyage** to get around. *Agences de voyage* provide fixed-priced – and sometimes timetabled – transport between most towns. Each agency runs certain routes, and finding out who goes where can be very time-consuming, especially as agencies and their routes change constantly. Even more confusingly, the agencies don't use official motor parks, but instead fill their vehicles outside their own ticket offices. Fortunately, booking offices for agencies going in the same general direction are often found in the same neighbourhood. Most agency vehicles are minibuses, but for connections between major towns and cities they run more comfortable buses. Both tend to pass police checkpoints with less trouble than share taxis and *clandos*.

Share taxis are government-licensed minibuses or saloon cars travelling from motor park to motor park at a fixed rate, though they often pile in extra passengers after leaving the motor park control.

Clandos (after *clandestin*) are ramshackle vehicles operating as unlicensed competition to the *agences* and share taxis. They tend to run on routes that none of the others cover, or snatch passengers from the share taxis outside the motor parks, piling people on top of each other and charging similar prices. They also tend to break down constantly

(take plenty of water if you're travelling by *clando*).

Within cities, **yellow taxis** are also shared and cost CFA150 for most short distances (a "drop" in English, or *ramassage* in French) – one of the few real bargains in Cameroon. Taxi drivers generally don't attempt to overcharge – it's hard to imagine why not – but be sure to agree on a fare before you get in.

Finally on the roads, in all the smaller towns and throughout most of the north – from Ngaoundéré northwards – plus Kribi and to the east, **motos** provide the easiest form of transport. For CFA100 these small motorcycles will take you anywhere you choose within the city limits and, for a bit more, outside the limits too. In some places – such as Ngaoundéré, Maroua and Batouri – they are organized and easily recognizable with their yellow numbered tabards. Elsewhere pretty much every young guy hanging out on the street with a motorcycle is a *moto* driver.

Car rental

You'll find **car rental** agencies only in the larger towns (Douala, Yaoundé, Maroua, Bafoussam and Ngaoundéré). Car **rental rates** are extremely high, especially with the main operators such as **Avis** – although they at least back up their high prices with reliable

Roadblocks

The one hazard even the most careful driver can't avoid in Cameroon is **police roadblocks**. These are usually on the outskirts of towns, often near a bar or café. They're not easy to spot, as they may consist of no more than a policeman fast asleep in camouflage fatigues and a piece of string stretched across the road (or, more worryingly, a nail-studded board). Cameroonian police are less troublesome to foreigners than they were a few years ago, but can still be drunk, abusive, surly, and alarmingly casual about pointing a gun at your stomach. The best precaution is always to travel with a full clutch of **documents**, whatever current regulations may say – it's easier to show an International Medical Certificate ("carte jaune") than to insist that you aren't required to carry it.

As a foreigner, you're permitted to move about with a certified photocopy of your passport, which avoids the fear of having it confiscated at a police check. Take the original and copies of the first five pages (as well as your visa) with a CFA1000 fiscal stamp (available from the Ministry of Finance) to any main police station, where it will be stamped and signed.

A more worrying development, which has become increasingly common in recent years, are the **fake roadblocks**, set up by armed bandits, usually at night. Local drivers know what's real and what's fake, so if your taxi suddenly accelerates to pass one, you'll know why.

cars. If you rent on a daily basis, without a driver, expect to pay about CFA50,000 per day for a small European or Japanese car, made up of a basic rate of around CFA25,000, plus CFA200 per kilometre and extra charges for taxes and insurance. For a 4x4, expect to pay the CFA50,000, plus CFA300 per kilometre plus extras. A driver will set you back around CFA10,000 per day and a further CFA2000 for any out-of-town trips that require an overnight stay.

By rail

There are two main railway lines. The first is the 93-kilometre western line from **Douala to Kumba**, which can take up to six hours – it's quicker to do this journey by road. The branch to **Kumba** from Mbanga can be useful, however, as the road into the Mamfé Depression can be very difficult, especially in the wet season.

The substantially longer **Transcamerounais** links Douala and Yaoundé with **Ngaoundéré** in the north. **Transcam I** covers the 308-kilometre stretch from **Douala to Yaoundé** with two services a day in each direction (CFA6000 1st class), leaving Douala at 7.15am and 1.40pm, and Yaoundé at 7.40am and 4pm. The journey takes more than three hours, so it's often faster to do it by road. **Transcam II** forges on for a further 620km from **Yaoundé to Ngaoundéré**, with a daily overnight service in each direction (6.10pm from Yaoundé and 6.30pm from Ngaoundéré; CFA17,000 1st class, CFA10,000 2nd class, CFA28,000 in a two-birth sleeper, CFA25,000 in a four-birth sleeper). This is a fairly quick trip – roughly twelve hours, assuming there are no delays – and substantially quicker than driving.

The train carriages are relatively comfortable, with couchettes (linen, blankets and pillows are provided), plus fans and washing facilities in the sleeper compartments, and an on-board stewardess who takes orders for dinner and breakfast. The seating carriages are often crowded, with food only available from vendors in the stations. Take plenty of water.

Due to the increased risk of **theft**, armed guards are now posted at the end of each carriage, it's still advisable, however, to keep your bags away from windows as thieves

have been known to perch on the train roof and fish for valuables.

By air

Cameroon Airlines' network is a mere skeleton of its former self, whittled down to just a **Douala–Yaoundé** service, three to four times daily, and occasional flights to **Garoua**. With a ramshackle fleet, flights are often either cancelled or have to make the odd emergency landing, and there's also a tendency to overbook flights. In short: arrive early and hope for the best. A second option between Yaoundé and Douala is Kenya Airways' Nairobi flight. which goes via Yaoundé roughly every other day. Following the 2007 crash near Douala, however, the future of this service is in doubt.

To reach more inaccessible areas, such as isolated national parks and game reserves, it's possible to charter **light planes** in Yaoundé or Douala, but you'll need deep pockets.

Accommodation

International-standard hotels in Cameroon are officially graded from one to five stars, and although it's hard to work out exactly how this system works, if a hotel has a star, it should guarantee some degree of comfort.

The majority of hotels and *auberges*, however, are **"unclassified"**. This doesn't necessarily mean that the place isn't fit to stay in – indeed you tend to get more for your money in the unclassified category. **Room rates** are usually negotiable, whatever the category; more expensive places in particular are often prepared to reduce their rates if you can give them a good reason – like staying more than one night or threatening to move to the hotel across the road.

Note that **boukarous** are bungalow-like thatched-roof huts, or *cases* in French.

Camping and missions

If you have your own transport, **camping** away from the major urban centres is a fine alternative to hotel living. The national parks and nature reserves are sometimes restricted, but elsewhere, there are tens of thousands of square kilometres of wild country which you can freely pitch a tent in.

All accommodation prices in this chapter are coded according to the following scale, whose equivalent in pounds sterling/US dollars is used throughout the book. Prices refer to the rate you can expect to pay for a room with two beds, including taxes. Single rooms, or single occupancy, will normally cost at least two-thirds of the twin-occupancy rate. For further details, see p.55.

❶ Under CFA5000 (under £5/$10)
❷ CFA5000–10,000 (£5–10/$10–20)
❸ CFA10,000–15,000 (£10–15/$20–30)
❹ CFA15,000–20,000 (£15–20/$30–40)
❺ CFA20,000–30,000 (£20–30/$40–60)
❻ CFA30,000–40,000 (£30–40/$60–80)
❼ CFA40,000–50,000 (£40–50/$80–100)
❽ Over CFA50,000 (over £50/$100)

The Christian **missions** scattered throughout Cameroon may put up travellers, but they don't have to – and don't always want to. In Douala and Yaoundé, the religious institutions are a literal godsend if you're travelling on your own and don't want to pay for a double room in a hotel. In the face of the ever-increasing demand, however, many missions have put up their prices and are starting to turn away all who are not visiting on church business. In recent years the government has tried to enforce this policy.

Staying with people

There's a large Western presence in Cameroon, so you won't be considered special or exotic, and you're unlikely to receive many offers to **stay with people**. You may find exceptions in the north, however, where the rocketing price of accommodation in out-of-the-way villages such as Mokolo has given enterprising young people the idea of "inviting" travellers to spend the night in their homes. If you stay a couple of days, they can earn a month's income, even for a contribution that is negligible compared to what you'd pay in a hotel. You might find this blend of commerce and camaraderie a little difficult to handle, but it's a solution that benefits both parties. Be very clear about prices and all that's included before agreeing to any such arrangements.

Eating and drinking

Cameroon has a rich and varied cuisine, with a heavy emphasis on maize, millet and groundnuts in the north, and on cassava, yams and plantains in the south. These staples can be boiled, pounded or even grilled, but invariably turn out bland – a characteristic which may put you off at first, though it complements the fiercely peppered sauces quite nicely.

Fruit and vegetables in Cameroon are probably the best in the whole of West Africa, and the variations in climate and altitude mean you can get nearly everything all year round – except the luscious and varied types of **mango** at which Cameroon excels, which are in season from February to May. There's a healthy demand for **salads**, too, though you'll have to be the judge on whether to risk the possibility of a tummy upset.

For cheap, freshly made food, you can't beat the **streetside stands**, usually rickety wooden counters lined by benches and with an array of delicacies on offer ranging from spicy bean stew to avocado salad and the unique spaghetti omelette, invariably served with – or in – a fresh baguette. Streetside stands tend to run out of food by early afternoon, after which grills take over. In the south especially, **grilled fish** is a popular evening meal, served with beer and *miondo* (fried plaintain). In the north, you'll find tasty little snack kebabs known as **soya** (exactly like the *suya* of Nigeria), which make a good meal with some chopped raw onion and French bread. Deriving from Nigeria, **Chicken DG** (Chicken Director General) is a celebratory dish consisting of a whole roast chicken with carrots, potatoes and other vegetables, served in its entirety on a big tray for all in the group to dig in, typically in bar-restaurants.

In common with much of Francophone West Africa, **French cuisine** dominates in the big hotels and expensive **restaurants**, where you can pay CFA10,000–20,000 per head – though all the fancy frills are no guarantee of a good meal. Restaurants in Yaoundé also serve a wide variety of more authentic **Cameroonian dishes** (although you're unlikely to find such specialized regional treats as fried termites, grasshoppers, dog, snake or cat). Beware, however, of upmarket restaurants serving **plats typiques** – they may simply be charging the earth for ordinary Cameroonian staples.

Dishes and staples in the south

Among various interesting local dishes served throughout southern Cameroon in small restaurants known as **chantiers** ("worksites"), run by *veuves joyeuses* ("merry widows") or *tantes* ("aunties"), the following stand out. Firstly, **bongo tchobi** is a memorable fish or meat dish, cooked in a black sauce made from various forest seeds and bark. **Bobolo**, from the South and Central provinces, is a heavy, nearly translucent, fermented cassava preparation served in a miniature baguette shape – a curiosity for most visitors rather than a rapidly acquired taste. **Miondo,** from Littoral province, is practically the same thing, but made with smaller strips of cassava wrapped in banana leaves. The most widely eaten southern dish is **ndolé**, made from a boiled and finely shredded **bitter leaf** plus groundnuts or **egusi** (pounded melon seeds). It's seasoned with hot oil and spices, cooked with fish or meat and eaten with one of the many starchy staples. The similar **kwem** is made from pounded cassava leaves and groundnuts, cooked in a red palm-oil sauce. **Folong** is another variation, a sauce of shredded, dark green leaves, with smoked fish, reckoned to be highly nutritious.

Bush meat is common, especially in the south, and undoubtedly threatens the survival of some species with the trade funneling forest wildlife onto city dinner plates. Bush rats and porcupines are still probably safe to eat (from the point of view of health as well as conservation), but any kind of primate should be strictly avoided on both counts. Porcupine **ndombas** (in which the meat is wrapped in plantain leaves to keep moist) are particularly delicious.

Buying your own food

A good range of food is available in the **markets**, and basic vegetables like potatoes, various cereals, onions, tomatoes and yams are roughly the same price throughout the country, with price reductions in the areas where they are grown. **Fruit and vegetables** for export, such as pineapples, avocados and mangoes, vary enormously in price depending on area and season. At harvest time in a growing area you can buy a sack of ten pineapples for CFA2000.

Good **bread and pastries** are available throughout the country at fixed prices, and there's a good selection of **supermarkets** in most major towns. One final bargain, wherever you might be in Cameroon, is locally produced **chocolate**.

Drinking

Brewing is the country's second biggest industry, something that is evident in the vast selection of **beer** (the largest in Africa) on sale pretty much everywhere. In the remotest corners, where public transport is sparse – you can be certain that even if everything else fails, the beer truck will get through. Brasseries du Cameroun produce the most popular brands: **33 Export** and **Castel**, while Guinness Cameroon produce a dark and bitter **Guinness FES** – stronger than its Irish counterpart, enjoyed in the north with kola nut to enhance its sweetness. They also brew the more expensive **Gold Harp**, considered the most prestigious of Cameroon's beers (hence the acronym: "**G**overnment **O**fficers **L**ike **D**rinking **H**eavily **A**fter **R**eceiving **P**ayment").

You can also find the usual international **soft drinks** everywhere, as well as plenty of local, sweet, brightly coloured carbonates. Pamplemousse (grapefruit) and Djino Cocktail (mixed fruits) are tasty carbonated fruit juices. **Bottled water** can be had anywhere that sells drinks, and from most grocery stores.

Of **traditional alcoholic** drinks, palm wine (*mimbo, matango* or *mbu*) is available throughout the south and west, hence the many names. Try to buy any wine as close to source as possible and make local enquiries to be sure that it hasn't been diluted with bad water, or artificially sweetened. The **distilled spirit** from palm wine is generally known as *afofo* (*arki* in Francophone areas) – this "African Gin" mixes well with a tonic. Other indigenous drinks include the millet beer of the north (*bilibili*) and *kwatcha* (or *sha*), a thick, opaque corn beer.

Communications

Post offices are open Mon–Fri 8am–3.30pm and Sat 8am–1pm. Letters to Europe take one to two weeks. The **poste restante** service operates well enough in Yaoundé and Douala, and costs CFA500 per letter.

Cameroon has embraced modern **telecommunications** with a vengeance. There is mobile phone (cell phone) coverage almost throughout the country – except in game parks and other remote corners – and a relatively sophisticated telecom system in the metropolitan areas that links up reams of Internet cafés.

Douala and Yaoundé have a sophisticated, generally reliable **telephone** system, with IDD to Europe and North America. Connections within and between the two cities are good, though phoning upcountry tends to be more reliable when using the mobile network. Most towns have fax/phone shops which can tell you the best times of day for connections to different areas, but streetside **mobile phone booths** are becoming an increasingly popular alternative. If you want to use your own mobile phone, Orange Cameroon and MTN Cameroon have roaming agreements with Orange, O2 and Vodafone. Alternatively, you can buy a Cameroonian SIM card from CFA5000 with Orange Cameroon or MTN Cameroon.

Internet access is spreading throughout the country and most towns are well provided with Internet cafés offering fast and efficient connections. At the moment, though, it's still at the stage where prices vary wildly – from CFA500/hr to CFA400/min – depending on whether landlines or mobile phone networks are being used.

Cameroon's **IDD** code is ☏237.

Opening hours, public holidays and festivals

Most businesses, banks and offices follow the practice of **continuous weekday opening** (Mon–Fri 7.30 or 8am–3pm, Sat 8am–1pm), but the old opening hours (Mon–Fri 8am–noon & 2.30–5.30pm) are also not uncommon. As a general rule, the further north you go, the higher the chances are that shops and businesses will be shut during the hot lunchtime hours.

As for public holidays, shops and administrative services all shut down for the major Muslim and Christian holidays. The most important of the official holidays, the Fête Nationale, takes place every May 20. National holidays include:

Youth Day February 11
Labour Day May 1
International Women's Day May 8
National Day May 20 (Parades and speeches commemorate the 1972 approval of the referendum for a united Cameroon.)
Assumption Day Aug 15

Local festivals take place too, the most well known of which are the Lela festival in **Bali** (mid-Dec); the grass-gathering ceremony in **Bafut** (end of April); and the End-of-Year festival, also in Bafut (late Dec); the Ngoun festival in **Foumban** (Dec); and the **harvest festivals** in the north (Jan–March).

Crafts and shopping

The most famous region for **artisanal work** is the Bamoun–Bamiléké district of West and North West provinces, known for carved statues, masks and bas-reliefs. The long tobacco pipes used by the Tikar and other people of the region have become popular tourist items and are widely available. Northern Cameroon is more renowned for leather and jewellery, fashioned primarily by the Fula. Samples from all the regions can be found at the *marchés artisanals* in Foumban and Yaoundé.

It's illegal to take antiques and certain works of art out of the country without government authorization. Many antiques are smuggled down the Gamana and Donga rivers from Nigeria, which has strict views about the export of its heritage, and imposes harsh penalties on smugglers.

If you are travelling overland, north from Cameroon, don't buy anything that even looks old; it will almost certainly be confiscated by Nigerian customs officers, whether antique or not. If you want to check, contact the **Délégation Provinciale du Tourisme** in Douala (℡33.42.14.22 or 33.42.11.91) or Yaoundé (℡22.22.44.11) and they'll direct you to the appropriate ministry, depending on what your item is – or what it's made of.

Crime and safety

Cameroon has serious crime and safety issues. Apart from the general security problems of the **eastern border districts** close to Chad and the Central African Republic, **Douala and Yaoundé** are becoming increasingly dangerous after dark. Robberies at knifepoint are not uncommon and it's not safe to carry anything of value in the street – preferably not even a bag. Follow carefully any local advice about which areas are dangerous, and always try to look as if you know where you are going. Cameroonian justice is rough: the death penalty exists in theory even for minor thefts, though few get as far as the courts. They may be dealt with by a roughing-up behind the police station or, if the cry of "*Voleur!*" is heard, by a beating from an angry crowd.

Emergencies

Police ℡017, fire ℡018.

Gender issues and sexual attitudes

Women's situations in Cameroon are hugely varied. The country's many ethnic groups, the range of religious beliefs, and the varying degrees of urbanization and westernization all have an impact on women's roles, which go all the way from

powerful matriarchs and professional women in southwestern towns, to submissive co-wives struggling on in traditional households in Extreme North province.

Perhaps because of the variations, **travelling as a woman** is relatively unproblematic – people are not unfamiliar with other cultures and traditions and generally treat you with respect.

Appearance can be important though: it's recommended that women cover knees and shoulders while in the Muslim areas of the north. The dress code is not nearly as strict as in neighbouring Nigeria, however, and it's not obligatory – certainly not in Kirdi areas, where locals customarily go stark naked (dressed only in a few nose spikes and a string around the waist). It's worth knowing that a strong streak of puritanism runs through the official psyche, especially in the Anglophone regions, and if you're a man, you'll attract the disdain of officials if you go bare-chested, wear earrings or have long hair – especially in dreadlocks.

Gay and lesbian travellers face a challenge, as **homosexuality** is a crime in Cameroon, and the law has recently begun to be enforced. However, sharing a room with a same-sex friend is generally not a problem if you stress that you are travelling with a friend/sister/brother/cousin and avoid using the word partner.

Entertainment and sport

Cameroon offers a feast for **music**-lovers, with some big names hailing from the country and an ongoing, lively nightlife scene in the big cities. **Cinema**, too, is significant, though economic conditions don't exactly encourage a solid local film industry. There's more background on music and cinema on p.1244–1249.

Sports

Football, always a wildly popular sport in Cameroon, had its status lifted almost to that of a religion by the national team, the Indomitable Lions' mighty result in the 1990 World Cup (they beat Argentina and Romania to reach the quarter-finals at odds of 100:1, only going out to England). Expectation now at fever pitch, they did less well in the 1994, 1998 and 2002 World Cups and didn't even qualify in 2006 (Pierre Wome, whose missed penalty denied Cameroon the place, hasn't played in the national team since) – all very disappointing given that they won the African Cup of Nations in 2000 and 2002.

Nationally, Cameroon have always appeared an efficient team in the general circus of West African football, and they have some of Africa's, and the world's, finest players to choose from, many of whom have given their careers to European clubs. Thanks to satellite TV, the entire country now watches with bated breath when the likes of Barcelona's **Samuel Eto'o** are playing.

The big teams in Cameroon are **Canon** of Yaoundé, **Bamboutos** of Mbouda, **PWD** of Bamenda and **Cotonsport** of Garoua.

⑮ Wildlife and national parks

Cameroon is blessed with a wonderful natural heritage, as author and naturalist Gerald Durrell discovered in the 1950s. In the north, the country's **grassland national parks** offer (or *could* offer) the closest thing to an East African safari to be found on this side of the continent, while its **rainforest parks** offer rare access to that environment. **Elephant**, **giraffe**, **buffalo**, several large **antelope** species, **lion** and – in the rain forests – **chimpanzee** and **western lowland gorilla**, give Cameroon the opportunity to be in the vanguard of conservation activity in Africa.

Unfortunately, the northern parks, in their remote and precariously located region close to troubled parts of Chad, have been subject to heavy poaching and habitat destruction, and it's believed that West Africa's last, tiny population of **black rhino** in the Bouba Ndjida and Bénoué national parks, has been wiped out.

The Cameroon government seems fairly committed to saving some of its wildlife – even at the expense of lucrative logging contracts and difficult decisions over local development. Most of the country's conservation initiatives are in partnership with the influential **WWF** (Worldwide Fund for Nature/ World Wildlife Fund; ⓦwww.panda.org). The country actively encourages paid-up hunting, as part of its conservation strategy.

A brief history of Cameroon

The first **Bantoid-speaking peoples** moved to the southern half of the Cameroon region from the Nigerian plateau by 200–100 BC, displacing the original inhabitants, the so-called "Pygmies", and pushing them deep into the forests. But the earliest clearly defined presence in Cameroon is that of the materially advanced **Sao culture**, which developed around Lake Chad and left archeological evidence in the form of bronze and terracotta human and animal figures, coins, dishes, jewellery and funeral jars. From the eighth century, the Sao evidently began mixing with peoples who had been pushed south by the powerful empire then forming in Kanem (the Kotoko who live along the banks of Lake Chad and the Logone River are thought to be their descendants).

Today, Cameroon is a complicated mixture of peoples, none of them really predominant. As the archetypal example of an artificial state, its present configuration derives in large part from the imposed colonial history of the last 120 years, a legacy from which it is still struggling to break free.

Arrival of the Portuguese

In 1472, the Portuguese navigator **Fernando Po** led an expedition around the Bay of Biafra, becoming the first European to penetrate the estuary of the **Wouri River**, which he called Río dos Camarões ("Prawn River"). From this time on, the coastal region gained influence, taking over from such northern powers as the **Bornu Empire** (which extended down to the Bénoué in the sixteenth century). The centre of trade shifted to the regions around Douala, Limbé and Bonaberi, where local chiefs signed consecutive trade agreements with the Portuguese, Dutch, English, French and Germans. These chiefs rounded up slaves and ivory which they traded for cloth, metal and other European products.

Although commerce flourished over the ensuing four centuries, the Europeans didn't settle on the Cameroonian coast until the nineteenth century,

when British missionaries began to protest against the **slave trade**. In 1845, an English pastor, **Alfred Saker**, founded the first European settlement in Cameroon at Douala. Although he set up churches and schools Saker was hardly a liberator. He recognized early on the strategic importance of **Douala** and **Victoria** and pushed for them to become crown colonies.

With the arrival of British, German and French **commercial houses**, trade shifted to "legitimate" exports of palm oil, ivory and gold. But the **Duala chiefs** became increasingly worried they would lose their role as middlemen between interior peoples and the Europeans and sought British guarantees that would have led to a protectorate. Queen Victoria hesitated. By the time she finally sent an envoy to make an arrangement, the Germans had beaten her to it. On July 12, 1884, **Gustav Nachtigal** signed a treaty with the Duala chiefs **Bell**, **Deïdo** and **Akwa**, who willingly ceded their sovereignty to Kaiser Wilhelm in exchange for trade advantages.

German, French and British occupations

In 1885, Baron von Soden became the first governor of Kamerun, and spent the next six years trying to quell rebellions in the interior. In 1895, **Jesco von Puttkamer**, the most notorious of the German governors, came to power. He ruled for twelve years and relied on brutality to provide forced labour for the southern plantations and to carve out the colony's first **railway line** in 1907. But the promising economic results of the German activities, which included building some roads, hospitals and schools, came to an abrupt halt with the outbreak of **World War I**. In 1916, after an arduous and bloody campaign, the Allies wrested control of the territory from Germany. In 1922 it was officially placed under French and British mandates – though only about one-fifth of the area was ceded to Britain.

The **British Cameroons** were joined to Nigeria in an administrative union, but lay outside the framework of development plans for Nigeria, and received only minimal funding. Ironically, much of the growth in the region after World War I was spurred by the **Germans**, who returned as private citizens to develop the plantations around the Victoria plains, in what is now the Limbé district. (When, in the 1930s, many of them rallied to the Nazis, they were expelled and their private development efforts consolidated into the Cameroon Development Corporation, today the country's second biggest employer.)

The **French** were more active in developing the infrastructure. Cultivation of the main export commodities of cocoa, palm oil, rubber and timber increased dramatically. French plans, however, relied heavily on exacting taxes or forced labour (in lieu of tax) to extend the road network, enlarge Douala's port and build up the vast plantations – activities which led to deep-seated grievances against French rule.

Nationalist beginnings

After World War II, the United Nations renewed the French and British

mandates, the **British sector** continuing to be ruled from Nigeria. On the eve of independence, two camps emerged: the first pushing to become a state within the Nigerian federation, the second calling for reunification with "the other" Cameroon.

In the **French territory**, calls for reunification were also heard. Political parties began to form, including the **Union des Populations Camerounais** (UPC) and the less radical Bloc Démocratique Camerounais of northerner **Ahmadou Ahidjo**.

The UPC was the first party to call both for unification of the two separate Cameroons and for **independence from France**. Prevented by force of opposition from attaining these demands legally, the UPC organized a **revolt** in the larger towns of the French colony in 1955. The uprising was put down, but at the cost of hundreds of lives and huge destruction. The UPC, using increasingly extreme and violent liberation tactics, was banned in 1956 by the French government, but its influence barely diminished, especially in the Bamiléké country and Sanaga region, where rebellion continued to be fomented and was brutally suppressed.

The UPC's actions were a catalyst to Cameroonian nationalism and focused the attention of more conservative parties on developing specific policies. Its influence was felt by leaders such as Ahidjo, who was still working with the political mechanisms put in place by the French. In 1958 he founded a new party, **l'Union Camerounaise**, and became the prime minister of the Assemblée Legislative du Cameroun. His platform called for reunification, total independence and national reconciliation.

Independence

Ahidjo met his first aim when he proclaimed **independence** on January 1, 1960. The following year, his goal of reunification was also partly satisfied. Following a UN plebiscite, the northern half of the former British territory voted to join Nigeria (and is today integrated into the states of Borno and Adamawa), while the southern British Cameroons voted to join the Francophone territory. But national reconciliation proved more difficult as the UPC problem dragged on, and it took a further twelve years before Ahidjo – with continued French assistance – prevailed over the rebels, when their last members were executed. In an astute piece of political manoeuvring, he then neutralized much of the internal opposition by integrating it into his government and the enlarged party, **l'Union Nationale Camerounaise**.

As the political wrinkles were being ironed out – symbolized by the adoption of a new constitution, the dissolution of the federal system and the formation of the **United Republic of Cameroon** in 1972 – progress was also being made on the economic front. Like Houphouët-Boigny in Côte d'Ivoire, Ahidjo focused first on developing agriculture and then moved on to basic industries. Thanks in part to the discovery of oil, the country's GNP nearly doubled in the first twenty years of independence. By the end of the 1970s, Cameroon was thus shaping up as one of the rare stable countries in the region. While reports of political prisoners and repression leaked out of the country, and Anglophone students (to single out just one obvious group) were extremely unhappy with the way Cameroon was going, the West turned a blind eye to the autocratic excesses of a reliable friend in the Cold War era.

A change of regime

As the years dragged on, however, Ahidjo appeared to be settling into a familiar, post-independence pattern in Africa – that of the powerful political leader who refuses to relinquish power or look to the future. He had been president for 22 years when he unexpectedly stepped down in 1982, citing ill-health as his reason. Just as Senghor had done in Senegal, he passed the sceptre to a young prime minister of his own grooming, though from a different background – the 49-year-old bilingual southerner, **Paul Biya**, a Béti. Despite being noted for his competence, Biya had barely been in office a year when his reputation, and that of Cameroon, took a beating in the international press.

The trouble started in 1983 when Biya fired the prime minister and several members of his cabinet, on the grounds that he had uncovered a **treasonous plot**. Ahidjo resigned as UNC party boss and, from his residence on the French Riviera, openly criticized his heir, claiming that Biya was turning Cameroon into a police state, and asserting that he had been tricked into relinquishing power by faked health reports (it seems the former president was resentful that Biya would not allow him to transfer his vast fortune out of Cameroon, and was sensitive to Muslim worries that the balance of power had shifted to southern Christians). The showdown had begun, but Biya seemed to have all the cards, and Ahidjo was sentenced to death in absentia. He died in Senegal in 1989.

Although Biya subsequently pardoned his predecessor, there was a **revolt** by units of the presidential guard formed by Ahidjo in Yaoundé in 1984. They were only put down by the army after three days of street fighting and a death toll estimated at as many as 1000. Ahidjo denied any involvement, but Biya cracked down on dissidents, and dozens of guard members were secretly tried and executed. Calm returned and Biya consolidated his position, but the incident showed that stability was fragile.

Consolidation of power

For months after the coup attempt, Biya rarely left the presidential palace. Many observers expected a further attempt to overthrow him, and it was widely believed that an irreparable rift between the north and the rest of the country had been opened. But after a series of purges within the government, military and public sector, the president seemed to gain confidence.

As the nation prepared for the five-year congress of the UNC, in 1985, expectations ran high that Biya would announce sweeping reforms, including the revival of a multiparty system. Such hopes were dashed when the president outlawed the opposition. Furthermore, he announced he was changing the UNC's name to the Rassemblement Démocratique du Peuple Camerounais (RDPC, or CPDM in English), apparently in a move to distance the party from its association with Ahidjo. At the same time, he moved towards a **cautious democratization** within the party, and in 1986 elections were held for members of RDPC bodies from the village level up to the *départements*, which saw the emergence of a number of new faces.

At the **international level**, relations improved with the West, and in 1985 Biya made a much-publicized official visit to France. This was viewed as a conciliatory move, as the two countries had been on bad terms since the attempted coup, due to the widely believed suspicion of French complicity. In 1986, Cameroon became the fourth African nation, after Zaire (now DR Congo), Liberia and Côte d'Ivoire, to restore diplomatic relations with Israel, partly in response to the wishes of the American government, with whom Biya was seeking closer ties after the cooling of relations with France.

These events, however, were largely overshadowed by the worst natural disaster in Cameroon's history. In late 1986, an eruption of underwater volcanic gases escaped at **Lake Nyos**, a crater lake in the Grassfields of North West Province. A cloud of deadly chemicals leaked into the atmosphere, suffocating as many as 3000 people in their sleep almost instantly and killing thousands of head of livestock. The catastrophe caused great insecurity among local people, who still depend heavily on the crater lakes for fish and drinking water, and even some of the country's Anglophone intelligentsia persisted in the belief that a crude American or Israeli chemical warfare experiment had been carried out at the lake site.

The 1990s

At the end of the 1980s, Biya's great strength – apart from skill at political manoeuvring – lay in the relative stability of the economy. Cameroon moved to the middle-bracket status of underdeveloped nations, with a gross national product per person considerably above West Africa's average. When coffee and cocoa prices dropped in the early 1980s, Cameroon was able to fall back on its rapidly growing oil exports, which actually pushed foreign trade into a surplus. But as the country entered its fourth decade of independence, economic and political stability were about to undergo serious challenges.

Not that the decade didn't start without optimism. In 1990, Biya indicated a willingness to go down the road to a multiparty system. However, Amnesty International's much publicized concern about **political detentions and torture** and steady pressure from Paris on reforms, explicitly tied to **debt relief**, made this announcement of measures to liberalize politics look like a response to unexpected events, rather than a planned programme of reform. Nonetheless, in anticipation of the changes, the newly formed, but unlicensed **Social Democratic Front** – the vanguard of the pro-democracy movement – proceeded, despite a government ban, with its inaugural rally in Bamenda in May 1990. The organizers managed to get more than 30,000 people onto the streets. After a peaceful demonstration, attempts to disperse the crowd met with stone-throwing and, in the ensuing rout, troops shot into fleeing marchers, killing six people and injuring dozens more. On the same day in Yaoundé, the university campus was the scene of brutal attacks on students supporting the rally.

Leaders of the SDF, not all of them from the Anglophone region, claimed that the Anglophone districts were being treated like a colony by the Francophone areas. As support withered for the government in North West and South West provinces, the Bamiléké of West Province – powerful in Cameroonian commerce – also lost enthusiasm after the murder of a senior lawyer, **Pierre Bouobda**, at a Bafoussam roadblock. The ill will from the West, added to continued resentment from the north about the treatment of Ahidjo's former circle, contributed to a heavy show of support for the opposition.

As pressure mounted, the national assembly adopted a draft law in December 1990 for the introduction of a multiparty political system. By early 1991, more than twenty opposition parties had registered and – under the banner of the **National Coordination Committee of Opposition Parties** (NCCOP) – collectively began calling for a national conference to outline the country's political future.

Biya flatly refused, and seemed taken aback that the opposition, with its ethnic, religious and political differences, had united so quickly against him. He placed seven of Cameroon's ten provinces under military rule, lashed out at the mushrooming **independent press**, and prohibited opposition gatherings. As security forces became increasingly violent in their crackdown on opposition rallies, the NCCOP tried a tougher tactic – a nationwide campaign of civil disobedience. **Operation Ghost Town** began in July 1991 as a highly effective strike that closed the ports and brought business and transport to a halt from Monday to Friday. The economic effect was crippling for the big towns and industries. Even in Douala, business slammed to a standstill.

The strikes dragged on through to November 1991, when the government, opposition and civilian organizations agreed on the formation of a constitutional committee. Biya finally consented to release all political prisoners, lifted

the ban on opposition meetings and set legislative elections for February 1992. Not everyone was happy, however. As Biya began tailoring the process to suit RDPC aims (he insisted on a single round of voting and forbade coalitions from participating), many opposition elements – including two of the four principal parties, the SDF and the Union Démocratique Camerounaise – called for an **election boycott**. The RDPC won 88 of 190 seats.

Biya's political support was clearly flagging, and a secret committee, set up to control every aspect of the poll, made a shameless attempt to influence the National Vote-Counting Commission and skew the voter register. The domestic media were tightly controlled, and the Douala-based printing house which published most of the independent newspapers was closed.

But the principal opposition contender – the SDF's **John Fru Ndi**, an Anglophone bookseller from Bamenda – was better organized than Biya expected and gathered widespread support throughout the country. Internationally, he scored high marks as he travelled to Germany, Britain and the US, and Nigeria openly backed his candidacy.

The opposition's momentum, however, was no match for Biya's tight control over the election process. After the polls of October 1992, the president claimed 39.9 percent of the vote to Fru Ndi's 35.9 percent. The US's National Democratic Institute, which had monitored the elections, wrote a scathing report of wilful fraud and widespread irregularities. Predictably, demonstrations broke out. Amnesty International reported mass arrests and related deaths as a **state of emergency** was declared in western Cameroon. John Fru Ndi and other prominent leaders were put under house arrest. Journalists were detained and tortured.

The bad press refocused international attention on Cameroon. South Africa's Nobel Prize–winning peacemaker **Desmond Tutu** tried to negotiate a settlement, but the government and opposition were too far apart to consider his proposals for a unity government. After his release, Fru Ndi flew to Washington, where President Bill Clinton quickly imposed economic sanctions on the Biya government. For his part Biya flew to Paris and negotiated a loan of $115 million to help stave off IMF pressure to resolve the growing **national debt crisis**.

Biya's recovery

Biya, who had spent years cultivating the image of a humane and stable leader, came out of the fight bruised and battered, with the international media describing him as a degenerate autocrat. Nonetheless, he slowly gathered support from the international community. His first major breakthrough came at the end of 1995 when, after protracted discussions, Cameroon was admitted into the **Commonwealth**, despite opposition objections that the country did not respect stipulated standards of human rights and democracy. Improved ties with Britain piqued the French, as did the fact that by the end of the 1990s, Cameroon was one of the few Central African countries that was not in complete crisis. Given the region's instability, foreign governments were reluctant to stir up divisions within Cameroon and resigned themselves to the status quo.

At home, the president was effective in dividing the opposition. Western Cameroonians increasingly called for a return to a federal system of government, while more radical members advocated **secession**. In 1995, the **Southern Cameroons National Council** (SCNC) emerged and called for an autonomous state. English-speaking representatives in the government criticized the demands, which also alienated Bamiléké support within the SDF. By focusing on regional rather than national issues, the movement estranged northerners from an opposition coalition; their principal party, the Union Nationale pour la Démocratie

et le Progrès (UNDP) had participated in the legislative elections and could therefore pursue regional aims in parliament.

By the time of legislative elections in 1997, there was little cohesion left within the opposition, but Biya took no chances of an upset, exercising a tight control over the proceedings and refusing once again to create an independent electoral commission. International observers substantiated opposition accusations of vote rigging and fraud, though there was little they could do about it. The RDPC claimed 109 of the 180 national assembly seats, the SDF took 43, and the UNDP saw its representation sink to 13 seats.

Despite the setback, the opposition failed to unite behind a single candidate for the presidential elections later that year, deciding instead to call a boycott, citing the country's history of corrupt elections and the lack of any meaningful reform. Criticism of the boycott by the US and France as "undemocratic" signalled the fact that Western countries had abandoned supporting change in Cameroon in favour of seven more years of Biya.

Only the **threat of war** shifted the focus from domestic politics. Throughout much of the 1990s and into the new millennium, hostilities with **Nigeria** flared over the long-disputed border at the **Bakassi Peninsula**. Though the conflict was originally limited to localized incidents, the military posturing on both sides led to clashes in 1996. Tensions eased in 1998, following an exchange of more than two hundred prisoners of war, but the 2002 ruling by the International Court of Justice in The Hague that sovereignty should be given to Cameroon caused tensions to rise again. Nigeria promptly rejected the ruling, and troops were re-posted on both sides of the border, while a joint commission was set up by the UN to negotiate a new settlement acceptable to both parties. The details of the handover was finally settled in the **Greentree Accord** in June 2006 thanks to direct intervention by UN Secretary General Kofi Annan, and Nigerian troops left the peninsula on August 14, 2006, under much pomp and circumstance, especially at Archibong Town, the peninsula's main settlement, where the majority of the population is Nigerian and will probably remain so.

At home, addressing the **economy** and keeping relations as smooth as possible with foreign creditors continued to be Biya's biggest task. By 1999, the IMF was financing its fifth structural adjustment agreement with Cameroon and, in a notable turnaround from ten years earlier, was lauding the country for its effective implementation of the programme. As 2000 approached, economic growth was above 5.5 percent, with inflation held at 3 percent. But despite the good news, Transparency International ranked Cameroon in 1998 as the **world's most corrupt country**. Biya downplayed the report, but still promised to crack down on those "who are well versed in cheating, fraud and even swindling" and sacked a few prominent managers of state-owned companies. In May 2006, international donors, including the World Bank, IMF and African Development Bank, cancelled 27 percent of the country's debt of $4.9 billion, under the Heavily Indebted Poor Countries initiative.

Despite the economic upswing, members of Biya's own cabinet have acknowledged that the country's economic growth has not brought benefits evenly to the country. One hope of reversing this trend is the building of a thousand-kilometre **pipeline** from the oilfields of southern Chad through Cameroon to the port at Kribi. Despite objections by international environmental lobbyists, the project was begun in 2000 and, since 2003, when oil started flowing through it, Cameroon is estimated to have earned $20 million a year. The timing is fortuitous since Cameroon's own oil industry has declined and the country will soon be a net oil importer, although plans to utilize the country's vast natural gas should play down the need. A new pipeline project, exporting excess natural gas from Cameroon to Equatorial Guinea for liquefaction, is also expected to create jobs and growth.

Election after election

Despite economic and social problems – unemployment, unpaid back-salaries, poor health and education services and rampant corruption – Biya's RDPC (CPDM) has easily triumphed at every **election** since the start of the millennium. In the parliamentary and municipal elections of 2002 the RDPC swept up most of the seats in parliament (the legislative council) and increased their municipal lead to take 85 percent of town councils, while John Fru Ndi's SDF lost heavily as he began to suffer criticism for his style. As usual, these elections were accompanied by widespread claims of fraud and vote-rigging – in many Anglophone areas election ballots simply never arrived.

At the presidential elections in 2004 Biya's victory was less overwhelming and in the eyes of most observers, slightly more credible than past elections, when he won with 71 percent of the vote to John Fru Ndi's 17.4 percent.

But the July 2007 parliamentary and council elections saw a return to form, as fraud on a massive scale was reported, using every trick in the book. In the Wouri East constituency of Douala, for example, more the 250,000 people registered to vote, of whom only 66,000 succeeded. More than one hundred High Court petitions were filed to annul the result. With reams of concrete evidence, the Supreme Court was forced finally to cancel the results for seventeen seats scattered across the country, but reruns in September were followed by months of controversy.

John Fru Ndi's **SDF** is losing ground, even allowing for fraudulent polls, and although he has support in other parts of the country, the SDF is overwhelmingly a party of North West Province. The other, smaller parties are real minority concerns, but since the opposition seems unable to unify, the dominance of the RDPC and Biya's leadership – complete with a large number of ministers from Biya's regional power base in the Centre and South provinces – seem all but guaranteed, even if by some miracle the government were to hold fair elections. Even if growth and development point in the right direction, there is a gaping division between rich and poor and, as long as Cameroon's political structure is mapped rigidly onto its regional divisions, there cannot be any happy prognosis for the future.

Music

Of all Cameroon's artists, it's been musicians who have most successfully put the country on the map for a world audience. **Francis Bebey**, who died in 2001, was Cameroon's honorary cultural ambassador to the world – a multi-talented artist in the broadest sense. More familiar in the music shops is the tireless saxophonist, singer, pianist and arranger **Manu Dibango**, who helped popularize **makossa**, Cameroon's biggest dance music, a sexy, fast-paced rhythm, now increasingly underscored by thunderous bass and, with the influence of Paris, only a squeeze away from **zouk**. Of the hundreds of musicians, **Sam Fan Thomas** and **Moni Bile** are the two other best-known exponents.

Less-enduring stars of recent decades were **Les Têtes Brulées**, who became internationally famous in 1989 with an album of the same name. Their music and wild cross-cultural appearance (day-glo "tribal paint", shaved and sculpted hair and the baddest trainers they could find) stirred up a whirlwind of excitement abroad, and confusion and controversy at home. If their success has now burnt itself out, their fast-paced musical style, **bikutsi**, is still very popular, especially in Yaoundé.

Folk music

There are hundreds of ethnic groups in Cameroon, many of them possessing a distinctive music and dance culture. More than two hundred different dances are still performed on a whole range of occasions, the majority accompanied by instrumental ensembles.

In the south, the **Bakweri**, **Bamiléké**, **Bamoun** and **Béti** have mostly xylophone or drum ensembles and their masked dance dramas are well worth seeing. The **Sultan of Bamoun's**

Musical Theatre (see p.1297) is a remarkable institution. Also in the south, the **Bulu**, **Fang**, **Eton** and **Mvele**, who play a wide diversity of musical instruments including the **ngkul**, a slit drum formerly used to convey messages but now only used to accompany the **ozila** or initiation dance; the **mendzan**, a small xylophone; and the **mvet**, a long stick-zither (*mvet* refers not only to the instrument but also the pantomime and dances associated with it). The **Baka** forest people have a range of fascinating instruments, including the earth bow, which uses the forest floor as a resonator.

The Baka Forest People *Heart of the Forest* (Hannibal). Showcase for the Baka "Pygmies'" extraordinary singing, and their various instruments – inspiration for the group Baka Beyond (whose Martin Cradick recorded this). Seamlessly stringing together trancey instrumental grooves, sploshing water-drum sessions, kids' campfire rhymes and wonderful *yelli* songs that draw you deep into the forest, the selection gives a generous overview of the Bakas' music without descending into ethnomusicology – and everyone on it gets a cut of the royalties. Check out their website ⓦ www.baka.co.uk, which also includes a full list of albums produced by Baka Beyond, the more recent ones with a strong Celtic influence.

Francis Bebey

Africa's "Renaissance man", Bebey worked his way through jazz and most of his country's roots music. A multi-instrumentalist and musicologist, amongst other things, he defied categorization, singing in English, French and Duala, experimenting with styles ranging from classical guitar and traditional rhythms to *makossa* and regular pop. He released some twenty albums, and you never quite know what you'll find on any of them.

Nandolo/With Love – Works 1963–1994 (Original Music). A fine sampling of Bebey's talents, from bamboo flute to wonderful guitar and thumb-piano pieces.

Travail au noir (Ozileka/Sonodisc). From melodic guitar to traditional Bantu lullaby, the texts are powerful and the music enchanting.

Dibiye (Pee Wee). The master's last album. Most of the tracks are sung in Duala and offer a nostalgic tribute to his African roots.

Makossa and other pop

Makossa, the pop music of Cameroon, was created in the 1950s but has its roots in the 1930s. Mission schools created their own bands to usher the pupils into assembly, using xylophones and percussion instruments. These bands performed at dances outside school hours, playing a mixture of Western and local styles. Guitars were introduced before World War II and guitarists would perform accompanied by a bottle player. There were three main dance styles at the time: *asiko* – percussion and xylophone music;

ambasse bey – a guitar-based dance with much faster rhythms; and the fledgling *makossa*, a popular folk dance, named after the word for "to strip off".

Although *makossa* endures (a recent star is **Sergio Polo**, who claims to be taking *makossa* back to roots), other styles are more ephemeral. In the early 1990s, the huge publicity given to **bikutsi** – the war rhythm of the Béti people zapped up for amps and guitars – was at least partly due to the ethnic provenance of President Paul Biya. Although still very much alive locally, it looked for a few months in 1994 as if **Les Têtes Brulées** would make it big on the world stage.

Bend-skin is a kind of percussion-led folk music, of which **Kouchoum Mbada** are the main protagonists. A wave of female singers such as **Sally Nyolo** and **Coco Mbassi** rose to international prominence in the late 1990s. A far cry from *makossa* and other energetic dance beats, their music is based on an adherence to simple melodies enhanced by searching lyrics.

It's no surprise of course that Cameroon has its own posse of eager **hip-hop** and R&B artists. **Koppo**'s pidgin rapping has brought him a big following. Check out ⓦ www.kamerhiphop.com.

Moni Bilé

Suave but exciting, Bilé is one of the best *makossa* musicians and was the most influential artist of the 1980s, his high-tech productions outselling all others.

10th Anniversary: Best of Moni Bilé (MAD Productions/Sonodisc). Enjoy the mellow growl and revisit those great dance-floor stirrers, "Bijou" and "O Si Tapa Lambo Lam".

Amour & Espérance (JPS). Mellow love lyrics, although still with an underlying *makossa* dance feel.

Richard Boma

Renowned session bassist, guitarist, percussionist and composer, Bona is known as the "African Sting". As a young boy in Adamawa he made his own instruments and performed at village weddings and religious ceremonies. Today his unique style sits on a crossroads of influences, including jazz, bossa nova, Afrobeat and folk traditional: he's one talented man.

Tiki (Decca). Samba meets soft jazz on a recent recording that also features US jazz guitarist Mike Stern and R&B star John Legend.

Révérence (Sony). Beautiful combination of native idioms with Western influences, ranging from sophisticated Pan-African syncopations of "Bisso Baba" and Cuban-style cha-cha-cha on "Ekwa Mwato" to the Americana-tinged melody of the title track.

Munia: The Tale (Verve). Packed with flavours and more collaborative songs, with guests including Salif Keita, Bailo Ba and Djely-Moussa Condé (flutes and *kora*).

Scenes from My Life (Sony). Bona's debut was considered the jazz album of the year when it came out in 1999.

Manu Dibango

Sax-player, composer, singer, pianist and arranger, Dibango's inspirations are diverse. He has lived and recorded in Brussels, Paris, Zaire, the US, Jamaica and Côte d'Ivoire. He started a whole wave of urban popular music with the release of his album *Soul Makossa* in 1973 (somewhat confusingly named, as it contains nothing that a Cameroonian musician would recognize as *makossa*). This record paved the way for a new generation of artists who now rely on a combination of traditional inspiration and high-tech recording facilities to produce the exportable dance music that has turned Douala into one of the dynamos of African music. Now in the superstar class – more than thirty years after his first single – Manu Dibango is one of the few African artists guaranteed to draw a full house anywhere in the world.

Live '91 (Stern's). The catalogue of Africa's foremost jazz sax-player is so vast, it's hard to know where to begin. If you find nothing to enjoy amongst the eclectic set on this old but representative CD, then you probably don't like him.

Homemade (Celluloid/Melodie). Classic cuts from the 1970s when Manu was really blowing up his own kind of Afrofusion into a massive sound. Includes the often reprised "Ah Freak son Fric".

CubAfrica (Celluloid/Melodie). Mellow versions of Cuban classics, accompanied on acoustic instruments by Cuarteto Patria and Manu's eternal guitar partner, Jerry Malekani.

Sax & Spiritual (Soul Paris). One of his more jazzy albums, made in faultless collaboration with Guinean pianist Lamabastani.

Anthology (Eagle Records). Triple CD covering Manu's best tracks and offering an excellent introduction to his unique range of styles.

Kamer Feeling (JPS). Once again the sax takes centre stage in a world of afro-soul-jazz.

Lapiro de Mbanga

Master of Cameroonian rap – Mbanga's music offers a tough blend of politics, rhythm and language couched in a range of styles from *makossa* to Congolese *soukous*.

Na wou go pay? (JPS). Featuring a tough mix of *makossa*, *zouk*, *soukous* and Afro-beat, Lapiro rebuts the criticism that he sold out to the powers that be – not very convincingly.

Coco Mbassi

Young and talented female artist who was nominated as best newcomer by BBC Radio 3 in 2003. Before starting her solo career, Mbassi worked as a vocalist for Salif Keita, Touré Kunda and Oumou Sangaré among others. Her music has gospel and jazzy tones to it, as well as deep African roots.

Sepia (Tropical). Debut album, with light drums and soft rhythms accompanying Mbassi's gripping and multi-nuanced voice.

Sally Nyolo

A former singer in the all-female a cappella group Zap Mama, Nyolo received the RFI's Prix Découverte for Tribu in 1996. Since then she has released three more albums showing a consistent stylistic development, with increasingly thoughtful lyrics and music searching for a link between her Cameroonian roots and Western influences.

Tribu (Lusafrica). Melodic first album, with Nyolo's strong voice accompanied by hypnotic drums and guitars.

Multiculti (Lusafrica). Thoughtful second album exploring the cultural contrast between the forests of Central Africa and the boulevards of Paris.

Béti (Lusafrica). Inspired by a trip back home, this homage to Béti women displays unmistakable *bikutsi* influences, but also uses traditional instruments such as the *kora*.

Zaione (Lusafrica). Nyolo's most recent album, this cocktail of *bikutsi* and reggae typifies her mix of autobiographical song-writing with a variety of musical styles.

Anne-Marie Nzie

"La voix d'or du Cameroun", Anne-Marie Nzie started singing at the age of 8 and was a national star by the 1950s. Though no longer a chart-topper, she remains one of the most respected and popular female singers in the country, still pumping out robust *bikutsi* music with her quavering, Piaf-like voice. Her semi-acoustic amalgam of traditional and modern instrumentation, and the variety of rhythms and moods, make a welcome change from *makossa*.

Beza Ba Dzo (Indigo). Anne-Marie's second album projects her folklore-based material with power and energy.

Petit-Pays

Initially fronted by the unmistakable voice of Sammy Diko, Petit-Pays became the best-known *makossa* band in the country. Diko left the band to pursue a solo career in the late 1990s and the band's fortunes took a bit of a dive before a new lead singer, Phillip Guy, brought them back into the limelight.

Coup d'état (JPS). Singalong party music, with electric guitars and a drum kit that gives the music a feverish pace.

Les Têtes Brulées

Les Têtes Brulées came to Europe on a high note, just when the national football team was showing promise in the 1994 World Cup (early shows had them playing football on stage).

Les Têtes Brulées (Bleu Caraïbes). The CD which broke *bikutsi* to the world, with lots of energy but little depth.

Sam Fan Thomas

Thomas recorded several albums with minor hits, but had to wait until 1984 and the release of *Makassi* to achieve a wider reputation. The album's single, "African Typic Collection", ignited his reputation when it became an international dance hit.

African Typic Collection (Virgin Earthworks). Four Cameroonian songs (and one stray Cape Verdean number) packaged around the mega-hit title song. With Charlotte Mbango.

No Satisfaction (JPS). Thomas's most recent and readily available album, with a wild tempo enhanced by powerful drums and bass.

15

CAMEROON | Basics

Cinema

Cameroonian cinema has often dealt with the conflict between living in the modern world and keeping old traditions alive. The country's cinematic profile has been boosted by internationally recognized directors such as **Jean-Marie Téno** and **Bassek ba Kobhio**. **Jean-Paul Ngassa** was one of the pioneers of Cameroonian cinema with his production of *Aventures en France* in 1962, followed by *La Grand Case Bamilékée* in 1965.

After Ngassa's *Une Nation est Née*, in 1970, Cameroonian film production went into a lull until **Daniel Kamwa** brought a new spark with his 1972 prize-winning short *Boubou Cravate*, based on a Francis Bebey story. The 1977 *Pousse Pousse* – a comical look at the conflict between traditional customs and modern urban lifestyles as expressed through the issue of bride price – established him as a director with wide public appeal.

During the same period **Jean-Pierre Dikongue-Pipa** began making waves. *Muna Moto*, made in 1975, won encouraging reviews in France. Pipa's other work includes *Prix de la Liberté* (1978) and *Badiaga* (1983).

Although Kamwa and Dikongue-Pipa are still the best-known Cameroonian producer-directors, a new generation began to emerge in the early and mid-1980s. After studying at the École Supérieure d'Études Cinématographiques in Paris, **Louis-Balthazar Amadangoleda** made his first full-length film, *Les trois petits cireurs*, in 1985. Based on the novel of the same name by Francis Bebey, it looks at delinquency and its consequences. As an actor, Amadangoleda starred in the 2007 FESPACO prize-winning film *Les Saignantes*, by compatriot director Jean-Pierre Bekolo.

A former professor of literature, **Arthur Sibita** turned to film in 1978. His first feature-length film, *Les Coopérants*, traces the adventures of six youths from the city who decide to return to the village.

With his first feature-length film, *L'Appât du Gain* (1982), **Jules Takam** broke away from common themes of bride price, marriage and tradition and offered instead a fast-paced political intrigue based in Paris.

Jean-Claude Tchuilen came out with a promising first feature film in 1984 – *Suicides* – a well-paced psycho-drama, set in Paris. It was banned for being inflammatory when first released in Cameroon and never bounced back commercially after the ban was lifted.

Of the new generation, **Jean-Marie Téno** has emerged as the most internationally recognized. Early shorts – *Schubbah* (1984), *Hommage* (1985) and *La Caresse et la Gifle* (1987) – earned him acclaim, but his feature, *Afrique, Je te Plumerai* (1991), thrust him into the spotlight. His follow-up to that documentary on the abuses of the Biya regime, *Clando* (1996), treats similar themes of corruption and chaos in modern Africa through the story of an unlicensed cab driver whose scrapes with the law lead him on a journey to Germany and back. The past few years have seen the prolific Téno direct *Chef!* (2000), exploring the failure of democracy and the exploitation of women in contemporary Cameroon; *Vacances au Pays* (1999), a personal documentary about his return to Bandjoun in West Province after thirty years; and *Le Mariage d'Alex* (2002), a subtly comic look at polygamy.

Also well known is **Bassek ba Kobhio**, whose *Sango Malo* (1990) examines a rural teacher's struggle to replace a strict and inappropriate European curriculum with education that the villagers can use to build a self-reliant community and shape their own future. He takes a revisionist view of Albert Schweitzer in *Le Grand Blanc* de Lambaréné (1995), shot on location in Gabon. *Le Silence de la Forêt* (2003), inspired by a novel by the Centrafricain writer Étienne Goyemide, tells the story of a teacher who meets a "pygmy" asking for food at a village party and finds himself embarking on a journey into the forest.

Finally, **Jean–Pierre Bekolo** directed his first feature, *Quartier Mozart* (1992), at the age of 25. This imaginative story features a young girl with magical gifts who transforms herself into a virile male, Mister Guy, and has a lot of fun with gender roles in the process. Bekolo is an emerging force in African cinema: *Le Complot d'Aristote* (1996) featured at the 1997 Sundance Festival and his gritty and all-too-topical *Les Saignantes* (*The Bloodiest*; 2005) won second overall prize at FESPACO in 2007 with Dorylia Calmel winning the award for Best Actress. *Les Saignantes* exposes life in Douala and the corruption of the Biya government in a way that no film has done before.

Books

There's a fair number of books about Cameroon, and the country has the advantage of a dual linguistic heritage which has inspired a relatively rich literature, though it is predominantly in French. Books marked 🏃 are especially recommended.

General accounts and travelogues

Nigel Barley *Innocent Anthropologist: Notes from a Mud Hut* and *A Plague of Caterpillars*. The two books that did for anthropology what Durrell did for animal collecting – and infuriated anthropologists.

🏃 **Gerald Durrell** *The Overloaded Ark*, *The Bafut Beagles* and *A Zoo in My Luggage*. Durrell's animal-collecting exploits in the British Cameroons – first freelance, and then for his Jersey Conservation Trust Zoo – are delightfully recounted and still funny, apart from an unexceptionally colonial attitude to quaint native behaviour. But it's hard indeed to recognize the present town of Mamfé – even less Bafut – in his misty pictures.

Susana Herrera *Mango Elephants in the Sun: How Life in an African Village Let Me Be in My Skin*. A light read describing a US Peace Corps volunteer's experiences in northern Cameroon in the 1990s. Aside from a sweet love story with the local doctor, the highlight is her dilemma over ongoing strikes and her enforced neutrality as a "Corper".

Dervla Murphy *In Cameroon with Egbert*. Entertaining account of the adventures of Murphy and daughter on horseback in Cameroon.

History, politics, art and society

Mark Delancey *Cameroon: Dependence and Independence*. Survey of history, economics and politics.

Philippe Gaillard *Le Cameroun* (two volumes). General political and economic survey in French from colonial times to the late 1980s.

Albert Mukong *Prisoner without a Crime*. The darker side of political life under Biya, this tells the story of six years of imprisonment with graphic details of arbitrary justice, brutality and torture. Leave at home.

Claude Njiké–Bergeret *La Sagesse de mon Village*. Cultural study of Bangangté in West Province. The author describes the difficulty of being part of two very different cultures, French and Cameroonian, and analyzes his roots in depth.

Tamara Northern *Art of Cameroon*. Large-format, colour-illustrated survey of regions and their art.

Joseph Sheppherd *Leaf of Honey*. An American anthropologist's study of the Ntuumu people of Cameroon, laced with their proverbs and views about life.

Colin Turnbull *The Forest People*. An account of the Ituri forest Bambuti ("Pygmies") in Congo; the best writing in English on the oldest African people. Essential, delightful reading for forest stays in Cameroon, though based on visits in the 1960s.

Fiction

Léon-Marie Ayissi *Contes et Berceuses Béti*. Satisfying collection of Béti folktales.

Francis Bebey *Agatha Moudio's Son* (translated from *Le Fils d'Agatha Moudio*). By someone better known as a musician (see p.1245), this debut novel is a tragicomic study of human relations in a traditional village society.

Mongo Beti *The Poor Christ of Bomba*. One of the senior figures of African literature – living in exile since 1959 – Beti's novels combine political satire with more basic human conflict. *Poor Christ*, the most cynical of his novels, deals with the perverse efforts of a French priest to convert the whole village, with disastrously ironic consequences. Later works, *Mission to Kala* and *King Lazarus*, established his mastery of social satire. After independence, Beti embarked on a long period of silence until the publication of his critique of the Ahidjo regime – *Main basse sur le Cameroon*, which he followed with *Remember Ruben* and *Perpetua and the Habit of Unhappiness*.

Calixthe Beyala *Your Name Shall be Tanga* and *The Sun Hath Looked Upon Me*. An emerging name in West African fiction, Beyala's heroes are women forced to act against poverty and the injustices of male-based societies.

Benjamin Matip *Afrique nous t'ignorons*. Matip contemplates the past from a young African's perspective – separated from tradition by Western education and World War II. The novel also hits out at the exploitation of Cameroonian planters: it contributed to an outpouring of anti-colonial literature in the 1950s. Matip's *À la Belle Etoile: Contes et Nouvelles d'Afrique* is a classic collection of folktales.

Ndeley Mokoso *Man Pass Man!* A string of darkly funny short stories. The subject of the title tale – maraboutic meddling on the football pitch – was rumoured as an explanation for Cameroon's success in the 1990 World Cup.

Jacques Mariel Nzouankeu *Le Souffle des Ancêtres*. Tales that illustrate the conflict between humans and the metaphysical forces that are believed to dominate their destinies.

Ferdinand Oyono *Houseboy* (translated from *Une Vie de Boy*). Oyono was one of the first satirical writers of the colonial period to break from an autobiographical form in this scathing satire. *The Old Man and the Medal* (translated from *Le Vieux Négre et la Médaille*) is less caustic, but equally effective, both in its criticism of colonial insensitivity, and of blind adherence to tradition.

Guillaume Oyônô-Mbia *Until Further Notice* and *Three Suitors, One Husband*. Written in English, these two plays are comic masterpieces. His later play in French, *Notre Fille ne se Mariera pas*, like *Three Suitors*, deals with the familiar theme of the bride price in a changing African society and was filmed by Daniel Kamwa in 1980.

René Philombe *Lettres de ma Cambuse*. Life in the urban slums described – even on the basis of personal experience – with humour.

Languages

Uniquely in Africa, Cameroon has **two official languages**, French and English, and a demanding but worthy policy of bilingualism in education and the civil service. In practice, French has always had the upper hand, as English is spoken only in the North West and South West provinces, which are inhabited by just 22 percent of the population. People tend to identify strongly with their Anglophone or Francophone heritage, and it's not uncommon for tempers to rise when a person from the Anglophone regions insists on speaking English to a taxi driver in Yaoundé, or vice versa. In North West and South West provinces, people in major towns usually speak **Pidgin**, which is a different language, not a bastardized English, which doesn't come easily to an outsider, though you'll recognize a few words. In the south, **Duala** and **Bassa** are often used as trading languages, while in the north, **Fulani** has taken on that role.

Glossary

Auberge Cheap hotel or *maison de passage*, usually with shared facilities

Ba- Means "people of" in the Bantu and Semi-Bantu languages, widely extended (by European geographers) to indicate their towns and villages. Place names, so many of which begin with Ba- are a good deal easier to remember if this prefix is mentally dropped.

Boukarou In hotel jargon, bungalow-like huts with thatched roofs

Chantier Literally a construction site. In Yaoundé's popular jargon "street food stands"

Chefferie Traditional chiefdom, and level of local administration

Circuit Northern name for a *chantier* or chop house

CPDM Cameroon People's Democratic Movement (RDPC in French), the ruling party

Dash Present, gift or bribe

FDS Front Social-Démocratique (SDF in English), the main opposition party

Fon In western Cameroon, a chief or king

Kirdi Collective name for the mountain people of the Mandara range. It means pagan, since most of these people are non-Muslim and non-Christian.

Lamidat In the north, equivalent to a sultanate. The sultan is the Lamido.

Mayo In the north, a river or dried riverbed

Ramassage "Collection" or "pick up". You take a taxi *en ramassage*, meaning you share it (and the fare) rather than rent it individually.

RDPC Rassemblement Démocratique du Peuple Camerounais (CPDM in English), the ruling party

SDF Social Democratic Front (FDS in French), the main opposition party

Saré Sudanic-style huts common in the north

Sauvetteurs Wandering vendors, hawkers

CAMEROON | Basics

15.1

Douala and South West Province

T he **economic capital** of Cameroon, **Douala** is a huge and energetic city abuzz with life twenty-four hours a day. The driving force behind its growth has been the **port**, which handles most of the nation's maritime traffic and has stimulated regional development in trade and industry. Douala's nonstop activity and relative prosperity is expressed in a relentless urban jungle, a cityscape distinguishable only by a clutch of mostly German colonial buildings which give the city its sense of history – something that's lacking in Yaoundé in the interior where modern-day urban planners have largely concentrated their efforts. A result of this neglect has been that Douala suffers from overpopulation and a worn-down and inadequate infrastructure. For **nightlife**, however, the city cannot be beaten: **live music** is always to be found somewhere nearby and its multitude of **restaurants** include some of the best in West Africa.

There is a wide variety of natural highlights within easy reach of the metropolis. For simple rest and recuperation, you can't beat the black-sand beaches around **Limbé**, a small town with a distinctly colonial flavour at the foot of **Mount Cameroon** – West Africa's highest peak. The colonial town of **Buéa** is only 70km away, 1000m up the slopes of the mountain, and makes a good base for climbing expeditions. Continuing north, **Kumba**, a vibrant commercial town located near beautiful **Lake Barombi Mbo**, is a good stopover on the way to **Korup National Park** and Nigeria. East of Kumba, and still only a few hours' drive from Douala, **Mount Kupé** and the **Manengouba twin crater lakes** provide enjoyable hiking.

Douala

Despite its status as the nation's largest and wealthiest city, **DOUALA** is not its most attractive. The relentless bustle and oppressive heat and humidity can be overwhelming, but if you can muster the energy to explore, the **old colonial buildings** in the Joss and Bonanjo districts give a powerful insight into the city's controversial history, the **market area** around the Lagos neighbourhood is the liveliest in Cameroon, and the Deïdo, Akwa and Bonapriso quarters offer some of the best **nightlife** in West Africa. Douala's many different facets are apparent in its many quarters, and with a population that has skyrocketed in recent years to more than two million, it has undergone some rapid changes. Although most of the city is fairly safe, crime is rampant in other areas, especially the area around the port – don't walk around with anything visibly valuable and aim to look as if you know where you are going.

Some history

Like so many settlements on the West African coast, the Douala area was once home to small fishing communities who first encountered Europeans when the **Portuguese** made contact at the end of the fifteenth century. Although trade – especially in slaves

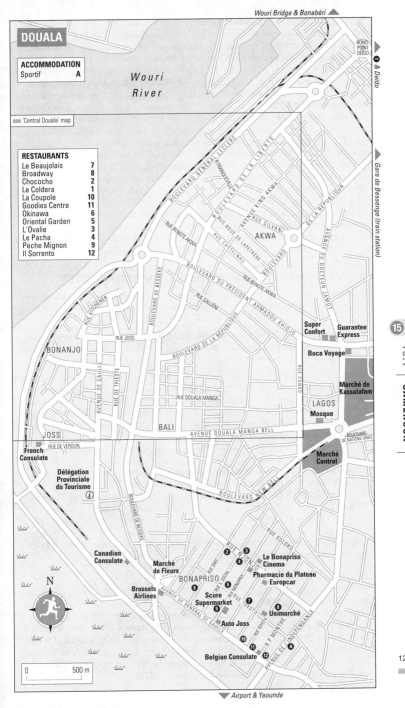

Wouri Bridge & Bonabéri

DOUALA

ACCOMMODATION
Sportif   **A**

Wouri River

see 'Central Douala' map

RESTAURANTS
Le Beaujolais   7
Broadway   8
Chococho   2
Le Coldera   1
La Coupole   10
Goodies Centre   11
Okinawa   6
Oriental Garden   5
L'Ovalie   3
Le Pacha   4
Peche Mignon   9
Il Sorrento   12

ROND-POINT DEÏDO

& Deïdo

Gare de Bessenge (train station)

BOULEVARD GÉNÉRAL LECLERC

BOULEVARD DE LA LIBERTÉ

BOULEVARD FRANÇOIS

AVENUE KING AKWA

RUE SILVANI

RUE BOUE DE LAPEYRERE

RUE BENOTE AKWA

RUE CASTELNAU

DE LA RÉPUBLIQUE

AKWA

AVENUE DU DOCTEUR JAMOT

BOULEVARD

BOULEVARD DE BESSÉKE

BOULEVARD DU PRÉSIDENT AHMADOU AHIDJO

RUE GALLIENI

RUE BENOTE AKWA

RUE KITCHENER

RUE JOSS

BONANJO

BOULEVARD DE LA RÉPUBLIQUE

Super Confort

Guarantee Express

Buca Voyage

Marché de Kassalafam

RUE CONGO

LAGOS
Mosque

AVENUE DE GAULLE

RUE DE TRIESTE

RUE DOUALA MANGA

BALI

AVENUE DOUALA MANGA BELL

JOSS

RUE DE VERDUN

French Consulate

Délégation Provinciale du Tourisme
ⓘ

BOULEVARD NEW BELL

Marché Central

BOULEVARD DE NATIONS UNIES

Canadian Consulate

Marché de Fleurs

RUE KOLOKO

RUE SNEC

③
②
④
Le Bonapriso Cinema

BONAPRISO

⑥

RUE SOCAL

⑤

RUE MINKOMBO

Pharmacie du Plateau
Europcar

Brussels Airlines

AVENUE DE GÉNÉRAL DE GAULLE

Score Supermarket
⑨

RUE TOYOTA

⑦

Unimarché
⑧

Auto Joss

⑩

⑪

RUE P. MONTHE

AVENUE DE INDEPENDANCE

Belgian Consulate   ⑫   Ⓐ

N

0   500 m

15

15.1

1253

Airport & Yaounde

– between local rulers and seafarers continued, Europeans only settled on the banks of the Wouri (or Cameroons) River in the nineteenth century. The first of these were **English missionaries** led by **Alfred Saker** who, in 1845, founded a small community at the site where the Temple du Centenaire stands today. By that time, the **Duala people** (who probably arrived in the estuary at the beginning of the seventeenth century) were established in two groups united around the **Bell** and **Akwa** families.

German trading companies followed in the footsteps of the missionaries and quickly persuaded Bismarck to protect their interests in the region. The German chancellor sent **Gustav Nachtigal** to claim the lands in the name of the Kaiser. In July 1884, Nachtigal signed treaties with the chiefs Bell, Akwa and Deïdo. With a flick of a pen, British designs in the region were wiped out, while the Duala chiefs had ceded legal rights to the territory (at least according to German law). In 1885, a German governor was appointed and **Kamerunstadt** became the capital. The name stuck until 1907, when it was changed to Douala. But before then, in 1901, the status of capital was transferred to Buéa, on the flanks of Mount Cameroon, which, to the Germans, had a much more agreeable climate.

After World War I, Douala became part of the French protectorate and although it did not regain its status as capital, the French began large-scale urban construction, and enlargement of the port. Industry followed, and Douala forged ahead to become the economic engine of the whole country and remains so today.

Arrival, information and city transport

The **airport** at Douala, a stone's throw southwest of the Bonapriso neighbourhood, handles the majority of **international** flights to Cameroon, though it's showing

---

Douala surface arrivals and departures

By road

Almost all of Douala's *agences de voyage* with services to **Yaoundé**, **Kribi and the east** are based around the junction of bd Ahidjo and av Jamot. The main companies for Yaoundé are Central Voyages and Garanti Express, with large stuffy coaches (CFA3500) as well as fast, nonstop luxury air-conditioned buses (CFA6000). These are supplemented by a new agency based at *Hôtel Sawa* called Le Car, which also runs a fast luxury service to Yaoundé.

The best agency for **Kribi** is Central Voyages, while agencies for **Ebolowa and the south** include Buca Voyage.

Agencies for **Bamenda, Bafoussam and the southwest** all have offices in the Bonabéri area. Garanti Express has a second outlet here. Other agencies include Amour Mezan for **Bamenda** and **Bafoussam**; Super Confort and Butsi Voyages for **Foumban** via **Bafoussam**; Mondial Express and Tonton for **Buéa** and **Kumba**.

Services stop in **Mutengene** en route to the west, northwest and southwest, where it's easy to find share taxis to **Limbé**.

Note that share taxis to **Limbé**, **Buéa**, **Mbanga** and **Kumba** leave from the Deïdo roundabout as well as Bonabéri motor park.

By train

You should make enquiries in advance to Camrail (☎33.40.24.13 or 33.40.14.22), since schedules change frequently. You can buy tickets to Yaoundé and Kumba, but in both cases you're likely to get to your destination a lot quicker if you do at least part of the journey by road. There are two daily trains to **Yaoundé** (7.15am & 1.30pm; 5hr; CFA6000 1st class, CFA3000 2nd class). There is one daily train to **Kumba** (7.30am; CFA1000) but it is extremely slow and unreliable – it's better, especially in the wet season, when the roads are bad, to take a share taxi on the good road to Mbanga and catch a train to Kumba from there (4 daily; 2–3hr; CFA500).

signs of age and is surprisingly small. There's an **ATM** (Visa only) in a secure booth. It costs CFA3000 to hire a **yellow taxi** into the centre during the day, and CFA5000 at night.

If you arrive **by train** from Yaoundé or Kumba you'll come in at the **Gare de Bessenge**, just off Boulevard de la République in the northeastern part of the city centre. The quickest way into town from here, and generally the best way of getting around, is to catch a yellow cab on a shared basis. The standard fare for a "drop" (a journey within the city limits in a share taxi) is CFA150.

Coming into central Douala **by bus** or **minibus** with an *agence de voyage* you usually end up at the company's booking office, although you can ask to be dropped off along the way. Most of the *agences de voyage* are based around the junction of Boulevard Ahmadou Ahidjo and Avenue du Docteur Jamot, less than a kilometre from the centre.

Agences arriving from West, North West and South West provinces are based around **Bonabéri**, about 6km north of the centre across the Wouri River. The journey to the centre in a hired cab costs CFA1500. Alternatively, for CFA200 you can catch share taxis from Bonabéri to **Rond-point Deïdo** (also known simply as "Rond-point"), which lies 2km to the north of the centre, from where a second drop will take you further into the centre. Long-distance drivers sometimes continue all the way into the centre. If this happens, ask to be dropped at the **Wouri Cinema**, which is a central landmark within walking distance of several moderately-priced hotels.

The **Délégation Provinciale du Tourisme** (☎33.42.14.22 or 33.42.14.10) is located on Avenue de Gaulle beyond the tennis club. As with tourist delegations elsewhere in the country, this is a government office and they don't provide tourist information as such, and asking any taxi driver will probably get you the information a lot more quickly. Some bookshops and street vendors sell **city maps** for CFA2000–5000, but many streets are unnamed – both on the map and on the ground. Locals and taxi drivers give directions by landmarks – hotels, nightclubs, roundabouts – rather than street names.

Accommodation

Cheap accommodation doesn't really exist in Douala – even the missions charge premium rent on rooms that in order to be bearable in the oppressive heat all have air conditioning. Although there are some decent places in the moderate category, the city seems to belong to the international hotels.

Hotels

Inexpensive to moderate

All the following hotels are keyed on the city-centre map on p.1257, except *Hôtel Sportif*, which is on the smaller-scale map of Douala on p.1253.

Astoria Prima rue Mermoz, Akwa ☎33.42.84.18 ⓦwww.hotelastoriacamroun .com. At the top end of the moderate scale, this romantic, small place in the heart of Akwa offers stylish s/c rooms with a/c, a cosy bar-restaurant, and free parking at the back. ❺

Auberge la Côte av King Akwa, Akwa ☎33.43.46.43. Small, box-like s/c rooms (some with a/c and a few also with TV), often rented out by the hour. There's also a good-value restaurant and a bar with TV. ❷

Beauséjour Mirabel rue Joffre, Akwa ☎33.42.38.85 ⓦwww.hbmdla.com. Elegant, Art-Nouveau-ish six-storey hotel in Akwa's main commercial area with some of the city's best nightclubs nearby. The hotel has bright, comfortable a/c s/c rooms, a streetfront café-restaurant (where breakfast, included in the price, is served), an Internet café free for guests, free and safe parking, and the promise of a refurbished rooftop swimming pool in the near future. ❺

Foyer du Marin end of rue Galliéni, off bd de la Liberté, Akwa ☎33.42.27.94 ⓔdoula@seemannsmission.org. Absolutely the best mid-range option (although in theory it's reserved for the use of seamen), with immaculate s/c a/c rooms – twin or double –

set around a small garden restaurant and an inviting pool. Fast Internet access in the lobby. Popular with expats, perhaps due to the draught beer and grilled sausages. Book in advance, as it's often full. ❹

La Côte off bd Ahmadou Ahidjo, Akwa ☎33.43.38.10 ✉grouplacote@hotmail.com. A new hotel branch of the same-named *auberge*, convenient for agency transport to Yaoundé, Kribi and the south, and the Togolese embassy. The spacious, clean, s/c a/c rooms all come with TV and cold showers, and there's a popular streetside a/c bar-restaurant. ❹

La Falaise rue Kitchener, Bonanjo ☎33.42.46.46 ✉hotelfalaise@cameroun-plus.com. Once one of the city's most stylish places, this has retained some of its colonial charm perched on a hill overlooking the Wouri River next to the old railway station. The a/c rooms – double or twin – are no longer as spotless as they once were. This is reflected in the prices, making it a good-value place to stay if you hanker for peace and quiet, away from bustling Akwa. Great views of the harbour from the pool but nowhere to sit nearby. ❺

Le Ndé bd de la Liberté, Akwa ☎33.42.70.34. Under new management, the once-popular *Ndé* is slowly getting back on track. With spacious, tiled, s/c a/c rooms standing in stark contrast to its dark corridors, it's the swimming pool out back that's the main pull with its fabulous views of the harbour. Also houses the Honorary British Consulate and has an excellent-value bar-restaurant. ❹

L'Oubangui on the corner of av King Akwa and rue Mermoz, Akwa ☎33.43.25.15 ✉houtelobangui@yahoo.fr. In the epicentre of the lively Akwa neighbourhood, this sparkling new hotel has excellent-value s/c a/c rooms – cold showers only – a streetside bar-restaurant, an Internet café and Wi-Fi throughout. Breakfast included. ❹

Procure Générale des Missions Catholiques rue Franqueville, Akwa ☎33.42.27.97. Poorly signposted (next to the orange AXA building), this mission guesthouse with pool is a godsend for lone travellers. Comfortable a/c s/c or non-s/c rooms with two to four single beds, and excellent-value meals in the restaurant on offer (not Sun). Missionaries get priority, and it's often full, so advance booking is essential. ❸

Sportif av des Palmiers, Bonapriso ☎33.43.76.40. Within easy reach of the airport (CFA200 for a drop) and walking distance of Bonapriso's nightlife, this none-too-luxurious hotel has a range of excellent-value s/c rooms of varying standards, some with

a/c and TV, others box-like with a fan. Rooms with fan ❷ or a/c ❹.

Expensive hotels

The following hotels are keyed on the city-centre map opposite.

Akwa Palace bd de la Liberté, Akwa ☎33.42.26.01 ⓦwww.hotel-akwa-palace.com. The oldest of the international hotels, still boasting a cheaper old colonial-style wing. Pleasant pool and gardens, casino, café-bar, and excellent restaurant. AVIS and Camair offices in the lobby and Wi-Fi throughout. Visa, MasterCard and Diners Club only. Old wing ❼, new wing ❽.

Ibis off av de Gaulle, Bonanjo ☎33.42.58.00 ⓦwww.ibishotel.com. Typical business-class hotel offering affordable luxury – though the rooms are on the small side – and abuzz with activity on the poolside terrace, and in the restaurants and shops. Major credit cards accepted. ❽

Méridien av des Cocotiers, Joss ☎33.43.50.00 ⓦwww.starwoodhotels.com. The classiest and most expensive hotel in town, with numerous restaurants, casino, pool, Wi-Fi, tennis courts, travel agent, and a well-stocked bookshop, plus free membership of a gym/health club (3km away). Small surcharge for sea-view rooms. Visa and Amex only. ❽

Parfait Garden bd de la Liberté, Akwa ☎33.42.63.57 ⓦwww.parfaitgarden.com. Following a complete makeover, once again among the city's most-favoured top-range places. Immaculately done-up rooms come with large tubs and grand city views. Rooms facing away from bd de la Liberté are somewhat quieter than balconied rooms facing the street. Good restaurant, bar, Internet café. No garden or pool. Visa only. ❼

Planet rue Boué de Lapeyère, off av Liberté, Akwa ☎33.43.31.31 ⓦwww.planethoteldouala .com. Fabulous new multistorey hotel in downtown Akwa within walking distance of a good selection of restaurants and nightclubs – opposite *Le Senate* (one of the best). Caters mainly for overseas NGO staff and business travellers. Spotless rooms include free broadband, flat-screen TVs and large tubs. Popular restaurant serves pricey buffet meals throughout the day. No cards. ❽

Sawa rue de Verdun, off av de Gaulle, Joss ☎33.42.08.66 ✉hotelsawa@hotelsawa.cm. With a fresh coat of pastel paint, this big, former *Novotel* is beginning to look smart again. Spacious rooms come with garden or car-park view (garden views have balconies with stunning harbour vistas). Large, clean pool and in-house massage service (CFA20,000/hr). Crafts, curios and nice jewellery sold in the foyer. Car rental and Internet café. Amex and Visa only. ❽

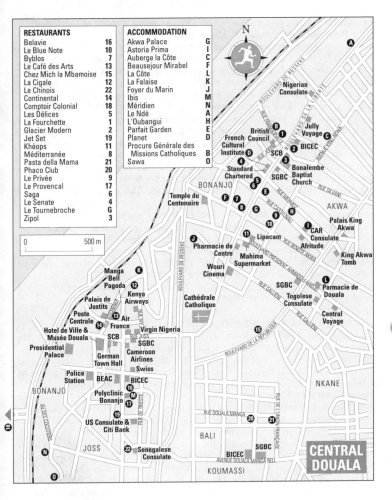

RESTAURANTS	
Belavie	16
Le Blue Note	10
Byblos	7
Le Café des Arts	13
Chez Mich la Mbamoise	15
La Cigale	12
Le Chinois	22
Continental	14
Comptoir Colonial	18
Les Délices	5
La Fourchette	1
Glacier Modern	2
Jet Set	19
Khéops	11
Méditerranée	8
Pasta della Mama	21
Phaco Club	20
Le Privée	9
Le Provencal	17
Saga	6
Le Senate	4
Le Tournebroche	G
Zipol	3

ACCOMMODATION	
Akwa Palace	G
Astoria Prima	I
Auberge la Côte	C
Beausejour Mirabel	F
La Côte	L
La Falaise	K
Foyer du Marin	J
Ibis	M
Méridien	N
Le Ndé	Z
L'Oubangui	A
Parfait Garden	H
Planet	E
Procure Générale des Missions Catholiques	D
Sawa	B

The City

Douala sprawls in every direction, with much of its industry on the far side of the Wouri Bridge, on the west bank of the river in the Bonabéri neighbourhood, which is also where most city workers live. Nonetheless, the various distinct quarters into which the city is divided – most of them named after local ruling families – aren't too difficult to work out.

Akwa: the modern centre

As the main commercial area, the **Akwa neighbourhood** is more or less the centre of the modern city. Its lifeline is the **Boulevard de la Liberté**, with the **Cathédrale Catholique** (daily 6.15am–6.30am; Sun choral mass 6.30am, English mass 8am, Duala mass 9.30am, French mass 11am) something of a landmark at its southern end. Built in the 1930s, this is one of the few attractive edifices in the neighbourhood, even if its neo-Romanesque style is a bit incongruous in this sweltering climate.

Continuing north, you pass the Wouri Cinema before arriving at the wide tree-lined **Boulevard du Président Ahmadou Ahidjo** (bd Ahidjo). Here, numerous department stores, supermarkets and boutiques provide an upmarket commercial backdrop for the street vendors selling clothes, shoes and accessories. North of here, along Boulevard de la République, stands the **Palais King Akwa**, an interesting palace built in a curious mishmash of styles for King Akwa XII, who died in 1976. A statue of him stands outside the palace, while his tomb-cum-monument can be found two streets south of here. Turning back down Boulevard Ahidjo and heading west, towards the river, takes you past the **Église Évangelique** (or Temple du Centenaire), built to commemorate the 100th anniversary of Alfred Saker's arrival. With great views down the hill to the **port**, this part of the Akwa neighbourhood has undergone massive developments in recent years, and now houses some very sought after multistorey real estate, tucked in between Boulevard Général Leclerc – also known as "the Beach" – and Boulevard de la Liberté.

Further north along bd de la Liberté you get to the **Akwa Palace** (now the hotel of the same name), a colonial pile that was Cameroon's ultimate luxury accommodation for many years, and still retains a certain charm. Beyond the hotel on the corner of rue Silvani stands another colonial relic, the small, German **Bonalembe Baptist Church** of 1899. Businesses become more sparse on Boulevard de la Liberté as it heads towards **Rond-point Deïdo** – aka Place de la Jeunesse – home to the much photographed *Statue de la Nouvelle Liberté*, a funky and enormous statue of a dancing man fashioned out of scrap iron. From the roundabout the road to the west heads towards the **Wouri Bridge** and over to the industrial **Bonabéri** neighbourhood on the west bank of the river.

Bonanjo and the administrative district

Heading south from the Cathédrale Catholique, Boulevard de la Liberté curves west across Boulevard de Besseke, a new, fast dual-carriageway connecting the port area to the south. After the bridge, Boulevard de la Liberté changes its name to rue Joss and continues downhill to **Place du Gouvernement** and Avenue de Gaulle. This is the heart of the administrative quarter and the **Bonanjo** district. The **Poste Centrale**, with a large monument commemorating the fallen of World War I, dominates the square. On one corner, you'll see the pagoda-shaped colonial house which was once the **palace** of Prince Rudolf Manga Bell. The grandson of a Duala signatory of the German treaty, the prince was later executed by the Germans for treason. The pagoda is still owned by the Manga Bell family and now houses a travel agency, a fancy French café and the **Musée Doual'art** (Mon–Fri 9am–7pm, Sat 9am–6.30pm; free), home to a small collection of modern African art.

The rather forlorn **Musée de Douala** (Mon–Fri 9am–4pm; CFA1000 with a guide) is housed in the **Hôtel de Ville** behind Place du Gouvernement. It's not signed anywhere; just walk into the City Hall and head upstairs and you'll find the museum on the first floor. As with all the government-run museums in Cameroon, the place lacks funding and is in a constant state of disarray. The collection consists of a dusty selection of poorly presented and inadequately explained national treasures, but has one or two rare pieces – potentially interesting, if you're going to be travelling around the country.

Southwest of the square, the impressive **Presidential Palace**, again from the German colonial era, is out of bounds, especially if you've got a camera – stories of innocent tourists being beaten up by the security police are not unheard of. However, if the colonial period's mark on the city interests you, there are plenty of other imposing **German colonial buildings** in the area around the Place du Gouvernement. These include the German hospital, which now houses the police station, the German law courts, and the central section of the Palais de Justice. Informative placards explaining the buildings' cultural and political significance have been erected in front of each, so you can basically treasure-hunt for placards and you'll find yourself in front of historical buildings. Continuing south along Avenue de Gaulle brings you to the **Joss** neighbourhood, with more colonial buildings. North of the *Hôtel Méridien*, **Avenue des Cocotiers** gives a good impression of German colonial residential architecture and city planning.

Markets

The districts of **Lagos** and **Kassalafam** are two of the liveliest neighbourhoods in town, and well worth visiting even if you don't want to buy anything from their bustling markets. From Bonanjo, Avenue Douala Manga Bell leads east through the Bali quarter and on to the Lagos quarter, where you'll find the **Marché Central** – the biggest market in the country. It spreads south of Avenue Douala Manga Bell and is hemmed in by the rue Congo to the west. The northeast corner is marked by the busy Place de l'Indépendance and the adjacent **mosque**, in front of which assorted barks, seeds and powders – the essential ingredients of the African pharmacy – are sold. Nearby, on rue Congo, the **Marché Congo** specializes in African and imported fabrics. The market area continues past Place de l'Indépendance up Boulevard des Nations Unies, where it merges with the **Marché de Kassalafam**, primarily a fruit and vegetable market.

Arts and crafts are sold at the **Marché des Fleurs**, off Avenue de Gaulle in the Bonapriso quarter. Foumban (see p.1295) has a reputation for being the best place in Cameroon to buy authentic artefacts (and high-quality reproductions), but this market rates a close second. They also sell good-quality jewellery as well as both real and fake antiques. The masks, both new and old (and it's pretty hard to tell which is which), are imported from all over West Africa, and are the same as those on sale in London or Paris at ten to twenty times the price.

Eating and drinking

Eating in Douala can be very expensive. Many of the upmarket restaurants are grouped in the **Bonapriso** quarter, Douala's prime residential area. The city also flaunts a number of Parisian-style **cafés**, where shoppers retire for a break and businesspeople do deals. You can relax in their air-conditioned comfort for as long as you like for the price of a coffee (CFA500–1000). *Akwa Palace*, *Les Délices* and *Glacier Moderne* take turns at being the in place of the moment and do superb pastries for CFA1000. A number of Greek bakeries – *Zipol*, *Chococho*, *Belavie* and *Goodie Centre* – also double as small but well-stocked grocery stores with take-out counters selling well-prepared fast food such as pizza slices and *chawarma*, and sometimes also have an eat-in café. At the other end of the city centre, the Akwa quarter is the best place for a large array of **street food**, especially near *Hôtel Beauséjour Mirabel* on rue Joffre, including crispy salads, spicy beans with fresh bread, and surprisingly tasty spaghetti omelettes. Don't go too late: the food usually runs out by about 4pm.

Restaurants

Cheap to moderate

You'll pay no more than CFA6000 a head (without drinks) to eat at the following restaurants and bars, and considerably less at some of them. All are keyed on the maps on p.1253 and p.1257.

Chez Mich la Mbamoise bd de la République, Bali ☎ 33.43.13.45. Lively, family-run restaurant with outdoor *paillote* seating, offering well-prepared Cameroonian and Western dishes. Open for lunch and dinner, the weekend speciality is couscous *maïs* with gombo, while chicken DG (CFA4000 for

half) and *ndolé* with prawns (CFA2000) are hits throughout the week. Booking recommended at weekends.

Chococho rue NjoNjo, Bonapriso (closed Sun). Popular bakery producing the best chocolate croissants in Douala. They can be devoured in the adjacent café where freshly made juices and sandwiches as well as home-made pizzas (CFA5000–7000 for a large one) are also on the menu.

Comptoir Colonial Youpewe Naval Base, Douala Port, Joss. Beautiful, trendy portside bar-restaurant in wood and bamboo, serving the likes of chicken and chips and grilled fish to accompany delightful drinks at sunset. On clear days you can see Mount Cameroon from the terrace.

Continental place du Gouvernement, Bonanjo. Small a/c restaurant in a container-like shed next to the Poste Centrale, serving outstanding *ndolé* and plantain chips (CFA1500) as well as the usual array of fish and chicken.

Foyer du Marin At the *Foyer du Marin*, Akwa. Tasty German sausages with salad (CFA1800), as well as a steak-and-chips-style menu, and cool draught beer served in a relaxing poolside atmosphere.

Glacier Moderne bd de la Liberté. Popular Greek ice cream and pastry place where arguably the best coffee in Douala makes breakfast (from CFA2500) a real treat. Throughout the day, filling burgers, steaks and chicken'n'chips, as well as delicious crispy salads, fill the place with hungry shoppers.

Il Sorrento av de Gaulle, Bonapriso (evenings only). Lively pizzeria with music at weekends. Count on around CFA5000 per head without drinks.

La Coupole 105 av de Gaulle, Bonapriso ℡33.42.29.60. Comfortable little corner bar with a restaurant section serving good-value Italian-style food (including pizzas) and take-outs. Expect to pay CFA4000–6000 per person.

Le Chinois av de Gaulle, Bonanjo ℡33.42.33.10. The oldest Chinese restaurant in town, and very affordable, even for the more expensive Sunday buffet (CFA9000).

Le Pacha rue NjoNjo between the church and the pharmacy, Bonapriso. Lebanese restaurant with salads and snacks like *chawarma* (CFA1700), plus more substantial meals.

Méditerranée bd de la Liberté, Akwa. Large, outdoor restaurant on one of the busiest streets in Douala serving excellent Greek dishes at reasonable prices – CFA4500 for moussaka. Tends to be patronized by prostitutes.

Pasta della Mama rue de l'Union Française, Bali ℡99.53.26.08. Italian-style food with a good-value *menu du jour* for CFA3500.

Phaco Club rue Douala Manga, near the Sonel building ℡99.55.30.08. As rumbustious as the warthog it's named after – but much friendlier. Tasty African food, including chicken wrapped in banana leaves and exotic bush meats. Dancers or musicians perform nightly. Allow CFA5000 per person, without drinks.

Saga bd de la Liberté, Akwa. Large new restaurant on Douala's busiest thoroughfare, serving well-prepared Cameroonian and Western dishes in comfortable surroundings. Mains start at CFA2500.

Expensive restaurants

Expensive Douala restaurants run CFA7000 to CFA20,000 per person, drinks excluded. The following are all keyed on the maps on p.1253 and p.1257.

Le Beaujolais rue Tokoto, Bonapriso ℡99.33.23.24. Also known as the Boj, this place does posh French cuisine at a price (from CFA10,000) and has a small bar and a pool table.

Le Café des Arts Manga Bell historical pagoda ℡99.81.10.87. Upmarket rustic French restaurant with good (mostly classical) music. There's also a pleasant garden, excellent for unwinding with a cool drink. Allow around CFA7000 per head without drinks.

La Cigale rue Kitchener, Joss, near *Hôtel La Falaise*. French–Lebanese place offering pizza and live music at weekends. There's also a good bar here.

La Fourchette rue Franqueville, Akwa ℡33.42.14.88. One of the few good French restaurants in Akwa – comfortable but expensive.

Okinawa rue SNEC, Bonapriso ℡33.42.69.10. High-quality Japanese sushi, as well as kebabs.

Oriental Garden rue S. Social, Bonapriso ℡33.42.69.38. Excellent Chinese restaurant with chefs from China. Allow CFA15,000 per head.

L'Ovalie rue NjoNjo, Bonapriso ℡99.06.05.11. Upmarket French cuisine, for which you pay dear, but it's all worth it.

Peche Mignon rue Monoprix opposite Score supermarket, Bonapriso. Excellent French food in pleasant surroundings.

Le Provençal av de Gaulle, Bonanjo ℡33.42.70.17 (weekday lunches only). Classy French lunchtime restaurant in Douala's banking district.

Le Tournebroche At the *Hôtel Akwa Palace* ℡33.42.05.40. Top-class French restaurant; allow CFA15,000 per person without drinks.

Nightlife

Douala's **clubs** open, close down and change hands quite frequently, but even if the name of a place changes, it generally remains a club, and the taxi drivers tend to know both past and present names. Clubs usually open around 11pm or midnight and close when they get quiet, some time between 3am and 5am. Entry **prices** vary enormously for foreigners, locals, men, and women, but once you're in you rarely come under pressure to buy drinks. If you do buy drinks, they'll cost anything from CFA3000–8000, or you can buy a bottle of whisky for about CFA25,000 to be kept for you behind the bar.

Le Blue Note rue Benote Akwa, Akwa. One of many nightclubs in the area behind *Hôtel Akwa*, playing a good mix of European and Cameroonian music and attracting a large crowd at weekends.
Broadway rue Toyota, Bonapriso. The Cameroonian version of a *Hard Rock Café*, with lots of dancing and different performers every night.
Byblos Across from *Hôtel Beauséjour Mirabel*, Akwa. Upmarket local club featuring mostly African music. Cheap entrance (CFA3000).
Le Coldera rue de la Joie, Deïdo. A popular locals' venue – you're likely to be the only foreigner here – on a street packed with bars and nightclubs.

Jet Set av de Gaulle, near Cameroon Airlines. Attracts a mainly young Cameroonian crowd with its good mix of African and Western music.
Khéops bd de Ahmadou Ahidjo, near bd de la Liberté junction. Flashy nightclub churning out Western and Cameroonian dance tunes.
La Privée rue Castelnau, behind *Hôtel Parfait Garden*. Hugely popular place where the DJ excels in spinning the best Cameroonian dance tunes.
Le Senat rue Boué de Lapeyère, across from *Hôtel Planet*, Akwa. The flavour of the month among expats, with live music most nights.

Listings

Airlines Most airline offices are in the Bonanjo neighbourhood. They include: Air France, 1 pl du Gouvernement ☎33.01.23.75 or 33.011279; Air Ivoire, bd de la Liberté ☎33.42.06.95 or 33.42.05.85; Bellview Airlines, rue Hôtel de Ville ☎33.43.21.31; Benin Golf Air ☎33.42.22.90 or 99.64.97.04; Brussels Airlines, av de Gaulle ☎33.42.05.15; Cameroon Airlines, 3 av de Gaulle ☎33.42.25.25 or 33.42.32.22 ☏33.42.49.49, and at the *Hôtel Akwa Palace* ☎33.42.26.01 (services to Garoua Mon 7pm & Fri 2pm, CFA85,500; services to Yaoundé Fri 2pm, CFA23,700); Kenya Airways, rue de Trieste ☎33.42.94.99 or 77.05.88.88; Swissair, rue Ivy ☎33.42.29.29; Virgin Nigeria, 123 rue Joss ☎33.42.78.69 or 33.42.76.27.
Banks and ATMs Major branches in the Bonanjo neighbourhood include: Banque Internationale du Cameroun pour l'Épargne et le Crédit (BICEC), av de Gaulle; Société Général de Banques au Cameroun (SGBC), rue Joss (which represents Thomas Cook); Société Commerciale de Banque Cameroun (SCB), rue Joss; Comercial Bank of Cameroon (CBC), av de Gaulle; and Citibank in the American Consulate building. All of these – apart from Citibank – also have branches in Akwa, where you'll find the head office of Standard Chartered Bank Cameroon, 57 bd de la Liberté. All the banks change euros; Citibank also change US dollars and Standard Chartered change pounds sterling. There are ATMs at all SGBC branches and most branches of SCB and BICEC. There are lots of exchange traders in front of the *Hôtel Akwa Palace* (usually offering better rates for US dollars than the banks, as well as a quicker service).
Books The bookshop at *Hôtel Méridien* sell international magazines and books in English. Lipacam,

27 bd Ahidjo, sells mainly educational books, but also has some fiction in French and a few maps. You can also usually find IGN maps at these places.
Car rental Avis, at *Hôtel Akwa Palace* (☎33.42.03.47 ☏33.42.70.56) and at Douala Airport (☎ & ☏33.43.96.29); Auto Joss, rue Monoprix near the Score supermarket ☎ & ☏33.42.86.19; Auto World, at *Hôtel Sawa* ☎ & ☏33.42.86.84; Hertz, bd de Général Leclerc ☎33.42.06.90 ☏342.42.60 and at Douala Airport ☎99.85.58.29.
Cinemas The two big air-conditioned cinemas are Le Bonapriso, on rue NjoNjo, and Le Wouri, on bd de la Liberté. The Centre Culturel Français shows French films.
Consulates Most main embassies are in Yaoundé, but a number of countries maintain consulates in Douala, including: Benin, Bepanda Collège Maturité ☎ & ☏33.40.21.53; Canada, 1726 av de Gaulle ☎33.43.31.03 ☏342.31.09; Central African Republic, next to King Akwa College, rue Castelnau ☎ & ☏ 33.43.45.47; Democratic Republic of Congo, 70 rue Sylvanie ☎33.43.20.29 ☏33.43.19.69; Equatorial Guinea, rue Tokoto, Bonapriso ☎99.93.84.24 or 33.42.96.09; France, av des Cocotiers ☎33.42.62.50 ☏33.43.31.05; Niger, next to the central mosque ☎33.42.63.69; Nigeria, bd de la Liberté ☎33.43.21.68 ☏33.43.07.66; Senegal, Galerie MAM, Bonanjo ☎33.42.28.63 ☏33.42.22.73; Togo, 490 rue Dicka Mpondo, Akwa ☎33.42.11.87; UK, *Hôtel le Ndé*, bd de la Liberté ☎33.43.97.32 or 77.71.36.51; USA, 3rd floor, Flatters Building, off av de Gaulle ☎33.42.03.03 ☏33.42.77.90.
Cultural centres British Council, rue Joffre, Akwa ☎33.42.51.45; Centre Culturel Français, bd de la

Liberté ☎ 33.42.69.96 🌐 www.francophone.net /ccfdouala; Centre Culturel Africain, in the Collège Liberman, rue des Écoles ☎ 33.42.28.90. The latter runs courses in African languages.

Doctors For emergencies, go to Polyclinic Bonanjo, av de Gaulle next to the *Ibis* hotel (☎ 33.43.99.10 or 33.42.17.80), or contact your consulate for advice.

Internet Internet cafés come and go quicker than you can mark them on a map. There are lots of them around and all hotels and most missions (except the Procure Générale des Missions Catholique) have in-house cafés and, in some cases, Wi-Fi.

Pharmacies Among the main 24-hour pharmacies are Pharmacie du Centre, 38 bd de la Liberté, and Pharmacie de Douala, bd Ahidjo.

Post office The Poste Centrale is on pl du Gouvernement in Bonanjo. Branches include: Poste de New Bell, av Douala Manga Bell, and Poste de Deïdo, rue Dibombé.

Supermarkets Score and Unimarché, both in Bonapriso, stock French delicacies flown in from Paris, but Mahima supermarket on bd Ahidjo is much cheaper, and sometimes has American goodies.

Swimming pools Non-guests can use the hotel pools at the *Akwa Palace* (CFA2000), *Sawa* (CFA4000) and *Méridien* (CFA5000). They're all expensive, but worth it when the humidity gets too much. Alternatively, try the smaller pool at the *Foyer du Marin* (CFA1000) or the newly refurbished rooftop pool at *Beauséjour Mirabel*.

Travel agencies Most travel agents offer a small selection of tours in Cameroon; they tend to be expensive (around CFA800,000 for a ten-day trip, including domestic flights) but are generally well organized. Agencies in Akwa include Jully Voyages, bd de la Liberté ☎ 33.42.32.09 📠 33.42.84.38; and Hemisphere Voyages, on the corner of bd de la Liberté and rue Galliéni ☎ 33.42.42.42. Agencies in Bonanjo include Cameroun Horizon, behind the Pagoda Manga Bell ☎ 33.42.94.24; Ébène Voyages ☎ 33.42.29.85, (ecotourism); and Delmas Voyages, rue Kitchener ☎ 33.42.11.84.

Limbé

LIMBÉ is everything Douala isn't – small, scenic and restful – with the mass of Mount Cameroon looming to the north. This is the nearest town to Douala on the open ocean, and it owes its popularity primarily to the surrounding beaches along the shore of **Ambas Bay**. There's a holiday feel to the place, with historical touches added in its well-preserved German and British **colonial buildings** and its shady **botanical garden**. Yet despite the influx of holiday-makers, expats and weekenders, English-speaking Limbé is not the expensive and overdone resort town you might expect, and there's enough economic life in the old **port** and the market, plus the nearby oil refinery and various agricultural projects, for the town not to rely wholly on its tourist industry.

Now that the **Bakassi border dispute** with Nigeria has been at least nominally resolved (see p.1242) the strong navy presence in Limbé is no more. The sailors' legacy in the shape of a hugely active nightlife, however, remains and the many holidaying Cameroonians from the Francophone part of the country do their best to keep it lively.

Some history

Limbé (called **Victoria** until 1983) was created by the London Baptist Missionary Society, after they were chased from Fernando Po by the Catholic Spanish in the mid-1850s. The missionaries turned to **Alfred Saker** – a former naval engineer converted to missionary work – and asked him to secure them a foothold on the mainland. Saker bought the lands around **Ambas Bay** from the Isubu king, William of Bimbia, and founded Victoria in 1858.

At first, Victoria was effectively an African Christian colony. The first inhabitants of the town were mostly **freed slaves** from Jamaica, Liberia and the Gold Coast, and converted Bakweri and Bimbia (indigenous peoples related to the Duala). From 1859, these townspeople were governed by their own tribunal, headed first by a Jamaican and then by a Sierra Leonean recaptive. At first, the town centred around the church, the school (established in 1860), and the missionary residences. But by

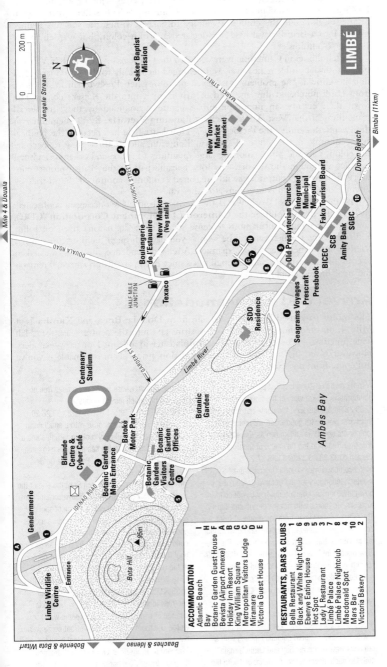

LIMBÉ

0 — 200 m

N

ACCOMMODATION
Atlantic Beach   I
Bay   H
Botanic Garden Guest House F
Bevista (Airport Annexe)   A
Holiday Inn Resort   B
King William Square   G
Metropolitan Visitors Lodge C
Miramare   D
Victoria Guest House   E

RESTAURANTS, BARS & CLUBS
Bella Restaurant   1
Black and White Night Club 6
Ebenye Eating House   9
Hot Spot   5
Lady L Restaurant   3
Limbé Palace   7
Limbé Palace Nightclub 8
Macdonald Spot   4
Mars Bar   10
Victoria Bakery   2

the 1870s, English and German **commercial enterprises** – John Holt, the Ambas Bay Trading Company and the Woermann Company – had established their own businesses alongside the church. Contrary to Saker's wishes, the site was neither turned into a British naval base nor declared a British colony, but was left to the Baptists to administer.

British holdings in Cameroon were ceded to the Germans on May 7, 1875. Victoria posed a special problem, however, as it belonged technically to the missionaries and not the Crown. The problem was solved in 1887 when Presbyterian missionaries from Basel purchased the land, and incorporated it into the Kaiser's colony. The town then became an important urban centre surrounded by the commercial plantations of the **West Afrikanische Pflanzung Victoria**. By the beginning of the twentieth century, the Victoria–Buéa–Douala triangle had become the political and economic nerve-centre of German Kamerun, and Victoria grew to become the colony's second port, exporting large quantities of cocoa and other agricultural produce. Although the Victoria territory became part of the British protectorate in 1915, German companies swiftly regained economic control of the district by buying back their old concessions after the war.

With the outbreak of World War II, the Germans' lands were once again confiscated. In 1947, the British founded the **Cameroon Development Corporation** (CDC), and the vast regional plantations – dense stands of cacao, banana trees, oil palms and rubber trees which can still be seen as you drive through the district – spurred Victoria into a new period of expansion. After independence, the CDC was taken over by the government, and although it has since been partially privatized, it remains the area's biggest employer.

⑮ Arrival and accommodation

The motor park used by vehicles to and from **Douala**, **Buéa** and **Kumba** is at **Mile 4**, on the Douala road. A drop by share taxi into the centre – ask for "Half Mile Junction" – costs CFA150. Most **hotels** cater to affluent Douala weekenders. However, given the standards of accommodation, prices seem reasonable if you've just come from that city.

Airport Annexe (Bevista) just past the gendarmerie, 1.5km west of the town centre ☎33.33.26.35. Although the name has changed, this basic place with good-sized s/c rooms with fans or a/c and TV is still known as *Bevista*. ②
Atlantic Beach at the town end of the Botanic Garden ☎33.33.23.32 ⓕ33.33.27.23 ⓔabhcomplex@yahoo.com. Originally the research laboratory for the Botanic Garden, this is now Limbé's most characterful hotel, with comfortable, s/c a/c rooms with hot water and satellite TV. The fabulous sea views from the rooms at front come at a price, while the slightly run-down former lab chalets at the back are much cheaper. The sea-view restaurant is popular, as is the pool (CFA1000 for non-guests). Breakfast is included in the room rate. Euros, dollars and pounds accepted. Chalet rooms and rooms with garden view ④, sea-view rooms ⑤.
Bay near the main roundabout ☎33.33.23.32 ⓕ33.33.27.23. Clean s/c rooms – twin or double – with fans in a restored colonial building with a fabulous view of Ambas Bay and Limbé's main nightlife spots down below. Co-managed with the

Atlantic Beach (whose pool can be used free of charge), but much less luxurious. ②
Botanic Garden Guest House ☎33.33.26.20. Scenically located guesthouse with a small dorm (CFA3000 per person) plus cooking facilities and a garden with access to the sea and space to pitch a tent (CFA1000 per person). Pay at the Botanic Garden Visitors' Centre.
Holiday Inn Resort off Church St at the end of the road ☎33.33.22.90 ⓦwww.holidayresortcmr.com. Luxurious establishment with a range of spotless, s/c a/c rooms with hot water. The restaurant does good, if expensive, fare, and there's a business centre with Internet access (CFA800/hr), an inviting pool (CFA1000 for non-guests) and a beer garden at the back. Booking essential at weekends. ③
King William Square off the main roundabout ☎33.33.29.99. Under new management, this centrally located, friendly two-storey hotel has a range of simple, clean s/c a/c rooms with hot water. The rooms upstairs at the front come with balcony and large bathtub. Breakfast included. ③
Metropolitan Visitors Lodge Church Rd, near the *Macdonald Spot* bar and *Lady L* restaurant

ⓣ 99.49.77.57. Small, inexpensive place with a range of basic s/c rooms with fan – some with TV – a good-value restaurant and safe parking. ②

🏃 **Miramare** west of the centre, on the Botanic Garden's seafront ⓣ & ⓕ 33.33.29.41. Co-managed by the *Atlantic Beach*, but much cheaper and friendlier, with beautiful views of Ambas Bay from its seaside position. Basic but clean s/c a/c *boukarous*

sleeping up to three, a pool (though it's sometimes infested with algae), and an excellent bar-restaurant. Breakfast included. ④

Victoria Guest House next to the *Bay Hotel* ⓣ 33.33.24.46. Friendly and homely place with a mixed bag of s/c, clean rooms with or without a/c, overlooking a peaceful garden that attracts many birds. Breakfast included. Rooms with fan ② or a/c ③.

The Town

The beachfront is the obvious place to start a visit. A main thoroughfare runs along the shoreline from **Down Beach**, the nearby **fish market** and German colonial-era **government school**, over to the *Atlantic Beach Hotel*. In between are most of the town's major **banks** and the Presbook and Prescraft centres, where you can buy books and regional **artwork**.

Looking out over Ambas Bay from the Down Beach area, you can see a group of small, recently depopulated **islands**, the foundations of buildings still visible, which continue to be used for traditional rituals and ceremonies. It's possible to visit the islands either by striking a deal with one of the fishermen at the port or (more safely) by arranging a trip through the Fako Tourism Board (Mon–Fri 7.30am–3.30pm; ⓣ 33.33.28.61 or 545.06.09 ⓔ fakotourism@yahoo.com), across the road from the SCB bank (around CFA50,000 for a boat carrying up to six, including food and guide fees, to visit three islands). Around the corner from the tourist board, the new **Integrated Municipal Museum** (Mon–Sat 8am to noon & 1–3pm; CFA500) is still at the embryonic stage with just a few, poorly described items on display. West of the *Atlantic Beach*, a road winds between the sea and the hills of the Botanic Garden to the *Miramare* and the garden's main entrance.

The **Botanic Garden** (ⓦ www.mcbcclimbe.org; CFA1000) was laid out by the Germans in the early nineteenth century to conduct agricultural experiments to improve productivity at the nearby CDC plantations, and originally covered most of present-day Limbé. It's now considered tropical Africa's most important botanic garden, with researchers coming from around the world to work here. Even for the nonspecialist it makes for a superb afternoon stroll, with hundreds of varieties of trees, and the Limbé River flowing through the middle. You can pick up a brochure of suggested trails at the visitors' centre when you arrive; they can also recommend guides and advice on things to do in the district. On your way around, don't miss the *Hot Spot* bar-restaurant (see overleaf) overlooking the bay.

Another excellent place to visit is the 🏃**Limbé Wildlife Centre** (daily 9am–5pm; CFA3000; ⓦ www.limbewildlife.org) across the Idenao Road past the oddly remote **post office**. This formerly dilapidated zoo is fast becoming the focus of primate conservation work in Cameroon, run jointly by the primate charity Pandrillus and the Government of Cameroon. In the spacious enclosures, orphans of apes and monkeys killed for bush meat are gently resocialized with members of their own age groups while recovering from their trauma, the long-term goal being to release them into the wild, once safe havens have been established in their natural habitats.

Heading back toward Limbé along Idenao Road, you'll pass the **Bifunde Centre** on your left-hand side. This shopping mall is a good place to stock up on supplies, not least from the excellent *Victoria Bakery* next door, and has Limbé's fastest Internet connections in the first-floor cybercafé.

Eating, drinking and nightlife

As well as the more expensive **European food** on offer in Limbé's hotel restaurants, there are quite a few good and inexpensive places in town. In the evening, the most popular area to head for is along the Bimbia road at **Down Beach**, next to where the daytime fish market is held. Here, the atmosphere is alive with blaring music and women lined up ready to grill your pick of freshly caught fish and then serve it with cool beer in concrete rondavels overlooking the sea, or on the beach itself. This fine combination of food and entertainment also used to take place on **Garden Street** but in an attempt to clean up the town, the council has torn down all the shacks, and there are now only a few ladies left selling fish and beer on solitary park benches – though things may well pick up again before too long.

There are a number of good **bars** around the King William Square roundabout, such as the classy, air-conditioned *Limbé Palace*, under *King William Square Hotel*, with its games room at the back. For **music** and **dancing**, choose between *Atlanta Inn*, playing mostly *makossa* mixes, *Bola's* across the road, with live music every night, the *Black and White Night Club* on the hill above the roundabout, and the *Limbé Palace Nightclub*, a block away. They all heave with party-goers every weekend.

Bella behind the wildlife centre in a quiet residential area. Well-prepared Cameroonian and European dishes served in a peaceful former villa, converted into one of Limbé's top restaurants.

Ebenye Eating House around the corner from the Presbyterian church. There's no signboard at the front, but mouthwatering smells and a steady stream of people heading behind the Nigerian Union building give this small traditional chop shop away. Local specialities include *eru* (a protein-rich forest vegetable) and water *fufu*.

Hot Spot in the Botanic Garden. Good and reasonably priced salads, seafood and other Western dishes, and possibly the town's best sea view.

Lady L Church St across from the *Metropolitan Visitors Lodge*. Large, open terrace where excellent Western and Cameroonian dishes are served from breakfast onwards.

Mars Bar on the sea wall. Perched precariously, this is a scenic spot for sundowners and slightly pricey seafood meals. The large-screen TV in the streetside bar at the front is the place to head for when Cameroon's football team or Samuel Eto'o are playing (or preferably both).

Around Limbé

West of Limbé, a string of **beaches** awaits, all with fine black sand (actually, a deep, bitter-chocolate colour), a result of the ocean's grinding of ancient lava flows from Mount Cameroon. The combination of lush tropical vegetation with the sea and the mountain produces a paradisiacal landscape, often enriched by the brooding purple and yellow of an impending storm or the green-and-gold sheen left behind by a recent downpour. Furthermore, the waters around here are perfect for swimming – unlike most places along the West African coast. You can get **transport to the beaches** from the Batoké motor park in front of the **stadium**. Either hire a cab direct to your destination, or take a shared taxi heading along the coast and, if you want to be sure to get back, arrange for it to pick you up again when you're ready to return.

Moving on from Limbé

The main *agences de voyage* in Limbé are Guarantee Express at Mile 2 (for **Bamenda**, **Bafoussam**, and **Yaoundé**), and Patience Express (opposite the hospital, for **Yaoundé**). Minibuses and share taxis for **Douala**, **Buéa** and **Kumba** leave continually from the Mile 4 motor park on the Douala road.

Twice weekly, the Achouka boat company runs a ferry service between Limbé and **Calabar** in Nigeria (p.1162) departing from the Bota wharf 2km west of the centre (CFA35,000). It's also possible to take a share taxi 48km up the coast to **Idenao** from the Batoké motor park and continue to Nigeria by motorized canoe from there (CFA10,000). Avoid the cheaper cargo vessels, which are unsafe and tend to bypass official exit and entry posts.

There are several fairly new **seafront hotels** in the area around **BOBENDE**, just north of Limbé past the CDC junction on Sonara road. The oldest and swankiest is the *FINI* (℡33.33.26.97 ☻www.finihotel.com ❻), which has a range of comfortable s/c a/c rooms in the main building and large bungalows sleeping four (CFA60,000) at the front. There's also an excellent restaurant that draws in crowds and a very popular nightclub (Tues–Sat). The more polished *Costal Beach Hotel* (℡ & ℻33.33.29.27 ❺) has immaculate s/c a/c rooms with satellite TV (some also have a sea view). A few hundred metres further north is the new *Costa Marina* (℡77.74.72.11 ❺), with accommodation in comfortable rondavels, plus a tennis court and pool. Unfortunately, none of these hotels have particularly attractive beaches.

To get to the most popular beach, where you can also **camp**, ask to be dropped at **Mile 6**; a signboard points through 500m of palm groves to the sea. Mile 6 is a public beach with a guardian, so you have to pay CFA1000 to use it, and more to camp. The nearby oil refinery isn't nearly as offputting as you might expect.

If you'd rather be watching fishing boats, head 3km further on to **BATOKÉ**, a fishing village with a stunning, free beach surrounded by mountains that drip with vegetation. A sign on the main road leads down to *Etisah Beach* (℡99.96.52.55 ☻www.etisah.com ❹), a small homely hotel, 300m from a pretty beach on the outskirts of Batoké, which offers basic rooms (fan or a/c), and a restaurant serving exotic bush-meat meals. Further along the coast, the road makes a small diversion around the tip of the massive 1999 **lava flow** before reaching **Mile 11 beach** and the natural Seme spring that flows with water so delicious and clean that it is bottled and sold throughout Cameroon. Next to the spring is the luxurious *Seme New Beach Resort* (℡77.93.45.48 ☻www.semebeach.com ❻), where you can use the guarded beach (CFA1000 including a soft drink) and eat at a slightly overpriced restaurant.

Beyond Mile 11, the paved road continues all the way to Idenao, passing numerous beautiful unspoiled beaches, as well as the second wettest place on earth, **DEBUND-SCHA**, 28km from Limbé (Mile 17). There's a **crater lake** at Cape Debundscha which is well worth exploring, while from **IDENAO** you can trek through the dense forest to the **Bomana falls**. If you want to visit **Korup National Park** (see p.1274) it's possible to reach Mundemba – the village at the main entrance – by boat from Idenao; this costs around CFA60,000 per day for a six-person boat (the trip only takes a few hours but departure times depend on the tides) – it's the same boat that plies between Idenao and Nigeria, plying through creeks and up the Ndian River through an area prolific with birds and monkeys.

Heading **south from Limbé**, after 10km you pass the army camp at Man O'War Bay (no photography) before reaching the quiet village of **BIMBIA** which today stands in stark contrast to its previous incarnation as one of the country's main slave markets. It later became site of the original **Camp Saker**, where the missionary first landed, and today houses a Baptist church and a small, basic holiday camping and chalet setup overlooking the ocean (bookings in Limbé through the Saker Baptist Mission just north of Market Street ℡33.33.23.23 ❷). Transport to the camp can be arranged at the mission, alternatively you'll have to wait for a share taxi from the fish market to fill up. Some 2km past Bimbia you'll find the start of the **Bimbia-Bonadikombo Nature Trail**, a two-hour hike which follows a river through mangroves and a variety of lowland forest types to **Bonadikombo**, from where you can catch a share taxi back to Limbé. Community Forest Guides from Bimbia will take you for CFA3000 per person plus CFA5000 community-development fee. Tours encompassing Bimbia and the nature trail are organized by BBNRMC in Limbé (℡33.33.33.25 ☻bbcommunityforest@yahoo.com), worth contacting, if only to organize a guide.

North of Limbé, heading inland from Bota, an enjoyable 5km trek up the **BONJONGO** road, leads to the impressive old German Palatine Mission Church and a great view of Ambas Bay. Bonjongo is one of three possible departure points for the walk up the 1713m **Small Mount Cameroon** (also known as Etinde). The other starting points are **Etomé**, just north of Batoké on the coast, and **Ekonjo**, a little closer to the top. Wherever you start from it's a hard day's trek up the steep slope, but you'll get a good impression of the montane forest. **Guides** for the climb can be found through the Botanic Garden Visitors' Centre (see p.1265), or through Cameroon Rev'Tours (☏33.42.10.05 ✉camrevtous@camnet.cm) at *Seme New Beach*. The tourist office in Limbé may also be able to help. Expect to pay a guide CFA5000–10,000 per day, plus extra fees such as the "village tax" (CFA10,000) which is paid to the village you set off from, as well as a bottle of whisky for the village chief and another bottle to appease the mountain spirits if you make it to the top.

Buéa and Mount Cameroon

Briefly the capital of German Kamerun, **BUÉA** is located on the slopes of **Mount Cameroon**, some 70km west of Douala (1½hr by road). Perched more than 1000m above the ocean, the town has a relatively cool and mosquito-free climate – something the Germans were always keen to seek out during their colonial days. Buéa's principal attraction for visitors today is as a base from which to climb Mount Cameroon; apart from this, the straggling town doesn't have a lot to offer.

The Germans began establishing military outposts in their new protectorate in 1895, with the arrival of colonial governor **Jesco von Puttkamer**. Buéa was one such spot, and was made capital in place of Douala from 1901 until 1909. It still retains many reminders of its **colonial past**, including administrative buildings, an old school, numerous villas built on piles and a magnificent **palace** built as von Puttkamer's residence. Today, this German *schloss* is used by the president – avoid photographing it.

During British rule, Buéa was placed under the authority of the Lieutenant Governor of the Southern Provinces of Nigeria. On the eve of independence, the town had dwindled to 3000 inhabitants and was primarily a colonial resort. But Buéa reacquired its prestige as an administrative centre when it became capital of English-speaking West Cameroon, in the post-independence federation. Over the next ten years, it received substantial public investment in the form of government buildings – including a university – and the population grew rapidly. Since then, Buéa has been demoted to capital of South West Province, and expansion has once more given way to stagnation. In recent years, Buéa has become an opposition stronghold and a focus of Anglophone resentment of Yaoundé's highhandedness.

Practicalities

All public transport to Buéa stops in the area around the **Mile 17 motor park** near the university. This is about 7km from an elusive town centre scattered along a dual carriageway climbing its way towards the foot of Mount Cameroon. It's CFA150 for a share taxi from the motor park to anywhere along this stretch. If you're heading on to Nigeria, there's a **Nigerian consulate** in town (☏33.32.25.28 or 33.32.26.56), where, with persistence, you should be able to get a visa. To find the consulate, turn left at the police station roundabout, at the top end of the dual carriageway as you're coming into town from Mile 17, from where it's around 300m past the *Parliamentarian Flats Hotel* on the left. The office of the **Provincial Delegation for Tourism**, on the dual carriageway (Mon–Fri 8am–3.30pm, but best before 2.00pm; ☏33.32.25.34 or 33.32.26.56), organizes guided ascents of the mountain (although it's better to organize your ascent through the Mount Cameroon Inter-communal Ecotourism Board, known as Mount CEO – see p.1270).

Accommodation

However you choose to do the climb, arranging the practicalities invariably requires you to spend the night in Buéa and there are several reasonably comfortable **places to stay**. The nostalgic old *Mountain Hotel* was closed on last check, but it's worth asking the tourist office if it's reopened, as it's potentially the nicest place in town.

Capital about 100m south of the main dual carriageway (follow the signposts) ☏ 33.32.33.31 or 33.32.33.32. Glitzy new place not far from *OIC*, with luxurious, clean tiled rooms all with a/c, TV, hot water and a balcony with views of dusty downtown Buéa. The classy, if pricey, restaurant has a good selection of French wine. ❹

Mermoz Long St (the old Limbé Rd) ☏ 33.32.23.49. Perhaps the best of the inexpensive places to stay in town, with comfortable s/c rooms with hot water and TV. Also has a good-value restaurant and bar. ❷

🏃 OIC (Opportunity Industrialization Centre) next to Soppo market on the main dual carriageway ☏ 33.32.25.86 or 33.32.25.22. The new section, with large, good-value rooms, all with hot showers and TV, far surpasses the old cheaper section with small and basic s/c rooms,

and cold showers. The popular restaurant is one of Buéa's best (mains CFA2500) and the outdoor barbecue bar gets very busy at weekends. ❸

Parliamentarian Flats 250m south of the police station roundabout ☏ 33.32.24.59. Government-owned hotel that looks decrepit from the outside. But the clean s/c rooms with hot water have stunning views of the slopes of Mount Cameroon. Although the restaurant is open 24/7 it's a good idea to order food in advance. ❷

Presbyterian Guest House turn right at the police station roundabout up the hill towards Buéa market, and then left through the Presbyterian grounds ☏ 99.80.20.03. Excellent-value sparklingly clean, basic rooms with two single beds (CFA4000 p/p), a few of them s/c, plus use of a well-equipped kitchen. Great views but no hot showers. CFA1000 to camp, or ❷.

Mount Cameroon

Buéa is the usual starting point for the ascent of the biodiverse and occasionally active volcano **Mount Cameroon** (the most recent **eruption**, in May 2000, lasted roughly three weeks; nobody was hurt). At 4095m high, and rising directly from sea level, Mount Cameroon – which is set to gain National Park status in the near future – is easily the tallest mountain in West and Central Africa, on a par with the higher peaks in the Alps and just lower than Mount Whitney in California. Despite the equatorial latitude, the highest slopes get freezing rain and occasional snow mixed in with unusually high winds, and the climate at the summit is alpine – conditions which, in conjunction with the very steep, stony slopes, can make it an arduous climb. You'll need a guide.

Determination, however, rather than super fitness or technique, is the attribute that will get you to the top – as most people do. Ideally you should go during the "dry" season (roughly mid-Nov to the end of April). The traditional route up the mountain – the direct and steep old **Guinness Track** – has now been supplemented by a number of other tracks that follow old hunter's trails. All these tracks are up the mountain's southeast face, avoiding the extremely heavy rainfall which afflicts the western slopes and the thunderstorms of the eastern and northern slopes. New descending trails follow an old elephant track on the northwestern slope, or the 1999 lava flow down to **Bakingili** on the coast.

The Race of Hope

Since its inception in 1973, the annual **Race of Hope** (formerly known as the Guinness Mountain Marathon) has achieved a reputation as one of the toughest athletic events in the world. On the last weekend in January or first of February, a field of about 350 runners slog 37km over tortuous terrain from the Buéa sports stadium up the Guinness Track's jungly lower slopes to the chilly summit of Mount Cameroon and back. Although Cameroonians dominate the competition, they have been joined by an international array of athletes, including Europeans and representatives of most African countries. Fifty thousand spectators watch the proceedings, with the men's winner usually completing the event in around four and a half hours and the women's winner in about five hours. If you want to take part, you'll have to be nominated by a sports club and complete the qualifying races. For more information contact the Athletics Federation (☏ 22.22.47.44) in Yaoundé.

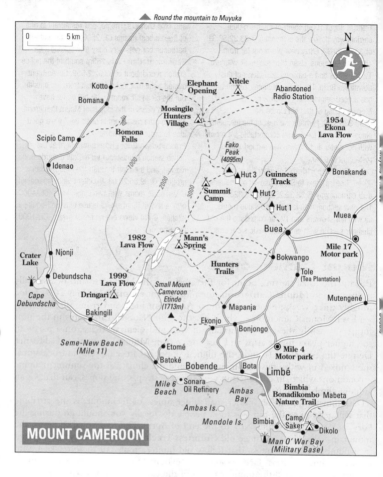

In the past the tourist office in Buéa has organized climbs up the Guinness Track, which gives only a limited impression of the mountain. These days they tend to refer potential climbers to the extremely professional 🏃 Mount Cameroon Inter-communal Ecotourism Board or **Mount CEO** (Mon–Fri 8am–5pm, Sat & Sun 7am–noon; ☎33.32.20.38 ⓦwww.mount-cameroon.org). Located at the top end of Buéa town, under the Buéa Local Council Office and opposite the market, Mount CEO's aim is to conserve the mountain's unique biodiversity by using knowledgeable local guides and porters (often ex-hunters), in order to support the local economy. By contrast, reps from a few private agencies down the road will approach you on the street (which Mount CEO do not) and try to lure you with sales patter about "ecotourism" without knowing what it entails or having adequate mountain experience. Be warned.

Every climber with Mount CEO pays CFA3000 per day towards a fund, a major proportion of which goes into village development projects. Every group must have a guide (CFA6000 per day) and porters (CFA5000 per day). For trips of two or more days you'll need at least one porter for every climber, especially if you're climbing to the summit, when they have to carry sufficient water for one and a half days of drinking and cooking.

Depending on which trail you choose, the climb to the summit and down again can be done over two to five days. It's possible, if you're extremely fit, to do the trek in a single day, making a pre-dawn start to be on the summit by mid-afternoon, and back down in Buéa shortly after dark, but obviously you won't have much time to absorb the mountain's moods and images. If you don't feel up to it, or don't have the time, Mount CEO have a list of excellent alternative treks on the mountain, that can involve overnight camps. In some ways, by not having the summit as a goal, these treks give you much more time to explore the unique mountain environment.

Equipment requirements need not be daunting. Footwear is the most important item: ideally you should wear waterproof hiking boots with ankle support. Plenty of people tackle the mountain in running shoes, but only the sturdiest will cushion your feet from jabbing rocks. Good **sleeping bags** and warm, **waterproof clothes** are necessary if you're staying a night on the mountain, and you'll also need to bring a tent if you're camping. Mount CEO has most of this kit to hire, but in limited supply, so it's a good idea to book it in advance. Depending on the arrangements you make with the guide and porters, you either bring a stove (also available at Mount CEO) and cook your own food, or eat together with them by paying for the supplies. Take plenty of **dried foods** (nuts, raisins and chocolate are recommended) and **water**, which is only available at Hut 1 and Mann's Spring on the way up, and at the Elephant Opening on your way down.

The climb

You can start the climb from several points – depending on how fit you are and how much time you have. The so-called **Guinness Track** takes a straight line from Buéa to the summit, along which there are three basic (and rat-infested) **mountain huts**, with a bare minimum of furnishings.

Most people prefer to ascend by one of the old **hunters' trails**, where there are basic **campsites**. From **BOKWANGO** or **MAPANJA**, you ascend through farmland and village plantations and then into primary rainforest, followed by montane forest before emerging into open savannah after about four hours. On clear days there are wonderful views of Small Mount Cameroon (Etinde), the ocean and Malabo Island, the sister volcano to Mount Cameroon and part of Equatorial Guinea. The first camp is in straw dome huts on the forest–savannah margin next to **Mann's Spring** (after German geographer Gustav Mann) where, if you're very lucky, you might find antelopes drinking. Mann's Spring is also the goal of a shorter one-day trek up the mountain, followed by a day's trek back down again looping via the 1982 lava flow, or two days down to **BAKINGILI** on the coast via the 1999 lava flow, and staying overnight at the new **Dringari** camp in the rainforest. If you push on up, the ascent continues past the 1999 lava flow. From here, the climb gets steeper as you move through colder **grasslands** to the Summit Camp, about 450m from the top. By now you're likely to be noticing minor altitude effects – shortness of breath and lassitude. Before sunrise on the third day you make the final ascent to **Fako peak** at 4095m, where you can sign the book to mark your triumph. Disappointingly, whatever the time of year it's rare to get a clear view from Fako, but early morning is the best bet.

The **descent** can be made into Buéa down the Guinness Track in just five leg-dissolving hours – with occasional encouragement from a "Guinness Is Good For You" sign. With more time available you can descend on the opposite side of the mountain through a completely different microclimate rich in wildlife. This descent starts down a steep, deep lava valley into a savannah region where there's a good chance you'll see antelopes. Close to the Bonakanda hunters' village you come across **Bat Cave** and, a little further on, the camp for the third night close to the Mosingile hunters' village.

Heading northwest from Mosingile takes you through forest towards Kotto, past the **Elephant Opening**, a clearing ploughed by forest elephants where they congregate to eat, drink and bathe. Forest elephants are extremely elusive, so it's unlikely you'll see the beasts themselves, though you may see their football-sized dung. This route continues west to meet the mountain ring road in Kotto, where you can arrange to be collected by vehicle or walk east to Nitele hunters' village. From Nitele it's a steep climb of four or five hours to an abandoned British radio station, now classified as an **industrial monument**. If the road has been repaired, you might be able to arrange for a good 4x4 vehicle to collect you here, or camp again and trek back to Buéa over the plateau and down a motorable road from **BONAKANDA**. An **alternative route** from Mosingile hunters' village follows the contours eastwards, direct to the radio station, avoiding the climb but also missing the Elephant Opening.

Kumba and around

Heading north from Buéa or Douala, the first major town of western Cameroon you reach is the agricultural and commercial centre of **KUMBA**. Although the town itself is oppressively hot, large and uninspiring, with a population approaching 140,000, it's in the heart of a beautiful region, while **Lake Barombi Mbo** – a picturesque crater lake just 5km out of town – is like another world.

Kumba's layout is disorientating: the town has no real centre – or rather it has several – and single-storey wooden-plank houses spread in all directions. There's a very big **market** here, specializing in goods imported from Nigeria (there's a large Igbo immigrant community in Kumba), and even if, like most travellers, you're just passing through, it's worth a look. Along Foncha Avenue, which runs west to east past the market, you'll find the **banks** and two **agences de voyage** (Tonton Express and Mondial) which have connections to Bamenda, Bafoussam, Douala and Yaoundé. Tonton also has a service to Mamfé (sometimes continuing to Ikom in Nigeria). Northeast of the market you'll find the **post office**, while the main **administrative quarter** is located a good 4km northwest of the market. Yet another centre has grown up around the **train station**.

Accommodation and eating

As you'd expect in a busy market centre such as this, there's a host of reasonably cheap hotels, most with decent **restaurants** and good selection of chop shops selling Nigerian delicacies such as *issi iwu*, the infamous goat's-head soup (look out for the eyes).

Gendarmerie Nationale & ▲ Lake Barombi Mbo

Tombel, Bafoussam, Bamenda, ▲
Train Station & Three Corners Motor park

KUMBA

Stadium

Tonton Express   Mondial

Catholic Mission   FONCHA AVENUE   SCB

Mbonge Motor park   Market   BICEC Bank

N

TREASURY STREET

ENGELE STREET

KRAMER AVENUE

ACCOMMODATION	
Azi Motel	E
Golden Bull	F
Kanton	D
Prestige Inn	A
Shamrock	B
Tavern Cross Junction	C

0   400 m

▼ Ekondo Titi, Mundemba & Korup National Park   ▼ Buea & Douala

Because Kumba is so spread out, share taxis from the centre to either of the motor parks cost CHA200. For share taxis to **Tombel**, **Bafoussam** and **Bamenda**, the Three Corners motor park is 3km northeast of the stadium. However, since the road north-east of Kumba is very rough, you can save time and discomfort by catching the train to **Mbanga** (two stops towards Douala) and from there catch one of the many buses plying the fast road north to Loum (7km from Tombel), Bafoussam and Bamenda. The Buéa motor park, on the Buéa road, has share taxis to **Limbé**, **Douala** and **Buéa**, while the Mbonge-road motor park, west of the town centre on the Ekondo Titi road, has share taxis to **Ekondo Titi** and **Mundemba** (for Korup National Park).

Azi Motel Buéa Rd ⊤ 33.35.42.91. Kumba's best hotel, offering good-value, clean s/c rooms with fans or a/c, all with hot showers and mosquito netting, a bar and an excellent restaurant. In front of the hotel is its business centre, with Kumba's most reliable Internet access and long-distance telephone. Rooms with fan ❷ or a/c ❸.

Golden Bull Mundemba Rd, on the outskirts of town. Formerly known as *Bridge Inn* and today only signposted with a board saying "hotel", this very basic place has dingy s/c rooms with a/c or fans, and a bar. You can camp in the grounds for CFA2000 per person. ❶

Kanton Kramer Ave, near Tavern Junction ⊤ 33.35.43.82. A funny, ramshackle place that looks from the outside as if it's still under construction but which has an array of spacious, nicely furnished and clean s/c rooms, with a/c or

fan. There's also a good-value restaurant and safe parking. ❷

Prestige Inn off Foncha Ave ⊤ 33.35.43.90. Small, unpretentious place a stone's throw from Tonton Express, offering a range of simple, clean s/c rooms with a/c or fan. ❷

Shamrock a short walk east of the Buéa road off Tavern Junction ⊤ 33.35.42.44. Spread over three floors with great views of the surrounding country-side, the s/c rooms here are smart, with a/c and shiny tiled floors, some with TV. ❸

Tavern Motel on the Buéa road/Kramer Ave junction ⊤ 33.35.43.39. With a glitzy new wing, the range of rooms on offer here is unusually wide, from basic, excellent-value, s/c fanned rooms in the old section, to gleaming balconied a/c rooms with TV in the new part. Inexpensive Cameroonian food is served in the restaurant and there's also a lively streetfront bar. Rooms with fan ❷ or a/c ❸.

Lake Barombi Mbo

You can walk from Kumba to **Lake Barombi Mbo** in about ninety minutes; in the dry season after the road has been graded it's also possible to reach the lakeshore by taxi (CFA500). Follow Lake Road (clearly signposted) which turns off to the left just after the SDO's (Senior Divisional Officer) office about 3km from the town

The **Barombi** people of the lakeshores are completely dependent on the lake and seem to have lived in a harmonious symbiosis with it for hundreds of years. The **fish** they catch are an obscure series of small cichlid species (mouth-breeding fish) called *pundu*, *kululu*, *dikume* and *pingu* – and a single type of catfish. All of them live only here, some at depths scientists haven't been able to account for in terms of normal fish physiology. Traditional hand-woven gill-nets and basket traps select only larger fish, ensuring their continued survival. Traditionally, the Barombi took further care to guar-antee their livelihood by actively appeasing the lake at their Ndengo cult grove. More and more young people, though, are installing themselves down in Kumba or further afield and leaving the old ways behind. Kumba itself is now drawing not just people but the lake's very water, which is piped to the town system. The surrounding forest is also under increasing pressure as areas are cleared for farming and the wood taken for fuel. It now remains to be seen if the road will improve the local economy or accelerate the destruction of the resource that locals have always depended upon.

centre past the German colonial administration buildings. Alternatively, take a taxi to the Lake Road junction from where it's a pleasant 2km walk to the lake. The area's dense forest crowds right down the inside of the crater to the lakeshore, providing an unbelievable green backdrop. The lake – 2.5km across and 110m deep – is crystal clear and most of it ideal for swimming. You'll see a couple of fishing boats when you arrive, and if their owners are around, they'll paddle you around the lake, or take you across it to the small village of **BAROMBI** on the other side. The price of the trip is negotiable, around CFA1000. Although most of the lake is safe for swimming, stay out of the water immediately around the village, as bilharzia is prevalent there.

The Mamfé Depression

The **Mamfé Depression** is a low-lying, thickly forested area bounded to the north, south and east by a semicircular mountain range. The area has its own unique flora and fauna, and contains several forest reserves and protected areas, including **Korup National Park** and **Mount Kupé**. Northeast of Mount Kupé is the **Manengouba Massif** and the beautiful **twin crater lakes**.

Passing through this area is the southernmost of the two principal overland routes from into Nigeria, via the somewhat isolated enclave of **Mamfé**, set amid dense forest about 65km short of the border. Only Nigeria-bound travellers (or those arriving from Nigeria) are likely to visit Mamfé, and even then only in the dry season, since during the rains the *piste* leading to Mamfé can become very difficult, even for 4x4s. If you can cope with its difficulties, however, the direct route from Kumba to Mamfé is quite a trip, as the road passes through dense rainforest, and occasionally yields spectacular views as it skirts the mountains.

Korup National Park

The **Korup National Park**, which adjoins Nigeria's Cross River National Park (see p.1166), contains Africa's oldest and most diverse rainforest, and is one of the continent's most important conservation sites, with a remarkably high number of **endemic species**. The park consists of 1260 square kilometres of ancient, mainly lowland, **tropical rainforest**, the southern part of which is primary. As a result of its inaccessibility, the infertility of its soils and the low density of commercially valuable tree species in it, the park has suffered very little disturbance in historic times. While other forests in the region have been affected by shifting cultivation and logging, Korup has remained largely untouched, and now boasts 410 different species of birds, 101 mammals, 92 amphibians, 82 reptiles, 130 fish, 950 butterflies, 620 trees and shrubs, and 480 herbs and climbers. It's a veritable hotspot of biodiversity.

As home to a quarter of all African **primate** species, Korup is a critically important site for the conservation of species including **chimpanzee** and **drill**, the rarest and most endangered primate in Africa. The park also boasts more **bird species** than any other site in Africa, including a number of rare and endangered species such as the red-headed rock fowl (*Picathartes oreas*), whilst its fast-flowing rivers are home to many varieties of **fish** previously unknown to zoologists – including a freshwater flying fish and a venomous, sand-burrowing catfish. In addition, new natural pharmacological products are being discovered all the time.

Getting to Korup National Park

The 90-kilometre *piste* leading from Kumba to the village of **Mundemba**, at the main entrance to the park, is reasonable in the dry season, when share taxis run regularly between the two towns, but can be very difficult in the rains. If you're coming all the way up from Douala, count on a full day's travel to the park, via Kumba and **EKONDO TITI**, even in the dry season. You can also reach Mundemba by boat from **Idenao**, on the coast west of Mount Cameroon. It's a

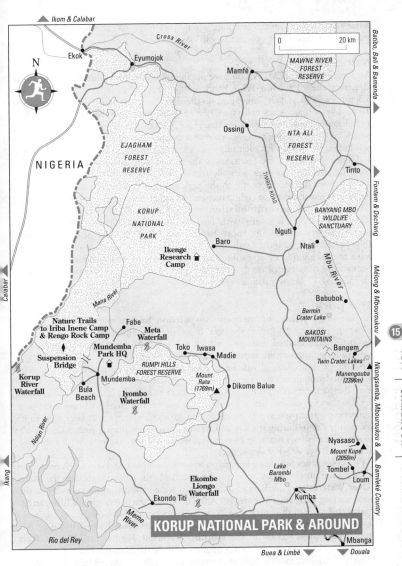

four- to six-hour trip by launch along the Mana River which brings you to Bulu Beach about 10km south of Mundemba.

Coming overland from Mamfé, the northernmost entrance to Korup is at **BARO**, which you reach via Nguti on the Mamfé–Kumba road. Public transport is hard to find for the 30km from Nguti to Baro, but there are occasional share taxis. However, while the park staff at Baro are welcoming, you can only hire porters, not guides and you'll need your own sleeping and cooking gear, all of which makes visiting the park from the southern sector far preferable.

Nevertheless, if you're heading to Korup from the north, and want to spend a night in **NGUTI**, the *Saint John of God Hospital Guesthouse* (2) has s/c rooms, running water and electricity in the evenings, while *Green Castle* (**1**) also has s/c rooms and a common room where you can buy drinks and order food.

Mundemba

Arriving in **MUNDEMBA**, you'll see the unmissable **Korup Tourist Information Centre** (June–Oct: Mon–Fri 7.30am–3.30pm, Sat & Sun 7.30–8.30am & 4.30–5.30pm; Nov–May: daily 7am–5pm) on the right-hand side of the road as you reach the middle of town. They collect a CFA5000 **park entrance fee** per day and assign an obligatory guide (CFA4000 per day, plus CFA2000 per day per porter as needed; with CFA1000 extra per porter or guide for overnight stays). An additional CFA3000 is collected per person for each night of camping. The guides are excellent company and, since they live in the forest, know the terrain well and are enthusiastic leaders. Note that visiting the park without a guide is illegal. Formalities out of the way, it's 8km from the tourist centre to the park entrance; a vehicle is available for hire (CFA8000 return for up to eight passengers including guide and porters).

There's modest **accommodation** at the popular *Marthas Guest House* (**2**), which has clean s/c rooms with fans, or the similar *Boseme Café Resort* (**2**) with a bar-restaurant. The more basic *Vista Palace* (**1**) has neat and reasonably priced rooms, some with shared facilities, and a good restaurant. If you want to make guide or accommodation arrangements before arriving at Korup, contact the conservator on ⊤77.78.78.83 or the WWF representatives in Limbé (⊤33.33.34.17 ⓦwww.panda.org).

The park

At the park entrance, an impressive **suspension bridge** spans the Mana River, allowing year-round access to the park. If you only have time for a **day-trip**, follow the nature trail marked with posts which point out the forest's interesting features – everything from termite mounds to an endless variety of plants and trees.

For longer visits, several **tourist camps** have been set up inside the park, with accommodation in insect-screened huts. The closest, *Iriba Inene Camp*, is only 1.5km from the park entrance on the nature trail. Each camp has a kitchen with firewood, drinking water, natural bathing points and latrine. You need to bring your own camping mattress, and insect repellent is a good idea: tiny sweat bees sometimes swarm the camps during the day, and swimming in rivers during your hikes is likely to attract blackflies, known in French as *mout-mout* – nasty creatures with a stinging, itchy bite. Beware too of driver ants.

The possibilities for exploring are pretty well unlimited, and two or three days of hiking is not unreasonable. In the southern sector of the park, trails lead to the **Mana River Waterfall**, to the **Rengo Rock** camp (cave explorations are possible in this area), and up to **Mount Yuhan** (1079m). The most attractive camp is **Chimpanzee camp**, 10km from the entrance. Hiking in the opposite direction (out of the park) leads to the **Meta Waterfall**, on the headwaters of the Mana River, half a day's trek from Mundemba, and on to the **Iyombo Waterfall**. Further east, **Mount Rata** rises to an elevation of 1769m, the highest peak in the **Rumpi Hills**. Despite the wealth of wildlife, your chances of seeing large animals are slim, though most people at least spot monkeys scampering through the canopy, and elusive duiker antelope in the undergrowth.

Mamfé and Ekok

MAMFÉ is basically a stopover point for travellers or traders, many of whom use the town as a base to unload goods they have smuggled from Nigeria on small boats up the Cross River. The constant comings and goings add energy to the otherwise sleepy town. Today the administrative headquarters of the Manyu district of South West Province, Mamfé (the name is a corruption of Mansfield, the settlement's first German district officer) was later part of the British Cameroons and subject to

Regular share taxis and minibuses to **Ekok**, **Bamenda** and **Kumba** leave from the main motor park in the centre of town. Tonton Voyages is the only *agence de voyage* with regular connections to Kumba (and occasionally Ikom in Nigeria; their office is near the motor park), but there are no agencies connecting Mamfé with Bamenda. During the wet season the road in both directions can be very bad, and you should expect a full day's strenuous journey.

To get to **Korup National Park** (see p.1274), take a taxi as far as Nguti for the northern entrance, or proceed to Kumba and change there for Mundemba, the main entrance.

You can catch a motorized pirogue, heading up the **Cross River** to Ekok, by the old German Bridge.

The beautiful mountain road to **Dschang** is difficult at any time of year, and generally impassable during the rains. Enquire at the motor park to see if any transport is headed along the road. Prepare to be terrified for much of the trip – wrecked vehicles strewn down the cliff sides attest to the danger of the route.

---

the policy of "indirect rule" expressed through the creation of Native Authorities. In 1959, the town hosted the Mamfé Conference, which tried (unsuccessfully) to establish voting rules for the upcoming UN plebiscite. In 1961 its inhabitants voted for unification with the Cameroon Republic, since when its status has declined. It's now mainly known as a centre for **witchcraft and traditional medicine**.

Practicalities

Considering its remoteness, Mamfé has a reasonable infrastructure – district buildings, hospital and missions. If you've just arrived from Nigeria, and have made it this far without CFA francs, you'll be relieved to discover that there's a BICEC **bank** here. In principle they should change traveller's cheques and cash, but you can only be certain of changing cash euros. There's also an active black market in Mamfé for changing naira, but the rate is better at the border.

If you've just arrived from Nigeria, Cameroonian prices are a shock. But **accommodation** seems pretty expensive in Mamfé even if you've come from the other direction, especially once you see what you actually get for your money.

Abunawa Lodge north of the centre near the river ☎33.34.12.47. Basic fanned accommodation in decent-sized s/c rooms. ❷

Data Guest House 1km north of the town centre ☎33.34.13.99. The best-value hotel in town, with friendly staff, good food and a range of clean s/c rooms (fan or a/c), all with TV, and a striking view over the Cross River. ❸

Eta Plaza Hotel Next to the colonial cemetery ☎33.34.13.93. Despite the grand name this small place is nothing to write home about, but it's got beds and a friendly atmosphere. ❶

Ekok: the Nigerian border

Some 36km west of Mamfé is the tiny border town of **EKOK**. In the dry season it's possible to cover this stretch in two to three hours; in the wet season the road is practically impassable, and often the only viable alternative is to reach Ekok by motorized pirogue. The border is open 24 hours a day, so there's no need **to stay** here, but if you do, several basic and cheap places (all ❶) survive from the times when the border closed every night. There's no **bank** in Ekok, but plenty of money-changers who give a better rate for naira than on the Nigerian side of the border.

Mount Kupé

In the southeastern part of the Manengouba range lies **Mount Kupé** (2050m), approximately 45km northeast of Kumba. Revered by the local Bakossi people as the home of their ancestral spirits, Mount Kupé is approached from the small village of **NYASOSO**, about 10km north of **TOMBEL**. Regular share taxis connect through from Kumba. The mountain is shrouded in a unique cloud forest which supports rich biodiversity, much of it endemic to the area. **Chimpanzees**, **drill** and several other species of threatened primate live on the mountain, but it's the diverse and unique **birdlife** that has given the mountain its international reputation – in an area of less than 50 square kilometres more than 320 species have been recorded to date. The most famous bird here, the Mount Kupé Bush shrike, is one of the world's rarest.

The WWF Mount Kupé Forest Site office is in Nyasoso; they can arrange **accommodation** in private homes in the village at a fixed rate of CFA3000 per person. The project also has information about the mountain's ecology, and they may be able to provide a species list if you're a keen bird-watcher. To climb the mountain you'll have to pay a Community Forest Fee of CFA2000 per person and take a guide at CFA3500 for the day. Optional porters cost CFA2500 per day.

The **climb** to the summit is steep, and slippery when wet, but can be done in six hours if you're reasonably fit. There are two marked routes, **Max's Trail** and **Shrike Trail**, which can be used to make a round trip. The trails lead through a fascinating forest, with fruits, orchids, mosses, lichens and epiphytes dangling from the trees. Once you've pushed your way up and out of the thickets onto the summit, you're rewarded with a spectacular view – if the weather is clear – and you may be lucky enough to hear chimps calling in the misty forest below. You can also go out **at night**, and with the aid of a guide and a good torch, there are good chances of spotting nocturnal primates, including **bush babies** and **loris**. It's also possible to camp for free on the mountain, having arranged for a porter to bring up food from the village. For this, prices are fixed: CFA2500 each for lunch and dinner, CFA1000 for breakfast.

As an alternative to the demanding climb, the project has created an informative 2km self-guided **nature trail**. With luck you may be able to get a free printed guide at the project office.

Manengouba twin crater lakes

Nestled in the huge grassy bowl of the Manengouba caldera, about 40km north of Mount Kupé, lie two spectacular **crater lakes**. The lakes, **Njeuh'edeub** (Male lake) and **Mwuah'edeub** (Female lake), are sacred to the local Bakossi people, who use the site for ancestor worship. The ancestral spirits are reckoned to have been responsible for giving the lakes their curiously different colours – the larger Female lake being blue and the smaller Male lake a vivid, algal green. Together, the twin lakes make for some wonderful hiking.

The most straightforward approach is from the small Anglophone administrative centre of **BANGEM** in the west. The road here from **Nyasoso** is difficult, but it's possible to drive almost all the way to the lakes, and accommodation in Bangem is cheap: choose from the shared toilets and bucket showers at *Farmers Bar* (❶) or go out of town on the Mélong road to try *Prestige Inn*'s tidy s/c rooms (❷). The *Catholic Mission* (❸), close to the town square, generally only accommodates missionaries.

From Bangem, **getting to the lakes** is easy and you don't need a guide. Either drive up along the relatively good dirt track which ends at the crater rim summit, or choose the more rewarding option of hiking up. Either way, you register and pay a fee of CFA2500 to the council clerk at the police station by the CPDM Party House in Bangem (get a receipt to avoid being charged twice; you can also pay the council guard in the shack next to Female lake). Buy provisions and drinking water in town, as there's nothing en route. To reach the lakes, head southeast out of town along Street Two and stick to the main track. The walk takes about three hours and is a steady climb until the final approach to the summit, where the track switchbacks up the steep crater rim and the motorable part ends. The track continues into and across the flat crater floor, but soon becomes indiscernible among the cattle tracks and grasses. Carry on in the same direction towards the peaks on the far side and the larger Female lake is revealed. Male lake is a short climb to the right, around a distinctive, small, steep hill. You can **camp**, **fish** and **swim** at Female lake, but swimming is forbidden in Male lake, and would be difficult anyway, as it's surrounded by steep, forested slopes.

The alternative eastern approach to the lakes – from **MBOUROUKOU**, off the fast Douala-to-Bafoussam road – involves staying at the former residence of the French colonial administrator for the region, a peaceful retreat called *Villa Luciole* (T 66.07.38.54 W www.villa-luciole.com ❻). With seven luxurious rooms in *boukarous*, and fresh produce from their own gardens, this small paradise provides an excellent base for some rewarding day-treks in the area, including the lakes. Getting to the lakes from here does requires a guide, however, which staff at the villa can organize (CFA8000/day). They also run treks on horseback (CFA25,000 guide included).

15.2

The western highlands

The landscapes of Cameroon's mountainous west are sometimes almost over-poweringly beautiful, ranging from the **volcanic hills** of the **Grassfields** to sheer cliffs with **waterfalls** and **crater lakes** hidden behind dense vegetation. The area is also interesting from a cultural point of view, with many of its old chiefdoms surviving into an era when increasing agricultural prosperity has brought one of the fastest rates of development in the country. In short, there's a wealth of sites and towns here which you could spend weeks or months exploring.

The western highlands region divides up fairly clearly into the **Bamiléké country** in the south, the **Bamenda Grassfields** in the north and the **Bamoun country** in the east. The main town in Bamiléké country – and the capital of the Francophone **Ouest** (West) Province – is the rapidly growing centre of **Bafoussam** – no longer a very soulful place, though it does make a convenient springboard for visiting more characterful regional towns. These include **Bandjoun**, which retains some of the traditional flavour of its old chiefdom and boasts the region's best-preserved **palace**; and the old German colonial resort of **Dschang**, situated in the mountains at an altitude of 1400m, which has an almost European climate.

Bamenda is the capital of the Anglophone **North West Province** and the starting point for the difficult **Ring Road**, which dips and bends through the mountainous **Grassfields**, a district of hilly, moist savannah, passing through a number of Tikar chiefdoms and Fula settlements along the route. Collapsed bridges and impassable stretches of road along the northern and eastern sections mean that, for years, it has been impossible to complete this circular trip by motor vehicle, and although repairing the routes has been a top priority for more than a decade, it somehow always seems to get missed out. You might speculate on whether this has anything to do with the Grassfield's reputation as an opposition stronghold.

In the Francophone **Pays Bamoun**, the cultural and historical highlight is **Foumban**, a town with a remarkable turn-of-the-century palace, notable museums and a thriving crafts industry.

Bafoussam

If you enjoy the hustle and bustle of a city on the move, **BAFOUSSAM** is the place for you. The **administrative capital** of the Province de l'Ouest, it's a noisy, vibrant centre of commercial hyperactivity, whose population has mushroomed to more than 300,000 in the last two decades. Situated on the edge of the Francophone zone, the Gallic influence is unmistakable, especially if you've just arrived from Bamenda. The Bamiléké, who dominate the city, are renowned throughout the country for their entrepreneurial energy. However, they never sell their land, so newcomers rarely integrate and the city is culturally very homogenous. The traditional **chefferie** (chief's compound) – to the southeast, off the route de Douala, may be worth a visit if you don't have time to visit the more impressive *chefferie* of Bandjoun, but in true Bamiléké style, people here tend to demand an extortionate entrance fee, and you'll have to haggle hard to be allowed in for what most other parts of the country would consider the standard CFA1000 per head plus CFA1500 for a camera.

Bafoussam owes its prosperity largely to **Arabica coffee**, which flourishes on farms in the surrounding hills. Various **industries**, stimulated by profits from coffee,

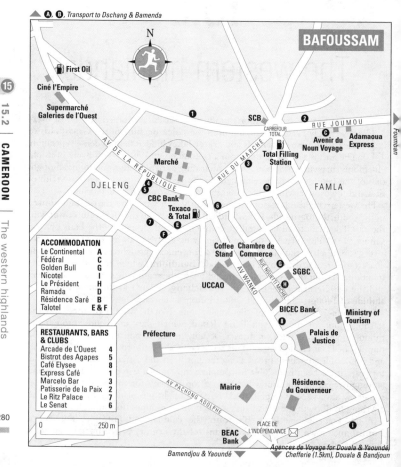

(A), (B), Transport to Dschang & Bamenda

BAFOUSSAM

First Oil
Ciné l'Empire
Supermarché Galeries de l'Ouest

AV DE LA RÉPUBLIQUE

Marché

DJELENG

CBC Bank
Texaco & Total

SCB

CARREFOUR TOTAL

RUE JOUMOU

Avenir du Noun Voyage
Adamaoua Express

RUE DU MARCHÉ

Total Filling Station

FAMLA

Foumban

Coffee Stand
Chambre de Commerce

SGBC

AV WANKO

RUE NGUETTI MICHEL

UCCAO

BICEC Bank
Ministry of Tourism

Préfecture

Palais de Justice

AV PACHONG ADOLPHE

Mairie
Résidence du Gouverneur

PLACE DE L'INDÉPENDANCE

BEAC Bank

ACCOMMODATION
Le Continental	A
Fédéral	C
Golden Bull	G
Nicotel	I
Le Président	H
Ramada	D
Résidence Saré	B
Talotel	E & F

RESTAURANTS, BARS & CLUBS
Arcade de L'Ouest	4
Bistrot des Agapes	5
Café Elysee	8
Express Café	1
Marcelo Bar	3
Patisserie de la Paix	2
Le Ritz Palace	7
Le Senat	6

0   250 m

Agences de Voyage for Douala & Yaoundé
Chefferie (1.5km), Douala & Bandjoun
Bamendjou & Yaoundé

have also made inroads in recent years. The Union des Coopératives du Café de l'Ouest (**UCCAO**) set up a processing plant in the 1970s, and a Brasseries du Cameroun brewery, a cigarette factory and a printing press have all started operations since then.

Accommodation

Bafoussam has a surprising lack of inexpensive **accommodation** for a town of its size. On the plus side, with its cooler climate, there's not much need for air conditioning.

Le Continental av de la République ☎33.44.14.58. One of the best-value options in town on the busy main road to Bamenda and Dschang. Spread over four floors, the comfortable s/c rooms are spacious and clean, with balcony, hot water and TV. There's a brilliant rooftop terrace from where you can take in the entire town layout. ❸

Fédéral 87 rue Joumou ☎33.44.13.09. Welcoming hotel on the main road to Foumban near the transport *agences* heading in that direction. The range of different-sized basic s/c rooms all come with hot water and TV, and there's also a good restaurant and a streetfront bar. ❷

Golden Bull two streets behind the Chambre de Commerce ☎33.44.28.85 ⓔhotelgoldenbull@ yahoo.fr. Sparkling new three-storey hotel with gleaming, tiled s/c rooms centred around a café-atrium, with more rooms in the neighbouring building, including a few cheaper triples sharing facilities. Behind the café is an excellent restaurant that always has a vegetarian option. ❹

Nicotel off pl de l'Indépendance, in the residential area behind the post office ☎33.44.24.18. Small,

friendly place in a quiet street offering large s/c rooms, all with hot water and TV, and a few with balconies. The cosy indoor bar-restaurant does good-value traditional Bamiléké fare. ❸

Le Président rue Nguetti Michel, near the BICEC bank ☎33.44.11.36. Once Bafoussam's grandest hotel, and though it's no longer very luxurious, the dark s/c rooms with hot water and TV are reasonably priced. ❸

Ramada off the Carrefour Total ☎77.95.54.87. Centrally located, this relatively inexpensive but rather seedy place has simple s/c rooms with cold water and a comfortable TV bar. ❷

Résidence Saré on the outskirts of town off the route de Bamenda ☎33.44.25.99. Slightly run-down chalets, with hot showers, fridge, satellite TV and a/c. ❹

Talotel off the Marché rond-point ☎77.76.95.15 ⓦwww.talotel.com. The most luxurious hotel in town, centrally located with beautifully carved doors and furniture. The a/c s/c rooms come with satellite TV and hot water, and there's a top-notch restaurant and lively outdoor bar. Car rental agency. ❺

The Town

Bafoussam's dual administrative and commercial functions are reflected in its layout. The broad avenues of the administrative quarter, where you'll find the Résidence du Gouverneur, *préfecture* and mairie, are neatly gathered on a hill in the **Tamdja neighbourhood**. From the roundabout where the Palais de Justice stands, the main **Avenue Wanko** heads downhill to the north towards the **market**. You'll find the major **banks**, including SGBC, CBC and BICEC either on or around Avenue Wanko, and SCB at the Carrefour Total near the Foumban road. SGBC and SCB have **ATMs**. The **Délégation du Tourisme** (☎33.44.77.82), behind the Palais de Justice, may be able to help with a few leaflets and advice. Bafoussam's **market**, held every four days, is in the middle of the older commercial neighbourhoods of Djeleng and Famla, and has a wide range of **crafts**.

Eating, drinking and nightlife

Unique to Bafoussam are the hexagonal UCCAO stands found around town. They sell quality **coffee** and local fast-food snacks – to be consumed standing – and you can find them all over, including just before the Dschang *gare routière* and in front of the UCCAO head office on Avenue Wanko. There are lines of good, cheap **eating places** on the road in front of the post office (off Place de l'Indépendance), and off Avenue de la République near the market. The *Pâtisserie de la Paix*, near

Agencies on the Foumban road, such as Avenir du Noun Voyage and Adamaoua Express, have numerous daily departures for **Foumban**. Adamaoua Express continues on to **Ngaoundéré** via **Banyo** and **Tibati**, on a very bad road (during the rains this trip can easily take two days). Alternatively, share taxis or *clandos* to Foumban and Foumbot can be found on the Foumban road down the road from Carrefour Total.

If you're heading **north**, Mazi Group Express, 2km northwest of the town centre on the Bamenda road, has regular departures to **Bamenda** and **Dschang**. Nearby, Mondial and Amour Mezan also have departures for Bamenda.

If you're heading **south**, you'll find a good number of agencies based at the southern end of town, beyond Place de l'Indépendance on the road to Bandjoun. Guarantee Express, Super Confort, Butsi and Central all have regular daily departures to **Douala** and **Yaoundé**. This stretch of road is also the best place to catch share taxis to **Bandjoun** (CFA300).

the Carrefour Total, just down the road from *Hôtel Fédéral*, is a good place to stop for fresh bread and pastries. During the day, there's good, inexpensive chop at the *Express Café*, on the Bamenda road west of Carrefour Total, which serves filling breakfasts and healthy portions of rice, beans, vegetables and chicken. Further out along the Bamenda road, there's a whole line of stalls selling cheap, freshly-made omelettes and salad (turn right after the Shell station).

Upmarket fare is found mostly at Bafoussam's better hotels. *Talotel*'s restaurant, *Masso*, does outstanding Cameroonian and Western dishes, at a price, and has a good wine list, while the restaurant at *Golden Bull* is known for its excellent buffet and range of pasta dishes. The *Arcade de l'Ouest*, on Avenue de la République, houses the *Bistrot des Agapes*, a fancy French restaurant serving *boeuf Bourguignon* and the like, as well as lunchtime salads and sandwiches.

A pleasant mid-budget spot to **eat and drink** is the laid-back *Café Elysée* on Avenue Wanko near the Palais de Justice. Open from early until late, the combination of traditional decor, chilled music and simple, inexpensive meals makes this a little haven away from the hectic street-life.

An excellent basic **bar** where you can watch the hustle and bustle of the street is the *Marcelo*, on rue du Marché. Food vendors pass here in a steady stream selling sausages and the like; alternatively, try anything from the day's menu from the nearby chop shops.

For **nightlife**, *Arcade de L'Ouest*, just off Avenue de la République across from the market, has live music every Wednesday, and most weekends. *Le Ritz Palace* nightclub, in front of *Talotel*, is the place to go dancing, along with *Le Senat*, a little further along on the same road.

The Bamiléké country

The **Bamiléké country** is roughly a triangle, delineated by the Noun River to the northeast and the Bamboutos Mountains to the west. The main roads in the area (all paved) pass through **Bafoussam**, **Bandjoun**, **Bangangté**, **Bafang**, **Dschang** and **Mbouda** – towns that are all easily accessible by public transport, and that can mostly be visited as day-trips from Bafoussam. The area has numerous **chefferies** (chiefdoms) and natural attractions including **crater lakes** and **waterfalls**.

Bandjoun

Some 15km south of Bafoussam, **BANDJOUN** is the largest and best preserved of the Bamiléké chiefdoms. The **chefferie** (chief's compound) is situated 3km south of Bandjoun on the route de Bangangté and you can reach it by catching a share taxi on the Douala road south of Place de l'Indépendance in Bafoussam. Bandjoun is the ideal place to admire traditional **Bamiléké architecture** at its best (see box, below) although a fire in 2005 meant that a large part of the old structures had to be rebuilt. Traditionally, the chief's compound was the largest in town, incorporating several huts encircled by a bamboo fence. Inside were rooms and granaries for the chief and each of his – sometimes numerous – wives. Larger public buildings used for assemblies, judicial gatherings or secret-society meetings also figured in the compound. Commonly, a large square preceded the entranceway to the "palace" and served as a **market** (market day in the Bamiléké country traditionally falls every eight days).

The Bandjoun chieftaincy follows this basic pattern more faithfully than others in the region, where cement and corrugated metal sheeting are replacing traditional building materials, though even here the chief lives in a modern palace built in 1994. Opposite, another colonial-style palace houses the **treasury** – the chief's collection of carved thrones, arms, pipes and other memorabilia which has now been converted into a **museum** (Ⓦwww.museumcam.org). There's an entrance fee of CFA2000 to visit the grounds and museum, and a further charge of CFA1500 to take photos.

When it comes to **accommodation**, Bandjoun hasn't got many options and you're probably best off staying in Bafoussam. The only worthwhile exception is the pricey *Centre Climatique de Bandjoun* (Ⓣ33.44.67.50 Ⓔccbandjoun@camnet .cm Ⓖ), three kilometres outside town on the Bafoussam road, with spacious s/c rooms with TV and hot water, and a popular restaurant packed with local Bamiléké businessmen.

From Bangangté to Bafang

There is a direct road from Bafoussam to Bafang, but it's worth going via Bangangté on the Bandjoun–Yaoundé road, as the road passes through one of the Bamiléké country's most spectacular stretches.

BANGANGTÉ is a fairly large town, with its share of administrative buildings and a wide avenue leading from the *préfecture* down to the modern Maison du Parti. When the **chefferie** here was renovated, modern buildings were replaced with traditional Bamiléké structures, and the complex may eventually rival that of Bandjoun. The road from Bangangté to Bafang (share taxis ply regularly between the two towns) passes the **Col de Bana**, or Bana Pass, which offers breathtaking panoramic views. Further along there's another traditional chiefdom, the **Chefferie de Bana**, located off the main road.

BAFANG in itself holds nothing worth staying around for. The scenery in the area is striking, however, with numerous **waterfalls**. One of these, the **Chute de la Mouenkeu**, is only a kilometre outside the town on the Douala road. A sign points to the falls, a short walk into the woods.

More spectacular (and famous from the early Tarzan movies) are the **Chutes d'Ekom**, 30km further down the Douala road. If you have your own vehicle, turn off the main road onto a dirt road heading southeast at a red sign indicating the Chefferie

Bamiléké architecture

Bamiléké houses characteristically consist of a square room topped with a roof varying in shape from cone to pyramid, covered with a thick layer of thatch. Although the principle seems simple enough, an elaborate framework is necessary to make the conical roof sit on square walls. The walls are built of palm fronds or bamboo filled in with mud, and a circular platform is then set on top of the walls. Finally, a frame is constructed on top of the platform and the thatch is added (though in recent years the trend has been to replace thatch with shiny corrugated-iron sheets). The exteriors of the buildings are often decorated with bamboo and intricately-carved wooden boards.

de Bayong and – in smaller writing – the *Chutes*. From this point, it's about 10km to the falls, though you have to walk the last few kilometres. At weekends, there are plenty of villagers from **EKOM NKAM** who will be keen to give you directions for a small fee; they'll know what you're looking for even before you tell them. In a beautiful forest setting, the **Nkam River** plunges eighty dramatic metres from the clifftop to the valley below. Unfortunately, the dirt road is almost impassable in the rainy season – ask about its condition before you head off from the main road.

Dschang and around

Three routes lead to the pleasant university town of **DSCHANG**: the paved road linked to the main Bafoussam–Bamenda road (less than an hour from Bafoussam and three hours from Bamenda and passing the Bamboutous Mountains); the steep and, in sections, terrifying road from Mamfé; and the German-built **route des Mbo**, a scenic but slow *piste* that starts in Mélong and winds its way through coffee and cocoa plantations. In 2007, this road was being paved.

Dschang was founded by the Germans in 1903. During the 1940s, Europeans forced by the war to stay in Africa all year round built a **vacation colony** here, attracted by the mild climate. The resulting complex, the *Centre Climatique* (☎33.45.10.58 ⓔ centreclimatique@hotmail.com ◉), still attracts numerous tourists with its landscaped gardens, first-class restaurant, swimming pool (CFA1000 for non-residents) and horse riding in the gardens. The centre offers some of the best – if these days slightly run-down – accommodation in the region, with various types of bungalows, including some with fireplaces and verandahs. The *Centre* is a short distance outside town, next to the internationally-recognized university, which is known especially for its ground-breaking agricultural faculty. As a result, Dschang attracts students from all over the world, giving the town a real student vibe.

Dschang also has Cameroon's only dedicated **tourist office** (Mon–Fri 8am–3pm ☎33.45.21.25), though it doesn't have a host of attractions to offer, apart from its large and colourful **market** and the **arts and crafts shops** at the university entrance. The surrounding countryside, however, is well worth exploring if you have a car. From Place de l'Indépendance, the route to **FONGO-TONGO** (towards Mamfé) leads through a series of hills and valleys, passing two waterfalls. The first, the **Cascade de Lingam**, 10km from Dschang, is signposted. The more impressive **Chute de la Mamy Wata** is roughly 10km past Fongo-Tongo and reached by a small side-road that ends at the top of the falls. Note, however, that towards the end of the dry season, neither waterfall is very impressive. Another excursion is to the **tea plantation** at **DSJUTITTSA**, a beautiful and tranquil place 20km north of Dschang, where it's sometimes possible to stay at the plantation lodge.

Practicalities

If you don't want to stay at the *Centre Climatique*, the town also has some reasonable-value smaller **hotels**. A good choice is the *Constellation* (☎33.45.10.61 ❷), near the Bafoussam *clando* minibus stop, with a range of clean s/c rooms, some with hot water. Two other reasonable options are the *Cendrillon* (☎33.45.18.98 ❷), behind the university administration building, with hot showers and a good restaurant; and the *Kemtsop* (☎22.34.14.95 ❷), near the rural council on the Bafoussam road, with basic rooms and a bar.

A good place to **eat** is the *Phenix Restaurant*, which does filling breakfasts, sandwiches and tasty local dishes such as rabbit stew. Of the town's **bars**, *La Maison Combatant* is a popular place and offers an unusual, not to say endangered, array of grilled meat (from elephant to rat) to accompany your beer. After dark, *Virgin* and *Conclusion* are the nightclubs to head for.

Moving on from Dschang, there are plenty of public-transport options. *Clando* minibuses heading for **Bafoussam** pick up passengers on the main road on the way. There are frequent buses to **Douala** and **Yaoundé** with a host of *agences de* *voyage* including the large Binam Voyages. Agencies such as Mazi Group Express link Dschang with **Bamenda** via **Mbouda**.

There aren't many vehicles on the beautiful mountain road down to **Mamfé**, but riding through this scenery on a mountain bike is a wonderful experience.

Bamenda and around

Apart from the glorious pines-and-bananas setting of the town, **BAMENDA** stands out as being at the centre of Cameroon's opposition movement. Home of the long-time presidential candidate, bookseller **John Fru Ndi**, it was here that the initial riots leading to the multiparty system took place, after police opened fire on the inaugural rally of the Social Democratic Front in 1990. Following the elections, security forces arrived *en masse* in the town, surrounding Fru Ndi's compound and arresting prominent party leaders. In 1995, members of the newly emerged Anglophone organization, the Southern Cameroon National Council (SCNC), demanded the establishment of an **Anglophone republic** – Southern Cameroon – and throughout the first half of the 1990s Bamenda was the site of numerous violent confrontations, driving local businesses to despair. This is not to say that Bamenda is dangerous, although it bubbles with political debate.

There are good excursions from Bamenda to the nearby fondom of **Bali**, a major crafts centre, and to **Awing Crater Lake**, near **Mount Lefo**, where you can swim.

The Town

The capital of North West Province and the heart of Anglophone Cameroon, Bamenda is really two towns – one administrative and the other commercial – separated by a steep escarpment. The **government buildings**, perched high on the clifftop, are in a neighbourhood known as **Up Station** (or Supply Station). German colonial forces initially settled in this spot and built a remarkably solid, red-brick **fortress** that today houses the Provincial Education Authority. You can walk inside to have a look around, but it's a good idea to introduce yourself first, especially as the building next door is occupied by the army. Next door to them is an old German, later British, colonial **cemetery**, that is worth seeing as it gives a real sense of colonial history. As you can read on the tombstones, the men resting here were killed in local battles that have since become legendary in Bali, Bafut and the villages around. You need to ask permission from the military post to visit the cemetery, and get them to show you where it is.

With sweeping views and cooler air, you can understand why Up Station was favoured by the German and British colonial administrators, and remains Bamenda's favoured **residential area**, and the stomping ground of expats, civil servants and the local business elite. Arriving in this part of town from the cities of the south, Bamenda seems to be nodding off, almost suburban. A tortuous road (Cameroon's most accident-prone highway) was carved out by the Germans at the beginning of the century, and snakes down to the hot valley and the Nkwen motor park, some three hundred metres below.

Downtown Bamenda, in complete contrast, is a sprawling conglomeration of small businesses and working neighbourhoods. A mid-morning stroll down Commercial Avenue, with its dual carriageway of workshops and pounding stereos, is a fitting introduction to the real heart of town, culminating in **City Chemist Roundabout**, locally known as Liberty Square in memory of pro-democracy marchers killed here by government forces on May 26, 1990. **Local crafts** are sold at the Prescraft Centre, next to the British Council Library, where you'll find a good selection of fixed-price bronzes, carvings and basketwork. A wider selection of crafts is found at the Handicraft Cooperative, located at the eastern end of town, along the road that climbs to Up Station. They have everything from extravagant masks and

BAMENDA

RESTAURANTS, BARS & CLUBS

Alisante Restaurant	3
Class Restaurant	2
Dallas	9
Dreamland	4
Fish Valley	1
Gracey's Restaurant	6
Mustard Seed	8
Reynam	5
Sam Soyer	7

ACCOMMODATION

Ayaba	E
Baptist Mission	A
Donga Palace	G
Ex-Serviceman's Guesthouse	D
Hotel Le Bien	J
Ideal Park	I
International	H
Mondial	C
Presbyterian Church Center	F
Skyline	B
Unity	K

Airport, Bafut & Wum

life-sized tribal warriors, to woven baskets and dinkey bottle-openers – sold at fixed prices. The **Main Market**, behind *Ideal Park Hotel*, is one of the biggest in the west, and offers cheap deals on goods smuggled in from Nigeria, and on local crafts.

Practicalities

The **Delegation for Tourism** (☎77.94.99.93), 250m west of City Chemist Roundabout on Commercial Avenue, is doing its best to get its act together, without much success. It can offer travel advice, but not much more. Two **travel agencies**,

Moving on from Bamenda

Agences de voyage

Bamenda has excellent onward connections, with numerous *agences de voyage* going in all directions. Most agencies have connections to **Douala** – the biggest two being Garanti Express and Amour Mezan. Amour Mezan has a large garage in Nkwen and Garanti is currently based at Up Station on the road towards Bafoussam but if you book in advance they pick up passengers at *Unity Hotel* (which they own). Both agencies also have frequent departures to **Bafoussam** and **Yaoundé**, and most major destinations in North West Province, including **Wum**, **Fundong**, **Nkambé**, **Ndu** and **Kumbo**. Symbol of Unity Express also has daily buses to Wum.

Minibuses for **Buéa** are run by Jeannot Express and Vatikan Express, while **Bafoussam** and **Dschang** are served by Mazi Group Express, from near the Hospital roundabout. Although many companies advertise connections to **Limbé**, you'll generally have to change bus along the way to another vehicle from the same agency. Similarly, there are no direct services to **Foumban**; you have to go via Bafoussam and change.

Share taxis and clandos

For certain regional destinations, **share taxis and minibuses** are the way to go, and leave from Bamenda's three motor parks: Nkwen park for **Bamessing**, **Ndop** and **Kumbo**; Ntarikon park, in the north of town, for **Mankon**, **Bafut** and **Wum**; and Bali park for **Bali**, **Batibo** and **Mamfé**.

ECO Travels & Tourism, at Up Station, close to Government junction (☏774.09.66 ✉nkembengsitepecot@hotmail.com), and Zwinkels Tours, next to Amour Mezan *agence de voyage* at Mile 2 Nkem (☏99.31.59.89 or ⓦwww.kameroenreizen.nl), do tours around North West Province with guides (CFA5000 per day) and can also help with 4x4 rental (CFA60,000 per day including driver).

All the major **banks** – Amity, BICEC and SGBC – are on Commercial Avenue and in principle they all change euro traveller's cheques and cash. There's also an **ATM** but it's *inside* the SGBC bank (which means that you can only withdraw cash during banking hours). At the southern end of Commercial Avenue is the **British Council Library** (Mon–Fri 9.30am–4.30pm, Sat 9.30–noon). Access is officially restricted to members, but they'll usually let you skim through their good range of periodicals and newspapers, all about two weeks out of date, and sometimes let you use their Internet for free. There are numerous other, constantly changing, **Internet** cafés in Bamenda along Commercial Avenue and Longla Street.

Accommodation

Bamenda offers **accommodation** of many descriptions, from mission dorms and cheery brothels to comfortable hotels, making it a good base for trips to nearby districts. Happily, room rates are somewhat cheaper than other large towns in Cameroon.

Ayaba Hotel Ayaba Rd ☏ 33.36.13.36 ✉ayabahotel@yahoo.co.uk. Bamenda's most luxurious hotel, in a peaceful part of town a short distance from bustling Commercial Ave. If you want to mingle with Cameroon's political elite, this is a good place to stay. Facilities include a cybercafé, tennis court, pool (non-guests CFA1500), restaurant with a good menu of mostly European food, and a nightclub (Fri & Sat). Rooms are comfortable with a/c and good views. ❹

Baptist Mission at the foot of the road to Up Station, near Nkwen motor park ☏55.32.14.27

(check-in Mon–Fri 6.30am–7pm, Sat 6.30am–6pm, Sun 6.30am–9am & 6–7pm). Quiet, clean and friendly, with simple two- to five-bed rooms (CFA3000 per person) with shared facilities, including hot showers. ❷

Clifton Mile 11, Nkwen, on the Bambui road ☏33.36.26.13. Glitzy new place with a range of stuffy s/c rooms, some with hot water and TV, and an excellent restaurant downstairs. Full of Cameroonian business travellers. ❸

Ideal Park off Commercial Ave, across from the Congress hall, behind the market ☏33.36.11.66.

Oldest and best-value hotel in town, with only nine rooms, organized around a courtyard. The s/c rooms are tidy, with hot water, and there's an excellent bar and a restaurant serving decent meals. For safety reasons, take a taxi to and from the hotel after dark, as the market area can be dodgy when deserted. ❷

International International St, a stone's throw from Commercial Ave ☎77.18.22.70. Owned by Garanti Express *agence de voyage*, there's a special drop-off and pick-up service at this centrally located place, which is very convenient if you arrive late at night. The slightly worn, s/c rooms are spacious, and have hot showers and TV, and there's a bar-restaurant and club (Fri & Sun). ❷

Le Bien off Wum Rd ☎33.36.12.06. Smart hotel a short walk from the Wum and Bafut motor parks, with a wide range of s/c rooms over two floors, set around a bar/courtyard. Rooms in the new section are only slightly bigger and better than the old section and not worth the extra. There's a good restaurant downstairs and safe parking. ❷

🏃 **Mondial** up the hill from the northern end of Hotel Ayaba Rd ☎33.36.18.32 📠33.36.28.84. Best in the mid-range, with large, clean s/c rooms (some with TV), and superb balconies overlooking town. Also the location of one of Bamenda's best nightclubs (Fri–Sun). ❸

New Look Unity off Wum Rd ☎33.36.37.82. Convenient for the Wum and Bafut motor parks, in a quiet residential area, with a range of inexpensive s/c rooms. The lively downstairs bar and breakfast restaurant can be noisy at night, so you may decide to opt for the upstairs rooms, which also have balconies and hot water. Rooms downstairs ❶ or upstairs ❷.

🏃 **Presbyterian Church Centre Mankon** off Longla St 1km north of Commercial Ave ☎33.36.40.70 or 777.77.80.63. In a residential neighbourhood a short walk from City Chemist Roundabout, this peaceful place offers dorm beds (CFA4000) and tidy s/c rooms with clean sheets, though couples wishing to share a room are supposed to be married. You can also camp here (CFA1000 per tent). ❷

Skyline Up Station ☎33.36.12.89. Set on a tremendous cliff-edge perch overlooking downtown Bamenda, this grand old pile suffered a serious setback with the building of the President's new residence, blocking the road leading to the hotel from downtown Bamenda, meaning that all access is now via the back route. The comfortable s/c rooms come with balconies with stunning views, but call in advance to check it's open. ❸

Eating, drinking and nightlife

Street eating is good in Bamenda. Besides street food like *soya* and grilled corn cobs, available all around town, more solid meals can be had at any of the numerous **roadside restaurants**, some of the best of which can be found by the town's many *agences de voyage*. There's also a health-food shack called *Reynam*, on Commercial Avenue, which does delicious, pricey fresh juices (drink in, or take out) and healthy sandwiches, and later in the day *Sam Soyer*, near the Municipal stadium, does fantastic *soya*, always best when washed down with cold beer. For more substantial or fancy sit-down meals, the larger hotels have good enough restaurants – the *Ayaba* is the most upmarket, but the *International* is good, too – and there's a handful of good, independent restaurants, listed below.

If you're **self-catering** you'll gravitate to the small *Princes Bakery* on Sonac road, for chocolate croissants and fresh bread, and the town's two supermarkets, Vatikan and New Life, which have a good range of stock.

Most **nightclubs** in Bamenda are connected to the bigger hotels and all of them only open from Friday to Sunday. The *Njang* at the *Ayaba Hotel* is the classiest in town, followed by the *Tropicana* at the *Mondial*, while the *Marakana* at the *International* is more affordable and very lively, but not as busy as *Dallas*, near Hospital roundabout, which is so rowdy that it's periodically shut down. For live cabaret, comedy or concerts, see what's on at the *Alliance Franco-Camerounaise* (☎99.43.13.38 or 33.36.31.45; CFA500–1000), a short walk from the *Mondial Hotel*.

Restaurants

Alizane basement, Tayim Building, Commercial Ave. Busy throughout the day, this is the place of the moment, serving delicious salads (from CFA800) and home-made fruit juices, and a good selection of mains at very reasonable prices. Only minus is that the food can sometimes be a little slow to show.

🏃 **Dreamland** on the first floor above National Financial Credit. Among the best places to eat, with tables outside on two large balconies overlooking Commercial Avenue. Open from early morning for breakfast (CFA1200 for continental), they also do an excellent-value lunchtime buffet (Mon–Fri noon–4pm; CFA2000) and à la carte (including a veggie option) throughout the day. Widescreen TV shows CNN and BBC.

Gracey's Commercial Ave in front of Prescraft (open Mon–Sat until 7pm). Tucked inside what appears to be a small shipping container, the filling and freshly-made dishes of omelette, salad and chips are excellent and very reasonably priced.

Handicraft Cooperative Station Road (open Mon–Sat until 8pm). After shopping in the cooperative, this is the perfect place to re-group and grab a bite to eat while enjoying the stunning views from the hillside terrace. Salads here are enormous and they do a festive Chicken DG (CFA6000 for an entire chicken) as well as mouthwatering burgers (CFA2800) and *ndolé* (CFA1200).

Sista Rosie's Bambui Rd, next to Clifton hotel (eves only). Legendary venue (now in a new location) serving probably the town's best grilled fish in spacious garden *boukarous*.

Bali

Of the region's main chiefdoms – Bafut, Bali and Nso – only **BALI** is not accessible by the Ring Road. A **Chamba** settlement (the Chamba are part of the Adamawa linguistic grouping), it was founded relatively late, around 1830. Its history is a series of wars and conflicts, notably with the nearby fondom of Bafut, and as recently as 2007, with the neighbouring Bawock. Only 20km west of Bamenda, Bali is an interesting stopover on the road to Mamfé, and a satisfying day's excursion from Bamenda, especially now that the road has been paved as far as Batibo (20km past Bali and the region's palm-wine capital). The beautiful **scenery** alone makes the trip worthwhile.

Bali's main attraction is the town's **Prescraft centre** where they make most of the wooden artefacts sold in the Prescraft shops in Bamenda and Limbé. If you arrive during the working week, you can see the skilled artists busy carving, weaving, and decorating calabashes. A shop at the centre sells a small selection of the results. Another good reason to stop is for the **Fon's palace**, not so much to see the modern palace (though that does have an interesting small exhibition), but more in the hope of having an audience with the Fon (chief) himself, a German–educated philosopher who is always keen to meet visitors to his fondom. If you're lucky he might even pull out some of his palm wine – reputedly the best in the area. The palace is also the place to get information and a guide for day-trips in the area, such as to the sacred cave where you'll see the skulls of Bali's many warrior enemies. Also recommended is **Forthung's Tower of Babel**, an incomplete 72-room building, which would have outdone the Fon's palace, had witchcraft not been used to prevent this grand treason from happening. Forthung died before it was completed.

With the completion of the new paved road, there's no reason to **stay overnight** in Bali. If you do, the *Prescraft Centre* has two rooms with a fully equipped kitchen in an old mission house (book at Prescraft in Bamenda ☏33.36.12.81 ; reduced price if you bring your own bedding).

Awing crater lake and Mount Lefo

Another possible excursion from Bamenda is to the tranquil **Awing crater lake**, off the Bafoussam road south of Bamenda, 7km north of **SANTA**, along a well maintained track that's accessible by car. A signpost points to a road leading east to the **Bafut Ngemba Forestry Reserve**; the lake is just beyond the reserve. Many Bamenda expats come here to swim at weekends, and Cameroonians to fish, although for superstitious reasons some prefer to steer clear of it altogether. If you ask the Fon of Awing for permission (a few kilometres further down a just-feasible road) you can **camp** in the beautiful hills surrounding the lake. A major **tourist resort** is planned for the area – but may not get built for many years yet.

Mount Lefo (2250m), the fourth highest mountain in Cameroon and West Africa, is a demanding day's climb from Lake Awing; the Fon of Awing will provide you with a guide (around CFA5000). On the lower slopes the climbing is easy, but the last few hundred metres to the peak are very steep. There are wonderful views of the Bamenda plateau from the summit, and of crater lakes in various stages of geological formation.

The Ring Road

The **Ring Road** comprises some 360km of difficult red–earth road interspersed by a few paved sections. Despite the demanding road conditions, this is a highly recommended route, bucking and swerving through some of the finest scenery in Africa, the verdant pasturelands of the **Grassfields**. But don't expect rolling savannah – for the most part the Grassfields are hilly meadows of rank herbage between stands of hardwood forest and patches of shifting agriculture. Natural sites in the region include the thundering **Menchum Falls**, a number of volcanoes such as **Mount Oku** (3011m), and nearly forty, crystal-clear **crater lakes**, many of them sacred, and at least one of them (Lake Nyos) potentially dangerous. Terraced farmlands defy the steep slopes; the mountain soils, ploughed along the contours, sustain crops like coco-yams, maize and plantains. Cash crops, such as coffee, grow at higher altitudes, and **Fula herders** roam the pastures to graze their cattle.

The best way to tour the Ring Road is by **car**, which allows you the freedom to stop between the route's main centres of **Bamenda**, **Wum**, **Nkambé** and **Kumbo**. Unfortunately, at the time of writing and for years now, the northern stretch of the road – between Nkambé and Wum – has been completely **impassable** to vehicles due to collapsed bridges at Nyos and Weh. With persistence it is sometimes possible to complete the route in a 4x4, either arriving at repaired bridges before they re-collapse, or avoiding the collapsed bridges and crossing the rivers elsewhere. Otherwise, until the bridges along the northern stretch are permanently repaired, the choice is between doing the Ring Road as a nearly-closed "U", or following an increasingly popular alternative route – **the small ring road** – via Bamenda, Wum, Weh, Fundong, Belo and Bambui. Drivers at the Bamenda motor parks can update you on road conditions. With a good 4x4 vehicle, and provided you are lucky with bridge repairs, you can drive round the entire Ring Road in two days, though this would be rushing it. The small ring road can be done, also in a bit of a rush, in one day.

All the larger towns on the two routes are accessible by **public transport** and offer basic accommodation. However, many of the most interesting sites described in the following accounts are off the main route, and you'll have to forgo them, unless you have your own transport or are willing to trek. Travelling by public transport also means it's very difficult to camp as you travel, and **camping** in the countryside – when you can find a flat space – is one of the Ring Road's greatest pleasures.

Should you choose to **cycle** some or all of the way round, beware that any rain will stop your machine dead in its tracks, horribly clogged with clay-like mud. In dry conditions, though, this is outstanding mountain-bike territory; allow around a week for the larger circuit. Whichever way you go, try to have a larger-scale **map** than the Michelin (try the tourist office in Bamenda); it's frustrating to try to follow a twisting, village-dotted route at a scale of 40km to 1cm. It's also a good idea to bring some bottles of local whisky, available in larger towns, to present to the fons (chiefs), if you visit any of the palaces in the various chiefdoms.

Bafut

The first stop along the Ring Road, heading in a clockwise direction from Bamenda, is the chiefdom of **BAFUT**, which acquired international fame in the 1950s and 60s as the site of two animal-collecting trips by the naturalist Gerald Durrell. His vividly descriptive account of the first, *The Bafut Beagles* (a reference to the team of hunters he assembled), makes amusing reading, though Bafut today feels a far cry from those slightly mythologized days of assistant district commissioners and pink gin.

Bafut is a **Tikar** community – people who migrated to Bafut in the fifteenth century from the northern Adamawa region following attacks by slave raiders. As one of the largest and most powerful of the traditional kingdoms in the Grassfields, it's divided into 26 **wards** on a ten-kilometre stretch of the Ring Road that trails along a ridge above the Menchum valley. The current fon of Bafut – **Abumbi II** – is a Paramount fon, the titular overlord of a large number of lesser fons in the region, and son of the fon featured in Gerald Durrell's book. Still quite young (he has only 55 wives, compared to his father's 152), Abumbi was chosen from his father's 100-odd offspring to ascend to the throne when the aged fon died in 1971. Although Abumbi II was educated in Yaoundé, he was allowed to succeed his father – in theory, upon pain of death if he broke local tradition. In **religion**, although the Tikar have long been dominated by Fula Muslims, and thus heavily Islamicized themselves, they have also (and perhaps not coincidentally) been the subjects of intense Presbyterian missionary work, so you'll meet a fair few Christians too.

Taxis continually ply the 20-kilometre paved stretch between Bamenda and Bafut in about half an hour, so there's no real reason to spend the night. The *Savanna Botanic Gardens*, 5km south of Bafut down the Bamenda road at Mile 11, is beautifully situated in park-like grounds and has a good but pricey **bar-restaurant**. They have a few spacious s/c rooms (☎77.76.10.51 ❷) – but also a persistent water problem, hence the low price. They allow **camping**.

Bafut's lively **market** takes place every eight days, with people coming from all over the region for its fruit, vegetables, spices, meat and livestock.

The Town

The main attraction in Bafut is the ♔ **Fon's Palace**, a large red-brick complex laid out in a quiet pattern of dark interiors and bright courtyards. The most sacred building in the complex is the **Achum**, the previous fon's palace, with its striking, pyramidal thatched roof. Dedicated to the ancestors, only the fon and other notables are allowed to enter this shrine. A visit to the royal compound and grounds costs CFA2500 per person and CFA1500 for a camera. The fon's wives or sons act as guides (call ☎77.41.23.57 to arrange tours in advance) and give an excellent insight into Bafut history and the many sacred rituals and traditions that are followed to this day. Beware, for example, when you hear the sound of the bugler by the main gate: it means that the fon's secret society is on the move and everyone has to scurry inside on pain of death if they set eyes on them. There are also strict rules about what may be touched, so it's best to keep your hands to yourself.

A highlight of a visit to the royal compound is the beautifully presented **museum**, housed in Gerald Durrell's old residence overlooking the palace grounds. Originally built by the Germans for the fon to reside in, it was recently refurbished with German assistance. Organized thematically, the topics covered range from the slave trade to Bafut ancestral spirits, and among the items are some beautiful carved sculptures, including a quirky one depicting the first European visitor. The Bafut people were not easily subdued by the German forces, and there's excellent insight into the depth of their resistance before they finally surrendered.

The yearly **grass-cutting ceremony** is still performed much as it was in the 1950s when described by Durrell. The entire community goes into the grasslands at the end of the dry season (usually late April) to collect bundles for rethatching the Achum and other important buildings, trooping in front of the fon with their offerings. It's a confirmation of community spirit and always ends up with tremendous feasting and the consumption of huge quantities of palm wine. A second annual **festival** takes place a week or so before Christmas, with formal, dressy presentations and much discharging of old guns, followed by a noisy series of dances and musical shows.

Wum and around

Travelling towards **Wum**, the last important town along the west side of the Ring Road from Bafut, the vegetation grows increasingly dense as the road follows the course of the **Menchum River**. This stretch of road has deteriorated drastically in recent years and is virtually impassable in the wet season. About 20km south of Wum, the **Menchum Falls** plunge spectacularly down a rocky cliffside, but they're set slightly off the road (on the west side) and you could easily pass right by without noticing them. If you have your own car, start looking out about 30km north of Bafut and listen for the thundering sound of falling water. At the exact spot, you'll probably see tyre marks where cars have pulled off the road. If you ask your taxi driver to pull off for a moment here, he's likely to oblige. There are no facilities of any kind here, nor anything to stop you boulder-hopping across the river in the dry season – except common sense; a French woman was swept over the edge a few years ago doing just that.

WUM is effectively a roadhead: beyond the town, public transport more or less fades out except on market days. The best **hotel** in town is the *Morning Star*, off the Bamenda road, which has a few s/c rooms, a top-floor verandah with a stunning view of the surrounding hills, and a bar (☎33.36.26.34; dorm beds CFA2000 or s/c ❶). Unless you arrange to have food prepared at the hotel, your best bet for **meals** is to head for the motor park. Try *New Deal* near Presbook, a popular drinking spot where you can also buy food.

Some 3km northwest of the town centre, **Lake Wum** is a fine crater lake nestled in the patchily cultivated hills. Fula herders graze their cattle in the open fields and bring them down to the lake to drink. The cool, green waters are immensely deep and you can swim here, although the banks can be muddy. If you're equipped to **camp**, contact the SDO (Senior Divisional Officer) in Wum for permission. Be aware of the justified paranoia of some locals about their crater lakes and read the advice about Lake Nyos opposite.

It's usually impossible to **move on** from Wum to Nkambé by public transport since bridges have collapsed at Weh and Nyos. If these are repaired, you might find extremely infrequent transport (maybe once a week) to Nkambé, although even this won't be running after the rains have started in April.

Fun with the Fundong Fon

"The Fon's palace near Fundong is great, very old fashioned, like a medieval courtyard. The Fon is old and speaks through an interpreter. Bring some booze as a present and make sure you can drink out of your hand. Remember the claps and low bowing!"

Verina Ingram, Netherlands

Wum to Bambui: the small ring road

Northeast of Wum, the Ring Road branches at **Weh**. If you head right (south), you get back to Bamenda via the **small ring road** and the town of Fundong. There's infrequent public transport along this route, but you can usually make progress. Alternatively you can hire a motorbike and driver in Wum (CFA5000) and do the bumpy, three-hour journey across magnificent highland savannah straight to Fundong, cutting out Weh in the process. En route you're likely to pass numerous Fula herders on horseback (many with mobile phones clipped onto their belts) and see some of the region's diverse birdlife.

In **FUNDONG** you'll find the **Chimney waterfalls,** the ancient Fon's palace – a twenty-minute drive up the hill behind the town centre (remember your whisky) – and good basic **accommodation** at the *Millennium Summer Hotel* (℡77.77.03.40 ❶). From here, there's daily Garanti Express and Amour Mezan Express transport back to Bamenda along a flawless paved road.

Along this road is **BELO** village, two hours from Bamenda, and home to an outstanding ecotourism setup which organizes a range of treks in the area, BERUDEP (Belo Rural Development Project ℡55.72.81.72 ⓦwww.berudep.org). Not only is Belo the starting point for a beautiful three-hour hike into the **Ijim Forest** – bordering the Kilum Forest and Mount Oku, but through BERUDEP you can also arrange trips in the area on horseback for around CFA10,000 for a full day including guide and lunch, and stay in local homes – allow CFA8000 per night including meals.

Wum to Nkambé

Continuing east on the main Ring Road, Weh offers the last chance until Nkambé of pumped water, market produce and chop-house food. After Weh, the road becomes wilder and switchbacks into a broad valley where a **collapsed bridge** abruptly stops all further traffic. Beyond here, the population diminishes drastically and the **landscape** becomes ravishingly beautiful and vibrant with colour – especially after the **rains** have started.

Lake Nyos

The dead village of **NYOS** is on the Ring Road (not, as marked on some maps, south of it) about 30km from Weh. The notorious **Lake Nyos** is a couple of kilometres to the south. The deep crater lake was the site of a mysterious natural **gas eruption** in 1986 which killed up to 3000 people when a cloud of suffocating gas, mainly carbon dioxide, billowed off its surface and rolled northwards down the valley towards Su-bum. Scientists believe that a reaction between the warmer surface waters and the cold carbon-dioxide-saturated waters of the lake depths caused the huge release of gas – something which could happen again at any of the deep lakes in the region. As a preventative measure scientists have begun venting a number of lakes to decrease gas pressures at the bottom. The crater lakes are supposed to be the homes of the spirits of the fons, and many locals still believe that Western scientific experimenting caused the event – foreigners are regarded suspiciously by some locals, who you may have to convince of your harmless intentions.

SU-BUM (Soumbon) – a scattering of houses and smoke-stained compounds looped along the valley about 30km from Weh – is now the only settlement of any size in the Nyos area. It too suffered a number of casualties from the gas disaster. More happily it boasts quite spectacular avocados. Camping or staying with people are the only options there.

Kimbi River Game Reserve

Some 50km from Weh, but currently only accessible from Nkambé in the east, lies the **Kimbi River Game Reserve** (a 2–3hr drive from Nkambé, only accessible in the rainy season by 4x4). The most abundant animals here are thought to be **waterbuck and buffalo**, though they have suffered severely from poaching. You'll need your own tent and supplies and a 4x4 to explore the park; there are no vehicles available for hire.

Dumbo: trekking into Nigeria

Around 74km from Weh (and 21km from Nkambé) at **MISANJE**, a pleasant market village with a small **auberge** (❶), a branch road heads north to **DUMBO** (17km) and the start of an exceptional trekking route – strictly foot traffic only – into Nigeria. There are customs and immigration posts in Dumbo, where officials are generally friendly, and may even help you find a guide-cum-porter to continue to Nigeria (normal rate about CFA5000). There's simple **accommodation** at *The Greenland* (❶).

The first quarter of the 40-kilometre trek to Nigeria is a gentle climb, which levels out for a few kilometres before reaching the edge of the escarpment and the steep, beautiful descent into Nigeria. The first small town you reach is **Bissaula** (see p.1216), where customs and immigration officials will be waiting. There are rudimentary rooms for foot-travellers at one or two settlements along the route.

Nkambé to Ndu and around

NKAMBÉ, on the northeast side of the Ring Road, is a large town by Grass-fields standards, signalling a return from remote regions with its filling stations, numerous eating and drinking houses, and a few hotels – the best are the inexpensive *Divisional Hotel* (T33.36.13.24 ❶) and the more comfortable *Millennium Star* (T77.51.68.70 ❷). If you're relying on public transport, Amour Mezan Express and Garanti Express have daily services linking Nkambé with Bamenda via Kumbo on the eastern Ring Road. You can also catch a share taxi heading north to **AKO** and a rough road to the Nigerian border town of Abong.

To the south, the Ring Road continues at an altitude of between 1500m and 2000m, soon becoming more densely populated and passing through the chiefdom of **MBOT**, which has its own fon and palace. **NDU**, a couple of kilometres further, is the site of Cameroon's largest tea plantation, an enterprise begun by the British in the 1950s. There's a filling station in Ndu, and with luck the *Dallas Hotel* (❶) will have reopened. It's a convenient if basic stopover, with bucket showers and electricity. A road leads east from Ndu towards **SABONGARI**, a motorable track connecting this road (18km east of Ndu) with a third Nigerian border crossing from the Grassfields, to Gembu in Nigeria. South of Ndu, about 10km before you reach the town of Kumbo, the region's largest cattle market takes place every Friday in the small village of **TAKIJA**.

Kumbo

KUMBO stands on a plateau 2000m above sea level. One of the biggest towns in the Grassfields, it has plenty of accommodation, banks and other facilities, including two of the best hospitals in the region. It's also the seat of another powerful **chiefdom**, as important as those of Bali and Bafut – that of the **Nso** linguistic group (the Banso). The Banso were defeated by the Germans in 1906, and their fon at the time executed in Bamenda – bitter history to which they have never been completely reconciled. The present fon lives here in a **palace** with both old and new sections (the latter with a decidedly Islamic flavour, as the last fon was from the Muslim side of the family). Though now predominantly a Catholic community, the Banso are traditionalists and certain behavioural norms are expected: for example, you shouldn't offer traditional office-holders your hand when greeting, nor cross your legs while seated, nor drink in their presence, nor pass the traditional policeman (*ngwerong*) on his left.

There's a large **market** in Kumbo every eight days, while once every year a spectacular **horse race** is held at the Tobin Stadium. Fula and Banso people from throughout the region assemble here for the event, which usually takes place in November. If you can plan to be here, it's exhilarating to watch their daredevil bareback riding; for more information, contact the tourist delegation in Bamenda (T77.94.99.93). On a slightly more offbeat note, there's a **cave** about half a kilometre east of Kumbo which is the resting place of a number of old skulls from long-ago traditional feuds. Find someone to take you.

As for **accommodation**, the bottom line is the *Central Inn Hotel*, overlooking the central motor park (T33.48.10.15 ❶). *Merry Land* is better and has a good range of rooms (T33.48.10.77 ❷), but the most comfortable and best-value hotel in town is the *Fomo 92*, off the Nkambé road just north of town (T33.48.16.16 F33.48.16.61 ❷). For **food**, the *Casablanca 2000* serves excellent chicken DG and cold beer at very reasonable prices. The *Samba* **nightclub** is a good place to shake off the Ring Road dust.

Elak

From Kumbo, you can detour off the Ring Road to **ELAK**, the principal village of the Oku fondom. The Oku people are renowned for their witchcraft and traditional medicines as well as their rich culture. The Oku cultural week, held at the **Fon's palace** around Easter, is a good opportunity to witness Oku masked dancing.

Elak is situated high on the northern slopes of **Mount Oku** – at 3011m, the second highest point in West Africa after Mount Cameroon. It's a pleasant climb to the summit, passing first through steep farmland and then into the **Kilum Forest** which, together with the neighbouring **Ijim Forest**, constitutes the largest remaining fragment of the montane forest that once covered much of the highlands. The forest is home to diverse birdlife: you may see the very localized and unmistakably red-headed **Bannerman's turaco** and the rare **banded wattle-eye**. At 2800m the forest gives way to subalpine grassland. From these cool heights you can sometimes see Mount Cameroon on exceptionally clear days.

On the western slopes of the mountain, at 2200m, is **Lake Oku**, a spectacular deep green crater lake encircled by a splendid dark forest. Lake Oku is sacred and tradition forbids fishing and swimming, though exceptions are sometimes made for foreigners. However, for the sake of protocol, you should ask the fon for permission before setting out to the lake. To do so, go to the **Fon's palace** at the far end of town equipped with the customary gift of a bottle of wine or local whisky and a fee of CFA1000 and you'll be given permission to climb the mountain. Someone will also be assigned as your guide, but make sure that you agree a guide price before setting off (around CFA3000). The Fon is a school headmaster and only at the palace during weekends and school holidays. If he's not in, one of the *nchindas* (palace officials) will be able to help.

There are several private houses in Elak with rooms available to rent (**1**), and bunk beds at the **Assofomi lodge** at the top end of town. While you're in Oku, check out the **Cultural and Touristic Centre** on the main street, which houses a large arts and crafts workshop where beautiful masks depicting local folk tales are carved in front of your eyes. There's also a small museum here (CFA300) which sells the extremely tasty local **honey**.

Kumbo to Bamenda

The leg from Kumbo to Bamenda (plied by Amour Mezan Express and Garanti Express) is the most heavily populated stretch of the Ring Road. South to **JAKIRI** you get panoramic views of the **Ndop Plains** and **Lake Bamendjing** reservoir. Jakiri was the headquarters of British troops from 1958 to 1961 when Southern Cameroon was on the verge of independence. A spectacular range of hills rears up near the town. If you decide to **stay** in Jakiri, the basic *Hotel Trans Afrique* (**1**) is adequate.

From Jakiri, you can branch off on a direct road to Foumban, 75km to the southeast. The main Ring Road continues on through superb scenery to **NDOP**, through the Sabga hills to **BAMBUI**, from where it's a 12km hop to Bamenda.

Foumban

Capital of the Bamoun people and seat of their sultan, the town of **FOUMBAN** is charged with history and culture. You're reminded of it at every turn as you pass monuments like the outstanding **Royal Palace**, built at the beginning of the twentieth century, the **Musée des Arts et des Traditions Bamoun**, or the ateliers of the talented **craftsmen** who turn out works in bronze, ebony and other materials.

These elements have given Foumban the most touristy feel of any town in the west, and you'll be the target of endless children who want to be your guide, shouting claims to be "sons of the sultan" (with such a prolific ruler, there may be an element of truth to many of them) and there can be intense pressure to spend money at every turn, with entreaties like "Come in to my shop, just for the pleasure of your eyes". But the atmosphere shouldn't deter you from visiting. Delving into Foumban's history and culture is a rewarding step towards an understanding of the whole region. And if you arrive in mid-December, in odd-numbered years, then the three day **Ngoun** festival, when the Bamoun people get the opportunity to vent their grievances with the sultan, will give you a great insight into the important role he plays in the lives of ordinary Bamoun people.

The Town

While the **administrative quarter** – with the town hall, post office, hospital and *préfecture* – clusters on the west of town, the sites more likely to draw your attention are all in the centre, within walking distance of the **Royal Palace**. Built in 1917 by Sultan Njoya, the old palace (the present sultan lives in a new one) is a notable architectural achievement, unique in Africa. The townspeople may tell you the king conceived his design in a dream, but he must have done some studying to enable him to combine assorted elements of German Baroque with such pure Romanesque forms – he was greatly influenced by a visit to the German castle at Buéa.

The Palace and Sultan's Museum

You approach the palace by means of a vast **courtyard** lined with *rônier* palms, tempering its blue tones with long shadows. Constructed entirely of locally made bricks, the mass is supported by strong pillars, the walls are carried by arcades and the structure is embellished with balconies worked with intricately carved wood. As you enter the building, you can't help but be impressed by the grandeur of the entrance hall, the armoury and the reception hall with its ceiling supported by four majestic columns. In the morning you can pass by to watch as the sultan holds court in the palace foyer. After prayers on Fridays, starting at around 1.30pm, you can also witness a colourful and deeply traditional event taking place, as court musicians play for the sultan while brilliantly dressed subjects pay their respects and seek his advice and good offices.

Tickets (CFA2000) for the 🏛 **Sultan's Museum** inside the palace, are sold in the reception building to the left of the courtyard as you enter. It's one of

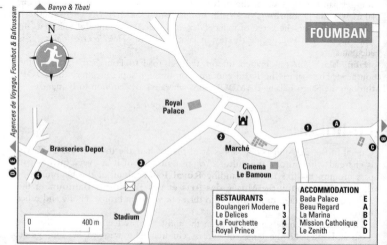

Village des Artisans & Musée des Arts et Traditions Bamoun

the most interesting museums in Cameroon and you'll be shown around by very knowledgeable bilingual guides. A private collection of memorabilia from the long line of kings gives a personal overview of Bamoun history. Among the eclectic assortment of objects are thrones decorated with beadwork, masks, weapons, shields made from hides and woven raffia palm, and a large collection of **sculptures**. One room contains the personal possessions of King Mbuémbué – his pipe, shields and dagger, and a calabash decorated with the jawbones of his enemies. Writings by Sultan Njoya are also on display – including the famous *History and Customs of the Bamouns* in the Shumom script he invented, which is still taught today.

The Village des Artisans

Don't listen to the small boys in Foumban's main square, who insist that the handful of little artisan shops clustered round the palace entrance constitute the town's main craft market. In fact, the real **Village des Artisans**, a major distribution centre for crafts and antiques from all over Cameroon and neighbouring countries, is a pleasant

The Bamoun Empire

The Bamoun Empire dates from the fourteenth century and was founded by **Nshare Yen**, the first of seventeen kings in the present dynasty. Son of a Tikar chief, Nshare led a faction of rebels away from the main territory and settled in the eastern country known as Pa-Mben. Here he consolidated his power and proclaimed himself king, establishing **Mfom-Ben** (from which the name Foumban derives) as his capital. The subsequent history has been carefully recorded, and today the accomplishments of all Nshare's successors are known in detail.

One of the most remarkable was **Mbuémbué**, a giant of a leader (he is said to have been 2.6m tall) whose first words were, "I will make the borders of the kingdom with blood and black iron; borders made with words are inevitably erased," Speaking at a normal volume, his voice is said to have carried for 2km. Not surprisingly, people listened. He fortified his capital (ruins of the old walls can be seen today), withstood Fulbe (Fula) invasions and expanded his empire while repulsing his Tikar and Bamiléké rivals.

Of all the kings, however, the greatest was the sixteenth in the dynasty, **Ibrahim Njoya** (reigned 1895–1924), under whose rule Bamoun culture experienced a golden age. A remarkable figure, he masterminded numerous inventions, not least of which was the **Bamoun alphabet** (one of only two in the whole West African region; the other was the Vai script in Liberia). Shumom, the language of the Bamoun, consists largely of monosyllabic roots, so Njoya's 510 original signs were easily converted, in 1909, into a syllabary and later refined into a true alphabet.

Once the alphabet was created, Njoya founded schools throughout the kingdom to teach the new writing. He also tried, less successfully, to design a printing press, and set about recording Bamoun tradition. It is thanks to his *History and Customs of the Bamouns* that so much is known about the empire (or, to be accurate, about his account of it, as related through oral tradition). Njoya also drew up a map of his kingdom, invented an electric mill and designed the outstanding **Royal Palace**.

Having converted to Islam, he was proclaimed Sultan of Bamoun, but with the arrival of Christian missionaries, he attempted to create a **new religion** fusing Islam, Christianity and traditional beliefs. The secular state (first colonial, later independent) tended to restrain this development, but Bamoun **court music and theatre** still reflect it and Islam remains an especially strong influence on Bamoun sculpture. Njoya was deposed by the French in 1924, and eventually exiled to Yaoundé, where he died in 1933, his pro-German views still mistrusted by the French. The present sultan is **Mbombo Njoya Ibrahim**. There's further background and news about the kingdom's affairs at ⊛ www.royaumebamoun.com.

Agences de voyage headed for **Douala** and **Yaoundé** via **Bafoussam** all have departure depots outside town, past the town gate, while, confusingly, their arrival depots are closer to the centre near the Jakiri road junction. Super Confort and Butsi Voyages have a few daily connections to Douala and Yaoundé, and, together with Avenir du Noun Voyage and Adamawa Express, regular daily departures to Bafoussam.

Adamawa Express also has a few weekly minibuses to **Ngaoundéré** via **Tibati** and **Banyo**, but this route is notoriously difficult; the *agences* advertise ten to twelve hours to get to Ngaoundéré, but in reality it can take several days, depending on the state of the road, and it's only possible during the dry season. An alternative is to stop in Banyo, at the end of the hardest part of the journey, spend the night at one of the inexpensive hostels near the market, and go on to **Tibati** the next day (half a day). From here you can get another taxi on the paved road to **Ngaoundal** (1½hr) or directly to **Ngaoundéré** (around half a day).

Share taxis for short distances like Foumban to **Foumbot** and **Bafoussam** stop in front of the market. Minibuses and *clandos* for longer distances can be found near the agencies outside town and will take you to **Kumbo** via **Jakiri**, **Nkongsamba** and **Bamenda**, leaving when full.

two-kilometre walk from the centre. Go west for 500m down the Bafoussam road and then turn left before the post office. Take the left fork after the stadium, and you'll find that each of the twenty or thirty houses lining the short road up to the village square contains a **workshop**. Here you can watch craftsmen from all over the country casting and beating metals, and carving wood.

Some of the finished artefacts are shiny-new, while some are tarnished to suit European tastes for distressed-looking "authenticity", but there's little attempt to fool you that you're buying a valuable antique when you can see identical items being manufactured alongside each other. Some shops do, nonetheless, sell genuine antiques, mainly smuggled from Nigeria, though such purchases of African heritage can't be recommended and may cause you real problems when you come to leave the country.

Musée des Arts et des Traditions Bamoun

On the square above the Village des Artisans is the **Musée des Arts et des Traditions Bamoun** (Mon–Sat 8am–5pm). You enter through two ornate carved doors, and begin your visit in the **Salle Mosé Yeyap** (Mosé Yeyap was a patron of the arts at the time of Sultan Njoya, and the museum started off as his private collection). Along the walls, a series of intricately carved wooden plaques portray important events in Bamoun history. Beside these are jugs for heating palm wine and clay masks. Notice the collection of clay and bronze pipes (some up to two metres long) used by dignitaries in traditional ceremonies, as well as the engraved gongs which the sultan would present to military heroes.

The **Salle du Guerrier** contains military relics recalling the many clashes between the Bamoun and their Bamiléké, Tikar and Fula neighbours. You'll see spears, *coupe-coupes* (engraved cups), protective charms and a calabash decorated with a skull and jawbones that was used in victory celebrations. In the **Salle du Notable**, carved wooden wall panels, a carved bed and table, weapons for fighting and hunting, riding gear, and a pot for palm wine, all evoke the lifestyle of the Bamoun elite. The **Salle du Danseur** is dedicated to music and dance, with costumes and unusual instruments including a xylophone embellished with carved snake heads. The Sultan's **court orchestra** still play these instruments to accompany elaborate theatrical pieces, and have toured abroad. The final room, the **Salle de la Cuisine Bamoun**, contains cooking utensils – pottery, baskets for smoking meat and mortars – used by Bamoun women.

The attendants are welcoming and helpful, not importunate but always ready to answer any questions, and a donation of around CFA1000 is expected. Don't forget to ask before taking pictures: permission is usually granted, but you cannot take it for granted, as they fear people will make postcards out of the photos.

Practicalities

There's nowhere official to **change money** in Foumban, though you can usually change cash dollars and euros at a few shops around the market. For **food**, apart from the few hotel restaurants, you might try the *Royal Prince*, across from the mosque, which sells well-prepared Cameroonian dishes and has the added bonus of a great view of the Foumban valley from its terrace. *Boulangerie Moderne*, not far from hotel *Beau Regard* on the main road, is a great place to sit and enjoy a pastry or yoghurt. *Restaurant les Délices*, on the Bafoussam road in front of the post office junction, serves excellent breakfasts and fresh salads and good helpings of rice, beans and meat for about CFA700. *La Fourchette*, further along the Bafoussam road, has burgers and pizzas.

Despite a heavy tourist presence, Foumban's **hotels** are a bit thin on the ground and surprisingly poor value, possibly because many visitors now come to Foumban on a day-trip from Bafoussam. The best places are on the outskirts of town. It's worth noting that water is a persistent problem in Foumban, and it's always a good idea to enquire about the current water situation before checking in at a hotel.

Accommodation

Baba Palace rte de Bafoussam, on the edge of town ☎ 33.48.27.48. Strange, large, new hotel complex with a range of comfortable s/c *boukarous* and rooms, but oddly devoid of clients. There's nowhere nearby to eat or drink, apart from the hotel's own bar-restaurant, so you'll have to head into town for any life. ❷

Beau Regard on the main commercial street ☎ 33.48.21.83. Once the pride of Foumban, this central hotel is now sadly run-down, although you can still glimpse its past glory in the carved woodwork decorating the walls and the well laid-out, mainly s/c, rooms. ❷

La Marina main street past the church, on the right-hand side ☎ 55.95.04.07. A small, friendly place in a less hectic part of town, with basic s/c rooms with cold showers (when there's water) and an excellent-value restaurant. ❶

Mission Catholique main street next to the church. Very central and potentially the best place in town, this recently extended place should now house a row of rooms – some s/c rooms with two single beds, others four-bed dorms with shared facilities. Dorm beds CFA3500 or s/c rooms ❷.

Rifum rte de Bafoussam ☎ 33.48.28.78. Shiny new multistorey place, next to the Butsi Voyages agency's arrivals depot. Rooms here are spacious, with large balconies and good baths. Overpriced bar-restaurant downstairs. ❸

Le Zenith off rte de Bafoussam, up a steep hill ☎ 33.48.24.25. Dusty, unpretentious place in a peaceful residential neighbourhood, within walking distance of the arrivals depots from Douala. Small but clean s/c rooms, and hot water if you're lucky. ❷

15.3

Yaoundé and the south

As the capital of Cameroon, Yaoundé has been consciously developed as a showcase, but remains essentially a large town interspersed with prestige buildings, not all of them finished. Still, you'll find it a city that's relatively easy to get around, with most of the facilities you might need, and plenty of good restaurants.

Only a few hours away to the southwest, spectacular **beaches** dot the Atlantic coastline between **Londji** and **Campo**, on the border of Equatorial Guinea. In between, Cameroon's second port, **Kribi**, has become something of a holiday centre and weekend retreat for Yaoundé's well-to-do residents. When you've had enough beach life, **Campo Ma'an National Park**, east of Campo, makes a satisfying day-trip into the rainforest. Elsewhere, the thick forest of sapele, mahogany, iroko and obiche which covers much of the southern interior makes travel difficult, though with time and determination, it's possible to explore the forest, using either **Ebolowa** or **Mbalmayo** as a base.

Yaoundé

Comparisons between the rival cities of **YAOUNDÉ** and Douala are inevitable, and most visitors prefer the capital. Set at an altitude of some 700m, and with a range of peaks, including **Mont Fébé**, as a backdrop, Yaoundé has a cooler climate than Douala and lies amid magnificent natural surroundings, heavy with green vegetation. The city's modern architecture adds to the positive impression and gives the city at least a superficial feeling of progress lacking in Douala. But where Yaoundé has acquired international credibility, it perhaps lacks soul.

Some history

The name **Yaoundé** is a corruption of **Ewondo**, the name of the ethnic group living in the area when the Germans arrived – and who still use the area's original name: Ongola. The Ewondo's history has them crossing the **Sanaga River** on the back of a giant snake before settling on the hilltops of the site of present-day Yaoundé. When the **Germans** crisscrossed the country at the end of the nineteenth century, setting up military posts to impose their rule in the new protectorate, they established a small presence here and their first commercial enterprises followed, in 1907. After World War I, the French chose the budding settlement as capital of their newly acquired territory. The British had claims to the former capital, Buéa, so Yaoundé became the administrative capital more or less by default. It has continued in that role ever since (except for a brief period during World War II), and while in terms of population (1.5 million) and industrialization, it comes some way behind Douala, it is fast catching up.

Arrival, information and city transport

Nsimalen International Airport is 18km south of Place Ahmadou Ahidjo down Boulevard de l'OCAM; hiring a cab into town costs CFA3500. For airline information, see "Listings" on p.1309.

Most of Yaoundé's *agences de voyage* are on the main road leading south to the **Mvan** neighbourhood, 3km south of the city centre on bd de l'OCAM. The main *agences* are: Garanti Express for Douala and Bamenda; Central Voyages for Douala, Bafoussam and Kribi; La Kribienne, for Kribi; Amour Mezan for Bamenda; Super Confort Voyages and Butsi Voyages for Bafoussam; Mondial Voyages for Kumba and Buéa; Tonton for Kumba; Alliance Voyage and Narral Voyages for Bertoua and the southeast; TransCam Voyages for Mbalmayo and Ebolowa.

Garanti Express and the new Le Car Agency based in front of the Omnisport stadium east of the centre, also run luxurious, fast a/c buses to Douala. For Bafoussam and Foumban, **share taxis** and **minibuses** leave from the *gare routière* **Etoudi** on the north side of the city, near the presidential palace.

By train

The night train to **Ngaoundéré** (departing daily at 6.10pm, arriving the next morning around 6am, if everything goes to plan, which it seldom does) via Bélabo (arriving around midnight) and Ngaoundal (for road routes to the Central African Republic) leaves from the **Gare Voyageurs**, off place Elig-Essono (enquiries ☏22.23.40.03). A one-way ticket to Ngaoundéré costs CFA28,000 in a 1st-class two-bunk sleeper, CFA25,000 in a 1st-class four-bunk sleeper, CFA17,000 for a 1st-class seat, and CFA10,000 for a 2nd-class seat. The two daily **Douala** trains leave at 7.40am and 4pm (5hr; CFA6000 1st class, CFA3000 2nd), but the journey is much quicker by road. For more information, see p.1231.

Arriving in Yaoundé with an *agence de voyage*, you're most likely to arrive at the booking office of your *agence*; most are based in the **Mvan** neighbourhood, about 3km south of **Place Ahmadou Ahidjo** (pl Ahidjo), better known as **Rond Point Score**. This is also where you're likely to find yourself if you're arriving from East Province by share taxi. From Rond Point Score, you can catch a yellow share taxi into town.

If you arrive by *agence* from the West or North West provinces – Bafoussam, Foumban or Bamenda – you'll be dropped off at one of the company offices near the *gare routière* in **Etoudi**, about 4km north of the centre.

If you come in by share taxi from Bamenda or South West Province, you'll arrive at Carrefour Obili, west of the city near the University of Earth Sciences. A few *agences* are based here as well.

By train, you'll arrive at the railway station known as **gare voyageurs**, just off **Place Elig-Essono**, about a kilometre north of Place Ahmadou Ahidjo. Several of the cheaper places to stay are located north of the station, away from the centre.

With its undulating hills spreading over an area of some forty square kilometres, and with few straight streets, orientation can be difficult (there's coverage of the city's neighbourhoods on p.1305). Unless you have your own transport or a healthy budget, you'll probably find yourself dependent on the omnipresent yellow **share taxis**. A drop within town officially costs CFA200 (less for short distances and more for trips off the main thoroughfares or late at night). Do like everyone else, shout out your destination and follow it by how much you're willing to pay: if they accept, they'll sound their horn once and stop. Remember that landmarks and buildings (*immeubles*, abbreviated to Imm) rather than street names are the usual method of orientation for cab drivers.

The **Ministère du Tourisme**, off Boulevard Rudolf Manga Bell (Mon–Fri 9am–noon & 1–5pm; ☏22.22.44.11 ⊛www.bcenter.fr/cameroun/index), should be able to help with a few leaflets and basic advice, although since it's a ministry and not a tourist office finding someone to speak to can sometimes be a problem. They find low-budget travel eccentric, though they're slowly coming round to the idea.

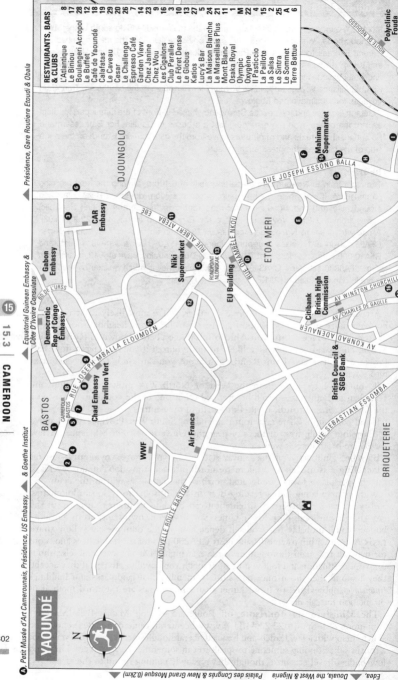

YAOUNDÉ

RESTAURANTS, BARS & CLUBS

L'Atlantique	8
Le Biniou	17
Boulangeri Acropol	28
Le Buffet	12
Café de Yaoundé	18
Calafatas	19
Le Caveau	29
Cesar	20
Le Challenge	26
Espresso Café	7
Garden View	14
Chez Janine	23
Chez Wou	9
Les Cigalons	16
Club Parallel	3
Le Fôret Dense	10
Le Globus	13
Katios	27
Lucy's Bar	5
La Maison Blanche	24
Le Marseillais Plus	21
Mont Blanc	11
Osaka Royal	1
Olympic	M
Oxygène	22
Il Pasticcio	4
La Paillote	15
La Salsa	2
Le Sintra	25
Le Sommet	A
Terre Battue	6

N

15.3 | CAMEROON

15

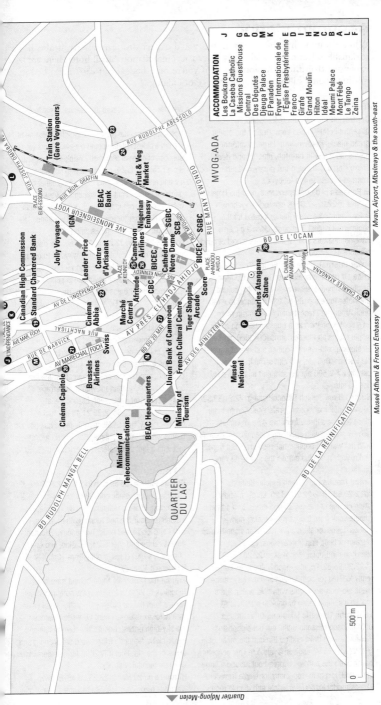

15

Museé Afhemi & French Embassy ▶

Mvan, Airport, Mbalmayo & the south-east ▶

◀ Quartier Ndjong-Melen

ACCOMMODATION

Les Boukarou	J
La Caseba Catholic Missions Guesthouse	G
Central	P
Des Députés	O
Dieuga Palace	M
El Panaden	K
Foyer Internationale de l'Église Presbytérienne	E
Franco	D
Girafe	I
Grand Moulin	N
Hilton	C
Idéal	B
Meumi Palace	A
Mont Fébé	L
Le Tango	F
Zeina	

Train Station (Gare Voyageurs)

Fruit & Veg Market

BEAC Bank

IGN

Jolly Voyages

Leader Price

Centre d'Artisanat

Cameroon Airlines

Nigerian Embassy

SGBC

SCB

BICEC

BICEC

Cathédrale Notre Dame

SGBC

Canadian High Commission

Standard Chartered Bank

Cinéma Abbia

Afritude

Marché Central

Score

Tiger Shopping Arcade

CBC

Place Ahmadou Ahidjo

Charles Atangana Statue

Cinéma Capitole

Brussels Airlines

Swiss

Union Bank of Cameroon

French Cultural Centre

Musée National

BEAC Headquarters

Ministry of Tourism

Ministry of Telecommunications

QUARTIER DU LAC

RUE JOSEPH MBALLA

RUE RUDOLPHE ABESSOLO

RUE MON. GRAFFIN

PLACE ELIG-ESSONO

AVE MONSEIGNEUR VOGT

RUE MANY ENONDO

MVOG-ADA

BD DE L'OCAM

RUE NDONG

AVE JOHN KENNEDY

PLACE JF KENNEDY

AV DE L'INDEPENDANCE

AVE PRES. EL HADJ AHIDJO

BD DU 20 MAI

AV DES MINISTERES

RUE NACHTIGAL

AVE MAR FOCH

RUE DE NARVICK

AV MARECHAL FOCH

L'INDEPENDANCE

BD RUDOLPH MANGA BELL

BD DE LA RÉUNIFICATION

AV CHARLES ATANGANA

PL. CHARLES ATANGANA

Footbridge

500 m

0

Accommodation

While Yaoundé has the luxury hotels you'd expect of a capital city, it also has a reasonable selection of moderately priced accommodation. Small hotels here are less expensive than those in Douala, and if you're on a budget but can't get a bed in a mission, there's still a pretty good choice of lodgings.

Inexpensive to moderate

Central off rue Jezouin ☎22.22.65.98 ✉centralhotel@yahoo.com. One of the oldest grand places in town, with large, comfortable rooms, all s/c with bathtub, plus TV and desk. There's an outstanding but pricey restaurant, and Internet access in the lobby. ⑥

El Panaden pl de l'Indépendance, near the Hôtel de Ville ☎22.22.27.65 ✉elpanaden@yahoo. fr. Excellent-value place ideally located for the commercial district. The large, clean a/c rooms have hot showers and TV, and there's a host of good restaurants nearby. ③

Foyer Internationale de l'Église Presbytérienne off rue Onembélé Nkou in the Etoa Meki neighbourhood, a short walk up the hill behind the water towers ☎99.85.23.76. Chilled-out redbrick American Presbyterian mission run more as a commune than as a guesthouse with a few single rooms and three dorms (CFA3000 per bed) all sharing cold-water facilities and use of a grand old kitchen. Outside, you can camp in the large garden (CFA1500 per person) and there's a cosy bonfire site. ②

Girafe off rue Joseph Essono Balla ☎22.21.39.32 ⓦwww.multimania.com/girafehotel. Comfortable place a stone's throw from the *gare voyageurs* railway station, with sparkling-clean s/c a/c rooms with hot water, a popular bar-restaurant out front, and a lively nightclub across the street. All very handy. ④

Grand Moulin rue Joseph Essono Balla ☎22.20.68.19 🖷22.20.68.20. Large, friendly place on one of the city's main drags, and a fifteenminute walk from the *gare voyageurs* railway station. Large, bright s/c a/c rooms and good-value restaurant belie first impressions. ④

Idéal on rond-point Nlongkak ☎22.20.98.52 🖷22.20.98.52. Popular, good-value hotel conveniently located for both Bastos and the city centre. Basic s/c, non-a/c rooms with cold water. Often full, so it's a good idea to book in advance. ②

La Caseba Catholic Missions Guesthouse off rue Joseph Essono Balla, but not signposted – follow a long drive and go through the metal gate ☎22.21.30.13 ✉resgispri@yahoo.fr. This peaceful haven, with the buildings spread out around a large courtyard, is a gem, especially for single travellers. The comfortable, non-s/c single and double rooms

are often full, so reserve in advance. Breakfast included. ③

Les Boukarous rue Narvick ☎22.23.39.06. One of the city's oldest hotels, spread over two floors with a smidgen of colonial charm still visible in the spacious, s/c a/c twin or double rooms, all with hot water and TV, and first-floor balconies overlooking either the garden bar-restaurant with its popular weekend cabaret, or one of the few quiet, downtown streets (choose the latter for a quiet night at weekends). ③

Le Tango off rue Joseph Essono Balla ☎22.23.27.90 🖷22.23.15.22. Near the *gare voyageurs* railway station, but awkward to get to from there – go via pl Elig Essono – this beautifully presented, new multistorey place is popular with Cameroonian business travellers. The a/c rooms all come with a fridge, TV, and plenty of hot water, and there's a classy bar-restaurant. Visa. ⑤

🏃 **Meumi Palace** rue Joseph Mballa Eloumden ☎22.20.92.11 🖷22.21.16.22. Hugely popular new place in the heart of Bastos with large, clean, tiled rooms, with TV, a/c and bathtubs, and large desks. Cybercafé in the lobby and a good bar-restaurant with front terrace. ⑤

🏃 **Zeina** off rue Joseph Essono Balla ☎22.21.22.35 🖷22.21.48.33. Tucked down an alley, this small, friendly place has tidy s/c rooms with hot water, some with TV and a/c, others just with a fan, and a pleasant restaurant. ③

Expensive

Djeuga Palace rue de Narvick ☎22.22.46.46 ⓦwww.djeuga-palace.com. New kid on the block downtown, offering real luxury in every area, including colour-themed rooms with minibars, safes and king-sized beds. Two pricey restaurants, fitness centre and sauna, 24hr casino, and one of the city's best clubs (nightly from 10pm). Wi-Fi throughout. Visa. ⑧

Franco rue Onembélé Nkou behind rond-point Nlongkak ☎22.20.13.07 ⓦwww.hotelfranco.net. Across from the EU building, this slick hotel caters mainly for expense-account EU visitors (hence the sky-high prices). Rooms are comfortable and super-clean, featuring fridges and safes and grand views of the city. Pool (CFA2000 for outsiders), plus Wi-Fi throughout. Visa. ⑧

Hilton bd du 20 Mai ☎22.23.36.46 ⓦwww .yaounde.hilton.com. Despite the steep competition this swanky hotel far outranks Yaoundé's other upmarket establishments, both in style and price (rooms start at CFA150,000). Facilities include extensive gardens with pool, fitness club, shops, Avis car rental, business centre, travel agent, seven bars and restaurants, tennis court and casino. Major credit cards. ❽

Hôtel des Députés in the administrative quarter next to the lake ⚏22.22.63.83 or 22.22.49.65 ⓦwww.hoteldeputes.com. After a major overhaul this modern state-run hotel now houses out-of-town MPs during parliamentary sessions (March & June–Nov) at which time it's necessary to book well in advance. Offers comfortable a/c rooms, pool (CFA2500 for non-guests), tennis courts, a bar-restaurant overlooking the lake, and a lively nightclub (Wed–Sun from 10pm). Visa and Amex. ❼

Mont Fébé on Mont Fébé ⚏22.21.40.02 ⓦwww .hotelmontfebe.com. A short cab ride from the centre, the main attraction here is the fabulous range of views (choose between mountain-view or golf-course-view rooms). Pleasant pool, tennis court, nightclub, casino and three restaurants. ❽

Yaoundé's neighbourhoods

There aren't many specific targets to aim for in Yaoundé, beyond the usual pleasures of sampling some good **restaurants** and visiting the main market or **marché centrale** (the city's museums are covered separately on p.1306). There are various **points of interest**, however, in each *quartier*, and it's worth knowing a little about the districts and their key sites and buildings when you're moving around the city.

The commercial centre

Despite the confusion caused by its asymmetrical layout, Yaoundé does have a walkable centre, with its heart at **Place Ahmadou Ahidjo** – better known as **Rond Point Score** or **Score Roundabout**. The most startling of the many buildings grouped around this square is the very 1950s **Cathédrale Notre Dame**, with its sloping roof that seems to go on forever. The city's main arteries shoot out from Place Ahidjo. To the east, Avenue Monseigneur Vogt runs uphill past many of the city's major banks. Avenue du Président El Hadj Ahidjo leads northwest of Place Ahidjo up to the colourful **marché central**, a building rife with innovative thieves – be careful. Avenue Kennedy, off Avenue Ahidjo, is one of the city's classier streets, flaunting a distinctly French flavour with its upmarket shops and a few nice lunchtime spots. This street ends in Place Kennedy, where you'll find the **Centre d'Artisanat**, the city's biggest crafts depot and a place well worth checking out. Avenue de l'Indépendance leads from Place Kennedy to Place de l'Indépendance, dominated by the futuristic **Hôtel de Ville**, the city hall.

The Lake Quarter and Melen

Most of the administrative buildings in the city are clumped to the west of place Ahidjo, between the city's lake – more like a stagnant pond really – and Boulevard du 20 Mai. This relatively sedate neighbourhood, the **Quartier du Lac**, cut through by imposing avenues, has long been a construction site for experiments in modern architecture, and buildings such as the **Ministère des Postes et Télécommunications** or the imaginative headquarters of the **Banque des États de l'Afrique Centrale** have gone a long way to shape Yaoundé's image in recent years. On Boulevard de la Réunification, which marks the southern fringe of this *quartier*, the **Monument de la Réunification** commemorating the union of Cameroon's French- and English-speaking communities, rises up in a helter-skelter spiral.

The northern suburbs

Yaoundé's poor and working-class districts are mostly tucked away in valleys, hidden from sight by the hilltops. Such neighbourhoods include **Briqueterie**, just northwest of town, site of the town's former Grande Mosquée, and **Messa**, also in the northwest, which houses **Marché Mokolo**, the liveliest and most approachable market in Yaoundé, where you can find fabrics, clothes and foodstuffs. The prestigious **Palais des Congrès** and the new **Grande Mosquée** are further north towards **Mont Fébé**. In the extreme north of town, the **Bastos** neighbourhood is the most exclusive residential area. The site of Cameroon's first factory (making the Bastos cigarettes which gave it its name), this quarter is now better known for its many embassies and the modern, and grandiose, **Présidence** – the presidential palace.

Museums and excursions

The **Musée National** is a recommended site for its recently installed permanent exhibits and its increasingly well presented collections. The city's two other collections are a taxi ride away: the immaculately presented **Petit Musée d'Art Camerounais**, one of West Africa's most worthwhile museums, and the outstanding **Musée Afhemi**, housing the vast private collection of a Bamiléké notable from West Province.

Petit Musée d'Art Camerounais

Located in a Benedictine monastery above *Hôtel Mont Fébé*, the **Petit Musée d'Art Camerounais** (Thurs, Sat & Sun 3–6pm; donation) is way out of the city centre – visiting offers a fantastic, panoramic view of the city. The museum is only accessible by taxi; expect to pay CFA2000 each way. The road up (first right after the hotel) ends at the monastery, and the entrance to the museum is down a narrow path past the monk's sanctuary. The museum itself is upstairs on the second floor and a monk will lead you to the exhibition. If you arrive outside museum hours and the reception is open, they'll normally let you in for CFA1000.

The museum's stark interior, with its clean, whitewashed walls, focuses attention on the displays. Although the collection is small, it contains many masterpieces, notably from the western provinces. First, the display of pipes (in ivory, wood and terracotta) includes some amazing **Bamoun bronze pipes**. Another room features **masks**, mainly from the Grassfields, and a superb, wooden **bas-relief** depicting a market scene. Notice, too, a king's carved wooden bed, and intricate wooden panels showing scenes from a hunt. A third room contains **Tikar bronzes** and includes pipes, bells used for calling the ancestors, and a king's throne. Finally, look out for some unusual **dice** made of fruit kernels, used by forest people of southern Cameroon as lucky charms.

Musée National

In the ministerial area, on Boulevard Rudolph Manga Bell, next to the High Court, the impressive and well-kept old presidential palace is now home to the 🏛 **Musée National** (Mon–Fri 10am–4pm, Sat 11am–4pm; CFA1000) which is very well worth visiting, not least for the stunning building. The museum itself has in recent years undergone massive changes and the exhibits are gradually becoming some of the best in the country.

The ground floor consists of three sections: the one on the left hosts changing contemporary-art exhibitions from home and abroad, while continuing through it, the next section contains the museum's **ethnological collection** and is packed with masks, musical instruments, seats and thrones, hunting and fishing tools, weaving and smithing tools, and a good selection of Fang sculptures. It's all rather disorganized, with minimal labelling, but improvements are continuing.

The museum's highlight is the section to the right of the entrance focusing on the **art and architecture** of specific cultural groups living in Cameroon's four distinct ecological zones: the Fang-Beti of the forest, the Bantu and Semi-Bantu, the Bamiléké of the Grassfields, and a range of peoples in the north. Beautifully set up, with colourful interactive panels, life-sized and miniature models, and a host of old photos, the exhibit's only drawback is that its in-depth explanations and descriptions are exclusively in French. Look out for the section on decorative arts, including body art, and details of how to build a pirogue.

The museum's final section is still unfinished. It's upstairs on the first floor, past two impressive Bamoun masks by the main staircase, and is set to house further temporary art exhibitions in the future. The view of the grounds and city is worth sneaking up for, in the meantime.

Musée Afhemi

Tucked away, 2km south of the centre in the Nsimeyong residential area, is one of Cameroon's finest museums, the privately run **Musée Afhemi** (Tues–Sat 9am–8pm, Sun 10am–8pm; CFA3000). Housed in a converted villa, the museum contains more than two thousand items of traditional art, antiquities and paintings, some more than nine hundred years old and made of everything from wood to bronze, copper, silver, brass and fired clay. The collection is extremely rich in traditional hand-woven fabric, hand-embroidered cloth, mud cloth, tie-dyed fabric, batik and beaded objects. The front porch has been made into an art gallery, and it's possible to have lunch here (book in advance on ☎22.31.90.38 or 99.94.46.56).

The exhibits are spread over five rooms, each with a distinct theme. The central room contains twenty or so mannequins wearing ritual or ceremonial **masks**. The second room is devoted to **charms and jujus**, with a jumble of healing artefacts, vectors of good omens, and repellents of dangerous charms – all powerful stuff. Room number three focuses on Bamiléké **women**, with traditionally dressed mannequins. The fourth room has an array of traditional **musical instruments**, while the fifth is packed with **pottery**.

Melen: mass at Ndjong-Melen and Mvog-Betsi Zoo

The animated **mass** at Ndjong-Melen is a famous outing, though it isn't staged for tourists. Every Sunday from 9.30am to noon the congregation in the **Catholic church** in this quarter on the western side of the city, work themselves into a state of high excitement during the Ewondo-language service. There's wonderful music, dancing and high-energy drumming, and everyone wears their most colourful outfits. It's a highly recommended experience.

For something equally audible, also in the *quartier* Melen, the **Mvog-Betsi Zoo** (daily 9am–6pm; CFA2000, camera CFA5000, video CDA10,000) is not the off-putting city menagerie you might expect, but in fact makes for an interesting afternoon visit. Built by the colonial government in the 1950s as a quarantine station, it is today managed by a British NGO (Cameroon Wildlife Aid Fund; ⒲www.cwaf.org) in conjunction with the Cameroonian government, and is concerned mainly with primate conservation, housing apes and monkeys that have suffered as a consequence of the illegal bush-meat trade. The zoo is now home to relatively content native primates, including mandrills, mangabeys, guenons and a group of highly endangered drills, along with the inevitable lion and hyenas, plus snakes and other reptiles.

CWAF and the Cameroonian government also co-manage a second site at **Mefou National Park** (daily 8am–4pm; CFA5000, camera CFA2000, video CFA5000), about an hour's drive from Yaoundé, heading south past the airport towards Mbalmayo. With some ten square kilometres of secondary forest, the park encompasses eight spacious, secure enclosures, sheltering orphaned native primates, including gorillas and chimps. The setting is beautiful, and well-informed guides are keen to show you around (CFA3000).

Eating, drinking and nightlife

The surest way of guaranteeing yourself **cheap eating** is to seek out Yaoundé's streetside food stalls. During working hours, there are lots of these around the administrative Quartier du Lac or Lake Quarter, catering for government employees. If you're staying at the *Presbyterian Mission* or *Hôtel Idéal*, there are numerous **small eateries** nearby on and around rue Ateba Ebé, serving good omelettes and Nescafé breakfasts, and filling rice and bean dishes later in the day. For good fresh pastries, croissants and *pain au chocolat*, as well as ice cream, head for *Boulangerie Calfatas*, on rue Nachtigal, just south of Place de l'Indépendance.

Restaurants

Inexpensive to moderate

Cheaper places are easy to stumble upon in the residential districts of Bastos, Messa and especially Briqueterie, though they are noticeably rarer in the centre. Some of these places also double as live-music venues.

Expresso Café rue Eloumden at the Carrefour Bastos junction above the Bastos Pharmacy ☏ 99.97.70.41. Stylish cybercafé that puts emphasis on the café. Good coffee, outstanding snacks and a fine array of home-made shakes and cold drinks – as well as eight laptops.

Garden View rue Joseph Essono Balla in the courtyard behind Mahima supermarket. The only place in Yaoundé that does a proper curry (from CFA3000), located next to a children's playground where shoppers relax and tank up while the kids burn off energy.

La Maison Blanche rue Rudolphe Abessolo. Lively outdoor nightspot with excellent grilled fish and plantain, washed down with cold beer, to the accompaniment of the latest Cameroonian hits.

La Paillote rue Joseph Essono Balla near Mahima supermarket ☏ 22.20.51.54. Sino-Vietnamese restaurant serving delicious, freshly made rice and noodle dishes on a verandah adorned with Chinese lanterns.

L'Atlantique rue Eloumden, Bastos ☏ 77.93.03.06. Good starters and excellent pizzas served in a pleasant courtyard at reasonable prices (CFA3500–5000).

Le Biniou rue de Gaulle, near *Hôtel El Panaden* ☏ 99.50.31.68 (closed Mon). Popular Breton restaurant serving crêpes with every imaginable topping (CFA1500–3800), plus standard French fare and fine French wines and cider.

Le Buffet rue Eloumden, just up from rond-point Nlongkak. Good and inexpensive counter meals (mains CFA1500). Very busy in the evenings.

Le Challenge av Kennedy. Self-service restaurant offering a good range of crunchy salads and well-prepared lunches of chicken, steak or stew (mains CFA2500) with tables inside or on the streetside terrace.

🏃 **Le Globus** on the hillside above rond-point Nlongkak. Watch the city's chaotic bustle from this outdoor bar-resto while tucking into well-made and reasonably priced fish or meat dishes (CFA2500).

Le Marseillais Plus av Foch. French-style eatery serving fantastic breakfasts and snacks as well as salads and full, three-course menus for CFA2600 – all very good value for the centre. There are other branches around the city, including one opposite Cinéma l'Abbia.

Le Sintra av Kennedy. Stylish French café serving really good coffee and simple, well-prepared French classics for lunch and dinner.

Terre Battue off rte d'Obala (rue Ateba Ebé). This, one of the best live-music spots in Yaoundé, also does good grilled food after 9pm, though the beers are expensive.

Expensive

As in Douala, upmarket restaurants can be extremely expensive – up to CFA30,000 per head, excluding drinks.

Café de Yaoundé av Winston Churchill ☏ 22.22.85.94. Superior Italian fare (including pizza and some unusual fried pasta appetizers) served on an upper level with a fine view of the neighbourhood.

Chez Wou rue Eloumden, Bastos ☏ 22.20.46.79. Across the street from the Pavilion Vert super-market, an authentic Chinese restaurant serving excellent but expensive food, with seating on a verandah or in the elegant dining room.

🏃 **La Salsa** off rue Eloumden behind the Nigerian ambassador's residence, Bastos ☏ 77.67.46.12. Currently Yaoundé's restaurant of choice, with a great range of seafood dishes and high-quality French and Italian fare, plus a good wine list.

Le Fôret Dense rue Eloumden, Bastos ☏ 22.20.53.08. Excellent Cameroonian food like *ndolé*, *folong*, tasty porcupine *ndombas* and other exotic dishes, served indoors or in pleasant outdoor *boukarous*.

Les Cigalons av Winston Churchill ☏ 22.23.41.25 (closed Sun). Down the hill from the British High Commission, serving classy French and Mediterranean food (mains around CFA7000).

Le Sommet at the *Hôtel Mont Fébé* ☏ 22.22.42.24. One of the best restaurants in town, with fabulous views and an especially popular Sun-morning poolside brunch.

Osaka Royal rue Eloumden behind Luc's Pressing ☏ 22.20.19.59. Popular new Japanese place serving fresh sushi (CFA17,000 for a platter) and a selection of mixed platters with sashimi and *maki* rolls, plus a few Korean classics.

Il Pasticcio off rue Eloumden ☏ 22.20.65.91. Italian restaurant in a peaceful villa, serving well-prepared classic cuisine including pizza fired up in the outdoor oven.

Nightlife

Yaoundé has less after-dark energy than Douala. Some restaurants double as music venues (see "Restaurants: inexpensive to moderate", opposite), while there are also bars and hotel discos and a few well-known clubs, but, apart from these, a number of bars and a few small places in Briqueterie and Messa are about all the city can offer. It's also dangerous to wander around after dark – take a taxi. The places listed below are geared towards dancing.

Bars and clubs

Le Caveau south of pl Ahidjo. Popular *boîte* with a good mix of Western music and the latest Central African hits, but a bit of a meat market. Occasional live bands. Free admission, but drinks around CFA5000.

Cesar rue Nachtigal next to the old Capital Cinema building. The most expensive place in town, with doormen dressed as Egyptian pharaohs, and packed with rich Cameroonians and Westerners dancing to predominantly Cameroonian music.

Chez Jeanine near *Maison Blanche*, rue Rudolphe Abessolo (see opposite). Bassa music played every weekend to raucous crowds – dress down rather than up.

Club Parallel near *Terre Battue* off rte d'Obala (see opposite). Inexpensive cabaret with live African, Western or traditional music every weekend. There's also excellent grilled chicken and a quieter outdoor area.

Katios av Ahidjo at rue Goker. One of the most expensive places in town, owned by Cameroon's most famous footballer, Samuel Eto'o. Pulsating lights, good music and several dance areas. Smart dress, CFA5000 admission.

Lucy's Bar rue Eloumden, near Carrefour Bastos. Popular bar with a glitzy Western atmosphere.

Olympic at *Hôtel Djeuga Palace*, rue de Narvick. Lively club, an expat favourite, with Western and African sounds. The casino next door offers a good retreat when the music gets too loud.

Listings

Airlines Air France, Nouvelle rte Bastos ☏ 33.01.12.75 or 33.01.12.79; Cameroon Airlines, av Monseigneur Vogt ☏ 22.23.03.04 or 22.23.40.01 (flights to Douala twice weekly, CFA23,700; Garoua Thurs, Sat & Sun CFA67,000); Kenya Airways, Imm Hajal ☏ 22.23.33.30 or 22.23.33.31; Brussels Airlines, av Foch in front of the police station ☏ 22.23.47.29 ℻ 22.23.47.40; Swissair, av Foch ☏ 22.22.97.37 ℻ 22.22.63.29. For additional flight information, including international carriers, call the airport on ☏ 22.23.36.02.

Banks The main banks are near place Ahidjo: BICEC, Union Bank of Cameroon, SGBC (agent for Thomas Cook), SCB, Commercial Bank of Cameroon (CDC). Standard Chartered is just south of Place de l'Indépendance. Citibank and SGBC are both on av de Gaulle. Most larger branches of SGBC, BICEC and SCB have ATMs. Street traders can be found on av Kennedy near the av Ahidjo junction.

Bookshops A limited selection of books can be found in the street stalls by Place Ahidjo. The little bookshop at the back of Tiger Arcade, on av

John Kennedy, has classic novels, books about Cameroon and Africa (mainly in French, though a few are in English), plus maps of Yaoundé and Douala.

Car rental The following are reliable but expensive: Avis, Hilton ☏ 22.23.36.46 ℻ 230.30.10 and rte de l'Aéroport ☏ 22.30.20.88; Hertz, rte de l'Aéroport ☏ 22.30.38.01 ℻ 33.42.42.60 and Yaoundé Airport ☏ 99.99.14.97; Sam Auto, *Hôtel Mont Fébé* ☏ 22.21.77.35.

Cinemas The best cinema with the latest films is Cinéma l'Abbia, rue Nachtigal. There's also a cinema at the French Cultural Centre.

Cultural centres British Council, av Charles de Gaulle ☏ 22.21.16.96 or 22.20.31.72; Centre Culturel Français, av Ahidjo ☏ 22.22.09.44 or 22.23.58.51; American Cultural Centre, US Embassy, av Rosa Parks, Bastos ☏ 22.20.15.00; Goethe Institute (German cultural centre), rue Joseph Mballa Eloumden, Bastos ☏ 22.21.44.09.

Dentists Adventist Clinic ☏ 22.22.11.10 and Polyclinic Fouda ☏ 22.22.93.68, rte de Ngousso, east of the railway tracks.

Doctors Polyclinic Fouda (see "Dentists"; General Hospital ☏22.20.28.02 or 22.21.20.18; University Hospital ☏22.23.21.03.

Embassies and consulates Canada, Imm Stamatiades, av de l'Indépendance ☏22.23.02.03 or ☏22.23.23.11; Central African Republic, off rue Albert Ateba Ebé ☏ & ℻22.20.51.55; Chad, rue Joseph Mballa Eloumden, Bastos ☏ & ℻22.21.06.24; Congo-Brazzaville, rue Restaurant la Riviera, Bastos ☏ & ℻22.21.24.58; Côte d'Ivoire, Bastos ☏ & ℻22.21.74.59; DR Congo, bd de l'URSS, Bastos ☏22.20.51.03; Equatorial Guinea, Bastos ☏22.21.08.04; France, Plateau Atémengué ☏22.20.79.50 ℻22.22.79.59; Gabon, off bd de l'URSS, Bastos Ekoudou ☏ & ℻22.21.02.24; Nigeria, off av Monseigneur Vogt ☏22.22.34.55 ℻22.23.55.51; UK, av Winston Churchill ☏22.22.07.96 or 22.22.05.45 ℻22.22.01.48, 24hr emergencies ☏77.71.30.53; USA, av Rosa Parks, Bastos ☏22.20.15.00 ✉yaounde.usembassy.gov.

Internet Yaoundé has a huge and ever-changing selection of cybercafés, most centred around av de l'Indépendance, rue Joseph Essono Balla and rue Joseph Balla Eloumden. Most hotels have so-called business centres with Internet access and a few have Wi-Fi networks throughout the premises. If your hotel isn't online, ask at reception.

Maps The Centre Géographique National, av Monseigneur Vogt (☏22.22.29.21), has city,

regional and national maps, but you'll probably have to order what you want since they don't have much stock. For basic city maps of Yaoundé and Douala, Tiger Arcade, on av Kennedy, has a stock of 1:15,000 and 1:20,000 sheets.

National parks For information about Campo Ma'an, Korup, Lobéké, Boumba Bek and Nki national parks, contact the WWF head office behind the BAT cigarette factory in Bastos (☏22.21.70.83 ⊛www.panda.org). The UNESCO office on av de l'Indépendance (☏22.22.57.63 ⊛www.unesco .org/yaounde) may be able to help with information about Dja Reserve.

Pharmacies Among the best stocked are the Pharmacie Française (☏22.22.14.76), on the corner of av Kennedy and av Ahidjo, and Provin-ciale, av Adenauer (☏22.20.94.93).

Post offices The main post office (Mon–Fri 7.30am–3.30pm, Sat & Sun 7.30am–noon) is on pl Ahidjo and has an international (only) phone and fax service. Poste restante costs CFA500 per letter.

Supermarkets The Niki chain is one of the cheapest; their three stores are in Mvog-bi (south of the Score roundabout), Messa and Nlongkak. Score, on pl Ahidjo, is well stocked, while Mahima, in the north of the city on rue Essono Bella, is the best place for one-stop shopping. For more expensive Western food, head for Pavilion Vert on rue Eloumden.

The Province du Sud

As an escape from Douala or Yaoundé, or from the rigours of overlanding, **Kribi** and the white-sand **beaches** of Cameroon's south coast are hard to beat. The quickest route from Douala or Yaoundé to Kribi is on the fast highway via **EDÉA**, an attractive town at the southernmost bridge over the broad **Sanaga River**. If you want to stay here, try the upmarket *La Sanaga* (☏33.46.49.62 ℻33.46.48.86 ④), which overlooks the river and the massive Sanaga hydroelectric plant. The town has a market, a post office and banks, and makes a good living from the passing Douala-Yaoundé-Kribi trade.

Three alternative routes from Yaoundé to Kribi run through the forests along tracks which, in the dry season at any rate, are usually passable in normal cars; two of these go first to **Ebolowa**, then continue either via **Lolodorf** or **Akom II**. The third goes by paved road to Eséka (37km south of the Yaoundé–Edéa road) and on to Lolodorf on a rugged *piste*. Travel can be painfully slow along these stretches, but the roads take in lush scenery punctuated with the occasional waterfall, and skirt a number of "Pygmy" villages. Thanks to pipeline money, a new fast road linking Yaoundé and Kribi via **Mvengue** is planned for the future.

Mbalmayo

Heading south through rich forests broken by plantations of coffee and cocoa, the fast N2 highway links the capital to Ebolowa, then continues to the borders of Gabon and Equatorial Guinea. The first major stop along the way is **MBALMAYO**,

Ebolowa's few *agences de voyage* are on the Yaoundé road, with frequent daily departures to **Yaoundé** via **Mbalmayo**. Most reliable is TransCam Voyages. From the main *gare routière*, there are also frequent share taxis to Yaoundé.

Minibuses to **Kribi** are less frequent and depend very much on the state of the roads, but **clandos** can usually be found at the Kribi *gare routière* on the route d'Ambam south of the town centre. During the rainy season the journey may take a couple of days, stopping overnight on the way in **Akom II** or **Lolodorf**, depending on which road is better.

If you're continuing to **Gabon** or **Equatorial Guinea**, you need to get to **Ambam** which is close to both frontiers (see below). Frequent minibuses leave daily from the Ambam *gare routière* just next to the Kribi motor park.

a prosperous town with a bank, post office and accommodation, though there's no real reason to stay here. If you do, the best option is about 10km out of town, on the Ebolowa road, at the *Ebogo Tourist Site* (❷), located on the western edge of the Mbalmayo Forest Reserve, which arranges day-trips up the **Nyong River** by pirogue.

To get to the coast or the borders, take the road that leads from Mbalmayo via **NGOULÉMAKONG** to **Ebolowa**.

Ebolowa and around

EBOLOWA is a lively provincial capital and important cocoa-marketing centre. While there's not much in the way of sights (though you could stop by the **Hôpital Enongal** to contemplate the dentist's chair where Albert Schweitzer had his teeth done) it's a pleasant stopping point in the forest region, with a large market that spreads out near the town's artificial **lake**. With more than 40,000 inhabitants, Ebolowa also has good services, including **banks** (SCB and BICEC), a **post office**, **pharmacies** and even a small **supermarket**.

There are several small **hotels** in Ebolowa. Most central and within easy reach of the *agences de voyage* is the basic *Ane Rouge* (☎22.28.34.38 ❷) with fanned rooms, a few s/c and the rest sharing facilities, and a great first-floor terrace. More upscale, 2km from the centre on the road to the border, and at the foot of the picturesque Mount Ebolowa, is *Le Ranch* (☎22.28.35.17 ℻22.28.49.34 ❸), with small, tidy *boukarous* boasting hot water and a/c. That said, water supplies are irregular in town, and even the best hotel can't guarantee enough pressure for a decent shower.

Ambam and on to Gabon and Equatorial Guinea

A good paved road continues south from Ebolowa through dense forest to **AMBAM**, the last major town before the borders of Equatorial Guinea and Gabon. There's a large market here with an international array of traders, and **accommodation** at rudimentary *auberges* or the more luxurious *La Couronne* (❸) with a/c and TV in all the rooms. But this is essentially a transit town, and your main objective will be to move on to somewhere else.

Share taxis **to Gabon** leave from Ambam's market and take little more than an hour to reach the border. On Saturdays, they stop at **ABAN MINKOO** for the eventful weekly market. Once at the border, there's a new bridge that crosses the Ntem River with taxis on the other side that assure regular transport to **BITAM** and Gabonese immigration.

Share taxis **to Equatorial Guinea** leave from the motor park across from the post office. Halfway to the border, vehicles cross the **Ntem River** on a regular ferry and then continue to the frontier town of **EBEBIYIN**. If you're travelling by public transport, you'll be dropped on Cameroonian territory, some 2km before reaching the town. After going through customs and immigration, you can board a waiting taxi to continue south.

Lolodorf and Akom II

From Ebolowa, it's 73km by a seasonal *piste* to **LOLODORF** (its name – "Lolo's village" – is about the only reminder of the German presence in the district, as most towns were renamed by the French). There's fuel here, along with accommodation in a few cheap *auberges* (❷) and a new hotel under construction. Only 110km separate Lolodorf from Kribi, with an initial paved stretch for the first 44km as far as **BIPINDI**. Some 20km from Lolodorf, you reach **BIDJOKA**, from where you can walk to the **Bidjoka Falls**.

From Bipindi, rough tracks wind through the hilly tropical forest making for a difficult trip. This route passes numerous "Pygmy" villages where, unlike in the extreme east of the country, the people have adopted a sedentary lifestyle.

If the road via Lolodorf isn't passable, an alternative, more southern route runs to Kribi via **AKOM II**, on the fringes of the **Campo Ma'an National Park** (see p.1316). Trekking into the reserve from here is difficult but very rewarding. There's basic accommodation at *Auberge Jacquie-Voyages* (❶) and they may also be able to help find a guide.

Kribi

Colonial reminders abound in **KRIBI**, giving it an air of nostalgia, tinged with a resort atmosphere brought in by city-weekenders scattered on the beaches. The home town of the Bassa, Kribi was a noted hotbed of UPC radicalism in the 1950s. The **port** in the town centre was built by the Germans and is today too shallow for larger vessels to enter the harbour: from the nearby hillside, crowned with its colonial **cathedral**, you can see ships anchored a few kilometres offshore as their cargo is docked by lighter. The former **German administrative buildings**, lining the beachfront on the northwest side of town, now house government offices such as the *préfecture* and the **tourist delegation** (☎33.46.10.80). Kribi's only **bank** (BICEC), on the rue de la Poste, has an **ATM** but doesn't change money.

Kribi is Cameroon's second-largest port, and, with the significant economic uplift the region has experienced since the completion in 2003 of the 1000-kilometre **Chad–Cameroon oil pipeline** – which runs to an off-shore terminal just south of here – it's beginning to feel like a town on the move, though the environmental impact of the pipeline has been considerable.

Accommodation

Because of the heavy tourist presence, **accommodation** tends to be relatively expensive in Kribi, especially at the beachside resorts, and particularly during weekends when booking is recommended. If you're on a tight budget, town hotels are a lot cheaper (although still expensive in Cameroon terms). Staying in town

> ### Kiridi – the short people
>
> Kribi's name is said to come from the word *kiridi*, which, roughly translated, means "short people" – a reminder that you're in **Pygmy country**. The "Pygmies" were the original inhabitants of the district, although nowadays Bantu-speakers like the **Batanga** and **Bakoko** predominate, and you might not see a single convincing "Pygmy". The "Pygmies", of course, don't call themselves by that term and every community is part of a small cluster of bands. Traditionally nomadic, they are now increasingly sedentary, and increasingly dependent upon the larger economy of Cameroon beyond the forest. All Africa's people of small stature have lost their original languages and now speak the local language of the dominant people – in this area that's Bassa.

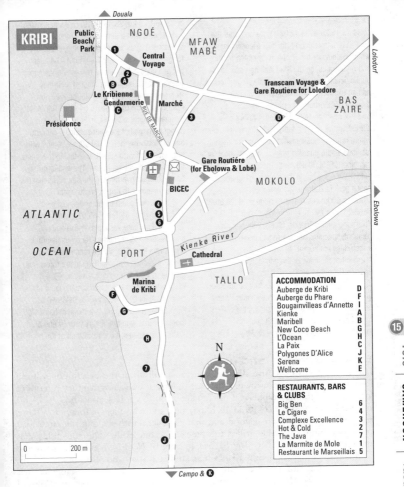

KRIBI

Douala

NGOÉ

MFAW MABÉ

Public Beach/ Park

Central Voyage

Le Kribienne

Gendarmerie

Marché

Présidence

RUE DE MARCHÉ

Transcam Voyage & Gare Routière for Lolodore

BAS ZAIRE

Lolodorf

Gare Routiére (for Ebolowa & Lobé)

BICEC

MOKOLO

Ebolowa

ATLANTIC

OCEAN

PORT

Kienke River

Cathedral

TALLO

Marina de Kribi

N

0   200 m

Campo & K

ACCOMMODATION

Auberge de Kribi	D
Auberge du Phare	F
Bougainvilleas d'Annette	I
Kienke	A
Maribell	B
New Coco Beach	G
L'Ocean	H
La Paix	C
Polygones D'Alice	J
Serena	K
Wellcome	E

RESTAURANTS, BARS & CLUBS

Big Ben	6
Le Cigare	4
Complexe Excellence	3
Hot & Cold	2
The Java	7
La Marmite de Mole	1
Restaurant le Marseillais	5

15

15.3 | **CAMEROON** | Yaoundé and the south

also makes it easier to enjoy inexpensive food and Kribi's buzzing nightlife. During the beachside hotels' "off-season", on weekdays, or if you're staying for some time", bargaining can knock up to thirty percent off the regular room rate. The places listed below are all within easy reach of town. For places further from the centre see beaches to the north or southern beaches (p.1315).

Auberge de Kribi on Lolodorf road, near TransCam Voyage ☏33.46.15.41. Very basic but superb-value rooms with fans and shared facilities in a busy commercial part of town, but a fair distance from the beach. ❶

Auberge du Phare just south of the bridge ☏55.64.04.64 or 44.75.00.52. Under new management, the former laid-back and characterful *auberge* is now a sleek, streamlined beach hotel hosting conferences and business travellers, with spotless rooms to match. The breezy beachfront

vista from the popular restaurant hasn't changed, though prices have gone up a notch. ❻

Bougainvilleas d'Annette south of the bridge just after the tarred road becomes dirt ☏66.06.85.16 or 99.44.72.41. Delightful place with a range of stylish s/c a/c rooms given minute attention to detail. Rooms in the main building are cheapest, the ones in the beachfront building with sea views and romantic French verandahs the dearest. Recommended bar-restaurant. ❺

La Kienke opposite Central Voyages ℡33.46.16.20 🖶33.42.93.41. Named after the river that runs through Kribi, this friendly place within walking distance of a lively clutch of bars and restaurants, on the road leading down to the public beach park, has comfortable s/c a/c rooms, and an excellent bar-restaurant serving ice-cold draught beer. Breakfast included. **④**

La Paix near the *Hôtel Maribell* in Kribi's quiet administrative quarter. Inexpensive motel-like place with a range of basic rooms, either s/c or sharing facilities, and a guarded front area that's ideal for camping (CFA5000 per tent). There's a large and potentially noisy bar in the main building and the beach park is 200m to the north. **②**

L'Océan 600m south of the bridge ℡99.28.85.35 or 66.23.83.43 📧mal_hocak@yahoo.fr. One of Kribi's most child-friendly hotels, with two rows of pleasant, spacious, s/c sea-facing bungalows, and a first-class restaurant. **⑤**

Maribell at the edge of the administrative quarter near *La Paix* ℡33.46.18.18 📧aboubello@yahoo .fr. Homely place in a large villa, 300m from Kribi's beach park, with tidy s/c rooms with a/c, TV and hot water, and a good-value restaurant. **④**

New Coco Beach on the beach south of the bridge next door to *Auberge du Phare*

℡33.46.15.84 🖶33.46.18.19. This small, rustic beach hotel, with a jumble of s/c rooms of different shapes and sizes, is excellent value, especially for groups (five sharing CFA40,000). The beach bar and good, albeit pricey, restaurant, keep many guests happily on-site for most of their stay. **⑤**

Polygone d'Alice south of the bridge, 1km from the centre ℡33.46.15.04 or 99.64.74.04 📧hotelpolygones@yahoo.fr. Funky, multistorey polygon-shaped place with spacious, colourful and meticulously decorated s/c a/c rooms with hot water, half with superb sea-facing balconies, the other half looking inland. The *boukarou*-style bar-restaurant overlooking the sea compensates for the distance to Kribi's bright lights. **⑤**

🏃 **Serena** south of the bridge just past *Polygone d'Alice* ℡66.52.71.07 📧serenakribi.com. A simple, stylish and unpretentious place, perfect for an undisturbed break from it all. The s/c a/c rooms have hot showers and the restaurant, a stone's throw from the sea, is excellent value for money. **⑤**

Wellcome just off the Hospital roundabout in the centre of Kribi ℡33.46.21.95 or 99.89.56.51. Friendly town lodgings with a range of basic s/c rooms – some with fan, others with TV and a/c – and an inexpensive bar-restaurant at the front. **②**

Eating, drinking and nightlife

For moderate-to-expensive **dining**, you can hardly beat the beachfront seafood restaurants of the hotels, many of which are so busy at weekends that they run out of food midway through dinner. Of the restaurants in town, *Le Cigare* (℡33.46.19.28) and *Restaurant le Marseillais* (℡33.46.18.63), next to each other on route de la Poste, are well known for their seafood and draught beer. Further along the same road you'll find more affordable grilled fish prepared at one of the numerous fish stands and served at the many bars. *Hot & Cold*, in front of *Hôtel La Kienke* and across the road from Central Voyages, is Kribi's best sandwich spot, and also does fresh fruit juice and ice cream. Further along the same road are a few new restaurants such as *La Marmite de Mole* (℡33.46.17.88), which does an excellent *steak au poivre* and other French dishes.

Kribi has a number of good **clubs** that keep going late into the night at weekends. *Big Ben*, near the bridge, is the town's golden oldie. *The Java*, at the big resort hotel, the *Palm Beach Plus*, is the upmarket place to go (CFA5000 entry fee), with a mix of African and European hits. The seafront bar gets busy here at the weekend, with a DJ playing until midnight. In town, at the livelier end of route de la Poste, a number of bars double up as dance venues, such as the packed *Complexe Excellence*.

The coast around Kribi

With their wild vegetation, white sand and safe swimming, the beaches along the coast north and south of Kribi are among the most beautiful anywhere in Africa. They stretch for more than 100km, from the small village of **Londji** to the town of **Campo** on the Equatorial Guinea border. If you're a beach bum, you'll be in your element, though the paradise is no longer a well-kept secret, and tourist facilities are gradually making their mark. Plans to build a natural-gas, fuelled power plant, somewhere between Kribi and Londji, may also ruin some of the appeal of this

There are frequent *agence* departures to **Yaoundé** and **Douala** with Kribi's three main companies, Central Voyages, La Kribienne and TransCam Voyage. La Kribienne and TransCam also have regular transport to **Grand Batanga** and further south to **Campo**. TransCam also runs to **Ebolowa** via **Lolodorf** and **Bipindi**. For Ebolowa via **Akom II** visit the *gare routière* on Lolodorf road. As ever, most departures leave early in the morning.

shore in the future. If you have transport, the **Campo Ma'an National Park**, east of Campo, is well worth exploring, protecting stretches of forest which are among the globe's most important sites of biodiversity.

Londji and the beaches to the north

North of Kribi, the road to Edéa hugs the coastline as it skirts some of the area's most picturesque strands, first passing the village of **MPALLA** and then, after 15km, **Cocotier Plage** (a beautiful beach where there are rudimentary bungalows for rent) before arriving at **LONDJI**. Some 25km north of Kribi – and 500m south of the Kribi tollgate – this small fishing village spreads round a large bay with calm, warm water, white sands and coconut trees. The *Auberge Jardinière* nestles on the beach and offers excellent seafood and the best **accommodation** in the village (☎99.91.72.69 ❸). It can get crowded with expats at weekends, though on other days you'll have the place to yourself. If you're on a budget, there are humbler *boukarous* for rent along the beach (❷). **Camping** is also possible on the beach for around CFA2500 per person, payable to the village chief, who employs guards to keep thieves at bay. You can order fresh fish from the guards, or fill up in town on fish, snail kebabs and rice. A couple of local bars sell beer, minerals and freshly tapped palm wine.

After midnight, **fishermen** set out in wooden canoes across the bay, stirring up phosphorescence in the water as they paddle out to the ocean. You can arrange with the beach guards to go along, though it's not always an eventful experience. If you're missing nightlife and restaurants, there are share taxis to and from Kribi throughout the daylight hours: they stop running in the early evening, however, after which time you can hire a cab back to Londji for CFA2000–3000.

The southern beaches to Campo

Another *piste* follows the coastline southwards from Kribi to the Equatorial Guinea border, passing more beaches lined with places to stay. Some 7km south of Kribi, just before **GRAND BATANGA**, a small signpost points down to the **Chutes de la Lobé**, where the river of the same name comes thrashing over a rocky descent as it plunges directly into the ocean. The force of these rapids stirs up an unappealing brownish foam in the bay, but the surrounding beaches are clean and have excellent swimming. A couple of **eating** places at the foot of the falls sell grilled shrimp and fish. If you want to stay, there are several good places close by. *Tara Plage* (☎33.46.20.83 ❸), about 2km before the waterfalls and 4km south of the bridge in Kribi, is the best budget hotel on the beachfront, with friendly staff and basic but comfortable s/c fanned or a/c rooms. It also has spacious four-person villas (CFA20,000), as well as tents for rent if you want to camp (CFA4000). The only drawback is the need to rely on the pricey restaurant if you don't want to travel the distance into town. The more luxurious and idyllically located ⚓ *Hotel Ilomba* is about 500m from the falls and has deluxe *boukarous* and a good but expensive restaurant (☎99.91.29.23 or 33.46.17.44 ❺). You can walk to the *chutes* from Kribi, but be aware that thieves try their luck along this stretch of the beach. You'll also get numerous offers for **pirogue trips** up the Lobé River (around three hours for CFA5000 per person), though these tend to be disappointing. While paddling upstream is picturesque and relaxing, the "Pygmy" villages you're supposed to be visiting are no such thing, and the "traditional hunting trips" feel like something out of a second-rate theme park.

The beaches between Grand Batanga and the fishing village of **EBOUNDJA**, 20km south of Kribi, are some of the most beautiful and isolated in the district. The local chief at Eboundja authorizes **camping** on the beach and can help arrange meals and fishing-boat excursions. Otherwise there are a few rooms at the excellent *Mimado* restaurant (☎99.97.79.17 ✉lobe61@hotmail.com ❷), run by two ex-Parisian restaurateurs, right on the beach. Alternatively you may be lucky and bag a **room** at the Catholic Mission.

Some 25km further south, a rocky formation, the **Rocher du Loup**, rises in a dramatic – if not wolf-like – fashion from the water. South of here, you're getting into very remote districts as the road reaches yet another fishing village, **EBODJÉ**, which is the site of a successful sea-turtle conservation and ecotourism initiative. Between November and January hundreds of turtles come ashore to lay their eggs. You can stay in private homes (❶) and have food prepared for you at the town's only restaurant (CFA1500 per meal).

Campo and the Campo Ma'an National Park

The southbound *piste* finally peters out at the two-bit border town of **CAMPO**, starting point for visits to the 2640-square-kilometre **Campo Ma'an National Park** (daily 8am–6pm) which is co-managed by WWF and the Cameroonian government. This is one of the world's most important biodiversity sites, protecting various types of rainforest, ranging in altitude from sea level to 800m. Currently it is also vying to become Africa's first trans-boundary Ramsar site as it links with Rio Campo National Park in Equatorial Guinea. Access to the area is agonizingly difficult as the logging companies that used to maintain the roads have moved on (check with WWF Yaoundé ☎22.21.62.67 or the park conservator ☎66.86.37.71 or 77.87.31.19 for details of their current condition).

You'll need your own 4x4 transport to get around, but once the old German road connecting Campo with **MA'AN** becomes drivable again you'll be able to spend a full day driving through the park past the picturesque waterfalls – the **Chutes Menve Élé** – with at least a theoretical chance of seeing buffalo and elephant if you make an early start. However, be warned that the dense forest makes animal-viewing extremely difficult.

Alternatively you can catch a motorized pirogue on Campo beach to the river-mouth **Île d'Ipikar**, which has no infrastructure but plenty of wildlife, including lowland gorilla, forest elephant, buffalo and chimpanzee. Once on the island you'll have to trek, and to stay overnight you'll need to camp. To visit the island you can pick up a **guide** (CFA3000) at Campo beach or the village of **MABIOGO** in the forest a few kilometres southeast of Campo. Otherwise there are also guides in **NKOÉLON**, west of the park, and **EBIANEMAYONG**, to the east, both of them on the old German road that runs through the park. The guides can also take you on short treks into clearings where there's a good chance you'll spot some of the many different monkey species living in the park, and maybe some unusual birdlife – you might even see the world's rarest bird, the colourful, small, bald *picatharte* or rock fowl. Park fees (CFA5000) should be paid at the clearly signposted forest office in Campo.

Accommodation in Campo is limited to a number of simple *auberges* (❶) plus a new ecolodge, funded by WWF as an ecotourism initiative, managed by the villagers. You can expect customs and immigration checks in the vicinity of the town, whether you're crossing into Equatorial Guinea or not. The town's beach stretches south to the mouth of the **Ntem River**, which marks the border.

From the beach you can negotiate with a *piroguier* to take you 10km up the Ntem River to **Yengue** in Equatorial Guinea. There's a frontier post here (make sure to get your passport stamped before continuing), and tracks leading to the road to the capital, **Bata**.

The Province de l'Est

Three hundred kilometres of partially paved road separate Yaoundé from **Bertoua**, the capital of East Province – a region which has changed dramatically due to gold prospecting and virtually unrestricted logging of the rainforest. Not long ago, places like **Yokadouma** and **Lomié** were isolated villages surrounded by undisturbed forest havens. Now, they have a boom-town atmosphere, with a ragtag assembly of bars, brothels and *auberges*.

The roads heading east from Yaoundé are largely maintained by the logging companies, but the pounding from the heavy trucks' suspension often corrugates the roads badly and from time to time they become impassable to ordinary vehicles. Formerly, the main N1 route to Bertoua followed the **Sanaga River** to **NANGA-EBOKO**, though a second road, the N10, following the course of the **Nyong River** is now more frequently used, since it's paved the whole way to Garoua Boulai. If you can drag your attention away from the hundreds of logging trucks, these routes provide some sense of being away from it all. Both **Somalomo**, 75km south of the town of **AYOS** on the N10, and **Lomié**, 127km south of **Abong Mbang**, are good bases for treks to the **Dja Faunal Reserve**, a large swathe of pristine rainforest to the south.

Most travellers press east towards **Bertoua**, passing through **DOUMÉ**, formerly the capital of the eastern region and site of some remarkable colonial vestiges, including a German cathedral and an imposing German fortress on top of a hill overlooking the town. Moving on from Bertoua towards the **Central African Republic**, a paved road heads northeast to **Garoua-Boulai**, a long journey through a great swathe of jungle and grassland to a busy crossing point and marketplace on the savannah fringes of central Cameroon.

Heading directly east from Bertoua you reach **Batouri**, a busy town en route to Berbérati in the Central African Republic, and to **YOKADOUMA**, the gateway to Cameroon's far-southeastern corner. The three **national parks** in this area – Lac Lobéké, Boumba Bek and Nki – are gradually becoming more accessible to visitors and offer some of the best rainforest game-viewing in Africa.

Dja Faunal Reserve

The **Dja Faunal Reserve**, bounded on its south, west and northern sides by the Dja River, is the largest area of intact primary rainforest in Cameroon, some 5200 square kilometres. After many years of relative obscurity it was made a UNESCO World Heritage Site in 1987 and is now set to become a national park. Accessing Dja is quite difficult, and you have to be entirely self-sufficient, bringing a tent and all equipment with you, but it's very much worth the effort: the **wildlife** includes large populations of lowland gorilla, chimpanzee, mandrill, forest elephant, sitatunga and buffalo; the **bird-watching** is excellent throughout the reserve; and there are opportunities for rewarding contacts with **Baka people** who live around the reserve boundaries.

In theory it's possible to visit Dja between about October and May though visibility is best between November and March. Reserve fees are CFA5000 per day and CFA2000 per camera. Before you set off, however, you should contact either the Ministry of Tourism (☏22.22.44.11) or UNESCO's Yaoundé field office (☏22.22.57.63) for the latest updates.

Beginning your trip from **SOMALOMO**, 220km from Yaoundé, is perhaps easiest. (Somalomo isn't marked on the Michelin map but is located on the north bank of the Dja, at the point where the map shows a five-tonne ferry crossing over the river, allowing access to the reserve.) You can stay at one of Somalomo's cheap hotels (❷) or at the reserve *campement* (❸), where staff can organize a guide (CFA3000/day), porters (CFA2000/day) and generally help with planning your visit. If you have time to spare, visit the town's extraordinary **orchid** *ombrière* (literally a "shader"), which is most impressive when the flowers are in bloom, mostly between July and September.

From Somalomo it's a long, 36km hike to a forest clearing called **Bouamir**, where you can set up camp while exploring the area on shorter day-trips. The reserve's **large mammals** are present in good numbers, but they are all difficult to see, partly because of the dense forest, partly as a result of intense hunting, though this is less of a problem in the vicinity of Bouamir. **Bird-watching**, however, can be extremely rewarding throughout the reserve, the northwest being especially good for hornbills and a Bouamir for the rare *picatharte*.

The eastern part of the reserve is home to **Baka** "Pygmies" or *gens du forêt*, who live along the boundary in relatively traditional camps. From **LOMIÉ**, you can arrange to trek into the forest with guides from their community, and stay in their villages. Baka guides are easiest to liaise with at the forest post, where the forest guards are stationed. The best place to **stay** in Lomié is the *Auberge de Raphia*, 1km out of town, which is basic but has a decent bar-restaurant (☎22.20.94.72 ②).

Bertoua

Situated on the borders of the savannah and the forest, Bertoua has grown rapidly in recent years to become the country's eighth-largest town, with a population of some 180,000. Growth has been largely thanks to logging and gold-mining, and there's a lively sense of commerce too, but the town is above all an **administrative centre**, seat of the East Province. It's an uninspiring place to visit, however, and for overland travellers, the most salient feature is likely to be its well-stocked shops, the **ATM** at the BICEC bank at the main junction in the town centre, and a good selection of **accommodation**, which makes it the obvious stopping point on the roads to and from East Province and Central African Republic – not that many travellers have been doing this route for several years, for security reasons.

The main **agences de voyage** are located near the market and town centre. Narral Voyages, Alliance Voyages and Woila Voyages have daily departures for **Yaoundé**. They, as well as Touristique Express, service the fast paved road to **Garoua-Boulai**. Narral and Alliance also have daily connections to **Batouri** and **Yokadouma** (a full day, leaving early morning) and to remote destinations such as the CAR border town of **Gamboula**, **Lomié** (for the eastern part of the Dja Reserve), and **Bélabo**, the closest town in the region on the **Transcam railway** line. Unfortunately, even when running to schedule trains heading both north and south reach Bélabo late at night.

Accommodation

Fanga north of the centre in the Mokolo neighbourhood, clearly signposted from the main road ☎22.23.10.63. Reasonably comfortable hotel with spacious a/c rooms with TV. ③

Mansa north of the centre ☎22.24.16.50 or 99.52.65.34. Hands down the town's top hotel, with a/c rooms, tennis court and an inviting pool (CFA2000 for non-guests). ⑤

Mirage down the road from the post office ☎22.24.26.47. Small place offering a range of s/c rooms, some with a/c and TV, and a

popular – and potentially noisy – cabaret at weekends. ②

Paris behind the market in *quartier* Élevage ☎22.24.20.46. Comfortable, middling place with a range of tidy s/c rooms with a/c or fan, some with TV. ③

Phenix Palace up the road from, and within walking distance of, the main *agences de voyage* offices ☎22.24.27.29. Friendly and good-value hotel with a range of clean s/c rooms, with a/c or fan, and a good bar-restaurant. ②

Garoua-Boulai

The state-of-the-art tarred road leading north of Bertoua to **GAROUA-BOULAI** is one of the most tangible benefits of the Chad–Cameroon oil pipeline, and takes in some fine mountain scenery near **NDOKAYO**, with panoramic views over the valley of the **Lom River**. The Adamawa Mountains are not far to the north, and many Fula herders pass through the one-horse border town of Garoua-Boulai. Inexpensive **accommodation** includes two basic places at the main junction: *La Forestière* (●) and the slightly better *Mission Catholique* (❷). Another option is to stay with the Sisters at the mission off the road to Meiganga; they have clean rooms (❷) as well as dormitory space.

The town's three *agences*, Narral, Alliance and Touristique Express, all have daily connections to **Ngaoundéré** on the fast road as far as **MEIGANGA**, where you can branch westwards to catch the train at **NGAOUNDAL**. These agencies also have regular daily connections to **Bertoua**.

Batouri

East of Bertoua, the forest yields to hilly savannah broken by rivers and woodlands. Travel is difficult along the poorly maintained *piste* leading to **BATOURI**, and a potential border crossing linking to the Central African Republic town of Berbérati. In Batouri, you can **stay** at the basic but pleasant *Hôtel Coopérant* (℡22.26.23.00 ❷) a hundred metres up the hill from the *agences de voyage* in the centre of town. There's also the *Belle Etoile* (℡22.26.25.18 ❸), south of the centre, with comfortable s/c rooms and a good restaurant. A CFA150 *moto* ride away from the centre, the *Mont Pandi* (℡22.26.25.77 ❸) has run-down s/c rooms, compensated for by the beautiful setting and the excellent bar-restaurant serving tasty local specialities such as porcupine. The most relaxing place to stay is with the welcoming sisters at the Catholic *Collège Bari* on the hilltop on the east side of town (leave a donation).

With **Mount Pandi** flanking the town, Batouri is base for some interesting excursions. The east is famous for its **gold mines**, which still attract prospectors from many parts of West and Central Africa; find a guide to take you to **KAMBELE**, a makeshift mining village 6km from Batouri. Seeing the river panners and the gold scales in the market (dominated by Hausa speculators), it's hard to avoid Wild West comparisons.

The town's two *agences de voyage*, Narral and Alliance, both leave before dawn to tackle the 102km of tortuous track to the frontier town of **KENTZOU**. They also run services throughout the day to **Bertoua** and down the long, slow road to **Yokadouma**. Before you travel, ask about the condition of the road – it's maintained frequently by logging companies, but it gets wrecked again just as rapidly and bridges often collapse.

The southeastern rainforests

The southeastern corner of Cameroon is covered by 27,000 square kilometres of dense, humid **Congo Basin rainforest** – part of the world's second richest forest region, only surpassed by the Amazon Basin. Of this area, some 8000 square kilometres are protected within three national parks (Lobéké, Boumba Bek and Nki) managed jointly by WWF and the Ministry of Forests and Fauna as the **Jengi Forest Project** – *jengi* meaning "spirit of the forest" in Baka (Ⓦtinyurl.com/32l3hj). The remaining area is split into logging and hunting concessions, community hunting areas and village areas. The population here – roughly half Baka, half various Bantu peoples – depends heavily on the forest for survival, and the region supports a rich variety of **wildlife**, including forest elephant, buffalo, bongo, chimpanzee, gorilla, and many species of monkey.

Yokadouma and around

The 200km *piste* from Batouri to **YOKADOUMA** is one of the worst in the country. The sense of achievement is almost tangible, when, caked in dust and/or mud, you finally arrive – and the mildly chaotic atmosphere in the isolated town tucked away in the jungle seems an appropriate mood music for surviving the trip.

There's a range of **places to stay**. In the centre of town are *La Cachette*, with clean, s/c rooms with fans and a bar-nightclub that gets noisy (T99.73.81.74 ❷), and *Libeta*, with slightly dingier, but quieter, s/c rooms without fans, and a few cheaper rooms sharing facilities (❶). The best place in town is the popular *L'Éléphant*, a five-minute walk from the centre towards the sports ground, with clean, s/c rooms with hot water, a few cheaper rooms sharing facilities, and a popular bar-restaurant (T22.24.28.77 or 77.89.65.59 ❸).

Your first stop should be the offices shared by the **WWF** and the **Ministère de Forêt et de la Faune** (Ministry of Forests and Wildlife/MINFOF) in the administrative quarter north of the centre (T66.29.59.31 or 55.29.24.84). They're in radio contact with their various bases throughout the forest and once you've decided how many days you want to spend, how far you're willing to hike, and which animals you're hoping to see, they will radio ahead to the relevant base to arrange for a Baka guide and porters to take you into the forest. They can also help with renting a 4x4 (CFA15,000 per day, including driver, plus CFA350/km). Your next stop should be Yokadouma's many provision stores – you'll need to stock up with water and supplies for the full length of your trip.

For road transport, Alliance and Narral are both located near the main roundabout and have regular departures to the Congo border town of **MOLOUNDOU**, via **Mambele** – where you'll find the main base for Lobéké National Park.

Lobéké National Park

Most accessible of the reserves is **Lobéké National Park**, contiguous with Dzanga-Sangha in the Central African Republic and Dzangha Ndoki in Congo, forming the tri-national Sangha Conservation Area, the largest area of protected rainforest in Africa. Its rich fauna can be viewed from raised platforms (**miradors**) constructed by the WWF for research purposes in forest clearings – *bais* in Baka. Staying overnight in a *mirador* offers a rare opportunity to watch birds with unparalleled visibility, while large mammals wander past seemingly unaware of your presence. *Miradors* can accommodate up to about five people. The two most popular and accessible *miradors* are *Petit Savanne*, a five-hour hike into the forest from the road, 47km south of the park headquarters at **Mambele** (160km south of Yokadouma), and *Djembe*, 115km east of Mambele, overlooking the Sangha River on the Central African Republic border, and accessible only by private 4x4.

Whatever your plans, you'll need to spend at least a day in the dusty junction town of **Mambele**, organizing the trip. There are two overnight possibilities: WWF's newly refurbished *Camp Kombo* (CFA7500/person) at the edge of the forest on the Yokadouma road, and the grandly named *Auberge Johannesburg Palace* (❷) near the main junction.

Before deciding which *bai* to head for, visit the park HQ in Mambele to check the *mirador* is free and has been unoccupied for at least three days (a cool-down period to allow wildlife to recover from the human disturbance). You'll also need to hire camp beds and basic kit if necessary, find a guide (CFA3000/day) and porters (CFA1500/day), and make food arrangements with them all (CFA1500/day is standard). And you need to pay your park fees (CFA5000/person/day, plus CFA5000/day for an "eco-guard" – a game ranger).

Once you are in the rainforest, trekking through it is an unforgettable experience. Your Baka guide moves stealthily and rapidly through the dense forest, alert to every sound, and pointing out easily missed highlights every few minutes. It's not unusual to hear **gorillas** nearby, and it's important to do exactly as your guide tells you: they're dangerous as well as vulnerable. Close, visual encounters are, however, extremely rare and there are no properly habituated families.

Boumba Bek and Nki forests

The contiguous **Boumba Bek** and **Nki forests** are pristine, and protected by rivers. The westernmost reserve, Nki, is only accessible by boat up the Dja River (arrange through the WWF base in Moloundu, on the Congo-Brazzaville border) or by road to **NDONGO** (west of Moloundou) followed by a four-hour trek to Nki falls. It takes two days of strenuous hiking to reach the *miradors* in Boumba Bek, arranged through the WWF base in **NGATO**, 30km south of Yokadouma.

15.4

Northern Cameroon

Northern Cameroon is separated from the rest of the country by a vast, almost trackless region in the centre. This huge expanse of rolling savannah and forests – as big as Scotland or Maine – is thinly populated and crossed by just three *pistes* and the railway. On its northern edge, the **Adamawa Mountains** cut across the centre of Cameroon, effectively dividing the country into two quite distinct parts. Beyond here, the climate is harsher and nature less generous, and a flat plateau stretches over much of the north, with light forests and grasslands replacing the south's thick vegetation. It's a tough journey by road from Yaoundé, Bertoua or Bamenda to the first town of northern Cameroon, **Ngaoundéré** – good enough reason to use the train – though once you've made it this far, the mostly flat and sealed highway which runs from Ngaoundéré all the way to **Kousséri** makes the north one of the easiest regions to travel through. There are no less than six **game parks** in the north, ranging from the hilly **Bouba Ndjida National Park**, home to the (probably now extinct) West African **black rhinoceros**, to the popular **Waza National Park**, whose flat savannah is ideal for spotting herds of giraffe and elephant, as well as lions and numerous other species.

In the extreme northwest, the volcanic **Mandara Mountains** have been scoured by thousands of years of *harmattan* winds, and the people of the region squeeze their livelihood out of the dry rocky slopes. Although this region has been discovered by travel operators, you can, if you're determined enough, work your way off the more beaten tracks and away from such overrun sites as **Roumsiki** to villages which may not be any more authentic but are at least less tainted by organized tourism.

While the mountain people of the northwest have retained traditional religious beliefs, the rest of the region bears the stamp of **Islam**, brought by Fula migrants, who established principalities called **lamidats** in the eighteenth century. The Muslim influence is especially noticeable in **Garoua** and **Maroua**, which seem unusually large and dynamic towns in a region where you might expect climate and geography to reduce energy to a minimum.

Ngaoundéré and around

Coming from the south, **NGAOUNDÉRÉ**, with its mango-shaded streets and mild climate (the result of its location at a height of 1400m), proves a satisfying introduction to the north. Though rapidly growing, the old Fula settlement still thrives in the neighbourhood around the Lamido's Palace, and local dress and architecture bear witness to a Sudanic tradition that is very much alive.

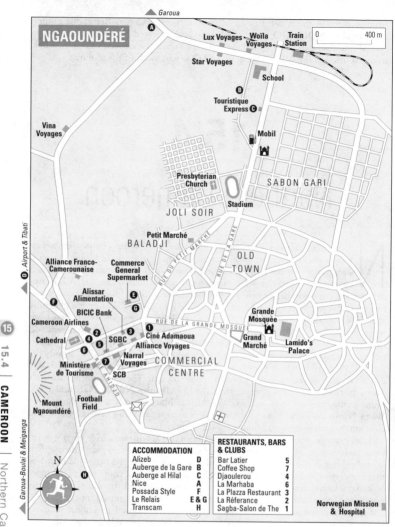

NGAOUNDÉRÉ

▲ Garoua

Lux Voyages • Woïla Voyages • Train Station

Star Voyages

School

Touristique Express ⒸⒷ

Mobil

Vina Voyages

Presbyterian Church

SABON GARI

JOLI SOIR

Stadium

Petit Marché

BALADJI

RUE DU PETIT MARCHÉ

OLD TOWN

RUE DE LA GARE

Alliance Franco-Camerounaise

Commerce General Supermarket

Alissar Alimentation

Ⓔ Ⓖ

BICIC Bank

Cameroon Airlines

RUE DE LA GRANDE MOSQUÉE

Grande Mosquée

Cathedral

❷ ❹ ❶ SGBC ❸ Ciné Adamaoua
❻ ❺
❼ Narral Voyages

Grand Marché

Lamido's Palace

Alliance Voyages

Ministère de Tourisme

COMMERCIAL CENTRE

SCB

Mount Ngaoundéré

Football Field

RUE D'ALOUDJI

N

Ⓗ

Garoua-Boulaï & Meiganga | Airport & Tibati

0 ——— 400 m

Norwegian Mission & Hospital

ACCOMMODATION
Alizeb	D
Auberge de la Gare	B
Auberge al Hilal	C
Nice	A
Possada Style	F
Le Relais	E & G
Transcam	H

RESTAURANTS, BARS & CLUBS
Bar Latier	5
Coffee Shop	7
Djaoulerou	4
La Marhaba	6
La Plazza Restaurant	3
La Réferance	2
Sagba-Salon de The	1

The first people to settle around Ngaoundéré – which means "mountain with a navel" in their language – were the **Mboum**, whose claims to the area were ceded to the Fula after a military siege in the early 1830s. By 1835, **Ardo Ndjobdji** had established the Muslim **lamidat** and the Mboum became Fula vassals. The city was surrounded by a protective wall in 1865 and extended its influence over a vast territory to the south and east; by the end of the nineteenth century, the town's population had grown to 10,000. Ngaoundéré changed little during the colonial period, and it wasn't until the **Trans-Cameroonian Railway** was extended here in 1974 that a real boom occurred; by 1983 the population had rocketed to nearly 60,000, and it may be close to 200,000 by now. New *quartiers* have grown up around the old centre, adding a sense of vitality to the traditional core, while growing economic activity now includes an industrial-scale slaughterhouse (livestock is a regional mainstay), a dairy and a tannery.

The **Ministère du Tourisme** on rue Ahidjo isn't worth visiting: staff appear completely disinterested. Instead, check out the events calendar at the **Alliance Franco–Camerounais de l'Adamaoua** (☎22.25.18.26 ⓦalliance.ngaoundere .free.fr), who put on excellent musical and cultural events that shouldn't be missed.

Accommodation

Alizés off the road to the airport, turn right at the signpost by the power station ☎22.25.16.89. In a quiet residential area on the outskirts of town, this little gem of a place offers excellent-value, basic s/c rooms – cold showers only – and has an excellent restaurant downstairs. ❷

Auberge de la Gare near the railway station ☎22.25.22.17 or 99.01.67.25. Friendly place with 24hr reception and well-maintained s/c rooms with hot water. Front garden with safe parking. Restaurant serves good cheap food. ❷

Auberge al Hilal rue de la Gare, next door to Touristique Express ☎22.25.19.97. Six simple s/c rooms with hot water; very convenient for the station and *agences de voyage*. No alcohol. ❷

Nice rte de Garoua, a 10min walk from the train station and *agences de voyage* ☎22.25.10.13. Should end up being the best in town when renovations are complete. Spacious s/c rooms with

TV and hot water. Pleasant garden restaurant, wonderfully scented by frangipani trees. ❸

Possada Style II off rue Ahidjo, north of the cathedral ☎22.25.17.03. A new sister establishment for the old *Possada Style I* further down the road. Clean s/c rooms with hot showers, and a good-value restaurant. The rooms at *Style 1* are cheaper and more basic. ❷

Le Relais behind the now defunct Cinéma Le Nord. With two wings around the corner from each other, an expensive new wing with spacious s/c rooms and a slightly run-down cheaper wing with s/c and non-s/c rooms. Both very convenient for the centre. Rooms in old wing ❷ or new wing ❹ .

Transcam off the rte de Garoua-Boulai ☎22.25.19.68 or 66.03.95.68 ⓔresahoteltranscam@yahoo.fr. Showy place with TV in a/c rooms and *boukarous*. Good service, and first-rate bar, restaurant and nightclub (Wed–Sun CFA3000) across the road. Visa. ❻

The Town

The **old town** centres around the **Lamido's Palace**, which is a *saré* – the Hausa word for this style of housing – made of *banco* huts with vast straw roofs swooping almost to the ground. A large wall surrounding the compound keeps the maze of courtyards, private dwellings and public rooms out of view from the street. For an **inside visit**, ask at the Lamido's Secretariat, housed in a new concrete building at the palace entrance (CFA3000 including guide, CFA1000 for camera use). By far the best time to visit the palace is on Fridays in time for **Friday prayers**. Dignitaries in brightly coloured *boubous* – magnificent accents of orange and red against the ochre tints of the town – come to pay their respects to the Lamido, who leads a procession to the mosque. Similar displays take place on Saturdays and Sundays.

Ngaoundéré's **Grand Marché** is down the main avenue from the palace, and surrounded by an arcaded wall. Despite the name, however, the **Petit Marché**, on the road of the same name, is now the town's main market, and is far more animated. The main avenue from both markets lead to the commercial centre, with its **banks** (BICEC and SGBC have **ATMs**) and **post office**.

Eating, drinking and nightlife

You'll find numerous cheap eating places around the *agences de voyage*. For something a little fancier, there are lots of options in the commercial centre. The rooftop terrace of *La Référance* is a nice place for an evening **drink** while the only two **nightclubs** are at *Marhaba* (CFA1500) and *Transcam* (CFA3000). To stock up on **supplies**, for the train or trips into the national parks, head to ETS Alissar Alimentation next to *Plazza Restaurant* or Commerce Général across the street from the new wing of *Hôtel le Relais*. They're both well-stocked with wine, cheese and other imported goods.

Bar Latier at the Marhaba end of the commercial centre's main street. Serves six varieties of locally produced yoghurt and milk, plus steaks, salads, and coffee and cake at reasonable prices.

Coffee Shop near the BICEC bank. Fresh coffee, plus *steak-frites* and large salads.

Djaoulerou Garden Court Square. New outdoor garden complex, with a small stage, featuring espresso and *dakkere* (yoghurt) throughout the day, plus the standard chicken-and-chips menu.

La Marhaba rue Ahidjo, next to *Le Motel*. A good bet for grilled fish and cold beer – and dancing at weekends.

La Plazza Restaurant next to Alissar Alimentation in the commercial centre. Good French and Lebanese cuisine at European prices.

Sagba Salon de Thé across from Ciné Adamaoua in the commercial centre. Laid-back place serving burger-type fast food and traditional *ndolé*-style dishes.

Around Ngaoundéré

If you have your own transport there are some easy side-trips in the environs of Ngaoundéré. The nearest scenic site is **Lac Tison**, just 10km from town. Take the Meiganga road south and after 6km a signpost points east to the crater lake, deep in the woods 3km further on. It's a pleasant trip along a *piste* bordered by awkward boulder formations, but forget swimming when you get there, as bilharzia is a real risk. Back on the Meiganga road, 15km from Ngaoundéré, just south of the village of **WAKWA**, the well-known waterfall, **Chute de la Vina**, tumbles thirty metres onto a table of rock.

A popular weekend getaway out of Ngaoundéré is the **Ngaoundaba Ranch** (℡99.59.54.06 ⓦwww.ngaoundaba.com ❹), 40km towards Meiganga, turning right (west) on a well-signposted dry-season road. Perched in the mountains by a beautiful **crater lake**, the main lodge recalls a Hemingway-esque vision of Africa, from where the now-deceased founder once led guests on hunting safaris. The image lives on as visitors gather for meals at a long trestle table with animal trophies on the heavy

Moving on from Ngaoundéré

Trains

Heading south to **Yaoundé**, your best bet is the **train**. The modern railway station (enquiries ℡22.25.12.71 or 22.25.12.30) is 1km north of the commercial centre. Couchette trains leave every evening at 6.30pm, arriving in Yaoundé, in theory, between 7.30am and 10am the following morning. If you're heading to **eastern Cameroon** or the **Central African Republic**, you can either take the Yaoundé train to **Bélabo**, arriving between 10pm and midnight, or the murderously slow Navette train, which leaves at 6.30am, stops at every station, and arrives at some point over the next two days. From Bélabo, Narral and Alliance Voyage continue to Bertoua.

Agences de voyage

Narral and Alliance ply the slow *piste* to **Meiganga**, where a paved road continues to the border town of **Garoua-Boulai** and on to **Bertoua**. Narral and Adamaoua Express also run west-bound services on the long and rugged road to **Foumban** via **Tibati**. Several *agences* operate daily services further north: Touristique Express has the smartest setup, with timetabled departures throughout the day in comfortable buses to **Garoua**, **Maroua** and **Kousséri**. They even sell bus tickets on board the train from Yaoundé, with buses connecting with the train on arrival, ideal if you want to continue north without pausing in Ngaoundéré.

For **Guidjiba** (connections to **Tcholliré** for **Bénoué** and **Bouba Ndjida** national parks), Lux, Star and Woila Voyage run several daily departures.

Flights

Cameroon Airlines (℡22.25.12.95) have suspended flights to Ngaoundéré. It might be worth calling the airport on ℡22.25.11.57.

stone and wood-beam walls. Most of the bougainvillea-bedecked *boukarous* have panoramic views of the area, which is great for **bird-watching**. Other diversions include swimming, fishing and boat trips on the lake.

Bénoué and Bouba Ndjida parks

Although often overshadowed by Waza National Park further north (see p.1336), there's rewarding **game-viewing** at the **Bénoué National Park**, and in the Bénoué conservation areas north of the park, and superb scenery in **Bouba Ndjida National Park**. The entire area is designated a UNESCO World Biosphere Reserve. The once-prolific wildlife of **Faro National Park** has been severely depleted by poaching, so unless you're interested in seeing the landscape (a mountain-dotted slab of bush) there is really no reason to visit it. Unfortunately, you can't get around the parks without your own transport, so if you don't have a vehicle you're left with the painfully expensive option of **renting a 4x4** in Ngaoundéré or Garoua, or the very uncertain option of hitching a lift in with mobile tourists.

The popular and tranquil **campements** in these areas provide a relaxing break away from it all; you should reserve in advance, especially for weekends or holidays. Contact the individual camp or the Délégation Provincial du Tourisme pour le Nord in Garoua (T22.27.22.90 F22.27.13.64). Note that Cameroonian conservation policy makes special provision for hunting in the designated national conservation areas, with head prices on every species, from elephant to monkey. The areas are well defined, and the paths of camera- and gun-users generally don't cross.

Bénoué National Park

Heading north from Ngaoundéré, you can enter the **Bénoué National Park** (Dec–May; entrance fee CFA5000/day, obligatory guide CFA3000/day, vehicle CFA2000/day) either at **MAYO ALIM** or **BANDA**. From both these small towns, tracks lead through the park to the *Campement du Buffle Noir* (T22.27.32.75). Situated on the banks of the Bénoué River, this camp has somewhat run-down s/c **rooms** grouped in simple *boukarous*. With prior permission you may be able to camp in the grounds. Meals at the restaurant cost CFA5000–8000.

Antelopes such as kob, waterbuck and hartebeest predominate in the park, but you may also see **buffalo** and Africa's largest antelope, the rare **Derby eland** – this is one of the few places in Africa where you have a realistic chance of seeing it. **Elephants** and **lions** are not as prolific as at Waza, but **hippos** and **crocodiles** are common in the river.

Fishing is possible in the conservation area northeast of the park (CFA5000/day), but you need to go with someone who has a fishing permit, or buy the permit yourself (CFA78,000, valid one year). A popular spot to fish is at the *Campement du Grand Capitaine* (c/o the Garoua tourist office on T22.27.22.90 ⑤), on the main road leading from **GUIDJIBA** to **TCHOLLIRÉ**, which offers luxurious, a/c *boukarous* and has a good restaurant.

Campement des Éléphants

Just north of Bénoué National Park, the thousand-square-kilometre **National Conservation Area No. 7** is an entirely different setup, managed single-handedly by a passionate wildlife enthusiast. The **Campement des Éléphants** (T99.86.08.00 Eperaarhaug@yahoo.fr; ⑥ including all meals) is a unique research station offering unusual wildlife experiences. Beautifully positioned on a rise overlooking a dry-season watering point on the Mayo Mbay River that flows north into Lake Lagdo, the camp arranges hugely informative treks and river trips into the fauna-rich surrounding area, home to a large population of elephants. What makes this place special is the level of knowledge the proprietor is keen to share about everything – from how to analyze elephant dung, to how carmine bee-eaters build their nests.

Excursions are expensive (around CFA50,000/person/day), but well organized and worth every penny. The camp, although a little rustic, has the enthusiasm of the proprietor painted all over it, and camp meals, enjoyed together at a central long table, are as educational as the treks in the bush. Book well in advance with emphasis on any special interest, and they'll try to accommodate your needs.

For information about helping out with wildlife surveys check out Ⓦwww .ecovolunteer.org. The zone also encompasses five villages which have benefited from camp-initiated **projects** such as oniongrowing and a health centre, and you can visit these to see progress.

Bouba Ndjida National Park

Possibly the most scenically stunning of the national parks, **Bouba Ndjida National Park** (Dec–May; entrance fee as for Bénoué National Park) was created in 1968 to protect the now extinct **black rhinoceros** and the increasingly rare **Derby eland**. The main access is via **KOUM**, 40km east of Tcholliré, where fees are paid. The rugged landscape, with rivers and relatively thick vegetation, makes this one of the country's most beautiful parks, and that's the most compelling reason to visit, because the thick bush in an area of 2200 square kilometres, with just 450km of *piste*, means that the animals are dispersed and very hard to spot. In addition, isolation and proximity to the Chadian border also mean that the risk of banditry is very real: you should talk to someone who has been recently before visiting.

Animals aren't seen much at Bouba Ndjida: the salt lick built to attract the rhinos never drew them often, and when a detailed IUCN rhino census was attempted in 2006, not a single animal was seen. The last of the western subspecies of the black rhino appear to have succumbed to poachers aiming to sell the valuable horns on the international Chinese-medicine market. There's more chance of seeing **elephant** and **buffalo** and, with luck, **lions** (which sometimes approach the *campement*) and **leopards**. The newly restored *Campement Bouba Ndjida camp* (reservations via the Garoua tourist office on ☏22.27.22.90; ❹, meals CFA6500) is 40km inside the park, overlooking the Mayo Lidi River.

Rey Bouba

REY BOUBA, west of Bouba Ndjida, is one of the most influential and traditional of the Fula *lamidats*. It's a worthwhile excursion to the village, where you can stay on the floor of a traditional resthouse (around CFA5000), but you may have to wait for days if you want an audience with the Lamido himself. Agencies plying the road between Ngaoundéré and Garoua stop in **Guidjiba**, where you can catch share taxis to **Tcholliré**, but you'll have to find a vehicle going north for the remaining 35km to Rey Bouba; your best chance is Friday – market day.

Garoua

The capital of North Province, **GAROUA** has grown rapidly since independence and now has a population nearing 500,000. Surprisingly, for a city situated so far into the interior, it has the country's fourth largest **port**, on the banks of the **Bénoué River**, not far upstream from the Nigerian border, where it becomes the Benue. This has helped smooth the way for local industrialization – though being former president Ahidjo's birthplace was no hindrance: he was always ready to invest in his home town. As the principal administrative and economic focus of the north, Garoua's more traditional aspects have been eclipsed to a large extent by its heterogeneous blend of northern Cameroonians, Nigerians and Chadians. Traditional *saré* buildings – quite common until the 1960s – have given way to cement homes with tin roofs, and the centre of town is dotted with modern blocks. Growth has brought increased facilities – banks, hotels and tourist information – making Garoua a convenient springboard for the far north.

Some history

Fali and Bata people were the first to settle along the banks of the Bénoué, in the eighteenth century. They were followed by **Kilba Fula** – herders who came in the early nineteenth century. After dan Fodio's jihad (see p.1206), the Fula built a fortification (*ribadou*) around the town they called Ribadou-Garoua, to stave off Fali invasions. Other Muslims – Hausa, Bornu and Shua Arabs – arrived in the second half of the nineteenth century, lending an early urbanism to the settlement. The present **lamidat** dates from 1839.

The **Germans** colonized Garoua in 1901 and set up a small port (British steamers from the Niger Company had been trading in ivory, salt and cloth since 1890). Enlarged in 1930, the port served as a vital link between Cameroon, Chad and Nigeria, even though it has only ever been able to function during the rainy season from mid-July to mid-October. As a result, Garoua became an important focus of international attention in Cameroon, and has always had a large expat community.

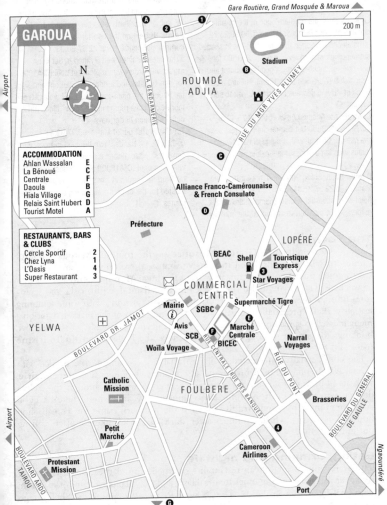

Gare Routière, Grand Mosquée & Maroua

GAROUA

0   200 m

Airport

N

ROUMDÉ ADJIA

Stadium

RUE DE LA GENDARMERIE

RUE DU MGR YVES PLUMEY

ACCOMMODATION
Ahlan Wassalan	E
La Bénoué	C
Centrale	F
Daoula	B
Hiala Village	G
Relais Saint Hubert	D
Tourist Motel	A

RESTAURANTS, BARS & CLUBS
Cercle Sportif	2
Chez Lyna	1
L'Oasis	4
Super Restaurant	3

Alliance Franco-Camérounaise & French Consulate

Préfecture

LOPÉRÉ

BEAC   Shell   Touristique Express

Star Voyages

COMMERCIAL CENTRE

Mairie   SGBC   Supermarché Tigre

YELWA

Avis   Marché Centrale

SCB   BICEC   Narral Voyages

Woïla Voyage

BOULEVARD DR. JAMOT

RUE CENTRALE-RUE DES BANQUES

RUE DU PONT

Catholic Mission

FOULBERE

Brasseries

BOULEVARD DU GÉNÉRAL DE GAULLE

Petit Marché

Cameroon Airlines

BOULEVARD ARDO TAMOU

Protestant Mission

Port

Airport

Ngaoundéré

After independence, the roads were improved, and investment increased in cotton, the regional cash crop, and related industries. In time, these were joined by a brewery and soap works. After some time in the bush, Garoua feels very much like the modern world again.

Accommodation

For a city this size, there are surprisingly few **hotels**, but there is some accommodation in all price ranges, including a couple of very comfortable international hotels. If you've just arrived from cool Ngaoundéré, the hot climate will have you gasping for air conditioning.

Ahlan Wassalan rue de la Gendarmerie, in the heart of the commercial centre ☏ 99.95.41.04. This small, friendly *auberge* near the main *agences de voyages* has a few hot, box-like rooms, some s/c. No alcohol. ❶

La Bénoué on the northern edge of the commercial centre, after *Relais St Hubert* ☏ 99.99.25.72 ✉ hotelbenoue@yahoo.fr. Aging but okay, in shaded surroundings with an inviting pool (CFA1500 for non-guests), tennis courts, a good restaurant and a nightclub (Wed–Sun from 10pm). The a/c rooms come in varying degrees of disrepair. Ask to see several. ❺

Centrale rue Adamou Amar ☏ 99.90.75.72 or 55.77.06.95. Basic but central *auberge*, just behind the Marché Central, with a range of twenty-odd rooms with fan or a/c, some s/c, and no two rooms alike. ❷

Daoula rte du Stade Omnisport, not far from the stadium ☏ 22.27.27.84 or 77.75.73.30. Friendly hotel with motel-like a/c s/c rooms encircling a garden, and a pleasant restaurant at the front. ❸

Hiala Village rue Boumaré in front of Cinéma Le Bénoué (formerly the Cinéma Étoile) ☏ 22.27.24.07. Centrally located near the port, this friendly and well-maintained *auberge* has small but clean s/c rooms (a/c or fan), some with TV, and an excellent-value bar-restaurant. ❷

Relais Hubert on the northern edge of the commercial centre ☏/℻ 22.27.30.33 ✉ hotelrelaissainthubert@yahoo.fr. Set in an attractive garden with a pleasant pool (CFA1000 for non-guests) and a decent restaurant and bar, though the once-luxurious a/c *boukarous* or more expensive rooms in the "new" block have definitely seen better days. ❹

Tourist Motel bd 20 Mai ☏ 99.97.92.41 ℻ 227.32.44. Hands down the best in town, with comfortable a/c rooms, a good restaurant and a very nice pool (CFA1000 for non-guests). A little far from the centre of town, but conveniently located for the airport – assuming there are any planes. ❻

The Town

Besides the monumental **Grande Mosquée** on the route de Maroua – one of Cameroon's largest, but closed to non-Muslims – there's nothing around town worth going out of your way for, apart from the huge **Marché Central**, at its best at weekends. Here you'll also find the **Centre Artisanal**, with masks and sculptures (though they tend towards airport-art anonymity) along with some tempting leatherwork. Be prepared to bargain vigorously. Just north of the market, traditional medicine-sellers spread out their wares under the neem trees, while across the street, bookings for game-park lodgings can be made at the **Délégation du Tourisme** (Mon–Fri 8am–3.30pm; ☏ 22.27.22.90 ℻ 22.27.13.64).

The commercial centre includes, all the usual suspects among the **banks**, with several **ATMs**, plus the **post office**, and administrative buildings such as the **mairie**, with its obligatory fountain. It's more interesting to wander through the **Yelwa** district, where the **Petit Marché** keeps things lively and where there's a good concentration of bars and **circuits** (*circuit* is the northern name for a small chop house). The energy, which continues **after dark**, makes it a likeable place to hang out in the evening.

Eating, drinking and nightlife

There are quite a few cheap restaurants grouped around the central cluster of *agences de voyage*, all serving omelette breakfasts, and rice, plantains, yams or macaroni with beef sauce later in the day. The ♨ *Super Restaurant*, opposite the Shell garage, serves the same sort of hunger-stoppers, but with freshly blended fruit juices and outstanding salads it's a couple of notches above the rest. Popular bar-restaurants include the *Cercle Sportif* and *Chez Lyna*, on the northern side of the Roumdé Adjia *quartier*. The beer is very reasonably priced, and both serve decent food for about CFA2000 a plate. There are cheap snacks aplenty in the *circuits* and food stalls around the animated Petit Marché. For something a bit more upmarket, *L'Oasis*, near the port, does excellent fish and steak. Best of the bunch among the hotel restaurants is the *Tourist Motel*, while *Hiala Village* is probably the best value. If you're pining for tastes from home, various **imported foods** are sold at the Supermarché Tigre near the Marché Central. And if you're looking for somewhere to **dance**, head for the nightclub at the *Hôtel Bénoué*. For **live music** check out what's on at the Alliance Franco-Camerounaise.

Lake Lagdo

About 50km south of Garoua at the town of **NGONG** is the German-run *Lagon Blue* resort, set on the beautiful Lac Lagdo (℡99.53.53.53 ❹). This is one of the most tranquil hotels in Cameroon, with a choice of *boukarous* (fan or a/c), all with terraces overlooking the picturesque lake and colourful gardens. The lakeside beach is delightful, although there's no guarantee that the waters are completely bilharzia-free. There's also a good bar-restaurant, and if you come during the week, chances are you'll have the entire place to yourself.

Maroua

One of Cameroon's few pre-colonial cities, **MAROUA** already had a population of some 25,000 when French administrators took their first census in 1916, and four times that number lived within 20km of the town. It's now the north's second-largest city, with some 300,000 inhabitants. It has retained a much more traditional flavour than Garoua, with old neighbourhoods spread out on both banks of the **Mayo Kaliao River** (a dry expanse of sand for half the year) and crisscrossed with streets shaded by sweet-smelling neem trees.

The best way to shuttle between sites in town is on the back of a **moto** (CFA150); they're quicker and easier to flag down than shared or private taxis and easily identified with their numbered, yellow bibs. From the main market, a broad avenue leads several hundred metres southeast to the Founangué Bridge (also known as Pont Vert), while Avenue du Kakataré stretches southwest nearly 2km past the Lamido's Palace to the very colonial **post office**. From the post office roundabout, the road heading

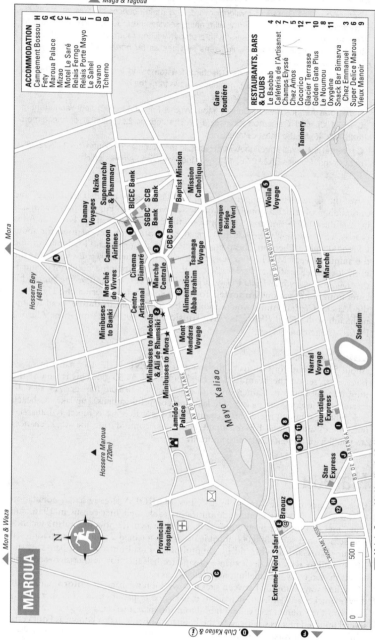

MAROUA

ACCOMMODATION
Campement Bossou H
Fety G
Maroua Palace A
Mizao C
Motel Le Saré F
Relais Ferngo J
Relais Porte Mayo E
Le Sahel I
Savano D
Tcherno B

RESTAURANTS, BARS & CLUBS
Le Baobab 4
Cafétéria de l'Artisanat 2
Champs Elyssé 7
Chez Amos 5
Cocorico 12
Glacier Terrasse 1
Golden Gate Plus 10
Le Noumou 8
Oxygène 11
Snack Bar Bimarva 3
Chez Emmanuel 6
Super Delice Maroua 9
Vieux Manoir

Maga & Yagoua

Mora

Mora & Waza

Mokolo, Garoua, Meskine Hospital & Airport

Hossere Bey (481m)

Hossere Maroua (720m)

Provincial Hospital

Gare Routière

Tannery

Mayo Kaliao

Stadium

Lamido's Palace

AV DU LAMIDO

AV DU KAKATARE

BD DE DIRENGAL

BD DU RENOUVEAU

CANON NE ASSO

Extrême-Nord Safari

Star Express

Touristique Express

Narral Voyage

Petit Marché

Foungangue Bridge (Pont Vert)

Mont Mandara Voyage

Tsanaga Voyage

Alimentation Abba Ibrahim

Marché Centrale

CBC Bank

SGBC Bank

SCB Bank

BICEC Bank

Baptist Mission

Mission Catholique

Cameroon Airlines

Cinema Diamaré

Marché de Vivres

Centre Artisanal

Damay Voyages

Nziko Supermarché & Pharmacy

Minibuses to Banki

Minibuses to Mokola & Ali de Rhumsiki

Minibuses to Mora

N

500 m

0, Club Kaliao & i

Club Kaliao & i

uphill to the northwest takes you to the **hospital**. The new **tourist office**, the Syndicat d'Initiative du Tourisme (Mon–Fri 9am–noon & 2–5pm; ☎99.85.50.47), which is setting up a guides service for Maroua, is reached by crossing the bridge and heading on a further 2km southwest.

Accommodation

Most of Maroua's **inexpensive auberges** can be found on the south side of the river near the stadium. **Upmarket hotels** are in the west, near the river and the Kaygama district. Most hotels charge CFA1500 for non-guests to use their pools, though the *Sahel* only charges CFA800.

Campement Bossou off bd de Diarenga, south of the river. Six basic *boukarous* in a quiet location with fans, cold s/c showers and shared toilets. Popular with budget travellers. ❶

Fety bd de Diarenga next to Narral Voyages ☎66.10.33.06. Welcoming small place with bright, clean s/c rooms with a/c and hot water, and, for a little extra, also TV. Small bar and good-value restaurant ideal for the bus – they'll call you when it's ready to leave. ❷

Maroua Palace qtr Djoudandou, 1km north of the centre ☎22.29.32.52 ☎22.29.15.25. International-class government-run hotel rising from the base of the Hosséré Bey hills where the Germans first planted their flag. Spacious a/c rooms with hot water and TV, pool and good restaurant. ❹

Mizao north of the river, behind the hospital ☎99.83.26.09. Former *Novotel*, hence the 1970s retro look (refurbishment imminent). The a/c rooms come with TV and hot water, and the restaurant offers a menu at CFA6000. Tennis courts and pool. ❹

Motel Le Saré south of the river towards the tourist office ☎77.22.18.98 or 99.02.90.91 ✉hotellesare@yahoo.fr. As spacious as the *Mizao*, but more likeable, in a large shaded garden with a small zoo (ostriches, monkeys, goats…), an inviting pool and a good restaurant. The pleasant s/c, motel-like rooms all come with private terraces, a/c and hot water. ❹

Procure Catholic Maroua south of the river, off bd de Diarenga ☎99.20.48.53 (canteen closed Sun). Catholic mission guesthouse in a large leafy compound that includes a school and church. Rooms are basic but tidy, all sharing facilities.

There's also a good canteen open throughout the day. ❷

Relais Ferngo off bd de Diarenga, south of the river. A peaceful, airy compound housing basic, run-down s/c *boukarous* with fans, and a quiet corner reserved for camping (CFA1000 per person) with a shower/toilet block. ❷

🏃 **Relais Porte Mayo** near the river ☎22.29.26.92 or 99.84.14.77 ✉portemayo@braouz.net. The town's best mid-range place, with comfortable s/c a/c *boukarous* in a garden setting, plus a pleasant courtyard restaurant, shops and a steady stream of crafts vendors. Popular expat rendezvous and a good place to seek information, hire vehicles or arrange tours. ❹

Le Sahel bd de Diarenga, next to Touristique Express ☎22.29.29.60. Modern hotel with good-sized, clean a/c rooms with hot water and TV. As well as friendly staff, assets are a good restaurant (CFA6000 for a three-course menu), a small but nice pool and fast Internet. ❸

Savano south of the river past the tourist office ☎22.29.22.55 or 77.32.84.24 ✉hotelsavano @hotmail.com. New hotel occupying three buildings around a junction in a quiet residential neighbourhood, with a range of smart, tidy s/c rooms with a/c, fan, hot water and TV. There's also a good-value bar-restaurant. Popular with Chadian business travellers. ❸

Tcherno across from the Central Market, next to Alimentation Abba Ibrahim ☎99.52.78.97 or 99.81.82.55. Grey multistorey hotel with basic s/c rooms (fan or a/c), TV and hot showers, plus an inexpensive restaurant and bar with street terrace. ❷

The markets

The **centre artisanal**, near the main market, is a large craft market with innumerable stands. The emphasis is on the locally made **leather goods** for which Maroua is famous (sandals, bags, round floor cushions) but there are goods from throughout Central and West Africa as well. Jewellery and hand-woven cloth can be good value here, but bargain astutely and take your time choosing;

there's a vast selection. If you can overcome the smell, the **tannery**, to the southeast of town on the road to **MINDIF** (CFA1000 for an obligatory guide), is another interesting place to visit.

Maroua's large **market** spreads out behind the Centre Artisanal. Although it's held daily, the busiest market day is Monday, when **Kirdi** ("pagan") peoples come from all over the region to trade. Everything from car parts and Japanese electrical goods to locally made cloth and traditional medicines is sold here. Just north of the market, the **Marché de Vivres** sells fresh produce.

Eating and drinking

Maroua offers a good range of **eating places**, from inexpensive *circuits* to the more formal restaurants of the big hotels. **L'Avion Me Laisse**, a street close to the western end of Boulevard du Renouveau, has a collection of small but lively bars where you can eat grilled fish. The street was named by the first woman who started a business there – after her German boyfriend had left her. A number of cheap restaurants also cluster around the *centre artisanal*. The greatest concentration of **bars** and **clubs** is along Boulevard du Renouveau; better ones include the *Golden Gate Plus*, *Champs Elysées*, *Vieux Manoir* and *Oxygène*, which has a smart little disco. For **live music**, *Cocoriko* hosts Cameroonian blues bands nightly except Mondays.

Le Baobab east of the market, across the street from the CBC Bank ☎77.56.64.50. Good Cameroonian dishes, like chicken in groundnut sauce (CFA2800) and a good-value three-course menu (CFA4000), served in thatched *boukarous*.
Cafétéria de l'Artisanat directly opposite the Centre Artisanal. Ice-cold yoghurt, and meals for around CFA1000 a plate.
Chez Amos at the eastern end of bd du Renouveau, next to Woila Voyages. Small place serving delicious vegetarian food as well as yoghurt and fresh juices.
Glacier Terrasse east of the market, by Cameroon Airlines. A likeable place where you can sit outside in the peaceful courtyard and eat fresh salads and well-made mains (CFA2000) washed down with excellent, fresh juice.
Le Noumou at the western end of bd du Renouveau, near some of the town's best

nightlife spots. A new place, under the same management as *l'Artisanat*, serving roughly the same good menu but in nicer, peaceful surroundings.
Relais Porte Mayo at the same-named hotel, near the river. Popular place with a good and varied menu, including Vietnamese specialities, which fills nightly with a lively expat crowd. Mains CFA4000–5000.
Snack Bar Bimarva Chez Emmanuel next to the old CDG supermarket building, just east of the market. A popular, moderately-priced snack bar with a good range of offerings, cold beer and satellite-TV news.
Super Delice Maroua near the Relais Porte Mayo end of bd du Renouveau. A small, busy restaurant with indoor and outdoor seating, serving well-prepared *ndolé* and *brochette* de capitaine at very reasonable prices.

Listings

Banks There are ATMs at SGBC and SCB, at the western end of the market. They, and BICEC, change euros (cash and traveller's cheques). To change US dollars cash go to Alimentation Abba Ibrahim (see "Supermarkets").
Car rental and tour organizers Maroua's three most professional and reliable setups are the Swiss-run Fagus Voyages (☎99.86.18.71 Ⓦwww.fagusvoyages.com), the agency at the *Relais Porte Mayo* hotel, and Extrême-Nord Safari (☎99.98.73.91 Ⓔdeli_teri@yahoo.fr), next door. They all offer reliable 4x4s with driver from around

CFA50,000 per day excluding fuel.
Hospitals CNPS Hospital ☎22.29.12.74 or 22.29.12.71; Hôpital Meskine ☎22.29.25.79.
Internet The two best places with fast connections are Braouz, around the corner from *Relais Porte Mayo* (Mon–Sat 9am–10pm, Sun 10am–6pm) and the cybercafé at *Hôtel Le Sahel*.
Supermarkets Best places to stock up on supplies are Nziko, opposite Cameroon Airlines, and Alimentation Abba Ibrahim next to *Hôtel Tcherno*. The latter may also change money.

Agences de voyage

If you're heading south to **Garoua** and **Ngaoundéré**, use one of the *agences*. Touristique Express is best, with regular timetabled departures in large comfortable coaches (they also sell Camrail train tickets to **Yaoundé**, though not first-class sleeper tickets). Touristique also has regular departures to **Kousséri**.

Narral has services to **Moubi** in Nigeria and major towns en route to **Garoua**, such as **Guider** and **Fingil** on the Chadian border.

Star Express, off boulevard du Renouveau, has regular services to **Garoua**, plus **Mora**, **Yagua**, **Kaele**, **Guidiguis** and **Toloum**.

Mont Mandara Voyages, just off avenue du Kakataré, has minibuses for **Mora** throughout the day, as well as regular services to **Kousséri**, and to **Banki** on the Nigerian border. Tsanaga Voyages, near the market, has regular departures for **Mokolo**.

Gare routières and clandos

There are two main **gares routières**: the one east of the Founangué Bridge has regular transport to destinations throughout the north, as far as **Kousséri** (for Chad; see p.1337), while the one at the southern end of boulevard de Diarenga past the *Procure Catholic*, has minibuses for **Mokolo**.

In the centre, on a corner of avenue du Kakataré, *clando* minibuses leave for **Mora** when full; *clandos* for **Banki** leave from the corner two streets north; while Ali de Rhumsiki has rickety minibuses for **Roumsiki** at noon on Monday, Wednesday and Fri. Travelling to **Roumsiki by moto** will set you back CFA3500.

Flights

Cameroon Airlines (☏22.29.15.15) has suspended flights to Maroua. Call the airport (☏22.29.10.21) for current flight information.

Mokolo, Mora and the Mandara Mountains

Beautiful and haunting, the denuded volcanic plugs of the **Mandara Mountains** rise up to the west of Maroua like stony brown fingers. They form the backdrop to some of the country's most fascinating and desolate scenery, and are home to communities who have come to be known as the "mountain people" – staunch non-Muslims who were pushed to the extremities of the inhabitable areas during the Muslim wars of the nineteenth century. Today, the region highlights Cameroon's most striking contrasts in the cultural diversity of Kirdi, Fula and Shua Arabs from the far north. In its ethnolinguistic complexity, highland setting and stone buildings – as well as the rise of organized adventure tourism – the Mokolo district bears superficial similarities to the Dogon country in Mali.

Crédit du Sahel in Mokolo is the only **bank** in the Mokolo area that changes money, and only cash euros, so you'll be better off changing money in Maroua. The only pumped **fuel** available in the district is from filling stations in Mokolo and Mora.

Mokolo and around

The main point of entry to the region, **MOKOLO** is the capital of the **Mafa** people (also called Matakam by the Fula) – one of the most populous groups in the mountains. Mokolo is a quiet, spread-out town with a small, modern trading centre (market day Wed), a motor park and not much else. You can **stay** at the expensive *Campement du Flamboyant*, which has a/c *boukarous* – some with hot water – a restaurant and bar (☎22.29.55.85 ❸), and where you may be able to camp in the compound. There's also the new modern *SunSet* (❸) next to the Crédit du Sahel bank, with bright a/c rooms with hot water. Cheaper rooms are found at the *Dza Mokolo Bar*, off the Maroua road to the right as you enter Mokolo (☎22.29.54.46 ❷); however, they don't serve any food. For **meals**, your best bet is the *Café Tout* at the Carrefour Elysée, run by an award-winning women's co-op who prepare excellent meals throughout the day.

The **Centre Artisanal** in the village of **DJINGLIYA**, 15km from Mokolo along the difficult road to Mora, has a few rooms (❶) and a restaurant and bar. They sell excellent basketwork at fixed, rock-bottom prices.

For an off-beat introduction to local culture stop off at the **Musée Malima** in the village of **GOURIA** 30km from Mokolo on the road to Roumsiki (ⓦwww.malima-project.org; CFA1000) with photos of local customs – weddings, funerals etc – on display alongside local artefacts that have been donated to the museum for safekeeping by the people of Gouria. If the museum is shut, a key is kept at the shop on the corner.

Exploring the district

There are numerous villages in the mountains where, if you go with a guide, you can stay in people's homes for a small fee. A guide should charge about CFA5000 per day, and if you manage to find a donkey not working in the fields or carrying water, you can hire it with its owner to carry your luggage for CFA10,000 a day. If you're here on a Thursday, head for the isolated mountain village of **TOUROU** – two days on foot, a couple of hours by *moto*, northwest of Mokolo and close to the Nigerian border – and witness the unusual sight of calabash-capped women milling around the weekly market selling traditional beer from their clay pots. As elsewhere in the region, people here are used to tourists, so be prepared to pay to take photos.

It's also possible to explore the area on **horseback**; Fagus Voyages in Maroua (see p.1332) run good tours, but you need to arrange everything well in advance. On the highest paths you can safely cross undetected and unmolested into Nigerian territory (see p.1214), but you should be wary of going further into Nigeria without making a formal exit from Cameroon.

Roumsiki

A brief visit to **ROUMSIKI**, 50km southwest of Mokolo, is very much a standard item on Cameroon's tourist circuit. It's a small and fairly ordinary village in itself, but wherever you look, the scenery is breathtaking. Roumsiki lies deep in the mountains, surrounded by magnificent time-worn peaks, the highest of which is much-photographed **Zivi**. Houses built of local stone in the traditional style blend in with the gothic backdrop, their colours changing shades from ochre and orange to umber and russet as the sun moves over the horizon.

The appeal of the visit is in theory to get a taste of the "real" Cameroon, and the built-in flaw is that the more people come, the more distorted and unreal life in Roumsiki becomes. You have no other option when arriving here than to allow the young men who greet you to act as your guides (unless you brought a paid companion with you or you brush straight past them and head for one of the hotels – all of which arrange guided trips in the area). The guides follow their own rigid programme in showing you what they imagine every tourist wants to see. There's no point resisting their help and trying to explore the village on your own; you'll just be made to feel like an unwelcome voyeur. So let the boys show you the **féticheur**, who tells your future by watching the way river crabs move pieces of wood; the **weavers**, who make cloth by hand; the **potters** and the **blacksmiths**. The guides also explain how the huts are constructed and the best of them will give you an interesting account of local customs and history. The people of Roumsiki are called **Margui**, or **Kapsikis** – "those who have grown tall". In the evening, your guides even accompany you to a nearby peak to get a better view of the sunset. Your every question, in fact, is answered before you ask it. It's all quite interesting on a superficial level, but it's about as personal as watching a television documentary. The bottom line is definitely money, and you'll just have to accept that (bring lots of small change). For **longer treks** into the mountains – up to a couple of days – your best bet is to head for one of the hotels. All offer pre-planned tours at a cost of anything between CFA7500 and CFA12,500 per day, all-inclusive. If you opt to ride, hiring a horse and tack costs around CFA3000 per hour.

There is an ever-increasing number of good **places to stay** in the village. The best of the lot is the 🏚 *Campement de Rhumsiki*, on the right as you enter town from Mokolo, with s/c a/c *boukarous* with hot water, breathtaking mountain views from the pool terrace, and an outstanding restaurant (☏22.29.11.65 ❹). Also good is the *Maison de l'Amitié* with stylish and spacious s/c a/c *boukarous* and a pleasant outdoor restaurant (call Lara Voyages in Maroua for booking ☏22.29.21.13 ❹). Less-expensive options include *Tour d'Argent*, which is primarily a good restaurant, with a few basic s/c rooms at the back (☏77.40.12.69; rooms with fan ❷ or a/c ❸), and *Auberge Le Kapsiki*, aka *La Casserole*, with s/c fanned rooms, plus a bar and restaurant overlooking the town centre (aka *La Casserole* ❷), whose friendly English-speaking proprietor used to guide overlanders through the Dogon country in Mali.

For **food**, the *Kirdi* at the town entrance has earned something of a reputation for its excellent pizzas and fresh home-made millet bread. *Baobab* at the other end of town does lovely couscous and *folleré*, and has a small stage and dance floor.

Mora and around

On market days (Wed in Mokolo and Sun in Mora) you can get a share taxi from Mokolo to **MORA** via **KOZA** – a *piste* that cuts through the heart of the **Mafa and Podoko country**, including Oudjilla (see overleaf). Even on these days, you will have to leave Mora very early in the afternoon to get back to Mokolo with the last taxi. On other days, you'll probably have to go by the less scenic but faster route that passes through Maroua. Mora is the last stop en route to **BANKI** on the Nigerian border, and an excellent spot to have your last cold beer before facing *sharia* rule in Borno State next door.

Capital of the **Wandala** (also called Mandara) – a people who accepted Islam in the late seventeenth century after their contact with the Bornu Empire – Mora is especially known for a **market** which attracts a wide range of peoples from throughout the region. Muslim Fula, Wandala and Shua women sell their goods alongside the traditionalist mountain people – **Podoko**, **Guizica** and **Mofou** – who retain their own firm views on suitable dress and headgear. It's a colourful mixture of cultures, and the market produce ranges from goat's milk to mangoes and millet. Donkeys and goats are sold in the **animal market**, and you'll also find jewellery and carved calabashes. If you've got time to spare, and fancy a little exercise, a half-day trek up the Mora Massif brings you to an interesting site from **World War I**. When war broke out, the German soldiers at Kousséri were blissfully unaware of events taking place in Europe. Upon being attacked by French and British soldiers the company fled to a small outpost above Mora and defended themselves until long after Germany had surrendered. There's a grave up here for a fallen British soldier, and the views are stupendous. You'll need a guide: the hotels listed below can help.

The best **accommodation** is at the *Auberge Mora Massif* (rooms with fan ❶ or a/c ❷), located in a tranquil part of town, clearly signposted a few blocks east of the motor park; turn right at the communal water pump. The s/c rooms, with fan or a/c, are kept clean by attentive staff, and the bar-restaurant serves meals (if you order well in advance) and cold drinks. The slightly cheaper *Campement Sanga de Podoko* (rooms with fan ❶ or a/c ❷), off the main road to Maroua, offers s/c *boukarous* with fans or a/c and a good bar-restaurant (again, order food well in advance).

Oudjilla

Mora is the departure point for the eleven-kilometre trip to the village of **OUDJILLA** in the mountains (midway between Mora and Mokolo), a spot which, like Roumsiki, has become a magnet for tourism. You can barely set foot in Mora without a posse of gushing teenagers racing up to you on motorbikes and asking, "Mistah, tu vas où, à Oudjilla?"

Oudjilla is an authentic **Podoko village**, though once again your experience there may seem a bit contrived. You're led on arrival to the *saré* of the chief, who lives in a walled compound encompassing a maze of roofed passageways which connect the many huts housing his fifty-plus wives and countless children. For a negotiable price, you get to visit the chief's compound and see the hut that serves for public deliberations; another where the chief's father is buried and where jugs of millet beer are stored; and the sacrificial pen where the chosen cow awaits slaughter during the harvest festival. You're taken into the hut of one of the wives to see the kitchen and the utensils used for pounding millet, storing water and so on.

At the end, you're "invited" to take photos of the chief and some of his wives with shaved heads and bare breasts. For just a little more money, the wives might even do a harvest dance. It may give you wonderful photos, but, at the same time, is liable to leave you feeling rather empty. To get beyond the performance would take more time and dedication than most people have, but there's nothing to stop you putting your feelings back in balance by exploring some of the other roads in this region; or by saying, "Non, merci, Oudjilla ne m'intéresse pas, mais pourrais-tu me diriger à…?" (then picking a small name from the map).

Waza National Park

With a minimum of vegetation cover, **Waza National Park** (open all year; fees per day: entrance CFA5000, obligatory guide CFA3000, camera CFA2000, vehicle CFA2000) spreads over 1700 square – and flat – kilometres of acacia-dotted grassland and seasonal marsh. For decades it has been considered one of the best sites for savannah game-viewing in West Africa and is also excellent for **bird-watching**, with specialities including the Sennar Penduline-tit and quail-plover.

Since Waza is the most popular of the game parks, it's also the one you have the best chance of hitching into, though chances of catching a ride are still pretty slim. Your only other option, if you don't have your own transport, is to hire a 4x4 in Maroua. The main park entrance, just outside the small town of **WAZA**, is marked by two crumbling Mousgoum huts. Pay your fees here, before heading to the nearby *Campement de Waza* (☎55.09.86.50 ❸), which you should book in advance. Set on a hill, this excellent camp offers a range of a/c *boukarous* equipped with running water and electricity and grouped around a clean pool (CFA4000 for non-guests). Expect to pay about CFA6000 for meals at the restaurant, which has a splendid panorama of the surrounding park. Alternatively, the hot and basic *Centre d'Accueil* (❷), near the park entrance, has *boukarous* with mosquito nets and shared facilities. You can also camp here for CFA2500 per tent, and there's a restaurant which does Cameroonian and standard tourist food if ordered in advance (CFA2500). In Waza village itself, *Chez Madame Bamenda*, a bar-restaurant, has a limited number of boxlike rooms (❶).

Giraffe are quite plentiful here, and congregate near the gate. There's a substantial **elephant** population too, which, with luck, you should have no problem seeing: indeed they're notorious in the district outside the park for trampling crops during the summer floods. Your chances of finding **lions** are also pretty good. **Ostriches**

tend to be shy, but **antelopes** such as waterbuck and roan are often spotted. The throng of water birds at the end of the dry season, as the marshes recede, can be spectacular.

Mourla

"A place you do not mention at all but should is Mourla, near Pouss on the Chadian border northeast of Maroua. Fabulous torpedo-shaped houses hand-built of clay mixed with straw (referred to as "cases obus"), a disappearing traditional style"

Hilary Dennison, UK

Kousséri and the northern extremity

At the confluence of the **Logone** and **Chari** rivers, **KOUSSÉRI** lies directly opposite the capital of Chad – **Ndjamena**. The bridge and pirogues linking them are the main *raison d'être* for a town – the former **Fort-Foureau** – that would otherwise be right off the beaten track. Principal sites in town include the **port** and **market** where, not surprisingly, fish is the mainstay (market day is Thursday). There is an increasing number of **places to stay** in Kousséri. Best is *Relais du Logone* (☎22.29.46.97 ❸) on the banks of the Logone River, with great sunset panoramas of Ndjamena on the opposite bank, and a/c or fanned rooms in *boukarous*. *La Terrasse* (❷), in front of the Elf petrol station, is also good, with clean s/c rooms (fan or a/c) and a pretty, terraced restaurant. Crédit du Sahel is the only **bank** in Kousséri, and they sometimes change cash euros, but you may find it easier to use moneychangers at the market. A potholed tar road links Kousséri to Maroua. It is serviced by two *agences de voyage*: Touristique Express and Damay Voyages. Boats still provide an important link with **Ndjamena**, but

---

Leaving Cameroon

Chad
From Kousséri, you can enter Chad – directly into its capital, **Ndjamena** – across the bridge, which closes promptly at 6pm every day. Taxis across are cheap and frequent, but officials of both countries are notoriously corrupt here and routinely try to sting those crossing the border for several thousand CFA. The unstable situation in Chad, with refugees pouring into Cameroon, doesn't help. The hotel *Relais Porte Mayo* in Maroua is *au fait* with the latest news and runs an airport shuttle to Ndjamena airport.

Nigeria
If you're continuing into Nigeria, **Gamboru** is your entry point If you happen to be travelling direct from Ndjamena to Maiduguri in Nigeria, you need a free transit visa (*visa de passage*) to cross the 100km or so of Cameroonian territory from Kousséri to Gamboru.

Niger
Making for **Niger**, while circumventing Nigeria, there are no straightforward places to cross into Chad north of Ndjamena. There's a pirogue crossing and exit/entrance formalities at Blangoua (Cameroon) for Mani (Chad), but you have to be coming from Makari (the *piste* closer to the river is difficult most of the year). In short, there's no advantage in avoiding Ndjamena, where you can, a) find other travellers doing the same and b) meet travellers coming in the other direction, having arrived from Niger with the latest news.

the bridge across the Logone, 2km upstream from the centre of Kousséri, offers an easier crossing.

Northern villages and Lake Chad

In the small towns and villages along the route to **Lake Chad**, you're at the mercy of the local authorities (police or *lamidos*) as there are no formal accommodation facilities. It's usually possible to park or camp with permission more or less wherever you want, for a negotiable fee. The problem, if you want to get close to the lake itself, is that the elusive waters have receded well to the north of most settlements.

From Kousséri, take a share taxi to Makari, which has a market on Wednesdays, when transport is easiest to arrange. It's a scenic *piste* that follows the **Chari River**, then veers westward through desert landscapes to **MALTAM**, before heading north. Once in **MAKARI**, you may be able to get a share taxi on to **BLANGOUA** on the river, where you'll need to declare yourself to the police before continuing to the shore. Between July and October, the only months when the river isn't dry, you can charter a motorized pirogue for the hour-long journey to Lake Chad (around CFA5000). An alternative is to charter a **moto** – but this can prove expensive.

Downstream from Kousséri, the sultanate of **GOULFEY** makes an interesting detour. A scenic *piste* leads here from Maltam along the Chari River to a small settlement of mostly *banco* houses that seems right in the back-of-beyond. Visitors hardly ever make it this far – it's nothing like Oudjilla or Roumsiki – and the Sultan is very welcoming and will probably invite you to stay at his palace. There is also a newly opened **museum** that details the region's history. From Goulfey a dry-season *piste* leads to Makari, but note that the *piste* direct from Goulfey to Blangoua is impassable most of the year.

Kalamaloué National Park

Just outside Kousséri on the road to Maltam, you'll pass through the smallest and most recently created of Cameroon's northern reserves, the five-square-kilometre **Kalamaloué National Park**, which stretches along the road from Kousséri to Maltam. Pay your fees at the park gate in the village of Moroko (open all year; fees per day: entrance CFA5000, obligatory guide CFA3000, camera CFA2000, vehicle CFA2000) and you can take guided **walking tours** to see crocodiles, elephants (only Jan–May, then they head back to Waza) and hippos in the Chari River that borders the park. There's a *campement* in the park, but it hasn't been open for years (the closest accommodation is in Kousséri and Waza).

Afridisiac?

If you're planning a trip to Africa, or would just like to learn more about it, *Travel Africa* magazine is the ideal read for you.

Published in the UK four times a year, each edition comprises atleast 128 pages of travel ideas, practical information and features on Africa's attractions, wildlife and cultures.

The magazine is supported by an extensive website with our full back issue archive and a Safari Planner to help you plan your next adventure.

Explore Africa in your own home. Subscribe today.

www.travelafricamag.com

tel: +44 (0)1844 278883   subs@travelafricamag.com
fax: +44 (0)1844 278893   4 Rycote Lane Farm, Milton Common, OX9 2NZ, UK

The GAMBIA

The smiling coast of Africa

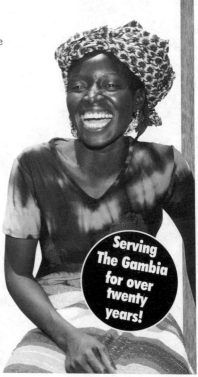

MANY HAPPY RETURNS

Fair Fares from
North South Travel

Return prices from*

Bangkok	**£275**	Kolkata	**£300**
Beijing	**£360**	Mumbai	**£287**
Delhi	**£237**	Nairobi	**£192**
Ho Chi Minh City	**£375**	New York	**£199**
Hong Kong	**£275**	Rio de Janiero	**£425**
Islamabad	**£302**	San Francisco	**£190**
Johannesburg	**£299**	Sydney	**£415**
Kathmandu	**£469**	Washington DC	**£185**

* all other European and long-haul destinations
available, taxes not included

For great air fares with all profits going to development, use North
South Travel. Call 01245 608 291 to speak to a real person or visit
www.northsouthtravel.co.uk
Free Rough Guide of your choice for every booking over £300
(quote "NI Rough Guide offer")

EVERY FLIGHT A FIGHT AGAINST POVERTY

Small print and

Index

A Rough Guide to Rough Guides

Published in 1982, the first Rough Guide – to Greece – was a student scheme that became a publishing phenomenon. Mark Ellingham, a recent graduate in English from Bristol University, had been travelling in Greece the previous summer and couldn't find the right guidebook. With a small group of friends he wrote his own guide, combining a highly contemporary, journalistic style with a thoroughly practical approach to travellers' needs.

The immediate success of the book spawned a series that rapidly covered dozens of destinations. And, in addition to impecunious backpackers, Rough Guides soon acquired a much broader and older readership that relished the guides' wit and inquisitiveness as much as their enthusiastic, critical approach and value-for-money ethos.

These days, Rough Guides include recommendations from shoestring to luxury and cover more than 200 destinations around the globe, including almost every country in the Americas and Europe, more than half of Africa and most of Asia and Australasia. Our ever-growing team of authors and photographers is spread all over the world, particularly in Europe, the USA and Australia.

In the early 1990s, Rough Guides branched out of travel, with the publication of Rough Guides to World Music, Classical Music and the Internet. All three have become benchmark titles in their fields, spearheading the publication of a wide range of books under the Rough Guide name.

Including the travel series, Rough Guides now number more than 350 titles, covering: phrasebooks, waterproof maps, music guides from Opera to Heavy Metal, reference works as diverse as Conspiracy Theories and Shakespeare, and popular culture books from iPods to Poker. Rough Guides also produce a series of more than 120 World Music CDs in partnership with World Music Network.

Visit www.roughguides.com to see our latest publications.

Rough Guide travel images are available for commercial licensing at www.roughguidespictures.com

SMALL PRINT

Rough Guide credits

Text editor: Richard Trillo
Layout: Pradeep Thapliyal
Cartography: Ashutosh Bharti
Picture editor: Mark Thomas
Production: Vicky Baldwin
Proofreader: Diane Margolis
Cover design: Chloë Roberts
Editorial: London Ruth Blackmore, Alison
Murchie, Karoline Thomas, Andy Turner, Keith
Drew, Edward Aves, Alice Park, Lucy White,
Jo Kirby, James Smart, Natasha Foges, Róisín
Cameron, Emma Traynor, Emma Gibbs, Kathryn
Lane, Christina Valhouli, Monica Woods, James
Rice, Mani Ramaswamy, Joe Staines, Peter
Buckley, Matthew Milton, Tracy Hopkins, Ruth
Tidball; **New York** Andrew Rosenberg, Steven
Horak, AnneLise Sorensen, April Isaacs, Ella
Steim, Anna Owens, Sean Mahoney, Courtney
Miller, Paula Nevdorf; **Delhi** Madhavi Singh,
Karen D'Souza
Design & Pictures: London Scott Stickland,
Dan May, Diana Jarvis, Nicole Newman, Sarah
Cummins, Emily Taylor; **Delhi** Umesh Aggarwal,

Ajay Verma, Jessica Subramanian, Ankur Guha,
Sachin Tanwar, Anita Singh, Nikhil Agarwal
Production: Rebecca Short
Cartography: London Maxine Repath, Ed
Wright, Katie Lloyd-Jones; **Delhi** Jai Prakash
Mishra, Rajesh Chhibber, Rajesh Mishra, Animesh
Pathak, Jasbir Sandhu, Karobi Gogoi, Amod
Singh, Alakananda Bhattacharya, Swati Handoo
Online: Narender Kumar, Rakesh Kumar,
Amit Verma, Rahul Kumar, Ganesh Sharma,
Debojit Borah, Saurabh Sati, Ravi Yadav
Marketing & Publicity: London Liz Statham,
Niki Hanmer, Louise Maher, Jess Carter, Vanessa
Godden, Vivienne Watton, Anna Paynton, Rachel
Sprackett, Libby Jellie; **New York** Geoff Colquitt,
Katy Ball; **Delhi** Ragini Govind
Manager India: Punita Singh
Reference Director: Andrew Lockett
Operations Manager: Helen Phillips
PA to Publishing Director: Nicola Henderson
Publishing Director: Martin Dunford
Commercial Manager: Gino Magnotta
Managing Director: John Duhigg

Publishing information

This fifth edition published June 2008 by
Rough Guides Ltd,
80 Strand, London WC2R 0RL
345 Hudson St, 4th Floor,
New York, NY 10014, USA
14 Local Shopping Centre, Panchsheel Park,
New Delhi 110017, India
Distributed by the Penguin Group
Penguin Books Ltd,
80 Strand, London WC2R 0RL
Penguin Group (USA)
375 Hudson Street, NY 10014, USA
Penguin Group (Australia)
250 Camberwell Road, Camberwell,
Victoria 3124, Australia
Penguin Books Canada Ltd,
10 Alcorn Avenue, Toronto, Ontario,
Canada M4V 1E4
Penguin Group (NZ)
67 Apollo Drive, Mairangi Bay, Auckland 1310,
New Zealand

Cover concept by Peter Dyer.
Typeset in Bembo and Helvetica to an original
design by Henry Iles.
Printed and bound in China
© Richard Trillo 2008

1376pp includes index
A catalogue record for this book is available from
the British Library
ISBN: 978-1-84353-850-9

1   3   5   7   9   8   6   4   2

Help us update

We've gone to a lot of effort to ensure that the
fifth edition of **The Rough Guide to West Africa**
is accurate and up to date. However, things
change –restaurants and hotels alter their prices
and standards; bad roads become impassable
or are occasionally surfaced; new wildlife
reserves are established; and travel conditions
fluctuate with the political climate. If you feel
we've got it wrong or left something out, we'd
like to know, and if you can remember the
address, phone, hours and price, so much the
better. We'll credit all contributions received and
send a copy of the next edition (or any other

Rough Guide if you prefer) for the best emails
or letters.

Please mark contributions "**West Africa
Update**" and send emails to ©mail
@roughguides.com and letters to Rough Guides,
80 Strand, London WC2R 0RL, or Rough Guides,
4th Floor, 345 Hudson St, New York, NY 10014.

Have your questions answered and tell others
about your trip at: ⓦ www.roughguides
.atinfopop.com.

Check for West African updates and make
comments at the author's blog: **http://
theroughguidetowestafrica.blogspot.com**.

Acknowledgements

The authors, **Richard Trillo** and **Jim Hudgens**, thank everyone at Rough Guides, and particularly **Jo Kirby** (editorial), **Mark Thomas** (picture research), **Pradeep Thapliyal** (design and layout), **Ashutosh Bharti** (cartography) and **Diane Margolis** (proofreading) for their unflagging support and assistance. Many thanks also to **Chloë Roberts** for a fine cover.

Jim thanks: Apou Gata Djima, Lisa Washington, Kairn Kleiman, Vijitha and Ndede Eyango, Anthony Mainer, Julia Bromhead, Gotzon Zaratiegi, Conerly Casey, Kendahl Radcliffe, Shirley Radcliffe, Luc and Fati Denesle, Belinda Sunnu and Elvis Nya Ndjenou.

Richard thanks: Mike Senanu and Paul Akanmori for guidance in Ghana; Sam Baddoo for a new impression of Old Accra; Jules Brown for excellent Ghana road-testing; Elsie Owusu and JustGhana for the Ghana trip; Alex Trillo, for essential guidance on West African football; Rose Skelton in Dakar for news and information; Jim Taylor of the 153 club for timely and informative emails; Andy Graham of hobotraveler.com for news, feedback and lateral thinking; and especially, as ever, Teresa, Phoebe, David and Alex for putting up with all the work.

Most of all, we thank all our tireless updaters, including **Henry Stedman** (Mali, Niger) and **Anita Ferruzi** (Sierra Leone) and:

Alan Duncan (Sierra Leone) thanks: Cecil Williams at the Sierra Leone Tourist Board and Aaron Kortenhaven.

Emma Gregg (The Gambia, Cape Verde) thanks, in The Gambia: Geri Mitchell, Maurice Phillips and all at the Safari Garden Hotel; Patrick Sothern and all at West African Tours; Lawrence Williams and James English of Makasutu; Clive Barlow of Birds of the Gambia; Stella Brewer-Marsden OBE and David Marsden; David Talfryn-Griffiths; Suelle Nachif; May Rooney of PRSP; Foday Trawally and Ann Rivington; and all at the Gambia Tourism Authority and the Ministry of Tourism. In Cape Verde: all at Barracuda Tours and Qualitur. And in the UK: Jenny Adams at Serenity Holidays; and Nathan Pope for unstinting support.

Kate Hawkings (Togo) thanks: several Peace Corps volunteers, particularly Jane Coleman, Laura Rishel, Karen Ramsey, Jon Lascher, Lindsay Hubert and Charlie Gillig; Nigel and Julia Tickner from the British School of Lomé; Lena and Guillaime Fourcaut and Joseph Creppy at L'Arbre des Voyages; Moussa Agouda in Dapaong; everybody at Le Galion Hotel, Lomé; and Jack Diffily at the US Embassy.

Hilary Heuler (Guinea) thanks: Ignacio Oliver-Cruz, Christopher Dalton, Molly Byrne, Robert Rogoyski and Amanda Breitbach.

Nana Luckham (Ghana, Benin) would like to thank, in the UK, Joanna Kirby and Richard Trillo at Rough Guides; in Benin: Pierre Godonou and Jean-Claude Gaye; in Ghana: Elizabeth Oforiwa Duodu, Awura Adjua Awuku-Yeboah, Ben Swift, Kobin Luckham, Patrick Smith, everyone at the Kumasi Tourist Board, Frank Ofosu and, most of all, Yaa Yeboah for her endless advice and support.

Lone Mouritsen (Cameroon) would like to thank: my three faithful travel companions – Mette, Nana and Debbie – who took it in turn to follow me to the remotest corners of the country. It was fun. I also want to thank Bruno, Samuel and Ferdinand for taking us safely up Mount Cameroon – or at least as far as our unfit bodies would go! Thank you too to Constance Njike in Douala for in-depth info about eating and nightlife, and to the Foyer du Marin for storing my ever-increasing pile of stuff. Thanks to Per Aarhaug at Elephant Camp for peace and entertainment; Francois Favager for his omnipresent good spirits and many, many contacts; Rudi Witt, Karim Miyal, Sarah McTavish and Wassa Patrick for the lowdown on music and cinema, and Susy King in Gouria for sharing her inspirational ideas. Also thank you to the guys at WWF, especially Tabe Tanjong, for helping out with information about the country's many national parks and reserves, and for making it possible for us to experience actual gorillas in the wild, one unforgettable hot morning in the rainforest.

Roger Norum (Mauritania, Senegal, Guinea) thanks: the patient and understanding Joanna Kirby and Richard Trillo for providing guidance through some of the toughest but most rewarding Rough Guide research and writing yet. On the ground, I'd have remained immobile and ignorant without several close friends: Nat Parker in St-Louis, who was a font of information and intelligence about Senegal; Keri Barber and Rick Valenzuela, who allowed me to hermit up and commiserate with them in Dakar for probably far too long; and Alessandra Pelizzeri in Nouakchott, who was a generous friend and knew everybody in town. Thanks also to the US Marines, Embassy and UN folks in Nouakchott for throwing such great parties, especially Brian, Josh, Sebastian, Joelle and Federico. In Nouadhibou, I was happy to have Sam, Moustapha and Lina Teffahi regale me with their insights into Mauritanian society. In Chinguetti, Sylvie at the Maure Bleu offered assistance and companionship across the sands of the Tagant, while in Atar I was grateful for the insight of Patrice at the Tivoujar. In Senegal, I thank Giulia Calcagnini, Babette and Thierry, Patrice at Tama Lodge and Paolo at Chez Paolo and, in Casamance, Giuliana, Frank and Ousmane. In Guinea, my utmost gratitude goes to Hilary Heuler, Barbara Zeugler, Marie-Paul and Hélène Filion – and their friends Lena, Charlotte, Olga and Nikhil – for saving me with first-rate generosity, hospitality and the 411 on everything Conakrien. Thanks also to Moustapha Diallo at the Ministry of Tourism, Jean Luc at the Novotel, Christine from Air France, who, despite a near crash landing, never stopped raging about the virtues of Guinea, and Marion Simon at Business Week for a memorable day at the market. Honourable mention for travel companions goes to the Early Anthropologists – Patrick Alexander, Lyle Kane and A'isha – without whom I'd probably be stuck on the A40 *en panne*. And finally special thanks to future president of Poland Ania Szatkowska, who faithfully, if at times reluctantly, trekked alongside me across dune, slum, isthmus and car park, enduring car accident, vitriolic argument, linguistic frustration and long walks on the beach.

Ross Velton (Guinea-Bissau, Burkina Faso) thanks: Gilles Develay, Marcel Kuehn and Richard Trillo.

Jeremy Weate and **Alex Hannaford** (Nigeria) thank: Maneesh Garg, Chief Muraína Oyelami of the Obatala Centre for Creative Arts in Iragbiji and Tola Olateru-Olagbegi at Bogobiri House hotel.

Readers' letters

Many thanks to the following **readers and correspondents**, whose letters and emails about the fourth edition were indispensable in guiding us on our research trips (for details on how to help us update this edition, see p.1347). And apologies if we've inadvertently omitted or misspelt anyone's name:

Michael Asher, Peter Ayim, Lema Bah, Alex Baneke, Emmanuel K. Bensah, Justice K. Boakye, Kathy Bright, Danny Briottet, Matt Brown, Sarah Brown, Adrian Carr, Giuliana Cossi, Christopher Cripps, Liesbeth and Mamou Daffé, Hilary Dennison, David Dixon, Miranda Dodd, Grégoire Douxchamps, Elvis Dwamena, Susanne Elsas, Igor Fabjan, John Falkner, Joelle Fichter, Britta Fluevog, Fai Foen, Rob Ford, Michael Franke, Chris Frean, Andy Graham, Trish Graham, Ben Guerard, Lenja Günther, Chris Hall, Paul Hammond, Gail Hopkins, Yuri Horowitz, Verina Ingram, Tom Ireland, Tansy Jefferies, Lukas Jonkers, Bruce Kennedy, Mike Kovalsky, Jon Lascher, Hilary Lawther, Jack Love, Jonas Ludvigsson, Helen Kilner-MacPhee, Sadie Rose Mank, James McCarthy, David McDannald, Matt McLaughlin, Peter Musa Mangong, Alys Mathers, Marieke van Meerten, Piers and Shirley Miller, Roger Moore, Angus Neil, Derik Olson, Sarah Peters, Miriam Phillips, Ken Preston-Mafham, Jutta Ratschinske, Alan and Margaret Reynolds, Allan and Margaret Rickman, Flavia Robin, Sara Rosen, Marta Sabbadini, Sophie Sarin, Beat Schilliger, Ken Shaw, Kayo Shiraishi, Ezra Simon, Martin Smith, David Somers, Carolyn Spice, Moritz Steiger, Laura Stevens, Judy Struys, Sara Stuart, Sharon Swyer, Tony Tabbal, April Thompson, Claudio Vitor Vaz, Peter Verney, Nigel Watt, Gina Wells, We Were Bikers, David Zeitlyn.

Photo credits

Index

Map entries are in colour.

Country key

(B) Benin..................949	(Gh) Ghana 783	(Ni) Niger.................1007
(BF) Burkina Faso......705	(Gui) Guinea.................. 559	(N) Nigeria...............1069
(C) Cameroon 1217	(GB) Guinea-Bissau...... 511	(S) Senegal 153
(CV) Cape Verde........431	(M) Mali......................... 321	(SL) Sierra Leone.......639
(Gam) The Gambia 263	(Mau) Mauritania............. 91	(T) Togo.....................883

A

Aba (N).........................1156
Aban Minkoo (C).........1311
Abanze (Gh)...................834
Abéné (S)......................260
Abéné and Kafountine
..............................260
Abeokuta (N)...............1133
Abomey (B)...................993
Abomey........................993
Abomey–Calavi (B).......983
Abong Mbang (C).......1317
Abono (Gh)...................862
Abuja (N) 1172–1178
Abuja...............1174–1175
accommodation 1173
airlines...........................1177
airport...........................1172
arrivals..........................1172
banks 1177
couriers 1177
cultural centres 1177
embassies 1177
Guara Falls 1173
history 1172
hotels 1173
information 1173
Internet 1177
Millennium Park 1173
nightlife.........................1177
post offices 1178
restaurants 1176
spa 1177
swimming pools.............1173
tourist office 1173
travel agents 1178
Usman Dam 1173
Zoo................................1173
Zuma Rock.....................1173
Abuko Reserve (Gam) ..306
Aburi (Gh)......................830
Abutia Kloe (Gh) 868
accommodation 54–57
Accra (Gh)............. 815–832
Accra..................816–817

accommodation 820–822
airlines............................. 828
airport............................. 818
arrivals............................. 818
banks 828
beaches........................... 825
bookshops 828
car rental 828
cinemas........................... 829
coffins.............................. 825
couriers 829
crafts............................... 824
cultural centres 829
embassies........................ 829
galleries........................... 824
history 815
hospitals.......................... 829
hotels 820–822
Internet............................ 829
Jamestown....................... 823
Kwame Nkrumah
   Memorial Park 823
markets............................ 824
National Museum............. 822
nightlife........................... 827
photos.............................. 829
post office 829
restaurants 826
shops 825, 829
swimming pools............... 829
telephones 829
tourist information............ 820
transport.......................... 819
travel agents 829
visa extensions 829
Western Union 829
Achada Fazendo (CV).... 473
Achada Furna (CV) 478
Ada Foah (Gh) 831
Adaklu, Mount (Gh)
.............................867, 868
Adamawa State (N) 1214
Aderbissinat (Ni) 1055
Adéta (T)........................929
adinkra cloth (Gh).........862
adire cloth (N) 1134
Adjarra (B).....................992
Ado-Awaiye (N)...........1140

Adomi Abra (T) 933
Adrar region (Mau)
.... 145–152
Adrar region and
north............................146
Afadjato, Mount (Gh) 870
Affiniam (S) 262
Afi Mountain Drill
   Ranch (N).................1168
Aflao (Gh)......................832
Agadez (Ni) 1058–1063
Agadez.......................1059
Agalak Range (Ni).......1066
Agbo Kopé (T) 933
Agbodrafo (T)................921
Ago (N).......................1138
Agou, Mont (T)..............929
Agoua, Mont (B) 996
Agrijit (Mau) 141
Aguégué (B)..................992
Agyam (Gh)...................851
Ahémè, Lac (B)..............989
Ahwiaa (Gh) 863
Ahyiresu Nature
   Reserve (Gh)..............830
AIDS 42, 72
Aïr Mountains (Ni).......1066
airlines to West
   Africa 21–23
Aiyanasi (Gh) 852
Akamkpa (N).................1167
Akassato (B) 983
Akjoujt (Mau)..................145
Akloa Falls (T)................932
Ako (C)........................1294
Akom II (C)..................1312
Akosombo (Gh) 865
Akwapim Ridge (Gh).....830
Akwidaa (Gh) 849
Alavanyo
   Abehenease (Gh).......870
Alcatraz, Île (Gui) 609
Aledjo (T) 937
Aledjo, Faille d' (T)........937

Readers' quotes

A walk on São Vicente (CV) 491
Air Kanté (T) 945
Ask the female shopkeepers (Gui) 638
By bus from Ouaga to Bobo (BF) 765
Cash not in hand (Gam) 303
Conakry live (Gui) 606
Cool address (N) 1202
Cycling in The Gambia (Gam) 314
Cycling on Sal (CV) 501
Dissenting voice (M) 385
Doing good in the pays Dogon (M) 415
Dune alert (N) 1204
Faranah's phone failure (Gui) 626
French exchanges (B) 986
Friendliest country on the continent (BF) 753
Fun with the Fundong Fon (C) 1292
Helping the police (Mau) 128
Hotel prices (Gh) 820
Jungle-hiking (Gui) 621
Just go ape (S) 220
Kumasi post office (Gh) 853
Lebanese citizens (Gam) 301
Lock your room (GB) 539
Mourla (C) 1337
Osogbo's brand of Nike (N) 1146
Over-rated? (Gh) 842
Paúl (CV) 495
Plastic wilderness (M) 422
Second impressions at the museum (S) 207
Sister food (T) 918
Sun and heat (CV) 508
TC's TCs (BF) 745
The ubiquitous machete (Gh) 876
Toubab Dialao (S) 219
Travel in comfort (T) 929
Trust the boatman (GB) 549
Warm tips (S) 242
Who are you with? (Ni) 1050
"Yovo" (B) 988
Yo-yo alcohol (Mau) 134
Zemi tips (B) 977

Aleg (Mau) 138
Aleheride (T) 937
Alfa Kouara (B) 1000
Alikalia (SL) 694
Almadies, Pointe
    des (S) 216
alms-giving 68
Alok (N) 1167
Amani (M) 415
Ambam (C) 1311
Amedzofe (Gh) 868
Amogjar Pass (Mau) 149
Ampenyi (Gh) 845
Anaburu (GB) 553

Aného (T) 923
Angoulá (M) 372
Aningeje (N) 1167
Ankasa Reserve (Gh) 851
Anomabo (Gh) 835, 836
Ansongo (M) 429
antibiotics 42
Aoudaghost (Mau) 142
Aoukar depression (Mau)
    141
Apam (Gh) 834
Arbre du Ténéré (Ni) 1067
Areia Branca (GB) 549
Arfanya (SL) 693

Argungu (N) 1209
Arli (BF) 750
Arli, Parc National d' (BF)
    .... 750, 1006
Arlit (Ni) 1063
Asafo companies (Gh) ... 836
Ashaiman (Gh) 831
Asikuma (Gh) 868
Assamakka (Ni) 1065
Assirik, Mont (S) 242
Assodé (Ni) 1066
Assomada (CV) 472
Assop Falls (N) 1181
Atakora Mountains (B)
    1002
Atakpamé (T) 930–932
Atakpamé 930
Atar (Mau) 145–149
Atar 148
Atebubu (Gh) 864
Atimpoku (Gh) 865
Atlantika Mountain
    Range (N) 1215
Awing, Lake (C) 1289
Axim (Gh) 835, 850
Ayorou (Ni) 430, 1046
Ayos (C) 1317
Ayoun el Atrous (Mau)
    142
Azougui (Mau) 148

B

Baboon Islands (Gam)
    317
Badou (T) 932
Bafang (C) 1283
Bafatá (GB) 244, 555
Bafatá 556
Bafilo (T) 937
Bafilo Falls (T) 938
Bafing, Parc National
    de (M) 374
Bafodia (SL) 693
Bafoulabé (M) 372
Bafoussam (C)... 1280–1282
Bafoussam 1280
Bafut (C) 1290
Baga (N) 1214
Baga Sola (Chad) 1214
Bagale (Gh) 882
Baia das Gatas,
    Boa Vista (CV) 509
Baia das Gatas,
    São Vicente (CV) 490
Baïla (S) 262
Bakau (Gam) 294

Bakel (S) 237
Baki Island (SL)............. 700
Bakingili (C) 1271
Baleya (Gui) 634
Baleyara (Ni) 1044
Bali (C)....................... 1289
Ballor (S) 238
Bamako (M) ... 358–369
Bamako, Central... 362
Bamako environs........ 359
Bamako: Hippodrome,
  Niaréla &
  Quinzambougou 366
accommodation 361
airlines............................. 368
airport............................. 368
arrivals....................359–360
banks 368
bookshops 368
botanical gardens 365
car rental 368
centre artisanal 364
cinemas.......................... 368
clubs 367
cultural centres 368
embassies....................... 368
Grand Mosquée 364
history 358
hotels 361
Internet........................... 368
maps 368
markets 364
museums 364
music venues 367
nightlife.......................... 367
Point G 365
post office 368
restaurants 365
supermarkets 368
swimming pools 369
telephones 368
tourist information........... 359
travel agents 369
visa extensions 369
zoo 365
Bamba (M)....399, 404, 419
Bambadinca (GB)
  ....554, 555
Bambara-Maoundé (M)
 418
Bambawo (SL).............. 702
Bambaya (Gui).............. 634
Bambui (C)................... 1295
Bamenda (C)............. 1168,
  1285–1289
Bamenda.................... 1286
Bamendjing, Lake (C)
 1295
Bamiléké country (C)
 1282
Bamoun empire (C) 1297
Bana, Col de (C).........1283
Banana Island (SL) 687

Banani (M) 415, 419
Banc d'Arguin, Parc
  National du (Mau) 126
Banda (C).................... 1325
Banda Nkwanta (Gh) 877
Banda-Karafaia (SL) 694
Bandia Reserve (S)....... 220
Bandiagara (M) 410
Bandio (Ni).................. 1045
Bandjoun (C)............... 1282
Banfora (BF) 772–774
Banfora 773
Bangangté (C) 1283
Bangem (C)................. 1278
Bani (BF)..................... 751
Banikoara (B) 1002
Banjul Area (Gam)
  288–305
Banjul 290–291
Banjul & the Kombo
  Peninsula 295
Banjul: the resorts and
  Serrekunda........ 298–299
accommodation 292,
  296–300
airlines............................. 303
airport............................. 303

Albert market 293
Arch............................. 22, 293
arrivals............................. 289
Bakau 294
banks 303
beaches........................... 300
Bijilo 294
Bijilo forest 301
bike rental 304
bird-watching 304, 307
bookshops 304
car rental 304
clubs 293, 301–303
crafts 304
cultural centres 304
dentists 304
embassies....................... 304
emergencies.................... 304
Fajara 294
hospitals.......................... 304
Internet........................... 304
Katchikali crocodile pool. 301
Kerr Serign 294
Kololi 294
Kotu................................ 294
Manjai Kunda 294
music lessons 305
National Museum............. 292
nightlife............. 293, 301–303
post office 305

Travel guidance

A walk along the Niger (Ni)................................. 1046
Advice for women travellers............................... 75
Big-city survival 65
Bribery... 67
Canoeing down the Niger (Gui).......................... 625
Dental care 42
Dialling codes.. 62
Exchange rates.. 47
Guides (M) 327
Hiring a guide in the Dogon country (M).............. 386
Insurance... 39
Massage in Wolof (S)... 231
Medicine bag... 44
Hiking, biking and related practicalities (Gui)....... 611
Organized trips (Gam) 271
Organizing a desert adventure (Ni)..................... 1060
Overlanding in West Africa................................. 25
Roadblocks (C).. 1230
"Rurally integrated" campements (S).................. 251
Street names in Bakau and Fajara (Gam) 294
Student cards.. 45
The Iron-ore Trains (Mau) 125
The Race of Hope (C)... 1269
The source of the Niger (Gui)............................. 634
Tipping (Gam).. 271
Travel and climate change 20
Vegetarian West Africa 59
Wolof food terms (S)..(167)
Work and study (S).. 159

restaurants 293, 301–303
Serrekunda........................ 294
shopping 304, 305
street names 294
telephones 305
tourist information............ 289
travel agents 305
visas extensions............... 305
Bankass (M)................... 416
Banki (N) 1213
banks in West Africa 47
Bansang (Gam)............. 319
Bao Bolon Wetland
  Reserve (Gam)........... 316
Baoulé River (M)........... 372
Baoura Bawa (Ni) 1049
Bare (Gh) 882
bargaining...................... 45
Barlaventos
  Islands (CV) 483–509
Baro (C) 1275
Baro (Gui) 623
Barombi Mbo,
  Lake (C) 1273
Barra (Gam) 311
Barril (CV) 497
Bassamba (T) 944
Bassar (T) 938
Bassari, Pays (S) 243
Basse (Gam)................. 319
Basse Casamance (S)
  244–262
Basse Casamance,
  Southern 254
Basse Casamance: the
  Campement Circuit ... 252
Basse Casamance, Parc
  National de (S)........... 259
Bassila (B)..................... 997
Bathurst (SL)................. 688
Batia (B)...................... 1005
Batoké (C).................. 1267
Batouri (C) 1319
Bauchi (N).................. 1182
Bawku (Gh).................. 881
BBC broadcasts............ 34
beer in West Africa ... 60–61
beggars in West Africa ... 68
Begnimato (M).............. 414
Bel Air (Gui) 609
Belo (C)...................... 1293
Belo Hills (N)................ 1112
BENIN 949–1006
Benin highlights........... 950
Benin............................ 952
  accommodation 957
  banks and exchange........ 956
  books 969
  cinema 959
  climate........................... 953
  costs 956

crafts 958
crime 959
currency 956
emergencies.................... 959
entertainment.................. 959
facts and figures 951
festivals 958
food and drink.................. 957
glossary........................... 970
health 955
history 960–967
information 955
Internet........................... 958
languages........................ 970
mail................................. 958
maps 955
media 955
music.................... 959, 968
national parks 959
opening hours 958
people 951
photography..................... 954
public holidays 958
red tape and visas 955
sexual attitudes............... 959
shopping 958
sports 959
telephones 958
transport.......................... 956
travel from other African
  countries 954
websites.......................... 955
wildlife 959
Benin City (N) 1147–1151
Benin City 1148
Bénoué National
  Park (C)................... 1325
Bénoué River (C) 1325
Benue State (N) 1182
Bertoua (C) 1318
Besease (Gh)............... 861
Besoulé (BF) 747
Bétanti, Île de (S).......... 222
Beyin (Gh).............835, 851
Beyla (Gui) 631
Bia National Park (Gh)
  861
Biafra (N)...........1092, 1153
Biakpa (Gh)................... 869
bicycle travel 28
Bida (N)...................... 1171
Bidjoka Falls (C) 1312
Bignona (S).................. 260
Bijagós Islands (GB)
  545–553
Bijilo (Gam).................. 294
bilharzia 41
Billy, Chutes de (M) 373
Bilma (Ni) 1056, 1067
Bimbia (C).................. 1267
Bimbilla (Gh) 871
Binkolo (SL) 691
Bintang (Gam) 314

Bintumani, Mount (SL)... 693
Biriwa (Gh)................... 836
Birnin Gwari (N) 1191
Birnin Kebbi (N) 1210
Birnin-Konni (Ni) 1049
Bissandougou (Gui)......630
Bissau (GB).........537–543
Bissau 538
Bissau, Central 541
  accommodation 539
  airlines............................ 543
  arrivals............................ 537
  banks 543
  beaches.......................... 542
  bike rental 543
  bookshops 543
  cafés............................... 542
  car rental 543
  carnival 540
  crafts 540
  cultural centres 543
  embassies....................... 543
  entertainment.................. 543
  hospital........................... 543
  hotels 539
  Internet........................... 543
  markets 540
  museum 540
  music venues 543
  nightclubs 543
  pharmacy 543
  Pidjiguiti Memorial 540
  post office 543
  restaurants 542
  shops 543
  tourist information............ 537
  travel agents 543
  visa extensions 543
Bissaula (N) 1216
Bitam (Gabon) 1311
Bla (M) 379
Black Johnson
  beach (SL) 686
black market.................. 48
Blangoua (C)............... 1338
blood transfusions.......... 43
Bo (SL)................... 695–697
Bo.............................. 695
Boa Entrada (CV).......... 473
Boa Vista (CV) 506–509
Boa Vista..................... 506
Boabeng (Gh) 863
Boabeng-Fiema Monkey
  Sanctuary (Gh)........... 863
Boadé (T)..................... 948
Bobende (C) 1267
Bobiri Reserve (Gh) 861
Bobo-Dioulasso (BF)
  765–771
Bobo-Dioulasso........... 766
Boca de Coruja (CV)..... 493
body language............... 68
Boé (GB)...................... 554

Markets

Freetown markets (SL).. 679
Ibadan area markets (N).................................... 1136
Lagos markets (N).. 1125
Market days in the Burkinabe Sahel (BF)............ 751
Market days in western Burkina (BF)................... 772
Pays Dogon market days (M) 409

Boffa (Gui)..................... 609
Bofossou (Gui).............. 634
Bogué (Mau) 138
Bohicon (B)................... 993
Bokwango (C)............. 1271
Bolama (GB) 545–549
Bolama island 547
Bole (Gh)...................... 877
Bolgatanga (Gh) 879
Bolgatanga 880
Bomana Falls (C) 1267
Bomboli, Chutes de (Gui)
.... 616
Bonadikombo (C) 1267
Bongo (Gh) 881
Bonjongo (C) 1267
Bonkoukou (Ni).......... 1044
Bonthe (SL)................. 700
Bonwire (Gh)................ 862
books about
  West Africa 34–37, 82
Boré (M)........................ 420
Borgu Game Reserve (N)
.... 1171
Borko (M)...................... 417
Borkono Falls (N)........ 1184
Bossou (Gui)................ 638
Bosumtwe, Lake (Gh)... 862
Bouamir (C) 1318
Bouba Ndjida
  National Park (C) 1326
Boubon (Ni) 1045
Bouche du Roy (B) 988
Boucle du Baoulé, Parc
  National de la (M) 372
Boukoumbé (B)........... 1004
Bouliwel (Gui) 615
Bouma Bek
  Forest (C) 1320
Boundou (S)................ 240
Bourem (M)........... 399, 404
Boutilimit (Mau) 138
Bouza (Ni) 1057
Branco, Ilhéu (CV) 496
Brava island (CV)... 479–482
Brava............................ 480
Brefet (Gam) 314
Brenu-Akyinim (Gh) 845
bribery in West Africa..... 67

Brikama (Gam).............. 308
Brikama........................ 308
Brin (S)........................ 252
British Council 70
Brufut (Gam)................ 309
Buatong (N) 1168
Buba (GB) 554
Bubaque (GB)...... 549–551
Bubaque town 551
Buéa (C)..................... 1268
Bui National Park (Gh)... 861
Buiba (Gam)................ 317
Buipe (Gh)................... 866
Bukuru (N) 1181
Bula (GB) 544
Buluf (S) 262
Bumbuna (SL)............. 693
Bunce Island (SL) 687
Bureh (SL).................. 687
BURKINA FASO ...705–781
Burkina Faso
  highlights.................706
Burkina Faso........ 708–709
  accommodation.............. 715
  banks and exchange........ 714
  books 728
  cinema 719, 727
  climate............................ 710
  costs 714
  crafts 718
  crime 718
  currency 714
  emergencies.................... 718
  entertainment 719
  facts and figures 707
  festivals 717
  food and drink................. 716
  glossary.......................... 730
  health 713
  history 720–725
  information 713
  Internet........................... 716
  language 728
  mail................................. 716
  maps 713
  media 713
  music...................... 719, 726
  national parks 719
  opening hours................. 717
  people 707
  photography.................... 710
  public holidays................ 717

red tape and visas 712
sexual attitudes................ 718
shopping 718
sports 719
telephones 716
theatre 719
transport.......................... 714
travel from other African
  countries....................... 711
websites.......................... 713
wildlife 719
Buruntuma (GB)............ 558
buses in West Africa....... 50
bush taxis.................. 48–49
Busua (Gh).................... 849
Butre (Gh) 835
Bwari (N)..................... 1177

C

Cabeça da Tarafes (CV)
.... 509
Cabo de Ribeira
  Paúl (CV)..................... 495
Cacheu (GB) 544
Calabar (N) 1162–1166
Calabar.......................... 1163
Calavi (B) 983
Calhau (CV)................... 491
Calheta de São
  Miguel (CV) 473
Cambaju (GB) 556
camels 54
cameras.................... 67, 87
CAMEROON 1217–1338
Cameroon
  highlights................. 1218
Cameroon 1220-1221
  accommodation 1231
  banks and exchange...... 1228
  books 1030
  cinema 1235, 1248
  climate............................ 1224
  costs 1228
  crafts 1234
  crime 1235
  currency 1228
  emergencies................... 1235
  entertainment................. 1235
  facts and figures 1222
  festivals 1234
  food and drink................ 1232
  glossary......................... 1251
  health 1228
  history 1237–1244
  information 1227
  Internet........................... 1234
  languages....................... 1251
  mail................................. 1234
  maps 1227
  media 1227

music.......... 1235, 1244–1247
national parks 1235
opening hours 1234
people 1222
photography 1219
public holidays 1234
red tape and visas 1226
road blocks 1230
sexual attitudes............. 1235
shopping 1234
sports 1235
telephones 1234
transport........................ 1229
travel from other
    African countries........ 1225
websites........................ 1227
wildlife 1235

Cameroon, Mount (C)
.... 1269–1272
Cameroon, Mount...... 1270
Campement des
    Éléphants (C) 1325
campements................... 55
camping........................... 56
Campo (C) 1316
Campo Baixo (CV)........ 481
Campo Ma'an National
    Park (C).......... 1312, 1316
Canchungo (GB)........... 544
Canhabaque (GB)......... 552
Cap Skiring (S) 256
Cap Skiring and
    around 256
Cape Coast (Gh).......... 835,
    837–840
Cape Coast................. 837
CAPE VERDE 431–510
Cape Verde
    highlights.................. 432
Cape Verde Islands
    434
    accommodation 441
    banks and exchange........ 439
    books 458
    climate............................ 436
    costs 438

crafts 444
crime 445
currency 438
emergencies...................... 445
entertainment.................... 445
facts and figures 433
festivals 444
food and drink.................... 442
glossary 461
health 437
history 447–457
information 437
Internet............................. 444
language 459
mail.................................. 444
maps 437
media 437
music................................ 445, 457
national parks 446
opening hours 444
people 434
photography...................... 435
public holidays 444
red tape
    and visas 436
sexual attitudes................. 445
shopping 444
sports 446
telephones 444
transport........................... 439
travel from other African
    countries...................... 436
websites........................... 437
wildlife 446

car rental 52
Caravela (GB) 552
carbon offsetting 20
carnivals 64
Carriçal (CV) 499
Casa Florestal (CV)....... 493
Casamance
    conflict (S).......... 180, 246
Catió (GB).................... 555
cellphones 62
Chã das
    Caldeiras (CV)............ 478
Chad, Lake (C) 1338

Chad, Lake (N)
.... 1056, 1214
Chambula (N)........... 1214
changing money............ 47
Chari River (C) 1338
Chéguénaron (Ni)........ 1045
Chiana (Gh)................... 879
Chiana-Katiu
    caves (Gh)................ 879
Chinguetti (Mau) 149
cholera.................... 38–39
Choum (Mau)........ 124–125
Christian holidays........... 64
Chuchiliga (Gh)............. 879
Cidade Velha (CV)......... 471
climate change 20
climate 15
clothes..................... 69, 73
Cobras, Ilha das (GB)... 549
Cocotier Plage (C) 1315
coffee............................. 60
collect calls.................... 62
Combouroh (Gui).......... 617
communications 61–63
Conakry (Gui)....... 591–608
Conakry, Central
    596–597
Conakry, Greater
    602–603
Conakry and the
    Îles de Los 599
    accommodation 594
    airlines 606
    airport............................. 592
    arrivals......................592–593
    banks 606
    beach 598
    bookshops 607
    car rental 607
    cinemas.......................... 607
    clubs 604
    crafts 607
    embassies 607
    history 591
    hospital........................... 607
    hotels 594
    Île de Kassa 600
    Île Roume........................ 600
    Île Tamara 600
    Îles de Los................599–600
    Internet........................... 607
    live music 605–606
    markets 598
    National Museum 598
    nightlife........................... 604
    pharmacies 607
    photography.................... 607
    post office 608
    restaurants 601–604
    Rogbané beach............... 598
    security........................... 592
    shops 598, 607, 608
    street names 592

Arts and architecture

Adire cloth (N) 1134
Bamiléké architecture (C)...................................... 1283
Cases à impluvium and fetish shrines (S).............. 253
Ghana's forts and castles (Gh) 834–835
Gold (Gh).. 787
Kente cloth (Gh) 862
Kiffa beads (Mau) 142
Ntonso dye stamps (Gh).. 864
Silversmiths and saddle makers in Agadez (Ni) ... 1061
Tavares, writer of mornas (CV)............................... 481
The anatomy of Dogon villages (M) 412
The Osogbo school (N)... 1145

telephones 608
tourist information............ 593
transport........................... 593
travel agents 608
visa extensions 608
contraception 35
corruption 67
costs in West Africa 45
Côte d'Ivoire (see note on p.12)
Cotonou (B) 971–982
Cotonou 972–973
Cotonou, Central
.... 978–979
accommodation 975
airlines............................... 981
airport............................... 974
arrivals............................... 974
banks 981
beaches............................ 976
beaches............................ 981
bookshops 981
car rental 981
cinemas............................ 981
clubs 980
embassies........................ 981
hospitals........................... 981
hotels 975
Internet............................. 981
Maps 981
markets 976–977
nightlife............................. 980
pharmacies 982
photography.................... 982
post office 982
restaurants 977–980
shops 982
swimming pools............... 982
telephones 982
tourist office 974
transport........................... 974
travel agents 982
visa extensions 982
Cova crater (CV) 493
Cova Joana (CV)........... 481
Coyah (Gui).................... 609
credit cards 47
Creek Town (N) 1166
crime and safety....... 64–67
crocodiles of the Sahara 141
Cross River National Park (N).......... 1166–1168
Cruzinha da Garça (CV) 494
cultural hints 7, 68–70
culture shock................. 12
Cure Salée festival (Ni) 1064–1065
Curral Velho (CV) 509
currencies...................... 46
currency exchange......... 47
Cussilintra (GB)............. 554

cycling in West Africa..... 53
cycling to West Africa 28

D

Dabola (Gui).................. 623
Dafra (BF) 771
Dagana (S).................... 236
Dagara (N) 1191
Dagona Wildfowl Sanctuary (N)........... 1203
Dagoudane-Pikine (S)... 218
Dakar (S) 197–218
Dakar centre 204–205
Dakar.............................198
Dakar: Cap Vert Peninsula 217
accommodation 201
airlines............................... 212
arrivals............................... 199
banks 212
bars 211
beaches............................ 208
bookshops 212
car rental 212
cinemas............................ 212
clubs 211
corniches 207
cultural centres 213
Dakar rally 203
embassies........................ 213
gare routière.................... 200
Grand Mosquée 206
Hann Park 208
history 197
hospitals........................... 212
hotels 202
IFAN Museum 207
Internet............................. 213
markets 206
music venues 211
nightlife............................. 211
pharmacies 213
police............................... 213
post office 213
restaurants 209–210
security............................. 201
shopping ..203, 206, 212, 213
swimming pools............... 213
telephones 213
tourist information............ 200
transport........................... 200
travel agents 213
wrestling........................... 213
Dalaba (Gui)................... 615
Damaturu (N) 1210
Dambai (Gh) 871
Dame de Mali (Gui)....... 622
Dan-Homey kingdom (B) 995
Danyi plateau (T)........... 929
Dapaong (T)................. 945

Dapaong 946
Dar es Salaam (Mau).... 139
Dargol (Ni).................... 1045
Dassa (B) 997
Datori (T)....................... 943
debit cards 47
debt in West Africa.......... 7
Debundscha (C).......... 1267
Delta du Saloum, Parc National du (S)........... 222
dental care...................... 42
Denu/Aflao (Gh) 832
Deux Balés, Parc National des (BF)....... 747
Devil's Island (SL) 686
Diafarabé (M) 379, 380
Diaguissa, Mont (Gui)....616
Diama (S)....................... 236
diamond-mining (SL)....701, 703
Diana (S) 261
Diapaga (BF)................. 750
diarrhoea 41
Diawling National Park (Mau) 137
Diébougou (BF) 780
Diébougou 780
Diembéreng (S)............. 258
Diffa (Ni) 1055
Digya National Park (Gh).................... 861
Dilapao (S) 250
Dilmun 1167
Dindima (N)................... 1183
Dinguiraye (Gui) 624
Diohère (S) 253
Dionewar (S) 222
Diouloulou (S) 260
Diourbel (S).................... 225
Diré (M)........................... 380
disabled travellers 71–72
Ditinn, Chutes de (Gui) 616
Dixcove (Gh) 835, 848
Dja Faunal Reserve (C) 1317
Djalloumbéré (S) 227
Djenné (M) 389–395
Djenné 392
Djibelor (S).................... 252
Djibo (BF)...................... 752
Djifere (S)....................... 222
Djiguibombo (M)........... 414
Djingliya (C) 1334
Djougou (B)................... 1002
Djoûk Pass (Mau) 141
Djounkoun (Gui)............ 618
Dodi Island (Gh)........... 866

Dogon country (M).......386, 404–420

Dogon country............408

Dogondoutchi (Doutchi) (Ni)............1049

dogs in West Africa........43

Dominghia (Gui)............609

Donga River (N)..........1215

Dongol-Touma (Gui)......617

Dori (BF)......................751

Doro (M)......................422

Dosso (Ni)...................1047

Douala (C)........1252–1262

Douala............................1253

Douala, Central...........1257

accommodation 1255–1256

airlines............................1261

airport............................1254

Akwa............................1257

arrivals............................1254

banks 1261

Bonanjo............................1258

bookshops 1261

car rental......................1261

cinemas............................1261

clubs 1261

consulates......................1261

cultural centres 1261

doctors............................1262

Douala Museum............1258

history 1252

hotels 1255–1256

information 1255

Internet............................1262

markets............................1159

nightlife............................1260

pharmacies 1262

post office 1262

restaurants 1259–1260

shops 1262

swimming pools..............1262

tourist office 1255

travel agents 1262

Doucki (Gui)..................617

Douentza (M)........399, 417

Douentza, Réserve de (M) 422

Doumé (C) 1317

Doundjourou (M)............414

Dounkimania (Gui)........616

Dourou (M)...................414

dress in West Africa 69, 73

drinks..........................60–61

drinking water................60

driving in West Africa 53

driving to West Africa 26–27

drugs 66

Dschang (C)................1284

Dsjutittsa (C)...............1284

Dublin Island (SL) 687

Dubréka (Gui)................608

Dumbo (C) 1216, 1293

Dumbuto (Gam)............316

Dzogbégan (T)..............929

E

Easter 64

eating and drinking..............9, 57–61

Ebebiyin (Equatorial Guinea)........................1311

Ebianemayong (C)......1316

Ebnou Pass (Mau) 149

Ebodjé (C)...................1316

Ebolowa (C)................1311

Eboundja (C)................1316

Edéa (C).....................1310

Edioungou (S)...............255

Efok (S) 259

Eito (CV)........................495

Ejisu (Gh) 861

Ejura (Gh)......................864

Ekang (N)...................1167

Ekok (C)......................1168

Mamfé (C)..................1168

Ekok (C)......................1277

Ekom Nkam (C) 1284

Ekom, Chutes d' (C)...1283

Ekondo Titi (C)............1274

Ekonjo (C)...................1267

Elak (C) 1295

electricity 87

Elinkine (S)...................256

Elméki (Ni)...................1066

Elmina (Gh)....835, 843–845

Elmina 843

Elubo (Gh)....................851

embassies of West African countries................29–31

Enampore (S)................253

Endé (M) 414

Enugu (N)..........1153–1155

Enugu............................1154

Enxude (GB) 554

Esie (N) 1140

Espargos (CV)...............500

Essakane (M) 403

Etaconval (Gui) 615

Eticoga (GB) 553

Etindé (C)...................1267

Etiolo (S) 243

etiquette 7, 68–70

Etomé (C)...................1267

Ewe names (T)..............926

exchange rates..............47

eye contact....................68

F

Fachi (Ni) 1067

facts and figures...............7

Fada-Ngourma (BF)......748

Fadiout (S) 220

Fajā d'Agua (CV)...........481

Fajara (Gam) 294

Fajās (CV) 498

Falaba (SL) 693

Falémé River (M) 372

Farafenni (Gam)............316

Farako, Chutes de (M)...382

Faranah (Gui)................624

Farenghia (Gui) 609

Farié (Ni) 1045

Farim (GB) 555

Faro National Park (C) 1325

Fatoto (Gam) 320

Faune de Tamou, Réserve Totale de (Ni)............1048

Ethnography

Cape Verdean Society (CV).. 453

Kiridi – the short people (C) 1312

The Asafo companies and posubans (Gh) 836

The Guerzé (Gui) 636

The Igbo (N) 1153

The Jola (S) 245

The Kissi – and their stone figures (Gui)............. 632

The Koranko (SL) 692

The Mende and secret societies (SL) 698

The origin of the seven Hausa states (N) 1186

The people of Tichit (Mau) 140

The Toma (Gui)... 635

Yatenga ethnography (BF) 758

Fazao-Malfakassa, Parc
  National de (T) 937
Febedougou,
  Domes de (BF)..........775
Félou, Chutes de (M)....373
female "circumcision" 74
ferries.................................51
Festival au Désert (M)
 403
Festival sur le Niger (M)
 375
festivals 63–64
FGM in West Africa
 74
Filingué (Ni).................1045
Firawa (SL)....................693
Firgoun (Ni) 1046
fishing rights (Mau).......121
flights in West Africa.......51
flights to West Africa
 19–23
Fogo island (CV)....474–479
Fogo 475
Fombori (M) 419
Fongo-Tongo (C) 1284
Fontainhas (CV) 494
food in West Africa....57–60
forex bureaux 47
Formosa (GB) 552
Forokonia (Gui) 634
Fort Bullen (Gam) 311
Foula-Mori (Gui)....558, 621
Foumban (C)...............1295
Foumban......................1296
Foundiougne (S) 222
Fouta Djalon (Gui)
 610–622
Fouta Djalon
  theocracy (Gui) 618
Freetown (SL) 670–683
Freetown Peninsula
 684
Freetown, Central
 676–677
Freetown, Greater
 672–673
  accommodation 672–674
  airlines...............................682
  airport................................670
  arrivals...............................670
  banks 682
  beaches..............................679

Festivals and traditions

Festivals in Sokodé (T).. 935
Festivals in the Agadez region (Ni) 1064
Id al-Fitr in Kano (N).. 1199
Islamic festivals.. 63
The Fête de Mare (Gui) 623
The Nabayius Gou (BF).. 740
The Ogua Fetu harvest festival (Gh) 839
Wrestling (Gam)... 315

boat rental.......................682
car rental 682
churches 675
cinemas...........................682
clubs 681
conservation....................682
Cotton Tree 674
couriers 682
cultural centres 682
dentists 683
East End..........................678
embassies........................683
ferries 670
Fourah Bay College 675
hospitals...........................683
hotels 672–674
Internet.............................683
Lumley Beach 679
markets 679
mosques 675
museum 678
newspapers 683
nightlife............................681
pharmacies 683
police...............................683
post office 683
restaurants 680
shops 683
street names 672
tourist information............671
transport...........................672
travel agents 683
visa extensions 683
Western Union 683
French vocabulary.... 82–87
fruit 59–60
Fulacunda (GB).............554
Fundo de
  Figueiras (CV) 509
Fundong (C)................1292
Furna (CV)....................480

G

Gabú (GB)....................557
Gabú.............................557
Gadalougué (Gui) 622
Galinhas, Ilha das (GB)
 550
Gambaga (Gh) 882
Gambia Fado (GB)........549
Gambia River (Gam).....313
Gambia River (Gui) 622
GAMBIA, THE......263–320
Gambia highlights 264
Gambia, The 266–267
  accommodation 271
  banks and exchange........270
  books 285
  climate..............................267
  costs 270
  crafts 274
  crime 274
  currency 270
  emergencies.....................274
  entertainment...................275
  facts and figures 265
  festivals 273
  food and drink..................272
  glossary 287
  health 269
  history 277–283
  information 268
  Internet.............................272
  language 286
  mail...................................273
  maps 269
  media 269
  music................................284
  national parks 276
  opening hours 273
  people 265
  photography......................266
  public holidays.................273
  red tape and visas 268
  sexual attitudes................275
  shopping 274
  sports 276
  telephones 273
  tipping 270
  tipping 271
  transport...........................270

Food and drink

Ghanaian food terms and dishes (Gh)............... 795
Krio food and drink terms (SL)............................ 649
Nigerian food (N).. 1084
Portuguese and Kriolu food terms (CV).............. 443

INDEX

travel from other African
   countries 267
websites 269
wildlife 276
Gandamia Massif (M)
   .... 417, 420
Gandiol (S) 233
Gangan, Mont (Gui) 613
Ganvié (B) 982
Gao (M) 399, 404,
   415–420
Gao 426
Gaoua (BF) 776–778
Gaoua 777
Gaoual (Gui) 619, 621
Garoua (C) 1326–1329
Garoua 1327
Garoua-Boulai (C) 1318
Gashaka-Gumpti National
   Park (N) 1215
Gashua (N) 1204, 1213
gay life in West Africa 73
Gaya (Ni) 1047
Gbakoré (Gui) 638
Gban, Mont (Gui) 638
Gberia-Fotombu (Gui) ... 624
Gêba (GB) 556
Gembu (N) 1215
Gemi, Mount (Gh) 868
gender issues and sexual
   attitudes 72–75
Gerewol festivals (Ni) ... 1065
getting to West Africa
   19–28
GHANA 783–882
Ghana highlights 784
Ghana 786
   accommodation 792
   banks and exchange 791
   books 811–812
   cinema 799
   climate 788
   costs 791
   crafts 798
   crime 798
   currency 791
   emergencies 798
   entertainment 799
   facts and figures 785
   festivals 797
   food and drink 794
   glossary 814
   gold 787
   health 790
   history 801–807
   information 789
   Internet 796
   language 813
   mail 796
   maps 790
   media 790
   music 799, 808–810
   national parks 800

opening hours 796
people 787
photography 787
public holidays 796
red tape and visas 789
sexual attitudes 798
shopping 798
sports 799
telephones 796
theatre 799
transport 792
travel from other African
   countries 788
websites 790
wildlife 800
Ghana's forts and
   castles 834–835
Ghana Town (Gam) 309
gifts in West Africa 69
Glidji (T) 924
Gloucester (SL) 688
Gnimgnama (M) 417
Gnit (S) 236
Goderich beach (SL)
   685
Gogoli (M) 416
Going, Chaine du (Gui)
   630
Gola National Park (SL)
   702
Gold Coast Slave
   Trade (Gh) 840–841
Golmy (S) 238
Gombe (N) 1182
Gomoa Fetteh (Gh) 832
Gorée, Île de (S) 214
Gorée, Île de 214
Gorgoram Fishing
   Festival (N) 1203
Gorom-Gorom (BF) 753
Gossi (M) 422
Gothèye (Ni) 1045
Gouina, Chutes de (M)
   373
Goumbogo (M) 372
Goundam (M) 380
Gouray (Mau) 238
Gourcy (BF) 759
Gouré (Ni) 1055
Gouria (C) 1334
Gourma-Rharous (M) ... 404
Grand Batanga (C) 1315
Grand Popo (B) 988
Grande Côte (S) 225
Grassfields, the (C) 1290
greetings 7, 68
Guéckédou (Gui) 634
Guediyawe (S) 218
Guelb er Richat (Mau) ... 152
Guembeul, Réserve de (S)
   233

Guidjiba (C) 1325
Guiers, Lac de (S) 236
Guilongou (BF) 751
GUINEA 559–638
Guinea highlights 560
Guinea 562–563
   accommodation 570
   banks and exchange 567
   books 587
   cinema 587
   climate 564
   costs 568
   crafts 573
   crime 573
   currency 567
   emergencies 574
   entertainment 574
   facts and figures 565
   festivals 573
   food and drink 571
   glossary 590
   health 568
   history 576–583
   information 568
   Internet 573
   language 588–590
   mail 572
   maps 568
   media 569
   music 574, 583–586
   national parks 575
   opening hours 573
   people 561
   photography 561
   public holidays 573
   red tape and visas 567
   sexual attitudes 574
   shopping 573
   sports 574
   telephones 572
   theatre 574
   transport 569
   travel from other African
      countries 564
   websites 568
   wildlife 574
GUINEA-BISSAU
   511–558
Guinea-Bissau
   highlights 512
Guinea-Bissau 514–515
   accommodation 520
   banks and exchange 519
   books 535
   cinema 523
   climate 517
   costs 518
   crafts 522
   crime 522
   currency 518
   entertainment 5323
   facts and figures 513
   festivals 522
   food and drink 521
   glossary 535
   health 518

history 524–532
information 518
Internet.............................522
language 535
mail....................................521
maps 518
media 518
music.........................533–534
national parks 523
opening hours..................522
people 513
photography 516
public holidays.................522
red tape and visas 517
sexual attitudes...............523
shopping 522
sports................................523
telephones 521
transport............................519
travel from other African
     countries 516
websites............................518
wildlife...............................523
Guinguette, La (BF) 771
Guior, Île de (S)..............222
Gunjur (Gam) 310
Guthurbé (M) 238
Gwoza (N)...................1214

H

Hadejia-Nguru Wetlands
  Conservation
  Project (N)................1203
Hamale (BF)...................781
Hamale (Gh)...................878
Hamilton beach (SL).....685
harmattan 16
Hausa country (N).......1185
Haut Niger, Parc
  National du (Gui)........626
Haute Casamance (S) ...244
health.......................37–44
Helekpe (Gh)..................868
hepatitis...........................38
Hérèmakono (Gui) 624
Hihéatro (T)....................930
hiking in West Africa.......54
hitchhiking 28, 51
HIV.............................42, 72
Ho (Gh) 867
Ho..................................867
Hohoe (Gh) 869
Hombori (M)...................421
homosexuality 73
horse riding 54
hospitality 57
hospitals 43
hostels.............................55
hotels.......................54–56

I

Ibadan (N) 1134–1138
Ibadan 1135
Ibbi (N) 1170
Ibi (M)..............................419
IDD dialing codes...........62
Idenao (C) 1267, 1274
Idjeli (M) 415
Ife (N) 1141
Iferouâne (Ni) 1066
Igbeti (N).......................1140
Igbo country (N)..........1152
Ijim Forest (C) 1293, 1295
Ikom (N) 1140, 1167
immunizations 38
I-n-Adiattafene (M) 422
inoculations 38
insurance 39
Internet access..............61
Iouik (Mau)....................126
Ipikar, Île d' (C) 1316
Iragbiji (N) 1146
Ireli (M)..........................415
Irié (Gui) 636
iron-ore trains (Mau).....125
Iseyin (N).......................1140
Islamic festivals 63
ivory.................................76
Iwik (Mau) 126

J

Jakiri (C).......................1295
James Island (Gam)......312
Janjanbureh (Gam) 317
Janjanbureh 318
Jardin de Prof. Chevalier,
  Le (Gui) 616
Jarreng (Gam)...............317

Jebba (N)....................1170
Jegbwema (SL).............703
Jemberem (GB) 555
Jimeta (N) 1215
Jinack Island (Gam)......312
Jinack Kajata (Gam) 312
Joal-Fadiout (S) 220
João Galego (CV) 509
João Viera (GB) 553
João Viera-Poilão
  National Park (GB).....553
John Obey beach (SL)
 686
Jos (N) 1178–1182
Jos..................................1179
Juba beach (SL) 685
Juffureh (Gam).............311

K

Kabadio (S)....................260
Kabala (SL) 624, 691
Kabba River (SL) 691
Kabrousse (S) 259
Kabyé country (T) 943
Kachouane (S)...............259
Kaduna (N)........1186–1190
Kaduna............................1187
Kaédi (Mau) 138
Kafountine (S)................261
Kafountine......................260
Kainji Dam (N).............1170
Kainji Lake National
  Park (N)....................1170
Kakara (N)...................1216
Kakoulima, Mont (Gui)
 608
Kakrima River (Gui).......618
Kakum National
  Park (Gh)............840–842
Kalabougou (M) 376

History

Aoudaghost and the Ghana Empire (Mau) 142
Beaver's colony (GB) 548
Sundiata, Niani and the Mali Empire (Gui)...628–629
The Cape Verdean Slave Trade (CV)................... 448
The Dan-Homey Kingdom (B)............................ 995
The Gold Coast Slave Trade (Gh) 840–841
The Gourounsi country (BF) 761
The history of Yatenga (BF) 756–757
The Kanem-Bornu Empire (N).......................... 1211
The rise and fall of Ribeira Grande (CV) 471
The rise of the jihad state (Gui)........................... 618
The Songhai Empire (M) 424

Kalakpa Resource
  Reserve (Gh).............868
Kalamaloué National
  Park (C).....................1338
Kale, Chutes de (M)......373
Kali (M).........................371
Kaltungo (N).................1182
Kamakwie (SL).............691
Kamale (N)..................1214
Kambadaga,
  Chutes de (Gui)..........616
Kambama (SL).............698
Kambele (C).................1319
Kambui Hills (SL).........702
Kamsar (Gui)................609
Kamuku National
  Park (N).....................1191
Kandé (T).....................943
Kandi (B).....................1000
Kanem-Bornu
  empire (N).................1211
Kani-Kombolé (M)........414
Kanilai (Gam)..............314
Kankan (Gui).........626–629
Kankan........................627
Kano (N)...........1194–1203
Kano.................1196–1197
  accommodation.............1198
  airlines..........................1203
  airport...........................1195
  arrivals..........................1195
  banks............................1203
  bookshops.....................1203
  consulates.....................1203
  couriers.........................1203
  cultural centres..............1203
  Dala Hill.......................1201
  durbars.........................1199
  dye pits.........................1199
  emir's palace.................1200
  history...........................1194
  hospitals........................1203
  hotels............................1198
  Id-al-Fitr festival.............1199
  information.....................1197
  Internet.........................1203
  markets................1201, 1202
  National museum............1201
  New City........................1201
  nightlife.........................1202
  Old City.........................1199
  pharmacies....................1203
  post office.....................1203
  post offices....................1203
  restaurants....................1202
  telephones....................1203
  tourist office..................1197
  travel agents..................1203
Kantchari (BF)..............750
Kanyang (N).................1168
Kaolack (S)...................226
Kaouar Cliffs (Ni).........1067
Kaourar oasis (Ni).......1056

Kara (T)................940–942
Kara...........................940
Karabane, Île de (S)......256
Karfiguéla,
  Chutes de (BF)...........775
Kartong (Gam)..............310
Kassa, Île de (Gui)........600
Katabang (N)...............1168
Katsina (N)..................1204
Kau-Ur (Gam)...............319
Kaya (BF).....................751
Kayar (S)......................216
Kayes (M).....................369
Kaymor (S)...................227
Kédougou (S)...............240,
  243, 372
Kénédougou Empire (M)
 380
Kenema (SL)................700
Kenema......................701
Kéniéba (M)...243, 370, 371
Kent (SL)......................687
kente cloth (Gh)............862
Kentzou (C)..................1319
Kéran National Park (T)
 943
Kérémou (B)................1002
Kérouané (Gui).............630
Kerr Batch (Gam)..........319
Kerr Serign (Gam).........294
Keta (Gh).....................832
Kete Krachi (Gh)...866, 871
Keur Albé (S)................227
Keur Bakari (S).............227
Keur Massène (Mau)....137
Keur Moussa (S)...........218
Keur Samba Dia (S)......221
Kiang West National
  Park (Gam).................315
Kidira (S).....................238
Kiffa (Mau)...................141
Kiffa beads..................142
Kilum Forest (C)...........1295
Kimbi River Game
  Reserve (C)...............1293
Kindia (Gui)..........610–613
Kindia.........................612
Kinkon, Chutes de (Gui)
 616
Kissidougou (Gui)........632
Kissidougou................633
Kita (M).......................373
Kita Kourou,
  Mont (M)....................373
Klouto (T).....................928
Klouto, Mont (T)............928
Ko (Lama,
  Forêt de (B)................993
Koa (M)........................383

Kobikoro (Gui)..............592
Koidu-Sefadu (SL)........703
Koinadugu (SL)............693
Koindu (SL)..................703
Kokrobite (Gh)..............832
kola nuts (see colour
  section)
Kolda (S)..............244, 556
Kololi (Gam).................294
Komadougou River (Ni)
 1055
Kombissiri (BF)............761
Komenda (Gh)......835, 845
Kongany (S).................238
Kongoussi (BF)............753
Konkouré (Gui).............613
Konna (M).....................420
Kono (SL).....................703
Konsankoro (Gui).........631
Korienzé (M)................380
Koro (M).......................416
Korup National
  Park (C).........1274–1276
Korup National Park...1275
Kotu (Gam)..................294
Kou Forest (BF)............771
Kouakourou (M)............395
Koubalan (S)................262
Koudou,
  Chutes de (B)..........1002
Koudougou (BF)...........747
Kouffé, Mont (B)...........996
Koum (C).....................1326
Kouma-Konda (T).........928
Koumbi Saleh (Mau)....143
Koumbia (Gui).............558
Koumi (BF)..................771
Koundara (Gui).....558, 622
Koundou (M)................419
Koungheul (S)..............227
Kounsitel (Gui).............621
Koupéla (BF)................748
Kouré (Ni)...................1047
Kouroussa (Gui)...........624
Kousséri (C)................1337
Koussi (Gui)................618
Koutiala (M).................379
Koza (C).....................1335
Kpalimé (T)..........925–928
Kpalimé......................927
Kpandu (Gh)................866
Kpéwa (T)....................937
Kpimé falls (T).............929
Kreb Kreb (Ni).............1066
Kribi (C)............1312–1315
Kribi...........................1313
Ksar Torchane (Mau)....149
Kudang Tenda (Gam)...317
Kumasi (Gh).........852–860

Kumasi 854
Kumba (C) 1272
Kumba............................1272
Kumbo (C) 1294
Kundundu (SL).............. 703
Kuntanase (Gh)............. 862
Kuntaur (Gam) 319
Kupe, Mount (C) 1277
Kwa Falls (N) 1086
Kwinella (Gam) 316
Kyabobo National
    Park (Gh).................. 871

Language

Akan names (Gh)................................860
Ewe names (T) 926
Names (M)..324
Niger-Congo languages 80–81
The Reverend Koelle and his
    Polyglotta Africana (SL)..................675

L

La Tapoa (Ni) 1048
Labé (Gui) 240,
    370, 619–621
Labé 619
Labézanga (M).............. 430
Lagdo, Lac (C)............. 1327
Lago (BF) 760
Lago (SL) 702
Lagos (N) 1117–1132
Lagos, Greater........... 1120
Lagos: the islands
    1126–1127
accommodation 1121
airlines........................... 1131
airports........................... 1117
arrivals........................... 1117
Badagry......................... 1128
banks............................. 1131
Bar Beach 1128
beaches......................... 1128
bookshops 1131
Brazilian quarter............ 1123
car rental 1131
couriers 1132
cultural centres 1132
Eleko Beach 1128
embassies...................... 1132
Gbara 1128
history 1117
hospitals........................ 1132
hotels 1121
Ikoyi 1124
Ilashe Beach 1129
information 1119
Internet.......................... 1132
Kuramo Beach 1128
Lagos Island.................. 1123
Lekki Beach 1128
Lekki Peninsula 1125
Lighthouse Beach 1128
markets 1123, 1125
National Museum........... 1123
National Theatre............ 1125
nightlife......................... 1130
pharmacies 1132
post offices 1132

restaurants 1129–1131
shops 1132
Slave Museum 1129
swimming pools 1132
Tafawa Balewa square ... 1123
Tarkwa Bay.................... 1129
telephones 1132
tourist office 1119
transport........................ 1119
travel agents 1132
Victoria Island 1124
Lakka beach (SL)........... 685
Lama depression (B) 993
Lamin Koto (Gam) 319
Languages............... 77–82
language map 78
Afro-Asiatic languages... 77–80
Akan 860
Arabic 80
Bamana phrases 355
Bantoid languages 81
Bantu languages 81
Benin 970
Berber languages............. 80
Bijagó phrases 536
Burkina Faso 728
Cameroon 1251
Cape Verde 434
Chadic languages 80
Djerma phrases.............. 1046
Dogon phrases............... 356
Ewe phrases 905, 926
Fula phrases 589
Ghana............................. 813
Gourounsi phrases.......... 729
Guinea............................. 588
Guinea-Bissau................ 536
Hassaniya phrases....116–117
Hausa phrases 1031
Igbo phrases 1115
Jola phrases................... 193
Koranko phrases............ 692
Kotokoli phrases............ 905
Krio phrases 649, 669
Kriolu phrases 443, 459
Kwa languages 80
Lobi phrases 729
Mali 355
Malinké phrases.............. 588
Mande languages ... 77, 81–82
Mandinka phrases 270
Mauritania 116
Mende phrases 669
Mina phrases 905
More phrases 728

Niger............................... 1031
Niger-Congo languages
   77–81
Nigeria............................ 1114
Portuguese..................... 443
Saharan languages 80
Senegal 193
Serer phrases.................. 193
Sierra Leone 669
Songhai languages 84
Susu phrases 588
The Gambia 270
Togo 905
Twi phrases 813
West Atlantic languages 80
Wolof phrases... 167, 193–196
Yoruba phrases 1114
Langue de Barbarie,
    Parc National de (S)... 233
Larabanga (Gh)............. 875
La-Todin (BF)................ 759
laundry in West Africa 87
Lawra (Gh) 781
Lawra (Gh) 877
Leckcheb (Mau)............ 140
Lefo, Mount (C) 1289
left-hand rule 68
Legon (Gh).................... 830
Leicester Peak (SL) 688
Léi-Mîro (Gui).............. 618
Lélouma (Gui) 621
Léo (BF) 704
Léré (M) 379
Levuma beach (SL) 685
Liati Wote (Gh)............. 870
Liberia (see note on p.15)
libraries with African
    resources 33
Limbé (C) 1262–1266
Limbé 1263
Lingam, Cascade
    de (C) 1284
Linguère (S) 226
Linsan (Gui) 613
living and working 70–71
Lobé, Chutes
    de la (C) 1315
Lobéké National
    Park (C).................... 1320
Lobi country (BF)...776–780
Loghi (BF) 780

Logone River (C).........1337
Lokosso (BF) 780
Lola (Gui) 638
Lolodorf (C)................1312
Lom River (C).............1319
Lombo Comprido (CV)
................................495
Lomé (T) 907–921
Lomé 908–909
  accommodation 912–914
  airlines.............................919
  airport.............................910
  Akodessewa....................916
  arrivals............................910
  banks 919
  beaches...........................914
  bookshops 919
  camping 913
  car rental 920
  church services...............920
  cinemas...........................920
  cultural centres...............920
  dentists............................920
  embassies........................920
  fetish market 916
  history 907
  horse riding 920
  hospitals...........................920
  hotels 912–914
  Internet............................920
  maps 920
  markets 914–916
  mechanics........................920
  museum 916
  nightlife............................918
  opticians...........................920
  pharmacies 921
  post office 921
  restaurants 917
  security 912
  sports clubs 921
  swimming pools................921
  telephones 921
  tennis 921
  tourist office 911
  transport...........................911
  travel agents 921
  visa extensions 921
Lomié (C) 1318
Londji (C) 1315
Loropeni (BF)...............779
Los, Îles de (Gui) 599
Los, Îles de 599
Louba, Mont (Gui) 618
Loumbila (BF) 751
Loura, Mont (Gui) 622
Lugajole (GB)...............554

Ma'an (C)....................1316
Mabiogo (C)................1316

Macenta (Gui).......631, 635
Maci (Gui) 617
Madagli (N) 1214
Madeiral (CV)...............491
Madeleines, Îles des (S)215
Madina-Woula (Gui)......612
Magburaka (SL) 693
Maiduguri (N).... 1210–1213
Maiduguri 1212
mail in West Africa.........61
Main de Fatima, La (M) 421
Maïné-Soroa (Ni) 1055
Maio (GB) 552
Maio island (CV) 482
Maio 482
Makakura (SL) 693
Makari (C) 1338
Makasutu Culture
  Forest (Gam)..............308
Makeni (SL)..........689–691
Makeni 690
Makongo (Gh)..............864
Makurdi (N) 1182
Mala (N) 1210
Malanville (B) 1001
malaria 39–41
Malème Hodar (S) 227
MALI....................321–430
Mali highlights 322
Mali 324–325
  accommodation 335
  banks and exchange........331
  books 353–355
  cinema 338, 352
  climate.............................328
  costs 331
  crafts 337
  crime 337
  currency 331
  emergencies....................337
  entertainment..................338
  facts and figures 323
  festivals 336
  food and drink................335
  glossary............................356
  guides 327
  health 331
  history 339–347
  information 332
  Internet............................336
  language 355
  mail..................................336
  maps 332
  media 332
  music..............338, 347–351
  national parks 338
  opening hours 336
  people 326
  photography....................326
  public holidays................336
  red tape and visas 330
  sexual attitudes...............337
  shopping 337
  sports 338
  telephones 336
  transport...........................333
  travel from other African
    countries.......................328
  websites...........................332
  wildlife..............................338
Mali Empire 396,
  628–629
Maliville/Mali (Gui) 622
Maltam (C) 1338
Maluwe (Gh) 877
Mambele (C) 1320
Mambila Plateau (N) ...1215
Mamfé (C)...................1276
Mamfé Depression (C)
................................1274
Mamou (Gui)................613
Mamou 614
Mampong (Gh) 864
Mamy Wata,
  Chute de (C) 1284
Manantali (M)................372
Mandara Mountains (C)
................................1333
Mandara Mountains (N)
................................1214
Mandinari (Gam)...........306
Manengouba crater
  lakes (C)...................1278
Manjai Kunda (Gam).....294
Mansa Konko (Gam)......316
Mansôa (GB)................555
map suppliers................29
Mapanja (C) 1271
maps of West Africa.......34
marabouts (S).......184–186
Maradi (Ni) 1050
Maradi......................1051
Markoye (BF) 754
Mar-Lodj 224
Maroon Island (SL) 687
Maroua (C)........1329–1333
Maroua......................1330
Marshall Caves (N) 1184
Massina (M) 379
Matam (S) 237
Matas de
  Cantanhez (GB) 555
Mato Grande (CV).........481
MAURITANIA.........91–152
Mauritania highlights
................................92
Mauritania 94
  accommodation 102
  banks and exchange........100
  books 116
  cinema 105
  climate..............................96
  costs 100
  crafts 104

M

crime 104
currency 100
emergencies...................... 104
entertainment 105
facts and figures 94
festivals 103
food and drink................... 103
glossary............................ 118
health 99
history 107–114
information 98
Internet............................. 104
language 116
mail.................................... 103
maps 99
media 99
music...................... 105, 115
national parks 106
opening hours 103
people 93
photography....................... 95
public holidays 103
red tape and visas 98
sexual attitudes................ 104
shopping 104
sports 105
telephones 104
transport........................... 101
travel from other African
    countries......................... 95
websites............................. 98
wildlife 105
Mayo Alim (C) 1325
Mayo Kaliao River (C)
    1329
Mbacke (S) 226
Mbalmayo (C) 1310
Mbane (S) 236
Mboro-sur-Mer (S).......... 225
Mbot (C)........................ 1294
Mbour (S) 220
Mbouroukou (C).......... 1279
Mederdra (Mau) 137
medical resources
    43–44
medicine bag.................. 43
Medina Sabak (S) 227
Medina-Gounas (S) 240
Médine (M)................... 370
Mefou National
    Park (C)...................... 1307
Meiganga (C) 1319
Menchum Falls (C) 1292
Menegou (BF)............... 754
Mengao (BF)................. 760
meningitis...................... 39
Menve Élé,
    Chutes (C)................ 1316
Mes-Meheux
    Island (SL) 687
Mfaminyen (N) 1167
Mfum (N)........... 1167, 1168
Michika (N)................. 1214

Mildo Market (N)......... 1214
Mindelo (CV) 484–490
Mindelo 486
Mindif (C) 1332
Miria (Ni) 1055
Misanje (C).................. 1293
missions 56
Missirah (S).................. 223
Missirikoro,
    Grottes de (M) 382
Mitty, Chutes de (Gui)
    616
Mlomp (S) 255
mobile phones............... 62
Mokolo (C) 1333
Mokwa (N) 1170
Mole National
    Park (Gh).................... 874
Moloundou (C)........... 1320
money...................... 45–48
Monte Gordo (CV) 498
Monte Verde (CV) 490
Monts Nimba
    Reserve (Gui) 638
Mopti (M) 383–387,
    390, 399
Mopti 384
Mora (C)........... 1213, 1335
Morfil, Île à (S) 236
Morro (CV) 483
mosquitos................ 39–40
Mosteiros (CV) 479
motorbiking 52
Moudjéria (Mau).......... 138
Mouenkeu,
    Chute de la (C) 1283
Mouit (S) 234
Mount Cameroon (C)
    1269–1272
Mount Cameroon....... 1270
Mouri (Gh)................... 835
Mouri Mountains (N)....1182
Mouridism (S) 184–186
Mourla (C) 1337
Moyenne Casamance (S)
    244
Mpalla (C) 1315
Mpataba (Gh)............... 851
Mubi (N)..................... 1214
mules in West Africa.......54

Mundemba (C)............ 1276
Murdeira (CV)............... 502
Music in West Africa 13
    Afro-beat..................... 1105
    apala 1104
    Benin 968
    Burkina Faso 726
    Cameroon 1244–1247
    Cape Verde 457
    Cape Verde 481
    coladeira 457
    fuji 1104
    Fula 350
    galala............................ 1107
    Ghana............. 799, 808–810
    Guinea....................583–586
    Guinea Bissau............. 533
    gumbe........................... 533
    Hausa 1200
    highlife.......................... 809
    hip-hop......................... 1107
    hip-life 810
    Igbo 1103
    jelis 347
    juju 1103
    kuduru 533
    makossa....................... 1245
    Mali 347–351, 375, 403
    Manding 347
    Mauritania 105, 115
    Mauritania 115
    morna............................ 457
    morna............................ 481
    Niger............................. 1029
    Nigeria..................1103–1107
    Nigerian highlife 1105
    palm-wine 808
    ragga 1107
    Senegal 171, 187–190
    Sierra Leone..............665–666
    The Gambia 284
    Togo 903
    Tuareg 336
    Wassoulou...................... 350
    Yoruba 1103
Muti Island (SL) 700

N

N'gor (S) 216
N'gourti (Ni) 1056
Naboulgou (T).............. 943

Music

Ghanaian instruments (Gh) 808
Hausa music (N)... 1200
Live at the Bay of Sharks (CV)............................. 490
Lobi traditions (BF)... 778
Manding instruments (M) 348
Traditional Moorish Instruments (Mau) 115

Nadoba (T)............943, 944
Nago (GB)....................552
Nakpanduri (Gh) 882
Nalerigu (Gh)................882
Nampala (M) 379
Nanga-Eboko (C)........1317
Nangbéto,
    Barrage de (T)............930
Nangodi (Gh) 881
national holidays 63–64
national parks...........75–77
Natitingou (B)..............1003
Navrongo (Gh) 878
Nayé (S)......................238
Ndangane (S)...............223
Ndiass (S) 219
Ndiol (S)......................234
Ndjamena (Chad).......1213,
    1337
Ndongo (C) 1321
Ndop (C) 1295
Ndop Plains (C) 1295
Ndu (C) 1294
Négala (M) 373
Néma (Mau) 143
New Bussa (N)............1170
newspapers 34
Ngaoundaba Ranch (C)
   1324
Ngaoundal (C) 1319
Ngaoundéré (C)
   1321–1324
Ngaoundéré 1322
Ngato (C) 1321
Ngayène (S) 227
Ngelehun (SL)..............702
Ngong (C) 1327
NGOs in West Africa 56,
    70–71
Ngoulémakong (C)......1311
Nguekokh (S)...............219
Nguigmi (Ni)...............1055
Nguru (N) 1203
Nguti (C) 1275
Niafounké (M) 379
Niagézazou (Gui) 635
Niambalang (S).............255
Niamey (Ni) 1033–1043
Niamey, Central
   1036–1037
Niamey, Greater........1034
    accommodation 1038
    airlines..........................1042
    Arbre du Ténéré............1040
    arrivals..........................1033
    banks 1042
    bookshop 1043
    car rental 1043
    cinemas.........................1043
    clubs 1042

    cultural centres 1040
    embassies......................1043
    history 1033
    hotels 1038
    Internet..........................1043
    markets 1040
    Musée National 1039
    nightlife.........................1042
    pharmacies 1043
    post office 1043
    restaurants 1041
    security..........................1038
    shops 1043
    swimming pools.............1043
    telephones 1043
    tourist office 1038
    transport........................1038
    travel agents 1043
    visa extensions 1043
    wrestling........................1043
Niamtougou (T)............943
Niani (Gui)...................630
Niani Maru (Gam) 319
Nianing (S) 220
NIGER 1007–1067
Niger highlights 1008
Niger.................. 1010–1011
    accommodation 1018
    banks and exchange...... 1016
    books 1030
    cinema 1020,
    climate...........................1013
    costs 1016
    crafts 1019
    crime 1019
    currency 1016
    emergencies...................1019
    entertainment.................1020
    facts and figures 1009
    festivals 1019
    food and drink................1018
    glossary 1032
    health 1016
    history 1021–1028
    information.....................1015
    Internet..........................1019
    language 1031
    mail...............................1018
    maps 1015
    media 1015
    music.............................1020
    national parks 1020
    opening hours................1019
    people 1009
    photography...................1012
    public holidays...............1019
    red tape and visas 1014
    sexual attitudes..............1019
    shopping 1019
    sports 1020
    telephones 1019
    transport........................1016
    travel from other African
        countries....................1013
    websites.........................1015
    wildlife 1020

Niger River...............8, 326,
    383–404, 423–430, 625,
    1046
Niger River,
    source of the (Gui).....634
NIGERIA...........1069–1216
Nigeria highlights 1070
Nigeria.............. 1072–1073
    accommodation 1082
    banks and exchange...... 1080
    books 1109–1113
    cinema 1087, 1108
    climate...........................1076
    costs 1079
    crafts 1086
    crime 1086
    currency 1079
    electricity.......................1075
    emergencies...................1087
    entertainment.................1087
    facts and figures 1074
    festivals 1086
    food and drink................1084
    glossary 1116
    health 1079
    history 1089–1102
    information.....................1078
    Internet..........................1085
    language 1114–1116
    mail...............................1085
    maps 1078
    media 1078
    music.......... 1087, 1103–1107
    national parks 1088
    Niger Delta conflict 1158
    opening hours................1085
    people 1074
    photography...................1075
    public holidays...............1085
    red tape and visas 1078
    sexual attitudes..............1087
    shopping 1086
    sports 1088
    telephones 1085
    theatre...........................1087
    transport........................1080
    travel from other African
        countries....................1076
    universities 1075
    websites.........................1078
    wildlife 1088
Nimba, Monts (Gui) 638
Nini-Suhien
    Reserve (Gh)..............851
Niodior (S)....................222
Niogbozou (Gui)...........635
Niokolo-Badiar, Parc
    National (Gui).............622
Niokolo-Koba, Parc
    National de (S)...........241
Niokolo-Koba, Parc
    National de................241
Nioro du Rip (S)............227
Nioro du Sahel (M) 372

Njai Kunda (Gam) 319
Nkam River (C) 1284
Nkambé (C) 1294
Nki Forest (C).............1320
Nkoélon (C).................1316
Nkoransa (Gh) 863
Nobéré (BF) 762
Nokoué, Lac (B)............982
Nombori (M)................415
Nossa Senhora
    do Monte (CV) 481
Nouadhibou (Mau)
   119–124
Nouadhibou 123
Nouadhibou & the Cap
    Blanc Peninsula........120
Nouakchott (Mau)
   127–136
Nouakchott environs ...128
Nouakchott 130–131
    accommodation 129
    airlines............................. 134
    arrivals............................. 127
    banks 134
    beaches........................... 132
    bookshops 134
    car parts.......................... 134
    car rental 135
    cinemas............................ 135
    crafts 132
    embassies........................ 135
    emergencies..................... 135
    hospitals.......................... 135
    hotels 129
    information 129
    Internet access 135
    markets 132
    museum 132
    National park offices 135
    nightlife........................... 134
    orientation 128
    post office 135
    restaurants 133
    shops 132
    swimming pools............... 135
    telephones 135
    transport.......................... 129
    travel agents 135
    visa extensions 136
Nouamghar (Mau)........126
Ntem River (C) 1316
Ntonso (Gh) 863
Numan (N) 1182
Nyasoso (C) 1278
Nyikine (S) 259
Nyong River (C)
    ....1311, 1317
Nyos, Lake (C)............1293
Nzébéla (Gui) 636
Nzérékoré (Gui)..... 636–638
Nzérékoré....................637
Nzoo (Gui)...................638
Nzulezo (Gh) 851

O

Obiré (BF) 780
Obuasi (Gh) 861
Obudu (N) 1169
Obudu Cattle Ranch (N)
   1169
Ogbomosho (N)..........1140
Ogboro (N) 1140
Ogoja (N) 1169
Ogol-du-haut (M).........415
Oguaa Fetu
    harvest festival (Gh)....839
Ogundiran (N) 1140
Oiseaux du Djoudj, Parc
    National des (S) 234
Oiseaux, Île aux (S).......222
Oiseaux, Presqu'île
    aux (S)........................260
Okomu National Park (N)
   1151
Oku, Lake (C)..............1295
Oku, Mount (C)
    ....1290, 1295
Old Oyo National
    Park (N)....................1140
Onitsha (N).................1156
Orango (GB) 553
Orango National
    Park (GB) 553
Oro (N) 1140
Oron (N) 1166
Osogbo (N) 1142–1147
Osogbo 1144
Ouadane (Mau)............151
Ouagadougou (BF)
    731–746
Ouagadougou...... 736–737
Ouagadougou,
    Central.......................741
Ouagadougou,
    Greater 732
    accommodation 734–738
    airlines............................. 745
    airport.............................. 732
    arrivals............................. 732
    banks 745
    bicycles............................ 745
    bookshops 745
    car rental 745
    cinemas............................ 745
    clubs 744
    crafts 741–742
    cultural centres 745
    embassies........................ 746
    history 731
    horse riding 746
    hospital............................ 746
    hotels 734–738
    Internet............................ 746
    libraries............................ 746
    maps 746
    markets 740
    mobylettes 745
    museums 739
    Nabayius Gou ceremony
    740
    nightlife........................... 744
    pharmacies 746
    photography..................... 746
    post office 746
    restaurants 742–744
    Sankara's grave 739
    shops 746
    telephones 746
    tourist office 733
    transport.......................... 733
    travel agents 746
    visa extensions 746
    Western Union 746
Ouahigouya (BF)... 754–759
Ouahigouya....................755
Oualata (Mau) 143
Oudjilla (C) 1336
Ouidah (B)............. 983–988
Ouidah............................987
Oujeft (Mau) 145
Ouro Sogui (S) 237
Oursi (BF)....................754
Oussouye (S) 255
Outamba-Kilimi National
    Park (SL) 691
overland travel to
    West Africa 23–28
Owabi Wildlife
    Sanctuary (Gh)...........861
Oyo (N) 1138
Oyo-Ile National
    Park (N)....................1138
Oyono (BF) 780

P

package tours 23
packing list 87
Paga (Gh)....................879
Pakali Ba (Gam)..........317
Pakali Nding (Gam)......316
palm wine 60–61
Palmarin (S) 221
Palmeira harbour (CV)...500
Pama (BF) 750
Pandi, Mount (C) 1319
Pankronu (Gh)..............863
Panyam (N).................1182
Parakou (B)..................998
Parakou...........................998
Passagem, Santo
    Antão (CV) 495
Passi (S).......................222

Pastoria (Gui) 613
Paúl (CV) 495
Payoma (S) 227
Peace Corps.................. 71
Pedra Badejo (CV)........ 473
Pedra da Lume (CV) 501
Pellal (Gui) 622
Pendjari, Parc
   National de la (B) 1005
Peoples 77–82
Peoples map 78
Abid 140
Akan 787
Akposso 930
Aku 265
Ana................................ 930
Asante 787, 856–857
Baga 561
Baka 1318
Bakoko 1222
Balante 513
Bamana.......................... 326
Bamiléké 1223, 1283
Bamoun................ 1222, 1297
Banso............................ 1294
Bantu-speaking.............. 1222
Bariba 993, 1000
Barombi......................... 1273
Bassa 1222
Bassari 886, 938
Bata............................... 1223
Bella 327, 707
Beriberi................ 1012, 1067
Betammaribe................. 1004
Bidan 93
Bijagó 513
Bini 1147
Bobo 707
Bororo 1012
Builsa 787
Bullom 641
Bussa 1000
Chamba 1289
Chorfa 140
Dagarti........................... 787
Dagomba 787, 871, 878
Dendi.............................. 1000
Djerma............. 761, 764, 1012
Dogon 327, 406, 412, 707
Douala............................ 1222
Dyula 561
Edo...................... 1075, 1147
Efik 1075
Eton 1222
Ewe 787, 885
Ewondo 1222
Fali................................. 1223
Fang 1222
Fante 787, 836
Fon 951, 992
Frafra................... 787, 879
Fula 94, 155, 265,
   327, 514, 561, 618, 641,
   707, 758, 1000, 1012, 1223,
   1326, 1327
Fulani (N) 1204, 1205, 1322

Fulse.............................. 758
Fulup 513
Ga 787
Ga-Adangme................... 787
Gonja.................... 787, 871
Gourma 945
Gourmantché 707
Gourounsi................ 707, 761
Guerzé 561, 636
Guizica 1335
Gwari 1075, 1173
Hal-Pulaar 94
Haratin.................. 93, 140
Hausa 707, 1009,
   1049, 1185, 1186
Ibibio 1075
Idoma 1075
Igbo 1075, 1153
Ijaw 1075, 1158
Imragen 126
Jola 155, 245, 265
Kabyé 885, 939
Kanouri........ 1012, 1052, 1075
Kanuri 1210, 1211
Kapsiki 1223,1335
Kassena 787, 878
Kel Gress Tuareg........... 1055
Kirdi 1223, 1312, 1332
Kissi 632, 641
Kono 641
Koranko............. 641, 692, 694
Kotoko 1223
Kotokoli 886
Kotokoli 933
Kouranko 561
Krios 641
Kurumba 758
Lebanese 265, 301
Limba 692
Lobi 710, 778
Loko 641
Loma 561
Mafa 1223
Mafa 1333
Malinké 326, 561
Mamprusi 787, 871, 878
Mandara 1335
Mandinka 155, 265, 514
Manjago 265
Manjak 513
Manon 638
Maouri 1049
Margui 1335
Masena 140
Massa............................. 1223
Maxi 996
Mboum 1322
Mende 641
Mende 641, 698–699
Mina 885
Mofou 1335
Moors 93, 265, 327
Mossi 707, 758
Mousgoum 1223
Nupe 1075
Pana 707
Pepel 513

Podoko....... 1223, 1335, 1336
Pygmies 1222, 1312
Rehian 140
Samos 707
"Semi-Bantu" 1222
Senoufo 327, 710
Serahule 265
Serer 155, 265
Sherbro 641
Shua Arabs 1075, 1210,
   1223, 1335
Sissala 787
Somba................ 1002, 1004
Songhai 1012
Songhai 326
Soninké 94
Susu 561, 641
Talensi 787
Tamberma 885, 939, 944
Tchamba 886
Temne............................. 641
Tikar 1222, 1291
Tiv 1075
Tofinu............................. 982
Toma 635
Toupouri 1223
Tuareg 327, 1012, 1058
Tukulor 155
Twi 885
Wala 787, 876
Wandala 1335
Wodaabé 1012
Wolof 94, 155, 158, 265
Yalunka........................... 641
Yarse (BF) 761
Yoruba............. 992, 996, 1075
Pepel (SL) 688
Petite Côte (S) 219
Petite Côte 223
phones in West Africa 62
photography 67, 69, 87
pickpocketing 65
Pico de Fogo (CV) 477
Picos (CV)..................... 472
Pita (Gui)...................... 616
Pitche (GB) 558
Pô (BF) 761
Pô, Parc National de (BF)
   ....762, 764
Podor (S) 236
Pointe St-Georges (S)
   256
police 66–67
polio............................... 38
Ponta do Sol (CV)......... 493
Pontinha da
   Janela (CV) 494
Popenguine (S)............. 219
population 7
Porga (B)..................... 1005
Port Harcourt (N)
   1157–1161
Port Harcourt 1160

Port Loko (SL) 688, 689
Porteto (CV)..................482
Porto Novo (B)......989–992
Porto Novo 990
Porto Novo (CV) 492
Possotomè (B)..............989
post in West Africa.........61
Potiskum (N)...............1204
Potoru (SL) 698
Pouké (Gui)..................616
Poura (BF)....................747
Praia (CV).............463–472
Praia: Platô 467
Praia 465
  accommodation..............464
  airlines...............................469
  arrivals..............................464
  banks 469
  bars 469
  bookshops 469
  car rental 469
  clubs 469
  cultural centres 469
  embassies.........................469
  hospital..............................470
  hotels 465
  Internet..............................470
  museums 466
  nightlife..............................469
  pharmacies 470
  post office 470
  restaurants 468
  telephones 470
  tourist information............464
  travel agents 470
  visa extensions 470
Praia Baixo (CV) 473
Praia da Bruce (GB) 551
Praia de São Pedro (CV)
 491
Prang (Gh) 864

Preguiça (CV)................497
press in West Africa 34
prickly heat.....................42
Princestown (Gh)
  ....835, 850
prostitution 72
public holidays and
  festivals...................63–64
public transport 48–52
Pujangulo (GB) 549
Pusiga (Gh)...................878
Pya (T) 943

Q

Quaddaga (M)...............383

R

Rabil (CV)..............507, 509
Race of Hope (C)........1269
Rachid (Mau) 140
radio in West Africa........34
Ramadan 63
Ramatoulaye (BF).........760
Ranch de Gibier de
  Nazinga (BF)...............763
Rata, Mount (C) 1276
Razo, Ilhéu (CV)............496
red tape and visas..........29
Red Volta Valley (Gh)...880
Regent (SL)...................688
religion in West Africa.....14
restaurants................55, 57

Retba, Lac (S)...............218
Rey Bouba (C) 1326
Rhoko (N).....................1165
Ribeira Brava (CV) 498
Ribeira Grande, Santo
  Antão (CV) 493–494
Ribeira Grande, Santiago
  (CV)...........................470
Ribeira Ilheu (CV)..........479
Richard Toll (S) 235
Ricketts Island (SL).......687
Ring Road, the (C).....1290
River Gambia National
  Park (Gam).................317
River No. 2
  beach (SL) 686
road rules 53
Rocher du Loup (C)....1316
Rosso (Mau) 136
Rosso (S) 235
Roume, Île (Gui)...........600
Roumsiki (C) 1334
Route de l'Aïr (Ni) 1066
Route de
  l'Espoir (Mau).............136
Roxa (GB) 552
Rubane (GB) 552
Rufisque (S) 219
Rui Vaz (CV)..................472
Rumpi Hills (C)............1276

S

Saala, Chutes
  de la (Gui) 621
Sabongari (C)..............1294
Sabou (BF)....................747
Sadiola (M) 371
safety 64–67, 87
Sahara routes 25
Sakanbiriwa (SL)...........703
Sal island (CV) 499–506
Sal island 499
Sal Rei (CV) 507
Sal Rei, Ilhéu de (CV)....507
Salde (S).......................237
Saloum Delta (S)...........222
Saloum Delta and Petite
  Côte............................223
salt requirements............42
Saltinho,
  Ponte do (GB)............554
Saltpond (Gh) 835
Saly-Niakhniakhale (S)...220
Saly-Portudal (S) 219
Sambrungo (Gh)...........881
Samoé (Gui)..................636

Modern times

Achievements (Gui)..581
Armed conflict in the north (Ni).........................1057
"Barça ou barsax" – Spain's hellish allure (S)......182
Fishing rights (Mau)..121
Project Zaca (BF) 742
Sexual attitudes 73
Sharia law in the northern states (N) 1099
The Casamance Conflict (S) 180
The Dakar Rally (S) 203
The Gambian women's movement (Gam) 275
The permanent plot (Gui).....................................580
The status of West African Women 74
The Tuareg rebellion (M).......................................344
Trouble in the Delta (N) 1158–1159
Universities (N)..1075
Western Sahara and the Polisario
  War (Mau)..108–109

San (M) 379
Sanaga River (C) 1310
Sanam (Ni) 1045
Sandaré (M) 372
Sandenièr (S) 244
Sanga (M) 415
Sansanding (M) 379
Sansanné-Mango (T) 945
Santa Barbara (CV) 481
Santa Luzia (CV) 496
Santa Maria (CV) ... 502–506
Santa Maria 503
Santiaba Manjak (S) 259
Santiago island (CV)
.... 462–474
Santiago island (CV) 463
Santo Antão
  island (CV) 491–496
Santo Antão island 492
Sanyang (Gam) 310
São Domingos (CV) 470
São Domingos (GB) 544
São Filipe (CV) 475–477
São Francisco (CV) 470
São Jorge (CV) 479
São Jorge dos
  Orgãos (CV) 472
São Nicolau island (CV)
.... 496–499
São Nicolau island 497
São Pedro (CV) 491
São Vicente island (CV)
.... 484–491
São Vicente island 484
Sapu (Gam) 317
Saraya (S) 243
Saréboïdo (Gui) 558
Sarékali (Gui) 622
Sarpan, Îlot (S) 216
Satí (BF) 764
Satiri (BF) 772
Savalou (B) 997
Sawla (Gh) 877
Say (Ni) 1048
scams 64–65
schistosomiasis 41
scorpions 43
Sebhikotane (S) 218
Sebhory (Gui) 616
security 64–67
Sédhiou (S) 244
Sefadu (SL) 703
Ségou (M) 374–379
Ségou 377
Ségou kingdom (M) 375
Ségou (S) 622
Ségou-Koro (M) 376
Séguénéga (BF) 758
Segueya (Gui) 613
Sei island (SL) 700

Sekondi (Gh) 835
Séléki (S) 253
Séléti (S) 260
Sélibabi (Mau) 138
SENEGAL 153–262
Senegal highlights 154
Senegal 156–157
  accommodation 165
  banks and exchange 162
  books 191
  cinema 171, 190
  climate 160
  costs 162
  crafts 170
  crime 170
  currency 162
  emergencies 170
  entertainment 170
  facts and figures 158
  festivals 169–170, 186
  food and drink 166
  glossary 196
  health 162
  history 172–183
  information 161
  Internet 168
  language 193–196
  mail 168
  maps 161
  media 161
  music 171, 187–190
  national parks 171
  opening hours 169
  people 155
  photography 155
  public holidays 169
  red tape and visas 161
  sexual attitudes 170
  shopping 170
  sports 171
  telephones 168
  theatre 171
  transport 163
  travel from other African
    countries 159
  websites 161
  wildlife 171
  work and study 159
Senegal River (S) 234
Senneh-Mentering (Gam)
.... 309
Sennissa (M) 394
Senya Beraku (Gh)
.... 832, 834
Sepeteri (N) 1140
Sérédou (Gui) 635
Serpent, Vallée du (M) ... 372
Serrekunda (Gam) 294
Serrekunda 298–299
Serti (N) 1215
Sévaré (M) 387–390
Sévaré 388
sexual attitudes 72–75
sexually transmitted
  diseases 42, 72

Shai Hills Reserve (Gh)
.... 830
Shaki (N) 1140
shaking hands 7, 68
Shama (Gh) 835, 845
Sharia law (N) ... 1099, 1185
Shebshi Mountains (N)
.... 1215
Shendam (N) 1182
Sherbro Island (SL) 699
Sidakoro (Gui) 626
SIERRA LEONE ... 639–703
Sierra Leone
  highlights 640
Sierra Leone 644
  accommodation 647
  banks and exchange 646
  books 666–668
  cinema 652
  climate 643
  costs 646
  crafts 650
  crime 651
  currency 646
  electricity 643
  emergencies 651
  entertainment 651
  fact file 642
  festivals 650
  food and drink 648
  glossary 669
  health 646
  history 653–664
  information 645
  Internet 650
  language 668
  mail 650
  maps 645
  media 646
  music 651, 665
  national parks 652
  opening hours 650
  people 641
  photography 643
  public holidays 650
  red tape and visas 645
  sexual attitudes 651
  shopping 650
  sports 652
  telephones 650
  theatre 652
  transport 647
  travel from other African
    countries 643
  websites 646
  wildlife 652
Siguiri (Gui) 630
Sikasso (M) 380
SIM cards 62
Simenti (S) 242
Sindou, les
  Pics de (BF) 775
Sine-Saloum
  Stone Circles (S) 227
Sinikoro (SL) 694

Sinkassé (BF).................947
Sinkuniya (SL)...............693
Sissamba (BF) 760
Slave trade in West Africa
  Benin 960, 983, 995
  Burkina Faso....................761
  Cameroon 1237
  Cape Verde 448
  Gambia, The 311–312
  Ghana.........................840–841
  Guinea-Bissau................524
  Niger...............................1052
  Nigeria........1089, 1129, 1147
  Senegal 214
  Sierra Leone.... 653–655, 687
sleeping sickness 41
Small Mount
  Cameroon (C) 1267
snakes in West Africa.....43
Sobané (Gui)..................609
Soga (GB) 552
Sokodé (T) 933–936
Sokodé.........................934
Sokoto (N) 1205–1209
Sokoto..........................1206
solifugids 43
Soma (Gam) 316
Somalomo (C).............1317
Somba country (B) 1004
Somniaga (BF)...............759
Sonfon, Lake (SL).........693
Songhai Empire (M)......424
Songho (M)....................411
Sonkwala Mountains (N)
 1169
Sotaventos Islands (CV)
  462–483
Sotouboua (T)...............937
Soumba, Cascades
  de la (Gui) 608
Soumbon (C) 1293
spiders.............................43
spirits (liquor)............60–61
staying with people 57
STDs.........................42, 72
St-Louis (S)........... 228–234
St-Louis.........................229
student cards 45
Su-Bum (C)..................1293
Sukur (N).....................1214
Sula Mountains (SL) 693
Sulima (SL) 698
Sussex beach (SL)........686

Tabili (Gui)....................609
Tacharane (M)...............426

Tacugama Chimpanzee
  Reserve (SL) 688
Tafadek (Ni)................1066
Tafarit (Mau).................126
Tafi Atome (Gh)............869
Tagant region (Mau)
  138–141
Tagbo Falls (Gh)...........870
Tahoua (Ni).......1045, 1056
Takija (C) 1294
Takoradi (Gh) 845–848
Takoradi 846
Takum (N) 1216
Talcho (Ni)...................1045
Tamale (Gh)........... 872–874
Tamale..........................872
Tamara, Île (Gui)...........600
Tambacounda (S) 239
Tambacounda.............239
Tambaoura,
  Falaise de (M) 370
Tamchekket (Mau) 142
Tamgak Mountains (Ni)
 1066
Tamou (Ni) 1048
Tanaf (GB)....................555
Tanaf (S).......................244
Tanbi Wetlands (Gam)
 305
Tangale Hill (N)............1182
Tangama, Pont (Gui).....616
Tanguen-Dassouri (BF)
 746
Tanguiéta (B)...............1005
Tanguiéta,
  Cascade de (B)........1005
Tanji (Gam)....................310
Tanougou,
  Cascades de (B)......1005
Tanout (Ni) 1055
Tantum (CV) 481
Taraba State (N).........1215
Tarrafal,
  Santiago (CV)............473

Tarrafal,
  Santo Antão (CV).......495
Tarrafal, São
  Nicolau (CV)..............497
"Tarrafes" do Rio
  Cacheu, Parque
  Natural dos (GB)........544
taxis in West Africa... 48–50
Tazerzait (Ni) 1067
Tcholliré (C).................1325
tea in West Africa 60
Tébaram (Ni) 1045
Techiman (Gh)..............863
Tegbi (Gh) 832
Tegourou (M)................411
Tekrur (Mau).................142
Télé, Lac (M) 380
telephone dialling codes
 62
telephones.....................62
television 34
Teli (M) 414
Télimélé (Gui) 619
Téloua (Ni)..................1066
Tendaba Camp (Gam)...316
Tène Peul (S)................227
Ténéré Desert (Ni)......1067
Tengréla, Lac de (BF) ...775
Tengzug shrine (Gh)......882
tents...............................56
Téra (Ni) 1045
Terjit (Mau) 145
tetanus............................38
Tezirek (Ni) 1067
theft in West Africa
  64–65
Thiès (S)........................224
Thiès.............................224
Thilogne (S)...................237
Tiadiaye (S)...................224
Tiakané (BF)..................763
Tichit (Mau)...................141
Tidjikja (Mau) 139
Tiébélé (BF) 762
Tiguidit, Falaise de (Ni)
 1055

Natural history

Abuko birdlife (Gam) 307
Ivory 76
Pigs (GB) 544
The crocodiles of the Sahara (Mau)..................... 139
The Diafarabé cattle crossing (M)....................... 380
The ecology of Barombi Mbo (C)....................... 1273
The Guelb er Richat (Mau)................................... 152
The Imragen – fishing in the desert
  with dolphins (Mau).. 126

INDEX

Tikoba I (Gh)..................851
Tillabéri (Ni)................1046
Timbedgha (Mau) 143
Timbi-Touni (Gui) 617
Timbo (Gui)...................614
Timbuktu (M) ... 395–404
Timbuktu (M)................397
time zones 88
time-keeping 69
Timia (Ni).....................1066
Timia, Cascade de (Ni)
......................................1066
Tin Labbé (Mau) 152
Tinkisso,
    Chutes de (Gui)..........623
Tinsera (Gui) 622
Tionk Essil (S)...............262
Tirelli (M)..............415, 416
Tison, Lac (C) 1324
Tite (GB) 554
Tivaouane (S)................225
Tiwai Island (SL)...........697
Tiwai Island Nature
    Reserve....................697
TOGO..................883–948
Togo highlights 884
Togo 883
    accommodation........ 892
    banks and exchange........ 891
    books 904
    cinema 895
    climate.............................. 888
    costs 890
    crafts 894
    crime 895
    currency 890
    emergencies..................... 895
    entertainment................... 895
    facts and figures 885
    festivals 894
    food and drink.................. 892
    glossary............................ 906
    health 890
    history 897–903
    information 889
    Internet............................ 894
    language 905
    mail................................... 893
    maps 889
    media 890
    music......................895, 903
    national parks 896
    opening hours.................. 894
    people.............................. 885
    photography..................... 886
    public holidays................. 894
    red tape and visas 889
    sexual attitudes............... 895
    shopping 894
    sports............................... 896
    telephones 894
    transport........................... 891
    travel from other African
        countries....................... 888
    websites............................ 889
    wildlife.............................. 896
Togoville (T)..................922
toilet paper 88
Tokeh Beach (SL) 686
Tombel (C) 1278
Tondourou (M) 421
Tongo (Gh)...................882
Tono Lake (Gh) 879
Touaga (T)...................946
Touba (S) 226
Toubab Dialao (S).........219
Toubacouta (S) 223
Tougouri (BF)................751
Toukoto (M)...................372
Toungad (Mau)..............146
Tountouroun (Gui).........622
tour operators................23
Touré, Samory (Gui)......588
Tourou (C) 1334
Tourvine Pass (Mau) 145
Toya, Mare de (M)........372
trains..............................51
transport............. 10, 48–54
trans-Saharan routes......25
travel advisories 33
travel agents for
    West Africa 23
traveller's cheques 47
travellers with disabilities
......................................71–72
Treji (S) 236
tribes (see peoples)
Tristão, Île (Gui)...........609
trypanosomiasis 41
Tsatsudo Falls (Gh).......870
Tuareg rebellion (M)......344
Tujering (Gam)..............310
Tumani Tenda (Gam).....309
Turner's Peninsula (SL)
......................................699
Turtle Islands (SL) 700
typhoid 38

U

Udo (N) 1152
Ugep (N) 1167
Umuahia (N)................1156
Unhocuum (GB)............553
Uno (GB)......................553
Uracane (GB)................553

V

vaccinations 38

Vale dos Cavaleiros (CV)
......................................474
Varela (GB)...................544
vegetarian food 58
vehicle documents 27
Velingara (S).................244
Vila das Pombas (CV)... 495
Vila do Maio (CV).........482
Vila Igreja (CV) 479
Vila Nova de
    Sintra (CV) 480
Vina, Chute de la (C)
......................................1324
Vinagre (CV)..................481
visa touristique entente ... 32
visas 29–32
Voile de la Mariée,
    Chutes de la (Gui)......613
Volta, Lake (Gh) 865, 866
Volta, The......................865
voluntary work..........70–71
Vom (N).......................1181
voodoo 911, 923,
    924, 951
VSO 71
"W" du Niger, Parc
    National du (B).........1001
"W" du Niger, Parc
    National du (Ni)........1047
"W" du Niger, Parc
    National du............1048

W

Wa (Gh).................781, 876
Wa 877
Wakwa (C) 1324
Walewale (Gh)...............882
warri board game 69
Wassa Domama Rock
    Shrine (Gh).................842
Wassu stone
    circles (Gam)..............318
water in West Africa 60
Waterloo (SL)........685, 687
Wato Fula (GB) 549
Wawa (N) 1171
Waza (C) 1336
Waza National
    Park (C).....................1336
websites 33
Wechai hippo
    sanctuary (Gh)...........877
Weh (C) 1292
Wenchi (Gh) 861
West Africa 4–5
West African
    currencies 46

Spiritual life

A glossary of Yoruba religion (N) 1143
Catholic Mass (M) 376
Sex, speech and weaving: a Dogon
    cosmology (M)... 406
Voodoo (B) 984–985

Western Sahara 108
Western Union 48
Wikki Warm Springs (N)
    1184
wildlife and national
    parks 16, 75–77
Winneba (Gh) 833
wiring money 48
Wli Falls (Gh) 870
women in West Africa 74
women travellers 72–75
working 70–71
wrestling (Gam) 315
Wukari (N) 1216
Wum (C) 1292
Wum, Lake (C) 1292
Xitole (GB) 554
Xofa (Gh) 801

Yankari National Park (N)
    1183
Yaoundé (C) 1300–1310
Yaoundé 1302–1303
    accommodation 1304
    airlines 1309
    airport 1300
    arrivals 1300
    banks 1309
    Bastos 1306
    bookshops 1309
    Briqueterie 1305
    car rental 1309
    cinemas 1309
    clubs 1309
    cultural centres 1309
    dentists 1309
    doctors 1310
    embassies 1310
    history 1300
    hotels 1304
    information 1301
    Internet 1310
    maps 1310
    markets 1305
    Melen 1307
    Mont Fébé 1306
    museums 1306
    national park offices....... 1309
    nightlife.......................... 1309
    pharmacies 1310
    post office 1310
    Quartier du Lac 1305
    restaurants 1307
    shops 1310
    tourist office 1301
    zoo 1307
Yassine (S) 260
Yatenga (BF) 754–760
Yeji (Gh) 864, 865
Yékéyéké festival (T) 925
Yele Island (SL) 700
Yélimané (M) 372
yellow fever 38
Yelwa (N) 1182
Yembéring (Gui) 622
Yendi (Gh) 871
Yendouma (M) 419
Yengue (Equatorial Guinea)
    1316
Yérifoula (BF) 780
Yifin (SL) 694
Yipa-Dafo (Gh).............. 870
Yirafilaia Badala (SL)..... 694
Yoff (S) 217
Yokadouma (C) 1319
Yola (N) 1215
York (SL) 686
Yoro (BF) 764
Yoruba religion............ 1143
Youga (M) 419
Youkounkoun (Gui) 240
Youtou (S) 259

Y

Yako (BF) 760
Yalembe (SL) 694
Yalogo (BF) 751
Yang-Yang (S) 226
Yankai island (SL) 700

Z

Zandoma (BF)................ 760
Zaria (N) 1191–1193

QUICK REFERENCE

	Fact file	Climate	Price codes	Fuel prices	Photography
Benin	951	953	957	956	954
Burkina Faso	707	710	715	714	710
Cameroon	1222	1228	1232	1228	1219
Cape Verde	433	436	441	438	435
The Gambia	265	267	272	270	266
Ghana	785	788	794	791	787
Guinea	565	564	571	568	561
Guinea-Bissau	513	517	520	519	516
Mali	323	328	335	331	326
Mauritania	93	96	102	100	95
Niger	1009	1013	1018	1016	1012
Nigeria	1074	1076	1083	1078	1075
Senegal	158	160	165	160	155
Sierra Leone	642	643	648	647	643
Togo	885	888	892	892	887

Zaria 1192
Zebilla (Gh) 881
Ziama hills (Gui)............635
Ziguinchor (S) 247–251

Ziguinchor....................248
Zinder (Ni)..................1052
Zinder..........................1053
Zinzana (M)..................379

Zouérat (Mau) 125–126
Zugurma (N)................1170
Zuma Rock (N) 1172,
   1176

Map symbols

----	International boundary	℃	Telephone
— ···	Provincial boundary	⊠	Post office
----	Chapter division boundary	⊞	Hospital
▬▬	Motorway	♠	Museum
═══	Main paved road	⊙	Statue
═══	Minor paved road	🏛	Monument
⊪⊪⊪	Steps	∴	Ruin
——	Unpaved road	🏛	Fortress
-----	Footpath	🏌	Golf course
▬■▬	Railway	◉	Accommodation
⌐ — —	Ferry route	■	Restaurant
═══	River/canal	Λ	Campground
----	Seasonal river	🏠	Mountain refuge
——	Dyke	🏊	Swimming pool
▬▬▬	Wall/fortifications	✻	Windmill
⌣	Bridge	🗼	Lighthouse
⊠	Gate	✸	Shipwreck
🗻	Mountain range	⊓	Shrine
▲	Mountain peak	⚲	Church (regional maps)
🏔	Cliff	🕌	Mosque
❊	Crater	☐	Market
🌊	Waterfall	◯	Stadium
⌐	Escarpment	▬	Building
🌥	Saltpan	⊞	Church (town maps)
✷	Swamp	🗀	Cemetery
⌒	Dune	⌐⌐	Muslim cemetery
✈	Airport	▒	Park
★	Transport stop	🗺	Forest
🏧	Fuel station	⬚	Beach
◆	Point of interest	▨	Marshland
@	Internet access	▨	Lava flow
ⓘ	Information office		

Avoid Guilt Trips

Buy fair trade coffee + bananas ✓

Save energy – use low energy bulbs ✓

— don't leave tv on standby ✓

Offset carbon emissions from flight to Madrid

Send goat to Africa ✓

Join Tourism Concern today ✓

Slowly, the world is changing.
Together we can, and will, make a difference.

Tourism Concern is the only UK registered charity fighting exploitation in one of the largest industries on earth: people forced from their homes in order that holiday resorts can be built, sweatshop labour conditions in hotels and destruction of the environment are just some of the issues that we tackle.

Sending people on a guilt trip is not something we do. We know as well as anyone that holidays are precious. But you can help us to ensure that tourism always benefits the local communities involved.

Call 020 7133 3330
or visit **tourismconcern.org.uk** to find out how.

A year's membership of Tourism Concern costs just £20 (£12 unwaged)
– that's 38 pence a week, less than the cost of a pint of milk, organic of course.

TourismConcern